DATE DUE

~~FE 16 '93~~		
~~MY 19 95~~		
AP 11 '97		
~~		

DEMCO 38-296

The Great Song Thesaurus

The Great Song Thesaurus

ROGER LAX

FREDERICK SMITH

Second Edition
Updated and Expanded

New York
OXFORD UNIVERSITY PRESS
1989

Oxford University Press

Oxford   New York   Toronto
Delhi   Bombay   Calcutta   Madras   Karachi
Petaling Jaya   Singapore   Hong Kong   Tokyo
Nairobi   Dar es Salaam   Cape Town
Melbourne   Auckland

and associated companies in
Berlin   Ibadan

Published by Oxford University Press, Inc.
200 Madison Avenue, New York, New York 10016

Oxford is a registered trademark of Oxford University Press

Library of Congress Cataloging-in-Publication Data
Lax, Roger.
The great song thesaurus / Roger Lax, Frederick Smith.—2nd ed.,
updated and expanded.
p. cm.   Includes index.
ISBN 0-19-505408-3
1. Popular music—Indexes. I. Smith, Frederick. II. Title.
ML128.S3L4   1989
784.5'0016—dc19   88-31267   CIP MN

2 4 6 8 9 7 5 3

Printed in the United States of America
on acid-free paper

For my mother
and in memory of my father

R.L.

Acknowledgments

For her unswerving tenacity during the plague of crises surrounding the completion of this book, I thank my literary agent Maria Carvainis, who for five years served equally well in the capacity of dear friend.

At the American Society of Composers, Authors and Publishers, Michael Kerker offered continued assistance in locating oftentimes unpublished and almost unobtainable information through ASCAP's excellent indexing staff. I wish also to extend my appreciation to Sheldon Meyer, Leona Capeless, and Joellyn Ausanka for their suggestions and assistance during the preparation of the manuscript.

For the tolerance of those who during my last year of assembling research and preparing the manuscript patiently cooked my meals, withstood my endless complaints, and saved both sanity and spirit, my deepest appreciation to Toni Goldin, Ian Ross Jenkins, Christian Ghigliotti, and Edward Howard.

The preparation of this Revised Edition proved very much a different task, for which I would like to thank additionally David Ascher for his generosity and expertise in helping me prepare the final manuscript.

And for their limitless support and generosity, my parents, Harrison and Arline, and grandmother Rose displayed those family qualities reserved for only a lucky few. To them I will be forever grateful.

ROGER LAX

Contents

Authors' Notes
on the Titles, Dates, Classification, Popularity, and Numerical Rankings of Songs Included in This Book

SONG TITLES

The original intent of this book was to select, from all divisions of song literature, the 10,000 best-known popular and/or significant songs in English-speaking countries and to cross-index the pertinent data associated with each for immediate and accessible reference.

Our initial list totaled upwards of 40,000 songs and themes selected from the areas of folk songs and ballads, contemporary pop songs, nursery rhymes, sea chanteys, music-hall ballads, works from musical theatre, film, radio, and television, political campaign songs, church carillons, school, college, and university songs, bugle calls, and advertising and commercial jingles. Also included were certain classical, ballet and symphonic themes that are today world standards.

From the hundreds of volumes we read and collected in specific genres of song literature, trade magazines in the entertainment and recording industries over the last fifty years, materials published by major performance rights organizations including the American Society of Composers, Authors and Publishers (ASCAP) and Broadcast Music Inc. (BMI), and literature, media and "life" in general, we began our work.

In Part V, song titles are cross-referenced by alternate and multiple titles by which a song has become known, and in all other Parts by the actual title ultimately used in Part V designated as the standard or accepted title today.

In Part I, certain song titles qualify for inclusion in a specific year because they are amusing, apt, topical, or are of historical interest, although as songs they did not become truly popular. Such cases have received the notation *not indexed* immediately following the title, indicating that they were not selected for inclusion in Part V.

Song titles are alphabetized by ignoring the articles *a, an,* and *the;* and in songs with non-English titles by ignoring the articles *la, le, las,* and *el.* Thus, "The Perfect Song" is alphabetized under the letter *P,* so is "El Paso."

AUTHORS' NOTES
SONG DATES

Dates associated with songs listed in this book most often represent the dates of maximum popularity as contrasted with the actual publication (printing) date or date of copyright, which can sometimes precede the former by as much as a decade. On the other hand, dates of maximum popularity may well precede, particularly in the case of traditional folk songs, the year in which they finally appeared in printed form.

Quite often disparities between the dates of popularity of songs in Europe and in the United States may be noted. For example, "J'Attendrai" reached popularity in 1939 in Europe but not until 1945 in the United States. Conversely, "Shadrack" was popular in the United States in 1931, but not in England until 1938, seven years later. In all cases, unless indicated otherwise, dates of popularity will reflect those in the United States.

SONG CLASSIFICATION

Songs for the post-1900 era are classified in Part I as follows:

Top Hits, see *Top Hit Song Popularity,* below.

Adaptations. Top Hits derived from earlier songs with different titles are designated as Adaptations. These songs are also entered in Part IV under adapted title only and in Part V under both original and adapted titles.

Revivals. Top Hits that have reappeared with renewed popularity three years or more after the initial listing date in Part I are designated as Revivals. These songs are also entered in Part V and cited with the one or multiple dates of popular revival.

Notable. Songs which, in the opinion of the authors, deserve attention because of some special acclaim or historical significance during that year, or because they were important as part of a film or theatre score are in the *Notable* group. All songs in this classification are also entered in Part V.

TOP HIT SONG POPULARITY

Estimates of annual song popularity in Part I are based primarily but not exclusively on:

1535–1848	Survival and recognition today and literary reference
1848–1920	American sheet-music sales. The first more or less accurate notion of sheet-music sales developed around the time of Stephen Foster's dominance in American popular music.

1920–1935	American sheet-music sales, record sales, and after 1926 and the birth of the radio networks, radio "air play."
1935–1955	American record sales plus radio "air play" in general and the influence of the "Your Hit Parade" radio program in particular.
1955–	Annual cumulative weekly single (not album) record sales rankings and ASCAP and BMI "air play" and performance statistics.

NUMERICAL SONG RANKINGS IN PART I

By Record Sales (1940–——). Numerical indications of annual cumulative weekly single (not album) record sales rankings are placed beneath each Top Hit song title and are designated with the initials RS. Immediately below the RS rating is the name of the recording artist associated with the hit.

A primary authority on weekly single record sales rankings in the United States is Joel Whitburn, who publishes the most comprehensive compilation of record sales classified by artists for the period beginning with 1940.

By Air Play on "Your Hit Parade" (1935–1950). Numerical indications of annual song popularity rankings according to the radio program "Your Hit Parade" are placed beneath each Top Hit song title and are designated with the initials HP. The popularity rankings featured on the subsequent television program "Your Hit Parade" derived from the format of the original radio show no longer proved to be a significant factor in establishing the popularity of a song after 1950.

By Air Play According to the Peatman Survey (1942–1956). Numerical indications of annual song popularity rankings of songs broadcast on radio and TV according to the Peatman Survey of "Air Play" are placed beneath each Top Hit song title and are designated with the initials AP. This survey was conducted by Professor John G. Peatman of Columbia University based on a weekly survey of songs most often heard "on the air." After 1951, the survey was based on the combined audiences of radio and TV.

Abbreviations

ARTISTIC FUNCTION

w.   words

m.   music

a.   artist

b.   book (script, in the case of musical theatre)

Pr.   producer

A&R   artists and repertoire

MEDIA SOURCE

(MT)   Musical Theatre

(T)   Non-Musical Theatre

(MF)   Musical Film

(F)   Non-Musical Film

(R)   Radio

(TV)   Television

(OB)   Off-Broadway

SONG RANKINGS

(see Authors' Notes)

HP   Hit Parade

RS   Record Sales

AP   Air Play

The Great Song Thesaurus

I

The Greatest Songs

I have tunes in my head for every war I've been to, and
indee for every critical or exciting phase of my life.
Winston Churchill

How cruelly sweet are
The echoes that start
When memory plays an old
Tune on the heart!
Eliza Cook

Refer to the Authors' Notes at the beginning of this book for information concerning the song titles, dates, classification, popularity, and rankings incorporated in this section. For more complete information about a particular song, refer to Part V; all song titles in this Part may, unless otherwise specified, be found in Part V.

This Part is a chronicle of Top Hits and notable songs beginning with the sixteenth century to 1986. It also pursues the evolution of music on records and air play including data on the hit records and recording artists since 1940. Each group of songs is accompanied by major events in the development of the world of modern entertainment from that same year or era.

THE ELIZABETHAN EPOCH 1558–1603

"The Excellency of the English Tongue." William Harrison coined this praise in 1587. It expressed the development of the language from the early Chaucerian English to the felicitous, widely ranging, and concise instrument we now enjoy.* Its perfection set the stage for the emergence of our present hierarchy of entertainment media.

C.P. Snow explains: "First, there are more words in the English language [some 454,000] than in any other known to man. In Russian, the nearest competitor, there

*In 1473–74, William Caxton, the English printer, published his first book printed in English.

are lots of approximate synonyms as in English for almost anything. But Russian does not have *two* primary sources of vocabulary as, from its Celtic and Teutonic (Anglo-Saxon) basic structure and French (Norman) top dressing, has English. Second, and partly because of this linguistic good luck, one of the great literatures of the world has been written in English. Third, English is the most analytical of all the Indo-European languages, that is, the grammar has been more radically broken down."

William Shakespeare. By 1586, or certainly by 1588, Shakespeare, twenty-two, had arrived in London from Stratford-on-Avon. The language had matured and was ready for his poetic genius to enrich it. Collaterally, musical notation had been standardized enough to be understood throughout Europe. At Oxford, Shakespeare had access to one of the great libraries in the Western world. There the entire known historical literatures of Greece and Rome were available to him for plot and story research. In the Bodleian Library, a copy of Sir Thomas North's translation (the first into English) of Plutarch's *Parallel Lives* contains notes thought to be those of Shakespeare himself. In 1577, Raphael Holinshed, the English historian, completed his *Chronicles of England, Scotland, and Ireland,* aforementioned.

In the Elizabethan theatre, still so young that it had not developed the convention of drawing a curtain between scenes, Shakespeare was one of the first actor-dramatists. He was also one of the first to try to limit actors to their written parts and to abolish ''gagging.'' In the years between 1595 and 1601, he wrote twelve of the thirty-eight plays thought to be his. From 1599, these were performed on the south bank of the Thames at the new Globe Theatre, in which he became a partner. No building for play acting was permitted within the city limits of London. Thus, on the days when the flag was raised in the tower of the theatre, ''groundlings'' would cross the river via London Bridge to stand or sit in the yard of the theatre to see the plays, directed by and starring Dick Burbage.

The players' performances and Shakespeare's scripts must have been powerful indeed to compete with bearbaiting, an intensely popular diversion featured in the house next door to the Globe. Popular tastes of the time tended much more to bathos than pathos, and in his time, Shakespeare's *Pericles* was always more popular than his *Hamlet.*

Later, in 1827, composer Hector Berlioz could write without exaggeration in his memoirs of his own discovery of *Hamlet:* ''Shakespeare, coming upon me unawares, struck me like a thunderbolt. The lightning flash of that discovery revealed to me at a stroke the whole heaven of art, illuminating it to its remotest corners. I recognized the meaning of grandeur, beauty, dramatic truth . . .'' No better description of the Bard's impact on the arts has been offered.

Slavery. In 1564, John Hawkins, later hero of the English fleet against the Spanish Armada, received for the first time sanction from the Queen for the trading of African slaves.

Martin Luther and Popular Song. That the second selection in this chronicle of popular songs is a hymn, ''Ein' Feste Burg'' (A Mighty Fortress Is Our God) by Martin Luther, is worthy of note. Martin Luther was an Augustinian friar of the Roman Catholic Church. Lacey Baldwin Smith describes the dramatic events of 1517 in which Luther was a protagonist: ''Leo X was in need of silver to construct that magnificent monument to Renaissance grandeur, the new Cathedral of St. Peter. In order to raise the money, the Pope turned to the international banking house of Fuggers and, by way of collateral, issued a [Papal] bull of indulgences whereby the faithful might purchase, for the price of a single silver coin, remittance of the pains of purgatory. The Fuggers supervised the collection, and John Tetzel, a Dominican monk, acted as chief vendor and canvassed Germany, assuring his listeners that:

'As soon as the coin in the coffer rings
The soul from purgatory springs.'

When Tetzel approached Wittenberg, Luther struck out against the belief that remission of sin could be bought, and on October 31, 1517, he posted upon the collegiate church door his Ninety-Five Theses, offering to debate the purpose of the indulgences, their spiritual value, and the Pope's authority to issue them.'' *

The freedom to sing in church was a right previously restricted to the priests, and the songs were sung exclusively in Latin. But Luther was determined to change that. He wrote: ''It is my intention to make German psalms for the people—spiritual songs, that is, whereby the word of God may be kept alive in them by singing,'' and with ''Ein' Feste Burg'' he fulfilled his promise. Heine called this great paraphrase of Psalm 46 ''the Marseillaise of the Reformation.'' This hymn has been translated into fifty-three languages, and J.S. Bach liked it so much he made three separate arrangements of it. Many thousands of Protestant martyrs were to be burned at the stake singing this best-known of German chorales.

c. 1226

Summer Is Icumen In

1529

A Mighty Fortress Is Our God (Ein' Feste Burg)

1560

Old Hundredth (Doxology), or, **Praise God, from Whom All Blessings Flow.** The music for this song was originally com-

*Lacey Baldwin Smith, *The Elizabethan World* (Boston: American Heritage Publishing Co. and Houghton Mifflin Co., 1966).

posed by Louis Bourgeois for Psalm 134 in the *Genevan Psalter* of 1551. Mentioned in Shakespeare's *Merry Wives of Windsor,* act 2, scene 1.

1580

Auprès de Ma Blonde

Frog Went a-Courtin (Frog He Would-a-Wooing Go)

Greensleeves (Green Sleeves). Earliest words published 1580, earliest music published 1652, although possibly performed at least a century earlier; see Part V. This song is also men-

tioned in Shakespeare's *Merry Wives of Windsor,* act 2, scene 1, and act 5, scene 5.

1597 or earlier

The Prayer of Thanksgiving

c. 1598

It Was a Lover and His Lass. From Shakespeare's *As You Like It,* act 5, scene 3.

THE BAROQUE PERIOD IN MUSIC, 1600–1750

The classic music forms of the Baroque period were in some degree Florentine in origin. The development in Florence of a music based on major or minor harmonies with a single voice melodic lead supported by chords would greatly affect subsequent forms of popular music. The steady and consistent rhythms featured in this music would also be reflected in popular taste.

In the late sixteenth century, Florentine humanists were experimenting with ancient Greek musical declamation producing the first Italian opera, Emilio del Cavalieri's *Il Satiro.*

1606

Inigo Jones. The noted English architect of Elizabethan and post-Elizabethan English, Inigo Jones, begins to experiment with movable scenery and the proscenium for the theatre.

1609

In Padua, Galileo Galilei constructs the first telescope. It has a magnification of thirty and Galileo has already discerned what appear to be craters on the moon. In Prague, Johannes Kepler publishes his first two laws of planetary motion. In his new studio in Antwerp, Peter Paul Rubens is painting the "Adoration of the Magi." In London, William Shakespeare is completing *Cymbeline* and *The Winter's Tale.* Though he has just become a partner in the new Blackfriar's Theatre, the next year he retires to Stratford.

Three Blind Mice (earliest words and music published 1609)

c. 1666

Barbry (Barbara) **Allen**
Love Will Find Out the Way

1683–1728

1683

Thomas Cross, music engraver, printer, publisher, and music seller, publishes Henry Purcell's *Sonnatas of III Parts.* Cross may be called the inventor of sheet music and in London of the time he virtually monopolized the music-engraving industry.

1685

George Frederick Handel, the (naturalized) English composer, is born, as is Johann Sebastian Bach, organist and composer. Handel, very popular in his time, would produce his first opera, *Almira,* at the Opera House in Hamburg in 1705. It contained forty-one German and fifteen Italian airs. Fifteen years later the first opera sea-

son at the Royal Academy in London would begin Handel's great success with a series of operas over the next twenty-one years.

1696

Dutch music publisher Estienne Roger introduces in 1696 the practice of punching notes on copper as an alternative process for music engraving. Three years later in London, William Pearson, developing the work of Heptinstall, significantly improves the craft of musical typography.

c. 1700

Air for the G String
The Foggy Foggy Dew

Keeper of the Eddystone Light
O God, Our Help in Ages Past
Soldier, Soldier, Won't You Marry Me?
Twelve Days of Christmas

1711

Auld Lang Syne (earliest words published 1711, earliest music published 1687)

1715

Sally in Our Alley

1722

Bach is the first to explore fully the possibilities of "equal temperament" in the musical scale, and publishes Book I of his *Well-Tempered Clavier.*

1728

The first English ballad opera, John Gay's *The Beggar's Opera,* is staged at Lincoln's Inn Fields Theatre under the management of John Rich. Running sixty-two performances, it is rightly said to have made "Rich gay and Gay rich." In 1729 Bach's *St. Matthew's Passion* is performed for the first time at Köthen.

The Beggar's Opera (m. John Gay). Songs from this opera include: "Let Us Take to the Road"; "Lillibulero" (c. 1686); "Greensleeves" (see 1580), "Hither Dear Husband"; "When a Wife's in a Pout."
Country Gardens (Vicar of Bray)

1732

Franz Joseph Haydn is born in Lower Austria. He would develop the four-movement symphony as a popular form, and his students would include Wolfgang Amadeus Mozart and Ludwig van Beethoven. This year also sees the opening of the Covent Garden Theatre in London and the publication of the earliest printed music for the pianoforte, Ludovico Giustini's sonatas for piano. In 1733 the first London performance of Thomas Augustine Arne's opera *Rosamund* is staged.

1740

Rule, Britannia (earliest words and music published 1740–41)

1744

God Save the King (earliest publication of words and music possibly in *Thesaurus Musicus,* 1744)
London Bridge

1745

The Campbells Are Coming

1747

David Garrick. On assuming the management of the Theatre Royal at Drury Lane this year, Garrick recites the following prologue by Samuel Johnson:

> The stage but echoes back the public voice.
> The drama's laws the drama's patrons give,
> For we that live to please, must please to live.

Garrick's forty-year career in the theatre began as a playwright with his *Lethe; or, Aesop in the Shades,* which opened at Drury Lane in 1740. His major success as an actor began the following year at Goodman's Fields where he made his debut as Shakespeare's Richard III. His naturalistic style of performance, a novelty at the time, brought him great critical acclaim, and his actor-manager commitment to the Bard enabled him to mount at least twenty-four revivals of Shakespeare's plays: Garrick's *Hamlet, Richard III,* and *King Lear* were such major successes that when he played *Macbeth,* his enthusiasm allowed him to alter the script and insert a dying speech of his own. Garrick died in 1779 and was the first actor buried in Westminster Abbey.

1750

Bach dies. The Baroque period comes to an end.

Allan Water
Bobby Shafto
British Grenadiers
Cockles and Mussels, Alive, Alive O!, or, O, Sweet Molly Malone
Come, Landlord, Fill the Flowing Bowl (English student song)
The Harp That Once Thro' Tara's Halls
Lavender's Blue (Diddle Diddle, or, Dilly, Dilly)
My Love Is Like a Red, Red Rose
O Soldier, Won't You Marry Me?
Robin Adair (Eileen Aroon) (ancient Celtic)

1758–70

The Girl I Left Behind Me (Brighton Camp) (known as early as 1758–70, it did not appear in print until 1808)

1760

Lass with the Delicate Air (Young Molly Who Lives at the Foot of the Hill)

1763

At seven years of age, Wolfgang Amadeus Mozart plays before the court at Versailles. The following year in London he meets Johann Christian Bach, a composer whose work he much admires, and before the close of 1765 he will finish his first symphony. Franz Joseph Haydn's Symphony No. 22 in E-flat *(Philosopher)* is first performed in 1764, followed, in two years by his *Great Organ Mass* in E-flat. In 1766 he will also become Kapellmeister to Prince Esterházy of Hungary.

1765

Kol Nidre (possibly as early as the fifteen century)

Mother Goose's Melodies. These melodies with *English* words are published this year. The origin of the melodies is thought to be traditional French, and include among others: Baa, Baa, Black Sheep; Ding Dong Bell; Fiddle Dee Dee; Georgie Porgie; Hey, Diddle Diddle; Hickory, Dickory, Dock, Humpty Dumpty; I Love Little Pussy; I Saw Three Ships Come Sailing; Jack and Jill; Jack Sprat; The Jolly Miller; Little Bo-Peep; Little Boy Blue; Little Jack Horner; Little Miss Muffet; Little Tommy Tucker; Mistress Mary Quite Contrary; (Here We Go Round) The Mulberry Bush; Old King Cole; Please Porridge Hot; Peter Peter Pumpkin Eater; Polly Put the Kettle On; Rock-a-Bye (Hush-a-Bye) Baby (with English words, see 1884); Simple Simon; Sing a Song of Sixpence; There Was an Old Woman Who Lived in a Shoe; Tom, Tom, the Piper's Son; Upstairs Downstairs

Twinkle, Twinkle, Little Star, or, **Ah! Vous Diraije Maman,** or, **ABCDEFG** (The Alphabet Song) (an adaptation in 1834), or, **Baa, Baa, Black Sheep**

1767

Hallelujah Chorus (from the *Messiah*, m. Handel)

1770

Handel's *Messiah* receives its first New York performance and Ludwig van Beethoven is born in Bonn.

1775

Believe Me If All Those Endearing Young Charms
The World Turned Upside Down, or, **Derry Down**

1778

Oh! Dear, What Can the Matter Be?

1780

Drink to Me Only with Thine Eyes (words from Ben Jonson's "To Celia" published in 1616; music first published 1780)

1782

Adeste Fideles
Gaudeamus Igitur (some of the words are from 1267)

c.1782

Hunt Theme (Tantivy! Tantivy! Tantivy!) (A-Hunting We Will Go). This may be related to "Hi Ho the Merry-O" (A-Hunting We Will Go)

1783

For He's a Jolly Good Fellow, or, **Malbrouk,** or, **We Won't Go Home Until Morning,** or, **The Bear Went Over the Mountain.** Melody may date from the Crusades.

1784

All Through the Night (Ar Hyd y Nos)
Deck the Halls with Boughs of Holly (lyrics first published in 1881)

1786

Mozart's *The Marriage of Figaro* is first performed in Vienna.

1788

Ye Banks and Braes O' Bonnie Doon

1789

The French Revolution begins, while in the United States George Washington is inaugurated President. In 1788

Mozart had written his last three symphonies (E-flat, G-minor, and C *(Jupiter))* in six weeks. He would die two years later.

The Lass of Richmond Hill

1790

The Marriage of Figaro Overture (m. Mozart)

1792

Then living in Vienna, Beethoven publishes his first music, Piano Trios, op. 1, and composer Gioacchino Antonio Rossini is born in Italy.

Irish Washerwoman, or, **The Scotch Bagpipe Melody**
La Marseillaise (m. Rouget de Lisle)

1796

Comin' Thro' the Rye (If a Body Meet a Body)
Minuet in G (m. Beethoven)

1797

Austrian composer Franz Schubert and Italian opera composer Gaetano Donizetti are both born this year.

1798–1802

The Wearin' o' the Green

1799

Pathétique Sonata (m. Beethoven)

1801

High Barbaree

1802

Moonlight Sonata (m. Beethoven)

1803

In France, the Corsican artillery officer Napoleon Bonaparte overthrows the corrupt Directory which has governed France since the Revolution of 1789. He becomes First Consul, and, the next year, Emperor Napoleon I of France.

1805

Beethoven's Third Symphony, the *Eroica* (originally the *Bonaparte),* premieres in Vienna, followed that same year by his opera *Leonore,* the original version of *Fidelio.*

1809

Composer, pianist, conductor, and organist Felix (Bartholdy) Mendelssohn is born. In the next year are born German composer Robert Schumann, Polish pianist and composer Frédéric Chopin and, in 1811, Franz Liszt, also a pianist and composer.

1810

Für Elise (m. Beethoven)

1811

Au Clair de la Lune (probably traditional)
Frére Jacques (probably traditional)

1813

In England, the Royal Philharmonic Society is founded. In Germany, composer Wilhelm Richard Wagner is born, and in Italy, composer Giuseppe Verdi.

The Barber of Seville (m. Rossini)
'Tis the Last Rose of Summer

1815

Napoleon is exiled to Elba after the French defeat at Waterloo. Though not successful at first, Rossini's *Barber of Seville* is premiered at Rome in 1816, reaching New York a mere three years later.

1820

Du, Du, Liegst Mir im Herzen (folksong)

1821

Invitation to the Dance (m. Weber)

1823

Moment Musicale (m. Schubert)

1824

Billy Boy
Charlie Is My Darlin'
Serenade (m. Schubert)

c.1824

John Anderson, My Jo

[*Ed. Note:* Classical and popular compositions originating in Europe subsequent to 1824 should be sought in the American section of this chronicle, where they have been combined with the American section beginning *1826–1827.* In the two sections that follow, *Colonial Era in America, 1609–1775* and *Post-Colonial Era, 1776–1825,* primarily native American songs are listed.]

THE COLONIAL ERA IN AMERICA, 1609–1775

1609

In the New World in September, Manhattan, an island roughly 12 1/2 miles long and 2 1/2 miles at its greatest width, and the great natural harbor surrounding it have been claimed for the Dutch East India Company by the English explorer Hendrik Hudson sailing under the flag of the Netherlands. The island is a quiet wilderness. The only sound is the soughing of the wind in the branches of the abundant stands of chestnut, oak, walnut, and pine trees. The boughs of the wild apple and peach trees are depressed with the weight of their fruit. Bears, beaver, deer, foxes, elk, otters, raccoons, wolves, and other animals can be seen. The flights of passenger pigeons are thick enough to cast shadows like passing clouds, and fifty-pound wild turkeys flap in the bush. Whales, and porpoises cavort in the harbor. In some inlets the shellfish have been undisturbed for so long that some of the oysters found are a foot in length.

Writes Hudson in his quarters on the *Half Moon:* "It [Manna-hatin] is as beautiful a land as one can hope to tread upon." Robert Juet, Hudson's navigator adds in his log: "The people of the Countery came aboord of us making shew of love, and gave us Tabacco and Indian wheat."

In future years, the Dutch colonize the southern tip of Manhattan, which becomes the city of Nieuw Amsterdam, established by its first governor, Peter Minuit, in 1626. On the northern limit of the settlement, a wall is constructed to keep the cows from getting out at night and inebriated Indians from getting in. The site of this wall is later known as Wall Street.

In 1664, the English, no longer accepting the Connecticut River as the western boundary of their colony of New England,* colonize what is now known as New Haven, and then move southwest to seize Nieuw Amsterdam from its Dutch governor, Peter Stuyvesant, and the Dutch East India Company (an event commemorated in the 1938 Kurt Weill and Maxwell Anderson Broadway musical *Knickerbocker Holiday*). They rename the tiny city on the island New York after the Duke of York, brother of the king, and settle in the district beyond the village wall, naming it with English nostalgia, Greenwich Village.

There is an old Indian trail on Manhattan Island that soon begins to serve as a cowpath along which the cows of Nieuw Amsterdam are led to pasture north of the village. The only street which runs the full length of the island, it is later developed and named Broad Wagon Way, and then simply Broadway. In 1664 Broadway is barely 1664 feet long. But Broadway moves north about ten blocks every ten years and is ultimately extended on the mainland to Albany, the capital of New York State, 150 miles distant, making it the longest street in the world. Said Maurice Barrymore in the late nineteenth century: "This is Broadway, the longest street with the shortest memory."

The neighboring Dutch colony of Breukelen, on Long Island, later becomes Brooklyn. The northern part of Manhattan Island is named after the Dutch town of Haarlem. A favorite custom of the people of Nieuw Amsterdam is to cross the Haarlem River at the north end of the island to the mainland, where a picnic and some de-

*The first permanent English settlement in America was founded at Jamestown, Virginia, on May 13, 1607. It was also the site of the first representative government in North America (1619).

licious cold fresh milk might be enjoyed at the farm of the Dane, Jonas Bronck. Bronck's place later comes to be known as The Bronx.

1612–20 (Popular primarily in the American colonies)

Traditional English hymns are brought to America by the Pilgrims, who use "The Psalmbook of Miles Standish" (The Ainsworth Psalter) (see also *Ye Olde New England Psalm-Tunes, 1620–1820,* republished in Boston by Oliver Ditson, 1930).

1621

The First Thanksgiving. The First Thanksgiving Day and dinner are celebrated by the Pilgrims and some friendly Indians in Plymouth Colony, on 15 October. The hymn is "A Prayer of Thanksgiving" (1597), sung in Dutch. The more familiar English title and words "We Gather Together To Ask the Lord's Blessing" was not published until 1894. Originally English, the Pilgrims acquired their Dutch in the Netherlands, from which they were expelled by social pressure after fleeing England because of religious persecution.

1640

First American Book Published. The Bay Psalm Book of the Massachusetts Bay colony is the first book to be published in English-held colonial North America.

1697

Street Lights. The first street lighting in New York is provided this year by requiring lanterns to be hung on every seventh house.

1699

First Theatrical Performance. Richard Hunter this year receives the first license granted in New York for a theatrical performance.

1700

The Eighteenth Century. Residents of New York complain of the crush of the downtown crowds as the population of the city approaches five thousand.

1715

Benjamin Franklin's Broadside Ballads. While working at his older brother's press, Benjamin Franklin composes topical songs to be sold in broadside form: "My brother put me on composing occasional ballads. One was called the Lighthouse Tragedy; the other was a sailor's song on the taking of Teach (or Blackbeard the Pirate) . . . and when they were printed he sent me about the town to sell them. The first sold wonderfully, the event being recent, having made a great noise . . ."—*Autobiography*—Franklin is nine years old.

1731

Francis Hopkinson. Francis Hopkinson, "the first native poet-composer of the United States," is born in Philadelphia.

1732–50

Colonial Theatre. In 1732, the theatre is established in New York by an English troupe who rent a building owned by Rip Van Dam on Maiden Lane and Pearl Street. In 1735, there is a first performance of the ballad opera *Flora* in Charleston, South Carolina. In 1736, the first American acting company, in Williamsburg, Virginia, presents the play *The Busybody.* In 1750, true to its Puritan tradition, all stage plays and entertainment are banned in the city of Boston and fines specified: £20 for the performer and £5 for anyone attending the performance. In 1751, *The Beggar's Opera* (1728) is performed in New York at the Nassau Street Theatre, built by the Hallam family of English actors who came over from London that year.

1753–98

Yankee Doodle (melody published in Glasgow as early as 1782)

1774

Some Things Never Change. John Adams, no mean talker himself, visiting New York to urge the American revolution, complains about New Yorkers: "They talk very loud, very fast, and altogether. If they ask you a question, before you can utter three words of your answer, they will break out upon you again, and talk away."

1775

Yankee Doodle. In April, British troops march out of Boston to the tune of "Yankee Doodle" in relief of their comrades at Lexington, who have been under fire from the American colonial "Minute Men." American patriotic fervor is high, and a broadside, *An Alphabet for Little Masters and Misses,* distributed on the streets of New York, begins:

A stands for Americans who scorn to be slaves;
B for Boston, where fortitude their freedom saves;

C for Congress, which, though loyal, will be free;
D stands for defence, 'gainst force and tyranny.

Daniel Boone. American frontiersman Daniel Boone is hired this year to hack a road at the Cumberland Gap through the Appalachian Mountains north to the fertile Indian land of Kaintuck and the Kentucky River. By 1800 some 400,000 settlers have left the eastern seaboard states for the West, and three-fourths of them have taken Boone's trail. Lord Byron mentions him in his poem *Don Juan,* and soon all the world is to know about Daniel Boone.

POST-COLONIAL ERA, 1776–1825

1776

The Declaration of Independence and the Birth of the United States. On June 11, the Continental Congress, composed of delegates from all the British colonies in North America save Canada, appoints John Adams, Benjamin Franklin, Thomas Jefferson, Robert R. Livingston, and Roger Sherman to draft a declaration of independence. On July 4, the final text of the Declaration is adopted. A copy of the Declaration arrives in New York, on July 9, and is read to the troops assembled by General Washington on the Common. The enthusiastic populace rushes to the Bowling Green and tears down the lead statute of King George III. The lead scrap is later returned to the British as bullets.

Mrs. Murray, the Dearest Enemy. The nearly defeated remnant of the American army is trapped on Brooklyn Heights, and faces annihilation at the hands of the British. But in a heavy fog, Washington spirits his army across the East River to Manhattan and flees to the West Side in an effort to join the American General Putnam, who leads the other division of American troops already on Manhattan. They combine forces at what is now Broadway and Forty-third Street and steal north up the West Side to Washington Heights.

Only a half-mile away, the British General Howe pursuing Washington and Putnam, pauses in the broiling sun at the inviting green lawn of the Murray House at Murray Hill where Mrs. Murray, a loyal daughter of the American Revolution, invites him and his officers to stop for luncheon, and some say, for breakfast. While Howe dallies with Mrs. Murray, Washington and the American Revolution are saved.

This victory of Mrs. Murray's arms over British arms is told with great fun in the Rodgers and Hart and Her-

bert Fields Broadway musical *Dearest Enemy* (1925). See "Here in My Arms" (1925).

1777

The Stars and Stripes. The Stars and Stripes are adopted this year as the flag of the United States, an occasion commemorated since 1923 on June 14, Flag Day. See "The Star Spangled Banner" (1814) and "Stars and Stripes Forever" (1897).

1778

General Washington. On May 11 at Valley Forge, General George Washington, commander in chief of the Continental Army opposing the British, in an effort to raise morale arranges for a performance of Addison's play *Cato.*

Chester (colonial marching song). This is the first popular composition by an American writer, William Billings.

1780–83

To Anacreon in Heaven (melody the same as for "The Star Spangled Banner")

1781

General Washington Defeats the British. The Revolutionary War ends as Washington's army and the fleet of French Admiral De Grasse trap Lord Cornwallis and his British troops on the Yorktown Peninsula. The siege ends on October 19; at the surrender the American fifes and drums play "Yankee Doodle," whereas the British, with suitable irony, play "The World Turned Upside Down."

1789

President Washington Laughs. A little theatre on John Street in New York established in 1767 plays host this year to George Washington, now President of the United States. The President, whose grim visage reflected his self-consciousness about his false teeth, creates a minor sensation by actually laughing (the only such occasion on record) during a performance of *Darby's Return.*

1794

James Hewitt's *Tammany, or the Indian Chief,* the first opera written in America, is performed in New York.

1796

Sailor's Hornpipe

1798

Adams and Liberty, or, **The Boston Patriotic Song** (melody the same as for "The Star Spangled Banner")
Hail Columbia!

1800

The Nineteenth Century. The population of the sixteen United States is now more than five million.

c. 1800

Amazing Grace

1807

Robert Fulton and the Steamboat. On August 17, Robert Fulton's steamboat *Clermont* sets out from Manhattan on the 150-mile trip to Albany; she makes an average speed of five miles per hour. She also fulfills the conditions stipulated for establishing Robert Fulton and Robert R. Livingston's monopoly for steam navigation of the Hudson. Commodore Vanderbilt, however, ignores Fulton's exclusive right of steam navigation in New York waters and operates first a ferry from New Jersey to New York, and later a steamboat line to Albany. Fulton's in-

vention will lead to a new show business vehicle, the showboat (see 1817 and 1845).

1808

New Orleans Opera House. The first opera house in North America is built in New Orleans.

Believe Me If All Those Endearing Young Charms

1809

Washington Irving's Gotham. Author Washington Irving applies the name "Gotham" to New York. The "wise men" of twelfth-century Gotham in Nottinghamshire, England, pretended to be silly and stupid to keep King John from building a palace there, and so avoided the consequent increase in parish taxes. Irving publishes a satirical *"History of New York . . . by Diedrich Knickerbocker,"* an amusing account of New Amsterdam, and from which derives the sobriquet "Father Knickerbocker" for New York City. The name knickers for knee-length trousers gathered below the knee comes from Cruikshank's illustrations for the *History.*

1812

War of 1812. The tide of the war turns against the British in 1814 after their unsuccessful 25-hour bombardment of Fort McHenry. Francis Scott Key of Maryland observes the engagement from a British man-of-war and creates the lyrics for "The Star Spangled Banner" on September 13.

Hail to the Chief (Sir Walter Scott)

1813

The Minstrel Boy
'Tis the Last Rose of Summer
Ye Parliament of England

1814

The Star Spangled Banner (see 1780)

1815

O (Ach) Du Lieber Augustin. Both "Molly (Polly) Put the Kettle On" and "Did You Ever See a Lassie" have the same melody.

1817

Showboat. The first professional theatrical performance on a showboat is presented in Natchez, Mississippi, on December 10.

1818

The Banjo. Joel Sweeney develops the banjo from a gourd with strings to the familiar four string instrument known today (see ''Banjo Song'').

Banjo Song
Silent Night, Holy Night (Josef Mohr, M. Franz Gruber)

1819

Rossini's *Barber of Seville* (English version) plays New York only three years after its premiere in Rome, and six months before it is heard in Paris (see 1825).

1820

John Peel (D'Ye Ken John Peel)

1821

The Santa Fe Trail. As Mexico gains its freedom from Spain, the first reliable overland route to what is now New Mexico and California via Santa Fe in Old Mexico is established in November. By 1850, a monthly stage runs the Trail from Independence, Missouri, to Santa Fe, New Mexico (then Old Mexico), and by 1860, more than 9000 men, 6000 mules, 27,000 oxen, and 3000 wagons are employed on the Trail. This is supplanted in 1880 by the Atchison, Topeka and Santa Fe Railroad, which runs along a good part of the original Trail.

1823

Home Sweet Home

1824

Fifth Avenue. Fifth Avenue in New York now runs as far north as Thirteenth Street.

1825

The Erie Canal. The Erie Canal, connecting New York City and Albany on the Hudson River with Buffalo on Lake Erie is completed. It is over 350 miles long and cost seven million dollars to construct. The Canal expands New York City's financial base and opens markets to the farmers of the Great Lakes region while aiding migration to the Midwest. The ''Ca-naw-lers'' would later inspire the songs ''Fifteen Miles (Years) on the Erie Canal (Low Bridge!—Everbody Down)'' (pub. 1913) and ''The E-ri-ee Canal'' (*c.* 1850).

First Italian Opera in America. The Italian-language version of Rossini's *The Barber of Seville* is introduced to America in New York at the Park Row Theatre (see 1819).

1826–1875 ERA

1826

Fiftieth Anniversary of the United States. Native American writings and songs become popular as the United States turns fifty. On July 4, former Presidents John Adams and Thomas Jefferson die, and Stephen Collins Foster is born.

Theatre from England. Edmund Kean, widely acclaimed English actor, becomes popular in New York City; *A Midsummer Night's Dream* is first performed.

James Fenimore Cooper. James Fenimore Cooper publishes his highly popular *Last of the Mohicans.*

Ave Maria (m. Schubert)
Marche Militaire (m. Schubert)

c. 1826

Shenandoah (Across the Wide Missouri) (traditional American sea chantey, but later associated with the West)

1827

The Coal Black Rose
God Rest You Merry, Gentlemen (English, *c.* 1770)
My Long-Tail Blue

1829

Mike Fink and Paul Bunyan. The legendary exploits of Mike Fink, the Ohio and Mississippi river boatman, and Paul Bunyan and Babe, his blue ox, become popular.

Rails. The first steam locomotive arrives in the United States, imported from England. See "John Henry" (1873).

William Tell Overture (m. Rossini)

1830

Cape Cod Girls
Jim Crow
Old Colony Times

c. 1830

Blow Ye Winds, Heigh Ho (sea chantey)
Boston Come-All Ye. Mentioned by Rudyard Kipling in *Captain Courageous* under the title of "The Fishes", it was possibly known in Scotland as "Blow the Wind Southerly."
Rock-a My Soul (in the Bosom of Abraham)

1832

America (My Country 'Tis of Thee). The new lyrics are set to the music of "God Save the King" (1744).
Nocturne op. 9 no. 2 (m. Chopin)
Rock of Ages

1833

The First Noël
Long Long Ago

1834

Grande Valse Brilliante (m. Chopin)
Turkey in the Straw, or, **Old Zip Coon**

1835

Wond'rous Love

1836

Davy Crockett and the Alamo. Frontiersman and Indian fighter Davy Crockett, three-time member of Congress from Tennessee, loses his life this year in the heroic defense of the Alamo (the Cottonwood).

1837

Vaudeville. The first vaudeville show in New York City is presented at Niblo's Garden, on the east side of Broadway, between Prince and Houston Streets.

On Wings of Song (m. Mendelssohn)

1838

East Side, West Side. The numbered streets of New York City are divided into East and West this year, with the house numbering beginning at Fifth Avenue with one.

Annie Laurie
Flow Gently, Sweet Afton
She Wore a Yellow Ribbon (All Round My Hat I Wore a Yellow Ribbon)

1839

Joy to the World (Antioch). Hymn derived from Handel.
Prélude op. 28 no. 7 (m. Chopin)
Träumerei (m. Schumann)

1840

The Funeral March (m. Chopin)
Kathleen Mavourneen
Kemo-Kimo
Polonaise Militaire (m. Chopin)
Rocked in the Cradle of the Deep

1843

Quickstep. The new dance craze this year and for the next two decades is the quickstep, sometimes danced to such interesting titles as the "Yale Quickstep" (1843), the "Phoenix Quickstep" (1849), the "No. 1 Hook and Ladder Quickstep" (1853). "President Pierce's March and Quickstep" (1853), the "Millard Fillmore Quickstep" (1856), the "Lincoln Quickstep" (1860), and the "Emancipation Quickstep" (1863) (none of these popular enough to be indexed).

Minstrels in New York. The Original Virginia Minstrels troupe opens in New York City at the Bowery Amphitheater. The company includes Dan Emmett, a violinist and composer of "Old Dan Tucker" (1843), "The Blue Tail Fly" (1846) and, later, "Dixie" (1860) among others. This group popularizes the use of Mr. Bones and

Mr. Tambourine as endmen, and Mr. Interlocuter as middleman in the now familiar minstrel routines.

Columbia, the Gem of the Ocean (English music)
I Dreamt I Dwelt in Marble Halls (*The Bohemian Girl*)
Old Dan Tucker
The Old Oaken Bucket (melody from the English tune "Araby's Daughter," 1822, and the words from an American poem published in 1817)

1844

Samuel F.B. Morse and His Telegraph. Samuel F.B. Morse demonstrates to Congress the practicality of the telegraph, transmitting a message over wire from Washington to Baltimore. This invention is later celebrated in the song title "The Telegraph (Song)" (1865) (not indexed).

Buffalo Gals (Won't You Come Out Tonight?), or **Lubly Fan.** Sung by Ole Jim in Mark Twain's *Huckleberry Finn* (see 1876).
Flying Dutchman **Overture** (m. Wagner)
(Go Tell Aunt Rhody) The Old Grey Goose (Is Dead)
Open Thy Lattice Love
Spring Song (m. Mendelssohn)
Vive la Compagnie (Vive L'Amour; traditional, from the French)
Wedding March (*A Midsummer Night's Dream*) (m. Mendelssohn)

c. 1844
Lolly Too Dum
Skip to My Lou

1845

Showboat (II). First theatrical performance on a showboat in New York City is presented at the foot of Canal Street, April 2.
Baseball. The founding of baseball as a national game is furthered by the establishment of the Knickerbocker Baseball Club of New York, the first baseball club to be organized in America.

Blest Be the Tie That Binds
Pilgrims' Chorus (*Tannhäuser*) (m. Wagner)
Scenes That Are Brightest (*Maritana*)

1846

Christy's Minstrels. The original Christy's Minstrels make their New York debut April 27. Other troupes famous in the history of minstrel shows to play New York over the years were led by Al G. Fields, Primrose and West, Lew Dockstader, and George "Honey Boy" Evans. Evans is to co-author the song "In the Good Old Summertime" (1902) and is celebrated himself in the song "Honey Boy" (1907).

Green Grow the Lilacs
Jimmy Crack Corn, or, **The Blue Tail Fly**
Sur le Pont d'Avignon (traditional French round)

1847

Liebesträume (m. Liszt)

c. 1847
The Marine's Hymn

1848

The Night Before Christmas. Clement C. Moore's "The Night Before Christmas, or A Visit from Saint Nicholas" is published. There have been various references in popular song to this poem which has been continuously popular for more than 130 years. A recent addition to the legend of Santa Claus's eight reindeer: Dasher, Dancer, Prancer, Vixen, Comet, Cupid, Dunder, and Blixen, is Rudolph. See "Rudolph, the Red-Nosed Reindeer" (1949).

Ah! So Pure (*Martha*) (m. Flotow)
Oh! Susanna
Sweet Alice (Ben Bolt)
(Old) Uncle Ned

1849

The Forty-Niners' California Gold Rush and "Oh! Susanna." In January 1848 James Marshall, boss of John Sutter's mill on the Sacramento River in California, discovers traces of a shiny metal in the tailrace of the mill. He and Sutter hurriedly consult the *Encyclopedia Americana* at Sutter's house to make sure that it is, as they suspect, gold. They succeed in keeping the news secret for only a short time: There is gold in California.

By ship around Cape Horn, by ship to Panama and up the west coast, or by the Santa Fe Trail, the rush to California is on. Along the way the California-bound gold hunters were singing Stephen Foster's ''Oh! Susanna'' (1848), ''Sacramento'' (1849), and ''What Was Your Name in the States?'' (1849).

Actors' Feud at the Astor Place Opera. Appearance of the English actor William Charles Macready causes a riot killing twenty-two and injuring thirty-six at the Astor Place Opera House in New York City, incited by partisans of Irish-American actor Edwin Forrest.

Saxophone. A new brass instrument, the saxophone, arrives in America. Developed by Belgian instrument maker Adolphe Sax, it permanently alters the character of band music.

Coronation March (m. G. Meyerbeer)
The Happy Farmer (m. Schumann)
Nelly Bly
Nelly Was a Lady
What Was Your Name in the States?

1850

Jenny Lind and P.T. Barnum. Swedish opera star Jenny Lind is presented at the Castle Garden in New York City, September 11, by P.T. Barnum. Barnum charges $225 for an opening night seat.

New York Inventions. Elias Howe makes possible both the manufacture of clothing in quantity and the beginning of the New York City fashion industry with his invention this year of the sewing machine. At 201 Cherry Street, the Hecker brothers, who mill flour, install the first ''vertical screw railway,'' known to us now as the elevator, thus making possible the future skyline of New York.

De Camptown Races (Gwine To Run All Night)
It Came Upon a Midnight Clear
Juanita (from a Spanish air)
The Merry Wives of Windsor—**Overture** (m. Otto Nicolai)
Sacramento
Santa Lucia

c. 1850
The E-ri-ee Canal
I Gave My Love a Cherry (The Riddle Song)

1851

Melville, Hawthorne, and Stowe. Melville's *Moby Dick* and Hawthorne's *House of the Seven Gables* are pub-

lished, and Harriet Stowe's anti-slavery novel *Uncle Tom's Cabin* appears as a magazine serial.

Arkansas Traveler
Hungarian Rhapsody No. 2 (m. Liszt)
Old Folks at Home (Way Down Upon the Swanee River)
Ring De Banjo
Wait for the Wagon

1852

Stephen Collins Foster. Having earlier written the hit songs ''Open Thy Lattice Love'' (1844), ''Oh! Susanna'' (1848), ''(Old) Uncle Ned'' (1848), ''Nelly Was a Lady'' (1849), ''Nelly Bly'' (1849), ''De Camptown Races (Gwine To Run All Night)'' (1850) and ''Ring De Banjo'' (1851), Stephen Foster this year becomes America's best-selling popular composer having sold 130,000 copies of ''Old Folks at Home (Way Down Upon the Swanee River)'' (1851).

Britannia, the Gem of the Ocean (m. Thomas E. Williams)
Massa's in de Cold Ground
Row, Row, Row Your Boat (round). (Earliest words 1852, earliest music published 1881, but most surely performed before that.)
Wedding March (*Lohengrin*) (m. Wagner)

1853

Steinway. Heinrich Steinweg, a piano maker from Germany, establishes Steinway & Sons on March 5, in Astoria, New York City. The company slogan: ''The instrument of the immortals.''

Uncle Tom's Cabin. A dramatized version of *Uncle Tom's Cabin* (see 1851) runs for 200 performances at the Chatham Theatre, in Chatham Square, New York.

Drink It Down, Drink It Down (later known as ''Balm of Gilead,'' or, ''Bingo'')
Good Night Ladies (Merrily We Roll Along) (for first part of melody see ''Someone's in the Kitchen with Dinah''; for second part of melody see ''Mary Had a Little Lamb'' (1867))
My Old Kentucky Home
Old Dog Tray
Pop Goes the Weasel (probably English traditional)
Sweet Betsy from Pike (Vilikens and His Dinah) (First known printed version this year, although may date to 1840 or earlier.)

1853–67

Good King Wenceslas (from Swedish melody, 1582)

1854

Carnival of Venice (m. J. Bellak)
Hard Times Come Again No More
Jeanie with the Light Brown Hair
Poet and Peasant Overture (m. von Suppé)

1855

Come Where My Love Lies Dreaming
Fantaisie Impromptu op. 66 (m. Chopin)
(Oh) Happy Day (see also "How Dry I Am," c. 1921)
Hark the Herald Angels Sing (m. Mendelssohn)
Kamennoi-Ostrow (m. Anton Rubinstein)
Listen to the Mocking Bird
Londonderry Air (based on a traditional Irish melody from County Derry) Revived in 1913 as "Danny Boy."
The Lone Fish (Meat) Ball
Melody in F (m. Rubinstein)

1857

Mardi Gras. New Orleans celebrates its First Mardi Gras in the Vieux Carré (French Quarter.)

Jingle Bells (The One-Horse Open Sleigh)
Lorena
We Three Kings of Orient

1858

Can Can (*Orpheus in the Underworld*) (m. Offenbach)
(Here We Go 'Round) The Mulberry Bush
The Yellow Rose of Texas, or, **Song of the Texas Rangers**

1859

Ave Maria (m. Gounod)
Hungarian Dance No. 5 (Béla Kélar, arr. Brahms)
Nearer, My God, to Thee (words, 1841)
Soldiers' Chorus (*Faust*) (m. Gounod)

1860

Civil War. The American Civil war threatens between North and South over the issue of slavery. Of a population of almost 32 million, 4 million blacks are slaves.

Ironically, "Dixie (Dixie's Land)," a song written the previous year by a minstrel (a white entertainer in black face) living in the North, Daniel D. Emmett, becomes the most popular Southern marching song, along with "Maryland, My Maryland." "Dixie" was first performed in 1854 from the stage by Bryant's minstrels at 472 Broadway, in New York. Some of the more important songs that the North adopted were "Battle Hymn of the Republic (Glory Hallelujah)" (1862) as well as the "John Brown's Body" lyric variation of the same song, "Tenting on the Old Camp Ground" (1864), "Tramp, Tramp, Tramp" (1864), and "Marching Through Georgia" as the war comes to a close in 1865.

Annie Lisle (Far Above Cayuga's Waters)
Dixie (Dixie's Land)
Old Black Joe
When I Saw Sweet Nellie Home

c. 1860
Streets of Laredo (The Cowboy's Lament) (melody originally Irish)

1861

Abide with Me
Aura Lee
The Bonnie Blue Flag (based on the Irish tune "The Jaunting Car")
Holy! Holy! Holy! Lord God Almighty
John Brown's Body, see "Battle Hymn of the Republic" (1862)
Maryland, My Maryland (O Tannenbaum, O Tannenbaum!)
The Vacant Chair

1862

Battle Hymn of the Republic (melody known as "Glory Hallelujah" in 1856 or earlier; then in 1861 became "John Brown's Body" and finally given this title in 1862)
Killarney
Kingdom Coming

1863

Lewis Carroll. In England, Lewis Carroll (Charles L. Dodgson) writes for young Alice Liddell *Alice's Adventures Underground.* Actress Ellen Terry, of whom Lewis Carroll was a lifelong admirer, said: "He was as fond of me as he could ever be of anyone over the age of ten."

Johnny Schmoker
Just Before the Battle, Mother
Sweet and Low
When Johnny Comes Marching Home

1864

Barcarolle *(Tales of Hoffman)* (m. Offenbach)
Beautiful Dreamer
Father, Dear Father, Come Home with Me Now
Goober Peas
Oh Where, Oh Where, Has My Little Dog Gone (music based on the third movement of Beethoven's Sixth Symphony *(Pastorale)* (1809), and this, in turn, on an English traditional dance, *c.* 1260)
La Paloma (The Dove)
Tenting on the Old Camp Ground (Tenting Tonight)
Tramp, Tramp, Tramp (the Boys Are Marching)

1865

The American Civil War Ends. General Lee surrenders to General Grant at Appomattox Court House in Virginia on April 9. Dead on both sides: almost 525,000 men out of a white population of approximately 27 million.

Lincoln. On April 14, President Lincoln attends Ford's Theatre and is shot during a performance of "Our American Cousin." He dies the next morning.

Vaudeville and Tony Pastor. Vaudeville (five-a-day) or "variety" becomes even more popular. Tony Pastor opens "legitimate" vaudeville at his Opera House in New York, August 14.

Hans Brinker. Mary M. Dodge publishes *Hans Brinker, or, The Silver Skates.* It receives a prize from the French Academy.

Ich Liebe Dich (m. Grieg)
Johnny Is My Darling
The Little Brown Church (in the Vale)
Marching Through Georgia

Negro spirituals begin to appear in printed form this year. (See also 1917, 1918, 1921, 1922, 1927, and 1930 for Negro spirituals arranged and printed by black musician Harry Thacker Burleigh.)

All God's Chillun Got Wings
Down by the Riverside (Ain't Gwine Study War No More)
Dry Bones
Ezekiel Saw de Wheel
Go Tell It on the Mountain
(O) Hand Me Down My Walking Cane
I Ain't Gonna Grieve My Lord No More
I Got (a Robe) Shoes (All God's Chillun Got Shoes)
Joshua Fit de Battle of Jericho
Look Down, Look Down That Lonesome Road

Never Said a Mumblin' Word
Oh, Mary, Don't You Weep, Don't You Mourn
(Gimme Dat) Old Time Religion
One More River To Cross
Roll, Jordan, Roll
Were You There When They Crucified My Lord

1866

The Black Crook and the Invention of the Broadway Musical. The first long-run American musical, *The Black Crook,* with libretto by Charles Barras, opens at Niblo's Garden (see 1837) on September 12. An amalgam of an acting company and a ballet troupe, it combined for the first time ladies in tights with melodrama. The show, which introduced the high-kicking French can-can and the "split" to American audiences, ran for 475 performances. The story of *The Black Crook* was retold in the 1954 Broadway musical *The Girl in Pink Tights,* with words and music by Leo Robin and Sigmund Romberg.

Song Royalties. For the first time a popular composer receives royalties from a publisher on the sale of individual copies of the composer's work (as opposed to outright sale of a song for a flat fee). See "Come Back to Erin," by Claribel (Charlotte Barnard).

More Baseball. Popular in the Union Army during the Civil War, this new game is celebrated in the song "Baseball Fever" (not indexed).

Come Back to Erin
Elégie (m. J. Massenet)
Now I Lay Me Down To Sleep
Tom Dula (Tom Dooley)
When You and I Were Young Maggie

1867

Nursery Rhymes. Sarah Josepha Hale wrote (1830) what have been described as the four best-known lines of verse in the English language, "Mary had a little lamb." These are set to the second melody of "Good Night Ladies (Merrily We Roll Along)."

Angel's Serenade (m. Gaetano Braga)
Artist's Life (m. J. Strauss)
The Blue Danube (m. J. Strauss)
I Was Seeing Nellie Home, *see* "When I Saw Sweet Nellie Home"
Mary Had a Little Lamb

Song of the Volga Boatman (traditional Russian folksong, probably much earlier than this date)

When I Saw Sweet Nellie Home (Aunt Dinah's Quilting Party)

1868

Buffalo Bill. General Phil Sheridan, U.S. Cavalry, employs William Frederick Cody, then twenty-two, as his regimental chief of scouts in the West. At twenty-two Cody had already been a Pony Express rider, stagecoach driver, guide, hunter, and trapper, and he was a good friend of Wild Bill Hickok. The extra wide hats he ordered from John B. Stetson of Philadelphia led to the tradition of "ten-gallon" hats. Buffalo Bill Cody introduced the word "cowboy" into the lexicon (see also 1883).

The Daring Young Man (on the Flying Trapeze)

Light Cavalry Overture (m. von Suppé)

O Little Town of Bethlehem

Sweet By and By

Tales from the Vienna Woods (m. J. Strauss)

Whispering Hope

1869

Transcontinental Railroad. The Union Pacific Railroad and the Central Pacific Railroad are joined at Promontory Point, Utah, to complete the first American transcontinental rail line. The delivery of each hammer blow on the final, gold spike completing the track is reported by telegraph throughout the nation.

Hungarian Dances (m. Brahms)

Little Brown Jug

None But the Lonely Heart (m. Tchaikovsky)

Now the Day Is Over

Shoo Fly, Don't Bother Me

Sweet Genevieve

Wine, Women and Song (m. J. Strauss)

1870

The Buffalo. The vast herds of buffalo on the American plains begin to be exterminated by white hunters who receive fifty cents to $1.25 for each hide. Buffalo, slaughtered at the rate of 1,200,000 per year, by 1883 are almost extinct.

Safe in the Arms of Jesus

Waltz Coppélia (m. Délibes)

c. 1870

Paddle Your Own Canoe

c. 1870–1875

Frankie and Johnny (Were Lovers)

c. 1870–1890

Goodbye Ol' Paint (I Ride an Old Paint, or, I'm a-Leavin' Cheyenne)

Little Old Sod Shanty

Strawberry Roan

1871

The Fisk Singers. The Jubilee Singers, a black choral group from Fisk University in Nashville, Tennessee, specializing in Negro spirituals, tour the east coast of the United States on a successful fund-raising tour.

P.T. Barnum. P.T. Barnum organizes his legendary circus, "The Greatest Show On Earth."

Goodbye, Liza Jane

Onward, Christian Soldiers (m. Sir Arthur Sullivan)

Reuben and Rachel (Reuben, Reuben, I've Been Thinking)

Romeo and Juliet (m. Tchaikovsky)

Sing a Song of Sixpence

A Thousand and One Nights (m. J. Strauss)

1872

World Peace Jubilee. Johann Strauss is invited to America to serve as conductor of the World Peace Jubilee in Boston. Participating are the Fisk University Jubilee Singers, 20,000 vocalists, forty brass bands, and a 1000-piece orchestra.

The Bartered Bride (m. Smetana)

Dance Macabre (m. Saint-Saëns)

Funeral March of a Marionette (m. Gounod)

1873

John Henry

The Mulligan Guard

Piano Concerto (m. Grieg)

Silver Threads Among the Gold

Vienna Life (Wiener Blut) (m. J. Strauss)

c. 1873

Home on the Range (Oh, Give Me a Home Where the Buffalo Roam)
The official Kansas state song.

1874

Du und Du *(Die Fledermaus; m. J. Strauss)*

1875

Maurice Barrymore. Maurice Barrymore (Herbert Blythe) arrives from London. Born in Agra, India, and educated at Cambridge, he abandons the bar for the theatre. In America, he is to co-star with such leading ladies as Mrs. Fiske, Modjeska, Olga Nethersole, and Lily Langtry. His marriage (1876) to Georgiana Drew was to produce those three talented luminaries of the American theatre, Lionel, Ethel (see 1901), and John (see 1903). The Edna Ferber-George S. Kaufman play, *The Royal Family* (1934), is more or less based on the exploits of the Barrymore family.

Piano Concerto No. 1 (m. Tchaikovsky)
Toreador Song *(Carmen;* m. Bizet)

1876–1889 ERA

1876

The United States Centennial. The United States is one hundred years old this year. The event is celebrated with the Centennial Exposition in Philadelphia. Young John Philip Sousa plays the violin in an orchestra conducted by French composer Jacques Offenbach at the Exposition.

Alexander Graham Bell's System. On March 10, in Boston, Alexander Graham Bell, twenty-nine, utters the first complete sentence to be transmitted by his invention, the telephone. The device is introduced to the public at the Philadelphia Centennial Exposition, where it greatly interests Dom Pedro II, Emperor of Brazil, who later produces worldwide publicity for Bell. Bell's instrument is sound-powered (has no amplification) and the earpiece (receiver) also serves as the mouthpiece (transmitter). He receives a $10,000 reward from the French government for his invention. The nation's songwriters respond with the "Telephone March" (not indexed) and countless other songs thereafter.

Mark Twain. Mark Twain (Samuel Langhorne Clemens), lecturer, author, newspaperman and wit, publishes *The Adventures of Tom Sawyer.* His *A Connecticut Yankee in King Arthur's Court* would later become the basis for the Rodgers and Hart Broadway musical *A Connecticut Yankee* (1927).

Hammerstein I. Oscar Hammerstein I, former German cigarmaker, enters show business in New York City in the German-language theatre.

Dance of the Hours *(La Gioconda;* m. Amilcare Ponchielli)
Grandfather's Clock
The Hat Father Wore
I'll Take You Home Again Kathleen

March Slav (m. Tchaikovsky)
My Heart at Thy Sweet Voice *(Samson and Delilah;* m. Saint-Saëns)
Pizzicati (from the ballet *Sylvia;* m. Délibes)
The Rose of Killarney
What a Friend We Have in Jesus

1877

Thomas Edison, Sound Recording, and the Phonograph. In 1650, Rostand had the poet Cyrano de Bergerac describe "books made wholly for the ears and not the eyes, in which anybody having a mind to read in it, winds up the machine with a great many little springs and straight, as from the mouth of a man, or a musical instrument, proceed all the distinct and different sounds." Two hundred twenty-seven years later Thomas Alva Edison recites "Mary Had a Little Lamb" into his new dictating machine. As he does so, he becomes the first actually to make, rather than theorize about, a sound recording (on a cylinder) and to play it back successfully.

The Microphone. Emile Berliner of Germany invents the microphone. Berliner's microphone design operates on the loose contact principle originally suggested but never implemented by Count du Moncel of France. The rights to the microphone are acquired by the Bell Telephone Company from Berliner for $50,000 in an effort to defeat the Western Union Telegraph Company's attempt to invade the telephone field. The Bell system prevailed and is today one of the world's largest corporations.

Disc Recording Duplication. Charles Cros of France suggests recording on flat discs rather than on cylinders (as in the Edison method), to permit molding, etching, or engraving copies (see 1887).

Abdulla Bulbul Ameer

Chopsticks (original title ''The Celebrated Chop Waltz'')

In the Gloaming

The Lost Chord (m. Sir Arthur Sullivan)

1878

Aloha Oe (Farewell to Thee)

Carry Me Back to Old Virginny

Emmet's Lullaby

He Is an Englishman (H.M.S. Pinafore)

I Am the Captain of the Pinafore (What Never) (H.M.S. Pinafore)

I'm Called Little Buttercup (H.M.S. Pinafore)

In the Evening by the Moonlight

The Kerry Dance (an adaptation based on the first eight bars of the melody ''The Cuckoo,'' w.m. Margaret Casson, published in England 1790)

Simple Aveu (m. Francis Thomé)

Skidmore Fancy Ball

When I Was a Lad (H.M.S. Pinafore)

Where Was Moses When the Lights Went Out?

1879

Thomas Edison and the Electric Light. Edison constructs the first incadescent lamp this year. Instead of an exposed electric arc, it has a filament of luminous carbonized cotton thread mounted in an evacuated glass bulb.

Gilbert and Sullivan. Last year's London success of *H.M.S. Pinafore* is topped in America. On December 1, Sullivan conducted the original D'Oyly Carte production from the pit of Daly's Fifth Avenue Theatre. Gilbert appeared for that performance as a member of the sailors' chorus. On December 31 they premiered their new operetta *The Pirates of Penzance* at the same theatre.

Alouette (earliest words and music published in Montreal, 1879, but most surely performed before that as a traditional French-Canadian folksong)

Atisket, Ataset

The Babies on Our Block

(Oh Dem) Golden Slippers

The Moldau (m. Smetana)

1880

The Old Chisholm Trail. The Chisholm Trail takes its name from Jesse Chisholm, a half-Cherokee Indian trader who, in 1866, with a cargo of buffalo hides, blazed a trail through the Indian territory from what is now Okla-homa to a trading post near Wichita, Kansas. Hundreds of thousands of Texas long-horns are driven over the trail each year. Sections of it can still be seen along the line of the Atchison, Topeka and Santa Fe Railroad. See ''The Old Chisholm Trail.''

Blow (Knock) the Man Down (sea chantey); first known printed version this year, probably traditional, c. 1830)

Cradle's Empty Baby's Gone

Funiculi—Funicula (m. Luigi Denza)

Hear Dem Bells

Sailing (,Sailing) (over the Bounding Main)

Songs My Mother Taught Me (m. A. Dvořák)

Stéphanie-Gavotte (m. Alphons Czibulka)

Waves of the Danube (Danube Waves) (m. Ivanovici)

c. 1880

The Old Chisholm Trail

1881

Fourteenth Street and Tony Pastor. 14th Street, the predecessor of Broadway, becomes New York City's theatrical center with the opening of Tony Pastor's House on October 24. To attract a feminine clientele for his theatre, Tony Pastor promises that nothing on stage will offend and that there will be no smoking or drinking by the audience. The ladies are often to be offered such door prizes as dress patterns, bags of flour, or half a ton of coal.

Dar's One More Ribber To Cross

Estudiantina (m. P. Lacombe)

Loch Lomond (The Bonnie Bonnie Banks, or, Oh! Ye'll Tak' the High Road) (earliest known printing this year, but possibly from 1746 Scotch traditional)

My Bonnie Lies Over the Ocean (Bring Back My Bonnie to Me)

The Norwegian Dance (m. Grieg)

Peek-a-Boo

The Spanish Cavalier

1882

Jumbo. The legendary elephant, Jumbo, makes his first appearance in P.T. Barnum's Circus. In 1935 he will be the inspiration for the Rodgers and Hart Broadway musical *Jumbo*.

Yiddish Theatre. First performance of Yiddish theatre begins in New York City on August 18.

Goodbye, My Lover, Goodbye
The Skaters (Waltz) (m. Emil Waldteufel)
Sweet Violets
When the Clock in the Tower Strikes Twelve

1883

Buffalo Bill. Buffalo Bill's first *Wild West*, a circus and rodeo featuring for the first time genuine cowboys and Indians, begins its tour of America at the Omaha, Nebraska, Fair Grounds, May 19. An early apprentice and careful student of this extravaganza is Florenz Ziegfeld, age fourteen. He has become quite proficient with a six-shooter in each hand when his father arrives and takes him back home.

Hollywood. Mr. and Mrs. Wilcox acquire a farm in Southern California for $1.25 an acre. Mrs. Wilcox plants the two pots of holly she has brought to the West and decides to name the farm Hollywood.

Edison on Broadway. The Hungarian Kiralfy Brothers' musical production *Excelsior* at Niblo's Garden on Broadway features ''spectacular electric lighting effects under the personal supervision of Thomas A. Edison'' (see also 1885).

The Farmer in the Dell (The Bride Cuts the Cake)
La Golondrina (m. Narciso Serradell)
A Handful of Earth from Mother's Grave
My Nellie's Blue Eyes
Only a Pansy Blossom
Polly Wolly Doodle
Strolling on the Brooklyn Bridge
There Is a Tavern in the Town
Voices of Spring (m. J. Strauss)
When the Robins Nest Again

1884

Always Take Mother's Advice
A Boy's Best Friend Is His Mother
Clementine
Climbing Up the Golden Stairs
España (Rhapsody) (m. Chabrier)
Listen to My Tale of Woe
Love's Old Sweet Song
Rock-a-Bye (Hush-a-Bye) Baby (words from *Mother Goose*, 1765)
While Strolling Through the Park One Day (The Fountain in the Park)
White Wings

1885

Electric Stage Lighting. Six years after Edison's invention of the incandescent electric light, the Lyceum Theatre in New York City is the first to be fully equipped with electricity on April 6.

Annie Oakley. Annie Oakley (Phoebe Ann Moses), who was adopted into his tribe by the great Sioux Indian chief Sitting Bull and given the name ''Watanya Cicilla'' or ''Little Sure Shot,'' joins Buffalo Bill's *Wild West*. Annie once at a distance of thirty feet put a shot through a ten-cent piece held between the thumb and forefinger, and was an expert rider who could accurately shoot a rifle while standing on the back of a galloping horse. Touring Europe in Buffalo Bill's *Wild West*, she once shot the ashes from the end of a cigarette held in the lips of Kaiser Wilhelm II. Unerring as ever, she thus failed to avert World War I.

There was a pigeon shooting match on Thanksgiving in 1875 which paired Frank Butler against fifteen-year-old Annie. He lost the match, but won Annie. They were married the next year and toured together in a partnership that lasted for the remaining fifty years of their lives.

Annie was the inspiration for the Irving Berlin hit Broadway musical *Annie Get Your Gun* (1946), starring Ethel Merman. The show was to have had a score by Jerome Kern, but Kern died shortly before the show was to go into rehearsal. Under the great pressure of replacing Kern at short notice, Berlin produced most of the *Annie Get Your Gun* score in ten days.

American Patrol (The version with the lyrics ''We Must Be Vigilant'' was popular in 1943.)
The Big Rock Candy Mountain
Remember Boy, You're Irish

1886

Statue of Liberty. The Statue of Liberty (its full title is ''Liberty Enlightening the World'') by sculptor Frédéric Bartholdi, standing 305 1/2 feet tall, is presented to the United States by France. It is dedicated on October 28, 1867, at Bedloes Island in New York harbor.

The Gladiator (March)
An Irishman's Home Sweet Home
Johnny Get Your Gun
The Letter That Never Came
What the Dickie-Birds Say

1887

Flat Disc Sound Recordings. Emil Berliner patents the "gramophone" in which the sound is recorded on a lateral cut flat disc. In Berliner's scheme, to improve on Edison's cylinders, lateral grooves are cut by the recording stylus into wax-coated flat zinc discs, which are electroplated to produce "stampers." These stampers then provide a means for the mass producing of disc records, a design used with very little change today.

Muybridge. Eadweard Muybridge's prints of locomotion are published by the University of Pennsylvania and provide the bridge between photography and motion pictures. His sequential technique of photographing animal and human locomotion, called electrophotography, provides a set of twenty-four pictures which, if viewed rapidly in succession, produce moving images. Muybridge's research is sponsored by Leland Stanford, California senator and founder of Stanford University.

"Give Me Your Tired, Your Poor, . . ." Some 371,619 steerage passengers debark at Manhattan's immigration station, Castle Garden.

Away in the Manger
La Cinquantaine (m. Gabriel-Marie)
Comrades
If You Love Me Darling, Tell Me with Your Eyes
Minuet in G (m. Paderewski)
A Night on Bald Mountain (m. Mussorgsky)
Pictures at an Exhibition (m. Mussorgsky)
Slavonic Dances (m. Dvořák)
The Swan (m. Saint-Saëns)

1888

Sousa. Then musical director for eight years of the United States Marine Band, composer John Philip Sousa writes "Semper Fidelis" at the request of President Chester A. Arthur. The piece was soon premiered in front of a reviewing stand on Pennsylvania Avenue with President Harrison and most of the House and Senate. A year later he would write two other early march hits, "The Washington Post" and "The Thunderer."

Berceuse *(Jocelyn)* (m. B. Godard)
Capriccio Espagnol (m. Rimsky-Korsakov)
Drill Ye Tarriers Drill
L'Internationale
Over the Waves (m. Juventino Rosas)
Peer Gynt Suite (m. Grieg)
Polovetsian Dances *(Prince Igor;* m. Borodin)
Scarf Dance (m. Chaminade)
Semper Fidelis
Where Did You Get That Hat?
With All Her Faults I Love Her Still

1889

Kodak. Amateur photography becomes popular as George Eastman advertises the "Kodak" box camera.

Motion Pictures. The final laboratory development of the "Kinetoscope" is completed by Edison. This device is a "peep-show" motion picture machine which projects an image through a slot to be viewed by the individual.

Magnetic Recording. Valdemar Poulson, Danish inventor, makes the first rudimentary experiments with the magnetic recording of sound on steel wire.

Down Went McGinty
Playmates
Slide Kelly Slide
The Thunderer (March)
The Washington Post (March)

1890–1899 ERA (THE GAY NINETIES)

1890

España (Tango) (m. Albéniz)
Intermezzo *(Cavalleria Rusticana;* m. Mascagni)
Little Annie Roonie
Love Will Find a Way (Morse)
Maggie Murphy's Home
Oh, Promise Me
Passing By
Scheherazade (m. Rimsky-Korsakov)
Sleeping Beauty Waltz (m. Tchaikovsky)
Throw Him Down McCloskey

1891

International Copyright Agreement. The first international copyright agreement is adopted. Prior to this year, songs of all composers were pirated with impunity in countries other than their own. Particularly victimized in this respect were British writers Gilbert and Sullivan.

Carnegie Hall. On May 5, Carnegie Hall, the gift to New York City of industrialist Andrew Carnegie, opens at 57th Street and Seventh Avenue, incorporating a brilliant architectural acoustic design by William Tuttle.

Bare Feet on Broadway. This year, a light opera, *The Tar and the Tartar,* features barefoot dancers on Broadway for the first time.

Brown October Ale
Death and Transfiguration (m. R. Strauss)
(What Shall We Do with) The Drunken Sailor (traditional sea chantey)
Hey, Rube!
Little Boy Blue
March of the Dwarfs (m. Grieg)
Molly O!
Narcissus
The Pardon Came Too Late
The Picture That's Turned to the Wall
Ta-ra-ra-boom-der-é (de-ay)

1892

Sheet Music Multi-Million Sales. The multi-million seller epoch of pop music begins as the sheet music sales of the song "After the Ball" amount to $5 million.

Sousa. John Phillip Sousa retires from the Marine Corps and forms his own band of one hundred players, marking the beginning of band concert popularity.

After the Ball
The Bowery
Daddy Wouldn't Buy Me a Bow-Wow
Daisy Bell (A Bicycle Built for Two)
The Man That Broke the Bank at Monte Carlo
My Sweetheart's the Man in the Moon
The Sweetest Story Every Told (Tell Me That You Love Me)
Vesti la Giubba (*Pagliacci;* m. Leoncavallo)
Waltz of the Flowers (*The Nutcracker Suite;* m. Tchaikovsky)

1893

First Movie Studio. Thomas Edison builds the first motion picture film studio, nicknamed "The Black Maria," in West Orange, New Jersey.

Irving Berlin. Irving Berlin (Israel Baline) arrives in the U.S. from Temun, Siberia. Born May 11, 1888, he is one of eight children living with his parents in a four-room cold-water flat at 330 Cherry Street in New York.

Eighteen years later Irving Berlin, a graduate of second grade, has written *four* of the hit songs for that year (see 1911).

Hoochy-Koochy. The Chicago Columbian Exposition celebrating the 400th anniversary of the discovery of America by Columbus opens May 1. It features the exotic dancer Little Egypt who does her famous hoochy-koochy dance, inspiring the song "The Streets of Cairo" (1895). Famous parody words with this music are "Oh, they don't wear pants in the southern part of France."

Lillian Russell. Lillian Russell, the doyenne of Broadway, is required to sing eight high Cs at each performance of this year's comic opera *Princess Nicotine.* See "Airy, Fairy Lillian" (1894).

The Cat Came Back
Do, Do, My Huckleberry Do
From the New World (Symphony) (m. Dvořák)
(Whoopee Ti Yi Yo) Git Along Little Doggies (traditional cowboy song, probably as early as 1880)
Happy Birthday to You (Good Morning to All)
Prelude in C # minor (m. Rachmaninoff)
See, Saw, Margery Daw
Two Little Girls in Blue
When the Roll Is Called Up Yonder

1894

Billboard. Billboard, the authoritative amusement trades' weekly, begins publication in November.

The Passing Show. The first of a series of shows incorporating the modern Broadway musical revue format entitled *The Passing Show* is presented. Productions with the same title appeared annually at the Winter Garden Theatre after 1900.

Victor Herbert. Formerly a cellist at the "Met," Victor Herbert leaves the string section to write eight comic operas and one farce during the period beginning with this year to the end of the century.

Airy, Fairy Lillian
And Her Golden Hair Was Hanging Down Her Back
Dunderbeck, or, Rambling Wreck from Georgia Tech
Forgotten
His Last Thoughts Were of You
The Honeymoon March
Humoresque (m. Dvořák)
I Don't Want To Play in Your Yard
I've Been Working on the Railroad, or, **The Levee Song,** or **Someone's in the Kitchen with Dinah,** (with new words in 1903 as "The Eyes of Texas" (Are Upon You)

Kathleen

The Little Lost Child

Mazel Tov

Meditation (Thaïs; m. Massenet)

My Friend the Major

My Pearl's a Bowery Girl

She Is More To Be Pitied Than Censured

She May Have Seen Better Days

The Sidewalks of New York (East Side, West Side)

(Prayer of Thanksgiving) We Gather Together (first published with English words; based on a traditional Dutch tune from 1597)

You Can't Play in Our Yard Any More

1895

Afternoon of a Faun (m. Debussy)

America, the Beautiful

(Casey Would Waltz with the Strawberry Blonde While) The Band Played On

The Belle of Avenoo A

Down in Poverty Row

A Dream

The Hand That Rocks the Cradle

The Handicap (March)

Just Tell Them That You Saw Me

King Cotton March

My Best Girl's a New Yorker (Corker)

Paupée Valsante (m. Poldini)

Put Me Off at Buffalo

Rastus on Parade

Reverie (m. Debussy)

The Streets of Cairo ("Hoochy-Koochy" is the verse)

The Sunshine of Paradise Alley

Till Eulenspiegel (m. R. Strauss)

1896

Maud Nugent. Maud Nugent writes the lyrics and music for "Sweet Rosie O'Grady," the first song written by a woman that sells a million copies.

Cakewalk. The cakewalk, a syncopated dance popular since plantation times when dancing black couples competed for a cake, is once again in vogue. See "Eli Green's Cakewalk" and later "De Cake Walk Queen" (1900) (not indexed). The first cakewalk hit "Rastus on Parade" (1895) is followed by the most popular cakewalk song "At a Georgia Camp Meeting" (1897).

Ragtime Songs. Possibly the first ragtime song, "My Gal Is a High Born Lady" appears this year. By 1899 songs with the word "rag" in the title become popular. See Scott Joplin's "Maple Leaf Rag" (1899).

All Coons Look Alike to Me

The Amorous Goldfish

El Capitan (March)

Chin, Chin, Chinaman

Eli Green's Cakewalk

Elsie from Chelsea

Going for a Pardon

Happy Days in Dixie

(There'll Be) A Hot Time in the Old Town (Tonight)

I Love You in the Same Old Way—Darling Sue

In a Persian Garden

In the Baggage Coach Ahead

I'se Your Nigger If You Want Me, Liza Jane

Kentucky Babe

Laugh and the World Laughs with You

Love Makes the World Go 'Round

Mister Johnson, Turn Me Loose

Mother Was a Lady, or, If Jack Were Only Here

My Gal Is a High Born Lady

The Red River Valley (based on James Kerrigan's "In the Bright Mohawk Valley," in its turn based on a traditional Canadian folksong)

Rustle of Spring (m. Sinding)

Sweet Rosie O'Grady

To a Wild Rose (Woodland Sketches)

When the Saints Go Marching In

You're Not the Only Pebble on the Beach

1897

Shellac Records. Plastic disc records for phonographs, introduced by Emile Berliner, are composed of shellac with an abrasive added to shape the needle to the groove. They are played with steel, cactus, or thorn needles that have to be changed by the user regularly. Shellac remains the standard until 1950.

Asleep in the Deep

At a Georgia Camp Meeting

Badinage

Beautiful Isle of Somewhere

Break the News to Mother

Danny Deever

Song of India (m. Rimsky-Korsakov)

The Sorcerer's Apprentice (m. Dukas)

Stars and Stripes Forever

Take Back Your Gold

1898

Spanish American War. George Dewey, hero of the naval engagement at Manila, is later celebrated in the song ''Come Home, Dewey, We Won't Do a Thing to You'' (1899).

Deutsche Gramaphon. Emile Berliner and his phonograph design employing the flat disc provide the basis for the establishment of the first disc record company, Deutsche Gramaphon, and shortly thereafter, the British Gramaphone Company.

Telegrams, Telephone Calls, and Baby. Telegraph and telephone songs are all the rage this year and next with ''I Guess I'll Have To Telegraph My Baby,'' ''I've Just Received a Telegram from Baby'' (1899), ''Telephone Me, Baby'' (1899), and ''Kissing Papa Through the Telephone'' (1899) (the last three not indexed).

First Black Broadway Musical. The production of *Clorindy, or, The Origin of the Cake Walk* is the first musical with an all-black cast to play Broadway. See ''Who Dat Say Chicken in Dis Crowd?''

Because (m. Bowers)

Boola Boola (possibly from Hawaii, with new words as the ''Yale Boola'' in 1901)

The Boy Guessed Right

Ciribiribin (m. Pestalozza)

The Fortune Teller

Gold Will Buy Most Anything But a True Girl's Heart

Goodnight, Little Girl, Goodnight

Gypsy Love Song (Slumber On)

I Guess I'll Have To Telegraph My Baby

It's Always Fair Weather When Good Fellows Get Together (A Stein Song)

Just One Girl

Kiss Me, Honey, Do

Mister Johnson, Don't Get Gay

The Moth and the Flame

Musetta's Waltz (*La Bohème;* m. Puccini)

My Old New Hampshire Home

Recessional (m. Reginald De Koven)

The Rosary

Salome

She Is the Belle of New York

She Was Bred in Old Kentucky

When You Were Sweet Sixteen

Who Dat Say Chicken in Dis Crowd?

You're Just a Little Nigger, Still You're Mine, All Mine

1899

Scott Joplin. Scott Joplin, black composer and pianist at the Maple Leaf Club in Sedalia, Missouri, writes ''Maple Leaf Rag''

More Amateur Photography. The amateur photographer and his Brownie box camera are celebrated this year in the song ''Snap Shot Sal'' and later in ''Katie and Her Kodak'' (1904) (neither indexed.)

Florenz Ziegfeld and Anna Held. The early Florenz Ziegfeld Broadway musical production *Papa's Wife* stars Ziegfeld's future wife, Anna Held, and displays for the first time Ziggy's exquisite taste in feminine figures by featuring a chorus line of sixteen fabulous beauties.

Absent

Always (m. Bowers)

Ben Hur Chariot Race (March)

Come Home, Dewey, We Won't Do a Thing to You

Doan Ye Cry, Mah Honey

The Girl I Loved in Sunny Tennessee

Hands Across the Sea (March)

Heart of My Heart (The Story of the Rose)

Hearts and Flowers (melody from 1893.)

Hello! Ma Baby

I'd Leave My Happy Home for You

If You Were Only Mine

Mandy Lee

Maple Leaf Rag

My Little Georgia Rose

My Wild Irish Rose

'O Sole Mio

On the Banks of the Wabash Far Away

Pavanne for a Dead Infanta (Princess) (m. Ravel)

A Picture No Artist Can Paint

She Was Happy Till She Met You

She'll Be Comin' Round the Mountain (based on the traditional Negro melody ''When the Chariot Comes'')

Smoky Mokes

Stay in Your Own Back Yard

There's Where My Heart Is Tonight

Where the Sweet Magnolias Grow

Whistling Rufus

THE TWENTIETH CENTURY
1900

The Twentieth Century. The twentieth century arrives. The United States has forty-five states and a $46 million surplus (!) in its Treasury. Quartets sing in barber shops on Saturday night, and the young ladies who operate the typing machines *are* the "typewriters." There are as yet no refrigerators and the iceman cometh daily.

Shave and a haircut (with bay rum)	25¢ (two bits)
One dozen eggs	12¢
Complete turkey dinner	20¢
One suit (tailor made)	$10.
Shirt	23¢
Mahogany parlor table	$ 3.95
Sofa	$ 9.98
Corned Beef	8¢/pound
Brass Bed	$ 3

Cylinder Records. The Graphophone record player, a cylinder machine, and Columbia Records, its manufacturer, are awarded the Grand Prize at the Paris Exposition.

Little Nipper. The French artist François Barraud paints the little dog Nipper listening to the gramophone and entitles it "His Master's Voice." Emile Berliner sees the painting in a gallery window, acquires it for his British Gramophone Company, and registers the painting and the slogan as a trademark in the U.S. Patent Office on July 10.

Casey. Engineer John Luther "Casey" Jones, born in Cayce, Kentucky, is killed at Vaughn, Mississippi, when his Cannonball Express collides with the rear of a freight train. (See "Casey Jones," 1909, also 1947.)

Automobiles. At the first of three Madison Square Gardens in New York, the first National Automobile Show opens.

Top Hits
A Bird in a Gilded Cage
Down South
The Gladiator's Entry (*not* "The Gladiator March")
Goodbye Dolly Gray
I Can't Tell Why I Love You, But I Do
Just Because She Made Dem Goo-Goo Eyes
Ma Blushin' Rosie
Strike Up the Band—Here Comes a Sailor
Tell Me Pretty Maiden

Notable
Absence Makes the Heart Grow Fonder
The Bridge of Sighs (m. Thornton)
Creole Belle
Flight of the Bumble Bee (m. Rimsky-Korsakov)

For Old Times' Sake
Lift Ev'ry Voice and Sing
Old Flag Never Touched the Ground
Valse Bleue
Violets

1901

Wireless. Gugliemo Marconi, the Italian inventor, in Newfoundland, hears the letter *s* sent to him by radio across the Atlantic from a transmitter in Wales.

New York Theatre. Broadway leads the world in legitimate theatres with forty-one; London has thirty-nine, and Paris, twenty-four.

C.B. De Mille. Cecil B. De Mille, later famous as a motion picture director, begins his career as an actor on Broadway in *Alice of Old Vincennes*.

Ethel Barrymore. Playwright Clyde Fitch provides Miss Ethel Barrymore, twenty-two, with a vehicle for Broadway stardom in his *Captain Jinks of the Horse Marines*. Winston Churchill later proposed marriage to Miss Barrymore; she declined.

Top Hits
Finlandia (m. Sibelius)
Hiawatha
I Love You Truly
Just A-Wearyin' for You
Mighty Lak' a Rose
Serenade (m. Drigo)

Notable
Any Old Place I Can Hang My Hat Is
Home Sweet Home to Me
The Billboard (March)
Blaze Away (March)
Concerto for Piano, No. 2 (m. Rachmaninoff)
Davy Jones' Locker
Don't Put Me Off at Buffalo Any More
Down Where the Cotton Blossoms Grow
Go Way Back and Sit Down
Hello, Central, Give Me Heaven
High Society (March)
The Honeysuckle and the Bee
I've Grown So Used to You
Josephine, My Jo
The Maiden with the Dreamy Eyes
My Castle on the Nile
O Dry Those Tears
Panamericana

Serenade (m. Toselli)
The Swan of Tuonela (m. Sibelius)
That's Where My Money Goes (possibly earlier)

1902

The Movies. Movie theatres become popular in New York City as Thomas Lally presents *New York in a Blizzard* and *The Capture of the Biffler Brothers.*

Caruso. Enrico Caruso becomes the first operatic star to make records, but he agrees to make only discs rather than cylinders because discs can be duplicated by the Berliner stamping process, producing a better sound quality.

J. Rosamond Johnson. Black composer J. Rosamond Johnson and writer Bob Cole have a great success this year with their hit "Under the Bamboo Tree" which is interpolated in the score *Sally in Our Alley.* With lyrics by his brother James Weldon Johnson, he is also the composer of "Lift Every Voice and Sing" (1900) (not indexed) and "Dry Bones" (1938). With writer Bob Cole he wrote, among others, "Oh, Didn't He Ramble" (1902) and "Lazy Moon" (1903). James Weldon Johnson was later appointed U.S. Consul to Venezuela and Nicaragua by President Theodore Roosevelt and served as national secretary of the N.A.A.C.P.

Football. The first Rose Bowl game is played at Pasadena.

Life at Home with the Baileys. As soon as word was out of the domestic difficulties of the William Bailey family (see "Bill Bailey, Won't You Please Come Home"), speculation mounted about his return in "I Wonder Why Bill Bailey Don't Come Home" and what happened once he did in "Since Bill Bailey Came Home" (the last two not indexed).

Beer Songs. Perhaps the first singing commercials began this year with a series of beer songs. The first, "Down Where the Wurzburger Flows" is followed by "Under the Anheuser Bush" (1903) and later "Budweiser's a Friend of Mine" (1907).

Top Hits
Because (m. d'Hardelot)
Bill Bailey, Won't You Please Come Home
Down Where the Wurzburger Flows
In the Good Old Summertime
In the Sweet Bye and Bye
Oh, Didn't He Ramble
On a Sunday Afternoon
Please Go 'Way and Let Me Sleep

Pomp and Circumstance (March) (m. Elgar)
Under the Bamboo Tree

Notable
Come Down Ma Evenin' Star
Down on the Farm
The Entertainer
If Money Talks, It Ain't on Speaking Terms with Me
Mister Dooley
The Morris Dance (m. German)
Since Sister Nell Heard Paderewski Play
When It's All Goin' Out, and Nothin' Comin' In
Where the Sunset Turns the Ocean's Blue to Gold

1903

Flying. At Kitty Hawk, N.C., Orville and Wilbur Wright take wing on December 18 for the world's first successful airplane flight. Their plane is powered with a twelve-horsepower engine and has been carefully tested in every detail in the world's first wind tunnel of the Wright brothers' own design. See "Come Take a Trip in My Airship" (1904).

Motion Pictures with Visual Story Line. The Great Train Robbery, directed by Edwin S. Porter, is filmed by the Edison Company. For the first time, a film has a story line developed in successive shots of different scenes. *The Great Train Robbery* takes all of twelve minutes.

Amusement Parks. At Coney Island, Dreamland opens at a cost of $2,000,000. See "Meet Me Tonight in Dreamland" (1909).

Oz and Pan on Broadway. The first Wizard of Oz, with lyrics by L. Frank Baum, and music by Paul Tietjens and A. Baldwin Sloane, opens as a musical on Broadway on January 21, while Sir James Barrie's *Peter Pan* opens also with Maude Adams starring as Peter.

Quaker City Four. The world's greatest barbershop quartet of all time, the Quaker City Four, achieves immortality this year with their smash rendition of "(You're the Flower of My Heart) Sweet Adeline" at Hammerstein's Victoria Theatre in New York City. "Sweet Adeline" is adopted as a campaign song by John J. ("Honey Fitz") Fitzgerald. He is elected mayor of Boston for two terms beginning the political dynasty of his Kennedy grandchildren: Joseph Jr., John, Robert, and Edward (Ted).

Tin Pan Alley. Songwriter Monroe H. Rosenfield is the first to apply the sobriquet "Tin Pan Alley" to the cluster of song publishers located on 28th Street between Sixth Avenue and Broadway in New York City.

Hawaii. The first wave of Hawaii genre songs hits the mainland with ''My Hula Lula Girl'' and ''My Honolulu Tomboy'' (1905) (not indexed).

More Caruso. Enrico Caruso makes his debut this year in *Rigoletto* at the original Metropolitan Opera House at Thirty-ninth Street in New York.

Immigration at Its Peak. Immigration from Europe peaks this year, as 857,046 future Americans arrive in New York.

Top Hits
Always Leave Them Laughing When You Say Goodbye
Bedelia
Dear Old Girl
Good-bye, Eliza Jane
I Can't Do the Sum
Ida, Sweet as Apple Cider
Kashmiri Love Song (Four Indian Love Lyrics)
The March of the Toys
(You're the Flower of My Heart) Sweet Adeline
Toyland

Adaptations
The Eyes of Texas (Are Upon You). (based on ''I've Been Working on the Railroad'' (1894))

Notable
Congo Love Song
I'm on the Water Wagon Now
Lazy Moon
Melody of Love
Mother o' Mine
Navajo
Spring, Beautiful Spring (Chimes of Spring) (m. Lincke)
The Temple Bells (Four Indian Love Lyrics)
Under the Anheuser Bush
Waltzing Matilda

1904

The Louisiana Purchase Exposition at St. Louis. This year's Exposition is immortalized in the song ''Meet Me in St. Louis, Louis,'' and much later in the MGM musical film *Meet Me in St. Louis* (1944), starring Judy Garland. At the Exposition, a new sausage in a roll sandwich called a ''frankfurter'' is an Exposition favorite.

Geronimo. Geronimo, mighty war chief of the Chiri-

cahuas tribe of the Apaches is captured in Arizona. He is taken under guard to appear at the St. Louis Exposition. There, Geronimo, who cost the United States government over a million dollars to capture, sells pictures of himself at twenty-five cents each.

George M. George M. Cohan (Kohane) opens on Broadway, this year, producing, directing, starring in, writing, and composing the musical *Little Johnny Jones,* which features George M. immortalizing ''Give My Regards to Broadway'' and ''(I Am) The Yankee Doodle Boy (Born on the Fourth of July).'' He was actually born on July 3, 1878.

Off-Broadway. Theatres with a capacity of three hundred or more are required by New York City to obtain an amusement license. This leads to the traditional seating capacity limit of 299 for the off-Broadway theatre classification.

Sexist Environmentalism. A woman is arrested for smoking a cigarette on New York's Fifth Avenue.

Top Hits
Give My Regards to Broadway
Goodbye, Little Girl, Goodbye
Goodbye, My Lady Love
Meet Me in St. Louis, Louis
Please Come and Play in My Yard
Stop Yer Tickling, Jock!
Teasing
(I Am) The Yankee Doodle Boy

Notable
Absinthe Frappé
Al Fresco
Alexander
Blue Bell
Come Back to Sorrento
Come Take a Trip in My Airship
Down on the Brandywine
Fascination (Valse Tzigane)
The Gold and Silver (Waltz) (m. Lehár)
Good-bye, Flo
In Zanzibar—My Little Chimpanzee
Life's a Funny Proposition After All
My Honey Lou
The Preacher and the Bear
Souvenir
Un Bel Dí (One Fine Day) (*Madame Butterfly;* m. Puccini)
Valse Triste
Valse Tzigane (Fascination)
Way Down in My Heart (I've Got a Feeling for You)

1905

Variety Hits the Newsstands. The first serious professional trade paper covering all of show business begins publication December 18.

The Hippodrome. The New York Hippodrome Theatre opens on April 12. Built by the owners of Luna Park at a cost of $1,750,000, this new theatrical palace has 5200 seats, a stage 100 feet deep with a 60-foot apron, two circus rings, and a swimming tank 14 feet deep with a secret underwater exit so that entire chorus lines can dive in and disappear. In the 1905 Hippodrome production *A Yankee Circus on Mars,* a man from Mars transports a bankrupt circus to Mars by airship, and a Civil War battle is staged in which the entire cavalry plunges into the tank. In the 1907 production of *The Auto Race and the Battle of Port Arthur,* the Hippodrome has room enough for Hagenbeck's elephants, the Vanderbilt Cup road race, and a naval battle in the huge tank. In 1908, another Hippodrome production, *Sporting Days,* features a bird ballet and a warplane "dogfight." The last show at the Hippodrome will be Billy Rose's 1935 circus musical *Jumbo,* with a score by Rodgers and Hart and starring Jimmy Durante.

Cars. The first automobile song hit, "In My Merry Oldsmobile," commemorates the first transcontinental auto race, which was won by the Oldsmobile entry.

James J. Walker. James J. Walker, future mayor of New York City, co-writes the song "Will You Love Me in December as You Do in May."

Eva Tanguay. Probably the most provocative and uninhibited vaudeville performer of this era, Canadian-born Eva Tanguay became one of the highest paid vaudeville performers at age twenty-seven. The "I Don't Care" Girl exploited her sexuality on stage, singing "Go as Far as You Like" and "It's All Been Done Before But Not the Way I Do It" while offstage was involved in numerous scandals, lawsuits, and feuds with booking agents and managers.

Top Hits
Clair de Lune (m. Debussy)
Everybody Works But Father
Forty-Five Minutes from Broadway
I Don't Care
I Want What I Want When I Want It
In My Merry Oldsmobile
In the Shade of the Old Apple Tree
Kiss Me Again
Mary's a Grand Old Name

My Gal Sal (They Call Her Frivolous Sal)
Nobody
Rufus Rastus Johnson Brown (What You Goin' To Do When the Rent Comes 'Round)
So Long Mary
Tammany
Wait 'til the Sun Shines, Nellie
The Whistler and His Dog
Will You Love Me in December (as You Do in May)

Notable
Daddy's Little Girl
Dearie (Kummer)
The Leader of the German Band
My Irish Molly-O
Parade of the Wooden Soldiers
When the Bell in the Lighthouse Rings Ding Dong
Where the River Shannon Flows
A Woman Is Only a Woman, But a Good Cigar Is a Smoke

1906

The New "Victrola." The Victor Company removes the familiar tin horn from the top of the phonograph; it is folded down into the wooden cabinet beneath.

Radio Music. In Massachusetts Reginald Fessenden transmits the first musical program by radio a distance of eleven miles.

The Astaires. The Astaires, Fred and Adele, make their stage debut as a dance team on the Orpheum vaudeville circuit. Miss Astaire is eight and Mr. Astaire is seven.

Murder on Broadway. On June 25, the opening night performance of the musical *Mam'zelle Champagne* at the Madison Square Garden Roof Theatre in New York City is interrupted when Harry K. Thaw shoots and kills fellow theatregoer, the noted architect Stanford White, because White's latest conquest, actress Evelyn Nesbitt Thaw, is Thaw's wife. Business improves enormously at *Mam'zelle Champagne,* as well as at Oscar Hammerstein I's Victoria Theatre, where Mrs. Thaw is headlining.

Top Hits
Anchors Aweigh
At Dawning
Because You're You
The (Little) Bird on Nellie's Hat
Chinatown, My Chinatown
Every Day Is Ladies' Day to Me
I Just Can't Make My Eyes Behave

I Love a Lassie (Ma Scotch Bluebell)

In Old New York (The Streets of New York)

Love Me and the World Is Mine

National Emblem (March) (parodied as "And the Monkey Wrapped Its Tail Around the Flagpole")

Sunbonnet Sue

Waiting at the Church (My Wife Won't Let Me)

Waltz Me Around Again, Willie—'Round, 'Round, 'Round

Won't You Come Over to My House

You're a Grand Old Flag

Adaptations
Schnitzelbank (based on "Johnny Schmoker" (1863))

Revivals
I Love You Truly (1901)

Notable
All In Down and Out

Cheyenne

College Life

Don't Go in the Lions' Cage Tonight

Eli Eli

He Walked Right In, Turned Around and Walked Right Out Again

He's a Cousin of Mine

I Was Born in Virginia (Ethel Levy's Virginia Song)

A Lemon in the Garden of Love

Moonbeams

My Mariuccia Take a Steamboat

Nellie Dean

Petite Tonkinoise

Since Father Went to Work

What's the Use of Dreaming

What's the Use of Loving If You Can't Love All the Time

When Love Is Young in the Springtime

1907

Movies Go West. The first company of "movie" actors arrives in Los Angeles from Chicago.

Ziegfeld Follies. Florenz Ziegfeld stages his first *Ziegfeld Follies* on the roof of the New York Theatre on July 9, starring Nora Bayes. Cost: $13,000. Noted for his taste in stunning women, Ziegfeld sets the following ideal standard this year for his Follies' beauties: bust, 36″; waist, 26″; hips, 38″. His settings and costumes frequently feature his favorite colors: white, pink, and gold. His Follies girls are paid $75 per week and many go on to fame or fortune.

Irving Berlin (II). Mr. Berlin's first published song lyrics for "Marie from Sunny Italy" appear. Total royalties: $.37.

The Two-Step. The predecessor dance craze to the ragtime dances this year is the two-step of "I'd Rather Two-Step Than Waltz" (not indexed) and "Everybody Two-Step" (1912) (not indexed).

The Glow Worm. The song "Glow Worm," an import from Germany, becomes popular this year. It will later be used by ballerina Anna Pavlova (see 1916) for her "Empire Gavotte."

Lily (Lillie) Langtry's Red Carpet. The actress Lily Langtry requests carpeting between her dressing room and the stage of the theatre to protect her dress hems.

The Merry Widow. Opening at the New Amsterdam on October 21, the hit of this season is Franz Lehár's new operetta *The Merry Widow,* which will run for 416 performances. Starring Donald Brian and Ethel Jackson, the hit waltz from this show was played everywhere that year from pirated sheet music in cheap editions as some of the music had no copyright.

Speeding. Theatre and vaudeville impresario Martin Beck is arrested for speeding in his new car at eighteen miles per hour within the city limits of New York. Mr. Beck founded the Orpheum (Western) vaudeville circuit from Chicago to San Francisco, and built the Palace Theatre in New York (see 1913).

Top Hits
Bell Bottom Trousers (probably traditional)

Glow Worm

Harrigan

I Wish I Had a Girl

It's Delightful To Be Married

Maxim's *(The Merry Widow)*

The Merry Widow Waltz (I Love You So) *(The Merry Widow)*

On the Road to Mandalay

Red Wing

School Days

Vilia *(The Merry Widow)*

Wal, I Swan!, or, Ebenezer Frye, or, Giddiap Napoleon, It Looks Like Rain

Notable
Because I'm Married Now

The Best I Get Is Much Obliged to You

Budweiser's a Friend of Mine

Come Along My Mandy

The Farewell (La Partida)

Honey Boy

I Love You So

I'm Afraid To Come Home in the Dark

Take Me Back to New York Town

That Lovin' Rag

There Never Was a Girl Like You

Tommy, Lad

Two Blue Eyes

Two Little Baby Shoes

Waltz Dream

When a Fellow's on the Level with a Girl That's on the Square

When We Are M-a-double-r-i-e-d

You Splash Me and I'll Splash You

1908

Both Sides Now. Columbia Phonograph Company advertises in *The Saturday Evening Post* the first two-sided phonograph disc on October 21.

Radio Stations. The first radio station goes "on the air" (later to become Station KQW) on January 16 in San Jose, California.

Movie Screens. For the first time, projection on a screen from a motion picture projector located at the rear of the theatre predominates in the motion picture industry, and the kinetoscope of nickelodeon fame falls into disuse (see 1889).

D.W. Griffith. At the age of thirty-three David Wark Griffith abandons his career as an actor when his first single-reel film as a director (with G.W. (Billy) Bitzer as chief cameraman) is released on July 14. *The Adventures of Dollie (Her Marvelous Experience at the Hands of Gypsies),* "one of the most remarkable cases of child-stealing," is depicted in this Biograph picture. It shows the thwarting by a kind Providence of the attempt by a Gypsy to kidnap a pretty little girl for revenge: Length 713 feet, price 14¢ per foot, #3454, produced at the Biograph Studios, 11 East 14th Street, New York City.

Nothing Changes. New Yorkers who complain that the city is not as safe as it used to be will be comforted by this year's ode to pedestrian safety entitled "I Used To Be Afraid To Go Home in the Dark, Now I'm Afraid To Go Home at All" (not indexed), an answer song to "I'm Afraid To Come Home in the Dark (1907).

Top Hits
Cuddle Up a Little Closer, Lovey Mine

Shine On, Harvest Moon

Smarty

Sweet Violets

Take Me Out to the Ball Game

Notable
All for the Love of You

Any Old Port in a Storm

Daisies Won't Tell

Down Among the Sugar Cane

Down in Jungle Town

Every Little Bit Added to What You've Got Makes Just a Little Bit More

Golliwogg's Cake Walk (*Children's Corner;* m. Debussy)

La Golondrina

Hoo-oo Ain't You Coming Out Tonight

If I Had a Thousand Lives To Live

In the Garden of My Heart

I've Taken Quite a Fancy to You

The Longest Way 'Round Is the Sweetest Way Home

Love Is Like a Cigarette

Roses Bring Dreams of You

She Sells Sea-Shells

A Vision of Salome

The Yama Yama Man

You Tell Me Your Dream (I Had a Dream, Dear)

You're in the Right Church, But the Wrong Pew

1909

Animated Cartoons. Experiments by Winsor McKay lead to the development of the animated cartoon. Ten thousand drawings are used to create McKay's *Gertie and the Dinosaur.*

North Pole. On April 6, after twenty years of effort, U.S. Admiral Robert Edwin Peary claims the discovery of the North Pole on this, his sixth attempt.

Model T. Henry Ford's Model T goes on the market; fifteen million of this design will be sold by 1928.

Diaghilev, Mahler, Stein. Serge Diaghilev brings Russian ballet to Paris for a summer season; Gustav Mahler completes his ninth and last symphony; and Gertrude Stein publishes her first book of fiction, *Three Lives.*

"Jelly Roll". Ferdinand "Jelly Roll" Morton, the father of the jazz piano, first appears at Anderson's Annex in New Orleans. He is later to write "Tiger Rag" (1917), "King Porter Stomp" (1924), "Wolverine Blues" (1923), "The Original Jelly Roll Blues" (not indexed) and "Buddy Bolden Blues" (c.1915).

Top Hits
By the Light of the Silvery Moon

Casey Jones

From the Land of the Sky Blue Water (Four American Indian Songs)

Has Anybody Here Seen Kelly

Heaven Will Protect the Working Girl

I Love My Wife, But Oh You Kid

I Wonder Who's Kissing Her Now

I've Got Rings on My Fingers (Mumbo Jumbo Jijjiboo J. O'Shea)

Meet Me Tonight in Dreamland

My Hero

My Pony Boy

On Wisconsin

Put on Your Old Grey Bonnet

That's A Plenty

Yip-I-Addy-I-Ay!

Notable

The Cubanola Glide

Dollar Princesses

I'm Awfully Glad I Met You

I've Got a Pain in My Sawdust

The Letter Song

Moving Day in Jungle Town

My Cousin Caruso

My Dream of Love

Next to Your Mother, Who Do You Love?

Nobody Knows, Nobody Cares

Rumanian Rhapsody (op. 11, no.1) (m. Georges Enesco)

Waltz (*The Count of Luxemburg*)

When I Dream in the Gloaming of You

Where My Caravan Has Rested

Yiddle on Your Fiddle

You Taught Me How To Love You, Now Teach Me To Forget

1910

The Ballroom Decade. The waltz is replaced as the standard dance as the decade of Ballroom Dancing begins. The trendier restaurants are equipped with dance floors, and the afternoon "thé dansant" becomes popular.

Sheet Music Sales. Encouraged by parlor piano sales, at least two billion copies of sheet music are sold for a high never again to be equalled. Single copy prices are 25¢ to 35¢.

Jerome Kern. Critic Alan Dale poses a question to be answered by three generations of theatre and filmgoers: "Who is this Jerome Kern whose music towers in an Eiffel way above the average primitive hurdy-gurdy ac-

companiment of the present day musical comedy?" Mr. Kern is twenty-five.

Fanny Brice. Miss Brice, nineteen years old, migrates from burlesque to the *Ziegfeld Follies of 1910,* starting at $18 per week.

Naughty Marietta. The New York Theatre opens on November 7 with Victor Herbert's newest operetta, *Naughty Marietta.* It will run 136 performances and star soprano Emma Trentini and tenor Orville Harrold. Its hit song "Ah! Sweet Mystery of Life" was originally an instrumental entr'acte until Orville Harrold encouraged its promotion to a tenor vocal number.

Boy Scouts and Camp Fire Girls. The Boy Scouts of America and the Camp Fire Girls of America are both founded this year.

Top Hits

Ah! Sweet Mystery of Life (*Naughty Marietta*)

Any Little Girl, That's a Nice Little Girl, Is the Right Little Girl for Me

Call Me Up Some Rainy Afternoon

Caprice Viennois

The Chicken Reel

Come, Josephine, in My Flying Machine

Don't Wake Me Up, I'm Dreaming

Down By the Old Mill Stream

Every Little Movement (Has a Meaning All Its Own)

Gee, But It's Great To Meet a Friend from Your Old Home Town

I'd Love To Live in Loveland (with a Girl Like You)

I'm Falling in Love with Someone (*Naughty Marietta*)

Italian Street Song (*Naughty Marietta*)

Let Me Call You Sweetheart

Liebesfreud

Liebeslied

Macushla

Mother Machree

A Perfect Day

Play That Barbershop Chord (Mister Jefferson Lord)

Put Your Arms Around Me, Honey

Some of These Days

Steamboat Bill

Stein Song (University of Maine)

That's Why They Call Me "Shine"

Washington & Lee Swing

What's the Matter with Father

Revivals

Passing By (1890)

Notable

All Aboard for Blanket Bay

All That I Ask of You Is Love

Alma, Where Do You Live

The Big Bass Viol

By the Saskatchewan

Day Dreams

(Beautiful) Garden of Roses

The Girl with the Flaxen Hair (m. Debussy)

Goodbye, Rose

Grizzly Bear

If He Comes In, I'm Going Out

If I Was a Millionaire

In All My Dreams I Dream of You

In the Shadows

I've Got the Time—I've Got the Place, But It's Hard To Find the Girl

Life Is Only What You Make It After All

Morning

Oh, That Beautiful Rag

On Mobile Bay

Plant a Watermelon on My Grave and Let the Juice Soak Through

Silver Bell

Tambourin Chinois

That Minor Strain

That's Yiddishe Love

Two Little Love Bees

Under the Yum-Yum Tree

Waltzes *(Der Rosenkavalier)*

You Are the Ideal of My Dreams

1911

Irving Berlin's Ragtime (III). Irving Berlin's "Alexander's Ragtime Band," "Everybody's Doin' It Now," "Ragtime Violin," and "That Mysterious Rag" are published (see below).

The Story of "Alexander's Ragtime Band." "Eddie Miller and Helen Vincent were appearing at the Garden Cafe, in New York City, and were the first to sing the song in public . . . I heard "Alexander's Ragtime Band" in (publisher) Ted Snyder's office and thought it would be a good number for the Garden. I asked Max Winslow, manager of the firm, to buy zobos (toy musical instruments) for the song, to be used at the Garden but he refused as he said the song wasn't worth it, and the toys would cost $5. Paul Salvin, owner of the Garden, put out the money for the zobos (himself) and the song was used the next night there. It was a sensation. Wins-

low . . . heard what a hit it was so (he) went to the Columbia Theatre and brought the manager of the show there over to the Garden to hear the song—next week it was in the burlesque show at the Columbia. The rest is history." (Ray Walker, composer, *Variety*, October 20, 1954.)

Ragtime Dances. The fish walk, grizzly bear, kangaroo dip, turkey-trot, walking the dog, ballin'-the-jack (1913) and bunny hug (1912) (see "Funny Bunny Hug") are the new dance steps.

Paderewski. Ignace Paderewski makes his first gramophone records at his home in Switzerland. See "Since Sister Nell Heard Paderewski Play" (1902).

Cole Porter. Mr. Porter's football rally song "Bulldog! Bulldog! Bow, Wow, Wow" is adopted by his fellow undergraduates, the faculty, and the alumni of Yale University. To this day it is sung at Yale football games with undiminished fervor. Mr. Porter is eighteen.

Jolson. Al Jolson makes his first appearance on the New York stage this year in *La Belle Paree*. Mr. Jolson is twenty-five.

O. Henry. The song "(Look Out For) Jimmy Valentine" is inspired by the society burglar immortalized in the O. Henry short story "A Retrieved Reformation."

Phone Calls. In "pop" argot, the telephone becomes simply the phone. See "A Ring on the Finger Is Worth Two on the Phone" and "Nora Malone (Call Me by Phone)" (1912, not indexed).

Top Hits

Alexander's Ragtime Band

All Alone (m. Von Tilzer)

Billy (For When I Walk)

Careless (Kelly's) Love (first printed version this year, but probably traditional *c.* 1895)

Down the Field (March)

Everybody's Doing It Now

I Want a Girl—Just Like the Girl That Married Dear Old Dad

(Look Out For) Jimmy Valentine

Little Grey Home in the West

My Beautiful Lady (The Kiss Waltz)

My Lovin' Honey Man

The Oceana Roll

Oh You Beautiful Doll

Ragtime Violin

Roamin' in the Gloamin'

Somewhere a Voice Is Calling

That Mysterious Rag

Too Much Mustard (Très Moutarde)

A Wee Deoch-an-Doris
The Whiffenpoof Song

Notable
Can't You Take It Back, and Change It for a Boy?
Daly's Reel
Daphnis et Chloé (m. Ravel)
The Fire Bird (m. Stravinsky; first performed 1910)
The Gaby Glide
If You Talk in Your Sleep, Don't Mention My Name
My Rosary of Dreams
A Ring on the Finger Is Worth Two on the Phone
The Spaniard That Blighted My Life
That Was Before I Met You
Till the Sands of the Desert Grow Cold
To the Land of My Small Romance
When I Was Twenty-one and You Were Sweet Sixteen
When You're Away
Woodman, Woodman, Spare That Tree

1912

Flat Round Records. Discs defeat cylinders in the popular market. Columbia Records adopts Berliner's new design and abandons the cylinder record business to the Edison Company.

The Blues. The political boss of Memphis, Tennessee, Edward H. Crump, asks black composer W.C. Handy for some special election night band music, and Handy writes "Mister Crump Don't 'Low No Easy Riders Roun' Here." An "easy rider" is a man who lives well and is supported financially by one or more working women. This Handy song proves even more popular retitled as "The Memphis Blues."

Mack Sennett. Mack Sennett, later celebrated in the Broadway musical *Mack and Mabel* (1974), produces his keystone comedies featuring the Keystone Kops and the Mack Sennett Bathing Beauties.

Top Hits
And the Green Grass Grew All Around
Be My Little Baby Bumblebee
Down South
Everybody Two-Step
Giannina Mia (Friml)
It's a Long Way to Tipperary
(Look Out For) Jimmy Valentine, *see* 1911
Lily of Laguna
(Just) A Little Love, a Little Kiss
Melody (Dawes)

The Memphis Blues
(On) Moonlight Bay
My Melancholy Baby
Ragtime Cowboy Joe
The Rose of Tralee
Row, Row, Row
Sweetheart of Sigma Chi
Sympathy
That's How I Need You
Tipperary, *see* It's a Long Way to Tipperary
Waiting for the Robert E. Lee
When I Lost You
When Irish Eyes Are Smiling
When the Midnight Choo-Choo Leaves for Alabam'
You Can't Stop Me from Loving You

Notable
After All That I've Been to You
Bagdad
Daddy Has a Sweetheart, and Mother Is Her Name
Funny Bunny Hug
Garland of Old Fashioned Roses
Hitchy-Koo
I'm the Lonesomest Gal in Town
Isle o' Dreams
Last Night Was the End of the World
Love Is Like a Firefly
On the Mississippi
Roll Dem Roly Boly Eyes
Sari Waltz
Take a Little Tip from Father
They Gotta Quit Kickin' My Dog Around
The Wedding Glide
When I Get You Alone Tonight
When It's Apple Blossom Time in Normandy
You're My Baby

1913

Feature Films. The first "four reel" feature films are produced. The Jesse Lasky Company (now Paramount) produces *Squaw Man* and *Brewster's Millions*.

Hollywood. D.W. Griffith moves to California and produces his feature film *Judith of Bethulia*.

Entertainer Unions. Actors' Equity is founded this year.

The New Theatre District. The center of legitimate theatre activity shifts to its present area around Broadway and Times Square as Shubert Alley opens October 2. The Shuberts later purchased the land beneath the Alley from the British branch of the Astor family, who owned the greater part of the block from Broadway to Eighth Avenue, 44th to 45th Street. The Alley is a private way that must be closed between Saturday midnight and Sunday midnight once each year to prevent it from reverting to public property. A brass plate in the pavement indicates that you tread on it as a privilege granted by the Shubert Organization.

Stravinsky. There is public rioting in Paris at the premiere of Igor Stravinsky's new experiment in musical dissonance, "Rites of Spring."

The Palace Theatre. The top vaudeville theatre of the world opens on Broadway, March 24, with the vaudeville team of McIntyre and Health headlining a bill that includes comedian Ed Wynn. Every major star of that period eventually played the Palace excepting two: Al Jolson and George M. Cohan.

Billboard Music Charts. Billboard magazine publishes its first list of sheet music best sellers: "Last Week's Ten Best Sellers Among the Popular Songs."

Ballroom Dancing and the Castles. Vernon and Irene Castle reach a $1000 per week salary in doing the two-step, the tango, the maxixe, and their new dance "The Castle Walk."

The Foxtrot. Mr. Harry Fox of vaudeville marries one of the two Dolly Sisters and introduces a new dance step, "Mr. Fox's Trot." In 1914 it will be danced by Vera Maxwell and Wallace McCutcheon in the Broadway musical *Century Girl.*

Modern Art. New Yorkers goggle at Marcel Duchamp's painting "Nude Descending a Staircase," exhibited at the Armory Show exhibit of European avant-garde painting.

Top Hits
Ballin' the Jack
Brighten the Corner Where You Are
El Choclo
The Curse of an Aching Heart
Destiny Waltz
(He'd Have To Get Under,) Get Out and Get Under (To Fix Up His Automobile)
Goodbye, Boys
If I Had My Way
My Wife's Gone to the Country (Hurrah! Hurrah!)
The Old Rugged Cross
Peg o' My Heart
Snooky Ookums
Sweethearts
The Teddy Bear's Picnic
That International Rag

There's a Long, Long Trail
The Trail of the Lonesome Pine
Where Did You Get That Girl
You Made Me Love You (I Didn't Want To Do It)

Adaptations
Danny Boy (based on a traditional old Irish air ("Londonderry Air")) of at least 1855, with added lyrics)
(Fifteen Miles [Years] on the) Erie Canal (Low Bridge!—Everybody Down) (based on a traditional folksong.)
Marcheta (based on Karl Nicolai's overture to the *Merry Wives of Windsor*)

Notable
All Aboard for Dixieland
The Angelus
Black and White Rag
Don't Blame It All on Broadway
I Miss You Most of All
Isle d'Amour
Nights of Gladness
On the Old Fall River Line
On the Shores of Italy
Panama
The Pullman Porters on Parade
Rites of Spring (m. Stravinsky)
Somebody's Coming to My House
Something Seems Tingle-Ingling
There's a Girl in the Heart of Maryland
What's the Good of Being Good—When No One's Good to Me
When You Play in the Game of Love
When You're All Dressed Up and No Place To Go
You're Here and I'm Here

1914

World War I. The first war to involve all of the major European powers begins.

Movie Serials. Adventures of Pauline (sometimes called *The Perils of Pauline)* is released, starring Pearl White. See "Poor Pauline."

ASCAP. Founded by the major American songwriters, the American Society of Composers, Authors and Publishers emerges as the first performing-rights organization on February 13, at Luchow's Restaurant on 14th Street in New York.

St. Louis Blues. W.C. Handy's song, published this year, will be featured five times in films: *St. Louis Blues*

(1928 and 1958), *Is Everybody Happy* (1929 and 1943), and *The Birth of the Blues* (1941).

Dolly Terris Morse. Dorothy (Theodora or Dolly) Terris Morse is the first woman writer to hold a membership card in the new performing rights society, ASCAP. She was later the author of lyrics of the hit songs "Three O'Clock in the Morning," "Wonderful One," and "Siboney."

Vernon and Irene Castle (II). The ballroom dancing exhibitions by the Castles continue to be the rage, and this year an engagement brings this couple $ 31,000 per week. They also appear in the Irving Berlin revue *Watch Your Step* which features "Show Me How To Do the Fox Trot" (not indexed). The story of the Castles is later celebrated in the motion picture *The Story of Vernon and Irene Castle* (1939), starring Ginger Rogers and Fred Astaire.

War Influence. Onset of World War I in Europe produces an American revulsion against German names. Sausages and rolls previously served at baseball games with the Germanic name "frankfurters" are renamed "hot dogs." This change is celebrated in the song "Fido Is a Hot Dog Now."

Silent Film Mood Music. By this year, certain songs find special favor with pianists and organists who provide mood music for silent film audiences: for example, for haunted houses and forbidding caves, "Mysterioso Pizzicato"; for the scene in which the villain demands payment of the mortgage OR ELSE from the poor widow who invariably has a beautiful young daughter, "Hearts and Flowers" (1899); for the scene in which someone desperately needing help tries to awaken the sleeping husband, sheriff, or fireman, "Please Go 'Way and Let Me Sleep" (1902); and for the chase, "The William Tell Overture" (1829). Songs associated with particular silent pictures: for *The Birth of a Nation,* "The Perfect Song" (1915); for *Mickey,* song of same title (1918); for *The Covered Wagon,* "Covered Wagon" and "Westward Ho!" (1923); for *What Price Glory?,* "Charmaine" (1926); for *Ramona,* song of same title (1927); and for *Lilac Time,* "Jeannine, I Dream of Lilac Time" (1928).

The Girl from Utah. Jerome Kern wrote about half the score to this English musical when he adapted it for performance in America. Julia Sanderson plays an American woman who leaves Utah for London to avoid Mormon polygamy. Kern wrote especially for her "They Didn't Believe Me" and with this song established his artistry, freely breaking all conventions of rhythm and key in a way that led to the creation of a new popular musical theatre.

Top Hits
The Aba Daba Honeymoon
By Heck
By the Beautiful Sea
By the Waters of Minnetonka
Can't Yo' Heah Me Callin', Caroline
Down Among the Sheltering Palms
Down on the Farm (Berlin), *see* "I Want To Go Back to Michigan—Down on the Farm"
Goodbye, Girls, I'm Through
He's a Devil in His Own Home Town
A Little Bit of Heaven, Sure They Call It Ireland
Love's Own Sweet Song (Sari Waltz)
Missouri Waltz
Play a Simple Melody
The Song of Songs
St. Louis Blues
Sylvia (Speaks)
They Didn't Believe Me
Too-ra-loo-ra-loo-ral, That's an Irish Lullaby
Twelfth Street Rag
When You Wore a Tulip and I Wore a Big Red Rose
When You're a Long, Long Way from Home
When You're Away

Revivals
That's A Plenty (1909)

Notable
Duna
Fido Is a Hot Dog Now
He's a Rag Picker
If You Don't Want My Peaches, You'd Better Stop Shaking My Tree
Mysterioso Pizzicato
On the 5:15
On the Good Ship Mary Ann
Pigeon Walk
Poor Pauline
Rebecca of Sunny-Brook Farm
Roll Them Cotton Bales
Shave and a Haircut, Bay Rum (probably traditional)
Sister Susie's Sewing Shirts for Soldiers
The Springtime of Life
There's a Little Spark of Love Still Burning
This Is the Life
Way Out Yonder in the Golden West
When It's Night Time in Dixieland
When the Angelus Is Ringing

Wien, Du Stadt Meiner Träume
You Planted a Rose in the Garden of Love

1915

The Birth of a Nation. Film director D.W. Griffith shoots his first major historical epic, *The Birth of a Nation,* starring Lillian Gish, produced at a cost of $100,000. The silent film was premiered at the Palace Theatre in New York City with a full pit orchestra to supply the musical background. Over the next fifteen years it grossed $20,000,000. The film blockbuster of all time, it is still being exhibited profitably.

Animated Cartoons (II). Max Fleischer creates Koko the clown in the cartoon *Out of the Inkwell.* In contrast to Walt Disney's realism (1928), Fleischer specializes in a surrealistic style in which solid objects are transformed into caterpillars playing saxophones or singing roller skates. Later he produces the first animated cartoon with recorded sound. Fleischer is the creator of the film cartoon characters Betty Boop (Boop boop-a-doop) and Popeye, Olive Oyl, and Wimpie, derived from the newspaper cartoon series (see 1931 and 1974).

Ukuleles and Hawaiian Guitars. Tin Pan Alley discovers Hawaii with ''Hello, Hawaii, How Are You'', ''On the Beach at Waikiki'', ''Song of the Islands'', ''Oh! How She Could Yacki, Hacki, Wicki, Wacki, Woo'' (1916), ''Since Maggie Dooley Learned the Hooley Hooley'' (1916), ''They're Wearing 'Em Higher in Hawaii'' (1916), ''Yaacka Hula Hickey Dula'' (1916), and ''Hawaiian Butterfly'' (1917).

The ''Flu.'' Influenza epidemic songs become popular. See ''Some Little Bug Is Going To Find You.''

Princess Theatre. Jerome Kern and Guy Bolton collaborate on *Nobody Home,* the first of their Princess Theatre shows written for manager Elisabeth Marbury. Budgeted at $7,500 with only two sets, a small cast, eight chorus girls and a ten-piece orchestra this show revolutionized musical theatre. The character situations resulted in a comedy that was not interjected. The placement of each song and the content of each lyric contributed to the development of the story line. Musical theatre became a play with music. The show's hits ''You Know and I Know'' and ''The Magic Melody'' began a new epoch. Their next show was *Very Good Eddie,* further developing the new style of non-spectacle intimacy, naturalism, where comedy and song evolved from plot and character. With P.G. Wodehouse in 1917, they wrote the very successful *Oh, Boy!* and in 1918, *Oh, Lady!*

Lady! The last Princess Theatre show was *Oh, My Dear!,* a Bolton-P.G. Wodehouse effort with music by Louis A. Hirsch which opened in 1918.

Top Hits
Are You from Dixie, 'Cause I'm from Dixie Too
Auf Wiederseh'n (Romberg)
By Heck (from 1914 with lyric added)
Canadian Capers
Fascination
Hello Frisco Hello
Hello, Hawaii, How Are You
How'd You Like To Spoon with Me
I Didn't Raise My Boy To Be a Soldier
I Love a Piano
If We Can't Be the Same Old Sweethearts, We'll Just Be the Same Old Friends
In a Monastery Garden
Jelly Roll Blues
Just Try To Picture Me (Back Home in Tennessee)
Keep the Home Fires Burning (Till the Boys Come Home)
Memories
M-O-T-H-E-R (A Word That Means the World to Me)
My Little Girl
My Mother's Rosary
Neapolitan Love Song
On the Beach at Waikiki
Pack Up Your Troubles in Your Old Kit Bag and Smile, Smile, Smile
Paper Doll
Ragging the Scale
Song of the Islands
There's a Broken Heart for Every Light on Broadway
When I Leave the World Behind

Adaptations
The Old Refrain (based on an 1887 Viennese song by Brandl; adaptation by Fritz Kreisler)

Revivals
Kiss Me Again (1905). Victor Herbert issued this song separately for the first time, not as part of the score of *Mile. Modiste.*

Notable
Alabama Jubilee
All for You
Along the Rocky Road to Dublin
America I Love You
Araby
Babes in the Wood

Beatrice Fairfax, Tell Me What To Do
Don't Bite the Hand That's Feeding You
Down in Bom-Bombay
Georgia Grind
The Girl on the Magazine Cover
I Love Coffee, I Love Tea (melody traditional)
Ireland Is Ireland to Me
It's Tulip Time in Holland
Ladder of Roses
The Little House Upon the Hill
Love, Here Is My Heart
Love Is the Best of All
The Magic Melody
My Sweet Adair
The Perfect Song
Put Me To Sleep with an Old-Fashioned Melody
She's the Daughter of Mother Machree
Siam
So Long Letty
Some Little Bug Is Going To Find You
The Sunshine of Your Smile
There's a Little Lane Without a Turning on the Way to Home Sweet Home
Underneath the Stars
We'll Have a Jubilee in My Old Kentucky Home
When You're in Love with Someone Who Is Not in Love with You
You Know and I Know
You'll Always Be the Same Sweet Girl

1916

Wilson. President Wilson campaigns for re-election on the "peace" platform: "He Kept Us Out of War." Topical songs are anti-war: "I Didn't Raise My Boy To Be a Soldier."

Jazz (Jass). From Basin Street (home of King Oliver and Louis Armstrong) in New Orleans, Beale Street in Memphis, the city of St. Louis, and the South generally, jazz players head for Chicago, San Francisco, and New York. As the U.S. Navy closes the bordellos in Storyville, in New Orleans (see "Farewell to Storyville" (1925)), girls, madams, and honky-tonk "barrelhouse" piano jazzists ("professors") scatter in the great Jazz Migration. By 1921 jazz has moved from the whorehouses of the South into the new "speakeasies" up North.

Diaghilev and the Ballet Russe. Serge Diaghilev and his ballet company arrive in New York from Paris. Later this year, his protégés, Naslov Nijinsky and ballerina prima donna Anna Pavlova, dance at the Hippodrome.

They are part of the first wave of cultural émigrés to flee Russia in the face of the oncoming Revolution of 1917.

Piano Rolls. Pianola rolls with imprinted song lyrics are an instant success.

Norman Rockwell. Rockwell paints his first cover for the *Saturday Evening Post* for May 20.

Top Hits
Allah's Holiday
Baby Shoes
Beale Street Blues
Bugle Call Rag (Blake, Morgan)
Colonel Bogey March
La Cumparsita
Good-bye, Good Luck, God Bless You
Goodbye Virginia
I Ain't Got Nobody
I Can Dance with Everyone But My Wife
If I Knock the "L" Out of Kelly
If You Were the Only Girl in the World
I'm Sorry I Made You Cry
Ireland Must Be Heaven, for My Mother Came from There
Li'l Liza Jane
M-I-S-S-I-S-S-I-P-P-I
Nat'an, Nat'an, Nat'an, Tell Me for What Are You Waitin', Nat'an
Nola
Poor Butterfly
Pretty Baby
Roses of Picardy
There's a Little Bit of Bad in Every Good Little Girl
There's a Quaker Down in Quaker Town
They're Wearing 'Em Higher in Hawaii
Throw Me a Rose
What Do You Want To Make Those Eyes at Me For?

Notable
Arrah Go On, I'm Gonna Go Back to Oregon
Down in Honky Tonky Town
'Forever' Is a Long, Long Time
Give a Little Credit to Your Dad
Have a Heart
He May Be Old, But He's Got Young Ideas
How's Every Little Thing in Dixie
If You Had All the World and Its Gold
I've a Shooting Box in Scotland
Joe Turner Blues
Katinka
Livery Stable Blues
Mammy's a Little Coal Black Rose

My Own Iona

Oh! How She Could Yacki, Hacki, Wicki, Wacki, Woo!

Rackety Coo!

Rolling Stones—All Come Rolling Home Again

She Is the Sunshine of Virginia

Since Maggie Dooley Learned the Hooley Hooley

Way Down in Iowa I'm Going To Hide Away

Where Did Robinson Crusoe Go with Friday on Saturday Night?

Yaacka Hula Hickey Dula

You Belong to Me (Herbert)

You Can't Get Along with 'Em or without 'Em

You're in Love

1917

Wilson (II). Wilson, safely re-elected on his "peace" platform, now discovers he wants war instead. America enters "The War To End All Wars" "To Make the World Safe for Democracy." Topical songs reflect this sudden change and are now pro-war. See "Over There," "Good-Bye Broadway, Hello France," "When Yankee Doodle Learns To Parlez Vous Francais," and "Joan of Arc, They Are Calling You."

ODJB. Columbia Records establishes jazz in America, and records its first "jass" (jazz) record on January 30. The Original Dixieland "Jass" Band led by Dominick (Nick) La Rocca (see 1908) in from Chicago, scouted there by Al Jolson, Fanny Brice, and others, stuns patrons of New York City's Riesenweber's Restaurant on Columbus Circle with its new music (see "Tiger Rag"). This may have been the first million-sale record of popular music. It was Columbia Record no. A2297 (A-side) "The Darktown Strutter's Ball" (B-side) "Indiana"; price 75¢.

Harry T. Burleigh. Black vocalist Harry Thacker Burleigh, who studied with and was a copyist for Antonin Dvorák, the composer from Bohemia, publishes a brilliant series of over fifty arrangements of traditional American black spirituals. See "Deep River," "Go Down, Moses," "Nobody Knows de Trouble I've Seen," "Swing Low, Sweet Chariot," "Oh Peter Go Ring Dem Bells" (1918), "Sometimes I Feel Like a Motherless Child" (1918), and " 'Tis Me, O Lord—Standin' in the Need of Pray'r" (1918). For ten years, beginning in 1900, Burleigh was baritone soloist at St. George's Church and the Temple Emanu-El in New York.

Billy Rose. Billy Rose, eighteen, future song writer and entertainment impresario is acclaimed world's champion stenographer using the Gregg system. He is able to take 200 words of dictation per minute and write forward or backward with either hand.

Vincent Youmans. At nineteen, composer Vincent Youmans begins his musical career with the U.S. Navy at the Great Lakes Naval Training Station. He becomes pianist for band leader John Phillip Sousa.

Fred Astaire. Mr. Astaire, now eighteen, makes his solo Broadway debut in *Over the Top* on November 28. Fifteen years later on November 29, 1932, he will open in his last Broadway musical *Gay Divorce,* before leaving the New York stage for Hollywood.

Over There. The sheet music for the George M. Cohan hit "Over There" features an Army campfire songfest scene illustrated by Norman Rockwell.

George Gershwin. The Guy Bolton-P.G. Wodehouse-Jerome Kern revue, *Miss 1917,* has a young new rehearsal pianist this year by the name of George Gershwin. Mr. Gershwin is nineteen.

Top Hits

The Bells of St. Mary's

The Darktown Strutters' Ball

Down in the Valley (Birmingham Jail) (probably traditional, *c.* 1845)

For Me and My Gal

Give Me the Moonlight, Give Me the Girl

Good-Bye Broadway, Hello France

I Don't Want To Get Well (I'm in Love with a Beautiful Nurse)

(Back Home Again in) Indiana

Indianola (instrumental)

Johnson Rag

Leave It to Jane

Little Mother of Mine

Love Will Find a Way (Fraser-Simson)

MacNamara's Band

Oh Johnny, Oh Johnny, Oh!

Out Where the West Begins

Over There

Rose Room

Smiles

Some Sunday Morning (Whiting)

They Go Wild Simply Wild Over Me

Thine Alone

Tiger Rag

'Till the Clouds Roll By (Kern)

Wait Till the Cows Come Home

Where Do We Go From Here

Will You Remember (Sweetheart)

Adaptations

Deep River (based on a traditional Negro spiritual, from at least 1875)

Go Down, Moses (based on a traditional Negro spiritual, from at least 1861)

Hail, Hail, the Gang's All Here (based on the tenor part "Come, friends, who plow the sea" and the chorus part "With catlike tread" from Act II, *The Pirates of Penzance,* by Gilbert and Sullivan; this melody was itself a parody of Verdi's "Anvil Chorus")

Nobody Knows de Trouble I've Seen (based on a traditional Negro spiritual, known as early as 1865)

The Old Grey Mare (She Ain't What She Used To Be) (melody based on the traditional "Got Out (Get Out of) the Wilderness," as early as 1858)

Old MacDonald Had a Farm (English words as early as 1706, American music as early as 1859)

Swing Low, Sweet Chariot (based on a traditional Negro spiritual, as early as 1872)

Notable

All the World Will Be Jealous of Me
The Bombo-shay
Bring Back My Daddy to Me
Come to the Fair
Eileen
Give a Man a Horse He Can Ride
Going Up
Good-Bye, Ma! Good-Bye, Pa! Good-Bye, Mule
Hawaiian Butterfly
Homing
I Don't Know Where I'm Going But I'm on My Way
I May Be Gone for a Long, Long Time
I'd Love To Be a Monkey in the Zoo
I'm All Bound 'Round with the Mason-Dixon Line
It Takes a Long, Tall, Brown-Skin Gal
It's a Long Lane That Has No Turning
Joan of Arc, They Are Calling You
Lily of the Valley
Little Sir Echo
Lorraine, My Beautiful Alsace Lorraine
Sailin' Away on the Henry Clay
Send Me Away with a Smile
Shim-Me-Sha-Wabble
The Siren's Song
Sweet Emalina, My Gal
(Everybody Ought To Know How To Do) The Tickle Toe
When the Boys Come Home
When Yankee Doodle Learns To Parlez Vous Francais
Where the Black-Eyed Susans Grow
Where the Morning Glories Grow (Whiting)

1918

More Vaudeville. 25,000 performers are now touring in 4000 vaudeville theatres in the U.S. They are booked on the Keith (eastern) or Orpheum (western) "circuit," with a gig at the Palace Theatre in New York City as the ultimate and most desirable goal.

Silent Film Title Themes. The title song "Mickey" associated with the silent film of the same name, starring Mabel Normand, becomes a top hit (see 1914).

Wartime Humor Songs. See "Oh! How I Hate To Get Up in the Morning," "Would You Rather Be a Colonel with an Eagle on Your Shoulder or a Private with a Chicken on Your Knee?," "There'll Be a Hot Time for the Old Men When the Young Men Go to War," "They Were All Out of Step But Jim," "Oh! Frenchy," "Keep Your Head Down, 'Fritzie Boy'," "If He Can Fight Like He Can Love, Good Night Germany!," "I Don't Want To Get Well (I'm in Love with a Beautiful Nurse)" (1917), "And He'd Say "Oo-La-La Wee-Wee'" (1919), "How Ya Gonna Keep 'Em Down on the Farm (After They've Seen Paree)" (1919), and "I've Got My Captain Working for Me Now" (1920).

K-K-K-Katy. The wartime hit song "K-K-K-Katy" by Geoffrey O'Hara was billed as "The Sensational Stammering Song Success Sung by the Soldiers and Sailors."

Tarzan. The first *Tarzan of the Apes* film is produced this year.

Top Hits

After You've Gone
Beautiful Ohio
The Daughter of Rosie O'Grady
Dear Little Boy of Mine
Dear Old Pal of Mine
Everything Is Peaches Down in Georgia
A Good Man Is Hard To Find
Good Morning, Mister Zip-Zip-Zip
Hello, Central, Give Me No Man's Land
Hindustan
Hinky Dinky Parlay Voo (Mad'moiselle from Armentières)
Ja-Da
K-K-K-Katy
Madelon
Mad'moiselle from Armentières, see "Hinky Dinky Parlay Voo"
Mickey
Oh! How I Hate To Get Up in the Morning
Rock-a-Bye Your Baby with a Dixie Melody

Somebody Stole My Gal

Till We Meet Again

The U.S. Field Artillery March (The Caissons Go Rolling Along)

Adaptations

I'm Always Chasing Rainbows (based on the Fantasie Impromptu in C-sharp minor by Chopin)

Oh, Peter, Go Ring Dem Bells (based on a traditional Negro spiritual)

Sometimes I Feel Like a Motherless Child (based on a traditional Negro spiritual, *c.* 1899)

('Tis Me, O Lord)—Standin' in the Need of Pray'r (based on a traditional Negro spiritual)

Notable

At the Jazz Band Ball

Bagdad

Bluin' the Blues

Chong, He Come from Hong Kong

Clarinet Marmalade

Dallas Blues

Garden of My Dreams

Have a Smile (for Everyone You Meet)

I Found the End of the Rainbow

I Hate To Lose You

If He Can Fight Like He Can Love, Good Night Germany

If You Look in Her Eyes

I'll Say She Does

In the Land of Beginning Again

Just a Baby's Prayer at Twilight

Keep Your Head Down, "Fritzie Boy"

Kisses—The Sweetest Kisses of All

Oh! Frenchy

Oh, How I Wish I Could Sleep Until My Daddy Comes Home

Original Dixieland One-Step

Ostrich Walk

Oui, Oui, Marie

The Rose of No Man's Land

Sunrise and You

That Tumble-Down Shack in Athlone

That Wonderful Mother of Mine

There'll Be a Hot Time for the Old Men When the Young Men Go to War

They Were All Out of Step But Jim

Tishomingo Blues

When You Look in the Heart of a Rose

Why Do They All Take the Night Boat to Albany

Would You Rather Be a Colonel with an Eagle on Your Shoulder, or a Private with a Chicken on Your Knee?

1919

Prohibition. Songwriter Harry Ruby anticipates the advent of Prohibition with his hit song "What'll We Do on a Saturday Night When the Town Goes Dry," and Irving Berlin adds "You Cannot Make Your Shimmy Shake on Tea" to the *Ziegfeld Follies of 1919*.

Actors' Strike and George M. This year sees the first Actors' Equity strike. George M. Cohan, facing a difficult choice as a theatre owner and manager, sides with the managers against the union. The resulting bitterness delays the placement of his statue in Times Square on Broadway for thirty years. During his career, Cohan wrote some 200 songs, eighty plays (forty in collaboration) and made at least 10,000 stage appearances. George M. never joined Equity, making him the only non-Equity professional actor ever permitted to appear with an Equity cast. Around the base of the Cohan statue at 46th Street and Broadway are inscribed the names of some of his alltime hit songs. Facing north is "You're a Grand Old Flag" and "Over There"; east, "Forty-Five Minutes from Broadway" and "Yankee Doodle Boy"; south, "Give My Regards to Broadway"; west, "Mary's a Grand Old Name" and "Harrigan."

The Shimmy. The new pre-Flapper dance is introduced by Bee Palmer and Gilda Gray. See "All the Quakers Are Shoulder Shakers down in Quaker Town" and "I Wish I Could Shimmy Like My Sister Kate," the latter sung in the *Ziegfeld Follies of 1922* by the great black comic, Bert Williams, remembered forever for his rendition of the song "Nobody" (1905).

Gershwin. Al Jolson stops the show nightly in the musical *Sinbad* at the Winter Garden Theatre on Broadway by singing "Swanee," with words by Irving Caesar and music by George Gershwin. Mr. Gershwin is now twenty-one.

Rodgers and Hart. Their first professional song, "Any Old Place with You," is interpolated in the score of Lew Fields's *A Lonely Romeo.* Mr. Rodgers is seventeen.

Alice Blue. Featured in the song "Alice Blue Gown" from the musical hit *Irene*, this shade of blue, selected by Alice Roosevelt Longworth, Teddy's daughter, is this year's rage.

Top Hits

(In My Sweet Little) Alice Blue Gown

Baby, Won't You Please Come Home

Blues My Naughty Sweetie Gives to Me

Cielito Lindo (Ay, Ay, Ay, Ay)

Dardanella

How Ya Gonna Keep 'Em Down on the Farm (After They've Seen Paree)

I Wish I Could Shimmy Like My Sister Kate

I'm Forever Blowing Bubbles

Indian Summer

Irene

Let the Rest of the World Go By

Love Sends a Little Gift of Roses

Mammy o' Mine

Mandy

"O" (Oh!)

Oh! What a Pal Was Mary

On Miami Shore

Peggy

A Pretty Girl Is Like a Melody

Royal Garden Blues

Sipping Cider Through a Straw

Smilin' Through

Some Day Sweetheart

Sugar Blues

Swanee

Sweet Sixteen

That Naughty Waltz

The World Is Waiting for the Sunrise

You'd Be Surprised

Your Eyes Have Told Me So

Adaptations

The Marine's Hymn (From the Halls of Montezuma to the Shores of Tripoli) (based on Offenbach's opera *Geneviève de Brabant* (1868)).

Notable

All the Quakers Are Shoulder Shakers down in Quaker Town

And He'd Say "Oo-La-La Wee-Wee"

Any Old Place with You

Barnyard Blues

Chinese Lullaby

Daddy Long Legs

I Ain't Gonna Give Nobody None o' This Jelly Roll

I Know What It Means To Be Lonesome

I Might Be Your "Once-in-a-While"

Just Like a Gypsy

The Love of Three Oranges (March) (m. Prokofiev)

Mexican Hat Dance

My Home Town Is a One Horse Town, But It's Big Enough for Me

My Isle of Golden Dreams

'N Everything

Nobody Knows and Nobody Seems To Care

Oh By Jingo, Oh By Gee, You're the Only Girl for Me

Oh! How I Laugh When I Think How I Cried About You

Old-Fashioned Garden

Take Your Girlie to the Movies If You Can't Make Love at Home

Tell Me

Tulip Time

The Vamp

Wait and See

Wait Till You Get Them Up in the Air, Boys

What'll We Do on a Saturday Night When the Town Goes Dry

You Ain't Heard Nothing Yet

You Are Free

You Cannot Make Your Shimmy Shake on Tea

You Didn't Want Me When You Had Me

You Said It

You're a Million Miles from Nowhere When You're One Little Mile from Home

1920

Prohibition (II). Prohibition, "the Noble Experiment" embodied in the Volstead Act, ratified January 16, 1919, and effective January 16 of this year, makes the sale of a drink that contains as much as one half-ounce of alcohol unlawful.

"Speakeasies." Hideaways serving illegal booze flourish in various guises, some even as funeral parlors. The most famous "speak" in New York City was Jack and Charlie's at 21 West 52nd Street. Habitués then and now refer to it as "21."

Radio Stations. Regularly scheduled radio broadcasts from stations with call letters begin. Station KDKA, Pittsburgh, reports the November 2 Presidential election results.

Stop! Designed by a black inventor, the first traffic light in the world is installed at Fifth Avenue and 42nd Street in New York.

Dialing. Dial telephones are introduced. The letters Q and Z are not used.

Top Hits

Alt Wien

Aunt Hagar's Blues

Avalon

Do You Ever Think of Me

Down by the O-Hi-O

Hold Me

I Never Knew I Could Love Anybody Like I'm Loving You

I Used To Love You, But It's All Over Now
I'll Be with You in Apple Blossom Time
The Japanese Sandman
Little Town in the Ould County Down
Look for the Silver Lining
Love Nest
Mah Lindy Lou
Margie
Mary (Hirsch)
My Mammy
Rose of Washington Square
San
So Long, Oo-Long, How Long You Gonna Be Gone?
When My Baby Smiles at Me
Whispering

Notable
All She'd Say Was Umh Hum
The Argentines, the Portuguese and the Greeks
Bright Eyes
Broadway Rose
Chanson
Chili Bean
Daddy, You've Been a Mother to Me
Feather Your Nest
Hiawatha's Melody of Love
Home Again Blues
I Belong to Glasgow
I Lost the Best Pal That I Had
I'd Love To Fall Asleep and Wake Up in My Mammy's Arms
I'll See You in C-U-B-A
In a Persian Market
I've Got My Captain Working for Me Now
Jazz Baby's Ball
Kalua
Left All Alone Again Blues
The Lilac Tree
The Moon Shines on the Moonshine
My Greenwich Village Sue
My Toreador (El Relicario)
Old Pal Why Don't You Answer Me
Pale Moon
(Lena from) Palesteena
Pretty Kitty Kelly
Tell Me Little Gypsy
That Old Irish Mother of Mine
Timbuctoo
Tripoli
La Veeda

Where Do They Go When They Row, Row, Row
Whose Baby Are You
Wild Rose
A Young Man's Fancy

1921

Sardi's. The restaurant on West 44th Street that is to become a theatre tradition opens March 5, in New York. Sardi's is to the American Theatre and the theatrical profession what the Mermaid Tavern must have been to Shakespeare and his confréres at the Globe. First called The Little Restaurant because of The Little Theatre next door, it was later moved from where the St. James Theatre is now to its present location. Artist Alex Gard will draw the first of the collection of caricatures of famous theatre personalities that line the walls inside. The tradition of holding first-night parties at Sardi's begins November 18, 1933, with the Otto Harbach and Jerome Kern musical *Roberta,* whose cast included George Murphy, Bob Hope, Allan Jones, and Fred MacMurray.

Valentino. Rudolph Valentino makes his first two motion pictures, *The Sheik and The Four Horsemen of the Apocalypse.* See ''The Sheik of Araby.''

Torch Songs. Fanny Brice sings ''My Man (Mon Homme)'' in *Ziegfeld Follies of 1921.*

The Wabash Blues. This song is played on a wind-up phonograph this year by actress Jeanne Eagles all through the Broadway play, *Rain,* as she portrays the character Sadie Thompson.

Top Hits
Ain't We Got Fun
All By Myself
And Her Mother Came Too
Any Time
April Showers
Bimini Bay
I'm Just Wild About Harry
I'm Nobody's Baby
Jazz Me Blues
Kitten on the Keys
Love Will Find a Way (Blake)
Ma! He's Making Eyes at Me
My Man (Mon Homme)
My Sunny Tennessee
Peggy O'Neil
Say It with Music
Second Hand Rose
The Sheik of Araby

Ten Little Fingers and Ten Little Toes—Down in Tennessee
There'll Be Some Changes Made
The Wabash Blues
The Wang-Wang Blues
When Buddha Smiles
When Francis Dances with Me

Adaptations
De Gospel Train (based on a traditional Negro spiritual)
Heav'n, Heav'n (Gonna Shout All Over God's Heaven) (based on a traditional Negro spiritual)
How Dry I Am (based on the hymn "(O) Happy Day," 1855)
Little David, Play on Your Harp (based on a traditional Negro spiritual)
Song of Love (based on the melodies of Schubert and Berte)
Steal Away to Jesus (based on a traditional Negro spiritual)

Notable
Bandana Days
Careless Love
Crazy Blues
Dancing Time
Dapper Dan
Dear Old Southland
Down Yonder
Everybody Step
I Ain't Nobody's Darling
I Found a Rose in the Devil's Garden
I Wonder If You Still Care for Me
I'll Forget You
I'm Missin' Mammy's Kissin'—And I Know She's Missin' Mine
Learn To Smile
Leave Me with a Smile
Ma Li'l Batteau (from "Bayou Songs")
Make Believe (Shilkret)
Mandy 'n' Me
Nichavo!
Sally
She's Mine, All Mine
Shuffle Along
Some Day I'll Find You (Parenteau)
Swanee River Moon
Sweet Lady
The Three-Cornered Hat (m. Manuel de Falla)
Tuck Me To Sleep in My Old 'Tucky Home
When Big Profundo Sang Low "C"
When Shall We Meet Again
Whip-poor-will

Wyoming
Yoo-Hoo

1922

Radio Commercials. The first commercially sponsored broadcast is heard on Station WEAF, New York (then owned by A.T.&T.).

Fletcher Henderson. Black composer and arranger Fletcher Henderson, later to become a driving force behind the Benny Goodman Orchestra, opens at the club Alabama in New York City. In his group of future star instrumentalists are Coleman Hawkins, Joe Smith, Louis Armstrong, and Don Redman. Mr. Henderson is twenty-four and Mr. Armstrong is twenty-two.

Lincoln and Tut. The Lincoln Memorial is dedicated in Washington, D.C.; in Egypt, Howard Carter and Lord Carnarvon open the tomb of King Tutankhamen.

Top Hits
L'Amour Toujours L'Amour
Carolina in the Morning
Chicago (That Toddlin' Town)
Do It Again
Georgia (*not* "Georgia On My Mind")
Hot Lips
I'll Build a Stairway to Paradise
A Kiss in the Dark
Lady of the Evening
Limehouse Blues
Mister Gallagher and Mister Shean
My Buddy
On the Alamo
Rose of the Rio Grande
Runnin' Wild
Stumbling
Three O'Clock in the Morning
Toot Toot Tootsie (Goo'Bye)
Trees
'Way Down Yonder in New Orleans
When Hearts Are Young
(My) Wonderful One

Adaptations
Couldn't Hear Nobody Pray (based on a traditional Negro spiritual)
Goin' Home (based on the largo from the "New World Symphony," op. 95, by Dvořák)

1923

Revivals

Ah! Sweet Mystery of Life (1910)

Frankie and Johnnie (Were Lovers) (*c.* 1870–75)

I Wish I Could Shimmy Like My Sister Kate (1919)

Parade of the Wooden Soldiers (1905)

Somebody Stole My Gal (1918)

Notable

Aggravatin' Papa (Don't You Try To Two-Time Me)

All Over Nothing at All

Angel Child

Baby Blue Eyes

Blue (and Broken Hearted)

A Brown Bird Singing

By the Shalimar

China Boy

Crinoline Days

Dancing Fool

Dearest (You're the Nearest to My Heart)

Dreamy Melody

Farewell Blues

Georgette

I Gave You Up Just Before You Threw Me Down

In the Little Red Schoolhouse

The John Henry Blues

The Lady in Ermine

The Little White Donkey (Le Petit Ane Blanc) (m. Ibert)

Lovesick Blues

Lovin' Sam, the Sheik of Alabam'

Mary, Dear, Some Day We Will Meet Again

My Honey's Lovin' Arms

My Rambler Rose

Neath the South Sea Moon

Nellie Kelly, I Love You

O-hi-o, see "Round on the End and High in the Middle, O-hi-o"

On the Gin, Gin, Ginny Shore

O-oo Ernest, Are You Earnest with Me?

Round on the End and High in the Middle, O-hi-o

Say It While Dancing

Some Sunny Day

Throw Me a Kiss

Water Boy

When the Leaves Come Tumbling Down

When the Sun Goes Down

Who Cares (Agar)

You Know You Belong to Somebody Else

You Remind Me of My Mother

You Tell Her, I S-t-u-t-t-e-r

Blacks and the Blues. Black artists singing the blues become popular. Bessie Smith, twenty-nine, begins to record for Columbia Records on February 16. Following the success of her first blues recording "Downhearted Blues," which sold 780,000 copies in less than six months, she will make twelve records a year for Columbia at $125 a side, with an option for twelve more at $150.

The Charleston. This new dance craze is inspired by the song "Charleston."

The Cotton Club. The legendary Harlem night spot, The Cotton Club, opens at 142nd Street and Lenox Avenue (see 1927).

Top Hits

Bambalina

Barney Google

Bugle Call Rag (Pettis, Meyers, Schoebel)

Charleston

Dizzy Fingers

Estrellita, see "Little Star"

Frasquita Serenade, see "My Little Nest of Heavenly Blue"

I Cried for You (Now It's Your Turn To Cry Over Me)

I Love Life

I Love You (Sweetheart of All My Dreams)

I'm Sitting Pretty in a Pretty Little City

It Ain't Gonna Rain No Mo'

Last Night on the Back Porch—I Loved Her Best of All

Linger Awhile

Little Star (Estrellita) (originally 1914 in Europe)

Louisville Lou, the Vampin' Lady

Mexicali Rose

My Little Nest of Heavenly Blue (Frasquita Serenade)

My Sweetie Went Away, She Didn't Say Where, When or Why

Nobody Knows You When You're Down and Out

On the Mall (March)

Sleep

A Smile Will Go a Long, Long Way

Some Sweet Day

Swingin' Down the Lane

That Old Gang of Mine

Who's Sorry Now

Yes! We Have No Bananas

You've Gotta See Mamma Ev'ry Night or You Can't See Mamma At All

Adaptations

Chansonette (based on Friml's "Chanson" of 1920, with lyrics)

Did You Ever Think as the Hearse Rolls By, or, **The Worms Crawl In, the Worms Crawl Out** (based on a traditional military song)

Who'll Buy My Violets (based on "La Violetera," 1918)

Revivals

Song of India (1897)

Sugar Blues (1919)

Notable

Angry

Annabelle

Beside a Babbling Brook

Chimes Blues

Come On, Spark Plug!

Covered Wagon Days (March)

Downhearted Blues

Gulf Coast Blues

I Won't Say I Will, But I Won't Say I Won't

I'm Goin' South

Indiana Moon

Just a Girl That Men Forget

Mama Goes Where Papa Goes

Mamma Loves Papa—Papa Loves Mamma

No, No, Nora

Oh! Didn't It Rain

Oh Gee, Oh Gosh, Oh Golly I'm in Love

Old Fashioned Love

(Home in) Pasadena

Raggedy Ann

Rememb'ring

La Rosita

Seven or Eleven—My Dixie Pair o'Dice

Sittin' in a Corner

Snake Rag

Sobbin' Blues

Stella

Tin Roof Blues

Weary Blues

Westward Ho!—The Covered Wagon March

When It's Night-Time in Italy, It's Wednesday Over Here

When You Walked Out Someone Else Walked Right In

Wild Flower

Wolverine Blues

1924

Electric Phonographs. Acoustical recordings, the standard since 1877, are replaced by electrical recordings made for the first time with a microphone, a process introduced by the Western Electric Company. In 1925 the Brunswick/General Electric Panotrope electric home phonograph will become available so that these recordings can also be played back electronically.

"Rhapsody in Blue." The first experiment in big band orchestrated jazz, George Gershwin's "Rhapsody in Blue," is performed by the Paul Whiteman Orchestra. Orchestrated by Ferde Grofé, it premiers at Aeolian Hall, New York, February 12.

Noel Coward. The twenty-five-year-old *enfant terrible* of the British theatre stuns London with his play *The Vortex.* He also introduces the twin fads—instantly adopted worldwide—of turtleneck sweaters and breakfasting in bed and making one's office there.

Billy Rose, Helen Morgan, and the Back Stage Club. Billy Rose opens the Back Stage Club over a garage on West 56th Street in New York, with Helen Morgan as the "chantootsie" and comedian Joe Frisco as emcee. The club is packed nightly and because of the crush of the crowd, Helen, illuminated with a baby blue spotlight, has to perch on the Steinway to sing.

Top Hits

All Alone (m. Berlin)

Amapola (Pretty Little Poppy)

California, Here I Come

Charley, My Boy

Copenhagen

Deep in My Heart, Dear

Doodle Doo Doo

Drinking Song

Everybody Loves My Baby, But My Baby Don't Love Nobody But Me

Fascinating Rhythm

Hard Hearted Hannah (The Vamp of Savannah)

How Come You Do Me Like You Do

I Want To Be Happy

I Wonder What's Become of Sally

I'll See You in My Dreams

Indian Love Call

It Had To Be You

Jealous

June Night

King Porter Stomp

(Oh) Lady Be Good
Let Me Linger Longer in Your Arms
The Man I Love
Memory Lane
My Time Is Your Time
Nobody's Sweetheart Now
The One I Love Belongs to Somebody Else
The Prisoner's Song
Rhapsody in Blue
Rose Marie
Serenade
S-H-I-N-E
Somebody Loves Me
Tea for Two
There's Yes, Yes, in Your Eyes
Totem-Tom-Tom
What'll I Do
When My Sugar Walks Down the Street
The Wreck of the Old '97

Notable
Bagdad (m. Ager)
Does the Spearmint Lose Its Flavor on the Bedpost Overnight
Doo Wacka Doo
Eccentric
Fidgety Feet
Follow the Swallow
Golden Days
Honest and Truly
I Wonder Who's Dancing with You Tonight
I'm a Little Blackbird Looking for a Bluebird
In Shadowland
Jimtown Blues
June Brought the Roses
Keep Smiling at Trouble
Lazy
Mandalay
Mandy Make Up Your Mind
My Best Girl
My Dream Girl, I Loved You Long Ago
Oh, Katharina
Parisian Pierrot
Prince of Wails
Ritual Fire Dance (from "El Amor Brujo," m. Manuel de Falla)
Sahara
So Am I
Spain
When You and I Were Seventeen

Where the Lazy Daisies Grow
Why Did I Kiss That Girl?

1925

Nashville. The first "Grand Ole Opry" radio broadcast originates from Station WSM, Nashville, November 28.

Follow the Bouncing Ball. Max Fleischer (see 1915, 1931, and 1974) produces silent sing-along film cartoons, which are accompanied by such silent movie organist maestros as Jesse Crawford and his wife at the Mighty Wurlitzer, or by full orchestras led by such eminent conductors as Erno Rapée and Boris Morros.

Spencer Williams and Josephine Baker. Baker opens this year in Paris at the Champs-Elysées Theatre with a repertoire of songs by black composer Spencer Williams, who for the next ten years is to write all of her numbers at the Folies Bergère. Williams is the author of such hits as "I Ain't Got Nobody" (1916), "Tishomingo Blues" (1918), "I Found a New Baby" (1919), "I Ain't Gonna Give Nobody None o' This Jelly Roll" (1919), "Royal Garden Blues" (with Clarence Williams, 1920), "Careless Love" (with W.C. Handy, 1921), "Everybody Loves My Baby" (1924), "Farewell to Storyville" (1925), and "Basin Street Blues" (1929).

Top Hits
Alabamy Bound
Always (m. Berlin)
Cecilia (Does Your Mother Know You're Out, Cecilia)
Cheatin' on Me
Clap Hands, Here Comes Charley
Collegiate
A Cup of Coffee, a Sandwich and You
Dinah
Don't Bring Lulu
Don't Wake Me Up, Let Me Dream
Drifting and Dreaming
Five Foot Two, Eyes of Blue (Has Anybody Seen My Gal?)
Here in My Arms
The Hills of Home
I Found a New Baby
I Love My Baby—My Baby Loves Me
I Never Knew (That Roses Grew)
If I Had a Girl Like You
If You Knew Susie, Like I Know Susie
I'm in Love Again
I'm Sitting on Top of the World
Jalousie
Just a Cottage Small—By a Waterfall

Looking for a Boy
Love Me Tonight
Manhattan
Milenberg Joys
My Sweetie Turned Me Down
Oh! How I Miss You Tonight
Only a Rose
Paddlin' Madelin' Home
Remember
Save Your Sorrow for Tomorrow
Show Me the Way To Go Home
Sleepy Time Gal
Sometimes I'm Happy
Song of the Vagabonds
Sunny
Sweet Georgia Brown
That Certain Feeling
That Certain Party
(I Wanna Go Where You Go, Do What You Do) Then I'll Be Happy
Ukulele Lady
Who
Why Do I Love You (Gershwin)
Yearning (Just for You)
Yes Sir, That's My Baby

Adaptations
Moonlight and Roses (based on "Andante" by Edwin Lemare)

Revivals
If You Were the Only Girl (in the World) (1916)

Notable
Bam, Bam, Bamy Shore
Boneyard Shuffle
Brown Eyes—Why Are You Blue
Bye and Bye
Davenport Blues
Down by the Winegar Woiks
D'Ye Love Me
Farewell to Storyville
Freshie
Grandpa's Spells
Headin' for Louisville
I Miss My Swiss, My Swiss Miss Misses Me
I Wonder Where My Baby Is Tonight
I'm Gonna Charleston Back to Charleston
Keep Your Skirts Down, Mary Ann
Let It Rain! Let It Pour! (I'll Be in Virginia in the Morning)

My Yiddishe Momme
Neapolitan Nights
Pal of My Cradle Days
Poor Little Rich Girl
Riverboat Shuffle
Sentimental Me
Some Day
Sometime
Song of the Flame
Squeeze Me
Sweet and Low-Down
Two Guitars
Two Little Bluebirds
Waltz Huguette
Waters of Perkiomen
Who Takes Care of the Caretaker's Daughter While the Caretaker's Busy Taking Care?

1926

"Talkies." The first moving picture with sound, *Don Juan,* starring John Barrymore, premieres at the Warner Theatre on Broadway, August 6.

Radio Networks. David Sarnoff's NBC goes "on the air" November 15, and William Paley's CBS follows on September 18, 1927.

Movie's Big Biz. As yet unaffected by radio, television, or the Depression, movies, still (for the most part) without sound, gross more than one billion dollars, domestic and foreign. More than 750 (!) feature films are made this year.

Flaming Youth of the Jazz Age. Modern youth seems to come complete with raccoon coats, stiff yellow slickers, unbuckled galoshes, hotcha Harlemania, rumble seats, and hip flasks filled with hooch supplied by Dutch Schultz and Al Capone. Flappers and their sheiks are dancing to the "Charleston" (1923), the "Black Bottom" (1926), and "The Varsity Drag" (1927).

Anti-war Films. The first major anti-war silent film, *What Price Glory?* (from the stage play), is released. The theme song associated with the film is "Charmaine."

Rodgers and Hart. This songwriting team has five shows running or opening on Broadway: *Dearest Enemy* (held over from 1925) at the Knickerbocker, *The Girl Friend* at the Vanderbilt, *Garrick Gaieties II* at the Garrick, *Peggy-Ann,* again at the Vanderbilt, *Betsy,* which also featured Irving Berlin's "Blue Skies," at the New Amsterdam. In London their *Lido Lady* is playing at the Gaiety Theatre.

THE GREATEST SONGS

Top Hits
(What Can I Say, Dear) After I Say I'm Sorry
All Alone Monday
Are You Lonesome Tonight
Baby Face
Birth of the Blues
Black Bottom
Blue Room
Breezin' Along with the Breeze
Bye Bye Blackbird
Charmaine
Clap Yo' Hands
Crazy Words (Vo-Do-De-O-Do)
'Deed I Do
The Desert Song
Dipper Mouth Blues, see ''Sugar Foot Stomp''
Do Do Do
Flapperette
The Gang That Sang Heart of My Heart
Gimme a Little Kiss, Will Ya, Huh?
The Girl Friend
Hey Gypsy (Play Gypsy)
Horses
I Can't Believe That You're in Love with Me
I Know That You Know
If I Could Be with You One Hour Tonight
In a Little Spanish Town
It All Depends on You
I've Found a New Baby
Lucky Day
Mary Lou
Moonlight on the Ganges
Mountain Greenery
Muskrat Ramble
One Alone
Play Gypsies—Dance Gypsies
Poor Papa (He's Got Nothin' At All)
The Ranger's Song
The Riff Song
Rio Rita
Romance
Someone To Watch Over Me
Sugar Foot Stomp (Dipper Mouth Blues)
Sunday
Tip Toe Through the Tulips (with Me)
Tonight You Belong to Me
Valencia
Valentine
What Can I Say, Dear, After I Say I'm Sorry, see ''After I Say I'm Sorry''

When Day Is Done
When the Red, Red Robin Comes Bob, Bob, Bobbin' Along
Where Do You Work-a John

Adaptations
Dark Eyes (Black Eyes) (based on the Russian gypsy song ''Otchi Tchornia,'' as early as 1884)

Revivals
La Cumparsita (1916)
My Toreador (El Relicario) (1920)

Notable
Am I Wasting My Time on You
Animal Crackers, see ''I'm Just Wild About Animal Crackers''
Barcelona
Because I Love You
The Big Butter and Egg Man
Black Eyes, see ''Dark Eyes,'' above
Bring Back Those Minstrel Days
Cherie, I Love You
Climbing Up the Ladder of Love
Cross Your Heart
Everything's Gonna Be All Right
Following the Sun Around
Gentlemen Prefer Blondes
The Girl Is You and the Boy Is Me
Harmony Blues
The Hawaiian Wedding Song
Heebie Jeebies
Hello, Aloha! How Are You?
Hello, Bluebird
I Left My Sugar Standing in the Rain
I'd Climb the Highest Mountain (If I Knew I'd Find You)
If You're in Love You'll Waltz
I'm Comin' Virginia
I'm Just Wild About Animal Crackers
Júrame (Promise, Love)
Katinka
The Kinkajou
A Little Birdie Told Me So
The Little White House (at the End of Honeymoon Lane)
Lonesome and Sorry
Looking at the World Through Rose Colored Glasses
Ma Curly-Headed Babby
Maybe (Gershwin)
Me Too
Mi Viejo Amor (An Old Love)
Mississippi Suite (m. Grofé)

Muddy Water

My Dream of the Big Parade

Our Director (March)

Reaching for the Moon

(I Don't Believe It But) Say It Again

Sleepy Head

Snag It

Song of the Wanderer

Sunny Disposish

Tamiami Trail

Ting-a-Ling (The Waltz of the Bells)

A Tree in the Park

Where'd You Get Those Eyes (*not* ''Jeepers Creepers'')

Why Do I

1927

Musical ''Talkies.'' The first musical ''talkie,'' *The Jazz Singer,* starring Al Jolson, premieres in New York on October 6. Jolson marks the occasion with his famous ''Wait a minute. You ain't heard nothin' yet, folks.'' This innovation of film plus sound was later celebrated in the song ''If I Had a Talking Picture of You'' (1929).

Oscar. The Academy of Motion Picture Arts and Sciences is established in Hollywood. The first Oscar-winning film in 1927–28 is the Paramount picture *Wings.* Best Actor is Emil Jennings in *The Way of All Flesh,* and Best Actress is Janet Gaynor in *Seventh Heaven.* Because of the advent of talking pictures, this is the only year the Academy grants an Oscar for Writing of the Best Titles in a Silent Film.

New York Theatre. Broadway reaches its all-time production peak as critics from the twenty-four New York City daily newspapers grapple with 268 attractions offered during this season. This compares with an average of fifty to sixty productions per season in the 1970–78 period.

Show Boat. Adapting Edna Ferber's novel for the musical stage, Jerome Kern and Oscar Hammerstein II open *Show Boat* at the Ziegfeld Theatre on December 27 to unanimous critical acclaim. Running 572 performances, this classic American musical introduces standards such as ''Make Believe,'' ''Why Do I Love You?,'' ''Can't Help Lovin' Dat Man,'' and ''Bill'' (lyrics by P.G. Wodehouse from an earlier collaboration with Kern) performed by Helen Morgan playing the role of Julie. Hammerstein describes his ''Ol' Man River'' as ''a song of resignation with a protest implied, sung by a character who is a rugged and untutored philospher.'' The music

and lyrics were faithful to the play and translated Ferber's novel with absolute integrity.

Duke Ellington. With the sponsorship of composer Jimmy McHugh, Duke Ellington, black composer and orchestra leader, opens at the Cotton Club in Harlem on December 4, for a five-year run. Mr. Ellington is twenty-eight.

Gene Austin. A million selling vocal record this year is ''My Blue Heaven,'' sung by Gene Austin.

The Astaires. Fred and Adele Astaire open the new Alvin Theatre starring in George and Ira Gershwin's musical hit *Funny Face.* The Alvin was built by the show's two producers, Alex Aarons and Vinton Freedley (ALex + VINton = ALVIN).

Texas Guinan. Texas (''Hello, Suckers!'') Guinan's ''300 Club'' is raided as Prohibition agents ''bust'' Broadway's foremost speakeasy operator again. It is her forty-seventh ''pinch.'' She is later aptly starred in a Broadway show titled *Padlocks of 1927,* and is remembered for introducing at her club ''the world's greatest dance team,'' George Raft and his brother Dick. She also popularized the description of her best customers as ''big butter and egg men'' (see ''The Big Butter and Egg Man'' (1926)).

Top Hits

Ain't She Sweet

Among My Souvenirs

At Sundown

Away Down South in Heaven

Back in Your Own Back Yard

The Best Things in Life Are Free

Bill

Bless This House

Blue Skies

Broken Hearted

Can't Help Lovin' Dat Man

Chloe

(What'll We Do on a) Dew-Dew-Dewy Day

Diane

The Doll Dance

Everywhere You Go

Funny Face

Girl of My Dreams

Gonna Get a Girl

Hallelujah!

Here Comes the Showboat

I'm Looking Over a Four Leaf Clover

Just a Memory

Let a Smile Be Your Umbrella on a Rainy Day

Lucky in Love
Make Believe
Me and My Shadow
Mississippi Mud
My Blue Heaven
My Heart Stood Still
Ol'Man River
Rain
Ramona
A Room with a View
Russian Lullaby
Sam, the Old Accordion Man
Shaking the Blues Away
Side By Side
The Song Is Ended But the Melody Lingers On
Soon (Gershwin)
Strike Up the Band
Sugar
'S Wonderful
Thinking of You
Thou Swell
The Varsity Drag
Why Do I Love You (Kern)
Your Land and My Land

Adaptations
He's Got the Whole World in His Hands (Hand) (based on a traditional Negro spiritual)
She'll Be Comin' 'Round the Mountain (When She Comes) (based on music of "When the Chariot Comes" (hymn) of 1899 or earlier)

Revivals
Down South (1912)
Frankie and Johnny (Were Lovers) (c. 1870–1875)
Little Town in the Ould County Down (1920)
My Melancholy Baby (1912)

Notable
Ay, Ay, Ay
Black and Tan Fantasy
Ça C'est Paris
C'est Vous (It's You)
Changes
Dancing Tambourine
Dancing the Devil Away
Forgive Me
Four or Five Times
Gid-ap, Garibaldi
The House by the Side of the Road

Jack in the Box
Just Another Day Wasted Away
Just Like the Butterfly (That's Caught in the Rain)
Lovely Lady
Miss Annabelle Lee
Mother
My One and Only
(Give Me) A Night in June
Paree! (Padilla)
Persian Rug
Preludes (Gershwin)
Red Lips Kiss My Blues Away
The Same Old Moon
She Don't Wanna
Silver Moon
So Tired
Soliloquy (Bloom)
Struttin' with Some Barbecue
(There's Something Nice About Everyone But) There's Everything Nice About You
Three Shades of Blue (Grofé)
To Keep My Love Alive
Up in the Clouds
We Two Shall Meet Again
What Does It Matter
Where's That Rainbow
Who's Wonderful, Who's Marvelous? Miss Annabelle Lee, see "Miss Annabelle Lee"
Wild Man Blues
You Don't Like It—Not Much

1928

Gershwin. The tone poem "An American in Paris" has its world premiere on December 13 by the New York Philharmonic-Symphony Society, Walter Damrosch conducting (see 1929). It is the first symphonic composition orchestrated solely by George Gershwin.

Disney and Mickey. Walt Disney, age twenty-seven, and Mickey Mouse, age one, produce the first Disney animated film, *Plane Crazy;* it is silent. Mickey did one more silent film, *Gallopin' Gaucho,* and then spoke at last (with Walt's voice) in *Steamboat Willie.*

Billboard Music Charts. Billboard magazine publishes its first list of radio and in-person song performances entitled "Popular Numbers Featured by Famous Singers and Leaders."

Pinetop Smith and Boogie Woogie. Black pianist Pinetop Smith, who invented the style, records his composition "Boogie Woogie" in Chicago, December 29.

Crosby. Bing has his first hit record with "I Surrender Dear" (see also 1929). Mr. Crosby is twenty-four.

Vallee. Rudy Vallee of Island Pond, Virginia, opens at the Heigh-Ho Club on East 53rd Street in New York City with his band, The Yale Collegians. He boosts his voice with a megaphone which was to become his trademark. The orchestra was later redubbed "The Connecticut Yankees," the name borrowed from the title of the Rodgers and Hart show current this year. Mr. Vallee is twenty-seven.

Boop Boop-a-Doop. Baby-voiced Helen Kane's squeaky and seductive rendition of the song "I Wanna Be Loved By You" (Boop boop-a-doop) in the Broadway show *Good Boy* identifies her forever after as "The Boop-a-Doop Girl." This character later became the basis of a movie cartoon series (see 1931) as well as a newspaper cartoon. Miss Kane's lawsuit for plagiarism in 1935 is unavailing.

Top Hits
An American in Paris (see 1929)
Button Up Your Overcoat
Carolina Moon
Constantinople
Coquette
Crazy Rhythm
Dance Little Lady
Dance of the Paper Dolls
Digga Digga Do
A Garden in the Rain
Get Out and Get Under the Moon
Good News
Honey
How About Me
How Long Has This Been Going On
I Can't Give You Anything But Love
I Get the Blues When It Rains
I Wanna Be Loved By You
If I Had You
I'll Get By
I'm a Ding Dong Daddy from Dumas
In a Mist
Jeannine, I Dream of Lilac Time
Just Imagine
Laugh, Clown, Laugh
Let's Do It (Let's Fall in Love)
The Lonesome Road
Love Me or Leave Me
Lover Come Back to Me
Makin' Whoopee

Manhattan Serenade
Marie
My Lucky Star
Nagasaki
One Kiss
(I Got a Woman Crazy for Me) She's Funny That Way
Shortnin' Bread
Softly, as in a Morning Sunrise
Sonny Boy
Stout Hearted Men
Sweet Lorraine
Sweet Sue (Just You)
(I Love You) Sweetheart of All My Dreams
Sweethearts on Parade
That's My Weakness Now
There's a Rainbow Round My Shoulder
Together
Wanting You
When You're Smiling—The Whole World Smiles with You
You Are Love
You Took Advantage of Me
You're the Cream in My Coffee

Adaptations
Hallelujah, I'm a Bum (a hobo version based on the traditional hymn "Revive Us Again")

Revivals
Marcheta (1913)
Moonlight and Roses (1925)
Original Dixieland One-Step (1918)
Sweetheart of Sigma Chi (1912)

Notable
The Alabama Song (Moon of Alabama)
Angela Mia
Avalon Town
Beloved
Boogie Woogie
Cherry
Chiquita
Doin' the New Lowdown
Doin' the Raccoon
Don't Hold Everything
Don't Look At Me That Way
Dusky Stevedore
Feeling I'm Falling
A Gay Caballero
Give Me One Hour
De Glory Road

Golden Gate
Goodnight
Half-Way to Heaven
High Upon a Hill Top
Hooray for Captain Spalding
Hot Heels
I Faw Down an' Go Boom
I Love To Dunk a Hunk of Spongecake
(I Scream, You Scream, We All Scream for) Ice Cream
I'm Bringing a Red, Red Rose
I'm Wild About Horns on Automobiles That Go "Ta-ta-ta-ta"
Just Like a Melody out of the Sky
K-ra-zy for You
Let's Misbehave
Lonesome in the Moonlight
Ma Belle
Mack the Knife (The Threepenny Opera)
March of the Musketeers
Marianne
Memories of France
The Mouche
Oh Baby Mine (I Get So Lonely)
Old Man Sunshine—Little Boy Bluebird
Once in a Lifetime
Pilot Me
A Precious Little Thing Called Love
Regimental Song
Revenge
Semper Paratus (Coast Guard March)
South
The Tartar Song
There's Something About a Rose
Washboard Blues
Watching the Clouds Roll By
When the White Lilacs Bloom Again
Where Is the Song of Songs for Me
Where the Shy Little Violets Grow
Yellow Dog Blues
You Wouldn't Fool Me

1929

The Crash. The stock market crashes in October and the Great Depression begins, marked by the *Variety* headline: "Wall Street Lays an Egg."

Radio Serials. "Amos 'n' Andy" begins network broadcasting, August 19. This team was previously known as "Sam and Henry," when heard over Station WGN, Chicago, 1926–28. Their opening theme, "The Perfect

Song" (1915), was originally associated with the silent film *The Birth of a Nation.*

Movie Palaces. Loew's Paradise in the Bronx, New York, costs MGM $1,500,000, with $34,500 for the console organ.

Modern Art. The Museum of Modern Art opens in New York.

Crooners Vallee, Crosby, and Colombo. Rudy Vallee (see also 1928), Bing Crosby, and Russ Colombo emerge as "crooner" singing stars aided by their recordings and network radio appearances. Not counting one-reelers made for Mack Sennett, Bing will star in fifty-five feature films beginning with *The King of Jazz* (1930) and ending with *Stagecoach* (1966). Russ Colombo, who was a discovery of composer Con Conrad, makes two million-selling records of Conrad's songs "(I'm Just a) Prisoner of Love" and "You Call It Madness But I Call It Love." Mr. Colombo is twenty-one.

Broadway Melody. On February 1, MGM's *The Broadway Melody* opens at Hollywood's Grauman's Theatre, the first "all talking, all singing, all dancing" screen musical. Production head Irving Thalberg hires writers Nacio Herb Brown and Arthur Freed to write a score especially for this film. It wins next year's Academy Award and launches the Hollywood musical era (fifty such films produced in 1930 alone).

Ethel Waters. Black actress and musical star Ethel Waters of Chester, Pennsylvania, appears in her first film, *On with the Show* (see "Am I Blue"). Miss Waters is twenty-nine.

Top Hits
Ain't Misbehavin'
Am I Blue
An American in Paris
Aren't We All, see "I'm a Dreamer"
Around the Corner and Under the Tree
Basin Street Blues
Bolero
Broadway Melody
Can't We Be Friends
Deep Night
Don't Ever Leave Me
Dream Lover
Glad Rag Doll
Great Day
Happy Days Are Here Again
Honeysuckle Rose
I Guess I'll Have To Change My Plan
I Kiss Your Hand, Madame

I May Be Wrong, But I Think You're Wonderful

If I Had a Talking Picture of You

I'll Always Be in Love with You

I'll See You Again

I'm a Dreamer (Aren't We All)

I'm Just a Vagabond Lover

Jericho

Just You, Just Me

Kansas City Kitty

Let Me Sing and I'm Happy

A Little Kiss Each Morning, a Little Kiss Each Night

Liza

Louise

Love (Your Magic Spell Is Everywhere)

Mean to Me

Miss You

Moanin' Low

More Than You Know

My Sin

The One Rose That's Left in My Heart

Orange Blossom Time

Pagan Love Song

Painting the Clouds with Sunshine

Paree (Porter)

Piccolo Pete

Puttin' on the Ritz

Romance

Should I (Reveal)

Siboney

Singin' in the Rain

Song of the Bayou

S'posin'

Stardust

Sunny Side Up

There'll Be Some Changes Made

There's Danger in Your Eyes, Cherie

(When) They Cut Down the Old Pine Tree

True Blue Lou

Underneath the Russian Moon

Wedding Bells Are Breaking Up That Old Gang of Mine

The Wedding of the Painted Doll

When It's Springtime in the Rockies

When the Organ Played at Twilight (The Song That Reached My Heart)

Why

Why Was I Born

With a Song in My Heart

Without a Song

The Woman in the Shoe

You Do Something to Me

You Were Meant for Me

You've Got That Thing

Zigeuner

Adaptations

You're in the Army Now (words known as early as 1917)

Revivals

If You Were the Only Girl (in the World) (1925)

Some Sweet Day (1923)

Song of the Islands (1915)

Tip Toe Through the Tulips (with Me) (1926)

Notable

Bilbao Song

Birmingham Bertha

Can't You Understand

Chant of the Jungle

Congratulations

Cross Your Fingers

Dear Little Cafe

Futuristic Rhythm

Green Eyes

Here Am I

How Long, How Long Blues

How Was I To Know

I Don't Want Your Kisses

I Got a "Code" in My "Dose"

If Love Were All

I've Got a Feeling I'm Falling

Keepin' Myself for You

Miss Hannah

My Kinda Love

My Love Parade

My Mother's Eyes

My Song of the Nile

My Sweeter Than Sweet

Satisfied

Seventh Heaven

She's Such a Comfort to Me

A Ship Without a Sail

Singing a Vagabond Song

Singin' in the Bathtub

The Song of the Shirt

To-Kay

Turn on the Heat

Weary River

When I'm Looking At You

Why Can't I

Wonderful You

You Don't Know Paree
Your Mother and Mine
Yours Sincerely

1930

Technicolor. The Vagabond King, starring Jeanette MacDonald and Dennis King, is the first feature film in Technicolor to be released.

Cole Porter Banned. Mr. Porter's "Love for Sale," his hit song about commercialized affection featured in the score of the Broadway revue *The New Yorkers,* is banned by the major radio networks.

Maurice Chevalier and Eleanor Powell. Maurice Chevalier presents an evening of French songs on Broadway assisted by a snappy young new tap dancer (eighteen) named Eleanor Powell, who later this year is featured in the Kay Swift revue *Fine and Dandy,* starring comedian Joe Cook (see also *Astaire,* 1940).

Marlene Dietrich. Mary Magdalene von Losch of Berlin, makes her American screen debut in Josef von Sternberg's *The Blue Angel,* starring Emil Jannings. Marlene, twenty-six, immortalized in this film the Sammy Lerner and Frederick Hollander song "Falling in Love Again."

Merman. Ethel Merman (née Zimmermann) leaves her $35 per week job as a secretary in Long Island City and starts at $350 a week as a featured player in George and Ira Gershwin's musical hit *Girl Crazy* at the Alvin Theatre. Holding the high C in the chorus of "I Got Rhythm" for sixteen measures, Miss Merman, twenty-one, stops the show.

Top Hits
All the King's Horses
Andalucia (m. Lecuona)
Betty Co-Ed
Beyond the Blue Horizon
Bidin' My Time
Body and Soul
But Not for Me
Bye Bye Blues
Can't We Talk It Over
Cheerful Little Earful
A Cottage for Sale
Cryin' for the Carolines
Dancing on the Ceiling
Dancing with Tears in My Eyes
Embraceable You
Exactly Like You

Falling in Love Again (Can't Help It)
Fine and Dandy
For You
Georgia on My Mind
Get Happy
I Got Rhythm
I Still Get a Thrill (Thinking of You)
I'm Confessin' That I Love You
I'm Yours
It Happened in Monterey
I've Got a Crush on You
Just a Gigolo
The Kiss Waltz
Lady Play Your Mandolin
Little White Lies
Love for Sale
Magic Is the Moonlight
Malagueña (m. Lecuona)
Memories of You
My Baby Just Cares for Me
My Future Just Passed
My Ideal
On the Sunny Side of the Street
Please Don't Talk About Me When I'm Gone
(Ol') Rockin' Chair
Sing Something Simple
Sing You Sinners
(By the) Sleepy Lagoon
So Beats My Heart for You
Something To Remember You By
St. James Infirmary (possibly known as early as 1890–99 as "Gambler's Blues")
Sweet and Hot
Ten Cents a Dance
Them There Eyes
Three Little Words
Time on My Hands
Two Hearts in Three Quarter Time
Walkin' My Baby Back Home
The Waltz You Saved for Me
What Is This Thing Called Love
When Your Hair Has Turned to Silver, I Will Love You Just the Same
With the Wind and the Rain in Your Hair
Would You Like To Take a Walk (Oo-Oo-Ooh)
You Brought a New Kind of Love to Me
You're Driving Me Crazy

Adaptations
(Joshua Fit De) Battle of Jericho (based on a traditional Negro spiritual)

Revivals
Stein Song (The University of Maine) (1910)

Notable
A Bench in the Park
Blue Again
Blue Is the Night
Can This Be Love
Come Out of the Kitchen, Mary Ann
Delishious
Down the River of Golden Dreams
The ''Free and Easy'' Hour of Parting
Go Home and Tell Your Mother
Goofus
Hangin' on the Garden Gate
Happy Feet
Have a Little Faith in Me
Hittin' the Bottle
Hora Staccato (arr. J. Heifetz)
I Love You So Much
If I Were King
I'm in the Market for You
In the Jailhouse Now
It Must Be True
The King's Horses
Lazy Lou'siana Moon
Lucky Seven
The March of Time
Moon Is Low (Brown)
Moonlight on the Colorado
Mysterious Mose
Ninety-Nine Out of a Hundred (Want To Be Loved)
Over Night
Reaching for the Moon
Ring Dem Bells
Rockin' in Rhythm
The Rogue Song
Sweet Jennie Lee
Swingin' in a Hammock
Where Have You Been?

1931

U.S. National Anthem. ''The Star Spangled Banner,'' lyrics by Francis Scott Key (see 1814) is adopted as the U.S. national anthem on March 3.

Stereo. British inventor Alan D. Blumlein patents two channels of audio in one record groove. In the first channel, sound recording is lateral (side-to-side), in the second, vertical (hill-and-dale).

Animated Cartoons. Max Fleischer creates the first of 112 cartoons with the leading character a flapper-like Helen Kane caricature (see 1928) called Betty Boop. The musical backgrounds are often by black jazz stars such as Cab Calloway and Louis Armstrong. Miss Boop's thighs drew great attention from Will Hays, the Hollywood censor during the thirties. At one time, Hays forced the Paramount studios to remove Betty's garter, which had been climbing higher and higher up her thigh, and over the years, Betty's neckline was slowly raised to reveal less and less of her very pronounced cleavage. In this same year Fleischer begins the film cartoon series *Popeye the Sailor,* an epoch that lasted until 1967—454 Popeye and Olive Oyl cartoons later.

Calypso Trend. From the Bahamas, see ''Mama Don't Want No Peas an' Rice an' Cocoanut Oil.''

Rhumba Trend. See ''Cuban Love Song,'' ''Mama Inez,'' ''The Night Was Made for Love,'' ''The Peanut Vendor,'' and ''When Yuba Plays the Rhumba on the Tuba.''

Rockin'. The phrase ''rockin''' makes an early appearance in the Duke Ellington song ''Rockin' in Rhythm'' (1930) popularized this year.

Top Hits
Adios
All of Me
As Time Goes By
Barnacle Bill the Sailor
Between the Devil and the Deep Blue Sea
Blues in My Heart
By the River Sainte Marie
Call Me Darling
Cuban Love Song
Dancing in the Dark
Dream a Little Dream of Me
Drums in My Heart
Goodnight, Sweetheart
Got a Date with an Angel
Guilty
Heartaches
Home
I Apologize
I Don't Know Why (I Just Do)
I Found a Million Dollar Baby in a Five and Ten Cent Store
I Love a Parade

THE GREATEST SONGS

I Love Louisa
I'm Through with Love
Just Friends
Just One More Chance
Lady of Spain
Lazy River
Life Is Just a Bowl of Cherries
Little Girl
Love Is Sweeping the Country
Love Letters in the Sand
Mad Dogs and Englishmen
Mama Inez
Marta
Minnie the Moocher
Mood Indigo
(There Ought To Be a) Moonlight Saving Time
My Song
Nevertheless
New Sun in the Sky
The Night Was Made for Love
Now's the Time To Fall in Love
Of Thee I Sing
Ooh That Kiss
(You Came to Me from) Out of Nowhere
Paradise (Waltz)
The Peanut Vendor (El Manisero)
Penthouse Serenade, see "When We're Alone"
Prisoner of Love
Quiéreme Mucho, see "Yours"
River, Stay 'Way from My Door
Shadrack
She Didn't Say Yes
Smile, Darn Ya, Smile
Someday I'll Find You (Coward)
Sweet and Lovely
Tell Me Why You Smile Mona Lisa
That's My Desire
The Thrill Is Gone
Through the Years
Till the Real Thing Comes Along
Two Loves Have I
Wabash Moon
Was That the Human Thing To Do
When I Take My Sugar to Tea
When It's Sleepy Time Down South
(When It's Roundup Time in Texas) When the Bloom Is on the Sage
When the Moon Comes Over the Mountain
When We're Alone (Penthouse Serenade)
When Your Lover Has Gone

When Yuba Plays the Rhumba on the Tuba
Where the Blue of the Night Meets the Gold of the Day
Whistling in the Dark
Wrap Your Troubles in Dreams, and Dream Your Troubles Away
You Call It Madness (Ah, But I Call It Love)
(I'll Be Glad When You're Dead) You Rascal You
You're My Everything
Yours (Quiéreme Mucho)
Yours Is My Heart Alone

Revivals
Alouette (1879)
Shine on Harvest Moon (1908)

Notable
At Your Command
Bend Down, Sister
Come to Me
Do the New York
Eleven More Months and Ten More Days
A Faded Summer Love
Got the Bench, Got the Park, But I Haven't Got You
Half Caste Woman
Ho-Hum
I'll Follow You
It's the Darndest Thing
I've Got Five Dollars
Jazz Nocturne
Kickin' the Gong Around
Lies
Mama Don't Want No Peas an' Rice an' Cocoanut Oil
Maria My Own (Maria La O)
Oh Monah
Poor Pierrot
(I'm) Popeye the Sailor Man
Running Between the Raindrops
She Lived Next Door to a Firehouse
Singin' the Blues
Street Scene
That's Why Darkies Were Born
This Is the Missus
The Torch Song
Try To Forget
Twentieth Century Blues
Under a Roof in Paree (Sous les Toits de Paris)
When I'm the President
While Hearts Are Singing
Who Cares
Who's Your Little Who-Zis

Why Dance
You Didn't Have to Tell Me—I Knew It All the Time
You Forgot Your Gloves
You Try Somebody Else, and I'll Try Somebody Else

1932

Pulitzer for a Musical. George S. Kaufman and Morrie Ryskind and Ira Gershwin receive the first Pulitzer Prize awarded to a Broadway musical for book and lyrics, respectively for *Of Thee I Sing.* George Gershwin's music does not receive the award.

Depression Songs. See ''Brother, Can You Spare a Dime'' and ''(In) A Shanty in Old Shanty Town.''

Record Sales Drop. As the Depression deepens, record sales fall to six million as compared with 107 million in 1927.

No More Vaudeville. Vaudeville is killed by the Depression, talking pictures, and radio. The Palace Theatre in New York closes as a vaudeville house on November 16 and reopens as the R.K.O. (Radio-Keith-Orpheum) Palace, a movie theatre.

Radio City Music Hall. The movie palace epoch climaxes as the last of the greats, Radio City Music Hall, opens December 27, with a capacity of 6200.

Shirley Temple. Shirley Temple of Santa Monica, California, makes her first screen appearance in the non-musical film *Red Haired Alibi.* Miss Temple is three.

Top Hits
Adios Muchachos
Alone Together
April in Paris
As You Desire Me
Auf Wiedersehn, My Dear
Brother, Can You Spare a Dime
Corrine Corrina
Crazy People
(When It's) Darkness on the Delta
Fit as a Fiddle (And Ready for Love)
A Ghost of a Chance, see ''I Don't Stand a Ghost of a Chance with You''
Granada
Have You Ever Been Lonely
How Deep Is the Ocean
I Don't Stand a Ghost of a Chance with You
I Gotta Right To Sing the Blues
I Guess I'll Have To Change My Plan
I Surrender Dear
If I Love Again

I'll Never Be the Same
I'm Getting Sentimental over You
Isn't It Romantic
It Don't Mean a Thing If It Ain't Got That Swing
It Was So Beautiful
I've Got the World on a String
I've Got You on My Mind
I've Told Ev'ry Little Star
Just an Echo in the Valley
Keepin' Out of Mischief Now
Let's All Sing Like the Birdies Sing
Let's Have Another Cup of Coffee
Let's Put Out the Lights and Go To Sleep
(Just a) Little Street Where Old Friends Meet
Louisiana Hayride
Lullaby of the Leaves
Mad About the Boy
Marching Along Together
Mimi
My Darling
My Silent Love
Night and Day
(I'd Love To Spend) One Hour with You
Play, Fiddle, Play
Please
Rise 'n' Shine
Say It Isn't So
A Sentimental Gentleman from Georgia
(In) A Shanty in Old Shanty Town
A Shine on Your Shoes
Smoke Rings
Snuggled on Your Shoulder, Cuddled in Your Arms
Soft Lights and Sweet Music
Somebody Loves You
The Song Is You
Speak to Me of Love (Parlez-moi d'Amour)
(On the) Street of Dreams
Take Me in Your Arms
Try a Little Tenderness
Underneath the Arches
We Just Couldn't Say Goodbye
Willow Weep for Me
Wintergreen for President
You Are Too Beautiful
You Can Depend on Me
You're an Old Smoothie
You're Blasé

Adaptations
Oh, Bury Me Not on the Lone Prairie (The Dying Cowboy)
  (based on a traditional cowboy song)

Revivals
La Cumparsita (1916)

Notable
All-American Girl
And So to Bed (m. Gordon, Revel)
(I Would Do) Anything for You
Butterflies in the Rain
By the Fireside
Cabin in the Cotton
Contented
Creole Love Call
Eadie Was a Lady
Happy-Go-Lucky You
I'll Never Have To Dream Again
Just Because You're You
Let's Call It a Day
Love Me Tonight
Masquerade
On a Roof in Manhattan
The Party's Over Now
So Do I
Strange Interlude
Three on a Match
Too Many Tears
Turn Out the Light
Underneath the Harlem Moon

1933

Prohibition Repealed. On December 5, speakeasies become night-clubs, cafés, bars, or just plain "gin mills."

Juke Joints. The juke box arrives in most of the above and at the local coffee shop or diner. On some, selections can be made directly from a coin box at your table.

Radio City and Rockefeller Center. In New York City, the complex surrounding the Music Hall is named Radio City after its principal occupants, the NBC Radio networks (Red and Blue), and is completed in November. The Blue network is later to become the ABC network.

Forty-Second Street. At twenty-four, Ruby Keeler (wife of Al Jolson) stars with Warner Baxter, Dick Powell, and Ginger Rogers in Busby Berkeley's imaginative movie musical, *Forty-Second Street.* Warner Brothers' Darryl Zanuck hired Al Dubin and Harry Warren to write the score which includes the hits "Forty-Second Street,"

"Shuffle Off to Buffalo," and "You're Getting To Be a Habit with Me."

The Three Little Pigs. Walt Disney's musical Technicolor cartoon short-subject film *The Three Little Pigs* featuring the song "Who's Afraid of the Big Bad Wolf" is a great success, inspiring Disney to attempt full-length animated cartoon features.

Irving Berlin. In the hit topical revue *As Thousands Cheer*, with score by Irving Berlin, the song "Easter Parade" is staged in stunning rotogravure and sung by Ziegfeld star Marilyn Miller (it was her last show) and Clifton Webb. Berlin had previously used the same melody in 1917 for "Smile and Show Your Dimple." In this show, Helen Broderick is also memorable as the Statute of Liberty. Each song in the show is preceded by a newspaper headline projected on a scrim, and in an innovation daring for the musical theatre at that time, the headline "Unknown Negro Lynched by Frenzied Mob" is followed by black actress Ethel Waters's poignant, show-stopping rendition of the Irving Berlin song "Supper Time."

Cole Porter, Divorce and Divorcée. The Cole Porter song "After You—Who" is sung by Fred Astaire in both the American and English editions of the Porter musical *Gay Divorce*, the show that also features "Night and Day." On its transmutation to film in Hollywood, however, the Hays Office of film censorship refuses to countenance indirect approval of divorces that are fun, and the show is retitled *The Gay Divorcée.* The film also features the first Academy Award winning song "The Continental" (see 1934).

Bob Hope. Mr. Hope, from Eltham, England, has a role in the Otto Harbach-Jerome Kern musical hit *Roberta.* Mr. Hope is thirty.

More Shirley Temple. This Wunderkind child star makes her musical film debut in *Stand Up and Cheer.* See "Stand Up and Cheer."

Flying Down to Rio. The first Fred Astaire-Ginger Rogers movie musical has a score written by Vincent Youmans, Gus Kahn, and Edward Eliscu and introduces the hits "Carioca" and "Orchids in the Moonlight."

Drive-In Theatres. Camden, New Jersey, features the first drive-in theatre with individual loudspeakers for each car.

Singing Telegrams. An innovation by The Postal Telegraph has its messengers singing birthday greetings in person.

Nelson Eddy. Nelson Eddy of Providence, Rhode Island, makes his Hollywood debut at thirty-two in the musical film *Broadway to Hollywood*, starring Frank

Morgan, Madge Evans, Jackie Cooper, Mickey Rooney, and Jimmy Durante. This film revived two songs by composer John Stromberg, ''Ma Blushin' Rosie'' (1900) and ''Come Down Ma Evenin' Star'' (1902), the latter of which he wrote for and dedicated to the Weber and Fields super-star, Lillian Russell. Stromberg was found dead in his apartment with the newly written manuscript of this song in his pocket.

Top Hits
Annie Doesn't Live Here Anymore
Blue Prelude
Boulevard of Broken Dreams
By a Waterfall
Carioca
Close Your Eyes
Did You Ever See a Dream Walking
Don't Blame Me
Down the Old Ox Road
Easter Parade
Everything I Have Is Yours
Flying Down to Rio
Forty-Second Street
The Gold Diggers' Song, see ''We're in the Money''
Heat Wave
Hey Young Fella Close Your Old Umbrella
I Cover the Waterfront
I Like Mountain Music
I Like the Likes of You
I Wanna Be Loved
It's Only a Paper Moon
It's the Talk of the Town
Jungle Drums
Keep Young and Beautiful
The Last Round-Up
Lazy Bones
Let's Fall in Love
Love Is the Sweetest Thing
Love Locked Out
Lover
Maria Elena
Mine
Moon Song (That Wasn't Meant for Me)
My Little Grass Shack in Kealakekua, Hawaii
Not for All the Rice in China
The Old Spinning Wheel
On the Trail (Grand Canyon Suite)
Orchids in the Moonlight
Pettin' in the Park
Rosetta

Shadow Waltz
Shuffle Off to Buffalo
Smoke Gets in Your Eyes
Sophisticated Lady
Stormy Weather
Tell Me Tonight
Temptation
Thanks
This Little Piggie Went to Market
Tony's Wife
The Touch of Your Hand
Two Tickets to Georgia
Under a Blanket of Blue
We'll Make Hay While the Sun Shines
We're in the Money (The Gold Diggers' Song)
What Is There To Say
Who's Afraid of the Big Bad Wolf
Yesterdays
You Gotta Be a Football Hero (To Get Along with the Beautiful Girls)
You're Devastating
You're Getting To Be a Habit with Me
You're Mine You
You've Got Me Crying Again

Adaptations
El Condor Pasa (If I Could) (based on a Peruvian folksong)
My Moonlight Madonna (based on ''Poème'' by Zden arek Fibich)

Revivals
(The Daring Young Man on) The Flying Trapeze (1868)

Notable
After All You're All I'm After
After You—Who
Ah, But Is It Love
Black Moonlight
Blue Lou (*not* ''True Blue Lou'')
Dinner at Eight
Doin' the Uptown Lowdown
The Eel
Evenin'
Experiment
Farewell to Arms
Happy as the Day Is Long
Hold Me
How Could We Be Wrong
How's Chances
A Hundred Years from Today

In the Valley of the Moon
Inka Dinka Doo
It Isn't Fair
Jimmy Had a Nickel
Keep on Doin' What You're Doin'
Knightsbridge March
Learn To Croon
Let 'Em Eat Cake
(The) Lorelei
Lovely
Moonlight and Pretzels
Music Makes Me
My Hat's on the Side of My Head
Once in a Blue Moon
One Morning in May
The Physician
Shanghai Lil
Stand Up and Cheer
Sweet Madness
There's Something About a Soldier
Young and Healthy
You're Gonna Lose Your Gal
You're My Past, Present and Future
You've Got Everything

1934

Bill Hill and Cowboy Songs. See "Cattle Call," "Tumbling Tumbleweeds," "Wagon Wheels"* (published in 1931), "The Last Round-Up"* (1933), "On the Trail" (1933), "Roll Along Prairie Moon" (1935), "Empty Saddles"* (1936), "I'm an Old Cowhand" (1936), and "Twilight on the Trail" (1936).

The songs with asterisks were written by Billy Hill, a *real* cowboy from Boston who actually *had* punched cattle in Montana and worked for a mining company in Death Valley. He was also the author of many other folksy hits including "They Cut Down the Old Pine Tree" (1929), "Have You Ever Been Lonely" (1933), "Old Spinning Wheel" (1933), "In the Chapel in the Moonlight" (1936), and "Call of the Canyon" (1942) from the film of the same title.

Anything Goes. Possibly Cole Porter's greatest achievement, the revised book of *Anything Goes* by Howard Lindsay and Russel Crouse was a big success. Starring Ethel Merman, Victor Moore, and William Gaxton, the hit songs include "All Through the Night," "Anything Goes," "I Get a Kick Out of You," "There'll Always Be a Lady Fair," "You're the Top," and "Blow,

Gabriel, Blow." Porter's score was uniformly brassy, witty, sexual, and sophisticated.

Cole Porter. Drugs are mentioned for the first time in the lyrics of a Top Hit. Things do not go better with Coke for Cole Porter; he gets no kick at all from cocaine. See "I Get a Kick Out of You."

The "Eyes" Have "It." In 1933–34 four top hit songs feature "eyes": "Close Your Eyes" (1933), "Smoke Gets in Your Eyes" (1933), "With My Eyes Wide Open" (1934), and "I Only Have Eyes for You" (1934).

Santa Claus. A reluctant Eddie Cantor introduces the Christmas classic "Santa Claus Is Coming to Town" on radio the week before Thanksgiving at the insistence of his wife, Ida.

All-Time Wittiest Song Titles. Having regaled us in 1932 with the intriguing song title "He Played His Ukulele as the Shop Went Down" (not indexed), songwriter Arthur Le Clerq's English wit prevails again this year as he offers two new songs: "What Can You Give a Nudist on His Birthday" and "Nobody Loves a Fairy When She's Forty." The former was a favorite of British artist Gracie Fields, and the latter is still sung by Tessie O'Shea.

Top Hits
All I Do Is Dream of You
All Through the Night (m. Porter)
Anything Goes
As Long As I Live (m. Arlen)
Autumn in New York
Be Still My Heart
The Beat of My Heart
Blow, Gabriel, Blow
Blue Moon
Carry Me Back to the Lone Prairie
Cattle Call
The Champagne Waltz
Cocktails for Two
The Continental
Deep Purple
Easy Come, Easy Go
Emaline
Fare Thee Well, Annabelle
Flirtation Walk
For All We Know
Goodnight My Love
Hands Across the Table
Hold My Hand
The House Is Haunted
I Get a Kick Out of You
I Only Have Eyes for You

I Saw Stars

If (Tolchard Evans)

If There Is Someone Lovelier Than You

I'll Follow My Secret Heart

(You May Not Be an Angel But) I'll String Along with You

Isle of Capri

(It's) June in January

Let's Take a Walk Around the Block

Little Dutch Mill

Little Man, You've Had a Busy Day

Love in Bloom

Love Is Just Around the Corner

Love Thy Neighbor

May I

Miss Otis Regrets

Mister and Mrs. Is the Name

The Moon Was Yellow

Moonglow

My Old Flame

My Shawl

No! No! A Thousand Times No!

The Object of My Affection

Ole Faithful

On the Good Ship Lollipop

One Night of Love

Out in the Cold Again

P.S. I Love You

El Rancho Grande

Santa Claus Is Coming to Town

Solitude

Stars Fell on Alabama

Stay as Sweet as You Are

Sweetie Pie

Thank You for a Lovely Evening

There Goes My Heart

True

Tumbling Tumbleweeds

Two Cigarettes in the Dark

The Very Thought of You

Wagon Wheels

What a Diff'rence a Day Made

Winter Wonderland

With Every Breath I Take

With My Eyes Wide Open, I'm Dreaming

You and the Night and the Music

You Oughta Be in Pictures

You're a Builder Upper

You're the Top

Adaptations

La Cucaracha (based on a Mexican folksong)

Notable

Baby, Take a Bow

Believe It Beloved

Blame It on My Youth

The Blue Bird of Happiness

The Breeze (That's Bringing My Honey Back to Me)

Butterfingers

Don't Let It Bother You

Everything Stops for Tea

Fair and Warmer

Fun To Be Fooled

The Gypsy in Me

Ha-Cha-Cha

Haunting Me

Here Comes the British

I Took My Harp to a Party

I Wish I Were Twins

Ill Wind (You're Blowin' Me No Good)

I'm Humming, I'm Whistling, I'm Singing

I'm on a See-Saw

Little Rock Getaway

Lost in a Fog

A Needle in a Haystack

Nobody Loves a Fairy When She's Forty

Pardon My Southern Accent

Play to Me, Gypsy

Rhythm Is Our Business

Rolling Home

Suddenly

The Sweetest Music This Side of Heaven

Take a Number from One to Ten

Thank You So Much Mrs. Lowsborough—Goodbye

Then I'll Be Tired of You

(Ooh) What a Little Moonlight Can Do

What Can You Give a Nudist on His Birthday

Wonder Bar

You're My Thrill

1935

Tape Recorder. At the Radio Exhibition in Berlin, the A.E.G. Company (Telefunken) exhibits a remarkable new recording machine, the Magnetophone. The machine records high-fidelity sound using for the first time tape consisting of carbonyl iron powder coated on cellulose acetate.

Your Hit Parade. Sponsored by Lucky Strike cigarettes, this new network radio show begins on Wednesday, April 20. Broadcast time is then shifted to Saturdays at 9 p.m., E.S.T. The theme song of the show is "(This Is My) Lucky Day" (1926), and the show opens with the chanting of tobacco auctioneer L. A. (Speed) Riggs. The program is enormously popular, and is soon celebrated in a feature film, *The Hit Parade* (1937). Somehow, the program slogan—"Have you tried a Lucky lately? So round, so firm, so fully packed, so free and easy on the draw"—escaped the eagle eyes of the network censors.

"Your Hit Parade" was the brainchild of the legendary long-time American Tobacco Company president George Washington Hill. Hill subscribed fanatically to the Calvin Coolidge credo: "Advertising is the spiritual side of business." There is a legend, which ought to be true even if it isn't, that limns Hill's style. Hill, the story goes, was offered by a promoter the chance to examine a fantastic new sales slogan consisting of only four words which were written on a slip of paper concealed in the promoter's fist. The cost for the look: $50,000. Hill agreed and unfolded the slip to read: "Be Happy—Go Lucky." Hill, the story goes, gladly paid.

With "Y.H.P." Hill not only moved Lucky Strikes across the sales counters of America, but with his concept of a weekly "song sweepstakes," he dramatically affected the course of American popular music.

Sydney Greenstreet's masterful characterization of the menacing, unctuous G. W. Hill in the film *The Hucksters* (1946) portrayed Hill as the ultimate example of the ogre-sponsor. Nevertheless, Hill, with his original idea of a weekly tabulation of current song popularity made "Your Hit Parade" the most popular show in radio networking with millions of loyal listeners.

Hill's personal whims of musical taste often seeped into "Your Hit Parade" survey statistics through his ad agency, Foote, Cone and Belding. Comparison of "Your Hit Parade" rankings and the popularity rankings of songs determined by record sales (RS) (included here from 1940) and general "air play" (AP) (included here from 1942) consequently often reveal wide divergences.

Drama Critics' Circle. The major critics of the New York City newspapers sponsor their own Drama Critics' Circle Awards because of dissatisfaction with the Pulitzer Prize selections.

Gershwin and Porgy. Porgy and Bess, an opera in English by George Gershwin, opens at the Alvin Theatre on Broadway on October 10. Based on the novel and play *Porgy* by Dorothy and Dubose Heyward, it features libretto and lyrics by Dubose Heyward and Ira Gershwin.

Porgy and Bess, produced by the Theatre Guild and directed by Reuben Mamoulian, ran for only 124 performances this year and received unfavorable critical notices.

The Apollo. The Apollo Theatre on 125th Street in Harlem opens March 3. (It had originally opened as the Lafayette Theatre May 17, 1925.)

Benny Goodman. Benny Goodman's orchestra becomes the rage after his opening at the Palomar Ballroom in Los Angeles in August, and Goodman is heralded The King of Swing. Thoroughly trained in the classics as well as swing, his opening theme song "Let's Dance" is a swinging version of Carl Maria von Weber's "Invitation to the Dance" (1821). His closing theme is "Goodbye" by Gordon Jenkins (1936).

Cole Porter and the Beguine. A new tropical jungle rhythm, the beguine, appears. Cole Porter presents "Begin the Beguine" in the Broadway show *Jubilee* (see also *Astaire and the Beguine,* 1940).

Bill Boyd. Silent film veteran Bill Boyd and his horse Topper create his perennial role of Hopalong Cassidy this year, adapted from the 1910 novel by Clarence Mulford.

Top Hits

["Your Hit Parade" song rankings (HP) begin this year.]

Alone HP 7 (1936)
Begin the Beguine
Bess, You Is My Woman Now
(Take Me Back to My) Boots and Saddle
Broadway Rhythm
The Broken Record
Chasing Shadows HP 6
Cheek to Cheek HP 3
East of the Sun and West of the Moon HP 9
From the Top of Your Head (to the Tip of Your Toes)
Here Comes Cookie
I Can't Get Started
I Dream Too Much
I Feel a Song Coming On
I Got Plenty o' Nuttin'
I'll Never Say "Never Again" Again
I'm Gonna Sit Right Down and Write Myself a Letter
I'm in the Mood for Love HP 5
I'm Shooting High
In a Little Gypsy Tea Room HP 1

In the Middle of a Kiss   HP 7
Isn't This a Lovely Day (To Be Caught in the Rain)
It Ain't Necessarily So
It's Easy To Remember
Just One of Those Things
Lovely To Look At
Lullaby of Broadway   HP 8
Lulu's Back in Town
Maybe
Moon Over Miami
The Music Goes 'Round and Around
My Romance
Old Timer
On Treasure Island   HP 4
Paris in the Spring
The Piccolino
Red Sails in the Sunset   HP 2
Soon (Maybe Not Tomorrow)
Stairway to the Stars
Summertime
Tell Me That You Love Me Tonight
Thanks a Million
These Foolish Things (Remind Me of You) (see 1936)
Top Hat, White Tie and Tails
Truckin'
Way Back Home
When I Grow Too Old To Dream
A Woman Is a Sometime Thing
You Are My Lucky Star   HP 10
Zing Went the Strings of My Heart

Notable
About a Quarter to Nine
Accent on Youth
Animal Crackers in My Soup
Beautiful Lady in Blue
Cockeyed Mayor of Kaunakakai
Cosi, Cosa
Darling, Je Vous Aime Beaucoup
Dinner for One, Please James
Dodging a Divorcee
Doin' the Ducky Wuck
Don't Give Up the Ship
Down by the River
Dust Off That Old Piano
Here's to Romance
Hooray for Love (Arlen)
I Got a Bran' New Suit
I Loves You Porgy
I Won't Dance

If I Should Lose You
If the Moon Turns Green
I'm Building Up to an Awful Let-Down
I'm Sittin' High on a Hill Top
In a Sentimental Mood
I've Got My Fingers Crossed
The Jockey on the Carousel
The Lady in Red
Let's Dance
Life Is a Song, Let's Sing It Together
A Little Bit Independent
Little Girl Blue
The Little Things You Used To Do
A Little White Gardenia
The Lord's Prayer
Love and a Dime
Love Is a Dancing Thing
Love Me Forever
The Loveliness of Your
Lovely Lady
Midnight in Paris
Miss Brown to You
(Don't Put Your Daughter on the Stage) Mrs. Worthington
My Man's Gone Now
My Very Good Friend the Milkman
No Strings (I'm Fancy Free)
Oh, Bess, Oh Where's My Bess
Please Believe Me
Rhythm of the Rain
Roll Along Covered Wagon
Roll Along Prairie Moon
She Shall Have Music
She's a Latin from Manhattan
So Long, It's Been Good To Know Ya
Song of the Open Road
There's a Boat Dat's Leavin' Soon for New York
This Time It's Love
Where Am I
Why Shouldn't I
With All My Heart
Without a Word of Warning
The Words Are in My Heart
You Let Me Down
Your Feet's Too Big
You're a Heavenly Thing

1936

Oscar for Dorothy Fields. In the Motion Picture Academy's first award to a female songwriter, Dorothy Fields receives an Oscar for the lyrics of "The Way You Look Tonight," with music by composer Jerome Kern, from the score of the picture *Swing Time*. The film stars Ginger Rogers and Fred Astaire with Helen Broderick and Victor Moore, and is directed by George Stevens.

Billboard Music Charts. Billboard magazine publishes its first list of the ten top-selling records of each of the record companies (as furnished by the record companies, and not by independent survey): "Ten Best Records For Week Ending. . . ."

Ballet in Musical Comedy. The ballet sequence "Slaughter on Tenth Avenue" is included in the Broadway musical *On Your Toes* on April 11.

Gloomy Sunday. The song "Gloomy Sunday" is banned from radio broadcasts in the U.S. after it is alleged to have caused suicides among radio listeners. This song, like its predecessor, "St. James Infirmary" (1930), is no longer heard on the air.

Loesser–Loewe. Contributors to an ephemeral revue dubbed *The Illustrator's Show* this season include fledgling lyricist Frank Loesser with his song "Bang the Bell Rang" (not indexed) and new composer Frederick Loewe with "The Waltz Was Born in Vienna" (not indexed).

Judy Garland. Frances Gumm of Grand Rapids, Michigan, makes her feature-length musical film debut in *Pigskin Parade,* starring Jack Haley and Betty Grable. She had previously appeared with her sisters in an earlier released short subject film. Miss Gumm is thirteen.

Top Hits
Bojangles of Harlem
Did I Remember   HP 1
Easy To Love
The Glory of Love
Goodbye (Jenkins)
Goody Goody   HP 8
I Wished on the Moon
I'm an Old Cowhand
In the Chapel in the Moonlight   HP 3
Is It True What They Say About Dixie   HP 4
It's a Sin To Tell a Lie
It's Been So Long
It's D'lovely   HP 9   (1937)
I've Got a Feeling You're Fooling
I've Got You Under My Skin
Let Yourself Go
Let's Face the Music and Dance
Lights Out   HP 10
Lost   HP 6

The Martins and the Coys
The Night Is Young and You're So Beautiful
No Greater Love, see "There Is No Greater Love" below
One, Two, Button Your Shoe
The Organ Grinder's Swing
Pennies from Heaven   HP 4   (1937)
Poinciana
San Francisco (Kaper)
Shoe Shine Boy
Stomping at the Savoy
There's a Small Hotel
These Foolish Things (Remind Me of You)   HP 5
To You Sweetheart Aloha
The Touch of Your Lips
Twilight on the Trail
(It Will Have To Do) Until the Real Thing Comes Along
The Way You Look Tonight   HP 2
When Did You Leave Heaven   HP 9
When My Dream Boat Comes Home
(I Would) Would You
You (Gee, But You're Wonderful)
You Can't Pull the Wool Over My Eyes

Adaptations
Hawaiian War Chant (based on a traditional Hawaiian song)
There Is No Greater Love (based on Concerto No. 1, B-flat minor by Tchaikovsky)

Revivals
Come Back to Sorrento (1904)
High Society (March) (1901)
The One Rose That's Left in My Heart (1929)
Waltzing Matilda (1903)
The Whiffenpoof Song (1909)

Notable
And My Life
And the Great Big Saw Came Nearer
As Long As You're Not in Love with Anyone Else
At the Codfish Ball
By Strauss
Caminito
Dancing Under the Stars
Does Your Heart Beat for Me
Empty Saddles
A Fine Romance
Friends
Glad To Be Unhappy
Gloomy Sunday
Goodnight Irene

Has Anybody Seen Our Ship
Hills of Old Wyoming
I Can't Escape from You
I Feel Like a Feather in the Breeze
I Like Bananas Because They Have No Bones
If You Can't Sing It You'll Have To Swing It
I'll Sing You a Thousand Love Songs
I'm in a Dancing Mood
I'm Putting All My Eggs in One Basket
Knock, Knock, Who's There
Last Night When We Were Young
Little Old Lady
The Love Bug Will Bite You
May I Have the Next Romance with You
Me and the Moon
A Melody from the Sky
Moonlight and Shadows
Moonrise in the Lowlands
The Most Beautiful Girl in the World
My Heart and I
No Regrets
(It Happened) On the Beach at Bali Bali
On Your Toes
Pick Yourself Up
Picture Me Without You (not Porter's "A Picture of Me Without You")
Play, Orchestra, Play
Rainbow on the River
Ridin' High
Say "Si Si"
Seal It with a Kiss
Sing, Baby, Sing
Slaughter on Tenth Avenue (Ballet)
So Do I
South Sea Island Magic
A Star Fell Out of Heaven
Stars in My Eyes
Summer Night
Take My Heart
Trust in Me
Twinkle, Twinkle, Little Star (not the traditional)
Waltz in Swing Time
We Saw the Sea
When a Lady Meets a Gentleman Down South
When I'm with You
Where Are You
With Plenty of Money and You
You Better Go Now
You Do the Darndest Things, Baby
You Gotta Eat Your Spinach, Baby

You Hit the Spot
You Turned the Tables on Me
You Were There

[*Note:* "Alone" was No. 7 on the Hit Parade (HP) for this year, but it was published in 1935.]

1937

Full-Length Animated Films. Walt Disney releases *Snow White and the Seven Dwarfs.* For this film Mr. Disney receives one regular size and seven miniature Oscars.

Jitterbugging. Teenagers line up at the Paramount Theatre in New York on March 10, to see Benny Goodman. Once inside, they dance the Big Apple and the Shag in the aisles. The earliest mention we could find of jitterbugs is in the title of the Fred Rose song "Jitterbug Tree" (1927).

Bing and Oscar Winning Songs. Bing Crosby achieves a record by introducing during his career more Academy Award winning songs than any other performer. He begins this year with "Sweet Leilani" from the film *Waikiki Wedding,* and later "White Christmas" from *Holiday Inn* (1942), "Swinging on a Star" from *Going My Way* (1944) (for which he also won a personal Oscar), and "In the Cool Cool Cool of the Evening" from *Here Comes the Groom* (1951).

Sonja Henie. Three-time Olympic figure-skating winner Sonja Henie of Oslo does for ice what Esther Williams does for chlorinated water in her first musical film *One in a Million.* Miss Henie is twenty-four.

Top Hits
Bei Mir Bist Du Schön
Blue Hawaii
Bob White (Whatcha Gonna Swing Tonight)
Boo-Hoo!   HP 5
Caravan
The Dipsy Doodle
A Foggy Day
A Gay Ranchero
Gone with the Wind
Gypsy in My Soul
Harbor Lights
Have You Met Miss Jones
Heigh-Ho
I Can Dream, Can't I
I'll Take Romance
In the Still of the Night
It Looks Like Rain in Cherry Blossom Lane   HP 2

I've Got My Love To Keep Me Warm
Johnny One Note
The Lady Is a Tramp
Lambeth Walk
Let's Call the Whole Thing Off
The Merry-Go-Round Broke Down
The Moon of Manakoora
My Funny Valentine
Nice Work If You Can Get It
Once in a While   HP 7
One Song
Remember Me
Rosalie
Sailboat in the Moonlight   HP 6
September in the Rain   HP 1
So Rare
Somebody Else Is Taking My Place
Sweet Leilani
Thanks for the Memory   HP 10 (1938)
That Old Feeling   HP 3
There's a Gold Mine in the Sky
There's a Lull in My Life
They All Laughed
They Can't Take That Away from Me
Too Marvelous for Words
Toy Trumpet
Vieni, Vieni   HP 10
Where or When
Whispers in the Dark   HP 8
Whistle While You Work
You Can't Have Everything
You're a Sweetheart

Adaptations
The Donkey Serenade (based on Friml's "Chanson" of 1920,
   with lyrics added)

Revivals
I'd Love To Live in Loveland (with a Girl Like You) (1910)
Muskrat Ramble (1926)
Song of India (1894–96)

Notable
Afraid To Dream
All At Once
All God's Chillun Got Rhythm
All This and Heaven Too
Am I in Love (m. Warren)
Blue Turning Grey Over You
By Myself

Can I Forget You
Did Your Mother Come from Ireland
Easy Living
The Folks Who Live on the Hill
Foolin' Myself
Georgianna
The Girl on the Police Gazette
Have You Got Any Castles Baby
Head Over Heels in Love
He's a Gypsy from Poughkeepsie
High, Wide and Handsome
I Can't Be Bothered Now
I Double Dare You
I Hit a New High
I Know Now
I See Your Face Before Me
I Used To Be Color Blind
I Wish I Were in Love Again
I'm the Good Humor Man
I'm Wishing
I've Got Beginner's Luck
Josephine
Lisbon Antigua
The Moon Got in My Eyes
The Moon Is Taking Lessons
My Little Buckaroo
Never in a Million Years
On the Sentimental Side
Our Penthouse on Third Avenue
Peckin'
Peter and the Wolf (m. Prokofiev)
Roses in the Rain
Sail Along, Silvery Moon
Satan Takes a Holiday
Serenade in the Night
Seventh Heaven
Shall We Dance (m. Gershwin)
Sing, Sing, Sing, Sing
Slap That Bass
Slumming on Park Avenue
Smarty
Snake Charmer
Snake Dreams
Some Day My Prince Will Come
Stop! You're Breaking My Heart
Sweet Heartache
Sweet Is the Word for You
Swing High, Swing Low
Things Are Looking Up
This Year's Kisses

True Confession
Twilight in Turkey
Wake Up and Live
Walter, Walter (Lead Me to the Altar)
Was It Rain
(She's the Girlfriend of) The Whirling Dervish
With a Smile and a Song
You Can't Stop Me from Dreaming
Yours and Mine

Note: "It's D'lovely" was No. 9 on the Hit Parade (HP) for this year, but was published in 1936. "Pennies from Heaven" was No. 4 on the Hit Parade (HP) for this year, but was published in 1936.

1938

Magnetic Tape Recordings. In January, magnetic tape is adopted as a future standard for radio broadcast recording in Germany.

Martin and Kelly. Adorned with a hooded fur parka, Mary Martin from Weatherford, Texas, stops the show *Leave It to Me* with the Cole Porter song "My Heart Belongs to Daddy" this November. She is sitting on a trunk with a French Line label next to a young chorus boy named Gene Kelly (see 1942). Miss Martin is twenty-five and Mr. Kelly is twenty-six.

Ella Fitzgerald. Chick Webb, legendary black drummer and orchestra leader, co-stars with Ella Fitzgerald, twenty, at the Savoy Ballroom in Harlem and Ella begins her rise to national stardom as a solo vocalist. See "Stomping at the Savoy" (1936).

More B.G. On January 16, Benny Goodman and his orchestra play the first jazz concert ever held in Carnegie Hall. Sidemen in the band include Harry James, Lionel Hampton, Gene Krupa, Jess Stacy, and Teddy Wilson, with vocalist Martha Tilton and arrangements by Fletcher Henderson and Benny Carter. Guest performers include Count Basie, Bobby Hackett, Johnny Hodges, Lester Young, and Cootie Williams.

Top Hits
Change Partners
Chiquita Banana
La Conga
Down Where the Trade Winds Blow
Falling in Love with Love
F.D.R. Jones
(The) Funny Old Hills
Get Out of Town

Heart and Soul
I Hadn't Anyone Till You
I Have Eyes
I Let a Song Go Out of My Heart   HP 9
I'll Be Seeing You
In My Little Red Book
Jeepers Creepers   HP 10 (1939)
(Our) Love Is Here To Stay
Love Walked In   HP 8
Music, Maestro, Please   HP 3
My Heart Belongs to Daddy
Now It Can Be Told
Oh Mama (The Butcher Boy)
Ol' Man Mose
One O'Clock Jump
Please Be Kind   HP 7
(I've Got) A Pocketful of Dreams   HP 2
San Antonio Rose (Rose of San Antone)
Says My Heart   HP 5
September Song
Small Fry
This Can't Be Love
Ti-Pi-Tin   HP 6
Two Sleepy People
You Go to My Head
You Must Have Been a Beautiful Baby
You're the Only Star in My Blue Heaven

Adaptations
Bach Goes to Town (based indirectly on a Bach prelude and fugue)
My Reverie (based on Debussy's "Rêverie" (1895))   HP 1

Revivals
A-Tisket A-Tasket (1879)   HP 4
Mexicali Rose (1923)

Notable
At Long Last Love
Between a Kiss and a Sigh
Boom
Cathedral in the Pines
Chiapanecas
Deep in a Dream
Don't Be That Way
Ferdinand the Bull
Flat Foot Floogie
From Now On
Hooray for Hollywood
I Fall in Love with You Every Day

I Married an Angel
I Was Doing All Right
It Never Was You
Jumpin' at the Woodside
Just a Kid Named Joe
The Latin Quarter
The Little Drummer Boy
Lullaby in Rhythm
Most Gentleman Don't Like Love
New Orleans
The Night Is Filled with Music
On the Bumpy Road to Love
Pavanne (Gould)
Penny Serenade
Prelude to a Kiss
Really the Blues
Sing for Your Supper
So Help Me
Spring Is Here
Sweet Little Headache, see "You're a Sweet Little Headache"
The Umbrella Man
Well All Right
While a Cigarette Was Burning
You Brought a New Kind of Love to Me
You Can Depend on Me
You Couldn't Be Cuter
You Leave Me Breathless
You're a Sweet Little Headache

[*Note:* "Thanks for the Memory" was No. 10 on the Hit Parade (HP) for this year, but was published in 1937.]

1939

World War II. America is not yet involved in this new war. No pro-war songs appear in the Top Hit list.

New York World's Fair. In this biggest and best of fairs, the world is introduced for the first time to the Trylon and the Perisphere, Nylon (by duPont), man-made lightning and the first practical dishwasher (by General Electric), and Elsie the Cow (by the Borden Co.), a purebred Jersey and queen of the automatic milking station. Investment in the Fair was $150,000,000. The official auto horns of the World's Fair were tuned to sound out the phrase "Boys and Girls Together" from the song "The Sidewalks of New York" (1893).

Television. Demonstrated by RCA-NBC at the New York World's Fair, television in mechanical form, had already been tested in London as early as 1925 by John L. Baird and in electronic form from 1935 by EMI (London) and the BBC. It was perfected in the U.S. not only by RCA but by CBS (New York) and G.E. (Station WRGB, Schenectady) based on early work in the 1920s by U.S. inventors Philo T. Farnsworth and Vladimir Zworykin.

More Juke Boxes. 225,000 jukes are installed and more records (13 million) are sold for juke-box use than for any other purpose.

Gone with the Wind. David O. Selznick's final cut of Margaret Mitchell's Civil War novel epic *Gone with the Wind,* starring Clark Gable, Vivien Leigh, Leslie Howard, and Olivia de Havilland, proves to be 3 hours and 42 minutes long, a record length at that time. So intrinsic to the success of this film is composer Max Steiner's Oscar-winning score, that of the 222 minutes of screenplay, only 30 minutes are without background music.

More Oz. In the continuing saga of *The Wizard of Oz,* the musical film version starring Judy Garland, Ray Bolger, Bert Lahr, Jack Haley, and Frank Morgan is released. The song "Over the Rainbow" by E.Y. Harburg and Harold Arlen wins the Academy Award.

Harlem Rides the Range. The first Hollywood western feature film with an all black cast, *Harlem Rides the Range,* appears this year.

Frank Sinatra. The epoch of big band star vocalists begins. A new vocalist, Francis Albert Sinatra, born December 12, 1917, in Hoboken, New Jersey, is hired by the Harry James Orchestra. His salary: $75 per week. He later joins the Tommy Dorsey Orchestra, backed by the vocal group The Pied Pipers.

The Samba. The Samba, the new dance from Brazil, arrives. See "Brazil."

God Bless America. The Irving Berlin song "God Bless America" is featured for the first time by Kate Smith on national network radio. First performed on Armistice Day, 1938, this song was written in 1917.

Top Hits
All the Things You Are, see 1940
And the Angels Sing   HP 6
An Apple for the Teacher
The Army Air Corps Song (The U.S. Air Force Song)
The Beer Barrel Polka   HP 9
Brazil
Careless (see 1940)
Cherokee
Darn That Dream
Frenesi (see 1940)
God Bless America
Good Morning

Hold Tight—Hold Tight

I Concentrate on You

I Didn't Know What Time It Was

If I Didn't Care

I'll Never Smile Again, see 1940

In the Mood

The Lady's in Love with You

La Mer (The Sea)

Moonlight Serenade

Over the Rainbow   HP 4

Scatterbrain   HP 3

South of the Border (Down Mexico Way)   HP 1

Stairway to the Stars   HP 8

Stay in My Arms, Cinderella

Sunrise Serenade

Tara's Theme

Three Little Fishes

We'll Meet Again

What's New

Wishing (Will Make It So)   HP 5

Adaptations

In an Eighteenth Century Drawing Room (based on Mozart's
    Piano Sonata No. 3, in C.)

The Lamp Is Low (based on Ravel's "Pavane")

Moon Love (based on the second movement of Tchaikovsky's
    Symphony No. 5, adapted by Andre Kostelanetz)   HP 7

My Prayer (based on Georges Boulanger's "Avant de Mourir,
    op.17" (1926)

Our Love (based on Tchaikovsky's tone poem "Romeo and
    Juliet" (1870))

Revivals

Adios, Muchachos (1932)

Begin the Beguine (1935)

By the Beautiful Sea (1919)

Chicago (That Toddlin' Town) (1922)

Deep Purple (1934)   HP 2

Little Brown Jug (1869)

Little Sir Echo (1917)

El Rancho Grande (1934)

The Very Thought of You (1934)

Notable

Adios, Mariquita Linda

Are You Having Any Fun

At the Balalaika

Baby Me

Bless You

Blue Orchids

Blue Rain

(See What the) Boys in the Back Room (Will Have)

Cavalry of the Steppes, see "Meadowlands"

Coffee in the Morning, Kisses at Night

Comes Love

Day In—Day Out

Ding Dong the Witch Is Dead

Do I Love You

Don't Worry 'Bout Me

East Side of Heaven

Faithful Forever

Flying Home

Follow the Yellow Brick Road

The Gaucho Serenade

Hang Your Heart on a Hickory Limb

Heaven Can Wait

Hong Kong Blues

Honky Tonk Train Blues

Honolulu

Huckleberry Duck

I Get Along Without You Very Well

I Like To Recognize the Tune

I Poured My Heart into a Song

If I Only Had a Brain

In an Old Dutch Garden

The Incredible Flutist

It's a Blue World

It's a Hap-Hap-Happy Day

I've Got My Eyes on You

Jumpin' Jive

Katie Went To Haiti

Lilacs in the Rain

The Masquerade Is Over

Meadowlands (Cavalry of the Steppes)

My Last Goodbye

Oh, You Crazy Moon

Old Mill Wheel

Old Soldiers Never Die

PEnnsylvania 6-5000

Run Rabbit Run

South American Way

Strange Fruit

'Tain't What You Do

There'll Always Be an England

That Sly Old Gentleman from Featherbed Lane

Undecided

We're Off To See the Wizard

Yours for a Song

[*Note:* "Jeepers Creepers" was No. 10 on the Hit Parade (HP) for this year, but was published in 1938.]

1940

World War II. War continues in Europe, as President Roosevelt campaigns on a "neutrality" peace pledge.

FM. The first regular broadcasts using the wideband system of Frequency Modulation, developed and promoted by Major Edwin H. Armstrong, begin Wednesday, January 5.

Billboard Music Charts. On July 20, *Billboard* magazine inaugurates "The Billboard Music Popularity Chart" including "Best Selling Singles" list. In the first of ten positions on the first singles chart is "I'll Never Smile Again" with artist Tommy Dorsey. Subsequent "Best Selling Singles" list modifications: after July 20, 1940, Top Ten; November 7, 1947, Top Fifteen; June 4, 1948, Top Thirty; November 8, 1953, Top Twenty; May 19, 1954, Top Thirty; June 15, 1955, Top Twenty-five. For a brief period, March 30 to October 26, 1955, both sides of a two-sided record were listed as one position.

Astaire and the Beguine. In the film *Broadway Melody of 1940,* Fred Astaire and Eleanor Powell immortalize "Begin the Beguine," dancing to it against a lustrous MGM ebony reflective floor and background in an incandescent performance that epitomizes, if a single dance could, Fred Astaire's coruscating and matchless choreography. Artie Shaw and his band sold two million disks of Jerry Gray's arrangement of this song, which was for Shaw "the real turning point of my life."

Billy Rose's Diamond Horseshoe. Starting with this year, Billy Rose's latest nightclub just off Broadway on 46th Street had a six-million-customer decade, and grossed $ 20,000,000. Twentieth Century-Fox Films paid Billy $ 175,000 for the use of the name as the title of the Betty Grable film *Diamond Horseshoe* (1945).

Cowboy Musicals. Films with singing cowboys hit their stride this year. Gene Autry and his horse Champion appear in six "oatuners" this year, and Roy Rogers and his horse Trigger in seven.

Recorded Music Sales. Total retail sales of recorded music, singles and albums combined, is estimated at $ 48 million.

Carmen Miranda. Maria Do Cormo Miranda da Cunha of Marco Canavozes, Portugal, goes *Down Argentine Way* this year with a fruit-laden hat, in her first musical film, starring Betty Grable and the new dance the conga. Miss Miranda is twenty-six.

Signs of the Times. The New York Times costs two cents per copy, a New York City subway ride five cents, and a gallon of gasoline seventeen cents.

Top Hits

[Record Sale song rankings (RS) begin this year.]

All or Nothing At All
All the Things You Are RS x HP 9
Along the Santa Fe Trail
Beat Me, Daddy, Eight to the Bar RS 4 (tie) HP x a. Will Bradley
Because of You
Blueberry Hill
Careless RS x HP 4
Do I Worry
Down Argentine Way RS 8 HP x a. Bob Crosby
Ferryboat Serenade
Fools Rush In
Frenesi RS 1 HP 3 (1941) a. Artie Shaw
Friendship
How High the Moon
I'll Never Smile Again RS 2 HP 2 a. Tommy Dorsey, vocalist Frank Sinatra
Imagination RS x HP 6
Intermezzo (A Love Story) (Souvenir de Vienne)
It Never Entered My Mind
It's a Big, Wide, Wonderful World
It's a Lovely Day Tomorrow
Just a Little Bit South of North Carolina
The Last Time I Saw Paris
The Nearness of You
A Nightingale Sang in Berkeley Square RS 7 HP x a. Glenn Miller
Only Forever RS 3 HP 7 a. Bing Crosby
Our Love Affair
Practice Makes Perfect RS x HP 8
San Antonio Rose (Rose of San Antone)
Sierra Sue RS 10 (tie) HP x a. Bing Crosby
Taking a Chance on Love
There I Go RS x HP 3
Trade Winds RS 4 (tie) HP x a. Bing Crosby
Tuxedo Junction
Wabash Cannon Ball
We Three—My Echo, My Shadow and Me RS 9 HP x a. Ink Spots
When You Wish Upon a Star RS x HP 5
You Are My Sunshine
You Stepped Out of a Dream
You Tell Me Your Dream
You Walk By

Adaptations

The Breeze and I (based on Lecuona's ''Andalucia'' of 1930) RS 6 HP x a. Jimmy Dorsey

On the Isle of May (based on Quartet in D by Tchaikovsky (1871))

The Woodpeckers' Song (based on ''Reginella Campagnola,'') RS x HP 1

Revivals

I'm Nobody's Baby (1921) RS 10 (tie) HP x a. Judy Garland

Indian Summer (1919) (lyrics added) RS x HP 10

Johnson Rag (1917) (lyrics added)

Maybe 91935(RS 5 HP x a. Ink Spots

Oh Johnny, Oh Johnny, Oh! (1917)

Notable

All This and Heaven Too (m. De Lange, Van Heusen)

April Played the Fiddle

Back in the Saddle Again

The Bad Humor Man

Between Eighteenth and Nineteenth on Chestnut Street

Big Noise from Winnetka

Bless 'Em All

Cabin in the Sky

The Call of the Canyon

Can't Get Indiana Off My Mind

Celery Stalks at Midnight

Clear Out of This World

El Cumbanchero

Down by the O-Hi-O

Falling Leaves

The Five O'Clock Whistle

Give a Little Whistle

Hi-Diddle-Dee-Dee (An Actor's Life for Me)

A House with a Little Red Barn

How Did He Look

I Hear Music

I'm Stepping Out with a Memory Tonight

In Chi-Chi Castenango

It's a Great Day for the Irish

It's the Same Old Shillelagh

I've Got No Strings

Java Jive (starts with two bars of ''I Love Coffee, I Love Tea,'' 1915)

Let There Be Love

Let's Be Buddies

Louisiana Purchase

Love Never Went to College

Love of My Life

Mama Yo Quiero (I Want My Mama)

Mister Meadowlark

On a Little Street in Singapore

One O'Clock Jump

Playmates

Rhumboogie

Say It (Over and Over Again)

Scrub Me Mama with a Boogie Beat

The Singing Hills

The Sky Fell Down

South Rampart Street Parade

Sweet Potato Piper

Symphony Moderne

This Is My Country

Until Tomorrow

We Could Make Such Beautiful Music

Well, Did You Evah

When the Sun Comes Out

When the Swallows Come Back to Capistrano

With the Wind and the Rain in Your Hair

1941

World War II. In March, without Congressional approval, President Roosevelt freezes the external monetary assets of Japan, completely cutting off Japan's oil supply. On December 7, 1941, Pearl Harbor in Hawaii is attacked by the Japanese; the United States enters World War II.

Pro-War Songs. With the entry of America into World War II, pro-war songs are rushed to the public, including ''We Did It Before and We Can Do It Again,'' ''He's 1-A in the Army (And A-1 in My Heart),'' and ''Remember Pearl Harbor'' (1942).

ASCAP War with the Networks, Birth of BMI. A quarrel in contract negotiations between the broadcasters and ASCAP, the composers' performing rights organization, leads to a nine-month blackout of ASCAP-licensed songs on 674 radio stations as well as to the birth of ASCAP's new competitor, BMI (Broadcast Music, Inc.). At the beginning, only songs in the public domain requiring no copyright clearance could be played on the air. Stephen Foster's songs were a favorite crutch for the broadcasters who could no longer use any of the songs in the ASCAP catalogue.

Fantasia by Disney. The first film, animated or otherwise, with stereo soundtrack, premieres November 13. The imagery of Mickey as the ''Sorcerer's Apprentice'' and the dancing hippos in La Gioconda's ''Dance of the Hours'' are today classics of animation art.

Glenn Miller. The Glenn Miller Orchestra recording of "Chattanooga Choo Choo" tops one million in sales. The distinctive sound of the band was achieved by using a clarinet lead over four saxes.

Gertrude Lawrence, Danny Kaye, and Lady in the Dark. Gertrude Lawrence stars and Danny Kaye is featured, in the Ira Gershwin-Kurt Weill Broadway musical *Lady in the Dark*. Mr. Kaye stunned the audience (and Messrs. Gershwin and Weill) by rattling off the names of the forty-nine Russian composers listed in the lyric of their song "Tschaikowsky" in thirty-nine seconds, and in later years, in thirty-one. The lyric was originally written as light verse by Ira Gershwin for the pre-pictorial weekly *Life* in June 1924 under his then pseudonym Arthur Francis (the names of his brother and sister).

Top Hits

The Anniversary Waltz

Autumn Nocturne

Babalu

Bewitched, Bothered and Bewildered

Blue Champagne   RS 6 (tie)   HP x   a. Jimmy Dorsey, vocalists Bob Eberle and Helen O'Connell

Blues in the Night

Chattanooga Choo Choo   RS 2   HP x   a. Glenn Miller

Cherry

Daddy   RS 3 (tie)   HP x   a. Sammy Kaye

Deep in the Heart of Texas

Dolores   RS 10 (tie)   HP x   a. Bing Crosby

Don't Take Your Love from Me

Everything Happens to Me

Ev'rything I Love

Flamingo

G'Bye Now

Hi Neighbor

High on a Windy Hill

How About You

Hut Sut Song   RS 10 (tie)   HP x   a. Freddy Martin

I Don't Want To Set the World on Fire   RS 9 (tie)   HP 7   a. Horace Heidt

I Don't Want To Walk Without You, Baby

I Got It Bad and That Ain't Good

I Hear a Rhapsody   RS 9 (tie)   HP 1   a. Charlie Barnet

I Know Why

I Remember April

I Understand

Intermezzo (from 1940)   RS x   HP 2

It All Comes Back to Me Now

It's Always You

It's So Peaceful in the Country

I've Got Sixpence (As I Go Rolling Home)

Jersey Bounce, see 1942

Jim

Kiss the Boys Goodbye

Let's Get Away from It All

Maria Elena   RS 5 (tie)   HP 5   a. Jimmy Dorsey, vocalists Bob Eberle and Helen O'Connell

The Music Makers

My Adobe Hacienda

My Sister and I   RS 5 (tie)   HP 8   a. Jimmy Dorsey, vocalists Bob Eberle and Helen O'Connell

Oh Look At Me Now   RS 8   HP x   a. Tommy Dorsey

Perfidia

Sand in My Shoes

Someone's Rocking My Dream Boat

Take the "A" Train

There! I've Said It Again

This Love of Mine

Time Was (Duerme)

Walking the Floor Over You

We Did It Before and We Can Do It Again

Yes My Darling Daughter

You and I   RS x   HP 9

Adaptations

I Think of You (based on the first movement of Rachmaninoff's Piano Concerto No. 2 (1901))

Song of the Volga Boatmen (based on a traditional Russian folksong)   RS 6 (tie)   HP x   a. Glenn Miller

(This Is) The Story of a Starry Night (based on the first movement of Symphony No. 6 *(Pathétique)* by Tchaikovsky (1893))

The Things I Love (based on Tchaikovsky's "Mélodie," op. 24, no. 3)

Tonight We Love (based on the first theme of Tchaikovsky's Piano Concerto No. 1 in B-flat minor (1875))   RS 3 (tie)   HP 6   a. Freddy Martin

Revivals

Amapola (1924)   RS 1   HP 4   a. Jimmy Dorsey, vocalists Bob Eberle and Helen O'Connell

Green Eyes (1929)   RS 4   HP x   a. Jimmy Dorsey, vocalists Bob Eberle and Helen O'Connell

I'll Be with You in Apple Blossom Time (1920)

Lazy River (1931)

There'll Be Some Changes Made (1929)

Waltzing Matilda (1903)

Yours (Quiéreme Mucho) (1931)   RS 7   HP 10   a. Jimmy Dorsey, vocalists Bob Eberle and Helen O'Connell

Notable

Aurora

Boogie Woogie Bugle Boy

Buckle Down, Winsocki
Chica Chica Boom Chic
Day Dreaming
Do You Care
Dream Dancing
Ev'rytime
Fan It
Flying Home
He's 1-A in the Army (and A-1 in My Heart)
I Came, I Saw, I Conga'd
I Could Write a Book
I Guess I'll Have To Dream the Rest
(Yi Yi Yi Yi) I Like You Very Much
I Said No
I See a Million People
It Happened in Sun Valley
London Pride
My Ship
A Sinner Kissed an Angel
Six Lessons from Madame La Zonga
Skylark
So Near and Yet So Far
Taboo
The Tenement Symphony
This Is New
This Is No Laughing Matter
This Time the Dream's on Me
Two Hearts That Pass in the Night
The Waiter and the Porter and the Upstairs Maid
A Weekend in Havana
We're the Couple in the Castle
When I Saw an Elephant Fly
Why Don't We Do This More Often
With a Twist of the Wrist
You Don't Know What Love Is
You Started Something

[*Note:* "Frenesi" was No. 3 on the Hit Parade (HP) for this year, but record sales peaked during 1940.]

1942

Pop Stop. Alarmed by the reduction in the employment of live musicians because of the use of recordings in broadcasting, James Caesar Petrillo, head of the musicians' union, bans all recording by musicians' union membership from August 1 to November 11, 1944. A cappella singing becomes a favorite arranging style on records.

Gordon and Warren. Writer Mack Gordon and com-poser Harry Warren break the record with four top tunes on the network radio show "Your Hit Parade" simultaneously: "There Will Never Be Another You," "I've Got a Gal in Kalamazoo," "Serenade in Blue," and "At Last." The last three were written for the Glenn Miller film *Orchestra Wives.* Gordon and Warren were the writer and composer most often represented over the years on "Your Hit Parade." Thirty-nine of Gordon's lyrics made the "Y.H.P." top ten, and forty-two of Warren's tunes.

This Is the Army. The theatre war morale production *This Is the Army* opens at the Broadway Theatre July 4 with an Irving Berlin score, and is adapted to the screen in 1943. Another Broadway war morale production is *Star and Garter* opening June 24 at the Music Box.

White Christmas. Irving Berlin's unbelievable success with "White Christmas" from the musical film *Holiday Inn,* is "probably the most valuable song . . . copyright in the world," according to *Variety.* It was the longest running hit song ever on "Your Hit Parade" totaling eighteen appearances (ten in first place) in 1942–43. This year it sells over a million copies of sheet music alone and in recording by the end of 1976 a total of over 108 million records in the United States and Canada and some twenty-five million foreign language disks throughout the world. Bing Crosby's recording for Decca sold over twenty-five million records, and both Victor's recording by Frank Martin and Columbia's recording by Frank Sinatra were enormous hits.

TOP HITS

[Peatman Survey of Air Play song rankings (AP) begins this year.]

Be Careful It's My Heart   RS x   HP x   AP 6
Be Honest with Me
Blues in the Night (from 1941)   RS 8 (tie)   HP 10   AP x   a. Woody Herman
Can't Get Out of This Mood
Cowboy Serenade
Dearly Beloved   RS x   HP x   AP 3
Don't Get Around Much Anymore, see 1943
Don't Sit Under the Apple Tree with Anyone Else But Me   RS x   HP 9   AP x
Easy Street
Elmer's Tune   RS 8 (tie)   HP 4   AP x   a. Glenn Miller, The Andrews Sisters
Happiness Is Just a Thing Called Joe
He Wears a Pair of Silver Wings   RS x   HP 6   AP 10
I Had the Craziest Dream, see 1943

I Left My Heart at the Stage Door Canteen RS x HP x AP 7

Idaho RS x HP x AP 1

I'll Be Around

In the Blue of Evening, see 1943

It Can't Be Wrong, see 1943

I've Got a Gal in Kalamazoo RS 4 HP x AP 2 a. Glenn Miller

Jersey Bounce RS 10 HP x AP x a. Benny Goodman

Jingle Jangle Jingle RS 3 HP 7 AP 5 a. Kay Kyser

The Lamplighter's Serenade

Moonlight Cocktail RS 2 HP x AP x a. Glenn Miller

My Devotion RS x HP 5 AP 4

One Dozen Roses RS x HP 8 AP x

Paper Doll, see 1943

Perdido (Lost)

Praise the Lord and Pass the Ammunition RS x HP x AP 9

Rose O'Day

Serenade in Blue

A String of Pearls RS 7 HP x AP x a. Glenn Miller

Tangerine RS 5 HP x AP x a. Jimmy Dorsey, vocalists Bob Eberle and Helen O'Connell

That Old Black Magic, see 1943

There Are Such Things

There Will Never Be Another You

This Is Worth Fighting For

(Theme from the) Warsaw Concerto

When the Lights Go On Again All Over the World

White Christmas RS 1 HP 1 AP x a. Bing Crosby

(There'll Be Blue Birds Over) The White Cliffs of Dover RS x HP 2 AP x

Who Wouldn't Love You RS 9 HP x AP x a. Kay Kyser

With My Head in the Clouds

You Were Never Lovelier

You'd Be So Nice To Come Home To

Adaptations

At the Crossroads (based on Lecuona's "Malagueña" of 1930)

Daybreak (based on Grofé's "The Mississippi Suite" of 1926)

Revivals

The Army Air Corps Song (The U.S. Air Force Song) (1939)

The Birth of the Blues (1926)

For Me and My Gal (1917)

In a Little Spanish Town (1926)

Miss You (1929)

My Gal Sal (1905)

Sleepy Lagoon (1930) RS 6 HP 3 AP 8

(When) They Cut Down the Old Pine Tree (1929)

What Is This Thing Called Love (1930)

Notable

(You Are) Always in My Heart

Arthur Murray Taught Me Dancing in a Hurry

At Last

Back to Donegal

Blue Shadows and White Gardenias

Conchita, Marquita, Lolita, Pepita, Rosita, Juanita Lopez

Cow-Cow Boogie

Dear Old Donegal

Everything I've Got Belongs to You

The Fleet's In

Goodbye Mama, I'm Off to Yokahama

Happy Holiday

He's My Guy

I Came Here To Talk for Joe

I Remember You

I Threw a Kiss in the Ocean

I'll Remember April

I'm Getting Tired So I Can Sleep

I'm Glad There Is You

I'm Old Fashioned

Johnny Doughboy Found a Rose in Ireland

Juke Box Saturday Night

Love Is a Song That Never Ends

Lover Man (Oh Where Can You Be)

Mister Five by Five

Moonlight Becomes You

My Paradise

Not Mine

Pennsylvania Polka

Put Your Dreams Away for Another Day

Remember Pearl Harbor

The Road to Morocco

There's a Star Spangled Banner Waving Somewhere

This Is the Army, Mister Jones

Three Little Sisters

Tweedle-O-Twill

Wait Till You See Her

Why Don't You Do Right

Yesterday's Roses

A Zoot Suit

1943

Oklahoma! Dejected by Hollywood and coming off five Broadway failures, Oscar Hammerstein II is asked by the Theatre Guild to collaborate with Richard Rodgers and make a musical of Lynn Riggs's folk play, *Green Grow the Lilacs.* Previewing in New Haven as *Away We Go,* all signs indicate disaster: "No Girls, No Gags, No

Chance.'' But after twenty days of rewrite and Boston previews, *Oklahoma!* opens in New York on March 31 to run for a record-breaking 2212 performances. Its cast includes unknowns Alfred Drake, Celeste Holm, Howard Keel, and Shelley Winters, among others. Agnes de Mille's sterling choreography reshapes dance in musical theatre and Rodgers's score contains one illustrious hit after another.

As Time Goes By. Humphrey Bogart and Ingrid Bergman immortalize *Casablanca* this year in the Michael Curtiz film which also stars Sydney Greenstreet, Peter Lorre, and Claude Rains. Herman Hupfeld's ''As Time Goes By'' (1931) is sung by Dooley Wilson. His character, Sam, is closely modeled after Spencer Williams, Josephine Baker's songwriter who toured Europe from Paris to Prague to Berlin and also the French colonies of Africa including Morocco.

Leonard Bernstein. Songwriter Lenny Amber in an emergency replaces Bruno Walter as conductor of the New York Philharmonic Orchestra at Carnegie Hall, November 13. This is his first major experience as a serious conductor. Mr. Bernstein is twenty-five.

Original Cast Albums for Broadway Shows. The Rodgers and Hammerstein hit Broadway musical *Oklahoma!* is released by Decca Records' Jack Kapp as a 78 r.p.m. record album. It sells over a million albums.

Gordon and Warren. Lyricist Mack Gordon and composer Harry Warren are given Oscars for their song ''You'll Never Know'' from the film *Hello, Frisco, Hello.* Harry Warren was an Oscar winner in 1935 and will be again in 1946.

Dinah Shore. Frances Rose Shore of Winchester, Tennessee, at twenty-six makes her musical film debut in *Thank Your Lucky Stars,* starring Eddie Cantor, Bette Davis, Olivia de Havilland, Errol Flynn, John Garfield, Joan Leslie, and Ann Sheridan. The score was by Frank Loesser and Arthur Schwartz. See ''They're Either Too Young or Too Old.'' Miss Shore was one of the early starring vocalists on ''Your Hit Parade'' and was then discovered by Eddie Cantor for his network radio show.

Frank Sinatra. Frank Sinatra makes his musical film debut in *Higher and Higher,* with a Harold Adamson and Jimmy McHugh score. See ''I Couldn't Sleep a Wink Last Night'' and ''(This Is) A Lovely Way To Spend an Evening.''

The Ninas. Artist and caricaturist Al Hirschfeld, who has been illustrating the drama page of *The New York Times* since 1923, begins to insinuate the name of Nina, his new-born daughter, into his theatre drawings. Because of a flood of phone calls and letters from exasper-ated Nina-hunters, the *Times* publisher Arthur Hays Sulzberger commanded Hirschfeld to let readers of his paper know when more than one Nina was to be found. He began to place a tiny number after his signature each week so signifying.

Top Hits

Amor, see 1944

Besame Mucho, see 1944

Comin' In on a Wing and a Prayer   RS 6 (tie)   HP 7   AP x   a. Song Spinners

Do Nothin' Till You Hear from Me

Don't Get Around Much Anymore   RS x   HP 10   AP 9

Don't Sweetheart Me

A Gay Ranchero

Goodbye, Sue

Holiday for Strings, see 1944

How Many Hearts Have You Broken

I Couldn't Sleep a Wink Last Night

I Had the Craziest Dream   RS 7   HP x   AP x   a. Harry James

I'll Be Seeing You, see 1944

In My Arms

In the Blue of Evening   RS 6 (tie)   HP 8   AP x   a. Tommy Dorsey

It Can't Be Wrong   RS x   HP x   AP 10

It's Love, Love, Love, see 1944

(It Seems to Me) I've Heard That Song Before   RS 1   HP 9   AP 8   a. Harry James

Let's Get Lost

(This Is) A Lovely Way To Spend an Evening

Mairzy Doats

My Heart Tells Me

My Shining Hour

Oh, What a Beautiful Morning

Oklahoma!

People Will Say We're in Love   RS x   HP 1   AP 1

Pistol Packing Mama   RS 8 (tie)   HP x   AP x   a. Al Dexter

Shoo-Shoo Baby, see 1944

Speak Low

Star Eyes

Sunday, Monday or Always   RS 3   HP 6   AP 6   a. Bing Crosby

The Surrey with the Fringe on Top

Take It Easy

Taking a Chance on Love   RS 6 (tie)   HP x   AP x   a. Benny Goodman

That Old Black Magic   RS 8 (tie)   HP x   AP 4   a. Glenn Miller

There Are Such Things (from 1942) RS 4 HP 5 AP x a. Tommy Dorsey

They're Either Too Young or Too Old

Tico Tico, see 1944

Walking the Floor Over You

What Do You Do in the Infantry?

You Keep Coming Back Like a Song

You'd Be So Nice To Come Home To (from 1942) RS x HP x AP 7

You'll Never Know RS 5 HP 2 AP 2 a. Dick Haymes

Adaptations

We Must Be Vigilant (based on ''American Patrol'' (1885))

Revivals

All or Nothing At All (1940) RS 10 HP x AP x a. Frank Sinatra

As Time Goes By (1931) RS x HP 4 AP 5 a. Perry Como; also Billy Eckstine

Big Noise from Winnetka (1940)

Brazil (1939) RS 9 HP x AP 3 a. Xavier Cugat

Ciribiribin (1898)

Cuddle Up a Little Closer (1908)

Paper Doll (1915) RS 2 HP 3 AP x a. Mills Brothers

Put Your Arms Around Me Honey (1910)

Somebody Else Is Taking My Place (1937)

Something To Remember You By (1930)

Notable

By the River of the Roses

Can't You Do a Friend a Favor

Close to You

Faithfully Yours

Der Fuehrer's Face

Gertie from Bizerte

Harlem Nocturne

Hit the Road to Dreamland

How Sweet You Are

I Can't Say No

I Heard You Cried Last Night

I Lost My Sugar in Salt Lake City

I Never Mention Your Name

I'll Be Home for Christmas

I'm Thinking Tonight of My Blue Eyes

It Must Be Jelly, 'Cause Jam Don't Shake Like That

Many a New Day

''Murder'' He Says

No Love, No Nothing

One for My Baby and One More for the Road

Out of My Dreams

Say a Prayer for the Boys Over There

So Tired

Wonder When My Baby's Coming Home

Yes Indeed

You've Got Me Where You Want Me

1944

D-Day. The Western Allies land troops on Normandy beaches on June 6 and soon fan out over northern France.

Glenn Miller. Captain Glenn Miller disappears in wartime flight over the English Channel.

End of Big Band Epoch. The big bands begin to give way to the star solo vocalists. By 1946, Tommy Dorsey, Harry James, Woody Herman, and Les Brown have disbanded their orchestras.

Bernstein on Broadway. Composer Leonard Bernstein's first Broadway musical production *On the Town,* with choreography by Jerome Robbins, opens December 28.

Sinatra at the Paramount. In October, 3000 teenagers scream ''We want Frankie'' at New York's Paramount Theatre, with over 20,000 outside spilling into Times Square. Within minutes the box office is destroyed, shop windows broken, and all pedestrian and vehicular traffic blocked. Inside the theatre girls swoon, scream, and wave their undergarments, while outside 421 policemen try in vain to restore order.

Meet Me in St. Louis. Vincent Minnelli's star-studded musical film introduces Ralph Blane and Hugh Martin's Academy Award-winning ''The Trolley Song'' and their popular ''Have Yourself a Merry Little Christmas'' and ''The Boy Next Door.'' The cast includes among others, Judy Garland, Margaret O'Brien, Mary Astor, Marjorie Main, and June Lockhart.

Going My Way. Paramount's Bing Crosby introduces the hit song ''Swinging On a Star'' and revives the 1914 ''Too-ra-loo-ra-loo-ral'' in Leo McCarey's film *Going My Way.*

Top Hits

Ac-cent-tchu-ate the Positive, see 1945

All of a Sudden

Amor RS x HP 6 AP 5

Besame Mucho RS 3 HP x AP 9 a. Jimmy Dorsey

Candy, see 1945

Don't Fence Me In RS 2 HP 7 (1945) AP x a. Bing Crosby and The Andrews Sisters

Down in the Valley

Dream, see 1945

Evalina

Going My Way

Holiday for Strings   RS 7   HP x   AP x   a. David Rose

How Blue the Night

I Dream of You

I Hear Music

I Love You   RS 4 (tie)   HP 8   AP 3   a. Bing Crosby

I Should Care, see 1945

I'll Get By   RS 5 (tie)   HP 4   AP 4   a. Harry James, vocalist Dick Haymes

I'll Walk Alone   RS 5 (tie)   HP 5   AP 6   a. Dinah Shore

I'm Making Believe   RS 6 (tie)   HP x   AP x   a. Ink Spots and Ella Fitzgerald

Is You Is or Is You Ain't My Baby?   RS 10 (tie)   HP x   AP x   a. Bing Crosby and The Andrews Sisters

It Could Happen to You

It's Love, Love, Love   RS 6 (tie)   HP x   AP x   a. Guy Lombardo

Jealous Heart

Lili Marlene

Long Ago and Far Away (Kern)   RS 9   HP 3   AP 1   a. Dick Haymes and Helen Forrest

My Heart Tells Me (from 1943)   RS 4 (tie)   HP 2   AP x   a. Glen Gray

Right as the Rain

Roll Me Over (Lay Me Down and Do It Again)

Rum and Coca-Cola, see 1945

San Fernando Valley   RS 8 (tie)   HP x   AP 8   a. Bing Crosby

Saturday Night Is the Loneliest Night of the Week

Sentimental Journey, see 1945

Shoo-Shoo Baby   RS x   HP 9   AP x

Spring Will Be a Little Late This Year

Swinging on a Star   RS 1   HP 7   AP x   a. Bing Crosby

Tico Tico

Till Then

Time Waits for No One   RS 10 (tie)   HP x   AP x   a. Helen Forrest

The Trolley Song   RS 8 (tie)   HP 10   AP 10   a. Pied Pipers

Twilight Time

You Always Hurt the One You Love   RS 4 (tie)   HP x   AP x   a. Mills Brothers

Adaptations

Dance with a Dolly (based on ''Lubly Fan, or, Buffalo Gals (Won't You Come Out Tonight?)'' (1844))

Skip to My Lou (based on the traditional (1844))

Strange Music (based on Grieg's ''Wedding Day in Troldhaugen'')

Revivals

Chiapanecas (1938)

I'll Be Seeing You (1938)   RS 5 (tie)   HP 1   AP 2   a. Bing Crosby

I'll Get By (1928)

It Had To Be You (1924)   RS x   HP x   AP 7

Magic Is the Moonlight (1930)

Meet Me in St. Louis, Louis (1904)

Poinciana (1936)

Together (1928)

Too-ra-loo-ra-loo-ral (1914)

What a Diff'rence a Day Made (1934)

Notable

And Her Tears Flowed Like Wine

As Long As I Live (Tobias, Simon (Steiner))

Baia

The Boy Next Door

Can't Help Singing

Close as Pages in a Book

Cornish Rhapsody

Cotton Tail

Ev'rytime We Say Goodbye

The G.I. Jive

Have Yourself a Merry Little Christmas

Here Come the Waves

His Rocking Horse Ran Away

How Little We Know

I Begged Her

I Didn't Know About You

I Don't Want To Love You

I Fall in Love Too Easily

I'm Gonna Move to the Outskirts of Town

Irresistible You

Let Me Love You Tonight

Let's Take the Long Way Home

A Little on the Lonely Side

Milkman Keep Those Bottles Quiet

Moonlight in Vermont

More and More

My Dreams Are Getting Better All the Time

Nancy (with the Laughing Face)

Opus Number One

Sleigh Ride in July

Some Other Time

Straighten Up and Fly Right

Suddenly It's Spring

Sure Thing

That's What I Like About the South

There Goes That Song Again

There's No You

The Three Caballeros

Up in Arms

When They Ask About You

You Belong to My Heart (Now and Forever)

You're Nobody 'Til Somebody Loves You

1945

World War II Ends. On May 6 Germany capitulates and two days later signs the articles of surrender in Berlin. Mussolini had been captured April 28 and shot by a firing squad. On April 30 Russian troops capture the Reichstag in Berlin and Hitler commits suicide the same day. In the Far East on August 6, Truman orders the A-Bomb dropped on Hiroshima, totally devastating the city; a second, three days later, destroys Nagasaki. August 14 is V-J Day, and Japan officially surrenders aboard the U.S.S. Missouri on September 2.

American servicemen say goodbye to their wartime buddies: ''Dig You Later (A Hubba-Hubba-Hubba)'' and return home on a ''Sentimental Journey'' anxious to see their girls: ''It's Been a Long Long Time.'' While ''Waitin' for the Train To Come In,'' girls for whom ''Saturday Night (Is the Loneliest Night of the Week),'' vow ''I'm Gonna Love That Guy (Like He's Never Been Loved Before).''

FDR and Truman. Only ninety-six days into his fourth term as President, Franklin Delano Roosevelt dies suddenly from a cerebral hemorrhage. Vice-President Harry S. Truman of Missouri is inaugurated 33rd President of the United States.

Aaron Copland. The Pulitzer Prize for music is awarded to Aaron Copland's ballet ''Appalachian Spring.''

Broadway and Hollywood. Among other shows, Broadway sees Tennessee Williams's *Glass Menagerie,* Howard Lindsay and Russel Crouse's Pulitzer Prize-winning *State of the Union,* and Maurice Evans's GI production of *Hamlet.* The two big musical productions were Sigmund Romberg's *Up in Central Park* and Rodgers and Hammerstein's *Carousel* (based on Ferenc Molnár's play *Liliom*).

In film the big movie musical was *Anchors Aweigh,* starring Frank Sinatra, Kathryn Grayson, and Gene Kelly. Other films included *The Bells of St. Mary's* with Bing Crosby and Ingrid Bergman, *The Corn Is Green* with Bette Davis, *Mildred Pierce* with Joan Crawford, Hitchcock's *Spellbound* with Ingrid Bergman and Gregory Peck, and *National Velvet* with Elizabeth Taylor.

The Price Is Right. A new automobile with optional extras can be bought for $950.

Top Hits

Ac-cent-tchu-ate the Positive RS 9   HP 10   AP 2   a. Bing Crosby and The Andrews Sisters; Johnny Mercer

All of My Life (m. Berlin)

Along the Navajo Trail

Aren't You Glad You're You, see 1946

Autumn Serenade

Candy RS 8 (tie)   HP x   AP 7   a. Johnny Mercer and Jo Stafford

Chickery Chick RS 5 (tie)   HP x   AP x   a. Sammy Kaye

Close as Pages in a Book, (from 1944)

Cruising Down the River

Doctor, Lawyer, Indian Chief, see 1946

Dream (When You're Feeling Blue) RS x   HP 2   AP 3

For Sentimental Reasons

Give Me the Simple Life

I Can't Begin To Tell You, see 1946

I Should Care RS x   HP x   AP 9

I Wish I Knew

If I Loved You RS 10   HP 3   AP 1   a. Perry Como

I'll Be Yours (J'Attendrai)

I'll Close My Eyes

I'm Beginning To See the Light RS x   HP x   AP 6

It Might As Well Be Spring, see 1946

It's a Grand Night for Singing

It's Been a Long, Long Time RS 5 (tie)   HP 6   AP x a. Harry James and Bing Crosby

J'Attendrai, see ''I'll Be Yours''

June Is Bustin' Out All Over

Just a Little Fond Affection

Laura RS x   HP 9   AP x

Let It Snow, Let It Snow, Let It Snow, see 1946

The More I See You

My Dreams Are Getting Better All the Time (from 1944) RS 4 (tie)   HP 7   AP 5   a. Les Brown

Oh What It Seemed To Be, see 1946

On the Atchison, Topeka, and the Santa Fe RS 4 (tie)   HP 8   AP x   a. Johnny Mercer

(You Came Along from) Out of Nowhere

Rum and Coca-Cola RS 3   HP x   AP x   a. The Andrews Sisters

Saturday Night (Is the Loneliest Night of the Week) (from 1944) RS x   HP x   AP 8

Seems Like Old Times

Sentimental Journey RS 2   HP 5   AP x   a. Les Brown, Doris Day

Symphony RS 6   HP 3 (1946)   AP 2 (1946)   a. Freddy Martin

That's for Me RS x HP x AP 10

There, I've Said It Again RS 7 HP x AP x a. Vaughn Monroe

While the Angelus Was Ringing (a.k.a. "The Three Bells" and "The Jimmy Brown Song" with different lyrics; see also 1948)

You'll Never Walk Alone

Adaptations

Bell Bottom Trousers (based on a traditional sea chantey from 1907) RS 8 (tie) HP x AP x a. Tony Pastor

If You Are But a Dream (based on Anton Rubinstein's "Romance in E-Flat")

One Meat Ball (based on "The Lone Fish Ball" of 1855)

Till the End of Time (based on Chopin's Polonaise in A-flat, op. 53, no. 6) RS 1 HP 1 AP 4 a. Perry Como

We Shall Overcome (based on the music from an early hymn of 1794, words from a second hymn of 1900)

Revivals

Cocktails for Two (1934)

My Shawl (1934)

These Foolish Things (Remind Me of You) (1936)

Notable

All At Once

All the Time

The Carousel Waltz

Did You Ever Get That Feeling in the Moonlight?

Dig You Later (A Hubba-Hubba-Hubba)

(Just Say I'm a) Friend of Yours

Gotta Be This or That

Here Comes Heaven Again

I'll Always Be With You

I'll Buy That Dream

I'm Gonna Love That Guy (Like He's Never Been Loved Before)

In Acapulco

Into Each Life Some Rain Must Fall

June Comes Around Every Year

Love

Love Is So Terrific

Love Letters

Matelot

Mister Snow

My Heart Sings

Negra Consentida (My Pet Brunette)

New York, New York

Nina

9:20 Special

No Can Do

Northwest Passage

Out of This World

Rodger Young

Sioux City Sue

Skyliner

Soliloquy

Some Sunday Morning, see 1946

(Theme from) Spellbound

There Must Be a Way

Waitin' for the Train To Come In

We'll Be Together Again

We'll Gather Lilacs

What's the Use of Wondrin'

You Won't Be Satisfied

[*Note:* "Don't Fence Me In" was No. 4 on the Hit Parade (HP) for this year, but record sales peaked during 1944.]

1946

Tape Recorders. German Magnetophon tape recorders, captured by the Allies during the occupation of Radio Luxembourg, are brought to the United States and demonstrated.

RCA and Sousa. John Philip Sousa's march "Stars and Stripes Forever" is honored by RCA Victor and selected to be the recording company's one billionth record.

Stravinsky and Herman. Igor Stravinsky's "Ebony Concerto" for clarinet and swing band is premiered at Carnegie Hall, performed by Woody Herman's band.

Annie Get Your Gun. Opening at the Imperial Theatre on May 16, Irving Berlin's *Annie Get Your Gun* starring Ethel Merman will be his greatest stage success and run for 1147 performances. Dinah Shore's recording of "Doin' What Comes Natur'lly" and Perry Como's "They Say It's Wonderful" become best sellers and three songs from this score are heard simultaneously for ten weeks on "Your Hit Parade." And of course, Miss Merman's rendition of "There's No Business Like Show Business" would be a signature song for her.

The Jolson Story. Columbia Pictures hires Larry Parks to play Al Jolson in the Alfred E. Green biopic of *The Jolson Story.* Jolson, now sixty, agrees to record the sound track himself, and Parks gives a sterling performance capturing the master showman. It opens on October 10 at Radio City Music Hall and Jolson's and Saul Chaplin's newly written "The Anniversary Song" sells two million disks: one million of Jolson's recording and a million for Bing Crosby's version, both recorded by Decca.

Top Hits

All Through the Day RS x HP 8 AP 5

Aren't You Glad You're You? RS x HP x AP 9

The Christmas Song (a.k.a. "Merry Christmas to You," or, "Chestnuts Roasting on an Open Fire")

Come Rain or Come Shine

Day By Day RS x HP x AP 4

Dear Old Donegal

Doctor, Lawyer, Indian Chief RS 8 (tie) HP x AP x a. Betty Hutton

Doin' What Comes Natur'lly

Five Minutes More RS 7 (tie) HP 7 AP x a. Frank Sinatra

The Girl That I Marry

Golden Earrings, see 1947

The Gypsy RS 1 HP 2 AP 10 a. Ink Spots

How Are Things in Glocca Morra, see 1947

Huggin' and Chalkin' RS 10 HP x AP x a. Hoagy Carmichael

I Can't Begin To Tell You RS 8 (tie) HP 9 AP 8 a. Bing Crosby

I Don't Know Enough About You

I Got the Sun in the Morning

If This Isn't Love

I'm a Big Girl Now RS 8 (tie) HP x AP x a. Sammy Kaye

In Love in Vain

It Might as Well Be Spring RS x HP 10 AP x

It's a Good Day

Linda, see 1947

Let It Snow, Let It Snow, Let It Snow RS 5 (tie) HP x AP 6 a. Vaughn Monroe

Oh, What It Seemed To Be RS 4 HP 5 AP 3 a. Frankie Carle

Old Devil Moon

The Old Lamp-Lighter RS 3 HP x AP x a. Sammy Kaye

Ole Buttermilk Sky RS 7 (tie) HP 6 AP x a. Kay Kyser

Personality RS 8 (tie) HP x AP x a. Johnny Mercer

Rumors Are Flying RS 2 HP x AP x a. Frank Carle

Shangri-La (neither from the film nor the later Broadway show)

Some Day You'll Want Me To Want You

South America Take It Away RS 9 HP x AP x a. Bing Crosby, The Andrews Sisters

Surrender RS 8 (tie) HP x AP x a. Perry Como

Tenderly, see 1947

There's No Business Like Show Business

They Say It's Wonderful RS x HP 1 AP 1

This Heart of Mine

To Each His Own RS 5 (tie) HP 4 AP x a. Eddy Howard; Freddy Martin; Ink Spots

When I'm Not Near the Girl I Love

You Always Hurt the One You Love

You're Nobody 'Til Somebody Loves You

Zip-A-Dee-Doo-Dah, see 1947

Adaptations

Full Moon and Empty Arms (based on Rachmaninoff's Piano Concerto No. 2 in C-minor)

Revivals

Chiquita Banana (1938)

I'm Always Chasing Rainbows (1918) RS x HP x AP 7

Jersey Bounce (1942)

Prisoner of Love (1931) RS 6 HP x AP x a. Perry Como

Puttin' on the Ritz (1929)

Temptation (1933)

You Keep Coming Back Like a Song (1943)

Notable

Along with Me

And So to Bed

Anything You Can Do

Aren't You Kind of Glad We Did

Atlanta, Ga.

The Begat

Caldonia

Canal Street Blues

Cement Mixer (Put-ti Put-ti)

Coax Me a Little Bit

Come Closer to Me (Acercate Mas)

A Couple of Song and Dance Men

Do You Know What It Means To Miss New Orleans

Either It's Love or It Isn't

Fifty-Second Street Theme

Hey-Ba-Ba-Re-Bop

I Got Lost in His Arms

I Guess I'll Get the Papers and Go Home

If I'm Lucky

It Couldn't Be True

It's a Pity To Say Goodnight

Laughing on the Outside (Crying on the Inside)

Linger in My Arms a Little Longer, Baby

Look to the Rainbow

Mama

Midnight Masquerade

My Defenses Are Down

On the Boardwalk in Atlantic City

Put It There Pal

Put the Blame on Mame
Rainy Night in Rio
(Get Your Kicks on) Route 66
Shoofly Pie and Apple Pan Dowdy
Some Sunday Morning (Jerome and Heindorf)
Somewhere in the Night
Sonata
Stella by Starlight
A Sunday Kind of Love
Tampico
That's Where I Came In
The Things We Did Last Summer
This Is Always
Through a Thousand Dreams
Till Then
Too Many Times
La Vie en Rose
When the Idle Poor Become the Idle Rich
Who Do You Love, I Hope
The Whole World Is Singing My Song
Wyoming (Oh Why, Oh Why Did I Ever Leave)
You Call Everybody Darlin'
You Can't Get a Man with a Gun
You Can't See the Sun When You're Crying
You Make Me Feel So Young

[*Note:* "Symphony" was No. 3 on the Hit Parade (HP), and No. 2 on Air Play (AP) for this year, but record sales (RS) peaked during 1945.]

1947

Television. Television emerges as a new medium and the great epochs of network radio broadcasting and Hollywood film companies with stables of expensive stars recede. Seven television stations begin regular broadcasts on the eastern seaboard of the U.S. The total number of viewers this year (black and white pictures only) is 14,000.

Stereo Tape Recorders. The first two-channel stereo audio tape machines are demonstrated.

The Tony. The American Theatre Wing Antoinette Perry Awards begin this year. The first award to the musical theatre will be bestowed on Cole Porter's *Kiss Me Kate* in 1949.

Broadway Fantasies. E.Y. Harburg and Burton Lane's *Finian's Rainbow* opens at the 46th Street Theatre on January 10, for a successful run of 725 performances. Masked by leprechauns and pots of gold, this show deals squarely with the issue of racism in America. It includes among other great songs "How Are Things in Glocca Morra?," "Old Devil Moon," "Look to the Rainbow," and "When I'm Not Near the Girl I Love." On March 13, the Ziegfeld Theatre opens Alan Jay Lerner and Frederick Loewe's first success, *Brigadoon,* which would run for 581 performances. Its three hits are "Almost Like Being in Love," "Come to Me, Bend to Me," and "The Heather on the Hill."

Top Hits
Almost Like Being in Love
As Long as I'm Dreaming
Ballerina   RS 2   HP 5 (1948)   AP x   a. Vaughn Monroe
Beyond the Sea
But Beautiful, see 1948
Chi-Baba Chi-Baba (My Bambino Go To Sleep)   RS 5   HP x   AP x   a. Perry Como
Civilization (Bongo Bongo Bongo)
Cool Water
Cuanto le Gusta
A Fellow Needs a Girl
Feudin' and Fightin'
(I Love You) For Sentimental Reasons   RS 7 (tie)   HP 5   AP 4   a. King Cole Trio
A Gal in Calico   RS x   HP x   AP 9
Golden Earrings   RS 8 (tie)   HP x   AP x   a. Peggy Lee
How Are Things in Glocca Morra   RS x   HP x   AP 6
How Soon   RS x   HP 10   AP x
I Wish I Didn't Love You So   RS 9   HP 6   AP 10 a. Vaughn Monroe
I'll Close My Eyes   RS x   HP x   AP 3
I'll Dance at Your Wedding
It's a Good Day (from 1946)   RS x   HP x   AP 2
Linda   RS x   HP 4   AP 5
Mam'selle   RS 6 (tie)   HP 7   AP x   a. Art Lund
Managua Nicaragua   RS 6 (tie)   HP x   AP 7   a. Freddy Martin
Near You   RS 1 (tie)   HP 3   AP x   a. Francis Craig
Open the Door, Richard   RS 7 (tie)   HP x   AP x   a. Count Basie
Papa Won't You Dance with Me
Sixteen Tons
Smoke! Smoke! Smoke! (That Cigarette)   RS 3   HP x   AP x   a. Tex Williams
Tenderly
That's My Desire   RS x   HP 8   AP x
Time After Time
Too Fat Polka   RS 8 (tie)   HP x   AP x   a. Arthur Godfrey
Woody Woodpecker, see 1948
You Are Never Away
Zip-A-Dee-Doo-Dah   RS x   HP x   AP 8

Adaptations
The Anniversary Song (based on Ivanovici's ''Danube Waves''
(1880)) RS 10 HP 2 AP 1 a. Al Jolson

Revivals
Guilty (1931)
Heartaches (1931) RS 1 (tie) HP 9 AP x a. Ted Weems
Just Imagine (1928)
Peg o' My Heart (1913) RS 4 HP 1 AP x a. Harmonicats; Three Suns
The Preacher and the Bear (1904)
That's What I Like About the South (1944)
There! I've Said It Again (1941)
There'll Be Some Changes Made (1921)
We Could Make Such Beautiful Music Together (1940)
We Three—My Echo, My Shadow and Me (1940)

Notable
Across the Alley from the Alamo
Ask Anyone Who Knows
Autumn Leaves
Big Brass Band from Brazil
Bloop Bleep
The Coffee Song
Come to the Mardi Gras, see 1948
Country Style
Dream, Dream, Dream
The Egg and I
For You, For Me, For Evermore
The Gentleman Is a Dope
The Heather on the Hill
The House of Blue Lights
I Do Do Do Like You
I Still Get Jealous
I Wonder, I Wonder, I Wonder
It's the Same Old Dream
Ivy
The Lady from Twenty-Nine Palms
Maybe You'll Be There
Midnight Sun
Misirlou
My Adobe Hacienda
Oh, But I Do
On Green Dolphin Street
Perhaps Perhaps Perhaps
Red Silk Stockings and Green Perfume
Serenade of the Bells
Smoke Dreams
So Far
Song of the South

Sooner or Later
The Stanley Steamer
There But for You Go I
Uncle Remus Said
The Wedding Samba
You Don't Have To Know the Language
You, You, You Are the One
You're My Girl

1948

LPs. On June 21, Dr. Peter Goldmark of the Columbia Broadcasting System demonstrates the first long playing record, which has twenty or more minutes of recording time per side. Within one year, the LP completely dominates the recording business and provides the most economical music storage density of any practical system. The new design represents a synthesis of the micro-groove approach used by Edison in 1926 and the 33 1/3 r.p.m. speed tried by Victor in 1931. The LP gives the average individual access to the complete classical and non-classical repertoire on a scale previously unimaginable, and it is not an exaggeration to say that it initiates a worldwide cultural revolution.

Easter Parade. MGM's feature musical starring Judy Garland and Fred Astaire with Peter Lawford and Ann Miller is a big success. With songs by Irving Berlin arranged and scored by John Green, this film includes among others ''A Fella with an Umbrella,'' ''It Only Happens When I Dance with You,'' ''Stepping Out with My Baby,'' ''A Couple of Swells,'' and of course ''Easter Parade.''

Kiss Me, Kate. Opening at the New Century on December 30 for a successful run of 1077 performances is Cole Porter's *Kiss Me, Kate,* based on Shakespeare's *The Taming of the Shrew* and starring Alfred Drake, Lisa Kirk, Harold Lang, and Patricia Morison. Porter proved himself most adept with his songs ''Always True to You in My Fashion,'' ''So in Love,'' ''Wunderbar,'' and ''Brush Up Your Shakespeare.''

Subway Fare Hike. The traditional five-cent subway fare in New York City is raised to ten cents.

Top Hits
''A''—You're Adorable
Baby, It's Cold Outside
Beg Your Pardon RS x HP x AP 9
But Beautiful RS x HP x AP 2
Buttons and Bows RS 1 HP 3 AP 4 a. Dinah Shore
Haunted Heart RS x HP x AP 7

Hurry on Down

It All Comes Back to Me Now

It's a Most Unusual Day

It's Magic   RS 10   HP 4   AP 5   a. Doris Day

A Little Bird Told Me, see 1949

Mañana (Is Soon Enough for Me)   RS 2   HP x   AP 8   a. Peggy Lee

My Darling, My Darling

My Happiness   RS x   HP 9   AP x

Nature Boy   RS 4   HP x   AP x   a. Nat King Cole

(I'd Like To Get You) On a Slow Boat to China   RS x   HP 6   AP x

Once in Love with Amy

Pass That Peace Pipe

Powder Your Face with Sunshine, see 1949

Sabre Dance (from "Gayaneh Ballet")

Serenade of the Bells (from 1947)   RS x   HP 8   AP x

Tennessee Waltz

A Tree in the Meadow   RS 7 (tie)   HP 1   AP 3   a. Margaret Whiting

While the Angelus Was Ringing (a.k.a. "The Three Bells" and "The Jimmy Brown Song")

Woody Woodpecker   RS 5   HP x   AP x   a. Kaye Kyser

You Call Everybody Darling (from 1946)   RS 7 (tie)   HP x   AP 10   a. Al Trace

You Can't Be True, Dear   RS 9   HP 7   AP x   a. Ken Griffin and Jerry Wayne

You're Breaking My Heart, see 1949

You've Changed

Adaptations

Lavender's Blue (Dilly, Dilly) (based on a traditional English folksong, *c.* 1750)

Now Is the Hour (based on the traditional New Zealand song, "Hearere Ra")   RS 8   HP 2   AP 1   a. Bing Crosby

Revivals

Easter Parade (1933)

Hora Staccato (1930)

I Love a Piano (1915)

I Wonder Who's Kissing Her Now (1909)

I'm Looking Over a Four Leaf Clover (1927)   RS 6   HP 10   AP 6   a. Art Mooney

Lazy (1924)

Snooky Ookums (1913)

That Old Gang of Mine (1923)

Twelfth Street Rag (1914)   RS 3   HP x   AP x   a. Pee Wee Hunt

Notable

Ah But It Happens

Be a Clown

Blue Shadows on the Trail

Bouquet of Roses

Candy Kisses, see 1949

Come to the Mardi Gras

A Couple of Swells

The Dickey Bird Song

The Dream of Olwen

A Fella with an Umbrella

Fiddle Faddle

For Every Man There's a Woman

Forever and Ever

Galway Bay

Hair of Gold, Eyes of Blue

Here I'll Stay

I Got Lucky in the Rain

I Love You So Much It Hurts

I Tipped My Hat and Slowly Rode Away

I Want To Thank Your Folks

I'm a-Comin' a-Courtin' Corabelle

It Only Happens When I Dance with You

It Was Written in the Stars

It's So Peaceful in the Country

It's You or No One

I've Got a Lovely Bunch of Cocoanuts

Laroo Laroo Lilli Bolero

Love Is So Terrific

Love of My Life

Matinee

The Night Has a Thousand Eyes (Brainin)

One Sunday Afternoon

Portrait of a Flirt

Put 'Em in a Box

Red Roses for a Blue Lady

Since I Fell for You

So in Love

So Tired

Stepping Out with My Baby

Sunday Kind of Love (from 1946)

Sun Flower

Swedish Pastry

This Is the Moment

Too Many Times (from 1946)

Tubby the Tuba

We'll Be Together Again (from 1945)

What's Good About Goodbye

You Say the Nicest Things, Baby

You Was

[*Note:* "Ballerina" was No. 5 on the Hit Parade (HP) for this year, but record sales peaked during 1947.]

1949

RCA 45s. RCA produces a 7-inch 45 r.p.m. disc with a large center hole to challenge the CBS LP announced last year. The challenge fails and the backlash inadvertently kills the 10-inch 78 r.p.m. record market.

Country and Western Enters Top Ten. The C & W song "Slippin' Around" crosses over from C & W charts to the Top Ten in record sales. Written by Floyd Tillman, it is sung by Margaret Whiting and Jimmy Wakely.

South Pacific. Rodgers and Hammerstein's Pulitzer Prize-winning musical adaptation of James A. Michener's *Tales of the South Pacific* opens at the Majestic Theatre on April 7 for a 1925-performance run. Its stars, Mary Martin and Ezio Pinza, introduce "This Nearly Was Mine," "I'm Gonna Wash That Man Right Outa My Hair," "A Wonderful Guy," "Happy Talk," "Carefully Taught," and "There Is Nothin' Like a Dame," "Bali Ha'i," "Younger Than Springtime," and "Some Enchanted Evening" which would all get to be Number 1 on "Your Hit Parade." The original cast recording (Columbia) would sell an unbelievable million albums. *South Pacific* would net a profit of over seven million dollars by 1970.

Doris Day. Doris von Kappelhoff of Cincinnati, Ohio, makes her film debut as Doris Day in *Romance on the High Seas,* in which she introduces her first hit song from a film, "It's Magic." Miss Day is twenty-five. In 1945 "Sentimental Journey" was her first big hit, recorded for Columbia with Les Brown and his orchestra, selling a million disks. This song later became Les Brown's orchestra theme.

Dean Martin and Jerry Lewis. Jerry Lewis of Newark, New Jersey, makes his first film appearance in the musical film *My Friend Irma Goes West* with Dean Martin of Steubenville, Ohio. Mr. Lewis is twenty-three and Mr. Martin is thirty-two.

Top Hits
Again RS 9 HP 2 AP 6 a. Gordon Jenkins
Bali Ha'i RS x HP 7 AP 9
Bibbidi-Bobbodi-Boo
Dear Hearts and Gentle People, see 1950
Diamonds Are a Girl's Best Friend
Dites-Moi Pourquoi
Don't Cry, Joe RS x HP 10 AP x
Far Away Places RS x HP 3 AP 5
Forever and Ever (from 1948) RS 10 (tie) HP 8 AP x a. Russ Morgan
Let's Take an Old-Fashioned Walk

A Little Bird Told Me RS 3 (tie) HP x AP 10 a. Evelyn Knight
Lovesick Blues
Mona Lisa, see 1950
Mule Train RS 4 HP x AP x a. Frankie Lane
Powder Your Face with Sunshine RS x HP x AP 3
Riders in the Sky RS 1 HP 9 AP x a. Vaughn Monroe
Rudolph, the Red-Nosed Reindeer RS 7 HP x AP x a. Gene Autry
Slippin' Around RS 10 (tie) HP x AP x a. Margaret Whiting and Jimmy Wakeley
So in Love (from 1948) RS x HP x AP 1
Some Enchanted Evening RS 5 HP 1 AP 2 a. Perry Como
Sun Flower (from 1948) RS x HP x AP 7
That Lucky Old Sun RS 2 HP x AP x a. Frankie Lane
Why Can't You Behave?
Younger Than Springtime

Adaptations
The Hot Canary (based on F. Poliakin's "Le Canari")
There's No Tomorrow (based on di Capua's "O Sole Mio" (1899)) RS 8 HP x AP x a. Tony Martin
You're Breaking My Heart (based on "La Mattinata" by Ruggiero Leoncavallo (1904)) RS 6 HP 5 AP x a. Vic Damone

Revivals
The Big Rock Candy Mountain (traditional)
Cruising Down the River (1945) RS 3 (tie) HP 4 AP 4 a. Russ Morgan, Blue Barron
Dry Bones (1865)
Everywhere You Go, 1927
How High the Moon (1940)
I Can Dream, Can't I, see 1950
I've Got My Love To Keep Me Warm (1937) RS x HP x AP 8
Jealous Heart (1944)
Johnson Rag (1917)
Lover (1933)
'Way Back Home (1935)

Notable
(I'm) Always True to You in My Fashion
Ballin' the Jack
Bloody Mary
Bonaparte's Retreat, see 1950
Brush Up Your Shakespeare
Bye Bye Baby
Candy Kisses
Careless Hands

Cigareets, Whusky and Wild Wild Women
Clancy Lowered the Boom
Clopin Clopant
A Cock-Eyed Optimist
Comme Ci, Comme Ça
Copper Canyon
The Cry of the Wild Goose
Daddy's Little Girl
Down by the Station
A Dream Is a Wish Your Heart Makes
Dreamer with a Penny
A Dreamer's Holiday
Early Autumn
Enjoy Yourself, It's Later Than You Think
The Four Winds and the Seven Seas
Ghost Riders in the Sky
Girls Were Made To Take Care of Boys
Happy Talk
He's a Real Gone Guy
Homework
Honey Bun
Hop Scotch Polka
How It Lies, How It Lies, How It Lies
Huckle-Buck
I Came Here To Talk for Joe (from 1942)
I Don't See Me in Your Eyes Anymore
I Hate Men
(Just One Way To Say) I Love You
I Love You Because
I Want You To Want Me To Want You
I'm Gonna Wash That Man Right Outa My Hair
I'm in Love with a Wonderful Guy, see "A Wonderful Guy"
It's a Big, Wide, Wonderful World
Jealous Heart (published in 1944, but popularized this year)
A Little Girl from Little Rock
Lost in the Stars
Lush Life
Maybe It's Because
Melodie d'Amour
Monday, Tuesday, Wednesday
My Foolish Heart
My One and Only Highland Fling
(Where Are You) Now That I Need You
The Old Master Painter
Perhaps Perhaps Perhaps (from 1947)
Peter Cottontail
Pigalle
Portrait of Jenny
Put Your Shoes On, Lucy
Room Full of Roses

Scarlet Ribbons for Her Hair
Room Full of Roses
La Seine
Sentimental Me
There Is Nothin' Like a Dame
This Nearly Was Mine
Through a Long Sleepless Night
Too Darn Hot
A Wonderful Guy
Wunderbar

[*Note:* "I Can Dream, Can't I?" was No. 6 on the Hit Parade (HP) for this year, but record sales peaked during 1950.]

1950

America's First Undeclared War. North Korea, financed and equipped by Soviet Russia, invades South Korea. The armed forces of the United States are sent into combat in the defense of South Korea by President Truman. Congress evades the responsibility of a formal declaration of war as required by the Constitution.

Records Predominate. Tabulations of record sales rather than broadcasts (air play) begin to determine song popularity. Sales chart ratings now begin to apply to individual single *recordings*, and not simply to the songs themselves.

Recorded Music Sales. Total retail sales of recorded music, singles and albums combined, is estimated at $200 million.

Your Hit Parade Says Goodbye. The last broadcast of the regular "Your Hit Parade" program is presented on network radio.

> So long for a while
> That's all the songs for a while
> So long from your Hit Parade
> And the beautiful music we played

The television version of "Your Hit Parade" ended several years later.

Color TV. Following years of debate between the Columbia Broadcasting System and the Radio Corporation of America, the Federal Communications Commission grants on October 11 to CBS the right to broadcast their form of color television.

Leadbelly. Huddie Ludbetter's "Goodnight, Irene" by Gordon Jenkins and The Weavers is this year's number one record. Discovered in Louisiana state prison by folksong archivist John A. Lomax, Leadbelly records for the Library of Congress and after his release in 1934 tours prisons and colleges and ultimately plays the Village Vanguard in New York's Greenwich Village. This year's Decca recording is followed by other successful releases by Frank Sinatra, Red Foley, and Ernest Tubb.

Guys and Dolls. The 46th Street Theatre, on November 24, opens Frank Loesser's *Guys and Dolls,* with book by Abe Burrows and Jo Swerling, directed by George S. Kaufman, and choreographed by Michael Kidd. The score includes such favorites as "Adelaide's Lament," "Fugue for Tinhorns," "I'll Know," "A Bushel and a Peck," "I've Never Been in Love Before," and "Take Back Your Mink."

Top Hits
All My Love RS 8 HP 6 AP 5 a. Patti Page
Autumn Leaves
A Bushel and a Peck
C'est Si Bon
Chattanoogie Shoe Shine Boy RS 5 (tie) HP x AP x a. Red Foley
Dear Hearts and Gentle People RS x HP 5 AP x
Dearie
End of a Love Affair
Gone Fishin'
Hoop-Dee-Doo RS x HP x AP 2
I Don't Care If the Sun Don't Shine RS x HP x AP 3
If (Evans; see 1951)
If I Knew You Were Comin' I'd've Baked a Cake RS 6 (tie) HP 10 AP 7 a. Eileen Barton
It Isn't Fair RS x HP x AP 8
It's a Lovely Day Today
It's So Nice To Have a Man Around the House
Mona Lisa RS x HP 2 AP 10 a. Nat King Cole
Music Music Music RS 5 (tie) HP x AP x a. Teresa Brewer
My Foolish Heart (from 1949) RS x HP 1 AP 1
My Heart Cries for You RS 9 HP x AP 9 (1951) a. Guy Mitchell
The Old Piano Roll Blues
Rag Mop RS 7 HP x AP x a. Lionel Hampton; Ames Brothers
Silver Bells
Sleigh Ride
The Thing RS 5 (tie) HP x AP x a. Phil Harris
The Third Man Theme (The Harry Lime Theme) RS 2 HP 8 AP 9 a. Anton Karas
Why Fight the Feeling?

Adaptations
She Wore a Yellow Ribbon (All 'Round My Hat I Wore a Yellow Ribbon) (based on the traditional folksong from 1885)

Tzena, Tzena, Tzena (based on a traditional Yiddish folksong) RS 10 HP x AP x a. Gordon Jenkins and The Weavers

Revivals
Bewitched, Bothered and Bewildered (1941) RS x HP 3 AP 6
Can't We Talk It Over (1931)
Goodnight Irene (1936) RS 1 HP 4 AP x a. Gordon Jenkins and The Weavers
Harbor Lights (1937) RS 6 (tie) HP 7 AP x a. Sammy Kaye
I Can Dream, Can't I (1937) RS 5 (tie) HP 6 (1949) AP x a. The Andrews Sisters
Moonlight in Vermont (1944)
Nevertheless (1931)
(Play a) Simple Melody (1914)
Thinking of You (1927)
La Vie en Rose (1946) RS x HP 9 AP 4
The Wedding Samba (1947)

Notable
Adelaide's Lament
All I Want for Christmas (Is My Two Front Teeth)
American Beauty Rose
The Best Thing for You (Would Be Me)
Bonaparte's Retreat
Can Anyone Explain (No! No! No!)
Candy and Cake
Christmas in Killarney
Come Dance with Me
Count Every Star
Every Day I Have the Blues
From This Moment On
Frosty the Snowman
Fugue for Tinhorns
(This Is) God's Country
Have I Told You Lately That I Love You
Hold My Hand
Home Cooking
I Almost Lost My Mind
I Am Loved
I Didn't Slip, I Wasn't Pushed, I Fell
I Like Ike
I Said My Pajamas (and Put on My Prayers)
I Taut I Taw a Puddy-Tat
I Wanna Be Loved
If I Were a Bell
I'll Know
I'll Never Be Free
I'm Gonna Live Till I Die

I've Never Been in Love Before
Life Is So Peculiar
Little White Duck
London by Night
Luck Be a Lady
Marrying for Love
A Marshmallow World
May the Good Lord Bless and Keep You
My Time of Day
Nobody's Chasing Me
Orange Colored Sky
Our Lady of Fatima
A Penny a Kiss, a Penny a Hug
Sam's Song
Sit Down, You're Rockin' the Boat
Something To Dance About
Stay with the Happy People
Sunshine Cake
There Must Be Somethin' Better Than Love
Use Your Imagination
Violins from Nowhere
Wanderin'
When the Wind Was Green
Wilhelmina
With These Hands
You Wonderful You
You're Just in Love

[*Note:* "Tennessee Waltz" was No.3 in record sales (RS) for this year, but air play (AP) peaked during 1951. This is the last year for the inclusion of the "Your Hit Parade" (HP) song rankings.]

1951

More Gershwin and Porgy. Lehman Engel conducts a specially recorded version of *Porgy and Bess* for Columbia Records (Grammy Hall of Fame Winner, 1976).

George Gershwin. The Oscar for the best picture this year is awarded to *An American in Paris,* a feature film with music by George Gershwin. Gene Kelly and Leslie Caron dance a spectacular ballet to Gershwin's tone poem which provides the film's title.

Menotti and Amahl. The first commissioned opera written exclusively for television is Gian-Carlo Menotti's fifty-minute *Amahl and the Night Visitors,* aired on December 24 by the National Broadcasting Company.

The King and I. Margaret Landon's book *Anna and the King of Siam* becomes Rodgers and Hammerstein's *The King and I,* opening March 29 at the St. James Theatre. Gertrude Lawrence, inspired by both the book and the 1948 non-musical film starring Rex Harrison and Irene Dunne, persuades the team to compose a score for adaptation. With Yul Brynner as the King and Gertrude Lawrence as Anna, the show runs 1246 performances. Top hits include "Hello, Young Lovers," "Getting To Know You," "I Whistle a Happy Tune," "I Have Dreamed," and "Shall We Dance." A high point is Jerome Robbins's choreography for the ballet "The Small House of Uncle Thomas."

Johnnie Ray. Columbia Records has Johnnie Ray record "Cry," a song written years before by a night watchman at a Pittsburgh dry-cleaning establishment (the B-side was Ray's "The Little White Cloud That Cried"), and it sells over two million disks.

Top Hits
Anytime, see 1952
Be My Love RS 7 AP 4 a. Mario Lanza
Belle, Belle, My Liberty Belle
Cold Cold Heart RS 4 AP x a. Tony Bennett
Come On-A-My House RS 4 (tie) AP x a. Rosemary Clooney
Cry, see 1952
Domino
Half as Much, see 1952
Hello Young Lovers
Hey Good Lookin'
(When We Are Dancing) I Get Ideas
I Talk to the Trees
I Whistle a Happy Tune
If You Go (Away) (Si Tu Partais)
In the Cool, Cool, Cool of the Evening
Jezebel RS 10 AP x a. Frankie Lane
Kisses Sweeter Than Wine
The Little White Cloud That Cried RS 9 (tie) AP x a. Johnnie Ray
Mocking Bird Hill RS x AP 6
The Old Soft Shoe
Please Mister Sun, see 1952
Roving Kind
Shall We Dance
Shanghai
Shrimp Boats
(It's No) Sin RS 6 AP x a. Eddy Howard
Slow Poke, see 1952
Sound Off
Sparrow in the Tree Top
Tell Me Why RS 8 AP x a. Four Aces
Too Late Now

Too Young RS 5 AP 1   a. Nat King Cole

We Kiss in a Shadow

While We're Young

Would I Love You (Love You Love You) RS x   AP 8

You're Just in Love (from 1950) RS x   AP 5

Adaptations

It's All in the Game (based on Dawes's instrumental, "Melody" (1912))

The Loveliest Night of the Year (based on J.P. Rosa's "Over the Waves" (1888))

On Top of Old Smokey (based on a traditional folksong, as early as 1916) RS 9 (tie) AP x   a. The Weavers

Rose, Rose I Love You (based on a traditional Chinese melody)

Revivals

The Aba Daba Honeymoon (1914)

Because of You (1940) RS 3 AP 3   a. Tony Bennett

Broken Hearted (1927)

Down Yonder (1921)

How High the Moon (1940) RS 2 AP 10   a. Les Paul and Mary Ford

If (Tolchard Evans; 1934) RS 4 (tie) AP 2   a. Perry Como

I'm in Love Again (1925)

(Our) Love Is Here To Stay (1938)

So Long, It's Been Good To Know Ya(1935)

Sweet Violets (1908)

Tennessee Waltz (1948) RS 3 (1950) AP 7   a. Patti Page

The World Is Waiting for the Sunrise (1919)

Notable

Alice in Wonderland

And So To Sleep Again

Be My Life's Companion

Blue Velvet

Boutonniere

Dance Me Loose

Getting To Know You

Got Her Off My Hands (But Can't Get Her Off My Mind)

Hold Me, Hold Me, Hold Me

A House Is a Home

How Could You Believe Me When I Said I Love You When You Know I've Been a Liar All My Life

I Have Dreamed

I Left My Hat in Haiti

I Like It—I Like It

I Ran All the Way Home

I Still See Elisa

I Won't Cry Anymore

I'd Like To Baby You

If You Catch a Little Cold

I'll Buy You a Star

I'm a Fool To Want You

I'm Late

It Is No Secret

A Kiss To Build a Dream On

(It's Gonna Be) A Long, Long Winter

Love Is the Reason

Mademoiselle de Paris

Make the Man Love Me

The March of the Siamese Children

Marshmallow Moon

Mister and Mississippi

Misto Cristofo Columbo

Mixed Emotions

My Beloved

My Resistance Is Low

My Truly, Truly Fair

Never

Somebody Bigger Than You and I

Something Wonderful

The Syncopated Clock

There Is No Christmas Like a Home Christmas

They Call the Wind Maria

The Typewriter

Unforgettable

A Very Merry Un-Birthday to You

The Waltzing Cat

[*Note:* "Cry" was No. 1 in record sales (RS) for this year, but air play (AP) peaked in popularity during 1952. "My Heart Cries for You" was No. 9 in air play (AP) for this year, but record sales (RS) peaked in popularity during 1950.]

1952

The Sound of Muzak. The U.S. Supreme Court rules that radio broadcasts to "captive" audiences are not an invasion of privacy.

I Like Ike. The first and possibly last successful political campaign song from a Broadway musical is Irving Berlin's "I Like Ike." It aids the election of President Eisenhower and is derived from the song "They Like Ike" featured in Berlin's Broadway musical success *Call Me Madam* (1950).

Cinerama. As demonstrated by inventor Fred Waller at the Broadway Theatre on September 30, this new development in three-dimensional motion picture projection was originally used during World War II for training Air Corps gunnery students.

Truman and Mozart. On May 3 President Truman performs Mozart's Piano Sonata No. 9 for 30 million people in a television broadcast from the East Room of the White House.

More Amos 'n' Andy. Broadcasting since 1929, the popular "Amos 'n' Andy" radio program celebrates its 10,000th broadcast.

Singin' in the Rain. This classic musical film satirizing Hollywood film-making during the late 1920s and the conversion to "talkies" is brilliantly performed by Gene Kelly, Donald O'Connor, Debbie Reynolds, and Jean Hagen. Its script, by Betty Comden and Adolph Green, employs many Arthur Freed-Nacio Herb Brown standards, and Gene Kelly's dancing of the title number becomes the signature of his career.

Top Hits

A-Round the Corner (Beneath the Berry Tree)

Auf Wiederseh'n Sweetheart

Be Anything (But Be Mine)   RS x   AP 6

Be My Life's Companion (from 1951)   RS x   AP 9

Because You're Mine

Blue Tango   RS 2 (tie)   AP 3   a. Leroy Anderson

Botch-A-Me   RS 10   AP x   a. Rosemary Clooney

Bunny Hop

Cry   RS 1 (1951)   AP 5   a. Johnnie Ray

Delicado   RS 6   AP x   a. Percy Faith

Do Not Forsake Me, see "High Noon"

Don't Let the Stars Get in Your Eyes

Gonna Get Along Without Ya Now

Half as Much   RS 7   AP x   a. Rosemary Clooney

Here in My Heart   RS 4   AP x   a. Al Martino

(Theme from) High Noon (Do Not Forsake Me, Oh My Darling)

I Saw Mommy Kissing Santa Claus   RS 5 (tie)   AP x   a. Jimmy Boyd

I Went to Your Wedding   RS 2 (tie)   AP x   a. Patti Page

I'm Yours

It's in the Book   RS 5 (tie)   AP x   a. Johnny Standley

Jambalaya (on the Bayou)

Meet Mister Callaghan

PIttsburgh, Pennsylvania

Please Mister Sun   RS x   AP 8

Pretend, see 1953

Slow Poke   RS x   AP 7

Somewhere Along the Way

Takes Two To Tango

That's All

Till I Waltz Again with You, see 1953

The Wheel of Fortune   RS 1   AP x   a. Kay Starr

When the World Was Young (Ah, the Apple Tree)

Why Don't You Believe Me   RS 3   AP x   a. Joni James

Wimoweh

Wish You Were Here   RS x   AP 2

You Belong to Me   RS 2 (tie)   AP 4   a. Jo Stafford

Your Cheatin' Heart, see 1953

Adaptations

Glow Worm (new lyric by Johnny Mercer added this year to this 1907 standard)   RS 8   AP x   a. Mills Brothers

Kiss of Fire (based on "El Choclo" (1913))   RS 9   AP x   a. Georgia Gibbs

Revivals

Anytime (1921)   RS x   AP 1

Forgive Me (1927)

I'm Glad There Is You (1942)

Lady of Spain (1931)

Trust in Me (1936)

Undecided (1939)

Walkin' My Baby Back Home (1930)   RS x   AP 10

Notable

Am I in Love (m. Brooks)

Anywhere I Wander

At Last, At Last

The Blacksmith Blues

Count Your Blessings Instead of Sheep

Early Autumn

The Gandy Dancers' Ball

Gone

A Guy Is a Guy

Hi Lili Hi Lo

The Hippopotamus Song (a.k.a. "Mud, Glorious Mud")

Hold Me, Thrill Me, Kiss Me

How Do You Speak to an Angel

I'm Hans Christian Andersen

Inchworm

Keep It a Secret

Love Is a Simple Thing

Lullaby of Birdland

Night Train

Nina Never Knew

No Moon At All

No Two People

One Little Candle

Padam, Padam

Petite Fleur

Serenade to a Lemonade

Thumbelina

To Know You (Is To Love You)
Too Old To Cut the Mustard
The Ugly Duckling
When I Fall in Love
Why Try To Change Me Now?
Wonderful Copenhagen
Zing a Little Zong

1953

Elizabeth II. Television film broadcasts to the American people on June 2 the coronation of Queen Elizabeth II from London's Westminster Abbey.

Cinema Stereo. In the first effort at cinema stereo since Walt Disney's *Fantasia,* stereo is again featured in the "Cinerama" religious epic film *The Robe,* starring Richard Burton, Jean Simmons, and Victor Mature. The 3-D thriller *House of Wax* had rudimentary stereo in 1951.

Hank Williams. Country and Western star Hank Williams, author of "You'll Never Get Out of This World Alive," dies of a drug overdose at twenty-nine. At fourteen he had been a star of the Grand Ole Opry in Nashville, Tennessee. During his career, he had eleven songs that sold over a million copies between 1949 and this year.

Top Hits
April in Portugal   RS 10 (tie)   AP 3   a. Les Baxter
C'est Magnifique
Crying in the Chapel
(How Much Is That) Doggie in the Window   RS 3 (tie)   AP x   a. Patti Page
Don't Let the Stars Get in Your Eyes (from 1952)   RS 5 (tie)   AP 6   a. Perry Como
Ebb Tide   RS 9 (tie)   AP x   a. Frank Chacksfield
Eternally (Terry's Theme from *Limelight*)
(Now and Then) A Fool Such As I
From Here to Eternity
From This Moment On
I Believe RS 9 (tie)   AP 1   a. Frankie Lane
I Love Paris
If You Love Me (I Won't Care)
I'm Walking Behind You   RS 7   AP x   a. Eddie Fisher
Istanbul, see 1954
It's All Right with Me
Limelight, see "Eternally"
Make Love to Me, see 1954
Moulin Rouge, see "Song from Moulin Rouge"
Non Dimenticar
O Mein Papa   RS 3   AP x   a. Eddie Fisher

Pretend   RS x   AP 8
Rags to Riches   RS 4   AP x   a. Tony Bennett
Ruby
Saint George and the Dragonet   (comedy)   RS 6   AP x   a. Stan Freeberg
Secret Love, see 1954
Song from Moulin Rouge (Where Is Your Heart)   RS 2   AP 2   a. Percy Faith
Tell Me You're Mine
That's Amore   RS 10 (tie)   AP x   a. Dean Martin
Till I Waltz Again with You   RS 5 (tie)   AP 7   a. Teresa Brewer
Vaya Con Dios   RS 1   AP 9   a. Les Paul and Mary Ford
Where Is Your Heart, see "Song from Moulin Rouge"
You, You, You   RS 8   AP x   a. Ames Brothers
Your Cheatin' Heart   RS x   AP 10

Adaptations
And This Is My Beloved, see 1954
Baubles, Bangles and Beads, see 1954
Eh Cumpari (based on a traditional Italian song)
No Other Love   RS 10 (tie)   AP 4   a. Perry Como
Stranger in Paradise, see 1954

Revivals
C'est Si Bon (1950)
Eighteenth Variation on a Theme by Paganini (Rachmaninoff (1934))
The Gang That Sang Heart of My Heart (1926)
Granada (1932)
"O" (Oh!) (1919)
P.S. I Love You (1934)
Side by Side (1927)   RS x   AP 5
With These Hands (1950)

Notable
Allez-Vous-En, Go Away
Anna
(Theme from) **The Bad and the Beautiful**
Blue Gardenia
Can Can
Changing Partners
Downhearted
(Theme from) **Dragnet**
Ev'ry Street's a Boulevard
Gambler's Guitar
Have You Heard
Here's That Rainy Day
I Am in Love
Just Another Polka

Keep It Gay
Lazy Afternoon
Love of My Life (from 1948)
Mexican Joe
Mobile
The Moon Is Blue
My Love, My Love
Oh Happy Day
Ohio
Quiet Girl
Return to Paradise
Ricochet
(We're Gonna) Rock Around the Clock, see 1955
Swedish Rhapsody
That's Entertainment
That's What Makes Paris Paree
Under Paris Skies (Sous le Ciel de Paris)
You'll Never Get Out of This World Alive

1954

Rock 'n' Roll. Alan Freed, disc jockey, popularizes the phrase ''rock 'n' roll'' as the theme of his show ''The Big Beat,'' broadcast over Station WINS, New York. (It may derive from the song ''Rock with Me, Henry, Roll with Me, Henry'' which was later cleaned up for broadcasting with the new title ''Dance with Me, Henry''; see 1955. However, there is an earlier song with the title ''Rock and Roll'' in the score of the film *Transatlantic Merry-Go-Round* (1934) starring Jack Benny.

More Television. The conquest of the United States by television is now complete. There are 517 television stations nationally, with an estimated 32,000,000 viewers.

Mambo. Dancing the mambo is made popular by Mexican band leader Perez Prado. Favorites include ''Cherry Pink and Apple Blossom White'' (1955), ''Mambo Italiano,'' ''Papa Loves Mambo,'' and ''They Were Doing the Mambo.''

More Jazz. The First Newport Jazz Festival is organized on July 17.

Sinatra and Eternity. Frank Sinatra receives an Academy Award for his performance in *From Here to Eternity* and begins his sensational comeback.

Top Hits
All of You
Anema e Core
Count Your Blessings (Instead of Sheep) (from 1952) RS x AP 10

Fanny
Fly Me to the Moon (In Other Words)
The Happy Wanderer
Hernando's Hideaway   RS x   AP 8
Hey There   RS 4   AP 3   a. Rosemary Clooney
The High and the Mighty
(There's No Place Like) Home for the Holidays
I Need You Now   RS 5 (tie)   AP x   a. Eddie Fisher
If I Give My Heart to You   RS x   AP 7
Istanbul (*not* Constantinople)
Let Me Go Lover, see 1955
The Little Shoemaker   RS 9   AP x   a. Gaylords
Little Things Mean a Lot   RS 1   AP x   a. Kitty Kallen
The Man That Got Away
Mister Sandman   RS 3 (tie)   AP 8 (1955)   a. Chordettes
Secret Love   RS 5 (tie)   AP 1   a. Doris Day
Shake, Rattle and Roll
Sh-Boom   RS 3 (tie)   AP x   a. Crew-Cuts
Smile
Teach Me Tonight
This Ole House   RS 6   AP x   a. Rosemary Clooney
Three Coins in the Fountain   RS 10   AP 9   a. Four Aces
Wanted   RS 2   AP 5   a. Perry Como
Young and Foolish
Young at Heart   RS 8   AP 2   a. Frank Sinatra

Adaptations
And This Is My Beloved (based on a theme from the third movement of Borodin's String Quartet No. 2)
Baubles, Bangles and Beads (based on a Borodin theme)
Make Love to Me (based on ''Tin Roof Blues'' (1923) by The New Orleans Rhythm Kings: Paul Mares, George Brunies, Mel Stitzel, Leon Rappalo, Ben Pollack, and Walter Melrose)   RS 5 (tie)   AP 6   a. Jo Stafford
Stranger in Paradise (based on a theme from the ''Polovtsian Dances'' from the opera *Prince Igor* by Borodin (1888))

Revivals
I Can't Believe That You're in Love with Me (1926)
Oh Baby Mine (I Get So Lonely) (1928)
Tara's Theme (1939)   (with lyrics added as ''My Own True Love.'')

Notable
Alone Too Long
Answer Me
Autumn in Rome
Belle of the Ball
Captain Hook's Waltz
Cara Mia
Cross Over the Bridge

Danger, Heartbreak Ahead

Dream, Dream, Dream

Fascination

The Finger of Suspicion Points at You

From the Vine Came the Grape (From the Grape Came the Wine)

Funny Thing

A Girl! A Girl! (Zoom Ba Di Alla Nella)

Green Years

Hold My Hand

Honey-Babe

Honeycomb

Hurt

I Could Be Happy with You

I Could Have Told You

I Left My Heart in San Francisco

I Speak to the Stars

I Won't Grow Up

I'll Walk with God

I'm Flying

It's a New World

It's Never Too Late To Fall in Love

I've Gotta Crow

Joey

The Jones Boy

Knock on Wood

Lost in Loveliness

Make Her Mine

Make Yourself Comfortable

The Mama Doll Song

Mambo Italiano

Misty

My Own True Love, see "Tara's Theme"

The Naughty Lady of Shady Lane

Never Never Land

Now and Forever

Papa Loves Mambo

Release Me

Skokiaan

Somebody Bad Stole De Wedding Bell

Song of the Barefoot Contessa

Steam Heat

Sur le Plage

Sway

They Were Doing the Mambo

Till We Two Are One

The Typewriter

Wendy

Won't You Charleston with Me?

[*Note:* "Melody of Love" was No. 7 in record sales (RS) for this year, but air play (AP) peaked during 1955.]

1955

More Rock. After being featured behind the titles of the film *Blackboard Jungle,* the record "(We're Gonna) Rock Around the Clock" by Bill Haley and the Comets makes Top Ten on the charts.

More Cinema Stereo. Six channels of stereo are used in the film version of *Oklahoma!*

The Ivor Novello Award. The first awards for recorded music begin in London as the Ivor Novello Awards are given this year by the Songwriters' Guild of Great Britain. The American Grammy Awards will follow three years later.

Billboard Music Charts. Billboard magazine expands its singles record list from the "Top Twenty-five" to the "Top One Hundred," later the "Hot Hundred."

Chuck Berry. A major influence in the origins of rock and roll, black recording artist Chuck Berry begins his career with the hit "Maybellene."

Top Hits

Ain't That a Shame   RS 7   AP x   a. Pat Boone

Ballad of Davy Crockett   RS 4 (tie)   AP 1   a. Bill Hayes

A Blossom Fell   RS 9 (tie)   AP x   a. Nat King Cole

Cherry Pink and Apple Blossom White   RS 1   AP 7   a. Perez Prado

The Crazy Otto Rag (Medley)   RS 9 (tie)   AP x   a. Johnny Maddox

Cry Me a River

Dance with Me Henry   RS 10   AP x   a. Georgia Gibbs

Heart

Hearts of Stone   RS 6   AP x   a. Fontane Sisters

I Hear You Knocking

I'll Never Stop Loving You

Learnin' the Blues   RS 9 (tie)   AP 10   a. Frank Sinatra

Let Me Go Lover   RS 5 (tie)   AP x   a. Joan Weber

Love and Marriage

Love Is a Many-Splendored Thing   RS 4 (tie)   AP 4   a. Four Aces

Maybellene

Moments To Remember

(We're Gonna) Rock Around the Clock   RS 2   AP x   a. Bill Haley

Sincerely   RS 3 (tie)   AP x   a. McGuire Sisters

Something's Gotta Give   RS x   AP 5

Tweedle Dee   RS x   AP 2

Unchained Melody   RS 8   AP 6   a. Les Baxter

Adaptations
Fooled (based on a theme by Franz Lehár)

Revivals
Autumn Leaves (1950) RS 5 (tie) AP x a. Roger Williams

Melody of Love (1903) RS 7 (1954) AP 3 a. Billy Vaughn

Sixteen Tons (1947) RS 3 (tie) AP x a. Tennessee Ernie Ford

The Yellow Rose of Texas (1858) RS 3 (tie) AP 9 a. Mitch Miller

Notable
All at Once You Love Her
Almost in Your Arms
The Bible Tells Me So
Blue Star
Can I Leave Off Wearin' My Shoes
Domani (Tomorrow)
Don't Be Angry
Everybody's Got a Home But Me
The Great Pretender
Happiness Street (Corner Sunshine Square)
He
Hey, Mister Banjo
How Important Can It Be
Humming Bird
I Never Has Seen Snow
The Impatient Years
Josephine
Ko Ko Mo
The Longest Walk
The Man from Laramie
The Night We Called It a Day
Only You (and You Alone)
Open Up Your Heart
Paper Roses
Paris Loves Lovers
Pete Kelly's Blues
Play Me Hearts and Flowers (I Wanna Cry)
Sailor Boys Have Talk to Me in English
Shifting, Whispering Sands
Siberia
(A) Sleepin' Bee
Smellin' of Vanilla
Stereophonic Sound
Strange Lady in Town
Take My Love
Teenage Prayer
(Love Is) The Tender Trap

Too Young To Go Steady
Two Ladies in De Shade of De Banana Tree
Two Lost Souls
Unsuspecting Heart
Wake the Town and Tell the People
Whatever Lola Wants, Lola Gets

[*Note:* "Mister Sandman" was No. 8 in air play (AP) for this year, but record sales (RS) peaked during 1954.]

1956

Elvis. This year marks the emergence of the first rock star, Elvis Presley. In January, Elvis records "Heartbreak Hotel," for RCA which rises to No. 1 on the sales charts February 22. Television censors decry his swiveling hip movements and forbid closeups below the waist. Later this year, Elvis appears in his first motion picture, Hal Wallis's *Love Me Tender*. He has nineteen hits this year, three reaching No. 1.

The Broadway musical *Bye Bye Birdie* (1960) is loosely based on his being drafted into the U.S. Army. Presley's synthesis of rhythm and blues and rock sweeps the pop culture and prepares the way for the rock epoch that follows. Mr. Presley is twenty-one.

Color TV. Color television, gestating since 1946, becomes a national influence.

American Bandstand. Dick Clark now hosts "American Bandstand," telecast six days a week since 1952 from Philadelphia on ABC-TV. Its estimated audience is twenty million teenagers and twenty million adults. This show discovers such stars as Bobby Darin, Frankie Avalon, Connie Francis, and Fabian.

Pygmalion, Galatea, and Shaw. The George Bernard Shaw play *Pygmalion* is an immense hit in musical form this year with an incomparable score by writers Alan Jay Lerner and composer Frederick Loewe. Its new name is *My Fair Lady*. Starring Julie Andrews as Eliza, Rex Harrison as Professor Higgins, and Stanley Holloway as Alfred P. Doolittle, the show opens at the Mark Hellinger on March 15, with direction by Moss Hart and choreography by Hanya Holm. Breaking all records in New York and London, it runs 2717 performances in New York. The score includes "The Rain in Spain," "Wouldn't It Be Loverly?," "I Could Have Danced All Night," "On the Street Where You Live," "I'm an Ordinary Man," "With a Little Bit of Luck," and "Get Me to the Church on Time." Gross income for *My Fair Lady* will exceed $80 million, excluding the Columbia original cast recording of five million albums and the

$5.5 million for the motion picture adaptation rights in 1964.

Top Hits
Allegheny Moon   RS 8 (tie)   AP x   a. Patti Page
Around the World
Blue Suede Shoes
Canadian Sunset   RS x   AP 8
Don't Be Cruel   RS 1 (tie)   AP x   a. Elvis Presley
Don't Forbid Me, see 1957
The Green Door   RS 5   AP x   a. Jim Lowe
Heartbreak Hotel   RS 1 (tie)   AP x   a. Elvis Presley
Honkey Tonk   RS 6   AP x   a. Bill Doggett
Hound Dog   RS 7 (tie)   AP x   a. Elvis Presley
I Could Have Danced All Night   RS x   AP 1
Just in Time
Just Walking in the Rain   RS 7 (tie)   AP x   a. Johnnie Ray
Memories Are Made of This   RS 3 (tie)   AP x   a. Dean Martin
Mister Wonderful
No, Not Much
On the Street Where You Live   RS x   AP 2
The Party's Over
(Theme from) Picnic, see also "Moonglow" *Revival* RS 8 (tie)   AP x   a. Morris Stoloff
The Poor People of Paris   RS 2   AP 3   a. Les Baxter
Que Será, Será, see "Whatever Will Be Will Be"
The Rain in Spain
Rock and Roll Waltz   RS 4 (tie)   AP 7   a. Kay Starr
Singin' the Blues, see 1957
Soft Summer Breeze
Standing on the Corner   RS x   AP 5
True Love   RS x   AP 10
The Wayward Wind   RS 1 (tie)   AP x   a. Gogi Grant
Whatever Will Be Will Be (Que Será, Será)   RS 8 (tie)   AP x   a. Doris Day
Why Do Fools Fall in Love

Adaptations
Hot Diggity   (based on Chabrier's "España" (Spanish Rhapsody) of 1884)   RS 9   AP 9   a. Dean Martin
Love Me Tender (based on the song "Aura Lee" of 1861) RS 4 (tie)   AP x   a. Elvis Presley

Revivals
Blueberry Hill (1940)
Green Grow the Lilacs (1846)
I Almost Lost My Mind (1950)
Lisbon Antigua (1937)   RS x   AP 4
Moonglow (1934)   RS 8 (tie)   AP x   a. Morris Stoloff

My Prayer (1939)   RS 3 (tie)   AP x   a. Platters
Scarlet Ribbons (for Her Hair) (1949)
Theme from *Threepenny Opera* (Mack the Knife) from "Mor-it'at" (1928)   RS x   AP 6
Tonight You Belong to Me (1926)
Well, Did You Evah (1940)

Notable
Anastasia
Band of Gold
Bells Are Ringing
Big "D"
Chain Gang
Cindy Oh Cindy
Friendly Persuasion
Get Me to the Church on Time
Glendora
Glitter and Be Gay
Gonna Get Along Without You Now
The Happy Whistler
Hey Jealous Lover
How Little It Matters, How Little We Know
I Love You Samantha
I Want You, I Need You, I Love You
It Only Hurts for a Little While
I've Grown Accustomed to Her Face
Ivory Tower
Joey, Joey, Joey
Juke Box Baby
Long Before I Knew You
Long Tall Sally
Mama from the Train
Mama Teach Me To Dance
The Man with the Golden Arm
Married I Can Always Get
The Money Tree
More (not "Mondo Cane")
The Most Happy Fella
Our Language of Love
Roll Over Beethoven
See You Later Alligator
Show Me
Somebody Up There Likes Me
Song for a Summer Night
(Theme from) La Strada
Sweet Heartaches
Teenage Crush
There's Never Been Anyone Else But You
This Could Be the Start of Something Big
Too Close for Comfort

Two Different Worlds
Walk Hand in Hand
When Sonny Gets Blue
Who Wants To Be a Millionaire
With a Little Bit of Luck
Wouldn't It Be Loverly
Wringle Wrangle
Written on the Wind
You're Sensational

[*Note:* "Young Love" was No. 10 in record sales (RS) for this year, but its sales peaked during 1957. This is the last year to include the Peatman Survey of Air Play (AP) song rankings.]

1957

Stereo Discs. Recordings having two stereo channels also compatible with mono players are first offered for sale in August.

Johnny Mathis. Johnny Mathis begins his career with the hit songs "Wonderful Wonderful" and "It's Not for Me To Say."

West Side Story. Shakespeare's *Romeo and Juliet* is retold on New York's upper West Side by book writer Arthur Laurents as conceived by Jerome Robbins. Lyrics are by Stephen Sondheim (his first show), music by Leonard Bernstein. Some songs from this masterwork include "America," "Tonight," "I Feel Pretty," and "Maria"; Jerome Robbins's choreography for "Cool," "The Rumble," and "Somewhere" brilliantly achieve their dramatic intent.

Tom and Jerry. A new songwriting team named Tom and Jerry appear on Dick Clark's "American Bandstand" with their best-selling record "Hey! School Girl." They are later to have other hits under the name of Simon and Garfunkel.

Calypso. Harry Belafonte records the West Indian folk tune "Jamaica Farewell" for Victor, securing with this recording and "The Banana Boat Song (Day-O)" that calypso will become a major craze.

Top Hits
All Shook Up   RS 2   a. Elvis Presley
All the Way
April Love   RS 8 (tie)   a. Pat Boone
Butterfly   RS 6 (tie)   a. Andy Williams
Bye Bye Love
Chances Are
The Day the Rains Came

Diana
Don't Forbid Me   RS 8 (tie)   a. Pat Boone
I Feel Pretty
It's Not for Me To Say
Jailhouse Rock   RS 4 (tie)   a. Elvis Presley
Jamaica Farewell
Kisses Sweeter Than Wine
Let Me Be Your Teddy Bear, see "Teddy Bear"
Little Darlin'
Maria
Old Cape Cod
Round and Round   RS 8 (tie)   a. Perry Como
Seventy-Six Trombones
Silhouettes
Singin' the Blues   RS 1   a. Guy Mitchell
Tammy   RS 5 (tie)   a. Debbie Reynolds
(Let Me Be Your) Teddy Bear   RS 3 (tie)   a. Elvis Presley
There's a Place for Us
Till There Was You
Tonight
Too Much
Wake Up Little Susie   RS 7 (tie)   a. Everly Brothers
Yellow Bird
You Send Me   RS 6 (tie)   a. Sam Cooke
Young Love (two recordings)   RS 10 (1956)   a. Sonny James   RS 4 (tie)   a. Tab Hunter

Adaptations
Fascination (based on F.D. Marchetti's "Valse Tzigane" of 1904)
The River Kwai March (based on "Colonel Bogie March" of 1916)

Revivals
Gone (1952)
Honeycomb (1954)   RS 7 (tie)   a. Jimmie Rodgers
I'm Gonna Sit Right Down and Write Myself a Letter (1935)
Love Letters in the Sand (1931)   RS 5 (tie)   a. Pat Boone
Melodie d'Amour (1949)
Shangri-La (1946)
So Rare (1937)   RS 9   a. Jimmy Dorsey

Notable
An Affair To Remember
America
Are You Sincere
The Banana Boat Song (Day-O)
Bee-Bop Baby
Blue Monday
A Boy Like That

Boy on a Dolphin
Ca, C'est L'Amour
Chantez Chantez
Cool
Dark Moon
Do I Love You (Because You're Beautiful)
The Four Walls
Gee, Officer Krupke!
Great Balls of Fire
Hey! School Girl
In My Own Little Corner
Ivy Rose
Let It Be Me
Lida Rose
Liechtensteiner Polka
Little Biscuit
Mama, Look a Booboo
Mangoes
Marian the Librarian
Matilda
Mountains Beyond the Moon
My Heart Reminds Me
My Special Angel
My White Knight
Napoleon
A New Fangled Tango
One Hand, One Heart
Party Doll
Peggy Sue
Promise Her Anything But Give Her Love
Raunchy
Rock and Roll Music
A Rose and a Baby Ruth
Sayonara
School Day
Search for Paradise
Send for Me
Something's Coming
Somewhere
Story of My Life
Ten Minutes Ago
That'll Be the Day
Till
Trouble (in River City)
The Twelfth of Never
A Very Special Love
A White Sport Coat and a Pink Carnation
Whole Lot-ta Shakin' Goin' On
Why Baby Why
Wild Is the Wind

Witchcraft
Wonderful Wonderful

[*Note:* "At the Hop" was No. 3 in record sales (RS) for this year, but its sales peaked during 1958.]

1958

Gigi. The Alan Jay Lerner-Frederick Loewe musical film *Gigi,* starring Leslie Caron, Louis Jourdan, Hermione Gingold, and Maurice Chevalier, wins Academy Awards in nine categories including Best Picture. The score includes "Thank Heaven for Little Girls," "I'm Glad I'm Not Young Anymore," "Gigi," "I Remember It Well," and "The Night They Invented Champagne."

Handy and the Blues. William Christopher Handy, black blues composer (1873–1958), dies at eighty-four. The last of the great blues writers, "Daddy of the Blues," he wrote "Memphis Blues" (1912), "St. Louis Blues" (1914), "Joe Turner Blues" (1916), "Beale Street Blues" (1916), "Aunt Hagar's Blues" (1920), "John Henry Blues" (1922), "Atlantic Blues" (1924), and "Last St. Louis Blues" (1937). In his struggle to get started as a composer, W.C. Handy once worked as a janitor and taught music at the Negro A. and M. College near Huntsville, Alabama. He was later to be honored by having a park in Memphis, Tennessee, named after him, and was proud to recall that King Edward VIII of England once asked the Scotch Highlander bagpipes to play that song about the "St. Louis woman with the diamond rings."

High Cost of Living. Letter writers are faced this year by a postal rate increase. First class goes from 3¢ to 4¢ and air mail from 6¢ to 7¢.

Top Hits
All I Have To Do Is Dream   RS 4 (tie)   a. Everly Brothers
At the Hop   RS 3 (tie) (1957)   a. Danny and The Juniors
Bird Dog   RS 10 (tie)   a. Everly Brothers
Catch a Falling Star
The Chipmunk Song   RS 3 (tie)   a. Chipmunks
Donna   RS 7   a. Richie Valens
Don't   RS 6 (tie)   a. Elvis Presley
Everybody Loves a Lover
Firefly
Get a Job   RS 5 (tie)   a. Silhouettes
Gigi
It's Only Make Believe   RS 5 (tie)   a. Conway Twitty
Jingle Bell Rock
Little Star   RS 6 (tie)   a. Elegants

Lollipop
Love Look Away
Magic Moments
Nel Blu, Dipinto Di Blu, see "Volare"
Patricia   RS 6 (tie)   a. Perez Prado
Poor Little Fool   RS 5 (tie)   a. Ricky Nelson
The Purple People Eater   RS 1 (tie)   a. Sheb Wooley
Return to Me
Rockin' Robin   RS 8 (tie)   a. Bobby Day
Satin Doll
Sixteen Candles   RS 8 (tie)   a. The Crests
Stagger Lee, see 1959
Sugartime
Summertime Summertime
Tequila   RS 2 (tie)   a. Champs
This Is All I Ask
To Know Him Is To Love Him   RS 4 (tie)   a. Teddy Bears
Volare (Nel Blu, Dipinto Di Blu)   RS 2 (tie)   a. Domenico Modugno
Witch Doctor   RS 4 (tie)   a. David Seville
Yakety Yak   RS 6 (tie)   a. Coasters

Adaptations
The Hawaiian Wedding Song (based on the same song from 1926, with new lyrics.)
It's All in the Game (based on an instrumental known as "Melody" (1912); this song also popular in 1951)   RS 1 (tie)   a. Tommy Edwards
Tom Dooley (based on the traditional folksong ("Tom Dula") of 1866))   RS 6 (tie)   a. Kingston Trio

Revivals
He's Got the Whole World (in His hands) (1927) RS 9   a. Laurie London
My Happiness (1948)   RS 10 (tie)   a. Connie Francis
Sail Along Silvery Moon (1937)
Twilight Time (1944)   RS 6 (tie)   a. Platters
Who's Sorry Now (1923)
You Always Hurt the One You Love (1946)

Notable
Aladdin
All American Boy
Another Time, Another Place
Arrivederci Roma
Beep Beep
Big Man
Born Too Late
A Certain Smile
Chanson d'Amour (Song of Love)
Chantilly Lace

Do You Want To Dance
The End
For the First Time (Como Prima)
Hard-Headed Woman
A Hundred Million Miracles
I Enjoy Being a Girl
I Remember It Well
If Dreams Come True
If I Had a Hammer
I'll Remember Tonight
I'm Glad I'm Not Young Anymore
Kewpie Doll
Left Right Out of Your Heart
Love Song from Houseboat
Maverick (TV theme)
Maybe Baby
The Night They Invented Champagne
Oh Lonesome Me
Padre
Pink Shoelaces
Queen of the Hop
The River Song (Something's Always Happening on the River)
Say a Prayer for Me Tonight
Secretly
She Is Not Thinking of Me (Waltz at Maxim's)
Short Shorts
Splish Splash
The Stroll
Sugarfoot
Sunday
Sweet Little Sixteen
The Swingin' Shepherd Blues
Tears on My Pillow
Thank Heaven for Little Girls
Topsy
A Very Precious Love
You Are Beautiful
Young and Warm and Wonderful

1959

The Grammy. The first Grammy Award honors are shared this year by "Nel Blu, Dipinto Di Blu" for best song and record, and "The Music from Peter Gunn" for best album. "Tequila" wins best R&B song; "Tom Dooley," best C&W song; *Gigi,* best motion picture soundtrack of an original score; and *The Music Man,* best original cast album of a Broadway production.

Gypsy. Opening on May 21 at the Broadway Theatre

for a run of 704 performances, Gypsy Rose Lee's autobiography is musicalized by Stephen Sondheim and Jule Styne's score to *Gypsy*. Ethel Merman introduces "Small World," "Together Wherever We Go," and "Some People" and brings the house down with "Everything's Coming Up Roses" and "Rose's Turn."

Rodgers and Hammerstein. The most successful Rodgers and Hammerstein musical, *The Sound of Music,* starring Mary Martin opens November 16 at the Lunt-Fontanne Theatre. It is eventually made into the largest grossing musical film up until *Grease* in 1978 (see 1965). Highlights of the score include "The Sound of Music," "Maria," "My Favorite Things," "Do Re Mi," "Climb Ev'ry Mountain," and "Edelweiss."

Cha-Cha. The latest dance in vogue this year is the Cha-Cha.

Alaska and Hawaii. The 49th and 50th states, Alaska and Hawaii, are added to the United States of America on, respectively, January 3 and August 21.

Top Hits

The Battle of New Orleans   RS 2   a. Johnny Horton
A Big Hunk of Love   RS 6 (tie)   a. Elvis Presley
Climb Ev'ry Mountain
Come Softly to Me   RS 4 (tie)   a. Fleetwoods
Do Re Mi
Dream Lover   RS 10   a. Bobby Darin
Everything's Coming Up Roses
Fever
The Happy Organ   RS 7 (tie)   a. Dave (Baby) Cortez
High Hopes
Kansas City   RS 6 (tie)   a. Wilbert Harrison
Lipstick on Your Collar
(I'm Just a) Lonely Boy   RS 4 (tie)   a. Paul Anka
Milord
Mister Blue   RS 7 (tie)   a. Fleetwoods
My Favorite Things
Personality   RS 8 (tie)   a. Lloyd Price
(Theme from) Peter Gunn
Put Your Head on My Shoulder   RS 9 (tie)   a. Paul Anka
Quiet Village
Sea of Love   RS 9 (tie)   a. Phil Phillips
Sleep Walk   RS 6 (tie)   a. Santo and Johnny
Small World
Some People
Sorry (I Ran All the Way Home)   RS 9 (tie)   a. Impalas
The Sound of Music
Stagger Lee   RS 4 (tie)   a. Lloyd Price
There Goes My Baby   RS 8 (tie)   a. Drifters
Venus   RS 3   a. Frankie Avalon

Adaptations

Don't You Know (based on Puccini's "Musetta's Waltz")   RS 9 (tie)   a. Della Reese
This Old Man (The Children's Marching Song) (based on a traditional nursery song)

Revivals

(Now and Then) A Fool Such As I (1953)
Mack the Knife (1928)   RS 1   a. Bobby Darin
Misty (1954)
(All of a Sudden) My Heart Sings (1945)
Petite Fleur (1952)
Smoke Gets in Your Eyes (1933)   RS 5   a. Platters
The Three Bells (While the Angelus Was Ringing) (1945) (not the 1945 version called "The Jimmy Brown Song")   RS 4 (tie)   a. Browns

Notable

All I Need Is the Girl
Alvin's Harmonica
Best of Everything
Big Hurt
Bobby Socks to Stockings
Breaking Up Is Hard To Do
Broken-Hearted Melody
Charlie Brown
Christmas Island
Ciao Ciao Bambina
Edelweiss
Frankie
French Foreign Legion
Goodbye Jimmy Goodbye
Hanging Tree
Happy Anniversary
Hawaiian Eye
Heartaches by the Number
Home Again
I Gotta Have You
('Til) I Kissed You
I Know
I Love a Cop
I Wanna Be Around
Kookie, Kookie, Lend Me Your Comb
Lawman
Let Me Entertain You
Like Young
The Little Drummer Boy
(In My) Little Tin Box
(The) Lonely Goatherd
Lonely Street

Maria
Memphis
Morgen—One More Sunrise
My Heart Is an Open Book
On the Beach
(I Don't Care) Only Love Me
Pillow Talk
La Plume de Ma Tante (theme)
Politics and Poker
Promise Me a Rose
(The Song of) Raintree County
Rawhide (TV theme)
Rose's Turn
See You in September
77 Sunset Strip (TV theme)
Since I Don't Have You
Sixteen Going on Seventeen
Strange Are the Ways of Love
Street of Love
Take Me Along
Teenager in Love
Till Tomorrow
Together Wherever We Go
Tomboy
Too Long at the Fair
Untouchables (TV theme)
Waterloo
When Did I Fall in Love
You'll Never Get Away from Me

1960

Motown. Black music producer Berry Gordy begins his Motown "music factory" in Detroit, Michigan, with Smokey Robinson and the Miracles, first on the record sales charts in 1959, and the Marvellettes in 1961. He is later responsible for the Supremes, on the charts in 1962, Dionne Warwick in 1962, Martha and the Vandellas in 1963, Stevie Wonder in 1963, The Temptations in 1964, The Four Tops in 1964, Diana Ross (billed separately from the Supremes) in 1967, and the Jackson 5 in 1969. It all came together for Motown and the Supremes with the 1964 No. 1 selling record (on the sales chart for fourteen weeks) of "Where Did Our Love Go?" This combined the talents of the Supremes with the songwriting and producing team of Eddie Holland, Lamont Dozier, and Brian Holland in the first of many million-selling records.

Recorded music sales. Total retail sales of recorded music, singles, albums, and tapes combined, is estimated at $600 million.

Actors' Equity. A strike by Actors' Equity closes all Broadway theatres for twelve days.

The Fantastic Fantasticks. The Off-Broadway musical *The Fantasticks,* with a score by Tom Jones and Harvey Schmidt and featuring Jerry Orbach, is adapted from Edmond Rostand's *Les Romantiques.* It opens at the Sullivan Theater in New York City on May 3 and will prove to be the longest running production in American theatre history. Hits include "Try To Remember," "Much More," and "Soon It's Gonna Rain," the last two popularized by Barbra Streisand's Columbia recording.

Ray Charles. A genius in all fields of popular music—jazz, blues, rock, country, gospel, Soul, and rhythm and blues—artist Ray Charles receives his first Grammy awards this year.

Top Hits
Alley-Oop RS 7 (tie) a. Hollywood Argyles
(Theme from) The Apartment
Beyond the Sea
Camelot
Cathy's Clown RS 3 (tie) a. Everly Brothers
Everybody's Somebody's Fool RS 6 (tie) a. Connie Francis
(Theme from) Exodus
Greenfields
Handy Man
He'll Have To Go RS 8 a. Jim Reeves
I Want To Be Wanted RS 7 (tie) a. Brenda Lee
If Ever I Would Leave You
I'm Sorry RS 5 (tie) a. Brenda Lee
Itsy Bitsy Teenie Weenie Yellow Polkadot Bikini RS 7 (tie) a. Brian Hyland
Last Date RS 10 a. Floyd Kramer
Mister Custer RS 7 (tie) a. Larry Verne
Mister Lucky
My Heart Has a Mind of Its Own RS 6 (tie) a. Connie Francis
Never on Sunday
Only the Lonely (Know the Way I Feel) RS 9 a. Roy Orbison
El Paso RS 6 (tie) a. Marty Robbins
Running Bear RS 5 (tie) a. Johnny Preston
Save the Last Dance for Me RS 5 (tie) a. Drifters
Stay RS 7 (tie) a. Maurice Williams and The Zodiacs
Stuck on You RS 4 a. Elvis Presley
(Theme from) A Summer Place RS 1 a. Percy Faith
Teen Angel RS 6 (tie) a. Mark Dinning

THE GREATEST SONGS

The Twist RS 7 (tie) a. Chubby Checker
Why RS 7 (tie) a. Frankie Avalon
You Talk Too Much

Adaptations

Clementine (based on a traditional folksong)
It's Now or Never (based on "O Sole Mio" (1899)) RS 3 (tie) a. Elvis Presley

Revivals

Are You Lonesome Tonight? (1926) RS 2 a. Elvis Presley
Chain Gang (1956)
Georgia on My Mind (1930)
Harbor Lights (1937)
Jealous Lover (1949)
The Old Lamp-Lighter (1946)
Paper Roses (1955)
We'll Meet Again (1939)
What a Diff'rence a Day Made (1934)

Notable

Any Way the Wind Blows
Artificial Flowers
Because They're Young
Bonanza
Calcutta
Dis Donc, Dis Donc
Dolce Far Niente
Follow Me
Footsteps
Give a Little Whistle
Good Timin'
The Green Leaves of Summer
Happy-Go-Lucky Me
He Don't Love You (He Will Break Your Heart)
Hey Look Me Over
How To Handle a Woman
I Ain't Down Yet
I Loved You Once in Silence
I Wonder What the King Is Doing Tonight
I'll Be There
Irma La Douce
Jump Over
Just Come Home
Kids
Let the Good Times Roll
A Lot of Livin' To Do
The Lusty Month of May
(Theme from) The Magnificent Seven
Make Someone Happy

Mama
Much More
Nice 'n' Easy
North to Alaska
O Dio Mio
One Boy
One of Us (Will Weep Tonight)
Our Language of Love
La Pachanga
Please Help Me I'm Falling
Poetry in Motion
Puppy Love
Put On a Happy Face
Rubber Ball
Sailor (Your Home Is the Sea)
The Second Time Around
Shazam
Sink the Bismarck
Soon It's Gonna Rain
Starlight
Swingin' School
Tell Laura I Love Her
This Is Your Life (Theme)
Tie Me Kangaroo Down Sport
Time and the River
Togetherness
Try To Remember
Twistin' U.S.A.
The Unforgiven (The Need for Love)
The Village of St. Bernadette
Wake Me When It's Over
Walk—Don't Run
What Do the Simple Folk Do
What Takes My Fancy
Wild One
Young Emotions
You're Sixteen

1961

How To Succeed. Frank Loesser's greatest theatrical success, *How To Succeed in Business Without Really Trying,* wins the Pulitzer, Tony, and Drama Critics Circle awards for best musical. Robert Morse introduces the hits "I Believe in You" and "Brotherhood of Man."

FM Stereo. Stereo broadcasting commences this year as FM stereo programs are approved by the Federal Communications Commission.

Surfing. Surfing emerges as a popular California sport with surfing music by the Beach Boys soon to follow.

See ''Surfin' U.S.A.'' (1963), ''I Get Around'' (1964), and ''Help Me Rhonda'' (1965).

Barbra Streisand. Barbra Streisand, nineteen, makes her first stage appearance in the off-off Broadway revue *Another Evening with Harry Stoones* (Get it?) in a cast that includes Diana Sands.

Jimmie Rodgers. Jimmie Rodgers is the first country music star to be elected to the Country Music Hall of Fame in Nashville, Tennessee.

Top Hits

Apache RS 8 (tie) a. Jorger Ingmann

The Boll Weevil Song RS 9 (tie) a. Brook Benton

Big Bad John RS 2 a. Jimmy Dean

Bristol Stomp RS 9 (tie) a. Davelles

Calcutta (from 1960) RS 6 (tie) a. Lawrence Welk

Can't Help Falling in Love (with You) RS 10 (tie) a. Elvis Presley

Corinna, Corinna

Cryin' RS 9 (tie) a. Roy Orbison

Daddy's Home RS 10 (tie) a. Shep and The Limelights

Hey Look Me Over (from 1960)

Hit the Road Jack RS 6 (tie) a. Ray Charles

I Like It Like That RS 8 (tie) a. Chris Kenner

The Lion Sleeps Tonight, see 1962

Moody River RS 5 (tie) a. Pat Boone

Moon River

Mother-in-Law RS 5 (tie) a. Ernie K-Doe

The Mountains High RS 10 (tie) a. Dick and Deedee

Please Mister Postman RS 5 (tie) a. Marvelettes

Pony Time RS 4 (tie) a. Chubby Checker

Quarter to Three RS 6 (tie) a. U.S. Bonds

Raindrops RS 9 (tie) a. Dee Clark

Run to Him RS 10 (tie) a. Bobby Vee

Runaround Sue RS 6 (tie) a. Dion

Runaway RS 3 a. Del Shannon

Running Scared RS 5 (tie) a. Roy Orbison

Surrender RS 6 (tie) a. Elvis Presley

Take Good Care of My Baby RS 4 (tie) a. Bobby Vee

Tossin' and Turnin' RS 1 a. Bobby Lewis

Travelin' Man RS 6 (tie) a. Ricky Nelson

The Wanderer RS 7 a. Dion

Where the Boys Are

Will You (Still) Love Me Tomorrow RS 6 (tie) a. Shirelles

Wimoweh, see ''The Lion Sleeps Tonight'' (1962)

Wonderland by Night RS 4 (tie) a. Bert Kaempfert

Wooden Heart RS 5 (tie) a. Joe Dowell

Adaptations

Michael (Row the Boat Ashore) (based on a traditional folk-song) RS 6 (tie) a. The Highwaymen

Revivals

The Bilbao Song (1929)

Blue Moon (1934) RS 4 (tie) a. Marcels

Perfidia (1941)

Yellow Bird (1958)

Notable

African Waltz

Al-Di-La

Baby, I Don't Care

(It's) Been a Long Day

Brotherhood of Man

Buzz Buzz A-Diddle-It

Cupid

Dedicated to the One I Love

The Doctor Kildare Theme (Three Stars Will Shine Tonight)

Ebony Eyes

Goodbye Cruel World

The Great Imposter

The Guns of Navarone

(Theme from) Hatari

A Hundred Pounds of Clay

Hurt

I Believe in You

I Love How You Love Me

It Was a Very Good Year

Let's Twist Again

Little Devil

Little Sister

Love Makes the World Go Round (theme from *Carnival*)

Milk and Honey

Muskrat

On the Rebound

Paris Original

Pocketful of Miracles

A Portrait of My Love

Sad Movies Make Me Cry

Sail Away

Shalom

Shop Around

Spanish Harlem

Take Five

Tender Is the Night

Theme from ''Ben Casey''

Theme from *Carnival*, see ''Love Makes the World Go Round''

Unchain My Heart

Voyage to the Bottom of the Sea
Walk On By
Wheels
Where Have All the Flowers Gone
Who Put the Bomp
Why Do the Wrong People Travel

[*Note:* "The Lion Sleeps Tonight" tied for No. 4 in record sales (RS) for this year, but its sales peaked during 1962.]

1962

America's Second Undeclared War. President Kennedy sends troops to establish the U.S. Military Assistance Command in South Vietnam. Kennedy instructs these forces "to fire to protect themselves if fired upon." Once again, as in 1950, Congress evades formal declaration of war as required by the Constitution. Time and again the constitutionality of the President's action is challenged in various Federal courts and in every case the courts refuse to rule on the merits of the question.

Liverpool. The Quarrymen Skiffle Group, a.k.a. the Moondogs, the Moonshiners, and the Silver Beatles, has gotten its act together, and on Saturday March 24 the following announcement is posted with pride:

The Heswall Jazz Club present their *All *Star *Bill starring The Beatles (Mersey Beat Poll Winners!)

Polydor Recording Artists! Prior to (their third) European (Hamburg, Germany) Tour! at the Barnston Women's Institute;

Admission: 7/6, 7:30 PM—11:15 PM.

Mr. Harrison is nineteen, Mr. McCartney is twenty, and Messrs. Lennon and Starr are twenty-two.

The Moog. The first practical electronic musical synthesizer is invented by Robert A. Moog (rhymes with vogue). This new synthetic (non-acoustical) music maker is a quantum leap advance from its rudimentary predecessor the Theremin, which was (and is) used to generate the eerie whining themes in monster movies. Unlike the Theremin, the Moog is a keyboard instrument, and the sounds synthesized can be repeated accurately and musically notated. The Theremin depends on the electronic hand capacitance of the operator and thus its operation is more dependent upon expressive technique. There had also appeared earlier, in France (1928), the Ondes Martenot, which resembles an electric harpsichord and sounds one note at a time.

The Twist. Chubby Checker's Cameo-Parkway recording of Hank Ballard's 1958 song "The Twist" is instantly a best seller. Born Ernest Evans, in admiration of his idol Fats Domino, he creates his own stage name, Chubby Checker. At the Peppermint Lounge in New York everybody is twisting, young and old, with jet setters and celebrities including Noël Coward and Judy Garland. The craze expands into marketing Twist skirts, Twist raincoats, and Twist nighties.

The Bossa Nova. The new Brazilian rhythm of the Bossa Nova becomes popular. See "Desafinado" (below), and "Blame It on the Bossa Nova" (1963), "How Insensitive" (1963), and "The Girl from Ipanema" (1964).

Auto Audio. The 8-track audio tape ridge for automobile tape players becomes available.

H.C. Deutchendorf, Jr. Chad Mitchell leaves the Chad Mitchell Trio and is replaced by H.C. Deutchendorf, Jr., composer of "Leavin' on a Jet Plane," see (1969). Later he is better known as John Denver.

Carole King. Songwriter and performer Carole King comes to attention this year with the hit song "It Might as Well Rain Until September." With her then husband songwriter Gerry Goffin, she is also responsible for "Loco-Motion," "Take Good Care of My Baby," "Up on the Roof," and "Will You Still Love Me Tomorrow."

Top Hits
Big Girls Don't Cry   RS 1 (tie)   a. Four Seasons
Cast Your Fate to the Wind
Days of Wine and Roses
Desafinado
Don't Break the Heart That Loves You   RS 5 (tie)   a. Connie Francis
Duke of Earl   RS 3 (tie)   a. Gene Chandler
Good Luck Charm   RS 4 (tie)   a. Elvis Presley
He's a Rebel   RS 4 (tie)   a. Crystals
Hey Baby   RS 3 (tie)   a. Bruce Channel
I Can't Stop Loving You   RS 1 (tie)   a. Ray Charles
Johnny Angel   RS 4 (tie)   a. Shelley Fabares
Limbo Rock   RS 6   a. Chubby Checker
The Loco-Motion   RS 5 (tie)   a. Little Eva
Mashed Potato Time   RS 7   a. Dee Dee Sharp
Monster Mash   RS 4 (tie)   a. Bobby (Boris) Pickett and The Crypt-Kickers
Only Love Can Break a Heart   RS 9 (tie)   a. Gene Pitney
The Peppermint Twist   RS 3 (tie)   a. Joey Dee and The Starlighters
Ramblin' Rose   RS 8 (tie)   a. Nat King Cole
Return to Sender   RS 8 (tie)   a. Elvis Presley

Roses Are Red, My Love   RS 2   a. Bobby Vinton

Sheila   RS 4 (tie)   a. Tommy Roe

Sherry   RS 1 (tie)   a. Four Seasons

Softly as I Leave You

Soldier Boy   RS 3 (tie)   a. Shirelles

Stranger on the Shore   RS 5 (tie)   a. Mister Acker Bilk

The Stripper   RS 5 (tie)   a. David Rose

A Taste of Honey

Telstar   RS 3 (tie)   a. Tornadoes

The Twist   RS 4 (tie)   a. Chubby Checker

The Wah-Watusi   RS 9 (tie)   a. Orlons

Walk On By (from 1961)

What Kind of Fool Am I

Wimoweh, see below "The Lion Sleeps Tonight" *(Adaptations)*

You Don't Know Me   RS 10   a. Ray Charles

Adaptations

Five Hundred Miles   (Railroader's Lament) (based on a traditional folksong)

The Lion Sleeps Tonight (Wimoweh) (based on a traditional African song)   RS 4 (tie) (1961)   a. Tokens

Loop de Loop (based on the traditional)

Midnight in Moscow (based on the Russian song "Padmas Koveeye Vietchera")   RS 9 (tie)   a. Kenny Ball

Revivals

Breaking Up Is Hard To Do (1959)   RS 4 (tie)   a. Neil Sedaka

Fly Me to the Moon (In Other Words) (1954)

I Left My Heart in San Francisco (1954)

If I Had a Hammer (1958)

Let There Be Love (1940)

Love Letters (1945)

Misty (1955)

The Night Has a Thousand Eyes (1948)

You Are My Sunshine (1940)

Notable

The Alley Cat

Baby Elephant Walk

Bobby's Girl

The Boy's Night Out

Break It to Me Gently

The Cha Cha Cha

Comedy Tonight

Do You Love Me

Everybody Ought To Have a Maid

Follow the Boys

Funny Way of Laughing

Gonna Build a Mountain

Green Onions

It Might as Well Rain Until September

I've Got Your Number

The James Bond Theme

(Theme from) Lawrence of Arabia

Let Me In

Lollipops and Roses

Lovely

Make It Easy on Yourself

The Man Who Shot Liberty Valance

My Coloring Book

No Strings

Nobody Told Me

Once in a Lifetime

Once Upon a Time

The One Who Really Loves You

Party Lights

Poor Little Hollywood Star

P.S. I Love You

Release Me

Sealed with a Kiss

Surfin' Safari

The Sweetest Sounds

To Be a Performer

Twist and Shout

Twistin' the Night Away

Walk on the Wild Side

What Now My Love (Et Maintenant)

Wolverton Mountain

1963

John F. Kennedy. On November 22, President Kennedy is assassinated in Dallas, Texas.

Protest Songs. Anti-war and social protest songs emerge as "Blowin' in the Wind" enters Top Ten list. Bob Dylan's song became a hymn for a generation rebelling against bigotry, racism, and nuclear war. Peter, Paul and Mary sell over two million disks in their Warner recording with two Grammy awards to support its place in recording history.

Bob Dylan. On November 4, 1961, Bob Dylan performed to an audience of fifty-three at the Carnegie Chapter Hall. On April 12 of this year he packs New York's Town Hall and on May 12 is invited to appear on the Ed Sullivan Show, an event which never happens because CBS authorities deny Dylan permission to perform his "Talking John Birch Society"; see above.

Stevie Wonder. Little Stevie Wonder, blind since birth,

debuts with his hit "Fingertips" and will prove to be the dominant performing artist of the early seventies.

Cassettes. Philips of Eindhoven, Netherlands, introduces the now universal compact audio cassette which runs at 1 7/8 inches per second, and has an audio tape only 0.15 inches wide.

Top Hits

All Over the World

Another Saturday Night

As Long as He Needs Me

Be My Baby   RS 10 (tie)   a. Ronettes

Blowin' in the Wind   RS 8 (tie)   a. Peter, Paul and Mary

Call Me Irresponsible

Can't Get Used To Losing You   RS 8 (tie)   a. Andy Williams

Charade

Dominique   RS 2 (tie)   a. The Singing Nun

Easier Said Than Done   RS 4 (tie)   a. Essex

The End of the World   RS 6   a. Skeeter Davis

Fingertips   RS 3 (tie)   a. (Little) Stevie Wonder

Go Away Little Girl   RS 4 (tie)   a. Steve Lawrence

(Love Is Like a) Heat Wave

He's So Fine   RS 2 (tie)   a. Chiffons

Hey Paula   RS 3 (tie)   a. Paul and Paula

I (Who Have Nothing)

I Will Follow Him   RS 3 (tie)   a. Little Peggy March

If You Wanna Be Happy   RS 4 (tie)   a. Jimmy Soul

I'm Leaving It Up to You   RS 4 (tie)   a. Dale and Grace

It's My Party   RS 4 (tie)   a. Lesley Gore

Louis Louis   RS 7 (tie)   a. The Kingsmen

More (theme from *Mondo Cane*)

My Boyfriend's Back   RS 3 (tie)   a. The Angels

One Note Samba

Our Day Will Come   RS 5 (tie)   a. Ruby and The Romantics

Puff the Magic Dragon   RS 9 (tie)   a. Peter, Paul and Mary

Rhythm of the Rain

Ruby Baby   RS 10 (tie)   a. Dion

So Much in Love   RS 5 (tie)   a. Tymes

Sugar Shack   RS 1   a. Jimmy Gilmer and The Fireballs

Sukiyaki   RS 3 (tie)   a. Kyu Sakamoto

Surf City   RS 4 (tie)   a. Jan and Dean

Surfin' U.S.A.

Theme from Mondo Cane, see "More"

Walk Like a Man   RS 3 (tie)   a. Four Seasons

Walk Right In   RS 4 (tie)   a. The Rooftop Singers

Washington Square   RS 9 (tie)   a. The Village Stompers

Wipeout   RS 7 (tie)   a. Surfaris

You Don't Own Me   RS 10 (tie)   a. Lesley Gore

Adaptations

Abilene (based on traditional song with new lyrics)

Hello Mudduh, Hello Faddah (parody) (based on the "Dance of the Hours," from Act III Ponchielli's *La Gioconda* (1876)

Revivals

Blue Velvet (1951)   RS 3 (tie)   a. Bobby Vinton

Deep Purple (1934)   RS 5 (tie)   a. Nino Tempo and April Stevens

Hava Nagila (Hebrew traditional)

I Love You Because (1949)

If I Had a Hammer (1958)

The Wayward Wind (1956)

We Shall Overcome (1945)

Notable

All I've Got To Do

Anyone Who Had a Heart

Be Back Soon

Blame It on the Bossa Nova

Blue on Blue

Busted

Consider Yourself

Da Doo Ron Ron

Danke Schön

Dear Friend

Detroit City

Do Wah Diddy Diddy, see 1964

Don't Think Twice, It's All Right

Food Glorious Food

Good Golly Miss Molly

The Good Life

Half a Sixpence

A Hard Rain's A-Gonna Fall

How Insensitive

I Wanna Be Your Man

I Wish You Love

I'd Do Anything

It's a Mad Mad Mad Mad World

It's All Right

Judy's Turn To Cry

The Lonely Bull

Losing You

Love's Been Good to Me

The Miss America Pageant

Mocking Bird

My Summer Love

The Night Has a Thousand Eyes (Garrett)

Nitty Gritty

Nobody's Darlin' But Mine

On Broadway
Painted Tainted Rose
The Patty Duke Theme (Cousins)
Sally Go Round the Roses
Saturday Night
South Street
Thank You Girl
Theme from *A New Kind of Love*
Those Lazy Hazy Crazy Days of Summer
The Times They Are A-Changin'
Up on the Roof
Where Is Love?
Who Will Buy?
Will He Like Me
Wives and Lovers
Young and in Love
You're the Reason I'm Living
You've Got To Pick a Pocket or Two

1964

Beatles. The Beatles' recording of "I Want To Hold Your Hand" is released on Friday, January 14, and three weeks later (February 9) they appear on the Ed Sullivan CBS television show and sing five songs to 728 screaming fans inside the Ed Sullivan Theatre on West 52nd Street. Their appearance on the show yields the highest Nielson rating in television history with an audience of 73 million people. On February 25 they appear at Carnegie Hall. "I Want To Hold Your Hand" becomes the No. 1 record in the U.S., and eight of their recordings are top sellers for this year. Beatlemania encouraged their first motion picture, *A Hard Day's Night,* a critical and, of course, financial success, which was also released this year.

R & B. In recognition of black music, *Billboard* magazine resumes separate listing of R & B (Rhythm and Blues) records as a category.

Fiddler on the Roof. Breaking all records and running 3242 performances, Sheldon Harnick and Jerry Bock's *Fiddler on the Roof* starring Zero Mostel will gross over $20 million in box office receipts in New York, plus at least $15 million in road company receipts, with companies all over the world. Some of the show's hits include "Sunrise, Sunset," "If I Were a Rich Man," "L'Chaim (To Life)," "Do You Love Me," and "Tradition."

Hello, Dolly! Adapting Thornton Wilder's 1955 play *The Matchmaker,* Jerry Herman's *Hello, Dolly!* settles in at the St. James for 2844 performances, with Carol Channing surrendering her Dolly Gallagher Levi to a chorus line of star replacements over the years, including Pearl Bailey in an all black company and Barbra Streisand in the 1969 film adaptation. Louis Armstrong's Kapp recording of the title song is a top seller this year. Other songs from the show include "Put on Your Sunday Clothes," "So Long, Dearie," and "Before the Parade Passes By."

Top Hits
Baby Love   RS 3 (tie)   a. Supremes
Bread and Butter   RS 9 (tie)   a. The Newbeats
Can't Buy Me Love   RS 2   a. Beatles
Chapel of Love   RS 4 (tie)   a. Dixie Cups
Chim Chim Cher-ee
Come See About Me   RS 5 (tie)   a. Supremes
Dancing in the Street   RS 8   a. Martha and The Vandellas
Dang Me
Do Wah Diddy Diddy   RS 5 (tie)   a. Manfred Mann
Do You Want To Know a Secret   RS 10 (tie)   a. Beatles
Downtown, see 1965
Everybody Loves Somebody   RS 6 (tie)   a. Dean Martin
Goin' Out of My Head
A Hard Day's Night   RS 5 (tie)   a. Beatles
Hello, Dolly!   RS 6 (tie)   a. Louis Armstrong
The House of the Rising Sun   RS 4 (tie)   a. Animals
I Feel Fine   RS 4 (tie)   a. Beatles
I Get Around   RS 5 (tie)   a. Beach Boys
I Want To Hold Your Hand   RS 1   a. Beatles
I Wish You Love (from 1963)
It Ain't Me, Babe
It's All Right (from 1963)
Last Kiss   RS 7 (tie)   a. J. Frank Wilson and The Cavaliers
Leader of the Pack   RS 6 (tie)   a. Shangri-Las
Love Me Do   RS 6 (tie)   a. Beatles
Love Me with All Your Heart
Mister Lonely   RS 6 (tie)   a. Bobby Vinton
My Boy Lollipop   RS 9 (tie)   a. Millie Small
My Guy   RS 5 (tie)   a. Mary Wells
Oh Pretty Woman   RS 4 (tie)   a. Roy Orbison
People
Please Please Me
Rag Doll   RS 5 (tie)   a. Four Seasons
Ringo   RS 6 (tie)   a. Lorne Greene
She Loves You   RS 5 (tie)   a. Beatles
She's Not There   RS 7 (tie)   a. The Zombies
Sunrise Sunset
Twist and Shout   RS 10 (tie)   a. Beatles
Under the Boardwalk
Walk On By

THE GREATEST SONGS

Where Did Our Love Go RS 5 (tie) a. Supremes
A World Without Love RS 6 (tie) a. Peter and Gordon

Revivals
Memphis (1959) RS 9 (tie) a. Johnny Rivers
Please Mister Postman (1961)
Roll Over Beethoven (1956)
Shangri-La (1946)
Slaughter on Tenth Avenue (1936)
There! I've Said It Again (1941) RS 3 (tie) a. Bobby Vinton
The Twelfth of Never (1957)

Notable
All Day and All of the Night
All I Really Want To Do
All My Loving
Amen
And I Love Her
Anyone Can Whistle
As Tears Go By
Before the Parade Passes By
Bits and Pieces
Clinging Vine
Dawn (Go Away)
Dear Heart
Do You Love Me?
Don't Let the Rain Come Down
Don't Let the Sun Catch You Crying
Don't Rain on My Parade
Don't Throw Your Love Away
From Russia with Love
The Girl from Ipanema
Girl Talk
Glad All Over
Good News
G.T.O.
High-Heel Sneakers
Home Sweet Heaven
A House Is Not a Home
How Glad I Am
Hush Hush Sweet Charlotte
I Only Want To Be with You
I Saw Her Standing There
I Should Have Known Better
If I Fell
If I Were a Rich Man
I'll Follow the Sun
I'm a Loser
I'm in Love

I'm the Greatest Star
It Only Takes a Moment
It Only Takes a Moment
Java
The Jerk
The Joker
Let It Be Me
Little Children
Loddy Lo
Look At That Face
Love with the Proper Stranger
Matchmaker, Matchmaker
My Kind of Town
The Name Game
On a Wonderful Day Like Today
Pink Panther Theme
P.S. I Love You
Put on Your Sunday Clothes
Reach Out for Me
Room without Windows
Sabbath Prayer
Seventh Dawn
Sha La La
She's a Fool
She's a Woman
So Long Dearie
Softly As I Leave You
A Spoonful of Sugar
Stockholm
Supercalifragilisticexpialidocious
Suspicion
Thank You Girl (from 1963)
That's Life
There's Always Something There To Remind Me
Time Is on My Side
To Life (L'Chaim)
Today
Tradition
Walk Away
Watch What Happens
We'll Sing in the Sunshine
Where Love Has Gone
White on White
Who Can I Turn To
Wishin' and Hopin'
The World I Used To Know
You Are Woman, I Am Man
You'd Better Love Me While You May
You'll Never Get to Heaven

1965

More Beatles. The Beatles fill Shea Stadium in New York to capacity on September 16.

Rolling Stones. The Rolling Stones, led by Mick Jagger, hit No. 1 on the charts with ''(I Can't Get No) Satisfaction.''

Bob Dylan. Dylan switches from acoustic to electric guitar at the Newport Folk Festival on July 25.

Hair. Through the influence of the Beatles, long hair, sometimes shoulder-length, comes into vogue as a male hair style for the first time since ''Buffalo Bill's Wild West and Congress of Rough Riders of the World.'' This trend is later celebrated in the musical *Hair* (1968).

The Sound of Music. The Rodgers and Hammerstein 1959 musical *The Sound of Music* is translated to film and stars Julie Andrews. It receives four Oscars including best picture and sells an almost unimaginable fifteen million albums between the original cast and motion picture soundtrack recordings. As of 1980 it is the eighth all-time rental champ earning $79,748,000 and is second only to *Grease* for musical film.

Blackout. On November 9, a massive electric power failure blacks out most of the northeastern United States and parts of Canada.

Top Hits

Back in My Arms Again RS 4 (tie) a. Supremes

Can't You Hear My Heartbeat RS 6 (tie) a. Herman's Hermits

Count Me In RS 8 (tie) a. Gary Lewis and The Playboys

Crying Time

Day Tripper

Downtown RS 3 (tie) a. Petula Clark

Eight Days a Week RS 3 (tie) a. Beatles

England Swings (Like a Pendulum Do)

The Eve of Destruction RS 4 (tie) a. Barry McGuire

The Game of Love RS 4 (tie) a. Wayne Fontana and The Mindbenders

Get Off My Cloud RS 3 (tie) a. Rolling Stones

(Theme from) Goldfinger

Hang on Sloopy RS 4 (tie) a. McCoys

Help! RS 2 (tie) a. Beatles

Help Me Rhonda RS 3 (tie) a. Beach Boys

I Can't Help Myself RS 3 (tie) a. Four Tops

I Got You Babe RS 2 (tie) a. Sonny and Cher

I Hear a Symphony RS 3 (tie) a. Supremes

(If It Takes Forever) I Will Wait for You

I'm Telling You Now RS 3 (tie) a. Freddie and The Dreamers

King of the Road

Like a Rolling Stone RS 7 a. Bob Dylan

Love Potion No. 9

A Lover's Concerto RS 6 (tie) a. Toys

Michelle

Mister Tambourine Man RS 4 (tie) a. Byrds

Mrs. Brown You've Got a Lovely Daughter RS 2 (tie) a. Herman's Hermits

My Girl RS 4 (tie) a. Temptations

One—Two—Three RS 6 (tie) a. Len Barry

Over and Over RS 4 (tie) a. Dave Clark Five

(I Can't Get No) Satisfaction RS 1 (tie) a. Rolling Stones

Save Your Heart for Me RS 8 (tie) a. Gary Lewis and The Playboys

The Shadow of Your Smile

The Sounds of Silence, see 1966

Stop in the Name of Love RS 3 (tie) a. Supremes

A Taste of Honey

This Diamond Ring RS 3 (tie) a. Gary Lewis and The Playboys

Ticket To Ride RS 4 (tie) a. Beatles

Treat Her Right RS 8 (tie) a. Roy Head

Turn! Turn! Turn! RS 2 (tie) a. Byrds

A Walk in the Black Forest

What the World Needs Now (Is Love)

Wooly Bully RS 5 a. Sam the Sham and The Pharaohs

Yesterday RS 1 (tie) a. Beatles

You Were on My Mind

You've Lost That Lovin' Feelin' RS 3 (tie) a. Righteous Brothers

Revivals

Crying in the Chapel (1953) RS 9 a. Elvis Presley

I'm Enery the Eighth (I Am) (1911) RS 4 (tie) a. Herman's Hermits

It Was a Very Good Year (1961)

Red Roses for a Blue Lady (1948)

Silhouettes (1957)

Unchained Melody (1955)

Notable

Ain't That Peculiar!

Baby the Rain Must Fall

Ballad of Cat Ballou

Blues in the Street

California Girls

Catch the Wind

Catch Us If You Can

Dindi

Do I Hear a Waltz

Do You Believe in Magic

Down in the Boondocks

Emily

Everyone's Gone to the Moon
For Lovin' Me
For Once in My Life
Forget Domani
Happiness Is
Heart Full of Soul
Houston
I Know a Place
If I Ruled the World
I'll Never Find Another You
I'm All Smiles
The "In" Crowd
It's Not Unusual
It's Only Love
The Jolly Green Giant
Lemon Tree
The Look of Love
Make It Easy on Yourself
Make the World Go Away
The Men in My Little Girl's Life
Papa's Got a Brand New Bag
Pass Me By
Positively Fourth Street
Queen of the House
Quiet Nights of Quiet Stars
Real Live Girl
She Touched Me
She's a Carioca
Somewhere
Spanish Eyes
Sunshine, Lollipops and Rainbows
The Sweetheart Tree
Take the Moment
Thunderball
Trains and Boats and Planes
Until It's Time for You To Go
We've Got To Get Out of This Place
What's New Pussycat
Why Did I Choose You
A World of Our Own
You've Got To Hide Your Love Away
You've Got Your Troubles

[*Note:* Because of the many ties this year, record sales are tabulated only to the ninth place.]

1966

More Beatles. The Beatles present their last live concert in San Francisco on August 29th.

Soft Rock. Soft Rock, newly called MOR (middle-of-the-road), becomes popular. Simon and Garfunkel's "The Sounds of Silence" hits the Top Ten in record sales with The Mamas and The Papas' "Monday Monday," Donovan's "Mellow Yellow," and the Association's "Cherish." The Supremes represent Motown with "You Can't Hurry Love" and The Beach Boys the California sound with "Good Vibrations."

Cabaret. John Kander and Fred Ebb's musical adaptation of Christopher Isherwood's *Berlin Stories* and subsequent non-musical play *I Am a Camera* successfully re-creates a lurid pre-Nazi Germany of the 1920s. It runs for 1165 performances with Lotte Lenya and Jack Gilford and in 1972 is adapted for an Academy Award-winning musical film, *Cabaret,* with Liza Minnelli and Joel Grey, who recreates his role in the Broadway production. ABC will pay $9 million for the television rights to the film. The title song was successfully recorded by Herb Alpert and the Tijuana Brass on A & M and by Marilyn Maye in a Victor recording. Other songs from the score include "Willkommen," "If You Could See Her," and "Why Should I Wake Up?"

Man of La Mancha. Opening at the Washington Square Theatre on November 22, 1965, by the beginning of this year the musical adaptation of Cervantes's *Don Quixote* is a smash hit thanks to feature recordings of "The Impossible Dream" (The Quest) by Jack Jones, Roger Williams, and The Hesitations. The combined run of its Off-Broadway and Broadway performances is 2328. Starring Richard Kiley, the original cast recording receives a gold record, and sheet music sales exceed two million copies.

Top Hits
Alfie
The Ballad of the Green Berets RS 1 a. Staff Sergeant Barry Sadler
Bang Bang (My Baby Shot Me Down) RS 10 (tie) a. Cher
Barbara Ann RS 10 (tie) a. Beach Boys
Born Free
California Dreamin'
Cherish RS 2 (tie) a. Association
Day Dream RS 9 (tie) a. Lovin' Spoonful
Did You Ever Have To Make Up Your Mind RS 10 (tie) a. Lovin' Spoonful
Eleanor Rigby
Free Again
Georgy Girl RS 5 a. Seekers
Good Lovin' RS 4 (tie) a. Young Rascals
Good Vibrations RS 4 (tie) a. Beach Boys
A Groovy Kind of Love RS 8 (tie) a. Mind Benders

Guantanamera

Hanky Panky RS 3 (tie) a. Tommy James and The Shondells

If I Were a Carpenter

The Impossible Dream (The Quest)

Lara's Theme, see "Somewhere My Love"

Last Train to Clarksville RS 4 (tie) a. Monkees

Lightnin' Strikes RS 4 (tie) a. Lou Christy

Lil' Red Riding Hood RS 7 (tie) a. Sam the Sham and The Pharaohs

Mellow Yellow RS 9 (tie) a. Donovan

Michelle (from 1965)

Monday Monday RS 2 (tie) a. The Mamas and The Papas

My Love RS 3 (tie) a. Petula Clark

96 Tears RS 4 (tie) a. ?[Question Mark] and The Mysterians

Nowhere Man

Paint It Black RS 3 (tie) a. Rolling Stones

Paperback Writer RS 3 (tie) a. Beatles

Parsley, Sage, Rosemary and Thyme, see "Scarborough Fair/Canticle"

Poor Side of Town RS 4 (tie) a. Johnny Rivers

The Quest, see "The Impossible Dream"

Reach Out I'll Be There RS 3 (tie) a. Four Tops

Red Rubber Ball RS 8 (tie) a. Cyrkle

Scarborough Fair/Canticle (Parsley, Sage, Rosemary and Thyme)

Snoopy vs. The Red Baron RS 9 (tie) a. Royal Guardsmen

Somewhere My Love (Lara's Theme)

(You're My) Soul and Inspiration RS 2 (tie) a. Righteous Brothers

The Sounds of Silence RS 3 (tie) a. Simon and Garfunkel

Strangers in the Night RS 4 (tie) a. Frank Sinatra

Summer in the City RS 2 (tie) a. Lovin' Spoonful

Sunny RS 6 a. Bobby Hebb

Sunshine Superman RS 4 (tie) a. Donovan

Tell It Like It Is RS 7 (tie) a. Aaron Neville

These Boots Are Made for Walkin' RS 4 (tie) a. Nancy Sinatra

We Can Work It Out RS 2 (tie) a. Beatles

When a Man Loves a Woman RS 3 (tie) a. Percy Sledge

Wild Thing RS 3 (tie) a. Troggs

Winchester Cathedral RS 2 (tie) a. New Vaudeville Band

Yellow Submarine

You Can't Hurry Love RS 3 (tie) a. Supremes

You Don't Have To Say You Love Me

You Keep Me Hangin' On RS 3 (tie) a. Supremes

Revivals

See You in September (1959)

What Now, My Love? (1962)

Notable

Almost Persuaded

Are You There (with Another Girl)

Baby Dream Your Dream

Batman Theme

(Hey) Big Spender

Bus Stop

Color My World

Come Back to Me

Cool Jerk

A Day in the Life of a Fool

Didn't We

Dulcinea

Elusive Butterfly

Girl

Gloria

Good Day, Sunshine

Got To Get You into My Life

Here, There and Everywhere

Homeward Bound

Hurry It's Lovely Up Here

I Couldn't Live Without Your Love

I Got You (I Feel Good)

If He Walked into My Life

I'm Looking Through You

I'm So Lonesome I Could Cry

In My Life

In the Arms of Love

It's Over

Just Like a Woman

Kicks

Listen People

Mame

A Man and a Woman

Message to Michael

Moment to Moment

Music To Watch Girls By

My Best Girl

19th Nervous Breakdown

Norwegian Wood

On a Clear Day You Can See Forever

Open a New Window

A Place in the Sun

Rainy Day Women #12 & 35

She Said She Said

Sloop John B.

Spanish Flea

Sugar Town

A Symphony for Susan

Time After Time

Tiny Bubbles
Turn Down Day
Uptight (Everything's Alright)
We Need a Little Christmas
What Did I Have That I Don't Have
Where Am I Going
You Wanna Bet
You're Gonna Hear from Me
You've Got Possibilities

1967

Rock Musicals on Broadway. The rock musicals *Hair* and *Your Own Thing* arrive Off-Broadway. *Hair* is presented on October 17 at The New York Shakespeare Festival Public Theatre, is moved to the discotheque Cheetah on December 22, and then opens uptown at the Biltmore Theatre on April 29, 1968. Eventually, fourteen touring companies of this show play concurrently in the U.S. and internationally; local companies appear from Tokyo to Rio de Janeiro. Cast members who later rise to stardom include Diane Keaton, Melba Moore, and Ben Vereen.

More Beatles. With *Sergeant Pepper's Lonely Hearts Club Band,* the Beatles overwhelm the recording industry and the world and create a song cycle of poetic musical genius. This year sees their *Magical Mystery Tour* album, which also becomes an instant best seller and ties in with their television movie of the same name. In six months, they write and record sixteen new songs, none of which have lost their freshness today. Their manager, Brian Epstein, dies of a drug overdose.

Aretha Franklin. Beginning with her first Atlantic recording "I Never Loved a Man," which stays on top of the R & B charts for seven weeks and brings her first gold record, she also records Otis Redding's "Respect" and Ronny Shannon's "Baby, I Love You." Her recording of "Respect" gets her two Grammys, a pattern not to be interrupted until 1975.

Top Hits
All You Need Is Love   RS 6 (tie)   a. Beatles
The Beat Goes On
By the Time I Get to Phoenix
Call Me
Can't Take My Eyes Off You   RS 8 (tie)   a. Frankie Vallie
Creque Alley
Daydream Believer   RS 3 (tie)   a. Monkees
Don't Sleep in the Subway
The 59th Street Bridge Song (Feelin' Groovy)

Gentle on My Mind
Georgy Girl (from 1966)
Groovin'   RS 3 (tie)   a. Young Rascals
The Happening   RS 6 (tie)   a. Supremes
Happy Together   RS 4 (tie)   a. Turtles
I Heard It Through the Grape Vine   RS 7   a. Gladys Knight and The Pips
I Was Made To Love Her   RS 9 (tie)   a. Stevie Wonder
I'm a Believer   RS 1   a. Monkees
Incense and Peppermints   RS 6 (tie)   a. Strawberry Alarm Clock
Kind of a Drag   RS 5 (tie)   a. Buckinghams
The Letter   RS 3 (tie)   a. Boxtops
Light My Fire   RS 4 (tie)   a. Doors
Little Bit o' Soul   RS 8 (tie)   a. Music Explosion
(With) A Little Help from My Friends
Love Is Here and Now You're Gone   RS 6 (tie)   a. Supremes
Lucy in the Sky with Diamonds
A Man and a Woman (from 1966)
My Beautiful Balloon, see "Up Up and Away"
Never My Love   RS 10   a. Association
Ode to Billie Joe   RS 3 (tie)   a. Bobbie Gentry
Penny Lane   RS 6 (tie)   a. Beatles
The Rain, the Park and Other Things   RS 8 (tie)   a. Cowsills
Respect   RS 5 (tie)   a. Aretha Franklin
Ruby Tuesday   RS 6 (tie)   a. Rolling Stones
Sergeant Pepper's Lonely Hearts Club Band
She's Leaving Home
Something Stupid   RS 3 (tie)   a. Frank Sinatra and Nancy Sinatra
Soul Man   RS 9 (tie)   a. Sam and Dave
Strangers in the Night (from 1966)
Strawberry Fields Forever
Sweet Soul Music   RS 9 (tie)   a. Arthur Conley
There's a Kind of Hush
To Sir with Love   RS 2   a. Lulu
Up Up and Away (My Beautiful Balloon)
Windy   RS 3 (tie)   a. Association

Revivals
Dedicated to the One I Love (1961)
Ding Dong, the Witch Is Dead (1939)
(Theme from) Elvira Madigan (m. Mozart, Piano Concerto No. 21 (1785))
Glad To Be Unhappy (1936)

Notable
Ain't No Mountain High Enough
Anyone Can Move a Mountain

Baby You're a Rich Man
Being for the Benefit of Mister Kite
Cabaret
California Nights
(Theme from) Casino Royale
Come Back When You Grow Up
A Day in the Life
Fixing a Hole
For Once in My Life
Getting Better
Go Where You Wanna Go
Good Morning, Good Morning
The Green Green Grass of Home
Honeymoon Is Over
I Dig Rock and Roll Music
I Say a Little Prayer
I Think We're Alone Now
I Will Wait for You
If You Could See Her
It Must Be Him
Lady Bird
A Little Bit Me, A Little Bit You
The Look of Love
Look Through My Window
Love Eyes
Lovely Rita (Meter Maid)
Mercy Mercy
The Money Song
My Cup Runneth Over
(You Make Me Feel Like) A Natural Woman
On the South Side of Chicago
Reflections
Release Me
San Francisco (Be Sure To Wear Some Flowers in Your Hair)
Spanish Eyes
Stop and Think It Over
Suzanne
Talk to the Animals
There Goes My Everything
This Is My Song
Thoroughly Modern Millie
The Tracks of My Tears
Twelve Thirty (Young Girls Are Coming to the Canyon)
(Theme from) Two For the Road
Wednesday's Child
When I'm Sixty-Four
A Whiter Shade of Pale
Willkommen
Windows of the World

You Only Live Twice
You're a Good Man, Charlie Brown

1968

More Beatles. By now, the Beatles have released some 230 versions of their work, with total record sales of more than 200 million worldwide and gross income of $175 million. In less than ten years they have sold 125 million singles and 85 million LPs.

President Johnson. President Johnson publicly announces on March 31 that he would neither seek nor accept the Democratic nomination for President.

Political Assassinations. On April 4, civil rights leader Rev. Dr. Martin Luther King, Jr. is fatally shot in Memphis, Tennessee. Senator Robert F. Kennedy is assassinated on June 5 at the Hotel Ambassador in Los Angeles after celebrating presidential primary victories in California and South Dakota.

Bette Midler. The future "Divine Miss M" is completing her second year playing Tzeitel in *Fiddler on the Roof.* In 1965 her first acting job was a small role in the film *Hawaii* (1966), the proceeds enabling her to leave the United States Naval Base where her father was employed as a house painter and come to New York.

Top Hits
Both Sides Now
Classical Gas
Cry Like a Baby   RS 10 (tie)   a. Boxtops
Do You Know the Way to San Jose
(Sittin' On) The Dock of the Bay   RS 4 (tie)   a. Otis Redding
The Good, the Bad and the Ugly   RS 8   a. Hugo Montenegro
Grazing in the Grass   RS 6 (tie)   a. Hugh Masekela
Green Tambourine   RS 7 (tie)   a. Lemon Pipers
Harper Valley P.T.A.   RS 7 (tie)   a. Jeannie Riley
Hello Goodbye   RS 5 (tie)   a. Beatles
Hello, I Love You (Won't You Tell Me Your Name)   RS 6 (tie)   a. Doors
Hey Jude   RS 1   a. Beatles
Honey   RS 3 (tie)   a. Bobby Goldsboro
I Heard It Through the Grape Vine   RS 2   a. Marvin Gaye
I'll Never Fall in Love Again
I've Got To Get a Message to You
Judy in Disguise (with Glasses)   RS 6 (tie)   a. John Fred and His Playboy Band
Lady Madonna
Little Green Apples   RS 9   a. O.C. Smith

Love Child   RS 6 (tie)   a. Diana Ross and The Supremes

Love Is Blue   RS 3 (tie)   a. Paul Mauriat

Love Theme from Romeo and Juliet (A Time for Us), see 1969

MacArthur Park

Mrs. Robinson   RS 5 (tie)   a. Simon and Garfunkel

Music To Watch Girls By

Over You

People Got To Be Free   RS 3 (tie)   a. Rascals

Sittin' on the Dock of the Bay, see ''The Dock of the Bay''

Son of a Preacher Man

Stoned Soul Picnic

Theme from The Thomas Crown Affair, see ''The Windmills of Your Mind''

This Guy's in Love with You   RS 4 (tie)   a. Herb Alpert

Tighten Up   RS 6 (tie)   a. Archie Bell and The Drells

A Time for Us, see ''Love Theme from Romeo and Juliet,'' 1969

Wichita Lineman

The Windmills of Your Mind (theme from The Thomas Crown Affair)

Young Girl   RS 10 (tie)   a. Gary Puckett and The Union Gap

Adaptations

Those Were the Days (based on a traditional East European tune)

Revivals

Down in the Depths on the Ninetieth Floor (1936)

He Don't Love You (He Will Break Your Heart) (1960)

I Get Along Without You Very Well (1939)

There's Always Something There To Remind Me (1964)

Notable

Abraham, Martin and John

Amsterdam

The Ballad of Bonnie and Clyde

A Beautiful Morning

Bend Me, Shake Me

Blackbird

Born To Be Wild

Carousel (Brel)

Cry Baby Cry

Dear Prudence

The Desperate Ones

Fire

Folsom Prison (Blues)

The Fool on the Hill

For Once in My Life

Good Night

Help Yourself

Helter Skelter

Hold Me Tight

The Horse

Hurdy Gurdy Man

I Am the Walrus

I Will

I Wish It Would Rain

If We Only Have Love

I'm Gonna Make You Love Me

I've Gotta Be Me

Julia

Jumpin' Jack Flash

Knowing When To Leave

Lady Willpower

(The) Last Thing on My Mind

The Life of the Party

(I'd) Like To Get To Know You

Loving You Has Made Me Bananas

Madeleine

Magical Mystery Tour

Man Without Love

Marieke

Mission: Impossible Theme

Mister Bojangles

Mony Mony

Old Folks

One Two Three Red Light

Promises Promises

Revolution

Season of the Witch

Simon Says

Sometimes Your Eyes Look Blue to Me

Sons Of

Stand By Your Man

Step to the Rear

Sunshine of Your Love

Timid Frieda

The Unicorn

Valleri

(Theme from) Valley of the Dolls

Wait Until Dark

The Weight

What a Wonderful World

When You're Young and in Love

While My Guitar Gently Weeps

White Room

Whoever You Are

Wild Honey Pie

Your Mother Should Know

Yummy Yummy Yummy

1969

Man On the Moon. U.S. astronaut Neil A. Armstrong, Commander of the Apollo II mission, is the first man to set foot on the moon on July 20. The event is broadcast live on television.

Woodstock. The outdoor arena, the road, and the tour come together near Woodstock, N.Y., on August 16. Attendance is 300,000, and the event makes the front page of the *New York Times*. The three-day festival of "peace, love and rock" took place on 600 acres of land and featured performances by all the great rock stars of the day, including Janis Joplin, Jefferson Airplane, Jimi Hendrix, Sly and the Family Stone, The Who, and Led Zeppelin. The film documentary of the 1967 Monterey International Pop Festival in California, focusing on performances by Otis Redding, The Mamas and the Papas, Jimi Hendrix, The Who, and Jefferson Airplane, is released this year. Artist Laura Nyro is poorly received and virtually given the hook. Two years later she would have a top-selling album on Columbia Records.

Dying Movie Palaces. Many become supermarkets, synagogues, twin theatres, or are simply torn down, as is the case of the legendary Roxy Theatre in New York City. In its palmiest days, the Roxy featured, in addition to a lush apartment for impresario Roxy, an orchestra of 110, five staff organists, six box offices, and a radio studio.

Still More Beatles. John Lennon marries Yoko Ono, Sunday, March 20.

Top Hits

And When I Die RS 10 (tie)   a. Blood, Sweat and Tears

Aquarius RS 1 (tie)   a. Fifth Dimension

Bad Moon Rising RS 9 (tie)   a. Creedence Clearwater Revival

A Boy Named Sue

Come Together RS 6 (tie)   a. Beatles

Crimson and Clover RS 5 (tie)   a. Tommy James and The Shondells

Crystal Blue Persuasion RS 8 (tie)   a. Tommy James and The Shondells

Dizzy RS 3 (tie)   a. Tommy Roe

Everyday People RS 3 (tie)   a. Sly and The Family Stone

Games People Play

Get Back RS 2   a. Beatles

Good Morning Starshine

Green River RS 10 (tie)   a. Creedence Clearwater Revival

Hair RS 8 (tie)   a. Cowsills

Hey There Lonely Girl RS 9 (tie)   a. Eddie Holman

Honky Tonk Women RS 3 (tie)   a. Rolling Stones

Hot Fun in the Summertime RS 7   a. Sly and The Family Stone

I Can't Get Next to You RS 5 (tie)   a. Temptations

In the Year 2525 RS 1 (tie)   a. Zager and Evans

It's Your Thing RS 9 (tie)   a. Isley Brothers

Jean RS 9 (tie)   a. Oliver

Lay Lady Lay

Leaving on a Jet Plane RS 6 (tie)   a. Peter, Paul and Mary

Let the Sunshine In RS 1 (tie)   a. The Fifth Dimension

Love Can Make You Happy RS 10 (tie)   a. Mercy

Love Theme from *Romeo and Juliet* (A Time for Us) RS 5(tie)   a. Henry Mancini

My Cherie Amor

My Way (Comme d'Habitude)

Na Na Hey Hey Kiss Him Goodbye RS 5 (tie)   a. Steam

Proud Mary RS 9 (tie)   a. Creedence Clearwater Revival

Something (In the Way She Moves) RS 6 (tie)   a. Beatles

Spinning Wheel RS 10 (tie)   a. Blood, Sweat and Tears

Sugar Sugar RS 3 (tie)   a. Archies

Suspicious Minds RS 6 (tie)   a. Elvis Presley

Take a Letter Maria RS 8 (tie)   a. R.B. Greaves

A Time for Us, see "Love Theme from *Romeo and Juliet*"

Wedding Bell Blues RS 4   a. The Fifth Dimension

You've Made Me So Very Happy RS 10 (tie)   a. Blood, Sweat and Tears

Revivals

Are You from Dixie (1915)

I Have Dreamed (1951)

Oh Happy Day (1953)

Put Your Head on My Shoulder (1959)

Notable

April Fools

Baby I Love You

Better Homes and Gardens

Build Me Up Buttercup

Coco

Color Him Father

Come Saturday Morning

Cream of the Crop

Day Is Done

Dear World

Didn't We

Do Your Own Thing

Don't Let Me Down

Easy To Be Hard

Everybody's Talkin' (theme from *Midnight Cowboy*)

Gabrielle

Galveston

(Let's) Get Together
Give Peace a Chance
Hawaii Five-O
He Ain't Heavy . . . He's My Brother
Here Comes the Sun
Hooked on a Feeling
Hurry on Down
Hurt So Bad
In the Ghetto
Is That All There Is
I've Got To Be Me
Kaw-Liga
Keem-O-Sabe
Kiss Her Now
Love's Been Good to Me
Midnight Cowboy
Momma Look Sharp
Move In a Little Closer Baby
Ob-La-Di Ob-La-Da
Odds and Ends (Of a Beautiful Love Affair)
One (Nilsson)
Only the Strong Survive
Put a Little Love in Your Heart
Ruby Don't Take Your Love to Town
See
She Belongs to Me
Someday Soon
Son of a Travelin' Man
Too Busy Thinking About My Baby
Traces
Tracy
Truck Stop
True Grit
Try a Little Kindness
What Does It Take To Win Your Love
Where Do I Go?
Where's the Playground Susie
Whole Lotta Love
Yesterday When I Was Young
Yester-me, Yester-you, Yesterday

1970

The End of the Beatles. The Beatles' last records, "Let It Be" and "The Long and Winding Road," make the Top Ten in record sales. Their last LP together, "Abbey Road," is released this year. In April, Paul McCartney officially announces that he is leaving the group and goes on to record independently. The Beatles' partnership is not legally dissolved until January 1975.

Rock Opera. Tommy, a rock opera composed by Peter Townshend (of The Who), is performed at the Metropolitan Opera House in New York City.

Rock and Drugs. Janis Joplin is found dead at age twenty-seven in her hotel room from an overdose of heroin mixed with a quart of tequila and two valium. Jim Morrison of The Doors and Jimi Hendrix, twenty-eight, also die of drug overdoses this year.

Rock and the Law. At the Altamont Speedway, California, last December 6, an audience member is killed, and others stabbed and beaten, when the Hell's Angels, hired for protection by the Rolling Stones, stampede into the audience on motorcycles. A direct result of that incident are court orders canceling scheduled rock performances notably the festival to occur in Powder Ridge, Connecticut.

Recorded Music Sales. Total retail sales of recorded music, singles, albums, and tapes combined, is estimated at $1.7 billion.

Earth Day. Nationwide anti-pollution demonstrations mark the first Earth Day, April 22.

Top Hits
ABC RS 5 (tie) a. Jackson Five
American Woman RS 4 (tie) a. Guess Who
Bridge Over Troubled Water RS 1 a. Simon and Garfunkel
(They Long To Be) Close to You RS 3 (tie) a. Carpenters
Cracklin' Rosie RS 6 (tie) a. Neil Diamond
Everything Is Beautiful RS 5 (tie) a. Ray Stevens
I Never Promised You a Rose Garden
I Think I Love You RS 4 (tie) a. Partridge Family
I Want You Back RS 6 (tie) a. Jackson Five
Let It Be RS 5 (tie) a. Beatles
The Long and Winding Road RS 5 (tie) a. Beatles
Long as I Can See the Light RS 9 (tie) a. Creedence Clearwater Revival
Lookin' Out My Back Door RS 9 (tie) a. Creedence Clearwater Revival
The Love You Save RS 5 (tie) a. Jackson Five
(I'd Like To) Make It with You RS 6 (tie) a. Bread
Mama Told Me (Not To Come) RS 5 (tie) a. Three Dog Night
No Sugar Tonight RS 4 (tie) a. Guess Who
One Less Bell To Answer RS 7 a. The Fifth Dimension
Raindrops Keep Fallin' on My Head RS 3 (tie) a. B.J. Thomas
Some Day We'll Be Together RS 6 (tie) (1969) a. Diana Ross and The Supremes
The Tears of a Clown RS 5 (tie) a. Smokey Robinson and The Miracles

Thank You Falettinme Be Mice Elf Again   RS 5 (tie) a. Sly and The Family Stone

Vehicle   RS 10   a. Ides of March

War   RS 4 (tie)   a. Edwyn Starr

We've Only Just Begun   RS 8 (tie)   a. Carpenters

Which Way You Goin' Billy   RS 8 (tie)   a. Poppy Family

The Wrapper   RS 9 (tie)   a. Jaggerz

Adaptations
El Condor Pasa (If I Could) (1933)   (based on a Peruvian folksong)

Revivals
Ain't No Mountain High Enough (1967)   RS 4 (tie)   a. Diana Ross

Band of Gold   (1956)

Before the Parade Passes By (1964)

For Once in My Life (1965)

If I Were a Carpenter (1966)

I'll Be There (1960)   RS 2   a. Jackson Five

Until It's Time for You To Go (1965)

Venus (1959)   RS 6 (tie)   a. Shocking Blue

A Whiter Shade of Pale (1967)

Notable
Across the Universe
Airport Love Theme
And the Grass Won't Pay No Mind
Another Hundred People
Applause
Barcelona
Being Alive
(Theme from) Borsalino
Candida
Company
Country Road
Daughter of Darkness
Do What You Wanna Do
Does Anybody Really Know What Time It Is
Domino
Dream Babies
Early in the Morning
Easy Come Easy Go
Fancy
Fire and Rain
For All We Know
Get Ready
Getting Married Today
Groovin'
Heaven Help Us All

Heed the Call
Holly Holy
I Got Love
I Who Have Nothing
If You Could Read My Mind
Isn't It a Pity
It's Impossible
Jerusalem
The Ladies Who Lunch
Lay Down (Candles in the Rain)
The Little Things You Do Together
Long Ago and Far Away (*not* kern)
Look What They've Done to My Song Ma
(Theme from) Love Story (Where Do I Begin)
(Song from) M.A.S.H.
My Woman, My Woman, My Wife
Okie from Muskogee
Paper Mache
Patches (I'm Depending on You)
Pieces of Dreams
Reach Out and Touch
Ride Captain Ride
Side By Side By Side
Snowbird
Sorry-Grateful
Stoney End
Sweet Caroline (Sweet Times Never Seemed So Good)
There's Enough To Go Around
Travelin' Band
What Are You Doing the Rest of Your Life
When Julie Comes Around
Who'll Stop the Rain
Why Can't I Touch You
Wild World
You Could Drive a Person Crazy
Your Song

1971

Gospel Rock. Rock shows based on the Bible are notable in the New York theatre this year. *Godspell,* with score by Stephen Schwartz, opens on May 17 Off-Broadway at the Cherry Lane Theater and *Jesus Christ Superstar,* with score by Tim Rice and Andrew Lloyd Webber, on October 12 at the Mark Hellinger Theater.

Super-Star Concert. George Harrison, Ravi Shankar, Eric Clapton, and Bob Dylan perform at the Concert for Bangladesh on August 1.

Carole King. With her husband co-writer Gerry Goffin, Carole King has been an active writer since 1960

with her Shirelles hit "Will You (Still) Love Me To-morrow" recorded on Scepter. Some of their hits would soon include "Up on the Roof" by the Drifters, "He's a Rebel" by The Crystals, "Go Away, Little Girl" by Steve Lawrence, "One Fine Day" by The Chiffons, and "Loco-Motion" by Little Eva. This year her second solo album, *Tapestry,* is an enormous success, selling over 13 1/2 million albums and making it the best-selling LP of all time. Carole King is honored with four Grammys this year.

Charles Manson. On January 26, Charles Manson and three of his followers are found guilty of first-degree murder in the brutal slaying of actress Sharon Tate and six others in 1969.

Top Hits

Brown Sugar   RS 5 (tie)   a. Rolling Stones
Family Affair   RS 4 (tie)   a. Sly and The Family Stone
For All We Know (from 1970)
Gypsies, Tramps and Thieves   RS 5 (tie)   a. Cher
How Can You Mend a Broken Heart   RS 3   a. Bee Gees
I Feel the Earth Move   RS 2 (tie)   a. Carole King
Indian Reservation   RS 6 (tie)   a. Raiders
It's Too Late   RS 2 (tie)   a. Carole King
Jesus Christ Superstar
Joy to the World   RS 1   a. Three Dog Night
Just My Imagination (Running Away with Me)   RS 5 (tie)   a. Temptations
Knock Three Times   RS 4 (tie)   a. Dawn
Maggie May (Reason To Believe)   RS 2 (tie)   a. Rod Stewart
Me and Bobby McGee   RS 5 (tie)   a. Janis Joplin
Mister Big Stuff   RS 8   a. Jean Knight
Mister Bo Jangles
My Sweet Lord   RS 3 (tie) (1970)   a. George Harrison
One Bad Apple   RS 2 (tie)   a. The Osmonds
Put Your Hand in the Hand   RS 10 (tie)   a. Ocean
Reason To Believe, see "Maggie May"
(Theme from) Shaft   RS 5 (tie)   a. Isaac Hayes
She's a Lady   RS 10 (tie)   a. Tom Jones
Take Me Home Country Roads   RS 7   a. John Denver
Uncle Albert (Admiral Halsey)   RS 6 (tie)   a. Paul and Linda McCartney
Want Ads   RS 6 (tie)   a. Honeycone
What's Goin' On   RS 9   a. Marvin Gaye
You've Got a Friend   RS 6 (tie)   a. Carole King

Revivals

Color My World (1966)
Go Away, Little Girl (1963)   RS 4 (tie)   a. Donny Osmond
Spanish Harlem (1961)

Notable

Ain't No Sunshine
Anticipation
(Hats Off, Here They Come, Those) Beautiful Girls
Bless the Beasts and Children
Broadway Baby
Could I Leave You
Day By Day
(The) God-Why-Don't-You-Love-Me Blues
Help Me Make It Through the Night
Here Comes the Sun
I Am, I Said
I Don't Know How To Love Him
I Won't Last a Day Without You
I'd Like To Teach the World To Sing
If
I'm Still Here
Kiss an Angel Good Mornin'
Losing My Mind
Mama's Pearl
Morning Has Broken
Never Can Say Goodbye
Peace Train
Rainy Days and Mondays
So Far Away
The Summer Knows (Theme from *Summer of '42*)
Superstar
Sweet Seasons
Waiting for the Girls Upstairs

1972

Watergate. Five men are arrested June 17 at the Watergate apartment complex in Washington, D.C., for breaking into the offices of the Democratic National Committee.

Grease. The 1950s' nostalgic "rock 'n' roll" musical *Grease,* opens Off-Broadway on February 14 at the Eden Theatre on Second Avenue, next at the Broadhurst Theatre on Broadway June 7, and moves later to the Royale Theatre on November 21. With lyrics and music by Warren Casey and Jim Jacobs, *Grease* has had an estimated total gross to 1978 of $40 million. In 1978, the musical film adaptation starring John Travolta and Olivia Newton-John would place itself at the close of 1980 as the top musical film rental and fourth all-time rental champ, bringing in $96,300,000 for Paramount.

Coal Miner's Daughter. On October 16, the Country Music Association names Loretta Lynn the first woman entertainer of the year (a title she would keep for the next three years). Receiving two more awards this year, her rise to national stardom encourages the writing of her autobiography, *Loretta Lynn: Coal Miner's Daughter,* in 1976 and later the film adaptation of the book in her successful biopic. Nashville, Tennessee, is by now the home of a $250 million-a-year country-and-western music industry.

Life. Ending thirty-six years as the leading weekly pictorial magazine, *Life* offers its last publication for sale with the December 29 issue.

Top Hits

Alone Again (Naturally)   RS 1 (tie)   a. Gilbert O'Sullivan

(Bye Bye) American Pie   RS 2 (tie)   a. Don McLean

Baby Don't Get Hooked on Me   RS 3 (tie)   a. Mack Davis

Ben   RS 5 (tie)   a. Michael Jackson

Black and White   RS 5 (tie)   a. Three Dog Night

Brand New Key   RS 4 (tie) (1971)   a. Melanie

Brandy (You're a Fine Girl)   RS 5 (tie)   a. Looking Glass

Burning Love   RS 10 (tie)   a. Elvis Presley

The Candy Man   RS 3 (tie)   a. Sammy Davis, Jr.

Clair   RS 9   a. Gilbert O'Sullivan

The First Time Ever I Saw Your Face   RS 1 (tie)   a. Roberta Flack

Heart of Gold   RS 5 (tie)   a. Neil Young

A Horse with No Name   RS 3 (tie)   a. America

I Am Woman   RS 5 (tie)   a. Helen Reddy

I Can See Clearly Now (The Rain Has Gone)   RS 2 (tie)   a. Johnny Nash

I Gotcha   RS 6   a. Joe Tex

I'll Take You There   RS 5 (tie)   a. Staple Singers

Lean on Me   RS 3 (tie)   a. Bill Withers

Let's Stay Together   RS 5 (tie)   a. Al Green

Long Cool Woman (in a Black Dress)   RS 10 (tie)   a. The Hollies

Me and Mrs. Jones   RS 3 (tie)   a. Billy Paul

My Ding-A-Ling   RS 4   a. Chuck Berry

Nights in White Satin   RS 7   a. Moody Blues

Oh Babe, What Would You Say

Oh Girl   RS 5 (tie)   a. Chi-lites

Outa-Space   RS 8   a. Billy Preston

Papa Was a Rollin' Stone   RS 5 (tie)   a. Temptations

Song Sung Blue   RS 5 (tie)   a. Neil Diamond

Without You   RS 2 (tie)   a. Nilsson

Revivals

Cabaret (1967)

The Lion Sleeps Tonight (Wimoweh) (1962)

Notable

Brian's Song

Could It Be I'm Falling in Love

Daddy Don't You Walk So Fast

Diamonds Are Forever

Don't Let Me Be Lonely Tonight

Freddy My Love

(Theme from) *The Godfather*

Hurting Each Other

I Saw the Light

It Never Rains in Southern California

Last Night I Didn't Get To Sleep At All

Layla

Look at Me, I'm Sandra Dee

Maybe This Time

Me and Julio Down by the Schoolyard

Money Money

Precious and Few

Rocky Mountain High

The Way of Love

1973

Elton John. Born Reginald Kenneth Dwight in Middlesex, England, son of a despotic military father responsible for a miserable, humiliating childhood, Elton Hercules John has three best-selling records this year and will become one of the wealthiest rock stars of all time. By 1976 he will have sold in six years 42 million albums and 18 million singles, with royalties exceeding $8 million. Ten of his albums will go platinum, and in 1974 his new contract with MCA Records guarantees him $8 million in royalties over the next five years.

Scott Joplin and The Sting. The Academy Award-winning film *The Sting* is released this year with a score derived from compositions by the black ragtime composer Scott Joplin, including "The Entertainer" (1902). But the Scott Joplin selections which are adapted to create the score are not cited, nor is his name mentioned. Before Joplin died on April 1, 1917, he opined: "When I'm dead twenty-five years people are going to recognize me." *The Sting* created a vogue for Joplin and revived interest in ragtime.

Night Music. Stephen Sondheim's *A Little Night Music,* three years after his successful *Company* and two years after his short-lived *Follies,* opens at the Shubert Theatre on February 25. Based on Ingmar Bergman's film *Smiles of a Summer Night,* the distinguished score includes among others, "The Miller's Son," "Liaisons," "Every Day a Little Death," and "The Glamorous Life.'' Glynis Johns's ''Send in the Clowns'' becomes the hit of the show and is successfully recorded by Judy Collins and Frank Sinatra, and earns a Grammy for ''song of the year'' in 1976.

McCartney and Wings. Paul McCartney and Wings, his new group, have two top records this year, ''My Love'' and ''Live and Let Die.''

Top Hits

Angie RS 5 (tie) a. Rolling Stones

Bad Bad Leroy Brown RS 4 (tie) a. Jim Croce

Brother Louie RS 4 (tie) a. Stories

The Cisco Kid RS 9 (tie) a. War

Crocodile Rock RS 3 (tie) a. Elton John

Daniel RS 9 (tie) a. Elton John

Delta Dawn RS 5 (tie) a. Helen Reddy

Dueling Banjos (*Deliverance* soundtrack) RS 10 (tie) a. Eric Weisberg and Steve Mandell

Frankenstein RS 5 (tie) a. Edgar Winter Group

Give Me Love (Give Me Peace on Earth) RS 5 (tie) a. George Harrison

Goodbye Yellow Brick Road RS 7 a. Elton John

Half-Breed RS 4 (tie) a. Cher

Keep on Truckin' RS 4 (tie) a. Eddie Kendricks

Killing Me Softly with His Song RS 1 a. Roberta Flack

Kodachrome RS 10 (tie) a. Paul Simon

Let's Get It On RS 4 (tie) a. Marvin Gaye

Live and Let Die (soundtrack) RS 10 (tie) a. Paul McCartney and Wings

Love Train RS 5 (tie) a. O'Jays

Loves Me Like a Rock RS 8 (tie) a. Paul Simon

Midnight Train to Georgia RS 4 (tie) a. Gladys Knight and The Pips

The Morning After (Song from *The Poseidon Adventure*) RS 4 (tie) a. Maureen McGovern

(If You Happen To See) The Most Beautiful Girl in the World RS 4 (tie) a. Charlie Rich

My Love RS 2 (tie) a. Paul McCartney and Wings

Neither One of Us (Wants To Be the First To Say Goodbye) RS 8 (tie) a. Gladys Knight and The Pips

The Night the Lights Went Out in Georgia RS 4 (tie) a. Vicki Lawrence

Photograph RS 5 (tie) a. Ringo Starr

Playground in My Mind RS 6 a. Clint Holmes

Ramblin' Man RS 8 (tie) a. Allman Brothers

Superstition RS 5 (tie) a. Stevie Wonder

Tie a Yellow Ribbon Round the Ole Oak Tree RS 2 (tie) a. Dawn featuring Tony Orlando

Top of the World RS 4 (tie) a. Carpenters

Touch Me in the Morning RS 5 (tie) a. Diana Ross

We're an American Band RS 5 (tie) a. Grand Funk

Will It Go Round in Circles RS 4 (tie) a. Billy Preston

Yesterday Once More RS 10 (tie) a. Carpenters

You Are the Sunshine of My Life RS 5 (tie) a. Stevie Wonder

You're So Vain RS 3 (tie) a. Carly Simon

Revivals

Also sprach Zarathustra (Theme from *2001: A Space Odyssey*) (1896)

Boogie Woogie Bugle Boy (1941)

Monster Mash (1962)

Paper Roses (1955)

The Twelfth of Never (1957)

Notable

Ain't No Woman (Like the One I've Got)

All I Know

Behind Closed Doors

Break Up To Make Up

Call Me (Come Back Home)

Danny's Song

Diamond Girl

Drift Away

Every Day a Little Death

Get Down

The Glamorous Life

Gypsy Man

Heartbeat—It's a Lovebeat

Helen Wheels

Hello It's Me

Here I Am (Come and Take Me)

Higher Ground

Hocus Pocus

I Got a Name

If You're Ready (Come Go with Me)

I'm Gonna Love You Just a Little More, Baby

I've Got To Use My Imagination

Jungle Boogie

Just You 'n' Me (Babe)

Keep Behind Closed Doors

Knockin' On Heaven's Door

Leave Me Alone (Ruby Red Dress)

Let Me Be There

Liaisons

Little Willy

Living for the City

Long Train Runnin'

The Love I Lost (Part 1)

Masterpiece

The Miller's Son

My Maria

(Say Has Anybody Seen) My Sweet Gypsy Rose

Natural High

Never Never Gonna Give You Up

Night Waltz

Put Your Hands Together

Right Place Wrong Time

The Right Thing To Do

Rock On

Send in the Clowns

Shamballa

Sing (Sing a Song)

Smoke on the Water

Smokin' in the Boys' Room

Space Race

Spiders and Snakes

Stuck in the Middle with You

That Lady

Uneasy Rider

Until You Come Back to Me (That's What I'm Gonna Do)

A Weekend in the Country

Wildflower

You Must Meet My Wife

1974

Nixon Resigns. President Richard M. Nixon resigns August 9 thus protecting himself from imminent impeachment proceedings by Congress.

John, Paul, George, Ringo. This year top hits are recorded individually by John Lennon with the Plastic Ono Nuclear Band, "Whatever Gets You Thru the Night"; Ringo Starr's revival of "You're Sixteen"; and Paul McCartney and Wings, "Band on the Run." In 1973 George Harrison's top hit was "Give Me Love (Give Me Peace on Earth)."

Animated Cartoon Nostalgia Revivals. Cartoon fans flock to see *Betty Boop Scandals of 1974* and a feature-length film anthology devoted to Bugs Bunny and his memorable tag line "What's Up, Doc?"

Top Hits

Angie Baby RS 3 (tie) a. Helen Reddy

Annie's Song RS 2 (tie) a. John Denver

Band on the Run RS 3 (tie) a. Paul McCartney and Wings

Bennie and the Jets RS 3 (tie) a. Elton John

Best Thing That Ever Happened to Me RS 9 (tie) a. Gladys Knight and The Pips

Billy Don't Be a Hero RS 2 (tie) a. Bo Donaldson and The Heywoods Boogie Down RS 6 (tie) a. Eddie Kendricks

Boogie on Reggae Women RS 9 (tie) a. Stevie Wonder

Can't Get Enough of Your Love, Babe RS 3 (tie) a. Barry White

Cat's in the Cradle RS 3 (tie) a. Harry Chapin

Dancing Machine RS 5 a. Jackson Five

Dark Lady RS 3 (tie) a. Cher

Do It ('Til You're Satisfied) RS 6 (tie) a. B.T. Express

Don't Let the Sun Go Down on Me RS 8 (tie) a. Elton John

Feel Like Makin' Love RS 3 (tie) a. Roberta Flack

(You're) Having My Baby RS 1 (tie) a. Paul Anka

Hooked on a Feeling RS 3 (tie) a. Blue Swede

I Can Help RS 2 (tie) a. Billy Swan

I Honestly Love You RS 2 (tie) a. Olivia Newton-John

I Shot the Sheriff RS 3 (tie) a. Eric Clapton

Jazz Man RS 7 a. Carole King

The Joker RS 3 (tie) a. Steve Miller Band

Kung Fu Fighting RS 2 (tie) a. Carl Douglas

Love's Theme RS 3 (tie) a. Love Unlimited Orchestra

My Melody of Love RS 9 (tie) a. Bobby Vinton

The Night Chicago Died RS 3 (tie) a. Paper Lace

Nothing from Nothing RS 3 (tie) a. Billy Preston

Rock Me Gently RS 3 (tie) a. Andy Kim

Rock the Boat RS 3 (tie) a. Hues Corporation

Rock Your Baby RS 2 (tie) a. George McCrae

Seasons in the Sun RS 1 (tie) a. Terry Jacks

Show and Tell RS 3 (tie) a. Al Wilson

The Streak RS 1 (tie) a. Ray Stevens

Sundown RS 3 (tie) a. Gordon Lightfoot

Sunshine on My Shoulders RS 3 (tie) a. John Denver

Tell Me Something Good RS 9 (tie) a. Rufus featuring Chaka Kahn

Then Came You RS 3 (tie) a. Dionne Warwick and The Spinners

Time in a Bottle RS 4 (tie) (1973) a. Jim Croce

TSOP The Sound of Philadelphia RS 2 (tie) a. MFSB featuring The Three Degrees

The Way We Were RS 1 (tie) a. Barbra Streisand

Whatever Gets You Thru the Night RS 3 (tie) a. John Lennon with the Plastic Ono Nuclear Band

When Will I See You Again RS 6 (tie) a. Three Degrees

You Ain't Seen Nothing Yet RS 3 (tie) a. Bachman-Turner Overdrive

You Haven't Done Nothin' RS 3 (tie) a. Stevie Wonder

You Make Me Feel Brand New RS 4 a. Stylistics

You're the First, My Last, My Everything RS 8 (tie) a. Barry White

Revivals

The Entertainer (Soundtrack from *The Sting*) (1902) RS 10 a. Marvin Hamlisch

The Loco-Motion (1962) RS 2 (tie) a. Grand Funk

You're Sixteen (1960) RS 3 (tie) a. Ringo Starr

Notable

The Air That I Breathe

All of My Life

The Bitch Is Back

Come and Get Your Love

It's Only Rock 'n Roll (But I Like It)

Jet

(Theme from) Murder on the Orient Express

Piano Man

Time Heals Everything

A Very Special Love Song

We May Never Love Like This Again

You and Me Against the World

1975

A Chorus Line. Conceived and directed by Michael Bennett, *A Chorus Line,* with music and lyrics by Marvin Hamlisch and Edward Kleban, opens downtown at Joseph Papp's Public (Newman) Theatre on Lafayette Street on May 21. On July 25 it moves to Broadway's Shubert Theatre and within weeks is considered a landmark in musical theatre history, securing nine Tonys and a Pulitzer. "What I Did for Love" becomes the hit of the show with other songs including "Dance: Ten; Looks: Three," "One," "At the Ballet," and "The Music and the Mirror."

More Oz. In the continuing saga of *The Wizard of Oz* another smash stage musical version, *The Wiz,* based on the original story by L. Frank Baum, opens with an all black cast at the Majestic Theatre on January 5. With music and lyrics by Charlie Smalls and starring Stephanie Mills, Ted Rose, and Mabel King, the score includes the hits "Ease On Down the Road" and "Home." In 1977, twenty miles of yellow vinyl floor covering will roll down Fifth Avenue and across the Brooklyn Bridge for the Diana Ross movie musical.

Disco Music. Disco dance melodies lead the Top Ten Singles list. "Touch" dancing returns with "The Hustle."

Top Hits

All By Myself RS 5 a. Eric Carmen

(Hey Won't You Play) Another Somebody Done Somebody Wrong Song RS 4 (tie) a. B.J. Thomas

Bad Blood RS 2 (tie) a. Neil Sedaka

Before the Next Teardrop Falls RS 4 (tie) a. Freddy Fender

Best of My Love RS 4 (tie) a. Eagles

Black Water RS 4 (tie) a. Doobie Brothers

Calypso RS 4 (tie) a. John Denver

Convoy RS 4 (tie) a. C.W. McCall

Ease on Down the Road

Fallin' in Love (Again) RS 4 (tie) a. Hamilton, Joe Frank and Reynolds

Fame RS 3 (tie) a. David Bowie

Fire RS 4 (tie) a. Ohio Players

Fly Robin Fly RS 2 (tie) a. Silver Convention

Get Down Tonight RS 4 (tie) a. K.C. and The Sunshine Band

Have You Never Been Mellow RS 4 (tie) a. Olivia Newton-John

He Don't Love You Like I Love You RS 2 (tie) a. Tony Orlando and Dawn

The Hustle RS 4 (tie) a. Van McCoy and The Soul City Symphony

I'm Not in Love RS 7 a. 10cc

I'M Sorry RS 4 (tie) a. John Denver

Island Girl RS 2 (tie) a. Elton John

Jackie Blue RS 10 (tie) a. Ozark Mountain Daredevils

Jive Talkin' RS 3 (tie) a. Bee Gees

Lady Marmalade RS 4 (tie) a. Labelle

Laughter in the Rain Rs 4 (tie) a. Neil Sedaka

Let's Do It Again RS 4 (tie) a. Staple Singers

Listen to What the Man Said RS 4 (tie) a. Paul McCartney and Wings

Love To Love You Baby RS 6 a. Donna Summer

Love Will Keep Us Together RS 1 a. The Captain and Tennille

Lovin' You RS 4 (tie) a. Minnie Riperton

Lyin' Eyes RS 9 a. Eagles

Mandy RS 4 (tie) a. Barry Manilow

My Eyes Adored You RS 4 (tie) a. Frankie Valli

One of These Nights RS 4 (tie) a. Eagles

Philadelphia Freedom RS 3 (tie) a. Elton John Band

Pick Up the Pieces RS 4 (tie) a. The Average White Band

Rhinestone Cowboy RS 3 (tie) a. Glen Campbell

Shining Star RS 4 (tie) a. Earth, Wind and Fire

Sister Golden Hair RS 4 (tie) a. America

Sky High RS 10 (tie) a. Jigsaw

Thank God I'm a Country Boy RS 4 (tie) a. John Denver

That's the Way (I Like It) RS 3 (tie) a. K.C. and The Sunshine Band

What I Did for Love

When Will I Be Loved RS 8 a. Linda Ronstadt

Where Is the Love

You Sexy Thing   RS 10 (tie)   a. Hot Chocolate
You're No Good   RS 4 (tie)   a. Linda Ronstadt

Revivals
Brazil (1943)
Breaking Up Is Hard To Do (1959)
Help Me, Rhonda (1965)
Lucy in the Sky with Diamonds (1967)   RS 3 (tie)   a. Elton John
Please Mister Postman (1961)
Ruby Baby (1963)
What a Diff'rence a Day Made (Makes) (1934)

Notable
Ain't No Way To Treat a Lady
All That Jazz
At Seventeen
At the Ballet
Bad Time
Ballroom Blitz
Carolina in the Pines
Chevy Van
Could It Be Magic
Country Boy You Got Your Feet in L.A.
Dance: Ten; Looks: Three
Dance with Me
Don't Nobody Bring Me No Bad News
Emma
Evergreen
Every Time You Touch Me (I Get High)
Express
Feelings
Fox on the Run
Freedom
Get Down Get Down (Get on the Floor)
Gone at Last
Heat Wave
Home
How Long?
How Sweet It Is (To Be Loved by You)
I Believe There's Nothing Stronger Than Our Love
I Don't Like To Sleep Alone
I Love Music (Part 1)
I'll Play for You
I'm Easy
I'm Not Lisa
The Immigrant
It Only Takes a Minute
It's a Miracle
It's a Sin When You Love Somebody

Lady Blue
Long Tall Glasses (I Can Dance)
Love Hurts
Love Won't Let Me Wait
Magic
Midnight Blue
Miracles
Mister Jaws
Mornin' Beautiful
Movin' On
My Little Town
My Own Best Friend
Nightingale
Nights on Broadway
No No Song
Old Days
One
Only Women Bleed
Only Yesterday
Pinball Wizard
Please Mister Please
Poetry Man
Razzle Dazzle
Rockin' Chair
Rocky
Run Joey Run
Send in the Clowns (see also 1973)
Snookeroo
Solitaire
Someone Saved My Life Tonight
Something Better To Do
SOS
Supernatural Thing—Part 1
Swearin' to God
Sweet Love
Take It to the Limit
Take Me in Your Arms (Rock Me a Little While)
That's When the Music Takes Me
They Just Can't Stop It (The Games People Play)
This Will Be
Times of Your Life
Walk Away from Love
Walking in Rhythm
Wasted Days and Wasted Nights
The Way I Want To Touch You
What Am I Gonna Do with You
Who Loves You
Why Am I Me
Why Can't We Be Friends

Wildfire
You Are So Beautiful

1976

The U.S. Bicentennial. America celebrates two hundred years as a nation on July 4. Six million people and Gerald Ford, President of the United States, gather for Operation Sail on the west side of the island of Manhattan to observe a fleet of hundreds of sailing boats led by an armada of sixteen windjammers from around the globe.

More Gershwin and Porgy. On September 25, the George Gershwin opera *Porgy and Bess* is revived by Sherwin M. Goldman and the Houston Grand Opera at the Uris Theatre in New York. For the first time, this Gershwin work is performed with its entire original score intact, recitative included.

Black Musical Theatre. As black audiences bring their patronage to Broadway, the trend to musicals with black casts continues. *Bubbling Brown Sugar* and *Guys and Dolls,* open this year, and *The Wiz* is held over from 1975. Recent major musicals with black casts have included *Purlie* (1970), *Raisin* (1973), and a revival of *Hello, Dolly!* starring Pearl Bailey (1967).

Barbra Streisand. Miss Streisand shares the Motion Picture Academy Award as composer with writer Paul Williams for their song "Evergreen" from her film version of *A Star Is Born.*

Top Hits
Afternoon Delight RS 5 (tie) a. Starland Vocal Band
Boogie Fever RS 6 (tie) a. The Sylvers
December 1963 (Oh What a Night) RS 4 (tie) a. Four Seasons
Disco Duck (Part 1) RS 6 (tie) a. Rick Dees and His Cast of Idiots
Disco Lady RS 3 (tie) a. Johnny Taylor
Do You Know Where You're Going To, see "Theme from *Mahogany*"
Don't Go Breaking My Heart RS 3 (tie) a. Elton John and Kiki Dee
Dream Weaver RS 10 (tie) a. Gary Wright
Fifty Ways To Leave Your Lover RS 4 (tie) a. Paul Simon
Fly Like an Eagle RS 10 (tie) a. Steve Miller
Get Up and Boogie RS 9 (tie) a. Silver Convention
I Write the Songs RS 6 (tie) a. Barry Manilow
I'd Really Love To See You Tonight RS 8 a. England Dan and John Ford Coley
If You Leave Me Now RS 5 (tie) a. Chicago
Kiss and Say Goodbye RS 5 (tie) a. The Manhattans
Let Your Love Flow RS 6 (tie) a. Bellamy Brothers

Love Hangover RS 5 (tie) a. Diana Ross
Love Is Alive RS 7 a. Gary Wright
Love Machine (Part 1) RS 6 (tie) a. The Miracles
Love Rollercoaster RS 6 (tie) a. Ohio Players
Play That Funky Music RS 4 (tie) a. Wild Cherry
Right Back Where We Started From RS 10 (tie) a. Maxine Nightingale
Rock 'n Me RS 6 (tie) a. Steve Miller
Rubberband Man RS 9 (tie) a. The Spinners
Saturday Night RS 6 (tie) a. Bay City Rollers
(Shake Shake Shake) Shake Your Booty RS 6 (tie) a. K.C. and The Sunshine Band
Silly Love Songs RS 2 a. Wings
Theme from *Mahogany* (Do You Know Where You're Going To) RS 6 (tie) a. Diana Ross
Theme from S.W.A.T. RS 6 (tie) a. Rhythm Heritage
Tonight's the Night (Gonna Be Alright) RS 1 a. Rod Stewart
Welcome Back RS 6 (tie) a. John Sebastian
The Wreck of the Edmund Fitzgerald RS 9 (tie) a. Gordon Lightfoot
You Should Be Dancing RS 6 (tie) a. Bee Gees
You'll Never Find Another Love Like Mine RS 9 (tie) a. Lou Rawls

Adaptations
A Fifth of Beethoven (based on themes from Beethoven's Fifth Symphony (1808) RS 6 (tie) a. Walter Murphy and The Big Apple Band

Revivals
Rock and Roll Music (1957)
That'll Be the Day (1957)

Notable
After the Lovin'
Beth
Bohemian Rhapsody
Broken Candy
Come on Over
Cupid
Dazz
Detroit Rock City
Devil Woman
Don't Pull Your Love
Dream On
Enjoy Yourself
Fooled Around and Fell in Love
Get Closer
A Good-Hearted Woman
Happy Days

Heaven Must Be Missing an Angel
Hot Line
I Do, I Do, I Do, I Do, I Do
I Like Dreamin'
I'll Be Good to You
Junk Food Junkie
Just To Be Close to You
Let 'Em In
Lonely Night (Angel Face)
Lost Without Your Love
Love in the Shadows
Love So Right
Low Down
Magic Man
Misty Blue
Money Honey
Moonlight Feels Right
More More More (Part 1)
More Than a Feeling
Muskrat Love
Nadia's Theme (The Young and the Restless)
Never Gonna Fall in Love Again
Night Moves
One Piece at a Time
Only Sixteen
Rhiannon
Sara Smile
Say You Love Me
Shannon
She's Gone
Show Me the Way
Shower the People
Sorry Seems To Be the Hardest Word
Still the One
Strange Magic
Summer
Sweet Thing
This Masquerade
Tryin' To Get the Feelin' Again
With Your Love
You Are the Woman
You're My Best Friend

1977

End of an Era. Four greats of the music industry die this year: Maria Callas, the dynamic opera star of her era who was responsible for reviving interest in bel canto operas; Bing Crosby, the great popular entertainer of his time, who, during his lifetime, sold at least four hundred million records; Elvis Presley, the first major figure in rock 'n' roll, who sold close to six hundred million records during his lifetime; and Leopold Stokowski, who, still recording at ninety-five, had the longest professional recording career.

Centennial of Recorded Sound. July 18 marked the one hundredth anniversary of Edison's dictating machine, which was designed initially for letter dictation without a stenographer. With it people recorded messages to be sent later over telephone lines.

Saturday Night Fever. John Travolta rises to instant stardom for his performance in *Saturday Night Fever* and elevates the art of disco dancing in musical film. As of 1980, it will be the third musical all-time film rental champ and bring in $74,100,000 for Paramount. With a predominant score by the Bee Gees, the number one hit ''How Deep Is Your Love'' is introduced with ''More Than a Woman,'' ''Stayin' Alive,'' ''Jive Talkin','' and ''Night Fever.'' Classical adaptations include Walter Murphy's ''A Fifth of Beethoven'' (see *1976*) and David Shire's ''Night on Disco Mountain.''

Star Wars. 20th Century-Fox's ''Buck Rogers-style'' science fiction adventure film takes in a record $127,000,000 in domestic film rentals. Not since *Gone with the Wind* has the public taken to a film with such enthusiasm.

Country Music Month. President Carter signs on September 30 a proclamation designating October as Country Music Month. Carter termed country music ''as universal as a sunset and as personal as a baby's smile.''

More Signs of the Times. The cost of the *New York Times* this year is twenty cents per copy, the New York City subway ride is fifty cents, and a gallon of gasoline is sixty-eight cents.

Top Hits
Baby, Come Back RS 2 a. Players
Best of My Love RS 7 (tie) a. Emotions
Blinded By the Light RS 6 (tie) (1976) a. Mann's Earth Band
Car Wash (soundtrack) RS 6 (tie) (1976) a. Rose Royce
Dancing Queen RS 6 (tie) (1976) a. Abba
Don't Give Up On Us
Don't Leave Me This Way RS 6 (tie) (1976) a. Thelma Houston
Dreams
Evergreen, or, **Love Theme from *A Star Is Born*** RS x a. Barbra Streisand
Gonna Fly Now (theme from *Rocky*) RS 10 (tie) a. Bill Conti
Got To Give It Up

Hotel California

How Deep Is Your Love RS 1 a. Bee Gees

I Just Want To Be Your Everything RS 3 a. Andy Gibb

I Wish RS 6 (tie) (1976) a. Stevie Wonder

I'm Your Boogie Man RS 7 (tie) a. KC & The Sunshine Band

Just the Way You Are

Looks Like We Made It

More Than a Woman

New Kid in Town RS 6 (tie) (1976) a. Eagles

Nobody Does It Better

Rich Girl RS 10 (tie) a. Daryl Hall and John Oates

Sir Duke

Slip Slidin' Away

Southern Nights RS 9 a. Glen Campbell

Star Wars Theme (Cantina Band) RS 10 (tie) a. Meco

Stayin' Alive RS 5 a. Bee Gees

(Love Is) Thicker Than Water RS 4 a. Andy Gibb

Tomorrow

Torn Between Two Lovers RS 6 (tie) (1976) a. Mary MacGregor

Undercover Angel RS 6 (tie) a. Alan O'Day

When I Need You RS 10 (tie) a. Leo Sayer

You Don't Have To Be a Star (To Be in My Show) RS 6 (tie) (1976) a. Marilyn McCoo and Billy Davis Junior

You Light Up My Life RS 6 (tie) a. Debby Boone

You Make Me Feel Like Dancing RS 6 (tie) a. Leo Sayer

Adaptations

Disco Lucy (based on the television theme from ''I Love Lucy'')

A Fifth of Beethoven, see 1976

Night on Disco Mountain (based on Mussorgsky's ''Night on Bald Mountain'' (1887))

Revivals

Da Doo Ron Ron (1963) RS 8 a. Shawn Cassidy

Some Enchanted Evening (1949)

Notable

Angel in Your Arms

Baby, What a Big Surprise

(Every Time I Turn Around) Back in Love Again

Blue Bayou

Boogie Nights

Brick House

(Theme from) Close Encounters of the Third Kind

Cold As Ice

Come Sail Away

Couldn't Get It Right

Dance, Dance, Dance (Yowsah, Yowsah, Yowsah)

Do You Wanna Make Love

Don't It Make My Brown Eyes Blue

Don't Stop

Easy

Easy Street

Emotion

Feels Like the First Time

Float On

Go Your Own Way

Handy Man

(It's) The Hard-Knock Life

Heaven on the Seventh Floor

Here You Come Again

Hey Deanie

Hey There, Good Times

(Your Love Has Lifted Me) Higher and Higher

I Feel Love

I Go Crazy

I Wanna Get Next to You

I'm in You

It's Ecstasy When You Lay Down Next to Me

It's So Easy

I've Got Love on My Mind

Jet Airliner

Just a Song Before I Go

Keep It Comin' Love

Little Girls

Lonely Boy

Lucille

Margaritaville

Maybe

Maybe I'm Amazed

Miss You Nights

My Heart Belongs to Me

(Theme from) New York, New York

N.Y.C.

On and On

Right Time of the Night

Save It for a Rainy Day

Save Your Kisses for Me

Sentimental Lady

Short People

Smoke from a Distant Fire

So Into You

Sometimes When We Touch

Star Wars (main title)

Strawberry Letter #23

Swayin' to the Music (Slow Dancin')

Telephone Line

That's Rock 'n' Roll

Theme from a Non-Existent TV Series
The Things We Do for Love
Thunder Island
Tryin' To Love Two
We Are the Champions
We Do It
We're All Alone
You and Me
You Made Me Believe in Magic
You Make Lovin' Fun
You're in My Heart (The Final Acclaim)

Stayin' Alive, see 1977
(Love Is) Thicker Than Water, see 1977
Three Times a Lady RS 7 (tie) a. Commodores
Too Much Heaven, see 1979
Too Much, Too Little, Too Late RS 8 (tie) a. Johnny Mathis, Deniece Williams
With a Little Luck RS 8 (tie) a. Wings
You Don't Bring Me Flowers RS 9 (tie) a. Neil Diamond, Barbra Streisand
You Needed Me RS 2 a. Anne Murray
You're the One That I Want RS 4 a. John Travolta, Olivia Newton-John

1978

Broadway Dances. Along with the popular disco dancing craze, New York theatre audiences have taken to both classical ballet and Broadway theatre dancing styles. This year sees Rudolf Nureyev performing at the Minskoff Theatre on 45th Street, Mikhail Baryshnikov at the Plymouth Theatre on the same block, Bob Fosse's *Dancin'* at the Broadhurst Theatre on 44th Street, the longrunning *A Chorus Line* next door at the Shubert Theatre, and the American Dance Machine at the Century Theatre.

More "Fats". Thomas "Fats" Waller's music returns to Broadway this year in a Tony Award-winning Broadway musical revue, *Ain't Misbehavin'*. He was last produced in 1943 with his production *Early to Bed*. Among his earlier successes were *Keep Shufflin'* (1928) and *Hot Chocolates* (1929).

More "Gone with the Wind". Columbia Broadcasting System (CBS) acquires, for twenty years, exclusive television rights to *Gone with the Wind* for a cost of thirty-five million dollars. This is the largest license fee ever paid for TV film rights.

Top Hits
Baby, Come Back, see 1977
Boogie Oogie Oogie RS 5 (tie) a. Taste of Honey
Do Ya Think I'm Sexy, see 1979
Le Freak, see 1979
Grease RS 6 (tie) a. Frankie Valli
Hot Child in the City RS 1 a. Nick Gilder
I Will Survive, see 1979
If I Can't Have You RS 6 (tie) a. Yvonne Elliman
Kiss You All Over RS 5 (tie) a. Exile
Last Dance
Miss You RS 7 (tie) a. Rolling Stones
Night Fever RS 7 (tie) a. Bee Gees
Shadow Dancing RS 3 a. Andy Gibb

Revivals
Come a Little Bit Closer (1964)
Got To Get You into My Life (1966)
MacArthur Park (1968) RS 7 (tie) a. Donna Summer
My Way (1969)
On Broadway (1963)
Um, Um, Um, Um, Um, Um (1964)

Notable
Baby, I'm Yours
Baker Street
Beast of Burden
Can't Smile Without You
The Closer I Get to You
Copacabana (At the Copa)
Count On Me (Love)
Dance with Me
Don't Cry Out Loud
Don't Look Back
(Our Love) Don't Throw It All Away
Double Vision
Dust in the Wind
Even Now
An Everlasting Love
Everyone's a Winner
Feels So Good
Fire
The Gambler
Get Off
The Groove Line
Heartbreaker
Hold the Line
Hopelessly Devoted to You
Hot Blooded
How Much I Feel
I Just Wanna Stop
I Love the Nightlife (Disco 'Round)

I Was Made for Dancin'
Imaginary Lover
It's a Heartache
Jack and Jill
Lay Down Sally
A Little More Love
Lotta Love
Love Is in the Air
Love Is Like Oxygen
Love Will Find a Way
Magnet and Steel
My Life
Native New Yorker
Ooh Baby Baby
Our Love
Promises
Ready To Take a Chance Again
Reminiscing
Shake Your Groove Thing
Shame
Sharing the Night Together
Somewhere in the Night
Still the Same
Summer Nights
Sweet Talkin' Woman
Take a Chance on Me
Talkin' in Your Sleep
A Terrific Band and a Real Nice Crowd
This Time I'm in It for Love
Time Passages
Two Doors Down
Use Ta Be My Girl
We'll Never Have To Say Goodbye Again
What You Won't Do for Love
Whenever I Call You "Friend"
Y.M.C.A.
You Belong to Me
You Never Done It Like That

1979

Papal and Presidential Recordings. Pope John Paul II is elected for membership in ASCAP, thus making the Pontiff eligible for performance royalties, after recording an album on the Crystal label featuring his original folksongs. Also, former President Richard M. Nixon receives a Grammy nomination for the LP of his television interviews with David Frost.

Fantasy Features. The craze for science fiction feature films expands to include a comic-strip adaptation to create *Superman*, a film serial adaptation to create *Buck Rogers*, a television adaptation to create *Star Trek*, and original spectacles including *The Alien* and *Battlestar Galactica*.

Top Hits
After the Love Has Gone
Babe RS 9 (tie) a. Styx
Bad Girls RS 8 (tie) a. Donna Summer
Da Ya Think I'm Sexy RS 7 (tie) a. Rod Stewart
Don't Stop 'Till You Get Enough RS 7 (tie) a. Michael Jackson
Enough Is Enough, see ''No More Tears''
Escape (The Piña Colada Song) RS 7 (tie) a. Rupert Holmes
Le Freak RS 3 (tie) a. Chic
Good Times RS 9 (tie) a. Chic
Heart of Glass RS 7 (tie) a. Blondie
Heartache Tonight RS 10 (tie) a. Eagles
Hot Stuff RS 7 (tie) a. Donna Summer
I Will Survive RS 1 (tie) a. Gloria Gaynor
It Goes Like It Goes
Knock On Wood RS 8 (tie) a. Amii Stewart
Love You Inside and Out RS 9 (tie) a. Bee Gees
My Sharona RS 6 a. Knack
No More Tears (Enough Is Enough) RS 10 (tie) a. Barbra Streisand/Donna Summer
The Piña Colada Song, see ''Escape''
Please Don't Go RS 2 a. K.C. & The Sunshine Band
Pop Muzik RS 4 a. M
Reunited RS 5 a. Peaches & Herb
Ring My Bell RS 7 (tie) a. Anita Ward
Rise RS 3 (tie) a. Herb Alpert
Sad Eyes RS 1 (tie) a. Robert John
Still RS 8 (tie) a. Commodores
Too Much Heaven RS 7 (tie) a. Bee Gees
Tragedy RS 8 (tie) a. Bee Gees
What a Fool Believes RS 8 (tie) a. Doobie Brothers
You Decorated My Life

Revivals
Can't Help Falling in Love (1961)
Easy To Be Hard (1969)
Heartbreak Hotel (1956)
If You Leave Me Now (1976)
Riders in the Sky (1949)

Notable
Ain't No Stoppin' Us Now
All I Ever Need Is You
Amanda

1979

Anyone Who Isn't Me Tonight
Baby I'm Burning
Back on My Mind Again
Big Shot
Burgers and Fries
Can You Fool— (You Just Can't Forget Her)
Can You Read My Mind
Chase (theme from *Midnight Express)*
Chuck E's in Love
Coca-Cola Cowboy (Theme from *Every Which Way But Loose)*
Crazy Love
Dance (Disco Heat)
Different Worlds
Disco Nights
Do It Or Die
Dog and Butterfly
Don't Bring Me Down
(Theme from) *Every Which Way But Loose,* see "Coca-Cola Cowboy"
Fool (If You Think It's Over)
Fooled by a Feeling
Forever in Blue Jeans
Get Used to It
Golden Tears
Good Timin'
Goodbye Stranger
Goodnight Tonight
Got To Be Real
Half the Way
Heart of the Night
Heaven Knows
Heaven Must Have Sent You
Home and Dry
Honesty
How You Gonna See Me Now
(If Loving You Is Wrong) I Don't Want To Be Right
I Just Fall In Love Again
I Know a Heartache When I See One
I Want You To Want Me
I Will Be in Love with You
If I Said You Had a Beautiful Body (Would You Hold It Against Me)
If You Remember Me
I'll Never Love This Way Again
I'm Every Woman
I'm Gonna Love You
It Must Be Love
I've Had a Lovely Time
Just for Tonight
Just When I Needed You Most

Keep On Dancin'
Lady
Lead Me On
A Little Bit of Soap
Logical Song
Love Ballad
Love Is the Answer
Love Takes Time
Main Event (The Fight)
Makin' It
Minute by Minute
No Tell Lover
Part-Time Lover
Power of Gold
Precious Love
Renegade
Riders in the Sky
Rubber Biscuit
Sail Away
Sail On
Sarava
Say Maybe
September
Shadows in the Moonlight
Shake It
Shake Your Body (Down to the Ground)
Shine a Little Love
Song on the Radio
Sultans of Swing
Suspicions
Sweet Life
Take Me Home
Theme from Ice Castles (Through the Eyes of Love)
They're Playing Our Song
This Is Love
This Night Won't Last Forever
Through the Eyes of Love, see "Theme from Ice Castles"
Took the Last Train
Tulsa Time
Tusk
We Are Family
We've Got Tonight
When I Dream
When You're in Love with a Beautiful Woman
While She Lays
Where Were You When I Was Falling in Love
Why Have You Left the One You Left Me For?
You Can't Change That
You Take My Breath Away
You're the Only One

1980

Strawberry Fields. The world mourns the senseless killing of Beatle John Lennon outside his home at The Dakota, in New York City, on December 8th. Mayor Koch renames the Central Park meadow seen from the Lennons' apartment "Strawberry Fields" and the city block where the assassination took place "Penny Lane." Mr. Lennon was 40 years old.

Abscam. Legislative corruption links 31 U.S. public officials to the surreptitious Abscam investigative operation conducted by the F.B.I. This leads to the first expulsion of a Congressman from the House of Representatives in the history of the U.S.

Around the World in Eighty Days. Six-time Oscar nominee Harold C. Adamson passes away this year. Among the hundreds of songs he wrote for 45 films and 12 Broadway shows, his hits include the lyrics for "Around the World in Eighty Days," "Time On My Hands," and "It's a Most Unusual Day."

Tumbling Tumbleweeds. Composer Bob Nolan, writer of over 1,000 western, country and gospel songs, including such classics as "Tumbling Trumbleweeds" and "Cool Water," dies of a heart attack at the age of 72 in Costa Mesa, California. The founder of the quartet Sons of the Pioneers, he earlier formed a trio in 1931 with Tim Spencer and a young cowboy singer named Leonard Slye, who later changed his name to Roy Rogers and left the group to make movies.

A Boy Named Sue. Sue K. Hicks, the man who inspired Johnny Cash's million-selling hit record in 1969, dies this year, at the age of 84, in his home in Tennessee. Mr. Hicks was an attorney and was named for his mother, who died while giving birth to him.

Top Hits
African Sanctus
All Out of Love
All the Gold in California
An American Dream
Another Brick in the Wall   RS 5   a. Pink Floyd
Another One Bites the Dust   RS 10   a. Queen
Biggest Part of Me
Blue Side
The Boxer
Brass in Pocket
Breakdown Dead Ahead
Bright Eyes
Call Me   RS 2   a. Blondie
Caravans

Cool Change
Could I Have This Dance
Coward of the Country
Crackers
Crazy Little Thing Calls Love   RS 6   a. Queen
Deja Vu
Desire
Do That to Me One More Time
Don't Do Me Like That
Dreamin'
Drivin' My Life Away
(Theme from) Dukes of Hazzard (Good Ol' Boys)
(Theme from) The Empire Strikes Back
Escape
Fame
Fire in the Morning
Forgive Me Girl
Funkytown   RS 9   a. Lipps, Inc.
Give It All You Got
Gone Too Far
Good Ol' Boys, see "Dukes of Hazzard"
Good Ole Boys Like Me
He was Beautiful
Heart of Mine
He's So Shy
Hold On To My Love
Hot Rod Hearts
I Believe In You
I Can't Help It
I Don't Like Mondays
I Wanna Be Your Lover
I'd Rather Leave While I'm in Love
If You Ever Change Your Mind
In America
It's Still Rock and Roll to Me
I've Loved You for a Long Time
Jane
Jo Jo
Just Like Starting Over, see "(Just Like) Starting Over"
Ladies Night
Late in the Evening
Let Me Love You Tonight
Let My Love Open the Door
The Logical Song
Look What You've Done to Me
Lost in Love
Magic   RS 8   a. Olivia Newton-John
More Than I Can Say
Music Machine
Never Knew Love Like This Before

No More Tears (Enough Is Enough)
No Night So Long
Nunc Dimittis
Off the Wall
On the Radio
On the Road Again
One in a Million You
Rock with You   RS 7   a. Michael Jackon
The Rose
Sailing
Sara
Secret Army
Sexy Eyes
She's Out of My Life
Shining Star
Shoestring
Should've Never Let You Go
Special Lady
Stand By Me
(Just Like) Starting Over   RS 3   a. John Lennon
Steal Away
Stomp
Take Your Time (Do It Right)
Taking Somebody with Me When I Fall
That Lovin' You Feelin' Again
Theme from *The Rose,* see "The Rose"
Theme from *Yanks,* see "(Theme from) Yanks"
Think About Me
Three Times in Love
Tired of Toein' the Line
Too Hot
Too Much Heaven
True Love Ways
Upside Down   RS 4   a. Diana Ross
The Valley of Swords
Video Killed the Radio Star
Wait For Me
War of the Worlds
We Don't Talk Much Anymore
We Were Meant To Be Loved
When I Wanted You
Why Don't You Spend the Night
Why Not Me
With You I'm Born Again
Woman in Love
Wondering Where the Lions Are
Workin' My Way Back to You
Xanadu
(Theme from) Yanks
Years

Yes, I'm Ready
You're the Only Woman

Revivals
Cupid (1976)
Daydream Believer (1967)
Help Me Make It Through the Night (1971)
Hurts So Bad (1969)
I'm Happy Just To Dance with You (1964)

Notable
Caddyshack, see "I'm Alright"
The Colors of My Life
Come Follow the Band
Come On Down
Coming Up—Live at Glasgow
Cruisin'
Don't Fall in Love with a Dreamer
Emotional Rescue
Give Me the Night
Hello Again
Hungry Heart
I Have a Noble Cock
I Like Your Style
I'm Alright, or, (Theme from) Caddyshack
Just Like That
Little Jeannie
Longer
Master Blaster (Jammin')
Ride Like the Wind
Theme from *Caddyshack,* see "I'm Alright"
The Wanderer

1981

Royal Marriage. England's Prince Charles weds Lady Diana Spencer on international television, capturing the romantic hearts of millions worldwide.

Terrorism. Political and personal terrorism makes top headlines as Egypt's President Anwar el-Sadat is gunned down by Moslem extremists, and U.S. President Ronald Reagan and Pope John II fall victim to assassination attempts.

Over the Rainbow. Premier lyricist E.Y. "Yip" Harburg passes away this year leaving a legacy of 50 years of immortal standards including, among other, the scores to *The Wizard of Oz* and *Finian's Rainbow.* Yip dies peacefully in Hollywood on March 5 at the age of 84. A champion of causes demanding economic justice, racial equality, and personal integrity, his top hits include

"Brother, Can You Spare a Dime," "It's Only a Paper Moon," and "Over the Rainbow."

Salvatore Guaranga. This year also suffers the loss of Harry Warren, one of America's most distinguished composers, at the age of 87. His actual name at birth was Salvatore Guaragna, and he enjoyed his 60-year career as Harry Warren, writer of songs for more than 50 film musicals and co-author of some 40 standards. Among his myriad hits are included "Forty-Second Street," "Lullaby of Broadway," "Jeepers Creepers," and "You Must Have Been a Beautiful Baby."

Broadway Revivals. Broadway musicals this year pay tribute to the past. David Merrick's *42nd Street* attempts to recapture the classic movie musical alongside the Marx Brothers tribute in *A Day in Hollywood—A Night in the Ukraine,* featuring songs by Richard Whiting. The Duke Ellington songbook is presented in the lavish revue *Sophisticated Ladies,* inspired by the success of the Fats Waller revue *Ain't Misbehavin'.* Mickey Rooney and Ann Miller bring back burlesque and the old standards in *Sugar Babies,* while Off-Broadway celebrates black vaudeville in *One Mo' Time.*

Rock Concert Rule Upheld. An Ohio law that bans non-reserved seating at rock concerts has been upheld by Judge Reno Riley, Jr., of Common Pleas Court. The law was passed after 11 persons were trampled to death before a concert in Cincinnati on December 3, 1979.

Top Hits

All Those Years Ago

Angel Flying Too Close to the Ground

Arthur's Theme (Best That You Can Do) RS 4   a. Christopher Cross

Babooshka

Believe It or Not, see "Greatest American Hero"

Best That You Can Do, see "Arthur's Theme"

Bette Davis Eyes RS 2   a. Kim Carnes

Blessed Are the Believers

Boy from New York City

But You Know I Love You

By Now

Can I See You Tonight

Celebration

Cool Love

Dixie on My Mind

Don't Stand So Close to Me

Don't Wait On Me

Drifter

Elvira

Endless Love RS 3   a. Diana Ross/Lionel Richie

Every Little Thing She Does Is Magic

Every Woman in the World

Falling Again

Fancy Free

Feels So Right

Flash

For Your Eyes Only

Fox

Games People Play

Giving It Up for Your Love

Goodbye Marie

(Theme from) Greatest American Hero (Believe It or Not)

Guilty

Guitar Man

A Headache Tomorrow (Or a Heartache Tonight)

Hearts

Her Town Too

Here I Am (Just When I Thought I Was Over You)

Hooked on Music

How 'Bout Us

I Can't Stand It

I Could Be So Good for You

I Could Never Miss You (More Than I Do)

I Don't Need You

I Love a Rainy Night RS 7   a. Eddie Rabbitt

I Loved 'Em Everyone

I Made It Through the Rain

I Think I'll Just Stay Here and Drink

I Was Country When Country Wasn't Cool

I Wouldn't Have Missed It for the World

(I'm Just an Old Chunk of Coal But) I'll Be a Diamond Someday

I'm in the Mood for Dancing

I'm Just an Old Chunk of Coal But I'll Be a Diamond Someday, see "I'll Be a Diamond Someday"

Is It You

It's My Turn

January, February

Jessie's Girl RS 6   a. Rick Springfield

Just Once

Just the Two of Us

Kiss on My List RS 5   a. Daryl Hall/John Oates

Little in Love

Living in a Fantasy

Living Inside Myself

Loving Her Was Easier (Than Anything I'll Ever Do Again)

Miracles

Modern Girl

My Baby Thinks He's a Train

Never Been So Loved in All My Life

Night Owls
9 to 5
Older Women
The One That You Love
Party Time
Physical RS 1 a. Olivia Newton-John
Prisoner of Hope
Private Eyes RS 9 a. Daryl Hall/John Oates
(Theme from) Raiders of the Lost Ark
Rainbow Stew
Rapture RS 10 a. Blondie
Seven Bridges Road
Seven Year Ache
Share Your Love with Me
Silver Dream Machine
Sleepin' with the Radio On
Slow Hand
Smoky Mountain Rain
Some Days Are Diamonds (Some Days Are Stone)
Southern Rains
Step By Step
Still Right Here in My Heart
Stop the Cavalry
Suddenly
Surround Me with Love
Take That Look Off Your Face
Takin' It Easy
Texas in My Rear View Mirror
Texas Women
That's All That Matters
Theme from *Arthur*, see ''Arthur's Theme''
Theme from *Greatest American Hero*, see ''Greatest American Hero''
Theme from *Raiders of the Lost Ark*, see ''(Theme from) Raiders of the Lost Ark''
There's No One Quite Like Grandma
Time
Together We Are Beautiful
Too Many Lovers
Touch Me When We're Dancing
Watching the Wheels
We're in This Love Together
What Kind of Fool
What You're Proposing
While You See a Chance
Who's Cheatin' Who
Why Lady Why
Wish You Were Here
Woman
You Don't Know Me

You Make My Dreams
You're the Reason God Made Oklahoma

Adaptations
Juliet Bravo (based on themes by Johann Sebastian Bach)
The Same Old Auld Lang Syne (inspired by the song of 1711)

Revivals
Cryin' (1961)
(You've Got To Have) Heart (1955)
Memphis (1959)
Mister Sandman (1954)
Sukiyaki (1963)
Tell It Like It Is (1966)
Why Do Fools Fall in Love (1956)

Notable
Angel of the Morning
Beautiful Boy
Being with You
The Best of Times
Could I Have This Dance
Good Thing Going
The Grass Is Always Greener
Keep On Loving You
Let's Groove
Love on the Rocks
Merrily We Roll Along
Morning Train (Nine to Five)
(There's) No Gettin' Over Me
Not a Day Goes By
Oh No
Old Friends
One by One
Queen of Hearts
The Same Old Auld Lang Syne
Start Me Up
Start Draggin' My Heart Around
There's No Gettin' Over Me, see ''(There's) No Gettin' Over Me''
The Tide Is High
Urgent
Waiting For a Girl Like You
Who's Crying Now
A Woman Needs Love (Just Like You do)

1982

Ban the Bomb. The worldwide anti-nuclear movement rallies together June 12 for World Peace Day, as over

750,000 demonstrators march in New York City's Central Park, as do millions more in cities throughout the world.

No Equal Rights. Despite their efforts to keep the pressure on until the very end, supporters of the Equal Rights Amendment finally admit defeat when they lose several vital key votes before the ratification deadline.

Financial Foreshadows. The New York Stock Exchange suffers its biggest one-day loss since the crash of 1929.

Juvenile Musical Acts. This year's latest phenomenon credits the juvenile market, as represented by the international Spanish and Latin American groups ''El Group Menudo'' and ''Parchis.'' The English group ''Mini-Pops'' LP sells 400,000 units in the U.S. in only the first six weeks of sale. Overseas, the LP sells over 500,000 copies. Their hit single, a remake of Connie Francis's 1958 hit ''Stupid Cupid'' by 12-year-old Mini-Pop thrush Joanna Wyatt, generates sales passing the 1 million mark.

Lehman Engel. Broadway's favorite orchestra conductor, Lehman Engel, dies this year at 71. Lehman was musical director for *Showboat, Brigadoon, Annie Get Your Gun,* and *Guys and Dolls,* among many other productions. In addition to winning two Tony Awards for conducting, he composed incidental music for T.S. Eliot's *Murder in the Cathedral* and Tennessee Williams's *A Streetcar Named Desire.* In the 1930's he wrote music for the Martha Graham Dance Company and conducted the first American performance of Kurt Weill's *The Threepenny Opera.*

Headphone Hazards. The Institute of Environmental Health warns consumers of the potential dangers of stereo headphones: ''Their high sensitivity raises their potential for hearing damage above that of all other sources.''

Top Hits
Abracadabra RS 9 a. Steve Miller Band
All My Rowdy Friends Have Settled Down
All Roads Lead to You
Always on My Mind
American Music
Another Honkey Tonk Night on Broadway
Are the Good Times Really Over
Big City
Blaze of Glory
Blue Moon with Heartache
Bobbie Sue
Born To Run
(Theme from) Brideshead Revisited
Castles in the Air

(Theme from) Chariots of Fire
Close Enough to Perfect
Centerfold RS 4 a. J. Geils Band
The Clown
Cool Night
A Country Boy Can Survive
Dancin' Your Memory Away
Did It in a Minute
Do You Believe in Love
Don't Stop Believin'
Don't Talk to Strangers
Don't Worry 'Bout Me Baby
Don't You Want Me RS 7 a. Human League
Ebony and Ivory RS 2 a. Paul McCartney/Stevie Wonder
(Theme from) E.T. The Extra-Terrestrial
Even the Nights Are Better
Eye in the Sky
Eye of the Tiger RS 3 a. Survivor
(Theme from) Flame Trees of Thika
Fourteen Carat Mind
(Theme from) The French Lieutenant's Woman
The Girl Is Mine
Gypsy
Hard To Say I'm Sorry RS 10 a. Chicago
He Got You
Headed for Heartache
Heartbreak Express
Heartbreaker
Hold Me
Honky Tonkin'
I Can't Go For That (No Can Do)
I Don't Care
I Don't Know Where To Start
I Don't Think She's in Love Anymore
I Just Came Here to Dance
I Love Rock 'N Roll RS 1 a. Joan Jett & The Blackhearts
I Will Always Love You
I Wish You Could Have Turned My Head
I'm Gonna Hire a Wino To Decorate Our Home
In the Air Tonight
It's Gonna Take a Miracle
I've Never Been to Me
Jack and Diane RS 6 a. John Cougar Mellencamp
Just Another Day in Paradise
Just To Satisfy You
Kansas City Lights
Key Largo
The Land of Make Believe
Leather and Lace
Listen to the Radio

Lonely Nights
Love in the First Degree
Love Me Tomorrow
A Love Song
Love Will Turn You Around
Love's Found You and Me
Make a Move on Me
Making Love
Man on Your Mind
Maneater   RS 5   a. Daryl Hall/John Oates
Memory
Mountain Music
Mountain of Love
No Can Do, see "I Can't Go For That"
Nobody
On the Way to the Sky
One Hundred Ways
Only One You
Open Arms
Personally
Red Neckin' Love Makin' Night
Rosanna
Same Ole Me
She Got the Goldmine I Got the Shaft
Shillingbury Tales
Shine
Should I Do It
65 Love Affair
Some Memories Just Won't Quit
Someone Could Lose a Heart Tonight
Somewhere Down the Road
Stand and Deliver
Still Doin' Time
Sweet Dreams
Take It Easy On Me
Take Me Down
Theme from *Brideshead Revisited,* see "(Theme from) Brideshead Revisited"
Theme from *Chariots of Fire,* see "(Theme from) Chariots of Fire"
Theme from *E.T. The Extra-Terrestrial,* see "(Theme from) E.T. The Extra-Terrestrial"
Theme from *Flame Trees of Thika,* see "(Theme from) Flame Trees of Thika"
Theme from *The French Lieutenant's Woman,* see "(Theme from) The French Lieutenant's Woman"
Through the Years
Trouble
Turn Your Love Around
Up Where We Belong   RS 8   a. Joe Cocker/Jennifer Warnes
Vienna

Watchin' Girls Go By
What Are We Doing Lonesome
What's Forever For
When All Is Said and Done
When He Shines
Who Can It Be Now?
Wired For Sound
Without Your Love
Woman In Love
Women Do Know How to Carry On
Would You Catch a Falling Star
Years Ago
You Could Have Been with Me
You Drive Me Crazy
You Never Gave Up On Me
You Should Hear How She Talks About You
You'll Be Back Every Night in My Dreams
You're the Best Break This Old Heart Ever Had

Revivals
Daddy's Home (1961)
(Sittin' on) The Dock of the Bay (1968)
Hey Baby (1962)
Let's Hang On (1965)
Oh Girl (1972)
Wake Up Little Susie (1957)

Notable
And I Am Telling You I'm Not Going
Cadillac Car
Dreams Girls
867-5309/Jenny
Freeze-Frame
The Germans at the Spa
Gloria
Grizabella the Glamour Cat
Harden My Heart
Heart Attack
Heartlight
Heat of the Moment
Hurt So Good
I Keep Forgettin' (Every Time You're Near)
Let It Whip
Mickey
Mister Mistoffolees
My Husband Makes Movies
Nine
One More Angel in Heaven
One Night Only
Only with You

The Other Woman
Shake It Up
Simple
That Girl
Unusual Way
We Got the Beat
When I First Saw You

1983

Women in Space. Ms. Sally Ride joins the members of the crew of the space shuttle *Challenger,* thus becoming America's first woman astronaut.

Ragtime's Last. Just five days after celebrating his 100th birthday, beloved ragtime composer and pianist Eubie Blake passes away on February 12 in Brooklyn, New York. Among many others, Eubie's top hits include "Bugle Call Rag," "You Were Meant for Me," and "I'm Just Wild About Harry."

PTA Censorship. With all good intent to protect children and young adults from being exposed to record albums containing lyrics relating to sex, violence, and substance abuse, the National Parent Teachers Association in conjunction with the Parents Music Resource Center releases their good-guys/bad-guys list of principal offenders. The report criticizes some companies for using a warning disclaimer as a marketing tool or joke, as in Poison's "unanimously censored and disapproved of by parents everywhere," or Sigue Sigue Sputnik's "Warning—Do Not Play If Accompanied by an Adult."

More Helter Skelter. A Cleveland-based Hell's Angel informs a federal Senate Judiciary Panel that the California Chapter has had a contract out on Mick Jagger since the 1969 Stones' Altamont concert, in which a biker was jailed for stabbing a spectator to death.

Top Hits
Africa
All Night Long (All Night)   RS 5   a. Lionel Richie
All Right
All This Love
All Through the Night
American Made
Baby, Come to Me   RS 10   a. Patti Austin/James Ingram
Beat It   RS 8   a. Michael Jackson
Break It to Me Gently
Come on Eileen
Do You Really Want to Hurt Me
Down Under   RS 7   a. Men At Work
The Dreaming

Every Breath You Take   RS 1   a. Police
(Theme from) Flashdance (What a Feeling)   RS 3   a. Irene Cara
For All Mankind (Theme from *Gandhi*)
Golden Brown
(Theme from) Harry's Game
Have You Ever Been in Love
Heart of the Night
Heart to Heart
I Don't Wanna Dance
I.O.U.
I Won't Hold You Back
Igy (What a Beautiful World)
An Innocent Man
Inside
Islands in the Stream   RS 9   a. Kenny Rogers/Dolly Parton
It Might Be You
It's a Mistake
It's Raining Again
I've Got a Rock 'n' Roll Heart
Jose Cuervo
Let's Dance
Love Plus One
Make Love Stay
Maniac
My Love
Now Those Days Are Gone
Oh Julie
Omnibus
On the Wings of Love
One You Love
Our House
Our Love Is on the Fault Line
Private Investigations
The Safety Dance
Say It Isn't So
Say Say Say   RS 4.   a. Michael Jackson/Paul McCartney
Separate Ways
Smiley's People
Somebody's Baby
Sounds Like Love
Southern Cross
Steppin' Out
Stranger in My House
Sweet Dreams (Are Made of This)
Theme from *Gandhi*, see "For All Mankind"
Theme from *Harry's Game,* see "Harry's Game"
Theme from *Plague Dogs,* see "Time and Tide"
Time (Clock of the Heart)
Time and Tide (Theme from *Plague Dogs*)

Total Eclipse of the Heart   RS 6   a. Bonnie Tyler
We've Got Tonight
You and I
You Can Do Magic

Revivals
Arthur's Theme (Best That You Can Do) (1981)
Puttin' On the Ritz (1929)
Save the Last Dance for Me (1960)
Sea of Love (1954)
Stop! in the Name of Love (1965)

Notable
Baby Baby Baby
The Best of Times
Cuddle In
Dirty Laundry
Electric Avenue
Hangin' Out the Window
Hungry Like the Wolf
I Am What I Am
I Want It All
Jeopardy
Life Is
Little Shop of Horrors
Making Love Out of Nothing At All
Mr. Roboto
Never Gonna Let You Go
Overkill
Romance
Sexual Healing
Shame On the Moon
She Works Hard for the Money
Somewhere That's Green
The Story Goes On
Stray Cat Strut
Suddenly Seymour
Tell Her About It
The Top of the Hill
Truly
Union of the Snake
Uptown Girl
Why Can't I Speak
You Are

1984

Olympic Terrorism. The Soviet Union and most of the East European nations pull their athletes out of the Sum-

mer Olympics, assailing the planned security precautions in Los Angeles.

Top Hits
(Theme from) Against All Odds (Take a Look at Me Now)
    RS 6   a. Phil Collins
Alibis
All of You
All Time High
Almost Over You
Almost Paradise
Automatic
B B B Burnin' Up with Love
Baby I Lied
Borderline
Break My Stride
Brown Eyed Girl
Caribbean Queen (No More Love on the Run)
Church of the Poison Mind
City of New Orleans
Dancing in the Dark
Disenchanted
Don't Answer Me
Don't Count the Rainy Days
Eyes That See in the Dark
Footloose   RS 4   a. Kenny Loggins
Ghostbusters   RS 8   a. Ray Parker Jr.
God Bless the USA
Going Home
Got a Hold on Me
Heart and Soul
Heart of Rock and Roll
Hello
Human Nature
I Can Dream About You
I Don't Want To Lose Your Love
I Feel For You
I Guess It Never Hurts To Hurt Sometimes
I Guess That's Why They Call It the Blues
I Just Called To Say I Love You   RS 7   a. Stevie Wonder
I Still Can't Get Over Loving You
I Still Do
I Want a New Drug
If Anyone Falls
If Ever You're in My Arms Again
If This Is It
I'm So Excited
It's a Miracle
Jump   RS 3   a. Van Halen
Just Another Woman in Love

THE GREATEST SONGS

Karma Chameleon RS 9 a. Culture Club
King of Pain
Lady Love Me One More Time
The Language of Love
Leave a Tender Moment Alone
Let the Music Play
Let's Hear It for the Boy
Like a Virgin RS 1 a. Madonna
A Little Good News
The Longest Time
Love Is a Battlefield
Love Somebody
Make My Day
Miss Me Blind
Missing You (Fogelberg)
Missing You (Waite, Sanford, Leonard)
No More Love on the Run, see "Caribbean Queen"
Nobody Love Me Like You Do
Nobody Told Me
Nothing Like Falling in Love
One Thing Leads to Another
Out of Touch
Owner of a Lonely Heart
Prime Time
P.Y.T. (Pretty Young Thing)
Pretty Young Thing, see "P.Y.T."
Read 'Em and Weep
The Reflex
Roll On Eighteen Wheeler
Running with the Night
Sad Songs (Say So Much)
Sister Christian
The Sound of Goodbye
Stand Back
Take a Look at Me Now, see "Against All Odds"
Telefone
That's All
That's Livin' Alright
Theme from *Against All Odds*, see "Against All Odds"
They Don't Know
Think of Laura
This Woman
Three Times a Lady
Time After Time
Time Will Reveal
To All the Girls I've Loved Before
Tonight I Celebrate My Love
Twist of Fate
Wake Me Up Before You Go-Go RS 10 a. Wham!
Wanna Be Startin' Somethin'

What About Me
What's Love Got To Do with It RS 5. a. Tina Turner
When Doves Cry RS 2 a. Prince
When We Make Love
Wrapped Around Your Finger
Yah Mo B There
You Can't Get What You Want (Till You Know What You Want)
You Might Think

Revivals
Save the Last Dance for Me (1960)
Sea of Love (1959)

Notable
All I Need
Children and Art
Dancing Is Everything
Drive
Everybody Loves Louis
Eyes Without a Face
Fabulous Feet
Finishing the Hat
Girls Just Want To Have Fun
Hard Habit To Break
Here Comes the Rain Again
Hold Me Now
I Remember How It Was
Joanna
Jump (For My Love)
Let's Go Crazy
Man in the Moon
Move On
99 Luftballons
Oh Sherrie
Purple Rain
Putting It Together
Self Control
She Bop
Somebody's Watching Me
Stuck On You
Sunday
Talking in Your Sleep
Thriller
Under the Roller Coaster
Wallflower
We Do Not Belong Together
The Wild Boys
William's Song

1985

Live Aid. A 17-hour "Live Aid" rock concert is broadcast on simultaneous worldwide radio and television, in response to the plight of the starving people of Africa. Some of the biggest names in the recording industry help to raise $70 million for this worthy cause. See "We Are the World."

Rock Hudson. Actor Rock Hudson becomes the first major celebrity to die of AIDS, bringing home to millions of Americans concern and urgency over the deadly disease feared to develop globally in epidemic proportions.

Top Hits
After All
Along Comes a Woman
Better Be Good to Me
Born in the U.S.A.
Boys of Summer
Breakdance
Broken Wings   RS 7   a. Mr. Mister
Can't Fight This Feeling   RS 4   a. REO Speedwagon
Careless Whisper   RS 3   a. Wham!/George Michael
Cool It Now
Crazy
Crazy for You
Dance Hall Days
Desert Moon
Do They Know It's Christmas?
Do What You Do
Don't Call It Love
Don't You (Forget About Me)
Everybody Wants To Rule the World   RS 10   a. Tears For Fears
Everything She Wants
Everytime You Go Away
Foolish Heart
Forever
Freeway of Love
Fresh
Getcha Back
Glory Days
(It's Hard To) Go Down Easy
Heaven
High On You
Highwayman
Hold Me
I Don't Know Why You Don't Want Me
I Don't Think I'm Ready for You

I Wanna Hear It from Your Lips
I Want To Know What Love Is   RS 8   a. Foreigner
If You Love Somebody Set Them Free
I'm on Fire
Into the Groove
It's Hard To Go Down Easy, see "Go Down Easy"
(Theme from) Jewel in the Crown
Just As I Am
Keeping the Faith
Legs
Lost in the Fifties Tonight (In the Still of the Night)
Love Light in Flight
Love Theme from *White Nights,* see "Separate Lives"
The Lucky One
Lucky Star
Man in Motion, see "St. Elmo's Fire"
Method of Modern Love
Misled
Missing You
Money for Nothing   RS 5   a. Dire Straits
Mystery Lady
Neutron Dance
Never Surrender
Nightshift (Orange)
Nightshift (Goldie, Lambert)
No More Lonely Nights
On the Dark Side
One More Night
Penny Lover
The Power of Love   RS 9   a. Huey Lewis & The News
Real Love
Run to You
Say You, Say Me   RS 1   a. Lionel Richie
Search Is Over
Second Wind, see "You're Only Human"
Separate Lives (Love Theme from *White Nights*)
Shout   RS 6   a. Tears for Fears
Smooth Operator
Solid
Some Guys Have All the Luck
St. Elmo's Fire (Man in Motion)
State of Shock
Strut
Suddenly
Sussudio
Tell Me I'm Not Dreaming
Theme from *Jewel in the Crown,* see "Jewel in the Crown"
Things Can Only Get Better
Time Don't Run Out on Me
Too Late for Goodbyes

Turn Around
Two Tribes
Valotte
A View to a Kill
Walking on Sunshine
The Warrior
We All Stand Together
We Are the World   RS 2   a. USA for Africa
We Belong
We Built This City
What She Wants
Who's Holding Donna Now
You Give Good Love
You're Only Human (Second Wind)

Revivals
All I Need (1983)
California Girls (1965)
Out of Touch (1983)
Sea of Love (1959)
There Goes My Baby (1959)

Notable
Alive and Kicking
Axel F
Capped Teeth and Caesar Salad
Cherish
Easy Lover
Hand for the Hog
The Heat Is On
How Blest We Are
Just a Piece of Sky
Loverboy
Material Girl
(Theme from) Miami Vice
Miss Celie's Blues (Sister)
Muddy Water
New Attitude
Oh Sheila
Part Time Lover
Party All the Time
Raspberry Beret
Rhythm of the Night
Saving All My Love for You
Surprise, Surprise
Take On Me
Theme from Miami Vice, see "(Theme from) Miami Vice"
Theme from *Thunderdome,* see "We Don't Need Another Hero"
Thunderdome, see "We Don't Need Another Hero"

Unexpected Song
We Don't Need Another Hero
You Belong to the City
You're the Inspiration

1986

Nuclear Accident. Soviet authorities wait 3 days before reporting a major nuclear power plant accident at Chernobyl. The resultant cloud of radiation causes an evacuation of some 40,000 persons who live near the plant in the Ukraine, although the Soviet Union acknowledges only 23 deaths directly caused by the accident.

Space Tragedy. Only moments after liftoff, U.S. space shuttle *Challenger* explodes, killing 6 astronauts and Christa McAuliffe, a New Hampshire schoolteacher. Subsequent investigations found that NASA was aware of safety problems that caused the explosion, but was encouraged to continue with the launch in order to maintain an unrealistic, but required, schedule by the Department of Defense.

Top Hits
Addicted to Love   RS 8   a. Robert Palmer
Bad Boy
Be Near Me
Bop
Born to Each Other, see "Friends and Lovers"
Born Yesterday
Burning Heart
Crush on You
Cry
Dancing on the Ceiling
Dress You Up
Edge of Darkness
Everyday
Fortress Around Your Heart
Friends and Lovers (Born to Each Other)
Glory of Love (Theme from *The Karate Kid Part II*)
Go Home
Graceland
Grandpa (Tell Me 'Bout the Good Old Days)
Greatest Love of All   RS 3   a. Whitney Houston
Head Over Heels
Higher Love
Hold On
Holding Back the Years
How Will I Know   RS 7   a. Whitney Houston
Hurts To Be in Love
I Know Him So Well

140

If the Phone Doesn't Ring, It's Me
Invisible Touch
Janet
King for a Day
Kiss   RS 6   a. Prince & The Revolution
Kyrie   RS 5   a. Mr. Mister
Lay Your Hands on Me
Life in a Northern Town
Life in One Day
Live To Tell
Love Parade
Love Theme from St. Elmo's Fire
Love Touch (Theme from *Legal Eagles*)
Mad About You
Manic Monday
Modern Woman
Morning Desire
Move Away
My Toot Toot
Never
Nikita
19
Nothin' At All
Now and Forever (You and Me)
On My Own   RS 2   a. Patti LaBelle/Michael McDonald
Only One
(Theme from) Out of Africa
Papa Don't Preach
Possession Obsession
R.O.C.K. in the U.S.A. (A Salute to 60's Rock)
Rock Me Amadeus   RS 4   a. Falco
Sara
Secret Lovers
Sledgehammer
Small Town
Something About You
Stand By Me
Stuck with You
Summer of '69
Sweet Freedom
Sweet Love
Take My Breath Away
Tender Love
That's What Friends Are For   RS 1   a. Dionne Warwick & Friends
Theme from *The Karate Kid Part II*, see "Glory of Love"
Theme from *Legal Eagles*, see "Love Touch"

Theme from *Out of Africa*, see "(Theme from) Out of Africa"
There'll Be Sad Songs (To Make You Cry)   RS 10   a. Billy Ocean
These Dreams
West End Girls   RS 9   a. Pet Shop Boys
What About Love?
When the Going Gets Tough, the Tough Get Going
Who's Zoomin' Who
The Woo Woo Song, see "You Should Be Mine"
World Gets in the Way
A World Without Love
You Are My Lady
You Should Be Mine (The Woo Woo Song)
Your Secret's Safe with Me
Your Wildest Dreams
You're a Friend of Mine

Revivals
Ain't Misbehavin' (1929)
Happy, Happy Birthday, Baby (1956)
Somewhere (1957)

Notable
All I Need Is a Miracle
Harlem Shuffle
I Can't Wait
If You Leave
I'm Your Man
Let's Go All the Way
Life in a Looking Glass
Living in America
My Hometown
No One Is To Blame
Silent Running (On Dangerous Ground)
Somewhere Out There
The Sweetest Taboo
Take Me Home
Talk to Me
Theme from *Short Circuit*, see "Who's Johnny"
Tonight She Comes
Walk of Life
What Have You Done for Me Lately
What You Need
Who's Johnny ("Short Circuit" Theme)
Why Can't This Be Love
Your Love

II

The Award Winners

It is the best of all trades to make songs,
and the second best to sing them.

Hilaire Belloc

In this Part are listings of the major song Awards, American and British, from the film, theatre, and recording industries. Only those specific awards related to popular song and in agreement with the requirements for inclusion in Part V (see Authors' Notes) are entered here. All song titles in this Part may be found in Part V.

Listings are per annum and divisible by head-ings for Film, Theatre, and Recording. Thus, the Grammy Awards (for recording) will be found under each division as the award applies (e.g. "original score" (for FILM); "original cast album" (for THEATRE); "record," "album," "R&B song," and "C&W (country) song" (for RECORDING)). This is designed so that the reader can fully appreciate award trends within each industry.

AMERICAN AWARDS

The *Academy Award* of the Academy of Motion Picture Arts and Sciences is given annually for recognition of excellence in some twenty categories of motion picture achievement. Only films released in Los Angeles are eligible, although special honors are frequently awarded for outstanding contributions or services to cinema. There are five Oscar nominations per category selected by Academy members of that field, while the Board of Governors elects special honors. Full membership votes by secret ballot elect the Award. What began in 1928 as a small dinner for 250 persons is now a nationally telecast spectacle with an estimated viewing audience of more than 150 million.

The *Antoinette Perry Award* of the American Theatre Wing began in 1947. The Tony honors distinguished achievement in American theatre. Frequently multiple Tony Awards are granted in individual categories, and today upwards of 550 people involved in the theatre vote on various categories. Originally the Tony was an engraved compact for the female winner and a cigarette lighter for the male, while today the medallion, designed by Herman Rosse, is presented annually on nationwide television from one of forty-one eligible Broadway theatres. Since 1965 this award has been sponsored by the League of New York Theatres and Producers.

The *Grammy Award* of the National Academy of Recording Arts and Sciences is presented annually on nationwide television to recognize outstanding creativity in artistic and technical areas of recording. First presented in 1958, nominations are selected by recommendations from Academy members and recording companies. Five finalists in each category are selected by special committees, local governors, and national trusts of the Academy. Members may vote only in their area of expertise.

The *New York Drama Critics Circle Award* began in 1936 and was first awarded to the musical theatre in 1946. The top award of $1000 cash prize is selected by members of the Circle in the category of best play of the year, best American and/or foreign play, and best musical. Scrolls are presented to other honored playwrights.

The *Obie Award* for Off-Broadway and Off-Off-Broadway productions was initiated for Off-Broadway in the 1955–1956 season by the New York City publication *The Village Voice*. It was extended to O.O.B. productions in 1964, and first awarded to a musical production in 1963. On occasion a monetary prize is awarded with the Obie plaque of citation.

The *Pulitzer Prize* of the Columbia University Graduate School of Journalism was endowed by the will of publisher Joseph Pulitzer of the *St. Louis Post-Dispatch* and was first awarded in 1918. The Pulitzer is a $1000 cash award and winners are selected by the fifteen-member advisory board. This prize has thus far been awarded to the Broadway musical theatre for the years 1932, 1950, 1960, 1962, and 1976.

1932

THEATRE

PULITZER. **Of Thee I Sing,** b. George S. Kaufman, Morris Ryskind, w. Ira Gershwin, m. George Gershwin (George Gershwin's score was not included in the award)

1933

NO MUSICAL AWARDS

1934

FILM

OSCAR. (Song) **The Continental,** w. Herb Magidson, m. Con Conrad, from *The Gay Divorcée*
(Scoring) **One Night of Love,** Louis Silvers

1935

FILM

OSCAR. (Song) **Lullaby of Broadway,** w. Al Dubin, m. Harry Warren, from *Gold Diggers of 1935*
(Scoring) **The Informer,** Max Steiner

1936

FILM

OSCAR. (Song) **The Way You Look Tonight,** w. Dorothy Fields, m. Jerome Kern, from *Swingtime*
(Scoring) **Anthony Adverse,** Leo Forbstein

1937

FILM

OSCAR. (Song) **Sweet Leilani,** w.m. Harry Owens, from *Waikiki Wedding*
(Scoring) **A Hundred Men and a Girl,** Charles Previn

1938

FILM

OSCAR. (Song) **Thanks for the Memory,** w. Leo Robin, m. Ralph Rainger, from *The Big Broadcast of 1938*
(Scoring) **Alexander's Ragtime Band,** Alfred Newman
(Original score) **The Adventures of Robin Hood,** Eric Wolfgang Korngold

1939

FILM

OSCAR. (Song) **Over the Rainbow,** w. E.Y. Harburg, m. Harold Arlen, from *The Wizard of Oz*
(Scoring) **Stagecoach,** Richard Hageman, Frank Harling, John Leipold, Leo Shuken
(Scoring—Original score) **The Wizard of Oz,** Herbert Stothart

1940

FILM

OSCAR. (Song) **When You Wish Upon a Star,** w. Ned Washington, m. Leigh Harline, from *Pinocchio*
(Scoring) **Tin Pan Alley,** Alfred Newman
(Original score) **Pinocchio,** Leigh Harline, Paul J. Smith, Ned Washington

1941

FILM

OSCAR. (Song) **The Last Time I Saw Paris,** w. Oscar Hammerstein II, m. Jerome Kern, from *Lady Be Good*
(Scoring—musical) **Dumbo,** Frank Churchill, Oliver Wallace
(Scoring—drama) **All That Money Can Buy,** Bernard Hermann

1942

FILM

OSCAR. (Song) **White Christmas,** w.m. Irving Berlin, from *Holiday Inn*
(Scoring—musical) **Yankee Doodle Dandy,** Ray Heindorf, Heinz Roemheld
(Scoring—drama) **Now Voyager,** Max Steiner

1943

FILM

OSCAR. (Song) **You'll Never Know,** w. Mack Gordon, m. Harry Warren, from *Hello Frisco, Hello*
(Scoring—musical) **This Is the Army,** Ray Heindorf
(Scoring—drama) **The Song of Bernadette,** Alfred Newman

1944

FILM

OSCAR. (Song) **Swinging on a Star,** w. Johnny Burke, m. Jimmy Van Heusen, from *Going My Way*
(Scoring—musical) **Cover Girl,** Morris Stoloff, Carmen Dragon
(Scoring—drama) **Since You Went Away,** Max Steiner

1945

FILM

OSCAR. (Song) **It Might As Well Be Spring,** w. Oscar Hammerstein II, m. Richard Rodgers, from *State Fair*
(Scoring—musical) **Anchors Aweigh,** Georgie Stoll
(Scoring—drama) **Spellbound,** Miklos Rozsa

1946

FILM

OSCAR. (Song) **On the Atchison, Topeka and the Santa Fe,** w. Johnny Mercer, m. Harry Warren, from *The Harvey Girls*
(Scoring—musical) **The Jolson Story,** Morris Stoloff
(Scoring—drama) **The Best Years of Our Lives,** Hugo Friedhofer

THEATRE

N.Y. DRAMA CRITICS. **Carousel,** b. Oscar Hammerstein II, from the play *Liliom* by Ferenc Molnár, adapted by Benjamin F. Glazer, w. Oscar Hammerstein II, m. Richard Rodgers

1947

FILM

OSCAR. (Song) **Zip-A-Dee-Doo-Dah,** w. Ray Gilbert, m. Allie Wrubel, from *Song of the South*
(Scoring—musical) **Mother Wore Tights,** Alfred Newman
(Scoring—drama) **A Double Life,** Miklos Rozsa

THEATRE

N.Y. DRAMA CRITICS. **Brigadoon,** b. Alan Jay Lerner, w. Alan Jay Lerner, m. Frederick Loewe

1948

FILM

OSCAR. (Song) **Buttons and Bows,** w. Ray Evans, m. Jay Livingston, from *Paleface*
(Scoring—musical) **Easter Parade,** Johnny Green, Roger Edens
(Scoring—drama) **The Red Shoes,** Brian Easdale

THEATRE

N.Y. DRAMA CRITICS. No musical award

1949

FILM

OSCAR. (Song) **Baby, It's Cold Outside,** w.m. Frank Loesser, from *Neptune's Daughter*
(Scoring—musical) *On the Town,* Roger Edens, Lennie Hayton
(Scoring—drama) **The Heiress,** Aaron Copland

THEATRE

TONY. **Kiss Me, Kate,** b. Bella and Samuel Spewack, adapted from Shakespeare's *Taming of the Shrew,* w.m. Cole Porter
N.Y. DRAMA CRITICS. **South Pacific,** b. Oscar Hammerstein II, Joshua Logan, w. Oscar Hammerstein II, m. Richard Rodgers

1950

FILM

OSCAR. (Song) **Mona Lisa,** w. Ray Evans, m. Jay Livingston, from *Captain Carey, U.S.A.*
(Scoring—musical) **Annie Get Your Gun,** Adolph Deutsch, Roger Edens
(Scoring—drama) **Sunset Boulevard,** Franz Waxman

THEATRE

TONY. **South Pacific,** b. Oscar Hammerstein II, Joshua Logan, w. Oscar Hammerstein II, m. Richard Rodgers
N.Y. DRAMA CRITICS. **The Consul,** b.w.m. Gian-Carlo Menotti

PULITZER. **South Pacific**

1951

FILM

OSCAR. (Song) **In the Cool, Cool, Cool of the Evening,** w. Johnny Mercer, m. Hoagy Carmichael, from *Here Comes the Groom*
(Scoring—musical) **An American in Paris,** Saul Chaplin, Johnny Green
(Scoring—drama) **A Place in the Sun,** Franz Waxman

THEATRE

TONY. **Guys and Dolls,** b. Jo Swerling, Abe Burrows, w.m. Frank Loesser
N.Y. DRAMA CRITICS. **Guys and Dolls**

1952

FILM

OSCAR. (Song) **High Noon,** w. Ned Washington, m. Dimitri Tiomkin, from *High Noon*
(Scoring—musical) **With a Song in My Heart,** Alfred Newman
(Scoring—drama) **High Noon,** Dimitri Tiomkin

THEATRE

TONY. **The King and I,** b. Oscar Hammerstein II, w. Oscar Hammerstein II, m. Richard Rodgers

N.Y. DRAMA CRITICS. **Pal Joey,** b. John O'Hara, w. Lorenz Hart, m. Richard Rodgers

1953

FILM

OSCAR. (Song) **Secret Love,** w. Paul Francis Webster, m. Sammy Fain, from *Calamity Jane*
(Scoring—musical) **Call Me Madam,** Alfred Newman
(Scoring—drama) **Lili,** Bronislaw Kaper

THEATRE

TONY. **Wonderful Town,** b. Joseph Fields, Jerome Chodorov, w. Betty Comden and Adolph Green, m. Leonard Bernstein
N.Y. DRAMA CRITICS. **Wonderful Town**

1954

FILM

OSCAR. (Song) **Three Coins in the Fountain,** w. Sammy Cahn, m. Jule Styne, from *Three Coins in the Fountain*
(Scoring—musical) **Seven Brides for Seven Brothers,** Adolph Deutsch, Saul Chaplin
(Scoring—drama) **The High and the Mighty,** Dimitri Tiomkin

THEATRE

TONY. **Kismet,** b. Charles Lederer, Luther Davis, from the play by Edward Knoblock
N.Y. DRAMA CRITICS. **The Golden Apple,** b. John Latouche, w. John Latouche, m. Jerome Moross

1955

FILM

OSCAR. (Song) **Love Is a Many-Splendored Thing,** w. Paul Francis Webster, m. Sammy Fain, from *Love Is a Many-Splendored Thing*
(Scoring—musical) **Oklahoma!,** Robert Russell Bennett, Jay Blackton, Adolph Deutsch
(Scoring—drama) **Love Is a Many-Splendored Thing,** Alfred Newman

THEATRE

TONY. **The Pajama Game,** b. George Abbott, Richard Bissell, w.m. Richard Adler and Jerry Ross
N.Y. DRAMA CRITICS. **The Saint of Bleecker Street,** b.w.m. Gian-Carlo Menotti

1956

FILM

OSCAR. (Song) **Que Sera, Sera,** w. Ray Evans, m. Jay Livingston, from *The Man Who Knew Too Much*
(Scoring—musical) **The King and I,** Alfred Newman, Ken Darby

(Scoring—drama) **Around the World in Eighty Days,** Victor Young

THEATRE

TONY. **Damn Yankees,** b. George Abbott, Douglass Wallop, w.m. Richard Adler and Jerry Ross
N.Y. DRAMA CRITICS. **My Fair Lady,** b. Alan Jay Lerner from the play *Pygmalion* by George Bernard Shaw, w. Alan Jay Lerner, m. Frederick Loewe

1957

FILM

OSCAR. (Song) **All the Way,** w. Sammy Cahn, m. Jimmy Van Heusen, from *The Joker Is Wild*
(Scoring—drama) **The Bridge on the River Kwai,** Malcolm Arnold
(Scoring—musical) No award

THEATRE

TONY. **My Fair Lady,** b. Alan Jay Lerner from the play *Pygmalion* by George Bernard Shaw, w. Alan Jay Lerner, m. Frederick Loewe
N.Y. DRAMA CRITICS. **The Most Happy Fella,** b. Frank Loesser from the play *They Knew What They Wanted* by Sidney Howard, w.m. Frank Loesser

1958

FILM

OSCAR. (Song) **Gigi,** w. Alan Jay Lerner, m. Frederick Loewe, from *Gigi*
(Scoring—musical) **Gigi,** Andre Previn
(Scoring—drama) **The Old Man and the Sea,** Dimitri Tiomkin
GRAMMY. (original score/cast) **Gigi**

THEATRE

TONY. **The Music Man,** b. Meredith Willson, w.m. Meredith Willson
N.Y. DRAMA CRITICS. **The Music Man**
GRAMMY. (original cast) **The Music Man**

RECORDING

GRAMMY. (Song) **Nel Blu Dipinto Di Blu** (Volare), w.m. Domenico Modugno
(Record) **Nel Blu Dipinto Di Blu** (Volare), w.m. Domenico Modugno
(Album) **The Music from Peter Gunn,** a Henry Mancini
(R&B song) **Tequila,** w.m. Chuck Rio
(C&W song) **Tom Dooley,** w.m. Traditional

1959

FILM

OSCAR. (Song) **High Hopes,** w. Sammy Cahn, m. Jimmy Van Heusen, from *Hole in the Head*

(Scoring—musical) **Porgy and Bess,** Andre Previn, Ken Darby

(Scoring—drama) **Ben Hur,** Miklos Rozsa

GRAMMY. (Original score) **Anatomy of a Murder,** Duke Ellington

THEATRE

TONY. **Redhead,** b. Herbert and Dorothy Fields, Sidney Sheldon, David Shaw, w. Dorothy Fields, m. Albert Hague

N.Y. DRAMA CRITICS. **La Plume de Ma Tante,** b. Robert Dhery, w. Robert Dhery, m. Gerard Calvi

GRAMMY. (Original cast) **Gypsy,** b. Arthur Laurents, w. Stephen Sondheim, m. Jule Styne; tied with *Redhead* (see above)

RECORDING

GRAMMY. (Song) **The Battle of New Orleans,** w.m. Jimmy Driftwood

(Record) **Mack the Knife,** a. Bobby Darin, Pr. Ahmet Ertegun

(Album) **Come Dance with Me,** a. Frank Sinatra, Pr. Dave Cavanaugh

(R&B song) **What a Diff'rence a Day Makes,** w.m. Maria Grever (Spanish w.), Stanley Adams (English w.)

(C&W song) **The Battle of New Orleans,** w.m. Jimmy Driftwood

1960

FILM

OSCAR. (Song) **Never On Sunday,** w.m. Manos Hadjidakis, from *Never On Sunday*

(Scoring—musical) **Song Without End,** Morris Stoloff, Harry Sukman

(Scoring—drama) **Exodus,** Ernest Gold

GRAMMY. (Original score) **Exodus,** Ernest Gold

THEATRE

TONY. **Fiorello!,** b. Jerome Weidman, George Abbott, w. Sheldon Harnick, m. Jerry Bock

Tied with **The Sound of Music,** b. Howard Lindsay, Russel Crouse, w. Oscar Hammerstein II, m. Richard Rodgers

N.Y. DRAMA CRITICS. **Fiorello!**

PULITZER. **Fiorello!**

GRAMMY. (Original cast) **The Sound of Music**

RECORDING

GRAMMY. (Song) **Theme from Exodus,** m. Ernest Gold

(Record) **Theme from *A Summer Place*,** a. Percy Faith, Pr. Ernest Altschuler

(Album) **Button Down Mind,** a. Bob Newhart, Pr. George Avakian

(R&B song) **Let the Good Times Roll,** w.m. Leonard Lee

(C&W song) **El Paso,** w.m. Marty Robbins

1961

FILM

OSCAR. (Song) **Moon River,** w. Johnny Mercer, m. Henry Mancini, from *Breakfast At Tiffany's*

(Scoring—musical) **West Side Story,** Saul Chaplin, Johnny Green, Sid Ramin, Irwin Kostal

(Scoring—drama) **Breakfast At Tiffany's,** Henry Mancini

GRAMMY. (Original score) **Breakfast At Tiffany's,** Henry Mancini

THEATRE

TONY. **Bye Bye Birdie,** b. Michael Stewart, w. Lee Adams, m. Charles Strouse

N.Y. DRAMA CRITICS. **Carnival,** b. Michael Stewart, w.m. Bob Merrill

GRAMMY. (Original cast) **How To Succeed in Business Without Really Trying,** b. Abe Burrows, Jack Weinstock, Willie Gilbert, w.m. Frank Loesser

RECORDING

GRAMMY. (Song) **Moon River,** w.m. Johnny Mercer, Henry Mancini

(Record) **Moon River,** a. Henry Mancini, Pr. Dick Peirce

(Album) **Judy at Carnegie Hall,** a. Judy Garland, Pr. Andrew Wiswell

(R&B song) **Hit the Road Jack,** w.m. Percy Mayfield

(C&W song) **Big Bad John,** w.m. Jimmy Dean

1962

FILM

OSCAR. (Song) **Days of Wine and Roses,** w. Johnny Mercer, m. Henry Mancini, from *Days of Wine and Roses*

(Scoring—adaptation or treatment) **The Music Man,** Ray Heindorf

(Scoring—substantially original) **Lawrence of Arabia,** Maurice Jarre

GRAMMY. (Original score) No award

THEATRE

TONY. **How To Succeed in Business Without Really Trying,** b. Abe Burrows, Jack Weinstock, Willie Gilbert, w.m. Frank Loesser

N.Y. DRAMA CRITICS. **How To Succeed in Business Without Really Trying**

PULITZER. **How To Succeed in Business Without Really Trying**

GRAMMY. (Original cast) **No Strings,** b. Samuel Taylor, w.m. Richard Rodgers

RECORDING

GRAMMY. (Song) **What Kind of Fool Am I?,** w.m. Leslie Bricusse, Anthony Newley

(Record) **I Left My Heart in San Francisco,** a. Tony Bennett, Pr. Ernie Altschuler

(Album) **The First Family,** a. Vaughn Meader, Pr. Bob Booker, Earle Doud

(R&B song) **I Can't Stop Loving You,** w.m. Don Gibson

(C&W song) **Funny Way of Laughing,** w.m. Hank Cochran

1963

FILM

OSCAR. (Song) **Call Me Irresponsible,** w. Sammy Cahn, m. Jimmy Van Heusen, from *Papa's Delicate Condition*

(Scoring—adaptation or treatment) **Irma La Douce,** Andre Previn

(Scoring—substantially original) **Tom Jones,** John Addison

GRAMMY. (Original score) **Tom Jones,** John Addison

THEATRE

TONY. **A Funny Thing Happened on the Way to the Forum,** b. Burt Shevelove, Larry Gelbart, based on the plays of Plautus, w.m. Stephen Sondheim

N.Y. DRAMA CRITICS. No musical award

OBIE. **The Boys from Syracuse,** b. George Abbott, from Shakespeare's *The Comedy of Errors,* w. Lorenz Hart, m. Richard Rodgers

GRAMMY. (Original cast) **She Loves Me,** b. Joe Masteroff, from the play *Parfumerie* by Miklos Laszlo, w. Sheldon Harnick, m. Jerry Bock

RECORDING

GRAMMY. (Song) **The Days of Wine and Roses,** w.m. Johnny Mercer, Henry Mancini

(Record) **The Days of Wine and Roses,** a. Henry Mancini, Pr. Steve Sholes

(Album) **The Barbra Streisand Album,** a. Barbra Streisand, Pr. Mike Berniker

(R&B song) **Busted,** w.m. Harlan Howard

(C&W song) **Detroit City,** w.m. Danny Dill, Mel Tillis

1964

FILM

OSCAR. (Song) **Chim Chim Cher-ee,** w.m. Richard M. Sherman, Robert B. Sherman, from *Mary Poppins*

(Scoring—adaptation or treatment) **My Fair Lady,** Andre Previn

(Original score) **Mary Poppins,** Richard M. Sherman, Robert B. Sherman

GRAMMY. (Original score) **Mary Poppins,** Richard M. Sherman, Robert B. Sherman

THEATRE

TONY. **Hello, Dolly!,** b. Michael Stewart, from the play *The Matchmaker* by Thornton Wilder, w.m. Jerry Herman

N.Y. DRAMA CRITICS. **Hello, Dolly!**

OBIE. **Home Movies,** b. Rosalyn Drexler, w. Rosalyn Drexler, m. Al Carmines

GRAMMY. (Original cast) **Funny Girl** b. Isobel Lennart, w. Bob Merrill, m. Jule Styne

RECORDING

GRAMMY. (Song) **Hello, Dolly!,** w.m. Jerry Herman

(Record) **The Girl from Ipanema,** a. Stan Getz, Astrud Gilberto, Pr. Creed Taylor

(Album) **Getz/Gilberto,** a. Stan Getz, Joao Gilberto, Pr. Creed Taylor

(R&B song) **How Glad I Am,** w.m. Jimmy T. Williams, Larry Harrison

(C&W song) **Dang Me,** w.m. Roger Miller

1965

FILM

OSCAR. (Song) **The Shadow of Your Smile,** w. Paul Francis Webster, m. Johnny Mandel, from *The Sandpiper*

(Scoring—adaptation or treatment) **The Sound of Music,** Irwin Kostal

(Scoring—original score) **Doctor Zhivago,** Maurice Jarre

GRAMMY. (Original score) **The Sandpiper,** Johnny Mandel

THEATRE

TONY. **Fiddler on the Roof,** b. Joseph Stein, based on the stories of Sholom Aleichem, w. Sheldon Harnick, m. Jerry Bock

N.Y. DRAMA CRITICS. **Fiddler on the Roof**

OBIE. **The Cradle Will Rock,** b.w.m. Marc Blitzstein

GRAMMY. (Original cast) **On a Clear Day You Can See Forever,** b. Alan Jay Lerner, w. Alan Jay Lerner, m. Burton Lane

RECORDING

GRAMMY. (Song) **The Shadow of Your Smile,** w.m. Paul Francis Webster, Johnny Mandel

(Record) **A Taste of Honey,** a. Herb Alpert and the Tijuana Brass, Pr. Herb Alpert and Jerry Moss

(Album) **September of My Years,** a. Frank Sinatra, Pr. Sonny Burke

(R&B song) **Papa's Got a Brand New Bag,** w.m. James Brown

(C&W song) **King of the Road,** w.m. Roger Miller

1966

FILM

OSCAR. (Song) **Born Free,** w. Don Black, m. John Barry, from *Born Free*

(Scoring—adaptation or treatment) **A Funny Thing Happened on the Way to the Forum,** Ken Thorne

(Scoring—original score) **Born Free,** John Barry

GRAMMY. (Original score) **Doctor Zhivago,** Maurice Jarre

THEATRE

TONY. **Man of La Mancha,** b. Dale Wasserman, Albert Marre, based on the life and works of Miguel de Cervantes, w. Joe Darion, m. Mitch Leigh

N.Y. DRAMA CRITICS. **Man of La Mancha**

OBIE. No musical award

GRAMMY. (Original cast) **Mame,** b. Jerome Lawrence and Robert E. Lee from their play *Auntie Mame,* w.m. Jerry Herman

RECORDING

GRAMMY. (Song) **Michelle,** w.m. John Lennon, Paul McCartney

(Record) **Strangers in the Night,** a. Frank Sinatra, Pr. Jimmy Bowen

(Album) **Sinatra: A Man and His Music,** a. Frank Sinatra, Pr. Sonny Burke

(R&B song) **Crying Time,** w.m. Buck Owens

(C&W song) **Almost Persuaded,** w.m. Glen Sutton, Billy Sherrill

1967

FILM
OSCAR. (Song) **Talk to the Animals,** w.m. Leslie Bricusse, from *Doctor Dolittle*
(Scoring—adaptation or treatment) **Camelot,** Alfred Newman, Ken Darby
(Scoring—original score) **Thoroughly Modern Millie,** Elmer Bernstein
GRAMMY. (Original score) **Mission: Impossible,** Lalo Schifrin

THEATRE
TONY. **Cabaret,** b. Joe Masteroff from the play *I Am a Camera* by John Van Druten, based on Christopher Isherwood's *Berlin Stories* w. Fred Ebb, m. John Kander
N.Y. DRAMA CRITICS. **Cabaret**
OBIE. No musical award
GRAMMY. (Original cast) **Cabaret**

RECORDING
GRAMMY. (Song) **Up, Up and Away,** w.m. Jim Webb
(Record) **Up, Up and Away,** a. Fifth Dimension, Pr. Marc Gordon, Johnny Rivers
(Album) **Sergeant Pepper's Lonely Hearts Club Band,** a. The Beatles, Pr. George Martin
(R&B song) **Respect,** w.m. Otis Redding
(C&W song) **Gentle on My Mind,** w.m. John Hartford

1968

FILM
OSCAR. (Song) **The Windmills of Your Mind,** w. Alan and Marilyn Bergman, m. Michel Legrand, from *The Thomas Crown Affair*
(Scoring—adaptation or treatment) **Oliver,** Johnny Green
(Scoring—original score) **The Lion in Winter,** John Barry
GRAMMY. (Original score) **The Graduate,** Paul Simon, Dave Grusin

THEATRE
TONY. **Hallelujah, Baby!,** b. Arthur Laurents, w. Betty Comden, Adolph Green, m. Jule Styne
N.Y. DRAMA CRITICS. **Your Own Thing,** b. Donald Driver from Shakespeare's *Twelfth Night,* w.m. Hal Hester, Danny Apolinar
OBIE. **In Circles,** b. Gertrude Stein, w.m. Al Carmines
GRAMMY. (Original cast) **Hair,** b. Gerome Ragni, James Rado, w. Gerome Ragni, James Rado, m. Galt MacDermot

RECORDING
GRAMMY. (Song) **Little Green Apples,** w.m. Bobby Russell
(Record) **Mrs. Robinson,** a. Simon and Garfunkel, Pr. Paul Simon, Art Garfunkel, Roy Halee
(Album) **By the Time I Get to Phoenix,** a. Glen Campbell, Pr. Al de Lory

(R&B song) **(Sittin' on) The Dock of the Bay,** w.m. Steve Cropper, Otis Redding
(C&W song) **Little Green Apples,** w.m. Bobby Russell

1969

FILM
OSCAR. (Song) **Raindrops Keep Fallin' on My Head,** w. Hal David, m. Burt Bacharach, from *Butch Cassidy and the Sundance Kid*
(Scoring—adaptation or treatment) **Hello, Dolly!,** Lennie Hayton, Lionel Newman
(Scoring—original score) **Butch Cassidy and the Sundance Kid,** Burt Bacharach
GRAMMY. (Original score) **Butch Cassidy and the Sundance Kid,** Burt Bacharach

THEATRE
TONY. **1776,** b. Peter Stone, w.m. Sherman Edwards
N.Y. DRAMA CRITICS. **1776**
OBIE. No musical award
GRAMMY. (Original cast) **Promises, Promises,** b. Neil Simon, from the film *The Apartment,* w. Hal David, m. Burt Bacharach

RECORDING
GRAMMY. (Song) **Games People Play,** w.m. Joe South
(Record) **Aquarius/Let the Sunshine In,** a. Fifth Dimension, Pr. Bones Howe
(Album) **Blood, Sweat & Tears,** a. Blood, Sweat and Tears, Pr. James Guercio
(R&B song) **Color Him Father,** w.m. Richard Spencer
(C&W song) **A Boy Named Sue,** w.m. Shel Silverstein

1970

FILM
OSCAR. (Song) **For All We Know,** w. Arthur James, Robb Wilson, m. Fred Karlin, from *Lovers and Other Strangers*
(Scoring—adaptation or treatment) **Let It Be,** The Beatles
(Scoring—original score) **Love Story,** Frances Lai
GRAMMY. (Original score) **Let It Be,** John Lennon, Paul McCartney, George Harrison, Ringo Starr

THEATRE
TONY. **Applause,** b. Betty Comden, Adolph Green from the film, *All About Eve,* w. Lee Adams, m. Charles Strouse
N.Y. DRAMA CRITICS. **Company,** b. George Furth, w.m. Stephen Sondheim
OBIE. **The Last Sweet Days of Isaac,** b. Gretchen Cryer, w. Gretchen Cryer, m. Nancy Ford
Tied with **The Me Nobody Knows,** b. Spoken text written by children (ages 7–18) attending New York City public schools, edited by Stephen M. Joseph, w. Will Holt, m. Gary William Friedman
GRAMMY. (Original cast) **Company**

RECORDING

GRAMMY. (Song) **Bridge Over Troubled Water,** w.m. Paul Simon

(Record) **Bridge Over Troubled Water,** a. Simon and Garfunkel, Pr. Paul Simon, Art Garfunkel, Roy Halee

(Album) **Bridge Over Troubled Water,** a. Simon and Garfunkel, Pr. Paul Simon, Art Garfunkel, Roy Halee

(R&B song) **Patches (I'm Depending on You),** w.m. General Johnson, Ronald Dunbar

(C&W song) **My Woman, My Woman, My Wife,** w.m. Marty Robbins

1971

FILM

OSCAR. (Song) **Theme from Shaft,** w.m. Isaac Hayes, from *Shaft*

(Scoring—adaptation or treatment) **Fiddler on the Roof,** John Williams

(Scoring—original score) **Summer of '42,** Michel Legrand

GRAMMY. (Original score) **Shaft,** Isaac Hayes

THEATRE

TONY. **Company,** b. George Furth, w.m. Stephen Sondheim

N.Y. DRAMA CRITICS. **Follies,** b. James Goldman, w.m. Stephen Sondheim

OBIE. No musical award

GRAMMY. (Original cast) **Godspell,** b. John-Michael Tebelak, w.m. Stephen Schwartz

RECORDING

GRAMMY. (Song) **You've Got a Friend,** w.m. Carole King

(Record) **It's Too Late,** a. Carole King, Pr. Lou Adler

(Album) **Tapestry,** a. Carole King, Pr. Lou Adler

(R&B song) **Ain't No Sunshine,** w.m. Bill Withers

(C&W song) **Help Me Make It Through the Night,** w.m. Kris Kristofferson, Fred Foster

1972

FILM

OSCAR. (Song) **The Morning After,** w.m. Al Kasha, Joe Harschorn, from *The Poseidon Adventure*

(Scoring—adaptation or treatment) **Cabaret,** Ralph Burns

(Scoring—original score) No award

GRAMMY. (Original score) **The Godfather,** Nino Rota

THEATRE

TONY. **Two Gentlemen of Verona,** b. John Guare, Mel Shapiro from Shakespeare's play, w. John Guare, m. Galt MacDermot

N.Y. DRAMA CRITICS. **Two Gentlemen of Verona**

OBIE. **Don't Bother Me, I Can't Cope,** b. Vinnette Carroll, w.m. Micki Grant

GRAMMY. (Original cast) **Don't Bother Me, I Can't Cope**

RECORDING

GRAMMY. (Song) **The First Time Ever I Saw Your Face,** w.m. Ewan MacColl

(Record) **The First Time Ever I Saw Your Face,** a. Roberta Flack, Pr. Joel Dorn

(Album) **The Concert for Bangla Desh,** a. George Harrison, Ravi Shankar, Bob Dylan, Leon Russell, Ringo Starr, Billy Preston, Eric Clapton, Klaus Voormann, Pr. George Harrison, Phil Spector

(R&B song) **Papa Was a Rolling Stone,** w.m. Barrett Strong, Norman Whitfield

(C&W song) **Kiss an Angel Good Mornin',** w.m. Ben Peters

1973

FILM

OSCAR. (Song) **The Way We Were,** w. Allan and Marilyn Bergman, m. Marvin Hamlisch, from *The Way We Were*

(Scoring—adaptation) **The Sting,** Marvin Hamlisch

(Scoring—original) **The Way We Were,** Marvin Hamlisch

GRAMMY. (Original score) **Jonathan Livingston Seagull,** Neil Diamond

THEATRE

TONY. **A Little Night Music,** b. Hugh Wheeler from the Ingmar Bergman film *Smiles of a Summer Night,* w.m. Stephen Sondheim

N.Y. DRAMA CRITICS. **A Little Night Music**

OBIE. No musical award

GRAMMY. (Original cast) **A Little Night Music**

RECORDING

GRAMMY. (Song) **Killing Me Softly with His Song,** w.m. Charles Fox, Norman Gimbel

(Record) **Killing Me Softly with His Song,** a. Roberta Flack, Pr. Joel Dorn

(Album) **Innervisions,** a. Stevie Wonder, Pr. Stevie Wonder

(R&B song) **Superstition,** w.m. Stevie Wonder

(C&W song) **Behind Closed Doors,** w.m. Kenny O'Dell

1974

FILM

OSCAR. (Song) **We May Never Love Like This Again,** w.m. Al Kasha, Joel Hirschorn, from *The Towering Inferno*

(Scoring—adaptation) **The Great Gatsby,** Nelson Riddle

(Scoring—original) **The Godfather, Part II,** Nino Rota, Carmine Coppola

GRAMMY. (Original score) **The Way We Were,** Marvin Hamlisch, Alan and Marilyn Bergman

THEATRE

TONY. **Raisin,** b. Robert Nemiroff, Charlotte Zaltzberg from the play *Raisin in the Sun* by Lorraine Hansberry, w. Robert Brittan, m. Judd Woldin

N.Y. DRAMA CRITICS. **Candide,** b. Hugh Wheeler, w. Richard Wilbur, addl. John Latouche, Stephen Sondheim, m. Leonard Bernstein

OBIE. No musical award

GRAMMY. (Original cast) **Raisin**

RECORDING

GRAMMY. (Song) **The Way We Were,** w.m. Marilyn and Alan Bergman, Marvin Hamlisch

(Record) **I Honestly Love You,** a. Olivia Newton-John, Pr. John Farrar

(Album) **Fulfillingness' First Finale,** a. Stevie Wonder, Pr. Stevie Wonder

(R&B song) **Living for the City,** w.m. Stevie Wonder

(C&W song) **A Very Special Love Song,** w.m. Norris Wilson, Billy Sherrill

1975

FILM

OSCAR. (Song) **I'm Easy,** w.m. Keith Carradine, from *Nashville*

(Scoring—adaptation) **Barry Lyndon,** Leonard Rosenman

(Scoring—original) **Jaws,** John Williams

GRAMMY. (Original score) **Jaws,** John Williams

THEATRE

TONY. **The Wiz,** b. William F. Brown, w.m. Charlie Smalls

N.Y. DRAMA CRITICS. **A Chorus Line,** b. James Kirkwood, Nicholas Dante, w. Edward Kleban, m. Marvin Hamlisch

OBIE. No musical award

GRAMMY. (Original cast) **The Wiz**

RECORDING

GRAMMY. (Song) **Send in the Clowns,** w.m. Stephen Sondheim

(Record) **Love Will Keep Us Together,** a. Captain and Tennille, Pr. Daryl Dragon

(Album) **Still Crazy After All These Years,** a. Paul Simon, Pr. Paul Simon, Phil Ramone

(R&B song) **Where Is the Love,** w.m. Harry Wayne Casey, Richard Finch, Willie Clark, Betty Wright

(Country song) **(Hey Won't You Play) Another Somebody Done Somebody Wrong Song,** w.m. Chips Moman, Larry Butler

1976

FILM

OSCAR. (Song) **Evergreen,** w. Paul Williams, m. Barbra Streisand, from *A Star Is Born*

(Scoring—adaptation) **Bound for Glory,** Leonard Rosenman

(Scoring—original) **The Omen,** Jerry Goldsmith

GRAMMY. (Original score) **Car Wash,** Norman Whitfield

THEATRE

TONY. **A Chorus Line,** b. James Kirkwood, Nicholas Dante, w. Edward Kleban, m. Marvin Hamlisch

N.Y. DRAMA CRITICS. **Pacific Overtures,** b. John Weidman, addl. Hugh Wheeler, w.m. Stephen Sondheim

OBIE. No musical award

PULITZER. **A Chorus Line**

GRAMMY. (Original cast) **Bubbling Brown Sugar,** b. Loften

Mitchell, Rosetta Le Noire, w.m. Many authors period 1925–1950

RECORDING

GRAMMY. (Song) **I Write the Songs,** w.m. Bruce Johnston

(Record) **This Masquerade,** a. George Benson, Pr. Tommy Lipuma

(Album) **Songs in the Key of Life,** a. Stevie Wonder, Pr. Stevie Wonder

(R&B song) **Lowdown,** w.m. Boz Scaggs, David Paich

(Country song) **Broken Lady,** w.m. Larry Gatlin

1977

FILM

OSCAR. (Song) **You Light Up My Life,** w.m. Joseph Brooks, from *You Light Up My Life*

(Scoring—adaptation) **A Little Night Music,** Jonathan Tunick

(Scoring—original) **Star Wars,** John Williams

GRAMMY. (Original score) **Star Wars,** John Williams

THEATRE

TONY. **Annie,** b. Thomas Meehan, w. Martin Charnin, m. Charles Strouse

N.Y. DRAMA CRITICS. **Annie**

OBIE. No musical award

GRAMMY. (Original cast) **Annie**

RECORDING

GRAMMY. (Song) **Love Theme from A Star Is Born (Evergreen),** w.m. Barbra Streisand, Paul Williams; **You Light Up My Life,** Joseph Brooks

(Record) **Hotel California,** a. Eagles, Pr. Bill Szymczyk

(Album) **Rumours,** a. Fleetwood Mac, Pr. Fleetwood Mac, Richard Dashut, Ken Caillat

(R&B song) **You Make Me Feel Like Dancing,** w.m. Leo Sayer, Vini Poncia

(Country song) **Don't It Make My Brown Eyes Blue,** w.m. Richard Leigh

1978

FILM

OSCAR. (Song) **Last Dance,** w.m. Paul Jabara, from *Thank God It's Friday*

(Scoring—adaptation) **The Buddy Holly Story,** Joe Renzetti

(Scoring—original) **Midnight Express,** Giorgio Moroder

GRAMMY. (Original score) **Close Encounters of the Third Kind,** John Williams

THEATRE

TONY. **Ain't Misbehavin',** w.m., Thomas "Fats" Waller and others

N.Y. DRAMA CRITICS. **Ain't Misbehavin'**

OBIE. No musical award

GRAMMY. (Original cast) **Ain't Misbehavin'**

RECORDING

GRAMMY. (Song) **Just the Way You Are,** w.m. Billy Joel
(Record) **Just the Way You Are,** a. Billy Joel, Pr. Phil Ramone
(Album) **Saturday Night Fever** (motion picture sound track), a. Bee Gees, Pr. Bee Gees, Karl Richardson, Albhy Galuten, and others
(R&B song) **Last Dance,** w.m. Paul Jabara
(Country song) **The Gambler,** w.m. Don Schlitz

1979

FILM

OSCAR. (Song) **It Goes Like It Goes,** w.m. Norman Gimbel, David Shire, from *Norma Rae*
(Scoring—adaptation) **All That Jazz,** Ralph Burns
(Scoring—original) **A Little Romance,** George Delerue
GRAMMY. (Original score) **Superman,** John Williams

THEATRE

TONY. **Sweeney Todd,** b. Hugh Wheeler, w.m. Stephen Sondheim

N.Y. DRAMA CRITICS. **Sweeney Todd**

OBIE. No musical award

GRAMMY. (Original cast) **Sweeney Todd**

RECORDING

GRAMMY. (Song) **What a Fool Believes,** w.m. Kenny Loggins, Michael McDonald
(Record) **What a Fool Believes,** a. The Doobie Brothers, Pr. Ted Templeman
(Album) **52nd Street,** a. Billy Joel, Pr. Phil Ramone
(R&B song) **After the Love Has Gone,** w.m. David Foster, Jay Graydon, Bill Champlin
(Country song) **You Decorated My Life,** w.m. Bob Morrison, Debbie Hupp

1980

FILM

OSCAR. (Song) **Fame,** w. Dean Pitchford, m. Michael Gore, from *Fame*
(Scoring—original) **Fame,** Michael Gore
GRAMMY. (Original score) **The Empire Strikes Back,** John Williams

THEATRE

TONY. **Evita,** w. Tim Rice, m. Andrew Lloyd Webber
N.Y. DRAMA CRITICS. **Evita**

OBIE. No musical award

GRAMMY. (Original cast) **Evita**

RECORDING

GRAMMY. (Song) **Sailing,** w.m. Christopher Cross
(Record) **Sailing,** a. Christopher Cross, Pr. Michael Omartian
(Album) **Christopher Cross,** a. Christopher Cross, Pr. Michael Omartian

(R&B song) **Never Knew Love Like This Before,** w.m. Reggie Lucas, James Mtume
(Country song) **On the Road Again,** w.m. Willie Nelson

1981

FILM

OSCAR. (Song) **Arthur's Theme (Best That You Can Do),** w.m. Peter Allen, Burt Bacharach, Christopher Cross, from *Arthur*
(Scoring—original) **Chariots of Fire,** Vangelis
GRAMMY. (Original score) **Raiders of the Lost Ark,** John Williams

THEATRE

TONY. **Woman of the Year,** b. Peter Stone, w.m. John Kander, Fred Ebb

N.Y. DRAMA CRITICS. (Special citations) **Lena Horne: The Lady and Her Music** *and* **The Pirates of Penzance**

OBIE. No musical award

GRAMMY. (Original cast) **Lena Horne: The Lady and Her Music Live on Broadway,** w.m. Various composers and lyricists

RECORDING

GRAMMY. (Song) **Bette Davis Eyes,** w.m. Donna Weiss, Jackie DeShannon
(Record) **Bette Davis Eyes,** a. Kim Carnes, Pr. Val Garay
(Album) **Double Fantasy,** a. John Lennon, Yoko Ono, Pr. John Lennon, Yoko Ono, Jack Douglas
(R&B song) **Just the Two of Us,** w.m. Ralph MacDonald, William Salter, Bill Withers
(Country song) **9 to 5,** w.m. Dolly Parton

1982

FILM

OSCAR. (Song) **Up Where We Belong,** w. Will Jennings, m. Jack Nitszche, Buffy Sainte-Marie, from *An Officer and a Gentleman*
(Scoring—original song score) **Victor Victoria,** w.m. Leslie Bricusse, Henry Mancini
(Scoring—adaptation) **Victor Victoria,** Henry Mancini
(Scoring—original) **E.T. The Extra-Terrestrial,** John Williams
GRAMMY. (Original score) **E.T. The Extra-Terrestrial,** John Williams

THEATRE

TONY. (Book) **Dreamgirls,** Tom Eyen (Score) **Nine,** w.m. Maury Yeston

N.Y. DRAMA CRITICS. No musical award

OBIE. No musical award

GRAMMY. (Original cast) **Dreamgirls,** w. Tom Eyen, m. Henry Krieger

RECORDING

GRAMMY. (Song) **Always on My Mind,** w.m. Wayne Carson, Johnny Christopher, Mark James

(Record) **Rosanna,** a. Toto, Pr. Toto

(Album) **Toto IV,** a. Toto, Pr. Toto

(R&B song) **Turn Your Love Around,** w.m. Bill Champlin, Jay Graydon, Steve Lukather

(Country song) **Always on My Mind,** w.m. Wayne Carson, Johnny Christopher, Mark James

1983

FILM

OSCAR. (Song) **Flashdance (What a Feeling),** w.m. Irene Cara, Keith Forsey, Giorgio Moroder, from *Flashdance*

(Scoring—song score) **Yentl,** w. Alan Bergman, Marilyn Bergman, m. Michel Legrand

(Scoring—original) **The Right Stuff,** Bill Conti

GRAMMY. (Original score) **Flashdance,** w.m. Giorgio Moroder, Keith Forsey, Irene Cara, Shandi Sinnamon, Ronald Magness, Douglas Cotler, Richard Gilbert, Michael Boddicker, Jerry Hey, Phil Ramone, Michael Sembello, Kim Carnes, Duane Hitchings, Craig Krampf, Dennis Matkosky

THEATRE

TONY. **Cats,** b. T.S. Eliot, w.m. T.S. Eliot, Andrew Lloyd Webber

N.Y. DRAMA CRITICS. **Little Shop of Horrors,** b. Howard Ashman, w. Howard Ashman, m. Alan Menken

OBIE. No musical award

GRAMMY. (Original cast) **Cats**

RECORDING

(Song) **Every Breath You Take,** w.m. Sting

(Record) **Beat It,** a. Michael Jackson, Pr. Quincy Jones, Michael Jackson

(Album) **Thriller,** a. Michael Jackson, Pr. Quincy Jones

(R&B song) **Billie Jean,** w.m. Michael Jackson

(Country song) **Stranger in My House,** w.m. Mike Reid

1984

FILM

OSCAR. (Song) **I Just Called To Say I Love You,** w.m. Stevie Wonder, from *The Woman in Red*

(Scoring—song score) **Purple Rain,** w.m. Prince

(Scoring—original) **A Passage to India,** Maurice Jarre

GRAMMY. (Original score) **Purple Rain,** Prince, John L. Nelson, Lisa and Wendy

THEATRE

TONY. **La Cage aux Folles,** b. Harvey Fierstein, w.m. Jerry Herman

N.Y. DRAMA CRITICS. **Sunday in the Park with George,** b. James Lapine, w.m. Stephen Sondheim

PULITZER. **Sunday in the Park with George**

OBIE. No musical award

GRAMMY. (Original cast) **Sunday in the Park with George**

RECORDING

GRAMMY. (Song) **What's Love Got To Do with It,** w.m. Terry Britten, Graham Lyle

(Record) **What's Love Got To Do with It,** a. Tina Turner, Pr. Terry Britten

(Album) **Can't Slow Down,** a. Lionel Richie, pr. James Anthony Carmichael, Lionel Richie

(R&B song) **I Feel For You,** w.m. Prince

(Country song) **City of New Orleans,** w.m. Steve Goodman

1985

FILM

OSCAR. (Song) **Say You, Say Me,** w.m. Lionel Richie, from *White Nights*

(Scoring—original) **Out of Africa,** John Barry

GRAMMY. (Original score) **Beverly Hills Cop,** Sharon Robinson, Jon Gilutin, Bunny Hull, Hawk, Howard Hewett, Micki Free, Sue Sheridan, Howie Rice, Keith Forsey, Harold Faltemeyer, Allee Willis, Dan Sembello, Marc Benno, Richard Theisen

THEATRE

TONY. **Big River,** b. William Hauptman, w.m. Roger Miller

N.Y. DRAMA CRITICS. No musical award

OBIE. No musical award

GRAMMY. (Original cast) **West Side Story,** w. Stephen Sondheim, m. Leonard Bernstein

RECORDING

GRAMMY. (Song) **We Are the World,** w.m. Michael Jackson, Lionel Richie

(Record) **We Are the World,** a. U.S.A. For Africa, Pr. Quincy Jones

(Album) **No Jacket Required,** a. Phil Collins, Pr. Phil Collins, Hugh Padgham

(R&B song) **Freeway of Love,** w.m. Jeffrey Cohen, Narada Michael Walden

(Country song) **Highwayman,** w.m. Jimmy L. Webb

1986

FILM

OSCAR. (Song) **Take My Breath Away,** w. Tom Whitlock, m. Giorgio Moroder, from *Top Gun*

(Scoring—original) **'Round Midnight,** Herbie Hancock

GRAMMY. (Original score) **Out of Africa,** John Barry

THEATRE

TONY. **The Mystery of Edwin Drood,** b.w.m. Rupert Holmes

N.Y. DRAMA CRITICS. No musical award

OBIE. No musical award

GRAMMY. (Original cast) **Follies in Concert,** w.m. Stephen Sondheim

RECORDING

GRAMMY. (Song) **That's What Friends Are For,** w.m. Burt Bacharach, Carole Bayer Sager

(Record) **Higher Love,** a. Steve Winwood, Pr. Russ Titelman, Steve Winwood

(Album) **Graceland,** a. Paul Simon, Pr. Paul Simon

(R&B song) **Sweet Love,** w.m. Anita Baker, Gary Bias, Louis A. Johnson

(Country song) **Grandpa (Tell Me 'Bout the Good Old Days),** w.m. Jamie O'Hara

BRITISH AWARDS

What! All this for a song?

William Cecil, Lord Burghley (1520–1598),
when ordered by Queen Elizabeth I to give £100
to Edmund Spenser for his poetry.

The PRS Ivor Novello Awards were first presented in 1955. They were founded and are administered by the Songwriters' Guild of Great Britain in conjunction with the Performing Right Society, founded in 1914. Awards are listed here per annum from 1955–66, then by season 1967/68–1977/78.

Ivor Novello (David Ivor Davies) (1893–1951) was born in Cardiff and was an actor, manager, dramatic and musical comedy author, and composer much beloved of Londoners. He was part-composer of the London musical-comedy ''Theodore and Co.'' with Jerome Kern as early as 1916, and over the years was noted for such songs as ''Keep the Home Fires Burning'' (1915) and ''We'll Gather Lilacs'' (1945).

1955

MOST POPULAR SONG. 1. **Ev'rywhere,** w.m. Tolchard Evans, Larry Kahn; 2. **A Blossom Fell,** w.m. Howard Barnes, Harold Cornelius, Dominic John

OUTSTANDING SONG. 1. **In Love for the Very First Time,** w.m. Jack Woodman, Paddy Roberts; 2. **Man in a Raincoat,** w.m. Warwick Webster

OUTSTANDING COMEDY SONG. 1. **Got'n Idea,** w.m. Jack Woodman, Paddy Roberts; 2. **The Income Tax Collector,** w.m. Michael Flanders, Donald Swann

OUTSTANDING CONCERT BALLAD. No award in this Class, but a special personal Award to **Haydn Wood**

MOST EFFECTIVE MUSICAL PLAY SCORE. 1. **Salad Days,** w.m. Julian Slade, Dorothy Reynolds; 2. **The Water Gipsies,** w.m. Vivian Ellis, A.P. Herbert

OUTSTANDING 'SWING' COMPOSITION. 1. **Big City Suite,** w.m. Ralph Dollimore; 2. **Fanfare Boogie,** w.m. Max Kaye, Brian Fahey

OUTSTANDING PIECE OF LIGHT ORCHESTRAL MUSIC. 1. **The Dam Busters,** m. Eric Coates; 2. **John and Julie,** m. Philip Green

OUTSTANDING SERVICES IN THE FIELD OF POPULAR MUSIC. **Jack Payne**

1956

BEST SELLING AND MOST PERFORMED SONG. 1. **My September Love,** w.m. Tolchard Evans, Richard Mullan; 2. **Out of Town,** w.m. Leslie Bricusse, Robin Beaumont

OUTSTANDING SONG. 1. **By the Fountains of Rome,** w.m. Matyas Seiber, Norman Newell 2. **My Unfinished Symphony,** w.m. Milton Carson

OUTSTANDING NOVELTY SONG. 1. **Nellie the Elephant,** w.m. Peter Hart, Ralph Butler; 2. **Lift Boy,** w.m. Ken Hare, Ron Goodwin, Dick James

OUTSTANDING COMPOSITION IN 'RHYTHM' STYLE. 1. **Itinerary of an Orchestra,** w.m. Johnny Dankworth, Dave Lindup; 2. **Experiments with Mice,** w.m. Johnny Dankworth

OUTSTANDING LIGHT ORCHESTRAL COMPOSITION. 1. **The Westminster Waltz,** m. Robert Farnon; 2. **Toyshop Ballet,** m. A.P. Mantovani

OUTSTANDING SCORE OF A STAGE PLAY, FILM, TV PROGRAMME OR RADIO PRODUCTION. 1. **The March Hare,** w.m. Philip Green; 2. **You Are My First Love,** w.m. Paddy Roberts, Lester Powell

OUTSTANDING PERSONAL SERVICES TO POPULAR MUSIC. **A.P. Mantovani**

1957

BEST SELLING AND MOST PERFORMED SONG. 1. **We Will Make Love,** w.m. Ronald Hulme, (Russ Hamilton); 2. **I'll Find You,** w.m. Tolchard Evans, Richard Mullan

OUTSTANDING SONG. 1. **A Handful of Songs,** w.m. Lionel Bart, Michael Pratt, Tommy Steele; 2. **Your Love Is My Love,** w.m. Francis Edwards, (Johnny Brandon)

OUTSTANDING NOVELTY SONG. 1. **Three Brothers,** w.m. Paddy Roberts; 2. **Water, Water,** w.m. Lionel Bart, Michael Pratt, Tommy Steele

OUTSTANDING COMPOSITION IN 'RHYTHM' STYLE. 1. **Overdrive,** w.m. Tommy Watt; 2. **Skiffling Strings,** w.m. Ron Goodwin

OUTSTANDING LIGHT ORCHESTRAL COMPOSITION. 1. **Eliza-**

bethan Serenade, m. Ronald Binge; 2. **The Streets of Sorento,** m. Tony Osborne

OUTSTANDING SCORE OF A STAGE PLAY, FILM, TV PROGRAMME, OR RADIO PRODUCTION. 1. **Free As Air,** w.m. Dorothy Reynolds, Julian Slade; 2. **The Tommy Steele Story,** w.m. Lionel Bart, Michael Pratt, Tommy Steele

OUTSTANDING PERSONAL SERVICES TO BRITISH POPULAR MUSIC. **Ted Heath**

1958

BEST SELLING AND MOST PERFORMED ITEM. 1. **Trudie,** w.m. Joe Henderson 2. **You Need Hands,** w.m. Max Bygraves

OUTSTANDING SONG. 1. **The Wind Cannot Read,** w.m. Peter Hart; 2. **There Goes My Lover,** w.m. Leonard Taylor, Harold Shaper

OUTSTANDING NOVELTY SONG. 1. **I'm So Ashamed,** w.m. Ken Hare; 2. **The Army Game,** w.m. Pat Napper, Sid Colin

OUTSTANDING COMPOSITION IN JAZZ OR BEAT IDIOM. 1. **The Colonel's Tune,** w.m. Johnny Dankworth; 2. **Rock Bottom,** w.m. Tommy Watt, Jock Bain

OUTSTANDING LIGHT ORCHESTRAL COMPOSITION. 1. **Lingering Lovers,** m. Ron Goodwin; 2. **Melody from the Sea,** m. Donald Phillips

OUTSTANDING SCORE OF A STAGE PLAY, FILM, T.V. PROGRAMME OR RADIO PRODUCTION. 1. **Theme Music for the 'Inn of the Sixth Happiness',** w.m. Malcolm Arnold; 2. **Josita,** w.m. Philip Green

OUTSTANDING SERVICES TO BRITISH POPULAR MUSIC. **Billy Cotton**

1959

BEST SELLING AND MOST PERFORMED WORK. 1. **Side Saddle,** w.m. Trevor Stanford, (Russ Conway); 2. **Living Doll,** w.m. Lionel Bart

OUTSTANDING SONG. 1. **The Village of St. Bernadette,** w.m. Eula Parker; 2. **Maybe This Year,** w.m. Ronald Wakley, Marcel Stellman

OUTSTANDING NOVELTY ITEM. 1. **The Ballad of Bethnal Green,** w.m. Paddy Roberts; 2. **Little White Bull,** w.m. Michael Pratt, Lionel Bart, Jimmy Bennett, (Tommy Steele)

OUTSTANDING COMPOSITION IN 'JAZZ' OR 'BEAT' IDIOM. 1. **Beaulieu Festival Suite,** w.m. Kenny Graham; 2. **Jazzboat,** w.m. Joe Henderson

OUTSTANDING LIGHT ORCHESTRAL COMPOSITION. 1. **Windows of Paris,** m. Tony Osborne; 2. **Ring Ding,** m. Steve Race

OUTSTANDING SCORE OF A STAGE PLAY, FILM, T.V. PROGRAMME OR RADIO PRODUCTION. 1. **Lock Up Your Daughters,** w.m. Laurie Johnson, Lionel Bart; 2. **Meet the Family,** w.m. Peter Greenwell, Peter Wildeblood

OUTSTANDING PERSONAL SERVICES TO BRITISH POPULAR MUSIC. **Lionel Bart**

1960

BEST SELLING AND MOST PERFORMED WORK. 1. **As Long As He Needs Me,** w.m. Lionel Bart; 2. **Apache,** w.m. Jerry Lordan

OUTSTANDING SONG. 1. **Portrait of My Love,** w.m. Cyril Ornadel, Norman Newell; 2. **As Long As He Needs Me,** w.m. Lionel Bart

OUTSTANDING LIGHT ORCHESTRAL COMPOSITION. 1. **Seashore,** m. Robert Farnon; 2. **The Willow Waltz,** m. Cyril Watters

OUTSTANDING COMPOSITION IN 'JAZZ' OR 'BEAT' IDIOM. 1. **Apache,** w.m. Jerry Lordan; 2. **Hit and Miss,** w.m. John Barry

OUTSTANDING SCORE OF A STAGE PLAY, FILM, T.V. PROGRAMME OR RADIO PRODUCTION. 1. **Oliver,** w.m. Lionel Bart; 2. **The Gurney Slade Theme,** w.m. Max Harris

NOTABLE. 1. **Goodness Gracious Me,** w.m. David Lee, Herbert Kretzmer; 2. **The Belle of Barking Creek,** w.m. Paddy Roberts

OUTSTANDING PERSONAL SERVICES TO BRITISH POPULAR MUSIC. **Eric Maschwitz**

SPECIAL AWARD. **What Do You Want If You Don't Want Money?** w.m. Johnny Worth

1961

MOST PERFORMED WORK. 1. **My Kind of Girl,** w.m. Leslie Bricusse; 2. **Portrait of My Love,** w.m. Cyril Ornadel, Norman Newell

HIGHEST CERTIFIED BRITISH SALES. 1. **Walkin' Back To Happiness,** w.m. John Schroeder, Michael Hawker; 2. **Are You Sure,** w.m. Bob Allison, John Allison

OUTSTANDING SONG. 1. **What Kind of Fool Am I?,** w.m. Leslie Bricusse, Anthony Newley; 2. **No Greater Love,** w.m. Michael Carr, Bunny Lewis

OUTSTANDING LIGHT ORCHESTRAL COMPOSITION. 1. **The Secrets of the Seine,** m. Tony Osborne; 2. **Stranger on the Shore,** m. Acker Bilk

OUTSTANDING ORIGINAL JAZZ COMPOSITION. 1. **African Waltz,** m. Galt Macdermot; 2. **Duddly Dell,** m. Dudley Moore

OUTSTANDING SCORE OF A MUSICAL STAGE PLAY. **Stop the World I Want to Get Off,** w.m. Leslie Bricusse, Anthony Newley

OUTSTANDING COMPOSITION IN A FILM, RADIO PRODUCTION OR TELEVISION PROGRAMME. 1. **The Maigret Theme,** w.m. Ron Grainer; 2. **The Avengers' Theme,** w.m. Johnny Dankworth

OUTSTANDING SERVICES TO BRITISH MUSIC. **Cliff Richard and the Shadows**

1962

MOST PERFORMED WORK. 1. **Stranger on the Shore,** w.m. Acker Bilk; 2. **Wonderful Land,** w.m. Jerry Lordan

HIGHEST CERTIFIED BRITISH SALES. 1. **Telstar,** w.m. Joe Meek; 2. **Bachelor Boy,** w.m. Cliff Richard, Bruce Welch

OUTSTANDING SONG. 1. **My Love and Devotion**, w.m. Howard Barnes, Joe Roncoroni, Harold Fields; 2. **Jeannie**, w.m. Norman Newell, Russ Conway

OUTSTANDING LIGHT ORCHESTRAL OR OTHER NON-VOCAL COMPOSITION. 1. **Nicola**, m. Steve Race; 2. **Turkish Coffee**, m. Tony Osborne

OUTSTANDING ORIGINAL JAZZ COMPOSITION. 1. **Outbreak of Murder**, m. Gordon Franks; 2. **Revival**, m. Joe Harriott

OUTSTANDING SCORE OF A MUSICAL. 1. **Summer Holiday**, w.m. Cliff Richard, Bruce Welch, Stanley Black, Brian Bennett, Peter Myers, Ronald Cass, Hank Marvin, Mike Conlin; 2. **Blitz**, w.m. Lionel Bart

OUTSTANDING COMPOSITION IN A FILM, RADIO PRODUCTION, OR TELEVISION PROGRAMME. 1. **Steptoe and Son**, w.m. Ron Grainer; 2. **March from A Little Suite**, w.m. Trevor Duncan

SPECIAL AWARD. **Lawrence Wright**

1963

MOST BROADCAST WORK. 1. **She Loves You**, w.m. John Lennon, Paul McCartney; 2. **Dance On**, w.m. Elaine Murtagh, Valerie Murtagh, Ray Adams

HIGHEST CERTIFIED BRITISH SALES. 1. **She Loves You**, w.m. John Lennon, Paul McCartney; 2. **I Want To Hold Your Hand**, w.m. John Lennon, Paul McCartney

OUTSTANDING SONG. 1. **If I Ruled the World**, w.m. Cyril Ornadel, Leslie Bricusse; 2. **All My Loving**, w.m. John Lennon, Paul McCartney

OUTSTANDING ORCHESTRAL/INSTRUMENTAL COMPOSITION. 1. **Carlos' Theme**, m. Ivor Slaney; 2. **Scarlett O'Hara**, m. Jerry Lordan

OUTSTANDING JAZZ WORK. 1. **What the Dickens**, m. Johnny Dankworth; 2. **Sweet September**, m. Bill McGuffie

OUTSTANDING SCORE OF A MUSICAL SHOW, FOR STAGE, CINEMA, TELEVISION, OR RADIO. 1. **Theme from 'The Avengers'**, w.m. Johnny Dankworth; 2. **Half a Sixpence**, w.m. David Heneker

MOST AMUSING OR NOVEL COMPOSITION. 1. **Flash, Bang, Wallop**, w.m. David Heneker; 2. **Harvest of Love**, w.m. Benny Hill, Tony Hatch

SPECIAL AWARD. **The Beatles, Brian Epstein, George Martin**

SPECIAL AWARD IN RECOGNITION OF FIFTY YEARS' SERVICE TO THE MUSIC INDUSTRY. **The Performing Right Society**

1964

MOST PERFORMED WORK. 1. **Can't Buy Me Love**, w.m. John Lennon, Paul McCartney; 2. **A Hard Day's Night**, w.m. John Lennon, Paul McCartney

HIGHEST CERTIFIED BRITISH SALES. 1. **Can't Buy Me Love**, w.m. John Lennon, Paul McCartney; 2. **I Feel Fine**, w.m. John Lennon, Paul McCartney

OUTSTANDING SONGS. 1. **Downtown**, w.m. Tony Hatch; 2. **Losing You**, w.m. Tom Springfield, Clive Westlake

OUTSTANDING ORCHESTRAL/INSTRUMENTAL COMPOSITION. 1. **Bombay Duckling** (Kipling Theme), m. Max Harris

OUTSTANDING THEME FROM RADIO, T.V. OR FILM. 1. **Not So Much a Programme, More a Way of Life**, w.m. Ron Grainer, Ned Sherrin, Caryl Brahms; 2. **A Hard Day's Night**, w.m. John Lennon, Paul McCartney

OUTSTANDING SCORE OF A STAGE MUSICAL. 1. **Robert and Elizabeth**, w.m. Ron Grainer, Ronald Millar, 2. **Maggie May**, w.m. Lionel Bart

SPECIAL AWARD. **Paddy Roberts**

1965

MOST PERFORMED WORK. 1. **I'll Never Find Another You**, w.m. Tom Springfield; 2. **March of the Mods**, w.m. Tony Carr

HIGHEST CERTIFIED BRITISH SALES. 1. **We Can Work It Out**, w.m. John Lennon, Paul McCartney; 2. **Help**, w.m. John Lennon, Paul McCartney

OUTSTANDING SONG. 1. **Yesterday**, w.m. John Lennon, Paul McCartney; 2. **Where Are You Now My Love**, w.m. Tony Hatch, Jackie Trent

OUTSTANDING BEAT SONG. 1. **It's Not Unusual**, w.m. Gordon Mills, Les Reed; 2. **Look Through Any Window**, w.m. Graham Gouldman, Charles Silverman

OUTSTANDING NOVELTY COMPOSITION. 1. **A Windmill in Old Amsterdam**, w.m. Ted Dicks, Myles Rudge; 2. **Mrs. Brown, You've Got a Lovely Daughter**, w.m. Trevor Peacock

OUTSTANDING SCORE OF A STAGE MUSICAL. **Charlie Girl**, w.m. David Heneker, John Taylor

OUTSTANDING CONTEMPORARY FOLK SONG. **Catch the Wind**, w.m. Donovan

OUTSTANDING INSTRUMENTAL COMPOSITION. 1. **March of the Mods**, m. Tony Carr; 2. **The Kiss**, m. Jack Parnell

SPECIAL AWARD. **BBC-TV** (for the production of the series, 'A Song for Europe')

1966

MOST PERFORMED WORK. 1. **Michelle**, w.m. John Lennon, Paul McCartney; 2. **Yesterday**, w.m. John Lennon, Paul McCartney

HIGHEST CERTIFIED BRITISH SALES. 1. **Yellow Submarine**, w.m. John Lennon, Paul McCartney; 2. **What Would I Be**, w.m. Jackie Trent

BRITAIN'S INTERNATIONAL SONG. 1. **Winchester Cathedral**, w.m. Geoff Stephens; 2. **Call Me**, w.m. Tony Hatch

FILM SONG. 1. **Born Free**, w.m. John Barry, Don Black; 2. **Time Drags By**, w.m. Hank B. Marvin, Bruce Welch, Brian Bennett, John Rostill

NOVELTY SONG. 1. **Hev Yew Gotta Loight, Boy?**, w.m. Allan Smethurst; 2. **Dedicated Follower of Fashion**, w.m. Ray Davies

INSTRUMENTAL COMPOSITION. 1. **The Power Game**, m. Wayne Hill; 2. **Khartoum**, m. Frank Cordell

SPECIAL AWARD. **Joe Loss**

1967/1968

MOST PERFORMED WORK. **Puppet on a String,** w.m. Bill Martin, Phil Coulter; **This Is My Song,** w.m. Charles Chaplin

HIGHEST CERTIFIED BRITISH SALES FOR THE YEAR 1967. **The Last Waltz,** w.m. Les Reed, Barry Mason; **Hello Goodbye,** w.m. John Lennon, Paul McCartney

BRITAIN'S INTERNATIONAL SONG. **A Whiter Shade of Pale,** w.m. Gary Brooker, Keith Reid; **To Sir with Love,** w.m. Don Black, Mark London

BEST BRITISH SONG. **She's Leaving Home,** w.m. John Lennon, Paul McCartney; **Don't Sleep in the Subway,** w.m. Jackie Trent, Tony Hatch

NOVELTY SONG. **Grocer Jack,** w.m. Keith West, Mark Wirtz; **The Ballad of Bonnie and Clyde,** w.m. Mitch Murray, Peter Callander

BEST INSTRUMENTAL THEME. **Love in the Open Air,** m. Paul McCartney

SPECIAL AWARD. **Doctor Dolittle,** w.m. Leslie Bricusse

1968/1969

MOST PERFORMED WORK. **Congratulations,** w.m. Bill Martin, Phil Coulter; **Delilah,** w.m. Les Reed, Barry Mason

HIGHEST CERTIFIED BRITISH SALES FOR THE YEAR 1968. **Hey Jude,** w.m. John Lennon, Paul McCartney; **Delilah,** w.m. Les Reed, Barry Mason

BRITAIN'S INTERNATIONAL SONG. **Delilah,** w.m. Les Reed, Barry Mason; **Congratulations,** w.m. Bill Martin, Phil Coulter

MOST ROMANTIC SONG. **I Close My Eyes and Count To Ten,** w.m. Clive Westlake; **Jezamine,** w.m. Marty Wilde (Frere Manston), Ronnie Scott (Jack Gellar)

OUTSTANDING DANCE-BEAT SONG. **Build Me Up Buttercup.** w.m. Tony Macaulay, Michael D'Abo

NOVELTY SONG. **I'm the Urban Spaceman,** w.m. Neil Innes; **Rosie,** w.m. Don Partridge

LIGHT MUSIC COMPOSITION. **Ring of Kerry,** m. Peter Hope; **633 Squadron,** m. Ron Goodwin

CERTIFICATES OF HONOUR. **Abergavenny,** w.m. Marty Wilde (Frere Manston), Ronnie Scott (Jack Gellar); **Massachusetts,** w.m. Barry Gibb, Robin Gibb, Maurice Gibb; **The Fool On the Hill,** w.m. John Lennon, Paul McCartney

OUTSTANDING SERVICES TO BRITISH MUSIC. **Andrew Gold**

1969/1970

MOST PERFORMED WORK. Winner: **Ob-La-Di Ob-La-Da,** w.m. John Lennon, Paul McCartney; Runner-up: **Boom Bang-A-Bang,** w.m. Alan Moorhouse, Peter Warne

HIGHEST CERTIFIED BRITISH SALES FOR THE YEAR 1969. Winner: **Get Back,** w.m. John Lennon, Paul McCartney;

Runner-up: **Honky Tonk Woman,** w.m. Mick Jagger, Keith Richard

SONGWRITER OF THE YEAR. Winner: **Tony Macaulay**

BEST SONG. Winner: **Where Do You Go To My Lovely,** w.m. Peter Sarstedt; Runner-up: **Lights of Cincinnati,** w.m. Tony Macaulay, Geoff Stephens

BEST SCORE FROM A FILM OR MUSICAL PLAY. Winner: **Madwoman of Chaillot,** w.m. Michael Lewis; Runner-up: **Battle of Britain,** w.m. Ron Goodwin

OUTSTANDING LIGHT ORCHESTRAL. ARRANGER/COMPOSER. Winner: **Ernest Tomlinson**

BRITISH INTERNATIONAL HIT. Winner: **Love Is All,** w.m. Les Reed, Barry Mason; Runner-up: **Honky Tonk Woman,** w.m. Mick Jagger, Keith Richard

INTERNATIONAL ARTIST OF THE YEAR. Winner: **Tom Jones**

OUTSTANDING SERVICES TO BRITISH MUSIC. Winner: **Sir Noël Coward**

SPECIAL AWARD. Winner: **Space Oddity,** w.m. David Bowie

SPECIAL AWARD. Winner: **Melting Pot,** w.m. Roger Cook, Roger Greenaway; Runner-up: **Give Peace a Chance,** w.m. John Lennon, Paul McCartney

1970/1971

MOST PERFORMED WORK. Winner: **Yellow River,** w.m. Jeff Christie; Runner-up: **Knock, Knock, Who's There?** w.m. Geoff Stephens, John Carter

HIGHEST CERTIFIED BRITISH SALES FOR THE YEAR 1970. Winner: **In the Summertime,** w.m. Ray Dorset; Runner-up: **Love Grows,** w.m. Tony Macaulay, Barry Mason

SONGWRITERS OF THE YEAR. **Roger Cook, Roger Greenaway**

BEST SONG. Winner: **Something,** w.m. George Harrison; Runner-up: **We're Gonna Change the World,** w.m. David Matthews, Tim Harris

BEST THEME, FROM ANY FILM, TELEVISION PROGRAMME OR THEATRICAL PRODUCTION. Winner: **Who Do You Think You Are Kidding, Mr. Hitler,** w.m. Jimmy Perry, Derek Taverner; Runner-up: **Light Flight,** w.m. The Pentangle

BEST BALLAD OR ROMANTIC SONG. Winner: **Home Lovin' Man,** w.m. Tony Macaulay, Roger Greenaway; Runner-up: **Your Song,** w.m. Bernie Taupin, Elton John; Runner-up: **United We Stand,** w.m. Tony Hiller, Peter Simons

BEST 'POP' SONG. Winner: **Love Grows,** w.m. Barry Mason, Tony Macaulay; Runner-up: **When I'm Dead and Gone,** w.m. Bernard Gallagher, Graham Lyle

BEST NOVEL OR UNUSUAL SONG. Winner: **Grandad,** w.m. Ken Pickett, Herbie Flowers; Runner-up: **Gimme Dat Ding,** w.m. Albert Hammond, Mike Hazlewood

LIGHT MUSIC AWARD. Winner: **March from The Colour Suite,** w.m. Gordon Langford

INTERNATIONAL HIT BY BRITISH WRITERS. Winner: **In the Summertime,** w.m. Ray Dorset; Runner-up: **Let It Be,** w.m. John Lennon, Paul McCartney

OUTSTANDING SERVICES TO BRITISH MUSIC. Winner: **Cliff Richard**

SPECIAL AWARD. **Jesus Christ Superstar** (rock opera), w.m. Andrew Lloyd-Webber, Tim Rice

CERTIFICATES OF HONOUR: **Elton John, Bernie Taupin, Raymond Douglas Davies**

1971/1972

MOST PERFORMED WORK. Winner: **My Sweet Lord,** w.m. George Harrison; Runner-up: **Hot Love,** w.m. Marc Bolan

HIGHEST CERTIFIED BRITISH SALES FOR THE YEAR 1971. Winner: **My Sweet Lord,** w.m. George Harrison; Runner-up: **Ernie,** w.m. Benny Hill

SONGWRITERS OF THE YEAR. **Roger Cook, Roger Greenaway**

BEST SONG. Winner: **Don't Let It Die,** w.m. E. Smith; Runner-up: **Why,** w.m. Roger Whittaker, Joan Stanton

BEST SONG AND/OR THEME AND/OR SCORE FROM ANY FILM, TELEVISION PROGRAMME OR THEATRICAL PRODUCTION. Winner: **I Don't Know How To Love Him,** w.m. Tim Rice, Andrew Lloyd-Webber; Runner-up: **Sleepy Shores,** w.m. Johnny Pearson

BEST BALLAD OR ROMANTIC SONG. Winner: **No Matter How I Try,** w.m. Ray O'Sullivan; Runner-up: **When You Are a King,** w.m. John Hill, Roger Hill

BEST 'POP' SONG. Winner: **Simple Game,** w.m. Mike Pinder; Runner-up: **Freedom Come, Freedom Go,** w.m. Albert Hammond, Mike Hazlewood, Roger Cook, Roger Greenaway

BEST NOVEL OR UNUSUAL SONG. Winner: **Ernie,** w.m. Benny Hill; Runner-up: **Rosetta,** w.m. Mike Snow

INTERNATIONAL HIT BY BRITISH WRITERS. Winner: **Jesus Christ Superstar,** w.m. Andrew Lloyd-Webber, Tim Rice

Entertainment Music. **Ron Goodwin**

OUTSTANDING SERVICES TO BRITISH MUSIC. **Jimmy Kennedy**

1972/1973

MOST PERFORMED WORK. Winner: **Beg, Steal or Borrow,** w.m. Graeme Hall, Tony Cole, Steve Wolfe; Runner-up: **Meet Me on the Corner,** w.m. Roderick Clements

HIGHEST CERTIFIED BRITISH SALES FOR THE YEAR 1972. Winner: **Mouldy Old Dough,** w.m. Nigel Fletcher, Rob Woodward; Runner-up: **Solid Gold Easy Action,** w.m. Marc Bolan

SONGWRITER OF THE YEAR. **Gilbert O'Sullivan**

BEST SONG. Winner: **Without You,** w.m. Peter Ham, Tom Evans; Runner-up: **Alone Again (Naturally),** w.m. Gilbert O'Sullivan

BEST SONG AND/OR THEME OR SCORE FROM ANY FILM OR THEATRICAL PRODUCTION. Winner: **Diamonds Are Forever,** w.m. Don Black, John Barry; Runner-up: **Tommy** (Rock Opera), w.m. Peter Townshend

BEST SONG AND/OR THEME FROM ANY RADIO OR TELEVISION PROGRAMME. Winner: **Colditz,** w.m. Robert Farnon; Runner-up: **Country Matters,** w.m. Derek Hilton

BEST BALLAD OR ROMANTIC SONG. Winner: **The First Time Ever I Saw Your Face,** w.m. Ewan MacColl; Runner-up: **Claire,** w.m. Gilbert O'Sullivan

BEST 'POP' SONG. Winner: **Oh Babe What Would You Say,** w.m. Hurricane Smith; Runner-up: **Long Cool Woman in a Black Dress,** w.m. Roger Cook, Roger Greenaway, Alan Clark

BEST NOVEL OR UNUSUAL SONG. Winner: **The People Tree,** w.m. Leslie Bricusse, Anthony Newley; Runner-up: **Our Jackie's Getting Married,** w.m. Peter Skellern

INTERNATIONAL HIT BY BRITISH WRITERS. Winner: **Without You,** w.m. Peter Ham, Tom Evans; Runner-up. **Alone Again (Naturally),** w.m. Gilbert O'Sullivan

SPECIAL CERTIFICATES OF HONOUR. **Marc Bolan, Cat Stevens, Mitch Murray, Peter Callander, Elton John, Bernie Taupin**

OUTSTANDING SERVICES TO BRITISH MUSIC. **Vivian Ellis**

1973/1974

MOST PERFORMED SONG. Winner: **Get Down,** w.m. Gilbert O'Sullivan; Runner-up: **Power To All Our Friends,** w.m. Doug Flett, Guy Fletcher

BEST SELLING BRITISH RECORD OF 1973. Winner: **I Love You Love Me Love,** w.m. Gary Glitter, Mike Leander; Runner-up: **Merry Xmas Everybody,** w.m. Neville Holder, James Lea

SONGWRITERS OF THE YEAR. **Nicky Chinn, Mike Chapman**

BEST SONG. Winner: **Daniel,** w.m. Elton John, Bernie Taupin; Runner-up: **My Love,** w.m. Paul McCartney

BEST SCORE FROM ANY FILM OR THEATRICAL PRODUCTION. Winner: **Jesus Christ Superstar,** w.m. Andrew Lloyd Webber, Tim Rice; Runner-up: **Live and Let Die,** w.m. Paul McCartney

BEST SONG OR THEME FROM ANY RADIO OR T.V. PROGRAMME. Winner: **Galloping Home,** w.m. Denis King; Runner-up: **Children of Rome,** w.m. Stanley Myers

BEST BALLAD OR ROMANTIC SONG. Winner: **Won't Somebody Dance with Me,** w.m. Lynsey de Paul; Runner-up: **Like Sister and Brother,** w.m. Geoff Stephens, Roger Greenaway

BEST 'POP' SONG. Winner: **You Won't Find Another Fool Like Me,** w.m. Tony Macaulay, Geoff Stephens; Runner-up: **Get Down,** w.m. Gilbert O'Sullivan

BEST NOVEL OR UNUSUAL SONG. Winner: **Nice One Cyril,** w.m. Harold Spiro, Helen Clarke

BEST BEAT SONG. Winner: **Rubber Bullets,** w.m. K. Godley, L. Creme, G. Gouldman; Runner-up: **Blockbuster,** w.m. Mike Chapman, Nicky Chinn

INTERNATIONAL HIT BY BRITISH WRITERS. Winner: **Power To All Our Friends,** w.m. Doug Flett, Guy Fletcher; Runner-up: **Crocodile Rock,** w.m. Elton John, Bernie Taupin; Runner-up: **Angie,** w.m. Mick Jagger, Keith Richard

SPECIAL CERTIFICATES OF HONOUR. **David Bowie, Gary Glitter, Neville Holder, James Lea, Mike Leander, The Moody Blues, Roy Wood, Jackie Rae, BBC Radio 2**

OUTSTANDING SERVICES TO BRITISH MUSIC. **Tolchard Evans**

1974/1975

MOST PERFORMED SONG. Winner: **Wombling Song**, w.m. Mike Batt; Runner-up: **The Air That I Breathe**, w.m. Albert Hammond, Mike Hazlewood

BEST SELLING BRITISH RECORD. Winner: **Tiger Feet**, w.m. Nicky Chinn, Mike Chapman; Runner-up: **Billy—Don't Be a Hero**, w.m. Mitch Murray, Peter Callander

SONGWRITERS OF THE YEAR. **Bill Martin, Phil Coulter**

BEST SONG. Winner: **Streets of London**, w.m. Ralph McTell; Runner-up: **Sad Sweet Dreamer**, w.m. Des Parton

BEST NEW MUSICAL. Winner: **Treasure Island**, w.m. Hal Shaper, Cyril Ornadel; Runner-up: **Billy** w.m. John Barry, Don Black

BEST THEME FROM A FILM OR A STAGE, RADIO OR TELEVISION PRODUCTION. Winner: **No Honestly!**, w.m. Lynsey de Paul; Runner-up: **The Wombling Song**, w.m. Mike Batt

BEST 'POP' SONG. Winner: **Kung Fu Fighting**, w.m. Carl Douglas; Runner-up: **Killer Queen**, w.m. Freddie Mercury

BEST NOVEL OR UNUSUAL SONG (from last year). **Part of the Union**, w.m. Richard Hudson, John Ford

BEST LIGHT ORCHESTRAL WORK. Winner: **Four Dances from Aladdin**, m. Ernest Tomlinson; Runner-up: **Suite No.1 for Small Orchestra**, m. John Hall

BRITISH INTERNATIONAL HIT. Winner: **The Night Chicago Died**, w.m. Mitch Murray, Peter Callander; Runner-up: **Kung Fu Fighting**, w.m. Carl Douglas

SPECIAL CERTIFICATES OF HONOUR. **Mike Oldfield, Rick Wakeman, Nicky Chinn, Mike Chapman, Teddy Holmes, Pink Floyd, Peter Shelley, Wayne Bickerton, Tony Waddington, Mike Leander, Gary Glitter, BBC Radio 2, Radio Luxembourg, Capital Radio**

OUTSTANDING SERVICES TO BRITISH MUSIC. **Vera Lynn, O.B.E.**

1975/1976

MOST PERFORMED WORK. Winner: **I'm Not in Love**, w.m. Eric Stewart, Graham Gouldman; Runner-up: **Last Farewell**, w.m. Roger Whittaker, R.A. Webster

BEST SELLING BRITISH RECORD. Winner: **Bohemian Rhapsody**, w.m. Freddie Mercury; Runner-up: **Sailing**, w.m. Gavin Sutherland

SONGWRITERS OF THE YEAR. **Wayne Bickerton, Tony Waddington**

BEST MUSICAL. Winner: **Great Expectations**, w.m. Hal Shaper, Cyril Ornadel

BEST FILM SCORE. Winner: **Murder On the Orient Express**, w.m. Richard Rodney Bennett; Runner-up: **Tommy**, w.m. Peter Townshend

BEST THEME FROM A RADIO OR TELEVISION PRODUCTION. Winner: **Upstairs Downstairs Theme** (The Edwardians), m. Alexander Faris; Runner-up: **The Good Word** (Theme from Nationwide), m. Johnny Scott

BEST 'MIDDLE-OF-THE-ROAD' (MOR) SONG. Winner: **Harry**, w.m. Catherine Howe; Runner-up: **Last Farewell**, w.m. Roger Whittaker, R. A. Webster

BEST 'POP' SONG. Winner: **I'm Not in Love**, w.m. Eric Stewart, Graham Gouldman; Runner-up: **Bohemian Rhapsody**, w.m. Freddie Mercury

BEST INSTRUMENTAL WORK. Winner: **Introduction and Air to a Stained Glass Window**, w.m. John Gregory; Runner-up: **Fantasia on a Nursery Song**, w.m. Leo Norman

BEST MUSICAL WORK FOR CHILDREN. Winner: **Captain Noah and His Floating Zoo**, w.m. Michael Flanders, Joseph Horovitz; Runner-up: **Quilp**, w.m. Anthony Newley

INTERNATIONAL HIT OF THE YEAR. Winner: **I'm Not in Love**, w.m. Eric Stewart, Graham Gouldman; Runner-up: **Island Girl**, w.m. Elton John, Bernie Taupin; Runner-up: **Doctor's Orders**, w.m. Roger Greenaway, Roger Cook, Geoff Stephens; Runner-up: **Magic**, w.m. David Paton, William Lyall; Runner-up: **Sky High**, w.m. Clive Scott, Desmond Dyer; Runner-up: **Sailing**, w.m. Gavin Sutherland

OUTSTANDING SERVICES TO BRITISH MUSIC. **Dick James**

1976/1977

MOST PERFORMED WORK. Winner: **Save Your Kisses for Me**, w.m. Tony Hiller, Martin Lee, Lee Sheriden; Runner-up: **Don't Go Breaking My Heart**, w.m. Elton John, Bernie Taupin

BEST SELLING BRITISH RECORD. Winner: **Save Your Kisses for Me**, w.m. Tony Hiller, Martin Lee, Lee Sheriden; Runner-up: **Don't Go Breaking My Heart**, w.m. Elton John, Bernie Taupin

SONGWRITER OF THE YEAR. **Biddu**

BEST MUSICAL. **Teeth 'n' Smiles**, w.m. Nick Bicat, Tony Bicat; **The Comedy of Errors**, w.m. Guy Woolfenden

BEST THEME FROM RADIO OR TELEVISION PRODUCTION. Winner: **Sam**, w.m. John McCabe; Runner-up: **Bouquet of Barbed Wire**, w.m. Dennis Farnon; Runner-up: **The Sweeney**, w.m. Harry South

BEST 'MIDDLE-OF-THE-ROAD' (MOR) SONG. Winner: **Music**, w.m. John Miles; Runner-up: **Don't Cry For Me, Argentina**, w.m. Tim Rice, Andrew Lloyd Webber; Runner-up: **Miss You Nights**, w.m. Dave Townsend

BEST 'POP' SONG. Winner: **Don't Go Breaking My Heart**, w.m. Elton John, Bernie Taupin; Runner-up: **Heart on My Sleeve**, w.m. Benny Gallagher, Graham Lyle; Runner-up: **We Do It**, w.m. Russell Stone

BEST INSTRUMENTAL WORK. Winner: **Rain Forest**, m. Biddu; Runner-up: **Theme from a Non-Existent TV Series**, m. Elton John, Bernie Taupin; Runner-up: **The Sweeney**, m. Harry South

INTERNATIONAL HIT OF THE YEAR. Winner: **Save Your Kisses for Me**, w.m. Tony Hiller, Martin Lee, Lee Sheriden; Runner-up: **Don't Go Breaking My Heart**, w.m. Elton John, Bernie Taupin; Runner-up: **You Should Be Dancing**, w.m. Barry Gibb, Maurice Gibb, Robin Gibb

SPECIAL AWARDS. **Monty Norman, Led Zeppelin**

OUTSTANDING SERVICES TO BRITISH MUSIC. **Sir Adrian Boult CH**

1977/1978

MOST PERFORMED WORK. Winner: **Don't Cry for Me Argentina**, w.m. Tim Rice, Andrew Lloyd Webber; Runner-up: **Don't Give Up On Us**, w.m. Tony Macaulay; Runner-up: **I Don't Want To Put a Hold On You**, w.m. Berni Flint, Michael Flint

BEST SELLING BRITISH RECORD. Winner: **Mull of Kintyre**, w.m. Paul McCartney, Denny Laine; Runner-up: **Don't Cry for Me Argentina**, w.m. Tim Rice, Andrew Lloyd Webber; Runner-up: **Don't Give Up On Us**, w.m. Tony Macaulay

SONGWRITER OF THE YEAR. **Tony Macaulay**

BEST MUSICAL. **Privates On Parade**, w.m. Denis King, Peter Nicholls

BEST THEME FROM RADIO OR TELEVISION PRODUCTION. Winner: **Poldark**, w.m. Kenyon Emrys-Roberts, Runner-up: **Wings**, w.m. Alexander Faris; Runner-up: **Love for Lydia**, m. Harry Rabinowitz

BEST SONG MUSICALLY AND LYRICALLY. Winner: **Don't Cry for Me Argentina**, w.m. Tim Rice, Andrew Lloyd Webber; Runner-up: **Sam**, w.m. John Farrar, Hank Marvin, Don Black; Runner-up: **How Deep Is Your Love**, w.m. Barry Gibb, Robin Gibb, Maurice Gibb

BEST 'POP' SONG. Winner: **How Deep Is Your Love**, w.m. Barry Gibb, Robin Gibb, Maurice Gibb; Runner-up: **Mull of Kintyre**, w.m. Paul McCartney, Denny Laine; Runner-up: **Boogie Nights**, w.m. Rod Temperton; Runner-up: **Don't Cry for Me Argentina**, w.m. Tim Rice, Andrew Lloyd Webber

BEST INSTRUMENTAL OR POPULAR ORCHESTRAL WORK. Winner: **Cavatina**, w.m. Stanley Myers; Runner-up: **The Snow Goose**, w.m. Ed Welch, Spike Milligan; Runner-up: **Love Transformation**, w.m. Roger Greenaway

INTERNATIONAL HIT OF THE YEAR. Winner: **Don't Cry for Me Argentina**, w.m. Tim Rice, Andrew Lloyd Webber; Runner-up: **How Deep Is Your Love**, w.m. Barry Gibb, Robin Gibb, Maurice Gibb; Runner-up: **Angelo**, w.m. Tony Hiller, Lee Sheriden, Martin Lee

BEST FILM MUSIC OR SONG. Winner: **How Deep Is Your Love**, w.m. Barry Gibb, Robin Gibb, Maurice Gibb; Runner-up: **The Duelists**, w.m. Howard Blake; Runner-up: **The Scarlet Buccaneer**, w.m. John Addison

OUTSTANDING LYRIC OF THE YEAR. Winner: **Matchstalk Men and Matchstalk Cats and Dogs**, w.m. Michael Coleman, Brian Burke; Runner-up: **Heaven on the Seventh Floor**, w.m. Dominique Bugatti, Frank Musker

SPECIAL AWARD. **The Bee Gees**

OUTSTANDING SERVICES TO BRITISH MUSIC. **Harry Mortimer, OBE**

1978/1979

MOST PERFORMED WORK. Winner: **Night Fever**, w.m. Barry Gibb, Robin Gibb, Maurice Gibb; Runner-up: **Mull of Kintyre**, w.m. Paul McCartney; Runner-up: **The Floral Dance**, w.m. Kate Moss

BEST SELLING 'A' SIDE. Winner: **Night Fever**, w.m. Barry Gibb, Robin Gibb, Maurice Gibb; Runner-up: **Rat Trap**, w.m.

Bob Geldof; Runner-up: **Matchstalk Men and Matchstalk Cats and Dogs**, w.m. Michael Coleman, Brian Burke

SONGWRITER OF THE YEAR. **The Gibb Brothers**

BEST MUSICAL. **Evita**, w.m. Tim Rice, Andrew Lloyd Weber

BEST THEME FROM RADIO OR TELEVISION PRODUCTION. Winner: **Lillie**, m. Joseph Horovitz; Runner-up: **Fawlty Towers**, m. Dennis Wilson; Runner-up: **Hong Kong Beat**, m. Richard Denton, Martin Cook

BEST SONG MUSICALLY AND LYRICALLY. Winner: **Baker Street**, w.m. Gerry Rafferty; Runner-up: **Wuthering Heights**, w.m. Kate Bush; Runner-up: **Can't Smile Without You**, w.m. Chris Arnold, David Martin, Geoff Morrow

BEST 'POP' SONG. Winner: **Baker Street**, w.m. Gerry Rafferty; Runner-up: **Wuthering Heights**, w.m. Kate Bush; Runner-up: **Night Fever**, w.m. Barry Gibb, Robin Gibb, Maurice Gibb

BEST INSTRUMENTAL OR POPULAR ORCHESTRA WORK. Winner: **Song for Guy**, m. Elton John; Runner-up: **Dr. Who**, m. Ron Grainer; Runner-up: **Heartsong**, m. Gordon Giltrap

INTERNATIONAL HIT OF THE YEAR. Winner: **Stayin' Alive**, w.m. Barry Gibb, Robin Gibb, Maurice Gibb; Runner-up: **It's a Heartache**, w.m. Ronnie Scott, Steve Wolfe; Runner-up: **Dreadlock Holiday**, w.m. Eric Stewart, Graham Gouldman

BEST FILM SCORE. Winner: **The Silent Witness**, m. Alan Hawkshaw; Runner-up: **Watership Down**, m. Angela Morley, Mike Batt, Malcolm Williamson; Runner-up: **The 39 Steps**, m. Ed Welch

BEST FILM SONG. Winner: **Bright Eyes**, w.m. Mike Batt; Runner-up: **Grease**, w.m. Barry Gibb; Runner-up: **Stayin' Alive**, w.m. Barry Gibb, Robin Gibb, Maurice Gibb

OUTSTANDING BRITISH LYRIC. Winner: **The Man with the Child in His Eyes**, w. Kate Bush; Runner-up: **Railway Hotel**, w. Mike Batt; Runner-up: **Baker Street**, w. Gerry Rafferty

OUTSTANDING SERVICES TO BRITISH MUSIC. **George Martin**

OUTSTANDING CONTRIBUTION TO BRITISH MUSIC. **E.L.O.**

OUTSTANDING SERVICES TO BRITISH SONGWRITERS. **Victor Knight**

1979/1980

MOST PERFORMED WORK. Winner: **Bright Eyes**, w.m. Mike Batt; Runner-up: **We Don't Talk Anymore**, w.m. Alan Tarney; Runner-up: **Cavatina**, w.m. Stanley Myers

BEST SELLING 'A' SIDE. Winner: **Bright Eyes**, w.m. Mike Batt; Runner-up: **I Don't Like Mondays**, w.m. Bob Geldof; Runner-up: **Another Brick in the Wall**, w.m. Roger Waters

SONGWRITER OF THE YEAR. **Ben Findon**

BEST BRITISH MUSICAL. Winner: **Songbook**, Monty Norman, Julian More; Runner-up: **A Day in Hollywood, a Night in the Ukraine**, Dick Vosburgh, Frank Lazarus

BEST THEME FROM A RADIO OR TELEVISION PRODUCTION. Winner: **Nunc Dimittis**, m. Geoffrey Burgon; Runner-up: **Secret Army**, m. Robert Farnon; Runner-up: **Shoestring**, m. George Fenton

BEST SONG MUSICALLY AND LYRICALLY. Winner: **The Logical Song**, w.m. Rick Davies, Roger Hodgson; Runner-up:

Bright Eyes, w.m. Mike Batt; Runner-up: **We Don't Talk Anymore,** w.m. Alan Tarney

BEST 'POP' SONG. Winner: **I Don't Like Mondays,** w.m. Bob Geldof; Runner-up: **Video Killed the Radio Star,** w.m. Bruce Woolley, Trevor Horn, Geoff Downes; Runner-up: **Off the Wall,** w.m. Rodney Temperton

BEST INSTRUMENTAL OR POPULAR ORCHESTRAL WORK. Winner: **War of the Worlds,** m. Jeff Wayne; Runner-up: **The Valley of Swords,** m. Mike Batt; Runner-up: **African Sanctus,** m. David Fanshawe

INTERNATIONAL HIT OF THE YEAR. Winner: **We Don't Talk Anymore,** w.m. Alan Tarney; Runner-up: **Too Much Heaven,** w.m. Barry Gibb, Robin Gibb, Maurice Gibb; Runner-up: **I Don't Like Mondays,** w.m. Bob Geldof

BEST FILM SONG, THEME OR SCORE. Winner: **Caravans,** w.m. Mike Batt; Runner-up: **Music Machine,** w.m. Leslie Hurdle, Frank Ricotti; Runner-up: **Yanks,** m. Richard Rodney Bennett

OUTSTANDING BRITISH LYRIC. Winner: **I Don't Like Mondays,** w. Bob Geldof; Runner-up: **He Was Beautiful,** w. Cleo Laine; Runner-up: **Bright Eyes,** w. Mike Batt

OUTSTANDING SERVICES TO BRITISH MUSIC. **Sir Robert Mayer**

SPECIAL AWARD FOR INTERNATIONAL ACHIEVEMENT. **Paul McCartney**

SPECIAL AWARD FOR LIFE ACHIEVEMENT. **E.Y. Harburg, Jimmy Kennedy**

1980/1981

MOST PERFORMED WORK. Winner: **Together We Are Beautiful,** w.m. Ken Leray; Runner-up: **January, February,** w.m.. Alan Tarney; Runner-up: **I'm in the Mood for Dancing,** w.m. Ben Findon, Michael Myers, Robert Puzey

BEST SELLING 'A' SIDE. Winner: **There's No One Quite Like Grandma,** w.m. Gordon Lorenz; Runner-up: **Woman In Love,** w.m. Barry Gibb, Robin Gibb; Runner-up: **Don't Stand So Close to Me,** w.m. Sting

SONGWRITER OF THE YEAR. **Sting**

BEST THEME FROM A RADIO OR TELEVISION PRODUCTION. Winner: **I Could Be So Good for You,** w.m. Gerard Kenny, Pat Waterman; Runner-up: **Fox,** m. George Fenton; Runner-up: **Juliet Bravo,** m. J.S. Bach, Arr. Derek Goom

BEST SONG MUSICALLY AND LYRICALLY. Winner: **Woman In Love,** w.m. Barry Gibb, Robin Gibb; Runner-up: **Babooshka,** w.m. Kate Bush; Runner-up: **Together We Are Beautiful,** w.m. Ken Leray

BEST 'POP' SONG. Winner: **Stop the Cavalry,** w.m. Jona Lewie; Runner-up: **Don't Stand So Close to Me,** w.m. Sting; Runner-up: **What You're Proposing,** w.m. Francis Rossi, Bernard Frost

BEST INTERNATIONAL HIT OF THE YEAR. Winner: **Another Brick in the Wall,** w.m. Roger Waters; Runner-up: **Woman In Love,** w.m. Barry Gibb, Robin Gibb; Runner-up: **Another One Bites the Dust,** w.m. John Deacon

BEST FILM SONG, THEME OR SCORE. Winner: **Xanadu,** w.m. Jeff Lynne; Runner-up: **Flash,** m. Brian May; Runner-up: **Silver Dream Machine,** m. David Essex

OUTSTANDING BRITISH LYRIC. Winner: **Take That Look Off Your Face,** w. Don Black; Runner-up: **Stop the Cavalry,** w. Jona Lewie; Runner-up: **Woman in Love,** w. Barry Gibb, Robin Gibb

OUTSTANDING SERVICES TO BRITISH MUSIC. **Sir William Walton**

SPECIAL AWARD FOR OUTSTANDING CONTRIBUTION TO BRITISH MUSIC. **John Lennon**

1981/1982

MOST PERFORMED WORK. Winner: **You Drive Me Crazy,** w.m. Ronnie Harwood; Runner-up: **Woman,** w.m. John Lennon

BEST SELLING 'A' SIDE. Winner: **Stand and Deliver,** w.m. Adam Ant, Marco Pirroni; Runner-up: **Vienna,** w.m. Billy Currie, Chris Cross, Warren Cann, Midge Ure; Runner-up: **Don't You Want Me,** w.m. Phil Oakey, Adrian Wright, Jo Callis

SONGWRITERS OF THE YEAR. **Adam Ant, Marco Pirroni**

BEST BRITISH MUSICAL. **Cats,** Andrew Lloyd Webber, T.S. Eliot, Trevor Nunn

BEST THEME FROM A TELEVISION OR RADIO PRODUCTION. Winner: **Brideshead Revisited,** m. Geoffrey Burgon; Runner-up: **Flame Trees of Thika,** m. Ken Howard, Alan Blaikley; Runner-up: **Shillingbury Tales,** m. Ed Welch

BEST SONG MUSICALLY AND LYRICALLY. Winner: **Memory,** w.m. Andrew Lloyd Webber, Trevor Nunn, T.S. Eliot; Runner-up: **Woman,** w.m. John Lennon; Runner-up: **The Land of Make Believe,** w.m. Andy Hill, Pete Sinfield

BEST 'POP' SONG. Winner: **Every Little Thing She Does Is Magic,** w.m. Sting; Runner-up: **Don't You Want Me,** w.m. Phil Oakey, Adrian Wright, Jo Callis; Runner-up: **Wired for Sound,** w.m. Alan Tarney, B.A. Robertson

INTERNATIONAL HIT OF THE YEAR. Winner: **In the Air Tonight,** w.m. Phil Collins; Runner-up: **(Just Like) Starting Over,** w.m. John Lennon; Runner-up: **Woman in Love,** w.m. Barry Gibb, Robin Gibb; Runner-up: **Every Little Thing She Does Is Magic,** w.m. Sting

BEST FILM THEME OR SONG. Winner: **The French Lieutenant's Woman,** m. Carl Davis; Runner-up: **Without Your Love,** m. Billy Nicholls; Runner-up: **For Your Eyes Only,** w.m. Bill Conti, Mike Leeson

OUTSTANDING BRITISH LYRIC. Winner: **Woman,** w. John Lennon; Runner-up: **The One You Love,** w.m. Graham Russell; Runner-up: **When He Shines,** w.m. Florrie Palmer, Dominic Bugatti

OUTSTANDING SERVICES TO BRITISH MUSIC. **Sir Lennox Berkeley CBE Hon Mus D**

OUTSTANDING CONTRIBUTION TO BRITISH MUSIC. **Pete Townshend, Roger Daltrey, Kenney Jones, John Entwistle, Keith Moon**

1982/1983

MOST PERFORMED WORK. Winner: **Golden Brown,** w.m. Jean J. Burnell, Hugh A. Cornwell, Jet Black, David Greenfield;

Runner-up: **Oh Julie,** w.m. Shakin Stevens; Runner-up: **Love Plus One,** w.m. Nick Heyward

BEST SELLING 'A' SIDE. Winner: **Come On Eileen,** w.m. Kevin Rowland, Kevin Adams, James Paterson; Runner-up: **Do You Really Want To Hurt Me,** w.m. George O'Dowd, Michael Craig, John Moss, Roy Hay; Runner-up: **Ebony and Ivory,** w.m. Paul McCartney

SONGWRITER OF THE YEAR. **Andy Hill**

BEST BRITISH MUSICAL. **Windy City,** w.m. Dick Vosburgh, Tony Macauley

BEST THEME FROM A TELEVISION OR RADIO PRODUCTION. Winner: **Theme From Harry's Game,** m. Paul Brennan; Runner-up: **Omnibus,** m. George Fenton; Runner-up: **Smiley's People,** m. Patrick Gowers

BEST SONG MUSICALLY AND LYRICALLY. Winner: **Have You Ever Been in Love,** w.m. Andy Hill, Pete Sinfield, John Danter; Runner-up: **Now Those Days Are Gone,** w.m. Andy Hill, Nichola Martin; Runner-up: **Heartbreaker,** w.m. Barry Gibb, Robin Gibb, Maurice Gibb

BEST 'POP' SONG. Winner: **Our House,** w.m. Carl Smyth, C.J. Foreman; Runner-up: **I Don't Wanna Dance,** w.m. Eddy Grant; Runner-up: **Come On Eileen,** w.m. Kevin Rowland, Kevin Adams, James Paterson

INTERNATIONAL HIT OF THE YEAR. Winner: **Ebony and Ivory,** w.m. Paul McCartney; Runner-up: **Heartbreaker,** w.m. Barry Gibb, Robin Gibb, Maurice Gibb; Runner-up: **Don't You Want Me,** w.m. Jo Callis, Phil Oakey, Adrian Wright

BEST FILM THEME OR SONG. Winner: **For All Mankind,** m. Ravi Shankar, George Fenton; Runner-up: **Time and Tide,** m. Alan Price; Runner-up: **Another Brick in the Wall,** w.m. Roger Waters

OUTSTANDING BRITISH LYRIC. Winner: **Private Investigations,** w. Mark Knopfler; Runner-up: **The Dreaming,** w. Kate Bush; Runner-up: **Have You Ever Been in Love,** w.m. Andy Hill, Pete Sinfield, John Danter

LIFETIME ACHIEVEMENT IN BRITISH MUSIC. **Vivian Ellis**

OUTSTANDING CONTRIBUTION TO BRITISH MUSIC. **Genesis: Peter Gabriel, Phil Collins, Steve Hackett, Michael Rutherford, Tony Banks**

SPECIAL AWARD FOR 25 YEARS IN THE MUSIC BUSINESS. **The Shadows**

1983/1984

MOST PERFORMED WORK. **Every Breath You Take,** w.m. Gordon Sumner (Sting)

BEST SELLING 'A' SIDE. **Karma Chameleon,** w.m. George O'Dowd, John Moss, Michael Craig, Roy Hay, Phil Pickett

SONGWRITER OF THE YEAR. **Annie Lennox, Dave Stewart**

BEST BRITISH MUSICAL. **Blood Brothers,** w.m. Willie Russell

BEST THEME FROM TELEVISION OR RADIO PRODUCTION. **That's Livin' Alright.** w.m. David Mackay, Ken Ashby

BEST SONG MUSICALLY AND LYRICALLY. **Every Breath You Take,** w.m. Gordon Sumner (Sting)

BEST 'POP' SONG. **Karma Chameleon,** w.m. George O'Dowd, John Moss, Michael Craig, Roy Hay, Phil Pickett

BEST 'ROCK' SONG. **Let's Dance,** w.m. David Jones (David Bowie)

INTERNATIONAL HIT OF THE YEAR. **Let's Dance,** w.m. David Jones (David Bowie)

BEST FILM THEME OR SONG. **Going Home,** w.m. Mark Knopfler

OUTSTANDING SERVICES TO BRITISH MUSIC. **Andrew Lloyd Webber**

OUTSTANDING CONTRIBUTION TO BRITISH MUSIC. **Status Quo**

1984/1985

MOST PERFORMED WORK. **Careless Whisper,** w.m. George Michael, Andrew Ridgeley

BEST SELLING 'A' SIDE. **Do They Know It's Christmas?,** w.m. Bob Geldof, Midge Ure

SONGWRITER OF THE YEAR. **George Michael**

BEST BRITISH MUSICAL. **The Hired Man,** w.m. Howard Goodall

BEST THEME FROM TELEVISION OR RADIO PRODUCTION. **Jewel in the Crown,** m. George Fenton

BEST SONG MUSICALLY AND LYRICALLY. **Against All Odds (Take a Look at Me Now),** w.m. Phil Collins

BEST CONTEMPORARY SONG. **Two Tribes,** w.m. Holly Johnson, Peter Gill, Mark O'Toole

INTERNATIONAL HIT OF THE YEAR. **The Reflex,** w.m. Simon Le Bon, John Taylor, Roger Taylor, Andy Taylor, Nick Rhodes

BEST FILM THEME OR SONG. **We All Stand Together,** w.m. Paul McCartney

OUTSTANDING SERVICES TO BRITISH MUSIC. **Sir Michael Tippett**

OUTSTANDING CONTRIBUTION TO BRITISH MUSIC. **Moody Blues**

JIMMY KENNEDY AWARD. **Tommie Connor**

1985/1986

MOST PERFORMED WORK. **Easy Lover,** w.m. Phil Collins, Philip Bailey, Nathan East

BEST SELLING 'A' SIDE. **I Know Him So Well,** w.m. Tim Rice, Bjorn Ulvaeus, Benny Andersson

SONGWRITER OF THE YEAR. **Roland Orzabel (Tears for Fears)**

BEST BRITISH MUSICAL. **Me and My Girl,** Reginald Armitage, Douglas Furber

BEST THEME FROM TELEVISION OR RADIO PRODUCTION. **Edge of Darkness,** m. Eric Clapton, Michael Kamen

BEST SONG MUSICALLY AND LYRICALLY. **Nikita,** w.m. Elton John, Bernie Taupin

BEST CONTEMPORARY SONG. **We Don't Need Another Hero,** w.m. Graham Lyle, Terry Britten

BRITISH AWARDS, 1985/1986

INTERNATIONAL HIT OF THE YEAR. **19,** w.m. Paul Hardcastle, Mike Oldfield, Bill Couturie, Jonas McCormack

BEST FILM THEME OR SONG. **We Don't Need Another Hero,** w.m. Graham Lyle, Terry Britten

OUTSTANDING SERVICES TO BRITISH MUSIC. **Dr. Malcolm Arnold CBE**

OUTSTANDING CONTRIBUTION TO BRITISH MUSIC. **Elton John**

JIMMY KENNEDY AWARD. **Lionel Bart**

III

Themes, Trademarks, and Signatures

Never to talk of oneself is a form of hypocrisy.

Nietzsche

This Part contains six divisions of theme, trademark, and signature songs: (1) Performers and Entertainers (2) Colleges, Universities and Other Educational Institutions (3) Advertising Jingles and Songs Used To Promote Commercial Products (4) Political Campaign Songs (5) Church Chimes and Carillons (6) American Bugle Calls.

It is not the purpose of this Part to include all possible theme, trademark, and signature songs as that list is endless. Only those songs deemed popular enough for inclusion in Part V are entered here.

For reasons of space, however, not all titles cited as themes, trademarks, and signatures in Part V are included. For further information about song popularity, refer to Authors' Notes at the front of this book.

For more complete information about a particular song entered here, see Part V; all song titles in this Part are included in Part V. In most cases, classical and folk sources ("based on") are also included in Part V.

PERFORMERS AND ENTERTAINERS

In this division, songs associated with particular performers and entertainers are listed alphabetically under the artist's name.

Ambrose **When Day Is Done**

Amos and Andy **The Perfect Song**

The Andrews Sisters **Bei Mir Bist Du Schon**

Louis Armstrong **When It's Sleepy Time Down South**

Gene Austin **My Blue Heaven**

Bonnie Baker **Oh Johnny, Oh Johnny, Oh!**

Charlie Barnet **Skyliner**

James Barton **Miss Annabelle Lee**

Count Basie **One O'Clock Jump**

Nora Bayes **Shine On Harvest Moon**

Tony Bennett **Because of You; I Left My Heart in San Francisco**

Jack Benny **Love in Bloom**

Milton Berle **Near You**

Ben Bernie **Au Revoir, Pleasant Dreams**

Stanley Black **That Old Black Magic**

Jules Bledsoe **Ol' Man River**

Emile Boreo **Parade of the Wooden Soldiers**

Lucienne Boyer **Speak to Me of Love (Parlez-Moi d'Amour)**

Fanny Brice **My Man; Rose of Washington Square**

Carl Brisson **Cocktails for Two**

Les Brown **Sentimental Journey**

Cab Calloway **Minnie the Moocher**

Eddie Calvert **O Mein Papa**

Eddie Cantor **Ida, Sweet as Apple Cider; Makin' Whoopee**

Frankie Carle **Sunrise Serenade**

Maurice Chevalier **Louise; Mimi**

Maggie Cline **Throw Him Down McCloskey**

Rosemary Clooney **Tenderly**

George M. Cohan **Give My Regards to Broadway**

Nat "King" Cole **Straighten Up and Fly Right**

Russ Columbo **Sweet and Lovely**

Perry Como **Dream Along with Me (I'm on My Way to a Star)**

Billy Cotton **Somebody Stole My Gal**

Noël Coward **I'll See You Again**

Francis Craig **Near You**

Bing Crosby **Where the Blue of the Night; White Christmas**

Billy Daniels **That Old Black Magic**

Bessie McCoy Davis **The Yama Yama Man**

Marlene Dietrich **Falling in Love Again**

Reginald Dixon **I Do Like to Be Beside the Seaside**

Jimmy Dorsey **So Rare** (closing theme)

Tommy Dorsey **I'm Getting Sentimental Over You**

Morton Downey **Carolina Moon**

Eddy Duchin **My Twilight Dream**

Jimmy Durante **Inka Dinka Doo**

Nelson Eddy **Shortnin' Bread**

Duke Ellington **Take the "A" Train**

G.H. Elliott (The Chocolate Colored Coon) **I Used To Sigh for the Silvery Moon**

Benny Fields **Broadway Rhythm**

Gracie Fields **Sally**

Eddie Fisher **May I Sing to You**

Mary Ford **How High the Moon**

George Formby **Leaning on the Lamp Post**

Roy Fox **Whispering**

Judy Garland **Over the Rainbow**

Carroll Gibbons **On the Air**

Arthur Godfrey **(It) Seems Like Old Times**

Benny Goodman **Goodbye** (closing theme); **Let's Dance** (opening theme)

Glen Gray **Smoke Rings**

Phil Harris **The Preacher and the Bear; That's What I Like About the South**

Anna Held **I Just Can't Make My Eyes Behave**

Hildegarde **Darling, Je Vous Aime Beaucoup**

Libby Holman **Moanin' Low**

Bob Hope **Thanks for the Memory**

Harry Horlick **Two Guitars**

Lena Horne **Stormy Weather**

Joe E. Howard **I Wonder Who's Kissing Her Now**

Leslie (Hutch) Hutchinson **Begin the Beguine**

The Ink Spots **If I Didn't Care**

Harry James **Ciribiribin; You Made Me Love You**

George Jessel **My Mother's Eyes**

Al Jolson **My Mammy; Sonny Boy**

Charlie Kunz **Clap Hands, Here Comes Charley**

Frankie Laine **We'll Be Together Again**

Mario Lanza **Be My Love**

Harry Lauder **I Love a Lassie**

Gertrude Lawrence **Limehouse Blues**

Layton and Johnstone **Dear Old Southland**

Harry Leader **Music, Maestro, Please**

Peggy Lee **Mañana Is Soon Enough for Me**

Eddie Leonard **Roll Dem Roly Boly Eyes**

Ted Lewis **When My Baby Smiles at Me**

Beatrice Lillie **There Are Fairies at the Bottom of Our Garden**

Guy Lombardo **Auld Lang Syne; Coquette**

Vincent Lopez **Nola**

Joe Loss **In the Mood**

Bert Lown and his Hotel Biltmore Orchestra **Bye Bye Blues**

Nellie Lutcher **Hurry On Down**

Tommy Lyman **My Melancholy Baby**

Vera Lynn **Yours**

John MacCormack **Mother Machree**

The Mamas and the Papas **Monday Monday; California Dreamin'**

Dean Martin **Everybody Loves Somebody (Sometime); That's Amore**

Mary Martin **My Heart Belongs to Daddy**

Tony Martin **I'll See You in My Dreams; There's No Tomorrow**

Billy Mayerl **Marigold**

Clyde McCoy **Sugar Blues**

Raquel Meller **Who'll Buy My Violets**

Ethel Merman **I Got Rhythm; There's No Business Like Show Business**

Glenn Miller **In the Mood; Moonlight Serenade**

Florence Mills **I'm Just Wild About Harry**

The Mills Brothers **Paper Doll**

Vaughn Monroe **Racing with the Moon**

Helen Morgan **Bill**

Russ Morgan **So Tired**

Ray Noble **Good Night Sweetheart; The Very Thought of You**

Jack Norworth **Take Me Out to the Ball Game**

Cavan O'Connor **Goodnight**

Chauncey Olcott **My Wild Irish Rose**

"Our Gang" **The Whistler and His Dog**

Patti Page **This Is My Song**

Bert Parks **The Miss America Pageant**

Les Paul **How High the Moon**

Jack Payne **Say It with Music**

Ann Pennington **Black Bottom; Charleston**

Edith Piaf **La Vie en Rose**

The Pied Pipers **Dream**

Johnny Ray **Cry**

Monte Ray **The Donkey Serenade**

Harry Richman **Puttin' On the Ritz**

Edmundo Ros **Cuban Love Song**

Harry Roy **Bugle Call Rag**

Jean Sablon **J'Attendrai**

Fritzi Scheff **Kiss Me Again**

Artie Shaw **Begin the Beguine**

Dinah Shore **Dinah; Yes My Darling Daughter**

Ethel Shutta **I Found a Million Dollar Baby in a Five and Ten Cent Store**

Victor Silvester **You're Dancing on My Heart**

Frank Sinatra **All or Nothing At All**

Kate Smith **God Bless America; When the Moon Comes over the Mountain**

Bill Snyder **Bewitched, Bothered and Bewildered**

The Sons of the Pioneers **Tumbling Tumbleweeds**

Cyril Stapleton **Sleepy Serenade**

Kay Starr **The Wheel of Fortune**

Lew Stone **Oh Monah**

Barbra Streisand **People**

Eva Tanguay **I Don't Care**

Suzette Tarri **Red Sails in the Sunset**

Billy Ternent **She's My Lovely**

Lawrence Tibbett **Without a Song**

Arthur Tracy (The Street Singer) **Marta**

Charles Trenet **La Mer**

Sophie Tucker **Some of These Days**

Frankie Vaughan **Give Me the Moonlight**

Syd Walker **Rags, Bottles or Bones**

Ethel Waters **Stormy Weather**

Paul Whiteman **Rhapsody in Blue**

Jay Wilbur **Just Like a Melody Out of the Sky**

Bert Williams **I Ain't Got Nobody**

Hannah Williams **Cheerful Little Earful**

Maurice Winnick **The Sweetest Music This Side of Heaven**

Eric Winstone **Stage Coach**

Henny Youngman **Smoke Gets in Your Eyes**

COLLEGES, UNIVERSITIES, AND OTHER EDUCATIONAL INSTITUTIONS

In this division, songs originally written for, adapted for or later associated with particular colleges, universities, and other educational institutions are listed alphabetically under their school name.

Brown University **The Old Oaken Bucket**

Columbia University **Roar, Lion, Roar**

Cornell University **Amici** (based on "Annie Lisle"); **Far Above Cayuga's Waters** (based on "Annie Lisle")

Dartmouth University **As the Backs Go Tearing By; In Town Again**

Eton School **Carmen Etonense; Eton Boating Song**

Fordham University **Fordham Ram March** (based on "Robin Adair")

Georgia Institute of Technology **Rambling Wreck from Georgia Tech** (based on "Dunderbeck, or, Johnny Vorbeck" and the earlier "Son of a Gambolier")

Harrow School **Forty Years On**

Harvard University **Fair Harvard** (based on "Believe Me If All Those Endearing Young Charms"); **The Lone Fish (Meat) Ball; Our Director** (March)

Indiana University **Indiana Our Indiana**

New York University **Palisades**

Ohio State University **Across the Field**

Princeton University **The Cannon Song; Marching Through Georgia; Old Nassau** (based on "Auld Lang Syne"); **Princeton, That's All; Whoop'er Up** (Rah! Rah! Rah! Siss Boom Ah!) (based on "There's Music in the Air")

Purdue University **Hail Purdue**

Rutgers University **On the Banks of the Old Raritan**

St. Mary's College **The Bells of St. Mary's**

Texas A&M College **The Aggie War Hymn**

Tulane University **Roll On, Tulane** (The Olive and Blue)

University of Chicago **Wave the Flag**

University of Iowa **Iowa Corn Song**

University of Maine **(Maine) Stein Song** (based on Brahms, "Hungarian Dances")

University of Michigan **The Victors**

University of Minnesota **The Rouser**

University of Pennsylvania **'Twas off the Blue Canaries, or, My Last Cigar**

University of Southern California **Fight On**

University of Texas **The Eyes of Texas** (Are Upon You) (based on "I've Been Working on the Railroad," or, "The Levee Song," or, "Someone's in the Kitchen with Dinah")

University of Utah **A Utah Man Am I** (based on "Solomon Levi")

University of Washington **Bow Down to Washington**

University of Wisconsin **On Wisconsin**

Washington and Lee University **Washington and Lee Swing**

West Point **Benny Havens, Oh!; The Girl I Left Behind Me; Song of the Vagabonds**

Yale University **Bingo** (based on "Balm of Gilead"); **Bulldog! Bulldog! Bow, Wow, Wow; Down the Field** (March); **The Whiffenpoof Song; Yale Boola** (based on "Boola Boola")

Non-Specific and General School Songs **All American Girl; Betty Co-Ed; Buckle Down Winsocki; A Capital Ship; Come, Landlord, Fill the Flowing Bowl; Dummy Song** (I'll Take the Legs from Off the Table); **Gaudeamus Igitur; Old College Chum** (based on "Sweet Genevieve"); **The Sweetheart of Sigma Chi; There Is a Tavern in the Town**

ADVERTISING JINGLES AND SONGS USED TO PROMOTE COMMERCIAL PRODUCTS

The term "Gebrauchsmusik" or "music for use" was invented by composer Paul Hindemith during the 1920's. In this division, songs originally written for, adapted for or later associated with the promotion of particular commercial products are listed alphabetically under their product's commercial name.

Ajax Cleanser **Use Ajax the Foaming Cleanser**

Anheuser Beer **Under the Anheuser Bush**

Aqua Velva After Shave **Aqua Velva Man**

Aunt Jemima Pancakes **Aunt Jemima** (Silver Dollar)

Barbasol Shaving Cream **Tammany**

Bell Telephone Systems **Call Me; Friendship Is for Keeps**

Betty Crocker Cake Mixes **It's So Nice To Have a Cake Around the House** (based on "It's So Nice To Have a Man Around the House")

Bosco Chocolate Flavored Syrup **I Love Bosco**

Brylcreem Hair Cream **Brylcreem, a Little Dab'll Do Ya**

Budweiser Beer **Budweiser's a Friend of Mine; When You Say Bud, You've Said It All; Where There's Life, There's Bud**

Burger King Food Chains **Have It Your Way** (based on "Man's World")

Campbell's Soup **Give Me the Campbell Life** (based on "Give Me the Simple Life")

Carnation Milk **Contented**

Chesterfield Cigarettes **Sound Off for Chesterfield** (based on "Sound Off")

Chevrolet Automobiles **See the U.S.A. in Your Chevrolet**

Chicken of the Sea Tuna **Ask Any Mermaid**

Chiquita Banana **(I'm) Chiquita Banana**

Coca-Cola Soft Drink **Fifty Million Times a Day; I'd Like To Teach the World To Sing; It's the Real Thing. Coke; Things Go Better with Coke**

Comet Automobiles **Everything's Coming Up Comets** (based on "Everything's Coming Up Roses") **Your Overcoat**

Curad Band-Aid **Mommy Put a Curad On** (based on "O (Ach) Du Lieber Augustin")

Dairy Queen Ice Cream **A Scrumpdillyishus Day**

(Wrigley's) Doublemint Chewing Gum **Double Your Pleasure**

Gillette Razor Blades **To Look Sharp**

Green Giant Vegetables **The Jolly Green Giant**

Heinz Ketchup **Anticipation**

Honda **Help Me Honda** (based on "Help Me Rhonda")

International Ladies Garment Workers Union **(Look For the) Union Label**

Kentucky Fried Chicken **Real Goodness from Kentucky Fried Chicken**

Kodak Camera **The Times of Your Life**

Lucky Strike Cigarettes **Lucky Day**

McDonald's Food Chain **You Deserve a Break Today; You, You're the One**

Miller High Life Beer **If You've Got the Time, We've Got the Beer**

Nescafé Coffee **Let's Have Another Cup of Coffee**

Northeast Airlines **Yellow Bird**

Oldsmobile Automobiles **In My Merry Oldsmobile**

Pan American Air Lines **Pan Am Makes the Goin' Great**

Pepsi-Cola Soft Drink **Pepsi-Cola Hits the Spot** (based on "John Peel"); **Pepsi's Got a Lot To Give, You've Got a Lot To Live**

Perdue Chicken Products **Try a Little Tenderness**

Pillsbury Flour and Cake Mixes **Bake Someone Happy** (based on "Make Someone Happy"); **Pillsbury Says It Best**

Rheingold Beer **Let's Do It**

Robert Hall Clothes **When the Values Go Up**

Schaefer Beer **Schaefer Is the One Beer**

Studebaker Station Wagons **Wait for the Wagon**

Sunkist Oranges **Good Vibrations**

Texaco Petroleum Products **Texaco Star Theme** (The Man Who Wears the Star)

Viceroy Cigarettes **Viceroy Gives You All the Taste All the Time**

Wesson Oil **Wessonality** (based on "Personality")

Wildroot Cream-Oil Hair Dressing **Get Wildroot Cream-Oil Charlie**

Wurzburger Beer **Down Where the Wurzburger Flows**

POLITICAL CAMPAIGN SONGS

In this division, songs originally written for, adapted for, or later associated with the political campaign of particular American federal, state, and local politicians are listed alphabetically under the candidate's name.

POLITICAL CAMPAIGN SONGS

John Quincy Adams **Adams and Liberty; Straight-Out Democratic** (based on "Old Rosin the Beau")

James Buchanan **The White House Chair**

Champ Clark **They Gotta Quit Kickin' My Dog (Dawg) Around**

Henry Clay **Clay and Frelinghuysen; The Mill-Boy of the Slashes** (based on "Old Rosin the Beau"), **Old Hal of the West** (based on "Old Rosin the Beau"); **Yankee Doodle**

Grover Cleveland **The Boss of the Nation; Hurrah for Cleveland; When Grover Cleveland Gets a Boy**

Schuyler Colfax **Hurrah! For Grant and Colfax**

Calvin Coolidge **Coolidge and Country; Keep Cool and Keep Coolidge; Keep Cool-Idge; Keeping Cool with Coolidge**

Jefferson Davis **Dixie**

Charles Gates Dawes **It's All in the Game**

Dwight D. Eisenhower **Dwight D. Eisenhower March; I Like Ike** (based on "They Like Ike"); **Ike for Four More Years; We Want Eisenhower**

James A. Garfield **Garfield Now Will Guide the Nation**

Ulysses S. Grant **Hurrah! For Grant and Colfax; Keep the Ball A-Rolling, or, Grant in the Chair; The Man Who Saved the Nation; President Grant's March; Should Brave Ulysses Be Forgot** (based on "Auld Lang Syne"); **Ulysses Is His Name**

Horace Greeley **Horace and No Relations; Horace Greeley's March; Say! Have You Taken Your Medicine Yet?**

Horace Harding **Harding, You're the Man for Us; Mr. Harding, We're All for You**

William Henry Harrison **Tippecanoe and Tyler Too**

Rutherford B. Hayes **Hurrah! For Hayes and Honest Ways!**

Herbert Hoover **Hoover** (The Man for Uncle Sam); **Mr. Hoover and Mr. Smith**

Andrew Jackson **The Hunters of Kentucky**

Abraham Lincoln **Lincoln and Liberty** (based on "Old Rosin the Beau"); **Old Abe Lincoln** (based on "The Old Grey Mare"); **Uncle Sam and Mexico** (based on "Old Dan Tucker"); **Yankee Doodle for Lincoln**

William McKinley **McKinley**

James K. Polk **Old Rosin the Beau; Yankee Doodle**

Franklin D. Roosevelt **Happy Days Are Here Again; Home on the Range; On with Roosevelt**

Theodore Roosevelt **Goodbye, Teddy, You Must March, March, March; Moving Day in Jungle Town; Our Next President** (Roosevelt); **We Want You Teddy for Four Years More**

Alfred E. Smith **He's Our Al; In the Fall We'll All Go Voting for Al; Mr. Hoover and Mr. Smith; The Sidewalks of New York**

Adlai Stevenson **Believe in Stevenson**

William Howard Taft **Bi-I-Double L-Bill; Get In Line for Big Bill Taft; On a Raft with Taft; Will Taft, We're Looking to You**

Sam Tilden **Honest Sam Tilden**

Harry S. Truman **I'm Just Wild About Harry; The Missouri Waltz**

John Tyler **Tippecanoe and Tyler Too**

James J. Walker **It's a Walk-In for Walker; Will You Love Me in December as You Do in May**

George Washington **The President's March**

William A. Wheeler **Hurrah! For Hayes and Honest Ways!**

Woodrow Wilson **I Think We've Got Another Washington and Wilson Is His Name; We Take Our Hats Off to You, Mr. Wilson; We're All with You, Mr. Wilson; Wilson, That's All!**

CHURCH CHIMES AND CARILLONS

Good schools and good bells are two signs of a
well-managed city.

Dutch saying

The word *carillon* evolved from the old French *quadrilloner,* meaning three bells of the *Voorslag,* plus the hour bell, totaling four bells. This was later called the *carilloner.*

According to William DeTurk, Assistant Carilloneur at the University of Michigan,

A carillon, by definition, must have real, bronze bells and must have a minimum of two octaves of these bells. The average range of a carillon today (1976) is four octaves, and the largest and heaviest carillon today is the one in New York City in the tower of the Riverside Church. It has seventy-four bells, the heaviest weighing twenty tons.

In addition, the tower of this church is 392 feet above sea level, a twenty-story elevator ride plus roughly 150 steps to the observation platform circling the tower. The carillon was a gift of John D. Rockefeller, Jr., and the twenty-ton bell, the heaviest tuned in the world, is called the Bourdon. The smaller treble bells weigh roughly ten pounds each.

CHURCH CHIMES AND CARILLONS

Ther traditional nursery rhyme, "Oranges and Lemons" mentions all the bell towers in the square mile of the city of London. Its lyric read:

Oranges and lemons, say the bells of St. Clement's.
You owe me five farthings, say the bells of St. Martin's.
When will you pay me? say the bells of Old Bailey.
When I grow rich, say the bells of Shoreditch.
When will that be, say the bells of Stepney.
I do not know, says the great bell of Bow.

Here comes a candle to light you to bed,
And here comes a chopper to cut off your head.

Pancakes and fritters, say the bells of St. Peter's.
Two sticks and an apple, say the bells of Whitechapel.
Old Father Baldpate, say the slow bells of Aldgate.
Poker and tongs, say the bells of St. Ann's.
Brickbats and tiles, say the bells of St. Giles'.

Here comes a candle to light you to bed,
And here comes a chopper to cut off your head.

As only the chimes at Westminster have received special song recognition, this therefore, will be the only expansion cited here.

Westminster Chimes. Written originally by William Crotch in 1793 for St. Mary's Church (the Great) in Cambridge, England, these traditional chimes, now rung from the Victoria Clock of the Houses of Parliament are played on four tubular bells. The melodic inspiration appears in the fifth bar of Handel's "I Know That My Redeemer Liveth" of 1793–94.

These chimes are heard in the release of Robeldo's "Three O'Clock in the Morning" of 1921. Also heard in a clock tower of a bank at Third Avenue and Twenty-second Street in New York, Magistrate George Postel ruled that the melody was "of special note" and not disturbing, after a suit of its disturbing the peace was brought into his court.

The 20-foot Clock Tower housing Big Ben (which, incidentally, is not the clock, but the name of the bell inside) was completed in 1858. Big Ben was cast by Warner's in 1856, the twentieth year of reign of Majesty Queen Victoria, at Norton, near Stockton-on-Tees. It is nine feet in diameter, seven and a half feet high, and weighs 13.5 tons. Both clock and bells were designed by Edmund Beckett Denison, who later became Lord Grimthorpe. Having made a great fortune at the bar, Denison was also an amateur architect and the first to study mathematically the relation of the shape and weight of a bell to its note value. For thirty-seven years he was president of the Horological Institute in Great Britain.

There is an old tradition that the chimes of Westminster sing at every hour, "Lord, through this hour, be Thou my guide. So by Thy power, no foot will slide."

AMERICAN BUGLE CALLS

Little is known about the origin of most of America's traditional bugle calls. However, those described below may also be found in Part V.

Assembly. First published by George W. Behn in 1842, this call is often parodied beginning with the words "There's a monkey in the grass."

Call to Arms

Call to Quarters

Charge

First Call. First published by George W. Behn in 1842, this call is today popularly heard at horse-racing tracks.

In 1950, Frank Loesser employed this theme in his "Fugue for Tinhorns" in *Guy and Dolls*.

General Quarters

Mess Call

Retreat. This traditional call was first heard by armies during medieval times.

Reveille. Published in 1836, this call was possibly written by a Frenchman as early as 1831 and published as "Le Réveil." Thus, this becomes the only traditional American bugle call not written by an American and still employed today in a foreign country.

Taps. This call was composed by Daniel O. Butterfield on the banks of the James River while in command of a brigade in the Army of the Potomac in Confederate territory. Having just been wounded at the Battle of Gaines' Mill on June 21, 1862, he wrote the work and soon taught it to O.W. Norton, bugler at brigade headquarters. It was first performed at Harrison's Landing on the James River in July, 1862.

It is still unknown as to why years later the title "Taps" became associated with this traditional American bugle call, although it is possibly derived from the Dutch "taptoo."

Tattoo. This call is a possible adaptation of "Tap-zu," used in Wallenstein's army to announce the closing of the taps and hence the end of the night's beer drinking.

IV

Elegant Plagiarisms

It seems to me I've heard that song before.
Sammy Cahn

I want to thank my "collaborators"—Bach, Beethoven, Brahms, Debussy.
Dimitri Tiomkin, upon receiving his Oscar for The High and the Mighty
at the Academy Award presentations, Hollywood, 1954

This Part contains song titles, listed alphabetically, of songs that are based on classical, folk, or earlier popular music sources. It is not the purpose of this list to include all known plagiarisms in popular song as that list is endless. Only those songs deemed popular enough for inclusion in Part V are entered here. For reasons of space, however, not all titles cited as adaptations in Part V are included. For further information about song popularity, refer to the Authors' Notes at the front of this book.

For more complete information about a particular song entered here, see Part V; all song titles in this Part are included in Part V. In most cases, classical and folk sources ("based on") are also included in Part V.

Song adaptations during the Colonial Era in America, and folksongs in general, chiefly from contemporary sources, are so numerous that they are not included here. They are, however, given reasonably detailed histories under their song title in Part V.

This list of adaptations does not include direct or near-direct English translation from foreign languages. Original non-English song titles are, however, given under their English song title in Part V.

Songs adopted by colleges, universities, or other educational institutions are listed in Part III under the school's name, and in Part V under their adapted title.

Advertising jingles and songs adapted to promote commercial products are listed in Part III under their product's commercial name, and in Part V under their jingle title.

Political campaign songs that are adaptions are listed in Part III under the name of the political candidate, and in Part V under their adapted and/or original song title.

Satirical parodies and humorous adaptations are included in Part V under their original non-adapted title.

Abilene (1963)   Based on the traditional song, with new lyrics.

America (My Country 'Tis of Thee) (1832)   Based on the music of "God Save the King" from England, 1744; and that, in turn, based on a melody composed by H. Harris for the King of Denmark; later, Herr G.B. Schumacher wrote the German words and it became "Heil Dir im Siegeskranz," onetime official Prussian national anthem.

And This Is My Beloved (1954) Based on a theme from the third movement, "Nocturne," of Borodin's String Quartet No. 2, in D Major.

The Anniversary Song (1947) Based on Ivanovici's "Danube Waves" (Ueber den Wellen) of 1880.

As Years Go By (1947) Based on Brahms's "Hungarian Dance No. 4."

At the Crossroads (1942) Based on Ernesto Lecuona's "Malagueña" of 1930.

Avalon (1920) Based on Puccini's aria "E lucevan le stelle" from *Tosca*.

Bach Goes to Town (1938) Based indirectly on a Bach prelude and fugue.

Baubles, Bangles and Beads (1954) Based on the "Scherzo" from Borodin's String Quartet No. 2, in D Major.

The Bay of Biscay, O! (1805) Based on a theme from the black sailors of London.

Bell Bottom Trousers (1907) Based on a traditional sea chantey.

Besame Mucho (1944) Based on the Enrique Granados "nightingale" aria from *Goyescas*.

The Bonnie Blue Flag (1861) Based on the Irish tune "The Jaunting Car."

Boola Boola (1898) Based on Bob Cole and Billy Johnson's "La Hoola Boola" of 1897.

The Bowery (1892) Based on the Neapolitan folksong "La Spagnola."

The Breeze and I (1940) Based on Ernesto Lecuona's "Andalucia" of 1930.

Bumble Boogie (1946) Based on Rimsky-Korsakov's "Flight of the Bumble Bee" of 1900.

Buy a Broom (c.1825) Based on "O (Ach) Du Lieber Augustin" of 1815, adapted Alexander Lee.

Bye Bye Blues (1930) Based on James H. Rogers' "The Star" of 1912.

Castle of Dreams (1919) Based on the middle section of Chopin's "Minute Waltz."

Chansonette (1923) Based on Rudolph Friml's "Chanson" of 1920, with lyrics.

Concerto for Two (1941) Based on the first movement of Tchaikovsky's First Piano Concerto, in B-flat minor.

El Condor Pasa (1933) Based on a Peruvian folksong.

La Cucaracha (1934) Based on a traditional Mexican folksong.

Dance with a Dolly (1944) Based on "Lubly Fan, or, Buffalo Gals (Won't You Come Out Tonight?)" of 1844.

Danny Boy (1913) Based on the Irish traditional "Londonderry Air" of 1855, with new lyrics.

Dark Eyes (Black Eyes) (1926) Based on the Russian gypsy song "Otchi Tchorniya," as early as 1884.

Daybreak (1942) Based on Ferde Groté's "Mississippi Suite" of 1926.

Dear Old Pal of Mine (1918) Loosely based on Wagner's "Song to the Evening Star."

Dear Old Southland (1921) Based on the traditional black American spiritual "Deep River" of 1875.

Did You Ever Think As the Hearse Rolls By, or, **The Worms Crawl In, the Worms Crawl Out** (1923) Based on a traditional military song.

Disco Lucy (1977) Based on the television theme from "I Love Lucy."

The Donkey Serenade (1937) Based on Rudolph Friml's "Chanson" of 1920, and "Chansonette" of 1923.

Don't Sit Under the Apple Tree (1942) Based on "Long Long Ago" of 1833.

Don't You Know (1959) Based on Puccini's "Musetta's Waltz" from the opera *La Bohème*.

The Echo Told Me a Lie (1949) Based on the traditional Italian folksong "Bella Ragazza Dalle Frecce Bionde."

Eh Cumpari (1953) Based on a traditional Italian song.

(Fifteen Miles [Years] on the) Erie Canal (Low Bridge!—Everybody Down) (1913) Based on a traditional American folksong.

The Eyes of Texas (Are Upon You) (1903) Based on "I've Been Working on the Railroad," or, "The Levee Song" or, "Someone's in the Kitchen with Dinah" of 1894.

Fascination (1932) Based on Marchetti's "Valse Tzigane" of 1904.

A Fifth of Beethoven (1976) Based on Beethoven's Fifth Symphony.

Five Hundred Miles (Railroader's Lament) (1962) Based on a traditional folksong.

Fooled (1955) Based on a theme by Franz Lehár.

Full Moon and Empty Arms (1946) Based on a theme from the first movement of Rachmaninofi's Second Piano Concerto in C minor.

Glow Worm (1952) Based on the 1907 standard with a new lyric by Johnny Mercer.

God Save the King (1744) Based on a melody composed by H. Harris for the King of Denmark; later, Herr G.B. Schumacher wrote the German words and it became "Heil Dir im Siegeskranz," the ontime official Prussian national anthem.

Goin' Home (1922) Based on the Largo from Dvorák's symphony "From the New World," op. 95, of 1893.

Good Night Sweetheart (1931) Based on themes from Schubert's Symphony in C and the Liszt Preludes.

ELEGANT PLAGIARISMS

Goodbye, My Lady Love (1904) Based on Myddleton's "Down South" of 1900.

A Guy Is a Guy (1952) Based on the English broadside ballad "I Went to the Alehouse (A Knave Is a Knave)" of 1719.

Gypsy Love Song (1898) Based on Chopin's Piano Concerto in E minor.

Hail, Hail, the Gang's All Here (1917) Based on the tenor part "Come, friends, who plow the sea" and the chorus part "With catlike tread" from Act II, *The Pirates of Penzance*, by Gilbert and Sullivan. This melody, in turn, was itself a parody of Verdi's "Anvil Chorus."

Hallelujah, I'm a Bum (1928) Based on the traditional hymn "Revive Us Again."

Hawaiian War Chant (1936) Based on a traditional Hawaiian song.

Hearts and Flowers (1899) Based on Alphonse Czibulka's "Wintermärchen" (Winter Story) of 1891.

Hello Dolly (1964) Based on Mack David's "Sunflower" of 1948.

Hello Mudduh, Hello Faddah (1963) Based on Ponchielli's "Dance of the Hours" from Act III of *La Gioconda*, written in 1876.

Here (1954) Based on Verdi's soprano aria "Caro Nome" from the opera *Rigoletto*.

He's Got the Whole World in His Hands (1927) Based on a traditional black American spiritual.

Horses (1926) Based on Tchaikovsky's "Troika."

The Hot Canary (1949) Based on F. Poliakin's "Le Canari."

Hot Diggity (1956) Based on Chabrier's "España" (Spanish Rhapsody) of 1884.

How Dry I Am (1921) Based on the traditional hymn "(Oh) Happy Day" of 1855.

I Can't Begin To Tell You (1946) Based on Rida Johnson Young and Melville Ellis's "When Love Is Young in Springtime" of 1906.

I Didn't Raise My Boy To Be a Soldier (1915) Based on Cohalin's "How Much I Really Cared" of 1914.

I Found You in the Rain (1941) Based on Chopin's Prelude No. 7.

I Get Ideas (1951) Based on "Adios Muchachos" of 1932.

I Look at Heaven (1942) Based on a theme from Grieg's Piano Concerto in A minor.

I Think of You (1941) Based on the first movement of Rachmaninoff's Second Piano Concerto in C minor.

I'd Climb the Highest Mountain (If I Knew I'd Find You) (1926) Based on Dvorák's "Humoresque."

If You Are But a Dream (1945) Based on Anton Rubinstein's "Romance" in E-flat.

I'm Always Chasing Rainbows (1918) Based on Chopin's "Fantaisie Impromptu" in C-sharp minor.

In an Eighteenth Century Drawing Room (1939) Based on Mozart's Piano Sonata No. 3, in C (K.525).

In the Moon Mist (1946) Based on Godard's "Because" from *Jocelyn*.

In the Valley of the Moon (1933) Based on the Adagio from Mendelssohn's "Violin Concerto."

Intermezzo (A Love Story) (Souvenir de Vienne) (1941) Based on a theme from Wagner's *Tristan und Isolde*.

It's All in the Game (1951) Based on an instrumental by Dawes known as "Melody" from 1912.

It's Now or Never (1960) Based on de Capua's "O Sole Mio" of 1899.

Juanita (1850) Based on a traditional Spanish air; and that, in turn, on Handel's aria "Lascia Ch'io Pianga."

Johnny Get Your Gun (1886) Based on "Johnny Get Your Hair Cut" and "The Arkansas Traveler" of 1851.

Johnny Is the Boy for Me (1953) Based on the traditional Roumanian folksong "Sanie Cu Zurgalai."

Juliet Bravo (1981) Based on themes by Johann Sebastian Bach.

The Kerry Dance (1878) Based on the first eight bars of the melody "The Cuckoo", w.m. Margaret Casson, published 1790 in England.

Kiss of Fire (1952) Based on A.G. Villoldo's "El Choclo" of 1913.

The Lamp Is Low (1934) Based on Ravel's "Pavanne for a Dead Infanta" of 1899.

The Liberty Song, or, **Come, Join Hand in Hand** (1768) Based on William Boyce's "Heart of Oak" of 1759.

The Lion Sleeps Tonight, or, **Wimoweh** (1962) Based on a traditional African song.

Love Letters in the Sand (1931) Based on William D. Hendrickson's "The Spanish Cavalier" of 1881.

Love Me Tender (1956) Based on George Poulton's "Aura Lee" of 1861.

The Loveliest Night of the Year (1951) Based on Juventino P. Rosa's "Over the Waves" of 1888.

Lover Come Back to Me (1928) Based on Tchaikovsky's "June Barcarolle."

Lullaby of Broadway (1935) Based on a theme from one of Brahms's Hungarian Dances and Offenbach's "Barcarolle" from *Tales of Hoffman*.

Make Love to Me (1954) Based on "Tin Roof Blues" of 1923.

Marcheta (1913) Based on a theme from Nicolai's Overture to the *Merry Wives of Windsor*.

ELEGANT PLAGIARISMS

Marine's Hymn (1919) Based on a theme from the opera *Geneviève de Brabant* by Offenbach, in 1868.

Mazel Tov (1894) Based on a Serbian folksong and Tchaikovsky's "Marche Slave."

Midnight in Moscow (1962) Based on the Russian song "Padmas Koveeye Vietchera."

Minnie the Moocher (1931) Based on the traditional folksong, "Willy the Weeper."

Moon Love (1939) Based on the second movement of Tchaikovsky's Symphony No. 5 in E; adapted by Andre Kostelanetz.

Moonlight and Roses (Bring Mem'ries of You) (1925) Based on Edwin H. Lemare's Andantino in D-flat of 1892.

Moonlight Cocktail (1942) Based on C. Luckeyth Robert's "Ripples of the Nile."

Moonlight Masquerade (1941) Based on Isaac Albéniz' "Tango" in D minor.

Music Goes 'Round and 'Round (1935) Based on "If you want to know who we are" from Gilbert and Sullivan's *The Mikado*.

My Cousin Caruso (1909) Based on Leoncavallo's aria "Vesti la Giubba" from *Pagliacci*.

My Moonlight Madonna (1933) Based on "Poème" by Zdenek Fibich.

My Nellie's Blue Eyes (1883) The chorus of this song is based on the Venetian song "Vieni sul Mar" (Come to the Sea).

My Prayer (1939) Based on Georges Boulanger's "Avant de Mourir," op. 17, of 1926.

My Reverie (1938) Based on Debussy's "Reverie" of 1895.

My Sweet Lord (1971) Based on Ronald Mack's "He's So Fine" of 1962.

My Twilight Dream (1939) Based on Chopin's Nocturne in E-flat.

Nature Boy (1948) Possibly based on Herman Yablokoff's Yiddish song "Schweig Mein Hartz" (Be Calm, My Heart) and the black American spiritual "Sweet Jesus Boy."

Night on Disco Mountain (1977) Based on Modeste Mussorgsky's "Night on Bald Mountain" of 1887.

Now and Forever (1941) Based on the dominant theme from the "Symphonie Pathétique."

Now Is the Hour (1948) Based on the traditional New Zealand song "Hearere Ra."

Oh, Bury Me Not on the Lone Prairie (The Dying Cowboy) (1932) Based on "The Ocean Burial" by George N. Allen in 1850. This song was later adapted to become what is now considered a traditional American cowboy song.

Oh Where, Oh Where, Has My Little Dog Gone (1864) Based on Beethoven's "Symphony Pastorale," No. 6, third movement (1809), and this based, in turn, on an English traditional dance, c.1260.

Old-Fashioned Garden (1919) The melody for this song was inspired by "The Vacant Chair," which, in turn, was adapted from "When I Saw Sweet Nellie Home" (Aunt Dinah's Quilting Party).

The Old Grey Mare (She Ain't What She Used to Be) (1917) Based on the traditional "Got Out (Get Out of) the Wilderness," from as early as 1858.

Old Grimes (1822) Based on the melody of "Auld Lang Syne" of 1711.

Old MacDonald Had a Farm (1917) Based on English words from as early as 1706, American music from as early as 1859.

The Old Oaken Bucket (1943) Based on the English melody "Araby's Daughter" of 1822, and that, in turn, on the Scottish air "Jessie, the Flower o'Dumblane."

The Old Refrain (1915) Based on a Viennese song by Hugo Klein and Joseph Brandl, of 1887; adapted by Fritz Kreisler.

On the Isle of May (1940) Based on Tchaikovsky's Andante Cantabile from his String Quartet in D Major.

One Meat Ball (1945) Based on "The Lone Fish Ball" of 1855.

Our Love (1939) Based on a theme from Tchaikovsky's symphonic poem "Romeo and Juliet" of 1871.

Pepsi-Cola Hits the Spot (1940) Based on "John Peel" of 1820, and the traditional English tune "Bonnie Annie."

The Perfect Song (1915) Based on Gaetano Braga's "Angel's Serenade" of 1867.

Play, Fiddle, Play (1932) Based possibly on the verse of "Gypsy Love Song" by Victor Herbert and the first theme of the First Piano Concerto in E minor by Chopin.

Pomp and Circumstance (1902) The title to this work was extracted from a line in Shakespeare's *Othello*, Act III, Sc.3.

Question and Answer (Demande et Response) (1943) Based on Coleridge-Taylor's "Petite Suite de Concert," op.77.

The River Kwai March (1957) Based on "Colonel Bogie March" of 1916.

The Rose I Bring You (1950) Based on Gaetano Braga's "Angels Serenade."

Rose O'Day (1942) Based on "She Wore a Yellow Ribbon" of 1838.

The Rose of No Man's Land (1918) Loosely based on Beethoven's Minuet in G.

Rose, Rose I Love You (1951) Based on a traditional Chinese melody.

Rum and Coca-Cola (1945) Possibly based on Lionel Belasco's "L'Année Passée" of 1906, published originally in Trinidad.

Russian Rag (1919) Based on Rachmaninoff's Prelude in C-sharp minor.

Sabre Dance (1948) Based on Aram Khachaturian's ballet "Gayaneh," Third Suite.

Sailin' On (1927) Based on largo from Dvořák's symphony "From the New World."

Sally in Our Alley (1902) Based on "The Country Lass" of 1715.

San Fernando Valley (1944) Based on "Sweet and Hot" of 1930.

Schnitzelbank (1906) Based on "Johnny Schmoker" of 1863.

Serenade in the Night (1937) Based on A. Bixio and B. Cherubini's "Violino Tzigano."

She'll Be Comin' Round the Mountain (When She Comes) (1899) Based on the traditional black American melody "When the Chariot Comes" (hymn) of 1899 or earlier.

Shortnin' Bread (1928) Based on a traditional folksong; possibly written by black composer Reese D'Pree in 1905.

Sigh No More, Ladies (c.1795) The words are based on a passage from Shakespeare's *Much Ado About Nothing*.

Sloop John B. (1966) Based on a Bahamas traditional song, from as early as 1927.

Some of These Days (1910) Based on Frank Williams's "Some o' Dese Days" of 1905.

Somebody Else Is Taking My Place (1937) Based on "Please Go 'Way and Let Me Sleep" of 1902.

Song of Love (1921) Based on the second theme from the "Unfinished Symphony" of Schubert and a melody by H. Berte.

Song of the Volga Boatman (1867) Based on a traditional Russian folksong.

Song Without End (1960) Based on Liszt's "Un Sospiro."

Stagger Lee (1959) Based on a traditional folksong.

(Maine) Stein Song (1910) Based on a theme from one of Brahms's "Hungarian Dances."

(This Is) The Story of a Starry Night (1941) Based on Tchaikovsky's "Pathétique" Symphony.

Strange Music (1944) Based on Grieg's "Wedding Day in Troldhaugen" and Nocturne.

Stranger in Paradise (1954) Based on a theme from Borodin's "Polovetsian Dances" from his opera *Prince Igor*, from 1888.

The Streets of Cairo (1895) Based on an Algerian melody titled "Kradoutja," known in France since 1600.

The Sunshine of Paradise Alley (1895) Based on a theme from Mascagni's *Cavalleria Rusticana*.

Surrender (1961) Based on the Italian art song "Torna a Sorrento," original words and music G.B. de Curtis and Ernesto de Curtis.

Take My Love (1955) Based on a theme from the third movement of Brahms's Third Symphony.

That Mesmerizing Mendelssohn Tune (1909) Based on Mendelssohn's "Spring Song."

There Is a Tavern in the Town (1883) Loosely based on a traditional Cornish folksong and the "Butcher Boy."

There Is No Greater Love (1936) Based on a theme from Tchaikovsky's Concerto No.1.

There's No Other Love (1960) Based on "Rosita" of 1923.

There's No Tomorrow (1949) Based on de Capua's "O Sole Mio" of 1899.

There's Yes Yes in Your Eyes (1924) Based on Wolf's "Without You the World Doesn't Seem the Same."

The Things I Love (1941) Based on Tchaikovsky's "Melodie," op.24, no.3.

The Third Man Theme (1950) Based on an eight-measure melody found by Anton Karas in a zither etude book.

Those Wedding Bells Shall Not Ring Out (1896) Based on Gussie Davis's "Fatal Wedding."

Those Were the Days (1968) Based on a traditional East European tune.

Till the End of Time (1945) Based on Chopin's Polonaise in A-flat, op.53, no.6.

Time Waits for No One (1944) Based on a theme from J. Strauss's "Tales of the Vienna Woods."

Ti-Pi-Tin (1938) Based on Chabrier's "España" and Lalo's "Symphonie Espagnole."

'Tis the Last Rose of Summer (1813) Based on Richard Alfred Milliken's "The Groves of Blarney."

To a Wild Rose (1896) Based on Liszt's "Liebestraum."

Tonight We Love (1941) Based on the first movement of Tchaikovsky's First Piano Concerto, in B-flat minor.

Toreador Song (1875) The "Habanera" in Bizet's *Carmen* is directly based on Sebastian Yradier's "El Areglito."

Two Lovely Black Eyes (1886) Based on the Venetian folktune, "Vieni sul Mar" (Come to the Sea).

Two Silhouettes in the Moonlight (1941) Based on "Poème" by Fibich.

Tzena, Tzena, Tzena (1950) Based on a traditional Yiddish folksong.

Under the Bamboo Tree (1902) Based on Chaminade's "Flatterer" (La Lisonjera).

The Vamp (1919) The chorus of this song is based on Puccini's aria "One Fine Day" from *Madama Butterfly*.

Wagon Wheels (1934) Based on "Goin' Home" of 1922, and that, in turn, based on the largo from the "From the New World" symphony, op.95, by Anton Dvořák, 1893.

Waltzing Matilda (1903) Based on Robert Tannahill's "Craigielea."

Water Boy (1922) Based on "Till the Clouds Roll By" of 1917; also "César Cui: Orientale"; also "Marche Slave" by Tchaikovsky.

ELEGANT PLAGIARISMS

We Must Be Vigilant (1943) Based on "American Patrol" of 1885.

We Shall Overcome (1945) Based on the music from an early hymn of 1794, words from a second hymn of 1900.

Westminster Chimes (1793–94) Based on Handel's "I Know That My Redeemer Liveth."

When It's Apple Blossom Time in Normandy (1912) Based on Beethoven's Minuet in G.

When the Lights Go On Again (All Over the World) (1942) Based on Beethoven's Minuet in G.

When You're in Love (1948) Based on Serradell's "La Golondrina."

Where Did You Get That Hat (1888) Based on a theme from Wagner's *Lohengrin and Die Meistersinger*.

Where the Blue of the Night Meets the Gold of the Day (1931) Possibly based on "Tit-Willow" from Gilbert and Sullivan's *The Mikado of 1885*.

The Whiffenpoof Song (1911) The words are in part based on Kipling's poem "Gentlemen Rankers."

Who'll Buy My Violets (1923) Based on "La Violetera" of 1918.

Who's Afraid of the Big Bad Wolf (1933) Based on Johann Strauss's "Champagne Song" from *Die Fledermaus* and "Perpetual Motion."

Wild Horses (1953) Based on Robert Schumann's "Wilder Reiter."

(My) Wonderful One (1922) Based on a theme by Marshall Neilan.

The Woodpecker(s') Song (1940) Based on the Italian "Reginella Campagnola."

The Wreck of the Old '97 (1924) Based on Henry C. Work's "The Ship That Never Returned."

Yes! We Have No Bananas (1923) Based on the melodies of "The Vacant Chair" and the earlier "When I Saw Sweet Nellie Home" (Aunt Dinah's Quilting Party).

You Are My Lucky Star (1935) Loosely based on a theme from Liszt's Second Hungarian Rhapsody.

You Me and Us (1957) Based on "Cielito Lindo" of 1919.

You'd Be So Nice To Come Home To (1942) Based on Sarasate's "Gypsy Airs" (Zigeunerwetsen).

You're Breaking My Heart (1949) Based on Ruggiero Leoncavallo's "La Mattinata" of 1904.

Z Cars Theme (1962) Based on the Northumbrian tune "Johnny Todd."

V

Song Titles

For further information on song titles and dates, refer to the Authors' Notes at the front of this book. For a complete list of media abbreviations, refer to the List of Abbreviations, also at the front of this book. For Record Sale, Hit Parade, and Air Play ratings, and performing artist for a particular Top Hit song, see Part I Chronological Listings.

ABC 1970 w.m. Deke Richards, Berry Gordy, Jr., Frederick Perren, Alphonso Mizell

ABCDEFG, or, The Alphabet Song, *see* **Twinkle, Twinkle, Little Star**

A-Hunting We Will Go, *see* **Hunt Theme**

À la Bien-Aimée, or, Papillons d'Amour, op. 59, no. 2. 1900 m. Edouard Schütt

A-Round the Corner (Beneath the Berry Tree) 1952 w.m. Josef Marais

A-Tisket A-Tasket 1879 w.m. Ella Fitzgerald, Al Feldman. (MF) *Two Girls and a Sailor*. June Allyson, Van Johnson, and Lena Horne appeared in *Two Girls and a Sailor*. Based on the traditional nursery rhyme, c. 1879. This song was popularly adapted in 1938 and revived in 1944.

"A"—You're Adorable 1948 w.m. Buddy Kaye, Fred Wise, Sidney Lippman. This song is also often called "The Alphabet Song."

Aba Daba Honeymoon, The 1914 w.m. Arthur Fields, Walter Donovan. (F) *Two Weeks with Love*. Louis Calhern, Debbie Reynolds, and Jane Powell appeared in *Two Weeks with Love*. This song was popularly revived in 1951.

Abdulla Bulbul Ameer (Abdul Abulbul Amir) 1877 w.m. Percy French; arr. Frank Crumit in 1928. Based on a traditional English song, from the time of the Crimean War. This song was originally written for a smoking concert at Trinity College, Dublin. This song was popularly revived in 1928.

Abergavenny 1969 w.m. Marty Wilde (Frere Manston), Ronnie Scott (Jack Gellar). Ivor Novello Award winner 1968–69.

Abide with Me, or, Fast Falls the Eventide 1861 w. Henry Francis Lyte m. William Henry Monk

Abie My Boy 1920 w.m. L. Silberman, A. Grock, Herbert Rule, Tom McGhee

Abilene 1963 w.m. John D. Loudermilk, Bob Gibson, Lester Brown, Albert Stanton. Based on a traditional song, with new lyrics.

About a Quarter to Nine 1935 w. Al Dubin m. Harry Warren. (MT) *Forty-Second Street*. (MF) *Casino de Paree*. (MF) *Go Into Your Dance*. (MF) *The Jolson Story*. Jerry Ohrbach and Tammy Grimes appeared in *Forty-Second Street*. Al Jolson appeared in *Casino de Paree*. Al Jolson, Ruby Keeler, and Helen Morgan appeared in *Go Into Your Dance*. Larry Parks appeared in *The Jolson Story*.

Abracadabra 1944 w.m. Cole Porter. (MT) *Mexican Hayride*. (MF) *Mexican Hayride*. June Havoc and Bobby Clark appeared in the stage production of *Mexican Hayride*. Bud Abbott and Lou Costello appeared in the film production of *Mexican Hayride*.

Abracadabra 1982 w.m. Steve Miller

Abraham 1942 w.m. Irving Berlin. (MF) *Holiday Inn*. Bing Crosby and Fred Astaire appeared in *Holiday Inn*.

Abraham, Martin and John 1968 w.m. Dick Holler

Absence Makes the Heart Grow Fonder 1900 w.m. Arthur Gillespie, Herbert Dillea, Fred Fisher

Absence Makes the Heart Grow Fonder (for Somebody Else) 1929 w.m. Samuel M. Lewis, Harry Warren, Joseph Young

Absent 1899 w. Catherine Young Glen m. John W. Metcalf

Absinthe Frappé 1904 w. Glen MacDonough m. Victor Herbert. (MT) *It Happened in Nordland*. (MF) *The Great Victor Herbert*. Mary Martin and Allan Jones appeared in *The Great Victor Herbert*.

Accent on Youth 1935 w. Tot Seymour m. Vee Lawnhurst. (F) *Accent on Youth*. Sylvia Sidney and Herbert Marshall appeared in *Accent on Youth*.

Ac-cent-tchu-ate the Positive 1945 w. Johnny Mercer m. Harold Arlen. (MF) *Here Come the Waves*. Bing Crosby and Betty Hutton appeared in *Here Come the Waves*.

Accidentally on Purpose 1940 w.m. Don McCray, Ernest Gold

Ace in the Hole 1941 w.m. Cole Porter. (MT) *Let's Face It!* (MT) *Let's Face It!* Eve Arden, Vivian Vance, and Danny Kaye appeared in the stage production of *Let's Face It!* Betty Hutton and Bob Hope appeared in the film production of *Let's Face It!*

Acercate Mas, *see* **Come Closer to Me**

Ach Du Lieber Augustin, *see* **O Du Lieber Augustin**

Across the Alley from the Alamo 1947 w.m. Joe Greene

Across the Field 1915 w.m. W.A. Dougherty, Jr. School song of Ohio State University.

Across the Wide Missouri, *see* **Shenandoah**

Actions Speak Louder Than Words 1891 w. George Horncastle m. Felix McGlennon

Actor's Life for Me, An, *see* **Hi-Diddle-Dee-Dee**

Adams and Liberty, or, **The Boston Patriotic Song** 1798 w. Robert Thomas (Treat) Paine m. The melody for this song is the same as that of "To Anacreon in Heaven" and "The Star Spangled Banner." This song was written for the Boston banquet of the Massachusetts Charitable Fire Society, June 1798. See also "To Anacreon in Heaven" and "The Star Spangled Banner."

Addicted to Love 1986 w.m. Robert Palmer

Addio Addio, or, **Goodbye** 1962 It. w. Domenico Modugno, Francesco Migliacci Eng. w. Carl Sigman m. Domenico Modugno. This song was awarded first prize at the San Remo Music Festival in 1962.

Addio, Mia Bella Napoli 1868 w.m. Teodoro Cottrau

Adelaide 1955 w.m. Frank Loesser. (MF) *Guys and Dolls.* Frank Sinatra, Marlon Brando, and Stubby Kaye appeared in *Guys and Dolls.* This song did not appear in the original stage production of *Guys and Dolls.*

Adelaide's Lament 1950 w.m. Frank Loesser. (MT) *Guys and Dolls.* (MF) *Guys and Dolls.* Robert Alda and Vivian Blaine appeared in the stage production of *Guys and Dolls.* Frank Sinatra, Vivian Blaine, and Marlon Brando appeared in the film production of *Guys and Dolls.*

Adele, *see* **Sweet and Gentle**

Adeline 1931 w.m. Joe Gilbert, Horatio Nicholls

Adeste Fideles, or, **O Come All Ye Faithful** 1782 Latin w.m. John Francis Wade Eng. w. Frederick Oakeley (in 1852). Possibly written by Wade in 1750, known then as "Portuguese Hymn"; although the Latin words have often been ascribed to St. Bonaventura in the thirteenth century.

Adios 1931 w.m. Enrico Madriguera, M. Woods, C. R. Del Campo

Adios, Mariquita Linda 1939 Sp.w. Marcos A. Jimenez Eng. w. Ray Gilbert m. Marcos A. Jimenez. (MF) *Masquerade in Mexico.* (F) *Only Angels Have Wings.* Dorothy Lamour appeared in *Masquerade in Mexico.* Cary Grant and Jean Arthur appeared in *Only Angels Have Wings.* This song was originally published in 1925 in South America.

Adios Muchachos 1932 w.m. Julio Cesar A. Sanders. This song was popularly revived in 1939. See also "I Get Ideas."

Adios My Love, or, **The Song of Athens** 1961 w. Norman Newell m. Manos Hadjidakis. (F) *Dreamland of Desire*

Affair To Remember, An 1957 Fr.w. Tanis Chandler Eng.w. Harold Adamson, Leo McCarey m. Harry Warren. (F) *An Affair To Remember.* Cary Grant and Deborah Kerr appeared in *An Affair To Remember.*

Afraid To Dream 1937 w.m. Mack Gordon, Harry Revel.

(MF) *You Can't Have Everything.* Alice Faye, Don Ameche, and Tony Martin appeared in *You Can't Have Everything.*

Africa 1983 w.m. David Paich, Jeff Porcaro

African Lament (Lamento Africano) 1931 w. L. Wolfe Gilbert m. Ernesto Lecuona. (MF) *The Road to Singapore.* William Powell and Doris Kenyon appeared in *The Road to Singapore.*

African Sanctus 1980 m. David Fanshawe Ivor Novello Award winner 1979–80.

African Waltz 1961 w. Mel Mandel, Norman Sachs m. Galt MacDermott. Ivor Novello Award winner 1961.

After All 1985 w.m. David Foster, Al Jarreau, Jay Graydon

After All That I've Been to You 1912 w. Jack Drislane m. Chris Smith

After All, You're All I'm After 1933 w. Edward Heyman m. Arthur Schwartz. (MT) *She Loves Me Not.* (MF) *She Loves Me Not.* Bing Crosby and Miriam Hopkins appeared in the film production of *She Loves Me Not.*

(What Can I Say, Dear) After I Say I'm Sorry 1926 w.m. Walter Donaldson, Abe Lyman. (MF) *Pete Kelly's Blues.* Peggy Lee appeared in *Pete Kelly's Blues.*

After My Laughter Came Tears 1928 w. Charles Tobias, Roy Turk m. Roy Turk

After the Ball 1892 w.m. Charles K. Harris. (MT) *A Trip to Chinatown.* This song was written on special order for a minstrel show in Harris's hometown of Milwaukee. Sam Doctor first performed the song, but having forgotten the words, this standard was to find its first popularity with baritone J. Aldrich Libby. See also Part I, 1892.

After the Dance 1931 w.m. Irving Caesar, William Frisch, Otto Motzan

After the Lights Go Down Low 1954 w.m. Alan White, LeRoy Lovett

After the Love Has Gone 1979 w.m. David Foster, Jay Graydon, William Champlin. Grammy Award winner 1979.

After the Lovin' 1976 w.m. Alan Bernstein, Richard A. Ziegler

After the Roses Have Faded Away 1914 w. Bessie Buchanan m. Ernest R. Ball

After Tonight We Say "Goodbye" 1932 w.m. Leo Towers, Harry Leon

After You—Who 1933 w.m. Cole Porter. (MT) *Gay Divorce.* Grace Moore and Fred Astaire appeared in the stage production of *Gay Divorce.*

After You Get What You Want, You Don't Want It 1921 w.m. Irving Berlin. (MF) *There's No Business Like Show Business.* Ethel Merman and Marilyn Monroe appeared in *There's No Business Like Show Business.*

After You've Gone 1918 w.m. Henry Creamer, Turner Layton. (MT) *Me and Bessie.* (MF) *For Me and My Gal.* (MF) *Jolson Sings Again.* (F) *Unholy Partners.* Linda Hopkins appeared in *Me and Bessie.* Judy Garland and Gene Kelly appeared in *For Me and My Gal.* Larry Parks appeared in *Jolson Sings Again.* Edward G. Robinson and Edward Arnold appeared in *Unholy Partners.*

Afternoon Delight   1976   w.m. Bill Danoff

Afternoon of a Faun   1895   m. Claude Debussy. From the French "L'Aprés-Midi d'Un Faune."

Again   1949   w. Dorcas Cochran   m. Lionel Newman. (F) *Road House*. Celeste Holm, Ida Lupino, and Richard Widmark appeared in *Road House*.

(Theme from) Against All Odds (Take a Look at Me Now)   1984   w.m. Phil Collins.   (F) *Against All Odds*. Ivor Novello Award winner 1984–85.

Age of Gold Ballet   1941   m. Dmitri Shostakovich

Aggie War Hymn, The   1921   w.m. J.V. "Pinky" Wilson. School song of Texas A.&M. College.

Aggravatin' Papa (Don't You Try To Two-Time Me)   1922   w.m. Roy Turk, J. Russel Robinson, Addy Britt

Ah, But Is It Love   1933   w. E.Y. Harburg   m. Jay Gorney. (MF) *Moonlight and Pretzels*. William Frawley and Mary Brian appeared in *Moonlight and Pretzels*.

Ah But It Happens   1948   w.m. William D. Dunham, Walter Kent

Ah! So Pure   1848   w. W. Friedrich   m. F. von Flotow. From the ballet *Martha*. *Martha* was first performed in the Paris 1844 ballet *Lady Harriette*.

Ah! Sweet Mystery of Life   1910   w. Rida Johnson Young   m. Victor Herbert. (MT) *Naughty Marietta*. (MF) *Naughty Marietta*. (MF) *The Great Victor Herbert*. Emma Trentini and Orville Harrold appeared in the stage production of *Naughty Marietta*. Jeanette MacDonald and Nelson Eddy appeared in the film production of *Naughty Marietta*. Mary Martin appeared in *The Great Victor Herbert*. This song was popularly revived in 1922.

Ah, the Apple Tree, *see* **When the World Was Young**

Ah! Vous Diraije Maman, *see* **Twinkle, Twinkle Little Star**

Ain't Gonna Give Nobody None of My Jelly Roll, *see* **I Ain't Gonna Give Nobody None o' This Jelly Roll**

Ain't Gonna Kiss You   1953   w.m. James Smith

Ain't Got a Dime to My Name   1943   w.m. Jimmy Van Heusen, Johnny Burke. (MF) *The Road to Morocco*. Bing Crosby, Bob Hope, and Dorothy Lamour appeared in *The Road to Morocco*.

Ain't Gwine Study War No More, *see* **Down by the Riverside**

Ain't It a Shame   1922   w.m. W.A. Hann, Joseph Simms, Al W. Brown

Ain't It Funny What a Difference Just a Few Hours Make   1903   w. Henry M. Blossom, Jr.   m. Alfred G. Bobyn. (MT) *The Yankee Consul*

Ain't It Grand To Be Bloomin' Well Dead   1932   w.m. Leslie Sarony

Ain't It Ni-Ice   1908   w.m. R.P. Weston, Bert Lee

Ain't It the Truth   1957   w. E.Y. Harburg   m. Harold Arlen. (MT) *Jamaica*

Ain't Misbehavin'   1929   w. Andy Razaf   m. Thomas "Fats" Waller, Harry Brooks. (MT) *Hot Chocolates*. (MT) *Ain't Misbehavin'*. (MF) *Stormy Weather*. (MF) *You Were Meant for Me*. (MF) *Gentlemen Marry Brunettes*. Jazzlips Richardson and Jimmy Baskette appeared in *Hot Chocolates*.

Debbie Allen and Nell Carter appeared in *Ain't Misbehavin'*. Lena Horne and Fats Waller appeared in *Stormy Weather*. Dan Dailey and Oscar Levant appeared in *You Were Meant for Me*. Jane Russell appeared in *Gentlemen Marry Brunettes*. Ironically, the melody to this song was later to be lifted by Dmitri Shostakovitch for the first movement of his Seventh Symphony. This song was popularly revived in 1986.

Ain't No Mountain High Enough   1967   w.m. Nickolas Ashford, Valerie Simpson. This song was popularly revived in 1970.

Ain't No Stoppin' Us Now   1979   w.m. Jerry Cohen, Gene McFadden, John Whitehead

Ain't No Sunshine   1971   w.m. Bill Withers. Grammy Award winner 1971.

Ain't No Way To Treat a Lady   1975   w.m. Harriet Schoch

Ain't No Woman Like the One I've Got   1973   w.m. Dennis Lambert, Brian Potter

Ain't She Sweet   1927   w.m. Jack Yellen, Milton Ager. (MT) *The 1940's Radio Hour*. (MF) *You Were Meant for Me*. (MF) *You're My Everything*. Dan Dailey appeared in both *You Were Meant for Me* and *You're My Everything*.

Ain't That a Shame   1955   w.m. Antoine Domino, David Bartholomew

Ain't That Funny   1962   w.m. Les Vandyke

Ain't We Got Fun   1921   w.m. Richard A. Whiting, Gus Kahn, Raymond B. Egan. (MF) *By the Light of the Silvery Moon*. (MF) *I'll See You in My Dreams*. Doris Day and Gordon MacRae appeared in *By the Light of the Silvery Moon*. Doris Day and Danny Thomas appeared in *I'll See You in My Dreams*, biopic of song writer Gus Kahn.

Air for the G String   c. 1700   m. Johann Sebastian Bach

Air That I Breathe, The   1974   w.m. Albert Louis Hammond, Michael Hazlewood. Ivor Novello Award winner 1974–75.

Airport Love Theme   1970   w.m. Alfred Newman, Paul Francis Webster. (F) *Airport*

Airy, Fairy Lillian   1894   w. Tony Raymond   m. Maurice Levi. From the comic opera *Princess Nicotine*. Lillian Russell, the doyenne of Broadway, was required to sing eight high Cs at each performance of *Princess Nicotine*.

Al-Di-La   1961   It.w. Mogol   Eng.w. Ervin Drake   m. Carlo Donida

Al Fresco   1904   w. Glen MacDonough   m. Victor Herbert. (MT) *It Happened in Nordland*. (MF) *The Great Victor Herbert*. Walter Connolly and Mary Martin appeared in *The Great Victor Herbert*.

Alabama Blossoms, The   1874   w.m. Frank Dumont; arr. James E. Stewart

Alabama Jubilee   1915   w.m. Jack Yellen, George L. Cobb

Alabama Song, The, or, **Moon of Alabama**   1928   w.m. Berthold Brecht, Kurt Weill

Alabamy Bound   1925   w. B.G. De Sylva, Bud Green   m. Ray Henderson. (MT) *Kid Boots*. (MF) *Show Business*. (MF) *The Great American Broadcast*. (MF) *Broadway*. (MF) *With a Song in My Heart*. Eddie Cantor appeared in *Kid Boots*. Eddie Cantor and Joan Davis appeared in *Show Business*.

George Raft, Janet Blair and Pat O'Brien appeared in *Broadway*. Susan Hayward appeared in *With a Song in My Heart*, biopic of singer Jane Froman.

Aladdin 1958 w.m. Cole Porter. (TV) *Aladdin*

Albatross 1967 w.m. Judy Collins (F) *The Subject Was Roses*. Patricia Neal appeared in *The Subject Was Roses*.

Alcoholic Blues, The 1919 w.m. Edward Laska, Albert von Tilzer. This song was a popular Prohibition lament.

Alexander (Don't You Love Your Baby No More) 1904 w. Andrew B. Sterling m. Harry Von Tilzer

Alexander's Ragtime Band 1911 w.m. Irving Berlin. (MT) *Hullo Ragtime*. (MF) *Alexander's Ragtime Band*. (MF) *There's No Business Like Show Business*. Lew Hearn and Shirley Kellog appeared in *Hullo Ragtime*. Alice Faye, Jack Haley, and Don Ameche appeared in *Alexander's Ragtime Band*. Ethel Merman and Donald O'Connor appeared in *There's No Business Like Show Business*. For the complete history of this song, see Part I, 1911.

Alfie 1966 w. Hal David m. Burt F. Bacharach. (F) *Alfie*. Michael Caine, Shelley Winters, and Millicent Martin appeared in *Alfie*.

"Algy," the Piccadilly Johnny with the Little Glass Eye 1895 w.m. Harry B. Morris

Ali Baba's Camel 1931 w.m. Noel Gay

Alibis 1984 w.m. Tom Snow, Tony Macaulay

(In My Sweet Little) Alice Blue Gown 1919 w. Joseph McCarthy m. Harry Tierney. (MT) *Irene*. (MF) *Irene*. Edith Day appeared in the stage production of *Irene*. Ray Milland and Anna Neagle appeared in the film production of *Irene*. The narrative of this song describes Alice Roosevelt Longworth's favorite shade of blue. Alice, of course, is Teddy's daughter.

Alice in Wonderland 1951 w.m. Bob Hilliard, Sammy Fain. (MF) *Alice in Wonderland*. The voices of Ed Wynn and Jerry Colonna appeared in *Alice in Wonderland*.

Alice, Where Art Thou 1861 w. Wellington Guernsey m. Joseph Ascher

Alice's Restaurant 1969 w.m. Arlo Guthrie. (F) *Alice's Restaurant*. Arlo Guthrie appeared in *Alice's Restaurant*. This song was a tribute to Alice Brock and her famous diner in the Berkshires.

Alive and Kicking 1985 w.m. Charles Burchill, Jim Kerr, Michael MacNeil

Alknomook, or, The Death of the Cherokee Indian c.1800 w.m. anon. Royall Tyler used the lyrics in his comedy of 1790, *The Contrast*, and these same lyrics were later adapted by Mrs. Ann Julia Hatton for her libretto to James Hewitt's ballad opera *Tammany*.

All 1957 w.m. Alan Stranks, Reynall Wreford

All Aboard for Blanket Bay 1910 w. Andrew B. Sterling m. Harry Von Tilzer

All Aboard for Dixieland 1913 w. Jack Yellen m. George L. Cobb. (MT) *High Jinks*.

All Alone 1911 w. Will Dillon m. Harry Von Tilzer

All Alone 1924 w.m. Irving Berlin. (MT) *Music Box Re-*

vue. (MF) *Alexander's Ragtime Band*. Tyrone Power and Don Ameche appeared in *Alexander's Ragtime Band*.

All Alone Monday 1926 w. Bert Kalmar m. Harry Ruby. (MT) *The Ramblers*. (MF) *The Cuckoos*. (MF) *Three Little Words*. Bobby Clark and Paul McCullough appeared in *The Ramblers*. Fred Astaire, Debbie Reynolds, and Red Skelton appeared in *Three Little Words*, biopic of song writers Bert Kalmar and Harry Ruby.

All American Boy 1958 w.m. Bill Parsons, Orville Lunsford

All American Girl 1932 w.m. Al Lewis

All Around the Mulberry Bush, *see* **The Mulberry Bush**

All At Once 1937 w. Lorenz Hart m. Richard Rodgers. (MT) *Babes in Arms*. (MF) *Babes in Arms*. Mitzi Green and Ray Heatherton appeared in the stage production of *Babes in Arms*. Judy Garland and Mickey Rooney appeared in the film production of *Babes in Arms*.

All At Once 1945 w. Ira Gershwin m. Kurt Weill. (MF) *Where Do We Go from Here*. Fred MacMurray and Joan Leslie appeared in *Where Do We Go from Here*.

All at Once You Love Her 1955 w. Oscar Hammerstein II m. Richard Rodgers. (MT) *Pipe Dream*.

All by Myself 1921 w.m. Irving Berlin. (MF) *Blue Skies*. Bing Crosby and Fred Astaire appeared in *Blue Skies*.

All by Yourself in the Moonlight 1929 w.m. Jay Wallis

All Choked Up 1972 w.m. Jim Jacobs, Warren Casey. (MT) *Grease*. (MF) *Grease*. Olivia Newton-John and John Travolta appeared in the film production of *Grease*.

All Coons Look Alike to Me 1896 w.m. Ernest Hogan. Ernest Hogan, a black, was referring in the title to the dismissal of a black woman's lover. He never considered the generic meaning of the title and upon realization, regretted the song's success for the rest of his life.

All Day and All of the Night 1964 w.m. Ray Davies

All for a Shilling a Day 1935 w.m. Noel Gay, Clifford Grey. (MF) *Me and Marlborough*. Jack Hulbert and Cicely Courtneidge appeared in *Me and Marlborough*.

All for (the) Love of You 1908 w. Dave Reed m. Ernest R. Ball

All for You 1915 w. Henry Blossom m. Victor Herbert. (MT) *The Princess Pat*. (MF) *The Great Victor Herbert*. Mary Martin and Allan Jones appeared in *The Great Victor Herbert*.

All God's Chillun Got Rhythm 1937 w.m. Walter Jurmann, Bronislaw Kaper, Gus Kahn. (MF) *A Day At the Races*. The Marx Brothers and Allan Jones appeared in *A Day At the Races*.

All God's Chillun Got Shoes, *see* **I Got Shoes**

All God's Chillun Got Wings 1865 w.m. traditional black American spiritual

All Good Gifts 1971 w.m. Stephen Schwartz. (MT) *Godspell*. (MF) *Godspell*.

All Hail the Power of Jesus' Name c. 1779 w. Edward Perronet m. Oliver Holden. This song has the same melody as Oliver Holden's "Coronation" of 1793.

All I Ask of You Is Love, *see* **All That I Ask of You Is Love**

All I Do Is Dream of You　1934　w. Arthur Freed m. Nacio Herb Brown. (F) *Sadie McKee.* (MF) *Singin' in the Rain.* Joan Crawford appeared in *Sadie McKee.* Gene Kelly, Debbie Reynolds, and Donald O'Connor appeared in the 1952 film production of *Singin' in the Rain.*

All I Ever Need Is You　1979　w.m. James E. Holiday

All I Have To Do Is Dream　1958　w.m. Boudleaux Bryant. This song was popularly revived in 1976.

All I Know　1973　w.m. Jimmy Webb

All I Need　1984　w.m. Glen Ballard, Clif Magness, David Pack

All I Need Is a Miracle　1986　w.m. Christopher Neil, Mike Rutherford

All I Need Is the Girl　1959　w. Stephen Sondheim m. Jule Styne. (MT) *Gypsy.* (MF) *Gypsy.* Ethel Merman appeared in the stage production of *Gypsy.* Rosalind Russell appeared in the film production of *Gypsy.*

All I Really Want To Do　1964　w.m. Bob Dylan

All I Want for Christmas (Is My Two Front Teeth)　1950 w.m. Donald Yetter Gardner

All In Down and Out　1906　w. R.C. McPherson (Cecil Mack) m. Smith, Johnson, Elmer Bowman

All in Fun　1939　w. Oscar Hammerstein II m. Jerome Kern. (MT) *Very Warm for May.* Grace McDonald and Donald Brian appeared in *Very Warm for May.*

All My Life　1936　w. Sidney Mitchell m. Sam H. Stept. (MF) *Laughing Irish Eyes.* (MF) *Johnny Doughboy.* Walter Kelly and Phil Regan appeared in *Laughing Irish Eyes.* Jane Withers and Henry Wilcoxson appeared in *Johnny Doughboy.*

All My Love　1950　Fr. w. Henri Contet Eng. w. Mitchell Parish m. Paul Durand. From the French "Boléro."

All My Loving　1964　w.m. John Lennon, Paul McCartney. Ivor Novello Award winner 1963.

All My Rowdy Friends Have Settled Down　1982　w.m. Hank Williams, Jr.

All Night Long (All Night)　1983　w.m. Lionel Richie

All of a Sudden My Heart Sings, *see* **My Heart Sings**

All of Me　1931　w.m. Seymour Simons, Gerald Marks. (MF) *Carless Lady.* (MF) *Meet Danny Wilson.* (MF) *Lady Sings the Blues.* Joan Bennett and John Boles appeared in *Carless Lady.* Frank Sinatra and Shelley Winters appeared in *Meet Danny Wilson.* Diana Ross appeared in *Lady Sings the Blues.*

All of My Life　1945　w.m. Irving Berlin

All of My Life　1974　w.m. Michael Randall

All of You　1954　w.m. Cole Porter. (MT) *Silk Stockings.* (MF) *Silk Stockings.* Fred Astaire and Cyd Charisse appeared in the film production of *Silk Stockings.*

All of You　1984　w.m. Cynthia Weil, Tony Renis

All on Account of Liza　1881　w. Henry P. Stephens m. Edward Solomon. This song was originally ascribed to Billie Taylor.

All or Nothing At All　1940　w.m. Jack Lawrence, Arthur Altman. (MF) *This Is the Life.* (MF) *Weekend Pass.* Donald O'Connor and Susanna Foster appeared in *This Is the Life.*

Noah Beery and George Barbier appeared in *Weekend Pass.* This song was popularly revived in 1943. Theme song of Frank Sinatra.

All Our Tomorrows　1943　w.m. Jimmy Kennedy

All Out of Love　1980　w.m. Clive Davis, Graham Russell

All Over Italy　1933　w.m. Ralph Butler, Ronnie Munro

All Over Nothing at All　1922　w. J. Keirn Brennan, Paul Cunningham m. James Rule

All Over the Place　1941　w.m. Noel Gay, Frank Eyton. (MF) *Sailors Three.* Tommy Trinder appeared in *Sailors Three.*

All Over the World　1963　w.m. Al Frisch, Charles Tobias

All Pals Together　1914　w.m. Reginald Sloan

All Quiet Along the Potomac Tonight　1864　w. Lamar Fontaine m. John Hill Hewitt

All Right　1983　w.m. Christopher Cross

All Roads to You　1982　w.m. Rhonda J. Fleiming, Dennis Morgan

All Round My Hat I Wore a Yellow Ribbon, *see* **She Wore a Yellow Ribbon**

All She'd Say Was Umh Hum　1920　w.m. King Zany, MacEmery, Van, Schenck. (MT) *Ziegfeld Follies of 1920.* Fanny Brice and W.C. Fields appeared in *Ziegfeld Follies of 1920.*

All Shook Up　1957　w.m. Otis Blackwell, Elvis Presley

All That Glitters Is Not Gold　1946　w. Lee Kuhn m. Alice Cornett, Eddie Asherman

All That I Ask of You Is Love　1910　w. Edgar Selden m. Herbert Ingraham

All That Jazz　1975　w. Fred Ebb m. John Kander. (MT) *Chicago.* Chita Rivera and Gwen Verdon appeared in *Chicago.*

All the Gold in California　1980　w.m. Larry Gatlin

All the King's Horses　1930　w.m. Howard Dietz, Edward Brandt, Alec Wilder. (MT) *Three's a Crowd.* Fred MacMurray, Tamara Geva, and Libby Holman appeared in *Three's a Crowd.*

All the Live-Long Day (and the Long, Long Night)　1964 w. Ira Gershwin m. George Gershwin. (MF) *Kiss Me, Stupid.*

All the Quakers Are Shoulder Shakers Down in Quaker Town　1919　w. Bert Kalmar, Edgar Leslie m. Pete Wendling. This new pre-Flapper dance was introduced by Bee Palmer and Gilda Gray.

All the Things You Are　1940　w. Oscar Hammerstein II m. Jerome Kern. (MT) *Very Warm for May.* (MF) *Till the Clouds Roll By.* (MF) *Because You're Mine.* Grace McDonald appeared in *Very Warm for May.* Frank Sinatra, Judy Garland, and Van Johnson appeared in *Till the Clouds Roll By,* biopic of composer Jerome Kern. Mario Lanza appeared in *Because You're Mine.*

All the Time　1945　w.m. Ralph Freedom, Sammy Fain. (MF) *No Leave No Love.* Van Johnson, Xavier Cugat, and Pat Kirkwood appeared in *No Leave No Love.*

All the Way　1957　w. Sammy Cahn m. Jimmy Van Heusen (F) *The Joker is Wild.* Frank Sinatra and Mitzi Gaynor appeared in *The Joker Is Wild.* Academy Award winner 1957.

All the Way My Saviour Leads Me 1875 w. Frances Jane Crosby (Mrs. Alexander Van Alstyne) m. Reverend Robert Lowry

All the World Will Be Jealous of Me 1917 w. Al Dubin m. Ernest R. Ball

All Things Love Thee, So Do I 1838 w. anon. m. Charles Edward Horn

All This and Heaven Too 1937 m. Max Steiner. This fanfare became the trademark theme for hundreds of Warner Brothers films.

All This and Heaven Too 1940 w.m. Edgar De Lange, Jimmy Van Heusen

All This Love 1983 w.m. Eldra DeBarge

All Those Years Ago 1981 w.m. George Harrison

All Through the Day 1946 w. Oscar Hammerstein II m. Jerome Kern. (MF) *Centennial Summer.* Cornel Wilde and Jeanne Crain appeared in *Centennial Summer.*

All Through the Night 1784 w.m. traditional air, from Wales. From the Welch "Ar Hyd y Nos."

All Through the Night 1934 w.m. Cole Porter. (MT) *Anything Goes.* (MF) *Anything Goes* (1936). (MF) *Anything Goes* (1956). Victor Moore, William Gaxton, and Ethel Merman appeared in the American stage production of *Anything Goes* Jack Whiting appeared in the British stage production of *Anything Goes.* Bing Crosby and Ethel Merman appeared in the 1936 film production of *Anything Goes.* Bing Crosby and Mitzi Gaynor appeared in the 1956 film production of *Anything Goes.*

All Through the Night 1983 w.m. Jules Shear

All Time High 1984 w.m. John Barry, Tim Rice

All You Need Is Love 1967 w.m. John Lennon, Paul McCartney. (MT) *Beatlemania.* (MF) *Yellow Submarine.* The Beatles appeared in *Yellow Submarine.*

Allah's Holiday 1916 w. Otto Harbach m. Rudolf Friml. (MT) *Katinka.* Adele Rowland and Franklyn Ardell appeared in *Katinka.*

Allan Water c. 1750 w.m. traditional, from England

Allegheny Moon 1956 w.m. Al Hoffman, Dick Manning

Alley Cat 1962 w.m. Frank Bjorn

Alley-Oop 1960 w.m. Dallas Frazier

Allez-Vous En (Go Away) 1953 w.m. Cole Porter. (MT) *Can-Can.* (MF) *Can-Can.* Frank Sinatra and Shirley MacLaine appeared in the film production of *Can-Can.*

Allison's Theme from Parrish 1961 m. Max Steiner. (F) *Parrish.* Claudette Colbert appeared in *Parrish.*

Alma Mater of Brown University, *see* **The Old Oaken Bucket**

Alma Where Do You Live 1910 w. George V. Hobart m. Adolph Philipp. (MT) *Alma Where Do You Live.*

Almost in Your Arms 1955 w.m. Ray Evans, Jay Livingston. (F) *Houseboat.* Cary Grant and Sophia Loren appeared in *Houseboat.*

(It's) Almost Like Being in Love 1947 w. Alan Jay Lerner m. Frederick Loewe. (MT) *Brigadoon.* (MF) *Brigadoon.*

David Brooks and Marion Bell appeared in the stage production of *Brigadoon.* Gene Kelly and Cyd Charisse appeared in the film production of *Brigadoon.*

Almost Over You 1984 w.m. Ciny Richardson, Jennie Kimball

Almost Paradise 1956 w.m. Norman Petty

Almost Paradise 1984 w.m. Eric Carmen, Dean Pitchford

Almost Persuaded 1966 w.m. Glen Sutton, Billy Sherrill. Grammy Award winner 1966.

Almost There 1964 w.m. Jerry Keller, Gloria Shayne. (MF) *I'd Rather Be Rich.* Sandra Dee and Robert Goulet appeared in *I'd Rather Be Rich.*

Aloha Oe, or, **Farewell to Thee** 1878 w.m. Queen Liliuokalani. (F) *Aloha.* Thelma Todd and Ben Lyon appeared in *Aloha.* This song was popularly revived in 1938. See also "There's Music in the Air."

Alone 1935 w. Arthur Freed m. Nacio Herb Brown. (MF) *A Night At the Opera.* (MF) *Andy Hardy Meets a Debutante.* (MF) *Born To Sing.* The Marx Brothers, Allan Jones, and Kitty Carlisle appeared in *A Night at the Opera.* Judy Garland and Mickey Rooney appeared in *Andy Hardy Meets a Debutante.* Leo Gorcey appeared in *Born To Sing.*

Alone Again (Naturally) 1972 w.m. Gilbert O'Sullivan. Ivor Novello Award winner 1972–73.

Alone at a Table for Two 1935 w. Billy Hill, Daniel Richman m. Ted Fiorito

Alone Together 1932 w. Howard Dietz m. Arthur Schwartz. (MT) *Flying Colors.* Patsy Kelly, Clifton Webb, and Imogene Coca appeared in *Flying Colors.*

Alone Too Long 1954 w. Dorothy Fields m. Arthur Schwartz. (MT) *By the Beautiful Sea.* (MF) *By the Beautiful Sea.*

Along Came Caroline 1960 w.m. Paul Stephens, Michael Cox, Terence McGrath, M. Steel

Along Comes a Woman 1985 w.m. Mark Goldenberg

Along the Navajo Trail 1945 w.m. Dick Charles, Eddie De Lange, Larry Marks. (MF) *Along the Navajo Trail.* *Don't Fence Me In.* (F) *The Blazing Sun.* Roy Rogers appeared in both *Along the Navajo Trail* and *Don't Fence Me In.* Gene Autry and Pat Buttram appeared in *The Blazing Sun.*

Along the Rocky Road to Dublin 1915 w. Joe Young m. Bert Grant

Along the Santa Fe Trail 1940 w.m. Al Dubin, Will Grosz, Edwina Coolidge. (F) *Santa Fe Trail.* Errol Flynn and Olivia de Havilland appeared in *Santa Fe Trail.*

Along with Me 1946 w.m. Harold Rome. (MT) *Call Me Mister.* (MF) *Call Me Mister.* Betty Garrett and Jules Munshin appeared in the stage production of *Call Me Mister.* Betty Grable and Danny Thomas appeared in the film production of *Call Me Mister.*

Alouette 1879 Earliest words and music published in Montreal, Canada, in 1879, but most surely performed before that as a traditional French-Canadian folksong. (MF) *People Are Funny.* Jack Haley and Rudy Vallee appeared in *People Are Funny.* This song was popularly revived in 1931. Sung by women while plucking fowls, this melody was in its day a standard worksong.

Alphabet Song, The, *see* **Twinkle, Twinkle, Little Star**

Also sprach Zarathustra, or, **Theme from** *2001: A Space Odyssey* 1968 m. Richard Strauss; arr. Eumir Deodato. (F) *2001: A Space Odyssey.* Based on the same by Richard Strauss, "Also sprach Zarathustra," op. 30 (1896). This work was popularly revived in 1973.

Alt Wien 1920 m. Leopold Godowsky

Alvin's Harmonica 1959 w.m. Ross Bagdasarian

Always 1899 w. Charles Horwitz m. Frederick V. Bowers

Always 1925 w.m. Irving Berlin. (MF) *Christmas Holiday.* Deanna Durbin and Gene Kelly appeared in *Christmas Holiday.*

Always 1934 w.m. Kenneth Leslie Smith, James Dyrenforth

(It Was) Always Always You 1961 w.m. Bob Merrill. (MT) *Carnival.*

Always and Always 1937 w. Bob Wright, Chet Forrest m. Edward Ward. (F) *Mannequin.* Joan Crawford and Spencer Tracy appeared in *Mannequin.*

(You Are) Always in My Heart 1942 w.m. Ernesto Lecuona, Kim Gannon. (MF) *Always in My Heart.* Walter Huston and Kay Francis appeared in *Always in My Heart.*

Always in the Way 1903 w.m. Charles K. Harris

Always Leave Them Laughing When You Say Goodbye 1903 w.m. George M. Cohan. (MT) *Mother Goose.*

Always on My Mind 1982 w.m. Wayne Carson, Johnny Christopher, Mark James. Grammy Award winner 1982.

Always Take Mother's Advice 1884 w.m. Jennie Lindsay

(I'm) Always True to You in My Fashion 1949 w.m. Cole Porter. (MT) *Kiss Me, Kate.* (MF) *Kiss Me, Kate.* Alfred Drake and Patricia Morison appeared in the stage production of *Kiss Me, Kate.* Ann Miller appeared in the film production of *Kiss Me, Kate.*

Am I Blue 1929 w. Grant Clarke m. Harry Akst. (MF) *On With the Show.* (MF) *Is Everybody Happy.* (MF) *So Long Letty.* (MF) *The Hard Way.* (MF) *The Eddy Duchin Story.* (F) *To Have and Have Not.* Joe E. Brown and Ethel Waters appeared in *On with the Show.* Larry Parks appeared in *Is Everybody Happy,* biopic of bandleader Ted Lewis. Ida Lupino and Joan Leslie appeared in *The Hard Way.* Humphrey Bogart and Lauren Bacall appeared in *To Have and Have Not.*

Am I in Love 1937 w. Al Dubin m. Harry Warren. (MF) *Mr. Dodd Takes the Air.* Kenny Baker and Jane Wyman appeared in *Mr. Dodd Takes the Air.*

Am I in Love 1952 w.m. Jack Brooks. (MF) *Son of Paleface.* Bob Hope, Jane Russell, and Roy Rogers appeared in *Son of Paleface.*

Am I Wasting My Time on (over) You 1926 w.m. Howard Johnson, Irving Bibo

Amanda 1979 w.m. Bob McDill

Amapola, or, **Pretty Little Poppy** 1924 Sp.w. Joseph M. Lacalle Eng.w. Joseph M. Lacalle new Eng.w. Albert Gamse

m. Joseph M. Lacalle. (MF) *First Love.* (F) *Saddle Pals.* Deanna Durbin and Robert Stack appeared in *First Love.* Gene Autry and Sterling Holloway appeared in *Saddle Pals.* This song was popularly revived in 1941.

Amazing Grace c. 1800 w.m. Traditional

America (My Country 'Tis of Thee) 1832 w. Samuel Francis Smith (1831) m. same as "God Save the King," 1744. This song was first performed July 4, 1831, at a children's gathering at Park Street Church, Boston. See also "God Save the King."

America 1957 w. Stephen Sondheim m. Leonard Bernstein. (MT) *West Side Story.* (MF) *West Side Story.* Natalie Wood and Rita Moreno appeared in the film production of *West Side Story.*

America I Love You 1915 w. Edgar Leslie m. Archie Gottler

America, the Beautiful 1895 w. Katharine Lee Bates m. Samuel Augustus Ward. (MF) *Bells of Capistrano.* (MF) *With a Song in My Heart.* Gene Autry and Smiley Burnette appeared in *Bells of Capistrano.* Susan Hayward appeared in *With a Song in My Heart,* biopic of singer Jane Froman. The words to this song were written by poet Katherine Lee Bates at Pikes Peak in 1893. The melody to this song was based on "Materna" by Samuel Augustus Ward.

American Beauty Rose 1950 w.m. Hal David, Redd Evans, Arthur Altman

American Dream, An 1980 w.m. Rodney Crowell

American in Paris, An 1929 m. George Gershwin. (MF) *Rhapsody in Blue.* (MF) *An American in Paris.* Oscar Levant, Alexis Smith, and Robert Alda appeared in *Rhapsody in Blue,* biopic of composer George Gershwin. Gene Kelly and Leslie Caron appeared in *An American in Paris.* This work had its world premiere on December 13, 1928, by the New York Philharmonic Society, Walter Damrosch conducting.

American Made 1983 w.m. Bob DiPiero, Patrick McManus

American Music 1982 w.m. Parker McGee

American Patrol (We Must Be Vigilant) 1885 m. F.W. Meacham. (MF) *Orchestra Wives.* (MF) *The Glenn Miller Story.* Glenn Miller and Ann Rutherford appeared in *Orchestra Wives.* An adapted version of this song, with added lyrics, was popularized in 1943.

(Bye Bye) American Pie 1972 w.m. Don McLean

American Star, The 1800 w. John McCreery m. D.C. Hewitt. The melody to this song was originally called "The Wounded Hussar" (Huzzar); the words were often sung to the melody of "Humours of Glen."

Amina 1907 m. Paul Lincke

Among My Souvenirs 1927 w. Edgar Leslie m. Horatio Nicholls. (MF) *Paris.* (F) *The Best Years of Our Lives.* Irene Bordoni and Zasu Pitts appeared in *Paris.* Frederic March appeared in *The Best Years of Our Lives.*

Amor 1944 Sp.w. Ricardo Lopez Mendez Eng.w. Sunny Skylar m. Garbriel Ruiz. (MF) *Broadway Rhythm.* (MF) *Swing in the Saddle.* (MF) *Lights of Old Santa Fe.* Ben Blue, Lena Horne, and George Murphy appeared in *Broadway Rhythm.* Jane Frazee appeared in *Swing in the Saddle.* Roy

Rogers, Dale Evans, and Gabby Hayes appeared in *Lights of Old Santa Fe.*

Amorous Goldfish, The 1896 w. Harry Greenbank m. Sidney Jones. (MT) *The Geisha.*

L'Amour Toujours L'Amour, or, **Love Everlasting** 1922 w. Catherine Chisholm Cushing m. Rudolf Friml

Amsterdam 1968 Eng.w. Eric Blau, Mort Shuman m. Jacques Brel. (MT) *Jacques Brel Is Alive and Well and Living in Paris.*

Amy, Wonderful Amy 1930 w.m. Horatio Nicholls, Joe Gilbert

Anacreon in Heaven, *see* **To Anacreon in Heaven**

Anastasia 1956 w. Paul Francis Webster m. Alfred Newman. (F) *Anastasia.* Ingrid Bergman, Yul Brynner, and Helen Hayes appeared in *Anastasia.*

Anatevka 1964 w. Sheldon Harnick m. Jerry Bock. (MT) *Fiddler on the Roff.* (MF) *Fiddler on the Roof.* Zero Mostel and Bette Midler appeared in the stage production of *Fiddler on the Roof.*

Anchored 1888 w. Samuel K. Cowan m. Michael Watson

Anchored 1956 w.m. Michael Watson, Clifford N. Page

Anchors Aweigh 1906 w. Alfred Hart Miles, R. Lovell m. Charles A. Zimmerman. This Navy anthem was originally titled "Sail Navy Down the Field" and was a marching song for the Annapolis Class of 1907. Mr. Miles tell to his death from an attic window on October 8, 1956, at the age of seventy-two.

And . . . 1975 w. Edward Kleban m. Marvin Hamlisch. (MT) *A Chorus Line.* Donna McKechnie appeared in *A Chorus Line.*

And a Little Bit More 1907 w. Alfred Bryan m. Fred Fisher

And He'd Say "Oo-La-La Wee-Wee" 1919 w.m. Harry Ruby, George Jessel

And Her Golden Hair Was Hanging Down Her Back 1894 w. Monroe H. Rosenfeld m. Felix McGlennon

And Her Mother Came Too 1921 w.m. Ivor Novello, Dion Titheradge. (MT) *A to Z.* Jack Buchanan appeared in *A to Z.*

And Her Tears Flowed Like Wine 1944 w.m. Joe Greene, Stanley Kenton, Charles Lawrence. (F) *Two Guys from Milwaukee.* Dennis Morgan, Jack Carson, and Joan Leslie appeared in *Two Guys from Milwaukee.*

And I Am Telling You I'm Not Going 1982 w. Tom Eyen m. Henry Krieger. (MT) *Dream Girls.* Loretta Devine and Jennifer Holliday appeared in *Dream Girls.*

And I Love Her 1964 w.m. John Lennon, Paul McCartney

And I Was Beautiful 1968 w.m. Jerry Herman. (MT) *Dear World.* Angela Lansbury appeared in *Dear World.*

And Mimi 1947 w. Jimmy Kennedy m. Nat Simon

And Russia Is Her Name 1943 w. E.Y. Harburg m. Jerome Kern. (F) *Song of Russia.* Robert Taylor and Susan Peters appeared in *Song of Russia.*

And So Do I 1940 w.m. Stephan Weiss, Paul Mann, Edgar De Lange

And So to Bed 1932 w.m. Mack Gordon, Harry Revel

And So to Bed 1946 w. Johnny Mercer m. Robert Emmett Dolan

And So To Sleep Again 1951 w.m. Joe Marsala, Sunny Skylar

And That Reminds Me, *see* **My Heart Reminds Me**

And the Angels Sing 1939 w.m. Johnny Mercer, Ziggy Elman. (MF) *And the Angels Sing.* (MF) *The Benny Goodman Story.* Betty Hutton and Fred MacMurray appeared in *And the Angels Sing.*

And the Band Played On, *see* **The Band Played On**

And the Grass Won't Pay No Mind 1970 w.m. Neil Diamond

And the Great Big Saw Came Nearer 1936 w.m. Robert E. Harris, Dwight B. Latham, Bert Lee, R.P. Weston

And the Green Grass Grew All Around 1912 w. William Jerome m. Harry Von Tilzer

And the Monkey Wrapped Its Tail Around the Flagpole, *see* **National Emblem** (March)

And This Is My Beloved 1954 w.m. Robert Wright, George Forrest. Based on a theme from the third movement, "Nocturne," of Borodin's String Quartet No. 2 in D Major. (MT) *Kismet.* (MF) *Kismet.* Ann Blythe and Howard Keel appeared in the film production of *Kismet.*

And When I Die 1966 w.m. Laura Nyro. This song was most popular in 1969.

Andalucia 1930 m. Ernesto Lecuona. From the suite "Andalucia." See also "The Breeze and I."

Anema e Core (With All My Heart and Soul) 1954 It. w. Tito Manlio m. Salve d'Esposito Eng. w. Mann Curtis, Harry Akst

Angel Child 1922 w.m. George Price, Abner Silver, Benny Davis

Angel Flying Too Close to the Ground 1981 w.m. Willie Nelson

Angel Gabriel 1875 w. anon. m. James E. Stewart

Angel in Your Arms 1977 w.m. Herbert Ivey, Terry Woodford

Angel of the Great White Way 1937 w.m. Elton Box, Desmond Cox, Don Pelosi, Paddy Roberts

Angel of the Morning 1981 w.m. Chip Taylor

Angela Mia (My Angel) 1928 w. Lew Pollack m. Erno Rapee. (F) *Street Angel*

Angelina 1960 w. Carolyn Leigh m. Cy Coleman. (MT) *Wildcat.*

Angelina Baker 1850 w.m. Stephen Collins Foster

Angelo 1977 w.m. Tony Hiller, Lee Sheriden, Martin Lee. Ivor Novello Award winner 1977–78.

Angels from the Realms of Glory 1867 w. James Montgomery m. Henry Smart

Angels Meet Me at the Cross Roads 1875 w.m. William Shakespeare Hays

Angel's Serenade 1867 It. w. Marco Marcelliano Marcello Eng. w. Harrison Millard m. Gaetano Braga. From the Italian "La Serenata." See also "The Perfect Song."

Angelus, The 1913 w. Robert B. Smith m. Victor Herbert. (MT) *Sweethearts*. (MF) *Sweethearts*. Nelson Eddy, Jeanette MacDonald, and Ray Bolger appeared in the film production of *Sweethearts*.

Angie 1973 w.m. Mick Jagger, Keith Richard. Ivor Novello Award winner 1973–74.

Angie Baby 1974 w.m. Alan O'Day

Animal Crackers, *see* **I'm Just Wild About Animal Crackers**

Animal Crackers in My Soup 1935 w.m. Ted Koehler, Irving Caesar, Ray Henderson. (MF) *Curly Top*. Shirley Temple appeared in *Curly Top*.

Anitra's Dance, op. 46, no. 3 1888 m. Edvard Grieg. From "Peer Gynt Suite, No. 1."

Anna 1953 w.m. Vatro Roman, F. Giordano, William Engvick. (F) *Anna*. Silvana Mangano and Raf Vallone appeared in *Anna*.

Annabelle 1923 w. Lew Brown m. Ray Henderson

Annabelle Lee, *see* **Miss Annabelle Lee**

Annie Doesn't Live Here Anymore 1933 w. Joe Young, Johnny Burke m. Harold Spina

Annie Laurie 1838 w. William Douglas in 1688 m. Lady John Scott (Alicia Ann Spottiswoode), from Scotland. James Grant states "William Douglas of Finland is supposed to compose and sing the song when in Flanders. He is killed in battle by the side of his friend Walter Fenton. A ball pierces his breast and he expires holding a lock of Annie's bright brown hair in his hand and murmuring her name!" Annie was the daughter of Sir Robert Laurie and his second wife, Jean, daughter of Riddel of Minto. She never got to marry her lover William, but was wedded to Mr. Alexander Fergusson of Craigdarroch in 1709.

Annie Lisle 1860 w.m. H.S. Thompson. This song was popularly adapted by C.K. Urguhart in 1941. Adapted, it became the Alma Mater of Cornell University in 1872 with the title "Far Above Cayuga's Waters" and the alternate title "Amici." The words were written by Archibald C. Weeks and Wilmot M. Smith.

Annie Roonie, *see* **Little Annie Roonie**

Annie's Song 1974 w.m. John Denver

Anniversary Song, The 1947 w.m. Al Jolson, Saul Chaplin. (MF) *The Jolson Story*. Larry Parks appeared in *The Jolson Story*. Based on Ivanovici's "Danube Waves" (Ueber den Wellen) of 1880. This song is traditionally played when a circus performer requires special concentration during his act.

Anniversary Waltz, The 1941 w.m. Dave Franklin, Al Dubin

Another Brick in the Wall 1980 w.m. Roger Waters. (MF) *The Wall*. Ivor Novello Award winner 1979–80. Ivor Novello Award winner 1980–81. Ivor Novello Award winner 1982–83.

Another Day 1971 w.m. Paul McCartney, Linda McCartney

Another Honky Tonk Night on Broadway 1982 w.m. Milton Brown, Steve Dorff, Snuff Garrett

Another Hundred People 1970 w.m. Stephen Sondheim. (MT) *Company*. (MT) *Side by Side by Sondheim*. Elaine Stritch appeared in *Company*. Millicent Martin and Julie N. McKenzie appeared in *Side by Side by Sondheim*.

Another Little Drink Wouldn't Do Us Any Harm 1916 w.m. Nat D. Ayer, Clifford Grey. (MT) *The Bing Boys Are Here*. Alfred Lester and Violet Loraine appeared in *The Bing Boys Are Here*.

Another One Bites the Dust 1980 w.m. John Deacon. Ivor Novello Award winner 1980–81.

Another Op'nin, Another Show 1948 w.m. Cole Porter. (MT) *Kiss Me, Kate*. (MF) *Kiss Me, Kate*. Alfred Drake and Patricia Morison appeared in the stage production of *Kiss Me, Kate*. Ann Miller appeared in the film production of *Kiss Me, Kate*.

Another Saturday Night 1963 w.m. Sam Cooke

(Hey Won't You Play) Another Somebody Done Somebody Wrong Song 1975 w.m. Chips Moman, Larry Butler. Grammy Award winner 1975.

Another Spring 1973 w.m. Malcolm Barron, Steven Cairn

Another Suitcase in Another Hall 1977 w.m. Tim Rice, Andrew Lloyd Webber. (MT) *Evita*. Ivor Novello Award winner 1976–77. Ivor Novello Award winner 1977–78.

Another Time, Another Place 1958 w.m. Ray Evans, Jay Livingston. (F) *Another Time, Another Place*. Lana Turner and Sean Connery appeared in *Another Time, Another Place*.

Answer, The 1921 w.m. Robert Huntington Terry

Answer Me (My Love) 1954 Orig. w. Fred Rauch Eng. w. Carl Sigman m. Gerhard Winkler

Anticipation 1971 w.m. Carly Simon. This song was later used for a Heinz Ketchup commercial promotion campaign. Ms. Simon was paid $50,000 for this use of her song.

Antioch, *see* **Joy to the World**

Anvil Chorus 1853 w. Salvadore Cammarano m. Giuseppe Verdi. From the opera *Il Trovatore*. See also "Hail, Hail, the Gang's All Here."

Any Bonds Today? 1940 w.m. Irving Berlin. Berlin's celebration to help the war effort brought in more than $10,000 in royalties for the Army Ordance Association.

Any Little Girl, That's a Nice Little Girl, Is the Right Little Girl for Me 1910 w. Thomas J. Gray m. Fred Fisher

Any Little Kiss 1931 w.m. Noël Coward

Any Old Iron 1911 w.m. Charles Collins, Fred Terry, E.A. Sheppard

Any Old Place I Can Hang My Hat Is Home Sweet Home to Me 1901 w. William Jerome m. Jean Schwartz

Any Old Place with You 1919 w. Lorenz Hart m. Richard Rodgers. (MT) *A Lonely Romeo*. This song was the first published effort for the Rodgers and Hart collaboration.

Any Old Port in a Storm 1908 w. Arthur J. Lamb m. Kerry Mills

Any Place I Hang My Hat Is Home 1946 w. Johnny Mercer m. Harold Arlen. (MT) *St. Louis Woman*. Pearl Bailey and Rex Ingram appeared in *St. Louis Woman*.

Any Time 1921 w.m. Herbert Happy Lawson. This song was popularly revived in 1952.

Any Time Is Kissing Time   1916   w.m. Frederick Norton, Oscar Asche. (MT) *Chu Chin Chow*. Violet Essex and Courtice Pounds appeared in the British production of *Chu Chin Chow*. Tyrone Power and Tessa Kosta appeared in the American production of *Chu Chin Chow*. This show was designed for the British morale effort during World War I.

Any Time's the Time To Fall in Love   1931   w.m. Elsie Janis, Jack King. (MF) *Along Came Youth*. Charles "Buddy" Rogers and Frances Dee appeared in *Along Came Youth*.

Any Way the Wind Blows   1960   w.m. By Dunham, Marilyn Hooven, Joe Hooven

Anyone Can Be a Millionaire   1955   w.m. Ed Franks. (F) *Fun at Saint Fanny's*.

Anyone Can Move a Mountain   1967   w.m. John D. Marks

Anyone Can Whistle   1964   w.m. Stephen Sondheim. (MT) *Anyone Can Whistle*. (MT) *Side by Side by Sondheim*. Millicent Martin and Julie N. McKenzie appeared in *Side by Side by Sondheim*.

Anyone Who Had a Heart   1963   w.m. Hal David, Burt Bacharach

Anyone Who Isn't Me Tonight   1979   w.m. Julie Didier, Daniel Cohen

(I Would Do) Anything for You   1932   w.m. Alexander Hill, Claude Hopkins

Anything Goes   1934   w.m. Cole Porter. (MT) *Anything Goes*. (MF) *Anything Goes* (1936). (MF) *Anything Goes* (1956). (F) *Boys in the Band*. (F) *Evil Under the Sun*. Ethel Merman, Victor Moore, and William Gaxton appeared in the stage production of *Anything Goes*. Ethel Merman and Bing Crosby appeared in the 1936 film production of *Anything Goes*. Bing Crosby and Donald O'Connor appeared in the 1956 film production of *Anything Goes*. Maggie Smith and James Mason appeared in *Evil Under the Sun*.

Anything I Dream Is Possible   1948   w.m. Billy Reid

Anything You Can Do   1946   w.m. Irving Berlin. (MT) *Annie Get Your Gun*. (MF) *Annie Get Your Gun*. Ethel Merman and Ray Middleton appeared in the stage production of *Annie Get Your Gun*. Betty Hutton and Howard Keel appeared in the film production of *Annie Get Your Gun*.

Anyway, Anyhow, Anywhere   1965   w.m. Peter Townshend, Roger Daltry

Anywhere I Wander   1952   w.m. Frank Loesser. (MF) *Hans Christian Andersen*. Danny Kaye appeared in *Hans Christian Andersen*.

Apache   1961   m. Jerry Lordan. Ivor Novello Award winner 1960.

Apache Dance   1861   m. Jacques Offenbach. From the ballet *Le Papillon*.

Apalachicola, Florida   1947   w.m. Johnny Burke, Jimmy Van Heusen. (MF) *The Road to Rio*. Bob Hope, Bing Crosby, and Dorothy Lamour appeared in *The Road to Rio*.

(Theme from) Apartment, The   1960   m. Charles Williams. (F) *The Apartment*. Jack Lemmon and Shirley MacLaine appeared in *The Apartment*. This song was originally published as "Jealous Lover" in 1949.

Applause   1970   w. Lee Adams   m. Charles Strouse. (MT) *Applause*. Lauren Bacall appeared in *Applause*.

Apple Blossom Time, *see* **I'll Be with You in Apple Blossom Time**

Apple for the Teacher, An   1939   w.m. Johnny Burke, James V. Monaco. (MF) *The Star Maker*. Bing Crosby and Ned Sparks appeared in *The Star Maker*

Applejack   1963   w.m. Les Vandyke

April Blossoms   1923   w. Otto Harbach, Oscar Hammerstein II   m. Herbert Stothart, Vincent Youmans. (MT) *Wildflower*.

April Fools   1969   w.m. Hal David, Burt F. Bacharach

April in Paris   1932   w. E.Y. Harburg   m. Vernon Duke. (MT) *Walk a Little Faster*. (MF) *April in Paris*. (MF) *Both Ends of the Candle*. (MF) *Paris Holiday*. Beatrice Lillie appeared in *Walk a Little Faster*. Doris Day and Ray Bolger appeared in *April in Paris*. Bob Hope and Anita Ekberg appeared in *Paris Holiday*.

April in Portugal   1953   Port. w. José Galhardo   Eng w. Jimmy Kennedy   m. Raul Ferrão

April Love   1957   w. Paul Francis Webster   m. Sammy Fain. (MF) *April Love*. Pat Boone and Shirley Jones appeared in *April Love*.

April Played the Fiddle   1940   w.m. Jimmy Monaco, Johnny Burke. (MF) *If I Had My Way*.

April Showers   1921   w. B.G. DeSylva   m. Louis Silvers. (MT) *Bombo*. (MF) *The Jolson Story*. (MF) *April Showers*. (MF) *Jolson Sings Again*. (MF) *The Eddy Duchin Story*. Al Jolson received thirty-six curtain calls for this song on October 6, 1921, opening night of *Bombo*. Larry Parks appeared in both *The Jolson Story* and *Jolson Sings Again*. Ann Sheridan and Jack Carson appeared in *April Showers*.

Aqua Velva Man   1974   w.m. Alfred Eichler, Julian Eichler. This song was written for an Aqua Velva commercial promotion campaign.

Aquarius   1969   w. Gerome Ragni, James Rado   m. Galt MacDermot. (MT) *Hair*. (MF) *Hair*. Grammy Award winner 1969.

Araby   1915   w.m. Irving Berlin

Araby's Daughter   1822   w. Thomas Moore   m. George Kiallmark. The words are based on Moore's "The Fire Worshippers," from "Lalla Rookh." See also "The Old Oaken Bucket."

Aragonaise   1885   m. Jules Massenet. From the ballet *Le Cid*.

Arcady Is Ever Young   1909   w.m. Lionel Monckton, Arthur Wimperis, Howard Talbot. (MT) *The Arcadians*. Florence Smithson appeared in *The Arcadians*.

Are the Good Times Really Over   1982   w.m. Merle Haggard

Are We Downhearted?—No!   1914   w.m. Lawrence Wright, Worton David

Are We To Part Like This, Bill   1912   w.m. Harry Castling, Charles Collins

Are You from Dixie, Cause I'm from Dixie Too   1915   w.m. Jack Yellen, George L. Cobb. This song was popularly revived in 1969.

Are You Going to San Francisco, *see* **San Francisco**

Are You Havin' Any Fun   1939   w. Jack Yellen   m. Sammy

Fain. (MT) *George White's Scandals of 1939*. (MT) *The Little Dog Laughed*. Ben Blue and Ann Miller appeared in *George White's Scandals of 1939*. Flanagan and Allen appeared in *The Little Dog Laughed*.

Are You Lonesome Tonight 1926 w.m. Roy Turk, Lou Handman. This song was popularly revived in 1960.

Are You Making Any Money 1933 w.m. Herman Hupfeld. (MF) *Moonlight and Pretzels*. William Frawley and Leo Carrillo appeared in *Moonlight and Pretzels*.

Are You My Love 1936 w. Lorenz Hart m. Richard Rodgers. (MF) *Dancing Pirate*.

Are You Sincere 1957 w.m. Wayne Walker

Are You Sorry 1925 w. Benny Davis m. Milton Ager

Are You Sure 1961 w.m. Bob Allison, John Allison. Ivor Novello Award winner 1961.

Are You There (with Another Girl) 1966 w. Hal David m. Burt F. Bacharach

Aren't We All, *see* **I'm a Dreamer**

Aren't You Glad You're You 1946 w. Johnny Burke m. Jimmy Van Heusen. (F) *The Bells of St. Mary's*. Bing Crosby and Ingrid Bergman appeared in *The Bells of St. Mary's*.

Aren't You Kind of Glad We Did 1946 w. Ira Gershwin m. George Gershwin. (MF) *The Shocking Miss Pilgrim*. Dick Haymes and Gene Lockhart appeared in *The Shocking Miss Pilgrim*.

Argentines, the Portuguese and the Greeks, The 1920 w.m. Arthur M. Swanstrom, Carey Morgan

Arise, O Sun 1921 w.m. Maude Craske-Day

Arizona 1917 w.m. Melville Gideon, James Heard. (MT) *Flying Colours*. Melville Gideon appeared in *Flying Colours*.

Arkansas Traveler, The 1851 m. uncertain; erroneously credited to Joseph Tosso. This song inspired six Currier & Ives lithograph plates which describe the narrative of "The Arkansas Traveler." See also "Johnny Get Your Gun."

L'Arlésienne (March of the Kings) 1872 The melody to this song dates originally from the thirteenth century. Later it was used by Georges Bizet in the opening bars of his music for Alphonse Daudet's drama *L'Arlésienne*.

Arm in Arm 1932 w.m. Harry Leon, Leo Towers

Armorer's Song 1891 w. Harry B. Smith m. Reginald DeKoven. (MT) *Robin Hood*.

Army Air Corps Song, The, or, **The U.S. Air Force Song** 1939 w.m. Robert Crawford. (MT) *Winged Victory*. (MF) *Follow the Band*. (MF) *Ice Capades Revue*. (F) *Winged Victory*. Eddie Quillan and Leon Errol appeared in *Follow the Band*. Ellen Drew and Jerry Colonna appeared in *Ice Capades Revue*. Lon McCallister and Jeanne Crain appeared in the film production of *Winged Victory*. This song was popularly revived in 1942.

Army and Navy Song, The, *see* **Columbia, the Gem of the Ocean**

Army Blue, *see* **Aura Lee**

Army Game, The 1958 w.m. Pat Napper, Sid Colin. Ivor Novello Award winner 1958.

Army Goes (Marching) Rolling Along, The, *see* **The U.S. Field Artillery March**

Army of Today's Alright, The 1915 w.m. Fred W. Leigh, Kenneth Lyle. (MF) *After the Ball*. Pat Kirkwood and Laurence Harvey appeared in *After the Ball*, biopic of English music hall artist Vesta Tilley.

Army, the Navy and the Air Force, The 1939 w.m. Herman Darewski

Around the Corner and Under the Tree 1929 w.m. Gus Kahn, Art Kassel

Around the World (in Eighty Days) 1956 w. Harold Adamson m. Victor Young. (F) *Around the World in Eighty Days*. David Niven and Shirley MacLaine appeared in *Around the World in Eighty Days*.

Arrah Go On, I'm Gonna Go Back to Oregon 1916 w. Sam M. Lewis, Joe Young m. Bert Grant. (MF) *The Dolly Sisters*. June Haver and Betty Grable appeared in *The Dolly Sisters*.

Arrah Wanna 1906 w. Jack Drislane m. Theodore F. Morse

Arrivederci Roma 1958 w.m. Carl Sigman, Renato Rascel, S. Giovannini, P. Garinei, Jack Fishman. (F) *The Seven Hills of Rome*. Mario Lanza and Peggy Castle appeared in *The Seven Hills of Rome*.

Arrow and the Song, The 1856 w. Henry Wadsworth Longfellow m. Michael William Balfe

Arthur Murray Taught Me Dancing in a Hurry 1942 w.m. Johnny Mercer, Victor Schertzinger. (MF) *The Fleet's In*. Dorothy Lamour, William Holden, and Betty Hutton appeared in *The Fleet's In*.

Arthur's Theme (Best That You Can Do) 1981 w.m. Peter Allen, Burt Bacharach, Christopher Cross. (F) *Arthur*. Liza Minnelli and Dudley Moore appeared in *Arthur*. This song was popularly revived in 1983.

Artificial Flowers 1960 w. Sheldon Harnick m. Jerry Bock. (MT) *Tenderloin*.

Artist's Life 1867 m. Johann Strauss. This composition was first performed on February 18, 1867.

As Deep as the Deep Blue Sea 1910 w. René Bronner m. H.W. Petrie

As I Go Rolling Home, *see* **I've Got Sixpence**

As Long as He Needs Me 1963 w.m. Lionel Bart. (MT) *Oliver!* (MF) *Oliver!* Georgia Brown appeared in the stage production of *Oliver!* Shani Wallis appeared in the film production of *Oliver!* Ivor Novello Award winner 1960.

As Long as I Live 1934 w. Ted Koehler m. Harold Arlen. (MT) *Cotton Club Parade*. (MT) *Lena Horne: The Lady and Her Music*. Lena Horne appeared in *Lena Horne: The Lady and Her Music*.

As Long as I Live 1944 w.m. Charles Tobias, Howard Simon, (Max Steiner). (F) *Saratoga Trunk*. Gary Cooper and Ingrid Bergman appeared in *Saratoga Trunk*.

As Long as I'm Dreaming 1947 w.m. Jimmy Van Heusen, Johnny Burke. (MF) *Welcome Stranger*. Bing Crosby and Barry Fitzgerald appeared in *Welcome Stranger*.

As Long as the Shamrock Grows Green 1912 w. James Brockman m. Nat Osborne

As Long as the World Rolls On 1907 w. George Graff, Jr. m. Ernest R. Ball

As Long as There's Music 1944 w. Sammy Cahn m. Jule Styne. (MF) *Step Lively.* Frank Sinatra, Adolphe Menjou, and George Murphy appeared in *Step Lively.*

As Long as You're Not in Love with Anyone Else, Why Don't You Fall in Love with Me 1936 w.m. Al Lewis, Mabel Wayne (MT) *Hi-De-Hi.* (MF) *Honeymoon Lodge.* Ozzie Nelson and David Bruce appeared in *Honeymoon Lodge.*

As Tears Go By 1964 w.m. Mick Jagger, Andrew Oldham, Keith Richard

As the Backs Go Tearing By 1909 w. John Thomas Keady m. Carl W. Blaisdell. School song of Dartmouth University.

As the Girls Go 1948 w. Harold Adamson m. Jimmy McHugh. (MT) *As the Girls Go.* Irene Rich and Bill Callahan appeared in *As the Girls Go.*

As Time Goes By 1931 w.m. Herman Hupfeld. (MT) *Everybody's Welcome.* (F) *Casablanca.* (MF) *She's Working Her Way Through College.* Frances Williams and Oscar Shaw appeared in *Everybody's Welcome.* Humphrey Bogart and Ingrid Bergman appeared in *Casablanca.* Virginia Mayo, Gene Nelson, and Ronald Reagan appeared in *She's Working Her Way Through College.* This song was popularly revived in 1943.

As the Years Go By 1947 w.m. Charles Tobias, Peter DeRose. (F) *Song of Love.* Katharine Hepburn and Paul Henreid appeared in *Song of Love.* Based on Brahms's Hungarian Dance No. 4.

As You Desire Me 1932 w.m. Allie Wrubel

As You Like It 1962 w.m. Les Vandyke

Ascot Gavotte 1956 w. Alan Jay Lerner m. Frederick Loewe. (MT) *My Fair Lady.* (MF) *My Fair Lady.* Rex Harrison appeared in both the stage and film productions of *My Fair Lady.* Julie Andrews appeared in the stage production of *My Fair Lady.* Audrey Hepburn appeared in the film production of *My Fair Lady.*

Asia 1913 w. E. Ray Goetz m. John Lindsay. (MT) *All Aboard.*

Ask a Policeman 1889 w.m. E.W. Rogers, A. E. Durandeau. This song was popularly revived in 1901.

Ask Any Mermaid 1970 w.m. Dick Marx and Associates. This song was written for a Chicken of the Sea Tuna commercial promotion campaign.

Ask Anyone Who Knows 1947 w.m. Eddie Seiler, Sol Marcus, Al Kaufman. (F) *Wallflower.* Joyce Reynolds and Janis Paige appeared in *Wallflower.*

Ask Her While the Band Is Playing 1908 w. Glen MacDonough m. Victor Herbert. (MT) *The Rose of Algeria.*

Ask the Man in the Moon 1891 w. J. Cheever Goodwin m. Woolson Morse. (MT) *Wang.*

Ask the Stars 1919 w. Frank Stammers m. Harold Orlob. (MT) *Nothing But Love.*

Asleep in the Deep 1897 w. Arthur J. Lamb m. Henry W. Petrie

Assembly 1842 m. anon.; first published George W. Behn. This American bugle call, first published in 1842, is often parodied beginning with the words "There's a monkey in the grass."

At a Georgia Camp Meeting 1897 m. Kerry Mills. See also Part I, 1896.

At Dawning, op. 29, no. 1 1906 w. Nelle Richmond Eberhart m. Charles Wakefield Cadman

At Last 1935 w. Charles Tobias, Sam Lewis m. Henry Tobias. (MT) *Earl Carroll's Sketch Book of 1935.* Jack Haley and Ken Murray appeared in *Earl Carroll's Sketch Book of 1935.* See also Part I, 1942.

At Last 1942 w.m. Harry Warren, Mack Gordon. (MT) *The 1940's Radio Hour.* (MF) *Sun Valley Serenade.* (MF) *Orchestra Wives.* (MF) *The Glenn Miller Story.* Sonja Henie and Glenn Miller appeared in *Sun Valley Serenade.* Glenn Miller and Ann Rutherford appeared in *Orchestra Wives.*

At Long Last Love 1938 w.m. Cole Porter. (MT) *You Never Know.* Clifton Webb and Lupe Velez appeared in *You Never Know.*

At Midnight on My Pillow Lying 1886 w. Claxson Bellamy, Harry Paulton m. Edward Jakobowski. (MT) *Erminie.*

At Santa Barbara 1912 w.m. Frederick E. Weatherly, Kennedy Russell

At Seventeen 1975 w.m. Janis Ian

At Sundown 1927 w.m. Walter Donaldson. (MF) *Bells of Capistrano.* (MF) *Glorifying the American Girl.* (MF) *Music for Millions.* (MF) *The Fabulous Dorseys.* (MF) *Love Me or Leave Me.* (MF) *The Rat Race.* Gene Autry and Smiley Burnette appeared in *Bells of Capistrano.* Eddie Cantor, Rudy Vallee, and Helen Morgan appeared in *Glorifying the American Girl.* Margaret O'Brien and Jimmy Durante appeared in *Music for Millions.* Doris Day and James Cagney appeared in *Love Me or Leave Me,* biopic of singer Ruth Etting. Tony Curtis and Debbie Reynolds appeared in *The Rat Race.*

At the Balalaika 1939 orig. w. Eric Maschwitz new w. Bob Wright, Chet Forrest m. George Posford; arr. Herbert Stothart. (MT) *Balalaika.* (MF) *Balalaika.* Nelson Eddy and Charles Ruggles appeared in the film production of *Balalaika.*

At the Ballet 1975 w. Edward Kleban m. Marvin Hamlisch. (MT) *A Chorus Line.* Donna McKechnie appeared in *A Chorus Line.*

At the Cafe Continental 1936 w.m. Will Grosz, Jimmy Kennedy

At the Codfish Ball 1936 w.m. Guy Kibbe, Slim Summerville. (MF) *Captain January.* Shirley Temple and Guy Kibbe appeared in *Captain January.*

At the Cross 1885 w. Isaac Watts m. R.E. Hudson

At the Crossroads 1942 w. Bob Russell m. Ernesto Lecuona. Based on Lecuona's "Malagueña" of 1930.

At the Devil's Ball 1912 w.m. Irving Berlin

At the End of a Beautiful Day 1916 w.m. William H. Perkins

At the End of the Day 1951 w.m. Donald O'Keefe

At the Hop 1958 w.m. Artie Singer, David White, John Medora

At the Jazz Band Ball 1918 w.m. Edwin B. Edwards, James La Rocca, Anthony Sbarbaro, Larry Shields

At the Mardi Gras, *see* **Come to the Mardi Gras**

At the Mississippi Cabaret 1914 w.m. A.S. Brown, M. Gumble

At the Moving Picture Ball 1920 w.m. Howard E. Johnson, Joseph H. Santley

At Trinity Church I Met My Doom 1894 w.m. Fred Gilbert. This English music hall ballad was popularly sung by Tom Costello.

At Your Command 1931 w.m. Harry Barris, Bing Crosby, Harry Tobias

Atchison, Topeka and the Santa Fe, The, *see* **On the Atchison, Topeka, and the Santa Fe**

Atlanta, Ga. 1946 w.m. Sunny Skylar, Artie Shaftel

Atlantis 1963 w.m. Jerry Lordan

Au Clair de la Lune 1811 w. possibly Jean Lully m. probably an eighteenth-century traditional French folksong.

Au Revoir But Not Goodbye 1936 w.m. Joseph Gilbert

Au Revoir, But Not Good-Bye, Soldier Boy 1917 w. Lew Brown m. Albert Von Tilzer

Au Revoir, Pleasant Dreams 1930 w. Jack Meskill m. Jean Schwartz. Theme song of Ben Bernie.

Auf Wiedersehn 1915 w. Herbert Reynolds m. Sigmund Romberg. (MT) *The Blue Paradise.* (MF) *Deep in My Heart.* Jose Ferrer and Merle Oberon appeared in *Deep in My Heart,* biopic of composer Sigmund Romberg.

Auf Wiedersehn, My Dear 1932 w.m. Al Hoffman, Ed G. Nelson, Al Goodhart, Milton Ager

Auf Wiederseh'n Sweetheart 1952 w. John Sexton, John Turner m. Eberhard Storch

Auld Lang Syne 1711 w. adapted Robert Burns; earliest words published 1711 m. traditional, from Scotland; earliest music published 1687. This song was later adapted for variations by Beethoven, and was later parodied as "Should Brave Ulysses Be Forgot," in praise of Ulysses S. Grant. Theme song of Guy Lombardo. The music for this song served as inspiration for "Old Nassau," school song of Princeton University. See also "Old Grimes." This song was popularly adapted in 1981.

Auld Robin Gray, or, **When the Sheep Are in the Fold** 1780w. written in 1772 by Lady Anne Barnard (Lindsay) m. Rev. William Leeves

Aunt Dinah's Quilting Party, *see* **When I Saw Sweet Nellie Home**

Aunt Hagar's Blues 1920 m. W.C. Handy. (MF) *Hi Good Lookin'.* (MF) *St. Louis Blues.* Jack Teagarden and Harriet Hilliard appeared in *Hi Good Lookin'.* Nat "King" Cole and Eartha Kitt appeared in *St. Louis Blues,* biopic of composer W.C. Handy.

Aunt Jemima (Silver Dollar) 1939 w.m. Jack Palmer, Clarke Van Ness. This song was written for an Aunt Jemima Pancakes commercial promotion campaign.

Aunt Jemima and Your Uncle Cream of Wheat 1936 w. Johnny Mercer m. Rube Bloom. (MT) *Blackbirds of 1936.*

Aunt Rhody, *see* **The Ole Grey Goose**

Auprès de Ma Blonde 1580 w.m. traditional, from France

Aura Lee 1861 w. W.W. Fosdick m. George R. Poulton. (F) *The Last Musketeer.* Rex Allen appeared in *The Last Musketeer.* This song is also known as "Army Blue," the U.S. Military Academy song. See also "Love Me Tender."

Aurora 1941 w.m. Harold Adamson, Mario Lago, Roberto Roberti. (MF) *Hold That Ghost.* The Andrews Sisters and Abbott and Costello appeared in *Hold That Ghost.*

Automatic 1984 w.m. Mark Goldenberg, Brock Walsh

Autumn Concerto 1956 It.w. Danpa Eng.w. Paul Siegel m. C. Bargoni. From the Italian "Concerto D'Automno." See also "My Heart Reminds Me."

Autumn Crocus 1932 w.m. Billy Mayerl

Autumn in New York 1934 w.m. Vernon Duke. (MT) *Thumbs Up!.* Eddie Dowling, J. Harold Murray, and Rose King appeared in *Thumbs Up!*

Autumn in Rome 1954 w.m. Sammy Cahn, Paul Weston. (F) *Indiscretion of an American Wife.*

Autumn Leaves 1947 Fr.w. Jacques Prevert Eng.w. Johnny Mercer m. Joseph Kosma. (F) *Hey Boy, Hey Girl.* From the French "Les Feuilles Mortes." This song was also popular in 1950, and revived in 1955.

Autumn Nocturne 1941 w.m. Kim Gannon, Josef Myrow

Autumn Serenade 1945 w. Sammy Gallop m. Peter DeRose

Avalon 1920 w.m. Al Jolson, B.G. DeSylva, Vincent Rose. (MF) *The Jolson Story.* (MF) *The Benny Goodman Story.* (MF) *Both Ends of the Candle.* Based on Puccini's aria "E lucevan le stelle" from *Tosca.* A lawsuit resulting from this musical theft awarded Puccini and his publishers $25,000 in damages and all future royalties. The recording publisher of "Avalon" was forced to go out of business. Larry Parks appeared in *The Jolson Story.*

Avalon Town 1928 w. Grant Clarke m. Nacio Herb Brown

Ave Maria 1826 w. Sir Walter Scott m. Franz Schubert. (MF) *Fantasia.* The words are taken from Sir Walter Scott's "The Lady of the Lake."

Ave Maria 1859 w. Bible: Luke 1:28; Fr.w. Paul Bernard m. Charles Gounod, based on J.S. Bach's First Prelude in "The Well-Tempered Clavichord"

Avengers' Theme, The 1961 m. Johnny Dankworth. (TV) *The Avengers.* Diana Rigg appeared in *The Avengers.* Ivor Novello Award winner 1961.

Away Down South in Heaven 1927 w. Bud Green m. Harry Warren

Away in (a) the Manger, or, **Luther's Cradle Hymn** 1887 w. anon. m. James Ramsey Murray. The words to this song have been erroneously credited to Martin Luther. The melody is possibly based on "Flow Gently, Sweet Afton."

Away with Melancholy c. 1790 w. anon. m. Wolfgang Amadeus Mozart. The music for this duet is adapted from the Act I finale of Mozart's *The Magic Flute.*

Axel F 1985 w.m. Harold Faltermeyer

Ay, Ay, Ay 1913 w.m. Osman Perez Freire. This song, not to be confused with "Cielito Lindo," was popularly revived in 1927.

Ay, Ay, Ay, Ay, *see* **Cielito Lindo**

B B B Burnin' Up with Love 1984 w.m. Eddie Rabbitt, Even Stevens, Billy Joe Walker

B-I, Bi 1941 w.m. Sidney Keith Russell, Judy Freeland, Beverly Freeland

Baa, Baa, Black Sheep, *see* **Mother Goose's Melodies, Twinkle Twinkle Little Star**

Babalu 1941 w.m. Bob Russell, Marguerita Lecuona. (MF) *Pan-Americana.* (F) *Variety Time.* (F) *Havana Rose.* Robert Benchley and Eve Arden appeared in *Pan-Americana.* Leon Errol and Edgar Kennedy appeared in *Variety Time.* Bill Williams and Estelita Rodriguez appeared in *Havana Rose.*

Babbitt and the Bromide, The 1927 w. Ira Gershwin m. George Gershwin. (MT) *Funny Face.* (MF) *Funny Face.* (MF) *Ziegfeld Follies.* Fred Astaire and Audrey Hepburn appeared in the film production of *Funny Face.* Fred Astaire, Lucille Ball, Fanny Brice, and Judy Garland appeared in *Ziegfeld Follies.* In the original stage production, this number was performed at 10:50 and concluded with Fred and Adele Astaire doing their famous "run-around" to "show-stopping" applause.

Babes in Arms 1937 w. Lorenz Hart m. Richard Rodgers. (MT) *Babes in Arms.* (MF) *Babes in Arms.* Mitzi Green and Ray Heatherton appeared in the stage production of *Babes in Arms.* Judy Garland and Mickey Rooney appeared in the film production of *Babes in Arms.*

Babes in the Wood 1915 w. Schuyler Greene, Jerome Kern m. Jerome Kern. (MT) *Very Good Eddie*

Babes in the Wood, *see also* **Two Little Babes in the Wood**

Babes in Toyland, *see* **Toyland**

Babies on Our Block, The 1879 w. Edward Harrigan m. David Braham. (MT) *The Skidmore Fancy Ball.*

Babooshka 1981 w.m. Kate Bush. Ivor Novello Award winner 1980–81.

Baby 1925 w. B.G. DeSylva, Ira Gershwin m. George Gershwin. (MT) *Tell Me More.* The out-of-town title for *Tell Me More* was *My Fair Lady.*

Baby, Baby All the Time 1946 w.m. Bob Troup

Baby Baby Baby 1953 w.m. Jerry Livingston, Mack David. (MF) *Those Redheads from Seattle.* Rhonda Flemming and Gene Barry appeared in *Those Redheads from Seattle.*

Baby Baby Baby 1983 w. Richard Maltby, Jr. m. David Shire. (MT) *Baby.* Liz Callaway and Beth Fowley appeared in *Baby.*

Baby Blue Eyes 1922 w.m. Walter Hirsch, George Jessel, Jesse Greer

Baby Come Back 1977 w.m. John Crowley, Peter Beckett

Baby, Come to Me 1983 w.m. Rodney Temperton

Baby Doll 1945 w.m. Harry Warren, Johnny Mercer. (MF) *The Belle of New York.* Fred Astaire and Majorie Main appeared in *The Belle of New York.* This song was popularly revived in 1952.

Baby Don't Get Hooked on Me 1972 w.m. Mac Davis

Baby Dream Your Dream 1966 w. Dorothy Fields m. Cy Coleman. (MT) *Sweet Charity.* (MF) *Sweet Charity.* Gwen Verdon appeared in the stage production of *Sweet Charity.* Shirley MacLaine appeared in the film production of *Sweet Charity.*

Baby Elephant Walk 1962 m. Henry Mancini. (F) *Hatari.* John Wayne and Red Buttons appeared in *Hatari.*

Baby Face 1926 w.m. Benny Davis, Harry Akst. (MF) *Jolson Sings Again.* Larry Parks appeared in *Jolson Sings Again.*

Baby I Don't Care 1957 w.m. Mike Stoller, Jerry Leiber. (MF) *Jailhouse Rock.* Elvis Presley and Judy Tyler appeared in *Jailhouse Rock.* This song was popularly revived in 1961.

Baby I Lied 1984 w.m. Deborah Allen, Rafe Van Hoy, Rory Bourke

Baby I Love You 1969 w.m. Ronny Shannon

Baby I'm Burning 1979 w.m. Dolly Parton

Baby I'm Yours 1965 w.m. Van McCoy. This song was popularly revived in 1978.

Baby, It's Cold Outside 1948 w.m. Frank Loesser. (MF) *Neptune's Daughter.* Esther Williams and Ricardo Montalban appeared in *Neptune's Daughter.* Academy Award winner 1949.

Baby Love 1964 w.m. Eddie Holland, Brian Holland, Lamont Dozier

Baby Me 1939 w.m. Lou Handman, Harry Harris, Archie Gottler

Baby Mine 1878 w. Charles Mackay m. Archibald Johnston. Popularly sung by Belle Cole, a noted singer of her day.

Baby Rose 1911 w. Louis Weslyn m. George Christie

Baby Shoes 1916 w. Joe Goodwin, Ed Rose m. Al Piantadosi

Baby, Take a Bow 1934 w.m. Lew Brown, Jay Gorney. (MF) *Stand Up and Cheer.* Shirley Temple and Warner Baxter appeared in *Stand Up and Cheer.*

Baby the Rain Must Fall 1965 w.m. Elmer Bernstein, Ernie Sheldon

Baby We Can't Go Wrong 1974 w.m. J. Dunning

Baby, Won't You Please Come Home 1919 w.m. Charles Warfield, Clarence Williams. (MF) *That's the Spirit.* Jack Oakie and Peggy Ryan appeared in *That's the Spirit.*

Baby You're a Rich Man 1967 w.m. John Lennon, Paul McCartney

Baby's Prayer 1898 w. R.A. Mullen m. R.L. Halle

Bach Goes to Town 1938 m. Alec Templeton. Loosely based on a Bach prelude and fugue.

Bachelor Boy 1962 w.m. Cliff Richard, Bruce Welch. (MF) *Summer Holiday.* Cliff Richard and Lauri Peters appeared in *Summer Holiday.* Ivor Novello Award winner 1962.

Bachelor Gay, A 1917 w.m. James W. Tate, Clifford Harris, Arthur Valentine. (MT) *The Maid of the Mountains.* Thorpe Bates appeared in *The Maid of the Mountains.*

Bacio, II, or, **The Kiss Waltz** 1859 It.w. Aldighieri m.

Luigi Arditi. This song was written for Maria Piccolomini, famous Italian operatic soprano.

Back Again to Happy-Go-Lucky Days 1932 w.m. Raymond Wallace

Back, Back, Back to Baltimore 1904 w. Harry H. Williams m. Egbert Van Alstyne

Back Bay Polka, The 1946 w. Ira Gershwin m. George Gershwin. (MF) *The Shocking Miss Pilgrim*. Betty Grable appeared in *The Shocking Miss Pilgrim*.

Back Home Again in Indiana, *see* **Indiana**

Back Home in Tennessee, *see* **Just Try To Picture Me**

(Every Time I Turn Around) Back in Love Again 1977 w.m. Len Hanks, Zane Grey

Back in My Arms Again 1965 w.m. Eddie Holland, Brian Holland, Lamont Dozier

Back in the Saddle Again 1940 w.m. Gene Autry, Ray Whiteley. (MF) *Wagon Train*. Gene Autry and Pat Buttram appeared in *Wagon Train*.

Back in Your Own Back Yard 1927 w.m. Al Jolson, Billy Rose, Dave Dreyer. (MF) *Jolson Sings Again*. (MF) *Silver Spurs*. Larry Parks appeared in *Jolson Sings Again*. Roy Rogers and Smiley Burnette appeared in *Silver Spurs*.

Back on My Mind Again 1979 w.m. Conrad Pierce, Charles W. Quillen

Back to Donegal 1942 w.m. Steve Graham

Back to the Carolina You Love 1914 w.m. Grant Clarke, Jean Schwartz

Back to Those Happy Days 1935 w.m. Horatio Nicholls

Bad and the Beautiful, (Theme from) The 1953 w.m. David Raksin (F) *The Bad and the Beautiful*

Bad Bad Leroy Brown 1973 w.m. Jim Croce

Bad Blood 1975 w.m. Philip Cody, Neil Sedaka

Bad Boy 1960 w.m. Marty Wilde

Bad Boy 1986 w.m. Lawrence Dermer, Joe Galdo, Rafael Vigil

Bad Girls 1979 w.m. Joseph Esposito, Edward Hokenson, Bruce Subano, Donna Summer

Bad Humor Man, The 1940 w.m. Johnny Mercer, Jimmy McHugh. (MF) *You'll Find Out*. Peter Lorre, Boris Karloff, and Bela Lugosi appeared in *You'll Find Out*.

Bad Moon Rising 1969 w.m. John Fogerty

Bad Penny Blues 1956 w.m. Humphrey Lyttelton

Bad Time 1975 w.m. Mark Farner

Bad Timing 1945 w. Betty Comden, Adolph Green m. Morton Gould. (MT) *Billion Dollar Baby*. Mitzi Green and William Talbot appeared in *Billion Dollar Baby*.

Badge from Your Coat, The 1941 w.m. Horatio Nicholls, Annette Mills

Badinage 1897 m. Victor Herbert

Bagdad 1912 w. Anne Caldwell m. Victor Herbert. (MT) *The Lady of the Slipper*.

Bagdad 1918 w. Harold Atteridge m. Al Jolson. (MT) *Sinbad*.

Bagdad 1924 w. Jack Yellen m. Milton Ager

Baia (No Baixa Do Sapateiro) 1944 Eng.w. Ray Gilbert m. Ary Barroso. (MF) *The Three Caballeros*.

Bajour 1964 w.m. Walter Marks. (MT) *Bajour*

Bake Dat Chicken Pie 1906 w.m. Frank Dumont

Baker Street 1978 w.m. Gerry Rafferty

Bal Masque 1913 w.m. Percy E. Fletcher

Bali Ha'i 1949 w. Oscar Hammerstein II m. Richard Rodgers. (MT) *South Pacific*. (MF) *South Pacific*. Mary Martin appeared in the stage production of *South Pacific*. Mitzi Gaynor appeared in the film production of *South Pacific*.

Ballad for Americans 1940 w. John Latouche m. Earl Robinson. (MT) *Sing for Your Supper*. (MF) *Born To Sing*. Leo Gorcey and Rags Ragland appeared in *Born To Sing*.

Ballad of a Crystal Man 1965 w.m. Donovan

Ballad of Bethnal Green, The 1959 w.m. Paddy Roberts. Ivor Novello Award winner 1959.

Ballad of Bonnie and Clyde, The 1968 w.m. Mitch Murray, Peter Callander. (F) *Bonnie and Clyde*. Warren Beatty, Faye Dunaway, Estelle Parsons, and Gene Hackman appeared in *Bonnie and Clyde*. Ivor Novello Award winner 1967-68.

Ballad of Cat Ballou 1965 w.m. Mack David, Jerry Livingston

Ballad of Davy Crockett 1955 w. Tom Blackburn m. George Burns. (F) *Davy Crockett*. (TV) *Davy Crockett*. Fess Parker appeared in both the film and TV productions of *Davy Crockett*. See also Part I, 1836.

Ballad of Jed Clampett 1963 w.m. Paul Henning. (TV) *The Beverley Hillbillies*.

Ballad of Paladin, The 1962 w.m. Johnny Western, Sam Rolfe, Richard Boone. (TV) *Have Gun, Will Travel*. This song was first introduced by Johnny Western in the TV series *Have Gun, Will Travel*.

Ballad of Sweeney Todd, The 1979 w.m. Stephen Sondheim. (MT) *Sweeney Todd*. Angela Lansbury and Len Cariou appeared in *Sweeney Todd*.

Ballad of the Green Berets, The 1966 w.m. Barry Sadler, Robin Mooore

Ballerina 1947 w. Bob Russell m. Carl Sigman.

Ballin' the Jack 1913 w. James Henry Burris m. Chris Smith. (MT) *The Passing Show of 1915*. (MF) *For Me and My Gal*. (MF) *On the Riviera*. (MF) *Jazz Dance*. (F) *That's My Boy*. Basil Hallam and Elsie Janis appeared in *The Passing Show of 1915*. Judy Garland and Gene Kelly appeared in *For Me and My Gal*. Danny Kaye and Gwen Verdon appeared in *On the Riviera*. Dean Martin and Jerry Lewis appeared in *That's My Boy*. This song was popularly revived in 1949.

Balm of Gilead, or, Bingo 1861 w.m. arr. H.T. Bryant. This song was previously known as "Drink It Down, Drink It Down" of 1853, possibly written by Julien Carle. Adapted, this song with the title "Bingo," became the school song for Yale University.

Bam, Bam, Bamy Shore 1925 w. Mort Dixon m. Ray Henderson

Bambalina 1923 w. Otto Harbach, Oscar Hammerstein II

m. Vincent Youmans, Herbert Stothart. (MT) *Wildflower*. Edith Day and Guy Robertson appeared in *Wildflower*.

Banana Boat Song, The (Day-O) 1957 w.m. Erik Darling, Bob Carey, Alan Arkin

Band of Gold 1956 w. Bob Musel m. Jack Taylor. This song was popularly revived in 1970.

Band on the Run 1974 w.m. Paul McCartney, Linda McCartney

(Casey Would Waltz with the Strawberry Blonde While) The Band Played On 1895 w. John E. Palmer m. Charles B. Ward. (MF) *Lillian Russell*. (MF) *The Strawberry Blonde*. Rita Hayworth and James Cagney appeared in *The Strawberry Blonde*.

Bandana Babies 1928 w. Dorothy Fields m. Jimmy McHugh. (MT) *Lew Leslie's Blackbirds of 1928*. Ethel Waters, Cab Calloway, and Duke Ellington appeared in *Lew Leslie's Blackbirds of 1928*.

Bandana Days 1921 w.m. Noble Sissle, Eubie Blake. (MT) *Shuffle Along*. Noble Sissle and Florence Mills appeared in *Shuffle Along*.

Bandana Land 1905 w. Glen MacDonough m. Victor Herbert. (MT) *It Happened in Nordland*.

Bang Bang (My Baby Shot Me Down) 1966 w.m. Sonny Bono

Banjo Song 1818 w. R. C. Dallas in 1824. m. anon. The banjo was evolved in 1818 by Joel Sweeney from a gourd with strings to a four-stringed instrument. This song was originally a piano piece titled "Dedicated To Georgiana," its composer unknown.

Banjo Song, A 1910 w. Howard Weeden m. Sidney Homer

Barbara Allen, *see* **Barbry (Barbara) Allen**

Barbara Ann 1966 w.m. Fred Fassert

Barber of Seville, The (Overture) 1813 m. Gioacchino Rossini. *Il Barbiere di Siviglia* was first performed in Rome on February 20, 1816. A startling similar overture was also used for Rossini's *Aurerliano in Palmira*, first performed in Milan on December 26, 1813, and *Elisabetta*, first performed in Naples on October 4, 1815.

Barbry (Barbara) Allen c.1666 m. Traditional, from England. "Barbara Allen" is an early American borrowing from an English folksong. One of the earliest references to this Scottish pentatonic tune is Samuel Pepsy's diary entry for January 2, 1666: "(It was) perfect pleasure to hear a Mrs. Knipp sing her little Scotch song of Barbary Allen." It was once published in the United States in 1780 as a patriotic song called "Sergeant Champs," the story of an American soldier who pretended to desert to the British in order to capture Benedict Arnold. Today, its melody and narrative exist in some form from Italy to the Scandanavian countries.

Barcarolle 1864 m. Jacques Offenbach. This standard was first written by Offenbach for his opera *Die Rhein Nixen*, produced in Vienna on February 4, 1864. As the "Barcarolle" from the opera *Tales of Hoffman*, it was first published in 1881.

Barcelona 1970 w.m. Stephen Sondheim. (MT) *Company*. (MT) *Side by Side by Sondheim*. Elaine Stritch appeared in *Company*. Millicent Martin and Julie N. McKenzie appeared in *Side by Side by Sondheim*.

Barefoot in the Park 1967 w.m. Neal Hefti, Johnny Mercer. (F) *Barefoot in the Park*. Jane Fonda and Robert Redford appeared in *Barefoot in the Park*.

Barnacle Bill the Sailor 1931 w.m. Carson Robinson, Frank Luther

Barney Google 1923 w.m. Billy Rose, Con Conrad

Barnum Had the Right Idea 1911 w.m. George M. Cohan. (MT) *The Little Millionaire*.

Barnyard Blues 1919 w.m. Edwin B. Edwards, James D. LaRocca, Anthony Sbarbaro, Larry Shields

Bartered Bride, The (Overture) 1872 m. Bedrich Smetana

Barwick Green (The Archers) 1925 w.m. Arthur Wood

Basin Street Blues 1929 w.m. Spencer Williams. (MF) *The Glenn Miller Story*. (MF) *The Strip*. Mickey Rooney and Sallie Forrest appeared in *The Strip*.

Bathing in the Sunshine 1931 w.m. Horatio Nicholls, Joe Gilbert

Batman Theme 1966 w.m. Neal Hefti. (TV) *Batman*.

Battle Cry of Freedom, The 1863 w.m. George Frederick Root

Battle Hymn of the Republic 1862 w. Julia Ward Howe m. melody known as "Glory Hallelujah" in 1856 or earlier, possibly by William Steffe; then became "John Brown's Body" version in 1861; and finally given this title in 1862. See also "John Brown's Body."

Battle of Britain 1970 w.m. Ron Goodwin

Battle of Jericho, The, *see* **Joshua Fit de Battle of Jericho**

Battle of New Orleans, The 1959 w.m. Jimmy Driftwood. Grammy Award winner 1959.

Battle of the Kegs, The 1778 w. Francis Hopkinson m. adaptation of the melody "Yankee Doodle." This parody, written by a signer of the Declaration of Independence, pokes fun at the incident of the British firing upon kegs of gunpowder floating in the Delaware River near their fleet. Hopkinson was to become America's first popular writer of art songs.

Baubles, Bangles and Beads 1954 w.m. Robert Wright, George Forrest. (MT) *Kismet*. (MF) *Kismet*. Ann Blyth and Howard Keel appeared in the film production of *Kismet*. Based on the "Scherzo" from Borodin's String Quartet in D Major.

Bay of Biscay O!, The 1805 w. Andrew Cherry m. John Davy. From the English ballad opera *Spanish Dollars*. Based on a theme from the black sailors of London.

Bayou Songs, *see* **Ma Li'l Batteau**

Be a Clown 1948 w.m. Cole Porter. (MF) *The Pirate*. Judy Garland and Gene Kelly appeared in *The Pirate*.

(To) Be a Performer 1962 w. Carolyn Leigh m. Cy Coleman. (MT) *Little Me*.

Be Anything (But Be Mine) 1952 w.m. Irving Gordon

Be Back Soon 1963 w.m. Lionel Bart. (MT) *Oliver!* (MF) *Oliver!*. Georgia Brown appeared in the stage production of *Oliver!* Shani Wallis appeared in the film production of *Oliver!* Ron Moody appeared in both the stage and film productions of *Oliver!*

Be-Bop Baby 1957 w.m. Pearl Lenghurst

Be Careful It's My Heart 1942 w.m. Irving Berlin. (MF) *Holiday Inn*. Bing Crosby and Fred Astaire appeared in *Holiday Inn*.

Be Honest with Me 1942 w.m. Fred Rose, Gene Autry. (MF) *Strictly in the Groove*. (MF) *Sierra Sue*. Martha Tilton and Donald O'Connor appeared in *Strictly in the Groove*. Gene Autry and Gabby Hayes appeared in *Sierra Sue*.

Be-In 1969 w.m. Galt MacDermot, James Rado, Gerome Ragni. (MT) *Hair*. (MF) *Hair*.

Be Kind to the Loved Ones at Home 1847 w.m. Isaac Baker Woodbury

Be Like the Kettle and Sing 1943 w.m. Connor, O'Connor, Ridley

Be Mine Tonight 1935 w. Sunny Skylar m. Maria Teresa Lara. From the Spanish ''Noche de Ronda.''

Be My Baby 1963 w.m. Phil Spector, Ellie Greenwich, Jeff Barry. (OB) *Leader of the Pack*.

Be My Life's Companion 1951 w.m. Bob Hilliard, Milton De Lugg

Be My Little Baby Bumblebee 1912 w. Stanley Murphy m. Henry I. Marshall. (MT) *The Ziegfeld Follies of 1911*. (MF) *Hoppity Goes to Town*. (MF) *By the Light of the Silvery Moon*. Doris Day and Gordon MacRae appeared in *By the Light of the Silvery Moon*.

Be My Love 1951 w. Sammy Cahn m. Nicholas Brodszky. (MF) *The Toast of New Orleans*. Mario Lanza, Kathryn Grayson, and David Niven appeared in *The Toast of New Orleans*. Theme song of Mario Lanza.

Be Near Me 1986 w.m. Martin Fry, Mark White

Be Still My Heart 1934 w.m. Allan Flynn, Jack Egan

Be Sure To Wear Some Flowers in Your Hair, *see* **San Francisco**

Beale Street Blues 1916 w.m. W.C. Handy. (MF) *St. Louis Blues*. Ella Fitzgerald, Eartha Kitt, and Nat ''King'' Cole appeared in *St. Louis Blues,* biopic of composer William C. Handy.

Beans Beans Beans 1912 w. Elmer Bowman m. Chris Smith

Bear Went Over the Mountain, The, *see* **For He's a Jolly Good Fellow**

Beat It 1983 w.m. Michael Jackson. Grammy Award winner 1983.

Beat Me, Daddy, Eight to the Bar 1940 w.m. Hugh Prince, Don Raye, Eleanor Sheehy

Beat of My Heart, The 1934 w. Johnny Burke m. Harold Spina

Beatrice Fairfax, Tell Me What To Do 1915 w.m. Grant Clarke, Joseph McCarthy, James V. Monaco. This was the first popular advice columnist song.

Beaulieu Festival Suite 1959 w.m. Kenny Graham. Ivor Novello Award winner 1959.

Beautiful Bird, Sing On 1867 w.m. T.H. Howe

Beautiful Boy 1981 w.m. John Lennon

Beautiful Brown Eyes 1951 w. Arthur Smith m. Alton Delmore

Beautiful Dreamer 1864 w.m. Stephen Collins Foster. (MF) *Swanee River*. Al Jolson and Don Ameche appeared in *Swanee River*. This song was written only a few days before Foster's death on January 13, 1864, in the poverty ward at Bellevue Hospital in New York.

Beautiful Eyes 1909 w. George Whiting, Carter De Haven m. Ted Snyder. (MT) *Mr. Hamlet of Broadway*.

Beautiful Friendship, A 1956 w. Stanley Styne m. Donald Kahn

Beautiful Garden of Roses, *see* **Garden of Roses**

(Hats Off, Here They Come, Those) Beautiful Girls 1971 w.m. Stephen Sondheim. (MT) *Follies*. Alexis Smith and Yvonne De Carlo appeared in *Follies*.

Beautiful Isle of Somewhere 1897 w. Mrs. Jessie Brown Pounds m. John S. Fearis

Beautiful Isle of the Sea 1865 w. George Cooper m. John Rogers Thomas

Beautiful Lady in Blue 1935 w. Sam M. Lewis m. J. Fred Coots

Beautiful Love 1931 w.m. Haven Gillespie, Victor Young, Wayne King, Egbert van Alstyne. (MF) *Sing a Jingle*. Allan Jones and June Vincent appeared in *Sing a Jingle*.

Beautiful Morning, A 1968 w.m. Edward Brigati, Felix Cavaliere

Beautiful Ohio 1918 w. Ballard MacDonald m. Mary Earl (Robert A. King)

Beautiful People of Denver 1960 w.m. Meredith Willson. (MT) *The Unsinkable Molly Brown*. (MF) *The Unsinkable Molly Brown*. Tammy Grimes appeared in the stage production of *The Unsinkable Molly Brown*. Debbie Reynolds appeared in the film production of *The Unsinkable Molly Brown*.

Because 1898 w. Charles Horwitz m. Frederick V. Bowers

Because 1902 w. Edward Teschemacher m. Guy d'Hardelot (Mrs. W.I. Rhodes [Helen Guy]). (F) *Three Smart Girls Grow Up*. Deanna Durbin and Robert Cummings appeared in *Three Smart Girls Grow Up*.

Because I Love You 1926 w.m. Irving Berlin

Because I'm Married Now (I Would If I Could But I Can't) 1907 w.m. Herbert Ingraham

Because of Rain 1951 w.m. Ruth Poll, Nat Cole, Bill Harrington

Because of You 1940 w.m. Arthur Hammerstein, Dudley Wilkinson. (F) *I Was an American Spy*. This song was popularly revived in 1951. Theme song of Tony Bennett.

Because They're Young 1960 w.m. Don Costa, Wally Gold, Aaron Schroeder. (F) *Because They're Young*. Dick Clark and Tuesday Weld appeared in *Because They're Young*.

Because You're Mine 1952 w. Sammy Cahn m. Nicholas Brodszky. (MF) *Because You're Mine*. Mario Lanza and James Whitmore appeared in *Because You're Mine*.

Because You're You 1906 w. Henry Blossom m. Victor Herbert. (MT) *The Red Mill*.

Bedelia 1903 w. William Jerome m. Jean Schwartz

Bedouin Love Song 1888 w. Bayard Taylor m. Ciro Pinsuti

Bedtime Story, A 1932 w.m. Leo Towers, Harry Leon, Horatio Nicholls

(It's) Been a Long Day 1961 w.m. Frank Loesser. (MT) *How To Succeed in Business Without Really Trying.* (MF) *How To Succeed in Business Without Really Trying.* Robert Morse appeared in both the stage and film productions of *How To Succeed in Business Without Really Trying.*

Beep Beep 1958 w.m. Donald Clapps, Carl Cicchetti

Beer Barrel Polka, The 1939 w.m. Lew Brown, Wladimir A. Timm, Taromir Vejvoda. Possibly based on a traditional folksong from Czechoslovakia. (MT) *Yokel Boy.* (MF) *A Night in Casablanca.* Phil Silvers, Buddy Ebsen, and Judy Canova appeared in *Yokel Boy.* The Marx Brothers appeared in *A Night in Casablanca.*

Beer, Beer, Glorious Beer 1901 w.m. Harry Anderson, Steve Leggett, Will Godwin

Before the Next Teardrop Falls 1975 w.m. Vivian Keith, Ben Peters

Before the Parade Passes By 1964 w.m. Jerry Herman. (MT) *Hello, Dolly!.* (MT) *Jerry's Girls.* (MF) *Hello, Dolly!.* Dorothy Loudon, Chita Rivera, and Leslie Uggams appeared in *Jerry's Girls.* Barbra Streisand appeared in the film production of *Hello, Dolly!* This song was popularly revived in 1970.

Beg, Steal or Borrow 1973 w.m. Graeme Hall, Tony Cole, Steve Wolfe. Ivor Novello Award winner 1972–73.

Beg Your Pardon 1948 w.m. Beasley Smith, Francis Craig

Begat, The 1947 w. E.Y. Harburg m. Burton Lane. (MT) *Finian's Rainbow.* Albert Sharpe and David Wayne appeared in the stage production of *Finian's Rainbow.* Fred Astaire and Petula Clark appeared in the film production of *Finian's Rainbow.*

Beggar's Opera, The 1728 w.m. John Gay. Songs from this opera include: "Greensleeves," "Hither Dear Husband," "Let Us Take to the Road," "Lilliburlero," (c.1686), "When a Wife's in a Pout."

Begin the Beguine 1935 w.m. Cole Porter. (MT) *Jubilee.* (MF) *Broadway Melody of 1940.* (MF) *Night and Day.* Melville Cooper and Mary Boland appeared in *Jubilee.* Fred Astaire and Eleanor Powell appeared in *Broadway Melody of 1940.* Cary Grant, Alexis Smith, and Mary Martin appeared in *Night and Day,* biopic of song writer Cole Porter. This song was popularly revived in 1939. Theme song of Leslie Hutchinson and Artie Shaw. See also Part I, 1940.

(I've Got) Beginner's Luck 1937 w. Ira Gershwin m. George Gershwin. (MF) *Shall We Dance.* Fred Astaire and Ginger Rogers appeared in *Shall We Dance.*

Behind Closed Doors 1973 w.m. Kenny O'Dell. Grammy Award winner 1973.

Bei Mir Bist Du Schön (Means That You're Grand) 1937 Yiddish w. Jacob Jacobs Eng. w. Sammy Cahn, Saul Chaplin m. Sholom Secunda. (F) *Love, Honor and Behave.* Wayne Morris and Priscilla Lane appeared in *Love, Honor and Behave.* This song was written for the Yiddish musical comedy *I Would If I Could* of 1933 and was first performed by Aaron

Lebedeff. As recorded by The Andrews Sisters, it became the first million-selling record by a female vocal group. Theme song of The Andrews Sisters.

Being Alive 1970 w.m. Stephen Sondheim. (MT) *Company.* Elaine Stritch appeared in *Company.*

Being for the Benefit of Mister Kite 1967 w.m. John Lennon, Paul McCartney

Being with You 1981 w.m. Smokey Robinson

Believe 1971 w. Fred Ebb m. John Kander. (MT) *70, Girls, 70.*

Believe in Yourself 1975 w.m. Charlie Smalls. (MT) *The Wiz.* (MF) *The Wiz.* Stephanie Mills, Ted Ross, and Mabel King appeared in the stage production of *The Wiz.* Diana Ross appeared in the film production of *The Wiz.*

Believe It Beloved 1934 w.m. George Whiting, Nat Burton, J.C. Johnson

Believe It or Not, *see* **Greatest American Hero**

Believe Me If All Those Endearing Young Charms 1775–1808 w. Thomas Moore m. based on "My Lodging (It) Is on the Cold Ground," of English or Irish origin; possibly Matthew Locke. The melody of this song was first published in 1775; the words and music first published together 1807–8. See also "Fair Harvard" and "My Lodging It Is on the Cold Ground".

Bell Bottom Trousers 1907 w.m. possibly based on a traditional sea chantey. This song was popularly revived and adapted in 1945.

Belle, Belle, My Liberty Belle 1951 w.m. Bob Merrill

Belle of Avenoo A, The 1895 w.m. Safford Waters

Belle of Barking Creek, The 1960 w.m. Paddy Roberts Ivor Novello Award winner 1960.

Belle of Mohawk Vale, The, or, Bonny Eloise 1858 w. George W. Elliott m. John Rogers Thomas

Belle of Pittsburg, The (March) uncertain m. John Philip Sousa

Belle of the Ball 1954 w. Mitchell Parish m. Leroy Anderson

Bells Across the Meadow 1924 w.m. Albert Ketelbey

Bells Are Ringing 1956 w. Betty Comden, Adolph Green m. Jule Styne. (MT) *Bells Are Ringing.* (MF) *Bells Are Ringing.* Judy Holliday appeared in both the stage and film productions of *Bells Are Ringing.*

Bells of St. Mary's, The 1917 w. Douglas Furber m. A. Emmett Adams. (MF) *The Bells of St. Mary's.* Bing Crosby and Ingrid Bergman appeared in *The Bells of St. Mary's.* This was later adapted as the school song for St. Mary's College.

Beloved 1928 w.m. Gus Kahn, Joe Sanders

Beloved, It Is Morn 1896 w. Emily Hickey m. Florence Aylward

Ben 1972 w.m. Walter Scharf, Donald Black. (F) *Ben.*

Ben Bolt, *see* **Sweet Alice**

Ben Hur Chariot Race (March) 1899 w.m. E.T. Paull

Bench in the Park, A 1930 w. Jack Yellen m. Milton

Ager. (MF) *King of Jazz*. Bing Crosby and Paul Whiteman appeared in *King of Jazz*.

Ben Casey, *see* **Theme from Ben Casey**

Bend Down, Sister   1931   w. Ballard MacDonald, Dave Silverstein   m. Con Conrad. (MF) *Palmy Days*. Eddie Cantor, George Raft, and Charlotte Greenwood appeared in *Palmy Days*.

Bend Me, Shape Me   1968   w.m. Laurence Weiss, Scott English

Beneath the Cross of Jesus   1881   w. Elizabeth Clephane   m. Frederick Maker

Bennie and the Jets   1974   w.m. Elton John, Bernie Taupin

Benny Havens, Oh!   1838   w. O'Brien—Arnold   m. traditional street ballad from Ireland; based on ''The Wearin' o' the Green.'' Adapted, this later became the unofficial West Point song. Its lyric:

Come fill your glasses, fellows, and stand up in a row,
To singing sentimentally we're going for to go;
In the army there's sobriety, promotion's very slow,
So we'll sing our reminiscences of Benny Havens, Oh!

Berceuse   1888   Fr.w. Paul Armand Silvestre, Victor Capoul   m. Benjamin Godard. This song is the tenor aria, from the opening of Act II of the opera *Jocelyn*.

Besame Mucho (Kiss Me Much)   1944   Sp.w. Consuelo Velazquez   Eng.w. Sunny Skylar   m. Consuelo Velazquez. Based on the Granados ''nightingale'' aria from *Goyescas*. (MF) *Club Havana*. (MF) *Follow the Boys*. George Raft appeared in *Follow the Boys*.

Beside a Babbling Brook   1923   w. Gus Kahn   m. Walter Donaldson

Beside a Shady Nook, *see* **It Must Be True**

Beside an Open Fireplace   1929   w.m. Paul Denniker, Will Osborne

Beside My Caravan   1934   w.m. Karel Vacek, Jimmy Kennedy

Bess, You Is My Woman Now   1935   w. DuBose Heyward, Ira Gershwin   m. George Gershwin. (MT) *Porgy and B* (MF) *Porgy and Bess*. Todd Duncan and Anne Wiggins Brown appeared in the 1935 stage production of *Porgy and Bess*. Sidney Poitier and Dorothy Dandridge appeared in the film production of *Porgy and Bess*.

Best I Get Is Much Obliged to You, The   1907   w.m. Benjamin Hapgood Burt

Best of All   1949   w.m. Ray Sonin, Wally Dewar

Best of Everything, The   1959   w. Sammy Cahn   m. Alfred Newman. (F) *The Best of Everything*. Hope Lange and Joan Crawford appeared in *The Best of Everything*.

Best of My Love   1975   w.m. Glen Frey, Don Henley, J David Souther

Best of My Love   1977   w.m. Maurice White, Albert McKay

Best of Times, The   1981   w.m. Dennis De Young

Best of Times, The   1983   w.m. Jerry Herman. (MT) *La Cage aux Folles*. (MT) *Jerry's Girls*. Gene Barry and George Hearn

appeared in *La Cage aux Folles*. Dorothy Loudon, Chita Rivera and Leslie Uggams appeared in *Jerry's Girls*.

Best That You Can Do, *see* **Arthur's Theme**

Best Thing for You, The   1950   w.m. Irving Berlin. (MT) *Call Me Madam*. (MF) *Call Me Madam*. Ethel Merman appeared in both the stage and film productions of *Call Me Madam*.

(You're the) Best Thing That Ever Happened to Me   1974   w.m. Jim Weatherly

Best Thing You've Ever Done   1970   w.m. Martin Charnin

Best Things in Life Are Free, The   1927   w. B.G. DeSylva, Lew Brown   m. Ray Henderson. (MT) *Good News*. (MF) *Good News* (1930). (MF) *Good News* (1947). (MF) *The Best Things in Life Are Free*. Joseph Santley and Zelma O'Neal appeared in the stage production of *Good News*. June Allyson and Peter Lawford appeared in the 1947 film production of *Good News*. Gordon MacRae, Dan Dailey, Ernest Borgnine appeared in *The Best Things in Life Are Free*, biopic of song writers DeSylva, Brown, and Henderson.

Beth   1976   w.m. Robert Ezrin, Stan Penridge, Peter Criss

Bette Davis Eyes   1981   w.m. Jackie DeShannon, Donna Weiss. Grammy Award winner 1981.

Better Be Good to Me   1985   w.m. Mike Chapman, Nicky Chinn, Holly Knight

Better Homes and Gardens   1969   w.m. Bobby Russell

Better Luck Next Time   1948   w.m. Irving Berlin. (MF) *Easter Parade*. Judy Garland, Fred Astaire, and Ann Miller appeared in *Easter Parade*.

Betty Co-Ed   1930   w.m. J. Paul Fogarty, Rudy Vallee. (MF) *Betty Co-Ed*. Jean Porter and Shirley Mills appeared in *Betty Co-Ed*.

Between a Kiss and a Sigh   1938   w.m. Johnny Burke, Arthur Johnston

Between Eighteenth and Nineteenth on Chestnut Street   1940   w.m. Dick Rogers, Will Osborne

Between the Devil and the Deep Blue Sea   1931   w. Koehler m. Harold Arlen. (F) *Rhythmania*.

Beware My Foolish Heart, *see* **My Foolish Heart**

Bewitched, Bothered and Bewildered   1941   m. Lorenz Hart   m. Richard Rodgers. (MT) *Pal Joey*. (MF) *Pal Joey*. Gene Kelly, Van Johnson, Vivienne Segal appeared in stage production of *Pal Joey*. Frank Sinatra and Rita Hayworth appeared in the film production of *Pal Joey*. This song was popularly revived in 1950. Theme song of Bill Snyder

Beyond the Blue Horizon   1930   w. Leo Robin   m. Richard Whiting, W. Franke Harling. (MF) *Monte Carlo*. (MF) *Follow the Boys*. Jeanette MacDonald appeared in both *Monte Carlo* and *Follow the Boys*.

Beyond the Sea   1947   w. Jack Lawrence   m. Charles Trenet

Bibbidi-Bobbodi-Boo   1949   w.m. Mack David, Al Hoffman, Jerry Livingston. (MF) *Cinderella*.

Bible Tells Me So, The   1955   w.m. Dale Evans

Bicycle Built for Two, A, *see* **Daisy Bell**

Bid Me Discourse   1820   w. William Shakespeare   m. Sir

Henry Rowley Bishop. The words to this song are based on Shakespeare's poem ''Venus and Adonis.''

Bidin' My Time 1930 w. Ira Gershwin m. George Gershwin. (MT) *Girl Crazy.* (MF) *Girl Crazy* (1932). (MF) *Girl Crazy* (1943). (MF) *Rhapsody in Blue.* (MF) *The Glenn Miller Story.* (MF) *When the Boys Meet the Girls.* Ethel Merman and Ginger Rodgers appeared in the stage production of *Girl Crazy.* Judy Garland and Mickey Rooney appeared in the 1943 film production of *Girl Crazy.* Oscar Levant, Robert Alda, Alexis Smith, and Glenn Miller appeared in *Rhapsody in Blue,* biopic of composer George Gershwin. Connie Francis appeared in *When the Boys Meet the Girls.*

B-I-Double L-Bill 1908 w. Monroe H. Rosenfeld m. Rosie Lloyd. This song was written for Republican Presidential candidate William Howard Taft.

Big Back Yard, The 19454 w. Dorothy Fields m. Sigmund Romberg. (MT) *Up in Central Park.* (MF) *Up in Central Park.* Deanna Durbin appeared in the film production of *Up in Central Park.*

Big Bad John 1961 w.m. Jimmy Dean. Grammy Award winner 1961.

Big Bass Viol, The 1910 w.m. M.T. Bohannon

Big Ben Chimes, *see* **Westminister Chimes**

Big Brass Band from Brazil, The 1947 w. Bob Hilliard m. Carl Sigman. (MT) *Angel in the Wings.*

Big Brown Bear, The, op. 52, no. 1 1919 w. H.A. Weydt m. Mana-Zucca

Big Butter and Egg Man, The 1926 w.m. Sidney Clare, Cliff Friend, Joseph H. Santley. For a history of this song, see Part I, 1927.

Big City 1982 w.m. Dean Holloway, Merle Haggard

Big City Suite 1955 w.m. Ralph Dollimore. Ivor Novello Award winner 1955.

Big "D" 1956 w.m. Frank Loesser. (MT) *The Most Happy Fella.*

Big Girls Don't Cry 1962 w.m. Bob Crewe, Bob Gaudio

Big Head 1953 w.m. Jack Meadows

Big Hunk of Love, A 1959 w.m. Aaron Schroeder, Sid Wyche

Big Hurt 1959 w.m. Wayne Shanklin

Big Mamou 1953 w.m. Link Davis

Big Man 1958 w.m. Glen Larson, Bruce Belland

Big Noise from Winnetka 1940 w.m. Bob Haggart, Ray Bauduc, Bob Crosby, Gil Rodin. (MT) *Dancing.* (F) *Let's Make Music.* (MF) *Reveille with Beverly.* Bob Crosby and Jean Rogers appeared in *Let's Make Music.* Ann Miller and William Wright appeared in *Reveille with Beverly.* This song was popularly revived in 1943.

Big Rock Candy Mountain, The 1885 w.m. anon.; traditional American folksong. (F) *Nighttime in Nevada.* Roy Rogers and Andy Devine appeared in *Nighttime in Nevada.* This song was popularly revived in 1949.

Big Shot 1979 w.m. Billy Joel

(Hey) Big Spender 1966 w. Dorothy Fields m. Cy Coleman. (MT) *Sweet Charity.* (MF) *Sweet Charity.* Gwen Ver-

don appeared in the stage production of *Sweet Charity.* Shirley MacLaine appeared in the film production of *Sweet Charity.*

Big Sunflower, The c.1866 w.m. Billy Newcomb. This song was popularized by Billy Emerson.

Big Time 1974 w.m. Jerry Herman. (MT) *Mack and Mabel.* Bernadette Peters and Robert Preston appeared in *Mack and Mabel.*

Biggest Aspidistra in the World, The 1938 w.m. Jimmy Harper, Wil Haines, Tommie Connor

Biggest Part of Me 1980 w.m. David Pack

Bilbao Song 1929 Ger.w. Bertolt Brecht Eng.w. Johnny Mercer m. Kurt Weill. (MT) *Happy End.* This song was popularly revived in 1961.

Bill 1927 w. P.G. Wodehouse, Oscar Hammerstein II m. Jerome Kern. (MT) *Show Boat.* (MF) *Show Boat* (1929). (MF) *Show Boat* (1936). (MF) *Show Boat* (1951). (MF) *The Man I Love.* (MF) *Both Ends of the Candle.* Charles Winninger appeared in the stage production of *Show Boat.* Helen Morgan appeared in the stage production and the 1929 film production of *Show Boat.* Helen Morgan, Irene Dunne, and Paul Robeson appeared in the 1936 film production of *Show Boat.* Kathryn Grayson and Ava Gardner appeared in the 1951 film production of *Show Boat.* Ida Lupino and Robert Alda appeared in *The Man I Love.* Theme song of Helen Morgan.

Bill, *see also* **Wedding Bell Blues**

Bill Bailey, Won't You Please Come Home 1902 w.m. Hughie Cannon. (MF) *Five Pennies.* Louis Armstrong appeared in *Five Pennies.* The narrative of this song is possibly based on the life of ''real'' William Godfrey Bailey, a trombonist and music teacher. See also Part I, 1902.

Billboard, The (March) 1901 m. John N. Klohr

Billie Jean 1983 w.m. Michael Jackson. Grammy Award winner 1983.

Billy (For When I Walk) 1911 w. Joe Goodwin m. Kendis and Paley

Billy 1974 w. Don Black m. John Barry

Billy Boy 1824 w.m. traditional folksong, from England

Billy Don't Be a Hero 1974 w.m. Mitch Murray, Peter Robin Callander. Ivor Novello Award winner 1974–75.

Billy Muggins 1906 w.m. Charles Ridgewell

Bim Bam Boom 1941 w.m. Harold Adamson, Noro Morales, John A. Camacho

Bimini Bay 1921 w.m. Gus Kahn, Raymond B. Egan, Richard A. Whiting

Bing! Bang! Bing 'Em on the Rhine 1918 w. Jack Mahoney m. Allan Flynn

Bingo, *see* **Balm of Gilead**

Bird Dog 1958 w.m. Boudleaux Bryant

Bird in a Gilded Cage, A 1900 w. Arthur J. Lamb m. Harry Von Tilzer. (F) *Ringside Maizie.* Ann Sheridan and Robert Sterling appeared in *Ringside Maizie.*

Bird of Love Divine 1912 w.m. Haydn Wood

(Little) Bird on Nellie's Hat, The 1906 w. Arthur J. Lamb m. Alfred Solman

Bird on the Wing 1936 w.m. Jimmy Kennedy, Will Grosz

Bird Songs at Eventide 1926 w. Royden Barrie m. Eric Coates

Birds in the Night 1869 w. Lionel H. Lewin m. Arthur Sullivan

Birmingham Bertha 1929 w.m. Harry Akst, Grant Clarke. (MF) *On with the Show.* Joe E. Brown and Ethel Waters appeared in *On with the Show.*

Birmingham Jail, *see* **Down in the Valley**

Birmingham Rag 1960 w.m. Mort Garson

Birth of Passion, The 1910 w. Otto Harbach m. Karl Hoschna. (MT) *Madame Sherry.*

Birth of the Blues, The 1926 w. B.G. DeSylva, Lew Brown m. Ray Henderson. (MT) *George White's Scandals of 1926.* (MT) *One Dam Thing After Another.* (MF) *Birth of the Blues.* (MF) *Painting the Clouds with Sunshine.* (MF) *The Best Things in Life Are Free.* Harry Richman and Ann Pennington appeared in *George White's Scandals of 1926.* Edith Baker appeared in *One Dam Thing After Another.* Bing Crosby, Mary Martin, and Jack Teagarden appeared in *Birth of the Blues.* Virginia Mayo and Dennis Morgan appeared in *Painting the Clouds with Sunshine.* Gordon MacRae, Dan Dailey, and Ernest Borgnine appeared in *The Best Things in Life Are Free,* biopic of song writers DeSylva, Brown, and Henderson. This song was popularly revived in 1942.

Birthday, A 1909 w. Christina Rossetti m. Raymond Huntington Woodman

Birthday of a King, The 1890 w. anon. m. William Harold Neidlinger

Bitch Is Back, The 1974 w.m. Elton John, Bernie Taupin

Bits and Pieces 1964 w.m. Dave Clark, Mike Smith

(What Did I Do To Be So) Black and Blue, *see* **What Did I Do To Be So Black and Blue**

Black and Tan Fantasy 1927 w.m. Edward Kennedy Ellington

Black and White 1972 w.m. David Arkin, Earl Robinson

Black and White Rag 1913 w.m. George Botsford

Black Bottom 1926 w. B.G. DeSylva, Lew Brown m. Ray Henderson. (MT) *George White's Scandals of 1926.* (MF) *A Star Is Born.* Ann Pennington and Frances Williams appeared in *George White's Scandals of 1926.* Judy Garland and James Mason appeared in *A Star Is Born.* Theme song of Ann Pennington. See also Part I, 1926.

Black Denim Trousers 1955 w. Michael Stoller m. Jerry Leiber

Black Eyes, *see* **Dark Eyes**

Black Is the Color of My True Love's Hair c.1875 w.m. traditional American folk ballad

Black Moonlight 1933 w.m. Sam Coslow, Arthur Johnston. (MF) *Too Much Harmony.* Bing Crosby and Jack Oakie appeared in *Too Much Harmony.*

Black Water 1975 w.m. Pat Simmons

Blackberry Way 1969 w.m. Roy Wood

Blackbird 1968 w.m. John Lennon, Paul McCartney

Blacksmith Blues, The 1952 w.m. Jack Holmes

Blah, Blah, Blah 1931 w. Ira Gershwin m. George Gershwin. (MT) *My One and Only.* (MF) *Delicious.* Tommy Tune and Twiggy appeared in *My One and Only.*

Blame It on My Youth 1934 w. Edward Heyman m. Oscar Levant

Blame It on the Bossa Nova 1963 w.m. Barry Mann, Cynthia Weil

Blaze Away (March) 1901 m. Abe Holzmann

Blaze of Glory 1909 w.m. Abe Holzmann

Blaze of Glory 1982 w.m. Larry Keith, Danny Morrison, Johnny Slate

Bless 'Em All 1940 w.m. Al Stillman, J. Hughes, Frank Lake

Bless the Beasts and Children 1971 w.m. Billy Mumy, Paul Gordon

Bless This House 1927 w.m. Helen Taylor, Mary H. Morgan

Bless You (For Being an Angel) 1939 w.m. Edward Lane, Don Baker

Blessed Are the Believers 1981 w.m. Charlie Black, Rory Bourke, Sandy Pinkard

Blest Be the Tie That Binds 1845 w.m. John Fawcett, Hans G. Naegeli, Kurt Kaiser. See also "Dennis".

Blind Ploughman, The 1913 w. Marguerite Radclyffe-Hall m. Robert Coningsby Clarke

Blinded by the Light 1977 w.m. Bruce Springsteen

Blockbuster 1974 w.m. Mike Chapman, Nicky Chinn. Ivor Novello Award winner 1973–74.

Bloody Mary 1949 w. Oscar Hammerstein II m. Richard Rodgers. (MT) *South Pacific.* (MF) *South Pacific.* Mary Martin and Bill Tabbert appeared in the stage production of *South Pacific.* Mitzi Gaynor and Ray Walston appeared in the film production of *South Pacific.*

(When the) Bloom Is on the Rye, or, **My Pretty Jane** 1832 w. Edward Fitzball m. Sir Henry Rowley Bishop

Bloop Bleep 1947 w.m. Frank Loesser

Blossom Fell, A 1955 w.m. Howard Barnes, Harold Cornelius, Dominic John. Ivor Novello Award winner 1955.

Blow, Gabriel, Blow 1934 w.m. Cole Porter. (MT) *Anything Goes.* (MF) *Anything Goes* (1936). (MF) *Anything Goes* (1956). Ethel Merman and Victor Moore appeared in the stage production of *Anything Goes.* Bing Crosby and Ethel Merman appeared in the 1936 film production of *Anything Goes.* Bing Crosby, Mitzi Gaynor, and Donald O'Connor appeared in the 1956 film production of *Anything Goes.*

Blow Out the Candle 1951 w.m. Phil Moore

Blow (Knock) the Man Down 1880 w.m. traditional sea chantey, from England. First known printed version this year, probably traditional, c.1830.

Blow the Smoke Away 1906 w. Will M. Hough, Frank R. Adams m. Joseph E. Howard. (MT) *The Time, the Place and the Girl.*

Blow Ye Winds, Heigh Ho c.1830 w.m. traditional sea chantey

Blowin' Away 1966 w.m. Laura Nyro. This song was most popular in 1969.

Blowin' in the Wind 1963 w.m. Bob Dylan

Blue (and Broken Hearted) 1922 w. Grant Clarke, Edgar Leslie m. Lou Handman

Blue Again 1930 w. Dorothy Fields m. Jimmy McHugh. (MT) *Vanderbilt Revue*. Joe Penner and Lulu McConnell appeared in *Vanderbilt Revue*.

Blue Alsatian Mountains, The 1875 w. Claribel (Mrs. Charles C. Barnard [Charlotte Arlington]) m. Stephen Adams (Michael Maybrick)

Blue and the Gray, The, or, **A Mother's Gift to Her Country** 1900 w.m. Paul Dresser

Blue Bayou 1977 w.m. Joe Melson, Roy Orbison

Blue Bell 1904 w. Edward Madden, Dolly Morse m. Theodore F. Morse. (MF) *The Jolson Story*. Larry Parks, Evelyn Keyes, William Demarest, and Bill Goodwin appeared in *The Jolson Story*. Born in Washington, D.C., Morse ran away from the Maryland Military Academy at age fourteen to New York, where he published his first composition at age fifteen.

Blue Bell of Scotland, The 1800 w.m. anon. This song is usually miscalled "The Blue Bells of Scotland."

Blue Bell Polka 1952 w.m. F. Stanley

Blue Bird of Happiness, The 1934 w. Edward Heyman m. Sandor Harmati. This song was introduced and featured by Jan Peerce in a Leon Leonidoff production at the Radio City Music Hall.

Blue Champagne 1941 w.m. Frank Ryerson, H. Grady Watts, Jimmy Eaton

Blue Danube, The (On the Beautiful Blue Danube) 1867 m. Johann Strauss. From the German "An der Schönen Blauen Donau."

Blue Eyes 1916 w.m. Horatio Nicholls, Fred Godfrey

Blue Eyes, see also **I'm Thinking Tonight of My Blue Eyes**

Blue Gardenia 1953 w.m. Lester Lee, Sidney Keith Russel

Blue Hawaii 1937 w.m. Leo Robin, Ralph Rainger. (MF) *Waikiki Wedding*. Bing Crosby and Martha Raye appeared in *Waikiki Wedding*.

Blue Is the Night 1930 w.m. Fred Fisher. (F) *Their Own Desire*. Norma Shearer and Robert Montgomery appeared in *Their Own Desire*.

Blue Juniata, The 1844 w.m. Marion Dix Sullivan. The Juniata is a river in Pennsylvania.

Blue Lou (not "True Blue Lou") 1933 w.m. Edgar M. Sampson, Irving Mills

Blue Mirage 1954 w. Sam Coslow m. Lotar Olias

Blue Monday 1957 w.m. Dave Bartholomew, Antione Domino

Blue Moon 1934 w. Lorenz Hart m. Richard Rodgers. (MT) *The 1940's Radio Hour*. (MF) *Words and Music*. (MF) *With a Song in My Heart*. (MF) *Hollywood Revue*. (F) *Malaya*. (MF) *Torch Song*. (F) *This Could Be the Night*. (F) *Kiss Them for Me*. Mickey Rooney, Gene Kelly, and Judy Garland appeared in *Words and Music*, biopic of song writers Rodgers and Hart. Susan Hayward appeared in *With a Song in My Heart*, biopic of singer Jane Froman. This song appeared as "Prayer" in *Hollywood Revue*. Spencer Tracy and

James Stewart appeared in *Malaya*. Joan Crawford appeared in *Torch Song*. Jean Simmons appeared in *This Could Be the Night*. Cary Grant and Jayne Mansfield appeared in *Kiss Them for Me*. This song was popularly revived in 1961. With an earlier lyric by Lorenz Hart titled "Make Me a Star," this song was originally written for Jean Harlow, but was cut from the movie it was intended for.

Blue Moon with Heartache 1982 w.m. Rosanne Cash

Blue on Blue 1963 w. Hal David m. Burt F. Bacharach

Blue Orchids 1939 w.m. Hoagy Carmichael

Blue Pacific Moonlight 1930 w.m. Jack Payne, Wallace Herbert

Blue Prelude 1933 w. Joe Bishop m. Gordon Jenkins. (MT) *Singin' in the Rain*.

Blue Rain 1939 w.m. Johnny Burke, Jimmy Van Heusen

Blue Ribbon Gal 1949 w.m. Irwin Dash, Ross Parker

Blue Room, The 1926 w. Lorenz Hart m. Richard Rodgers. (MT) *The Girl Friend*. (MF) *Words and Music*. (MF) *The Eddy Duchin Story*. Eva Puck and Sam White appeared in *The Girl Friend*. Judy Garland, Gene Kelly, and Mickey Rooney appeared in *Words and Music*, biopic of song writers Rodgers and Hart.

Blue Shadows and White Gardenias 1942 w.m. Mack Gordon, Harry Owens. (MF) *Song of the Islands*. Victor Mature and Betty Grable appeared in *Song of the Islands*.

Blue Shadows on the Trail 1948 w.m. Johnny Lange, Eliot Daniel. (MF) *Melody Time*. Roy Rogers, Trigger, and the Andrews Sisters appeared in *Melody Time*.

Blue Side 1980 w.m. David Lasley, Allee Willis

Blue Skies 1927 w.m. Irving Berlin. (MT) *Betsy*. (MT) *Blue Skies*. (MF) *The Jazz Singer*. (MF) *Glorifying the American Girl*. (MF) *Alexander's Ragtime Band*. (MF) *Blue Skies*. (MF) *White Christmas*. Belle Baker and Al Shean appeared in *Betsy*. Jack Smith appeared in the stage production of *Blue Skies*. Al Jolson appeared in *The Jazz Singer*. Helen Morgan, Eddie Cantor, and Rudy Vallee appeared in *Glorifying the American Girl*. Tyrone Power appeared in *Alexander's Ragtime Band*. Bing Crosby and Fred Astaire appeared in the film production of *Blue Skies*. Bing Crosby and Danny Kaye appeared in *White Christmas*.

Blue Skies Are Round the Corner 1939 w.m. Hugh Charles, Ross Parker

Blue Star 1955 w.m. Edward Heyman, Victor Young

Blue Suede Shoes 1956 w.m. Carl Lee Perkins. (MF) *G.I. Blues*. Elvis Presley and Juliet Prowse appeared in *G.I. Blues*.

Blue Tail Fly, The, see **Jimmy Crack Corn**

Blue Tango 1952 m. Leroy Anderson

Blue Turning Grey Over You 1937 w.m. Andy Razaf, Thomas "Fats" Waller

Blue Velvet 1951 w.m. Bernie Wayne, Lee Morris. This song was popularly revived in 1963.

Blue Without You 1930 m. Fred Astaire, Mitchell Parish

Blueberry Hill 1940 w.m. Al Lewis, Larry Stock, Vincent Rose. (MF) *The Singing Hill*. Gene Autry and Smiley Burnette appeared in *The Singing Hill*. This song was popularly revived in 1956.

Bluebird (Vola Colomba) 1952 w.m. C. Concina

Blues in My Heart 1931 w.m. Benny Carter, Irving Mills

Blues in the Night 1941 w. Johnny Mercer m. Harold Arlen. (MF) *Blues in the Night.* Priscilla Lane and Richard Whorf appeared in *Blues in the Night.*

Blues My Naughty Sweetie Gives to Me 1919 w.m. Charles McCarron, Carey Morgan, Arthur Swanstrom

Blues Serenade, A 1935 w. Mitchell Parish m. Frank Signorelli

Bluin' the Blues 1918 w.m. Edwin B. Edwards, James D. La Rocca, Sidney D. Mitchell, Anthony Sbarbaro, Larry Shields

Boats of Mine 1919 w. Robert Louis Stevenson m. Anne Stratton Miller

Bob White (Whatcha Gonna Swing Tonight) 1937 w. Johnny Mercer m. Bernard Hanighen

Bobbie Sue w.m. Wood Newton, Adele Tyler, Daniel Tyler

Bobby Shafto c. 1750 w.m. traditional sea chantey. The Shaftos were a well-known Northumberland family. The narrative of this song concerns a particular family member who ran away to sea to escape the attention of another family member who had become an embarrassment.

Bobby Sox (Socks) to Stockings 1959 w.m. Russell Faith, Clarence Way Kehner, R. di Cicco

Bobby's Girl 1962 w.m. Gary Klein, Henry Hoffman

Body and Soul 1930 w. Edward Heyman, Robert Sour, Frank Eyton m. John Green. (MT) *Three's a Crowd.* (MF) *The Man I Love.* (F) *Her Kind of Man.* (MF) *The Eddy Duchin Story.* (MF) *Both Ends of the Candle.* Fred MacMurray, Fred Allen, and Alan Jones appeared in *Three's a Crowd.* Ida Lupino and Robert Alda appeared in *The Man I Love.* Dana Clark and Janis Paige appeared in *Her Kind of Man.*

Bohemia 1916 w.m. Paul Rubens, Adrian Ross. (MT) *Happy Day.* Jose Collins appeared in *Happy Day.*

Bohemian Rhapsody 1976 w.m. Freddie Mercury. Ivor Novello Award winner 1975–76.

Boiled Beef and Carrots 1910 w.m. Charles Collins, Fred Murray

Bojangles of Harlem 1936 w. Dorothy Fields m. Jerome Kern. (MF) *Swing Time.* Ginger Rogers, Fred Astaire, and Helen Broderick appeared in *Swing Time.*

Bolero 1929 m. Maurice Ravel. This work bears but a faint resemblance to the authentic Spanish dance of the same name.

Boll Weevil Song, The 1961 w.m. Clyde Otis, Brook Benton

Bombay Duckling (Kipling Theme) 1964 w.m. Max Harris

Bombo-Shay, The 1917 w.m. Henry Creamer, Henry Lewis, Turner Layton

Bon Bon Buddy 1907 w. Alex Rogers m. Will Marion Cook

Bonanza 1960 m. Jay Livingston, Ray Evans. (TV) *Bonanza.*

Bonaparte's Retreat 1950 w.m. Pee Wee King

Boneyard Shuffle 1925 w.m. Hoagy Carmichael, Irving Mills

Bongo Bongo Bongo, *see* **Civilization**

Bonne Nuit—Goodnight 1951 w.m. Jay Livingston, Ray Evans. (MF) *Here Comes the Groom.* Bing Crosby and Alexis Smith appeared in *Here Comes the Groom.*

Bonnie Blue Flag, The 1861 w. Mrs. Annie Chambers-Ketchum m. Harry MacCarthy. This was a popular song of the Confederate States during the American Civil War. It is based on the Irish tune "The Jaunting Car." MacCarthy and his sister, performing as a music-hall team in New Orleans, supposedly wrote this song as a finale to their act.

Bonnie Bonnie Banks, The, *see* **Loch Lomond**

Bonnie Doon c.1830 w. Robert Burns m. traditional, from Scotland

Bonnie Dundee c.1830 w. Sir Walter Scott m. traditional, from Scotland

Bonnie Eloise, or, **The Belle of Mohawk Vale** 1858 w. George W. Elliott m. John Rogers Thomas

Boo-Hoo 1937 w.m. Edward Heyman, John Jacob Loeb, carmen Lombardo

Boogie Down 1974 w.m. Anita Poree, Frank Wilson, Leonard Caston

Boogie Fever 1976 w.m. Frederick J. Perren, Kenny St. Lewis

Boogie Nights 1977 w.m. Rod Temperton. Ivor Norello Award winner 1977–78.

Boogie On Reggae Woman 1974 w.m. Stevie Wonder

Boogie Oogie Oogie 1978 w.m. Janice Johnson, Perry Kibble

Boogie Woogie 1928 m. Pinetop Smith. Invented by black pianist Pinetop Smith, this style of composition was first recorded in Chicago, on December 29, 1928.

Boogie Woogie Bugle Boy (from Company B) 1941 w.m. Hughie Prince, Don Raye, (MT) *The 1940's Radio Hour.* (MF) *Buck Privates.* (MF) *Swingtime Johnny.* The Andrews Sisters appeared in both *Buck Privates* and *Swingtime Johnny.* This song was popularly revived in 1973.

Book, The 1954 w.m. Hans Gottwald, Paddy Roberts

Boola Boola 1898 w.m. anon. Based on Bob Cole and Billy Johnson's "La Hoola Boola" of 1897. Possibly from Hawaii, with new words, as the "Yale Boola" of 1901.

Boom 1938 w.m. E. Ray Goetz, Charles Trenet

Boom Bang-A-Bang 1970 w.m. Alan Moorhouse, Peter Warne. Ivor Novello Award winner 1969–70.

Boomerang 1955 w.m. Mark Lotz, Alan Gold, Tom Harrison

Boomps-a-Daisy 1939 w.m. Annette Mills. (MT) *Hellzapoppin'.*

(Take Me Back to My) Boots and Saddle 1935 w.m. Walter Samuels, Leonard Whitcup, Teddy Powell. (MF) *Call of the Canyon.* Gene Autry and Smiley Burnette appeared in *Call of the Canyon.*

Bop 1986 w.m. Paul Davis

Borderline 1984 w.m. Reggie Grant Lucas

Born Free 1966 w. Don Black m. John Barry. (F) *Born Free.* Academy Award winner 1966. Ivor Novello Award winner 1966.

Born in the U.S.A. 1985 w.m. Bruce Springsteen

Born to Each Other, *see* **Friends and Lovers**

Born to Run 1982 w.m. Paul Kennerley

Born To Lose 1943 w.m. Frankie Brown

Born Too Late 1958 w.m. Charles Strouse, Fred Tobias

Born Yesterday 1986 w.m. Don Everly

(Theme from) Borsalino 1970 w.m. Claude Jean H. Bolling, Pierre C.M.N. LeRoyer

Bosom Buddies 1966 w.m. Jerry Herman. (MT) *Mame.* (MT) *Jerry's Girls.* (MF) *Mame.* Angela Lansbury appeared in the stage production of *Mame.* Dorothy Loudon, Chita Rivera, and Leslie Uggams appeared in *Jerry's Girls.* Lucille Ball appeared in the film production of *Mame.* Beatrice Arthur appeared in both the stage and film productions of *Mame.*

Boston Come-All Ye c.1830 w.m. anon. This song is mentioned by Rudyard Kipling in *Captains Courageous* under the title of "The Fishes." It was also possibly known in Scotland as "Blow the Wind Southerly."

Boston Patriotic Song, The, *see* **Adams and Liberty**

Botch-A-Me 1952 It.w. R. Morbelli, L. Astore Eng.w. Eddie Y. Stanley m. R. Morbelli, L. Astore

Both Sides Now 1968 w.m. Joni Mitchell

Boulevard of Broken Dreams 1933 w. Al Dubin m. Harry Warren. (MF) *Moulin Rouge* (1934). (F) *Moulin Rouge* (1953). Constance Bennett and Helen Wesley appeared in the 1934 film production of *Moulin Rouge.* Jose Ferrer and Zsa Zsa Gabor appeared in the 1953 film production of *Moulin Rouge.*

Bouquet (I Shall Always Think of You) 1925 w.m. Horatio Nicholls, Ray Morelle

Bouquet of Barbed Wire 1977 w.m. Dennis Farnon

Bouquet of Roses, A 1948 w.m. Steve Nelson, Bob Hilliard

Boutonniere 1951 w. Bob Hilliard m. Dave Mann

Bowery, The 1892 w. Charles H. Hoyt m. Percy Gaunt. Based on the Neapolitan folksong "La Spagnola." (MT) *A Trip to Chinatown.* (MF) *Sunbonnet Sue.* Gale Storm and Phil Regan appeared in *Sunbonnet Sue.* This song was so popular that real estate values along the Bowery dropped, and shopkeepers protested the performance of this song.

Bowl of Roses, A 1905 w. W.E. Healey m. Robert Coningby Clarke

Boxer, The 1980 w.m. Paul Simon. This song was originally written in 1980.

Boy and a Girl Were Dancing, A 1932 w. Mack Gordon m. Harry Revel

Boy from . . . , The 1966 w. Stephen Sondheim m. Mary Rodgers. (MT) *The Mad Show.* (MT) *Side by Side by Sondheim.* Millicent Martin and Julie N. McKenzie appeared in *Side by Side by Sondheim.*

Boy from New York City 1981 w.m. George Davis

Boy Guessed Right, The 1898 w.m. Lionel Monckton. (MT) *A Runaway Girl.*

Boy Like That, A 1957 w. Stephen Sondheim m. Leonard Bernstein. (MT) *West Side Story.* (MF) *West Side Story.*

Natalie Wood and Rita Moreno appeared in the film production of *West Side Story.*

Boy Named Sue, A 1969 w.m. Shel Silverstein. Grammy Award winner 1969.

Boy Next Door, The 1944 w. Hugh Martin m. Ralph Blane. (MF) *Meet Me in St. Louis.* Judy Garland, Marjorie Main, and Margaret O'Brien appeared in *Meet Me in St. Louis.*

Boy on a Dolphin 1957 w.m. Jean Fermanoglou, Hugo W. Friedhofer, Takis Morakis, Paul Francis Webster, François Depastas

Boy! What Love Has Done to Me! 1930 w. Ira Gershwin m. George Gershwin. (MT) *Girl Crazy.* (MF) *Girl Crazy* (1932). (MF) *Girl Crazy* (1943). Ethel Merman and Ginger Rogers both made their Broadway debuts in *Girl Crazy.* Judy Garland and Mickey Rooney appeared in the 1943 film production of *Girl Crazy.*

Boys Are Coming Home Today, The 1903 w.m. Paul Dresser

Boy's Best Friend Is His Mother, A 1884 w.m. Joseph P. Skelly. Mr. Skelly, a prolific writer of some 400 songs, was a plumber by trade and spent most of his composing earnings on liquor.

Boys Cry 1964 w.m. Buddy Kaye, Tommy Scott

(See What) Boys in the Back Room, The (Will Have) 1939 w. Frank Loesser m. Frederick Hollander. (F) *Destry Rides Again.* Marlene Dietrich and James Stewart appeared in *Destry Rides Again.*

Boy's Night Out, The 1962 w.m. Sammy Cahn, James Van Heusen. (F) *Boys' Night Out.* Kim Novak and Tony Randall appeared in *Boys' Night Out.*

Boys of Summer 1985 w.m. Michael Campbell, Don Henley

Brahms' Lullaby, *see* **Lullaby**

Brahn Boots 1940 w.m. R.P. Weston, Bert Lee

Brand New Key 1972 w.m. Melanie Safka

Brandy (You're a Fine Girl) 1972 w.m. Elliot Lurie

Brass in Pocket 1980 w.m. Chrissie Hynde, James Scott

Brave Old Oak, The 1837 w. Henry Fothergill Chorley m. Edward James Loder; arr. Henry Russell

Brazil 1939 Eng.w. Bob Russell m. Ary Barroso. From the Spanish "Arquela do Brasil." (MF) *Saludos Amigos.* (F) *Brazil.* (MF) *The Eddy Duchin Story.* (MF) *Jam Session.* Roy Rogers and Virginia Bruce appeared in *Brazil.* Ann Miller and Louis Armstrong appeared in *Jam Session.* This song was popularly revived in 1943, and later again in 1975.

Bread and Butter 1964 w.m. Larry Parks, Jay Turnbow

Break It to Me Gently 1962 w.m. Diane Lampert, Joe Seneca

Break It to Me Gently 1983 w.m. Diane Lampert, Joe Seneca

Break My Stride 1984 w.m. Greg Prestopine, Matthew Wilder

Break of Day 1943 w.m. Hans May, Alan Stranks (MT) *Old Chelsea*

Break the News to Mother 1897 w.m. Charles K. Harris.

(MF) *Wait Till the Sun Shines Nellie*. David Wayne appeared in *Wait Till the Sun Shines Nellie*.

Break Up To Make Up 1973 w.m. Thomas Bell, Kenneth Gamble, Linda Creed

Breakdance 1985 w.m. Bunny Hull

Breakdown Dead Ahead 1980 w.m. David Foster, Boz Scaggs

Breakfast at Tiffany's 1961 m. Henry Mancini. (F) *Breakfast at Tiffany's*. Audrey Hepburn appeared in *Breakfast at Tiffany's*.

Breaking in a Brand New Broken Heart 1961 w.m. Howard Greenfield, Jack Keller

Breaking Up Is Hard To Do 1959 w.m. Neil Sedaka, Howard Greenfield. This song was popularly revived in 1962, and again in 1975.

Breeze, The (That's Bringing My Honey Back to Me) 1934 w.m. Al Lewis, Tony Sacco, Richard B. Smith

Breeze and I, The 1940 w. Al Stillman m. Ernesto Lecuona. Based on Ernesto Lecuona's "Andalucia" of 1930. (MF) *Cuban Pete*. Desi Arnaz and Ethel Smith appeared in *Cuban Pete*.

Breezin' Along with the Breeze 1926 w.m. Haven Gillespie, Seymour Simons, Richard A. Whiting. (MF) *Both Ends of the Candle*.

Brian's Song 1972 w. Alan Bergman, Marilyn Bergman m. Michel Legrand. (F) *Brian's Song*.

Bridal Chorus, *see* **Wedding March** *(Lohengrin)*

Bride Cuts the Cake, The, *see* **The Farmer in the Dell**

Bride Elect, The 1896 w.m. John Philip Sousa

(Theme from) Brideshead Revisited 1982 m. Geoffrey Burgon. (TV) *Brideshead Revisited*. Jeremy Irons appeared in the BBC-TV production of *Brideshead Revisited*. Ivor Novello Award winner 1981–82.

Bridge of Sighs, The 1900 w.m. James Thornton

Bridge of Sighs, The 1953 w.m. Billy Reid

Bridge over Troubled Water 1970 w.m. Paul Simon. Grammy Award winner 1970.

Bright Eyes 1920 w. Harry B. Smith m. Otto Motzan, M.K. Jerome

Bright Eyes 1980 w.m. Mike Bart. (F) *Bright Eyes*. Ivor Novello Award winner 1978–79. Ivor Novello Award winner 1979–80.

Brighten the Corner Where You Are 1913 w. Ina Duley Ogdon m. Charles H. Gabriel

Brighter Than the Sun 1932 w.m. Ray Noble

Brighton Camp, *see* **The Girl I Left Behind Me**

Bring Back My Bonnie to Me, *see* **My Bonnie Lies over the Ocean**

Bring Back My Daddy to Me 1917 w. William Tracey, Howard Johnson m. George W. Meyer

Bring Back My Golden Dreams 1911 w. Alfred Bryan m. George W. Meyer

Bring Back Those Minstrel Days 1926 w. Ballard MacDonald m. Martin Broones. (MT) *Rufus Lemaire's Affairs*.

Bring Me a Rose 1909 w. Lionel Monckton, Arthur Wim-

peris m. Lionel Monckton. (MT) *The Arcadians*. Julia Sanderson and Grace Studdiford appeared in *The Arcadians*.

Bring Me a Rose 1916 w.m. Charles Shisler

Bring Me Sunshine 1966 w.m. Arthur Kent

Bringing in the Sheaves uncertain w. Knowles Shaw m. George Minor

Bristol Stomp 1961 w.m. Dave Appell, Kal Mann

Britannia Rag 1952 w.m. Winifred Atwell

Britannia the Gem of the Ocean, *see* **Columbia the Gem of the Ocean**

British Empire, The 1972 w.m. Wilfred Josephs. (TV-BBC) *The British Empire*.

British Grenadiers c. 1750 w.m. traditional, from England. This song was later adapted in 1775 by Joseph Warren as "Free America."

Broadway Baby 1971 w.m. Stephen Sondheim. (MT) *Follies*. (MT) *Side by Side by Sondheim*. Yvonne DeCarlo and Alexis Smith appeared in *Follies*. Millicent Martin and Julie N. McKenzie appeared in *Side by Side by Sondheim*.

Broadway Melody 1929 w. Arthur Freed m. Nacio Herb Brown. (MF) *Broadway Melody*. Charles King and Bessie Love appeared in *Broadway Melody*.

Broadway Rhythm 1935 w. Arthur Freed m. Nacio Herb Brown. (MF) *Broadway Melody of 1936*. (MF) *Presenting Lily Mars*. Eleanor Powell and Jack Benny appeared in *Broadway Melody of 1936*. Judy Garland, Van Heflin, and Spring Byington appeared in *Presenting Lily Mars*. Theme song of Benny Fields.

Broadway Rose 1920 w. Eugene West m. Otis Spencer, Martin Fried

Broken Doll 1916 w.m. James W. Tate. (MT) *Samples*.

Broken Hearted, *see* **Here Am I—Broken Hearted**

Broken Hearted Clown 1937 w.m. Don Pelosi, Harry Leon

Broken-Hearted Melody 1959 w. Hal David m. Sherman Edwards

Broken Lady 1976 w.m. Larry Gatlin. Grammy Award winner 1976.

Broken Melody, The 1901 w.m. August Van Biene

Broken Record, The 1935 w.m. Cliff Friend, Charles Tobias, Boyd Bunch

Broken Wings 1952 w.m. John Jerome, Bernard Grun

Broken Wings 1985 w.m. Steven George, John Lang, Richard Page

Brother Bill 1942 m. Louis Armstrong

Brother, Can You Spare a Dime 1932 w. E.Y. Harburg m. Jay Gorney. (MT) *Americana*. (MF) *Embarrassing Moments*. George Givot and Albert Carroll appeared in *Americana*. Marian Nixon and Chester Morris appeared in *Embarrassing Moments*.

Brother Louie 1973 w.m. Errol A.G. Brown, Anthony Wilson

Brotherhood of Man 1961 w.m. Frank Loesser. (MT) *How To Succeed in Business Without Really Trying*. (MF) *How To Succeed in Business Without Really Trying*. Robert Morse appeared in both the stage and film productions of *How To Succeed in Business Without Really Trying.*

Brown Bird Singing, A 1922 w. Royden Barrie m. Haydn Wood

Brown Eyed Girl 1984 w.m. Van Morrison

Brown Eyes—Why Are You Blue 1925 w. Alfred Bryan m. George W. Meyer

Brown October Ale 1891 w. Harry B. Smith m. Reginald DeKoven. (MT) *Robin Hood.*

Brush Up Your Shakespeare 1949 w.m. Cole Porter. (MT) *Kiss Me, Kate.* (MF) *Kiss Me, Kate.* Alfred Drake and Patricia Morison appeared in the stage production of *Kiss Me, Kate.* Ann Miller appeared in the film production of *Kiss Me, Kate.*

Brylcreem, A Little Dab'll Do Ya 1949 w.m. John P. Atherton. This song was written for a Brylcreem Hair Cream commercial promotion campaign.

Bubble, The 1913 w. Otto Harbach m. Rudolf Friml. (MT) *High Jinks.*

Buckle Down, Winsocki 1941 w.m. Hugh Martin, Ralph Blane. (MT) *Best Foot Forward.* (MF) *Best Foot Forward.* June Allyson and Nancy Walker appeared in the stage production of *Best Foot Forward.* Lucille Ball and June Allyson appeared in the film production of *Best Foot Forward.*

Buddha 1919 w. Ed Rose m. Lew Pollack

Budweiser's a Friend of Mine 1907 w. Vincent P. Bryan m. Seymour Furth. This song was later used for a Budweiser Beer commercial promotion campaign.

Buffalo Gals (Won't You Come Out Tonight?), or, **Lubly Fan** 1844 w.m. Cool White (John Hodges). This song was sung by Ole Jim in Chapter Two of Mark Twain's *The Adventures of Huckleberry Finn.* It was also heard in one of Will Rogers's last films, *Steamboat Round de Bend.*

Bugle Call (Rag) 1916 m. J. Hubert (Eubie) Blake, Carey Morgan

Bugle Call Rag 1923 w.m. Jack Pettis, Billy Meyers, Elmer Schoebel. (MF) *Orchestra Wives.* (MF) *The Benny Goodman Story.* Glenn Miller and Ann Rutherford appeared in *Orchestra Wives.* Theme song of Harry Roy.

Build Me Up Buttercup 1969 w.m. Tony Macaulay, Michael D'Abo. Ivor Novello Award winner 1968–69.

Bulldog! Bulldog! Bow, Wow, Wow 1911 w.m. Cole Porter. Mr. Porter wrote his football rally song at age eighteen, while an undergraduate at Yale.

Bumble Boogie 1946 m. Jack Fina. Based on Rimsky-Korsakov's ''Flight of the Bumble Bee'' (1900).

Bunch of Roses 1910 m. Ruperto Chapi y Lorente. From the Spanish ''El Puñoa de Rosas.''

Bunny Hop 1952 w.m. Ray Anthony, Leonard Auletti

Burgers and Fries 1979 w.m. Ben Peters

Burlington Bertie from Bow 1915 w.m. William Hargreaves. This English music hall ballad was popularly sung by Miss Ella Shields, who came to England from Philadelphia.

Burning Heart 1986 w.m. James Peterik, Frank Sullivan. (F) *Rocky IV.* Sylvester Stallone appeared in *Rocky IV.*

Burning Love 1972 w.m. Dennis Linde

Bury Me Not on the Lone Prairie, *see* **Oh, Bury Me Not on the Lone Prairie**

Bus Stop 1966 w.m. Graham Gouldman

Bushel and a Peck, A 1950 w.m. Frank Loesser. (MT) *Guys and Dolls.* (MF) *Guys and Dolls.* Robert Alda, Jean Simmons, and Vivian Blaine appeared in the stage production of *Guys and Dolls.* Marlon Brando and Frank Sinatra appeared in the film production of *Guys and Dolls.*

Busted 1963 w.m. Harlan Howard. Grammy Award winner 1963.

But Beautiful 1948 w. Johnny Burke m. Jimmy Van Heusen. (MF) *The Road to Rio.* Bob Hope, Bing Crosby, and Dorothy Lamour appeared in *The Road to Rio.*

But I Do—You Know I Do 1926 w. Gus Kahn m. Walter Donaldson

But Not for Me 1930 w. Ira Gershwin m. George Gershwin. (MT) *Girl Crazy.* (MF) *Girl Crazy* (1932). (MF) *Girl Crazy* (1943). Ethel Merman and Ginger Rogers both made their Broadway debuts in *Girl Crazy.* Bert Wheeler and Eddie Quillan appeared in the 1932 film production of *Girl Crazy.* Judy Garland, June Allyson, and Mickey Rooney appeared in the 1943 film production of *Girl Crazy.*

But You Know I Love You 1981 w.m. Mike Settle

Butcher Boy, The, *see* **Oh Mama**

Butterfingers 1934 w.m. Irving Berlin

Butterflies in the Rain 1932 w.m. Stanley Damerell, Robert Hargreaves, Sherman Myers

Butterfly 1957 w.m. Anthony September

Button Up Your Overcoat 1928 w. B.G. DeSylva, Lew Brown m. Ray Henderson. (MT) *Follow Thru.* (MF) *Follow Thru.* (MF) *The Best Things in Life Are Free.* Jack Haley, Zelma O'Neal, and Eleanor Powell appeared in the stage production of *Follow Thru.* Gordon MacRae, Dan Dailey, and Ernest Borgnine appeared in *The Best Things in Life Are Free,* biopic of song writers DeSylva, Brown, and Henderson. This song was used for a television advertising campaign for Contac cold medication.

Buttons and Bows 1948 w. Raymond Evans m. Jay Livingston. (F) *Paleface.* Bob Hope and Jane Russell appeared in *Paleface.* Academy Award winner 1948. A $600,000 plagiarism suit filed by bandleader Freddie Rich was decided by a jury in the Superior Court of Los Angeles to be unfounded, and established the basic melody to be in the public domain.

Buy a Broom, or, **The Bavarian Girl's Song** c.1825 w. D.O. Meara m. based on ''O (Ach) Du Lieber Augustin'' of 1815; adapted Alexander Lee

Buzz Buzz A-Diddle-It 1961 w.m. Robert S. Crewe, Jr., Frank C. Slay, Jr.

By a Waterfall 1933 w. Irving Kahal m. Sammy Fain. (MF) *Footlight Parade.* Dick Powell, Ruby Keeler, and James Cagney appeared in *Footlight Parade.*

By a Wishing Well 1938 w.m. Mack Gordon, Harry Revel. (F) *My Lucky Star.*

By Candlelight 1942 w.m. Sonny Miller, Hugh Charles

By Heck 1914 w. L. Wolfe Gilbert m. S.R. Henry (Henry

R. Stern). (MT) *Push and Go*. John Henning appeared in *Push and Go*. The words were added to this melody in 1915.

By Myself 1937 w. Howard Dietz m. Arthur Schwartz. (MT) *Between the Devil*. Jack Buchanan, Evelyn Laye, and Adele Dixon appeared in *Between the Devil*.

By Now 1981 w.m. Dean Dillon, Donald Pfrimmer, Charles Quillen

By Strauss 1936 w. Ira Gershwin m. George Gershwin. (MT) *The Show Is On*. (MF) *An American in Paris*. Bert Lahr, Mitzi Mayfair, and Beatrice Lillie appeared in *The Show Is On*. Gene Kelly and Leslie Caron appeared in *An American in Paris*.

By the Beautiful Sea 1914 w. Harold R. Atteridge m. Harry Carroll. (MF) *The Story of Vernon and Irene Castle*. (MF) *Some Like It Hot*. Ginger Rogers and Fred Astaire appeared in *The Story of Vernon and Irene Castle*. Marilyn Monroe, Jack Lemmon, and Tony Curtis appeared in *Some Like It Hot*. This song was popularly revived in 1939.

By the Bend of the River 1927 w. Bernhard Haig m. Clara Edwards

By the Fireside 1932 w.m. Ray Noble, James Campbell, Reginald Connelly

By the Fountains of Rome 1956 w.m. Matyas Seiber, Norman Newell. Ivor Novello Award winner 1956.

By the Light of the Silvery Moon 1909 w. Edward Madden m. Gus Edwards. (MT) *The Ziegfeld Follies* (1909). (MF) *Birth of the Blues*. (MF) *Sunbonnet Sue*. (MF) *The Jolson Story*. (MF) *Two Weeks with Love*. (MF) *By the Light of the Silvery Moon*. (MF) *Always Leave Them Laughing*. Bing Crosby and Mary Martin appeared in *Birth of the Blues*. Gale Storm and Phil Regan appeared in *Sunbonnet Sue*. Larry Parks appeared in *The Jolson Story*. Jane Powell and Debbie Reynolds appeared in *Two Weeks with Love*. Milton Berle and Bert Lahr appeared in *Always Leave Them Laughing*. This song was inspired by a 1905 moonlight gondola ride in Venice.

By the River of (the) Roses 1943 w.m. Marty Symes, Joe Burke. (MF) *Trail to San Antone*. Peggy Stewart and Sterling Holloway appeared in *Trail to San Antone*.

By the River Sainte Marie 1931 w. Edgar Leslie m. Harry Warren. (MF) *Swing in the Saddle*. Joan Frazee and the King Cole Trio appeared in *Swing in the Saddle*.

By the Sad Sea Waves 1850 w. Alfred Bunn m. Julius Benedict. From the English opera *The Brides of Venice*. This song was popularly sung by Jenny Lind during her American concert tour.

By the Sad Sea Waves 1895 w. Lester Barrett m. Lester Thomas

By the Saskatchewan 1910 w. C.M.S. McLellan m. Ivan Caryll. (MT) *The Pink Lady*.

By the Sea, *see* **By the Beautiful Sea**

By the Shalimar 1922 w.m. Ted Koehler, Frank Magine

By the Side of the Zuyder Zee 1907 w.m. Bennett Scott, A.J. Mills

By the Sleepy Lagoon, *see* **Sleepy Lagoon**

By the Sycamore Tree 1931 w. Haven Gillespie m. Pete Wendling

By the Time I Get to Phoenix 1967 w.m. Jim Webb

By the Watermelon Vine, Lindy Lou 1914 w.m. Thomas S. Allen

By the Waters of Minnetonka 1914 w. J.M. Cavanass m. Thurlow Lieurance

Bye and Bye 1925 w. Lorenz Hart m. Richard Rodgers. (MT) *Dearest Enemy*.

Bye Bye American Pie, *see* **American Pie**

Bye Bye Baby 1936 w. Walter Hirsch m. Lou Handman

Bye Bye Baby 1949 w. Leo Robin m. Jule Styne. (MT) *Gentlemen Prefer Blondes*. (MF) *Gentlemen Prefer Blondes*. Carol Channing appeared in the stage production of *Gentlemen Prefer Blondes*. Marilyn Monroe appeared in the film production of *Gentlemen Prefer Blondes*.

Bye Bye Blackbird 1926 w. Mort Dixon m. Ray Henderson. (MF) *Rainbow Round My Shoulder*. (MF) *The Eddie Cantor Story*. (MF) *Pete Kelly's Blues*. (F) *Isadora*. Frankie Laine appeared in *Rainbow Round My Shoulder*. Peggy Lee appeared in *Pete Kelly's Blues*. Vanessa Redgrave appeared in *Isadora*.

Bye Bye Blues 1930 w.m. Fred Hamm, Dave Bennett, Bert Lown, Chauncey Gray. Based on James H. Rogers's "The Star" of 1912. Theme song of Bert Lown and his Hotel Biltmore Orchestra.

Bye Bye Love 1957 w.m. Felice Bryant, Boudleaux Bryant

C-Jam Blues 1942 w.m. Edward Kennedy "Duke" Ellington

Ça C'est L'Amour 1957 w.m. Cole Porter. (MF) *Les Girls*. Gene Kelly, Kay Kendall, and Mitzi Gaynor appeared in *Les Girls*.

Ça C'est Paris 1927 w.m. Philip Moody, Doris Pony Sherrell

Cabaret 1967 w. Fred Ebb m. John Kander. (MT) *Cabaret*. (MF) *Cabaret*. Lotte Lenya and Joel Grey appeared in the stage production of *Cabaret*. Liza Minnelli and Joel Grey appeared in the film production of *Cabaret*. This song was popularly revived in 1972.

Cabin in the Cotton 1932 w. Irving Caesar, George White m. Harold Arlen. (MT) *George White's Music Hall Varieties*. Bert Lahr, Harry Richman, and Eleanor Powell appeared in *George White's Music Hall Varieties*.

Cabin in the Sky 1940 w. John Latouche m. Vernon Duke. (MT) *Cabin in the Sky*. (MF) *Cabin in the Sky*. Ethel Waters, Todd Duncan, and Katherine Dunbar appeared in the stage production of *Cabin in the Sky*. Ethel Waters and Lena Horne appeared in the film production of *Cabin in the Sky*.

Caddyshack, *see* **I'm Alright**

Cadillac Car 1982 w. Tom Eyen m. Henry Krieger. (MT) *Dream Girls*. Loretta Devine and Jennifer Holliday appeared in *Dream Girls*.

Cafe in Vienna 1934 w.m. Karel Vacek, Jimmy Kennedy

Cage in the Window, A 1934 w.m. Clark Gibson, Ray Morton

Caissons Go Rolling Along, The, *see* **The U.S. Field Artillery March**

Calcutta 1960 w. Lee Pockriss, Paul J. Vance m. Heino Gaze

Caldonia (What Makes Your Big Head So Hard) 1946 w.m. Fleecie Moore. (MF) *Swing Parade of 1946.*

Calendar Girl 1960 w.m. Howard Greenfield, Neil Sedaka

California Dreamin' 1966 w.m. John Phillips, Michele Gilliam Phillips. Theme song of The Mamas and the Papas.

California Girls 1965 w.m. Brian Wilson. This song was popularly revived in 1985.

California, Here I Come 1924 w.m. Al Jolson, B.G. DeSylva, Joseph Meyer. (MT) *Bombo.* (MT) *Big Boy.* (MF) *Lucky Boy.* (MF) *Rose of Washington Square.* (MF) *The Jolson Story.* (MF) *You're My Everything.* (MF) *Jolson Sings Again.* (MF) *With a Song in My Heart.* Al Jolson, Ralph Whitehead, and Franklyn Batie appeared in *Big Boy.* Al Jolson appeared in *Bombo* and *Rose of Washington Square.* George Jessel appeared in *Lucky Boy.* Larry Parks appeared in *The Jolson Story* and *Jolson Sings Again.* Dan Dailey and Anne Baxter appeared in *You're My Everything.* Susan Hayward appeared in *With a Song in My Heart,* biopic of singer Jane Froman.

California Nights 1967 w.m. Howard Leibling, Marvin Hamlisch

Call Me 1967 w.m. Tony Hatch. Ivor Novello Award winner 1966. This song was later used for a Bell Telephone Systems commercial promotion campaign.

Call Me 1980 w.m. Giorgio Moroder. (F) *American Gigolo.*

Call Me (Come Back Home) 1973 w.m. Al Green, Al Jackson, Jr.

Call Me Darling 1931 Ger.w. Bert Reisfeld, Mart Fryberg, Rolf Marbet Eng.w. Dorothy Dick m. Bert Reisfeld, Mort Fryberg, Rolf Marbet. From the German "Sag' Mir Darling."

Call Me Irresponsible 1963 w. Sammy Cahn m. Jimmy Van Heusen. (F) *Papa's Delicate Condition.* Jackie Gleason and Glynis Johns appeared in *Papa's Delicate Condition.* Academy Award winner 1963.

Call Me Mister 1946 w.m. Harold Rome. (MT) *Call Me Mister.* (MF) *Call Me Mister.* Betty Garrett and Bill Callahan appeared in the stage production of *Call Me Mister.* Betty Grable and Danny Thomas appeared in the film production of *Call Me Mister.*

Call Me Up Some Rainy Afternoon 1910 w.m. Irving Berlin

Call of the Canyon, The 1940 w.m. Billy Hill. (MF) *Call of the Canyon.* Gene Autry and Smiley Burnette appeared in *Call of the Canyon.*

Call of the Far-Away Hills, The 1952 w.m. Victor Young, Mack David. (F) *Shane.* Alan Ladd and Jean Arthur appeared in *Shane.*

Call Round Any Old Time 1908 w.m. Charles Moore, E.W. Rogers

Calling All Workers (March) 1940 w.m. Eric Coates

Calling to Her Boy Just Once Again 1900 w.m. Paul Dresser

Calvary 1887 w. Henry Vaughan m. Paul Rodney

Calypso 1975 w.m. John Denver

Camel Hop 1938 m. Mary Lou Williams

Camelot 1960 w. Alan Jay Lerner m. Frederick Loewe. (MT) *Camelot.* (MF) *Camelot.* Julie Andrews and Richard Burton appeared in the stage production of *Camelot.* Vanessa Redgrave and Richard Harris appeared in the film production of *Camelot.*

Caminito 1936 w.m. Penaloza Gabino Coria, Juan de Dios Filiberto

Campbells Are Coming, The 1745 w. Robert Burns. m. traditional, from Scotland. This song was possibly composed during the imprisonment of Mary Queen of Scots in Lochleven Castle in 1567; another version of the song's origin was that it was written about 1715 during the rebellion against George I. The hero of the rebellion was, of course, John Campbell. Possibly based on the traditional country dance "Hob or Nob."

Camptown Races, De see **De Camptown Races**

Can Anyone Explain? (No! No! No!) 1950 w.m. George Weiss, Bennie Benjamin

Can Can 1858 m. Jacques Offenbach. From the opera *Orphée dux Enfers (Orpheus in the Underworld),* which was first performed in Paris on October 21, 1858.

Can-Can 1953 w.m. Cole Porter. (MT) *Can-Can.* (MF) *Can-Can.* Frank Sinatra, Shirley MacLaine, and Juliet Prowse appeared in the film production of *Can-Can.*

Can I Forget You 1937 w. Oscar Hammerstein II m. Jerome Kern. (MF) *High, Wide and Handsome.* Irene Dunn and Randolph Scott appeared in *High, Wide and Handsome.*

Can I Leave Off Wearin' My Shoes 1955 w.m. Truman Capote, Harold Arlen. (MT) *House of Flowers*

Can I See You Tonight 1981 w.m. Deborah Allen, Rafe Van Hoy

Can It Be Love 1915 w.m. Paul Rubens, Adrian Ross. (MT) *Betty.*

Can This Be Love 1930 w. Paul James m. Kay Swift. (MT) *Fine and Dandy.* Joe Cook and Eleanor Powell appeared in *Fine and Dandy.*

Can This Be Love 1954 w.m. Irene Roper, Terence Roper, Robert Raglan

Can You Fool—(You Just Can't Forget Her) 1979 w.m. Michael Smotherman

Can You Imagine That, see **Mira**

Can You Read My Mind 1979 w.m. Leslie Bricusse, John Williams (F) *Superman.* Chris Reeves appeared in *Superman.*

Canadian Boat Song 1804 w. Thomas Moore m. French-Canadian tune of "Dans Mon Chemin." The lyric to this song was written by Moore while being towed down the St. Lawrence River and listening to the boatman who sang the melody "Dans Mon Chemin."

Canadian Capers 1915 w.m. Gus Chandler, Bert White, Henry Cohen. (MF) *My Dream Is Yours.* Doris Day and Jack Carson appeared in *My Dream Is Yours.*

Canadian Sunset 1956 w. Norman Gimbel m. Eddie Heywood

Canal Street Blues 1946 w.m. Joseph Oliver

Candida 1970 w.m. Toni Wine, Irwin Levine

Candlelight and Wine 1943 w.m. Harold Adamson, Jimmy McHugh. (MF) *Around the World*. Kay Kyser and Joan Davis appeared in *Around the World*.

Candles in the Rain, *see* **Lay Down**

Candy 1945 w.m. Mack David, Joan Whitney, Alex Kramer

Candy and Cake 1950 w.m. Bob Merrill

Candy Kisses 1949 w.m. George Morgan. (MF) *Down Dakota Way*. Roy Rogers and Dale Evans appeared in *Down Dakota Way*.

Candy Man, The 1972 w.m. Leslie Bricusse, Anthony Newley

Cannon Song, The 1907 w.m. Joseph Hewitt, Arthur Osborn. Princeton University fight song.

Canoe Song, The 1935 w.m. Micha Spoliansky, Arthur Wimperis. (MF) *Sanders of the River*. Paul Robeson appeared in *Sanders of the River*.

Can't Buy Me Love 1964 w.m. John Lennon, Paul McCartney. (MT) *Beatllemania*. Ivor Novello Award winner 1964.

Can't Fight This Feeling 1985 w.m. Kevin Cronin

Can't Get Enough of Your Love Babe 1974 w.m. Barry White

Can't Get Indiana Off My Mind 1940 w.m. Robert De Leon, Hoagy Carmichael

Can't Get Out of This Mood 1942 w. Frank Loesser m. Jimmy McHugh. (MF) *Seven Days Leave*. Victor Mature and Lucille Ball appeared in *Seven Days Leave*.

Can't Get Used To Losing You 1963 w.m. Doc Pomus, Mort Shuman

Can't Help Falling in Love (with You) 1961 w.m. George Weiss, Luigi Creatore, Hugo Peretti. (MF) *Blue Hawaii*. Elvis Presley and Angela Lansbury appeared in *Blue Hawaii*.

Can't Help Lovin' Dat Man 1927 w. Oscar Hammerstein II m. Jerome Kern. (MT) *Show Boat*. (MT) *Lena Horne: The Lady and Her Music. (MF) Show Boat* (1929). (MF) *Show Boat* (1936). (MF) *Show Boat* (1951). (MF) *Till the Clouds Roll By*. (MF) *Both Ends of the Candle*. Helen Morgan and Charles Winninger appeared in the American stage production of *Show Boat*. Marie Burke appeared in the British stage production of *Show Boat*. Lena Horne appeared in *Lena Horne: The Lady and Her Music*. Allan Jones and Irene Dunne appeared in the 1936 film production of *Show Boat*. Kathryn Grayson and Ava Gardner appeared in the 1951 film production of *Show Boat*. June Allyson, Frank Sinatra, Judy Garland, and Lena Horne appeared in *Till the Clouds Roll By*, biopic of composer Jerome Kern.

Can't Help Singing 1944 w. E.Y. Harburg m. Jerome Kern. (MF) *Can't Help Singing*. Deanna Durbin and Robert Paige appeared in *Can't Help Singing*.

Can't Smile Without You 1978 w.m. Geoff Morrow, Arnold Christian, David Isaacs

Can't Take My Eyes Off You 1967 w.m. Bob Crewe, Bob Gaudio

Can't We Be Friends 1929 w. Paul James m. Kay Swift. (MT) *The Little Show* (First Edition)

Can't We Talk It Over 1930 w. Ned Washington m. Victor Young. (F) *Illegal*. Edward G. Robinson and Jayne Mansfield appeared in *Illegal*. This song was popularly revived in 1950.

Can't Yo' Heah Me Callin', Caroline 1914 w.m. William H. Gardner, Caro Roma

Can't You Do a Friend a Favor 1943 w. Lorenz Hart m. Richard Rodgers. (MT) *A Connecticut Yankee. (MF) A Connecticut Yankee* (1949). This song was added to the 1943 stage production of *A Connecticut Yankee*. Bing Crosby appeared in the 1949 film production of *A Connecticut Yankee*.

Can't You Hear My Heart Beat 1965 w.m. Carter-Lewis

Can't You See That She's Mine 1964 w.m. Dave Clark, Mike Smith

Can't You Take It Back, and Change It for a Boy 1911 w.m. Thurland Chattaway

Can't You Understand 1929 w. Jack Osterman m. Victor Young

Cantique de Noël, *see* **Christmas Song**

Canto Siboney, *see* **Siboney**

Cape Ann 1843 w.m. anon. First performed in act 3, scene 5 of *The Two Noble Kinsmen*, this song was popularized by J.J. Hutchinson of the Hutchinson Family singers.

Cape Cod Girls 1830 w.m. traditional American sea chantey

Capital Ship, A c.1875 w.m. anon. This college song borrows its refrain ''Then blow ye winds, heigh-ho, a-roving I will go'' from Stephen Foster's ''De Camptown Races.''

Capitan, El (March) 1896 m. John Philip Sousa

Capped Teeth and Caesar Salad 1985 w. Don Black, Richard Maltby, Jr. m. Andrew Lloyd Webber. (MT) *Song and Dance*. Bernadette Peters appeared in *Song and Dance*.

Capriccio Espagnol, op. 34 1888 m. Nikolai Rimsky-Korsakov

Caprice Viennois 1910 m. Fritz Kreisler

Captain Gingah 1913 w.m. George Bastow, F.W. Leigh

Captain Hook's Waltz 1954 w. Betty Comden, Adolph Green m. Jule Styne. (MT) *Peter Pan*. Mary Martin and Cyril Ritchard appeared in *Peter Pan*.

Captain Jinks of the Horse Marines 1868 w.m. William Horace Lingard m. T. Maclagan. This song was first performed in America by the British Lingard Comedy Company, at the Theatre Comique in New York.

Captain Kidd, *see* **Wond'rous Love**

Captain Noah and His Floating Zoo 1976 w.m. Michael Flanders, Joseph Horovitz

Car Wash 1977 w.m. Norman Whitfield. (F) *Car Wash*. Richard Pryor appeared in *Car Wash*.

Cara Mia 1954 w.m. Tulio Tranpani, Lee Lange

Caramba It's the Samba 1948 w.m. George Wyle, Edward Pola, Irving Taylor

Caravan 1937 w. Irving Mills m. Duke Ellington, Juan Tizol. (MT) *Sophisticated Ladies*. Gregory Hines and Phyllis Hyman appeared in *Sophisticated Ladies*.

Caravans 1980 w.m. Mike Batt. Ivor Novello Award winner 1979–80.

Careless 1940 w.m. Lew Quadling, Eddy Howard, Dick Jurgens

Careless Hands 1949 w.m. Bob Hilliard, Carl Sigman

Careless (Kelly's) Love 1911 w.m. anon. First printed version this year, but probably traditional, 1840–95.

Careless Love 1921 w.m. W.C. Handy, Spencer Williams, Martha Koenig. (MF) *St. Louis Blues*. Nat "King" Cole and Eartha Kitt appeared in *St. Louis Blues*, biopic of W.C. Handy.

Careless Whisper 1985 w.m. George Michael, Andrew Ridgeley. Ivor Novello Award winner 1984–85.

Caribbean Queen (No More Love on the Run) 1984 w.m. Keith Diamond, Leslie Charles, Billy Ocean

Carioca 1933 w. Gus Kahn, Edward Eliscu m. Vincent Youmans. (MF) *Flying Down to Rio*. Dolores Del Rio and Fred Astaire appeared in *Flying Down to Rio*.

Carissima 1905 w.m. Arthur Penn

Carle Boogie 1945 w.m. Frankie Carle

Carlos' Theme 1963 w.m. Ivor Slaney

Carmen Etonense uncertain w.m. J. Barnby. Eton school song.

(Theme from) Carnival, *see* **Love Makes the World Go Round**

Carnival Is Over, The 1965 w.m. Tom Springfield

Carnival of Venice 1854 m. J. Bellak

Carol of the Bells 1936 Eng.w. Peter J. Wilhousky m. M. Leontovich. A popular Ukranian Christmas carol.

Carolina 1945 w.m. Max Nesbitt, Harry Nesbitt, Jack Stodel

Carolina in the Morning 1922 w. Gus Kahn m. Walter Donaldson. (MT) *Passing Show of 1922*. (MF) *The Dolly Sisters*. (MF) *April Showers*. (MF) *Jolson Sings Again*. (MF) *I'll See You In My Dreams*. Betty Grable and June Haver appeared in *The Dolly Sisters*. Ann Sheridan and Robert Alda appeared in *April Showers*. Larry Parks appeared in *Jolson Sings Again*. Doris Day and Danny Thomas appeared in *I'll See You in My Dreams*, biopic of song writer Gus Kahn.

Carolina in the Pines 1975 w.m. Michael Murphey

Carolina Moon 1928 w.m. Benny Davis, Joe Burke. Theme song of Morton Downey.

Carolina Sunshine 1919 w. Walter Hirsch m. Erwin R. Schmidt

Carousel 1968 Eng.w. Eric Blau, Mort Shuman m. Jacques Brel. (MT) *Jacques Brel Is Alive and Well and Living in Paris*.

Carousel Waltz 1945 m. Richard Rodgers. (MT) *Carousel*. (MF) *Carousel*. Gordon MacRae and Shirley Jones appeared in the film production of *Carousel*.

Carrie, or, **Carrie Marry Harry** 1909 w. Junie McCree m. Albert Von Tilzer. (F) *Flame of the Barbary Coast*. John Wayne and Ann Dvorak appeared in *Flame of the Barbary Coast*.

Carrier Dove, The 1836 w. anon. m. Daniel Johnson

Carry Me Back to Green Pastures 1933 w.m. Harry S. Pepper

Carry Me Back to Old Virginny 1878 w.m. James A. Bland. (F) *Hullabaloo*. Frank Morgan and Billie Burke appeared in *Hullabaloo*. This song later became the official state song of Virginia. Along with writing his seven hundred songs, James Bland was also the first black examiner in the U.S. Patent Office.

Carry Me Back to Ole Virginny, or, **De Floating Show** 1847 w.m. Charles T. White

Carry Me Back to Tennessee, *see* **Ellie Rhee**

Carry Me Back to the Lone Prairie 1934 w.m. Carson J. Robison. (MF) *Stars Over Broadway*. James Melton and Jane Froman appeared in *Stars Over Broadway*.

Casanova 1962 w.m. Karl Götz

Casey Jones 1909 w. T. Lawrence Seibert m. Eddie Newton. (MF) *Sunset in Wyoming*. Gene Autry and Smiley Burnette appeared in *Sunset in Wyoming*. The narrative of this song concerns the heroism of John Luther "Casey" Jones, engineer of the "Cannon Ball Express" on the Illinois Central Railroad. On the April 29, 1900, run, sensing an impending collision, Jones had everyone else aboard jump off, save himself. Wallace Saunders, his black engine-wiper, possibly wrote this ballad about his friend Casey. See also Part I, 1947.

Casey Would Waltz with the Strawberry Blonde, *see* **The Band Played On**

(Theme from) Casino Royale 1967 w. Hal David m. Burt Bacharach. (F) *Casino Royale*.

Cast Your Fate to the Wind 1962 w.m. Vince Guaraldi

Castle of Dreams 1919 w. Joseph McCarthy m. Harry Tierney. (MT) *Irene*. (MF) *Irene*. Anna Neagle and Ray Milland appeared in the British production of *Irene*. Based on the middle section of Chopin's Minute Waltz.

Castles in the Air 1982 w.m. Don McLean

Cat Came Back, The 1893 w.m. Henry S. Miller

Catch a Falling Star 1958 w.m. Paul Vance, Lee Pockriss

Catch the Wind 1965 w.m. Donovan. Ivor Novello Award winner 1965.

Catch Us If You Can 1965 w.m. Leonard Davidson, Dave Clark. (F) *Catch Us If You Can*.

Cathedral in the Pines 1938 w.m. Charles Kenny, Nick Kenny

Cathy's Clown 1960 w.m. Don Everly, Phil Everly

Cat's in the Cradle 1974 w.m. Harry Chapin, Sandra C. Chapin

Cattle Call 1934 w.m. Tex Owens

Cavalry of the Steppes, *see* **Meadowlands**

Cavatina 1861 m. Joachin Raff. No.3 in "Six Morceaux," op.85.

Cavatina 1977 w.m. Stanley Myers. Ivor Novello Award winner 1977–78.

Cecile Waltz 1914 m. Frank W. McKee

(Does Your Mother Know You're Out) Cecilia 1925 w. Herman Ruby m. Dave Dreyer

Celebratin' 1936 w.m. Harry Woods

Celebration 1981 w.m. Robert Earl Bell, Ronald Nathan Bell, George M. Brown, Eumir Deodato, Robert Mickens, Claydes Eugene Smith, James Warren Taylor, Dennis Ronald Thomas, Earl Eugene Toon, Jr.

Celery Stalks at Midnight 1940 w.m. Carl Sigman

Cement Mixer (Put-ti Put-ti) 1946 w.m. Slim Gaillard, Lee Ricks

Centerfold 1982 w.m. Seth Justman

Certain Smile, A 1958 w. Paul Francis Webster m. Sammy Fain. (F) *A Certain Smile.* Rosanno Brazzi appeared in *A Certain Smile.*

C'est Fini, *see* **Dark Is the Night**

C'est la Vie 1961 w. Carolyn Leigh m. Cy Coleman

C'est Magnifique 1953 w.m. Cole Porter. (MT) *Can-Can.* (MF) *Can-Can.* Frank Sinatra, Maurice Chevalier, and Shirley MacLaine appeared in the film production of *Can-Can.*

C'est Si Bon 1950 Fr.w. André Hornez Eng.w. Jerry Seelen m. Henri Betti, André Hornez. (MT) *Latin Quarter.* (MF) *New Faces.* Eartha Kitt appeared in *New Faces.* This song was popularly revived in 1953.

C'est Vous (It's You) 1927 w.m. Abner Greenberg, Abner Silver, Harry Richman

Cha Cha Cha, The 1962 w.m. Kal Mann, Dave Appell

Chain Gang 1956 w.m. Sam Cooke. This song was popularly revived in 1960.

Champagne Charley Was His Name 1867 w. H.J. Whymark m. Alfred Lee

Champagne Waltz, The 1934 w.m. Milton Drake, Ben Oakland, Con Conrad. (MF) *The Champagne Waltz.* Fred MacMurray and Jack Oakie appeared in *The Champagne Waltz.*

Chances Are 1957 w. Al Stillman m. Robert Allen

Change Partners 1938 w.m. Irving Berlin. (MF) *Carefree.* Fred Astaire and Ginger Rogers appeared in *Carefree.*

Changes 1927 w.m. Walter Donaldson

Changing My Tune 1946 w. Ira Gershwin m. George Gershwin (MF) *The Shocking Miss Pilgrim.* Betty Grable and Ann Revere appeared in *The Shocking Miss Pilgrim.*

Changing of the Guard, The 1932 w.m. Flotsam and Jetsam (B.C. Hilliam, Malcolm McEachern)

Changing Partners 1953 w. Joe Darion m. Larry Coleman

Chanson 1920 m. Rudolf Friml. See also "Chansonette."

Chanson d'Amour (Song of Love) 1958 w.m. Wayne Shanklin

Chansonette 1923 w. Sigmund Spaeth m. Rudolph Friml. Based on Friml's "Chanson" of 1920, with lyrics added. This song was included in Paul Whiteman's historic program a year later that introduced Gershwin's "Rhapsody in Blue" and it would reappear later in the screen version of Friml's *Firefly* as "The Donkey Serenade".

Chant of the Jungle 1929 w. Arthur Freed m. Nacio Herb Brown. (F) *Untamed.* Joan Crawford and Robert Montgomery appeared in *Untamed.*

Chant sans Paroles 1868 m. Peter Tchaikovsky

Chantez Chantez 1957 w. Albert Gamse m. Irving Fields

Chanticleer Rag, The 1910 w. Edward Madden m. Albert Gumble

Chantilly Lace 1958 w.m. J.P. Richardson. This song was popularly revived in 1973.

Chapel of Love 1964 w.m. Jeff Barry, Ellie Greenwich, Phil Spector. (OB) *Leader of the Pack.*

(Theme from) Charade 1963 w. Johnny Mercer m. Henry Mancini. (F) *Charade.* Cary Grant and Audrey Hepburn appeared in *Charade.*

(Theme from) Chariots of Fire 1982 m. Vangelis. (F) *Chariots of Fire.*

Charleston 1923 w.m. Cecil Mack, James Johnson. (MT) *Runnin' Wild.* (MF) *You're My Everything.* Anne Baxter appeared in *You're My Everything.* Theme song of Ann Pennington.

Charley, My Boy 1924 w.m. Gus Kahn, Ted Fiorito

Charlie Brown 1959 w.m. Jerry Leiber, Mike Stoller

Charlie Is My Darlin' 1824 w.m. traditional, from Scotland

Charmaine 1926 w.m. Erno Rapee, Lew Pollack. (F) *What Price Glory?* (F) *Sunset Boulevard.* Edmund Lowe and Victor McLaglen appeared in *What Price Glory?* Gloria Swanson appeared in *Sunset Boulevard.* This song was written for the piano and orchestra accompaniment of the earlier silent film classic *What Price Glory?*

Charming Young Widow I Met on the Train, The 1868 w.m. W.H. Gove

Chasing Rainbows, *see* **I'm Always Chasing Rainbows**

Chasing Shadows 1935 w.m. Abner Silver, Benny Davis

Chattanooga Choo Choo 1941 w. Mack Gordon m. Harry Warren. (MT) *The 1940's Radio Hour.* (MF) *Sun Valley Serenade.* (MF) *Springtime in the Rockies.* (MF) *The Glenn Miller Story.* Sonja Henie, Milton Berle, and Glenn Miller appeared in *Sun Valley Serenade.*

Chattanoogie Shoe Shine Boy 1950 w.m. Harry Stone, Jack Stapp (F) *Indian Territory* Gene Autry appeared in *Indian Territory.*

Cheatin' on Me 1925 w. Jack Yellen m. Lew Pollack

Cheek to Cheek 1935 w.m. Irving Berlin (MF) *Top Hat* Fred Astaire and Ginger Rogers appeared in *Top Hat.* This song bears a slight resemblance to Chopin's Polonaise in A-flat.

Cheer, Boys, Cheer 1843 w. Charles Mackay m. Henry Russell. This song became the traditional march of the British fifes and drums played for the departure of a regiment.

Cheer, Cheer for Old Notre Dame uncertain w.m. John Shea, Michael Shea. Victory march for Notre Dame.

Cheerful Little Earful 1930 w. Ira Gershwin, Billy Rose m. Harry Warren. (MT) *Sweet and Low.* James Barton, Fannie Brice, and George Jessel appeared in *Sweet and Low.* Theme song of Hannah Williams.

Chelsea Morning 1967 w.m. Joni Mitchell

Cherchez la Femme 1976 w.m. August Darnell, Stony Browder, Jr.

Cherie (Cherie, Je T'Aime) 1926 w.m. Lillian Rosedale Goodman

Cherish 1966 w.m. Terry Kirkman. This song was popularly revived in 1971.

Cherish 1985 w.m. Robert Bell, Ronald Bell, James Bonnefond, George Brown, Claydes Eugene Smith, James Taylor, Curtis Williams

Cherokee 1939 w.m. Ray Noble. (MF) *Jam Session.* (MF) *Drum Crazy.* Ann Miller and Louis Armstrong appeared in *Jam Session.*

Cherry 1928 w. Ray Gilbert, Don Redman m. Don Redman

Cherry 1941 w.m. Charles N. Daniels

Cherry Blossom Lane, *see* **It Looks Like Rain in Cherry Blossom Lane**

Cherry Pink and Apple Blossom White 1955 Fr.w. Jacques Larue Eng.w. Mack David m. "Louiquy." (F) *Underwater.* Jane Russell and Gilbert Roland appeared in *Underwater.*

Cherry Ripe 1825 w. Robert Herrick m. Charles Edward Horn

Chester (Let Tyrants Shake Their Iron Rod) 1778 w.m. William Billings. This colonial marching song was the first original popular song composition by an American; Billings was blind in one eye and short in one leg and believed that everyone should sing.

Chestnut Tree, The 1938 w.m. Jimmy Kennedy, Tommie Connor, Hamilton Kennedy

Chestnuts Roasting on an Open Fire, *see* **The Christmas Song**

Chevy Van 1975 w.m. Sammy Johns

Chewing a Piece of Straw 1945 w.m. Howard Barnes, Hedley Grey

Cheyenne 1906 w. Harry H. Williams m. Egbert Van Alstyne

Chi-Baba Chi-Baba (My Bambino Go to Sleep) 1947 w.m. Mack David, Al Hoffman, Jerry Livingston

Chiapanecas (While There's Music There's Romance) 1938 Sp.w. Emilio de Torre Eng.w. Albert Garuse m. V. de Campo; arr. Ricardo Romero. (F) *Girl from Mexico.* Lupe Velez and Donald Woods appeared in *Girl from Mexico.* This song was popularly revived in 1944.

Chica Chica Boom Chic 1941 w.m. Mack Gordon, Harry Warren. (MF) *That Night in Rio.* Carmen Miranda and Don Ameche appeared in *That Night in Rio.*

Chicago (That Toddlin' Town) 1922 w.m. Fred Fisher. (MF) *Oh You Beautiful Doll.* (MF) *With a Song in My Heart.* (MF) *The Joker Is Wild.* (MF) *The Story of Vernon and Irene Castle.* June Haver appeared in *Oh You Beautiful Doll.* Susan Hayward appeared in *With a Song in My Heart,* biopic of singer Jane Froman. Frank Sinatra appeared in *The Joker Is Wild,* biopic of Joe E. Lewis. Fred Astaire and Ginger Rog-

ers appeared in *The Story of Vernon and Irene Castle.* This song was popularly revived in 1939.

Chick 1959 w.m. Joe Henderson

Chick-a-Pen 1960 w.m. Meredith Willson. (MT) *The Unsinkable Molly Brown.* (MF) *The Unsinkable Molly Brown.* Tammy Grimes appeared in the stage production of *The Unsinkable Molly Brown.* Debbie Reynolds appeared in the film production of *The Unsinkable Molly Brown.*

Chick Chick Chicken 1925 w.m. Thomas McGhee, Fred Holt, Irving King

Chicken Reel, The 1910 m. Joseph M. Daly. This song was originally published as "Two-Step and Buck Dance."

Chickery Chick 1945 w.m. Sylvia Dee, Sidney Lippman

Child Love 1911 w. Dave Oppenheim m. Joe Cooper.

Children and Art 1984 w.m. Stephen Sondheim. (MT) *Sunday in the Park with George.* Mandy Patinkin and Bernadette Peters appeared in *Sunday in the Park with George.*

Children of Rome 1974 w.m. Stanley Myers. Ivor Novello Award winner 1973–74.

Children's Marching Song, The, *see* **This Old Man**

Chili Bean (Eenie Meenie Minie Mo) 1920 w. Lew Brown m. Albert Von Tilzer. (MT) *Pot Luck.*

Chim Chim Cher-ee 1964 w.m. Richard M. Sherman, Robert B. Sherman. (MF) *Mary Poppins.* Julie Andrews and Dick Van Dyke appeared in *Mary Poppins.* Academy Award winner 1964.

Chimes Blues 1923 w.m. Joe Oliver

Chimes of Spring, *see* **Spring, Beautiful Spring**

Chin, Chin, Chinaman 1896 w. Harry Greenbank m. Sidney Jones. (MT) *The Geisha.*

Chin Up, Ladies! 1961 w.m. Jerry Herman. (MT) *Milk and Honey.*

China Boy 1922 w.m. Dick Winfree, Phil Boutelje. (MF) *The Benny Goodman Story.*

China Tea 1959 w.m. Trevor Stanford

Chinaman's Song, The 1921 w.m. Percy Fletcher, Oscar Asche. (MT) *Cairo.* Frank Cochrane appeared in *Cairo.*

Chinatown, My Chinatown 1906 w. William Jerome m. Jean Schwartz. (MT) *Up and Down Broadway.* (MT) *Push and Go.* (MF) *Bright Lights.* (MF) *Is Everybody Happy.* (MF) *Jolson Sings Again.* (MF) *The Seven Little Foys.* Shirley Kellog appeared in *Push and Go.* Frank Fay and Noah Beery appeared in *Bright Lights.* Larry Parks appeared in *Is Everybody Happy,* biopic of bandleader Ted Lewis, and *Jolson Sings Again.* Bob Hope appeared in *The Seven Little Foys.*

Chinese Laundry Blues 1932 w.m. Jack Cottrell, George Formby

Chinese Lullaby 1919 w.m. Robert Hood Bowers. (MT) *East Is West.*

Ching A Ring Chaw, or, **Sambo's Address to His Bred'ren** 1833 w.m. anon. This song was adapted and arranged years later by Aaron Copland.

Chipmunk Song, The, or, **Christmas Don't Be Late** 1958 w.m. Ross Bagdasarian

Chiquita 1928 w. L. Wolfe Gilbert m. Mabel Wayne

(I'm) Chiquita Banana 1938 w.m. Len Mackenzie, Garth Montgomery, William Wirges. (MT) *The 1940's Radio Hour* This song was popularly revived in 1946. Beginning in 1946, it was used for a Chiquita Banana commercial promotion campaign.

Chirpy Chirpy, Cheep Cheep 1971 w.m. Larry Stott

Chrisholm Trail, *see* **The Old Chisholm Trail**

Chitty Chitty Bang Bang 1968 w.m. Richard Sherman, Robert Sherman. (F) *Chitty Chitty Bang Bang.* Dick Van Dyke appeared in *Chitty Chitty Bang Bang.*

Chloe 1927 w.m. Gus Kahn, Charles N. Daniels

Choclo, El 1913 w. Francice Luban m. A.G. Villoldo. The words to this song were not published in the original 1913 edition. This song is the classic, standard tango, of Argentine origin. See also "Kiss of Fire."

Chon Kina 1896 w. Harry Greenbank m. Sidney Jones. (MT) *The Geisha.*

Chong, He Come from Hong Kong 1919 w.m. Harold Weeks. (MT) *Bran Pie.* Beatrice Lillie and Odette Myrtil appeared in *Bran Pie.*

Choo-Choo Honeymoon 1968 w. George Haimsohn, Robin Miller m. Jim Wise. (MT) *Dames at Sea.* Bernadette Peters appeared in *Dames at Sea.*

Choo Choo Train 1953 Eng.w. Jack Lawrence m. Marc Fontenoy

Chopsticks 1877 m. Arthur de Lulli. The original title for this piece was "The Celebrated Chop Waltz." On page 3 of the original publication of this standard was written: "This part (primo part of the duet) must be played with both hands turned sideways, the little fingers the lowest, so that the movements of the hands imitate the chopping; from which the waltz gets its name." Arthur de Lulli was the pseudonym for Euphemia Allen. Variations of this theme were written by both Alexander Borodin and Rimsky-Korsakov.

Christmas in Killarney 1950 w.m. John Redmond, James Cavanaugh, Frank Weldon

Christmas Island 1959 w.m. Lyle L. Moraine

Christmas Song, or, O Holy Night 1858 Eng.w. John Sullivan Dwight m. Adolphe Adam. From the French "Cantique de Noël."

Christmas Song, The, or, Merry Christmas to You, or, Chestnuts Roasting on an Open Fire 1946 w.m. Mel Torme, Robert Wells

Christopher Columbus 1936 w. Andy Razaf m. Leon Berry

Christopher Robin at Buckingham Palace 1924 w.m. A.A. Milne, Harold Fraser-Simson

Christopher Robin Is Saying His Prayers 1935 w.m. A.A. Milne, Harold Fraser-Simson

Chrysanthemum Tea 1976 w.m. Stephen Sondheim. (MT) *Pacific Overtures.* Mako appeared in *Pacific Overtures.*

Chuck E's in Love 1979 w.m. Rickie Lee Jones

Church in the Wildwood, The, *see* **The Little Brown Church in the Vale**

Church of the Poison Mind 1984 w.m. Michael Craig, Boy George, Roy Hay, Jon Moss

Church's One Foundation, The 1864 w. Samuel Stone m. Samuel Wesley

Ciao Ciao Bambina 1959 w.m. Domenico Modugno, Mitchell Parish, Edoardo Verde

Cielito Lindo (Ay, Ay, Ay, Ay) 1919 w.m. Quirino Mendoza y Cortéz; arr. Neil Wilson, Carlo Fernandez, Sebastian Yradier. (MF) *Casa Mañana.* Robert Clarke and Virginia Welles appeared in *Casa Mañana.*

Cigarette 1905 w.m. Herbert Haines, Evelyn Baker, Charles Taylor (MT) *The Catch of the Season*

Cimarron (Roll On) 1942 w.m. Johnny Bond. (MF) *Twilight on the Trail.* (MF) *Heart of the Rio Grande.* Bill Boyd and Brand King appeared in *Twilight on the Trail.* Gene Autry and Smiley Burnette appeared in *Heart of the Rio Grande.*

Cinco Robles (Five Oaks) 1956 w.m. Larry Sullivan, Dorothy Wright

Cinderella 1949 w.m. Mack David, Al Hoffman, Jerry Livingston. (MF) *Cinderella.*

Cinderella Brown 1930 w. Dorothy Fields m. Jimmy McHugh. (MT) *Lew Leslie's International Revue.* Gertrude Lawrence and Florence Moore appeared in *Lew Leslie's International Revue.*

Cinderella, Stay in My Arms, *see* **Stay in My Arms, Cinderella**

Cinderella Sweetheart 1938 w.m. Art Strauss, Bob Dale

Cindy c.1840 w.m. traditional American folk ballad

Cindy Oh Cindy 1956 w.m. Bob Barron, Burt Long

Cinquantaine, La 1887 m. Gabriel Marie

Circus Is on Parade, The 1935 w. Lorenz Hart m. Richard Rodgers. (MT) *Jumbo.* (MF) *Jumbo.* Jimmy Durante and Gloria Grafton appeared in *Jumbo.*

Ciribiribin 1898 w. Rudolf Thaler m. Alberto Pestalozza. (MF) *One Night of Love.* (MF) *Hit the Deck.* (F) *Heaven Can Wait.* Grace Moore appeared in *One Night of Love.* Jane Powell and Debbie Reynolds appeared in *Hit the Deck.* Warren Beatty appeared in *Heaven Can Wait.* This song was popularly revived in 1943. Theme song of Harry James.

Cisco Kid, The 1973 w.m. Sylvester Allen, Harold Ray Brown, Morris D. Dickerson, Leroy L. Jordan, Lee Oskar Levitin, Charles Miller, Howard E. Scott

City Lights 1978 w. Fred Ebb m. John Kander. (MT) *The Act.* Liza Minnelli and Barry Nelson appeared in *The Act.*

City of Laughter, City of Tears 1920 w.m. Horatio Nicholls

City of New Orleans 1984 w.m. Steve Goodman. Grammy Award winner 1984.

Civilization (Bongo Bongo Bongo) 1947 w. Bob Hilliard m. Carl Sigman. (MT) *Angel in the Wings.*

Clair de Lune 1905 m. Claude Debussy. From "Suite Bergamesque."

Claire 1972 w.m. Gilbert O'Sullivan. Ivor Novello Award winner 1972–73.

Clancy Lowered the Boom 1949 w.m. Hy Heath, Johnny Lange

Clap Hands, Here Comes Charley 1925 w. Ballard

MacDonald, Billy Rose   m. Joseph Meyer. Theme song of Charlie Kunz.

Clap Yo' Hands 1926 w. Ira Gershwin m. George Gershwin. (MT) *Oh, Kay!.* (MF) *Rhapsody in Blue.* (MF) *Funny Face.* Victor Moore, Gerald Oliver Smith, and Gertrude Lawrence appeared in the American production of *Oh, Kay!.* Claude Hulbert and Gertrude Lawrence appeared in the British production of *Oh, Kay!.* Oscar Levant, Robert Alda, and Alexis Smith appeared in *Rhapsody in Blue,* biopic of George Gershwin. Fred Astaire, Audrey Hepburn, and Kay Thompson appeared in *Funny Face.*

Clapping Song, The, or, **My Mother Told Me** 1965 w.m. Lincoln Chase

Clare De Kitchen, or, **De Kentucky Screamer** c.1835 w.m. anon.

Clarinet Marmalade 1918 w.m. Edwin B. Edwards, D. James La Rocca, Anthony Sbarbaro, Larry Shields

Class 1975 w. Fred Ebb m. John Kander. (MT) *Chicago.* Chita Rivera and Gwen Verdon appeared in *Chicago.*

Classical Gas 1968 w.m. Mason Williams

Clavelitos (Carnations) 1909 Sp.w. Estic Valverde, Joaquin Valverde Eng.w. Mrs. M.T.E. Sandwith m. Estic Valverde, Joaquin Valverde

Clear Out of This World 1940 w. Al Dubin m. Jimmy McHugh. (MT) *Keep Off the Grass.* Jimmy Durante, Ray Bolger, and Jane Froman appeared in *Keep Off the Grass.*

(Oh, My Darling) Clementine 1884 w.m. Percy Montrose. This song was popularly revived in 1960.

Cleopatterer 1917 w. P.G. Wodehouse m. Jerome Kern. (MT) *Leave It to Jane.* (MF) *Till the Clouds Roll By.* Oscar Shaw and Georgia O'Ramey appeared in *Leave It to Jane.* Judy Garland, Robert Walker, and June Allyson appeared in *Till the Clouds Roll By,* biopic of composer Jerome Kern.

Climb Ev'ry Mountain 1959 w. Oscar Hammerstein II m. Richard Rodgers. (MT) *The Sound of Music.* (MF) *The Sound of Music.* Mary Martin appeared in the stage production of *The Sound of Music.* Julie Andrews appeared in the film production of *The Sound of Music.*

Climbing Up 1937 w.m. Eric Maschwitz, Mischa Spoliansky. (F) *King Solomon's Mines.* Steward Granger and Deborah Kerr appeared in *King Solomon's Mines.*

Climbing Up the Golden Stairs 1884 w.m. traditional black American spiritual, possibly from as early as 1860

Climbing Up the Ladder of Love 1926 w. Raymond Klages m. Jesse Greer. (MT) *Earl Carroll's Varieties (Fifth Edition).*

Clinging Vine 1964 w.m. Leon Carr, Grace Lane, Earl Shuman

Clopin Clopant 1949 w.m. Kermit Goell, Pierre Dudan, Bruno Coquatrix. (MT) *Latin Quarter.*

Close 1937 w.m. Cole Porter. (MF) *Rosalie.* This song was written for Nelson Eddy, who appeared with Eleanor Powell and Ray Bolger in *Rosalie.*

Close as Pages in a Book 1945 w. Dorothy Fields m. Sigmund Romberg. (MT) *Up in Central Park.* (MF) *Up in Central Park.* Maureen Cannon and Betty Bruce appeared in the stage production of *Up in Central Park.* Deanna Durbin appeared in the film production of *Up in Central Park.*

(Theme from) Close Encounters of the Third Kind 1977 m. John Williams. (F) *Close Encounters of the Third Kind.* Grammy Award winner 1978.

Close Enough to Perfect 1982 w.m. Carl Chambers

Close to My Heart 1915 w. Andrew B. Sterling m. Harry Von Tilzer

Close to You 1943 w.m. Al Hoffman, Carl G. Lampe, Jerry Livingston

(They Long To Be) Close to You 1970 w. Hal David m. Burt Bacharach

Close Your Eyes 1933 w.m. Bernice Petkere

Closer I Get to You, The 1978 w.m. Reggie Lucas, James Mtume

Clown, The 1982 w.m. Brenda Barnett, Charles Chalmer, Sandra Rhodes, Wayne Carson

Coal Black Mammy 1921 w. Laddie Cliff m. Ivy St. Helier. (MT) *The Co-Optimists.*

Coal Black Rose, The 1827 w.m. anon.; sometimes attributed to White Snyder. This song was made popular by black minstrel George Washington Dixon. He later wrote two afterpiece expansions as a result of his success, ''The Lottery Ticket'' of 1829 and ''Love in a Cloud'' of 1830.

Coax Me a Little Bit 1946 w. Charles Tobias m. Nat Simon

Cobbler's Song, The 1916 w. Oscar Asche m. Frederick Norton. (MT) *Chu Chin Chow.* Frank Cochrane and Violet Essex appeared in *Chu Chin Chow.*

Coca-Cola Cowboy (Theme from *Every Which Way But Loose*) 1979 w.m. Samuel Lee Atchley. (F) *Every Which Way But Loose.*

Cockeyed Mayor of Kaunakakai 1935 w.m. R. Alex Anderson, Al Stillman

Cockeyed Optimist, A 1949 w. Oscar Hammerstein II m. Richard Rodgers. (MT) *South Pacific.* (MF) *South Pacific.* Mary Martin appeared in the stage production of *South Pacific.* Mitzi Gaynor appeared in the film production of *South Pacific.*

Cockles and Mussels, Alive, Alive, O!, or, **Sweet Molly Malone** c.1750 w.m. traditional, from Ireland

Cocktails for Two 1934 w.m. Arthur Johnston, Sam Coslow. (MF) *Murder at the Vanities.* (MF) *Ladies' Man.* Carl Brisson and Jack Oakie appeared in *Murder at the Vanities.* Eddie Bracken and Spike Jones appeared in *Ladies' Man.* This song was popularly revived in 1945. Theme song of Carl Brisson.

Coco 1969 w. Alan Jay Lerner m. André Previn. (MT) *Coco.* Katharine Hepburn appeared in *Coco,* a musical based on the life of dress designer Gabrielle Chanel.

Cocoanut Grove 1938 w.m. Harry Owens. (MF) *Cocoanut Grove.* Fred MacMurray, Ben Blue, and Eve Arden appeared in *Cocoanut Grove.*

Cocoanut Sweet 1957 w. E.Y. Harburg m. Harold Arlen. (MT) *Jamaica.*

Coffee in the Morning, Kisses at Night 1934 w.m. Al Dubin, Harry Warren. (MF) *Moulin Rouge.* Constance Bennett and Helen Wesley appeared in *Moulin Rouge*. This song was most popular in 1939.

Coffee Song, The (They've Got an Awful Lot of Coffee in Brazil) 1947 w.m. Bob Hilliard, Dick Miles. (MT) *Piccadilly Hayride*

Cokey Cokey, The, or, **The Hokey Cokey** 1945 w.m. traditional; Eng.w. Jimmy Kennedy

Colas Breugnon 1946 m. Dmitri Kabalevsky

Cold Cold Heart 1951 w.m. Hank Williams. (MF) *Apache Country*. Gene Autry and Pat Buttram appeared in *Apache Country*.

Colditz 1973 w.m. Robert Farnon. Ivor Novello Award winner 1972–73.

(La La) Colette 1956 w.m. Leon Pober

Colette 1960 w.m. Billy Fury

College Life 1906 w. Porter Emerson Browne m. Henry Frantzen

College Rhythm 1934 w.m. Mack Gordon, Harry Revel. (MF) *College Rhythm*. Joe Penner and Lanny Ross appeared in *College Rhythm*

Collegiate 1925 w.m. Moe Jaffe, Nat Bonx. (MT) *Gay Paree*. (MF) *The Time, the Place and the Girl*. (MF) *Animal Crackers*. Grant Withers and James Kirkwood appeared in *The Time, the Place and the Girl*. The Marx Brothers appeared in *Animal Crackers*.

Colonel Bogey (Bogie) March 1916 m. Kenneth J. Alford (Major F.J. Ricketts). (F) *The Bridge on the River Kwai*. The composer of this song was the band master of the Second Battalion, Argyll and Sutherland Highlanders. See also "The River Kwai March."

Colonel's Tune, The 1958 w.m. Johnny Dankworth. Ivor Novello Award winner 1958.

Color Him Father 1969 w.m. Richard Spencer. Grammy Award winner 1969.

Color My World 1966 w.m. Jackie Trent, Tony Hatch. This song was popularly revived in 1971.

Colors of My Life, The 1980 w. Michael Stewart m. Cy Coleman. (MT) *Barnum*. Jim Dale and Glen Close appeared in *Barnum*.

Colours 1965 w.m. Donovan

Columbia, the Gem of the Ocean, or, **The Red, White and Blue** 1843 w.m. David T. Shaw, T.A. Beckett. The earliest English edition of "Britannia the Gem of the Ocean" is dated at 1852; w. Stephen Joseph Meany (1842) m. Thomas E. Williams.

The American version of this song, originally copyrighted under the title "Columbia the Land of the Brave," is dated at 1843; its authors are listed above. This song is also known as "The Army and Navy Song."

Comancheros, The 1961 w.m. Tillman Franks

Come a Little Bit Closer 1964 w.m. Wes Farrell, Bobby Hart, Tommy Boyce. This song was popularly revived in 1978.

Come After Breakfast, Bring 'Long Your Lunch and Leave 'Fore Supper Time 1909 w.m. J. Tim Bryman, Chris Smith, James Henry Burris

Come Along My Mandy 1907 w.m. Tom Mellor, Alfred J. Lawrence, Harry Gifford; also credited to Jack Norworth and Nora Bayes. (MT) *The Jolly Bachelors*. Jack Norworth and Nora Bayes appeared in *The Jolly Bachelors*. This song was most popular in 1910.

Come and Get Your Love 1974 w.m. Lolly Vegas

Come and Have a Swing with Me 1917 w. Anne Caldwell m. Ivan Caryll. (MT) *Jack o' Lantern*.

Come Back and Shake Me 1970 w.m. Kenny Young

Come Back to Erin 1866 w.m. Claribel (Charlotte Barnard)

Come Back to Me 1966 w. Alan Jay Lerner m. Burton Lane. (MT) *On a Clear Day You Can See Forever*. (MF) *On a Clear Day You Can See Forever*. Barbra Streisand appeared in the film production of *On a Clear Day You Can See Forever*.

Come Back to Sorrento 1904 w.m. Ernesto de Curtis, Claude Aveling. (MF) *Paramount on Parade*. (MF) *On the Sunny Side of the Street*. Maurice Chevalier and Kay Francis appeared in *Paramount on Parade*. Frankie Laine and Billy Daniels appeared in *On the Sunny Side of the Street*. This song was popularly revived in 1936.

Come Back When You Grow Up 1967 w.m. Martha Sharp

Come Closer to Me 1946 Sp.w. Osvaldo Farres Eng.w. Al Stewart m. Osvaldo Farres. From the Spanish "Accercate Mas." (MF) *Easy To Wed*. Lucille Ball, Esther Williams, and Van Johnson appeared in *Easy To Wed*.

Come Dance with Me 1950 w.m. George Blake, Richard Leibert

Come Dancing 1962 w.m. Downes, David

Come Down Ma Evenin' Star 1902 w. Robert B. Smith m. John Stromberg. (MT) *Twirly Whirly*. (MF) *Broadway to Hollywood*. (MF) *My Wild Irish Rose*. This song was immortalized by Lillian Russell in *Twirly Whirly*. Mickey Rooney, Jimmy Durante, and Nelson Eddy appeared in *Broadway to Hollywood*. Dennis Morgan and Arlene Dahl appeared in *My Wild Irish Rose*. Stromberg wrote this song for and dedicated it to the Weber and Fields super-star, Lillian Russell. He was found dead in his apartment with the newly written manuscript of this song in his pocket.

Come Follow the Band 1980 w. Michael Stewart m. Cy Coleman. (MT) *Barnum*. Jim Dale and Glen Close appeared in *Barnum*.

Come Go with Me 1957 w.m. C.E. Quick

Come Home, Dewey, We Won't Do a Thing to You 1899 w.m. Paul Dresser. See also Part I, 1898.

Come Home, Father, *see* **Father, Dear Father, Come Home with Me Now**

Come Home to My Arms 1956 w.m. Leslie Baguley, Emily Jane

Come into the Garden, Maud 1857 w. Alfred Lord Tennyson m. Michael William Balfe

Come, Josephine, in My Flying Machine 1910 w. Alfred Bryan m. Fred Fisher. (MF) *The Story of Vernon and Irene Castle*. (MF) *Oh You Beautiful Doll*. Fred Astaire and Ginger Rogers appeared in *The Story of Vernon and Irene Castle*. June Haver appeared in *Oh You Beautiful Doll*.

Come, Landlord, Fill the Flowing Bowl c.1750 w.m. traditional, from England. This song later became a traditional English student song.

Come, Oh, Come to Me 1887 w. Mrs. James G. Johnson m. James McGranahan

Come, Oh Come with Me, the Moon is Beaming 1842 w. B.S. Barclay m. traditional, from Italy

Come On Down 1980 w.m. Alex Bradford. (MT) *Your Arms Too Short To Box with God.* Jennifer-Yvette Holliday appeared in *Your Arms Too Short To Box with God.*

Come on Down Town 1908 w.m. George M. Cohan. (MT) *The Yankee Prince.*

Come On Eileen 1983 w.m. Kevin Adams, James Paterson, Kevin Rowland. Ivor Novello Award winner 1982–83.

Come On Over 1976 w.m. Barry Gibb, Robin Gibb

Come On, Papa 1918 w.m. Edgar Leslie, Harry Ruby

Come On, Spark Plug! 1923 w.m. Billy Rose, Con Conrad

Come On-A-My House 1951 w.m. Ross Bagdasarian, William Saroyan

Come Out of the Kitchen, Mary Ann 1930 w.m. James Kendis, Charles Bayha

Come Outside 1962 w.m. Charles Blackwell

Come Prima, *see* **For the First Time**

Come Rain or Come Shine 1946 w. Johnny Mercer m. Harold Arlen. (MT) *St. Louis Woman.* Pearl Bailey and Ruby Hill appeared in *St. Louis Woman.*

Come Saturday Morning 1969 w.m. Fred Karlin, Dory Previn. (F) *The Sterile Cuckoo.* Liza Minnelli appeared in *The Sterile Cuckoo.*

Come See About Me 1964 w.m. Eddie Holland, Brian Holland, Lamont Dozier

Come Softly to Me 1959 w.m. Gary Troxel, Gretchen Christopher, Barbara Ellis

Come Sta' 1961 w.m. Harry Gordon

Come Take a Trip in My Airship 1904 w. Ren Shields m. George Evans. See also Part I, 1903.

Come Tell Me What's Your Answer, Yes or No 1898 w.m. Paul Dresser. (MF) *My Gal Sal.* Rita Hayworth and Victor Mature appeared in *My Gal Sal.*

Come, Thou Almighty King 1757 w. anon. m. Felice de Giardini

Come to Me 1931 w.m. B.G. DeSylva, Lew Brown, Ray Henderson. (F) *Indiscreet.* Gloria Swanson and Ben Lyon appeared in *Indiscreet.*

Come to Me 1957 w. Peter Lind Hayes m. Robert Allen. (TV) *Come to Me.*

Come to Me, Bend to Me 1947 w. Alan Jay Lerner m. Frederick Loewe. (MT) *Brigadoon.* (MF) *Brigadoon.* David Brooks and Marion Bell appeared in the stage production of *Brigadoon.* Gene Kelly and Cyd Charisse appeared in the film production of *Brigadoon.*

Come to the Ball 1911 w.m. Lionel Monckton, Adrian Ross, Percy Greenbank. (MT) *The Quaker Girl.* Gracie Leigh, Gertie Millar, and George Carvey appeared in *The Quaker Girl.*

Come to the Fair 1917 w.m. Helen Taylor, Easthope Martin

Come to the Land of Bohemia 1907 w.m. Ren Shields, George Evans

Come to the Mardi Gras 1937 w. Ervin Drake, Jimmy Shirl m. Max Bulhoes, Milton de Oliveira. This song was popularly revived in 1948.

Come to the Moon 1919 w. Ned Wayburn, Lou Paley m. George Gershwin

Come Together 1969 w.m. John Lennon, Paul McCartney. (MT) *Beatlemania.*

Come What May (Après Toi) 1973 w.m. Panas, Munro

Come Where My Love Lies Dreaming 1855 w.m. Stephen Collins Foster. (MF) *I Dream of Jeanie.* Bill Shirley and Ray Middleton appeared in *I Dream of Jeanie.*

Come, Ye Blessed 1917 w. biblical m. John Prindle Scott

Come, Ye Faithful, Raise the Strain 1872 w. John Mason Neale, translated from the Greek of St. John of Damascus, 8th century m. Arthur Sullivan adaptation to "St. Kevin"

Come, Ye Saints 1848 w.m. William Clayton

Comedy of Errors, The 1977 w.m. Guy Woolfenden

Comedy Tonight 1962 w.m. Stephen Sondheim (MT) *A Funny Thing Happened on the Way to the Forum* (MF) *A Funny Thing Happened on the Way to the Forum* (MT) *Side by Side by Sondheim.* Zero Mostel and Jack Gilford appeared in the stage and film productions of *A Funny Thing Happened on the Way to the Forum.* Millicent Martin and Julie N. McKenzie appeared in *Side by Side by Sondheim.*

Comes Love 1939 w. Lew Brown, Charles Tobias m. Sam Stept. (MT) *Yokel Boy.* (MT) *Funny Side Up.* (F) *Yokel Boy.* Phil Silvers, Judy Canova, and Buddy Ebsen appeared in the stage production of *Yokel Boy.* Joan Davis appeared in the film production of *Yokel Boy.*

Coming Home 1945 w.m. Billy Reid

Comin' In on a Wing and a Prayer 1943 w. Harold Adamson m. Jimmy McHugh

Comin' Round the Mountain, *see* **She'll Be Comin' Round the Mountain**

Comin' Thro' the Rye, or, **If a Body Meet a Body** 1796 w. Robert Burns m. traditional, from Scotland. This song was popularly performed by Mrs. Henly at the Royal Circus in the pantomime *Harlequin Mariner,* with music adapted by J. Sanderson.

Coming Up—Live at Glasgow 1980 w.m. Paul McCartney

Comme Ci, Comme Ça 1949 w.m. Bruno Coquatrix, Pierre Dudan, Alex Kramer, Joan Whitney

Company 1970 w.m. Stephen Sondheim. (MT) *Company.* (MT) *Side by Side by Sondheim.* Elaine Stritch appeared in *Company.* Millicent Martin and Julie N. McKenzie appeared in *Side by Side by Sondheim.*

Company Sergeant Major, The 1918 w.m. Wilfrid Sanderson

Comrades 1887 w.m. Felix McGlennon

Concert in the Park 1939 w. David Franklin m. Clifford Friend

Concerto for Piano, No.2, *see* **Piano Concerto, No.2**

Concerto for Two 1941 w.m. Jack Lawrence; arr. Robert C. Haring. Based on the first movement of Tchaikovsky's First Piano Concerto, in B-flat minor.

Concerto in F 1925 m. George Gershwin. (MF) *An American in Paris.* (MF) *Rhapsody in Blue.* Gene Kelly and Leslie Caron appeared in *An American in Paris.* Oscar Levant and Alexis Smith appeared in *Rhapsody in Blue,* biopic of composer George Gershwin.

Conchita, Marquita, Lolita, Pepita, Rosita, Juanita Lopez 1942 w.m. Herb Magidson, Jule Styne. (MF) *Priorities on Parade.* Ann Miller, Johnny Johnston, and Jerry Colonna appeared in *Priorities on Parade.*

Concrete and Clay 1965 w.m. Tommy Moeller, Brian Parker

Condor Pasa, El (If I Could) 1933 w.m. Based on a Peruvian folksong. This song was popularly adapted in 1970.

Confessin', *see* **I'm Confessin'**

Confession 1931 w. Howard Dietz m. Arthur Schwartz. (MT) *The Band Wagon.* (MF) *The Band Wagon.*

Confidentially 1949 w.m. Reg Dixon

Conga Atomica, La 1938 w.m. Eliseo Grenet

Congo Love Song 1903 w.m. Bob Cole, J. Rosamond Johnson

Congratulations 1929 w.m. Maceo Pinkard, Coleman Goeta, Bud Green, Sam H. Stept

Congratulations 1969 w.m. Bill Martin, Phil Coulter. Ivor Novello Award winner 1968–69.

Connecticut 1946 w. Hugh Martin m. Ralph Blane

Consider Yourself 1963 w.m. Lionel Bart. (MT) *Oliver!* (MF) *Oliver!.* Ron Moody appeared in both the stage and film productions of *Oliver!.*

Consolation 1908 w. Edward Madden m. Theodore F. Morse

Constantinople 1928 w.m. Harry Carlton

Constantly 1910 w. Chris Smith, James Henry Burris m. Bert Williams

Contented 1932 w. Roy Turk m. Don Bestor. This song later became the commercial radio theme used to promote Carnation Milk and their "contented" cows.

Continental, The 1934 w. Herb Magidson m. Con Conrad. (MF) *The Gay Divorcée.* Fred Astaire and Ginger Rogers appeared in the film production of *The Gay Divorcée.* This song did not appear in the original 1932 stage production of *Gay Divorce.* Academy Award winner 1934.

Conversation on Park Avenue 1946 w.m. Willie ("The Lion") Smith

Convict and the Bird, The 1888 w.m. Paul Dresser

Convoy 1975 w.m. Clifford Twemlow

Cool 1957 w. Stephen Sondheim m. Leonard Bernstein. (MT) *West Side Story.* (MF) *West Side Story.* Carol Lawrence and Chita Rivera appeared in the stage production of *West Side Story.* Natalie Wood and Rita Moreno appeared in the film production of *West Side Story.*

Cool Change 1980 w.m. Glenn Shorrock

Cool It Now 1985 w.m. Vincent Brantley, Ricky Timas

Cool Jerk 1966 w.m. Donald Storball

Cool Love 1981 w.m. Donald Jenkins, Cory Lerios, John Pierce

Cool Night 1982 w.m. Paul Davis

Cool Water 1936 w.m. Bob Nolan. (MF) *Hands Across the Border.* (MF) *Along the Navajo Trail.* Roy Rogers and Bob Nolan appeared in *Hands Across the Border.* Roy Rogers and Gabby Hayes appeared in *Along the Navajo Trail.* This song was popularly revived in 1947.

Coom Pretty One 1934 w.m. Leslie Sarony. (MF) *Rolling in Money.* Leslie Sarony appeared in *Rolling in Money.*

Coon! Coon! Coon! 1901 w.m. Gene Jefferson, Leo Friedman

Copacabana (At the Copa) 1978 w.m. Barry Manilow, Bruce Sussman, Jack Feldman

Copenhagen 1924 m. Charlie Davis

Copper Canyon 1949 w.m. Jay Livingston, Raymond B. Evans (F) *Copper Canyon.* Ray Milland and Hedy Lamarr appeared in *Copper Canyon.*

Coquette 1928 w. Gus Kahn m. Carmen Lombardo, John W. Green (MF) *Cockeyed Cavaliers.* Bert Wheeler and Thelma Todd appeared in *Cockeyed Cavaliers.* Theme song of Guy Lombardo.

Corabelle, *see* **I'm a-Comin' a-Courtin' Corabelle**

Cornish Rhapsody 1944 m. Hubert Bath. (MF) *Love Story.* (MF) *Sincerely Yours.* Liberace appeared in *Sincerely Yours.*

Coronation 1793 m. Oliver Holden. See also "All Hail the Power of Jesus' Name."

Coronation March 1849 m. Giacomo Meyerbeer

Coronation Scot 1948 w.m. Vivian Ellis

Coronation Street 1961 w.m. Eric Spear

Coronation Waltz, The 1937 w.m. Jimmy Kennedy

Corrine Corrina 1932 w.m. Bo Chatman, Mitchell Parish, J.M. Williams. This song was popularly revived in 1961.

Cosi Cosa 1935 w. Ned Washington m. Bronislaw Kaper, Walter Jurmann. (MF) *A Night at the Opera.* The Marx Brothers, Allan Jones, and Kitty Carlisle appeared in *A Night at the Opera.*

Cossack Love Song, or, **Don't Forget Me** 1926 w. Otto Harbach, Oscar Hammerstein II m. Herbert Stothart, George Gershwin. (MT) *Song of the Flame.*

Cottage by the Sea, The 1856 w.m. John Rogers Thomas

Cottage for Sale, A 1930 w. Larry Conley m. Willard Robison

Cottage of My Mother, The 1848 w. Jesse Hutchinson m. Judson Hutchinson. This song was popularly performed by the Hutchinson Family singers.

Cotton Fields c.1850 w.m. traditional American ballad. This song was popularly revived in 1961.

Cotton Tail 1944 w.m. Edward Kennedy "Duke" Ellington

Could I Have This Dance 1980 w.m. Wayland Holyfield, Bob House. (F) *Urban Cowboy.*

Could I Leave You 1971 w.m. Stephen Sondheim. (MT)

Follies. (MT) *Side by Side by Sondheim.* Yvonne DeCarlo and Alexis Smith appeared in *Follies.* Millicent Martin and Julie N. McKenzie appeared in *Side by Side by Sondheim.*

Could It Be I'm Falling in Love 1972 w.m. Melvin Steals, Mervin Steals

Could It Be Magic 1975 w.m. Barry Manilow

Couldn't Hear Nobody Pray 1922 w.m. traditional Black American spiritual; arr. Henry Thacker Burleigh in 1922

Count Every Star 1950 w. Sammy Gallop m. Bruno Coquatrix

Count Me In 1965 w.m. Glen D. Hardin

Count on Me Love 1978 w.m. Jesse Barish

Count Your Blessings 1948 w.m. Edith Temple, Reginald Morgan

Count Your Blessings Instead of Sheep 1952 w.m. Irving Berlin. (MF) *White Christmas.* Bing Crosby, Danny Kaye, and Rosemary Clooney appeared in *White Christmas.* This song was most popular in 1954.

Country Boy Can Survive, A 1982 w.m. Hank Williams, Jr.

Country Boy You Got Your Feet in L.A. 1975 w.m. Dennis Lambert, Brian Potter

Country Dance 1890 m. Edward German

Country Gardens 1728 (MT) *The Quaker's Opera* m. Percy Grainger

Country Matters 1973 w.m. Derek Hilton. Ivor Novello Award winner 1972–73.

Country Road 1970 w.m. Mary Catherine Danoff, William Danoff, Henri John Deutschend

Country Style 1947 w.m. Jimmy Van Heusen, Johnny Burke. (MF) *Welcome Stranger.* Bing Crosby and Barry Fitzgerald appeared in *Welcome Stranger.*

Couple of Song and Dance Men, A 1946 w.m. Irving Berlin. (MF) *Blue Skies.* Bing Crosby appeared in *Blue Skies.*

Couple of Swells, A 1948 w.m. Irving Berlin. (MF) *Easter Parade.* Judy Garland and Fred Astaire appeared in *Easter Parade.*

Cousin Jedediah 1863 w.m. H.S. Thompson

Covered Wagon Days (March) 1923 w.m. Will Morrissey, Joe Burrows. (F) *The Covered Wagon.* This song was written for the piano and orchestra accompaniment to this classic silent film.

Coward of the County 1980 w.m. Roger Bowling, Billy Edd Wheeler

Cowboy 1937 w.m. Michael Carr

Cowboy Serenade, or, My Last Cigarette 1942 w.m. Rich Hall. (MF) *Cowboy Serenade.* Gene Autry and Smiley Burnette appeared in *Cowboy Serenade.*

Cowboy's Lament, The, *see* **Streets of Laredo**

Cow-Cow Boogie 1942 w.m. Benny Carter, Don Raye, Gene de Paul. (MF) *Reveille with Beverly.* Ann Miller and William Wright appeared in *Reveille with Beverly.* This song was originally sung by Ella Fitzgerald in a film, from which it was cut before the picture was released.

Coz I Love You 1972 w.m. Neville Holder, James Lea

Crackers 1980 w.m. Kye Fleming, Dennis Morgan

Cracklin' Rosie 1970 w.m. Neil Diamond

Cracovienne Fantastique 1840 m. Ignace Paderewski

Cradle Song, *see* **Lullaby** (Brahms)

Cradle's Empty, Baby's Gone 1880 w.m. Harry Kennedy. This song was soon parodied with William Delaney's "Empty Is the Bottle, Father's Tight," and Tommy Tucker's "Bottle's Empty, Whiskey's Gone."

Crazy 1985 w.m. Richard Marx, Kenny Rogers

Crazy Blues 1921 w.m. Perry Bradford

Crazy for You, *see* **K-Ra-Zy for You**

Crazy for You 1985 w.m. John Bettis, Jon Lind

Crazy Heart 1951 w.m. Fred Rose, Maurice Murray

Crazy Little Thing Called Love 1980 w.m. Frederick Mercury

Crazy Love 1979 w.m. Russell Young

Crazy Otto Rag (Medley), The 1955 w. Edward R. White, m. Mack Wolfson

Crazy People 1932 w.m. Edgar Leslie, James Monaco. (MF) *The Big Broadcast.* Bing Crosby and Kate Smith appeared in *The Big Broadcast.*

Crazy Rhythm 1928 w. Irving Caesar m. Joseph Meyer, Roger Wolfe Kahn. (MT) *Here's Howe.* (MT) *Lucky Girl.* (MF) *You Were Meant for Me.* (MF) *Tea for Two.* Dan Dailey and Oscar Levant appeared in *You Were Meant for Me.* Doris Day and Gordon MacRae appeared in *Tea for Two,* based on *No, No, Nanette.*

Crazy Words (Crazy Tune) (Vo-Do-De-O-Do) 1926 w.m. Jack Yellen, Milton Ager

Cream of the Crop 1969 w.m. Dick Hyman

Creole Belle 1900 w. George Sidney m. J. Bodewalt Lampe

Creole Love Call 1932 w.m. Edward Kennedy "Duke" Ellington

Creque Alley 1967 w.m. John Phillips, Michele Gilliam Phillips

Crest of a Wave, The 1934 w.m. Ralph Reader

Cricket on the Hearth, The 1913 w. Robert B. Smith m. Victor Herbert. (MT) *Sweethearts.*

Crimson and Clover 1969 w.m. Peter Lucia, Jr., Tommy James

Crinoline Days 1922 w.m. Irving Berlin. (MT) *Music Box Revue.*

Crocodile Rock 1973 w.m. Elton John, Bernie Taupin. Ivor Novello Award winner 1973–74.

Croquet 1867 w. C.H. Webb m. John Rogers Thomas

Cross Over the Bridge 1954 w.m. Bennie Benjamin, George Weiss

Cross Your Fingers 1929 w. Arthur Swanstrom, Benny Davis m. J. Fred Coots. (MT) *Sons o' Guns.* (MF) *Sons o' Guns.*

Cross Your Heart 1926 w. B.G. DeSylva m. Lewis E. Gensler. (MT) *Queen High.*

Crucifix 1879 Eng. w. Theodore T. Barker; second version F.W. Rosier m. Jean Baptiste Faure

Crucifixion, The 1887 w. selected and written by the Rev. W.J. Sparrow-Simpson m. John Stainer

Cruel Sea, The 1963 w.m. Mike Maxfield

Cruisin' 1980 w.m. William Robinson, Marvin Tarplin

Cruising Down the River 1945 w.m. Eily Beadell, Nell Tollerton. This song was popularly revived in 1949.

Crusader's Hymn, or, **Fairest Lord Jesus** 1850 w. anon. m. Silesian folksong. This hymn has been incorrectly dated to the time of the Crusades.

Crush on You 1986 w.m. Aaron Zigman, Jerry Knight

Cry 1952 w.m. Churchill Kohlman. Theme song of Johnnie Ray. The author of this song was a night watchman at a Pittsburgh dry-cleaning establishment.

Cry 1986 w.m. Lol Creme, Kevin Godley

Cry Like a Baby 1968 w.m. Spooner Oldham, Dan Penn

Cry Me a River 1955 w.m. Arthur Hamilton

Cry of the Wild Goose, The 1950 w.m. Terry Gilkyson

Cry, the Beloved Country 1949 w. Maxwell Anderson m. Kurt Weill. (MT) *Lost in the Stars.* (MF) *Lost in the Stars.* Todd Duncan, Warren Coleman, and William Grewes appeared in the stage production of *Lost in the Stars.* Melba Moore appeared in the film production of *Lost in the Stars.*

Cryin' 1961 w.m. Roy Orbison, Joe Melson. This song was popularly revived in 1981.

Cryin' for the Carolines 1930 w. Sam M. Lewis, Joe Young m. Harry Warren. (MF) *Spring Is Here.* Alexander Gray and Bernice Claire appeared in *Spring Is Here.*

Crying Game, The 1964 w.m. Geoff Stephens

Crying in the Chapel 1953 w.m. Artie Glenn. This song was popularly revived in 1965.

Crying Time 1965 w.m. Buck Owens. Grammy Award winner 1966.

Crystal Blue Persuasion 1969 w.m. Tommy James, Mike Vale, Ed J. Gray

Crystal Gazer, The 1949 w.m. Frank Petch

Cu-Tu-Gu-Ru (Jack, Jack, Jack) 1946 Sp.w. Armando Castro Eng.w. Joe Davis m. Armando Castro

Cuanto Le Gusta 1947 w. Ray Gilbert m. Gabriel Ruiz. (MF) *A Date with Judy.* Elizabeth Taylor and Jane Powell appeared in *A Date with Judy.*

Cuban Love Song 1931 w.m. Herbert Stothart, Jimmy McHugh, Dorothy Fields. (MT) *Sugar Babies.* (MF) *The Cuban Love Song.* Ann Miller and Mickey Rooney appeared in *Sugar Babies.* Lawrence Tibbett and Jimmy Durante appeared in *The Cuban Love Song.* Theme song of Edmundo Ros.
Cuban Overture 1932 m. George Gershwin. This work was originally entitled "Rhumba."

Cuban Pete 1936 w.m. Norman Henderson. (MF) *Cuban Pete.* Desi Arnaz and Ethel Smith appeared in *Cuban Pete.* This song was popularly revived in 1946.

Cubanola Glide, The 1909 w. Vincent P. Bryan m. Harry Von Tilzer. (F) *Flame of the Barbary Coast.* John Wayne

and William Frawley appeared in *Flame of the Barbary Coast.* This song was the forerunner to the craze dances Grizzly Bear, Turkey Trot, and Bunny Hug.

Cucaracha, La 1916 w.m. arr. Hawley Ader; another arr. Stanley Adams; another arr. words Mitchell Parish. Based on a traditional Mexican folksong. (F) *Viva Villa.* (F) *La Cucaracha.* (F) *Romance of the Rio Grande.* Cesar Romero and Lynne Roberts appeared in *Romance of the Rio Grande.* This song was popularly revived in 1934.

Cuckoo, The, *see* **The Kerry Dance**

Cuckoo in the Clock 1938 w. Johnny Mercer m. Walter Donaldson

Cuddle In 1983 w.m. Roger Lax. (OB) *Weekend.*

Cuddle Up a Little Closer, Lovey Mine 1908 w. Otto Harbach m. Karl Hoschna. (MT) *The Three Twins.* (MF) *The Story of Vernon and Irene Castle.* (MF) *Birth of the Blues.* (MF) *Is Everybody Happy.* (MF) *On Moonlight Bay.* Fred Astaire and Ginger Rogers appeared in *The Story of Vernon and Irene Castle.* Bing Crosby and Mary Martin appeared in *Birth of the Blues.* Bob Haymes appeared in *Is Everybody Happy,* biopic of bandleader Ted Lewis. Doris Day and Gordon MacRae appeared in *On Moonlight Bay.* This song was popularly revived in 1943.

Cumbanchero, El 1940 w.m. Rafael Hernandez. (MF) *Cuban Pete.* Desi Arnaz and Ethel Smith appeared in *Cuban Pete.* This song was popularly revived in 1946, and again in 1952.

Cumparsita, La 1916 w. Carol Raven m. G.H. Matos Rodriguez. The words to this song were not added until 1932. This song was popularly revived in 1926, and again in 1932.

Cup of Coffee, a Sandwich and You, A 1925 w. Al Dubin, Billy Rose m. Joseph Meyer. (MT) *Charlot's Revue of 1925.* (MT) *The Charlot Show of 1926.* Gertrude Lawrence and Jack Buchanan appeared in *Charlot's Revue of 1925.* This song was parodied by Richard Connell as "An Oyster, a Cloister and You."

Cupboard Love 1963 w.m. Les Vandyke

Cupid 1976 w.m. Sam Cooke. This song was popularly revived in 1980.

Cupid and I 1897 w. Harry B. Smith m. Victor Herbert. (MT) *The Serenade.*

Curse of an Aching Heart, The 1913 w. Henry Fink m. Al Piantadosi. (MF) *Show Business.*

Curse of the Dreamer, The 1899 w.m. Paul Dresser.

Cynthia's in Love 1942 w. Jack Owens m. Gish-White

Czardas 1904 m. Vittorio Monti

Da-Da, Da-Da 1928 w.m. W. Dore

Da Doo Ron Ron (When He Walked Me Home) 1963 w.m. Phil Spector, Jeff Barry, Ellie Greenwich. (OB) *Leader of the Pack.* This song was popularly revived in 1977.

Daddy 1880 w. Mary Mark Lemon m. Arthur Henry Behrend

Daddy 1941 w.m. Lou Klein, Robert Trout. (MF) *Two Latins from Manhattan.* (MF) *Gentlemen Marry Brunettes.* Joan Davis and Joan Woodbury appeared in *Two Latins from*

Manhattan. Anita Ellis and Jane Russell appeared in *Gentlemen Marry Brunettes.*

Daddy Don't You Walk So Fast 1972 w.m. Peter Robin Callander, Geoff Stephens

Daddy Has a Sweetheart, and Mother Is Her Name 1912 w. Gene Buck m. Dave Stamper

Daddy Long Legs 1919 w. Sam M. Lewis, Joe Young m. Harry Ruby

Daddy Wouldn't Buy Me a Bow-Wow 1892 w.m. Joseph Tabrar. This English music hall song, popularly sung by Vesta Victoria, was an early ode to the "sugar daddy." See also, of course, the American "My Heart Belongs to Daddy."

Daddy, You've Been a Mother to Me 1920 w.m. Fred Fisher

Daddy's Home 1961 w.m. Jimmy Sheppard, William Miller. This song was popularly revived in 1973. This song was popularly revived in 1982.

Daddy's Little Girl 1905 w. Edward Madden m. Theodore F. Morse

Daddy's Little Girl 1949 w.m. Bobby Burke, Horace Gerlach

Dagger Dance 1911 m. Victor Herbert. From the opera *Natoma.*

Daisies Won't Tell 1908 w.m. Anita Owen

Daisy Bell, or, **A Bicycle Built for Two,** or, **Daisy, Daisy** 1892 w.m. Harry Dacre. (F) *I'll Be Your Sweetheart.* This song was first popularly performed by English music hall singer Katie Lawerence in London.

Daisy, Daisy, *see* **Daisy Bell**

Daisy Deane 1863 w. T.F. Winthrop m. James Ramsey Murray.

Dallas Blues 1918 w.m. Spencer Williams

Daly's Reel 1911 m. Joseph M. Daly

Dam Busters (March), The 1955 w.m. Eric Coates. (F) *The Dam Busters.* Michael Redgrave appeared in *The Dam Busters.* Ivor Novello Award winner 1955.

Dance, *see also* **Danse**

Dance (Disco Heat) 1979 w.m. Victor R. Osborne, Eric Jay Robinson

Dance, Dance, Dance (Yowsah, Yowsah, Yowsah) 1977 w.m. Nile Rodgers, Bernard Edwards, Kenny Lehman

Dance Hall Days 1985 w.m. Jack Hues

Dance Little Lady 1928 w.m. Noël Coward. (MT) *This Year of Grace.* Beatrice Lillie and Noël Coward appeared in *This Year of Grace.*

Dance Macabre, *see* **Danse Macabre**

Dance Me Loose 1951 w.m. Mel Howard, Lee Erwin

Dance, My Darlings 1935 w. Oscar Hammerstein II m. Sigmund Romberg. (MT) *May Wine.* Walter Slezak and Nancy McCord appeared in *May Wine.*

Dance of the Hours 1876 m. Amilcare Ponchielli. From the opera *La Gioconda.* (MF) *Fantasia.* See also "Hello Mudduh, Hello Faddah."

Dance of the Paper Dolls 1928 w.m. Johnny Tucker, Joe Schuster, John Siras

Dance of the Spanish Onion 1942 m. David Rose

Dance On 1963 w.m. Elaine Murtagh, Valerie Murtagh, Ray Adams. Ivor Novello Award winner 1963.

Dance: Ten; Looks: Three 1975 w. Edward Kleban m. Marvin Hamlisch. (MT) *A Chorus Line.* Donna McKechnie appeared in *A Chorus Line.*

Dance with a Dolly 1944 w.m. Terry Shand, Jimmy Eaton, Mickey Leader. Based on "Lubly Fan, or, Buffalo Gals (Won't You Come Out Tonight?)" of 1844. (MF) *On Stage Everybody.* Peggy Ryan and Johnny Coy appeared in *On Stage Everybody.*

Dance with Me 1975 w.m. John J. Hall, Johanna Hall

Dance with Me 1978 w.m. Peter Brown, Robert Rans

Dance with Me Henry 1955 w.m. Etta James

Dance with Your Uncle Joseph 1915 w.m. Liston, William Hargreaves

Dancing 1963 w.m. Jerry Herman. (MT) *Hello, Dolly!.* (MF) *Hello, Dolly!* Carol Channing appeared in the stage production of *Hello, Dolly!.* Barbra Streisand appeared in the film production of *Hello, Dolly!.*

Dancing Fool 1922 w. Harry B. Smith, Francis Wheeler m. Ted Snyder

Dancing Honeymoon 1922 w.m. Philip Braham

Dancing in the Dark 1931 w. Howard Dietz m. Arthur Schwartz. (MT) *The Band Wagon.* (MF) *Dancing in the Dark.* (MF) *The Band Wagon.* Fred and Adele Astaire appeared in the stage production of *The Band Wagon.* William Powell and Betsy Drake appeared in *Dancing in the Dark.* Fred Astaire, Cyd Charisse, and Nanette Fabray appeared in the film production of *The Band Wagon.*

Dancing in the Dark 1984 w.m. Bruce Springsteen

Dancing in the Streets 1964 w.m. William Stevenson, Marvin Gaye, Ivory Joe Hunter

Dancing Is Everything 1984 w. Robert Lorick m. Henry Krieger. (MT) *The Tap Dance Kid.* Alfonso Ribiero appeared in *The Tap Dance Kid.*

Dancing Lesson, The 1918 w.m. Herbert Oliver

Dancing Machine 1974 w.m. Weldon Parks

Dancing on a Dime 1941 w. Frank Loesser m. Burton Lane. (MF) *Dancing on a Dime.* Grace McDonald and Robert Paige appeared in *Dancing on a Dime.*

Dancing on the Ceiling 1930 w. Lorenz Hart m. Richard Rodgers. (MT) *Simple Simon.* (MT) *Evergreen.* (MF) *Evergreen.* This song was written for, but did not appear in, the New York production of *Simple Simon.* Jessie Matthews appeared in both the stage and film productions of *Evergreen.*

Dancing on the Ceiling 1986 w.m. Michael Frenchik, Carlos Rios

Dancing Queen 1977 w.m. Benny Anderson, Bjorn Ulvaeus, Stig Anderson

Dancing Shoes 1963 w.m. Hank Brian Marvin, Bruce Welch

Dancing Tambourine 1927 w. Phil Ponce m. W.C. Polla. This song was originally published without words in 1927.

Dancing the Devil Away 1927 w. Otto Harbach, Bert Kalmar m. Harry Ruby. (MT) *Lucky.* (MF) *The Cuckoos.* Ruby

Keeler and Josephine Santley appeared in *Lucky*. Bert Wheeler, Bob Woolsey, and Dorothy Lee appeared in *The Cuckoos*.

Dancing Time 1921 w.m. Jerome Kern, George Grossmith. (MT) *The Cabaret Girl*. Dorothy Dickson appeared in *The Cabaret Girl*.

Dancing Under the Stars 1936 w.m. Harry Owens

Dancing with a Dolly, *see* **Dance with a Dolly**

Dancing with My Shadow 1935 w.m. Harry Woods

(I'm) Dancing with Tears in My Eyes 1930 w. Al Dubin m. Joe Burke

Dancin' Your Memory Away 1982 w.m. Eddie Burton, Tom Grant

Dandy Jim of Caroline 1843 w. Silas S. Steele m. Dan Myers (J. Richard Myers). This song was written for Cool White, organizer of the "Virginia Serenaders," in 1843; his real name was John Hodges.

Dang Me 1964 w.m. Roger Miller. Grammy Award winner 1964.

Danger, Heartbreak Ahead 1954 w.m. Carl Stutz, Nathan Carl Barefoot, Jr.

Daniel 1973 w.m. Elton John, Bernie Taupin. (F) *Alice Doesn't Live Here Anymore*. Ellen Burstyn appeared in *Alice Doesn't Live Here Anymore*. Ivor Novello Award winner 1973–74.

Danke Schön 1963 w.m. Bert Kaempfert, Kurt Schwabach, Milt Gabler

Dankgebet, *see* **We Gather Together**

Danny Boy 1913 w.m. Frederick Edward Weatherly. Based on the Irish traditional "Londonderry Air" of 1855.

Danny by My Side 1891 w. Ned Harrigan m. David Braham. (MT) *The Last of the Hogans*. This song was performed by Al Smith in 1933 at the fiftieth anniversary celebration of the opening of the Brooklyn Bridge.

Danny Deever 1897 w. Rudyard Kipling m. Walter Damrosch

Danny's Song 1973 w.m. Ken Loggins

Danse Macabre 1872 w. Henri Cazalis m. Camille Saint-Saëns

Danse Nègre, op. 58, no.5 1908 m. Cyril Scott

Danube Waves, *see* **Waves of the Danube**

Daphnis et Chloé 1911 m. Maurice Ravel

Dapper Dan 1921 w. Lew Brown m. Albert Von Tilzer. (MT) *A to Z*. Jack Buchanan and the Trix Sisters appeared in *A to Z*.

Dardanella 1919 w. Fred Fisher m. Felix Bernard, Johnny S. Black. This song was originally titled "Turkish Tom Toms." (MT) *Afgar*. Alice Delysia appeared in *Afgar*. A lawsuit was filed by Fred Fisher against composer Jerome Kern for Kern's song "Ka-Lu-A," claiming that Kern had stolen the bass accompaniment from "Dardanella." Kern won indisputably and was offered a suit of clothes as token payment. Kern declined.

Daring Young Man, The (on the Flying Trapeze) 1868 w. George Leybourne m. Alfred Lee. This song was popularly revived in 1933. In 1869, an answer song, "The Flying Velocipede," was published.

Dark Eyes, or, **Black Eyes** 1926 w.m. arr. Harry Horlick, Gregory Stone. Based on the traditional Russian gypsy song "Otchi Tchorniya," as early as 1884.

Dark Is the Night (C'est Fini) 1951 w. Sammy Cahn m. Nicholas Brodszky. (MF) *Rich, Young and Pretty*. Jane Powell and Vic Damone appeared in *Rich, Young and Pretty*.

Dark Lady 1974 w.m. John Durrill

Dark Moon 1957 w.m. Ned Miller

Darkest the Hour 1886 w. Claxson Bellamy, Harry Poulton m. Edward Jakobowski. (MT) *Erminie*.

(When It's) Darkness on the Delta 1932 w.m. Jerry Livingston, Al Neiburg, Marty Symes. (MF) *South of Dixie*. David Bruce and Ann Gwynne appeared in *South of Dixie*.

Darktown Strutters' Ball, The 1917 w.m. Shelton Brooks. (MF) *The Story of Vernon and Irene Castle*. (MF) *Broadway*. (MF) *The Dolly Sisters*. (MF) *Incendiary Blonde*. Fred Astaire and Ginger Rogers appeared in *The Story of Vernon and Irene Castle*. George Raft, Pat O'Brien, and Janet Blair appeared in *Broadway*. Betty Grable appeared in *The Dolly Sisters*. Betty Hutton appeared in *Incendiary Blonde*, biopic of speakeasy owner Texas Guinan. See also Part I, 1917.

Darling, Je Vous Aime Beaucoup 1935 w.m. Anna Sosenko. Theme song of Hildegarde.

Darling Nelly Gray 1856 w.m. Benjamin Russell Hanby

Darling Sue, *see* **I Love You in the Same Old Way**

Darn That Dream 1939 w. Eddie De Lange m. Jimmy Van Heusen. (MT) *Swingin' the Dream* Louis Armstrong appeared as "Bottom" in *Swingin' the Dream*, based on William Shakespeare's *A Midsummer Night's Dream*.

Dar's One More Ribber To Cross 1881 w.m. traditional black American spiritual, possibly from as early as 1870.

Dashing White Sergeant, The 1826 w. General Burgoyne m. Sir Henry Rowley Bishop

Dat's Where My Money Goes, *see* **That's Where My Money Goes**

Daughter of Darkness 1970 w.m. Les Reed, Geoff Stephens

Daughter of Rosie O'Grady, The 1918 w. Monty C. Bricem. Walter Donaldson. (F) *The Daughter of Rosie O'Grady*. June Haver and Gordon MacRae appeared in *The Daughter of Rosie O'Grady*.

Davenport Blues 1927 w.m. Bix Beiderbecke

Davy Crockett, *see* **The Ballad of Davy Crockett**

Davy Jones' Locker 1901 w.m. H.W. Petrie

Dawn (Go Away) 1964 w.m. Bob Gaudio, Sandy Linzer

Dawn of a New Day 1938 w. Ira Gershwin m. George Gershwin

Day After Tomorrow, The 1962 w.m. Lionel Bart

Day Before Spring, The 1945 w. Alan Jay Lerner m. Frederick Loewe. (MT) *The Day Before Spring*. Irene Manning and Bill Johnson appeared in *The Day Before Spring*.

Day by Day 1946 w.m. Sammy Cahn, Axel Stordahl, Paul Weston

Day by Day 1971 w.m. Stephen Schwartz. (MT) *Godspell*. (MF) *Godspell*. Stephen Nathan and Sonia Manzano appeared in the stage production of *Godspell*.

Day Dreaming 1938 w.m. Johnny Mercer, Harry Warren. (MF) *The Gay Imposter*.

Day Dreaming 1941 w. Gus Kahn m. Jerome Kern

Day Dreams 1910 w. Harry B. Smith, Robert B. Smith m. Heinrich Reinhardt. (MT) *The Spring Maid*.

Day In—Day Out 1939 w.m. Johnny Mercer, Rube Bloom

Day in the Life, A 1967 w.m. John Lennon, Paul McCartney. (MT) *Beatlemania*.

Day in the Life of a Fool, A 1966 orig.w. Antonio Maria, François Llenas Eng.w. Carl Sigman m. Luiz Bonfa

Day Is Done 1969 w.m. Peter Yarrow

Day-O, *see* **The Banana Boat Song**

Day the Rains Came, The 1957 Fr. w. Pierre Delanoe Eng. w. Carl Sigman m. Gilbert Becaud

Day Tripper 1965 w.m. John Lennon, Paul McCartney. (MT) *Beatlemania*.

Day You Came Along, The 1933 w. Arthur Johnston m. Sam Coslow. (MF) *Too Much Harmony*. Bing Crosby appeared in *Too Much Harmony*.

Daybreak 1942 w. Harold Adamson m. Ferde Grofé. (MF) *Thousands Cheer*. Judy Garland, Mickey Rooney, and Lucille Ball appeared in *Thousands Cheer*. Based on Ferde Grofé's "Mississippi Suite" of 1926.

Daydream 1966 w.m. John B. Sebastian

Daydream Believer 1967 w.m. John C. Stewart. This song was popularly revived in 1980.

Days of Wine and Roses 1962 w. Johnny Mercer m. Henry Mancini. (F) *Days of Wine and Roses*. Jack Lemmon and Lee Remick appeared in *Days of Wine and Roses*. Academy Award winner 1962. Grammy Award winner 1963.

Dazz 1976 w.m. Reginald J. Hargis, Edward D. Frans, Jr., R.L. Ransom, Jr.

De, *see also word that follows*

De Boatman's Dance 1843 w.m. Old Dan D. Emmitt (Daniel Decatur Emmitt)

De Camptown Races (Gwine To Run All Night) 1850 w.m. Stephen Collins Foster. (MF) *Swanee River*. (F) *Colorado*. (MF) *I Dream of Jeanie*. Al Jolson and Don Ameche appeared in *Swanee River*. Roy Rogers and Gabby Hayes appeared in *Colorado*. Ray Middleton and Bill Shirley appeared in *I Dream of Jeanie*. A bastardized version of this song, "Sacramento," was invented by the California fortyniners. See also Part I, 1849. See also "A Capital Ship."

De Gospel Train 1921 w.m. Based on a traditional black American spiritual, c.1871; arr. Henry Thacker Burleigh

Deadwood Stage, The 1954 w. Paul Francis Webster m. Sammy Fain. (MF) *Calamity Jane*. Doris Day appeared in *Calamity Jane*.

Dear Eyes That Haunt Me 1927 w. Harry B. Smith m. Emmerich Kalman. (MT) *The Circus Princess*

Dear Friend 1963 w. Sheldon Harnick m. Jerry Bock. (MT) *She Loves Me*.

Dear Heart 1964 w.m. Ray Evans, Jay Livingston, Henry Mancini. (F) *Dear Heart*. Angela Lansbury, Geraldine Page, and Glenn Ford appeared in *Dear Heart*.

Dear Hearts and Gentle People 1950 w. Bob Hilliard m. Sammy Fain

Dear John Letter 1953 w.m. Billy Barton, Lewis Talley, Fuzzy Owen

Dear Little Boy of Mine 1918 w. J. Keirn Brennan m. Ernest R. Ball

Dear Little Café 1929 w.m. Noël Coward. (MT) *Bitter Sweet*. (MF) *Bitter Sweet*. Jeanette MacDonald and Nelson Eddy appeared in the film production of *Bitter Sweet*.

Dear Little Girl 1926 w. Ira Gershwin m. George Gershwin. (MT) *Oh, Kay!*.

Dear Mother, in Dreams I See Her 1886 w. Claxson Bellamy, Harry Paulton m. Edward Jakobowski. (MT) *Erminie*.

Dear Old Donegal 1942 w.m. Steve Graham. This song was popularly revived in 1946.

Dear Old Girl 1903 w. Richard Henry Buck m. Theodore F. Morse

Dear Old Pal of Mine 1918 w. Harold Robé m. Lieutenant Gitz Rice. Loosely based on Wagner's "Song to the Evening Star."

Dear Old Rose 1912 w. Jack Drislane m. George W. Meyer

Dear Old Southland 1921 w. Henry Creamer m. Turner Layton. Based on the traditional black American spiritual "Deep River" of 1875. Theme song of Layton and Johnstone.

Dear Prudence 1968 w.m. John Lennon, Paul McCartney

Dear World 1969 w.m. Jerry Herman. (MT) *Dear World*. Angela Lansbury appeared in *Dear World*.

Dearest, You're the Nearest to My Heart 1922 w. Benny Davis m. Harry Akst

Dearie 1905 w.m. Clare Kummer

Dearie 1950 w.m. Bob Hilliard, Dave Mann

Dearly Beloved 1942 w. Johnny Mercer m. Jerome Kern. (MF) *You Were Never Lovelier*. Rita Hayworth, Fred Astaire, and Xavier Cugat appeared in *You Were Never Lovelier*.

Death and Transfiguration 1891 m. Richard Strauss. From the German "Tod und Verklärung," op.24.

Death of Nelson, The 1811 w. Samuel James Arnold m. John Braham. (MT) *The Americans*. During its premiere performance by tenor John Braham in *The Americans*, one Lady Hamilton took ill in a private box, stopping the performance with screams and sobs.

December and May, or, **Mollie Newell Don't Be Cruel** 1893 w. Edward B. Marks m. William Lorraine

December 1963 (Oh What a Night) 1976 w.m. Robert Gaudio, Judy Parker

Deck the Halls with Boughs of Holly 1784 w. anon.; first published 1881 m. traditional, from Wales

Decoration Day, *see* **I Was Looking for My Boy, She Said**

Dedicated Follower of Fashion 1966 w.m. Ray Davies. Ivor Novello Award winner 1966.

Dedicated to the One I Love 1961 w.m. Lowman Pauling, Ralph Bass. This song was popularly revived in 1967.

'Deed I Do 1927 w. Walter Hirsch m. Fred Rose

Deep in a Dream 1938 w.m. Eddie De Lange, Jimmy Van Heusen

Deep in My Heart, Dear 1924 w. Dorothy Donnelly m. Sigmund Romberg. (MT) *The Student Prince.* (MF) *The Student Prince.* (MF) *Deep in My Heart.* Howard Marsh and George Hassell appeared in the American stage production of *The Student Prince.* Harry Welchman and Rose Hignell appeared in the British stage production of *The Student Prince.* The voice of Mario Lanza appeared in the 1954 film production of *The Student Prince.* Merle Oberon and Jose Ferrer appeared in *Deep in My Heart,* biopic of composer Sigmund Romberg.

Deep in the Heart of Texas 1941 w. June Hershey m. Don Swander. (MF) *Hi Neighbor.* (MF) *Heart of the Rio Grande.* (MF) *With a Song in My Heart.* Jean Parker and John Archer appeared in *Hi Neighbor.* Gene Autry and Smiley Burnette appeared in *Heart of the Rio Grande.* Susan Hayward appeared in *With a Song in My Heart,* biopic of singer Jane Froman. Ms. Hershey had not been to Texas prior to writing the words to this song.

Deep in Your Eyes 1920 w. William Le Baron m. Victor Jacobi. (MT) *The Half Moon.* Edna May Oliver and Ivy Sawyer appeared in *The Half Moon.*

Deep Night 1929 w. Rudy Vallee m. Charlie Henderson. (MF) *Both Ends of the Candle.*

Deep Purple 1934 w. Mitchell Parish m. Peter DeRose. The words to this song were added in 1939. This song was popularly revived in 1939, and again in 1963.

Deep River 1917 w.m. based on a traditional black American spiritual from at least 1875; arr. Henry Thacker Burleigh. See also "Dear Old Southland."

Deja Vu 1980 w.m. Adrienne Anderson, Isaac Hayes

Delicado 1952 w. Jack Lawrence m. Waldyr Azevedo

Delilah 1917 w.m. Horatio Nicholls

Delilah 1969 w.m. Les Reed, Barry Mason. Ivor Novello Award winner 1968–69.

Delishious 1930 w. Ira Gershwin m. George Gershwin. (MF) *Delicious.* (MF) *Rhapsody in Blue.* Janet Gaynor and Charles Farrell appeared in *Delicious.* Robert Alda, Alexis Smith, and Al Jolson appeared in *Rhapsody in Blue,* biopic of composer George Gershwin.

Deliverance, *see* **Dueling Banjos**

Delta Dawn 1973 w.m. Alex Harvey, Larry Collins

Delyse 1937 w.m. Horatio Nicholls, Joseph Gilbert

Dennis 1845 m. Hans Georg Nägeli. This melody was later used for the hymn "Blest Be the Tie That Binds."

Der Deitcher's Dog, *see* **Oh Where, Oh Where, Has My Little Dog Gone**

Derry Down, *see* **The World Turned Upside Down**

Desafinado (Slightly Out of Tune) 1962 orig. w. Newton Mendonca Eng. w. Jon Hendricks, Jessie Cavanaugh m. Antonio Carlos Jobim

Desert Moon 1985 w.m. Dennis De Young

Desert Song, The 1926 w. Otto Harbach, Oscar Hammerstein II m. Sigmund Romberg. (MT) *The Desert Song.* (MF) *The Desert Song* (1929). (MF) *The Desert Song* (1943). (MF) *The Desert Song* (1953). (MF) *Deep in My Heart.* Vivienne Segal and Robert Halliday appeared in the American stage production of *The Desert Song.* Edith Day and Harry Welchman appeared in the British stage production of *The Desert Song.* John Boles and Myrna Loy appeared in the 1929 film production of *The Desert Song.* Dennis Morgan and Irene Manning appeared in the 1943 film production of *The Desert Song.* Kathryn Grayson and Gordon MacRae appeared in the 1953 film production of *The Desert Song.* Jose Ferrer and Merle Oberon appeared in *Deep in My Heart,* biopic of composer Sigmund Romberg.

Desire 1980 w.m. Barry Gibb, Maurice Gibb, Robin Gibb

Desperate Ones 1968 Eng. w. Eric Blau, Mort Shuman m. Jacques Brel. (MT) *Jacques Brel Is Alive and Well and Living in Paris.*

Detroit City 1963 w.m. Danny Dill, Mel Tillis. Grammy Award winner 1963.

Detroit Rock City 1976 w.m. Stanley Eisen, Bob Ezrin

Devil and the Deep Blue Sea, The, *see* **Between the Devil and the Deep Blue Sea**

Devil Woman 1976 w.m. Christine Authors, Terry Britten

Devil's Gallop, *or,* **Dick Barton Theme** 1948 w.m. Charles Williams

(What'll We Do on a) Dew-Dew-Dewy Day 1927 w.m. Howard Johnson, Charles Tobias, Al Sherman

Di! Di! Di! 1908 w.m. F.C. Carr

Diamond Girl 1973 w.m. Jimmy Seals, Dash Crofts

Diamonds 1963 w.m. Jerry Lordan

Diamonds Are a Girl's Best Friend 1949 w. Leo Robin m. Jule Styne. (MT) *Gentlemen Prefer Blondes.* (MF) *Gentlemen Prefer Blondes.* Carol Channing appeared in the stage production of *Gentlemen Prefer Blondes.* Marilyn Monroe appeared in the film production of *Gentlemen Prefer Blondes.*

Diamonds Are Forever 1972 w.m. Don Black, John Barry. (F) *Diamonds Are Forever.* Ivor Novello Award winner 1972–73.

Diana 1957 w.m. Paul Anka

Diane 1927 w.m. Erno Rapee, Lew Pollack. (F) *Seventh Heaven.* James Stewart appeared in *Seventh Heaven.*

Dickey Bird Song, The 1948 w.m. Howard Dietz, Sammy Fain. (F) *Three Daring Daughter.* Jeanette MacDonald, Jose Iturbi, and Jane Powell appeared in *Three Daring Daughters.*

Dick's Maggot 1951 w.m. based on a seventeenth-century dance; arr. Ernest Tomlinson. (TV-BBC) *Steve Race.*

Dicky Bird Hop, The 1926 w.m. Ronald Gourlay, Leslie Sarony

Did I Remember 1936 w. Harold Adamson m. Walter Donaldson. (F) *Suzy.* Jean Harlow and Cary Grant appeared in *Suzy.*

Did It in a Minute 1982 w.m. Janna Allen, Sara Allen, Daryl Hall

Did Tosti Raise His Bowler Hat When He Said Goodbye 1925 w.m. Billy Mayerl, Gene Paul

Did You Close Your Eyes (When We Kissed) 1957 w.m. Bob Merrill. (MT) *New Girl in Town.*

Did You Ever Get That Feeling in the Moonlight 1945 w.m. James Cavanaugh, Larry Stock, Ira Schuster

Did You Ever Have To Make Up Your Mind 1966 w.m. John B. Sebastian

Did You Ever Ride on a Rainbow 1956 w.m. Leo Robin, Jule Styne. (MF) *Ruggles of Red Gap.*

Did You Ever See a Dream Walking 1933 w. Mack Gordon m. Harry Revel. (MF) *Sitting Pretty.* Jack Oakie, Jack Haley, and Ginger Rogers appeared in *Sitting Pretty.*

Did You Ever See a Lassie, *see* **O Du Lieber Augustin**

Did You Ever Think as the Hearse Rolls By, or, **The Worms Crawl In, the Worms Crawl Out** 1923 w.m. possibly based on a traditional military song popularly sung by British soldiers between 1854 and 1856 during the Crimean War. This song was later arranged for children in 1948 with the title ''The Elephant Walk.''

Did Your Mother Come from Ireland 1937 w.m. Jimmy Kennedy, Michael Carr

Didn't We 1966 w.m. Jimmy L. Webb. This song was also popular in 1969.

Different Worlds 1979 w.m. Charles Fox, Norman Gimbel. (TV) *Angie.*

Dig You Later (A Hubba-Hubba-Hubba) 1945 w. Harold Adamson m. Jimmy McHugh. (MF) *Doll Face.* Perry Como, Carmen Miranda, and Vivian Blaine appeared in *Doll Face.* See also Part I, 1945.

Diga Diga Do 1928 w. Dorothy Fields m. Jimmy McHugh. (MT) *Blackbirds of 1928* (MF) *Stormy Weather.* Adelaide Hall and Aida Ward appeared in *Blackbirds of 1928.* Lena Horne and Fats Waller appeared in *Stormy Weather.*

Dimples 1962 w. Carolyn Leigh m. Cy Coleman. (MT) *Little Me.* Sid Caesar appeared in *Little Me.*

Dinah 1925 w. Sam M. Lewis, Joe Young m. Harry Akst. (MT) *Kid Boots.* (MF) *Broadway.* (MF) *Show Business.* (MF) *Rose Marie.* Eddie Cantor appeared in both *Kid Boots* and *Show Business.* George Raft, Pat O'Brien, and Janet Blair appeared in *Broadway.* Nelson Eddy and Jeanette MacDonald appeared in *Rose Marie.* Theme song of Dinah Shore.

Dindi 1965 w.m. Ray Gilbert, Antonio Carlos Jobim, Louis Oliveria

Ding Dong Bell, *see* **Mother Goose's Melodies**

Ding Dong! The Witch Is Dead 1939 w. E.Y. Harburg m. Harold Arlen. (MF) *The Wizard of Oz.* Judy Garland, Ray Bolger, and Bert Lahr appeared in *The Wizard of Oz.* This song was popularly revived in 1967.

Dinner at Eight 1933 w. Dorothy Fields m. Jimmy McHugh. (F) *Dinner at Eight.* John Barrymore, Wallace Beery, and Lionel Barrymore appeared in *Dinner at Eight.*

Dinner for One, Please James 1935 w.m. Michael Carr

Dipper Mouth Blues, *see* **Sugar Foot Stomp**

Dipsy Doodle, The 1937 w.m. Larry Clinton. (MF) *Since You Went Away.* Claudette Colbert and Shirley Temple appeared in *Since You Went Away.*

Dirty Hands, Dirty Face 1923 w.m. James Monaco, Edgar Leslie, Grant Clarke, Al Jolson. (MT) *Bombo.* (MF) *The Jazz Singer.* Al Jolson appeared in both *Bombo* and *The Jazz Singer.*

Dirty Laundry 1983 w.m. Donald Henley, Daniel Kortchmer

Dis-Donc, Dis-Donc 1960 w. Marguerite Monnot m. Julian More, David Heneker, Monte Norman. (MT) *Irma La Douce.* (MF) *Irma La Douce.* Shirley MacLaine appeared in the film production of *Irma La Douce.*

Disco Duck (Part 1) 1976 w.m. Rick Dees

Disco Lady 1976 w.m. Harvey Scales, Albert Vance, Don Davis

Disco Nights 1979 w.m. Keith Crier, Paul Service

Disenchanted 1984 w.m. Michael Martin Murphey, Jim Ed Norman, Chick Rains

Distant Dreams 1966 w.m. Cindy Walker

Dites-Moi Pourquoi 1949 w. Oscar Hammerstein II m. Richard Rodgers. (MT) *South Pacific.* (MF) *South Pacific.* Mary Martin appeared in the stage production of *South Pacific.* Mitzi Gaynor appeared in the film production of *South Pacific.*

(I Wish I Was in) Dixie, or, **Dixie's Land** 1860 w.m. Daniel Decatur Emmett. (MF) *With a Song in My Heart.* Susan Hayward appeared in *With a Song in My Heart,* biopic of singer Jane Froman. ''Dixie,'' the outstanding song of the American Civil War period, was composed by Dan D. Emmett as a ''walk-around'' for the closing number of a minstrel show at Bryant's Theatre, during which the entire company would parade. The origin of the word Dixie is in dispute, but all agree that Emmett, a black, effectively renamed the South with his masterpiece. Both the North and South rewrote the song with lyrics favoring its side. We could find no positive substantiation that makes conclusive the origin of ''Dixie'' as deriving from the Mason-Dixon line, the ten-dollar bills printed in New Orleans that were called ''Dixies'' because ''Dix'' (French for ten) was printed on them, or the branch of the Dixie family (Johann Dixye) that settled in Harlem, New York, and after an unsuccessful attempt to cultivate tobacco, moved South after selling its eight slaves to a harsh master in South Carolina (they may have written the song). The name ''Dixie'' can be traced back to the era of Elizabeth I of England. The first Wolstan Dixie rallied to the cause of Charles I, providing him with funds to field a regiment for three years for which he received a baronetcy in 1660. Recently, Lady Penelope Dixie of Bodsworth Park in Leicestershire, England, offered for sale her family estate (the family motto is ''Quod dixi, dixi (What I have said, I have said)''). The sale of her estate was the result of there being no male survivors to the Dixie baronetcy in England and the prohibitive cost of tracing an American Dixie's lineage to Bosworth Park. Whether the Dixie family name contributed to the song title is moot, but the power of the name is unarguable as the popularity of ''Dixie Cups'' and musical phrase ''Dixieland'' will attest. At the age of eighty, Dan

Emmett was still making triumphal tours with Al G. Fields Minstrels, ''bringing the house down'' every time he appeared. Sadly, he died a poor man, because the publisher of this all-time smash hit had persuaded Emmett to turn over his copyright for a flat fee of $500. This song was played at Jefferson Davis's inauguration in Montgomery, Alabama, in February 1861.

Dixie on My Mind 1981 w.m. Hank Williams, Jr.

Dizzy 1969 w.m. Fred Weller, Tommy Roe

Dizzy Fingers 1923 m. Zez Confrey

D'Lovely, *see* **It's D'Lovely**

Do Do Do 1926 w. Ira Gershwin m. George Gershwin. (MT) *Oh, Kay!*. (MF) *Tea for Two*. (MF) *Both Ends of the Candle*. Gertrude Lawrence and Victor Moore appeared in the American production of *Oh, Kay!*. Harold French and Claude Hulbert appeared in the British production of *Oh, Kay!*. Doris Day and Gordon MacRae appeared in *Tea for Two*, based on *No, No, Nanette*.

Do, Do, My Huckleberry Do 1893 w. Harry Dillon m. John Dillon. (MT) *A Trip to Chinatown (Second Edition)*.

Do I Hear a Waltz?. 1965 w. Stephen Sondheim m. Richard Rodgers. (MT) *Do I Hear a Waltz?*.

Do I Hear You Saying ''I Love You'' 1928 w. Lorenz Hart m. Richard Rodgers. (MT) *Present Arms*.

Do I Love You 1925 w. E. Ray Goetz m. Henri Christine, E. Ray Goetz. (MT) *Naughty Cinderella*.

Do I Love You 1939 w.m. Cole Porter. (MT) *Du Barry Was a Lady*. (MT) *Black Vanities*. (MF) *Du Barry Was a Lady*. Lucille Ball, Red Skelton, and Gene Kelly appeared in the film production of *Du Barry Was a Lady*.

Do I Love You Because You're Beautiful 1957 w. Oscar Hammerstein II m. Richard Rodgers. (TV) *Cinderella*.

Do I Worry 1940 w.m. Stanley Cowan, Bobby North. (MF) *Pardon My Sarong*. (MF) *Honeymoon Lodge*. Bud Abbott and Lou Costello appeared in *Pardon My Sarong*. David Bruce and Ozzie Nelson appeared in *Honeymoon Lodge*.

Do It (Till You're Satisfied) 1974 w.m. Billy Nichols

Do It Again 1912 w.m. Irving Berlin

(Please) Do It Again 1922 w. B.G. DeSylva m. George Gershwin. (MT) *The French Doll*. (MT) *Mayfair and Montmartre*. (MF) *Rhapsody in Blue*. Alice Delysia appeared in *Mayfair and Montmartre*. Robert Alda, Oscar Levant, and Alexis Smith appeared in *Rhapsody in Blue,* biopic of composer George Gershwin.

Do It Again 1968 w.m. Brian Wilson, Mike Love

Do It Or Die 1979 w.m. Buddy Buie, J.R. Cobb, Ronnie Hammond

Do It the Hard Way 1940 w. Lorenz Hart m. Richard Rodgers. (MT) *Pal Joey*. (MF) *Pal Joey*. Gene Kelly, Van Johnson, and June Havoc appeared in the stage production of *Pal Joey*. Frank Sinatra and Kim Novak appeared in the film production of *Pal Joey*.

Do Not Forsake Me, Oh My Darling, *see* **High Noon**

Do Nothin' Till You Hear from Me 1943 w. Bob Russell m. Duke Ellington. Based on Duke Ellington's ''Concerto for Cootie.''

Do-Re-Mi 1959 w. Oscar Hammerstein II m. Richard Rodgers. (MT) *The Sound of Music*. (MF) *The Sound of Music*. Mary Martin appeared in the stage production of *The Sound of Music*. Julie Andrews appeared in the film production of *The Sound of Music*.

Do Something 1929 w.m. Bud Green, Sammy Stept. (MF) *Nothing But the Truth*. (MF) *Syncopation*. Bob Hope and Paulette Goddard appeared in *Nothing But the Truth*. Ian Hunter and Adolphe Menjou appeared in *Syncopation*.

Do That to Me One More Time 1980 w.m. Toni Tennille

Do the New York 1931 w. Jack P. Murray, Barry Trivers m. Ben Oakland. (MT) *Ziegfeld Follies of 1931*.

Do They Know It's Christmas? 1985 w.m. Bob Geldof, Midge Ure. Ivor Novello Award winner 1984–85.

Do They Miss Me at Home 1852 w. Mrs. Caroline A. Mason m. S.M. Grannis

Do Wah Diddy Diddy 1964 w.m. Ellie Greenwich, Jeff Barry

Do What You Do 1985 w.m. Larry Di Tommaso, Ralph Palladino

Do What You Wanna Do 1970 w.m. J.B. Bingham, Jr.

Do You Believe in Love 1982 w.m. Robert Lang

Do You Believe in Magic 1965 w.m. John B. Sebastian

Do You Care 1941 w.m. John M. Elliott, Lew Quadling

Do You Ever Think of Me 1920 w.m. Harry D. Kerr, Earl Burtnett

Do You Know the Way to San Jose 1968 w. Hal David m. Burt Bacharach

Do You Know What It Means to Miss New Orleans 1946 w. Eddie De Lange m. Louis Alter. (MF) *New Orleans*. Dorothy Patrick and Louis Armstrong appeared in *New Orleans*.

Do You Know Where You're Going To, or, **Theme from Mahogany** 1976 w.m. Gerry Goffin, Michael Masser. (F) *Mahogany*. Diana Ross and Anthony Perkins appeared in *Mahogany*.

Do You Love Me 1946 w.m. Harry Ruby. (MF) *Do You Love Me?*. Maureen O'Hara, Dick Haymes, and Harry James appeared in *Do You Love Me?*.

Do You Love Me 1964 w. Sheldon Harnick m. Jerry Bock. (MT) *Fiddler on the Roof*. (MF) *Fiddler on the Roof*. Zero Mostel and Bette Midler appeared in the stage production of *Fiddler on the Roof*.

Do You Mind 1960 w.m. Lionel Bart. (F) *Let's Get Married*.

Do You Really Want To Hurt Me 1983 w.m. Michael Craig, Roy Hay, Jon Moss, George O'Dowd (Boy George). Ivor Novello Award winner 1982–83.

Do You Remember the Last Waltz 1911 w.m. Bennett Scott, A.J. Mills

Do You Take This Woman for Your Lawful Wife? 1913 w. Andrew B. Sterling m. Harry Von Tilzer. (MT) *The Passing Show of 1913*.

Do You Want To Dance 1958 w.m. Robert Freeman. This song was popularly revived in 1975.

Do You Want To Know a Secret 1964 w.m. John Lennon, Paul McCartney

Do Your Own Thing 1969 w.m. Hal Hester, Danny Apolinar. (MT) *Your Own Thing*.

Doan Ye Cry, Mah Honey 1899 w.m. Albert W. Noll

(Sittin' on) Dock of the Bay, The 1968 w.m. Steve Cropper, Otis Redding. Grammy Award winner 1968. This song was popularly revived in 1982.

(Theme from) Doctor Kildaire, or, Three Stars Will Shine Tonight 1961 w.m. Peter Rugolo, Jerry Goldsmith. (TV) *Doctor Kildaire*. Richard Chamberlain appeared in *Doctor Kildaire*.

Doctor, Lawyer, Indian Chief 1946 w. Paul Francis Webster m. Hoagy Carmichael. (MF) *Stork Club*. Betty Hutton and Barry Fitzgerald appeared in *Stork Club*.

Doctor Tinkle Tinker 1910 w. Otto Harbach m. Karl Hoschna. (MT) *The Girl of My Dreams*.

Doctor Who Theme 1964 w.m. Ron Grainer

Doctor's Orders 1976 w.m. Roger Greenaway, Roger Cook, Geoff Stephens. Ivor Novello Award winner 1975–76.

Dodging a Divorcee 1935 m. Reginald Forsythe

Does Anybody Really Know What Time It Is 1970 w.m. Robert William Lamm

Does Santa Claus Sleep with His Whiskers 1934 w.m. Billy Bray, Fred Gibson

Does the Spearmint Lose Its Flavor on the Bedpost Overnight 1924 w. Billy Rose, Marty Bloom m. Ernest Breuer

Does Your Heart Beat for Me 1936 w. Mitchell Parish m. Russ Morgan, Arnold Johnson

Dog and Butterfly 1979 w.m. Susan Ennis, Ann Wilson, Nancy Wilson

(How Much Is That) Doggie in the Window 1953 w.m. Bob Merrill

Doin' the Ducky Wuck 1935 w.m. Joe Penner, Hal Raynor

Doin' the New Low-Down 1928 w. Dorothy Fields m. Jimmy McHugh. (MT) *Blackbirds of 1928*. Adelaide Hall, Bill Robinson, and Aida Ward appeared in *Blackbirds of 1928*.

Doin' the Raccoon 1928 w. Raymond Klages m. J. Fred Coots. (MF) *The Time, the Place and the Girl*. Grant Withers and James Kirkwood appeared in *The Time, the Place and the Girl*.

Doin' the Uptown Lowdown 1933 w. Mack Gordon m. Harry Revel. (MF) *Broadway Through a Keyhole*. Constance Cummings and Texas Guinan appeared in *Broadway Through a Keyhole*.

Doin' What Comes Natur'lly 1946 w.m. Irving Berlin. (MT) *Annie Get Your Gun*. (MF) *Annie Get Your Gun*. Ethel Merman appeared in the stage production of *Annie Get Your Gun*. Betty Hutton appeared in the film production of *Annie Get Your Gun*.

Dolce Far Niente 1960 w.m. Meredith Wilson. (MT) *The Unsinkable Molly Brown*. (MF) *The Unsinkable Molly Brown*. Tammy Grimes appeared in the stage production of *The Un-*

sinkable Molly Brown. Debbie Reynolds appeared in the film production of *The Unsinkable Molly Brown*.

Doll Dance, The 1927 m. Nacio Herb Brown

Dollar Princesses 1909 w.m. Adrian Ross, Leo Fall. (MT) *The Dollar Princess*.

Dolores 1941 w. Frank Loesser m. Louis Alter. (MF) *Las Vegas Nights*. (MF) *The Gay City*. Constance Moore and Bert Wheeler appeared in *Las Vegas Nights*.

Domani (Tomorrow) 1955 w. Tony Velona m. Ulpio Minucci

Dominique 1963 orig.w. Soeur Sourire Eng.w. Noel Regney m. Soeur Sourire. (F) *The Singing Nun*. Debbie Reynolds and Greer Garson appeared in *The Singing Nun*.

Domino 1951 Fr.w. Jacques Plante Eng.w. Don Raye m. Louis Ferrari

Domino 1970 w.m. Van Morrison

Don Juan, op.20 1880 m. Richard Strauss

Donkey Serenade, The 1937 w. Robert Wright, George Forrest m. Rudolf Friml, Herbert Stothart. Based on Friml's "Chanson" of 1920, with lyrics added. (MF) *The Firefly*. Allan Jones and Jeanette MacDonald appeared in the film production of *The Firefly*. Theme song of Monte Ray. See also "Chansonette."

Donna 1958 w.m. Ritchie Valens

Don't 1958 w.m. Jerry Leiber, Mike Stoller

Don't Answer Me 1984 w.m. Alan Parsons, Eric Woolfson

Don't Ask Me Why 1943 w.m. Robert Stolz, Joe Young

Don't Be Angry 1955 n.m. Napoleon Brown, Rose Marie McCoy, Fred Mendelssohn

Don't Be That Way 1938 w.m. Mitchell Parish, Benny Goodman, Edgar Sampson

Don't Bite the Hand That's Feeding You 1915 w. Thomas Hoier m. James Morgan. (MF) *Bells of Capistrano*. Gene Autry and Smiley Burnette appeared in *Bells of Capistrano*.

Don't Blame It All on Broadway 1913 w. Joe Young, Harry Williams m. Bert Grant

Don't Blame Me 1933 w. Dorothy Fields m. Jimmy McHugh. (MT) *Sugar Babies*. (F) *Dinner at Eight*. (MF) *Freddie Steps Out*. (F) *Big City*. (MF) *The Strip*. Ann Miller and Mickey Rooney appeared in *Sugar Babies*. John Barrymore, Lionel Barrymore, and Wallace Beery appeared in *Dinner at Eight*. Freddie Stewart appeared in *Freddie Steps Out*. Margaret O'Brien and Robert Preston appeared in *Big City*. Mickey Rooney appeared in *The Strip*. **Don't Break the Heart That Loves You** 1962 w.m. Benny Davis, Ted Murry

Don't Bring Lulu 1925 w. Billy Rose, Lew Brown m. Ray Henderson

Don't Bring Me Down 1964 w.m. Johnnie Dee

Don't Bring Me Down 1979 w.m. Jeff Lynne

Don't Bring Me Your Heartaches 1965 w.m. Robin Conrad, Les Reed

Don't Call It Love 1985 w.m. Dean Pitchford, Tom Snow

Don't Count the Rainy Days 1984 w.m. Jerry Careaga, Wayland Holyfield

Don't Cry for Me, Argentina 1977 w.m. Tim Rice, Andrew Lloyd Webber. (MT) *Evita*. Ivor Novello Award winner 1976–77. Ivor Novello Award winner 1977–78.

Don't Cry, Frenchy, Don't Cry 1919 w.m. Sam M. Lewis, Joe Young m. Walter Donaldson

Don't Cry, Joe 1949 w.m. Joe Marsala

Don't Dilly Dally on the Way 1919 w.m. Fred W. Leigh, Charles Collins. In Victorian England, a not unusual circumstance was "shooting the moon," that is, decamping by night with the furniture to avoid paying the arrears of rent. This activity is the subject of this satirical music hall ballad. This English music hall song was popularly sung by Marie Lloyd, a most famous music hall singer, and a star at sixteen years of age.

Don't Do Me Like That 1980 w.m. Tom Petty

Don't Do That to the Poor Puss Cat 1928 w.m. Leslie Sarony, Frank Eyton

Don't Ever Be Afraid To Go Home 1952 w. Bob Hilliard m. Carl Sigman

Don't Ever Leave Me 1929 w. Oscar Hammerstein II m. Jerome Kern. (MT) *Sweet Adeline*. (MF) *Sweet Adeline*. (MF) *Both Ends of the Candle*. Irene Dunne and Ned Sparks appeared in the film production of *Sweet Adeline*.

Don't Explain 1946 w.m. Billie Holiday. (MF) *Lady Sings the Blues*. Diana Ross appeared in *Lady Sings the Blues*.

Don't Fall in Love with a Dreamer 1980 w.m. David Ellingson, Kim Carnes Ellingson

Don't Fence Me In 1944 w.m. Cole Porter. (MF) *Hollywood Canteen*. (MF) *Don't Fence Me In*. Bette Davis and Joan Crawford appeared in *Hollywood Canteen*. Roy Rogers and Gabby Hayes appeared in *Don't Fence Me In*. See also Part I, 1944.

Don't Forbid Me 1957 w.m. Charles Singleton

Don't Get Around Much Anymore 1943 w. Bob Russell m. Duke Ellington. (MT) *Sophisticated Ladies*. Gregory Hines and Phyllis Hyman appeared in *Sophisticated Ladies*. Based on Ellington's "Never No Lament."

Don't Give Up On Us 1977 w.m. Tony Macaulay. Ivor Novello Award winner 1977–78.

Don't Give Up the Old Love for the New 1896 w.m. James Thornton

Don't Give Up the Ship 1935 w. Al Dubin m. Harry Warren. (MF) *Shipmates Forever*. James Melton and Jane Froman appeared in *Shipmates Forever*.

Don't Go Breaking My Heart 1976 w.m. Elton John, Bernie Taupin. Ivor Novello Award winner 1976–77.

Don't Go Down the Mine 1910 w.m. William Geddes, Robert Donnelly

Don't Go in the Lion's Cage Tonight 1906 w.m. E. Ray Goetz, John Gilroy

Don't Go Out Tonight, Boy 1895 w. George Cooper m. Charles E. Pratt

Don't Go to Strangers 1954 w. Redd Evans m. Arthur Kent, Dave Mann

Don't Have Any More, Mrs. Moore 1926 w.m. Harry Castling, James Walsh

Don't Hold Everything 1928 w. B.G. DeSylva, Lew Brown m. Ray Henderson. (MT) *Hold Everything!*. Bert Lahr and Ona Munson appeared in *Hold Everything!*.

Don't It Make My Brown Eyes Blue 1977 w.m. Richard Leigh. Grammy Award winner 1977.

Don't Laugh at Me ('Cause I'm a Fool) 1952 w.m. Norman Wisdom, June Tremayne. (MF) *Trouble in Store*.

Don't Leave Me, Dolly 1898 w. William H. Gardner m. Harry Weill

Don't Leave Me This Way 1977 w.m. Cary Gilbert, Kenny Gamble, Leon Huff

Don't Let It Bother You 1934 w. Mack Gordon m. Harry Revel. (MF) *The Gay Divorcee*. Ginger Rogers, Fred Astaire, and Edward Everett Horton appeared in *The Gay Divorcee*. This song did not appear in the stage production *Gay Divorce*.

Don't Let It Die 1972 w.m. E.S. Smith. Ivor Novello Award winner 1971–72.

Don't Let Me Be Lonely Tonight 1972 w.m. James Taylor

Don't Let the Stars Get in Your Eyes 1952 w.m. Slim Willet

Don't Let the Sun Catch You Crying 1964 w.m. Gerrard Marsden

Don't Let the Sun Go Down on Me 1974 w.m. Elton John, Bernie Taupin

Don't Look At Me That Way 1928 w.m. Cole Porter. (MT) *Paris*.

Don't Marry Me 1958 w. Oscar Hammerstein II m. Richard Rodgers. (MT) *Flower Drum Song*. (MF) *Flower Drum Song*.

Don't Pull Your Love 1976 w.m. Dennis Lambert, Brian Potter

Don't Put Me Off at Buffalo Any More 1901 w. William Jerome m. Jean Schwartz

Don't Put Your Daughter on the Stage, *see* **Mrs. Worthington**

Don't Rain on My Parade 1964 w. Bob Merrill m. Jule Styne. (MT) *Funny Girl*. (MF) *Funny Girl*. Barbra Streisand appeared in both the stage and film productions of *Funny Girl*.

Don't Ring-a Da Bell 1956 w.m. Johnny Reine, Sonny Miller

Don't Sit Under the Apple Tree (with Anyone Else But Me) 1942 w.m. Sammy Stept, Charles Tobias, Lew Brown. Based on "Long Long Ago" of 1833. (MF) *Private Buckaroo*. (MF) *With a Song in My Heart*. (MF) *Kiss Them for Me*. The Andrews Sisters and Joe E. Lewis appeared in *Private Buckaroo*. Susan Hayward appeared in *With a Song in My Heart*, biopic of singer Jane Froman. Cary Grant and Jayne Mansfield appeared in *Kiss Them for Me*.

Don't Sleep in the Subway 1967 w.m. Jackie Trent, Tony Hatch. Ivor Novello Award winner 1967–68.

Don't Stand So Close to Me   1981   w.m. Sting. Ivor Novello Award winner 1980–81.

Don't Stay Away Too Long   1955   w.m. Al Hoffman, Dick Manning

Don't Stop   1977   w.m. Christine McVie

Don't Stop Believin'   1982   w. Jonathan Cain, Stephen Perry, Neal Schon

Don't Stop 'Til You Get Enough   1979   w.m. Michael Jackson

Don't Stop—Twist   1962   w.m. Frankie Vaughan

Don't Sweetheart Me   1943   w.m. Clifford Friend, Charles Tobias. (F) *Hi Beautiful*. Noah Beery appeared in *Hi Beautiful*.

Don't Take Me Home   1908   w. Vincent Bryan   m. Harry Von Tilzer

Don't Take Your Love from Me   1941   w.m. Henry Nemo

Don't Talk to Him   1963   w.m. Cliff Richard, Bruce Welch

Don't Talk to Strangers   1982   w.m. Rick Springfield

Don't Tell a Soul   1931   w.m. Harry S. Pepper

Don't Tell Her (What's Happened to Me)   1930   w.m. B.G. DeSylva, Lew Brown, Ray Henderson. (MF) *Lover Come Back*. Lucille Ball and George Brent appeared in *Lover Come Back*. This song was popularly revived in 1946.

Don't Tell Her That You Love Her   1896   w.m. Paul Dresser

Don't That Beat All   1962   w.m. Les Vandyke

Don't Think Twice, It's All Right   1963   w.m. Bob Dylan

(Our Love) Don't Throw It All Away   1978   w.m. George Blake, David Richard Mindel

Don't Throw Your Love Away   1964   w.m. B. Jackson, J. Wisner

Don't Treat Me Like a Child   1961   w.m. Mike Hawker, John Schroeder

Don't Turn Around   1964   w.m. Peter Lee Stirling, Barry Mason

Don't Wait On Me   1981   w.m. Donald Reid, Harold Reid

Don't Wait 'Til the Night Before Christmas   1938   w. Sam M. Lewis   m. Abel Baer

Don't Wake Me Up, I'm Dreaming   1910   w. Beth Slater Whitson   m. Herbert Ingraham

Don't Wake Me Up, Let Me Dream   1925   w. L. Wolfe Gilbert   m. Mabel Wayne, Abel Baer

Don't Worry   1955   w.m. Ed Franks

Don't Worry   1960   w.m. Marty Robbins

Don't Worry 'Bout Me   1939   w. Ted Koehler   m. Rube Bloom

Don't Worry 'Bout Me Baby   1982   w.m. Deborah Allen, Bruce Channel, Kieran Kane

Don't You Cry, My Honey, *see* **Doan Ye Cry, Mah Honey**

Don't You (Forget About Me)   1985   w.m. Keith Forsey, Steve Schiff

Don't You Know   1959   w.m. Bobby Worth. Based on Puccini's "Musetta's Waltz" from the opera *La Bohème*.

Don't You Know It   1961   w.m. Les Vandyke

Don't You Rock Me Daddy-O   1957   w.m. Wally Whyton, Bill Varley

Don't You Think It's Time   1963   w.m. Geoffrey Goddard, Joe Meek

Don't You Want Me   1982   w.m. Jo Callis, Phil Oakey, Adrian Wright. Ivor Novello Award winner 1981–82. Ivor Novello Award winner 1982–83.

Doo Wacka Doo   1924   w.m. Clarence Gaskill, Will Donaldson, George Horther

Doodle Doo Doo   1924   w.m. Art Kassel, Mel Stitzel

Door of My (Her) Dreams, The   1924   w. Otto Harbach, Oscar Hammerstein II   m. Rudolf Friml. (MT) *Rose Marie*.

Double Vision   1978   w.m. A. Van, C. Phillips

Double Your Pleasure   1959   w.m. Mike Chan, Dick Cunliffe. This song was written for a Wrigley's Doublemint Chewing Gum commercial promotion campaign.

Dove, The, *see* **La Paloma**

Down Among the Sheltering Palms   1914   w. James Brockman   m. Abe Olman. (MF) *That Midnight Kiss*. (MF) *Some Like It Hot*. Kathryn Grayson and Mario Lanza appeared in *That Midnight Kiss*. Marilyn Monroe, Jack Lemmon, and Tony Curtis appeared in *Some Like It Hot*.

Down Among the Sugar Cane   1908   w. Avery, Hart   m. Cecil Mack, Chris Smith

Down Among the Sugar-Cane   1929   w. Charles Tobias, Sidney Clare   m. Peter DeRose. (MF) *So Long Letty*. Grant Withers and Patsy Ruth Miller appeared in *So Long Letty*.

Down and Out, *see* **Silver Dollar**

Down Argentine Way   1940   w.m. Mack Gordon, Harry Warren. (MF) *Down Argentine Way*. Betty Grable and Carmen Miranda appeared in *Down Argentine Way*.

Down at the Huskin' Bee   1909   w. Monroe H. Rosenfeld   m. S.R. Henry (Henry R. Stern). This song was originally published as an instrumental only in 1908, with the title "S.R. Henry's Barn Dance."

Down at the Old Swimming Hole   1921   w.m. Al Wilson, Jim Brennan

Down Below   1958   w.m. Sydney Carter

Down by the O-Hi-O   1920   w.m. anon. This song was popularly revived in 1940.

Down by the Old Mill Stream   1910   w.m. Earl K. Smith, Tell Taylor. Though authorship is still in debate, journalist Gary Pakulski concludes that co-authorship was likely. Smith, in a 1940 letter to a Findlay man, said he thought up the title and wrote the chorus. Taylor added the two verses a year later. Smith describes the chorus as "the hit part of the song." Taylor, however, later embarked on a new venture: a golf course he affectionately named the Old Mill Stream Course. A relative has vivid recollections of Taylor driving around the course with a lawn mower hitched to the rear of his Cadillac.

Down by the River   1935   w. Lorenz Hart   m. Richard Rodgers. (MF) *Mississippi*. Bing Crosby, W.C. Fields, and Joan Bennett appeared in *Mississippi*.

Down by the Riverside, or, **Ain't Gwine Study War No More**   1865   w.m. traditional black American spiritual. (F) *Colo-*

rado Sundown. Slim Pickens and Rex Allen appeared in *Colorado Sundown.*

Down by the Silvery Rio Grande 1913 w. Dave Weisberg, Robert F. Roden m. Charles Speidel

Down by the Station 1949 w.m. arr. 1959 Glen Larson, Bruce Belland

Down by the Winegar Woiks 1925 w.m. Don Bestor, Roger Lewis, Walter Donovan

Down Forget-Me-Not Lane 1941 w.m. Horatio Nicholls, Charlie Chester, Reg Morgan

Down Home in Tennessee, *see* **Just Try To Picture Me**

Down in Bom-Bombay 1915 w. Ballard MacDonald m. Harry Carroll

Down in Dear Old New Orleans 1912 w. Joe Young m. Conrad and Whidden. (MF) *Ziegfeld Follies of 1912.*

Down in Honky Tonky Town 1916 w.m. Charles McCarron, Chris Smith

Down in Jungle Town 1908 w. Edward Madden m. Theodore F. Morse

Down in Poverty Row 1895 w. Gussie L. Davis m. Arthur Trevelyan

Down in Tennessee, *see* **Ten Little Fingers and Ten Little Toes—Down in Tennessee**

Down in the Boondocks 1965 w.m. Joe South

Down in the Depths on the Ninetieth Floor 1936 w.m. Cole Porter. (MT) *Red, Hot and Blue!.* (MF) *Red, Hot and Blue!.* Ethel Merman, Jimmy Durante, and Bob Hope appeared in the stage production of *Red, Hot and Blue!* Betty Hutton and Victor Mature appeared in the film production of *Red, Hot and Blue!.*

Down in the Forest 1906 w.m. Landon Ronald

Down in the Glen 1949 w.m. Harry Gordon, Tommie Connor

Down in the Old Cherry Orchard 1907 w. Alfred Bryan m. Henry Stern (S.R. Henry)

Down in the Valley, or, **Birmingham Jail,** or, **Bird in a Cage,** or, **Down on the Levee** 1917 w.m. traditional mountain song, c. 1845. (MF) *Moonlight and Cactus.* (F) *The Last Musketeer.* (F) *Montana Territory.* The Andrews Sisters appeared in *Moonlight and Cactus.* Rex Allen appeared in *The Last Musketeer.* Wanda Hendrix appeared in *Montana Territory.* This song was popularly revived in 1944.

Down Mexico Way, *see* **South of the Border**

Down on the Brandywine 1904 w. Vincent P. Bryan m. J.B. Mullen

Down on the Farm (They All Ask for You) 1902 w. Raymond A. Browne m. Harry Von Tilzer

Down on the Farm, *see also* **I Want To Go Back to Michigan—Down on the Farm**

Down on the Farm in Harvest Time 1913 w. Andrew K. Allison m. Dick Richards

Down South 1900 w. Sigmund Spaeth m. W.H. Myddleton. The words to this song were added in 1927. (F) *Big Boy.* Al Jolson and Claudia Dell appeared in *Big Boy.* This song

was reissued in 1912, and popularly revived in 1927. See also "Goodbye, My Lady Love."

Down Sweetheart Avenue 1948 w.m. Frank Chacksfield, Cedric Rushworth

Down the Field (March) 1911 w. Caleb W. O'Connor m. Stanleigh P. Friedman. Fight song for Yale University. For his fiftieth class reunion, Yale honored Stanleigh P. Friedman by carving into Welch Hall, where he roomed as a student, the following inscription: " 'Down the Field' was written within these walls by Stanleigh P. Friedman, '05.''

Down the Mall 1937 m. John Belton

Down the Old Ox Road 1933 w.m. Sam Coslow, Arthur Johnston. (MF) *College Humor.* Bing Crosby and Burns and Allen appeared in *College Humor.*

Down the River of Golden Dreams 1930 w.m. John Klenner, Nathaniel Shilkret

Down the Winding Road of Dreams 1922 w. Margaret Cantrell m. Ernest R. Ball

Down Under 1982 w.m. Colin Hay, Ron Strykert

Down Vauxhall Way 1912 w.m. Edward Teschemacher, Herbert Oliver

Down Went McGinty 1889 w.m. Joseph Flynn

Down Where the Cotton Blossoms Grow 1901 w. Andrew B. Sterling m. Harry Von Tilzer

Down Where the Silv'ry Mohawk Flows 1905 w. Monroe H. Rosenfeld m. John Heinzman, Otto Heinzman

Down Where the Swanee River Flows 1916 w. Charles McCarron, Charles S. Alberte m. Albert Von Tilzer

Down Where the Trade Winds Blow 1938 w.m. Harry Owens. (MF) *Hawaii Calls.* Bobby Breen and Ned Sparks appeared in *Hawaii Calls.*

Down Where the Wurzburger Flows 1902 w. Vincent P. Bryan m. Harry Von Tilzer. This song renamed Nora Bayes the ''Wurzburger Girl,'' after she introduced it at Percy Williams's Orpheum Theatre in Brooklyn. It was later adapted for a Wurzburger Beer commercial promotion campaign.

Down with Love 1937 w. E.Y. Harburg m. Harold Arlen. (MT) *Hooray for What!.* Ed Wynn and Jack Whiting appeared in *Hooray for What!.*

Down Yonder 1921 w.m. L. Wolfe Gilbert. This song was popularly revived in 1951.

Downhearted 1953 w.m. Bob Hilliard, David A. Mann

Downhearted Blues 1923 w.m. Alberta Hunter. For a complete history of this song, see Part I, 1923.

Downtown 1965 w.m. Tony Hatch. Ivor Novello Award winner 1964.

Doxology, *see* **Old Hundred(th) Doxology**

Dr., *see* **Doctor**

(Theme from) Dragnet 1953 m. Walter Schumann. (TV) *Dragnet.*

Dream (When You're Feeling Blue) 1945 w.m. Johnny Mercer. (F) *Her Highness and the Bellboy.* (MF) *Daddy Long Legs.* Hedy Lamarr and June Allyson appeared in *Her Highness and the Bellboy.* Fred Astaire and Leslie Caron appeared in *Daddy Long Legs.* Theme song of The Pied Pipers.

Dream, A   1895   w. Charles B. Cory   m. J.C. Bartlett

Dream a Little Dream of Me   1931   w. Gus Kahn   m. Wilbur Schwandt, Fabian Andre

Dream Along with Me (I'm on My Way to a Star)   1955   w.m. Carl Sigman. Theme song of Perry Como.

Dream Babies   1970   w. Herb Schapiro   m. Gary William Friedman. (MT) *The Me Nobody Knows.*

Dream Dancing   1941   w.m. Cole Porter. (MF) *You'll Never Get Rich.* Fred Astaire and Rita Hayworth appeared in *You'll Never Get Rich.*

Dream, Dream, Dream   1947   w.m. Louis Ricca, John Redmond

Dream, Dream, Dream   1954   w. Mitchell Parish   m. Jimmy McHugh

Dream Girls   1982   w. Tom Eyen   m. Henry Krieger. (MT) *Dream Girls.* Loretta Devine and Jennifer Holliday appeared in *Dream Girls.*

Dream Is a Wish Your Heart Makes, A   1949   w.m. Jerry Livingston, Mack David, Al Hoffman. (MF) *Cinderella.*

Dream Lover   1929   w. Clifford Grey   m. Victor Schertzinger. (MF) *The Love Parade.* (MF) *Lady in the Dark.* Maurice Chevalier and Jeanette MacDonald appeared in *The Love Parade.* Ginger Rogers and Ray Milland appeared in *Lady in the Dark.*

Dream Lover   1959   w.m. Bobby Darin

Dream of My Boyhood Days, A   1896   w.m. Paul Dresser

Dream of Olwen, The   1948   w.m. Charles Williams. (MF) *While I Live.*

Dream On   1976   w.m. Steve Tallarico

Dreamer with a Penny   1949   w. Lester Lee   m. Allan Roberts. (MT) *All for Love*

Dreamer's Holiday, A   1949   w.m. Kim Gannon, Mabel Wayne

Dreamin'   1980   w.m. Alan Tarney, Leo Sayer

Dreaming   1906   w. L.W. Heiser   m. J. Anton Dailey

Dreaming   1932   w.m. Reginald Connelly, Bud Flanagan

Dreaming, *see also* **Time Was**

Dreaming, The   1983   w. Kate Bush. Ivor Novello Award winner 1982–83.

Dreams   1977   w.m. Stevie Nicks

Dreams of Long Ago   1912   It.w.   John Focacci   Eng.w. Earl Carroll   m. Enrico Caruso. From the Italian "Sogni d'altra Età."

Dreamy Alabama   1919   w.m. Mary Earl (Robert A. King)

Dreamy Melody   1922   w.m. Ted Koehler, Frank Magine, C. Naset

Dress You Up   1986   w.m. Andrea La Russo

Drift Away   1973   w.m. Mentor Williams

Drifter   1981   w.m. Archie Jordan, Donald Pfrimmer

Drifting Along with the Tumbling Tumbleweeds, *see* **Tumbling Tumbleweeds**

Drifting and Dreaming (Sweet Paradise)   1925   w. Haven Gillespie   m. Egbert van Alstyne, Erwin R. Schmidt, Loyal Curtis

Drill Ye Tarriers Drill   1888   w.m. anon., possibly Thomas F. Casey. (MT) *A Brass Monkey.* "Tarrier" is slang for ruffian. Casey performed this number as a topper to his vaudeville act at Tony Pastor's.

Drink It Down, Drink It Down, *see* **Balm of Gilead**

Drink, Puppy, Drink   1874   w.m. C.J. Whyte Melville

Drink to Me Only with Thine Eyes   1780   w. earliest words published 1616 in the poem "To Celia" by Ben Jonson   m. earliest music published 1780; sometimes attributed to Colonel R. Mellish

Drinking Song   1924   w. Dorothy Donnelly   m. Sigmund Romberg. (MT) *The Student Prince.* (MF) *The Student Prince.* Raymond Marlowe and Paul Clemon appeared in the British stage production of *The Student Prince.* The voice of Mario Lanza was used in the film production of *The Student Prince.*

Drive   1984   w.m. Ric Ocasek

Drivin' My Life Away   1980   w.m. David Malloy, Eddie Rabbitt, Even Stevens. (F) *Roadie.*

Drummer Boy of Shiloh, The   1862   w.m. Will Hays. During the American Civil War, this song was popular with both the North and the South.

Drums in My Heart   1932   w. Edward Heyman   m. Vincent Youmans. (MT) *Through the Years.* Natalie Hall, Michael Bartlett, and Charles Winninger appeared in *Through the Years.*

(What Shall We Do with) Drunken Sailor, The, or, **Columbus,** or, **John Brown Had a Little Injun,** or, **Ten Little Indians**   1891   w.m. traditional sea chantey. See also "Ten Little Indians."

Dry Bones   1865   w. James Weldon Johnson   m. J. Rosamond Johnson. Based on a traditional black American spiritual. This song was popularly revived in 1949. See also Part I, 1902.

Du, Du, Liegst Mir im Herzen   1820   w.m. traditional folksong from Germany

Du und Du (You and You Waltz)   1874   m. Johann Strauss. (MF) *The Great Waltz.* Words were added to this melody by Oscar Hammerstein II for the musical film *The Great Waltz.*

Duddly Dell   1961   w.m. Dudley Moore

Dueling Banjos   1973   w.m. Arthur Smith. (F) *Deliverance.*

Duelists, The   1977   w.m. Howard Blake. Ivor Novello Award winner 1977–78.

Duerme, *see* **Time Was**

Duke of Earl, The   1962   w.m. Earl Edwards, Bernie Williams, Eugene Dixon

(Theme from) Dukes of Hazzard (Good Ol' Boys)   1980   w.m. Waylon Jennings. (TV) *Dukes of Hazzard.*

Dulcinea   1966   w. Joe Darion   m. Mitch Leigh. (MT) *Man of La Mancha.* (MF) *Man of La Mancha.* Richard Kiley appeared in the stage production of *Man of La Mancha.* Sophia Loren appeared in the film production of *Man of La Mancha.*

Dum Dum   1961   w.m. Jackie DeShannon, Sharon Sheeley

Dummy Song, or, **I'll Take the Legs from off the Table**   1920   w.m. anon. This traditional college song is based on "Washington and Lee Swing," school song for Washington and Lee University.

Duna 1914 w. Marjorie Pickhall m. Josephine McGill

Dunderbeck, *see* **Rambling Wreck from Georgia Tech**

Dungaree Doll 1955 w. Ben Raleigh m. Sherman Edwards

Durham Town 1970 w.m. Roger Whittaker

Dusky Stevedore 1928 w. Andy Razaf m. J.C. Johnson

Dust in the Wind 1978 w.m. Kerry Livgren

D'Ya Love Me? 1925 w. Oscar Hammerstein II m. Jerome Kern. (MT) *Sunny.* (MF) *Sunny* (1930). (MF) *Sunny* (1941). Marilyn Miller, Jack Donahue, and Clifton Webb appeared in the stage production of *Sunny.* Marilyn Miller and Lawrence Gray appeared in the first film production of *Sunny.*

D'Ye Ken John Peel, *see* **John Peel**

Dying Cowboy, The, *see* **Oh, Bury Me Not on the Lone Prairie**

Dying Poet, The 1864 m. Seven Octaves (Louis Moreau Gottschalk)

Each Tomorrow Morning 1968 w.m. Jerry Herman. (MT) *Dear World.* Angela Lansbury appeared in *Dear World.*

Eadie Was a Lady 1932 w. B.G. DeSylva m. Nacio Herb Brown, Richard Whiting. (MT) *Take a Chance.* (MF) *Take a Chance.* Ethel Merman, Jack Whiting, and Jack Haley appeared in the stage production of *Take a Chance.* Charles "Buddy" Rogers and James Dunn appeared in the film production of *Take a Chance.*

Early Autumn 1949 w. Johnny Mercer m. Ralph Burns, Woody Herman. This song was also popular in 1952.

Early in de Mornin' 1877 w.m. William Shakespeare Hays

Early in the Morning 1970 w.m. Mike Leander, Eddie Seago

Earth Angel 1955 w.m. Curtis Williams

Ease On Down the Road 1975 w.m. Charlie Smalls. (MT) *The Wiz.* (MF) *The Wix.* Stephanie Mills, Ted Ross, and Mabel King appeared in the stage production of *The Wiz.* Diana Ross appeared in the film production of *The Wiz.*

Easier Said Than Done 1963 w.m. William B. Linton, Larry F. Huff

East of the Moon, West of the Stars 1927 w. Fleta Jan Brown m. Herbert Spencer

East of the Sun and West of the Moon 1935 w.m. Brooks Bowman. (MT) *Stags at Bay.*

East Side of Heaven 1939 w. Johnny Burke m. James V. Monaco. (MF) *East Side of Heaven.* Bing Crosby and Joan Blondell appeared in *East Side of Heaven.*

East Side, West Side, *see* **The Sidewalks of New York**

Easter Parade 1933 w.m. Irving Berlin. (MT) *As Thousands Cheer.* (MT) *Stop Press.* (MF) *Alexander's Ragtime Band.* (MF) *Holiday Inn.* (MF) *Easter Parade.* Clifton Webb and Marilyn Miller appeared in *As Thousands Cheer.* Dorothy Dixon appeared in *Stop Press.* Tyrone Power appeared in *Alexander's Ragtime Band.* Fred Astaire and Bing Crosby appeared in *Holiday Inn.* Judy Garland, Fred Astaire, and Ann Miller appeared in *Easter Parade.* This song was popularly revived in 1948. This song was originally titled in 1917

"Smile and Show Your Dimple"; the melody was later used for "Easter Parade."

Easy Come, Easy Go 1934 w. Edward Heyman m. John W. Green. (MF) *Bachelor of Arts.* Anita Louise and Tom Brown appeared in *Bachelor of Arts.*

Easy Come, Easy Go 1970 w.m. Diane W. Hilderbrand, Jack Keller

Easy Going Me 1961 w.m. Lionel Bart

Easy Living 1937 w.m. Leo Robin, Ralph Ranger. (F) *Easy Living.* Jean Arthur and Edward Arnold appeared in *Easy Living.*

Easy Lover 1985 w.m. Phil Collins, Philip Bailey, Nathan East. Ivor Novello Award winner 1985–86.

Easy Rider 1933 w.m. Shelton Brooks. (MF) *She Done Him Wrong.* Mae West and Cary Grant appeared in *She Done Him Wrong.*

Easy Street 1942 w.m. Alan Rankin Jones

Easy Street 1977 w. Martin Charnin m. Charles Strouse. (MT) *Annie.* Dorothy Louden and Andrea McArdle appeared in *Annie.*

Easy To Be Hard 1969 w. Gerome Ragni, James Rado m. Galt MacDermot. (MT) *Hair.* (MF) *Hair.*

Easy To Love 1936 w.m. Cole Porter. (MF) *Born To Dance.* (MF) *Night and Day.* (MF) *Easy To Love.* Eleanor Powell and James Stewart appeared in *Born To Dance.* Cary Grant, Alexis Smith, and Mary Martin appeared in *Night and Day,* biopic of song writer Cole Porter.

Easy To Remember, *see* **It's Easy To Remember**

Easy To Say, *see* **Prove It by the Things You Do**

Easy Winners 1903 m. Scott Joplin

Ebb Tide 1953 w.m. Carl Sigman, Robert Maxwell. (F) *Sweet Bird of Youth.* Paul Newman and Geraldine Page appeared in *Sweet Bird of Youth.*

Ebenezer Frye, *see* **Wal, I Swan!**

Ebony and Ivory 1982 w.m. Paul McCartney. Ivor Novello Award winner 1982–83.

Ebony Eyes 1961 w.m. John D. Loudermilk

Echo Told Me a Lie, The 1949 w.m. Howard Barnes, Harold Fields, Dominic John. Based on the traditional Italian folksong "Bella Ragazza Dalle Trecce Bionde."

Ecstasy Tango 1952 w.m. Jose Belmonte

Eddystone Light, The, *see* **The Keeper of the Eddystone Light**

Edelweiss 1959 w. Oscar Hammerstein II m. Richard Rodgers. (MT) *The Sound of Music.* (MF) *The Sound of Music.* Mary Martin appeared in the stage production of *The Sound of Music.* Julie Andrews appeared in the film production of *The Sound of Music.*

Edge of Darkness 1986 w.m. Eric Clapton, Michael Kamen. Ivor Novello Award winner 1985–86.

Edwardians, The *see* **Upstairs Downstairs**

Eel, The 1933 w.m. Bud Freeman

Eeny Meeny Miney Mo 1935 w. Johnny Mercer m. Matty Malneck. (MF) *To Beat the Band.* Hugh Herbert and Helen Broderick appeared in *To Beat the Band.*

Egg and I, The 1947 w.m. Harry Akst, Herman Ruby, Bert Kalmar, Al Jolson. (F) *The Egg and I.*

Eh Cumpari 1953 w.m. arr. Julius La Rosa, Archie Bleyer. Based on a traditional Italian song.

Eight by Ten 1963 w.m. Bill Anderson, Walter Haynes

Eight Days a Week 1965 w.m. John Lennon, Paul McCartney

867–5309/Jenny 1982 w.m. James Keller, Alexander Call

1812 Overture, op. 49 1882 m. Peter Tchaikovsky. (MF) *Help!.* Completed November 19, 1880, this work was first performed in Moscow on August 20, 1882.

Eighteenth Variation on a Theme by Paganini 1953 m. Sergei Rachmaninoff. This classical standard was popularly adapted and revived in 1953.

Eileen (Alanna Asthore) 1917 w. Henry Blossom m. Victor Herbert. (MT) *Eileen.*

Eileen Allanna 1873 w. E.S. Marble m. John Rogers Thomas

Eileen Aroon, *see* **Robin Adair**

Ein' Feste Burg, *see* **A Mighty Fortress Is Our God**

Either It's Love or It Isn't 1946 w.m. Doris Fisher, Allan Roberts. (MF) *Dead Reckoning.* Humphrey Bogart and Lizabeth Scott appeared in *Dead Reckoning.*

El Capitan, *see* **Capitan, El**

El Choclo, *see* **Choclo, El**

El Cumbanchero, *see* **Cumbanchero, El**

El Rancho Grande, *see* **Rancho Grande, El**

El Relicario, *see* **My Toreador**

Eleanor Rigby 1966 w.m. John Lennon, Paul McCartney. (MT) *Beatlemania.* (MF) *Yellow Submarine.*

Electric Avenue 1983 w.m. Eddy Grant

Élégie 1866 m. Jules Massenet

Eleven More Months and Ten More Days 1931 w.m. Arthur Fields, Fred Hall. (MF) *Ride Tenderfoot Ride.* Gene Autry and June Storey appeared in *Ride Tenderfoot Ride.*

Eleventh Hour Melody 1956 w. Carl Sigman m. King Palmer

Eli Eli 1906 w. Bible; second verse of the twenty-second Psalm of David m. probably Jacob Sandler. This song was first published with the title "Eli, Eli, Lomo Ozavtoni (My God, My God, Why Has Thou Forsaken Me?)". Mr. Sandler claimed to have written the song for the 1896 play *Brocha,* in which it was performed by Sophia Karp.

Eli Green's Cakewalk 1896 w.m. David Reed, Sadie Koninsky

Elizabeth 1931 w. Irving Caesar m. Robert Katscher. (MT) *The Wonder Bar.* Elise Randolph appeared in the British production of *The Wonder Bar.*

Elizabethan Serenade 1952 w.m. Ronald Binge. Ivor Novello Award winner 1957. This song was popularly revived in 1957.

Ellen Bayne 1854 w.m. Stephen Collins Foster

Ellie Rhee, or, **Carry Me Back to Tennessee** 1865 w.m. Septimus Winner. Based originally on "Ella Ree," by C.E. Stewart and James W. Porter, from 1853.

Elmer's Tune 1942 w.m. Sammy Gallop, Dick Jurgens, Elmer Albrecht. (MF) *Strictly in the Groove.* Martha Tilton and Donald O'Connor appeared in *Strictly in the Groove.*

Elsie from Chelsea 1896 w.m. Harry Dacre

Elusive Butterfly 1966 w.m. Bob Lind

Elvira 1981 w.m. Dallas Frazier

(Theme from) Elvira Madigan 1967 m. Wolfgang Amadeus Mozart. (F) *Elvira Madigan.* Based on Mozart's op. 29 of 1785.

Emaline 1934 w. Mitchell Parish m. Frank Perkins

Embraceable You 1930 w. Ira Gershwin m. George Gershwin. (MT) *Girl Crazy.* (MF) *Girl Crazy* (1932). (MF) *Girl Crazy* (1949). (MF) *Always Leave Them Laughing.* (MF) *Nancy Goes to Rio.* (MF) *Rhapsody in Blue.* (MF) *An American in Paris.* (MF) *With a Song in My Heart.* (MF) *Sincerely Yours.* (MF) *When the Boys Meet the Girls.* Ethel Merman and Ginger Rogers both made their Broadway debuts in the stage production of *Girl Crazy.* Bert Wheeler appeared in the 1932 film production of *Girl Crazy.* Judy Garland, June Allyson, and Mickey Rooney appeared in the 1949 film production of *Girl Crazy.* Milton Berle and Bert Lahr appeared in *Always Leave Them Laughing.* Jane Powell and Ann Sothern appeared in *Nancy Goes to Rio.* Alexis Smith, Robert Alda, and Oscar Levant appeared in *Rhapsody in Blue,* biopic of composer George Gershwin. Gene Kelly and Leslie Caron appeared in *An American in Paris.* Susan Hayward appeared in *With a Song in My Heart,* biopic of singer Jane Froman. Liberace appeared in *Sincerely Yours.* Connie Francis appeared in *When the Boys Meet the Girls.*

Emergency Ward 10 Theme 1959 w.m. Peter Yorke. (TV-BBC) *Emergency Ward 10.*

Emily 1965 w.m. John Mandel, Johnny Mercer

Emma 1975 w.m. Errol Brown, Tony Wilson

Emmet's Lullaby, or, **Fritz, Our Cousin German,** or, **Brother's Lullaby** 1878 w.m. Joseph Kline Emmet. This lullaby contains the popular refrain "Go to sleep my baby, my baby, my baby."

Emotion 1977 w.m. Barry Gibb, Robin Gibb

Emotional Rescue 1980 w.m. Keith Richards, Mick Jagger

Emotions 1960 w.m. Mel Tillis, Ramsey Kearney

(Theme from) Empire Strikes Back, The 1980 m. John Williams. (F) *The Empire Strikes Back.* Harrison Ford and Carrie Fisher appeared in *The Empire Strikes Back.* Grammy Award winner 1980.

Empty Saddles 1936 w.m. Billy Hill. (MF) *Rhythm on the Range.* Bing Crosby and Martha Raye appeared in *Rhythm on the Range.*

Enchanted Island 1958 w. Al Stillman m. Robert Allen

End, The (of the Rainbow) 1958 w. Sid Jacobson m. Jimmy Krondes

End of a Love Affair 1950 w.m. Edward C. Redding

End of the Road, The 1926 w.m. Harry Lauder, William Dillon

End of the World, The 1963 w.m. Fred Rose

Endless Love 1981 w.m. Lionel Richie

England Swings (Like a Pendulum Do) 1965 w.m. Roger Miller

English Country Gardens 1962 w.m. traditional; new words Robert Jordan

English Rose 1902 w.m. Edward German. (MT) *Merrie England.* Robert Evett and Henry Lytton appeared in *Merrie England.*

Enjoy Yourself 1976 w.m. Kenny Gamble, Leon Huff

Enjoy Yourself, It's Later Than You Think 1949 w.m. Herb Magidson m. Carl Sigman

Entertainer, The 1902 m. Scott Joplin; arr. Marvin Hamlisch. (F) *The Sting.* Paul Newman and Robert Redford appeared in *The Sting.* This song was popularly adapted in 1974. See also Part I, 1973.

Entire History of the World in Two Minutes and Thirty-Two Seconds 1955 w. Mike Stewart m. Charles Strouse. (MT) *Shoestring Revue.*

Entry of the Gladiators, *see* **The Gladiator's Entry**

Eres Tu 1932 w.m. Miguel Sandoval

(Fifteen Miles [Years] on the) Erie Canal (Low Bridge!—Everybody Down) 1913 w.m. Thomas S. Allen. Based on a traditional American folksong. The Erie Canal was opened in 1825. See also Part I, 1825.

E-ri-ee, The c. 1850 w.m. traditional American folksong. The Erie Canal was opened in 1825. See also Part I, 1825.

Ernie 1972 w.m. Benny Hill. Ivor Novello Award winner 1971–72.

Escape 1980 w.m. Rupert Holmes

España (Rhapsody) 1884 m. Emmanuel Chabrier

España (Tango) 1890 m. Isaac M.F. Albéniz

Estrellita, *see* **Little Star**

Estudiantina 1881 w. J. de Lau Lusignan m. Paul Lacome; arr. Emile Waldteufel

(Theme from) E.T. The Extra-Terrestrial m. John Williams. (F) *E.T. The Extra-Terrestrial.* Grammy Award winner 1982.

Et Maintenant, *see* **What Now My Love**

Eternally, or, **Terry's Theme** 1953 w. Geoffrey Parsons m. Charles Chaplin. (F) *Limelight.* Charles Chaplin and Claire Bloom appeared in *Limelight.*

Ethel Levy's Virginia Song, *see* **I Was Born in Virginia**

Evangeline 1862 w.m. William Shakespeare Hays

Eve Cost Adam Just One Bone 1921 w.m. Charles Bayha

Eve of Destruction, The 1965 w.m. P.F. Sloan, Steve Barri, V. Buggy, C. Francoia

Evelina 1944 w. E.Y. Harburg m. Harold Arlen. (MT) *Bloomer Girl.*

Even Now 1978 w.m. Barry Manilow, Marty Panzer

Even the Nights Are Better 1982 w.m. Kenneth Bell, Terry Skinner, J.L. Wallace

Evening in Caroline, An 1931 w.m. Walter Donaldson

Evensong 1911 w.m. Easthope Martin

Ever of Thee 1852 w. George Linley m. Foley Hall

Ever So Goosey 1929 w.m. Ralph Butler, Raymond Wallace, Julian Wright

Evergreen, or, **Love Theme from** *A Star Is Born* 1975 w. Paul Williams m. Barbra Streisand. (MF) *A Star Is Born.* Barbra Streisand and Kris Kristofferson appeared in *A Star Is Born.* Academy Award winner 1976. Grammy Award winner 1977.

Everlasting Love, An 1978 w.m. Barry Gibb

Evermore 1955 w.m. Gerry Levine, Paddy Roberts

Every Breath You Take 1983 w.m. Sting (Gordon Sumner). Grammy Award winner 1983. Ivor Novello Award winner 1983–84.

Every Day a Little Death 1973 w.m. Stephen Sondheim. (MT) *A Little Night Music.* (MF) *A Little Night Music.* Glynis Johns, Hermione Gingold, and Len Cariou appeared in the stage production of *A Little Night Music.* Len Cariou, Elizabeth Taylor, and Hermione Gingold appeared in the film production of *A Little Night Music.*

Ev'ry Day Away from You 1929 w. Charles Tobias m. Jay Mills

Every Day I Have the Blues 1950 w.m. Peter Chatman

Every Day Is Ladies' Day with Me 1906 w. Henry Blossom m. Victor Herbert. (MT) *The Red Mill.*

Every Day Will Be Sunday When the Town Goes Dry 1918 w.m. William Jerome, Jack Mohoney. A popular Prohibition song.

Every Girl Loves Me But the Girl I Love 1910 w. Otto Harbach m. Karl Hoschna. (MT) *The Girl of My Dreams.*

Every Little Bit Added to What You've Got Makes Just a Little Bit More 1908 w.m. William A. Dillon, Lawrence M. Dillon

Every Little Movement (Has a Meaning All Its Own) 1910 w. Otto Harbach m. Karl Hoschna. (MT) *Madame Sherry.* (MF) *On Moonlight Bay.* Doris Day and Gordon MacRae appeared in *On Moonlight Bay.*

Every Little Thing She Does Is Magic 1981 w.m. Sting. Ivor Novello Award winner 1981–82.

Ev'ry Little While 1916 w.m. James W. Tate. (MT) *Some.*

Ev'ry Little While 1928 w. Clifford Grey, P.G. Wodehouse m. Rudolf Friml. (MT) *The Three Musketeers.*

Every Night There's a Light 1898 w.m. Paul Dresser

Every Race Has a Flag But the Coon 1900 w.m. Will A. Heelan, J. Fred Helf

Ev'ry Street's a Boulevard in Old New York 1953 w. Bob Hilliard m. Jule Styne. (MT) *Hazel Flagg.* (MF) *Living It Up.* Dean Martin, Jerry Lewis, and Janet Leigh appeared in *Living It Up.*

Ev'ry Sunday Afternoon 1940 w. Lorenz Hart m. Richard Rodgers. (MT) *Higher and Higher.* (MF) *Higher and Higher.* Frank Sinatra appeared in the film production of *Higher and Higher.*

Ev'ry Time 1941 w.m. Hugh Martin, Ralph Blane. (MT) *Best Foot Forward.* (MF) *Best Foot Forward.* Lucille Ball and June Allyson appeared in the film production of *Best Foot Forward.*

Every Time I Feel the Spirit c.1865 w.m. traditional black American spiritual

Ev'ry Time We Say Goodbye 1944 w.m. Cole Porter. (MT) *Seven Lively Arts.* Beatrice Lillie, Bert Lahr, and Benny Goodman appeared in *Seven Lively Arts.*

Every Time You Touch Me (I Get High) 1975 w.m. Billy Sherrill, Charlie Rich

Every Which Way But Loose 1979 w.m. Thomas "Snuff" Garrett, Milton Brown, Stephen Dorff. (F) *Every Which Way But Loose.*

Every Woman in the World 1981 w.m. Dominic Bugatti, Frank Musker

Ev'rybody Has a Laughing Place 1946 w. Ray Gilbert m. Allie Wrubel. (MF) *Song of the South.*

Everybody Loves a Lover 1958 w. Richard Adler m. Robert Allen

Everybody Loves Louis 1984 w.m. Stephen Sondheim. (MT) *Sunday in the Park with George.* Mandy Patinkin and Bernadette Peters appeared in *Sunday in the Park with George.*

Everybody Loves My Baby, But My Baby Don't Love Nobody But Me 1924 w.m. Jack Palmer, Spencer Williams

Everybody Loves Somebody 1952 w.m. Harold Rome. (MT) *Wish You Were Here.*

Everybody Loves Somebody 1964 w.m. Ken Lane, Irving Taylor

Everybody Ought To Have a Maid 1962 w.m. Stephen Sondheim. (MT) *A Funny Thing Happened on the Way to the Forum.* (MF) *A Funny Thing Happened on the Way to the Forum.* Zero Mostel and Jack Gilford appeared in the film production of *A Funny Thing Happened on the Way to the Forum.*

Everybody Ought To Know How To Do the Tickle Toe, *see* **The Tickle Toe**

Everybody Says Don't 1964 w.m. Stephen Sondheim. (MT) *Anyone Can Whistle.* (MT) *Side by Side by Sondheim.* Millicent Martin and Julie N. McKenzie appeared in *Side by Side by Sondheim.*

Everybody Step 1921 w.m. Irving Berlin. (MT) *The Music Box Revue.* (MF) *Alexander's Ragtime Band.* (MF) *Blue Skies.* Willie Collier and Sam Bernard appeared in *The Music Box Revue,* opening show of the new Music Box Theatre. Tyrone Power and Ethel Merman appeared in *Alexander's Ragtime Band.* Bing Crosby and Fred Astaire appeared in *Blue Skies.*

Everybody Two-Step 1912 w. Earl C. Jones m. Wallie Herzer

Everybody Wants To Rule the World 1985 w.m. Roland Orzabal, Ian Stanley

Everybody Works But Father 1905 w.m. Jean Havez

Everybody's Crazy on the Foxtrot 1916 w.m. Bennett Scott, A.J. Mills

Everybody's Doing It (Now) 1911 w.m. Irving Berlin. (MT) *Everybody's Doing It.* (MF) *Alexander's Ragtime Band.* (MF) *The Fabulous Dorseys.* (MF) *Easter Parade.* Robert Hale and Ida Crispi appeared in *Everybody's Doing It.* Tyrone Power, Alice Faye, and Ethel Merman appeared in *Alexan-*

der's Ragtime Band. Fred Astaire, Judy Garland, and Ann Miller appeared in *Easter Parade.*

Ev'rybody's Got a Home But Me 1955 w. Oscar Hammerstein II m. Richard Rodgers. (MT) *Pipe Dream.*

Everybody's Somebody's Fool 1960 w. Jack Keller m. Howard Greenfield

Everybody's Talkin', or, **Theme from** *Midnight Cowboy* 1969 w.m. Fred Neil. (F) *Midnight Cowboy.* Dustin Hoffman and John Voight appeared in *Midnight Cowboy.*

Everyday 1986 w.m. Buddy Holly, Norman Petty

Everyday People 1969 w.m. Sly Stewart

Ev'ryone Says "I Love You" 1932 w.m. Harry Ruby, Bert Kalmar. (MF) *Horse Feathers.* The Marx Brothers appeared in *Horse Feathers.*

Everyone's Gone to the Moon 1965 w.m. Kenneth King

Everything Happens to Me 1941 w.m. Thomas M. Adair, Matt Dennis

Everything I Have Is Yours 1933 w. Harold Adamson m. Burton Lane. (MF) *Dancing Lady.* (F) *Strictly Dishonorable.* (MF) *Everything I Have Is Yours.* Joan Crawford, Clark Gable, and Fred Astaire appeared in *Dancing Lady.* Ezio Pinza and Janet Leigh appeared in *Strictly Dishonorable.* Gower Champion and Monica Lewis appeared in *Everything I Have Is Yours.* See also Part I, 1917.

Everything I Love 1941 w.m. Cole Porter. (MT) *Let's Face It.* (MF) *Let's Face It.* Eve Arden, Vivian Vance, and Danny Kaye appeared in the stage production of *Let's Face It.* Betty Hutton and Bob Hope appeared in the film production of *Let's Face It.*

Everything Is Beautiful 1970 w.m. Ray Stevens

Everything Is Peaches Down in Georgia 1918 w. Grant Clarke m. Milton Ager, George W. Meyer. (MT) *U.S.*

Ev'rything I've Got (Belongs to You) 1942 w. Lorenz Hart m. Richard Rodgers. (MT) *By Jupiter.* Constance Moore and Ray Bolger appeared in *By Jupiter.*

Everything She Wants 1985 w.m. George Michael

Everything Stops for Tea 1934 w.m. Maurice Sigler, Al Goodhart, Al Hoffman. (MF) *Come Out of the Pantry.* Jack Buchanan appeared in *Come Out of the Pantry.*

Everything's Al'Right 1964 w.m. Nicholas Crouch, John Conrad, Simon Stavely, Stuart James, Keith Karlson

Everything's Alright 1971 w. Timothy Rice m. Andrew Lloyd Webber. (MT) *Jesus Christ Superstar.* (MF) *Jesus Christ Superstar.*

Everything's Alright, *see also* **Uptight**

Everything's Coming Up Roses 1959 w. Stephen Sondheim m. Jule Styne. (MT) *Gypsy.* (MF) *Gypsy.* Ethel Merman appeared in the stage production of *Gypsy.* Rosalind Russell appeared in the film production of *Gypsy.* The melody for this song was originally written by Jule Style more than a dozen years earlier. This song was later adapted for a commercial promotion campaign for "Comet" automobiles, with the title "Everything's Coming Up Comets."

Everything's Gonna Be All Right 1926 w.m. Benny Davis, Harry Akst

Everything's in Rhythm with My Heart 1935 w.m.

Maurice Sigler, Al Goodhart, Al Hoffman. (MF) *First a Girl*. Jessie Matthews appeared in *First a Girl*.

Everytime You Go Away 1985 w.m. Daryl Hall

Ev'rywhere 1955 w.m. Tolchard Evans, Larry Kahn. Ivor Novello Award winner 1955.

Everywhere You Go 1927 w.m. Larry Shay, Mark Fisher, Joe Goodwin. This song was popularly revived in 1947.

Evil Hearted You 1965 w.m. Graham Gouldman

Exactly Like You 1930 w. Dorothy Fields m. Jimmy McHugh. (MT) *Lew Leslie's International Revue*. (MT) *Sugar Babies*. (MF) *The Eddy Duchin Story*. Gertrude Lawrence and Florence Moore appeared in *Lew Leslie's International Revue*. Ann Miller and Mickey Rooney appeared in *Sugar Babies*.

Excelsior 1843 w. Henry Wadsworth Longfellow m. Michael William Balfe. This song was popularized by the Hutchinson Family singers, and described by Oliver Wendell Holmes as "a trumpet call to the energies of youth."

Excelsior 1862 w. Henry Wadsworth Longfellow m. John Blockley

(Theme from) Exodus 1960 w. Pat Boone m. Ernest Gold. (F) *Exodus*. Paul Newman and Sal Mineo appeared in *Exodus*. Grammy Award winner 1960.

Experiment 1933 w.m. Cole Porter. (MT) *Nymph Errant*. Gertrude Lawrence appeared in *Nymph Errant*.

Experiments with Mice 1956 w.m. Johnny Dankworth. Ivor Novello Award winner 1956.

Express 1975 w.m. Louis Risbrook, Barbara Lomas, William Risbrook, Orlando Woods, Richard Thompson, Carlos Ward

Eye in the Sky 1982 w.m. Alan Parsons, Eric Woolfson

Eye of the Tiger 1982 w.m. James Peterik, Frank Sullivan

Eyes of Blue, Eyes of Brown 1901 w.m. Costen, Andrew B. Sterling

Eyes of Texas (Are Upon You), The 1903 w. John L. Sinclair m. anon. Melody based on "I've Been Working on the Railroad," or "The Levee Song," or, "Someone's in the Kitchen with Dinah" of 1894. (F) *Night Stage to Galveston*. Gene Autry appeared in *Night Stage to Galveston*. Fight song of the University of Texas, this song was written by Sinclair for a campus minstrel show. See also "I've Been Working on the Railroad."

Eyes That See in the Dark 1984 w.m. Barry Gibb, Maurice Gibb

Eyes Without a Face 1984 w.m. Billy Idol, Steve Stevens

Ezekiel Saw De Wheel 1865 w.m. traditional black American spiritual. (F) *Barbed Wire*. Gene Autry and Pat Buttram appeared in *Barbed Wire*.

Fabulous Feet 1984 w. Robert Lorick m. Henry Krieger. (MT) *The Tap Dance Kid*. Alfonso Ribiero appeared in *The Tap Dance Kid*.

Face to Face 1897 w.m. Herbert Johnson

Face to Face 1899 w. Mrs. Frank A. Breck m. Grant Colfax Tullar

Face to Face with the Girl of My Dreams 1914 w.m. Richard Howard

Fact Can Be a Beautiful Thing, A 1968 w. Hal David m. Burt Bacharach. (MT) *Promises, Promises*.

Fade Out—Fade In 1964 w. Betty Comden, Adolph Green m. Jule Styne. (MT) *Fade Out—Fade In*.

Faded Summer Love, A 1931 w.m. Phil Baxter

Fair and Warmer 1934 w. Al Dubin m. Harry Warren. (MF) *Twenty Million Sweethearts*. Dick Powell and Ginger Rogers appeared in *Twenty Million Sweethearts*.

Fair Harvard 1836 w. Samuel Gilman m. based on the melody of "Believe Me If All Those Endearing Young Charms." Samuel Gilman, a Unitarian minister, wrote these words to celebrate the 200th anniversary of his Alma Mater. See also "Believe Me If All Those Endearing Young Charms."

Fair Rosmarin, see **Schön Rosmarin**

Fairy on the Clock 1929 w.m. Erell Reaves, Montague Ewing

Faith 1934 w.m. Tolchard Evans, Stanley J. Damerell, Floyd Huddleston

Faith of Our Fathers 1864 w. Frederick Faber m. H.F. Hemy

Faithful Forever 1939 w.m. Leo Robin, Ralph Rainger. (MF) *Gulliver's Travels*. Jessica Dragonette and Lanny Ross appeared in *Gulliver's Travels*.

Faithfully Yours 1943 w.m. Sigmund Romberg, Charles Tobias

Fall In and Follow Me 1911 w.m. A.J. Mills, Bennett Scott

Fall in Love with You 1960 w.m. Ian Samwell

Falling Again 1981 w.m. Bob McDill

Fallin' in Love (Again) 1975 w.m. Dan Hamilton, Ann Hamilton

Falling in Love Again 1930 w.m. Fredrich Hollander, Reginald Connelly. (F) *The Blue Angel* (1930). (F) *The Blue Angel* (1959). Marlene Dietrich and Emil Jannings appeared in the 1930 film production of *The Blue Angel*. May Britt appeared in the 1959 film production of *The Blue Angel*. Theme song of Marlene Dietrich. See also Part I, 1930.

Falling in Love with Love 1938 w. Lorenz Hart m. Richard Rodgers. (MT) *The Boys from Syracuse*. (MT) *Up and Doing*. (MF) *The Boys from Syracuse*. Teddy Hart and Jimmy Savo appeared in the stage production of *The Boys from Syracuse*. Allan Jones and Martha Raye appeared in the film production of *The Boys from Syracuse*.

Falling in Love with You 1926 w.m. Joseph Meyer

Falling Leaves 1940 w.m. Mack David, Frankie Carle

Fame 1975 w.m. John Lennon, David Bowie

Fame 1980 w.m. Dean Pitchford, Michael Gore. (F) *Fame*.

Family Affair 1971 w.m. Sly Stewart

Fancy 1970 w.m. Bobbie Gentry

Fancy Free 1981 w.m. Roy August, Jimbeau Hinson

Fanfare Boogie 1955 w.m. Max Kaye, Brian Fahey. Ivor Novello Award winner 1955.

Fanny 1954 w.m. Harold Rome. (MT) *Fanny*. (F) *Fanny*.

Leslie Caron and Maurice Chevalier appeared in the non-musical film production of *Fanny*.

Fantasia on a Nursery Song 1976 w.m. Leo Norman

Fantaisie Impromptu, op.66 1855 m. Frédéric Chopin

Far Above Cayuga's Waters, *see* **Annie Lisle**

Far Away Places 1949 w.m. Joan Whitney, Alex Kramer

Far Off I Hear a Lover's Flute 1909 w. Nelle Richmond Eberhart m. Charles Wakefield Cadman. From "Four American Indian Songs."

Fare Thee Well, Annabelle 1934 w. Mort Dixon m. Allie Wrubel. (MF) *Sweet Music*. Rudy Vallee, Ann Sothern, and Helen Morgan appeared in *Sweet Music*.

Farewell, The 1907 w. E. Blasco m. F.M. Alvarez. From the Spanish "La Partida."

Farewell Blues 1922 w.m. Elmer Schoebel, Paul Mares, Leon Rappolo

Farewell to Arms 1933 w.m. Abner Silver, Allie Wrubel

Farewell to Storyville 1925 w.m. Spencer Williams, Clarence Williams. In 1916 the U.S. Navy closed the bordellos in Storyville, New Orleans.

Farewell to Thee, *see* **Aloha Oe**

Farmer in the Dell, The 1883 w.m. traditional. Based on the German children's game "Der Kirmessbauer." This song has been traditionally adapted to the words "The Bride Cuts the Cake."

Fascinating Rhythm 1924 w. Ira Gershwin m. George Gershwin. (MT) *Lady, Be Good*. (MF) *Lady, Be Good*. (MF) *Girl Crazy* (1943). (MF) *Rhapsody in Blue*. Fred Astaire and Adele Astaire appeared in the stage production of *Lady, Be Good*. Robert Young, Red Skeleton, annd Eleanor Powell appeared in the film production of *Lady, Be Good*. Judy Garland, Micky Rooney, and June Allyson appeared in the 1943 film production of *Girl Crazy*. Oscar Levant appeared in *Rhapsody in Blue*, biopic of composer George Gershwin.

Fascination, or, **Valse Tzigane** 1904 m. F.D. Marchetti

Fascination 1915 w.m. Harold Atteridge, Sigmund Romberg

Fascination 1932 w. Dick Manning m. F.D. Marchetti. (F) *Love in the Afternoon*. Audrey Hepburn and Gary Cooper appeared in *Love in the Afternoon*. This song was popularly adapted in 1957, and based originally on Marchetti's "Valse Tzigane" of 1904.

Fashionette 1928 w.m. Jack Glogau, Robert King. (MF) *The Time, the Place and the Girl*. Vivian Oakland and James Kirkwood appeared in *The Time, the Place and the Girl*.

Fat Li'l' Feller Wid His Mammy's Eyes 1913 w.m. Sheridan Gordon, F.L. Stanton

Fatal Rose of Red, The 1900 w.m. J. Fred Helf, Edward Gardenier

Fatal Wedding, The 1893 w. W.H Windom m. Gussie L. Davis

Father, Dear Father, Come Home with Me Now, or, **Come Home, Father** 1864 w.m. Henry Clay Work. This famous temperance song first appeared in the Timothy Shay Arthur melodrama *Ten Nights in a Barroom*.

F.B.I. 1961 w.m. Peter Gormley. (TV) *The F.B.I.*

F.D.R. Jones 1938 w.m. Harold J. Rome. (MT) *Sing Out the News*. June Allyson and Philip Loeb appeared in *Sing Out the News*.

Fear Ye Not, O Israel 1889 w. Biblical m. Dudley Buck

Feather in Her Tyrolean Hat, The 1937 w.m. Annette Mills

Feather Your Nest 1920 w.m. James Kendis, James Brockman, Howard Johnson

Federal Street, *see* **See, Gentle Patience Smiles on Pain**

(That's the Time I) Feel Like Makin' Love 1974 w.m. Gene McDaniels

Feelin' Groovy, *see* **The 59th Street Bridge Song**

Feeling I'm Falling 1928 w. Ira Gershwin m. George Gershwin. (MT) *Treasure Girl*.

Feeling We Once Had, The 1975 w.m. Charlie Smalls. (MT) *The Wiz*. (MF) *The Wiz*. Stephanie Mills, Tiger Haymes, and Ted Ross appeared in the stage production of *The Wiz*. Diana Ross appeared in the film production of *The Wiz*.

Feelings 1975 w.m. Morris Albert

Feels So Good 1978 w.m. Chuck Mangione

Feels So Right 1981 w.m. Randy Owen

Felix Kept on Walking 1924 w.m. Edward E. Bryant, Hubert W. David

Fella with an Umbrella, A 1948 w.m. Irving Berlin. (MF) *Easter Parade*. Judy Garland, Ann Miller, and Fred Astaire appeared in *Easter Parade*.

Fellow Needs a Girl, A 1947 w. Oscar Hammerstein II m. Richard Rodgers. (MT) *Allegro*. William Ching, John Battles, and Anna Mary Dickey appeared in *Allegro*.

Ferdinand the Bull 1938 w. Larry Morey m. Albert Hay Malotte. (MF) *Ferdinand the Bull*.

Ferry Boat Inn, The 1950 w.m. Don Pelosi, Jimmy Campbell

Ferry 'Cross the Mersey 1965 w.m. Gerry Marsden. (F) *Ferry Across the Mersey*.

Ferryboat Serenade 1940 orig. w. M. Panzeri Eng.w. Harold Adamson m. Eldo di Lazzaro

Feudin' and Fightin' 1947 w. Al Dubin, Burton Lane m. Burton Lane. (MT) *Laffing Room Only*. (MF) *Feudin', Fussin' and A-Fightin'*. Olsen and Johnson and Betty Garrett appeared in *Laffing Room Only*. Donald O'Connor and Marjorie Main appeared in *Feudin', Fussin, and A-Fightin'*.

Fever 1959 w.m. Eddie Cooley, John R. Davenport. (F) *Hey Boy! Hey Girl!*

Fiddle Dee Dee, *see* **Mother Goose's Melodies**

Fiddle Faddle 1948 m. Leroy Anderson

Fidgety Feet 1924 w. Ira Gershwin m. George Gershwin. (MT) *Oh, Kay!*. Gertrude Lawrence, Victor Moore, and Gerald Oliver Smith appeared in *Oh, Kay!*.

Fido Is a Hot Dog Now 1914 w. Charles McCarron, Thomas J. Gray m. Raymond Walker. World War I in Europe produced an American revulsion against German names. Sausages and rolls previously served at baseball games with the Germanic name "frankfurters" are renamed hot dogs.

Field Artillery March, The, *see* **The U.S. Field Artillery March**

Fifteen Cents 1913 w.m. Chris Smith

Fifteen Men on the Dead Man's Chest—Yo! Ho! Ho! and a Bottle of Rum, *see* **Pirate Song**

Fifteen Miles (Years) on the Erie Canal *see* **Erie Canal**

Fifth of Beethoven, A 1976 w.m. Walter Murphy. Based on Beethoven's Fifth Symphony. (MF) *Saturday Night Fever.* John Travolta appeared in *Saturday Night Fever.*

Fifty Million Frenchmen Can't Be Wrong 1927 w. Billy Rose, Willie Raskin m. Fred Fisher

Fifty Million Times a Day 1955 w.m. Ben Ludlow. This song was written for a Coca-Cola commercial promotion campaign.

Fifty Ways To Leave Your Lover 1976 w.m. Paul Simon

59th Street Bridge Song, The, or, **Feelin' Groovy** 1967 w.m. Paul Simon. See also Part I, 1909.

Fifty-Second Street Theme 1948 m. Theolonius Monk

Fight On uncertain w.m. Milo Sweet, Glen Grant. Fight song for the University of Southern California.

Fine and Dandy 1930 w. Paul James m. Kay Swift. (MT) *Fine and Dandy.* Joe Cook and Eleanor Powell appeared in *Fine and Dandy.*

Fine Romance, A 1936 w. Dorothy Fields m. Jerome Kern. (MF) *Swing Time.* (MF) *Till the Clouds Roll By.* Fred Astaire and Ginger Rogers appeared in *Swing Time.* June Allyson, Frank Sinatra, Judy Garland, and Van Johnson appeared in *Till the Clouds Roll By,* biopic of composer Jerome Kern.

Finger of Suspicion Points at You, The 1954 w.m. Paul Mann, Al Lewis

Fingertips (Part II) 1963 w.m. Henry Cosby, Clarence Paul

Finishing the Hat 1984 w.m. Stephen Sondheim. (MT) *Sunday in the Park with George.* Mandy Patinkin and Bernadette Peters appeared in *Sunday in the Park with George.*

Finlandia 1901 m. Jean Sibelius. From the suite "Finland Awakes," op. 26, no. 7.

Fire 1975 w.m. Jim Williams, Clarence Satchell, Leroy Bonner, Marshall Jones, R. Middlebrooks, Marvin Pierce, William Beck

Fire and Rain 1970 w.m. James Taylor

Fire Brigade 1969 w.m. Roy Wood

Fire in the Morning 1980 w.m. Stephen Dorff, Larry Herbstritt, Gary Harju

Firebird Ballet Suite, The 1911 m. Igor Stravinsky

Firefly 1958 w. Carolyn Leigh m. Cy Coleman

First Call 1842 m. anon.; first published George W. Behn. This American bugle call is today heard at horse-racing tracks. In 1950, Frank Loesser employed this theme in his "Fugue for Tinhorns" in *Guys and Dolls.*

First, Last and Always 1923 w. Benny Davis m. Harry Akst

First Love, Last Love, Best Love 1918 w.m. Nat D. Ayer, Clifford Grey. (MT) *The Bing Boys on Broadway.* Violet Loraine, George Rubey, and Clara Evelyn appeared in *The Bing Boys on Broadway.*

First Lullaby, The 1941 w.m. Michael Carr, Jack Popplewell

First Noël, The 1833 w.m. traditional English Christmas carol

First Thing Monday Mornin' 1970 w. Peter Udell m. Gary Geld. (MT) *Purlie.* Melba Moore and Sherman Hensley appeared in *Purlie.*

First Time 1963 w.m. Chris Andrews

First Time Ever I Saw Your Face, The 1972 w.m. Ewan MacColl. Grammy Award winner 1972. Ivor Novello Award winner 1972–73.

Fishermen of England, The 1921 w.m. Montague F. Phillips, Gerald Dodson. (MT) *The Rebel Maid.* Thorpe Bates appeared in *The Rebel Maid.*

Fit as a Fiddle (And Ready for Love) 1932 w. Arthur Freed m. Al Hoffman, Al Goodhart. (MT) *Singin' in the Rain.* (MF) *Singing in the Rain.* Gene Kelly, Donald O'Connor, and Debbie Reynolds appeared in the 1952 film production of *Singing in the Rain.*

Five Cent Shave, The 1880 w.m. Thomas Cannon

Five Foot Two, Eyes of Blue (Has Anybody Seen My Girl?) 1925 w. Sam M. Lewis, Joe Young m. Ray Henderson. (MF) *Has Anybody Seen My Gal.* Rock Hudson appeared in *Has Anybody Seen My Gal.*

Five-Four-Three-Two-One 1964 w.m. Paul Jones, Mike Hugg, Manfred Mann

Five Hundred Miles, or, **Railroad's Lament** 1962 w.m. traditional American ballad

Five Minutes More 1946 w. Sammy Cahn m. Jule Styne. (MT) *Piccadilly Hayride.* (F) *Sweetheart of Sigma Chi.* Phil Regan and Elyse Knox appeared in *Sweetheart of Sigma Chi.*

Five O'Clock Whistle, The 1940 w.m. Kim Gannon, William C.K. Irwin, Josef Myrow

Fixing a Hole 1967 w.m. John Lennon, Paul McCartney

(Theme from) Flame Trees of Thika m. Alan Blaikley, Ken Howard. (TV) *Flame Trees of Thika.* Ivor Novello Award winner 1981–82.

Flamingo 1941 w. Edmund Anderson m. Ted Grouya. (MT) *Big Top.*

Flanagan 1892 w.m. C.W. Murphy, William Letters. This song was popularly revived in 1910.

Flapperette 1926 w. John Murray m. Jesse Greer. This song was originally published in 1926 without lyrics.

Flash 1981 m. Brian May. Ivor Novello Award winner 1980–81.

Flash, Bang, Wallop 1963 w.m. David Heneker. (MT) *Half a Sixpence.* Ivor Novello Award winner 1963.

(Theme from) Flashdance (What a Feeling) w.m. Irene Cara, Keith Forsey, Giorgio Moroder. (MF) *Flashdance.* Grammy Award winner 1983.

Flat Foot Floogie (with the Floy Floy) 1938 w.m. Slim Gaillard, Sam Stewart, Bud Green

Flee as a Bird 1857 w. Mrs. Mary S. B. Dana m. George Frederick Root

Fleet's In, The 1942 w.m. Johnny Mercer, Victor Schertzinger. (MF) *The Fleet's In.* Dorothy Lamour, William Holden, and Betty Hutton appeared in *The Fleet's In.*

Fleet's in Port Again, The 1936 w.m. Noel Gay. (MT) *Okay for Sound.*

Flies Crawled Up the Window, The 1932 w.m. Vivian Ellis, Douglas Furber. (MF) *Jack's the Boy.* Jack Hulbert appeared in *Jack's the Boy.*

Flight of the Bumble Bee 1900 m. Rimsky-Korsakov. From the opera *The Tale of Tsar Saltan.* See also "Bumble Boogie."

Flirtation Walk 1934 w.m. Mort Dixon, Allie Wrubel. (MF) *Flirtation Walk.* Ruby Keeler and Dick Powell appeared in *Flirtation Walk.*

Flirtation Waltz, The 1952 w.m. R. Heywood, Leslie Sarony

Float On 1977 w.m. Arnold Ingram, James Mitchell, Jr., Marvin Willis

Floating Down the Sleepy Lagoon, *see* **Waters of Venice**

Floral Dance, The 1911 w.m. Katie Moss

Florida, the Moon and You 1926 w. Gene Buck m. Rudolf Friml. (MT) *Ziegfeld's American Revue of 1926.*

Florodora Sextet, *see* **Tell Me Pretty Maiden**

Flow Gently, Sweet Afton, or **Afton Water** 1838 w. Robert Burns m. James E. Spilman. (F) *Pursuit to Algiers.* Basil Rathbone and Nigel Bruce appeared in *Pursuit to Algiers.*

Flower from Mother's Grave, A 1878 w.m. Harry Kennedy

Flower Song (Blumenlied) 1890 m. Gustav Lange

Flowers for Madame 1935 w.m. Charles Tobias, Charles Newman, Murray Mencher

Fly Home, Little Heart 1949 w.m. Ivor Novello. From *King's Rhapsody.*

Fly Like an Eagle 1976 w.m. Charles D. Merriam

Fly Me to the Moon, or, **In Other Words** 1954 w.m. Bart Howard. This song was popularly revived in 1962.

Fly Robin Fly 1975 w.m. Sylvester Levay, Stephen Prager

Flying Down to Rio 1933 w. Gus Kahn, Edward Eliscu m. Vincent Youmans. (MF) *Flying Down to Rio.* Dolores Del Rio and Fred Astair appeared in *Flying Down to Rio.*

Flying Dutchman (Overture) 1844 m. Richard Wagner

Flying Dutchman, The 1907 w.m. Paul Rubens. (MT) *Miss Hook of Holland.*

Flying Home 1939 w. Sid Robin m. Benny Goodman, Lionel Hampton. This song was again popular in 1941.

Flying Trapeze, The, *see* **The Daring Young Man**

Foggy Day, A 1937 w. Ira Gershwin m. George Gershwin. (MF) *Damsel in Distress.* Fred Astaire, George Burns and Gracie Allen appeared in *Damsel in Distress.*

Foggy, Foggy Dew, The c.1700 w.m. traditional folksong, from England

Fold Your Wings 1935 w.m. Ivor Novello, Christopher Hassell. (MT) *Glamorous Night.* (MF) *Glamorous Night.* Trefor Jones and Mary Ellis appeared in both the stage and film productions of *Glamorous Night.*

Folks Are All Waiting To See the Fast Steamer, The 1848

w. Benjamin A. Baker m. Based on "Jolly Young Waterman." (MT) *A Glance at New York.*

Folks That Put On Airs 1863 w.m. W.H. Coulston, E.F. Dixey, H. Angelo

Folks Who Live on the Hill, The 1937 w. Oscar Hammerstein II m. Jerome Kern. (MF) *High, Wide and Handsome.* Irene Dunne and Dorothy Lamour appeared in *High, Wide and Handsome.*

Follow Me 1960 w. Alan Jay Lerner m. Frederick Loewe. (MT) *Camelot.* (MF) *Camelot.* Julie Andrews and Richard Burton appeared in the stage production of *Camelot.* Vanessa Redgrave and Richard Harris appeared in the film production of *Camelot.*

Follow the Boys 1962 w.m. Benny Davis, Ted Murry. (F) *Follow the Boys.*

Follow the Gleam 1915 w. Helen Miller m. Sallie Douglas

Follow the Swallow 1924 w. Billy Rose, Mort Dixon m. Ray Henderson

Follow the Yellow Brick Road, *see* **We're Off To See the Wizard**

Follow Thru 1928 w. B.G. DeSylva, Lew Brown m. Ray Henderson. (MT) *Follow Thru.* Jack Haley and Eleanor Powell appeared in *Follow Thru.*

Following in Father's Footsteps 1905 w.m. E. W. Rogers, Vesta Tilley. (MF) *After the Ball.* Pat Kirkwood appeared in *After the Ball,* biopic of Vesta Tilley, famed English music hall girl.

Following the Sun Around 1926 w. Joseph McCarthy m. Harry Tierney. (MT) *Rio Rita.* (MF) *Rio Rita* Murray, and Bert Wheeler appeared in the stage production of *Rio Rita.* John Boles and Bert Wheeler appeared in the 1929 film production of *Rio Rita.*

Folsom Prison (Blues) 1968 w.m. Johnny Cash

Food Glorious Food 1963 w.m. Lionel Bart. (MT) *Oliver!.* (MF) *Oliver!.* Georgia Brown and Ron Moody appeared in the stage production of *Oliver!.* Shani Wallis and Ron Moody appeared in the film production of *Oliver!.*

Fool (If You Think It's Over) 1979 w.m. Chris Rea

Fool Number One 1961 w.m. Kathryn R. Fulton

Fool On the Hill, The 1968 w.m. John Lennon, Paul McCartney. (MT) *Beatlemania.* Ivor Novello Award winner 1968–69.

(Now and Then) Fool Such As I, A 1953 w.m. Bill Trader. This song was popularly revived in 1959.

Fool Was I, A 1951 w.m. Roy Alfred, Kurt Adams

Fooled 1955 w.m. Mann Curtis, Doris Tauber. Based on a theme by Franz Lehár

Fooled Around and Fell in Love 1976 w.m. Elvin Bishop

Fooled by a Feeling 1979 w.m. Kye Fleming, Dennis Morgan

Foolin' Myself 1937 w.m. Jack Lawrence, Peter Tinturin

Foolish Heart 1985 w.m. Randy Goodrum, Steve Perry

Fools Rush In 1940 w. Johnny Mercer m. Rube Bloom

Foot Tapper 1963 w.m. Hank B. Marvin, Bruce Welch. (MF) *Summer Holiday*. Cliff Richard and Lauri Peters appeared in *Summer Holiday*.

Footloose 1984 w.m. Dean Pitchford, Kenny Loggins. (F) *Footloose*.

Footsteps 1960 w.m. Barry Mann, Hank Hunter

For All Eternity 1891 It.w. Pietro Mazzoni Fr.w. Gabriel Leprevost Ger.w. A.L. Mackechnie Eng.w. S.A. Herbert m. Angelo Mascheroni. From the Italian "Eternamente." From the French "A Jamais." From the German "In alle Ewigkeit."

For All Mankind (Theme from *Gandhi*) 1983 m. Ravi Shankar, George Fenton. (F) *Gandhi*. Ben Kingsley appeared in *Gandhi*. Ivor Novello Award winner 1982–83.

For All We Know 1934 w. Sam M. Lewis m. J. Fred Coots

For All We Know 1970 w. Arthur James, Robb Wilson m. Fred Karlin. (F) *Lovers and Other Strangers*. Academy Award winner 1970.

For Every Day Is Ladies' Day, *see* **Every Day Is Ladies' Day to Me**

For Every Man There's a Woman 1948 w. Leo Robin m. Harold Arlen. (MF) *Casbah*. Tony Martin, Yvonne DeCarlo, and Peter Lorre appeared in *Casbah*.

For He's a Jolly Good Fellow, or, **Malbrouk (Malbrough),** or, **We Won't Go Home Until Morning,** or, **The Bear Went Over the Mountain** 1783 w. traditional m. the melody for this song may date from the Crusades. This song was sung as a lullaby by Marie Antoinette and later employed by Beethoven in his 1813 "Battle Symphony." Chateaubriand heard the tune sung by Arabs in Palestine, supporting the theory that Crusaders at the time of Godfrey de Bouillon or Louis IX introduced the song there. "There is reason, however, to believe that the couplets 'Mort et convoi de l'invincible Malbrough' were improvised on the night of the battle of Malplaquet, September 11, 1709, in the bivouack of Marshal de Villars at Quesnoy, three miles from the scene of the fight" (S.J. Adair Fitz-Gerald, 1901). In 1812, Napoleon hummed the military air "Marlborough" as he "crossed the Niemen in setting out upon his disastrous Russian campaign . . ."

For Lovin' Me 1965 w.m. Gordon Lightfoot

For Me and My Gal 1917 w. Edgar Leslie, E. Ray Goetz m. George W. Meyer. (MT) *Here and There*. (MF) *For Me and My Gal*. (MF) *Jolson Sings Again*. Judy Garland and Gene Kelly appeared in *For Me and My Gal*. Larry Parks appeared in *Jolson Sings Again*. This song was popularly revived in 1942.

For My Sweetheart 1926 w. Gus Kahn m. Walter Donaldson

For Old Times' Sake 1900 w.m. Charles K. Harris

For Once in My Life 1965 w.m. Ronald Miller, Orlando Murden. This song was also popular in 1967, 1968, and 1970.

(I Love You) For Sentimental Reasons 1945 w. Deke Watson m. William Best. This song was also popular in 1947.

For the Beauty of the Earth 1864 w. Folliott Pierpoint m. Conrad Kocher

For the First Time (Come Prima) 1958 It.w. M. Panzeri Eng. w. Buck Ram m. S. Paola Taccani, V. di Paola, Mary Bond

For the Good Times 1970 w.m. Kris Kristofferson. This song was popularly revived in 1974, and again in 1978.

For the Noo, or **Something in the Bottle for the Morning** 1905 w. Harry Lauder, Gerald Grafton m. Harry Lauder

For You 1930 w.m. Al Dubin, Joe Burke. (MF) *Holy Terror*. Humphrey Bogart and James Kirkwood appeared in *Holy Terror*.

For You Alone 1909 w. P.J. O'Reilly m. Henry E. Geeh!

For You Alone 1965 w.m. Graham Gouldman

For You, For Me, For Evermore 1947 w. Ira Gershwin m. George Gershwin. (MF) *The Shocking Miss Pilgrim*. Betty Grable appeared in *The Shocking Miss Pilgrim*.

For Your Eyes Only 1981 w.m. Bill Conti, Mike Leeson. Ivor Novello Award winner 1981–82.

For Your Love 1958 w.m. Ed Townsend

Fordham Ram March, *see* **Robin Adair**

Forever 1985 w.m. David Foster

Forever and Ever 1948 w.m. Malia Rosa, Franz Winkler

Forever in Blue Jeans 1979 w.m. Richard Winchell Bennett, Neil Diamond

"Forever" Is a Long, Long Time 1916 w. Darl MacBoyle m. Albert Von Tilzer

Forever with the Lord 1886 w. James Montgomery m. Charles Gounod

Forget Domani 1965 w.m. Norman Newell, Riz Ortolani

Forget Him 1963 w.m. Mark Anthony

Forget-Me-Not 1883 m. Allan Macbeth

Forget Me Not 1962 w.m. Les Vandyke

Forgive Me 1927 w. Jack Yellen m. Milton Ager. (MF) *Bells of Capistrano*. Gene Autry and Smiley Burnette appeared in *Bells of Capistrano*. This song was popularly revived in 1952.

Forgive Me Girl 1980 w.m. Michael Zager

Forgive My Heart 1955 w. Sammy Gallop m. Chester Conn

Forgotten 1894 w. Flora Wulschner m. Eugene Cowles

Fortress Around Your Heart 1986 w.m. Sting

Fortune Teller, The 1898 w. Harry B. Smith m. Victor Herbert. (MT) *The Fortune Teller*.

Fortunio's Song (Fortunio) 1929 Fr.w. Alfred de Musset Eng.w. Adrian Ross m. André Messager

Forty-Five Minutes from Broadway 1905 w.m. George M. Cohan. (MT) *Forty-Five Minutes from Broadway*. (MT) *George M!*. (MF) *Yankee Doodle Dandy*. Fay Templeton and Victor Moore appeared in *Forty-Five Minutes from Broadway*. Joel Grey and Bernadette Peters appeared in *George M!*. James Cagney and Joan Leslie appeared in *Yankee Doodle Dandy*. The "libelous statements" made by George M. Cohan in this title song of the show about New Rochelle, New York, encouraged the calling of an emergency session of the Chamber of Commerce of that township, after which an official boycott of the show was immediately called. See also Part I, 1919.

Forty-Second Street 1932 w. Al Dubin m. Harry Warren. (MT) *Forty-Second Street.* (MF) *Forty-Second Street.* Jerry Ohrbach and Tammy Grimes appeared in *Forty-Second Street.* Dick Powell and Ruby Keeler, while dancing on top of a taxi cab, appeared in *Forty-Second Street.*

Forty-Seven Ginger Headed Sailors 1928 w.m. Leslie Sarony. (MT) *Clowns in Clover.* Cicely Courtneidge appeared in *Clowns in Clover.*

Forty Years On uncertain w.m. John Farmer, E.E. Bowen. This tune became the Harrow school song.

Fountain Fay 1910 w. Robert B. Smith m. Heinrich Reinhardt (MT) *The Spring Maid.*

Fountain in the Park, The, *see* **While Strolling Through the Park One Day**

Four American Indian Songs, *see* **Far Off I Hear a Lover's Flute, From the Land of the Sky Blue Water, The Moon Drops Low, The White Dawn Is Stealing**

Four and Twenty Blackbirds, *see* **Sing a Song of Sixpence**

Four Dances from Aladdin 1975 w.m. Ernest Tomlinson

Four Indian Love Lyrics, *see* **Kashmiri Love Song, Less Than the Dust, The Temple Bells, Till I Wake**

Four or Five Times 1927 w.m. Byron Gay

Four Walls, The 1957 w.m. Marvin Moore, George Campbell

Four Winds and the Seven Sea, The 1949 w. Hal David m. Don Rodney

Fourteen Carat Mind 1982 w.m. Dallas Frazier, Larry Lee

Fox 1981 w.m. George Fenton. Ivor Novello Award winner 1980–81.

Fox on the Run 1975 w.m. Brian Connolly, Stephen Priest, Andrew Scott, Michael Tucker

Frank Mills 1968 w. Gerome Ragni, James Rado m. Galt MacDermot. (MT) *Hair.* This song did not appear in the 1979 film production of *Hair.*

Frankenstein 1973 w.m. Edgar Winter

Frankie 1959 w. Howard Greenfield m. Neil Sedaka

Frankie and Johnnie (Johnny) (Were Lovers) c.1870–75 w.m. anon. Thomas Beer dates this song from an actual incident from as early as 1850 and claims it to have been sung at the siege of Vicksburg. However early it may have been written, it was not fully published until 1912. This song was popularly revived in 1922 and again in 1927.

Franklin D. Roosevelt Jones 1939 w.m. Harold Rome. (MT) *Sing Out the News.* (MT) *The Little Dog Laughed.* (MF) *Babes On Broadway.* Mickey Rooney and Judy Garland appeared in *Babes on Broadway.*

Frasquita Serenade, *see* **My Little Nest of Heavenly Blue**

Freddy My Love 1972 w.m. Warren Casey, Jim Jacobs. (MT) *Grease.* (MF) *Grease.* John Travolta and Olivia Newton-John appeared in the film production of *Grease.*

Free Again 1966 w.m. Jos Baselli, Armand Canfora, Robert Colby, Michel Jourdan

Free America, *see* **British Grenadiers**

Free and Easy Hour of Parting, The 1930 w. Roy Turk m. Fred E. Ahlert. (MF) *Free and Easy.* (MF) *Dance Fools Dance.* Buster Keaton, Anita Paige, and Robert Montgomery appeared in *Free and Easy.* Joan Crawford and Cliff Edwards appeared in *Dance Fools Dance.*

Free as Air 1957 w.m. Dorothy Reynolds, Julian Slade

Freedom Come, Freedom Go 1972 w.m. Albert Hammond, Mike Hazlewood, Roger Cook, Roger Greenaway. Ivor Novello Award winner 1971–72.

Freeway of Love 1985 w.m. Jeffrey Cohen, Narada Michael Walden. Grammy Award winner 1985.

Freeze-Frame 1982 w.m. Peter Wolf, Seth Justman

French Foreign Legion 1959 w.m. Aaron Schroeder, Guy Wood

French Lesson, The 1947 w. Betty Comden, Adolph Green m. Roger Edens. (MF) *Good News.* June Allyson and Peter Lawford appeared in *Good News.*

(Theme from) French Lieutenant's Woman, The 1982 m. Carl Davis. (F) *The French Lieutenant's Woman.* Meryl Streep and Jeremy Irons appeared in *The French Lieutenant's Woman.* Ivor Novello Award winner 1981–82.

Frenesi 1940 Sp.w. Alberto Dominguez Eng.w. Ray Charles, S.K. Russell m. Albert Dominguez

Frère Jacques 1811 w.m. probably traditional folksong, from France

Fresh 1985 w.m. Robert Bell, Ronald Bell, James Bonnefond, George Brown, Sandy Linzer, Claydes Eugene Smith, James Taylor, Curtis Williams

Freshie 1925 w. Jesse Greer, Harold Berg m. Jesse Greer

Friend o' Mine 1913 w. Frederick Edward Weatherly m. Wilfred Sanderson

(Just Say I'm a) Friend of Yours 1945 w. Johnny Burke m. Jimmy Van Heusen. (F) *A Man Called Sullivan.* (F) *The Great John L.* Greg McClure appeared in *The Great John L.*

Friendly Persuasion, or, **Thee I Love** 1956 w. Paul Francis Webster m. Dimitri Tiomkin. (F) *Friendly Persuasion.* Gary Cooper and Tony Perkins appeared in *Friendly Persuasion.*

Friends 1971 w.m. Terry Reid

Friends and Lovers (Born to Each Other) 1986 w.m. Paul Gordon, Jay Gruska

Friends and Neighbours 1954 w.m. Malcolm Lockyer, Marvin Scott

Friendship 1940 w.m. Cole Porter. (MT) *Du Barry Was a Lady.* (MF) *Du Barry Was a Lady.* Ethel Merman, Bert Lahr, and Betty Grable appeared in the stage production of *Du Barry Was a Lady.* Lucille Ball, Red Skelton, and Gene Kelly appeared in the film production of *Du Barry Was a Lady.* Ethel Merman sang this standard for a Friendship Cottage Cheese 1981 television advertising promotion campaign.

Friendship Is for Keeps 1974 w.m. John Lieberman. This song was written for a Bell Telephone Systems commercial promotion campaign.

Frightened City, The 1961 w.m. Norrie Paramor. (F) *The*

Frightened City. Herbert Lom appeared in *The Frightened City.*

Frog He Would a-Wooing Go, *see* **Frog Went a-Courtin'**

Frog Went a-Courtin', or, **Frog He Would a-Wooing Go,** or, **Mister Frog Went a-Courtin'** 1580 w.m. anon. This song is possibly a reference to Queen Elizabeth's suitor the Duke of Anjou.

From Another World 1940 w. Lorenz Hart m. Richard Rodgers. (MT) *Higher and Higher.* (MF) *Higher and Higher.* Frank Sinatra appeared in the film production of *Higher and Higher.*

From Greenland's Icy Mountains 1829 w. Reginald Heber m. Lowell Mason

From Here to Eternity 1953 w.m. Bob Wells, Fred Karger. (F) *From Here to Eternity.* Montgomery Clift, Deborah Kerr, and Frank Sinatra appeared in *From Here to Eternity.*

From Now On 1938 w.m. Cole Porter. (MT) *Leave It to Me.* Mary Martin, Sophie Tucker, William Gaxton, and Victor Moore appeared in *Leave It to Me.*

From Russia with Love 1964 w.m. Lionel Bart. (F) *From Russia with Love.* Sean Connery and Lotte Lenya appeared in *From Russia with Love.*

From the Halls of Montezuma, *see* **The Marine's Hymn**

From the Land of the Sky Blue Water 1909 w. Nelle Richmond Eberhart m. Charles Wakefield Cadman. From ''Four American Indian Songs.''

From the New World Symphony 1893 m. Anton Dvorák. From the German ''Aus Der Neuen Welt.'' See also ''Goin' Home.''

From the Time We Say Goodbye 1952 w.m. Leslie Sturdy

From the Top of Your Head to the Tip of Your Shoes 1935 w. Mack Gordon m. Harry Revel. (MF) *Two for Tonight.* Bing Crosby appeared in *Two for Tonight.*

From the Vine Came the Grape (From the Grape Came the Wine) 1949 w.m. Leonard Whitcup. Paul Cunningham. This song was popularly revived in 1954.

From This Moment On 1950 w.m. Cole Porter. (MT) *Lena Horne: The Lady and Her Music.* (MT) *Out of This World.* (MF) *Kiss Me, Kate.* This song was dropped from the New York production of *Out of This World.* Lena Horne appeared in *Lena Horne: The Lady and Her Music.* Ann Miller, Kathryn Grayson, and Howard Keel appeared in the film production of *Kiss Me, Kate.* This song did not appear in the original stage production of *Kiss Me, Kate.* This song was popularly revived in 1953.

Frosty the Snow Man 1950 w.m. Steve Nelson, Walter E. Rollins

Fuehrer's Face, Der 1943 w.m. Oliver Wallace. (MF) *Der Fuehrer's Face.*

Fugue for Tinhorns 1950 w.m. Frank Loesser. (MT) *Guys and Dolls.* (MF) *Guys and Dolls.* Robert Alda and Vivian Blaine appeared in the stage production of *Guys and Dolls.* Frank Sinatra, Marlon Brando, and Stubby Kaye appeared in the film production of *Guys and Dolls.* This piece employs the 1842 American bugle call, ''First Call,'' traditionally heard at horse races today.

Full Moon 1936 orig. w. Gonzalo Curiel Eng.w. Bob Russell m. Gonzalo Curiel, Marcelene Odette

Full Moon and Empty Arms 1946 w.m. Buddy Kaye, Ted Mossman. Based on a theme from the first movement of Rachmaninoff's Piano Concerto No. 2 in C-minor.

Full Moon Union, The 1880 w. Edward Harrigan m. David Braham. (MT) *The Mulligan Guards' Surprise.*

Fully Persuaded 1875 w. Rev. J.B. Atchinson m. William F. Sherwin

Fun To Be Fooled 1934 w. Ira Gershwin, E.Y. Harburg m. Harold Arlen. (MT) *Life Begins at 8:40.* Frances Williams, Ray Bolger, and Bert Lahr appeared in *Life Begins at 8:40.*

Funeral March 1840 m. Frédéric Chopin. This work was published in May of 1840 as the Adagio movement of his ''Sonate,'' op. 35, for piano.

Funeral March of a Marionette 1872 m. Charles Gounod. (TV) *Alfred Hitchcock Presents.*

Funiculì—Funiculà 1880 w.m. Luigi Denza. This song immortalized the opening of the Mount Vesuvius funicular railway.

Funkytown 1980 w.m. Steve Greenberg

Funny Bunny Hug 1912 w.m. William Tracey, Ray Walker, Dave Ringle. (MT) *Sing Out Sweet Land.* In 1912, when Bill Tracey attempted to collect his royalty check from J. Fred Helf at the Winter Garden Theatre, he learned of Helf's filing for bankruptcy. It was not until 1945, thirty-three years later, that Tracey made any money from this song, at which time the Theatre Guild used it in *Sing Out Sweet Land.*

Funny Face 1927 w. Ira Gershwin m. George Gershwin. (MT) *Funny Face.* (MF) *Funny Face.* Fred Astaire and Adele Astaire appeared in the stage production of *Funny Face.* Fred Astaire and Audrey Hepburn appeared in the film production of *Funny Face.*

Funny, Familiar, Forgotten Feelings 1966 w.m. M. Newbury

Funny Girl 1968 w. Bob Merrill m. Jule Styne. (MF) *Funny Girl.* Barbra Streisand appeared in both the stage and film productions of *Funny Girl.* This song did not appear in the New York stage production of *Funny Girl.*

Funny How Love Can Be 1965 w.m. ''Carter-Lewis''

Funny Old Hills, The 1938 w. Leo Robin m. Ralph Rainger. (MF) *Paris Honeymoon.* (F) *Twilight On the Trail.* Bing Crosby and Shirley Ross appeared in *Paris Honeymoon.* Bill Boyd and Brad King appeared in *Twilight on the Trail.*

Funny Thing 1954 w.m. Carl Sigman, Arthur Williams

Funny Way of Laughing 1962 w.m. Hank Cochran. Grammy Award winner 1962.

Für Elise (Albumblatt) 1810 m. Ludwig van Beethoven. Nohl, who found the manuscript, titled it ''Für Elise,'' although he probably misread Beethoven's writing of the name ''Therese.''

Future Mrs. 'Awkins, The c. 1890 w.m. Albert Chevalier

Futuristic Rhythm 1929 w. Dorothy Fields m. Jimmy

McHugh. (MT) *Hello Daddy*. Betty Starbuck, Mary Lawlor, and George Hassell appeared in *Hello Daddy*.

Gabrielle 1969 w. Alan Jay Lerner m. André Previn. (MT) *Coco*. Katharine Hepburn appeared in *Coco*, a musical based on the life of dress designer Gabrielle Chanel.

Gaby Glide, The 1911 w. Harry Pilcer m. Louis A. Hirsch. (MT) *Vera Violetta*. (MT) *Hullo Ragtime*. Al Jolson and Mae West appeared in *Vera Violetta*. Young French actress Gaby Deslys, while the girlfriend of King Alphonso of Spain, quickly became known to New Yorkers as ''Chicken à la King.''

Gal in Calico, A 1947 w. Leo Robin m. Arthur Schwartz. (MF) *The Time, the Place and the Girl*. Dennis Morgan and Jack Carson appeared in *The Time, the Place and the Girl*.

Galloping Home 1974 w.m. Denis King. Ivor Novello Award winner 1973–74.

Galloping Major, The 1907 w.m. George Bastow, F.W. Leigh. (MF) *The Galloping Major*. Basil Radford appeared in *The Galloping Major*.

Galveston 1969 w.m. Jimmy Webb

Galway Bay 1948 w.m. Arthur Colahan

Gambler, The 1978 w.m. Don Schlitz. Ivor Novello Award winner 1978.

Gambler's Blues, *see* **St. James Infirmary**

Gambler's Guitar 1953 w.m. Jim Lowe

Games People Play 1969 w.m. Joe South. Grammy Award winner 1969.

Games People Play 1981 w.m. Alan Parsons, Eric Woolfson

Gandy Dancers' Ball, The 1952 w.m. Paul Weston, Paul Mason Howard

Gang That Sang Heart of My Heart, The 1926 w.m. Ben Ryan. This song was popularly revived in 1953.

Gangway 1937 w.m. Sol Lerner, Al Goodhart, Al Hoffman. (MF) *Gangway*. Jessie Matthews appeared in *Gangway*.

Garden in the Rain, A 1928 w. James Dyrenforth m. Carroll Gibbons

Garden of Eden, The 1956 w.m. Dennise Norwood

Garden of Love, The 1904 w.m. André Messager, Lilian Eldee, Percy Greenbank. (MT) *Veronique*.

Garden of My Dreams 1918 w.m. Gene Buck, Dave Stamper

(Beautiful) Garden of Roses 1910 w. J.E. Dempsey m. Johann C. Schmid

Garden of Your Heart, The 1914 w. Edward Teschemacher m. Francis Dorel

Garfield Now Will Guide the Nation 1880 w.m. Thomas P. Westendorf. This song was written to support the Republican Presidential candidate James A. Garfield in the 1880 election.

Garland of Old Fashioned Roses 1912 w.m. E. Clinton Keithley

Gary, Indiana 1957 w.m. Meredith Willson. (MT) *The Music Man*. (MF) *The Music Man*. Robert Preston appeared in both the stage and film productions of *The Music Man*.

Gasoline Alley Bred 1971 w.m. Tony Macaulay, Roger Cook, Roger Greenaway

Gather the Rose 1928 w. Brian Hooker m. Rudolph Friml. (MT) *The White Eagle*.

Gaucho Serenade, The 1939 w.m. James Cavanaugh, John Redmond, Nat Simon

Gaudeamus Igitur 1782 w. some of the words are possibly suggested from a 1287 Latin manuscript. m. the melody, of unknown origin, was fully popularized by 1782. This standard is thought to be the oldest student song, epitomizing the luxuries of the carefree student life.

Gay Caballero, A 1928 w.m. Frank Crumit, Lou Klein. (MF) *Dance Fools Dance*. Joan Crawford and Cliff Edwards appeared in *Dance Fools Dance*.

Gay Ranchero, A 1937 w.m. Abe Tuvin, Francia Lubin, J.J. Espinoza. (MF) *King of the Cowboys*. (MF) *The Gay Ranchero*. Roy Rogers and Smiley Burnette appeared in *King of the Cowboys*. Roy Rogers and Andy Devine appeared in *The Gay Ranchero*. This song was popularly revived in 1943.

Gee! 1953 w.m. Viola Watkins, Daniel Norton, William Davis

Gee, But I'd Like To Make You Happy 1930 w.m. Larry Shay, George Ward, Reggie Montgomery. (MF) *Good News*.

Gee, But It's Great To Meet a Friend from Your Old Home Town 1910 w. William Tracey m. James McGavisk

Gee, Officer Krupke! 1957 w. Stephen Sondheim m. Leonard Bernstein. (MT) *West Side Story*. (MF) *West Side Story*. Martin Charnin, Carol Lawrence, and Chita Rivera appeared in the stage production of *West Side Story*. Natalie Wood and Rita Moreno appeared in the film production of *West Side Story*. The last three bars of this song are the traditional ''Shave and a Haircut, Bay Rum.''

Gee Whiz, It's You 1961 w.m. Hank B. Marvin, Ian Samwell

General's Fast Asleep, The 1935 w.m. Jimmy Kennedy, Michael Carr

Genie with the Light Brown Lamp 1965 w.m. Hank B. Marvin, Bruce Welch, John Rostill, Brian Bennett

Gentle Annie 1856 w.m. Stephen Collins Foster

Gentle on My Mind 1967 w.m. John Hartford. Grammy Award winner 1967.

Gentle Zitella, *see* **Love's Ritornella**

Gentleman Is a Dope, The 1947 w. Oscar Hammerstein II m. Richard Rodgers. (MT) *Allegro*. Annamary Dickey, William Ching, and Gloria Wills appeared in *Allegro*.

Gentlemen Prefer Blondes 1926 w. B.G. DeSylva m. Lewis E. Gensler. (MT) *Queen High*. Charles Ruggles and Mary Lawlor appeared in *Queen High*.

Gentlemen, the King 1935 w.m. Cyril Ray, Ivor McLaren

Georgette 1922 w. Lew Brown m. Ray Henderson. (MT) *Greenwich Village Follies*.

Georgia 1922 w. Howard Johnson m. Walter Donaldson. This song is not to be confused with ''Georgia on My Mind.''

Georgia Grind 1915 w.m. Spencer Williams

Georgia on My Mind 1930 w. Stuart Gorrell m. Hoagy Carmichael. This song was popularly revived in 1960.

Georgian Rumba 1956 w.m. Ivor Slaney

Georgia's Gotta Moon 1938 w.m. Max Nesbitt, Harry Nesbitt

Georgie Porgie, *see* **Mother Goose's Melodies**

Georgy Girl 1966 w. Jim Dale m. Tom Springfield. (F) *Georgy Girl.* Lynn Redgrave and James Mason appeared in *Georgy Girl.*

Germans at the Spa, The 1982 w.m. Maury Yeston. *Nine.* Liliane Montevecchi and Anita Morris appeared in *Nine.*

Geronimo 1963 w.m. Hank B. Marvin

Gertie from Bizerte 1943 w.m. James Cavanaugh, Walter Kent, Bob Cutter

Gertie the Girl with the Gong 1935 w.m. Ray Sonin, Ronnie Munro

Gesù Bambino 1917 It.w. Pietro A. Yon Eng.w. Frederick Herman Martens m. Pietro A. Yon

Get a Job 1958 w.m. Earl T. Beal, Raymond W. Edwards, William F. Horton, Richard A. Lewis

Get a Load of That 1947 w. Langston Hughes m. Kurt Weill. (MT) *Street Scene.* Anne Jeffreys and Norman Cordon appeared in *Street Scene.*

Get Along Little Doggies, *see* **Git Along Little Doggies**

Get Back 1969 w.m. John Lennon, Paul McCartney. (MT) *Beatlemania.* Ivor Novello Award winner 1969–70.

Get Closer 1976 w.m. Jimmy Seals, Dash Crofts

Get Down 1973 w.m. Gilbert O'Sullivan. Ivor Novello Award winner 1973–74.

Get Down Get Down (Get on the Floor) 1975 w.m. Joe Simon, Caeford Gerald

Get Down Tonight 1975 w.m. Harry Casey, Richard Finch

Get Happy 1930 w. Ted Koehler m. Harold Arlen. (MT) *Nine-Fifteen Revue.* (MF) *Summer Stock.* (MF) *If You Feel Like Singing.* (MF) *With a Song in My Heart.* Ruth Etting and Fred Keating appeared in *Nine-Fifteen Revue.* Judy Garland and Gene Kelly appeared in *Summer Stock.* Frank Sinatra appeared in *If You Feel Like Singing.* Susan Hayward appeared in *With a Song in My Heart,* biopic of singer Jane Froman.

Get Lost 1961 w.m. Les Vandyke

Get Me to the Church on Time 1956 w. Alan Jay Lerner m. Frederick Loewe. (MT) *My Fair Lady.* (MF) *My Fair Lady.* Julie Andrews and Rex Harrison appeared in the stage production of *My Fair Lady.*

Get Off My Cloud 1965 w.m. Mick Jagger, Keith Richard

(He'd Have To Get Under,) Get Out and Get Under (To Fix Up His Automobile) 1913 w. Grant Clarke, Edgar Leslie m. Maurice Abrahams. (MT) *The Pleasure Seekers.* (MT) *Hullo Tango.* Gerald Kirby appeared in *Hullo Tango.*

Get Out and Get Under the Moon 1928 w. Charles Tobias, William Jerome m. Larry Shay

Get Out of Town 1938 w.m. Cole Porter. (MT) *Leave It to Me.* William Gaxton and Victor Moore appeared in *Leave It to Me.*

Get Out Those Old Records 1951 w.m. Carmen Lombardo, John Jacob Loeb

Get Ready 1970 w.m. Eric Clapton, Yvonne Elliman

Get Thee Behind Me, Satan 1936 w.m. Irving Berlin. (MF) *Follow the Fleet.* Fred Astaire and Ginger Rogers appeared in *Follow the Fleet.*

(Let's) Get Together 1969 w.m. Chester Powers, Jr.

Get Up and Boogie 1976 w.m. Sylvester Levay, Stephen Prager

Get Used to It 1979 w.m. Michael S. Omartian, Roger Voudouris

Get Wildroot Cream-Oil Charlie 1947 w.m. J. Ward Maurer. This song was written for a Wildroot Cream Oil Hair Dressing commercial promotion campaign.

Get Your Kicks on Route 66, *see* **Route 66**

Getcha Back 1985 w.m. Mike Love, Terry Melcher

Getting Around and About 1935 w.m. Lewis Ilda, Michael Carr

Getting Better 1967 w.m. John Lennon, Paul McCartney

Getting Married Today 1970 w.m. Stephen Sondheim. (MT) *Company.* (MT) *Side by Side by Sondheim.* Elaine Stritch appeared in *Company.* Millicent Martin and Julie N. McKenzie appeared in *Side by Side by Sondheim.*

Getting To Know You 1951 w. Oscar Hammerstein II m. Richard Rodgers. (MT) *The King and I.* (MF) *The King and I.* Gertrude Lawrence and Yul Brynner appeared in the stage production of *The King and I.* Deborah Kerr and Yul Brynner appeared in the film production of *The King and I.*

Ghost Herd in the Sky, The, *see* **Riders in the Sky**

Ghost of a Chance, A *see* **I Don't Stand a Ghost of a Chance with You**

Ghost of the Violin, The 1912 w. Bert Kalmar m. Ted Snyder

Ghost Riders in the Sky, or, **A Cowboy Legend** 1949 w.m. Stan Jones. (F) *Riders in the Sky.* Gene Autry and Gloria Henry appeared in *Riders in the Sky.*

Ghostbusters 1984 w.m. Ray Parker, Jr. (F) *Ghostbusters.*

G.I. Jive, The 1943 w.m. Donald Kahn, Johnny Mercer

Giannina Mia 1912 w. Otto Harbach m. Rudolf Friml. (MT) *The Firefly.* (MF) *The Firefly.* Emma Trentini and Ray Atwell appeared in the stage production of *The Firefly.* Allan Jones and Jeanette MacDonald appeared in the film production of *The Firefly.*

Gid-ap, Garibaldi 1927 w. Howard Johnson, Billy Moll m. Harry Warren

Giddiap Napoleon, It Looks Like Rain, *see* **Wal, I Swan!**

Gigi 1958 w. Alan Jay Lerner m. Frederick Loewe. (MF) *Gigi.* Leslie Caron, Maurice Chevalier, and Hermione Gingold appeared in *Gigi.* Academy Award winner 1958.

Gigolo, *see* **I'm a Gigolo**

Gilbert the Filbert 1914 w.m. Arthur Wimperis, Herman Finck. (MT) *The Passing Show.* Basil Hallam appeared in *The Passing Show.*

Gilly Gilly Ossenfeffer 1954 w.m. Al Hoffman, Dick Manning

Gimme a Little Kiss, Will Ya, Huh? 1926 w.m. Roy Turk, Jack Smith, Maceo Pinkard. (F) *Lady on a Train*. (MF) *Has Anybody Seen My Gal*. Deanna Durbin and Ralph Bellamy appeared in *Lady on a Train*. Rock Hudson appeared in *Has Anybody Seen My Gal*.

Gimme a Pigfoot (and a Bottle of Beer) w.m. Wesley Wilson. (MT) *Me and Bessie*. (MF) *Lady Sings the Blues*. Linda Hopkins appeared in *Me and Bessie*. Diana Ross appeared in *Lady Sings the Blues*.

Gimme Dat Ding 1971 w.m. Albert Hammond, Mike Hazlewood. Ivor Novello Award winner 1970–71.

Ginger You're Barmy 1912 w.m. Fred Murray

Gipsy, *see* **Gypsy**

Girl 1966 w.m. John Lennon, Paul McCartney

Girl! A Girl!, A, or, **Zoom Ba Di Alli Nella** 1954 w.m. Bennie Benjamin, George Weiss, Al Bandini

Girl at the Ironing Board, The 1934 w. Al Dubin m. Harry Warren. (MF) *Dames*. Joan Blondell, Ruby Keeler, and Dick Powell appeared in *Dames*.

Girl Don't Come 1965 w.m. Chris Andrews

Girl Friend, The 1926 w. Lorenz Hart m. Richard Rodgers. (MT) *The Girl Friend*.

Girl Friend of the Whirling Dervish, The 1938 w. Al Dubin m. Harry Warren. (MF) *Garden of the Moon*. Jerry Colonna and Pat O'Brien appeared in *Garden of the Moon*.

Girl from Ipanema, The 1964 w.m. Antonio Carlos Jobim, Norman Gimbel, Vinicius de Moraes. (F) *The Color of Money*. Paul Newman appeared in *The Color of Money*. Grammy Award winner 1964.

Girl I Left Behind Me, The, or, **Brighton Camp** 1758–70 w. possibly Thomas Moore m. anon.; based on the Hibernian tune "Brighton Camp." While this standard was known as early as 1758–70, it did not appear in print until 1808. This song is performed at West Point graduations and roots an army tradition in its story about an Irish bandmaster serving with the British, who left behind a woman in every city, town, and village.

Girl I Loved in Sunny Tennessee, The 1899 w. Harry Braisted m. Stanley Carter

Girl in the Alice Blue Gown, The 1938 w.m. Ross Parker

Girl in the Crinoline Gown, The 1924 w.m. Melville Gideon, Clifford Seyler. (MT) *The Co-Optimists*. Melville Gideon appeared in *The Co-Optimists*.

Girl Is Mine, The 1982 w.m. Michael Jackson

Girl Is You and the Boy Is Me, The 1926 w. B.G. DeSylva, Lew Brown m. Ray Henderson. (MT) *George White's Scandals of 1926*. Ann Pennington and Frances Williams appeared in *George White's Scandals of 1926*.

Girl Like You, A 1961 w.m. Jerry Lordan

Girl of My Dreams 1927 w.m. Sunny Clapp

Girl of the Pi Beta Phi, A 1927 w. B.G. DeSylva, Lew Brown m. Ray Henderson. (MT) *Good News*. (MF) *Good News*.

Girl on the Magazine Cover, The 1915 w.m. Irving Berlin. (MT) *Stop! Look! Listen!*. (MT) *Follow the Crowd*. (MF) *Easter Parade*. Joseph Coyne and Ethel Levey appeared in

Follow the Crowd. Judy Garland and Fred Astaire appeared in *Easter Parade*.

Girl on the Police Gazette, The 1937 w.m. Irving Berlin. (MT) *Star and Garter*. (MF) *On the Avenue*. Dick Powell and the Ritz Brothers appeared in *On the Avenue*.

Girl Talk 1964 w.m. Mort Lindsey

Girl That I Marry, The 1946 w.m. Irving Berlin. (MT) *Annie Get Your Gun*. (MF) *Annie Get Your Gun*. Ray Middleton appeared in the stage production of *Annie Get Your Gun*. Howard Keel appeared in the film production of *Annie Get Your Gun*.

Girl with a Brogue, The 1909 w. Arthur Wimperis m. Lionel Monckton. (MT) *The Arcadians*.

Girl with the Dreamy Eyes, The 1935 w.m. Michael Carr, Eddie Pola

Girl with the Flaxen Hair, The 1910 m. Claude Debussy. From "La Fille aux Cheveux de Lin," Prelude No. 8.

Girl with the Golden Braids, The 1957 w.m. Stanley Kahan, Eddie Snyder

Girlie Was Made To Love, A 1911 w. Joe Goodwin m. George W. Meyer

Girls, Girls, Girls 1907 w. Adrian Ross m. Franz Lehár. (MT) *The Merry Widow*. (MF) *The Merry Widow* (1934). (MF) *The Merry Widow* (1952). New lyrics for this song were written by Gus Kahn and Lorenz Hart for the 1934 film production of *The Merry Widow*. Jeanette MacDonald and Maurice Chevalier appeared in the 1934 film production of *The Merry Widow*. Lana Turner and Fernando Lamas appeared in the 1952 film production of *The Merry Widow*.

Girls Just Want To Have Fun 1984 w.m. Robert Hazard

Girls Were Made To Take Care of Boys 1949 w.m. Ralph Blane. (MF) *One Sunday Afternoon*. Dennis Morgan and Janis Paige appeared in *One Sunday Afternoon*.

(Whoopee Ti Yi Yo) Git Along Little Dog(g)ies 1893 w.m. traditional cowboy song, from probably as early as 1880. (F) *Maisie*. Ann Sothern and Robert Young appeared in *Maisie*. "Dogie" is the cowboy term for an undersized motherless calf.

Give a Little Credit to Your Dad 1916 w. William Tracey m. Nat Vincent

Give a Little Whistle 1940 w.m. Ned Washington, Leigh Harline. (MF) *Pinocchio*.

Give a Little Whistle 1960 w. Carolyn Leigh m. Cy Coleman. (MT) *Wildcat*.

Give a Man a Horse He Can Ride 1917 w. James Thomson m. Geoffrey O'Hara

Give Her My Love 1956 w.m. Leslie Baguley, Tommie Connor, Michael Reine

Give It All You Got 1980 w.m. Chuck Mangione

Give It Back to the Indians 1939 w. Lorenz Hart m. Richard Rodgers. (MT) *Too Many Girls*. (MF) *Too Many Girls*. Van Johnson and Desi Arnaz appeared in the stage production of *Too Many Girls*. Lucille Ball appeared in the film production of *Too Many Girls*.

Give Me a Little Cosy Corner 1918 w.m. James W. Tate, Clifford Harris

Give Me a Moment Please 1930 w. Leo Robin m. Richard A. Whiting, W. Franke Harling. (MF) *Monte Carlo*. Jeanette MacDonald and Zasu Pitts appeared in *Monte Carlo*.

Give Me a Night in June, *see* **A Night in June**

Give Me Love (Give Me Peace on Earth) 1973 w.m. George Harrison

Give Me One Dozen Roses, *see* **One Dozen Roses**

Give Me One Hour 1928 w. Brian Hooker m. Rudolf Friml. (MT) *The White Eagle*.

Give Me Something To Remember You By, *see* **Something To Remember You By**

Give Me That Old Time Religion, *see* **Old Time Religion**

Give Me the Moonlight, Give Me the Girl 1917 w. Lew Brown m. Albert Von Tilzer. (MT) *Hullo America*. (MF) *The Dolly Sisters*. Betty Grable and June Haver appeared in *The Dolly Sisters*, biopic of the famous sister act. Theme song of Frankie Vaughan.

Give Me the Night 1980 w.m. Rodney Temperton

Give Me the Old Soft Shoe, *see* **The Old Soft Shoe**

Give Me the Simple Life 1945 w. Harry Ruby m. Rube Bloom. (MF) *Give Me the Simple Life*. (MF) *Wake Up and Dream*. June Haver and John Payne appeared in *Give Me the Simple Life*. June Haver and John Payne appeared in *Wake Up and Dream*. The music from this song was later used for the 1977 Campbell's Soup commercial promotion campaign and retitled "Give Me the Campbell Life."

Give Me Your Tired, Your Poor 1949 w. Emma Lazarus m. Irving Berlin. (MT) *Miss Liberty*. The poem by Emma Lazarus appears at the base of the Statue of Liberty.

Give My Regards to Broadway 1904 w.m. George M. Cohan. (MT) *Little Johnny Jones*. (MT) *George M!*. (MF) *Little Johnny Jones*. (MF) *Broadway Melody*. (MF) *The Great American Broadcast*. (MF) *Yankee Doodle Dandy*. (MF) *Jolson Sings Again*. (MF) *With a Song in My Heart*. (F) *Give My Regards to Broadway*. Bernadette Peters and Joel Grey appeared in *George M!*. James Cagney and Joan Leslie appeared in *Yankee Doodle Dandy*. Larry Parks appeared in *Jolson Sings Again*. Susan Hayward and David Wayne appeared in *With a Song in My Heart*, biopic of singer Jane Froman. Dan Dailey and Charles Ruggles appeared in *Give My Regards to Broadway*. Theme song of George M. Cohan. See also Part I, 1919.

Give Peace a Chance 1969 w.m. John Lennon, Paul McCartney. Ivor Novello Award winner 1969–70.

Give Yourself a Pat on the Back 1930 w.m. Ralph Butler, Raymond Wallace

Givin' It Up for Your Love 1981 w.m. Jerry Williams

Glad All Over 1964 w.m. Dave Clark, Mike Smith

Glad Rag Doll 1929 w.m. Jack Yellen, Milton Ager, Dan Dougherty. (MF) *Glad Rag Doll*. Dolores Costello and Ralph Graves appeared in *Glad Rag Doll*.

Glad To Be Unhappy 1936 w. Lorenz Hart m. Richard Rodgers. (MT) *On Your Toes*. (MF) *On Your Toes*. Ray Bolger appeared in the stage production of *On Your Toes*. This song was popularly revived in 1967.

Gladiator('s) March, The 1886 m. John Philip Sousa. This march is traditionally performed in circuses throughout the world.

Gladiator's Entry, The 1900 m. Julius Fuarcik. (F) *Heaven Can Wait*. Warren Beatty and Julie Christie appeared in *Heaven Can Wait*. This melody is performed traditionally at circuses and wrestling matches throughout the world.

Glamorous Life, The 1973 w.m. Stephen Sondheim. (MT) *A Little Night Music*. (MF) *A Little Night Music*. Len Cariou, Glynis Johns, and Hermione Gingold appeared in the stage production of *A Little Night Music*. Elizabeth Taylor, Len Cariou, and Hermione Gingold appeared in the film production of *A Little Night Music*.

Glamorous Night 1935 w.m. Ivor Novello, Christopher Hassell. (MT) *Glamorous Night*. (MF) *Glamorous Night*. Trevor Jones and Mary Ellis appeared in both the stage and film productions of *Glamorous Night*.

Glendora 1956 w.m. Ray Stanley

Glendy Burke, The 1860 w.m. Stephen Collins Foster

Glitter and Be Gay 1956 w. Richard Wilbur m. Leonard Bernstein. (MT) *Candide*.

Globetrotter 1963 w.m. Joe Meek

Gloomy Sunday 1936 Hung.w. Laszlo Javor Eng.w. Sam M. Lewis m. Rezso Seress. This song was banned from radio broadcasts in the U.S. after allegedly causing suicides among radio listeners. This song, like "St. James Infirmary" of 1930, is no longer heard on the air.

Gloria, or, **Theme from** *Butterfield 8* 1960 w. Mack Davidm. Bronislaw Kaper. (F) *Butterfield 8*.

Gloria 1966 w.m. Van Morrison

Gloria 1982 w.m. Umberto Tozzi, Giancarlo Bigazzi, Trevor Veitch

Glory Days 1985 w.m. Bruce Springsteen

Glory (Glory) Hallelujah, *see* **Battle Hymn of the Republic**

Glory of Love (Theme from *The Karate Kid Part II*) 1986 w.m. Peter Cetera, David Foster, Diane Nini. (F) *The Karate Kid Part II*.

Glory of Love, The 1936 w.m. William Hill

Glory Road, De 1928 w. Clement Wood m. Jacques Wolfe

Glory Song, The, *see* **O That Will Be Glory for Me**

Glow Worm (,The) 1907 Ger.w. Paul Lincke Eng.w. Lilla Cayley Robinson m. Paul Lincke. (MT) *The Girl Behind the Counter*. This song was first published in 1902. A new lyric by Johnny Mercer was added in 1952 to this standard. In a yellow satin dress, ballerina Anna Pavlova danced to this song in her Empire Gavotte, in 1916.

Go Away Little Girl 1963 w.m. Gerry Goffin, Carole King. This song was popularly revived in 1971.

Go Call the Doctor, or, **Anti-Calomel** 1843 w.m. Judson Hutchinson. This song was popularly performed by the Hutchinson Family singers.

(It's Hard To) Go Down Easy 1985 w.m. Jay Bolotin

Go Down, Moses 1917 w.m. arr. Harry Thacker Burleigh. Based on a traditional black American spiritual, from at least 1861.

Go Fly a Kite 1939 w.m. James V. Monaco, Johnny Burke.

(MF) *The Star Maker*. Bing Crosby and Ned Sparks appeared in *The Star Maker*.

Go, Go, Go, Go 1951 w. Mack David m. Jerry Livingston

Go Home 1986 w.m. Stevie Wonder

Go Home and Tell Your Mother 1930 w. Dorothy Fields m. Jimmy McHugh. (MF) *Love in the Rough*. (MF) *Dance Fools Dance*. Robert Montgomery and Dorothy Jordon appeared in *Love in the Rough*. Joan Crawford and Lester Vail appeared in *Dance Fools Dance*.

Go, Little Boat 1917 w. P.G. Wodehouse m. Jerome Kern. (MT) *Miss 1917*. (MF) *Till the Clouds Roll By*. Robert Walker, Judy Garland, and June Allyson appeared in *Till the Clouds Roll By*, biopic of composer Jerome Kern.

Go Now 1963 w.m. Banks, Bennett

Go Tell Aunt Rhody, *see* **The Ole Grey Goose**

Go Tell It on the Mountain 1865 w.m. traditional black American spiritual.

Go To Sleep My Baby, My Baby, My Baby, *see* **Emmet's Lullaby**

Go Way Back and Sit Down 1901 w. Elmer Bowman m. Al Johns

Go Where You Wanna Go 1967 w.m. John Phillips

Go Your Own Way 1977 w.m. Lindsey Buckingham

God Be with You Till We Meet Again 1883 w. Jeremiah Eames Rankin m. William Gould Tomer

God Bless America 1939 w.m. Irving Berlin. (MF) *This Is the Army*. Ronald Reagan and Kate Smith appeared in *This Is the Army*. This song was first performed on public radio by Kate Smith on Armistice Day, 1938. Irving Berlin signed over his royalties for this song to the Boy and Girl Scouts of America. *The New York Times* reports: ''. . . both the song and Miss [Kate] Smith experienced a curious resurgence of popularity beginning in 1969 when the Philadelphia Flyers professional hockey team began to substitute her recording of the song for 'The Star-Spangled Banner' before games. The team began to win on nights the song was played. As the team improved the record was reserved for crucial games and, at the end of the 1975–76 playing season the Flyers' record was 41 wins, 5 losses and 1 tie on nights Kate Smith Sang 'God Bless America,' either on record or in person. The first three of the five or so times she appeared in person, the Flyers' opponents were scoreless.''

God Bless Our Native Land 1844 w. Rev. Charles Timothy Brooks m. Based on ''America'' of 1832

God Bless the Child 1941 w.m. Arthur Herzog, Jr., Billie Holiday. (MT) *Bubbling Brown Sugar*. (MF) *Lady Sings the Blues*. Avon Long and Vivian Reed appeared in *Bubbling Brown Sugar*. Diana Ross appeared in *Lady Sings the Blues*.

God Bless the USA 1984 w.m. Lee Greenwood

God Only Knows 1966 w.m. Wilson, Asher

God Rest You Merry Gentlemen 1827 w.m. traditional carol, from England

God Save the King (Queen) 1744 w. possibly Henry Careym. possibly Dr. John Bull in 1619; probably Henry Carey. Based on a melody composed by H. Harris for the King of Denmark; later, Herr G.B. Schumacher wrote the German words and it became ''Heil Dir im Seigeskranz,'' the one-time official Prussian National Anthem. This song was also the Russian state anthem until Czar Nicholas commissioned Lwoff in 1833 to write ''God Preserve the Czar.'' Beethoven composed a set of seven variations on this theme in 1804, and later used it again in his ''Battle Symphony.'' Weber also employed the theme in his cantata ''Kampf und Sieg'' and his ''Jubel Overture.'' Dr. Bull was one of the organists for the Chapel Royal during the reign of James I. See also ''America (My Country 'Tis of Thee).''

God, That's Good 1979 w.m. Stephen Sondheim. (MT) *Sweeney Todd*. Angela Lansbury and Len Cariou appeared in *Sweeney Todd*.

God-Why-Don't-You-Love-Me Blues, The 1971 w.m. Stephen Sondheim. (MT) *Follies*. Alexis Smith and Yvonne De Carlo appeared in *Follies*.

(Theme from) Godfather, The (Waltz) 1972 w.m. Billy Meshel, Larry Kusik, Nino Rota. (F) *The Godfather*. Al Pacino, Marlon Brando, and Diane Keaton appeared in *The Godfather*. See also ''Michael's Theme,'' ''Speak Softly Love.''

(Theme from) Godfather, The (Part II) 1974 m. Nino Rota. (F) *The Godfather Part II*. Al Pacino, Diane Keaton, and Robert DeNiro appeared in *The Godfather Part II*.

(This Is) God's Country 1938 w. E.Y. Harburg m. Harold Arlen. (MT) *Hooray for What!* (MF) *Babes in Arms*. Ed Wynn and Paul Haakon appeared in *Hooray for What!* Mickey Rooney and Judy Garland appeared in *Babes in Arms*. This song was popularly revived in 1950.

God's Green World 1945 w. Alan Jay Lerner m. Frederick Loewe. (MT) *The Day Before Spring*. Bill Johnson and Irene Manning appeared in *The Day Before Spring*.

Goin' Home 1922 w. William Arms Fisher m. based on the Largo from Anton Dvorák's 1893 symphony ''From the New World,'' op. 95. See also ''Wagon Wheels.''

Going Home 1984 w.m. Mark Knopfler. (F) *Local Hero*. Ivor Novello Award winner 1983–84.

Goin' Out of My Head 1964 w.m. Teddy Randazzo, Bobby Weinstein

Going for a Pardon 1896 w. James Thornton, Clara Havenschild m. James Thornton

Going My Way 1944 w. Johnny Burke m. Jimmy Van Heusen. (MF) *Going My Way*. Bing Crosby and Barry Fitzgerald appeared in *Going My Way*.

Going to Memphis 1960 new w.m. Johnny Cash

Going Up 1917 w. Otto Harbach m. Louis Hirsch. (MT) *Going Up*. Joseph Coyne and Marjorie Gordon appeared in the British production of *Going Up*.

Gold and Silver (Waltz), The 1904 m. Franz Lehár from the German ''Gold und Silber,'' op. 75. This waltz was written for a gala ball given by Princess Metternich on January 27, 1902.

Gold Diggers' Song, The, *see* **We're in the Money**

Gold Will Buy Most Anything But a True Girl's Heart 1898 w. Charles E. Foreman m. Monroe H. Rosenfeld

Golden Brown 1983 w.m. Jet Black, Jean J. Burnell, Hugh

A. Cornwell, David Greenfield. Ivor Novello Award winner 1982–83.

Golden Days 1924 w. Dorothy Donnelly m. Sigmund Romberg. (MT) *The Student Prince.* (MF) *The Student Prince.* Herbert Waterous and Rose Hishell appeared in the British production of *The Student Prince.* Ann Blyth appeared in the 1954 film production of *The Student Prince.*

Golden Earrings 1947 w. Jay Livingston, Ray Evans m. Victor Young. (F) *Golden Earrings.* Ray Milland and Marlene Dietrich appeared in *Golden Earrings.*

Golden Gate 1928 w. Billy Rose, Dave Dreyer m. Al Jolson, Joseph Meyer

(Oh Dem) Golden Slippers 1879 w.m. James A. Bland. (F) *Tulsa Kid.* Luana Walters and Noah Beery appeared in *Tulsa Kid.*

Golden Song, The 1923 w. Adrian Ross m. Franz Schubert. (MT) *Lilac Time.* Clara Butterworth and Courtice Pounds appeared in *Lilac Time.*

Golden Tango, The 1953 w.m. Victor Sylvester, Ernest Wilson

Golden Tears 1979 w.m. John Arthur Schweers

Golden Wedding, De 1880 w.m. James A. Bland

Golden West, The 1925 w.m. Horatio Nicholls

(Theme from) Goldfinger 1965 w.m. Leslie Bricusse, Anthony Newley, John Barry. (F) *Goldfinger.* Sean Connery and Honor Blackman appeared in *Goldfinger.*

Golliwogg's Cake Walk 1908 m. Claude Debussy from ''The Children's Corner''

Golondrina, La 1883 w. L. Wolfe Gilbert m. Narciso Serradell. (MF) *Happy Days.* (MF) *Fiesta.* Anne Ayars appeared in *Fiesta.* The words to this Mexican song were added in 1908.

Gone 1952 w.m. Smokey Rogers. This song was popularly revived in 1957.

Gone at Last 1975 w.m. Paul Simon

Gone Fishin' 1950 w.m. Charles Kenny, Nick Kenny

Gone Too Far 1980 w.m. David Malloy, Eddie Rabbitt, Even Stevens

Gone with the Wind 1937 w. Herbert Magidson, Allie Wrubel

Gonna Be Alright, *see* **Tonight's the Night**

Gonna Build a Mountain 1962 w.m. Leslie Bricusse, Anthony Newley. (MT) *Stop the World—I Want To Get Off.* Anthony Newley appeared in *Stop the World—I Want To Get Off.*

Gonna Fly Now, or, **Theme from** *Rocky* 1977 w.m. Ayn Robbins, Bill Conti, Carol Connors. (F) *Rocky.* Sylvester Stallone appeared in *Rocky.*

Gonna Get a Girl 1927 w.m. Howard Simon, Al Lewis

Gonna Get Along Without Ya Now 1952 w.m. Milton Kellem. This song was popularly revived in 1956.

Gonna Shout All Over God's Heav'n, *see* **I Got Shoes**

Goober Peas 1864 w.m. Johnny Reb; erroneously credited to A. Pindar, Esq. ''Goober peas'' is a slang term for peanuts; this song serves as a complaint against meager food rations for soldiers. Georgian soldiers during the Civil War were often known as ''goober grabbers.''

Good Bye-ee 1918 w.m. R.P. Weston, Bert Lee

Good Companions, The 1957 w.m. C.A. Rossi, Paddy Roberts, Geoffrey Parsons. (F) *The Good Companions.*

Good Day Sunshine 1966 w.m. John Lennon, Paul McCartney

Good Evening, Caroline 1908 w. Jack Norworth m. Albert Von Tilzer

Good Golly Miss Molly 1963 w.m. Robert Blackwell, John Marascalco

Good Hearted Woman, A 1976 w.m. Waylon Jennings, Willie Nelson

Good King Wenceslas 1853–1867 w. Rev. John Mason Neale m. anon., based on a Swedish melody of 1582. During the tenth century, the Duke of Bohemia, Wenceslas, was legendary for his abounding generosity.

Good Life, The 1963 w.m. Sacha Distel, Jack Reardon

Good Lovin' 1966 w.m. Rudy Clark, Arthur Resnick

Good Luck Charm 1962 w.m. Wally Gold, Aaron Schroeder

Good Luck, Good Health, God Bless You 1951 w.m. Charles Adams, A. Le Royal

Good Man Is Hard To Find, A 1918 w.m. Eddie Green. (MT) *Back Again.* (MT) *Me and Bessie.* (MF) *Meet Danny Wilson.* Lee White appeared in *Back Again.* Linda Hopkins appeared in *Me and Bessie.* Frank Sinatra and Shelly Winters appeared in *Meet Danny Wilson.*

Good Morning 1939 w. Arthur Freed m. Nacio Herb Brown. (MF) *Babes in Arms.* (MF) *Singin' in the Rain.* Mickey Rooney and Judy Garland appeared in *Babes in Arms.* Gene Kelly, Debbie Reynolds, and Donald O'Connor appeared in the 1952 film production of *Singin' in the Rain.*

Good Morning, Good Morning 1967 w.m. John Lennon, Paul McCartney

Good Morning Heartache 1946 w.m. Irene Higginbotham, Ervin Drake, Dan Fisher. (MF) *Lady Sings the Blues.* Diana Ross appeared in *Lady Sings the Blues.*

Good Morning, Mister Zip-Zip-Zip 1918 w.m. Robert Lloyd

Good Morning Starshine 1969 w. Gerome Ragni, James Rado m. Galt MacDermot. (MT) *Hair.* (MF) *Hair.*

Good Morning to All, *see* **Happy Birthday to You**

Good News 1928 w. B.G. DeSylva, Lew Brown m. Ray Henderson. (MT) *Good News.* (MF) *Good News* (1930). (MF) *Good News* (1947). (MF) *The Best Things in Life Are Free.* George Olsen and Joseph Santley appeared in the stage production of *Good News.* Bessie Love and Mary Lawlor appeared in the 1930 film production of *Good News.* Gordon MacRae, Dan Dailey, and Ernest Borgnine appeared in *The Best Things in Life Are Free,* biopic of song writers DeSylva, Brown, and Henderson.

Good News 1964 w.m. Sam Cooke

Good Night 1968 w.m. John Lennon, Paul McCartney

Good Night Angel 1937 w. Herb Magidson m. Allie

Wrubel. (MF) *Radio City Revels.* Jack Oakie and Ann Miller appeared in *Radio City Revels.*

Good Night Dear   1908   w.m. Will R. Anderson. (MT) *Love Watches.*

Good Night Ladies, or, **Merrily We Roll Along**   1853   w. E.P. Christy as early as 1847; also Ferd V.D. Garretson   m. for the first part of this melody, see ''Someone's in the Kitchen with Dinah''; for the second part, see also ''Mary Had a Little Lamb.''

Good Night, Nurse (Kiss Your Little Patient)   1912   w. Thomas J. Gray   m. Raymond Walker

Good Night, Sweetheart   1931   w.m. Ray Noble, Jimmy Campbell, Reginald Connelly; based on themes from Schubert's Symphony in C and the Liszt Preludes; Amer.w. Rudy Vallee. (MT) *Earl Carroll's Vanities of 1930.* (MT) *Earl Carroll's Vanities of 1931.* (MT) *Americana.* (MF) *You Were Meant for Me.* (MF) *Stardust on the Sage.* Jack Benny and Patsy Kelly appeared in *Earl Carroll's Vanities of 1930.* Rudy Vallee and his Connecticut Yankees appeared in *Americana.* Jeanne Crain and Dan Dailey appeared in *You Were Meant for Me.* Gene Autry and Gabby Hayes appeared in *Stardust on the Sage.* Closing theme of Ray Noble.

Good Old Bad Days, The   1972   w.m. Leslie Bricusse, Anthony Newley

Good Ol' Boys, *see* (Theme from) Dukes of Hazzard

Good Ole Boys Like Me   1980   w.m. Bob McDill

Good Old U.S.A., The   1906   w. Jack Drislane   m. Theodore F. Morse

Good Ship Lollipop, *see* **On the Good Ship Lollipop**

Good Sweet Ham   1873   w.m. Henry Hart; arr. James E. Stewart

Good, the Bad and the Ugly, The   1968   w.m. Ennio Morricone. (F) *The Good, the Bad and the Ugly.* Clint Eastwood and Eli Wallach appeared in *The Good, the Bad and the Ugly.*

Good Thing Going   1981   w.m. Stephen Sondheim. (MT) *Merrily We Roll Along.* Ann Morrison appeared in *Merrily We Roll Along.*

Good Times   1979   w.m. Bernard Edwards, Nile Rodgers

Good Timin'   1960   w.m. Clint Ballard, Jr., Fred Tobias

Good Timin'   1979   w.m. Brian Wilson, Carl Wilson

Good Vibrations   1966   w.m. Brian Wilson, Mike Love. This song was used in 1979 for a major television advertising campaign for Sunkist Oranges.

Good Word, The (Theme from *Nationwide)*   1976   m. Johnny Scott. (TV-BBC) *Nationwide.* Ivor Novello Award winner 1975–1976.

Goodbye   1881   w. G.T. Whyte-Melville   m. Francesco Paolo Tosti

Goodbye   1936   m. Gordon Jenkins. Closing theme of the Benny Goodman Orchestra.

Goodbye, Au Revoir, Auf Wiedersehn   1936   w. Irving Caesar   m. Eric Coates, based on his ''Knightsbridge March.'' (MT) *White Horse Inn.* William Gaxton and Kitty Carlisle appeared in *White Horse Inn.*

Goodbye, Boys   1913   w. Andrew B. Sterling, William Dillon   m. Harry Von Tilzer

Good-Bye Broadway, Hello France   1917   w. C. Francis

Reisner, Benny Davis   m. Billy Baskette. (MT) *The Passing Show of 1917.*

Goodbye Cruel World   1961   w.m. Gloria Shayne

Goodbye Dolly Gray   1900   w.m. Will D. Cobb, Paul Barnes. (MF) *Wait Till the Sun Shines Nellie.* David Wayne appeared in *Wait Till the Sun Shines Nellie.*

Good-bye, Eliza Jane   1903   w. Andrew B. Sterling   m. Harry Von Tilzer

Good-bye, Flo   1904   w.m. George M. Cohan. (MT) *Little Johnny Jones.*

Goodbye, Girls, I'm Through   1914   w. John Golden   m. Ivan Caryll. (MT) *Chin-Chin.*

Good-bye, Good Luck, God Bless You   1916   w. J. Keirn Brennan   m. Ernest R. Ball

Goodbye Hawaii   1935   w.m. Harry Leon, Vic Robbins, Leo Towers, Dave Appollon

Goodbye Jimmy Goodbye   1959   w.m. Jack Vaughn

Goodbye, Little Girl, Goodbye   1904   w. Will D. Cobb   m. Gus Edwards

Goodbye, Little Girl of My Dreams   1913   w. Richard Howard   m. A. Fred Phillips

Goodbye, Liza Jane   1871   w.m. traditional minstrel song; arr. Eddie Fox

Good-Bye, Ma! Good-Bye, Pa! Good-Bye, Mule, or, **Long Boy**   1917   w. William Herschell   m. Barclay Walker

Goodbye Marie   1981   w.m. Dennis Linde, Mel McDaniel

Goodbye, My Lady Love   1904   w.m. Joseph E. Howard. Based on Myddleton's ''Down South'' of 1900.

Good-Bye, My Lover, Good-Bye   1882   w.m. traditional, from England; erroneously credited to T.H. Allen

G'Bye Now   1941   w.m. Jay Levison, Ray Evans, Chic Johnson, Ole Olsen. (MF) *Hellzapoppin'.* Olsen and Johnson and Martha Raye appeared in *Hellzapoppin'.*

Goodbye Ol' Paint, or, **I Ride an Old Paint,** or, **I'm a-Leavin' Cheyenne**   c. 1870–90   w.m. traditional

Goodbye, Rose   1910   w. Addison Burkhart   m. Herbert Ingraham

Goodbye Sally   1940   w.m. Arthur Risco, J. Borelli

Goodbye Stranger   1979   w.m. Richard Davies, Roger Hodgson

Goodbye Sue   1943   w.m. Jimmy Rule, Lou Ricca, Jules Loman.

Goodbye to All That   1930   w.m. Harry S. Pepper

Goodbye to All That   1946   w. Ira Gershwin   m. Arthur Schwartz. (MT) *Park Avenue.*

Goodbye to Rome, *see* **Arrivederci Roma**

Goodbye Virginia   1916   w.m. Grant Clarke, Jean Schwartz

Goodbye Yellow Brick Road   1973   w.m. Elton John, Bernie Taupin

Goodness Gracious Me   1960   w.m. David Lee, Herbert Kretzmer. Ivor Novello Award winner 1960.

Goodness Knows How I Love You   1929   w. Billy Hays, Ray Bretz   m. Ted Weitz

Goodnight (I'm Only a Strolling Vagabond)   1928   w.m.

Edward Kunneke, Adrian Ross. (MT) *The Cousin from Nowhere*. This song was originally published in 1923 in Germany. Theme song of Cavan O'Connor.

Goodnight and God Bless You 1941 w.m. Morton Fraser

Goodnight Children, Everywhere 1940 w.m. Gabby Rogers, Harry Phillips

Goodnight Irene 1936 w.m. Huddie Ledbetter, John Lomax. This song was popularly revived in 1950.

Goodnight, Little Girl, Goodnight 1898 w. Julia M. Hays m. J.C. Macy

Goodnight My Love 1934 w. Mack Gordon m. Harry Revel. (MF) *Stowaway*. (MF) *We're Not Dressing*. Shirley Temple, Robert Young, and Alice Faye appeared in *Stowaway*.

Goodnight My Someone 1957 w.m. Meredith Wilson. (MT) *The Music Man*. (MF) *The Music Man*. Robert Preston appeared in both the stage and film productions of *The Music Man*.

Goodnight to You All 1937 w.m. John G. Watson, Muriel Watson

Goodnight Tonight 1979 w.m. Paul McCartney

Goodnight Vienna 1932 w.m. Eric Maschwitz, George Posford. (MF) *Goodnight Vienna*. Jack Buchanan appeared in *Goodnight Vienna*.

Goodnight Wherever You Are 1944 w.m. Dick Robertson, Al Hoffman, Frank Weldon

Goodtime Charley 1975 w. Hal Hackady m. Larry Grossman. (MT) *Goodtime Charley*. Joel Grey and Susan Browning appeared in *Goodtime Charley*.

Goodwin, *see* '**Tis Dawn, the Lark Is Singing**

Goody Goody 1936 w.m. Johnny Mercer, Matt Malneck. (MF) *The Benny Goodman Story*.

Goofus 1930 w. Gus Kahn m. Wayne King, William Harold

Gordon for Me, A 1950 w.m. Robert Wilson

Gospel Train, De, *see* **De Gospel Train**

Gossip Calypso 1963 w.m. Trevor Peacock

Got a Bran' New Suit 1935 w. Howard Dietz m. Arthur Schwartz. (MT) *At Home Abroad*. Beatrice Lillie appeared in *At Home Abroad*.

Got a Date with an Angel 1931 w. Clifford Grey, Sonnie Miller m. Jack Waller, Joseph Tunbridge. (MT) *For the Love of Mike*. Bobby Howes appeared in *For the Love of Mike*.

Got a Hold on Me 1984 w.m. Christine McVie, Todd Sharp

Got Her Off My Hands (But Can't Get Her Off My Mind) 1951 w.m. Sam Lewis, Joseph Young, Fred Phillips

Got the Bench, Got the Park, But I Haven't Got You 1931 w.m. Al Lewis, Al Sherman, Fred Phillips

Got the Jitters 1934 w. Billy Rose, Paul Francis Webster m. John Jacob Loeb

Got To Be Real 1979 w.m. David Paich, David Foster, Cheryl Lynn

Got To Get You into My Life 1966 w.m. John Lennon, Paul McCartney. (MT) *Beatlemania*. (This song was popularly revived in 1978.

Got'n Idea 1955 w.m. Jack Woodman, Paddy Roberts. Ivor Novello Award winner 1955.

Gotta Be This or That 1945 w.m. Sunny Skylar

Graceland 1986 w.m. Paul Simon. Grammy Award winner 1986.

Graduation Day 1956 w. Noel Sherman m. Joe Sherman

Grafted into the Army 1862 w.m. Henry Clay Work

Granada 1932 Sp.w. Augustin Lara Eng.w. Dorothy Dodd m. Augustin Lara. (MF) *The Gay Ranchero*. (MF) *Because You're Mine*. (MF) *I'll Be Yours*. Roy Rogers and Andy Devine appeared in *The Gay Ranchero*. Mario Lanza appeared in *Because You're Mine*. Deanna Durbin, Tom Drake, and Adolphe Menjou appeared in *I'll Be Yours*. This song was popularly revivied in 1953.

Grand Canyon Suite, *see* **On the Trail**

Grand Old Flag, *see* **You're a Grand Old Flag**

Grand Old Ivy 1961 w.m. Frank Loesser. (MT) *How To Succeed in Business Without Really Trying*. (MF) *How To Succeed in Business Without Really Trying*. Robert Morse appeared in both the stage and film productions of *How To Succeed*.

Grandad 1971 w.m. Ken Pickett, Herbie Flowers. Ivor Novello Award winner 1970–71.

Grande Valse Brilliante 1834 m. Frédéric Chopin

Grandfather's Clock 1876 w.m. Henry Clay Work. This song was first performed by Sam Lucas of the Hyer Sisters Colored Minstrels in New Haven, Connecticut. Henry Clay Work was an abolitionist, inventor of toys, and skilled typesetter. A self-taught musician, Mr. Work wrote many Prohibitionist and Unionist songs during his lifetime.

Grandpa (Tell Me 'Bout the Good Old Days) 1986 w.m. Jamie O'Hara. Grammy Award winner 1986.

Grandpa's Spells 1925 w.m. Ferdinand Joseph Morton

Granny's Old Arm-Chair 1932 w.m. John Read

Grass Is Always Greener, The 1981 w. Fred Ebb m. John Kander. (MT) *Woman of the Year*. Lauren Bacall appeared in *Woman of the Year*.

Grasshopper's Dance, The 1907 w.m. Bucalossi

Grave of Bonaparte, The 1843 w. Henry S. Washburne m. Lyman Health. A member of the Massachusetts Senate, Washburne graduated from Brown University in 1840.

Grazin' in the Grass 1968 w.m. Philemon Hou, Harry Elston

Grease 1978 w.m. Barry Gibb. Ivor Novello Award winner 1978–79.

Great Balls of Fire 1957 w.m. Jack Hammer, Otis Blackwell. (MF) *Jamboree*. Jerry Lee Lewis and Kay Medford appeared in *Jamboree*.

Great Day 1929 w. Billy Rose, Edward Eliscu m. Vincent Youmans. (MT) *Great Day!*. Mayo Method and Allan Pryor appeared in *Great Day!*.

Great Imposter, The 1961 m. Henry Mancini. (F) *The Great Imposter*. Tony Curtis appeared in *The Great Imposter*.

Great Indoors, The 1930 w.m. Cole Porter. (MT) *The New Yorkers.*

Great Pretender, The 1955 w.m. Buck Ram. (MF) *Rock Around the Clock.* Bill Haley appeared in *Rock Around the Clock.*

(Theme from) Greatest American Hero (Believe It or Not) 1981 w.m. Stephen Geyer, Mike Post. (F) *Greatest American Hero.*

Greatest Love of All 1986 w.m. Linda Creed, Michael Masser

Greatest Mistake of My Life, The 1937 w.m. James Netson

Green Cockatoo, The 1946 w.m. Don Rellegro

Green Door, The 1956 w. Marvin Moore m. Bob Davie

Green Eyes (Aquellos Ojos Verdes) 1929 Sp.w. Adolfo Utrera Eng. w. L. Wolfe Gilbert m. Nilo Menendez. (MF) *The Fabulous Dorseys.* This song was popularly revived in 1941.

Green Green Grass of Home, The 1967 w.m. Curly Putman

Green Grow the Lilacs 1846 w.m. anon. This song was popularly revived in 1956. Dating back to the release of Mexican soldiers from U.S. jails after the war of 1846–47, this song was originally sung as "Gringo the Lilacs," introducing the term to American vernacular.

Green Leaves of Summer, The 1960 w. Paul Francis Webster m. Dimitri Tiomkin. (F) *The Alamo.* John Wayne and Richard Widmark appeared in *The Alamo.*

Green Mountain Farmer, The 1798 w. (Robert) Thomas Paine m. William Shield. This song was one of the most popular patriotic songs of its day.

Green Onions 1962 w.m. Steve Cropper, Al Jackson, Jr., Lewis Steinberg, Booker T. Jones

Green Sleeves, *see* **Greensleeves**

Green-Up Time 1948 w. Alan Jay Lerner m. Kurt Weill. (MT) *Love Life.* Nanette Fabray and Ray Middleton appeared in *Love Life.*

Green Years 1954 w.m. Don Reid, Arthur Altman

Greenfields 1960 w.m. Terry Gilkyson, Richard Dehr, Frank Miller

Greensleeves (Green Sleeves) 1580 w.m. anon.; traditional, from England. Earliest words published 1580, earliest music published 1652, although possibly performed at least one hundred years earlier. King Henry VIII, a known song writer, is often credited as the true author. This song is mentioned twice in Shakespeare's *Merry Wives of Windsor,* Act II, Sc.2, c.1596. During Elizabethan times, this was originally a vigorous dance tune, and in 1596, one diary reports a young girl "was footing it aloft on the green, with foot out, and foot in."

Grizabella the Glamour Cat 1982 w. T.S. Eliot m. Andrew Lloyd Webber. (MT) *Cats.* Betty Buckley appeared in *Cats.*

Grizzly Bear 1910 w.m. George Botsford, Irving Berlin

Grocer Jack 1968 w.m. Keith West, Mark Wirtz. Ivor Novello Award winner 1967–68.

Groovin' 1967 w.m. Eddie Brigati, Felix Cavaliere. This song was popularly revived in 1970.

Groovy Kind of Love, A 1966 w.m. Toni Wine, Carole Bayer

G.T.O. 1964 w.m. John Wilkin

Guantanamera 1966 w.m. Pete Seeger, Hector Angulo

Guilty 1931 w.m. Gus Kahn, Harry Akst, Richard A. Whiting. This song was popularly revived in 1947.

Guilty 1981 w.m. Barry Gibb, Maurice Gibb, Robin Gibb

Guitar Man 1981 w.m. Jerry Reid

Gulf Coast Blues 1923 w.m. Clarence Williams

Gum Tree Canoe, The (On Tom-Big-Bee River) 1885 w. S.S. Steele m. A.F. Winnemore

Guns of Navarone, The 1961 w.m. Paul Francis Webster, Dimitri Tiomkin. (F) *The Guns of Navarone.*

Gurney Slade Theme, The 1960 w.m. Max Harris. (TV-BBC) *The Strange World of Gurney Slade.* Ivor Novello Award winner 1960.

Guy Is a Guy, A 1952 w.m. Oscar Brand, based on the English broadside ballad "I Went to the Alehouse (A Knave Is a Knave)" of 1719.

Guys and Dolls 1950 w.m. Frank Loesser. (MT) *Guys and Dolls.* (MF) *Guys and Dolls.* Robert Alda and Vivian Blaine appeared in the stage production of *Guys and Dolls.* Frank Sinatra and Stubby Kaye appeared in the film production of Guys and Dolls.

Gwine To Run All Night, *see* **De Camptown Races**

Gypsy 1982 w.m. Stevie Nicks

Gypsy, The 1946 w.m. Billy Reid

Gypsy Dream Rose 1929 w. James Kendis, Frank Samuels m. Meyer Gusman

Gypsy in Me, The 1934 w.m. Cole Porter. (MT) *Anything Goes.* (MT) *Anything Goes* (1936). (MF) *Anything Goes* (1956). Ethel Merman, Victor Moore, and William Gaxton appeared in the stage production of *Anything Goes.* Bing Crosby and Ethel Merman appeared in the 1936 film production of *Anything Goes.* Bing Crosby and Mitzi Gaynor appeared in the 1956 film production of *Anything Goes.*

Gypsy in My Soul 1937 w. Moe Jaffe, Clay Boland m. Clay Boland

Gypsy Love Song, or, **Slumber On** 1898 w. Harry B. Smith m. Victor Herbert. Based on Chopin's Piano Concerto in E minor. See also "Play, Fiddle, Play." (MT) *The Fortune Teller.* (MF) *Love Happy.*

Gypsy Maiden 1912 w.m. Adrian Ross, Franz Lehár. (MT) *Gypsy Love.*

Gypsy Man 1973 w.m. Sylvester Allen, Harold Ray Brown, Morris D. Dickerson, Leroy L. Jordan, Lee Oskar Levitin, Charles Miller, Howard E. Scott

Gypsy Melody 1930 w.m. Horatio Nicholls

Gypsy Sabre Dance, *see* **Sabre Dance**

Gypsys, Tramps and Thieves 1971 w.m. Robert Stone

Ha-Cha-Cha 1934 w. Otto Harbach m. Jerome Kern. (MT) *The Cat and the Fiddle.* (MF) *The Cat and the Fiddle.*

Jeanette MacDonald, Charles Butterworth, and Frank Morgan appeared in the film production of *The Cat and the Fiddle*. Written in 1931, this song was most popular in 1934.

Haydn's Ox Minuet 1853 m. anon.; erroneously credited to Franz Joseph Haydn

Hail Columbia, or, **New Federal Song** 1978 w. Joseph Hopkinson m. Philip Phile. The words were written for actor Gilbert Fox to sing in the finale of Broaden's comedy *The Italian Monk*. The music is based on Philip Phile's "The President's March" of 1789.

Hail, Hail, the Gang's All Here 1917 w. D.A. Esrom (Morse) (1917); Theodora Morse (1904) m. Theodore Morse (husband of Theodora). Based on the tenor part "Come, friends, who plow the sea" and the chorus part "With catlike tread" from Act II, *The Pirates of Penzance,* by Gilbert and Sullivan. This melody, in turn, was itself a parody of Verdi's "Anvil Chorus."

Hail Purdue 1913 w. J. Morrison m. E.J. Wotawa. School song of Purdue University.

Hail to the Chief 1812 w. Sir Walter Scott m. possibly James Sanderson. The words are extracted from Scott's 1810 narrative poem "The Lady of the Lake." This march is traditionally played to announce the arrival of the President of the United States; when this custom began still remains a mystery, although we know the march was performed at the inauguration of President Polk on March 4, 1845.

Hair 1969 w. Gerome Ragni, James Rado m. Galt MacDermot. (MT) *Hair*. (MT) *Hair*.

Hair of Gold, Eyes of Blue 1948 w.m. Sunny Skylar. (MF) *Riders of the Whistling Pines*. Gene Autry and Patricia White appeared in *Riders of the Whistling Pines*.

Half Sixpence 1963 w.m. David Heneker. (MT) *Half a Sixpence*.

Half as Much 1952 w.m. Curley Williams

Half-Breed 1973 w.m. Mary Dean, Al Capps

Half-Caste Woman 1931 w.m. Noël Coward. (MT) *Ziegfeld Follies of 1931*.

Half of It, Dearie, Blues, The 1924 w. Ira Gershwin m. George Gershwin. (MT) *Lady, Be Good*.

Half the Way 1979 w.m. Bobby Wood, Ralph Murphy

Half-Way to Heaven 1928 w. Al Dubin m. J. Russell Robinson

Hallelujah! 1927 w. Clifford Grey, Leo Robin m. Vincent Youmans. (MT) *Hit the Deck*. (MF) *Hit the Deck* (1929). (MF) *Hit the Deck* (1955). Jack Oakie and Polly Walker appeared in the 1929 film production of *Hit the Deck*. Tony Martin and Vic Damone appeared in the 1955 film production of *Hit the Deck*. This was the first published song of Vincent Youmans.

Hallelujah Chorus 1767 w. compiled and adapted Charles Jennens m. George Frederic Handel from "Messiah." This work was first performed in Dublin on April 13, 1742, and first published in 1767.

Hallelujah, I'm a Bum 1928 w.m. Harry Kirby McClintock, based on the traditional hymn "Revive Us Again." (MF) *Hallelujah, I'm a Bum*.

Halls of Montezuma, The, *see* **The Marine's Hymn**

Hambone 1952 w.m. Leon Washington, Red Saunders

Hammacher Schlemmer, I Love You 1948 w. Howard Dietz m. Arthur Schwartz. This song was the first success for this collaboration team.

Hand for the Hog 1985 w.m. Roger Miller. (MT) *Big River*.

(O) Hand Me Down My Walking Cane 1865 w.m. traditional black American spiritual

Hand That Rocks the Cradle, The 1895 w. Charles W. Berkeley m. William H. Holmes

Handful of Earth from (My Dear) Mother's Grave, A 1883 w.m. Joseph Murphy. (MT) *Kerry Gow*. Joseph Murphy appeared in *Kerry Gow*.

Handful of Songs, A 1957 w.m. Lionel Bart, Michael Pratt, Tommy Steele. (MF) *The Tommy Steele Story*. Ivor Novello Award winner 1957.

Handicap March, The 1895 w. Dave Reed, Jr. m. George Rosey (George M. Rosenberg). (MF) *Big Boy*. Al Jolson and Claudia Dell appeared in *Big Boy*. The words were first added in 1923.

Hands Across the Sea (March) 1899 m. John Philip Sousa

Hands Across the Table 1934 w. Mitchell Parish m. Jean Delettre (MT) *Continental Varieties*. Lucienne Boyer appeared in *Continental Varieties*.

Handsome Territorial, A 1939 w.m. Jimmy Kennedy, Michael Carr

Handy Man 1960 w.m. Otis Blackwell, Jimmy Jones, Charles Merenstein. This song was popularly revived in 1977.

Hang On Sloopy 1965 w.m. Bert Russell, Wes Farrell

Hang On the Bell Nellie 1949 w.m. Clive Erard, Ross Parker, Tommie Connor

Hang Your Heart on a Hickory Limb 1939 w. Johnny Burke m. James V. Monaco. (MF) *East Side of Heaven*. Bing Crosby and Joan Blondell appeared in *East Side of Heaven*.

Hangin' on the Garden Gate 1930 w. Gus Kahn m. Ted Fiorito

Hangin' Out the Window 1983 w.m. Roger Lax. (OB) *Weekend*.

Hanging Tree 1959 w.m. Mack David, Jerry Livingston

Hanky Panky 1966 w.m. Jeff Barry, Ellie Greenwich

Hannah! 1903 w. Joseph C. Farrell m. Henry Frantzen

Hannah, Won't You Open That Door? 1904 w. Andrew B. Sterling m. Harry Von Tilzer

Happening, The 1967 w.m. Eddie Holland, Brian Holland, Lamont Dozier

Happiness 1963 w.m. Bill Anderson

Happiness Is 1965 w.m. Paul Parnes, paul Evans

Happiness Is (Just) a Thing Called Joe 1942 w. E.Y. Harburg m. Harold Arlen. (MF) *Cabin in the Sky*. (F) *I'll Cry Tomorrow*. This song did not appear in the original 1940 stage production of *Cabin in the Sky*. Ethel Waters and Lena Horne appeared in the film production of *Cabin in the Sky*. Susan Hayward appeared in *I'll Cry Tomorrow*.

Happiness Street (Corner Sunshine Square) 1955 w.m. Mack Wolfson, Edward R. White

Happy, or, **Love Theme from** *Lady Sings the Blues* 1972 w. Smokey Robinson m. Michel Legrand. (MF) *Lady Sings the Blues.* Diana Ross appeared in *Lady Sings the Blues,* biopic of singer Billie Holiday.

Happy Anniversary 1959 w.m. Robert Allen, Al Stillman. (F) *Happy Anniversary.* David Niven, Mitzi Gaynor, and Patty Duke appeared in *Happy Anniversary.*

Happy as the Day Is Long 1933 w.m. Ted Koehler, Harold Arlen

Happy Birds 1887 w. C.T. Steele m. Edward Holst

Happy Birthday to You, or, **Good Morning to All** 1893 w. Patty Smith Hill m. Mildred J. Hill. (MT) *As Thousands Cheer.* A lawsuit resulted in the unauthorized use of Ms. Hill's standard in *As Thousands Cheer,* for which her estate still receives active royalties. Born in Louisville, Kentucky, in 1854, Ms. Hill was a prodigy concert pianist who became an organist, choir leader, and teacher.

Happy Christmas, Little Friend 1952 w. Oscar Hammerstein II m. Richard Rodgers. This song was first published in *Life* Magazine.

(Oh) Happy Day 1855 w.m. traditional. See also "How Dry I Am."

Happy Days 1976 w.m. Norman Gimbel, Charles Fox. (TV) *Happy Days.* Henry Winkler appeared in *Happy Days.*

Happy Days Are Here Again 1929 w. Jack Yellen m. Milton Ager. (MF) *Chasing Rainbows.* (MF) *Rain or Shine.* (R) *Your Hit Parade.* Bessie Love, Charles Ring, and Marie Dressler appeared in *Chasing Rainbows.* Joe Cook and Tom Howard appeared in *Rain or Shine.* This song was popularly revived in 1963. Ironically, this became the theme of Franklin D. Roosevelt's New Deal effort in 1933.

Happy Days in Dixie 1896 m. Kerry Mills

Happy Ending 1933 w.m. Harry Parr-Davies. (MF) *This Week of Grace.* Gracie Fields appeared in *This Week of Grace.*

Happy Farmer, The, op.68, No. 10 1849 m. Robert Schumann. This melody is also known as "The Merry Peasant."

Happy Feet 1930 w. Jack Yellen m. Milton Ager. (MF) *King of Jazz.* Bing Crosby and Paul Whiteman appeared in *King of Jazz.*

Happy Go Lucky Lane 1928 w. Sam M. Lewis, Joe Young m. Joseph Meyer

Happy Go Lucky Me 1960 w.m. Paul Evans, Al Byron

Happy-Go-Lucky You and Broken-Hearted Me 1932 w.m. Jack Murray, Al Goodhart, Al Hoffman

Happy, Happy Birthday, Baby 1956 w.m. Margo Sylvia, Gilbert Lopez. This song was popularly revived in 1986.

Happy Holiday 1942 w.m. Irving Berlin. (MF) *Holiday Inn.* Fred Astaire and Bing Crosby appeared in *Holiday Inn.*

Happy in Love 1941 w. Jack Yellen m. Sammy Fain. (MT) *Sons o' Fun.* Carmen Miranda and Ella Logan appeared in *Sons o' Fun.*

Happy Organ, The 1959 w.m. Ken Wood (Walter R. Moody), David Clowney

Happy Talk 1949 w. Oscar Hammerstein II m. Richard Rodgers. (MT) *South Pacific.* (MF) *South Pacific.* Mary Martin and Bill Tabbert appeared in the stage production of *South Pacific.* Mitzi Gaynor and Ray Walston appeared in the film production of *South Pacific.*

Happy Time, The 1967 w. Fred Ebb m. John Kander. (MT) *The Happy Time.* Robert Goulet appeared in *The Happy Time.*

Happy To Keep His Dinner Warm 1961 w.m. Frank Loesser. (MT) *How To Succeed in Business Without Really Trying.* (MF) *How To Succeed in Business Without Really Trying.* Robert Morse appeared in both the stage and film productions of *How To Succeed.*

Happy Together 1967 w.m. Alan Lee Gordon, Garry Bonner

Happy Wanderer, The 1954 Eng. w. Antonia Ridge m. Friedrich Möller

Happy Whistler, The 1956 w.m. Don Robertson

Harbor Lights 1937 w. Jimmy Kennedy m. Hugh Williams (Will Grosz). This song was popularly revived in 1950 and again in 1960.

Harbor of Love, The 1911 w. Earl C. Jones m. Charlotte Blake

Hard Day's Night, A 1964 w.m. John Lennon, Paul McCartney. (MF) *A Hard Day's Night.* (MF) *Help!* The Beatles appeared in both *A Hard Day's Night and Help!* Ivor Novello Award winner 1964.

Hard Habit To Break 1984 w.m. John Parker, Stephen Kipner

Hard-Headed Woman 1958 w.m. Claude de Metruis. (F) *King Creole.* Elvis Presley and Carolyn Jones appeared in *King Creole.*

Hard Hearted Hannah (The Vamp of Savannah) 1924 w.m. Jack Yellen, Milton Ager, Bob Bigelow, Charles Bates. (MF) *Pete Kelly's Blues.* Ella Fitzgerald and Peggy Lee appeared in *Pete Kelly's Blues.*

(It's) Hard-Knock Life, The 1977 w. Martin Charnin m. Charles Strouse. (MT) *Annie.* Dorothy Loudon and Andrea McArdle appeared in *Annie.*

Hard Rain's A-Gonna Fall, A 1963 w.m. Bob Dylan

Hard Times Come Again No More 1854 w.m. Stephen Collins Foster

Hard to Get 1955 w.m. Jack Segal. This song was introduced by Giselle Mackenzie on the dramatic television program *Justice.*

Hard To Say I'm Sorry 1982 w.m. Peter Cetera, David Foster

Harden My Heart 1984 w.m. Marvin Webster Ross

Harding, You're the Man for Us 1920 w.m. Al Jolson. This song was written for the Presidential campaign of Warren G. Harding in 1920.

Hark the Herald Angels Sing 1855 w. Charles Wesley m. Felix Mendelssohn; based on his "Festgesang" for two male choirs and brass instruments. This work was written to celebrate the 400th anniversary of Gutenberg's invention of the printing press.

Harlem Moon 1931 w. Mann Holiner m. Alberta Nichols. (MT) *Rhapsody in Black.*

Harlem Nocturne 1943 w. Dick Rogers m. Earle H. Hagen

Harlem Shuffle 1986 w.m. Bob Relf, Earl Nelson

Harp That Once Thro' Tara's Halls, The 1750 w. Thomas Moore m. traditional Irish melody, entitled "Gramachree."

Harper Valley P.T.A. 1968 w.m. Tom T. Hall

Harriet 1945 w.m. Abel Baer, Paul Cunningham. (MF) *My Pal Trigger*. Roy Rogers, Dale Evans, and Gabby Hayes appeared in *My Pal Trigger*.

Harrigan 1907 w.m. George M. Cohan. (MT) *Fifty Miles from Boston*. (MT) *George M!* (MF) *Yankee Doodle Dandy*. George M. Cohan appeared in *Fifty Miles from Boston*. Joel Grey and Bernadette Peters appeared in *George M!* James Cagney and Joan Leslie appeared in *Yankee Doodle Dandy*. See also Part 1, 1919.

Harry 1976 w.m. Catherine Howe. Ivor Novello Award winner 1975–76.

Harry Lime Theme, The, *see* **The Third Man Theme**

(Theme from) Harry's Game 1983 m. Paul Brennan. Ivor Novello Award winner 1982–83.

Harvest of Love 1963 w.m. Benny Hill, Tony Hatch. Ivor Novello Award winner 1963.

Has Anybody Here Seen Kelly 1909 w.m. C.W. Murphy, Will Letters, John Charles Moore, William C. McKenna. (MT) *The Jolly Bachelors*. Nora Bayes and Jack Norworth appeared in *The Jolly Bachelors*.

Has Anybody Seen My Gal (Girl), *see* **Five Foot Two, Eyes of Blue**

Has Anybody Seen Our Ship 1936 w.m. Noël Coward. (MT) *Tonight at 8:30* (Red Peppers) Noël Coward and Gertrude Lawrence appeared in the British production of *Tonight at 8:30*.

Hat Me Father Wore, The 1876 w.m. Ferguson, Daniel McCarthy

(Theme from) Hatari 1961 m. Henry Mancini. (F) *Hatari*.

Hatikva 1895 w. Naphtali Herz Imber m. anon. The words to this song were written in 1886, and in 1897. "Hatikva" was adopted as the Zionist anthem of Israel. See also "Moldau."

Hats Off to Me 1891 w. Edward Harrigan m. David Braham

Haunted Ball Room 1953 w.m. Harold Spina

Haunted Heart 1948 w. Howard Dietz m. Arthur Schwartz. (MT) *Inside U.S.A.*

Haunting Me 1934 w. Eddie De Lange m. Joe Myrow

Hava Nagila 1963 w.m. Traditional Jewish song. During the black protest movement, this song was popularly adapted in 1963, with new words by Betty Comden and Adolph Green, musically adapted by Jule Styne and introduced by Lena Horne.

Have a Drink on Me 1936 w.m. Donegan, Buchanan

Have a Heart 1916 w. P.G. Wodehouse m. Jerome Kern. (MT) *Have a Heart*.

Have a Little Faith in Me 1930 w.m. Harry Warren, Sam Lewis, Joe Young. (MF) *Spring Is Here*. Alexander Gray and Bernice Claire appeared in *Spring Is Here*.

Have a Smile (For Everyone You Meet) 1918 w.m. J. Keirn Brennan, Paul Cunningham, Bert L. Rule

Have I Stayed Too Long at the Fair, *see* **Too Long at the Fair**

Have I the Right 1964 w.m. Howard Blaikley

Have I Told You Lately That I Love You 1946 w.m. Scott Wiseman. This song was popularly revived in 1950.

Have It Your Way 1974 w.m. Dennis Berger. This song was written for a Burger King commercial promotion campaign. Based on Michael Schwartz's 1968 "Man's World" jingle written for a non-profit advertising campaign for the Big Brothers of America. Mr. Schwartz filed suit for $9500.

Have You Ever Been in Love 1983 w.m. John Danter, Andy Hill, Pete Sinfield. Ivor Novello Award winner 1982–83.

Have You Ever Been Lonely (Have You Ever Been Blue) 1932 w.m. George Brown, Peter DeRose. (F) *Oklahoma Annie*. Judy Canova and John Russell appeared in *Oklahoma Annie*.

Have You Forgotten So Soon 1938 w. Edward Heyman, Sam Coslow m. Abner Silver

Have You Got Any Castles, Baby 1937 w. Johnny Mercer m. Richard A. Whiting. (MF) *Varsity Show*. Dick Powell and Ted Healy appeared in *Varsity Show*.

Have You Heard 1953 w. Lew Douglas m. Frank Lavere, Leroy W. Rodde

Have You Met Miss Jones 1937 w. Lorenz Hart m. Richard Rodgers. (MT) *I'd Rather Be Right*. (MT) *All Clear*. (MF) *Gentlemen Marry Brunettes*. George M. Cohan and Joy Hodges appeared in *I'd Rather Be Right*. Jane Russell and Rudy Vallee appeared in *Gentlemen Marry Brunettes*.

Have You Never Been Mellow 1975 w.m. John Farrar

Have Yourself a Merry Little Christmas 1944 w.m. Hugh Martin, Ralph Blane. (MT) *The 1940's Radio Hour*. (MF) *Meet Me in St. Louis*. Judy Garland, Margaret O'Brien, and Mary Astor appeared in *Meet Me in St. Louis*.

(Theme from) Hawaii Five-O 1969 w.m. Mort Stevens. (TV) *Hawaii Five-O*.

Hawaiian Butterfly 1917 w. George A. Little m. Billy Baskette, Joseph H. Santley. (MT) *Bubbly*. Teddie Gerrard appeared in *Bubbly*.

Hawaiian Eye 1959 w.m. Jerry Livingston, Mack David

Hawaiian War Chant 1936 Eng.w. Ralph Freed m. John Noble, Leleiohaku, based on a traditional Hawaiian song. (MF) *It's a Date*. (MF) *Song of the Islands*. Deanna Durbin appeared in *It's a Date*. Victor Mature and Betty Grable appeared in *Song of the Islands*.

Hawaiian Wedding Song, The 1926 Hawaiian w. Charles E. King Eng.w. Al Hoffman, Dick Manning m. Charles E. King. The original Hawaiian song was titled "KaKali Nei Au," and recorded in 1951 by Bing Crosby with the title "Here Ends the Rainbow." This song was popularly adapted in 1958 with new lyrics.

Hazel Dell, The 1853 w.m. Wurzel (George Frederick Root)

He 1955 w. Richard Mullan m. Jack Richards

He Ain't Heavy . . . He's My Brother 1969 w.m. Bob Russell, Bobby Scott

He Brought Home Another 1896 w.m. Paul Dresser

He Don't Love You Like I Love You 1975 w.m. Curtis Mayfield, Calvin Carter

He Fought for a Cause He Thought Was Right 1896 w.m. Paul Dresser

He Goes to Church on Sunday 1907 w. Vincent P. Bryan m. E. Ray Goetz. (MT) *The Orchid.*

He Got You 1982 w.m. Ralph Murphy, Bobby Wood

He Is an Englishman 1878 w. William S. Gilbert m. Arthur Sullivan. From the operetta *H.M.S. Pinafore.*

He May Be Old, But He's Got Young Ideas 1916 w.m. Howard Johnson, Alex Gerber, Harry Jentes

He Needs Me 1955 w.m. Arthur Hamilton. (MF) *Pete Kelly's Blues.* Peggy Lee appeared in *Pete Kelly's Blues.*

He Walked Right In, Turned Around and Walked Right Out Again 1906 w. Edward Rose m. Maxwell Silver

He Walks with Me, *see* **In the Garden**

He Was Beautiful 1980 w.m. Cleo Laine. Ivor Novello Award winner 1979–80.

He Wears a Pair of Silver Wings 1942 w.m. Eric Maschwitz, Michael Carr

He Who His Country's Liv'ry Wears 1803 w. William Dunlap m. Victor Pellesier. (MT) *The Glory of Columbia, Her Yeomanry.*

Head Low 1929 w. Willard Robison m. Frank Skinner

Head Over Heels 1986 w.m. Roland Orzabal, Curt Smith

Head Over Heels in Love 1937 w.m. Harry Revel, Mack Gordon. (MF) *Head Over Heels.* Jessie Matthews appeared in *Head Over Heels.*

Headache Tomorrow, A (Or a Heartache Tonight) 1981 w.m. Chuck Rains

Headed for Heartache 1982 w.m. Kent Blazy, Jim Dowell

Headin' for Louisville 1925 w. B.G. DeSylva m. Joseph Meyer

Hear Dem Bells 1880 w.m. D.S. McCosh

(You've Got to Have) Heart 1955 w.m. Richard Adler, Jerry Ross. (MT) *Damn Yankees.* (MF) *Damn Yankees.* (F) *Only When I Laugh.* Gwen Verdon appeared in both the stage and film productions of *Damn Yankees.* Marsha Mason and James Coco appeared in *Only When I Laugh.* This song was popularly revived in 1981.

Heart and Soul 1938 w. Frank Loesser m. Hoagy Carmichael. (MF) *A Song Is Born.* Danny Kaye and Virginia Mayo appeared in *A Song Is Born.*

Heart and Soul 1984 w.m. Mike Chapman, Nicky Chinn

Heart Attack 1982 w.m. Paul Bliss, Stephen Kipner

Heart Bow'd Down, The 1843 w. Alfred Bunn m. Michael William Balfe. From the opera *The Bohemian Girl.*

Heart Full of Soul 1965 w.m. Graham Gouldman

Heart of a Fool, The 1954 w. Hal David m. Frank Weldon

Heart of a Man, The 1959 w.m. Peggy Cochrane, Paddy Roberts. (MF) *The Heart of a Man.* Frankie Vaughan and Anne Heywood appeared in *The Heart of a Man.*

Heart of a Rose 1918 w.m. Horatio Nicholls, Worton David

Heart of a Teenage Girl 1960 w.m. Bill Crompton, Morgan Jones

Heart of Glass 1979 w.m. Deborah Harry, Christopher Stein

Heart of Gold 1972 w.m. Neil Young

Heart of Mine 1980 w.m. Mike Foster

Heart of My Heart, *see* **The Gang That Sang Heart of My Heart**

Heart of My Heart (I Love You), or, **The Story of the Rose** 1899 w. "Alice" m. Andrew Mack

Heart of Oak 1759 w. David Garrick m. William Boyce. This song appeared in the pantomime production *Harlequin's Invasion* in London, in 1759. It later served as inspiration for "The Liberty Song" in 1768.

Heart of Rock and Roll 1984 w.m. John Colla, Huey Lewis

Heart of the Night 1979 w.m. Norman Paul Cotton

Heart of the Night 1983 w.m. John Bettis, Michael Clark

Heart on My Sleeve 1977 w.m. Benny Gallagher, Graham Lyle. Ivor Novello Award winner 1976–77.

Heart to Heart 1983 w.m. David Foster, Kenny Loggins, Michael McDonald

Heartaches 1931 w. John Klenner m. Al Hoffman. This song was popularly revived in 1947.

Heartaches By the Number 1959 w.m. Harlan Howard

Heartbeat—It's a Lovebeat 1973 w.m. William G. Hudspeth, Michael Kennedy

Heartbreak Express 1982 w.m. Dolly Parton

Heartbreak Hotel 1956 w.m. Mae Boren Axton, Tommy Durden, Elvis Presley

Heartbreaker 1978 w.m. Carole Bayer Sager, David Wolfert

Heartbreaker 1982 w.m. Barry Gibb, Maurice Gibb, Robin Gibb. Ivor Novello Award winner 1982–83.

Heartlight 1982 w.m. Burt Bacharach, Neil Diamond, Carole Bayer Sager

Hearts 1981 w.m. Jesse Barish

Hearts and Flowers 1899 w. Mary D. Brine m. Theodore Moses Tobani, based on Alphonse Czibulka's "Wintermärchen (Winter Story)" of 1891. See also Part 1, 1914.

Hearts of Stone 1955 w.m. Rudy Jackson, Edward Ray

Heat Is On, The 1985 w.m. Harold Faltermeyer, Keith Forsey

Heat of the Moment 1982 w.m. John Wetton, Geoffrey Downes

Heat Wave 1933 w.m. Irving Berlin. (MT) *As Thousands Cheer.* (MF) *Alexander's Ragtime Band.* (MF) *Thousands Cheer.* (MF) *Blue Skies.* (MF) *There's No Business Like Show Business.* Ethel Waters and Marilyn Miller appeared in *As Thousands Cheer.* Tyrone Power appeared in *Alexander's Ragtime Band.* Kathryn Grayson and Gene Kelly appeared in *As Thousands Cheer.* Bing Crosby and Fred Astaire appeared in *Blue Skies.* Ethel Merman and Marilyn Monroe appeared in *There's No Business Like Show Business.*

(Love Is Like a) Heat Wave 1963 w.m. Eddie Holland,

Brian Holland, Lamont Dozier. This song was popularly revived in 1975.

Heather on the Hill, The 1947 w. Alan Jay Lerner m. Frederick Loewe. (MT) *Brigadoon.* (MF) *Brigadoon.* David Brooks and Marion Bell appeared in the stage production of *Brigadoon.* Gene Kelly and Cyd Charisse appeared in the film production of *Brigadoon.*

Heaven 1985 w.m. Bryan Adams, Jim Vallance

Heaven Can Wait 1939 w.m. Edgar De Lange, Jimmy Van Heusen

Heav'n, Heav'n, *see* **I Got Shoes**

Heaven Help Us All 1970 w.m. Ronald Miller

Heaven Knows 1979 w.m. Peter Bellotte, Giorgio Moroder, Donna Summer, Gregg Mathieson

Heaven Must Be Missing an Angel 1976 w.m. Kenny St. Lewis, Frederick Perren

Heaven Must Have Sent You 1979 w.m. Lamont Dozier, Brian Holland, Eddie Holland

Heaven on Earth 1926 w. Ira Gershwin, Howard Dietz m. George Gershwin. (MT) *Oh, Kay!*

Heaven on the Seventh Floor 1977 w.m. Dominique Bugatti, Frank Musker. Ivor Novello Award winner 1977–78.

Heaven Will Protect the Working Girl 1909 w. Edgar Smith m. A. Baldwin Sloane. (MT) *Tillie's Nightmare.* This song was popularly performed by Marie Dressler.

He'd Have To Get Under, Get Out and Get Under, To Fix Up His Automobile, *see* **Get Out and Get Under**

Heebie Jeebies 1926 w.m. Boyd Atkins

Heed the Call 1970 w.m. Kin Vassy

Heidelberg Stein Song 1902 w. Frank Pixley m. Gustav Luders. (MT) *The Prince of Pilsen.*

Heigh-Ho 1937 w. Larry Morey m. Frank Churchill. (MF) *Snow White and the Seven Dwarfs.*

Heigh-Ho Everybody, Heigh-Ho 1929 w.m. Harry Woods. (MF) *The Vagabond Lover.* Rudy Vallee and Sally Blane appeared in *The Vagabond Lover.*

Helen Wheels 1973 w.m. Paul McCartney, Linda McCartney

He'll Have To Go 1960 w.m. Joe Allison, Audrey Allison

Hello 1984 w.m. Lionel Richie

Hello, Aloha! How Are You? 1926 w. L. Wolfe Gilbert m. Abel Baer

Hello, Bluebird 1926 w.m. Cliff Friend

Hello, Central, Give Me Heaven 1901 w.m. Charles K. Harris

Hello, Central, Give Me No Man's Land 1918 w. Sam M. Lewis, Joe Young m. Jean Schwartz. (MT) *Sinbad.* Al Jolson appeared in *Sinbad.*

Hello Dolly 1964 w.m. Jerry Herman. (MT) *Hello, Dolly!* (MT) *Jerry's Girls.* (MF) *Hello, Dolly!* Carol Channing appeared in the stage production of *Hello, Dolly!* Dorothy Loudon, Chita Rivera and Leslie Uggams appeared in *Jerry's Girls.* Barbra Streisand appeared in the film production of *Hello, Dolly!* Grammy Award winner 1964. Based on Mack David's "Sunflower" of 1948. More than half a million dol-

lars was awarded to Mr. David for this note-for-note copyright infringement, though Mr. Herman was to retain legal authorship of the song.

Hello Frisco Hello 1915 w. Gene Buck m. Louis A. Hirsch. (MT) *Ziegfeld Follies of 1915.* (MF) *Wharf Angel.* Dorothy Dell and Preston Foster appeared in *Wharf Angel.*

Hello Goodbye 1968 w.m. John Lennon, Paul McCartney. Ivor Novello Award winner 1967–68.

Hello, Hawaii, How Are You 1915 w. Bert Kalmar, Edgar Leslie m. Jean Schwartz

Hello, Hello There 1956 w. Betty Comden, Adolph Green m. Jule Styne. (MT) *Bells Are Ringing.* (MF) *Bells Are Ringing.* Judy Holliday appeared in both the stage and film productions of *Bells Are Ringing.*

Hello, Hello, Who's Your Lady Friend 1914 w.m. Worton David, Bert Lee, Harry Fragson. (MF) *The Story of Vernon and Irene Castle.* Ginger Rogers and Fred Astaire appeared in *The Story of Vernon and Irene Castle.*

Hello, I Love You (Won't You Tell Me Your Name) 1968 w.m. John Densmore, Robert Krieger, Raymond Manzarek, James Morrison

Hello It's Me 1973 w.m. Todd Rundgren

Hello Little Girl 1963 w.m. John Lennon, Paul McCartney

Hello! Ma Baby 1889 w.m. Ida Emerson, Joseph E. Howard

Hello Mudduh, Hello Faddah 1963 w.m. Alan Sherman. This parody is based on Ponchielli's "Dance of the Hours," from Act III of *La Gioconda,* written in 1876.

Hello, My Lover, Goodbye 1931 w. Edward Heyman m. John Green. (MT) *Here Goes the Bride.*

Hello Swanee, Hello 1926 w.m. Sam Coslow, Addy Britt

Hello Twelve, Hello Thirteen, Hello Love, 1975 w. Edward Kleban m. Marvin Hamlisch. (MT) *A Chorus Line.* Donna McKechnie appeared in *A Chorus Line.*

Hello Young Lovers 1951 w. Oscar Hammerstein II m. Richard Rodgers. (MT) *The King and I.* (MF) *The King and I.* Yul Brynner and Gertrude Lawrence appeared in the stage production of *The King and I.* Yul Brynner and Deborah Kerr appeared in the film production of *The King and I.*

Help! 1965 w.m. John Lennon, Paul McCartney. (MT) *Beatlemania.* (MF) *Help!.* The Beatles appeared in *Help!* Ivor Novello Award winner 1965.

Help Me Make It Through the Night 1971 w.m. Kris Kristofferson, Fred Foster. Grammy Award winner 1971. This song was popularly revived in 1980.

Help Me Rhonda 1965 w.m. Brian Wilson. This song was popularly revived in 1975.

Help Yourself 1968 w.m. C. Donida, Jack Fishman, Mongol

Helter Skelter 1968 w.m. John Lennon, Paul McCartney. (MT) *Beatlemania.*

Her Bright Smile Haunts Me Still 1868 w. J.E. Carpenter m. W.T. Wrighton

Her Eyes Don't Shine Like Diamonds 1894 w.m. Dave Marion

Her Golden Hair Was Hanging Down Her Back, *see* **And Her Golden Hair Was Hanging Down Her Back**

Her Name Is Mary 1933 w.m. Bruce Sievier, Harold Ramsey

Her Town Too 1981 w.m. James Taylor, Robert Wachtel

Here 1954 w.m. Dorcas Cochran, Harold Grant. Based on Verdi's soprano aria "Caro Nome," from the opera *Rigoletto*.

Here Am I 1929 w. Oscar Hammerstein II m. Jerome Kern. (MT) *Sweet Adeline*. (MF) *Sweet Adeline*. Irene Dunne and Donald Woods appeared in the film production of *Sweet Adeline*.

Here Am I—Broken Hearted 1927 w. B.G. DeSylva, Lew Brown m. Ray Henderson. (MT) *Artists and Models* (1927). (MF) *The Best Things in Life Are Free*. Ernest Borgnine, Gordon MacRae, and Dan Dailey appeared in *The Best Things in Life Are Free*, biopic of song writers DeSylva, Brown, and Henderson. This song was popularly revived in 1951.

Here Come the British (Bang! Bang!) 1934 w. John Mercer m. Bernard Hanighan

Here Come the Waves 1944 w.m. Johnny Mercer, Harold Arlen. (MF) *Here Come the Waves*. Bing Crosby and Betty Hutton appeared in *Here Come the Waves*.

(Lookie, Lookie, Lookie) Here Comes Cookie 1935 w.m. Mack Gordon, Harry Revel. (MF) *Love in Bloom*. George Burns and Gracie Allen appeared in *Love in Bloom*.

Here Comes Heaven Again 1945 w. Harold Adamson m. Jimmy McHugh. (MF) *Doll Face*. (MF) *Come Back to Me*. Vivian Blaine and Perry Como appeared in *Doll Face*.

Here Comes My Daddy Now—Oh Pop—Oh Pop—Oh Pop 1912 w. L. Wolfe Gilbert m. Lewis F. Muir.

Here Comes Peter Cottontail, *see* **Peter Cottontail**

Here Comes Santa Claus 1947 w.m. Gene Autry, Oakley Haldeman

Here Comes Summer 1959 w.m. Jerry Keller

Here Comes the Rain Again 1984 w.m. Annie Lennox, Dave Stewart

Here Comes the Showboat 1927 w. Billy Rose m. Maceo Pinkard. (MT) *Africana*. (MF) *Show Boat*. Alma Rubens, Otis Harlan, and Laura LaPlante appeared in *Show Boat*.

Here Comes the Sun 1971 w.m. George Harrison

Here I Am (Come and Take Me) 1973 w.m. Al Green, Mabon Hodges

Here I Am (Just When I Thought I Was Over You) 1981 w.m. Norman Sallit

Here I Go Again 1964 w.m. Mort Shuman, Clive Westlake

Here I'll Stay 1948 w. Alan Jay Lerner m. Kurt Weill. (MT) *Love Life*. Nanette Fabray and Ray Middleton appeared in *Love Life*.

Here in My Arms 1925 w. Lorenz Hart m. Richard Rodgers. (MT) *Dearest Enemy*. (MT) *Lido Lady*. (MF) *Tea for Two*. Helen Hart and Charles Purcell appeared in *Dearest Enemy*. Phyllis Dave and Jack Hulbert appeared in *Lido Lady*. Doris Day, Gordon MacRae, and Eve Arden appeared in *Tea for Two*, based on *No, No, Nanette*.

Here in My Heart 1952 w.m. Pat Genaro, Lou Levinson, Bill Borrelli

Here It Comes Again 1965 w.m. Barry Mason, Les Reed

Here Lies Love 1933 w.m. Leo Robin, Ralph Rainger. (MF) *The Big Broadcast*. Bing Crosby and Kate Smith appeared in *The Big Broadcast*.

Here, There and Everywhere 1966 w.m. John Lennon, Paul McCartney

Here We Are 1929 w. Gus Kahn m. Harry Warren

Here We Are, Here We Are, Here We Are Again 1914 w.m. Charles Knight, Kenneth Lyle

Here We Go Round the Mulberry Bush, *see* **The Mulberry Bush**

Here You Come Again 1977 w.m. Barry Mann, Cynthia Weil. (MT) *Dancin'*

Here's That Rainy Day 1953 w. Johnny Burke m. Jimmy Van Heusen (MT) *Carnival in Flanders*.

Here's to Love 1912 w.m. Paul Rubens, Arthur Wimperis. (MT) *The Sunshine Girl*.

Here's to Romance 1935 w. Herb Magidson m. Con Conrad. (F) *Here's to Romance*. Nino Martini and Genevieve Tobin appeared in *Here's to Romance*.

Here's to the Next Time 1932 w.m. Henry Hall

Here's to Us 1962 w. Carolyn Leigh m. Cy Coleman. (MT) *Little Me*. Sid Caesar appeared in *Little Me*.

Hernando's Hideaway 1954 w.m. Richard Adler, Jerry Ross. (MT) *The Pajama Game*. (MF) *The Pajama Game*. Doris Day and John Raitt appeared in the film production of *The Pajama Game*.

He's a Cousin of Mine 1906 w. Cecil Mack m. Chris Smith, Silvio Hein. (MT) *Marrying Mary*.

He's a Devil in His Own Home Town 1914 w. Grant Clarke, Irving Berlin m. Irving Berlin

He's a Gypsy from Poughkeepsie 1937 w.m. Bud Green, Emery Deutsch

He's a Humdinger 1934 w.m. Maurice Sigler, Al Goodhart, Al Hoffman

He's a Rag Picker 1914 w.m. Irving Berlin. (MT) *5064 Gerard*. Jack Morrison and Jack Norworth appeared in *5064 Gerard*.

He's a Real Gone Guy 1947 w.m. Nellie Lutcher

He's a Rebel 1962 w.m. Gene Pitney

He's a Right Guy 1942 w.m. Cole Porter. (MT) *Something for the Boys*. (MF) *Something for the Boys*. Ethel Merman, Paula Laurence and Betty Bruce appeared in the stage production of *Something for the Boys*. Carmen Miranda, Phil Silvers and Perry Como appeared in the film production of *Something for the Boys*.

He's a Tramp 1952 w.m. Peggy Lee, Sonny Burke. (MF) *Lady and the Tramp*.

He's Dead But He Won't Lie Down 1932 w.m. Will E. Haines, Maurice Beresford, James Harper

He's Funny That Way, *see* **She's Funny That Way**

He's Got the Whole World in His Hand (Hands) 1927

w.m. Based on a traditional black American spiritual. This song was popularly revived in 1958.

He's Me Pal   1905   w. Vincent P. Bryan   m. Gus Edwards

He's My Guy   1942   w.m. Don Raye, Gene De Paul. (F) *Who Done It?* (MF) *Follow the Band.* (MF) *Hi' Ya Chum.* Bud Abbott and Lou Costello appeared in *Who Done It?* Leon Errol and Skinny Ennis appeared in *Follow the Band.* The Ritz Brothers and Jane Frazee appeared in *Hi' Ya Chum.*

He's 1-A in the Army (and A-1 in My Heart)   1941   w.m. Redd Evans

He's Our Al   1928   w.m. Albert Von Tilzer, A. Seymour Brown. This song was written for the 1928 Presidential campaign of Al Smith.

He's So Fine   1963   w.m. Ronald Mack. See also "My Sweet Lord."

He's So Shy   1980   w.m. Tom Snow, Cynthia Weil

He's the Wizard   1975   w.m. Charlie Smalls. (MT) *The Wiz.* (MF) *The Wiz.* Stephanie Mills, Mabel King, and Tiger Haynes appeared in the stage production of *The Wiz.* Diana Ross appeared in the film production of *The Wiz.*

Hev Yew Gotta Loight, Boy?   1966   w.m. Allan Smethurst. Ivor Novello Award winner 1966.

Hey-Ba-Ba-Re-Bop   1945   w.m. Lionel Hampton, Curley Hamner, Gladys Hampton

Hey, Babe, Hey (I'm Nuts About You)   1936   w.m. Cole Porter. (MF) *Born To Dance.* Eleanor Powell appeared in *Born To Dance.*

Hey Baby   1962   w.m. Margaret Cobb, Bruce Channel. This song was popularly revived in 1982.

Hey Big Spender, *see* **Big Spender**

Hey, Diddle, Diddle, *see* **Mother Goose's Melodies**

Hey Good Lookin'   1951   w.m. Hank Williams

Hey Gypsy (Play Gypsy) (Komm Tzizany)   1926   w.m. Emmerich Kalman, Clifford Grey, "N. Foley." (MT) *Countess Maritza.* John Garrick appeared in the British production of *Countess Maritza.*

Hey Jealous Lover   1956   w.m. Sammy Cahn, Kay Twomey, Bee Walker

Hey Jude   1968   w.m. John Lennon, Paul McCartney. (MT) *Beatlemania.* Ivor Novello Award winner 1968–69.

Hey Little Hen   1941   w.m. Ralph Butler, Noel Gay

Hey Look Me Over   1960   w. Carolyn Leigh   m. Cy Coleman. (MT) *Wildcat.*

Hey Mister Banjo   1955   w.m. Freddy Morgan, Norman Malkin

Hey Paula   1963   w.m. Ray Hildebrand

Hey, Rube!   1891   w. J. Sherrie Matthews   m. Harry Bulger

Hey There   1954   w.m. Richard Adler, Jerry Ross. (MT) *The Pajama Game.* (MF) *The Pajama Game.* Doris Day and John Raitt appeared in the film production of *The Pajama Game.*

Hey There, Good Times   1977   w. Michael Stewart   m. Cy Coleman. (MT) *I Love My Wife.*

Hey Won't You Play Another Somebody Done Somebody Wrong Song, *see* **Another Somebody Done Somebody Wrong Song**

Hey Young Fella Close Your Old Umbrella   1933   w. Dorothy Fields   m. Jimmy McHugh. (MT) *Radio City Music Hall's First New York Production.*

Hi-Diddle-Dee-Dee (An Actor's Life for Me)   1940   w.m. Ned Washington, Leigh Harline. (MF) *Pinocchio.*

Hi-Diddle-Diddle   1926   w.m. Carleton A. Coon, Hal Keidel

Hi Ho the Merry-O (A-Hunting We Will Go), *see* **Hunt Theme**

Hi Lili Hi Lo   1952   w. Helen Deutsch   m. Bronislaw Kaper. (F) *Lili.* Leslie Caron appeared in *Lili.*

Hi Neighbor   1941   w.m. Jack Owens. (MF) *San Antonio Rose.* (MF) *Hi Neighbor.* Jane Frazee and Robert Paige appeared in *San Antonio Rose.* John Archer and Jean Parker appeared in *Hi Neighbor.*

Hi Tiddley Hi Ti Island   1937   w.m. Ralph Stanley, Leslie Alleyn

Hiawatha   1901   w. James O'Dea   m. Neil Moret. The words to this song were added in 1903.

Hiawatha's Melody of Love   1920   w. Alfred Bryan, Artie Mehlinger   m. George W. Meyer

Hic, Haec, Hoc   1963   w. Sidney Michaels   m. Mark Sandrich, Jr. (MT) *Ben Franklin in Paris.*

Hickory, Dickory, Dock, *see* **Mother Goose's Melodies**

Hide Thou Me   1880   w. Frances Jane Crosby (Mrs. Alexander Van Alstyne)   m. Reverend Robert Lowry

Hideaway   1966   w.m. Howard Blaikley

Hiding in Thee   1877   w. William O. Cushing   m. Ira David Sankey

High and the Mighty, The   1954   w. Ned Washington   m. Dimitri Tiomkin. (F) *The High and the Mighty.* John Wayne appeared in *The High and The Mighty.*

High Barbaree   1801   w.m. Charles Dibdin. Charles Dibdin was employed as full-time songwriter by the British Navy and was officially "song writer for the Royal Navy." The song narrates how the "Prince of Luther," a British vessel, defeated the Barbary pirates.

High Class Baby   1958   w.m. Ian Samwell

High Heel Sneakers   1964   w.m. Robert Higginbotham

High Hopes   1959   w. Sammy Cahn   m. Jimmy Van Heusen. (F) *Hole in the Head.* Frank Sinatra and Edward G. Robinson appeared in *Hole in the Head.* Academy Award winner 1959.

(Theme from) High Noon (Do Not Forsake Me, Oh My Darling)   1952   w. Ned Washington   m. Dimitri Tiomkin. (F) *High Noon.* Gary Cooper and Grace Kelly appeared in *High Noon.*

High on a Windy Hill   1941   w.m. Alex C. Kramer, Joan Whitney

High on You   1985   w.m. Frankie Sullivan

High School Cadets   1891   m. John Philip Sousa

High Society (March)   1901   w.m. Walter Melrose, Porter Steele. This song was popularly revived in 1936.

High Upon a Hill Top   1928   w.m. Abel Baer, Ivan Campbell, George Whiting

High, Wide and Handsome   1937   w. Oscar Hammerstein

II m. Jerome Kern. (MF) *High, Wide and Handsome*. Irene Dunne, Randolph Scott, and Dorothy Lamour appeared in *High, Wide and Handsome*.

(Your Love Has Lifted Me) Higher and Higher 1977 w.m. Carl Smith, Gary Jackson, Raynard Miner

Higher Ground 1973 w.m. Stevie Wonder

Higher Love 1986 w.m. Will Jennings, Steve Winwood. Grammy Award winner 1986.

Highway Patrol 1956 w.m. Ray Llewellyn

Highwayman 1985 w.m. Jimmy L. Webb. Grammy Award winner 1985.

Hills of Home, The 1925 w. Floride Calhoun m. Oscar J. Fox

Hills of Old Wyomin', The 1936 w.m. Leo Robin, Ralph Rainger, Earl Robinson. (MF) *Palm Springs*. (F) *Song of Old Wyoming*. Frances Langford and Smith Ballew appeared in *Palm Springs*. Eddie Dean and Jennifer Holt appeared in *Song of Old Wyoming*.

Hindustan 1918 w.m. Oliver G. Wallace, Harold Weeks. (MT) *Joy Bells*.

Hinky Dinky Parlay Voo, or, Mad'moiselle from Armentières 1918 w. anon.; possibly Edward Rowland m. anon.; possibly Gitz, Rice. Popular World War I song.

(What Has Become of) Hinky Dinky Parlay Voo 1924 w.m. Al Dubin, Jimmy McHugh, Irving Mills, Irwin Dash. (MF) *The Cockeyed World*. Joe E. Brown and Stuart Erwin appeared in *The Cockeyed World*.

Hippopotamus Song, The, or, Mud, Glorious Mud 1952 w. David Ormont, Henry H. Tobias

His Last Thoughts Were of You 1894 w. Edward B. Marks m. Joseph W. Stern

(And) His Rocking Horse Ran Away 1944 w.m. Jimmy Van Heusen, Johnny Burke. (MF) *And the Angels Sing*. Betty Hutton and Fred MacMurray appeared in *And the Angels Sing*.

Hit and Miss 1960 w.m. John Barry. Ivor Novello Award winner 1960.

Hit the Road Jack 1961 w.m. Percy Mayfield. Grammy Award winner 1961.

Hit the Road to Dreamland 1943 w. Johnny Mercer m. Harold Arlen. (MF) *Star Spangled Rhythm*. (MF) *That Certain Feeling*. Bing Crosby, Mary Martin, Fred MacMurray, and Dick Powell appeared in *Star Spangled Rhythm*. Bob Hope and Eva Marie Saint appeared in *That Certain Feeling*.

Hitchy-Koo 1912 w. L. Wolfe Gilbert m. Lewis F. Muir, Maurice Abrahams. (MT) *Hullo Ragtime*. Lew Hearn and Shirley Kellog appeared in *Hullo Ragtime*.

Hither Dear Husband, see **The Beggar's Opera**

Hitting the Bottle 1930 w. Ted Koehler m. Harold Arlen. (MT) *Earl Carroll's Vanities* of 1930. Jack Benny and Patsy Kelly appeared in *Earl Carroll's Vanities of 1930*.

Ho! Ho! Ha! Ha! Me Too, see **Me Too**

Ho Hum 1931 w.m. Edward Heyman, Dana Suesse. (MF) *Monkey Business*. The Marx Brothers and Thelma Todd appeared in *Monkey Business*.

Hoch, Caroline 1932 w. R.P. Weston, Bert Lee m. Jack

Waller, Joseph Tunbridge. (MT) *Tell Her the Truth*. Lillian Emerson and John Sheehan, Jr. appeared in *Tell Her the Truth*.

Hocus Pocus 1973 w.m. Jan Akkerman, Thys Van Leer

Hold Back the Dawn 1944 w.m. Hedley Grey

Hold 'Em Joe 1954 w.m. Harry Thomas. (MT) *John Murray Anderson's Almanac*. Harry Belafonte appeared in *John Murray Anderson's Almanac*.

Hold Me 1920 w.m. Art Hickman, Ben Black. (MT) *Ziegfeld Follies of 1920*.

Hold Me 1933 w.m. Jack Little, David Oppenheim, Ira Schuster

Hold Me 1982 w.m. Christie McVie, Robin Patton

Hold Me 1985 w.m. Linda Creed

Hold Me, Hold Me, Hold Me 1951 w. Betty Comden, Adolph Green m. Jule Styne. (MT) *Two on the Isle*.

Hold Me Now 1984 w.m. Tom Bailey, Alannah Currie, Joe Leeway

Hold Me, Thrill Me, Kiss Me 1952 w.m. Harry Noble

Hold Me Tight 1968 w.m. Johnny Nash

Hold My Hand 1934 w.m. Jack Yellen, Irving Caesar, Ray Henderson. (MF) *George White's Scandals*. Rudy Vallee, Jimmy Durante, and Alice Faye appeared in *George White's Scandals*.

Hold My Hand 1950 w.m. Jack Lawrence, Richard Meyers. (MF) *Susan Slept Here*. Debbie Reynolds and Dick Powell appeared in *Susan Slept Here*. This song was popularly revived in 1954.

Hold On 1986 w.m. Rosanne Cash

Hold On to My Love 1980 w.m. Robin Gibb, Derek Weaver

Hold Tight—Hold Tight 1939 w.m. L. Ware, L. Kent, J. Brandow, E. Robinson, W. Spotswood

Hold Your Hand Out Naughty Boy 1914 w.m. C.W. Murphy, Worton David

Holding Back the Years 1986 w.m. Mick Hucknall, Neil Moss

Hole in the Ground 1962 w.m. Ted Dicks, Myles Rudge

Holiday for Strings 1944 m. David Rose. (MF) *Ladies' Man*. (F) *The Unfinished Dance*. Eddie Bracken, Cass Daley, and Virginia Weekes appeared in *Ladies' Man*. Margaret O'Brien, Cyd Charisse, and Danny Thomas appeared in *The Unfinished Dance*.

Holly Holy 1970 w.m. Neil Diamond

Hollyhock 1927 w.m. Billy Mayerl

Holy City, The 1892 w. Frederick Edward Weatherly m. Stephen Adams (Michael Maybrick)

Holy Cow 1966 w.m. A. Toussaint

Holy! Holy! Lord God Almighty 1861 w. Reginald Heber m. from the hymn "Nicaea" by John Bacchus Dykes

Home 1931 w.m. Harry Clarkson, Peter Van Steeden, Jeff Clarkson. (MF) *Moonlight and Cactus*. The Andrews Sisters and Leo Carrillo appeared in *Moonlight and Cactus*.

Home 1975 w.m. Charlie Smalls. (MT) *The Wiz*. (MF) *The Wiz*. Stephanie Mills, Ted Ross, and Mabel King appeared in the stage production of *The Wiz.* Diana Ross and Mabel King appeared in the film production of *The Wiz.*

Home Again 1851 w.m. Marshall S. Pike

Home Again 1959 w. Sheldon Harnick   m. Jerry Bock. (MT) *Fiorello!*

Home Again Blues 1920   w.m. Harry Akst, Irving Berlin

Home and Dry 1979   w.m. Gerry Rafferty

Home Cooking 1950   w.m. Ray Evans, Jay Livingston. (MF) *Fancy Pants.* Bob Hope and Lucille Ball appeared in *Fancy Pants.*

(There's No Place Like) Home for the Holidays 1954   w. Al Stillman   m. Robert Allen

Home in Pasadena, *see* **Pasadena**

Home Lovin' Man 1971   w.m. Tony Macaulay, Roger Greenaway. Ivor Novello Award winner 1970–71.

Home on the Range, or, **Oh, Give Me a Home Where the Buffalo Roam** c.1873   w. possibly Brewster Higley   m. possibly Dan Kelly. (F) *The Fighting Coast Guard.* Brian Donlevy and Forrest Tucker appeared in *The Fighting Coast Guard.* The official Kansas state song. The original title to this song was "My Western Home." First popularized by John A. Lomax and David Guion, this song was years later to become the favorite of President Franklin D. Roosevelt.

Home Sweet Heaven 1964   w.m. Hugh Martin, Timothy Gray. (MT) *High Spirits.*

Home Sweet Home 1823   w. John Howard Payne   m. based on "Sicilian Air"; arr. Sir Henry Rowley Bishop. From the English opera *Clari, or, The Maid of Milan.* This song was later to appear in the lesson scene of Rossini's *Barber of Seville.* Sadly, Payne was to be denied authorship and royalty to this song, and had no home or income for most of his last years. This song became a favorite encore number for singer Jenny Lind to perform.

Home Town 1937   w.m. Jimmy Kennedy, Michael Carr. (MT) *London Rhapsody.*

Homecoming Waltz, The 1943   w.m. Bob Musel, Ray Sonin Reginald Connelly

Homesick 1923   w.m. Irving Berlin

Homesick—That's All 1945   w.m. Gordon Jenkins

Homeward Bound 1966   w.m. Paul Simon

Homework 1949   w.m. Irving Berlin. (MT) *Miss Liberty.*

Homing 1917   w. Arthur L. Salmon   m. Teresa del Riego

Homing Waltz, The 1952   w.m. Tommie Connor, Michael Reine

Honest and Truly 1924   w.m. Fred Rose; revised Leo Wood (1946)

Honesty 1979   w.m. Billy Joel

Honey 1928   w.m. Seymour Simons, Haven Gillespie, Richard A. Whiting. (MF) *Her Highness and the Bellboy.*

Honey 1968   w.m. Bobby Russell

Honey—Babe 1954   w. Paul Francis Webster   m. Max Steiner. (F) *Battle Cry.* The words are based on a traditional folksong.

Honey Boy 1907   w. Jack Norworth   m. Albert Von Tilzer

Honey Bun 1949   w. Oscar Hammerstein II   m. Richard Rodgers. (MT) *South Pacific.* (MF) *South Pacific.* Mary Martin appeared in the stage production of *South Pacific.* Mitzi Gaynor appeared in the film production of *South Pacific.*

Honey-Love 1911   w. Jack Drislane   m. George W. Meyer

Honey That I Love So Well 1898   w.m. Harry Freeman

Honeycomb 1954   w.m. Bob Merrill. This song was popularly revived in 1957.

Honeymoon 1908   w. Frank Adams, Will Hough   m. Joseph Howard

Honeymoon, The (March) 1894   m. George Rosey (George M. Rosenberg)

Honeymoon Is Over, The 1967   w. Tom Jones   m. Harvey Schmidt. (MT) *I Do! I Do!*

Honeysuckle and the Bee, The 1901   w.m. Albert Fitz, William Penn. (F) *I'll Be Your Sweetheart.*

Honeysuckle Rose 1929   w. Andy Razaf   m. Thomas "Fats" Waller. (MT) *Load of Coal.* (MT) *Bubbling Brown Sugar.* (MT) *Ain't Misbehavin'.* (MF) *Tin Pan Alley.* (MF) *Thousands Cheer.* Avon Long and Josephine Premice appeared in *Bubbling Brown Sugar.* Nell Carter and Debbie Allen appeared in *Ain't Misbehavin'.* Betty Grable appeared in *Tin Pan Alley.* Kathryn Grayson, Judy Garland, and Gene Kelly appeared in *Thousands Cheer.*

Hong Kong Blues 1939   w.m. Hoagy Carmichael

Honkey Tonk 1956   w. Henry Glover   m. Bill Doggett, Billy Butler, Shep Sheppard, Clifford Scott

Honky Tonk Train Blues 1939   w.m. Meade Lewis

Honky Tonk Women 1969   w.m. Mick Jagger, Keith Richard. Ivor Novello Award winner 1969–70.

Honky Tonkin' 1982   w.m. Hank Williams

Honolulu 1939   w.m. Gus Kahn, Harry Warren. (MF) *Honolulu.*

Hoo-oo Ain't You Coming Out Tonight 1908   w.m. Herbert Ingraham

Hoochy-Koochy, *see* **The Streets of Cairo**

Hooked on a Feeling 1969   w.m. Mark James. This song was popularly revived in 1974.

Hooked on Music 1981   w.m. Mac Davis

Hook's Waltz, *see* **Captain Hook's Waltz**

Hoop-Dee-Doo 1950   w. Frank Loesser   m. Milton De-Lugg

Hooray for Captain Spalding 1928   w. Bert Kalmar   m. Harry Ruby. (MT) *Animal Crackers.* (MF) *Animal Crackers.* (MF) *Three Little Words.* The Marx Brothers appeared in both the stage and film productions of *Animal Crackers.* Fred Astaire and Red Skelton appeared in *Three Little Words,* biopic of song writers Bert Kalmar and Harry Ruby.

Hooray for Hollywood 1938   w.m. Richard Whiting, Johnny Mercer. (MF) *Hollywood Hotel.* Benny Goodman and his band, Gene Krupa, and Dick Powell appeared in *Hollywood Hotel.*

Hooray for Love 1935   w. Dorothy Fields   m. Jimmy McHugh. (MF) *Hooray for Love.* Ann Sothern and "Fats" Waller appeared in *Hooray for Love.*

Hooray for Love 1948 w. Leo Robin m. Harold Arlen. (MF) *Casban.* Tony Martin, Yvonne DeCarlo, and Peter Lorre appeared in *Casbah*

Hootchy Kootchy Dance, *see* **The Streets of Cairo**

Hoots Mon 1959 w.m. Harry Robinson

Hop Scotch Polka 1949 w.m. William Whitlock, Carl Sigman, Gene Rayburn

Hope Told a Flattering Tale 1793 w. Peter Pindar (John Wolcott) m. Giovanni Paisiello. This song from Paisiello's opera *La Molinara* was adapted by Beethoven, who composed a set of variations on the melody.

Hopelessly Devoted to You 1978 w.m. John Farrar. (MF) *Grease.* John Travolta and Olivia Newton-John appeared in *Grease.*

Hora Staccato 1930 m. Grigoras Dinicu; arr. Jascha Heifetz. This song was popularly revived in 1948. Written for violin and piano, this work was composed in 1906, but first published in 1930 when it was transcribed by Jascha Heifetz.

Horace and No Relations 1872 w.m. W.O. Fiske. This song, written for New York editor Horace Greeley's Presidential campaign against incumbent President Grant, was a commentary on the misdeeds of Grant's first administration. Its lyric:

> Next their eyes so very wistful,
> Cast around to get a fist full
> Of the needful cash to fill their empty purses;
> And they fell on cheap relations,
> Who soon filled the public stations—
> Carpet-baggers, uncles, aunts and e'en their nurses.

Hors D'Oeuvres 1915 w.m. David Comer. (MT) *5064 Gerard.* Jack Norworth and Murray's Ragtime Trio appeared in *5064 Gerard.*

Horse, The 1968 w.m. Jesse James

Horse with No Name, A 1972 w.m. Lee Bunnell

Horses 1926 w.m. Byron Gay, Richard A. Whiting. Based on Tchaikovsky's "Troika."

Horsey, Horsey 1938 w.m. Elton Box, Desmond Cox, Paddy Roberts, Ralph Butler

Horsey, Keep Your Tail Up 1923 w.m. Walter Hirsch, Bert Kaplan

Hosanna 1891 Fr.w. Julien Didée Eng.w. Nathan Haskel Dole m. Jules Granier

Hostess with the Mostes' on the Ball 1950 w.m. Irving Berlin. (MT) *Call Me Madam.* (MF) *Call Me Madam.* Ethel Merman appeared in both the stage and film productions of *Call Me Madam.*

Hot Canary, The 1949 w. Ray Gilbert m. Paul Nero. Based on F. Poliakin's "Le Canari."

Hot Child in the City 1978 w.m. James McCulloch, Nick Gilder

Hot Cross Buns, *see* **Mother Goose's Melodies**

Hot Diggity (Dog Ziggity Boom) 1956 w.m. Al Hoffman, Dick Manning. Based on Chabrier's "España (Spanish Rhapsody)" of 1884.

Hot Fun in the Summertime 1969 w.m. Sly Steward

Hot Heels 1928 w. Billy Rose, Ballard MacDonald m. Lee David. (MT) *Padlocks of 1927.*

Hot Line 1976 w.m. Kenny St. Lewis, Frederic Perren

Hot Lips 1922 w.m. Henry Busse, Henry Lange, Lou Davis. (MT) *The Rat Race.* Tony Curtis and Debbie Reynolds appeared in *The Rat Race.*

Hot Love 1972 w.m. Marc Bolan. Ivor Novello Award winner 1971–72.

Hod Rod Hearts 1980 w.m. Stephen Geyer, Bill La Bounty

Hot Stuff 1979 w.m. Peter Bellotte, Harold Faltermeier, Keith Forsey

(There'll Be) A Hot Time in the Old Town, (Tonight) 1896 w. Joseph Hayden m. Theodore M. Metz. (MT) *Me and Bessie.* Linda Hopkins appeared in *Me and Bessie.* Written for minstrels McIntyre & Heath, this song was played as Theodore Roosevelt's Rough Riders charged up San Juan Hill.

Hound Dog 1956 w.m. Jerry Leiber, Mike Stoller

Hour Never Passes, An 1944 w.m. Jimmy Kennedy

Hour of Parting, The 1931 w. Gus Kahn m. Mischa Spoliansky

House By the Side of the Road, The 1927 w. Sam Walter Foss m. Mrs. M.H. Gulesian

House I Live In, The 1942 w. Lewis Allan m. Earl Robinson

House Is a Home, A 1951 w. Hal David m. Leon Carr

House Is Haunted, The 1934 w.m. Basil G. Adlam, Billy Rose. (MT) *The Ziegfeld Follies of 1934.*

House Is Not a Home, A 1964 w. Hal David m. Burt F. Bacharach

House of Bamboo, The 1958 w.m. Norman Murrells, Bill Crompton

House of Blue Lights, The 1947 w.m. Freddie Slack, Don Raye

House of Flowers 1954 w. Truman Capote, Harold Arlen m. Harold Arlen. (MT) *House of Flowers.*

House of the Rising Sun, The 1964 w.m. Alan Price. This song was popularly revived in 1974.

House That Jack Built, The 1967 w.m. Alan Price

House with a Little Red Barn, A 1940 w. Nancy Hamilton m. Morgan Lewis. (MT) *Two for the Show.* Betty Hutton, Keenan Wynn, and Richard Haydn appeared in *Two for the Show.*

Houseboat, *see* **Love Song from** *Houseboat*

Houston 1965 w.m. Lee Hazlewood

How About Me 1928 w.m. Irving Berlin

How About That 1960 w.m. Les Vandyke

(I Like New York in June) How About You 1941 w. Ralph Freed m. Burton Lane. (MF) *Babes on Broadway.* (MF) *Kiss Them for Me.* Judy Garland and Mickey Rooney appeared in *Babes on Broadway.* Cary Grant and Suzy Parker appeared in *Kiss Them for Me.*

How Am I To Know 1929 w.m. Dorothy Parker, Jack King. (F) *Dynamite.* (F) *Pandora and the Flying Dutchman.* Charles Bickford and Conrad Nagel appeared in *Dynamite.* James

Mason and Ava Gardner appeared in *Pandora and the Flying Dutchman.*

How Are Things in Glocca Morra 1947 w. E.Y. Harburg m. Burton Lane. (MT) *Finian's Rainbow.* (MF) *Finian's Rainbow.* Albert Sharpe and David Wayne appeared in the stage production of *Finian's Rainbow.* Fred Astaire and Petula Clark appeared in the film production of *Finian's Rainbow.*

How Blest We Are 1985 w.m. Roger Miller. (MT) *Big River.*

How Blue the Night 1944 w. Harold Adamson m. Jimmy McHugh. (MF) *Four Jills and a Jeep.*

How 'Bout Us 1981 w.m. Dana Walden

How Can I Be Sure 1968 w.m. Felix Cavaliere, Edward J. Brigati, Jr.

How Can I Leave Thee 1851 w.m. anon., from the German "Ach Wie 1st's Möglich."

How Can You Buy Killarney 1949 w.m. Hamilton Kennedy, Ted Steels, Freddie Grant, Gerard Morrison

How Can You Forget 1938 w. Lorenz Hart m. Richard Rodgers. (F) *Fools for Scandal.* (F) *The World of Susie Wong.* Carole Lombard and Ralph Bellamy appeared in *Fools for Scandal.* William Holden and Nancy Kwan appeared in *The World of Susie Wong.*

How Can You Mend a Broken Heart 1971 w.m. Barry Gibb, Robin Gibb

How Can You Say We're Through, *see* **Through**

How Can You Tell 1918 w. Ned Wayburn m. Harold Orlob. (MT) *Demi-Tasse Revue.*

How Come You Do Me Like You Do 1924 w.m. Gene Austin, Roy Bergere. (MF) *That's the Spirit.* (MF) *Three for the Show.* Jack Oakie and Peggy Ryan appeared in *That's the Spirit.* Betty Grable and Jack Lemmon appeared in *Three for the Show.*

How Could I Be So Wrong 1968 w.m. Walter Marks. (MT) *Golden Rainbow.*

How Could We Be Wrong 1933 w.m. Cole Porter

How Could You Believe Me When I Said I Love You When You Know I've Been a Liar All My Life 1951 w. Alan Jay Lerner m. Burton Lane. (MF) *Royal Wedding.* (MF) *Wedding Bells.* Fred Astaire and Jane Powell appeared in *Royal Wedding.*

How Deep Is the Ocean 1932 w.m. Irving Berlin. (MF) *Blue Skies.* (MF) *Meet Danny Wilson.* Bing Crosby and Fred Astaire appeared in *Blue Skies.* Frank Sinatra and Shelley Winters appeared in *Meet Danny Wilson.*

How Deep Is Your Love 1977 w.m. Barry Gibb, Robin Gibb, Maurice Gibb. (MF) *Saturday Night Fever.* John Travolta appeared in *Saturday Night Fever.* Ivor Novello Award winner 1977–1978.

How Did He Look 1940 w. Gladys Shelley m. Abner Silver

How Do You Do It 1963 w.m. Mitch Murray

How Do You Speak to an Angel 1953 w. Bob Hilliard m. Jule Styne. (MT) *Hazel Flagg.*

How Dry I Am 1921 w. Phillip Dodridge m. Edward F.

Rimbault. This adaptation of 1921 is based originally on the traditional hymn "(Oh) Happy Day" of 1855. An adapted version of "Oh Happy Day" was popular in 1953, and again in 1969.

How Glad I Am 1964 w.m. Jimmy T. Williams, Larry Harrison. Grammy Award winner 1964.

How High the Moon 1940 w. Nancy Hamilton m. Morgan Lewis. (MT) *Two for the Show.* Betty Hutton and Richard Haydn appeared in *Two for the Show.* This song was popularly revived in 1949, and again in 1951. Theme song of Les Paul and Mary Ford.

How I Love You (I'm Tellin' the Birds, I'm Tellin' the Bees) 1926 w. Lew Brown m. Cliff Friend. (MT) *Big Boy.*

How Important Can It Be 1955 w.m. Bennie Benjamin, George Weiss

How It Lies, How It Lies, How It Lies 1949 w. Paul Francis Webster m. Sonny Burke

How Little It Matters, How Little We Know 1956 w. Carolyn Leigh m. Philip Springer

How Little We Know 1944 w. Johnny Mercer m. Hoagy Carmichael. (F) *To Have and Have Not.* (F) *Dark Passage.* Lauren Bacall and Humprey Bogart appeared in *To Have and Have Not.* Humphrey Bogart and Lauren Bacall appeared in *Dark Passage.*

How Long 1975 w.m. Paul Carrack

How Long Has This Been Going On 1928 w. Ira Gershwin m. George Gershwin. (MT) *Rosalie.* (MT) *My One and Only.* (MF) *Funny Face.* Tommy Tune and Twiggy appeared in *My One and Only.* Marilyn Miller and Gladys Glad appeared in *Rosalie.* Fred Astaire and Audrey Hepburn appeared in *Funny Face.*

How Long, How Long Blues 1929 w.m. Ann Engberg Conniff

How Lucky You Are 1947 w.m. Eddie Cassen, Desmond O'Connor

How Many Hearts Have You Broken 1943 w. Marty Symes m. Al Kaufman

How Much I Feel 1978 w.m. David Pack

How Much Is That Doggie in the Window, *see* **Doggie in the Window**

How Soon 1947 w.m. Jack Owens, Carrol Lucas

How Stands the Glass Around, or, **Wolfe's Song,** or, **Why, Soldiers, Why,** or, **The Duke of Berwick's March** 1710–1729 w.m. traditional drinking song, from England. The melody to this song is often erroneously ascribed to Handel. In 1729, this melody was found in the ballad opera *The Patron.* Sung for his officers by General James Wolfe on the eve before Quebec was attacked in 1759.

How Strange 1939 w.m. Gus Kahn, Herbert Stothart. (F) *Idiot's Delight.* Clark Gable, Norma Shearer, and Burgess Meredith appeared in *Idiot's Delight.*

How Sweet It Is (to Be Loved By You) 1975 w.m. Eddie Holland, Brian Holland, Lamont Dozier

How Sweet You Are 1943 w. Frank Loesser m. Arthur Schwartz. (MF) *Thank Your Lucky Stars.* Eddie Cantor and Bette Davis appeared in *Thank Your Lucky Stars.*

How To 1961 w.m. Frank Loesser. (MT) *How To Succeed in Business Without Really Trying.* (MF) *How To Succeed in Business Without Really Trying.* Robert Morse appeared in both the stage and film productions of *How To Succeed.*

How To Handle a Woman 1960 w. Alan Jay Lerner m. Frederick Loewe. (MT) *Camelot.* (MF) *Camelot.* Julie Andrews and Richard Burton appeared in the stage production of *Camelot.* Vanessa Redgrave and Richard Harris appeared in the film production of *Camelot.*

How Was I To Know 1928 w. Lorenz Hart m. Richard Rodgers. (MT) *She's My Baby.* This song did not appear in the New York production of *She's My Baby,* and subsequently was rewritten in 1929 for the stage musical *Heads Up!* with the new title "Why Do You Suppose."

How Will I Know 1986 w.m. George Merrill, Shannon Rubicam, Narada Michael Walden

How Ya Gonna Keep 'Em Down on the Farm (After They've Seen Paree) 1919 w. Sam M. Lewis, Joe Young m. Walter Donaldson. (MF) *For Me and My Gal.* (MF) *The Eddie Cantor Story.* Judy Garland and Gene Kelly appeared in *For Me and My Gal.*

How You Gonna See Me Now 1979 w.m. Alice Cooper, Dick Wagner, Bernie Taupin

How'd You Like To Be My Daddy 1918 w. Sam M. Lewis, Joe Young m. Ted Snyder. (MT) *Sinbad.*

How'd You Like To Spoon with Me 1915 w. Edward Laska m. Jerome Kern. (MT) *The Earl and the Girl.* (MF) *Till the Clouds Roll By.* Judy Garland, Robert Walker, and Van Johnson appeared in *Till the Clouds Roll By,* biopic of composer Jerome Kern.

How'm I Doin' (Hey Hey) 1932 w.m. Lem Fowler, Don Redman

How's Chances 1933 w.m. Irving Berlin. (MT) *As Thousands Cheer.* (MT) *Stop Press.* (MF) *Thousands Cheer.* Marilyn Miller, Ethel Waters, and Clifton Webb appeared in *As Thousands Cheer.* Kathryn Grayson and Gene Kelly appeared in *Thousands Cheer.*

How's Every Little Thing in Dixie 1916 w. Jack Yellen m. Albert Gumble

How's Your Romance 1932 w.m. Cole Porter. (MT) *Gay Divorce.* (MF) *The Gay Divorcee.* Fred Astaire and Grace Moore appeared in the stage production of *Gay Divorce.* Ginger Rogers and Fred Astaire appeared in the film production of *The Gay Divorcee.*

Hubba-Hubba-Hubba, A, *see* **Dig You Later**

Huckle-Buck 1949 w. Roy Alfred m. Andy Gibson

Huckleberry Duck 1939 w.m. Jack Lawrence, Raymond Scott

Huckleberry Finn 1917 w.m. Cliff Hess, Sam M. Lewis, Joe Young

Huggin' and Chalkin' 1946 w.m. Kermit Goell, Clarence Leonard Hayes

Hugs and Kisses 1926 w. Raymond Klages m. Louis Alter. (MT) *Earl Carroll's Vanities of 1926.*

Huguette Waltz, *see* **Waltz Huguette**

Human Nature 1984 w.m. John Bettis, Steve Porcaro

Humming Bird 1955 w.m. Don Robertson

Humoresque 1894 m. Anton Dvorák

Humpty Dumpty, *see* **Mother Goose's Melodies**

Hundred Million Miracles, A 1958 w. Oscar Hammerstein II m. Richard Rodgers. (MT) *Flower Drum Song.* (MF) *Flower Drum Song.*

Hundred Pounds of Clay, A 1961 w.m. Bob Elgin, Luther Dixon, Kay Rogers

Hundred Years from Now, A 1928 w.m. Sid Silvers, Phil Baker

Hundred Years from Today, A 1933 w. Joseph Young, Ned Washington m. Victor Young. (MT) *Blackbirds of 1933.* (MF) *The Girl from Missouri.* (F) *Straight Is the Way.* Bill Robinson appeared in *Blackbirds of 1933.* Jean Harlow and Lionel Barrymore appeared in *The Girl from Missouri.* Gladys George and Franchot Tone appeared in *Straight Is the Way.*

Hungarian Dance No. 1 1869 m. Johannes Brahms

Hungarian Dance No. 5 1859 m. Béla Kélar; arr. Johannes Brahams, 1869

Hungarian Dances 1869 m. Johannes Brahams; No. 17–21 arr. Anton Dvorák. Twenty-one pieces for piano, four hands.

Hungarian Rhapsody No. 2 1851 m. Franz Liszt

Hungry Heart 1980 w.m. Bruce Springsteen

Hungry Like the Wolf 1983 w.m. Simon LeBon, Nick Rhodes, Andy Taylor, John Taylor, Roger Taylor

Hunt Theme (Tantivy! Tantivy! Tantivy!), or, **A-Hunting We Will Go** c. 1782 w.m. traditional; possibly Procida Bucalossi. This song may be related to "Hi Ho the Merry-O (A-Hunting We Will Go)."

Hunters of Kentucky, The 1826 w. Samuel Woodworth m. based on the traditional English ballad "Miss Bailey's Ghost" of c.1550. This song, written for tenor Arthur Keene's American tour, was to become a campaign song for Andrew Jackson. Its lyric celebrates the exploits of the Kentucky riflemen at the battle of New Orleans, January 8, 1815.

Hurdy Gurdy Man 1968 w.m. Harold Levey

Hurrah! for Grant and Colfax 1868 w.m. George Cooper, R. Goerdler. This song was written for General Ulysses S. Grant and Schuyler Colfax for their 1868 Republican campaign for President and Vice President.

Hurrah! for Hayes and Honest Ways! 1876 w.m. E.W. Foster. This song was written for the Republican Presidential and Vice Presidential candidates Rutherford B. Hayes and William A. Wheeler. Its lyric:

> Come on ye jolly boys in gray,
>   And you my boys in blue;
> We'll clasp the hand all o'er the land,
>   For gallant Hayes and Wheeler true.

This vote in the electoral college was such that the winner was not officially decided until two days before inauguration day, March 4, 1877.

Hurray for Baffin's Bay 1903 w. Vincent Bryan m. Theodore F. Morse. (MT) *The Wizard of Oz.*

Hurry It's Lovely Up Here 1966 w. Alan Jay Lerner m.

Burton Lane. (MT) *On a Clear Day You Can See Forever*. (MF) *On a Clear Day You Can See Forever*. Barbara Streisand appeared in the film production of *On a Clear Day You Can See Forever*.

Hurry on Down (to my House) 1948 w.m. Nellie Lutcher. This song was popularly revived in 1969. Theme song of Nellie Lutcher.

Hurt 1954 w.m. Jimmy Crane, Al Jacobs. This song was popularly revived in 1961.

Hurt So Good 1982 w.m. John Cougar Mellencamp, George Greer

Hurting Each Other 1972 w.m. Gary Geld, Peter Udell

Hurts So Bad 1969 w.m. Teddy Randazzo, Bobby Weinstein, Robert L. Harshman. This song was popularly revived in 1980.

Hurts To Be in Love 1986 w.m. Gino Vannelli

Hush Hush Sweet Charlotte 1964 w.m. Frank De Vol, Mack David. (F) *Hush Hush Sweet Charlotte*. Bette Davis and Olivia de Havilland appeared in *Hush Hush Sweet Charlotte*.

Hush-a-Bye Baby see **Rock-a-Bye Baby**

Hustle, The 1975 w.m. Van McCoy. This song, which was responsible for the revitalization of "touch" dancing, was written practically as a throwaway. Well after the song was produced, McCoy saw his first hustle at the Monastery discotheque in Queens, New York.

Hut Sut Song 1941 w.m. Leo Killion, Ted McMichael, Jack Owens. (MF) *San Antonio Rose*. Lon Chaney, Jr., and Robert Paige appeared in *San Antonio Rose*.

Hymn to Him, A 1956 w. Alan Jay Lerner m. Frederick Loewe. (MT) *My Fair Lady*. (MF) *My Fair Lady*. Rex Harrison and Julie Andrews appeared in the stage production of *My Fair Lady*. Rex Harrison and Audrey Hepburn appeared in the film production of *My Fair Lady*.

I Ain't Down Yet 1960 w.m. Meredith Willson. (MT) *The Unsinkable Molly Brown*. (MF) *The Unsinkable Molly Brown*. Tammy Grimes appeared in the stage production of *The Unsinkable Molly Brown*. Debbie Reynolds appeared in the film production of *The Unsinkable Molly Brown*.

I Ain't Gonna Give Nobody None o' This Jelly Roll 1919 w.m. Clarence Williams, Spencer Williams

I Ain't Gonna Grieve My Lord No More 1865 w.m. traditional black American spiritual

I Ain't Got Nobody 1916 w. Roger Graham m. Spencer Williams, Dave Peyton. (MF) *Paris Honeymoon*. Bing Crosby appeared in *Paris Honeymoon*. Theme song of Bert Williams.

I Ain't Nobody's Darling 1921 w. Elmer Hughes m. Robert A. King

I Almost Lost My Mind 1950 w.m. Ivory Joe Hunter. This song was popularly revived in 1956.

I Am a Poor Wayfaring Stranger, see **Wayfarin' Stranger**

I Am Coming 1881 w. Helen R. Young m. Ira David Sankey

I Am, I Said 1971 w.m. Neil Diamond

I Am in Love 1953 w.m. Cole Porter. (MT) *Can-Can*. (MF) *Can-Can*. Frank Sinatra and Shirley MacLaine appeared in the film production of *Can-Can*.

I Am Just a Little Girl, see **Looking for a Boy**

I Am Loved 1950 w.m. Cole Porter. (MT) *Out of This World*. Charlotte Greenwood and William Redfield appeared in *Out of This World*.

I Am the Captain of the Pinafore (What Never) 1878 w. William S. Gilbert m. Arthur Sullivan. (MT) *H.M.S. Pinafore*.

I Am the Monarch of the Sea 1878 w. William S. Gilbert m. Arthur Sullivan. (MT) *H.M.S. Pinafore*.

I Am the Walrus 1968 w.m. John Lennon, Paul McCartney. (MT) *Beatlemania*.

I Am the Yankee Doodle Boy, see **The Yankee Doodle Boy**

I Am What I Am 1983 w.m. Jerry Herman. (MT) *La Cage aux Folles*. Gene Barry and George Hearn appeared in *La Cage aux Folles*.

I Am Woman 1972 w.m. Helen Reddy, Ray Burton

I Apologize 1931 w.m. Al Hoffman, Al Goodhart, Ed Nelson

I Beg of You 1957 w.m. Rose Marie McCoy, Kelly Owens

I Begged Her 1944 w. Sammy Cahn m. Jule Styne. (MF) *Anchors Aweigh*. Frank Sinatra and Gene Kelly appeared in *Anchors Aweigh*.

I Believe 1953 w.m. Ervin Drake, Irvin Graham, Jimmy Shirl, Al Stillman

I Believe in You 1961 w.m. Frank Loesser. (MT) *How To Succeed in Business Without Really Trying*. (MF) *How To Succeed in Business Without Really Trying*. Robert Morse appeared in both the stage and film productions of *How To Succeed*.

I Believe in You 1980 w.m. Roger Cook, Samuel Hogin

I Believe There's Nothing Stronger Than Our Love 1975 w.m. Paul Anka

I Belong to Glasgow 1920 w.m. Will Fyffe

I Bought Myself a Bottle of Ink 1934 w.m. Arthur le Clerq, Stanley Damerell, Tolchard Evans

I Cain't Say No 1943 w. Oscar Hammerstein II m. Richard Rodgers. (MT) *Oklahoma!*. (MF) *Oklahoma!*. Alfred Drake and Celeste Holm appeared in the stage production of *Oklahoma!*. Gordon MacRae and Shirley Jones appeared in the film production of *Oklahoma!*.

I Came Here To Talk for Joe 1942 w.m. Charles Tobias, Lew Brown, Sam H. Stept. This song was popularly revived in 1949.

I Came, I Saw, I Congad 1941 w.m. James Cavanaugh, John Redmond, Frank Weldon

I Can Dance with Everyone But My Wife 1916 w. Joseph Cawthorn, John L. Golden m. John L. Golden. (MT) *Sybil*.

I Can Do That 1975 w. Edward Kleban m. Marvin Hamlisch. (MT) *A Chorus Line*. Donna McKechnie appeared in *A Chorus Line*.

I Can Dream About You 1984 w.m. Dan Hartman

I Can Dream, Can't I 1937 w. Irving Kahal m. Sammy Fain. (MT) *Right This Way.* Joe E. Lewis appeared in *right This Way.* This song was popularly revived in 1950 and again in 1968.

I Can Get It for You Wholesale 1929 w.m. Charles Tobias, Jack Ellis

I Can Give You the Starlight 1939 w.m. Ivor Novello, Christopher Hassell. (MT) *The Dancing Years.* (MF) *The Dancing Years.* Mary Ellis appeared in *The Dancing Years.*

I Can Help 1974 w.m. Billy Swan

I Can See Clearly Now (the Rain Has Gone) 1972 w.m. Johnny Nash

I Can't Be Bothered Now 1937 w. Ira Gershwin m. George Gershwin. (MT) *My One and Only.* (MF) *Damsel in Distress.* Tommy Tune and Twiggy appeared in *My One and Only.* Fred Astaire, Joan Fontaine, George Burns, and Gracie Allen appeared in *Damsel in Distress.*

I Can't Begin To Tell You 1946 w. Mack Gordon m. James V. Monaco. Based on Rida Johnson Young and Melville Ellis's "When Love Is Young in Springtime" of 1906. (MF) *The Dolly Sisters.* (MF) *You're My Everything.* Betty Grable and June Haver appeared in *The Dolly Sisters.* Dan Dailey and Anne Baxter appeared in *You're My Everything.*

I Can't Believe That You're in Love with Me 1926 w. Clarence Gaskill m. Jimmy McHugh. (MT) *On With the Show.* (F) *The Caine Mutiny.* Humphrey Bogart appeared in *The Caine Mutiny.* This song was popularly revived in 1954.

I Can't Do My Belly Bottom Button Up 1916 w.m. J.P. Long

I Can't Do the Sum 1903 w. Glen MacDonough m. Victor Herbert. (MT) *Babes in Toyland.* (MF) *Babes in Toyland.* Laurel and Hardy appeared in the film production of *Babes in Toyland.*

I Can't Escape from You 1936 w.m. Leo Robin, Richard A. Whiting. (MF) *Rhythm On the Range.* Bing Crosby and Martha Raye appeared in *Rhythm On the Range.*

I Can't Get Next to You 1969 w.m. Barrett Strong, Norman Whitfield

I Can't Get No Satisfaction, *see* **Satisfaction**

I Can't Get Started (with You) 1935 w. Ira Gershwin m. Vernon Duke. (MT) *Ziegfeld Follies of 1936–1937.* Fanny Brice and Gypsy Rose Lee appeared in *Ziegfeld Follies of 1936–1937.*

I Can't Get the One I Want (Those I Get I Don't Want) 1924 w. Billy Rose, Herman Ruby m. Lou Handman

I Can't Give You Anything But Love 1928 w. Dorothy Fields m. Jimmy McHugh. (MT) *Blackbirds of 1928.* (MT) *Ain't Misbehavin'.* (MT) *Sugar Babies.* (MF) *I Can't Give You Anything But Love Baby.* (F) *Bringing Up Baby.* (MF) *True to the Army.* (MF) *Stormy Weather.* (MF) *Jam Session.* (F) *Born Yesterday.* (MF) *Both Ends of the Candle.* This song was dropped from the 1927 score *Harry Delmar's Revels.* Adelaide Hall and Bill Robinson appeared in *Blackbirds of 1928.* Debbie Allen and Nell Carter appeared in *Ain't Misbehavin'.* Ann Miller and Mickey Rooney appeared in *Sugar Babies.* Katharine Hepburn and Cary Grant appeared in *Bringing Up Baby.* Jerry Colonna and Ann Miller appeared in *True to the Army.* Lena Horne and Fats Waller appeared

in *Stormy Weather.* Ann Miller and Louis Armstrong appeared in *Jam Session.* Judy Holliday and William Holden appeared in *Born Yesterday.* This song, the last written for the score of *Blackbirds of 1928,* was inspired by writers Fields and McHugh when eavesdropping on a poor couple window shopping in front of Tiffany's. Overhearing the near title of the song, they raced home and completed it within one hour.

I Can't Go for That (No Can Do) 1982 w.m. Sara Allen, Daryl Hall, John Oates

I Can't Help It 1980 w.m. Barry Gibb

I Can't Help Myself 1965 w.m. Eddie Holland, Brian Holland, Lamont Dozier

I Can't Say No, *see* **I Cain't Say No**

I Can't Stand It 1981 w.m. Eric Clapton

I Can't Stop Loving You 1962 w.m. Don Gibson. Grammy Award winner 1962.

I Can't Tell Why I Love You, But I Do 1900 w. Will D. Cobb m. Gus Edwards. (MF) *In Old Sacramento.* (MF) *Somebody Loves Me.* Bill Elliott and Constance Moore appeared in *In Old Sacramento.* Betty Hutton appeared in *Somebody Loves Me.*

I Can't Think Ob Nuthin' Else But You 1896 w.m. Harry Dacre

I Can't Wait 1986 w.m. John Smith

I Close My Eyes and Count to Ten 1969 w.m. Clive Westlake. Ivor Novello Award winner 1968–1969.

I Concentrate on You 1939 w.m. Cole Porter. (MF) *Broadway Melody of 1940.* Fred Astaire and Eleanor Powell appeared in *Broadway Melody of 1940.*

I Could Be Happy with You 1954 w.m. Sandy Wilson. (MT) *The Boy Friend.*

I Could Be So Good for You 1981 w.m. Gerard Kenny, Pat Waterman. Ivor Novello Award winner 1980–81.

I Could Easily Fall 1965 w.m. Hank B. Marvin, Bruce Welch, John Rostill, Brian Bennett

I Could Go On Singing (Till the Cows Come Home) 1963 w. E.Y. Harburg m. Harold Arlen. (MF) *I Could Go On Singing.* Judy Garland appeared in *I Could Go On Singing.*

I Could Have Danced All Night 1956 w. Alan Jay Lerner m. Frederick Loewe. (MT) *My Fair Lady.* (MF) *My Fair Lady.* Julie Andrews appeared in the stage production of *My Fair Lady.* Audrey Hepburn appeared in the film production of *My Fair Lady.*

I Could Have Told You 1954 w.m. Carl Sigman, Arthur Williams

I Could Never Miss You (More Than I Do) 1981 w.m. Neil Harrison

I Could Write a Book 1941 w. Lorenz Hart m. Richard Rodgers. (MT) *Pal Joey.* (MF) *Pal Joey.* Vivienne Segal, Gene Kelly, and Van Johnson appeared in the stage production of *Pal Joey.* Frank Sinatra, Rita Hayworth, and Kim Novak appeared in the film production of *Pal Joey.*

I Couldn't Live without Your Love 1966 w.m. Tony Hatch, Jackie Trent

I Couldn't Sleep a Wink Last Night 1943 w. Harold Adamson m. Jimmy McHugh. (MF) *Higher and Higher.*

(F) *The Blue Veil*. Frank Sinatra, Michele Morgan, and Jack Haley appeared in *Higher and Higher*. Charles Laughton and Joan Blondell appeared in *The Blue Veil*.

I Cover the Waterfront 1933 w. Edward Heyman m. John W. Green. (F) *I Cover the Waterfront*. Claudette Colbert and Ben Lyon appeared in *I Cover the Waterfront*.

I Cried for You (Now It's Your Turn To Cry over Me) 1923 w.m. Arthur Freed, Gus Arnheim, Abe Lyman. (MF) *Babes in Arms*. (MF) *Somebody Loves Me*. (MF) *Lady Sings the Blues*. Mickey Rooney and Judy Garland appeared in *Babes in Arms*. Betty Hutton appeared in *Somebody Loves Me*, biopic of song spinners Blossom Seeley and Benny Fields. Diana Ross appeared in *Lady Sings the Blues*, biopic of singer Billie Holiday.

I Didn't Know About You 1944 w. Bob Russell m. Duke Ellington. Based on Duke Ellington's "Sentimental Lady."

I Didn't Know I Loved You 1973 w.m. Garry Glitter, Mike Lauder

I Didn't Know What Time It Was 1939 w. Lorenz Hart m. Richard Rodgers. (MT) *Too Many Girls*. (MF) *Too Many Girls*. (MF) *Pal Joey*. Van Johnson and Desi Arnaz appeared in the stage production of *Too Many Girls*. Lucille Ball and Ann Miller appeared in the film production of *Too Many Girls*. Frank Sinatra and Kim Novak appeared in *Pal Joey*.

I Didn't Raise My Boy To Be a Soldier 1915 w. Alfred Bryan m. Al Piantadosi. Based on Cohalin's "How Much I Really Cared" of 1914. This song was parodied also in 1915 as "I Didn't Raise My Ford To Be a Jitney," with words and music by Jack Frost. See also Part I, 1916.

I Didn't Slip, I Wasn't Pushed, I Fell 1950 w.m. Eddie Pola, George Wyle

I Dig Rock and Roll Music 1967 w.m. Dave Dixon, James H. Mason, Paul Stookey

I Do Do Do Like You 1947 w.m. Allie Wrubel

I Do, I Do, I Do, I Do, I Do 1976 w.m. Benny Andersson, Stig Anderson, Bjorn Ulvaeus

I Do Like To Be Beside the Seaside 1909 w.m. John A. Glover Kind. (F) *The Adventures of Sherlock Holmes*. Theme song of Reginald Dixon.

I Don't Believe It, But Say It Again, *see* **Say It Again**

I Don't Care 1905 w. Jean Lenox m. Harry O. Sutton. (MF) *In the Good Old Summertime*. Judy Garland, Van Johnson, and Buster Keaton appeared in *In the Good Old Summertime*. Theme song of Eva Tanguay.

I Don't Care 1982 w.m. Webb Pierce, Cindy Walker

I Don't Care If the Sun Don't Shine 1950 w.m. Mack David

I Don't Care Who Knows It 1944 w. Harold Adamson m. Jimmy McHugh. (F) *Nob Hill*. Vivian Blaine appeared in *Nob Hill*.

I Don't Know Enough About You 1946 w.m. Peggy Lee, Dave Barbour

I Don't Know How To Love Him 1971 w. Tim Rice m. Andrew Lloyd Webber. (MT) *Jesus Christ Superstar*. (MF) *Jesus Christ Superstar*. Ben Vereen appeared in the stage production of *Jesus Christ Superstar*. Ivor Novello Award winner 1971–72.

I Don't Know Where I'm Going But I'm on My Way 1917 w.m. George Fairman

I Don't Know Where To Start 1982 w.m. Thom Schuyler

I Don't Know Why (I Just Do) 1931 w. Roy Turk m. Fred E. Ahlert. (F) *Faithful in My Fashion*. Donna Reed and Edward Everett Horton appeared in *Faithful in My Fashion*.

I Don't Know Why You Don't Want Me 1985 w.m. Rosanne Cash

I Don't Like Mondays 1980 w.m. Bob Geldof. Ivor Novello Award winner 1979–80.

I Don't Like To Sleep Alone 1975 w.m. Paul Anka

I Don't Need You 1981 w.m. Rick Christian

I Don't See Me in Your Eyes Anymore 1949 w.m. George Weiss, Bennie Benjamin

I Don't Stand a Ghost of a Chance with You 1932 w. Bing Crosby, Ned Washington m. Victor Young. (MF) *Follies Bergere*. Maurice Chevalier and Merle Oberon appeared in *Follies Bergere*.

I Don't Think I'll End It All Today 1957 w. E.Y. Harburg m. Harold Arlen. (MT) *Jamaica*.

I Don't Think I'm Ready for You 1985 w.m. Milton Brown, Steve Dorff, Snuff Garrett, Burt Reynolds

I Don't Think She's in Love Anymore 1982 w.m. Kent Robbins

I Don't Wanna Dance 1983 w.m. Eddy Grant. Ivor Novello Award winner 1982–83.

I Don't Want Another Sister 1908 w. Leroi Scarlett m. Edna Williams

(If Loving You Is Wrong) I Don't Want To Be Right 1979 w.m. Homer Banks, Carl Hampton, Raymond Jackson

I Don't Want To Get Well (I'm in Love with a Beautiful Nurse) 1917 w. Howard Johnson, Harry Pease m. Harry Jentes. (MF) *Show Business*. Eddie Cantor and Joan Davis appeared in *Show Business*.

I Don't Want To Know 1969 w.m. Jerry Herman. (MT) *Dear World*. (MT) *Jerry's Girls*. Angela Lansbury appeared in *Dear World*. Dorothy Loudon, Chita Rivera, and Leslie Uggams appeared in *Jerry's Girls*.

I Don't Want To Love You (Like I Do) 1944 w.m. Henry Pritchard

I Don't Want To Lose Your Love 1984 w.m. Joey Carbone

I Don't Want To Play in Your Yard 1894 w. Philip Wingate m. H.W. Petrie. See also Part I, 1899.

I Don't Want To Put a Hold on You 1977 w.m. Bernie Flint, Michael Flint. Ivor Novello Award winner 1977–78.

I Don't Want To Set the World on Fire 1941 w.m. Eddie Seiler, Sol Marcus, Bennie Benjamin, Eddie Durham

I Don't Want To Walk Without You, Baby 1941 w. Frank Loesser m. Jule Styne. (MF) *Sweater Girl*. Eddie Bracken and Betty Rhodes appeared in *Sweater Girl*.

I Don't Want Your Kisses 1929 w.m. Martin M. Broones, Fred Fisher. (MF) *So This Is College*. Elliott Nugent and Robert Montgomery appeared in *So This Is College*.

I Double Dare You 1937 w.m. Jimmy Eaton, Terry Shand

I Dream of Jeanie with the Light Brown Hair, *see* **Jeanie with the Light Brown Hair**

I Dream of You 1944 w.m. Marjorie Goetschius, Edna Osser

I Dream Too Much 1935 w. Dorothy Fields m. Jerome Kern. (MF) *I Dream Too Much.* Lily Pons, Henry Fonda, and Lucille Ball appeared in *I Dream Too Much.*

I Dreamed 1956 w.m. Charles Grean, Marvin Moore

I Dreamt I Dwelt in Marble Halls 1843 w. Alfred Bunn m. Michael William Balfe. From the opera *The Bohemian Girl.*

I Enjoy Being a Girl 1958 w. Oscar Hammerstein II m. Richard Rodgers. (MT) *Flower Drum Song.* (MF) *Flower Drum Song.* Nancy Kwan appeared in the film production of *Flower Drum Song.*

I Fall in Love Too Easily 1944 w. Sammy Cahn m. Jule Styne. (MF) *Anchors Aweigh.* Frank Sinatra, Gene Kelly, and Kathryn Grayson appeared in *Anchors Aweigh.*

I Fall in Love with You Every Day 1946 w.m. Sam H. Stept

I Faw Down an' Go Boom 1928 w.m. James Brockman, Leonard Stevens, B.B.B. Donaldson

I Feel a Song Coming On 1935 w. Dorothy Fields, George Oppenheimer m. Jimmy McHugh. (MT) *Sugar Babies.* (MF) *Every Night at Eight.* (MF) *Follow the Boys.* (MF) *The Stooge.* Ann Miller and Mickey Rooney appeared in *Sugar Babies.* Frances Langford and George Raft appeared in *Every Night at Eight.* George Raft and Marlene Dietrich appeared in *Follow the Boys.* Dean Martin appeared in *The Stooge.*

I Feel Fine 1964 w.m. John Lennon, Paul McCartney. Ivor Novello Award winner 1964.

I Feel for You 1984 w.m. Prince. (MF) *Purple Rain.* Prince appeared in *Purple Rain.* Grammy Award winner 1984.

I Feel Like a Feather in the Breeze 1936 w.m. Mack Gordon, Harry Revel. (MF) *Collegiate.* (MF) *The Charm School.* (MF) *The Stooge.* Joe Penner, Betty Grable, and Jack Oakie appeared in *Collegiate.* Dean Martin appeared in *The Stooge.*

I Feel Love 1977 w.m. Donna Summer, Giorgio Moroder, Peter Bellotte

I Feel Pretty 1957 w. Stephen Sondheim m. Leonard Bernstein. (MT) *West Side Story.* (MF) *West Side Story.* Carol Lawrence appeared in the stage production of *West Side Story.* Natalie Wood appeared in the film production of *West Side Story.*

I Feel the Earth Move 1971 w.m. Carole King

I Forgive You 1932 w.m. Jack Yellen, Harold Arlen

I Found a Million Dollar Baby in a Five and Ten Cent Store 1931 w. Mort Dixon, Billy Rose m. Harry Warren. (MT) *Crazy Quilt.* (MF) *Million Dollar Baby.* Fanny Brice and Ted Healy appeared in *Crazy Quilt.* Ronald Reagan and Jimmy Fay appeared in *Million Dollar Baby.* Theme song of Ethel Shutta.

I Found a New Baby 1925 w.m. Jack Palmer, Spencer Williams. (MF) *Sweet and Low-Down.* This song was popularly revived in 1944.

I Found a Rose in the Devil's Garden 1921 w.m. Willie Raskin, Fred Fisher

I Found the End of the Rainbow 1918 w.m. John Mears, Harry Tierney, Joseph McCarthy

I Found You 1931 w.m. Ray Noble, James Campbell, Reginald Connelly

I Found You and You Found Me 1918 w. P.G. Wodehouse m. Jerome Kern. (MT) *Oh, Lady, Lady.*

I Found You in the Rain 1941 w.m. H. Barlow. Based on Chopin's Prelude No.7.

I Gave My Love a Cherry, or, **The Riddle Song** c.1850 w.m. traditional folksong

I Gave You Up Just Before You Threw Me Down 1922 w.m. Bert Kalmar, Harry Ruby, Fred E. Ahlert

I Get a Kick Out of You 1934 w.m. Cole Porter. (MT) *Anything Goes.* (MF) *Anything Goes* (1936). (MF) *Anything Goes* (1956). (MF) *Night and Day.* (MF) *On the Sunny Side of the Street.* Ethel Merman and Victor Moore appeared in the stage production of *Anything Goes.* Bing Crosby and Ethel Merman appeared in the 1936 film production of *Anything Goes.* Bing Crosby and Mitzi Gaynor appeared in the 1956 film production of *Anything Goes.* Cary Grant, Alexis Smith, and Mary Martin appeared in *Night and Day.* biopic of Cole Porter. Frankie Laine and Billy Daniels appeared in *On the Sunny Side of the Street.*

I Get Along Without You Very Well 1939 w.m. Hoagy Carmichael. (F) *The Las Vegas Story.* Jane Russell and Victor Mature appeared in *The Las Vegas Story.* This song was popularly revived in 1968.

I Get Around 1964 w.m. Brian Wilson

(When We Are Dancing) I Get Ideas 1951 w. Dorcas Cochran m. Sanders. Based on "Adios Muchachos" of 1932.

I Get So Lonely, *see* **Oh Baby Mine**

I Get the Blues When It Rains 1928 w.m. Marcy Klauber, Harry Stoddard

I Give My Heart 1931 w. Rowland Leigh m. Carl Millöcker (revised Theo MacKeben). (MT) *The Dubarry.* Grace Moore appeared in the American production of *The Dubarry.* Anny Ahlers appeared in the British production of *The Dubarry.*

I Give Thanks for You 1943 w.m. Peter Young

I Give You My Word 1940 w.m. Al Kavelin, Merril Lyn

I Go Crazy 1977 w.m. Paul Davis

I Got a "Code" in My "Dose" (Cold in My Nose) 1929 w.m. Arthur Fields, Fred Hall, Billy Rose

I Got a Name 1973 w.m. Norman Gimbel, Charles Fox. (MT) *Lena Horne: The Lady and Her Music.* Lena Horne appeared in *Lena Horne: The Lady and Her Music.*

I Got a Robe, *see* **I Got Shoes**

I Got a Song 1944 w. E.Y. Harburg m. Harold Arlen. (MT) *Bloomer Girl.* Celeste Holm and David Brooks appeared in *Bloomer Girl.*

I Got a Woman Crazy for Me, *see* **She's Funny That Way**

I Got It Bad and That Ain't Good 1941 w. Paul Francis Webster m. Edward Kennedy "Duke" Ellington. (MT) *The 1940's Radio Hour.* (MT) *Sophisticated Ladies.* (MF) *The Benny Goodman Story.* (MT) *This Could Be the Night.* Gregory Hines and Phyllis Hyman appeared in *Sophisticated Ladies*.

I Got Lost in His Arms 1946 w.m. Irving Berlin. (MT) *Annie Get Your Gun.* (MF) *Annie Get Your Gun.* Ethel Merman appeared in the stage production of *Annie Get Your Gun.* Betty Hutton appeared in the film production of *Annie Get Your Gun.*

I Got Love 1970 w. Peter Udell m. Gary Geld. (MT) *Purlie.* Melba Moore and Sherman Hensley appeared in *Purlie.*

I Got Lucky in the Rain 1948 w. Harold Adamson m. Jimmy McHugh. (MT) *As the Girls Go.* Irene Rich and Bill Callahan appeared in *As the Girls Go.*

I Got Plenty o' Nuttin' 1935 w. Ira Gershwin, DuBose Heyward m. George Gershwin. (MT) *Porgy and Bess.* (MF) *Porgy and Bess.* (MF) *Rhapsody in Blue.* Todd Duncan and Anne Wiggins Brown appeared in the original stage production of *Porgy and Bess.* Sidney Poitier and Sammy Davis, Jr., appeared in the film production of *Porgy and Bess.* Robert Alda, Alexis Smith, and Oscar Levant appeared in *Rhapsody in Blue,* biopic of composer George Gershwin.

I Got Rhythm 1930 w. Ira Gershwin m. George Gershwin. (MT) *Girl Crazy.* (MF) *Girl Crazy* (1932). (MF) *Girl Crazy* (1943). (MF) *Rhapsody in Blue.* (MF) *An American in Paris.* (MF) *When the Boys Meet the Girls.* Ethel Merman and Ginger Rogers both made their Broadway debuts in the stage production of *Girl Crazy.* Judy Garland, June Allison, and Mickey Rooney appeared in the film production of *Girl Crazy.* Oscar Levant, Robert Alda, and Alexis Smith appeared in *Rhapsody in Blue,* biopic of composer George Gershwin. Gene Kelly and Leslie Caron appeared in *An American in Paris.* Connie Francis appeared in *When the Boys Meet the Girls.* Theme song of Ethel Merman.

I Got (a Robe) Shoes, or, **All God's Chillun Got Shoes** 1865 w.m. traditional black American spiritual. This song was adapted in 1921 by Harry Thacker Burleigh with the title "Heav'n Heav'n (Gonna Shout All Over God's Heav'n)."

I Got Spurs, *see* **Jingle Jangle Jingle**

I Got the Sun in the Morning 1946 w.m. Irving Berlin. (MT) *Annie Get Your Gun.* (MF) *Annie Get Your Gun.* Ethel Merman and Ray Middleton appeared in the stage production of *Annie Get Your Gun.* Betty Hutton and Howard Keel appeared in the film production of *Annie Get Your Gun.*

I Got You (I Feel Good) 1966 w.m. James Brown

I Got You Babe 1965 w.m. Sonny Bono

I Gotcha 1972 w.m. Don Redman, Herman Stein

I Gotta Have You 1959 w. Arnold B. Horwitt m. Richard Lewine. (MT) *The Girls Against the Boys.*

I Gotta (I've Got a) Right To Sing the Blues 1932 w. Ted Koehler m. Harold Arlen. (MT) *Earl Carroll's Vanities of 1932.* Milton Berle and Helen Broderick appeared in *Earl Carroll's Vanities of 1932.*

I Guess I'll Get the Papers and Go Home 1946 w.m. Hughie Prince, Dick Rogers, Hal Kanner

I Guess I'll Have To Change My Plan 1929 w. Howard Dietz m. Arthur Schwartz. (MT) *The Little Show (First Edition).* (MF) *The Band Wagon.* Fred Astaire, Nanette Fa-

bray, and Oscar Levant appeared in *The Band Wagon.* This song was popularly revived in 1932. This song was originally the official Brandt Lake Camp Song, composed by Arthur Schwartz when he worked at the camp with lyricist Lorenz Hart. The melody was later used with a new lyric by Howard Deitz for *The Little Show* with the new title "I Guess I'll Have To Change My Plan."

I Guess I'll Have To Dream the Rest 1941 w.m. Michael Stoner

I Guess I'll Have To Telegraph My Baby 1898 w.m. George M. Cohan

I Guess It Never Hurts To Hurt Sometimes 1984 w.m. Randy Van Warmer

I Guess That's Why They Call It the Blues 1984 w.m. Elton John, Davey Johnstone, Bernie Taupin

I Had a Dream, Dear, *see* **You Tell Me Your Dream**

I Had Myself a True Love, *see* **True Love**

I Had the Craziest Dream 1943 w. Mack Gordon m. Harry Warren. (MF) *Springtime in the Rockies.* Harry James, Betty Grable, and Carmen Miranda appeared in *Springtime in the Rockies.*

I Hadn't Anyone Till You 1938 w.m. Ray Noble. (MF) *On the Sunny Side of the Street.* (F) *In a Lonely Place.* Frankie Laine and Billy Daniels appeared in *On the Sunny Side of the Street.* Humphrey Bogart appeared in *In a Lonely Place.*

I Happen To Like New York 1930 w.m. Cole Porter. (MT) *The New Yorkers.* Charles King, Hope Williams, and Jimmy Durante appeared in *The New Yorkers.*

I Hate Men 1949 w.m. Cole Porter. (MT) *Kiss Me, Kate.* (MF) *Kiss Me, Kate.* Alfred Drake and Patricia Morrison appeared in the stage production of *Kiss Me, Kate.* Kathryn Grayson, Howard Keel, and Ann Miller appeared in the film production of *Kiss Me, Kate.*

I Hate To Lose You 1918 w. Grant Clarke m. Archie Gottler. (MF) *The Merry Monihans.* Donald O'Connor and Peggy Ryan appeared in *The Merry Monihans.*

I Have a Noble Cock 1980 w. Nevill Coghill m. Richard Hill, John Hawkins. (MT) *Canterbury Tales.*

I Have But One Heart 1945 w.m. Johnny Farrow, Marty Symes

I Have Dreamed 1951 w. Oscar Hammerstein II m. Richard Rodgers. (MT) *The King and I.* (MF) *The King and I.* Yul Brynner and Gertrude Lawrence appeared in the stage production of *The King and I.* Yul Brynner and Gertrude Lawrence appeared in the stage production of *The King and I.* Yul Brynner and Deborah Kerr appeared in the film production of *The King and I.* This song was popularly revived in 1969.

I Have Eyes (To See With) 1938 w.m. Leo Robin, Ralph Rainger. (MF) *Artists and Models.* (MF) *Paris Honeymoon.* Jack Benny, Ida Lupino, and Martha Raye appeared in *Artists and Models.* Bing Crosby and Shirley Ross appeared in *Paris Honeymoon.*

I Haven't Got a Worry in the World 1946 w. Oscar Hammerstein II m. Richard Rodgers. (T) *Happy Birthday.*

I Hear a Rhapsody 1941 w.m. George Frajos, Jack Baker,

Dick Gasparre. (MF) *Casa Mañana*. (F) *Clash By Night*. Robert Clarke and Virginia Welles appeared in *Cash By Night*. This song was popularly revived in 1952.

I Hear a Symphony 1965 w.m. Eddie Holland, Brian Holland, Lamont Dozier

I Hear a Thrush at Eve 1913 w. Nelle Richmond Eberhart m. Charles Wakefield Cadman

I Hear Music 1940 w.m. Frank Loesser, Burton Lane. (MF) *Dancing on a Dime*. Grace McDonald and Robert Paige appeared in *Dancing on a Dime*. This song was popularly revived in 1956.

I Hear Music 1944 w.m. Fred Waring, Jack Dolph, Roy Ringwald

I Hear Music When I Look at You, *see* **The Song Is You**

I Hear You Calling Me 1908 w.m. Harold Herford, Charles Marshall

I Hear You Knocking 1955 w.m. Dave Bartholomew, Pearl King

I Heard It Through the Grapevine 1967 w.m. Norman Whitfield, Barrett Strong

I Heard the Bells on Christmas Day 1956 w. Henry Wadsworth Longfellow (adapted) m. John Marks

I Heard You Cried Last Night 1943 w.m. Jerry Kruger, Ted Grouya. (F) *Cinderella Swings It*. Gloria Warren and Guy Kibbe appeared in *Cinderella Swings It*.

I Hit a New High 1937 w. Harold Adamson m. Jimmy McHugh. (MF) *Hitting a New High*. Lili Pons and Edward Everett Horton appeared in *Hitting a New High*.

I Honestly Love You 1974 w.m. Peter Allen, Jeff Barry. Grammy Award winner 1974.

I Hope I Get It 1975 w. Edward Kleban m. Marvin Hamlisch. (MT) *A Chorus Line*. Donna McKechnie appeared in *A Chorus Line*.

I Just Called To Say I Love You 1984 w.m. Stevie Wonder. (F) *The Woman in Red*. Academy Award winner 1984.

I Just Came Here To Dance 1982 w.m. Kenneth Bell, Terry Skinner, J.L. Wallace

I Just Can't Make My Eyes Behave 1906 w.m. Will D. Cobb, Gus Edwards. (MT) *The Parisian Model*. Anna Held and Truly Shattuck appeared in *The Parisian Model*. Theme song of Anna Held.

I Just Fall in Love Again 1979 w.m. Stephen Dorff, Larry Herbstritt, Harry Lloyd, Gloria Sklerov

I Just Roll Along Havin' My Ups and Downs 1927 w. Jo' Trent m. Peter DeRose

I Just Wanna Stop 1978 w.m. Ross Vannelli

I Just Want To Be Your Everything 1977 w.m. Barry Gibb

I Just Want To Go Back and Start the Whole Thing Over 1901 w.m. Paul Dresser

I Keep Forgettin' (Every Time You're Near) 1982 w.m. Jerry Leiber, Mike Stoller

I Kiss Your Hand, Madame 1929 Germ. w. Fritz Rotter Eng.w. Samuel Lewis, Joseph Young m. Ralph Erwin. (MF) *The Emperor Waltz*. Bing Crosby and Joan Fontaine appeared in *The Emperor Waltz*.

('Til) **I Kissed You** 1959 w.m. Don Everly

I Know 1959 w.m. Carl Stutz, Edith Lindeman

I Know a Bank Where the Wild Thyme Blows 1830 w. William Shakespeare m. Charles Edward Horn. The lyric for this song was adapted from Shakespeare's *A Midsummer Night's Dream*.

I Know a Heartache When I See One 1979 w.m. Charles F. Black, Rory Bourke, Kerry Chater

I Know a Lovely Garden 1907 w.m. Guy d'Hardelot, Edward Teschemacher

I Know a Place 1965 w.m. Tony Hatch

I Know Him So Well 1986 w.m. Benny Andersson, Tim Rice, Bjorn Ulvaeus. Ivor Novello Award winner 1985–86.

I Know I Got More Than My Share 1916 w.m. Grant Clarke, Howard Johnson

I Know Now 1937 w. Al Dubin m. Harry Warren. (MF) *The Singing Marine*. Dick Powell and Doris Weston appeared in *The Singing Marine*.

I Know That Someday You'll Want Me, *see* **Some Day You'll Want Me To Want You**

I Know That You Know 1926 w. Anne Caldwell m. Vincent Youmans. (MT) *Oh, Please!* (MF) *Tea for Two*. (MF) *Hit the Deck*. Doris Day and Gordon MacRae appeared in *Tea for Two*, based on *No, No, Nanette*. Jane Powell and Vic Damone appeared in *Hit the Deck*.

I Know What It Means To Be Lonesome 1919 w.m. James Kendis, James Brockman, Nathaniel H. Vincent

I Know Where the Files Go in the Wintertime 1920 w.m. Sam Mayo, J.P. Harrington

I Know Why 1941 w.m. Harry Warren, Mack Gordon. (MF) *Sun Valley Serenade*. (MF) *The Glenn Miller Story*. Sonja Henie, Milton Berle, and Glenn Miller appeared in *Sun Valley Serenade*.

I Leave My Heart in an English Garden 1950 w.m. Harry Parr-Davies, Christopher Hassall. (MT) *Dear Miss Phoebe*.

I Left My Hat in Haiti 1951 w. Alan Jay Lerner m. Burton Lane. (MF) *Royal Wedding*. Fred Astaire and Jane Powell appeared in *Royal Wedding*.

I Left My Heart at the Stage Door Canteen 1942 w.m. Irving Berlin. (MT) *This Is the Army*. (MF) *This Is the Army*. Kate Smith and Ronald Reagan appeared in the film production of *This Is the Army*.

I Left My Heart in San Francisco 1954 w. Douglass Crossm. George Cory. Grammy Award winner 1962. This song was popularly revived in 1962. Theme song of Tony Bennett.

I Left My Sugar Standing in the Rain (and She Melted Away) 1926 w. Irving Kahal m. Sammy Fain

I Let a Song Go Out of My Heart 1938 w. Irving Mills, Henry Nemo, John Redmond m. Duke Ellington. (MT) *Sophisticated Ladies*. Gregory Hines and Phyllis Hyman appeared in *Sophisticated Ladies*.

I Lift Up My Finger and I Say Tweet Tweet 1929 w.m. Leslie Sarony. (MT) *Love Lies*. Stanley Lupino appeared in *Love Lies*.

I Like Bananas Because They Have No Bones 1936 w.m. Chris Yacich

I Like Dreamin' 1976 w.m. Kenny Nolan

I Like IKE 1950 w.m. Irving Berlin

I Like It 1963 w.m. Mitch Murray

I Like It—I Like It 1951 w.m. Mack David, Jerry Livingston

I Like It Like That 1961 w.m. Chris Kenner, Allen Tousaint

I Like Mountain Music 1933 w. James Cavanaugh m. Frank Weldon

I Like the Likes of You 1933 w. E.Y. Harburg m. Vernon Duke. (MT) *Ziegfeld Follies of 1934*. Fanny Brice and Jane Froman appeared in *Ziegfeld Follies of 1934*.

I Like To Recognize the Tune 1939 w. Lorenz Hart m. Richard Rodgers. (MT) *Too Many Girls*. (MF) *Too Many Girls*. (MF) *Meet the People*. Van Johnson and Desi Arnaz appeared in the stage production of *Too Many Girls*. Lucille Ball appeared in the film production of *Too Many Girls*. Lucille Ball, Dick Powell, and Bert Lahr appeared in *Meet the People*.

(Yi Yi Yi Yi) I Like You Very Much 1941 w.m. Mack Gordon, Harry Warren. (MF) *That Night in Rio*. Carmen Miranda and Alica Faye appeared in *That Night in Rio*.

I Like Your Old French Bonnet 1906 w.m. Mellor, Lawrence, Gifford

I Like Your Style 1980 w. Michael Stewart m. Cy Coleman. (MT) *Barnum*. Jim Dale and Glenn Close appeared in *Barnum*.

I Live in Trafalgar Square c. 1898 w.m. C.W. Murphy

I Long To See the Girl I Left Behind 1893 w.m. John T. Kelly

I Look at Heaven 1942 w.m. Bobby Worth, Ray Austin, Freddy Martin. Based on a theme from Grieg's Piano Concerto in A minor.

I Lost My Sugar in Salt Lake City 1943 w.m. Leon Rene, Johnny Lange. (MF) *Stormy Weather*. Lena Horne and Fats Waller appeared in *Stormy Weather*.

I Lost the Best Pal That I Had 1920 w.m. Dick Thomas

I Love a Cop 1959 w. Sheldon Harnick m. Jerry Bock. (MT) *Fiorello!*

I Love a Lassie, or **Ma Scotch Bluebell** 1906 w.m. Harry Lauder, Gerald Grafton. Theme song of Harry Lauder.

I Love a Parade 1931 w. Ted Koehler m. Harold Arlen. (MF) *Manhattan Parade*. Charles Butterworth and Walter Miller appeared in *Manhattan Parade*.

I Love a Piano 1915 w.m. Irving Berlin. (MT) *Stop! Look! Listen!* (MT) *Follow the Crowd*. (MF) *Easter Parade*. Joseph Coyne and Ethel Levey appeared in *Follow the Crowd*. Judy Garland and Fred Astaire appeared in *Easter Parade*. This song was popularly revived in 1948.

I Love a Rainy Night 1981 w.m. David Malloy, Eddie Rabbitt, Even Stevens

I Love Bosco 1951 w.m. Joan Edwards, Lyn Duddy. This song was written for a Bosco Chocolate Flavored Syrup commercial promotion campaign.

I Love Coffee, I Love Tea 1915 w.m. anon. The melody to this song is traditional. See also "Java Jive."

I Love How You Love Me 1961 w.m. Barry Mann, Larry Kolber

I Love, I Love, I Love My Wife, But Oh You Kid 1909 w. Jimmy Lucas m. Harry von Tilzer

I Love Life, op.83 1923 w. Irwin M. Cassel m. Mlle. Mana Zucca

I Love Little Pussy, *see* **Mother Goose's Melodies**

I Love Louisa 1931 w. Howard Dietz m. Arthur Schwartz. (MT) *The Band Wagon*. (MF) *Dancing in the Dark*. (MF) *The Band Wagon*. Fred Astaire, Adele Astaire, and Frank Morgan appeared in the stage production of *The Band Wagon*. William Powell, Betsy Drake, and Adolphe Menjou appeared in *Dancing in the Dark*. Fred Astaire and Nanette Fabray appeared in the film production of *The Band Wagon*.

I Love Love 1911 w. Channing Pollack, Rennold Wolf m. Charles J. Gebest. (MT) *The Red Widow*.

I Love Lucy w.m. Eliot Daniel, Harold Adamson. (TV) *I Love Lucy*. Lucille Ball, Desi Arnaz, Vivian Vance, and William Frawley appeared in *I Love Lucy*.

I Love Music (Part 1) 1975 w.m. Kenneth Gamble, Leon Huff

I Love My Baby—My Baby Loves Me 1925 w. Bud Green m. Harry Warren. (MF) *Drum Crazy*. Ruby Lane appeared in *Drum Crazy*.

I Love My Wife, But Oh You Kid 1909 w.m. Harry Armstrong, Billy Clark

I Love Paris 1953 w.m. Cole Porter. (MT) *Can-Can*. (MF) *Can-Can*. Frank Sinatra, Shirley MacLaine, and Juliet Prowse appeared in the film production of *Can-Can*.

I Love Rock 'n Roll 1982 w.m. Alan Merrill, Jerry Mamberg

I Love the Ladies 1914 w. Grant Clarke m. Jean Schwartz

I Love the Little Things 1964 w.m. Tony Hatch

I Love the Moon 1912 w.m. Paul Rubens

I Love the Name of Mary 1913 w.m. Richard Oldham, Helen Taylor

I Love the Nightlife (Disco 'Round) 1978 w.m. Alicia Bridges, Susan Hutcheson

I Love the Way You Say "Goodnight" 1951 w.m. Eddie Pola, George Wyle. (MF) *Lullaby of Broadway*. Doris Day and Billy DeWolf appeared in *Lullaby of Broadway*.

I Love Thee, *see* **Ich Liebe Dich**

I Love To Dunk a Hunk of Sponge Cake 1928 w.m. Clarence Gaskill

I Love To Rhyme 1938 w. Ira Gershwin m. George Gershwin. (MF) *The Goldwyn Follies*. Adolphe Menjou and the Ritz Brothers appeared in *The Goldwyn Follies*.

I Love To Sing 1938 w.m. Paul Misraki, Tommie Connor, Michael Carr. (MF) *Rhythm Serenade*.

I Love To Tell the Story 1874 w. Catherine Hankey m. William G. Fischer

I Love You (Sweetheart of All My Dreams) 1923 w.m. Art Fitch, Kay Fitch, Bert Lowe. (F) *Thirty Seconds over Tokyo*. Spencer Tracy and Van Johnson appeared in *Thirty Seconds over Tokyo*.

I Love You (Je t'aime) 1923 Fr.w. Paul Combis Eng.w. Harlan Thompson m. Harry Archer. (MT) *Little Jessie James*. (F) *The Sun Also Rises*. Errol Flynn and Ava Gardner appeared in *The Sun Also Rises*. This song was popularly revived in 1928.

I Love You 1944 w.m. Cole Porter. (MT) *Mexican Hayride*. (MF) *Mexican Hayride*. June Havoc and Bobby Clark appeared in the stage production of *Mexican Hayride*. Bud Abbott and Lou Costello appeared in the film production of *Mexican Hayride*.

(Just One Way To Say) I Love You 1949 w.m. Irving Berlin

I Love You 1960 w.m. Bruce Welch

I Love You Because 1963 w.m. Leon Payne

I Love You for Sentimental Reasons, *see* **For Sentimental Reasons**

I Love You in the Same Old Way—Darling Sue 1896 w. Walter H. Ford m. John W. Bratton

I Love You Love Me Love 1974 w.m. Garry Glitter, Mike Leander. Ivor Novello Award winner 1973/1974.

I Love You Samantha 1956 w.m. Cole Porter. (MF) *High Society*. Bing Crosby, Frank Sinatra, and Grace Kelly appeared in High Society, based on the film *The Philadelphia Story*.

I Love You So, *see* **Merry Widow Waltz**

I Love You So Much 1930 w. Bert Kalmar m. Harry Ruby. (MF) *The Cuckoos*. (MF) *Three Little Words*. Bert Wheeler and Robert Woolsey appeared in *The Cuckoos*. Fred Astaire and Red Skelton appeared in *Three Little Words*, biopic of song writers Bert Kalmar and Harry Ruby.

I Love You So Much It Hurts 1948 w.m. Floyd Tillman

I Love You This Morning 1945 w. Alan Jay Lerner m. Frederick Loewe. (MT) *The Day Before Spring*.

I Love You Truly 1901 w.m. Carrie Jacobs-Bond. This song was popularly revived in 1906, and again in 1934.

I Loved 'Em Everyone 1981 w.m. Phil Sampson

I Loved Her Best of All, *see* **Last Night On the Back Porch**

I Loved You Once in Silence 1960 w. Alan Jay Lerner m. Frederick Loewe. (MT) *Camelot*. (MF) *Camelot*. Julie Andrews appeared in the stage production of *Camelot*. Vanessa Redgrave appeared in the film production of *Camelot*.

I Loves You Porgy 1935 w. DuBose Heyward, Ira Gershwin m. George Gershwin. (MT) *Porgy and Bess*. (MF) *Porgy and Bess*. Todd Duncan and Anne Brown appeared in the original stage production of *Porgy and Bess*. Sidney Poitier and Dorothy Dandridge appeared in the film production of *Porgy and Bess*.

I Made It Through the Rain 1981 w.m. Jack Feldman, Gerard Kenny, Barry Manilow, Drey Sheppard, Bruce Sussman

I Married an Angel 1938 w. Lorenz Hart m. Richard Rodgers. (MT) *I Married an Angel*. (MF) *I Married an Angel*. Vera Zorina and Walter Slezak appeared in the stage production of *I Married an Angel*. Jeanette MacDonald, Nelson Eddy, and Edward Everett Horton appeared in the film production of *I Married an Angel*.

I May Be Crazy 1902 w.m. Leslie Stuart

I May Be Crazy, But I Ain't No Fool 1904 w.m. Alexander Rogers

I May Be Gone for a Long, Long Time 1917 w. Lew Brown m. Albert Von Tilzer. (MT) *Hitchy-Koo*.

I May Be Wrong, But I Think You're Wonderful 1929 w. Harry Ruskin m. Henry Sullivan. (MT) *John Murray Anderson's Almanac*. (MF) *Wallflower*. (MF) *You're My Everything*. (MF) *Swingtime Johnny*. (MF) *Young Man of Music*. (MF) *On the Sunny Side of the Street*. (MF) *Starlift*. Jimmy Savo and Roy Atwell appeared in *John Murray Anderson's Almanac*. Janis Paige and Joyce Reynolds appeared in *Wallflower*. Dan Dailey and Anne Baxter appeared in *You're My Everything*. The Andrews Sisters and Harriet Hilliard appeared in *Swingtime Johnny*. Doris Day appeared in *Young Man of Music* and *Starlift*. Frankie Laine and Billy Daniels appeared in *On the Sunny Side of the Street*.

I Met Her on Monday 1942 w.m. Lionel Newman, Allie Wrubel

I Might Be Your "Once-in-a-While" 1919 w. Robert B. Smith m. Victor Herbert. (MT) *Angel Face*. (MF) *The Great Victor Herbert*. Mary Martin and Allan Jones appeared in *The Great Victor Herbert*.

I Miss My Swiss, My Swiss Miss Misses Me 1925 w. L. Wolfe Gilbert m. Abel Baer. (MT) *Chauve Souris*.

I Miss You Most of All 1913 w.m. Joseph McCarthy, Sr., James V. Monaco

I Must See Annie Tonight 1938 w.m. Dave Franklin, Cliff Friend

I Need Thee Every Hour 1872 w. Annie S. Hawks m. Reverend Robert Lowry

I Need You Now 1954 w.m. Jimmie Crane, Al Jacobs

I Never Do Anything Twice 1976 w.m. Stephen Sondheim. (MT) *Side by Side by Sondheim*. (F) *The 7% Solution*. Millicent Martin and Julie N. McKenzie appeared in *Side by Side by Sondheim*. Regine appeared in *The 7% Solution*.

I Never Drank Behind the Bar 1882 w. Edward Harrigan m. David Braham. (MT) *The McSorleys*.

I Never Had a Chance 1934 w.m. Irving Berlin

I Never Had a Mammy 1923 w.m. Duncan Sisters. (MT) *Topsy & Eva*. The Duncan Sisters appeared in *Topsy & Eva*.

I Never Has Seen Snow 1955 w. Truman Capote, Harold Arlen m. Harold Arlen. (MT) *House of Flowers*.

I Never Knew I Could Love Anybody Like I'm Loving You 1920 w.m. Tom Pitts, Ray Egan, Roy K. Marsh. (MF) *Honeymoon Lodge*. Ozzie Nelson and Rod Cameron appeared in *Honeymoon Lodge*.

I Never Knew (That Roses Grew) 1925 w. Gus Kahn m. Ted Fiorito. (MF) *Pete Kelly's Blues*. (MF) *I'll See You in My Dreams*. Peggy Lee and Ella Fitzgerald appeared in *Pete Kelly's Blues*. Doris Day and Danny Thomas appeared in *I'll See You in My Dreams*, biopic of song writer Gus Kahn.

I Never Meant To Hurt You 1966 w.m. Laura Nyro. This song was most popular in 1969.

I Never Mention Your Name (Oh No) 1943 w.m. Mack Davis, Don George, Walter Kent

I Never Promised You a Rose Garden 1970 w.m. Joe South

I Never See Maggie Alone   1926   w.m. Harry Tilsley, Everett Lynton

I.O.U.   1983   w.m. Kerry Chater, Austin Roberts

I Once Had a Heart, Margarita   1935   w.m. Joseph Schmitz, Thomas Connor, Kurt Feltz, Edward B. Lisbona

I Only Have Eyes for You   1934   w. Al Dubin   m. Harry Warren. (MF) *Dames*. (MF) *Tea for Two*. (MF) *Jolson Sings Again*. (F) *The Girl from Jones Beach*. Dick Powell and Ruby Keeler appeared in *Dames*. Doris Day and Gordon MacRae appeared in *Tea for Two*, based on *No, No, Nanette*. Larry Parks appeared in *Jolson Sings Again*. Ronald Reagan and Virginia Mayo appeared in *The Girl from Jones Beach*. This song was popularly revived in 1975.

I Only Want To Be with You   1964   w.m. Mike Hawker, Ivor Raymonde

I Passed By Your Window   1917   w.m. May Brahe

I Pitch My Lonely Caravan at Night   1921   w.m. Eric Coates, Annette Horey

I Played Fiddle for the Czar   1932   w. Mack Gordon   m. Harry Revel

I Poured My Heart into a Song   1939   w.m. Irving Berlin. (MF) *Second Fiddle*. Rudy Vallee and Sonja Henie appeared in *Second Fiddle*.

I Ran All the Way Home   1951   w.m. George David Weiss, Bennie Benjamin

I Ran All the Way Home, *see also* **Sorry**

I Remember April, *see* **I'll Remember April**

I Remember How It Was   1984   w. Robert Lorick   m. Henry Krieger. (MT) *The Tap Dance Kid*. Alfonso Ribiero appeared in *The Tap Dance Kid*.

I Remember It Well   1958   w. Alan Jay Lerner   m. Frederick Loewe. (MF) *Gigi*. Maurice Chevalier and Hermione Gingold appeared in *Gigi*.

I Remember the Cornfields   1950   w.m. Martyn Mayne, Harry Ralton

I Remember You   1942   w. Johnny Mercer   m. Victor Schertzinger. (MF) *The Fleet's In*. Dorothy Lamour and Betty Hutton appeared in *The Fleet's In*.

I Ride an Old Paint, *see* **Goodbye Ol' Paint**

I Said My Pajamas (and Put On My Prayers)   1950   w.m. Eddie Pola, George Wyle

I Said No   1941   w. Frank Loesser   m. Jule Styne. (MF) *Sweater Girl*. Eddie Bracken and Betty Jane Rhodes appeared in *Sweater Girl*.

I Saw Her Standing There   1964   w.m. John Lennon, Paul McCartney

I Saw Mommy Kissing Santa Claus   1952   w.m. Tommie Connor

I Saw Stars   1934   w.m. Maurice Sigler, Al Goodhart, Al Hoffman

I Saw the Light   1972   w.m. Todd Rundgren

I Saw Three Ships Come Sailing   uncertain   w.m. traditional carol. See also ''Mother Goose's Melodies.''

I Say a Little Prayer   1967   w. Hal David   m. Burt Bacharach

I Scream, You Scream, We All Scream for Ice Cream, *see* **Ice Cream**

I See a Million People   1941   w.m. Una Mae Carlisle, Robert Sour

I See Your Face Before Me   1937   w. Howard Dietz   m. Arthur Schwartz. (MT) *Between the Devil*. Jack Buchanan and Evelyn Laye appeared in *Between the Devil*.

I Shall Always Remember You Smiling   1939   w.m. Ross Parker, Hugh Charles

I Shall Be Waiting   1940   w.m. Ross Parker, Hugh Charles, Joe Irwin

I Shot the Sheriff   1974   w.m. Bob Marley

I Should Care   1945   w.m. Sammy Cahn, Axel Stordahl, Paul Weston. (MF) *Thrill of a Romance*. Van Johnson and Esther Williams appeared in *Thrill of a Romance*.

I Should Have Known Better   1964   w.m. John Lennon, Paul McCartney

I Speak to the Stars   1954   w.m. Paul Francis Webster, Sammy Fain

I Stayed Too Long at the Fair, *see* **Too Long at the Fair**

I Still Believe   1954   w.m. Billy Reid

I Still Can't Get Over Loving You   1984   w.m. Ray Parker, Jr.

I Still Do   1984   w.m. J.D. Martin, John Jarrard

I Still Get a Thrill (Thinking of You)   1930   w.m. Benny Davis, J. Fred Coots

I Still Get Jealous   1947   w. Sammy Cahn   m. Jule Styne. (MT) *High Button Shoes*. Phil Silvers and Nanette Fabray appeared in *High Button Shoes*.

I Still Love To Kiss You Goodnight   1937   w. Walter Bullock   m. Harold Spina. (MF) *Fifty-Second Street*. Ian Hunter and Zasu Pitts appeared in *Fifty-Second Street*.

I Still See Elisa   1951   w. Alan Jay Lerner   m. Frederick Loewe. (MT) *Paint Your Wagon*. (MF) *Paint Your Wagon*.

I Surrender Dear   1932   w. Gordon Clifford   m. Harry Barris. (MF) *I Surrender Dear*. Gloria Jean and David Street appeared in *I Surrender Dear*. This song, Bing Crosby's first popular hit, was recorded by him at age twenty-four.

I Talk to the Trees   1951   w. Alan Jay Learner   m. Frederick Loewe. (MT) *Paint Your Wagon*. (MF) *Paint Your Wagon*. Lee Marvin appeared in the film production of *Paint Your Wagon*.

I Taut I Taw a Puddy-Tat   1950   w.m. Alan W. Livingston, Warren Foster

I Think I Love You   1970   w.m. Tony Romeo

I Think I'll Just Stay Here and Drink   1981   w.m. Merle Haggard

I Think of You   1941   w.m. Jack Elliot, Don Marcotte. (MF) *Holiday in Mexico*. Walter Pigeon and Jose Iturbi appeared in *Holiday in Mexico*. Based on the first movement of Rachmaninoff's Second Piano Concerto in C-minor. This song was first recorded by Tommy Dorsey and his orchestra, with the vocal by Frank Sinatra.

I Think of You   1964   w.m. Peter Lee Stirling

I Think When I Read That Sweet Story   1841   w. Jemima Luke   m. traditional, from England

I Threw a Kiss in the Ocean   1942   w.m. Irving Berlin. Irving Berlin signed the royalties for this song over to Navy Relief.

I Tipped My Hat and Slowly Rode Away   1948   w.m. Dick Charles, Lawrence W. Markes

I Took My Harp to a Party   1934   w. Desmond Carter   m. Noel Gay

I Travel the Road   1925   w.m. Pat Thayer, Donovan Parsons. This song was popularly revived in 1932.

I Understand   1941   w.m. Kim Gannon, Mabel Wayne

I Understand Just How You Feel   1953   w.m. Pat Best

I Used To Be Color Blind   1937   w.m. Irving Berlin. (MF) *Carefree*. Fred Astaire and Ginger Rogers appeared in *Carefree*.

I Used To Love You, But It's All Over Now   1920   w. Lew Brown   m. Albert Von Tilzer

I Used to Sigh for the Silvery Moon   1909   w.m. Herman Darewski, Lester Barnett. Theme song of G.H. Elliott (The Chocolate Colored Coon).

I Wanna Be a Friend of Yours, *see* **And a Little Bit More**

I Wanna Be Around   1959   w.m. Johnny Mercer, Sadie Vimmerstedt

I Wanna Be Loved   1933   w. Billy Rose, Edward Heyman   m. Johnny Green

I Wanna Be Loved by You   1928   w. Bert Kalmar   m. Herbert Stothart, Harry Ruby. (MT) *Good Boy*. (MF) *Three Little Words*. (MF) *Gentlemen Marry Brunettes*. (MF) *Some Like It Hot*. Helen Kane and Effie Shannon appeared in *Good Boy*. Fred Astaire and Red Skelton appeared in *Three Little Words*, biopic of song writers Harry Ruby and Bert Kalmar. Jane Russell appeared in *Gentlemen Marry Brunettes*. Marilyn Monroe, Jack Lemmon, and Tony Curtis appeared in *Some Like It Hot*. For a complete history of this song, see Part I, 1928.

I Wanna Be Your Lover   1980   w.m. Prince Nelson

I Wanna Get Married   1944   w. Dan Shapiro, Milton Pascal   m. Philip Charig. (MT) *Follow the Girls*. Gertrude Niesen and Jackie Gleason appeared in *Follow the Girls*.

I Wanna Get Next to You   1977   w.m. Norman Whitfield

I Wanna Go Where You Go, *see* **Then I'll Be Happy**

I Wanna Hear It from Your Lips   1985   w.m. Eric Carmen, Dean Pitchford

I Want a Girl—Just Like the Girl That Married Dear Old Dad   1911   w. William Dillon   m. Harry Von Tilzer. (MF) *Show Business*. (MF) *The Jolson Story*. Larry Parks appeared in *The Jolson Story*.

I Want a Man   1931   w. Lorenz Hart   m. Richard Rodgers. (MT) *America's Sweetheart*.

I Want a New Drug   1984   w.m. Christopher Hayes, Huey Lewis

I Want It All   1983   w.m. Richard Maltby, Jr.   m. David Shire. (MT) *Baby*. Liz Callaway and Beth Fowler appeared in *Baby*.

I Want My Mama, *see* **Mama Yo Quiero**

I Want Some Money   1922   w.m. Herbert Rule, Fred Holt, L. Silberman, Tom McGhee

I Want To Be a Military Man   1900   w.m. Leslie Stuart, Owen Hall. (MT) *Florodora*.

I Want To Be Happy   1924   w. Irving Caesar   m. Vincent Youmans. (MT) *No, No, Nanette*. (MT) *Lena Horne: The Lady and Her Music*. (MF) *No, No, Nanette*. (MF) *Tea for Two*. Louise Groody and Mary Lawlor appeared in the American stage production of *No, No, Nanette*. Joseph Coyne and Bennie Hale appeared in the British stage production of *No, No, Nanette*. Lena Horne appeared in *Lena Horne: The Lady and Her Music*. Anna Neagle and Victor Mature appeared in the film production of *No, No, Nanette*. Doris Day and Gordon MacRae appeared in *Tea for Two*, the American film version of *No, No, Nanette*.

I Want To Be Wanted   1960   It.w. A. Testa   Eng.w. Kim Gannon   m. Pino Spotti. From the Italian "Per Tutta la Vita."

I Want To Go Back to Michigan—Down on the Farm   1914   w.m. Irving Berlin. (MT) *5064 Gerard*. (MF) *Easter Parade*. Judy Garland and Fred Astaire appeared in *Easter Parade*.

I Want To Go Home   1938   w.m. Cole Porter. (MT) *Leave It to Me*. William Gaxton and Victor Moore appeared in *Leave It to Me*.

I Want To Hold Your Hand   1964   w.m. John Lennon, Paul McCartney. (MT) *Beatlemania*. Ivor Novello Award winner 1963. For a complete history of this song, see Part I, 1964.

I Want To Know What Love Is   1985   w.m. Mick Jones

I Want To Marry a Male Quartette   1916   w. Otto Harbach   m. Rudolf Friml. (MT) *Katinka*. Adele Rowland and Franklyn Ardell appeared in *Katinka*.

I Want To Marry a Man   1906   w.m. Howard Talbot. (MT) *The Girl Behind the Counter*. Isobel Jay appeared in *The Girl Behind the Counter*.

I Want To Thank Your Folks   1948   w.m. Bennie Benjamin, George Weiss

I Want What I Want When I Want It   1905   w. Henry Blossom   m. Victor Herbert. (MT) *Mlle. Modiste*.

I Want You   1907   w.m. George M. Cohan. (MT) *The Talk of New York*.

I Want You Back   1970   w.m. Berry Gordy, Alphonso J. Mizell, Frederick J. Perren, Deke Richards

I Want You, I Need You, I Love You   1956   w. Maurice Mysels   m. Ira Kosloff

I Want You To Want Me   1979   w.m. Rick Nielsen

I Want You To Want Me To Want You   1949   w.m. Alfred Bryan, Fred Fisher, Bob Shafer. (MF) *Oh You Beautiful Doll*. June Haver appeared in *Oh You Beautiful Doll*.

I Was a Good Little Girl Till I Met You   1914   w.m. Clifford Harris, James W. Tate

I Was a Very Good Baby   1909   w. Harry L. Cort, George E. Stoddard   m. Harold Orlob. (MT) *Listen Lester*. This song was popularly revived in 1918.

I Was Born in Virginia, or, **Ethel Levy's Virginia Song**   1906   w.m. George M. Cohan. (MT) *George Washington, Jr.* (MF) *Yankee Doodle Dandy*. James Cagney and Joan Leslie appeared in *Yankee Doodle Dandy*.

I Was Country When Country Wasn't Cool   1981   w.m. Kye Fleming, Dennis Morgan

I Was Doing All Right 1938 w. Ira Gershwin m. George Gershwin. (MF) *The Goldwyn Follies.* Adolphe Menjou appeared in *The Goldwyn Follies.*

I Was in the Mood 1933 w.m. Eddie Pola, Michael Carr

I Was Looking for My Boy, She Said, or, **Decoration Day** 1895 w.m. Paul Dresser

I Was Made To Love Her 1967 w.m. Henry Cosby, Sylvia Moy, Lulu Hardaway, Stevie Wonder

I Was Never Kissed Before 1947 w.m. Vivian Ellis. (MT) *Bless the Bride.* George Guetary appeared in *Bless the Bride.*

I Was Seeing Nellie Home, *see* **When I Saw Sweet Nellie Home**

I Was Standing at the Corner of the Street 1910 w.m. George Formby, Hunt

I Watch the Love Parade 1931 w. Otto Harbach m. Jerome Kern. (MT) *The Cat and the Fiddle.* (MF) *The Cat and the Fiddle.* Jeanette MacDonald, Frank Morgan, and Vivienne Segal appeared in the film production of *The Cat and the Fiddle.*

I Went Out of My Way 1941 w.m. Helen Bliss. This song was popularly revived in 1954.

I Went to a Marvelous Party 1939 w.m. Noël Coward. (MT) *Set to Music.* Beatrice Lillie appeared in *Set to Music.*

I Went to Your Wedding 1952 w.m. Jessie Mae Robinson

I Whistle a Happy Tune 1951 w. Oscar Hammerstein II m. Richard Rodgers. (MT) *The King and I.* (MF) *The King and I.* Gertrude Lawrence and Yul Brynner appeared in the stage production of *The King and I.* Deborah Kerr and Yul Brynner appeared in the film production of *The King and I.*

I Who Have Nothing 1963 Orig. w. Mogol Eng.w. Jerry Leiber, Mike Stoller m. Carlo Donida. From the original "Uno Dei Tanti." This song was popularly revived in 1970.

I Will 1968 w.m. John Lennon, Paul McCartney

I Will Always Love You 1982 w.m. Dolly Parton

I Will Be in Love with You 1979 w.m. Livingston Taylor

I Will Drink the Wine 1971 w.m. Paul Ryan

I Will Follow Him 1963 w.m. Arthur Altman, Norman Gimbel, Del Roma, J.W. Stole

I Will Survive 1978 w.m. Frank Collins

If It Takes Forever) I Will Wait for You 1965 w.m. Michel Legrand, Norman Gimbel, Jacques Demy. (F) *The Umbrellas of Cherbourg.* Catherine Deneuve appeared in *The Umbrellas of Cherbourg.* This song was also popular in 1967.

I Wish 1977 w.m. Stevie Wonder

I Wish I Could Shimmy Like My Sister Kate 1919 w.m. Armand J. Piron. This pre-Flapper dance was introduced by Bee Palmer and Gilda Gray, and was later popularly revived in 1922.

I Wish I (We) Didn't Have To Say Good Night 1944 w.m. Frank Loesser, Harold Adamson, Jimmy McHugh. (MF) *Something for the Boys.* Carmen Miranda and Perry Como appeared in the film production of *Something for the Boys.* This song did not appear in the original 1943 stage production of *Something for the Boys.*

I Wish I Didn't Love You So 1947 w.m. Frank Loesser. (MF) *The Perils of Pauline.* Betty Hutton, John Lund, and Billy DeWolfe appeared in *The Perils of Pauline.*

I Wish I Had a Girl 1907 w. Gus Kahn m. Grace LeBoy Kahn. (MF) *I'll See You in My Dreams.* Doris Day and Danny Thomas appeared in *I'll See You in My Dreams,* biopic of song writer Gus Kahn.

I Wish I Had My Old Girl Back Again 1909 w. Ballard MacDonald m. Paul Wallace

I Wish I Knew 1945 w. Mack Gordon m. Harry Warren. (MF) *Diamond Horseshoe.*

I Wish I Was in Dixie's Land, see **Dixie**

I Wish I Were in Love Again 1937 w. Lorenz Hart m. Richard Rodgers. (MT) *Babes in Arms.* (MF) *Babes in Arms.* (MF) *Words and Music.* Mitzi Green and Ray Heatherton appeared in the stage production of *Babes in Arms.* Judy Garland and Mickey Rooney appeared in the film production of *Babes in Arms.* Mickey Rooney, Judy Garland, and Gene Kelly appeared in *Words and Music,* biopic of song writers Rodgers and Hart.

I Wish I Were Twins 1934 w.m. Edgar De Lange, Frank Loesser, Joseph Meyer

I Wish It Would Rain 1968 w.m. Rodger Penzabene, Barrett Strong, Norman Whitfield

I Wish That You Were Here Tonight 1896 w.m. Paul Dresser

I Wish You Could Have Turned My Head 1982 w.m. Sonny Throckmorton

I Wish You Love 1963 w.m. Charles Trenet. From the French "Que Restetil de Nos Amours."

I Wished on the Moon 1936 w.m. Dorothy Parker, Ralph Rainger. (MF) *The Big Broadcast of 1936.* Bing Crosby and Amos and Andy appeared in *The Big Broadcast of 1936.*

I Wonder, I Wonder, I Wonder 1947 w.m. Daryl Hutchins

I Wonder If Love Is a Dream 1915 w.m. Dorothy Foster, Edward Teschemacher

I Wonder If She'll Ever Come Back to Me 1896 w.m. Paul Dresser

I Wonder If She's Waiting 1899 w. Andrew B. Sterling m. Harry Von Tilzer

I Wonder If You Still Care for Me 1921 w. Harry B. Smith, Francis Wheeler m. Ted Snyder

I Wonder What Became of Me 1946 w. Johnny Mercer m. Harold Arlen. (MT) *St. Louis Woman.* This song did not appear in the original New York stage production.

I Wonder What the King Is Doing Tonight 1960 w. Alan Jay Lerner m. Frederick Loewe. (MT) *Camelot.* (MF) *Camelot.* Julie Andrews appeared in the stage production of *Camelot.* Vanessa Redgrave appeared in the film production of *Camelot.*

I Wonder What's Become of Sally 1924 w. Jack Yellen m. Milton Ager

I Wonder Where My Baby Is Tonight 1925 w.m. Gus Kahn, Walter Donaldson. (MT) *The Co-Optimists.* Melville Gideon appeared in *The Co-Optimists.*

I Wonder Where My Lovin' Man Has Gone 1914 w. Earl C. Jones m. Richard Whiting, Charles L. Cooke

I Wonder Where She Is Tonight 1899 w.m. Paul Dresser

I Wonder Who's Dancing with You Tonight 1924 w. Mort Dixon, Billy Rose m. Ray Henderson

I Wonder Who's Kissing Her Now 1909 w. Will M. Hough, Frank R. Adams m. Joseph E. Howard, Harold Orlob. (MT) *The Prince of Tonight.* (MF) *The Time, the Place and the Girl.* (MF) *I Wonder Who's Kissing Her Now.* Grant Withers and James Kirkwood appeared in *The Time, the Place and the Girl.* June Haver and Martha Stewart appeared in *I Wonder Who's Kissing Her Now,* biopic of song writer Joe Howard. This song was popularly revived in 1948. Theme song of Joe E. Howard. For years, this song was attributed to Joe Howard only. After an intense legal battle, Harold Orlob was awarded co-authorship.

I Won't Cry Anymore 1951 w.m. Fred Wise, Al Frisch

I Won't Dance 1935 w. Dorothy Fields, Oscar Hammerstein II, Otto Harbach, Jimmy McHugh m. Jerome Kern. (MF) *Roberta.* (MF) *Till the Clouds Roll By.* (MF) *Lovely To Look At.* Fred Astaire and Ginger Rogers appeared in the film production of *Roberta.* Frank Sinatra, Judy Garland and Van Johnson appeared in *Till the Clouds Roll By,* biopic of composer Jerome Kern. Kathryn Grayson, Howard Keel and Red Skelton appeared in *Lovely To Look At,* remake of *Roberta.* This song did not appear in the original 1933 stage production of *Roberta.*

I Won't Grow Up 1954 w. Carolyn Leigh m. Mark Charlap. (MT) *Peter Pan.* Mary Martin appeared in *Peter Pan.*

I Won't Hold You Back 1983 w.m. Steve Lukather

I Won't Last a Day Without You 1971 w.m. Roger Nicholls, Paul Williams

I Won't Say I Will, But I Won't Say I Won't 1923 w. B.G. DeSylva, Arthur Francis (Ira Gershwin) m. George Gershwin. (MT) *Little Miss Bluebeard.* (MT) *Nifties of 1923.* Irene Bordoni and Eric Blore appeared in *Little Miss Bluebeard.* Frank Crumit and Hazel Dawn appeared in *Nifties of 1923.*

I Won't Tell a Soul (That I Love You) 1938 w.m. Ross Parker, Hugh Charles

I Would Be True 1911 w.m. Howard Walter, Joseph Peek

I Would Do Anything for You, *see* **Anything for You**

I Would, Would You, *see* **Would You**

I Wouldn't Have Missed It for the World 1981 w.m. Kye Fleming, Dennis Morgan, Charles Quillen

I Wouldn't Leave My Little Wooden Hut for You 1905 w.m. Tom Mellor, Charles Collins

I Write the Songs 1976 w.m. Bruce Johnston. Grammy Award winner 1976.

(I Scream, You Scream, We All Scream for) Ice Cream 1928 w.m. Howard Johnson, Billy Moll, Robert King (Bob Keiser). The narrative of this song tells of the prowess of the gridiron warriors of the Eskimo college team of Oogie Wa Wa.

Ice Cream Man 1963 w.m. Joe Meek. (F) *Farewell Performance.*

Ich Liebe Dich (I Love Thee) 1865 Danish w. Hans Christian Andersen m. Edvard Grieg. From the Norwegian "Jes Elsker Dig." The music for this song was inspired by Grieg's love for his cousin Nina Hagerup.

I'd Be a Butterfly 1826 w.m. Thomas Haynes Bayly

I'd Be Lost Without You 1937 w. Bob Wright, Chet Forrest m. Walter Donaldson. (F) *Sinner Take All.* Bruce Cabot and Margaret Lindsay appeared in *Sinner Take All.*

I'd Climb the Highest Mountain (If I Knew I'd Find You) 1926 w.m. Lew Brown, Sidney Clare. Based on Dvorák's "Humoresque."

I'd Do Anything 1963 w.m. Lionel Bart. (MT) *Oliver!* (MF) *Oliver!* Georgia Brown appeared in the stage production of *Oliver!* Shani Wallace appeared in the film production of *Oliver!*

I'd Leave My Happy Home for You 1899 w. Will A. Heelan m. Harry Von Tilzer. (MF) *The Naughty Nineties.* Abbott and Costello and Rita Johnson appeared in *The Naughty Nineties.* This song was popularly performed by Blanche Ring.

I'd Like To Baby You 1951 w.m. Jay Livingston, Ray Evans. (MF) *Aaron Slick from Punkin Crick.* Alan Young, Dinah Shore, and Robert Merrill appeared in *Aaron Slick from Punkin Crick.*

I'd Like To Be a Sister to a Brother Just Like You 1918 w.m. Will Morrissey. "Elizabeth Brice, while in France for the America Over There Theatre League in 1918, sang Will Morrissey's song 'I'd Like To Be a Sister to a Brother Just Like You.' In hospital wards she would pick out the most bashful soldier, sing to him, and for a finish she'd kiss him. One soldier lying in bed in one ward was so embarrassed and bashful that he pulled the bed sheet over his head when she serenaded him. Everyone laughed. At the finish of the song, when she started to kiss him, she discovered he had died while she was singing to him. She never sang the song again."—Ray Walker, *Variety,* Oct. 20, 1954.

I'd Like To Get You on a Slow Boat to China, *see* **On a Slow Boat to China**

I'd Like To Make It with You, *see* **Make It with You**

I'd Like To See the Kaiser with a Lily in His Hand 1918 w.m. Henry Leslie, Howard Johnson, Billy Frisch. (MT) *Doing Our Bit.*

I'd Like To Teach the World To Sing 1971 w.m. Billy Davis, Dottie West, Bill Backer. This song was written for a Coca-Cola commercial promotion campaign.

I'd Love To Be a Monkey in the Zoo 1917 w. Bert Hanlon m. Willie White

I'd Love To Fall Asleep and Wake Up in My Mammy's Arms 1920 w.m. Sam M. Lewis, Joseph Young, Fred E. Ahlert

I'd Love To Live in Loveland (with a Girl Like You) 1910 w.m. W.R. Williams (Rossiter). This song was popularly revived in 1937.

I'd Love To Meet That Old Sweetheart of Mine 1926 w.m. Benny Davis, Joe Burke

I'd Love To Spend One Hour with You, *see* **One Hour with You**

I'd Rather Be a Lobster Than a Wise Guy 1907 w.m. Edward Madden, Theodore F. Morse. This song appeared during a craze of several "I'd Rather Be" songs, including "I'd Rather Be a Farmer Than a Soldier," "I'd Rather Be a Lemon Than a Grapefruit," "I'd Rather Two-Step Than Waltz, Bill," and "I'd Rather Be on the Outside Lookin' In Than on the Inside Lookin' Out."

I'd Rather Be Blue Over You (Than Happy with Somebody Else) 1928 w.m. Billy Rose, Fred Fisher. (MF) *My Man.* (MF) *Funny Girl.* Fanny Brice and Guinn Williams appeared in *My Man.* Barbra Streisand and Omar Shariff appeared in *Funny Girl.*

I'd Rather Be Right 1937 w. Lorenz Hart m. Richard Rodgers. (MT) *I'd Rather Be Right.* George M. Cohan and Joy Hodges appeared in *I'd Rather Be Right.*

I'd Rather Leave While I'm in Love 1980 w.m. Peter Allen, Carole Bayer Sager

I'd Really Like To Get To Know You, *see* **Like To Get To Know You**

I'd Really Love To See You Tonight 1976 w.m. Parker McGee

I'd Still Believe You True 1900 w.m. Paul Dresser

Ida, Sweet As Apple Cider 1903 w. Eddie Leonard m. Eddie Munson. (MT) *Roly Boly Eyes.* (MF) *Babes in Arms.* (MF) *Incendiary Blonde.* (MF) *The Eddie Cantor Story.* Eddie Leonard and Queenie Smith appeared in *Roly Boly Eyes.* Mickey Rooney and Judy Garland appeared in *Babes in Arms.* Betty Hutton appeared in *Incendiary Blonde,* biopic of speakeasy hostess Texas Guinan. Theme song of Eddie Cantor.

Idaho 1942 w.m. Jesse Stone. (MF) *Idaho.* Roy Rogers and Smiley Burnette appeared in *Idaho.*

I'd've Baked a Cake, *see* **If I Knew You Were Comin' I'd've Baked a Cake**

If 1934 w. Robert Hargreaves, Stanley J. Damerell m. Tolchard Evans. This song was popularly revived in 1951.

If 1971 w.m. David A. Gates. This song was most popular in 1973.

If a Body Meet a Body, *see* **Comin' Thro' the Rye**

If a Girl Like You Loved a Boy Like Me 1905 w.m. Will D. Cobb, Gus Edwards

If Anyone Falls 1984 w.m. Stevie Nicks, Sandy Stewart

If Dreams Come True 1958 w. Al Stillman m. Robert Allen

If Ever I Would Leave You 1960 w. Alan Jay Lerner m. Frederick Loewe. (MT) *Camelot.* (MF) *Camelot.* Julie Andrews and Richard Burton appeared in the stage production of *Camelot.* Vanessa Redgrave and Richard Harris appeared in the film production of *Camelot.*

If Ever You're in My Arms Again 1984 w.m. Tom Snow, Cynthia Weil, Michael Masser

If He Can Fight Like He Can Love, Good Night Germany 1918 w. Grant Clarke m. Howard E. Rogers

If He Comes In, I'm Going Out 1910 w. Cecil Mack m. Chris Smith

If He Walked into My Life 1966 w.m. Jerry Herman. (MT) *Mame.* (MT) *Jerry's Girls.* (MF) *Mame.* Angela Lansbury appeared in the stage production of *Mame.* Dorothy Loudon, Chita Rivera and Leslie Uggams appeared in *Jerry's Girls.* Lucille Ball appeared in the film production of *Mame.*

If I Can't Have You 1978 w.m. Barry Gibb, Maurice Gibb, Robin Gibb (F) *Saturday Night Fever.* John Travolta appeared in *Saturday Night Fever.*

If I Could Be with You One Hour Tonight 1926 w.m. Henry Creamer, Jimmy P. Johnson. (MF) *The Man I Love.* (F) *Flamingo Road.* Ida Lupino and Robert Alda appeared in *The Man I Love.* Joan Crawford appeared in *Flamingo Road.*

If I Didn't Care 1939 w.m. Jack Lawrence. Theme song of The Ink Spots.

If I Fell 1964 w.m. John Lennon, Paul McCartney. (MT) *Beatlemania.*

If I Give My Heart to You 1954 w.m. Jimmie Crane, Al Jacobs, Jimmy Brewster

If I Had a Girl Like You 1925 w.m. Billy Rose, Mort Dixon, Ray Henderson. (MF) *Children of Dreams.* Paul Gregory and Margaret Schilling appeared in *Children of Dreams.*

If I Had a Hammer 1958 w.m. Lee Hays, Pete Seeger. This song was popularly revived in 1962 and 1963.

If I Had a Talking Picture of You 1929 w. B.G. DeSylva, Lew Brown m. Ray Henderson. (MF) *Sunny Side Up.* (MF) *The Best Things in Life Are Free.* Janet Gaynor and Joe E. Brown appeared in *Sunny Side Up.* Gordon MacRae, Dan Dailey, and Ernest Borgnine appeared in *The Best Things in Life Are Free,* biopic of song writers DeSylva, Brown, and Henderson.

If I Had a Thousand Lives To Live 1908 w. Sylvester Maguire m. Alfred Solman

If I Had My Druthers 1956 w. Johnny Mercer m. Gene De Paul. (MT) *Li'l Abner.* (MF) *Li'l Abner.* Stubby Kaye appeared in the film production of *Li'l Abner.*

If I Had My Life To Live Over 1950 w.m. Larry Vincent, Harry Tobias, Moe Jaffe

If I Had My Way 1913 w. Lou Klein m. James Kendis. (MF) *If I Had My Way.* (MF) *Sunbonnet Sue.* Bing Crosby and Blanche Ring appeared in *If I Had My Way.* Gale Storm and Phil Regan appeared in *Sunbonnet Sue.*

If I Had the Wings of an Angel, *see* **The Prisoner's Song**

If I Had You 1928 w.m. Ted Shapiro, Jimmy Campbell, Reginald Connelly. (MF) *Under the Clock.* (MF) *You Were Meant for Me.* Dan Dailey and Oscar Levant appeared in *You Were Meant for Me.*

If I Knew You Were Comin' I'd've Baked a Cake 1950 w.m. Al Hoffman, Robert Merrill, Clem Watts. Robert Merrill, whose real name is Henry Lavan, claims to have written some three thousand songs prior to this, his first hit.

If I Knock the "L" Out of Kelly 1916 w. Sam M. Lewis, Joe Young m. Bert Grant

If I Lost You 1957 w.m. Tolchard Evans, Richard Mullan

If I Love Again 1932 w. John P. Murray m. Ben Oakland. (MT) *Hold Your Horses.* Ona Munson, Joe Cook and Harriet Hoctor appeared in *Hold Your Horses.*

If I Loved You 1945 w. Oscar Hammerstein II m. Richard Rodgers. (MT) *Carousel.* (MF) *Carousel.* Jan Clayton and John Raitt appeared in the stage production of *Carousel.* Gordon MacRae and Shirley Jones appeared in the film production of *Carousel.*

If I May 1955 w.m. Rose Marie McCoy, Charles Singleton

If I Only Had a Brain 1939 w. E.Y. Harburg m. Harold Arlen. (MF) *The Wizard of Oz.* Jack Haley, Ray Bolger, Bert Lahr, and Judy Garland appeared in *The Wizard of Oz.*

If I Only Had Wings 1940 w.m. Sid Colin, Ronnie Aldrich

If I Ruled the World 1965 w. Leslie Bricusse m. Cyril Ornadel. (MT) *Pickwick.* Harry Secombe appeared in *Pickwick.* Ivor Novello Award winner 1963.

If I Said You Had a Beautiful Body (Would You Hold It Against Me) 1979 w.m. David Bellamy

If I Should Fall in Love Again 1940 w.m. Jack Popplewell

If I Should Lose You 1935 w.m. Leo Robin, Ralph Rainger. (MF) *Rose of the Rancho.* John Boles and Gladys Sworthout appeared in *Rose of the Rancho.*

If I Should Plant a Tiny Seed of Love 1909 w.m. James W. Tate, Ballard MacDonald

If I Thought You'd Ever 1970 w.m. John Cameron

If I Was a Millionaire 1910 w. Will D. Cobb m. Gus Edwards

If I Were a Bell 1950 w.m. Frank Loesser. (MT) *Guys and Dolls.* (MF) *Guys and Dolls.* Robert Alda and Vivian Blaine appeared in the stage production of *Guys and Dolls.* Frank Sinatra, Jean Simmons, and Marlon Brando appeared in the film production of *Guys and Dolls.*

If I Were a Blackbird 1950 w.m. traditional, from England. This song was popularly revived in 1950.

If I Were a Carpenter 1966 w.m. Tim Hardin. This song was popularly revived in 1970.

If I Were a Rich Man 1964 w. Sheldon Harnick m. Jerry Bock. (MT) *Fiddler on the Roof.* (MF) *Fiddler on the Roof.* Zero Mostel appeared in the stage production of *Fiddler on the Roof.*

If I Were King 1930 w.m. Newell Chase, Leo Robin, Sam Coslow. (MF) *The Vagabond King.* (F) *If I Were King.* Jeanette MacDonald and Dennis King appeared in the 1930 film production of *The Vagabond King.* Ronald Colman and Basil Rathbone appeared in *If I Were King.*

If I'm Going To Die I'm Going To Have Some Fun 1907 w.m. George M. Cohan. (MT) *The Honeymooners*

If I'm Lucky 1946 w. Edgar De Lange m. Josef Myrow. (MF) *If I'm Lucky.* Vivian Blaine, Perry Como, Harry James, and Carmen Miranda appeared in *If I'm Lucky.*

If It Takes Forever, *see* **I Will Wait for You**

If It Wasn't for the 'ouses in Between 1900 w.m. Edgar Bateman, George Le Brunn

If Jack Were Only Here, *see* **Mother Was a Lady**

If Love Were All 1929 w.m. Noël Coward. (MT) *Bitter Sweet.* (MF) *Bitter Sweet.* Jeanette MacDonald and Nelson Eddy appeared in the film production of *Bitter Sweet.*

If Momma Was Married 1959 w. Stephen Sondheim m. Jule Styne. (MT) *Gypsy.* (MT) *Side by Side by Sondheim.* (MF) *Gypsy.* Ethel Merman appeared in the stage production of *Gypsy.* Millicent Martin and Julie N. McKenzie appeared in *Side by Side by Sondheim.* Rosalind Russell appeared in the film production of *Gypsy.*

If Money Talks, It Ain't on Speaking Terms with Me 1902 w.m. J. Fred Helf

If Only You Were Mine 1899 w. Harry B. Smith m. Victor Herbert. (MT) *The Singing Girl.*

If the Moon Turns Green 1935 w.m. Bernard D. Hanighan

If the Phone Doesn't Ring, It's Me 1986 w.m. Jimmy Buffett, Will Jennings

If the Rain's Got To Fall 1965 w.m. David Heneker. (MT) *Half a Sixpence.*

If the Waters Could Speak As They Flow 1887 w.m. Charles Graham

If There Is Someone Lovelier Than You 1934 w. Howard Dietz m. Arthur Schwartz. (MT) *Revenge With Music.* Libby Holman and Ilka Chase appeared in *Revenge With Music.*

If This Is It 1984 w.m. John Colla, Huey Lewis

If This Isn't Love 1946 w. E.Y. Harburg m. Burton Lane. (MT) *Finian's Rainbow.* Albert Sharpe and David Wayne appeared in *Finian's Rainbow.*

If Those Lips Could Only Speak 1907 w.m. Charles Ridgewell, Will Godwin

If Washington Should Come to Life 1906 w.m. George M. Cohan. (MT) *George Washington, Jr.*

If We Can't Be the Same Old Sweethearts, We'll Just Be the Same Old Friends 1915 w. Joe McCarthy m. James V. Monaco

If We Only Have Love 1968 Eng.w. Eric Blau, Mort Shuman m. Jacques Brel. (MT) *Jacques Brel Is Alive and Well and Living in Paris.*

If Winter Comes 1922 w.m. Melville Gideon, Clifford Grey

If You Are But a Dream 1945 w.m. Moe Jaffe, Jack Fulton, Nat Bonx. Based on Anton Rubinstein's "Romance" in E-flat.

If You Believe (MT) *Lena Horne: The Lady and Her Music.* Lena Horne appeared in *Lena Horne: The Lady and Her Music.*

If You Can't Sing It You'll Have To Swing It (Mister Paganini) 1936 w.m. Sam Coslow. (MF) *Rhythm on the Range.* Bing Crosby and Martha Raye appeared in *Rhythm on the Range.*

If You Catch a Little Cold 1951 w.m. Hal Borne, Buddy Kaye

If You Could Care for Me 1918 w.m. Herman Darewski, E. Ray Goetz, Arthur Wimperis. (MT) *As You Were.* (MF) *The Time, the Place and the Girl.* (F) *Task Force.* John Humphries and Alice Delysia appeared in the British production of *As You Were*. James Kirkwood and Betty Compson appeared in *The Time, the Place and the Girl*. Gary Cooper appeared in *Task Force*.

If You Could Read My Mind　1970　w.m. Gordon Lightfoot

If You Could See Her　1967　w. Fred Ebb　m. John Kander. (MT) *Cabaret*. (MF) *Cabaret*. Joel Grey and Lotte Lenya appeared in the stage production of *Cabaret*. Liza Minnelli and Joel Grey appeared in the film production of *Cabaret*.

If You Don't Want My Peaches, You'd Better Stop Shaking My Tree　1914　w.m. Irving Berlin

If You Ever Change Your Mind　1980　w.m. Parker McGee, Bob Gundry

If You Ever Go to Ireland　1944　w.m. Art Noel

If You Go (Away)　1951　w.m. Geoffrey Parsons, Michael Ember. (F) *Night Without Stars*. David Farrar appeared in *Night Without Stars*. From the French ''Si Tu Partais.''

If You Had All the World and Its Gold　1916　w.m. Bartley Costello, Harry Edelheit, Al Piantadosi

If You Happen To See the Most Beautiful Girl in the World, *see* **The Most Beautiful Girl in the World**

If You Knew Susie, Like I Know Susie　1925　w.m. B.G. DeSylva, Joseph Meyer. (MT) *Big Boy*. (MT) *Kid Boots*. (MF) *The Great Ziegfeld*. (MF) *The Eddie Cantor Story*. (MF) *The Benny Goodman Story*.

If You Leave　1986　w.m. Andy McCluskey, Paul David Humphreys, Martin Cooper

If You Leave Me Now　1976　w.m. Peter Cetera

If You Look in Her Eyes　1918　w. Otto Harbach　m. Louis A. Hirsch. (MT) *Going Up*. Frank Craven and Ruth Donnelly appeared in the American production of *Going Up*. Marjorie Gordon and Evelyn Laye appeared in the British production of *Going Up*.

If You Love Me (I Won't Care)　1953　w.m. Marguerite Monnot, Edith Piaf, Geoffrey Parsons. This song was popularly revived in 1959.

If You Love Me Darling, Tell Me with Your Eyes　1887　w. Samuel Minturn Peck　m. Hubbard T. Smith

If You Love Somebody Set Them Free　1985　w.m. Gordon ''Sting'' Sumner

If You Please　1943　w. Johnny Burke　m. Jimmy Van Heusen. (MF) *Dixie*. Bing Crosby and Dorothy Lamour appeared in *Dixie*.

If You Remember Me　1979　w.m. Carole Bayer Sager, Marvin Hamlisch. (F) *The Champ*.

If You See My Sweetheart　1897　w.m. Paul Dresser

If You Should Ever Need Me (You'll Always Find Me Here)　1931　w. Al Dubin　m. Joe Burke

If You Talk in Your Sleep, Don't Mention My Name　1911　w. A. Seymour Brown　m. Nat D. Ayer

If You Wanna Be Happy　1963　w.m. Frank J. Guida, Carmela Guida, Joseph Royster

If You Want the Rainbow (You Must Have the Rain)　1929　w.m. Billy Rose, Mort Dixon, Oscar Levant. (MF) *My Man*. Fanny Brice and Guinn Williams appeared in *My Man*.

If You Were I and I Were You　1908　w. Henry Blossom　w. Victor Herbert. (MT) *Prima Donna*.

If You Were Mine　1935　w.m. Johnny Mercer, Matt Malneck. (MF) *To Beat the Band*. Helen Broderick and Hugh Herbert appeared in *To Beat the Band*.

If You Were Only Mine　1932　w. Charles Newman　m. Isham Jones

If You Were the Only Girl in the World　1916　w. Clifford Grey　m. Nat D. Ayer. (MT) *The Bing Boys Are Here*. (MF) *The Vagabond Lover*. (MF) *Both Ends of the Candle*. George Robey and Violet Loraine appeared in *The Bing Boys Are Here*. Rudy Vallee appeared in *The Vagabond Lover*. This song was popularly revived in 1925 and again in 1929.

If You're a Viper, *see* **The Viper's Drag**

If You're in Love You'll Waltz　1926　w. Joseph McCarthy　m. Harry Tierney. (MT) *Rio Rita*. (MF) *Rio Rita* (1929). (MF) *Rio Rita* (1942). Ethelind Terry and J. Harold Murray appeared in the stage production of *Rio Rita*. Bert Wheeler and John Boles appeared in the 1929 film production of *Rio Rita*. Kathryn Grayson, Bud Abott, and Lou Costello appeared in the 1942 film production of *Rio Rita*.

If You're Irish Come into the Parlour　1920　w.m. Shaun Glenville, Frank Miller

If You're Ready (Come Go with Me)　1973　w.m. Ray Jackson, Carl Hampton, Homer Banks

If You've Got the Time, We've Got the Beer　1971　w.m. Bill Backer. This song was written for a Miller High Life Beer commercial promotion campaign.

Igy (What a Beautiful World)　1983　w.m. Donald Fagen

II Bacio, *see* **Bacio, II**

I'll Always Be in Love with You　1929　w.m. Bud Green, Herman Ruby, Sam H. Stept. (MF) *Stepping High*. (MF) *Syncopation*. Dorothy Lee, Ian Hunter, and Adolphe Menjou appeared in *Syncopation*.

I'll Always Be with You　1945　w.m. Marjorie Goetschius, Edna Osser

(I'm Just an Old Chunk of Coal But) I'll Be a Diamond Someday　1981　w.m. Billy Joe Shaver

I'll Be Around　1942　w.m. Alec Wilder. (MF) *The Joe Louis Story*.

I'll Be Glad When You're Dead, You Rascal You, *see* **You Rascal You**

I'll Be Good Because of You　1931　w.m. Ray Noble, Alan Murray

I'll Be Good to You　1976　w.m. Louis Johnson, George Johnson, Senora Sam

I'll Be Happy When the Preacher Makes You Mine　1919　w. Sam M. Lewis, Joe Young　m. Walter Donaldson

I'll Be Home　1956　w.m. Ferdinand Washington, Stan Lewis

I'll Be Home for Christmas　1943　w.m. Kim Gannon, Walter Kent, Buck Ram

I'll Be in Virginia in the Morning, *see* **Let It Rain! Let It Pour!**

I'll Be Ready When the Great Day Comes　1882　w.m. James S. Putman

I'll Be Seeing You 1938 w. Irving Kahal m. Sammy Fain. (MT) *Right This Way.* (MT) *The 1940's Radio Hour.* (F) *I'll Be Seeing You.* Joe E. Lewis and Guy Robertson appeared in *Right This Way.* Ginger Rogers and Shirley Temple appeared in *I'll Be Seeing You.* This song was popularly revived in 1944.

I'll Be There 1955 w.m. Jerry Wayne

I'll Be with You in Apple Blossom Time 1920 w. Neville Fleeson m. Albert Von Tilzer. (MF) *Buck Privates.* The Andrews Sisters appeared in *Buck Privates.* This song was popularly revived in 1941.

I'll Be with You When the Roses Bloom Again 1901 w. Will D. Cobb m. Gus Edwards

I'll Be Your Sweetheart 1900 w.m. Harry Dacre. (MF) *I'll Be Your Sweetheart.*

I'll Be Yours (J'Attendrai) 1938 Fr.w. Louis Poterat. Eng.w. Anna Sosenko m. Dino Olivieri. This song was popularly revived in 1945. Theme song of Jean Sablon.

I'll Build a Stairway to Paradise 1922 w. B.G. DeSylva, Ira Gershwin (Arthur Francis) m. George Gershwin. (MT) *George White's Scandals of 1922.* (MT) *Stop Flirting.* (MF) *Rhapsody in Blue.* (MF) *An American in Paris.* Paul Whiteman, W.C. Fields, and Ed Wynn appeared in *George White's Scandals of 1922.* Oscar Levant, Robert Alda, and Alexis Smith appeared in *Rhapsody in Blue,* biopic of composer George Gershwin. Gene Kelly and Leslie Caron appeared in *An American in Paris.*

I'll Buy That Dream 1945 w. Herb Magidson m. Allie Wrubel. (MF) *Sing Your Way Home.* Jack Haley and Anne Jeffreys appeared in *Sing Your Way Home.*

I'll Buy You a Star 1951 w. Dorothy Fields m. Arthur Schwartz. (MT) *A Tree Grows in Brooklyn.* Shirley Booth and Johnny Johnston appeared in *A Tree Grows in Brooklyn.*

I'll Close My Eyes 1945 w. Buddy Kaye m. Billy Reid. (MF) *Six Five Special.* This song was also popular in 1947.

I'll Come When You Call 1955 w.m. Josephine Caryll, David Caryll

I'll Dance at Your Wedding 1947 w. Herb Magidson m. Ben Oakland

I'll Find You 1957 w.m. Tolchard Evans, Richard Mullan. (F) *Sea Wife.* Richard Burton appeared in *Sea Wife.* Ivor Novello Award winner 1957.

I'll Follow My Secret Heart 1934 w.m. Noël Coward. (MT) *Conversation Piece.* Noël Coward and Yvonne Printemps appeared in *Conversation Piece.*

I'll Follow the Sun 1964 w.m. John Lennon, Paul McCartney

I'll Follow You 1931 w.m. Fred E. Ahlert, Roy Turk

I'll Forget You 1921 w.m. Annelu Burns, Ernest R. Ball

I'll Get By (As Long As I Have You) 1928 w. Roy Turk m. Fred E. Ahlert. (F) *A Guy Named Joe.* (MF) *Follow the Boys.* (MF) *You Were Meant for Me.* (MF) *I'll Get By.* (MF) *A Star Is Born.* (MF) *Both Ends of the Candle.* Spencer Tracy and Irene Dunne appeared in *A Guy Named Joe.* Marlene Dietrich and Dinah Shore appeared in *Follow the Boys.* Jeanne Crain and Dan Dailey appeared in *You Were Meant for Me.*

Gloria De Haven and Dennis Day appeared in *I'll Get By.* Judy Garland and James Mason appeared in *A Star Is Born.* This song was popularly revived in 1944.

I'll Go Home with Bonnie Jean 1947 w. Alan Jay Lerner m. Frederick Loewe. (MT) *Brigadoon.* (MF) *Brigadoon.* Gene Kelly and Cyd Charisse appeared in the film production of *Brigadoon.*

I'll Keep You Satisfied 1963 w.m. John Lennon, Paul McCartney

I'll Know 1950 w.m. Frank Loesser. (MT) *Guys and Dolls.* (MF) *Guys and Dolls.*

I'll Make a Man of You 1914 w.m. Herman Finck, Arthur Wimperis. (MT) *The Passing Show of 1914.*

I'll Make Up for Everything 1947 w.m. Ross Parker

I'll Miss You in the Evening 1932 w.m. Irving Berlin

I'll Never Be Free 1950 w.m. Bennie Benjamin, George Weiss

I'll Never Be Jealous Again 1954 w.m. Richard Adler, Jerry Ross. (MT) *The Pajama Game.* (MF) *The Pajama Game.* Doris Day appeared in the film production of *The Pajama Game.*

I'll Never Be the Same 1932 w.m. Gus Kahn, Matt Malneck, Frank Signorelli

I'll Never Fall in Love Again 1968 w. Hal David m. Burt Bacharach. (MT) *Promises, Promises.*

I'll Never Find Another You 1965 w.m. Tom Springfield. Ivor Novello Award winner 1965.

I'll Never Get Over You 1963 w.m. Gordon Mills

I'll Never Have To Dream Again 1932 w.m. Isham Jones, Charles Newman

I'll Never Let a Day Pass By 1941 w. Frank Loesser m. Victor Schertzinger. (MF) *Kiss the Boys Goodbye.* Mary Martin, Oscar Levant, and Don Ameche appeared in *Kiss the Boys Goodbye.*

I'll Never Love Again (La Borrachita) 1920 Sp.w. Ignacio F. Esperon Eng.w. Al Stewart m. Ignacio F. Esperon

I'll Never Love This Way Again 1979 w.m. Will Jennings, Richard Kerr

I'll Never Say "Never Again" Again 1935 w.m. Harry Woods

I'll Never Smile Again 1940 w.m. Ruth Lowe (MT) *The 1940's Radio Hour.*

I'll Never Stop Loving You 1955 w. Sammy Cahn m. Nicholas Brodszky. (MF) *Love Me or Leave Me.* Doris Day and James Cagney appeared in *Love Me or Leave Me,* biopic of singer Ruth Etting.

I'll Only Miss Her When I Think of Her 1965 w. Sammy Cahn m. Jimmy Van Heusen. (MT) *Skyscraper.* Julie Harris appeared in *Skyscraper.*

I'll Play for You 1975 w.m. Jimmy Seals, Dash Crofts

I'll Pray for You 1940 w.m. Roy King, Stanley Hill

I'll (I) Remember April 1942 w.m. Don Raye, Gene De Paul, Patricia Johnston. (MF) *Ride 'Em Cowboy.* (MF) *I'll Remember April.* Bud Abbott, Lou Costello, and Ella Fitzgerald appeared in *Ride 'Em Cowboy.*

I'll Remember Tonight 1958 w.m. Paul Francis Webster, Sammy Fain

I'll Remember You 1919 w. Frank Stammers m. Harold Orlob. (MT) *Nothing But Love.*

I'll Say She Does 1918 w.m. B.G. DeSylva, Gus Kahn, Al Jolson. (MT) *Sinbad.*

I'll See You Again 1929 w.m. Noeël Coward. (MT) *Bitter Sweet.* (MF) *Bitter Sweet.* Noël Coward and Evelyn Laye appeared in the American stage production of *Bitter Sweet.* Peggy Wood and George Metaxa appeared in the British stage production of *Bitter Sweet.* Jeanette MacDonald and Nelson Eddy appeared in the film production of *Bitter Sweet.* Theme song of Noël Coward.

I'll See You in C-U-B-A 1920 w.m. Irving Berlin. (MT) *The Greenwich Village Follies.* (MF) *Blue Skies.* Fred Astaire, Bing Crosby, and Trudy Irwin appeared in *Blue Skies.*

I'll See You in My Dreams 1924 w. Gus Kahn m. Isham Jones. (MF) *Follow the Boys.* (MF) *I'll See You in My Dreams.* (MF) *Keep Your Powder Dry.* George Raft appeared in *Follow the Boys.* Doris Day appeared in *I'll See You in My Dreams,* biopic of song writer Gus Kahn. Lana Turner appeared in *Keep Your Powder Dry.* Theme song of Tony Martin.

I'll Sing Thee Songs of Araby 1877 w. William Gorman Wills m. Frederic Clay

I'll Sing You a Thousand Love Songs 1936 w.m. Al Dubin, Harry Warren. (MF) *Cain and Mabel.* Marion Davies and Clark Gable appeared in *Cain and Mabel.*

I'll Stop at Nothing 1965 w.m. Chris Andrews

(You May Not Be an Angel But) I'll String Along with You 1934 w. Al Dubin m. Harry Warren. (MF) *Twenty Million Sweethearts.* (MF) *My Dream Is Yours.* Dick Powell, Ruby Keeler, and Ginger Rogers appeared in *Twenty Million Sweethearts.* Jack Carson and Doris Day appeared in *My Dream Is Yours.*

I'll Take Romance 1937 w. Oscar Hammerstein II m. Ben Oakland. (MF) *I'll Take Romance.* (MF) *Holiday in Havana.* (MF) *The Eddy Duchin Story.* (MF) *Manhattan Angel.* Grace Moore and Melvyn Douglas appeared in *I'll Take Romance.* Desi Arnaz appeared in *Holiday in Havana.* Gloria Jean and Ross Ford appeared in *Manhattan Angel.*

I'll Take You Home Again Kathleen 1876 w.m. Thomas P. Westendorf. This song is often erroneously believed to be a traditional Irish ballad. In fact, it was written in Kentucky (some say Plainfield, Indiana) by Westendorf to cheer up his homesick wife who wished to return East. Her name, though, was Jennie, not Kathleen.

I'll Take You There 1972 w.m. Alvertis Isbell

I'll Tell the Man in the Street 1938 w. Lorenz Hart m. Richard Rodgers. (MT) *I Married an Angel.* (MF) *I Married an Angel.* Vera Zorina and Walter Slezak appeared in the stage production of *I Married an Angel.* Jeanette MacDonald and Nelson Eddy appeared in the film production of *I Married an Angel.*

I'll Think of You 1941 w.m. Gerry Mason

I'll Walk Alone 1944 w. Sammy Cahn m. Jule Styne. (MF) *Follow the Boys.* (MF) *With a Song in My Heart.* (F)

Three Cheers for the Boys. W.C. Fields, Marlene Dietrich, and Sophie Tucker appeared in *Follow the Boys.* Susan Hayward appeared in *With a Song in My Heart,* biopic of singer Jane Froman.

I'll Walk beside You 1939 w.m. Alan Murray, Edward Lockton

I'll Walk with God 1954 w.m. Paul Francis Webster, Nicholas Brodszky

Ill Wind (You're Blowin' Me No Good) 1934 w.m. Ted Koehler, Harold Arlen

I'm a Believer 1967 w.m. Neil Diamond

I'm a Big Girl Now 1946 w.m. Al Hoffman, Milton Drake, Jerry Livingston

I'm a-Comin' a-Courtin' Corabelle 1948 w.m. Charles Newman, Allie Wrubel

I'm a Ding Dong Daddy from Dumas 1928 w.m. Phil Baxter

I'm a Dreamer (Aren't We All) 1929 w. B.G. DeSylva, Lew Brown m. Ray Henderson. (MF) *Sunny Side Up.* (MF) *Holy Terror.* (MF) *The Best Things in Life Are Free.* Janet Gaynor and Joe E. Brown appeared in *Sunny Side Up.* Humphrey Bogart and James Kirkwood appeared in *Holy Terror.* Gordon MacRae, Dan Dailey, and Ernest Borgnine appeared in *The Best Things in Life Are Free,* biopic of song writers DeSylva, Brown, and Henderson.

I'm a Fool To Care 1954 w.m. Ted Daffan

I'm a Fool To Want You 1951 w.m. Frank Sinatra, Joel Herron, Jack Wolf

I'm a Gigolo 1929 w.m. Cole Porter. (MT) *Wake Up and Dream.* Jack Buchanan and Jessie Matthews appeared in *Wake Up and Dream.*

I'm a-Leavin' Cheyenne, *see* **Goodbye Ol' Paint**

I'm a Little Bit Fonder of You 1925 w.m. Irving Caesar

I'm a Little Blackbird Looking for a Bluebird 1924 w.m. George Meyer, Arthur Johnston, Roy Turk, Grant Clarke. (MT) *Dixie to Broadway.* Florence Mills and Shelton Brooks appeared in *Dixie to Broadway.*

I'm a Loser 1964 w.m. John Lennon, Paul McCartney

I'm a Popular Man 1907 w.m. George M. Cohan. (MT) *The Honeymooners.*

I'm a Rambling Wreck from Georgia Tech, *see* **Rambling Wreck from Georgia Tech**

I'm a Yankee Doodle Dandy, *see* **Yankee Doodle Boy**

I'm Afraid To Come Home in the Dark 1907 w. Harry H. Williams m. Egbert Van Alstyne. See also Part I, 1908.

I'm All Bound 'Round with the Mason—Dixon Line 1917 w. Sam M. Lewis, Joe Young m. Jean Schwartz

I'm All Smiles 1965 w. Herbert Martin m. Michael Leonard. (MT) *The Yearling.*

I'm Alright, or, **(Theme from) Caddyshack** 1980 w.m. Kenny Loggins. (F) *Caddyshack.*

I'm Always Chasing Rainbows 1918 w. Joseph McCarthy m. Harry Carroll. Based on the ''Fantaisie Impromptu'' in C-sharp minor by Chopin. (MT) *Oh, Look!.* (MF) *Ziegfeld Girl.* (MF) *The Dolly Sisters.* (MF) *The Merry Monihans.*

Judy Garland, James Stewart and Lana Turner appeared in *Ziegfeld Girl*. June Haver and Betty Grable appeared in *The Dolly Sisters*. Donald O'Connor and Peggy Ryan appeared in *The Merry Monihans*. This song was popularly revived in 1946.

I'm Always True to You in My Fashion, *see* **Always True to You in My Fashion**

I'm an Airman 1926 w.m. McGhee, Russell

I'm an Indian Too 1946 w.m. Irving Berlin. (MT) *Annie Get Your Gun*. (MF) *Annie Get Your Gun*. Ethel Merman and Ray Middleton appeared in the stage production of *Annie Get Your Gun*. Betty Hutton and Howard Keel appeared in the film production of *Annie Get Your Gun*.

I'm an Old Cowhand (from the Rio Grande) 1936 w.m. Johnny Mercer. (MF) *Rhythm On the Range*. (MF) *King of the Cowboys*. Bing Crosby and Martha Raye appeared in *Rhythm On the Range*. Roy Rogers and Smiley Burnette appeared in *King of the Cowboys*.

I'm an Ordinary Man 1956 w. Alan Jay Lerner m. Frederick Loewe. (MT) *My Fair Lady*. (MF) *My Fair Lady*. Rex Harrison appeared in both the stage and film productions of *My Fair Lady*.

I'm Awfully Glad I Met You 1909 w. Jack Drislane m. George W. Meyer

I'm Beginning To See the Light 1945 w.m. Harry James, Duke Ellington, Johnny Hodges, Don George. (MF) *The Man from Oklahoma*.

I'm Bringing a Red, Red Rose 1928 w. Gus Kahn m. Walter Donaldson. (MT) *Whoopee*. Eddie Cantor and Ruth Etting appeared in *Whoopee*.

I'm Building Up to an Awful Let-Down 1935 w. Johnny Mercer m. Fred Astaire

I'm Called Little Buttercup 1878 w. William S. Gilbert m. Arthur Sullivan. (MT) *H.M.S. Pinafore*.

I'm Comin' Virginia 1926 w.m. Will Marion Cook, Donald Heywood. (MT) *Africana*. (MT) *Miss Calico*. (MF) *The Benny Goodman Story*. Ethel Waters appeared in *Miss Calico*.

I'm Confessin' That I Love You 1930 w. A.J. Neiburg m. Doc Dougherty, Ellis Reynolds

I'm Crying 1964 w.m. Alan Price, Eric Burdon

I'm Dancing with Tears in My Eyes, *see* **Dancing with Tears in My Eyes**

I'm Depending on You, *see* **Patches**

I'm Dreaming Tonight of My Blue Eyes, *see* **I'm Thinking Tonight of My Blue Eyes**

I'm Easy 1975 w.m. Keith Carradine. (F) *Nashville*. Academy Award winner 1975.

I'm Falling in Love with Someone 1910 w. Rida Johnson Young m. Victor Herbert. (MT) *Naughty Marietta*. (MF) *Naughty Marietta* (1934). (MF) *The Great Victor Herbert*. Jeanette MacDonald, Nelson Eddy, and Elsa Lanchester appeared in the film production of *Naughty Marietta*. Mary Martin and Allan Jones appeared in *The Great Victor Herbert*.

I'm Flying 1954 w. Carolyn Leigh m. Mark Charlap. (MT) *Peter Pan*. Mary Martin appeared in *Peter Pan*.

I'm Forever Blowing Bubbles 1919 w.m. Jean Kenbrovin, John William Kellette. (MT) *Passing Show of 1918*. (MF) *On Moonlight Bay*. Doris Day and Gordon MacRae appeared in *On Moonlight Bay*.

I'm Getting Sentimental over You 1932 w. Ned Washington m. George Bassman. Theme song of Tommy Dorsey.

I'm Getting Tired So I Can Sleep 1942 w.m. Irving Berlin. (MT) *This Is the Army*. (MF) *This Is the Army*. Kate Smith and Ronald Reagan appeared in the film production of *This Is the Army*.

I'm Glad I Waited for You 1945 w. Sammy Cahn m. Jule Styne. (MF) *Tars and Spars*. Janet Blair, Alfred Drake, and Sid Caesar appeared in *Tars and Spars*.

I'm Glad I'm Not Young Anymore 1958 w. Alan Jay Lerner m. Frederick Loewe. (MF) *Gigi*. Maurice Chevalier and Hermione Gingold appeared in *Gigi*.

I'm Glad There Is You 1942 w.m. Paul M. Mertz, Jimmy Dorsey. (MT) *Lena Horne: The Lady and Her Music*. Lena Horne appeared in *Lena Horne: The Lady and Her Music*. This song was popularly revived in 1952.

I'm Going Back to Himazas 1927 w.m. Fred Austin

I'm Going Back to Kentucky Sue, *see* **Kentucky Sue**

I'm Goin' South 1923 w.m. Abner Silver, Harry Woods. (MT) *Bombo*. (MT) *Kid Boots*.

I'm Going To See You Today 1942 w.m. Joyce Grenfell, Richard Addinsell

I'm Gonna Charleston Back to Charleston 1925 w.m. Roy Turk, Lou Handman

I'm Gonna Get Lit Up (When the Lights Go On in London) 1943 w.m. Hubert Gregg

I'm Gonna Get Married 1959 w.m. Lloyd Price, Harold Logan

I'm Gonna Hire a Wino To Decorate Our Home 1982 w.m. DeWayne Blackwell

I'm Gonna Live till I Die 1950 w.m. Walter Kent, Mann Curtis, Al Hoffman. (MF) *On the Sunny Side of the Street*. (F) *This Could Be the Night*. Frankie Laine and Billy Daniels appeared in *On the Sunny Side of the Street*. Jean Simmons and Anthony Franciosa appeared in *This Could Be the Night*.

I'm Gonna Love That Guy (Like He's Never Been Loved Before) 1945 w.m. Frances Ash. See also Part I, 1945.

I'm Gonna Love You 1979 w.m. Michael Smotherman

I'm Gonna Love You Just a Little More Baby 1973 w.m. Barry White

I'm Gonna Move to (the) Outskirts of Town 1944 w.m. Roy Jordan

I'm Gonna Pin My Medal On the Girl I Left Behind 1918 w.m. Irving Berlin

I'm Gonna Ring the Bell Tonight 1953 w. Sammy Cahn m. Vernon Duke. (MF) *April in Paris*. Doris Day and Ray Bolger appeared in *April in Paris*.

I'm Gonna Sit Right Down and Write Myself a Letter 1935 w. Joe Young m. Fred E. Ahlert. (MT) *Ain't Misbehavin'*. (MT) *Lena Horne: The Lady and Her Music*. Debbie Allen and Nell Carter appeared in *Ain't Misbehavin'*. Lena Horne appeared in *Lena Horne: The Lady and Her Music*. This song was popularly revived in 1957.

I'm Gonna Wash My Hands of You 1935 w.m. Franz Vienna, Eddie Pola

I'm Gonna Wash That Man Right Outa My Hair 1949 w. Oscar Hammerstein II m. Richard Rodgers. (MT) *South Pacific*. (MF) *South Pacific*. Mary Martin appeared in the stage production of *South Pacific*. Mitzi Gaynor appeared in the film production of *South Pacific*.

I'm Hans Christian Andersen 1952 w.m. Frank Loesser. (MF) *Hans Christian Andersen*. Danny Kaye appeared in *Hans Christian Andersen*.

I'm Happy When I'm Hiking 1931 w.m. Ralph Butler, Raymond Wallace, Reginald Connelly, James Campbell

I'm Henery the Eighth (I Am) 1911 w.m. R.P. Weston, Fred Murray. This song was popularly revived in 1965. English music hall artist Harry Champion popularly sang this song with "almost desperate gusto, his face bathed with sweat and his arms and legs flying."

I'm Humming, I'm Whistling, I'm Singing 1934 w.m. Mack Gordon, Harry Revel. (MF) *She Loves Me Not*. Bing Crosby and Miriam Hopkins appeared in *She Loves Me Not*.

I'm in a Dancing Mood 1936 w.m. Maurice Sigler, Al Goodhart, Al Hoffman. (MT) *This'll Make You Whistle*. (MF) *This'll Make You Whistle*. Jack Buchanan and Elsie Randolph appeared in both the stage and film productions of *This'll Make You Whistle*.

I'm in Love 1919 w. William Le Baron m. Fritz Kreisler. (MT) *Apple Blossoms*.

I'm in Love Again 1925 w.m. Cole Porter. (MT) *The Greenwich Village Follies* (1924). (MT) *Up with the Lark*. This song was popularly revived in 1951.

I'm in Love Again 1956 w.m. Antoine "Fats" Domino, Dave Bartholomew

I'm in Love with a Wonderful Guy 1949 w. Oscar Hammerstein II m. Richard Rodgers. (MT) *South Pacific*. (MF) *South Pacific*. Mary Martin appeared in the stage production of *South Pacific*. Mitzi Gaynor appeared in the film production of *South Pacific*.

I'm in Love with Miss Logan 1952 w.m. Ronny Graham. (MT) *New Faces of 1952*.

I'm in Love with Two Sweethearts 1945 w.m. Elton Box, Desmond Cox, Lewis Ilda

I'm in the Market for You 1930 w.m. Joseph McCarthy, James Hanley. (MF) *High Society Blues*. Janet Gaynor and William Collier, Sr., appeared in *High Society Blues*.

I'm in the Mood for Dancing 1981 w.m. Ben Findon, Michael Myers, Robert Puzey. Ivor Novello Award winner 1980–81.

I'm in the Mood for Love 1935 w. Dorothy Fields m. Jimmy McHugh. (MF) *Every Night at Eight*. (F) *Between Two Women*. (MF) *People Are Funny*. (F) *That's My Boy*. Frances Langford and George Raft appeared in *Every Night At Eight*. Van Johnson and Lionel Barrymore appeared in *Between Two Women*. Jack Haley and Rudy Vallee appeared in *People Are Funny*. Dean Martin and Jerry Lewis appeared in *That's My Boy*.

I'm Just a Baby 1962 w.m. Jerry Lordan

I'm Just a Lonely Boy, *see* **Lonely Boy**

I'm Just a Vagabond Lover 1929 w.m. Rudy Vallee, Leon Zimmerman. (MF) *The Vagabond Lover*. (MF) *Glorifying the American Girl*. Rudy Vallee appeared in both *The Vagabond Lover* and *Glorifying the American Girl*. Helen Morgan, Rudy Vallee, and Eddie Cantor appeared in *Glorifying the American Girl*.

I'm Just an Old Chunk of Coal But I'll Be a Diamond Someday, *see* **I'll Be a Diamond Someday**

I'm Just Wild About Animal Crackers 1926 w.m. Sam Coslow, Fred Rich, Harry Link

I'm Just Wild About Harry 1921 w. Noble Sissle m. Eubie Blake. (MT) *Shuffle Along*. (MT) *Eubie!*. (MF) *Babes in Arms*. (MF) *Rose of Washington Square*. (MF) *Broadway*. (MF) *Is Everybody Happy*. (MF) *Jolson Sings Again*. Noble Sissle and Florence Mills appeared in *Shuffle Along*. Judy Garland and Mickey Rooney appeared in *Babes in Arms*. Al Jolson and Tyrone Power appeared in *Rose of Washington Square*. George Raft, Pat O'Brien, and Janet Blair appeared in *Broadway*. Bob Haymes appeared in *Is Everybody Happy*, biopic of bandleader Ted Lewis. Larry Parks appeared in *Jolson Sings Again*. Theme song of Florence Mills. This song was used in 1948 for Harry Truman's Presidential campaign theme song.

I'm Late 1951 w.m. Bob Hilliard, Sammy Fain. (MF) *Alice in Wonderland*. The voices of Sterling Holloway and Richard Haydn appeared in *Alice in Wonderland*.

I'm Leaving It All Up to You 1963 w.m. Dewey Terry, Jr., Don F. Harris. This song was popularly revived in 1974.

I'm Like a Fish Out of Water 1937 w.m. Richard A. Whiting, Johnny Mercer. (MF) *Hollywood Hotel*. Dick Powell and Rosemary Lane performed this song in *Hollywood Hotel*, wading fully clothed in a small fountain.

I'm Looking for a Guy Who Plays Alto and Baritone and Doubles on a Clarinet and Wears a Size Thirty-seven Suit 1941 w.m. Ox Nelson. This is, apparently, the longest song title ever published.

I'm Looking for a Nice Young Fellow Who Is Looking for a Nice Young Girl 1910 w. Jeff T. Branen m. S.R. Henry, Jeff T. Branen

I'm Looking Over a Four Leaf Clover 1927 w. Mort Dixonm. Harry Woods. (MF) *Jolson Sings Again*. Larry Parks appeared in *Jolson Sings Again*. This song was popularly revived in 1948.

I'm Looking Through You 1966 w.m. John Lennon, Paul McCartney

I'm Making Believe 1944 w. Mack Gordon m. James V. Monaco. (MF) *Sweet and Low Down*. Benny Goodman and Jack Oakie appeared in *Sweet and Low Down*.

I'm Missin' Mammy's Kissin'—And I Know She's Missin' Mine 1921 w. Sidney Clare m. Lew Pollack

I'm Nobody's Baby 1921 w.m. Benny Davis, Milton Ager, Lester Santly. (MF) *Andy Hardy Meets a Debutante*. Judy Garland and Mickey Rooney appeared in *Andy Hardy Meets a Debutante*. This song was popularly revived in 1940.

I'm Not at All in Love 1954 w.m. Richard Adler, Jerry

Ross. (MT) *The Pajama Game.* (MF) *The Pajama Game.* Doris Day appeared in the film production of *The Pajama Game.*

I'm Not in Love 1975 w.m. Eric Stewart, Graham Gouldman. Ivor Novello Award winner 1975–76.

I'm Not Lisa 1975 w.m. Jessie Colter

I'm Old Fashioned 1942 w. Johnny Mercer m. Jerome Kern. (MF) *You Were Never Lovelier.* Rita Hayworth, Fred Astaire, and Xavier Cugat appeared in *You Were Never Lovelier.*

I'm on a See-Saw 1934 w. Desmond Carter m. Vivian Ellis. (MT) *Jill Darling.* Louise Brown and John Mills appeared in *Jill Darling.*

I'm on Fire 1985 w.m. Bruce Springsteen

I'm on My Way 1935 w. DuBose Heyward m. George Gershwin. (MT) *Porgy and Bess.* (MF) *Porgy and Bess.*

I'm on the Water Wagon Now 1903 w. Paul West m. John W. Bratton

I'm Only Thinking of Him 1965 w. Joe Darion m. Mitch Leigh. (MT) *Man of La Mancha.* (MF) *Man of La Mancha.* Richard Kiley appeared in the stage production of *Man of La Mancha.* Sophia Loren appeared in the film production of *Man of La Mancha.*

I'm Painting the Clouds with Sunshine, *see* **Painting the Clouds with Sunshine**

I'm Playing with Fire 1932 w.m. Irving Berlin

I'm Popeye the Sailor Man, *see* **Popeye the Sailor Man**

I'm Putting All My Eggs in One Basket 1936 w.m. Irving Berlin. (MF) *Follow the Fleet.* Fred Astaire and Ginger Rogers appeared in *Follow the Fleet.*

I'm Shooting High 1935 w. Ted Koehler m. Jimmy McHugh. (MT) *Sugar Babies.* (MF) *King of Burlesque.* Ann Miller and Mickey Rooney appeared in *Sugar Babies.* Alice Faye, Warner Baxter, and Jack Oakie appeared in *King of Burlesque.*

I'm Shy, Mary Ellen, I'm Shy 1911 w.m. Charles Ridgewell, George Stevens

I'm Sittin' High on a Hill Top 1935 w.m. Gus Kahn, Arthur Johnston. (MF) *Thanks a Million.* Dick Powell and Fred Allen appeared in *Thanks a Million.*

I'm Sitting on Top of the World (Just Rolling Along—Just Rolling Along) 1925 w. Sam M. Lewis, Joe Young m. Ray Henderson. (MF) *The Singing Fool.* (MF) *The Jolson Story.* (F) *I'll Cry Tomorrow.* Al Jolson appeared in *The Singing Fool.* Larry Parks appeared in *The Jolson Story.* Susan Hayward appeared in *I'll Cry Tomorrow.*

I'm Sitting Pretty in a Pretty Little City 1923 w.m. Lou Davis, Henry Santly, Abel Baer

I'm So Ashamed 1958 w.m. Ken Hare. Ivor Novello Award winner 1958.

I'm So Excited 1984 w.m. Trevor Lawrence, Anita Pointer, June Pointer, Ruth Pointer

I'm So Lonesome I Could Cry 1949 w.m. Hank Williams. This song was popularly revived in 1966.

I'm Sorry 1960 w.m. Ronnie Self, Dub Albritton

I'm Sorry 1975 w.m. John Denver

I'm Sorry I Made You Cry 1916 w.m. N.J. Clesi. (MF) *Rose of Washington Square.* (MF) *Somebody Loves Me.* Al Jolson and Alice Faye appeared in *Rose of Washington Square.* Betty Hutton appeared in *Somebody Loves Me,* biopic of song spinners Blossom Seeley and Benny Fields.

I'm Stepping Out with a Memory Tonight 1940 w. Herb Magidson m. Allie Wrubel

I'm Still Here 1971 w.m. Stephen Sondheim. (MT) *Follies.* (MT) *Side by Side by Sondheim.* Alexis Smith and Yvonne DeCarlo appeared in *Follies.* Millicent Martin and Julie N. McKenzie appeared in *Side by Side by Sondheim.*

I'm Still Your Mother, Dear, *see* **You're Going Far Away, Lad**

I'm Telling You Now 1965 w.m. Freddie Garrity, Mitch Murray

I'm the Greatest Star 1964 w. Bob Merrill m. Jule Styne. (MT) *Funny Girl.* (MF) *Funny Girl.* Barbra Streisand appeared in both the stage and film productions of *Funny Girl.*

I'm the Last of the Red-Hot Mamas 1929 w.m. Jack Yellen, Milton Ager. (MF) *Honky Tonk.* Sophie Tucker and Audrey Ferris appeared in *Honky Tonk.*

I'm the Lonely One 1964 w.m. Gordon Mills

I'm the Lonesomest Gal in Town 1912 w. Lew Brown m. Albert Von Tilzer. (MF) *Make Believe Ballroom.* (F) *South Sea Sinner.* Shelley Winters and MacDonald Carey appeared in *South Sea Sinner.*

I'm the One 1964 w.m. Gerry Marsden

I'm the Urban Spaceman 1969 w.m. Neil Innes. Ivor Novello Award winner 1968–69.

I'm (Dreaming) Thinking Tonight of My Blue Eyes 1943 w.m. Don Marcotte, A.P. Carter. (MF) *The Man from Music Mountain.* Roy Rogers and Ruth Terry appeared in *The Man from Music Mountain.*

I'm Through with Love 1931 w. Gus Kahn m. Matt Malneck, Fud Livingston. (MF) *Honeymoon Lodge.* (MF) *With a Song in My Heart.* (MF) *Some Like It Hot.* Ozzie Nelson and David Bruce appeared in *Honeymoon Lodge.* Susan Hayward appeared in *With a Song in My Heart,* biopic of singer Jane Froman. Marilyn Monroe, Jack Lemmon and Tony Curtis appeared in *Some Like It Hot.*

I'm Tickled to Death I'm Single 1923 w.m. Melville Gideon, Clifford Seyler

I'm Twenty-One Today 1912 w.m. Alec Kendal

I'm Tying the Leaves So They Won't Come Down 1907 w.m. E.S.S. Huntington, J.F. Helf

I'm Unlucky 1902 w. William Jerome m. Jean Schwartz. (MT) *The Wild Rose.*

I'm Waiting for Ships That Never Come In 1923 w. Jack Yellen, William Raskin m. Abe Ulman

I'm Walkin' 1957 w.m. Antoine "Fats" Domino, Dave Bartholomew

I'm Walking Behind You 1953 w.m. Billy Reid

I'm Wild About Horns on Automobiles That Go "Ta-Ta-Ta-Ta" 1928 w.m. Clarence Gaskill

I'm Wishing 1937 w.m. Larry Morey, Frank Churchill. (MF) *Snow White and the Seven Dwarfs.*

I'm Your Boogie Man 1977 w.m. Harry Casey, Richard Finch

I'm Your Man 1986 w.m. George Michael

I'm Yours 1930 w. E.Y. Harburg m. John W. Green. (F) *Leave It to Lester.* (MF) *The Stooge.* Dean Martin, Jerry Lewis, and Polly Bergen appeared in *The Stooge.*

I'm Yours 1952 w.m. Robert Mellin

Imaginary Lover 1978 w.m. Buddy Buie, Robert Nix, Dean Daughtry

Imagination 1940 w. Johnny Burke m. Jimmy Van Heusen

Immigrant, The 1975 w.m. Neil Sedaka, Phil Cody

Impatient Years, The 1955 w. Sammy Cahn m. James Van Heusen

Imperial Echoes w.m. Arnold Safroni. (R) *BBC Radio News.*

Impossible Dream, The, or, **The Quest** 1966 w. Joe Darion m. Mitch Leigh. (MT) *Man of La Mancha.* (MF) *Man of La Mancha.* Richard Kiley appeared in the stage production of *Man of La Mancha.* Sophia Loren appeared in the film production of *Man of La Mancha.*

In a Chinese Temple Garden 1920 w.m. Albert Ketèlbey

In a Cozy Corner 1901 w. Walter Ford m. John W. Bratton

In a Golden Coach 1953 w.m. Ronald Jamieson, Harry Leon

In a Little Dutch Mill, *see* **Little Dutch Mill**

In a Little Gypsy Tea Room 1935 w. Edgar Leslie m. Joe Burke

In a Little Spanish Town 1926 w. Sam M. Lewis, Joe Young m. Mabel Wayne. (MF) *Ridin' Down the Canyon.* Roy Rogers and Gabby Hayes appeared in *Ridin' Down the Canyon.* This song was popularly revived in 1942.

In a Mist 1928 m. Bix Beiderbecke

In a Monastery Garden 1915 m. Albert William Ketèlbey

In a Party Mood 1943 w.m. Jack Strachey

In a Persian Garden 1896 w. Edward Fitzgerald m. Liza Lehmann. The words are translated from Omar Khayyam's ''Rubáiyát.''

In a Persian Market 1920 w.m. Albert W. Ketèlbey. Albert W. Ketèlbey was a pseudonym for William Aston.

In a Sentimental Mood 1935 w.m. Duke Ellington, Irving Mills, Manny Kurtz. (MT) *Sophisticated Ladies.* Gregory Hines and Phyllis Hyman appeared in *Sophisticated Ladies.*

In a Shanty in Old Shanty Town, *see* **A Shanty in Old Shanty Town**

In Acapulco 1945 w. Mack Gordon m. Harry Warren. (MF) *Diamond Horseshoe.*

In All My Dreams I Dream of You 1910 w.m. Joseph McCarthy, Sr., Al Piantadosi

In America 1980 w.m. Tom Crain, Charlie Daniels, Taz Di Gregorio, Fred Edwards, Charlie Hayward, Jim Marshall

In an Eighteenth Century Drawing Room 1939 w. Jack Lawrence m. Raymond Scott. Based on Mozart's Piano Sonata No. 3, in C, (K.525).

In an Old Dutch Garden 1939 w.m. Mack Gordon, Will Grosz

In Chichicastenango 1940 w. Henry Myers m. Jay Gorney. (MT) *Meet the People.* Nanette Fabray, Marion Colby, and Peggy Ryan appeared in *Meet the People.*

In Dear Old Illinois 1902 w.m. Paul Dresser

In Dulci Jubilo c.1350 w.m. medieval carol, from Germany

In Egern on the Tegern See 1932 w. Oscar Hammerstein II m. Jerome Kern. (MT) *Music in the Air.* Al Shean, Reginald Werrenrath, and Walter Slezak appeared in *Music in the Air.*

In Every Woman 1979 w.m. Nickolas Ashford, Valerie Simpson

In Good Old New York Town 1899 w.m. Paul Dresser

In Heavenly Love Abiding 1864 w. Anna Waring, Sam Wesley m. John Rogers Thomas

In Love for the Very First Time 1955 w.m. Jack Woodman, Paddy Roberts. (F) *An Alligator Named Daisy.* Diana Dors appeared in *An Alligator Named Daisy.* Ivor Novello Award winner 1955.

In Love in Vain 1946 w. Leo Robin m. Jerome Kern. (MF) *Centennial Summer.* Jeanne Crain and Cornel Wilde appeared in *Centennial Summer.*

In Love with Love 1923 w. Anne Caldwell m. Jerome Kern. (MT) *The Stepping Stones.* Fred Stone appeared in *The Stepping Stones.*

In My Arms 1943 w.m. Frank Loesser, Ted Grouya. (F) *See Here, Private Hargrove.* Robert Walker and Donna Reed appeared in *See Here, Private Hargrove.*

In My Harem 1913 w.m. Irving Berlin

In My Life 1966 w.m. John Lennon, Paul McCartney

In My Little Bottom Drawer 1934 w.m. Will Haines, Jimmy Harper, Maurice Beresford. (MF) *Sing As We Go.* Gracie Fields appeared in *Sing As We Go.*

In My Little Red Book 1938 w.m. Al Stillman, Ray Bloch, Nat Simon

In My Little Snapshot Album 1938 w.m. Harry Parr-Davies, Jimmy Harper, Will E. Haines. (MF) *I See Ice.* George Formby appeared in *I See Ice.*

In My Little Tin Box, *see* **Little Tin Box**

In My Merry Oldsmobile 1905 w. Vincent P. Bryan m. Gus Edwards. (MF) *The Merry Monihans.* Peggy Ryan and Donald O'Connor appeared in *The Merry Monihans.* This song, later used for an Oldsmobile commercial promotion campaign, commemorates the first transcontinental auto race of 1904, in which an Oldsmobile won first prize.

In My Own Little Corner 1957 w. Oscar Hammerstein II m. Richard Rodgers. (TV) *Cinderella.*

In My Sweet Little Alice Blue Gown, *see* **Alice Blue Gown**

In Old New York, *or,* **The Streets of New York** 1906 w. Henry Blossom m. Victor Herbert. (MT) *The Red Mill.*

In Other Words, *see* **Fly Me to the Moon**

In Our Little Den of Iniquity 1940 w. Lorenz Hart m. Richard Rodgers. (MT) *Pal Joey.* (MF) *Pal Joey.* Gene Kelly, Van Johnson, and Vivienne Segal appeared in the stage production of *Pal Joey.* Frank Sinatra and Kim Novak appeared in the film production of *Pal Joey.*

In San Francisco, *see* **I Left My Heart in San Francisco**

In Shadowland 1924 w. Sam M. Lewis, Joe Young m. Ruth Brooks, Fred E. Ahlert

In Summer 1963 w.m. Elaine Murtagh, Valerie Murtagh, Ray Adams

In Summertime On Brendon 1911 w.m. Graham Peel, A.E. Housman

In the Air Tonight 1982 w.m. Phil Collins. Ivor Novello Award winner 1981–82.

In the Arms of Love 1966 w.m. Ray Evans, Jay Livingston, Henry Mancini

In the Baggage Coach Ahead 1896 w.m. Gussie L. Davis

In the Blue of Evening 1943 w. Thomas Adair m. Alfred A. D'Artega

In the Bosom of Abraham, *see* **Rock-a My Soul**

In the Chapel in the Moonlight 1936 w.m. William Hill

In the Cool, Cool, Cool of the Evening 1951 w. Johnny Mercer m. Hoagy Carmichael. (MF) *Here Comes the Groom.* Bing Crosby and Alexis Smith appeared in *Here Comes the Groom.* Academy Award winner 1951.

In the Evening by the Moonlight 1878 w.m. James Bland

In the Evening by the Moonlight, Dear Louise 1912 w. Andrew B. Sterling m. Harry Von Tilzer

In the Fall We'll All Go Voting for Al 1928 w.m. Irving Berlin. This song was written for Al Smith's Presidential campaign of 1928.

(He Walks with Me) In the Garden 1912 w.m. C. Austin Miles. According to the most recent poll conducted by *The Christian Herald,* this gospel hymn rates third in popularity among Protestant churchgoers, over 1,666 hymn contenders. Firt and second places were awarded to "The Old Rugged Cross" and "What a Friend We Have in Jesus."

In the Garden of My Heart 1908 w. Caro Roma m. Ernest R. Ball

In the Garden of Tomorrow 1924 w. George Graff, Jr. m. Jessie L. Deppen

In the Ghetto 1969 w.m. Mac Davis

In the Gloaming 1877 w.m. Annie Fortesque Harrison. The composer of this song was later to wed Lord Alfred Hill, the comptroller of Queen Victoria's household.

In the Gold Fields of Nevada 1915 w. Edgar Leslie m. Archie Gottler

In the Good Old Summer Time 1902 w. Ren Shields m. George Evans. (MT) *The Defender.* (MF) *In the Good Old Summertime.* Blanche Ring and Harry Davenport appeared in *The Defender.* Judy Garland and Van Johnson appeared in *In the Good Old Summertime.* This song was inspired by an afternoon outing at Brighton Beach with Shields, Evans, and vaudeville singer Blanche Ring. Miss Ring soon after introduced the song in *The Defender.* See also Part I, 1846.

In the Great Somewhere 1901 w.m. Paul Dresser

In the Heart of the Dark 1939 w. Oscar Hammerstein II m. Jerome Kern. (MT) *Very Warm for May.*

In the House of Too Much Trouble 1900 w.m. Will A. Heelan, J. Fred Helf

In the Land of Beginning Again 1918 w. Grant Clarke m. George W. Meyer. (F) *The Bells of St. Mary's.* Bing Crosby and Ingrid Bergman appeared in *The Bells of St. Mary's.*

In the Land of Harmony 1911 w. Bert Kalmar m. Ted Snyder

In the Little Red Schoolhouse 1922 w.m. Al Wilson, James Brennan

In the Louisiana Lowlands 1859 w.m. anon.

In the Luxembourg Gardens 1925 w.m. Kathleen Lockhart Manning

In the Merry Month of June 1903 w.m. Ren Shields, George Evans

In the Middle of a Kiss 1935 w.m. Sam Coslow. (F) *College Scandal.* (MF) *The Clock Strikes Eight.* William Frawley and Arline Judge appeared in *College Scandal.*

In the Middle of an Island 1957 w.m. Ted Varnick, Nick Acquaviva

In the Middle of the Night 1925 w. Billy Rose m. Walter Donaldson

In the Midnight Hour 1965 w.m. Steve Cropper

In the Mood 1939 w.m. Andy Razaf, Joseph Garland. (MF) *Sun Valley Serenade.* (MF) *The Glenn Miller Story.* Sonja Henie and Glenn Miller appeared in *Sun Valley Serenade.* Theme song of Joe Loss and Glenn Miller.

In the Moon Mist 1946 w.m. Jack Lawrence. Based on Godard's "Berceuse" from *Jocelyn.*

In the Morning by the Bright Light 1879 w.m. James A. Bland

In the Quartermaster's Stores 1940 w.m. traditional; adapted Elton Box, Desmond Cox, Bert Reed

In the Shade of the Old Apple Tree 1905 w. Harry H. Williams m. Egbert Van Alstyne

In the Shadows 1910 w. E. Ray Goetz m. Herman Finck. The words to this song were added in 1911.

In the Still of the Night 1937 w.m. Cole Porter. (MF) *Rosalie.* (MF) *Night and Day.* Nelson Eddy and Eleanor Powell appeared in *Rosalie.* Cary Grant, Alexis Smith, and Mary Martin appeared in *Night and Day,* biopic of song writer Cole Porter.

In the Summertime 1971 w.m. Ray Dorset. Ivor Novello Award winner 1970–71.

In the Sweet Bye and Bye 1902 w. Vincent P. Bryan m. Harry Von Tilzer

In the Town Where I Was Born 1914 w. Dick Howard, Billy Tracey m. Al Harriman. (MF) *Old Homestead.* The Weaver Brothers appeared in *Old Homestead.*

In the Twi-Twi-Twi-Light 1906 w.m. Herman Darewski, Charles Wilmot. (MT) *The Dairymaids.*

In the Valley of the Moon 1933 w.m. Charles Tobias, Joe Burke. Based on the Adagio from Mendelssohn's Violin Concerto.

In the Wildwood Where the Bluebells Grew 1907 w.m. Herbert H. Taylor

In the Year 2525 1969 w.m. Richard S. Evans

In Thoughts of You 1965 w.m. Geoff Morrow, Chris Arnold

In Twilight Town 1912 m. C.M. Denison m. E.F. Dusenberry

In Zanzibar—My Little Chimpanzee 1904 w. Will D. Cobb m. Gus Edwards. (MT) *The Medal and the Maid.*

Incense and Peppermints 1967 w.m. John Carter, Tim Gilbert

Inchworm 1952 w.m. Frank Loesser. (MF) *Hans Christian Andersen.* Danny Kaye appeared in *Hans Christian Andersen.*

Income Tax Collector, The 1955 w.m. Michael Flanders, Donald Swann. Ivor Novello Award winner 1955.

Incredible Flutist, The 1939 m. Walter Piston. From the ballet "The Incredible Flutist."

Indian Love Call 1924 w. Otto Harbach, Oscar Hammerstein II m. Rudolf Friml. (MT) *Rose Marie.* (MF) *Rose Marie* (1936). (MF) *Rose Marie* (1954). Derek Oldham and Edith Day appeared in the British stage production of *Rose Marie.* Nelson Eddy and Jeanette MacDonald appeared in the 1936 film production of *Rose Marie.* Fernando Lamas and Ann Blyth appeared in the 1954 film production of *Rose Marie.* This song was supposedly the favorite of President Eisenhower.

Indian Reservation 1971 w.m. John D. Loudermilk

Indian Summer 1919 m. Victor Herbert. This song was popularly revived in 1940, with lyrics added that year by Al Dubin.

(Back Home Again in) Indiana 1917 w. Ballard MacDonald m. James F. Hanley. (MF) *With a Song in My Heart.* (MF) *Satchmo the Great.* (MF) *Drum Crazy.* (MF) *The Five Pennies.* Susan Hayward appeared in *With a Song in My Heart,* biopic of singer Jane Froman. The Louis Armstrong All Stars appeared in *Satchmo the Great.* Danny Kaye appeared in *The Five Pennies,* biopic of jazzman Red Nichols. See also Part I, 1917.

Indiana Moon 1923 w. Benny Davis m. Isham Jones

Indianola 1917 w. Frank Warren m. S.R. Henry, D. Onivas (Domenico Savino). This song was published in 1917 as a piano solo only.

Ingle Side, The c.1840 w. Hew Ainslie m. T.V. Wiesenthal

Inka Dinka Doo 1933 w.m. Jimmy Durante, Ben Ryan, Harry Donnelly. (MF) *The Great Schnozzle.* (MF) *This Time for Keeps.* (MF) *Palooka.* Jimmy Durante appeared in *The Great Schnozzle.* Esther Williams and Jimmy Durante appeared in *This Time for Keeps.* Jimmy Durante appeared in *Palooka.* Theme song of Jimmy Durante.

Inn of the Sixth Happiness 1958 m. Malcolm Arnold

Innocent Man, An 1983 w.m. Billy Joel

Inside 1983 w.m. Michael Reid

Intermezzo 1890 m. Pietro Mascagni. From the opera *Cavalleria Rusticana.*

Intermezzo (A Love Story) (Souvenir de Vienne) 1941 w. Robert Henning m. Heinz Provost. (MF) *Intermezzo.* (F) *Escape to Happiness.* Ingrid Bergman and Leslie Howard appeared in *Intermezzo.* Based on a theme from *Tristan and Isolde,* by Richard Wagner.

International Rag, *see* **That International Rag**

Internationale, L' 1888 Fr.w. Eugène Pottier m. Pierre Degeyter, Adolphe Degeyter. This song was the official anthem of the Soviet Union from 1917 to 1944.

Into Each Life Some Rain Must Fall 1945 w.m. Allan Roberts, Doris Fisher

Into the Groove 1985 w.m. Stephen Bray, Madonna

Introduction and Air to a Stained Glass Window 1976 w.m. John Gregory

Invisible Touch 1986 w.m. Tony Banks, Phil Collins, Mike Rutherford

Invitation 1952 w. Paul Francis Webster m. Bronislaw Kaper. (F) *Invitation.* Van Johnson and Dorothy McGuire appeared in *Invitation.*

Invitation to a Broken Heart 1951 w.m. Phil Baker, Paul Mann, Al Lewis

Invitation to the Dance 1821 m. Carl Maria von Weber. From the German "Aufforderung zum Tanze." See also "Let's Dance" of 1935.

Iowa Corn Song uncertain w.m. E. Riley, G. Botsford, R. Lockard, G. Hamilton. Fight song for the University of Iowa.

Ireland Is Ireland to Me 1915 w. Fiske O'Hara, J. Keirn Brennan m. Ernest R. Ball

Ireland Must Be Heaven, for My Mother Came from There 1916 w.m. Joseph McCarthy, Howard Johnson, Fred Fisher. (MF) *Oh You Beautiful Doll.*

Irene 1919 w. Joseph McCarthy m. Harry Tierney. (MT) *Irene.* (MF) *Irene.* Edith Day appeared in the stage production of *Irene.* Ray Milland and Anna Neagle appeared in the film production of *Irene.*

Irene's Lullaby, *see* **Sleep, Baby, Sleep**

Irish Jubilee, The 1890 w. James Thornton m. Charles Lawlor. James Thornton was a singing waiter at Allen's Bal Mabille in New York City before his success as a song writer.

Irish Washerwoman, or, The Scotch Bagpipe Melody 1792 m. traditional Irish folk dance

Irma La Douce 1960 w. Julian More, David Heneker, Monte Norman m. Marguerite Monnot. (MT) *Irma La Dance.* (MF) *Irma La Douce.* Jack Lemmon and Shirley MacLaine appeared in the film production of *Irma La Douce.*

Irresistible You 1944 w.m. Don Raye, Gene De Paul. (MF) *Broadway Rhythm.* Lena Horne and George Murphy appeared in *Broadway Rhythm.*

Is I In Love? I Is 1932 w. Mercer Cook m. J. Russell Robinson

Is It a Sin?, *See* **Guilty**

Is It Always like This 1943 w.m. Alec Wilder

Is It True What They Say About Dixie 1936 w.m. Irving Caesar, Sammy Lerner, Gerald Marks. (MF) *Jolson Sings Again.* Larry Parks appeared in *Jolson Sings Again.*

Is It You 1981 w.m. Bill Champlin, Lee Ritenour, Eric Tagg

Is That All There Is 1969 w. Jerry Leiber m. Mike Stoller

Is You Is or Is You Ain't My Baby 1944 w. Billy Austin

m. Louis Jordan. (MF) *Follow the Boys.* George Raft, Marlene Dietrich, and W.C. Fields appeared in *Follow the Boys.*

I'se Gwine Back to Dixie 1874 w.m. Charles T. White. (F) *Overland Telegraph.* Tim Holt and Richard Martin appeared in *Overland Telegraph.*

I'se Your Nigger If You Want Me, Liza Jane 1896 w.m. Paul Dresser

Island Girl 1975 w.m. Elton John, Bernie Taupin. Ivor Novello Award winner 1975–76.

Island of Dreams 1963 w.m. Tom Springfield

Islands in the Stream 1983 w.m. Barry Gibb, Maurice Gibb, Robin Gibb

Isle d'Amour (Isle of Love) 1913 w. Earl Carroll m. Leo Edwards. (MT) *Ziegfeld Follies of 1913.* (MF) *The Merry Monihans.* Donald O'Connor and Peggy Ryan appeared in *The Merry Monihans.*

Isle of Capri 1934 w. Jimmy Kennedy m. Will Grosz

Isle o' Dreams 1912 w. George Graff, Jr., Chauncey Olcott m. Ernest R. Ball. (MT) *The Isle o' Dreams.*

Isle of Innisfree 1952 w.m. Richard Farrelly

Isle of Love, *see* **Isle d'Amour**

Isle of Our Dreams, The 1906 w. Henry Blossom m. Victor Herbert. (MT) *The Red Mill.*

Isn't It a Pity 1933 w. Ira Gershwin m. George Gershwin. (MT) *Pardon My English.* Barbara Newberry and Carl Randall appeared in *Pardon My English.*

Isn't It Kinda Fun 1945 w. Oscar Hammerstein II m. Richard Rodgers. (MF) *State Fair.* Vivian Blaine, Jeanne Crain, and Dana Andrews appeared in *State Fair.*

Isn't It Romantic 1932 w. Lorenz Hart m. Richard Rodgers. (MF) *Love Me Tonight.* Maurice Chevalier and Jeanette MacDonald appeared in *Love Me Tonight.*

Isn't Love the Grandest Thing 1935 w. Jack Scholl m. Louis Alter. (F) *The Rainmakers.* Bert Wheeler and Robert Woolsey appeared in *The Rainmakers.*

Isn't She the Sweetest Thing 1925 w. Gus Kahn m. Walter Donaldson

Isn't This a Lovely Day (To Be Caught in the Rain) 1935 w.m. Irving Berlin. (MF) *Top Hat.* Fred Astaire and Ginger Rogers appeared in *Top Hat.*

Istanbul (Not Constantinople) 1954 w. Jimmy Kennedy m. Nat Simon

It Ain't Gonna Rain No Mo' 1923 w.m. Wendell Hall. (MT) *The Punch Bowl.* (MF) *Has Anybody Seen My Gal.* Gwen Farrar and Norah Blaney appeared in *The Punch Bowl.* Rock Hudson and Piper Laurie appeared in *Has Anybody Seen My Gal.* Based on a traditional folksong from Kentucky, as early as 1870.

It Ain't Me Babe 1964 w.m. Bob Dylan

It Ain't Necessarily So 1935 w. Ira Gershwin m. George Gershwin. (MT) *Porgy and Bess.* (MF) *Porgy and Bess.* (MF) *Rhapsody in Blue.* Todd Duncan and Anne Wiggins Brown appeared in the stage production of *Porgy and Bess.* Sammy Davis, Jr., and Sidney Poitier appeared in the film production of *Porgy and Bess.* Oscar Levant and Alexis Smith appeared in *Rhapsody in Blue,* biopic of composer George Gershwin.

It All Belongs to You (The Laugh of the Town) 1938 w.m. Cole Porter. (F) *Break the News.* Maurice Chevalier and Jack Buchanan appeared in *Break the News.*

It All Comes Back to Me Now 1941 w.m. Alex C. Kramer, Joan Whitney, Hy Zaret. This song was popularly revived in 1948.

It All Depends on You 1926 w.m. B.G. DeSylva, Lew Brown, Ray Henderson. (MT) *Big Boy.* (MT) *Lido Lady.* (MF) *The Singing Fool.* (MF) *The Best Things in Life Are Free.* (MF) *Love Me or Leave Me.* Al Jolson appeared in *Big Boy* and *The Singing Fool.* Phyllis Dave appeared in *Lido Lady.* Ernest Borgnine, Gordon MacRae, and Dan Dailey appeared in *The Best Things in Life Are Free,* biopic of song writers DeSylva, Brown, and Henderson. Doris Day and James Cagney appeared in *Love Me or Leave Me,* biopic of singer Ruth Etting. This song was added to *Big Boy* in 1926.

It Came upon a Midnight Clear 1850 w. Rev. Edmund Hamilton Sears m. Richard Storrs Willis. The words and music to this now traditional hymn were not written together, but were edited into one work for a book of hymns.

It Can't Be Wrong 1943 w. Kim Gannon m. Max Steiner. (F) *Now Voyager.* Bette Davis and Paul Henreid appeared in *Now Voyager.*

It Costs So Little 1942 w.m. Horatio Nicholls, Alf Ritter, J. Lester Smith

It Could Happen to You 1944 w. Johnny Burke m. Jimmy Van Heusen. (MF) *And the Angels Sing.* Betty Hutton and Fred MacMurray appeared in *And the Angels Sing.*

It Couldn't Be True (Or Could It) 1946 w.m. Sylvia Dee, Sidney Lippman

It Don't Mean a Thing If It Ain't Got That Swing 1932 w. Irving Mills m. Duke Ellington. (MT) *Bubbling Brown Sugar.* (MT) *Sophisticated Ladies.* Vivian Reed and Avon Long appeared in *Bubbling Brown Sugar.* Gregory Hines and Phyllis Hyman appeared in *Sophisticated Ladies.*

It Goes Like It Goes 1979 w.m. Norman Gimbel, David Shire. (F) *Norma Rae.* Academy Award winner 1979. Sally Fields appeared in *Norma Rae.*

It Had To Be You 1924 w. Gus Kahn m. Isham Jones. (MF) *Show Business.* (MF) *Incendiary Blonde.* (MF) *I'll See You in My Dreams.* (F) *South Sea Sinner.* Eddie Cantor and Joan Davis appeared in *Show Business.* Betty Hutton appeared in *Incendiary Blonde,* biopic of speakeasy owner Texas Guinan. Doris Day and Danny Thomas appeared in *I'll See You in My Dreams,* biopic of song writer Gus Kahn. Shelley Winters and MacDonald Carey appeared in *South Sea Sinner.* This song was popularly revived in 1944.

It Happened in Adano 1949 w.m. Don Pelosi, Harold Fields

It Happened in Monterey 1930 w. Billy Rose m. Mabel Wayne. (MF) *King of Jazz.* Bing Crosby and Paul Whiteman appeared in *King of Jazz.*

It Happened in Sun Valley 1941 w. Mack Gordon m. Harry Warren. (MF) *Sun Valley Serenade.* (MF) *It Happened in Sun Valley.* Sonja Henie, Milton Berle, and Glenn Miller appeared in *Sun Valley Serenade.*

It Happened On the Beach at Bali Bali, *see* **On the Beach at Bali Bali**

It Is No Secret 1951 w.m. Stuart Hamblen

It Is Only a Tiny Garden 1916 w.m. Haydn Wood, Lillian Glanville

It Is Well with My Soul 1876 w. H.C. Spafford m. Paul P. Bliss

It Isn't Fair 1933 w. Richard Himber m. Richard Himber, Frank Warshauer, Sylvester Sprigato. This song was popularly revived in 1950.

It Looks (to Me) Like a Big Night Tonight 1908 w. Harry Williams m. Egbert Van Alstyne

It Looks Like Rain in Cherry Blossom Lane 1937 w.m. Edgar Leslie, Joseph Burke

It Might As Well Be Spring 1946 w. Oscar Hammerstein II m. Richard Rodgers. (MF) *State Fair* (1945). (MF) *State Fair* (1962). Vivian Blaine and Dick Haymes appeared in the 1945 film production of *State Fair*. Pat Boone and Ann Margret appeared in the 1962 film production of *State Fair*. Academy Award winner 1945.

It Might Be You 1983 w.m. Alan Bergman, Marilyn Bergman, Dave Grusin

It Must Be Him 1967 w.m. Gilbert Becaud. From the French "Seul Su Son Etgle."

It Must Be Jelly, 'Cause Jam Don't Shake Like That 1943 w.m. J. Chalmers MacGregor, Sunny Skylar

It Must Be Love 1930 w.m. Mack Gordon, Abner Silver, Ted Snyder. (MF) *Swing High*. Fred Scott and Helen Twelvetrees appeared in *Swing High*.

It Must Be Love 1979 w.m. Bob McDill

It Must Be True (You Are Mine, All Mine) 1930 w. Gus Arnheim, Gordon Clifford m. Harry Barris. (MF) *The Eddy Duchin Story*.

It Never Entered My Mind 1940 w. Lorenz Hart m. Richard Rodgers. (MT) *Higher and Higher* . (MF) *Higher and Higher*. Jack Haley and Shirley Ross appeared in the stage production of *Higher and Higher*. Frank Sinatra appeared in the film production of *Higher and Higher*.

It Never Rains in Southern California 1972 w.m. Michael Hazlewood, Albert Hammond

It Never Was You 1938 w. Maxwell Anderson m. Kurt Weill. (MT) *Knickerbocker Holiday*. (MF) *Knickerbocker Holiday*. Nelson Eddy appeared in the film production of *Knickerbocker Holiday*.

It Only Happens When I Dance with You 1948 w.m. Irving Berlin. (MF) *Easter Parade*. Fred Astaire, Ann Miller, and Judy Garland appeared in *Easter Parade*.

It Only Hurts for a Little While 1956 w. Mack David m. Fred Spielman

It Only Takes a Minute 1975 w.m. Dennis Lambert, Brian Potter

It Only Takes a Moment 1964 w.m. Jerry Herman. (MT) *Hello, Dolly!*. (MT) *Jerry's Girls*. (MF) *Hello, Dolly!*. Carol Channing appeared in the stage production of *Hello Dolly!* Dorothy Loudon, Chita Rivera and Leslie Uggams appeared in *Jerry's Girls*. Barbra Streisand appeared in the film production of *Hello, Dolly!*

It Seems Like Old Times 1937 w.m. Charles Tobias, Sam H. Stept. Theme song of Arthur Godfrey's radio show.

It Seems to Me I've Heard That Song Before, *see* **I've Heard That Song Before**

It Takes a Little Rain with the Sunshine To Make the World Go Round 1913 w. Ballard MacDonald m. Harry Carroll

It Takes a Long, Tall, Brown-Skin Gal 1917 w.m. Will E. Skidmore

It Takes a Woman 1964 w.m. Jerry Herman. (MT) *Hello, Dolly!*. (MT) *Jerry's Girls*. (MF) *Hello, Dolly!*. Carol Channing appeared in the stage production of *Hello, Dolly!*. Dorothy Loudon, Chita Rivera and Leslie Uggams appeared in *Jerry's Girls*. Barbra Streisand and Walter Matthau appeared in the film production of *Hello, Dolly!*

It Was a Dream 1875 w. Robert Edward Francillon m. Frederick Hymen Cowen

It Was a Lover and His Lass c.1598 w.m. traditional, from England. From Shakespeare's *As You Like It*.

It Was a Very Good Year 1961 w.m. Ervin Drake. This song was popularly revived in 1965.

It Was Always You, *see* **Always Always You**

It Was Only a Sun Shower 1927 w.m. Irving Kahal, Francis Wheeler

It Was So Beautiful (and You Were Mine) 1932 w. Arthur Freed m. Harry Barris (MF) *The Big Broadcast*. Bing Crosby and Kate Smith appeared in *The Big Broadcast*.

It Was Written in the Stars 1948 w. Leo Robin m. Harold Arlen. (MF) *Casbah*. Yvonne DeCarlo, Tony Martin, and Peter Lorre appeared in *Casbah*.

Italian Street Song 1910 w. Rida Johnson Young m. Victor Herbert. (MT) *Naughty Marietta*. (MF) *Naughty Marietta*. Emma Trentini and Orville Harrold appeared in the stage production of *Naughty Marietta*. Jeanette MacDonald and Nelson Eddy appeared in the film production of *Naughty Marietta*.

Itchycoo Park 1968 w.m. Steve Marriott, Ronnie Lane

Itinerary of an Orchestra 1956 w.m. Johnny Dankworth, Dave Lindup. Ivor Novello Award winner 1956.

It's a Big, Wide, Wonderful World 1940 w.m. John Rox. (MF) *All in Fun*. (MF) *Rhythm Inn*. Imogene Coca and Bill Robinson appeared in *All in Fun*. Jane Frazee and Kirby Grant appeared in *Rhythm Inn*. This song was popularly revived in 1949.

It's a Blue World 1939 w.m. Robert Wright, Chet Forrest. (MF) *Music in My Heart*. Tony Martin and Rita Hayworth appeared in *Music in My Heart*.

It's a Boy 1958 w.m. Paddy Roberts

It's a Good Day 1946 w.m. Peggy Lee, Dave Barbour (MF) *With a Song in My Heart*. Susan Hayward appeared in *With a Song in My Heart*, biopic of singer Jane Froman.

It's a Grand Night for Singing 1945 w. Oscar Hammerstein II m. Richard Rodgers. (MF) *State Fair* (1945). (MF) *State Fair* (1962). Jeanne Crain and Dana Andrews appeared in the 1945 film production of *State Fair*. Pat Boone, Anne

Margret, and Bobby Darin appeared in the 1962 film production of *State Fair*.

It's a Great Big Shame 1900 w.m. Edgar Bateman, George Le Brunn

It's a Great Day for the Irish 1940 w.m. Roger Edens. (MF) *Little Nellie Kelly*. Judy Garland and George Murphy appeared in *Little Nellie Kelly*.

It's a Hap-Hap-Happy Day 1939 w.m. Sammy Timberg, Winston Sharples, Al Neiburg. (MF) *Gulliver's Travels*. Lanny Ross and Jessica Dragonette appeared in *Gulliver's Travels*.

It's a Heartache 1978 w.m. Ronnie Scott, Victor Batty

It's a Lonesome Old Town (When You're Not Around) 1930 w.m. Harry Tobias, Charles Kisco

It's a Long Lane That Has No Turning 1917 w. Arthur A. Penn m. Manuel Klein

It's a Long (Long) Way to Tipperary 1912 w.m. Jack Judge, Harry H. Williams (MT) *Chin-Chin*. (MT) *Dancing Around*. (MF) *Wait Till the Sun Shines Nellie*. (F) *What Price Glory?* Montgomery and Stone and Belle Story appeared in *Chin-Chin*. David Wayne appeared in *Wait Till the Sun Shines Nellie*. James Cagney appeared in *What Price Glory?*

It's a Lovely Day Today 1950 w.m. Irving Berlin. (MT) *Call Me Madam*. (MF) *Call Me Madam*. Ethel Merman appeared in both the stage and film productions of *Call Me Madam*.

It's a Lovely Day Tomorrow, *see* **Tomorrow Is a Lovely Day**

It's a Mad, Mad, Mad, Mad World 1963 w.m. Ernest Gold, Mack David. (F) *It's a Mad, Mad, Mad, Mad World*. Spencer Tracy, Jimmy Durante, Mickey Rooney, and Ethel Merman appeared in *It's a Mad, Mad, Mad, Mad World*.

It's a Marshmallow World, *see* **Marshmallow World**

It's a Miracle 1975 w.m. Barry Manilow, Marty Panzer

It's a Miracle 1984 w.m. Phil Pickett, Mickey Craig, Roy Ernest Hay, Jon Moss, George O'Dowd

It's a Mistake 1983 w.m. Colin Hay

It's a Most Unusual Day 1948 w. Harold Adamson m. Jimmy McHugh. (MF) *A Date with Judy*. Elizabeth Taylor and Jane Powell appeared in *A Date with Judy*.

It's a New World 1954 w. Ira Gershwin m. Harold Arlen. (MF) *A Star Is Born*. Judy Garland and James Mason appeared in *A Star Is Born*.

It's a Pity To Say Goodnight 1946 w.m. Billy Reid

It's a Sin To Tell a Lie 1933 w.m. Billy Mayhew. (MT) *Ain't Misbehavin'*. Debbie Allen and Nell Carter appeared in *Ain't Misbehavin'*. This song was most popular in 1936.

It's a Sin When You Love Somebody 1973 w.m. Jimmy Webb

It's a Woman's World 1954 w. Sammy Cahn m. Cyril Mockridge

It's a Wonderful World 1931 w. Oscar Hammerstein II m. Sigmund Romberg. (MT) *East Wind*.

It's All in the Game 1951 w. Carl Sigman m. General Charles Gates Dawes. Based on an instrumental by Dawes known as "Melody," from 1912, adapted in 1951 and again in 1958. Charles Dawes was Vice-President of the United States from 1925 to 1929. At the time of this song's publication, he was afraid of becoming the target of puns. Said Mr. Dawes: "My business is that of a banker, and few bankers have won renown as composers of music. I know that I will be the target of punster friends. They will say that if all the notes in my bank are as bad as my musical ones, they are not worth the paper they are written on."

It's All Right 1963 w.m. Curtis Mayfield

It's All Right with Me 1953 w.m. Cole Porter. (MT) *Can-Can*. (MF) *Can-Can*. Frank Sinatra, Shirley MacLaine, and Juliet Prowse appeared in the film production of *Can-Can*.

It's Almost Like Being in Love, *see* **Almost Like Being in Love**

It's Almost Tomorrow 1953 w. Wade Buff m. Gene Adkinson

It's Always Fair Weather When Good Fellows Get Together, or **A Stein Song** 1898 w. Richard Hovey m. Frederic Field Bullard

It's Always You 1941 w. Johnny Burke m. Jimmy Van Heusen. (MF) *The Road to Zanzibar*. Bing Crosby, Bob Hope, and Dorothy Lamour appeared in *The Road to Zanzibar*.

It's an Open Secret 1964 w.m. Joy Webb

It's Been a Long, Long Time 1945 w. Sammy Cahn m. Jule Styne. (MF) *I'll Get By!* June Haver and Dennis Day appeared in *I'll Get By*. See also Part I, 1945.

It's Been So Long 1936 w. Harold Adamson, Walter Donaldson. (MF) *The Great Ziegfeld*. (MF) *The Benny Goodman Story*. William Powell, Fanny Brice, and Virginia Bruce appeared in *The Great Ziegfeld*.

It's Beginning To Look (a Lot) Like Christmas 1951 w.m. Meredith Willson

It's Dark on Observatory Hill 1934 w. Johnny Burke m. Harold Spina

It's Delightful To Be Married 1907 w. Anna Held m. Vincent Scotto. (MT) *The Parisian Model*.

It's De-Lovely 1936 w.m. Cole Porter. (MT) *Red, Hot and Blue!* (MT) *The Fleet's Lit Up*. (MF) *Red, Hot and Blue!* (MF) *Anything Goes*. (F) *Evil Under the Sun*. Ethel Merman, Jimmy Durante, and Bob Hope appeared in the stage production of *Red, Hot and Blue!* Frances Day appeared in *The Fleet's Lit Up*. Betty Hutton and Victor Mature appeared in the film production of *Red, Hot and Blue!* Maggie Smith and Peter Ustinov appeared in *Evil Under the Sun*.

It's Easy to Remember (and So Hard to Forget) 1935 w. Lorenz Hart m. Richard Rodgers. (MF) *Mississippi* Bing Crosby, W.C. Fields, and Queenie Smith appeared in *Mississippi*.

It's Easy To Say, *see* **Prove It By the Things You Do**

It's Foolish But It's Fun 1934 w.m. Robert Stolz, Gus Kahn. (MF) *Spring Parade*. Deanna Durbin appeared in *Swing Parade*. This song was popularly revived in 1941.

It's Gonna Be a Long, Long Winter, *see* **A Long, Long Winter**

It's Gonna Take a Miracle 1982 w.m. Teddy Randazzo, Lou Stallman, Brian Weinstein

It's Good News Week 1965 w.m. Kenneth King

It's Good To Be Alive 1957 w.m. Bob Merrill. (MT) *New Girl in Town.*

It's Got To Be Love 1936 w. Lorenz Hart m. Richard Rodgers. (MT) *On Your Toes.* (MF) *On Your Toes.*

It's Gotta Be This or That, *see* **Gotta Be This or That**

It's Great To Be a Soldier Man 1907 w. Jack Drislane m. Theodore F. Morse

It's Great To Be in Love 1931 w.m. Cliff Friend. (MT) *Earl Carroll's Vanities of 1930.* (MT) *Earl Carroll's Vanities of 1931.* Jack Benny and Patsy Kelly appeared in *Earl Carroll's Vanities of 1930.* Will Mahoney and William Demarest appeared in *Earl Carroll's Vanities of 1931.*

It's Hard To Go Down Easy, *see* **Go Down Easy**

It's Impossible 1970 Eng.w. Sid Wayne m. Canche A. Manzanero

It's in the Air 1939 w.m. Harry Parr-Davies. (MF) *It's In the Air.*

It's in the Book 1952 w.m. J. Standley, Art Thorsen

It's June in January, *see* **June in January**

It's Just a Little Street Where Old Friends Meet, *see* **A Little Street Where Old Friends Meet**

It's Just a Matter of Time 1958 w.m. Clyde Otis, Brook Benton, Belford Hendricks

It's Just the Gypsy in My Soul, *see* **Gypsy in My Soul**

It's Later Than You Think, *see* **Enjoy Yourself, It's Later Than You Think**

It's Like Old Times, *see* **Seems Like Old Times**

It's Love 1953 w. Betty Comden, Adolph Green m. Leonard Bernstein. (MT) *Wonderful Town.*

It's Love Again 1936 w.m. Sam Coslow. (MF) *It's Love Again.* Jessie Matthews and Robert Young appeared in *It's Love Again.*

It's Love, Love, Love 1944 w.m. Joan Whitney, Mack David, Alex Kramer. Based loosely on "The Duke and Duchess of Kent." (MF) *Stars on Parade.* (MF) *That Wonderful Urge.* Tyrone Power and Gene Tierney appeared in *That Wonderful Urge.*

It's Magic 1948 w. Sammy Cahn m. Jule Styne. (MF) *Romance On the High Seas.* (MF) *It's Magic.* (MF) *Starlift.* Doris Day and Jack Carson appeared in *Romance On the High Seas.* Doris Day and Gordon MacRae appeared in *Starlift.*

It's Make Believe Ballroom Time 1936 w.m. Paul Denniker, Andy Razaf, Michael Stoner

It's My Mother's Birthday Today 1935 w.m. Eddie Lisbona, Tommie Connor

It's My Party 1963 w.m. Wally Gold, John Gluck, Herb Wiener

It's My Turn 1981 w.m. Michael Masser, Carole Bayer Sager

It's Never Too Late To Fall in Love 1954 w.m. Sandy Wilson. (MT) *The Boy Friend.*

It's Nice To Get Up in the Morning 1913 w.m. Harry Lauder

It's No Secret, *see* **It Is No Secret**

It's No Sin 1951 w. Chester R. Shull m. George Hoven

It's Not for Me To Say 1957 w. Al Stillman m. Robert Allen. (F) *Lizzie.* Eleanor Parker and Joan Blondell appeared in *Lizzie.*

It's Not Unusual 1965 w.m. Gordon Mills, Les Reed. Ivor Novello Award winner 1965.

It's Now or Never 1960 w.m. Aaron Schroeder, Wally Gold. Based on de Capua's "O Sole Mio" of 1899.

It's Only a Paper Moon 1933 w. E.Y. Harburg, Billy Rose m. Harold Arlen. (T) *The Great Magoo.* (MF) *Take a Chance.* (F) *Too Young to Know.* (F) *Paper Moon.* Cliff Edwards and Charles "Buddy" Rogers appeared in *Take a Chance.* June Leslie and Robert Hutton appeared in *Too Young to Know.* Ryan O'Neal and Tatum O'Neal appeared in *Paper Moon.*

It's Only Love 1965 w.m. John Lennon, Paul McCartney

It's Only Make Believe 1958 w.m. Conway Twitty, Jack Nance

It's Only Rock 'n Roll (But I Like It) 1974 w.m. Mick Jagger, Keith Richard

It's Over 1966 w.m. Jimmie Rodgers

It's Raining Again 1983 w.m. Richard Davies, Roger Hodgson

It's So Easy 1977 w.m. Buddy Holly, Norman Petty

It's So Nice To Have a Man Around the House 1950 w. Jack Elliott m. Harold Spina. This song was later adapted for the Betty Crocker Cake Mixes commercial promotion campaign with the new lyric "It's so nice to have a cake around the house."

It's So Peaceful in the Country 1941 w.m. Alec Wilder. This song was popularly revived in 1948.

It's Still Rock and Roll to Me 1980 w.m. Billy Joel

It's the Darndest Thing 1931 w. Dorothy Fields m. Jimmy McHugh. (T) *Singin' the Blues.* (MF) *Singin' the Blues.*

It's the Irish in Your Eye, (It's the Irish in Your Smile) 1916 w. William Dillon m. Albert Von Tilzer

It's the Loveliest Night of the Year, *see* **Over the Waves**

It's the Real Thing. Coke. 1969 w.m. Bill Backer. This song was written for a Coca-Cola commercial promotion campaign.

It's the Same Old Dream 1947 w. Sammy Cahn m. Jule Styne. (MF) *It Happened in Brooklyn.* Frank Sinatra, Kathryn Grayson, and Jimmy Durante appeared in *It Happened in Brooklyn.*

It's the Same Old Shillelagh 1940 w.m. P. White

It's the Talk of the Town 1933 w. Marty Symes, Al J. Neiburg m. Jerry Livingston

It's Time to Say Goodnight 1934 w.m. Jack Yellen, Herb Magidson, Joseph Meyer. (MF) *George White's Scandals.* Alice Faye, Cliff Edwards, and Eleanor Powell appeared in *George White's Scandals.*

It's Too Late 1971 w.m. Carole King. Grammy Award winner 1971.

It's Too Soon To Know 1948 w.m. Deborah Chessler. This song was popularly revived in 1958.

It's Tulip Time in Holland 1915 w. Dave Radford m.

Richard A. Whiting. (MF) *April Showers*. Ann Sheridan and Jack Carson appeared in *April Showers*.

It's You 1957 w.m. Meredith Wilson. (MT) *The Music Man*. (MF) *The Music Man*. Robert Preston appeared in both the stage and film productions of *The Music Man*.

It's You, *see also* **C'est Vous**

It's You or No One 1948 w. Sammy Cahn m. Jule Styne. (MF) *It's Magic*. (MF) *Romance On the High Seas*. Doris Day and Jack Carson appeared in *Romance On the High Seas*.

It's Your Thing 1969 w.m. Rudolph Isley, Ronald Isley, O'Kelly Isley

Itsy Bitsy Teenie Weenie Yellow Polkadot Bikini 1960 w.m. Paul J. Vance, Lee Pockriss

I've a Longing in My Heart for You, Louise 1900 w.m. Charles K. Harris

I've a Shooting Box in Scotland 1916 w. T. Lawrason Riggs, Cole Porter m. Cole Porter (MT) *See America First*. Clifton Webb, Red Eagle and Jeanne Cartier appeared in *See America First*.

I've Been Floating Down the Old Green River 1915 w. Bert Kalmar m. Joe Cooper. (MT) *Maid in America*.

I've Been Working on the Railroad, or, **The Levee Song**, or, **Someone's in the Kitchen with Dinah** 1894 w.m. traditional American folksong, c. 1880. Also known with new words in 1903 as ''The Eyes of Texas (Are Upon You).''

I've Come Here To Stay 1890 w. Edward Harrigan m. David Braham. (MT) *Reilly and the Four Hundred*.

I've Found a New Baby, *see* **I Found a New Baby**

I've Got a Crush on You 1930 w. Ira Gershwin m. George Gershwin. (MT) *Treasure Girl*. (MT) *Strike Up the Band*. (MF) *Strike Up the Band*. (MF) *Meet Danny Wilson*. (MF) *Three for the Show*. (MF) *Both Ends of the Candle*. (F) *Alice Doesn't Live Here Anymore*. Gertrude Lawrence and Clifton Webb appeared in *Treasure Girl*. Blanche Ring appeared in the stage production of *Strike Up the Band*. Judy Garland and Mickey Rooney appeared in the film production of *Strike Up the Band*. Frank Sinatra and Shelly Winters appeared in *Meet Danny Wilson*. Betty Grable and Jack Lemmon appeared in *Three for the Show*.

I've Got a Feeling for You, *see* **Way Down in My Heart**

I've Got a Feeling I'm Falling 1929 w. Billy Rose m. Harry Link, Thomas ''Fats'' Waller. (MT) *Ain't Misbehavin'*. (MF) *Applause*. Debbie Allen and Nell Carter appeared in *Ain't Misbehavin'*. Helen Morgan and Joan Peters appeared in *Applause*.

I've Got a Feeling You're Fooling 1936 w.m. Arthur Freed, Nacio Herb Brown. (MT) *Singin' in the Rain*. (MF) *Broadway Melody of 1936*. (MF) *Singin' in the Rain*. (MF) *With a Song in My Heart*. Eleanor Powell and Jack Benny appeared in *Broadway Melody of 1936*. Gene Kelly, Debbie Reynolds, and Donald O'Connor appeared in the 1952 film production of *Singin' in the Rain*. Susan Hayward appeared in *With a Song in My Heart*, biopic of singer Jane Froman.

I've Got a Gal in Kalamazoo 1942 w.m. Mack Gordon, Harry Warren. (MF) *Orchestra Wives*. (MF) *Kiss Them for Me*. Glenn Miller and Ann Rutherford appeared in *Orchestra Wives*. Cary Grant and Jayne Mansfield appeared in *Kiss Them for Me*. See also Part I, 1942.

I've Got a Lovely Bunch of Cocoanuts 1948 w.m. Fred Heatherton

I've Got a Pain in My Sawdust 1909 w. Henry Edward Warner m. Herman Avery Wade

I've Got a Pocketful of Dreams, *see* **A Pocketful of Dreams**

I've Got a Right To Sing the Blues, *see* **I Gotta Right To Sing the Blues**

I've Got a Rock 'n' Roll Heart 1983 w.m. Steve Diamond, Troy Seals, Ed Setser

I've Got Beginner's Luck, *see* **Beginner's Luck**

I've Got Five Dollars 1931 w. Lorenz Hart m. Richard Rodgers (MT) *America's Sweetheart*. (MT) *The Show Is On*. (MF) *Gentlemen Marry Brunettes*. Harriet Lake and Jack Whiting appeared in *America's Sweetheart*. Beatrice Lillie, Bert Lahr, and Mitzi Mayfair appeared in *The Show Is On*. Jane Russell and Jeanne Crain appeared in *Gentlemen Marry Brunettes*.

I've Got It Bad and That Ain't Good, *see* **I Got It Bad and That Ain't Good**

I've Got My Captain Working for Me Now 1920 w.m. Irving Berlin. (MF) *Blue Skies*. Bing Crosby and Fred Astaire appeared in *Blue Skies*.

I've Got My Eyes on You 1939 w.m. Cole Porter. (MF) *Broadway Melody of 1940*. (F) *Andy Hardy's Private Secretary*. Fred Astaire and Eleanor Powell appeared in *Broadway Melody of 1940*. Lewis Stone, Mickey Rooney, and Fay Holden appeared in *Andy Hardy's Private Secretary*.

I've Got My Fingers Crossed 1935 w. Ted Koehler m. Jimmy McHugh. (MT) *Ain't Misbehavin'*. (MF) *King of Burlesque*. Nell Carter and Debbie Allen appeared in *Ain't Misbehavin'*. Warner Baxter, Alice Faye, and ''Fats'' Waller appeared in *King of Burlesque*.

I've Got My Love To Keep Me Warm 1937 w.m. Irving Berlin. (MF) *On the Avenue*. Dick Powell and the Ritz Brothers appeared in *On the Avenue*. This song was popularly revived in 1949.

I've Got No Strings 1940 w.m. Ned Washington, Leigh Harline. (MF) *Pinocchio*.

I've Got Rings on My Fingers, or, **Mumbo Jumbo Jijjiboo J. O'Shea** 1909 w. R.P. Weston, F.J. Barnes m. Maurice Scott. (MT) *The Midnight Sons*. (MT) *The Yankee Girl*. Blanche Ring and Harry Gilfoil appeared in *The Yankee Girl*.

I've Got Sixpence (As I Go Rolling Home) 1941 w.m. Elton Box, Desmond Cox

I've Got the Time—I've Got the Place, but It's Hard To Find the Girl 1910 w. Ballard MacDonald m. S.R. Henry

I've Got the World on a String 1932 w. Ted Koehler m. Harold Arlen. (MF) *I'll Get By*. June Haver and Dennis Day appeared in *I'll Get By*.

I've Got To Be Me 1968 w.m. Walter Marks. (MT) *Golden Rainbow*.

288

I've Got To Use My Imagination 1973 w.m. Gerry Goffin, Barry Goldberg

I've Got You on My Mind 1932 w.m. Cole Porter. (MT) *Gay Divorce*. (MF) *The Gay Divorce*. Grace Moore and Fred Astaire appeared in the stage production of *Gay Divorce*. Ginger Rogers and Fred Astaire appeared in the film production of *The Gay Divorcee*.

I've Got You Under My Skin 1936 w.m. Cole Porter. (MF) *Born To Dance*. (MF) *Night and Day*. (F) *This Could Be the Night*. (F) *Evil Under the Sun*. Eleanor Powell and James Stewart appeared in *Born To Dance*. Cary Grant, Alexis Smith, and Mary Martin appeared in *Night and Day*, biopic of song writer Cole Porter. Jean Simmons appeared in *This Could Be the Night*. Maggie Smith and Peter Ustinov appeared in *Evil Under the Sun*.

I've Got Your Number 1962 w. Carolyn Leigh m. Cy Coleman. (MT) *Little Me*. Sid Caesar appeared in *Little Me*.

I've Gotta Be Me, *see* **I've Got To Be Me**

I've Gotta Crow 1954 w. Carolyn Leigh m. Mark Charlap. (MT) *Peter Pan*. Mary Martin appeared in *Peter Pan*.

I've Grown Accustomed to Her Face 1956 w. Alan Jay Lerner m. Frederick Loewe. (MT) *My Fair Lady*. (MF) *My Fair Lady*. Rex Harrison and Julie Andrews appeared in the stage production of *My Fair Lady*. Rex Harrison and Audrey Hepburn appeared in the film production of *My Fair Lady*.

I've Grown So Used to You 1901 w.m. Thurland Chattaway

I've Had a Lovely Time 1979 w.m. Don Cook, James Fron Throckmorton

I've Had My Moments 1934 w.m. Walter Donaldson, Gus Kahn. (MF) *The Girl from Missouri*. (MF) *Hollywood Party*. Jean Harlow and Lionel Barrymore appeared in *The Girl from Missouri*. Laurel and Hardy and Jimmy Durante appeared in *Hollywood Party*.

(It Seems to Me) I've Heard That Song Before 1943 w. Sammy Cahn m. Jule Styne. (F) *Youth On Parade*. John Hubbard and Ruth Terry appeared in *Youth on Parade*.

I've Just Come Back To Say Goodbye 1897 w.m. Charles K. Harris

I've Lost All My Love for You 1926 w. Lewis and Young m. Harry Akst, Al Piantadosi

I've Loved You for a Long Time 1980 w.m. Michael Zager

I've Never Been in Love Before 1950 w.m. Frank Loesser. (MT) *Guys and Dolls*. (MF) *Guys and Dolls*. Robert Alda and Vivian Blaine appeared in the stage production of *Guys and Dolls*. Frank Sinatra, Jean Simmons, and Marlon Brando appeared in the film production of *Guys and Dolls*.

I've Never Been to Me 1982 w.m. Kenneth Hirsch, Ron Miller

I've Never Seen a Straight Banana 1926 w.m. Ted Waite

I've Taken Quite a Fancy to You 1908 w. Edward Madden m. Theodore F. Morse

I've Told Every Little Star 1932 w. Oscar Hammerstein II m. Jerome Kern (MT) *Music in the Air*. (MF) *Music in the Air*. Walter Slezak and Katherine Carrington appeared in the American stage production of *Music in the Air*. Mary Ellis appeared in the British stage production of *Music in the Air*. Gloria Swanson and Reginald Owen appeared in the film production of *Music in the Air*.

I've Waited Honey, Waited Long for You 1899 w.m. George A. Nichols

I've Waited So Long 1959 w.m. Jerry Lordan. (F) *Idle On Parade*.

Ivory Tower 1956 w.m. Jack Fulton, Lois Steele

Ivy 1947 w.m. Hoagy Carmichael. (F) *Ivy*. Joan Fontaine and Patric Knowles appeared in *Ivy*.

Ivy Rose 1957 w.m. Al Hoffman, Dick Manning. Possibly based on a traditional Russian song.

Ja-Da 1918 w.m. Bob Carleton. (MT) *Bran Pie*. Beatrice Lillie appeared in *Bran Pie*.

Jack and Diane 1982 w.m. John Cougar Mellencamp

Jack and Jill, *see* **Mother Goose's Melodies**

Jack in the Box 1927 m. Zez Confrey

Jack in the Box 1972 w.m. David Myers, John Worsley

Jack of Diamonds, *see* **Water Boy**

Jack Sprat, *see* **Mother Goose's Melodies**

Jackie Blue 1975 w.m. Larry Lee, Steve Cash

Jacques D'Iraq (Jock D'Rock) 1956 w.m. Jerry Bock, Larry Holofcener, George Weiss. (MT) *Mr. Wonderful*.

Jailhouse Rock 1957 w.m. Jerry Leiber, Mike Stoller. (MF) *Jailhouse Rock*. Elvis Presley appeared in *Jailhouse Rock*.

Jalousie (Jealousy) 1925 (Br.) Eng.w. Winifred May (U.S.A.) Eng.w. Vera Bloom m. Jacob Gade. (MF) *Anchors Aweigh*. (MF) *Painting the Clouds with Sunshine*. Frank Sinatra and Gene Kelly appeared in *Anchors Aweigh*. Lucille Norman and Virginia Mayo appeared in *Painting the Clouds with Sunshine*.

Jamaica Farewell 1957 w.m. Herbie Lovell, Roy McIntyre, Lillian Keyser

Jamaican Rumba 1948 m. Arthur Benjamin

Jambalaya (on the Bayou) 1952 w.m. Hank Williams

James Bond Theme, The 1962 m. Morty Norman. (F) *Doctor No*. (F) *From Russia with Love*. Sean Connery appeared in *Doctor No*. Sean Connery and Lotte Lenya appeared in *From Russia with Love*.

Jane 1980 w.m. Craig Chaquico, David Feiberg, Paul Kantner, James McPherson

Janet 1986 w.m. Bobby Caldwell, Franne Golde

Janet's Choice 1860 w.m. Claribel (Mrs. Charlotte Barnard [Arlington])

Janette 1928 w.m. Horatio Nicholls

January, February 1981 w.m. Alan Tarney. Ivor Novello Award winner 1980–81.

Japanese Sandman, The 1920 w. Raymond B. Egan m. Richard A. Whiting

Japanese Sunset, A 1924 w. Archie Bell m. Jessie L. Deppen

J'Attendrai, *see* **I'll Be Yours**

Java 1964 w.m. Allen Toussaint, Alvin O. Tyler, Murray Sporn, Marilyn Schack

Java Jive 1940 w. Milton Drake m. Ben Oakland. This song starts with two opening bars of ''I Love Coffee, I Love Tea'' of 1915.

Jazz Baby's Ball 1920 w. Charles Bayha m. Maceo Pinkard. (MT) *Shubert Gaieties of 1919*.

Jazz Man 1974 w.m. Carole King, Donald Palmer

Jazz Me Blues 1921 m. Tom Delaney

Jazz Nocturne 1931 m. Dana Suesse

Jazzboat 1959 w.m. Joe Henderson. Ivor Novello Award winner 1959.

Je Vous Aime 1947 w.m. Sam Coslow. (MF) *Copacabana*. Groucho Marx and Carmen Miranda appeared in *Copacabana*.

Jealous 1924 w. Dick Finch, Tommie Malie m. Jack Little. (F) *The Feminine Touch*. (MF) *Somebody Loves Me*. (F) *Don't Trust Your Husband*. Rosalind Russell appeared in *The Feminine Touch*. Betty Hutton appeared in *Somebody Loves Me*. Fred MacMurray and ''Buddy'' Rogers appeared in *Don't Trust Your Husband*.

Jealous Heart 1944 w.m. Jenny Lou Carson. This song was most popular in 1949.

Jealous Lover, *see* **The Apartment**

Jealousy, *see* **Jalousie**

Jean 1895 w.m. Paul Dresser

Jean 1969 w.m. Rod McKuen. (F) *The Prime of Miss Jean Brodie*. Maggie Smith appeared in *The Prime of Miss Jean Brodie*.

Jeanie with the Light Brown Hair 1854 w.m. Stephen Collins Foster. (MF) *Swanee River*. (MF) *I Dream of Jeanie*. Don Ameche and Al Jolson appeared in *Swanee River*. Ray Middleton and Bill Shirley appeared in *I Dream of Jeanie*. Foster wrote this song for his new wife, Jane McDowell; the marriage, however, proved unsuccessful, with countless separations over the years. See also Part I, 1941.

Jeannie 1962 w.m. Norman Newell, Russ Conway. Ivor Novello Award winner 1962.

Jeannine, I Dream of Lilac Time 1928 w. L. Wolfe Gilbert m. Nathaniel Shilkret. (F) *Lilac Time*. Colleen Moore appeared in *Lilac Time*. This song was written for the piano and orchestra accompaniment to this classic silent film.

Jeepers Creepers 1938 w. Johnny Mercer m. Harry Warren. (MF) *Going Places*. This song was sung by Louis Armstrong in *Going Places* to a racehorse named, coincidentally, Jeepers Creepers.

Jelly Roll Blues 1915 w.m. Fred Morton

Jemmy Boker, *see* **Johnny Schmoker**

Jennie Lee 1902 w. Arthur J. Lamb m. Harry Von Tilzer

Jennie, the Flower of Kildare 1873 w. Frank Dumont m. James E. Stewart

Jenny, *see* **Saga of Jenny**

Jeopardy 1983 w.m. Greg Kihn, Stephen Wright

Jericho 1929 w. Leo Robin m. Richard Myers. (MT) *Hello, Yourself!* (MF) *I Dood It*. Red Skelton, Lena Horne and Eleanor Powell appeared in *I Dood It*.

Jerk, The 1964 w.m. Don Julian

Jersey Bounce 1942 w. Buddy Feyne, Robert B. Wright m. Bobby Plater, Tiny Bradshaw, Edward Johnson, Robert B. Wright. (MF) *The Benny Goodman Story*. The words to this song were not added until 1946. This song was popularly revived in 1946.

Jerusalem 1887 w. Nella m. Henry Parker

Jerusalem 1970 w.m. Herb Alpert

Jerusalem the Golden 1861 w. John Mason Neale, based on a work by Bernard of Cluny, twelfth century

Jesse 1973 w.m. Janis Ian

Jessie, the Flow'r o'Dumblane 1808 w. Robert Tannahill m. Robert Archibald Smith

Jessie's Girl 1981 w.m. Rick Springfield

Jesus Christ Superstar 1971 w.m. Andrew Lloyd Webber, Tim Rice. (MT) *Jesus Christ Superstar*. (MF) *Jesus Christ Superstar*. Ben Vereen appeared in the stage production of *Jesus Christ Superstar*. Ivor Novello Award winner 1971–72.

Jesus, Keep Me Near the Cross, *see* **Near the Cross**

Jesus, Lover of My Soul 1834 w. Charles Wesley m. Simeon Butler Marsh

Jet 1974 w.m. Paul McCartney, Linda McCartney

Jet Song 1957 w. Stephen Sondheim m. Leonard Bernstein. (MT) *West Side Story*. (MF) *West Side Story*. Carol Lawrence and Larry Kert appeared in the stage production of *West Side Story*. Natalie Wood and Rita Moreno appeared in the film production of *West Side Story*.

(Theme from) Jewel in the Crown 1985 m. George Fenton. (TV) *Jewel in the Crown*. Ivor Novello Award winner 1984–85.

Jewel of Asia, The 1896 w. Harry Greenbank m. James Philp. (MT) *The Geisha*.

Jezamine 1969 w.m. Marty Wilde (Irene Manston) Ronnie Scott (Jack Gellar). Ivor Novello Award winner 1968–69.

Jezebel 1951 w.m. Wayne Shanklin. (MF) *Seven Hills of Rome*. Mario Lanza appeared in *Seven Hills of Rome*.

Jilted 1954 w.m. Robert Colby, Dick Manning

Jim 1941 w. Nelson Shawn m. Caesar Petrillo, Edward Ross. (MF) *Yokel Boy*. Albert Dekker appeared in *Yokel Boy*.

Jim Along, Josey 1840 w.m. Edward Harper. This song was performed by the playwright in *The Free Nigger of New York*, of 1838.

Jim Crack Corn, *see* **Jimmy Crack Corn**

(Jump) Jim Crow 1830 w.m. anon.; possibly black minstrel Thomas Dartmouth ''Daddy'' Rice, who popularized this song and dance

Jimmy Brown Song, The, *see* **While the Angelus Was Ringing**

Jimmy Crack Corn, or, The Blue Tail Fly 1846 w.m. accredited to Daniel Decatur Emmett. President Lincoln requested this song be played when he went to speak at Gettysburg.

Jimmy Had a Nickel 1933 w. Al Hoffman, Maurice Sigler, Al Goodhart

(Look Out For) Jimmy Valentine 1911 w. Edward Madden m. Gus Edwards. The narrative of this song was inspired by the society burglar immortalized in the O. Henry short story ''A Retrieved Reformation.''

Jimtown Blues 1924 w.m. Fred Rose

Jingle Bell Rock 1958 w.m. Joseph Carleton Beal, James Ross Boothe

Jingle Bells, or, **The One Horse Open Sleigh** 1857 w.m. J.S. Pierpont. (MT) *The 1940's Radio Hour.*

Jingle Jangle Jingle 1942 w. Frank Loesser m. Joseph J. Lilley. (F) *Forest Rangers.* Fred MacMurray, Susan Hayward, and Paulette Goddard appeared in *Forest Rangers.*

Jive Talkin' 1975 w.m. Barry Gibb, Robin Gibb, Maurice Gibb. (F) *Saturday Night Fever.*

Jo Jo 1980 w.m. David Foster, Boz Scaggs, David Lasley

Joan of Arc, They Are Calling You 1917 w. Alfred Bryan, Willie Weston m. Jack Wells

Joanna 1969 w.m. Tony Hatch, Jackie Trent

Joanna 1984 w.m. Clifford Adams, Robert Bell, Ronald Bell, James Bonneford, George Brown, Claydes Eugene Smith, James Taylor, Curtis Williams

Jock, *see* **Stop Yer Tickling, Jock!**

Jockey on the Carousel, The 1935 w. Dorothy Fields m. Jerome Kern. (MF) *I Dream Too Much.* Lily Pons, Henry Fonda, and Lucille Ball appeared in *I Dream Too Much.*

Joe Turner Blues 1916 w.m. William C. Handy, Walter Hirsch

Joey 1954 w.m. Herb Wiener, James J. Kriegsman, Salmirs-Bernstein

Joey, Joey, Joey 1956 w.m. Frank Loesser. (MT) *The Most Happy Fella.*

Jogging Along the Highway 1917 w.m. Harold Samuel

John and Julie 1955 w.m. Philip Green. (F) *John and Julie.* Constance Cummings appeared in *John and Julie.* Ivor Novello Award winner 1955.

John Anderson, My Jo c.1824 w.m. Robert Burns, Josef Marais

(The Wreck of the) John B 1951 w.m. adapted Lee Hays. This song was revived in 1966 as ''Sloop John B.''

John Brown's Body 1861 w. anon.; attributed to Charles S. Hall; Henry Howard Brownell; Thomas Brigham Bishop m. melody based on ''Glory, Glory Hallelujah.'' The words to this song were inspired by the hanging of abolitionist John Brown on Dec. 2, 1859. Sung by the Boston Light Infantry at Fort Marion in 1861. See also ''Battle Hymn of the Republic.''

John Henry 1873 w.m. traditional

John Henry Blues, The 1922 w.m. William C. Handy

(D'Ye Ken) John Peel 1820 w. John Woodcock Graves. m. traditional Old English tune ''Bonnie Annie.'' John Peel was a famous Cumberland hunting man who died in 1854, age 78 years. The melody for this song was later used for a Pepsi-Cola commercial promotion campaign with the lyric ''Pepsi-Cola hits the spot, twelve full ounces that's a lot.'' See also ''Pepsi-Cola Hits the Spot.''

Johnny Angel 1962 w.m. Lyn Duddy, Lee Pockriss

Johnny Doughboy Found a Rose in Ireland 1942 w. Kay Twomey m. Allan Roberts, Al Goodhart. (MF) *Johnny Doughboy.* Jane Withers and Henry Wilcoxson appeared in *Johnny Doughboy.*

Johnny Get Your Gun 1886 w.m. Monroe Rosenfeld. Based on ''Johnny Get Your Hair Cut'' and ''The Arkansas Traveler'' of 1851. The line of lyric ''Johnny get your gun, your sword and pistol'' was added years later by Rosenfeld's publisher, Ellcott Shapiro.

Johnny Is My Darling 1865 w.m. Traditional

Johnny Is the Boy for Me 1953 w.m. Paddy Roberts, Marcel Stellman. Based on the traditional Roumanian folksong ''Sanie Cu Zurgalai.''

Johnny One Note 1937 w. Lorenz Hart m. Richard Rodgers. (MT) *Babes in Arms.* (MF) *Babes in Arms.* (MF) *Words and Music.* Mitzi Green and Ray Heatherton appeared in the stage production of *Babes in Arms.* Judy Garland and Mickey Rooney appeared in the film production of *Babes in Arms.* Mickey Rooney, Judy Garland, and Gene Kelly appeared in *Words and Music,* biopic of song writers Rodgers and Hart.

Johnny Remember Me 1961 w.m. Geoffrey Goddard

Johnny Schmoker 1863 w.m. anon. The melody for this song was adapted as ''Schnitzelbank'' in 1906.

Johnny Vorbeck, *see* **Rambling Wreck from Georgia Tech**

Johnny's Theme, or, **Here's Johnny** 1962 m. Paul Anka, Johnny Carson. (TV) *The Tonight Show.*

Johnson Rag 1917 w. Jack Lawrence m. Guy Hall, Henry Kleinauf. This song was popularly revived in 1940 (with lyrics added) and again in 1949.

Joint Is Jumpin', The 1938 w. Andy Razaf, J.C. Johnson m. Thomas ''Fats'' Waller. (MT) *Ain't Misbehavin'.* Debbie Allen and Nell Carter appeared in *Ain't Misbehavin'.*

Joker, The 1964 w.m. Leslie Bricusse, Anthony Newley. (MT) *The Roar of the Greasepaint—The Smell of the Crowd.* Anthony Newley and Cyril Ritchard appeared in *The Roar of the Greasepaint—The Smell of the Crowd.*

Joker, The 1974 w.m. Eddie Curtis, Steve Miller

Jollity Farm 1930 w.m. Leslie Sarony

Jolly Commodore 1890 w. Edward Harrigan m. David Braham. (MT) *Reilly and the Four Hundred.*

Jolly Farmer, The, *see* **The Happy Farmer**

Jolly Good Company 1931 w.m. Raymond Wallace

Jolly Good Luck to the Girl Who Loves a Soldier 1915 w.m. Fred W. Leigh, Kenneth Lyle. (MF) *After the Ball.* Laurence Harvey appeared in *After the Ball,* biopic of English music hall artist, Vesta Tilley.

Jolly Green Giant, The 1965 w.m. Don F. Harris, Lynn Easton, Dewey Terry, Jr. This song pays homage to the advertising promotion campaign hero for Green Giant canned vegetables.

Jolly Miller, The *see* **Mother Goose's Melodies**

Jones Boy, The 1954 w.m. Manny Curtis, Vic Mizzy

Jose Cuervo 1983 w.m. Cindy Jordan

Josephine 1937 w. Gus Kahn m. Wayne King, Burke Bivens

Josephine 1955 w.m. Cole Porter. (MT) *Silk Stockings*. (MF) *Silk Stockings*. Fred Astaire and Cyd Charisse appeared in the film production of *Silk Stockings*.

Josephine, My Jo 1901 w. R.C. McPherson m. James T. Bryman

Josephine Please No Lean on the Bell 1945 w.m. Edward G. Nelson, Harry Pease, Duke Leonard

Josh-Ua 1912 w.m. George Arthurs, Bert Lee

Joshua Fit (Fought) de Battle of Jericho 1865 w.m. traditional black American spiritual. This song was popularly revived in 1930, with a new arrangement by Marshall Bartholomew.

Josita 1958 w.m. Philip Green

Joy to the World, or, **Antioch** 1839 w. Isaac Watts m. hymn derived from Handel; arr. Lowell Mason 1836

Joy to the World 1971 w.m. Hoyt Axton

Juanita 1850 w.m. traditional; w. possibly Carolina Norton. Based on a traditional Spanish air, and that, in turn, on Handel's aria "Lascia Ch'io Pianga." (F) *The Rodeo King and the Senorita*. Mary Ellen Kay and Rex Allen appeared in *The Rodeo King and the Senorita*.

Juba Dance 1913 w.m. R. Nathaniel Dett. From the suite "In the Bottoms."

Jubilation T. Cornpone 1956 w. Johnny Mercer m. Gene De Paul. (MT) *Li'l Abner*. (MF) *Li'l Abner*. Stubby Kaye appeared in the film production of *Li'l Abner*.

Judy in Disguise (with Glasses) 1968 w.m. John Fred, Andrew Bernard

Judy's Turn To Cry 1963 w.m. Edna Lewis, Beverly Ross

Juke Box Baby 1956 w. Noel Sherman m. Joe Sherman

Juke Box Saturday Night 1942 w. Al Stillman m. Paul McGrane. (MT) *Stars On Ice*.

Julia 1968 w.m. John Lennon, Paul McCartney

Juliet 1964 w.m. Mike Wilsh, Fritz Fryer, Lionel Morton

Juliet Bravo 1981 m. Johann Sebastian Bach, Arr. Derek Goom. Ivor Novello Award winner 1980–81.

Jump 1984 w.m. Michael Anthony, David Lee Roth, Alex Van Halen, Eddie Van Halen

Jump (for My Love) 1984 w.m. Steve Mitchell, Marti Sharron-Humak, Gary P. Skardina

Jump Jim Crow 1917 w. Rida Johnson Young m. Sigmund Romberg. (MT) *Maytime*. (MF) *Maytime*. Peggy Wood, Charles Purcell, and William Norris appeared in the stage production of *Maytime*. Jeanette MacDonald, Nelson Eddy, and John Barrymore appeared in the film production of *Maytime*.

Jump, Jim Crow, *see also* **Jim Crow**

Jump Over 1960 w.m. Bob Crewe, Frank C. Slay, Jr.

Jumpin' at the Woodside 1938 w.m. William "Count" Basie

Jumping Bean 1949 w.m. Robert Farnon

Jumpin' Jive 1939 w.m. Cab Calloway, Jack Palmer

June Brought the Roses 1924 w. Ralph Stanley m. John Openshaw

June Comes Around Every Year 1945 w. Johnny Mercer m. Harold Arlen. (MF) *Out of This World*. Eddie Bracken and Veronica Lake appeared in *Out of This World*.

(It's) June in January 1934 w.m. Leo Robin, Ralph Rainger. (MF) *Here Is My Heart*. Bing Crosby appeared in *Here Is My Heart*.

June Is Bustin' Out All Over 1945 w. Oscar Hammerstein II m. Richard Rodgers. (MT) *Carousel*. (MF) *Carousel*. Jan Clayton and John Raitt appeared in the stage production of *Carousel*. Gordon MacRae and Shirley Jones appeared in the film production of *Carousel*.

June Moon 1929 w.m. Ring Lardner. (T) *June Moon*. (F) *June Moon*. Harry Akst and Jack Oakie appeared in the film production of *June Moon*.

June Night (Just Give Me a June Night, the Moonlight and You) 1924 w. Cliff Friend m. Abel Baer. (MF) *Somebody Loves Me*. Betty Hutton appeared in *Somebody Loves Me*, biopic of song spinners Blossom Seeley and Benny Fields.

Jungle Boogie 1973 w.m. Robert D. Mersey

Jungle Drums (Canto Karabali) 1933 Eng.w. Carmen Lombardo, Charles O'Flynn m. Ernesto Lecuona. (F) *Dancing Co-Ed*. Lana Turner appeared in *Dancing Co-Ed*.

Júrame (Promise, Love) 1926 Sp.w. Maria Grever Eng.w. Frederick Herman Martens m. Maria Grever

Just a Baby's Prayer at Twilight 1918 w. Sam M. Lewis, Joe Young m. M.K. Jerome

Just a Closer Walk with Thee 1950 w.m. Red Foley

Just a Cottage Small—By a Waterfall 1925 w. B.G. DeSylva m. James F. Hanley

Just a Dream 1958 w.m. Jimmy Clanton, C. Matassa

Just a Gigolo 1930 Ger.w. Julius Brammer Eng.w. Irving Caesar m. Leonello Casucci. From the German "Schöner Gigolo". (MF) *Lover Come Back*. Lucille Ball appeared in *Lover Come Back*.

Just a Girl That Men Forget 1923 Fr.w. R. Beaudry Eng.w.m. Al Dubin, Fred Rath, Joe Garren

Just a Kid Named Joe 1938 w.m. Mack David, Jerry Livingston

Just a Little Bit South of North Carolina 1940 w.m. Sunny Skylar, Arthur Shaftel

Just a Little Fond Affection 1945 w.m. Elton Box, Desmond Cox, Lewis Ilda

Just a Little Love, a Little Kiss, *see* **A Little Love, a Little Kiss**

Just a Little Lovin' 1912 w. Andrew B. Sterling m. Harry Von Tilzer

Just a Little Rocking Chair and You 1905 w. Bert Fitzgibbon, Jack Drislane m. Theodore F. Morse

Just a Little Street Where Old Friends Meet, *see* **Little Street Where Old Friends Meet**

Just a Memory 1927 w. B.G. DeSylva, Lew Brown m. Ray Henderson. (MF) *Look for the Silver Lining*. (MF) *The Best Things in Life Are Free*. (MF) *Both Ends of the Candle*. June Haver and Ray Bolger appeared in *Look for the Silver Lining*, biopic of Marilyn Miller. Gordon MacRae, Dan

Dailey, and Ernest Borgnine appeared in *The Best Things in Life Are Free*, biopic of song writers DeSylva, Brown, and Henderson.

Just a Piece of Sky 1985 w. Alan Bergman, Marilyn Bergman m. Michel Legrand. (MF) *Yentl*. Barbra Streisand appeared in *Yentl*.

Just a Song At Twilight, *see* **Love's Old Sweet Song**

Just a Voice To Call Me, Dear 1917 w. P.G. Wodehouse m. Emmerich Kalman. (MT) *The Riviera Girl*.

Just A-Wearyin' for You 1901 w. Frank Stanton m. Carrie Jacobs-Bond

Just an Echo in the Valley 1932 w.m. Jimmy Campbell, Reginald Connelly, Harry M. Woods

Just Another Day in Paradise 1982 w.m. Columbia Jones, Sonny Limbo

Just Another Day Wasted Away 1927 w.m. Charles Tobias, Roy Turk

Just Another Polka 1953 w.m. Frank Loesser, Milton DeLugg

Just Another Woman in Love 1984 w.m. Wanda Mallette, Patti Ryan

Just As I Am 1985 w.m. Robert Eric Hegel, Richard Allen Wagner

Just As I Am Without One Plea 1849 w. Charlotte Elliot m. William Batchelder Bradbury

Just As the Sun Went Down 1898 w. Karl Kennett m. Lyn Udall

Just Because She Made Dem Goo-Goo Eyes 1900 w.m. John Queen, Hughie Cannon

Just Because You're You 1932 w.m. Cliff Friend

Just Before the Battle, Mother 1863 w.m. George Frederick Root

Just Born To Be Your Baby 1957 w. Luther Dixon m. Billy Dawn Smith

Just Come Home 1960 Fr.w. Edith Piaf Eng.w. Carl Sigman m. Marguerite Monnot

Just for Once 1959 w. Dorothy Fields m. Albert Hague. (MT) *Redhead*.

Just for the Sake of Our Daughter 1897 w.m. Monroe H. Rosenfeld

Just for Tonight 1979 w. Carole Bayer Sager m. Marvin Hamlisch. (MT) *They're Playing Our Song*. Robert Klein and Lucie Arnaz appeared in *They're Playing Our Song*.

Just for You, *see* **Yearning**

Just Friends 1931 w. Sam M. Lewis m. John Klenner

Just Humming Along 1932 w.m. Montague Ewing, Sherman Myers

Just Imagine 1928 w. B.G. DeSylva, Lew Brown m. Ray Henderson. (MT) *Good News*. (MF) *Good News* (1947). (MF) *The Best Things in Life Are Free*. June Allyson and Peter Lawford appeared in the 1947 film production of *Good News*. Gordon MacRae, Dan Dailey, and Ernest Borgnine appeared in *The Best Things in Life Are Free*, biopic of song writers DeSylva, Brown, and Henderson. This song was popularly revived in 1947.

Just In Time 1956 w. Betty Comden, Adolph Green m. Jule Styne. (MT) *Bells Are Ringing*. (MF) *Bells Are Ringing*. Judy Holiday appeared in both the stage and film productions of *Bells Are Ringing*.

Just Let Me Look at You 1938 w. Dorothy Fields m. Jerome Kern. (MF) *The Joy of Living*. Irene Dunne, Douglas Fairbanks, Jr., and Lucille Ball appeared in *The Joy of Living*.

Just Like a Butterfly (That's Caught in the Rain) 1927 w. Mort Dixon m. Harry Woods

Just Like a Gypsy 1919 w.m. Seymour B. Simons, Nora Bayes. (MT) *Ladies First*.

Just Like a Melody Out of the Sky 1928 w.m. Walter Donaldson. Theme song of Jay Wilbur.

Just Like a Thief 1923 w.m. Horatio Nicholls

Just Like a Woman 1966 w.m. Bob Dylan

Just Like Eddie 1963 w.m. Geoffrey Goddard

Just Like Starting Over, *see* **(Just Like) Starting Over**

Just Like That 1980 w. Dick Vosburgh m. Frank Lazarus. (MT) *A Day in Hollywood—a Night in the Ukraine*. David Garrison and Priscilla Lopez appeared in *A Day in Hollywood—a Night in the Ukraine*.

Just Like the Butterfly (That's Caught in the Rain), *see* **Just Like a Butterfly**

Just Like the Ivy 1903 w.m. A.J. Mills, Harry Castling

Just Like Washington Crossed the Delaware, General Pershing Will Cross the Rhine 1918 w. Howard Johnson m. George W. Meyer

Just My Imagination (Running Away with Me) 1971 w.m. Norman Whitfield, Barrett Strong

Just Once 1981 w.m. Barry Mann, Cynthia Weil

Just Once for All Time 1931 w.m. Werner Heymann, Robert Gilbert, Rowland Leigh. (F) *Congress Dances*. Lilian Harvey and Lil Dagover appeared in *Congress Dances*.

Just One Girl 1898 w. Karl Kennett m. Lyn Udall

Just One More Chance 1931 w.m. Sam Coslow, Arthur Johnston. (MF) *College Coach*. (MF) *The Stooge*. Dean Martin, Jerry Lewis, and Polly Bergen appeared in *The Stooge*.

Just One of Those Things 1935 w.m. Cole Porter. (MT) *Jubilee*. (MT) *Lena Horne: The Lady and Her Music*. (MF) *Night and Day*. (MF) *Lullaby of Broadway*. (MF) *The Young At Heart*. (MF) *The Eddy Duchin Story*. (MF) *Can-Can*. The title for this song was used five years earlier in a song from Porter's 1930 musical *The New Yorkers*, but was dropped from the New York production. Melville Cooper and May Boland appeared in *Jubilee*. Lena Horne appeared in *Lena Horne: The Lady and Her Music*. Cary Grant and Mary Martin appeared in *Night and Day*, biopic of composer Cole Porter. Doris Day and Billy DeWolf appeared in *Lullaby of Broadway*. Frank Sinatra and Doris Day appeared in *The Young at Heart*. Frank Sinatra and Shirley MacLaine appeared in *Can-Can*.

Just One Way To Say I Love You 1949 w.m. Irving Berlin. (MT) *Miss Liberty*. Eddie Albert, Allyn McLerie, and Mary McCarthy appeared in *Miss Liberty*.

Just Say I'm a Friend of Yours, *see* **Friend of Yours**

Just Tell Them That You Saw Me 1895 w.m. Paul Dresser

Just the Two of Us 1981 w.m. Ralph MacDonald, William Salter, Bill Withers. Grammy Award winner 1981.

Just the Way You Are 1977 w.m. Billy Joel. Grammy Award winner 1978.

Just To Be Close to You 1976 w.m. Lionel Richie

Just to Satisfy You 1982 w.m. Don Bowman, Waylon Jennings

Just Try To Picture Me (Back [Down] Home in Tennessee) 1915 w. William Jerome m. Walter Donaldson

Just Walking in the Rain 1956 w.m. Johnny Bragg, Robert S. Riley

Just We Two 1924 w. Dorothy Donnelly m. Sigmund Romberg. (MT) *The Student Prince.* Howard Marsh, Ilsa Marvenga, and George Hassell appeared in *The Student Prince.*

Just When I Needed You Most 1979 w.m. Randy Van Warmer

Just You, Just Me 1929 w. Raymond Klages m. Jesse Greer. (MF) *Marianne.* (F) *This Could Be the Night.* Marion Davies and Lawrence Gray appeared in *Marianne.* Jean Simmons and Anthony Franciosa appeared in *This Could Be the Night.*

Just You 'N' Me (Babe) 1973 w.m. James C. Pankow

Just You Wait 1956 w. Alan Jay Lerner m. Frederick Loewe. (MT) *My Fair Lady.* (MF) *My Fair Lady.* Julie Andrews appeared in the stage production of *My Fair Lady.* Audrey Hepburn appeared in the film production of *My Fair Lady.*

Kafoozelum 1866 w. S. Oxon m. arr. F. Blume

Kalamazoo, *see* **I've Got a Gal in Kalamazoo**

Ka-Lu-A 1920 w. Anne Caldwell m. Jerome Kern. (MT) *Good Morning, Dearie.* (MT) *The Cabaret Girl.* (MF) *Till the Clouds Roll By.* Dorothy Dickson appeared in *The Cabaret Girl.* June Allyson and Judy Garland appeared in *Till the Clouds Roll By,* biopic of composer Jerome Kern. A lawsuit was filed by Fred Fisher against Jerome Kern, claiming that Kern had stolen the bass accompaniment for his "Ka-Lu-A" from Fisher's "Dardanella" of 1919. Kern won indisputably and was offered a suit of clothes as a token payment. Kern declined.

Kamennoi Ostrow 1855 m. Artur Rubinstein

Kansas City 1943 w. Oscar Hammerstein II m. Richard Rodgers. (MT) *Oklahoma!* (MF) *Oklahoma!* Celeste Holm, Alfred Drake, and Betty Garde appeared in the stage production of *Oklahoma!* Shirley Jones and Gordon MacRae appeared in the film production of *Oklahoma!*

Kansas City 1959 w. Mike Stoller m. Jerry Leiber

Kansas City Kitty 1929 w. Edgar Leslie m. Walter Donaldson. (MF) *Kansas City Kitty.* Joan Davis and Bob Crosby appeared in *Kansas City Kitty.*

Kansas City Lights 1982 w.m. Rhonda J. Fleming, Dennis Morgan

Karma Chameleon 1984 w.m. Michael Craig, Roy Hay, John Moss, George O'Dowd, Phil Pickett. Ivor Novello Award winner 1983–84.

Kashmiri Love Song 1903 w. Lawrence Hope m. Amy Woodeforde-Finden. From "Four Indian Love Lyrics." The narrative of this song tells the true story of Adela Florence Cory, who, while married to a British general in India, fell in love with the son of an Indian rajah in Kashmir.

Kathleen 1894 w.m. Helene Mora

Kathleen Mavourneen 1840 w. Annie Crawford (Barry) m. Frederick William Nichols Crouch

Katie Went to Haiti 1939 w.m. Cole Porter. (MT) *Du Barry Was a Lady.* (MF) *Du Barry Was a Lady.* Ethel Merman, Bert Lahr, and Betty Grable appeared in the stage production of *Du Barry Was a Lady.* Lucille Ball, Red Skelton, and Gene Kelly appeared in the film production of *Du Barry Was a Lady.*

Katinka 1916 w. Otto Harbach m. Rudolf Friml. (MT) *Katinka.*

Katinka 1926 w. Ben Russell m. Henry Tobias

Kattie (Katy) Avourneen 1856 w.m. Desmond Ryan, Frederick Nicholls Crouch, S.T. Gordon

Katy Bell 1863 w.m. Stephen Collins Foster

Kaw-Liga 1969 w.m. Fred Rose, Hank Williams

Keem-O-Sabe 1969 w.m. Bernard Binnick, Bernice Borisoff

Keep-A-Hoppin' 1960 w.m. Meredith Willson. (MT) *The Unsinkable Molly Brown.* (MF) *The Unsinkable Molly Brown.* Tammy Grimes appeared in the stage production of *The Unsinkable Molly Brown.* Debbie Reynolds appeared in the film production of *The Unsinkable Molly Brown.*

Keep a Little Cozy Corner in Your Heart for Me 1905 w. Jack Drislane m. Theodore F. Morse

Keep It a Secret 1952 w.m. Jessie Mae Robinson

Keep It Comin' Love 1977 w.m. Harry Casey, Richard Finch

Keep It Gay 1953 w. Oscar Hammerstein II m. Richard Rodgers. (MT) *Me and Juliet.*

Keep On Dancin' 1979 w.m. Joseph William Tucci, Gary R. Turnier

Keep On Doin' What You're Doin' 1933 w.m. Bert Kalmar, Harry Ruby. (MF) *Hips Hips Hooray.* Ruth Etting and Thelma Todd appeared in *Hips Hips Hooray.*

Keep On Loving You 1981 w.m. Kevin Cronin

Keep on the Sunny Side 1906 w. Jack Drislane m. Theodore F. Morse

Keep On Truckin' 1973 w.m. Frank Wilson, Anita Poree, Leonard Caston

Keep Smiling at Trouble 1924 w. Al Jolson, B.G. DeSylva m. Lewis Gensler. (MT) *Big Boy.* Al Jolson, Ralph Whitehead, and Franklyn Batie appeared in *Big Boy.*

Keep Sweeping the Cobwebs Off the Moon 1927 w. Sam M. Lewis, Joe Young m. Oscar Levant

Keep the Home Fires Burning (Till the Boys Come Home) 1915 w. Lena Guilbert Ford m. Ivor Novello

Keep Young and Beautiful 1933 w. Al Dubin m. Harry Warren. (MF) *Roman Scandals.* Eddie Cantor and Ruth Etting appeared in *Roman Scandals.*

Keep Your Head Down, "Fritzie Boy" 1918 w.m. Gitz Rice

Keep Your Skirts Down, Mary Ann 1925 w. Andrew B. Sterling m. Ray Henderson, Robert A. King

Keep Your Sunny Side Up, *see* **Sunny Side Up**

Keeper of the Eddystone Light, The, or, **The Eddystone Light** c.1700 w.m. traditional sea chantey

Keepin' Myself for You 1929 w. Sidney Clare m. Vincent Youmans. (MF) *Hit the Deck*. Jack Oakie and Polly Walker appeared in the 1929 film production of *Hit the Deck*.

Keepin' Out of Mischief Now 1932 w. Andy Razaf m. Thomas "Fats" Waller. (MT) *Ain't Misbehavin'*. Debbie Allen and Nell Carter appeared in *Ain't Misbehavin'*.

Keeping the Faith 1985 w.m. Billy Joel

Kemo-Kimo 1840 w.m. traditional

Kentucky 1944 w.m. Henry Pritchard

Kentucky Babe 1896 w. Richard Buck m. Adam Geibel

Kentucky Screamer, De, *see* **Clare De Kitchen**

Kentucky Sue 1912 w. Lew Brown m. Albert Von Tilzer

Kentucky Waltz 1934 w.m. Bill Monroe. This song was popularly revived in 1951.

Kerry Dance, The 1878 w. James Lyman Molloy m. anon.; based on the first eight bars of the melody "The Cuckoo", w.m. Margaret Casson, published 1790 in England.

Kewpie Doll 1958 w.m. Sid Tepper, Roy C. Bennett

Key Largo 1982 w.m. Bertie Higgins, Sonny Limbo

Khartoum 1966 w.m. Frank Cordell

Kickin' the Clouds Away 1925 w. B.G. DeSylva, Ira Gershwin m. George Gershwin. (MT) *Tell Me More*. (MT) *My One and Only*. Tommy Tune and Twiggy appeared in *My One and Only*. The original out-of-town title for *Tell Me More* was *My Fair Lady*.

Kickin' the Gong Around 1931 w.m. Ted Koehler, Harold Arlen. (MF) *The Big Broadcast*. Cab Calloway, Bing Crosby, and Kate Smith appeared in *The Big Broadcast*.

Kicks 1966 w.m. Barry Mann, Cynthia Weil

Kid Days 1919 w. Jesse G.M. Glick m. Irving M. Wilson

Kids 1960 w. Lee Adams m. Charles Strouse. (MT) *Bye Bye Birdie*. (MF) *Bye Bye Birdie*. Dick Van Dyke, Janet Leigh, and Ann Margret appeared in the film production of *Bye Bye Birdie*.

Killarney 1862 w. Edmund Falconer m. Michael William Balfe

Killer Queen 1975 w.m. Freddie Mercury. Ivor Novello Award winner 1974–75.

Killing Me Softly with His Song 1973 w.m. Charles Fox, Norman Gimbel Grammy Award winner 1973.

Kind of a Drag 1967 w.m. James Holvay

Kinda Like You 1932 w. Edward Heyman m. Vincent Youmans. (MT) *Through the Years*.

King Cotton March 1895 m. John Philip Sousa. This march was specially written for the Cotton States Exposition at Atlanta in 1895.

King for a Day 1986 w.m. Tom Bailey, Alannah Currie, Joe Leeway

King of Pain 1984 w.m. Gordon "Sting" Sumner

King of the Road 1965 w.m. Roger Miller. Grammy Award winner 1965. See also Part I, 1965.

King Porter Stomp 1924 m. Ferdinand "Jelly Roll" Morton

Kingdom Coming, or, **The Year of Jubilo** 1862 w.m. Henry Clay Work

King's Horses, The 1930 w.m. Noel Gay, Harry Graham. (MT) *Folly To Be Wise*.

King's Navee, The 1936 w.m. Charles Dunn

Kinkajou, The 1926 w. Joseph McCarthy m. Harry Tierney. (MT) *Rio Rita*. (MF) *Rio Rita* (1929). (MF) *Rio Rita* (1942). Ethelind Terry and J. Harold Murray appeared in the stage production of *Rio Rita*. Bert Wheeler and John Boles appeared in the 1929 film production of *Rio Rita*.

Kiss 1986 w.m. Prince

Kiss, The 1965 w.m. Jack Parnell

Kiss a Four Leaf Clover 1926 w. Anne Caldwell, Otto Harbach m. Jerome Kern. (MT) *Criss-Cross*.

Kiss an Angel Good Mornin' 1971 w.m. Ben Peters. Grammy Award winner 1972.

Kiss and Let's Make Up 1891 w.m. Charles K. Harris

Kiss and Run 1953 w.m. Jack Ledru, Rene Dononcin, Bill Engvick

Kiss and Say Goodbye 1976 w.m. Winfred Lovett

Kiss Her Now 1969 w.m. Jerry Herman. (MT) *Dear World*. (MT) *Jerry's Girls*. Angela Lansbury appeared in *Dear World*. Dorothy Loudon, Chita Rivera, and Leslie Uggams appeared in *Jerry's Girls*.

Kiss in the Dark, A 1922 w. B.G. DeSylva m. Victor Herbert. (MT) *Orange Blossoms*. (MF) *The Great Victor Herbert*. (MF) *Look for the Silver Lining*. Mary Martin and Allan Jones appeared in *The Great Victor Herbert*. Ray Bolger and June Haver appeared in *Look for the Silver Lining*. biopic of Marilyn Miller.

Kiss Me 1979 w.m. Stephen Sondheim. (MT) *Sweeney Todd*. Angela Lansbury and Len Cariou appeared in *Sweeney Todd*.

Kiss Me Again, or, **If I Were on the Stage** 1905 w. Henry Blossom m. Victor Herbert. (MT) *Mlle. Modiste*. (MF) *The Great Victor Herbert*. Mary Martin appeared in *The Great Victor Herbert*. This song was originally titled "If I Were on the Stage." This song was popularly revived in 1915, when Victor Herbert issued it separately for the first time, and not as part of the score of *Mlle. Modiste*. While *Mlle. Modiste* was in rehearsal, Fritzi Scheff, star of the show, asked Victor Herbert to kiss her, thus inspiring this song. Theme song of Fritzi Scheff.

Kiss Me, Honey, Do 1898 w. Edgar Smith m. John Stromberg

Kiss Me, Honey Honey, Kiss Me 1958 w.m. Al Timothy, Michael Julien

Kiss Me, My Honey, Kiss Me 1910 w. Irving Berlin m. Ted Snyder

Kiss Me Sweet 1949 w.m. Milton Drake

Kiss of Fire 1952 w.m. Lester Allen, Robert B. Hill. Based on A.G. Villoldo's "El Choclo" of 1913.

Kiss on My List 1981 w.m. Janna Allen, Daryl Hall

Kiss That You've Forgotten, The (Is the Kiss I Can't Forget) 1931 w. Dorothy Dick m. Harry Link

Kiss the Boys Goodbye 1941 w. Frank Loesser m. Victor Schertzinger. (MF) *Kiss the Boys Goodbye*. Mary Martin and Don Ameche appeared in *Kiss the Boys Goodbye*.

Kiss To Build a Dream On, A 1935 w.m. Bert Kalmar, Harry Ruby, Oscar Hammerstein II. (MF) *The Strip*. Mickey Rooney and Louis Armstrong appeared in *The Strip*. This song was popularly revived in 1951.

Kiss Waltz, The 1930 w. Al Dubin m. Joe Burke. (MF) *Dancing Sweeties*. (F) *Three Flights Up*. Sue Carol and Grant Withers appeared in *Dancing Sweeties*.

Kiss Waltz, The, *see also* **Il Bacio** *and* **My Beautiful Lady**

Kiss You All Over 1978 w.m. Nicky Chinn, Mike Chapman

Kisses Sweeter Than Wine 1951 w. Paul Campbell m. Joel Newman. This song was popularly revived in 1957.

Kisses—The Sweetest Kisses of All 1918 w. Alex Sullivan m. Lynn Cowan

Kitten on the Keys 1921 w. Sam Coslow m. Edward (Zez) Confrey. This song was published in 1921 as a piano solo only.

Kitty the Telephone Girl 1915 w.m. A.J. Lawrence, Huntley Trevor, Tom Mellor, Harry Gifford. (MT) *5064 Gerard*. Jack Norworth and Murray's Ragtime Trio appeared in *5064 Gerard*.

K-K-K-Katy 1918 Fr.w. A. Bollaert Eng.w. Geoffrey O'Hara m. Geoffrey O'Hara (MT) *Buzz*. (MT) *The Glorious Days*. (MF) *The Cockeyed World*. (MF) *Tin Pan Alley*. Walter Williams and Dan O'Neill appeared in *Buzz Buzz*. Anna Neagle appeared in *The Glorious Days*. Joe E. Lewis appeared in *The Cockeyed World*. Betty Grable appeared in *Tin Pan Alley*. This wartime hit was billed as "The Sensational Stammering Song Success Sung by the Soldiers and Sailors."

Knees Up Mother Brown 1938 w.m. Harris Weston, Bert Lee, Irving Taylor

Knights of the Mystic Star 1891 w. Edward Harrigan m. David Braham. (MT) *The Last of the Hogans*.

Knightsbridge March, or, **In Town Tonight** 1933 m. Eric Coates. From "London Suite."

Knock, Knock, Who's There 1936 w.m. William Henry Davies, Vincent Lopez

Knock, Knock, Who's There 1971 w.m. Geoff Stephens, John Carter. Ivor Novello Award winner 1970–71.

Knock On Wood 1954 w.m. Sylvia Fine. (MF) *Knock On Wood*. Danny Kaye and Mai Zetterling appeared in *Knock On Wood*.

Knock On Wood 1979 w.m. Steve Cropper, Eddie Floyd

Knock Three Times 1971 w.m. Irwin Levine, L. Russell Brown

Knocked 'Em in the Old Kent Road 1901 w. Albert Chevalier m. Charles Ingle

Knockin' on Heaven's Door 1973 **w.m. Bob Dylan**

Knot of Blue, A 1905 w. Glen MacDonough m. Victor Herbert. (MT) *It Happened in Nordland*.

Knowing When To Leave 1968 w. Hal David m. Burt Bacharach. (MT) *Promises, Promises*

Ko Ko Mo (I Love You So) 1955 w.m. Jake Porter, Eunice Levy, Forrest Wilson

Kodachrome 1973 w.m. Paul Simon

Kol Nidre 1765 w. possibly as early as the ninth century m. possibly as early as the fifteenth century. (MF) *The Jazz Singer*. Al Jolson appeared in *The Jazz Singer*.

Kon-Tiki 1961 w.m. Michael Carr

Kookie, Kookie, Lend Me Your Comb 1959 w.m. Irving Taylor. (TV) *77 Sunset Strip*.

K-ra-zy for You 1928 w. Ira Gershwin m. George Gershwin. (MT) *Treasure Girl*. Gertrude Lawrence and Clifton Webb appeared in *Treasure Girl*.

Kung Fu Fighting 1974 w.m. Carl Douglas. Ivor Novello Award winner 1974–75.

Kyrie 1986 w.m. Steven George, John Lang, Richard Page

La-Di-Da-Di-Da 1934 w.m. Noel Gay, Desmond Carter. (MT) *That's a Pretty Thing*. Bobbie Comber appeared in *That's a Pretty Thing*.

Ladder of Roses 1915 w. R.H. Burnside m. Raymond Hubbell. (MT) *Hip, Hip, Horray*.

Ladies in Waiting 1957 w.m. Cole Porter. (MF) *Les Girls*.

Ladies Night 1980 w.m. Robert Earl Bell, Ronald Nathan Bell, George M. Brown, Claydes Eugene Smith, James Warren Taylor, Dennis Ronald Thomas, Earl Eugene Toon, Jr., Muhammed Meekaaeel

Ladies Who Lunch, The 1970 w.m. Stephen Sondheim. (MT) *Company*. Elaine Stritch appeared in *Company*.

Ladies Who Sing with the Band, The 1943 w.m. Thomas "Fats" Waller, George Marion, Jr. (MT) *Early to Bed*. (MT) *Ain't Misbehavin'*. Richard Kolmar and Muriel Angelus appeared in *Early to Bed*. Debbie Allen and Nell Carter appeared in *Ain't Misbehavin'*.

Lady 1979 w.m. Graham Goble

Lady Be Good, *see* **Oh, Lady Be Good**

Lady Bird 1967 w.m. Lee Hazelwood. This song pays tribute to Lady Bird Johnson, then First Lady of the United States.

Lady Blue 1975 w.m. Leon Russell

Lady from Twenty-Nine Palms, The 1947 w.m. Allie Wrubel

Lady in Ermine, The 1922 w. Cyrus Wood m. Alfred Goodman. (MT) *The Lady in Ermine*.

Lady in Red, The 1935 w.m. Mort Dixon, Allie Wrubel. (MF) *In Caliente*. Dolores Del Rio and Edward Everett Horton appeared in *In Caliente*.

Lady Is a Tramp, The 1937 w. Lorenz Hart m. Richard Rodgers. (MT) *Babes in Arms*. (MF) *Babes in Arms*. (MF) *Words and Music*. (MF) *Pal Joey*. Mitzi Green and Ray Heatherton appeared in the stage production of *Babes in Arms*.

Judy Garland and Mickey Rooney appeared in the film production of *Babes in Arms*. Lena Horne appeared in *Words and Music*, biopic of song writers Rodgers and Hart. Frank Sinatra and Kim Novak appeared in *Pal Joey*. This song was written by Rodgers and Hart in one day.

Lady Love Me One More Time 1984 w.m. James Howard, David Paitch

Lady Luck Show 1929 w.m. Ray Perkins. (MT) *Show of Shows*. (MF) *Show of Shows*. Beatrice Lillie and Loretta Young appeared in both the stage and film productions of *Show of Shows*.

Lady Madonna 1968 w.m. John Lennon, Paul McCartney. (MT) *Beatlemania*.

Lady Marmalade 1975 w.m. Kenny Nolan, Bob Crewe

Lady of Spain 1931 w. Erell Reaves m. Tolchard Evans. This song was popularly revived in 1952.

Lady of the Evening 1922 w.m. Irving Berlin. (MT) *Music Box Revue*.

Lady Play Your Mandolin 1930 w. Irving Ceasar m. Oscar Levant

Lady Willpower 1968 w.m. Jerry Fuller

Lady's in Love with You, The 1939 w. Frank Loesser m. Burton Lane. (MF) *Some Like It Hot*. Bob Hope and Shirley Ross appeared in the 1939 film production of *Some Like It Hot*.

Lafayette—We Hear You Calling 1918 w.m. Mary Earl (Robert A. King)

Lambeth Walk 1937 w.m. Douglas Furber, Noel Gay, Arthur Rose. (MT) *Me and My Girl*. Lupino Lane appeared in *Me and My Girl*.

Lament of the Irish Emigrant, The 1843 w. Mrs. Price Blackwood m. William Richardson Dempster

Lamp Is Low, The 1939 w. Mitchell Parish m. Peter DeRose, Bert Shefter. Based on Ravel's ''Pavanne for a Dead Infanta'' of 1899.

Lamplighter's Serenade, The 1942 w. Paul Francis Webster m. Hoagy Carmichael

Lamplit Hour, The 1919 w. Thomas Burke m. Arthur A. Penn

Land of Golden Dreams, The 1912 w. C.M. Denison m. E.F. Dusenberry

Land of Hope and Glory, The 1902 w. Arthur C. Benson m. Edward Elgar

Land of Make Believe, The 1982 w.m. Andy Hill, Pete Sinfield. Ivor Novello Award winner 1981–82.

Land of My Best Girl, The 1914 w. Ballard MacDonald m. Harry Carroll

Landing of the Pilgrims, The, or, **The Pilgrim Fathers** 1830 w. Felicia Dorothea Hemans m. Augusta Browne (Garrett)

Landlord, Fill the Flowing Bowl, *see* **Come, Landlord, Fill the Flowing Bowl**

Language of Love, The 1984 w.m. Dan Fogelberg

Lanky Yankee Boys in Blue, The 1908 w. Edward Madden m. Theodore F. Morse

Lara's Theme, *see* **Somewhere My Love**

Laroo Laroo Lilli Bolero 1948 w.m. Sylvia Dee, Sidney Lippman, Elizabeth Evelyn Moore

Lass of Richmond Hill, The 1789 w. Leonard McNally m. James Hook. James Hook, a noted organist of his day, wrote some two thousand songs.

Lass with the Delicate Air, The, or, **Young Molly Who Lives at the Foot of the Hill** 1760 w. anon. m. Michael Arne *(not* Thomas Arne)

Last Dance 1978 w.m. Paul Jabara. (F) *Thank God It's Friday*. Grammy Award winner 1978. Academy Award winner 1978.

Last Date 1960 w.m. Floyd Cramer

Last Farewell 1976 w.m. Roger Whittaker, R.A. Webster. Ivor Novello Award winner 1975–76.

Last Hope, The 1856 m. Louis Moreau Gottschalk

Last Kiss 1964 w.m. Wayne Cochran

Last Night I Didn't Get to Sleep At All 1972 w.m. Tony Macaulay

Last Night On the Back Porch—I Loved Her Best of All 1923 w.m. Lew Brown, Carl Schraubstader

Last Night Was Made for Love 1962 w.m. Alan Fielding

Last Night Was the End of the World 1912 w. Andrew B. Sterling m. Harry Von Tilzer

Last Night When We Were Young 1936 w. E.Y. Harburg m. Harold Arlen

Last of the Hogans, The 1891 w. Edward Harrigan m. David Braham

Last Rose of Summer, The *see* **'Tis the Last Rose of Summer**

Last Round-Up, The 1933 w.m. William Hill. (MT) *Ziegfeld Follies of 1934*. (MF) *The Singing Hill*. (MF) *Don't Fence Me In*. Fanny Brice and Jane Froman appeared in *Ziegfeld Follies of 1934*. Gene Autry and Smiley Burnette appeared in *The Singing Hill*. Roy Rogers and Dale Evans appeared in *Don't Fence Me In*. This song was first popularly sung by Joe Morrison at New York's Paramount Theatre.

Last Thing On My Mind, (The) 1968 w.m. Tom Paxton

Last Time I Saw Paris, The 1940 w. Oscar Hammerstein II m. Jerome Kern. (MF) *Lady, Be Good*. (MF) *Till the Clouds Roll By*. (MF) *Paris Holiday*. Eleanor Powell, Robert Young, and Ann Sothern appeared in *Lady, Be Good*. June Allyson, Frank Sinatra, and Judy Garland appeared in *Till the Clouds Roll By*, biopic of composer Jerome Kern. Bob Hope and Anita Ekberg appeared in *Paris Holiday*. Academy Award winner 1941. This song did not appear in the 1924 stage production of *Lady, Be Good*. The impending fall of Paris to the Nazis inspired Hammerstein to write these words.

Last Train to Clarksville 1966 w.m. Tommy Boyce, Bobby Hart

Last Waltz, The 1968 w.m. Les Reed, Barry Mason. Ivor Novello Award winner 1967/1968.

Late in the Evening 1980 w.m. Paul Simon

Late Show, The, *see* **The Syncopated Clock**

Latin Quarter, The 1938 w.m. Al Dubin, Harry Warren. (MF) *Gold Diggers in Paris*. Rudy Vallee and Hugh Herbert appeared in *Gold Diggers in Paris*.

Laugh and the World Laughs with You 1896 w. Ella Wheeler Wilcox m. Louis Gottschalk

Laugh, Clown, Laugh 1928 w. Sam M. Lewis, Joe Young m. Ted Fiorito

Laughing Irish Eyes 1936 w.m. Sidney Mitchell, Sammy Stept. (MF) *Laughing Irish Eyes*. Phil Regan and Evelyn Knapp appeared in *Laughing Irish Eyes*.

Laughing On the Outside (Crying On the Inside) 1946 w. Ben Raleigh m. Bernie Wayne

Laughing Policeman, The 1938 w.m. Billy Grey

Laughing Water 1903 w. George Totten Smith m. Frederick W. Hager. (MT) *Mother Goose*.

Laughter in the Rain 1975 w.m. Neil Sedaka

Laura 1945 w. Johnny Mercer m. David Raksin. (F) *Laura*. Dana Andrews and Clifton Webb appeared in *Laura*.

Lavender's Blue (Diddle Diddle, or, Dilly Dilly) c.1750 w.m. traditional folksong, from England. (MF) *So Dear to My Heart*. This song was popularly adapted in 1948 by Eliot Daniel and Larry Morey.

Lawman 1959 w.m. Jerry Livingston, Mack David

(Theme from) Lawrence of Arabia 1962 m. Maurice Jarre. (F) *Lawrence of Arabia*. Peter O'Toole and Omar Sharif appeared in *Lawrence of Arabia*.

Lay Down (Candles in the Rain) 1970 w.m. Melanie Safka

Lay Down Sally 1978 w.m. Eric Clapton, Marcy Levy, George Terry

Lay Down Sally 1978 w.m. Eric Clapton, Marcy Levy, Gerhard Eng.w. Paddy Roberts m. Leon Land, Ake Gerhard

Lay, Lady, Lay 1969 w.m. Bob Dylan

Lay Your Hands on Me 1986 w.m. Tom Bailey, Alannah Currie, Joe Leeway

Layla 1972 w.m. Eric Clapton, James Beck Gordon

Lazy 1924 w.m. Irving Berlin. (MF) *Alexander's Ragtime Band*. This song was popularly revived in 1948.

Lazy Afternoon 1954 w. John Latouche m. Jerome Moross. (MT) *The Golden Apple*.

Lazy Bones 1933 w.m. Johnny Mercer, Hoagy Carmichael

Lazy Lou'siana Moon 1930 w.m. Walter Donaldson

Lazy Moon 1903 w. Bob Cole m. J. Rosamond Johnson. (MF) *Here Comes Cookie*. George Burns, Gracie Allen and Betty Furness appeared in *Here Comes Cookie*. See also Part 1, 1903.

(Up a) Lazy River 1931 w.m. Hoagy Carmichael, Sidney Arodin. (F) *The Best Years of Our Lives*. (MF) *Hey Boy, Hey Girl*. (MF) *Cowboy Canteen*. Frederic March and Myrna Loy appeared in *The Best Years of Our Lives*. Keely Smith appeared in *Hey Boy, Hey Girl*. Tex Ritter and Charles Starrett appeared in *Cowboy Canteen*. This song was popularly revived in 1941.

Lead, Kindly Light 1868 w. John Henry Newman m. John Bacchus Dykes

Lead Me On 1979 w.m. Allee Willis, David Lasley

Leader of the German Band, The 1905 w. Edward Madden m. Theodore F. Morse

Leader of the Pack, The 1964 w.m. Ellie Greenwich, Jeff Barry, George Morton. (OB) *Leader of the Pack*.

Lean On Me 1972 w.m. Bill Withers

Lean On Me 1972 w. Fred Bluth m. Steven Metcalf. (MT) *Drat!*

Leaning on a Lamp Post 1937 w.m. Noel Gay. (MF) *Feather Your Nest*. George Formby appeared in *Feather Your Nest*. Theme song of George Formby.

Leanin' on the Ole Top Rail 1939 w.m. Nick Kenny, Charles Kenny. (MF) *Ride Tenderfoot Ride*. Gene Autry and Smiley Burnette appeared in *Ride Tenderfoot Ride*.

Learn To Croon 1933 w.m. Sam Coslow, Arthur Johnston. (MF) *College Humor*. Bing Crosby and Burns and Allen appeared in *College Humor*.

Learn To Smile 1921 w. Otto Harbach m. Louis A. Hirsch. Loosely based on "Sari Waltz" and a theme from Beethoven's Fifth Symphony. (MT) *The O'Brien Girl*.

Learn Your Lessons Well 1971 w.m. Stephen Schwartz. (MT) *Godspell*. (MF) *Godspell*.

Learnin' the Blues 1955 w.m. Dolores Vicki Silvers

Leather and Lace 1982 w.m. Stevie Nicks

Leave a Little Love 1965 w.m. Robin Conrad, Les Reed

Leave a Tender Moment Alone 1984 w.m. Billy Joel

Leave It to Jane 1917 w. P.G. Wodehouse m. Jerome Kern. (MT) *Leave It to Jane*. (MF) *Till the Clouds Roll By*. Judy Garland, Van Johnson, Robert Walker, and Kathryn Grayson appeared in *Till the Clouds Roll By*, biopic of composer Jerome Kern.

Leave Me Alone (Ruby Red Dress) 1973 w.m. Linda Laurie

Leave Me with a Smile 1921 w.m. Charles Koehler, Earl Burtnett

Leaving on a Jet Plane 1969 w.m. John Denver. See also Part I, 1962.

Leetle Bateese 1921 w.m. William Drummond, Geoffrey O'Hara

Left All Alone Again Blues 1920 w. Anne Caldwell m. Jerome Kern. (MT) *The Night Boat*. Louise Groody and John E. Hazzard appeared in *The Night Boat*.

Left Right Out of Your Heart 1958 w. Earl Shuman m. Mort Garson

Legalize My Name 1946 w. Johnny Mercer m. Harold Arlen. (MT) *St. Louis Woman*. Pearl Bailey, Rex Ingram, and Harold and Fayard Nicholas appeared in *St. Louis Woman*.

Legend of the Glass Mountain, The 1949 w.m. Nino Rota. (MF) *The Glass Mountain*.

Legs 1985 w.m. Frank Beard, Billy Gibbons, Dusty Hill

Leicester Square Rag 1949 w.m. Harry Roy

Lemon in the Garden of Love, A 1906 w. M.E. Rourke m. Richard Carle. (MT) *The Spring Chicken*. (F) *Ma, He's Making Eyes at Me*. Tom Brown and Constance Moore appeared in *Ma, He's Making Eyes at Me*.

Lemon Tree 1965 w.m. Will Holt

Lena from Palesteena, *see* **Palesteena**

Less Than the Dust 1903 w. Laurence Hope m. Amy Woodeforde-Finden. From ''Four Indian Love Lyrics.''

Let a Smile Be Your Umbrella on a Rainy (Rainy) Day 1927 w. Irving Kahal, Francis Wheeler m. Sammy Fain. (MF) *It's a Great Life.*

Let Bygones Be Bygones 1897 w. Charles Shackford m. Kerry Mills

Let Bygones Be Bygones 1933 w.m. Joseph Gilbert

Let 'Em Eat Cake 1933 w. Ira Gershwin m. George Gershwin. (MT) *Let 'Em Eat Cake.* Lois Moran, Victor Moore, and William Gaxton appeared in *Let 'Em Eat Cake.*

Let 'Em In 1976 w.m. Paul McCartney, Linda McCartney

Let Erin Remember the Days of Old 1808 w. Thomas Moore m. based on the melody to ''The Red Fox''

Let It Alone 1906 w. Alex Rogers m. Bert A. Williams

Let It Be 1970 w.m. John Lennon, Paul McCartney. (MT) *Beatlemania.* Ivor Novello Award winner 1970–71.

Let It Be Me 1957 Fr.w. Pierre Delanoe Eng.w. Mann Curtis m. Gilbert Becaud. This song was popularly revived in 1964.

Let It Be Soon 1946 w.m. Dick Hurran, Hugh Wade

Let It Rain! Let It Pour! (I'll Be in Virginia in the Morning) 1925 w. Cliff Friend m. Walter Donaldson

Let It Snow, Let It Snow, Let It Snow 1946 w. Sammy Cahn m. Jule Styne

Let It Whip 1982 w.m. Reggie Andrews, Leon Chancler

Let Me Be the One 1971 w.m. Roger Nicholls

Let Me Be There 1973 w.m. John Rostill

Let Me Be Your Sugar Baby 1979 w.m. Arthur Malvin. (MT) *Sugar Babies.* Ann Miller and Mickey Rooney appeared in *Sugar Babies.*

Let Me Be Your Teddy Bear, *see* **Teddy Bear**

Let Me Call You Sweetheart 1910 w.m. Beth Slater Whitson, Leo Friedman

Let Me Dream Again 1875 w. B.C. Stevenson m. Arthur Sullivan

Let Me Entertain You 1959 w. Stephen Sondheim m. Jule Styne. (MT) *Gypsy.* (MF) *Gypsy.* Ethel Merman appeared in the stage production of *Gypsy.* Rosalind Russell appeared in the film production of *Gypsy.*

Let Me Go Lover 1955 w.m. Jenny Lou Carson; special w. Al Hill. This song was originally ''Let Me Go Devil'' in 1953 and rewritten at the suggestion of Mitch Miller for use in a CBS production of *Studio One.*

Let Me In 1962 w.m. Yvonne Baker

Let Me Linger Longer in Your Arms 1924 w. Cliff Friend m. Abel Baer

Let Me Love You Tonight 1944 w.m. Mitchell Parish, Rene Touzet

Let Me Love You Tonight 1980 w.m. George Greer, Jeffrey Wilson, Stgug Woodard

Let Me Shake the Hand That Shook the Hand of Sullivan 1898 w. Monroe Rosenfeld m. Alfred Williams

Let Me Sing and I'm Happy 1929 w.m. Irving Berlin. (MF) *Mammy.* (MF) *The Jolson Story.* Al Jolson and Louise Dresser appeared in *Mammy.* Larry Parks appeared in *The Jolson Story.*

Let My Love Open the Door 1980 w.m. Peter Townshend

Let My Song Fill Your Heart 1936 w.m. Ernest Charles

Let the Good Times Roll 1960 w.m. Leonard Lee. Grammy Award winner 1960.

Let the Great Big World Keep Turning 1917 w.m. Nat D. Ayer, Clifford Grey. (MT) *The Bing Girls Are There.* Violet Loraine appeared in *The Bing Girls Are There.*

Let the Heartaches Begin 1968 w.m. Tony Macaulay, Marilyn McLeod

Let the Music Play 1984 w.m. Chris Barbosa, Ed Chisolm

Let the People Sing 1940 w.m. Noel Gay, Ian Grant, Frank Eyton. (MT) *Lights Up.* Evelyn Laye appeared in *Lights Up.*

Let the Rest of the World Go By 1919 w. J. Keirn Brennan m. Ernest R. Ball

Let the Sunshine In 1969 w. Gerome Ragni, James Rado m. Galt MacDermot. (MT) *Hair.* (MF) *Hair.* Grammy Award winner 1969.

Let There Be Love 1940 w.m. Ian Grant, Lionel Rand. This song was popularly revived in 1962.

Let Us Be Sweethearts Over Again 1937 w.m. Joseph Gilbert

Let Us Take to the Road, *see* **The Beggar's Opera**

Let Your Love Flow 1976 w.m. Lawrence Williams

Let Yourself Go 1936 w.m. Irving Berlin. (MF) *Follow the Fleet.* Fred Astaire and Ginger Rogers appeared in *Follow the Fleet.*

Let's All Go Down the Strand 1910 w.m. Harry Castling, C.W. Murphy

Let's All Go the Music Hall 1934 w.m. Horatio Nicholls

Let's All Sing Like the Birdies Sing 1932 w. Robert Hargreaves, Stanley J. Damerell m. Tolchard Evans

Let's Be Buddies 1940 w.m. Cole Porter. (MT) *Panama Hattie.* (MT) *Black Vanities.* (MF) *Panama Hattie.* Ethel Merman, Betty Hutton, and Joan Carroll appeared in the stage production of *Panama Hattie.* Ann Sheridan, Ben Blue, and Red Skelton appeared in the film production of *Panama Hattie.*

Let's Call It a Day 1932 w. B.G. DeSylva, Lew Brown m. Ray Henderson. (MT) *Strike Me Pink.* (MF) *Strike Me Pink.* Jimmy Durante and Roy Atwell appeared in the stage production of *Strike Me Pink.* Eddie Cantor and Ethel Merman appeared in the film production of *Strike Me Pink.*

Let's Call the Whole Thing Off 1937 w. Ira Gershwin m. George Gershwin. (MF) *Shall We Dance.* Fred Astaire and Ginger Rogers appeared in *Shall We Dance.*

Let's Dance 1935 w.m. Fanny Baldridge, Joseph Bonine, Gregory Stone. Based on Carl Maria Von Weber's ''Invitation to the Dance'' of 1821. Theme song of Benny Goodman.

Let's Dance 1962 w.m. Jim Lee

Let's Dance 1983 w.m. David Jones (David Bowie). Ivor Novello Award winner 1983–84.

Let's Do It (Let's Fall in Love) 1928 w.m. Cole Porter.

(MT) *Paris.* (MT) *Wake Up and Dream.* (MF) *Night and Day.* Irene Bordoni and Albert Morgetson appeared in *Paris.* Cary Grant, Alexis Smith, and Mary Martin appeared in *Night and Day,* biopic of song writer Cole Porter. This song was later adapted for a Rheingold Beer commercial promotion campaign.

Let's Do It Again   1975   w.m. Curtis Mayfield

Let's Face the Music and Dance   1936   w.m. Irving Berlin. (MF) *Follow the Fleet.* Fred Astaire and Ginger Rogers appeared in *Follow the Fleet.*

Let's Fall in Love   1933   w. Ted Koehler   m. Harold Arlen. (MF) *Let's Fall in Love.* (MF) *On the Sunny Side of the Street.* (MF) *Strictly French.* (MF) *The Eddy Duchin Story.* (MF) *Can-Can.* Ann Sothern and Edmund Lowe appeared in *Let's Fall In Love.* Frankie Laine and Billy Daniels appeared in *On the Sunny Side of the Street.* Dorothy Lamour and Don Ameche appeared in *Slightly French.* Frank Sinatra, Juliet Prowse, and Shirley MacLaine appeared in *Can-Can.*

Let's Fall in Love, *see also* **Let's Do It**

Let's Get Away from It All   1941   w.m. Thomas Adair, Matt Dennis

Let's Get It On   1973   w.m. Ed Townsend

Let's Get Lost   1943   w. Frank Loesser   m. Jimmy McHugh. (MF) *Happy Go Lucky.* Mary Martin, Dick Powell, and Betty Hutton appeared in *Happy Go Lucky.*

Let's Get Together   1961   w.m. Robert Sherman, Richard Sherman. (F) *The Parent Trap.* Hayley Mills appeared in *The Parent Trap.*

Let's Get Together, *see also* **Get Together**

Let's Go All the Way   1986   w.m. Gary Lee Cooper

Let's Go Crazy   1984   w.m. Prince

Let's Go Into a Picture Show   1909   w.m. Junie McCree, Albert Von Tilzer

Let's Groove   1981   w.m. Maurice White, Wayne Vaughn

Let's Hang On   1965   w.m. Bob Crewe, Sandy Linzer, Denny Randell. This song was popularly revived in 1982.

Let's Have a Tiddley at the Milk Bar   1936   w.m. Noel Gay

Let's Have Another Cup of Coffee   1932   w.m. Irving Berlin. (MT) *Face the Music.* J. Harold Murray and Mary Boland appeared in *Face the Music.* This song was later adapted for a Nescafé commercial promotion campaign.

Let's Hear It for the Boy   1984   w.m. Dean Pitchford, Tom Snow

Let's Keep It That Way   1946   w.m. Desmond O'Connor, Jack Denby, Muriel Watson

Let's Kiss and Make Up   1927   w. Ira Gershwin   m. George Gershwin. (MT) *Funny Face.* (MF) *Funny Face.* Fred and Adele Astaire and Victor Moore appeared in the stage production of *Funny Face.* Fred Astaire and Audrey Hepburn appeared in the film production of *Funny Face.*

Let's Misbehave   1928   w.m. Cole Porter. (MT) *Paris.* Irene Bordoni and Albert Margetson appeared in *Paris.* This song did not appear in the New York production of *Paris.*

Let's Put Out the Lights and Go to Sleep   1932   w.m. Herman Hupfeld. (MT) *George White's Music Hall Varieties.*

Let's Start the New Year Right   1942   w.m. Irving Berlin. (MF) *Holiday Inn.* Fred Astaire and Bing Crosby appeared in *Holiday Inn.*

Let's Stay Together   1972   w.m. Al Green, Willie Mitchell, Al Jackson

Let's Take a Walk Around the Block   1934   w. Ira Gershwin, E.Y. Harburg   m. Harold Arlen. (MT) *Life Begins at 8:40.* Frances Williams, Bert Lahr, and Ray Bolger appeared in *Life Begins at 8:40.*

Let's Take an Old-Fashioned Walk   1949   w.m. Irving Berlin. (MT) *Miss Liberty.* Eddie Albert, Mary McCarthy, and Charles Dingle appeared in *Miss Liberty.*

Let's Take the Long Way Home   1944   w. Johnny Mercer   m. Harold Arlen. (MF) *Here Come the Waves.* Bing Crosby and Betty Hutton appeared in *Here Come the Waves.*

Let's Talk About Love   1962   w.m. Norrie Paramor, Bunny Lewis

Let's Twist Again   1961   w.m. Dave Appell, Kal Mann

Let's Work Together   1970   w.m. Wilbert Harrison

Letter, The   1967   w.m. Wayne Thompson

Letter Song, The   1909   w. Stanislaus Stange   m. Oscar Straus. (MT) *The Chocolate Soldier.* (MF) *The Chocolate Soldier.* Evelyn d'Alroy and C.H. Workman appeared in the British stage production of *The Chocolate Soldier.* Nelson Eddy, Nigel Bruce, and Risé Stevens appeared in the film production of *The Chocolate Soldier.*

Letter Song   1919   w. William Le Baron   m. Fritz Kreisler. (MT) *Apple Blossoms.*

Letter That Never Came, The   1886   w.m. Paul Dresser

Letter to a Soldier, A   1956   w.m. Gee Langdon

Levee Song, The, *see* **I've Been Working On the Railroad**

Liaisons   1973   w.m. Stephen Sondheim. (MT) *A Little Night Music.* (MF) *A Little Night Music.* Hermione Gingold, Glynis Johns, and Len Cariou appeared in the stage production of *A Little Night Music.* Elizabeth Taylor, Hermione Gingold, and Len Cariou appeared in the film production of *A Little Night Music.*

Liberty Bell, The   1893   m. John Philip Sousa. A series of concerts at the Trocadero in Chicago inspired Sousa to compose this composition.

Liberty Bell—It's Time To Ring Again   1917   w. Joe Goodwin   m. Halsey K. Mohr

Liberty Song, The, or, **Come, Join Hand in Hand,** or, **In Freedom We're Born**   1768   w. Mrs. Mercy Warren; also John Dickinson   m. William Boyce. The melody is based on William Boyce's "Heart of Oak" of 1759. This was probably America's first patriotic song.

Lida Rose   1957   w.m. Meredith Willson. (MT) *The Music Man.* (MF) *The Music Man.* Robert Preston appeared in both the stage and film productions of *The Music Man.*

Liebesfreud   1910   m. Fritz Kreisler

Liebeslied   1910   m. Fritz Kreisler

Liebesträume   1847   w. F. Freiligrath   m. Franz Liszt. The music to this standard first appeared with words as a song titled "O Lieb." The music was published separately for the first time in 1850.

Liechtensteiner Polka 1957 w.m. Edmund Kötscher, R. Lindt

Lies 1931 w. George E. Springer m. Harry Barris

Life in a Looking Glass 1986 w. Leslie Bricusse m. Henry Mancini. (F) *That's Life.*

Life in a Northern Town 1986 w.m. Gilbert Alexander Gabriel, Nicholas William Laird-Clowes

Life in One Day 1986 w.m. Howard Jones

Life Is 1983 w. Fred Ebb m. John Kander. (MT) *Zorba.* Anthony Quinn and Debbie Shapiro appeared in *Zorba.*

Life Is a Song, Let's Sing It Together 1935 w. Joe Young m. Fred E. Ahlert

Life Is Just a Bowl of Cherries 1931 w. Lew Brown m. Ray Henderson. (MT) *George White's Scandals of 1931 (Eleventh Edition).* (MF) *George White's Scandals of 1931.* (MF) *The Best Things in Life Are Free.* (MF) *George White's Scandals of 1945.* Ethel Merman and Ray Bolger appeared in the stage production of *George White's Scandals of 1931.* Gordon MacRae, Dan Dailey, and Ernest Borgnine appeared in *The Best Things in Life Are Free,* biopic of song writers DeSylva, Brown, and Henderson. Joan Davis and Jack Haley appeared in *George White's Scandals of 1945.*

Life Is Nothing Without Music 1939 w.m. Fred Hartley

Life Is Only What You Make It After All 1910 w. Edgar Smith m. A. Baldwin Sloane. (MT) *Tillie's Nightmare.*

Life Is So Peculiar 1950 w.m. Johnny Burke, James Van Heusen. (MF) *Mr. Music.* Bing Crosby and Peggy Lee appeared in *Mr. Music.*

Life Let Us Cherish, or, **Snatch Fleeting Pleasures** 1796 w. anon. m. Hans Georg Naegeli. From the German ''Freut euch des Lebens.''

Life, Love and Laughter 1945 w. Ira Gershwin m. Kurt Weill

Life of the Party, The 1968 w. Fred Ebb m. John Kander. (MT) *The Happy Time.*

Life On the Ocean Wave, A 1838 w. Epes Sargent m. Henry Russell. Sargent wrote the words to this song by expanding S.J. Arnold's poem ''The Death of Nelson.'' This song was made the official march of the Royal Marines in 1889.

Life's a Funny Proposition After All 1904 w.m. George M. Cohan. (MT) *Little Johnny Jones.*

Life's Desire 1932 w.m. Tolchard Evans, Stanley J. Damerell, Robert Hargreaves

Life's Railway to Heaven 1891 w. M.E. Abbey m. Charles D. Tillman

Lift Boy 1956 w.m. Ken Hare, Ron Goodwin, Dick James. Ivor Novello Award winner 1956.

Lift Ev'ry Voice and Sing 1900 w.m. James Weldon Johnson, J. Rosamond Johnson

Light Cavalry (Overture) 1868 m. Franz von Suppé. From the German ''Leichte Cavallerie.''

Light My Fire 1967 w.m. John Densmore, Robert Krieger, Raymond Manzarek, James Morrison

Light of Other Days, The 1836 w. Alfred Bunn m. Michael William Balfe. From Balfe's opera *The Maid of Artois.*

Lighterman Tom 1911 w.m. Francis J. Barron, W.H. Squire

Lightnin' Strikes 1966 w.m. Lou Christie, Twyla Herbert

Lightning Tree, The 1972 w.m. Stephen Francis

Lights of Cincinnati 1970 w.m. Tony Macaulay, Geoff Stephens. Ivor Novello Award winner 1969–70.

Lights Out 1936 w.m. Billy Hill

Like a Rolling Stone 1965 w.m. Bob Dylan

Like a Virgin 1984 w.m. Tom Kelly, Bill Steinberg

Like Sister and Brother 1974 w.m. Geoff Stephens, Roger Greenaway. Ivor Novello Award winner 1973–74.

(I'd Really) Like To Get To Know You 1968 w.m. Stuart Scharf

Like Young 1959 w. Paul Francis Webster m. André Previn

Li'l Darlin' (Don't Dream of Anybody But Me) 1959 w.m. Neal Hefti

Li'l Liza Jane 1916 w.m. Countess Ada de Lachau. This song remains a favorite of Rotary organizations.

Lil' Ole Bitty Pissant Country Place, A 1978 w.m. Carol Hall. (MT) *The Best Little Whorehouse in Texas.* Delores Hall appeared in *The Best Little Whorehouse in Texas.*

Li'l Red Riding Hood 1966 w.m. Ronald Blackwell

Lilac Tree, The, or, **Perspicacity** 1920 w.m. George H. Gartlan

Lilacs in the Rain 1939 w. Mitchell Parish m. Peter DeRose

Lili (Lilli) Marlene 1944 w.m. Hans Leip, Norbert Schultze, Tommie Connor. Most popularly sung by Marlene Dietrich, the words to this song were written by German soldier Hans Leip in 1915 on his way to the Russian front. ''Leip said he was stationed in Berlin with the German Army in 1914 and had two girlfriends—Lili and Marlene. Lili was the daughter of a Berlin businessman and Marlene an army nurse. Standing guard one night under a lamppost, the first three verses came to the author but he failed to finish it until 1937.'' This song was originally titled ''My Lili of the Lamppost.''

Lilliburlero c.1686 w. First Marquess of Wharton m. possibly Henry Purcell. The words to this song are a direct attack on the Earl of Tyroconne (General Talbot) when he was appointed Lord Lieutenant of Ireland by the Roman Catholic James II. Included in John Gay's *The Beggar's Opera* in 1728, this song was later adapted as ''There Was an Old Woman Tossed Up in a Basket.''

Lily Dale 1852 w.m. H.S. Thompson; add'l w. Alan Skelly

Lily of Laguna 1912 w.m. Leslie Stuart. (MF) *Lilacs in the Spring.* Errol Flynn appeared in *Lilacs in the Spring.* Originally published in 1898 in England, this English music hall ballad was popularly sung in England by an American. The subject of the song, Lily, is a southern American black girl. When Leslie Stuart was asked the exact whereabouts of Laguna, the reply was ''If you are going from New Orleans to California it lies about a hundred miles on your left.''

Lily of the Valley 1917 w. L. Wolfe Gilbert m. Anatole Friedland

Lily the Pink 1969 w.m. John Henry, Peter Michael McCarthey, Roger McGough

Limbo Rock 1962 w.m. Jon Sheldon, William E. Strange

Limehouse Blues 1922 w. Douglas Furber m. Philip Braham. (MT) *A to Z.* (MT) *Andre Charlot's Revue of 1924.* (MF) *Ziegfeld Follies.* Gertrude Lawrence appeared in both *A to Z* and *Charlot's Revue of 1924.* Beatric Lillie appeared in *Andre Charlot's Revue of 1924.* Judy Garland, Fred Astaire, Lucille Ball, and Fanny Brice appeared in *Ziegfeld Follies.* Theme song of Gertrude Lawrence. "Limehouse" refers to London's East End.

Limelight, *see* **Eternally**

Lincoln, Grant or Lee 1903 w.m. Paul Dresser

Linda 1947 w.m. Jack Lawrence, Ann Ronell. (F) *The Story of G.I. Joe.* Burgess Meredith and Robert Mitchum appeared in *The Story of G.I. Joe.*

Lindy Lou, *see* **By the Watermelon Vine**

Linger a Little Longer in the Twilight 1932 w.m. Harry Woods, James Campbell, Reginald Connelly

Linger Awhile 1923 w. Harry Owens m. Vincent Rose. (MF) *Belles on Their Toes.* Myrna Loy appeared in *Belles on Their Toes.*

Linger in My Arms a Little Longer Baby 1946 w.m. Herbert Magidson

Lingering Lovers 1958 w.m. Ron Goodwin

Lion and Albert, The 1933 w.m. Marriott Edgar

Lion Sleeps Tonight, The, or, **Wimoweh** 1962 new w.m. Hugo Peretti, Luigi Creatore, George Weiss, Albert Stanton. Originally released by Paul Campbell as "Wimoweh" in 1952, but first popularized in 1962. Based on a traditional African song. This song was popularly revived in 1972.

Lipstick on Your Collar 1959 w. Edna Lewis m. George Goehring

Lisbon Antigua, or, **In Old Lisbon** 1937 Port.w. Jose Galhardo, Amadeu do Vale Eng.w. Harry Dupree m. Raul Portela. This song was popularly revived in 1956.

Listen People 1966 w.m. Graham Gouldman. (MF) *When the Boys Meet the Girls.*

Listen to My Tale of Woe 1884 w. Eugene Field m. Hubbard F. Smith

Listen to the Mocking Bird 1855 w. Septimus Winner (pseud. Alice Hawthorne) m. Richard Milburn. "Listen to the Mocking Bird" was dedicated to Harriet Lane, the most sociable First Lady since Dolley Madison and niece of bachelor President James Buchanan. This song was compared by President Lincoln to "the laughter of a little girl at play." Richard Milburn was a poor black barber from Philadelphia, whose music was overheard and published by Septimus winner. Winner sold his publishing rights for fifty dollars. Septimus winner was actually tried, but acquitted, for treason for writing the song "Give Us Back Our Old Commander" in 1862, thus becoming the only songwriter whose work was deemed treasonous by the Secretary of War.

Listen to the Radio 1982 w.m. Frederic Knipe

Listen to What the Man Said 1975 w.m. Paul McCartney, Linda McCartney

Liszt, Chopin and Mendelssohn 1932 w.m. Horatio Nicholls, Leo Towers, Harry Leon

Little Alabama Coon 1893 w.m. Hattie Starr

Little Annie Roonie 1890 w.m. Michael Nolan. This British music-hall favorite was introduced in America by Annie Hart, known as "The Bowery Girl," at the London Theatre in New York City. Nolan was so embittered at the piracy of his song by American publishers (it was written prior to the international copyright law), that he never wrote another song. This song was republished for a picture starring Mary Pickford with the new title "America's Sweetheart."

Little Bird On Nellie's Hat, The, *see* **The Bird On Nellie's Hat**

Little Bird Told Me, A 1949 w.m. Harvey O. Brooks

Little Birdie Told Me So, A 1926 w. Lorenz Hart m. Richard Rodgers. (MT) *Peggy-Ann.*

Little Birdies Learning How To Fly 1898 w. Hugh Morton m. Gustave Kerker. (MT) *The Telephone Girl.*

Little Biscuit 1957 w. E.Y. Harburg m. Harold Arlen. (MT) *Jamaica.*

Little Bit Independent, A 1935 w.m. Edgar Leslie, Joseph A. Burke

Little Bit Me, A Little Bit You, A 1967 w.m. Neil Diamond

Little Bit of Heaven, Sure They Call It Ireland, A 1914 w. J. Keirn Brennan m. Ernest R. Ball. (MT) *The Heart of Paddy Whack.* (MF) *A Little Bit of Heaven.* (MF) *My Wild Irish Rose.* Robert Stack and Gloria Jean appeared in *A Little Bit of Heaven.* Dennis Morgan and Arlene Dahl appeared in *My Wild Irish Rose.*

Little Bit of Soap, A 1979 w.m. Bert Russell

Little Bit o' Soul 1967 w.m. Kenneth Alan J. Hawker, John Nichola Shakespeare

Little Bit off the Top 1901 w.m. Fred Murray, Fred W. Leigh

Little Bit South of North Carolina, *see* **Just a Little Bit South of North Carolina**

Little Bo-Peep, *see* **Mother Goose's Melodies**

Little Boy Blue 1891 w. Eugene Field m. Ethelbert Nevin

Little Boy Blue, *see also* **Mother Goose's Melodies**

Little Boy Called "Taps", A 1904 w. Edward Madden m. Theodore F. Morse

Little Boy That Santa Claus Forgot, The 1937 w.m. Tommie Connor, Jimmy Leach, Michael Carr

Little Brains—A Little Talent, A 1955 w.m. Richard Adler, Jerry Ross. (MT) *Damn Yankees.* (MF) *Damn Yankees.*

Little Brown Church (in the Vale), The 1865 w.m. William S. Pitts

Little Brown Jug 1869 w.m. Joseph E. Winner (pseud. R.A. Eastburn), (MT) *The 1940's Radio Hour.* (F) *Hired Wife.* Rosalind Russell, Brian Aherne, and Virginia Bruce appeared in *Hired Wife.* "Little Brown Jug" was popularized by the Weatherwax Brothers Quartet in 1911, and was popularly revived in 1939 by Glenn Miller and his orchestra.

Little Bunch of Shamrocks, A 1913 w. William Jerome, Andrew B. Sterling m. Harry Von Tilzer

Little by Little 1929 w.m. Walter O'Keefe, Bobby Dolan.

(F) *The Sophomore.* Sally O'Neil and Eddie Quillan appeared in *The Sophomore.*

Little Children 1964 w.m. Mort Shuman, Leslie McFarland

Little Church Around the Corner, The 1919 w. Alexander Gerber m. Sigmund Romberg. (MT) *The Magic Melody.*

Little Co-operation from You, A 1937 w.m. Samuel Lerner, Al Goodhart, Al Hoffman. (MT) *Going Greek.* Roy Royston and Louise Brown appeared in *Going Greek.*

Little Damozel, The 1912 w.m. Ivor Novello

Little Darlin' 1957 w.m. Maurice Williams

Little David, Play on Your Harp 1921 w.m. traditional black American spiritual, c.1871; arr. Henry Thacker Burleigh in 1921.

Little Devil 1961 w.m. Neil Sedaka, Howard Greenfield

Little Dolly Daydream 1900 w.m. Leslie Stuart

Little Donkey 1959 w.m. Eric Boswell

Little Drops of Rain 1961 w. E.Y. Harburg m. Harold Arlen. (MF) *Gay Purr-ee.*

Little Drummer Boy, The 1938 w.m. Harry Leon, Don Pelosi

Little Drummer Boy, The 1959 w.m. Harry Simeone, Henry Onorati

Little Dutch Mill 1934 w.m. Ralph Freed, Harry Barris

Little Footsteps 1868 w. Michael Bennett Leavitt m. James A. Barney

Little Girl 1931 w.m. Francis Henry, Madeline Hyde

Little Girl 1969 w.m. Reg Presley

Little Girl Blue 1935 w. Lorenz Hart m. Richard Rodgers. (MT) *Jumbo.* (MF) *Jumbo.* Jimmy Durante and Gloria Grafton appeared in the stage production of *Jumbo.*

Little Girl from Little Rock, A 1949 w. Leo Robin m. Jule Styne. (MT) *Gentlemen Prefer Blondes.* (MF) *Gentlemen Prefer Blondes.* Carol Channing appeared in the stage production of *Gentlemen Prefer Blondes.* Marilyn Monroe appeared in the film production of *Gentlemen Prefer Blondes.*

Little Girls 1977 w. Martin Charnin m. Charles Strouse. (MT) *Annie.* Dorothy Loudon and Andrea McArdle appeared in *Annie.*

Little Girls, Good Bye 1919 w. William Le Baron m. Victor Jacobi. (MT) *Apple Blossoms.*

Little Good News, A 1984 w.m. Charlie Black, Rory Bourke, Tommy Rocco

Little Green Apples 1968 w.m. Bobby Russell. Grammy Award winner 1968.

Little Grey Home in the West 1911 w. Wilmot D. Eardley m. Hermann Löhr. This song was played for Queen Elizabeth when she visited Paris with her fiancé, the Duke of Edinburgh.

Little Grey House, The 1949 w. Maxwell Anderson m. Kurt Weill. (MT) *Lost in the Stars.* (MF) *Lost in the Stars.* Todd Duncan, William Greaves, and Herbert Coleman appeared in the stage production of *Lost in the Stars.* Melba Moore appeared in the film production of *Lost in the Stars.*

(With) Little Help from My Friends, A 1967 w.m. John Lennon, Paul McCartney. (MT) *Beatlemania.* (MF) *Yellow Submarine.*

Little House upon the Hill, The 1915 w. Ballard MacDonald, Joe Goodwin m. Harry Puck

Little in Love 1981 w.m. Alan Tarney

Little Jack Frost Get Lost 1947 w.m. Al Stillman, Seger Ellis

Little Jack Horner, *see* **Mother Goose's Melodies**

Little Jeannie 1980 w.m. Elton John, Gary Osborne

Little Kiss Each Morning, a Little Kiss Each Night, A 1929 w.m. Harry Woods. (MF) *The Vagabond Lover.* Rudy Vallee and Marie Dressler appeared in *The Vagabond Lover.*

Little Lamb 1959 w. Stephen Sondheim m. Jule Styne. (MT) *Gypsy.* (MF) *Gypsy.* Ethel Merman appeared in the stage production of *Gypsy.* Rosalind Russell appeared in the film production of *Gypsy.* The melody of this song was written by Jule Styne for a lyric by Styne's son, Stanley, for a Zanuck film from which it was cut.

Little Liza Jane, *see* **Li'l Liza Jane**

Little Lost Child, The 1894 w. Edward B. Marks m. Joseph W. Stern. This song was the first to be illustrated, during performance, with slides on a projection screen; the moving picture was to emerge not far in the future.

(Just) Little Love, a Little Kiss, A 1912 Fr.w. Nilson Fysher Eng.w. Adrian Ross m. Lao Silesu. From the French ''Un Peu D'Amour.'' (MT) *Ziegfeld Follies of 1913.*

Little Lovin', A 1964 w.m. Russell Alquist

Little Lulu 1943 w.m. Buddy Kaye, Sidney Lippman, Fred Wise

Little Man, You've Had a Busy Day 1934 w. Maurice Sigler, Al Hoffman m. Mabel Wayne

Little Mary Sunshine 1959 w.m. Rick Besoyan. (MT) *Little Mary Sunshine.*

Little Miss Lonely 1962 w.m. Mike Hawker, John Schroeder

Little Miss Melody 1917 w.m. Lionel Monckton, Adrian Ross, Percy Greenbank. (MT) *The Boy.* Nellie Taylor appeared in *The Boy.*

Little Miss Muffet, *see* **Mother Goose's Melodies**

Little Mohee, *see* **On Top of Old Smokey**

Little More Love, A 1978 w.m. Al Jacobs, Joseph Meyer

Little Mother of Mine 1917 w. Walter H. Brown m. Henry Thacker Burleigh

Little of What You Fancy, A 1915 w.m. Fred W. Leigh, George Arthurs

Little Old Lady 1936 w. Stanley Adams m. Hoagy Carmichael. (MT) *The Show Is On.*

Little Old Log Cabin in the Lane, The 1871 w.m. William Shakespeare Hays

Little Old Mill 1947 w.m. Don Pelosi, Lewis Ilda, Leo Towers

Little Old Sod Shanty 1870–1890 w.m. Traditional

Little on the Lonely Side, A 1944 w.m. Dick Robertson, James Cavanaugh, Frank Weldon

Little One 1956 w.m. Cole Porter. (MF) *High Society.* Frank Sinatra and Bing Crosby appeared in *High Society.*

Little Pink Petty from Peter 1907 w.m. Paul Rubens. (MT) *Miss Hook of Holland.*

Little Priest, A 1979 w.m. Stephen Sondheim. (MT) *Sweeney Todd.* Angela Lansbury and Len Cariou appeared in *Sweeney Todd.*

Little Princess, *see* **Princesita**

Little Red Monkey 1953 w.m. Jack Jordan

Little Red Rooster 1961 w.m. Willie Dixon

Little Rock Getaway 1934 w.m. Carl Sigman, Joe Sullivan

Little Shoemaker, The 1954 Eng.w.m. Geoffrey Parsons, Rudi Revil, Nathan Korb, James John T. Phillips

Little Shop of Horrors 1983 w. Howard Ashman m. Alan Menken. (OB) *Little Shop of Horrors.* Ellen Green appeared in *Little Shop of Horrors.*

Little Sir Echo 1917 w.m. Joe Marsala, Laura Smith, J.S. Fearis; arr. Adele Girard. This song was popularly revived in 1939.

Little Sister 1961 w.m. Jerome "Doc" Pomus, Mort Shuman

Little Star, or, **Estrellita** 1923 m. Manuel M. Ponce; arr. Frank LaForge. This work was originally published in 1914 in Europe.

Little Star 1958 w.m. Arthur Venosa, Vito Picone

Little Star, *see also* **I've Told Ev'ry Little Star**

(Just a) Little Street Where Old Friends Meet 1932 w.m. Gus Kahn, Harry M. Woods

Little Surplus Me, or, **Surplus Blues** 1946 w.m. Harold Rome. (MT) *Call Me Mister.*

Little Things Mean a Lot 1954 w.m. Edith Lindeman, Carl Stutz

Little Things You Do Together, The 1970 w.m. Stephen Sondheim. (MT) *Company.* (MT) *Side by Side by Sondheim.* Elaine Stritch appeared in *Company.* Julie N. McKenzie and Millicent Martin appeared in *Side by Side by Sondheim.*

Little Things You Used To Do, The 1935 w. Al Dubin m. Harry Warren. (MF) *Go Into Your Dance.*

(In My) Little Tin Box 1959 w. Sheldon Harnick m. Jerry Bock. (MT) *Fiorello!*

Little Tommy Tucker, *see* **Mother Goose's Melodies**

Little Town in the Ould County Down 1920 w. Richard W. Pasco m. Monto Carlo, Alma M. Sanders. This song was popularly revived in 1927.

Little White Bull, The 1959 w.m. Michael Pratt, Lionel Bart, Jimmy Bennett (Tommy Steele). (F) *Tommy the Toreador.* Ivor Novello Award winner 1959.

Little White Cloud That Cried, The 1951 w.m. Johnnie Ray

Little White Cottage 1857 w. Marshall S. Pike m. G.S.P.; arr. J.S. Pierpont

Little White Donkey, The 1922 m. Jacques Ibert. From the French "Le Petit Âne Blanc," from *Histoires.*

Little White Duck 1950 w.m. Walt Barrows, Bernard Zaritsky

Little White Gardenia, A 1935 w.m. Sam Coslow. (MT) *All the King's Horses.* (MF) *All the King's Horses.* Carl Brisson, Edward Everett Horton, and Mary Ellis appeared in *All the King's Horses.*

Little White House, The (at the End of Honeymoon Lane) 1926 w. Eddie Dowling, Irving Caesar m. James F. Hanley (MT) *Honeymoon Lane.* (MF) *Honeymoon Lane.* Kate Smith playing the role of Tiny Little made her stage debut in *Honeymoon Lane.* Eddie Dowling and June Collyer appeared in the film production of *Honeymoon Lane.*

Little White Lies 1930 w.m. Walter Donaldson. (MF) *Lover Come Back.*

Little Yellow Bird 1903 w.m. C.W. Murphy, William Hargreaves. (MT) *The Cherry Girl.* (F) *The Picture of Dorian Gray.* George Sanders and Donna Reed appeared in *The Picture of Dorian Gray.*

Live and Let Die 1973 w.m. Paul McCartney, Linda McCartney. (F) *Live and Let Die.*

Live, Laugh and Love 1931 w.m. Werner Heymann, Rowland Leigh. (F) *Congress Dances.* Liddell Peddieson and Lilian Harvey appeared in *Congress Dances.*

Live To Tell 1986 w.m. Patrick Leonard, Madonna

Lively 1960 w.m. Peter Buchanan, Lonnie Donegan

Livery Stable Blues 1916 w.m. Marvin Lee, Ray Lopez, Alcide Nunez

Living Doll 1959 w.m. Lionel Bart. (F) *Serious Charge.* Ivor Novello Award winner 1959.

Living for the City 1973 w.m. Stevie Wonder. Grammy Award winner 1974.

Living in a Fantasy 1981 w.m. Leo Sayer, Alan Tarney

Living in America 1986 w.m. Dan Hartman, Charlie Midnight

Living Inside Myself 1981 w.m. Gino Vanelli

Liza (All the Clouds'll Roll Away) 1929 w. Ira Gershwin, Gus Kahn m. George Gershwin. (MT) *Show Girl.* (MF) *Rhapsody in Blue.* (MF) *The Man I Love.* (MF) *The Jolson Story.* (MF) *An American in Paris.* (MF) *Starlift.* Jimmy Durante, Ruby Keeler, and Joseph Macauley appeared in *Show Girl.* Oscar Levant, Robert Alda, and Alexis Smith appeared in *Rhapsody in Blue,* biopic of composer George Gershwin. Ida Lupino appeared in *The Man I Love.* Larry Parks appeared in *The Jolson Story.* Gene Kelly and Leslie Caron appeared in *An American in Paris.* Doris Day and Gordon MacRae appeared in *Starlift.*

Liza Johnson 1902 w.m. Edgar Bateman, George Le Brunn. (F) *No Trees in the Street.* Stanley Holloway appeared in *No Trees in the Street.*

Lizzie Borden 1952 w.m. Michael Brown. (MT) *New Faces of 1952.*

Lo! Here the Gentle Lark 1819 w. William Shakespeare m. Sir Henry Rowley Bishop. (MF) *I Dream of Jeanie.* Ray Middleton and Bill Shirley appeared in *I Dream of Jeanie.* The words are based on Shakespeare's poem "Venus and

Adonis.'' This title is often misquoted as ''Lo! *Hear* the Gentle Lark.''

Lo, How a Rose E'er Blooming   1894   Ger.w. anon. Eng.w. Theodore Baker   m. traditional, from the sixteenth century; arr. Michael Praetorius. From the German ''Es Ist Ein' Ros' Entsprungen.''

Load of Hay, A   1950   w.m. Michael Feahy, Howard Barnes. Based on Ethelbert Nevin's ''Narcissus.''

Lobster Quadrille, The   1953   w.m. Joseph Horovitz

Loch Lomond, or, **The Bonnie Bonnie Banks,** or, **Oh! Ye'll Take the High Road**   1881   w.m. traditional, from Scotland. (F) *Pursuit to Algiers.* Sung by Nigel Bruce in the Sherlock Holmes mystery *Pursuit to Algiers.* Earliest known printing this year, but possibly 1746.

Lock Up Your Daughters   1959   w.m. Laurie Johnson, Lionel Bart

Locked Out After Nine   1880   w. Edward Harrigan   m. David Braham. (MT) *The Mulligan Guards' Picnic.*

Loco-Motion, The   1962   w.m. Gerry Goffin, Carole King. This song was popularly revived in 1974.

Loddy Lo   1964   w.m. Dave Appell, Kal Mann

Logical Song   1979   w.m. Richard Davies, Roger Hodgson. Ivor Novello Award winner 1979–80.

Lollipop   1958   w.m. Julius Dixon, Beverly Ross

Lollipops and Roses   1962   w.m. Tony Velona

Lolly Too Dum   c.1844   w.m. traditional mountain song

London Bridge   1744   w.m. traditional children's song, from England. The words were first published in London in 1744; the music and words were first published together in Philadelphia in 1879.

London by Night   1950   w.m. Carroll Coates

London I Love, The   1941   w.m. George Posford

London Pride   1941   w.m. Noël Coward

Londonderry Air   1855   w.m. based on a traditional air from County Derry, Ireland. This song was later revived in 1913 as ''Danny Boy.''

Lone Fish (Meat) Ball, The   1855   w.m. Richard Storrs Willis. This popular college song is credited by B.A. Botkin to be actually the work of Harvard Latin Professor George Martin Lane. See also ''One Meat Ball.''

Loneliness of Evening   1965   w. Oscar Hammerstein II   m. Richard Rodgers. (TV) *Cinderella.* This song was originally in the score written for *South Pacific,* but did not appear in the New York production.

Lonely   1962   w.m. Norrie Paramor, Acker Bilk. (F) *Band of Thieves.*

Lonely Ballerina   1954   w.m. Michael Carr, ''Lambrecht.''

(I'm Just a) Lonely Boy   1959   w.m. Paul Anka. (MF) *Girl's Town.* Paul Anka and Mel Torme appeared in *Girl's Town.*

Lonely Boy   1977   w.m. Andrew Gold

Lonely Bull, The   1963   w.m. Sol Lake

Lonely Footsteps   1945   w.m. Howard Barnes, Lucia Ravenge

Lonely Goatherd, The   1959   w. Oscar Hammerstein II   m.

Richard Rodgers. (MT) *The Sound of Music.* (MF) *The Sound of Music.* Mary Martin appeared in the stage production of *The Sound of Music.* Julie Andrews appeared in the film production of *The Sound of Music.*

Lonely Heart   1933   w.m. Irving Berlin. (MT) *As Thousands Cheer.*

Lonely House   1947   w. Langston Hughes   m. Kurt Weill. (MT) *Street Scene.* Anne Jeffreys, Norman Cordon, and Hope Emerson appeared in *Street Scene.*

Lonely Little Robin   1951   w.m. Cy Coben

Lonely Night (Angel Face)   1976   w.m. Neil Sedaka

Lonely Nights   1982   w.m. Stewart Harris, Keith Stegall

Lonely Pup (in a Christmas Shop)   1960   w.m. Archie Alexander

Lonely Street   1959   m. Phil Villipigue

Lonesome and Sorry   1926   w.m. Benny Davis, Con Conrad

Lonesome in the Moonlight   1928   w. Ben Russell   m. Abel Baer

Lonesome Old Town, *see* **It's a Lonesome Old Town**

(Look Down That) Lonesome Road   1928   w. Gene Austin   m. Nathaniel Shilkret. (MF) *Show Boat.*

Lonesome Road, *see also* **Look Down, Look Down That Lonesome Road**

Long Ago, The, *see* **Long Long Ago**

Long Ago and Far Away   1944   w. Ira Gershwin   m. Jerome Kern. (MF) *Cover Girl.* (MF) *Till the Clouds Roll By.* Gene Kelly, Rita Hayworth, and Phil Silvers appeared in *Cover Girl.* June Allyson, Frank Sinatra, Judy Garland, and Van Johnson appeared in *Till the Clouds Roll By,* biopic of composer Jerome Kern.

Long Ago in Alcala   1894   w. Frederick Edward Weatherly, Adrian Ross   m. André Messager. From the British comic opera *Mirette.*

Long and Winding Road, The   1970   w.m. John Lennon, Paul McCartney. (MT) *Beatlemania.*

Long Before I Knew You   1956   w. Betty Comden, Adolph Green   m. Jule Styne. (MT) *Bells Are Ringing.* (MF) *Bells Are Ringing.* Judy Holliday appeared in both the stage and film productions of *Bells Are Ringing.*

Long Boy, *see* **Good-Bye, Ma! Good-Bye, Pa! Good-Bye, Mule**

Long Cool Woman (in a Black Dress)   1972   w.m. Roger Cook, Roger Greenaway, Harold Clark. Ivor Novello Award winner 1972–1973.

Long Day Closes, The   1868   w. Henry Fothergill Chorley   m. Arthur Sullivan

Long-Haired Lover from Liverpool   1970   w.m. C. Dowden

Long Live Love   1965   w.m. Chris Andrews

Long Long Ago, or, **The Long Ago**   1833   w.m. Thomas Haynes Bayly. (F) *Calling Wild Bill Elliott.* Bill Elliott and Gabby Hayes appeared in *Calling Wild Bill Elliott.* See also ''Don't Sit Under the Apple Tree.''

Long, Long Trail, *see* **There's a Long, Long Trail**

(It's Gonna Be) Long, Long Winter, A 1951 w.m. Buddy Kaye, Jule Styne

Long Tall Glasses (I Can Dance) 1975 w.m. David Alexandra Courtney, Leo Sayer

Long Tall Sally 1956 w.m. Enotris Johnson. (MF) *Don't Knock the Rock.* Bill Haley appeared in *Don't Knock the Rock.*

Long Time Ago, or, **Shinbone Alley** 1833 w.m. anon. This song was popularized by Thomas "Daddy" Rice.

Long Train Runnin' 1973 w.m. Tom Johnston

Longer 1980 w.m. Dan Fogelberg

Longest Time, The 1984 w.m. Billy Joel

Longest Walk, The 1955 w.m. Edward Pola, Fred Spielman

Longest Way 'Round Is the Sweetest Way Home, The 1908 w. Ren Shields m. Kerry Mills

Longing for You 1905 w. Jack Drislane m. Theodore F. Morse

Longing for You 1955 w. Bernard Jansen m. Walter Dana Based on Oscar Straus's "A Waltz Dream."

Look Around (You'll Find Me There) 1971 w.m. Francis Albert Lai, Lowell Mark, Norman J. Simon

Look At 'Er 1957 w.m. Bob Merrill. (MT) *New Girl in Town.*

Look at Me, I'm Sandra Dee 1972 w.m. Jim Jacobs, Warren Casey. (MT) *Grease.* (MF) *Grease.* John Travolta and Olivia Newton-John appeared in the film production of *Grease.*

Look at Me Now, *see* **Oh Look at Me Now**

Look at That Face 1964 w.m. Leslie Bricusse, Anthony Newley. (MT) *The Roar of the Greasepaint—The Smell of the Crowd.* Anthony Newley and Cyril Ritchard appeared in *The Roar of the Greasepaint—The Smell of the Crowd.*

Look Down, Look Down That Lonesome Road 1865 w.m. traditional black American spiritual. (F) *Old Oklahoma Plains.* Rex Allen and Slim Pickens appeared in *Old Oklahoma Plains.*

Look for a Star 1960 w.m. Mark Anthony. (F) *Circus of Horrors.* Anton Diffring and Erica Remberg appeared in *Circus of Horrors.*

Look for the Silver Lining 1920 w. B.G. DeSylva m. Jerome Kern. (MT) *Good Morning, Dearie.* (MT) *Sally.* (MT) *The Wild Rose.* (MF) *Sally.* (MF) *Till the Clouds Roll By.* (MF) *Look for the Silver Lining.* (MF) *Meet Me in St. Louis.* Marilyn Miller and Mary Hay appeared in the American stage production of *Sally.* Dorothy Dickson and Gregory Stroud appeared in the British stage production of *Sally.* Jessie Matthews appeared in *The Wild Rose.* Marilyn Miller and Joe E. Brown appeared in the film production of *Sally.* June Allyson, Judy Garland, and Frank Sinatra appeared in *Till the Clouds Roll By,* biopic of composer Jerome Kern. Ray Bolger, June Haver, and Gordon MacRae appeared in *Look for the Silver Lining,* biopic of Marilyn Miller.

Look into Your Heart 1976 w.m. Curtis Mayfield. (MF) *Sparkle.*

Look of Love, The 1965 w. Hal David m. Burt Bacharach. (F) *The Boys in the Band.* (F) *Casino Royale.*

Look Out for Jimmy Valentine, *see* **Jimmy Valentine**

Look Through Any Window 1965 w.m. Graham Gouldman, Charles Silverman. Ivor Novello Award winner 1965.

Look Through My Window 1967 w.m. John Phillips

Look to the Rainbow 1946 w. E.Y. Harburg m. Burton Lane. (MT) *Finian's Rainbow.* Albert Sharpe and David Wayne appeared in *Finian's Rainbow.*

Look What They've Done to My Song Ma 1970 w.m. Melanie Safka

Look What You've Done to Me 1980 w.m. David Foster, Boz Scaggs

Look Who's Dancing 1951 w. Dorothy Fields m. Arthur Schwartz. (MT) *A Tree Grows in Brooklyn.* Shirley Booth and Johnny Johnston appeared in *A Tree Grows in Brooklyn.*

Lookie, Lookie, Lookie, Here Comes Cookie, *see* **Here Comes Cookie**

Looking Around w.m. Colin Smith. (TV-BBC) *Looking Around.*

Looking At the World Through Rose Colored Glasses 1926 w.m. Tommy Malie, Jimmie Stieger

Looking Back 1870 w. Louisa Gray m. Arthur Sullivan

Looking for a Boy 1925 w. Ira Gershwin m. George Gershwin. (MT) *Tip-Toes.* Queenie Smith and Robert Halliday appeared in the American production of *Tip-Toes.* Dorothy Dickson appeared in the British production of *Tip-Toes.*

Looking High, High, High 1960 w.m. John Watson

Lookin' Out My Back Door 1970 w.m. John C. Fogerty

Looks Like We Made It 1977 w.m. Will Jennings, Richard Kerr

Loop de Loop 1962 w.m. Teddy Vann.; Based on the traditional song.

Lord Is My Light, The 1897 w. Biblical m. Frances Allitsen

Lord Randall c.1745 w.m. traditional ballad, from Scotland

Lord Thomas and Fair Elinore c.1725 w.m. traditional ballad, from England

Lords of the Air 1939 w.m. Davy Burnaby, Michael North

Lord's Prayer, The 1935 w. Biblical adaptation m. Albert Hay Malotte. (MF) *Because You're Mine.* Mario Lanza appeared in *Because You're Mine.*

Lorelei 1933 w. Ira Gershwin m. George Gershwin. (MT) *Pardon My English.* Carl Randall and Barbara Newbury appeared in *Pardon My English.*

Lorena 1857 w. Rev. H.D.L. Webster m. Joseph Philbrick Webster. This ballad was often sung by homesick soldiers of the South, and was all but forgotten until Margaret Mitchell mentioned it in her epic novel *Gone With the Wind.*

Lorraine, My Beautiful Alsace Lorraine 1917 w. Alfred Bryan m. Fred Fisher

Losing My Mind 1971 w.m. Stephen Sondheim. (MT) *Follies.* (MT) *Side by Side by Sondheim.* Alexis Smith and

Yvonne DeCarlo appeared in *Follies*. Millicent Martin and Julie N. McKenzie appeared in *Side by Side by Sondheim*.

Losing You 1963 Orig.w. Pierce Havet Eng.w. Carl Sigman w. Jean Renard

Losing You 1963 w.m. Tom Springfield, Clive Westlake. Ivor Novello Award winner 1964.

Lost 1936 w.m. Phil Ohman, Johnny Mercer, Macy O. Teetor

Lost Barber Shop Chord 1926 w. Ira Gershwin m. George Gershwin. (MT) *Americana*. Helen Morgan, Roy Atwell, and Lew Brice appeared in *Americana*.

Lost Chord, The 1877 w. Adelaide Procter m. Sir Arthur Sullivan. This song concerns the brother of Arthur Sullivan, Fred, an actor and singer destined for success who became ill and died three weeks later, his brother at his side. This song was first performed at a Boosey Ballad Concert in London.

Lost in a Fog 1934 w. Dorothy Fields m. Jimmy McHugh. (F) *Have a Heart*. Jean Parker and James Dunn appeared in *Have a Heart*.

Lost in Love 1980 w.m. Graham Russell

Lost in Loveliness 1954 w. Leo Robin m. Sigmund Romberg (developed by Don Walker). (MT) *The Girl in Pink Tights*.

Lost in the Fifties Tonight (In the Still of the Night) 1985 w.m. Fredericke L. Parris

Lost in the Stars 1949 w. Maxwell Anderson m. Kurt Weill. (MT) *Lost in the Stars*. (MF) *Lost in the Stars*. Todd Duncan, Warren Coleman, and William Greaves appeared in the stage production of *Lost in the Stars*. Melba Moore appeared in the film production of *Lost in the Stars*.

(I've Got) Lot of Livin' To Do, A 1960 w. Lee Adams m. Charles Strouse. (MT) *Bye Bye Birdie*. (MF) *Bye Bye Birdie*. Ann-Margret and Dick Van Dyke appeared in the film production of *Bye Bye Birdie*.

Lotus Land 1905 m. Cyril Scott

Louie Louie 1963 w.m. Richard Berry

Louise 1929 w. Leo Robin m. Richard A. Whiting. (MF) *Innocents of Paris*. (F) *Halfway to Heaven*. (MF) *You Can't Ration Love*. (MF) *The Stooge*. Maurice Chevalier and George Fawcett appeared in *Innocents of Paris*. Buddy Rogers and Jean Arthur appeared in *Halfway to Heaven*. Betty Jane Rhodes and Johnny Johnston appeared in *You Can't Ration Love*. Dean Martin and Jerry Lewis appeared in *The Stooge*. Theme song of Maurice Chevalier.

Lou(i)siana Belle 1847 w.m. Stephen Collins Foster. An original signed copy of this song manuscript was discovered on Aug. 11, 1956. Foster, who characteristically drew his stems on the wrong side of the notes, wrote this song at age twenty-one.

Louisiana Hayride 1932 w. Howard Dietz m. Arthur Schwartz. (MT) *Flying Colors*. (MT) *Please*. (MF) *The Band Wagon*. Clifton Webb, Patsy Kelly, and Imogene Coca appeared in *Flying Colors*. Fred Astaire and Cyd Charisee appeared in *The Band Wagon*.

Louisiana Purchase 1940 w.m. Irving Berlin. (MT) *Loui-siana Purchase*. (MF) *Louisiana Purchase*. Victor Moore, William Gaxton, and Irene Bordoni appeared in the stage production of *Louisiana Purchase*. Bob Hope and Irene Bordoni appeared in the film production of *Louisiana Purchase*.

Louisville Lou, the Vampin' Lady 1923 w. Jack Yellen m. Milton Ager

Lounging at the Waldorf 1936 w. Richard Maltby, Jr. m. Thomas "Fats" Waller. (MT) *Ain't Misbehavin'*. Debbie Allen and Nell Carter appeared in *Ain't Misbehavin'*. This song was most popular in 1938.

Love 1945 w.m. Hugh Martin, Ralph Blane. (MF) *Ziegfeld Follies*. Fred Astaire, Judy Garland, and Lena Horne appeared in *Ziegfeld Follies*.

Love (Your Magic Spell Is Everywhere) 1929 w. Elsie Janism. Edmund Goulding. (F) *The Trespasser*. Gloria Swanson and Robert Ames appeared in *The Trespasser*.

Love and a Dime 1935 w.m. Brooks Bowman. From the Princeton University Triangle Club production *Stags at Bay*.

Love and Marriage 1955 w. Sammy Cahn m. James Van Heusen. (TV) *Our Town*.

Love and Wine 1912 w.m. Franz Lehár, Adrian Ross. (MT) *Gypsy Love*.

Love Ballad 1979 w.m. Skip Scarborough

Love Boat, The 1920 w. Gene Buck m. Victor Herbert. (MT) *Ziegfeld Follies of 1920*.

Love Bug Will Bite You, The 1936 w.m. Pinky Tomlin

Love Can Make You Happy 1969 w.m. Jack Sigler, Jr.

Love Child 1968 w.m. Frank E. Wilson, Deke Richards, Pam Sawyer, R. Dean Taylor

Love Everlasting, *see* L'Amour Toujours L'Amour

Love Eyes 1967 w.m. Lee Hazlewood

Love for Lydia 1977 m. Harry Rabinowitz. (TV-BBC) *Love for Lydia*. Ivor Novello Award winner 1977–78.

Love for Sale 1930 w.m. Cole Porter. (MT) *The New Yorkers*. This song was banned from public broadcasting by the major radio networks.

Love Forever I Adore You 1929 w.m. G. de Micheli

Love from a Heart of Gold 1961 w.m. Frank Loesser. (MT) *How To Succeed In Business Without Really Trying*. (MF) *How To Succeed In Business Without Really Trying*. Robert Morse appeared in both the stage and film productions of *How To Succeed*.

Love Grows 1971 w.m. Tony Macaulay, Barry Mason. Ivor Novello Award winner 1970/1971.

Love Hangover 1976 w.m. Marilyn McLeod, Pamela Joan Sawyer

Love Has Eyes 1814 w. Charles Dibdin m. Sir Henry Rowley Bishop

Love Has Wings 1913 w. C.C.S. Cushing, E.P. Heath m. Emmerich Kalman. (MT) *Sari*.

Love, Here Is My Heart 1915 Fr.w. Louis Delamarre Eng.w. Adrian Ross m. Lao Silesu. (F) *Young Eagles* Charles "Buddy" Rogers and Virginia Bruce appeared in *Young Eagles*.

Love Hurts 1975 w.m. Boudleaux Bryant

Love I Long For, The 1944 w. Howard Dietz m. Vernon Duke. (MT) *Sadie Thompson.*

Love I Lost, The (Part I) 1973 w.m. Leon Huff, Kenneth Gamble

Love in a Home 1956 w. Johnny Mercer m. Gene De Paul. (MT) *Li'l Abner.* (MF) *Li'l Abner.* Stubby Kaye appeared in the film production of *Li'l Abner.*

Love in an Automobile 1899 w.m. Alfred R. Dixon. This song is probably the first published "automobile" genre song.

Love in Bloom 1934 w.m. Leo Robin, Ralph Rainger. (MF) *She Loves Me Not.* (F) *New York Town.* (MF) *True to the Army.* Bing Crosby and Miriam Hopkins appeared in *She Loves Me Not.* Mary Martin and Fred MacMurray appeared in *New York Town.* Judy Canova, Ann Miller, and Jerry Colonna appeared in *True to the Army.* Theme song of Jack Benny.

Love in the First Degree 1982 w.m. Tim DuBois, Jim Hurt

Love in the Open Air 1968 w.m. Paul McCartny

Love in the Shadows 1976 w.m. Neil Sedaka, Phil Cody

Love Is 1958 w.m. Leslie Bricusse

Love Is a Battlefield 1984 w.m. Mike Chapman, Holly Knight

Love Is a Dancing Thing 1935 w. Howard Dietz m. Arthur Schwartz. (MT) *At Home Abroad.* (F) *Follow the Sun.* Beatrice Lillie, Ethel Waters, and Eleanor Powell appeared in *At Home Abroad.*

Love Is a Many-Splendored Thing 1955 w. Paul Francis Webster m. Sammy Fain. (F) *Love Is a Many-Splendored Thing.* Jennifer Jones and William Holden appeared in *Love Is a Many-Splendored Thing.* Academy Award winner 1955.

Love Is a Simple Thing 1952 w. June Carroll m. Arthur Siegel. (MT) *New Faces of 1952.*

Love Is a Song That Never Ends 1942 w.m. Frank Churchill, Edward Plumb. (MF) *Bambi.*

Love Is Alive 1976 w.m. Gary Wright

Love Is All 1940 w.m. Pinky Tomlin, Harry Tobias. (MF) *It's a Date.* Deanna Durbin appeared in *It's a Date.*

Love Is All 1970 w.m. Les Reed, Barry Mason. Ivor Novello Award winner 1969–70.

Love Is Blue 1968 w.m. Bryan Blackburn, Pierre Cour, Andre Popp

Love Is Here and Now You're Gone 1967 w.m. Eddie Holland, Brian Holland, Lamont Dozier

Love Is Here To Stay, *see* **Our Love Is Here To Stay**

Love Is in the Air 1978 w.m. Harry Vanda, George Young

Love Is Just Around the Corner 1934 w. Leo Robin m. Lewis E. Gensler. (MF) *Here Is My Heart.* Bing Crosby appeared in *Here Is My Heart.*

Love Is Like a Cigarette 1908 w. Glen MacDonough m. Victor Herbert. (MT) *The Rose of Algeria.*

Love Is Like a Firefly 1912 w. Otto Harbach m. Rudolf Friml. (MT) *The Firefly.* (MF) *The Firefly.* Jeanette MacDonald and Allan Jones appeared in the film production of *The Firefly.*

Love Is Like a Heat Wave, *see* **Heat Wave**

Love Is Like a Violin 1945 w.m. Miarka Laparcerie, Jimmy Kennedy. (F) *Little Boy Lost.* Bing Crosby and Claude Dauphin appeared in *Little Boy Lost.* This song was popularly revived in 1953 and later again in 1960.

Love Is My Reason 1945 w.m. Ivor Novello. (MT) *Perchance To Dream.* Muriel Barron appeared in *Perchance To Dream.*

Love Is So Terrific 1945 w.m. Sunny Skylar, Artie Shaftel. This song was also popular in 1948.

Love Is Strange 1957 w.m. Mickey Baker, Ethel Smith

Love Is Sweeping the Country 1931 w. Ira Gershwin m. George Gershwin. (MT) *Of Thee I Sing.* William Gaxton and Victor Moore appeared in *Of Thee I Sing.*

Love Is the Answer 1979 w.m. Todd Rundgren

Love Is the Best of All 1915 w. Henry Blossom m. Victor Herbert. (MT) *The Princess Pat.*

Love Is the Darndest Thing 1946 w.m. Johnny Burke, Jimmy Van Heusen. (MF) *Cross My Heart.* Betty Hutton and Sonny Tufts appeared in *Cross My Heart.*

Love Is the Reason 1951 w. Dorothy Fields m. Arthur Schwartz. (MT) *A Tree Grows in Brooklyn.* Shirley Booth and Johnny Johnston appeared in *A Tree Grows in Brooklyn.*

Love Is The Sweetest Thing 1933 w.m. Ray Noble. (MF) *Say It With Music.* (F) *Confidential Agent.* Jack Payne appeared in *Say It with Music.* Charles Boyer and Lauren Bacall appeared in *Confidential Agent.*

Love Is the Tender Trap, *see* **The Tender Trap**

Love Is Thicker Than Water, *see* **Thicker Than Water**

Love Is Where You Find It 1938 w.m. Johnny Mercer, Harry Warren. (MT) *Singin' in the Rain.* (MF) *Garden of the Moon.* Pat O'Brien and John Payne appeared in *Garden of the Moon.*

Love Is Where You Find It 1948 w.m. Earl Brent, Nacio Herb Brown. (MF) *The Kissing Bandit.* Frank Sinatra and Kathryn Grayson appeared in *The Kissing Bandit.*

Love Letters 1945 w. Edward Heyman m. Victor Young. (F) *Love Letters.* Jennifer Jones and Joseph Cotten appeared in *Love Letters.* This song was popularly revived in 1962.

Love Letters in the Sand 1931 w. Nick Kenny, Charles Kenny m. J. Fred Coots. Loosely based on William D. Hendrickson's "The Spanish Cavalier" of 1881. This song was popularly revived in 1957.

Love Light in Flight 1985 w.m. Stevie Wonder

Love Locked Out 1933 w. Max Kester m. Ray Noble

Love Look Away 1958 w. Oscar Hammerstein II m. Richard Rodgers. (MT) *Flower Drum Song.* (MF) *Flower Drum Song.* Nancy Kwan appeared in the film production of *Flower Drum Song.*

Love Makes the World Go 'Round 1896 w. Clyde Fitch m. arr. William Furst. (MT) *Bohemia.*

Love Makes the World Go Round, or, **Theme from** *Carnival* 1961 w.m. Bob Merrill. (MT) *Carnival.*

Love Me and the World Is Mine 1906 w. Dave Reed, Jr. m. Ernest R. Ball

Love Me Do 1964 w.m. John Lennon, Paul McCartney

Love Me Forever 1935 w. Gus Kahn m. Victor Schertzinger. (F) *On Wings of Song.* (F) *Love Me Forever.* Grace Moore appeared in *On Wings of Song.* Grace Moore and Spring Byington appeared in *Love Me Forever.*

Love Me Forever 1950 w.m. Harry Leon, Don Pelosi

Love Me Little, Love Me Long 1893 w.m. Percy Gaunt

Love Me or Leave Me 1928 w. Gus Kahn m. Walter Donaldson. (MT) *Whoopee.* (MT) *Simple Simon.* (MF) *I'll See You in My Dreams.* (MF) *Love Me or Leave Me.* Ruth Etting and Eddie Cantor appeared in *Whoopee.* Ed Wynn and Harriet Hoctor appeared in *Simple Simon.* Doris Day and Danny Thomas appeared in *I'll See You in My Dreams,* biopic of song writer Gus Kahn. Doris Day and James Cagney appeared in *Love Me or Leave Me,* biopic of singer Ruth Etting.

Love Me Tender 1956 w.m. Elvis Presley, Vera Matson. (F) *Love Me Tender.* Elvis Presley appeared in *Love Me Tender.* Based on George Poulton's "Aura Lee" of 1861.

Love Me Tomorrow 1982 w.m. Peter Cetera, David Foster

Love Me Tonight 1925 w. Brian Hooker m. Rudolf Friml. (MT) *The Vagabond King.* (MF) *The Vagabond King* (1930). (MF) *Love Me Tonight.* (MF) *The Vagabond King* (1956). Carolyn Thompson and Dennis King appeared in the stage production of *The Vagabond King.* Dennis King and Jeanette MacDonald appeared in the 1930 film production of *The Vagabond King.* Maurice Chevalier appeared in *Love Me Tonight.* This song was popularly revived in 1932.

Love Me with All Your Heart 1964 w.m. Carlos Rigual, Mario Rigual, Sunny Skylar, Carlos Martinoli

Love Must Be Free 1943 w.m. Alan Paul

Love Nest, The 1920 w. Otto Harbach m. Louis A. Hirsch. (MT) *Mary.* (MF) *Both Ends of the Candle.*

Love Never Went to College 1940 w. Lorenz Hart m. Richard Rodgers. (MT) *Too Many Girls.* (MF) *Too Many Girls.* Lucille Ball and Ann Miller appeared in the film production of *Too Many Girls.*

Love of My Life 1940 w. Johnny Mercer m. Artie Shaw. (MF) *Second Chorus.* Fred Astaire, Paulette Goddard, and Burgess Meredith appeared in *Second Chorus.*

Love of My Life 1948 w.m. Cole Porter. (MF) *The Pirate.* Gene Kelly and Judy Garland appeared in *The Pirate.* This song was popularly revived in 1953.

Love of Three Oranges (March), op. 33 1919 m. Serge Prokofieff. From "L'Amour des Trois Oranges."

Love on a Dime, *see* **Love and a Dime**

Love on a Greyhound Bus 1945 w. Ralph Blane, Kay Thompson m. George Stoll. (MF) *No Leave, No Love.* Pat Kirkwood appeared in *No Leave, No Love.*

Love on the Rocks 1981 w.m. Neil Diamond

Love Parade, *see* **My Love Parade**

Love Parade 1986 w.m. Gilbert Alexander Gabriel, Nicholas William Laird-Clowes

Love Plus One 1983 w.m. Nick Heyward. Ivor Novello Award winner 1982–83.

Love Potion Number Nine 1965 w.m. Mike Stoller, Jerry Leiber

Love Rollercoaster 1976 w.m. Clarence Satchell, Leroy Bonner, Ralph Middlebrooks, Willie Beck, Marvin Pierce, Marshall Jones, James Williams

Love Sends a Little Gift of Roses 1919 w. Leslie Cooke m. John Openshaw

Love So Right 1976 w.m. Barry Gibb, Robin Gibb, Maurice Gibb

Love Somebody 1948 w.m. Alex C. Kramer, Joan Whitney. Based on a traditional American folk ballad.

Love Somebody 1984 w.m. Rick Springfield

Love Song, A 1982 w.m. Lee Greenwood

Love Song from *Houseboat,* or, **Almost in Your Arms** 1958 w.m. Ray Evans, Jay Livingston. (F) *Houseboat.* Sophia Loren and Cary Grant appeared in *Houseboat.*

Love Songs of the Nile 1933 w. Arthur Freed m. Nacio Herb Brown. (F) *The Barbarian.* Ramon Novarro and Myrna Loy appeared in *The Barbarian.*

Love Steals Your Heart 1946 w.m. HansMay, Alan Stranks. (F) *The Wicked Lady.* James Mason and Margaret Lockwood appeared in *The Wicked Lady.*

(Theme from) Love Story, or, **Where Do I Begin** 1970 w.m. Carl Sigman, Francis Lai. (F) *Love Story.* Ryan O'Neal and Ali McGraw appeared in *Love Story.*

Love Story, A, *see* **Intermezzo**

Love Takes Times 1979 w.m. Larry Hoppen, Marilyn Mason.

Love Tales 1923 w. Ben Ryan m. Vincent Rose

Love Theme from *A Star Is Born,* *see* **Evergreen**

Love Theme from *Romeo and Juliet,* or, **A Time for Us** 1969 w.m. Larry Kusik, Eddie Snyder, Nino Rota. (F) *Romeo and Juliet.* Olivia Hussey appeared in *Romeo and Juliet.*

Love Theme from *St. Elmo's Fire* 1986 m. David Foster. (F) *St. Elmo's Fire.* Emilio Estevez and Andrew McCarthy appeared in *St. Elmo's Fire.*

Love Theme from *White Nights,* *see* **Separate Lives.**

Love Thy Neighbor 1934 w. Mack Gordon m. Harry Revel. (MF) *We're Not Dressing.* Bing Crosby appeared in *We're Not Dressing.*

Love To Love You Baby 1975 w.m. Peter Bellotte, Donna Summer, Giorgio Moroder

Love Touch (Theme from *Legal Eagles*) 1986 w.m. Gene Black, Mike Chapman, Holly Knight. (F) *Legal Eagles.*

Love Transformation 1977 w.m. Roger Greenaway. Ivor Novello Award winner 1977–78.

Love Walked In 1938 w. Ira Gershwin m. George Gershwin. (MF) *The Goldwyn Follies.* (MF) *Rhapsody in Blue.* Adolphe Menjou and the Ritz Brothers appeared in *The Goldwyn Follies.* Oscar Levant, Robert Alda, and Alexis Smith appeared in *Rhapsody in Blue,* biopic of composer George Gershwin.

Love—What Are You Doing to My Heart 1933 w.m. Tibor Barczi, Samuel M. Lewis

Love Will Find a Way 1890 w. J. Cheever Goodwin m. Woolson Morse

Love Will Find a Way 1917 w. Harry Graham m. Harold

Fraser-Simson. (MT) *The Maid of the Mountains.* Jose Collins and Thorpe Bates appeared in *The Maid of the Mountains.*

Love Will Find a Way 1921 w. Noble Sissle m. Eubie Blake. (MT) *Shuffle Along of 1921.* (MT) *Bubbling Brown Sugar.* Noble Sissle and Florence Mills appeared in *Shuffle Along,* Avon Long and Vivian Reed appeared in *Bubbling Brown Sugar.*

Love Will Find a Way 1978 w.m. Cory Lerios, David Jenkins

Love Will Find Out the Way c. 1666 w.m. traditional, from England

Love Will Keep Us Together 1975 w.m. Neil Sedaka, Howard Greenfield. Grammy Award winner 1975.

Love Will Turn You Around 1982 w.m. Dave Malloy, Kenny Rogers, Tom Schuyler, Even Stevens

Love with the Proper Stranger 1964 w.m. Johnny Mercer, Elmer Bernstein. (F) *Love with the Proper Stranger.* Natalie Wood and Steve McQueen appeared in *Love with the Proper Stranger.*

Love Won't Let Me Wait 1975 w.m. Vinnie Barrett, Bobby Eli

Love Ya 1951 w. Charles Tobias m. Peter DeRose

Love You Inside and Out 1979 w.m. Barry Gibb, Maurice Gibb, Robin Gibb

Loveliest Night of the Year, The 1951 w. Paul Francis Webster m. arr. Irving Aaronson. (MF) *The Great Caruso.* Mario Lanza appeared in *The Great Caruso.* Based on Juventino P. Rosa's ''Over the Waves'' of 1888.

Loveliness of You, The 1935 w. Mack Gordon m. Harry Revel. (MF) *You Can't Have Everything.* Don Ameche and Tony Martin appeared in *You Can't Have Everything.*

Lovely 1933 w. Edgar Leslie m. Fred E. Ahlert

Lovely 1962 w.m. Stephen Sondheim. (MT) *A Funny Thing Happened on the Way to the Forum.* (MF) *A Funny Thing Happened on the Way to the Forum.* Zero Mostel and Jack Gilford appeared in the film production of *A Funny Thing Happened on the Way to the Forum.*

Lovely Bunch of Cocoanuts, *see* **I've Got a Lovely Bunch of Cocoanuts**

Lovely Lady 1927 w. Harry A. Steinberg, Eddie Ward, Cyrus Wood m. Dave Stamper, Harold Levey. (MT) *Lovely Lady.* Edna Leedom and Guy Robertson appeared in *Lovely Lady.*

Lovely Lady 1935 w. Ted Koehler m. Jimmy McHugh. (MT) *The Glorious Days.* (MF) *King of Burlesque.* Anna Neagle appeared in *The Glorious Days.* Warner Baxter, ''Fats'' Waller, and Alice Faye appeared in *King of Burlesque.*

Lovely Lady Let the Roses See You Today 1935 w.m. Norman Hardy

Lovely Luana 1945 w.m. Don Raye, Gene De Paul. (MF) *Song of the Sarong.* Nancy Kelly and Fuzzy Knight appeared in *Song of the Sarong.*

Lovely Night, A 1957 w. Oscar Hammerstein II m. Richard Rodgers. (TV) *Cinderella.*

Lovely Rita (Meter Maid) 1967 w.m. John Lennon, Paul McCartney

Lovely To Look At 1935 w. Dorothy Fields, Jimmy McHugh m. Jerome Kern. (MF) *Roberta.* (MF) *Lovely To Look At.* Irene Dunne and Fred Astaire appeared in *Roberta.* Kathryn Grayson, Gower Champion and Howard Keel appeared in *Lovely To Look At,* remake of *Roberta.* This song did not appear in the original 1933 stage production of *Roberta.*

(This Is) Lovely Way to Spend an Evening, A 1943 w. Harold Adamson m. Jimmy McHugh. (MF) *Higher and Higher.* (F) *The Racket.* Frank Sinatra, Michele Morgan, and Jack Haley appeared in *Higher and Higher.* Robert Mitchum and Lizabeth Scott appeared in *The Racket.*

Lover 1933 w. Lorenz Hart m. Richard Rodgers. (MF) *Love Me Tonight.* (MF) *Words and Music.* (MF) *The Jazz Singer* (1953). (MF) *The Rat Race.* Maurice Chevalier and Jeanette MacDonald appeared in *Love Me Tonight.* Mickey Rooney, Judy Garland, and Gene Kelly appeared in *Words and Music,* biopic of song writers Rodgers and Hart. Danny Thomas and Peggy Lee appeared in *The Jazz Singer.* Tony Curtis and Debbie Reynolds appeared in *The Rat Race.* This song was popularly revived in 1949.

Lover Come Back to Me 1928 w. Oscar Hammerstein II m. Sigmund Romberg. (MT) *The New Moon.* (MF) *The New Moon* (1930). (MF) *The New Moon* (1940). (MF) *Deep In My Heart.* Evelyn Herbert and Robert Halliday appeared in the American stage production of *The New Moon.* Evelyn Laye appeared in the British stage production of *The New Moon.* Nelson Eddy and Jeanette MacDonald appeared in the 1940 film production of *The New Moon.* Jose Ferrer and Merle Oberon appeared in *Deep in My Heart,* biopic of composer Sigmund Romberg. The release of this song is based on Tchaikovsky's ''June Barcarolle.''

Lover Man (Oh Where Can You Be) 1942 w.m. Jimmy Davis, Roger ''Ram'' Ramirez, Jimmy Sherman. (MF) *Lady Sings the Blues.* Diana Ross appeared in *Lady Sings the Blues,* biopic of singer Billie Holiday.

Lover of My Dreams, or, **Mirabelle Waltz** 1931 w.m. Noël Coward

Loverboy 1985 w.m. Robert ''Mutt'' Lange, Billy Ocean, Keith Diamond

Lover's Concerto, A 1965 w.m. Denny Randell, Sandy Linzer. Based on Beethoven's ''Minuet in G.''

Love's Been Good to Me 1963 w.m. Rod McKuen. This song was popularly revived in 1969.

Love's Eyes 1825 w. Samuel Woodworth m. based on the traditional Scottish air ''Roy's Wife''; arr. John Davies. From the ballad opera *The Forest Rose.*

Love's Found You and Me 1982 w.m. Ed Bruce, Randall Jay Rogers

Love's Garden of Roses 1915 w.m. Haydn Wood, Ruth Rutherford

Loves Me Like a Rock 1973 w.m. Paul Simon

Love's Old Sweet Song 1884 w.m. G. Clifton Bingham, James Lyman Molloy. (MF) *Wait Till the Sun Shines Nellie.* David Wayne appeared in *Wait Till the Sun Shines Nellie.* James Molloy, an Irish lawyer who wrote three operettas, later edited (with J.L. Hatton) a collection of folksongs of his country. This song was popularly performed by Antoinette Sterling.

Love's Own Sweet Song, or, **Sari Waltz** 1914 w. C.C.S. Cushing, E.P. Heath m. Emmerich Kalman. (MT) *Sari.*

Love's Ritornella, or, **Gentle Zitella** 1829 w. James Robinson Planché m. Thomas Simpson Cooke. (MT) *The Brigand.*

Love's Roundelay 1908 w. Joseph W. Herbert m. Oscar Straus. (MT) *A Waltz Dream.*

Love's Theme 1974 w.m. Barry White

Lovesick Blues 1922 w.m. Cliff Friend, Irving Mills

Lovesick Blues 1949 w.m. Hank Williams

Loving Her Was Easier (Than Anything I'll Ever Do Again) 1981 w.m. Kris Kristofferson

Lovin' Sam, the Sheik of Alabam' 1922 w. Jack Yellen m. Milton Ager

Lovin' You 1975 w.m. Richard Rudolph, Minnie Riperton

Loving You Has Made Me Bananas 1968 w.m. Guy Marks

Low-Backed Car, The 1846 w. Samuel Lover m. based on the traditional Irish melody "The Jolly Ploughman"

Low Bridge!—Everybody Down, *see* Erie Canal

Lowdown 1976 w.m. Boz Scaggs, David Paich. Grammy Award winner 1976.

Lubly Fan, *see* Buffalo Gals

Lucille 1977 w.m. Hal Bynum, Roger Bowling

Luck Be a Lady 1950 w.m. Frank Loesser. (MT) *Guys and Dolls.* (MF) *Guys and Dolls.* Robert Alda and Vivian Blaine appeared in the stage production of *Guys and Dolls.* Frank Sinatra and Marlon Brando appeared in the film production of *Guys and Dolls.*

Lucky Day 1926 w. B.G. DeSylva, Lew Brown m. Ray Henderson (MT) *George White's Scandals of 1926.* (MT) *Shake Your Feet.* (MF) *The Best Things in Life Are Free.* (R) *Your Hit Parade.* Gordon MacRae, Ernest Borgnine, and Dan Dailey appeared in *The Best Things in Life Are Free,* biopic of song writers DeSylva, Brown, and Henderson. This song was played on the radio program "Your Hit Parade" broadcasts to advertise Lucky Strike cigarettes.

Lucky Five 1960 w.m. Trevor Stanford

Lucky in Love 1927 w. B.G. DeSylva, Lew Brown m. Ray Henderson. (MT) *Good News.* (MF) *Good News* (1947). Mary Lawlor and Zelma O'Neal appeared in the stage production of *Good News.* June Allyson and Peter Lawford appeared in the film production of *Good News.*

Lucky Jim 1896 w. Charles Horwitz m. Frederick V. Bowers

Lucky One, The 1985 w.m. Bruce Roberts

Lucky Seven 1930 w. Howard Dietz m. Arthur Schwartz. (MT) *The Second Little Show.*

Lucky Star 1985 w.m. Madonna

Lucky to Be Me 1944 w. Betty Comden, Adolph Green m. Leonard Bernstein. (MT) *On the Town.* (MF) *On the Town.* Gene Kelly, Frank Sinatra, and Ann Miller appeared in the film production of *On the Town.*

Lucy in the Sky with Diamonds 1967 w.m. John Lennon, Paul McCartney. (MT) *Beatlemania.* (MF) *Yellow Submarine.* During the drug culture of the late 1960s, this song's initials supposedly alluded to the taking of LSD for hallucinogenic experiences. This song was popularly revived in 1975.

Lucy Neale, *see* Miss Lucy Neale

Lucy's Theme from Parrish 1961 m. Max Steiner. (F) *Parrish.*

Lullaby 1868 Ger.w. anon. Eng. w. Mrs. Natalia MacFarren m. Johannes Brahms. From the German "Wiegenlied," op.49.

Lullaby 1886 w.m. Claxson Bellamy, Harry Paulton, Edward Jakobowski. (MT) *Erminie.*

Lullaby, *see also* Emmet's Lullaby

Lullaby in Rhythm 1938 w.m. Benny Goodman, Edgar Sampson, Clarence Prift, Walter Hirsch. (MF) *The Benny Goodman Story.*

Lullaby of Birdland 1952 w.m. George Shearing, George Weiss

Lullaby of Broadway 1935 w. Al Dubin m. Harry Warren. Based on a theme from a "Hungarian Dance" by Brahms and Offenbach's "Barcarolle" from *Tales of Hoffman.* (MT) *Forty-Second Street.* (MF) *The Gold Diggers of 1935.* (MF) *Lullaby of Broadway.* Jerry Ohrbach and Tammy Grimes appeared in *Forty-Second Street.* Dick Powell, Adolphe Menjou, and Wini Shaw appeared in *The Gold Diggers of 1935;* this was one of the longest and most spectacular Busby Berkeley production numbers, running almost fifteen minutes of film. Doris Day and Billy DeWolf appeared in *Lullaby of Broadway.* Academy Award winner 1935.

Lullaby of the Leaves 1932 w.m. Bernice Petkere, Joe Young

Lulu's Back in Town 1935 w. Al Dubin m. Harry Warren. (MF) *Broadway Gondolier.* Dick Powell, Joan Blondell, and Adolphe Menjou appeared in *Broadway Gondolier.*

Lush Life 1949 w.m. Billy Strayhorn

Lusty Month of May, The 1960 w. Alan Jay Lerner m. Frederick Loewe. (MT) *Camelot.* (MF) *Camelot.* Julie Andrews appeared in the stage production of *Camelot.* Vanessa Redgrave appeared in the film production of *Camelot.*

Lydia 1941 m. Miklos Rozsa (F) *Lydia.* Merle Oberon and Joseph Cotten appeared in *Lydia.*

Lydia the Tattooed Lady 1939 w E.Y. Harburg m. Harold Arlen. (MF) *A Day at the Circus.* The Marx Brothers and Eve Arden appeared in *A Day at the Circus.*

Lyin' Eyes 1975 w.m. Glen Frey, Don Henley

M-Squad 1958 m. William "Count" Basie. (TV) *M-Squad.*

Ma Belle 1928 w. P.G. Wodehouse, Clifford Grey m. Rudolf Friml. (MT) *The Three Musketeers.*

Ma Belle Marguerita 1947 w.m. A.P. Herbert, Vivian Ellis. (MT) *Bless the Bride.* George Guetary appeared in *Bless the Bride.*

Ma Blushin' Rosie 1900 w. Edgar Smith m. John Stromberg. (MF) *The Jolson Story.* (MF) *Broadway to Hollywood.* (MF) *Jolson Sings Again.* Larry Parks appeared in *The Jolson Story.* Jackie Cooper, Mickey Rooney, and Nelson Eddy appeared in *Broadway to Hollywood.* Larry Parks appeared in *Jolson Sings Again.*

Ma Curly Headed Babby 1926 w.m. George H. Clutsam. This song was popularly revived in 1932.

Ma! He's Making Eyes at Me 1921 w. Sidney Clare m. Con Conrad. (MT) *The Midnight Rounders.* (MF) *Singin' in the Corn.* (F) *Ma, He's Making Eyes at Me.* Eddie Cantor appeared in *The Midnight Rounders.* Judy Canova and Allen Jenkins appeared in *Singin' in the Corn.* Anne Nagel and Constance Moore appeared in *Ma, He's Making Eyes at Me.*

Ma Li'l Batteau 1921 w. Michael de Longpré (Lily Strickland) m. Lily Strickland. From "Bayou Songs."

Ma, Look At Charlie 1927 w.m. Elven Hedges

Ma Scotch Bluebell, *see* **I Love a Lassie**

MacArthur Park 1968 w.m. Jim Webb. This song was popularly revived in 1978.

MacNamara's Band 1917 w. John J. Stamford m. Shamus O'Connor. (MF) *I'll Get By.* (F) *Bad Lands of Dakota.* Gloria De Haven and Dennis Day appeared in *I'll Get By. Robert Stack and Ann Rutherford appeared in Bad Lands of Dakota.*

Mack the Knife, or, **Theme from *The Threepenny Opera,* or, Morit'at** 1928 Ger.w. Bertolt Brecht Eng.w. Marc Blitzstein m. Kurt Weill. (MT) *The Threepenny Opera.* (MF) *Satchmo the Great.* Grammy Award winner 1959. This song was popularly revived in 1954, 1956, and 1959. The melody of this song was used by Billy Rose in 1935 for his nightclub with a lyric he had written encouraging patrons to throw quarters into a wishing well in which was situated a nude girl.

Macushla 1910 w. Josephine V. Rowe m. Dermot MacMurrough

Mad About the Boy 1932 w.m. Noël Coward. (MT) *Words and Music.* (MT) *Set to Music.* Gertrude Lawrence appeared in *Words and Music.* Beatrice Lillie appeared in *Set to Music.*

Mad About You 1986 w.m. Paula J. Brown, Mitchel Y. Evans, James F. Whelan, III

Mad Dogs and Englishmen 1931 w.m. Noël Coward. (MT) *The Third Little Show.* (MT) *Words and Music.* Beatrice Lillie and Eddie Arnold appeared in *The Third Little Show.* Gertrude Lawrence appeared in *Words and Music.*

Made for Each Other 1945 w.m. Ervin Drake, Jimmy Shirl, Rene Touzet. (MF) *Holiday in Havana.* Desi Arnaz and Marty Hatcher appeared in *Holiday in Havana.* From the Spanish "Tu Felicidad."

Made You 1960 w.m. John Barry. (F) *Beat Girl.*

Madeleine 1968 Eng.w. Eric Blau, Mort Shuman m. Jacques Brel. (MT) *Jacques Brel Is Alive and Well and Living in Paris.*

Madelon 1918 Fr.w. Louis Bousquet Eng.w. Alfred Bryan m. Camille Robert. (MT) *Hullo America.*

Mademoiselle de Paris 1951 w.m. Henri Alexandre Contet, Paul Jules Durand, Eric Maschwitz, Mitchell Parish

Mad'moiselle from Armentières, *see* **Hinky Dinky Parlay Voo**

Madrid 1929 w. J. Danielson, F. Vimont m. L.E. DeFrancesco

Maggie May 1964 w.m. Lionel Bart

Maggie May/Reason To Believe 1971 w.m. Martin Quittenton, Rod Stewart

Maggie Murphy's Home 1890 w. Edward Harrigan m. David Braham. (MT) *Reilly and the Four Hundred.* This song was first performed by Emma Pollock in *Reilly and the Four Hundred.*

Maggie, the Cows Are in the Clover 1886 w.m. Albert W. Filson

Magic 1975 w.m. David Payton, William Lyall. Ivor Novello Award winner 1975–76.

Magic 1980 w.m. John Farrar. (MF) *Xanadu.* Olivia Newton-John appeared in *Xanadu.*

Magic Is the Moonlight 1930 Sp.w. Maria Grever Eng.w. Charles Pasquale m. Maria Grever. (MF) *Nancy Goes to Rio.* Jane Powell and Ann Sothern appeared in *Nancy Goes to Rio.* From the Spanish "Te Quiero Dijiste." This song was popularly revived in 1944.

Magic Man 1976 w.m. Ann Wilson, Nancy Wilson

Magic Moments 1958 w. Hal David m. Burt F. Bacharach

Magic of Your Eyes, The 1917 w.m. Arthur A. Penn

Magic to Do 1972 w.m. Stephen Schwartz. (MT) *Pippin.* Ben Vereen and Jill Clayburgh appeared in *Pippin.*

(You've Got) Magic Touch, The 1956 w.m. Buck Ram

Magical Mystery Tour 1968 w.m. John Lennon, Paul McCartney. (MT) *Beatlemania.*

(Theme from) Magnificent Seven, The 1960 w.m. Elmer Bernstein. (F) *The Magnificent Seven.* Yul Brynner and Eli Wallach appeared in *The Magnificent Seven.*

Mah Lindy Lou 1920 w.m. Lily Strickland

Mahzel 1948 w.m. Artie Wayne, Jack Beekman

Maiden with the Dreamy Eyes, The 1901 w. J. Rosamond Johnson m. Bob Cole. (MT) *The Little Duchess.* This song was most popularly performed by Anna Held, Mrs. Florenz Ziegfeld.

Maiden's Prayer, A 1858 m. Thecla Badarczewska. From the French "La Prière d'une Vierge."

Maigret Theme, The 1961 w.m. Ron Grainer. (TV-BBC) *Maigret.* Ivor Novello Award winner 1961.

Main Event/The Fight 1979 w.m. Paul Jabara, Bob Esty, Bruce Roberts. (F) *The Main Event.* Barbra Streisand appeared in *The Main Event.*

Maine Stein Song, *see* **Stein Song**

Mairzy Doats 1943 w.m. Milton Drake, Al Hoffman, Jerry Livingston. The meaning of the title may be found in the lyric "Mares eat oats and does eat oats and little lambs eat ivy."

Make a Miracle 1948 w.m. Frank Loesser. (MT) *Where's Charley?.* (MF) *Where's Charley?.* Ray Bolger appeared in both the stage and film productions of *Where's Charley?.*

Make a Move on Me 1982 w.m. John Farrar, Tom Snow

Make Believe 1921 w. Benny Davis m. Jack Shilkret

Make Believe 1927 w. Oscar Hammerstein II m. Jerome Kern. (MT) *Show Boat.* (MF) *Show Boat* (1936). (MF) *Show Boat* (1951). (MF) *Till the Clouds Roll By.* Helen Morgan and Charles Winninger appeared in the original American stage production of *Show Boat*. Edith Day and Howett Worster appeared in the British stage production of *Show Boat*. Allan Jones and Helen Morgan appeared in the 1936 film production of *Show Boat*. Kathryn Grayson and Ava Gardner appeared in the 1951 film production of *Show Boat*. June Allyson and Judy Garland appeared in *Till the Clouds Roll By*, biopic of composer Jerome Kern.

Make Believe Ballroom, *see* **It's Make Believe Ballroom Time**

Make Believe Island 1940 w. Nick Kenny, Charles Kenny, Sam Coslow m. Will Grosz

Make 'Em Laugh 1952 w.m. Arthur Freed, Nacio Herb Brown. (MT) *Singin' in the Rain*. (MF) *Singin' in the Rain*. Donald O'Connor, Gene Kelly, and Debbie Reynolds appeared in the 1952 film production of *Singin' in the Rain*.

Make Her Mine 1954 w.m. Sammy Gallop, Chester Conn

Make It Easy On Yourself 1962 w. Hal David m. Burt F. Bacharach. This song was popularly revived in 1965.

(I'd Like To) Make It with You 1970 w.m. David Gates. This song was most popular in 1972.

Make Love Stay 1983 w.m. Dan Fogelberg

Make Love to Me 1954 w. Bill Norvas, Allan Copeland m. Leon Roppolo, Paul Mares, Benny Pollack, George Brunies, Mel Stitzel, Walter Melrose. Based on "Tin Roof Blues" of 1923.

Make Mine Music 1946 w.m. Eliot Daniel, Ken Darby. (MF) *Make Mine Music*. The voices of Dinah Shore and Jerry Colonna appeared in *Make Mine Music*.

Make My Day 1984 w.m. Dewayne Blackwell

Make Someone Happy 1960 w. Betty Comden, Adolph Green m. Jule Styne (MT) *Do Re Mi*. This song was popularly adapted in 1978 as "Bake Someone Happy" for the television commercial promotion campaign for Pillsbury Flour and cake mixes.

Make the Man Love Me 1951 w. Dorothy Fields m. Arthur Schwartz. (MT) *A Tree Grows in Brooklyn*. Shirley Booth and Marcia van Dyke appeared in *A Tree Grows in Brooklyn*.

Make the World Go Away 1965 w.m. Hank Cochran

Make Yourself Comfortable 1954 w.m. Bob Merrill

Makin' It 1979 w.m. Dino Fekaris, Freddie Perren. (TV) *Makin' It*.

Making Love 1982 w.m. Burt Bacharach, Bruce Roberts, Carole Bayer Sager

Making Love Out of Nothing At All 1983 w.m. Jim Steinman

Makin' Whoopee 1928 w. Gus Kahn m. Walter Donaldson. (MT) *Whoopee*. (MF) *Whoopee*. (MF) *Show Business*. (MF) *I'll See You in My Dreams*. (MF) *The Eddie Cantor Story*. Eddie Cantor appeared in both the stage and film productions of *Whoopee*. Ruth Etting appeared in the stage production of *Whoopee*. Eddie Cantor and Joan Davis appeared in *Show Business*. Doris Day and Danny Thomas appeared in *I'll See You in My Dreams*, biopic of song writer Gus Kahn. Theme song of Eddie Cantor.

Malagueña 1930 Sp.w. Ernesto Lecuona Eng.w. Marian Banks m. Ernesto Lecuona. From the suite "Andalucia." The English words did not appear with the original publication in 1929.

Malbrouk (Malbrough), *see* **For He's a Jolly Good Fellow**

Malinda 1912 w. Stanley Murphy m. Henry I. Marshall

Mama 1946 w. Geoffrey Parsons, John Turner m. C.A. Bixio. This song was popularly revived in 1960.

Mama Doll Song, The 1954 w.m. Nat Simon, Charles Tobias

Mama Don't Allow No Easy Riders Here 1929 w.m. Charles "Cow-Cow" Davenport

Mama Don't Want No Peas an' Rice an' Cocoanut Oil 1931 w. L. Wolfe Gilbert m. Charlie Lofthouse (L. Charles). Based on a traditional folk melody from the Bahamas.

Mama from the Train, or, **A Kiss, A Kiss** 1956 w.m. Irving Gordon

Mama Goes Where Papa Goes 1923 w.m. Milton Ager, Jack Yellen

Mama Inez 1931 w. L. Wolfe Gilbert m. Eliseo Grenet

Mama, Look a Booboo 1957 w.m. Lord Melody (Fitzroy Alexander)

Mama Teach Me To Dance 1956 w.m. Al Hoffman, Dick Manning

Mama Told Me Not To Come 1970 w.m. Randy Newman

Mama Yo Quiero (I Want My Mama) 1940 Sp.w. Jararaca Paiva, Vincente Paiva Eng.w. Al Stillman m. Jararaca Paiva, Vincente Paiva. (MT) *Earl Carroll's Vanities*. (MF) *Down Argentine Way*. (MF) *Babes On Broadway*. (MF) *Ladies' Man*. Betty Grable and Carmen Miranda appeared in *Down Argentine Way*. Mickey Rooney and Judy Garland appeared in *Babes on Broadway*. Eddie Bracken, Cass Daley and Virginia Weekes appeared in *Ladies' Man*.

Mama's Pearl 1971 w.m. Berry Gordy, Alphonso J. Mizell, Frederick J. Perren, Deke Richards

Mambo Italiano 1954 w.m. Bob Merrill

Mame 1966 w.m. Jerry Herman. (MT) *Mame*. (MT) *Jerry's Girls*. (MF) *Mame*. Angela Lansbury appeared in the stage production of *Mame*. Dorothy Loudon, Chita Rivera, and Leslie Uggams appeared in *Jerry's Girls*. Lucille Ball appeared in the film production of *Mame*.

Mamie (Don't You Feel Ashamie) 1901 w. Will D. Cobb m. Gus Edwards

Mamie, Come Kiss Your Honey 1893 w.m. May Irwin. (MT) *A Country Sport*.

Mamma Loves Papa—Papa Loves Mamma 1923 w.m. Cliff Friend, Abel Baer

Mammy, *see* **My Mammy**

Mammy Jinny's Jubilee 1913 w. L. Wolfe Gilbert m. Lewis F. Muir

Mammy o' Mine 1919 w. William Tracey m. Maceo Pinkard

Mammy's Chocolate Soldier 1918 w. Sidney Mitchell m. Archie Gottler

Mammy's (a) Little Coal Black Rose 1916 w. Raymond Egan m. Richard A. Whiting

Mammy's Little Kinky Headed Boy 1926 w. Joseph M. White m. George J. Tinkaus

Mammy's Little Pumpkin Colored Coon(s) 1897 w.m. Hillman, Perrin. (MT) *The Good Mister Best*.

Mam'selle 1947 w. Mack Gordon m. Edmund Goulding. (F) *The Razor's Edge*. Tyrone Power and Gene Tierney appeared in *The Razor's Edge*.

Man and a Woman, A 1966 Fr.w. Pierre Barouch Eng.w. Jerry Keller m. Francis Lai. (F) *A Man and a Woman*. Anouk Aimee appeared in *A Man and a Woman*.

Man Chases a Girl, A 1955 w.m. Irving Berlin. (MF) *There's No Business Like Show Business*. Ethel Merman, Marilyn Monroe, and Donald O'Connor appeared in *There's No Business Like Show Business*.

Man from Laramie, The 1955 w.m. Ned Washington, Lester Lee. (F) *The Man from Laramie*. James Stewart appeared in *The Man from Laramie*.

(Theme from) Man from U.N.C.L.E., The 1965 m. Jerry Goldsmith. (TV) *The Man from U.N.C.L.E.*

Man I Love, The 1924 w. Ira Gershwin m. George Gershwin. (MT) *Lady, Be Good*. (MT) *Strike Up the Band*. (MT) *Will o' the Whispers*. (MF) *Rhapsody in Blue*. (MF) *The Man I Love*. (MF) *Sincerely Yours*. (MF) *Young at Heart*. (MF) *The Eddy Duchin Story*. (MF) *Both Ends of the Candle*. This song did not appear in the New York stage production of *Lady Be Good*. Blanche Ring appeared in the stage production of *Strike Up the Band*. Jack Smith appeared in *Will o' the Whispers*. Oscar Levant, Robert Alda, and Alexis Smith appeared in *Rhapsody in Blue*, biopic of composer George Gershwin. Ida Lupino and Robert Alda appeared in *The Man I Love*. Liberace appeared in *Sincerely Yours*. Frank Sinatra and Doris Day appeared in *Young at Heart*, based on John Garfield's film *Four Daughters*.

Man in a Raincoat 1955 w.m. Warwick Webster. Ivor Novello Award winner 1955.

Man in Motion, *see* **St. Elmo's Fire**

Man in the Moon 1984 w. Robert Lorick m. Henry Krieger. (MT) *The Tap Dance Kid*. Alfonso Ribiero appeared in *The Tap Dance Kid*.

Man of La Mancha 1965 w. Joe Darion m. Mitch Leigh. (MT) *Man of La Mancha*. (MF) *Man of La Mancha*. Richard Kiley appeared in the stage production of *Man of La Mancha*. Sophia Loren appeared in the film production of *Man of La Mancha*.

Man of My Heart 1943 w.m. Ivor Novello

Man of Mystery 1960 w.m. Michael Carr

Man on the Flying Trapeze, The, *see* **The Daring Young Man**

Man on Your Mind 1982 w.m. Glenn Shorrock, Kerryn Tolhurst

Man That (Who) Broke the Bank at Monte Carlo, The 1892 w.m. Fred Gilbert. (MF) *In Old Sacramento*. Bill Elliott and Constance Moore appeared in *In Old Sacramento*. The inspiration for the narrative of this song comes from gambler Arthur DeCourcey Bower, who referred to himself as the man in the title of this song. This song was first popularly performed by the English music hall artist Charles Corborn.

Man That Got Away, The 1954 w. Ira Gershwin m. Harold Arlen. (MF) *A Star Is Born*. Judy Garland and James Mason appeared in *A Star Is Born*.

Man to Man Talk 1959 w. Marshall Barer m. Mary

Rodgers. (MT) *Once Upon a Mattress*. Carol Burnette appeared in *Once Upon a Mattress*.

Man Who Shot Liberty Valance, The 1962 w. Hal David m. Burt Bacharach. (F) *The Man Who Shot Liberty Valance*. James Stewart and John Wayne appeared in *The Man Who Shot Liberty Valance*.

Man With the Golden Arm, The 1956 w. Sammy Cahn m. James Van Heusen. (F) *The Man With the Golden Arm*. Frank Sinatra and Kim Novak appeared in *The Man With the Golden Arm*.

Man With the Ladder and the Hose, The 1904 w.m. T. Mayo Geary

Man Without Love, A 1968 Orig.w. R. Livraghi, D. Pace, M. Panzeri Eng.w. Barry Mason m. R. Livraghi, D. Pace, M. Panzeri

Managua Nicaragua 1947 w.m. Albert Gamse, Irving Fields

Mañana (Is Soon Enough for Me) 1948 w.m. Peggy Lee, David Barbour. Theme song of Peggy Lee.

Mañana Pasado Mañana 1962 w.m. Norrie Paramor

Manchester 1968 w. Gerome Ragni, James Rado m. Galt MacDermot. (MT) *Hair*. (MF) *Hair*.

Mandalay 1924 w.m. Earl Burtnett, Abe Lyman, Gus Arnheim

Mandolin Serenade 1957 w.m. Charles Chaplin, John Turner, Geoffrey Parsons. (F) *A King in New York*. Charles Chaplin and Dawn Addams appeared in *A King in New York*.

Mandolins in the Moonlight 1958 w.m. George Weiss, Aaron Schroeder

Mandy 1919 w.m. Irving Berlin. (MT) *Yip! Yip! Yaphank*. (MT) *The Ziegfeld Follies of 1919*. (MT) *This Is the Army*. (MF) *Kid Millions*. (MF) *White Christmas*. Kate Smith and Ronald Reagan appeared in *This Is the Army*. Eddie Cantor, Ethel Merman, and Ann Sothern appeared in *Kid Millions*. Bing Crosby and Danny Kaye appeared in *White Christmas*.

Mandy 1975 w.m. Scott English, Richard Kerr

Mandy 'n' Me 1921 w. Bert Kalmar m. Con Conrad, Otto Motzan

Mandy Lee 1899 w.m. Thurland Chattaway

Mandy Make Up Your Mind 1924 w. Grant Clarke, Roy Turk m. George W. Meyer, Arthur Johnston. (MT) *Dixie to Broadway*.

Maneater 1982 w.m. Sara Allen, Daryl Hall, John Oates

Mangos 1957 w.m. Dee Libbey, Sid Wayne. (MT) *Ziegfeld Follies of 1957*.

Manhattan 1925 w. Lorenz Hart m. Richard Rodgers. (MT) *The Garrick Gaieties* (First Edition). (MF) *Words and Music*. Sterling Holloway and Betty Starbuck appeared in *The Garrick Gaieties* (First Edition). Judy Garland, Gene Kelly, and Mickey Rooney appeared in *Words and Music*, biopic of song writers Rodgers and Hart.

Manhattan Beach 1893 m. John Philip Sousa. With this march, Sousa celebrated a year's engagement at that resort.

Manhattan Madness 1932 w.m. Irving Berlin. (MT) *Face the Music*. J. Harold Murray and Katherine Carrington appeared in *Face the Music*.

Manhattan Serenade 1928 w. Harold Adamson m. Louis Alter. The words to this song were not added until 1942.

Maniac 1983 w.m. Dennis Matkosky, Michael Sembello. (MF) *Flashdance*.

Manic Monday 1986 w.m. Prince Nelson

Manisero, El, *see* **The Peanut Vendor**

Mansion of Aching Hearts, The 1902 w. Arthur J. Lamb m. Harry Von Tilzer

Many a New Day 1943 w. Oscar Hammerstein II m. Richard Rodgers. (MT) *Oklahoma!* (MF) *Oklahoma!* Betty Garde, Celeste Holm, and Alfred Drake appeared in the stage production of *Oklahoma!*. Shirley Jones and Gordon MacRae appeared in the film production of *Oklahoma!*.

Many Happy Returns of the Day 1931 w.m. Al Dubin, Joe Burke

Many Long Years Ago, *see* **The Old Grey Mare**

Many Moons Ago 1933 w. Mack Gordon m. Harry Revel. (MF) *Sitting Pretty*. Jack Oakie, Jack Haley, and Ginger Rogers appeared in *Sitting Pretty*.

Many Times 1953 w. Jessie Barnes m. Felix Stahl

Maple Leaf Rag 1899 m. Scott Joplin

Marahuana 1934 w.m. Johnny Burke, Sam Coslow, Arthur Johnston. (MF) *Murder at the Vanities*. Duke Ellington and Carl Brisson appeared in *Murder at the Vanities*.

March from "A Little Suite" 1962 w.m. Trevor Duncan. (TV-BBC) *Doctor Finlay's Case-Book*.

March from "The Colour Suite" 1971 w.m. Gordon Langford

March Hare, The 1956 w.m. Philip Green. Ivor Novello Award winner 1956.

March of the Dwarfs 1891 m. Edvard Greig. This melody is performed traditionally at circuses throughout the world.

March of the Men of Harlech 1825 w. Thomas Love Peacock m. traditional, from Wales

March of the Mods 1965 w.m. Tony Carr. Ivor Novello Award winner 1965.

March of the Musketeers 1928 w. P.G. Wodehouse, Clifford Grey m. Rudolf Friml. (MT) *The Three Musketeers*.

March of the (Royal) Siamese Children 1951 m. Richard Rodgers. (MT) *The King and I*. (MF) *The King and I*. Gertrude Lawrence and Yul Brynner appeared in the stage production of *The King and I*. Deborah Kerr and Yul Brynner appeared in the film production of *The King and I*.

March of the Tin Soldiers 1887 m. Gabriel Pierné. From the French "Marche de Petits Soldats de Plomb," op.14, no.6.

March of the Toys, The 1903 m. Victor Herbert. (MT) *Babes in Toyland*. (MF) *Babes in Toyland*. (MF) *The Great Victor Herbert*. Laurel and Hardy appeared in the film production of *Babes in Toyland*. Mary Martin appeared in *The Great Victor Herbert*.

March of Time, The 1930 w. Ted Koehler m. Harold Arlen. (MT) *Earl Carroll's Vanities of 1930*.

Marche Militaire, op. 51, no. 1 1826 m. Franz Schubert

Marche Slave, op. 31 1876 m. Peter Tchaikovsky. Based on a Serbian folksong. See also "Water Boy."

Marcheta 1913 w.m. Victor Schertzinger. Based on a theme from Nicolai's overture to *The Merry Wives of Windsor*. This song was popularly revived in 1928.

Marching Along Together 1932 w.m. Mort Dixon, Edward Pola, Franz K.W. Steininger

Marching Strings 1952 w.m. Marshall Ross. (F) *It's Great To Be Young*.

Marching Through Georgia 1865 w.m. Henry Clay Work. This song was later adapted to become the Princeton University football song.

Margaritaville 1977 w.m. Jimmy Buffett

Margie 1920 w. Benny Davis m. Con Conrad, J. Russel Robinson. (F) *Margie*. (MF) *The Eddie Cantor Story*. Tom Brown appeared in *Margie*.

Marguerite 1883 w.m. Charles A. White. Performed by the writer for actor Denman Thompson backstage at the Old Boston Theatre; the "echo" line was so impressive it was immediately placed in the current play *The Old Homestead*.

Maria 1957 w. Stephen Sondheim m. Leonard Bernstein. (MT) *West Side Story*. (MF) *West Side Story*. Carol Lawrence and Chita Rivera appeared in the stage production of *West Side Story*. Natalie Wood and Rita Moreno appeared in the film production of *West Side Story*.

Maria 1959 w. Oscar Hammerstein II m. Richard Rodgers. (MT) *The Sound of Music*. (MF) *The Sound of Music*. Mary Martin appeared in the stage production of *The Sound of Music*. Julie Andrews appeared in the film production of *The Sound of Music*.

Maria Elena 1933 Sp.w. Lorenzo Barcelata Eng.w.S.K. Russell m. Lorenzo Barcelata. (F) *Down Mexico Way*. This song was popularly revived in 1941.

Maria My Own 1931 Eng.w. L. Wolfe Gilbert m. Ernesto Lecuona. From the Spanish "Maria La O."

Maria Wiegenlied 1912 Ger.w. Martin Boelitz m. Max Reger. An American version of this song was published in 1912 with the title "The Virgin's Slumber Song" with English words by Edward Teschemacher.

Marian the Librarian 1957 w.m. Meredith Wilson. (MT) *The Music Man*. (MF) *The Music Man*. Robert Preston appeared in both the stage and film productions of *The Music Man*.

Marianne 1928 w. Oscar Hammerstein II m. Sigmund Romberg. (MT) *The New Moon*. (MF) *The New Moon* (1930). (MF) *The New Moon* (1940). Evelyn Herbert and Robert Halliday appeared in the stage production of *The New Moon*. Grace Moore and Lawrence Tibbett appeared in the 1930 film production of *The New Moon*. Jeanette MacDonald and Nelson Eddy appeared in the 1940 film production of *The New Moon*.

Marianne 1955 w.m. Richard Dehr, Frank Miller, Terry Gilkyson. This song was most popular in 1957.

Marie 1928 w.m. Irving Berlin. (F) *The Awakening*. (MF) *Alexander's Ragtime Band*. (MF) *The Fabulous Dorseys*. Vilma Banky appeared in *The Awakening*. Tyrone Power,

Alice Faye, and Ethel Merman appeared in *Alexander's Ragtime Band.*

Marie from Sunny Italy 1909 w. Irving Berlin m. M. Nicholson. This, Irving Berlin's first published song, grossed him a total of thirty-seven cents in royalties.

Marieke 1968 Eng.w. Eric Blau, Mort Shuman m. Jacques Brel. (MT) *Jacques Brel Is Alive and Well and Living in Paris.*

Marigold 1928 w.m. Billy Mayerl. Theme song of Billy Mayerl.

Marine's Hymn, The, or, **From the Halls of Montezuma to the Shores of Tripoli** 1919 w. anon.; possibly Henry C. Davis m. based on a theme from Jacques Offenbach's opera *Geneviève de Brabant,* 1868

Market on Saturday Night, The 1882 w. Edward Harrigan m. David Braham

Marriage of Figaro, The (Overture) 1790 m. Wolfgang Amadeus Mozart. From the opera *Die Hochzeit des Figaro.* The *Marriage of Figaro* was first performed in Vienna on May 1, 1786. Its overture was first published separately in June 1790.

Married 1966 w. Fred Ebb m. John Kander. (MT) *Cabaret.* (MF) *Cabaret.* Joel Grey and Lotte Lenya appeared in the stage production of *Cabaret.* Liza Minnelli and Joel Grey appeared in the film production of *Cabaret.*

Married I Can Always Get 1956 w.m. Gordon Jenkins. (MF) *Manhattan Tower.*

Marry Me 1961 w.m. Lawrence Jacks

Marrying for Love 1950 w.m. Irving Berlin. (MT) *Call Me Madam.* (MF) *Call Me Madam.* Ethel Merman appeared in both the stage and film productions of *Call Me Madam.*

Marseillaise, La 1792 w.m. Claude Joseph Rouget de Lisle. The French national anthem was written in Strasbourg by an engineer-officer upon the French declaration of war against Austria's Emperor Francis and Prussia's King Frederick Wilhelm II.

Marshmallow Moon 1951 w.m. Jay Livingston, Ray Evans. (MF) *Aaron Slick from Punkin Crick.* Alan Young, Robert Merrill, and Dinah Shore appeared in *Aaron Slick from Punkin Crick.*

Marshmallow World, A 1950 w. Carl Sigman m. Peter DeRose

Marta, or, **Rambling Rose of the Wildwood** 1931 Eng.w. L. Wolfe Gilbert m. Moises Simon. Theme song of Arthur Tracy.

Martins and the Coys, The 1936 w.m. Ted Weems, Al Cameron

Mary 1920 w. Otto Harbach m. Louis A. Hirsch. (MT) *Mary.*

Mary Ann 1946 Sp.w. Jamie Yamin Eng.w. Joe Davis m. traditional, from the Caribbean. This song was later adapted as "Marianne" in 1955.

Mary, Dear, Some Day We Will Meet Again 1922 w.m. Harry DeCosta, M.K. Jerome

Mary Had a Little Lamb 1867 w. Sarah Josepha Hale m. combined with the first part and second melody of "Good Night Ladies" from 1853. The song in this form was first published in 1867. "Mary Had a Little Lamb," described by E.V. Lucas as the best-known four-line verse in the English language, was written by Mrs. Sarah Josepha Hale of Boston, and published over her initials, September 1830, in the juvenile magazine of which she was editor. See also "Good Night Ladies."

Mary Lou 1926 w.m. Abe Lyman, George Waggner, J. Russell Robinson. (MT) *High Time.* (MF) *Mary Lou.* Robert Lowery and Joan Barton appeared in *Mary Lou.*

Mary, Mary, Quite Contrary, *see* **Mistress Mary, Quite Contrary**

Mary of Argyle 1838 w. Charles Jeffreys m. Sidney Nelson

Mary Rose 1920 w.m. Philip Braham

Mary Rose 1933 w.m. Harry Parr-Davies. (MF) *This Week of Grace.* Gracie Fields appeared in *This Week of Grace.*

Mary, You're a Little Bit Old Fashioned 1914 w. Marion Sunshine m. Henry I. Marshall. (MF) *One Sunday Afternoon.* Dennis Morgan and Janis Paige appeared in *One Sunday Afternoon.*

Maryland, My Maryland, or, **Tannenbaum, O Tannenbaum!** 1861 w. James Ryder Randall m. based earliest on the drinking song "Mini est Propositum" by Walter de Mapes, a deacon at Oxford in the twelfth century, and the later German folksong "Tannenbaum, O Tannenbaum!" The words were written by twenty-two-year-old Randall at Paydras College, Pointe-Coupée, Louisiana, on April 23, 1861.

Mary's a Grand Old Name 1905 w.m. George M. Cohan. (MT) *Forty-Five Minutes from Broadway.* (MF) *Yankee Doodle Dandy.* (MF) *The Seven Little Foys.* James Cagney and Joan Leslie appeared in *Yankee Doodle Dandy.* Bob Hope appeared in *The Seven Little Foys.* See also Part I, 1919.

Mary's Boy Child 1956 w.m. Jester Hairston

Mary's Dream, or, *Sandy's Ghost* 1793 w. anon. m. John Relfe

Mary's Tears 1817 w. Thomas Moore m. Oliver Shaw. This song was performed for President Monroe in Boston on July 5, 1817.

Mascot of the Troop, The 1905 w. Henry Blossom m. Victor Herbert. (MT) *Mlle. Modiste.*

(Song from) M*A*S*H 1970 w.m. Michael Altman, John Mandel. (F) *M*A*S*H.* (TV) *M*A*S*H.* Donald Sutherland, Elliott Gould, and Sally Kellerman appeared in the film production of *M*A*S*H.* Alan Alda and Loretta Swit appeared in the television production of *M*A*S*H.*

Mashed Potato Time 1962 w.m. Robert Bateman, Georgia Dobbins, William Garrett, Frederick C. Gorman, Brian Holland

Masquerade 1932 w. Paul Francis Webster m. John Jacob Loeb

(I'm Afraid) Masquerade Is Over, The 1939 w. Herb Magidson m. Allie Wrubel

Massachusetts 1969 w.m. Barry Gibb, Robin Gibb, Maurice Gibb. Ivor Novello Award winner 1968–69.

Massa's in De Cold (Cold) Ground   1852   w.m. Stephen Collins Foster. "Massa" might possibly have been Judge Rowan of Bardstown, Kentucky, a cousin of the composer's father. Mr. Foster, sometimes forced to write his words and music on brown wrapping paper for lack of funds, died with thirty-eight cents on his person in the poverty ward of Bellevue Hospital in New York City on January 13, 1864.

Master Blaster (Jammin')   1980   w.m. Stevie Wonder

Masterpiece   1973   w.m. Norman Whitfield

Match of the Day   1972   m. Rhet Stoller

Matchmaker, Matchmaker   1964   w. Sheldon Harnick   m. Jerry Bock. (MT) *Fiddler on the Roof.* (MF) *Fiddler on the Roof.* Zero Mostel and Bette Midler appeared in the stage production of *Fiddler on the Roof.*

Matchstalk Men and Matchstalk Cats and Dogs   1977   w.m. Michael Coleman, Brian Burke. Ivor Novello Award winner 1977–78. Ivor Novello Award winner 1978–79.

Mate o' Mine   1914   w.m. Leslie Cooke, Percy Elliott

Matelot   1945   w.m. Noël Coward. (MT) *Sigh No More.* Graham Payne appeared in *Sigh No More.*

Material Girl   1985   w.m. Peter Brown, Robert Rans

Materna, *see* **America, the Beautiful**

Matilda   1957   w.m. Norman Span ("King Radio"). This song was ascribed in 1953 to Harry Belafonte and Millard Thomas; possibly based on a traditional folksong from Trinidad.

Matinee   1948   w. Bob Russell   m. Carl Sigman

Mattinata, La ('Tis the Day)   1904   It.w. Ruggiero Leoncavallo Eng.w. Edward Teschemacher   m. Ruggiero Leoncavallo. See also "You're Breaking My Heart."

Maverick   1958   w.m. Paul Francis Webster, David Buttolph. (TV) *Maverick.*

Maxim's   1907   w. Adrian Ross   m. Franz Lehár. (MT) *The Merry Widow.* (MF) *The Merry Widow* (1934). (MF) *The Merry Widow* (1952). Maurice Chevalier and Jeanette MacDonald appeared in the 1934 film production of *The Merry Widow.* Lana Turner and Fernando Lamas appeared in the 1952 film production of *The Merry Widow.*

Maxina   1919   w.m. M. Boissonade, W.F. Hurndall

May I   1934   w. Mack Gordon   m. Harry Revel. (MF) *We're Not Dressing.* Bing Crosby, Carole Lombard, and George Burns and Gracie Allen appeared in *We're Not Dressing.*

May I Have the Next Romance with You   1936   w. Mack Gordon   m. Harry Revel. (MF) *Head Over Heels.* Jessie Matthews appeared in *Head Over Heels.*

May I Sing to You   1953   w.m. Charles Tobias, Harry Akst, Eddie Fisher. Theme song of Eddie Fisher.

May the Good Lord Bless and Keep You   1950   w.m. Meredith Willson

Maybe   1926   w. Ira Gershwin   m. George Gershwin. (MT) *Oh, Kay!.* Gertrude Lawrence and Victor Moore appeared in *Oh, Kay!.*

Maybe   1935   w.m. Allan Flynn, Frank Madden. This song was popularly revived in 1940.

Maybe   1977   w. Martin Charnin   m. Charles Strouse. (MT) *Annie.* Dorothy Loudon and Andrea McArdle appeared in *Annie.*

Maybe I Love You Too Much   1933   w.m. Irving Berlin

Maybe I'm Amazed   1977   w.m. Paul McCartny

Maybe It's Because   1949   w. Harry Ruby   m. Johnnie Scott. (MT) *Along Fifth Avenue.* Jackie Gleason and Nancy Walker appeared in *Along Fifth Avenue.*

Maybe It's Because I'm a Londoner   1949   w.m. Hubert Gregg

Maybe This Time   1972   w. Fred Ebb   m. John Kander. (MF) *Cabaret.* Liza Minnelli and Joel Grey appeared in the film production of *Cabaret.* This song was written for the 1972 film production of *Cabaret.*

Maybe This Year   1959   w.m. Ronald Wakley, Marcel Stellman. Ivor Novello Award winner 1959.

Maybe You'll Be There   1947   w. Sammy Gallop   m. Rube Bloom

Maybellene   1955   w.m. Chuck Berry, Russel D. Fratto, Alan Freed

Mazel Tov   1894   w. Sigmund Mogulesco, Joseph Lateiner   m. Sigmund Mogulesco. Based on a Serbian folksong and Tchaikovsky's "Marche Slave." This song was written for the Jewish operetta *Blihmele* (Little Flower).

Mazel Tov   1961   w.m. Jerry Herman. (MT) *Milk and Honey.*

McNally's Row of Flats   1882   w. Edward Harrigan   m. David Braham

McNamara's Band, *see* **MacNamara's Band**

Me   1931   w.m. Irving Berlin

Me and Bobby McGee   1971   w.m. Kris Kristofferson, Fred L. Foster

Me and Jane in a Plane   1927   w.m. Edgar Leslie, Joe Gilbert

Me and Julio Down by the Schoolyard   1972   w.m. Paul Simon

Me and Mrs. Jones   1972   w.m. Leon Huff, Kenneth Gamble, Cary Gilbert

Me and My Dog   1936   w.m. Vivian Ellis. (MF) *Public Nuisance No. 1.*

Me and My Girl   1938   w.m. Noel Gay, Douglas Furber. (MT) *Me and My Girl.* Lupino Lane appeared in *Me and My Girl.*

Me and My Melinda   1942   w.m. Irving Berlin

Me and My Shadow   1927   w. Billy Rose   m. Al Jolson, Dave Dreyer. (MF) *Feudin', Fussin' and Fightin'.* Donald O'Connor and Marjorie Main appeared in *Feudin', Fussin' and Fightin'.*

Me and the Moon   1936   w. Walter Hirsch   m. Lou Handman

Me and the Old Folks at Home   1935   w.m. Rodd Arden, Leo Towers, Harry Leon

Me and You and a Dog Named Boo   1972   w.m. Kent La Voie

(Ho! Ho! Ha! Ha!) Me Too   1926   w.m. Harry Woods, Charles Tobias, Al Sherman

Meadowlands, or, **Cavalry of the Steppes** 1939 Rus.w. Victor Gussev Eng.w. Olga Paul; also M.L. Korr; also Harold J. Rome m. Lev Knipper (F) *Mission to Moscow*. The Soviet Army song.

Mean to Me 1929 w.m. Roy Turk, Fred E. Ahlert. (MT) *Ain't Misbehavin'*. (MF) *Love Me or Leave Me*. (MF) *Lady Sings the Blues*. Debbie Allen and Nell Carter appeared in *Ain't Misbehavin'*. Doris Day and James Cagney appeared in *Love Me or Leave Me*, biopic of singer Ruth Etting. Diana Ross appeared in *Lady Sings the Blues*, biopic of singer Billie Holiday.

Méditation 1894 m. Jules Massenet. From *Thaïs*.

Meeskite 1966 w. Fred Ebb m. John Kander. (MT) *Cabaret*. Jack Gilford and Lotte Lenya appeared in the stage production of *Cabaret*. This song did not appear in the 1972 film production of *Cabaret*.

Meet Me at the Station, Dear 1917 w. Sam M. Lewis, Joe Young m. Ted Snyder

Meet Me by Moonlight Alone 1826 w.m. Joseph Augustine Wade. This song was popularly sung by Mme. Lucia Elizabeth Vestris.

Meet Me in Bubble Land 1919 w. Caspar Nathan, Joe Manne m. Isham Jones

Meet Me in St. Louis, Louis 1904 w. Andrew B. Sterling m. Kerry Mills. (MF) *Meet Me in St. Louis*. Judy Garland, Mary Astor and Marjorie Main appeared in *Meet Me in St. Louis*. This song was popularly revived in 1944. 1904 was the year of the St. Louis Exposition.

Meet Me Jenny When the Sun Goes Down 1908 w.m. Harry Castling, Fred Godfrey

Meet Me on the Corner 1955 w.m. Peter Hart, Paddy Roberts

Meet Me on the Corner 1973 w.m. Roderick Clements. Ivor Novello Award winner 1972/1973.

Meet Me Tonight in Dreamland 1909 w. Beth Slater Whitson m. Leo Friedman. (MF) *In the Good Old Summertime*. Judy Garland and Van Johnson appeared in *In the Good Old Summertime*. This song most likely referred to the opening in 1902 of "Dreamland," the original amusement section of Coney Island. See also Part I, 1902.

Meet Mister Callaghan 1952 w.m. Jimmy Shirl, Ervin Drake, Eric Spear. (MT) *Meet Mister Callaghan*. (MF) *Meet Mister Callaghan*.

Meet the Family 1959 w.m. Peter Greenwell, Peter Wildeblood

Meeting of the Waters of Hudson and Erie, The 1825 w.m. Samuel Woodworth. This song celebrates the opening, in 1825, of the Erie Canal.

Mein Herr 1972 w. Fred Ebb m. John Kander. (MF) *Cabaret*. Liza Minnelli and Joel Grey appeared in *Cabaret*. This song did not appear in the original stage production of *Cabaret*.

Melancholy Baby, *see* **My Melancholy Baby**

Melba Waltz, The 1953 w.m. Mischa Spoliansky, Norman Newell

Melba Waltz, *see also* **Se Saran Rose**

Melisands in the Wood 1902 w.m. Alma Goetz, Ethel Clifford

Mellow Yellow 1966 w.m. Donovan. This song supposedly alluded to the craze smoking of banana peels for hallucinogenic experiences.

Melodie d'Amour (Melody of Love) 1949 w. Leo Johns m. Henri Salvador. This song was popularly revived in 1957.

Melody 1912 m. Charles Gates Dawes. The composer of this song later became Vice-President of the United States for the years 1925 through 1929. See also "It's All in the Game."

Melody from the Sea 1958 w.m. Donald Phillips

Melody from the Sky, A 1936 w. Sidney D. Mitchell m. Louis Alter. (F) *The Trail of the Lonesome Pine*. Sylvia Sidney, Fred MacMurray, and Henry Fonda appeared in *The Trail of the Lonesome Pine*.

Melody in F 1855 m. Anton Rubinstein

Melody Lingers On, The *see* **The Song Is Ended But the Melody Lingers On**

Melody of Love 1903 w. Tom Glazer m. H. Engelmann. This song was popularly revived in 1955.

Melody of Love, *see also* **Melodie d'Amour**

Melting Pot 1970 w.m. Roger Cook, Roger Greenaway. Ivor Novello Award winner 1969–70.

Memories 1915 w. Gustave Kahn m. Egbert Van Alstyne. (MF) *I'll See You in My Dreams*. Doris Day and Danny Thomas appeared in *I'll See You in My Dreams*, biopic of song writer Gus Kahn.

Mem'ries, or, **Golden Memory Days** 1928 w. Henry M. Neely m. Harold Sanford

Memories Are Made of This 1956 w.m. Terry Gilkyson, Richard Dehr, Frank Miller. (MF) *The Seven Hills of Rome*. Mario Lanza appeared in *The Seven Hills of Rome*.

Memories Live Longer Than Dreams 1940 w.m. Ross Parker

Memories of France 1928 w. Al Dubin m. J. Russell Robinson

Memories of You 1930 w. Andy Razaf m. Eubie Blake. (MT) *Blackbirds of 1930*. (MT) *Eubie!*. (MF) *The Benny Goodman Story*. (MF) *Drum Crazy*. Anita O'Day appeared in *Drum Crazy*.

Memory 1982 w. T.S. Eliot m. Andrew Lloyd Webber. (MT) *Cats*. Betty Buckley appeared in *Cats*. Ivor Novello Award winner 1981–82.

Memory Lane 1924 w. B.G. DeSylva m. Larry Spier, Con Conrad. (MF) *In Society*. Abbott and Costello appeared in *In Society*.

Memphis 1959 w.m. Chuck Berry. This song was popularly revived in 1964 and later again in 1981.

Memphis Blues, The 1912 w. George A. Norton m. William Christopher Handy. (MF) *Birth of the Blues*. (MF) *St. Louis Blues* (1958). Bing Crosby and Mary Martin appeared in *Birth of the Blues*. Nat "King" Cole and Eartha Kitt appeared in *St. Louis Blues*, biopic of composer W.C. Handy. The words to this song were added in 1913. This song was written for the political campaign of Memphis political boss Edward H. Crump, with the obvious title ''Mr. Crump.''

Memphis in June 1945 w. Paul Francis Webster m. Hoagy Carmichael. (F) *Johnny Angel*. Hoagy Carmichael and George Raft appeared in *Johnny Angel*.

Men in My Little Girl's Life, The 1965 w.m. Mary Candy, Eddie V. Deane, Gloria Shayne

Mer, La (The Sea) 1939 w.m. Charles Trenet. (MF) *Together Again*. Charles Boyer and Irene Dunne appeared in *Together Again*. Theme song of Charles Trenet.

Mercy Mercy Mercy 1967 w.m. Joe Zawinul

Merrily We Roll Along, *see* **Good Night Ladies**

Merrily We Roll Along 1981 w.m. Stephen Sondheim. (MT) *Merrily We Roll Along*. Ann Morrison appeared in *Merrily We Roll Along*.

Merry Christmas to You, *see* **The Christmas Song**

Merry-Go-Round Broke Down, The 1937 w.m. Cliff Friend, Dave Franklin

Merry Peasant, The, *see* **The Happy Farmer**

Merry Swiss Boy, The 1927 w. translated William Ball m. based on a Tyrolean melody; arr. Ignaz Moscheles

Merry Widow Waltz, The, or, **I Love You So** 1907 w. Adrian Ross m. Franz Lehár. (MT) *The Merry Widow*. (MF) *The Merry Widow* (1934). (MF) *The Merry Widow* (1952). Maurice Chevalier and Jeanette MacDonald appeared in the 1934 film production of *The Merry Widow*. Lana Turner and Fernando Lamas appeared in the 1952 film production of *The Merry Widow*.

Merry Wives of Windsor, The (Overture) 1850 m. Otto Nicolai. From the opera *Die Lustigen Weiber von Windsor*. *The Merry Wives of Windsor* was first performed on March 9, 1849, in Berlin.

Merry Xmas Everybody 1974 w.m. Neville Holder, James Lea. Ivor Novello Award winner 1973–74.

Message of the Violet, The 1902 w. Frank Pixley m. Gustav Luders. (MT) *The Prince of Pilsen*.

Message to Michael 1966 w. Hal David m. Burt F. Bacharach

Message Understood 1965 w.m. Chris Andrews

Messing About on the River 1960 w.m. Mark Anthony

Method of Modern Love 1985 w.m. Janna Allen, Daryl Hall

Mexicali Rose 1923 w. Helen Stone m. Jack B. Tenny. (MF) *Rhythm on the Range*. (MF) *Mexicali Rose*. (MF) *Song of Texas*. (F) *Barbed Wire*. Bing Crosby and Martha Raye appeared in *Rhythm on the Range*. Gene Autry and Luana Walters appeared in *Mexicali Rose*. Roy Rogers and Bob Nolan appeared in *Song of Texas*. Gene Autry and Pat Buttram appeared in *Barbed Wire*. This song was popularly revived in 1938.

Mexican Hat Dance 1919 m. arr. F.A. Partichela. From the Spanish ''Jarabe Tapatío.'' This melody to the national dance of Mexico was first performed at the Coliseo in Mexico City on July 9, 1790.

Mexican Joe 1953 w.m. Mitchell Torok

Mexico 1961 w.m. Boudleaux Bryant

Mi Viejo Amor (An Old Love) 1926 Sp.w. F. Fernandez Bustament Eng. w. Romney Brent m. Alfonso Esparza Oteo

Miami Beach Rumba 1946 Sp.w. Johnnie Camacho Eng.w. Albert Gamse m. Irving Fields

(Theme from) Miami Vice 1985 m. Jan Hammer. (TV) *Miami Vice*.

Michael (Row the Boat Ashore) 1961 w.m. based on a traditional folksong; arr. Albert Gamse; also Dave Fisher

Michael from Mountains 1968 w.m. Joni Mitchell

Michael's Theme 1972 m. Nino Rota. (F) *The Godfather*. Marlon Brando, Al Pacino, and Diane Keaton appeared in *The Godfather*.

Michelle 1965 w.m. John Lennon, Paul McCartney. (MT) *Beatlemania*. Grammy Award winner 1966. Ivor Novello Award winner 1966.

Michigan, *see* **I Want To Go Back to Michigan**

Mick McGilligan's Ball 1948 w.m. Michael Casey

Mickey 1918 w. Harry H. Williams m. Neil Moret. (F) *Mickey*. Mabel Normand appeared in *Mickey*. This song was written for the piano and orchestra accompaniment to this classic silent film.

Mickey 1982 w.m. Nicholas Chinn, Michael Chapman

'Mid the Green Fields of Virginia 1898 w.m. Charles K. Harris

Midnight Blue 1975 w.m. Melissa Manchester, Carole Bayer Sager

Midnight Cowboy 1969 w.m. John Barry, Jacob Gold. (F) *Midnight Cowboy*. Dustin Hoffman appeared in *Midnight Cowboy*.

Midnight Fire-Alarm 1900 m. Harry J. Lincoln; arr. E.T. Paull

Midnight in Moscow, or, **Moscow Nights** 1962 w.m. Vassili Soloviev-Sedoi; adapted Kenny Ball. Based on the Russian song ''Padmas Koveeye Vietchera.''

Midnight in Paris 1935 w.m. Herb Magidson, Con Conrad. (F) *Here's to Romance*. Nino Martini and Genevieve Tobin appeared in *Here's to Romance*.

Midnight Masquerade 1946 w.m. Jack Manus, Bernard Bierman, Arthur Bierman

Midnight Sun 1947 w.m. Johnny Mercer, Francis J. Burke

Midnight Train to Georgia 1973 w.m. Jim Weatherly

Midshipmite, The 1875 w. Frederick Edward Weatherly m. Stephen Adams (Michael Maybrick)

Mifanwy 1913 w.m. Dorothy Foster, Frederick Edward Weatherly

Mighty Fortress Is Our God, A, or, **Ein' Feste Burg** 1529 w.m. Martin Luther; words based on Psalm 46. According to Hübner, Luther wrote this hymn on the Wartburg ''and having finished upset the inkstand over it, whereupon the devil laughed, and Luther threw the inkpot at him.'' Meyerbeer used the melody in his opera *Les Huguenots;* Bach adapted it into a cantata; Mendelssohn adapted it for his ''Reformation Symphony,'' and Wagner for his ''Kaiser March.'' In 1631 King Gustavus Adolphus of Sweden commanded it to be sung by the entire army just prior to the battle of Leipzig. See Part I for additional information on this title.

Mighty Lak' a Rose 1901 w. Frank L. Stanton m. Ethelbert Nevin. This song was written in the last year of Nevin's life.

Milenberg Joys 1925 m. Leon Rappolo, Paul Mares, "Jelly Roll" Morton

Military Life, or, **The Jerk Song** 1946 w.m. Harold Rome. (MT) *Call Me Mister.* (MF) *Call Me Mister.* Betty Grable and Danny Thomas appeared in the film production of *Call Me Mister.*

Milk and Honey 1961 w.m. Jerry Herman. (MT) *Milk and Honey.* (MT) *Jerry's Girls.* Dorothy Loudon, Chita Rivera, and Leslie Uggams appeared in *Jerry's Girls.*

Milkman Keep Those Bottles Quiet 1944 w.m. Don Raye, Gene De Paul. (MF) *Broadway Rhythm.* Lena Horne, Ben Blue, and George Murphy appeared in *Broadway Rhythm.*

Miller's Son, The 1973 w.m. Stephen Sondheim. (MT) *A Little Night Music.* (MF) *A Little Night Music.* Len Cariou, Glynnis Johns, and Hermione Gingold appeared in the stage production of *A Little Night Music.* Len Cariou, Elizabeth Taylor, and Hermione Gingold appeared in the film production of *A Little Night Music.*

Milord 1959 w.m. Marguerite A. Monnot, Joseph Mustacchi

Mimi 1932 w. Lorenz Hart m. Richard Rodgers. (MF) *Love Me Tonight.* Maurice Chevalier, Charles Ruggles, and Jeanette MacDonald appeared in *Love Me Tonight.* Theme song of Maurice Chevalier.

Mind If I Make Love to You 1956 w.m. Cole Porter. (MF) *High Society.* Frank Sinatra and Bing Crosby appeared in *High Society.*

Mine 1933 w. Ira Gershwin m. George Gershwin. (MT) *Let 'Em Eat Cake.*

Mine Eyes Have Seen the Glory, *see* **Battle Hymn of the Republic**

Miner's Dream of Home, The 1900 w.m. Will Godwin, Leo Dryden

Minnie from Trinidad 1941 w.m. Roger Edens. (MF) *Ziegfeld Girl.* James Stewart, Eve Arden, and Judy Garland appeared in *Ziegfeld Girl.*

Minnie the Mermaid, or, **A Love Song in Fish Time** 1923 w.m. B.G. De Sylva

Minnie the Moocher, or, **The Ho De Ho Song** 1931 w.m. Cab Calloway, Irving Mills, Clarence Gaskill. (MT) *The Blues Brothers.* (F) *When You're in Love.* Cab Calloway, Aretha Franklin, and Ray Charles appeared in *The Blues Brothers.* Based on the traditional folksong "Willy the Weeper." Theme song of Cab Calloway.

(To the War Has Gone) Minstrel Boy, The 1813 w. Thomas Moore m. based on the melody of "The Moreen"

Minstrel's Return from the War, The 1827 w.m. James Hill Hewitt

Minuet in G 1796 m. Ludwig van Beethoven

Minuet in G 1887 m. Ignace Paderewski

Minute by Minute 1979 w.m. Lester Abrams

Minute Waltz, The 1964 w.m. arr. Lan O'Kun. Based on Chopin's "Minute Waltz," op. 64, no. 1 in D flat.

Mira 1961 w.m. Bob Merrill. (MT) *Carnival.*

Miracle Song 1964 w.m. Stephen Sondheim. (MT) *Anyone Can Whistle.* (MT) *Side by Side by Sondheim.* Julie N. McKenzie and Millicent Martin appeared in *Side by Side by Sondheim.*

Miracles 1975 w.m. Marty Balin

Miracles 1981 w.m. Roger Cook

Mirame Asi, or, **Grant Those Glances,** or, **Look At Me** 1928 Sp.w.m. Eduardo Sanchez de Fuentes. This Spanish song was also set to English words with new titles: "Grant Those Glances" had Eng.w. by Frederick Herman Martens, and "Look At Me" (1931) had Eng.w. by Carol Raven.

Misery Farm 1929 w.m. C. Jay Wallis

Misirlou 1947 w.m. Milton Leeds, Fred Wise, R.N. Roubanis

Misled 1985 w.m. Robert Bell, Ronald Bell, James Bonnefond, George Brown, Claydes Eugene Smith, James Taylor, Curtis Williams

Miss America Pageant, The 1963 w.m. Abe Osser. Theme song of Bert Parks and the Miss America competition.

(Who's Wonderful, Who's Marvelous?) Miss Annabelle Lee 1927 w.m. Sidney Clare, Lew Pollack, Harry Richman. (MT) *Will o' the Whispers.* (MF) *Gentlemen Marry Brunettes.* Jack Smith appeared in *Will o' the Whispers.* Jane Russell appeared in *Gentlemen Marry Brunettes.* Theme song of James Barton.

Miss Bailey's Ghost, *see* **The Hunters of Kentucky**

Miss Brown to You 1935 w.m. Leo Robin, Richard A. Whiting, Ralph Rainger. (MF) *The Big Broadcast of 1936.* Bing Crosby, George Burns and Gracie Allen, and Amos and Andy appeared in *The Big Broadcast of 1936.*

Miss Celie's Blues (Sister) 1985 w.m. Quincy Jones, Lionel Richie, Rod Temperton. (F) *The Color Purple.* Whoopie Goldberg appeared in *The Color Purple.*

Miss Hannah, *see* **Oh Miss Hannah**

Miss Lucy Long, *see* **Take Your Time, Miss Lucy**

Miss Lucy Neale 1844 w.m. James Sanford. James Sanford's melody was popularly adapted during the Mexican War of 1846–47 by patriotic song writers.

Miss Marmelstein 1962 w.m. Harold Rome. (MT) *I Can Get It for You Wholesale.* Barbra Streisand appeared in *I Can Get It for You Wholesale.*

Miss Me Blind 1984 w.m. Michael Craig, Boy George, Roy Hay, Jon Moss

Miss Otis Regrets 1934 w.m. Cole Porter. (MT) *Hi Diddle Diddle.* (MF) *Night and Day.* Douglas Byng appeared in *Hi Diddle Diddle.* Cary Grant, Alexis Smith, and Mary Martin appeared in *Night and Day,* biopic of song writer Cole Porter.

Miss You 1929 w. Charles Tobias, Harry Tobias m. Henry Tobias. (MF) *Strictly in the Groove.* Martha Tilton and Donald O'Connor appeared in *Strictly in the Groove.* This song was popularly revived in 1942.

Miss You Nights 1977 w.m. Dave Townsend. Ivor Novello Award winner 1976–77.

Missing You 1984 w.m. Dan Fogelberg

Missing You 1984 w.m. John Waite, Chaz Sanford, Mark Leonard

Missing You 1985 w.m. Lionel Richie

(Theme from) Mission: Impossible 1968 m. Lalo Schifrin. (TV) *Mission: Impossible.*

M-I-S-S-I-S-S-I-P-P-I 1916 w. Bert Hanlon, Ben Ryan m. Harry Tierney. (MT) *Hitchy-Koo.* (MT) *The Beauty Spot.*

Mississippi Mud 1927 w.m. Harry Barris

Mississippi Suite 1926 m. Ferde Grofé. See also "Daybreak."

Missouri Houn' Dawg Song, The, *see* **They Gotta Quit Kickin' My Dog Around**

Missouri Waltz, The 1914 w. James Royce Shannon m. Frederick Knight Logan. Based on "an original melody procured by John Valentine Eppell . . ." A favorite song of President Harry Truman, this song remains the top sheet music seller of all time, and is the official state song of Missouri. Fred Logan willed the royalties of this song to his mother, onetime prima donna of the old American Opera Company.

Mistakes 1928 w.m. Horatio Nicholls, Edgar Leslie

Mister and Mississippi 1951 w.m. Irving Gordon

Mister (Mr.) and Mrs. Is the Name 1934 w. Mort Dixon m. Allie Wrubel. (MF) *Flirtation Walk.* Ruby Keeler and Dick Powell appeared in *Flirtation Walk.*

Mister Big Stuff 1971 w.m. Joseph Broussard, Ralph G. Williams, Carrol Washington

Mister Blue 1959 w.m. DeWayne Blackwell

Mister Bo Jangles (Bojangles) 1968 w.m. Jerry Jeff Walker. (MT) *Dancin'.* This song was also popular in 1971.

Mister Cellophane 1975 w. Fred Ebb m. John Kander. (MT) *Chicago.* Chita Rivera and Gwen Verdon appeared in *Chicago.*

Mister Christopher Columbus, *see* **Misto Cristofo Columbo**

Mister Custer 1960 w.m. Fred Darian, Al De Lory, Joseph Van Winkle

Mister Dooley 1902 w. William Jerome m. Jean Schwartz. (MT) *The Chinese Honeymoon.*

Mister Dumpling 1955 w.m. Joe Heathcote

Mister Five by Five 1942 w.m. Gene De Paul, Don Raye. (MF) *Behind the Eight Ball.* (MF) *Off the Beaten Track.* (F) *Who Done It?.* Carol Bruce and Dick Foran appeared in *Behind the Eight Ball.* Bud Abbott and Lou Costello appeared in *Who Done It?.*

Mister Frog Went a-Courtin', *see* **Frog Went a-Courtin'**

Mister Gallagher and Mister Shean 1922 w.m. Ed Gallagher, Al Shean. (MT) *Ziegfeld Follies of 1922.* (MF) *Ziegfeld Girl.* Judy Garland, James Stewart, and Lana Turner appeared in *Ziegfeld Girl.*

Mister Goldstone 1959 w. Stephen Sondheim m. Jule Styne. (MT) *Gypsy.* (MF) *Gypsy.* Ethel Merman appeared in the stage production of *Gypsy.* Rosalind Russell appeared in the film production of *Gypsy.*

Mister Jefferson Lord, *see* **Play That Barbershop Chord**

Mister Johnson, Don't Get Gay 1898 w.m. Dave Reed, Jr.

Mister Johnson, Turn Me Loose 1896 w.m. Ben R. Harney. (MT) *Courted Into Court.*

Mister Kiss Kiss Bang Bang 1965 w.m. John Barry

Mister Lonely 1964 w.m. Gene Allan, Bobby Vinton. This song was popularly revived in 1969.

(Mister) Mr. Lucky 1960 w. Ray Evans, Jay Livingston. m. Henry Mancini. (TV) *Mr. Lucky.*

Mister Meadowlark 1940 w.m. Walter Donaldson, John H. Mercer

Mister Mistoffolees 1982 w. T.S. Eliot m. Andrew Lloyd Webber. (MT) *Cats.* Betty Buckley appeared in *Cats.*

Mister Moon You've Got a Million Sweethearts 1946 w.m. Charlie Chester, Ken Morris

Mister Paganini, *see* **If You Can't Sing It You'll Have To Swing It**

Mister Roboto 1983 w.m. Dennis De Young

Mister Sandman 1954 w.m. Pat Ballard. This song was popularly revived in 1981.

Mister Snow, *see* **When I Marry Mister Snow**

Mister Tambourine Man 1965 w.m. Bob Dylan

Mister Volunteer, or, **You Don't Belong to the Regulars, You're Just a Volunteer** 1901 w.m. Paul Dresser. (MF) *My Gal Sal.* Rita Hayworth and Victor Mature appeared in *My Gal Sal.*

Mister Wonderful 1956 w.m. Jerry Bock, Larry Holofcener, George Weiss. (MT) *Mr. Wonderful.*

Mistletoe and Holly 1957 w.m. Frank Sinatra, Dok Stanford, Henry Sanicola

Misto Cristofo Columbo 1951 w.m. Ray Evans, Jay Livingston. (MF) *Here Comes the Groom.* Bing Crosby and Alexis Smith appeared in *Here Comes the Groom.*

Mistress Mary Quite Contrary, *see* **Mother Goose's Melodies**

Misty 1954 w. Johnny Burke m. Erroll Garner. This song was popularly revived in 1959 and again in 1962.

Misty Blue 1976 w.m. Bob Montgomery

Misty Islands of the Highlands 1935 w.m. Jimmy Kennedy, Michael Carr

Mixed Emotions 1951 w.m. Stuart F. Loucheim

Moanin' 1959 w.m. Bobby Timmons

Moanin' in the Mornin' 1937 w. E.Y. Harburg m. Harold Arlen. (MT) *Hooray for What!.* Ed Wynn and Paul Haakon appeared in *Hooray for What!.*

Moanin' Low 1929 w. Howard Dietz m. Ralph Rainger. (MT) *The Little Show* (First Edition). (F) *Key Largo.* Edward G. Robinson, Humphrey Bogart, and Lauren Bacall appeared in *Key Largo.* Theme song of Libby Holman.

Mobile 1954 w.m. Robert Wells, David Holt

Mocking Bird 1963 w.m. Charlie Foxx, Inez Foxx

Mocking Bird Hill 1951 w.m. Vaughn Horton

Modern Girl 1981 w.m. Dominic Bugatti, Frank Musker

Modern Woman 1986 w.m. Billy Joel

Mogul Theme, The 1965 w.m. Tom Springfield

Moldau 1879 m. Bedrich Smetana. Possibly based on a Dutch and/or Swedish folksong. The Israeli national anthem, "Hatikva," is based on this song. See also "Hatikva."

Mollie Darling 1871 w.m. William Shakespeare Hays

Molly and I and the Baby 1892 w.m. Harry Kennedy

Molly Malone, see **Cockles and Mussels**

Molly O!, or, **Mavourneen** 1891 w.m. William J. Scanlan

Molly O'Morgan 1910 w.m. William Letters, Fred Godfrey

Molly on the Shore 1911 m. arr. percy Aldridge Grainger

Molly Put the Kettle On, see **O Du Lieber Augustin**

Moment I Saw You, The 1945 w. Harold Purcell m. Manning Sherwin. (MT) *Under the Counter*. Cicely Courtneidge appeared in *Under the Counter*.

Moment Musicale 1823 m. Franz Schubert

Moment to Moment 1966 w. Johnny Mercer m. Henry Mancini

Moments To Remember 1955 w. Al Stillman m. Robert Allen

Momma Look Sharp 1969 w.m. Sherman Edwards. (MT) *1779*. John Cullum appeared in *1776*.

Mon Homme, see **My Man**

Mona Lisa 1932 w.m. Henry Sullivan, Desmond Carter. (MT) *Bow Bells*. Binnie Hale and Andre Randall appeared in *Bow Bells*.

Mona Lisa 1950 w. Raymond Evans m. Jay Livingston. (F) *Captain Carey, U.S.A.* (F) *After Midnight*. Alan Ladd appeared in *Captain Carey, U.S.A.* Academy Award winner 1950.

Monastery Bells, The 1854 m. Louis Alfred Lefébure-Wély. From the French "Les Cloches du Monastère," op.54, no.1.

Monday Monday 1966 w.m. John E. A. Phillips. This song was popularly revived in 1971. Theme song of The Mamas and the Papas.

Monday, Tuesday, Wednesday 1949 w.m. Ross Parker

Money (Money) 1972 w. Fred Ebb m. John Kander. (MF) *Carbaret*. Liza Minnelli and Joel Grey appeared in the film production of *Cabaret*. This song was added to the 1972 film production of *Cabaret*.

Money for Nothing 1985 w.m. Mark Knopfler, Sting

Money Honey 1976 w.m. Eric Faulkner, Stuart Woods

Money Song, The 1948 w.m. Harold J. Rome. (MT) *That's the Ticket*.

Money Song, The 1967 w. Fred Ebb m. John Kander. (MT) *Cabaret*. This song is not to be confused with "Money," which was added to the 1972 film production of *Cabaret*.

Money Tree, The 1956 w. Cliff Ferre m. Mark McIntyre

Monkey Doodle Dandy 1909 w. Jack Drislane m. Henry Frantzen

Monkey's Wedding, The 1836 w.m. Alfred Williams. The melody for this song is loosely based on the English traditional "Pop Goes the Weasel."

Monotonous 1952 w. June Carroll m. Arthur Siegel. (MT) *New Faces of 1952*. (MF) *New Faces*. Eartha Kitt was featured in both the stage and film productions of *New Faces of 1952* and *New Faces*.

Monsieur Dupont 1968 w.m. Pruhn, Peter Robin Callander

Monster Mash 1962 w.m. Bobby Pickett, Leonard Capizzi. This song was popularly revived in 1973.

Mony Mony 1968 w.m. Bobby Bloom, Ritchie Cordell, Bo Gentry, Tommy James

Mood Indigo 1931 w.m. Duke Ellington, Irving Mills, Albany Bigard. (MT) *Sophisticated Ladies*. Gregory Hines and Phyllis Hyman appeared in *Sophisticated Ladies*.

Moody River 1961 w.m. Gary D. Bruce

Moon Drops Low, The 1909 w. Nelle Richmond Eberhart m. Charles Wakefield Cadman. From "Four American Indian Songs."

Moon Got in My Eyes, The 1937 w. John Burke m. Arthur Johnston. (MF) *Double or Nothing*. Bing Crosby, Martha Raye, and Andy Devine appeared in *Double or Nothing*.

Moon Has His Eyes on You, The 1905 w. Billy Johnson m. Albert Von Tilzer

Moon Is Blue, The 1953 w.m. Sylvia Fine, Herchel B. Gilbert

Moon Is Low, The 1930 w.m. Arthur Freed, Nacio Herb Brown. (F) *Montana Moon*. Joan Crawford and Cliff Edwards appeared in *Montana Moon*.

Moon Love 1939 w.m. Mack David, Mack Davis, Andre Kostelanetz. Based on the second movement of Tchaikovsky's Symphony no. 5 in E, adapted by Andre Kostelanetz.

Moon of Alabama, see **The Alabama Song**

Moon of Manakoora, The 1937 w. Frank Loesser m. Alfred Newman. (F) *The Hurricane*. Dorothy Lamour, Mary Astor, and Raymond Massey appeared in *The Hurricane*.

Moon of My Delight 1928 w. Lorenz Hart m. Richard Rodgers. (MT) *Chee-Chee*.

Moon Over Miami 1935 w. Edgar Leslie m. Joe Burke

Moon River 1961 w. Johnny Mercer m. Henry Mancini. (F) *Breakfast at Tiffany's*. Audrey Hepburn appeared in *Breakfast at Tiffany's*. Academy Award winner 1961. Grammy Award winner 1961.

Moon Shines on the Moonshine, The 1920 w. Francis DeWitt m. Robert Hood Bowers. (MT) *Broadway Brevities of 1920*.

Moon Song (That Wasn't Meant for Me) 1933 w.m. Sam Coslow, Arthur Johnston. (MF) *Hello Everybody*. Randolph Scott and Sally Blane appeared in *Hello Everybody*.

Moon Was Yellow, The 1934 w. Edgar Leslie m. Fred E. Ahlert

Moonbeams 1906 w. Henry Blossom m. Victor Herbert. (MT) *The Red Mill*.

Moonglow 1934 w.m. Will Hudson, Eddie De Lange, Irving Mills. (MT) *Blackbirds of 1934*. (F) *Picnic*. (MF) *The Benny Goodman Story*. Kim Novak and William Holden appeared in *Picnic*. This song was popularly revived in 1956.

Eddie DeLange died ten years before this song achieved any popular success.

Moonlight and Pretzels 1933 w. E.Y. Harburg m. Jay Gorney. (MF) *Moonlight and Pretzels*. William Frawley and Roger Pryor appeared in *Moonlight and Pretzels*.

Moonlight and Roses (Bring Mem'ries of You) 1925 w.m. Ben Black, Neil Moret (Charles N. Daniels). (MF) *Song of Texas*. Roy Rogers and Bob Nolan appeared in *Song of Texas*. Based on Edwin H. Lemare's Andantino in D-flat, of 1892. This song was popularly revived in 1928.

Moonlight and Shadows 1936 w.m. Leo Robin, Frederick Hollander. (F) *Jungle Princess*. Dorothy Lamour and Ray Milland appeared in *Jungle Princess*.

(On) Moonlight Bay 1912 w. Edward Madden m. Percy Wenrich. (MF) *Tin Pan Alley*. (MF) *On Moonlight Bay*. Alice Faye and Betty Grable appeared in *Tin Pan Alley*. Doris Day and Gordon MacRae appeared in *On Moonlight Bay*.

Moonlight Becomes You 1942 w. Johnny Burke m. Jimmy Van Heusen. (MF) *The Road to Morocco*. Bob Hope, Bing Crosby, and Dorothy Lamour appeared in *The Road to Morocco*.

Moonlight Cocktail 1942 w.m. Kim Gannon, C. Luckeyth Roberts. (MF) *A Night in Casablanca*. The Marx Brothers appeared in *A Night in Casablanca*. Based on C. Luckeyth Roberts' ''Ripples of the Nile.''

Moonlight Feels Right 1976 w.m. Michael Bruce Blackman

Moonlight Gambler 1956 w. Bob Hilliard m. Philip Springer

Moonlight in Vermont 1944 w. John Blackburn m. Karl Suessdorf. This song was popularly revived in 1950.

Moonlight Masquerade 1941 w. Jack Lawrence m. Toots Camarata. Based on Isaac Albéniz' ''Tango'' in D-minor.

Moonlight Mood 1942 w.m. Harold Adamson, Peter DeRose

Moonlight On the Colorado 1930 w. Billy Moll m. Robert A. King

Moonlight On the Ganges 1926 w. Chester Wallace m. Sherman Myers

Moonlight On the Rhine 1914 w. Bert Kalmar, Edgar Leslie m. Ted Snyder. (MT) *One Girl in a Million*.

(There Ought To Be a) Moonlight Saving Time 1931 w.m. Irving Kahal, Harry Richman

Moonlight Serenade 1939 w. Mitchell Parish m. Glenn Miller. (MF) *The Glenn Miller Story*. Theme song of Glenn Miller.

Moonlight Sonata, op.27, no.2. 1802 m. Ludwig van Beethoven. Critic Ludwig Rellstab supposedly named this work the ''Moonlight Sonata'' in 1850.

Moonrise On the Lowlands 1936 w.m. Jerry Livingston, Al J. Neiburg

Moonstruck 1909 w.m. Ivan Caryll, Lionel Monckton. (MT) *Our Miss Gibbs*. Gertie Millar appeared in *Our Miss Gibbs*.

More 1956 w. Tom Glazer m. Alex Alstone. This is *not* the ''Theme from *Mondo Cane*.''

More, or, **Theme from** *Mondo Cane* 1963 w.m. Norman Newell, Riz Ortolani, N. Oliviero. (F) *Mondo Cane*.

More and More 1944 w. E.Y. Harburg m. Jerome Kern. (MF) *Can't Help Singing*. Deanna Durbin and Robert Paige appeared in *Can't Help Singing*.

More I See You, The 1945 w. Mack Gordon m. Harry Warren. (MF) *Diamond Horseshoe*. Betty Grable and Dick Haymes appeared in *Diamond Horseshoe*.

More Love Than Your Love 1954 w. Dorothy Fields m. Arthur Schwartz. (MT) *By the Beautiful Sea*.

More More More (Part I) 1976 w.m. Gregg Diamond

More Than a Feeling 1975 w.m. Tom Scholz

More Than a Woman 1977 w.m. Barry Gibb, Robin Gibb, Maurice Gibb. (MF) *Saturday Night Fever*. John Travolta appeared in *Saturday Night Fever*.

More Than I Can Say 1980 w.m. Jerry Allison, Sonny Curtis

More Than You Know 1929 w. Billy Rose, Edward Eliscu m. Vincent Youmans. (MT) *Great Day!* (MF) *Hit the Deck*. (F) *Encore*. (MF) *Both Ends of the Candle*. (MF) *Funny Lady*. Mayo Methot appeared in *Great Day!* Tony Martin appeared in *Hit the Deck*. Barbra Streisand and James Caan appeared in *Funny Lady*, biopic of Fanny Brice.

More We Are Together, The 1926 w.m. Irving King

Morgen—One More Sunrise 1959 Ger.w. Peter Mösser Eng.w. Noel Sherman m. Peter Mösser

Morit'at, *see* **Mack the Knife**

Morning 1910 w. Frank L. Stanton m. Oley Speaks

Morning After, The, or, **Song From** *The Poseidon Adventure* 1973 w.m. Al Kasha, Joe Harschorn. (F) *The Poseidon Adventure*. Shelley Winters appeared in *The Poseidon Adventure*. Academy Award winner 1972.

Morning After the Night Before, The 1910 w. Ed Moran m. J. Fred Helf

Mornin' Beautiful 1975 w.m. Sandy Linzer, Dave Appell

Morning Desire 1986 w.m. Dave Loggins

Morning Dew 1964 w.m. Bonnie Dobson

Morning Has Broken 1971 w.m. Eleanor Farjeon, Cat Stevens

Morning of My Life 1966 w.m. Barry Alan Gibb

Morning, Please Don't Come 1970 w.m. Tom Springfield

Morning Side of the Mountain, The 1951 w.m. Dick Manning, Larry Stock

Morning Train (Nine to Five) 1981 w.m. Florrie Palmer

Morris Dance, The 1902 w.m. Sir Edward German, Hugo Frey

Mosquito's Parade, The 1899 m. Howard Whitney; arr. Theodore Bendix

(If You Happen To See) Most Beautiful Girl, The (in the World) 1973 w.m. Rory Bourke, Billy Sherrill, Norro Wilson

Most Beautiful Girl in the World, The 1936 w. Lorenz Hart m. Richard Rodgers. (MT) *Jumbo*. (MF) *Jumbo*. Jimmy Durante and Gloria Grafton appeared in the stage production of *Jumbo*.

Most Gentlemen Don't Like Love 1938 w.m. Cole Porter. (MT) *Leave It to Me*. (MT) *Black Velvet*. William Gaxton, Victor Moore, Mary Martin, and Sophie Tucker appeared in *Leave It to Me*. Pat Kirkwood appeared in *Black Velvet*.

Most Happy Fella, The 1956 w.m. Frank Loesser. (MT) *The Most Happy Fella*.

Moth and the Flame, The 1898 w. George Taggart m. Max S. Witt

Mother 1916 w. Rida Johnson Young m. Sigmund Romberg. (MT) *Her Soldier Boy*.

Mother 1927 w. Dorothy Donnelly m. Sigmund Romberg. (MT) *My Maryland*.

M-O-T-H-E-R (A Word That Means the World to Me) 1915 w. Howard Johnson m. Theodore F. Morse

Mother Goose's Melodies 1765 w.m. After Boston printer Thomas Fleet married Elizabeth Goose, his mother-in-law sang endless nursery rhymes to his infant son. He soon published *Mother Goose's Melodies for Children*, which states, "Mother Goose's maiden name was Elizabeth Foster, and was born in Massachusetts in 1665. She married Isaac Goose when about twenty years old, and died in 1757." These melodies with *English* words include the following: "Baa, Baa, Black Sheep," "Ding Dong Bell," "Fiddle Dee Dee," "Georgie Porgie," "Hey Diddle Diddle," "Hickory, Dickory, Dock," "Hot Cross Buns," "Humpty Dumpty," "I Love Little Pussy," "I Saw Three Ships Come Sailing," "Jack and Jill," "Jack Sprat," "The Jolly Miller," "Little Bo-Peep," "Little Boy Blue," "Little Jack Horner," "Little Miss Muffet," "Little Tommy Tucker," "Mary Had a Little Lamb" (included in the new collection in 1867), "Mistress Mary Quite Contrary," "(Here We Go Round) The Mulberry Bush" (also 1858), "The North Wind Doth Blow" (1715), "Old King Cole," "Pease Porridge Hot," "Peter Peter Pumpkin Eater," "Polly Put the Kettle On," "Rock-a-Bye (Hush-a-Bye) Baby" (with English words, 1884), "See Saw Marjory Daw," "Simple Simon," "Sing a Song of Sixpence" (also 1871), "There Was an Old Woman Who Lived in a Shoe," "Three Little Kittens," "Tom, Tom, the Piper's Son" and "Upstairs Downstairs." Many were based on traditional French melodies.

Mother Machree 1910 w. Rida Johnson Young m. Ernest R. Ball, Chauncey Olcott. (MT) *Barry of Ballymore*. (MF) *My Wild Irish Rose*. Dennis Morgan and Arlene Dahl appeared in *My Wild Irish Rose*. Theme song of Irish tenor John McCormack.

Mother o' Mine 1903 w. Rudyard Kipling m. Frank E. Tours

Mother Was a Lady, or, **If Jack Were Only Here** 1896 w. Edward B. Marks m. Joseph W. Stern

Mother-in-Law 1961 w.m. Allen Toussaint

Mother's Gift to Her Country, A, *see* **The Blue and the Gray**

Mottoes Framed upon the Wall, The 1888 w. William Devere m. W.S. Mullaly

Mouldy Old Dough 1973 w.m. Nigel Fletcher, Rob Woodward. Ivor Novello Award winner 1972–73.

Moulin Rouge, *see* **Song from Moulin Rouge**

Mountain Greenery 1926 w. Lorenz Hart m. Richard Rodgers. (MT) *The Garrick Gaieties (Second Edition)*. (MT) *The Girl Friend*. (MF) *Words and Music*. Betty Starbuck and Sterling Halloway appeared in *The Garrick Gaieties (Second Edition)*. Mickey Rooney, Judy Garland, and Gene Kelly appeared in *Words and Music*, biopic of song writers Rodgers and Hart.

Mountain Music 1982 w.m. Randy Owen

Mountain of Love 1982 w.m. Harold Dorman

Mountains Beyond the Moon 1957 w.m. Carl Sigman, Franz Waxman

Mountains High, The 1961 w.m. Dick St. John

Mountains of Mourne 1910 w.m. traditional. This song was popularly revived in 1910.

Move Away 1986 w.m. Phil Pickett

Move In a Little Closer Baby 1969 w.m. Arnold Capitanelli, Robert O'Connor

Move On 1984 w.m. Stephen Sondheim. (MT) *Sunday in the Park with George*. Mandy Patinkin and Bernadette Peters appeared in *Sunday in the Park with George*.

Move Over Darling 1963 w.m. Joe Lubin, Hal Kanter, Terry Melcher. (F) *Move Over Darling*. Doris Day and James Garner appeared in *Move Over Darling*.

Movies Were Movies (MT) *Jerry's Girls*. Dorothy Loudon, Chita Rivera, and Leslie Uggams appeared in *Jerry's Girls*.

Moving Day in Jungle Town 1909 w. A. Seymour Brown m. Nat D. Ayer. This song concerned Theodore Roosevelt's African safari.

Movin' On 1975 w.m. Merle Haggard

Mr., *see* **Mister**

Mrs. Brown You've Got a Lovely Daughter 1965 w.m. Trevor Peacock. Ivor Novello Award winner 1965.

Mrs. Robinson 1968 w.m. Paul Simon. (F) *The Graduate*. Anne Bancroft and Dustin Hoffman appeared in *The Graduate*. Grammy Award winner 1968.

(Don't Put Your Daughter on the Stage) Mrs. Worthington 1935 w.m. Noël Coward

Much Binding in the Marsh 1946 w.m. Richard Murdoch, Sidney Torch

Much More 1960 w. Tom Jones m. Harvey Schmidt. (MT) *The Fantasticks*.

Much Obliged to You, *see* **The Best I Get Is Much Obliged to You**

Mucking About the Garden 1929 w.m. Q. Cumber (Leslie Sarony)

Mud, Glorious Mud, *see* **The Hippopotamus Song**

Muddy Water 1926 w. Jo' Trent m. Peter DeRose, Harry Richman

Muddy Water 1985 w.m. Roger Miller. (MT) *Big River*.

(Here We Go Round) Mulberry Bush, The, *see* **Mother Goose's Melodies**

Mule Skinner Blues 1931 w.m. Jimmie Rodgers, George Vaughn

Mule Train 1949 w.m. Johnny Lange, Hy Heath, Fred Glickman. (F) *Mule Train*. (MF) *Singing Guns*. Gene Autry and Pat Buttram appeared in *Mule Train*. Vaughan Monroe and Walter Brennan appeared in *Singing Guns*.

Mull of Kintyre 1977 w.m. Paul McCartney, Denny Laine. Ivor Novello Award winner 1977–1978. Ivor Novello Award winner 1978–79.

Mulligan Braves, The 1880 w. Edward Harrigan m. David Braham. (MT) *The Mulligan Guards' Nominee*.

Mulligan Guard, The 1873 w. Edward Harrigan m. David Braham. (MT) *The Mulligan Guard*.

Mumbo Jumbo Jijjiboo J. O'Shea, *see* **I've Got Rings on My Fingers**

"Murder" He Says 1943 w. Frank Loesser m. Jimmy McHugh. (MF) *Happy Go Lucky*. (MF) *Jam Session*. Mary Martin, Dick Powell, and Betty Hutton appeared in *Happy Go Lucky*. Ann Miller and Louis Armstrong appeared in *Jam Session*.

(Theme from) Murder On the Orient Express 1974 m. Richard Rodney Bennett. (F) *Murder On the Orient Express*. Albert Finney and Ingrid Bergman appeared in *Murder on the Orient Express*. Ivor Novello Award winner 1975–76.

Musetta's Waltz 1898 w. Giuseppe Giacosa, Luigi Illica m. Giacomo Puccini. From the opera *La Bohème*.

Music 1977 w.m. John Miles. Ivor Novello Award winner 1976–77.

Music and the Mirror, The 1975 w. Edward Kleban m. Marvin Hamlisch. (MT) *A Chorus Line*. Donna McKechnie appeared in *A Chorus Line*.

Music Machine 1980 w.m. Leslie Hurdle, Frank Ricotti. Ivor Novello Award winner 1979–80.

Music Goes 'Round and 'Round, The 1935 w. "Red" Hodgson m. Edward Farley, Michael Riley. (MF) *The Music Goes Round*. (MF) *The Five Pennies*. Danny Kaye appeared in *The Five Pennies*, biopic of jazzman Red Nichols. Based on "If You Want To Know Who We Are," from Gilbert and Sullivan's *The Mikado*.

Music in May (Careless Rapture) 1936 w.m. Ivor Novello

Music, Maestro, Please 1938 w. Herb Magidson m. Allie Wrubel. (MT) *These Foolish Things*. Frances Day appeared in *These Foolish Things*. Theme song of Harry Leader.

Music Makers, The 1941 w. Don Raye m. Harry James

Music Makes Me 1933 w. Gus Kahn, Edward Eliscu m. Vincent Youmans. (MF) *Flying Down to Rio*. Dolores Del Rio and Fred Astaire appeared in *Flying Down to Rio*.

Music Music Everywhere (But Not a Song in My Heart) 1932 w. Ted Koehler m. Harold Arlen

Music Music Music 1950 w.m. Stephen Weiss, Bernie Baum

Music Stopped, The 1944 w.m. Harold Adamson, Jimmy McHugh. (MF) *Higher and Higher*. Frank Sinatra, Michele Morgan, and Victor Borge appeared in *Higher and Higher*.

Music To Watch Girls By 1966 w.m. Sid Ramin, Tony Velona. This song was also popular in 1968.

Musica Prohibita, La (Forbidden Music) 1905 w. N. Malpadi m. Stanislao Gastoldon. This song was published earlier in Italy, between 1883 and 1887.

Muskrat Ramble 1926 w.m. Ray Gilbert, Edward Ory. This song was popularly revived in 1937.

Must Be Madison 1962 w.m. Jack Woodman

Mutual Admiration Society 1957 w. Matt Dubey m. Harold Karr. (MT) *Happy Hunting*.

My Adobe Hacienda 1941 w.m. Louise Massey, Lee Penny. (MF) *The Big Sombrero*. Gene Autry appeared in *The Big Sombrero*. This song was popularly revived in 1947.

My Ain Folk 1905 w. Wilfred Mills m. Laura G. Lemon

My Angel, *see* **Angela Mia**

My Angeline 1895 w. Harry B. Smith m. Victor Herbert. (MT) *The Wizard of the Nile*.

My Baby Just Cares for Me 1930 w.m. Gus Kahn, Walter Donaldson. (MT) *Whoopee*. (MF) *Whoopee*. (MF) *Big City Blues*. Eddie Cantor appeared in both the stage and film productions of *Whoopee*. Joan Blondell and Lyle Talbot appeared in *Big City Blues*.

My Baby Thinks He's a Train 1981 w.m. Leroy Prestone

My Baby's Arms 1919 w. Joseph McCarthy m. Harry Tierney. (MT) *Ziegfeld Follies of 1919*.

My Baby's Comin' Home 1952 w.m. William Leavitt, John Grady, Sherm Feller

My Barney Lies Over the Ocean (Just the Way He Lied to Me) 1919 w. Sam M. Lewis, Joe Young m. Bert Grant

My Beautiful Alsace Lorraine, *see* **Lorraine**

My Beautiful Balloon, *see* **Up Up and Away**

My Beautiful Lady, or, **The Kiss Waltz** 1911 w. C.M.S. McLellan m. Ivan Caryll. (MT) *The Pink Lady*. (F) *The Actress*. Spencer Tracy and Jean Simmons appeared in *The Actress*.

My Beautiful Sarie Marais 1945 w.m. Michael Carr, Tommie Connor

My Belgian Rose 1918 Fr.w. Louis Delamarre Eng.w.m. George Benoit, Robert Levenson, Ted Garton

My Beloved 1951 w.m. Jay Livingston, Ray Evans. (F) *Marshmallow Moon*.

My Best Girl 1924 w.m. Walter Donaldson

My Best Girl 1966 w.m. Jerry Herman. (MT) *Mame*. (MF) *Mame*. Angela Lansbury appeared in the stage production of *Mame*. Lucille Ball appeared in the film production of *Mame*.

My Best Girl's a New Yorker (Corker) 1895 w.m. John Stromberg

My Blackbirds Are Bluebirds Now 1929 w.m. Irving Caesar, Cliff Friend. (MT) *Whoopee*. (MF) *Lucky Boy*. Eddie Cantor and Ruth Etting appeared in *Whoopee*. George Jessel and Margaret Quimby appeared in *Lucky Boy*.

My Blue Bird Was Caught in the Rain 1930 w. Henry Creamer m. Max Rich

My Blue Heaven 1927 w. George Whiting m. Walter Donaldson. (MT) *Will o' the Whispers*. (F) *Never a Dull Moment*. (MF) *Moon Over Las Vegas*. (MF) *My Blue Heaven*. Jack Smith appeared in *Will o' the Whispers*. The Ritz Brothers and Frances Langford appeared in *Never a Dull Moment*. David Bruce and Anne Gwynne appeared in *Moon Over Las Vegas*. Betty Grable and Dan Dailey appeared in *My Blue Heaven*. Theme song of Gene Austin.

My Blushing Rosie, *see* **Ma Blushin' Rosie**

My Bonnie Lies Over the Ocean, or, **Bring Back My Bonnie to Me** 1881 w.m. traditional, from Scotland; erroneously attributed to Charles E. Pratt (H.J. Fulmer)

My Boomerang Won't Come Back 1961 w.m. Max Diamond, Charlie Drake

My Boy Lollipop 1964 w.m. Johnny Roberts, Robert Spencer, Morris Levy

My Boyfriend's Back 1963 w.m. Robert Feldman, Gerald Goldstein, Richard Gottehrer

My British Buddy 1943 w.m. Irving Berlin. (MT) *This Is the Army.* (MF) *This Is the Army.*

My Buddies 1919 w.m. B.C. Hilliam. (MT) *Buddies.* Peggy Wood, Donald Brian, and Roland Young appeared in *Buddies.*

My Buddy 1922 w. Gus Kahn m. Walter Donaldson. (MF) *I'll See You in My Dreams.* Doris Day and Danny Thomas appeared in *I'll See You in My Dreams,* biopic of song writer Gus Kahn.

My Cabin of Dreams 1937 w.m. Nick Kenny, Al Frazzini, Nat Madison

My Castle on the Nile 1901 w. Robert Cole, J.W. Johnson m. J. Rosamond Johnson

My Cherie Amor 1969 w.m. Henry Cosby, Sylvia Moy, Stevie Wonder

My Coloring Book 1962 w.m. John Kander, Fred Ebb

My Country 'Tis of Thee, *see* **America**

My Cousin Caruso 1909 w. Edward Madden m. Gus Edwards. Based on Leoncavallo's aria "Vesti la Giubba" from *Pagliacci.*

My Creole Sue 1898 w.m. Gussie L. Davis

My Cup Runneth Over 1967 w. Tom Jones m. Harvey Schmidt. (MT) *I Do! I Do!.*

My Dad's Dinner Pail 1883 w. Edward Harrigan m. David Braham. (MT) *Cordelia's Aspirations.*

My Darling 1932 w. Edward Heyman m. Richard Myers. (MT) *Earl Carroll's Vanities of 1932.* Milton Berle and Helen Broderick appeared in *Earl Carroll's Vanities of 1932.*

My Darling Clementine, *see* **Clementine**

My Darling, My Darling 1948 w.m. Frank Loesser. (MT) *Where's Charley?.* (MF) *Where's Charley?.* Ray Bolger appeared in both the stage and film productions of *Where's Charley?.*

My Dear Little Cingalee 1904 w.m. Lionel Monckton, Adrian Ross, Percy Greenbank. (MT) *The Cingalee.*

My Dearest Dear 1939 w.m. Ivor Novello, Christopher Hassall. (MT) *The Dancing Years.* May Ellis appeared in *The Dancing Years.*

My Dearest Heart 1876 w. anon. m. Arthur Sullivan

My Defenses Are Down 1946 w.m. Irving Berlin. (MT) *Annie Get Your Gun.* (MF) *Annie Get Your Gun.* Ethel Merman and Ray Middleton appeared in the stage production of *Annie Get Your Gun.* Betty Hutton and Howard Keel appeared in the film production of *Annie Get Your Gun.*

My Devotion 1942 w.m. Roc Hillman, Johnny Napton. (MF)

Follow the Band. Leon Errol and Eddie Quillan appeared in *Follow the Band.*

My Dixie Pair o' Dice, *see* **Seven or Eleven**

My Dream Girl, I Loved You Long Ago 1924 w. Rida Johnson Young m. Victor Herbert. (MT) *The Dream Girl.*

My Dream Is Yours 1949 w.m. Harry Warren, Ralph Blane. (MF) *My Dream Is Yours.* Doris Day and Jack Carson appeared in *My Dream Is Yours.*

My Dream of Love 1909 w.m. Adrian Ross, Leo Fall. (MT) *The Dollar Princess.*

My Dream of the Big Parade 1926 w. Al Dubin m. Jimmy McHugh

My Dreams Are Getting Better All the Time 1944 w.m. Vic Mizzy, Mann Curtis. (MF) *In Society.* Bud Abbott and Lou Costello appeared in *In Society.*

My Elusive Dreams 1968 w.m. Curly Putman, Billy Sherrill. This song was popularly revived in 1975.

My Eyes Adored You 1975 w.m. Bob Crewe, Kenny Nolan

My Faith Looks Up to Thee 1832 w. Ray Palmer m. based on "Olivet" by Lowell Mason

My Faithful Stradivari 1913 w. C.C.S. Cushing, E.P. Heath m. Emmerich Kalman. (MT) *Sari.*

My Favorite Things 1959 w. Oscar Hammerstein II m. Richard Rodgers. (MT) *The Sound of Music.* (MF) *The Sound of Music.* Mary Martin appeared in the stage production of *The Sound of Music.* Julie Andrews appeared in the film production of *The Sound of Music.*

My First Thrill 1936 w.m. Maurice Sigler, Al Hoffman, Al Goodhart. (MF) *She Shall Have Music.* Jack Hylton appeared in *She Shall Have Music.*

My Foolish Heart 1949 w. Ned Washington m. Victor Young. (F) *My Foolish Heart.* Susan Hayward and Dana Andrews appeared in *My Foolish Heart.*

My Friend the Major 1894 w.m. E.W. Rogers

My Friend the Sea 1961 w.m. Ron Goodwin, Jack Fishman

My Funny Valentine 1937 w. Lorenz Hart m. Richard Rodgers. (MT) *Babes in Arms.* (MF) *Babes in Arms.* (MF) *Gentlemen Marry Brunettes.* (MF) *Pal Joey.* Mitzi Green and Ray Heatherton appeared in the stage production of *Babes in Arms.* Judy Garland and Mickey Rooney appeared in the film production of *Babes in Arms.* Jane Russell and Jeanne Crain appeared in *Gentlemen Marry Brunettes.* Frank Sinatra, Rita Hayworth, and Kim Novak appeared in the film production of *Pal Joey.*

My Future Just Passed 1930 w. George Marion m. Richard A. Whiting. (MF) *Safety in Numbers.* Charles "Buddy" Rogers and Carole Lombard appeared in *Safety in Numbers.*

My Gal Is a High Born Lady 1896 w.m. Barney Fagan; arr. Gustav Luders. (MF) *In Old Sacramento.* Bill Elliott and Constance Moore appeared in *In Old Sacramento.* This was possibly the first popular ragtime song.

My Gal Sal, or, **They Call Her Frivolous Sal** 1905 w.m. Paul Dresser. (MF) *My Gal Sal.* Rita Hayworth and Victor

Mature appeared in *My Gal Sal*. This song was popularly revived in 1942.

My Generation 1965 w.m. Peter Townshend

My Girl Has Gone 1965 w.m. William "Smokey" Robinson, Jr., Marvin Tarplin, Warren Moore, Robert E. Rogers

My Girl's a Yorkshire Girl 1908 w.m. C.W. Murphy, Dan Lipton

My Grandma's Advice 1857 w.m. arr. Edward Kanski

My Greenwich Village Sue 1920 w.m. Carey Morgan, Arthur Swanstrom

My Guiding Star 1905 w. Thurland Chattaway m. Jean Schwartz

My Guy 1964 w.m. William "Smokey" Robinson, Jr.

My Guy's Come Back 1945 w.m. Mel Powell, Ray McKinley

My Happiness 1933 w. Betty Peterson m. Borney Bergantine. This song was popularly revived in 1948 and again in 1958.

My Hat's on the Side of My Head 1933 w.m. Claude Hurlbert, Harry Woods. (F) *Jack Ahoy*. Jack Hurlbert appeared in *Jack Ahoy*.

My Heart and I 1936 w.m. Leo Robin, Frederick Hollander. (MF) *Anything Goes* (1936). Ethel Merman, Bing Crosby, and Ida Lupino appeared in the 1936 film production of *Anything Goes*. This song did not appear in the original stage production of *Anything Goes*.

My Heart and I 1943 w.m. Frederick Tysh, Richard Tauber, Walter Ellis. (MT) *Old Chelsea*. Richard Tauber appeared in *Old Chelsea*.

My Heart and Lute 1830 w. Thomas Moore m. Sir Henry Rowley Bishop. The words to this song are often erroneously credited to J.P. Kemble.

My Heart at Thy Sweet Voice 1876 m. Camille Saint-Saëns. From the opera *Samson and Delilah*.

My Heart Belongs to Daddy 1938 w.m. Cole Porter. (MT) *Leave It to Me*. (MT) *Black Velvet*. (MF) *Night and Day*. William Gaxton, Sophie Tucker, Victor Moore, and Mary Martin appeared in *Leave It to Me*. Cary Grant, Alexis Smith, and Mary Martin appeared in *Night and Day*, biopic of song writer Cole Porter. Theme song of Mary Martin.

My Heart Belongs to Me 1977 w.m. Alan Gordon

My Heart Cries for You 1950 w.m. Percy Faith, Carl Sigman

My Heart Goes Crazy 1946 w. Johnny Burke m. James Van Heusen. (MF) *My Heart Goes Crazy*. (MF) *London Town*. Syd Field and Greta Gynt appeared in *My Heart Goes Crazy*. Syd Field and Kay Kendall appeared in *London Town*.

My Heart Has a Mind of Its Own 1960 w. Howard Greenfield m. Jack Keller

My Heart Has Learned To Love You, Now Do Not Say Goodbye 1910 w. David Reed m. Ernest R. Ball

My Heart Is a Hobo 1947 w. Johnny Burke m. Jimmy Van Heusen. (MF) *Welcome Stranger*. Bing Crosby and Barry Fitzgerald appeared in *Welcome Stranger*.

My Heart Is an Open Book 1959 w. Hal David m. Lee Pockriss

My Heart Is Taking Lessons 1937 w.m. Jimmy Monaco, Johnny Burke. (MF) *Doctor Rhythm*. Bing Crosby, Beatrice Lillie, and Andy Devine appeared in *Doctor Rhythm*.

My Heart Reminds Me, or, And That Reminds Me 1957 w. Al Stillman m. Camillo Bargoni. Based on "Autumn Concerto" of 1956. See also "Autumn Concerto."

(All of a Sudden) My Heart Sings 1945 w.m. Harold Rome, "Jamblan" Henri Herpin. (MF) *Anchors Aweigh*. (MF) *Junior Prom*. Frank Sinatra, Gene Kelly, and Kathryn Grayson appeared in *Anchors Aweigh*. Freddie Stewart and June Preisser appeared in *Junior Prom*. This song was popularly revived in 1959.

My Heart Still Clings to the Old First Love 1901 w.m. Paul Dresser

My Heart Stood Still 1927 w. Lorenz Hart m. Richard Rodgers. (MT) *A Connecticut Yankee*. (MT) *One Dam Thing After Another*. (MF) *A Connecticut Yankee* (1931). William Gaxton and William Norris appeared in the stage production of *A Connecticut Yankee*. Edith Baker and Jessie Matthews appeared in *One Dam Thing After Another*. Will Rogers and Maureen O'Sullivan appeared in the 1931 film production of *A Connecticut Yankee*. This song was inspired by a reckless Parisian taxi ride in which one female traveler exclaimed the title of the song to Mr. Hart.

My Heart Tells Me 1943 w. Mack Gordon m. Harry Warren. (MF) *Sweet Rosie O'Grady*. Betty Grable and Robert Young appeared in *Sweet Rosie O'Grady*.

My Heart's To Let 1933 w.m. Jack Waller, Joe Tunbridge

My Hero 1909 w. Stanislaus Stange m. Oscar Straus. (MT) *The Chocolate Soldier*. (MF) *The Chocolate Soldier*. (MF) *Two Weeks with Love*. Evelyn d'Alroy and C.H. Workman appeared in the British stage production of *The Chocolate Soldier*. Nelson Eddy, Nigel Bruce, and Risé Stevens appeared in the film production of *The Chocolate Soldier*. Jane Powell and Debbie Reynolds appeared in *Two Weeks with Love*.

My Home Town Is a One Horse Town, But It's Big Enough for Me 1919 w. Alex Gerber m. Abner Silver

My Hometown 1986 w.m. Bruce Springsteen

My Honey Lou 1904 w.m. Thurland Chattaway

My Honey's Lovin' Arms 1922 w. Herman Ruby m. Joseph Meyer

My Husband Makes Movies 1982 w.m. Maury Yeston. (MT) *Nine*. Liliane Montevecchi and Anita Morris appeared in *Nine*.

My Ideal 1884 It.w. Carmelo Errica Eng.w. Harrison Millard m. Francesco Paolo Tostí. From the Italian "Ideale."

My Ideal 1930 w. Leo Robin m. Richard A. Whiting, Newell Chase. (MF) *Playboy of Paris*. (MF) *Along Came Youth*. Maurice Chevalier and Frances Dee appeared in *Playboy of Paris*. Charles "Buddy" Rogers and Frances Dee appeared in *Along Came Youth*.

My Inspiration Is You 1928 w.m. Horatio Nicholls. (MF) *Stepping High*.

My Irish Molly O 1905 w. William Jerome m. Jean Schwartz. (MT) *Sergeant Brue*. Frank Daniels and Blanche Ring appeared in *Sergeant Brue*.

My Isle of Golden Dreams 1919 w. Gus Kahn m. Walter Blaufuss

My Kid's a Crooner 1935 w.m. Marion Harris, Reg Montgomery

My Kind of Girl 1961 w.m. Leslie Bricusse. Ivor Novello Award winner 1961.

My Kind of Town 1964 w.m. Sammy Cahn, Jimmy Van Heusen

My Kinda Love 1929 w. Jo' Trent m. Louis Alter. (MT) *Americana of 1928.*

My Laddie 1906 w. Princess Troubetzkay m. William Armour Thayer

My Lady Lou 1899 w. Charles Doty m. E.S. Brill

My Lady Loves To Dance 1953 w. Sammy Gallop m. Milton DeLugg

My Last Cigar, see **'Twas off the Blue Canaries**

My Last Cigarette, see **Cowboy Serenade**

My Last Date with You 1960 w. Boudleaux Bryant, Skeeter Davis m. Floyd Cramer

My Last Go 'Round, see **Blue Prelude**

My Last Goodbye 1939 w.m. Eddy Howard

My Life Belongs to You 1939 w.m. Ivor Novello, Christopher Hassall. (MT) *The Dancing Years.* Mary Ellis appeared in *The Dancing Years.*

My Little Buckaroo 1937 w. Jack Scholl m. M.K. Jerome. (F) *Cherokee Strip.* (MF) *Don't Fence Me In.* (MF) *Ridin' Down the Canyon.* Florence Rice and Richard Dix appeared in *Cherokee Strip.* Roy Rogers and Dale Evans appeared in *Don't Fence Me In.* Roy Rogers and Gabby Hayes appeared in *Ridin' Down the Canyon.*

My Little Chimpanzee, see **In Zanzibar**

My Little Deitcher Girl 1908 w.m. Bert Lee

My Little Georgia Rose 1899 w. Robert F. Roden m. Max S. Witt

My Little Girl 1915 w. Sam M. Lewis, William Dillon m. Albert Von Tilzer

My Little Grass Shack in Kealakekua, Hawaii 1933 w.m. John Avery Noble, Thomas J. Harrison

My Little Gypsy Sweetheart, see **Gypsy Love Song**

My Little Nest of Heavenly Blue, or **Frasquita Serenade (Blaues Himmelbett),** or, **Farewell, My Love, Farewell** 1923 Ger.w. Dr. A.M. Willner, Heinz Reichart Eng.w. Sigmund Spaeth m. Franz Lehár. (MT) *Frasquita.* Jose Collins appeared in the British production of *Frasquita.*

My Little Town 1975 w.m. Paul Simon

My Lodging (It) Is on the Cold Ground 1775 w. Sir William Davenant m. traditional, from England or Ireland; possibly Matthew Locke. This song was so popularly sung by Moll Davies, one of the earliest English actresses, that she gained the attention of Charles II, who married her. Their daughter was Mary Tudor who married the second Earl of Derwentwater. See also "Believe Me If All Those Endearing Young Charms" and "Fair Harvard."

My Long-Tail Blue 1827 w.m. anon. This song was made popular by black minstrels George Washington Dixon and William Pennington.

My Love 1966 w.m. Tony Hatch

My Love 1973 w.m. Paul McCartney, Linda McCartney. Ivor Novello Award winner 1973–1974.

My Love 1983 w.m. Lionel Richie

My Love and Devotion 1951 w.m. Milton Carson

My Love and Devotion 1962 w.m. Howard Barnes, Joe Roncoroni, Harold Fields. Ivor Novello Award winner 1962.

My Love for You 1960 w. Sid Wayne m. Abner Silver

My Love Is Like a Red, Red Rose c.1750 w. Robert Burns m. traditional, from Scotland. Based on the old Scottish tune "Low Down in the Broom."

My Love, My Love 1953 w. Bob Haymes m. Nick Acquaviva

(This Is) My Love Parade 1929 w. Clifford Grey m. Victor Schertzinger. (MF) *The Love Parade.* Maurice Chevalier appeared in *The Love Parade.*

My Lover Is a Fisherman 1922 w.m. Lily Strickland

My Lovin' Honey Man 1911 w.m. Joe McCarthy, Al Piantadosi

My Lucky Star 1928 w. B.G. DeSylva, Lew Brown m. Ray Henderson. (MT) *Follow Thru.*

My Lucky Star 1928 w. Lorenz Hart m. Richard Rodgers. (MT) *She's My Baby.* Beatrice Lillie, Irene Dunne, and Clifton Webb appeared in *She's My Baby.*

My Lucky Star, see also **You Are My Lucky Star**

My Mammy 1920 w. Sam Lewis, Joe Young m. Walter Donaldson. (MT) *Sinbad.* (MF) *The Jazz Singer.* (MF) *Rose of Washington Square.* (MF) *The Jolson Story.* (MF) *Jolson Sings Again.* Al Jolson appeared in *Sinbad, The Jazz Singer, Rose of Washington Square.* Larry Parks appeared in *The Jolson Story* and *Jolson Sings Again.* Theme song of Al Jolson.

My Man 1921 Fr.w. Albert Willemetz, Jacques Charles Eng.w. Channing Pollock m. Maurice Yvain. (MT) *Ziegfeld Follies of 1921.* (MF) *My Man.* (MF) *The Great Ziegfeld.* (MF) *Rose of Washington Square.* (MF) *Funny Girl.* (MF) *Lady Sings the Blues.* Fanny Brice appeared in both *Ziegfeld Follies of 1921* and *My Man.* William Powell appeared in *The Great Ziegfeld.* Al Jolson appeared in *Rose of Washington Square.* Barbra Streisand appeared in *Funny Girl,* biopic of Fanny Brice. Diana Ross appeared in *Lady Sings the Blues.* From the French "Mon Homme." Theme song of Fanny Brice.

My Man's Gone Now 1935 m. DuBose Heyward m. George Gershwin. (MT) *Porgy and Bess.* (MF) *Porgy and Bess.*

My Maria 1973 w.m. Daniel Moore

My Mariuccia Take a Steamboat 1906 w. George Ronklyn m. Al Piantodosi

My Melancholy Baby 1912 w. George A. Norton m. Ernie Burnett. (MF) *Birth of the Blues.* (MF) *Both Ends of the Candle.* Bing Crosby and Mary Martin appeared in *Birth of the Blues.* This song was popularly revived in 1927. This song was originally titled "Melancholy" and was first performed at Denver's Dutch Mill. Theme song of Tommy Lyman.

My Melody of Love 1974 w.m. Bobby Vinton, Henry Mayer, George Buschor

My Moonlight Madonna 1933 w. Paul Francis Webster m. William Scotti. Based on ''Poème'' by Zdenek Fibich.

My Mother Bids Me Bind My Hair 1799 w. Mrs. Anne Hunter (Home) m. Joseph Haydn

My Mother Was a Lady, *see* **Mother Was a Lady**

My Mother's Bible 1841 w. George Pope Morris m. Henry Russell

My Mother's Bible 1893 w. M.B. Williams m. Charles D. Tillman

My Mother's Eyes 1929 w. L. Wolfe Gilbert m. Abel Baer. (MF) *Lucky Boy*. George Jessel and Gwen Lee appeared in *Lucky Boy*. Theme song of George Jessel.

My Mother's Lullaby 1917 w. Charles Louis Ruddy m. Harold Brown Freeman

My Mother's Rosary 1915 w. Sam M. Lewis m. George W. Meyer

My Nellie's Blue Eyes 1883 w.m. William J. Scanlan. (MF) *My Wild Irish Rose*. Dennis Morgan and Arlene Dahl appeared in *My Wild Irish Rose*. The chorus of this song is based on the Venetian folksong ''Vieni sul Mar'' (Come to the Sea).

My Old Aunt Sally 1843 w.m. Old Dan D. Emmit (Daniel Decatur Emmett)

My Old Dutch 1901 w.m. Albert Chevalier, Charles Ingle

My Old Flame 1934 w.m. Arthur Johnston, Sam Coslow. (MF) *Belle of the Nineties*. Mae West and Duke Ellington appeared in *Belle of the Nineties*.

My Old Kentucky Home (Good Night) 1853 w.m. Stephen Collins Foster. (MF) *Swanee River*. (MF) *I Dream of Jeanie*. Al Jolson and Don Ameche appeared in *Swanee River*. Ray Middleton and Bill Shirley appeared in *I Dream of Jeanie*.

My Old Man's a Dustman 1960 w.m. Lonnie Donegan

My Old New Hampshire Home 1898 w. Andrew B. Sterling m. Harry Von Tilzer

My One and Only 1927 w. Ira Gershwin m. George Gershwin. (MT) *Funny Face*. (MT) *My One and Only*. (MF) *Funny Face*. Fred Astaire, Adele Astaire, and Victor Moore appeared in the stage production of *Funny Face*. Tommy Tune and Twiggy appeared in *My One and Only*. Fred Astaire and Audrey Hepburn appeared in the film production of *Funny Face*.

My One and Only Heart 1953 w. Al Stillman w. Robert Allen

My One and Only Highland Fling 1949 w. Ira Gershwin m. Harry Warren. (MF) *The Barkleys of Broadway*. Fred Astaire, Ginger Rogers, and Billie Burke appeared in *The Barkleys of Broadway*.

My One and Only Love 1953 w.m. Guy Wood, Robert Mellin. Based on Anton Rubinstein's ''Romance.''

My Own 1938 w. Harold Adamson m. Jimmy McHugh. (MF) *That Certain Age*. Deanna Durbin and Jackie Cooper appeared in *That Certain Age*.

My Own Best Friend 1975 w. Fred Ebb m. John Kan-

der. (MT) *Chicago*. Chita Rivera and Gwen Verdon appeared in *Chicago*.

My Own Iona 1916 w. L. Wolfe Gilbert m. Anatole Friedland, Carey Morgan

My Own True Love, *see* **Tara's Theme**

My Own United States 1909 w. Stanislaus Stange m. Julian Edwards. (MT) *When Johnny Comes Marching Home*.

My Paradise 1942 w.m. Harry Parr-Davies. (MT) *Gangway*. Anne Ziegler and Webster Booth appeared in *Gangway*.

My Pearl's a Bowery Girl 1894 w. William Jerome m. Andrew Mack

My Pet Brunette, *see* **Negra Consentida**

My Pony Boy 1909 w. Bobby Health m. Charles O'Donnell. (MT) *Miss Innocence*.

My Prayer 1939 w. Jimmy Kennedy m. Georges Boulanger. Based on Georges Boulanger's ''Avant de Mourir,'' op. 17, of 1926. This song was popularly revived in 1956.

My Pretty Jane, *see* **The Bloom Is on the Rye**

My Quiet Village 1959 w. Mel Leven m. Les Baxter

My Rambler Rose 1922 w. Gene Buck m. Louis A. Hirsch, Dave Stamper. (MT) *Ziegfeld Follies of 1922*.

My Resistance Is Low 1951 w. Harold Adamson m. Hoagy Carmichael. (F) *The Las Vegas Story*. Jane Russell and Victor Mature appeared in *The Las Vegas Story*.

My Restless Lover 1954 w.m. Pembroke Davenport

My Reverie 1938 w.m. Larry Clinton. Based on Claude Debussy's ''Reverie'' of 1895.

My Rocking Horse Ran Away, *see* **His Rocking Horse Ran Away**

My Romance 1935 w. Lorenz Hart m. Richard Rodgers. (MT) *Jumbo*. (MF) *Jumbo*. Jimmy Durante and Gloria Grafton appeared in the stage production of *Jumbo*.

My Rosary of Dreams 1911 w.m. E.F. Dusenberry, C.M. Denison

My San Domingo Maid 1903 w. Henry Blossom m. Alfred George Robyn. (MT) *The Yankee Consul*.

My Scotch Bluebell, *see* **I Love a Lassie**

My September Love 1956 w.m. Tolchard Evans, Richard Mullan. Ivor Novello Award winner 1956.

My Sharona 1979 w.m. Berton Averre, Douglas Fieger

My Shawl 1934 Sp.w. Pedro Berrios Eng.w. Stanley Adams m. Xavier Cugat. This song was popularly revived in 1945.

My Shining Hour 1943 w. Johnny Mercer m. Harold Arlen. (MF) *The Sky's the Limit*. Fred Astaire, Robert Benchley, and Joan Leslie appeared in *The Sky's the Limit*.

My Ship 1941 w. Ira Gershwin m. Kurt Weill. (MT) *Lady in the Dark*. (MF) *Lady in the Dark*. Gertrude Lawrence, Victor Mature, and Danny Kaye appeared in the stage production of *Lady in the Dark*. Ginger Rogers appeared in the film production of *Lady in the Dark*.

My Silent Love 1932 w.m. Edward Heyman, Dana Suesse

My Sin 1929 w.m. B.G. DeSylva, Lew Brown, Ray Henderson. (MF) *The Best Things in Life Are Free*. Gordon

MacRae, Dan Dailey, and Ernest Borgnine appeared in *The Best Things in Life Are Free,* biopic of song writers DeSylva, Brown, and Henderson.

My Sister and I   1941   w.m. Alex C. Kramer, Joan Whitney, Hy Zaret

My Son, My Son   1954   w.m. Eddie Calvert, Melville Farley, Bob Howard

My Song   1931   w. B.G. DeSylva, Lew Brown   m. Ray Henderson. (MT) *George White's Scandals of 1931 (Eleventh Edition).* (MF) *Chip off the Old Block.* Donald O'Connor and Helen Broderick appeared in *Chip off the Old Block.*

My Song Goes Round the World   1933   w.m. Hans May, Ernst Neubach, Jimmy Kennedy. (MF) *My Song Goes Round the World.* Josef Schmidt appeared in *My Song Goes Round the World.*

My Song of the Nile   1929   w. Al Bryan   m. George W. Meyer. (F) *Drag.*

My Southern Rose   1909   w.m. Earl Taylor

My Spanish Rose   1920   w. Anne Caldwell   m. Jose Padilla. (MT) *The Night Boat.*

My Special Angel   1957   w.m. Jimmy Duncan

My Sugar Is So Refined   1946   w. Sylvia Dee, Josephine Proffitt   m. Sidney Lippman

My Summer Love   1963   w.m. Mort Garson, Bob Hilliard

My Sunny Tennessee   1921   w.m. Bert Kalmar, Harry Ruby, Herman Ruby. (MT) *The Midnight Rounders, 1921.* (MF) *Three Little Words.* Eddie Cantor and Jane Green appeared in *The Midnight Rounders, 1921.* Fred Astaire and Red Skelton appeared in *Three Little Words,* biopic of song writers Bert Kalmar and Harry Ruby.

My Sunshine Jane   1917   w. J. Keirn Brennan   m. Ernest R. Ball

My Sweet Adair   1915   w.m. L. Wolfe Gilbert, Anatole Friedland

(Say Has Anybody Seen) My Sweet Gypsy Rose   1973   w.m. Irwin Levine, L. Russell Brown

My Sweet Lord   1971   w.m. George Harrison. Ivor Novello Award winner 1971–72. George Harrison was judged responsible for unintentional infringement of copyright in a lawsuit filed on behalf of Ronald Mack for his song "He's So Fine," the 1962 hit recording by The Chiffons.

My Sweeter Than Sweet   1929   w. George Marion, Jr.   m. Richard A. Whiting. (MF) *Sweetie.* Nancy Carroll and Helen Kane appeared in *Sweetie.*

My Sweetheart's the Man in the Moon   1892   w.m. James Thornton

My Sweetie Turned Me Down   1925   w. Gus Kahn   m. Walter Donaldson

My Sweetie Went Away (She Didn't Say Where, When or Why)   1923   w.m. Roy Turk, Lou Handman

My Task   1903   w. Maude Louise Ray   m. Emma L. Ashford (Hindle)

My Thanks to You   1950   w.m. Norman Newell, Noel Gay

My Time Is Your Time   1924   w.m. R.S. Hooper, H.M. Tennat. (R) *Fleischmann Hour.* This song was used as the opening and closing theme by Rudy Vallee for the radio broadcast program the *Fleischmann Hour,* beginning in October 1929.

My Time of Day   1950   w.m. Frank Loesser. (MT) *Guys and Dolls.* (MF) *Guys and Dolls.* Frank Sinatra and Marlon Brando appeared in the film production of *Guys and Dolls.*

My Toot Toot   1986   w.m. Sidney Simien

My Toreador   1920   Sp.w. Armando Oliveros Millan, José Na Castellvi García Eng.w. William Cary Duncan   m. José Padilla. From the Spanish "El Relicario." This song was popularly revived in 1926.

My Truly, Truly Fair   1951   w.m. Bob Merrill

My Trundle Bed, or, **Recollections of Childhood**   1860   w. anon.   m. John C. Baker

My Twilight Dream   1939   w.m. Lew Sherwood, Eddy Duchin. Based on Chopin's Nocturne in E-flat. Theme song of Eddy Duchin.

My Unfinished Symphony   1956   w.m. Milton Carson. Ivor Novello Award winner 1956.

My Very Good Friend the Milkman   1935   w.m. Johnny Burke, Harold Spina

My Way   1969   w. Paul Anka   m. Claude François, Jacques Revaux, Giles Thibaut. From the French "Mon Habitude." This song was popularly revived in 1978.

My White Knight   1957   w.m. Meredith Wilson. (MT) *The Music Man.* (MF) *The Music Man.* Robert Preston appeared in both the stage and film productions of *The Music Man.*

My Wife's Gone to the Country (Hurrah! Hurrah!)   1913   w. George Whiting, Irving Berlin   m. Ted Snyder

My Wild Irish Rose   1899   w.m. Chauncey Olcott. (MT) *A Romance of Athlone.* (MF) *My Wild Irish Rose.* Dennis Morgan and Arlene Dahl appeared in *My Wild Irish Rose.* Theme song of Chauncey Olcott.

My Woman, My Woman, My Wife   1970   w.m. Marty Robbins. Grammy Award winner 1970.

My Wonderful Dream Girl   1913   w. Oliver Morosco   m. Victor Schertzinger

My Wonderful One, *see* **Wonderful One**

My Word You Do Look Queer   1922   w.m. R.P. Weston, Bert Lee

My Yiddishe Momme   1925   w. Jack Yellen   m. Jack Yellen, Lew Pollack

Mysterioso Pizzicato   1914   m. edited J. Bodewalt Lampe. This melody was traditionally used as backround music for scary scenes during the silent movie era.

Mysterious Mose   1930   w.m. Walter Doyle

Mystery Girl   1961   w.m. Trevor Peacock

Mystery Lady   1985   w.m. Keith Diamond

'N Everything   1919   w.m. Al Jolson, B.G. DeSylva, Gus Kahn. (MT) *Tails Up.*

Na Na Hey Hey Kiss Him Goodbye   1969   w.m. Gary De Carlo, Paul Leka, Dale Frashver

Nadia's Theme, or, **The Young and the Restless**   1976   w.m. Perry Botkin, Jr., Barry De Vorzon

Nagasaki   1928   w. Mort Dixon   m. Harry Warren

Name Game, The 1964 w.m. Lincoln Chase, Shirley El-liston

Namely You 1956 w. Johnny Mercer m. Gene De Paul. (MT) *Li'l Abner*. (MF) *Li'l Abner*. Stubby Kaye appeared in the film production of *Li'l Abner*.

Nancy (with the Laughing Face) 1944 w.m. Phil Silvers, Jimmy Van Heusen

Nancy Brown 1901 w.m. Clifton Crawford

Nancy Lee 1875 w. Frederick Edward Weatherly m. Ste-phen Adams (Michael Maybrick)

Nancy Till 1851 w.m. anon.; erroneously credited to Ste-phen Collins Foster

Napoleon's a Pastry 1937 w. E.Y. Harburg m. Harold Arlen. (MT) *Hooray for What!* (MT) *Jamaica*. Ed Wynn and Paul Haakon appeared in *Hooray for What!* The original words to this song from the 1937 score *Hooray for What!* were adapted for the 1957 *Jamaica*, by the same team.

Narcissus 1891 m. Ethelbert Nevin. From "Water Scenes," op.13, no.4.

Nat'an, Nat'an, Nat'an, Tell Me for What Are You Wai-tin', Nat'an 1916 w.m. James Kendis

National Emblem (March) 1906 m. E.E. Bagley. This melody is performed traditionally at circuses throughout the world. Parodied as "And (When) the Monkey Wrapped Its Tail Around the Flagpole."

Native New Yorker 1978 w.m. Sandy Linzer, Denny Ran-dell

Natural High 1973 w.m. Charles McCormick

(You Make Me Feel Like) Natural Woman, A 1967 w.m. Jerry Wexler, Gerry Goffin, Carole King

Nature Boy 1948 w.m. Eden Ahbez. Possibly based on Herman Yablokoff's Yiddish song "Schweig Mein Hartz" (Be Calm, My Heart) and a traditional black American spir-itual, "Sweet Jesus Boy."

Naughty Lady of Shady Lane, The 1954 w.m. Sid Tep-per, Roy C. Bennett

Naughty Naughty Naughty 1916 w.m. Egbert Van Al-styne, Harry H. Williams. (MT) *Show of Wonders*.

Navajo 1903 w. Harry H. Williams m. Egbert Van Al-styne. (MT) *Nancy Brown*.

Navy Gets the Gravy and the Army Gets the Beans, The 1950 w.m. Mack David, Jerry Livingston. (MF) *At War with the Army*. Dean Martin, Jerry Lewis, and Polly Bergen appeared in *At War with the Army*.

Nazareth 1862 Fr.w. A. Porte Eng.w. Henry Fothergill Chorley m. Charles Gounod. From the French "Jésus de Nazareth."

Neapolitan Love Song 1915 w. Henry Blossom, Jr. m. Victor Herbert. (MT) *The Princess Pat*. (MF) *The Great Vic-tor Herbert*. Eleanor Painter and Sam Hardy appeared in *The Princess Pat*. Mary Martin and Allan Jones appeared in *The Great Victor Herbert*.

Neapolitan Nights 1925 w. Harry D. Kerr m. J.S. Za-mecnik

(Jesus Keep Me) Near the Cross 1867 w. Frances Jane Crosby (Mrs. Alexander Van Alstyne) m. William Howard Doane

Near You 1947 w. Kermit Goell m. Francis Craig. (TV) *Texaco Hour*. Theme song of Francis Craig and Milton Berle.

Nearer, My God, to Thee 1859 w. Sarah Adams (Flower); words from 1841 m. based on the hymn "Bethany"; arr. Lowell Mason

Nearness of You, The 1940 w. Ned Washington m. Hoagy Carmichael

'Neath the South Sea Moon 1922 w.m. Gene Buck, Louis A. Hirsch, Dave Stamper. (MT) *Ziegfeld Follies of 1922*.

Necessity 1946 w. E.Y. Harburg m. Burton Lane. (MT) *Finian's Rainbow*.

Needle in a Haystack, A 1934 w. Herb Magidson m. Con Conrad. (MF) *The Gay Divorcee*. This song did not appear in the original stage production of *Gay Divorce*.

Negra Consentida (My Pet Brunette) 1929 Eng.w. Mar-jorie Harper Sp.w.m. Joaquin Pardove. This song was pop-ularly revived in 1945.

Neither One of Us (Wants To Be the First To Say Goodbye) 1973 w.m. Jim Weatherly

Nel Blu Dipinto Di Blu, *see* Volare

Nellie Dean 1906 w.m. Harry Armstrong

Nellie Kelly, I Love You 1922 w.m. George M. Cohan. (MT) *Little Nellie Kelly*. (MT) *George M!*. George M. Co-han appeared in *Little Nellie Kelly*. Joel Grey and Bernadette Peters appeared in *George M!*.

Nellie the Elephant 1956 w.m. Peter Hart, Ralph Butler. Ivor Novello Award winner 1956.

Nelly Bly 1849 w.m. Stephen Collins Foster. (F) *Overland Telegraph*. Tim Holt and Richard Martin appeared in *Over-land Telegraph*.

Nelly Was a Lady 1849 w.m. Stephen Collins Foster

Nestin' Time in Flatbush 1917 w. P.G. Wodehouse m. Jerome Kern. (MT) *Oh, Boy!*.

Neutron Dance 1985 w.m. Danny Sembello, Allee Willis

Never 1951 w.m. Eliot Daniel, Lionel Newman. (MF) *Golden Girl*. Mitzi Gaynor, Dale Robertson, and Dennis Day appeared in *Golden Girl*.

Never 1986 w.m. Gene Black, Holly Knight, Ann Wilson, Nancy Wilson

Never Be Anyone Else But You 1959 w.m. Baker Knight

Never Been So Loved in All My Life 1981 w.m. Wayland Holyfield, Norro Wilson

Never Can Say Goodbye 1971 w.m. Clifton Davis

Never Do a Tango with an Eskimo 1956 w.m. Tommie Connor

Never Ending Song of Love 1972 w.m. D. Bramlett

Never Gonna Fall in Love Again 1976 w.m. Eric Carmen

Never Gonna Let You Go 1983 w.m. Cynthia Weil, Barry Mann

Never Goodbye 1962 w.m. Jimmy Kennedy

Never in a Million Years 1937 w. Mack Gordon m. Harry Revel. (MF) *Wake Up and Live*. Walter Winchell and Alice Faye appeared in *Wake Up and Live*.

Never Knew Love Like This Before 1980 w.m. Reggie Lucas, James Mtume. Grammy Award winner 1980.

Never Let Her Go 1952 w.m. Kay Twomey, Fred Wise, Ben Weisman

Never Mind 1959 w.m. Ian Samwell

Never My Love 1967 w.m. Donald J. Addrisi, Richard P. Addrisi

Never Never Land 1954 w. Betty Comden, Adolph Green m. Jule Styne. (MT) *Peter Pan.* Mary Martin appeared in *Peter Pan.*

Never on Sunday 1960 Greek w. Manos Hadjidakis Eng.w. Billy Towne m. Manos Hadjidakis. (F) *Never on Sunday.* (MT) *Illya Darling.* Melina Mercouri appeared in *Never on Sunday.* Academy Award winner 1960.

Never Said a Mumblin' Word 1865 w.m. traditional black American spiritual

Never Say Goodbye 1943 w.m. Harry Parr-Davies, Harold Purcell. (MT) *Lisbon Story.* (MF) *Lisbon Story.* Patricia Burke appeared in the stage production of *Lisbon Story.* Richard Tauber appeared in the film production of *Lisbon Story.*

Never Say No 1960 w. Tom Jones m. Harvey Schmidt. (MT) *The Fantasticks.*

Never Surrender 1985 w.m. Corey Hart

Never Take No for an Answer 1886 w.m. J.F. Mitchell

Never Take the Horse Shoe from the Door 1880 w. Edward Harrigan m. David Braham. (MT) *The Mulligan Guards' Surprise.*

Nevertheless (I'm In Love with You) 1931 w.m. Bert Kalmar, Harry Ruby. (MF) *Three Little Words.* Red Skelton, Fred Astaire, and Debbie Reynolds appeared in *Three Little Words,* biopic of song writers Bert Kalmar and Harry Ruby.

New Attitude 1985 w.m. Bunny Hull, Sharon Robinson, Jonathan Gilutin. (F) *Beverly Hills Cop.* Eddie Murphy appeared in *Beverly Hills Cop.*

New-Fangled Tango, A 1957 w. Matt Dubey m. Harold Karr. (MT) *Happy Hunting.*

(Theme from) New Kind of Love, A 1963 w.m. Erroll Garner. (F) *A New Kind of Love.* Paul Newman and Joanne Woodward appeared in *A New Kind of Love.*

New Kind of Love, A see also **You Brought a New Kind of Love to Me**

New Sun in the Sky 1931 w. Howard Dietz m. Arthur Schwartz. (MT) *The Band Wagon.* (MF) *Dancing in the Dark.* (MF) *The Band Wagon.* Fred Astaire, Adele Astaire, and Frank Morgan appeared in the stage production of *The Band Wagon.* William Powell, Betsy Drake, and Adolphe Menjou appeared in *Dancing in the Dark.* Fred Astaire and Nanette Fabray appeared in the film production of *The Band Wagon.*

New World in the Morning 1970 w.m. Roger Whittaker

New World Symphony, see **From the New World Symphony**

New York, New York 1945 w. Betty Comden, Adolph Green m. Leonard Bernstein. (MT) *On the Town.* (MF) *On the Town.* Nancy Walker and Chris Alexander appeared in the stage production of *On the Town.* Gene Kelly, Ann Miller, and Frank Sinatra appeared in the film production of *On the Town.*

Next Time 1963 w.m. Buddy Kaye, Philip Springer. (MF) *Summer Holiday.* Cliff Richard and Lauri Peters appeared in *Summer Holiday.*

Next to Your Mother, Who Do You Love? 1909 w. Irving Berlin m. Ted Snyder

Nicaea, see **Holy! Holy! Holy! Lord God Almighty**

Nice 'n' Easy 1960 w.m. Lew Spence, Alan Bergman, Marilyn Keith

Nice Cup of Tea, A 1937 w.m. A.P. Herbert, Henry Sullivan. (MT) *Home and Beauty.* Binnie Hale appeared in *Home and Beauty.*

Nice One Cyril 1974 w.m. Harold Spiro, Helen Clarke. Ivor Novello Award winner 1973–74.

Nice People (with Nice Habits) 1938 w.m. Nat Mills, Fred Malcolm. (MT) *These Foolish Things.*

Nice To Know You Care 1948 w.m. Norman Newell, Leslie Baguley

Nice Work If You Can Get It 1937 w. Ira Gershwin m. George Gershwin. (MT) *My One and Only.* (MF) *A Damsel in Distress.* (MF) *An American in Paris.* Tommy Tune and Twiggy appeared in *My One and Only.* Fred Astaire and George Burns and Gracie Allen appeared in *A Damsel in Distress.* Leslie Caron and Gene Kelly appeared in *An American in Paris.*

Nichavo!, op.66 1921 w. Helene Jerome m. Mlle. Mana Zucca

Nicodemus Johnson 1865 w. anon. m. J.B. Murphy

Nicola 1962 w.m. Steve Race. Ivor Novello Award winner 1962

Night 1960 w.m. Johnny Lehman, Herb Miller

Night and Day 1932 w.m. Cole Porter. (MT) *Gay Divorce.* (MF) *The Gay Divorcee.* (MF) *Night and Day.* (F) *Lady on a Train.* Grace Moore and Fred Astaire appeared in the stage production of *Gay Divorce.* Fred Astaire Ginger Rogres, Ginger Rogers, and Edward Everett Horton appeared in the film production of *The Gay Divorcee.* Cary Grant, Alexis Smith, and Mary Martin appeared in *Night and Day.* Deanna Durbin and Ralph Bellamy appeared in *Lady on a Train.*

Night Chicago Died, The 1974 w.m. Mitch Murray, Peter Callander. Ivor Novello Award winner 1974–75.

Night Fever 1978 w.m. Barry Gibb, Maurice Gibb, Robin Gibb. (MF) *Saturday Night Fever.* John Travolta appeared in *Saturday Night Fever.*

Night Has a Thousand Eyes, The 1948 w. Buddy Bernier m. Jerry Brainin. (F) *The Night Has a Thousand Eyes.* Edward G. Robinson and Virginia Bruce appeared in *The Night Has a Thousand Eyes.* This song was popularly revived in 1962.

Night Has a Thousand Eyes, The 1963 w.m. Marilyn Garrett, Dottie Wayne, Ben Weisman. (F) *Just for Fun.*

(Give Me) Night in June, A 1927 w.m. Cliff Friend

Night Is Filled with Music, The 1938 w.m. Irving Berlin. (MF) *Carefree.* Fred Astaire and Ginger Rogers appeared in *Carefree.*

Night Is Young and You're So Beautiful, The 1936 w. Irving Kahal, Billy Rose m. Dana Suesse. (MT) *And On We Go.*

Night May Have Its Sadness 1921 w.m. Ivor Novello, Collie Knox. (MT) *Andre Charlot's Revue of 1924.* Gertrude Lawrence and Beatrice Lillie appeared in *Andre Charlot's Revue of 1924.*

Night on Bald Mountain, A 1887 m. Modeste Mussorgsky. (MF) *Fantasia.* See also ''Night on Disco Mountain.''

Night on Disco Mountain 1977 w.m. arr. David Shire. (MF) *Saturday Night Fever.* John Travolta appeared in *Saturday Night Fever.* Based on Modeste Mussorgsky's ''Night on Bald Mountain'' of 1887.

Night the Floor Fell In, The 1950 w.m. Ken Wheeley

Night the Lights Went Out in Georgia, The 1973 w.m. Bobby Russell

Night They Invented Champagne, The 1958 w. Alan Jay Lerner m. Frederick Loewe. (MF) *Gigi.* Leslie Caron, Hermione Gingold, and Maurice Chevalier appeared in *Gigi.*

Night Train 1952 w.m. Jimmy Forrest, Oscar Washington, Lewis C. Simpkins

Night Waltz 1973 w.m. Stephen Sondheim. (MT) *A Little Night Music.* (MF) *A Little Night Music.* Glynnis Johns, Len Cariou, and Hermione Gingold appeared in the stage production of *A Little Night Music.* Elizabeth Taylor, Len Cariou, and Hermione Gingold appeared in the film production of *A Little Night Music.*

Night Was Made for Love, The 1931 w. Otto Harbach m. Jerome Kern. (MT) *The Cat and the Fiddle.* (MF) *The Cat and the Fiddle.* Bettina Hall and George Metaxa appeared in the American stage production of *The Cat and the Fiddle.* Peggy Wood appeared in the British stage production of *The Cat and the Fiddle.* Jeanette MacDonald and Charles Butterworth appeared in the film production of *The Cat and the Fiddle.*

Night We Called It a Day, The 1944 w.m. Thomas Adair, Matt Dennis. (MF) *Sing a Jingle.* Allan Jones and Edward Norris appeared in *Sing a Jingle.* This song was popularly revived in 1955.

Nightingale 1942 w.m. Xavier Cugat, George Rosner, Fred Wise

Nightingale 1975 w.m. Carole King, David Palmer

Nightingale Sang in Berkeley Square, A 1940 w.m. Eric Maschwitz, Manning Sherwin, Jack Strachey

Nightowls 1981 w.m. Graham Goble

Nights in White Satin 1972 w.m. David Justin Hayward

Nights of Gladness 1913 w. Ballard MacDonald m. Charles Ancliffe

Nights of Splendor, *see* **Neapolitan Nights**

Nightshift 1985 w.m. Walter Orange

Nightshift 1985 w.m. Franhie Goldie, Dennis Lambert

Nikita 1986 w.m. Elton John, Bernie Taupin. Ivor Novello Award winner 1985–86.

Nina 1945 w.m. Noël Coward. (MT) *Sigh No More.* (MF) *The Pirate.* Judy Garland and Gene Kelly appeared in *The Pirate.*

Nina Never Knew 1952 w.m. Louis Alter, Milton Drake

Nina Rosa 1929 w. Irving Caesar m. Sigmund Romberg. (MT) *Nina Rosa.* Ethelind Terry and Guy Robertson appeared in *Nina Rosa.*

Nine 1982 w.m. Maury Yeston. (MT) *Nine.* Liliane Montevecchi and Anita Morris appeared in *Nine.*

9 to 5 1981 w.m. Dolly Parton. (F) *9 to 5.* Jane Fonda, Dolly Parton, and Lilly Tomlin appeared in *9 to 5.* Grammy Award winner 1981.

19 1986 w.m. Bill Couturie, Paul Hardcastle, Jonas McCormick, Mike Oldfield. Ivor Novello Award winner 1985–86.

Nineteenth Nervous Breakdown 1966 w.m. Mick Jagger, Keith Richard

Ninety and Nine, The 1876 w. Elizabeth C. Clephane m. Ira David Sankey

99 Luftballons 1984 w.m. Carlos Karges, Petersen Fahrenkrog, Kevin MacAlea

Ninety-Nine Out of a Hundred (Want To Be Loved) 1930 w.m. Al Lewis, Al Sherman

Ninety-Six Tears 1966 w.m. Rudy Martins

Nitty Gritty, The 1963 w.m. Lincoln Chase

No Bad News 1975 w.m. Charlie Smalls. (MT) *The Wiz.* (MF) *The Wiz.* Stephanie Mills, Mabel King, and Ted Ross appeared in the stage production of *The Wiz.* Diana Ross and Mabel King appeared in the film production of *The Wiz.*

No Can Do 1945 w. Charlie Tobias m. Nat Simon

No Can Do, *see also* **I Can't Go for That**

(There's) No Gettin' Over Me 1981 w.m. Tom Brasfield, James Walton Aldridge, Jr.

No Greater Love 1961 w.m. Michael Carr, Bunny Lewis. Ivor Novello Award winner 1961.

No Greater Love, *see also* **There Is No Greater Love**

No Honestly! 1975 w.m. Lynsey de Paul. Ivor Novello Award winner 1974–75.

No Love, No Nothing 1943 w. Leo Robin m. Harry Warren. (MF) *The Girls He Left Behind.* (MF) *The Gang's All Here.* Alice Faye appeared in *The Girls He Left Behind.* Alice Faye and Carmen Miranda appeared in *The Gang's All Here.*

No Matter How I Try 1972 w.m. Ray O'Sullivan. Ivor Novello Award winner 1971–72.

No Milk Today 1948 w.m. Graham Goodman

No Moon at All 1948 w. Redd Evans m. Dave Mann. This song was most popular in 1952.

No More 1955 w.m. Leo De John, Julie De John, Dux De John

No More Love on the Run, *see* **Caribbean Queen**

No More Lonely Nights 1985 w.m. Paul McCartney

No More Tears (Enough Is Enough) 1980 w.m. Paul Jabara, Bruce Roberts

No Night So Long 1980 w.m. Will Jennings, Richard Kerr

No! No! A Thousand Times No! 1934 w.m. Al Sherman, Al Lewis, Abner Silver

No, No, Nora 1923 Fr.w. Paul Combis Eng.w. Gus Kahn

m. Ted Fiorito, Ernie Erdman. (MF) *I'll See You in My Dreams.* Doris Day and Danny Thomas appeared in *I'll See You in My Dreams,* biopic of song writer Gus Kahn. From the French "Non, Non, Nora."

No No Song   1975   w.m. Hoyt Axton, David Jackson, Jr.

No, Not Much   1956   w. Al Stillman   m. Robert Allen

No One Ever Loved You More Than I   1896   w. Edward B. Marks   m. Joseph W. Stern

No One Is To Blame   1986   w.m. Howard Jones

No Orchids for My Lady   1948   w.m. Jack Strachey, Alan Stranks. (MT) *Bolton's Revue.*

No Other Arms, No Other Lips   1959   w.m. Joan Whitney, Alex Kramer, Hy Zaret

No Other Love   1953   w. Oscar Hammerstein II   m. Richard Rodgers. (MT) *Me and Juliet.* (TV) *Cinderella.* Based on Rodgers's "Beneath the Southern Cross" from the TV documentary *Victory at Sea.*

No Regrets   1936   w. Harry Tobias   m. Roy Ingraham

No Strings (I'm Fancy Free)   1935   w.m. Irving Berlin. (MF) *Top Hat.* Fred Astaire, Ginger Rogers, and Helen Broderick appeared in *Top Hat.*

No Strings   1962   w.m. Richard Rodgers. (MT) *No Strings.* Diahann Carroll appeared in *No Strings.*

No Tell Lover   1979   w.m. Peter Cetera, Lee Loughnane, Daniel Seraphine

No Two People   1952   w.m. Frank Loesser. (MF) *Hans Christian Andersen.* Danny Kaye appeared in *Hans Christian Andersen.*

No Wedding Bells for Me   1907   w.m. E.P. Moran, Will A. Heelan, Seymour Furth. At the end of this song is a direct quotation from Mendelssohn's "Wedding March."

Noah's Ark, *see* **There's One Wide River To Cross**

Nobody   1905   w. Alex Rogers   m. Bert A. Williams

Nobody   1982   w.m. Rhonda J. Fleming, Dennis Morgan

Nobody But You   1919   w. B.G. DeSylva   m. George Gershwin. (MT) *La La Lucille.*

Nobody Does It Better   1977   w.m. Carole Bayer Sager, Marvin Hamlisch

Nobody Else But Me   1946   w. Oscar Hammerstein II   m. Jerome Kern. (MT) *Show Boat* (1945 revival). (MF) *Show Boat* (1951). This song was added to the 1945 revival production of *Show Boat,* and was the last song written by Jerome Kern.

Nobody Knows and Nobody Seems To Care   1919   w.m. Irving Berlin

Nobody Knows De Trouble I've Seen   1917   w.m. based on a traditional black American spiritual known as early as 1865; arr. Henry Thacker Burleigh

Nobody Knows, Nobody Cares   1909   w.m. Charles K. Harris

Nobody Knows the Trouble I've Seen, *see* **Nobody Knows De Trouble I've Seen**

Nobody Knows What a Red Head Mama Can Do   1925   w.m. Irving Mills, Al Dubin, Sammy Fain

Nobody Knows You When You're Down and Out   1923

w.m. James Cox. (MT) *Me and Bessie.* Linda Hopkins appeared in *Me and Bessie.*

Nobody Loves a Fairy When She's Forty   1934   w.m. Arthur W.D. Henley

Nobody Loves Me Like You Do   1984   w.m. James Dunne, Pam Phillips

Nobody Told Me   1962   w.m. Richard Rodgers. (MT) *No Strings.*

Nobody Told Me   1984   w.m. John Lennon

Nobody Wants Me   1926   w.m. Morrie Ryskind, Henry Souvaine. (MT) *Americana, 1926.*

Nobody's Chasing Me   1950   w.m. Cole Porter. (MT) *Out of This World.* Charlotte Greenwood and William Redfield appeared in *Out of This World.*

Nobody's Heart (Belongs to Me)   1942   w. Lorenz Hart   m. Richard Rodgers. (MT) *By Jupiter.* Constance Moore and Ray Bolger appeared in *By Jupiter.*

Nobody's Little Girl   1907   w. Jack Drislane   m. Theodore F. Morse

Nobody's Sweetheart Now   1924   w.m. Gus Kahn, Ernie Erdman, Billy Meyers, Elmer Schoebel. (MF) *I'm Nobody's Sweetheart Now.* (MF) *Red-Headed Woman.* (MF) *I'll See You in My Dreams.* Dennis O'Keefe and Constance Moore appeared in *I'm Nobody's Sweetheart Now.* Jean Harlow and Chester Morris appeared in *Red-Headed Woman.* Doris Day and Danny Thomas appeared in *I'll See You in My Dreams,* biopic of song writer Gus Kahn.

Nocturne, op. 9, no. 2   1832   m. Frédéric Chopin

Nodding Roses   1916   w. Schuyler Greene, Herbert Reynolds   m. Jerome Kern. (MT) *Very Good Eddie.*

Nola   1916   m. Felix Arndt. (MF) *That's the Spirit.* Peggy Ryan and Jack Oakie appeared in *That's the Spirit.* Theme song of Vincent Lopez. Words to this song were later added by Sunny Skylar and another version by James Burns.

Non Dimenticar (Don't Forget)   1953   It.w. Michele Galdieri   Eng.w. Shelley Dobbins   m. P.G. Redi. (F) *Anna.* Silvana Mangano appeared in *Anna.*

Non È Ver, *see* **'Tis Not True**

None But the Lonely Heart, op.6, no.6   1869   m. Peter Tchaikovsky

Nora Malone (Call Me By Phone)   1912   w.m. Albert von Tilzer, Junie McCree. (MF) *The Naughty Nineties.* Abbott and Costello and Rita Johnson appeared in *The Naughty Nineties.*

North to Alaska   1960   w.m. Mike Phillips. (F) *North to Alaska.* John Wayne and Stewart Granger appeared in *North to Alaska.*

North Wind Doth Blow, The, *see* **Mother Goose's Melodies**

Northwest Passage   1945   w.m. Ralph Burns, Woody Herman, Greig Stewart Jackson

Norway   1915   w. Joe McCarthy   m. Fred Fisher

Norwegian Dance, The   1881   m. Edvard Grieg

Norwegian Wood   1966   w.m. John Lennon, Paul McCartney

Not a Day Goes By   1981   w.m. Stephen Sondheim. (MT)

Merrily We Roll Along. Ann Morrison appeared in *Merrily We Roll Along.*

Not for All the Rice in China   1933   w.m. Irving Berlin. (MT) *As Thousands Cheer.*

Not Mine   1942   w.m. Johnny Mercer, Victor Schertzinger. (MF) *The Fleet's In.* Dorothy Lamour, William Holden, and Betty Hutton appeared in *The Fleet's In.*

Not Since Nineveh   1953   w.m. Robert Wright, George Forrest. (MT) *Kismet.* (MF) *Kismet.* Based on the melodies of Alexander Borodin.

Not So Much a Programme, More a Way of Life   1964   w.m. Ron Grainer, Ned Sherrin, Caryl Brahms

Not While I'm Around   1979   w.m. Stephen Sondheim. (MT) *Sweeney Todd.* Angela Lansbury and Len Cariou appeared in *Sweeney Todd.*

Nothing   1975   w. Edward Kleban   m. Marvin Hamlisch. (MT) *A Chorus Line.* Donna McKechnie appeared in *A Chorus Line.*

Nothin' At All   1986   w.m. Mark Mueller

Nothing Can Stop Me Now!   1965   w.m. Leslie Bricusse, Anthony Newley. (MT) *The Roar of the Greasepaint—The Smell of the Crowd.* Cyril Ritchard and Anthony Newley appeared in *The Roar of the Greasepaint—The Smell of the Crowd.*

Nothing from Nothing   1974   w.m. Billy Preston

Nothing Like Falling in Love   1984   w.m. Thom Schuyler, James Schnaars

Nothing New Beneath the Sun   1906   w.m. George M. Cohan

Nothing Rhymed   1971   w.m. Ray O'Sullivan

Now   1936   w. Ted Fetter   m. Vernon Duke. (MT) *The Show Is On.* Beatrice Lillie and Bert Lahr appeared in *The Show Is On.*

Now   1944   w.m. Robert Wright, George Forrest. (MT) *Song of Norway.* Based on the melodies of Grieg.

Now   1968   w.m. Henry Mayer

Now   1973   w.m. Stephen Sondheim. (MT) *A Little Night Music.* (MF) *A Little Night Music.* Glynis Johns, Len Cariou, and Hermione Gingold appeared in the stage production of *A Little Night Music.* Elizabeth Taylor, Len Cariou, and Hermione Gingold appeared in the film production of *A Little Night Music.*

Now and Forever   1941   w.m. Al Stillman, Jan Savitt. Based on the dominant theme from the "Symphonie Pathétique."

Now and Forever (You and Me)   1986   w.m. David Foster, Randy Goodrum, Jim Vallance

Now and Forever   1954   w.m. Johnny May, Walter Rothenberg, Peter Hanse

Now I Lay Me Down To Sleep   1866   w.m. Hattie A. Fox, A.D. Walbridge

Now Is the Hour   1948   w.m. Dorothy Stewart, Maewa Kaihau, Clement Scott. Based on the traditional New Zealand song "Hearere Ra."

Now Is the Month of Maying   1598   w.m. Thomas Morley

Now It Can Be Told   1938   w.m. Irving Berlin. (MF) *Alex-*

ander's Ragtime Band. Tyrone Power and Alice Faye appeared in *Alexander's Ragtime Band.*

Now Sleeps the Crimson Petal   1904   w. Alfred Lord Tennyson   m. Roger Quilter

(Where Are You) Now That I Need You   1949   w.m. Frank Loesser. (MF) *Red, Hot and Blue.* Betty Hutton and Victor Mature appeared in *Red, Hot and Blue.*

Now the Day Is Over   1869   w. Sabine Baring-Gould   m. Joseph Barnby

Now Those Days Are Gone   1983   w.m. Andy Hill, Nichola Martin. Ivor Novello Award winner 1982–83.

Nowhere Man   1966   w.m. John Lennon, Paul McCartney. (MT) *Beatlemania.* (MF) *Yellow Submarine.*

(Potatoes Are Cheaper—Tomatoes Are Cheaper) Now's the Time To Fall in Love   1931   w. Al Lewis   m. Al Sherman. (MF) *The Eddie Cantor Story.*

Number Something Far Away Lane   1943   w.m. Howard Barnes, Hedley Grey, Ord Hamilton

Nunc Dimittis   1980   m. Geoffrey Burgon. Ivor Novello Award winner 1979–80.

Nursie   1939   w.m. Art Noel, Don Pelosi

Nutcracker Suite, The   1892   m. Peter Tchaikovsky. (MF) *Fantasia.* This popular Christmas ballet includes, among other dances, "Dance of the Sugar-Plum Fairy," "Arabian Dance," "Chinese Dance," and "Waltz of the Flowers"; employed by Walt Disney in his animated film *Fantasia.*

N.Y.C.   1977   w. Martin Charnin   m. Charles Strouse. (MT) *Annie.* Dorothy Loudon and Andrea McArdle appeared in *Annie.*

O (Oh!)   1919   w. Byron Gay   m. Byron Gay, Arnold Johnson. This song was popularly revived in 1953.

O Come All Ye Faithful, *see* **Adeste Fidelis**

O Cuba (Tu)   1928   Sp.w. Fernan Sanchez   Eng.w. Frederick Herman Martens   m. Eduardo Sanchez de Fuentes; arr. Charles F. Manney

O Dio Mio   1960   w.m. Al Hoffman, Dick Manning

O Dry Those Tears   1901   w.m. Teresa del Riego

O (Arch) Du Lieber Augustin   1815   w. anon.; published in Austria in 1815   m. anon.; published as early as 1788. The words and music were first published together in 1877. The melody for this song is the same as that for "Molly (Polly) Put the Kettle On" and "Did You Ever See a Lassie." Apparently, in 1679, minstrel Augustin lay stone drunk in the plague pit and yet somehow survived. This song was later adapted for a Curad commercial promotion campaign with the lyric "Mommy put a Curad on."

O Flower Divine   1914   w.m. Edward Teschemacher, Haydn Wood

O God, Our Help in Ages Past   c.1700   w. Isaac Watts   m. William Croft

O Hand Me Down My Walking Cane, *see* **Hand Me Down My Walking Cane**

O (Oh) Happy Day, *see* **How Dry I Am**

O Holy Night, *see* **Christmas Song**

O, Katharina, *see* **Oh, Katharina**

O Leo 1935 w. Howard Dietz m. Arthur Schwartz. (MT) *At Home Abroad.* Beatrice Lillie appeared in *At Home Abroad.*

O Little Town of Bethlehem 1868 w. Phillips Brooks m. Lewis H. Redner. This song was first popularly published in 1920. The words to this hymn were written by the Reverend Mr. Brooks for his Sunday school program at Trinity Church in Boston.

O Mein Papa, *see* **Oh My Papa**

O Sanctissima, *see* **Sicilian Hymn**

O Soldier, Won't You Marry Me? c.1750 w.m. anon.

'O Sole Mio 1899 w. Giovanni Capurro m. Edoardo di Capua. See also "It's Now or Never" and "There's No Tomorrow."

O Tannenbaum, O Tannenbaum!, *see* **Maryland, My Maryland**

O That Will Be Glory for Me, or, **The Glory Song** 1900 w.m. Charles H. Gabriel

O Word of God Incarnate 1867 w. William Walsham How m. Felix Mendelssohn (in 1693)

Oh Babe, What Would You Say 1972 w.m. Hurricane Smith. Ivor Novello Award winner 1972–73.

Oh Baby Mine (I Get So Lonely) 1928 w.m. Pat Ballard. This song was popularly revived in 1954.

Oh, Bess, Oh Where's My Bess 1935 w. Ira Gershwin m. George Gershwin. (MT) *Porgy and Bess.* (MF) *Porgy and Bess.* Sidney Poitier and Sammy Davis, Jr. appeared in the film production of *Porgy and Bess.*

Oh! Boy, What a Girl 1925 w. Bud Green m. Wright, Bessinger. (MT) *Gay Paree.*

Oh Boys Carry Me 'Long 1851 w.m. Stephen Collins Foster

Oh, Bury Me Not on the Lone Prairie, or, **The Dying Cowboy** 1849 w.m. based on the poem "The Ocean Burial" of 1839 by E.H. Chapin, and set to music by George N. Allen in 1849. This song was later adapted to become what is considered now a traditional American cowboy song. This song was popularly revived in 1932.

Oh But I Do 1947 w. Leo Robin m. Arthur Schwartz. (MF) *The Time, the Place and the Girl.* Dennis Morgan and Janis Paige appeared in *The Time, the Place and the Girl.*

Oh By Jingo, Oh By Gee, You're the Only Girl for Me 1919 w.m. Lew Brown, Albert Von Tilzer. (MT) *Linger Longer Letty.* (MF) *Incendiary Blonde.* (MF) *Skirts Ahoy.* Betty Hutton appeared in *Incendiary Blonde,* biopic of speakeasy owner Texas Guinan. Esther Williams and Vivian Blaine appeared in *Skirts Ahoy.*

Oh Charley Take It Away 1925 w.m. Elvin Hedges, Frederick Malcolm, Arthur W.D. Henley

Oh! Dear, What Can the Matter Be 1778 w.m. traditional, from England

Oh Dem Golden Slippers, *see* **Golden Slippers**

Oh, Didn't He Ramble 1902 w.m. Bob Cole, J. Rosamond Johnson; arr. Will Handy in 1945. See also Part I, 1902.

Oh! Didn't It Rain 1923 w.m. Eddie Leonard

Oh Donna Clara 1931 w. Irving Caesar; also Jimmy Kennedy; also Rowland Leigh m. Robert Katscher. (MT) *The Wonder Bar.* Al Jolson and Arthur Treacher appeared in *The Wonder Bar.*

Oh! Frenchy 1918 w. Sam Ehrlich m. Con Conrad. (MF) *The Dolly Sisters.* June Haver and Betty Grable appeared in *The Dolly Sisters.*

Oh Gee, Oh Gosh, Oh Golly I'm in Love 1923 w. Ole Olsen, Chic Johnson m. Ernest Breuer. (MT) *The Ziegfeld Follies* (1923). Eddie Cantor appeared in *The Ziegfeld Follies* (1923)

Oh Girl 1972 w.m. Eugene Record. This song was popularly revived in 1982.

Oh, Give Me a Home Where the Buffalo Roam, *see* **Home on the Range**

Oh, Give Me Something To Remember You By, *see* **Something To Remember You By**

Oh Happy Day 1953 w.m. Nancy Binns Reed, Don Howard Koplow

Oh Happy Day, *see also* **Happy Day**

Oh, How I Hate To Get Up in the Morning 1918 w.m. Irving Berlin. (MT) *Yip! Yip! Yaphank.* (MT) *This Is the Army.* (MF) *Alexander's Ragtime Band.* (MF) *This Is the Army.* Irving Berlin appeared in *Yip! Yaphank* and *This Is the Army.* Tyrone Power and Alice Faye appeared in *Alexander's Ragtime Band.* Ronald Reagan and Kate Smith appeared in *This Is the Army.* Irving Berlin signed the royalties of this song over to Army Emergency Relief.

Oh! How I Laugh When I Think How I Cried About You 1919 w. Roy Turk, George Jessel m. Willy White

Oh! How I Miss You Tonight 1925 w.m. Benny Davis, Joe Burke, Mark Fisher

Oh, How I Wish I Could Sleep Until My Daddy Comes Home 1918 w. Sam M. Lewis, Joe Young m. Pete Wendling

Oh! How She Could Yacki, Hacki, Wicki, Wacki, Woo 1916 w. Stanley Murphy, Charles McCarron m. Albert Von Tilzer. (MT) *The Ziegfeld Follies* (1916). (MT) *Houp-La.* Gertie Millar appeared in *Houp-La.*

Oh, I Can't Sit Down 1935 w. Ira Gershwin m. George Gershwin. (MT) *Porgy and Bess.* (MF) *Porgy and Bess.*

Oh I Love Society, *see* **Society**

Oh! I Must Go Home Tonight 1910 w.m. William Hargreaves

Oh Isn't It Singular 1903 w. J.P. Harrington m. George Le Brunn

Oh Johnny, Oh Johnny, Oh! 1917 w. Ed Rose m. Abe Olman. (MT) *Follow Me.* This song was popularly revived in 1940. Theme song of Bonnie Baker.

Oh Julie 1983 w.m. Shakin Stevens. Ivor Novello Award winner 1982–83.

Oh, Katharina 1924 w. L. Wolfe Gilbert m. Richard Fall. (MT) *Chauve Souris.*

Oh, Lady Be Good 1924 w. Ira Gershwin m. George Gershwin. (MT) *Lady, Be Good.* (MF) *Lady, Be Good.* (MF) *Rhapsody in Blue.* Fred Astaire and Adele Astaire appeared in the stage production of *Lady, Be Good.* Robert Young,

Lionel Barrymore, and Ann Sothern appeared in the film production of *Lady, Be Good*. Oscar Levant, Robert Alda, and Alexis Smith appeared in *Rhapsody in Blue*, biopic of George Gershwin.

Oh Listen to the Band, *see* **Soldiers in the Park**

Oh Lonesome Me 1958 w.m. Don Gibson. This song was popularly revived in 1969.

Oh Look At Me Now 1941 w.m. John de Vries, Joe Bushkin. (MF) *Disc Jockey*. This song was popularly revived in 1952.

Oh Mama, or, **The Butcher Boy** 1938 w.m. Lew Brown, Rudy Vallee

Oh Mamma Mia 1940 w.m. Roma Campbell-Hunter, Freddy Grant

Oh, Mary, Don't You Weep, Don't You Mourn 1865 w.m. traditional black American spiritual

Oh Me! Oh My! Oh You! 1921 w. Arthur Francis (Ira Gershwin) m. Vincent Youmans. (MT) *Two Little Girls in Blue*. (MF) *Tea for Two*. Madeline and Marion Fairbanks and Evelyn Law appeared in *Two Little Girls in Blue*. Doris Day and Gordon MacRae appeared in *Tea for Two*, based on the stage production *No, No, Nanette*.

Oh Me, Oh My, Oh You 1934 w.m. Harold Adamson, Burton Lane. (MF) *Strictly Dynamite*. Jimmy Durante and Lupe Velez appeared in *Strictly Dynamite*.

Oh Miss Hannah 1924 w. Thekla Hollingsworth m. Jessie L. Deppen. This song was popularly revived in 1929.

Oh Monah 1931 w.m. Ted Weems, Country Washburn. Theme song of Lew Stone.

Oh Murphy 1926 w. B.G. DeSylva, Lew Brown m. Ray Henderson

Oh, My Darling Clementine, *see* **Clementine**

Oh My Papa, or, **O Mein Papa** 1953 Ger.w. Paul Burkhard Eng.w. John Turner, Geoffrey Parsons m. Paul Burkhard. (F) *Fireworks*. *Fireworks* was a Swiss film. Theme song of Eddie Calvert.

Oh Nicholas Don't Be So Ridiculous 1939 w.m. Jimmy Kennedy, Harry Castling

Oh No 1981 w.m. Lionel Richie

Oh No, We Never Mention Her 1828 w.m. Thomas Haynes Bayly

Oh Oh Antonio 1908 w.m. C.W. Murphy, Dan Lipton

Oh Peter Go Ring Dem Bells 1918 w.m. based on a traditional black American spiritual, c.1865; arr. Henry Thacker Burleigh

Oh Pretty Woman 1964 w.m. Roy Orbison, William Dees

Oh Promise Me 1890 w. Clement Scott m. Reginald DeKoven. (MT) *Robin Hood*. This song was introduced in the operetta *Robin Hood*, by singer Jessie Bartlett Davis.

Oh Sam 1872 w.m. William Shakespeare Hays

Oh Sheila 1985 w.m. Gerald Valentine, Melvin Riley

Oh Sherrie 1984 w.m. Bill Cuomo, Craig Krampf, Randy Goodrum, Steve Perry

Oh Star of Eve 1922 w.m. Hubert W. David, Ed Bryant

Oh! Susanna 1848 w.m. Stephen Collins Foster. (MF)

Swanee River. (F) *Colorado*. (F) *Overland Telegraph*. (MF) *I Dream of Jeanie*. Al Jolson and Don Ameche appeared in *Swanee River*. Roy Rogers and Gabby Hayes appeared in *Colorado*. Tim Holt and Richard Martin appeared in *Overland Telegraph*. Ray Middleton and Bill Shirley appeared in *I Dream of Jeanie*. This was very popular during the 1849 California Gold Rush. See also Part I, 1849.

Oh, That Beautiful Rag 1910 w. Irving Berlin m. Ted Snyder. (MT) *Up and Down Broadway*.

Oh That We Two Were Maying 1888 w. Charles Kingsley m. Ethelbert Nevin

Oh, the Fairies, Whoa, the Fairies 1878 w.m. W.G. Eaton

Oh What a Beautiful Mornin' 1943 w. Oscar Hammerstein II m. Richard Rodgers (MT) *Oklahoma!*. (MF) *Oklahoma!*. Betty Garde, Alfred Drake, and Celeste Holm appeared in the stage production of *Oklahoma!*. Gordon MacRae and Shirley Jones appeared in the film production of *Oklahoma!*

Oh What a Night I Spent (Time I Had) with Minnie the Mermaid, *see* **Minnie the Mermaid**

Oh! What a Pal Was Mary 1919 w. Edgar Leslie, Bert Kalmar m. Pete Wendling

Oh What It Seemed To Be 1946 w.m. Bennie Benjamin, George Weiss, Frankie Carle

Oh Where, Oh Where, Has My Little Dog Gone, or, **Der Deitcher's Dog** 1864 Eng.w. Septimus Winner m. based on Beethoven's "Symphony Pastorale," 3rd movement (1809), and this based, in turn, on an English traditional dance, c.1260. From the German "Zu Lauterbach."

Oh Why, Oh Why Did I Ever Leave Wyoming, *see* **Wyoming**

Oh You Beautiful Doll 1911 w. A. Seymour Brown m. Nat D. Ayer. (MF) *Wharf Angel*. (MF) *The Story of Vernon and Irene Castle*. (MF) *For Me and My Gal*. (MF) *Oh You Beautiful Doll*. Victor McLaglen and Dorothy Dell appeared in *Wharf Angel* Fred Astaire and Ginger Rogers appeared in *The Story of Vernon and Irene Castle*. Judy Garland and Gene Kelly appeared in *For Me and My Gal*. June Haver appeared in *Oh You Beautiful Doll*. This melody was heard on the Gabriel-trumpet car horns during the 1920s.

Oh You Circus Day 1911 w.m. Edith Lessing, James V. Monaco. (MT) *Hanky Panky*.

Oh You Crazy Moon 1939 w.m. Johnny Burke, Jimmy Van Heusen

Oh You Cutie (You Ever Loving Child) 1912 w. Harry H. Williams m. Nat D. Ayer

Oh You Million Dollar Baby 1912 w. Eddie Doerr m. Lou S. Lashley

Oh You Million Dollar Doll 1913 w. Grant Clarke, Edgar Leslie m. Maurice Abrahams

Ob-La-Di Ob-La-Da 1969 w.m. John Lennon, Paul McCartney. Ivor Novello Award winner 1969–70.

Object of My Affection, The 1934 w.m. Pinky Tomlin, Coy Poe, Jimmie Grier. (F) *Times Square Lady*. (MF) *The Fabulous Dorseys*. Robert Taylor and Virginia Bruce appeared in *Times Square Lady*.

Occasional Man, An 1955 w. Ralph Blane m. Hugh Martin. (MF) *Girl Rush.*

Ocean Burial, The, *see* **Oh Bury Me Not on the Lone Prairie**

Oceana Roll, The 1911 w. Roger Lewis m. Lucien Denni (F) *Mildred Pierce.* Joan Crawford appeared in *Mildred Pierce.*

(Theme from) Odd Couple, The 1968 w.m. Sammy Cahn, Neal Hefti. (F) *The Odd Couple.* (TV) *The Odd Couple.* Jack Lemmon and Walter Matthau appeared in the film production of *The Odd Couple.* Tony Randall and Jack Klugman appeared in the TV production of *The Odd Couple.*

Odds and Ends (of a Beautiful Love Affair) 1969 w. Hal David m. Burt Bacharach

Ode to Billie Joe 1967 w.m. Bobbie Gentry

Of Thee I Sing 1931 w. Ira Gershwin m. George Gershwin. (MT) *Of Thee I Sing.* William Gaxton and Victor Moore appeared in *Of Thee I Sing.*

Off the Wall 1980 w.m. Rodney Temperton. Ivor Novello Award winner 1979–80.

Oft in the Stilly Night 1818 w. Thomas Moore m. traditional, from Scotland; arr. Sir John Stevenson. This song was one of the favorites of Abraham Lincoln.

Ogo-Pogo, The 1925 w.m. Ralph Butler, Mark Strong, Cumberland Clark

Ohio 1953 w. Betty Comden, Adolph Green m. Leonard Bernstein. (MT) *Wonderful Town.*

O-hi-o, *see also* **Round on the End and High in the Middle, O-hi-o**

Okie from Muskogee 1970 w.m. Merle Haggard, Roy Edward Burris

Oklahoma 1943 w. Oscar Hammerstein II m. Richard Rodgers. (MT) *Oklahoma!.* (MF) *Oklahoma!.* Betty Garde, Alfred Drake, and Celeste Holm appeared in the stage production of *Oklahoma!.* Shirley Jones and Gordon MacRae appeared in the film production of *Oklahoma!*

Old Abe Lincoln, *see* **The Old Grey Mare**

Old Ark's a-Moverin', De c.1871 w.m. traditional black American spiritual

Old Arm Chair, The 1840 w. Eliza Cook m. Henry Russell

Old Black Joe 1860 w.m. Stephen Collins Foster. (MF) *Swanee River.* Al Jolson and Don Ameche appeared in *Swanee River.* This song was melodically referred to in the Finale of Ippolitoff-Ivanoff's "Caucasian Sketches" (March of the Sardar).

Old Cape Cod 1957 w.m. Claire Rothrock, Milt Yakus, Allan Jeffrey

Old Chisholm Trail, The c.1880 w.m. anon. (F) *Mule Train.* (F) *Old Oklahoma Plains.* Gene Autry and Pat Buttram appeared in *Mule Train.* Rex Allen and Slim Pickens appeared in *Old Oklahoma Plains.* The Chisholm Trail was actually an Indian-haunted cattle trace stretching from the southern tip of Texas to the middle of Kansas, terminating at Abilene.

Old Colony Times 1830 w.m. anon. This song was taught by John Lothron Motley to schoolmate Bismarck, while studying at Göttingen in 1832. Bismarck later quoted words

to this song in a speech before the Reichstag on February 6, 1888. The lyrics were later quoted in Part IV, Chapter 2 of Hardy's *Under the Greenwood Tree.*

Old Dan Tucker 1843 w.m. probably Old Dan D. Emmit (Daniel Decatur Emmett). This song was parodied in 1846 as "Uncle Sam and Mexico," a campaign song supporting Abraham Lincoln. Emmett composed this song at age fifteen.

Old Days 1975 w.m. James C. Pankow

Old Devil Moon 1946 w. E.Y. Harburg m. Burton Lane. (MT) *Finian's Rainbow.* Albert Sharpe and David Wayne appeared in *Finian's Rainbow.*

Old Dog Tray 1853 w.m. Stephen Collins Foster. (MF) *I Dream of Jeanie.* Ray Middleton and Bill Shirley appeared in *I Dream of Jeanie.* In its day, this song was the third most popular of Foster's hits, after "Old Folks at Home" and "Kentucky Home."

Old Faithful, *see* **Ole Faithful**

Old-Fashioned Garden 1919 w.m. Cole Porter. (MT) *Hitchy-Koo of 1919.* (MF) *Night and Day.* Charles Howard and Joe Cook appeared in *Hitchy-Koo of 1919.* Cary Grant, Mary Martin, and Alexis Smith appeared in *Night and Day.* The melody for this song was inspired by "The Vacant Chair," which in turn was adapted from "When I Saw Sweet Nellie Home" (Aunt Dinah's Quilting Party).

Old-Fashioned Love 1923 w. Cecil Mack m. James Johnson. (MT) *Runnin' Wild.*

Old-Fashioned Walk, An, *see* **Let's Take an Old-Fashioned Walk**

Old-Fashioned Wife, An 1917 w. P.G. Wodehouse m. Jerome Kern. (MT) *Oh, Boy!.*

Old Father Thames 1933 w.m. Raymond Wallace, Betsy O'Hogan

Old Flag Never Touched the Ground 1900 w.m. J. Rosamond Johnson, James W. Johnson

Old Flame Flickers and I Wonder Why, The 1898 w.m. Paul Dresser

Old Folks 1968 Eng.w. Eric Blau, Mort Shuman m. Jacques Brel. (MT) *Jacques Brel Is Alive and Well and Living in Paris.*

Old Folks At Home (Way Down Upon the Swanee River) 1851 w.m. Stephen Collins Foster. (MF) *I Dream of Jeanie.* Ray Middleton and Bill Shirley appeared in *I Dream of Jeanie.* Stephen Collins Foster received only $15.00 for sale of this song to E.P. Christy. This song is today the official state song of Florida.

Old Friends 1981 w.m. Stephen Sondheim. (MT) *Merrily We Roll Along.* Ann Morrison appeared in *Merrily We Roll Along.*

Old Friends and Old Times 1856 w. Charles Swain m. John Rogers Thomas

Old Granite State, The 1843 w. Jesse Hutchinson m. based on "The Old Church Yard." This song was popularized by the Hutchinson Family Singers.

Old Grey Goose, The, *see* **The Ole Grey Goose**

Old Grey Mare, The (She Ain't What She Used to Be) 1917 w. possibly Gus Bailey m. arr. Frank Panella. Based on

J. Warner's 1858 "Down in Alabam," also known as "Got Out (Get Out of) the Wilderness." This song with the new title "Old Abe Lincoln" was used in Lincoln's Presidential campaign of 1860.

Old Grimes 1822 w. Albert Gorton Greene m. based on the melody of "Auld Lang Syne" of 1711. Greene wrote this song at age sixteen while a sophomore at Brown University. A parody of this song was written by the young Walt Whitman.

Old House, The 1937 w.m. Frederick O'Connor

Old Hundred(th) Doxology, or, Praise God, from Whom All Blessings Flow 1551–1561 w. Psalm 134 of the Genevan Psalter, 1551 edition m. Louis Bourgeouis; possibly adapted from a French secular song. This song is mentioned in Shakespeare's *Merry Wives of Windsor,* Act II, Sc.2.

Old King Cole, *see* **Mother Goose's Melodies**

Old Kitchen Kettle, The 1932 w.m. Harry Woods, James Campbell, Reginald Connelly

Old Lamp-Lighter, The 1946 w. Charles Tobias m. Nat Simon. This song was popularly revived in 1960.

Old Love, An, *see* **Mi Viejo Amor**

Old MacDonald Had a Farm 1917 w.m. based on English words by Thomas D'Urfey as early as 1706; American music from as early as 1859 with the title "Litoria! Litoria!" This song was first known in America as "The Gobble Family," and first published in 1917 with the title "Ohio." In this version, the owner of the farm is named MacDougal.

Ol' Man Mose 1938 w.m. Louis Armstrong, Zilner Trenton Randolph

Ol' Man River 1927 w. Oscar Hammerstein II m. Jerome Kern. (MT) *Show Boat.* (MF) *Show Boat* (1929). (MF) *Show Boat* (1936). (MF) *Show Boat* (1951). (MF) *Till the Clouds Roll By.* Helen Morgan and Charles Winninger appeared in the original stage production of *Show Boat.* Otis Harlan and Alma Rubens appeared in the 1929 film production of *Show Boat.* Irene Dunne and Allan Jones appeared in the 1936 film production of *Show Boat.* Kathryn Grayson and Howard Keel appeared in the 1951 film production of *Show Boat.* Judy Garland, Van Johnson, and Dinah Shore appeared in *Till the Clouds Roll By,* biopic of composer Jerome Kern. Theme song of Jules Bledsoe.

Old Man Sunshine—Little Boy Bluebird 1928 w. Morton Dixon m. Harry Warren

Old Master Painter, The 1949 w. Haven Gillespie m. Beasley Smith

Old Mill Wheel 1939 w.m. Benny Davis, Milton Ager, Jesse Greer

Old Nassau, *see* **Auld Lang Syne**

Old Oaken Bucket, The 1843 w. Samuel Woodworth m. George Kiallmark. Based on the English melody "Araby's Daughter" of 1822; the words were first published as an American poem in 1817. The music was originally the Scottish air "Jessie, the Flower o' Dumblane." In 1864, this song was the subject of a Currier and Ives colored lithograph. The original well was located at Old Oaken Bucket Road at Scituate, Massachusetts. This song, with new lyrics, later became Brown University's Alma Mater.

Old Ox Road, The, *see* **Down the Old Ox Road**

Old Paint, *see* **Goodbye Ol' Paint**

Old Pal Why Don't You Answer Me 1920 w. Sam M. Lewis, Joe Young m. M.K. Jerome

Old Pi-anna Rag, The 1955 w.m. Don Phillips

Old Piano Roll Blues, The 1950 w.m. Cy Coben

Old Refrain, The 1915 m. Fritz Kreisler. Based on a Viennese song by Hugo Klein and Joseph Brandl, of 1887; adapted Fritz Kreisler. From the German "Du Alter Stefansthurm" from the operetta *Der Liebe Augustine.*

Ol' Rockin' Chair, *see* **Rockin' Chair**

Old Rosin the Beau 1835 w.m. traditional, from Scotland. Between 1840 and 1875 this song was used for four political campaigns: the Presidential campaign of James K. Polk; two songs supporting Henry Clay ("The Mill-Boy of the Slashes" and "Old Hal of the West"); the Republican campaign supporting "Lincoln and Liberty"); and John Quincy Adams's campaign song "Straight-Out Democrat."

Old Rugged Cross, The 1913 w.m. Reverend George Bennard. In the most recent poll conducted by *The Christian Herald,* Protestant churchgoers chose this gospel hymn as their favorite of 1,666 hymns and songs. Second, third, and fourth places went to "What a Friend We Have in Jesus," "In the Garden," and "How Great Thou Art," respectively.

Old Sam (Pick Up Tha' Musket) 1932 w.m. Stanley Holloway, Wolseley Charles. (MF) *D'Ye Ken John Peel.* Stanley Holloway appeared in *D'Ye Ken John Peel.*

Old Ship of Mine 1935 w.m. Don Pelosi, Rodd Arden

Old Soft Shoe, The 1951 w. Nancy Hamilton m. Morgan Lewis. (MT) *Three To Make Ready.* Ray Bolger, Gordon MacRae, and Arthur Godfrey appeared in *Three To Make Ready.* This song, written in 1946, was most popular in 1951.

Old Soldiers Never Die 1939 w.m. Frank C. Westphal

"Ol" Song, The 1933 w.m. Harry Carlton

Old Spinning Wheel, The 1933 w.m. Billy Hill

(Gimme Dat) Old Time Religion 1865 w.m. traditional black American spiritual

Old Timer 1935 w.m. Richard Carr, Lewis Ilda

Old Uncle Ned, *see* **Uncle Ned**

Old Violin, An 1929 w.m. Helen Taylor, Howard Fisher

Old Water Mill, An 1934 w.m. Charles Tobias, Jack Scholl, Murray Mencher

Old Zip Coon, *see* **Turkey in the Straw**

Older and Wiser 1960 w. Lee Adams m. Charles Strouse. (MT) *Bye Bye Birdie.* (MF) *Bye Bye Birdie.* Dick Van Dyke and Ann-Margret appeared in the film production of *Bye Bye Birdie.*

Older Women 1981 w.m. James O'Hara

Oldest Established, The (Permanent Floating Crap Game in New York) 1950 w.m. Frank Loesser. (MT) *Guys and Dolls.* (MF) *Guys and Dolls.* Marlon Brando and Frank Sinatra appeared in the film production of *Guys and Dolls.*

Ole Buttermilk Sky 1946 w.m. Hoagy Carmichael, Jack Brooks. (F) *Canyon Passage.* Dana Andrews, Susan Hayward, and Hoagy Carmichael appeared in *Canyon Passage.*

Ole Faithful 1934 w.m. Michael Carr, Hamilton Kennedy. (MF) *My Pal Trigger*. Roy Rogers, Dale Evans, and Gabby Hayes appeared in *My Pal Trigger*.

(Go Tell Aunt Rhody) Ole Grey Goose, The (Is Dead) 1844 w.m. traditional American folksong. (MF) *Disc Jockey*.

Ole Shady, or, **The Song of the Contraband** 1861 w.m. Benjamin Russell Hanby

Olga Pulloffski 1935 w.m. R.P. Weston, Bert Lee. (F) *The Beautiful Spy*.

Omaha 1919 w.m. Horatio Nicholls, Worton David

Omnibus 1983 m. George Fenton. Ivor Novello Award winner 1982–83.

On a Bicycle Built for Two, *see* **Daisy Bell**

On a Clear Day You Can See Forever 1966 w. Alan Jay Lerner m. Burton Lane. (MT) *On a Clear Day You Can See Forever*. (MF) *On a Clear Day You Can See Forever*. Barbra Streisand appeared in the film production of *On a Clear Day You Can See Forever*.

On a Desert Island with Thee 1927 w. Lorenz Hart m. Richard Rodgers. (MT) *A Connecticut Yankee*. (MF) *A Connecticut Yankee* (1931). (MF) *A Connecticut Yankee* (1949). William Gaxton and William Norris appeared in the stage production of *A Connecticut Yankee*. Will Rogers and Maureen O'Sullivan appeared in the 1931 film production of *A Connecticut Yankee*. Bing Crosby appeared in the 1949 film poduction of *A Connecticut Yankee*.

On a Dew-Dew-Dewy Day, *see* **Dew-Dew-Dewy Day**

On a Little Street in Singapore 1940 w.m. William J. Hill, Peter DeRose

On a Roof in Manhattan 1932 w.m. Irving Berlin (MT) *Face the Music*. Mary Roland and Katherine Carrington appeared in *Face the Music*.

(I'd Like To Get You) On a Slow Boat to China 1948 w.m. Frank Loesser

On a Street of Chinese Lanterns 1927 w.m. James Campbell, Reginald Connelly

On a Sunday Afternoon 1902 w. Andrew B. Sterling m. Harry Von Tilzer. (F) *Atlantic City*. (MF) *The Naughty Nineties*. Constance Moore and Jerry Colonna appeared in *Atlantic City*. Bud Abbott, Lou Costello, and Rita Johnson appeared in *The Naughty Nineties*.

On a Wonderful Day Like Today, *see* **A Wonderful Day Like Today**

On and On 1977 w.m. Stephen Bishop

On Broadway 1963 w.m. Barry Mann, Cynthia Weil, Jerry Leiber, Mike Stoller. This song was popularly revived in 1978.

On Green Dolphin Street 1947 w.m. Ned Washington, Bronislaw Kaper. (F) *Green Dolphin Street*. Lana Turner and Van Heflin appeared in *Green Dolphin Street*.

On Miami Shore, or, **Golden Sands of Miami** 1919 w. William Le Baron m. Victor Jacobi

On Mobile Bay 1910 w. Earl C. Jones m. Charles N. Daniels (Neil Moret)

On Moonlight Bay, *see* **Moonlight Bay**

On Mother Kelly's Doorstep 1925 w.m. G.A. Stevens

On My Own 1986 w.m. Carole Bayer Sager

On Springfield Mountain, *see* **The Pesky Sarpent**

On the Air 1932 w.m. Carroll Gibbons. Theme song of Carroll Gibbons.

On the Alamo 1922 w. Gus Kahn m. Isham Jones

On the Atchison, Topeka, and the Sante Fe 1945 w. Johnny Mercer m. Harry Warren. (MF) *The Harvey Girls*. Judy Garland, Ray Bolger, and Angela Lansbury appeared in *The Harvey Girls*. Academy Award winner 1946.

On the Banks of Allen Water 1815 w. Matthew Gregory Lewis m. "Lady C.S."; arr. Charles Edward Horn

On the Banks of the Old Raritan 1938 w.m. arr. Thornton W. Allen. School song of Rutgers University.

On the Banks of the Wabash Far Away 1899 w.m. Paul Dresser. (MF) *My Gal Sal*. (MF) *The Jolson Story*. (MF) *Wait Till the Sun Shines Nellie*. Larry Parks appeared in *The Jolson Story*. David Wayne appeared in *Wait Till the Sun Shines Nellie*. This song became the official state song of Indiana. This song was inspired by Paul Dresser's brother, novelist Theodore Dreiser.

On the Bayou, *see* **Jambalaya**

On the Beach 1959 w.m. Steve Allen, Ernest Gold. (F) *On the Beach*. While the score to *On the Beach* failed to win an Academy Award, he did receive the Golden Globe Award and the Downbeat award for best dramatic film score.

On the Beach 1964 w.m. Bruce Welch, Hank B. Marvin, Cliff Richard. (F) *Wonderful Life*.

(It Happened) On the Beach at Bali Bali 1936 w.m. Al Sherman, Abner Silver, Jack Meskill

On the Beach at Waikiki 1915 w. G.H. Stover m. Henry Kailimai. (MT) *The Bird of Paradise*.

On the Beautiful Blue Danube, *see* **The Blue Danube**

On the Benches in the Park 1896 w.m. James Thornton

On the Boardwalk in Atlantic City 1946 w. Mack Gordon m. Josef Myrow. (MF) *Three Little Girls in Blue*, June Haver, George Montgomery, and Vivian Blaine appeared in *Three Little Girls in Blue*.

On the Bumpy Road to Love 1938 w. Al Hoffman, Al Lewis, Murray Mencher. (MF) *Listen Darling*. Judy Garland and Freddie Bartholemew appeared in *Listen Darling*.

On the Crest of a Wave 1934 w.m. Ralph Reader

On the Dark Side 1985 w.m. John Cafferty

On the 5:15 1914 w. Stanley Murphy m. Henry I. Marshall. (MT) *5064 Gerard*. Jack Morrison and Lee White appeared in *5064 Gerard*.

On the Flying Trapeze, *see* **The Daring Young Man**

On the Gin, Gin, Ginny Shore 1922 w. Edgar Leslie m. Walter Donaldson

On the Good Ship Lollipop 1934 w.m. Sidney Clare, Richard A. Whiting. (F) *Bright Eyes*. (MF) *You're My Everything*. Shirley Temple and James Dunn appeared in *Bright Eyes*. Dan Dailey and Anne Baxter appeared in *You're My Everything*.

On the Good Ship Mary Ann 1914 w. Gus Kahn m. Grace LeBoy

On the Isle of May   1940   w.m. Mack David, André Kostelanetz. Based on the Andante Cantabile from Tchaikovsky's String Quartet in D-Major.

On the Mall (March)   1923   m. Edwin Franko Goldman

On the Mississippi   1912   w. Ballard MacDonald   m. Harry Carroll, Arthur Fields. (MF) *The Dolly Sisters*. Betty Grable and June Haver appeared in *The Dolly Sisters*.

On the Old Fall River Line   1913   w. William Jerome, Andrew B. Sterling   m. Harry Von Tilzer.

On the Other Side of the Tracks, *see* **The Other Side of the Tracks**

On the Outside Looking In   1939   w.m. Michael Carr. (MT) *The Little Dog Laughed.*

On the Radio   1980   w.m. Giorgio Moroder, Donna Summer

On the Rebound   1961   w.m. Floyd Cramer

On the Road Again   1980   w.m. Willie Nelson. Grammy Award winner 1980.

On the Road to Mandalay   1907   w. Rudyard Kipling   m. Oley Speaks

On the Sentimental Side   1937   w.m. Johnny Burke, James V. Monaco. (MF) *Doctor Rhythm*. Bing Crosby, Beatrice Lillie, and Andy Devine appeared in *Doctor Rhythm*.

On the Shore at Lei Lei   1916   w.m. Henry Kalimar, Herbert Reynolds, Jerome Kern. (MT) *Very Good Eddie.*

On the Shores of Italy   1913   w.m. Jack Glogau, Al Piantadosi

On the Shores of Tripoli, *see* **Tripoli**

On the South Side of Chicago   1967   w.m. Phil Zeller

On the Street of Dreams, *see* **Street of Dreams**

On the Street Where You Live   1956   w. Alan Jay Lerner   m. Frederick Loewe. (MT) *My Fair Lady*. (MF) *My Fair Lady*. Rex Harrison and Julie Andrews appeared in the stage production of *My Fair Lady*. Rex Harrison and Audrey Hepburn appeared in the film production of *My Fair Lady*.

On the Sunny Side of the Street   1930   w. Dorothy Fields   m. Jimmy McHugh. (MT) *Lew Leslie's International Revue*. (MT) *Sugar Babies*. (MF) *Is Everybody Happy*. (MF) *Swing Parade of 1946*. (MF) *The Sunny Side of the Street*. (MF) *Two Blondes and a Red Head*. (MF) *The Benny Goodman Story*. (MF) The Eddy Duchin Story. (MF) *Both Ends of the Candle*. Florence Moore, Gertrude Lawrence, and Harry Richman appeared in *Lew Leslie's International Revue*. Ann Miller and Mickey Rooney appeared in *Sugar Babies*. Larry Parks and Ted Lewis appeared in *Is Everybody Happy*, biopic of bandleader Ted Lewis. Jean Porter, Jimmy Lloyd, and June Preisser appeared in *Two Blondes and a Red Head*. Frankie Laine and Billy Daniels appeared in *On the Sunny Side of the Street.*

On the Trail   1933   m. Ferde Grofé. From "Grand Canyon Suite."

On the Trail of the Lonesome Pine, *see* **The Trail of the Lonesome Pine**

On the Twentieth Century   1978   w. Betty Comden, Adolph Green   m. Cy Coleman. (MT) *On the Twentieth Century*. John Cullum, Imogene Coca, and Quitman Flood III appeared in *On the Twentieth Century.*

On the Way to the Sky   1982   w.m. Neil Diamond, Carole Bayer Sager

On the Wings of Love   1983   w.m. Jeffrey Osborne, Peter Schless

On Tom-Big-Bee River, *see* **The Gum Tree Canoe**

On Top of Old Smokey   1951   w.m. based on the traditional folksong "Little Mohee," as early as 1916; arr. Fred Barovick. (F) *Valley of Fire*. Gene Autry and Gail Davis appeared in *Valley of Fire.*

On Treasure Island   1935   w.m. Edgar Leslie, Joseph Burke

On Wings of Song, op.39, no.2   1837   m. Felix Mendelssohn. (MF) *I Dream of Jeanie*. Ray Middleton and Bill Shirley appeared in *I Dream of Jeanie.*

On Wisconsin   1909   w. Carl Beck   m. W.T. Purdy. School song of the university of Wisconsin.

On with Roosevelt   1935   w.m. Louise Graeser. This song was written for Franklin D. Roosevelt's Presidential campaign.

On Your Toes   1936   w. Lorenz Hart   m. Richard Rodgers. (MT) *On Your Toes*. (MF) *On Your Toes*. (MF) *Words and Music*. Ray Bolger and Luella Gear appeared in the stage production of *On Your Toes*. Zorina and Eddie Albert appeared in the film production of *On Your Toes*. Mickey Rooney, Judy Garland, and Gene Kelly appeared in *Words and Music,* biopic of song writers Rodgers and Hart.

Once Ev'ry Year   1894   w.m. Paul Dresser

Once in a Blue Moon   1923   w. Anne Caldwell   m. Jerome Kern. (MT) *The Stepping Stones*. This song was popularly revived in 1933.

Once in a Lifetime   1928   w. Raymond Klages   m. Jesse Greer. (MT) *Earl Carroll's Vanities of 1928 (Seventh Edition)*. W.C. Fields and Joe Frisco appeared in *Earl Carroll's Vanities of 1928 (Seventh Edition).*

Once in a Lifetime   1962   w.m. Leslie Bricusse, Anthony Newley. (MT) *Stop the World—I Want To Get Off*. Anthony Newley appeared in *Stop the World—I Want To Get Off.*

Once in a While   1937   w. Bud Green   m. Michael Edwards. (MF) *I'll Get By*. Gloria De Haven and Dennis Day appeared in *I'll Get By.*

Once in Every Lifetime   1960   w.m. Guy Magenta

Once in Love with Amy   1948   w.m. Frank Loesser. (MT) *Where's Charley?*. (MF) *Where's Charley?*. Ray Bolger appeared in both the stage and film productions of *Where's Charley?*.

Once Knew a Fella   1959   w.m. Harold Rome. (MT) *Destry Rides Again*. (F) *Destry Rides Again*. James Stewart and Marlene Dietrich appeared in the film production of *Destry Rides Again.*

Once Upon a Dream   1962   w.m. Norrie Paramor, Richard Rowe. (F) *Play It Cool*. Billy Fury and Helen Shapiro appeared in *Play It Cool.*

Once Upon a Time   1962   w. Lee Adams   m. Charles Strouse. (MT) *All American*. Ray Bolger appeared in *All American.*

Once Upon a Wintertime 1947 w.m. Johnny Brandon, R. Martin

One 1975 w. Edward Kleban m. Marvin Hamlisch. (MT) *A Chorus Line.* Donna McKechnie appeared in *A Chorus Line.*

One Alone 1926 w. Oscar Hammerstein II, Otto Harbach m. Sigmund Romberg. (MT) *The Desert Song.* (MF) *The Desert Song* (1943). (MF) *The Desert Song* (1953). Vivienne Segal and Robert Halliday appeared in the American stage production of *The Desert Song.* Harry Welchman and Edith Day appeared in the British stage production of *The Desert Song.* Irene Manning and Dennis Morgan appeared in the 1943 film production of *The Desert Song.* Kathryn Grayson and Gordon MacRae appeared in the 1953 film production of *The Desert Song.*

One Bad Apple (Don't Spoil the Whole Bunch) 1971 w.m. George H. Jackson

One Boy 1960 w. Lee Adams m. Charles Strouse. (MT) *Bye Bye Birdie.* (MF) *Bye Bye Birdie.* Dick Van Dyke and Ann-Margret appeared in *Bye Bye Birdie.*

One by One 1981 w.m. Bobby LaKind, Michael McDonald

One Called "Mother" and the Other "Home Sweet Home" 1905 w. William Cahill m. Theodore F. Morse

One Dozen Roses 1942 w. Roger Lewis, Country Washburn m. Dick Jergens, Walter Donovan

One Fine Day, or, **Un Bel Dì** 1904 w. Luigi Illica, Giuseppe Giacosa m. Giacomo Puccini. From the opera *Madama Butterfly.*

One for My Baby (and One More for the Road) 1943 w. Johnny Mercer m. Harold Arlen. (MF) *The Sky's the Limit.* (F) *Macao.* Fred Astaire, Robert Benchley, and Joan Leslie appeared in *The Sky's the Limit.* Robert Mitchum and Jane Russell appeared in *Macao.*

One Hand, One Heart 1957 w. Stephen Sondheim m. Leonard Bernstein. (MT) *West Side Story.* (MF) *West Side Story.* Natalie Wood and Rita Moreno appeared in the film production of *West Side Story.*

One-Horse Open Sleigh, The, *see* **Jingle Bells**

(I'd Love To Spend) One Hour with You 1932 w.m. Leo Robin, Richard A. Whiting. (MF) *One Hour with You.* Maurice Chevalier and Jeanette MacDonald appeared in *One Hour with You.*

One Hundred Ways 1982 w.m. Tony Coleman, Kathy Wakefield, Benjamin Wright

One I Love Belongs to Somebody Else, The 1924 w. Gus Kahn m. Isham Jones. (MF) *I'll See You in My Dreams.* (MF) *Both Ends of the Candle.* Doris Day and Danny Thomas appeared in *I'll See You in My Dreams,* biopic of song writer Gus Kahn.

One in a Million You 1980 w.m. Sam Dees

One Kiss 1928 w. Oscar Hammerstein II m. Sigmund Romberg. (MT) *The New Moon.* (MF) *The New Moon* (1930). (MF) *The New Moon* (1940). (MF) *Deep in My Heart.* Evelyn Laye appeared in the British stage production of *The New Moon.* Adolphe Menjou and Grace Moore appeared in the 1930 film production of *The New Moon.* Nelson Eddy and Jeanette MacDonald appeared in the 1940 film production of *The New Moon.* Jose Ferrer and Merle Oberon appeared in *Deep in My Heart,* biopic of composer Sigmund Romberg.

One Less Bell To Answer 1970 w. Hal David m. Burt Bacharach

One Little Candle 1952 w.m. Joseph Maloy Roach, George Mysels

One Little, Two Little, Three Little Indians, *see* **Ten Little Indians**

One Love 1946 w. Leo Robin m. David Rose

One Love Forever 1942 w.m. Jimmy Dyrenforth, Kenneth Leslie-Smith

One Meat Ball 1945 w.m. Louis C. Singer, Hy Zaret. Based on "The Lone Fish Ball" of 1855.

One Moment Alone 1931 w. Otto Harbach m. Jerome Kern. (MT) *The Cat and the Fiddle.* (MF) *The Cat and the Fiddle.* Jeanette MacDonald, Frank Morgan, and Charles Butterworth appeared in the film production of *The Cat and the Fiddle.*

One More Angel in Heaven 1982 w. Tim Rice m. Andrew Lloyd Webber. (MT) *Joseph and the Amazing Technicolor Dreamcoat.* Laurie Beechman appeared in *Joseph and the Amazing Technicolor Dreamcoat.*

One More Dance 1932 w. Oscar Hammerstein II m. Jerome Kern. (MT) *Music in the Air.* (MF) *Music in the Air.* (MF) *Till the Clouds Roll By.* Gloria Swanson and Al Shean appeared in the film production of *Music in the Air.* Judy Garland, Dinah Shore, and June Allyson appeared in *Till the Clouds Roll By,* biopic of composer Jerome Kern.

One More Kiss 1942 w.m. Morton Morrow

One More Night 1985 w.m. Phil Collins

One More River To Cross 1865 w.m. traditional black American spiritual

One More Time 1931 w.m. B.G. DeSylva, Lew Brown, Ray Henderson

One Morning in May 1933 w.m. Mitchell Parish, Hoagy Carmichael

One Night in June 1899 w.m. Charles K. Harris

One Night of Love 1934 w. Gus Kahn m. Victor Schertzinger. (MF) *One Night of Love.* Grace Moore and Tullio Carminati appeared in *One Night of Love.*

One Night Only 1982 w. Tom Eyen m. Henry Krieger. (MT) *Dream Girls.* Loretta Devine and Jennifer Holliday appeared in *Dream Girls.*

One O'Clock Jump 1938 w.m. William "Count" Basie, Harry James. (MF) *Reveille with Beverly.* (MF) *Night Club Girl.* (MF) *The Benny Goodman Story.* Frank Sinatra and Ann Miller appeared in *Reveille with Beverly.* Vivian Austin and Edward Norris appeared in *Night Club Girl.* Theme song of Count Basie.

One of the Ruins That Cromwell Knocked About a Bit 1912 w.m. Harry Bedford, Terry Sullivan

One of These Nights 1975 w.m. Glenn Frey, Don Henley

One of Us Will Weep Tonight 1960 w.m. Clint Ballard, Jr., Fred Tobias

One Piece at a Time 1976 w.m. Wayne Kemp

One Rose That's Left in My Heart, The 1929 w.m. Del Lyon, Lani McIntyre. This song was popularly revived in 1936.

One Song 1937 w. Larry Morey m. Frank Churchill. (MF) *Snow White and the Seven Dwarfs.*

One Sunday Afternoon 1948 w.m. Ralph Blane. (MF) *One Sunday Afternoon.* Dennis Morgan and Janis Paige appeared in *One Sunday Afternoon.*

One That You Love, The 1981 w. Graham Russell. Ivor Novello Award winner 1981–82.

One Thing Leads to Another 1984 w.m. Alfred Agius, Cy Curnin, Rupert Greenall, Jamie West-Oram, Adam Woods

One, Two, Button Your Shoe 1936 w. John Burke m. Arthur Johnston. (MF) *Pennies from Heaven.* Bing Crosby and Louis Armstrong appeared in *Pennies from Heaven.*

One, Two, Three 1946 w. Ira Gershwin m. George Gershwin. (MF) *The Shocking Miss Pilgrim.* Dick Haymes and Ann Revere appeared in *The Shocking Miss Pilgrim.*

One—Two—Three 1965 w.m. John Madara, David White, Eddie Holland, Brian Holland, Leonard Broisoff

One Two Three Red Light 1968 w.m. Sal Trimachi, Bobbi Trimachi

One Way Love 1964 w.m. Bert Russell, Norman Meade

One Who Really Loves You, The 1962 w.m. William Robinson, Jr.

One You Love 1983 w.m. Glenn Frey, Jack Tempchin

Only a Bowery Boy 1894 w. Charles B. Ward m. Gussie L. Davis

Only a Pansy Blossom 1883 w. Eben Rexford m. Frank Howard

Only a Rose 1925 w. Brian Hooker m. Rudolf Friml. (MT) *The Vagabond King.* (MF) *The Vagabond King* (1930). (MF) *The Vagabond King* (1956). Carolyn Thomson and Dennis King appeared in the American stage production of *The Vagabond King.* Derek Oldham and Winnie Melville appeared in the British stage production of *The Vagabond King.* Dennis King and Jeanette MacDonald appeared in the 1930 film production of *The Vagabond King.* Kathryn Grayson and Rita Moreno appeared in the 1956 film production of *The Vagabond King.*

Only Forever 1940 w. Johnny Burke m. James V. Monaco. (MF) *Rhythm on the River.* Bing Crosby and Mary Martin appeared in *Rhythm on the River.*

Only Love Can Break a Heart 1962 w. Hal David m. Burt Bacharach

(I Don't Care) Only Love Me 1959 It.w. Pinchi Eng.w. Mann Curtis m. V. Panzuti

Only Make Believe, *see* **Make Believe**

Only Me 1894 w. Walter H. Ford m. John W. Bratton

Only One 1986 w.m. James Taylor

Only One Girl in the World for Me 1895 w.m. Dave Marion

Only One You 1982 w.m. Michael Garvin, Kenneth Jones

Only Sixteen 1958 w.m. Barbara Campbell

Only Sixteen 1976 w.m. Sam Cooke

Only the Heartaches 1960 w.m. Wayne P. Walker

Only the Lonely (Know the Way I Feel) 1960 w.m. Roy Orbison, Joe Melson

Only the Strong Survive 1969 w.m. Kenneth Gamble, Leon Huff, Jerry Butler

Only with You 1982 w.m. Maury Yeston. (MT) *Nine.* Liliane Montevecchi and Anita Morris appeared in *Nine.*

Only Women Bleed 1975 w.m. Alice Cooper, Dick Wagner

Only Yesterday 1975 w.m. John Bettis, Richard Carpenter

Only You (and You Alone) 1955 w.m. Buck Ram, Ande Rand. (MF) *Rock Around the Clock.* Bill Haley appeared in *Rock Around the Clock.*

Onward, Christian Soldiers 1871 w. Sabine Baring-Gould m. Sir Arthur Sullivan

Ooh Baby 1974 w.m. Gilbert O'Sullivan

Ooh That Kiss 1931 w. Mort Dixon, Joe Young m. Harry Warren. (MT) *The Laugh Parade.* Ed Wynn and Eunice Healy appeared in *The Laugh Parade.*

O-oo Ernest, Are You Earnest With Me? 1922 w. Sidney Clare, Harry Tobias m. Cliff Friend

Open a New Window 1966 w.m. Jerry Herman. (MT) *Mame.* (MF) *Mame.* Angela Lansbury appeared in the stage production of *Mame.* Lucille Ball appeared in the film production of *Mame.*

Open Arms 1982 w.m. Jonathan Cain, Stephen Perry

Open the Door, Richard 1947 w. "Dusty" Fletcher, John Mason m. Jack McVea, Dan Howell

Open the Gates of the Temple 1903 w. Fanny Crosby (Mrs. Alexander Van Alstyne) m. Phoebe Palmet (Mrs. Joseph F. Knapp)

Open Thy Lattice Love 1844 w. George P. Morris m. Stephen Collins Foster. This was the first published song by the eighteen-year-old Stephen Foster. The words were found by Foster in an article in the *New Mirror.*

Open Up Your Heart (and Let the Sunshine In) 1955 w.m. Stuart Hamblen

Opus (Number) One 1944 w.m. Sy Oliver

Orange Blossom Time 1929 w.m. Joe Goodwin, Gus Edwards. (MF) *Hollywood Revue.* Jack Benny, Joan Crawford, Buster Keaton, and the young Judy Garland appeared in *Hollywood Revue.*

Orange Colored Sky 1950 w.m. William Stein, Milton DeLugg

Orange Grove in California, An 1923 w.m. Irving Berlin. (MT) *The Music Box Revue of 1923.* Robert Benchley, Frank Tinney and Grace Moore appeared in *The Music Box Revue of 1923.*

Oranges and Lemons, *see* **The Bells of St. Clements**

Orchids in the Moonlight 1933 w. Gus Kahn, Edward Eliscu m. Vincent Youmans. (MF) *Flying Down to Rio.* Dolores Del Rio and Fred Astaire appeared in *Flying Down to Rio.*

Ordinary People 1951 w.m. George Posford

Organ Grinder, The 1932 w. Herb Magidson m. Sam H. Stept

Organ Grinder's Swing, The 1936 w. Mitchell Parish, Irving Mills m. Will Hudson

Origin of Gunpowder, The, or, **When Vulcan Forg'd the Bolts of Jove** 1805 w. Thomas John Dibdin m. John Braham. From the British comic opera *The English Fleet in 1342.*

Original Dixieland One-Step 1918 w.m. Joe Jordan, James D. La Rocca, J. Russell Robinson. This song was popularly revived in 1928.

Ostrich Walk 1918 w.m. Edwin B. Edwards, James D. La Rocca, Anthony Sbarbaro, Larry Shields

Other Man's Grass, The (Is Always Greener) 1968 w.m. Jackie Trent, Tony Hatch

Other People's Babies 1934 w.m. Vivian Ellis, A.P. Herbert. (MT) *Streamline.* Norah Howard appeared in *Streamline.*

(On) Other Side of the Tracks, The 1962 w. Carolyn Leigh m. Cy Coleman. (MT) *Little Me.*

Other Woman, The 1982 w.m. Ray Parker, Jr.

Oui, Oui, Marie 1918 w. Alfred Bryan, Joe McCarthy m. Fred Fisher. (F) *What Price Glory?* James Cagney and Dan Dailey appeared in *What Price Glory?*

Our Country, May She Always Be Right 1898 w.m. Paul Dresser

Our Day Will Come 1963 w.m. Mort Garson, Bob Hilliard

Our Director (March) 1926 m. F.E. Bigelow. This tune later became the Harvard fight song.

Our Favourite Melodies 1962 w.m. Bob Elgin, Kay Rogers, Wes Farrell

Our House 1983 w.m. Carl Smyth, C.J. Foreman. Ivor Novello Award winner 1982–83.

Our Jackie's Getting Married 1973 w.m. Peter Skellern. Ivor Novello Award winner 1972–73.

Our Lady of Fatima 1950 w.m. Gladys Gollahon

Our Language of Love 1956 w.m. Monte Norman, David Heneker, Julian More, Alexander Breffort, Marguerite Monnot. (MT) *Irma La Douce.* (MF) *Irma La Douce.* Jack Lemmon and Shirley MacLaine appeared in the film production of *Irma La Douce.* This song was most popular in 1960.

Our Lodger's Such a Nice Young Man 1901 w.m. Fred Murray, L. Barclay

Our Love 1939 w.m. Buddy Bernier, Bob Emmerich, Larry Clinton. Based on Tchaikovsky's symphonic poem "Romeo and Juliet" of 1871.

Our Love (Don't Throw It All Away) 1978 w.m. Barry Gibb, Blue Weaver

Our Love Affair 1940 w.m. Arthur Freed, Roger Edens. (MF) *Strike Up the Band.* Mickey Rooney and Judy Garland appeared in *Strike Up the Band.*

Our Love Is Here To Stay 1938 w. Ira Gershwin m. George Gershwin (MF) *The Goldwyn Follies.* (MF) *An American in Paris.* Adolphe Menjou and the Ritz Brothers appeared in *The Goldwyn Follies.* Gene Kelly and Leslie Caron appeared in *An American in Paris.* This song was popularly revived in 1951.

Our Love Is on the Fault Line 1983 w.m. Reece Kirk

Our Love Story 1949 w.m. Norman Newell, William Harrison

Our Penthouse on Third Avenue 1937 w.m. Lew Brown, Sammy Fain. (MF) *New Faces of 1937.* Joe Penner and Milton Berle appeared in *New Faces of 1937.*

Our Song 1937 w. Dorothy Fields m. Jerome Kern. (F) *When You're in Love.* Cary Grant and Grace Moore appeared in *When You're in Love.*

Our Waltz 1943 w. Nat Burton m. David Rose

Ours Is a Nice 'ouse Ours Is 1921 w.m. Herbert Rule, Fred Holt. (MT) *Fun of the Fayre.* Alfred Lester appeared in *Fun of the Fayre.*

Out in the Cold Again 1934 w.m. Rube Bloom, Ted Koehler

Out in the Cold Cold Snow 1934 w.m. W.G. Haines, James S. Hancock. (MF) *Love, Life and Laughter.* Gracie Fields appeared in *Love, Life and Laughter.*

(Theme from) Out of Africa 1986 m. John Barry. (F) *Out of Africa.* Meryl Streep and Robert Redford appeared in *Out of Africa.* Academy Award winner 1985. Grammy Award winner 1986.

Out of My Dreams 1943 w. Oscar Hammerstein II m. Richard Rodgers. (MT) *Oklahoma!.* (MF) *Oklahoma!.* Celeste Holm, Afred Drake, and Betty Garde appeared in the stage production of *Oklahoma!.* Shirley Jones and Gordon MacRae appeared in the film production of *Oklahoma!.*

(You Came Along from) Out of Nowhere 1931 w. Edward Heyman m. John W. Green. (F) *Dude Ranch.* (F) *You Came Along.* (MF) *The Rat Race.* Mitzi Green and Jack Oakie appeared in *Dude Ranch.* Helen Forrest appeared in *You Came Along.* Tony Curtis and Debbie Reynolds appeared in *The Rat Race.* This song was popularly revived in 1945.

Out of This World 1945 w. Johnny Mercer m. Harold Arlen. (MF) *Out of This World.* Bing Crosby and Veronica Lake appeared in *Out of This World.*

Out of Touch 1984 w.m. Daryl Hall, John Oates. This song was popularly revived in 1985.

Out of Town 1956 w.m. Leslie Bricusse, Robin Beaumont. (F) *Charlie Moon.* Max Bygraves and Dennis Price appeared in *Charlie Moon.* Ivor Novello Award winner 1956.

Out on the Edge of Beyond 1972 w.m. Mike Sammes

Out There in the Sunshine with You 1923 w. J. Keirn Brennan m. Ernest R. Ball

Out Where the West Begins 1917 w. Arthur Chapman m. Estelle Philleo

Outa-Space 1972 w.m. Joseph Arthur Greene, Billy Preston

Outbreak of Murder 1962 w.m. Gordon Franks

Outcast Unknown, The 1887 w.m. Paul Dresser

Outside of Heaven 1952 w. Sammy Gallop m. Chester Conn

Over and Over 1965 w.m. Robert Byrd

Over and Over Again 1929 w. Bert Kalmar m. Harry Ruby

Over and Over Again 1935 w. Lorenz Hart m. Richard Rodgers. (MT) *Jumbo.* (MF) *Jumbo.*

Over and Over Again, *see also* **Say It**

Over My Shoulder 1934 w.m. Harry Woods. (MF) *Evergreen*. Jessie Matthews appeared in *Evergreen*.

Over the Bounding Main, *see* **Sailing**

Over the Garden Wall 1930 w.m. Leslie Sarony, Cecil Harrington

Over the Hill 1974 w. Peter Udell m. Gary Geld. (MT) *Shenandoah*. John Cullum and Penelope Milford appeared in *Shenandoah*.

Over the Rainbow 1939 w. E.Y. Harburg m. Harold Arlen. (MF) *The Wizard of Oz*. Judy Garland, Ray Bolger, and Bert Lahr appeared in *The Wizard of Oz*. Academy Award winner 1939. Theme song of Judy Garland. This song was deleted three times from the final print of the film but restored largely from the efforts of Arthur Freed coming to its defense against the front office and the publisher who objected to the octave leap in the melody.

Over the Waves 1888 w.m. Juventino Rosas

Over There 1917 w.m. George M. Cohan. (MT) *Zig-Zag*. (MT) *George M!.* (MF) *The Cockeyed World*. (MF) *Yankee Doodle Dandy*. Shirley Kellog appeared in *Zig-Zag*. Joel Grey and Bernadette Peters appeared in *George M!.* Joe E. Brown and Stuart Erwin appeared in *The Cockeyed World*. James Cagney and Joan Leslie appeared in *Yankee Doodle Dandy*. This song was first performed by Charles King at a New York Hippodrome Red Cross benefit and found its first popular success with Nora Bayes. The original sheet music for this song featured a cover illustration by Norman Rockwell. See also Part I, 1919.

Over You 1964 w.m. Derek Quinn, Alan Jones

Over You 1968 w.m. Jerry Fuller

Overdrive 1957 w.m. Tommy Watt. Ivor Novello Award winner 1957.

Overkill 1983 w.m. Colin Hay

Overnight 1930 w. Billy Rose, Charlotte Kent m. Louis Alter. (MT) *Sweet and Low*.

Owner of a Lonely Heart 1984 w.m. Jon Anderson, Trevor Horn, Trevor Rabin, Chris Squire

Pachanga, La 1960 Sp.w. Eduardo Davidson Eng.w. Jeanne Pollack m. Eduardo Davidson

Pack Up Your Trouble in Your Old Kit Bag and Smile, Smile, Smile 1915 w. George Asaf m. Felix Powell. (MT) *Her Soldier Boy*. (MT) *Dancin'*. (MF) *It's a Great Life*. (MF) *What's Cooking?* (MF) *Wait Till the Sun Shines Nellie*. (MF) *On Moonlight Bay*. (F) *What Price Glory?* Benny Rubin and Lawrence Gray appeared in *It's a Great Life*. The Andrews Sisters and Billy Burke appeared in *What's Cooking?*. David Wayne appeared in *Wait Till the Sun Shines Nellie*. Doris Day and Gordon MacRae appeared in *On Moonlight Bay*. James Cagney appeared in *What Price Glory?*

Padam, Padam 1952 w.m. Henri Alexander Contet, Norbert Glanzberg, Mann Holiner, Alberta Nichols

Paddlin' Madelin' Home 1925 w.m. Harry Woods. (MT) *Sunny*.

Paddy Duffy's Cart 1881 w. Edward Harrigan m. David Braham. (MT) *Squatter Sovereignty*.

Paddy McGinty's Goat 1917 w.m. R.P. Weston, Bert Lee

Padre 1958 Fr.w. Jacque Larue Eng.w. Paul Francis Websterm. Jacque Larue

Pagan Love Song 1929 w. Arthur Freed m. Nacio Herb Brown. (F) *The Pagan*. (MF) *Pagan Love Song*. Ramon Novarro and Dorothy Janis appeared in *The Pagan*. Howard Keel and Esther Williams appeared in *Pagan Love Song*.

Paint It Black 1966 w.m. Mick Jagger, Keith Richard

Painted Tainted Rose 1963 w.m. Peter DeAngelis, Jean Sawyer

Painting the Clouds with Sunshine 1929 w. Al Dubin m. Joe Burke. (MF) *Gold Diggers of Broadway*. (MF) *Little Johnny Jones*. (MF) *Painting the Clouds with Sunshine*. Nancy Welford and Ann Pennington appeared in *Gold Diggers of Broadway*. Virginia Mayo and Dennis Morgan appeared in *Painting the Clouds with Sunshine*.

Pal Like You, A 1917 w. P.G. Wodehouse m. Jerome Kern. (MT) *Oh, Boy!*

Pal of My Cradle Days 1925 w. Marshall Montgomery m. Al Piantadosi

Pal That I Loved Stole the Gal That I Loved, The 1924 w.m. Harry Pease, Edward G. Nelson

Pale Moon 1920 w. Jesse Glick m. Frederick Knight Logan

(Lena from) Palesteena 1920 w.m. Con Conrad, J. Russell Robinson

Pallisers, The w.m. Herbert Chappell. (TV-BBC) *The Pallisers*.

Palm Trees, The, or, **The Palms** 1872 Fr.w. anon. m. Jean Baptiste Faure. From the French "Les Rameaux."

Paloma, La (The Dove) 1864 Sp.w. anon. Eng.w. anon. m. Sebastian Yradier. First published in the United States in 1877.

Pan Am Makes the Goin' Great 1967 w. Warren Pfaff m. Stan Applebaum. This song was written for the Pan Am Air Lines commercial promotion campaign.

Panamericana 1901 m. Victor Herbert. This song celebrates the Pan-American Exposition of 1901.

Papa Don't Preach 1986 w.m. Brian Elliot

Papa Loves Mambo 1954 w.m. Al Hoffman, Dick Manning, Bix Reichner. This song was popularized by Perry Como on his network television show.

Papa Was a Rollin' Stone 1972 w.m. Barrett Strong, Norman Whitfield. Grammy Award winner 1972.

Papa Won't You Dance with Me 1947 w. Sammy Cahn m. Jule Styne. (MT) *High Button Shoes*. Phil Silvers and Nanette Fabray appeared in *High Button Shoes*.

Papa's Got a Brand New Bag 1965 w.m. James Brown. Grammy Award winner 1965.

Paper Doll 1915 w.m. Johnny S. Black. (MF) *Hi Good Lookin'*. Kirby Grant and Harriet Hilliard appeared in *Hi Good Lookin'*. This song was popularly revived in 1943. Theme song of the Mills Brothers.

Paper Kisses 1955 w.m. John Jerome

Paper Mache 1970 w. Hal David m. Burt Bacharach

Paper Roses 1955 w. Janice Torre m. Fred Spielman. This song was popularly revived in 1960 and in 1973.

Paperback Writer 1966 w.m. John Lennon, Paul McCartney

Papillons d'Amour, *see* **À la Bien-Aimée**

Parade of the Wooden Soldiers 1905 w. Ballard MacDonald m. Leon Jessel. (MT) *Chauve-Souris.* From the German "Die Parade der Holzsoldaten (Zinnsoldaten)." This song was popularly revived in 1922. Theme song of Emile Boreo.

Paradise (Waltz) 1931 w. Nacio Herb Brown, Gordon Clifford m. Nacio Herb Brown. (F) *A Woman Commands.* Basil Rathbone and Pola Negri appeared in *A Woman Commands.*

Paradise for Two 1917 w.m. James W. Tate, Clifford Harris, Arthur Valentine. (MT) *The Maid of the Mountains.* Thorpe Bates and Jose Collins appeared in *The Maid of the Mountains.*

Pardon Came Too Late, The 1891 w.m. Paul Dresser

Pardon Me, My Dear Alphonse, After You, My Dear Gaston 1902 w. Vincent P. Bryan m. Harry Von Tilzer

Pardon My Southern Accent 1934 w. Johnny Mercer m. Matt Malneck

Paree! 1927 w. Leo Robin m. José Padilla

Paree 1929 w.m. Cole Porter. (MT) *Fifty Million Frenchmen.* (MF) *Fifty Million Frenchmen.* Helen Broderick and William Gaxton appeared in the film production of *Fifty Million Frenchmen.*

Paris In the Spring 1935 w.m. Mack Gordon, Harry Revel. (MF) *Paris Love Song.* (MF) *Paris in the Spring.* (MF) *The Princess Comes Across.* Mary Ellis and Tullio Carmanati appeared in *Paris in the Spring.* Carole Lombard and Fred MacMurray appeared in *The Princess Comes Across.*

Paris Loves Lovers 1955 w.m. Cole Porter. (MT) *Silk Stockings.* (MF) *Silk Stockings.* Fred Astaire and Cyd Charisse appeared in the film production of *Silk Stockings.*

Paris Original 1961 w.m. Frank Loesser. (MT) *How To Succeed in Business Without Really Trying.* (MF) *How To Succeed in Business Without Really Trying.* Robert Morse appeared in both the stage and film productions of *How To Succeed.*

Parisian Pierrot 1924 w.m. Noël Coward. (MT) *London Calling.* (MT) *Andre Charlot's Revue of 1924.* Noël Coward appeared in *London Calling.* Beatrice Lillie and Gertrude Lawrence appeared in *Andre Charlot's Revue of 1924.*

(I Don't Understand) Parisians, The 1958 w. Alan Jay Lerner m. Frederick Loewe. (MF) *Gigi.* Leslie Caron and Maurice Chevalier appeared in *Gigi.*

Park Avenue Fantasy, *see* **Stairway to the Stars**

Parlez-Moi d'Amour, *see* **Speak to Me of Love**

Parliament of England, *see* **Ye Parliament of England**

Parsley, Sage, Rosemary and Thyme, *see* **Scarborough Fair/Canticle**

Part of the Union 1974 w.m. Richard Hudson, John Ford. Ivor Novello Award winner 1974–75.

Part Time Lover 1985 w.m. Stevie Wonder

Partida, La, *see* **The Farewell**

Part-Time Lover 1979 w.m. Gary Anthony Osborne, Reginald K. Dwight

Party All the Time 1985 w.m. Rick James

Party Doll 1957 w.m. James Bowen, Buddy Knox

Party Lights 1962 w.m. Claudine Clark

Party Time 1981 w.m. Bruce Channel

Party's Over, The 1956 w. Betty Comden, Adolph Green m. Jule Styne. (MT) *Bells Are Ringing.* (MF) *Bells Are Ringing.* Judy Holliday appeared in both the stage and film productions of *Bells Are Ringing.*

Party's Over Now, The 1939 w.m. Noël Coward. (MT) *Set to Music.*

(Home In) Pasadena 1923 w.m. Harry Warren, Grant Clarke, Edgar Leslie

Paso, El 1960 w.m. Marty Robbins. Grammy Award winner 1960.

Pass Me By 1965 w. Carolyn Leigh m. Cy Coleman. (F) *Father Goose.* Cary Grant and Leslie Caron appeared in *Father Goose.*

Pass That Peace Pipe 1948 w.m. Hugh Martin, Roger Edens, Ralph Blane. (MF) *Good News.* June Allyson and Peter Lawford appeared in *Good News.*

Passé 1942 Fr.w. Jean Sablon, Jean Geiringer Eng.w.m. Eddie De Lange, Carl Sigman, Joseph Meyer

Passing Breeze 1960 w.m. Trevor Stanford

Passing By 1890 w. Robert Herrick, seventeenth century. m. Edward C. Purcell (Edward Purcell Cockram). This song was popularly revived in 1910.

Passing Strangers 1957 w.m. Rita Mann

Patches 1962 w.m. Larry Kolber, Barry Mann

Patches (I'm Depending on You) 1970 w.m. General Johnson, Ronald Dunbar. Grammy Award winner 1970.

Path That Leads the Other Way, The 1898 w.m. Paul Dresser

Pathfinder's March 1973 w.m. Malcolm Lockyer

Patricia 1958 m. Perez Prado. (F) *La Dolce Vita.* Marcello Mastroianni, Anita Ekberg, and Anouk Aimee appeared in *La Dolce Vita.*

Patrick's Day Parade. 1874 w. Edward Harrigan m. David Braham. (MT) *Patrick's Day Parade.*

Patsy Ory Ory Aye (A-Workin' on the Railroad) 1955 w.m. Hal Moore, Billy Mure

Patty Duke Theme, The (Cousins) 1963 w. Bob Welles m. Sid Ramin. (TV) *The Patty Duke Show.*

Paul Temple Theme 1970 w.m. Ron Grainer

Pavanne 1938 m. Morton Gould. From "American Symphonette No.2."

Pavanne for a Dead Infanta (Princess) 1899 m. Maurice Ravel. From the French "Pavane pour une Infante Défunte." See also "The Lamp Is Low."

Pavo Real, *see* **The Peacock**

Peace Train 1971 w.m. Cat Stevens

Peacock, The 1931 Sp.w. Ernesto Lecuona Eng.w. Carol Raven m. Ernesto Lecuona. From the Spanish "Pavo Real."

Peal Out the Watchword, *see* **True-Hearted, Whole-Hearted**

Peanut Vendor, The 1931 w. Marion Sunshine, L. Wolfe Gilbert m. Moises Simon. (MF) *A Star Is Born.* (F) *Only Angels Have Wings.* Judy Garland and James Mason appeared in *A Star Is Born.* Cary Grant and Jean Arthur appeared in *Only Angels Have Wings.* From the Spanish ''El Manisero.''

Pearl of Sweet Ceylon, The 1904 w.m. Lionel Monckton, Adrian Ross, Percy Greenbank. (MT) *The Cingalee.*

Pease Porridge Hot, *see* **Mother Goose's Melodies**

Peckin' 1937 w.m. Ben Pollack, Harry James. (MF) *New Faces of 1937.* Milton Berle and Joe Penner appeared in *New Faces of 1937.*

Pedro the Fisherman 1943 w.m. Harry Parr-Davies, Harold Purcell. (MT) *Lisbon Story.* (MF) *Lisbon Story.* Richard Tauber appeared in the film production of *Lisbon Story.*

Peek-a-Boo 1881 w.m. William J. Scanlan. (MT) *Friend and Foe.* This song was echoed in 1883 by Robert Keiser (later Bob King) as ''Peep-boo.'' At thirteen, Scanlan was already known as ''The Temperance Boy Songster.''

Peer Gynt Suite, op.46, no.1 1888 m. Edvard Grieg. This suite included ''Anitra's Dance,'' ''Ase's Death,'' ''In the Hall of Mountain King,'' ''March of the Dwarfs,'' and ''Morning'' and was used as incidental music to Ibsen's *Peer Gynt.*

Peg o' My Heart 1913 w. Alfred Bryan m. Fred Fisher. (MT) *The Ziegfeld Follies of 1913.* (MF) *Oh You Beautiful Doll.* June Haver appeared in *Oh You Beautiful Doll.* This song was popularly revived in 1947.

Peggy 1919 w. Harry Williams m. Neil Moret

Peggy O'Neil 1921 w.m. Harry Pease, Edward G. Nelson, Gilbert Dodge

Peggy Sue 1957 w.m. Jerry Allison, Norman Petty, Buddy Holly

Pennies from Heaven 1936 w. John Burke m. Arthur Johnston. (MF) *Pennies from Heaven.* Bing Crosby and Louis Armstrong appeared in *Pennies from Heaven.*

Pennsylvania Polka 1942 w.m. Lester Lee, Zeke Manners. (MF) *Give Out Sisters.* The Andrews Sisters and Charles Butterworth appeared in *Give Out Sisters.*

Pennsylvania 6-5000 1939 w.m. Carl Sigman, Jerry Gray. (MF) *The Glenn Miller Story.*

Penny a Kiss, A Penny a Hug, A 1950 w.m. Buddy Kaye

Penny Lane 1967 w.m. John Lennon, Paul McCartney. (MT) *Beatlemania.*

Penny Lover 1985 w.m. Brenda Harvey-Richie, Lionel Richie

Penny Serenade 1938 w.m. Arthur William Hallifax, Melle Weersma

Penthouse Serenade, *see* **When We're Alone**

People 1964 w. Bob Merrill m. Jule Styne. (MT) *Funny Girl.* (MF) *Funny Girl.* Barbra Streisand appeared in both the stage and film productions of *Funny Girl.* Theme song of Barbra Streisand.

People Got To Be Free 1968 w.m. Edward Brigati, Jr., Felix Cavaliere

People Tree, The 1973 w.m. Leslie Bricusse, Anthony Newley. Ivor Novello Award winner 1972–73.

People Will Say We're in Love 1943 w. Oscar Hammerstein II m. Richard Rodgers. (MT) *Oklahoma!.* (MF) *Oklahoma!.* Afred Drake, Celeste Holm and Betty Garde appeared in the stage production of *Oklahoma!.* Shirley Jones and Gordon MacRae appeared in the film production of *Oklahoma!.*

Pepe 1961 w.m. Dory Langdon, Hans Wittstatt. (F) *Pepe.* Shirley Jones and Cantinflas appeared in *Pepe.*

Peppermint Twist, The 1962 w.m. Joey Dee, Henry Glover

Pepsi-Cola Hits the Spot 1940 m. traditional, from England. This song was adapted for a Pepsi-Cola commercial promotion campaign. Based on ''John Peel'' of 1820 and the traditional English tune ''Bonnie Annie.'' See also ''John Peel.''

Pepsi's Got a Lot To Give, You've Got a Lot To Live 1969 w.m. Batten, Barton Durstine, Osborn m. Joe Brooks. This song was written for a Pepsi-Cola commercial promotion campaign.

Perdido (Lost) 1942 w.m. Ervin M. Drake, Hans Lengsfelder, Juan Tizol. (MT) *Sophisticated Ladies.* Gregory Hines and Phyllis Hyman appeared in *Sophisticated Ladies.*

Perfect Day, A 1910 w.m. Carrie Jacobs-Bond

Perfect Song, The 1915 w. Clarence Lucas m. Joseph Carl Breil. (F) *The Birth of a Nation.* (R) *Amos 'n' Andy.* Lillian Gish and Henry B. Walthall appeared in *The Birth of a Nation.* This song was written for the piano and orchestra accompaniment to this silent film classic. Based on Bragas's ''Angel's Serenade'' of 1867. Theme song of the ''Amos 'n' Andy'' radio show in 1928.

Perfidia 1941 w.m. Milton Leeds, Alberto Dominguez. (MF) *Stardust on the Sage.* Gene Autry and Gabby Hayes appeared in *Stardust on the Sage.* This song was popularly revived in 1961.

Perhaps, Perhaps, Perhaps 1947 w.m. Joseph M. Davis, Osvaldo Farres. This song was also popular in 1949.

Pernambuco 1948 w.m. Frank Loesser. (MT) *Where's Charley?.* (MF) *Where's Charley?.* Ray Bolger appeared in both the stage and film productions of *Where's Charley?.*

Persian Rosebud 1928 w.m. Horatio Nicholls

Persian Rug 1927 w.m. Charles N. Daniels, Neil Moret, Gus Kahn

Personality 1946 w. Johnny Burke m. Jimmy Van Heusen. (MF) *The Road to Utopia.* Bing Crosby, Bob Hope, and Dorothy Lamour appeared in *The Road to Utopia.* This song was later adapted as ''Wessonality'' for the Wesson Oil television advertising campaign.

Personality 1959 w.m. Harold Logan, Lloyd Price

Personally 1982 w.m. Paul Kelly

Perspicacity, *see* **The Lilac Tree**

(Theme from) Persuaders, The 1971 m. John Barry

Pesky Sarpent, The, or, **(On) Springfield Mountain** 1840 w. anon.; possibly Nathan Torrey, or Daniel or Jesse Carpenter m. based on ''Old Hundred.'' The narrative of this song was based on the death of twenty-two-year-old Leiutenant Thomas Merrick (Myrick) of Springfield from a rattlesnake bite in 1761. His gravestone is still in existence.

Pete Kelly's Blues 1955 w. Sammy Cahn m. Ray Heindorf. (MF) *Pete Kelly's Blues*. Peggy Lee, Paul Newman, and Janet Leigh appeared in *Pete Kelly's Blues*.

Peter and the Wolf, op.67 1937 m. Serge Prokofieff

Peter Cottontail 1949 w.m. Steve Nelson, Walter E. Rollins

Peter Go Ring Dem Bells, *see* **Oh Peter Go Ring Dem Bells**

(Theme from) Peter Gunn 1959 m. Henry Mancini. (TV) *Peter Gunn*. This theme won two Grammys for ''best album'' and ''best arrangement'' of the year, was nominated for, but did not win, an Emmy in 1959, and was Henry Mancini's first popular composition. It sold almost a million albums and in a *Down Beat* disc jockey poll was selected as ''best jazz record of the year.''

Peter Peter Pumpkin Eater, *see* **Mother Goose's Melodies**

Petersbourgh Sleighride 1887 w. Richard Eilenberg

Petite Fleur 1952 m. Sidney Bechet. This song was popularly revived in 1959.

Petite Tonkinoise 1906 w.m. Henri Marius Christine, George H. Sanders, Vincent Baptiste Scotto

Petite Waltz, The 1950 m. Joe Heyne

Petticoats of Portugal 1956 w.m. Michael Durso, Mel Mitchell, Murl Kahn

Pettin' in the Park 1933 w.m. Al Dubin, Harry Warren. (MF) *Gold Diggers of 1933*. Dick Powell, Warren Williams, and Ruby Keeler appeared in *Gold Diggers of 1933*.

Peu d'Amour, Un, *see* **A Little Love, a Little Kiss**

Phil the Fluter's Ball 1912 w.m. Percy French

Philadelphia Freedom 1975 w.m. Elton John, Bernie Taupin

Photo of the Girl I Left Behind, The 1911 w.m. Billy Merson

Photograph 1973 w.m. George Harrison, Ringo Starr

Physical 1981 w.m. Stephen Kipner, Terry Shaddick

Physician, The 1933 w.m. Cole Porter. (MT) *Nymph Errant*. Gertrude Lawrence appeared in *Nymph Errant*.

Pianissimo 1961 w.m. Alex Alstone

Piano Concerto, op. 16 1873 m. Edvard Grieg

Piano Concerto, No. 1 1875 m. Peter Tchaikovsky

Piano Concerto, No. 2 1901 m. Sergei Rachmaninoff

Piano Man 1974 w.m. Billy Joel

Picador 1926 w.m. Horatio Nicholls

Piccolino, The 1935 w.m. Irving Berlin. (MF) *Top Hat*. Fred Astaire, Ginger Rogers, and Edward Everett Horton appeared in *Top Hat*.

Piccolo Pete 1929 w.m. Phil Baxter. (MF) *The Vagabond Lover*. Rudy Vallee and Sally Blane appeared in *The Vagabond Lover*.

Pick Up the Pieces 1975 w.m. Roger Ball, Malcolm Duncan, Alan Gorrie, Robbie McIntosh, Owen McIntyre, Jamie Stuart

Pick Yourself Up 1936 w. Dorothy Fields m. Jerome Kern.

(MF) *Swing Time*. Fred Astaire, Helen Broderick, and Ginger Rogers appeared in *Swing Time*.

Pickin' a Chicken 1956 w.m. Garfield de Mortimer, Derek Bernfield, Paddy Roberts

(Theme from) Picnic 1956 w. Steve Allen m. George W. Duning. (F) *Picnic*. Kim Novak and Rosalind Russell appeared in *Picnic*.

Picnic for Two, A 1905 w. Arthur J. Lamb m. Albert Von Tilzer

Picture Me Without You 1936 w. Ted Koehler m. Jimmy McHugh. (MF) *Dimples*. Shirley Temple and Frank Morgan appeared in *Dimples*. (*Not* ''A Picture of Me Without You'' by Porter).

Picture No Artist Can Paint, A 1899 w.m. J. Fred Helf. (MT) *Hodge Podge and Co.*

Picture of Me Without You, A 1935 w.m. Cole Porter. (MT) *Jubilee*.

Picture of You, A 1962 w.m. Johnny Beveridge, Peter Oakman

Picture Parade w.m. Jack Beaver. (TV-BBC) *Picture Parade*.

Picture That's Turned to (Toward) the Wall, The 1891 w.m. Charles Graham

Pictures at an Exhibition 1887 m. Modeste Mussorgsky. An 1873 exhibition of the paintings of Victor Alexander Hartmann served as the inspiration for this work.

Pictures In the Sky 1972 w.m. John Fiddler

Pieces of Dreams 1970 w.m. Alan Bergman, Marilyn Bergman, Michel Legrand. (F) *Pieces of Dreams*.

Pied Piper, The 1965 w.m. A. Kernfeld, Steve Duboff

Pierette and Pierrot 1911 w.m. Franz Lehàr, Robert Bodansky, A.M. Willner. (MT) *The Count of Luxembourg*. May de Sousa appeared in *The Count of Luxembourg*.

Pigalle 1949 w.m. Georges Konyn, Charles Newman, Georges Ulmer

Pigeon Walk 1914 m. James V. Monaco

Pilgrim Fathers, The, *see* **The Landing of the Pilgrims**

Pilgrim's Chorus 1845 w.m. Richard Wagner. From the opera *Tannhäuser*. *Tannhäuser* was first performed in Dresden on October 19, 1845.

Pillow Talk 1959 w.m. Inez James, Buddy Pepper. (F) *Pillow Talk*. Doris Day and Rock Hudson appeared in *Pillow Talk*.

Pillsbury Says It Best 1957 w.m. Leo Burnett Company, Inc. This song was written for a Pillsbury Flour commerical promotion campaign.

Pilot Me 1928 w.m. Gregory Dane Brown

Pinball Wizard 1975 w.m. Peter Townshend

Piney Ridge 1915 w. Ballard MacDonald m. Halsey K. Mohr

(Theme from) Pink Panther, The 1964 m. Henry Mancini. (MF) *The Blues Brothers*. (F) *The Pink Panther*. Cab Calloway, Aretha Franklin, and Ray Charles appeared in *The Blues Brothers*. Peter Sellers and Claudia Cardinale appeared in *The Pink Panther*.

Pink Shoelaces   1958   w.m. Mickie Grant

Pipes of Pan, The   1909   w.m. Lionel Monckton, Arthur Wimperis, Howard Talbot. (MT) *The Arcadians.* Florence Smithson appeared in *The Arcadians.*

Pipes of Pan Are Calling, The   1905   w.m. Lionel Monckton

Pirate Jenny   1933   Ger.w. Bertolt Brecht. Eng.w. Marc Blitzstein   m. Kurt Weill. (MT) *The Threepenny Opera.*

Pirate Song, or, Fifteen Men on a (the) Dead Man's Chest—Yo! Ho! Ho! and a Bottle of Rum   uncertain   w.m. anon.; arr. Henry F. Gilbert

Pirate's Chorus, *see* **Hail, Hail, the Gang's All Here**

Pistol Packin' Mama   1943   w.m. Al Dexter

Pittsburgh, Pennsylvania   1952   w.m. Bob Merrill

Pizzicati   1876   m. Léo Délibes. From the ballet *Sylvia.*

Place in the Sun, A   1966   w.m. Ronald Miller, Bryan Wells

Plant a Watermelon on My Grave and Let the Juice Soak Through   1910   w.m. Frank Dumont, R.P. Lilly

Play a Simple Melody   1914   w.m. Irving Berlin. (MT) *Watch Your Step.* (MF) *There's No Business Like Show Business.* Vernon and Irene Castle appeared in *Watch Your Step.* Ethel Merman and Dan Dailey appeared in *There's No Business Like Show Business.* This song was popularly revived in 1950.

Play, Fiddle, Play   1932   w. Jack Lawrence   m. Arthur Altman, Emergy Deutsch. Possibly based on the verse of "Gypsy Love Song" by Victor Herbert and the first theme of the First Piano Concerto in E-minor by Chopin.

Play Gypsies—Dance Gypsies   1926   w. Harry B. Smith   m. Emmerich Kalman. (MT) *Countess Maritza.* Yvonne D'Arle and Walter Woolf appeared in *Countess Maritza.*

Play Me Hearts and Flowers (I Wanna Cry)   1955   w.m. Mann Curtis, Sanford Green. This song was introduced by Johnny Desmond on the *Philco Playhouse* television program.

Play Orchestra Play   1936   w.m. Noël Coward. (MT) *Tonight at 8:30 (Shadow Play).* Noël Coward and Gertrude Lawrence appeared in the British production of *Tonight at 8:30.*

Play That Barbershop Chord (Mister Jefferson Lord)   1910   w. Ballard MacDonald, William Tracey   m. Lewis F. Muir. (MF) *In the Good Old Summertime.* Judy Garland, Van Johnson, Spring Byington, and Buster Keaton appeared in *In the Good Old Summertime.*

Play That Funky Music   1976   w.m. Robert Parissi

Play to Me, Gypsy   1934   Orig. w. Beda   Eng.w. Jimmy Kennedy   m. Karel Vacek

Playground in My Mind   1973   w.m. Lee Pockriss, Paul Vance

Playmates   1889   w.m. Harry Dacre

Playmates   1940   w.m. Saxie Dowell

Playthings   1921   w.m. Horatio Nicholls, Worton David

Please   1932   w. Leo Robin   m. Ralph Rainger. (MF) *The Big Broadcast.* (F) *From Hell to Heaven.* Bing Crosby and Kate Smith appeared in *The Big Broadcast.* Carole Lombard and Jack Oakie appeared in *From Hell to Heaven.*

Please Be Kind   1938   w.m. Sammy Cahn, Saul Chaplin

Please Believe Me   1935   w. Larry Yoell   m. Al Jacobs

Please Come and Play in My Yard   1904   w. Edward Madden   m. Theodore F. Morse

Please Don't Go   1979   w.m. Harry Casey, Richard Finch

Please Don't Mention It   1932   w.m. Harry S. Pepper

Please Don't Say No   1944   w. Ralph Freed   m. Sammy Fain. (MF) *Thrill of a Romance.* Van Johnson and Ester Williams appeared in *Thrill of a Romance.*

Please Don't Take My Lovin' Man Away   1912   w. Lew Brown   m. Albert Von Tilzer

Please Don't Talk About Me When I'm Gone   1930   w.m. Sidney Clare, Sam H. Stept, Bee Palmer. (MF) *Lullaby of Broadway.* Doris Day and Billy DeWolf appeared in *Lullaby of Broadway.*

Please Don't Tease   1960   w.m. Bruce Welch, Peter Chester

Please Go 'Way and Let Me Sleep   1902   w.m. J. Tim Bryman; erroneously credited to Harry Von Tilzer. See also "Somebody Else Is Taking My Place." See also Part I, 1914.

Please Hello   1976   w.m. Stephen Sondheim. (MT) *Pacific Overtures.* Mako appeared in *Pacific Overtures.*

Please Help Me I'm Falling   1960   w.m. Hal Blair, Don Robertson

Please Mister Please   1975   w.m. John Henry Rostill, Bruce Welch

Please Mister Postman   1961   w.m. Brian Holland, Robert Bateman, Fred Gorman. This song was popularly revived in 1964, and later again in 1975.

Please Mister Sun   1952   w. Sid Frank   m. Ray Getzov

Please Please Me   1964   w.m. John Lennon, Paul McCartney

Plenty To Be Thankful For   1942   w.m. Irving Berlin. (MF) *Holiday Inn.* Bing Crosby and Fred Astaire appeared in *Holiday Inn.*

Plink, Plank, Plunk   1952   m. Leroy Anderson

Plum Pudding   1884   w. Edward Harrigan   m. David Braham

Plume de Ma Tante, La (The Pen of My Aunt)   1959   w.m. Al Hoffman, Dick Manning

(I've Got) Pocketful of Dreams, A   1938   w.m. John Burke, James Monaco. (MF) *Sing You Sinners.* Bing Crosby and Fred MacMurray appeared in *Sing You Sinners.*

Pocketful of Miracles   1961   w. Sammy Cahn   m. James Van Heusen. (F) *Pocketful of Miracles.* Glenn Ford, Bette Davis, and Hope Lange appeared in *Pocketful of Miracles.*

Poet and Peasant Overture   1854   m. Franz von Suppé. From the German "Dichter und Bauer."

Poetry in Motion   1960   w.m. Mike Anthony, Paul Kaufman

Poetry Man   1975   w.m. Phoebe Snow

Poinciana   1936   w.m. Buddy Bernier, Nat Simon. This song was popularly revived in 1944.

Point of No Return, The   1960   w.m. John Harris, Derek New

Poldark 1977 w.m. Kenyon Emrys-Roberts. Ivor Novello Award winner 1977–78.

Policeman's Holiday, The 1911 w.m. Montague Ewing, Earl Berwick. The words to this song were added in 1932.

Polish Dance 1872 m. Xavier Scharwenka

Politics and Poker 1959 w. Sheldon Harnick m. Jerry Bock. (MT) *Fiorello!*.

Polk Salad Annie 1969 w.m. Tony Joe White

Polka Dots and Moonbeams 1940 w. Johnny Burke m. Jimmy Van Heusen

Polly Perkins of Paddington Green 1912 w.m. Harry Clifton

Polly Put the Kettle On, *see* **Mother Goose's Melodies** *and* **O Du Lieber Augustin**

Polly Wolly Doodle 1883 w.m. traditional black American minstrel song. (F) *Tangier*. Maria Montez and Preston Foster appeared in *Tangier*.

Polonaise Militaire, op. 40, no. 1 in A 1840 m. Frédéric Chopin

Polovetsian Dances 1888 m. Alexander Borodin. From the opera *Prince Igor. Prince Igor* was first performed in St. Petersburg on November 4, 1890, shortly after Borodin's death. See also "Stranger in Paradise."

Pomp and Circumstance, op.39, no. 1 1902 w. Arthur Benson m. Edward Elgar. This song was performed at the coronation ceremonies of King Edward VII. Its title is from a line in Shakespeare's *Othello,* Act III, Scene 3.

Pony Boy, *see* **My Pony Boy**

Pony Time 1961 w.m. Don Covay, John Berry

Poor Butterfly 1916 w. John L. Golden m. Raymond Hubbell. (MT) *The Big Show*.

Poor John 1906 w. Fred W. Leigh m. Henry E. Pether

Poor Jud (Is Daid) 1943 w. Oscar Hammerstein II m. Richard Rodgers. (MT) *Oklahoma!*. (MF) *Oklahoma!*. Alfred Drake, Betty Garde, and Celeste Holm appeared in the stage production of *Oklahoma!*. Shirley Jones and Gordon MacRae appeared in the film production of *Oklahoma!*.

Poor Little Angeline 1936 w.m. Will Grosz, Jimmy Kennedy

Poor Little Fool 1958 w.m. Shari Sheeley

Poor Little Hollywood Star 1962 w. Carolyn Leigh m. Cy Coleman. (MT) *Little Me*. Sid Caesar appeared in *Little Me*.

Poor Little Rich Girl 1925 w.m. Noël Coward, Philip Braham. (MT) *On with the Dance*. (MT) *Andre Charlot's Revue of 1926*. Alice Delysia appeared in *On with the Dance*.

Poor Me 1960 w.m. Les Vandyke

Poor Old Slave 1851 w.m. anon.

Poor Papa (He's Got Nuthin' At All) 1926 w. Billy Rose m. Harry Woods

Poor Pauline 1914 w. Charles McCarron m. Raymond Walker. (F) *The Adventures of Pauline*. (MF) *The Perils of Pauline*. Pearl White appeared in *The Adventures of Pauline*. Betty Hutton, John Lund, and Billy DeWolfe appeared in *The Perils of Pauline*. This song was written for the piano

and orchestra accompaniment to Pauline's weekly perils in the silent serial, *The Adventures of Pauline*.

Poor People of Paris, The 1956 Fr.w. René Rouzaud Eng.w. Jack Lawrence m. Marguerite Monnot. From the French "La Goulant du Pauvre Jean."

Poor Pierrot 1931 w. Otto Harbach m. Jerome Kern. (MT) *The Cat and the Fiddle*. (MF) *The Cat and the Fiddle*. Jeanette MacDonald, Charles Butterworth, and Vivienne Segal appeared in the film production of *The Cat and the Fiddle*.

Poor Side of Town 1966 w.m. Johnny Rivers, Lou Adler

Poor Tom, *see* **Tom Bowling**

Poor Wayfaring Stranger, *see* **Wayfarin' Stranger**

Pop Goes the Weasel 1853 w.m. possibly Charles Twiggs. The melody to this standard is based on a traditional English dance. In London of 1853, hatters would pawn ("pop") their instrument of trade ("weasels") on Saturday nights.

Popcorn 1970 w.m. Gershon Kingsley

Pope He Leads a Happy Life, The 1842 w.m. anon.

(I'm) Popeye the Sailor Man 1931 w.m. Sammy Lerner. See also Part I, 1931.

Poppa Won't You Dance with Me, *see* **Papa Won't You Dance with Me**

Portrait of a Flirt 1948 w.m. Robert J. Farnon

Portrait of Jennie 1949 w.m. Dimitri Tiomkin

Portrait of My Love, A 1961 w.m. Cyril Ornadel, Norman Newell. Ivor Novello Award winner 1960. Ivor Novello Award winner 1961.

Portuguese Washerwomen, The 1955 w.m. André Popp, Roger Lucchesi

Positively Fourth Street 1965 w.m. Bob Dylan

Possession Obsession 1986 w.m. Sara Allen, Daryl Hall, John Oates

Possibly 1927 w.m. Carroll Gibbons, James Dyrenforth

Potatoes Are Cheaper—Tomatoes Are Cheaper, *see* **Now's the Time To Fall In Love**

Poupée Valsante (Waltzing Doll) 1903 m. Eduard Poldini. This piece was written in 1895, and first published in 1903 by G. Schirmer.

Poverty's Tears Ebb and Flow 1885 w. Edward Harrigan m. David Braham. (MT) *Old Lavender*.

Powder Your Face with Sunshine 1949 w.m. Carmen Lombardo, Stanley Rochinski. (MF) *Cow Town*. Gene Autry and Gail Davis appeared in *Cow Town*.

Power Game, The 1966 w.m. Wayne Hill

Power of Gold 1979 w.m. Dan Fogelberg

Power of Love, The 1985 w.m. Johnny Colla, Chris Hayes, Huey Lewis. (F) *Back To the Future*.

Power to All Our Friends 1974 w.m. Doug Flett, Guy Fletcher. Ivor Novello Award winner 1973–74.

Practice Makes Perfect 1940 w.m. Ernest Gold

Praeludium 1919 w.m. Armas Jarnefelt

Praise God from Whom All Blessings Flow, *see* **Old Hundred(th) Doxology**

Praise the Lord and Pass the Ammunition 1942 w.m.

Frank Loesser. Possibly inspired by the melody of "The Old Grey Mare" and certainly by the words of Chaplain Maguire aboard a U.S. Navy warship en route to Pearl Harbor. See also "The Old Grey Mare."

Prayer of Thanksgiving, *see* **We Gather Together**

Preacher and the Bear, The 1904 w.m. George Fairman; arr. Joe Arzonia (Arthur Longbrake). This song was popularly revived in 1947. George Fairman wrote this song while playing the piano at The Harp tavern in Columbus, Ohio, and later sold it to Joe Arzonia in an attempt to raise cash to leave town. Theme song of Phil Harris's radio show.

Precious and Few 1972 w.m. Walter Nims

Precious Little Thing Called Love, A 1928 w.m. Lou Davis, J. Fred Coots. (F) *Shopworn Angel.* Gary Cooper and Nancy Carroll appeared in *Shopworn Angel.*

Precious Love 1979 w.m. Robert L. Welch

Prelude, op.28, no.7 1839 m. Frédéric Chopin

Prelude in C# minor, op.3, no.2 1893 m. Sergei Rachmaninoff. This work was composed by Rachmaninoff at age nineteen.

Prelude to a Kiss 1938 w.m. Irving Gordon, Irving Mills, Edward Kennedy "Duke" Ellington

Prelude to the Stars 1945 w.m. Vic Oliver

Preludes (nos. 1,2,3) 1927 m. George Gershwin

President Grant's March 1868 m. Patrick S. Gilmore. Written on Grant's election to the Presidency, this march is still played at the White House.

President's March, The 1789 m. Philip Phile. This work was supposedly played at George Washington's inauguration. See also "Hail Columbia."

Pretend 1953 w.m. Lew Douglas, Cliff Parman, Frank Lavere

Pretty Baby 1916 w. Gus Kahn m. Egbert Van Alstyne, Tony Jackson. (MT) *The Passing Show of 1916.* (MT) *Houp-La.* (MF) *Rose of Washington Square.* (MF) *Is Everybody Happy.* (MF) *Broadway Rhythm.* (MF) *Jolson Sings Again.* (MF) *I'll See You in My Dreams.* (MF) *The Eddie Cantor Story.* Gertie Millar appeared in *Houp-La.* Al Jolson appeared in *Rose of Washington Square.* Larry Parks appeared in *Is Everybody Happy,* biopic of bandleader Ted Lewis, and *Jolson Sings Again.* Lena Horne and Charles Winninger appeared in *Broadway Rhythm.* Doris Day and Danny Thomas appeared in *I'll See You in My Dreams,* biopic of song writer Gus Kahn.

Pretty Edelweiss 1915 w. Matthew Woodward, Joseph Herbert m. Franz Lehár. (MT) *Alone at Last.* Elizabeth Goodhall, Madame Namara, and Roy Atwell appeared in *Alone at Last.*

Pretty Flamingo 1966 w.m. Mark Barkan

Pretty Girl, A 1891 w. J. Cheever Goodwin m. Woolson Morse. (MT) *Wang.*

Pretty Girl Is Like a Melody, A 1919 w.m. Irving Berlin. (MT) *Ziegfeld Follies of 1919.* (MF) *The Great Ziegfeld.* (MF) *Alexander's Ragtime Band.* (MF) *Blue Skies.* (MF) *There's No Business Like Show Business.* William Powell, Frank Morgan, and Virginia Bruce appeared in *The Great Ziegfeld.*

Don Ameche and Ethel Merman appeared in *Alexander's Ragtime Band.* Bing Crosby and Fred Astaire appeared in *Blue Skies.* Ethel Merman and Marilyn Monroe appeared in *There's No Business Like Show Business.*

Pretty Kitty Kelly 1920 w. Harry Pease m. Ed G. Nelson

Pretty Lady 1976 w.m. Stephen Sondheim. (MT) *Pacific Overtures.* (MT) *Side by Side by Sondheim.* Mako appeared in *Pacific Overtures.* Millicent Martin and Julie N. McKenzie appeared in *Side by Side by Sondheim.*

Pretty Little Poppy, *see* **Amapola**

Pretty Women 1979 w.m. Stephen Sondheim. (MT) *Sweeney Todd.* Angela Lansbury and Len Cariou appeared in *Sweeney Todd.*

Pretty Young Thing, *see* **P.Y.T.**

Prime Time 1984 w.m. Alan Parsons, Eric Woolfson

Primrose 1939 w.m. Ivor Novello, Christopher Hassall. (MT) *The Dancing Years.* Roma Beaumont appeared in *The Dancing Years.*

Primrose Hill 1946 w.m. Charlie Chester, Ken Morris, Everett Lynton

Prince of Wails 1924 w.m. Elmer Schoebel

Princesita 1928 Sp.w. M.E. Palomero Eng.w. Frederick Herman Martens m. José Padilla

Princeton Cannon Song, *see* **The Cannon Song**

Princeton, That's All 1904 w.m. Kenneth Clark. School song of Princeton University.

Prisoner of Hope 1981 w.m. Sterling Whipple, Gerald Metcalf

Prisoner of Love 1931 w. Leo Robin m. Russ Columbo, Clarence Gaskill. This song was popularly revived in 1946.

Prisoner's Song, The 1924 w.m. Guy Massey. See also Part I, 1924.

Private Eyes 1981 w.m. Joanna Allen, Sara Allen, Daryl Hall, Warren Pash

Private Investigations 1983 w. Mark Knopfler. Ivor Novello Award winner 1982–83.

Promise Her Anything But Give Her Love 1957 w.m. Roy Alfred

Promise, Love, *see* **Júrame**

Promise Me a Rose 1959 w.m. Bob Merrill. (MT) *Take Me Along.* Jackie Gleason, Walter Pidgeon, and Eileen Herlie appeared in *Take Me Along.*

Promises Promises 1968 w. Hal David m. Burt Bacharach. (MT) *Promises, Promises.*

Proud Mary 1969 w.m. John C. Fogerty

Prove It by the Things You Do (It's Easy To Say) 1945 w.m. Allan Roberts, Doris Fisher

P.S. I Love You 1934 w. Johnny Mercer m. Gordon Jenkins. This song was popularly revived in 1953.

P.S. I Love You 1962 w.m. John Lennon, Paul McCartney. This song was most popular in 1964.

Pucker Up Your Lips, Miss Lindy 1912 w. Eli Dawson m. Albert Von Tilzer

Puddin' Head Jones 1933 w.m. Alfred Bryan, Lou Handman

Puff the Magic Dragon 1963 w.m. Leonard Lipton, Peter Yarrow. During the drug culture of the late 1960s, this song supposedly alluded to the smoking of marijuana and the taking of hallucinogenic drugs.

Pullman Porters on Parade, The 1913 w. Ren. G. May (Irving Berlin) m. Maurice Abrahams. Irving Berlin's pseudonym, Ren G. May, is an anagram for "Germany"; Berlin is, of course, the capital of Germany, and ironically, his songs were banned there during World War II.

Puppchen 1935 w.m. Bert Kalmar, Harry Ruby

Puppet on a String 1968 w.m. Bill Martin, Phil Coulter. Ivor Novello Award winner 1967–68.

Puppy Love 1960 w.m. Paul Anka

Purple People Eater, The 1958 w.m. Sheb Wooley

Purple Rain 1984 w.m. Prince. (MF) *Purple Rain*. Prince appeared in *Purple Rain*. Grammy Award winner 1984.

Push De Button 1957 w. E.Y. Harburg m. Harold Arlen. (MT) *Jamaica*. (MT) *Lena Horne: The Lady and Her Music*. Lena Horne appeared in *Lena Horne: The Lady and Her Music*.

Push Dem Clouds Away 1892 w.m. Percy Gaunt. (MT) *A Trip to Chinatown*.

Pushbike Song, The 1971 w.m. Idris Jones, Evan Jones

Put a Little Love in Your Heart 1969 w.m. Randy James Myers, Jackie De Shannon, Jimmy Holiday

Put Away a Little Ray of Golden Sunshine 1924 w. Sam M. Lewis, Joe Young m. Fred E. Ahlert

Put 'Em in a Box, Tie 'Em with a Ribbon (And Throw 'Em In the Deep Blue Sea) 1948 w. Sammy Cahn m. Jule Styne. (MF) *Romance on the High Seas*. (MF) *It's Magic*. Doris Day and Jack Carson appeared in *Romance on the High Seas*. Doris Day appeared in *It's Magic*.

Put It There Pal 1946 w.m. Jimmy Van Heusen, Johnny Burke. (MF) *The Road to Utopia*. Bing Crosby, Bob Hope, and Dorothy Lamour appeared in *The Road to Utopia*.

Put Me Amongst the Girls 1908 w.m. C.W. Murphy, Dan Lipton

Put Me Off at Buffalo 1895 w. Harry Dillon m. John Dillon. See also Part I, 1901.

Put Me To Sleep with an Old-Fashioned Melody 1915 w. Sam M. Lewis, Dick Howard m. Harry Jentes

Put On a Happy Face 1960 w. Lee Adams m. Charles Strouse. (MT) *Bye Bye Birdie*. (MF) *Bye Bye Birdie*. Dick Van Dyke and Ann-Margret appeared in the film production of *Bye Bye Birdie*.

Put On Your Old Grey Bonnet 1909 w. Stanley Murphy m. Percy Wenrich

Put On Your Slippers and Fill Up Your Pipe 1916 w. Edward P. Moran, Will A. Heelan m. Albert Von Tilzer

Put On Your Sunday Clothes 1964 w.m. Jerry Herman. (MT) *Hello, Dolly!* (MT) *Jerry's Girls*. (MF) *Hello, Dolly!* Carol Channing appeared in the stage production of *Hello, Dolly!* Dorothy Loudon, Chita Rivera, and Leslie Uggams appeared in *Jerry's Girls*. Barbra Streisand appeared in the film production of *Hello, Dolly!*

Put On Your Ta Ta Little Girlie 1911 w.m. Fred W. Leigh

Put the Blame on Mame 1946 w.m. Allan Roberts, Doris Fisher. (MF) *Gilda*. (MF) *Betty Co-Ed*. Rita Hayworth and Glenn Ford appeared in *Gilda*. Jean Porter and Shirley Mills appeared in *Betty Co-Ed*.

Put Your Arms Around Me Honey (Hold Me Tight) 1910 w. Junie McCree m. Albert Von Tilzer. (MF) *Coney Island*. (MF) *Louisiana Hayride*. (MF) *In the Good Old Summertime*. Betty Grable and Caesar Romero appeared in *Coney Island*. Judy Canova and Ross Hunter appeared in *Louisiana Hayride*. Judy Garland, Van Johnson, and Spring Byington appeared in *In the Good Old Summertime*. This song was popularly revived in 1943.

Put Your Dreams Away for Another Day 1942 w. Ruth Lowe m. Paul Mann, Stephan Weiss

Put Your Hand in the Hand 1971 w.m. Gene MacLellan

Put Your Hands Together 1973 w.m. Kenneth Gamble, Leon Huff

Put Your Head on My Shoulder 1959 w.m. Paul Anka. This song was popularly revived in 1969.

Put Your Shoes On, Lucy 1949 w.m. Hank Fort

Put-ti Put-ti, *see* **Cement Mixer**

Puttin' On the Ritz 1929 w.m. Irving Berlin. (MF) *Puttin' On the Ritz*. (MF) *Blue Skies*. Joan Bennett and Harry Richman appeared in *Puttin' On the Ritz*. Bing Crosby and Fred Astaire appeared in *Blue Skies*. This song was popularly revived in 1946 and later again in 1983. Theme song of Harry Richman.

Putting It Together 1984 w.m. Stephen Sondheim. (MT) *Sunday in the Park with George*. Mandy Patinkin and Bernadette Peters appeared in *Sunday in the Park with George*.

P.Y.T. (Pretty Young Thing) 1984 w.m. James Ingram, Quincy Jones

Quarter to Three Waltz 1961 w.m. Gene Barge, Frank J. Guida, Gary Anderson, Joseph Royster

Que Será, Será, *see* **Whatever Will Be Will Be**

Queen of Hearts 1981 w.m. Henry Devito

Queen of the Hop 1958 w.m. Woody Harris

Queen Was in the Parlour, The 1931 w.m. Sherman Myers

Quest, The, *see* **The Impossible Dream**

Question and Answer (Demande et Reponse) 1943 w.m. Samuel Coleridge-Taylor, Stanley Arthur. Based on Coleridge-Taylor's "Petite Suite de Concert," op.77.

Quiéreme Mucho, *see* **Yours**

Quiet Girl, A 1953 w. Betty Comden, Adolph Green m. Leonard Bernstein. (MT) *Wonderful Town*.

Quiet Girl, A 1966 w.m. John Hanson

Quiet Night 1936 w. Lorenz Hart m. Richard Rodgers. (MT) *On Your Toes*. (MF) *On Your Toes*. Zorina and Eddie Albert appeared in the film production of *On Your Toes*.

Quiet Village, *see* **My Quiet Village**

Quiller Has the Brains 1900 w. Harry B. Smith m. Reginald DeKoven. (MT) *Foxy Quiller*.

Quilting Party, The *see* **When I Saw Sweet Nellie Home**

Race Is On, The 1964 w.m. Don Rollins

(When You're) Racing with the Clock 1954 w.m. Richard Adler, Jerry Ross. (MT) *The Pajama Game.* (MF) *The Pajama Game.* Doris Day appeared in the film production of *The Pajama Game.*

Racing with the Moon 1941 w.m. Vaughn Monroe, Pauline Pope, Johnny Watson. Theme song of the Vaughn Monroe orchestra.

Rackety-Coo! 1916 w. Otto Harbach m. Rudolf Friml. (MT) *Katinka.* Adele Rowland and Franklyn Ardell appeared in *Katinka.*

Rag Doll 1964 w.m. Robert Crewe, Jr., Robert Gaudio

Rag Mop 1950 w.m. Johnnie Lee Wills, Deacon Anderson. (MF) *Honeychile.* Judy Canova and Eddie Foy, Jr. appeared in *Honeychile.*

Raggedy Ann 1923 w. Anne Caldwell m. Jerome Kern (MT) *The Stepping Stones.*

Ragging the Scale 1915 w. Dave Ringle m. Edward B. Claypoole. This song was published in 1915 without words.

Rags, Bottles or Bones 1938 w.m. Stanley Holloway, Harry S. Pepper. Theme song of Syd Walker.

Rags to Riches 1953 w.m. Richard Adler, Jerry Ross

Ragtime Cowboy Joe 1912 w.m. Lewis F. Muir, Grant Clarke, Maurice Abrahams. (MF) *Hello Frisco Hello.* (MF) *Incendiary Blonde.* Alice Faye and John Payne appeared in *Hello Frisco Hello.* Betty Hutton appeared in *Incendiary Blonde,* biopic of speakeasy hostess Texas Guinan.

Ragtime Violin 1911 w.m. Irving Berlin

(Theme from) Raiders of the Lost Ark 1981 m. John Williams. (F) *Raiders of the Lost Ark.* Harrison Ford and Karen Allen appeared in *Raiders of the Lost Ark.* Grammy Award winner 1981.

Railroad Jim 1915 w.m. Nat H. Vincent

Railroader's Lament, *see* **Five Hundred Miles**

Rain 1927 w.m. Eugene Ford. With this song Rudy Vallee first used a megaphone, later to become his professional trademark, to amplify his weak voice.

Rain 1934 w. William Hill m. Peter DeRose

Rain Forest 1977 w.m. Biddu

Rain in Spain, The 1956 w. Alan Jay Lerner m. Frederick Loewe. (MT) *My Fair Lady.* (MF) *My Fair Lady.* Julie Andrews and Rex Harrison appeared in the stage production of *My Fair Lady.* Audrey Hepburn and Rex Harrison appeared in the film production of *My Fair Lady.*

Rain, the Park and Other Things, The 1967 w.m. Artie Kornfeld, Steve Duboff

Rainbow 1908 w.m. Percy Wenrich

Rainbow 1957 w.m. Ronald Hulme, (Russ Hamilton)

Rainbow on the River 1936 w. Paul Francis Webster m. Louis Alter. (MF) *Rainbow on the River.* Bobby Breen and Charles Butterworth appeared in *Rainbow on the River.*

Rainbow Road, De 1891 w. Edward Harrigan m. David Braham

Rainbow Round My Shoulder, *see* **There's a Rainbow Round My Shoulder**

Rainbow Stew 1981 w.m. Merle Haggard

Raindrops 1961 w.m. Dee Clark

Raindrops Keep Fallin' on My Head 1970 w. Hal David m. Burt Bacharach. (F) *Butch Cassidy and the Sundance Kid.* Paul Newman and Robert Redford appeared in *Butch Cassidy and the Sundance Kid.* Academy Award winner 1969.

(The Song of) Raintree County 1959 w.m. Paul Francis Webster, Johnny Green. (F) *Raintree County.*

Rainy Day, The 1847 w. Henry Wadsworth Longfellow m. Isaac Baker Woodbury

Rainy Day Women #12 & 35 1966 w.m. Bob Dylan

Rainy Days and Mondays 1971 w.m. Roger Nicholls, Paul Williams

Rainy Night in Rio 1946 w. Leo Robin m. Arthur Schwartz. (MF) *The Time, the Place and the Girl.* Dennis Morgan and Jack Carson appeared in *The Time, the Place and the Girl.*

Ramblin' Man 1973 w.m. Dicky Betts

Rambling Rose 1948 w.m. Joseph McCarthy, Joe Burke

Ramblin' Rose 1962 w.m. Joe Sherman, Noel Sherman

Rambling Wreck from Georgia Tech 1919 w.m. Frank Roman. Based on the 1894 version of the traditional "Dunderbeck," or, "Johnny Vorbeck," and the earlier "Son of a Gambolier." This song was popularly revived in 1936. School song for the Georgia Institute of Technology.

Rameaux, Les, *see* **The Palm Trees**

Ramona 1927 w. L. Wolfe Gilbert m. Mabel Wayne. (F) *Ramona.* Dolores Del Rio appeared in *Ramona.* This song, written for the piano and orchestra accompaniment to the silent film, was performed by Dolores Del Rio on a national tour to help promote the film.

Rancho Grande, El 1934 Sp.w. Silvano R. Ramos Eng.w. Bartley Costello m. Silvano R. Ramos. (MF) *Mexicali Rose.* (MF) *My Pal Trigger.* Gene Autry appeared in *Mexicali Rose.* Roy Rogers, Dale Evans, and Gabby Hayes appeared in *My Pal Trigger.* This song was popularly revived in 1939.

Ranger's Song, The 1926 w. Joseph McCarthy m. Harry Tierney. (MT) *Rio Rita.* (MF) *Rio Rita* (1929). (MF) *Rio Rita* (1942). Bert Wheeler, John Boles, and Dorothy Lee appeared in the 1929 film production of *Rio Rita.* Bud Abbott, Lou Costello, and Kathryn Grayson appeared in the 1942 film production of *Rio Rita.*

Rap Tap on Wood 1936 w.m. Cole Porter. (MF) *Born To Dance.* Eleanor Powell, James Stewart, and Una Merkel appeared in *Born To Dance.*

Rapture 1981 w.m. Deborah Harry, Chris Stein

Raspberry Beret 1985 w.m. Prince

Rastus on Parade 1895 w. George Marion m. Kerry Mills. This song was so popular in its day that a resident of Troy, New York, requested that it be played at his funeral. See also Part I, 1896.

Raunchy 1957 w.m. William Justis, Sidney Manker

(Theme from) Rawhide 1959 w.m. Ned Washington, Dimitri Tiomkin. (MF) *The Blues Brothers.* (TV) *Rawhide.* Cab Calloway, Aretha Franklin, and Ray Charles appeared in *The Blues Brothers*. This theme was sung by Frankie Laine during the opening credits for *Rawhide*.

Razzazza Mazzazza 1905 m. Arthur Pryor

Razzle Dazzle 1975 w. Fred Ebb m. John Kander. (MT) *Chicago*. Gwen Verdon and Chita Rivera appeared in *Chicago*.

Reach Out and Touch 1970 w.m. Charles F. Brown

Reach Out for Me 1964 w. Hal David m. Burt F. Bacharach

Reach Out I'll Be There 1966 w.m. Eddie Holland, Brian Holland, Lamont Dozier

Reaching for the Moon 1926 w.m. Benny Davis, Jesse Greer

Reaching for the Moon 1930 w.m. Irving Berlin. (F) *Reaching for the Moon*. Douglas Fairbanks, Bebe Daniels, and Edward Everett Horton appeared in *Reaching for the Moon*.

Read 'Em and Weep 1984 w.m. Jim Steinman

Ready To Take a Chance Again 1978 w.m. Charles Fox, Norman Gimbel

Ready, Willing and Able 1955 w.m. Al Rinker, Floyd Huddleston, Dick Gleason. (MF) *Young at Heart*. Frank Sinatra, Doris Day, and Ethel Barrymore appeared in *Young at Heart*.

Real Goodness from Kentucky Fried Chicken 1975 w. Hal Kome m. Comtrack, Inc. This song was written for a Kentucky Fried Chicken commercial promotion campaign.

Real Live Girl 1962 w. Carolyn Leigh m. Cy Coleman. (MT) *Little Me*. This song was most popular in 1965.

Real Love 1985 w.m. David Malloy, Randy McCormick

Real Nice Clambake, A, *see* **This Was a Real Nice Clambake**

Rebecca of Sunny-Brook Farm 1914 w. A. Seymour Brown m. Albert Gumble

Recessional 1898 w. Rudyard Kipling m. Reginald DeKoven. The words to this song celebrate Queen Victoria's Diamond Jubilee.

Red Balloon, The 1969 w.m. Raymond Froggatt

Red Lips Kiss My Blues Away 1927 w.m. Alfred Bryan, James V. Monaco, Pete Wendling

Red Neckin' Love Makin' Night 1982 w.m. Max Barnes, Troy Seals

Red River Valley, The 1896 w.m. anon.; based on James Kerrigan's "In the Bright Mohawk Valley," and that in turn based on a traditional Canadian folksong. (MF) *King of the Cowboys*. Roy Rogers and Smiley Burnette appeared in *King of the Cowboys*. This song refers to the Red River of Lake Winnipeg, Manitoba, Canada.

Red Roses for a Blue Lady 1948 w.m. Sid Tepper, Roy Brodsky. This song was popularly revived in 1965.

Red Rubber Ball 1966 w.m. Paul Simon, Bruce Woodley

Red Sails In the Sunset 1935 w. Jimmy Kennedy m. Hugh Williams (Will Grosz). (MT) *Provincetown Follies*. Billy Green and Beatrice Kay appeared in *Provincetown Follies*. Theme song of Suzette Tarri.

Red Silk Stockings and Green Perfume 1947 w.m. Bob Hilliard, Sammy Mysels, Dick Sanford

Red, White and Blue, The, *see* **Columbia, the Gem of the Ocean**

Red Wing 1907 w. Thurland Chattaway m. Kerry Mills

Reflections 1967 w.m. Eddie Holland, Brian Holland, Lamont Dozier

Reflections In the Water 1933 w. Paul Francis Webster m. John Loeb

Reflections on the Water 1948 w.m. Billy Reid

Reflex, The 1984 w.m. Simon Le Bon, Andy Taylor, John Taylor, Roger Taylor. Ivor Novello Award winner 1984–85.

Regency Rakes 1934 w.m. Noël Coward. (MT) *Conversation Piece*.

Regiment of Sambre and Meuse, The 1917 Fr.w. Paul Cezano Eng.w. George Harris, Jr. m. Robert Planquette. From the French "Le Regiment de Sambre et Meuse."

Regimental Song 1928 w. Brian Hooker m. Rudolf Friml. (MT) *The White Eagle*.

Release Me 1954 w.m. Eddie Miller, W.S. Stevenson. This song was popularly revived in 1962 and 1967.

Relicario, El, *see* **My Toreador**

Remember 1925 w.m. Irving Berlin. (MT) *The Co-Optimists*. (MF) *Alexander's Ragtime Band*. (MF) *There's No Business Like Show Business*. Melville Gideon appeared in *The Co-Optimists*. Tyrone Power and Ethel Merman appeared in *Alexander's Ragtime Band*. Ethel Merman and Marilyn Monroe appeared in *There's No Business Like Show Business*.

Remember Boy, You're Irish (Shane na Lown) 1885 w.m. William J. Scanlan

Remember Me 1937 w. Al Dubin m. Harry Warren. (MF) *Mr. Dodd Takes the Air*. (F) *Never Say Goodbye*. Kenny Baker and Jane Wyman appeared in *Mr. Todd Takes the Air*. Eleanor Parker and Errol Flynn appeared in *Never Say Goodbye*.

Remember Pearl Harbor 1942 w.m. Don Reid, Sammy Kaye

Rememb'ring 1923 w.m. Vivian Duncan, Rosetta Duncan. (MT) *Topsy and Eva*. The Duncan Sisters appeared in *Topsy and Eva*.

Reminiscing 1978 w.m. Graham Goble

Renegade 1979 w.m. Tommy Shaw

Rescue the Perishing 1870 w. Mrs. Alexander Van Alstyne (Frances Jane Crosby) m. William Howard Doane

Respect 1967 w.m. Otis Redding. Grammy Award winner 1967.

Retreat uncertain w.m. anon. This traditional "American" bugle call actually was first heard by armies during medieval times.

Return to Me 1958 w. Danny Di Minno m. Carmen Lombardo

Return to Paradise 1953 w.m. Ned Washington, Dimitri Tiomkin

(Theme from) Return to Peyton Place, or, **The Wonderful Season of Love** 1958 w. Paul Francis Webster m. Franz Waxman. (F) *Return to Peyton Place*.

Return to Sender 1962 w.m. Winfield Scott, Otis Blackwell. (MF) *Girls! Girls! Girls!*. Elvis Presley and Stella Stevens appeared in *Girls! Girls! Girls!*.

Reuben and Rachel, or, **Reuben, Reuben, I've Been Thinking** 1871 w. Harry Birch m. William Gooch

Reunited 1979 w.m. Dino Fekaris, Freddie Perren

Reveille 1836 m. This standard bugle call was possibly written by a Frenchman as early as 1831 and published as "Le Réveil." This is the only traditional American bugle call not written by an American and still employed today in a foreign country.

Revenge 1928 w. Sam M. Lewis, Joe Young m. Harry Akst

Reverie 1895 m. Claude Debussy. See also "My Reverie."

Revival 1962 w.m. Joe Harriott

Revolution 1968 w.m. John Lennon, Paul McCartney. (MT) *Beatlemania*.

Rhapsody in Blue 1924 m. George Gershwin. (MT) *Blackbirds of 1934*. (MF) *King of Jazz*. (MF) *Rhapsody in Blue*. Bing Crosby and Paul Whiteman appeared in *King of Jazz*. Oscar Levant, Alexis Smith, and Robert Alda appeared in *Rhapsody in Blue*, biopic of composer George Gershwin. This work premiered at Aeolian Hall, New York, on February 12, 1924; it was arranged by Ferde Grofé and conducted by paul Whiteman. Theme song of Paul Whiteman.

Rhiannon 1976 w.m. Stephanie Nicks

Rhinestone Cowboy 1975 w.m. Larry Weiss

Rhumboogie, *see* **Rum Boogie**

Rhymes 1931 w.m. Leslie Sarony

(If I had) Rhythm in My Nursery Rhymes 1935 w. Sammy Cahn, Don Raye m. Jimmie Lunceford, Saul I. Chaplin

Rhythm Is Our Business 1934 w.m. Jimmie Lunceford, Saul Kaplan, Sammy Cahn. (MF) *It's Great To Be Young*.

Rhythm of the Night 1985 w.m. Diane Warren

Rhythm of the Rain 1935 w.m. Jack Meskill, Jack Stern. (MF) *Folies Bergère*. Maurice Chevalier and Merle Oberon appeared in *Folies Bergère*.

Rhythm of the Rain 1963 w.m. John Gummoe

Rhythm on the River 1940 w.m. Johnny Burke, James V. Monaco. (MF) *Rhythm on the River*. Bing Crosby and Mary Martin appeared in *Rhythm on the River*.

Rich and Rare Were the Gems She Wore 1807 w. Thomas Moore m. based on the traditional "The Summer Is Coming."

Rich Girl 1977 w.m. Daryl Hall

Ricochet 1953 w.m. Larry Coleman, Joe Darion, Norman Gimbel

Riddle Song, The, *see* **I Gave My Love a Cherry**

Ride Captain Ride 1970 w.m. Frank Konte, Carlos Pinera

Ride Like the Wind 1980 w.m. Christopher Cross

Ride On, Ride On 1918 w. Henry Hart Milman m. John Prindle Scott

Ride, Tenderfoot Ride. 1938 w.m. Johnny Mercer, Richard A. Whiting. (MF) *Romance and Rhythm*. (MF) *Ride Tenderfoot Ride*. (MF) *Cowboy from Brooklyn*. Dick Powell appeared in *Romance and Rhythm*. Gene Autry appeared in *Ride Tenderfoot Ride*. Dick Powell, Pat O'Brien, and Priscilla Lane appeared in *Cowboy from Brooklyn*.

Riders in the Sky, *see* **Ghost Rides in the Sky**

Ridin' High 1936 w.m. Cole Porter. (MT) *Red, Hot and Blue!* (MF) *Red, Hot and Blue!* Ethel Merman, Jimmy Durante, and Bob Hope appeared in the stage production of *Red, Hot and Blue!* Betty Hutton and Victor Mature appeared in the film production of *Red, Hot and Blue!*

Ridin' on the Moon 1946 w. Johnny Mercer m. Harold Arlen. (MT) *St. Louis Woman*. Pearl Bailey, Rex Ingram, and Ruby Hill appeared in *St. Louis Woman*.

Riff Song, The 1926 w. Otto Harbach, Oscar Hammerstein II m. Sigmund Romberg. (MT) *The Desert Song*. (MF) *The Desert Song* (1929). (MF) *The Desert Song* (1953). Harry Welchman and Edith Day appeared in the British stage production of *The Desert Song*. John Boles and Myrna Loy appeared in the 1929 film production of *The Desert Song*. Kathryn Grayson and Gordon MacRae appeared in the 1953 film production of *The Desert Song*.

Right as the Rain 1944 w. E.Y. Harburg m. Harold Arlen. (MT) *Bloomer Girl*.

Right Back Where We Started From 1976 w.m. Pierre Tubbs, Vincent Edwards

Right Place Wrong Time 1973 w.m. Dr. John (Malcolm Rebennack)

Right Said Fred 1962 w.m. Ted Dicks, Myles Rudge

Right Thing To Do, The 1973 w.m. Carly Simon

Rimpianto, *see* **Serenade**

Ring-a-Ding Girl 1962 w.m. Stan Butcher, Syd Cordell

Ring De Banjo 1851 w.m. Stephen Collins Foster. (MF) *Swanee River*. (F) *Colorado*. (MF) *I Dream of Jeanie*. Al Jolson and Don Ameche appeared in *Swanee River*. Roy Rogers and Gabby Hayes appeared in *Colorado*. Ray Middleton and Bill Shirley appeared in *I Dream of Jeanie*.

Ring Dem Bells 1930 w.m. Duke Ellington, Irving Mills. (MF) *Check and Double Check*. Duke Ellington and Amos and Andy appeared in *Check and Double Check*.

Ring Ding 1959 w.m. Steve Race

Ring of Kerry 1969 w.m. Peter Hope

Ring on the Finger Is Worth Two on the Phone, A 1911 w. Jack Mahoney m. George W. Meyer

Ringo 1964 w.m. Hal Blair, Don Robertson

Rio Rita 1926 w. Joseph McCarthy m. Harry Tierney. (MT) *Rio Rita*. (MF) *Rio Rita* (1929). (MF) *Rio Rita* (1942). Ethelind Terry and Bert Wheeler appeared in the American stage production of *Rio Rita*. Edith Day appeared in the British stage production of *Rio Rita*. Bert Wheeler and John Boles appeared in the 1929 film production of *Rio Rita*. Kathryn Grayson, Bud Abbott, and Lou Costello appeared in the 1942 film production of *Rio Rita*.

Rip Van Winkle Was a Lucky Man 1901 w. William Jerome m. Jean Schwartz

Rise 1979 w.m. Andy Armer, Randy W. Alpert

Rise and Fall of Flingle Bunt 1964 w.m. Bruce Welch, Hank B. Marvin, John Rostill, Brian Bennett

Rise and Shine 1932 w. B.G. DeSylva m. Vincent Youmans. (MT) *Take a Chance.* (MT) *Rise and Shine.* (MF) *Take a Chance.* Ethel Merman, Jack Whiting, and Jack Haley appeared in the stage production of *Take a Chance.* Charles "Buddy" Rogers and James Dunn appeared in the film production of *Take a Chance.*

Rise, Gentle Moon 1833 w. James Robinson Planché m. John Braham

Rites of Spring 1911 m. Igor Stravinsky. (MF) *Fantasia.*

Ritual Fire Dance 1924 (Sp.w. G. Martinez Sierra) m. Manuel de Falla. From the Spanish "Danza Ritual del Fuego," from de Falla's *El Amor Brujo* of 1921.

River Boat 1959 w.m. Bill Anderson

River Kwai March, The 1957 w.m. Malcolm Arnold. (F) *The Bridge On the River Kwai.* William Holden and Alec Guinness appeared in *The Bridge On the River Kwai.* Based on "Colonel Bogie March" of 1916.

River Song, The, or, **Something's Always Happening On the River** 1958 w. Betty Comden, Adolph Green m. Jule Styne

River, Stay 'Way from My Door 1931 w. Mort Dixon m. Harry Woods

Riverboat Shuffle 1925 w. Mitchell Parish, Dick Voynow, Irving Mills m. Hoagy Carmichael. The words to this song were not added until 1939.

Riviera Rose 1924 w.m. Horatio Nicholls

Road to Morocco, The 1942 w.m. Jimmy Van Heusen, Johnny Burke. (MF) *The Road to Morocco.* Bing Crosby, Bob Hope, and Dorothy Lamour appeared in *The Road to Morocco.*

Road to Paradise, The 1917 w. Rida Johnson Young m. Sigmund Romberg. (MT) *Maytime.* (MF) *Maytime.* Jeanette MacDonald, Nelson Eddy, and John Barrymore appeared in the film production of *Maytime.*

Roadways 1917 w. John Masefield m. John Hopkins Densmore

Roam On, (My) Little Gipsy Sweetheart 1927 w.m. Francis Wheeler, Irving Kahal, Ted Snyder

Roamin' in the Gloamin' 1911 w.m. Harry Lauder. This English music hall song was popularly sung by its Scottish author, Sir Harry Lauder.

Roar, Lion, Roar uncertain w. Corey Ford m. Roy Webb, Morris W. Watkins. School song for Columbia University.

Robbers' Chorus, The 1916 w. Oscar Asche m. Frederick Norton. (MT) *Chu Chin Chow.*

Robbers' March, The 1916 w. Oscar Asche m. Frederick Norton. (MT) *Chu Chin Chow.*

Robert and Elizabeth 1964 w.m. Ron Grainer, Ronald Miller

Robert E. Lee, *see* **Waiting for the Robert E. Lee**

Robin Adair c.1750 w. Lady Caroline Keppell m. traditional Celtic melody. This song was originally known as "Robin Aroon" with different lyrics. Lady Keppell's lyric concerned her extended engagement to her lover, a surgeon, Robert Adair. This song later became the "Fordham Ram March" for Fordham University.

Robins and Roses 1936 w. Edgar Leslie m. Joe Burke

Robot 1963 w.m. Joe Meek

Rock-A-Billy 1957 w.m. Woody Harris, Eddie V. Deane

Rock-a-Bye (Hush-a-Bye) Baby 1884 w.m. Effie I. Canning (Effie I. Crockett). Words from *Mother Goose's Melodies,* 1765. This song was written by Ms. Crockett, a relative of Davy Crockett, at age fifteen.

Rock-a-Bye Your Baby with a Dixie Melody 1918 w. Sam M. Lewis, Joe Young m. Jean Schwartz. (MT) *Sinbad.* (MF) *Show of Shows.* (MF) *Rose of Washington Square.* (MF) *The Jolson Story.* (MF) *Jolson Sings Again.* (MF) *The Merry Monihans.* Al Jolson appeared in both *Sinbad* and *Rose of Washington Square.* Beatrice Lillie and Loretta Young appeared in *Show of Shows.* Larry Parks appeared in both *The Jolson Story* and *Jolson Sings Again.* Donald O'Connor and Peggy Ryan appeared in *The Merry Monihans.*

Rock-a My Soul (in the Bosom of Abraham) c.1830 w.m. traditional black American spiritual

Rock 'n Me 1976 w.m. Steve Miller

Rock and Roll Music 1957 w.m. Chuck Berry. This song was popularly revived in 1976.

Rock and Roll Waltz 1956 w. Dick Ware m. Shorty Allen

(We're Gonna) Rock Around the Clock 1955 w.m. Max C. Freedman, Jimmy De Knight. (F) *Blackboard Jungle.* (MF) *Rock Around the Clock.* Glenn Ford, Sidney Poitier, and Anne Francis appeared in *Blackboard Jungle.* Bill Haley appeared in *Rock Around the Clock.*

Rock Beside the Sea, The 1852 w. anon. m. Charles Crozat Converse

Rock Bottom 1958 w.m. Tommy Watt, Jock Bain. Ivor Novello Award winner 1958.

R.O.C.K. in the U.S.A. (A Salute to 60's Rock) w.m. John Cougar Mellencamp

Rock Island Line 1956 w.m. based on a traditional theme; new w.m. Lonnie Donegan

Rock Love 1954 w.m. Henry Glover

Rock Me Amadeus 1986 w.m. Robert Bolland, Ferdinand Bolland, Johann Hoelzel

Rock Me Gently 1974 w.m. Andy Kim

Rock Me To Sleep, Mother 1860 w. Florence Percy, (Elizabeth Allen) m. Ernest Leslie

Rock of Ages 1832 w. Augustus Montague Toplady m. Thomas Hasting's hymn "Toplady"

Rock On 1973 w.m. David Essex

Rock the Boat 1974 w.m. Waldo Holmes

Rock with the Cavemen 1957 w.m. Michael Pratt, Lionel Bart, Tommy Steele

Rock with You 1980 w.m. Rodney Temperton

Rock Your Baby 1974 w.m. Harry Casey, Richard Finch

Rockaway 1917 w.m. Howard Johnson, Alex Rogers, C. Luckeyth Roberts

Rocked in the Cradle of the Deep 1840 w. Mrs. Willard m. Joseph Philip Knight. Inspired by a view of the Bristol Channel, this song was later parodied as "Locked in the Stable with the Sheep."

(Ol') Rockin' Chair 1930 w.m. Hoagy Carmichael

Rockin' Chair 1975 w.m. Willie Clarke, Clarence Reid

Rockin' Good Way, A (To Mess Around and Fall in Love) 1960 w.m. Clyde Otis, Brook Benton, Luchi DeJesus

Rockin' in Rhythm 1930 w.m. Duke Ellington, Harry Carney, Irving Mills. (MT) *Sophisticated Ladies.* Gregory Hines and Phyllis Hyman appeared in *Sophisticated Ladies.*

Rockin' Robin 1958 w.m. Jimmie Thomas. This song was popularly revived in 1972.

Rocky 1975 w.m. Ronald Jay Johnson

Rocky Mountain High 1972 w.m. John Denver, Michael C. Taylor

Rodger Young 1945 w.m. Frank Loesser

Rogue Song, The 1930 w.m. Clifford Grey, Herbert Stothart. (MF) *The Rogue Song.* Lawrence Tibbett, Stan Laurel, and Oliver Hardy appeared in *The Rogue Song.*

Roll Along Covered Wagon 1935 w.m. Jimmy Kennedy

Roll Along Prairie Moon 1935 w.m. Ted Fiorito, Harry MacPherson, Albert Von Tilzer. (MF) *Here Comes the Band.* (MF) *King of the Cowboys.* Virginia Bruce, Ted Healy, and Harry Stockwell appeared in *Here Comes the Band.* Roy Rogers and Smiley Burnette appeared in *King of the Cowboys.*

Roll Away Clouds 1928 w.m. Jack Waller, Joe Tunbridge. (MT) *Virginia.*

Roll Dem Roly Boly Eyes 1912 w.m. Eddie Leonard. (MF) *Melody Lane.* Eddie Leonard and Josephine Dunn appeared in *Melody Lane.* Theme song of Eddie Leonard.

Roll, Jordan, Roll 1865 w.m. traditional black American spiritual

Roll Me Over 1944 w.m. Desmond O'Connor

Roll On Eighteen Wheeler 1984 w.m. Dave Loggins

Roll On Silver Moon, or, **The Silver Moon** 1847 w.m. traditional, from England

Roll On, Tulane, or, **The Olive and Blue** 1925 w.m. Marten Ten Hoor, Walter Goldstein. School song of Tulane University.

Roll Out! Heave Dat Cotton 1877 w.m. William Shakespeare Hays

Roll Out the Barrel, *see* **The Beer Barrel Polka**

Roll Over Beethoven 1956 w.m. Chuck Berry. (MT) *Beatlemania.* This song was popularly revived in 1964.

Roll Them Cotton Bales 1914 w. James W. Johnson m. J. Rosamond Johnson

Rolled into One 1917 w. P.G. Wodehouse m. Jerome Kern. (MT) *Oh, Boy!*

Rolling Home 1934 w.m. Cole Porter. (MF) *Born To Dance.* Eleanor Powell, James Stewart, and Virginia Bruce appeared in *Born To Dance.* This song was most popular in 1936.

Rolling Round the World 1926 w.m. Scott Sanders

Rolling Stones—All Come Rolling Home Again 1916 w. Edgar Leslie m. Archie Gottler

Roly Boly Eyes, *see* **Roll Dem Roly Boly Eyes**

Romance 1926 w. Otto Harbach, Oscar Hammerstein II m. Sigmund Romberg. (MT) *The Desert Song.* (MF) *The Desert Song* (1929). (MF) *The Desert Song.* (1943). (MF) *The Desert Song* (1953). Vivienne Segal and Robert Halliday appeared in the stage production of *The Desert Song.* Myrna Loy and John Boles appeared in the 1929 film production of *The Desert Song.* Irene Manning and Dennis Morgan appeared in the 1943 film production of *The Desert Song.*

Romance 1929 w. Edgar Leslie m. Walter Donaldson. (F) *Cameo Kirby.* (F) *It's a Pleasure.* Norman Terris and J. Harold Murray appeared in *Cameo Kirby.* Sonja Henie appeared in *It's a Pleasure.*

Romance 1983 w. Richard Maltby, Jr. m. David Shire. (MT) *Baby.* Liz Callaway and Beth Fowley appeared in *Baby.*

Romantica 1960 w. Edorado Verde, Rascal

Romany Life 1898 w. Harry Smith m. Victor Herbert. (MT) *The Fortune Teller.*

Romany Rose 1924 w.m. Horatio Nicholls

Romeo and Juliet 1871 m. Peter Tchaikovsky. See also "Our Love."

Room Five Hundred and Four 1941 w.m. Eric Maschwitz, George Posford

Room Full (Roomful) of Roses 1949 w.m. Tim Spencer. (F) *Mule Train.* Gene Autry and Pat Buttram appeared in *Mule Train.*

Room in Bloomsbury, A 1954 w.m. Sandy Wilson. (MT) *The Boy Friend.*

Room with a View, A 1927 w.m. Noël Coward. (MT) *This Year of Grace.* Noël Coward and Beatrice Lillie appeared in *This Year of Grace.*

Room Without Windows, A 1964 w.m. Ervin Drake. (MT) *What Makes Sammy Run?*

Root, Hog, or Die 1856 w.m. Richard J. McGowan

Ro-Ro-Rollin' Along 1930 w.m. Murray Mencher, Billy Moll, Harry Richman. (F) *Near the Rainbow's End.* Bob Steele and Al Ferguson appeared in *Near the Rainbow's End.*

Rosalie 1937 w.m. Cole Porter. (MF) *Rosalie.* Nelson Eddy and Eleanor Powell appeared in *Rosalie.*

Rosalie the Prairie Flower 1855 w.m. Wurzel (George Frederick Root)

Rosanna 1982 w.m. David Paich. Grammy Award winner 1982.

Rosary, The 1898 w. Robert Cameron Rogers m. Ethelbert Nevin

Rose, The 1980 w.m. Amanda McBroom. (MF) *The Rose.* Bette Midler appeared in *The Rose,* biopic of singer Janis Joplin.

Rose and a Baby Ruth, A 1957 w.m. John Loudermilk

Rose Colored Glasses, *see* **Looking At the World Through Rose Colored Glasses**

Rose Garden, *see* **I Never Promised You a Rose Garden**

Rose I Bring You, The 1950 w.m. Tommie Connor, Michael Reine. Based on Gaetano Braga's "Angels' Serenade."

Rose in a Garden of Weeds, A 1926 w.m. R.B. Saxe, Hubert W. David. This song was popularly revived in 1949.

Rose in Her Hair, The 1935 w. Al Dubin m. Harry Warren. (MF) *The Broadway Gondolier*. Dick Powell, Joan Blondell, and Adolphe Menjou appeared in *The Broadway Gondolier*.

Rose in the Bud 1907 w.m. Dorothy Foster, P.J. Barrow

Rose Marie 1924 w. Otto Harbach, Oscar Hammerstein II m. Rudolf Friml. (MT) *Rose Marie*. (MF) *Rose Marie* (1936). (MF) *Rose Marie* (1954). Mary Ellis, Dennis King, and Arthur Deagon appeared in the American stage production of *Rose Marie*. Derek Oldham appeared in the British stage production of *Rose Marie*. Nelson Eddy and Jeanette MacDonald appeared in the 1936 film production of *Rose Marie*. Ann Blyth, Howard Keel, and Fernando Lamas appeared in the 1954 film production of *Rose Marie*.

Rose O'Day 1942 w.m. Charles Tobias, Al Lewis. Based on "She Wore a Yellow Ribbon" of 1838.

Rose of Alabama, The 1846 w. S.S. Steele m. anon.

Rose of Allandale, The 1832 w. Charles Jeffreys m. Sidney Nelson

Rose of England 1938 w.m. Ivor Novello, Christopher Hassall. (MT) *Crest of the Wave*. Olive Gilbert and Edgar Elmes appeared in *Crest of the Wave*.

Rose of Killarney, The 1876 w. George Cooper m. John Rogers Thomas

Rose of Lucerne, or, The Swiss Toy Girl 1823 w. anon. m. John Barnett.

Rose of My Heart 1911 w.m. Hermann Löhr

Rose of No Man's Land, The 1918 w. Jack Caddingan m. Joseph A. Brennan. (MF) *The Cockeyed World*. Joe E. Brown and Stuart Erwin appeared in *The Cockeyed World*. Loosely based on Beethoven's "Minuet in G."

Rose of San Antone, *see* **San Antonio Rose**

Rose of the Rio Grande 1922 w. Edgar Leslie m. Harry Warren, Ross Gorman. (MT) *The 1940's Radio Hour*.

Rose of the World 1909 w. Glen MacDonough m. Victor Herbert. (MT) *The Rose of Algeria*. (MF) *The Great Victor Herbert*. Mary Martin and Allan Jones appeared in *The Great Victor Herbert*.

Rose of Tralee, The 1912 w.m. Charles Glover, C. Mordaunt Spencer. (MF) *Song of My Heart*. John McCormack and Maureen O'Sullivan appeared in *Song of My Heart*.

Rose of Washington Square 1920 w. Ballard MacDonald m. James F. Hanley. (MT) *Ziegfeld Midnight Frolic*. (MF) *Rose of Washington Square*. Fanny Brice and W.C. Fields appeared in *Ziegfeld Midnight Frolic*. Alice Faye appeared in *Rose of Washington Square*. Theme song of Fanny Brice.

Rose Room 1917 w.m. Harry Williams, Art Hickman. (MF) *Somebody Loves Me*. (MF) *The Merry Monihans*. Betty Hutton appeared in *Somebody Loves Me*. Donald O'Connor and Peggy Ryan appeared in *The Merry Monihans*.

Rose, Rose I Love You 1951 w. Wilfred Thomas m. arr. Chris Langdon. Based on a traditional Chinese melody.

Rose Tattoo, The 1955 w. Jack Brooks m. Harry Warren. (F) *The Rose Tattoo*.

Roses Are Forget-Me-Nots 1930 w.m. Al Hoffman, Charles O'Flynn, Will Osborne

Roses Are Red, My Love 1962 w.m. Al Byron, Paul Evans

Roses Bring Dreams of You 1908 w.m. Herbert Ingraham

Roses for Remembrance 1926 w.m. Gus Kahn, Loyal Curtis

Roses in the Rain 1937 w.m. Remus Harris, Irving Melsner

Roses of Picardy 1916 w. Frederick Edward Weatherly m. Haydn Wood

Rose's Turn 1959 w. Stephen Sondheim m. Jule Styne. (MT) *Gypsy*. (MF) *Gypsy*. Ethel Merman appeared in the stage production of *Gypsy*. Rosalind Russell appeared in the film production of *Gypsy*.

Rosetta 1933 w.m. Earl Hines, Henri Woode

Rosetta 1972 w.m. Mike Snow. Ivor Novello Award winner 1971–72.

Rosie 1960 w. Lee Adams m. Charles Strouse. (MT) *Bye Bye Birdie*. (MF) *Bye Bye Birdie*. Dick Van Dyke and Janet Leigh appeared in the film production of *Bye Bye Birdie*.

Rosie 1969 w.m. Don Partridge. Ivor Novello Award winner 1968–69.

Rosita, La 1923 w. Allan Stuart m. Paul Dupont

Rotten Row w.m. Walter Scott. (R-BBC) *Rotten Row*.

Roulette 1959 w.m. Trevor Stanford

Round and Round 1957 w.m. Lou Stallman, Joe Shapiro

Round Her Neck She Wore a Yellow Ribbon, *see* **She Wore a Yellow Ribbon**

Round on the End and High in the Middle, O-hi-o 1922 w.m. Alfred Bryan, Bert Hanlon

Round the Marble Arch 1932 w.m. Noel Gay, Ralph Butler

Rouser, The 1938 w.m. Floyd M. Hutsell. School song for the University of Minnesota.

Rousseau's Dream 1812 w.m. Jean Jacques Rousseau, arr. Johann Baptist Cramer. Based on a song from Rousseau's one-act opera *Le Devin du Village*.

(Get Your Kicks On) Route 66 1946 w.m. Bob Troup

Roving Kind, The 1951 w.m. Arnold Stanton, Jessie Cavanaugh. (MF) *Disc Jockey*.

Row, Row, Row 1912 w. William Jerome m. James V. Monaco. (MT) *The Ziegfeld Follies* (1912). (MF) *Incendiary Blonde*. (MF) *Two Weeks with Love*. (MF) *The Seven Little Foys*. Betty Hutton appeared in *Incendiary Blonde,* biopic of speakeasy hostess Texas Guinan. Debbie Reynolds and Carleton Carpenter appeared in *Two Weeks with Love*. Bob Hope appeared in *The Seven Little Foys*.

Row, Row, Row Your Boat (Round) 1852 w.m. anon; earliest words 1852, earliest music published 1881, but most surely performed before that.

Row Thy Boat Lightly 1847 w. H.F. Woodman m. Isaac Baker Woodbury

Royal Event 1960 w.m. Trevor Stanford

Royal Garden Blues 1919 w.m. Spencer Williams, Clarence Williams. (MF) *Jazz Dance*. (MF) *Drum Crazy*. Gene Krupa and his orchestra appeared in *Drum Crazy*.

Rubber Ball   1960   w.m. Anne Orlowski, Aaron Schroeder

Rubber Bullets   1974   w.m. Kevin Godley, Lawrence Creme, Graham Keith Gouldman. Ivor Novello Award winner 1973–74.

Rubberband Man   1976   w.m. Thomas Bell, Linda Creed

Ruby   1953   w. Mitchell Parish   m. Heinz Roemheld. (F) *Ruby Gentry*. Charlton Heston appeared in *Ruby Gentry*.

Ruby Baby   1963   w.m. Jerry Leiber, Mike Stoller. This song was popularly revived in 1975.

Ruby, Don't Take Your Love to Town   1969   w.m. Mel Tillis

Rudolph the Red-Nosed Reindeer   1949   w.m. Johnny Marks. Based on the Robert L. May story written in 1939 for Montgomery Ward & Co. See also Part I, 1848.

Rufus Rastus Johnson Brown (What You Goin' To Do When the Rent Comes 'Round)   1905   w. Andrew B. Sterling m. Harry Von Tilzer

Rule, Britannia   1740–1741   w. James Thomson; possibly David Mallet   m. Thomas Arne. From the English masque, *Alfred*. The opening phrase of this melody was quoted by Handel in his 1746 "Occasional Oratorio." It was later found in a set of variations by Beethoven and in a Wagner Overture in 1836.

Rum and Coca-Cola   1945   Sp.w. Clotilde Arias Eng.w. Morey Amsterdam   m. Jeri Sullavan, Paul Baron. This song was first introduced at the Versailles night club in New York, and is possibly based on Lionel Belasco's "L'Année Passée" of 1906, published originally in Trinidad. A plagiarism suit ensued in which Belasco's publisher sued the authors and won. Belasco settled for a large financial payment and sacrificed all future property rights of the song as well as writer credit.

Rum Boogie (Rhumboogie)   1940   w.m. Don Raye, Hughie Prince. (MF) *Argentine Nights*. Constance Moore and the Andrews Sisters appeared in *Argentine Nights*.

Rumanian Rhapsody, op.11, no.1   1909   m. Georges Enesco. This work was first performed in Paris on February 7, 1908.

Rumba Rhapsody   1946   m. Rafael Audinot, Alberto de Bru

Rumba Rumba   1942   m. J. Pafumy

Rumors Are Flying   1946   w.m. Bennie Benjamin, George Weiss

Run Joey Run   1975   w.m. Jack A. Perricone, Paul Vance

Run Rabbit Run   1939   w.m. Noel Gay, Ralph Butler. (MT) *The Little Dog Laughed*. Flanagan and Allen appeared in *The Little Dog Laughed*.

Run to Him   1961   w.m. Gerry Goffin, Jack Keller

Run to You   1985   w.m. Bryan Adams, Jim Vallance

Runaround Sue   1961   w.m. Ernie Maresca, Dion Di Mucci

Runaway   1961   w.m. Max T. Crook, Charles Westover

Runaway Train, The   1925   w.m. Carson Robison

Running Bear   1960   w.m. J.P. Richardson

Running Between the Raindrops   1931   w. James Dyrenforth   m. Carroll Gibbons

Running Scared   1961   w.m. Roy Orbison, Joe Melson

Runnin' Wild   1922   w. Joe Grey, Leo Wood   m. A. Harrington Gibbs. (MF) *Running Wild*. (MF) *Some Like It Hot*. (MF) *The Five Pennies*. Marilyn Monroe, Jack Lemmon, and Tony Curtis appeared in *Some Like It Hot*. Red Nichols's Five Pennies and Danny Kaye appeared in *The Five Pennies*.

Running with the Night   1984   w.m. Cynthia Weil, Lionel Richie

Russian Lullaby   1927   w.m. Irving Berlin. (MF) *Blue Skies*. Bing Crosby and Fred Astaire appeared in *Blue Skies*.

Russian Rag   1919   w.m. George L. Cobb. Based on Rachmaninoff's Prelude in C-sharp minor.

Russian Rose   1941   w.m. Sonny Miller, Hughie Charles

Rustle of Spring   1896   m. Christian Sinding. From the German "Frühlingsrauschen," op.32, no.3.

Sabbath Prayer   1964   w. Sheldon Harnick   m. Jerry Bock. (MT) *Fiddler on the Roof*. (MF) *Fiddler on the Roof*. Zero Mostel appeared in the stage production of *Fiddler on the Roof*.

Sabre Dance   1948   w.m. Allan Roberts, Lester Lee. Based on Aram Khachaturian's ballet "Gayaneh," Third Suite.

Sacramento, *see* **De Camptown Races**

Sad Eyes   1979   w.m. Robert John

Sad Movies Make Me Cry   1961   w.m. John D. Loudermilk

Sad Songs (Say So Much)   1984   w.m. Elton John, Bernie Taupin

Sad Sweet Dreamer   1975   w.m. Des Parton. Ivor Novello Award winner 1974–75.

Sadie Salome, Go Home   1909   w.m. Irving Berlin, Edgar Leslie

Safe in the Arms of Jesus   1870   w. Frances Jane Crosby (Mrs. Alexander Van Alstyne)   m. William Howard Doane

Safely Through Another Week   1824   w. John Newton   m. Lowell Mason

Safety Dance, The   1983   w.m. Ivan Doroschuk

Saga of Jenny   1941   w. Ira Gershwin   m. Kurt Weill. (MT) *Lady in the Dark*. (MF) *Lady in the Dark*. Gertrude Lawrence, Danny Kaye, and Victor Mature appeared in the stage production of *Lady in the Dark*. Ginger Rogers appeared in the film production of *Lady in the Dark*.

Sahara   1924   w.m. Herman Finck

Sail Along Silvery Moon   1937   w. Harry Tobias   m. Percy Wenrich. This song was popularly revived in 1958.

Sail Away   1961   w.m. Noël Coward. (MT) *Sail Away*.

Sail Away   1979   w.m. Rafe Van Hoy

Sail On   1979   w.m. Lionel Richie

Sailboat in the Moonlight   1937   w.m. Carmen Lombardo, John Jacob Loeb

Sailing or, **Sailing, Sailing over the Bounding Main**   1880   w.m. Godfrey Marks (James Frederick Swift)

Sailing 1976 w.m. Gavin Sutherland. Ivor Novello Award winner 1975–76.

Sailing 1980 w.m. Christopher Cross. Grammy Award winner 1980.

Sailin' Away on the Henry Clay 1917 w. Gus Kahn m. Egbert Van Alstyne

Sailing Down the Chesapeake Bay 1913 w. Jean C. Havez m. George Botsford

Sailin' On 1927 w. Gus Kahn m. based on Dvorák's Largo from his "From the New World" symphony.

Sailing, Sailing, *see* **Sailing**

Sailor (Your Home Is the Sea) 1960 Fr.w. Fini Busch Eng.w. Alan Holt m. Werner Scharfenberger

Sailor Boys Have Talk to Me in English 1955 w.m. Milton DeLugg, Bob Hilliard

Sailor of My Dreams, The 1968 w. George Haimsohn, Robin Miller m. Jim Wise. (MT) *Dames At Sea.*

Sailor Who Are You Dreaming of Tonight 1944 w.m. Stanley Damerell, Reg Butler, Tolchard Evans

Sailor's Epitaph, The, *see* **Tom Bowling**

Sailor's Hornpipe 1796 m. based on a traditional dance of English or Irish origin and possibly on an old sailor's song, "Jack's the Lad." (MF) *For Me and My Gal.*

Saint, *see* **St.**

Saints Go Marching In, The, *see* **When the Saints Go Marching In**

Salad Days 1955 w.m. Julian Slade, Dorothy Reynolds

Sally 1921 w. Clifford Grey, (Al Dubin, Joe Burke) m. Jerome Kern. (MT) *Sally.* (MF) *Sally.* Marilyn Miller and Leon Errol appeared in the stage production of *Sally.* Marilyn Miller and Joe E. Brown appeared in the film production of *Sally.*

Sally 1931 w.m. William Haines, Harry Leon, Leo Towers. (MF) *Sally in Our Alley.* Gracie Fields appeared in *Sally in Our Alley.* Theme song of Gracie Fields.

Sally Go Round the Roses 1963 w.m. Lona Spector, Zell Sanders

Sally in Our Alley 1902 w.m. Henry Carey. (MT) *Sally in Our Alley.* Marie Cahill and Harry Fairleigh appeared in *Sally in Our Alley.* Based on "The Country Lass" of 1715. The last line of this song is traditionally used by barber-shop quartets to tag such songs as "Sweet Adeline."

Sally, Irene and Mary 1922 w.m. Arthur Lange, Paul Van Loan

Sally, You Brought the Sunshine to Our Alley 1922 w.m. Wynn Stanley, Andrew Allen

Salome 1898 m. William Lorraine

Salut d'Amour 1889 m. Edward Elgar

Sam 1977 w.m. John Farrar, Hank Marvin, Don Black. Ivor Novello Award winner 1977–78.

Sam, the Old Accordion Man 1927 w.m. Walter Donaldson. (MF) *Glorifying the American Girl.* (MF) *Love Me or Leave Me.* Rudy Vallee, Helen Morgan, and Eddie Cantor appeared in *Glorifying the American Girl.* Doris Day and James Cagney appeared in *Love Me or Leave Me,* biopic of singer Ruth Etting.

Sam, You Made the Pants Too Long 1940 w.m. Sam Lewis, Victor Young; new words Milton Berle. This parody written by Milton Berle was based on Sam Lewis and Victor Young's "Lawd, You Made the Night Too Long" of 1932; it was popularized by Joe E. Lewis.

Sambo's Address to His Bred'ren, *see* **Ching A Ring Chaw**

Same Old Auld Lang Syne, The 1981 w.m. Dan Fogelberg. This song was loosely inspired by the 1711 standard "Auld Lang Syne".

Same Old Moon, The 1927 w. Otto Harbach, Bert Kalmar m. Harry Ruby. (MT) *Lucky.* Ruby Keeler and Joseph Santley appeared in *Lucky.*

Same Ole Me 1982 w.m. Paul Overstreet

Same Sort of Girl 1914 w. Harry B. Smith m. Jerome Kern. (MT) *The Girl from Utah.*

Same Sweet Girl Today, The 1895 w.m. Dan W. Quinn

Sammy 1903 w. James O'Dea m. Edward Hutchison. (MT) *The Wizard of Oz.*

Sam's Song 1950 w. Jack Elliott m. Lew Quadling

Samson and Delilah, *see* **My Heart At Thy Sweet Voice**

San 1920 w.m. Lindsay McPhail, Walter Michels

San Antonio 1907 w. Harry H. Williams m. Egbert Van Alstyne

San Antonio Rose, or, **Rose of San Antone** 1938 w.m. Bob Wills. (MF) *San Antonio Rose.* Jane Frazee appeared in *San Antonio Rose.* This song was also popular in 1940.

San Fernando Valley 1944 w.m. Gordon Jenkins. (MF) *San Fernando Valley.* Roy Rogers, Dale Evans, and Bob Nolan appeared in *San Fernando Valley.* Based on "Sweet and Hot" of 1930.

San Francisco 1936 w.m. Gus Kahn, Walter Jurmann, Bronislaw Kaper. (F) *San Francisco.* Jeanette MacDonald, Clark Gable, and Spencer Tracy appeared in *San Francisco.*

(Are You Going to) San Francisco (Be Sure To Wear Some Flowers in Your Hair) 1967 w.m. John Phillips

Sand in My Shoes 1941 w. Frank Loesser m. Victor Schertzinger. (MF) *Kiss the Boys Goodbye.* Mary Martin, Don Ameche, and Oscar Levant appeared in *Kiss the Boys Goodbye.*

Sandy's Ghost, *see* **Mary's Dream**

Santa Claus Is Coming to Town 1934 w. Haven Gillespie m. J. Fred Coots

Santa Lucia 1850 It.w. Teodoro Cottrau Eng.w. Thomas Oliphant m. Teodoro Cottrau

Sara 1980 w.m. Stevie Nicks

Sara 1986 w.m. Ina Wolf, Peter Wolf

Sara Smile 1976 w.m. Daryl Hall, John Oates

Sarava 1979 w. N. Richard Nash m. Mitch Leigh. (MT) *Sarava.* Tovah Feldshuh appeared in *Sarava.*

Sarawaki 1935 w.m. Val Gordon

Sari Waltz, *see* **Love's Own Sweet Song**

Satan Takes a Holiday 1937 w.m. Larry Clinton

Satin Doll 1958 w. Johnny Mercer m. Billy Strayhorn, Duke Ellington. (MT) *Sophisticated Ladies.* Gregory Hines and Phyllis Hyman appeared in *Sophisticated Ladies.*

(I Can't Get No) Satisfaction 1965 w.m. Mick Jagger, Keith Richard

Satisfied 1929 w. Irving Caesar m. Cliff Friend

Saturday Night 1963 w.m. Randy Sparks

Saturday Night 1976 w.m. Philip Coulter, Bill Martin

Saturday Night Is the Loneliest Night of the Week 1944 w. Sammy Cahn m. Jule Styne. See also Part I, 1945.

Savage, The 1961 w.m. Norrie Paramor. (F) *The Young Ones.*

Savanna 1957 w. E.Y. Harburg m. Harold Arlen. (MT) *Jamaica.*

Save It for a Rainy Day 1977 w.m. Stephen Bishop

Save the Country 1969 w.m. Laura Nyro

Save the Last Dance for Me 1960 w.m. Jerome "Doc" Pomus, Mort Shuman. This song was popularly revived in 1983 and 1984.

Save Your Heart for Me 1965 w.m. Gary Geld, Peter David Udell

Save Your Kisses for Me 1965 w.m. Tony Hiller, Martin Lee, Lee Sheriden. Ivor Novello Award winner 1976–77.

Save Your Sorrow for Tomorrow 1925 w. B.G. DeSylva m. Al Sherman

Saved by Grace 1894 w. Mrs. Alexander Van Alstyne (Frances Jane Crosby) m. George Coles Stebbins

Saving All My Love for You 1985 w.m. Gerald Goffin, Michael Masser

Savior, Breathe an Evening Blessing 1878 w. James Edmeston m. George Coles Stebbins; erroneously attributed to Dmitri Bortnyanski.

Say a Prayer for Me Tonight 1958 w. Alan Jay Lerner m. Frederick Loewe. (MF) *Gigi.* Leslie Caron, Maurice Chevalier, and Hermione Gingold appeared in *Gigi.*

Say a Prayer for the Boys Over There 1943 w.m. Jimmy McHugh, Herb Magidson. (F) *Hers To Hold.* Deanna Durbin and Joseph Cotten appeared in *Hers to Hold.*

Say "Au Revoir" But Not "Goodbye" 1893 w.m. Harry Kennedy. This song was performed at Harry Kennedy's funeral by Helene Mora.

Say, Darling 1958 w. Adolph Green, Betty Comden m. Jule Styne. (MT) *Say, Darling.*

Say! Have You Taken Your Medicine Yet? 1872 w.m. W.S. Trask. This song was written for newspaper editor Horace Greeley's 1872 Presidential campaign against then President Grant. Its lyric:

> Don't You know Greeley you hated of late?
> Swallow him down! Swallow him down!
> He is your candidate, swallow him "straight"
> Swallow him, swallow him down!
> Never complain that your stomach revolts!
> Greeley (swallow him down)
> Cleared your convention like senna and salts
> Can't you swallow him down?

Say I Won't Be There 1963 w.m. Tom Springfield

Say It (Over and Over Again) 1940 w. Frank Loesser m.

Jimmy McHugh. (MF) *Buck Benny Rides Again.* Jack Benny and Andy Devine appeared in *Buck Benny Rides Again.*

(I Don't Believe It But) Say It Again 1926 w. Harry Richman m. Abner Silver

Say It Isn't So 1932 w.m. Irving Berlin

Say It Isn't So 1983 w.m. Daryl Hall

Say It While Dancing 1922 w. Benny Davis m. Abner Silver

Say It with Music 1921 w.m. Irving Berlin. (MT) *Music Box Revue.* (MT) *Mayfair and Montmartre.* (MF) *Alexander's Ragtime Band.* Willie Collier and Sam Bernard appeared in *The Music Box Revue,* the opening show in the new Music Box Theatre. Alice Faye and Don Ameche appeared in *Alexander's Ragtime Band.* Theme song of Jack Payne.

Say Maybe 1979 w.m. Neil Diamond

Say Not Love Is a Dream 1912 w. Basil Hood m. Franz Lehár. (MT) *The Count of Luxembourg.*

Say Say Say 1983 w.m. Michael Jackson, Paul McCartney

Say "Si Si" 1936 Sp.w. Francia Lubin Eng.w. Al Stillman m. Ernesto Lecuona

Say Wonderful Things 1963 w.m. Norman Newell, Philip Green

Say You Love Me 1976 w.m. Christine McVie

Say You, Say Me 1985 w.m. Lionel Richie. (F) *White Nights.*

Say You're Mine Again 1953 w.m. Charles Nathan, Dave Heisler

Sayonara 1957 w.m. Irving Berlin

Says My Heart 1938 w. Frank Loesser m. Burton Lane. (MF) *Cocoanut Grove.* Fred MacMurray, Ben Blue, and Eve Arden appeared in *Cocoanut Grove.*

Scandal of Little Lizzie Ford, The 1921 w. Billy Curtis m. Harry Von Tilzer

Scarborough Fair/Canticle, or, **Parsley, Sage, Rosemary and Thyme** 1966 w.m. Paul Simon, Arthur Garfunkel. (F) *The Graduate.* Dustin Hoffman and Anne Bancroft appeared in *The Graduate.*

Scarf Dance 1888 m. Cécile Chaminade. From the ballet "Callirhoë." From the French "Pas des Echarpes," op.73.

Scarlet Buccaneer, The 1977 w.m. John Addison. Ivor Novello Award winner 1977-78.

Scarlet O'Hara 1963 w.m. Jerry Lordan

Scarlet Ribbons (for Her Hair) 1949 w. Jack Segal m. Evelyn Danzig. This song was popularly revived in 1956.

Scatterbrain 1939 w.m. Johnny Burke, Frankie Masters, Keene-Bean. (MF) *That's Right, You're Wrong.* Kay Kyser, Adolphe Menjou, and Lucille Ball appeared in *That's Right, You're Wrong.*

Scenes de Ballet 1944 m. Igor Stravinsky. (MT) *The Seven Lively Arts.*

Scenes That Are Brightest 1845 w. Edward Fitzball m. Vincent Wallace. From the English opera *Maritana.*

Schaefer Is the One Beer 1961 w. Jim Jordan m. Joe Hornsby, Ted German. This song was written for a Schaefer Beer commercial promotion campaign.

Scheherazade, op.35   1890   m. Nikolai Rimsky-Korsakov

Schnitzelbank   1906   w.m. anon. Based on the melody of "Johnny Schmoker" of 1863.

Schön Rosmarin (Fair Rosmarin)   1910   m. Fritz Kreisler

School Day (Ring! Ring! Goes the Bell)   1957   w.m. Chuck Berry

School Days   1907   w. Will D. Cobb   m. Gus Edwards. (MF) *Sunbonnet Sue.* Gale Storm and Phil Regan appeared in *Sunbonnet Sue.*

Scotch Bagpipe Melody, The *see* **Irish Washerwoman**

Scots Wha Hae Wi' Wallace Bled   c.1820   w. Robert Burns m. traditional, from Scotland

Scottish Samba   1949   w.m. Johnny Reine

Scottish Soldier Green Hill   1961   w.m. Andy Stewart, Iaian A. MacFadyen

Scrub Me Mama with a Boogie Beat   1940   w.m. Don Raye

Scrumpdillyishus Day, A   1976   w. Robert Larranaga, Dale Menten   m. Dale Menten. This song was written for a Dairy Queen commercial promotion campaign.

Se Saran Rose, *or,* **Melba Waltz**   1888   It.w. Pietro Mazzini   m. Luigi Arditi

Sea, The, *see* **La Mer**

Sea Hath Its Pearls, The   1871   w. Henry Wadsworth Longfellow; translated from the German of Heinrich Heine. m. Charles Gounod. Longfellow's translation was set to new music in 1884 by Ciro Pinsuti.

(Theme from) Sea Hunt   1959   m. David Rose. (TV) *Sea Hunt.*

Sea of Love   1959   w.m. G. Khoury, P. Baptiste. This song was popularly revived in 1984.

Seal It with a Kiss   1936   w. Edward Heyman   m. Arthur Schwartz. (MF) *That Girl From Paris.* Lucille Ball and Lili Pons appeared in *That Girl From Paris.*

Sealed with a Kiss   1962   w.m. Gary Geld, Peter Udell

Search for Paradise   1957   w.m. Ned Washington, Dimitri Tiomkin

Search Is Over   1985   w.m.. Jim Peterik, Frank Sullivan

Seashore   1960   w.m. Robert Farnon

Seasons in the Sun   1974   w.m. Jacques Brel, Rod McKuen

Second Hand Rose   1921   w. Grant Clarke   m. James F. Hanley. (MT) *Ziegfeld Follies of 1921.* (MF) *My Man.* Fanny Brice appeared in *Ziegfeld Follies of 1921* and *My Man.*

Second Minuet, The   1924   w.m. Maurice Besly

Second Rhapsody, The   1931   m. George Gershwin

Second Star to the Right, The   1953   w. Sammy Cahn   m. Sammy Fain. (MF) *Peter Pan.*

Second Time Around, The   1960   w. Sammy Cahn   m. James Van Heusen. (F) *High Time.* Bing Crosby and Fabian appeared in *High Time.*

Second Wind, *see* **You're Only Human**

Secret Army   1980   m. Robert Farnon. Ivor Novello Award winner 1979–80.

Secret Lovers   1986   w.m. David Lewis, Wayne Lewis

Secret Love   1954   w. Paul Francis Webster   m. Sammy Fain

(MF) *Calamity Jane.* Doris Day appeared in *Calamity Jane.* Academy Award winner 1953. See also Part I, 1872.

Secretary Is Not a Toy, A   1961   w.m. Frank Loesser. (MT) *How To Succeed In Business Without Really Trying.* (MF) *How To Succeed In Business Without Really Trying.* Robert Morse appeared in both the stage and film productions of *How To Succeed.*

Secretly   1958   w.m. Al Hoffman, Dick Manning, Mark Markwell

Secrets of the Seine, The   1961   w.m. Tony Osborne

See   1969   w.m. Felix Cavaliere

See Emily Play   1968   w.m. Syd Barrett

See, Gentle Patience Smiles on Pain   1835   w. Anne Steele m. Henry Kemble Oliver. Based on the traditional hymn "Federal Street."

See, Saw, Margery Daw   1893   w.m. Arthur West

See Saw Marjory Daw, *see also* **Mother Goose's Melodies**

See the U.S.A. in Your Chevrolet   1948   w.m. Leon Carr, Leo Corday. This advertising song was performed by Dinah Shore on her television *Chevrolet Hour.*

See What the Boys in the Back Room Will Have, *see* **Boys in the Back Room**

See You in September   1959   w.m. Sherman Edwards, Sid Wayne. This song was popularly revived in 1966.

See You Later Alligator   1956   w.m. Robert Guidry

Seeing Nellie Home, *see* **When I Saw Sweet Nellie Home**

Seems Like Old Times   1945   w.m. Carmen Lombardo, John Jacob Loeb. Theme song of Arthur Godfrey.

Seine, La   1949   w.m. Geoffrey Parsons, Guy Lafarge, F. Monod. (MT) *Sauce Tartare.*

Self Control   1984   w.m. Giancarlo Bigazzi, Stephen Piccolo, Raffaele Riefoli

Semper Fidelis   1888   m. John Philip Sousa. (MF) *The Cockeyed World.* Joe E. Brown and Stuart Erwin appeared in *The Cockeyed World.* Sousa sold this song, including full piano, brass band, and orchestra arrangements, to publisher Harry Coleman for $ 35.00.

Semper Paratus   1928   w.m. Francis Saltus Van Boskerck. (F) *The Fighting Coast Guard.* Brian Donlevy and Forrest Tucker appeared in *The Fighting Coast Guard.* Popularly revived in 1938, this song is the official U.S. Coast Guard March.

Send for Me   1957   w.m. Ollie Jones

Send in the Clowns   1973   w.m. Stephen Sondheim. (MT) *A Little Night Music.* (MT) *Side by Side by Sondheim.* (MF) *A Little Night Music.* Len Cariou, Glynis Johns, and Hermione Gingold appeared in the stage production of *A Little Night Music.* Millicent Martin and Julie N. McKenzie appeared in *Side by Side by Sondheim.* Elizabeth Taylor, Len Cariou, and Hermione Gingold appeared in the film production of *A Little Night Music.* Grammy Award winner 1975. This song was most popular in 1975.

Send Me Away with a Smile   1917   w.m. Al Piantadosi, Louis Weslyn

Señora   1922   w.m. Owen Murphy

Sensation Rag 1908 m. Joseph Lamb

Sentimental Gentleman from Georgia, A 1932 w. Mitchell Parish m. Frank Perkins

Sentimental Journey 1945 w.m. Bud Green, Les Brown, Ben Homer. (F) *Sentimental Journey*. Maureen O'Hara and William Bendix appeared in *Sentimental Journey*. Theme song of Les Brown and his orchestra. See also Part I, 1945.

Sentimental Me 1925 w. Lorenz Hart m. Richard Rodgers. (MT) *The Garrick Gaieties (First Edition)*.

Sentimental Me 1949 w.m. Jim Morehead, Jimmy Cassin

Sentimental Touch, The 1958 w. Sammy Gallop m. Albert Van Dam

Separate Lives (Love Theme from *White Nights*) w.m. Stephen Bishop. (F) *White Nights*.

Separate Ways 1983 w.m.. Jonathan Cain, Steve Perry

September in the Rain 1937 w. Al Dubin m. Harry Warren. (MF) *Stars over Broadway*. (MF) *Melody for Two*. James Melton and Jane Froman appeared in *Stars over Broadway*. James Melton appeared in *Melody for Two*. Mr. Melton later became the leading tenor of the Metropolitan Opera.

September Song 1938 w. Maxwell Anderson m. Kurt Weill. (MT) *Knickerbocker Holiday*. (MF) *Knickerbocker Holiday*. (F) *September Affair*. Ray Middleton and Walter Huston appeared in the stage production of *Knickerbocker Holiday*. Nelson Eddy appeared in the film production of *Knickerbocker Holiday*. Joan Fontaine and Joseph Cotten appeared in *September Affair*.

Serenade 1824 m. Franz Schubert

Serenade 1901 w. Jerry Gray, Herb Hendler m. Riccardo Drigo. From the ballet *Les Millions d'Arlequin*. *Les Millions d'Arlequin* was choreographed in St. Petersburg in 1900 by Marius Petipa.

Serenade 1901 w.m. Enrico Toselli, Leon E.S. Young

Serenade, or, **Rimpianto** 1923 It.w. Alfred Silvestri Eng.trans. Sigmund Spaeth m. Enrico Toselli. Based on "Serenade" of 1901.

Serenade 1924 w. Dorothy Donnelly m. Sigmund Romberg. (MT) *The Student Prince*. (MF) *The Student Prince*. (MF) *Deep in My Heart*. Jose Ferrer and Merle Oberon appeared in *Deep in My Heart,* biopic of composer Sigmund Romberg.

Serenade for Strings (Suite), op.3 1888 m. Victor Herbert

Serenade In Blue 1942 w. Mack Gordon m. Harry Warren. (MF) *Orchestra Wives*. Glenn Miller, George Montgomery, and Ann Rutherford appeared in *Orchestra Wives*. See also Part 1, 1942.

Serenade in the Night 1937 Eng.w.m. Jimmy Kennedy. Based on C.A. Bixio and B. Cherubini's "Violino Tzigano."

Serenade of Love 1929 w. Irving Caesar m. Sigmund Romberg. (MT) *Nina Rosa*.

Serenade of the Bells 1947 w.m. Kay Twomey, Al Urbano, Al Goodhart

Serenade to a Lemonade 1952 w. Sammy Gallop m. David Rose

Serenata 1949 w. Mitchell Parish m. Leroy Anderson

Serenata, La, *see* **Angel's Serenade**

Sergeant Pepper's Lonely Hearts Club Band 1967 w.m. John Lennon, Paul McCartney. (MF) *Yellow Submarine*.

Set Me Free 1965 w.m. Ray Davies

Seven Bridges Road 1981 w.m. Stephen Young

7-1/2 Cents 1954 w.m. Richard Adler, Jerry Ross. (MT) *The Pajama Game*. (MF) *The Pajama Game*. Doris Day appeared in the film production of *The Pajama Game*.

Seven Lonely Days 1953 w.m. Alden Shuman, Earl Shuman, Marshall Brown

Seven or Eleven—My Dixie Pair o' Dice 1923 w. Lew Brown m. Walter Donaldson

Seven Year Ache 1981 w.m. Rosanne Cash

Seventeen 1955 w.m. Boyd Bennett, John Young, Jr., Chuck Gorman

Seventeen, *see also* **When You and I Were Seventeen**

Seventeen Candles 1940 w.m. Art Strauss, Bob Dale, Sonny Miller

Seventh Dawn 1964 w.m. Riziero Ortolani, Paul Francis Webster

Seventh Heaven 1929 w.m. Al Jolson, B.G. De Sylva, Lew Brown, Ray Henderson. (MF) *Say It with Songs*. (F) *Little Pal*. Al Jolson and Davey Lee appeared in *Say It with Songs*.

Seventh Heaven 1937 w. Sidney D. Mitchell m. Lew Pollack. (F) *Seventh Heaven*. James Stewart appeared in *Seventh Heaven*.

77 Sunset Strip, *see* **Kookie, Kookie, Lend Me Your Comb**

Seventy-Six Trombones 1957 w.m. Meredith Willson. (MT) *The Music Man*. (MF) *The Music Man*. Robert Preston appeared in both the stage and film productions of *The Music Man*.

Sexual Healing 1983 w.m. Odell Brown, Marvin Gaye

Sexy Eyes 1980 w.m. Robert Mather, Keith Stegall, Chris Waters

Sha La La 1964 w.m. Robert Mosley, Robert Taylor, Frances Hycock

Shade of the Palm, The 1900 w. Owen Hall m. Leslie Stuart. (MT) *Florodora*. Based on a Nocturne by Chopin.

Shades of Night 1916 w. L. Wolfe Gilbert m. Anatole Friedland, Malvin Franklin

Shadow Dancing 1978 w.m. Robin Gibb, Maurice Gibb, Barry Gibb, Andy Gibb

Shadow of the Moon 1924 w. P.G. Wodehouse m. Jerome Kern. (MT) *Sitting Pretty*.

Shadow of Your Smile, The 1965 w. Paul Francis Webster m. Johnny Mandel. (F) *The Sandpiper*. Elizabeth Taylor and Richard Burton appeared in *The Sandpiper*. Academy Award winner 1965. Grammy Award winner 1965.

Shadow Waltz 1933 w. Al Dubin m. Harry Warren. (MT) *Forty-Second Street*. (MF) *Gold Diggers of 1933*. Jerry Ohrbach and Tammy Grimes appeared in *Forty-Second Street*. Dick Powell and Ned Sparks appeared in *Gold Diggers of 1933*.

Shadowland 1914 m. Lawrence B. Gilbert

Shadows in the Moonlight 1979 w.m. Charles F. Black, Rory Burke

Shadrack (Meshack, Abednigo) 1931 w.m. Robert MacGimsey

Shady Lady Bird 1941 w.m. Hugh Martin, Ralph Blane. (MT) *Best Foot Forward*. (MF) *Best Foot Forward*. June Allyson and Nancy Walker appeared in the stage production of *Best Foot Forward*. Lucille Ball and June Allyson appeared in the film production of *Best Foot Forward*.

(Theme from) Shaft 1971 w.m. Isaac Hayes. (F) *Shaft*. Academy Award winner 1971.

Shake It 1979 w.m. Terence Boylan

Shake It Off 1935 w. Lew Brown m. Harold Arlen. (MF) *Strike Me Pink*. Eddie Cantor and Ethel Merman appeared in *Strike Me Pink*.

Shake It Up 1982 w.m. Richard Otcasek

Shake, Rattle and Roll 1954 w.m. Charles Calhoun

Shake the Hand That Shook the Hand of Sullivan, *see* **Let Me Shake the Hand That Shook the Hand of Sullivan**

Shake Your Body (Down to the Ground) 1979 w.m. Marlon Jackson, Michael Jackson, Sigmund Jackson, Steven Jackson, Tariano Jackson

(Shake Shake Shake) Shake Your Booty 1976 w.m. Harry Casey, Richard Finch

Shakin' All Over 1960 w.m. Johnny Kidd

Shaking the Blues Away 1927 w.m. Irving Berlin. (MT) *Ziegfeld Follies of 1927*. (MF) *Easter Parade*. Eddie Cantor and Ruth Etting appeared in *Ziegfeld Follies of 1927*. Ann Miller, Judy Garland, and Fred Astaire appeared in *Easter Parade*.

Shall I Have It Bobbed or Shingled 1924 w.m. Weston, Lee

Shall We Dance 1937 w. Ira Gershwin m. George Gershwin. (MF) *Shall We Dance*. Fred Astaire and Ginger Rogers appeared in *Shall We Dance*.

Shall We Dance 1951 w. Oscar Hammerstein II m. Richard Rodgers. (MT) *The King and I*. (MF) *The King and I*. Gertrude Lawrence and Yul Brynner appeared in the stage production of *The King and I*. Deborah Kerr and Yul Brynner appeared in the film production of *The King and I*.

Shalom 1961 w.m. Jerry Herman. (MT) *Milk and Honey*.

Shambala 1973 w.m. Daniel Moore

Shame 1978 w.m. John Fitch, Reuben Cross

Shame On the Moon 1983 w.m. Rodney Crowell

Shanghai 1925 w.m. Horatio Nicholls

Shanghai 1951 w. Bob Hilliard m. Milton DeLugg

Shanghai Lil 1933 w. Al Dubin m. Harry Warren. (MF) *Footlight Parade*. James Cagney, Ruby Keeler, and Joan Blondell appeared in *Footlight Parade*.

Shangri-La 1946 w.m. Matt Molneck, Robert Maxwell. *Not* from the film and later Broadway show. This song was popularly revived in 1957, and later again in 1964.

Shannon 1976 w.m. Henry Gross

(In) Shanty in Old Shanty Town, A 1932 w. Joe Young m. Little Jack Little, John Siras. (MF) *Lullaby of Broadway*. Doris Day and Billy DeWolf appeared in *Lullaby of Broadway*.

Share Your Love with Me 1981 w.m. Alfred Braggs, Don Robey

Sharing the Night Together 1978 w.m. Ava Aldridge

Shave and a Haircut, Bay Rum 1914 w. Joe McCarthy m. Jimmie V. Monaco. Published in 1914 as the song "Rum Diddle-de-um Bum, That's It," based on "Hot Scotch Rag" of 1911. This song was popularly revived in 1939. See also "Gee, Officer Krupke."

Shazam 1960 w.m. Lee Hazlewood, Duane Eddy. (F) *Because They're Young*. Dick Clark and Tuesday Weld appeared in *Because They're Young*.

Sh-Boom 1954 w.m. James Keyes, Claude Feaster, Carl Feaster, Floyd F. McRae, James Edwards

She Belongs to Me 1969 w.m. Bob Dylan

She Bop 1984 w.m. Gary Corbett, Cyndi Lauper, Stephen Broughton Lunt

She Didn't Say Yes (She Didn't Say No) 1931 w. Otto Harbach m. Jerome Kern. (MT) *The Cat and the Fiddle*. (MF) *The Cat and the Fiddle*. (MF) *Till the Clouds Roll By*. Bettina Hall and George Metaxa appeared in the stage production of *The Cat and the Fiddle*. Jeanette MacDonald and Charles Butterworth appeared in the film production of *The Cat and the Fiddle*. June Allyson, Frank Sinatra, Judy Garland, and Van Johnson appeared in *Till the Clouds Roll By*, biopic of composer Jerome Kern.

She Don't Wanna 1927 w.m. Jack Yellen, Milton Ager

She Got the Goldmine I Got the Shaft 1982 w.m. Tim DuBois

She Is Ma Daisy 1905 w.m. Harry Lauder, J.D. Harper

She Is More To Be Pitied Than Censured 1894 w.m. William B. Gray

She Is Not Thinking of Me (Waltz at Maxim's) 1958 w. Alan Jay Lerner m. Frederick Loewe. (MF) *Gigi*. Leslie Caron, Maurice Chevalier, and Hermione Gingold appeared in *Gigi*.

She Is the Belle of New York 1898 w. Hugh Morton m. Gustave Kerker. (MT) *The Belle of New York*.

She Is the Sunshine of Virginia 1916 w. Ballard MacDonald m. Harry Carroll

She Lived Next Door to a Firehouse 1931 w.m. Lou Klein, Fred Phillips

She Loves Me 1963 w. Sheldon Harnick m. Jerry Bock. (MT) *She Loves Me*.

She Loves You 1964 w.m. John Lennon, Paul McCartney. (MT) *Beatlemania*. Ivor Novello Award winner 1963.

She May Have Seen Better Days 1894 w.m. James Thornton

She Reminds Me of You 1934 w. Mack Gordon m. Harry Revel. (MF) *We're Not Dressing*. Bing Crosby and Carole Lombard appeared in *We're Not Dressing*.

She Said She Said 1966 w.m. John Lennon, Paul McCartney

She Sells Sea-Shells (on the Seashore) 1908 w. Terry Sullivan m. Harry Gifford. (MT) *The Beauty Shop*.

She Shall Have Music 1935 w.m. Maurice Sigler, Al

Goodhart, Al Hoffman. (MF) *She Shall Have Music.* Jack Hylton and June Clyde appeared in *She Shall Have Music.*

She Took Mother's Advice 1910 w. Stanley Murphy m. Percy Wenrich

She Touched Me 1965 w. Ira Levin m. Milton Schafer. (MT) *Drat! The Cat!.*

She Waits by the Deep Blue Sea 1905 w. Edward Madden m. Theodore F. Morse

She Walks Like You, She Talks Like You, *see* **She Reminds Me of You**

She Was Bred in Old Kentucky 1898 w. Harry Braisted m. Stanley Carter

She Was Happy Till She Met You 1899 w. Charles Graham m. Monroe H. Rosenfeld

She Was One of the Early Birds 1917 w.m. T.W. Conner

She Went to the City 1904 w.m. Paul Dresser

She Wore a Yellow Ribbon, or, **All Round My Hat (Round Her Neck) I (She) Wore a Yellow Ribbon** 1838 w.m. traditional. This song was adapted and popularly revived in 1950.

She Works Hard for the Money 1983. w.m. Michael Omartian, Donna Summer

She Wouldn't Do What I Asked Her To 1923 w.m. Sidney D. Mitchell, Sam Gottlieb, Philip Boutelje, Al Burt

Sheik of Araby, The 1921 w. Harry B. Smith, Francis Wheeler m. Ted Snyder. (MT) *Make It Snappy.* (MF) *Tin Pan Alley.*

Sheila 1962 w.m. Tommy Roe

She'll Be Comin' Round the Mountain (When She Comes) 1899 w.m. based on the traditional black American melody ''When the Chariot Comes'' (hymn) of 1899 or earlier. (F) *Tangier.* Maria Montez and Preston Foster appeared in *Tangier.* This adaptation was popularly revived in 1927.

Shenandoah, or, **Across the Wide Missouri** c.1826 w.m. traditional American sea chantey, but later associated with the West. See also ''Theme from Peyton Place.''

Shepherd of the Hills 1927 w.m. Horatio Nicholls, Edgar Leslie

Shepherd Serenade, The 1941 w.m. Kermit Goell, Fred Spielman

Sherry 1962 w.m. Bob Gaudio

She's a Carioca 1965 w.m. Ray Gilbert, Antonio Carlos Jobim, Vinicus de Moraes

She's a Fool 1964 w.m. Ben Raleigh, Mark Barkan

She's a Lady 1971 w.m. Paul Anka

She's a Lassie from Lancashire 1908 w.m. C.W. Murphy, Dan Lipton, John Neat

She's a Latin from Manhattan 1935 w. Al Dubin m. Harry Warren. (MF) *Casino de Paris.* (MF) *Go into Your Dance.* (MF) *The Jolson Story.* Al Jolson appeared in *Casino de Paris.* Al Jolson, Ruby Keeler, and Patsy Kelly appeared in *Go into Your Dance.* Larry Parks appeared in *The Jolson Story.*

She's a Woman 1964 w.m. John Lennon, Paul McCartney

(I Got a Woman Crazy for Me) She's Funny That Way 1928 w.

Richard A. Whiting m. Neil Moret. (F) *The Postman Always Rings Twice. (MF) Rainbow Round My Shoulder.* (MF) *Meet Danny Wilson.* Lana Turner and John Garfield appeared in *The Postman Always Rings Twice.* Frankie Laine and Billy Daniels appeared in *Rainbow Round My Shoulder.* Frank Sinatra and Shelley Winters appeared in *Meet Danny Wilson.*

She's Gone 1976 w.m. Daryl Hall, John Oates

She's Leaving Home 1967 w.m. John Lennon, Paul McCartney. Ivor Novello Award winner 1967–68.

She's Mine, All Mine 1921 w.m. Bert Kalmar, Harry Ruby. (MF) *Three Little Words.* Fred Astaire and Red Skelton appeared in *Three Little Words,* biopic of song writers Bert Kalmar and Harry Ruby.

She's My Lovely 1937 w.m. Vivian Ellis. (MT) *Hide and Seek.* Bobby Howes appeared in *Hide and Seek.* Theme song of Billy Ternent.

She's Not There 1964 w.m. Rod Argent

She's Out of My Life 1980 w.m. Tom Bahler

She's Such a Comfort to Me 1929 w. Douglas Furber, Max Lief, Nathaniel Lief, Donovan Parsons m. Arthur Schwartz. (MT) *Wake Up and Dream.*

She's the Daughter of Mother Machree 1915 w. Jeff T. Branen m. Ernest R. Ball.

She's the Fairest Little Flower Dear Old Dixie Ever Grew (Knew) 1907 w. Ashley S. Johnson m. Theodore F. Morse

She's the Girlfriend of the Whirling Dervish, *see* **The Whirling Dervish**

Shew (Shoo) Fly, Don't Bother Me 1869 w. Billy Reeves m. Frank Campbell; arr. Rollin Howard

Shifting, Whispering Sands 1955 w. V.C. Gilbert m. Mary M. Hadler

Shillingbury Tales 1982 m. Ed Welch. Ivor Novello Award winner 1981–82.

Shim-Me-Sha-Wabble 1917 w.m. Spencer Williams

Shinaniki Da 1929 w.m. Harry Carlton

Shinbone Alley, *see* **Long Time Ago**

Shindig 1963 w.m. Hank B. Marvin, Bruce Welch

S-H-I-N-E 1924 w. Cecil Mack, Lew Brown m. Ford Dabney. (MF) *Birth of the Blues.* (MF) *The Benny Goodman Story.* (MF) *The Eddy Duchin Story.* (MF) *Cabin in the Sky.* Bing Crosby and Mary Martin appeared in *Birth of the Blues.* Ethel Waters and Lena Horne appeared in the film production of *Cabin in the Sky.*

Shine 1982 w.m. Waylon Jennings

Shine a Little Love 1979 w.m. Jeff Lynne

Shine On Harvest Moon 1908 w. Jack Norworth m. Nora Bayes, Jack Norworth. (MT) *Ziegfeld Follies* (1908). (MT) *Miss Innocence.* (MT) *Ziegfeld Follies of 1931.* (MF) *Ever Since Eve.* (MF) *Nancy Goes to Rio.* (MF) *Shine On Harvest Moon.* (MF) *The Eddy Duchin Story.* Marion Davies and Robert Montgomery appeared in *Ever Since Eve.* Jane Powell and Ann Sothern appeared in *Nancy Goes to Rio.* Ann Sheridan appeared in *Shine On Harvest Moon,* biopic of entertainer Nora Bayes. Carmen Cavallaro appeared in *The Eddy Duchin Story.* This song was popularly revived in 1931.

Shine On Victory Moon   1944   w.m. Joe Gilbert

Shine on Your Shoes, A   1932   w. Howard Dietz   m. Arthur Schwartz. (MT) *Flying Colors.* (MF) *The Band Wagon.* Clifton Webb, Patsy Kelly, and Imogene Coca appeared in *Flying Colors.* Fred Astaire, Cyd Charisse, Nanette Fabray, and Oscar Levant appeared in *The Band Wagon.*

Shine Through My Dreams   1935   w.m. Ivor Novello, Christopher Hassall. (MT) *Glamorous Night.* (MF) *Glamorous Night.* Trefor Jones appeared in both the stage and film productions of *Glamorous Night.*

Shining Star   1975   w.m. Maurice White, Philip Bailey, Larry Dunn

Shining Star   1980   w.m. Leo Graham, Jr., Paul Richmond

Ship Ahoy, or, **All the Nice Girls Love a Sailor**   1909   w.m. A.J. Mills, Bennett Scott

Ship Without a Sail, A   1929   w. Lorenz Hart   m. Richard Rodgers. (MT) *Heads Up!.* (MF) *Heads Up!.* Charles "Buddy" Rogers and Helen Kane appeared in the film production of *Heads Up!*

Shipmates Forever, *see* **Don't Give Up the Ship**

Shipmates of Mine   1913   w.m. Wilfrid Sanderson

Shiralee   1957   w.m. Tommy Steele. (F) *Shiralee.*

Shoe Shine Boy   1936   w. Sammy Cahn   m. Saul Chaplin

Shoeless Joe from Hannibal, Mo.   1955   w.m. Richard Adler, Jerry Ross. (MT) *Damn Yankees.* (MF) *Damn Yankees.* Gwen Verdon appeared in both the stage and film productions of *Damn Yankees.*

Shoemaker's Serenade, The   1947   w.m. Joe Lubin, Edward M. Lisbona

Shoestring   1980   m. George Fenton. Ivor Novello Award winner 1979–80.

Shoo Fly, Don't Bother Me, *see* **Shew Fly, Don't Bother Me**

Shoofly Pie and Apple Pan Dowdy   1946   w. Sammy Gallop   m. Guy Woods

Shoo-Shoo Baby   1944   w.m. Phil Moore. (MF) *Three Cheers for the Boys.* (MF) *Follow the Boys.* (MF) *Trocadero.* George Raft and Marlene Dietrich appeared in *Follow the Boys.* Rosemary Lane and Cliff Nazarro appeared in *Trocadero.*

Shop Around   1961   w.m. Berry Gordy, Jr., Bill "Smokey" Robinson

Shores of Tripoli, The, *see* **The Marine's Hymn**

Short, Fat and 4F   1943   w.m. Don Raye, Gene De Paul. (MF) *What's Buzzin' Cousin.* Ann Miller and Eddie "Rochester" Anderson appeared in *What's Buzzin' Cousin.*

Short People   1977   w.m. Randy Newman

Short Shorts   1958   w.m. Thomas Austin, Bill Crandall, Bill Dalton, Bob Gaudio

Shortnin' Bread   1928   w.m. Jacques Wolfe. Based on a traditional folksong; possibly written by black composer Reese D'Pree in 1905. (MF) *Louisiana Hayride.* Judy Canova and Ross Hunter appeared in *Louisiana Hayride.* Theme song of Nelson Eddy.

Should I (Reveal)   1929   w. Arthur Freed   m. Nacio Herb Brown. (MF) *Lord Byron of Broadway.* (MF) *Singin' in the Rain.* Ethelind Terry and Cliff Edwards appeared in *Lord Byron of Broadway.* Gene Kelly, Debbie Reynolds, and Donald O'Connor appeared in *Singin' in the Rain.*

Should I Do It   1982   w.m. Layng Martine, Jr.

Should I Tell You I Love You   1946   w.m. Cole Porter. (MT) *Around the World in Eighty Days.* Arthur Margetson and Mary Healy appeared in *Around the World in Eighty Days.*

Should've Never Let You Go   1980   w.m. Neil Sedaka, Phillip Cody

Shout   1985   w.m. Roland Orzabal, Ian Stanley

Show and Tell   1974   w.m. Jerry Fuller

Show Business, *see* **There's No Business Like Show Business**

Show Me   1956   w. Alan Jay Lerner   m. Frederick Loewe. (MT) *My Fair Lady.* (MF) *My Fair Lady.* Julie Andrews and Rex Harrison appeared in the stage production of *My Fair Lady.* Audrey Hepburn and Rex Harrison appeared in the film production of *My Fair Lady.*

Show Me the Town   1926   w. Ira Gershwin   m. George Gershwin. (MT) *Oh, Kay!.* (MT) *Rosalie.* This song did not appear in the New York production of *Oh, Kay!.*

Show Me the Way   1896   w.m. Paul Dresser

Show Me the Way   1976   w.m. Peter Frampton

Show Me the Way To Go Home   1925   w.m. Irving King. Based on the title only of Archie Morrow's 1901 "Show Me the Way To Go Home, Babe." "Irving King" is a pseudonym for the team of Reginald Connelly and Jimmy Campbell.

Show the White of Yo' Eye   1903   w.m. Stanley Crawford

Shower the People   1976   w.m. James Taylor

Shrimp Boats   1951   w.m. Paul Mason Howard, Paul Weston

Shuffle Along   1921   w.m. Noble Sissle, Eubie Blake. (MT) *Shuffle Along.* (MT) *Eubie!.*

Shuffle Off to Buffalo   1932   w. Al Dubin   m. Harry Warren. (MT) *Forty-Second Street.* (MF) *Forty-Second Street.* Jerry Ohrbach and Tammy Grimes appeared in *Forty-Second Street.* Ruby Keeler and Ginger Rogers appeared in *Forty-Second Street,* dancing and singing aboard the sleeper train, the Niagara Limited.

Shufflin' Along   1922   w.m. Nat D. Ayer, Ralph Stanley. (MT) *Snap.*

Shufflin' Sam   1924   w. P.G. Wodehouse   m. Jerome Kern. (MT) *Sitting Pretty.*

Shut the Door, (They're Comin' Through the Window)   1926 w.m. Billy Mann, Wally Ives, Dick Howard, Jim Kern

Shy Serenade   1938   w.m. George Scott-Wood

Siam   1915   w. Howard Johnson   m. Fred Fisher

Siamese Patrol   1912   m. Paul Lincke

Siberia   1955   w.m. Cole Porter. (MT) *Silk Stockings.* (MF) *Silk Stockings.* Fred Astaire and Cyd Charisse appeared in the film production of *Silk Stockings.*

Siboney   1929   Sp.w. Ernesto Lecuona   Eng.w. Theodora Morse (Dolly Morse, Dorothy Terriss)   m. Ernesto Lecuona. (MF) *Get Hep to Love.* Gloria Jean and Donald O'Connor appeared in *Get Hep to Love.* The original Spanish title was "Canto Siboney."

Sicilian Hymn (O Sanctissima) 1819 w.m. anon.

Side by Side 1927 w.m. Harry Woods. This song was popularly revived in 1953.

Side by Side by Side 1970 w.m. Stephen Sondheim. (MT) *Company*. (MT) *Side by Side by Sondheim*. Elaine Stritch appeared in *Company*. Millicent Martin and Julie N. McKenzie appeared in *Side by Side by Sondheim*.

Side Saddle 1959 w.m. Trevor Stanford (Russ Conway). Ivor Novello Award winner 1959.

Sidewalks of Cuba 1935 w.m. Mitchell Parish, Irving Mills, Ben Oakland

Sidewalks of New York, The, or, **East Side, West Side** 1894 w.m. Charles B. Lawlor, James W. Blake. (MF) *Beau James*. Bob Hope and Alexis Smith appeared in *Beau James*. This song was used for Al Smith's Presidential campaign of 1928.

Sierra Sue 1916 w.m. Joseph B. Carey. (MF) *Sierra Sue*. Gene Autry and Gabby Hayes appeared in *Sierra Sue*. This song was popular for the first time in 1940.

Sigh by Night 1945 w. George Marion, Jr. m. Emmerich Kalman. (MT) *Marinka*.

Sigh No More, Ladies c.1795 w. William Shakespeare m. Richard John Samuel Stevens. The words to this song are adapted from a passage in Shakespeare's *Much Ado About Nothing*.

Silent Night, Holy Night 1818 Ger.w. Joseph Mohr Eng.w. anon.; standard translation 1871 m. Franz Gruber. From the German "Stille Nacht, Heilige Nacht." This song was popularly performed by the Strasser Sisters, Tyrolean singers in Germany in the 1830s. This song was first performed at midnight mass on Christmas Eve, 1818, in the village church at Oberndorf in the Austrian Tyrol. It was written to compensate for a broken church organ and was performed on guitar.

Silent Running (On Dangerous Ground) 1986 w.m. Brian A. Robertson, Mike Rutherford

Silhouettes 1957 w.m. Frank C. Slay, Jr., Bob Crewe. This song was popularly revived in 1965.

Silly Love Songs 1976 w.m. Paul McCartney, Linda McCartney

Silver Bell 1910 w. Edward Madden m. Percy Wenrich

Silver Bells 1950 w.m. Jay Livingston, Ray Evans. (F) *The Lemon Drop Kid*. Bob Hope and Lloyd Nolan appeared in *The Lemon Drop Kid*.

Silver Dollar (Down and Out) 1950 w.m. Clarke Van Ness, Jack Palmer

Silver Dream Machine 1981 m. David Essex. Ivor Novello Award winner 1980–81.

Silver Hair and Heart of Gold 1932 w.m. Peter Maurice, Joe Gilbert

Silver Moon 1927 w. Dorothy Donnelly m. Sigmund Romberg. (MT) *My Maryland*.

Silver Moon, The, *see also* **Roll On Silver Moon**

Silver Threads Among the Gold 1873 w. Eben E. Rexford m. Hart Pease Danks. This song was most popularly sung by tenor Richard José.

Silver Wings in the Moonlight 1942 w.m. Sonny Miller, Hugh Charles, Leo Towers

Simon Says 1968 w.m. Elliot Chiprut

Simon the Cellarer 1860 w. anon. m. John Liptrot Hatton

Simonetta 1953 w. Irving Caesar m. Belle Fenstock

Simple 1982 w.m. Maury Yeston. (MT) *Nine*. Liliane Montevecchi and Anita Morris appeared in *Nine*.

Simple Aveu 1878 m. Francis Thomé

Simple Game 1972 w.m. Mike Pinder. Ivor Novello Award winner 1971–72.

Simple Joys of Maidenhood, The 1960 w. Alan Jay Lerner m. Frederick Loewe. (MT) *Camelot*. (MF) *Camelot*. Julie Andrews appeared in the stage production of *Camelot*. Vanessa Redgrave appeared in the film production of *Camelot*.

Simple Melody, *see* **Play a Simple Melody**

Simple Simon, *see* **Mother Goose's Melodies**

Sin, *see* **It's No Sin**

Since Father Went to Work 1906 w.m. William Cahill

Since I Don't Have You 1959 w. James Beaumont, Janet Vogel, Joseph Verscharen, Walter Lester, John Taylor m. Joseph Rock, Lennie Martin

Since I Fell for You 1948 w.m. Buddy Johnson

Since I Met You Baby 1956 w.m. Ivory Joe Hunter

Since Maggie Dooley Learned the Hooley Hooley 1916 w. Bert Kalmar, Edgar Leslie m. George W. Meyer

Since Sister Nell Heard Paderewski Play 1902 w. William Jerome m. Jean Schwartz. See also Part I, 1911.

Sincerely 1955 w.m. Harvey Fuqua, Alan Freed

Sing (Sing a Song) 1973 w.m. Joe Raposo. (TV) *Sesame Street*.

Sing a Rainbow 1955 w.m. Arthur Hamilton

Sing a Song of Freedom 1972 w.m. Guy Fletcher, Doug Flett

Sing a Song of Sixpence, *see* **Mother Goose's Melodies**

Sing an Old Fashioned Song (To a Young Sophisticated Lady) 1935 w. Joe Young m. Fred E. Ahlert

Sing As We Go 1934 w.m. Harry Parr-Davies, Gracie Fields. (MF) *Sing As We Go*. Gracie Fields appeared in *Sing As We Go*.

Sing, Baby, Sing 1936 w. Jack Yellen m. Lew Pollack. (MF) *Sing Baby Sing*. Adolphe Menjou, Ted Healy, and Dixie Dunbar appeared in *Sing Baby Sing*.

Sing Brothers 1932 w. R.P. Weston, Bert Lee m. Jack Waller, Joe Tunbridge. (MT) *Tell Her the Truth*.

Sing, Everybody Sing 1942 w.m. John P. Long

Sing for Your Supper 1938 w. Lorenz Hart m. Richard Rodgers. (MT) *The Boys from Syracuse*. (MF) *Up and Doing*. (MF) *The Boys from Syracuse*. Teddy Hart, Jimmy Savo, and Eddie Albert appeared in the stage production of *The Boys from Syracuse*. Allan Jones and Martha Raye appeared in the film production of *The Boys from Syracuse*. This song was popularly revived in 1967.

Sing Joyous Bird 1914 w.m. Montague Phillips

Sing Little Birdie 1957 w.m. Syd Cordell, Stan Butcher

Sing, Sing, Sing, Sing 1937 w.m. Louis Prima. (MF) *The*

Benny Goodman Story. Steve Allen and Donna Reed appeared in *The Benny Goodman Story.*

Sing Something Simple 1930 w.m. Herman Hupfeld. (MT) *The Second Little Show.*

Sing You Sinners 1930 w. Sam Coslow m. W. Franke Harling. (MF) *Honey.* (MF) *I'll Cry Tomorrow.* Zasu Pitts and Nancy Carroll appeared in *Honey.* Susan Hayward appeared in *I'll Cry Tomorrow.*

Singer and the Song, The 1899 w. Will D. Cobb m. Gus Edwards

Singing a Vagabond Song 1929 w.m. Sam Messenheimer, Harry Richman, Val Burton. (MF) *Puttin' On the Ritz.* Harry Richman appeared in *Puttin' On the Ritz.*

Singing Hills, The 1940 w.m. Mack David, Dick Sanford, Sammy Mysels

Singin' in the Bathtub 1929 w.m. Herb Magidson, Ned Washington, Michael H. Cleary. (MT) *Show of Shows.* (MF) *Show of Shows.* Beatrice Lillie and Loretta Young appeared in *Show of Shows.*

Singin' in the Rain 1929 w. Arthur Freed m. Nacio Herb Brown. (MT) *Singing' in the Rain.* (MF) *Hollywood Revue.* (MF) *Little Nellie Kelly.* (F) *Hi Beautiful.* (MF) *Singin' in the Rain.* (F) *A Clockwork Orange.* Lionel Barrymore, Jack Benny, and Marion Davies appeared in *Hollywood Revue.* Judy Garland and George Murphy appeared in *Little Nellie Kelly.* Noah Beery appeared in *Hi Beautiful.* Gene Kelly, Debbie Reynolds, and Donald O'Connor appeared in *Singing' in the Rain.*

Singing Piano, The 1959 w.m. Tolchard Evans

Singin' the Blues 1931 w. Dorothy Fields m. Jimmy McHugh. (MT) *Singin' the Blues.* (MF) *Singin' the Blues.*

Singin' the Blues 1957 w.m. Melvin Endsley

Sink Red Sun 1909 w.m. Teresa del Riego

Sink the Bismarck 1960 w.m. Johnny Horton, Tillman Franks. (F) *Sink the Bismarck.*

Sinner Kissed an Angel, A 1941 w.m. Mack David, Larry Shay

Sioux City Sue 1945 w. Ray Freedman m. Dick Thomas. (F) *Sioux City Sue.*

Sipping Cider Thru' (Through) a Straw 1919 w.m. Carey Morgan, Lee David

Siren's Song, The 1917 w. P.G. Wodehouse m. Jerome Kern. (MT) *Leave It to Jane.* Oscar Shaw and Georgia O'Ramey appeared in *Leave It to Jane.*

Sister Christian 1984 w.m. Kelly Keagy

Sister Golden Hair 1975 w.m. Gerald L. Beckley

Sister Kate, *see* **I Wish I Could Shimmy Like My Sister Kate**

Sister Susie's Sewing Shirts for Soldiers 1914 w. R.P. Weston m. Herman E. Darewski

Sit Down, You're Rocking the Boat 1913 w.m. William Jerome, Grant Clarke, Jean Schwartz

Sit Down, You're Rockin' the Boat 1950 w.m. Frank Loesser. (MT) *Guys and Dolls.* (MF) *Guys and Dolls.* Robert Alda and Vivian Blaine appeared in the stage production

of *Guys and Dolls.* Frank Sinatra, Stubby Kaye, and Marlon Brando appeared in the film production of *Guys and Dolls.*

Sitting by the Window 1949 w.m. Paul Insetta

Sittin' in a Corner 1923 w. Gus Kahn m. George W. Meyer

Sitting in the Back Seat 1959 w.m. Lee Pockriss

Sitting on a Fire Barred Gate 1931 w.m. Stanley Damerell, Reginald Hargreaves

Sittin' on the Dock of the Bay, *see* **The Dock of the Bay**

633 Squadron 1969 w.m. Ron Goodwin

Six Lessons from Madame LaZonga 1941. w. Charles Newman m. James V. Monaco. (F) *Six Lessons from Madame LaZonga.* Lupe Velez and William Frawley appeared in *Six Lessons from Madame LaZonga.*

Six Little Wives 1899 w. Harry Greenbank, Adrian Ross m. Sidney Jones. (MT) *San Toy.*

Sixteen Candles 1958 w.m. Luther Dixon, Allyson R. Khent

Sixteen Going on Seventeen 1959 w. Oscar Hammerstein II m. Richard Rodgers. (MT) *The Sound of Music.* (MF) *The Sound of Music.* Mary Martin appeared in the stage production of *The Sound of Music.* Julie Andrews appeared in the film production of *The Sound of Music.*

Sixteen Tons 1947 w.m. Merle Travis. This song was popularly revived in 1955.

65 Love Affair 1982 w.m. Paul Davis

Sixty Seconds Every Minute, I Think of You 1922 w. Irving Caesar, John Murray Anderson m. Louis A. Hirsch. (MT) *Greenwich Village Follies.*

Skaters, The (Waltz) 1882 m. Emile Waldteufel

Skidmore Fancy Ball, The 1878 w. Edward Harrigan m. David Braham. (MT) *Mulligan Guard.* (MT) *The Skidmore Fancy Ball.*

Skidmore Guard, The 1874 w. Edward Harrigan m. David Braham

Skidmore Masquerade, The 1880 w. Edward Harrigan m. David Braham. (MT) *The Mulligan Guards' Nominee.*

Skiffling Strings 1957 w.m. Ron Goodwin. Ivor Novello Award winner 1957.

Skip to My Lou c.1844 w.m. traditional American folksong. (MF) *Meet Me in St. Louis.* Judy Garland, Mary Astor, and Margaret O'Brien appeared in *Meet Me in St. Louis*

Skirt Dance 1890 m. Meyer W. Lutz (Wilhelm Meyer-Lutz). (MT) *Faust Up-to-Date.*

Skokiaan 1954 w. Tom Glazer m. August Machon Musarurgwa

Sky Fell Down, The 1940 w. Edward Heyman m. Louis Alter

Sky High 1975 w.m. Clive Scott, Desmond Dyer. Ivor Novello Award winner 1975–76.

Skylark 1941 w.m. Johnny Mercer, Hoagy Carmichael

Skyliner 1945 w.m. Charlie Barnet. Theme song of Charlie Barnet.

Slap That Bass 1937 w. Ira Gershwin m. George Gershwin. (MF) *Shall We Dance.* Fred Astaire and Ginger Rogers appeared in *Shall We Dance.*

Slaughter on Tenth Avenue (Ballet) 1936 m. Richard Rodgers. (MT) *On Your Toes.* (MF) *On Your Toes.* (MF) *Words and Music.* Ray Bolger and Luella Gear appeared in the stage production of *On Your Toes.* Zorina and Eddie Albert appeared in the film production of *On Your Toes.* Judy Garland, Gene Kelly, and Mickey Rooney appeared in *Words and Music,* biopic of song writers Rodgers and Hart. This work was popularly revived in 1964.

Slavonic Dances 1887 m. Anton Dvorák

Sledgehammer 1986 w.m.. Peter Gabriel

Sleep 1923 w.m. Earl Lebieg

Sleep, Baby, Sleep, or, Irene's Lullaby 1885 w.m. John J. Handley

Sleep Walk 1959 w. Don Wolf m. Johnny Santo, Ann Farina

Sleeping Beauty Waltz, op.66, no.6 1890 m. Peter Tchaikovsky

Sleepin' Bee, A 1955 w. Harold Arlen, Truman Capote m. Harold Arlen. (MT) *House of Flowers.* Pearl Bailey and Diahann Carroll appeared in *House of Flowers.*

Sleepin' with the Radio On 1981 w.m. Steve Davis

Sleepy Head 1926 w.m. Benny Davis, Jesse Greer

(By the) Sleepy Lagoon (Valse Serenade) 1930 w. Jack Lawrence m. Eric Coates. (MF) *Sleepy Lagoon.* Judy Canova and Dennis Day appeared in *Sleepy Lagoon.* This song was popularly revived in 1942.

Sleepy Serenade 1941 w.m. Mort Greene, Lou Singer. (MF) *Hold That Ghost.* The Andrews Sisters, Bud Abbott, and Lou Costello appeared in *Hold That Ghost.* Theme song of Cyril Stapleton.

Sleepy Shores 1972 w.m. Johnny Pearson. (TV-BBC) *Owen MD.*

Sleepy Time Down South, *see* **When It's Sleepy Time Down South**

Sleepy Time Gal 1925 w. Joseph R. Alden, Raymond B. Egan m. Ange Lorenzo, Richard A. Whiting. (MF) *Sleepy Time Gal.* Judy Canova and Tom Brown appeared in *Sleepy Time Gal.*

Sleigh, The 1926 w. Ivor Tchervanow m. Richard Kountz

Sleigh Ride 1950 w. Mitchell Parish m. Leroy Anderson

Sleigh Ride in July 1944 w.m. Johnny Burke, James Van Heusen. (MF) *Belle of the Yukon.* Gypsy Rose Lee and Dinah Shore appeared in *Belle of the Yukon.*

Slide Kelly Slide 1889 w.m. John W. Kelly. Kelly was nicknamed "The Rolling Mill Man."

Slip Slidin' Away 1977 w.m. Paul Simon

Slippin' Around 1949 w.m. Floyd Tillman

Sloop John B. 1966 w.m. Brian Wilson. Based on a traditional Bahamian song from as early as 1927.

Slow Boat to China, *see* **On a Slow Boat to China**

Slow Hand 1981 w.m. John Bettis, Michael Clark

Slow Poke 1952 w.m. Pee Wee King, Redd Stewart, Chilton Price

Slumber On, My Little Gypsy Sweetheart, *see* **Gypsy Love Song**

Slumming on Park Avenue 1937 w.m. Irving Berlin. (MF) *On the Avenue.* Alice Faye and Dick Powell appeared in *On the Avenue.*

Small Fry 1938 w. Frank Loesser m. Hoagy Carmichael. (MF) *Sing You Sinners.* Bing Crosby and Fred MacMurray appeared in *Sing You Sinners.*

Small Town 1986 w.m. John Cougar Mellencamp

Small World 1959 w. Stephen Sondheim m. Jule Styne. (MT) *Gypsy.* (MF) *Gypsy.* Ethel Merman appeared in the stage production of *Gypsy.* Rosalind Russell appeared in the film production of *Gypsy.*

Smarty 1908 w. Jack Norworth m. Albert Von Tilzer

Smellin' of Vanilla (Bamboo Cage) 1955 w. Harold Arlen, Truman Capote m. Harold Arlen. (MT) *House of Flowers.* Pearl Bailey and Diahann Carroll appeared in *House of Flowers.*

Smile 1954 w. John Turner, Geoffrey Parsons m. Charles Chaplin. (F) *Modern Times.*

Smile, Darn Ya, Smile 1931 w. Charles O'Flynn, Jack Meskill m. Max Rice

Smile, Smile, Smile, *see* **Pack Up Your Troubles in Your Old Kit Bag and Smile, Smile, Smile**

Smile When You Say "Goodbye" 1937 w.m. Harry Parr-Davies

Smile Will Go a Long, Long Way, A 1923 w.m. Benny Davis, Harry Akst

Smiles 1917 w. J. Will Callahan m. Lee G. Roberts. (MT) *The Passing Show of 1918.* (MF) *The Dolly Sisters.* (MF) *Somebody Loves Me.* (MF) *Wait Till the Sun Shines Nellie.* (MF) *The Eddy Duchin Story.* (F) *What Price Glory?* Betty Hutton appeared in *The Dolly Sisters,* biopic of the famous sister team. Betty Hutton appeared in *Somebody Loves Me.* David Wayne appeared in *Wait Till the Sun Shines Nellie.* James Cagney appeared in *What Price Glory?* Supposedly, Roberts wrote this song on the back of a package of cigarettes.

Smiley's People 1983 m. Patrick Gowers. Ivor Novello Award winner 1982–83.

Smilin' Through 1919 w.m. Arthur A. Penn. (F) *Smilin' Through.*

Smoke Dreams 1947 w.m. John Klenner, Lloyd Schaefer, Ted Steele

Smoke from a Distant Fire 1977 w.m. Ed Sanford, John Townsend, Steven Stewart

Smoke Gets in Your Eyes 1933 w. Otto Harbach m. Jerome Kern. (MT) *Roberta.* (MF) *Roberta.* (MF) *Till the Clouds Roll By.* (MF) *Lovely To Look At.* Bob Hope appeared in the stage production of *Roberta.* Irene Dunne, Fred Astaire, and Ginger Rogers appeared in the film production of *Roberta.* Frank Sinatra, Judy Garland, and Van Johnson appeared in *Till the Clouds Roll By,* biopic of composer Jerome Kern. Kathryn Grayson and Howard Keel appeared in *Lovely To Look At.* This song was popularly revived in 1959. The Director of *Roberta* attempted to have this song cut from the stage production, leading to a dispute that Kern fortunately won. Theme song of Henny Youngman.

Smoke on the Water 1973 w.m. Richard Blackmore, Ian Gillan, Roger David Glover, Jon Lord, Ian Paice

Smoke Rings 1932 w. Ned Washington m. H. Eugene Gifford. Theme song of Glen Gray.

Smoke! Smoke! Smoke! (That Cigarette) 1947 w.m. Merle Travis, Tex Williams

Smokin' in the Boys Room 1973 w.m. Michael Koda, Michael G. Lutz

Smoky Mokes 1899 m. Abe Holzmann. This melody was the standard cakewalk of its day.

Smoky Mountain, see **On Top of Old Smokey**

Smoky Mountain Rain 1981 w.m. Kye Fleming

Smooth Operator 1985 w.m. Ray St. John, Sade

Snag It 1926 w.m. Joseph Oliver

Snake Charmer 1937 w.m. Leonard Whitcup, Teddy Powell

Snake Rag 1923 w.m. Joseph Oliver

Snookeroo 1975 w.m. Bernard Taupin, Dwight K. Reginald

Snook(e)y Ookums 1913 w.m. Irving Berlin. (MT) *Hullo Ragtime.* (MF) *Easter Parade.* Shirley Kellog and Lew Hearn appeared in *Hullo Ragtime.* Judy Garland and Fred Astaire appeared in *Easter Parade.* This song was popularly revived in 1948.

Snoopy vs. The Red Baron 1966 w.m. Dick Holler, Phil Gernhard

Snow Coach 1959 w.m. Trevor Stanford

Snow Goose, The 1977 w.m. Ed Welch, Spike Milligan. Ivor Novello Award winner 1977–78.

Snowbird 1970 w.m. Gene MacLellan

Snowy White Snow and Jingle Bells 1949 w.m. Billy Reid

Snuggled on Your Shoulder, Cuddled in Your Arms 1932 w. Joe Young m. Carmen Lombardo

So Am I 1924 w. Ira Gershwin m. George Gershwin. (MT) *Lady, Be Good.* Fred Astaire and Adele Astaire appeared in the American stage production of *Lady, Be Good.* George Vollaire appeared in the British stage production of *Lady, Be Good.* This song did not appear in the film production of *Lady, Be Good.*

So Beats My Heart for You 1930 w.m. Pat Ballard, Charles Henderson, Tom Waring. (F) *Rah-Rah-Daze.* Fred Waring and His Pennsylvanians appeared in *Rah-Rah-Daze.*

So Blue 1927 w.m. B.G. DeSylva, Lew Brown, Ray Henderson. Based on a theme by Helen Crawford.

So Do I 1932 w. B.G. De Sylva m. Vincent Youmans. (MT) *Take a Chance.*

So Do I 1936 w. John Burke m. Arthur Johnston. (MF) *Pennies from Heaven.* Bing Crosby and Louis Armstrong appeared in *Pennies from Heaven.*

So Far 1947 w. Oscar Hammerstein II m. Richard Rodgers. (MT) *Allegro.* Roberta Jonay, William Ching, and Annamary Dickey appeared in *Allegro.*

So Far Away 1971 w.m. Carole King

So Help Me 1934 w.m. Irving Berlin

So Help Me 1938 w. Edward DeLange m. Jimmy Van Heusen

So In Love (Am I) 1948 w.m. Cole Porter. (MT) *Kiss Me, Kate.* (MF) *Kiss Me, Kate.* Alfred Drake and Patricia Morison appeared in the stage production of *Kiss Me, Kate.* Kathryn Grayson, Howard Keel, and Ann Miller appeared in the film production of *Kiss Me, Kate.*

So Into You 1977 w.m. Buddy Buie, Dean Daughtry, Robert Nix

So Long Dearie 1964 w.m. Jerry Herman. (MT) *Hello, Dolly!* (MT) *Jerry's Girls.* (MF) *Hello, Dolly!* Carol Channing appeared in the stage production of *Hello, Dolly!* Dorothy Loudon, Chita Rivera, and Leslie Uggams appeared in *Jerry's Girls.* Barbra Streisand appeared in the film production of *Hello, Dolly!*

So Long, Farewell 1959 w. Oscar Hammerstein II m. Richard Rodgers. (MT) *The Sound of Music.* (MF) *The Sound of Music.* Mary Martin appeared in the stage production of *The Sound of Music.* Julie Andrews appeared in the film production of *The Sound of Music.*

So Long (It's Been Good To Know Yuh) 1935 w.m. Woody Guthrie. This song was popularly revived in 1951.

So Long Letty 1915 w.m. Earl Carroll. (MT) *So Long Letty.* Grant Withers and Patsy Roth Miller appeared in *So Long Letty.*

So Long Mary 1905 w.m. George M. Cohan. (MT) *Forty-Five Minutes from Broadway.* (MT) *George M!* (MF) *Yankee Doodle Dandy.* George M. Cohan appeared in *Forty-Five Minutes from Broadway.* Joel Grey and Bernadette Peters appeared in *George M!* James Cagney and Joan Leslie appeared in *Yankee Doodle Dandy.*

So Long, Oo-Long, How Long You Gonna Be Gone? 1920 w.m. Bert Kalmar, Harry Ruby. (MF) *Three Little Words.* Fred Astaire, Debbie Reynolds, and Red Skelton appeared in *Three Little Words,* biopic of song writers Bert Kalmar and Harry Ruby.

So Many Memories 1937 w.m. Harry Woods

So Much in Love 1963 w.m. Roy Straigis, William Jackson III, George Williams

So Near and Yet So Far 1941 w.m. Cole Porter. (MF) *You'll Never Get Rich.* Fred Astaire and Rita Hayworth appeared in *You'll Never Get Rich.*

So Rare 1937 w. Jack Sharpe m. Jerry Herst. This song was popularly revived in 1957. Closing theme of the Jimmy Dorsey Orchestra.

So Tired 1927 w.m. Russ Morgan, John B. Soell

So Tired 1943 w.m. Russ Morgan, Jack Staurt. This song was popularly revived in 1948. Theme song of Russ Morgan.

So You're the One 1941 w.m. Joan Whitney, Hy Zaret

Sobbin' Blues 1923 w.m. Art Kassel

Sobbin' Women 1954 w.m. Gene De Paul, Johnny Mercer. (MF) *Seven Brides for Seven Brothers.* Jane Powell and Howard Keel appeared in *Seven Brides for Seven Brothers.*

(Oh I Love) Society 1898 w. Aubrey Hopwood, Harry Greenbank m. Lionel Monckton. (MT) *A Runaway Girl.*

Soft Lights and Sweet Music 1932 w.m. Irving Berlin. (MT) *Face the Music.* Hugh O'Connell and Mary Boland appeared in *Face the Music.*

Soft Shoe Shuffle, The 1942 w.m. Spencer Williams, Maurice Burman

Soft Summer Breeze 1956 w. Judy Spencer m. Eddie Heywood

Soft Winds 1940 w. Fred Royal m. Benny Goodman

Softly As I Leave You 1962 Orig.w. G. Calabrese Eng.w. Hal Shaper m. A. deVita. This song was most popular in 1964.

Softly, As in a Morning Sunrise 1928 w.m. Oscar Hammerstein II m. Sigmund Romberg. (MT) *The New Moon*. (MF) *The New Moon* (1930). (MF) *The New Moon* (1930). (MF) *The New Moon* (1940). (MF) *Deep in My Heart*. Evelyn Herbert and Robert Halliday appeared in the American stage production of *The New Moon*. Ben Williams appeared in the British stage production of *The New Moon*. Grace Moore and Adolphe Menjou appeared in the 1930 film production of *The New Moon*. Nelson Eddy and Jeanette MacDonald appeared in the 1940 film production of *The New Moon* Jose Ferrer and Merle Oberon appeared in *Deep in My Heart*, biopic of composer Sigmund Romberg.

Softly, Softly 1955 w.m. Pierre Dudan, Paddy Roberts, Mark Paul

Softly, Softly Theme 1966 w.m. Bridget Fry. (TV-BBC) *Softly, Softly*.

Softly Thro' the Summer Night 1913 w. C.C.S. Cushing, E.P. Heath m. Emmerich Kalman. (MT) *Sari*.

Solamente Una Vez, *see* **You Belong to My Heart**

Soldier Boy 1962 w.m. Luther Dixon, Florence Green

Soldier, Soldier, Won't You Marry Me? c.1700 w.m. traditional, from England. (F) *New Mexico*. Lew Ayres and Marilyn Maxwell appeared in *New Mexico*.

Soldiers' Chorus 1859 w. Jules Barbier, Michel Carré m. Charles Gounod. From the opera *Faust. Faust* was first performed in Paris on March 19, 1859.

Soldiers in the Park, The 1898 w. Lionel Monckton, Aubrey Hopwood, Harry Greenbank m. Ivan Caryll. (MT) *A Runaway Girl*.

Soldier's Life, A 1886 w. Claxson Bellamy, Harry Paulton m. Edward Jakobowski. (MT) *Erminie*.

Soldiers of the Queen 1900 w.m. Leslie Stuart

Solid 1985 w.m. Nickolas Ashford, Valerie Simpson

Solid Gold Easy Action 1973 w.m. Marc Bolan. Ivor Novello Award winner 1972–73.

Soliloquy 1927 m. Rube Bloom

Soliloquy 1945 w. Oscar Hammerstein II m. Richard Rodgers. (MT) *Carousel*. (MF) *Carousel*. Jan Clayton and John Raitt appeared in the stage production of *Carousel*. Gordon MacRae and Shirley Jones appeared in the film production of *Carousel*.

Solitaire 1975 w.m. Philip Cody, Neil Sedaka

Solitude 1934 w. Eddie De Lange, Irving Mills m. Duke Ellington. (MT) *Sophisticated Ladies*. Gregory Hines and Phyllis Hyman appeared in *Sophisticated Ladies*.

Some Day, *see also* **Someday**

Some Day 1925 w. Brian Hooker m. Rudolf Friml. (MT) *The Vagabond King*. (MF) *The Vagabond King* (1930). (MF) *The Vagabond King* (1956). Derek Oldham and Winnie Melville appeared in the British stage production of *The Vagabond King*. Jeanette MacDonald and Dennis King appeared in the 1930 film production of *The Vagabond King*. Kathryn Grayson and Rita Moreno appeared in the 1956 film production of *The Vagabond King*.

Some Day I'll Find You 1921 w. Schuyler Greene m. Zoel Parenteau. (MT) *Kiki*.

Some Day I'll Find You 1931 w.m. Noël Coward. (T) *Private Lives*. Noël Coward and Gertrude Lawrence appeared in *Private Lives*.

Some Day My Heart Will Awake 1949 w.m. Ivor Novello. (MT) *King's Rhapsody*. (MF) *King's Rhapsody*. Anna Neagle and Errol Flynn appeared in the film production of *King's Rhapsody*.

Some Day My Prince Will Come 1937 w. Larry Morey m. Frank Churchill. (MF) *Snow White and the Seven Dwarfs*.

Some Day Soon 1944 w.m. Jimmy Leach

Some Day Sweetheart 1919 w.m. John C. Spikes, Benjamin Spikes

Some Day We'll Be Together 1970 w.m. Harvey Fuqua, Jackey Beavers, Johnny Bristol. This song was the last recorded by Diana Ross and the Supremes.

Some Day You'll Want Me To Want You 1946 w.m. Jimmie Hodges. (MF) *Sioux City Sue*. Gene Autry and Lynne Roberts appeared in *Sioux City Sue*.

Some Days Are Diamonds (Some Days Are Stone) 1981 w.m. Dick Feller

Some Enchanted Evening 1949 w. Oscar Hammerstein II m. Richard Rodgers. (MT) *South Pacific*. (MF) *South Pacific*. Mary Martin appeared in the stage production of *South Pacific*. Mitzi Gaynor appeared in the film production of *South Pacific*. This song was popularly revived in 1977.

Some Folks 1855 w.m. Stephen Collins Foster. The death of Foster's parents in 1855 provoked his severe depression and eventual nervous collapse.

Some Guys Have All the Luck 1985 w.m. Jeff Fortgang

Some Little Bug Is Going To Find You (Some Day) 1915 w. Benjamin Hapgood Burt, Roy Atwell m. Silvio Hein. (MT) *Alone At Last*. Elizabeth Goodhall, Madame Namara and Roy Atwell appeared in *Alone At Last*. This song celebrates the influenza epidemic of that year.

Some Memories Just Won't Quit 1982 w.m. Bobby Springfield

Some of These Days 1910 w.m. Shelton Brooks. (MF) *Animal Crackers*. (MF) *Broadway*. (MF) *Follow the Boys*. (MF) *Rose Marie*. The Four Marx Brothers appeared in *Animal Crackers*. George Raft, Pat O'Brien, and Janet Blair appeared in *Broadway*. George Raft, W.C. Fields, and Marlene Dietrich appeared in *Follow the Boys*. Nelson Eddy and Jeanette MacDonald appeared in *Rose Marie*. Based on Frank Williams' "Some o' Dese Days" of 1905. Journalist Gary Pakulski relates: Black composer Shelton Brooks received only a $30 one-time payment. When later adopted by entertainer Sophie Tucker as her theme song, it made millions. As the original copyright was expiring, Vogel Music mounted a successful legal challenge on behalf of Brooks. The composer and his heirs received royalties for many years later. Theme song of Sophie Tucker.

Some Other Time 1944 w. Betty Comden, Adolph Green m. Leonard Bernstein. (MT) *On the Town.* (MF) *On the Town.* Gene Kelly, Ann Miller, and Frank Sinatra appeared in the film production of *On the Town.*

Some People 1959 w. Stephen Sondheim m. Jule Styne. (MT) *Gypsy.* (MF) *Gypsy.* Ethel Merman appeared in the stage production of *Gypsy.* Rosalind Russell appeared in the film production of *Gypsy.*

Some Sort of Somebody 1915 w. Elsie Janis m. Jerome Kern. (MT) *Very Good Eddie.*

Some Sunday Morning 1917 w. Gus Kahn, Raymond Egan m. Richard A. Whiting

Some Sunday Morning 1946 w. Ted Koehler m. M.K. Jerome, Ray Heindorf. (F) *San Antonio.* Errol Flynn and Alexis Smith appeared in *San Antonio.*

Some Sunny Day 1922 w.m. Irving Berlin

Some Sweet Day 1923 w. Gene Buck m. Dave Stamper, Louis A. Hirsch. (MT) *Ziegfeld Follies of 1922.* This song was popularly revived in 1929.

Somebody 1954 w.m. Joe Henderson

Somebody Bad Stole De Wedding Bell 1954 w. Bob Hilliard m. Dave Mann

Somebody Bigger Than You and I 1951 w.m. Johnny Lange, Hy Heath, Sonny Burke. (F) *The Old West.* Gene Autry and Pat Buttram appeared in *The Old West.*

Somebody Else Is Taking My Place 1937 w.m. Richard Howard, Bob Ellsworth, Russ Morgan. (MF) *Call of the Canyon.* (MF) *Strictly in the Groove.* Gene Autry appeared in *Call of the Canyon.* Martha Tilton and Donald O'Connor appeared in *Strictly in the Groove.* Based on "Please Go 'Way and Let Me Sleep" of 1902. This song was popularly revived in 1943.

Somebody Else, It's Always Somebody Else 1910 w. Jack Drislane m. George W. Meyer

Somebody Loves Me 1924 w. B.G. DeSylva, Ballard MacDonald m. George Gershwin. (MT) *George White's Scandals of 1924.* (MF) *Rhapsody in Blue.* (MF) *Lullaby of Broadway.* (MF) *Somebody Loves Me.* (MF) *Pete Kelly's Blues.* Lester Allen and Will Mahoney appeared in *George White's Scandals of 1924.* Oscar Levant and Alexis Smith appeared in *Rhapsody in Blue,* biopic of composer George Gershwin. Betty Hutton appeared in *Somebody Loves Me.* Peggy Lee and Ella Fitzgerald appeared in *Pete Kelly's Blues.*

Somebody Loves You 1932 w.m. Charles Tobias, Peter DeRose

Somebody, Somewhere 1956 w.m. Frank Loesser. (MT) *The Most Happy Fella.*

Somebody Stole My Gal 1918 w.m. Leo Wood. This song was popularly revived in 1922. Theme song of Billy Cotton.

Somebody Up There Likes Me 1956 w. Sammy Cahn m. Bronislaw Kaper. (F) *Somebody Up There Likes Me.* Paul Newman appeared in *Somebody Up There Likes Me.*

Somebody's Baby 1983 w.m. Jackson Browne, Danny Kortchmar

Somebody's Coming to My House 1913 w.m. Irving Berlin

Somebody's Watching Me 1984 w.m. Rockwell

Someday I'll Find You, *see* **Some Day I'll Find You**

Someday Soon 1969 w.m. Ian Tyson

Somehow 1930 w.m. Frederick Loewe, Earle Crooker. (MF) *Life of the Party.* Winnie Lightner and Jack Whiting appeared in *Life of the Party.*

Someone Could Lose a Heart Tonight 1982 w.m. David Malloy, Eddie Rabbitt, Even Stevens

Someone Else's Baby 1960 w.m. Les Vandyke, Perry Ford

Someone in a Tree 1976 w.m. Stephen Sondheim. (MT) *Pacific Overtures.* Mako appeared in *Pacific Overtures.*

Someone Like You 1919 w. Robert B. Smith m. Victor Herbert. (MT) *Angel Face.* (MF) *My Dream Is Yours.* Doris Day appeared in *My Dream Is Yours.*

Someone Nice Like You 1961 w.m. Leslie Bricusse, Anthony Newley. (MT) *Stop the World—I Want To Get Off.* Anthony Newley appeared in *Stop the World—I Want To Get Off.*

Someone Saved My Life Tonight 1975 w.m. Elton John, Bernie Taupin

Someone To Watch Over Me 1926 w. Ira Gershwin m. George Gershwin. (MT) *Oh, Kay!.* (MF) *Rhapsody in Blue.* (MF) *Young at Heart.* (MF) *Three for the Show.* (MF) *Beau James.* (MF) *Both Ends of the Candle.* Gertrude Lawrence and Victor Moore appeared in *Oh, Kay!.* Robert Alda, Alexis Smith, and Oscar Levant appeared in *Rhapsody in Blue,* biopic of composer George Gershwin. Frank Sinatra appeared in *Young at Heart.* Betty Grable and Jack Lemmon appeared in *Three for the Show,* remake of *Too Many Husbands,* with Jean Arthur. Bob Hope and Vera Miles appeared in *Beau James.*

Someone's in the Kitchen with Dinah, *see* **Good Night Ladies** *and* **I've Been Working on the Railroad**

Someone's Rocking My Dream Boat 1941 w.m. Emerson Scott, Otis Rene, Leon Rene. (MF) *Juke Girl.* Ann Sheridan and Ronald Reagan appeared in *Juke Girl.*

Something (In the Way She Moves) 1969 w.m. George Harrison. Ivor Novello Award winner 1970–71.

Something About You 1986 w.m. Boon Gould, Phil Gould, Mark King, Mike Lindup, Wally Badarou

Something Better To Do 1975 w.m. John Farrar

Something for Jesus 1871 w. S.D. Phelps m. Reverend Robert Lowry

Something in the Bottle for the Morning, *see* **For the Noo**

Something Is Happening 1969 w.m. R. Del Turco, G. Bigazzi

Something Seems Tingle-Ingling 1913 w. Otto Harbach m. Rudolf Friml. (MT) *High Jinks.* Peter Gawthorne appeared in *High Jinks.*

Somethin' Stupid 1967 w.m. C. Carson Parks

Something To Dance About 1950 w.m. Irving Berlin. (MT) *Call Me Madam.* (MF) *Call Me Madam.* Ethel Merman appeared in both the stage and film productions of *Call Me Madam.*

Something To Remember You By 1930 w. Howard Dietz m. Arthur Schwartz. (MT) *Three's a Crowd.* (F) *His Kind of Man.* (MF) *Dancing in the Dark.* (MF) *Both Ends of the Candle.* Fred MacMurray and Fred Allen appeared in *Three's a Crowd.* Dana Clark and Janis Paige appeared in *Her Kind of Man.* William Powell and Adolphe Menjou appeared in *Dancing in the Dark.* This song was popularly revived in 1943. The melody for this song was originally written by Schwartz for a Leslie Henson production in England, with a lyric by Desmond Carter titled ''I Have No Words To Say How Much I Love You.''

Something Wonderful 1951 w. Oscar Hammerstein II m. Richard Rodgers. (MT) *The King and I.* (MF) *The King and I.* Gertrude Lawrence and Yul Brynner appeared in the stage production of *The King and I.* Deborah Kerr and Yul Brynner appeared in the film production of *The King and I.*

Something's Always Happening on the River 1958 w. Betty Comden, Adolph Green m. Jule Styne. (MT) *Say, Darling.*

Something's Coming 1957 w. Stephen Sondheim m. Leonard Bernstein. (MT) *West Side Story.* (MF) *West Side Story.* Carol Lawrence appeared in the stage production of *West Side Story.* Natalie Wood appeared in the film production of *West Side Story.*

Something's Gotta Give 1955 w.m. Johnny Mercer. (MF) *Daddy Long Legs.* Fred Astaire and Leslie Caron appeared in *Daddy Long Legs.*

Sometime 1918 w. Rida Johnson Young m. Rudolf Friml. (MT) *Sometime.*

Sometime 1925 w. Gus Kahn m. Ted Fiorito

Sometime We'll Understand 1891 w. Maxwell N. Cornelius, D.D. m. James McGranahan

Sometime You'll Wish Me Back Again 1924 w.m. E. Austin Keith

Sometimes I Feel Like a Motherless Child 1918 w.m. based on a traditional black American spiritual, c.1899; arr. Henry Thacker Burleigh

Sometimes I'm Happy 1925 w. Irving Caesar m. Vincent Youmans. (MT) *Hit the Deck.* (MF) *Hit the Deck* (1929). (MF) *Hit the Deck* (1955). Louise Groody and Stella Mayhew appeared in the stage production of *Hit the Deck.* Polly Walker and Jack Oakie appeared in the 1929 film production of *Hit the Deck.* Jane Powell appeared in the 1955 film production of *Hit the Deck.* This song was first performed by Miss Toots Pounds in the 1925 stage production of *Hit the Deck;* the melody was written for the score of *Mary Jane McKane* with words by Oscar Hammerstein II and William Cary Duncan and titled ''Come On and Pet Me.''

Sometimes Your Eyes Look Blue to Me, *see* **Whoever You Are**

Somewhere 1957 w. Stephen Sondheim m. Leonard Bernstein. (MT) *West Side Story.* (MF) *West Side Story.* Carol Lawrence, Larry Kert, and Chita Rivera appeared in the stage production of *West Side Story.* Natalie Wood and Rita Moreno appeared in the film production of *West Side Story.* This song was popularly revived in 1965 and later again in 1986.

Somewhere a Voice Is Calling 1911 w. Eileen Newton m. Arthur F. Tate

Somewhere Along the Way 1952 w. Sammy Gallop m. Kurt Adams

Somewhere Down the Road 1982 w.m. Tom Snow, Cynthia Weil

Somewhere in France with You 1918 w.m. James W. Tate, A. Anderson, Arthur Valentine

Somewhere in France with You 1940 w.m. Michael Carr

Somewhere in Old Wyoming 1930 w.m. Charles Tobias, Peter DeRose

Somewhere in the Night 1946 w.m. Mack Gordon, Joseph Myrow. (MF) *Three Little Girls in Blue.* June Haver, Celeste Holm, and Vivian Blaine appeared in *Three Little Girls in Blue.*

Somewhere My Love, or, **Lara's Theme** 1966 w.m. Paul Francis Webster, Maurice Jarre

Somewhere Out There 1986 w. Cynthia Weil m. James Horner, Barry Mann. (F) *An American Tail.*

Somewhere That's Green 1983 w. Howard Ashman m. Alan Menken. (OB) *Little Shop of Horrors.* Ellen Green appeared in *Little Shop of Horrors.*

Son of a Preacher Man 1968 w.m. John Hurley, Ronnie Wilkins

Son of a Travelin' Man 1969 w.m. R.I. Allen, Mauro Lusini, Francesco Migliacci

Son of God Goes Forth to War, The 1872 w. Reginald Heber m. based on Henry Stephen Cutler's ''All Saints New.''

Son of My Father 1972 w.m. Giorgio Moroder

Son, This Is She 1962 w.m. Geoffrey Goddard

Sonata 1946 w. Ervin Drake, Jimmy Shirl m. Alex Alstone

Sonata Pathétique 1799 m. Ludwig van Beethoven

Song for a Summer Night 1956 w.m. Robert Allen. (TV) *Song for a Summer Night (Studio One).* This song was recorded for *Song for a Summer Night* by Mitch Miller and his orchestra.

Song from M*A*S*H, *see* **M*A*S*H**

Song from Moulin Rouge, The, or, **Where Is Your Heart** 1953 w. William Engvick m. Georges Auric. (F) *Moulin Rouge.* Jose Ferrer appeared in *Moulin Rouge.*

Song Is Ended But the Melody Lingers On, The 1927 w.m. Irving Berlin. (MT) *Will o' the Whispers.* Jack Smith appeared in *Will o' the Whispers.*

Song Is You, The 1932 w. Oscar Hammerstein II m. Jerome Kern. (MT) *Music In the Air.* (MF) *Music in the Air.* Al Shean and Ann Barry appeared in the American stage production of *Music in the Air.* Marry Ellis appeared in the British stage production of *Music in the Air.* Gloria Swanson and Reginald Owen appeared in the film production of *Music In the Air.*

Song of Athens, The, *see* **Adios My Love**

Song of Capri 1949 w.m. Mischa Spoliansky, Norman Newell. (MF) *That Dangerous Age.*

Song of India 1897 m. Nikolai Rimsky-Korsakov. (MF) *Drum Crazy.* (MF) *Song of Scheherazade.* Yvonne DeCarlo and Eve Arden appeared in *Song of Scheherazade.* From the French "Chanson Indoue," from the opera *Sadko.* This work was popularly revived in 1923 and 1937.

Song of Love 1921 w. Dorothy Donnelly m. Sigmund Romberg. (MT) *Blossom Time.* Based on the second theme of the "Unfinished Symphony" of Schubert, and on a melody by H. Berte.

Song of Old Hawaii, A 1938 w.m. Gordon Beecher, Johnny Noble

Song of Songs, The 1914 Fr. Maurice Vancaire Eng.w. Clarence Lucas m. Moya (Harold Vicars). From the French "Chanson du Coeur Brisé."

Song of the Barefoot Contessa 1954 w.m. Mario Nascimbene

Song of the Bayou 1929 m. Rube Bloom

Song of the Blacksmith 1934 w.m. Peter DeRose, Al Stillman

Song of the Clyde 1958 w.m. Ian Gourlay, Robert Yeudall

Song of the Contraband, The, *see* **Ole Shady**

Song of the Dawn 1930 w.m. Jack Yellen, Milton Ager. (MF) *The King of Jazz.* Paul Whiteman and John Boles appeared in *The King of Jazz.*

Song of the Flame 1925 w. Otto Harbach, Oscar Hammerstein II m. George Gershwin, Herbert Stothart. (MT) *Song of the Flame.* Tessa Kosta and Guy Robertson appeared in *Song of the Flame.*

Song of the Islands 1915 w.m. Charles E. King, (Harry Kerr). (MF) *Melody Lane.* (MF) *Ice-Capades Revue.* Eddie Leonard and Josephine Dunn appeared in *Melody Lane.* Jerry Colonna and Richard Denning appeared in *Ice-Capades Revue.* From the Hawaiian "Na Lei Hawaii." This song was popularly revived in 1929.

Song of the Open Road 1935 w.m. Albert Hay Malotte. (MF) *Hi Gaucho.* John Carroll and Steffi Duna appeared in *Hi Gaucho.*

Song of the Rose 1932 w.m. Eddie Cherkose, Charles Rosoff. (F) *Rose of the Rio Grande.* John Carroll appeared in *Rose of the Rio Grande.*

Song of the Shirt, The 1843 w.m. Thomas Hood. This song was first published anonymously in the 1843 Christmas edition of *Punch* magazine. In its day, it was so popular that it was written on cotton pocket handkerchiefs and sold at drapers' shops.

Song of the Shirt, The 1929 w. Clifford Grey m. Herbert Stothart. (MF) *The Rogue Song.*

Song of the Soul 1909 w. Edward Locke m. Joseph Carl Breil. (T) *The Climax.*

Song of the South 1947 w. Sam Coslow m. Arthur Johnston. (MF) *Song of the South.*

Song of the Texas Ranger, *see* **The Yellow Rose of Texas**

Song of the Trees, The 1935 w.m. Tolchard Evans, Stanley Damerell, Robert Hargreaves

Song of the Vagabonds 1925 w. Brian Hooker m. Rudolf Friml. (MF) *The Vagabond King.* (MF) *The Vagabond King* (1930). (MF) *The Vagabond King* (1956). Dennis King and Carolyn Thomson appeared in the American stage production of *The Vagabond King.* Derek Oldham appeared in the British stage production of *The Vagabond King.* Jeanette MacDonald and Dennis King appeared in the 1930 film production of *The Vagabond King.* Kathryn Grayson and Rita Moreno appeared in the 1956 film production of *The Vagabond King.* This song is also used by West Point for their football anthem.

Song of the Volga Boatman (Boatmen) 1867 w.m. based on a traditional folksong from Russia, probably much earlier than this date. This adaptation was popularly revived in 1941.

Song of the Wanderer 1926 w.m. Neil Moret.

Song on the Radio 1979 w.m. Al Stewart

Song Sung Blue 1972 w.m. Neil Diamond

Song That Reached My Heart, The 1887 w.m. Julian Jordan

Song That Reached My Heart, The, *see also* **When the Organ Played at Twilight**

Song Without End 1960 w.m. Ned Washington, Morris Stoloff, George W. Duning. Based on Liszt's "Un Sospiro."

Song Without Words 1868 m. Peter Tchaikovsky

Songs My Mother Taught Me 1880 Ger.w. Adolph Heyduk Eng.w. Mrs. Natalia MacFarren m. Anton Dvorák. From the German "Als die Alte Mutter," op.55, no.4, from "Zigeunermelodien."

Sonny Boy 1928 w.m. Al Jolson, B.G. DeSylva, Lew Brown, Ray Henderson (MF) *The Singing Fool.* (MF) *Jolson Sings Again.* (MF) *The Best Things in Life Are Free.* Al Jolson appeared in *The Singing Fool.* Larry Parks appeared in *Jolson Sings Again.* Gordon MacRae, Dan Dailey, and Ernest Borgnine appeared in *The Best Things in Life Are Free,* biopic of song writers DeSylva, Brown, and Henderson. Theme song of Al Jolson.

Song Of 1968 Eng.w. Eric Blau, Mort Shuman m. Jacques Brel. (MT) *Jacques Brel Is Alive and Well and Living in Paris.*

Sons of the Sea 1902 w.m. Felix McGlennon. This English music hall ballad was popularly performed by Arthur Reece.

Soon 1927 w. Ira Gershwin m. George Gershwin. (MT) *Strike Up the Band.* (MT) *My One and Only.* (MF) *Strike Up the Band.* Tommy Tune and Twiggy appeared in *My One and Only.* Judy Garland and Mickey Rooney appeared in the film production of *Strike Up the Band.*

Soon (Maybe Not Tomorrow) 1935 w. Lorenz Hart m. Richard Rodgers. (MF) *Mississippi.* Bing Crosby, Queenie Smith, and W.C. Fields appeared in *Mississippi.*

Soon It Will Be Sunday 1946 w.m. James Bunting, Peter Hart

Soon It's Gonna Rain 1960 w. Tom Jones m. Harvey Schmidt. (MT) *The Fantasticks.*

Sooner or Later (You're Gonna Be Comin' Around) 1947 w. Ray Gilbert m. Charles Wolcott. (MF) *Song of the South.*

Sooty 1955 w.m. Harry Corbett

Sophisticated Lady 1933 w. Irving Mills, Mitchell Parish m. Duke Ellington. (MT) *Bubbling Brown Sugar.* (MT) *So-*

phisticated Ladies. Avon Long and Vivian Reed appeared in *Bubbling Brown Sugar.* Gregory Hines and Phyllis Hyman appeared in *Sophisticated Ladies.* This song was published in 1933 as an instrumental only.

Sophisticated Swing 1936 w. Mitchell Parish m. Will Hudson

Sorcerer's Apprentice, The 1897 m. Paul Dukas. (MF) *Fantasia.* Mickey Mouse appeared in *Fantasia.* From the French "L'Apprenti Sorcier."

Sorry (I Ran All the Way Home) 1959 w.m. Harry Giosasi, Artie Zwirn

Sorry—Grateful 1970 w.m. Stephen Sondheim. (MT) *Company.* Elaine Stritch appeared in *Company.*

Sorry Seems To Be the Hardest Word 1976 w.m. Elton John, Bernie Taupin

SOS 1975 w.m. Stig Anderson, Bjorn Ulvaeus, Benny Andersson

(You're My) Soul and Inspiration 1966 w.m. Barry Mann, Cynthia Weil

Soul Man 1967 w.m. Isaac Lee Hayes, Jr., David Porter

Sound of Goodbye, The 1984 w.m. Hugh Prestwood

Sound of Music, The 1959 w. Oscar Hammerstein II m. Richard Rodgers. (MT) *The Sound of Music.* (MF) *The Sound of Music.* Mary Martin appeared in the stage production of *The Sound of Music.* Julie Andrews appeared in the film production of *The Sound of Music.*

Sound of Philadelphia, The, *see* **TSOP**

Sound Off 1951 w.m. Willie Lee Duckworth. This song was later used for the famous "Sound Off for Chesterfield" commercial promotion campaign with additional words by Bernard Lentz.

Sounds Like Love 1983 w.m. Charlie Black, Tommy Rocco

Sounds of Silence, The 1966 w.m. Paul Simon. (F) *The Graduate.* Dustin Hoffman and Anne Bancroft appeared in *The Graduate.*

South America Take It Away 1946 w.m. Harold Rome. (MT) *Call Me Mister.* (MT) *Starlight Roof.* (MF) *Call Me Mister.* Betty Garrett, Bill Callahan, and Jules Munshin appeared in the stage production of *Call Me Mister.* Betty Grable and Danny Thomas appeared in the film production of *Call Me Mister.*

South American Way 1939 w. Al Dubin m. Jimmy McHugh. (MT) *Streets of Paris.* (MF) *Down Argentine Way.* Carmen Miranda appeared in both *Streets of Paris* and *Down Argentine Way.* Bud Abbott and Lou Costello appeared in *Streets of Paris.*

South of the Border (Down Mexico Way) 1939 w.m. Jimmy Kennedy, Michael Carr

South Rampart Street Parade 1940 w.m. Steve Allen, Ray Bauduc, Robert Haggart

South Sea Island Magic 1936 w.m. Andy Iona Long

South Street 1963 w.m. Dave Appell, Kal Mann

Southern Cross 1982 w.m. Michael Curtis, Richard Curtis, Stephen Stills

Southern Nights 1977 w.m. Allen Toussaint

Southern Rains 1981 w.m. Roger Murrah

Souvenir 1904 m. Frantisek Drdla

Souvenir de Vienne, *see* **Intermezzo**

Space Oddity 1970 w.m. David Bowie

Space Race 1973 w.m. Billy Preston

Spacious Firmament on High, The 1850 w. Joseph Addison m. based on the chorus "The heavens are telling" from Franz Joseph Haydn's oratorio "The Creation."

Spain 1924 w. Gus Kahn m. Isham Jones

Spaniard That (Who) Blighted My Life, The 1911 w.m. Billy Merson. (MF) *The Jolson Story.* Larry Parks appeared in *The Jolson Story.*

Spanish Cavalier, The 1881 w.m. William D. Hendrickson. This song possibly inspired the later "Love Letters in the Sand" by Nick Kenny.

Spanish Eyes 1965 w.m. Bert Kaempfert, Eddie Snyder, Charles Singleton. This song was most popular in 1967.

Spanish Flea 1966 w.m. Jerry Leiber, Phil Spector. This song was popularly revived in 1971.

Sparkle 1976 w.m. Curtis Mayfield. (MF) *Sparkle.*

Sparkling and Bright c.1830 w. Charles Fenno Hoffman m. James B. Taylor

Sparrow in the Tree Top 1951 w.m. Bob Merrill

Speak Low 1943 w. Ogden Nash m. Kurt Weill. (MT) *One Touch of Venus.* (MF) *One Touch of Venus.* Mary Martin and John Boles appeared in the stage production of *One Touch of Venus.* Ava Gardner and Eve Arden appeared in the film production of *One Touch of Venus.*

Speak Softly 1962 w.m. Jimmy Fontana

Speak Softly Love 1972 w. Larry Kusik m. Nino Rota. (F) *The Godfather.* Marlon Brando, Al Pacino, and Diane Keaton appeared in *The Godfather.*

Speak to Me of Love 1932 Fr.w. Jean Lenoir Eng.w. Bruce Siever m. Jean Lenoir. (MF) *Both Ends of the Candle.* (F) *Her Kind of Man.* (MF) *In Old Sacramento.* Dane Clark and Janis Paige appeared in *Her Kind of Man.* Bill Elliott and Constance Moore appeared in *In Old Sacramento.* From the French "Parlez-Moi d'Amour." Theme song of Lucienne Boyer.

Special Lady 1980 w.m. Willie Goodman, Harry Ray, Lee Walter

(Theme from) Spellbound 1945 w.m. Stanley Adams, Alfred Newman. (F) *Spellbound.* Gregory Peck and Ingrid Bergman appeared in *Spellbound.*

Spice of Life, The 1937 w.m. Jimmy Kennedy, Michael Carr

Spiders and Snakes 1973 w.m. David Bellamy, Jim Stafford

Spinning Wheel 1935 w.m. Maryan Rawicz. Signature theme of Rawicz and Landauer.

Spinning Wheel 1969 w.m. David Clayton-Thomas

Spirit of Independence 1912 m. Abe Holzmann

Splish Splash 1958 w.m. Bobby Darin, Jean Murray

Spooky Ookum 1918 w. Henry Blossom m. Victor Herbert. (MT) *The Velvet Lady.* This is *not* Irving Berlin's "Snooky Ookums" of 1913.

Spoonful of Sugar, A 1964 w.m. Richard M. Sherman, Robert B. Sherman. (MF) *Mary Poppins.* Julie Andrews and Dick Van Dyke appeared in *Mary Poppins.*

S'posin' 1929 w. Andy Razaf m. Paul Denniker. (MF) *Feudin', Fussin' and A-Fightin'.* Donald O'Connor and Marjorie Main appeared in *Feudin', Fussin' and A-Fightin'.*

Spread a Little Happiness 1929 w.m. Vivian Ellis, Richard Myers, Greatrex Newman. (MT) *Mister Cinders.* Binnie Hale appeared in *Mister Cinders.*

Spread a Little Sunshine 1972 w.m. Stephen Schwartz. (MT) *Pippin.* Ben Vereen and Jill Clayburgh appeared in *Pippin.*

Spring, Beautiful Spring, or, **Chimes of Spring** 1903 m. Paul Lincke. From the German "O Frühling, Wie Bist Du So Schön."

Spring Is Here 1938 w. Lorenz Hart m. Richard Rodgers. (MT) *I Married an Angel.* (MF) *I Married an Angel.* Vera Zorina and Vivienne Segal appeared in the stage production of *I Married an Angel.* Jeanette MacDonald and Nelson Eddy appeared in the film production of *I Married an Angel.*

Spring Song 1844 m. Felix Mendelssohn

Spring, Spring, Spring 1955 w.m. Gene De Paul, Johnny Mercer. (MF) *Seven Brides for Seven Brothers.* Jane Powell and Howard Keel appeared in *Seven Brides for Seven Brothers.*

Spring Will Be a Little Late This Year 1944 w.m. Frank Loesser. (F) *Christmas Holiday.* Deanna Durbin and Gene Kelly appeared in *Christmas Holiday.*

Springfield Mountain, *see* **The Pesky Sarpent**

Springtime of Life, The 1914 w. Robert B. Smith m. Victor Herbert. (MT) *The Debutante.*

Squeeze Me 1925 w. Clarence Williams m. Thomas "Fats" Waller. (MT) *Ain't Misbehavin'.* Debbie Allen and Nell Carter appeared in *Ain't Misbehavin'.*

St. Elmo's Fire (Man in Motion) w.m. John Parr, David Foster. (F) *St. Elmo's Fire.* Rob Lowe and Judd Nelson appeared in *St. Elmo's Fire.*

St. (Saint) George and the Dragonet 1953 w. Stan Freeberg. This comedy piece was No. 6 in record sales for 1953.

St. James Infirmary 1930 w.m. Joe Primrose. (MT) *Blackbirds of 1934.* (MF) *The Birth of the Blues.* Bing Crosby and Mary Martin appeared in *The Birth of the Blues.* This song was possibly known as early as 1890–99 as "Gambler's Blues."

St. Kevin, *see* **Come, Ye Faithful, Raise the Strain**

St. Louis Blues 1914 w.m. W.C. Handy. (MF) *St. Louis Blues.* (MF) *Is Everybody Happy.* (MF) *The Birth of the Blues.* (MF) *Jam Session.* (F) *Glory Alley.* Bessie Smith appeared in the 1928 film production of *St. Louis Blues.* Nat "King" Cole appeared in the 1958 film production of *St. Louis Blues.* Ted Lewis appeared in both the 1929 and 1943 film productions of *Is Everybody Happy.* Bing Crosby and Mary Martin appeared in *The Birth of the Blues.* Louis Armstrong and Ann Miller appeared in *Jam Session.* Leslie Caron appeared in *Glory Alley.*

St. Louis Woman 1935 w.m. Betty Laidlow, Bob Lively. (MF) *St. Louis Woman.* Roberta Gale and Jeanette Loff appeared in *St. Louis Woman.*

St. Mary's in the Twilight 1941 w.m. Jimmy Kennedy

Stage Coach 1942 w.m. Eric Winstone. Theme song of Eric Winstone.

Stagger Lee 1959 w.m. Harold Logan, Lloyd Price. Based on a traditional folksong.

Stairway to Paradise, *see* **I'll Build a Stairway to Paradise**

Stairway to the Stars (Park Avenue Fantasy) 1935 w. Mitchell Parish m. Matt Malneck, Frank Signorelli. This song was popularly revived in 1939.

Stand and Deliver 1982 w.m. Adam Ant, Marco Pirroni. Ivor Novello Award winner 1981–82.

Stand Back 1984 w.m. Stevie Nicks, Prince Nelson

Stand By Me 1980 w.m. Ben E. King, Jerry Leiber, Mike Stoller. (F) *Stand By Me.* This song was popularly revived in 1986.

Stand By Your Man 1968 w.m. Tammy Wynette, Billy Sherrill

Stand Up and Cheer 1933 w.m. Lew Brown, Harry Akst. (MF) *Stand Up and Cheer.* Shirley Temple in her musical film debut and Nigel Bruce appeared in *Stand Up and Cheer.*

Stand Up and Fight Like H--- 1905 w.m. George M. Cohan. (MT) *Forty-Five Minutes from Broadway.*

Stand Up, Stand Up for Jesus, *see* **'Tis Dawn, the Lark Is Singing**

('Tis Me, O Lord) Standin' In the Need of Pray'r 1918 w.m. based on a traditional black American spiritual; arr. Henry Thacker Burleigh

Standing on the Corner 1956 w.m. Frank Loesser. (MT) *The Most Happy Fella.*

Stanley Steamer, The 1947 w. Ralph Blane m. Harry Warren. (MF) *Summer Holiday.* Mickey Rooney and Frank Morgan appeared in *Summer Holiday,* based on Eugene O'Neill's *Ah, Wilderness.*

Star, The 1912 w. Charles F. Lummis m. James H. Rogers. See also "Bye Bye Blues."

Star Dust 1929 w. Mitchell Parish m. Hoagy Carmichael. (MF) *The Eddy Duchin Story.* The melody of this song was written by Carmichael in 1927 while walking the campus of Indiana University.

Star Eyes 1943 w.m. Don Raye, Gene De Paul. (MF) *I Dood It.* Red Skelton, Lena Horne, and Eleanor Powell appeared in *I Dood It.*

Star Fell Out of Heaven, A 1936 w. Mack Gordon m. Harry Revel

Star in the East 1835 w.m. William Walker

Star Light, Star Bright 1895 w. Harry B. Smith m. Victor Herbert. (MT) *The Wizard of the Nile.*

Star of the Evening 1855 w.m. James M. Sayles; arr. Henry Tucker

Star Spangled Banner, The 1814 w. Francis Scott Key m. John Stafford Smith. The melody for this song is based on the traditional English "To Anacreon in Heaven" and is the same as that used for ''Adams and Liberty,'' or ''The Boston Patriotic Song.'' This song was first sung publicly by Ferdinand Durang in a tavern run by Colonel MacConkey, next door to the Holiday Street Theatre. It was not until March 3, 1931, that President Hoover signed the bill declaring this our national anthem. See also ''Adams and Liberty'' and ''To Anacreon in Heaven.''

(Theme from) Star Wars 1977 m. John Williams. (F) *Star Wars*. Alec Guinness and Carrie Fisher appeared in *Star Wars*. Academy Award winner 1977. Grammy Award winner 1977.

Stardust on the Moon 1937 w.m. Emery Deutsch, Jimmy Rogan

Starlight 1905 w. Edward Madden m. Theodore F. Morse

Starlight 1960 w.m. Lee Pockriss, Paul J. Vance

Starlight Serenade 1941 w.m. Hans May, Frederick Tysh, Sonny Miller

Stars and Stripes Forever 1897 m. John Philip Sousa. (MT) *Dancin'*. Words, written by Sousa, were added in a new published ''song'' version in 1898. The melody to this song was written by Sousa aboard ship from England to the United States in 1896.

Stars Fell on Alabama 1934 w. Mitchell Parish m. Frank Perkins

Stars in My Eyes 1936 w. Dorothy Fields m. Fritz Kreisler. (MF) *The King Steps Out*. Grace Moore appeared in *The King Steps Out*. Based on ''Who Can Tell'' from 1919.

Stars in Your Eyes 1941 Sp.w. Ricardo Lopez Mendez Eng.w. Mort Greene m. Gabriel Ruiz. (MF) *Pan-Americana*. Robert Benchley and Eve Arden appeared in *Pan-Americana*. This song was popularly revived in 1945.

Stars of the Summer Night 1856 w. Henry Wadsworth Longfellow m. Isaac Baker Woodbury

Stars Shine in Your Eyes, *see* **La Strada**

Stars Will Remember, The 1946 w.m. Leo Towers, Don Pelosi. (F) *Smart Girls Don't Talk*. Virginia Mayo and Bruce Bennett appeared in *Smart Girls Don't Talk*.

Start Me Up 1981 w.m. Keith Richards, Mick Jagger

(Just Like) Starting Over 1980 w.m. John Lennon. Ivor Novello Award winner 1981–82.

Startime 1956 w.m. Eric Rogers

State of Shock 1985 w.m. Randy Lee Hansen, Michael Jackson

Stately Homes of England, The 1938 w.m. Noël Coward. (MT) *Set to Music*. Beatrice Lillie appeared in *Set to Music*.

Stay 1960 w.m. Maurice Williams

Stay as Sweet as You Are 1934 w. Mack Gordon m. Harry Revel. (MF) *College Rhythm*. Joe Penner and Lanny Ross appeared in *College Rhythm*.

Stay Awhile 1964 w.m. Mike Hawker, Ivor Raymonde

Stay in My Arms, Cinderella 1939 w.m. Jimmy Kennedy, Michael Carr

Stay in Your Own Back Yard 1899 w. Karl Kennett m. Lyn Udall

Stay with the Happy People 1950 w. Bob Hilliard m. Jule Styne. (MT) *Michael Todd's Peep Show*.

Stayin' Alive 1977 w.m. Barry Gibb, Robin Gibb, Maurice Gibb. (MF) *Saturday Night Fever*. John Travolta appeared in *Saturday Night Fever*. Ivor Novello Award winner 1978–79.

Staying Young 1959 w.m. Bob Merrill. (MT) *Take Me Along*. Jackie Gleason, Walter Pidgeon, and Eileen Herlie appeared in *Take Me Along*.

Steal Away 1980 w.m. Robbie Dupree

Steal Away to Jesus 1921 w.m. traditional black American spiritual, c.1871; arr. Henry Thacker Burleigh in 1921.

Steam Heat 1954 w.m. Richard Adler, Jerry Ross. (MT) *The Pajama Game*. (MF) *The Pajama Game*. Doris Day and John Raitt appeared in the film production of *The Pajama Game*.

Steamboat Bill 1910 w. Ren Shields m. Leighton Brothers. (F) *Ridin' on a Rainbow*. Gene Autry and Smiley Burnette appeared in *Ridin' on a Rainbow*.

(Maine)Stein Song 1910 w. Lincoln Colcord m. E.A. Fenstad. (MF) *With a Song in My Heart*. Susan Hayward appeared in *With a Song in My Heart,* biopic of singer Jane Froman. This song was first published with the title ''Opie—The University of Maine Song'' on June 23, 1910. School song for the University of Maine. Based on one of Brahms's Hungarian Dances. This song was popularly revived in 1930.

Stein Song, A (Bullard), *see* **It's Always Fair Weather When Good Fellows Get Together**

Stein Song, *see also* **Heidelberg Stein Song**

Stella 1923 w.m. Al Jolson, Benny Davis, Harry Akst

Stella by Starlight 1946 w. Ned Washington m. Victor Young. (F) *The Uninvited*. Ray Milland and Ruth Hussey appeared in *The Uninvited*.

Step by Step 1959 w.m. Ollie Jones, Billy Dawn Smith

Step by Step 1981 w.m. David Malloy, Eddie Rabbitt, Even Stevens

Step to the Rear 1968 w. Carolyn Leigh m. Elmer Bernstein. (MT) *How Now, Dow Jones*.

Stephanie—Gavotte 1880 m. Alphons Czibulka

Steppin' Out 1983 w.m. Joe Jackson

Steppin' Out with My Baby 1948 w.m. Irving Berlin. (MF) *Easter Parade*. Judy Garland, Fred Astaire, and Ann Miller appeared in *Easter Parade*.

Steptoe and Son 1962 w.m. Ron Grainer

Stereophonic Sound 1955 w.m. Cole Porter. (MT) *Silk Stockings*. (MF) *Silk Stockings*. Fred Astaire and Cyd Charisse appeared in the film production of *Silk Stockings*.

Still as the Night 1885 Ger.w. anon. Eng.w. Mrs. John P. Morgan m. Karl Bohm. From the German ''Still Wie Die Nacht.''

Still Doin' Time 1982 w.m. Michael Heeney, John Moffat

Still I'm Sad 1965 w.m. Paul Samwell-Smith, James McCarthy

Still Right Here in My Heart 1981 w.m. George Greer, Jeffrey Wilson

Still the One 1976 w.m. John Hall, Johanna Hall

Sting, The, *see* **The Entertainer**

Stockholm 1964 w.m. George Cates

Stomp 1980 w.m. Val Johnson, Rodney Temperton, George Johnson, Louis Johnson

Stomping at the Savoy 1936 w. Andy Razaf m. Benny Goodman, Edgar Sampson, Chick Webb. (MT) *Bubbling Brown Sugar.* (MF) *The Benny Goodman Story.* Josephine Premice and Avon Long appeared in *Bubbling Brown Sugar.* This song was originally published in 1936 as an instrumental only. See also Part I, 1938.

Stone Cold Dead in the Market 1946 w.m. Wilmoth Houdini

Stoned Soul Picnic 1968 w.m. Laura Nyro. This song was most popular in 1969.

Stoney End 1970 w.m. Laura Nyro

Stop and Shop at the Co-Op Shop 1930 w.m. R.P. Weston, Bert Lee

Stop and Think It Over 1967 w.m. Jake Graffagnino

Stop Beating 'Round the Mulberry Bush 1938 w.m. Bickley Reichner, Clay Boland. Based on the traditional Mother Goose melody, "The Mulberry Bush."

Stop Dat Knocking at My Door 1843 w.m. A.F. Winnemore, Charles T. White

Stop Draggin' My Heart Around 1981 w.m. Tom Petty, Michael Campbell

Stop! in the Name of Love 1965 w.m. Eddie Holland, Brian Holland, Lamont Dozier. This song was popularly revived in 1983.

Stop the Cavalry 1981 w.m. Jona Lewie. Ivor Novello Award winner 1980–81.

Stop Yer Tickling, Jock! 1904 w. Harry Lauder, Frank Folley m. Harry Lauder

Stop! You're Breaking My Heart 1937 w. Ted Koehler m. Burton Lane. (MF) *Artists and Models.* Jack Benny, Martha Raye, and Ida Lupino appeared in *Artists and Models.*

Stormy Weather 1933 w. Ted Koehler m. Harold Arlen. (MT) *Cotton Club Revue.* (MT) *On with the Show.* (MT) *Lena Horne: The Lady and Her Music.* (MF) *Stormy Weather.* (MF) *Swing Parade of 1946.* (F) *Amarcord.* Lena Horne appeared in *Lena Horne: The Lady and Her Music.* Jimmy Campbell appeared in *On with the Show.* Lena Horne and "Fats" Waller appeared in *Stormy Weather.* Gale Storm and Lonnee Boswell appeared in *Swing Parade of 1946.* Theme song of Lena Horne and Ethel Waters. This song was originally written for Cab Calloway.

Story Goes On, The 1983 w. Richard Maltby, Jr. m. David Shire. Liz Callaway and Beth Fowley appeared in *Baby.*

(This Is) Story of a Starry Night, The 1941 w.m. Jerry Livingston, Al Hoffman, Mann Curtis. Based on Tchaikovsky's "Pathétique" Symphony No. 6.

Story of My Life 1957 w. Hal David m. Burt Bacharach

Story of the Rose, The, *see* **Heart of My Heart**

Story of Tina, The 1945 w.m. D. Katrivanov

Stouthearted Men 1928 w. Oscar Hammerstein II m. Sigmund Romberg. (MT) *The New Moon.* (MT) *Dancin'.* (MF) *The New Moon* (1930). (MF) *The New Moon* (1940). (MF) *Deep in My Heart.* Evelyn Herbert and Robert Halliday appeared in the American stage production of *The New Moon.* Ben Williams appeared in the British stage production of *The New Moon.* Adolphe Menjou and Grace Moore appeared in the 1930 film production of *The New Moon.* Nelson Eddy and Jeanette MacDonald appeared in the 1940 film production of *The New Moon.* Jose Ferrer, Merle Oberon, and Walter Pidgeon appeared in *Deep in My Heart,* biopic of composer Sigmund Romberg.

(Theme from) Strada, La, or, **Stars Shine in Your Eyes** 1956 w.m. John Turner, Geoffrey Parsons, Nino Rota. (F) *La Strada.*

Straighten Up and Fly Right 1944 w.m. Irving Mills, Nat Cole. Theme song of Nat "King" Cole.

Strange Are the Ways of Love 1959 w.m. Ned Washington, Dimitri Tiomkin

Strange Enchantment 1939 w. Frank Loesser m. Frederick Hollander. (MF) *Man About Town.* Jack Benny, Rochester, and Dorothy Lamour appeared in *Man About Town.*

Strange Fruit 1939 w.m. Lewis Allen. (MF) *Lady Sings the Blues.* Diana Ross appeared in *Lady Sings the Blues,* biopic of singer Billie Holiday. Billie Holiday is often erroneously credited with being the co-author of this song. The subject of the narrative is the lynching of a black man in the southern United States.

Strange Interlude 1932 w. Ben Bernie, Walter Hirsch m. Phil Baker

Strange Lady in Town 1955 w. Ned Washington m. Dimitri Tiomkin. (F) *Strange Lady in Town.* Greer Garson and Dana Andrews appeared in *Strange Lady in Town.*

Strange Magic 1976 w.m. Jeff Lynne

Strange Music 1944 w.m. George Forrest, Robert Wright. (MT) *Song of Norway.* Lawrence Brooks appeared in the American stage production of *Song of Norway.* John Hargreaves appeared in the British stage production of *Song of Norway.* Based on Grieg's "Wedding Day in Troldhaugen" and "Nocturne."

Stranger, The 1960 w.m. Bill Crompton, Morgan Jones

Stranger in My House 1983 w.m. Michael Reid. Grammy Award winner 1983.

Stranger in Paradise 1954 w.m. Robert Wright, George Forrest. (MT) *Kismet.* (MF) *Kismet.* Ann Blyth and Howard Keel appeared in the film production of *Kismet.* Based on a theme from Borodin's "Polovetsian Dances" from his opera *Prince Igor* of 1888.

Stranger in Town, A 1945 w.m. Mel Torme

Stranger on the Shore 1962 w.m. Acker Bilk, Robert Mellin. (TV-BBC) *Stranger on the Shore.* Ivor Novello Award winner 1961. Ivor Novello Award winner 1962.

Stranger Than Fiction 1955 w.m. Howard Shaw

Strangers 1967 w.m. Richard Rodgers. (TV) *Androcles and the Lion.*

Strangers in the Night 1966 w.m. Bert Kaempfert, Eddie Snyder, Charles Singleton. (F) *A Man Could Get Killed.* Grammy Award winner 1966.

Strawberry Fair 1960 w.m. traditional; new words Nolly Clapton

Strawberry Fields Forever 1967 w.m. John Lennon, Paul McCartney. (MT) *Beatlemania.*

Strawberry Letter #23 1977 w.m. Shuggie Otis

Strawberry Roan c.1870–1890 w.m. traditional. (F) *The Rodeo King and the Señorita.* Rex Allen and Mary Ellen Kay appeared in *The Rodeo King and the Señorita.*

Streak, The 1974 w.m. Ray Stevens. This song celebrates the craze that year of students running naked across college campuses.

(On the) Street of Dreams 1932 w.m. Samuel M. Lewis, Victor Young

Strada Del' Amore, La (The Street of Love) 1959 w.m. Jack Reardon

Stray Cat Strut 1983 w.m. Brian Fitzer

Streets of Cairo, The 1895 w.m. James Thornton. "Hoochy-Koochy" is the verse to this song. This song is popularly parodied with the words "Oh they don't wear pants in the Southern parts of France." In America, this song was popularized by the dancing of "Little Egypt" at the 1893 Chicago World's Columbian Exposition. Based on the Algerian melody titled "Kradoutja," known in France since 1600. See also Part I, 1893.

Streets of Laredo, or, **The Cowboy's Lament** c.1860 w.m. anon.; arr. Ray Evans, Jay Livingston. (F) *Streets of Laredo.* (F) *Utah Wagon Train.* William Holden and William Bendix appeared in *Streets of Laredo.* Rex Allen and Penny Edwards appeared in *Utah Wagon Train.* The melody is traditional, from Ireland. The narrative of this song is actually about a dying British soldier.

Streets of London 1975 w.m. Ralph McTell. Ivor Novello Award winner 1974–75.

Streets of New York, The, *see* **In Old New York**

Streets of Sorrento, The 1957 w.m. Tony Osborne

Strike Me Pink 1933 w. B.G. DeSylva, Lew Brown m. Ray Henderson. (MT) *Strike Me Pink.* (MF) *Strike Me Pink.* Jimmy Durante and Roy Atwell appeared in the stage production of *Strike Me Pink.* Eddie Cantor and Ethel Merman appeared in the film production of *Strike Me Pink.*

Strike the Cymbal 1814 w. Reverend William Slaughton m. Vincenzo Puccitta, adapted Benjamin Carr

Strike Up the Band 1927 w. Ira Gershwin m. George Gershwin. (MT) *Strike Up the Band.* (MT) *The 1940's Radio Hour.* (MT) *My One and Only.* (MF) *Strike Up the Band.* Blanche Ring appeared in the stage production of *Strike Up the Band.* Tommy Tune and Twiggy appeared in *My One and Only.* Judy Garland and Mickey Rooney appeared in the film production of *Strike Up the Band.*

Strike Up the Band—Here Comes a Sailor 1900 w. Andrew B. Sterling m. Charles B. Ward. (MF) *In Old Sacramento.* Bill Elliott and Constance Moore appeared in *In Old Sacramento.*

String of Pearls, A 1942 w.m. Eddie De Lange, Jerry Gray. (MF) *The Glenn Miller Story.*

Stripper, The 1962 m. David Rose. (F) *The Stripper.* Joanne Woodward appeared in *The Stripper.*

Stroll, The 1958 w.m. Nancy Lee, Clyde Otis

Strollers We 1901 w.m. Harry B. Smith, Ludwig Englander. (MT) *The Strollers.*

Strollin' 1959 w.m. Ralph Reader

Strolling on the Brooklyn Bridge 1883 w. George Cooper m. Joseph P. Skelly.

Strut 1985 w.m. Charlie Dore, Julian Littman

Struttin' with Some Barbecue 1927 w.m. Louis Armstrong, Lil Hardin

Stuck in the Middle (with You) 1973 w.m. Gerry Rafferty, Joe Egan

Stuck on You 1960 w.m. Aaron Schroeder, J. Leslie McFarland

Stuck on You 1984 w.m. Lionel Richie

Stuck with You 1986 w.m. Christopher Hayes, Huey Lewis

Stumbling 1922 w.m. Zez Confrey

Such a Li'l Fellow 1913 w. Frances Lowell m. William Dichmont

Such an Education, Has My Mary Ann, or, **Sweet Mary Ann** 1878 w. Edward Harrigan m. David Braham. (MT) *Malone's Night Off, or The German Turnverein.*

Suddenly 1934 w. E.Y. Harburg, Billy Rose m. Vernon Duke. (MT) *The Ziegfeld Follies of 1934.*

Suddenly 1981 w.m. John Farrar

Suddenly 1985 w.m. Billy Ocean, Keith Diamond

Suddenly It's Spring 1944 w. Johnny Burke m. Jimmy Van Heusen. (MF) *Lady in the Dark.* Ginger Rogers appeared in the film production of *Lady in the Dark.* This song did not appear in the original 1941 stage production, but was added to the 1944 film production.

Suddenly Seymour 1983 w. Howard Ashman m. Alan Menken (OB) *Little Shop of Horrors.* Ellen Green appeared in *Little Shop of Horrors.*

Suddenly There's a Valley 1955 w. Charles Meyer m. Biff Jones

Sugar 1927 w.m. Maceo Pinkard, Sidney D. Mitchell. (MF) *Pete Kelly's Blues.* Peggy Lee appeared in *Pete Kelly's Blues.* This song was popularly revived in 1955.

Sugar and Spice 1963 w.m. Fred Nightingale

Sugar Blues 1923 w. Lucy Fletcher m. Clarence Williams. This song was originally written in 1919. Theme song of Clyde McCoy.

Sugar Foot Stomp, or, **Dipper Mouth Blues** 1926 w.m. Joseph Oliver

Sugar Shack 1963 w.m. Keith McCormack, Faye Voss

Sugar Sugar 1969 w.m. Jeff Barry, Andy Kim

Sugar Town 1966 w.m. Lee Hazlewood

Sugarfoot 1958 w.m. Paul Francis Webster, Ray Heindorf, Max Steiner

Sugartime 1958 w.m. Charlie Phillips, Odis Echols

Suite No. 1 for Small Orchestra 1975 w.m. John Hall

Sukiyaki 1963 w.m. El Rohusuke, Hachidai Nakamura. From the Japanese "Ueo Muite Aruku." This song was popularly revived in 1981.

Sultans of Swing 1979 w.m. Mark Knopfler

Summer Is Icumen In c.1250 w.m. traditional, from England. This English round is possibly the first example of truly harmonized music, being the oldest six-part composition and the oldest canon.

Summer 1976 w.m. Sylvester Allen, Harold Ray Brown, Morris D. Dickerson, Gerald Goldstein, Leroy Jordan, Lee Oskar Levitin, Charles Miller, Howard E. Scott

Summer Dreams 1958 w. Rae H. Seymour, Dorcas Cochran, Frank LaForge m. Manuel M. Ponce

Summer Evening in Santa Cruz, A 1939 w.m. Fred Hartley, Jose Payan

Summer Holiday 1963 w.m. Bruce Welch, Brian Bennett. (MF) *Summer Holiday.* Cliff Richard and Lauri Peters appeared in *Summer Holiday.*

Summer in the City 1966 w.m. John B. Sebastian, Mark Sebastian, Steve Boone

Summer Is A-Comin' In 1958 w.m. Leslie Bricusse

Summer Knows, The, or, **Theme from** *Summer of '42* 1971 w. Alan Bergman, Marilyn Bergman m. Michel Legrand. (F) *Summer of '42.* Jennifer O'Neill and Gary Grimes appeared in *Summer of '42.*

Summer Night 1936 w. Al Dubin m. Harry Warren. (MF) *Sing Me a Love Song.* Patricia Ellis and Zasu Pitts appeared in *Sing Me a Love Song.*

Summer of '69 1986 w.m. Bryan Adams, Jim Vallance

(Theme from) Summer Place, A 1960 m. Max Steiner. (F) *A Summer Place.* Richard Egan and Sandra Dee appeared in *A Summer Place.* Grammy Award winner 1960.

Summer Set 1960 w.m. Acker Bilk, David Collett

Summertime 1935 w. DuBose Heyward m. George Gershwin. (MT) *Porgy and Bess.* (MF) *Porgy and Bess.* (MF) *Rhapsody in Blue.* Todd Duncan, Anne Wiggins Brown, and Warren Coleman appeared in the original stage production of *Porgy and Bess.* Sidney Poitier and Sammy Davis, Jr., appeared in the film production of *Porgy and Bess.* Oscar Levant, Alexis Smith, and Robert Alda appeared in *Rhapsody in Blue,* biopic of composer George Gershwin.

Summertime Summertime 1958 w.m. Sherm Feller, Tom Jameson

Sun Has Got His Hat On, The 1932 w.m. Ralph Butler, Noel Gay

Sun Shines Brighter, The 1917 w. P.G. Wodehouse m. Jerome Kern. (MT) *Leave It to Jane.*

Sunbonnet Sue 1906 w. Will D. Cobb m. Gus Edwards. (MF) *The Star Maker.* (MF) *Sunbonnet Sue.* Bing Crosby appeared in *The Star Maker.* Gale Storm and Phil Regan appeared in *Sunbonnet Sue.*

Sunday 1926 w.m. Ned Miller, Chester Cohn, Jules Stein, Bennie Krueger

Sunday 1958 w. Oscar Hammerstein II m. Richard Rodgers. (MT) *Flower Drum Song.* (MF) *Flower Drum Song.*

Sunday 1984 w.m. Stephen Sondheim (MT) *Sunday in the Park with George.* Mandy Patinkin and Bernadette Peters appeared in *Sunday in the Park with George.*

Sunday Kind of Love, A 1946 w.m. Barbara Belle, Anita Leonard, Louis Prima, Stan Rhodes

Sunday, Monday or Always 1943 w. Johnny Mercer m. Jimmy Van Heusen. (MF) *Dixie.* Bing Crosby and Dorothy Lamour appeared in *Dixie.*

Sundown 1974 w.m. Gordon Lightfoot

Sunflower 1948 w.m. Mack David. This song was popularized in 1949 by Russ Morgan. Mack David filed suit against writer Jerry Herman claiming that ''Hello Dolly'' was note-for-note identical with his song. While authorship was to remain Mr. Herman's, Mr. David was awarded more than half a million dollars—the highest financial settlement ever for song theft. The state song of Kansas.

Sunny 1925 w. Oscar Hammerstein II m. Jerome Kern. (MT) *Sunny.* (MF) *Sunny* (1930). (MF) *Sunny* (1941). (MF) *Till the Clouds Roll By.* (MF) *Look for the Silver Lining.* Jack Donahue and Clifton Webb appeared in the American stage production of *Sunny,* Jack Hobbs appeared in the British stage production of *Sunny.* Marilyn Miller appeared in the 1930 film production of *Sunny.* Anna Neagle and Ray Bolger appeared in the 1941 film production of *Sunny.* Judy Garland, Van Johnson, and Dinah Shore appeared in *Till the Clouds Roll By,* biopic of composer Jerome Kern. June Haver and Ray Bolger appeared in *Look for the Silver Lining,* biopic of Marilyn Miller.

Sunny 1966 w.m. Bobby Hebb

Sunny Days 1931 w.m. Reginald Connelly, Will Jason, Val Burton

Sunny Disposish 1926 w. Ira Gershwin m. Philip Charig. (MT) *Americana.* Helen Morgan, Roy Atwell, and Lew Brice appeared in *Americana.*

Sunny Havana 1925 w.m. Horatio Nicholls

Sunny Side of the Street, The, *see* **On the Sunny Side of the Street**

(Keep Your) Sunny Side Up 1929 w.m. B.G. DeSylva, Lew Brown, Ray Henderson. (MF) *Sunny Side Up.* (MF) *The Best Things in Life Are Free.* Janet Gaynor and Joe E. Brown appeared in *Sunny Side Up.* Dan Dailey, Gordon MacRae, and Ernest Borgnine appeared in *The Best Things in Life Are Free,* biopic of song writers DeSylva, Brown, and Henderson.

Sunrise and You 1918 w.m. Arthur A. Penn. (F) *Young Eagles.* Charles ''Buddy'' Rogers and Virginia Bruce appeared in *Young Eagles.*

Sunrise Serenade 1939 w. Jack Lawrence m. Frankie Carle. Theme song of Frankie Carle.

Sunrise Sunset 1964 w. Sheldon Harnick m. Jerry Bock. (MT) *Fiddler on the Roof.* (MF) *Fiddler on the Roof.* Zero Mostel appeared in the stage production of *Fiddler on the Roof.*

Sunset Trail, The 1936 w.m. Jimmy Kennedy, Michael Carr

Sunshine Cake 1950 w. Johnny Burke m. James Van Heusen. (MF) *Riding High.* Bing Crosby and Coleen Gray appeared in *Riding High.*

Sunshine Girl 1957 w.m. Bob Merrill. (MT) *New Girl in Town.*

Sunshine, Lollipops and Rainbows 1965 w. Howard Liebling m. Marvin Hamlisch

Sunshine of Paradise Alley, The 1895 w. Walter H. Ford

m. John W. Bratton. Based on a theme from Mascagni's *Cavalleria Rusticana*.

Sunshine of Your Smile, The 1915 w. Leonard Cooke m. Lillian Ray

Sunshine on My Shoulders 1974 w.m. John Denver, Richard L. Kniss, Michael C. Taylor

Supercalifragilisticexpialidocious 1964 w.m. Richard M. Sherman, Robert B. Sherman. (MF) *Mary Poppins*. Julie Andrews and Dick Van Dyke appeared in *Mary Poppins*.

Superstition 1973 w.m. Stevie Wonder. Grammy Award winner 1973.

Suppose I Had Never Met You 1921 w. Harlan Thompson m. Harry Archer. (MT) *Little Jessie James*.

Sur La Plage 1954 w.m. Sandy Wilson. (MT) *The Boy Friend*.

Sur le Pont d'Avignon 1846 w.m. traditional French round. This song was danced to on Pont St. Bénézet, a bridge over the Rhone River. This bridge, completed in 1185, inspired the writing of this round in a tavern on the island of Barthelesse.

Sure Thing 1944 w. Ira Gershwin m. Jerome Kern. (MF) *Cover Girl*. Rita Hayworth, Gene Kelly, and Phil Silvers appeared in *Cover Girl*.

Surf City 1963 w.m. Brian Wilson, Jan Berry

Surfin' Safari 1962 w.m. Mike Love, Brian Wilson

Surfin' U.S.A. 1963 w.m. Chuck Berry

Surprise, Surprise 1985 w. Edward Kleban m. Marvin Hamlisch. (MF) *A Chorus Line*. This song was added to the film adaptation of *A Chorus Line*.

Surrender 1946 w.m. Bennie Benjamin, George David Weiss

Surrender 1961 w.m. Jerome ''Doc'' Pomus, Mort Shuman. Based on the Italian art song ''Torna a Sorrento,'' original words and music G.B. de Curtis and Ernesto de Curtis.

Surrey with the Fringe on Top, The 1943 w. Oscar Hammerstein II m. Richard Rodgers. (MT) *Oklahoma!*. (MF) *Oklahoma!*. Alfred Drake, Betty Garde, and Celeste Holm appeared in *Oklahoma!*. Shirley Jones and Gordon MacRae appeared in the film production of *Oklahoma!*.

Surround Me with Love 1981 w.m. Wayland Holyfield, Norro Wilson

Susan Jane 1871 w.m. William Shakespeare Hays

Susannah's Squeaking Shoes 1923 w. Arthur Weigall m. Muriel Lillie. (MT) *Andre Charlot's Revue of 1925*.

Susie, *see* **If You Knew Susie, Like I Know Susie**

Suspicion 1964 w.m. ''Doc'' Pomus, Mort Shuman

Suspicions 1979 w.m. David Malloy, Randy McCormick, Eddie Rabbitt, Even Stevens

Suspicious Minds 1969 w.m. Mark James

Sussex by the Sea 1908 w.m. Ward-Higgs

Sussudio 1985 w.m. Phil Collins

Suzanne 1967 w.m. Leonard Cohen

Swan, The 1887 m. Camille Saint-Saëns. From the French

''Le Cygne,'' from the collection ''Le Carnaval des Animaux.''

Swan of Tuonela, The, op.22, no. 3 1901 m. Jean Sibelius

Swanee 1919 w. Irving Caesar m. George Gershwin. (MT) *Sinbad*. (MT) *Jigsaw*. (MT) *The Glorious Days*. (MF) *Rhapsody in Blue*. (MF) *The Jolson Story*. (MF) *Jolson Sings Again*. (MF) *Sincerely Yours*. (MF) *A Star Is Born*. Al Jolson appeared in *Sinbad*. Anna Neagle appeared in *The Glorious Days*. Robert Alda and Alexis Smith appeared in *Rhapsody in Blue*, biopic of composer George Gershwin. Larry Parks appeared in both *The Jolson Story* and *Jolson Sings Again*. Liberace appeared in *Sincerely Yours*. Judy Garland and James Mason appeared in *A Star Is Born*.

Swanee River Moon 1921 w.m. H. Pitman Clarke

S.W.A.T., *see* **Theme from S.W.A.T.**

Sway 1954 w.m. Norman Gimbel, Pablo Ruiz

Swearin' to God 1975 w.m. Bob Crewe, Denny Randell

Swedish Pastry 1948 w.m. Barney Kessel

Swedish Rhapsody 1953 w.m. Erik Leidzen

Sweeney, The 1977 w.m. Harry South

Sweep 1933 w.m. Vivian Ellis

Sweeping the Clouds Away 1930 w.m. Sam Coslow. (MF) *Paramount on Parade*. Maurice Chevalier and Gary Cooper appeared in *Paramount on Parade*.

(You're the Flower of My Heart) Sweet Adeline 1903 w. Richard H. Gerard (Richard Gerard Husch) m. Henry W. Armstrong. The original title of this song was ''Down Home in New England.'' The name Adeline was inspired by the farewell tour of Italian opera singer Adelina Patti. Henry Armstrong was seventeen years old when he wrote this standard. See also Part I, 1902.

Sweet Afton, *see* **Flow Gently, Sweet Afton**

Sweet Alice, or, **Ben Bolt,** or, **Don't You Remember** 1848 w. Thomas Dunn English m. Nelson Kneass, from an old German melody.

Sweet and Gentle 1955 w.m. Otillio Portal, George Thorn. From the Spanish ''Me Lo Dijo Adela.''

Sweet and Hot 1930 w. Jack Yellen m. Harold Arlen. (MT) *You Said It*. See also ''San Fernando Valley.''

Sweet and Lovely 1931 w.m. Gus Arnheim, Harry Tobias, Jules Lemare. (MF) *Two Girls and a Sailor*. Van Johnson, June Allyson, and Jimmy Durante appeared in *Two Girls and a Sailor*. Theme song of Russ Columbo.

Sweet and Low. 1863 w. Alfred Tennyson m. Joseph Barnby. The words are from Tennyson's ''Medley,'' from *The Princess*.

Sweet and Low-Down 1925 w. Ira Gershwin m. George Gershwin. (MT) *Tip-Toes*. Queenie Smith and Robert Halliday appeared in the American stage production of *Tip-Toes*. Peggy Beatty and Laddie Cliff appeared in the British stage production of *Tip-Toes*.

Sweet Annie Moore 1901 w.m. John H. Flynn. (MT) *The Casino Girl*.

Sweet as a Song 1937 w.m. Mack Gordon, Harry Revel. (MF) *Sally, Irene and Mary*. Alice Faye appeared in *Sally, Irene and Mary*.

Sweet Betsy from Pike, or, Vilikens and His Dinah 1853 w. possibly John A. Stone m. anon. First known printed version 1853, although this song may date from 1840 or earlier. This song was parodied by Stephen Collins Foster during the 1856 Presidential campaign with the title "The Great Baby Show, or, The Abolition Show."

Sweet Blindness 1967 w.m. Laura Nyro. This song was most popular in 1969.

Sweet Bunch of Daisies 1894 w.m. Anita Owen

Sweet By and By 1868 w. S. Fillmore m. Joseph P. Webster

Sweet Caroline (Sweet Times Never Seemed So Good) 1970 w.m. Neil Diamond

Sweet Danger 1961 w.m. Robert Wright, George Forrest. (MT) *Kean.*

Sweet Dreams 1982 w.m. Graham Russell

Sweet Dreams (Are Made of This) 1983 w.m. Annie Lennox, David Stewart

Sweet Emalina, My Gal 1917 w.m. Henry Creamer, Turner Layton

Sweet Freedom 1986 w.m. Rodney Temperton

Sweet Genevieve 1869 w. George Cooper m. Henry Tucker. (MF) *Incendiary Blonde.* Betty Hutton appeared in *Incendiary Blonde,* biopic of speakeasy hostess Texas Guinan. The story of this song concerns Cooper's wife Genevieve, who died shortly after their marriage. He sold the lyrics to Tucker for a flat five dollars, and this song remains today one of the world's standards. This song was later adapted into a popular college song, "Old College Chum."

Sweet Georgia Brown 1925 w.m. Kenneth Casey, Maceo Pinkard. (MT) *Bubbling Brown Sugar.* (MF) *Broadway.* (MF) *Follow the Boys.* (MF) *Some Like It Hot.* Josephine Premice and Vivian Reed appeared in *Bubbling Brown Sugar.* George Raft, Pat O'Brien, and Janet Blair appeared in *Broadway.* George Raft appeared in *Follow the Boys.* Marilyn Monroe, Jack Lemmon, and Tony Curtis appeared in *Some Like It Hot.* Authorship of this song has erroneously been credited to Ben Bernie.

Sweet Hawaiian Moonlight 1917 w. Harold G. Frost m. F. Henri Klickmann

Sweet Heartache 1937 w.m. Ned Washington, Sammy Stept. (MF) *Hit Parade.* Frances Langford and Duke Ellington appeared in *Hit Parade.*

Sweet Heartaches 1956 w.m. Jimmy Kennedy, Nat Simon

Sweet Is the Word for You 1937 w. Leo Robin m. Ralph Rainger. (MF) *Waikiki Wedding.* Bing Crosby and Martha Raye appeared in *Waikiki Wedding.*

Sweet Jennie Lee 1930 w.m. Walter Donaldson. (MF) *Lover Come Back.* Lucille Ball and George Brent appeared in *Lover Come Back.*

Sweet Kentucky Babe, *see* **Kentucky Babe**

Sweet Kentucky Lady 1914 w. William Jerome m. Louis A. Hirsch

Sweet Lady 1921 w. Howard Johnson m. Frank Crumit, Dave Zoob. (MT) *Tangerine.*

Sweet Leilani 1937 w.m. Harry Owens. (MF) *Waikiki Wedding.* Bing Crosby and Martha Raye appeared in *Waikiki Wedding.* Academy Award winner 1937.

Sweet Life 1979 w.m. Susan M. Collins

Sweet Little Buttercup 1917 w. Alfred Bryan m. Herman Paley

Sweet Little Headache, *see* **You're a Sweet Little Headache**

Sweet Little Sixteen 1958 w.m. Chuck Berry

Sweet Lorraine 1928 w. Mitchell Parish m. Clifford Burwell

Sweet Love 1975 w.m. William Atwell King, Jr., Ronald LaPread, Sr., Thomas McClary, Walter Lee Orange, Lionel Richie, Jr., Milan Williams

Sweet Love 1986 w.m. Anita Baker, Gary Bias, Louis A. Johnson. Grammy Award winner 1986.

Sweet Madness 1933 w. Ned Washington m. Victor Young. (MT) *Murder at the Vanities.* James Rennie appeared in *Murder at the Vanities.*

Sweet Marie 1893 w. Cy Warman m. Raymond Moore

Sweet Mary Ann, *see* **Such an Education Has My Mary Ann**

Sweet Old Fashioned Girl, A 1956 w.m. Bob Merrill

Sweet Paradise, *see* **Drifting and Dreaming**

Sweet Peter 1925 w. Lorenz Hart m. Richard Rodgers. (MT) *Dearest Enemy.*

Sweet Potato Piper 1940 w. Johnny Burke m. James V. Monaco. (MF) *The Road to Singapore* Bing Crosby and Bob Hope appeared in *The Road to Singapore.*

Sweet Rosie O'Grady 1896 w.m. Maude Nugent. This was the first million-copy selling song written by a woman. Ms. Nugent introduced the song herself at Tony Pastor's, on Fourteenth Street in New York City.

Sweet Savannah 1898 w.m. Paul Dresser

Sweet Seasons 1971 w.m. Carole King, Toni Stern

Sweet September 1963 w.m. Bill McGuffie

Sweet Sixteen 1919 w. Gene Buck m. Dave Stamper. (MT) *Ziegfeld Follies of 1919.*

Sweet Sixteen Bars 1958 m. Ray Charles

Sweet Soul Music 1967 w.m. Sam Cooke, Otis Redding, Jr., Arthur Conley

Sweet Spirit, Hear My Prayer 1860 w. Edward Fitzball m. William Vincent Wallace. From the English opera *Lurline.*

Sweet Sue (Just You) 1928 w. Will J. Harris m. Victor Young. (MF) *Rhythm Parade.* The Mills Brothers and Gale Storm appeared in *Rhythm Parade.*

Sweet Talkin' Guy 1966 w.m. Doug Morris, Eliot Greenberg, Barbara Baer, Robert Schwartz

Sweet Talkin' Woman 1978 w.m. Jeff Lynne

Sweet Thing 1976 w.m. Chaka Khan, Tony Maiden

Sweet Thoughts of Home 1904 w. Stanislaus Stange m. Julian Edwards. (MT) *Love's Lottery.*

Sweet Times Never Seemed So Good, *see* **Sweet Caroline**

Sweet Violets 1882 w.m. Joseph Emmet; adapted 1951 Cy Coben, Charles Green. (MT) *Fritz Among the Gypsies.*

Sweet Violets 1908 m. W.C. Powell. This song was popularly revived in 1951.

Sweet William 1964 w.m. Buddy Kaye, Philip Springer

Sweetest Flower the Garden Grew, The 1907 w.m. Thurland Chattaway

Sweetest Maid of All 1908 w. Joseph Herbert m. Oscar Straus. (MT) *A Waltz Dream*.

Sweetest Music This Side of Heaven, The 1934 w.m. Carmen Lombardo, Cliff Friend. (MF) *Many Happy Returns*. George Burns, Gracie Allen, and Ray Milland appeared in *Many Happy Returns*. Theme song of Maurice Winnick.

Sweetest Sight That I Have Ever Seen, The 1937 w. Oscar Hammerstein II m. Jerome Kern. (MF) *High, Wide and Handsome*. Irene Dunne and Randolph Scott appeared in *High, Wide, and Handsome*.

Sweetest Song in the World, The 1938 w.m. Harry Parr-Davies. (MF) *We're Going To Be Rich*. Gracie Fields appeared in *We're Going To Be Rich*.

Sweetest Sounds, The 1962 w.m. Richard Rodgers. (MT) *No Strings*.

Sweetest Story Ever Told, The, or, **Tell Me That You Love Me** 1892 w.m. R.M. Stults. This song was originally written for Miss Myra Mirella.

Sweetest Taboo, The 1986 w.m. Martin Ditcham, Sade

Sweetest Thing in Life, The 1924 w. B.G. DeSylva m. Jerome Kern. (MT) *Peter Pan*.

Sweetheart, *see* **Will You Remember**

Sweetheart of All My Dreams, *see* **I Love You**

Sweetheart of Sigma Chi, The 1912 w. Byron D. Stokes m. F. Dudleigh Vernor. (MF) *The Sweetheart of Sigma Chi*. This song was popularly revived in 1928. This song was written as a love song to the Sigma Chi chapter of Albion College for its twenty-fifth anniversary at the school.

Sweetheart Tree, The 1965 w. Johnny Mercer m. Henry Mancini (F) *The Great Race*. Tony Curtis and Natalie Wood appeared in *The Great Race*.

Sweetheart, We'll Never Grow Old 1946 w.m. Jack Denby, Muriel Watson

Sweethearts 1913 w. Robert B. Smith m. Victor Herbert. (MT) *Sweethearts*. (MF) *Sweethearts*. Tom MacNaughton and Christie MacDonald appeared in the stage production of *Sweethearts*. Nelson Eddy and Jeanette MacDonald appeared in the film production of *Sweethearts*.

Sweethearts on Parade 1928 w. Charles Newman m. Carmen Lombardo. (MF) *Sweethearts on Parade*. Marie Provost and Alice White appeared in *Sweethearts on Parade*.

Sweetie Pie 1934 w.m. John Jacob Loeb

Swing High, Swing Low 1937 w. Ralph Freed m. Burton Lane. (MF) *Swing High, Swing Low*. Dorothy Lamour, Fred MacMurray, and Carole Lombard appeared in *Swing High, Swing Low*.

Swing Low, Sweet Chariot 1917 w.m. based on a traditional black American spiritual as early as 1872; arr. Henry Thacker Burleigh. (MT) *Bubbling Brown Sugar*. Josephine Premice and Vivian Reed appeared in *Bubbling Brown Sugar*.

Swingin' Down the Lane 1923 w. Gus Kahn m. Isham Jones. (MF) *I'll See You in My Dreams*. Doris Day and Danny Thomas appeared in *I'll See You in My Dreams*, biopic of song writer Gus Kahn.

Swingin' in a Hammock 1930 w. Tot Seymour, Charles O'Flynn m. Pete Wendling

Swinging on a Star 1944 w. Johnny Burke m. Jimmy Van Heusen. (MF) *Going My Way*. Bing Crosby and Barry Fitzgerald appeared in *Going My Way*. Academy Award winner 1944.

Swingin' School 1960 w.m. Dave Appell, Bernie Lowe, Kal Mann

Swingin' Shepherd Blues, The 1958 w. Rhoda Roberts, Kenny Jacobson m. Moe Kossman

Swingin' the Jinx Away 1936 w.m. Cole Porter. (MF) *Born To Dance*. (MF) *I Dood It*. Eleanor Powell, James Stewart, and Una Merkel appeared in *Born To Dance*. Red Skelton and Lena Horne appeared in *I Dood It*.

Swiss (Echo) Song 1852 w. anon. m. Carl Eckert

Swiss Toy Girl, The, *see* **Rose of Lucerne**

'S Wonderful 1927 w. Ira Gershwin m. George Gershwin. (MT) *Funny Face*. (MT) *My One and Only*. (MF) *Rhapsody in Blue*. (MF) *An American in Paris*. (MF) *Starlift*. (MF) *Funny Face*. Fred Astaire, Adele Astaire, and Victor Moore appeared in the stage production of *Funny Face*. Tommy Tune and Twiggy appeared in *My One and Only*. Oscar Levant and Alexis Smith appeared in *Rhapsody in Blue*, biopic of composer George Gershwin. Gene Kelly and Leslie Caron appeared in *An American in Paris*. Doris Day and Gordon MacRae appeared in *Starlift*. Fred Astaire and Audrey Hepburn appeared in the film production of *Funny Face*.

Sword of Bunker Hill, The 1855 w. William Ross Wallace m. Bernard Covert

Sylvia 1914 w. Clinton Scollard m. Oley Speaks

Sympathy 1912 w. Otto Harbach m. Rudolf Friml. (MT) *The Firefly*. (MF) *The Firefly*. Jeanette MacDonald and Allan Jones appeared in the film production of *The Firefly*.

Symphony 1945 Orig.w. Andre Tabet, Roger Bernstein Eng.w. Jack Lawrence m. Alex Alstone

Symphony for Susan, A 1966 w.m. Bill Stegmeyer

Symphony Moderne 1940 m. Max Steiner

Syncopated Clock, The 1951 m. Leroy Anderson. (TV) *The Late Show*.

Taboo 1941 w. S.K. Russell m. Marguerita Lecuona

'Tain't Nobody's Business If I Do 1922 w.m. Porter Grainger, Everett Robbins. (MT) *Me and Bessie*. (MT) *Ain't Misbehavin'*. (MF) *Lady Sings the Blues*. Linda Hopkins appeared in *Me and Bessie*, the stage biography of singer Bessie Smith. Nell Carter and Debbie Allen appeared in *Ain't Misbehavin'*. Diana Ross appeared in *Lady Sings the Blues*, biopic of singer Billie Holiday. This was the first song recorded by Thomas "Fats" Waller.

'Tain't What You Do (It's the Way That You Do It) 1939 w.m. James Oliver Young

Take a Car 1905 w.m. Ed Rose, Ted Snyder. This song

was written in praise of the trolley, claiming "it beats all your hansoms and automobiles."

Take a Day Off, Mary Ann 1891 w. Edward Harrigan m. David Braham. (MT) *The Last of the Hogans.*

Take a Letter, Maria 1969 w.m. R.B. Greaves

Take a Little Tip from Father 1912 w.m. Ted Snyder, Irving Berlin

Take a Look At Me Now, *see* **Against All Odds**

Take a Number from One to Ten 1934 w.m. Mack Gordon, Harry Revel. (MF) *College Rhythm.* Joe Penner and Lanny Ross appeared in *College Rhythm.*

Take a Seat, Old Lady 1894 w.m. Paul Dresser

Take Back the Heart You Gave 1864 w.m. Claribel (Mrs. Charles C. Barnard [Charlotte Arlington])

Take Back Your Gold 1897 w.m. Monroe H. Rosenfeld; w. erroneously credited to Louis W. Pritzkow. This song was popularly sung by both Emma Carus and Imogene Comer.

Take Back Your Mink 1950 w.m. Frank Loesser. (MT) *Guys and Dolls.* (MF) *Guys and Dolls.* Robert Alda and Vivian Blaine appeared in the stage production of *Guys and Dolls.* Vivian Blaine and Marlon Brando appeared in the film production of *Guys and Dolls.*

Take Care (When You Say "Te Quiero") 1945 w.m. Henry Pritchard

Take Five 1961 m. Dave Brubeck

Take Good Care of My Baby 1961 w.m. Gerry Goffin, Carole King

Take It Easy 1943 w.m. Alberto de Bru, Irving Taylor, Vic Mizzy. (MF) *Two Girls and a Sailor.* Van Johnson, June Allyson, and Jimmy Durante appeared in *Two Girls and a Sailor.*

Take It Easy on Me 1982 w.m. Graham Goble

Take It Slow, Joe 1957 w. E.Y. Harburg m. Harold Arlen. (MT) *Jamaica.*

Take It to the Limit 1975 w.m. Don Henley, Randy Meisner

Take Me Along 1959 w.m. Bob Merrill. (MT) *Take Me Along.* Jackie Gleason, Walter Pidgeon, and Eileen Herlie appeared in *Take Me Along.*

Take Me Around Again 1907 w. Edward Rose m. Kerry Mills

Take Me Back to Dear Old Blighty 1917 w.m. A.J. Mills, Fred Godfrey, Bennett Scott

Take Me Back to My Boots and Saddle, *see* **Boots and Saddle**

Take Me Back to New York Town 1907 w. Andrew B. Sterling m. Harry Von Tilzer

Take Me Back to the Garden of Love 1911 w. E. Ray Goetz m. Nat Osborne

Take Me Back to Your Heart Again 1905 w. Collin Davis m. Frank J. Richmond

Take Me Down 1982 w.m. Mark Gray, James Pennington

Take Me High 1974 w.m. Tony Cole

Take Me Home 1979 w.m. Michele Allen, Bob Esty

Take Me Home 1986 w.m. Phil Collins

Take Me Home Country Roads 1971 w.m. Bill Danoff, Taffy Danoff, John Denver

Take Me in Your Arms 1932 w.m. Mitchell Parish, Fritz Rotter, Fred Markush. (MF) *Hi, Buddy.* (MF) *On Stage Everybody.* Harriet Hilliard and Marjorie Lord appeared in *Hi, Buddy.* Peggy Ryan and Johnny Coy appeared in *On Stage Everybody.*

Take Me in Your Arms (Rock Me a Little While) 1975 w.m. Eddie Holland, Brian Holland, Lamont Dozier

Take Me Out to the Ball Game 1908 w. Jack Norworth m. Albert Von Tilzer. (MF) *Everybody's Cheering.* Theme song of Jack Norworth. Supposedly, Jack Norworth had never seen a major league baseball game until after this song was published. Mr. Norworth, whose real name was John Klem, had five wives: Louise Dresser, Nora Bayes, Mary Johnson, Emma Dorothy Adelphi, and Beatrice Amy Archer. See also Part I, 1845.

Take Me to the Midnight Cake Walk Ball 1915 w.m. Eddie Cox, Arthur Jackson, Maurice Abrahams

Take Me Up with You, Dearie 1909 w. Junie McCree m. Albert Von Tilzer

Take My Breath Away 1986 w. Tom Whitlock m. Giorgio Moroder. (F) *Top Gun.*

Take My Heart 1936 w. Joe Young m. Fred E. Ahlert

Take My Love 1955 w.m. Helen Deutsch, Bronislaw Kaper. Based on a theme from the third movement of Brahms's Third Symphony.

Take On Me 1985 w.m. Magne Furuholmer, Morten Harket, Pål Waaktaar

Take That Look Off Your Face 1981 w.m. Don Black. Ivor Novello Award winner 1980–81.

Take the "A" Train 1941 w.m. Billy Strayhorn. (MT) *Bubbling Brown Sugar.* (MT) *Sophisticated Ladies.* (MF) *Reveille with Beverly.* Avon Long and Josephine Premice appeared in *Bubbling Brown Sugar.* Gregory Hines and Phyllis Hyman appeared in *Sophisticated Ladies.* Ann Miller and William Wright appeared in *Reveille with Beverly.* Theme song of Duke Ellington.

Take the Moment 1965 w. Stephen Sondheim m. Richard Rodgers. (MT) *Do I Hear a Waltz?*

Take Your Girl 1949 w.m. Ivor Novello, Christopher Hassall. (MT) *King's Rhapsody.* (MF) *King's Rhapsody.* Anna Neagle and Errol Flynn appeared in the film production of *King's Rhapsody.*

Take Your Girlie to the Movies If You Can't Make Love at Home 1919 w. Edgar Leslie, Bert Kalmar m. Pete Wendling

Take Your Time (Do It Right) 1980 w.m. Sigidi, Harold Clayton

Take Your Time, Miss Lucy 1842 w.m. William Whitlock

Takes Two To Tango 1952 w.m. Al Hoffman, Dick Manning

Taking a Chance on Love 1940 w. John Latouche, Ted Fetter m. Vernon Duke. (MT) *Cabin in the Sky.* (MF) *Cabin in the Sky.* (MF) *I Dood It.* (MF) *I'll Get By.* (MF) *The Benny Goodman Story.* (MF) *This Could Be the Night.* Ethel Waters,

Rex Ingram, and Katherine Dunbar appeared in the stage production of *Cabin in the Sky*. Ethel Waters, Rochester, and Lena Horne appeared in the film production of *Cabin in the Sky*. Red Skelton, Lena Horne, and Eleanor Powell appeared in *I Dood It*. June Haver and Dennis Day appeared in *I'll Get By*. Jean Simmons and Anthony Franciosa appeared in *This Could Be the Night*. Popularly revived in 1943, this song was originally titled "Fooling Around with Love."

Taking In the Town 1890 w. Edward Harrigan m. David Braham. (MT) *Reilly and the Four Hundred*.

Takin' It Easy 1981 w.m. Lucy Dalton, Billy Sherrill, Mark Sherrill

Taking Somebody with Me When I Fall 1980 w.m. Larry Gatlin

Tale of a Bumble Bee, The 1901 w. Frank Pixley m. Gustav Luders. (MT) *King Dodo*.

Tale of the Kangaroo, The 1900 w. Frank Pixley m. Gustav Luders. (MT) *The Burgomaster*.

Tale of the Seashell, The 1902 w. Frank Pixley m. Gustav Luders. (MT) *The Prince of Pilsen*.

Tale of the Turtle Dove, The 1904 w. Frank Pixley m. Gustav Luders. (MT) *Woodland*.

Tales from (of) the Vienna Woods 1868 m. Johann Strauss. (MF) *The Great Waltz*. Words were added to this melody by Oscar Hammerstein II for the film production, *The Great Waltz*. From the German "Geschichten aus dem Wienerwald," op.325.

Talk of the Town, The, *see* **It's the Talk of the Town**

Talk to Me 1986 w.m. Chaz Sanford

Talk to the Animals 1967 w.m. Leslie Bricusse. (MF) *Doctor Dolittle*. Academy Award winner 1967.

Talkin' in Your Sleep 1978 w.m. Roger Cook, Bobby Ray Wood

Talking in Your Sleep 1984 w.m. Coz Canler, Jimmy Marinos, Wally Palmar, Mike Skill, Pete Solley

Tallahassee 1947 w.m. Frank Loesser. (MF) *Variety Girl*. Mary Hatcher, William Demarest, and DeForest Kelley appeared in *Variety Girl*.

Tambourin Chinois 1910 m. Fritz Kreisler

Tamiami Trail 1926 w.m. Cliff Friend, Joseph H. Santley

Tammany 1905 w. Vincent P. Bryan m. Gus Edwards. (MT) *Fantana*. This song was first popularly performed by Lee Harrison in *Fantana*, and is now the official anthem for the Tammany Society, for whom the song was written. It soon became associated with "Big Bill" Devery, a police chief fired by Tammany. The melody of this song was later used for a Barbasol shaving cream commercial promotion campaign.

Tammany Quickstep 1794 m. James Hewitt. From the opera *Tammany*.

Tammy 1957 w.m. Jay Livingston, Ray Evans. (F) *Tammy and the Bachelor*. Debbie Reynolds and Walter Brennan appeared in *Tammy and the Bachelor*.

Tampico 1946 w.m. Walter Ruick

Tangerine 1942 w. Johnny Mercer m. Victor Schertzin-

ger. (MF) *The Fleet's In*. Dorothy Lamour, William Holden, and Betty Hutton appeared in *The Fleet's In*.

Tantivy! Tantivy! Tantivy! (A-Hunting We Will Go), *see* **Hunt Theme**

Taps 1862 m. Daniel O. Butterfield. This standard American bugle call was composed by Daniel O. Butterfield on the banks of the James River when he was in command of a brigade in the Army of the Potomac in Confederate territory. He wrote the work after having been wounded at the Battle of Gaines's Mill in June 1862, and soon taught it to O.W. Norton, bugler at Brigade Headquarters, who first performed it at Harrison's Landing on the James River in July 1862. It is still unknown as to why years later the title "Taps" was given to this traditional American bugle call, although it is possibly derived from the Dutch "taptoo."

Ta-Ra-Ra-Boom-Der-É (De-Ay) 1891 w.m. Henry J. Sayers. This song was popularly introduced in England by Lottie Collins.

Tara's Theme 1939 w. Mack David m. Max Steiner. (F) *Gone with the Wind*. (TV) *Million Dollar Movie*. Clark Gable, Vivien Leigh, and Olivia de Havilland appeared in *Gone with the Wind*. This song, with lyrics added, was released as "My Own True Love" in 1954.

Tartar Song, The 1928 w. Lorenz Hart m. Richard Rodgers. (MT) *Chee-Chee*. Betty Starbuck and Helen Ford appeared in *Chee-Chee*.

Taste of Honey, A 1962 w. Ric Marlow m. Bobby Scott. Grammy Award winner 1965.

Tattoo uncertain m. anon. This traditional American bugle call is a possible adaptation of "Tap-zu," used in Wallenstein's army to announce the closing of the taps and hence the end of the night's beer drinking.

Te Quiero Dijiste, *see* **Magic Is the Moonlight**

Tea for Two 1924 w. Irving Caesar m. Vincent Youmans. (MT) *No, No, Nanette*. (MF) *No, No, Nanette*. (MF) *Tea for Two*. (MF) *With a Song in My Heart*. (MF) *Sincerely Yours*. (MF) *Jazz on a Summer's Day*. Louise Groody and Mary Lawlor appeared in the American stage production of *No, No, Nanette*. Seymour Beard appeared in the British stage production of *No, No, Nanette*. Anna Neagle and Victor Mature appeared in the film production of *No, No, Nanette*. Doris Day appeared in *Tea for Two*, the remake of *No, No, Nanette*. Susan Hayward appeared in *With a Song in My Heart*, biopic of singer Jane Froman. Liberace and Dorothy Mallone appeared in *Sincerely Yours*. Anita O'Day appeared in *Jazz on a Summer's Day*.

Teach Me How To Kiss 1900 w.m. Gustave Kerker, Hugh Morton. (MT) *The Belle of New York*.

Teach Me Tonight 1954 w. Sammy Cahn m. Gene De Paul

Tear Fell, A 1956 w.m. Dorian Burton, Eugene Randolph

Tears 1935 w.m. Billy Uhr

Tears of a Clown, The 1970 w.m. Henry Cosby, Steveland Morris, William "Smokey" Robinson, Jr.

Tears on My Pillow 1939 w.m. Max Nesbitt, Harry Nesbitt

Tears on My Pillow 1958 w.m. Sylvester Bradford, Al Lewis

Tease Me 1960 w.m. Keith Kelly

Teasing 1904 w. Cecil Mack m. Albert Von Tilzer. (MT) *The Catch of the Season.*

(Let Be Be Your) Teddy Bear 1957 w.m. Kal Mann, Bernie Lowe. (MF) *Loving You.* Elvis Presley appeared in *Loving You.*

Teddy Bear's Picnic, The 1913 w.m. John W. Bratton, James B. Kennedy

Teen Angel 1960 w.m. Jean Surrey, Red Surrey

Teenage Crush 1956 w.m. Audrey Allison, Joe Allison. This song was first performed by Tommy Sands on the Kraft Theater for NBC.

Teenage Prayer 1955 w.m. Bix Reichner, Bernie Lowe

Teenager in Love 1959 w.m. Jerome "Doc" Pomus, Mort Shuman

Teeth 'n' Smiles 1977 w.m. Nick Bicat, Tony Bicat

Telefone 1984 w.m. Gregory Mathieson, Trevor Veitch

Telephone Hour, The 1960 w. Lee Adams m. Charles Strouse. (MT) *Bye Bye Birdie.* (MF) *Bye Bye Birdie.* Dick Van Dyke and Ann-Margret appeared in the film production of *Bye Bye Birdie.***Telephone Line** 1977 w.m. Jeff Lynne

Tell All the World 1961 w.m. Mark Anthony

Tell Her About It 1983 w.m. Billy Joel

Tell It All Over Again 1914 w. Henry Blossom m. Victor Herbert. (MT) *The Only Girl.*

Tell It Like It Is 1966 w.m. George Davis, Lee Diamond. This song was popularly revived in 1981.

Tell It Out Among the Nations (Heathen) That the Lord Is King 1881 w. Frances Ridley Havergal m. arr. Ira David Sankey

Tell Laura I Love Her 1960 w.m. Jeff Barry, Ben Raleigh

Tell Me 1919 w. J. Will Callahan m. Max Kortlander. (MF) *On Moonlight Bay.* Doris Day and Gordon MacRae appeared in *On Moonlight Bay.*

Tell Me a Story 1948 w.m. Maurice Sigler, Larry Stock

Tell Me, Babbling Echo, or, The Request c.1775 w. poss. Clarke m. Gerard Vogler

Tell Me I'm Forgiven 1930 w.m. Robert Katscher, Rowland Leigh. (MT) *The Wonder Bar.* Carl Brisson and Gwen Farrar appeared in the British production of *The Wonder Bar.*

Tell Me I'm Not Dreaming 1985 w.m. Bruce Sudano

Tell Me Little Gypsy 1920 w.m. Irving Berlin. (MT) *Ziegfeld Follies of 1920.*

Tell Me More 1925 w. B.G. DeSylva, Ira Gershwin m. George Gershwin. (MT) *Tell Me More.*

Tell Me Pretty Maiden (Are There Any More At Home Like You) 1900 w. Owen Hall m. Leslie Stuart (Thomas A. Barrett). (MT) *Florodora.*

Tell Me Something Good 1974 w.m. Stevie Wonder

Tell Me That You Love Me, *see* **The Sweetest Story Ever Told**

Tell Me That You Love Me Tonight 1935 w. Al Silverman m. C.A. Bixio. Based on the Italian "Parlami d'Amore Mariù," w. Ennio Neri.

Tell Me the Old, Old Story 1878 w. Catherine Hankey m. William Howard Doane

Tell Me Tonight 1933 w.m. Mischa Spoliansky, Frank Eyton. (MF) *Tell Me Tonight.* Jan Kiepura and Sonnie Hale appeared in *Tell Me Tonight.*

Tell Me When 1964 w.m. Geoff Stephens, Les Reed

Tell Me Why 1951 w. Al Alberts m. Marty Gold

Tell Me Why You Smile Mona Lisa 1931 Ger.w. Walter Reisch Eng.w. Raymond B. Egan m. Robert Stolz. From the German "Warum Lächelst Du Mona Lisa."

Tell Me You're Mine 1953 w.m. R. Fredianelli, D. Ravasino

Tell Mother I'll Be There 1890 w.m. Charles M. Fillmore

Telstar 1962 w.m. Joe Meek. Ivor Novello Award winner 1962.

Temple Bell, The 1911 w.m. Lionel Monckton, Arthur Wimperis. (MT) *The Mousme.* Florence Smithson appeared in *The Mousme.*

Temple Bells, The 1903 w. Laurence Hope m. Amy Woodeforde-Finden. From "Four Indian Love Lyrics."

Temptation 1933 w. Arthur Freed m. Nacio Herb Brown. (MF) *Going Hollywood.* (MF) *Kiss Them for Me.* (F) *Written on the Wind.* (MF) *The Seven Hills of Rome.* (F) *Malaya.* Bing Crosby appeared in *Going Hollywood.* Rock Hudson and Lauren Bacall appeared in *Written on the Wind.* Mario Lanza appeared in *The Seven Hills of Rome.* Spencer Tracy and James Stewart appeared in *Malaya.* This song was popularly revived in 1946.

Temptation Rag 1909 w.m. Henry Lodge

Ten Cents a Dance 1930 w. Lorenz Hart m. Richard Rodgers. (MT) *Simple Simon.* (MF) *Ten Cents a Dance.* (MF) *Love Me or Leave Me.* Ruth Etting, Ed Wynn, and Harriet Hoctor appeared in *Simple Simon.* Doris Day and James Cagney appeared in *Love Me or Leave Me,* biopic of singer Ruth Etting. This song was written by Rodgers and Hart in two hours.

Ten Little Fingers and Ten Little Toes—Down In Tennessee 1921 w. Harry Pease, Johnny White m. Ira Schuster, Ed G. Nelson

Ten Little Indians, or, Ten Little Injuns, or, Ten Little Niggers (in England) 1868 w.m. Septimus Winner. Possibly based on "The Drunken Sailor." See also "The Drunken Sailor."

Ten Minutes Ago 1957 w. Oscar Hammerstein II m. Richard Rodgers. (TV) *Cinderella.*

Ten Pretty Girls 1937 w.m. Will Grosz, Jimmy Kennedy

Ten Thousand Years from Now 1923 w. J. Keirn Brennan m. Ernest R. Ball

Tender Is the Night 1961 w.m. Paul Francis Webster, Sammy Fain. (F) *Tender Is the Night.*

Tender Love 1986 w.m. Jimmy Jam, Terry Lewis

Tender Shepherd 1954 w. Carolyn Leigh m. Mark Charlap. (MT) *Peter Pan.* Mary Martin appeared in *Peter Pan.*

(Love Is) Tender Trap, The 1955 w. Sammy Cahn m. James Van Heusen. (F) *The Tender Trap*. (F) *This Could Be the Night*. Frank Sinatra, Celeste Holm, and Debbie Reynolds appeared in *The Tender Trap*. Jean Simmons and Anthony Franciosa appeared in *This Could Be the Night*.

Tenderly 1926 w. Abe Lyman m. Joe Dale

Tenderly 1947 w. Jack Lawrence m. Walter Gross. (MF) *Torch Song*. Joan Crawford and Gig Young appeared in *Torch Song*. Theme song of Rosemary Clooney.

Tenderly Calling 1890 w. Frances Jane Crosby (Mrs. Alexander Van Alstyne) m. Ira David Sankey

Tenement Symphony, The 1941 w.m. Sid Kuller, Ray Golden, Hal Borne. (MF) *The Big Store*. The Marx Brothers and Tony Martin appeared in *The Big Store*.

Tennessee Waltz 1948 w.m. Redd Stewart, Pee Wee King. This song was popularly revived in 1951.

Tenting on the Old Camp Ground, or, **Tenting Tonight** 1864 w.m. Walter Kittredge. Because of a childhood bout with rheumatic fever, Kittredge could not become a Union soldier. He wrote this song as his personal plea for peace. This song was most popularly performed by the Hutchinson Family singers.

Tenting Tonight, *see* **Tenting on the Old Camp Ground**

Tequila 1958 m. Chuck Rio. Grammy Award winner 1958.

Terrific Band and a Real Nice Crowd, A 1978 w. Alan Bergman, Marilyn Bergman m. Billy Goldenberg. (MT) *Ballroom*. Dorothy Loudon and Vincent Gardenia appeared in *Ballroom*.

Terry 1965 w.m. "Twinkle"

Terry's Theme, *see* **Eternally**

Tessie, You Are the Only, Only, Only 1902 w.m. Will R. Anderson. (MT) *The Silver Slipper*.

Texaco Star Theme (The Man Who Wears the Star) 1961 w.m. W.A. Fredricks. This song was written for a Texaco petroleum products commercial promotion campaign.

Texas in My Rear View Mirror 1981 w.m. Mac Davis

Texas Women 1981 w.m. Hank Williams, Jr.

Thank God for a Garden 1915 w.m. Teresa del Riego

Thank God I'm a Country Boy 1975 w.m. John Martin Sommers

Thank Heaven for Little Girls 1958 w. Alan Jay Lerner m. Frederick Loewe. (MF) *Gigi*. Leslie Caron, Maurice Chevalier, and Hermione Gingold appeared in *Gigi*.

Thank U Very Much 1968 w.m. M. McGear

Thank You Falettin Me Be Mice Elf Again 1970 w.m. Sly Stewart

Thank You for a Lovely Evening 1934 w. Dorothy Fields m. Jimmy McHugh. (MF) *The Girl from Missouri*. (F) *Have a Heart*. Jean Harlow and Franchot Tone appeared in *The Girl from Missouri*. Jean Parker and James Dunn appeared in *Have a Heart*.

Thank You Girl 1963 w.m. John Lennon, Paul McCartney

Thank You So Much Mrs. Lowsborough—Goodbye 1934 w.m. Cole Porter

Thank You Very Much 1971 w.m. Leslie Bricusse

Thank Your Father 1930 w. B.G. DeSylva, Lew Brown m. Ray Henderson. (MT) *Flying High*.

Thanks 1933 w.m. Sam Coslow, Arthur Johnston. (MF) *Too Much Harmony*. Bing Crosby and Jack Oakie appeared in *Too Much Harmony*.

Thanks a Million 1935 w. Gus Kahn m. Arthur Johnston. (MF) *Thanks a Million*. Fred Allen and Dick Powell appeared in *Thanks a Million*.

Thanks for the Buggy Ride 1925 w.m. Jules Buffano. (MF) *Always a Bridesmaid*. The Andrews Sisters and Charles Butterworth appeared in *Always a Bridesmaid*.

Thanks for the Memory 1937 w. Leo Robin m. Ralph Rainger. (MF) *The Big Broadcast of 1938*. Bob Hope, Martha Raye, and Shirley Ross appeared in *The Big Broadcast of 1938*. Academy Award winner 1938. Theme song of Bob Hope.

That Beautiful Rag 1910 w.m. Irving Berlin, Ted Snyder

That Certain Feeling 1925 w. Ira Gershwin m. George Gershwin. (MT) *Tip-Toes*. (F) *That Certain Feeling*. Queenie Smith and Robert Halliday appeared in the American production of *Tip-Toes*. Dorothy Dickson and Allen Kearns appeared in the British production of *Tip-Toes*. Bob Hope and Eva Marie Saint appeared in *That Certain Feeling*.

That Certain Party 1925 w. Gus Kahn m. Walter Donaldson

That Daffydill Rag 1912 w.m. Bill Meuller, Frank Mueller

That Dear Old Gentleman 1956 w.m. Paddy Roberts

That Feeling in the Moonlight, *see* **Did You Ever Get That Feeling in the Moonlight**

That Girl 1982 w.m. Stevie Wonder

That Great Come and Get It Day 1946 w. E.Y. Harburg m. Burton Lane. (MT) *Finian's Rainbow*. (MF) *Finian's Rainbow*. Albert Sharpe and David Wayne appeared in the stage production of *Finian's Rainbow*. Fred Astaire and Petula Clark appeared in the film production of *Finian's Rainbow*.

That International Rag 1913 w.m. Irving Berlin. (MF) *Alexander's Ragtime Band*. (MF) *Call Me Madam*. Tyrone Power appeared in *Alexander's Ragtime Band*. Ethel Merman appeared in *Call Me Madam*. This song was written, says Berlin, "practically to order, in one sitting, for an Albert de Courville revue. Bonita and Lew Hearn and Ethel Levey (ex-Mrs. George M. Cohan) introduced the song. I had been booked by the London Palladium as "the American ragtime King.' I was young and brash, and it all came so fast and I didn't care." The song speaks of "dukes and lords and Russian czars—men who own their motor cars."

That Lady 1973 w.m. Christopher H. Jasper, Ernest Isley, Marvin Isley

That Lonesome Road, *see* **Look Down, Look Down That Lonesome Road**

That Lost Barbershop Chord 1926 w. Ira Gershwin m. George Gershwin. (MT) *Americana* (1926).

That Lovely Weekend 1942 w.m. Ted Heath, Moira Heath

That Lovin' Rag 1907 w. Victor H. Smalley m. Bernie Adler

That Lovin' You Feelin' Again 1980 w.m. Roy Orbison, Roma Price

That Lucky Old Sun 1949 w. Haven Gillespie m. Beasley Smith

That Mellow Melody 1912 w. Sam M. Lewis m. George W. Meyer

That Mesmerizing Mendelssohn Tune 1909 w.m. Irving Berlin. Based on Mendelssohn's "Spring Song."

That Minor Strain 1910 w. Cecil Mack m. Ford Dabney

That Mysterious Rag 1911 w.m. Irving Berlin, Ted Snyder

That Naughty Waltz 1919 w. Edwin Stanley m. Sol P. Levy

That Old Black Magic 1943 w. Johnny Mercer m. Harold Arlen. (MT) *The 1940's Radio Hour.* (MF) *Star Spangled Rhythm.* (MF) *Here Come the Waves.* (MF) *Meet Danny Wilson.* Bing Crosby, Bob Hope, Mary Martin, and Veronica Lake appeared in *Star Spangled Rhythm.* Bing Crosby and Betty Hutton appeared in *Here Come the Waves.* Frank Sinatra and Shelley Winters appeared in *Meet Danny Wilson.* Theme song of Billy Daniels and Stanley Black.

That Old Fashioned Mother of Mine 1919 w.m. Horatio Nicholls, Worton David

That Old Feeling 1937 w.m. Lew Brown, Sammy Fain. (MF) *Vogues of 1938.* (MF) *With a Song in My Heart.* Warner Baxter and Joan Bennett appeared in *Vogues of 1938.* Susan Hayward appeared in *With a Song in My Heart,* biopic of singer Jane Froman.

That Old Gang of Mine 1923 w. Billy Rose, Mort Dixon m. Ray Henderson. This song was popularly revived in 1948.

That Old Girl of Mine 1912 w. Earl C. Jones m. Egbert Van Alstyne

That Old Irish Mother of Mine 1920 w. William Jerome m. Harry Von Tilzer

That Same Old Feeling 1971 w.m. Tony Macaulay, Marilyn McLeod

That Silver-Haired Daddy of Mine 1937 w.m. Gene Autry, Jimmy Long

That Sly Old Gentleman from Featherbed Lane 1939 w. Johnny Burke m. James V. Monaco. (MF) *East Side of Heaven.* Bing Crosby and Joan Blondell appeared in *East Side of Heaven.*

That Tumble-Down Shack in Athlone 1918 w. Richard W. Pascoe m. Monte Carlo, Alma M. Sanders

That Was Before I Met You 1911 w. Alfred Bryan m. George W. Meyer

That Wan't Meant for Me, *see* **Moon Song**

That Wonderful Mother of Mine 1918 w. Clyde Hager m. Walter Goodwin

That'll Be the Day 1957 w.m. Buddy Holly, Norman Petty. This song was popularly revived in 1976.

That's A Plenty 1909 w. Henry Creamer m. Bert A. Williams. This song was popularly revived in 1914.

That's All 1952 w.m. Bob Haymes, Alan Brandt

That's All 1984 w.m. Tony Banks, Phil Collins, Mike Rutherford

That's All I Want from You 1954 w.m. M. Rotha, Fritz Rotter

That's All That Matters 1981 w.m. Hank Cochran

That's Amore (That's Love) 1953 w. Jack Brooks m. Harry Warren. (F) *The Caddy.* Dean Martin and Jerry Lewis appeared in *The Caddy.* Theme song of Dean Martin.

That's an Irish Lullaby, *see* **Too-ra-loo-ra-loo-ral, That's an Irish Lullaby**

That's Entertainment 1953 w. Howard Dietz m. Arthur Schwartz. (MF) *The Band Wagon.* Fred Astaire and Nanette Fabray appeared in *The Band Wagon.* This song did not appear in the original 1931 stage production of *The Band Wagon.*

That's for Me 1941 w.m. Jimmy Monaco, Johnny Burke. (MF) *Rhythm on the River.* Bing Crosby and Mary Martin appeared in *Rhythm on the River.*

That's for Me 1945 w. Oscar Hammerstein II m. Richard Rodgers. (MF) *State Fair* (1945). (MF) *State Fair* (1962). Vivian Blaine and Jeanne Crain appeared in the 1945 film production of *State Fair.* Pat Boone and Ann-Margret appeared in the 1962 film production of *State Fair.*

That's Good Enough for Me 1946 w.m. Allan Roberts, Doris Fisher. (MF) *The Thrill of Brazil.* (MF) *Little Miss Broadway.* Evelyn Keyes, Keenan Wynn, Ann Miller, and Allyn Joslyn appeared in *The Thrill of Brazil.* Jean Porter and John Shelton appeared in *Little Miss Broadway.*

That's Gratitude 1908 w.m. George A. Norton, Sheppard Camp

That's How a Love Song Was Born 1955 w.m. Norman Newell, Philip Green

That's How I Love the Blues 1941 w.m. Hugh Martin, Ralph Blane. (MT) *Best Foot Forward.* (MF) *Best Foot Forward.* June Allyson and Nancy Walker appeared in the stage production of *Best Foot Forward.* Lucille Ball and June Allyson appeared in the film production of *Best Foot Forward.*

That's How I Need You 1912 w. Joe McCarthy, Joe Goodwin m. Al Piantadosi

That's How Much I Love You 1946 w.m. Eddy Arnold, Wally Fowler, J. Graydon Hall

That's Life 1964 w. E.Y. Harburg m. Vernon Duke

That's Livin' Alright 1984 w.m. David Mackay, Ken Ashby. Ivor Novello Award winner 1983–84.

That's My Desire 1931 w. Carroll Loveday m. Helmy Kresa. This song was popularly revived in 1947.

That's My Weakness Now 1928 w.m. Bud Green, Sam H. Stept

That's Rock 'N' Roll 1977 w.m. Eric Carmen

That's the Beginning of the End 1946 w.m. Joan Whitney, Alex Kramer

That's the Reason Noo I Wear a Kilt 1906 w. Harry Lauder, A.B. Kendal m. Harry Lauder

That's the Time I Feel Like Makin' Love, *see* **Feel Like Makin' Love**

That's the Way 1965 w.m. Howard Blaikley

That's the Way I Like It 1975 w.m. Harry Casey, Richard Finch

That's What Friends Are For 1986 w.m. Burt Bacharach, Carole Bayer Sager. Grammy Award winner 1986. Proceeds from this song were generously donated to an AIDS campaign for patients, support groups, and medical research.

That's What I Like about the South 1944 w.m. Andy Razaf. This song was popularly revived in 1947. Theme song of Phil Harris.

That's What I Want for Christmas 1936 w.m. Irving Caesar, Gerald Marks. (MF) *Stowaway*. Shirley Temple, Robert Young, and Alice Faye appeared in *Stowaway*.

That's What Love Will Do 1963 w.m. Trevor Peacock

That's What Makes Paris Paree 1953 w. Sammy Cahn m. Vernon Duke. (MF) *April in Paris*. Doris Day and Ray Bolger appeared in *April in Paris*.

That's What the Daisy Said 1903 w.m. Albert Von Tilzer

That's When the Music Takes Me 1975 w.m. Neil Sedaka

That's Where I Came In 1946 w.m. Charles Tobias, Peter DeRose

That's Where My Money Goes 1901 w.m. Walter Daniels, R.P. Lilly. This song was most popular in 1901, but was possibly published several years earlier.

That's Why Darkies Were Born 1931 w. B.G. DeSylva, Lew Brown m. Ray Henderson. (MT) *George White's Scandals of 1931 (Eleventh Edition)*. (MF) *George White's Scandals*. Ethel Merman and Ray Bolger appeared in *George White's Scandals of 1931*.

That's Why They Call Me ''Shine'' 1910 w. Cecil Mack m. Ford Dabney. (MF) *The Birth of the Blues*. Bing Crosby and Mary Martin appeared in *The Birth of the Blues*.

That's Yiddishe Love 1910 w.m. James Brockman

Thee I Love, *see* **Friendly Persuasion**

Them There Eyes 1930 w.m. Maceo Pinkard, Doris Tauber, William Tracey. (MF) *Lady Sings the Blues*. Diana Ross appeared in *Lady Sings the Blues*, biopic of singer Billie Holiday.

Theme for Young Lovers 1964 w.m. Bruce Welch

Theme from *A New Kind of Love*, *see* **A New Kind of Love**

Theme from a Non-Existent TV Series 1977 w.m. Elton John, Bernie Taupin

Theme from *A Summer Place*, *see* **A Summer Place**

Theme from *Against All Odds*, *see* **Against All Odds**

Theme from *All In the Family*, *see* **Those Were the Days**

Theme from *Arthur*, *see* **Arthur's Theme**

Theme from *Ben Casey* 1961 w.m. David Raksin. (TV) *Ben Casey*.

Theme from *Bonnie and Clyde*, *see* **The Ballad of Bonnie and Clyde**

Theme from *Brideshead Revisited*, *see* **Brideshead Revisited**

Theme from *Butterfield 8*, *see* **Gloria**

Theme from *Caddyshack*, *see* **I'm Alright**

Theme from *Carnival*, *see* **Love Makes the World Go Round**

Theme from *Chariots of Fire*, *see* **Chariots of Fire**

Theme from *Dukes of Hazzard*, *see* **Dukes of Hazzard**

Theme from *Elvira Madigan*, *see* **Elvira Madigan**

Theme from *Exodus*, *see* **Exodus**

Theme from *Flame Trees of Thika*, *see* **Flame Trees of Thika**

Theme from *Flashdance*, *see* **Flashdance**

Theme from *Footloose*, *see* **Footloose**

Theme from *Gandhi*, *see* **For All Mankind**

Theme from *Ghostbusters*, *see* **Ghostbusters**

Theme from *Goldfinger*, *see* **Goldfinger**

Theme from *Greatest American Hero*, *see* **Greatest American Hero**

Theme from *Harry's Game*, *see* **Harry's Game**

Theme from *High Noon*, *see* **High Noon**

Theme from *Ice Castles* (Through the Eyes of Love) 1979 w.m. Carol Bayer Sager, Marvin Hamlisch. (F) *Ice Castles*.

Theme from *Jewel in the Crown*, *see* **Jewel in the Crown**

Theme from *La Strada*, *see* **La Strada**

Theme from *Lady Sings the Blues*, *see* **Happy**

Theme from *Lawrence of Arabia*, *see* **Lawrence of Arabia**

Theme from *Legal Eagles*, *see* **Love Touch**

Theme from *Love Story*, *see* **Love Story**

Theme from *Mahogany*, *see* **Do You Know Where You're Going To**

Theme from *Miami Vice*, *see* **Miami Vice**

Theme from *Midnight Cowboy*, *see* **Everybody's Talkin'**

Theme from *Million Dollar Movie*, *see* **Tara's Theme**

Theme from *Mondo Cane*, *see* **More**

Theme from *Murder on the Orient Express*, *see* **Murder on the Orient Express**

Theme from *Out of Africa*, *see* **Out of Africa**

Theme from *Peyton Place* 1958 w.m. Paul Francis Webster, Franz Waxman. Based on the traditional American folksong ''Shenandoah.'' (TV) *Peyton Place*. Mia Farrow appeared in *Peyton Place*.

Theme from *Picnic*, *see* **Picnic**

Theme from *Raiders of the Lost Ark*, *see* **(Theme from) Raiders of the Lost Ark**

Theme from *Rocky*, *see* **Gonna Fly Now**

Theme from *Shaft*, *see* **Shaft**

Theme from *Short Circuit*, *see* **Who's Johnny**

Theme from *Spellbound*, *see* **Spellbound**

Theme from *Star Wars*, *see* **Star Wars**

Theme from *Summer of '42*, *see* **The Summer Knows**

Theme from *S.W.A.T.* 1976 m. Jack Elliott. (TV) *S.W.A.T.*

Theme from *The Apartment*, *see* **The Apartment**

Theme from *The Bad and the Beautiful*, *see* **The Bad and the Beautiful**

Theme from *The Eleventh Hour* 1962 m. Harry Sukman. (TV) *The Eleventh Hour*.

Theme from *The Empire Strikes Back*, *see* **The Empire Strikes Back**

Theme from *The French Lieutenant's Woman*, *see* **The French Lieutenant's Woman**

Theme from *The Godfather, see* **The Godfather**

Theme from *The Godfather Part II, see* **The Godfather Part II**

Theme from *The Karate Kid Part II, see* **Glory of Love**

Theme from *The Late Show, see* **The Syncopated Clock**

Theme from *The Odd Couple, see* **The Odd Couple**

Theme from *The Persuaders, see* **The Persuaders**

Theme from *The Pink Panther, see* **The Pink Panther**

Theme from *The Poseidon Adventure, see* **The Morning After**

Theme from *The Rose, see* **The Rose**

Theme from *The Thomas Crown Affair, see* **The Windmills of Your Mind**

Theme from *The Tonight Show, see* **Johnny's Theme**

Theme from *The Untouchables* 1960 m. Nelson Riddle. (TV) *The Untouchables.*

Theme from the Warsaw Concerto, *see* **Warsaw Concerto**

Theme from *The Way to the Stars, see* **The Way to the Stars**

Theme from *The Wonderful World of the Brothers Grimm* 1962 m. Bob Merrill. (F) *The Wonderful World of the Brothers Grimm.*

Theme from *The Three Penny Opera, see* **Mack the Knife**

Theme from *Thunderdome, see* **We Don't Need Another Hero**

Theme from *Two for the Road, see* **Two for the Road**

Theme from *2001: A Space Odyssey, see* **Also Sprach Zarathustra**

Theme from *Upstairs Downstairs, see* **Upstairs Downstairs**

Theme from *Valley of the Dolls, see* **Valley of the Dolls**

Theme from *Yanks, see* **(Theme from) Yanks**

Theme from *Zorba the Greek, see* **Zorba the Greek**

Then Came You 1974 w.m. Sherman Marshall, Phillip Pugh

Then He Kissed Me 1963 w.m. Phil Spector, Ellie Greenwich, Jeff Barry

(I Wanna Go Where You Go, Do What You Do) Then I'll Be Happy 1925 w. Sidney Clare, Lew Brown m. Cliff Friend

Then I'll Be Tired of You 1934 w.m. E.Y. Harburg, Arthur Schwartz

Then I'll Have Time for You 1928 w. B.G. DeSylva, Lew Brown m. Ray Henderson. (MT) *Follow Thru.*

Then You May Take Me to the Fair 1960 w. Alan Jay Lerner m. Frederick Loewe. (MT) *Camelot.* (MF) *Camelot.* Julie Andrews appeared in the stage production of *Camelot.* Vanessa Redgrave appeared in the film production of *Camelot.*

Then You'll Remember Me 1843 w. Alfred Bunn m. Michael William Balfe. (MT) *The Bohemian Girl.*

There Are Angels Outside Heaven 1943 w.m. Frederick Tysh, Richard Tauber, Walter Ellis. (MT) *Old Chelsea.* Carole Lynn and Richard Tauber appeared in *Old Chelsea.*

There Are Fairies at the Bottom of Our Garden 1917 w.m. Liza Lehmann. Theme song of Beatrice Lillie.

There Are Such Things 1942 w.m. Stanley Adams, Abel Baer, George W. Meyer

There But For You Go I 1947 w. Alan Jay Lerner m. Frederick Loewe. (MT) *Brigadoon.* (MF) *Brigadoon.* David Brooks and Marion Bell appeared in the stage production of *Brigadoon.* Gene Kelly and Cyd Charisse appeared in the film production of *Brigadoon.*

There Goes My Baby 1959 w.m. Benjamin Nelson, Lover Patterson, George Teadwell, Jerry Leiber, Mike Stoller. This song was popularly revived in 1985.

There Goes My Everything 1967 w.m. Dallas Frazier

There Goes My Heart 1934 w. Benny Davis m. Abner Silver

There Goes My Lover 1958 w.m. Leonard Taylor, Harold Shaper. Ivor Novello Award winner 1958.

There Goes That Song Again 1944 w. Sammy Cahn m. Jule Styne. (MF) *Carolina Blues.* Kay Kyser, Ann Miller, and Victor Moore appeared in *Carolina Blues.*

There I Go 1940 w. Hy Zaret m. Irving Weiser

There Is a Green Hill Far Away 1871 w. Mrs. Cecil Frances Alexander (Humphreys) m. Charles Gounod. The words to this song have been incorrectly attributed to Henry Wadsworth Longfellow.

There Is a Tavern in the Town 1883 w.m. anon.; erroneously credited to William H. Hills. Loosely based on a Cornish folksong and the "Butcher Boy."

One of the popular standard college songs of the Ivy League colleges.

There Is No Christmas Like a Home Christmas 1951 w.m. Mickey J. Addy, Carl Sigman

There Is No Death 1919 w. Gordon Johnstone m. Geoffrey O'Hara

There Is No Greater Love 1936 w. Marty Symes m. Isham Jones. Based on a theme from Tchaikovsky's Concerto no. 1.

There Is Nothin' Like a Dame 1949 w. Oscar Hammerstein II m. Richard Rodgers. (MT) *South Pacific.* (MF) *South Pacific.* Mary Martin appeared in the stage production of *South Pacific.* Mitzi Gaynor appeared in the film production of *South Pacific.*

There Isn't Any Limit to My Love 1936 w.m. Maurice Sigler, Al Hoffman, Al Goodhart. (MF) *This'll Make You Whistle.* Jack Buchanan appeared in *This'll Make You Whistle.*

There! I've Said It Again 1941 w.m. Redd Evans, Dave Mann. This song was most popular in 1945, and revived in 1947 and 1964.

There Must Be a Way 1945 w.m. sammy Gallop, David Saxon, Robert S. Cook

There Must Be Something Better Than Love 1950 w. Dorothy Fields m. Morton Gould. (MT) *Arms and the Girl.* Pearl Bailey and Nanette Fabray appeared in *Arms and the Girl.*

There Never Was a Girl Like You 1907 w. Harry H. Williams m. Egbert Van Alstyne

There Once Was an Owl 1904 w. Harry B. Smith m. Victor Herbert. (MT) *Babette.* (MF) *The Great Victor Herbert.* Mary Martin and Allan Jones appeared in *The Great Victor Herbert.*

There Ought To Be a Moonlight Saving Time, *see* **Moonlight Saving Time**

There Was an Old Woman Who Lived in a Shoe, *see* **Mother Goose's Melodies**

There Will Never Be Another You   1942   w. Mack Gordon m. Harry Warren. (MF) *Iceland.* (MF) *I'll Get By.* Sonja Henie and John Payne appeared in *Iceland.* Dennis Day and June Haver appeared in *I'll Get By.* See also Part I, 1942.

There You Are Then   1921   w.m. L. Silberman

There'll Always Be an England   1939   w.m. Ross Parker, Hughie Charles

There'll Be a Hot Time for the Old Men When the Young Men Go to War   1918   w.m. Grant Clarke, George W. Meyer

There'll Be a Hot Time in the Old Town Tonight, *see* **A Hot Time in the Old Town**

There'll Be Bluebirds over the White Cliffs of Dover, *see* **The White Cliffs of Dover**

There'll Be No Teardrops Tonight   1949   w.m. Hank Williams

There'll Be Sad Songs (To Make You Cry)   1986   w.m. Wayne Brath Waite, Barry Eastmond, Billy Ocean

There'll Be Some Changes Made   1921   w.m. W. Benton Overstreet, Billy Higgins. (MT) *Bubbling Brown Sugar.* (F) *Designing Woman.* (F) *The Blue Veil.* Avon Long and Josephine Premice appeared in *Bubbling Brown Sugar.* Dolores Gray and Gregory Peck appeared in *Designing Woman.* Charles Laughton and Joan Blondell appeared in *The Blue Veil.* This song was popularly revied in 1929, 1941, and 1947.

There'll Come a Time   1895   w.m. Charles K. Harris

There'll Come a Time   1911   w.m. Shelton Brooks

There's a Boat Dat's Leavin' Soon for New York   1935   w. Ira Gershwin   m. George Gershwin. (MT) *Porgy and Bess.* (MF) *Porgy and Bess.* Todd Duncan, Anne Wiggins Brown, and Warren Coleman appeared in the original stage production of *Porgy and Bess.* Sammy Davis, Jr., and Sidney Poitier appeared in the film production of *Porgy and Bess.*

There's a Boy Coming Home on Leave   1940   w.m. Jimmy Kennedy

There's a Broken Heart for Every Light on Broadway   1915   w. Howard Johnson   m. Fred Fisher. (MF) *Oh You Beautiful Doll.* June Haver appeared in *Oh You Beautiful Doll,* biopic of composer Fred Fisher.

There's a Church in the Valley by the Wildwood, *see* **The Little Brown Church**

There's a Cradle in Caroline   1927   w. Sam M. Lewis, Joe Young   m. Fred E. Ahlert. (MF) *Stepping High.*

There's a Dixie Girl Who's Longing for a Yankee Doodle Boy   1911   w. Robert F. Roden   m. George W. Meyer

There's a Garden in Old Italy   1916   w. Joseph McCarthy m. Jack Glogau

There's a Girl in the Heart of Maryland (With a Heart That Belongs to Me)   1913   w. Ballard MacDonald   m. Harry Carroll

There's a Girl in This World for Every Boy and a Boy for Every Girl   1907   w. Will D. Cobb   m. Ted Snyder

There's a Gold Mine in the Sky   1937   w.m. Charles Kenny, Nick Kenny. (F) *Gold Mine in the Sky.* (F) *An Affair To Remember.* Gene Autry appeared in *Gold Mine in the Sky.* Cary Grant and Deborah Kerr appeared in *An Affair To Remember.*

There's a Good Time Coming   1930   w.m. Ralph Butler, Raymond Wallace.

There's a Great Day Coming, Mañana   1940   w. E.Y. Harburg   m. Burton Lane. (MT) *Hold On to Your Hats.* Al Jolson, Martha Raye, and Jack Whiting appeared in *Hold On to Your Hats.*

There's a Kind of Hush   1967   w.m. Reed Stephens, Geoff Stephens

There's a Land of Begin Again   1942   w.m. Ross Parker, Hugh Charles

There's a Light in Your Eyes   1918   w. P.G. Wodehouse m. Ivan Caryll. (MT) *The Girl Behind the Gun.*

There's a Little Bit of Bad in Every Good Little Girl   1916 w. Grant Clarke   m. Fred Fisher

There's a Little Lane Without a Turning on the Way to Home Sweet Home   1915   w. Sam M. Lewis   m. George W. Meyer

There's a Little Spark of Love Still Burning   1914   w. Joe McCarthy   m. Fred Fisher

There's a Little Star Shining for You   1897   w.m. James Thornton

There's a Long, Long Trail   1913   w. Stoddard King   m. Zo Elliott. This song was popular with the British troops during World War I.

There's a Lovely Lake in London   1935   w.m. Tolchard Evans, Stanley Damerell, Ralph Butler

There's a Lull in My Life   1937   w. Mack Gordon   m. Harry Revel. (MF) *Wake Up and Live.* Walter Winchell and Alice Faye appeared in *Wake Up and Live.*

There's a Million Girlies Lonesome Tonight, and Still I'm All Alone   1921   w. William Tracey, Alfred Jentes, Murray Roth   m. James F. Hanley

There's a New World   1969   w.m. Michael Carr

There's a Place for Us, *see* **Somewhere**

There's a Quaker Down in Quaker Town   1916   w. David Berg   m. Alfred Solman

There's a Rainbow Round My Shoulder   1928   w.m. Al Jolson, Billy Rose, Dave Dreyer. (MF) *The Singing Fool.* (MF) *The Jolson Story.* (MF) *Rainbow Round My Shoulder.* Al Jolson appeared in *The Singing Fool.* Larry Parks appeared in *The Jolson Story.* Frankie Laine appeared in *Rainbow Round My Shoulder.*

There's a Small Hotel   1936   w. Lorenz Hart   m. Richard Rodgers. (MT) *On Your Toes.* (MF) *On Your Toes.* (MF) *Words and Music.* (MF) *Pal Joey.* Ray Bolger and Luella Gear appeared in the stage production of *On Your Toes.* Zorina and Eddie Albert appeared in the film production of *On Your Toes.* Judy Garland, Gene Kelly, and Mickey Rooney appeared in *Words and Music,* biopic of song writers Rodgers and Hart. Frank Sinatra appeared in *Pal Joey.* The lyrics for this song were written by Larry Hart in the men's room of the Shubert Theatre in Boston.

There's a Star Spangled Banner Waving Somewhere 1942 w.m. Paul Roberts, Shelby Darnell

There's a Tavern in the Town, *see* **There Is a Tavern in the Town**

There's Always Something There To Remind Me 1964 w. Hal David m. Burt Bacharach. This song was popularly revived in 1968.

There's Always Tomorrow 1931 w.m. Phil Charig, Vivian Ellis, Douglas Furber. (MT) *Stand Up and Sing.* Elsie Randolph and Jack Buchanan appeared in *Stand Up and Sing.*

There's an Old Spinning Wheel, *see* **The Old Spinning Wheel**

There's Danger in Your Eyes, Cherie 1929 w.m. Harry Richman, Jack Meskill, Peter Wendling. (MF) *Puttin' On the Ritz.* (MF) *Rich, Young and Pretty.* Harry Richman and Joan Bennett appeared in *Puttin' On the Ritz.* Jane Powell and Vic Damone appeared in *Rich, Young and Pretty.*

There's Egypt in Your Dreamy Eyes 1917 w. Fleta Jan Brown m. Herbert Spencer

There's Enough To Go Around 1970 w. Alan Bergman, Marilyn Bergman m. Henry Mancini. (F) *Gaily Gaily.*

(There's Something Nice About Everyone But) There's Everything Nice About You 1927 w. Arthur Terker, Alfred Bryan m. Pete Wendling

There's Gonna Be a Great Day, *see* **Great Day**

There's Life in the Old Dog Yet 1918 w. P.G. Wodehouse m. Ivan Caryll. (MT) *The Girl Behind the Gun.*

There's Music in the Air 1854 w. Frances Jane Crosby (Mrs. Alexander Van Alstyne) m. George Frederick Root. The melody of this song inspired a phrase in "Aloha Oe." This song was later used by Princeton University in their "Whoop'er Up" song ("Rah!Rah!Rah! Siss Boom Ah!").

There's Never Been Anyone Else But You 1956 w.m. Paul Francis Webster, Dimitri Tiomkin

There's No Business Like Show Business 1946 w.m. Irving Berlin. (MT) *Annie Get Your Gun.* (MF) *Annie Get Your Gun.* (MF) *There's No Business Like Show Business.* Ethel Merman belted out this song in the stage production of *Annie Get Your Gun* and the film production *There's No Business Like Show Business.* Betty Hutton appeared in the film production of *Annie Get Your Gun.* Theme song of Ethel Merman.

There's No Gettin' Over Me, *see* **No Gettin' Over Me**

There's No Holding Me 1946 w. Ira Gershwin m. Arthur Schwartz. (MT) *Park Avenue.* Raymond Walburn and Leonora Corbett appeared in *Park Avenue.*

There's No North or South Today 1901 w.m. Paul Dresser

There's No One Quite Like Grandma 1981 w.m. Gordon Lorenz. Ivor Novello Award winner 1980–81.

There's No Other Love 1960 new w. Jimmy Kennedy m. Lester O'Keefe, Gus Haenschen. Based on "Rosita" of 1923.

There's No Place Like Home, *see* **Home Sweet Home**

There's No Place Like Home for the Holidays, *see* **Home for the Holidays**

There's No Tomorrow 1949 w.m. Al Hoffman, Leo Corday, Leon Carr. (MF) *Two Tickets to Broadway.* Janet Leigh, Tony Martin, and Ann Miller appeared in *Two Tickets to Broadway.* Based on deCapua's "O Sole Mio" of 1899. Theme song of Tony Martin.

There's No Two Ways About Love 1943 w.m. James P. Johnson, Ted Keohler, Irving Mills. (MF) *Stormy Weather.* Lena Horne and "Fats" Waller appeared in *Stormy Weather.*

There's No You 1944 w.m. Harold S. Hopper, Thomas M. Adair

There's Nothing True But Heaven 1829 w. Thomas Moore m. Oliver Shaw

There's One Wide River to Cross, or, **Noah's Ark** c.1865 w.m. traditional black American spiritual

There's Something About a Rose (That Reminds Me of You) 1928 w. Irving Kahal, Francis Wheeler m. Sammy Fain

There's Something About a Solider 1933 w.m. Noel Gay. (MF) *Me and Marlborough.* Cicely Courtneidge appeared in *Me and Marlborough.*

There's Something About a Uniform 1908 w.m. George M. Cohan. (MT) *The Man Who Owns Broadway.*

There's Something Nice About Everyone But There's Everything Nice About You, *see* **There's Everything Nice About You**

There's Where My Heart Is Tonight 1899 w.m. Paul Dresser

There's Yes, Yes, in Your Eyes 1924 w. Joseph H. Santley m. Cliff Friend. Based on Wolf's "Without You the World Doesn't Seem the Same."

These Are My Mountains 1966 w.m. James Copeland

These Boots Are Made for Walking 1966 w.m. Lee Hazlewood

These Dreams 1986 w.m. Martin Page, Bernie Taupin

These Foolish Things (Remind Me of You) 1936 w. Holt Marvell m. Jack Strachey, Harry Link. (MT) *Spread It Abroad.* (MF) *Ghost Catchers.* Dorothy Dickson appeared in *Spread It Abroad.* Gloria Jean and Leo Carrillo appeared in *Ghost Catchers.* This song was popularly revived in 1945.

These Things I Offer You (for a Lifetime) 1951 w. Morty Nevins m. Bennie Benjamin, George Weiss

They All Laughed 1937 w. Ira Gershwin m. George Gershwin. (MF) *Shall We Dance.* Fred Astaire and Ginger Rogers appeared in *Shall We Dance.*

They Always Pick on Me 1911 w. Stanley Murphy m. Harry Von Tilzer

They Call Her Frivolous Sal, *see* **My Gal Sal**

They Call the Wind Maria 1951 w. Alan Jay Lerner m. Frederick Loewe. (MT) *Paint Your Wagon.* (MF) *Paint Your Wagon.* Lee Marvin appeared in the film production of *Paint Your Wagon.*

They Can't Take That Away from Me 1937 w. Ira Gershwin m. George Gershwin. (MF) *Shall We Dance.* (MF) *The Barkleys of Broadway.* Fred Astaire, Ginger Rogers, and Billie Burke appeared both in *Shall We Dance* and *The Barkleys of Broadway.*

(When) They Cut Down the Old Pine Tree 1929 w.m. William Raskin, Edward Eliscu, George Brown. (MF) *King of the Cowboys.* Roy Rogers and Smiley Burnette appeared in *King of the Cowboys*. This song was popularly revived in 1942.

They Didn't Believe Me 1914 w. Herbert Reynolds m. Jerome Kern. (MT) *The Girl from Utah*. (MT) *Tonight's the Night*. (MF) *Till the Clouds Roll By*. (MF) *That Midnight Kiss*. Julia Sanderson and Donald Brian appeared in *The Girl from Utah*. George Grossmith and Haidee de Rance appeared in *Tonight's the Night*. Judy Garland, Frank Sinatra, and June Allyson appeared in *Till the Clouds Roll By*, biopic of composer Jerome Kern. Mario Lanza and Kathryn Grayson appeared in *That Midnight Kiss*.

They Don't Know 1984 w.m. Kirsty MacColl

They Go Wild Simply Wild over Me 1917 w. Joe McCarthy m. Fred Fisher

They Gotta Quit Kickin' My Dog (Dawg) **Around, or, The Missouri Houn' Dawg Song** 1912 w. Webb M. Oungst m. Cy Perkins. This song was used by Senator Champ Clark, a Missouri Democrat, in his Presidential nomination campaign against Woodrow Wilson.

They Just Can't Stop It (The Games People Play) 1975 w.m. Joseph Jefferson, Bruce Hawes, Charles Simmons

They Kissed, I Saw Them Do It 1889 w.m. Charles Beach Hawley

They Never Tell All What They Know 1893 w. Edward Harrigan m. David Braham

They Say 1938 w. Edward Heyman m. Paul Mann, Stephan Weiss

They Say It's Wonderful 1946 w.m. Irving Berlin. (MT) *Annie Get Your Gun*. (MF) *Annie Get Your Gun*. Ethel Merman and Ray Middleton appeared in the stage production of *Annie Get Your Gun*. Betty Hutton and Howard Keel appeared in the film production of *Annie Get Your Gun*.

They Were All Out of Step But Jim 1918 w.m. Irving Berlin

They Were Doing the Mambo 1954 w.m. Sonny Burke, Don Raye

They're All Sweeties 1919 w. Andrew B. Sterling m. Harry Von Tilzer

They're Either Too Young or Too Old 1943 w. Frank Loesser m. Arthur Schwartz. (MF) *Thank Your Lucky Stars*. (MF) *With a Song in My Heart*. Eddie Cantor and Bette Davis appeared in *Thank Your Lucky Stars*. Susan Hayward appeared in *With a Song in My Heart*, biopic of singer Jane Froman.

They're Playing Our Song 1979 w. Carole Bayer Sager m. Marvin Hamlisch. (MT) *They're Playing Our Song*. Robert Klein and Lucie Arnaz appeared in *They're Playing Our Song*.

They're Wearing 'Em Higher in Hawaii 1916 w. Joe Goodwin m. Halsey K. Mohr. (MF) *Show Business*.

(Love Is) Thicker Than Water 1977 w.m. Barry Gibb, Andy Gibb

Thine Alone 1917 w. Henry Blossom m. Victor Herbert. (MT) *Eileen*. (MF) *The Great Victor Herbert*. Walter Scanlan and Grace Breen appeared in *Eileen*. Mary Martin and Allan Jones appeared in *The Great Victor Herbert*. After destruction by fire of the theatre, scenery, and costumes for

Hearts of Erin while it was still in rehearsal in Toronto, the producers, fearing arson, changed the name of the show to *Eileen* for its New York opening.

Thing, The 1950 w.m. Charles Randolph Green. (F) *The Wild Blue Yonder*. Phil Harris appeared in *The Wild Blue Yonder*.

Things Are Looking Up 1934 w.m. Noel Gay. (MF) *Things Are Looking Up*. Cicely Courtneidge appeared in *Things Are Looking Up*.

Things Are Looking Up 1937 w. Ira Gershwin m. George Gershwin. (MF) *Damsel in Distress*. Fred Astaire, Joan Fontaine, and Burns and Allen appeared in *Damsel in Distress*.

Things Can Only Get Better 1985 w.m. Howard Jones

Things Go Better with Coke 1963 w.m. Bill Backer. This song was written for a Coca-Cola commercial promotion campaign.

Things I Love, The 1941 w.m. Lew Harris, Harold Barlow. (F) *I Wake Up Screaming*. Betty Grable and Victor Mature appeared in *I Wake Up Screaming*. Based on Tchaikovsky's "Melodie," op.24, no.3.

Things I Want, The 1937 w. Oscar Hammerstein II m. Jerome Kern. (MF) *High, Wide and Handsome*. Irene Dunne and Randolph Scott appeared in *High, Wide and Handsome*.

Things We Did Last Summer, The 1946 w. Sammy Cahn m. Jule Styne

Things We Do for Love, The 1977 w.m. Graham Gouldman, Eric Stewart

Think About Me 1980 w.m.. Christine McVie

Think of Laura 1984 w.m. Christopher Cross

Thinking of You 1927 w. Bert Kalmar m. Harry Ruby. (MT) *Five O'Clock Girl*. (MF) *Three Little Words*. Mary Eaton and Oscar Shaw appeared in *Five O'Clock Girl*. Fred Astaire, Red Skelton, and Debbie Reynolds appeared in *Three Little Words*, biopic of song writers Bert Kalmar and Harry Ruby. This song was popularly revived in 1950.

Third Man Theme, The, or, The Harry Lime Theme 1950 m. Anton Karas. (F) *The Third Man*. Orson Wells and Joseph Cotten appeared in *The Third Man*. Based on an eight-measure melody found by Karas in a zither étude book.

This Can't Be Love 1938 w. Lorenz Hart m. Richard Rodgers. (MT) *The Boys from Syracuse*. (MT) *Funny Side Up*. (MT) *Up and Doing*. (MF) *The Boys from Syracuse*. (MF) *Words and Music*. Eddie Albert and Teddy Hart appeared in the stage production of *The Boys from Syracuse*. Patricia Burke appeared in *Up and Doing*. Allan Jones and Martha Raye appeared in the film production of *The Boys from Syracuse*. Mickey Rooney, Judy Garland, and Gene Kelly appeared in *Words and Music*, biopic of composers Rodgers and Hart.

This Could Be the Start of Something (Big) 1956 w.m. Steve Allen

This Diamond Ring 1965 w.m. Bob Brass, Irwin Levine, Al Kooper

This Guy's in Love with You 1968 w. Hal David m. Burt Bacharach

This Heart of Mine 1946 w.m. Arthur Freed, Harry Warren. (MF) *Ziegfeld Follies*. Fred Astaire, Fanny Brice, Lena Horne, and Lucille Ball appeared in *Ziegfeld Follies*.

This Is a Lovely Way To Spend an Evening, *see* **A Lovely Way To Spend an Evening**

This Is All I Ask 1958 w.m. Gordon Jenkins

This Is Alwlays 1946 w. Mack Gordon m. Harry Warren. (MF) *Three Little Girls in Blue*. June Haver, George Montgomery, and Vivian Blaine appeared in *Three Little Girls in Blue*.

This Is God's Country, *see* God's Country

This Is It 1939 w. Dorothy Fields m. Arthur Schwartz. (MT) *Stars in Your Eyes*. Ethel Merman, Jimmy Durante, and Mildred Natwick appeared in *Stars in Your Eyes*.

This Is Love 1979 w.m. Madeline Sunshine

This Is My Country 1940 w. Don Raye m. Al Jacobs

This Is My Love Parade, *see* **My Love Parade**

This Is My Lovely Day 1947 w.m. Vivian Ellis. (MT) *Bless the Bride*. George Guetary appeared in *Bless the Bride*.

This Is My Mother's Day 1948 w.m. Billy Reid

This Is My Song 1967 w.m. Charles Chaplin. Ivor Novello Award winner 1967–68.

This Is My Song Theme 1950 w.m. Dick Charles. Theme song of Patti Page.

This Is New 1941 w. Ira Gershwin m. Kurt Weill. (MT) *Lady in the Dark*. (MF) *Lady in the Dark*. Gertrude Lawrence appeared in the stage production of *Lady in the Dark*. Ginger Rogers appeared in the film production of *Lady in the Dark*.

This Is No Laughing Matter 1941 w.m. Al Frisch, Buddy Kaye

This Is Romance 1933 w. Edward Heyman m. Vernon Duke

This Is the Army Mister Jones 1942 w.m. Irving Berlin. (MT) *This Is the Army*. (MF) *This Is the Army*. Kate Smith and Ronald Reagan appeared in the film production of *This Is the Army*.

This Is the Life 1914 w.m. Irving Berlin

This Is the Missus 1931 w. B.G. DeSylva, Lew Brown m. Ray Henderson. (MT) *George White's Scandals of 1931 (Eleventh Edition)*. Ethel Merman and Ray Bolger appeared in *George White's Scandals of 1931*.

This Is the Moment 1948 w. Leo Robin m. Frederick Hollander. (MF) *That Lady in Ermine*. Betty Grable and Douglas Fairbanks, Jr. appeared in *That Lady in Ermine*.

This Is the Mrs., *see* **This Is the Missus**

This Is the Story of a Starry Night, *see* **The Story of a Starry Night**

This Is Worth Fighting For 1942 w.m. Sammy Stept, Edgar De Lange. (MF) *When Johnny Comes Marching Home*. Allan Jones and Donald O'Connor appeared in *When Johnny Comes Marching Home*.

This Is Your Life 1960 w.m. Joseph S. Dubin

This Little Piggie Went to Market 1933 w.m. Sam Coslow, Harold Lewis

This Love of Mine 1941 w. Frank Sinatra m. Sol Parker, Henry Sanicola

This Masquerade 1976 w.m. Leon Russell. Grammy Award winner 1976.

This Nearly Was Mine 1949 w. Oscar Hammerstein II m. Richard Rodgers. (MT) *South Pacific*. (MF) *South Pacific*. Mary Martin appeared in the stage production of *South Pacific*. Mitzi Gaynor appeared in the film production of *South Pacific*.

This Night Won't Last Forever 1979 w.m. Roy Freirich, Bill La Bounty

This Old Man, or, **The Children's Marching Song** (Nick, Nack, Paddy Whack) 1959 w.m. anon.; adapted Malcolm Arnold. (F) *The Inn of the Sixth Happiness*. Ingrid Bergman appeared in *The Inn of the Sixth Happiness*. Based on a traditional nursery song.

This Ole House 1954 w.m. Stuart Hamblen

This Time I'm in It for Love 1978 w.m. Steve Pippin, Larry Keith

This Time It's Love 1935 w. Sam M. Lewis m. J. Fred Coots

This Time the Dream's on Me 1941 w. Johnny Mercer m. Harold Arlen. (MF) *Blues in the Night*. Priscilla Lane and Richard Whorf appeared in *Blues in the Night*.

This Was a Real Nice Clambake 1945 w. Oscar Hammerstein II m. Richard Rodgers. (MT) *Carousel*. (MF) *Carousel*. Jan Clayton and John Raitt appeared in the stage production of *Carousel*. Gordon MacRae and Shirley Jones appeared in the film production of *Carousel*.

This Will Be (An Everlasting Love) 1975 w.m. Chuck Jackson, Marvin Yancy

This Woman 1984 w.m. Albhy Galuten, Barry Gibb

This Year's Kisses 1937 w.m. Irving Berlin. (MF) *On the Avenue*. Dick Powell and Alice Faye appeared in *On the Avenue*.

This'll Make You Whistle 1936 w.m. Maurice Sigler, Al Hoffman, Al Goodhart. (MT) *This'll Make You Whistle*. (MF) *This'll Make You Whistle*. Jack Buchanan and Elsie Randolph appeared in both the stage and film productions of *This'll Make You Whistle*.

Thoroughly Modern Millie 1967 w.m. Sammy Cahn, James Van Heusen. (MF) *Thoroughly Modern Millie*. Julie Andrews and Beatrice Lillie appeared in *Thoroughly Modern Millie*.

Those Lazy Hazy Crazy Days of Summer 1963 w.m. Hans Carste, Charles Tobias

Those Wedding Bells Shall Not Ring Out 1896 w.m. Monroe H. Rosenfeld. Based on Gussie Davis's "Fatal Wedding." On the cover to the sheet music of this song was the following: "*Note*: The incidents in this song are based upon a tragedy which occurred in a western city. The author does not seek to glorify the event. He has simply tried to portray the tragedy in a simple tale, which in its truth to nature may serve a useful moral and an interesting dramatic episode."

Those Were the Days, or, **Theme from** *All in the Family* 1971 w.m. Charles Strouse, Lee Adams. (TV) *All in the Family*. Carroll O'Connor and Jean Stapleton appeared in *All in the Family*.

Those Were the Days 1968 w.m. Gene Raskin. Based on a traditional Eastern European tune.

Thou Art Gone from My Gaze 1852 w.m. George Linley

Thou Art So Near and Yet So Far 1858 w.m. Alexander Reichardt. From the German "Du Bist Mir Nah und Doch So Fern."

Thou Swell 1927 w. Lorenz Hart m. Richard Rodgers. (MT) *A Connecticut Yankee.* (MT) *A Yankee at the Court of King Arthur.* (MF) *A Connecticut Yankee* (1931). (MF) *Words and Music.* William Gaxton and William Norris appeared in the stage production of *A Connecticut Yankee.* Maureen O'Sullivan and Will Rogers appeared in the 1931 film production of *A Connecticut Yankee.* Mickey Rooney, Judy Garland, and Gene Kelly appeared in *Words and Music,* biopic of song writers Rodgers and Hart.

Though Your Sins Be as Scarlet 1887 w. Frances Jane Crosby (Mrs. Alexander Van Alstyne) m. William Howard Doane

Thousand and One Nights, A 1871 m. Johann Strauss. From the German "Tausend und Eine Nacht," op.346.

Three Bells, The, *see* **While the Angelus Was Ringing**

Three Blind Mice 1609 w.m. anon. The earliest known words and music were published in 1609, making this probably the earliest printed popular secular, i.e. nonreligious, song.

Three Brothers 1957 w.m. Paddy Roberts. Ivor Novello Award winner 1957.

Three Caballeros, The 1944 w.m. Ray Gilbert, Manuel Esperon. (MF) *The Three Caballeros.*

Three Coins in the Fountain 1954 w. Sammy Cahn m. Jule Styne. (F) *Three Coins in the Fountain.* Clifton Webb and Louis Jourdan appeared in *Three Coins in the Fountain.* Academy Award winner 1954.

Three-Cornered Hat, The 1921 m. Manuel de Falla

Three for Jack 1904 w. Frederick Edward Weatherly m. W.H. Squire

Three Kings of Orient, *see* **We Three Kings of Orient**

Three Little Fishes 1939 w.m. Saxie Dowell

Three Little Kittens, *see* **Mother Goose's Melodies**

Three Little Sisters 1942 w.m. Irving Taylor, Vic Mizzy. (MF) *Private Buckaroo.* The Andrews Sisters and Joe E. Lewis appeared in *Private Buckaroo.*

Three Little Words 1930 w. Harry Ruby m. Bert Kalmar. (MT) *Folly To Be Wise.* (MF) *Check and Double Check.* (MF) *Three Little Words.* Amos and Andy appeared in *Check and Double Check.* Fred Astaire and Red Skelton appeared in *Three Little Words,* biopic of song writers Bert Kalmar and Harry Ruby.

Three O'Clock in the Morning 1921 w. Dorothy Terris (Theodora Morse) m. Julian Robeldo. (MF) *Margie* (MF) *Belles on Their Toes.* (MF) *The Eddy Duchin Story.* Jeanne Crain and Glenn Langan appeared in *Margie.* Myrna Loy appeared in *Belles on their Toes.* The Westminster Chimes are heard in this song. See "Westminster Chimes." See also Part I, 1914.

Three on a Match 1932 w. Raymond B. Egan m. Ted Fiorito. (MF) *Blondie of the Follies.* Marion Davies, Jimmy Durante, and Zasu Pitts appeared in *Blondie of the Follies.*

Three Shades of Blue 1927 m. Ferde Grofé. This work included "Indigo," "Alice Blue," and "Heliotrope."

Three Stars Will Shine Tonight, *see* **The Doctor Kildare Theme**

Three Times a Lady 1984 w.m. Lionel Richie

Three Times in Love 1980 w.m. Tommy James, Ronald Serota

Three Wonderful Letters from Home 1918 w. Joe Goodwin, Ballard MacDonald m. James F. Hanley

Three's a Crowd 1932 w. Al Dubin, Irving Kahal m. Harry Warren. (MF) *The Crooner.* Rudy Vallee and his Connecticut Yankees appeared in *The Crooner.*

Thrill Is Gone, The 1931 w. B.G. DeSylva, Lew Brown m. Ray Henderson. (MT) *George White's Scandals of 1913 (Eleventh Edition).* (MF) *The Best Things in Life Are Free.* Ethel Merman and Ray Bolger appeared in *George White's Scandals of 1931.* Gordon MacRae, Dan Dailey, and Ernest Borgnine appeared in *The Best Things in Life Are Free,* biopic of song writers DeSylva, Brown, and Henderson.

Thriller 1984 w.m. Rodney Temperton

Through 1929 w.m. James V. Monaco

Through a Long and Sleepless Night 1949 w.m. Mack Gordon, Alfred Newman. (F) *Come to the Stable.* Loretta Young and Celeste Holm appeared in *Come to the Stable.*

Through a Thousand Dreams 1946 w. Leo Robin m. Arthur Schwartz. (MF) *The Time, the Place and the Girl.* Dennis Morgan and Jack Carson appeared in *The Time, the Place and the Girl.*

Through All the World, *see* **Wond'rous Love**

Through the Years 1931 w. Edward Heyman m. Vincent Youmans. (MT) *Through the Years.* (MF) *Smiling Through.* Natalie Hall and Michael Bartlett appeared in *Through the Years.*

Through the Years 1982 w.m. Steve Dorff, Marty Panzer

Throw Another Log on the Fire 1934 w.m. Charles Tobias, Jack Scholl, Ted Murry (Murray Mencher)

Throw Him Down McCloskey 1890 w.m. John W. Kelly. This song was popularly sung by Maggie Cline. Loosely based on Foster's "Oh! Susanna" of 1848. Theme song of Maggie Cline.

Throw Me a Kiss 1922 w.m. Louis A. Hirsch, Gene Buck, Dave Stamper, Maurice Yvain. (MT) *Ziegfeld Follies of 1922.*

Throw Me a Rose 1916 w. P.G. Wodehouse, M.E. Rourke m. Emmerich Kalman. (MT) *Miss Springtime.*

Throw Open Wide Your Window 1932 w.m. Hans May

Thumb Marks 1923 w. based on "Ballads of Immortality" m. John Barnes Wells

Thumbelina 1952 w.m. Frank Loesser. (MF) *Hans Christian Andersen.* Danny Kaye appeared in *Hans Christian Andersen.*

Thunder Island 1977 w.m. Jay Ferguson

Thunderbirds Theme 1965 w.m. Barry Gray

Thunderdome, *see* **We Don't Need Another Hero**

Thunderer, The 1889 m. John Philip Sousa

Thy Beaming Eyes 1890 w. William Henry Gardner m. Edward MacDowell

Thy Sentinel Am I 1889 w. Edward Oxenford m. Michael Watson

Ticket To Ride 1965 w.m. John Lennon, Paul McCartney. (MF) *Help!* The Beatles appeared in *Help!*

(Everybody Ought To Know How to Do) Tickle Toe, The 1917 w. Otto Harbach m. Louis A. Hirsch. (MT) *Going Up.* Henry de Bray and Marjorie Gordon appeared in the British production of *Going Up.*

Tico Tico 1944 Port.w. Aloysio Oliveira Eng.w. Ervin Drake m. Zequinha Abreu. (MF) *Saludos Amigos.* (MF) *Bathing Beauty.* (MF) *Copacabana.* (MF) *Club Havana.* (F) *It's a Pleasure.* (MF) *Kansas City Kitty.* Red Skelton and Esther Williams appeared in *Bathing Beauty.* Carmen Miranda appeared in *Copacabana.* Joan Davis and Bob Crosby appeared in *Kansas City Kitty.*

Tide Is High, The 1981 w.m. John Holt

Tie a Yellow Ribbon Round the Ole Oak Tree 1973 w.m. Irwin Levine, L. Russell Brown

Tie Me Kangaroo Down Sport 1960 w.m. Rolf Harris

Tiger Feet 1975 w.m. Nicky Chinn, Mike Chapman. Ivor Novello Award winner 1974–75.

Tiger Rag 1917 w. Harry DeCosta m. Original Dixieland Jazz Band. (MF) *Is Everybody Happy.* (MF) *The Big Broadcast.* (MF) *Birth of the Blues.* (MF) *Has Anybody Seen My Gal.* (MF) *Night Club Girl.* Ted Lewis appeared in *Is Everybody Happy.* The Mills Brothers, Bing Crosby, and Kate Smith appeared in *The Big Broadcast.* Bing Crosby and Mary Martin appeared in *Birth of the Blues.* Rock Hudson appeared in *Has Anybody Seen My Gal.* Edward Norris and Vivian Austin appeared in *Nightclub Girl.* Possible claims to authorship have been assigned to "Jelly Roll" Morton, Jack Carey, and Ernest Miller. See also Part I, 1917.

Tiger Rose 1917 w.m. Gene Buck

Tiggerty Boo 1940 w.m. Hal Halifax

Tighten Up 1968 w.m. Billy H. Buttier, Archie Bell

Till 1957 w.m. Pierre Buisson, Charles Sananes, Carl Sigman

Till All Our Dreams Come True 1949 w.m. H.C. Bonocini, Desmond O'Connor

Till Eulenspiegel 1895 m. Richard Strauss. From the German "Till Eulenspiegels Lustige Streiche," op.28. This work was first performed on November 5, 1895, in Cologne.

Till I Wake 1903 w. Laurence Hope m. Amy Woodeforde-Finden. From "Four Indian Love Lyrics."

Till I Waltz Again with You 1953 w.m. Sidney Prosen

Till Stars Forget To Shine 1944 w.m. Joe Lubin, Sonny Miller, Hugh Charles

Till the Boys Come Home, *see* **Keep the Home Fires Burning**

Till ('Til) the Clouds Roll By 1917 w. Jerome Kern, Guy Bolton, P.G. Wodehouse m. Jerome Kern. (MT) *Oh, Boy!.* (MT) *Oh Joy.* (MF) *Till the Clouds Roll By* Marion Davies and Anna Wheaton appeared in *Oh, Boy!.* Beatrice Lillie and Tom Powers appeared in *Oh Joy.* June Allyson, Judy Gar-

land, and Frank Sinatra appeared in *Till the Clouds Roll By,* biopic of composer Jerome Kern. Based on a traditional Bohemian hymn. See also "Water Boy."

Till the End of Time 1945 w.m. Buddy Kaye, Ted Mossman. (F) *Till the End of Time.* Dorothy McGuire, Guy Madison, and Robert Mitchum appeared in *Till the End of Time.* Based on Chopin's Polonaise in A-Flat, op.53, no.6.

Till the Lights of London Shine Again 1940 w.m. Tommie Connor, Eddie Pola

Till the Real Thing Comes Along 1931 w. Mann Holiner, Sammy Cahn m. Alberta Nichols. (MT) *Rhapsody in Black.* Ethel Waters appeared in *Rhapsody in Black.*

Till the Sands of the Desert Grow Cold 1911 w. George Graff, Jr. m. Ernest R. Ball

Till Then 1933 w. Ira Gershwin m. George Gershwin

Till Then 1944 w.m. Eddie Seiler, Sol Marcus, Guy Wood. This song was also popular in 1946.

Till There Was You 1957 w.m. Meredith Willson. (MT) *The Music Man.* (MF) *The Music Man.* Robert Preston appeared in both the stage and film productions of *The Music Man.*

Till Tomorrow 1959 w. Sheldon Harnick m. Jerry Bock. (MT) *Fiorello!.*

Till We Meet Again 1918 w. Raymond B. Egan m. Richard A. Whiting. (MF) *On Moonlight Bay.* (MF) *The Eddy Duchin Story.* Doris Day and Gordon MacRae appeared in *On Moonlight Bay.*

Till We Two Are One 1954 w.m. Tom Glazer, Larry Martin, Billy Martin

Timbuctoo 1920 w.m. Bert Kalmar, Harry Ruby

Time 1981 w.m. Alan Parson, Eric Woolfson

Time (Clock of the Heart) 1983 w.m. Michael Craig, Boy George, Roy Hay, John Moss

Time After Time 1947 w. Sammy Cahn m. Jule Styne. (MF) *It Happened in Brooklyn.* Frank Sinatra, Katherine Grayson, and Jimmy Durante appeared in *It Happened in Brooklyn.* This song was popularly revived in 1966.

Time After Time 1984 Cyndi Lauper, Rob Hyman

Time and Tide (Theme from *Plague Dogs*) 1983 m. Alan Price. (F) *Plague Dogs.* Ivor Novello Award winner 1982–83.

Time Alone Will Tell 1948 w.m. Eve Lynd

Time and Love 1966 w.m. Laura Nyro. This song was most popular in 1969.

Time and the River 1960 w.m. Wally Gold, Aaron Schroeder

Time Don't Run Out on Me 1985 w.m. Gerald Goffin

Time Drags By 1966 w.m. Hank B. Marvin, Bruce Welch, Brian Bennett, John Rostill. Ivor Novello Award winner 1966.

Time for Us, A, *see* **Love Theme from** *Romeo and Juliet*

Time Has Come, The 1961 w.m. Les Vandyke. (F) *What a Whopper.*

Time Heals Everything 1974 w.m. Jerry Herman. (MT) *Mack and Mabel.* (MT) *Jerry's Girls.* Bernadette Peters and

Robert Preston appeared in *Mack and Mabel*. Dorothy Loudon, Chita Rivera, and Leslie Uggams appeared in *Jerry's Girls*.

Time in a Bottle 1974 w.m. Jim Croce

Time Is on My Side 1964 w.m. Jerry Ragovoy

Time Marches On 1946 m. John Belton

Time May Change 1948 w.m. Hugh Wade

Time on My Hands 1930 w. Harold Adamson, Mack Gordon m. Vincent Youmans. (MT) *Smiles*. (MT) *One Girl*. (MF) *Look For the Silver Lining*. (MF) *The Eddy Duchin Story*. Marilyn Miller and Fred and Adele Astaire appeared in *Smiles*. June Haver, Ray Bolger, and Gordon MacRae appeared in *Look For the Silver Lining*, biopic of Marilyn Miller. Marilyn Miller refused to perform this song in the short-lived run of *Smiles*.

Time Passages 1978 w.m. Al Stewart, Peter White

Time Waits for No One 1944 w.m. Clifford Friend, Charles Tobias. (MF) *Shine On Harvest Moon*. Ann Sheridan and Dennis Morgan appeared in *Shine On Harvest Moon*, biopic of entertainers Nora Bayes and Jack Norworth. Based on a theme from Strauss's "Tales of the Vienna Woods."

Time Was, or, **Dreaming** 1941 Sp.w. Gabriel Luna. Eng. w. S.K. Russell (Sidney Keith) m. Miguel Prado From the Spanish "Duerme."

Time Will Reveal 1984 w.m. Bunny DeBarge, Eldra DeBarge

Timer 1967 w.m. Laura Nyro. This song was most popular in 1969.

Times of Your Life, The 1975 w.m. Paul Anka. This song was written for the an Eastman Kodak commercial promotion campaign.

Times They Are A-Changin', The 1963 w.m. Bob Dylan

Timid Frieda 1968 Eng.w. Eric Blau, Mort Shuman m. Jacques Brel. (MT) *Jacques Brel Is Alive and Well and Living in Paris*.

Tin Roof Blues 1923 m. Leon Roppolo, Paul Mares, Benny Pollack, George Brunies, Mel Stitzel, Walter Melrose

Tina 1934 w.m. Will Grosz, Hamilton Kennedy

Tina Marie 1955 w.m. Robert Merrill

Ting-a-Ling, or, **The Waltz of the Bells** 1926 w. Addy Britt m. Jack Little

Tiny Bubbles 1966 w.m. Leon Pober

Ti-Pi-Tin 1938 Sp.w. Maria Grever Eng.w. Raymond Leveen m. Maria Grever Based on Chabrier's "España" and Lalo's "Symphonie Espagnole."

Tip Toe Through the Tulips (with Me) 1926 w. Al Dubin m. Joe Burke. (MF) *Gold Diggers of Broadway*. (F) *Confidential Agent*. (MF) *Painting the Clouds with Sunshine*. Ann Pennington and Nancy Welford appeared in *Gold Diggers of Broadway*. Charles Boyer and Lauren Bacall appeared in *Confidential Agent*. Virginia Mayo appeared in *Painting the Clouds with Sunshine*. This song was popularly revived in 1929.

Tip-Top Tipperary Mary 1914 w. Ballard MacDonald m. Harry Carroll

Tippecanoe and Tyler Too 1840 w. Alexander C. Ross m. based on the tune "Little Pigs." Used in the Presidential campaign of General William Henry Harrison with John Tyler as his running mate; this became the official song of the Whig Party.

Tipperary, *see* **It's a Long Way to Tipperary**

Tired 1945 w.m. Allan Roberts, Doris Fisher. (MF) *Varsity Girl*. This song was popularized by Pearl Bailey at the Blue Angel nightclub on New York's Upper East Side, and later in the film *Varsity Girl* in 1947.

Tired of Toein' the Line 1980 w.m. Rocky Burnette, Ronald Coleman

'Tis But a Little Faded Flower 1860 w. Frederick Enoch m. John Rogers Thomas. (F) *Reap the Wild Wind*. Ray Milland, Paulette Goddard, and Raymond Massey appeared in *Reap the Wild Wind*.

'Tis Dawn, the Lark Is Singing 1837 w. anon. m. George James Webb. The music for this song was later used for the hymns "Stand Up, Stand Up for Jesus" (w. George Duffield), "Webb," and "Goodwin."

'Tis Home Where'er the Heart Is 1838 w. Robert Dale Owens m. traditional. (T) *Pochahontas*. *Pochahontas* was an American drama originally produced in New York.

'Tis Me, O Lord, *see* **Standin' In the Need of Pray'r**

'Tis Not True 1875 It.w. anon. Eng.w. Theodore T. Barker m. Titto Mattei. From the Italian "Nonè Ver."

'Tis the Last Rose of Summer 1813 w. Thomas Moore m. based on "The Groves of Blarney," by Richard Alfred Milliken. (MF) *Rainbow Round My Shoulder*. Frankie Laine appeared in *Rainbow Round My Shoulder*. This melody was later to be heard in Flotow's opera *Martha*. It was later interpolated by Beethoven and by Mendelssohn for piano. This song was most popularly performed by soprano Catherine Hays.

Tishomingo Blues 1918 w.m. Spencer Williams

Tit-Willow 1885 w. William S. Gilbert m. Arthur Sullivan. (MT) *The Mikado*.

Tits and Ass 1975 w. Edward Kleban m. Marvin Hamlisch. (MT) *A Chorus Line*.

T'morra, T'morra 1944 w. E.Y. Harburg m. Harold Arlen. (MT) *Bloomer Girl*. Celeste Holm and David Brooks appeared in *Bloomer Girl*.

To a Sweet Pretty Thing 1937 w. Joe Young m. Fred E. Ahlert

To a Water Lily 1896 m. Edward MacDowell. From *Woodland Sketches*.

To a Wild Rose 1896 m. Edward MacDowell. From *Woodland Sketches*. Based on Liszt's "Liebestraum."

To All the Girls I've Loved Before 1984 w.m. Hal David, Albert Hammond

To Anacreon in Heaven 1780–1783 w. Ralph Tomlinson m. John Stafford Smith, or, Samuel Arnold. The melody for this song is the same as that used for "The Star Spangled Banner." This was originally the song of the Anacreontic Society of London. *See also* "The Star Spangled Banner" and "Adams and Liberty."

To Be a Performer, *see* **Be a Performer**

To Be Forgotten 1928 w.m. Irving Berlin

To Each His Own 1946 w.m. Jay Livingston, Ray Evans. (F) *To Each His Own.* Olivia de Havilland appeared in *To Each His Own.*

To Have, To Hold, To Love 1913 w. Darl MacBoyle m. Ernest R. Ball

To Keep My Love Alive 1927 w. Lorenz Hart m. Richard Rodgers. (MT) *A Connecticut Yankee.* (MF) *A Connecticut Yankee.* This song was added to the 1943 stage production of *A Connecticut Yankee.* Maureen O'Sullivan and Will Rogers appeared in the 1931 film production of *A Connecticut Yankee.*

To Know Him Is To Love Him 1958 w.m. Philip Spector

To Know You (Is To Love You) 1952 w.m. Allan Roberts, Robert Allen

To Know You Is To Love You 1928 w. B.G. DeSylva, Lew Brown m. Ray Henderson. (MT) *Hold Everything!*

To Life, or, **L'Chaim** 1964 w. Sheldon Harnick m. Jerry Bock. (MT) *Fiddler on the Roof.* (MF) *Fiddler on the Roof.* Zero Mostel appeared in the stage production of *Fiddler on the Roof.*

To Look Sharp 1953 w.m. Mahlon Merrick. This song was written for a Gillette commercial promotion campaign.

To Sing for You 1965 w.m. Donovan

To Sir with Love 1967 w.m. Don Black, Mark London. (F) *To Sir with Love.* Sidney Poitier and Lulu appeared in *To Sir with Love.* Ivor Novello Award winner 1967–68.

To the Land of My Own (Small) Romance 1911 w. Harry B. Smith m. Victor Herbert. (MT) *The Enchantress.* (MF) *The Great Victor Herbert.* Mary Martin and Alan Jones appeared in *The Great Victor Herbert.*

To Whom It Concerns 1965 w.m. Chris Andrews

To You Sweetheart, Aloha 1936 w.m. Harry Owens

Tobacco's But an Indian Weed 1699 w.m. anon.

Tobermory 1901 w.m. Harry Lauder

Today 1964 w.m. Randy Sparks

Today I Feel So Happy 1931 w.m. Paul Abrahams, Desmond Carter, Frank Eyton. (MF) *Sunshine Susie.* Renata Muller appeared in *Sunshine Susie.*

Today I Met My Love 1972 w.m. Johnny Pearson

Together 1928 w. B.G. DeSylva, Lew Brown m. Ray Henderson. (MF) *Since You Went Away.* (MF) *The Best Things in Life Are Free.* Claudette Colbert and Shirley Temple appeared in *Since You Went Away.* Gordon MacRae, Dan Dailey, and Ernest Borgnine appeared in *The Best Things in Life Are Free,* biopic of song writers DeSylva, Brown, and Henderson. This song was popularly revived in 1944.

Together We Are Beautiful 1981 w.m. Ken Leray. Ivor Novello Award winner 1980–81.

Together Wherever We Go 1959 w. Stephen Sondheim m. Jule Styne. (MT) *Gypsy.* (MF) *Gypsy.* Ethel Merman appeared in the stage production of *Gypsy.* Rosalind Russell appeared in the film production of *Gypsy.*

Togetherness 1960 w.m. Russell Faith

Tokay (To-Kay) 1929 w.m. Noël Coward. (MT) *Bitter Sweet.* (MF) *Bitter Sweet.* Peggy Wood and Gerald Nodin appeared in the stage production of *Bitter Sweet.* Jeanette MacDonald and Nelson Eddy appeared in the film production of *Bitter Sweet.*

Tokyo Melody 1964 w.m. Helmut Zacharias, Heinz Hellmer, Lionel Bart

Tom-Big-Bee River, *see* **The Gum Tree Canoe**

(Poor) Tom Bowling, or, **The Sailor's Epitaph** 1790 w.m. Charles Dibdin. This song was written about Dibdin's brother Captain Thomas Dibdin, who died at sea soon after being struck by lighting.

Tom Dooley, or, **Tom Dula** 1866 w.m. traditional American folksong; adapted Alan Lomax, Frank Warner, 1958. This song is about Blue Ridge Mountain hero Tom Dula, who was hanged for murder in 1868. After having fought in the Civil War with Zeb Vance's 26th Regiment, he became the lover of both Laura Fester and her cousin Ann Melton. In 1866 Laura was found in a shallow grave, and Tom was tried and found guilty of her murder. Years later, just before her death, Ann Melton confessed to having murdered her cousin. This song was popularly adapted by Dave Guard in 1958.

Tom, Tom, the Piper's Son, *see* **Mother Goose's Melodies**

Tomboy 1959 w.m. Jim Conway, Joe Farrell

Tommy, Lad 1907 w. Edward Teschemacher m. E.J. Margetson

Tommy, Make Room for Your Uncle 1875 w.m. T.S. Lonsdale

Tomorrow 1938 w.m. Cole Porter. (MT) *Leave It to Me.* William Gaxton and Victor Moore appeared in *Leave It to Me.*

Tomorrow 1977 w. Martin Charnin m. Charles Strouse. (MT) *Annie.* Dorothy Loudon and Andrea McArdle appeared in *Annie.*

Tomorrow Is a Lovely Day 1940 w.m. Irving Berlin. (MT) *Louisiana Purchase.* (MF) *Louisiana Purchase.* Victor Moore, William Gaxton, and Irene Bordoni appeared in the stage production of *Louisiana Purchase.* Bob Hope and Irene Bordoni appeared in the film production of *Louisiana Purchase.*

Tonight 1957 w. Stephen Sondheim m. Leonard Bernstein. (MT) *West Side Story.* (MF) *West Side Story.* Carol Lawrence and Larry Kert appeared in the stage production of *West Side Story.* Natalie Wood and Rita Moreno appeared in the film production of *West Side Story.*

Tonight I Celebrate My Love 1984 w.m. Michael Masser, Gerald Goffin

Tonight or Never 1931 w.m. Harold Adamson, Burton Lane. (MT) *Earl Carroll's Vanities of 1930.* (MT) *Earl Carroll's Vanities of 1931.* Jack Benny and Patsy Kelly appeared in *Earl Carroll's Vanities of 1930.* will Mahoney and William Demarest appeared in *Earl Carroll's Vanities of 1931.*

Tonight She Comes 1986 w.m. Richard Otcasek

Tonight We Love 1941 w. Bobby Worth m. Ray Austin, Freddy Martin. Based on the first movement of Tchaikovsky's First Piano Concerto, in B-flat minor.

Tonight You Belong to Me 1926 w. Billy Rose m. Lee David. This song was popularly revived in 1956.

Tonight's the Night (It's Gonna Be Alright) 1976 w.m. Rod Stewart

Tony from America 1910 w.m. Lionel Monckton, Arthur Wimperis. (MT) *The Quaker Girl*. Gracie Leigh, Gertie Millar, and George Carvey appeared in *The Quaker Girl*.

Tony's Wife 1933 w. Harold Adamson m. Burton Lane

Too Bad 1955 w.m. Cole Porter. (MT) *Silk Stockings*. (MF) *Silk Stockings*. Fred Astaire and Cyd Charisse appeared in the film production of *Silk Stockings*.

Too Beautiful To Last 1972 w.m. Richard rodney Bennett

Too Busy Thinking About My Baby 1969 w.m. Norman Whitfield, Barrett Strong, Janie Bradford

Too Close for Comfort 1956 w.m. Jerry Bock, Larry Holofcener, George Weiss. (MT) *Mr. Wonderful*. Sammy Davis, Jr., appeared in *Mr. Wonderful*.

Too Darn Hot 1949 w.m. Cole Porter. (MT) *Kiss Me, Kate*. (MF) *Kiss Me, Kate*. Alfred Drake and Patricia Morrison appeared in the stage production of *Kiss Me, Kate*. Kathryn Grayson, Howard Keel, and Ann Miller appeared in the film production of *Kiss Me, Kate*.

Too Fat Polka 1947 w.m. Ross MacLean, Arthur Richardson

Too Good for the Average Man 1936 w. Lorenz Hart m. Richard Rodgers. (MT) *On Your Toes*. (MF) *On Your Toes*. Luella Gear and Ray Bolger appeared in the stage production of *On Your Toes*.

Too Hot 1980 w.m. George M. Brown

Too Late for Goodbyes 1985 w.m. Julian Lennon

Too Late Now 1951 w. Alan Jay Lerner m. Burton Lane. (MF) *Royal Wedding*. (MF) *Wedding Bells*. Fred Astaire, Jane Powell, and Peter Lawford appeared in *Royal Wedding*.

(Have I Stayed) Too Long at the Fair 1959 w.m. Billy Barnes. (MT) *The Billy Barnes Revue*.

Too Many Irons in the Fire 1933 w.m. Johnny S. Black

Too Many Lovers 1981 w.m. Samuel Hogin, Ted Lindsey, Mark True

Too Many Mornings 1971 w.m. Stephen Sondheim. (MT) *Follies*. Alexis Smith and Yvonne DeCarlo appeared in *Follies*.

Too Many Parties and Too Many Pals 1925 w. Billy Rose, Mort Dixon m. Ray Henderson

Too Many Rings Around Rosie 1925 w. Otto Harbach, Irving Caesar m. Vincent Youmans. (MT) *No, No, Nanette*. Louise Groody and Mary Lawlor appeared in *No, No, Nanette*.

Too Many Tears 1932 w.m. Al Dubin, Harry Warren

Too Many Times 1946 w.m. Sunny Skylar

Too Marvelous for Words 1937 w. Johnny Mercer m. Richard A. Whiting. (MF) *Ready, Willing and Able*. (MF) *Young Man of Music*. (MF) *On the Sunny Side of the Street*. Doris Day appeared in *Young Man of Music*. Frankie Laine and Billy Daniels appeared in *On the Sunny Side of the Street*.

Too Much 1957 w.m. Lee Rosenberg, Bernard Weinman

Too Much Heaven 1980 w.m. Barry Gibb, Maurice Gibb, Robin Gibb. Ivor Novello Award winner 1979–80.

Too Much Mustard (Très Moutarde) 1911 m. Cecil Macklin. (MF) *The Story of Vernon and Irene Castle*. Ginger Rogers and Fred Astaire appeared in *The Story of Vernon and Irene Castle*.

Too Much, Too Little, Too Late 1978 w.m. Nat Kipner, John Vallins

Too Old To Cut the Mustard 1952 w.m. Bill Carlisle

Too Romantic 1940 w.m. Johnny Burke, James V. Monaco. (MF) *The Road to Singapore*. Bing Crosby, Bob Hope, and Dorothy Lamour appeared in *The Road to Singapore*.

Too Young 1951 w. Sylvia Dee m. Sid Lippman

Too Young To Go Steady 1955 w.m. Jimmy McHugh, Harold Adamson

Took the Last Train 1979 w.m. David Gates

Too-ra-loo-ra-loo-ral, That's an Irish Lullaby 1914 w.m. James R. Shannon. (MT) *Shameen Dhu*. (MF) *Going My Way*. Bing Crosby and Barry Fitzgerald appeared in *Going My Way*. This song was popularly revived in 1944.

Toor-ie On His Bonnet, The 1947 w.m. Noel Gay, George Brown

Toot Toot Tootsie (Goo'Bye) 1922 w.m. Gus Kahn, Ernie Erdman, Dan Russo. (MT) *Bombo*. (MF) *The Jazz Singer*. (MF) *Rose of Washington Square*. (MF) *The Jolson Story*. (MF) *Jolson Sings Again*. (MF) *I'll See You in My Dreams*. Al Jolson appeared in *Bombo, The Jazz Singer* and *Rose of Washington Square*. Larry Parks appeared in *The Jolson Story* and *Jolson Sings Again*. Doris Day and Danny Thomas appeared in *I'll See You in My Dreams*, biopic of song writer Gus Kahn.

Top Hat, White Tie and Tails 1935 w.m. Irving Berlin. (MF) *Top Hat*. Fred Astaire and Ginger Rogers appeared in *Top Hat*.

Top of the Hill, The 1983 w. Fred Ebb m. John Kander. (MT) *Zorba*. Anthony Quinn and Debbie Shapiro appeared in *Zorba*.

Top of the World 1973 w.m. Richard Carpenter, John Bettis

Toplady, *see* **Rock of Ages**

Topsy 1958 w.m. Edgar William Battle, Eddie Durham

Torch Song, The 1931 w. Joe Young, Mort Dixon m. Harry Warren. (MT) *The Laugh Parade*. Ed Wynn and Bartlett Simmons appeared in *The Laugh Parade*.

Toreador Song 1875 w. H. Meilhac, Ludovic Halévy m. Georges Bizet. From the opera *Carmen*. *Carmen* had its premiere in Paris on March 3, 1875. The ''Habañera'' in Bizet's *Carmen* is directly based on Sebastian Yradier's ''El Areglito.''

Torn Between Two Lovers 1977 w.m. Phil Jarrell, Peter Yarrow

Torpedo and the Whale, The 1881 w. Henry Bougham Farnie m. Edmond Audran. (MT) *Olivette*.

Tossin' and Turnin' 1961 w.m. Malou Rene, Ritchie Adams

Tossing and Turning 1965 w.m. John Carter, Ken Lewis, Perry Ford

Total Eclipse of the Heart 1983 w.m. Jim Steinman

Totem Tom-Tom 1924 w. Oscar Hammerstein II, Otto harbach m. Rudolf Friml. (MT) *Rose Marie.* (MF) *Rose Marie.* Mary Ellis, Dennis King, and Arthur Deagon appeared in the stage production of Rose Marie. Nelson Eddy and Jeanette MacDonald appeared in the 1936 film production of *Rose Marie.*

Touch Me in the Morning 1973 w.m. Michael Masser, Ron Miller

Touch Me When We're Dancing 1981 w.m. Kenneth Bell, Terry Skinner, J.L. Wallace

Touch of Your Hand, The 1933 w. Otto Harbach m. Jerome Kern. (MT) *Roberta.* (MF) *Roberta.* (MF) *Lovely To Look At.* Bob Hope and Fay Templeton appeared in the stage production of *Roberta.* Fred Astaire, Ginger Rogers, and Irene Dunn appeared in the film production of *Roberta.* Howard Keel and Kathryn Grayson appeared in *Lovely To Look At.*

Touch of Your Lips, The 1936 w.m. Ray Noble

Town Where I Was Born, The 1905 w.m. Paul Dresser

Toy Drum Major, The 1925 w.m. Horatio Nicholls

Toy Monkey, The, or, **I'm a Monkey On a Stick** 1896 w. Harry Greenbank m. Lionel Monckton. (MT) *The Geisha.*

Toy Town 1915 w.m. Lionel Monckton, Herman Finck. (MT) *Bric-a-Brac.* Gertie Millar appeared in *Bric-a-Brac.*

Toy Trumpet 1937 w.m. Sidney Mitchell, Lew Pollack m. Raymond Scott (Harry Warnow). (MF) *Rebecca of Sunnybrook Farm.* Shirley Temple, Jack Haley, and Randolph Scott appeared in *Rebecca of Sunnybrook Farm.* This song was published in 1937 as an instrumental only.

Toyland 1903 w. Glen MacDonough m. Victor Herbert. (MT) *Babes in Toyland.* (MF) *Babes in Toyland.* Laurel and Hardy appeared in the film production of *Babes in Toyland. Babes in Toyland* opened on June 17, 1903, in Chicago.

Toyshop Ballet 1956 w.m. A.P. Mantovani

Trabling Back to Georgia 1874 w. Arthur W. French m. Charles D. Blake

Traces 1969 w.m. Buddy Buie, Emory Gordy, Jr., James B. Cobb, Jr.

Tracks of My Tears, The 1967 w.m. Warren Moore, William "Smokey" Robinson, Marvin Tarpin. This song was popularly revived in 1976.

Tracy 1969 w.m. Lee Pockriss, Paul Vance

Tracy's Theme 1960 w. Roz Gordon m. Robert Ascher. (TV) *The Philadelphia Story.*

Trade Winds 1940 w.m. Cliff Friend, Charles Tobias

Tradition 1964 w. Sheldon Harnick m. Jerry Bock. (MT) *Fiddler on the Roof.* (MF) *Fiddler on the Roof.* Zero Mostel appeared in the stage production of *Fiddler on the Roof.*

Traffic Jam 1939 w.m. Artie Shaw, Teddy McRae. (MF) *Dancing Co-Ed.* Lana Turner, Richard Carlson, and Artie Shaw and his band appeared in *Dancing Co-Ed.*

Tragedy 1979 w.m. Barry Gibb, Maurice Gibb, Robin Gibb

Trial of Dreams 1926 w. Raymond Klages m. Einar Swan

Trail of the Lonesome Pine, The 1913 w. Ballard MacDonald m. Harry Carroll

Trains and Boats and Planes 1965 w. Hal David m. Burt Bacharach

Tramp, Tramp, Tramp 1864 w.m. George Frederick Root

Tramp! Tramp! Tramp! Along the Highway 1910 w. Rida Johnson Young m. Victor Herbert. (MT) *Naughty Marietta.* (MF) *Naughty Marietta.* Emma Trentini and Orville Harrold appeared in the stage production of *Naughty Marietta.* Jeanette MacDonald, Nelson Eddy, and Elsa Lanchester appeared in the film production of *Naughty Marietta.*

Transatlantic Lullaby 1939 w.m. Diana Morgan, Robert McDermott, Geoffrey Wright. (MT) *The Gate Revue.*

Transfusion 1956 w.m. Jimmy Drake

Träumerei 1839 m. Robert Schumann. From "Kinderscenen" (Children's Scenes), op. 15, no.7.

Traveling Back to Georgia, *see* **Trabling Back to Georgia**

Travelin' Band 1970 w.m. Basil G. Adlam, Jay Milton, Henry Russell

Travelin' Man 1961 w.m. Jerry Fuller

Travellin' Light 1959 w.m. Sid Tepper, Roy C. Bennett

Treat Her Right 1965 w.m. Roy Head

Treat Me Rough 1930 w. Ira Gershwin m. George Gershwin. (MT) *Girl Crazy.* (MF) *Girl Crazy.* Judy Garland, Mickey Rooney, and June Allyson appeared in the 1943 film production of *Girl Crazy.*

Treble Chance 1959 w.m. Joe Henderson

Tree in the Meadow, A 1948 w.m. Billy Reid

Tree in the Park, A 1926 w. Lorenz Hart m. Richard Rodgers. (MT) *Peggy-Ann.* Helen Ford and Betty Starbuck appeared in the American stage production of *Peggy-Ann.* Dorothy Dickson appeared in the British stage production of *Peggy-Ann.*

Trees 1922 w. Joyce Kilmer m. Oscar Rasbach. The actual oak tree serving as inspiration for Joyce Kilmer's poem was at Ryder's Lane and Route 1, New Brunswick, N.J.

(On the Shores of) Tripoli 1920 w. Paul Cunningham, Al Dubin m. Irving Weill

Trois Cloches, Les, *see* **While the Angelus Was Ringing**

Trolley Song, The 1944 w.m. Hugh Martin, Ralph Blane. (MF) *Meet Me in St. Louis.* Judy Garland, Tom Drake, and Margaret O'Brien appeared in *Meet Me in St. Louis.*

Trouble 1982 w.m. Lindsey Buckingham

Trouble (in River City) 1957 w.m. Meredith Willson. (MT) *The Music Man.* (MF) *The Music Man.* Robert Preston appeared in both the stage and film productions of *The Music Man.*

Truck Stop 1969 w.m. Jerry Dean Smith

Truckin' 1935 w. Ted Koehler m. Rube Bloom. (MT) *Cotton Club Parade, 26th Edition.*

Trudie 1958 w.m. Joe Henderson. Ivor Novello Award winner 1958.

True 1934 w.m. Walter G. Samuels, Leonard Whitcup

True Blue Lou 1929 w.m. Sam Coslow, Leo Robin, Richard A. Whiting. (MF) *The Dance of Life.* Hal Skelly, Nancy Carroll, and Oscar Levant appeared in *The Dance of Life.*

True Confession 1937 w.m. Sam Coslow, Frederick Hollander. (F) *True Confession*. Carole Lombard and Fred MacMurray appeared in *True Confession*.

True Grit 1969 w. Don Black m. Elmer Bernstein. (F) *True Grit*. John Wayne appeared in *True Grit*.

True-Hearted, Whole-Hearted, or, **Peal Out the Watchword** 1890 w. Frances Ridley Havergal m. George Coles Stebbins

(I Had Myself a) True Love 1946 w. Johnny Mercer m. Harold Arlen. (MT) *St. Louis Woman*. Pearl Bailey and Rex Ingram appeared in *St. Louis Woman*.

True Love 1956 w.m. Cole Porter. (MF) *High Society*. Bing Crosby, Grace Kelly, and Frank Sinatra appeared in *High Society*, the musical version of *The Philadelphia Story*.

True Love Ways 1980 w.m. Norman Petty, Buddy Holly

Truly 1983 w.m. Lionel Richie

Trumpeter, The 1904 w. Francis J. Barron m. J. Airlie Dix

Trust in Me 1936 w.m. Ned Wever, Jean Schwartz, Milton Ager. This song was popularly revived in 1952.

Trusting Jesus, That Is All 1876 w. E.P. Stites m. Ira David Sankey

Try a Little Kindness 1969 w.m. Bobby Austin, Thomas Sapaugh

Try a Little Tenderness 1932 w.m. Harry Woods, Jimmy Campbell, Reginald Connelly. This song was used for the 1980 Perdue Chicken Parts television promotion campaign.

Try Again Johnnie 1902 w.m. Lionel Monckton, Adrian Ross. (MT) *A Country Girl*. Evie Greene appeared in the British production of *A Country Girl*.

Try To Forget 1931 w. Otto Harbach m. Jerome Kern. (MT) *The Cat and the Fiddle*. (MF) *The Cat and the Fiddle*. Jeanette MacDonald and Charles Butterworth appeared in the film production of *The Cat and the Fiddle*.

Try To Remember 1960 w. Tom Jones m. Harvey Schmidt. (MT) *The Fantasticks*.

Trying 1952 w.m. Billy Vaughn

Tryin' To Get the Feelin' Again 1976 w.m. David Pomeranz

Tryin' To Love Two 1977 w.m. Paul Mitchell, William Bell

Tschaikowsky 1941 w. Ira Gershwin m. Kurt Weill. (MT) *Lady in the Dark*. (MF) *Lady in the Dark*. Gertrude Lawrence, Danny Kaye, and Victor Mature appeared in the stage production of *Lady in the Dark*. Ginger Rogers appeared in the film production of *Lady in the Dark*.

T.S.O.P. (The Sound of Philadelphia) 1974 w.m. Kenneth Gamble, Leon Huff

Tu, *see* **O Cuba**

Tu Felicidad, *see* **Made for Each Other**

Tubby the Tuba 1948 w.m. George Kleinsinger, Paul Tripp

Tuck Me To Sleep in My Old 'Tucky Home 1921 w.m. Sam M. Lewis, Joe Young m. George W. Meyer

Tulip Time 1919 w. Gene Buck m. Dave Stamper. (MT) *Ziegfeld Follies of 1919*.

Tulsa Time 1979 w.m. Danny Flowers

Tumbling Tumbleweeds 1934 w.m. Bob Nolan. (MF) *Tumbling Tumbleweeds*. (MF) *Don't Fence Me In*. (MF) *Silver Spurs*. (MF) *Hollywood Canteen*. Gene Autry and Lucille Brown appeared in *Tumbling Tumbleweeds*. Roy Rogers and Gabby Hayes appeared in *Don't Fence Me In*. Roy Rogers and Smiley Burnette appeared in *Silver Spurs*. Joan Crawford, Bette Davis, and Eddie Cantor appeared in *Hollywood Canteen*. Theme song of The Sons of the Pioneers.

Turkey in the Straw, or, **Old Zip Coon** 1834 w.m. anon.; possibly of Irish origin, sometimes ascribed to Bob Farrell and/or George Washington Dixon. ''There Was an Old Soldier Who Had a Wooden Leg'' is an adaptation of the melody of this song.

Turkish Coffee 1962 w.m. Tony Osborne

Turn Around 1968 w.m. Les Reed, Barry Mason

Turn Around 1985 w.m. Carole Bayer Sager

Turn Back the Universe and Give Me Yesterday 1916 w. J. Keirn Brennan m. Ernest R. Ball

Turn Down Day 1966 w.m. David Blume, Jerry Keller

Turn 'Erbert's Face to the Wall, Mother 1935 w.m. William Ellis, Max Kester, Ronald Hill

Turn On the Heat 1929 w. B.G. DeSylva, Lew Brown m. Ray Henderson. (MF) *Sunny Side Up*. Janet Gaynor and Charles Farrell appeared in *Sunny Side Up*.

Turn Out the Light 1932 w. B.G. DeSylva m. Nacio Herb Brown, Richard Whiting. (MT) *Take a Chance*. (MF) *Take a Chance*. Ethel Merman, Jack Whiting, and Jack Haley appeared in the stage production of *Take a Chance*. Charles ''Buddy'' Rogers and James Dunn appeared in the film production of *Take a Chance*.

Turn! Turn! Turn! 1965 w.m. Pete Seeger

Turn Your Love Around 1982 w.m. Bill Champlin, Jay Graydon, Steve Lukather. Grammy Award winner 1982.

Turn Your Radio On 1959 w.m. Albert E. Brumley

Turned Up 1924 w.m. Herbert Rule, Harry Castling

Tusk 1979 w.m. Lindsey Buckingham

Tuxedo Junction 1940 w.m. Buddy Feyne, William Johnson, Erskin Hawkins, Julian Dash. (MF) *The Glenn Miller Story*.

'Twas Not So Long Ago 1929 w. Oscar Hammerstein II m. Jerome Kern. (MT) *Sweet Adeline*. (MF) *Sweet Adeline*.

'Twas Off the Blue Canaries, or, **My Last Cigar** 1848 w.m. James M. Hubbard. This song is today the school song of the University of Pennsylvania.

Tweedle Dee 1955 w.m. Winfield Scott

Tweedle Dee—Tweedle Dum 1972 w.m. Mario Capuano, Giosafatte Capuano, H. Scott

Tweedle-O-Twill 1942 w.m. Gene Autry, Fred Rose. (F) *Home in Wyoming*. (F) *Whirlwind*. Gene Autry and Smiley Burnette appeared in both *Home in Wyoming and Whirlwind*.

Twelfth of Never, The 1957 w.m. Jerry Livingston, Paul Francis Webster. This song was popularly revived in 1964 and 1973.

Twelfth Street Rag 1914 m. Euday L. Bowman. This song was published with words by James S. Summer in 1919; with words by Spencer Williams in 1929; and with words by Andy Razaf in 1942. This song was popularly revived in 1948.

Twelve Days of Christmas c.1700 w.m. traditional, from England. One source reports: "A Partridge in a Pear Tree" is a carol of great antiquity. It has been sung in many places and in many ways. Once its singing was accompanied by dancing and the asking of alms. At other times it has been part of a game of forfeits, each error in the song being paid for by penance of some kind. (This is still a practice in the North of England). The partridge in chuch symbolism indicates abandonment of faith, the partridge being known as a bird that deserts its young. (Here it may imply fickleness.) The pear tree possibly refers to a one-time Christmas custom wherein a young girl, upon backing into a pear tree, then circling it three times, was to be rewarded by seeing the image of her true love. The three French hens are Breton hens, the four colly birds are "collied," or coal-black. The five golden rings refer to the ringed pheasant. The twelve days, of course, are those between Christmas and Epiphany. Since this is traditionally a time of great ceremony, it is thought by some that the gifts of the song refer slyly to penances exacted for failure to observe certain fine points of ritual.

Twelve Thirty, or, **Young Girls Are Coming to the Canyon** 1967 w.m. John Phillips

Twentieth Century Blues 1931 w.m. Noël Coward. (MF) *Cavalcade.*

Twickenham Ferry 1875 w.m. Theophile Marzials

Twilight in Turkey 1937 m. Raymond Scott (Harry Warnow). (MF) *Ali Baba Goes to Town.* Eddie Cantor and Tony Martin appeared in *Ali Baba Goes to Town.*

Twilight on the Trail 1936 w. Sidney D. Mitchell m. Louis Alter. (MF) *The Trail of the Lonesome Pine.* Sylvia Sidney, Fred MacMurray, and Henry Fonda appeared in *The Trail of the Lonesome Pine.*

Twilight Time 1944 w.m. Buck Ram, Morty Nevins, Al Nevins, Artie Dunn. This song was popularly revived in 1958.

Twinkle Twinkle, Little Star, or, **Ah! Vous Diraije Maman,** or, **ABCDEFG** (The Alphabet Song, an adaptation in 1835), or, **Baa, Baa, Black Sheep** 1765 w. Jane Taylor; published 1806 with the title "The Star," from *Rhymes for the Nursery* m. traditional, from France.

Twinkle Twinkle, Little Star 1936 w. Herb Magidson m. Ben Oakland. (MF) *Hats Off.* Mae Clarke and John Payne appeared in *Hats Off.* Not the traditional song with this title.

Twinkling Stars Are Laughing Love 1855 w.m. John P. Ordway

Twist, The 1960 w.m. Hank Ballard. This song was most popular in 1962.

Twist and Shout 1962 w.m. Bert Russell, Philip Medley. This song was most popular in 1964.

Twist of Fate 1984 w.m. Peter Beckett, Steve Kipner

Twistin' the Night Away 1962 w.m. Sam Cooke

Twistin' U.S.A. 1960 w.m. Kal Mann

Two Blue Eyes 1907 w. Edward Madden m. Theodore F. Morse

Two Cigarettes in the Dark 1934 w. Paul Francis Webster

m. Lew Pollack. (F) *Kill That Story.* Gloria Grafton appeared in *Kill That Story.*

Two Different Worlds 1956 w. Sid Wayne m. Al Frisch

Two Doors Down 1978 w.m. Dolly Parton

Two Faces in the Dark 1959 w. Dorothy Fields m. Albert Hague. (MT) *Redhead.*

(Theme from) Two for the Road 1967 m. Henry Mancini. (F) *Two for the Road.* Audrey Hepburn and Albert Finney appeared in *Two for the Road.*

Two Grenadiers, The 1840 w. Heinrich Heine m. Robert Schumann. From the German "Die Beiden Grenadiere."

Two Guitars 1925 m. based on a traditional gypsy folksong from Russia. (R) *Atlantic & Pacific Radio Hour.* This piece was first published in 1912 in Russia, after its winning the 1911 Rome Grand Prize. Theme song of Harry Horlick.

Two Hearts Are Better Than One 1946 w. Leo Robin m. Jerome Kern. (MF) *Centennial Summer.* Walter Brennan, Jeanne Crain, and Cornel Wilde appeared in *Centennial Summer.*

Two Hearts in Three Quarter Time 1930 Ger.w. Walter Reisch, A. Robinson Eng.w. Joe Young m. Robert Stolz. From the German film operetta *Zwei Herzen im Dreivierteltakt (Two Hearts in Waltz Time).* Walter Janseen and Willy Forst appeared in *Two Hearts in Waltz Time.*

Two Hearts That Pass in the Night 1941 w. Forman Brown m. Ernesto Lecuona. Based on "Dame de Tus Rosas."

Two Ladies 1972 w. Fred Ebb m. John Kander. (MF) *Cabaret.* Liza Minnelli and Joel Grey appeared in the film production of *Cabaret.* This song did not appear in the original stage production of *Cabaret.*

Two Ladies in De Shade of De Banana Tree 1955 w. Harold Arlen, Truman Capote m. Harold Arlen. (MT) *House of Flowers.*

Two Laughing Irish Eyes 1915 w. Henry Blossom m. Victor Herbert. (MT) *The Princess Pat.*

Two Little Babes in the Wood 1928 w.m. Cole Porter. (MT) *Paris.*

Two Little Baby Shoes 1907 w. Edward Madden m. Theodore F. Morse

Two Little Bluebirds 1925 w. Oscar Hammerstein II m. Jerome Kern. (MT) *Sunny* (MF) *Sunny.* Kitty Reidy and Howett Worster appeared in the American stage production of *Sunny.* Elsie Randolph and Jack Buchanan appeared in the British stage production of *Sunny.*

Two Little Boys 1903 w.m. Theodore F. Morse

Two Little Girls In Blue 1893 w.m. Charles Graham

Two Little Love Bees 1910 w. Harry B. Smith, Robert B. Smith m. Heinrich Reinhardt. (MT) *The Spring Maid.*

Two Little Magpies 1923 w. anon. m. John Barnes Wells

Two Lost Souls 1955 w.m. Richard Adler, Jerry Ross. (MT) *Damn Yankees.* (MF) *Damn Yankees.* Gwen Verdon appeared in both the stage and film productions of *Damn Yankees.*

Two Lovely Black Eyes 1886 w.m. Charles Coborn. Based on the Venetian folk tune "Vieni sul Mar" (Come to the Sea).

Two Loves Have I 1931 w.m. Georges Konyn, Jack Murray, Vincent Baptiste Scotto, Barry Trivers, Henri Eugene Vantard

Two of Us, The 1936 w.m. Van Phillips, James Campbell, Reginald Connelly

Two Silhouettes 1945 w. Ray Gilbert m. Charles Wolcott. (MF) *Make Mine Music*.

Two Silhouettes in the Moonlight 1941 m. C. Kelley. Based on ''Poème'' by Fibich.

Two Sleepy People 1938 w. Frank Loesser m. Hoagy Carmichael. (MT) *Ain't Misbehavin'*. (F) *Thanks for the Memory*. Debbie Allen and Nell Carter appeared in *Ain't Misbehavin'*. Bob Hope and Shirley Ross appeared in *Thanks for the Memory*.

Two Tickets to Georgia 1933 w.m. Joe Young, Charles Tobias, J. Fred Coots

Two Tribes 1985 w.m. Peter Gill, Holly Johnson, Mark O'Toole. Ivor Novello Award winner 1984–85.

Tying Apples on a Lilac Tree, *see* **The Lilac Tree**

Typewriter, The 1951 m. Leroy Anderson. This song was also popular in 1954.

Tyrolese Evening Hymn 1828 w. Felicia Dorothea Hemans m. Augusta Browne (Garrett)

Tzena, Tzena, Tzena 1950 w. Gordon Jenkins m. arr. Spencer Ross; also w. Mitchell Parish m. Issacher Miron (Michrovsky), Julius Grossman.

Ugly Chile (You're Some Pretty Doll) 1917 w.m. Clarence Williams

Ugly Duckling, The 1952 w.m. Frank Loesser. (MF) *Hans Christian Andersen*. Danny Kaye appeared in *Hans Christian Andersen*.

Ukulele Lady 1925 w. Gus Kahn m. Richard A. Whiting. (MF) *I'll See You in My Dreams*. Doris Day and Danny Thomas appeared in *I'll See You in My Dreams*, biopic of song writer Gus Kahn.

Ulysses Is His Name 1868 w.m. Dexter Smith. This song was written for the Presidential campaign supporting Ulysses S. Grant.

Um, Um, Um, Um, Um, Um 1964 w.m. Curtis Mayfield. This song was popularly revived in 1978.

Umbrella Man, The 1938 w.m. James Cavanaugh, Vincent Rose, Larry Stock. (MT) *These Foolish Things*. (MF) *Garden of the Moon*. Pat O'Brien and Margaret Lindsay appeared in *Garden of the Moon*.

(Theme from) Umbrellas of Cherbourg, The, *see* **I Will Wait for You**

Un Bel Dì, or, **One Fine Day** 1904 w. Luigi Illica, Giuseppe Giacosa m. Giacomo Puccini. From the opera *Madama Butterfly*. *Madama Butterfly* was first produced in Milan on February 17, 1904, to an unappreciative audience.

Unchain My Heart 1961 w.m. Freddy James, Agnes Jones

Unchained Melody 1955 w. Hy Zaret m. Alex North. (F) *Unchained*. Elroy Hirsch appeared in *Unchained*. This song was popularly revived in 1965.

Uncle Albert/Admiral Halsey 1971 w.m. Paul McCartney, Linda McCartney

(Old) Uncle Ned 1848 w.m. Stephen Collins Foster

Uncle Remus Said 1947 w.m. Johnny Lange, Hy Heath, Eliot Daniel. (MF) *Song of the South*.

Undecided 1939 w. Sid Robin m. Charles Shavers. This song was popularly revived in 1952.

Under a Blanket of Blue 1933 w. Marty Symes, Al J. Neiburg m. Jerry Levinson

Under a Roof in Paree 1931 Fr.w. René Nazelles Eng.w. Irving Caesar m. Raoul Moretti. (F) *Sous les Toits de Paris*.

Under Any Old Flag at All 1907 w.m. George M. Cohan. (MT) *The Talk of New York*.

Under Hawaiian Skies 1920 Fr.w. Z. Renaud Eng.w. Ernie Erdman m. Fred Rose. From the French ''Sous les Cieux d'Hawaii.''

Under Paris Skies 1953 w. Fr.w. Jean Drejac Eng.w. Kim Gannon m. Hubert Giraud. From the French ''Sous le Ciel de Paris.''

Under the Anheuser Bush 1903 w.m. Andrew B. Sterling, Harry Von Tilzer. This song was later used for an Anheuser Beer commercial promotion campaign.

Under the Bamboo Tree 1902 w.m. Robert Cole, J. Rosamond Johnson. (MT) *Sally in Our Alley*. (MT) *Nancy Brown*. (MF) *Meet Me in St. Louis*. Marie Cahill and Dan McAvoy appeared in *Sally in Our Alley*. Judy Garland and Mary Astor appeared in *Meet Me in St. Louis*. Based on Chaminade's ''Flatterer'' (La Lisonjera).

Under the Boardwalk 1964 w.m. Arthur Resnick, Kenny Young

Under the Bridges of Paris 1931 w.m. Vincent Scotto, Jean Rodor, Dorcas Cochram. From the French ''Sous les Ponts de Paris.''

Under the Deodar 1902 w.m. Lionel Monckton, Adrian Ross. (MT) *A Country Girl*. Evie Greene appeared in the British production of *A Country Girl*.

Under the Double Eagle (March) uncertain m. Josef Franz Wagner. (MT) *Dancin'*.

Under the Roller Coaster 1984 w. Fred Ebb m. John Kander. (MT) *The Rink*. Liza Minnelli and Chita Rivera appeared in *The Rink*.

Under the Yum Yum Tree 1910 w. Andrew B. Sterling m. Harry Von Tilzer. (MF) *Wharf Angel*. Dorothy Dell and Preston Foster appeared in *Wharf Angel*.

Underneath the Arches 1932 w.m. Bud Flanagan; add'l w. Joseph McCarthy

Underneath the Harlem Moon 1932 w.m. Mack Gordon, Harry Revel

Underneath the Russian Moon 1929 w. James Kendis, Frank Samuels m. Meyer Gusman

Underneath the Stars 1915 w. Fleta Jan Brown m. Herbert Spencer

Unexpected Song 1985 w. Don Black, Richard Maltby, Jr. m. Andrew Lloyd Webber. (MT) *Song and Dance*. Bernadette Peters appeared in *Song and Dance*.

Unforgettable   1951   w.m. Irving Gordon

Unforgiven, The (The Need for Love)   1960   w. Ned Washington   m. Dimitri Tiomkin. (F) *The Unforgiven.* Burt Lancaster, Audrey Hepburn, and Lillian Gish appeared in *The Unforgiven.*

Unicorn, The   1968   w.m. Shel Silverstein

(Look For the) Union Label   1975   w. Paula Green   m. Malcolm Dodds. This song was written for an International Ladies Garment Workers Union commercial promotion campaign.

Union of the Snake   1983   w.m. Nicholas James Bates, Simon John Charles Le Bon, Andrew Taylor, Nigel John Taylor, Roger Andrew Taylor

United We Stand   1971   w.m. Tony Hiller, Peter Simons. Ivor Novello Award winner 1970–71.

Unless   1934   w.m. Tolchard Evans, Robert Hargreaves, Stanley Damerell

Unlucky in Love   1924   w.m. Irving Berlin. (MT) *The Music Box Revue of 1924.* Oscar Shaw, Fanny Brice, and Grace Moore appeared in *The Music Box Revue of 1924.*

Unsuspecting Heart   1955   w. Freddy James   m. Joe Beal, Bob Singer, Joe Shank

Until   1911   w. Edward Teschemacher   m. Wilfrid Sanderson

Until It's Time for You To Go   1965   w.m. Buffy Sainte-Marie. This song was popularly revived in 1970.

(It Will Have To Do) Until the Real Thing Comes Along, *see also* **Till the Real Thing Comes Along.**   1936   w.m. Sammy Cahn, Saul Chaplin, L.E. Freeman, Mann Holiner, Alberta Nichols.

Until Tomorrow   1940   w.m. Sammy Kaye

Until You Come Back to Me (That's What I'm Gonna Do)   1973   w.m. Clarence Paul, Morris Broadnax

(Theme from) Untouchables, The   1959   m. Nelson Riddle. (TV) *The Untouchables.*

Unusual Way   1982   w.m. Maury Yeston. (MT) *Nine.* Liliane Montevecchi and Anita Morris appeared in *Nine.*

Up a Lazy River, *see* **Lazy River**

Up Cherry Street   1964   w.m. Julius Wechter

Up in a Balloon   1908   w. Ren Shields   m. Percy Wenrich

Up in the Clouds   1927   w. Bert Kalmer   m. Harry Ruby. (MT) *Five O'Clock Girl.* Mary Eaton and Oscar Shaw appeared in *Five O'Clock Girl.*

Up on the Roof   1963   w.m. Gerry Goffin, Carole King

Up Up and Away, or, **My Beautiful Balloon**   1967   w.m. Jim Webb. Grammy Award winner 1967. The inspiration for this song came when Webb's girlfriend left him to marry another man. The song was written for a film that was never produced.

Up Where We Belong   1982   w.m. Will Jennings, Jack Nitzsche, Buffy Sainte-Marie. (F) *An Officer and a Gentleman.* Richard Gere appeared in *An Officer and a Gentleman.*

Up with the Lark   1946   w. Leo Robin   m. Jerome Kern. (MF) *Centennial Summer.* Cornel Wilde and Linda Darnell appeared in *Centennial Summer.*

Upside Down   1980   w.m. Bernie Edwards, Nile Rodgers

(Theme from) Upstairs Downstairs, or, **The Edwardians**   1976   m. Alexander Faris. (TV-BBC) *Upstairs Downstairs.* Ivor Novello Award winner 1975–76.

Upstairs Downstairs, *see also* **Mother Goose's Melodies**

Uptight (Everything's Alright)   1966   w.m. Sylvia Moy, Henry Cosby, Stevie Wonder

Uptown Girl   1983   w.m. Billy Joel

Urgent   1981   w.m. Michael Jones

U.S. Air Force Song, The, *see* **The Army Air Corps Song**

U.S. Field Artillery March, The, or, **The Caissons Go Rolling Along**   1918   w.m. Edmund L. Gruber; erroneously attributed to John Philip Sousa. (MF) *Ice-Capades Revue.* (MF) *The Heat's On.* Ellen Drew and Jerry Colonna appeared in *Ice-Capades Revue.* Mae West, Victor Moore, and Xavier Cugat appeared in *The Heat's On.* This song was later adapted in 1956 with new words by Harold W. Arberg as "The Army Goes (Marching) Rolling Along," and soon became the official song of the United States Army. John Philip Sousa performed this song at a special Liberty Loan benefit concert at the New York Hippodrome. Brigadier General Edmund L. Gruber wrote the standard "Over hill, over dale" passage.

Use Ajax the Foaming Cleanser   1950   w.m. Joe Rines. This song was written for an Ajax Cleanser commercial promotion campaign.

Use Ta Be My Girl   1978   w.m. Kenneth Gamble, Leon Huff

Use Your Imagination   1950   w.m. Cole Porter. (MT) *Out of This World.* Charlotte Greenwood and William Redfield appeared in the stage production of *Out of This World.*

Utah Man Am I, A   1936   w.m. based on the tune "Solomon Levi"; adapted Thornton W. Allen. School song for the University of Utah.

Vacant Chair, The, or, **We Shall Meet But We Shall Miss Him**   1861   w. Henry S. Washburne   m. George Frederick Root. The narrative of this song refers to the death of Lt. John William Grout of the Fifteenth Massachusetts Volunteer Infantry. Its melody probably was inspired by "When I Saw Sweet Nellie Home (Aunt Dinah's Quilting Party)." The same tune later influenced Cole Porter's "Old-Fashioned Garden" and "Yes, We Have No Bananas."

Vagabond, The   1884   w. Charles Lamb Kenney   m. traditional; arr. James Lyman Molloy, J.L. Hatton. (MT) *The Student's Frolic.* The melody, as it appeared in the operetta *The Student's Frolic,* was originally titled "Beer, Beer, Beautiful Beer."

Vagabond Dreams   1939   w. Jack Lawrence   m. Hoagy Carmichael

Vagabond King Waltz, The, *see* **Waltz Huguette**

Vagabond Lover, *see* **I'm Just a Vagabond Lover**

Vagabond Song, *see* **Singing a Vagabond Song**

Valencia   1926   Fr.w. Lucienne Boyer, Jacques Charles   Eng.w. Clifford Grey   m. José Padilla. (MT) *The Great Temptations.*

Valentine   1926   w. Albert Willemetz   m. H. Christine. (MF)

Innocents of Paris. Maurice Chevalier appeared in *Innocents of Paris.*

Valleri 1968 w.m. Tommy Boyce, Bobby Hart

Valley of Swords, The 1980 m. Mike Batt. Ivor Novello Award winner 1979–80.

(Theme from) Valley of the Dolls 1968 w.m. Dory Previn, Andre Previn. (F) *Valley of the Dolls.* Patty Duke appeared in *Valley of the Dolls.*

Valley Valparaiso 1955 w.m. René Denoncin, José Gomera

Valotte 1985 w.m. Justin Clayton, Julian Lennon, Carlton Morales

Valse, *see* **Waltz**

Vamp, The 1919 w.m. Byron Gay. This song paid tribute to Theda Bara. The chorus of this song is based on Puccini's aria "One Fine Day" from *Madama Butterfly.*

Vanessa 1952 w.m. Bernie Wayne

Varsity Drag, The 1927 w. B.G. DeSylva, Lew Brown m. Ray Henderson. (MT) *Good News.* (MF) *Good News* (1930). (MF) *Good News* (1947). Zelma O'Neal and Mary Lawlor appeared in the stage production of *Good News.* Bessie Love and Mary Lawlor appeared in the 1930 film production of *Good News.* June Allyson and Peter Lawford appeared in the 1947 film production of *Good News.* See also Part I, 1926.

Vaya Con Dios 1953 w.m. Larry Russell, Inez James, Buddy Pepper

Veeda, La 1920 w. Nat Vincent m. John Alden

Vehicle 1970 w.m. James M. Peterik

Venus 1959 w.m. Ed Marshall. This song was popularly revived in 1970.

(Theme from) Vertigo 1958 w.m. Jay Livingston, Ray Evans. (F) *Vertigo.* James Stewart and Kim Novak appeared in *Vertigo.*

Very Merry Un-Birthday to You, A 1951 w.m. Mack David, Al Hoffman, Jerry Livingston. (MF) *Alice in Wonderland.* The voices of Ed Wynn and Jerry Colonna appeared in *Alice in Wonderland.*

Very Precious Love, A 1958 w. Paul Francis Webster m. Sammy Fain. (MF) *Majorie Morningstar.* Gene Kelly, Natalie Wood, and Ed Wynn appeared in *Majorie Morningstar.*

Very Soft Shoes 1959 w. Marshall Barer m. Mary Rodgers. (MT) *Once Upon a Mattress.* Carol Burnette appeared in *Once Upon a Mattress.*

Very Special Love, A 1957 w.m. Robert Allen

Very Special Love Song, A 1974 w.m. Norro Wilson, Billy Sherrill. Grammy Award winner 1974.

Very Thought of You, The 1934 w.m. Ray Noble. (MF) *Young Man of Music.* (MF) *Young Man with a Horn.* Doris Day and Lauren Bacall appeared in *Young Man of Music* and *Young Man with a Horn.* This song was popularly revived in 1939. Opening theme of the Ray Noble Orchestra.

Vesti la Giubba 1892 w.m. Ruggiero Leoncavallo. From the opera *Pagliacci.* This aria, most popularly performed by Enrico Caruso, was recorded on February 1, 1904, and was the first million-selling classical recording.

Vicar of Bray, *see* **Country Gardens**

Viceroy Gives You All the Taste All the Time 1969 w. Richard Delia m. Stan Applebaum. This song was written for a Viceroy Cigarettes commercial promotion campaign

Victors, The 1936 w.m. Louis Elbel. School song of the University of Michigan.

Victory March, *see* **Cheer, Cheer for Old Notre Dame**

Video Killed the Radio Star 1980 w.m. Geoff Downes, Trevor Horn, Bruce Woolley. Ivor Novello Award winner 1979–80.

Vie en Rose, La 1946 Fr.w. Edith Piaf Eng.w. Mack David m. R.S. Louiguy (Luis Guglielmi). (F) *To the Victor.* (MF) *The Eddy Duchin Story.* Dennis Morgan appeared in *To the Victor.* This song is alternately called "Take Me to Your Heart Again." Its original title was "You're Too Dangerous, Cherie." This song was popularly revived in 1950. Theme song of Edith Piaf.

Vieni, Vieni 1937 It.w. George Koger, H. Varna Eng.w. Rudy Vallee m. Vincent Scotto

Vienna 1982 w.m. Warren Cann, Christopher Cross, Billy Currie, Midge Ure. Ivor Novello Award winner 1981–82.

Vienna Dreams 1937 Ger.w. Rudolf Sieczynski Eng.w. Irving Caesar m. Rudolf Sieczynski (MF) *Painting the Clouds with Sunshine.* Virginia Mayo and Dennis Morgan appeared in *Painting the Clouds with Sunshine.* From the German "Wien du Stadt Meiner Träume," op.1.

Vienna Life 1873 m. Johann Strauss. From the German "Weiner Blut," op.354.

View to a Kill, A 1985 w.m. John Barry, Simon Le Bon, Nick Rhodes, Andy Taylor, John Taylor, Roger Taylor

Vilia 1907 w. Adrian Ross m. Franz Lehár. (MT) *The Merry Widow.* (MF) *The Merry Widow* (1934). (MF) *The Merry Widow* (1952). Maurice Chevalier and Jeanette MacDonald appeared in the 1934 film production of *The Merry Widow.* Lana Turner and Fernando Lamas appeared in the 1952 film production of *The Merry Widow.* New words were written for the 1934 film production by Lorenz Hart.

Vilikens and His Dinah, *see* **Sweet Betsy from Pike**

Village Blacksmith, The 1857 w. Henry Wadsworth Longfellow m. Willoughby Hunter Weiss

Village of Saint Bernadette, The 1960 w.m. Eula Parker. Ivor Novello Award winner 1959.

Vincent 1972 w.m. Don McLean

Violetera, La, *see* **Who'll Buy My Violets**

Violets 1900 w. Julian Fane m. Ellen Wright. (MT) *The Little Duchess.*

Violin Began To Play, The 1949 w.m. Ivor Novello

Violin Song, The 1915 w.m. Paul Rubens, Percy Greenbank. (MT) *Tina.* Phyllis Dare appeared in *Tina.*

Violins from Nowhere 1950 w.m. Herb Magidson m. Sammy Fain. (MT) *Michael Todd's Peep Show.* June Allen and Lilly Christine appeared in *Michael Todd's Peep Show.*

Viper's Drag, The 1934 w.m. Thomas "Fats" Waller. (MT) *Ain't Misbehavin'.* Debbie Allen and Nell Carter appeared in *Ain't Misbehavin'.* This song was written as an ode to a reefer of marijuana.

Virgin's Slumber Song, The, *see* **Maria Wiegenlied**

Vision of Salome, A 1908 m. J. Bodewalt Lampe. This song was the first "mystery tune" of the radio production "Stop the Music."

Viva I'America: Home of the Free 1859 w.m. Harrison Millard

Vive La Compagnie, or, **Vive L'Amour** 1844 w.m. traditional, from France. Based on the 1840 "Lincolnshire Poacher" and the earlier "Bucks A-Hunting Go." This song was first published in 1838.

Vive L'Amour, *see* **Vive La Compagnie**

Voice in the Wilderness, A 1960 w.m. Norrie Paramor, Bunny Lewis. (F) *Expresso Bongo.* Laurence Harvey and Sylvia Sims appeared in *Expresso Bongo.*

Voice of R.K.O., The 1929 w.m. Tom Kennedy. (R) *R.K.O. Radio Hour.*

Voice of the Hudson, The 1903 w.m. Paul Dresser

Voices of Spring 1883 m. Johann Strauss. (MF) *The Great Waltz.* Words were added to this song by Oscar Hammerstein II for the musical film *The Great Waltz.*

Voices of the Woods, or, **Welcome, Sweet Springtime** 1884 w. anon. m. Based on Rubinstein's "Melody in F"; arr. Michael Watson

Volare, or, **Nel Blu, Dipinto Di Blu** 1958 It.w. Domenico Modugno, Francesco Migliacci Eng.w. Mitchell Parish m. Domenico Modugno. Grammy Award winner 1958.

Volunteer Organist, The 1893 w. William B. Gray (Glenroy) m. Henry Lamb (Spaulding)

Voyage to the Bottom of the Sea 1961 w.m. Russell Faith. (F) *Voyage to the Bottom of the Sea.* Walter Pidgeon and Joan Fontaine appeared in *Voyage to the Bottom of the Sea.*

Wabash Blues, The 1921 w. Dave Ringle m. Fred Meinken. (F) *Joan of the Ozarks.* Judy Canova and Joe E. Brown appeared in *Joan of the Ozarks.*

Wabash Cannonball 1940 w.m. A.P. Carter. (F) *Rolling Home to Texas.* Tex Ritter and Slim Andrews appeared in *Rolling Home to Texas.*

Wabash Moon 1931 w.m. Dave Dreyer, Morton Downey

Wagon Wheels 1934 w. Billy Hill m. Peter DeRose. (MT) *Ziegfeld Follies of 1934.* (MT) *The New Ziegfeld Follies.* Fanny Brice and Jane Froman appeared in *Ziegfeld Follies of 1934.* Based on "Goin' Home" of 1922, and that, in turn, based on the Largo from the "From the New World" Symphony, op.95, by Anton Dvorak, 1893.

Wah Hoo 1936 w.m. Cliff Friend

Wah-Watusi, The 1962 w.m. Dave Appell, Kal Mann

Wait 1916 w.m. Guy d'Hardelot

Wait and See 1945 w. Johnny Mercer m. Harry Warren. (MF) *The Harvey Girls.* Judy Garland, Angela Lansbury, and Ray Bolger appeared in *The Harvey Girls.*

Wait For Me 1980 w.m. Daryl Hall

Wait for the Wagon 1851 w. possibly R. Bishop Buckley m. George P. Knauff. This song was used in 1884 to promote the Studebaker Wagon. R. Bishop Buckley organized Buckley's Minstrels in 1843.

Wait 'Til the Sun Shines, Nellie 1905 w. Andrew B. Sterling m. Harry Von Tilzer. (MF) *Birth of the Blues.* (MF) *Rhythm Parade.* (MF) *In the Good Old Summertime.* (MF) *Wait Till the Sun Shines Nellie.* Bing Crosby and Mary Martin appeared in *Birth of the Blues.* Gale Storm and Robert Lowey appeared in *Rhythm Parade.* Judy Garland and Van Johnson appeared in *In the Good Old Summertime.* David Wayne appeared in *Wait Till the Sun Shines Nellie.*

Wait Till the Clouds Roll By 1881 w. J.T. Wood m. H.T. Fulmer

Wait Till the Cows Come Home 1917 w. Anne Caldwell m. Ivan Caryll. (MT) *Jack O'Lantern.* Fred Stone appeared in *Jack O'Lantern.*

Wait Till the Tide Comes In 1887 w. George Propheter m. Gussie L. Davis

Wait Till You Get Them Up in the Air, Boys 1919 w. Lew Brown m. Albert Von Tilzer

Wait Till You See Her 1942 w. Lorenz Hart m. Richard Rodgers. (MT) *By Jupiter.*

Wait Until Dark 1968 w.m. Ray Evans, Henry Mancini, Jerry Livingston. (F) *Wait Until Dark.* Audrey Hepburn appeared in *Wait Until Dark.*

Wait Until Your Daddy Comes Home 1912 w.m. Irving Berlin

Waiter and the Porter and the Upstairs Maid, The 1941 w.m. Johnny Mercer. (MF) *Birth of the Blues.* Bing Crosby and Mary Martin appeared in *Birth of the Blues.*

Waiting 1867 w. Ellen H. Flagg m. Harrison Millard

Waiting 1909 w. Harry L. Cort, George E. Stoddard m. Harold Orlob. (MT) *Listen Lester.*

Waiting at the Church, or **My Wife Won't Let Me** 1906 w. Fred W. Leigh m. Henry E. Pether. (MF) *Birth of the Blues.* Bing Crosby and Mary Martin appeared in *Birth of the Blues.* This song was originally written for Vesta Victoria.

Waiting For a Girl Like You 1981 w.m. Michael Jones, Louis Grammatico

Waiting for the Girls Upstairs 1971 w.m. Stephen Sondheim. (MT) *Follies.* Yvonne DeCarlo and Alexis Smith appeared in *Follies.*

Waiting for the Robert E. Lee 1912 w. L. Wolfe Gilbert m. Lewis F. Muir. (MF) *The Story of Vernon and Irene Castle.* (MF) *The Jolson Story.* Fred Astaire and Ginger Rogers appeared in *The Story of Vernon and Irene Castle.* Larry Parks appeared in *The Jolson Story.*

Waitin' for the Train To Come In 1945 w.m. Sunny Skylar, Martin Block

Wake Me Up Before You Go-Go 1984 w.m. George Michael

Wake Me When It's Over 1960 w.m. Sammy Cahn, James Van Heusen

Wake Nicodemus 1864 w.m. Henry Clay Work

Wake the Town and Tell the People 1955 w. Sammy Gallop m. Jerry Livingston

Wake Up and Live 1937 w. Mack Gordon m. Harry Revel. (MF) *Wake Up and Live.* Walter Winchell and Alice Faye appeared in *Wake Up and Live.*

Wake Up Little Susie 1957 w.m. Boudleaux Bryant, Felice Bryant. This song was popularly revived in 1982.

Waking Or Sleeping 1943 w.m. Ivor Novello

Wal, I Swan!, or, **Ebenezer Frye,** or, **Giddiap Napoleon, It Looks Like Rain** 1907 w.m. Benjamin Hapgood Burt

Walk Away from Love 1975 w.m. Charles Kipps, Jr.

Walk Away, Renee 1966 w.m. Mike Lookofsky, Tony Sansone, Bob Calilli

Walk—Don't Run 1960 w.m. Johnny Smith

Walk Hand in Hand 1956 w.m. Johnny Cowell

Walk in the Black Forest, A 1965 w.m. Horst Jankowski

Walk Like a Man 1963 w.m. Bob Crewe, Bob Gaudio

Walk of Life 1986 w.m. Mark Knopfler

Walk On By 1961 w. Hal David m. Burt Bacharach. This song was most popular in 1964.

Walk on the Wild Side 1962 w. Mack David m. Elmer Bernstein. (F) *Walk on the Wild Side*. Laurence Harvey and Jane Fonda appeared in *Walk on the Wild Side*.

Walk Right In 1930 w.m. Gus Cannon in 1929; arr. 1962 Erik Darling, W. Svanoc. This song was popularly revived in 1963.

Walkin' Back to Happiness 1961 w.m. John Schroeder, Michael Hawker. Ivor Novello Award winner 1961.

Walkin' by the River 1940 w. Robert Sour m. Una Mae Carlisle

Walking Happy 1966 w. Sammy Cahn m. Jimmy Van Heusen. (MT) *Walking Happy*. Norman Wisdom appeared in *Walking Happy*.

Walking in Rhythm 1975 w.m. Barney Perry

Walkin' My Baby Back Home 1930 w.m. Roy Turk, Fred E. Ahlert, Harry Richman. This song was popularly revived in 1952.

Walking on Sunshine 1985 w.m. Kimberley Rew

Walkin' to Missouri 1952 w.m. Bob Merrill

Wallflower 1984 w. Fred Ebb m. John Kander. (MT) *The Rink*. Liza Minnelli and Chita Rivera appeared in *The Rink*.

Walter, Walter (Lead Me to the Altar) 1937 w.m. E.G. Butler, W.G. Haines, James S. Hancock

Waltz: included at the end of the "Waltz" listings are compositions whose titles begin with the French "Valse"

Waltz 1909 m. Franz Lehár. (MT) *The Count of Luxembourg*. *The Count of Luxembourg* premiered in Vienna on November 12, 1909.

Waltz Coppélia 1870 w. Léo Délibes. From the ballet *Coppélia*. *Coppélia* was first performed in Paris on May 25, 1870.

Waltz Dream, A 1907 w.m. Oscar Straus, Adrian Ross. (MT) *A Waltz Dream*.

Waltz Huguette, or, **The Vagabond King Waltz** 1925 w. Brian Hooker m. Rudolf Friml. (MT) *The Vagabond King*. (MF) *The Vagabond King* (1930). (MF) *The Vagabond King* (1956). Carolyn Thomson and Dennis King appeared in the stage production of *The Vagabond King*. Jeanette MacDonald and Dennis King appeared in the 1930 film production of *The Vagabond King*.

Waltz in Swing Time 1936 w. Dorothy Fields m. Jerome Kern. (MF) *Swing Time*. Fred Astaire, Ginger Rogers, and Victor Moore appeared in *Swing Time*.

Waltz Me Around Again Willie—'Round, 'Round, 'Round 1906 w. Will D. Cobb m. Ren Shields. (MT) *His Honour the Mayor*.

Waltz of My Heart 1939 w.m. Ivor Novello, Christopher Hassall. (MT) *The Dancing Years*. (MF) *The Dancing Years*. Mary Ellis appeared in *The Dancing Years*.

Waltz of the Bells, The, see **Ting-a-Ling**

Waltz of the Flowers 1892 m. Peter Tchaikovsky. (MF) *Fantasia*. From *The Nutcracker Suite*. See also *The Nutcracker Suite*.

Waltz of the Gypsies, The 1937 w.m. Michael Carr

Waltz Song 1902 w.m. Edward German

Waltz Theme 1945 m. Richard Addinsell. (F) *Blithe Spirit*.

Waltz You Saved for Me, The 1930 w. Gus Kahn m. Wayne King, Emil Flindt

Waltzes 1910 m. Richard Strauss. From *Der Rosenkavalier*. *Der Rosenkavalier* was first performed in Dresden, January 26, 1911.

Valse Bleue 1900 m. Alfred Margis

Valse Lente 1870 m. Léo Délibes. From the ballet *Coppélia*.

Valse Septembre 1909 w.m. Felix Godwin

Valse Serenade, see **Sleepy Lagoon**

Valse Triste 1904 m. Jean Sibelius

Valse Tzigane, see **Fascination**

Waltzing Cat, The 1951 m. Leroy Anderson

Waltzing Doll, see **Poupée Valsante**

Waltzing Matilda 1903 w. A.B. "Banjo" Paterson m. Marie Cowan; arr. Orrie Lee. (F) *On the Beach*. Gregory Peck and Fred Astaire appeared in *On the Beach*. Based on Robert Tannahill's "Craigielea." This traditional Australian song was popularly revived in 1936 and 1941. First performed at a horse race in 1895, this song's "matilda" refers to a knapsack, and not a girl. This song later became the unofficial national anthem of Australia; the official anthem, as of May 22, 1977, is "Advance Australia Fair."

Wanderer, The 1961 w.m. Ernest Maresca

Wanderer, The 1980 w.m. Donna Summer, Giorgio Moroder

Wanderin' 1950 w.m. traditional. (F) *Heart of the Rockies*. Roy Rogers and Penny Edwards appeared in *Heart of the Rockies*. Two new arrangements were published in 1950: the first, arranged by Sammy Kaye; the second, by Ed Jackson.

Wang, Wang Blues, The 1921 w.m. Gus Mueller, "Buster" Johnson, Henry Busse. (MF) *Somebody Loves Me*. (MF) *The Rat Race*. Betty Hutton appeared in *Somebody Loves Me*, biopic of song spinners Blossom Seeley and Benny Fields. Tony Curtis and Debbie Reynolds appeared in *The Rat Race*.

Wanna Be Startin' Somethin' 1984 w.m. Michael Jackson

Want Ads 1971 w.m. General Johnson, Barney Perkins, Greg S. Perry

Wanted 1954 w.m. Jack Fulton, Lois Steele

Wanting You 1928 w. Oscar Hammerstein II m. Sigmund Romberg. (MT) *The New Moon*. (MF) *The New Moon* (1930). (MF) *The New Moon* (1940). Grace Moore and Lawrence Tibbett appeared in the 1930 film production of *The New Moon*. Jeanette MacDonald and Nelson Eddy appeared in the 1940 film production of *The New Moon*.

War 1970 w.m. Norman Whitfield, Barrett Strong

War of the Worlds 1980 m. Jeff Wayne. Ivor Novello Award winner 1979–80.

Warblings at Eve 1858 m. Henry Brinley Richards

Warrior, The 1985 w.m. Nick Gilder

Warrior Bold, A 1875 w. Edwin Thomas m. Stephen Adams (Michael Maybrick)

(Theme from The) Warsaw Concerto 1942 m. Richard Addinsell. (F) *Dangerous Moonlight*. Anton Walbrook and Sally Gray appeared in *Dangerous Moonlight*.

Was It a Dream 1928 w.m. Sam Coslow, Larry Spier, Addy Britt

Was It Rain 1937 w. Walter Hirsch m. Lou Handman. (MF) *The Hit Parade*. Phil Regan and Frances Langford appeared in *The Hit Parade*.

Was That the Human Thing To Do 1931 w.m. Joseph Young, Sammy Fain

Washboard Blues 1928 w.m. Hoagy Carmichael, Fred B. Callahan

Washing on the Siegfried Line 1939 w.m. Jimmy Kennedy, Michael Carr. This song was popularly performed all over Britain by the comedy team of Flanagan and Allen. Parodied by Nazi Germany, it was played over the radio in every occupied country in its newer aggressive version, until 1945 and the defeat of Germany.

Washington and Lee Swing 1910 w. Thornton W. Allen, C.A. Robbins m. Thornton W. Allen, M.W. Sheafe. This song at a slower tempo resembles "Chinatown, My Chinatown." School song for Washington & Lee University. See "Dummy Song."

Washington Post 1889 m. John Philip Sousa. This standard was written on commission for *The Washington Post* award ceremonies for promising journalists and essayists.

Washington Square 1963 w.m. Bob Goldstein, David Shire

Wasted Days Wasted Nights 1975 w.m. Freddy Fender, Wayne Duncan

Watch What Happens 1964 w.m. Norman Gimbel, Michel Legrand. (MT) *Lena Horne: The Lady and Her Music*. Lena Horne appeared in *Lena Horne: The Lady and Her Music*.

Watchin' Girls Go By 1982 w.m. Buddy Killen, Ronnie McDowell

Watching the Clouds Roll By 1928 w. Bert Kalmar m. Harry Ruby. (MT) *Animal Crackers*. (MF) *Animal Crackers*. The Marx Brothers appeared in both the stage and film productions of *Animal Crackers*.

Watching the Trains Come In 1916 w.m. Frank Leo

Watching the Wheels 1981 w.m. John Lennon

Water Boy 1922 w.m. Avery Robinson. This popular black American convict song is based on "Till the Clouds Roll By" of 1917, "César Cui: Orientale," and "Marche Slav" by Tchaikovsky.

Water Gypsies, The 1955 w.m. Vivian Ellis, A.P. Herbert

Water, Water 1957 w.m. Lionel Bart, Michael Pratt, Tommy Steele. Ivor Novello Award winner 1957.

Waterloo 1959 w.m. John Loudermilk, Marijohn Wilkin

Waters of Perkiomen 1925 w. Al Dubin m. F. Henri Klickmann

Waters of Venice, or, **Floating Down the Sleepy Lagoon** 1918 w. Neville Fleeson m. Albert Von Tilzer

Waves of the Danube, or, **Danube Waves** 1880 m. Ion Ivanovici. See also "The Anniversary Song."

Way Back Home 1935 w.m. Al Lewis, Tom Waring. This song was popularly revived in 1949.

Way Down in Iowa I'm Going To Hide Away 1916 w. Sam M. Lewis, Joe Young m. George W. Meyer

Way Down in My Heart, or, **I've Got a Feeling for You** 1904 w. Edward Madden m. Theodore F. Morse

Way Down in Old Indiana 1901 w.m. Paul Dresser

Way Down Upon the Swanee River, *see* **Old Folks at Home**

Way Down Yonder in New Orleans 1922 w.m. Henry Creamer, J. Turner Layton. (MT) *Spices of 1922*. (MF) *Is Everybody Happy*. (MF) *Somebody Loves Me*. (MF) *Drum Crazy*. Bob Haymes appeared in *Is Everybody Happy*, biopic of bandleader Ted Lewis. Betty Hutton appeared in *Somebody Loves Me*.

Way Down Yonder in the Cornfield 1901 w.m. Will D. Cobb, Gus Edwards

Way I Want To Touch You, The 1975 w.m. Toni Tennille

Way of Love, The 1972 w.m. Al Stillman, Jacques J.J. Dieval, Mariano Ruiz

Way Out West 1937 w. Lorenz Hart m. Richard Rodgers. (MT) *Babes in Arms*. (MF) *Babes in Arms*. Mitzi Green and Ray Heatherton appeared in the stage production of *Babes in Arms*. Judy Garland and Mickey Rooney appeared in the film production of *Babes in Arms*.

Way Out Yonder in the Golden West 1914 w.m. Percy Wenrich

Way That the Wind Blows, The 1946 w.m. Joan Whitney, Alex Kramer

(Theme from) Way to the Stars, The 1945 w.m. Nicholas Brodszky

Way We Were, The 1974 w. Alan Bergman, Marilyn Bergman m. Marvin Hamlisch. (F) *The Way We Were*. Academy Award winner 1973. Grammy Award winner 1974. Barbra Streisand and Robert Redford appeared in *The Way We Were*.

Way You Look Tonight, The 1936 w. Dorothy Fields m. Jerome Kern. (MF) *Swing Time*. Fred Astaire and Ginger Rogers appeared in *Swing Time*. Academy Award winner 1936.

Wayfarin' Stranger c.1800 w.m. traditional American folk ballad

Wayward Wind, The 1956 w.m. Stan Lebowsky, Herb Newman. This song was popularly revived in 1963.

Wayworn Traveller, The 1794 w. G. Colman m. Samuel Arnold. From the English ballad opera *The Mountaineers*.

We All Stand Together 1985 w.m. Paul McCartney. Ivor Novello Award winner 1984–85.

We All Went Up Up Up the Mountain 1933 w.m. Elton Box, Desmond Cox, Ralph Butler

We Are Coming, Father Abraham, 300,000 More 1862 w.m. James Sloan Gibbons, erroneously credited to Stephen Collins Foster and William Cullen Bryant. When this song was performed for President Abraham Lincoln, he remarked that it "contained an excellent sentiment and was sung in a manner worthy of the sentiment."

We Are Family 1979 w.m. Bernard Edwards, Nile Rodgers

We Are in Love 1964 w.m. Chris Andrews

We Are the World 1985 w.m. Michael Jackson, Lionel Richie. Proceeds from this song were donated to help feed the starving peoples of Africa. Grammy Award winner 1985.

We Belong 1985 w.m. Eric Lowen, Dan Navarro

We Built This City 1985 w.m. Dennis Lambert, Martin Page, Bernie Taupin, Peter Wolf

We Came from the Same Old State 1899 w.m. Paul Dresser

We Can Work It Out 1966 w.m. John Lennon, Paul McCartney. (MT) *Beatlemania*. Ivor Novello Award winner 1965.

We Could Make Such Beautiful Music (Together) 1940 w. Robert Sour m. Henry Manners. This song was popularly revived in 1947.

We Did It Before (and We Can Do It Again) 1941 w.m. Charles Tobias, Cliff Friend. (MT) *Banjo Eyes*. (F) *Sweetheart of the Fleet*. Joan Davis and Joan Woodbury appeared in *Sweetheart of the Fleet*.

We Do It 1977 w.m. Russell Stone. Ivor Novello Award winner 1976–77.

We Do Not Belong Together 1984 w.m. Stephen Sondheim. (MT) *Sunday in the Park with George*. Mandy Patinkin and Bernadette Peters appeared in *Sunday in the Park with George*.

We Don't Need Another Hero 1985 w.m. Graham Lyle, Terry Britten. (F) *Thunderdome*. Mel Gibson and Tina Turner appeared in *Thunderdome*. Ivor Novello Award winner 1985–86.

We Don't Talk Anymore 1980 w.m. Alan Tarney. Ivor Novello Award winner 1979–80.

We Don't Want the Bacon, What We Want Is a Piece of the Rhine 1918 w.m. Howard Carr, Harry Russell, Jimmie Havens

We Fight Tomorrow, Mother 1898 w.m. Paul Dresser

We Gather Together (To Ask the Lord's Blessing), or, **Prayer of Thanksgiving** 1597 or earlier w.m. anon.; first published with English words in 1894; this standard is based on the traditional Dutch hymn "Dankgebet." According to Al-

bert F. Robinson, organist and choirmaster, Chapel of St. Cornelius the Centurion, "the words of this hymn were written by an unknown author in celebration of Dutch freedom from sovereignty at the end of the sixteenth century. It was first published in 1626."

We Got the Beat 1982 w.m. Charlotte Caffey

We Just Couldn't Say Goodbye 1932 w.m. Harry Woods

We Kiss in a Shadow 1951 w. Oscar Hammerstein II m. Richard Rodgers. (MT) *The King and I*. (MF) *The King and I*. Gertrude Lawrence and Yul Brynner appeared in the stage production of *The King and I*. Deborah Kerr and Yul Brynner appeared in the film production of *The King and I*.

We May Never Love Like This Again 1974 w.m. Al Kasha, Joel Hirschorn. (F) *The Towering Inferno*. Academy Award winner 1974.

We Must Be Vigilant, *see* **American Patrol**

We Need a Little Christmas 1966 w.m. Jerry Herman. (MT) *Mame*. (MT) *Jerry's Girls*. (MF) *Mame*. Angela Lansbury appeared in the stage production of *Mame*. Dorothy Loudon, Chita Rivera, and Leslie Uggams appeared in *Jerry's Girls*. Lucille Ball appeared in the film production of *Mame*.

We Never Talk Much 1951 w. Sammy Cahn m. Nicholas Brodszky. (MF) *Rich, Young and Pretty*. Jane Powell and Vic Damone appeared in *Rich, Young and Pretty*.

We Parted By the River 1866 w.m. William Shakespeare Hays

We Parted on the Shore 1934 w.m. Harry Lauder

We Saw the Sea 1936 w.m. Irving Berlin. (MF) *Follow the Fleet*. Fred Astaire and Ginger Rogers appeared in *Follow the Fleet*.

We Shall Meet But We shall Miss Him, *see* **The Vacant Chair**

We Shall Overcome 1945 w.m. anon.; based on the music from the early hymn "O Sanctissima" of 1794, and words from the C. Albert Findley hymn "I'll Overcome Some Day" of 1901. This song was popularly revived in 1946 by black tobacco workers seeking to raise their forty-five cents per hour wage, and in 1963 during the black Civil Rights movement.

We Three Kings of Orient (Are) 1857 w.m. John Henry Hopkins

We Three—My Echo, My Shadow and Me 1940 w.m. Nelson Cogne, Sammy Mysels, Dick Robertson. This song was popularly revived in 1947.

We Two Shall Meet Again 1927 w. Harry B. Smith m. Emmerich Kalman. (MT) *The Circus Princess*.

We Were Meant To Be Loved 1980 w.m. James Photoglou, Brian Neary

We Were Sweethearts for Many Years 1895 w.m. Paul Dresser

We Will Always Be Sweethearts 1932 w. Leo Robin m. Oscar Straus. (MF) *One Hour with You*. Jeanette MacDonald and Maurice Chevalier appeared in *One Hour with You*.

We Will Make Love 1957 w.m. Ronald Hulme (Russ Hamilton). Ivor Novello Award winner 1957.

We Won't Go Home Until Morning, *see* **For He's a Jolly Good Fellow**

Wear My Ring Around Your Neck 1958 w.m. Bert Carroll, Russell Moody

Wearin' o' the Green, The 1798–1802 w.m. traditional street ballad, from Ireland. See also "Benny Havens, Oh!"

Weary Blues 1956 w.m. Artie Matthews, Mort Greene, George Cates

Weary River 1929 w. Grant Clarke m. Louis Silvers. (F) *Weary River*. Richard Barthelmess and William Holden appeared in *Weary River*.

Webb, *see* 'Tis Dawn, the Lark Is Singing

Wedding Bell Blues 1966 w.m. Laura Nyro. This song was most popular in 1969.

Wedding Bells Are Breaking Up That Old Gang of Mine 1929 w. Irving Kahal, Willie Raskin m. Sammy Fain

Wedding Glide, The 1912 w.m. Louis Hirsch. (MT) *The Passing Show of 1912*. (MT) *Hullo Ragtime*. Gerald Kirby, Lew Hearn, and Shirley Kellog appeared in *Hullo Ragtime*.

Wedding March 1844 m. Felix Mendelssohn. From the German "Ein Sommernachtstraum," the opera *A Midsummer Night's Dream*. See also "Wedding March (Bridal Chorus)" by Wagner.

Wedding March (Bridal Chorus) 1852 m. Richard Wagner. From the opera *Lohengrin*. This theme and Mendelssohn's "Wedding March" from the opera *A Midsummer Night's Dream* were first performed together at the royal wedding of Princess Victoria of England and Prince Frederick William of Prussia in 1858; this began the still popular tradition of these wedding marches being performed together.

Wedding of Lilli Marlene, The 1949 w.m. Michael Reine, Tommie Connor

Wedding of Mister Mickey Mouse, The 1933 w.m. Eddie Pola, Franz Vienna

Wedding o' Sandy McNab 1908 w.m. Harry Lauder

Wedding of the Painted Doll, The 1929 w. Arthur Freed m. Nacio Herb Brown. (MT) *Singin' in the Rain*. (MF) *Broadway Melody*. (MF) *Singin' in the Rain*. Bessie Love appeared in *Broadway Melody*. Gene Kelly, Debbie Reynolds, and Donald O'Connor appeared in *Singin' in the Rain*.

Wedding of the Rose 1911 w.m. Leon Jessel

Wedding of the Winds 1897 m. John T. Hall

Wedding Ring 1957 w.m. Ronald Hulme (Russ Hamilton)

Wedding Samba, The 1947 w.m. Abraham Ellstein, Allan Small, Joseph Leibowitz. (MF) *On an Island with You*. Esther Williams, Peter Lawford, and Jimmy Durante appeared in *On an Island with You*. This song, originally known as "The Wedding Rhumba," was popularly revived in 1950.

Wednesday's Child 1967 w.m. Mack David

Wee Deoch-an-Doris, A 1911 w.m. Gerald Grafton, Harry Lauder

Weekend in Havana, A 1941 w.m. Mack Gordon, Harry Warren. (MF) *A Weekend in Havana*. Carmen Miranda, Cesar Romero, and Alice Fáye appeared in *A Weekend in Havana*.

Weekend in the Country, A 1973 w.m. Stephen Sondheim. (MT) *A Little Night Music*. (MF) *A Little Night Music*. Len Cariou, Glynis Johns, and Hermione Gingold appeared in the stage production of *A Little Night Music*. Len Cariou, Elizabeth Taylor, and Hermione Gingold appeared in the film production of *A Little Night Music*.

Weeping, Sad and Lonely, or, **When This Cruel War Is Over** 1863 w. Charles Carroll Sawyer m. Henry Tucker. This song inspired Septimus Winner to write his answer song "Yes, I Would the War Were Over." One critic of the time wrote "there is nothing in this sentimental song that enables one to read the riddle of its remarkable popularity during the Civil War. It has no poetic merit; its rhythm is commonplace, and the tune to which it was sung was of the flimsiest musical structure, without even a trick of melody to commend it."

Weeping Saviour 1835 w.m. William Walker

Weeping Willer, The 1865 w.m. Harry Clifton

Weight, The 1968 w.m. Jaime Robertson

Welcome Back 1976 w.m. John Sebastian. (TV) *Welcome Back Kotter*.

Welcome Sweet Springtime, see Voices of the Woods

Welcome to My World 1962 w.m. Winkler, Hathcock

We'll Be Together Again 1945 w.m. Carl Fischer, Frankie Laine. This song was also popular in 1948. Theme song of Frankie Laine.

Well, Did You Evah 1940 w.m. Cole Porter. (MT) *Du Barry Was a Lady* (MF) *Du Barry Was a Lady* (MF) *High Society*. Ethel Merman, Bert Lahr, and Betty Grable appeared in the stage production of *Du Barry Was a Lady*. Gene Kelly and Lucille Ball appeared in the film production of *Du Barry Was a Lady*. Bing Crosby, Grace Kelly, and Frank Sinatra appeared in *High Society*. This song was popularly revived in 1956.

We'll Gather Lilacs 1945 w.m. Ivor Novello. (MT) *Perchance To Dream*. (MF) *Lilacs in the Spring*. Olive Gilbert appeared in *Perchance To Dream*. Errol Flynn appeared in *Lilacs in the Spring*.

We'll Have a Jubilee in My Old Kentucky Home 1915 w. Coleman Goetz m. Walter Donaldson

We'll Have a Kingdom 1926 w. Otto Harbach, Oscar Hammerstein II m. Rudolf Friml. (MT) *The Wild Rose*.

We'll Have To Go 1960 w. Charles Green m. Joe Allison, Audrey Allison

Well, I Swan, *see* Wal, I Swan!

We'll Keep a Welcome 1949 w.m. Mai Jones, Lyn Joshua, James Harper

We'll Knock the Heligo—Into Heligo—Out of Heliogoland 1917 w. John O'Brien m. Theodore F. Morse

We'll May Hay While The Sun Shines 1933 w. Arthur Freed m. Nacio Herb Brown. (MF) *Going Hollywood*. Bing Crosby appeared in *Going Hollywood*.

We'll Meet Again 1939 w.m. Ernie Burnett, Gerald Griffin. This song was popularly revived in 1960.

We'll Never Have To Say Goodbye Again 1978 w.m. Jeffrey Comanor

We'll Sing in the Sunshine 1964 w.m. Gale Garnett

Well-a-Day 1846 w. anon. m. George Linley

Wendy 1954 w. Betty Comden, Adolph Green m. Jule Styne. (MT) *Peter Pan*. Mary Martin appeared in *Peter Pan*.

We're Going Over 1917 w.m. Andrew B. Sterling, Bernie Grossman, Arthur Lange

We're Gonna Be All Right 1965 w. Stephen Sondheim. Richard Rodgers. (MT) *Do I Hear a Waltz?* (MT) *Side by Side by Sondheim.* Millicent Martin and Julie N. McKenzie appeared in *Side by Side by Sondheim.*

We're Gonna Change the World 1971 w.m. David Matthews, Tim Harris. Ivor Novello Award winner 1970–71.

We're Having a Baby 1941 w. Harold Adamson m. Vernon Duke. (MT) *Banjo Eyes.* (MF) *Hollywood Canteen.* Bette Davis, Joan Crawford, and Eddie Cantor appeared in *Hollywood Canteen.*

We're in the Money, or, **The Gold Diggers' Song** 1933 w. Al Dubin m. Harry Warren. (MT) *Forty-Second Street.* (MF) *The Gold Diggers of 1933.* (MF) *Painting the Clouds with Sunshine.* Jerry Ohrbach and Tammy Grimes appeared in *Forty-Second Street.* Ginger Rogers appeared in *The Gold Diggers of 1933,* dancing in an outfit consisting entirely of silver coins; 1933 was also the most severe period of the Depression. Virginia Mayo appeared in *Painting the Clouds With Sunshine,* the 1951 remake of *The Gold Diggers of 1933.*

We're in This Love Together 1981 w.m. Roger Murrah, Keith Stegall

We're Marching to Zion 1867 w. Isaac Watts m. Reverend Robert Lowry

We're Off To See the Wizard 1939 w. E.Y. Harburg m. Harold Arlen. (MF) *The Wizard of Oz.* Judy Garland, Ray Bolger, Bert Lahr, and Jack Haley appeared in *The Wizard of Oz.*

We're the Couple in the Castle 1941 w. Frank Loesser m. Hoagy Carmichael. (MF) *Mr. Bug Goes to Town.*

We're Through 1964 w.m. Lee Rainsford

Were You There When They Crucified My Lord? 1865 w.m. traditional black American spiritual

West End Blues 1928 w.m. Joseph Oliver, Clarence Williams

West End Girls 1986 w.m. Chris Lowe, Neil Tennant

West of the Great Divide 1924 w. George Whiting m. Ernest R. Ball

West of Zanzibar (Jambo) 1954 w.m. Jack Fishman. (F) *West of Zanzibar.*

Westminster Chimes 1793–1794 Written by William Crotch in 1793 for St. Mary's Church (the Great) in Cambridge, England, these traditional chimes now are played on four tubular balls in the Victoria Clock of the Houses of Parliament. The melodic inspiration is the fifth bar of Handel's ''I Know That My Redeemer Liveth'' of 1793–94. These chimes are heard in the release of Robeldo's ''Three O'Clock in the Morning'' of 1921. Magistrate George Postel ruled that the melody which was also heard in a New York clock tower, was ''of special note'' and not a disturbance, after a suit of disturbing the peace was brought into his court. The 320-foot clock tower housing Big Ben (which is not the name of the clock, but of the 13.5-ton bell inside) was completed in 1858. See also ''Bells of St. Clement's.''

Westminster Waltz 1956 w.m. Robert Farnon. Ivor Novello Award winner 1956.

Westward Ho!—The Covered Wagon March 1923 w. R.A. Barnet m. Hugo Riesenfeld. (F) *The Covered Wagon.* This song was written for the piano and orchestra accompaniment to this classic silent film.

Wet Sheet and a Flowing Sea, A 1825 w. Allan Cunningham m. based on ''Le Petit Tambour''

We've a Million in the Field 1862 w.m. Stephen Collins Foster

We've Been Chums for Fifty Years 1905 w.m. Thurland Chattaway

We've Got To Keep Up with the Joneses 1935 w.m. Leslie Elliot, Robert Rutherford

We've Got Tonight 1979 w.m. Bob Seger. This song was popularly revived in 1983.

We've Only Just Begun 1970 w.m. Paul Williams. This song originally was a bank advertising jingle.

Weymouth Chimes, The 1905 w.m. J.S. Howgill

Whar Did You Cum From, or, **Knock a Nigger Down** 1840 w.m. anon. Popularly sung by Joel W. Sweeney, possibly the first banjo-playing black minstrel.

What a Diff'rence a Day Made (Makes) 1934 Sp.w. Maria Grever Eng.w. Stanley Adams m. Maria Grever. Grammy Award winner 1959. This song was popularly revived in 1944, 1960, and 1975. From the Spanish ''Cuando Vuelva a Tu Lado.''

What a Feeling, *see* **Flashdance**

What a Fool Believes 1979 w.m. Kenny Loggins, Michael McDonald. Grammy Award winner 1979.

What a Friend We Have in Jesus 1876 w. Horatius Bonar m. Charles Crozat Converse. According to a poll conducted by *The Christian Herald,* this gospel hymn rates second in popularity among Protestant churchgoers polled concerning 1,666 hymn and song contenders. First honors went to ''The Old Rugged Cross.''

(Ooh) What a Little Moonlight Can Do 1934 w.m. Harry Woods. (F) *Road House.* Ida Lupino appeared in *Road House.*

What a Mouth 1960 w.m. R.P. Weston

What a Wonderful Mother You'd Be 1915 w. Joe Goodwin m. Al Piantadosi

What a Wonderful World 1968 w.m. George Douglas, George David Weiss

What About Love? 1986 w.m. Jim Vallance

What About Me 1984 w.m. David Foster, Richard Marx, Kenny Rogers

What Am I Gonna Do with You 1975 w.m. Barry White

What Are the Wild Waves Saying 1850 w. Joseph Edwards Carpenter m. Stephen Glover. The deathbed scene of Little Paul in the Dickens novel *Dombey and Son* inspired Joseph Carpenter's haunting lyric of memories of the sea.

What Are We Doing Lonesome 1982 w.m. Larry Gatlin

What Are You Doing the Rest of Your Life 1944 w. Ted Koehler m. Burton Lane. (MF) *Hollywood Canteen.* Joan Crawford, Bette Davis, and Eddie Cantor appeared in *Hollywood Canteen.*

What Are You Doing the Rest of Your Life 1970 w. Alan

Bergman, Marilyn Bergman m. Michel Legrand. (F) *The Happy Ending.*

What Can I Say, Dear, After I Say I'm Sorry, *see* **After I Say I'm Sorry**

What Cher, *see* **Knocked 'Em in the Old Kent Road**

What Did I Do To Be So Black and Blue 1933 w.m. Andy Razaf, Thomas "Fats" Waller, Harry Brooks. (MT) *Hot Chocolates.* (MT) *Ain't Misbehavin'.* (MF) *Satchmo the Great.* Jazzlips Richardson and Jimmy Baskette appeared in *Hot Chocolates.* Debbie Allen and Nell Carter appeared in *Ain't Misbehavin'.* Louis Armstrong appeared in *Satchmo the Great.* Written in 1929, this song was first popularized in 1933.

What Did I Have That I Don't Have 1966 w. Alan Jay Lerner m. Burton Lane. (MT) *On a Clear Day You Can See Forever.* (MF) *On a Clear Day You Can See Forever.* Barbra Streisand appeared in the film production of *On a Clear Day You Can See Forever.*

What Do I Care 1929 w.m. Raymond Klages, Jesse Greer, Harry Carroll

What Do I Care, *see also* **My Sweetie Turned Me Down**

What Do (the) Simple Folk Do 1960 w. Alan Jay Lerner m. Frederick Loewe. (MT) *Camelot.* (MF) *Camelot.* Julie Andrews appeared in the stage production of *Camelot.* Vanessa Redgrave appeared in the film production of *Camelot.*

What Do We Do on a Dew-Dew-Dewy Day, *see* **Dew-Dew-Dewy Day**

What Do You Do in the Infantry? 1943 w.m. Frank Loesser

What Do You Want 1959 w.m. Les Vandyke. Ivor Novello Award winner 1959.

What Do You Want To Make Those Eyes at Me For 1916 w.m. Joe McCarthy, Howard Johnson, James V. Monaco. (MT) *The Better 'Ole.* (MF) *Incendiary Blonde.* (MF) *The Merry Monihans.* Betty Hutton appeared in *Incendiary Blonde,* biopic of speakeasy hostess Texas Guinan. Donald O'Connor and Peggy Ryan appeared in *The Merry Monihans.*

What Does It Matter 1927 w.m. Irving Berlin

What Does It Take (To Win Your Love) 1969 w.m. Harvey Fuqua, Vernon Bullock, Johnny Bristol

What D'Yer Think of That 1922 w.m. J.P. Long

What Good Does It Do 1957 w. E.Y. Harburg m. Harold Arlen (MT) *Jamaica.*

What Have You Done for Me Lately 1986 w.m. Jimmy Jam, Terry Lewis

What Ho She Bumps 1900 w.m. A.J. Mills, Harry Castling

What I Did for Love 1975 w. Edward Kleban m. Marvin Hamlisch. (MT) *A Chorus Line.* Donna McKechnie appeared in *A Chorus Line.*

What Is Home Without a Mother 1854 w.m. Septimus Winner (Alice Hawthorne)

What Is There To Say 1933 w. E.Y. Harburg m. Vernon Duke. (MT) *Ziegfeld Follies of 1934.* Fanny Brice and Jane Froman appeared in *Ziegfeld Follies of 1934.*

What Is This Thing Called Love 1930 w.m. Cole Porter. (MT) *Wake Up and Dream.* (MF) *Wake Up and Dream.* (MF) *Night and Day.* (MF) *Starlift.* (MF) *The Eddy Duchin Story.* Jack Buchanan and Jessie Matthews appeared in the American stage production of *Wake Up and Dream.* George Metaxa appeared in the British stage production of *Wake Up and Dream.* Cary Grant and Mary Martin appeared in *Night and Day,* biopic of song writer Cole Porter. Doris Day appeared in *Starlift.* This song was popularly revived in 1942.

What Kind of Fool 1981 w.m. Albhy Galuten, Barry Gibb

What Kind of Fool Am I 1962 w.m. Leslie Bricusse, Anthony Newley. (MT) *Stop the World—I Want To Get Off.* Anthony Newley appeared in *Stop the World—I Want To Get Off.* Grammy Award winner 1962. Ivor Novello Award winner 1961.

What More Can I Say 1942 w.m. Art Noel

What Now My Love 1962 Fr.w. Pierre Delanoe Eng.w. Carl Sigman m. Gilbert Becaud From the French "Et Maintenant." This song was popularly revived in 1966.

What Shall We Do with the Drunken Sailor, *see* **The Drunken Sailor**

What She Wants 1985 w.m. Kerry Chater, Renee Armand

What Take My Fancy 1960 w. Carolyn Leigh m. Cy Coleman. (MT) *Wildcat.*

What the Dickens 1963 w.m. Johnny Dankworth

What the Dickie-Birds Say 1886 w. Claxson Bellamy, Harry Paulton m. Edward Jakobowski. (MT) *Erminie.*

What the World Needs Now Is Love 1965 w. Hal David m. Burt Bacharach

What Was Your Name in the States? 1849 w.m. possibly John Philip Sousa. See also Part I, 1849.

What Will I Tell My Heart 1937 w.m. Peter Tinturin, Jack Lawrence

What Would I Be 1966 w.m. Jackie Trent. Ivor Novello Award winner 1966.

What Would We Do Without You 1970 w.m. Stephen Sondheim. (MT) *Company.* Elaine Stritch appeared in *Company.*

What You Goin' To Do When the Rent Comes 'Round, *see* **Rufus Rastus Johnson Brown**

What You Need 1986 w.m. Andrew Farris, Michael Hutchence

What You're Proposing 1981 w.m. Francis Rossi, Bernard Frost. Ivor Novello Award winner 1980–81.

Whatever Gets You Thru the Night 1974 w.m. John Lennon, Yoko Ono

Whatever Lola Wants 1955 w.m. Richard Adler, Jerry Ross. (MT) *Damn Yankees.* (MF) *Damn Yankees.* Gwen Verdon appeared in both the stage and film productions of *Damn Yankees.*

Whatever Will Be, Will Be, or, **Que Sera, Sera** 1956 w. Raymond Evans m. Jay Livingston. (F) *The Man Who Knew Too Much.* James Stewart and Doris Day appeared in *The Man Who Knew Too Much.* Academy Award winner 1956.

What'll I Do 1924 w.m. Irving Berlin. (MT) *Music Box Revue.* (MT) *The Punch Bowl.* Gwen Farrar and Norah Blaney appeared in *The Punch Bowl.*

What'll We Do on a Dew-Dew-Dewy Day, *see* **Dew-Dew-Dewy Day**

What'll We Do on a Saturday Night When the Town Goes Dry 1919 w.m. Harry Ruby. This song anticipated Prohibition.

What's Forever For 1982 w.m. Rafe Van Hoy

What's Going On 1971 w.m. Renaldo Benson, Al Cleveland, Marvin Gaye

What's Good about Good Night 1938 w. Dorothy Fields m. Jerome Kern. (MF) *Joy of Living*. Irene Dunne, Lucille Ball, and Douglas Fairbanks, Jr. appeared in *Joy of Living*.

What's Good about Goodbye 1948 w. Leo Robin m. Harold Arlen. (MF) *Casbah*. Tony Martin, Peter Lorre, and Yvonne DeCarlo appeared in *Casbah*.

What's Good for General Bullmoose 1956 w. Johnny Mercer m. Gene De Paul. (MT) *Li'l Abner*. (MF) *Li'l Abner*. Stubby Kaye appeared in the film production of *Li'l Abner*.

What's Love Got To Do with It 1984 w.m. Terry Britten, Graham Lyle. Grammy Award winner 1984.

What's New 1939 w.m. Johnny Burke, Robert Haggart

What's New Pussycat 1965 w. Hal David m. Burt Bacharach. (F) *What's New Pussycat*.

What's the Good of Being Good—When No One's Good to Me 1913 w. Stanley Murphy m. Harry Von Tilzer

What's the Matter with Father 1910 w. Harry H. Williams m. Egbert Van Alstyne

What's the Reason (I'm Not Pleasin' You) 1935 w. Coy Poe, Jimmy Grier m. Pinky Tomlin, Earl Hatch. This song was popularly revived in 1957.

What's the Use of Dreaming 1906 w.m. Joseph E. Howard

What's the Use of Loving If You Can't Love All the Time 1906 w. Joseph Mittenthal m. Harry Armstrong

What's the Use of Wond'rin' 1945 w. Oscar Hammerstein II m. Richard Rodgers. (MT) *Carousel*. (MF) *Carousel*. Jan Clayton and John Raitt appeared in the stage production of Carousel. Gordon MacRae and Shirley Jones appeared in the film production of *Carousel*.

Wheel of Fortune, The 1952 w.m. Bennie Benjamin, George Weiss. Theme song of Kay Starr.

Wheel of the Wagon Is Broken, The 1935 w.m. Elton Box, Desmond Cox, Michael Carr

Wheels 1961 w.m. Jimmy Tomes, Richard Stephens

Wheezy Anna 1933 w.m. Leslie Sarony

When a Fellah Has Turned Sixteen 1898 w.m. E.W. Rogers

When a Fellow's on the Level with a Girl That's on the Square 1907 w.m. George M. Cohan. (MT) *The Talk of New York*.

When a Gypsy Makes His Violin Cry 1935 w. Dick Smith, Frank Winegar, Jimmy Rogan m. Emergy Deutsch

When a Lady Meets a Gentleman Down South 1936 w.m. Michael Cleary, David Oppenheim

When a Maid Comes Knocking at Your Heart 1912 w. Otto Harbach m. Rudolf Friml. (MT) *The Firefly*. (MF)

The Firefly. Jeanette MacDonald and Allan Jones appeared in the film production of *The Firefly*.

When a Man Loves a Woman 1966 w.m. Calvin H. Lewis, Andrew Wright

When a Soldier's on Parade 1934 w.m. Leslie Sarony. (MT) *On with the Show*.

When a Wife's in a Pout, *see* **The Beggar's Opera**

When a Woman Hears the Sound of the Drum and Fife 1803 w. William Dunlap m. Victor Pellesier. (MT) *The Glory of Columbia, Her Yeomanry*.

When a Woman Loves a Man 1938 w.m. Johnny Mercer, Bernard Hanighan, Gordon Jenkins

When Alexander Takes His Ragtime Band to France 1918 w.m. Alfred Bryan, Cliff Hess, Edgar Leslie

When All Is Said and Done 1982 w.m. Benny Anderson, Bjorn Ulvaeus

When Big Profundo Sang Low "C" 1921 w. Marion T. Bohannon m. George Botsford

When Buddha Smiles 1921 w. Arthur Freed m. Nacio Herb Brown

When Day Is Done 1926 w. B.G. DeSylva m. Robert Katscher. (MT) *Will o' the Whispers*. Jack Smith appeared in *Will o' the Whispers*. Theme song of Ambrose.

When De Moon Comes Up Behind De Hill 1900 w.m. Paul Dresser

When Did I Fall in Love 1959 w. Sheldon Harnick m. Jerry Bock. (MT) *Fiorello!*

When Did You Leave Heaven 1936 w. Walter Bullock m. Richard A. Whiting. (MF) *Sing Baby Sing*. Adolphe Menjou, Ted Healy, and Dixie Dunbar appeared in *Sing Baby Sing*.

When Doves Cry 1984 w.m. Prince

When Father Papered the Parlour 1909 w.m. R.P. Weston, F.J. Barnes

When Francis Dances with Me 1921 w. Benny Ryan m. Sol Violinsky (Sol Ginsberg). (F) *Give My Regards to Broadway*. Dan Dailey and Charles Winninger appeared in *Give My Regards to Broadway*.

When Good Fellows Get Together, *see* **It's Always Fair Weather When Good Fellows Get Together**

When He Shines 1982 w.m. Florrie Palmer, Dominic Bugatti. Ivor Novello Award winner 1981–82.

When Hearts Are Young 1922 w. Cyrus Wood m. Sigmund Romberg, Alfred Goodman. (MT) *The Lady in Ermine*.

When I Dream 1979 w.m. Sandy Mason Theoret

When I Dream in the Gloaming of You 1909 w.m. Herbert Ingraham

When I Fall in Love 1951 w.m. Edward Heyman, Victor Young. (F) *One Minute to Zero*. (F) *Istanbul*. Robert Mitchum and Ann Blyth appeared in *One Minute to Zero*. Errol Flynn appeared in *Istanbul*. This song was popularly revived in 1951.

When I Fall in Love 1952 w.m. Albert Selden. (MT) *Small Wonder*. Tom Elwell and Mary McCarthy appeared in *Small Wonder*. Written in 1948, this song was most popular in 1952.

When I First Saw You 1982 w. Tom Eyen m. Henry Krieger. (MT) *Dream Girls.* Loretta Devine and Jennifer Holliday appeared in *Dream Girls.*

When I Get You Alone Tonight 1912 w.m. Joseph Mc-Carthy, Joe Goodwin, Fred Fisher. (MF) *Oh You Beautiful Doll.* June Have appeared in *Oh You Beautiful Doll,* biopic of composer Fred Fisher.

When I Grow Too Old To Dream 1935 w. Oscar Hammerstein II m. Sigmund Romberg. (MF) *The Night Is Young.* (MF) *Deep in My Heart.* Evelyn Laye and Rosalind Russell appeared in *The Night Is Young.* Jose Ferrer and Merle Oberon appeared in *Deep in My Heart.*

When I Have Sung My Songs 1934 w.m. Ernest Charles

When I Leave the World Behind 1915 w.m. Irving Berlin

When I Lost You 1912 w.m. Irving Berlin. The subject of this song is Irving Berlin's first wife, Dorothy Goetz, who died of typhoid fever shortly after their marriage.

When I Marry Mister Snow 1945 w. Oscar Hammerstein II m. Richard Rodgers. (MT) *Carousel.* (MF) *Carousel.* Jan Clayton and John Raitt appeared in the stage production of *Carousel.* Shirley Jones and Gordon MacRae appeared in the film production of *Carousel.*

When I Need You 1977 w.m. Carole Bayer Sager, Albert Hammond

When I Saw an Elephant Fly 1941 w.m. Oliver Wallace, Ned Washington. (MF) *Dumbo.*

When I Saw Sweet Nellie Home, or, **I Was Seeing Nellie Home,** or, **Aunt Dinah's Quilting Party** 1860–1867 w. J. Fletcher m. Frances Kyle. The melody for this song was adapted for ''The Vacant Chair'' and years later inspired Cole Porter's ''Old-Fashioned Garden'' and ''Yes, We Have No Bananas.''

When I See an Elephant Fly, *see* **When I Saw an Elephant Fly**

When I Take My Sugar to Tea 1931 w.m. Sammy Fain, Irving Kahal, Pierre Norman. (MF) *Monkey Business.* (F) *The Mating Season.* The Four Marx Brothers and Ruth Hall appeared in *Monkey Business.* Gene Tierney and Miriam Hopkins appeared in *The Mating Season.*

When I Wanted You 1980 w.m. Gino Cunico

When I Was a Lad 1878 w. William S. Gilbert m. Arthur Sullivan. From the operetta *H.M.S. Pinafore.*

When I Was a Little Cuckoo 1944 w.m. Cole Porter. (MT) *Seven Lively Arts.*

When I Was Twenty-One and You Were Sweet Sixteen 1911 w.m. Harry H. Williams m. Egbert Van Alstyne

When I'm Cleaning Windows 1937 w.m. George Formby, Fred E. Cliffe, Harry Gifford. (MF) *Keep Your Seats Please.* George Formby appeared in *Keep Your Seats Please.*

When I'm Dead and Gone 1971 w.m. Bernard Gallagher, Graham Lyle. Ivor Novello Award winner 1970–71.

When I'm Gone I Won't Forget 1920 w. Ivan Reid m. Peter DeRose

When I'm Gone You'll Soon Forget 1920 w. E. Austin Keith

When I'm Looking at You 1929 w. Clifford Grey m.

Herbert Stothart. (MF) *The Rogue Song.* Lawrence Tibbett and Laurel and Hardy appeared in *The Rogue Song.*

When I'm Not Near the Girl I Love 1946 w. E.Y. Harburg m. Burton Lane. (MT) *Finian's Rainbow.* Albert Sharpe and David Wayne appeared in *Finian's Rainbow.*

When I'm Sixty-Four 1967 w.m. John Lennon, Paul McCartney

When I'm the President (We Want Cantor) 1931 w.m. Al Lewis, Al Sherman

When I'm with My Baby, *see* **I Don't Care if the Sun Don't Shine**

When I'm with You 1936 w. Mack Gordon m. Harry Revel. (MF) *Poor Little Rich Girl.* Shirley Temple, Jack Haley, and Alice Faye appeared in *Poor Little Rich Girl.*

When Irish Eyes Are Smiling 1912 w. Chauncey Olcott, George Graff, Jr. m. Ernest R. Ball (MT) *The Isle o' Dreams.*

When It's All Goin' Out, and Nothin' Comin' In 1902 w.m. Bert Williams, George Walker

When It's Apple Blossom Time in Normandy 1912 w.m. Harry Gifford, Huntley Trevor, Tom Mellor. (MF) *Shine On Harvest Moon.* Ann Sheridan appeared in *Shine on Harvest Moon,* biopic of entertainer Nora Bayes. Based on Beethoven's ''Minuet in G.''

When It's Darkness on the Delta, *see* **Darkness on the Delta**

When It's Night Time Down in Burgundy 1914 w. Alfred Bryan m. Herman Paley

When It's Night Time in Dixie Land 1914 w.m. Irving Berlin

When It's Night-Time in Italy, It's Wednesday Over Here 1923 w.m. James Kendis, Lew Brown

When It's Roundup Time in Texas, *see* **When the Bloom Is on the Sage**

When It's Sleepy Time Down South 1931 w.m. Leon Rene, Otis Rene, Clarence Muse. Theme song of Louis Armstrong.

When It's Springtime in the Rockies 1929 w. Mary Hale Woolsey, Milton Taggart m. Robert Sauer. (MF) *Silver Spurs.* Roy Rogers and Smiley Burnette appeared in *Silver Spurs.*

When Johnny Comes Marching Home 1863 w.m. Patrick Sarsfield Gilmore (Louis Lambert); arr. 1945 Buddy Kaye. (MT) *Dancin'.* (MF) *When Johnny Comes Marching Home.* Allan Jones and Donald O'Connor appeared in *When Johnny Comes Marching Home.* This song was originally published as ''Johnny Fill Up the Bowl'' in 1863. Gilmore was bandmaster of the Union Army attached to General Butler's command in New Orleans.

When Julie Comes Around 1970 w.m. Lee Pockriss, Paul Vance

When Kate and I Were Coming Thro' the Rye 1902 w. Andrew B. Sterling m. Harry Von Tilzer

When Lights Are Low 1923 Fr.w. R. Brisson Eng.w.m. Gus Kahn, Ted Koehler, Ted Fiorito

When Love Is Young in Springtime 1906 w.m. Rida Johnson Young, Melville Ellis. (T) *Brown of Harvard.* This song was used as incidental music only in *Brown of Harvard.* See also ''I Can't Begin To Tell You.''

When My Baby Smiles at Me 1920 w. Andrew B. Sterling, Ted Lewis m. Bill Munro. (MT) *The Greenwich Village Follies.* (MF) *When My Baby Smiles at Me.* Betty Grable and Dan Dailey appeared in *When My Baby Smiles at Me.* Theme song of Ted Lewis.

When My Dream Boat Comes Home 1936 w.m. Cliff Friend, Dave Franklin

When My Ship Comes In 1935 w.m. Walter Donaldson, Gus Kahn. (MF) *Kid Millions.* Eddie Cantor, Ethel Merman, and Ann Sothern appeared in *Kid Millions.*

When My Sugar Walks Down the Street, All the Birdies Go Tweet-Tweet-Tweet 1924 w.m. Irving Mills, Gene Austin, Jimmy McHugh

When Shadows Fall, *see* **Home**

When Shall I Again See Ireland 1917 w. Henry Blossom m. Victor Herbert. (MT) *Eileen.* Walter Scanlon and Grace Breen appeared in *Eileen.* After destruction by fire of the theatre, scenery, and costumes for *Hearts of Erin* while it was still in rehearsal in Toronto, the producers, fearing arson, changed the name of the show to *Eileen* for its New York opening.

When Shall We Meet Again 1921 w. Raymond B. Egan m. Richard A. Whiting

When She Walks in the Room 1945 w. Dorothy Fields m. Sigmund Romberg. (MT) *Up in Central Park.* (MF) *Up in Central Park.* Deanna Durbin and Vincent Price appeared in the film production of *Up in Central Park.*

When Someone You Love Loves You 1948 w.m. Charles Gaynor. (MT) *Lend an Ear.*

When Sonny Gets Blue 1956 w.m. Marvin Fisher, Jack Segal

When Stars Are in the Quiet Skies 1838 w. E.L. Bulwer (Edward George Earle Lytton Bulwer-Lytton) m. Alexander Ball

When Sweet Marie Was Sweet Sixteen 1907 w. Raymond Moore m. Ernest R. Ball

When the Angelus Is Ringing 1914 w. Joe Young m. Bert Grant. (MT) *Business As Usual.* Henri Leoni appeared in *Business As Usual.* See also "While the Angelus Was Ringing."

When the Apples Grow on a Lilac Tree, *see* **The Lilac Tree**

When the Bees Are in the Hive 1904 w. Alfred Bryan m. Kerry Mills

When the Bell in the Lighthouse Rings Ding Dong 1905 w. Arthur J. Lamb m. Alfred Solman

When the Birds Have Sung Themselves To Sleep 1901 w.m. Paul Dresser

When the Birds in Georgia Sing of Tennessee 1907 w. Arthur J. Lamb m. Ernest R. Ball

When the Black Sheep Returns to the Fold 1916 w.m. Irving Berlin

(When It's Roundup Time in Texas) When the Bloom Is on the Sage 1931 w.m. Nathaniel H. Vincent, Fred Howard Wright

When the Blue Sky Turns to Gold 1901 w.m. Thurland Chattaway

When the Boys Come Home 1917 w. John Hay m. Oley Speaks

When the Chariot Comes, *see* **She'll Be Comin' Round the Mountain**

When the Cherry Blossoms Fall 1919 w. Stephen Ivor Szinnyey, William Cary Duncan m. Anselm Goetzel. (MT) *The Royal Vagabond.*

When the Children Are Asleep 1945 w. Oscar Hammerstein II m. Richard Rodgers. (MT) *Carousel.* (MF) *Carousel.* Jan Clayton and John Raitt appeared in the stage production of *Carousel.* Gordon MacRae and Shirley Jones appeared in the film production of *Carousel.*

When the Circus Came to Town 1938 w.m. Jimmy Eaton, Terry Shand, Julian Kay

When the Clock in the Tower Strikes Twelve 1882 w. Edward Harrigan m. David Braham

When the Corn Is Waving, Annie Dear 1860 w.m. Charles Blamphin

When the Going Gets Tough, the Tough Get Going 1986 w.m. Wayne Brath Waite, Barry Eastmond, Robert John "Mutt" Lange, Billy Ocean

When the Guards Are on Parade 1931 w.m. Horatio Nicholls, Leslie Sarony

When the Guardsman Started Crooning on Parade 1936 w.m. Eddie Lisbona, Tommie Connor

When the Gypsy Played 1935 w.m. Ivor Novello, Christopher Hassall. (MT) *Glamorous Night.* (MF) *Glamorous Night.* Trefor Jones and Mary Ellis appeared in both stage and film productions of *Glamorous Night.*

When the Harvest Days Are Over, Jessie Dear 1900 w. Howard Graham m. Harry Von Tilzer

When the Honeymoon Was Over 1921 w.m. Fred Fisher

When the Idle Poor Become the Idle Rich 1946 w. E.Y. Harburg m. Burton Lane. (MT) *Finian's Rainbow.* Albert Sharpe and David Wayne appeared in *Finian's Rainbow.*

When the Leaves Come Tumbling Down 1922 w.m. Richard Howard

When the Lights Are Low 1936 w.m. Benny Carter, Spencer Williams

When the Lights Go On Again (All Over the World) 1942 w.m. Edward Seiler, Sol Marcus, Bennie Benjamin. (F) *When the Lights Go On Again.* James Lydon and Regis Toomey appeared in *When the Lights Go On Again.* Based on Beethoven's "Minuet in G."

When the Midnight Choo-Choo Leaves for Alabam' 1912 w.m. Irving Berlin. (MF) *Alexander's Ragtime Band.* (MF) *Easter Parade.* (MF) *There's No Business Like Show Business.* Judy Garland, Ann Miller, and Fred Astaire appeared in *Easter Parade.* Ethel Merman, Marilyn Monroe, and Donald O'Connor appeared in *There's No Business Like Show Business.*

When the Mists Have Cleared Away 1880 w. Annie Herbert m. Arthur Henshaw

When the Mists Have Rolled Away 1883 w. Annie Herbert m. Ira David Sankey

When the Mocking Birds Are Singing in the Wildwood 1905 w. Arthur J. Lamb m. H.B. Blake

When the Monkey Wrapped Its Tail Around the Flagpole, *see* **National Emblem**

When the Moon Comes Over the Mountain 1931 w. Howard Johnson m. Harry Woods. Theme song of Kate Smith.

When the Nylons Bloom Again 1943 w. George Marion, Jr. m. Thomas "Fats" Waller. (MT) *Early to Bed.* (MT) *Ain't Misbehavin'.* Mary Small and Muriel Angelus appeared in *Early to Bed.* Nell Carter and Debbie Allen appeared in *Ain't Misbehavin'.*

When the One You Love (Simply Won't Love Back) 1945 w. Sammy Cahn m. Jule Styne. (MF) *Cinderella Jones.* Joan Leslie and Robert Alda appeared in *Cinderella Jones.*

When the Organ Played at Twilight (The Song That Reached My Heart) 1929 w. Raymond Wallace m. James Campbell, Reginald Connelly

When the Poppies Bloom Again 1936 w.m. Don Pelosi, Leo Towers, Morton Morrow

When the Red, Red Robin Comes Bob, Bob, Bobbin' Along 1926 w.m. Harry Woods. (MF) *The Jolson Story.* (MF) *Has Anybody Seen My Gal.* (F) *I'll Cry Tomorrow.* Larry Parks appeared in *The Jolson Story.* Piper Laurie and Rock Hudson appeared in *Has Anybody Seen My Gal.* Susan Hayward appeared in *I'll Cry Tomorrow.*

When the Robins Nest Again 1883 w.m. Frank Howard

When the Roll Is Called Up Yonder 1893 w.m. James M. Black

When the Saints Go Marching In 1896 w. Katharine E. Purvis m. James M. Black

When the Sergeant Major's on Parade 1925 w.m. Ernest Longstaffe

When the Spring Is in the Air 1932 w. Oscar Hammerstein II m. Jerome Kern. (MT) *Music in the Air.*

When the Sun Comes Out 1940 w. Ted Koehler m. Harold Arlen

When the Sun Goes Down 1922 w.m. Melville Gideon. (MT) *The Co-Optimists.* Melville Gideon appeared in *The Co-Optimists.*

When the Swallows Come Back to Capistrano 1940 w.m. Leon Rene

When the Values Go Up 1946 w.m. anon. This song was written for a Robert Hall Clothes commercial promotion campaign.

When the War Is Over, Mary 1864 w. George Cooper m. John Rogers Thomas

When the White Lilacs Bloom Again 1928 w.m. Fritz Rotter, Franz Doelle

When the Wind Was Green 1950 w.m. Donald Henry Stinson

When the World Was Young (Ah, the Apple Tree) 1952 w.m. Johnny Mercer, Philippe Gerald Block

When They Ask About You 1944 w.m. Sam Stept. (MF) *Stars on Parade.* Larry Parks and Ray Walker appeared in *Stars on Parade.*

When They Cut Down the Old Pine Tree, *see* **They Cut Down the Old Pine Tree**

When They Sound the Last All Clear 1941 w.m. Hugh Charles, Louis Elton

When This Cruel War Is Over, *see* **Weeping, Sad and Lonely**

When Vulcan Forg'd the Bolts of Jove, *see* **The Origin of Gunpowder**

When We Are M-a-double-r-i-e-d 1907 w.m. George M. Cohan. (MT) *Fifty Miles from Boston.*

When We Make Love 1984 w.m. Troy Seals, Mentor Williams

When We're Alone, or, **Penthouse Serenade** 1931 w.m. Will Jason, Val Burton. (MF) *Beau James.* Bob Hope and Vera Miles appeared in *Beau James.*

When We've Wound Up the Watch on the Rhine 1914 w.m. Herman Darewski, E.V. Lucas. (MT) *Business As Usual.* Ambrose Thorne and Violet Loraine appeared in *Business As Usual.*

When Will I Be Loved 1960 w.m. Phil Everly. This song was popularly revived in 1976.

When Will I See You Again 1974 w.m. Kenneth Gamble, Leon Huff

When Will You Say I Love You 1963 w.m. Alan Fielding

When Yankee Doodle Learns To Parlez Vous Français 1917 w. William Hart m. Edward Nelson

When You Ain't Got No Money, Well, You Needn't Come 'Round 1898 w. Clarence S. Brewster m. A. Baldwin Sloane

When You and I Were Dancing 1924 w.m. H.M. Tennat, Graham Jones

When You and I Were Seventeen 1924 w. Gus Kahn m. Charles Rosoff

When You and I Were Young, Maggie 1866 w. George W. Johnson m. James Austin Butterfield. (MF) *Swing Time Johnny.* The Andrews Sisters and Tim Ryan appeared in *Swing Time Johnny.* This song is based on the actual story of Maggie Clark, a schoolgirl, and her teacher, George W. Johnson, who was courting her. Johnson wrote a poem for Miss Clark at the hill where they would meet, near her home in Canada. Johnson published the poem and they were soon married, but Maggie died that same year.

When You Are a King 1972 w.m. John Hill, Roger Hill. Ivor Novello Award winner 1971–72.

When You Are in Love 1912 w.m. Lionel Monckton, Percy Greenbank. (MT) *The Dancing Mistress.*

When You Come Back 1918 w.m. George M. Cohan

When You Come Back They'll Wonder Who the----You Are 1902 w.m. Paul Dresser

When You Come Home 1912 w.m. W.H. Squire

When You Come to the End of the Day 1929 w.m. Frank C. Westphal, Gus Kahn

When You First Kissed the Last Girl You Loved 1908 w. Will M. Hough, Frank R. Adams m. Joseph E. Howard. (MT) *A Stubborn Cinderella.*

When You Know You're Not Forgotten 1943 w.m. Elton Box, Desmond Cox

When You Know You're Not Forgotten by the Girl You Can't Forget 1906 w. Edward Gardenier m. J. Fred Helf

When You Look in the Heart of a Rose 1918 w. Marian Gillespie m. Florence Methven. (MT) *The Better 'Ole*. Charles McNaughton appeared in *The Better 'Ole*.

When You Lose the One You Love 1955 w.m. Don Pelosi, Rodd Arden, Jimmy Harper

When You Play in the Game of Love 1913 w. Joe Goodwin m. Al Piantadosi

When You Played the Organ and I Sang "The Rosary" 1927 w.m. Edgar Leslie, Joseph Gilbert

When You Say Bud, You've Said It All 1974 w.m. Steve Karmen. This song was written for a Budweiser Beer commercial promotion campaign.

When You Walk in the Room, *see* When She Walks in the Room

When You Walked Out Someone Else Walked Right In 1923 w.m. Irving Berlin. (MT) *The Music Box Revue of 1923*. Robert Benchley and Grace Moore appeared in *The Music Box Revue of 1923*.

When You Were Sweet Sixteen 1898 w.m. James Thornton. (F) *A Man Called Sullivan*. (MF) *The Jolson Story*. Larry Parks appeared in *The Jolson Story*. Thornton sold this song simultaneously to two publishers, and received fifteen dollars from each, followed by the inevitable lawsuit.

When You Wish Upon a Star 1940 w. Ned Washington m. Leigh Harline. (MF) *Pinocchio*. Academy Award winner 1940.

When You Wore a Pinafore 1908 w. Edward Madden m. Theodore F. Morse.

When You Wore a Tulip and I Wore a Big Red Rose 1914 w. Jack Mahoney m. Percy Wenrich. (MF) *For Me and My Gal*. (MF) *Belles on Their Toes*. (MF) *The Merry Monihans*. Judy Garland and Gene Kelly appeared in *For Me and My Gal*. Myrna Loy appeared in *Belles on Their Toes*. Donald O'Connor and Peggy Ryan appeared in *The Merry Monihans*.

When Your Hair Has Turned to Silver, I Will Love You Just the Same 1930 w. Charles Tobias m. Peter De Rose

When Your Love Grows Cold 1895 w.m. Charles Miller

When Your Lover Has Gone 1931 w.m. E.A. Swan. (MF) *Blonde Crazy*. James Cagney, Joan Blondell, and Louis Calhern appeared in *Blonde Crazy*.

When Your Old Wedding Ring Was New 1935 w. Charles McCarthy, Joe Solieri m. Bert Douglas

When You're a Long, Long Way from Home 1914 w. Sam M. Lewis m. George W. Meyer

When You're All Dressed Up and No Place To Go 1913 w. Benjamin Hapgood Burt m. Silvio Hein. (MT) *The Beauty Shop*. (MT) *Mr. Manhattan*. Raymond Hitchcock appeared in *The Beauty Shop* and later again in *Mr. Manhattan*.

When You're Away 1911 w. A. Seymour Brown, Joe Young m. Bert Grant

When You're Away 1914 w. Henry Blossom m. Victor Herbert. (MT) *The Only Girl*.

When You're in Love 1948 w.m. Desmond O'Connor, Harold Fields, Dominic John. Based on Serradell's "La Golondrina."

When You're in Love with a Beautiful Woman 1979 w.m. Even Stevens

When You're in Love with Someone Who Is Not in Love with You 1915 w.m. Grant Clarke, Al Piantadosi

When You're Pretty 1906 w.m. Henry Blossom, Victor Herbert. (MT) *The Red Mill*.

When You're Smiling (The Whole World Smiles with You) 1928 w.m. Mark Fisher, Joe Goodwin, Larry Shay. (MF) *Meet Danny Wilson*. Frank Sinatra and Shelley Winters appeared in *Meet Danny Wilson*.

When You're Wearing the Ball and Chain 1914 w. Harry B. Smith m. Victor Herbert. (MT) *The Only Girl*.

When You're Young and in Love 1968 w.m. Hal Hester, Danny Apolinar. (MT) *Your Own Thing*.

When You've Had a Little Love You Want a Little More 1912 w. Arthur Lamb m. John T. Hall

When Yuba Plays the Rumba on His Tuba 1931 w.m. Herman Hupfeld. (MT) *The Third Little Show*.

Whenever I Call You "Friend" 1978 w.m. Melissa Manchester

Where Am I 1935 w. Al Dubin m. Harry Warren. (MF) *Stars Over Broadway*.

Where Am I Going 1966 w. Dorothy Fields m. Cy Coleman. (MT) *Sweet Charity*. (MF) *Sweet Charity*. Gwen Verdon appeared in the stage production of *Sweet Charity*. Shirley MacLaine appeared in the film production of *Sweet Charity*.

Where Are the Friends of Other Days 1903 w.m. Paul Dresser

Where Are You 1936 w. Harold Adamson m. Jimmy McHugh. (MT) *Top of the Town*. Gertrude Niesen appeared in *Top of the Town*.

Where Are You Now My Love 1965 w.m. Tony Hatch, Jackie Trent. Ivor Novello Award winner 1965.

Where Are You Now That I Need You, *see* Now That I Need You

Where Did My Snowman Go 1952 w.m. Freddie Poser, Geoffrey Venis

Where Did Our Love Go 1964 w.m. Eddie Holland, Brian Holland, Lamont Dozier

Where Did Robinson Crusoe Go with Friday on Saturday Night? 1916 w. Sam M. Lewis, Joe Young m. George W. Meyer. (MT) *Robinson Crusoe, Jr.* (MT) *Follow the Crowd*. Al Jolson appeared in *Robinson Crusoe, Jr.* Ethel Levey appeared in *Follow the Crowd*.

Where Did You Come From, *see* Whar Did You Cum From

Where Did You Get That Girl 1913 w. Bert Kalmar m. Harry Puck. (MF) *Three Little Words*. Fred Astaire and Red Skelton appeared in *Three Little Words*, biopic of song writers Bert Kalmar and Harry Ruby.

Where Did You Get That Hat 1888 w.m. Joseph J. Sullivan. Based on a theme from Wagner's *Lohengrin* and *Die Meistersinger*. This song was introduced by Joseph J. Sullivan in New York City at the Miner's Eighth Avenue Theatre. The song's narrative was inspired by Sullivan's wearing old clothes found in his attic, to the obvious delight of the neighborhood children.

Where Do Flies Go in the Winter Time? 1919 w.m. Frank Leo

Where Do I Begin, *see Love Story*

Where Do I Go 1969 w. Gerome Ragni, James Rado m. Galt MacDermot. (MT) *Hair.* (MF) *Hair.*

Where Do I Go from Here 1968 w.m. Voices, Inc. (MT) *The Believers.*

Where Do They Go When They Row, Row, Row 1920 w. Bert Kalmar, George Jessel m. Harry Ruby

Where Do We Go from Here 1917 w.m. Howard Johnson, Percy Wenrich. (MF) *For Me and My Gal.* Judy Garland and Gene Kelly appeared in *For Me and My Gal.*

Where Do You Go to My Lovely 1970 w.m. Peter Sarstedt. Ivor Novello Award winner 1969–70.

Where Do You Work-a John 1926 w.m. Mortimer Weinberg, Charley Marks, Harry Warren

Where Have All the Flowers Gone 1961 w.m. Pete Seeger

Where Have You Been 1930 w.m. Cole Porter. (MT) *The New Yorkers.*

Where Is Love? 1963 w.m. Lionel Bart. (MT) *Oliver!* (MF) *Oliver!* Georgia Brown and Ron Moody appeared in the stage production of *Oliver!* Shani Wallis and Ron Moody appeared in the film production of *Oliver!*

Where Is My (Wand'ring) Boy Tonight 1877 w.m. Reverend Robert Lowry

Where Is the Love 1975 w.m. Harry Wayne Casey, Richard Finch, Willie Clark, Betty Wright. Grammy Award winner 1975.

Where Is the (That) Song of Songs for Me 1928 w.m. Irving Berlin. (F) *Lady of the Pavements.* (MF) *Lover Come Back.* Lupe Velez and William Boyd appeared in *Lady of the Pavements.* Lucille Ball and George Brent appeared in *Lover Come Back.*

Where Is Your Heart, *see The Song from Moulin Rouge*

Where Love Has Gone 1964 w.m. Sammy Cahn, James Van Heusen. (F) *Where Love Has Gone.* Susan Hayward and Bette Davis appeared in *Where Love Has Gone.*

Where My Caravan Has Rested 1909 w. Edward Teschemacher m. Hermann Löhr. From "Romany Songs."

Where, Oh Where, Has My Little Dog Gone, *see Oh Where, Oh Where, Has My Little Dog Gone*

Where or When 1937 w. Lorenz Hart m. Richard Rodgers. (MT) *Babes in Arms.* (MT) *Lena Horne: The Lady and Her Music.* (MF) *Babes in Arms.* (MF) *Words and Music.* (F) *Alice Doesn't Live Here Anymore.* Mitzi Green and Ray Heatherton appeared in the stage production of *Babes in Arms.* Lena Horne appeared in *Lena Horne: The Lady and Her Music.* Mickey Rooney and Judy Garland appeared in the film production of *Babes in Arms.* Lena Horne appeared in *Words and Music,* biopic of song writers Rodgers and Hart. Ellen Burstyn appeared in *Alice Doesn't Live Here Anymore.*

Where the Black-Eyed Susans Grow 1917 w. Dave Radford m. Richard A. Whiting. (MT) *Robinson Crusoe, Jr.* (MT) *Cheep.* Al Jolson appeared in *Robinson Crusoe, Jr.* Beatrice Lillie appeared in *Cheep.*

Where the Blue Begins 1940 w.m. Harry Parr-Davies

Where the Blue of the Night Meets the Gold of the Day 1931 w.m. Roy Turk, Bing Crosby, Fred E. Ahlert. (MF) *The Big Broadcast.* Bing Crosby appeared in *The Big Broadcast.* Possibly based on "Tit-Willow" from Gilbert and Sullivan's score *The Mikado* of 1885. Theme song of Bing Crosby.

Where the Boys Are 1961 w. Howard Greenfield m. Neil Sedaka. (F) *Where the Boys Are.* Connie Francis appeared in *Where the Boys Are.*

Where the Chicken Got the Axe 1893 w.m. Will H. Mayo, William Glenroy

Where The Lazy Daisies Grow 1924 w.m. Cliff Friend

Where the Morning Glories Grow 1917 w. Gus Kahn, Raymond Egan m. Richard A. Whiting

Where the Morning Glories Twine Around the Door 1905 w. Andrew B. Sterling m. Harry Von Tilzer

Where the River Shannon Flows 1905 w.m. James J. Russell

Where the Shy Little Violets Grow 1928 w.m. Gus Kahn, Harry Warren

Where the Silv'ry Colorado Wends Its Way 1901 w. C.H. Scoggins m. Charles Avril

Where the Southern Roses Grow 1904 w. Richard H. Buck m. Theodore F. Morse

Where the Sunset Turns the Ocean's Blue to Gold 1902 w. Eva Fern Buckner m. Henry W. Petrie

Where the Sweet Magnolias Grow 1899 w. Andrew B. Sterling m. Harry Von Tilzer

Where the Twilight Comes To Kiss the Rose Goodnight 1912 w. Robert F. Roden m. Henry W. Petrie

Where the Waters Are Blue 1942 w.m. Hugh Charles, Sonny Miller

Where There's Life, There's Bud 1959 w. Bob Johnson m. Russ David. This song was written for a Budweiser commercial promotion campaign.

Where Was Moses When the Lights Went Out 1878 w.m. anon.; arr. Max Vernor

Where Were You When I Was Falling in Love 1979 w.m. Steve Jobe, Jeff Alan Silbar, John Samuel Lorber

Where Would You Be Without Me 1965 w.m. Leslie Bricusse, Anthony Newley. (MT) *The Roar of the Greasepaint—The Smell of the Crowd.* Anthony Newley and Cyril Ritchard appeared in *The Roar of the Greasepaint—The Smell of the Crowd.*

Where'd You Get Those Eyes (*not* "Jeepers Creepers") 1926 w.m. Walter Donaldson

Where's That Rainbow 1927 w. Lorenz Hart m. Richard Rodgers. (MT) *Peggy-Ann.* (MF) *Words and Music.* Mickey Rooney, Judy Garland, and Gene Kelly appeared in *Words and Music,* biopic of song writers Rodgers and Hart.

Where's the Boy? Here's the Girl! 1928 w. Ira Gershwin m. George Gershwin. (MT) *Treasure Girl.*

Where's the Playground Susie 1969 w.m. Jim Webb

Which Way You Goin' Billy 1970 w.m. Terry Jacks

Whiffenpoof Song, The 1911 w. Meade Minnigerode, George S. Pomeroy m. Tod B. Galloway. (F) *Winged Victory.* Lee J. Cobb, Red Buttons, and Judy Holliday appeared in *Winged Victory.* This song was popularly revived in 1936. Theme song of the The Whiffenpoof Society, a division of the Yale Glee Club, from 1909. The words are in part based on Kipling's poem "Gentlemen Rankers." The name "Whiffenproof" is based on a fantasy creature from Victor Herbert's operetta *Little Nemo,* of 1908.

While a Cigarette Was Burning 1938 w.m. Charles Kenny, Nick Kenny

While Hearts Are Singing 1931 w. Clifford Grey m. Oscar Straus. (MF) *The Smiling Lieutenant.* Maurice Chevalier and Claudette Colbert appeared in *The Smiling Lieutenant.*

While My Guitar Gently Weeps 1968 w.m. George Harrison

While Others Are Building Castles in the Air (I'll Build a Cottage for Two) 1919 w. Jack Mahoney m. Fred Fisher

While She Lays 1979 w.m. Stephen M. Gibb

While Strolling Through the Park One Day, or, **The Fountain in the Park** 1884 w.m. Ed Haley, Robert A. Keiser (King). (MF) *Hollywood Revue.* (MF) *Sunbonnet Sue.* Joan Crawford, Marion Davies, and Norma Shearer appeared in *Hollywood Revue.* Gale Storm and Phil Regan appeared in *Sunbonnet Sue.* This song was first performed by the Du Rell Twin Brothers.

While the Angelus Was Ringing, or, **The Three Bells** (Les Trois Cloches), or, **The Jimmy Brown Song** [with different lyrics] 1945 Fr.w. Jean Villard (Gilles) m. Eng.w. Bert Reisfeld ("The Three Bells") Dick Manning ("While the Angelus Was Ringing") m. Jean Villard (Gilles). This song was popular again in 1948 and 1959, although not the version called "The Jimmy Brown Song." See also "When the Angelus Is Ringing."

While the Bloom Is on the Rye, *see* **The Bloom Is on the Rye**

While We Are (Were) Dancing, *see* **I Get Ideas**

While We're Young 1943 w. Bill Engvick m. Alec Wilder, Morty Palitz. This song was popularly revived in 1951.

While You Danced, Danced, Danced 1951 w.m. Stephan Weiss

While You See a Chance 1981 w.m. Steve Winwood, Will Jennings

Whip-Poor-Will 1921 w. B.G. DeSylva m. Jerome Kern. (MT) *Sally.* (MF) *Look For the Silver Lining.* June Haver, Gordon MacRae, and Ray Bolger appeared in *Look For the Silver Lining,* biopic of Marilyn Miller.

Whisper That You Love Me 1942 w. John Klenner m. Hans Engelmann

Whisper to Me 1917 w.m. Lionel Monckton, Herman Finck, Adrian Ross (MT) *Airs and Graces.* Gertie Millar and Ernest Pike appeared in *Airs and Graces.*

Whisper Your Mother's Name 1896 w. Harry Braisted m. Stanley Carter

Whispering 1920 w. Malvin Schonberger; possibly Richard Coburn m. John Schonberger. (MF) *Ziegfeld Girl.* (MF) *Belles on Their Toes.* (MF) *The Eddy Duchin Story.* Judy Garland, James Stewart, and Hedy Lamarr appeared in *Zieg-*

feld Girl. Myrna Loy appeared in *Belles on Their Toes.* Carmen Cavallaro appeared in *The Eddy Duchin Story.* Theme song of Roy Fox.

Whispering Bells 1957 w.m. F. Lowry, Boudleaux Bryant

Whispering Hope 1868 w.m. Alice Hawthorne (Septimus Winner)

Whispering Pines of Nevada, The 1927 w.m. Horatio Nicholls

Whispers in the Dark 1937 w.m. Leo Robin, Frederick Hollander. (F) *Desire.* (MF) *Artists and Models.* Marlene Dietrich and Gary Cooper appeared in *Desire.* Jack Benny, Ida Lupino, and Martha Raye appeared in *Artists and Models.*

(Just) Whistle While You Work 1937 w. Larry Morey m. Frank Churchill. (MF) *Snow White and the Seven Dwarfs.*

Whistler and His Dog, The 1905 m. Arthur Pryor. (MF) *The Emperor Waltz.* Bing Crosby and Joan Fontaine appeared in *The Emperor Waltz.* Theme song of the "Our Gang" serials.

Whistling Boy, The 1937 w. Dorothy Fields m. Jerome Kern. (F) *When You're in Love.* Grace Moore appeared in *When You're in Love.*

Whistling Coon, The 1888 w.m. Sam Devere

Whistling in the Dark 1931 w.m. Allen Boretz, Dana Suesse

Whistling Rufus 1899 w. W. Murdock Lind m. Kerry Mills

White Christmas 1942 w.m. Irving Berlin. (MF) *Holiday Inn.* (MF) *Blue Skies.* (MF) *White Christmas.* Bing Crosby and Fred Astaire appeared in both *Holiday Inn* and *Blue Skies.* Bing Crosby, Danny Kaye, and Rosemary Clooney appeared in *White Christmas.* Academy Award winner 1942. Theme song of Bing Crosby.

(There'll Be Blue Birds Over) White Cliffs of Dover, The 1942 w. Nat Burton m. Walter Kent

White Dawn Is Stealing, The 1909 w. Nelle Richmond Eberhart m. Charles Wakefield Cadman. From "Four American Indian Songs."

White Dove, The 1930 w. Clifford Grey m. Franz Lehár. (MF) *The Rogue Song.* Lawrence Tibbett and Laurel and Hardy appeared in *The Rogue Song.*

White Horse Inn, The 1931 w.m. Robert Stolz, Irving Caesar, Ralph Benatsky, Harry Graham. (MT) *White Horse Inn.* Greta Hoffman appeared in the British production of *White Horse Inn.* Kitty Carlisle and William Gaxton appeared in the American 1936 production of *White Horse Inn.*

White House Chair, The 1856 w.m. Stephen Collins Foster. This song was written for the Presidential campaign of James Buchanan, Foster's sister's brother-in-law.

White on White 1964 w.m. Bernice Ross, Lor Crane

White Peacock, The 1917 m. Charles Tomlinson Griffes

White Rose of Athens, The 1961 Eng.w. Norman Newell, Archie Bleyer m. Manos Hadjidakis

White Silver Sands 1957 w.m. Red-Chuck Matthews. A claim to half-authorship of this song was filed by Mrs. Gladys Reinhardt against Clarence "Red" Matthews; she contended that he put the song on the market without her knowledge although she had written all the music and part of the words.

White Sport Coat and a Pink Carnation, A 1957 w.m. Marty Robbins

White Suit Samba, The 1951 w.m. Jack Parnell, T.E.B. Clarke. (F) *The Man in the White Suit*. Alec Guinness and Joan Greenwood appeared in *The Man in the White Suit*.

White Wings 1884 w.m. Banks, Winter

Whiter Shade of Pale, A 1967 w.m. Gary Brooker, Keith Reid. Ivor Novello Award winner 1967–68. This song was popularly revived in 1970.

Whittington Chimes uncertain Played by eight bells, the melody for these chimes first belonged to the Church of St. Mary le Bow. Dick Whittington, inspired by their magnificence, received the call to return and become "Lord Mayor of Londontown."

Who 1925 w. Oscar Hammerstein II m. Jerome Kern. (MT) *Sunny*. (MF) *Sunny*. (MF) *Till the Clouds Roll By*. (MF) *Look For the Silver Lining*. Marilyn Miller and Jack Donahue appeared in the American stage production of *Sunny*. Binnie Hale appeared in the British stage production of *Sunny*. Judy Garland and Frank Sinatra appeared in *Till the Clouds Roll By*, biopic of composer Jerome Kern. Gordon MacRae and Ray Bolger appeared in *Look For the Silver Lining*, biopic of Marilyn Miller.

Who Am I 1961 w.m. Les Vandyke

Who Ate Napoleons with Josephine When Bonaparte Was Away 1920 w. Alfred Bryan m. E. Ray Goetz. (MT) *As You Were*.

Who Can I Turn To (When Nobody Needs Me) 1964 w.m. Leslie Bricusse, Anthony Newley. (MT) *The Roar of the Greasepaint—The Smell of the Crowd*. Anthony Newley and Cyril Ritchard appeared in *The Roar of the Greasepaint— The Smell of the Crowd*.

Who Can It Be Now? 1982 w.m. David Colin Hay

Who Can Tell 1919 w. William Le Baron m. Fritz Kreisler. (MT) *Apple Blossoms*. (MF) *The King Steps Out*. This song was rewritten as "Stars in My Eyes" for the 1936 film *The King Steps Out*, with new words by Dorothy Fields.

Who Cares 1922 w. Jack Yellen m. Milton Ager. (MT) *Bombo*.

Who Cares 1931 w. Ira Gershwin m. George Gershwin. (MT) *Of Thee I Sing*.

Who Could Be Bluer 1960 w.m. Jerry Lordan

Who Dat Say Chicken in Dis Crowd 1898 w. Paul Lawrence Dunbar m. Will Marion. (MT) *Clorindy, or, The Origin of the Cake Walk*. See also Part I, 1898.

Who Do You Love, I Hope 1946 w.m. Irving Berlin. (MT) *Annie Get Your Gun*. (MF) *Annie Get Your Gun*. Ethel Merman appeared in the stage production of *Annie Get Your Gun*. Betty Hutton appeared in the film production of *Annie Get Your Gun*.

Who Do You Think You Are 1947 w. Sylvia Dee m. Sidney Lippman. (MT) *Barefoot Boy with Cheek*. Nancy Walker, Red Buttons, and Billy Redfield appeared in *Barefoot Boy with Cheek*.

Who Do You Think You Are Kidding Mister Hitler 1971 w.m. Jimmy Perry, Derek Taverner

Who Hit Me 1948 w.m. Charles Gaynor. (MT) *Lend an Ear*.

Who Knows Where the Times Goes 1967 w.m. Sandy Denny. (F) *The Subject Was Roses*. Patricia Neal appeared in *The Subject Was Roses*.

Who Loves You 1975 w.m. Bob Gaudio, Judy Parker

Who Needs You 1956 w. Al Stillman m. Robert Allen

Who Put the Bomp (in the Bomp Ba Bomp Ba Bomp) 1961 w.m. Barry Mann, Gerry Goffin

Who Takes Care of the Caretaker's Daughter While the Caretaker's Busy Taking Care? 1925 w.m. Chick Endor

Who Threw the Overalls in Mrs. Murphy's Chowder 1899 w.m. George L. Giefer

Who Wants To Be a Millionaire 1956 w.m. Cole Porter. (MF) *High Society*. Frank Sinatra, Grace Kelly, and Bing Crosby appeared in *High Society*.

Who Were You with Last Night 1912 w.m. Fred Godfrey, Mark Sheridan

Who Will Buy? 1963 w.m. Lionel Bart. (MT) *Oliver!*. (MF) *Oliver!*. Georgia Brown and Ron Moody appeared in the stage production of *Oliver!*. Shani Wallis and Ron Moody appeared in the film production of *Oliver!*.

Who Wouldn't Love You 1942 w.m. Bill Carey, Carl Fischer

Whoa, Emma 1877 w.m. John Read, T.S. Lonsdale. (MT) *The Streets of New York*. When "Whoa, Emma" was revived in *The Streets of New York*, Jimmy Walker and Al Smith, two singing politicians, heartily joined in the chorus. This song was revived again years later by Rudy Vallee in an updated fox-trot arrangement.

Whoever You Are, or, **Sometimes Your Eyes Look Blue to Me** 1968 w. Hal David m. Burt Bacharach. (MT) *Promises, Promises*.

Whole Lotta Love 1969 w.m. John Bonham, John Paul Jones, James Page, Robert Plant

Whole Lot-ta Shakin' Goin' On 1957 w.m. Dave Williams, Sunny David

Whole World Is Singing My Song, The 1946 w. Manny Kurtz m. Vic Mizzy

Who'll Buy My Violets 1923 Eng.w. E. Ray Goetz m. José Padilla. (MT) *Little Miss Bluebeard*. (F) *City Lights*. Irene Bordoni and Eric Blore appeared in *Little Miss Bluebeard*. Charlie Chaplin appeared in *City Lights*. Based on "La Violetera" of 1918. Theme song of Raquel Meller.

Who'll Stop the Rain 1970 w.m. John C. Fogerty

Whoopee Ti Yi Yo, *see* **Git Along Little Doggies**

Who's Afraid of the Big Bad Wolf 1933 w.m. Frank E. Churchill, Ann Ronell. (MF) *The Three Little Pigs*. (MF) *Babes in Toyland*. Stan Laurel and Oliver Hardy appeared in *Babes in Toyland*. Based on Johann Strauss's "Champagne Song" from *Die Fledermaus* and "Perpetual Motion." This song was written during the depths of the Depression, and became a sort of anti-Depression anthem.

Who's Been Polishing the Sun 1935 w.m. Noel Gay. (MF)

The Camels Are Coming. Jack Hulbert appeared in *The Camels Are Coming.*

Who's Cheatin' Who 1981 w.m. Jerry Hayes

Who's Crying Now 1981 w.m. Jonathan Cain, Stephen Perry

Who's Holding Donna Now 1985 w.m. Randy Goodrum, Jay Graydon, David Foster

Who's Johnny ("Short Circuit" Theme) 1986 w.m. Ina Wolf

Who's Sorry Now 1923 w. Bert Kalmar, Harry Ruby m. Ted Snyder. (F) *A Night in Casablanca.* (MF) *Three Little Words.* The Marx Brothers appeared in *A Night in Casablanca.* Fred Astaire, Debbie Reynolds, and Red Skelton appeared in *Three Little Words,* biopic of song writers Bert Kalmar and Harry Ruby. This song was popularly revived in 1958.

Who's Taking You Home Tonight 1940 w.m. Manning Sherwin, Tommie Connor. (MT) *Shephard's Pie.*

Who's Wonderful, Who's Marvelous? Miss Annabelle Lee, *see* **Miss Annabelle Lee**

Who's Your Little Who-Zis 1931 w.m. Walter Hirsch, Al Goering, Ben Bernie. (MF) *The Stooge.* Dean Martin, Jerry Lewis, and Polly Bergen appeared in *The Stooge.*

Who's Zoomin' Who 1986 w.m. Aretha Franklin, Preston Glass, Narada Michael Walden

Whose Baby Are You 1920 w. Anne Caldwell m. Jerome Kern. (MT) *The Night Boat.* (MT) *Fun of the Fayre.* Alfred Lester appeared in *Fun of the Fayre.*

Whose Little Heart Are You Breaking Now 1917 w.m. Irving Berlin

Whosoever Will May Come 1891 w. A. Montieth m. Ira David Sankey

Why (Is There a Rainbow in the Sky) 1929 w. Arthur Swanstrom, Benny Davis m. J. Fred Coots. (MT) *Sons o' Guns.* (MF) *Sons o' Guns.*

Why 1960 w.m. Peter DeAngelis, Robert P. Marcucci

Why 1972 w.m. Roger Whittaker, Joan Stanton. Ivor Novello Award winner 1971–72.

Why Am I Always the Bridesmaid 1917 w.m. Fred W. Leigh, Charles Collins, Lily Morris

Why Am I Me 1975 w. Peter Udell m. Gary Geld. (MT) *Shenandoah.* John Cullum appeared in *Shenandoah.*

Why Baby Why 1957 w.m. Luther Dixon, Larry Harrison

Why Can't I 1929 w. Lorenz Hart m. Richard Rodgers. (MT) *Spring Is Here.*

Why Can't I Speak 1983 w. Fred Ebb m. John Kander. (MT) *Zorba.* Anthony Quinn and Debbie Shapiro appeared in *Zorba.*

Why Can't I Touch You 1970 w.m. C.C. Courtney, Peter Link. (MT) *Salvation.*

Why Can't the English 1956 w. Alan Jay Lerner m. Frederick Loewe. (MT) *My Fair Lady.* (MF) *My Fair Lady.* Rex Harrison appeared in both the stage and film productions of *My Fair Lady.*

Why Can't This Be Love 1986 w.m. Sammy Hagar, Michael Anthony, Alex Van Halen, Edward Van Halen

Why Can't We Be Friends 1975 w.m. Sylvester Allen, Harold Ray Brown, Morris D. Dickerson, Gerald Goldstein, Leroy L. Jordan, Lee Oskar Levitin, Charles Miller, Howard E. Scott

Why Can't We Live Together 1973 w.m. Tim Thomas

Why Can't You Behave 1949 w.m. Cole Porter. (MT) *Kiss Me, Kate.* (MF) *Kiss Me, Kate.* Alfred Drake and Patricia Morison appeared in the stage production of *Kiss Me, Kate.* Ann Miller, Kathryn Grayson, and Howard Keel appeared in the film production of *Kiss Me, Kate.*

Why Dance 1931 w. Roy Turk m. Fred E. Ahlert

Why Did I Choose You 1965 w. Herbert Martin m. Michael Leonard. (MT) *The Yearling.*

Why Did I Kiss That Girl 1924 w. Lew Brown m. Robert King, Ray Henderson

Why Did I Leave My Little Back Room 1901 w.m. A.J. Mills, Frank W. Carter

Why Did She Fall for the Leader of the Band 1936 w.m. Jimmy Kennedy, Michael Carr. (MF) *She Shall Have Music.* Jack Hylton appeared in *She Shall Have Music.*

Why Did They Dig Ma's Grave So Deep 1880 w.m. Joseph P. Skelly

Why Do Fools Fall in Love 1956 w.m. Frank Lymon, George Goldner. This song was popularly revived in 1981.

Why Do I 1926 w. Lorenz Hart m. Richard Rodgers. (MT) *The Girl Friend.* Eva Puck and Sam White appeared in *The Girl Friend.*

Why Do I Love You 1925 w. B.G. DeSylva, Ira Gershwin m. George Gershwin. (MT) *Tell Me More.* The original out-of-town title for *Tell Me More* was *My Fair Lady.*

Why Do I Love You 1927 w. Oscar Hammerstein II m. Jerome Kern. (MT) *Show Boat.* (MF) *Show Boat* (1951). Howett Worster and Edith Day appeared in the British stage production of *Show Boat.* Howard Keel, Kathryn Grayson, and Ava Gardner appeared in the 1951 film production of *Show Boat.*

Why Do the Wrong People Travel 1961 w.m. Noël Coward. (MT) *Sail Away.* This song was banned from British radio for the reason that it was "thought to offend on the grounds of general taste."

Why Do They All Take the Night Boat to Albany 1918 w. Joe Young, Sam M. Lewis m. Jean Schwartz

Why Do You Suppose 1929 w. Lorenz Hart m. Richard Rodgers. (MT) *Heads Up!* See also "How Was I To Know."

Why Do You Treat Me Like You Do 1965 w.m. Donovan

Why Does It Get So Late So Early 1946 w. Allie Wrubel, John Lehman m. Allie Wrubel

Why Don't They Dance the Polka Anymore 1914 w. Harry B. Smith m. Jerome Kern. (MT) *The Girl from Utah.*

Why Don't They Understand 1958 w.m. Jack Fishman, Joe Henderson

Why Don't We Do This More Often 1941 w.m. Charles Newman, Allie Wrubel

Why Don't You Answer Me 1920 w.m. Sam M. Lewis, Joe Young, M.K. Jerome

Why Don't You Believe Me 1952 w.m. Lew Douglas, King Laney, Roy Rodde

Why Don't You Do Right 1942 w.m. Joe McCoy

Why Don't You Fall in Love With Me, see **As Long As You're Not in Love with Anyone Else**

Why Don't You Spend the Night 1980 w.m. Bob McDill

Why Fight the (That) Feeling 1950 w.m. Frank Loesser. (MF) *Let's Dance.* Betty Hutton and Fred Astaire appeared in *Let's Dance.*

Why Have You Left the One You Left Me For? 1979 w.m. Christopher Mark True

Why Is the Bacon So Tough 1929 w.m. Reginald Arkell, Charles Prentice

Why Lady Why 1981 w.m. Teddy Gentry, Richard Scott

Why Not Me 1980 w.m. Carson Whitsett, Fred Knobloch

Why Oh Why Did I Ever Leave Wyoming, see **Wyoming**

Why Oh Why Oh Why? 1974 w.m. Gilbert O'Sullivan

Why Should I Care 1937 w.m. Cole Porter. (MF) *Rosalie.* Eleanor Powell, Nelson Eddy, and Frank Morgan appeared in *Rosalie.*

Why Should I Cry Over You 1922 w.m. Ned Miller, Chester Cohn

Why Shouldn't I 1935 w.m. Cole Porter. (MT) *Jubilee.* Melville Cooper and Mary Boland appeared in *Jubilee.*

Why, Soldiers, Why, see **How Stands the Glass Around**

Why Try To Change Me Now 1952 w.m. Cy Coleman, Joseph A. McCarthy

Why Was I Born 1929 w. Oscar Hammerstein II m. Jerome Kern. (MT) *Sweet Adeline.* (MF) *Sweet Adeline.* (MF) *Till the Clouds Roll By.* (MF) *The Man I Love.* (MF) *Both Ends of the Candle.* Helen Morgan, Irene Franklin, and Charles Butterworth appeared in the stage production of *Sweet Adeline.* Irene Dunne and Hugh Herbert appeared in the film production of *Sweet Adeline.* June Allyson, Frank Sinatra, Judy Garland, and Van Johnson appeared in *Till the Clouds Roll By,* biopic of composer Jerome Kern. Ida Lupino and Robert Alda appeared in *The Man I Love.*

Why Worry 1952 w.m. Ralph Edwards, John Sexton

Wichita Lineman 1968 w.m. Jim Webb

Widow Machree 1842 w.m. Samuel Lover

Wiegenlied, see **Lullaby**

Wien, Du Stadt Meiner Träume 1914 w.m. Rudolf Sieczynski

Wiener Blut, see **Vienna Life**

Wig Wam Bam 1973 w.m. Nicky Chinn, Mike Chapman

Wild Boys, The 1984 w.m. Roger Taylor, Nigel Taylor, Andrew Taylor, Nick Rhodes, Simon Le Bon

Wild Flower, see **Wildflower**

Wild Honey Pie 1968 w.m. John Lennon, Paul McCartney

Wild Horses 1953 w.m. Johnny Burke. Based on Robert Schumann's "Wilder Reiter."

Wild Is the Wind 1957 w.m. Ned Washington, Dimitri Tiomkin

Wild Man Blues 1927 w.m. Louis Armstrong, Ferdinand Joseph Morton

Wild One 1960 w.m. Dave Appell, Bernie Lowe, Kal Mann

Wild Rose, The 1910 w. George V. Hobart m. Victor Herbert. (MT) *When Sweet Sixteen.*

Wild Rose 1920 w. Clifford Grey m. Jerome Kern. (MT) *Sally.* (MT) *The Wild Rose.* (MF) *Sally.* (MF) *Look For the Silver Lining.* Dorothy Dickson appeared in the British stage production of *Sally.* Marilyn Miller and Joe E. Brown appeared in the film production of *Sally.* Ray Bolger and June Haver appeared in *Look For the Silver Lining,* biopic of Marilyn Miller.

Wild Thing 1966 w.m. Chip Taylor

Wild Wind 1961 w.m. Geoffrey Goddard

Wild World 1970 w.m. Cat Stevens

Wildfire 1975 w.m. Michael Murphey, Larry Cansler

Wildflower 1923 w. Otto Harbach, Oscar Hammerstein II m. Herbert Stothart, Vincent Youmans. (MT) *The Wildflower.* Edith Day and Guy Robertson appeared in *The Wildflower.*

Wildflower 1973 w.m. David Richardson, Doug Edwards

Wilhelmina 1950 w. Mack Gordon m. Josef Myrow. (MF) *Wabash Avenue.* Betty Grable and Victor Mature appeared in *Wabash Avenue.*

Will He Like Me 1963 w. Sheldon Harnick m. Jerry Bock. (MT) *She Loves Me.*

Will I What 1962 w.m. Johnny Powell, Nick Shakespear, Ken Hawker

Will It Go Round in Circles 1973 w.m. Bruce Fisher, Billy Preston

Will You Love Me in December As You Do in May 1905 w. James J. Walker m. Ernest R. Ball. (MF) *The Eddy Duchin Story.* (MF) *Beau James.* Bob Hope and Alexis Smith appeared in *Beau James.*

Will You (Still) Love Me Tomorrow 1961 w.m. Gerry Goffin, Carole King

Will You Marry Me Tomorrow, Maria 1937 w. Oscar Hammerstein II m. Jerome Kern. (MF) *High, Wide and Handsome.* Irene Dunne appeared in *High, Wide and Handsome.*

Will You Remember (Sweetheart) 1917 w. Rida Johnson Young m. Sigmund Romberg. (MT) *Maytime.* (MF) *Maytime.* (MF) *Deep in My Heart.* Peggy Wood, Charles Purcell and William Norris appeared in *Maytime.* Jeanette MacDonald and Nelson Eddy appeared in the film production of *Maytime.* Jose Ferrer and Merle Oberon appeared in *Deep in My Heart,* biopic of composer Sigmund Romberg.

William Tell Overture 1829 m. Gioacchino Rossini. From the French "Guillaume Tell." Performance time for the original "Guillaume Tell" was four and one-half hours. See also Part I, 1914.

William's Song 1984 w. Robert Lorick m. Henry Krieger. (MT) *The Tap Dance Kid.* Alfonso Ribiero appeared in *The Tap Dance Kid.*

Willie We Have Missed You 1854 w.m. Stephen Collins Foster

Willkommen 1967 w. Fred Ebb m. John Kander. (MT) *Cabaret.* (MF) *Cabaret.* Lotte Lenya and Joel Grey appeared in the stage production of *Cabaret.* Liza Minnelli and Joel Gray appeared in the film production of *Cabaret.*

Willow Waltz, The 1960 w.m. Cyril Watters

Willow Weep for Me 1932 w.m. Ann Ronell. (MF) *Love Happy.* The Marx Brothers appeared in *Love Happy.*

Wilson, That's All! 1912 w. Ballard MacDonald m. George Walter Brown. This song was used for the Presidential campaign of Woodrow Wilson.

Wimoweh, *see* **The Lion Sleeps Tonight**

Winchester Cathedral 1966 w.m. Geoff Stephens. Ivor Novello Award winner 1966.

Wind Cannot Read, The 1958 w.m. Peter Hart. Ivor Novello Award winner 1958.

Windmill in Old Amsterdam, A 1965 w.m. Ted Dicks, Myles Rudge. Ivor Novello Award winner 1965.

Windmills of Your Mind, The, or, **Theme from** *The Thomas Crown Affair* 1968 w. Alan Bergman, Marilyn Bergman m. Michel Legrand. (F) *The Thomas Crown Affair.* Academy Award winner 1968.

Windmill's Turning, The 1938 w.m. Jan van Laar, Sr., Leo Fuld

Windows of Paris 1959 w.m. Tony Osborne. Ivor Novello Award winner 1959.

Windows of the World 1967 w. Hal David m. Burt Bacharach

Windsor Waltz, The 1953 w.m. Hans May, Michael Reine

Windy 1967 w.m. Ruthann Friedman

Wine of France 1904 w.m. Ivan Caryll. (MT) *The Duchess of Dantzig.*

Wine, Women and Song 1869 m. Johann Strauss. From the German "Wein, Weid und Gesang," op.333.

Wings 1977 w.m. Alexander Faris. (R) *Wings.* Ivor Novello Award winner 1977–78. Constance Cummings appeared in *Wings.*

Winter 1910 w. Alfred Bryan m. Albert Gumble

Winter Wonderland 1934 w. Richard Smith m. Felix Bernard

Wintergreen for President 1932 w. Ira Gershwin m. George Gershwin. (MT) *Of Thee I Sing.* Victor Moore and William Gaxton appeared in *Of Thee I Sing.*

Wipe Out 1963 w.m. Ron Wilson, James Fuller, Robert Berryhill, Patrick Connolly

Wired for Sound 1982 w.m. Alan Tarney, B.A. Robertson. Ivor Novello Award winner 1981–82.

Wise Old Owl, A 1903 w.m. Edward Madden, Theodore F. Morse

Wish I May 1963 w.m. Hugh Martin, Ralph Blane (MT) *Best Foot Forward.* (MF) *Best Foot Forward.* Lucille Ball and June Allyson appeared in the film production of *Best Foot Forward.* This song did not appear in the original 1941 stage production, but was added to the 1963 Off-Broadway stage production.

Wish Me Luck As You Wave Me Goodbye 1939 w.m. Harry Parr-Davies, Phil Park. (F) *Shipyard Sally.* Gracie Fields appeared in *Shipyard Sally.*

Wish You Were Here 1952 w.m. Harold Rome. (MT) *Wish You Were Here.*

Wish You Were Here 1981 w.m. Kye Fleming, Dennis Morgan

Wishing (Will Make It So) 1939 w.m. B.G. DeSylva. (F) *Love Affair.* (MF) *George White's Scandals.* Irene Dunne and Charles Boyer appeared in *Love Affair.*

Wishin' and Hopin' 1964 w. Hal David m. Burt Bacharach

Witch Doctor 1958 w.m. Ross Bagdasarian

Witchcraft 1957 w. Carolyn Leigh m. Cy Coleman

With a Little Bit of Luck 1956 w. Alan Jay Lerner m. Frederick Loewe. (MT) *My Fair Lady.* (MF) *My Fair Lady.* Julie Andrews and Rex Harrison appeared in the stage production of *My Fair Lady.* Audrey Hepburn and Rex Harrison appeared in the film production of *My Fair Lady.*

With a Little Help from My Friends, *see* **A Little Help from My Friends**

With a Smile and a Song 1937 w. Larry Morey m. Frank Churchill. (MF) *Snow White and the Seven Dwarfs.*

With a Song in My Heart 1929 w. Lorenz Hart m. Richard Rodgers. (MT) *Spring Is Here.* (MT) *Cochrane's 1930 Revue.* (MF) *Spring Is Here.* (MF) *This Is the Life.* (MF) *Words and Music.* (MF) *Young Man of Music.* (MF) *Young Man with a Horn.* (MF) *Painting the Clouds with Sunshine.* (MF) *With a Song in My Heart.* Charles Ruggles and Lillian Taiz appeared in the stage production of *Spring Is Here.* Alexander Gray and Bernice Claire appeared in the film production of *Spring Is Here.* Donald O'Connor and Susanna Foster appeared in *This Is the Life.* Dennis Morgan and Virginia Mayo appeared in *Painting the Clouds with Sunshine.* Susan Hayward and Thelma Ritter appeared in *With a Song in My Heart,* biopic of singer Jane Froman.

With a Twist of the Wrist 1941 w.m. Irvin Graham. (MT) *Crazy with the Heat.* (MF) *Rhythm Inn.* Carl Randall and Willie Howard appeared in *Crazy with the Heat.* Jane Frazee and Kirby Grant appeared in *Rhythm Inn.*

With All Her Faults I Love Her Still 1888 w.m. Monroe H. Rosenfeld. Popularly sung by minstrel tenor Richard Jose. This song belongs to the tradition of "echo" songs that includes, among others, "How Dry I Am," "Say Au Revoir," and, of course, "Sweet Adeline."

With All My Heart 1931 w. Desmond Carter m. Johann Strauss. (MT) *The Great Waltz.* (MF) *The Great Waltz.* This song was most popular in 1934.

With All My Heart 1935 w. Gus Kahn m. Jimmy McHugh. (F) *Her Master's Voice.* Edward Everett Horton and Peggy Conklin appeared in *Her Master's Voice.*

With Every Breath I Take 1934 w.m. Leo Robin, Ralph Rainger. (MF) *Here Is My Heart.* Bing Crosby appeared in *Here Is My Heart.*

With Her Head Tucked Underneath Her Arm 1934 w.m. R.P. Weston, Bert Lee

With My Eyes Wide Open I'm Dreaming 1934 w.m. Mack Gordon, Harry Revel. (MF) *Shoot the Works.* (MF) *The Stooge.* Ben Bernie, Dorothy Dell, and Jack Oakie appeared in *Shoot the Works.* Dean Martin, Jerry Lewis, and Polly Bergen appeared in *The Stooge.*

With My Head in the Clouds 1942 w.m. Irving Berlin. (MT) *This Is the Army.*

With My Shillelagh Under My Arm 1937 w.m. Billy O'Brien, Raymond Wallace

With Plenty of Money and You 1936 w. Al Dubin m. Harry Warren. (MF) *Gold Diggers of 1937.* (MF) *She's Working Her Way Through College.* Dick Powell, Victor Moore, and Joan Blondell appeared in *Gold Diggers of 1937.* Virginia Mayo and Gene Nelson appeared in *She's Working Her Way Through College.*

With the Wind and the Rain in Your Hair 1930 w.m. Jack Lawrence, Clara Edwards. This song was popularly revived in 1940.

With These Hands 1950 w. Benny Davis m. Abner Silver. This song was popularly revived in 1953.

With You I'm Born Again 1980 w.m. Carol Connors, David Shire

With Your Love 1976 w.m. Martyn Buchwald, Joey Covington, Victor Smith

Within a Mile of Edinburgh 1794 w. adapted from Thomas D'Urfey m. James Hook. (MT) *Harlequin and Faustus (in London)*

Within the Cellar's Depth I Sit 1875 Eng.w. Louis Charles Elson m. Karl Ludwig Fischer. From the German "Der Rheinweinzecher." This song is also known in English as "Drinking" and "In Cellar Cool."

Without a Song 1929 w. Billy Rose, Edward Eliscu m. Vincent Youmans. (MT) *Great Day!* Mayo Methot and Allan Pryor appeared in *Great Day!* Theme song of Lawrence Tibbett.

Without a Word of Warning 1935 w.m. Mack Gordon, Harry Revel. (MF) *Two for Tonight.* Bing Crosby and Joan Bennett appeared in *Two for Tonight.*

Without Love 1955 w.m. Cole Porter. (MT) *Silk Stockings.* (MF) *Silk Stockings.* Fred Astaire and Cyd Charisse appeared in the film production of *Silk Stockings.*

Without That Certain Thing 1933 w.m. Max Nesbitt, Harry Nesbitt

Without You 1942 Sp.w. Osvaldo Farres Eng.w. Ray Gilbert; also Charles Wolcott m. Osvaldo Farres. (MF) *Make Mine Music.* The voices of Dinah Shore and Jerry Colonna appeared in *Make Mine Music.* From the Spanish "Tres Palabres."

Without You 1956 w. Alan Jay Lerner m. Frederick Loewe. (MT) *My Fair Lady.* (MF) *My Fair Lady.* Rex Harrison and Julie Andrews appeared in the stage production of *My Fair Lady.* Rex Harrison and Audrey Hepburn appeared in the film production of *My Fair Lady.*

Without You 1972 w.m. Peter Ham, Tom Evans. Ivor Novello Award winner 1972–73.

Without You I'm Nothing 1956 w.m. Jerry Bock, George Weiss, Larry Holofcener. (MT) *Mr. Wonderful.*

Without Your Love 1982 m. Billy Nicholls. Ivor Novello Award winner 1981–82.

(Theme from) Wives and Lovers 1963 w. Hal David m. Burt Bacharach. (F) *Wives and Lovers.* Van Johnson, Janet Leigh, and Shelley Winters appeared in *Wives and Lovers.*

Wolfe's Song, *see* How Stands the Glass Around

Wolverine Blues 1923 w.m. Ferdinand ("Jelly Roll") Morton, Benjamin Spikes, John C. Spikes

Wolverton Mountain 1962 w.m. Merle Kilgore, Claude King

Woman 1981 w.m. John Lennon. Ivor Novello Award winner 1981–82.

Woman in Love 1980 w.m. Barry Gibb, Robin Gibb. Ivor Novello Award winner 1980–81. Ivor Novello Award winner 1981–82.

Woman in Love, A 1955 w.m. Frank Loesser. (MF) *Guys and Dolls.* Marlon Brando, Jean Simmons, and Frank Sinatra appeared in *Guys and Dolls.* This song did not appear in the original 1950 stage production of *Guys and Dolls.*

Woman in the Shoe, The 1929 w. Arthur Freed m. Nacio Herb Brown. (MF) *Lord Byron of Broadway.* Ethelind Terry and Cliff Edwards appeared in *Lord Byron of Broadway.*

Woman Is a Sometime Thing, A 1935 w. DuBose Heyward m. George Gershwin. (MT) *Porgy and Bess.* (MF) *Porgy and Bess.* Todd Duncan, Anne Wiggins Brown, and Warren Coleman appeared in the original stage production of *Porgy and Bess.* Sidney Poitier, Pearl Bailey, and Sammy Davis, Jr., appeared in the film production of *Porgy and Bess.*

Woman Is Only a Woman, But a Good Cigar Is a Smoke, A 1905 w. Harry B. Smith m. Victor Herbert. (MT) *Miss Dolly Dollars.*

Woman Needs Love, A (Just Like You Do) 1981 w.m. Ray Parker, Jr.

Wombling Song 1975 w.m. Mike Batt. Ivor Novello Award winner 1974–75.

Women Do Know How To Carry On 1982 w.m. Bobby Emmons, Waylon Jennings

Wonder Bar 1934 w. Al Dubin m. Harry Warren. (MF) *Wonder Bar.* Al Jolson, Dolores Del Rio, and Dick Powell appeared in *Wonder Bar.*

Wonder of You, The 1971 w.m. Baker Knight

Wonder When My Baby's Coming Home 1943 w.m. Kermit Goell, Arthur Kent

Wonder Why 1951 w. Sammy Cahn m. Nicholas Brodszky. (MF) *Rich, Young and Pretty.* Jane Powell and Vic Damone appeared in *Rich, Young and Pretty.*

Wonderful Copenhagen 1952 w.m. Frank Loesser. (MF) *Hans Christian Andersen.* Danny Kaye appeared in *Hans Christian Andersen.*

(On) Wonderful Day Like Today, A 1965 w.m. Leslie Bricusse, Anthony Newley. (MT) *The Roar of the Greasepaint—The Smell of the Crowd.* Anthony Newley and Cyril

Ritchard appeared in *The Roar of the Greasepaint—The Smell of the Crowd*.

Wonderful Eyes 1914 w.m. Paul Rubens, Percy Greenbank. (MT) *After the Girl*.

Wonderful Guy, A, *see* **I'm In Love with a Wonderful Guy**

Wonderful Land 1962 w.m. Jerry Lordan. Ivor Novello Award winner 1962.

(My) Wonderful One 1922 w. Dorothy Terris m. Paul Whiteman, Ferde Grofé. (F) *Margie*. Glenn Langan and Lynn Bari appeared in *Margie*. Based on a theme by Marshall Neilan.

Wonderful Time Up There, A 1947 w.m. Lee Roy Abernathy

Wonderful Wonderful 1957 w. Ben Raleigh m. Sherman Edwards

Wonderful You 1929 w. Jack Meskill, Max Rich m. Pete Wendling

Wondering Where the Lions Are 1980 w.m. Bruce Cockburn

Wonderland by Night 1961 w. Lincoln Chase m. Klaus Gunter Neumann

Wond'rous Love, or, **Captain Kidd,** or, **Through All the World** 1835 w.m. based on a traditional English ballad, c.1700

Won't Somebody Dance with Me 1974 w.m. Lynsey de Paul. Ivor Novello Award winner 1973–74.

Won't You Be My Honey 1907 w. Jack Drislane m. Theodore F. Morse

Won't You Be My Little Girl 1896 w. Isaac G. Reynolds m. Homer Tourjee

Won't You Be My Sweetheart 1893 w. J.G. Judson m. H.C. Verner

Won't You Change Partners and Dance with Me, *see* **Change Partners**

Won't You Charleston with Me 1954 w.m. Sandy Wilson. (MT) *The Boy Friend*.

Won't You Come Home Bill Bailey, *see* **Bill Bailey Won't You Please Come Home**

Won't You Come Over to My House 1906 w. Harry H. Williams m. Egbert Van Alstyne

Won't You Fondle Me 1904 w.m. James Kendis, Herman Paley

Won't You Play a Simple Melody, *see* **Play a Simple Melody**

Won't You Tell Me Why, Robin 1861 w.m. Claribel (Mrs. Charlotte Arlington Barnard)

Won't You Waltz "Home Sweet Home" with Me 1907 w.m. Herbert Ingraham

Woo Woo Song, The, *see* **You Should Be Mine**

Wooden Heart 1961 w.m. Fred Wise, Benjamin Weisman, Kathleen G. Twomey, Berthold Kaempfert. (MF) *G.I. Blues*. Elvis Presely and Juliet Prowse appeared in *G.I. Blues*. Based on the traditional German folksong "Muss I Denn."

Wooden Soldier and the China Doll, The 1932 w. Charles Newman m. Isham Jones

Woodland Sketches 1896 m. Edward MacDowell. This volume of piano sketches included "To a Wild Rose," "Will o' the Wisp," "At an Old Trysting Place," "In Autumn," "From an Indian Lodge," "To a Water Lily," "From Uncle Remus," "A Deserted Farm," "By a Meadow Brook," and "Told At Sunset."

Woodman Spare That Tree 1837 w. George Pope Morris m. Henry Russell. In 1868 a college parody by John Love, Jr. of New York University was titled "Barber, Spare Those Hairs."

Woodman, Woodman, Spare That Tree 1911 w.m. Irving Berlin. Based on George P. Morris's poem of the same name, this song was written as special material for Bert Williams.

Woodpecker(s') Song, The 1940 It.w. C. Bruno Eng.w. Harold Adamson m. Eldo di Lazzaro (MF) *Ride Tenderfoot Ride*. Gene Autry appeared in *Ride Tenderfoot Ride*. Based on the Italian "Reginella Campagnola."

Woody Woodpecker 1948 w.m. George Tibbles, Ramey Idriss

Wooing of the Violin, The 1920 w. Robert B. Smith m. Victor Herbert. (MT) *Some Colonel*.

Wooly Bully 1965 w.m. Domingo Samudio

Words 1968 w.m. Barry Gibb, Robin Gibb, Maurice Gibb

Words Are in My Heart, The 1935 w. Al Dubin m. Harry Warren. (MF) *Gold Diggers of 1935*. Dick Powell, Adolphe Menjou, and Glenda Farrell appeared in *Gold Diggers of 1935*.

Words without Music 1935 w. Ira Gershwin m. Vernon Duke. (MT) *Ziegfeld Follies of 1936–1937*. Fanny Brice and Gypsy Rose Lee appeared in *Ziegfeld Follies of 1936–1937*.

Words, Words, Words 1965 w.m. Walter Marks. (MT) *Bajour*. Chita Rivera and Nancy Dussault appeared in *Bajour*.

Work for the Night Is Coming 1864 w. Annie L. Walker m. Lowell Mason

Workin' My Way Back to You 1980 w.m. Sandy Linzer, Denny Randell

World Cup March, The 1966 w.m. Alan Moorhouse, Mansfield

World Gets in the Way 1986 w.m. Gloria Estefan

World I Used To Know, The 1964 w.m. Rod McKuen

World Is Mine (Tonight), The 1935 w.m. George Posford, Holt Marvell. (F) *The Gay Desperado*. Nino Martini and Ida Lupino appeared in *The Gay Desperado*.

World Is Singing My Song, The 1946 w. Mann Curtis m. Vic Mizzy

World Is Waiting for the Sunrise, The 1919 w. Eugene Lockhart m. Ernest Seitz. This song was popularly revived in 1951.

World of Our Own, A 1965 w.m. Tom Springfield

World Owes Me a Living, The 1934 w. Larry Morey m. Leigh Harline. (MF) *The Grasshopper and the Ants*.

World Turned Upside Down, The, or, **Derry Down** 1775 w.m. traditional march, from England

World Weary 1928 w.m. Noël Coward. (MT) *This Year of Grace*. Beatrice Lillie and Noël Coward appeared in *This Year of Grace*.

World Without Love, A 1964 w.m. John Lennon, Paul McCartney

World Without Love, A 1986 w.m. Eddie Rabbitt, Even Stevens

Worms Crawl In, the Worms Crawl Out, The, *see* **Did You Ever Think As the Hearse Rolls By**

Worst Pies in London, The 1979 w.m. Stephen Sondheim. (MT) *Sweeney Todd.* Angela Lansbury and Len Cariou appeared in *Sweeney Todd.*

Would God I Were a Tender Apple Blossom 1894 w. Katherine Hinkson (Tyman) m. traditional, from Ireland

Would I Love You (Love You Love You) 1951 w. Bob Russell m. Harold Spina

(I Would) Would You 1936 w.m. Arthur Freed, Nacio Herb Brown. (F) *San Francisco.* (MF) *Singing in the Rain.* Clark Gable, Spencer Tracy, and Jeanette MacDonald appeared in *San Francisco.* Gene Kelly, Debbie Reynolds, and Donald O'Connor appeared in *Singing in the Rain.*

Would You Care 1905 w.m. Charles K. Harris

Would You Catch a Falling Star 1982 w.m. Bobby Braddock

Would You Like To Take a Walk 1930 w. Mort Dixon, Billy Rose m. Harry Warren. (MT) *Sweet and Low.* (MT) *Crazy Quilt.* (MF) *You're My Everything.* Fanny Brice and James Barton appeared in the American stage production of *Sweet and Low.* Julia Sanderson and Frank Crumit appeared in the British stage production of *Sweet and Low.* Fanny Brice and Ted Healy appeared in *Crazy Quilt.* Dan Dailey and Anne Baxter appeared in *You're My Everything.*

Would You Rather Be a Colonel with an Eagle on Your Shoulder, or a Private with a Chicken on Your Knee? 1918 w. Sidney D. Mitchell m. Archie Gottler. (MT) *Ziegfeld Follies* (of 1919).

Wouldn't It Be Loverly 1956 w. Alan Jay Lerner m. Frederick Loewe. (MT) *My Fair Lady.* (MF) *My Fair Lady.* Julie Andrews and Rex Harrison appeared in the stage production of *My Fair Lady.* Audrey Hepburn and Rex Harrison appeared in the film production of *My Fair Lady.*

Wrap Your Troubles in Dreams (and Dream Your Troubles Away) 1931 w.m. Ted Koehler, Harry Barris, Billy Moll. (MF) *Rainbow Round My Shoulder.* (F) *Top Man.* Frankie Laine appeared in *Rainbow Round My Shoulder.* Donald O'Connor and Lillian Gish appeared in *Top Man.*

Wrap Yourself in Cotton Wool 1942 w.m. Val Guest, Manning Sherwin. (MT) *Get a Load of This.* Celia Lipton appeared in *Get a Load of This.*

Wrapped Around Your Finger 1984 w.m. Gordon "Sting" Sumner

Wreck of the Edmund Fitzgerald, The 1976 w.m. Gordon Lightfoot. This song is based on the actual disappearance in November 1975 of the ship *Edmund Fitzgerald* in the "Whitefish trapezium" area of Lake Superior. At least a dozen vessels have disappeared in storms in that region, claiming nearly two hundred lives.

Wreck of the John B, The, *see* **John B**

Wreck of the "Julie Plante," The 1920 w. William Henry Drummond m. Geoffrey O'Hara

Wreck of (on) the Old (Southern) '97, The 1924 w.m. anon. Based on Henry C. Work's "The Ship That Never Returned." See also Part I, 1924.

Wringle Wrangle 1956 w.m. Stan Jones

Written on the Wind 1956 w.m. Sammy Cahn

WRNS March, The 1942 m. Richard Addinsell

Wunderbar 1949 w.m. Cole Porter. (MT) *Kiss Me, Kate.* (MF) *Kiss Me, Kate.* Alfred Drake and Patricia Morison appeared in the stage production of *Kiss Me, Kate.* Kathryn Grayson, Howard Keel, and Ann Miller appeared in the film production of *Kiss Me, Kate.*

(Oh Why, Oh Why Did I Ever Leave) Wyoming 1946 w.m. Morey Amsterdam

Wyoming Lullaby 1920 w.m. Gene Williams

Xanadu 1980 w.m. Jeff Lynne. (MF) *Xanadu.* Olivia Newton-John and Gene Kelly appeared in *Xanadu.* Ivor Novello Award winner 1980–81.

Ya Got Me 1945 w. Betty Comden, Adolph Green m. Leonard Bernstein. (MT) *On the Town.* (MF) *On the Town.*

Yaaka Hula Hickey Dula 1916 w.m. E. Ray Goetz, Joe Young, Pete Wendling. (MT) *Robinson Crusoe, Jr.* (MF) *Applause.* Al Jolson appeared in *Robinson Crusoe, Jr.* Helen Morgan and Joan Peters appeared in *Applause.*

Yah Mo B There 1984 w.m. James Ingram, Quincy Jones, Michael McDonald, Rodney Temperton

Yakety Yak 1958 w.m. Jerry Leiber, Mike Stoller

Yale Boola, *see* **Boola Boola**

Yama Yama Man, The 1908 w. George Collin Davis m. Karl Hoschna. (MT) *The Three Twins.* (MF) *The Story of Vernon and Irene Castle.* (MF) *Look For the Silver Lining.* Sung by Ginger Rogers in the 1939 musical film *The Story of Vernon and Irene Castle.* Ray Bolger appeared in *Look For the Silver Lining.* Theme song of Bessie McCoy Davis.

Yankee Doodle 1753–1798 w.m. traditional, from England, Scotland, or Ireland; words added by countless contributors in the early years in America, among them British army surgeon Dr. Richard Schuckburgh in 1758 while he was camping with General Abercrombie on the old Van Rensselaer estate near Albany. The melody was published in Glasgow as early as 1782; another early London publication possibly from as early as 1777. This song's origins have been claimed by music historians to be everything from a Dutch reapers' ballad to a Hungarian folksong. The pay for the Dutch harvesters was all the buttermilk they could drink and one tenth of the grain they reaped. Their lyric was the following:

> Yankee Dudel, Dodel down,
> Diddle, dudel, lanther,
> Yanke vivor, vover vown,
> Botermilk und tanther.

Over fifty possible sources have been cited but proved false. However, we do know that the song was included in Andrew Barton's libretto for the American opera *The Disappointment, or, The Force of Credulity,* in 1767. It was also known in its day as "The Lexington March" and was definitely played at Bunker Hill, Cornwallis's surrender at Yorktown, the battle of Lexington and Burgoyne's surrender at Saratoga in 1777. This theme appears in compositions by Anton Rubinstein, Henri Vieuxtemps, and Paderewski, and suggestions of it are in the Finale of Dvorak's "From the New World" Symphony. See also "Battle of the Kegs."

Yankee Doodle Blues, The 1922 w. Irving Caesar, B.G. DeSylva m. George Gershwin. (MF) *Rhapsody in Blue.* (MF) *I'll Get By.* Robert Alda, Alexis Smith, and Al Jolson appeared in *Rhapsody in Blue,* biopic of composer George Gershwin. June Haver and Dennis Day appeared in *I'll Get By.*

(I Am) Yankee Doodle Boy, The 1904 w.m. George M. Cohan. (MT) *Little Johnny Jones.* (MT) *George M!* (MT) *Dancin'.* (MF) *Little Johnny Jones.* (MF) *Yankee Doodle Dandy.* (MF) *The Seven Little Foys.* Joel Grey and Bernadette Peters appeared in *George M!* James Cagney appeared in *Yankee Doodle Dandy.* Bob Hope appeared in *The Seven Little Foys.* See also Part I, 1919.

Yankee Rose 1926 w. Sidney Holden m. Abe Frankel

Yankee Ship and a Yankee Crew, A 1837 w. J.S. Jones, Esq. m. C.M. King, Esq.

(Theme from) Yanks 1980 m. Richard Rodney Bennett. (F) *Yanks.* Vanessa Redgrave appeared in *Yanks.* Ivor Novello Award winner 1979–80.

Ye Banks and Braes O' Bonnie Doon 1788 w. Robert Burns m. traditional air, from Scotland. This song was also known in its day as "The Caledonian Hunt's Delight."

Ye Parliament of England 1813 w.m. traditional, from England

Yeah Yeah 1963 w.m. Grand, Patrick, Hendrick

Year from Today, A 1924 w. P.G. Wodehouse m. Jerome Kern. (MT) *Sitting Pretty.*

Year of Jubilo, The, *see* **Kingdom Coming**

Yearning (Just for You) 1925 w.m. Benny Davis, Joe Burke. (MF) *Sweethearts on Parade.* Ray Middleton and Alice White appeared in *Sweethearts on Parade.*

Years 1980 w.m. Kye Fleming, Dennis Morgan

Years Ago 1982 w.m. Donald Reid

Year's At the Spring, The 1900 w. Robert Browning m. Mrs. H.H.A. Beach

Yellow Bird 1957 w.m. Norman Luboff, Marilyn Keith, Alan Bergman. This song was popularly revived in 1961, and was later adapted for the Northeast Airlines television commercial advertising campaign.

Yellow Dog Blues 1928 w.m. W.C. Handy. (MF) *St. Louis Blues.* Nat "King" Cole and Eartha Kitt appeared in *St. Louis Blues,* biopic of composer W.C. Handy.

Yellow River 1971 w.m. Jeff Christie. Ivor Novello Award winner 1970–71.

Yellow Rose of Texas, The, or, **Song of the Texas Rangers** 1858 w. J.K.; adapted Don George, 1955. (F) *Night Stage to Galveston.* Gene Autry and Pat Buttram appeared in *Night Stage to Galveston.* This song was popularly revived in 1955. This was one of Franklin D. Roosevelt's favorite songs. AS-CAP ruled in 1956 that the royalty payments for this song

would be 20 percent of that for an original song since it was based on a song in the public domain.

Yellow Submarine 1966 w.m. John Lennon, Paul McCartney. (MF) *Yellow Submarine.* Ivor Novello Award winner 1966.

Yeoman of England 1902 w.m. Edward German. (MT) *Merrie England.* Henry Lytton and Robert Evett appeared in *Merrie England.*

Yeoman's Wedding Song, The 1875 w. Maria X. Hayes m. Prince Josef Poniatowski

Yes, I'm Ready 1980 w.m. Barbara Mason

Yes Indeed 1943 w.m. Sy Oliver. This song was written in 1941.

Yes, Let Me Like a Soldier Fall 1845 w. Edward Fitzball m. Vincent Wallace. From the English opera *Maritana.*

Yes My Darling Daughter 1941 w.m. Jack Lawrence. Theme song of Dinah Shore.

Yes Sir, That's My Baby 1925 w. Gus Kahn m. Walter Donaldson. (MF) *Broadway.* (MF) *The Eddie Cantor Story.* (MF) *I'll See You in My Dreams.* George Raft, Pat O'Brien, and Janet Blair appeared in *Broadway.* Doris Day and Danny Thomas appeared in *I'll See You in My Dreams,* biopic of song writer Gus Kahn.

Yes! We Have No Bananas 1923 w.m. Frank Silver, Irving Cohn. The melody for this song was inspired by "The Vacant Chair," which, in turn, was adapted from "When I Saw Sweet Nellie Home (Aunt Dinah's Quilting Party)."

Yesterday 1965 w.m. John Lennon, Paul McCartney. (MT) *Beatlemania.* Ivor Novello Award winner 1965. Ivor Novello Award winner 1966.

Yesterday Man 1965 w.m. Chris Andrews

Yesterday Once More 1973 w.m. John Bettis, Richard Carpenter

Yesterday When I Was Young 1969 w.m. Charles Aznavour, Herbert Kretzmer

Yesterdays 1933 w. Otto Harbach m. Jerome Kern. (MT) *Roberta.* (MF) *Roberta.* (MF) *Till the Clouds Roll By.* (MT) *Lovely To Look At.* Bob Hope and Fay Templeton appeared in the stage production of *Roberta.* Fred Astaire and Ginger Rogers appeared in the film production of *Roberta.* June Allyson, Frank Sinatra, Judy Garland, and Van Johnson appeared in *Till the Clouds Roll By,* biopic of composer Jerome Kern. Kathryn Grayson and Howard Keel appeared in *Lovely To Look At,* remake of *Roberta.*

Yesterday's Roses 1942 w.m. Peter DeAngelis, Noel Sherman

Yester-Me, Yester-You, Yesterday 1969 w.m. Ronald Miller, Bryan Wells

Yi Yi Yi Yi *see* **I Like You Very Much**

Yiddle on Your Fiddle, or, **Play Some Ragtime** 1909 w.m. Irving Berlin

Yield Not to Temptation 1868 w.m. Horatio Richmond Palmer

Yip-I-Addy-I-Ay! 1909 w. Will D. Cobb m. John H. Flynn. (MT) *Our Miss Gibbs.* (F) *New York Town.* (MF) *Sunbonnet Sue.* Gertie Millar and George Grossmith, Jr., appeared in *Our Miss Gibbs*. Fred MacMurray and Mary Martin appeared in *New York Town*. Gale Storm and Phil Regan appeared in *Sunbonnet Sue*.

Yoo-Hoo 1921 w. B.G. DeSylva . Al Jolson

You (Gee But You're Wonderful) 1936 w. Harold Adamson m. Walter Donaldson. (MF) *The Great Ziegfeld*. William Powell appeared in *The Great Ziegfeld*.

You Ain't Heard Nothing Yet 1919 w.m. Al Jolson, Gus Kahn, B.G. DeSylva

You Ain't Seen Nothing Yet 1974 w.m. Randy Bachman

You Alone, or, **Solo Tu** 1953 w. Al Stillman m. Robert Allen

You Always Hurt the One You Love 1944 w.m. Doris Fisher, Allan Roberts. This song was also popular in 1946, and revived in 1958.

You and I 1941 w.m. Meredith Willson

You and I 1983 w.m. Frank Myers

You and Me 1977 w.m. Alice Cooper, Dick Wagner

You and Me Against the World 1974 w.m. Kenneth Lee Asher, Paul Williams

You and the Night and the Music 1934 w. Howard Dietz m. Arthur Schwartz. (MT) *Revenge with Music*. (MT) *Stop Press*. Libby Holman and Ilka Chase appeared in *Revenge with Music*.

You and You Waltz, *see* **Du and Du**

You Are Always in My Heart, *see* **Always in My Heart**

You Are Beautiful 1958 m. Oscar Hammerstein II m. Richard Rodgers. (MT) *Flower Drum Song*. (MF) *Flower Drum Song*.

You Are 1983 w.m. Brenda Harvey-Richie, Lionel Richie

You Are Free 1919 w. William Le Baron m. Victor Jacobi. (MT) *Apple Blossoms*. Fred Astaire, Adele Astaire, and Wilda Bennett appeared in *Apple Blossoms*.

You Are Love 1928 w. Oscar Hammerstein II m. Jerome Kern. (MT) *Show Boat*. (MF) *Show Boat* (1936). Irene Dunne, Allan Jones, and Helen Morgan appeared in the 1936 film production of *Show Boat*.

You Are Mine, All Mine, *see* **It Must Be True**

You Are Mine Evermore 1927 w. Harry B. Smith m. Emmerich Kalman. (MT) *The Circus Princess*.

You Are My First Love 1956 w.m. Paddy Roberts, Lester Powell. (F) *It's Great To Be Young*. Ivor Novello Award winner 1956.

You Are My Lady 1986 w.m. Barry Eastmond

You Are My Lucky Star 1935 w. Arthur Freed m. Nacio Herb Brown. (MT) *Singin' in the Rain*. (MF) *Broadway Melody of 1936*. (MF) *Babes in Arms*. (MF) *Born To Sing*. (MF) *Singin' in the Rain*. Jack Benny and Eleanor Powell appeared in *Broadway Melody of 1936*. Mickey Rooney and Judy Garland appeared in *Babes in Arms*. Leo Gorcey appeared in *Born To Sing*. Gene Kelly, Debbie Reynolds, and Donald O'Connor appeared in *Singin' in the Rain*. Loosely based on a theme from Liszt's Second Hungarian Rhapsody.

You Are My Sunshine 1940 w.m. Jimmie Davis, Charles Mitchell. (MF) *Take Me Back to Oklahoma*. (MF) *Strictly in the Groove*. Tex Ritter appeared in *Take Me Back to Okla-*

homa. Martha Tilton and Donald O'Connor appeared in *Strictly in the Groove*. This song was popularly revived in 1962. Jimmy Davis ran for and was elected governor of Louisiana in 1944.

You Are Never Away 1947 w. Oscar Hammerstein II m. Richard Rodgers. (MT) *Allegro*. John Battles, William Ching, and Annamary Dickey appeared in *Allegro*.

You Are Sixteen 1959 w. Oscar Hammerstein II m. Richard Rodgers. (MT) *The Sound of Music*. (MF) *The Sound of Music*. Mary Martin appeared in the stage production of *The Sound of Music*. Julie Andrews appeared in the film production of *The Sound of Music*.

You Are So Beautiful 1975 w.m. Bruce Fisher, Billy Preston

You Are the Ideal of My Dreams 1910 w.m. Herbert Ingraham

You Are the Sunshine of My Life 1973 w.m. Stevie Wonder

You Are the Woman 1976 w.m. Richard Roberts

You Are Too Beautiful 1932 w. Lorenz Hart m. Richard Rodgers. (MF) *Hallelujah, I'm a Bum*. Al Jolson and Frank Morgan appeared in *Hallelujah, I'm a Bum*. This song was popularly revived in 1945.

You Are Woman (I Am Man) 1964 w. Bob Merrill m. Jule Styne. (MT) *Funny Girl*. (MF) *Funny Girl*. Barbra Streisand appeared in both the stage and film productions of *Funny Girl*.

You Beautiful So and So 1929 w. Billy Rose m. Ted Snyder. (MT) *Earl Carroll's Sketch Book of 1929*. Will Mahoney and William Demarest appeared in *Earl Carroll's Sketch Book of 1929*.

You Belong To Me 1916 w. Harry B. Smith m. Victor Herbert. (MT) *The Century Girl*.

You Belong to Me 1952 w.m. Pee Wee King, Redd Stewart, Chilton Price

You Belong to Me 1978 w.m. Michael McDonald

You Belong to My Heart (Now and Forever), or, **Solamente Una Vez** 1944 w. Ray Gilbert m. Augustin Lara (MF) *The Three Caballeros*. (MF) *The Gay Ranchero*. (MF) *You Belong to My Heart*. (MF) *Mr. Imperium*. Roy Rogers and Andy Devine appeared in *The Gay Ranchero*. Lana Turner and Ezio Pinza appeared in *Mr. Imperium*.

You Belong to the City 1985 w.m. Glenn Frey, Jack Tempchin

You Better Go Now 1936 w.m. Irvin Graham, Bix Reichner. (MT) *New Faces of 1936*. Van Johnson and Imogene Coca appeared in *New Faces of 1936*.

You Better Keep Babying Baby (Or Baby's Gonna Bye-Bye You) 1923 w. William Tracey m. Jack Stanley

You Bring Out the Lover in Me 1956 w. Carolyn Leigh m. Philip Springer

You Brought a New Kind of Love to Me 1930 w.m. Sammy Fain, Irving Kahal, Pierre Norman. (MF) *The Big Pond*. (MF) *Monkey Business*. Maurice Chevalier and Claudette Colbert appeared in *The Big Pond*. The Marx Brothers and Thelma Todd appeared in *Monkey Business*. This song was popularly revived in 1938.

You Call Everybody Darling 1946 w.m. Sam Martin, Ben L. Trace, Clem Watts, Albert J. Trace. This song was also popular in 1948.

You Call It Madness (Ah, But I Call It Love) 1931 w.m. Con Conrad

You Came a Long Way from St. Louis 1948 w.m. John Benson Brooks, Sidney Keith Russell

You Came Along from Out of Nowhere, see **Out of Nowhere**

You Came to Me from Out of Nowhere, see **Out of Nowhere**

You Can Depend on Me 1932 w.m. Charles Carpenter, Louis Dunlap, Earl Hines. This song was popularly revived in 1938.

You Can Do Magic 1983 w.m. Russ Ballard

You Can Do No Wrong 1948 w.m. Cole Porter. (MF) *The Pirate.* Judy Garland and Gene Kelly appeared in *The Pirate.*

You Can Have Broadway 1906 w.m. George M. Cohan. (MT) *George Washington, Jr.*

You Can Never Stop Me Loving You 1963 w.m. Ian Samwell, Jean Slater

You Cannot Make Your Shimmy Shake on Tea 1919 w.m. Irving Berlin, Rennold Wolf. This song anticipated Prohibition.

You Can't Be True, Dear 1948 w. Hal Cotton m. Ken Griffen. From the German ''Du Kannst Nicht Treu Sein,'' Ger. w. Gerhard Ebeler, orig. m. Hans Otten.

You Can't Change That 1979 w.m. Ray Parker, Jr.

You Can't Chop Your Poppa Up in Massachusetts 1952 w.m. Michael Brown

You Can't Do That 'Ere 1935 w.m. Raymond Wallace, Jack Rolls

You Can't Get a Man with a Gun 1946 w.m. Irving Berlin. (MT) *Annie Get Your Gun.* (MF) *Annie Get Your Gun.* Ethel Merman and Ray Middleton appeared in the stage production of *Annie Get Your Gun.*

You Can't Get Along With 'Em or Without 'Em 1916 w. Grant Clarke m. Fred Fisher

You Can't Get What You Want (Till You Know What You Want) w.m. Joe Jackson

You Can't Have Everything 1937 w.m. Mack Gordon, Harry Revel. (MF) *You Can't Have Everything.* Alice Faye, the Ritz Brothers, and Don Ameche appeared in *You Can't Have Everything.*

You Can't Hurry Love 1966 w.m. Eddie Holland, Brian Holland, Lamont Dozier

You Can't Keep a Good Man Down 1900 w.m. M. F. Carey

You Can't Play Every Instrument in the Band 1913 w. Joseph Cawthorn m. John L. Golden. (MT) *The Sunshine Girl.*

You Can't Play in Our Yard Any More 1894 w. Philip Wingate m. H.W. Petrie

You Can't Pull the Wool over My Eyes 1936 w.m. Milton Ager, Charles Newman, Murray Mencher

You Can't See the Sun When You're Crying 1946 w.m. Allan Roberts, Doris Fisher

You Can't Stop Me from Dreaming 1937 w.m. Dave Franklin, Cliff Friend

You Can't Stop Me from Loving You 1912 w. Alexander Gerber, Murphy m. Henry I. Marshall

You Could Drive a Person Crazy 1970 w.m. Stephen Sondheim. (MT) *Company.* (MT) *Side by Side by Sondheim.* Elaine Stritch appeared in *Company.* Millicent Martin and Julie N. McKenzie appeared in *Side by Side by Sondheim.*

You Could Have Been with Me 1982 w.m. Lea Maalfrid

You Couldn't Be Cuter 1938 w. Dorothy Fields m. Jerome Kern. (MF) *Joy of Living.* Irene Dunne, Lucille Ball, and Douglas Fairbanks, Jr., appeared in *Joy of Living.*

You Decorated My Life 1979 w.m. Bob Morrison, Debbie Hupp. Grammy Award winner 1979.

You Deserve a Break Today 1971 w. Keith Reinhard, Richard Hazlett, Ed Farran m. Sid Woloshin, Kevin Gavin. This song was written for a McDonald's commercial promotion campaign.

You Did It 1956 w. Alan Jay Lerner m. Frederick Loewe. (MT) *My Fair Lady.* (MF) *My Fair Lady.* Julie Andrews and Rex Harrison appeared in the stage production of *My Fair Lady.* Audrey Hepburn and Rex Harrison appeared in the film production of *My Fair Lady.*

You Didn't Have To Tell Me—I Knew It All the Time 1931 w.m. Walter Donaldson

You Didn't Want Me When You Had Me 1919 w.m. George J. Bennett, Bernie Grossman, Benee Russell

You Die If You Worry 1930 w.m. Stanley Damerell, Robert Hargreaves

You Do 1947 w.m. Mack Gordon, Josef Myrow. (MF) *Mother Wore Tights.* Dan Dailey and Betty Grable appeared in *Mother Wore Tights.*

You Do Something to Me 1929 w.m. Cole Porter. (MT) *Fifty Million Frenchmen.* (MF) *Fifty Million Frenchmen.* (MF) *Night and Day.* (MF) *Starlift.* (MF) *Because You're Mine.* (MF) *Can-Can.* (F) *Evil Under the Sun.* William Gaxton and Betty Compton appeared in the film production of *Fifty Million Frenchmen.* Cary Grant, Alexis Smith, and Mary Martin appeared in *Night and Day,* biopic of song writer Cole Porter. Doris Day and Virginia Mayo appeared in *Starlift.* Mario Lanza appeared in *Because You're Mine.* Frank Sinatra and Shirley MacLaine appeared in *Can-Can.* Maggie Smith and Peter Ustinov appeared in *Evil Under the Sun.*

You Do the Darndest Things, Baby 1936 w. Sidney D. Mitchell m. Lew Pollack. (MF) *Pigskin Parade.* Judy Garland, Betty Grable, Patsy Kelly, and Jack Haley appeared in *Pigskin Parade.*

You Don't Belong to the Regulars, You're Just a Volunteer, see **Mister Volunteer**

You Don't Have To Be a Star (To Be in My Show) 1977 w.m. James Dean, John Henry Glover, Jr.

You Don't Have To Know the Language 1947 w.m. Jimmy Van Heusen, Johnny Burke. (MF) *The Road to Rio.* Bob Hope, Bing Crosby, and Dorothy Lamour appeared in *The Road to Rio.*

You Don't Have To Say You Love Me 1966 Orig.w. V.

Pollavicini Eng.w. Vicki Wickham, Simon Napier-Bell m. P. Donaggio

You Don't Have To Tell Me, I Know 1941 w.m. Don Pelosi, Art Noel

You Don't Know 1961 w.m. Mike Hawker, John Schroeder

You Don't Know Me 1962 w.m. Cindy Walker, Eddy Arnold

You Don't Know Paree 1929 w.m. Cole Porter. (MT) *Fifty Million Frenchmen*. (MF) *Fifty Million Frenchmen*. William Gaxton and Helen Broderick appeared in the film production of *Fifty Million Frenchmen*.

You Don't Know What Love Is 1941 w.m. Don Raye, Gene De Paul. (MF) *Keep 'Em Flying*. Abbott and Costello and Martha Raye appeared in *Keep 'Em Flying*.

You Don't Like It—Not Much 1927 w.m. Ned Miller, Art Kahn, Chester Cohn

You Don't Own Me 1963 w.m. John Madara, David White

You Drive Me Crazy 1982 w.m. Ronnie Harwood. Ivor Novello Award winner 1981–82.

You Dropped Me Like a Red Hot Penny 1936 w. Joe Young m. Fred E. Ahlert

You Find the Time, I'll Find the Place 1929 w.m. B.G. DeSylva, Lew Brown, Ray Henderson. (MF) *Sunny Side Up*. Janet Gaynor and Charles Farrell appeared in *Sunny Side Up*.

You Forgot Your Gloves 1931 w. Edward Eliscu m. Ned Lehak. (MT) *The Third Little Show*. Beatrice Lillie, Eddie Arnold, and Carl Randall appeared in *The Third Little Show*.

You Give Good Love 1985 w.m. Lala

You Go to My Head 1938 w. Haven Gillespie m. J. Fred Coots

You Gotta Be a Football Hero (To Get Along with the Beautiful Girls) 1933 w.m. Al Sherman, Buddy Fields, Al Lewis

You Gotta Eat Your Spinach, Baby 1936 w.m. Mack Gordon, Harry Revel. (MF) *Poor Little Rich Girl*. Shirley Temple, Jack Haley, and Gloria Stewart appeared in *Poor Little Rich Girl*.

You Gotta Have a Gimmick 1959 w. Stephen Sondheim m. Jule Styne. (MT) *Gypsy*. (MT) *Side by Side by Sondheim*. (MF) *Gypsy*. Ethel Merman appeared in the stage production of *Gypsy*. Millicent Martin and Julie N. McKenzie appeared in *Side by Side by Sondheim*. Rosalind Russell appeared in the film production of *Gypsy*.

You Gotta Quit Kickin' My Dawg Around, *see* **They Gotta Quit Kickin' My Dog Around**

You Happen Once in a Lifetime 1943 w.m. Manning Sherwin, Harold Purcell

You Have Cast Your Shadow on the Sea 1938 w. Lorenz Hart m. Richard Rodgers. (MT) *The Boys from Syracuse*. (MF) *The Boys from Syracuse*.

You Have Everything 1937 w. Howard Dietz m. Arthur Schwartz. (MT) *Between the Devil*.

You Have Taken My Heart 1933 w. Johnny Mercer m. Gordon Jenkins

You Haven't Changed At All 1945 w. Alan Jay Lerner m. Frederick Loewe. (MT) *The Day Before Spring*. Bill Johnson and Irene Manning appeared in *The Day Before Spring*.

You Haven't Done Nothing Yet 1974 w.m. Stevie Wonder

You Hit the Spot 1936 w.m. Mack Gordon, Harry Revel. (MF) *Collegiate*. (MF) *The Charm School*. Joe Penner, Jack Oakie, and Betty Grable appeared in *Collegiate*. Frances Langford appeared in *The Charm School*.

You Irritate Me So 1941 w.m. Cole Porter. (MT) *Let's Face It*. (MF) *Let's Face It*. Eve Arden, Vivian Vance, and Danny Kaye appeared in the stage production of *Let's Face It*. Betty Hutton and Bob Hope appeared in the film production of *Let's Face It*.

You Keep Coming Back Like a Song 1943 w.m. Irving Berlin. (MF) *Blue Skies*. Bing Crosby and Fred Astaire appeared in *Blue Skies*. This song was popularly revived in 1946.

You Keep Me Hangin' On 1966 w.m. Eddie Holland, Brian Holland, Lamont Dozier

You Know and I Know (and We Both Understand) 1915 w. Schuyler Greene m. Jerome Kern. (MT) *Nobody Home*.

You Know You Belong to Somebody Else 1922 w. Eugene West m. James V. Monaco

You Leave Me Breathless 1938 w.m. Ralph Freed, Frederick Hollander. (MF) *Cocoanut Grove*. Fred MacMurray, Ben Blue, and Eve Arden appeared in *Cocoanut Grove*.

You Let Me Down 1935 w. Al Dubin m. Harry Warren. (MF) *Stars Over Broadway*.

You Light Up My Life 1977 w.m. Joseph Brooks. (F) *You Light Up My Life*. Academy Award winner 1977. Grammy Award winner 1977.

You Made Me Care When I Wasn't in Love 1940 w.m. Joseph George Gilbert

You Made Me Love You (I Didn't Want To Do It) 1913 w. Joseph McCarthy m. James V. Monaco. (MF) *Wharf Angel*. (MF) *Broadway Melody of 1938*. (MF) *Syncopation*. (MF) *Private Buckaroo*. (MF) *The Jolson Story*. (MF) *Jolson Sings Again*. (MF) *Love Me or Leave Me*. Dorothy Dell and Preston Foster appeared in *Wharf Angel*. Judy Garland appeared in *Broadway Melody of 1938*. Adolphe Menjou and Jackie Cooper appeared in *Syncopation*. The Andrews Sisters and Joe E. Lewis appeared in *Private Buckaroo*. Larry Parks appeared in *The Jolson Story* and *Jolson Sings Again*. Doris Day appeared in *Love Me or Leave Me*. Theme song of Harry James.

You Make Lovin' Fun 1977 w.m. Christine McVie

You Make Me Feel Brand New 1974 w.m. Linda Creed, Thomas Bell

You Make Me Feel Like a Natural Woman, *see* **A Natural Woman**

You Make Me Feel Like Dancing 1977 w.m. Vini Poncia, Leo Sayer. Grammy Award winner 1977.

You Make Me Feel So Young 1946 w. Mack Gordon m. Josef Myrow. (MF) *Three Little Girls in Blue*. (MF) *I'll Get By*. June Haver, George Montgomery, and Vivian Blaine appeared in *Three Little Girls in Blue*. June Haver and Dennis Day appeared in *I'll Get By*.

You Make My Dreams 1981 w.m. Sara Allen, Daryl Hall, John Oates

You May Not Be An Angel, *see* **I'll String Along with You**

You Me and Us 1957 w.m. John Jerome. Based on "Cielito Lindo" of 1919.

You Might Think 1984 w.m. Ric Ocasek

You Must Have Been a Beautiful Baby 1938 w. Johnny Mercer m. Harry Warren. (F) *Hard To Get*. (MF) *The Eddie Cantor Story*. Dick Powell and Olivia DeHaviland appeared in *Hard To Get*.

You Must Meet My Wife 1973 w.m. Stephen Sondheim. (MT) *A Little Night Music*. (MT) *Side by Side by Sondheim*. (MF) *A Little Night Music*. Glynis Johns, Len Cariou, and Hermione Gingold appeared in the stage production of *A Little Night Music*. Millicent Martin and Julie N. McKenzie appeared in *Side by Side by Sondheim*. Elizabeth Taylor, Len Cariou, and Hermione Gingold appeared in the film production of *A Little Night Music*.

You Mustn't Kick It Around 1940 w. Lorenz Hart m. Richard Rodgers. (MT) *Pal Joey*. (MF) *Pal Joey*. Gene Kelly, Van Johnson, and June Havoc appeared in the stage production of *Pal Joey*. Frank Sinatra and Kim Novak appeared in the film production of *Pal Joey*.

You Naughty, Naughty Men 1866 w. T. Kennick m. G. Bicknell. (MT) *The Black Crook*. This song was performed by Milly Cavendish in the original stage production of *The Black Crook*. Its subject is the weakness of the male animal, and is one of the earliest feminist songs. As premiered on September 12, 1866, performance time for this first extravaganza was five and a half hours; it ran for 474 performances.

You Need Hands 1958 w.m. Max Bygraves. Ivor Novello Award winner 1958.

You Never Done It Like That 1978 w.m. Howard Greenfield, Neil Sedaka

You Never Gave Up on Me 1982 w.m. Leslie Pearl

You Never Knew About Me 1917 w. P.G. Wodehouse m. Jerome Kern. (MT) *Oh, Boy!*

You Never Miss the Water Till the Well Runs Dry, or, **Waste Not, Want Not** 1874 w.m. Rollin Howard. The writers to this song have erroneously been credited as Harry Linn and D. Angelo. Made popular by Fred Walz, this song was popular with Bryant's minstrels.

(Theme from) You Only Live Twice 1967 w.m. Leslie Bricusse, John Barry. (F) *You Only Live Twice*. Sean Connery appeared in *You Only Live Twice*.

You Oughta Be in Pictures 1934 w. Edward Heyman m. Dana Suesse. (F) *New York Town*. (MF) *Starlift*. Fred MacMurray and Mary Martin appeared in *New York Town*. Doris Day and Gordon MacRae appeared in *Starlift*.

You Oughta See My Baby 1920 w. Roy Turk m. Fred E. Ahlert

You Planted a Rose in the Garden of Love 1914 w. J. Will Callahan m. Ernest R. Ball

(I'll Be Glad When You're Dead) You Rascal You 1931 w.m. Charles Davenport

You Really Got Me 1964 w.m. Ray Davies

You Remind Me of My Mother 1922 w.m. George M. Cohan. (MT) *Little Nellie Kelly*. (MF) *Fifty Million Frenchmen*. Elizabeth Hines and Charles King appeared in *Little Nellie Kelly*. William Gaxton and Helen Broderick appeared in *Fifty Million Frenchmen*.

You Remind Me of the Girl That Used To Go to School with Me 1910 w. Jack Drislane m. Charles Miller

You Said It 1919 w. Bert Kalmar, Eddie Cox m. Henry W. Santly

You Said Something 1917 w. Jerome Kern P.G. Wodehouse m. Jerome Kern. (MT) *Have a Heart*.

You Say the Nicest Things, Baby 1948 w. Harold Adamson m. Jimmy McHugh. (MT) *As the Girls Go*. Irene Rich and Bill Callahan appeared in *As the Girls Go*.

You Send Me 1957 w.m. L.C. Cook. This song was popularly revived in 1985.

You Sexy Thing 1975 w.m. Errol A.G. Brown, Tony Wilson

You Should Be Dancing 1976 w.m. Barry Gibb, Maurice Gibb, Robin Gibb. (MF) *Saturday Night Fever*. Ivor Novello Award winner 1976–77. John Travolta appeared in *Saturday Night Fever*.

You Should Be Mine (The Woo Woo Song) 1986 w.m. Andy Goldmark, Bruce Roberts

You Should Hear How She Talks About You 1982 w.m. Dean Pitchford, Tom Snow

You Splash Me and I'll Splash You 1907 w. Arthur J. Lamb m. Alfred Solman

You Started Something 1941 w.m. Ralph Rainger, Leo Robin. (MF) *Moon over Miami*. Betty Grable and Robert Cummings appeared in *Moon over Miami*.

You Stepped Out of a Dream 1940 w. Gus Kahn m. Nacio Herb Brown. (MF) *Ziegfeld Girl*. James Stewart, Judy Garland, and Hedy Lamarr appeared in *Ziegfeld Girl*.

You Take My Breath Away 1979 w.m. Bruce Hart, Stephen Lawrence. (F) *Sooner or Later*.

You Talk Too Much 1960 w.m. Joseph Jones, Reginald Hall

You Taught Me How To Love You, Now Teach Me To Forget 1909 w. Jack Drislane, Alfred Bryan m. George W. Meyer

You Tell Her, I S-t-u-t-t-e-r 1922 w.m. Billy Rose, Cliff Friend. (MF) *Millions in the Air*. Robert Cummings and Inez Courtney appeared in *Millions in the Air*.

You Tell Me Your Dream, or, **I Had a Dream, Dear** 1908 w.m. Charles N. Daniels, Jay Blackton, Albert H. Brown, Seymoure Rice

You Took Advantage of Me 1928 w. Lorenz Hart m. Richard Rodgers. (MT) *Present Arms*. (MF) *A Star Is Born*. Charles King and Florence LeBreton appeared in *Present Arms*. Judy Garland and James Mason appeared in *A Star Is Born*. This song was a favorite of the Prince of Wales while he was courting Wallis Simpson. See also Part I, 1928.

You Try Somebody Else, and I'll Try Somebody Else (We'll Be Back Together Again) 1931 w.m. B.G. DeSylva, Lew Brown, Ray Henderson

You Turned the Tables on Me 1936 w. Sidney D. Mitchell m. Louis Alter. (MF) *Sing Baby Sing*. (MF) *The Benny Goodman Story*. (MF) *Kiss Them for Me*. Alice Faye and Adolphe Menjou appeared in *Sing Baby Sing*. Cary Grant and Jayne Mansfield appeared in *Kiss Them for Me*.

You Walk By 1940 w.m. Ben Raleigh, Bernie Wayne

You Wanna Bet 1966 w.m. Dorothy Fields, Cy Coleman

You Was 1948 w.m. Paul Francis Webster, Francis ''Sonny'' Burke

You Were Meant for Me 1924 w. Noble Sissle m. Eubie Blake. (MT) *Andre Charlot's Revue of 1924*.

You Were Meant for Me 1929 w. Arthur Freed m. Nacio Herb Brown. (MF) *Broadway Melody*. (MF) *Hollywood Revue*. (MF) *Show of Shows*. (MF) *You Were Meant for Me*. (MF) *Singin' in the Rain*. Bessie Love appeared in *Broadway Melody*. Conrad Nagel and Marie Dressler appeared in *Hollywood Revue*. Loretta Young and Beatrice Lillie appeared in *Show of Shows*. Dan Dailey and Jeanne Crain appeared in *You Were Meant for Me*. Gene Kelly, Debbie Reynolds, and Donald O'Connor appeared in *Singin' in the Rain*.

You Were Never Lovelier 1942 w. Johnny Mercer m. Jerome Kern. (MF) *You Were Never Lovelier*. Rita Hayworth and Fred Astaire appeared in *You Were Never Lovelier*.

You Were on My Mind 1965 w.m. Sylvia Fricker

You Were Only Foolin' 1947 w. Billy Faber, Fred Meadows m. Larry Fotine

You Were There 1936 w.m. Noël Coward. (MT) *Tonight at 8:30 (Shadow Play)*. Noël Coward and Gertrude Lawrence appeared in the British production of *Tonight at 8:30*.

You Wonderful You 1950 w. Saul Chapin, Jack Brooks m. Harry Warren. (MF) *Summer Stock*. Judy Garland and Gene Kelly appeared in *Summer Stock*.

You Won't Be Satisfied (Until You Break My Heart) 1945 w.m. Freddy James, Larry Stock

You Won't Find Another Fool Like Me 1974 w.m. Tony Macaulay, Geoff Stephens. Ivor Novello Award winner 1973–74.

You Wouldn't Fool Me, Would You 1928 w. B.G. DeSylva, Lew Brown m. Ray Henderson. (MT) *Follow Thru*. Zelma O'Neal and Jack Haley appeared in *Follow Thru*.

You, You, You 1953 w. Robert Mellin m. Lotar Olias

You, You, You Are the One 1947 w. Milton Leeds, Fred Wise m. Tetos Demey

You, You're the One 1975 w. Keith Reinhard, Dan Nicholsm. Ginny Redington. This song was written for a McDonald's commercial promotion campaign.

You'd Be So Easy To Love, *see* Easy To Love

You'd Be So Nice To Come Home To 1942 w.m. Cole Porter. (MF) *Something To Shout About*. Don Ameche, Janet Blair, and William Gaxton appeared in *Something To Shout About*. Based on Sarasate's ''Gypsy Airs (Zigeunerweisen).''

You'd Be Surprised 1919 w.m. Irving Berlin. (MT) *The Ziegfeld Follies (1919)*. (MT) *Afgar*. (MF) *Blue Skies*. (MF) *There's No Business Like Show Business*. Eddie Cantor appeared in *The Ziegfeld Follies (1919)*. Alice Delysia appeared in *Afgar*. Bing Crosby and Fred Astaire appeared in *Blue Skies*. Ethel Merman and Marilyn Monroe appeared in *There's No Business Like Show Business*.

You'd Better Love Me (While You May) 1964 w.m. Hugh Martin, Timothy Gray. (MT) *High Spirits*.

You'd Never Know the Old Home Town of Mine 1915 w. Howard Johnson m. Walter Donaldson

You'll Always Be My Lifetime Sweetheart 1955 w. K.C. Rogan m. Bobby Day

You'll Always Be the One I Love 1946 w. Sunny Skylar m. Ticker Freeman. (MF) *Song of the South*.

You'll Always Be the Same Sweet Girl 1915 w. Andrew B. Sterling m. Harry Von Tilzer

You'll Be Back Every Night in My Dreams 1982 w.m. Wayland Holyfield, Johnny Russell

You'll Have To Swing It, *see* If You Can't Sing It, You'll Have To Swing It

You'll Meet Me, Won't You 1852 w. S.J. Burr m. James Gaspard Maeder. From the American opera *The Peri*.

You'll Never Find Another Love Like Mine 1976 w.m. Kenneth Gamble, Leon Huff

You'll Never Get Away from Me 1959 w. Stephen Sondheim m. Jule Styne. (MT) *Gypsy*. (MF) *Gypsy*. Ethel Merman appeared in the stage production of *Gypsy*. Rosalind Russell appeared in the film production of *Gypsy*. The music for this song was written by Jule Styne for a television production with a lyric by Leo Robin, titled ''In Pursuit of Happiness.''

You'll Never Get to Heaven 1964 w. Hal David m. Burt Bacharach

You'll Never Know 1943 w. Mack Gordon m. Harry Warren. (MF) *Hello Frisco, Hello*. John Payne and Alice Faye appeared in *Hello Frisco, Hello*. Academy Award winner 1943.

You'll Never Walk Alone 1945 w. Oscar Hammerstein II m. Richard Rodgers. (MT) *Carousel*. (MF) *Carousel*. Jan Clayton and John Raitt appeared in the stage production of *Carousel*. Shirley Jones and Gordon MacRae appeared in the film production of *Carousel*.

Young and Foolish 1954 w. Arnold B. Horwitt m. Albert Hague. (MT) *Plain and Fancy*

Young and Healthy 1932 w. Al Dubin m. Harry Warren. (MT) *Forty-Second Street*. (MF) *Forty-Second Street*. Jerry Ohrbach and Tammy Grimes appeared in *Forty-Second Street*. Ruby Keeler and Dick Powell appeared in *Forty-Second Street*.

Young and in Love 1963 w.m. Dick St. John

Young and the Restless, The, *see* Nadia's Theme

Young and Warm and Wonderful 1958 w. Hy Zaret m. Lou Singer

Young at Heart 1954 w. Carolyn Leigh m. Johnny Richards. (MF) *Young at Heart*. Frank Sinatra, Doris Day, and Ethel Barrymore appeared in *Young at Heart*, based on the film *Four Daughters*, which starred John Garfield.

Young Emotions 1960 w. Mack David m. Jerry Livingston

Young Folks at Home, The 1852 w Frank Spencer m. Miss Hattie Livingston

Young Girl 1968 w.m. Jerry Fuller

Young Girls Are Coming to the Canyon, *see* **Twelve Thirty**

Young Ideas 1955 w.m. Moose Charlap, Chuck Sweeney

Young Love 1957 w.m. Carole Joyner, Ric Cartey

Young Man's Fancy, A 1920 w. John Murray Anderson, Jack Yellen m. Milton Ager. (MT) *What's in a Name* (MT) *League of Notions.*

Young Molly Who Lives at the Foot of the Hill, *see* **The Lass with the Delicate Air**

Younger Than Springtime 1949 w. Oscar Hammerstein II m. Richard Rodgers. (MT) *South Pacific.* (MF) *South Pacific.* Mary Martin appeared in the stage production of *South Pacific.* Mitzi Gaynor appeared in the film production of *South Pacific.*

Your Cheatin' Heart 1953 w.m. Hank Williams

Your Dad Gave His Life for His Country 1903 w. Harry J. Breen m. T. Mayo Geary

Your Eyes 1931 w.m. Robert Stolz, Ralph Benatsky, Harry Graham. (MT) *White Horse Inn.*

Your Eyes Have Told Me So 1919 w. Gus Kahn, Walter Blaufuss m. Egbert Van Alstyne. (MF) *Sing Me a Love Song.* (MF) *I'll See You in My Dreams.* James Melton, Patricia Ellis, and Zasu Pitts appeared in *Sing Me a Love Song.* Doris Day and Danny Thomas appeared in *I'll See You in My Dreams,* biopic of song writer Gus Kahn.

Your Feet's Too Big 1935 w.m. Ada Benson, Fred Fisher. (MT) *Ain't Misbehavin'.* Debbie Allen and Nell Carter appeared in *Ain't Misbehavin'.*

Your God Comes First, Your Country Next, Then Mother Dear 1898 w.m. Paul Dresser

Your Heart and My Heart 1950 w.m. Ross Parker. (MT) *Knights of Madness.*

Your King and Country Want You 1914 w.m. Paul Rubens

Your Land and My Land 1927 w. Dorothy Donnelly m. Sigmund Romberg. (MT) *My Maryland.* Evelyn Herbert and Nathaniel Wagner appeared in *My Maryland.*

Your Love 1986 w.m. John Spinks

Your Love Is My Love 1957 w.m. Francis Edwards (Johnny Brandon). Ivor Novello Award winner 1957.

Your Mother and Mine 1929 w.m. Joe Goodwin, Gus Edwards. (MF) *Hollywood Revue.* (MF) *Show of Shows.* Marion Davies, Joan Crawford, Jack Benny, Lionel Barrymore, Buster Keaton, and the Brox Sisters (among them Judy Garland) appeared in *Hollywood Revenue.* Beatrice Lillie and Loretta Young appeared in *Show of Shows.*

Your Mother Should Know 1968 w.m. John Lennon, Paul McCartney

Your Secret's Safe with Me 1986 w.m. Michael Franks

Your Song 1970 w.m. Bernie Taupin, Elton John. Ivor Novello Award winner 1970–71.

Your Wildest Dreams 1986 w.m.. Justin Hayward

You're a Builder Upper 1934 w. Ira Gershwin, E.Y. Harburg m. Harold Arlen. (MT) *Life Begins at 8:40.* Frances Williams, Ray Bolger, and Bert Lahr appeared in *Life Begins at 8:40.*

You're a Friend of Mine 1986 w.m. Jeffrey Cohen

You're a Good Man, Charlie Brown 1967 w.m. Clark Gesner. (MT) *Your're a Good Man, Charlie Brown.*

You're a Grand Old Flag 1906 w.m. George M. Cohan. (MT) *George Washington, Jr.* (MT) *George M!.* (MF) *Yankee Doodle Dandy.* George M. Cohan appeared in *George Washington, Jr.* Joel Grey and Bernadette Peters appeared in *George M!.* James Cagney and Joan Leslie appeared in *Yankee Doodle Dandy.* The original word "rag" was deemed disrespectful and was changed to "flag." See also Part I, 1919.

You're a Great Big Blue Eyed Baby 1913 w.m. A. Seymour Brown

You're a Heavenly Thing 1935 w.m. Little Jack Little, Joe Young

You're a Million Miles from Nowhere When You're One Little Mile from Home 1919 w. Sam M. Lewis, Joe Young m. Walter Donaldson

You're a Pink Toothbrush 1953 w.m. Ralph Ruvin, Bob Halfin, Harold Irving

You're a Sweet Little Headache 1938 w.m. Leo Robin, Ralph Rainger. (MF) *Paris Honeymoon.* Bing Crosby and Shirley Ross appeared in *Paris Honeymoon.*

You're a Sweetheart 1937 w. Harold Adamson m. Jimmy McHugh. (MF) *You're a Sweetheart.* (MF) *Meet Danny Wilson.* Alice Faye and George Murphy appeared in *You're a Sweetheart.* Frank Sinatra and Shelley Winters appeared in *Meet Danny Wilson.*

You're Always in My Arms (but Only in My Dreams) 1929 w. Joseph McCarthy m. Harry Tierney. (MF) *Rio Rita.* Bert Wheeler and John Boles appeared in *Rio Rita.* This song did not appear in the original 1927 stage production of *Rio Rita.*

You're an Angel 1935 w.m. Jimmy McHugh, Dorothy Fields. (MF) *Hooray for Love.* Ann Sothern and "Fats" Waller appeared in *Hooray for Love.*

You're an Old Smoothie 1932 w. B.G. DeSylva m. Nacio Herb Brown, Richard Whiting. (MT) *Take a Chance.* (MT) *Nice Goings On.* Ethel Merman, Jack Haley, and Jack Whiting appeared in *Take a Chance.*

You're as Welcome as the Flowers in May 1901 w.m. Dan J. Sullivan

You're Blasé 1932 w. Bruce Sievier m. Ord Hamilton. (MT) *Bow Bells.* Binnie Hale appeared in *Bow Bells.*

You're Breaking My Heart 1949 w.m. Pat Genaro, Sunny Skylar. Based on Ruggiero Leoncavallo's "La Mattinata" of 1904.

You're Clear Out of this World, *see* **Out of This World**

You're Dancing on My Heart 1932 w.m. George Meyer, Al Bryan. Theme song of Victor Silvester.

You're De Apple of My Eye 1896 w. George H. Emerick m. Herbert Dillea

You're Devastating 1933 w. Otto Harbach m. Jerome Kern. (MT) *Roberta.* (MF) *Roberta.* (MF) *Lovely To Look At.* Bob Hope and Fay Templeton appeared in the stage production of *Roberta.* Kathryn Grayson, Red Skelton, Howard Keel, and Ann Miller appeared in *Lovely To Look At,* remake of *Roberta.*

You're Driving Me Crazy (What Did I Do) 1930 w.m. Walter Donaldson. (MT) *Smiles*. (MF) *Gentlemen Marry Brunettes*. Jane Russell appeared in *Gentlemen Marry Brunettes*.

You're Getting To Be a Habit with Me 1932 w. Al Dubin m. Harry Warren. (MT) *Forty-Second Street*. (MF) *Forty-Second Street*. (MF) *Lullaby of Broadway*. Jerry Ohrbach and Tammy Grimes appeared in *Forty-Second Street*. Ruby Keeler, Dick Powell, and Ginger Rogers appeared in *Forty-Second Street*. Doris Day and Billy DeWolf appeared in *Lullaby of Broadway*.

You're Going Far Away, Lad, or, **I'm Still Your Mother, Dear** 1897 w.m. Paul Dresser

You're Gonna Hear from Me 1966 w.m. Dory Previn, Andre Previn

You're Gonna Lose Your Gal 1933 w.m. Joe Young, James V. Monaco. (MF) *Starlift*. Doris Day, Gordon MacRae, and Virginia Mayo appeared in *Starlift*.

You're Having My Baby, see **Having My Baby**

You're Here and I'm Here 1913 w. Harry B. Smith m. Jerome Kern. (MT) *The Marriage Market*. (MT) *The Laughing Husband*. (MT) *The Passing Show*. Basil Hallam and Elsie Janis appeared in *The Passing Show*.

You're in Love 1916 w. Otto Harbach, Edward Clark m. Rudolf Friml. (MT) *You're in Love*.

You're in Love with Everyone 1924 m. Ray Henderson

You're in the Army Now 1929 w. Tell Taylor, Ole Olsen m. Isham Jones. This song possibly was based on ''I'm in the Army,'' w.m. Victor Ormond, and ''We're in the Army Now,'' both 1917.

You're in the Right Church, But the Wrong Pew 1908 w. Cecil Mack m. Chris Smith

You're (You'se) Just a Little Nigger, Still You're Mine, All Mine 1898 w.m. Paul Dresser

You're Just in Love 1950 w.m. Irving Berlin. (MT) *Call Me Madam*. (MF) *Call Me Madam*. Ethel Merman appeared in both the stage and film productions of *Call Me Madam*.

You're Just Too Too 1957 w.m. Cole Porter

You're Lonely and I'm Lonely 1941 w.m. Irving Berlin. (MF) *Louisiana Purchase*. Bob Hope, Victor Moore, and Irene Bordoni appeared in *Louisiana Purchase*.

You're Mine You 1933 w.m. Edward Heyman, Johnny Green

You're More Than the World to Me 1914 w. Jeff Branen m. Alfred Solman

You're My Baby 1912 w. A. Seymour Brown m. Nat D. Ayer. (MT) *Hullo Ragtime*. Lew Hearn and Gerald Kirby appeared in *Hullo Ragtime*.

You're My Best Friend 1976 w.m. John Deacon

You're My Everything 1931 w. Mort Dixon, Joe Young m. Harry Warren. (MT) *The Laugh Parade*. (MF) *You're My Everything*. (MF) *Painting the Clouds with Sunshine*. (MF) *The Eddy Duchin Story*. Ed Wynn and Eunice Healy appeared in *The Laugh Parade*. Dan Dailey and Anne Baxter appeared in *You're My Everything*. Virginia Mayo and Dennis Morgan appeared in *Painting the Clouds with Sunshine*. Carmen Cavallaro appeared in *The Eddy Duchin Story*.

You're My Girl 1947 w. Sammy Cahn m. Jule Styne. (MT) *High Button Shoes*. Phil Silvers and Nanette Fabray appeared in *High Button Shoes*.

You're My Past, Present, and Future 1933 w. Mack Gordon m. Harry Revel. (MF) *Broadway Through a Keyhole*. Texas Guinan and Constance Cummings appeared in *Broadway Through a Keyhole*.

You're My Soul and Inspiration, see **Soul and Inspiration**

You're My Thrill 1934 w.m. Sidney Clare, Jay Gorney. (MF) *Jimmy and Sallie*. James Dunn and Claire Trevor appeared in *Jimmy and Sallie*.

You're My World 1964 w.m. Umberto Bindi, Carl Sigman, Gino Paoli

You're No Good 1975 w.m. Clint Ballard, Jr.

You're Nobody 'Til Somebody Loves You 1944 w.m. Russ Morgan, Larry Stock, James Cavanaugh. This song was also popular in 1946.

You're Not the Only Pebble on the Beach 1896 w. Harry Braisted m. Stanley Carter. (F) *Trail Street*. Randolph Scott and Anne Jeffreys appeared in *Trail Street*.

You're Only Human (Second Wind) 1985 w.m. Billy Joel

You're Sensational 1956 w.m. Cole Porter. (MF) *High Society*. Bing Crosby, Frank Sinatra, and Grace Kelly appeared in *High Society*, the musical version of *The Philadelphia Story*.

You're Sixteen 1960 w.m. Richard Sherman, Robert Sherman. This song was popularly revived in 1974.

You're So Vain 1973 w.m. Carly Simon

You're Some Pretty Doll, see **Ugly Chile**

You're Such a Comfort to Me 1933 w. Mack Gordon m. Harry Revel. (MF) *Sitting Pretty*. Jack Oakie, Jack Haley, and Ginger Rogers appeared in *Sitting Pretty*.

You're the Best Break This Old Heart Ever Had 1982 w.m. Robert Hatch, Wayland Holyfield

You're the Cream in My Coffee 1928 w. B.G. DeSylva, Lew Brown m. Ray Henderson. (MT) *Hold Everything!* (MF) *The Cockeyed World*. Bert Lahr and Ona Munson appeared in *Hold Everything!*. Joe E. Brown and Stuart Erwin appeared in *The Cockeyed World*.

You're the First, the Last, My Everything 1974 w.m. Barry White

You're the Flower of My Heart, Sweet Adeline, see **Sweet Adeline**

You're the Inspiration 1985 w.m. Peter Cetera, David Foster

You're the One (You Beautiful Son-of-a-Gun) 1932 w.m. Buddy Fields, Gerald Marks

You're the One I Care For 1930 w. Harry Link m. Bert Lown, Chauncey Gray

You're the One That I Want 1978 w.m. John Farrar. (MF) *Grease*. John Travolta and Olivia Newton-John appeared in *Grease*.

You're the Only One 1979 w.m. Bruce Roberts, Carole Bayer Sager

You're the Only Star in My Blue Heaven 1938 w.m. Gene Autry. (F) *The Old Barn Dance*. (MF) *Mexicali Rose*. (F)

Rim of the Canyon. Gene Autry appeared in *The Old Barn Dance, Mexicali Rose,* and *Rim of the Canyon.*

You're the Only Woman 1980 w.m. David Pack

You're the Reason God Made Oklahoma 1981 w.m. Larry Collins, Sandy Pinkard

You're the Reason I'm Living 1963 w.m. Bobby Darin

You're the Top 1934 w.m. Cole Porter. (MT) *Anything Goes.* (MF) *Anything Goes* (1936). (MF) *Anything Goes* (1956). (MF) *Night and Day.* (F) *Evil Under the Sun.* Ethel Merman, Victor Moore, and William Gaxton appeared in the American stage production of *Anything Goes.* Jack Whiting and Jeanne Aubert appeared in the British stage production of *Anything Goes.* Bing Crosby and Ethel Merman appeared in the 1936 film production of *Anything Goes.* Bing Crosby and Mitzi Gaynor appeared in the 1956 film production of *Anything Goes.* Cary Grant, Alexis Smith, and Mary Martin appeared in *Night and Day,* biopic of song writer Cole Porter. Maggie Smith and Peter Ustinov appeared in *Evil Under the Sun.*

Yours, or, Quiéreme Mucho 1931 Sp.w. Augustin Rodriquez Eng.w. Jack Sherr m. Gonzalo Roig. (MF) *Orchestra Wives.* (F) *Sioux City Sue.* Gene Autry and Lynne Roberts appeared in *Sioux City Sue.* This song was popularly revived in 1941. Theme song of Vera Lynn.

Yours and Mine 1937 w.m. Arthur Freed, Nacio Herb Brown. (MF) *Broadway Melody of 1937.* Eleanor Powell, Sophie Tucker, and Judy Garland appeared in *Broadway Melody of 1937.*

Yours for a Song 1939 w. Billy Rose, Ted Fetter m. Dana Suesse. (MT) *Billy Rose's Aquacade* (at the New York World's Fair, 1939).

Yours Is My Heart Alone 1931 Ger.w. Ludwig Herzer, Fritz Lohner Eng.w. Harry B. Smith m. Franz Lehár. (MT) *Yours Is My Heart.* Richard Tauber, Alexander D'Arcy, and Fred Keating appeared in *Yours Is My Heart.* From the German ''Dein Ist Mein Ganzes Herz,'' from the operetta *Die Gelbe Jacke.*

Yours Sincerely 1929 w. Lorenz Hart m. Richard Rodgers. (MT) *Spring Is Here.* Alexander Gray and Bernice Claire appeared in *Spring Is Here.*

You've Changed 1942 w. Bill Carey m. Carl Fischer. (MF) *Lady Sings the Blues.* Diana Ross appeared in *Lady Sings the Blues.* This song was most popular in 1948.

You've Done Something to My Heart 1940 w.m. Noel Gay, Ian Grant, Frank Eyton. (MT) *Lights Up.* Evelyn Laye appeared in *Lights Up.*

You've Got a Friend 1971 w.m. Carole King. Grammy Award winner 1971.

You've Got Everything 1933 w.m. Gus Kahn, Walter Donaldson. (F) *The Prize Fighter and the Lady.* Jack Dempsey and Myrna Loy appeared in *The Prize Fighter and the Lady.*

You've Got Me Crying Again 1933 w. Charles Newman m. Isham Jones

You've Got Me Dangling on a String 1971 w.m. Ronald Dunbar, Wayne

You've Got Me Where You Want Me 1943 w.m. Johnny Mercer, Harry Warren

You've Got Possibilities 1966 w. Lee Adams m. Charles Strouse. (MT) *(It's a Bird, It's a Plane) It's Superman.* Jack Cassidy appeared in *(It's a Bird, It's a Plane) It's Superman.*

You've Got That Thing 1929 w.m. Cole Porter. (MT) *Fifty Million Frenchmen.* (MF) *Fifty Million Frenchmen.* William Gaxton, Jack Thompson, and Helen Broderick appeared in the film production of *Fifty Million Frenchmen.*

You've Got To Be (Carefully) **Taught** 1949 w. Oscar Hammerstein II m. Richard Rodgers. (MT) *South Pacific.* (MF) *South Pacific.* Mary Martin and Bill Tabbert appeared in the stage production of *South Pacific.* Mitzi Gaynor and Ray Walston appeared in the film production of *South Pacific.*

You've Got To Hide Your Love Away 1965 w.m. John Lennon, Paul McCartney. (MF) *Help!* The Beatles appeared in *Help!*

You've Got To Pick a Pocket or Two 1963 w.m. Lionel Bart. (MT) *Oliver!.* (MF) *Oliver!.* Ron Moody appeared in both the stage and film productions of *Oliver!.*

You've Got Your Mother's Big Blue Eyes 1913 w.m. Irving Berlin

You've Got Your Troubles 1965 w.m. Roger Cook, Roger Greenaway

You've Gotta (Got to) See Mamma Ev'ry Night, Or You Can't See Mamma At All 1923 w.m. Billy Rose, Con Conrad. (MT) *Dover Street to Dixie.*

You've Lost That Lovin' Feelin' 1965 w.m. Barry Mann, Cynthia Weil, Phil Spector. This song was popularly revived in 1980.

You've Made Me So Very Happy 1969 w.m. Berry Gordy, Jr., Frank E. Wilson, Brenda Holloway, Patrice Holloway

Yuletide, Park Avenue 1946 w.m. Harold Rome. (MT) *Call Me Mister.* (MF) *Call Me Mister.* Betty Garrett and Bill Callahan appeared in the stage production of *Call Me Mister.* Betty Grable and Danny Thomas appeared in the film production of *Call Me Mister.*

Yummy Yummy Yummy 1968 w.m. Arthur Resnick, Joe Levine

Z Cars Theme 1962 w.m. traditional; arr. Bridget Fry. (TV-BBC) *Z Cars.* Based on the Northumbrian tune ''Johnny Todd.''

Zampa (Overture) 1831 m. Louis Joseph Ferdinand Herold. *Zampa* was first performed in Paris on May 3, 1831.

Zenda Waltzes 1895 m. Frank M. Witmark

Zigeuner 1929 w.m. Noël Coward. (MT) *Bitter Sweet.* (MF) *Bitter Sweet.* Peggy Wood and Evelyn Laye appeared in the stage production of *Bitter Sweet.* Jeanette MacDonald and Nelson Eddy appeared in the film production of *Bitter Sweet.*

Zing a Little Zong 1952 w. Leo Robin m. Harry Warren. (MF) *Just for You.* Bing Crosby, Ethel Barrymore and Natalie Wood appeared in *Just for You.*

Zing Went the Strings of My Heart 1935 w.m. James F. Hanley. (MT) *Thumbs Up!* (MF) *Listen Darling.* (MF) *Lullaby of Broadway.* (MF) *Thumbs Up.* Eddie Dowling and Ray Dooley appeared in the stage production of *Thumbs Up!* Judy Garland and Mary Astor appeared in *Listen Darling.*

Doris Day and Billy DeWolf appeared in *Lullaby of Broadway*. Elsa Lancaster and Brenda Joyce appeared in the film production of *Thumbs Up*.

Zip 1940 w. Lorenz Hart m. Richard Rodgers. (MT) *Pal Joey*. (MF) *Pal Joey*. Gene Kelly, Van Johnson, and June Havoc appeared in the stage production of *Pal Joey*. Frank Sinatra, Rita Hayworth, and Kim Novak appeared in the film production of *Pal Joey*.

Zip-A-Dee-Doo-Dah 1947 w. Ray Gilbert m. Allie Wrubel. (MF) *Song of the South*. Academy Award winner 1947.

Zip Coon, *see* **Turkey in the Straw**

Zizzy, Ze Zum, Zum 1898 w. Karl Kennett m. Lyn Udall

Zoot Suit, A 1942 w.m. Ray Gilbert, Bob O'Brien

(Theme from) Zorba the Greek 1965 m. Mikos Theodorakis. (F) *Zorba the Greek*. Anthony Quinn and Alan Bates appeared in *Zorba the Greek*.

Zuyder Zee 1944 w. Sammy Cahn m. Jule Styne. (MF) *Knickerbocker Holiday*. Nelson Eddy and Constance Dowling appeared in *Knickerbocker Holiday*.

VI
British Song Titles

This part contains titles of songs originating from or primarily popular only in the British Isles, listed chronologically, including winners of the Ivor Novello Award (see Part II). Songs originating from or popular in the British Isles that also achieved popularity in the United States are listed chronologically in Part I and alphabetically in Part V and not entered here. Selected titles prior to 1900 and all titles after 1900 are also listed in Part V.

This Part contains the following sections:

Prior to 1900
Traditional.
    Folk Song and Folk Dances
    Old Welsh or Welsh Folk
Traditional Irish (Old Irish, Irish Folk, and Folk Dances)
Traditional Scottish (Scottish Folk, Folk Dances, and Highland Tunes) Hebridean
Sea Chanteys and Broadside Ballads
School Songs
1870–1890
Victorian
Music Hall
1900 to and including 1986

PRIOR TO 1900

TRADITIONAL

Agincourt (song on the British victory of c. 1415)
All on the Road to Brighton
L'Amour Demoi (15th century)
And When I Die (old army marching song)
The Animals Went in Two by Two
The Bailiff's Daughter of Islington
Begone! Dull Care (17th century)
Bonnie Charlie's Now Awa' (c. 1820) w.m. Nell Gow
Bonnie Dundee

The British Grenadiers (c. 1785)
Buttercups and Daisies
The Cheerful 'Arn (The Fox Jumped)
The Chesapeake and the Shannon
The Cooper o' Fife
The Cottage Well Thatch'd with Straw
Down Among the Dead Men (c.1660)
An Eriskay Lullaby
A Fairy's Love Song (old Celtic air)
Farmer Giles (see Villikins and His Dinah, Part V)
Fisher's Hornpipe
Gaily the Troubador
The Gipsy's Warning
The Golden Vanity
Green Grow the Rushes, O!
Gypsy Lament
Here's a Health Unto His Majesty
The Hunt Is Up
Hunt Theme (Tantivy!)
I Know Where I'm Going
I'll Bid My Heart Be Still (Old Border)
I'll Give You a Paper of Pins (1869)
I'm Ninety-Five (March of the Rifle Brigade)
The Island
It Was a Lover and His Lass
I've Gone Out for the Day
The Laughing Policeman
The Leafy Cool-Kellure (The White-Breasted Boy)
The Leather Bottel
The Licolnshire Poacher
A Man's a Man for a' That
The Massacre of MacPherson
The Mermaid (Oh! 'Twas in the Broad)
Now Is the Month of Maying (1598) w.m. Thomas Morley
O, Can Ye Sew Cushions (Heigh O'Heugh O')
O, Good Ale (For 'Tis, O, Good Ale)
Oh Ilkley Moor Baht'at (Yorkshire)
One Man Went To Mow
Pretty Polly Oliver (17th century)
The Queen's Mary's
The Road to the Isles

BRITISH SONG TITLES

The Roast Beef of Old England (1670–1750) w.m. A. Leveridge

Roses for Remembrance

Sing a Song of Sunbeams

Song of the Western Men (Old Cornish)

Sound the Pibroch

Under the Greenwood Tree

The Vicar of Bray

Who Killed Cock Robin?

Widdicombe Fair (West County)

Willie's Gone to Melville Castle

Won't You Buy My Pretty Flowers?

The Yellow Ribbon

You Gentlemen of England (pre-17th century)

Folk Song and Folk Dances

Amid the New-Mown Hay

Amo, Amas, I Love a Lass

The Arethusa (pre-1730 country dance)

As I Walked Out

Aye Waukin' O!

The Barley Mow

Bobby Shaftoe (North Country)

Cockles and Mussels

Come Lasses and Lads (17th century)

De'il Among the Tailors (eightsome reel)

Dick's Maggot

Early One Morning

A Fairy's Love Song (Old Celtic)

Fishers Hornpipe

Flowers in the Valley

Flowers of Edinburgh (country dance)

The Foggy, Foggy Dew

The Fox Jumped Over the Parson's Gate

High Germany (West Country)

I Will Give My Love an Apple

John Peel (c. 1820)

The Keel Row

Let Him Go, Let Him Tarry

The Miller of the Dee (pre-1762)

O, No, John

O, the Oak and the Ash (Northumbrian)

Oh! Breathe Not His Name

Sir Roger de Coverly (country dance)

Strawberry Fair (15th century)

Twankydillo (Sussex)

The Twelve Days of Christmas

Old Welsh or Welsh Folk

Adieu to Dear Cambria (Llandyfri)

The Ash Grove

The Black Monk (Y Mynach Du)

Brown Haired Maiden

David of the White Rock (Dafydd y Gareg Wen)

The Dove (Y Denyn Pur)

The Exile of Cambria (Yr Alltud o Gymru)

Gwendoleen's Repose (Hun Gwenllian)

The Mistletoe (Cnot y Coed)

The Rising of the Lark (Codiad Yr Hedydd)

TRADITIONAL IRISH (Old Irish, Irish Folk and Folk Dances)

Come Haste to the Wedding

Eileen Oge

Garry Owen

The Gentle Maiden

The Harp That Once Thro' Tara's Halls

Jack O'Hazeldean (poem by Sir Walter Scott)

The Lark in the Clear Air

The Minstrel Boy

My Love's an Arbutus

Robin Adair (Eileen Aroon) (c.1750)

Rory O'Moore

The Snowy-Breasted Pearl

Speed the Plough

Tee Birks o' Aberfeldy   w. Burns

TRADITIONAL SCOTTISH (Scottish Folk, Folk Dances, and Highland Tunes)

Aignish on the Machair

As I Gaed Down Glenmoriston

The Auld Hoose

Blue Bonnets Over the Border

Bonnie Dundee

The Bonnie Earl o' Morray

Bonnie George Campbell

Bonnie Mary of Argyll

Bonnie Strathyre

The Campbells Are Coming (1745)

Charlie Is My Darling

The Circassian Circle

The Cooper o' Fife

The Dashing White Sergeant

The De'il Among the Tailors (reel)

BRITISH SONG TITLES, 1870–1900

Ae Fond Kiss w. Burns
Glasgow Highlanders
Ho-Ro My Nut-Brown Maiden
How Can Ye Gang Lassie?
Lament for Maclean of Ardgour
The Land o' the Leal (c. 1798)
Leezie Lindsay
Maiden of Morven
Miss MacLeod's Reel
Monymusk (foursome reel)
My Faithful Fond One
My Love's in Germanie
O Can Ye Sew Cushions
O Gin I Were Where Gowdie Rins
The Piper of Dundee
The Praise of Islay
Scots, Whae Hae wi' Wallace Bled
Scottish Hornpipe
She Moved Thro' the Fair (Donegal)
Sir Patrick Spens
Skye Boat Song
Sound the Pibroch
Tee Birks o' Aberfeldy w. Burns
Wi' a Hundred Pipes an a'
Ye Banks and Braes

Hebridean

Deirdre's Farewell to Scotland
Eriskay Love Lilt
Kishmul's Galley
Land of Heart's Desire
The Mull Fisher's Love Song
The Road to the Isles
The Sea Tangle
Sleeps the Noon

SEA CHANTEYS AND BROADSIDE BALLADS

Blow the Man Down (c. 1879)
Drake's Drum w.m. C. V. Stanford
Johnny Come Down to Hilo

SCHOOL SONGS

Carmen Etonense (Eton school song) w.m. J. Barnby
Eton Boating Song w.m. A.D.E.W.
Forty Years On (Harrow school song) w.m. J. Farmer

1870–1890

Drink, Puppy, Drink (1874) w.m. C.J. Whyte Melville
Oh, the Fairies, Whoa, the Fairies (1878) w.m. W. G. Eaton

VICTORIAN

At Trinity Church I Met My Doom (1894) w.m. Fred Gilbert
Father, Dear Father w.m. H.C. Work
Flanagan (1892) w.m. C. Murphy, W. Letters
She Was Poor But She Was Honest
The Tarpaulin Jacket w.m. Charles Coote

MUSIC HALL

Ask a Policeman (1889) w.m. E. W. Rogers
Captain Ginjan w.m. Fred W. Leigh; Edwardian
Come Along Home, Papa w.m. James W. Tate
Dear Old Pals w.m. G. W. Hunt
Down Went the Captain w.m. Kate Royle
'E Dunno Where 'E Are
The German Band w.m. Arthur Lloyd
He's Going To Marry Mary Ann w.m. Jos Tabrar
The Honeysuckle and the Bee w.m. W. H. Penn
Hullo, Tu-Tu! w.m. C. Scott Gatty
I Live in Trafalgar Square (c. 1898) w.m. C. W. Murphy
I Shall Get in Such a Row When Martha Knows
I Want To Be a Lidy w.m. A. W. Malbert
I'll Be Your Sweetheart w.m. Harry Dacre
Lily of Laguna (1898) w.m. Leslie Stuart
Little Annie Roonie (Rooney) (1890) w.m. Michael Nolan
A Little Bit off the Top w.m. Murray, Leigh
My Son, My Son, My Only One w.m. George le Brunn
Now I Have To Call Him Father w.m. Fred Godfrey
Rosie's Young Man
She Was One of the Early Birds w.m. T. W. Connor
Swing Me Higher, Obadiah w.m. Maurice Scott
Two Lovely Black Eyes (1886) w.m. Charles Coborn
The Weeping Willer (1865) w.m. Harry Clifton

1900

Comrades w.m. Felix McGlennon, Tom Costello
For Old Times' Sake w.m. Charles Osborne
I Want To Be a Military Man w.m. Leslie Stuart, Owen Hall

If It Wasn't for the 'ouses in Between w.m. Edgar Bateman, George Le Brunn

I'll Be Your Sweetheart w.m. Harry Dacre

It's a Great Big Shame w.m. Edgar Bateman, George Le Brunn

Little Dolly Daydream w.m. Leslie Stuart

The Miner's Dream of Home w.m. Will Godwin, Leo Dryden

The Shade of the Palm w.m. Leslie Stuart, Owen Hall

The Soldiers in the Park w.m. Lionel Monckton, Ivan Caryll

Soldiers of the Queen w.m. Leslie Stuart

The Valeta (round dance)

What Ho She Bumps w.m. A. J. Mills, Harry Castling

1901

Ask a Policeman w.m. A. E. Durandeau, E. W. Rogers

Beer, Beer, Glorious Beer w.m. Harry Anderson, Steve Leggett, Will Godwin

The Broken Melody w.m. August Van Biene

Knocked 'Em in the Old Kent Road w.m. Albert Chevalier, Charles Ingle

Little Bit off the Top w.m. Fred Murray, Fred W. Leigh

My Old Dutch w.m. Albert Chevalier, Charles Ingle

Our Lodger's Such a Nice Young Man w.m. F. Murray, L. Barclay

Why Did I Leave My Little Back Room w.m. A. J. Mills, Frank W. Carter

1902

English Rose w.m. Edward German

I May Be Crazy w.m. Leslie Stuart

Liza Johnson w.m. Edgar Bateman, George Le Brunn

Melisands in the Wood w.m. Alma Goetz, Ethel Clifford

Sons of the Sea w.m. Felix McGlennon

Try Again Johnnie w.m. Lionel Monckton, Adrian Ross

Under the Deodar w.m. Lionel Monckton, Adrian Ross

Waltz Song w.m. Edward German

Yeoman of England w.m. Edward German

1903

Just Like the Ivy w.m. A. J. Mills, Harry Castling

Little Yellow Bird w.m. C. W. Murphy, William Hargreaves

Mother o' Mine w.m. Frank Tours, Rudyard Kipling

Two Little Boys w.m. T. F. Morse

1904

My Dear Little Cingalee w.m. Lionel Monckton, Adrian Ross, Percy Greenbank

The Pearl of Sweet Ceylon w.m. Lionel Monckton, Adrian Ross, Percy Greenbank

Wine of France w.m. Ivan Caryll

1905

Cigarette w.m. Herbert Haines, Evelyn Baker, Charles Taylor

Following in Father's Footsteps w.m. E. W. Rogers, Vesta Tilley

I Wouldn't Leave My Little Wooden Hut for You w.m. Tom Mellor, Charles Collins

My Ain Folk w.m. Wilfred Mills, Laura G. Lemon

The Pipes of Pan Are Calling w.m. Lionel Monckton

The Weymouth Chimes w.m. J. S. Howgill

1906

Billy Muggins w.m. Charles Ridgewell

Down in the Forest w.m. Landon Ronald

I Like Your Old French Bonnet w.m. Mellor, Lawrance, Gifford

I Want To Marry a Man w.m. Howard Talbot

In the Twi-Twi-Twi-Light w.m. Herman Darewski, Charles Wilmot

Poor John w.m. Fred Leigh, Henry Pether

She Is Ma Daisy w.m. Harry Lauder, J. D. Harper

Waiting at the Church w.m. Fred Leigh, Henry Pether

1907

By the Side of the Zuyder Zee w.m. Bennett Scott, A. J. Mills

The Flying Dutchman w.m. Paul Rubens

The Galloping Major w.m. George Bastow, F. W. Leigh

The Grasshopper's Dance w.m. Bucalossi

I Know a Lovely Garden w.m. Guy d'Hardelot, E. Teschemacher

If Those Lips Could Only Speak w.m. Charles Rigewell, Will Godwin

Little Pink Petty from Peter w.m. Paul Rubens

Rose in the Bud w.m. Dorothy Foster, P. J. Barrow

1908

Ain't It Ni-Ice   w.m. R. P. Weston, B. Lee

Call Round Any Old Time   w.m. Charles Moore, E. W. Rogers

Di! Di! Di! (music hall)   w.m. F. C. Carr

I Hear You Calling Me   w.m. Harold Herford, Charles Marshall

Meet Me Jenny When the Sun Goes Down   w.m. Harry Castling, Fred Godfrey

My Girl's a Yorkshire Girl   w.m. C. W. Murphy, Dan Lipton

My Little Deitcher Girl   w.m. Bert Lee

Oh Oh Antonio   w.m. C. W. Murphy, Dan Lipton

Put Me Amongst the Girls   w.m. C. W. Murphy, Dan Lipton

She's a Lassie from Lancashire   w.m. C. W. Murphy, Dan Lipton, John Neat

Sussex by the Sea   w.m. Ward-Higgs

Wedding o'Sandy McNab   w.m. Harry Lauder

1909

Arcady Is Ever Young   w.m. Lionel Monckton, Arthur Wimperis, Howard Talbot

I Do Like To Be Beside the Seaside   w.m. John A. Glover Kind

I Used To Sigh for the Silvery Moon   w.m. Herman Darewski, Lester Barrett

If I Should Plant a Tiny Seed of Love   w.m. James W. Tate, Ballard MacDonald

Moonstruck   w.m. Ivan Caryll, Lionel Monckton

The Pipes of Pan   w.m. Lionel Monckton, Arthur Wimperis, Howard Talbot

Ship Ahoy   w.m. A. J. Mills, Bennett Scott

Sink Red Sun   w.m. Teresa del Riego

Temptation Rag   w.m. Henry Lodge

Valse Septembre   w.m. Felix Godwin

When Father Papered the Parlour   w.m. R. P. Weston, F. J. Barnes

Where My Caravan Has Rested   w.m. Edward Teschemacher, Herman Lohr

1910

Boiled Beef and Carrots   w.m. Charles Collins, Fred Murray

Come to the Ball   w.m. Lionel Monckton, Adrian Ross, Percy Greenbank

Don't Go Down the Mine   w.m. William Geddes, Robert Donnelly

Flanagan   w.m. C. W. Murphy, William Letters

I Was Standing at the Corner of the Street   w.m. Formby, Hunt

Let's All Go Down the Strand   w.m. Harry Castling, C. W. Murphy

Molly O'Morgan   w.m. William Letters, Fred Godfrey

Mountains of Mourne   w.m. Traditional

Oh! I Must Go Home Tonight   w.m. William Hargreaves

Tony from America   w.m. Lionel Monckton, Arthur Wimperis

1911

Any Old Iron   w.m. Charles Collins, Fred Terry, E. A. Sheppard

Do You Remember the Last Waltz   w.m. Bennett Scott, A. J. Mills

Evensong   w.m. Easthope Martin

Fall In and Follow Me   w.m. A. J. Mills, Bennett Scott

The Floral Dance   w.m. Katie Moss

I'm Henery the Eighth (I Am)   w.m. R. P. Weston, Fred Murray

I'm Shy, Mary Ellen, I'm Shy   w.m. Charles Ridgewell, George Stevens

In Summertime on Brendon   w.m. Graham Peel, A. E. Housman

Lighterman Tom   w.m. Francis J. Barron, W. H. Squire

Macushla   w.m. Josephine V. Rowe, Dermot MacMurrough

The Photo of the Girl I Left Behind   w.m. Billy Merson

The Policeman's Holiday   w.m. Montague Ewing, Earl Berwick

Put On Your Ta Ta Little Girlie   w.m. Fred W. Leigh

Rose of My Heart   w.m. Herman Lohr

The Temple Bell   w.m. Lionel Monckton, Arthur Wimperis

Until   w.m. Edward Teschemacher, Wilfred Sanderson

Wedding of the Rose   w.m. Leon Jessel

1912

Are We To Part Like This, Bill   w.m. Harry Castling, Charles Collins

At Santa Barbara   w.m. Frederick E. Weatherley, Kennedy Russell

Bird of Love Divine   w.m. Haydn Wood

Down Vauxhall Way   w.m. Edward Teschemacher, Oliver

Ginger You're Barmy   w.m. Fred Murray

Here's to Love   w.m. Paul Rubens, Arthur Wimperis

I Love the Moon   w.m. Paul Rubens

I'm Twenty-one Today   w.m. Alec Kendal

Josh-Ua   w.m. George Arthurs, Bert Lee

The Little Damozel   w.m. Ivor Novello

Nights of Gladness   w.m. Charles Ancliffe

One of the Ruins That Cromwell Knocked About a Bit   w.m. Harry Bedford, Terry Sullivan

Phil the Fluter's Ball   w.m. Percy French

Polly Perkins of Paddington Green   w.m. Harry Clifton

When You Are in Love   w.m. Lionel Monckton, Percy Greenbank

When You Come Home   w.m. W. H. Squire

Who Were You with Last Night   w.m. Fred Godfrey, Mark Sheridan

1913

Bal Masque   w.m. Percy E. Fletcher

Captain Gingah   w.m. George Bastow, F. W. Leigh

Fat Li'l' Feller Wid His Mammy's Eyes   w.m. Sheridan Gordon, F. L. Stanton

Friend o' Mine   w.m. F. E. Weatherly, Wilfred Sanderson

I Love the Name of Mary   w.m. Richard Oldham, Helen Taylor

It's Nice To Get Up in the Morning   w.m. Harry Lauder

Mifanwy   w.m. Dorothy Foster, F. E. Weatherly

Shipmates of Mine   w.m. Wilfrid Sanderson

1914

All Pals Together   w.m. Reginald Sloan

Are We Downhearted?—No!   w.m. Lawrence Wright, Worton David

Gilbert the Filbert   w.m. Arthur Wimperis, Herman Finck

Hello, Hello, Who's Your Lady Friend   w.m. Worton David, Bert Lee, Harry Fragson

Here We Are, Here We Are, Here We Are Again   w.m. Charles Knight, Kenneth Lyle

Hold Your Hand Out Naughty Boy   w.m. C. W. Murphy, Worton David

I Was a Good Little Girl Till I Met You   w.m. Clifford Harris, James W. Tate

I'll Make a Man of You   w.m. Herman Finck, Arthur Wimperis

Mate o' Mine   w.m. Leslie Cooke, Percy Elliott

O Flower Divine   w.m. Edward Teschemacher, Haydn Wood

Sing Joyous Bird   w.m. Montague Phillips

When We've Wound Up the Watch on the Rhine   w.m. Herman Darewski, E. V. Lucas

Wonderful Eyes   w.m. Paul Rubens, Percy Greenbank

Your King and Country Want You   w.m. Paul Rubens

1915

The Army of Today's Alright   w.m. Fred W. Leigh, Kenneth Lyle

Burlington Bertie from Bow   w.m. William Hargreaves

Can It Be Love   w.m. Paul Rubens, Adrian Ross

Dance with Your Uncle Joseph   w.m. Liston, William Hargreaves

Hors D'Oeuvres   w.m. David Comer

I Wonder If Love Is a Dream   w.m. Dorothy Foster, Edward Teschemacher

Jolly Good Luck to the Girl Who Loves a Soldier   w.m. Fred W. Leigh, Kenneth Lyle

Kitty the Telephone Girl   w.m. A. J. Lawrence, Huntley Trevor, Tom Mellor, Harry Gifford

A Little of What You Fancy   w.m. Fred W. Leigh, George Arthurs

Love's Garden of Roses   w.m. Haydn Wood, Ruth Rutherford

Sister Susie's Sewing Shirts for Soldiers   w.m. R. P. Weston, Herman Darewski

Thank God for a Garden   w.m. Teresa del Riego

Toy Town   w.m. Lionel Monckton, Herman Finck

The Violin Song   w.m. Paul Rubens, Percy Greenbank

1916

Another Little Drink   w.m. Nat D. Ayer

Any Time's Kissing Time   w.m. Frederick Norton, Oscar Asche

Blue Eyes   w.m. Horatio Nicholls, Fred Godfrey

Bohemia   w.m. Paul Rubens, Adrian Ross

Broken Doll   w.m. James W. Tate

The Cobbler's Song   w.m. Frederick Norton, Oscar Asche

Ev'ry Little While   w.m. James W. Tate

Everybody's Crazy on the Foxtrot   w.m. Bennett Scott, A. J. Mills

I Can't Do My Belly Bottom Button Up   w.m. J. P. Long

It Is Only a Tiny Garden   w.m. Haydn Wood, Lillian Glanville

The Robbers' Chorus   w.m. Frederick Norton, Oscar Asche

Underneath the Stars   w.m. Herbert Spencer, F. Brown

Wait   w.m. Guy d'Hardelot

Watching the Trains Come In   w.m. Frank Leo

1917

Arizona   w.m. Melville Gideon, James Heard

A Bachelor Gay   w.m. James W. Tate, Clifford Harris, Arthur Valentine

Come to the Fair   w.m. Helen Taylor, Easthope Martin

Delilah   w.m. Horatio Nicholls

I Passed By Your Window   w.m. May Brahe

Jogging Along the Highway   w.m. Harold Samuel

Let the Great Big World Keep Turning   w.m. Nat D. Ayer, Clifford Grey

Little Miss Melody   w.m. Lionel Monckton, Adrian Ross, Percy Greenbank

Love Will Find a Way (*The Maid of the Mountains*)   w.m. Harold Fraser-Simson

Paddy McGinty's Goat   w.m. R. P. Weston, Bert Lee

Paradise for Two (*The Maid of the Mountains*)   w.m. James W. Tate, Clifford Harris, Arthur Valentine

She Was One of the Early Birds   w.m. T. W. Conner

Take Me Back to Dear Old Blighty   w.m. A. J. Mills, Fred Godfrey, Bennett Scott

There Are Fairies at the Bottom of Our Garden   w.m. Liza Lehmann

Whisper to Me   w.m. Lionel Monckton, Herman Finck, Adrian Ross

Why Am I Always the Bridesmaid   w.m. Fred W. Leigh, Charles Collins, Lily Morris

1918

The Company Sergeant Major   w.m. Wilfrid Sanderson

The Dancing Lesson   w.m. Herbert Oliver

First Love, Last Love, Best Love   w.m. Nat D. Ayer, Clifford Grey

Give Me a Little Cosy Corner   w.m. James W. Tate, Clifford Harris

Good Bye-ee   w.m. R. P. Weston, Bert Lee

Heart of a Rose   w.m. Horatio Nicholls, Worton David

If You Could Care for Me   w.m. Herman Darewski, Arthur Wimperis

Somewhere in France with You   w.m. James W. Tate, A. Anderson, Arthur Valentine

1919

Don't Dilly Dally on the Way   w.m. Fred W. Leigh, Charles Collins

Maxina   w.m. M. Boissonade, W. F. Hurndall

Omaha   w.m. Horatio Nicholls, Worton David

Praeludium   w.m. Järnfelt

That Old Fashioned Mother of Mine   w.m. Horatio Nicholls, Worton David

Where Do Flies Go in the Winter Time?   w.m. Frank Leo

1920

Abie My Boy   w.m. L. Silberman, A. Grock, Herbert Rule, Tom McGhee

City of Laughter, City of Tears   w.m. Horatio Nicholls

I Know Where the Flies Go in the Wintertime   w.m. Sam Mayo, J. P. Harrington

If You're Irish Come into the Parlour   w.m. Shaun Glenville, Frank Miller

Mary Rose   w.m. Philip Braham

Wyoming Lullaby   w.m. Gene Williams

1921

Arise, O Sun   w.m. Maude Craske-Day

The Chinaman's Song   w.m. Percy Fletcher, Oscar Asche

Coal Black Mammy   w.m. Ivy St. Helier, Laddie Cliff

The Fishermen of England   w.m. Montague F. Phillips, Gerald Dodson

I Pitch My Lonely Caravan at Night   w.m. Eric Coates, Annette Horey

Night May Have Its Sadness   w.m. Ivor Novello

Ours Is a Nice 'ouse Ours Is   w.m. Herbert Rule, Fred Holt

Playthings   w.m. Horatio Nicholls, Worton David

There You Are Then   w.m. L. Silberman

1922

Dancing Honeymoon   w.m. Philip Braham

I Want Some Money   w.m. Herbert Rule, Fred Holt, L. Silberman, Tom McGhee

If Winter Comes   w.m. Melville Gideon, Clifford Grey

My Word You Do Look Queer   w.m. R. P. Weston, Bert Lee

Oh Star of Eve   w.m. Hubert W. David, Ed Bryant

Sally, You Brought the Sunshine to Our Alley   w.m. Wynn Stanley, Andrew Allen

Señora   w.m. Owen Murphy

Shufflin' Along   w.m. Nat D. Ayer, Ralph Stanley

What D'Yer Think of That   w.m. J. P. Long

1923

Horsey, Keep Your Tail Up

I'm Tickled to Death I'm Single   w.m. Melville Gideon, Clifford Seyler

Just Like a Thief   w.m. Horatio Nicholls

Susannah's Squeaking Shoes

1924

Bells Across the Meadow   w.m. Albert William Ketèlbey

Christopher Robin at Buckingham Palace   w.m. A. A. Milne, Harold Fraser-Simson

Felix Kept On Walking   w.m. Edward E. Bryant, Hubert W. David

Girl in the Crinoline Gown, The   w.m. Melville Gideon Clifford Seyler

Riviera Rose   w.m. Horatio Nicholls

Romany Rose   w.m. Horatio Nicholls

Sahara   w.m. Horatio Nicholls, Jean Frederick

Second Minuet, The   w.m. Maurice Besly

Shall I Have It Bobbed or Shingled   w.m. Weston, Lee

Turned Up   w.m. Rule, Castling

When You and I Were Dancing   w.m. H. M. Tennent, Graham Jones

1925

Barwick Green (The Archers)   w.m. Arthur Wood

Bouquet (I Shall Always Think of You)   w.m. Horatio Nicholls, Ray Morelle

Chick Chick Chicken   w.m. Thomas McGhee, Fred Holt, Irving King

Did Tosti Raise His Bowler Hat When He Said Goodbye   w.m. Billy Mayerl, Gene Paul

Golden West, The   w.m. Horatio Nicholls

I Travel the Road   w.m. Pat Thayer

I'm a Little Bit Fonder of You

Ogo-Pogo, The   w.m. Ralph Butler, Mark Strong, Cumberland Clark

Oh Charley Take It Away   w.m. Hedges, Malcolm, le Clerq

On Mother Kelly's Doorstep   w.m. G. A. Stevens

Runaway Train, The   w.m. Carson Robison

Shanghai   w.m. Horatio Nicholls

Sunny Havana   w.m. Horatio Nicholls

The Toy Drum Major   w.m. Horatio Nicholls

When the Sergeant Major's on Parade   w.m. Ernest Longstaffe

1926

Bird Songs at Eventide   w.m. Eric Coates, Royden Barrie

The Dickey Bird Hop   w.m. Ronald Gourlay, Leslie Sarony

Don't Have Any More Mrs. Moore   w.m. Harry Castling, James Walsh

End of the Road, The   w.m. Harry Lauder, William Dillon

I Never See Maggie Alone   w.m. Harry Tilsley, Everett Lynton

I'm an Airman   w.m. McGhee, Russell

I've Never Seen a Straight Banana   w.m. Ted Waite

More We Are Together, The   w.m. Irving King

Picador   w.m. Horatio Nicholls

Rolling Round the World   w.m. Scott Sanders

Rose in a Garden of Weeds, A   w.m. R. B. Saxe, H. W. David

1927

Hollyhock   w.m. Billy Mayerl

I'm Going Back to Himazas   w.m. Fred Austin

Ma, Look at Charlie   w.m. Elven Hedges

Me and Jane in a Plane   w.m. Edgar Leslie, Joe Gilbert

On a Street of Chinese Lanterns   w.m. James Campbell, Reginald Connelly

Possibly   w.m. Carrol Gibbons, James Dyrenforth

Shepherd of the Hills   w.m. Horatio Nicholls, Edgar Leslie

When You Played the Organ and I Sang "The Rosary"   w.m. Edgar Leslie, Joseph Gilbert

The Whispering Pines of Nevada   w.m. Horatio Nicholls

1928

Da-Da, Da-Da   w.m. W. Dore

Don't Do That to the Poor Puss Cat   w.m. Leslie Sarony, Frank Eyton

Fashionette   w.m. Glogau, King

Forty-seven Ginger Headed Sailors   w.m. Leslie Sarony

Janette   w.m. Horatio Nicholls

Marigold   w.m. Billy Mayerl

Mistakes   w.m. Horatio Nicholls, Edgar Leslie

My Inspiration Is You   w.m. Horatio Nicholls

Persian Rosebud   w.m. Horatio Nicholls

Roll Away Clouds   w.m. Jack Waller, Joe Tunbridge

1929

All by Yourself in the Moonlight   w.m. Jay Wallis

Ever So Goosey   w.m. Ralph Butler, Raymond Wallace, Julian Wright

Fairy on the Clock   w.m. E. Reeves, S. Myers

I Lift Up My Finger and I Say Tweet Tweet   w.m. Leslie Sarony

Love Forever I Adore You   w.m. G. de Micheli

Misery Farm   w.m. C. Jay Wallis

Mucking About the Garden   w.m. Q. Cumber (Leslie Sarony)

Old Violin, An   w.m. Helen Taylor, Howard Fisher

Shinaniki Da   w.m. Harry Carlton

Spread a Little Happiness   w.m. Vivian Ellis, Richard Myers, Greatrex Newman

Why Is the Bacon So Tough   w.m. Reginald Arkell, Charles Prentice

1930

Amy, Wonderful Amy   w.m. Horatio Nicholls, Joe Gilbert

Blue Pacific Moonlight   w.m. Jack Payne, Wallace Herbert

Gipsy Melody   w.m. Horatio Nicholls

Give Yourself a Pat on the Back   w.m. Ralph Butler, Raymond Wallace

Goodbye to All That   w.m. Harry S. Pepper

Jollity Farm   w.m. Leslie Sarony

King's Horses, The   w.m. Noel Gay, Harry Graham

Oh, Donna Clara   w.m. J. Petersburski

Over the Garden Wall   w.m. Leslie Sarony, Cecil Harrington

Ro-Ro-Rollin' Along   w.m. Mencher, Moll, Richman

Stop and Shop at the Co-Op Shop   w.m. R. P. Weston, Bert Lee

Tell Me I'm Forgiven (*Wonder Bar*)   w.m. Robert Katscher

There's a Good Time Coming   w.m. Ralph Butler, Raymond Wallace

You Die If You Worry   w.m. Stanley Damerell, Robert Hargreaves

1931

Adeline   w.m. Joe Gilbert, Horatio Nicholls

Ali Baba's Camel   w.m. Noel Gay

Any Little Kiss   w.m. Noel Coward

Bathing in the Sunshine   w.m. Horatio Nicholls, Joe Gilbert

Don't Tell a Soul   w.m. Harry S. Pepper

I Found You   w.m. Ray Noble, James Campbell, Reginald Connelly

I Give My Heart   w.m. C. Millocker

I'll Be Good Because of You   w.m. Ray Noble, Alan Murray

I'm Happy When I'm Hiking   w.m. Ralph Butler, Raymond Wallace, Reginald Connelly, James Campbell

Jolly Good Company   w.m. Raymond Wallace

Just Once for All Time   w.m. Werner Heyman

Live, Laugh and Love   w.m. Werner Heymann

Lover of My Dreams (*Cavalcade*)   w.m. Noel Coward

The Queen Was in the Parlour   w.m. Sherman Myers

Rhymes   w.m. Leslie Sarony

Sally   w.m. William Haines, Harry Leon, Leo Towers

Sitting on a Five Barred Gate   w.m. Stanley Damerell, Reginald Hargreaves

Sunny Days   w.m. Reginald Connelly, Will Jason, Val Burton

There's Always Tomorrow   w.m. Phil Charig, Vivian Ellis, Douglas Furber

Today I Feel So Happy   w.m. Paul Abraham

When the Guards Are on Parade   w.m. Horatio Nicholls, Leslie Sarony

You're Eyes (*White Horse Inn*)   w.m. Robert Stolz

1932

After Tonight We Say "Goodbye"   w.m. Powers, Leon

Ain't It Grand To Be Bloomin' Well Dead   w.m. Leslie Sarony

Arm in Arm   w.m. Harry Leon, Leo Towers

Autumn Crocus   w.m. Billy Mayerl

Back Again to Happy-Go-Lucky Days   w.m. Raymond Wallace

Bedtime Story, A   w.m. Leo Towers, Harry Leon, Horatio Nicholls

Brighter Than the Sun   w.m. Ray Noble

By the Fireside   w.m. Ray Noble, James Campbell, Reginald Connelly

Changing of the Guard, The   w.m. Flotsam & Jetsam (B. C. Hilliam, Malcolm McEachern)

Chinese Laundry Blues   w.m. Jack Cottrell, George Formby

Dreaming   w.m. Reginald Connelly, Bud Flanagan

The Flies Crawled Up the Window   w.m. Vivian Ellis, Douglas Furber

Goodnight Vienna   w.m. Eric Maschwitz, George Posford

Granny's Old Arm-Chair   w.m. John Read

Here's to the Next Time   w.m. Henry Hall

He's Dead But He Won't Lie Down   w.m. Will E. Haines, Maurice Beresford, James Harper

Hoch, Caroline   w.m. Jack Waller, Joe Tunbridge

How Do You Do, Mr. Brown?

I Travel the Road   w.m. Donovan Parsons, Pat Thayer

Just Humming Along   w.m. Montague Ewing, Sherman Myers

Life's Desire   w.m. Tolchard Evans, Stanley J. Damerell, Robert Hargreaves

Linger a Little Longer in the Twilight   w.m. Harry Woods, James Campbell, Reginald Connelly

Liszt, Chopin and Mendelssohn   w.m. Horatio Nicholls, Leo Towers, Harry Leon

Ma Curly Headed Babby   w.m. George Clutsam

Mona Lisa   w.m. Henry Sullivan, Desmond Carter

Old Kitchen Kettle, The   w.m. Harry Woods, James Campbell, Reginald Connelly

Old Sam (*Pick Up Tha' Musket*)   w.m. Stanley Holloway, Wolseley Charles

On the Air   w.m. Carroll Gibbons

Please Don't Mention It   w.m. Harry S. Pepper

Round the Marble Arch   w.m. Noel Gay, Ralph Butler

Silver Hair and Heart of Gold   w.m. Peter Maurice, Joe Gilbert

Sing Brothers   w.m. Jack Waller, Joe Tunbridge

Song of the Rose   w.m. Cherkose, Rosoff

The Sun Has Got His Hat On   w.m. Ralph Butler, Noel Gay

Throw Open Wide Your Window   w.m. Hans May

You're Dancing on My Heart   w.m. Meyer

1933

All Over Italy   w.m. Ralph Butler, Ronnie Munro

Butterflies in the Rain   w.m. Stanley Damerell, Robert Hargreaves, Sherman Myers

Carry Me Back to Green Pastures   w.m. Harry S. Pepper

Happy Ending   w.m. Harry Parr-Davies

Her Name Is Mary   w.m. Bruce Sievier, Harold Ramsey

I Was in the Mood   w.m. Eddie Pola, Michael Carr

Let Bygones Be Bygones   w.m. Joseph Gilbert

Lion and Albert, The   w.m. Marriott Edgar

Mary Rose   w.m. Harry Parr-Davies

My Hat's on the Side of My Head   w.m. Harry Woods, Claude Hulbert

My Heart's To Let   w.m. Jack Waller, Joe Tunbridge

My Song Goes Round the World   w.m. Hans May

Old Father Thames   w.m. Raymond Wallace, Betsy O'Hogan

The "Ol'" Song   w.m. Harry Carlton

Sweep   w.m. Vivian Ellis

We All Went Up Up Up the Mountain   w.m. Elton Box, Desmond Cox, Ralph Butler

Wedding of Mr. Mickey Mouse, The   w.m. Eddie Pola, Franz Vienna

Wheezy Anna   w.m. Leslie Sarony

1934

Always   w.m. Kenneth Leslie Smith, James Dyrenforth

Beside My Caravan   w.m. Karel Vacek, Jimmy Kennedy

Cafe in Vienna   w.m. Karel Vacek, Jimmy Kennedy

A Cage in the Window   w.m. Clark Gibson, Ray Morton

Coom Pretty One   w.m. Leslie Sarony

The Crest of a Wave   w.m. Ralph Reader

Does Santa Clause Sleep with His Whiskers   w.m. Billy Bray, Fred Gibson

Faith   w.m. Tolchard Evans

I Bought Myself a Bottle of Ink   w.m. Arthur le Clerq, Stanley Damerell, Tolchard Evans

I'm on a See-Saw   w.m. Vivian Ellis, Desmond Carter

In My Little Bottom Drawer   w.m. Will Haines, Jimmy Harper, Maurice Beresford

It's Foolish But It's Fun

It's Time To Say Goodnight   w.m. Henry Hall, Kate Gibson

La-Di-Da-Di-Da   w.m. Noel Gay, Desmond Carter

Let's All Go to the Music Hall   w.m. Horatio Nicholls

On the Crest of a Wave   w.m. Ralph Reader

Other People's Babies   w.m. Vivian Ellis, A. P. Herbert

Out in the Cold Cold Snow   w.m. W. E. Haines, J. Harper

Over My Shoulder   w.m. Harry Woods

Play to Me Gipsy   w.m. Karel Vacek, Jimmy Kennedy

Sing As We Go   w.m. Harry Parr-Davies, Gracie Fields

Things Are Looking Up   w.m. Noel Gay

Tina   w.m. Will Grosz, Hamilton Kennedy

Unless   w.m. Tolchard Evans, Robert Hargreaves, Stanley Damerell

We Parted on the Shore   w.m. Harry Lauder

When a Soldier's on Parade   w.m. Leslie Sarony

With Her Head Tucked Underneath Her Arm   w.m. R. P. Weston, Bert Lee

1935

All for a Shilling a Day   w.m. Noel Gay, Clifford Grey

Back to Those Happy Days   w.m. Horatio Nicholls

Canoe Song, The   w.m. Micha Spoliansky, Arthur Wimperis

Christopher Robin Is Saying His Prayers   w.m. A.A. Milne, Harold Fraser-Simson

Dancing with My Shadow   w.m. Harry Woods

Everything's in Rhythm with My Heart   w.m. Maurice Sigler, Al Goodhart, Al Hoffman

Fold Your Wings   w.m. Ivor Novello, Christopher Hassell

General's Fast Asleep, The   w.m. Jimmy Kennedy, Michael Carr

Gentlemen the King   w.m. Cyril Ray, Ivor McLaren

Gertie the Girl with the Gong   w.m. Ray Sonin, Ronnie Munro

Getting Around and About   w.m. Lewis Ilda, Michael Carr

Girl with the Dreamy Eyes, The   w.m. Michael Carr, Eddie Pola

Glamorous Night   w.m. Ivor Novello, Christopher Hassall

Goodbye Hawaii   w.m. Harry Leon, Vic Robbins, Leo Towers, Dave Appollon

I Once Had a Heart, Margarita   w.m. J. Schmitz

I'm Gonna Wash My Hands of You   w.m. Franz Vienna, Eddie Pola

It's My Mother's Birthday Today   w.m. Eddie Lisbona, Tommie Connor

Lovely Lady Let the Roses See You Today w.m. Norman Hardy

Me and the Old Folks at Home w.m. Rodd Arden, Leo Towers, Harry Leon

Misty Islands of the Highlands w.m. Jimmy Kennedy, Michael Carr

My Kid's a Crooner w.m. Marion Harris, Reg Montgomery

Old Ship of Mine w.m. Don Pelosi, Rodd Arden

Olga Pulloffski *(The Beautiful Spy)* w.m. R. P. Weston, Bert Lee

Roll Along Covered Wagon w.m. Jimmy Kennedy

Sarawaki w.m. Val Gordon

Shine Through My Dreams w.m. Ivor Novello, Christopher Hassall

Song of the Trees, The w.m. Tolchard Evans, Stanley Damerell, Robert Hargreaves

Spinning Wheel (Rawicz and Landauer signature tune) w.m. Maryan Rawicz

Tears w.m. Billy Uhr

There's a Lovely Lake in London w.m. Tolchard Evans, Stanley Damerell, Ralph Butler

Turn 'Erbert's Face to the Wall, Mother w.m. William Ellis, Max Kester, Ronald Hill

We've Got To Keep Up with the Joneses w.m. Leslie Elliot, Robert Rutherford

Wheel of the Wagon Is Broken, The w.m. Elton Box, Desmond Cox, Michael Carr

When the Gypsy Played w.m. Ivor Novello, Christopher Hassall

Who's Been Polishing the Sun w.m. Noel Gay

World Is Mine Tonight, The w.m. George Posford, Holt Marvell

You Can't Do That 'Ere w.m. Raymond Wallace, Jack Rolls

1936

At the Cafe Continental w.m. Will Grosz, Jimmy Kennedy

Au Revoir But Not Goodbye w.m. Joseph Gilbert

Bird on the Wing w.m. Jimmy Kennedy, Will Grosz

Celebratin' w.m. Harry Woods

Fleet's in Port Again, The w.m. Noel Gay

Have a Drink on Me w.m. Donegan, Buchanan

Hear My Song *(Violetta)*

It's Love Again w.m. Sam Coslow

King's Navee, The w.m. Charles Dunn

Let's Have a Tiddley at the Milk Bar w.m. Noel Gay

Me and My Dog w.m. Vivian Ellis

Music in May *(Careless Rapture)* w.m. Ivor Novello

My First Thrill w.m. Maurice Sigler, Al Hoffman, Al Goodhart

Poor Little Angeline w.m. Will Grosz, Jimmy Kennedy

The Sunset Trail w.m. Jimmy Kennedy, Michael Carr

There Isn't Any Limit to My Love w.m. Maurice Sigler, Al Hoffman, Al Goodhart

This'll Make You Whistle w.m. Maurice Sigler, Al Hoffman, Al Goodhart

Two of Us, The w.m. Van Phillips, James Campbell, Reginald Connelly

When the Guardsman Started Crooning on Parade w.m. Eddie Lisbona, Tommie Connor

When the Lights Are Low w.m. Benny Carter, Spencer Williams

When the Poppies Bloom Again w.m. Don Pelosi, Leo Towers, Morton Morrow

Why Did She Fall for the Leader of the Band w.m. Jimmy Kennedy, Michael Carr

1937

Angel of the Great White Way w.m. Elton Box, Desmond Cox, Don Pelosi, Paddy Roberts

Broken Hearted Clown w.m. Don Pelosi, Art Noel

Climbing Up w.m. Eric Maschwitz, Mischa Spoliansky

The Coronation Waltz w.m. Jimmy Kennedy

Cowboy w.m. Michael Carr

Delyse w.m. Horatio Nicholls, Joseph Gilbert

Down the Mall (piano solo) m. John Belton

The Feather in Her Tyrolean Hat w.m. Annette Mills

Gangway w.m. Sol Lerner, Al Goodhart, Al Hoffman

Goodnight to You All w.m. Denby, Watson

The Greatest Mistake of My Life w.m. James Netson

Hi Tiddley Hi Ti Island w.m. Ralph Stanley, Leslie Alleyn

Home Town w.m. Jimmy Kennedy, Michael Carr

Leaning on a Lamp Post w.m. Noel Gay

Let Us Be Sweethearts Over Again w.m. Joseph Gilbert

Little Boy That Santa Claus Forgot, The w.m. Tommie Connor, Jimmy Leach, Michael Carr

Little Co-operation from You, A w.m. Samuel Lerner, Al Goodhart, Al Hoffman

Nice Cup of Tea, A w.m. A. P. Herbert, Henry Sullivan

Old House, The w.m. Frederick O'Connor

She's My Lovely w.m. Vivian Ellis

Smile When You Say "Goodbye" w.m. Harry Parr-Davies

Spice of Life, The w.m. Jimmy Kennedy, Michael Carr

Ten Pretty Girls w.m. Will Grosz, Jimmy Kennedy

Walter, Walter (Lead Me to the Altar) w.m. W. E. Haines, J. Harper, Eugene Butler

Waltz of the Gipsies, The w.m. Michael Carr

When I'm Cleaning Windows w.m. Cliffe, Gifford, Formby

With My Shillelagh Under My Arm w.m. Billy O'Brien, Raymond Wallace

1938

The Biggest Aspidistra in the World w.m. Jimmy Harper, Will Haines, Tommie Connor

Chestnut Tree, The w.m. Jimmy Kennedy, Tommie Connor, Hamilton Kennedy

Cinderella Stay in My Arms w.m. Jimmy Kennedy, Michael Carr

Cinderella Sweetheart w.m. Art Strauss, Bob Dale

Georgia's Gotta Moon w.m. Max Nesbitt, Harry Nesbitt

Girl in the Alice Blue Gown, The w.m. Ross Parker

Horsey, Horsey w.m. Elton Box, Desmond Cox, Paddy Roberts, Ralph Butler

I Love To Sing w.m. P. Misraki

I Won't Tell a Soul (That I Love You) w.m. Ross Parker, Hugh Charles

In My Little Snapshot Album w.m. Harry Parr-Davies, Jimmy Harper, Will E. Haines

Knees Up Mother Brown w.m. Harris Weston, Bert Lee, Irving Taylor

The Laughing Policeman w.m. Billy Grey

Me and My Girl w.m. Noel Gay, Douglas Furber

'Neath the Spreading Chestnut Tree

Nice People (with Nice Habits) w.m. Nat Mills, Fred Malcolm

Rags, Bottles or Bones w.m. Stanley Holloway, Harry S. Pepper

Rose of England w.m. Ivor Novello, Christopher Hassall

Shy Serenade w.m. George Scott-Wood

Stately Homes of England, The w.m. Noël Coward

Sweetest Song in the World, The w.m. Harry Parr-Davies

Windmill's Turning, The w.m. J. van Laar, Sr.

1939

Army, the Navy and the Air Force, The w.m. Herman Darewski

Blue Skies Are Round the Corner w.m. Hugh Charles, Ross Parker

Boomps-a-Daisy w.m. Annette Mills

Handsome Territorial, A w.m. Jimmy Kennedy, Michael Carr

I Can Give You the Starlight w.m. Ivor Novello, Christopher Hassall

I Shall Always Remember You Smiling w.m. Ross Parker, Hugh Charles

I'll Walk Beside You w.m. Alan Murray, Edward Lockton

It's in the Air w.m. Harry Parr-Davies

Life Is Nothing Without Music w.m. Fred Hartley

Lords of the Air w.m. Davy Burnaby, Michael North

My Dearest Dear w.m. Ivor Novello, Christopher Hassall

My Life Belongs to You w.m. Ivor Novello, Christopher Hassall

Nursie w.m. Art Noel, Don Pelosi

Oh Nicholas Don't Be So Ridiculous w.m. Jimmy Kennedy, Harry Castling

On the Outside Looking In w.m. Michael Carr

Primrose w.m. Ivor Novello, Christopher Hassall

Summer Evening in Santa Cruz, A w.m. Fred Hartley, Jose Payan

Tears on My Pillow w.m. Max Nesbitt, Harry Nesbitt

Transatlantic Lullaby w.m. Diana Morgan, Robert McDermott, Geoffrey Wright

Waltz of My Heart w.m. Ivor Novello, Christopher Hassall

Washing on the Siegfried Line w.m. Jimmy Kennedy, Michael Carr

Wish Me Luck As You Wave Me Goodbye w.m. Harry Parr-Davies, Phil Park

1940

Brahn Boots w.m. R. P. Weston, Bert Lee

Calling All Workers (March) w.m. Eric Coates

Goodbye Sally w.m. Arthur Risco, J. Borelli

Goodnight Children, Everywhere w.m. Gabby Rogers, Harry Phillips

I Shall Be Waiting w.m. Ross Parker, Hugh Charles, Joe Irwin

If I Only Had Wings w.m. Sid Colin, Ronnie Aldrich

If I Should Fall in Love Again w.m. Jack Popplewell

I'll Pray for You w.m. Roy King, Stanley Hill

In the Quartermaster's Stores w.m. traditional; adapted by Elton Box, Desmond Cox, Bert Reed

Let the People Sing w.m. Noel Gay, Ian Grant, Frank Eyton

Memories Live Longer Than Dreams w.m. Ross Parker

Oh Mamma Mia w.m. Roma Campbell-Hunter, Freddy Grant

Seventeen Candles w.m. Art Strauss, Bob Dale, Sonny Miller

Shake Down the Stars

Somewhere in France with You w.m. Michael Carr

There's a Boy Coming Home on Leave w.m. Jimmy Kennedy

Tiggerty Boo w.m. Hal Halifax

Till the Lights of London Shine Again w.m. Tommie Connor, Eddie Pola

Where the Blue Begins w.m. Harry Parr-Davies

Who's Taking You Home Tonight w.m. Manning Sherwin, Tommie Connor

You Made Me Care When I Wasn't in Love w.m. Joseph George Gilbert

You've Done Something to My Heart w.m. Noel Gay, Ian Grant, Frank Eyton

1941

All Over the Place   w.m. Noel Gay, Frank Eyton

Badge from Your Coat, The   w.m. Horatio Nicholls, Annette Mills

Down Forget-Me-Not Lane   w.m. Horatio Nicholls, Charlie Chester, Reg Morgan

First Lullaby, The   w.m. Michael Carr, Jack Popplewell

Goodnight and God Bless You   w.m. Morton Fraser

Hey Little Hen   w.m. Ralph Butler, Noel Gray

I'll Think of You   w.m. Gerry Mason

London I Love, The   w.m. George Posford

Remember Me (The Girl in the Wood)

Room Five Hundred and Four   w.m. Eric Maschwitz, George Posford

Russian Rose   w.m. Sonny Miller, Hughie Charles

Saint Mary's in the Twilight   w.m. Jimmy Kennedy

Starlight Serenade   w.m. Hans May, Frederick Tysh, Sonny Miller

When They Sound the Last All Clear   w.m. Hugh Charles, Louis Elton

You Don't Have To Tell Me, I Know   w.m. Don Pelosi, Art Noel

1942

By Candlelight   w.m. Sonny Miller, Hugh Charles

I'm Going To See You Today   w.m. Joyce Grenfell, Richard Addinsell

It Costs So Little   w.m. Horatio Nicholls, Alf Ritter, J. Lester Smith

One Love Forever   w.m. Jimmy Dyrenforth, Kenneth Leslie-Smith

One More Kiss   w.m. Morton Morrow

Silver Wings in the Moonlight   w.m. Sonny Miller, Hugh Charles, Leo Towers

Sing, Everybody Sing   w.m. John P. Long

Soft Shoe Shuffle, The   w.m. Spencer Williams, Maurice Burman

Stage Coach   w.m. Eric Winstone

That Lovely Weekend   w.m. Ted and Moira Heath

There's a Land of Begin Again   w.m. Ross Parker, Hugh Charles

What More Can I Say   w.m. Art Noel

Where the Waters Are Blue   w.m. Hugh Charles, Sonny Miller

Wrap Yourself in Cotton Wool   w.m. Val Guest, Manning Sherwin

WRNS March, The   w.m. Richard Addinsell

1943

All Our Tomorrows   w.m. Jimmy Kennedy

Be Like the Kettle and Sing   w.m. Connor, O'Connor, Ridley

Break of Day   w.m. Hans May, Alan Stranks

Homecoming Waltz, The   w.m. Bob Musel, Ray Sonin, Reginald Connelly

I Give Thanks for You   w.m. Peter Young

I'm Gonna Get Lit Up (When the Lights Go On in London)   w.m. Hubert Gregg

In a Party Mood   w.m. Jack Strachey

Love Must Be Free   w.m. Alan Paul

Man of My Heart   w.m. Ivor Novello

My Heart and I   w.m. Frederick Tysh, Richard Tauber, Walter Ellis

Never Say Goodbye   w.m. Harry Parr-Davies, Harold Purcell

Number Something Far Away Lane   w.m. Howard Barnes, Hedley Grey, Ord Hamilton

Pedro the Fisherman   w.m. Harry Parr-Davies, Harold Purcell

Question and Answer (Demande et Reponse)   w.m. Samuel Coleridge-Taylor, Stanley Arthur. Based on ''Petite Suite de Concert'', Opus 77, by Coleridge-Taylor.

There Are Angels Outside Heaven   w.m. Frederick Tysh, Richard Tauber, Walter Ellis

Waking or Sleeping   w.m. Ivor Novello

When You Know You're Not Forgotten   w.m. Elton Box, Desmond Cox

You Happen Once in a Lifetime   w.m. M. Sherwin

1944

Hold Back the Dawn   w.m. Hedley Grey

Hour Never Passes, An   w.m. Jimmy Kennedy

If You Ever Go to Ireland   w.m. Art Noel

Sailor Who Are You Dreaming of Tonight   w.m. Stanley Damerell, Reg Butler, Tolchard Evans

Shine on Victory Moon   w.m. Joe Gilbert

Some Day Soon   w.m. Jimmy Leach

Till Stars Forget to Shine   w.m. Joe Lubin, Sonny Miller, Hugh Charles

1945

Carolina   w.m. Max Nesbitt, Harry Nesbitt, Jack Stodel

Chewing a Piece of Straw   w.m. Howard Barnes, Hedley Grey

Cokey Cokey, The   w.m. Jimmy Kennedy

Coming Home   w.m. Billy Reid

Gipsy, The   w.m. Billy Reid

I'm in Love with Two Sweethearts   w.m. Elton Box, Desmond Cox, Lewis Ilda

Lonely Footsteps   w.m. Howard Barnes, Lucia Ravenge

Love Is Like a Violin   w.m. Laparcerie

Love Is My Reason   w.m. Ivor Novello

Moment I Saw You, The   w.m. Harold Purcell, Manning Sherwin

My Beautiful Sarie Marais   w.m. Carr, Connor

My Guy's Come Back   w.m. Mel Powell, Ray McKinley

Prelude to the Stars   w.m. Vic Oliver

Story of Tina, The   w.m. D. Katrivanou

Theme from "The Way to the Stars"   w.m. N. Brodsky

1946

Green Cockatoo, The   w.m. Don Rellegro

Let It Be Soon   w.m. Dick Hurran, Hugh Wade

Let's Keep It That Way   w.m. Desmond O'Connor, Jack Denby, Muriel Watson

Love Steals Your Heart   w.m. Hans May, Alan Stranks

Mister Moon You've Got a Million Sweethearts   w.m. Charlie Chester, Ken Morris

Much Binding in the Marsh   w.m. Murdoch, Horne, Torch

Primrose Hill   w.m. Charlie Chester, Ken Morris, Everett Lynton

Soon It Will Be Sunday   w.m. James Bunting, Peter Hart

The Stars Will Remember   w.m. Don Pelosi, Leo Towers

Sweetheart, We'll Never Grow Old   w.m. Jack Denby, Muriel Watson

Time Marches On (instrumental)   m. John Belton

1947

How Lucky You Are   w.m. Eddie Cassen, Desmond O'Connor

I Was Never Kissed Before   w.m. Vivian Ellis

I'll Make Up for Everything   w.m. Ross Parker

Little Old Mill   w.m. Don Pelosi, Lewis Ilda, Leo Towers

Ma Belle Marguerita   w.m. A.P. Herbert, Vivian Ellis

Once Upon a Wintertime   w.m. Johnny Brandon, R. Martin

Shoemaker's Serenade, The   w.m. Lubin, Lisbona

This Is My Lovely Day   w.m. Vivian Ellis

Toor-ie on His Bonnet, The   w.m. Noel Gay, George Brown

1948

Anything I Dream Is Possible   w.m. Billy Reid

Coronation Scot   w.m. Vivian Ellis

Count Your Blessings   w.m. Edith Temple, Reginald Morgan

Devil's Gallop (Dick Barton theme)   w.m. Charles Williams

Down Sweetheart Avenue   w.m. Frank Chacksfield, Cedric Rushworth

Dream of Olwen, The   w.m. Charles Williams

Jamaican Rumba   w.m. Arthur Benjamin

Mick McGilligan's Ball   w.m. Michael Casey

Nice To Know You Care   w.m. Norman Newell, Leslie Baguley

No Milk Today   w.m. Graham Goodman

No Orchids for My Lady   w.m. Jack Strachey, Alan Stranks

Reflections on the Water   w.m. Billy Reid

This Is My Mother's Day   w.m. Billy Reid

Time Alone Will Tell   w.m. Eve Lynd

Time May Change   w.m. Hugh Wade

When You're in Love   w.m. Desmond O'Connor, Harold Fields, Dominic John

1949

Best of All   w.m. Ray Sonin, Wally Dewar

Blue Ribbon Gal   w.m. Irwin Dash, Ross Parker

Confidentially   w.m. Reg Dixon

Crystal Gazer, The   w.m. Frank Petch

Down in the Glen   w.m. Harry Gordon, Tommie Connor

Echo Told Me a Lie, The   w.m. Howard Barnes, Harold Fields, Dominic John

Fly Home, Little Heart (King's Rhapsody)   w.m. Ivor Novello

Hang on the Bell Nellie   w.m. Clive Erard, Ross Parker, Tommie Connor

How Can You Buy Killarney   w.m. Hamilton Kennedy, Ted Steels, Freddie Grant, Gerard Morrison

I Love You Because   w.m. Leon Payne

It Happened in Adano   w.m. Don Pelosi, Harold Fields

Jumping Bean   w.m. Robert Farnon

Leicester Square Rag   w.m. Harry Roy

Maybe It's Because I'm a Londoner   w.m. Hubert Greg

Our Love Story   w.m. Norman Newell, William Harrison

Rose in a Garden of Weeds, A   w.m. R. B. Saxe, Hubert W. David

Scottish Samba   w.m. Johnny Reine

Snowy White Snow and Jingle Bells   w.m. Billy Reid

Some Day My Heart Will Awake (King's Rhapsody)   w.m. Ivor Novello

Song of Capri   w.m. Mischa Spoliansky, Norman Newell

Take Your Girl   w.m. Ivor Novello, Christopher Hassall

Till All Our Dreams Come True   w.m. H. C. Bonocini, Desmond O'Connor

Violin Began To Play, The   w.m. Ivor Novello

Wedding of Lilli Marlene, The   w.m. Michael Reine, Tommie Connor

We'll Keep a Welcome   w.m. Mai Jones, Lyn Joshua, James Harper

Where Did My Snowman Go   w.m. Freddie Poser, Geoffrey Venis

Why Worry   w.m. Ralph Edwards, John Sexton

1950

The Ferry Boat Inn   w.m. Don Pelosi, Jimmy Campbell

A Gordon for Me   w.m. Robert Wilson

I Leave My Heart in an English Garden   w.m. Harry Parr-Davies, Christopher Hassall

I Remember the Cornfields   w.m. Martyn Mayne, Harry Ralton

If I Were a Blackbird   w.m. traditional

Load of Hay, A   w.m. Michael Feahy, Howard Barnes

Love Me Forever   w.m. Noel, Pelosi

My Thanks to You   w.m. Norman Newell, Noel Gay

Night the Floor Fell In, The   w.m. Ken Wheeley

Petite Waltz, The   w.m. Joe Heyne

Rose I Bring You, The   w.m. Tommie Connor, Michael Reine

Your Heart and My Heart   w.m. Ross Parker

1951

At the End of the Day   w.m. Donald O'Keefe

Good Luck, Good Health, God Bless You   w.m. Charles Adams, A. Le Royal

My Love and Devotion   w.m. Milton Carson

Ordinary People   w.m. G. Posford

White Suit Samba, The   w.m. Jack Parnell, T. E. B. Clarke

1952

Blue Bell Polka   w.m. F. Stanley

Bluebird (Vola Colomba)   w.m. C. Concina

Britannia Rag   w.m. Winifred Atwell

Broken Wings   w.m. John Jerome, Bernard Grun

Don't Laugh at Me ('Cause I'm a Fool)   w.m. Norman Wisdom, June Tremayne

Ecstasy Tango   w.m. Jose Belmonte

Elizabethan Serenade   w.m. Ronald Binge

Flirtation Waltz, The   w.m. R. Heywood, Leslie Sarony

From the Time We Say Goodbye   w.m. Leslie Sturdy

Homing Waltz, The   w.m. Tommie Connor, Michael Reine

Isle of Innisfree   w.m. Richard Farrelly

Marching Strings   w.m. Marshall Ross

My Baby's Comin' Home   w.m. William Leavitt, John Grady, Sherm Feller

1953

Ain't Gonna Kiss You   w.m. James Smith

Big Head   w.m. Jack Meadows

Bridge of Sighs, The   w.m. Billy Reid

Golden Tango, The   w.m. Victor Sylvester, Ernest Wilson

In a Golden Coach   w.m. Ronald Jamieson, Harry Leon

It's Almost Tomorrow   w.m. Gene Adkinson

Johnny Is the Boy for Me   w.m. Paddy Roberts, Marcel Stellman

Little Red Monkey   w.m. Jack Jordan

Lobster Quadrille, The   w.m. J. Horowitz

Melba Waltz, The   w.m. Mischa Spoliansky, Norman Newell

Windsor Waltz, The   w.m. Hans May, Michael Reine

You're a Pink Toothbrush   w.m. Ralph Ruvin, Bob Halfin, Harold Irving

1954

Book, The   w.m. Hans Gottwald, Paddy Roberts

Can This Be Love   w.m. Irene Roper, Terence Roper, Robert Raglan

Friends and Neighbours   w.m. Malcolm Lockyer, Marvin Scott

I Still Believe   w.m. Billy Reid

Lonely Ballerina   w.m. Michael Carr, "Lambrecht"

My Son, My Son   w.m. Eddie Calvert, Melville Farley, Bob Howard

Somebody   w.m. Joe Henderson

West of Zanzibar (Jambo)   w.m. Jack Fishman

1955

Anyone Can Be a Millionaire   w.m. Ed Franks

Big City Suite   w.m. Ralph Dollimore

Boomerang   w.m. Mark Lotz, Alan Gold, Tom Harrison

Dam Busters, The (March)   w.m. Eric Coates

Don't Worry   w.m. Ed Franks

Evermore   w.m. Gerry Levine, Paddy Roberts

Ev'rywhere   w.m. Larry Kahn, Tolchard Evans

Fanfare Boogie   w.m. Max Kaye, Brian Fahey

Got'n Idea   w.m. Jack Woodman, Paddy Roberts

I'll Be There   w.m. Jerry Wayne

I'll Come When You Call w.m. Josephine Caryll, David Caryll

In Love for the Very First Time w.m. Jack Woodman, Paddy Roberts

Income Tax Collector, The w.m. Michael Flanders, Donald Swann

John and Julie w.m. Philip Green

Man in a Raincoat w.m. Warwick Webster

Meet Me on the Corner w.m. Peter Hart, Paddy Roberts

Mr. Dumpling w.m. Joe Heathcote

Old Pi-anna Rag, The w.m. Don Philips

Paper Kisses w.m. John Jerome

Salad Days w.m. Julian Slade, Dorothy Reynolds

Sing a Rainbow w.m. Arthur Hamilton

Softly, Softly w.m. Pierre Dudan, Paddy Roberts, Mark Paul

Sooty w.m. Harry Corbett

Stranger Than Fiction w.m. Howard Shaw

That's How a Love Song Was Born w.m. Norman Newell, Philip Green

Water Gipsies, The w.m. Vivian Ellis, A.P. Herbert

When You Lose the One You Love w.m. Don Pelosi, Rodd Arden, Jimmy Harper

1956

Anchored w.m. M. Watson

Bad Penny Blues w.m. Humphrey Lyttelton

Come Home to My Arms w.m. Leslie Baguley, Emily Jane

Don't Ring-a Da Bell w.m. Johnny Reine, Sonny Miller

Experiments with Mice w.m. Johnny Dankworth

Garden of Eden, The w.m. Dennise Norwood

Georgian Rumba w.m. Ivor Slaney

Give Her My Love w.m. Leslie Baguley, Tommie Connor, Michael Reine

Highway Patrol w.m. Ray Llewellyn

Itinerary of an Orchestra w.m. Johnny Dankworth, Dave Lindup

Lay Down Your Arms w.m. Leon Land, Ake Gerhard, Paddy Roberts

Letter to a Soldier, A w.m. Gee Langdon

Lift Boy w.m. Ken Hare, Ron Goodwin, Dick James

March Hare, The w.m. Philip Green

Mary's Boy Child w.m. Jester Hairston

My September Love w.m. Tolchard Evans, Richard Mullan

My Unfinished Symphony w.m. Milton Carson

Nellie the Elephant w.m. Peter Hart, Ralph Butler

Never Do a Tango with an Eskimo w.m. Tommie Connor

Out of Town w.m. Leslie Bricusse, Robin Beaumont

Pickin' a Chicken w.m. Garfield de Mortimer, Derek Bernfield, Paddy Roberts

Startime w.m. Eric Rogers

That Dear Old Gentleman w.m. Paddy Roberts

Toyshop Ballet m. A. P. Mantovani

Westminster Waltz, The w.m. Robert Farnon

You Are My First Love w.m. Paddy Roberts, Lester Powell

1957

All w.m. Alan Stranks, Reynall Wreford

Don't You Rock Me Daddy-O w.m. Wally Whyton, Bill Varley

Elizabethan Serenade w.m. Ronald Binge

Free As Air w.m. Dorothy Reynolds, Julian Slade

Good Companions, The w.m. C. A. Rossi, Paddy Roberts, Geoffrey Parsons

Handful of Songs, A w.m. Tommy Steele, Lionel Bart, Michael Pratt

If I Lost You w.m. Tolchard Evans, Richard Mullan

I'll Find You w.m. Tolchard Evans, Richard Mullan

Mandolin Serenade w.m. Charles Chaplin, John Turner, Geoffrey Parsons

Overdrive w.m. Tommy Watt

Passing Strangers w.m. Rita Mann

Rainbow w.m. Ronald Hulme (Russ Hamilton)

Rock with the Cavemen w.m. Michael Pratt, Lionel Bart, Tommy Steele

Shiralee w.m. Tommy Steele

Sing Little Birdie w.m. Syd Cordell, Stan Butcher

Skiffling Strings w.m. Ron Goodwin

Streets of Sorrento, The w.m. Tony Osborne

Three Brothers w.m. Paddy Roberts

Tommy Steele Story, The w.m. Lionel Bart, Michael Pratt, Tommy Steele

Water, Water w.m. Lionel Bart, Michael Pratt, Tommy Steele

We Will Make Love w.m. Ronald Hulme (Russ Hamilton)

Wedding Ring w.m. Ronald Hulme (Russ Hamilton)

You Me and Us w.m. John Jerome

Your Love Is My Love w.m. Francis Edwards (Johnny Brandon)

1958

The Army Game w.m. Pat Napper, Sid Colin

Colonel's Tune, The w.m. Johnny Dankworth

Down Below w.m. Sydney Carter

For Your Love w.m. Ed Townsend

High Class Baby w.m. Ian Samwell

House of Bamboo, The w.m. Norman Murrells, Bill Crompton

I'm So Ashamed   w.m. Ken Hare

Inn of the Sixth Happiness (theme music)   m. Malcolm Arnold

It's a Boy   w.m. Paddy Roberts

Josita   w.m. Philip Green

Kiss Me, Honey Honey, Kiss Me   w.m. Al Timothy, Michael Julien

Lingering Lovers   w.m. Ron Goodwin

Love Is   w.m. Leslie Bricusse

Melody from the Sea   w.m. Donald Phillips

Only Sixteen   w.m. Barbara Campbell

Rock Bottom   w.m. Tommy Watt, Jock Bain

Song of the Clyde   w.m. Bell, Gourlay

Summer Is A-Comin' In   w.m. Leslie Bricusse

There Goes My Lover   w.m. Leonard Taylor, Harold Shaper

Trudie   w.m. Joe Henderson

Why Don't They Understand   w.m. Jack Fishman, Joe Henderson

Wind Cannot Read, The   w.m. Peter Hart

You Need Hands   w.m. Max Bygraves

1959

Ballad of Bethnal Green, The   w.m. Paddy Roberts

Beaulieu Festival Suite   w.m. Kenny Graham

Chick   w.m. Joe Henderson

China Tea   w.m. Trevor Stanford

Emergency Ward 10 Theme   w.m. Peter Yorke

Heart of a Man   w.m. Peggy Cochrane, Paddy Roberts

He'll Have To Go   w.m. J. Allison, A. Allison

Here Comes Summer   w.m. Jerry Keller

Hoots Mon   w.m. Harry Robinson

If You Love Me (I Won't Care)   w.m. M. Monnot

I've Waited So Long   w.m. Jerry Lordan

Jazzboat   w.m. Joe Henderson

Li'l Darlin' (Don't Dream of Anybody But Me)   w.m. N. Hefti

Little Donkey   w.m. Eric Boswell

Little White Bull, The   w.m. Lionel Bart, Michael Pratt, Jimmy Bennett, Tommy Steele

Living Doll   w.m. Lionel Bart

Lock Up Your Daughters   w.m. Laurie Johnson, Lionel Bart

Maybe This Year   w.m. Ronald Wakley, Marcel Stellman

Meet the Family   w.m. Peter Greenwell, Peter Wildeblood

Moanin'   w.m. Bobby Timmons

Never Mind   w.m. Ian Samwell

Ring Ding   w.m. Steve Race

River Boat   w.m. Bill Anderson

Roulette   w.m. Trevor Stanford

Side Saddle   w.m. Trevor Stanford, (Russ Conway)

Sing Little Birdie   w.m. Stan Butcher, Syd Cordell

Singing Piano, The   w.m. Tolchard Evans

Sitting in the Back Seat   w.m. Lee Pockriss

Snow Coach   w.m. Trevor Stanford

Strollin'   w.m. Ralph Reader

Treble Chance   w.m. Joe Henderson

Turn Your Radio On   w.m. Albert E. Brumley

Village of Saint Bernadette, The   w.m. Eula Parker

What Do You Want   w.m. Les Vandyke

Windows of Paris   w.m. Tony Osborne

1960

Along Came Caroline   w.m. Paul Stephens, Michael Cox, Terence McGrath, M. Steel

Apache   w.m. Jerry Lordan

Bad Boy   w.m. Marty Wilde

Belle of Barking Creek, The   w.m. Paddy Roberts

Birmingham Rag   w.m. Mort Garson

Colette   w.m. Billy Fury

Do You Mind   w.m. Lionel Bart

Fall in Love with You   w.m. Ian Samwell

Goodness Gracious Me   w.m. Herbert Kretzmer, Dave Lee

Gurney Slade Theme, The   w.m. Max Harris

Heart of a Teenage Girl   w.m. Bill Crompton, Morgan Jones

Hit and Miss   w.m. John Barry

How About That   w.m. Les Vandyke

I Love You   w.m. Bruce Welch

Lively   w.m. Peter Buchanan, Lonnie Donegan

Lonely Pup (in a Christmas Shop)   w.m. Archie Alexander

Look for a Star   w.m. Mark Anthony

Looking High, High, High   w.m. John Watson

Lucky Five   w.m. Trevor Stanford

Made You   w.m. John Barry

Man of Mystery   w.m. Michael Carr

Messing About on the River   w.m. Mark Anthony

My Old Man's a Dustman   w.m. Lonnie Donegan

Nice 'n' Easy   w.m. Lew Spence

Once in Every Lifetime   w.m. Guy Magenta

Only the Heartaches   w.m. Wayne P. Walker

Passing Breeze   w.m. Trevor Stanford

Please Don't Tease   w.m. Bruce Welch, Peter Chester

Point of No Return, The   w.m. John Harris, Derek New

Poor Me   w.m. Les Vandyke

Romantica   w.m. Verde, Rascal

Royal Event   w.m. Trevor Stanford

Seashore   w.m. Robert Farnon

Shakin' All Over   w.m. Johnny Kidd

Someone Else's Baby   w.m. Les Vandyke, Perry Ford

Stranger, The w.m. Bill Crompton, Morgan Jones

Strawberry Fair w.m. traditional; new lyric by Nolly Clapton.

Summer Set w.m. Acker Bilk, David Collett

Tease Me w.m. Keith Kelly

Voice in the Wilderness, A w.m. Norrie Paramor, Bunny Lewis

What a Mouth R. P. Weston

Wheels (Cha Cha) w.m. Norman Petty

Who Could Be Bluer w.m. Jerry Lordan

Willow Waltz, The w.m. Cyril Watters

Secrets of the Seine, The w.m. Tony Osborne

Stranger on the Shore w.m. Acker Bilk

Tell All the World w.m. Mark Anthony

Time Has Come, The w.m. Les Vandyke

Walking Back to Happiness w.m. Mike Hawker, John Schroeder

Who Am I w.m. Les Vandyke

Wild Wind w.m. Geoffrey Goddard

You Don't Know w.m. Mike Hawker, John Schroeder

1961

African Waltz w.m. Galt MacDermot, Mel Mandel, Norman Sachs

Are You Sure w.m. Bob Allison, John Allison

Avengers' Theme, The w.m. Johnny Dankworth

Barbara Ann w.m. Fred Fassert

Comancheros, The w.m. Tillman Franks

Come Sta' w.m. Harry Gordon

Coronation Street w.m. Eric Spear

Don't Treat Me Like a Child w.m. Mike Hawker, John Schroeder

Don't You Know It w.m. Les Vandyke

Duddley Dell w.m. Dudley Moore

Easy Going Me w.m. Lionel Bart

F.B.I. w.m. Peter Gormley

Frightened City, The w.m. Norrie Paramor

Gee Whiz, It's You w.m. Hank B. Marvin, Ian Samwell

Get Lost w.m. Les Vandyke

Girl Like You, A w.m. Jerry Lordan

I (Who Have Nothing) w.m. C. Donida

Johnny Remember Me w.m. Geoffrey Goddard

Kon-Tiki w.m. Michael Carr

Little Red Rooster w.m. Willie Dixon

Maigret Theme, The w.m. Ron Grainer

Marry Me w.m. Lawrence Jacks

Midnight in Moscow (Moscow Nights) w.m. Vassili Soloviev-Sedoi; adapted Kenny Ball

My Boomerang Won't Come Back w.m. Max Diamond, Charlie Drake

My Friend the Sea w.m. Ron Goodwin, Jack Fishman

My Kind of Girl w.m. Leslie Bricusse

Mystery Girl w.m. Trevor Peacock

No Greater Love w.m. Michael Carr, Bunny Lewis

Once in a Lifetime w.m. Leslie Bricusse, Anthony Newley

Pianissimo w.m. Alex Alstone

Savage, The w.m. Norrie Paramor

Scottish Soldier, A w.m. Stewart, MacFadyen

1962

Ain't That Funny w.m. Les Vandyke

As You Like It w.m. Les Vandyke

Casanova w.m. Karl Glauotz

Clinging Vine

Come Dancing w.m. Downes, David

Come Outside w.m. Charles Blackwell

Day After Tomorrow, The w.m. Lionel Bart

Don't Stop—Twist w.m. Frankie Vaughan

Don't That Beat All w.m. Les Vandyke

English Country Gardens w.m. traditional; new lyric Robert Jordan

Forget Me Not w.m. Les Vandyke

Hole in the Ground w.m. Ted Dicks, Myles Rudge

I'm Just a Baby w.m. Jerry Lordan

Jeannie w.m. Russ Conway, Norman Newell

Last Night Was Made for Love w.m. Alan Fielding

Let's Dance w.m. Jim Lee

Let's Talk About Love w.m. Norrie Paramor, Bunny Lewis

Little Miss Lonely w.m. Mike Hawker, John Schroeder

Lonely w.m. Norrie Paramor, Acker Bilk

Mañana Pasado Mañana w.m. Norrie Paramor

March from "A Little Suite" w.m. Trevor Duncan

Must Be Madison w.m. Jack Woodman

My Love and Devotion w.m. Howard Barnes, Joe Roncoroni, Harold Fields

Never Goodbye w.m. Jimmy Kennedy

Nicola w.m. Steve Race

Once Upon a Dream w.m. Norrie Paramor, Richard Rowe

Our Favourite Melodies w.m. Bob Elgin, Kay Rogers, Wes Farrell

Outbreak of Murder w.m. Gordon Franks

Picture of You, A w.m. Johnny Beveridge, Peter Oakman

Revival w.m. Joe Harriott

Right Said Fred w.m. Ted Dicks, Myles Rudge

Ring-a-Ding Girl w.m. Stan Butcher, Syd Cordell

Son, This Is She w.m. Geoffrey Goddard

Speak Softly w.m. Jimmy Fontana

Steptoe and Son w.m. Ron Grainer

Stranger on the Shore w.m. Acker Bilk, Robert Mellin

Telstar w.m. Joe Meek

Turkish Coffee w.m. Tony Osborne

Welcome to My World w.m. Winkler, Hathcock

When Love Comes Along

Will I What w.m. Johnny Powell, Nick Shakespear, Ken Hawker

Wonderful Land w.m. Jerry Lordan

Z Cars Theme w.m. traditional; arranged Bridget Fry. Based on the Northumbrian tune ''Johnny Todd.''

1963

Applejack w.m. Les Vandyke

Atlantis w.m. Jerry Lordan

Bachelor Boy w.m. Cliff Richard, Bruce Welch

Carlos' Theme w.m. Ivor Slaney

Cruel Sea, The w.m. Mike Maxfield

Cupboard Love w.m. Les Vandyke

Dance On w.m. Valerie Murtagh, Elaine Murtagh, Ray Adams

Dancing Shoes w.m. Marvin, Welch

Diamonds w.m. Jerry Lordan

Don't Talk to Him w.m. Cliff Richard, Bruce Welch

Don't You Think It's Time w.m. Geoffrey Goddard, Joe Meek

Eight by Ten w.m. Anderson, Haynes, Turner

First Time w.m. Chris Andrews

Flash, Bang, Wallop w.m. David Heneker

Foot Tapper w.m. Hank B. Marvin, Bruce Welch

Forget Him w.m. Mark Anthony

Geronimo w.m. Hank B. Marvin

Globetrotter w.m. Joe Meek

Go Now w.m. Banks, Bennett

Gossip Calypso w.m. Trevor Peacock

Half a Sixpence w.m. David Heneker

Happiness w.m. Bill Anderson

Harvest of Love w.m. Benny Hill, Tony Hatch

Hello Little Girl w.m. John Lennon, Paul McCartney

How Do You Do It w.m. Mitch Murray

I Like It w.m. Mitch Murray

Ice Cream Man w.m. Joe Meek

I'll Keep You Satisfied w.m. John Lennon, Paul McCartney

I'll Never Get Over You w.m. Gordon Mills

I'm Telling You Now w.m. Freddie Garrity, Mitch Murray

In Summer w.m. Elaine Murtagh, Valerie Murtagh, Ray Adams

Island of Dreams w.m. Tom Springfield

Just Like Eddie w.m. Geoffrey Goddard

Make the World Go Away w.m. Hank Cochran

Next Time w.m. Buddy Kaye, Phillip Springer

Robot w.m. Joe Meek

Say I Won't Be There w.m. Tom Springfield

Say Wonderful Things w.m. Norman Newell, Phillip Green

Scarlet O'Hara w.m. Jerry Lordan

Shindig w.m. Hank B. Marvin, Bruce Welch

Sugar and Spice w.m. Fred Nightingale

Summer Holiday w.m. Bruce Welch, Brian Bennett

Sweet September w.m. Bill McGuffie

That's What Love Will Do w.m. Trevor Peacock

Then He Kissed Me w.m. Spector, Greenwich, Barry

What the Dickens w.m. Johnny Dankworth

When Will You Say I Love You w.m. Alan Fielding

Yeah Yeah w.m. Grand, Patrick, Hendrick

You Can Never Stop Me Loving You w.m. Ian Samwell, Jean Slater

1964

All Day and All of the Night w.m. Ray Davies

Almost There w.m. Keller, Shayne

Bits and Pieces w.m. Dave Clark, Mike Smith

Bombay Duckling (Kipling Theme) w.m. Max Harris

Boys Cry w.m. Buddy Kaye, Tommy Scott

Can't You See That She's Mine w.m. Dave Clark, Mike Smith

Crying Game, The w.m. Geoff Stephens

Don't Bring Me Down w.m. Johnnie Dee

Don't Let the Sun Catch You Crying w.m. Gerry Marsden, Fred Marsden, Les Chadwick, Les Maguire

Don't Turn Around w.m. Peter Lee Stirling, Barry Mason

Dr. Who Theme w.m. Ron Grainer

Everything's Al'Right w.m. Nicholas Crouch, John Conrad, Simon Stavely, Stuart James, Keith Karlson

Five-Four-Three-Two-One w.m. Paul Jones, Mike Hugg, Manfred Mann

Glad All Over w.m. Dave Clark, Mike Smith

Have I the Right w.m. Howard Blaikley

Here I Go Again w.m. Mort Shuman, Clive Westlake

I Feel Fine w.m. John Lennon, Paul McCartney

I Love the Little Things w.m. Tony Hatch

I Only Want To Be with You w.m. Mike Hawker, Ivor Raymonde

I Think of You w.m. Peter Lee Stirling

I'm Crying w.m. Alan Price, Eric Burdon

I'm the Lonely One w.m. Gordon Mills

I'm the One w.m. Gerry Marsden

It's an Open Secret w.m. Joy Webb

It's Over

Juliet w.m. Mike Wilsh, Fritz Fryer, Lionel Morton

Little Lovin', A w.m. Russell Alquist

Losing You w.m. Tom Springfield, Clive Westlake

Maggie May w.m. Lionel Bart

Morning Dew w.m. Bonnie Dobson

Not So Much a Programme, More a Way of Life w.m. Ron Grainer, Ned Sherrin, Caryl Brahms

On the Beach w.m. Bruce Welch, Hank B. Marvin, Cliff Richard

One Way Love w.m. Bert Russell, Norman Meade

Over You w.m. Derek Quinn, Alan Jones

Race Is On, The w.m. Don Rollins

Rise and Fall of Flingle Bunt w.m. Bruce Welch, Hank B. Marvin, John Rostill, Brian Bennett

Robert and Elizabeth w.m. Ron Grainer, Ronald Millar

Stay Awhile w.m. Mike Hawker, Ivor Raymonde

Sweet William w.m. Buddy Kaye, Philip Springer

Tell Me When w.m. Geoff Stephens, Les Reed

Theme for Young Lovers w.m. Bruce Welch

Tokyo Melody w.m. Helmut Zacharias, Heinz Hellmer, Lionel Bart

Up Cherry Street w.m. Julius Wechter

We Are in Love w.m. Chris Andrews

We're Through w.m. Lee Rainsford

You Really Got Me w.m. Ray Davies

You're My World w.m. Bindi, Sigman

1965

Anyway, Anyhow, Anywhere w.m. Peter Townshend, Roger Daltry

Ballad of a Crystal Man w.m. Donovan

Carnival Is Over, The w.m. Tom Springfield

Catch the Wind w.m. Donovan

Clapping Song, The (My Mother Told Me) w.m. Lincoln Chase

Colours w.m. Donovan

Concrete and Clay w.m. Tommy Moeller, Brian Parker

Don't Bring Me Your Heartaches w.m. Robin Conrad, Les Reed

Everyone's Gone to the Moon w.m. Kenneth King

Evil Hearted You w.m. Graham Gouldman

Ferry 'Cross the Mersey w.m. Gerry Marsden

For You Alone w.m. Graham Gouldman

Funny How Love Can Be w.m. "Carter-Lewis"

Genie with the Light Brown Lamp w.m. Hank B. Marvin, Bruce Welch, John Rostill, Brian Bennett

Get Off My Cloud w.m. Mick Jagger, Keith Richards

Girl Don't Come w.m. Chris Andrews

Green Green Grass of Home, The w.m. Curly Patman

Heart Full of Soul w.m. Graham Gouldman

Here It Comes Again w.m. Barry Mason, Les Reed

I Could Easily Fall w.m. Hank B. Marvin, Bruce Welch, John Rostill, Brian Bennett

I'll Never Find Another You w.m. Tom Springfield

I'll Stop at Nothing w.m. Chris Andrews

In the Midnight Hour w.m. Steve Cropper

In Thoughts of You w.m. Geoff Morrow, Chris Arnold

It's Good News Week w.m. Kenneth King

It's Not Unusual w.m. Gordon Mills, Les Reed

Kiss, The w.m. Jack Parnell

Leave a Little Love w.m. Robin Conrad, Les Reed

Let's Hang On w.m. Crewe, Linzer, Randell

Long Live Love w.m. Chris Andrews

Look Through Any Window w.m. Graham Gouldman, Charles Silverman

March of the Mods w.m. Tony Carr

Message Understood w.m. Chris Andrews

Mister Kiss Kiss Bang Bang w.m. John Barry

Mogul Theme, The w.m. Tom Springfield

Mrs. Brown, You've Got a Lovely Daughter w.m. Trevor Peacock

My Generation w.m. Peter Townshend

Pied Piper, The w.m. A. Kernfeld, Steve Duboff

Set Me Free w.m. Ray Davies

Still I'm Sad w.m. Paul Samwell-Smith, James McCarthy

Terry w.m. "Twinkle"

That's the Way w.m. Howard Blaikley

Thunderbirds Theme w.m. Barry Gray

To Sing for You w.m. Donovan

To Whom It Concerns w.m. Chris Andrews

Tossing and Turning w.m. John Carter, Ken Lewis, Perry Ford

Where Are You Now (My Love) w.m. Tony Hatch, Jackie Trent

Why Do You Treat Me Like You Do w.m. Donovan

Windmill in Old Amsterdam, A w.m. Ted Dicks, Myles Rudge

World of Our Own, A w.m. Tom Springfield

Yesterday Man w.m. Chris Andrews

1966

Bring Me Sunshine w.m. Arthur Kent

Dedicated Follower of Fashion w.m. Ray Davies

Distant Dreams w.m. Cindy Walker

Funny, Familiar, Forgotten Feelings w.m. M. Newbury

God Only Knows w.m. Wilson, Asher

Hev Yew Gotta Loight, Boy? w.m. Allan Smethurst

Hideaway w.m. H. Blaikley

Holy Cow w.m. A. Toussaint

Khartoum w.m. Frank Cordell

Man Without Love, A   w.m. Livraghi, Pace, Panzeri

Morning of My Life   w.m. Barry Alan Gibb

Paint It Black   w.m. Mick Jagger, Keith Richard

Power Game, The   w.m. Wayne Hill

Pretty Flamingo   w.m. Mark Barkan

Quiet Girl, A   w.m. John Hanson

Ruby, Don't Take Your Love to Town   w.m. Mel Tillis

Sloop John B.   w.m. Brian Wilson

Softly, Softly Theme (BBC TV series)   w.m. Bridget Fry

These Are My Mountains   **w.m. James Copeland**

Time Drags By   w.m. Hank B. Marvin, Bruce Welch, Brian Bennett, John Rostill

What Would I Be   w.m. Jackie Trent

World Cup March, The   w.m. Moorhouse, Mansfield

I'm the Urban Spaceman   w.m. Neil Innes

Jezamine   w.m. Marty Wilde (Frere Manston), Ronnie Scott, (Jack Gellar)

Joanna   w.m. Tony Hatch, Jackie Trent

Lily the Pink   w.m. Gorman, McGear, McGough

Little Girl   w.m. Reg Presley

Massachusetts   w.m. Barry Gibb, Robin Gibb, Maurice Gibb

Polk Salad Annie   w.m. Tony Joe White

Red Balloon, The   w.m. Raymond Froggatt

Ring of Kerry   w.m. Peter Hope

Rosie   w.m. Don Partridge

633 Squadron   w.m. Ron Goodwin

Something Is Happening   w.m. R. Del Turco, G. Bigazzi

There's a New World   w.m. Michael Carr

Young Girl   w.m. Jerry Fuller

1967–1968

Ballad of Bonnie and Clyde, The   w.m. Mitch Murray, Peter Callander

Doctor Dolittle (score)   w.m. Leslie Bricusse

Grocer Jack   w.m. Keith West, Mark Wirtz

House That Jack Built, The   w.m. Alan Price

How Can I Be Sure   w.m. Cavaliere, Brigati

Itchycoo Park   w.m. Steve Marriott, Ronnie Lane

Last Waltz, The   w.m. Les Reed, Barry Mason

Let the Heartaches Begin   w.m. Macaulay, MacLeod

Love in the Open Air   w.m. Paul McCartney

Monsieur Dupont   w.m. Pruhn, Callander

Now   w.m. Henry Mayer

Other Man's Grass, The (Is Always Greener)   w.m. Jackie Trent, Tony Hatch

Puppet on a String   w.m. Bill Martin, Phil Coulter

See Emily Play   w.m. Syd Barrett

Thank U Very Much (Aintree Iron)   w.m. M. McGear

This Is My Song   w.m. Charles Chaplin

Turn Around   w.m. Les Reed, Barry Mason

Words   w.m. Barry Gibb, Robin Gibb, Maurice Gibb

1968–1969

Abergavenny   w.m. Marty Wilde (Frere Manston), Ronnie Scott, (Jack Gellar)

Blackberry Way   w.m. Roy Wood

Build Me Up Buttercup   w.m. Tony Macaulay, Michael D'Abo

Congratulations   w.m. Bill Martin, Phil Coulter

Delilah   w.m. Les Reed, Barry Mason

Fire Brigade   w.m. Roy Wood

I Close My Eyes and Count to Ten   w.m. Clive Westlake

1969–1970

Battle of Britain (theme)   w.m. Ron Goodwin

Boom Bang-a-Bang   w.m. Alan Moorhouse, Peter Warne

Come Back and Shake Me   w.m. K. Young

Durham Town   w.m. Roger Whittaker

Early in the Morning   w.m. Leander, Seago

If I Thought You'd Ever   w.m. John Cameron

Let's Work Together   w.m. Wilbert Harrison

Lights of Cincinnati   w.m. Tony Macaulay, Geoff Stephens

Long-Haired Lover from Liverpool   w.m. C. Dowden

Love Is All   w.m. Les Reed, Barry Mason

Madwoman of Chaillot (score)   w.m. Michael Lewis

Melting Pot   w.m. Roger Cook, Roger Greenaway

Morning, Please Don't Come   w.m. Tom Springfield

New World in the Morning   w.m. Roger Whittaker

Paul Temple Theme   w.m. Ron Grainer

Popcorn   w.m. Gershon Kingsley

Space Oddity   w.m. David Bowie

Where Do You Go to My Lovely   w.m. Peter Sarstedt

1970–1971

Chirpy Chirpy, Cheep Cheep   w.m. Larry Stott

Everything's Alright (*Jesus Christ Superstar*)   w.m. Andrew Lloyd-Webber, Tim Rice

Friends   w.m. Terry Reid

Gasoline Alley Bred   w.m. Tony Macaulay, Roger Cook, Roger Greenaway

Gimme Dat Ding   w.m. Albert Hammond, Mike Hazlewood

Grandad   w.m. Ken Pickett, Herbie Flowers

Home Lovin' Man   w.m. Tony Macaulay, Roger Greenaway

I Will Drink the Wine   w.m. Paul Ryan

In the Summertime   w.m. Ray Dorset

Jesus Christ Superstar (rock opera)   w.m. Andrew Lloyd-Webber, Tim Rice

Knock, Knock, Who's There?   w.m. Geoff Stephens, John Carter

Let Me Be the One   w.m. Roger Nicholls

Light Flight   w.m. The Pentangle

Look Around You and You'll Find Me There   w.m. F. Lai

Love Grows   w.m. Tony Macaulay, Barry Mason

March from "The Colour Suite"   w.m. Gordon Langford

Nothing Rhymed   w.m. Ray O'Sullivan

Patches   w.m. R. Dunbar, N. Johnson

Pieces of Dreams   w.m. Michel Legrand

Pushbike Song, The   w.m. Idris Jones, Evan Jones

Rupert   w.m. Roker, Weston

Thank You Very Much (*Scrooge*)   w.m. Leslie Bricusse

That Same Old Feeling   w.m. Tony Macaulay, Marilyn McLeod

Theme from "The Persuaders"   w.m. John Barry

United We Stand   w.m. Tony Hiller, Peter Simons

We're Gonna Change the World   w.m. David Matthews, Tim Harris

When I'm Dead and Gone   w.m. Bernard Gallagher, Graham Lyle

Who Do You Think You Are Kidding Mr. Hitler (BBC TV signature theme)   w.m. Jimmy Perry, Derek Taverner

Wonder of You, The   w.m. Baker Knight

Yellow River   w.m. Jeff Christie

Your Song   w.m. Bernie Taupin, Elton John

You've Got Me Dangling on a String   w.m. Dunbar, Wayne

1971–1972

British Empire, The (TV theme)   w.m. Wilfred Josephs

Coz I Love You   w.m. Holder, Lea

Don't Let It Die   w.m. E. Smith

Ernie   w.m. Benny Hill

Freedom Come, Freedom Go   w.m. Albert Hammond, Mike Hazlewood, Roger Cook, Roger Greenaway

Good Old Bad Days, The   w.m. Leslie Bricusse, Anthony Newley

Hot Love   w.m. Marc Bolan

Jack in the Box   w.m. David Myers, John Worsley

Lightning Tree, The   w.m. Stephen Francis

Match of the Day (instrumental)   m. Rhet Stoller

Me and You and a Dog Named Boo   w.m. Kent La Voie

Never Ending Song of Love   w.m. D. Bramlett

No Matter How I Try   w.m. Ray O'Sullivan

Out on the Edge of Beyond   w.m. Mike Sammes

Pictures in the Sky   w.m. John Fiddler

Rosetta   w.m. Mike Snow

Simple Game   w.m. Mike Pinder

Sing a Song of Freedom   w.m. Guy Fletcher, Doug Flett

Sleepy Shores ("Owen MD" TV signature tune)   w.m. Johnny Pearson

Son of My Father   w.m. Giorgio Moroder

Today I Met My Love   w.m. Johnny Pearson

Too Beautiful To Last   w.m. Richard Rodney Bennett

Tweedle Dee-Tweedle Dum   w.m. M. Cubuano, G. Cubuano

Vincent   w.m. Don McLean

When You Are a King   w.m. John Hill, Roger Hill

Why   w.m. Roger Whittaker, Joan Stanton

1972–1973

Another Spring   w.m. Malcolm Barron, Steven Cairn

Beg, Steal or Borrow   w.m. Graeme Hall, Tony Cole, Steve Wolfe

Colditz (March)   w.m. Robert Farnon

Come What May (Après Toi)   w.m. Panas, Munro

Country Matters   w.m. Derek Hilton

First Time Ever I Saw Your Face, The   w.m. Ewan MacColl

I Didn't Know I Loved You   w.m. Garry Glitter, Mike Lauder

Long Cool Woman in a Black Dress   w.m. Roger Cook, Roger Greenaway, Alan Clark

Meet Me on the Corner   w.m. Roderick Clements

Mouldy Old Dough   w.m. Nigel Fletcher, Rob Woodward

Oh Babe, What Would You Say   w.m. Hurricane Smith

Our Jackie's Getting Married   w.m. Peter Skellern

Pathfinder's March   w.m. Malcolm Lockyer

People Tree, The   w.m. Leslie Bricusse, Anthony Newley

Solid Gold Easy Action   w.m. Marc Bolan

Tommy (rock opera)   w.m. Peter Townshend

Wig Wam Bam   w.m. Nicky Chinn, Mike Chapman

Without You   w.m. Peter Ham, Tom Evans

1973–1974

All of My Life   w.m. Michael Randall

Angie   w.m. Mick Jagger, Keith Richard

Baby We Can't Go Wrong   w.m. J. Dunning

Blockbuster   w.m. Mike Chapman, Nicky Chinn

Children of Rome   w.m. Stanley Myers

Crocodile Rock   w.m. Elton John, Bernie Taupin

Daniel   w.m. Elton John, Bernie Taupin

Galloping Home   w.m. Denis King

I Love You Love Me Love w.m. Garry Glitter, Mike Leander

Like Sister and Brother w.m. Geoff Stephens, Roger Greenaway

Merry Xmas Everybody w.m. Neville Holder, James Lea

My Love w.m. Paul McCartney

Nice One Cyril w.m. Harold Spiro, Helen Clarke

Ooh Baby w.m. Gilbert O'Sullivan

Part of the Union w.m. Richard Hudson, John Ford

Power to All Our Friends w.m. Doug Flett, Guy Fletcher

Rubber Bullets w.m. K. Godley, L. Creme, G. Gouldman

Take Me High w.m. Tony Cole

Why Oh Why Oh Why? w.m. Gilbert O'Sullivan

Won't Somebody Dance With Me w.m. Lynsey de Paul

You Won't Find Another Fool Like Me w.m. Tony Macaulay, Geoff Stephens

1974–1975

Air That I Breathe, The w.m. Albert Hammond, Mike Hazlewood

Billy (score) w.m. John Barry, Don Black

Billy Don't Be a Hero w.m. Mitch Murray, Peter Callander

Four Dances from Aladdin w.m. Ernest Tomlinson

Killer Queen w.m. Freddie Mercury

Kung Fu Fighting w.m. Carl Douglas

Night Chicago Died, The w.m. Mitch Murray, Peter Callander

No Honestly? w.m. Lynsey de Paul

Sad Sweet Dreamer w.m. Des Parton

Streets of London w.m. Ralph McTell

Suite No. 1 for Small Orchestra w.m. John Hall

Tiger Feet w.m. Nicky Chinn, Mike Chapman

Treasure Island (score) w.m. Hal Shaper, Cyril Ornadel

Wombling Song w.m. Mike Batt

1975–1976

Bohemian Rhapsody w.m. Freddie Mercury

Captain Noah and His Floating Zoo w.m. Michael Flanders, Joseph Horovitz

Doctor's Orders w.m. Roger Greenaway, Roger Cook, Geoff Stephens

Fantasia on a Nursery Song w.m. Leo Norman

Good Word, The (theme from "Nationwide") w.m. Johnny Scott

Great Expectations (score) w.m. Hal Shaper, Cyril Ornadel

Harry w.m. Catherine Howe

I'm Not in Love w.m. Eric Stewart, Graham Gouldman

Introduction and Air to a Stained Glass Window w.m. John Gregory

Island Girl w.m. Elton John, Bernie Taupin

Last Farewell w.m. Roger Whittaker, R. A. Webster

Magic w.m. David Paton, William Lyall

Murder on the Orient Express (score) w.m. Richard Rodney Bennett

Quilp w.m. Anthony Newley

Sailing w.m. Gavin Sutherland

Sky High w.m. Clive Scott, Desmond Dyer

"Upstairs Downstairs" Theme (The Edwardians) w.m. Alexander Faris

1976–1977

Bouquet of Barbed Wire w.m. Dennis Farnon

Comedy of Errors, The w.m. Guy Woolfenden

Don't Cry for Me, Argentina w.m. Tim Rice, Andrew Lloyd-Webber

Don't Go Breaking My Heart w.m. Elton John, Bernie Taupin

Heart on My Sleeve w.m. Benny Gallagher, Graham Lyle

Miss You Nights w.m. Dave Townsend

Music w.m. John Miles

Rain Forest w.m. Biddu

Sam w.m. John McCabe

Save Your Kisses for Me w.m. Tony Hiller, Martin Lee, Lee Sheriden

Sweeney, The w.m. Harry South

Teeth'n' Smiles w.m. Nick Bicat, Tony Bicat

Theme from a Non-Existent TV Series m. Elton John, Bernie Taupin

We Do It w.m. Russell Stone

You Should Be Dancing w.m. Barry Gibb, Maurice Gibb, Robin Gibb

1977–1978

Angelo w.m. Tony Hiller, Lee Sheriden, Martin Lee

Boogie Nights w.m. Rod Temperton

Cavatina w.m. Stanley Myers

Don't Cry for Me Argentina w.m. Tim Rice, Andrew Lloyd-Webber

Don't Give Up on Us w.m. Tony Macaulay

The Duelists w.m. Howard Blake

Heaven on the Seventh Floor w.m. Dominique Bugatti, Frank Musker

How Deep Is Your Love w.m. Barry Gibb, Robin Gibb, Maurice Gibb

I Don't Want To Put a Hold on You   w.m. Berni Flint, Michael Flint

Love for Lydia   w.m. Harry Rabinowitz

Love Transformation   w.m. Roger Greenaway

Matchstalk Men and Matchstalk Cats and Dogs   w.m. Michael Coleman, Brian Burke

Mull of Kintyre   w.m. Paul McCartney, Denny Laine

Poldark   w.m. Kenyon Emrys-Roberts

Sam   w.m. John Farrar, Hank Marvin, Don Black

The Scarlet Buccaneer   w.m. John Addison

The Snow Goose   w.m. Ed Welch, Spike Milligan

Wings   w.m. Alexander Faris

Cavatina   w.m. Stanley Myers

He Was Beautiful   w. Cleo Laine

I Don't Like Mondays   w.m. Bob Geldof

The Logical Song   w.m. Rick Davies, Roger Hodgson

Music Machine   w.m. Leslie Hurdle, Frank Ricotti

Nunc Dimittis   m. Geoffrey Burgon

Off the Wall   w.m. Rodney Temperton

Secret Army   w.m. Robert Farnon

Shoestring   m. George Fenton

Too Much Heaven   w.m. Barry Gibb, Robin Gibb, Maurice Gibb

The Valley of Swords   m. Mike Batt

Video Killed the Radio Star   w.m. Bruce Woolley, Trevor Horn, Geoff Downes

War of the Worlds   m. Jeff Wayne

We Don't Talk Anymore   w.m. Alan Tarney

Yanks   m. Richard Rodney Bennett

1978–1979

Baker Street   w.m. Gerry Rafferty

Bright Eyes   w.m. Mike Batt

Can't Smile Without You   w.m. Chris Arnold, David Martin, Geoff Morrow

Dr. Who   m. Ron Grainer

Dreadlock Holiday   w.m. Eric Stewart, Graham Gouldman

Fawlty Towers   m. Dennis Wilson

The Floral Dance   w.m. Kate Moss

Grease   w.m. Barry Gibb

Heartsong   m. Gordon Giltrap

Hong Kong Bear   m. Richard Denton, Martin Cook

It's a Heartache   w.m. Ronnie Scott, Steve Wolfe

Lillie   m. Joseph Horovitz

The Man with the Child in His Eyes   w. Kate Bush

Matchstalk Men and Matchstalk Cats and Dogs   w.m. Michael Coleman, Brian Burke

Mull of Kintyre   w.m. Paul McCartney

Night Fever   w.m. Barry Gibb, Robin Gibb, Maurice Gibb

Railway Hotel   w. Mike Batt

Rat Trap   w.m. Bob Geldof

The Silent Witness   m. Alan Hawkshaw

Song For Guy   m. Elton John

Stayin' Alive   w.m. Barry Gibb, Robin Gibb, Maurice Gibb

The 39 Steps   m. Ed Welch

Watership Down   m. Angela Morley, Mike Batt, Malcolm Williamson

Wuthering Heights   w.m. Kate Bush

1979–1980

African Sanctus   m. David Fanshawe

Another Brick in the Wall   w.m. Roger Waters

Bright Eyes   w.m. Mike Batt

Caravans   w.m. Mike Batt

1980–1981

Another Brick in the Wall   w.m. Roger Waters

Another One Bites the Dust   w.m. John Deacon

Babooshka   w.m. Kate Bush

Don't Stand So Close to Me   w.m. Sting

Flash   m. Brian May

Fox   m. George Fenton

I Could Be So Good for You   w.m. Gerard Kenny, Pat Waterman

I'm in the Mood for Dancing   w.m. Ben Findon, Michael Myers, Robert Puzey

January, February   w.m. Alan Tarney

Juliet Bravo   m. J.S. Bach, Arr. Derek Goom

Silver Dream Machine   m. David Essex

Stop the Cavalry   w.m. Jona Lewie

Take That Look Off Your Face   w. Don Black

There's No One Quite Like Grandma   w.m. Gordon Lorenz

Together We Are Beautiful   w.m. Ken Leray

What You're Proposing   w.m. Francis Rossi, Bernard Frost

Woman in Love   w.m. Barry Gibb, Robin Gibb

Xanadu   w.m. Jeff Lynne

1981–1982

Brideshead Revisited   m. Geoffrey Burgon

Don't You Want Me   w.m. Phil Oakey, Adrian Wright, Jo Callis

Every Little Thing She Does Is Magic   w.m. Sting

Flame Trees of Thika   m. Ken Howard, Alan Blaikley

For Your Eyes Only   w.m. Bill Conti, Mike Leeson

BRITISH SONG TITLES, 1982–1986

The French Lieutenant's Woman   m. Carl Davis

In the Air Tonight   w.m. Phil Collins

The Land of Make Believe   w.m. Andy Hill, Pete Sinfield

Memory   w.m. Andrew Lloyd Webber, Trevor Nunn, T.S. Eliot

The One You Love   w.m. Graham Russell

Shillingbury Tales   m. Ed Welch

Stand and Deliver   w.m. Adam Ant, Marco Pirroni

(Just Like) Starting Over   w.m. John Lennon

Vienna   w.m. Billy Currie, Chris Cross, Warren Cann, Midge Ure

When He Shines   w.m. Florrie Palmer, Dominic Bugatti

Wired for Sound   w.m. Alan Tarney, B.A. Robertson

Without Your Love   m. Billy Nicholls

Woman   w.m. John Lennon

Woman in Love   w.m. Barry Gibb, Robin Gibb

You Drive Me Crazy   w.m. Ronnie Harwood

1982–1983

Another Brick in the Wall   w.m. Roger Waters

Come on Eileen   w.m. Kevin Rowland, Kevin Adams, James Paterson

Do You Really Want To Hurt Me   w.m. George O'Dowd, Michael Craig, John Moss, Roy Hay

Don't You Want Me   w.m. Jo Callis, Phil Oakey, Adrian Wright

The Dreaming   w. Kate Bush

Ebony and Ivory   w.m. Paul McCartney

For All Mankind   Ravi Shankar, George Fenton

Golden Brown   w.m. Jean J. Burnell, Hugh A. Cornwell, Jet Black, David Greenfield

Have You Ever Been in Love   w.m. Andy Hill, Pete Sinfield, John Danter

Heartbreaker   w.m. Barry Gibb, Robin Gibb, Maurice Gibb

I Don't Wanna Dance   w.m. Eddy Grant

Love Plus One   w.m. Nick Heyward

Now Those Days Are Gone   w.m. Andy Hill, Nichola Martin

Oh Julie   w.m. Shakin Stevens

Omnibus   m. George Fenton

Our House   w.m. Carl Smyth, C.J. Foreman

Private Investigations   w. Mark Knopfler

Smiley's People   m. Patrick Gowers

Theme From Harry's Game   Paul Brennan

Time and Tide   m. Alan Price

1983–1984

Every Breath You Take   w.m. Gordon Sumner (Sting)

Going Home   w.m. Mark Knopfler

Karma Chameleon   w.m. George O'Dowd, John Moss, Michael Craig, Roy Hay, Phil Pickett

Let's Dance   w.m. David Jones (David Bowie)

That's Livin' Alright   w.m. David Mackay, Ken Ashby

1984–1985

Against All Odds (Take a Look at Me Now)   w.m. Phil Collins

Careless Whisper   w.m. George Michael, Andrew Ridgeley

Do They Know It's Christmas?   w.m. Bob Geldof, Midge Ure

Jewel in the Crown   m. George Fenton

The Reflex   w.m. Simon Le Bon, John Taylor, Roger Taylor, Andy Taylor, Nick Rhodes

Two Tribes   w.m. Holly Johnson, Peter Gill, Mark O'Toole

We All Stand Together   w.m. Paul McCartney

1985–1986

Easy Lover   w.m. Phil Collins, Philip Bailey, Nathan East

Edge of Darkness   w.m. Eric Clapton, Michael Kamen

I Know Him So Well   w.m. Tim Rice, Bjorn Ulvaeus, Benny Andersson

Nikita   w.m. Elton John, Bernie Taupin

19   w.m. Paul Hardcastle, Mike Oldfield, Bill Couturie, Jonas McCormack

We Don't Need Another Hero   w.m. Graham Lyle, Terry Britten

VII

Lyricists and Composers

A total of 6,163 contributing lyricists and composers are listed alphabetically in this part. All song titles are listed alphabetically under their respective author(s). It is not the purpose of these listings to indicate the complete body of work of any given author. Only those songs selected for inclusion in Part V are entered here. For more complete information about a particular song, refer to Part V; all song titles in this part are listed alphabetically in Part V. Co-authorship is not indicated in this compilation and readers are advised to refer to Part V where they may confirm sole or co-authorship.

Aaronson, Irving   The Loveliest Night of the Year

Abbey, M.E.   Life's Railway to Heaven

Abernathy, Lee Roy   A Wonderful Time Up There

Abrahams, Maurice   (He'd Have To Get Under,) Get Out and Get Under (To Fix Up His Automobile); Hitchy-Koo; Oh You Million Dollar Doll; The Pullman Porters on Parade; Ragtime Cowboy Joe; Take Me to the Midnight Cake Walk Ball

Abrahams, Paul   Today I Feel So Happy

Abrams, Lester   Minute by Minute

Abreu, Zequinha   Tico Tico

Acquaviva, Nick   In the Middle of an Island; My Love, My Love

Adair, Thomas M.   Everything Happens to Me; In the Blue of Evening; Let's Get Away from It All; The Night We Called It a Day; There's No You

Adam, Adolphe   Christmas Song, or, O Holy Night

Adams, A. Emmett   The Bells of St. Mary's

Adams, Bryan   Heaven; Run To You; Summer of '69

Adams, Charles   Good Luck, Good Health, God Bless You

Adams, Clifford   Joanna

Adams, Frank R.   Blow the Smoke Away; Honeymoon; I Wonder Who's Kissing Her Now; When You First Kissed the Last Girl You Loved

Adams, Kevin   Come On Eileen

Adams, Kurt   A Fool Was I; Somewhere Along the Way

Adams, Lee   Applause; Kids; (I've Got) A Lot of Livin' To Do; Older and Wiser; Once Upon a Time; One Boy; Put On a Happy Face; Rosie; The Telephone Hour; Those Were the Days, or, Theme from *All in the Family;* You've Got Possibilities

Adams, Ray   Dance On; In Summer

Adams, Ritchie   Tossin' and Turnin'

Adams (Flower), Sarah   Nearer, My God, to Thee

Adams, Stanley   La Cucaracha; Little Old Lady; My Shawl; (Theme from) Spellbound; There Are Such Things; What a Diff'rence a Day Made (Makes)

Adams, Stephen (Michael Maybrick)   The Blue Alsation Mountains; The Holy City; The Midshipmite; Nancy Lee; A Warrior Bold

Adamson, Harold   An Affair To Remember; Around the World (in Eighty Days); As the Girls Go; Aurora; Bim Bam Boom; Candlelight and Wine; Comin' In on a Wing and a Prayer; Daybreak; Did I Remember; Dig You Later (A Hubba-Hubba-Hubba); Everything I Have Is Yours; Ferryboat Serenade; Here Comes Heaven Again; How Blue the Night; I Couldn't Sleep a Wink Last Night; I Don't Care Who Knows It; I Got Lucky in the Rain; I Hit a New High; I Love Lucy; I Wish I (We) Didn't Have To Say Good Night; It's a Most Unusual Day; It's Been So Long; (This Is) A Lovely Way To Spend an Evening; Manhattan Serenade; Moonlight Mood; The Music Stopped; My Own; My Resistance Is Low; Oh Me, Oh My, Oh You; Time on My Hands; Tonight Or Never; Tony's Wife; Too Young To Go Steady; We're Having a Baby; Where Are You; The Woodpecker(s') Song; You (Gee But You're Wonderful); You Say the Nicest Things, Baby; You're a Sweetheart

Addinsell, Richard   I'm Going To See You Today; Waltz Theme; (Theme From The) Warsaw Concerto; The WRNS March

Addison, John   The Scarlet Buccaneer

Addison, Joseph   The Spacious Firmament on High

Addrisi, Donald J.   Never My Love

Addrisi, Richard P.   Never My Love

Addy, Mickey J.   There Is No Christmas Like a Home Christmas

Ader, Hawley   La Cucaracha

Adkinson, Gene   It's Almost Tomorrow

Adlam, Basil G.   The House Is Haunted; Travelin' Band

Adler, Bernie   That Lovin' Rag

Adler, Lou   Poor Side of Town

Adler, Richard   Everybody Loves a Lover; (You've Got To Have) Heart; Hernando's Hideaway; Hey There; I'll Never Be Jealous Again; I'm Not at All in Love; A Little Brains—A Little Talent; (When You're) Racing with the Clock; Rags to Riches; 7 1/2 Cents; Shoeless Joe from Hannibal, Mo.; Steam Heat; Two Lost Souls; Whatever Lola Wants

Ager, Milton   Ain't She Sweet; Are You Sorry; Auf Wiedersehn, My Dear; Bagdad; A Bench in the Park; Crazy Words (Crazy Tune) (Vo-Do-De-O-Do); Everything Is Peaches Down in Georgia; Forgive Me; Glad Rag Doll; Happy Days Are Here Again; Happy Feet; Hard-Hearted Hannah (the Vamp of Savannah); I Wonder What's Become of Sally; I'm Nobody's Baby; I'm the Last of the Red-Hot Mamas; Louisville Lou, the Vampin' Lady; Lovin' Sam, the Sheik of Alabam'; Mama Goes Where Papa Goes; Old Mill Wheel; She Don't Wanna; Song of the Dawn; Trust In Me; Who Cares; You Can't Pull the Wool over My Eyes; A Young Man's Fancy

Agius, Alfred   One Thing Leads to Another

Ahbez, Eden   Nature Boy

Ahlert, Fred E.   The Free and Easy Hour of Parting; I Don't Know Why (I Just Do); I Gave You Up Just Before You Threw Me Down; I'd Love To Fall Asleep and Wake Up in My Mammy's Arms; I'll Follow You; I'll Get By (as Long as I Have You); I'm Gonna Sit Right Down and Write Myself a Letter; In Shadowland; Life Is a Song, Let's Sing It Together; Lovely; Mean to Me; The Moon Was Yellow; Put Away a Little Ray of Golden Sunshine; Sing an Old-Fashioned Song (to a Young Sophisticated Lady); Take My Heart; There's a Cradle in Caroline; To a Sweet Pretty Thing; Walkin' My Baby Back Home; Where the Blue of the Night Meets the Gold of the Day; Why Dance; You Dropped Me Like a Red Hot Penny; You Oughta See My Baby

Ainslie, Hew   The Ingle Side

Akkerman, Jan   Hocus Pocus

Akst, Harry   Am I Blue; Anema e Core (with All My Heart and Soul); Baby Face; Birmingham Bertha; Dearest, You're the Nearest to My Heart; Dinah; The Egg and I; Everything's Gonna Be All Right; First, Last and Always; Guilty; Home Again Blues; I've Lost All My Love for You; May I Sing to You; Revenge; A Smile Will Go a Long, Long Way; Stand Up and Cheer; Stella

Albéniz, Isaac M.F.   España (Tango)

Albert, Morris   Feelings

Alberte, Charles S.   Down Where the Swanee River Flows

Alberts, Al   Tell Me Why

Albrecht, Elmer   Elmer's Tune

Albritton, Dub   I'm Sorry

Alden, John   La Veeda

Alden, Joseph R.   Sleepy Time Gal

Aldrich, Ronnie   If I Only Had Wings

Aldridge, Ava   Sharing the Night Together

Aldridge, James Walton Jr.   (There's) No Gettin' Over Me

Alexander, Archie   Lonely Pup (in a Christmas Shop)

Alexander, Fitzroy (Lord Melody)   Mama, Look a Booboo

Alexander (Humphreys), Mrs. Cecil Frances   There Is a Green Hill Far Away

Alford, Kenneth J. (Major F.J. Ricketts)   Colonel Bogey (Bogie) March

Alfred, Roy   A Fool Was I; Huckle-Buck; Promise Her Anything But Give Her Love

Allan, Gene   Mister Lonely

Allan, Lewis   The House I Live In

Allen, Andrew   Sally, You Brought the Sunshine to Our Alley

Allen, Deborah   Baby I Lied; Can I See You Tonight; Don't Worry 'Bout Me Baby

Allen, Elizabeth   Rock Me to Sleep, Mother (as Florence Percy)

Allen, George N.   Oh, Bury Me Not on the Lone Prairie, or, The Dying Cowboy

Allen, Janna   Did It in a Minute; Kiss on My List; Method of Modern Love; Private Eyes

Allen, Lester   Kiss of Fire

Allen, Lewis   Strange Fruit

Allen, Michele   Take Me Home

Allen, Peter   Arthur's Theme (Best That You Can Do); I Honestly Love You; I'd Rather Leave While I'm in Love

Allen, R.I.   Son of a Travelin' Man

Allen, Robert   Chances Are; Come to Me; Enchanted Island; Everybody Loves a Lover; Happy Anniversary; (There's No Place Like) Home for the Holidays; If Dreams Come True; It's Not for Me To Say; Moments To Remember; My One and Only Heart; No, Not Much; Song for a Summer Night; To Know You (Is To Love You); A Very Special Love; Who Needs You; You Alone, or, Solo Tu

Allen, Sara   Did It in a Minute; I Can't Go for That (No Can Do); Maneater; Possession Obsession; Private Eyes; You Make My Dreams

Allen, Shorty   Rock and Roll Waltz

Allen, Steve   On the Beach; (Theme from) Picnic; South Rampart Street Parade; This Could Be the Start of Something (Big)

Allen, Sylvester   The Cisco Kid; Gypsy Man; Summer; Why Can't We Be Friends

Allen, Thomas S.   By the Watermelon Vine, Lindy Lou; (Fifteen Miles (Years) on the) Erie Canal (Low Bridge!—Everybody Down)

Allen, Thornton W.   On the Banks of the Old Raritan; A Utah Man Am I; Washington and Lee Swing

Alleyn, Leslie   Hi Tiddley Hi Ti Island

Allison, Andrew K.   Down on the Farm in Harvest Time

Allison, Audrey   He'll (We'll) Have To Go; Teenage Crush

Allison, Bob   Are You Sure

Allison, Jerry   Peggy Sue; More Than I Can Say

Allison, Joe   He'll (We'll) Have to Go; Teenage Crush

Allison, John   Are You Sure

Allitsen, Frances   The Lord Is My Light

Alpert, Herb   Jerusalem

Alpert, Randy W.   Rise

Alquist, Russell   A Little Lovin'

Alstone, Alex   More; Pianissimo; Sonata; Symphony

Alter, Louis   Do You Know What It Means To Miss New Orleans; Dolores; Hugs and Kisses; Isn't Love the Grandest Thing; Manhattan Serenade; A Melody from the Sky; My Kinda Love; Nina Never Knew; Overnight; Rainbow on the River; The Sky Fell Down; Twilight on the Trail; You Turned the Tables on Me

Altman, Arthur   All or Nothing at All; American Beauty Rose; Green Years; I Will Follow Him; Play, Fiddle, Play

Altman, Michael   (Song from) M*A*S*H

Alvarez, F.M.   The Farewell

Amsterdam, Morey   Rum and Coca-Cola; (Oh Why, Oh Why Did I Ever Leave) Wyoming

Ancliffe, Charles   Nights of Gladness

Andersen, Hans Christian   Ich Liebe Dich (I Love Thee)

Anderson, A.   Somewhere in France with You

Anderson, Adrienne   Deja Vu

Anderson, Bill   Eight By Ten; Happiness; River Boat

Anderson, Deacon   Rag Mop

Anderson, Edmund   Flamingo

Anderson, Gary   Quarter to Three Waltz

Anderson, Harry   Beer, Beer, Glorious Beer

Anderson, John Murray   Owner of Lonely Heart; Sixty Seconds Every Minute, I Think of You; A Young Man's Fancy

Anderson, Leroy   Belle of the Ball; Blue Tango; Fiddle Faddle; Plink, Plank, Plunk; Serenata; Sleigh Ride; The Syncopated Clock; The Typewriter; The Waltzing Cat

Anderson, Maxwell   Cry, the Beloved Country; It Never Was You; The Little Grey House; Lost in the Stars; September Song

Anderson, R. Alex   Cockeyed Mayor of Kaunakakai

Anderson, Stig   Dancing Queen; I Do, I Do, I Do, I Do, I Do; SOS

Anderson, Will R.   Good Night Dear; Tessie, You Are the Only, Only, Only

Andersson, Benny   Dancing Queen; I Do, I Do, I Do, I Do, I Do; I Know Him So Well; SOS; When All Is Said and Done

Andre, Fabian   Dream a Little Dream of Me

Andrews, Chris   First Time; Girl Don't Come; I'll Stop at Nothing; Long Live Love; Message Understood; To Whom It Concerns; We Are in Love; Yesterday Man

Andrews, Reggie   Let It Whip

Angelo, H.   Folks That Put On Airs

Angulo, Hector   Guantanamera

Anka, Paul   Diana; I Believe There's Nothing Stronger Than Our Love; I Don't Like To Sleep Alone; Johnny's Theme, or, Here's Johnny; (I'm Just a) Lonely Boy; My Way; Puppy Love; Put Your Head on My Shoulder; She's a Lady; The Times of Your Life

Ant, Adam   Stand and Deliver

Anthony, Mark   Forget Him; Look for a Star; Messing About on the River; Tell All the World

Anthony, Mike   Jump; Poetry in Motion; Why Can't This Be Love

Anthony, Ray   Bunny Hop

Apolinar, Danny   Do Your Own Thing; When You're Young and in Love

Appell, Dave   Bristol Stomp; The Cha Cha Cha; Let's Twist Again; Loddy Lo; Mornin' Beautiful; South Street; Swingin' School; The Wah-Watusi; Wild One

Applebaum, Stan   Pan Am Makes the Goin' Great; Viceroy Gives You All the Taste All the Time

Appollon, Dave   Goodbye Hawaii

Archer, Harry   I Love You (Je t' Aime); Suppose I Had Never Met You

Arden, Rodd   Me and the Old Folks at Home; Old Ship of Mine; When You Lose the One You Love

Arditi, Luigi   Il Bacio, or, The Kiss Waltz; Se Saran Rose, or, Melba Waltz

Argent, Rod   She's Not There

Arias, Clotilde   Rum and Coca-Cola

Arkell, Reginald   Why Is the Bacon So Tough

Arkin, Alan   The Banana Boat Song (Day-O)

Arkin, David   Black and White

Arlen, Harold   Ac-cent-tchu-ate the Positive; Ain't It the Truth; Any Place I Hang My Hat Is Home; As Long As I Live; Between the Devil and the Deep Blue Sea; Blues in the Night; Cabin in the Cotton; Can I Leave Off Wearin' My Shoes; Cocoanut Sweet; Come Rain or Come Shine; Ding Dong! The Witch Is Dead; Down with Love; Evelina; For Every Man There's a Woman; Fun To Be Fooled; Get Happy; (This Is) God's Country; Happiness Is (Just) a Thing Called Joe; Happy as the Day Is Long; Here Come the Waves; Hit the Road to Dreamland; Hitting the Bottle; Hooray for Love; House of Flowers; I Could Go On Singing (Till the Cows Come Home); I Don't Think I'll End It All Today; I Forgive You; I Got a Song; I Gotta (I've Got a) Right To Sing the Blues; I Love a Parade; I Never Has Seen Snow; I Wonder What Became of Me; If I Only Had a Brain; Ill Wind (You're Blowin' Me No Good); It Was Written in the Stars; It's a New World; It's Only a Paper Moon; I've Got the World on a String; June Comes Around Every Year; Kickin' the Gong Around; Last Night When We Were Young; Legalize My Name; Let's Fall in Love; Let's Take a Walk Around the Block; Let's Take the Long Way Home; Little Biscuit; Little Drops of Rain; Lydia the Tattooed Lady; The Man That Got Away; The March of Time; Moanin' in the Mornin'; Music Music Everywhere (But Not a Song in My Heart); My Shining Hour; Napoleon's a Pastry; One for My Baby (and One More for the Road); Out of This World; Over the Rainbow; Push De Button; Ridin' on the Moon; Right as the Rain; Savanna; Shake It Off; A Sleepin' Bee; Smellin' of Vanilla (Bamboo Case); Stormy Weather; Sweet and Hot; Take It Slow, Joe; That Old Black Magic; This Time the Dream's on Me; T'morra, T'morra; (I Had Myself a) True Love; Two Ladies in de Shade of de Banana Tree; We're Off To See the

Wizard; What Good Does It Do; What's Good About Good-bye; When the Sun Comes Out; You're a Builder Upper

Armand, Renee   What She Wants

Armer, Andy   Rise

Armstrong, Harry   I Love My Wife, But Oh You Kid; Nellie Dean; What's the Use of Loving If You Can't Love All the Time

Armstrong, Henry W.   (You're the Flower of My Heart) Sweet Adeline

Armstrong, Louis   Brother Bill; Ol' Man Mose; Struttin' with Some Barbecue; Wild Man Blues

Arndt, Felix   Nola

Arne, Michael   The Lass with the Delicate Air, or, Young Molly Who Lives at the Foot of the Hill

Arne, Thomas   Rule, Britannia

Arnheim, Gus   I Cried for You (Now It's Your Turn To Cry over Me); It Must Be True (You Are Mine, All Mine); Mandalay; Sweet and Lovely

Arnold, Chris   In Thoughts of You

Arnold, Eddy   That's How Much I Love You; You Don't Know Me

Arnold, Malcolm   Inn of the Sixth Happiness; The River Kwai March; This Old Man, or, The Children's Marching Song (Nick, Nack, Paddy Whack)

Arnold, Samuel James   The Death of Nelson; To Anacreon in Heaven; The Wayworn Traveller

Arodin, Sidney   (Up a) Lazy River

Arthur, Stanley   Question and Answer (Démande et Réponse)

Arthurs, George   Josh-Ua; A Little of What You Fancy

Arzonia, Joe   The Preacher and the Bear (as Arthur Longbrake)

Asaf, George   Pack Up Your Trouble in Your Old Kit Bag and Smile, Smile, Smile

Asche, Oscar   Any Time Is Kissing Time; The Chinaman's Song; The Cobbler's Song; The Robbers' Chorus; The Robbers' March

Ascher, Joseph   Alice, Where Art Thou

Ascher, Robert   Tracy's Theme

Ash, Frances   I'm Gonna Love That Guy (Like He's Never Been Loved Before)

Ashby, Ken   That's Livin' Alright

Asher, Kenneth Lee   You and Me Against the World

Asherman, Eddie   All That Glitters Is Not Gold

Ashford (Hindle), Emma L.   My Task

Ashford, Nickolas   Ain't No Mountain High Enough; In Every Woman; Solid

Ashman, Howard   Little Shop of Horrors; Somewhere That's Green; Suddenly Seymour

Astaire, Fred   Blue Without You; I'm Building Up to an Awful Let-Down

Astore, L.   Botch-A-Me

Atchinson, Reverend J.B.   Fully Persuaded

Atchley, Samuel Lee   Coca Cola Cowboy (Theme from *Every Which Way But Loose*)

Atherton, John P.   Brylcreem, A Little Dab'll Do Ya

Atkins, Boyd   Heebie Jeebies

Atteridge, Harold R.   Bagdad; By the Beautiful Sea; Fascination

Atwell, Roy   Some Little Bug Is Going To Find You (Some Day)

Atwell, Winifred   Britannia Rag

Audinot, Rafael   Rumba Rhapsody

Audran, Edmond   The Torpedo and the Whale

August, Roy   Fancy Free

Auletti, Leonard   Bunny Hop

Auric, Georges   The Song from Moulin Rouge, or, Where Is Your Heart

Austin, Billy   Is You Is or Is You Ain't My Baby

Austin, Bobby   Try a Little Kindness

Austin, Fred   I'm Going Back to Himazas

Austin, Gene   How Come You Do Me Like You Do; (Look Down That) Lonesome Road; When My Sugar Walks down the Street, All the Birdies Go Tweet-Tweet-Tweet

Austin, Ray   I Look at Heaven; Tonight We Love

Austin, Thomas   Short Shorts

Authors, Christine   Devil Woman

Autry, Gene   Back in the Saddle Again; Be Honest with Me; Here Comes Santa Claus; That Silver-Haired Daddy of Mine; Tweedle-O-Twill; You're the Only Star in My Blue Heaven

Aveling, Claude   Come Back to Sorrento

Averre, Berton   My Sharona

Avril, Charles   Where the Silv'ry Colorado Wends Its Way

Axton, Hoyt   Joy to the World; No No Song

Axton, Mae Boren   Heartbreak Hotel

Ayer, Nat D.   Another Little Drink Wouldn't Do Us Any Harm; First Love, Last Love, Best Love; If You Talk in Your Sleep, Don't Mention My Name; If You Were the Only Girl in the World; Let the Great Big World Keep Turning; Moving Day in Jungle Town; Oh You Beautiful Doll; Oh You Cutie (You Ever Loving Child); Shufflin' Along; You're My Baby

Aylward, Florence   Beloved, It Is Morn

Azevedo, Waldyr   Delicado

Aznavour, Charles   Yesterday When I Was Young

Bach, Johann Sebastian   Air for the G String; Juliet Bravo

Bacharach, Burt F.   Alfie; Anyone Who Had a Heart; April Fools; Are You There (with Another Girl); Arthur's Theme (Best That You Can Do); Blue on Blue; (Theme from) Casino Royale; (They Long To Be) Close to You; Do You Know the Way to San Jose; A Fact Can Be a Beautiful Thing; Heartlight; A House Is Not a Home; I Say a Little Prayer; I'll Never Fall in Love Again; Knowing When To Leave; The Look of Love; Magic Moments; Make It Easy on Yourself; Making Love; The Man Who Shot Liberty Valance; Message to Michael; Odds and Ends (of a Beautiful Love Affair); One

Less Bell To Answer; Only Love Can Break a Heart; Paper Maché; Promises Promises; Raindrops Keep Fallin' on My Head; Reach Out for Me; Story of My Life; That's What Friends Are For; There's Always Something There To Remind Me; This Guy's in Love with You; Trains and Boats and Planes; Walk On By; What the World Needs Now Is Love; What's New Pussycat; Whoever You Are, or, Sometimes Your Eyes Look Blue to Me; Windows of the World; Wishin' and Hopin'; (Theme from) Wives and Lovers; You'll Never Get to Heaven

Bachman, Randy   You Ain't Seen Nothing Yet

Backer, Bill   I'd Like To Teach the World To Sing; If You've Got the Time, We've Got the Beer; It's the Real Thing. Coke.; Things Go Better with Coke

Badarczewska, Thecla   A Maiden's Prayer

Badarou, Wally   Something About You

Baer, Abel   Don't Wait 'Til the Night Before Christmas; Don't Wake Me Up, Let Me Dream; Harriet; Hello, Aloha! How Are You?; High upon a Hill Top; I Miss My Swiss, My Swiss Miss Misses Me; I'm Sitting Pretty in a Pretty Little City; June Night (Just Give Me a June Night, the Moonlight and You); Let Me Linger Longer in Your Arms; Lonesome in the Moonlight; Mamma Loves Papa—Papa Loves Mamma; My Mother's Eyes; There Are Such Things

Baer, Barbara   Sweet Talkin' Guy

Bagdasarian, Ross   Alvin's Harmonica; The Chipmunk Song, or, Christmas Don't Be Late; Come On-A-My House; Witch Doctor

Bagley, E.E.   National Emblem (March)

Baguley, Leslie   Come Home to My Arms; Give Her My Love; Nice To Know You Care

Bahler, Tom   She's Out of My Life

Bailey, Gus   The Old Grey Mare (She Ain't What She Used To Be)

Bailey, Philip   Easy Lover; Shining Star

Baily, Tom   Hold Me Now; King for a Day; Lay Your Hands on Me

Bain, Jock   Rock Bottom

Baker, Anita   Sweet Love

Baker, Benjamin A.   The Folks Are All Waiting To See the Fast Steamer

Baker, Don   Bless You (for Being an Angel)

Baker, Evelyn   Cigarette

Baker, Jack   I Hear a Rhapsody

Baker, John C.   My Trundle Bed, or, Recollections of Childhood

Baker, Mickey   Love Is Strange

Baker, Phil   A Hundred Years from Now; Invitation to a Broken Heart; Strange Interlude

Baker, Theodore   Lo, How a Rose E'er Blooming

Baker, Yvonne   Let Me In

Baldridge, Fanny   Let's Dance

Balfe, Michael William   The Arrow and the Song; Come into the Garden, Maud; Excelsior; The Heart Bow'd Down; I Dreamt I Dwelt in Marble Halls; Killarney; The Light of Other Days; Then You'll Remember Me

Balin, Marty   Miracles

Ball, Alexander   When Stars Are in the Quiet Skies

Ball, Ernest R.   After the Roses Have Faded Away; All for (the) Love of You; All the World Will Be Jealous of Me; As Long as the World Rolls On; Dear Little Boy of Mine; Down the Winding Road of Dreams; Goodbye, Good Luck, God Bless You; I'll Forget You; In the Garden of My Heart; Ireland Is Ireland to Me; Isle o' Dreams; Let the Rest of the World Go By; A Little Bit of Heaven, Sure They Call It Ireland; Love Me and the World Is Mine; Mother Machree; My Heart Has Learned To Love You, Now Do Not Say Goodbye; My Sunshine Jane; Out There in the Sunshine with You; She's the Daughter of Mother Machree; Ten Thousand Years from Now; Till the Sands of the Desert Grow Cold; To Have, To Hold, To Love; Turn Back the Universe and Give Me Yesterday; West of the Great Divide; When Irish Eyes Are Smiling; When Sweet Marie Was Sweet Sixteen; When the Birds in Georgia Sing of Tennessee; Will You Love Me in December as You Do in May; You Planted a Rose in the Garden of Love

Ball, Kenny   Midnight in Moscow, or, Moscow Nights

Ball, Roger   Pick Up the Pieces

Ball, William   The Merry Swiss Boy

Ballard, Clint Jr.   Good Timin'; One of Us Will Weep Tonight; You're No Good

Ballard, Glenn   All I Need

Ballard, Hank   The Twist

Ballard, Pat   Mister Sandman; Oh Baby Mine (I Get So Lonely); So Beats My Heart for You

Ballard, Russ   You Can Do Magic

Bandini, Al   A Girl! A Girl!, or, Zoom Ba Di Alli Nella

Banks, Homer   (If Loving You Is Wrong) I Don't Want To Be Right; If You're Ready (Come Go with Me)

Banks, Marian   Malagueña

Banks, Tony   Invisible Touch; That's All

Baptiste, P.   Sea of Love

Barbier, Jules   Soldier's Chorus

Barbosa, Chris   Let the Music Play

Barbour, Dave   I Don't Know Enough About You; It's a Good Day; Mañana (Is Soon Enough for Me)

Barcelata, Lorenzo   Maria Elena

Barclay, B.S.   Come, Oh Come with Me, the Moon Is Beaming

Barclay, L.   Our Lodger's Such a Nice Young Man

Barczi, Tibor   Love—What Are You Doing to My Heart

Barefoot, Nathan Carl, Jr.   Danger, Heartbreak Ahead

Barer, Marshall   Man to Man Talk; Very Soft Shoes

Barge, Gene   Quarter to Three Waltz

Bargoni, Camillo   Autumn Concerto; My Heart Reminds Me, or, And That Reminds Me

Baring-Gould, Sabine   Now the Day Is Over; Onward, Christian Soldiers

Barish, Jesse Count on Me Love; Hearts

Barkan, Mark Pretty Flamingo; She's a Fool

Barker, Theodore T. Crucifix; 'Tis Not True

Barlow, Harold I Found You in the Rain; The Things I Love

Barnard (Lindsay), Lady Anne Auld Robin Gray, or, When the Sheep Are in the Fold

Barnby, Joseph Carmen Etonense; Now the Day Is Over; Sweet and Low

Barnes, Billy (Have I Stayed) Too Long at the Fair

Barnes, F.J. I've Got Rings on My Fingers, or, Mumbo Jumbo Jijjiboo J. O'Shea; When Father Papered the Parlour

Barnes, Howard A Blossom Fell; Chewing a Piece of Straw; The Echo Told Me a Lie; A Load of Hay; Lonely Footsteps; My Love and Devotion; Number Something Far Away Lane

Barnes, Jessie Many Times

Barnes, Max Red Neckin' Love Makin' Night

Barnes, Paul Goodbye Dolly Gray

Barnet, Charlie Skyliner

Barnet, R.A. Westward Ho!—The Covered Wagon March

Barnett, Brenda The Clown

Barnett, John Rose of Lucerne, or, The Swiss Toy Girl

Barnett, Lester I Used To Sigh for the Silvery Moon

Barney, James A. Little Footsteps

Baron, Paul Rum and Coca-Cola

Barouch, Pierre A Man and a Woman

Barrett, Lester By the Sad Sea Waves

Barrett, Syd See Emily Play

Barrett, Thomas A., *see* **Leslie Stuart**

Barrett, Vinnie Love Won't Let Me Wait

Barri, Steve The Eve of Destruction

Barrie, Royden Bird Songs at Eventide; A Brown Bird Singing

Barris, Harry At Your Command; I Surrender Dear; It Must Be True (You Are Mine, All Mine); It Was So Beautiful (and You Were Mine); Lies; Little Dutch Mill; Mississippi Mud; Wrap Your Troubles in Dreams (and Dream Your Troubles Away)

Barron, Bob Cindy Oh Cindy

Barron, Francis J. Lighterman Tom; The Trumpeter

Barron, Malcolm Another Spring

Barroso, Ary Baia (No Baixa Do Sapateiro); Brazil

Barrow, P.J. Rose in the Bud

Barrows, Walt Little White Duck

Barry, Jeff Be My Baby; Chapel of Love; Da Doo Ron Ron (When He Walked Me Home); Do Wah Diddy Diddy; Hanky Panky; I Honestly Love You; The Leader of the Pack; Sugar Sugar; Tell Laura I Love Her; Then He Kissed Me

Barry, John All Time High; Billy; Born Free; Diamonds Are Forever; (Theme from) Goldfinger; Hit and Miss; Made You; Midnight Cowboy; Mister Kiss Kiss Bang Bang; (Theme from) Out of Africa; (Theme from) The Persuaders; A View To a Kill; (Theme from) You Only Live Twice

Bart, Lionel As Long as He Needs Me; Be Back Soon; Consider Yourself; The Day After Tomorrow; Do You Mind; Easy Going Me; Food Glorious Food; From Russia with Love; A Handful of Songs; I'd Do Anything; The Little White Bull; Living Doll; Lock Up Your Daughters; Maggie May; Rock with the Cavemen; Tokyo Melody; Water, Water; Where Is Love?; Who Will Buy?; You've Got To Pick a Pocket or Two

Bartholomew, David Ain't That a Shame; Blue Monday; I Hear You Knocking; I'm in Love Again; I'm Walkin'

Bartlett, J.C. A Dream

Barton, Billy Dear John Letter

Baselli, Joss Free Again

Basie, William "Count" Jumpin' at the Woodside; M-Squad; One O'Clock Jump

Baskette, Billy Goodbye Broadway, Hello France; Hawaiian Butterfly

Bass, Ralph Dedicated to the One I Love

Bassman, George I'm Getting Sentimental over You

Bastow, George Captain Gingah; The Galloping Major

Bateman, Edgar If It Wasn't for the 'ouses in Between; It's a Great Big Shame; Liza Johnson

Bateman, Robert Mashed Potato Time; Please Mister Postman

Bates, Charles Hard Hearted Hannah (The Vamp of Savannah)

Bates, Katharine Lee America, the Beautiful

Bates, Nicholas James Union of the Snake

Bath, Hubert Cornish Rhapsody

Batt, Mike Bright Eyes; Caravans; The Valley of Swords; Wombling Song

Battle, Edgar William Topsy

Batty, Victor It's a Heartache

Bauduc, Ray Big Noise from Winnetka; South Rampart Street Parade

Baum, Bernie Music Music Music

Baxter, Les My Quiet Village

Baxter, Phil A Faded Summer Love; I'm a Ding Dong Daddy from Dumas; Piccolo Pete

Bayes, Nora Come Along My Mandy; Just Like a Gypsy; Shine On Harvest Moon

Bayha, Charles Come Out of the Kitchen, Mary Ann; Eve Cost Adam Just One Bone; Jazz Baby's Ball

Bayly, Thomas Haynes I'd Be a Butterfly; Long Long Ago, or, The Long Ago; Oh No, We Never Mention Her

Beach, Mrs. H.H.A. The Year's at the Spring

Beadell, Eily Cruising Down the River

Beal, Earl T. Get a Job

Beal, Joseph Carleton Jingle Bell Rock; Unsuspecting Heart

Beard, Frank Legs

Beaudry, R. Just a Girl That Men Forget

Beaumont, James Since I Don't Have You

Beaumont, Robin Out of Town

Beaver, Jack Picture Parade

Beavers, Jackey Some Day We'll Be Together

Becaud, Gilbert The Day the Rains Came; It Must Be Him; Let It Be Me; What Now My Love

Bechet, Sidney Petite Fleur

Beck, Carl On Wisconsin

Beck, William Fire; Love Rollercoaster

Beckett, Peter Baby Come Back; Twist of Fate

Beckett, T.A. Columbia, the Gem of the Ocean, or, The Red, White and Blue

Beckley, Gerald L. Sister Golden Hair

Bedford, Harry One of the Ruins That Cromwell Knocked About a Bit

Beecher, Gordon A Song of Old Hawaii

Beekman, Jack Mahzel

Beethoven, Ludwig van Für Elise (Albumblatt); Minuet in G; Moonlight Sonata; Sonata Pathétique

Behn, George W. Assembly

Behrend, Arthur Henry Daddy

Beiderbecke, Bix Davenport Blues; In a Mist

Bell, Archie A Japanese Sunset; Tighten Up

Bell, Kenneth Even the Nights Are Better; I Just Came Here To Dance; Touch Me When We're Dancing

Bell, Robert Earl Celebration; Cherish; Fresh; Joanna; Ladies Night; Misled

Bell, Ronald Nathan Celebration; Cherish; Fresh; Joanna; Ladies Night; Misled

Bell, Thomas Break Up To Make Up; Rubberband Man; You Make Me Feel Brand New

Bell, William Tryin' To Love Two

Bellak, J. Carnival of Venice

Bellamy, Claxson At Midnight on My Pillow Lying; Darkest the Hour; Dear Mother, in Dreams I See Her; Lullaby; A Soldier's Life; What the Dickie-Birds Say

Bellamy, David If I Said You Had a Beautiful Body (Would You Hold It Against Me); Spiders and Snakes

Belland, Bruce Big Man; Down by the Station

Belle, Barbara A Sunday Kind of Love

Bellotte, Peter Heaven Knows; Hot Stuff; I Feel Love; Love To Love You Baby

Belmonte, Jose Ecstasy Tango

Belton, John Down the Mall; Time Marches On

Benatsky, Ralph The White Horse Inn; Your Eyes

Bendix, Theodore The Mosquito's Parade

Benedict, Julius By the Sad Sea Waves

Benjamin, Arthur Jamaican Rumba

Benjamin, Bennie Can Anyone Explain? (No! No! No!); Cross over the Bridge; A Girl! A Girl!, or, Zoom Ba Di Alli Nella; How Important Can It Be; I Don't See Me in Your Eyes Anymore; I Don't Want To Set the World on Fire; I Ran All the Way Home; I Want To Thank Your Folks; I'll Never Be Free; Oh What It Seemed To Be; Rumors Are Flying; Surrender; These Things I Offer You (for a Lifetime); The Wheel of Fortune; When the Lights Go On Again (All Over the World)

Bennard, Reverend George The Old Rugged Cross

Bennett, Boyd Seventeen

Bennett, Brian Genie with the Light Brown Lamp; I Could Easily Fall; Rise and Fall of Flingle Bunt; Summer Holiday; Time Drags By

Bennett, Dave Bye Bye Blues

Bennett, George J. You Didn't Want Me When You Had Me

Bennett, Jimmy The Little White Bull

Bennett, Richard Rodney (Theme from) Murder on the Orient Express; Too Beautiful To Last; (Theme from) Yanks

Bennett, Richard Winchell Forever in Blue Jeans

Bennett, Roy C. Kewpie Doll; The Naughty Lady of Shady Lane; Travellin' Light

Benoit, George My Belgian Rose

Benson, Ada Your Feet's Too Big

Benson, Arthur C. The Land of Hope and Glory; Pomp and Circumstance

Benson, Renaldo What's Going On

Benton, Brook The Boll Weevil Song; It's Just a Matter of Time; A Rockin' Good Way (To Mess Around and Fall in Love)

Beresford, Maurice He's Dead But He Won't Lie Down; In My Little Bottom Drawer

Berg, David There's a Quaker Down in Quaker Town

Berg, Harold Freshie

Bergantine, Borney My Happiness

Berger, Dennis Have It Your Way

Bergere, Roy How Come You Do Me Like You Do

Bergman, Alan Brian's Song; It Might Be You; Just a Piece of Sky; Nice 'n' Easy; Pieces of Dreams; The Summer Knows, or, Theme from *Summer of '42;* A Terrific Band and a Real Nice Crowd; There's Enough To Go Around; The Way We Were; What Are You Doing the Rest of Your Life; The Windmills of Your Mind, or, Theme from *The Thomas Crown Affair;* Yellow Bird

Bergman, Marilyn Brian's Song; It Might Be You; Just a Piece of Sky; Pieces of Dreams; The Summer Knows, or, Theme from *Summer of '42;* A Terrific Band and a Real Nice Crowd; There's Enough To Go Around; The Way We Were; What Are You Doing the Rest of Your Life; The Windmills of Your Mind, or, Theme from *The Thomas Crown Affair*

Berkeley, Charles W. The Hand That Rocks the Cradle

Berle, Milton Sam, You Made the Pants Too Long

Berlin, Irving Abraham; After You Get What You Want, You Don't Want It; Alexander's Ragtime Band; All Alone; All By Myself; All of My Life; Always; Any Bonds Today?; Anything You Can Do; Araby; At the Devil's Ball; Be Careful It's My Heart; Because I Love You; The Best Thing for You; Better Luck Next Time; Blue Skies; Butterfingers; Call Me Up Some Rainy Afternoon; Change Partners; Cheek To Cheek; Count Your Blessings Instead of Sheep; A Couple of Song and Dance Men; A Couple of Swells; Crinoline Days; Do It Again; Doin' What Comes Natur'lly; Easter Parade; Everybody Step; Everybody's Doing It (Now); A Fella with an Umbrella; Get Thee Behind Me, Satan; The Girl on the

Magazine Cover; The Girl on the Police Gazette; The Girl That I Marry; Give Me Your Tired, Your Poor; God Bless America; Grizzly Bear; Happy Holiday; Heat Wave; He's a Devil in His Own Home Town; He's a Rag Picker; Home Again Blues; Homesick; Homework; Hostess with the Mostes' on the Ball; How About Me; How Deep Is the Ocean; How's Chances; I Got Lost in His Arms; I Got the Sun in the Morning; I Left My Heart at the Stage Door Canteen; I Like IKE; I Love a Piano; (Just One Way To Say) I Love You; I Never Had a Chance; I Poured My Heart into a Song; I Threw a Kiss in the Ocean; I Used To Be Color Blind; I Want To Go Back to Michigan—Down on the Farm; If You Don't Want My Peaches, You'd Better Stop Shaking My Tree; I'll Miss You in the Evening; I'll See You in C-U-B-A; I'm an Indian Too; I'm Getting Tired So I Can Sleep; I'm Gonna Pin My Medal on the Girl I Left Behind; I'm Playing with Fire; I'm Putting All My Eggs in One Basket; In My Harem; In the Fall We'll All Go Voting for Al; Isn't This a Lovely Day (To Be Caught in the Rain); It Only Happens When I Dance with You; I've Got a Lovely Day Today; I've Got My Captain Working for Me Now; I've Got My Love To Keep Me Warm; Just One Way To Say I Love You; Kiss Me, My Honey, Kiss Me; Lady of the Evening; Lazy; Let Me Sing and I'm Happy; Let Yourself Go; Let's Face the Music and Dance; Let's Have Another Cup of Coffee; Let's Start the New Year Right; Let's Take an Old-Fashioned Walk; Lonely Heart; Louisiana Purchase; A Man Chases a Girl; Mandy; Manhattan Madness; Marie; Marie from Sunny Italy; Marrying for Love; Maybe I Love You Too Much; Me; Me and My Melinda; My British Buddy; My Defenses Are Down; My Wife's Gone to the Country (Hurrah! Hurrah!); Next to Your Mother, Who Do You Love?; The Night Is Filled with Music; No Strings (I'm Fancy Free); Nobody Knows and Nobody Seems To Care; Not for All the Rice in China; Now It Can Be Told; Oh, How I Hate To Get Up in the Morning; Oh, That Beautiful Rag; On a Roof in Manhattan; An Orange Grove in California; The Piccolino; Play a Simple Melody; Plenty To Be Thankful For; A Pretty Girl Is Like a Melody; The Pullman Porters on Parade (as Ren G. May); Puttin' On the Ritz; Ragtime Violin; Reaching for the Moon; Remember; Russian Lullaby; Sadie Salome, Go Home; Say It Isn't So; Say It with Music; Sayonara; Shaking the Blues Away; Slumming on Park Avenue; Snook(e)y Ookums; So Help Me; Soft Lights and Sweet Music; Some Sunny Day; Somebody's Coming to My House; Something To Dance About; The Song Is Ended But the Melody Lingers On; Steppin' Out with My Baby; Take a Little Tip from Father; Tell Me Little Gypsy; That Beautiful Rag; That International Rag; That Mesmerizing Mendelssohn Tune; That Mysterious Rag; There's No Business Like Show Business; They Say It's Wonderful; They Were All Out of Step But Jim; This Is the Army Mister Jones; This Is the Life; This Year's Kisses; To Be Forgotten; Tomorrow Is a Lovely Day; Top Hat, White Tie and Tails; Unlucky in Love; Wait Until Your Daddy Comes Home; We Saw the Sea; What Does It Matter; What'll I Do; When I Leave the World Behind; When I Lost You; When It's Night Time in Dixie Land; When the Black Sheep Returns to the Fold; When the Midnight Choo-Choo Leaves for Alabam'; When You Walked Out Someone Else Walked Right In; Where Is the (That) Song of Songs for Me; White Christmas; Who Do You Love, I Hope; Whose Little Heart Are You Breaking Now; With

My Head in the Clouds; Woodman, Woodman, Spare That Tree; Yiddle on Your Fiddle, or, Play Some Ragtime; You Cannot Make Your Shimmy Shake on Tea; You Can't Get a Man with a Gun; You Keep Coming Back Like a Song; You'd Be Surprised; You're Just in Love; You're Lonely and I'm Lonely; You've Got Your Mother's Big Blue Eyes

Bernard, Andrew Judy in Disguise (with Glasses)

Bernard, Felix Dardanella; Winter Wonderland

Bernard, Paul Ave Maria

Bernfield, Derek Pickin' a Chicken

Bernie, Ben Strange Interlude; Who's You Little Who-Zis

Bernier, Buddy The Night Has a Thousand Eyes; Our Love; Poinciana

Bernstein, Alan After the Lovin'

Bernstein, Elmer Baby the Rain Must Fall; Love with the Proper Stranger; (Theme from) The Magnificent Seven; Step to the Rear; True Grit; Walk on the Wild Side

Bernstein, Leonard America; A Boy Like That; Cool; Gee, Officer Krupke!; Glitter and Be Gay; I Feel Pretty; It's Love; Jet Song; Lucky To Be Me; Maria; New York, New York; Ohio; One Hand, One Heart; A Quiet Girl; Some Other Time; Something's Coming; Somewhere; Tonight; Ya Got Me

Bernstein, Roger Symphony

Berrios, Pedro My Shawl

Berry, Charles Edward "Chuck" Maybellene; Memphis; Rock and Roll Music; Roll Over Beethoven; School Day (Ring! Ring! Goes the Bell); Surfin' U.S.A.; Sweet Little Sixteen

Berry, Jan Surf City

Berry, John Pony Time

Berry, Leon Christopher Columbus

Berry, Richard Louie Louie

Berryhill, Robert Wipe Out

Berwick, Earl The Policeman's Holiday

Besly, Maurice The Second Minuet

Besoyan, Rick Little Mary Sunshine

Best, Pat I Understand Just How You Feel

Best, William (I Love You) For Sentimental Reasons

Bestor, Don Contented; Down by the Winegar Woiks

Betti, Henri C'est Si Bon

Bettis, John Crazy for You; Heart of the Night; Human Nature; Only Yesterday; Slow Hand; Top of the World; Yesterday Once More

Betts, Dicky Ramblin' Man

Beveridge, Johnny A Picture of You

Bias, Gary Sweet Love

Bibo, Irving Am I Wasting My Time on (over) You

Bicat, Nick Teeth 'n' Smiles

Bicat, Tony Teeth 'n' Smiles

Bicknell, G. You Nuaghty, Naughty Men

Bierman, Arthur Midnight Masquerade

Bierman, Bernard Midnight Masquerade

Bigard, Albany Mood Indigo

Bigazzi, Giancarlo   Gloria; Self Control; Something Is Happening

Bigelow, Bob   Hard Hearted Hannah (the Vamp of Savannah)

Bigelow, F.E.   Our Director (March)

Bilk, Acker   Lonely; Stranger on the Shore; Summer Set

Billings, William   Chester (Let Tyrants Shake Their Iron Rod)

Bindi, Umberto   You're My World

Binge, Ronald   Elizabethan Serenade

Bingham, G. Clifton   Love's Old Sweet Song

Bingham, J.B. Jr.   Do What You Wanna Do

Binnick, Bernard   Keem-O-Sabe

Birch, Harry   Reuben and Rachel, or, Reuben, Reuben, I've Been Thinking

Bishop, Elvin   Fooled Around and Fell in Love

Bishop, Joe   Blue Prelude

Bishop, Sir Henry Rowley   Bid Me Discourse; (When the) Bloom Is on the Rye, or, My Pretty Jane; The Dashing White Sergeant; Home Sweet Home; Lo! Here the Gentle Lark; Love Has Eyes; My Heart and Lute

Bishop, Stephen   On and On; Save It for a Rainy Day; Separate Lives (Love Theme from *White Nights*)

Bishop, Thomas Brigham   John Brown's Body

Bivens, Burke   Josephine

Bixio, C.A.   Mama; Tell Me That You Love Me Tonight

Bizet, Georges   Toreador Song

Bjorn, Frank   Alley Cat

Black, Ben   Hold Me; Moonlight and Roses (Bring Mem'ries of You)

Black, Charles F.   Blessed Are the Believers; I Know a Heartache When I See One; A Little Good News; Shadows in the Moonlight; Sounds Like Love

Black, Donald   Ben; Billy; Born Free; Capped Teeth and Caesar Salad; Diamonds Are Forever; Sam; Take That Look Off Your Face; To Sir with Love; True Grit; Unexpected Song

Black, Gene   Love Touch (Theme from *Legal Eagles*); Never

Black, James M.   When the Roll Is Called Up Yonder; When the Saints Go Marching In

Black, Jet   Golden Brown

Black, Johnny S.   Dardanella; Paper Doll; Too Many Irons in the Fire

Blackburn, Bryan   Love Is Blue

Blackburn, John   Moonlight in Vermont

Blackburn, Tom   Ballad of Davy Crockett

Blackman, Michael Bruce   Moonlight Feels Right

Blackmore, Richard   Smoke on the Water

Blackton, Jay   You Tell Me Your Dream, or, I Had a Dream, Dear

Blackwell, Charles   Come Outside

Blackwell, DeWayne   I'm Gonna Hire a Wino To Decorate Our Home; Make My Day; Mister Blue

Blackwell, Otis   All Shook Up; Don't Be Cruel; Great Balls of Fire; Handy Man; Return to Sender

Blackwell, Robert   Good Golly Miss Molly

Blackwell, Ronald   Li'l Red Riding Hood

Blackwood, Mrs. Price   The Lament of the Irish Emigrant

Blaikley, Alan   (Theme from) Flame Trees of Thika

Blaikley, Howard   Have I the Right; Hideaway; That's the Way

Blair, Hal   Please Help Me I'm Falling; Ringo

Blaisdell, Carl W.   As the Backs Go Tearing By

Blake, Charles D.   Trabling Back to Georgia

Blake, Charlotte   The Harbor of Love

Blake, Eubie   Bandana Days; Bugle Call (Rag); I'm Just Wild About Harry; Love Will Find a Way; Memories of You; Shuffle Along; You Were Meant for Me

Blake, George   Come Dance with Me; (Our Love) Don't Throw It All Away

Blake, H.B.   When the Mocking Birds Are Singing in the Wildwood

Blake, Howard   The Duelists

Blake, James W.   The Sidewalks of New York, or, East Side, West Side

Blamphin, Charles   When the Corn Is Waving, Annie Dear

Bland, James A.   Carry Me Back to Old Virginny; (Oh Dem) Golden Slippers; De Golden Wedding; In the Evening by the Moonlight; In the Morning by the Bright Light

Blane, Ralph   The Boy Next Door; Buckle Down, Winsocki; Connecticut; Ev'ry Time; Girls Were Made To Take Care of Boys; Have Yourself a Merry Little Christmas; Love; Love on a Greyhound Bus; My Dream Is Yours; An Occasional Man; One Sunday Afternoon; Pass That Peace Pipe; Shady Lady Bird; The Stanley Steamer; That's How I Love the Blues; The Trolley Song; Wish I May

Blasco, E.   The Farewell

Blau, Eric   Amsterdam; Carousel; Desperate Ones; If We Only Have Love; Madeleine; Marieke; Old Folks; Sons Of; Timid Frieda

Blaufuss, Walter   My Isle of Golden Dreams; Your Eyes Have Told Me So

Blazy, Kent   Headed for Heartache

Bleyer, Archie   Eh Cumpari; The White Rose of Athens

Bliss, Helen   I Went Out of My Way

Bliss, Paul P.   Heart Attack; It Is Well with My Soul

Blitzstein, Marc   Mack the Knife, or, Theme from The Threepenny Opera, or, Morit'at; Pirate Jenny

Bloch, Ray   In My Little Red Book

Block, Martin   Waitin' for the Train To Come In

Block, Philippe Gerard   When the World Was Young (Ah, the Apple Tree)

Blockley, John   Excelsior

Bloom, Bobby   Mony, Mony

Bloom, Marty   Does the Spearmint Lose Its Flavor on the Bedpost Overnight

Bloom, Rube   Aunt Jemima and Your Uncle Cream of Wheat; Day In—Day Out; Don't Worry 'Bout Me; Fools Rush In; Give Me the Simple Life; Maybe You'll Be There; Out in the Cold Again; Soliloquy; Song of the Bayou; Truckin'

Bloom, Vera   Jalousie (Jealousy)

Blossom, Henry M., Jr.   Ain't It Funny What a Difference Just a Few Hours Make; All for You; Because You're You; Eileen (Alanna Asthore) Every Day Is Ladies' Day with Me; I Want What I Want When I Want It; If You Were I and I Were You; In Old New York, or, The Streets of New York; The Isle of Our Dreams; Kiss Me Again, or, If I Were on the Stage; Love Is the Best of All; The Mascot of the Troop; Moonbeams; My San Domingo Maid; Neapolitan Love Song; Spooky Ookum; Tell It All Over Again; Thine Alone; Two Laughing Irish Eyes; When Shall I Again See Ireland; When You're Away; When You're Pretty

Blume, David   Turn Down Day

Blume, F.   Kafoozelum

Bluth, Fred   Lean On Me

Bobyn, Alfred G.   Ain't It Funny What a Difference Just a Few Hours Make

Bock, Jerry   Anatevka; Artificial Flowers; Dear Friend; Do You Love Me; Home Again; I Love a Cop; If I Were a Rich Man; Jacques D'Iraq (Jock D'Rock); (In My) Little Tin Box; Matchmaker, Matchmaker; Mister Wonderful; Politics and Poker; Sabbath Prayer; She Loves Me; Sunrise Sunset; Till Tomorrow; To Life, or, L'Chaim; Too Close for Comfort; Tradition; When Did I Fall in Love; Will He Like Me; Without You I'm Nothing

Bodansky, Robert   Pierette and Pierrot

Boelitz, Martin   Maria Wiegenlied

Bohannon, Marion T.   The Big Bass Viol; When Big Profundo Sang Low "C"

Bohm, Karl   Still As the Night

Boissonade, M.   Maxina

Bolan, Marc   Hot Love; Solid Gold Easy Action

Boland, Clay   Gypsy in My Soul; Stop Beating 'Round the Mulberry Bush

Bollaert, A.   K-K-K-Katy

Bolland, Ferdinand   Rock Me Amadeus

Bolland, Robert   Rock Me Amadeus

Bolling, Claude Jean H.   (Theme from) Borsalino

Bolotin, Jay   (It's Hard To) Go Down Easy

Bolton, Guy   Till ('Til) the Clouds Roll By

Bonar, Horatius   What a Friend We Have in Jesus

Bond, Johnny   Cimarron (Roll On)

Bond, Mary   For the First Time (Come Prima)

Bonfa, Luiz   A Day in the Life of a Fool

Bonham, John   Whole Lotta Love

Bonine, Joseph   Let's Dance

Bonnefond, James   Cherish; Fresh; Joanna; Misled

Bonner, Garry   Happy Together

Bonner, Leroy   Fire; Love Rollercoaster

Bono, Sonny   Bang Bang (My Baby Shot Me Down); I Got You Babe

Bonocini, H.C.   Till All Our Dreams Come True

Bonx, Nat   Collegiate; If You Are But a Dream

Boone, Pat   (Theme from) Exodus

Boone, Richard   The Ballad of Paladin

Boone, Steve   Summer in the City

Boothe, James Ross   Jingle Bell Rock

Borelli, J.   Goodbye Sally

Boretz, Allen   Whistling in the Dark

Borisoff, Bernice   Keem-O-Sabe

Born, Lew   Button Up Your Overcoat

Borne, Hal   If You Catch a Little Cold; The Tenement Symphony

Borodin, Alexander   Polovetsian Dances

Borrelli, Bill   Here in My Heart

Boswell, Eric   Little Donkey

Botkin, Perry, Jr.   Nadia's Theme, or, The Young and the Restless

Botsford, George   Black and White Rag; Grizzly Bear; Iowa Corn Song; Sailing Down the Chesapeake Bay; When Big Profundo Sang Low "C"

Boulanger, Georges   My Prayer

Bourgeois, Louis   Old Hundred(th) Doxology, or, Praise God, from Whom All Blessings Flow

Bourke, Rory   Baby I Lied; Blessed Are the Believers; I Know a Heartache When I See One; A Little Good News; (If You Happen To See) The Most Beautiful Girl (in the World)

Bousquet, Louis   Madelon

Boutelje, Philip   China Boy; She Wouldn't Do What I Asked Her To

Bowen, E.E.   Forty Years On

Bowen, James   Party Doll

Bowers, Frederick V.   Always; Because; Lucky Jim

Bowers, Robert Hood   Chinese Lullaby; The Moon Shines on the Moonshine

Bowie, David   Fame; Let's Dance; Space Oddity

Bowling, Roger   Coward of the County; Lucille

Bowman, Brooks   East of the Sun and West of the Moon; Love and a Dime

Bowman, Don   Just To Satisfy You

Bowman, Elmer   All In Down and Out; Beans Beans Beans; Go Way Back and Sit Down

Bowman, Euday L.   Twelfth Street Rag

Box, Elton   Angel of the Great White Way; Horsey, Horsey; I'm in Love with Two Sweethearts; In the Quartermaster's Stores; I've Got Sixpence (As I Go Rolling Home); Just a Little Fond Affection; We All Went Up Up Up the Mountain; The Wheel of the Wagon Is Broken; When You Know You're Not Forgotten

Boy George, *see* George O'Dowd

Boyce, Tommy   Come a Little Bit Closer; Last Train to Clarksville; Valleri

Boyce, William   Heart of Oak; The Liberty Song, or, Come, Join Hand in Hand, or, In Freedom We're Born

Boyer, Lucienne   Valencia

Boylan, Terence   Shake It

Bradbury, William Batchelder   Just as I Am Without One Plea

Braddock, Bobby Would You Catch a Falling Star

Bradford, Alex Come on Down

Bradford, Janie Too Busy Thinking About My Baby

Bradford, Perry Crazy Blues

Bradford, Sylvester Tears on My Pillow

Bradshaw, Tiny Jersey Bounce

Braga, Gaetano Angel's Serenade

Bragg, Johnny Just Walking in the Rain

Braggs, Alfred Share Your Love with Me

Braham, David The Babies on Our Block; Danny by My Side; The Full Moon Union; Hats Off to Me; I Never Drank Behind the Bar; I've Come Here To Stay; Jolly Commodore; Knights of the Mystic Star; The Last of the Hogans; Locked Out After Nine; Maggie Murphy's Home; The Market on Saturday Night; McNally's Row of Flats; The Mulligan Braves; The Mulligan Guard; My Dad's Dinner Pail; Never Take the Horse Shoe from the Door; Paddy Duffy's Cart; Patrick's Day Parade; Plum Pudding; Poverty's Tears Ebb and Flow; De Rainbow Road; The Skidmore Fancy Ball; The Skidmore Guard; The Skidmore Masquerade; Such an Education, Has My Mary Ann, or, Sweet Mary Ann; Take a Day Off, Mary Ann; Taking In the Town; They Never Tell All What They Know; When the Clock in the Tower Strikes Twelve

Braham, John The Death of Nelson; The Origin of Gunpowder, or, When Vulcan Forg'd the Bolts of Jove; Rise, Gentle Moon

Braham, Philip Dancing Honeymoon; Limehouse Blues; Mary Rose; Poor Little Rich Girl

Brahe, May I Passed By Your Window

Brahms, Caryl Not So Much a Programme, More a Way of Life

Brahms, Johannes Hungarian Dance No. 1; Hungarian Dance No. 5; Lullaby

Brainin, Jerry The Night Has a Thousand Eyes

Braisted, Harry The Girl I Loved in Sunny Tennessee; She Was Bred in Old Kentucky; Whisper Your Mother's Name; You're Not the Only Pebble on the Beach

Bramlett, D. Never Ending Song of Love

Brammer, Julius Just a Gigolo

Brand, Oscar A Guy Is a Guy

Brandon, Johnny Once Upon a Wintertime; Your Love Is My Love

Brandow, J. Hold Tight—Hold Tight

Brandt, Alan That's All

Brandt, Edward All the King's Horses

Branen, Jeff T. I'm Looking for a Nice Young Fellow Who Is Looking for a Nice Young Girl; She's the Daughter of Mother Machree; You're More Than the World to Me

Brantley, Vincent Cool It Now

Brasfield, Tom (There's) No Gettin' Over Me

Brass, Bob This Diamond Ring

Bratton, John W. I Love You in the Same Old Way—Darling Sue; I'm on the Water Wagon Now; In a Cozy Corner; Only Me; The Sunshine of Paradise Alley; The Teddy Bear's Picnic

Bray, Billy Does Santa Claus Sleep with His Whiskers

Bray, Stephen Into the Groove

Brecht, Bertolt The Alabama Song, or, Moon of Alabama; Bilbao Song; Mack the Knife, or, Theme from The Threepenny Opera, or, Morit'at; Pirate Jenny

Breck, Mrs. Frank A. Face to Face

Breen, Harry J. Your Dad Gave His Life For His Country

Breffort, Alexandre Our Language of Love

Breil, Joseph Carl The Perfect Song; Song of the Soul

Brel, Jacques Amsterdam; Carousel; Desperate Ones; If We Only Have Love; Madeleine; Marieke; Old Folks; Seasons in the Sun; Sons Of; Timid Frieda

Brennan, J. Keirn All Over Nothing at All; Dear Little Boy of Mine; Down At the Old Swimming Hole; Good-bye, Good Luck, God Bless You; Have a Smile (for Everyone You Meet); In the Little Red Schoolhouse; Ireland Is Ireland to Me; Let the Rest of the World Go By; A Little Bit of Heaven, Sure They Call It Ireland; My Sunshine Jane; Out There in the Sunshine with You; Ten Thousand Years from Now; Turn Back the Universe and Give Me Yesterday

Brennan, Joseph A. The Rose of No Man's Land

Brennan, Paul (Theme from) Harry's Game

Brent, Earl Love Is Where You Find It

Brent, Romney Mi Viejo Amor

Bretz, Ray Goodness Knows How I Love You

Breuer, Ernest Does the Spearmint Lose Its Flavor on the Bedpost Overnight; Oh Gee, Oh Gosh, Oh Golly I'm in Love

Brewster, Clarence S. When You Ain't Got No Money, Well, You Needn't Come 'Round

Brewster, Jimmy If I Give My Heart to You

Brice, Monty C. The Daughter of Rosie O'Grady

Bricusse, Leslie Can You Read My Mind (Theme from *Superman*); The Candy Man; (Theme from) Goldfinger; Gonna Build a Mountain; The Good Old Bad Days; If I Ruled the World; The Joker; Life in a Looking Glass; Look At That Face; Love Is; My Kind of Girl; Nothing Can Stop Me Now!; Once in a Lifetime; Out of Town; The People Tree; Someone Nice Like You; Summer Is A-Comin' In; Talk to the Animals; Thank You Very Much; What Kind of Fool Am I; Where Would You Be Without Me; Who Can I Turn To (When Nobody Needs Me); (On) A Wonderful Day Like Today; (Theme from) You Only Live Twice

Bridges, Alicia I Love the Nightlife (Disco 'Round)

Brigati, Edward J., Jr. A Beautiful Morning; Groovin'; How Can I Be Sure; People Got To Be Free

Brill, E.S. My Lady Lou

Brine, Mary D. Hearts and Flowers

Brisson, R. When Lights Are Low

Bristol, Johnny Some Day We'll Be Together; What Does It Take (To Win Your Love)

Britt, Addy Aggravatin' Papa (Don't You Try To Two-Time Me); Hello Swanee, Hello; Ting-a-Ling, or, The Waltz of the Bells; Was It a Dream

Britten, Terry Devil Woman; We Don't Need Another Hero; What's Love Got To Do with It

Broadnax, Morris Until You Come Back to Me (That's What I'm Gonna Do)

Brockman, James As Long as the Shamrock Grows Green; Down Among the Sheltering Palms; Feather Your Nest; I Faw Down an' Go Boom; I Know What It Means To Be Lonesome; That's Yiddishe Love

Brodsky, Roy Red Roses for a Blue Lady

Brodszky, Nicholas Be My Love; Because You're Mine; Dark Is the Night (C'est Fini); I'll Never Stop Loving You; I'll Walk with God; (Theme from) The Way to the Stars; We Never Talk Much; Wonder Why

Broisoff, Leonard One—Two—Three

Bronner, René As Deep as the Deep Blue Sea

Brooker, Gary A Whiter Shade of Pale

Brooks, Harry Ain't Misbehavin'; What Did I Do To Be So Black and Blue

Brooks, Harvey O. A Little Bird Told Me

Brooks, Jack Am I in Love; Ole Buttermilk Sky; The Rose Tattoo; That's Amore; You Wonderful You

Brooks, Joe Pepsi's Got a Lot To Give, You've Got a Lot To Live

Brooks, John Benson You Came a Long Way from St. Louis

Brooks, Joseph You Light Up My Life

Brooks, Phillips O Little Town of Bethlehem

Brooks, Reverend Charles Timothy God Bless Our Native Land

Brooks, Ruth In Shadowland

Brooks, Shelton The Darktown Stutters' Ball; Easy Rider; Some of These Days; There'll Come a Time

Broones, Martin M. Bring Back Those Minstrel Days; I Don't Want Your Kisses

Broussard, Joseph Mister Big Stuff

Browder, Stony Jr. Cherchez la Femme

Brown, A. Seymour At the Mississippi Cabaret; He's Our Al; If You Talk in Your Sleep, Don't Mention My Name; Moving Day in Jungle Town; Oh You Beautiful Doll; Rebecca of Sunny-Brook Farm; When You're Away; You're a Great Big Blue-Eyed Baby; You're My Baby

Brown, Al W. Ain't It a Shame

Brown, Albert H. You Tell Me Your Dream, or, I Had a Dream, Dear

Brown, Charles F. Reach Out and Touch

Brown, Errol A.G. Brother Louie; Emma; You Sexy Thing

Brown, Fleta Jan East of the Moon, West of the Stars; There's Egypt in Your Dreamy Eyes; Underneath the Stars

Brown, Forman Two Hearts That Pass in the Night

Brown, Frankie Born To Lose

Brown, George Celebration; Cherish; Fresh; Have You Ever Been Lonely (Have You Ever Been Blue); Joanna; Ladies Night; Misled; (When) They Cut Down the Old Pine Tree; Too Hot; The Toor-ie on His Bonnet; Wilson, That's All!

Brown, Gregory Dane Pilot Me

Brown, Harold Ray The Cisco Kid; Gypsy Man; Summer; Why Can't We Be Friends

Brown, James I Got You (I Feel Good); Papa's Got a Brand New Bag

Brown, L. Russell Knock Three Times; (Say Has Anybody Seen) My Sweet Gypsy Rose; Tie a Yellow Ribbon Round the Ole Oak Tree

Brown, Lester Abilene; Sentimental Journey

Brown, Lew Annabelle; Au Revoir, But Not Good-Bye, Soldier Boy; Baby, Take a Bow; The Beer Barrel Polka; The Best Things in Life Are Free; The Birth of the Blues; Black Bottom; Chili Bean (Eenie Meenie Minie Mo); Come to Me; Comes Love; Dapper Dan; Don't Bring Lulu; Don't Hold Everything; Don't Sit Under the Apple Tree (with Anyone Else But Me); Don't Tell Her (What's Happened to Me); Follow Thru; Georgette; The Girl Is You and the Boy Is Me; A Girl of the Pi Beta Phi; Give Me the Moonlight, Give Me the Girl; Good News; Here Am I—Broken Hearted; How I Love You (I'm Tellin' the Birds, I'm Tellin' the Bees); I Came Here To Talk for Joe; I May Be Gone for a Long, Long Time; I Used To Love You, But It's All Over Now; I'd Climb the Highest Mountain (If I Knew I'd Find You); If I Had a Talking Picture of You; I'm a Dreamer (Aren't We All); I'm the Lonesomest Gal in Town; It All Depends on You; Just a Memory; Just Imagine; Kentucky Sue; Last Night on the Back Porch—I Loved Her Best of All; Let's Call It a Day; Life Is Just a Bowl of Cherries; Lucky Day; Lucky in Love; My Lucky Star; My Sin; My Song; Oh By Jingo, Oh By Gee, You're the Only Girl for Me; Oh Mama, or, The Butcher Boy; Oh Murphy; One More Time; Our Penthouse on Third Avenue; Please Don't Take My Lovin' Man Away; Seven or Eleven—My Dixie Pair o'Dice; Seventh Heaven; Shake It Off; S-H-I-N-E; So Blue; Sonny Boy; Stand Up and Cheer; Strike Me Pink; (Keep Your) Sunny Side Up; Thank Your Father; That Old Feeling; That's Why Darkies Were Born; (I Wanna Go Where You Go, Do What You Do) Then I'll Be Happy; Then I'll Have Time for You; This Is the Missus; The Thrill Is Gone; To Know You Is To Love You; Together; Turn On the Heat; The Varsity Drag; Wait Till You Get Them Up in the Air, Boys; When It's Night-Time in Italy, It's Wednesday Over Here; Why Did I Kiss That Girl; You Find the Time, I'll Find the Place; You Try Somebody Else, and I'll Try Somebody Else (We'll Be Back Together Again); You Wouldn't Fool Me, Would You; You're the Cream in My Coffee

Brown, Marshall Seven Lonely Days

Brown, Michael Lizzie Borden (You Can't Chop Your Poppa Up in Massachusetts)

Brown, Milton Another Honky Tonk Night On Broadway; Every Which Way But Loose; I Don't Think I'm Ready For You

Brown, Nacio Herb All I Do Is Dream of You; Alone; Avalon Town; Broadway Melody; Broadway Rhythm; Chant of the Jungle; The Doll Dance; Eadie Was a Lady; Good Morning; I've Got a Feeling You're Fooling; Love Is Where You Find It; Love Songs of the Nile; Make 'Em Laugh; The Moon Is Low; Pagan Love Song; Paradise (Waltz); Should I (Reveal); Singin' in the Rain; Temptation; Turn Out the Light; The Wedding of the Painted Doll; We'll Make Hay While the Sun Shines; When Buddha Smiles; The Woman in the Shoe; (I Would) Would You; You Are My Lucky Star; You

Stepped Out of A Dream; You Were Meant for Me; You're An Old Smoothie; Yours and Mine

Brown, Napoleon   Don't Be Angry

Brown, Odell   Sexual Healing

Brown, Paula J.   Mad About You

Brown, Peter   Dance with Me; Material Girl

Brown, Walter H.   Little Mother of Mine

Brown (Garrett), Augusta   The Landing of the Pilgrims, or, The Pilgrim Fathers; Tyrolese Evening Hymn

Browne, Porter Emerson   College Life

Brown, Raymond A.   Down on the Farm (They All Ask for You)

Browne, Jackson   Somebody's Baby

Brownell, Henry Howard   John Brown's Body

Browning, Robert   The Year's at the Spring

Brubeck, Dave   Take Five

Bruce, Ed   Love's Found You and Me

Bruce, Gary D.   Moody River

Brumley, Albert E.   Turn Your Radio On

Brunies, George   Make Love to Me; Tin Roof Blues

Bruno, C.   The Woodpecker(s') Song

Bruns, George   Ballad of Davy Crockett

Bryan, Alfred   And a Little Bit More; Bring Back My Golden Dreams; Brown Eyes—Why Are You Blue; Come, Josephine, in My Flying Machine; Down in the Old Cherry Orchard; Hiawatha's Melody of Love; I Didn't Raise My Boy To Be a Soldier; I Want You To Want Me To Want You; Joan of Arc, They Are Calling You; Lorraine, My Beautiful Alsace Lorraine; Madelon; My Song of the Nile; Oui, Oui, Marie; Peg o' My Heart; Puddin' Head Jones; Red Lips Kiss My Blues Away; Round on the End and High in the Middle, O-hi-o; Sweet Little Buttercup; That Was Before I Met You; (There's Something Nice About Everyone But) There's Everything Nice About You; When Alexander Takes His Ragtime Band to France; When It's Night Time Down in Burgundy; When the Bees Are in the Hive; Who Ate Napoleons with Josephine When Bonaparte Was Away; Winter; You Taught Me How To Love You, Now Teach Me To Forget; You're Dancing on My Heart

Bryan, Vincent P.   Budweiser's a Friend of Mine; The Cubanola Glide; Don't Take Me Home; Down on the Brandywine; Down Where the Wurzburger Flows; He Goes to Church on Sunday; He's Me Pal; Hurray for Baffin's Bay; In My Merry Oldsmobile; In the Sweet Bye and Bye; Pardon Me, My Dear Alphonse, After You, My Dear Gaston; Tammany

Bryant, Boudleaux   All I Have To Do Is Dream; Bird Dog; Bye Bye Love; Love Hurts; Mexico; My Last Date with You; Wake Up Little Susie; Whispering Bells

Bryant, Edward E.   Felix Kept On Walking; Oh Star of Eve

Bryant, Felice   Bye Bye Love; Wake Up Little Susie

Bryant, H.T.   Balm of Gilead, or, Bingo

Bryman, James Tim   Come After Breakfast, Bring 'Long Your Lunch and Leave 'Fore Supper Time; Josephine, My Jo; Please Go 'Way and Let Me Sleep

Buchanan, Bessie   After the Roses Have Faded Away

Buchanan, Peter   Lively

Buchwald, Martyn   With Your Love

Buck, Dudley   Fear Ye Not, O Israel

Buck, Gene   Daddy Has a Sweetheart, and Mother Is Her Name; Florida, the Moon and You; Garden of My Dreams; Hello Frisco Hello; The Love Boat; My Rambler Rose; 'Neath the South Sea Moon; Some Sweet Day; Sweet Sixteen; Throw Me a Kiss; Tiger Rose; Tulip Time

Buck, Richard Henry   Dear Old Girl; Kentucky Babe; Where the Southern Roses Grow

Buckingham, Lindsey   Go Your Own Way; Trouble; Tusk

Buckley, R. Bishop   Wait for the Wagon

Buckner, Eva Fern   Where the Sunset Turns the Ocean's Blue to Gold

Buff, Wade   It's Almost Tomorrow

Buffano, Jules   Thanks for the Buggy Ride

Buffett, Jimmy   If the Phone Doesn't Ring, It's Me; Margaritaville

Bugatti, Dominic   Every Woman in the World; Heaven on the Seventh Floor; Modern Girl; When He Shines

Buggy, V.   The Eve of Destruction

Buie, Buddy   Do It or Die; Imaginary Lover; So Into You; Traces

Buisson, Pierre   Till

Bulger, Harry   Hey, Rube!

Bulhoes, Max   Come to the Mardi Gras

Bull, Dr. John   God Save the King (Queen)

Bullard, Frederic Field   It's Always Fair Weather When Good Fellows Get Together, or, A Stein Song

Bullock, Vernon   What Does It Take (To Win Your Love)

Bullock, Walter   I Still Love To Kiss You Goodnight; When Did You Leave Heaven

Bulwer, E.L. (Edward George Earle Lytton Bulwer-Lytton)   When Stars Are in the Quiet Skies

Bunch, Boyd   The Broken Record

Bunn, Alfred   By the Sad Sea Waves; The Heart Bow'd Down; I Dreamt I Dwelt in Marble Halls; The Light of the Other Days; Then You'll Remember Me

Bunnell, Lee   A Horse with No Name

Bunting, James   Soon It Will Be Sunday

Burchill, Charles   Alive and Kicking

Burdon, Eric   I'm Crying

Burgon, Geoffrey   (Theme from) Brideshead Revisited; Nunc Dimittis

Burgoyne, General   The Dashing White Sergeant

Burke, Bobby   Daddy's Little Girl

Burke, Brian   Matchstalk Men and Matchstalk Cats and Dogs

Burke, Francis J.   Midnight Sun

Burke, Johnny   Ain't Got a Dime to My Name; Annie Doesn't Live Here Anymore; Apalachicola, Florida; An Apple for the Teacher; April Played the Fiddle; Aren't You Glad You're You; As Long as I'm Dreaming; The Beat of My Heart; Between a Kiss and a Sigh; Blue Rain; But Beautiful; Country

Style; East Side of Heaven; (Just Say I'm a) Friend of Yours; Go Fly a Kite; Going My Way; Hang Your Heart on a Hickory Limb; Here's That Rainy Day; (And) His Rocking Horse Ran Away; If You Please; Imagination; It Could Happen to You; It's Always You; It's Dark on Observatory Hill; Life Is So Peculiar; Love Is the Darndest Thing; Marahuana; Misty; The Moon Got in My Eyes; Moonlight Becomes You; My Heart Goes Crazy; My Heart Is a Hobo; My Heart Is Taking Lessons; My Very Good Friend the Milkman; Oh You Crazy Moon; On the Sentimental Side; One, Two, Button Your Shoe; Only Forever; Pennies from Heaven; Personality; (I've Got) A Pocketful of Dreams; Polka Dots and Moonbeams; Put It There Pal; Rhythm on the River; The Road to Morocco; Scatterbrain; Sleigh Ride in July; So Do I; Suddenly It's Spring; Sunshine Cake; Sweet Potato Piper; Swinging on a Star; That Sly Old Gentleman from Featherbed Lane; That's for Me; Too Romantic; What's New; Wild Horses; You Don't Have To Know the Language

Burke, Joseph A. By the River of (the) Roses; Carolina Moon; (I'm) Dancing with Tears in My Eyes; For You; I'd Love To Meet That Old Sweetheart of Mine; If You Should Ever Need Me (You'll Always Find Me Here); In a Little Gypsy Tea Room; In the Valley of the Moon; It Looks Like Rain in Cherry Blossom Lane; The Kiss Waltz; A Little Bit Independent; Many Happy Returns of the Day; Moon Over Miami; Oh! How I Miss You Tonight; On Treasure Island; Painting the Clouds with Sunshine; Rambling Rose; Robins and Roses; Sally; Tip Toe Through the Tulips (with Me); Yearning (Just for You)

Burke, Rory Shadows in the Moonlight

Burke, Sonny He's a Tramp; How It Lies, How It Lies; How It Lies; Somebody Bigger Than You and I; They Were Doing the Mambo; You Was

Burke, Thomas The Lamplit Hour

Burkhard, Paul Oh My Papa, or, O Mein Papa

Burkhart, Addison Goodbye, Rose

Burleigh, Henry Thacker Little Mother of Mine

Burman, Maurice The Soft Shoe Shuffle

Burnaby, Davy Lords of the Air

Burnell, Jean J. Golden Brown

Burnett, Ernie My Melancholy Baby; We'll Meet Again

Burnette, Rocky Tired of Toein' the Line

Burns, Annelu I'll Forget You

Burns, Ralph Early Autumn; Northwest Passage

Burns, Robert Auld Lang Syne; Bonnie Doon; The Campbells Are Coming; Comin' Thro' the Rye, or, If a Body Meet a Body; Flow Gently, Sweet Afton, or, Afton Water; John Anderson, My Joe; My Love Is Like a Red, Red Rose; Scots What Hae Wi' Wallace Bled; Ye Banks and Braes O'Bonnie Doon

Burnside, R.H. Ladder of Roses

Burr, S.J. You'll Meet Me, Won't You

Burris, James Henry Ballin' the Jack; Come After Breakfast, Bring 'Long Your Lunch and Leave 'Fore Supper Time; Constantly

Burris, Roy Edward Okie from Muskogee

Burrows, Joe Covered Wagon Days (March)

Burt, Al She Wouldn't Do What I Asked Her To

Burt, Benjamin Hapgood The Best I Get Is Much Obliged to You; Some Little Bug Is Going To Find You (Some Day); Wal, I Swan!, or, Ebenezer Frye, or, Giddiap Napoleon, It Looks Like Rain; When You're All Dressed Up and No Place To Go

Burtnett, Earl Do You Ever Think of Me; Leave Me with a Smile; Mandalay

Burton, Dorian A Tear Fell

Burton, Eddie Dancin' Your Memory Away

Burton, Nat Believe It Beloved; Our Waltz; (There'll Be Blue Birds over) The White Cliffs of Dover

Burton, Ray I Am Woman

Burton, Val Singing a Vagabond Song; Sunny Days; When We're Alone, or, Penthouse Serenade

Burwell, Clifford Sweet Lorraine

Busch, Fini Sailor (Your Home Is the Sea)

Buschor, George My Melody of Love

Bush, Kate Babooshka; The Dreaming

Bushkin, Joe Oh Look At Me Now

Busse, Henry Hot Lips; The Wang, Wang Blues

Bustament, F. Fernandez Mi Viejo Amor

Butcher, Stan Ring-a-Ding Girl; Sing Little Birdie

Butler, Billy Honkey Tonk

Butler, E.G. Walter, Walter (Lead Me to the Altar)

Butler, Jerry Only the Strong Survive

Butler, Larry (Hey Won't You Play) Another Somebody Done Somebody Wrong Song

Butler, Ralph All Over Italy; Ever So Goosey; Give Yourself a Pat on the Back; Hey Little Hen; Horsey, Horsey; I'm Happy When I'm Hiking; Nellie the Elephant; The Ogo-Pogo; Round the Marble Arch; Run Rabbit Run; The Sun Has Got His Hat On; There's a Good Time Coming; There's a Lovely Lake in London; We All Went Up Up Up the Mountain

Butler, Reg Sailor Who Are You Dreaming of Tonight

Butterfield, Daniel O. Taps

Butterfield, James Austin When You and I Were Young, Maggie

Buttier, Billy H. Tighten Up

Buttolph, David Maverick

Bygraves, Max You Need Hands

Bynum, Hal Lucille

Byrd, Robert Over and Over

Byron, Al Happy Go Lucky Me; Roses Are Red, My Love

Caddingan, Jack The Rose of No Man's Land

Cadman, Charles Wakefield At Dawning; Far Off I Hear a Lover's Flute; From the Land of the Sky Blue Water; I Hear a Thrush at Eve; The Moon Drops Low; The White Dawn Is Stealing

Caesar, Irving After the Dance; Animal Crackers in My Soup; Cabin in the Cotton; Crazy Rhythm; Elizabeth; Goodbye, Au Revoir, Auf Wiedersehn; Hold My Hand; I Want To Be Happy; I'm a Little Bit Fonder of You; Is It True What They Say About Dixie; Just a Gigolo; Lady Play Your Mandolin; The Little White House (at the End of Honeymoon Lane); My Blackbirds Are Bluebirds Now; Nina Rosa; Oh Donna Clara; Satisfied; Serenade of Love; Simonetta; Sixty Seconds Every Minute, I Think of You; Sometimes I'm Happy; Swanee; Tea for Two; That's What I Want for Christmas; Too Many Rings Around Rosie; Under a Roof in Paree; Vienna Dreams; The White Horse Inn; The Yankee Doodle Blues

Cafferty, John On the Dark Side

Caffey, Charlotte We Got the Beat

Cahill, William One Called "Mother" and the Other "Home Sweet Home"; Since Father Went To Work

Cahn, Sammy All the Way; As Long As There's Music; Autumn in Rome; Be My Love; Because You're Mine; Bei Mir Bist Du Schön (Means That You're Grand); The Best of Everything; The Boy's Night Out; Call Me Irresponsible; Dark Is the Night (C'est Fini); Day by Day; Five Minutes More; Hey Jealous Lover; High Hopes; I Begged Her; I Fall in Love Too Easily; I Should Care; I Still Get Jealous; I'll Never Stop Loving You; I'll Only Miss Her When I Think of Her; I'll Walk Alone; I'm Glad I Waited for You; I'm Gonna Ring the Bell Tonight; The Impatient Years; It's a Woman's World; It's Been a Long, Long Time; It's Magic; It's the Same Old Dream; It's You or No One; (It Seems to Me) I've Heard That Song Before; Let It Snow, Let It Snow, Let It Snow; Love and Marriage; The Man with the Golden Arm; My Kind of Town; (Theme from) The Odd Couple; Papa Won't You Dance with Me; Pete Kelly's Blues; Please Be Kind; Pocketful of Miracles; Put 'Em in a Box, Tie 'Em with a Ribbon (and Throw 'Em in the Deep Blue Sea); (If I Had) Rhythm in My Nursery Rhymes; Rhythm Is Our Business; Saturday Night Is the Loneliest Night of the Week; The Second Star to the Right; The Second Time Around; Shoe Shine Boy; Somebody Up There Likes Me; Teach Me Tonight; (Love Is) The Tender Trap; That's What Makes Paris Paree; There Goes That Song Again; The Things We Did Last Summer; Thoroughly Modern Millie; Three Coins in the Fountain; (It Will Have To Do (Until)) Till the Real Thing Comes Along; Time After Time; Wake Me When It's Over; Walking Happy; We Never Talk Much; When the One You Love (Simply Won't Love Back) Where Love Has Gone; Wonder Why; Written on the Wind; You're My Girl; Zuyder Zee

Cain, Jonathan Don't Stop Believin'; Open Arms; Separate Ways; Who's Crying Now

Cairn, Steven Another Spring

Calabrese, G. Softly As I Leave You

Caldwell, Anne Bagdad; Come and Have a Swing with Me; I Know That You Know; In Love with Love; Ka-Lu-A; Kiss a Four Leaf Clover; Left All Alone Again Blues; My Spanish Rose; Once in a Blue Moon; Raggedy Ann; Wait Till the Cows Come Home; Whose Baby Are You

Caldwell, Bobby Janet

Calhoun, Charles Shake, Rattle and Roll

Calhoun, Floride The Hills of Home

Calilli, Bob Walk Away, Renee

Call, Alexander 867-5309/Jenny

Callahan, Fred B. Washboard Blues

Callahan, J. Will Smiles; Tell Me; You Planted a Rose in the Garden of Love

Callander, Peter Robin The Ballad of Bonnie and Clyde; Billy Don't Be a Hero; Daddy Don't You Walk So Fast; Monsieur Dupont; The Night Chicago Died

Callis, Jo Don't You Want Me

Calloway, Cab Jumpin' Jive; Minnie the Moocher, or, The Ho De Ho Song

Calvert, Eddie My Son, My Son

Camacho, John A. Bim Bam Boom; Miami Beach Rumba

Camarata, Toots Moonlight Masquerade

Cameron, Al The Martins and the Coys

Cameron, John If I Thought You'd Ever

Cammarano, Salvadore Anvil Chorus

Camp, Sheppard That's Gratitude

Campbell, Barbara Only Sixteen

Campbell, Frank Shew (Shoo) Fly, Don't Bother Me

Campbell, George The Four Walls

Campbell, Ivan High Upon a Hill Top

Campbell, James By the Fireside; The Ferry Boat Inn; Good Night, Sweetheart; I Found You; If I Had You; I'm Happy When I'm Hiking; Just an Echo in the Valley; Linger a Little Longer in the Twilight; The Old Kitchen Kettle; On a Street of Chinese Lanterns; Show Me the Way To Go Home; Try a Little Tenderness; The Two of Us; When the Organ Played at Twilight (the Song That Reached My Heart)

Campbell, Michael Boys of Summer; Stop Draggin' My Heart Around

Campbell, Paul Kisses Sweeter Than Wine

Campbell-Hunter, Roma Oh Mamma Mia

Cancler, Coz Talking in Your Sleep

Candy, Mary The Men in My Little Girl's Life

Canfora, Armand Free Again

Cann, Warren Warren

Canning, Effie I. (Effie I. Crockett) Rock-a-Bye (Hush-a-Bye) Baby

Cannon, Gus Walk Right In

Cannon, Hughie Bill Bailey, Won't You Please Come Home; Just Because She Made Dem Goo-Goo Eyes

Cannon, Thomas The Five Cent Shave

Cansler, Larry Wildfire

Cantrell, Margaret Down the Winding Road of Dreams

Capitanelli, Arnold Move In a Little Closer Baby

Capizzi, Leonard Monster Mash

Capli, Erdogan (She's the Girlfriend of) The Whirling Dervish

Capote, Truman Can I Leave Off Wearin' My Shoes; House of Flowers; I Never Has Seen Snow; A Sleepin' Bee; Smellin' of Vanilla (Bamboo Cage); Two Ladies in De Shade of De Banana Tree

Capoul, Victor Berceuse

Capps, Al Half-Breed

Capuano, Giosafatte Tweedle Dee—Tweedle Dum

Capuano, Mario Tweedle Dee—Tweedle Dum

Capurro, Giovanni 'O Sole Mio

Cara, Irene Flashdance (What a Feeling)

Carbone, Joey I Don't Want To Lose Your Love

Careaga, Jerry Don't Count the Rainy Days

Carey, Bill Who Wouldn't Love You; You've Changed

Carey, Bob The Banana Boat Song (Day-O)

Carey, Henry God Save the King (Queen); Sally in Our Alley

Carey, Joseph B. Sierra Sue

Carey, M.F. You Can't Keep a Good Man Down

Carle, Frankie Carle Boogie; Falling Leaves; Oh What It Seemed To Be; Sunrise Serenade

Carle, Richard A Lemon in the Garden of Love

Carleton, Bob Ja-Da

Carlisle, Bill Too Old To Cut the Mustard

Carlisle, Una Mae I See a Million People; Walkin' by the River

Carlo, Monte Little Town in the Ould County Down; That Tumble-Down Shack in Athlone

Carlton, Harry Constantinople; The ''Ol'' Song; Shinaniki Da

Carmen, Eric Almost Paradise; I Wanna Hear It from Your Lips; Never Gonna Fall in Love Again; That's Rock 'N' Roll

Carmichael, Hoagy Blue Orchids; Boneyard Shuffle; Can't Get Indiana Off My Mind; Doctor, Lawyer, Indian Chief; Georgia On My Mind; Heart and Soul; Hong Kong Blues; How Little We Know; I Get Along Without You Very Well; In the Cool, Cool, Cool of the Evening; Ivy; The Lamplighter's Serenade; Lazy Bones; (Up a) Lazy River; Little Old Lady; Memphis In June; My Resistance Is Low; The Nearness of You; Ole Buttermilk Sky; One Morning in May; Riverboat Shuffle; (Ol') Rockin' Chair; Skylark; Small Fry; Star Dust; Two Sleepy People; Vagabond Dreams; Washboard Blues; We're the Couple in the Castle

Carney, Harry Rockin' in Rhythm

Carpenter, Charles You Can Depend on Me

Carpenter, Joseph Edwards Her Bright Smile Haunts Me Still; What Are the Wild Waves Saying

Carpenter, Richard Only Yesterday; Top of the World; Yesterday Once More

Carr, Benjamin Strike the Cymbal

Carr, F.C. Di! Di! Di!

Carr, Howard We Don't Want the Bacon, What We Want Is a Piece of the Rhine

Carr, Leon Clinging Vine; A House Is a Home; See the U.S.A. in Your Chevrolet; There's No Tomorrow

Carr, Michael Cowboy; Did Your Mother Come from Ireland; Dinner for One, Please James; The First Lullaby; The General's Fast Asleep; Getting Around and About; The Girl with the Dreamy Eyes; A Handsome Territorial; He Wears a Pair of Silver Wings; Home Town; I Love To Sing; I Was in the Mood; Kon-Tiki; The Little Boy That Santa Claus Forgot; Lonely Ballerina; Man of Mystery; Misty Islands of the Highlands; My Beautiful Sarie Marais; No Greater Love; Ole Faithful; On the Outside Looking In; Somewhere in France with You; South of the Border (Down Mexico Way); The Spice of Life; Stay in My Arms, Cinderella; The Sunset Trail; There's a New World; The Waltz of the Gypsies; Washing on the Siegfried Line; The Wheel of the Wagon Is Broken; Why Did She Fall for the Leader of the Band

Carr, Richard Old Timer

Carr, Tony March of the Mods

Carrack, Paul How Long

Carradine, Keith I'm Easy

Carré, Michel Soldier's Chorus

Carroll, Bert Wear My Ring Around Your Neck

Carroll, Earl Dreams of Long Ago; Isle d'Amour (Isle of Love); So Long Letty

Carroll, Harry By the Beautiful Sea; Down in Bom-Bombay; I'm Always Chasing Rainbows; It Takes a Little Rain with the Sunshine To Make the World Go Round; The Land of My Best Girl; On the Mississippi; She Is the Sunshine of Virginia; There's a Girl in the Heart of Maryland (with a Heart That Belongs to Me); Tip-Top Tipperary Mary; The Trail of the Lonesome Pine; What Do I Care

Carroll, June Love Is a Simple Thing; Monotonous

Carson, Jenny Lou Jealous Heart; Let Me Go Lover

Carson, Johnny Johnny's Theme, or, Here's Johnny

Carson, Milton My Love and Devotion; My Unfinished Symphony

Carson, Wayne Always on My Mind; The Clown

Carste, Hans Those Lazy Hazy Crazy Days of Summer

Carter, A.P. I'm (Dreaming) Thinking Tonight of My Blue Eyes; Wabash Cannonball

Carter, Benny Blues in My Heart; Cow-Cow Boogie; When the Lights Are Low

Carter, Calvin He Don't Love You Like I Love You

Carter, Desmond I Took My Harp to a Party; I'm on a See-Saw; La-Di-Da-Di-Da; Mona Lisa; Today I Feel So Happy; With All My Heart

Carter, Frank W. Why Did I Leave My Little Back Room

Carter, John Incense and Peppermints; Knock, Knock, Who's There; Tossing and Turning

Carter, Stanley The Girl I Loved in Sunny Tennessee; She Was Bred in Old Kentucky; Whisper Your Mother's Name; You're Not the Only Pebble on the Beach

Carter, Sydney Down Below

Cartey, Ric Young Love

Caruso, Enrico Dreams of Long Ago

Caryll, David I'll Come When You Call

Caryll, Ivan By the Saskatchewan; Come and Have a Swing with Me; Goodbye, Girls, I'm Through; Moonstruck; My Beautiful Lady, or, The Kiss Waltz; There's a Light in Your Eyes; There's Life in the Old Dog Yet; Wait Till the Cows Come Home; Wine of France

Caryll, Josephine   I'll Come When You Call

Casey, Harry Wayne   Get Down Tonight; I'm Your Boogie Man; Keep It Comin' Love; Please Don't Go; Rock Your Baby; (Shake Shake Shake) Shake Your Booty; That's the Way I Like It; Where Is the Love

Casey, Kenneth   Sweet Georgia Brown

Casey, Michael   Mick McGilligan's Ball

Casey, Thomas F.   Drill Ye Tarriers Drill

Casey, Warren   All Choked Up; Freddy My Love; Look At Me, I'm Sandra Dee

Cash, Johnny   Folsom Prison (Blues); Going to Memphis

Cash, Rosanne   Blue Moon with Heartache; Hold On; I Don't Know Why You Don't Want Me; Seven Year Ache

Cash, Steve   Jackie Blue

Cassel, Irwin M.   I Love Life

Cassen, Eddie   How Lucky You Are

Cassin, Jimmy   Sentimental Me

Casson, Margaret   The Cuckoo

Castling, Harry   Are We To Part Like This, Bill; Don't Have Any More, Mrs. Moore; Just Like the Ivy; Let's All Go Down the Strand; Meet Me Jenny When the Sun Goes Down; Oh Nicholas Don't Be So Ridiculous; Turned Up; What Ho She Bumps

Caston, Leonard   Boogie Down; Keep on Truckin'

Castro, Armando   Cu-Tu-Gu-Ru (Jack, Jack, Jack)

Casucci, Leonello   Just a Gigolo

Cates, George   Stockholm; Weary Blues

Cavaliere, Felix   A Beautiful Morning; Groovin'; How Can I Be Sure; People Got To Be Free; See

Cavanass, J.M.   By the Waters of Minnetonka

Cavanaugh, James   Christmas in Killarney; Did You Ever Get That Feeling in the Moonlight; The Gaucho Serenade; Gertie from Bizerte; I Came, I Saw, I Congad; I Like Mountain Music; A Little on the Lonely Side; The Umbrella Man; You're Nobody 'Til Somebody Loves You

Cavanaugh, Jessie   Desafinado (Slightly Out of Tune); The Roving Kind

Cawthorn, Joseph   I Can Dance with Everyone But My Wife; You Can't Play Every Instrument in the Band

Cazalis, Henri   Danse Macabre

Cetera, Peter   Glory of Love (Theme from *The Karate Kid Part II*); Hard To Say I'm Sorry; If You Leave Me Now; Love Me Tomorrow; No Tell Lover; You're the Inspiration

Cezano, Paul   The Regiment of Sambre and Meuse

Chabrier, Emmanuel   España (Rhapsody)

Chacksfield, Frank   Down Sweetheart Avenue

Chalmer, Charles   The Clown

Chambers, Carl   Close Enough to Perfect

Chambers-Ketchum, Mrs. Annie   The Bonnie Blue Flag

Chaminade, Cécile   Scarf Dance

Champlin, William   After the Love Has Gone; Is It You; Turn Your Love Around

Chan, Mike   Double Your Pleasure

Chancler, Leon   Let It Whip

Chandler, Gus   Canadian Capers

Chandler, Tanis   An Affair To Remember

Channel, Bruce   Don't Worry 'Bout Me Baby; Hey Baby; Party Time

Chapin, Harry   Cat's in the Cradle

Chapin, Sandra C.   Cat's in the Cradle

Chapin, Saul   You Wonderful You

Chaplin, Charles   Eternally, or, Terry's Theme; Mandolin Serenade; Smile; This Is My Song

Chaplin, Saul I.   The Anniversary Song; Bei Mir Bist Du Schön (Means That You're Grand); Please Be Kind; (If I Had) Rhythm in My Nursery Rhymes; Shoe Shine Boy; (It Will Have To Do) Until the Real Thing Comes Along

Chapman, Arthur   Out Where the West Begins

Chapman, Michael   Better Be Good to Me; Blockbuster; Heart and Soul; Kiss You All Over; Love Is a Battlefield; Love Touch (Theme from *Legal Eagles*); Mickey; Tiger Feet; Wig Wam Bam

Chappell, Herbert   The Pallisers

Chaquico, Craig   Jane

Charig, Philip   I Wanna Get Married; Sunny Disposish; There's Always Tomorrow

Charlap, Mark   I Won't Grow Up; I'm Flying; I've Gotta Crow; Tender Shepherd; Young Ideas

Charles, Dick   Along the Navajo Trail; I Tipped My Hat and Slowly Rode Away; This Is My Song Theme

Charles, Ernest   Let My Song Fill Your Heart; When I Have Sung My Songs

Charles, Hugh   Blue Skies Are Round the Corner; By Candlelight; I Shall Always Remember You Smiling; I Shall Be Waiting; I Won't Tell a Soul (That I Love You); Russian Rose; Silver Wings in the Moonlight; There'll Always Be an England; There's a Land of Begin Again; Till Stars Forget To Shine; When They Sound the Last All Clear; Where the Waters Are Blue

Charles, Jacques   My Man; Valencia

Charles, Leslie   Caribbean Queen (No More Love on the Run)

Charles, Ray   Frenesi; Sweet Sixteen Bars

Charles, Wolseley   Old Sam (Pick Up Tha' Musket)

Charnin, Martin   Best Thing You've Ever Done; Easy Street; (It's) The Hard-Knock Life; Little Girls; Maybe; N.Y.C.; Tomorrow

Chase, Lincoln   The Clapping Song, or, My Mother Told Me; The Name Game; The Nitty Gritty; Wonderland by Night

Chase, Newell   If I Were King; My Ideal

Chater, Kerry   I Know a Heartache When I See One; I.O.U.; What She Wants

Chatman, Bo   Corrine Corrina

Chatman, Peter   Every Day I Have the Blues

Chattaway, Thurland   Can't You Take It Back and Change It for a Boy; I've Grown So Used to You; Mandy Lee; My Guiding Star; My Honey Lou; Red Wing; The Sweetest Flower the Garden Grew; we've Been Chums for Fifty Years; When the Blue Sky Turns to Gold

Cherkose, Eddie Song of the Rose

Cherry, Andrew The Bay of Biscay O!

Chessler, Deborah It's Too Soon To Know

Chester, Charlie Down Forget-Me-Not Lane; Mister Moon You've Got a Million Sweethearts; Primrose Hill

Chester, Peter Please Don't Tease

Chevalier, Albert The Future Mrs. 'Awkins; Knocked 'Em in the Old Kent Road; My Old Dutch

Chinn, Nicholas Better Be Good to Me; Blockbuster; Heart and Soul; Kiss You All Over; Mickey; Tiger Feet; Wig Wam Bam

Chiprut, Elliot Simon Says

Chisolm, Ed Let the Music Play

Chopin, Frédéric Fantaisie Impromptu; Funeral March; Grande Valse Brilliante; The Minute Waltz; Nocturne; Polonaise Militari; Prelude

Chorley, Henry Fothergill The Brave Old Oak; The Long Day Closes; Nazareth

Christian, Arnold Can't Smile Without You

Christian, Rick I Don't Need You

Christie, George Baby Rose

Christie, Jeff Yellow River

Christie, Lou Lightnin' Strikes

Christine, Henri Marius Do I Love You; Petite Tonkinoise; Valentine

Christopher, Gretchen Come Softly to Me

Christopher, Johnny Always on My Mind

Christy, E.P. Good Night Ladies, or, Merrily We Roll Along

Churchill, Frank E. Heigh-Ho; I'm Wishing; Love Is a Song That Never Ends; One Song; Some Day My Prince Will Come; (Just) Whistle While You Work; Who's Afraid of the Big Bad Wolf; with a Smile and a Song

Cicchetti, Carl Beep Beep

Clanton, Jimmy Just a Dream

Clapp, Sunny Girl of My Dreams

Clapps, Donald Beep Beep

Clapton, Eric Edge of Darkness; Get Ready; I Can't Stand It; Lay Down Sally; Layla

Clapton, Nolly Strawberry Fair

Clare, Sidney The Big Butter and Egg Man; Down Among the Sugar-Cane; I'd Climb the Highest Mountain (If I Knew I'd Find You); I'm Missin' Mammy's Kissin'—and I Know She's Missin' Mine; Keepin' Myself for You; Ma! He's Making Eyes at Me; (Who's Wonderful, Who's Marvelous?) Miss Annabelle Lee; On the Good Ship Lollipop; O-oo Ernest, Are You Earnest With Me?; Please Don't Talk About Me When I'm Gone; (I Wanna Go Where You Go, Do What You Do) Then I'll Be Happy; You're My Thrill

Claribel (Mrs. Charles C. Barnard (Charlotte Arlington)) The Blue Alsation Mountains; Come Back to Erin; Janet's Choice; Take Back the Heart You Gave; Won't You Tell Me Why, Robin

Clark, Billy I Love My Wife, But Oh You Kid

Clark, Claudine Party Lights

Clark, Cumberland The Ogo-Pogo

Clark, Dave Bits and Pieces; Can't You See That She's Mine; Catch Us If You Can; Glad All Over

Clark, Dee Raindrops

Clark, Edward You're in Love

Clark, Harold Long Cool Woman (in a Black Dress)

Clark, Kenneth Princeton, That's All

Clark, Michael Heart of the Night; Slow Hand

Clark, Rudy Good Lovin'

Clark, Willie Where Is the Love

Clarke, Grant Am I Blue; Avalon Town; Back to the Carolina You Love; Beatrice Fairfax, Tell Me What To Do; Birmingham Bertha; Blue (and Broken Hearted); Dirty Hands, Dirty Face; Everything Is Peaches Down in Georgia; (He'd Have To Get Under,) Get Out and Get Under (To Fix Up His Automobile); Goodbye Virginia; He's a Devil in His Own Home Town; I Hate To Lose You; I Know I Got More Than My Share; I Love the Ladies; If He Can Fight Like He Can Love, Good Night Germany; I'm a Little Blackbird Looking for a Bluebird; In the Land of Beginning Again; Mandy Make Up Your Mind; Oh You Million Dollar Doll; (Home in) Pasadena; Ragtime Cowboy Joe; Second Hand Rose; Sit Down, You're Rocking the Boat; There'll Be a Hot Time for the Old Men When the Young Men Go to War; There's a Little Bit of Bad in Every Good Little Girl; Weary River; When You're in Love with Someone Who Is Not in Love with You; You Can't Get Along With 'Em or Without 'Em

Clarke, H. Pitman Swanee River Moon

Clarke, Helen Nice One Cyril

Clarke, Robert Coningsby The Blind Ploughman; A Bowl of Roses

Clarke, T.E.B. The White Suite Samba

Clarke, Willie Rockin' Chair

Clarkson, Harry Home

Clarkson, Jeff Home

Clay, Frederic I'll Sing Thee Songs of Araby

Claypoole, Edward B. Ragging the Scale

Clayton, Harold Take Your Time (Do It Right)

Clayton, Justin Valotte

Clayton, William Come, Ye Saints

Clayton-Thomas, David Spinning Wheel

Cleary, Michael H. Singin' in the Bathtub; When a Lady Meets a Gentleman Down South

Clements, Roderick Meet Me On the Corner

Clephane, Elizabeth C. Beneath the Cross of Jesus; The Ninety and Nine

Clesi, N.J. I'm Sorry I Made You Cry

Cleveland, Al What's Going On

Cliff, Laddie Coal Black Mammy

Cliffe, Fred E. When I'm Cleaning Windows

Clifford, Ethel Melisands in the Wood

Clifford, Gordon I Surrender Dear; It Must Be True (You Are Mine, All Mine); Paradise (Waltz)

Clifton, Harry Polly Perkins of Paddington Green; The Weeping Willer

Clinton, Larry The Dipsy Doodle; My Reverie; Our Love; Satan Takes a Holiday

Clowney, David The Happy Organ

Clutsam, George H. Ma Curly-Headed Babby

Coates, Carroll London by Night

Coates, Eric Bird Songs at Eventide; Calling All Workers (March); The Dam Busters (March); Goodbye, Au Revoir, Auf Wiedersehn; I Pitch My Lonely Caravan at Night; Knightsbridge March, or, In Town Tonight; (By the) Sleepy Lagoon (Valse Serenade)

Cobb, George L. Alabama Jubilee; All Aboard for Dixieland; Are You from Dixie, 'Cause I'm from Dixie Too; Russian Rag

Cobb, James B., Jr. Do It or Die; Traces

Cobb, Margaret Hey Baby

Cobb, Will D. Goodbye Dolly Gray; Goodbye, Little Girl, Goodbye; I Can't Tell Why I Love You, But I Do; I Just Can't Make My Eyes Behave; If a Girl Like You Loved a Boy Like Me; If I Was a Millionaire; I'll Be with You When the Roses Bloom Again; In Zanzibar—My Little Chimpanzee; Mamie (Don't You Feel Ashamie); School Days; The Singer and the Song; Sunbonnet Sue; There's a Girl in This World for Every Boy and a Boy for Every Girl; Waltz Me Around Again Willie—'Round, 'Round, 'Round; Way Down Yonder in the Cornfield; Yip-I-Addy-I-Ay!

Coben, Cy Lonely Little Robin; The Old Piano Roll Blues; Sweet Violets

Coborn, Charles Two Lovely Black Eyes

Coburn, Richard Whispering

Cochran, Dorcas Again; Here; (When We Are Dancing) I Get Ideas; Summer Dreams; Under the Bridges of Paris

Cochran, Hank Funny Way of Laughing; Make the World Go Away; That's All That Matters

Cochran, Wayne Last Kiss

Cochrane, Peggy The Heart of a Man

Cockburn, Bruce Wondering Where the Lions Are

Cody, Philip Bad Blood; The Immigrant; Love in the Shadows; Solitaire

Cody, Phillip Should've Never Let You Go

Coghill, Nevill I Have a Noble Cock

Cogne, Nelson We Three—My Echo, My Shadow and Me

Cohan, George M. Always Leave Them Laughing When You Say Goodbye; Barnum Had the Right Idea; Come on Down Town; Forty-Five Minutes from Broadway; Give My Regards to Broadway; Good-bye, Flo; Harrigan; I Guess I'll Have To Telegraph My Baby; I Want You; I Was Born in Virginia, or, Ethel Levy's Virginia Song; If I'm Going To Die I'm Going To Have Some Fun; If Washington Should Come to Life; I'm a Popular Man; Life's a Funny Proposition After All; Mary's a Grand Old Name; Nellie Kelly, I Love You; Nothing New Beneath the Sun; Over There; So Long Mary; Stand Up and Fight Like H——; There's Something About a Uniform; Under Any Old Flag At All; When a Fellow's on the Level with a Girl That's on the Square; When

We Are M-a-double-r-i-e-d; When You Come Back; (I Am) The Yankee Doodle Boy; You Can Have Broadway; You Remind Me of My Mother; You're a Grand Old Flag

Cohen, Henry Canadian Capers

Cohen, Daniel Anyone Who Isn't Me Tonight

Cohen, Jeffrey Freeway of Love; You're a Friend of Mine

Cohen, Jerry Ain't No Stoppin' Us Now

Cohen, Leonard Suzanne

Cohn, Chester Sunday; Why Should I Cry over You; You Don't Like It—Not Much

Cohn, Irving Yes! We Have No Bananas

Colahan, Arthur Galway Bay

Colby, Robert Free Again; Jilted

Colcord, Lincoln (Maine) Stein Song

Cole, Bob Congo Love Song; Lazy Moon; The Maiden with the Dreamy Eyes; My Castle on the Nile; Oh, Didn't He Ramble

Cole, Nat "King" Because of Rain; Straighten Up and Fly Right

Cole, Robert Under the Bamboo Tree

Cole, Tony Beg, Steal or Borrow; Take Me High

Coleman, Cy Angelina; Baby Dream Your Dream; (To) Be a Performer; (Hey) Big Spender; C'est la Vie; The Colors of My Life; Come Follow the Band; Dimples; Firefly; Give a Little Whistle; Here's to Us; Hey Look Me Over; Hey There, Good Times; I Like Your Style; I've Got Your Number; On the Twentieth Century; (On) The Other Side of the Tracks; Pass Me By; Poor Little Hollywood Star; Real Live Girl; What Takes My Fancy; Where Am I Going; Why Try To Change Me Now; Witchcraft; You Wanna Bet

Coleman, Larry Changing Partners; Ricochet

Coleman, Michael Matchstalk Men and Matchstalk Cats and Dogs

Coleman, Ronald Tired of Toein' the Line

Coleman, Tony One Hundred Ways

Coleridge-Taylor, Samuel Question and Answer (Démande et Réponse)

Colin, Sid The Army Game; If I Only Had Wings

Colla, John Heart of Rock and Roll; If This Is It; The Power of Love

Collett, David Summer Set

Collins, Charles Any Old Iron; Are We To Part Like This, Bill; Boiled Beef and Carrots; Don't Dilly Dally on the Way; I Wouldn't Leave My Little Wooden Hut for You; Why Am I Always the Bridesmaid

Collins, Frank I Will Survive

Collins, Judy Albatross; My Father

Collins, Larry Delta Dawn; You're the Reason God Made Oklahoma

Collins, Phil Against All Odds (Take a Look at Me Now); Easy Lover; In the Air Tonight; Invisible Touch; One More Night; Sussudio; Take Me Home; That's All

Collins, Susan M. Sweet Life

Colman, G. The Wayworn Traveller

Colter, Jessie   I'm Not Lisa

Columbo, Russ   Prisoner of Love

Comanor, Jeffrey   We'll Never Have To Say Goodbye Again

Combis, Paul   I Love You (Je T'Aime); No, No, Nora

Comden, Betty   Bad Timing; Bells Are Ringing; Captain Hook's Waltz; Fade Out—Fade In; The French Lesson; Hello, Hello There; Hold Me, Hold Me, Hold Me; It's Love; Just in Time; Long Before I Knew You; Lucky To Be Me; Make Someone Happy; Never Never Land; New York, New York; Ohio; On the Twentieth Century; The Party's Over; A Quiet Girl; The River Song, or, Something's Always Happening on the River; Say, Darling; Some Other Time; Ya Got Me

Comer, David   Hors D'Oeuvres

Concina, C.   Bluebird (Vola Colomba)

Confrey, Edward "Zez"   Dizzy Fingers; Jack in the Box; Kitten on the Keys; Stumbling

Conley, Arthur   Sweet Soul Music

Conley, Larry   A Cottage for Sale

Conn, Chester   Forgive My Heart; Make Her Mine; Outside of Heaven

Connelly, Reginald   By the Fireside; Dreaming; Falling in Love Again; Good Night, Sweetheart; The Homecoming Waltz; I Found You; If I Had You; I'm Happy When I'm Hiking; Just an Echo in the Valley; Linger a Little Longer in the Twilight; The Old Kitchen Kettle; On a Street of Chinese Lanterns; Show Me the Way To Go Home; Sunny Days; Try a Little Tenderness; The Two of Us; When the Organ Played at Twilight (The Song That Reached My Heart)

Conner, T.W.   She Was One of the Early Birds

Conniff, Ann Engberg   How Long, How Long Blues

Connolly, Brian   Fox on the Run

Connolly, Patrick   Wipe Out

Connor, Tommie   The Biggest Aspidistra in the World; The Chestnut Tree; Down in the Glen; Give Her My Love; Hang on the Bell Nellie; The Homing Waltz; I Love To Sing; I Once Had a Heart, Margarita; I Saw Mommy Kissing Santa Claus; It's My Mother's Birthday Today; Lili (Lilli) Marlene; The Little Boy That Santa Claus Forgot; My Beautiful Sarie Marais; Never Do a Tango with an Eskimo; The Rose I Bring You; Till the Lights of London Shine Again; The Wedding of Lilli Marlene; When the Guardsman Started Crooning on Parade; Who's Taking You Home Tonight

Connors, Carol   Gonna Fly Now, or, Theme from Rocky; With You I'm Born Again

Conrad, Con   Barney Google; Bend Down, Sister; The Champagne Waltz; Come On, Spark Plug!; The Continental; Here's to Romance; Lonesome and Sorry; Ma! He's Making Eyes At Me; Mandy 'n' Me; Margie; Memory Lane; Midnight in Paris; A Needle in a Haystack; Oh! Frenchy; (Lena from) Palesteena; You Call It Madness (Ah, But I Call It Love); You've Gotta (Got to) See Mamma Ev'ry Night, or You Can't See Mamma At All

Conrad, John   Everything's Al' Right

Conrad, Robin   Don't Bring Me Your Heartaches; Leave a Little Love

Contet, Henri Alexandre   All My Love; Mademoiselle de Paris; Padam, Padam

Conti, Bill   For Your Eyes Only; Gonna Fly Now, or, Theme from Rocky

Converse, Charles Crozat   The Rock Beside the Sea; What a Friend We Have in Jesus

Conway, Jim   Tomboy

Conway, Russ   Jeannie; Side Saddle

Cook, Don   I've Had a Lovely Time

Cook, Eliza   The Old Arm Chair

Cook, L.C.   You Send Me

Cook, Mercer   Is I In Love? I Is

Cook, Robert S.   There Must Be a Way

Cook, Roger   Doctor's Orders; Freedom Come, Freedom Go; Gasoline Alley Bred; I Believe in You; Long Cool Woman (in a Black Dress); Melting Pot; Miracles; Talkin' in Your Sleep; You've Got Your Troubles

Cook, Will Marion   Bon Bon Buddy; I'm Comin' Virginia

Cooke, Charles L.   I Wonder Where My Lovin' Man Has Gone

Cooke, Leonard   The Sunshine of Your Smile

Cooke, Leslie   Love Sends a Little Gift of Roses; Mate o' Mine

Cooke, Sam   Another Saturday Night; Chain Gang; Cupid; Good News; Only Sixteen; Sweet Soul Music; Twistin' the Night Away

Cooke, Thomas Simpson   Love's Ritornella, or, Gentle Zitella

Cooley, Eddie   Fever

Coolidge, Edwina   Along the Santa Fe Trail

Coon, Carleton A.   Hi-Diddle-Diddle

Cooper, Alice   How You Gonna See Me Now; Only Women Bleed; You and Me

Cooper, Gary Lee   Let's Go All the Way

Cooper, George   Beautiful Isle of the Sea; Don't Go Out Tonight, Boy; Hurrah! for Grant and Colfax; The Rose of Killarney; Strolling on the Brooklyn Bridge; Sweet Genevieve; When the War Is Over, Mary

Cooper, Joe   Child Love; I've Been Floating Down the Old Green River

Cooper, Martin   If You Leave

Coots, J. Fred   Beautiful Lady in Blue; Cross Your Fingers; Doin' the Raccoon; For All We Know; I Still Get a Thrill (Thinking of You); Love Letters in the Sand; A Precious Little Thing Called Love; Santa Claus Is Coming to Town; This Time It's Love; Two Tickets to Georgia; Why (Is There a Rainbow in the Sky); You Go to My Head

Copeland, Allan   Make Love to Me

Copeland, James   These Are My Mountains

Coquatrix, Bruno   Clopin Clopant; Comme Çi, Comme Ça; Count Every Star

Corbett, Gary   She Bop

Corbett, Harry   Sooty

Corday, Leo See the U.S.A. in Your Chevrolet; There's No Tomorrow

Cordell, Frank Khartoum

Cordell, Ritchie Mony, Mony

Cordell, Syd Ring-a-Ding Girl; Sing Little Birdie

Coria, Penaloza Gabino Caminito

Cornelius, Harold A Blossom Fell

Cornelius, Maxwell N., D.D. Sometime We'll Understand

Cornett, Alice All That Glitters Is Not Gold

Cornwell, Hugh A. Golden Brown

Cort, Harry L. I Was a Very Good Baby; Waiting

Cory, Charles B. A Dream

Cory, George I Left My Heart in San Francisco

Cosby, Henry Fingertips (Part II); I Was Made To Love Her; My Cherie Amor; The Tears of a Clown; Uptight (Everything's Alright)

Coslow, Sam Black Moonlight; Blue Mirage; Cocktails for Two; The Day You Came Along; Down the Old Ox Road; Have You Forgotten So Soon; Hello Swanee, Hello; If I Were King; If You Can't Sing It You'll Have To Swing It (Mister Paganini); I'm Just Wild About Animal Crackers; In the Middle of a Kiss; It's Love Again; Je Vous Aime; Just One More Chance; Kitten on the Keys; Learn To Croon; A Little White Gardenia; Make Believe Island; Marahuana; Moon Song (That Wasn't Meant for Me); My Old Flame; Sing You Sinners; Song of the South; Sweeping the Clouds Away; Thanks; This Little Piggie Went to Market; True Blue Lou; True Confession; Was It a Dream

Costa, Don Because They're Young

Costello, Bartley If You Had All the World and Its Gold; El Rancho Grande

Cotton, Hal You Can't Be True, Dear

Cotton, Norman Paul Heart of the Night

Cottrau, Teodoro Addio, Mia Bella Napoli; Santa Lucia

Cottrell, Jack Chinese Laundry Blues

Coulston, W.H. Folks That Put On Airs

Coulter, Phil Congratulations; Puppet on a String; Saturday Night

Cour, Pierre Love Is Blue

Courtney, C.C. Why Can't I Touch You

Courtney, David Alexandra Long Tall Glasses (I Can Dance)

Couturie, Bill 19

Covay, Don Pony Time

Covert, Bernard The Sword of Bunker Hill

Covington, Joey With Your Love

Cowan, Lynn Kisses—The Sweetest Kisses of All

Cowan, Marie Waltzing Matilda

Cowan, Samuel K. Anchored

Cowan, Stanley Do I Worry

Coward, Noél Any Little Kiss; Dance Little Lady; Dear Little Café; Half-Caste Woman; Has Anybody Seen Our Ship; I Went to a Marvelous Party; If Love Were All; I'll Follow My Secret Heart; I'll See You Again; London Pride; Lover of My Dreams, or, Mirabelle Waltz; Mad About the Boy; Mad Dogs and Englishmen; Matelot; (Don't Put Your Daughter on the Stage) Mrs. Worthington; Nina; Parisian Pierrot; The Party's Over Now; Play Orchestra Play; Poor Little Rich Girl; Regency Rakes; A Room with a View; Sail Away; Some Day I'll Find You; The Stately Homes of England; Tokay (ToKay); Twentieth Century Blues; Why Do the Wrong People Travel; World Weary; You Were There; Zigeuner

Cowell, Johnny Walk Hand in Hand

Cowen, Frederick Hymen It Was a Dream

Cowles, Eugene Forgotten

Cox, Desmond Angel of the Great White Way; Horsey, Horsey; I'm in Love with Two Sweethearts; In the Quartermaster's Stores; I've Got Sixpence (As I Go Rolling Home); Just a Little Fond Affection; We All Went Up Up Up the Mountain; The Wheel of the Wagon Is Broken; When You Know You're Not Forgotten

Cox, Eddie Take Me to the Midnight Cake Walk Ball; You Said It

Cox, James Nobody Knows You When You're Down and Out

Cox, Michael Along Came Caroline

Craig, Francis Beg Your Pardon; Near You

Craig, Michael Church of the Poison Mind; Do You Really Want To Hurt Me; It's a Miracle; Karma Chameleon; Miss Me Blind; Time (Clock of the Heart)

Crain, Tom In America

Cramer, Floyd My Last Date with You; On the Rebound

Cramer, Johann Baptist Rousseau's Dream

Crandall, Bill Short Shorts

Crane, Jimmie Hurt; I Need You Now; If I Give My Heart to You

Crane, Lor White On White

Craske-Day, Maude Arise, O Sun

Crawford (Barry), Annie Kathleen Mavourneen

Crawford, Clifton Nancy Brown

Crawford, Robert The Army Air Corps Song, or, The U.S. Air Force Song

Crawford, Stanley Show the White of Yo' Eye

Creamer, Henry After You've Gone; The Bombo-Shay; Dear Old Southland; If I Could Be with You One Hour Tonight; My Blue Bird Was Caught in the Rain; Sweet Emalina, My Gal; That's A Plenty;' Way Down Yonder in New Orleans

Creatore, Luigi Can't Help Falling in Love (with You); The Lion Sleeps Tonight, or, Wimoweh

Creed, Linda Break Up To Make Up; Greatest Love of All; Hold Me; Rubberband Man; You Make Me Feel Brand New

Creme, Lawrence Rubber Bullets

Creme, Lol Cry

Crewe, Bob Big Girls Don't Cry; Buzz Buzz A-Diddle-It; Can't Take My Eyes Off of You; Jump Over; Lady Marmalade; Let's Hang On; My Eyes Adored You; Rag Doll; Silhouettes; Swearin' to God; Walk Like a Man

Crier, Keith   Disco Nights

Criss, Peter   Beth

Croce, Jim   Bad Bad Leroy Brown; Time in a Bottle

Croft, William   O God, Our Help in Ages Past

Crofts, Dash   Diamond Girl; Get Closer; I'll Play for You

Crompton, Bill   Heart of a Teenage Girl; The House of Bamboo; The Stranger

Cronin, Kevin   Can't Fight This Feeling; Keep On Loving You

Crook, Max T.   Runaway

Crooker, Earle   Somehow

Cropper, Steve   (Sittin' on) The Dock of the Bay; Green Onions; In the Midnight Hour; Knock On Wood

Crosby, Bing   At Your Command; I Don't Stand a Ghost of a Chance with You; Where the Blue of the Night Meets the Gold of the Day

Crosby, Bob   Big Noise from Winnetka

Crosby, Frances Jane (Mrs. Alexander Van Alstyne)   All the Way My Saviour Leads Me; Hide Thou Me; (Jesus Keep Me) Near the Cross; Open the Gates of the Temple; Rescue the Perishing; Safe in the Arms of Jesus; Saved by Grace; Tenderly Calling; There's Music in the Air; Though Your Sins Be as Scarlet

Cross, Christopher   All Right; Arthur's Theme (Best That You Can Do); Ride Like the Wind; Sailing; Think of Laura; Vienna

Cross, Douglass   I Left My Heart in San Francisco

Cross, Reuben   Shame

Crotch, William   Westminster Chimes

Crouch, Frederick William Nichols   Kathleen Mavourneen; Kattie (Katty) Avourneen

Crouch, Nicholas   Everything's Al'Right

Crowell, Rodney   An American Dream; Shame On the Moon

Crowley, John   Baby Come Back

Crumit, Frank   Abdulla Bulbul Ameer (Abdul Abulbul Amir); A Gay Caballero; Sweet Lady

Cugat, Xavier   My Shawl; Nightingale

Cunico, Gino   When I Wanted You

Cunliffe, Dick   Double Your Peasure

Cunningham, Allan   A Wet Sheet and a Flowing Sea

Cunningham, Paul   All Over Nothing at All; From the Vine Came the Grape (from the Grape Came the Wine); Harriet; Have a Smile (for Everyone You Meet); (On the Shores of) Tripoli

Cuomo, Bill   Oh Sherrie

Curiel, Gonzalo   Full Moon

Curnin, Cy   One Thing Leads to Another

Currie, Alannah   Hold Me Now; King for a Day; Lay Your Hands on Me

Currie, Billy   Vienna

Curtis, Billy   The Scandal of Little Lizzie Ford

Curtis, Eddie   The Joker

Curtis, Loyal   Drifting and Dreaming (Sweet Paradise); Roses for Remembrance

Curtis, Mann   Anema e Core (With All My Heart and Soul); Fooled; I'm Gonna Live Till I Die; The Jones Boy; Let It Be Me; My Dreams Are Getting Better All the Time; (I Don't Care) Only Love Me; Play Me Hearts and Flowers (I Wanna Cry); (This Is) The Story of a Starry Night; The World Is Singing My Song

Curtis, Michael   Southern Cross

Curtis, Richard   Southern Cross

Curtis, Sonny   More Than I Can Say

Cushing, Catherine Chisholm   L'Amour Toujours L'Amour, or, Love Everlasting; Love Has Wings; Love's Own Sweet Song, or, Sari Waltz; My Faithful Stradivari; Softly Thro' the Summer Night

Cushing, William O.   Hiding in Thee

Cutler, Henry Stephen   All Saints New; The Son of God Goes Forth to War

Cutter, Bob   Gertie from Bizertie

Czibulka, Alphons   Stephanie-Gavotte

Dabney, Ford   S-H-I-N-E; That Minor Strain; That's Why They Call Me "Shine"

D'Abo, Michael   Build Me Up Buttercup

Dacre, Harry   Daisy Bell, or, A Bicycle Built for Two, or, Daisy, Daisy; Elsie from Chelsea; I Can't Think Ob Nuthin' Else But You; I'll Be Your Sweetheart; Playmates

Daffan, Ted   I'm a Fool To Care

Dailey, J. Anton   Dreaming

Dale, Bob   Cinderella Sweetheart; Seventeen Candles

Dale, Jim   Georgy Girl

Dale, Joe   Tenderly

Dallas, R.C.   Bonja Song

Dalton, Bill   Short Shorts

Dalton, Lucy   Takin' It Easy

Daltry, Roger   Anyway, Anyhow, Anywhere

Daly, Joseph M.   The Chicken Reel; Daly's Reel

Damerell, Stanley J.   Butterflies in the Rain; Faith; I Bought Myself a Bottle of Ink; If; Let's All Sing Like the Birdies Sing; Life's Desire; Sailor Who Are You Dreaming of To-night; Sitting on a Fire Barred Gate; The Song of the Trees; There's a Lovely Lake in London; Unless; You Die If You Worry

Damrosch, Walter   Danny Deever

Dana, Mrs. Mary S.B.   Flee as a Bird

Dana, Walter   Longing for You

Daniel, Eliot   Blue Shadows on the Trail; I Love Lucy; Make Mine Music; Never; Uncle Remus Said

Daniels, Charles N., *see* **Neil Moret**

Daniels, Charlie   In America

Daniels, Walter   That's Where My Money Goes

Danielson, J.   Madrid

Danks, Hart Pease   Silver Threads Among the Gold

Dankworth, Johnny   The Avengers' Theme; The Colonel's Tune; Experiments with Mice; Itinerary of an Orchestra; What the Dickens

Danoff, Bill   Afternoon Delight; (Take Me Home) Country Road

Danoff, Mary Catherine   (Take Me Home) Country Road

Danoff, Taffy   (Take Me Home) Country Road

Danter, John   Have You Ever Been in Love

Danzig, Evelyn   Scarlet Ribbons (for Her Hair)

Darby, Ken   Make Mine Music

Darewski, Herman   The Army, the Navy and the Air Force; I Used To Sigh for the Silvery Moon; If You Could Care for Me; In the Twi-Twi-Twi-Light; Sister Susie's Sewing Shirts for Soldiers; When We've Wound Up the Watch on the Rhine

Darian, Fred   Mister Custer

Darin, Bobby   Dream Lover; Splish Splash; You're the Reason I'm Living

Darion, Joe   Changing Partners; Dulcinea; I'm Only Thinking of Him; The Impossible Dream, or, The Quest; Man of La Mancha; Ricochet

Darling, Erik   The Banana Boat Song (Day-O); Walk Right In

Darnell, August   Cherchez la Femme

Darnell, Shelby   There's a Star Spangled Banner Waving Somewhere

D'Artega, Alfred A.   In the Blue of Evening

Dash, Irwin   Blue Ribbon Gal; (What Has Become of) Hinky Dinky Parlay Voo

Dash, Julian   Tuxedo Junction

Daughtry, Dean   Imaginary Lover; So Into You

Davenant, Sir William   My Lodging (It) Is on the Cold Ground

Davenport, Charles "Cow-Cow"   Mama Don't Allow No Easy Riders Here; (I'll Be Glad When You're Dead) You Rascal You

Davenport, John R.   Fever

Davenport, Pembroke   My Restless Lover

David, Hal   Alfie; American Beauty Rose; Anyone Who Had a Heart; April Fools; Are You There (with Another Girl); Blue on Blue; Broken-Hearted Melody; (Theme from) Casino Royale; (They Long To Be) Close to You; Do You Know the Way to San Jose; A Fact Can Be a Beautiful Thing; The Four Winds and the Seven Seas; The Heart of a Fool; A House Is a Home; A House Is Not a Home; I Say a Little Prayer; I'll Never Fall in Love Again; Knowing When To Leave; The Look of Love; Magic Moments; Make It Easy on Yourself; The Man Who Shot Liberty Valance; Message to Michael; My Heart Is an Open Book; Odds and Ends (of a Beautiful Love Affair); One Less Bell To Answer; Only Love Can Break a Heart; Paper Mache; Promises Promises; Raindrops Keep Fallin' on My Head; Reach Out for Me; Story of My Life; There's Always Something There To Remind Me; This Guy's in Love with You; To All the Girls I've Loved Before; Trains and Boats and Planes; Walk On By; What the World Needs Now Is Love; What's New Pussycat; Whoever You Are, or, Sometimes Your Eyes Look Blue to Me; Windows of the World; Wishin' and Hopin'; (Theme from) Wives and Lovers; You'll Never Get to Heaven

David, Hubert W.   Felix Kept On Walking; Oh Star of Eve; A Rose in a Garden of Weeds

David, Lee   Hot Heels; Sipping Cider Thru' (Through) a Straw; Tonight You Belong to Me

David, Mack   Baby Baby Baby; Ballad of Cat Ballou; Bibbidi-Bobbodi-Boo; The Call of the Far-Away Hills; Candy; Cherry Pink and Apple Blossom White; Chi-Baba Chi-Baba (My Bambino Go To Sleep); Cinderella; A Dream Is a Wish Your Heart Makes; Falling Leaves; Gloria, or, Theme from Butterfield 8; Go, Go, Go, Go; Hanging Tree; Hawaiian Eye; Hush Hush Sweet Charlotte; I Don't Care If the Sun Don't Shine; I Like It—I Like It; It Only Hurts for a Little While; It's a Mad, Mad, Mad, Mad World; It's Love, Love, Love; Just a Kid Named Joe; Lawman; Moon Love; The Navy Gets the Gravy and the Army Gets the Beans; On the Isle of May; The Singing Hills; A Sinner Kissed an Angel; Sunflower; Tara's Theme; A Very Merry Un-Birthday to You; La Vie en Rose; Walk on the Wild Side; Wednesday's Child; Young Emotions

David, Russ   Where There's Life, There's Bud

David, Sunny   Whole Lot-ta Shakin' Goin' On

David, Worton   Are We Downhearted?—No!; Heart of a Rose; Helllo, Hello, Who's Your Lady Friend; Hold Your Hand Out Naughty Boy; Omaha; Playthings; That Old Fashioned Mother of Mine

Davidson, Eduardo   La Pachanga

Davidson, Leonard   Catch Us If You Can

Davie, Bob   The Green Door

Davies, John   Love's Eyes

Davies, Ray   All Day and All of the Night; Dedicated Follower of Fashion; Set Me Free; You Really Got Me

Davies, Richard   Goodbye Stranger; It's Raining Again; The Logical Song

Davies, William Henry   Knock, Knock, Who's There

Davis, Benny   Angel Child; Are You Sorry; Baby Face; Carolina Moon; Chasing Shadows; Cross Your Fingers; Dearest, You're the Nearest to My Heart; Don't Break the Heart That Loves You; Everything's Gonna Be All Right; First, Last and Always; Follow the Boys; Good-bye Broadway, Hello France; I Still Get a Thrill (Thinking of You); I'd Love To Meet That Old Sweetheart of Mine; I'm Nobody's Baby; Indiana Moon; Lonesome and Sorry; Make Believe; Margie; Oh! How I Miss You Tonight; Old Mill Wheel; Reaching for the Moon; Say It While Dancing; Sleepy Head; A Smile Will Go a Long, Long Way; Stella; There Goes My Heart; Why (Is There a Rainbow in the Sky); With These Hands; Yearning (Just for You)

Davis, Carl   (Theme from) The French Lieutenant's Woman

Davis, Charlie   Copenhagen

Davis, Clifton   Never Can Say Goodbye

Davis, Clive   All Out of Love

Davis, Collin   Take Me Back to Your Heart Again

Davis, Don   Disco Lady

Davis, George   Boy from New York City; Tell It Like It Is; The Yama Yama Man

Davis, Gussie L.   Down in Poverty Row; The Fatal Wedding; In the Baggage Coach Ahead; My Creole Sue; Only a Bowery Boy; Wait Till the Tide Comes In

Davis, Henry C.   The Marine's Hymn, or, From the Halls of Montezuma to the Shores of Tripoli

Davis, Jimmie   Lover Man (Oh Where Can You Be); You Are My Sunshine

Davis, Joe   Cu-Tu-Gu-Ru (Jack, Jack, Jack); Mary Ann; Perhaps, Perhaps, Perhaps

Davis, Link   Big Mamou

Davis, Lou   Hot Lips; I'm Sitting Pretty in a Pretty Little City; A Precious Little Thing Called Love

Davis, Mac   Baby Don't Get Hooked on Me; Hooked on Music; In the Ghetto; Texas in My Rear View Mirror

Davis, Mack   I Never Mention Your Name (Oh No); Moon Love

Davis, Paul   Bop; Cool Night; I Go Crazy; 65 Love Affair

Davis, Skeeter   My Last Date with You

Davis, Steve   Sleepin' with the Radio On

Davis, William   Gee! I'd Like To Teach the World To Sing

Davy, John   The Bay of Biscay O!

Dawes, General Charles Gates   It's All in the Game; Melody

Dawson, Eli   Pucker Up Your Lips, Miss Lindy

Day, Bobby   You'll Always Be My Lifetime Sweetheart

Deacon, John   Another One Bites the Dust; You're My Best Friend

Dean, Jimmy   Big Bad John; You Don't Have To Be a Star (To Be in My Show)

Dean, Mary   Half-Breed

Deane, Eddie V.   The Men in My Little Girl's Life; Rock-A-Billy

DeAngelis, Peter   Painted Tainted Rose; Why; Yesterday's Roses

Debarge, Bunny   Time Will Reveal

Debarge, Eldra   All This Love; Time Will Reveal

de Bru, Alberto   Rumba Rhapsody; Take It Easy

Debussy, Claude   Afternoon of a Faun; Clair de Lune; The Girl with the Flaxen Hair; Golliwogg's Cake Walk; Reverie

de Campo, V.   Chiapanecas (While There's Music There's Romance)

De Carlo, Gary   Na Na Hey Hey Kiss Him Goodbye

DeCosta, Harry   Mary, Dear, Some Day We Will Meet Again; Tiger Rag

de Curtis, Ernesto   Come Back to Sorrento

Dee, Joey   The Peppermint Twist

Dee, Johnnie   Don't Bring Me Down

Dee, Sylvia   Chickery Chick; It Couldn't Be True (or Could It); Laroo Laroo Lilli Bolero; My Sugar Is So Refined; Too Young; Who Do You Think You Are

Dees, Rick   Disco Duck (Part 1)

Dees, Sam   One in a Million You

Dees, William   Oh Pretty Woman

de Falla, Manuel   Ritual Fire Dance; The Three-Cornered Hat

DeFrancesco, L.E.   Madrid

de Fuentes, Eduardo Sanchez   Mirame Así, or, Grant Those Glances, or, Look At Me; O Cuba (Tu)

Degeyter, Adolphe   L'Internationale

Degeyter, Pierre   L'Internationale

de Giardini, Felice   Come, Thou Almighty King

De Haven, Carter   Beautiful Eyes

Dehr, Richard   Greenfields; Marianne; Memories Are Made of This

DeJesus, Luchi   A Rockin' Good Way (To Mess Around and Fall in Love)

De John, Dux   No More

De John, Julie   No More

De John, Leo   No More

De Knight, Jimmy   (We're Gonna) Rock Around the Clock

DeKoven, Reginald   Armorer's Song; Brown October Ale; Oh Promise Me; Quilter Has the Brains; Recessional

de Lachau, Countess Ada   Li'l Liza Jane

Delamarre, Louis   Love, Here Is My Heart; My Belgian Rose

Delaney, Tom   Jazz Me Blues

De Lange, Eddie   All This and Heaven Too; Along the Navajo Trail; And So Do I; Darn That Dream; Deep in a Dream; Do You Know What It Means To Miss New Orleans; Haunting Me; Heaven Can Wait; I Wish I Were Twins; If I'm Lucky; Moonglow; Passé; So Help Me; Solitude; A String of Pearls; This Is Worth Fighting For

Delanoe, Pierre   The Day the Rains Came; Let It Be Me; What Now My Love

de Lau Lusignan, J.   Estudiantina

Del Campo, C.R.   Adios

De Leon, Robert   Can't Get Indiana off My Mind

Delettre, Jean   Hands Across the Table

Delia, Richard   Viceroy Gives You All the Taste All the Time

Délibes, Léo   Pizzicati; Waltz Coppélia; Valse Lente

de Lisle, Claude Joseph Rouget   La Marseillaise

Delmore, Alton   Beautiful Brown Eyes

de Longpré, Michael   Ma Li'l Batteau

De Lory, Al   Mister Custer

del Riego, Teresa   Homing; O Dry Those Tears; Sink Red Sun; Thank God for a Garden

Del Turco, R.   Something Is Happening

DeLugg, Milton   Be My Life's Companion; Hoop-Dee-Doo; Just Another Polka; My Lady Loves To Dance; Orange Colored Sky; Sailor Boys Have Talk to Me in English; Shanghai

de Lulli, Arthur (Euphemia Allen)   Chopsticks

de Metruis, Claude   Hard-Headed Woman

Demey, Tetos   You, You, You Are the One

de Micheli, G.   Love Forever I Adore You

de Moraes, Vincius   The Girl from Ipanema; She's a Carioca

de Mortimer, Garfield   Pickin' a Chicken

Dempsey, J.E.   (Beautiful) Garden of Roses

Dempster, William Richardson   The Lament of the Irish Emigrant

de Musset, Alfred   Fortunio's Song (Fortunio)

Demy, Jacques   (If It Takes Forever) I Will Wait for You

Denby, Jack   Let's Keep It That Way; Sweetheart, We'll Never Grow Old

Denison, C.M.   In Twilight Town; The Land of Golden Dreams; My Rosary of Dreams

Denni, Lucien   The Oceana Roll

Denniker, Paul   Beside an Open Fireplace; It's Make Believe Ballroom Time; S'posin'

Dennis, Matt   Everything Happens to Me; Let's Get Away from It All; The Night We Called It a Day

Denny, Sandy   Who Knows Where the Time Goes

Denoncin, René   Valley Valparaiso

Densmore, John   Hello, I Love You (Won't You Tell Me Your Name); Light My Fire

Densmore, John Hopkins   Roadways

Denver, John   Annie's Song; Calypso; I'm Sorry; Leaving on a Jet Plane; Rocky Mountain High; Sunshine on My Shoulders; Take Me Home Country Roads

Denza, Luigi   Funiculì—Funiculà

Deodato, Eumir   Celebration; Theme from 2001: A Space Odyssey

de Oliveira, Milton   Come to the Mardi Gras

Depastas, Francois   Boy on a Dolphin

de Paul, Gene   Cow-Cow Boogie; He's My Guy; If I Had My Druthers; I'll (I) Remember April; Irresistible You; Jubilation T. Cornpone; Love in a Home; Lovely Luana; Milkman Keep Those Bottles Quiet; Mister Five by Five; Namely You; Short, Fat and 4F; Sobbin' Women; Spring, Spring, Spring; Star Eyes; Teach Me Tonight; What's Good for General Bullmoose; You Don't Know What Love Is

de Paul, Lynsey   No Honestly!; Won't Somebody Dance with Me

Deppen, Jessie L.   In the Garden of Tomorrow; A Japanese Sunset; Oh Miss Hannah

Dermer, Lawrence   Bad Boy

DeRose, Peter   As the Years Go By; Autumn Serenade; Deep Purple; Down Among the Sugar-Cane; Have You Ever Been Lonely (Have You Ever Been Blue); I Just Roll Along Havin' My Ups and Downs; The Lamp Is Low; Lilacs in the Rain; Love Ya; A Marshmallow World; Moonlight Mood; Muddy Water; On a Little Street in Singapore; Rain; Somebody Loves You; Somewhere in Old Wyoming; Song of the Blacksmith; That's Where I Came In; Wagon Wheels; When I'm Gone I Won't Forget; When Your Hair Has Turned to Silver, I Will Love You Just the Same

DeShannon, Jackie   Bette Davis Eyes; Dum Dum; Put a Little Love in Your Heart

d'Esposito, Salve   Anema e Core (With All My Heart and Soul)

DeSylva, B.G.   Alabamy Bound; April Showers; Avalon; Baby; The Best Things in Life Are Free; The Birth of the Blues; Black Bottom; Button Up Your Overcoat; California, Here I Come; Come to Me; Cross Your Heart; (Please) Do It Again; Don't Hold Everything; Don't Tell Her (What Happened to Me); Eadie Was a Lady; Follow Thru; Gentlemen Prefer Blondes; The Girl Is You and the Boy Is Me; A Girl of the Pi Beta Phi; Good News; Headin' for Louisville; Here Am I—Broken Hearted; I Won't Say I Will, But I Won't Say I Won't; If I Had a Talking Picture of You; If You Knew Susie, Like I Know Susie; I'll Build a Stairway to Paradise; I'll Say She Does; I'm a Dreamer (Aren't We All); It All Depends On You; Just a Cottage Small—by a Waterfall; Just a Memory; Just Imagine; Keep Smiling At Trouble; Kickin' the Clouds Away; A Kiss in the Dark; Let's Call It a Day; Look for the Silver Lining; Lucky Day; Lucky in Love; Memory Lane; Minnie the Mermaid, or, A Love Song in Fish Time; My Lucky Star; My Sin; My Song; 'N Everything; Nobody But You; Oh Murphy; One More Time; Rise and Shine; Save Your Sorrow for Tomorrow; Seventh Heaven; So Blue; So Do I; Somebody Loves Me; Sonny Boy; Strike Me Pink; (Keep Your) Sunny Side Up; The Sweetest Thing in Life; Tell Me More; Thank Your Father; That's Why Darkies Were Born; Then I'll Have Time for You; This Is the Missus; The Thrill Is Gone; To Know You Is To Love You; Together; Turn On the Heat; Turn Out the Light; The Varisty Drag; When Day Is Done; Whip-Poor-Will; Why Do I Love You; Wishing (Will Make It So); The Yankee Doodle Blues; Yoo-Hoo; You Ain't Heard Nothing Yet; You Find the Time, I'll Find the Place; You Try Somebody Else, and I'll Try Somebody Else (We'll Be Back Together Again); You Wouldn't Fool Me, Would You; You're an Old Smoothie; You're the Cream in My Coffee

de Torre, Emilio   Chiapanecas (While There's Music There's Romance)

Dett, R. Nathaniel   Juba Dance

Deutsch, Emery   He's a Gypsy from Poughkeepsie; Play, Fiddle, Play; Stardust on the Moon; When a Gypsy Makes His Violin Cry

Deutsch, Helen   Hi Lili Hi Lo; Take My Love

Deutschend, Henri John   Country Road

Devere, Sam   The Whistling Coon

Devere, William   The Mottoes Framed upon the Wall

deVita, A.   Softly as I Leave You

Devito, Henry   Queen of Hearts

De Vol, Frank   Hush Hush Sweet Charlotte

De Vorzon, Barry   Nadia's Theme, or, The Young and the Restless

de Vries, John   Oh Look At Me Now

Dewar, Wally   Best of All

DeWitt, Francis   The Moon Shines on the Moonshine

Dexter, Al   Pistol Packin' Mama

De Young, Dennis   The Best of Times; Desert Moon; Mr. Roboto

d'Hardelot, Guy   Because; I Know a Lovely Garden; Wait

Diamond, Gregg   More More More (Part 1)

Diamond, Keith   Caribbean Queen (No More Love on the Run); Loverboy; Mystery Lady; Suddenly

Diamond, Lee   Tell It Like It Is

Diamond, Max   My Boomerang Won't Come Back

Diamond, Neil   And the Grass Won't Pay No Mind; Cracklin' Rosie; Forever in Blue Jeans; Heartlight; Hello Again; Holly Holy; I Am, I Said; I'm a Believer; A Little Bit Me, a Little Bit You; Love on the Rocks; On the Way to the Sky; Say Maybe; Song Sung Blue; Sweet Caroline (Sweet Times Never Seemed So Good)

Diamond, Steve   I've Got a Rock 'n' Roll Heart

Dibdin, Charles   High Barbaree; Love Has Eyes; (Poor) Tom Bowling, or, The Sailor's Epitaph

Dibdin, Thomas John   The Origin of Gunpowder, or, When Vulcan Forg'd the Bolts of Jove

di Capua, Edoardo   'O Sole Mio

Dichmont, William   Such a Li'l Fellow

di Cicco, R.   Bobby Sox (Socks) to Stockings

Dick, Dorothy   Call Me Darling; The Kiss That You've Forgotten (Is the Kiss I Can't Forget)

Dickerson, Morris D.   The Cisco Kid; Gypsy Man; Summer; Why Can't We Be Friends

Dickinson, John   The Liberty Song, or, Come, Join Hand in Hand, or, In Freedom We're Born

Dicks, Ted   Hole in the Ground; Right Said Fred; A Windmill in Old Amsterdam

Didée, Julien   Hosanna

Didier, Julie   Anyone Who Isn't Me Tonight

Dietz, Howard   All the King's Horses; Alone Together; By Myself; Confession; Dancing in the Dark; The Dickey Bird Song; Got a Bran' New Suit; Hammacher Schlemmer, I Love You; Haunted Heart; Heaven on Earth; I Guess I'll Have To Change My Plan; I Love Louisa; I See Your Face Before Me; If There Is Someone Lovelier Than You; Louisiana Hayride; The Love I Long For; Love Is a Dancing Thing; Lucky Seven; Moanin' Low; New Sun in the Sky; O Leo; A Shine on Your Shoes; Something To Remember You By; That's Entertainment; You and the Night and the Music; You Have Everything

Dieval, Jacques J.J.   The Way of Love

Di Gregorio, Taz   In America

di Lazzaro, Eldo   Ferryboat Serenade; The Woodpecker(s') Song

Dill, Danny   Detroit City

Dillea, Herbert   Absence Makes the Heart Grow Fonder; You're De Apple of My Eye

Dillon, Dean   By Now

Dillon, Harry   Do, Do, My Huckleberry Do; Put Me Off at Buffalo

Dillon, John   Do, Do, My Huckleberry Do; Put Me Off at Buffalo

Dillon, Lawrence M.   Every Little Bit Added to What You've Got Makes Just a Little Bit More

Dillon, William A.   All Alone; The End of the Road; Every Little Bit Added to What You've Got Makes Just a Little Bit More; Goodbye, Boys; I Want a Girl—Just Like the Girl That Married Dear Old Dad; It's the Irish in Your Eye, (It's the Irish in Your Smile); My Little Girl

Di Minno, Danny   Return to Me

Di Mucci, Dion   Runaround Sue

Dinicu, Grigoras   Hora Staccato

Di Paola, V.   For the First Time (Come Prima)

DiPiero, Bob   American Made

Distel, Sacha   The Good Life

Ditchman, Martin   The Sweetest Taboo

Di Tommaso, Larry   Do What You Do

Dix, J. Airlie   The Trumpeter

Dixey, E.F.   Folks That Put On Airs

Dixon, Alfred R.   Love in an Automobile

Dixon, Dave   I Dig Rock and Roll Music

Dixon, Eugene   The Duke of Earl

Dixon, Julius   Lollipop

Dixon, Luther   A Hundred Pounds of Clay; Just Born To Be Your Baby; Sixteen Candles; Soldier Boy; Why Baby Why

Dixon, Mort   Bam, Bam, Bamy Shore; By Bye Blackbird; Fare Thee Well, Annabelle; Flirtation Walk; Follow the Swallow; I Found a Million Dollar Baby in a Five and Ten Cent Store; I Wonder Who's Dancing with You Tonight; If I Had a Girl Like You; If You Want the Rainbow (You Must Have the Rain); I'm Looking Over a Four Leaf Clover; Just Like a Butterfly (That's Caught in the Rain); The Lady in Red; Marching Along Together; Mister (Mr.) and Mrs. Is the Name; Nagasaki; Old Man Sunshine—Little Boy Bluebird; Ooh That Kiss; River, Stay 'Way from My Door; That Old Gang of Mine; Too Many Parties and Too Many Pals; The Torch Song; Would You Like To Take a Walk; You're My Everything

Dixon, Reg   Confidentially

Dixon, Willie   Little Red Rooster

Doane, William Howard   (Jesus Keep Me) Near the Cross; Rescue the Perishing; Safe in the Arms of Jesus; Tell Me the Old, Old Story; Though Your Sins Be as Scarlet

Dobbins, Georgia   Mashed Potato Time

Dobbins, Shelley   Non Dimenticar

Dobson, Bonnie   Morning Dew

Dodd, Dorothy   Granada

Dodds, Malcolm   (Look For the) Union Label

Dodge, Gilbert   Peggy O'Neil

Dodridge, Phillip   How Dry I Am

Dodson, Gerald   The Fishermen of England

Doelle, Franz   When the Whites Lilacs Bloom Again

Doerr, Eddie   Oh You Million Dollar Baby

Doggett, Bill   Honkey Tonk

Dolan, Robert Emmett   And So to Bed; Little By Little

Dole, Nathan Haskel   Hosanna

Dollimore, Ralph   Big City Suite

Dolph, Jack   I Hear Music

Dominguez, Alberto   Frenesi; Perfidia

Domino, Antoine "Fats"   Ain't That a Shame; Blue Monday; I'm in Love Again; I'm Walkin'

Donaggio, P.   You Don't Have To Say You Love Me

Donaldson, B.B.B.   I Faw Down an' Go Boom

Donaldson, Walter   (What Can I Say, Dear) After I Say I'm Sorry; At Sundown; Beside a Babbling Brook; But I Do— You Know I Do; Carolina in the Morning; Changes; Cuckoo in the Clock; The Daughter of Rosie O'Grady; Did I Remember; Don't Cry, Frenchy, Don't Cry; Doo Wacka Doo; An Evening in Caroline; For My Sweetheart; Georgia; How Ya Gonna Keep 'Em Down on the Farm (After They've Seen Paree); I Wonder Where My Baby Is Tonight; I'd Be Lost Without You; I'll Be Happy When the Preacher Makes You Mine; I'm Bringing a Red, Red Rose; In the Middle of the Night; Isn't She the Sweetest Thing; It's Been So Long; I've Had My Moments; Just Like a Melody Out of the Sky; Just Try To Picture Me (Back (Down) Home in Tennessee); Kansas City Kitty; Lazy Lou'siana Moon; Let It Rain! Let It Pour! (I'll Be in Virginia in the Morning); Little White Lies; Love Me or Leave Me; Makin' Whoopee; Mister Meadowlark; My Baby Just Cares for Me; My Best Girl; My Blue Heaven; My Buddy; My Mammy; My Sweetie Turned Me Down; On the Gin, Gin, Ginny Shore; Romance; Sam, the Old Accordion Man; Seven or Eleven—My Dixie Pair o' Dice; Sweet Jennie Lee; That Certain Party; We'll Have a Jubilee in My Old Kentucky Home; When My Ship Comes In; Where'd You Get Those Eyes; Yes Sir, That's My Baby; You (Gee But You're Wonderful); You Didn't Have To Tell Me—I Knew It All the Time; You'd Never Know the Old Home Town of Mine; You're a Million Miles from Nowhere When You're One Little Mile from Home; You're Driving Me Crazy (What Did I Do); You've Got Everything

Donaldson, Will   Doo Wacka Doo

Donegan, Lonnie   Lively; My Old Man's a Dustman; Rock Island Line

Donida, Carlo   Al-Di-La; Help Yourself; I Who Have Nothing

Donnelly, Dorothy   Deep in My Heart, Dear; Drinking Song; Golden Days; Just We Two; Mother; Serenade; Silver Moon; Song of Love; Your Land and My Land

Donnelly, Harry   Inka Dinka Doo

Donnelly, Robert   Don't Go Down the Mine

Dononcin, Rene   Kiss and Run

Donovan   Ballad of a Crystal Man; Catch the Wind; Colours; Mellow Yellow; To Sing for You; Why Do You Treat Me Like You Do

Donovan, Walter   The Aba Daba Honeymoon; Down by the Winegar Woiks; One Dozen Roses

Dore, Charlie   Strut

Dore, W.   Da-Da, Da-Da

Dorel, Francis   The Garden of Your Heart

Dorff, Stephen   Another Honky Tonk Night on Broadway; Every Which Way But Loose; Fire in the Morning; I Don't Think I'm Ready for You; I Just Fall in Love Again; Through the Years

Dorman, Harold   Mountain of Love

Doroschuk, Ivan   The Safety Dance

Dorset, Ray   In the Summertime

Dorsey, Jimmy   I'm Glad There Is You

Doty, Charles   My Lady Lou

Dougherty, Dan   Glad Rag Doll

Dougherty, Doc   I'm Confessin' That I Love You

Dougherty, W.A., Jr.   Across the Field

Douglas, Bert   When Your Old Wedding Ring Was New

Douglas, Carl   Kung Fu Fighting

Douglas, George   What a Wonderful World

Douglas, Lew   Have You Heard; Pretend; Why Don't You Believe Me

Douglas, Sallie   Follow the Gleam

Douglas, William   Annie Laurie

do Vale, Amadeu   Lisbon Antigua, or, In Old Lisbon

Dowden, C.   Long-Haired Lover from Liverpool

Dowell, Jim   Headed for Heartache

Dowell, Saxie   Playmates; Three Little Fishes

Dowling, Eddie   The Little White House (at the End of Honeymoon Lane)

Downes, David   Come Dancing

Downes, Geoffrey   Heart of the Moment; Video Killed the Radio Star

Downey, Morton   Wabash Moon

Doyle, Walter   Mysterious Mose

Dozier, Lamont   Baby Love; Back in My Arms Again; Come See About Me; The Happening; (Love Is Like a) Heat Wave; Heaven Must Have Sent You; How Sweet It Is (To Be Loved By You); I Can't Help Myself; I Hear a Symphony; Love Is Here and Now You're Gone; Reach Out I'll Be There; Reflections; Stop! In the Name of Love; Take Me in Your Arms (Rock Me a Little While); Where Did Our Love Go; You Can't Hurry Love; You Keep Me Hangin' On

Drake, Charlie   My Boomerang Won't Come Back

Drake, Ervin   Al-Di-La; Come to the Mardi Gras; Good Morning Heartache; I Believe; It Was a Very Good Year; Made for Each Other; Meet Mister Callaghan; Perdido; A Room Without Windows; Sonata; Tico Tico

Drake, Jimmy   Transfusion

Drake, Milton   The Champagne Waltz; I'm a Big Girl Now; Java Jive; Kiss Me Sweet; Mairzy Doats; Nina Never Knew

Drdla, Frantisek   Souvenir

Drejac, Jean   Under Paris Skies

Dresser, Paul   The Blue and the Gray, or, A Mother's Gift to Her Country; The Boys Are Coming Home Today; Calling to Her Boy Just Once Again; Come Home, Dewey, We Won't Do a Thing to You; Come Tell Me What's Your Answer, Yes or No; The Convict and the Bird; The Curse of the Dreamer; Don't Tell Her That You Love Her; A Dream of My Boyhood Days; Every Night There's a Light; He Brought Home Another; He Fought for a Cause He Thought Was Right; I Just Want To Go Back and Start the Whole Thing Over; I Was Looking for My Boy, She Said, or, Decoration Day; I Wish That You Were Here Tonight; I Wonder If She'll Ever Come Back to Me; I Wonder Where She Is Tonight; I'd Still Believe You True; If You See My Sweetheart; In Dear Old Illinois; In Good Old New York Town; In the Great Somewhere; I'se Your Nigger If You Want Me, Liza Jane; Jean; Just Tell Them That You Saw Me; The Letter That Never Came; Lincoln, Grant or Lee; Mister Volunteer, or, You Don't

Belong to the Regulars, You're Just a Volunteer; My Gal Sal, or, They Call her Frivolous Sal; My Heart Still Clings to the Old First Love; The Old Flame Flickers and I Wonder Why; On the Banks of the Wabash Far Away; Once Ev'ry Year; Our Country, May She Always Be Right; The Outcast Unknown; The Pardon Came Too Late; The Path That Leads the Other Way; She Went to the City; Show Me the Way; Sweet Savannah; Take a Seat, Old Lady; There's No North or South Today; There's Where My Heart Is Tonight; The Town Where I Was Born; The Voice of the Hudson; Way Down in Old Indiana; We Came from the Same Old State; We Fight Tomorrow, Mother; We Were Sweethearts for Many Years; When De Moon Comes Up Behind De Hill; When the Birds Have Sung Themselves to Sleep; When You Come Back They'll Wonder Who the——You Are; Where Are the Friends of Other Days; Your God Comes First, Your Country Next, Then Mother Dear; You're Going Far Away, Lad, or, I'm Still Your Mother, Dear; You're (You'se) Just a Little Nigger, Still You're Mine, All Mine

Dreyer, Dave   Back in Your Own Back Yard; (Does Your Mother Know You're Out) Cecilia; Golden Gate; Me and My Shadow; There's a Rainbow Round My Shoulder; Wabash Moon

Driftwood, Jimmy   The Battle of New Orleans

Drigo, Riccardo   Serenade

Drislane, Jack   After All That I've Been to You; Arrah Wanna; Dear Old Rose; The Good Old U.S.A.; Honey-Love; I'm Awfully Glad I Met You; It's Great To Be a Soldier Man; Just a Little Rocking Chair and You; Keep a Little Cozy Corner in Your Heart for Me; Keep on the Sunny Side; Longing for You; Monkey Doodle Dandy; Nobody's Little Girl; Somebody Else, It's Always Somebody Else; Won't You Be My Honey; You Remind Me of the Girl That Used To Go to School with Me; You Taught Me How To Love You, Now Teach Me To Forget

Drummond, William Henry   Leetle Bateese; The Wreck of the "Julie Plante"

Dryden, Leo   The Miner's Dream of Home

Dubey, Matt   Mutual Admiration Society; A New-Fangled Tango

Dubin, Al   About a Quarter to Nine; All the World Will Be Jealous of Me; Along the Santa Fe Trail; Am I in Love; The Anniversary Waltz; Boulevard of Broken Dreams; Clear Out of This World; Coffee in the Morning, Kisses at Night; A Cup of Coffee, a Sandwich and You; (I'm) Dancing with Tears in My Eyes; Don't Give Up the Ship; Fair and Warmer; Feudin' and Fightin' For You; Forty-Second Street; The Girl at the Ironing Board; The Girl Friend of the Whirling Dervish; Half-Way to Heaven; (What Has Become of) Hinky Dinky Parlay Voo; I Know Now; I Only Have Eyes for You; If You Should Ever Need Me (You'll Always Find Me Here); I'll Sing You a Thousand Love Songs; (You May Not Be an Angel But) I'll String Along with You; Indian Summer; Just a Girl That Men Forget; Keep Young and Beautiful; The Kiss Waltz; The Latin Quarter; The Little Things You Used To Do; Lullaby of Broadway; Lulu's Back in Town; Many Happy Returns of the Day; Memories of France; My Dream of the Big Parade; Nobody Knows What a Red Head Mama Can Do; Painting the Clouds with Sunshine; Pettin' in the Park;

Remember Me; The Rose in Her Hair; Sally; September in the Rain; Shadow Waltz; Shanghai Lil; She's a Latin from Manhattan; Shuffle Off to Buffalo; South American Way; Summer Night; Three's a Crowd; Tip Toe Through the Tulips (with Me); Too Many Tears; (On the Shores of) Tripoli; Waters of Perkiomen; We're in the Money, or, The Gold Diggers' Song; Where Am I; With Plenty of Money and You; Wonder Bar; The Words Are in My Heart; You Let Me Down; Young and Healthy; You're Getting To Be a Habit with Me

Dubin, Joseph S.   This Is Your Life

Duboff, Steve   The Pied Piper; The Rain, the Park and Other Things

DuBois, Tim   Love in the First Degree; She Got the Goldmine I Got the Shaft

Duchin, Eddy   My Twilight Dream

Duckworth, Willie Lee   Sound Off

Dudan, Pierre   Clopin Clopant; Comme Ci, Comme Ca; Softly, Softly

Duddy, Lyn   I Love Bosco; Johnny Angel

Dukas, Paul   The Sorcerer's Apprentice

Duke, Vernon   April in Paris; Autumn in New York; Cabin in the Sky; I Can't Get Started (with You); I Like the Likes of You; I'm Gonna Ring the Bell Tonight; The Love I Long For; Now; Suddenly; Taking a Chance on Love; That's Life; That's What Makes Paris Paree; This Is Romance; We're Having a Baby; What Is There To Say; Words Without Music

Dumont, Frank   The Alabama Blossoms; Bake Dat Chicken Pie; Jennie, the Flower of Kildare; Plant a Watermelon on My Grave and Let the Juice Soak Through

Dunbar, Paul Lawrence   Who Dat Say Chicken in Dis Crowd

Dunbar, Ronald   Patches (I'm Depending on You); You've Got Me Dangling on a String

Duncan, Jimmy   My Special Angel

Duncan, Malcolm   Pick Up the Pieces

Duncan, Rosetta   Rememb'ring

Duncan, Trevor   March from "A Little Suite"

Duncan, Vivian   Rememb'ring

Duncan, Wayne   Wasted Days Wasted Nights

Duncan, William Cary   My Toreador; When the Cherry Blossoms Fall

Dunham, William D.   Ah But It Happens

Duning, George W.   (Theme from) Picnic; Song Without End

Dunlap, Louis   You Can Depend on Me

Dunlap, William   He Who His Country's Liv'ry Wears; When a Woman Hears the Sound of the Drum and Fife

Dunn, Artie   Twilight Time

Dunn, Charles   The King's Navee

Dunn, Larry   Shining Star

Dunne, James   Nobody Loves Me Like You Do

Dunning, J.   Baby We Can't Go Wrong

Dupont, Paul   La Rosita

Dupree, Harry   Lisbon Antigua, or, In Old Lisbon

Dupree, Robbie   Steal Away

Durand, Paul Jules   All My Love; Mademoiselle de Paris

Durandeau, A.E.   Ask a Policeman

Durante, Jimmy   Inka Dinka Doo

Durden, Tommy   Heartbreak Hotel

D'Urfey, Thomas   Within a Mile of Edinburgh

Durham, Eddie   I Don't Want To Set the World on Fire; Topsy

Durrill, John   Dark Lady

Durso, Michael   Petticoats of Portugal

Durstine, Barton   Pepsi's Got a Lot To Give, You've Got a Lot To Live

Dusenberry, E.F.   In Twilight Town; The Land of Golden Dreams; My Rosary of Dreams

Dvořák, Anton   From the New World Symphony; Goin' Home; Humoresque; Hungarian Dances; Slavonic Dances; Songs My Mother Taught Me

Dwight, John Sullivan   Christmas Song, or, O Holy Night

Dwight, Reginald K.   Part-Time Lover

Dyer, Desmond   Sky High

Dykes, John Bacchus   Holy! Holy! Lord God Almighty; Lead, Kindly Light

Dylan, Bob   All I Really Want To Do; Blowin' in the Wind; Don't Think Twice, It's All Right; A Hard Rain's a-Gonna Fall; It Ain't Me Babe; Just Like a Woman; Knockin' on Heaven's Door; Lay, Lady, Lay; Like a Rolling Stone; Mister Tambourine Man; Positively Fourth Street; Rainy Day Women #12 & 35; She Belongs to Me; The Times They Are A-Changin'

Dyrenforth, James   Always; A Garden in the Rain; One Love Forever; Possibly; Running Between the Raindrops

Eardley, Wilmot D.   Little Grey Home in the West

Earl, Mary   Beautiful Ohio; Dreamy Alabama; Lafayette—We Hear You Calling

East, Nathan   Easy Lover

Eastburn, R.A., *see* **Joseph E. Winner**

Eastmond, Barry   There'll Be Sad Songs (To Make You Cry); When the Going Gets Tough, the Tough Get Going

Easton, Lynn   The Jolly Green Giant

Eaton, Jimmy   Blue Champagne; Dance with a Dolly; I Double Dare You; When the Circus Came to Town

Eaton, W.G.   Oh, the Fairies, Whoa, the Fairies

Ebb, Fred   All That Jazz; Believe; Cabaret; City Lights; Class; The Grass Is Always Greener; The Happy Time; If You Could See Her; The Life of the Party; Life Is; Married; Maybe This Time; Meeskite; Mein Herr; Mister Cellophane; Money (Money); The Money Song; My Coloring Book; My Own Best Friend; Razzle Dazzle; The Top of the Hill; Two Ladies; Under the Roller Coaster; Wallflower; Why Can't I Speak; Willkommen

Eberhart, Nelle Richmond   At Dawning; Far Off I Hear a Lover's Flute; From the Land of the Sky Blue Water; I Hear a Thrush at Eve; The Moon Drops Low; The White Dawn Is Stealing

Echols, Odis   Sugartime

Eckert, Carl   Swiss (Echo) Song

Eddy, Duane   Shazam

Edelheit, Harry   If You Had All the World and Its Gold

Edens, Roger   The French Lesson; It's a Great Day for the Irish; Minnie from Trinidad; Our Love Affair; Pass That Peace Pipe

Edgar, Marriott   The Lion and Albert

Edmeston, James   Saviour, Breathe an Evening Blessing

Edwards, Bernard   Dance, Dance, Dance (Yowsah, Yowsah, Yowsah); Good Times; Upside Down; We Are Family

Edwards, Clara   By the Bend of the River; With the Wind and the Rain in Your Hair

Edwards, Doug   Wildflower

Edwards, Earl   The Duke of Earl

Edwards, Edwin B.   At the Jazz Band Ball; Barnyard Blues; Bluin' the Blues; Clarinet Marmalade; Ostrich Walk

Edwards, Francis   Your Love Is My Love

Edwards, Fred   In America

Edwards, Gus   By the Light of the Silvery Moon; Goodbye, Little Girl, Goodbye; He's Me Pal; I Can't Tell Why I Love You, But I Do; I Just Can't Make My Eyes Behave; If a Girl Like You Loved a Boy Like Me; If I Was a Millionaire; I'll Be with You When the Roses Bloom Again; In My Merry Oldsmobile; In Zanzibar—My Little Chimpanzee; (Look Out For) Jimmy Valentine; Mamie (Don't You Feel Ashamie); My Cousin Caruso; Orange Blossom Time; School Days; The Singer and the Song; Sunbonnet Sue; Tammany; Way Down Yonder in the Cornfield; Your Mother and Mine

Edwards, James   Sh-Boom

Edwards, Joan   I Love Bosco

Edwards, Julian   My Own United States; Sweet Thoughts of Home

Edwards, Leo   Isle d'Amour (Isle of Love)

Edwards, Michael   Once in a While

Edwards, Ralph   Why Worry

Edwards, Raymond W.   Get a Job

Edwards, Sherman   Broken-Hearted Melody; Dungaree Doll; Momma Look Sharp; See You in September; Wonderful Wonderful

Edwards, Vincent   Right Back Where We Started From

Egan, Jack   Be Still My Heart

Egan, Joe   Stuck in the Middle (with You)

Egan, Raymond B.   Ain't We Got Fun; Bimini Bay; I Never Knew I Could Love Anybody Like I'm Loving You; The Japanese Sandman; Mammy's (a) Little Coal Black Rose; Sleepy Time Gal; Some Sunday Morning; Tell Me Why You Smile Mona Lisa; Three on a Match; Till We Meet Again; When Shall We Meet Again; Where the Morning Glories Grow

Ehrlich, Sam   Oh! Frenchy

Eichler, Alfred   Aqua Velva Man

Eichler, Julian   Aqua Velva Man

Eilenberg, Richard   Petersbourgh Sleighride

Eisen, Stanley   Detroit Rock City

Elbel, Louis   The Victors

Eldee, Lilian   The Garden of Love

Elgar, Edward   The Land of Hope and Glory; Pomp and Circumstance; Salut d'Amour

Elgin, Bob   A Hundred Pounds of Clay; Our Favourite Melodies

Eli, Bobby   Love Won't Let Me Wait

Eliot, T.S.   Grizabella the Glamour Cat; Memory; Mister Mistoffolees

Eliscu, Edward   Carioca; Flying Down to Rio; Great Day; More Than You Know; Music Makes Me; Orchids in the Moonlight; (When) They Cut Down the Old Pine Tree; Without a Song; You Forgot Your Gloves

Elliman, Yvonne   Get Ready

Ellingson, David   Don't Fall in Love with a Dreamer

Ellingson, Kim Carnes   Don't Fall in Love with a Dreamer

Ellington, Edward Kennedy "Duke"   Black and Tan Fantasy; C-Jam Blues; Caravan; Cotton Tail; Creole Love Call; Do Nothin' Till You Hear from Me; Don't Get Around Much Anymore; I Didn't Know About You; I Got It Bad and That Ain't Good; I Let a Song Go Out of My Heart; I'm Beginning To See the Light; In a Sentimental Mood; It Don't Mean a Thing If It Ain't Got That Swing; Mood Indigo; Prelude to a Kiss; Ring Dem Bells; Rockin' in Rhythm; Satin Doll; Solitude; Sophisticated Lady

Elliot, Brian   Papa Don't Preach

Elliot, Charlotte   Just As I Am Without One Plea

Elliot, Leslie   We've Got To Keep Up with the Joneses

Elliott, George W.   The Belle of Mohawk Vale, or, Bonny (ie) Eloise

Elliott, Jack   I Think of You; It's So Nice To Have a Man Around the House; Sam's Song; Theme from S.W.A.T.

Elliott, John M.   Do You Care

Elliott, Percy   Mate o' Mine

Elliott, Zo   There's a Long, Long Trail

Ellis, Barbara   Come Softly to Me

Ellis, Jack   I Can Get It for You Wholesale

Ellis, Melville   When Love Is Young in Springtime

Ellis, Seger   Little Jack Frost Get Lost

Ellis, Vivian   Coronation Scot; The Flies Crawled Up the Window; I Was Never Kissed Before; I'm on a See-Saw; Ma Belle Marguerita; Me and My Dog; Other People's Babies; She's My Lovely; Spread a Little Happiness; Sweet; There's Always Tomorrow; This Is My Lovely Day; The Water Gypsies

Ellis, Walter   My Heart and I; There Are Angels Outside Heaven

Ellis, William   Turn 'Erbert's Face to the Wall, Mother

Elliston, Shirley   The Name Game

Ellstein, Abraham   The Wedding Samba

Ellsworth, Bob   Somebody Else Is Taking My Place

Elman, Ziggy   And the Angels Sing

Elson, Louis Charles   Within the Cellar's Depth I Sit

Elston, Harry   Grazin' in the Grass

Elton, Louis   When They Sound the Last All Clear

Ember, Michael   If You Go (Away)

Emerick, George H.   You're De Apple of My Eye

Emerson, Ida   Hello! Ma Baby

Emmerich, Bob   Our Love

Emmet, Joseph Kline   Emmet's Lullaby, or, Fritz, Our Cousin German, or, Brother's Lullaby; Sweet Violets

Emmett, Daniel Decatur (Old Dan D. Emmit(t))   De Boatman's Dance; (I Wish I Was in) Dixie, or, Dixie's Land; Jimmy Crack Corn, or, The Blue Tail Fly; My Old Aunt Sally; Old Dan Tucker

Emmons, Bobby   Women Do Know How To Carry On

Emrys-Roberts, Kenyon   Poldark

Endor, Chick   Who Takes Care of the Caretaker's Daughter While the Caretaker's Busy Taking Care?

Endsley, Melvin   Singin' the Blues

Enesco, Georges   Rumanian Rhapsody

Engelmann, Hans   Melody of Love; Whisper That You Love Me

Englander, Ludwig   Strollers We

English, Scott   Bend Me, Shape Me; Mandy

English, Thomas Dunn   Sweet Alice, or, Ben Bolt, or, Don't You Remember

Engvick, William   Anna; Kiss and Run; The Song from Moulin Rouge, or, Where Is Your Heart; While We're Young

Ennis, Susan   Dog and Butterfly

Enoch, Frederick   'Tis But a Little Faded Flower

Erard, Clive   Hang on the Bell Nellie

Erdman, Ernie   No, No, Nora; Nobody's Sweetheart Now; Toot Toot Tootsie (Goo'Bye); Under Hawaiian Skies

Errica, Carmelo   My Ideal

Erwin, Lee   Dance Me Loose

Erwin, Ralph   I Kiss Your Hand, Madame

Esperon, Ignacio F.   I'll Never Love Again (La Borrachita)

Esperon, Manuel   The Three Caballeros

Espinoza, J.J.   A Gay Ranchero

Esposito, Joseph   Bad Girls

Esrom, D.A., *see* **Theodore F. Morse**

Essex, David   Rock On; Silver Dream Machine

Estefan, Gloria   World Gets in the Way

Esty, Bob   Main Event/The Fight; Take Me Home

Evans, Dale   The Bible Tells Me So

Evans, George   Come Take a Trip in My Airship; Come to the Land of Bohemia; In the Good Old Summer Time; In the Merry Month of June

Evans, Mitchel Y.   Mad About You

Evans, Paul   Happiness Is; Happy Go Lucky Me; Roses Are Red, My Love

Evans, Raymond B.   Almost in Your Arms; Another Time, Another Place; Bonanza; Bonne Nuit-Goodnight; Buttons and Bows; Copper Canyon; Dear Heart; Golden Earrings; G'Bye Now; Home Cooking; I'd Like To Baby You; In the Arms of Love; Love Song from *Houseboat,* or, Almost in Your Arms;

Marshmallow Moon; Mr. Lucky; Misto Cristofo Columbo; Mona Lisa; My Beloved; Silver Bells; Streets of Laredo, or, The Cowboy's Lament; Tammy; To Each His Own; (Theme from) Vertigo; Wait Until Dark; Whatever Will Be, Will Be, or, Que Sera, Sera

Evans, Redd   American Beauty Rose; Don't Go to Strangers; He's 1-A in the Army (and A-1 in My Heart); No Moon At All; There! I've Said It Again

Evans, Richard S.   In the Year 2525

Evans, Tolchard   Ev'rywhere; Faith; I Bought Myself a Bottle of Ink; If; If I Lost You; I'll Find You; Lady of Spain; Life's Desire; My September Love; Sailor Who Are You Dreaming of Tonight; The Singing Piano; The Song of the Trees; There's a Lovely Lake in London; Unless

Evans, Tom   Without You

Everly, Don   Born Yesterday; Cathy's Clown; ('Til) I Kissed You

Everly, Phil   Cathy's Clown; When Will I Be Loved

Ewing, Montague   Fairy on the Clock; Just Humming Along; The Policeman's Holiday

Eyen, Tom   And I Am Telling You I'm Not Going; Cadillac Car; Dream Girls; One Night Only; When I First Saw You

Eyton, Frank   All over the Place; Body and Soul; Don't Do That to the Poor Puss Cat; Let the People Sing; Tell Me Tonight; Today I Feel So Happy; You've Done Something to My Heart

Ezrin, Robert   Beth; Detroit Rock City

Faber, Billy   You Were Only Foolin'

Faber, Frederick   Faith of Our Fathers

Fagan, Barney   My Gal Is a High Born Lady

Fagen, Donald   Igy (What a Beautiful World)

Fahey, Brian   Fanfare Boogie

Fahrenkrog, Petersen   99 Luftballons

Fain, Sammy   Alice in Wonderland; All the Time; April Love; Are You Havin' Any Fun; By a Waterfall; A Certain Smile; The Deadwood Stage; Dear Hearts and Gentle People; The Dickey Bird Song; Happy in Love; I Can Dream, Can't I; I Left My Sugar Standing in the Rain (and She Melted Away); I Speak to the Stars; I'll Be Seeing You; I'll Remember Tonight; I'm Late; Let a Smile Be Your Umbrella on a Rainy (Rainy) Day; Love Is a Many-Splendored Thing; Nobody Knows What a Red Head Mama Can Do; Our Penthouse on Third Avenue; Please Don't Say "No"; The Second Star to the Right; Secret Love; Tender Is the Night; That Old Feeling; There's Something About a Rose (That Reminds Me of You); A Very Precious Love; Violins from Nowhere; Was That the Human Thing To Do; Wedding Bells Are Breaking Up That Old Gang of Mine; When I Take My Sugar to Tea; You Brought a New Kind of Love to Me

Fairman, George   I Don't Know Where I'm Going But I'm on My Way; The Preacher and the Bear

Faith, Percy   My Heart Cries for You

Faith, Russell   Bobby Sox (Socks) to Stockings; Togetherness; Voyage to the Bottom of the Sea

Falconer, Edmund   Killarney

Fall, Leo   Dollar Princesses; My Dream of Love

Fall, Richard   Oh, Katharina

Faltermeyer, Harold   Axel F; The Heat Is On; Hot Stuff

Fane, Julian   Violets

Fanshawe, David   African Sanctus

Farina, Ann   Sleep Walk

Faris, Alexander   (Theme from) Upstairs Downstairs, or, The Edwardians; Wings

Farjeon, Eleanor   Morning Has Broken

Farley, Edward   The Music Goes 'Round and 'Round

Farley, Melville   My Son, My Son

Farmer, John   Forty Years On

Farner, Mark   Bad Time

Farnie, Henry Bougham   The Torpedo and the Whale

Farnon, Dennis   Bouquet of Barbed Wire

Farnon, Robert J.   Colditz; Jumping Bean; Portrait of a Flirt; Seashore; Secret Army; Westminster Waltz

Farran, Ed   You Deserve a Break Today

Farrar, John   Have You Never Been Mellow; Hopelessly Devoted to You; Magic; Make a Move on Me; Sam; Something Better To Do; Suddenly; You're the One That I Want

Farrell, Joe   Tomboy

Farrell, Joseph C.   Hannah!

Farrell, Wes   Come a Little Bit Closer; Hang On Sloopy; Our Favourite Melodies

Farrelly, Richard   Isle of Innisfree

Farres, Osvaldo   Come Closer to Me; Perhaps, Perhaps, Perhaps; Without You

Farris, Andrew   What You Need

Farrow, Johnny   I Have But One Heart

Fassert, Fred   Barbara Ann

Faulkner, Eric   Money Honey

Faure, Jean Baptiste   Crucifix; The Palm Trees, or, The Palms

Fawcett, John   Blest Be the Tie That Binds

Feahy, Michael   A Load of Hay

Fearis, John S.   Beautiful Isle of Somewhere; Little Sir Echo

Feaster, Carl   Sh-Boom

Feaster, Claude   Sh-Boom

Feiberg, David   Jane

Fekaris, Dino   Makin' It; Reunited

Feldman, Al   A-Tisket A-Tasket

Feldman, Jack   Copacabana (At the Copa); I Made It Through the Rain

Feldman, Robert   My Boyfriend's Back

Feller, Dick   Some Days Are Diamonds (Some Days Are Stone)

Feller, Sherm   My Baby's Comin' Home; Summertime Summertime

Feltz, Kurt   I Once Had a Heart, Margarita

Fender, Freddy   Wasted Days Wasted Nights

Fenstad, E.A.   (Maine) Stein Song

Fenstock, Belle Simonetta

Fenton, George For All Mankind (Theme from *Gandhi*); Fox; (Theme from) Jewel in the Crown; Omnibus; Shoestring

Ferguson, Jay Thunder Island

Fermanoglou, Jean Boy on a Dolphin

Fernandez, Carlo Cielito Lindo (Ay, Ay, Ay, Ay)

Ferrão, Raul April in Portugal

Ferrari, Louis Domino

Ferre, Cliff The Money Tree

Fetter, Ted Now; Taking a Chance on Love; Yours for a Song

Feyne, Buddy Jersey Bounce; Tuxedo Junction

Fiddler, John Pictures in the Sky

Fieger, Douglas My Sharona

Field, Eugene Listen to My Tale of Woe; Little Boy Blue

Fielding, Alan Last Night Was Made for Love; When Will You Say I Love You

Fields, Arthur The Aba Daba Honeymoon; Eleven More Months and Ten More Days; I Got a "Code" in My "Dose"; On the Mississippi

Fields, Buddy You Gotta Be a Football Hero (To Get Along with the Beautiful Girls); You're the One (You Beautiful Son-of-a-Gun)

Fields, Dorothy Alone Too Long; Baby Dream Your Dream; Bandana Babies; The Big Back Yard; (Hey) Big Spender; Blue Again; Bojangles of Harlem; Cinderella Brown; Close as Pages in a Book; Cuban Love Song; Diga Diga Do; Dinner at Eight; Doin' the New Low-Down; Don't Blame Me; Exactly Like You; A Fine Romance; Futuristic Rhythm; Go Home and Tell Your Mother; Hey Young Fella Close Your Old Umbrella; Hooray for Love; I Can't Give You Anything But Love; I Dream Too Much; I Feel a Song Coming On; I Won't Dance; I'll Buy You a Star; I'm in the Mood for Love; It's the Darndest Thing; The Jockey on the Carousel; Just for Once; Just Let Me Look At You; Look Who's Dancing; Lost in a Fog; Love Is the Reason; Lovely To Look At; Make the Man Love Me; More Love Than Your Love; On the Sunny Side of the Street; Our Song; Pick Yourself Up; Singin' the Blues; Stars in My Eyes; Thank You for a Lovely Evening; There Must Be Something Better Than Love; This Is It; Two Faces in the Dark; Waltz in Swing Time; The Way You Look Tonight; What's Good About Good Night; When She Walks In the Room; Where Am I Going; The Whistling Boy; You Couldn't Be Cuter; You Wanna Bet; You're an Angel

Fields, Gracie Sing as We Go

Fields, Harold The Echo Told Me a Lie; It Happened in Adano; My Love and Devotion; When You're in Love

Fields, Irving Chantez Chantez; Managua Nicaragua; Miami Beach Rumba

Filiberto, Juan de Dios Caminito

Fillmore, Charles M. Tell Mother I'll Be There

Fillmore, S. Sweet By and By

Filson, Albert W. Maggie, the Cows Are in the Clover

Fina, Jack Bumble Boogie

Finch, Richard Get Down Tonight; I'm Your Boogie Man; Jealous; Keep It Comin' Love; Please Don't Go; Rock Your Baby; (Shake Shake Shake) Shake Your Booty; That's the Way I Like It; Where Is the Love

Finck, Herman Gilbert the Filbert; I'll Make a Man of You; In the Shadows; Sahara; Toy Town; Whisper to Me

Findon, Ben I'm in the Mood For Dancing

Fine, Sylvia Knock On Wood; The Moon Is Blue

Fink, Henry The Curse of an Aching Heart

Fiorito, Ted Alone at a Table for Two; Charley, My Boy; Hangin' on the Garden Gate; I Never Knew (That Roses Grew); Laugh, Clown, Laugh; No, No, Nora; Roll Along Prairie Moon; Sometime; Three on a Match; When Lights Are Low

Fischer, Carl We'll Be Together Again; Who Wouldn't Love You; You've Changed

Fischer, Karl Ludwig Within the Cellar's Depth I Sit

Fischer, William G. I Love To Tell the Story

Fisher, Bruce With It Go Round in Circles; You Are So Beautiful

Fisher, Dan Good Morning Heartache

Fisher, Dave Michael (Row the Boat Ashore)

Fisher, Doris Either It's Love or It Isn't; Into Each Life Some Rain Must Fall; Prove It by the Things You Do (It's Easy To Say); Put the Blame on Mame; That's Good Enough for Me; Tired; You Always Hurt the One You Love; You Can't See the Sun When You're Crying

Fisher, Eddie May I Sing to You

Fisher, Fred Absence Makes the Heart Grow Fonder; And a Little Bit More; Any Little Girl, That's a Nice Little Girl, Is the Right Little Girl for Me; Blue Is the Night; Chicago (That Toddlin' Town); Come, Josephine, in My Flying Machine; Daddy, You've Been a Mother to Me; Dardanella; Fifty Million Frenchmen Can't Be Wrong; I Don't Want Your Kisses; I Found a Rose in the Devil's Garden; I Want You To Want Me To Want You; I'd Rather Be Blue over You (Than Happy with Somebody Else); Ireland Must Be Heaven, for My Mother Came from There; Lorraine, My Beautiful Alsace Lorraine; Norway; Oui, Oui, Marie; Peg o' My Heart; Siam; There's a Broken Heart for Every Light on Broadway; There's a Little bit of Bad in Every Good Little Girl; There's a Little Spark of Love Still Burning; They Go Wild Simply Wild over Me; When I Get You Alone Tonight; When the Honeymoon Was Over; While Others Are Building Castles in the Air (I'll Build a Cottage for Two); You Can't Get Along With 'Em or Without 'Em; Your Feet's Too Big

Fisher, Howard An Old Violin

Fisher, Mark Everywhere You Go; Oh! How I Miss You Tonight; When You're Smiling (The Whole World Smiles with You)

Fisher, Marvin When Sonny Gets Blue

Fisher, William Arms Goin' Home

Fishman, Jack Arrivederci Roma; Help Yourself; My Friend the Sea; West of Zanzibar (Jambo); Why Don't They Understand

Fiske, W.O. Horace and No Relations

Fitch, Art I Love You (Sweetheart of All My Dreams)

Fitch, Clyde   Love Makes the World Go 'Round

Fitch, John   Shame

Fitch, Kay   I Love You (Sweetheart of All My Dreams)

Fitz, Albert   The Honeysuckle and the Bee

Fitzball, Edward   (When the) Bloom Is on the Rye, or, My Pretty Jane; Scenes That Are Brightest; Sweet Spirit, Hear My Prayer; Yes, Let Me Like a Soldier Fall

Fitzer, Brian   Stray Cat Strut

Fitzgerald, Edward   In a Persian Garden

Fitzgerald, Ella   A-Tisket A-Tasket

Fitzgibbon, Bert   Just a Little Rocking Chair and You

Flagg, Ellen H.   Waiting

Flanagan, Bud   Dreaming; Underneath the Arches

Flanders, Michael   Captain Noah and His Floating Zoo; The Income Tax Collector

Fleeson, Neville   I'll Be with You in Apple Blossom Time; Waters of Venice, or, Floating Down the Sleepy Lagoon

Fleming, Kye   Crackers; Fooled by a Feeling; I Was Country When Country Wasn't Cool; I Wouldn't Have Missed It for the World; Smoky Mountain Rain; Wish You Were Here; Years

Fleming, Rhonda J.   All Roads Lead to You; Kansas City Lights; Nobody

Fletcher, "Dusty"   Open the Door, Richard

Fletcher, Guy   Power to All Our Friends; Sing a Song of Freedom

Fletcher, J.   When I Saw Sweet Nellie Home, or, I Was Seeing Nellie Home, or, Aunt Dinah's Quilting Party

Fletcher, Lucy   Sugar Blue

Fletcher, Nigel   Mouldy Old Dough

Fletcher, Percy E.   Bal Masque; The Chinaman's Song

Flett, Doug   Power to All Our Friends; Sing a Song of Freedom

Flindt, Emil   The Waltz You Saved for Me

Flint, Bernie   I Don't Want To Put a Hold on You

Flint, Michael   I Don't Want To Put a Hold on You

Flowers, Danny   Tulsa Time

Flowers, Herbie   Grandad

Floyd, Eddie   Knock On Wood

Flynn, Allan   Be Still My Heart; Bing! Bang! Bing 'Em on the Rhine; Maybe

Flynn, John H.   Sweet Annie Moore; Yip-I-Addy-I-Ay!

Flynn, Joseph   Down Went McGinty

Focacci, John   Dreams of Long Ago

Fogarty, J. Paul   Betty Co-Ed

Fogelberg, Dan   The Language of Love; Longer; Make Love Stay; Missing You; Power of Gold; The Same Old Auld Lang Syne

Fogerty, John C.   Bad Moon Rising; Lookin' Out My Back Door; Proud Mary; Who'll Stop the Rain

Foley, Red   Just a Closer Walk with Thee

Folley, Frank   Stop Yer Tickling, Jock!

Fontaine, Lamar   All Quiet Along the Potomac Tonight

Fontana, Jimmy   Speak Softly

Fontenoy, Marc   Choo Choo Train

Ford, Corey   Roar, Lion, Roar

Ford, Eugene   Rain

Ford, John   Part of the Union

Ford, Lena Guilbert   Keep the Home Fires Burning (Till the Boys Come Home)

Ford, Perry   Someone Else's Baby; Tossing and Turning

Ford, Walter H.   I Love You in the Same Old Way—Darling Sue; In a Cozy Corner; Only Me; The Sunshine of Paradise Alley

Foreman, Charles E.   Gold Will Buy Most Anything But a True Girl's Heart

Foreman, C.J.   Our House

Formby, George   Chinese Laundry Blues; I Was Standing at the Corner of the Street; When I'm Cleaning Windows

Forrest, Chet   Always and Always; At the Balalaika; I'd Be Lost Without You; It's a Blue World

Forrest, George   And This Is My Beloved; Baubles, Bangles and Beads; The Donkey Serenade; Not Since Nineveh; Now; Strange Music; Stranger in Paradise; Sweet Danger

Forrest, Jimmy   Night Train

Forsey, Keith   Don't You (Forget About Me); Flashdance (What a Feeling); The Heat Is On; Hot Stuff

Forsythe, Reginald   Dodging a Divorcee

Fort, Hank   Put Your Shoes On, Lucy

Fortgang, Jeff   Some Guys Have All the Luck

Fosdick, W.W.   Aura Lee

Foss, Sam Walter   The House by the Side of the Road

Foster, David   After All; After the Love Has Gone; Forever; Glory of Love (Theme from *The Karate Kid Part II*); Got To Be Real; Hard To Say I'm Sorry; Heart to Heart; Jo Jo; Look What You've Done to Me; Love Me Tomorrow; Love Theme from St. Elmo's Fire; Now and Forever (You and Me); St. Elmo's Fire (Man in Motion); What About Me; Who's Holding Donna Now; You're the Inspiration

Foster, Dorothy   I Wonder If Love Is a Dream; Mifanwy; Rose in the Bud

Foster, E.W.   Hurrah! for Hayes and Honest Ways!

Foster, Fred L.   Help Me Make It Through the Night; Me and Bobby McGee

Foster, Mike   Heart of Mine

Foster, Stephen Collins   Angelina Baker; Beautiful Dreamer; Come Where My Love Lies Dreaming; De Camptown Races (Gwine To Run All Night); Ellen Bayne; Gentle Annie; The Glendy Burke; Hard Times Come Again No More; Jeanie with the Light Brown Hair; Katy Bell; Lou(i)siana Belle; Massa's in De Cold (Cold) Ground; My Old Kentucky Home (Good Night); Nelly Bly; Nelly Was a Lady; Oh Boys Carry Me 'Long; Oh! Susanna; Old Black Joe; Old Dog Tray; Old Folks at Home (Way Down upon the Swance River); Open Thy Lattice Love; Ring De Banjo; Some Folks; (Old) Uncle Ned; We've a Million in the Field; The White House Chair; Willie We Have Missed You

Foster, Warren   I Taut I Taw a Puddy-Tat

Fotine, Larry   You Were Only Foolin'

Fowler, Lem   How'm I Doin' (Hey Hey)

Fowler, Wally   That's How Much I Love You

Fox, Charles   Different Worlds; Happy Days; I Got a Name; Killing Me Softly with His Song; Ready To Take a Chance Again

Fox, Hattie A.   Now I Lay Me Down To Sleep

Fox, Oscar J.   The Hills of Home

Foxx, Charlie   Mocking Bird

Foxx, Inez   Mocking Bird

Fragson, Harry   Hello, Hello, Who's Your Lady Friend

Frajos, George   I Hear a Rhapsody

Frampton, Peter   Show Me the Way

Francillon, Robert Edward   It Was a Dream

Francis, Arthur, *see* **Ira Gershwin**

Francis, Stephen   The Lightning Tree

Francoia, C.   The Eve of Destruction

Francois, Claude   My Way

Frank, Sid   Please Mister Sun

Frankel, Abe   Yankee Rose

Franklin, Aretha   Who's Zoomin' Who

Franklin, David   The Anniversary Waltz; Concert in the Park; I Must See Annie Tonight; The Merry-Go-Round Broke Down; When My Dream Boat Comes Home; You Can't Stop Me from Dreaming

Franklin, Malvin   Shades of Night

Franks, Ed   Anyone Can Be a Millionaire; Don't Worry

Franks, Gordon   Outbreak of Murder

Franks, Michael   Your Secret's Safe with Me

Franks, Tillman   The Comancheros; Sink the Bismarck

Frans, Edward D. Jr.   Dazz

Frantzen, Henry   College Life; Hannah!; Monkey Doodle Dandy

Fraser, Morton   Goodnight and God Bless You

Fraser-Simson, Harold   Christopher Robin at Buckingham Palace; Christopher Robin Is Saying His Prayers; Love Will Find a Way

Frashver, Dale   Na Na Hey Hey Kiss Him Goodbye

Fratto, Russel D.   Maybellene

Frazier, Dallas   Alley-Oop; Elvira; Fourteen Carat Mind; There Goes My Everything

Frazzini, Al   My Cabin of Dreams

Fred, John   Judy in Disguise (with Glasses)

Fredianelli, R.   Tell Me You're Mine

Fredericks, W.A.   Texaco Star Theme (The Man Who Wears the Star)

Freeberg, Stan   St. (Saint) George and the Dragonet

Freed, Alan   Maybellene; Sincerely

Freed, Arthur   All I Do Is Dream of You; Alone; Broadway Melody; Broadway Rhythm; Chant of the Jungle; Fit as a Fiddle (and Ready for Love); Good Morning; I Cried for You (Now It's Your Turn To Cry over Me); It Was So Beautiful (and You Were Mine); I've Got a Feeling You're Fooling; Love Songs of the Nile; Make 'Em Laugh; The Moon Is Low; Our Love Affair; Pagan Love Song; Should I (Reveal); Singin' in the Rain; Temptation; This Heart of Mine; The Wedding of the Painted Doll; We'll Make Hay While the Sun Shines; When Buddha Smiles; The Woman in the Shoe; (I Would) Would You; You Are My Lucky Star; You Were Meant for Me; Yours and Mine

Freed, Ralph   Hawaiian War Chant; (I Like New York in June) How About You; Little Dutch Mill; Please Don't Say "No"; Swing High, Swing Low; You Leave Me Breathless

Freedman, Max C.   (We're Gonna) Rock Around the Clock

Freedman, Ray   Sioux City Sue

Freedom, Ralph   All the Time

Freeland, Beverly   B-I, Bi

Freeland, Judy   B-I, Bi

Freeman, Bud   The Eel

Freeman, Harold Brown   My Mother's Lullaby

Freeman, Harry   Honey That I Love So Well

Freeman, L.E.   (It Will Have To Do) Until the Real Thing Comes Along

Freeman, Robert   Do You Want To Dance

Freeman, Ticker   You'll Always Be the One I Love

Freiligrath, F.   Liebesträume

Freire, Osman Perez   Ay, Ay, Ay

Freirich, Roy   This Night Won't Last Forever

French, Arthur W.   Trabling Back to Georgia

French, Percy   Abdulla Bulbul Ameer (Abdul Abulbul Amir); Phil the Fluter's Ball

Frenchik, Michael   Dancing on the Ceiling

Frey, Glenn   Best of My Love; Lyin' Eyes; Once You Love; One of These Nights; You Belong to the City

Frey, Hugo   The Morris Dance

Fricker, Sylvia   You Were on My Mind

Fried, Martin   Broadway Rose

Friedhofer, Hugo W.   Boy on a Dolphin

Friedland, Anatole   Lily of the Valley; My Own Iona; My Sweet Adair; Shades of Night

Friedman, Gary William   Dream Babies

Friedman, Leo   Coon! Coon! Coon!; Let Me Call You Sweetheart; Meet Me Tonight in Dreamland

Friedman, Ruthann   Windy

Friedman, Stanleigh P.   Down the Field (March)

Friedrich, W.   Ah! So Pure

Friend, Cliff   The Big Butter and Egg Man; The Broken Record; Concert in the Park; Don't Sweetheart Me; Hello, Bluebird; How I Love You (I'm Tellin' the Birds, I'm Tellin' the Bees); I Must See Annie Tonight; It's Great To Be in Love; June Night (Just Give Me a June Night, the Moonlight and You); Just Because You're You; Let It Rain! Let It Pour! (I'll Be in Virginia in the Morning); Let Me Linger Longer in Your Arms; Lovesick Blues; Mamma Loves Papa—Papa Loves Mamma; The Merry-Go-Round Broke Down; My

Blackbirds Are Bluebirds Now; O-oo Ernest, Are You Earnest with Me?; Satisfied; The Sweetest Music This Side of Heaven; Tamiami Trail; (I Wanna Go Where You Go, Do What You Do) Then I'll Be Happy; There's Yes, Yes, in Your Eyes; Time Waits For No One; Trade Winds; Wah Hoo; We Did It Before (and We Can Do It Again); When My Dream Boat Comes Home; Where the Lazy Daisies Grow; You Can't Stop Me from Dreaming; You Tell Her, I S-t-u-t-t-e-r

Friml, Rudolf   Allah's Holiday; L'Amour, Toujours L'Amour, or, Love Everlasting; The Bubble; Chanson; Chansonette; The Donkey Serenade; The Door of My (Her) Dreams; Ev'ry Little Smile; Florida, the Moon and You; Gather the Rose; Giannina Mia; Give Me One Hour; I Want To Marry a Male Quartet; Indian Love Call; Katinka; Love Is Like a Firefly; Love Me Tonight; Ma Belle; March of the Musketeers; Only a Rose; Rackety-Coo!; Regimental Song; Rose Marie; Some Day; Something Seems Tingle-Ingling; Sometime; Song of the Vagabonds; Sympathy; Totem Tom-Tom; Waltz Huguette, or, The Vagabond King Waltz; We'll Have a Kingdom; When a Maid Comes Knocking at Your Heart; You're in Love

Frish, Al   All Over the World; I Won't Cry Anymore; This Is No Laughing Matter; Two Different Worlds

Frisch, William   After the Dance; I'd Like To See the Kaiser with a Lily in His Hand

Froggatt, Raymond   The Red Balloon

Frost, Bernard   What You're Proposing

Frost, Harold G.   Sweet Hawaiian Moonlight

Fry, Bridget   Softly, Softly Theme; Z Cars Theme

Fry, Martin   Be Near Me

Fryberg, Mart   Call Me Darling

Fryer, Fritz   Juliet

Fučik, Julius   The Gladiator's Entry

Fuld, Leo   The Windmill's Turning

Fuller, James   Wipe Out

Fuller, Jerry   Lady Willpower; Over You; Show and Tell; Travelin' Man; Young Girl

Fulmer, H.T.   Wait Till the Clouds Roll By

Fulton, Jack   If You Are But a Dream; Ivory Tower; Wanted

Fulton, Kathryn R.   Fool Number One

Fuqua, Harvey   Sincerely; Some Day We'll Be Together; What Does It Take (To Win Your Love)

Furber, Douglas   The Bells of St. Mary's; The Flies Crawled Up the Window; Lambeth Walk; Limehouse Blues; Me and My Girl; She's Such a Comfort to Me; There's Always Tomorrow

Furst, William   Love Makes the World Go 'Round

Furth, Seymour   Budweiser's a Friend of Mine; No Wedding Bells for Me

Furuholmen, Magne   Take On Me

Fury, Billy   Colette

Fyffe, Will   I Belong to Glasgow

Fysher, Nilson   (Just) A Little Love, a Little Kiss

Gabler, Milt   Danke Schön

Gabriel, Charles H.   Brighten the Corner Where You Are; O That Will Be Glory for Me, or, The Glory Song

Gabriel, Gilbert Alexander   Life in a Northern Town; Love Parade

Gabriel, Peter   Sledgehammer

Gade, Jacob   Jalousie (Jealousy)

Gaillard, Slim   Cement Mixer (Put-ti Put-ti); Flat Foot Floogie (with the Floy Floy)

Galdieri, Michele   Non Dimenticar

Galdo, Joe   Bad Boy

Galhardo, José   April in Portugal; Lisbon Antigua, or, In Old Lisbon

Gallagher, Benny   Heart on My Sleeve

Gallagher, Bernard   When I'm Dead and Gone

Gallagher, Ed   Mister Gallagher and Mister Shean

Gallop, Sammy   Autumn Serenade; Count Every Star; Elmer's Tune; Forgive My Heart; Make Her Mine; Maybe You'll Be There; My Lady Loves To Dance; Outside of Heaven; The Sentimental Touch; Serenade to a Lemonade; Shoofly Pie and Apple Pan Dowdy; Somewhere Along the Way; There Must Be a Way; Wake the Town and Tell the People

Galloway, Tod B.   The Whiffenpoof Song

Galuten, Albhy   This Woman; What Kind of Fool

Gamble, Kenneth   Break Up To Make Up; Don't Leave Me This Way; Enjoy Yourself; I Love Music (Part 1); The Love I Lost (Part 1); Me and Mrs. Jones; Only the Strong Survive; Put Your Hands Together; T.S.O.P. (The Sound of Philadelphia); Use Ta Be My Girl; When Will I See You Again; You'll Never Find Another Love Like Mine

Gamse, Albert   Amapola, or, Pretty Little Poppy; Chantez Chantez; Managua Nicaragua; Miami Beach Rumba; Michael (Row the Boat Ashore)

Gannon, Kim   (You Are) Always in My Heart; Autumn Nocturne; A Dreamer's Holiday; The Five O'Clock Whistle; I Understand; I Want To Be Wanted; I'll Be Home for Christmas; It Can't Be Wrong; Moonlight Cocktail; Under Paris Skies

García, José Na Castellvi   My Toreador

Gardenier, Edward   The Fatal Rose of Red; When You Know You're Not Forgotten by the Girl You Can't Forget

Gardner, Donald Yetter   All I Want for Christmas (Is My Two Front Teeth)

Gardner, William Henry   Can't Yo' Heah Me Callin', Caroline; Don't Leave Me, Dolly; Thy Beaming Eyes

Garfunkel, Arthur   Scarborough Fair/ Canticle, or, Parsley, Sage, Rosemary and Thyme

Garinei, P.   Arrivederci Roma

Garland, Joseph   In the Mood

Garner, Erroll   Misty; (Theme from) A New Kind of Love

Garnett, Gale   We'll Sing in the Sunshine

Garren, Joe   Just a Girl That Men Forget

Garretson, Ferd V.D.   Good Night Ladies, or, Merrily We Roll Along

Garrett, Marilyn   The Night Has a Thousand Eyes

Garrett, Thomas "Snuff"   Another Honky Tonk Night on Broadway; I Don't Think I'm Ready for You; Every Which Way But Loose

Garrett, William   Mashed Potato Time

Garrick, David   Heart of Oak

Garrity, Freddie   I'm Telling You Now

Garson, Mort   Birmingham Rag; Left Right Out of Your Heart; My Summer Love; Our Day Will Come

Gartlan, George H.   The Lilac Tree, or, Perspicacity

Garton, Ted   My Belgian Rose

Garuse, Albert   Chiapanecas (While There's Music There's Romance)

Garvin, Michael   Only One You

Gaskill, Clarence   Doo Wacka Doo; I Can't Believe That You're in Love with Me; I Love To Dunk a Hunk of Sponge Cake; I'm Wild About Horns on Automobiles That Go "Ta-Ta-Ta-Ta"; Minnie the Moocher, or, The Ho De Ho Song; Prisoner of Love

Gasparre, Dick   I Hear a Rhapsody

Gastoldon, Stanislao   La Musica Prohibita

Gates, David A.   If; (I'd Like To) Make It with You; Took the Last Train

Gatlin, Larry   All the Gold in California; Broken Lady; Taking Somebody with Me When I Fall; What Are We Doing Lonesome

Gaudio, Robert   Big Girls Don't Cry; Can't Take My Eyes off You; Dawn (Go Away); December 1963 (Oh What a Night); Rag Doll; Sherry; Short Shorts; Walk Like a Man; Who Loves You

Gaunt, Percy   The Bowery; Love Me Little, Love Me Long; Push Dem Clouds Away

Gavin, Kevin   You Deserve a Break Today

Gay, Byron   Four or Five Times; Horses; O (Oh!); The Vamp

Gay, John   The Beggar's Opera (*including* a version of Greensleeves; Hither Dear Husband; Let Us Take to the Road; Lilliburlero; When a Wife's in a Pout)

Gay, Noel   Ali Baba's Camel; All for a Shilling a Day; All Over the Place; The Fleet's in Port Again; Hey Little Hen; I Took My Harp to a Party; The King's Horses; La-Di-Da-Di-Da; Lambeth Walk; Leaning On a Lamp Post; Let the People Sing; Let's Have a Tiddley at the Milk Bar; Me and My Girl; My Thanks to You; Round the Marble Arch; Run Rabbit Run; The Sun Has Got His Hat On; There's Something About a Soldier; Things Are Looking Up; The Toor-ie on His Bonnet; Who's Been Polishing the Sun; You've Done Something to My Heart

Gaye, Marvin   Dancing in the Streets; Sexual Healing; What's Going On

Gaynor, Charles   When Someone You Love Loves You; Who Hit Me

Gaze, Heino   Calcutta

Geary, T. Mayo   The Man with the Ladder and the Hose; Your Dad Gave His Life for His Country

Gebest, Charles J.   I Love Love

Geddes, William   Don't Go Down the Mine

Geehl, Henry E.   For You Alone

Geibel, Adam   Kentucky Babe

Geiringer, Jean   Passé

Geld, Gary   First Thing Monday Mornin'; Hurting Each Other; I Got Love; Over the Hill; Save Your Heart for Me; Sealed with a Kiss; Why Am I Me

Geldof, Bob   Do They Know It's Christmas?; I Don't Like Mondays

Gellar, Jack   Abergavenny; Jezamine

Genaro, Pat   Here in My Heart; You're Breaking My Heart

Gensler, Lewis E.   Comes Your Heart; Gentleman Prefer Blondes; keep Smiling at Trouble; Love Is Just Around the Corner

Gentry, Bobbie   Fancy; Mony, Mony; Ode to Billie Joe

Gentry, Teddy   Why Lady Why

George, Boy, *see* George O'Dowd

George, Don   I Never Mention Your Name (Oh No); I'm Beginning To See the Light; The Yellow Rose of Texas, or, Song of the Texas Rangers

George, Steven   Broken Wings; Kyrie

Gerald, Caeford   Get Down Get Down (Get on the Floor)

Gerard, Richard H., *see* **Richard Gerard Husch**

Gerber, Alexander   He May Be Old, But He's Got Young Ideas; The Little Church Around the Corner; My Home Town Is a One Horse Town, But It's Big Enough for Me; You Can't Stop Me from Loving You

Gerhard, Ake   Lay Down Your Arms

Gerlach, Horace   Daddy's Little Girl

German, Edward   Country Dance; English Rose; The Morris Dance; Waltz Song; Yeoman of England

German, Ted   Schaefer Is the One Beer

Gernhard, Phil   Snoopy vs. The Red Baron

Gershwin, George   All the Live-Long Day (and the Long, Long Night); An American in Paris; Aren't You Kind of Glad We Did; The Babbitt and the Bromide; Baby; The Back Bay Polka; (I've Got) Beginner's Luck; Bess, You Is My Woman Now; Bidin' My Time; Blah, Blah, Blah; Boy! What Love Has Done to Me!; But Not for Me; By Strauss; Changing My Tune; Clap Yo' Hands; Come to the Moon; Concerto in F; Cossack Love Song, or, Don't Forget Me; Cuban Overture; Dawn of a New Day; Dear Little Girl; Delishious; Do Do Do; (Please) Do It Again; Embraceable You; Fascinating Rhythm; Feeling I'm Falling; Fidgety Feet; A Foggy Day; For You, for Me, for Evermore; Funny Face; The Half of It, Dearie, Blues, Heaven on Earth; How Long Has This Been Going On; I Can't Be Bothered Now; I Got Plenty o' Nuttin'; I Got Rhythm; I Love To Rhyme; I Loves You Porgy; I Was Doing All Right; I Won't Say I Will, But I Won't Say I Won't; I'll Build a Stairway to Paradise; I'm on My Way; Isn't It a Pity; It Ain't Necessarily So; I've Got a Crush on You; Kickin's the Clouds Away; K-ra-zy for You; Let 'Em Eat Cake; Let's Call the Whole Thing Off; Let's Kiss and Make Up; Liza (All the Clouds'll Roll Away); Looking for a Boy; Lorelei; Lost Barber Shop Chord; Love Is Sweeping the Country; Love Walked In; The Man I Love; Maybe; Mine;

My Man's Gone Now; My One and Only; Nice Work If You Can Get It; Nobody But You; Oh, Bess, Oh Where's My Bess; Oh, I Can't Sit Down; Oh, Lady Be Good; Of Thee I Sing; One, Two, Three; Our Love Is Here To Stay; Preludes; Rhapsody in Blue; The Second Rhapsody; Shall We Dance; Show Me the Town; Slap That Bass; So Am I; Somebody Loves Me; Someone To Watch Over Me; Song of the Flame; Soon; Strike Up the Band; Summertime; Swanee; Sweet and Low-Down; 'S Wonderful; Tell Me More; That Certain Feeling; That Lost Barbershop Chord; There's a Boat Dat's Leavin' Soon for New York; They All Laughed; They Can't Take That Away from Me; Things Are Looking Up; Till Then; Treat Me Rough; Where's the Boy? Here's the Girl!; Who Cares; Why Do I Love You; Wintergreen for President; A Woman Is a Sometime Thing; The Yankee Doodle Blues

Gershwin, Ira   All At Once; All the Live-Long Day (and the Long, Long Night); Aren't You Kind of Glad We Did; The Babbitt and the Bromide; Baby; The Back Bay Polka; (I've Got) Beginner's Luck; Bess, You Is My Woman Now; Bidin' My Time; Blah, Blah, Blah; Boy! What Love Has Done to Me!; But Not for Me; By Strauss; Changing My Tune; Cheerful Little Earful; Clap Yo' Hands; Dawn of a New Day; Dear Little Girl; Delishious; Do Do Do; Embraceable You; Fascinating Rhythm; Feeling I'm Falling; Fidgety Feet; A Foggy Day; For You, for Me, for Evermore; Fun To Be Fooled; Funny Face; Goodbye to All That; The Half of It, Dearie, Blues; Heaven on Earth; How Long Has This Been Going On; I Can't Be Bothered Now; I Can't Get Started (with You); I Got Plenty o' Nuttin'; I Got Rhythm; I Love To Rhyme; I Loves You Porgy; I Was Doing All Right; I Won't Say I Will, But I Won't Say I Won't (*as* Arthur Francis); I'll Build a Stairway to Paradise (*as* Arthur Francis); Isn't It a Pity; It Ain't Necessarily So; It's a New World; I've Got a Crush on You; Kickin' the Clouds Away; K-ra-zy for You; Let 'Em Eat Cake; Let's Call the Whole Thing Off; Let's Kiss and Make Up; Let's Take a Walk Around the Block; Life, Love and Laughter; Liza (All the Clouds'll Roll Away); Long Ago and Far Away; Looking for a Boy; Lorelei; Lost Barber Shop Chord; Love Is Sweeping the Country; Love Walked In; The Man I Love; The Man That Got Away; Maybe; Mine; My One and Only; My One and Only Highland Fling; My Ship; Nice Work If You Can Get It; Oh, Bess, Oh Where's My Bess; Oh, I Can't Sit Down; Oh, Lady Be Good; Oh Me! Oh My! Oh You! (*as* Arthur Francis); Of Thee I Sing; One, Two, Three; Our Love Is Here To Stay; Saga of Jenny; Shall We Dance; Show Me the Town; Slap That Bass; So Am I; Someone To Watch over Me; Soon; Strike Up the Band; Sunny Disposish; Sure Thing; Sweet and Low-Down; 'S Wonderful; Tell Me More; That Certain Feeling; That Lost Barbershop Chord; There's a Boat Dat's Leavin' Soon for New York; There's No Holding Me; They All Laughed; They Can't Take That Away from Me; Things Are Looking Up; This Is New; Till Then; Treat Me Rough; Tschaikowsky; Where's The Boy? Here's the Girl; Who Cares; Why Do I Love You; Wintergreen for President; Words Without Music; You're a Builder Upper

Gesner, Clark   You're a Good Man, Charlie Brown

Getzov, Ray   Please Mister Sun

Geyer, Stephen   Greatest American Hero (Believe It or Not); Hot Rod Hearts

Giacosa, Giuseppe   Musetta's Waltz; One Fine Day, or, Un Bel Dì

Gibb, Andy   Shadow Dancing; (Love Is) Thicker Than Water

Gibb, Barry   Come On Over; Desire; Emotion; An Everlasting Love; Eyes That See in the Dark; Grease; Guilty; Heartbreaker; How Can You Mend a Broken Heart; How Deep Is Your Love; I Can't Help It; I Just Want To Be Your Everything; If I Can't Have You; Islands in the Stream; Jive Talkin'; Love So Right; Love You Inside and Out; Massachusetts; More Than a Woman; Morning of My Life; Night Fever; Our Love (Don't Throw It All Away); Shadow Dancing; Stayin' Alive; (Love Is) Thicker Than Water; This Woman; Too Much Heaven; Tragedy; Words; What Kind of Fool; Woman in Love; You Should Be Dancing

Gibb, Maurice   Desire; Eyes That See in the Dark; Guilty; Heartbreaker; How Deep Is Your Love; If I Can't Have You; Islands in the Stream; Jive Talkin'; Love So Right; Love You Inside and Out; Massachusetts; More Than a Woman; Night Fever; Shadow Dancing; Stayin' Alive; Too Much Heaven; Tragedy; Words; You Should Be Dancing

Gibb, Robin   Come On Over; Desire; Emotion; Guilty; Heartbreaker; Hold On to My Love; How Can You Mend a Broken Heart; How Deep Is Your Love; If I Can't Have You; Islands in the Stream; Jive Talkin'; Love So Right; Love You Inside and Out; Massachusetts; More Than a Woman; Night Fever; Shadow Dancing; Stayin' Alive; Too Much Heaven; Tragedy; Woman in Love; Words; You Should Be Dancing

Gibb, Stephen M.   While She Lays

Gibbons, Billy   Legs

Gibbons, Carroll   A Garden in the Rain; On the Air; Possibly; Running Between the Raindrops

Gibbons, James Sloan   We Are Coming, Father Abraham, 300,000 More

Gibbs, A. Harrington   Runnin' Wild

Gibson, Andy   Huckle-Buck

Gibson, Bob   Abilene

Gibson, Clark   A Cage in the Window

Gibson, Don   I Can't Stop Loving You; Oh Lonesome Me

Gibson, Fred   Does Santa Claus Sleep with His Whiskers

Gideon, Melville   Arizona; The Girl in the Crinoline Gown; If Winter Comes; I'm Tickled to Death I'm Single; When the Sun Goes Down

Giefer, George L.   Who Threw the Overalls in Mrs. Murphy's Chowder

Gifford, H. Eugene   Smoke Rings

Gifford, Harry   Come Along My Mandy; Kitty the Telephone Girl; She Sells Sea-Shells (on the Seashore); When I'm Cleaning Windows; When It's Apple Blossom Time in Normandy

Gilbert, Cary   Don't Leave Me This Way; Me and Mrs. Jones

Gilbert, Fred   At Trinity Church I Met My Doom; The Man That (Who) Broke the Bank at Monte Carlo

Gilbert, Henry F.   Pirate Song, or, Fifteen Men on a (the) Dead Man's Chest—Yo! Ho! Ho! and a Bottle of Rum

Gilbert, Herchel B.   The Moon Is Blue

Gilbert, Joseph Adeline; Amy, Wonderful Amy, Au Revoir But Not Goodbye; Bathing in the Sunshine; Delyse; Let Bygones Be Bygones; Let Us Be Sweethearts Over Again; Me and Jane in a Plane; Shine On Victory Moon; Silver Hair and Heart of Gold; When You Played the Organ and I Sang "The Rosary"; You Made Me Care When I Wasn't in Love

Gilbert, L. Wolfe African Lament (Lamento Africano); By Heck; Chiquita; Don't Wake Me Up, Let Me Dream; Down Yonder; La Golondrina; Green Eyes; Hello, Aloha! How Are You?; Here Comes My Daddy Now—Oh Pop—Oh Pop— Oh Pop; Hitchy-Koo; I Miss My Swiss, My Swiss Miss Misses Me; Jeannine, I Dream of Lilac Time; Lily of the Valley; Mama Don't Want No Peas an' Rice an' Cocoanut Oil; Mama Inez; Mammy Jinny's Jubilee; Maria My Own; Marta, or, Rambling Rose of the Wildwood; My Mother's Eyes; My Own Iona; My Sweet Adair; Oh, Katharina; The Peanut Vendor; Ramona; Shades of Night; Waiting For the Robert E. Lee

Gilbert, Lawrence B. Shadowland

Gilbert, Ray Adios, Mariquita Linda; Baia (No Baixa Do Sapateiro); Cherry; Cuanto Le Gusta; Dindi; Ev'rybody Has a Laughing Place; The Hot Canary; Muskrat Ramble; She's a Carioca; Sooner or Later (You're Gonna Be Comin' Around); The Three Caballeros; Two Silhouettes; Without You; You Belong to My Heart (Now and Forever), or, Solamente Una Vez; Zip-A-Dee-Doo-Dah; A Zoot Suit

Gilbert, Robert Just Once for All Time

Gilbert, Tim Incense and Peppermints

Gilbert, V.C. Shifting, Whispering Sands

Gilbert, William S. He Is an Englishman; I Am the Captain of the Pinafore (What Never); I Am the Monarch of the Sea; I'm Called Little Buttercup; Tit-Willow; When I Was a Lad

Gilder, Nick Hot Child in the City; The Warrior

Gilkyson, Terry The Cry of the Wild Goose; Greenfields; Marianne; Memories Are Made of This

Gill, Peter Two Tribes

Gillan, Ian Smoke on the Water

Gillespie, Arthur Absence Makes the Heart Grow Fonder

Gillespie, Haven Beautiful Love; Breezin' Along with the Breeze; By the Sycamore Tree; Drifting and Dreaming (Sweet Paradise); Honey; The Old Master Painter; Santa Claus Is Coming to Town; That Lucky Old Sun; You Go to My Head

Gillespie, Marian When You Look in the Heart of a Rose

Gilman, Samuel Fair Harvard

Gilmore, Patrick Sarsfield President Grant's March; When Johnny Comes Marching Home (as Louis Lambert)

Gilroy, John Don't Go in the Lions' Cage Tonight

Gilutin, Jonathan New Attitude

Gimbel, Norman Canadian Sunset; Different Worlds; The Girl from Ipanema; Happy Days; I Got a Name; I Will Follow Him; (If It Takes Forever) I Will Wait for You; It Goes Like It Goes; Killing Me Softly with His Song; Ready To Take a Chance Again; Ricochet; Sway; Watch What Happens

Ginsberg, Sol When Frances Dances with Me (as Sol Violinsky)

Giordano, F. Anna

Giosasi, Harry Sorry (I Ran All the Way Home)

Giovannini, S. Arrivederci Roma

Girard, Adele Little Sir Echo

Giraud, Hubert Under Paris Skies

Glanville, Lillian It Is Only a Tiny Garden

Glanzberg, Norbert Padam, Padam

Glass, Preston Who's Zoomin' Who

Glazer, Tom Melody of Love; More; Skokiaan; Till We Two Are One

Gleason, Dick Ready, Willing and Able

Glen, Catherine Young Absent

Glenn, Artie Crying in the Chapel

Glenroy, William Where the Chicken Got the Axe

Glenville, Shaun If You're Irish Come into the Parlour

Glick, Jesse G.M. Kid Days; Pale Moon

Glickman, Fred Mule Train

Glitter, Garry I Didn't Know I Loved You; I Love You Love Me Love

Glogau, Jack Fashionette; On the Shores of Italy; There's a Garden in Old Italy

Glover, Charles The Rose of Tralee

Glover, Henry Honkey Tonk; The Peppermint Twist; Rock Love

Glover, John Henry, Jr. You Don't Have To Be a Star (To Be in My Show)

Glover, Roger David Smoke on the Water

Glover, Stephen What Are the Wild Waves Saying

Gluck, John It's My Party

Goble, Graham Lady; Nightowls; Reminiscing; Take It Easy on Me

Godard, Benjamin Berceuse

Goddard, Geoffrey Don't You Think It's Time; Johnny Remember Me; Just Like Eddie; Son, This Is She; Wild Wind

Godfrey, Fred Blue Eyes; Meet Me Jenny When the Sun Goes Down; Molly O'Morgan; Take Me Back to Dear Old Blighty; Who Were You with Last Night

Godley, Kevin Rubber Bullets

Godowsky, Leopold Alt Wien

Godwin, Felix Valse Septembre

Godwin, Will Beer, Beer, Glorious Beer; If Those Lips Could Only Speak; The Miner's Dream of Home

Goehring, George Lipstick on Your Collar

Goell, Kermit Clopin Clopant; Huggin' and Chalkin'; Near You; The Shepherd Serenade; Wonder When My Baby's Coming Home

Goerdler, R. Hurrah! for Grant and Colfax

Goering, Al Who's Your Little Who-Zis

Goeta, Coleman Congratulations

Goetschius, Marjorie I Dream of You; I'll Always Be with You

Goetz, Alma   Melisands in the Wood

Goetz, Coleman   We'll Have a Jubilee in My Old Kentucky Home

Goetz, E. Ray   Asia; Boom; Do I Love You; Don't Go in the Lions' Cage Tonight; For Me and My Gal; He Goes to Church on Sunday; If You Could Care for Me; In the Shadows; Take Me Back to the Garden of Love; Who Ate Napoleons with Josephine When Bonaparte Was Away; Who'll Buy My Violets; Yaaka Hula Hickey Dula

Goetzel, Anselm   When the Cherry Blossoms Fall

Goffin, Gerry   Do You Know Where You're Going To, or, Theme from *Mahogany;* Go Away Little Girl; I've Got To Use My Imagination; The Loco-Motion; (You Make Me Feel Like) A Natural Woman; Run to Him; Saving All My Love for You; Take Good Care of My Baby; Time Don't Run Out on Me; Tonight I Celebrate My Love; Up on the Roof; Who Put the Bomp (in the Bomp Ba Bomp Ba Bomp); Will You (Still) Love Me Tomorrow

Gold, Alan   Boomerang

Gold, Andrew   Lonely Boy

Gold, Ernest   Accidentally on Purpose; (Theme from) Exodus; It's a Mad, Mad, Mad, Mad World; On the Beach; Practice Makes Perfect

Gold, Jacob   Midnight Cowboy

Gold, Marty   Tell Me Why

Gold, Wally   Because They're Young; Good Luck Charm; It's My Party; It's Now or Never; Time and the River

Goldberg, Barry   I've Got To Use My Imagination

Golde, Franne   Janet

Golden, John L.   Goodbye, Girls, I'm Through; I Can Dance with Everyone But My Wife; Poor Butterfly; You Can't Play Every Instrument in the Band

Golden, Ray   The Tenement Symphony

Goldenberg, Billy   A Terrific Band and a Real Nice Crowd

Goldenberg, Mark   Along Comes a Woman; Automatic

Goldie, Frankie   Nightshift

Goldman, Edwin Franko   On the Mall (March)

Goldmark, Andy   You Should Be Mine (The Woo Woo Song)

Goldner, George   Why Do Fools Fall in Love

Goldsmith, Jerry   (Theme from) Doctor Kildaire, or, Three Stars Will Shine Tonight; (Theme from) The Man from U.N.C.L.E.

Goldstein, Bob   Washington Square

Goldstein, Gerald   My Boyfriend's Back; Summer; Why Can't We Be Friends

Goldstein, Walter   Roll On, Tulane, or, The Olive and Blue

Gollahon, Gladys   Our Lady of Fatima

Gomera, José   Valley Valparaiso

Gooch, William   Reuben and Rachel, or, Reuben, Reuben, I've Been Thinking

Goodhart, Al   Auf Wiedersehn, My Dear; Everything Stops for Tea; Everything's in Rhythm with My Heart; Fit As a Fiddle (and Ready for Love); Gangway; Happy-Go-Lucky You and Broken-Hearted Me; He's a Humdinger; I Apologize; I Saw Stars; I'm in a Dancing Mood; Jimmy Had a Nickel; Johnny Doughboy Found a Rose in Ireland; A Little Co-operation from You; My First Thrill; Seranade of the Bells; She Shall Have Music; There Isn't Any Limit to My Love; This'll Make You Whistle

Goodman, Alfred   The Lady in Ermine; When Hearts Are Young

Goodman, Benny   Don't Be That Way; Flying Home; Lullaby in Rhythm; Soft Winds; Stomping at the Savoy

Goodman, Graham   No Milk Today

Goodman, Lillian Rosedale   Cherie (Cherie, Je T'Aime)

Goodman, Steve   City of New Orleans

Goodman, Willie   Special Lady

Goodrum, Randy   Foolish Heart; Now and Forever (You and Me); Oh Sherrie; Who's Holding Donna Now

Goodwin, J. Cheever   Ask the Man in the Moon; Love Will Find a Way; A Pretty Girl

Goodwin, Joe   Baby Shoes; Billy (for When I Walk); Everywhere You Go; A Girlie Was Made To Love; Liberty Bell—It's Time To Ring Again; The Little House upon the Hill; Orange Blossom Time; That's How I Need You; They're Wearing 'Em Higher in Hawaii; Three Wonderful Letters from Home; What a Wonderful Mother You'd Be; When I Get You Alone Tonight; When You Play in the Game of Love; When You're Smiling (The Whole World Smiles with You); Your Mother and Mine

Goodwin, Ron   Battle of Britain; Lift Boy; Lingering Lovers; My Friend the Sea; 633 Squadron; Skiffling Strings

Goodwin, Walter   That Wonderful Mother of Mine

Gordon, Alan Lee   Happy Together; My Heart Belongs to Me

Gordon, Harry   Come Sta'; Down in the Glen

Gordon, Irving   Be Anything (But Be Mine); Mama from the Train, or, A Kiss, A Kiss; Mister and Mississippi; Prelude to a Kiss; Unforgettable

Gordon, James Beck   Layla

Gordon, Mack   Afraid To Dream; And So to Bed; At Last; Blue Shadows and White Gardenias; A Boy and a Girl Were Dancing; By a Wishing Well; Chattanooga Choo Choo; Chica Chica Boom Chic; College Rhythm; Did You Ever See a Dream Walking; Doin' the Uptown Lowdown; Don't Let It Bother You; Down Argentine Way; From the Top of Your Head to the Tip of Your Shoes; Goodnight My Love; Head Over Heels in Love; (Lookie, Lookie, Lookie,) Here Comes Cookie; I Can't Begin To Tell You; I Feel Like a Feather in the Breeze; I Had the Craziest Dream; I Know Why; (Yi Yi Yi Yi) I Like You Very Much; I Played Fiddle for the Czar; I Wish I Knew; I'm Humming, I'm Whistling, I'm Singing; I'm Making Believe; In Acapulco; In an Old Dutch Garden; It Happened in Sun Valley; It Must Be Love; I've Got a Gal in Kalamazoo; Love Thy Neighbor; The Loveliness of You; Mam'selle; Many Moons Ago; May I; May I Have the Next Romance with You; The More I See You; My Heart Tells Me; Never in a Million Years; On the Boardwalk in Atlantic City; Paris in the Spring; Serenade in Blue; She Reminds Me of You; Somewhere in the Night; A Star Fell Out of Heaven; Stay as Sweet as You Are; Sweet as a Song; Take a Number from One to Ten; There Will Never Be Another You; There's a Lull in My Life; This Is Always; Through a Long and Sleepless Night; Time on My Hands; Underneath the Harlem Moon; Wake Up and Live; A Weekend in Havana; When I'm with You; Wilhelmina; With My Eyes Wide Open I'm Dreaming; Without a Word of Warning; You Can't Have Everything; You Do; You Gotta Eat Your Spinach, Baby; You Hit the Spot; You Make Me Feel So Young; You'll Never Know; You're My Past, Present and Future; You're Such a Comfort to Me

Gordon, Paul   Bless the Beasts and Children; Friends and Lovers (Born to Each Other)

Gordon, Roz   Tracy's Theme

Gordon, S.T.   Kattie (Katty) Avourneen

Gordon, Sheridan   Fat Li'l' Feller Wid His Mammy's Eyes

Gordon, Val   Sarawaki

Gordy, Berry Jr.   ABC; I Want You Back; Mama's Pearl; Shop Around; You've Made Me So Very Happy

Gordy, Emory, Jr.   Traces

Gore, Michael   Fame

Gorman, Chuck   Seventeen

Gorman, Frederick C.   Mashed Potato Time; Please Mister Postman

Gorman, Ross   Rose of the Rio Grande

Gormley, Peter   F.B.I.

Gorney, Jay   Ah, But Is It Love; Baby, Take a Bow; Brother, Can You Spare a Dime; In Chichicastenango; Moonlight and Pretzels; You're My Thrill

Gorrell, Stuart   Georgia On My Mind

Gorrie, Alan   Pick Up the Pieces

Gottehrer, Richard   My Boyfriend's Back

Gottler, Archie   America I Love You; Baby Me; I Hate To Lose You; In the Gold Fields of Nevada; Mammy's Chocolate Soldier; Rolling Stones—All Come Rolling Home Again; Would You Rather Be a Colonel with an Eagle on Your Shoulder or a Private with a Chicken on Your Knee?

Gottlieb, Sam   She Wouldn't Do What I Asked Her To

Gottschalk, Louis Moreau   The Dying Poet; The Last Hope; Laugh and the World Laughs with You

Gottwald, Hans   The Book

Götz, Karl   Casanova

Gould, Boon   Something About You

Gould, Morton   Bad Timing; Pavanne; There Must Be Something Better Than Love

Gould, Phil   Something About You

Goulding, Edmund   Love (Your Magic Spell Is Everywhere); Mam'selle

Gouldman, Graham Keith   Bus Stop; Evil Hearted You; For You Alone; Heart Full of Soul; I'm Not in Love; Listen People; Look Through Any Window; Rubber Bullets; The Things We Do for Love

Gounod, Charles   Ave Maria; Forever with the Lord; Funeral March of a Marionette; Nazareth; The Sea Hath Its Pearls; Soldier's Chorus; There Is a Green Hill Far Away

Gourlay, Ian   Song of the Clyde

Gourlay, Ronald   The Dicky Bird Hop

Gove, W.H.   The Charming Young Widow I Met on the Train

Gowers, Patrick   Smiley's People

Grady, John   My Baby's Comin' Home

Graeser, Louise   On with Roosevelt

Graff, George Jr.   As Long as the World Rolls On; In the Garden of Tomorrow; Isle o' Dreams; Till the Sands of the Desert Grow Cold; When Irish Eyes Are Smiling

Graffagnino, Jake   Stop and Think It Over

Grafton, Gerald   For the Noo, or, Something in the Bottle for the Morning; I Love a Lassie, or, Ma Scotch Bluebell; A Wee Deoch-an-Doris

Graham, Charles   If the Waters Could Speak as They Flow; The Picture That's Turned to (Toward) the Wall; She Was Happy Till She Met You; Two Little Girls in Blue

Graham, Harry   The King's Horses; Love Will Find a Way; The White Horse Inn; Your Eyes

Graham, Howard   When the Harvest Days Are Over, Jessie Dear

Graham, Irvin   I Believe; With a Twist of the Wrist; You Better Go Now

Graham, Kenny   Beaulieu Festival Suite

Graham, Leo Jr.   Shining Star

Graham, Roger   I Ain't Got Nobody

Graham, Ronny   I'm in Love with Miss Logan

Graham, Steve   Back to Donegal; Dear Old Donegal

Grainer, Ron   Doctor Who Theme; The Maigret Theme; Not So Much a Programme, More a Way of Life; Paul Temple Theme; Robert and Elizabeth; Steptoe and Son

Grainer, Percy Aldridge   Country Gardens; Molly on the Shore

Grainger, Porter   'Tain't Nobody's Business If I Do

Grainer, Jules   Hosanna

Grannis, S.M.   Do They Miss Me at Home

Grant, Bert   Along the Rocky Road to Dublin; Arrah Go On, I'm Gonna Go Back to Oregon; Don't Blame It All on Broadway; If I Knock the ''L'' Out of Kelly; My Barney Lies Over the Ocean (Just the Way He Lied to Me); When the Angelus Is Ringing; When You're Away

Grant, Eddy   Electric Avenue; I Don't Wanna Dance

Grant, Freddie(y)   How Can You Buy Killarney; Oh Mamma Mia

Grant, Glen   Fight On

Grant, Harold   Here

Grant, Ian   Let the People Sing; Let There Be Love; You've Done Something to My Heart

Grant, Mickie   Pink Shoelaces

Grant, Tom   Dancin' Your Memory Away

Graves, John Woodcock   (D'Ye Ken) John Peel

Gray, Barry   Thunderbirds Theme

Gray, Chauncey   Bye Bye Blues; You're the One I Care For

Gray, Ed J.   Crystal Blue Persuasion

Gray, Jerry   Pennsylvania 6-5000; Serenade: A String of Pearls

Gray, Louisa   Looking Back

Gray, Mark   Take Me Down

Gray, Thomas J.   Any Little Girl, That's a Nice Little Girl, Is the Right Little Girl for Me; Fido Is a Hot Dog Now; Good Night, Nurse (Kiss Your Little Patient)

Gray, Timothy   Home Sweet Heaven; You'd Better Love Me (While You May)

Gray, William B.   She Is More To Be Pitied Than Censured; The Volunteer Organist (as William B. Glenroy)

Graydon, Jay   After All; After the Love Has Gone; Turn Your Love Around; Who's Holding Donna Now

Grean, Charles   I Dreamed; Sweet Violets

Greaves, R.B.   Take a Letter, Maria

Green, Adolph   Bad Timing; Bells Are Ringing; Captain Hook's Waltz; Fade Out—Fade In; The French Lesson; Hello, Hello There; Hold Me, Hold Me, Hold Me; It's Love; Just in Time; Long Before I Knew You; Lucky To Be Me; Make Someone Happy; Never Never Land; New York, New York; Ohio; On the Twentieth Century; The Party's Over; A Quiet Girl; The River Song, or, Something's Always Happening on the River; Say, Darling; Some Other Time; Ya Got Me

Green, Al   Call Me (Come Back Home); Here I Am (Come and Take Me); Let's Stay Together

Green, Bud   Alabamy Bound; Away Down South in Heaven; Congratulations; Do Something; Flat Foot Floogie (with the Floy Floy); He's a Gypsy from Poughkeepsie; I Love My Baby—My Baby Loves Me; I'll Always Be in Love with You; Oh! Boy, What a Girl; Once in a While; Sentimental Journey; That's My Weakness Now

Green, Charles Randolph   The Thing; We'll Have To Go

Green, Eddie   A Good Man Is Hard To Find

Green, Florence   Soldier Boy

Green, John W.   Body and Soul; Coquette; Easy Come, Easy Go; Hello, My Lover, Goodbye; I Cover the Waterfront; I Wanna Be Loved; I'm Yours; (You Came Along from) Out of Nowhere; (The Song of) Raintree County; You're Mine You

Green, Paula   (Look For the) Union Label

Green, Philip   John and Julie; Josita; The March Hare; Say Wonderful Things; That's How a Love Song Was Born

Green, Sanford   Play Me Hearts and Flowers (I Wanna Cry)

Greenall, Rupert   One Thing Leads to Another

Greenaway, Roger   Doctor's Orders; Freedom Come, Freedom Go; Gasoline Alley Bred; Home Lovin' Man; Like Sister and Brother; Long Cool Woman (in a Black Dress); Love Transformation; Melting Pot; You've Got Your Troubles

Greenbank, Harry   The Amorous Goldfish; Chin, Chin, Chinaman; Chon Kina; The Jewel of Asia; Six Little Wives; (Oh I Love) Society; The Soldiers in the Park; The Toy Monkey, or, I'm a Monkey on a Stick

Greenbank, Percy   Come to the Ball; The Garden of Love; Little Miss Melody; My Dear Little Cingalee; The Pearl of Sweet Ceylon; The Violin Song; When You Are in Love; Wonderful Eyes

Greenberg, Abner   C'est Vous (It's You)

Greenberg, Eliot   Sweet Talkin' Guy

Greenberg, Steve   Funkytown

Greene, Albert Gordon   Old Grimes

Greene, Joe   Across the Alley from the Alamo; And Her Tears Flowed Like Wine

Greene, Joseph Arthur   Outa-Space

Greene, Mort   Sleepy Serenade; Stars in Your Eyes; Weary Blues

Greene, Schuyler   Babes in the Wood; Nodding Roses; Some Day I'll Find You; You Know and I Know (and We Both Understand)

Greenfield, David   Golden Brown

Greenfield, Howard   Breaking in a Brand New Broken Heart; Breaking Up Is Hard To Do; Calendar Girl; Everybody's Somebody's Fool; Frankie; Little Devil; Love Will Keep Us Together; My Heart Has a Mind of Its Own; Where the Boys Are; You Never Done It Like That

Greenwell, Peter   Meet the Family

Greenwich, Ellie   Be My Baby; Chapel of Love; Da Doo Ron Ron (When He Walked Me Home); Do Wah Diddy Diddy; Hanky Panky; The Leader of the Pack; Then He Kissed Me

Greenwood, Lee   God Bless the USA; A Love Song

Greer, George   Hurt So Good; Let Me Love You Tonight; Still Right Here in My Heart

Greer, Jesse   Baby Blue Eyes; Climbing Up the Ladder of Love; Flapperette; Freshie; Just You, Just Me; Old Mill Wheel; Once in a Lifetime; Reaching for the Moon; Sleepy Head; What Do I Care

Gregg, Hubert   I'm Gonna Get Lit Up (When the Lights Go On in London); Maybe It's Because I'm a Londoner

Gregory, John   Introduction and Air to a Stained Glass Window

Grenet, Eliseo   La Conga Atomica; Mama Inez

Grenfell, Joyce   I'm Going To See You Today

Grever, Maria   Júrame (Promise, Love); Magic Is the Moonlight; Ti-Pi-Tin; What a Diff'rence a Day Made (Makes)

Grey, Billy   The Laughing Policeman

Grey, Clifford   All for a Shilling a Day; Another Little Drink Wouldn't Do Us Any Harm; Dream Lover; Ev'ry Little While; First Love, Last Love, Best Love; Got a Date with an Angel; Hallelujah! Hey Gypsy (Play Gypsy) (Komn Tzizany); If Winter Comes; If You Were the Only Girl in the World; Let the Great Big World Keep Turning; Ma Belle; March of the Musketeers; (This Is) My Love Parade; The Rogue Song; Sally; The Song of the Shirt; Valencia; When I'm Looking at You; While Hearts Are Singing; The White Dove; Wild Rose

Grey, Hedley   Chewing a Piece of Straw; Hold Back the Dawn; Number Something Far Away Lane

Grey, Joe   Runnin' Wild

Grey, Zane   (Every Time I Turn Around) Back in Love Again

Grieg, Edvard   Anitra's Dance; Ich Liebe Dich (I Love Thee); March of the Dwarfs; The Norwegian Dance; Peer Gynt Suite; Piano Concerto

Grier, Jimmy   The Object of My Affection; What's the Reason (I'm Not Pleasin' You)

Griffen, Ken   You Can't Be True, Dear

Griffes, Charles Tomlinson   The White Peacock

Griffen, Gerald   We'll Meet Again

Grock, A.   Abie My Boy

Grofé, Ferde   Daybreak; Mississippi Suite; On the Trail; Three Shades of Blue; (My) Wonderful One

Gross, Henry   Shannon

Gross, Walter   Tenderly

Grossman, Bernie   We're Going Over; You Didn't Want Me When You Had Me

Grossman, Julius   Tzena, Tzena, Tzena

Grossman, Larry   Goodtime Charley

Grossmith, George   Dancing Time

Grosz, Will   Along the Santa Fe Trail; At the Cafe Continental; Bird on the Wing; Harbor Lights; In an Old Dutch Garden; Isle of Capri; Make Believe Island; Poor Little Angeline; Red Sails in the Sunset; Ten Pretty Girls; Tina

Grouya, Ted   Flamingo; I Heard You Cried Last Night; In My Arms

Gruber, Edmund L.   The U.S. Field Artillery March, or, The Caissons Go Rolling Along

Gruber, Franz   Silent Night, Holy Night

Grun, Bernard   Broken Wings

Grusin, Dave   It Might Be You

Gruska, Jay   Friends and Lovers (Born to Each Other)

Guaraldi, Vince   Cast Your Fate to the Wind

Guernsey, Wellington   Alice, Where Art Thou

Guest, Val   Wrap Yourself in Cotton Wool

Guglielmi, Luis (R.S. Louiguy)   Cherry Pink and Apple Blossom White; La Vie en Rose

Guida, Carmela   If You Wanna Be Happy

Guida, Frank J.   If You Wanna Be Happy; Quarter to Three Waltz

Guidry, Robert   See You Later Alligator

Gulesian, Mrs. M.H.   The House by the Side of the Road

Gumble, Albert   The Chanticleer Rag; How's Every Little Thing in Dixie; Rebecca of Sunny-Brook Farm; Winter

Gumble, M.   At the Mississippi Cabaret

Gummoe, John   Rhythm of the Rain

Gundry, Bob   If You Ever Change Your Mind

Gusman, Meyer   Gypsy Dream Rose; Underneath the Russian Moon

Gussev, Victor   Meadowlands, or, Cavalry of the Steppes

Guthrie, Arlo   Alice's Restaurant

Guthrie, Woody   So Long (It's Been Good To Know Yuh)

Hackady, Hal   Goodtime Charley

Hadjidakis, Manos   Adios My Love, or, The Song of Athens; Never on Sunday; The White Rose of Athens

Hadler, Mary M.   Shifting, Whispering Sands

Haenschen, Gus   There's No Other Love

Hagar, Sammy   Why Can't This Be Love

Hagen, Earle H.   Harlem Nocturne

Hager, Clyde   That Wonderful Mother of Mine

Hager, Frederick W.   Laughing Water

Haggard, Merle   Are the Good Times Really Over; Big City; I Think I'll Just Stay Here and Drink; Movin' On; Okie from Muskogee; Rainbow Stew

Haggart, Robert   Big Noise from Winnetka; South Rampart Street Parade; What's New

Hague, Albert   Just for Once; Two Faces in the Dark; Young and Foolish

Haig, Bernhard   By the Bend of the River

Haimsohn, George   Choo-Choo Honeymoon; The Sailor of My Dreams

Haines, Herbert   Cigarette

Haines, Will   The Biggest Aspidistra in the World; He's Dead But He Won't Lie Down; In My Little Bottom Drawer; In My Little Snapshot Album; Out in the Cold Cold Snow; Sally; Walter, Walter (Lead Me to the Altar)

Hairston, Jester   Mary's Boy Child

Haldeman, Oakley   Here Comes Santa Claus

Hale, Sarah Josepha   Mary Had a Little Lamb

Halévy, Ludovic   Toreador Song

Haley, Ed   While Stolling Through the Park One Day, or, The Fountain in the Park

Halfin, Bob   You're a Pink Toothbrush

Halifax, Hal   Tiggerty Boo

Hall, Carol   A Lil' Ole Bitty Pissant Country Place

Hall, Charles S.   John Brown's Body

Hall, Daryl   Did It in a Minute; Everytime You Go Away; I Can't Go for That (No Can Do); Kiss on My List; Maneater; Method of Modern Love; Out of Touch; Possession Obsession; Private Eyes; Rich Girl; Sara Smile; Say It Isn't So; She's Gone; Wait For Me; You Make My Dreams

Hall, Foley   Ever of Thee

Hall, Fred   Eleven More Months and Ten More Days; I Got a "Code" in My "Dose"

Hall, Graeme   Beg, Steal or Borrow

Hall, Guy   Johnson Rag

Hall, Henry   Here's to the Next Time

Hall, J. Graydon   That's How Much I Love You

Hall, Johanna   Dance with Me; Still the One; Suite No. 1 for Small Orchestra

Hall, John T.   Wedding of the Winds; When You've Had a Little Love You Want a Little More

Hall, Owen   I Want To Be a Military Man; The Shade of the Palm; Tell Me Pretty Maiden (Are There Any More at Home Like You)

Hall, Reginald   You Talk Too Much

Hall, Rich   Cowboy Serenade, or, My Last Cigarette

Hall, Tom T.   Harper Valley P.T.A.

Hall, Wendell   It Ain't Gonna Rain No Mo'

Halle, R.L.   Baby's Prayer

Hallifax, Arthur William   Penny Serenade

Ham, Peter   Without You

Hamblen, Stuart   It Is No Secret; Open Up Your Heart (and Let the Sunshine In); This Ole House

Hamilton, Ann   Fallin' in Love (Again)

Hamilton, Arthur   Cry Me a River; He Needs Me; Sing a Rainbow

Hamilton, Dan   Fallin' in Love (Again)

Hamilton, G.   Iowa Corn Song

Hamilton, Nancy   A House with a Little Red Barn; How High the Moon; The Old Soft Shoe

Hamilton, Ord   Number Something Far Away Lane; You're Blasé

Hamilton, Russ   Rainbow; We Will Make Love; Wedding Ring

Hamlisch, Marvin   And . . . ; At the Ballet; California Nights; Dance:Ten, Looks:Three; The Entertainer; Hello Twelve, Hello Thirteen, Hello Love; I Can Do That; I Hope I Get It; If You Remember Me; Just for Tonight; The Music and the Mirror; Nobody Does It Better; Nothing; One; Sunshine, Lollipops and Rainbows; Surprise, Surprise; Theme from Ice Castles (Through the Eyes of Love); They're Playing Our Song; Tits and Ass; The Way We Were; What I Did for Love

Hamm, Fred   Bye Bye Blues

Hammer, Jack   Great Balls of Fire

Hammer, Jan   (Theme from) Miami Vice

Hammerstein, Arthur   Because of You

Hammerstein II, Oscar   All At Once You Love Her; All in Fun; All the Things You Are; All Through the Day; April Blossoms; Bali Ha'i; Bambalina; Bill; Bloody Mary; Can I Forget You; Can't Help Lovin' Dat Man; Climb Ev'ry Mountain; A Cockeyed Optimist; Cossack Love Song, or, Don't Forget Me; Dance, My Darlings; The Desert Song; Dites-moi Pourquoi; Do I Love You Because You're Beautiful; Do-Re-Mi; Don't Ever Leave Me; Don't Marry Me; The Door of My (Her) Dreams; D'Ya Love Me?; Edelweiss; Ev'rybody's Got a Home But Me; A Fellow Needs a Girl; The Folks Who Live on the Hill; The Gentleman Is a Dope; Getting To Know You; Happy Christmas, Little Friend; Happy Talk; Hello Young Lovers; Here Am I; High, Wide and Handsome; Honey Bun; A Hundred Million Miracles; I Cain't Say No; I Enjoy Being a Girl; I Have Dreamed; I Haven't Got a Worry in the World; I Whistle a Happy Tune; I Won't Dance; If I Loved You; I'll Take Romance; I'm Gonna Wash That Man Right Outa My Hair; I'm in Love with a Wonderful Guy; In Egern on the Tegern See; In My Own Little Corner; In the Heart of the Dark; Indian Love Call; Isn't It Kinda Fun; It Might As Well Be Spring; It's a Grand Night for Singing; It's a Wonderful World; I've Told Every Little Star; June Is Bustin' Out All Over; Kansas City; Keep It Gay; A Kiss To Build a Dream On; The Last Time I Saw Paris; Loneliness of Evening; The Lonely Goatherd; Love Look Away; A Lovely Night; Lover Come Back to Me; Make Believe; Many a New Day; Maria; Marianne; My Favorite Things; No Other Love; Nobody Else But Me; Oh What a Beautiful Mornin'; Oklahoma; Ol' Man River; One Alone; One Kiss;

One More Dance; Out of My Dreams; People Will Say We're in Love; Poor Jud (Is Daid); The Riff Song; Romance; Rose Marie; Shall We Dance; Sixteen Going on Seventeen; So Far; So Long, Farewell; Softly, As in a Morning Sunrise; Soliloquy; Some Enchanted Evening; Something Wonderful; The Song Is You; Song of the Flame; The Sound of Music; Stouthearted Men; Sunday; Sunny; The Surrey with the Fringe on Top; The Sweetest Sight That I Have Ever Seen; Ten Minutes Ago; That's For Me; There Is Nothin' Like a Dame; The Things I Want; This Nearly Was Mine; This Was a Real Nice Clambake; Totem Tom-Tom; 'Twas Not So Long Ago; Two Little Bluebirds; Wanting You; We Kiss in a Shadow; We'll Have a Kingdom; What's the Use of Wond'rin'; When I Grow Too Old To Dream; When I Marry Mister Snow; When the Children Are Asleep; When the Spring Is in the Air; Who; Why Do I Love You; Why Was I Born; Wildflower; Will You Marry Me Tomorrow, Maria; You Are Beautiful; You Are Love; You Are Never Away; You Are Sixteen; You'll Never Walk Alone; Younger Than Springtime; You've Got To Be (Carefully) Taught

Hammond, Albert Louis   (The) Air That I Breathe; Freedom Come, Freedom Go; Gimme Dat Ding; It Never Rains in Southern California; To All the Girls I've Loved Before; When I Need You

Hammond, Ronnie   Do It or Die

Hamner, Curley   Hey-Ba-Ba-Re-Bop

Hampton, Carl   (If Loving You Is Wrong) I Don't Want To Be Right; If You're Ready (Come Go with Me)

Hampton, Gladys   Hey-Ba-Ba-Re-Bop

Hampton, Lionel   Flying Home; Hey-Ba-Ba-Re-Bop

Hanby, Benjamin Russell   Darling Nelly Gray; Ole Shady, or, The Song of the Contraband

Hancock, James S.   Out in the Cold Cold Snow; Walter, Walter (Lead Me to the Altar)

Handel, George Frederic   Hallelujah Chorus; Joy to the World, or, Antioch

Handley, John J.   Sleep, Baby, Sleep, or, Irene's Lullaby

Handman, Lou   Are You Lonesome Tonight; Baby Me; Blue (and Broken Hearted); Bye Bye Baby; I Can't Get the One I Want (Those I Get I Don't Want); I'm Gonna Charleston Back to Charleston; Me and the Moon; My Sweetie Went Away (She Didn't Say Where, When or Why); Puddin' Head Jones; Was It Rain

Handy, William Christopher   Aunt Hagar's Blues; Beale Street Blues; Careless Love; Joe Turner Blues; The John Henry Blues; The Memphis Blues; St. Louis Blues; Yellow Dog Blues

Hanighan, Bernard   Bob White (Whatcha Gonna Swing Tonight); Here Come the British (Bang! Bang!); If the Moon Turns Green; When a Woman Loves a Man

Hankey, Catherine   I Love To Tell the Story; Tell Me the Old, Old Story

Hanks, Len   (Every Time I Turn Around) Back in Love Again

Hanley, James F.   I'm in the Market for You; (Back Home Again in) Indiana; Just a Cottage Small—by a Waterfall; The Little White House (at the End of Honeymoon Lane); Rose of Washington Square; Second Hand Rose; There's a Million

Girlies Lonesome Tonight, and Still I'm All Alone; Three Wonderful Letters from Home; Zing Went the Strings of My Heart

Hanlon, Bert I'd Love To Be a Monkey in the Zoo; M-I-S-S-I-S-S-I-P-P-I; Round on the End and High in the Middle, O-hi-o

Hann, W.A. Ain't It a Shame

Hanse, Peter Now and Forever

Hansen, Randy Lee State of Shock

Hanson, John A Quiet Girl

Harbach, Otto Allah's Holiday; April Blossoms; Bambalina; The Birth of Passion; The Bubble; Cossack Love Song, or, Don't Forget Me; Cuddle Up a Little Closer, Lovey Mine; Dancing the Devil Away; The Desert Song; Doctor Tinkle Tinker; The Door of My (Her) Dreams; Every Girl Loves Me But the Girl I Love; Every Little Movement (Has a Meaning All Its Own); Giannina Mia; Going Up; Ha-Cha-Cha; I Want To Marry a Male Quartet; I Watch the Love Parade; I Won't Dance; If You Look in Her Eyes; Indian Love Call; Katinka; Kiss a Four Leaf Clover; Learn To Smile; Love Is Like a Firefly; The Love Nest; Mary; The Night Was Made for Love; One Alone; One Moment Alone; Poor Pierrot; Rackety-Coo!; The Riff Song; Romance; Rose Marie; The Same Old Moon; She Didn't Say Yes (She Didn't Say No); Smoke Gets in Your Eyes; Something Seems Tingle-Ingling; Song of the Flame; Sympathy; (Everybody Ought To Know How To Do) The Tickle Toe; Too Many Rings Around Rosie; Totem Tom-Tom; The Touch of Your Hand; Try To Forget; We'll Have a Kingdom; When a Maid Comes Knocking at Your Heart; Wildflower; Yesterdays; You're Devastating; You're in Love

Harburg, E.Y. "Yip" Ah, But Is It Love; Ain't It the Truth; And Russia Is Her Name; April in Paris; The Begat; Brother, Can You Spare a Dime; Can't Help Singing; Cocoanut Sweet; Ding Dong! The Witch Is Dead; Down with Love; Evelina; Fun To Be Fooled; (This Is) God's Country; Happiness Is (Just) a Thing Called Joe; How Are Things in Glocca Morra; I Could Go On Singing (Till the Cows Come Home); I Don't Think I'll End It All Today; I Got a Song; I Like the Likes of You; If I Only Had a Brain; If This Isn't Love; I'm Yours; It's Only a Paper Moon; Last Night When We Were Young; Let's Take a Walk Around the Block; Little Biscuit; Little Drops of Rain; Look to the Rainbow; Lydia the Tattooed Lady; Moanin' in the Mornin'; Moonlight and Pretzels; More and More; Napoleon's a Pastry; Necessity; Old Devil Moon; Over the Rainbow; Push de Button; Right As the Rain; Savanna; Suddenly; Take It Slow, Joe; That Great Come and Get It Day; That's Life; Then I'll Be Tired of You; There's a Great Day Coming, Mañana; T'morra, T'morra; We're Off To See the Wizard; What Good Does It Do; What Is There To Say; When I'm Not Near the Girl I Love; When the Idle Poor Become the Idle Rich; You're a Builder Upper

Hardaway, Lulu I Was Made To Love Her

Hardcastle, Paul 19

Hardin, Glen D. Count Me In

Hardin, Lil Struttin' with Some Barbecue

Hardin, Tim If I Were a Carpenter

Hardy, Norman Lovely Lady Let the Roses See You Today

Hare, Ken I'm So Ashamed; Lift Boy

Hargis, Reginald J. Dazz

Hargreaves, Reginald Sitting on a Fire Barred Gate

Hargreaves, Robert Butterflies in the Rain; If; Let's All Sing Like the Birdies Sing; Life's Desire; The Song of the Trees; Unless; You Die If You Worry

Hargreaves, William Burlington Bertie from Bow; Dance with Your Uncle Joseph; Little Yellow Bird; Oh! I Must Go Home Tonight

Haring, Robert C. Concerto for Two

Harju, Gary Five in the Morning

Harket, Morten Take On Me

Harline, Leigh Give a Little Whistle; Hi-Diddle-Dee-Dee (an Actor's Life for Me); I've Got No Strings; When You Wish upon a Star; The World Owes Me a Living

Harling, W. Franke Beyond the Blue Horizon; Give Me a Moment Please; Sing You Sinners

Harmati, Sandor The Blue Bird of Happiness

Harney, Ben R. Mister Johnson, Turn Me Loose

Harnick, Sheldon Anatevka; Artificial Flowers; Dear Friend; Do You Love Me; Home Again; I Love a Cop; If I Were a Rich Man; (In My) Little Tin Box; Matchmaker, Matchmaker; Politics and Poker; Sabbath Prayer; She Loves Me; Sunrise Sunset; Till Tomorrow; To Life, or, L'Chaim; Tradition; When Did I Fall in Love; Will He Like Me

Harold, William Goofus

Harper, Edward Jim Along, Josey

Harper, James The Biggest Aspidistra in the World; He's Dead But He Won't Lie Down; In My Little Bottom Drawer; In My Little Snapshot Album; She Is Ma Daisy; We'll Keep a Welcome; When You Lose the One You Love

Harper, Marjorie Negra Consentida (My Pet Brunette)

Harrigan, Edward The Babies on Our Block; Danny by My Side; The Full Moon Union; Hats Off to Me; I Never Drank Behind the Bar; I've Come Here To Stay; Jolly Commodore; Knights of the Mystic Star; The Last of the Hogans; Locked Out After Nine; Maggie Murphy's Home; The Market on Saturday Night; McNally's Row of Flats; The Mulligan Braves; The Mulligan Guard; My Dad's Dinner Pail; Never Take the Horse Shoe from the Door; Paddy Duffy's Cart; Patrick's Day Parade; Plum Pudding; Poverty's Tears Ebb and Flow; De Rainbow Road; The Skidmore Fancy Ball; The Skidmore Guard; The Skidmore Masquerade; Such an Education, Has My Mary Ann, or, Sweet Mary Ann; Take a Day Off, Mary Ann; Taking in the Town; They Never Tell All What They Know; When the Clock in the Tower Strikes Twelve

Harriman, Al In the Town Where I Was Born

Harrington, Bill Because of Rain

Harrington, Cecil Over the Garden Wall

Harrington, J.P. I Know Where the Flies Go in the Wintertime; Oh Isn't It Singular

Harriott, Joe Revival

Harris, Charles K. After the Ball; Always in the Way; Break the News to Mother; For Old Times' Sake; Hello, Central, Give Me Heaven; I've a Longing in My Heart for You, Louise; I've Just Come Back To Say Goodbye; Kiss and Let's Make Up; 'Mid the Green Fields of Virginia; Nobody Knows, Nobody Cares; One Night in June; There'll Come a Time; Would You Care

Harris, Clifford   A Bachelor Gay; Give Me a Little Cosy Corner; I Was a Good Little Girl Till I Met You; Paradise for Two

Harris, Don F.   I'm Leaving It All Up to You; The Jolly Green Giant

Harris, George Jr.   The Regiment of Sambre and Meuse

Harris, Harry   Baby Me

Harris, John   The Point of No Return

Harris, Lew   The Things I Love

Harris, Marion   My Kid's a Crooner

Harris, Max   Bombay Duckling (Kipling Theme); The Gurney Slade Theme

Harris, Remus   Roses in the Rain

Harris, Robert E.   And the Great Big Saw Came Nearer

Harris, Rolf   Tie Me Kangaroo Down Sport

Harris, Stewart   Lonely Nights

Harris, Tim   We're Gonna Change the World

Harris, Will J.   Sweet Sue (Just You)

Harris, Wood   Queen of the Hop; Rock-A-Billy

Harrison, Annie Fortesque   In the Gloaming

Harrison, George   All Those Years Ago; Give Me Love (Give Me Peace on Earth); Here Comes the Sun; My Sweet Lord; Photograph; Something (in the Way She Moves); While My Guitar Gently Weeps

Harrison, Larry   How Glad I Am; Why Baby Why

Harrison, Neil   I Could Never Miss You (More Than I Do)

Harrison, Tom   Boomerang; My Little Grass Shack in Kealakekua, Hawaii

Harrison, Wilbert   Let's Work Together

Harrison, William   Our Love Story

Harry, Deborah   Heart of Glass; Rapture

Harschorn, Joe   The Morning After, or, Song from *The Poseidon Adventure*

Harshman, Robert L.   Hurts So Bad

Hart, Bobby   Come a Little Bit CLoser; Last Train to Clarksville; Valleri

Hart, Bruce   You Take My Breath Away

Hart, Corey   Never Surrender

Hart, Henry   Good Sweet Ham

Hart, Lorenz   All At Once; Any Old Place with You; Are You My Love; Babes in Arms; Bewitched, Bothered and Bewildered; Blue Moon; The Blue Room; Bye and Bye; Can't You Do a Friend a Favor; The Circus Is on Parade; Dancing on the Ceiling; Do I Hear You Saying "I Love You"; Do It the Hard Way; Down By the River; Ev'ry Sunday Afternoon; Ev'rything I've Got (Belongs to You); Falling in Love with Love; From Another World; The Girl Friend; Give It Back to the Indians; Glad To Be Unhappy; Have You Met Miss Jones; Here in My Arms; How Can You Forget; How Was I To Know; I Could Write a Book; I Didn't Know What Time It Was; I Like To Recognize the Tune; I Married an Angel; I Want a Man; I Wish I Were in Love Again; I'd Rather Be

Right; I'll Tell the Man in the Street; In Our Little Den of Iniquity; Isn't It Romantic; It Never Entered My Mind; It's Easy To Remember (and So Hard To Forget); It's Got To Be Love; I've Got Five Dollars; Johnny One Note; The Lady Is a Tramp; A Little Birdie Told Me So; Little Girl Blue; Love Never Went to College; Lover; Manhattan; Mimi; Moon of My Delight; The Most Beautiful Girl in the World; Mountain Greenery; My Funny Valentine; My Heart Stood Still; My Lucky Star; My Romance; Nobody's Heart (Belongs to Me); On a Desert Island with Thee; On Your Toes; Over and Over Again; Quiet Night; Sentimental Me; A Ship Without a Sail; Sing for Your Supper; Soon (Maybe Not Tomorrow); Spring Is Here; Sweet Peter; The Tartar Song; Ten Cents a Dance; There's a Small Hotel; This Can't Be Love; Thou Swell; To Keep My Love Alive; Too Good for the Average Man; A Tree in the Park; Wait Till You See Her; Way Out West; Where Or When; Where's That Rainbow; Why Can't I; Why Do I; Why Do You Suppose; With a Song in My Heart; You Are Too Beautiful; You Have Cast Your Shadow on the Sea; You Mustn't Kick It Around; You Took Advantage of Me; Yours Sincerely; Zip

Hart, Peter   Meet Me on the Corner; Nellie the Elephant; Soon It Will Be Sunday; The Wind Cannot Read

Hart, William   When Yankee Doodle Learns To Parlez-Vous Francais

Hartford, John   Gentle on My Mind

Hartley, Fred   Life Is Nothing Without Music; A Summer Evening in Santa Cruz

Hartman, Dan   I Can Dream About You; Living in America

Harvey, Alex   Delta Dawn

Harvey-Richie, Brenda   Penny Lover; You Are

Harwood, Ronnie   You Drive Me Crazy

Hassall, Christopher   Fold Your Wings; Glamorous Night; I Can Give You the Starlight; I Leave My Heart in an English Garden; My Dearest Dear; My Life Belongs to You; Primrose; Rose of England; Shine Through My Dreams; Take Your Girl; Waltz of My Heart; When the Gypsy Played

Hasting, Thomas   Toplady; Rock of Ages

Hatch, Earl   What's the Reason (I'm Not Pleasin' You)

Hatch, Robert   You're the Best Break This Old Heart Ever Had

Hatch, Tony   Call Me; Color My World; Don't Sleep in the Subway; Downtown; Harvest of Love; I Couldn't Live Without Your Love; I Know a Place; I Love the Little Things; Joanna; My Love; The Other Man's Grass (Is Always Greener); Where Are You Now My Love

Hatton, John Liptrot   Simon the Cellarer; The Vagabond

Havens, Jimmie   We Don't Want the Bacon, What We Want Is a Piece of the Rhine

Havenschild, Clara   Going for a Pardon

Havergal, Frances Ridley   Tell It Out Among the Nations (Heathen) That the Lord Is King; True-Hearted, Whole-Hearted, or, Peal Out the Watchword

Havet, Pierce   Losing You

Havez, Jean C.   Everybody Works But Father; Sailing Down the Chesapeake Bay

Hawes, Bruce   They Just Can't Stop It (The Games People Play)

Hawker, Kenneth Alan J.   Little Bit o'Soul; Will I What

Hawker, Mike   Don't Treat Me Like a Child; I Only Want To Be with You; Little Miss Lonely; Stay Awhile; Walkin' Back to Happiness; You Don't Know

Hawkins, Erskin   Tuxedo Junction

Hawkins, John   I Have a Noble Cock

Hawks, Annie S.   I Need Thee Every Hour

Hawley, Charles Beach   They Kissed, I Saw Them Do It

Hawthorne, Alice, *see* **Septimus Winner**

Hay, Colin   Down Under; It's a Mistake; Overkill; Who Can It Be Now

Hay, John   When the Boys Come Home

Hay, Roy   Church of the Poison Mind; Do You Really Want To Hurt Me; It's a Miracle; Karma Chameleon; Miss Me Blind; Time (Clock of the Heart)

Hayden, Joseph   (There'll Be) A Hot Time in the Old Town (Tonight)

Haydn, Joseph   My Mother Bids Me Bind My Hair

Hayes, Christopher   I Want a New Drug; The Power of Love; Stuck with You

Hayes, Clarence Leonard   Huggin' and Chalkin'

Hayes, Isaac Lee Jr.   Deja Vu; (Theme from) Shaft; Soul Man

Hayes, Jerry   Who's Cheatin' Who

Hayes, Maria X.   The Yeoman's Wedding Song

Hayes, Peter Lind   Come to Me

Haymes, Bob   My Love, My Love; That's All

Haynes, Walter   Eight by Ten

Hays, Billy   Goodness Knows How I Love You

Hays, Julia M.   Goodnight, Little Girl, Goodnight

Hays, Lee   If I Had a Hammer; (The Wreck of the) John B

Hays, William Shakespeare   Angels Meet Me at the Cross Roads; The Drummer Boy of Shiloh; Early in de Mornin'; Evangeline; The Little Old Log Cabin in the Lane; Mollie Darling; Oh Sam; Roll Out! Heave Dat Cotton; Susan Jane; We Parted by the River

Hayward, Charlie   In America

Hayward, David Justin   Nights in White Satin

Hayward, Justin   Your Wildest Dreams

Hazard, Robert   Girls Just Want To Have Fun

Hazlett, Richard   You Deserve a Break Today

Hazlewood, Lee   Houston; Lady Bird; Love Eyes; Shazam; Sugar Town; These Boots Are Made for Walking

Hazlewood, Michael   (The) Air That I Breathe; Freedom Come, Freedom Go; Gimme Dat Ding; It Never Rains in Southern California

Head, Roy   Treat Her Right

Healey, W.E.   A Bowl of Roses

Heard, James   Arizona

Heath, Bobby   My Pony Boy

Heath, E.P.   Love Has Wings; Love's Own Sweet Song, or,

Sari Waltz; My Faithful Stradivari; Softly Thro' the Summer Night

Heath, Hy   Clancy Lowered the Boom; Mule Train; Somebody Bigger Than You and I; Uncle Remus Said

Heath, Lyman   The Grave of Bonaparte

Heath, Moira   That Lovely Weekend

Heath, Ted   That Lovely Weekend

Heathcote, Joe   Mister Dumpling

Heatherton, Fred   I've Got a Lovely Bunch of Cocoanuts

Hebb, Bobby   Sunny

Heber, Reginald   From Greenland's Icy Mountains; Holy! Holy! Lord God Almighty; The Son of God Goes Forth to War

Hedges, Elven   Ma, Look At Charlie; Oh Charley Take It Away

Heelan, Will A.   Every Race Has a Flag But the Coon; I'd Leave My Happy Home for You; In the House of Too Much Trouble; No Wedding Bells for Me; Put On Your Slippers and Fill Up Your Pipe

Heeney, Michael   Still Doin' Time

Hefti, Neal   Barefoot in the Park; Batman Theme; Li'l Darlin' (Don't Dream of Anybody But Me); (Theme from) The Odd Couple

Hegel, Robert Eric   Just As I Am

Heifetz, Jascha   Hora Staccato

Hein, Silvio   He's a Cousin of Mine; Some Little Bug Is Going To Find You (Some Day); When You're All Dressed Up and No Place to Go.

Heindorf, Ray   Pete Kelly's Blues; Some Sunday Morning; Sugarfoot

Heine, Heinrich   The Sea Hath Its Pearls; The Two Grenadiers

Heinzman, John   Down Where the Silv'ry Mohawk Flows

Heinzman, Otto   Down Where the Silv'ry Mohawk Flows

Heiser, L.W.   Dreaming

Heisler, Dave   Say You're Mine Again

Held, Anna   It's Delightful To Be Married

Helf, J. Fred   Every Race Has a Flag But the Coon; The Fatal Rose of Red; If Money Talks, It Ain't on Speaking Terms with Me; I'm Tying the Leaves So They Won't Come Down; In the House of Too Much Trouble; The Morning After the Night Before; A Picture No Artist Can Paint; When You Know You're Not Forgotten by the Girl You Can't Forget

Hellmer, Heinz   Tokyo Melody

Hemans, Felicia Dorothea   The Landing of the Pilgrims, or, The Pilgrim Fathers; Tyrolese Evening Hymn

Hemy, H.F.   Faith of Our Fathers

Henderson, Charlie   Deep Night; So Beats My Heart for You

Henderson, Joe   Chick; Jazzboat; Somebody; Treble Chance; Trudie; Why Don't They Understand

Henderson, Norman   Cuban Pete

Henderson, Ray   Alabamy Bound; Animal Crackers in My Soup; Annabelle; Bam, Bam, Bamy Shore; The Best Things in Life Are Free; The Birth of the Blues; Black Bottom; Button Up Your Overcoat; Bye Bye Blackbird; Come Home;

Don't Bring Lulu; Don't Hold Everything; Don't Tell Her (What's Happened to Me); Five Foot Two, Eyes of Blue (Has Anybody Seen My Girl?); Follow the Swallow; Follow Thru; Georgette; The Girl Is You and the Boy Is Me; A Girl of the Pi Beta Phi; Good News; Here Am I—Broken Hearted; Hold My Hand; I Wonder Who's Dancing with You Tonight; If I Had a Girl Like You; If I Had a Talking Picture of You; I'm a Dreamer (Aren't We All); I'm Sitting on Top of the World (Just Rolling Along—Just Rolling Along); It All Depends on You; Just a Memory; Just Imagine; Keep Your Skirts Down, Mary Ann; Let's Call It a Day; Life Is Just a Bowl of Cherries; Lucky Day; Lucky in Love; My Lucky Star; My Sin; My Song; Oh Murphy; One More Time; Seventh Heaven; So Blue; Sonny Boy; Strike Me Pink; (Keep Your) Sunny Side Up; Thank Your Father; That Old Gang of Mine; That's Why Darkies Were Born; Then I'll Have Time for You; This Is the Missus; The Thrill Is Gone; To Know You Is To Love You; Together; Too Many Parties and Too Many Pals; Turn on the Heat; The Varsity Drag; Why Did I Kiss That Girl; You Find the Time, I'll Find the Place; You Try Somebody Else, and I'll Try Somebody Else (We'll Be Back Together Again); You Wouldn't Fool Me, Would You; You're in Love with Everyone; You're the Cream in My Coffee

Hendler, Herb   Serenade

Hendricks, Belford   It's Just a Matter of Time

Hendricks, Jon   Desafinado (Slightly Out of Tune)

Hendrickson, William D.   The Spanish Cavalier

Heneker, David   Dis-Donc, Dis-Donc; Flash, Bang, Wallop; Half a Sixpence; If the Rain's Got To Fall; Irma La Douce; Our Language of Love

Henley, Arthur W.D.   Nobody Loves a Fairy When She's Forty; Oh Charley Take It Away

Henley, Don   Best of My Love; Boys of Summer; Dirty Laundry; Lyin' Eyes; One of These Nights; Take It to the Limit

Henning, Paul   Ballad of Jed Clampett

Henning, Robert   Intermezzo (A Love Story) (Souvenir de Vienne)

Henry, Francis   Little Girl

Henry, John   Lily the Pink

Henry, S.R. (Henry R. Stern)   By Heck; Down at the Huskin' Bee; Down in the Old Cherry Orchard; I'm Looking for a Nice Young Fellow Who Is Looking for a Nice Young Girl; Indianola; I've Got the Time—I've Got the Place, But It's Hard To Find the Girl

Henshaw, Arthur   When the Mists Have Cleared Away

Herbert, A.P.   Ma Belle Marguerita; A Nice Cup of Tea; Other People's Babies; The Water Gypsies

Herbert, Annie   When the Mists Have Cleared Away; When the Mists Have Rolled Away

Herbert, Joseph W.   Love's Roundelay; Pretty Edelweiss; Sweetest Maid of All

Herbert, S.A.   For All Eternity

Herbert, Twyla   Lightnin' Strikes

Herbert, Victor   Absinthe Frappé; Ah! Sweet Mystery of Life; Al Fresco; All for You; The Angelus; Ask Her While the Band Is Playing; Badinage; Bagdad; Bandana Land; Because You're You; The Cricket on the Heath; Cupid and I; Dagger Dance; Eileen (Alanna Asthore); Every Day Is Ladies' Day With Me; The Fortune Teller; Gypsy Love Song, or, Slumber On; I Can't Do the Sum; I Might Be Your "Once-in-a-While"; I Want What I Want When I Want It; If Only You Were Mine; If You Were I and I Were You; I'm Falling in Love with Someone; In Old New York, or, The Streets of New York; Indian Summer; The Isle of Our Dreams; Italian Street Song; A Kiss in the Dark; Kiss Me Again, or, If I Were on the Stage; A Knot of Blue; The Love Boat; Love Is Like a Cigarette; Love Is the Best of All; The March of the Toys; The Mascot of the Troop; Moonbeams; My Angeline; My Dream Girl, I Loved You Long Ago; Neapolitan Love Song; Panamericana; Romany Life; Rose of the World; Serenade for Strings; Someone Like You; Spooky Ookum; The Springtime of Life; Star Light, Star Bright; Sweethearts; Tell It All Over Again; There Once Was an Owl; Thine Alone; To the Land of My Own (Small) Romance; Toyland; Tramp! Tramp! Tramp! Along the Highway; Two Laughing Irish Eyes; When Shall I Again See Ireland; When You're Away; When You're Pretty; When You're Wearing the Ball and Chain; The Wild Rose; A Woman Is Only a Woman, But a Good Cigar Is a Smoke; The Wooing of the Violin; You Belong to Me

Herbert, Wallace   Blue Pacific Moonlight

Herbstritt, Larry   Fire in the Morning; I Just Fall in Love Again

Herford, Harold   I Hear You Calling Me

Herman, Jerry   And I Was Beautiful; Before the Parade Passes By; The Best of Times; Big Time; Bosom Buddies; Chin Up, Ladies!; Dancing; Dear World; Each Tomorrow Morning; Hello Dolly; I Am What I Am; I Don't Want To Know; If He Walked into My Life; It Only Takes a Moment; It Takes a Woman; Kiss Her Now; Mame; Mazel Tov; Milk and Honey; My Best Girl; Open a New Window; Put On Your Sunday Clothes; Shalom; So Long Dearie; Time Heals Everything; We Need a Little Christmas

Herman, Woody   Early Autumn; Northwest Passage

Hernandez, Rafael   El Cumbanchero

Herold, Louis Joseph Ferdinand   Zampa (Overture)

Herpin, Henri "Jamblan"   (All of a Sudden) My Heart Sings

Herrick, Robert   Cherry Ripe; Passing By

Herron, Joel   I'm a Fool To Want You

Herschell, William   Good-Bye, Ma! Good-Bye, Pa! Good-Bye, Mule, or, Long Boy

Hershey, June   Deep in the Heart of Texas

Herst, Jerry   So Rare

Herzer, Ludwig   Yours Is My Heart Alone

Herzer, Wallie   Everybody Two-Step

Herzog, Arthur Jr.   God Bless the Child

Hess, Cliff   Huckleberry Finn; When Alexander Takes His Ragtime Band to France

Hester, Hal   Do Your Own Thing; When You're Young and in Love

Hewitt, D.C.   The American Star

Hewitt, James Hill   The Minstrel's Return from the War; Tammany Quickstep

Hewitt, John Hill   All Quiet Along the Potomac Tonight

Hewitt, Joseph   The Cannon Song

Heyduk, Adolph   Songs My Mother Taught Me

Heyman, Edward   After All, You're All I'm After; Blame It on My Youth; The Blue Bird of Happiness; Blue Star; Body and Soul; Boo-Hoo; Drums in My Heart; Easy Come, Easy Go; Have You Forgotten So Soon; Hello, My Lover, Goodbye; Ho Hum; I Cover the Waterfront; I Wanna Be Loved; Kinda Like You; Love Letters; My Darling; My Silent Love; (You Came Along from) Out of Nowhere; Seal It with a Kiss; The Sky Fell Down; They Say; This Is Romance; Through the Years; When I Fall in Love; You Oughta Be in Pictures; You're Mine You

Heymann, Werner   Just Once for All Time; Live, Laugh and Love

Heyne, Joe   The Petite Waltz

Heyward, DuBose   Bess, You Is My Woman Now; I Got Plenty o' Nuttin'; I Loves You Porgy; I'm on My Way; My Man's Gone Now; Summertime; A Woman Is a Sometime Thing

Heyward, Nick   Love Plus One

Heywood, Donald   I'm Comin' Virginia

Heywood, Eddie   Canadian Sunset; Soft Summer Breeze

Heywood, R.   The Flirtation Waltz

Hickey, Emily   Beloved, It Is Morn

Hickman, Art   Hold Me; Rose Room

Higginbotham, Irene   Good Morning Heartache

Higginbotham, Robert   High Heel Sneakers

Higgins, Bertie   Key Largo

Higgins, Billy   There'll Be Some Changes Made

Higley, Brewster   Home on the Range, or, Oh, Give Me a Home Where the Buffalo Roam

Hilderbrand, Ray   Hey Paula

Hilderbrand, Diane W.   Easy Come, Easy Go

Hill, Alexander   (I Would Do) Anything for You; Let Me Go Lover

Hill, Andy   Have You Ever Been in Love; The Land of Make Believe; Now Those Days Are Gone

Hill, Benny   Ernie; Harvest of Love

Hill, Billy   Alone at a Table for Two; The Call of the Canyon; Empty Saddles; The Glory of Love; In the Chapel in the Moonlight; The Last Round-Up; Lights Out; The Old Spinning Wheel; On a Little Street in Singapore; Rain; Wagon Wheels

Hill, Dusty   Legs

Hill, John   When You Are a King

Hill, Mildred J.   Happy Birthday to You, or, Good Morning to All

Hill, Patty Smith   Happy Birthday to You, or, Good Morning to All

Hill, Richard   I Have a Noble Cock

Hill, Robert B.   Kiss of Fire

Hill, Roger   When You Are a King

Hill, Ronald   Turn 'Erbert's Face to the Wall, Mother

Hill, Stanley   I'll Pray for You

Hill, Wayne   The Power Game

Hiller, Tony   Angelo; Save Your Kisses for Me; United We Stand

Hilliam, B.C.   The Changing of the Guard; My Buddies

Hilliard, Bob   Alice in Wonderland; Be My Life's Companion; The Big Brass Band from Brazil; A Bouquet of Roses; Boutonniere; Careless Hands; Civilization (Bongo Bongo Bongo); The Coffee Song (They've Got an Awful Lot of Coffee in Brazil); Dear Hearts and Gentle People; Dearie; Don't Ever Be Afraid To Go Home; Downhearted; Ev'ry Street's a Boulevard in Old New York; How Do You Speak to an Angel; I'm Late; Moonlight Gambler; My Summer Love; Our Day Will Come; Red Silk Stockings and Green Perfume; Sailor Boys Have Talk to Me in English; Shanghai; Somebody Bad Stole De Wedding Bell; Stay with the Happy People

Hillman, Roc   My Devotion

Hills, William H.   There Is a Tavern in the Town

Hilton, Derek   Country Matters

Himber, Richard   It Isn't Fair

Hines, Earl   Rosetta; You Can Depend On Me

Hinkson (Tyman), Katherine   Would God I Were a Tender Apple Blossom

Hinson, Jimbeau   Fancy Free

Hirsch, Kenneth   I've Never Been to Me

Hirsch, Louis A.   The Gaby Glide; Going Up; Hello Frisco Hello; If You Look in Her Eyes; Learn To Smile; The Love Nest; Mary; My Rambler Rose; 'Neath the South Sea Moon; Sixty Seconds Every Minute, I Think of You; Some Sweet Day; Sweet Kentucky Lady; Throw Me a Kiss; (Everybody Ought To Know How To Do) The Tickle Toe; The Wedding Glide

Hirsch, Walter   Baby Blue Eyes; Bye Bye Baby; Carolina Sunshine; 'Deed I Do; Horsey, Keep Your Tail Up; Joe Turner Blues; Lullaby in Rhythm; Me and the Moon; Strange Interlude; Was It Rain; Who's Your Little Who-Zis

Hirschorn, Joel   We May Never Love Like This Again

Hobart, George V.   Alma Where Do You Live; The Wild Rose

Hodges, Jimmie   Some Day You'll Want Me To Want You

Hodges, John, *see also* **Cool White**

Hodges, Johnny   I'm Beginning To See the Light

Hodges, Mabon   Here I Am (Come and Take Me)

Hodgson, "Red"   The Music Goes 'Round and 'Round

Hodgson, Roger   Goodbye Stranger; It's Raining Again; Logical Song

Hoelzel, Johann   Rock Me Amadeus

Hoffman, Al   Allegheny Moon; Auf Wiedersehn, My Dear; Bibbidi-Bobbodi-Boo; Chi-Baba Chi-Baba (My Bambino Go To Sleep); Cinderella; Close to You; Don't Stay Away Too Long; A Dream Is a Wish Your Heart Makes; Everything Stops for Tea; Everything's in Rhythm with My Heart; Fit as a Fiddle (and Ready for Love); Gangway; Gilly Gilly Ossenfeffer; Goodnight Wherever You Are; Happy-Go-Lucky You and Broken-Hearted Me; The Hawaiian Wedding Song; Heartaches; He's a Humdinger; Hot Diggity (Dog Ziggity Boom); I Apologize; I Saw Stars; If I Knew You Were Comin' I'd've Baked a Cake; I'm a Big Girl Now; I'm Gonna Live Till I Die; I'm in a Dancing Mood; Ivy Rose; Jimmy Had a Nickel; A Little Co-operation from You; Little Man, You've Had a Busy Day; Mairzy Doats; Mama Teach Me To Dance; My First Thrill; O Dio Mio; On the Bumpy Road to Love; Papa Loves Mambo; La Plume de Ma Tante; Roses Are Forget-Me-Nots; Secretly; She Shall Have Music; (This Is) The Story of a Starry Night; Takes Two To Tango; There Isn't Any Limit to My Love; There's No Tomorrow; This'll Make You Whistle; A Very Merry Un-Birthday to You

Hoffman, Charles Fenno   Sparkling and Bright

Hoffman, Henry   Bobby's Girl

Hogan, Ernest   All Coons Look Alike to Me

Hogin, Samuel   I Believe in You; Too Many Lovers

Hoier, Thomas   Don't Bite the Hand That's Feeding You

Hokenson, Edward   Bad Girls

Holden, Oliver   All Hail the Power of Jesus' Name; Coronation

Holden, Sidney   Yankee Rose

Holder, Neville   Coz I Love You; Merry Xmas Everybody

Holiday, Billie   Don't Explain; God Bless the Child

Holiday, Jimmy E.   All I Ever Need Is You; Put a Little Love in Your Heart

Holiner, Mann   Harlem Moon; Padam, Padam; (It Will Have To Do) Till (Until) the Real Thing Comes Along

Holland, Brian   Baby Love; Back in My Arms Again; Come See About Me; The Happening; (Love Is Like a) Heat Wave; Heaven Must Have Sent You; How Sweet It Is (To Be Loved by You); I Can't Help Myself; I Hear a Symphony; Love Is Here and Now You're Gone; Mashed Potato Time: One-Two-Three; Please Mister Postman; Reach Out I'll Be There: Reflections; Stop! In the Name of Love; Take Me in Your Arms (Rock Me a Little While); Where Did Our Love Go; You Can't Hurry Love; You Keep Me Hangin' On

Holland, Eddie   Baby Love; Back in My Arms Again; Come See About Me; The Happening; (Love Is Like a) Heat Wave; Heaven Must Have Sent You; How Sweet It Is (To Be Loved By You); I Can't Help Myself; I Hear a Symphony; Love Is Here and Now You're Gone; One-Two-Three; Reach Out I'll Be There; Reflections; Stop! In the Name of Love; Take Me in Your Arms (Rock Me a Little While); Where Did Our Love Go; You Can't Hurry Love; You Keep Me Hangin' On

Hollander, Frederick   (See What) The Boys in the Back Room (Will Have); Falling in Love Again; Moonlight and Shadows; My Heart and I; Strange Enchantment; This Is the Moment; True Confession; Whispers in the Dark; You Leave Me Breathless

Holler, Dick   Abraham, Martin and John; Snoopy vs. The Red Baron

Hollingsworth, Thekla   Oh Miss Hannah

Holloway, Brenda   You've Made Me So Very Happy

Holloway, Dean   Big City

Holloway, Patrice   You've Made Me So Very Happy

Holloway, Stanley   Old Sam (Pick Up Tha' Musket); Rags, Bottles or Bones

Holly, Buddy   Everyday; It's So Easy; Peggy Sue; That'll Be the Day; True Love Ways

Holmes; Jack   The Blacksmith Blues

Holmes, Rupert   Escape

Holmes, Waldo   Rock the Boat

Holmes, William H.   The Hand That Rocks the Cradle

Holofcener, Larry   Jacques D'Iraq (Jock D'Rock); Mister Wonderful; Too Close for Comfort; Without You I'm Nothing

Holst, Edward   Happy Birds

Holt, Alan   Sailor (Your Home Is the Sea)

Holt, David   Mobile

Holt, Fred   Chick Chick Chicken; I Want Some Money; Ours Is a Nice 'ouse Ours Is

Holt, John   The Tide Is High

Holt, Will   Lemon Tree

Holvay, James   Kind of a Drag

Holyfield, Wayland   Could I Have This Dance; Don't Count the Rainy Days; Never Been So Loved in All My Life; Surround Me with Love; You'll Be Back Every Night in My Dreams; You're the Best Break This Old Heart Ever Had

Holzmann, Abe   Blaze Away (March); Blaze of Glory; Smoky Mokes; Spirit of Independence

Homer, Sidney   A Banjo Song

Hood, Basil   Say Not Love Is a Dream

Hood, Thomas   The Song of the Shirt

Hook, James   The Lass of Richmond Hill; Within a Mile of Edinburgh

Hooker, Brian   Gather the Rose; Give Me One Hour; Love Me Tonight; Only a Rose; Regimental Song; Some Day; Song of the Vagabonds; Waltz Huguette, or, The Vagabond King Waltz

Hooper, R.S.   My Time Is Your Time

Hoor, Marten Ten   Roll On, Tulane, or, The Olive and Blue

Hooven, Joe   Any Way the Wind Blows

Hope, Laurence   Kashmiri Love Song; Less Than the Dust; The Temple Bells; Till I Wake

Hope, Peter   Ring of Kerry

Hopkins, Claude   (I Would Do) Anything for You

Hopkins, John Henry   We Three Kings of Orient (Are)

Hopkinson, Francis   The Battle of the Kegs

Hopkinson, Joseph   Hail Columbia, or, New Federal Song

Hoppen, Larry   Love Takes Time

Hopper, Harold S.   There's No You

Hopwood, Aubrey   (Oh I Love) Society; The Soldiers in the Park

Horey, Annette   I Pitch My Lonely Caravan at Night

Horlick, Harry   Dark Eyes, or, Black Eyes

Horn, Charles Edward   All Things Love Thee, So Do I; Cherry Ripe; I Know a Bank Where the Wild Thyme Blows; On the Banks of Allan Water

Horn, Trevor   Owner of a Lonely Heart; Video Killed the Radio Star

Horncastle, George   Actions Speak Louder Than Words

Horner, James   Somewhere Out There

Hornez, André   C'est Si Bon

Hornsby, Joe   Schaefer Is the One Beer

Horowitz, Joseph   Captain Noah and His Floating Zoo; The Lobster Quadrille

Horther, George   Doo Wacka Doo

Horton, Johnny   Sink the Bismarck

Horton, Vaughn   Mocking Bird Hill

Horton, William F.   Get a Job

Horwitt, Arnold B.   I Gotta Have You; Young and Foolish

Horwitz, Charles   Always; Because; Lucky Jim

Hoschna, Karl   The Birth of Passion; Cuddle Up a Little Closer, Lovey Mine; Doctor Tinkle Tinker; Every Girl Loves Me But the Girl I Love; Every Little Movement (Has a Meaning All Its Own); The Yama Yama Man

Hou, Philemon   Grazin' in the Grass

Houdini, Wilmoth   Stone Cold Dead in the Market

Hough, Will M.   Blow the Smoke Away; Honeymoon; I Wonder Who's Kissing Her Now; When You First Kissed the Last Girl You Loved

House, Bob   Could I Have This Dance

Housman, A.E.   In Summertime on Brendon

Hoven, George   It's No Sin

Hovey, Richard   It's Always Fair Weather When Good Fellows Get Together, or, A Stein Song

How, William Walsham   O Word of God Incarnate

Howard, Bart   Fly Me to the Moon, or, In Other Words

Howard, Bob   My Son, My Son

Howard, Eddy   Careless; My Last Goodbye

Howard, Frank   Only a Pansy Blossom; When the Robins Nest Again

Howard, Harlan   Busted; Heartaches by the Number

Howard, James   Lady Love Me One More Time

Howard, Joseph E.   Blow the Smoke Away; Goodbye, My Lady Love; Hello! Ma Baby; Honeymoon; I Wonder Who's Kissing Her Now; What's the Use of Dreaming; When You First Kissed the Last Girl You Loved

Howard, Ken   (Theme from) Flame Trees of Thika

Howard, Mel   Dance Me Loose

Howard, Paul Mason   The Gandy Dancers' Ball; Shrimp Boats

Howard, Richard   Face to Face with the Girl of My Dreams; Goodbye, Little Girl of My Dreams; In the Town Where I Was Born; Put Me to Sleep with an Old-Fashioned Melody; Shut the Door (They're Coming Through the Window); Somebody Else Is Taking My Place; When the Leaves Come Tumbling Down

Howard, Rollin   Shew (Shoo) Fly, Don't Bother Me; You Never Miss the Water Till the Well Runs Dry, or, Waste Not, Want Not

Howe, Catherine   Harry

Howe, Julia Ward   Battle Hymn of the Republic

Howard, T.H.   Beautiful Bird, Sing On

Howell, Dan   Open the Door, Richard

Howgill, J.S.   The Weymouth Chimes

Hoyt, Charles H.   The Bowery

Hubbard, James M.   'Twas off the Blue Canaries, or, My Last Cigar

Hubbell, Raymond   Ladder of Roses; Poor Butterfly

Hucknall, Mick   Holding Back the Years

Huddleston, Floyd   Faith; Ready, Willing and Able

Hudson, R.E.   At the Cross

Hudson, Richard   Part of the Union

Hudson, Will   Moonglow; The Organ Grinder's Swing; Sophisticated Swing

Hudspeth, William G.   Heartbeat—It's a Lovebeat

Hues, Jack   Dance Hall Days

Huff, Larry F.   Easier Said Than Done

Huff, Leon   Don't Leave Me This Way; Enjoy Yourself; Love Music (Part 1); The Love I Lost (Part 1); Me and Mrs Jones; Only the Strong Survive; Put Your Hands Together T.S.O.P. (The Sound of Philadelphia); Use Ta Be My Girl; When Will I See You Again; You'll Never Find Another Love Like Mine

Hugg, Mike   Five-Four-Three-Two-One

Hughes, Elmer   I Ain't Nobody's Darling

Hughes, J.   Bless 'Em All

Hughes, Langston   Get a Load of That; Lonely House

Hull, Bunny   Breakdance; New Attitude

Hulme, Ronald   Rain; We Will Make Love; Wedding Ring

Humphreys, Paul David   If You Leave

Hunter, Alberta   Downhearted Blues

Hunter, Hank   Footsteps

Hunter, Ivory Joe   Dancing in the Streets; I Almost Lost My Mind; Since I Met You Baby

Hunter (Home), Mrs. Anne   My Mother Bids Me Bind My Hair

Huntington, E.S.S.   I'm Tying the Leaves So They Won't Come Down

Hupfeld, Herman   Are You Making Any Money; As Time Goes By; Let's Put Out the Lights and Go To Sleep; Sing Something Simple; When Yuba Plays the Rumba on His Tuba

Hurdle, Leslie   Music Machine

Hurlbert, Claude   My Hat's on the Side of My Head

Hurley, John   Son of a Preacher Man

Hurndall, W.F.   Maxina

Hurran, Dick   Let It Be Soon

Hurt, Jim   Love in the First Degree

Husch, Richard Gerard (Richard H. Gerard)   (You're the Flower of My Heart) Sweet Adeline

Hutchence, Michael   What You Need

Hutcheson, Susan   I Love the Nightlife (Disco 'Round)

Hutchins, Daryl   I Wonder, I Wonder, I Wonder

Hutchinson, Jesse   The Cottage of My Mother; The Old Granite State

Hutchinson, Judson   The Cottage of My Mother; Go Call the Doctor, or, Anti-Calomel

Hutchison, Edward   Sammy

Hutsell, Floyd M.   The Rouser

Hycock, Frances   Sha La La

Hyde, Madeline   Little Girl

Hyman, Dick   Cream of the Crop

Hyman, Rob   Time After Time

Hynde, Chrissie   Brass in Pocket

Ian, Janis   At Seventeen; Jesse

Ibert, Jacques   The Little White Donkey

Idol, Billy   Eyes Without a Face

Idriss, Ramey   Woody Woodpecker

Ilda, Lewis   Getting Around and About; I'm in Love with Two Sweethearts; Just a Little Fond Affection; Little Old Mill; Old Timer

Illica, Luigi   Musetta's Waltz; One Fine Day, or, Un Bel Dì

Imber, Naphtali Herz   Hatikva

Ingle, Charles   Knocked 'Em in the Old Kent Road; My Old Dutch

Ingraham, Herbert   All That I Ask of You Is Love; Because I'm Married Now (I Would If I Could But I Can't); Don't Wake Me Up, I'm Dreaming; Goodbye, Rose; Hoo-oo Ain't You Coming Out Tonight; Roses Bring Dreams of You; When I Dream in the Gloaming of You; Won't You Waltz "Home Sweet Home" with Me; You Are the Ideal of My Dreams

Ingraham, Roy   No Regrets

Ingram, Arnold   Float On

Ingram, James   P.Y.T. (Pretty Young Thing); Yah Mo B There

Innes, Neil   I'm the Urban Spaceman

Insetta, Paul   Sitting by the Window

Irving, Harold   You're a Pink Toothbrush

Irwin, Joe   I Shall Be Waiting

Irwin, May   Mamie, Come Kiss Your Honey

Irwin, William C.K.   The Five O'Clock Whistle

Isaacs, David   Can't Smile Without You

Isbell, Alvertis   I'll Take You There

Isley, Ernest   That Lady

Isley, Marvin   That Lady

Isley, O'Kelly   It's Your Thing

Isley, Ronald   It's Your Thing

Isley, Rudolph   It's Your Thing

Ivanovici, Ion   Waves of the Danube, or, Danube Waves

Ives, Wally   Shut the Door (They're Comin' Through the Window)

Ivey, Herbert   Angel in Your Arms

Jabara, Paul   Last Dance; Main Event/The Fight; No More Tears (Enough Is Enough)

Jacks, Lawrence   Marry Me

Jacks, Terry   Which Way You Goin' Billy

Jackson, Al, Jr.   Call Me (Come Back Home); Green Onions; Let's Stay Together

Jackson, Arthur   Take Me to the Midnight Cake Walk Ball

Jackson, B.   Don't Throw Your Love Away

Jackson, Chuck   This Will Be (an Everlasting Love)

Jackson, David Jr.   No No Song

Jackson, Gary   (Your Love Has Lifted Me) Higher and Higher

Jackson, George H.   One Bad Apple (Don't Spoil the Whole Bunch)

Jackson, Greig Stewart   Northwest Passage

Jackson, Joe   Steppin' Out; You Can't Get What You Want (Till You Know What You Want)

Jackson, Marlon   Shake Your Body (Down to the Ground)

Jackson, Michael   Beat It; Billie Jean; Don't Stop 'Til You Get Enough; The Girl Is Mine; Say Say Say; Shake Your Body (Down to the Ground); State of Shock; Wanna Be Startin' Something; We Are the World

Jackson, Raymond   (If Loving You Is Wrong) I Don't Want To Be Right; If You're Ready (Come Go with Me)

Jackson, Rudy   Hearts of Stone

Jackson, Sigmund   Shake Your Body (Down to the Ground)

Jackson, Steven   Shake Your Body (Down to the Ground)

Jackson, Tariano   Shake Your Body (Down to the Ground)

Jackson, Tony   Pretty Baby

Jackson III, William   So Much in Love

Jacobi, Victor   Deep in Your Eyes; Little Girls, Good Bye; On Miami Shore, or, Golden Sands of Miami; You Are Free

Jacobs, Al   Hurt; I Need You Now; If I Give My Heart to You; A Little More Love; Please Believe Me; This Is My Country

Jacobs, Jacob   Bei Mir Bist Du Schön (Means That You're Grand)

Jacobs, Jim   All Choked Up; Freddy My Love; Look At Me, I'm Sandra Dee

Jacobs-Bond, Carrie   I Love You Truly; Just A-Wearyin' for You; A Perfect Day

Jacobson, Kenny   The Swingin' Shepherd Blues

Jacobson, Sid   The End (of the Rainbow)

Jaffe, Moe   Collegiate; Gypsy in My Soul; If I Had My Life To Live Over; If You Are But a Dream

Jagger, Mick   Angie; As Tears Go By; Emotional Rescue; Get Off My Cloud; Honky Tonk Women; It's Only Rock 'n Roll (But I Like It); Nineteenth Nervous Breakdown; Paint It Black; (I Can't Get No) Satisfaction; Start Me Up

Jakobowski, Edward   At Midnight on My Pillow Lying; Darkest the Hour; Dear Mother, in Dreams I See Her; Lullaby; A Soldier's Life; What the Dickie-Birds Say

Jam, Jimmy   Tender Love; What Have You Done for Me Lately

James, Arthur   For All We Know

James, Dick   Lift Boy

James, Etta   Dance with Me Henry

James, Freddy   Unchain My Heart; Unsuspecting Heart; You Won't Be Satisfied (Until You Break My Heart)

James, Harry   I'm Beginning To See the Light; The Music Makers; One O'Clock Jump; Peckin'

James, Inez   Pillow Talk; Vaya Con Dios

James, Jesse   The Horse

James, Mark   Always On My Mind; Hooked on a Feeling; Suspicious Minds

James, Paul   Can This Be Love; Can't We Be Friends; Fine and Dandy

James, Rick   Party All the Time

James, Stuart   Everything's Al'Right

James, Tommy   Crimson and Clover; Crystal Blue Persuasion; Mony, Mony; Three Times in Love

Jameson, Tom   Summertime Summertime

Jamieson, Ronald   In a Golden Coach

Jane, Emily   Come Home to My Arms

Janis, Elsie   Any Time's the Time To Fall in Love; Love (Your Magic Spell Is Everywhere); Some Sort of Somebody

Jankowski, Horst   A Walk in the Black Forest

Jansen, Bernard   Longing for You

Jarnefelt, Armas   Praeludium

Jarrard, John   I Still Do

Jarre, Maurice   (Theme from) Lawrence of Arabia; Somewhere My Love, or, Lara's Theme

Jarreau, Al   After All

Jarrell, Phil   Torn Between Two Lovers

Jason, Will   Sunny Days; When We're Alone, or, Penthouse Serenade

Jasper, Christopher H.   That Lady

Javor, Laszlo   Gloomy Sunday

Jefferson, Gene   Coon! Coon! Coon!

Jefferson, Joseph   They Just Can't Stop It (The Games People Play)

Jeffrey, Allan   Old Cape Cod

Jeffreys, Charles   Mary of Argyle; The Rose of Allandale

Jenkins, David   Love Will Find a Way

Jenkins, Donald   Cool Love

Jenkins, Gordon   Blue Prelude; Goodbye; Homesick—That's All; Married I Can Always Get; P.S. I Love You; San Fernando Valley; This Is All I Ask; Tzena, Tzena, Tzena; When a Woman Loves a Man; You Have Taken My Heart

Jennens, Charles   Hallelujah Chorus

Jennings, Waylon   Dukes of Hazzard (Good Ol' Boys); A Good Hearted Woman; Just To Satisfy You; Shine; Women Do Know How To Carry On

Jennings, Will   Higher Love; If the Phone Doesn't Ring, It's Me; I'll Never Love This Way Again; Looks Like We Made It; No Night So Long; Up Where We Belong; While You See a Chance

Jentes, Alfred   There's a Million Girlies Lonesome Tonight, and Still I'm All Alone

Jentes, Harry   He May Be Old, But He's Got Young Ideas; I Don't Want To Get Well (I'm in Love with a Beautiful Nurse); Put Me To Sleep with an Old-Fashioned Melody

Jergens, Dick   One Dozen Roses

Jerome, Helene   Nichavo!

Jerome, John   Broken Wings; Paper Kisses; You Me and Us

Jerome, M.K.   Bright Eyes; Just a Baby's Prayer at Twilight; Mary, Dear, Some Day We Will Meet Again; My Little Buckaroo; Old Pal Why Don't You Answer Me; Some Sunday Morning; Why Don't You Answer Me

Jerome, William   And the Green Grass Grew All Around; Any Old Place I Can Hang My Hat Is Home Sweet Home to Me; Bedelia; Chinatown, My Chinatown; Don't Put Me Off at Buffalo Any More; Every Day Will Be Sunday When the Town Goes Dry; Get Out and Get Under the Moon; I'm Unlucky; Just Try To Picture Me (Back (Down) Home in Tennessee); A Little Bunch of Shamrocks; Mister Dooley; My Irish Molly O; My Pearl's a Bowery Girl; On the Old Fall River Line; Rip Van Winkle Was a Lucky Man; Row, Row, Row; Since Sister Nell Heard Paderewski Play; Sit Down, You're Rocking the Boat; Sweet Kentucky Lady; That Old Irish Mother of Mine

Jessel, George   And He'd Say "Oo-La-La Wee-Wee"; Baby Blue Eyes; Oh! How I Laugh When I Think How I Cried About You; Where Do They Go When They Row, Row, Row

Jessel, Leon   Parade of the Wooden Soldiers; Wedding of the Rose

Jimenez, Marcos A.   Adios, Mariquita LInda

Jobe, Steve   Where Were You When I Was Falling in Love

Jobim, Antonio Carlos   Desafinado (Slightly Out of Tune); Dindi; The Girl from Ipanema; She's a Carioca

Joel, Billy   Big Shot; Honesty; An Innocent Man; It's Still Rock and Roll to Me; Just the Way You Are; Keeping the Faith; Leave a Tender Moment Alone; The Longest Time; Modern Woman; Piano Man; Tell Her About It; Uptown Girl; You're Only Human (Second Wind)

John, Dominic   A Blossom Fell; The Echo Told Me a Lie; When You're in Love

John, Dr., *see* **Malcolm Rebennack**

John, Elton   Bennie and the Jets; The Bitch Is Back; Crocodile Rock; Daniel; Don't Go Breaking My Heart; Don't Let the Sun Go Down on Me; Goodbye Yellow Brick Road; I Guess That's Why They Call It the Blues; Island Girl; Little Jeannie; Nikita; Philadelphia Freedom; Sad Songs (Say So Much); Someone Saved My Life Tonight; Sorry Seems To Be the Hardest Word; Theme from a Non-Existent TV Series; Your Song

John, Robert   Sad Eyes

Johns, Al   Go Way Back and Sit Down

Johns, Leo   Melodie d'Amour (Melody of Love)

Johns, Sammy   Chevy Van

Johnson, Arnold   Does Your Heart Beat for Me; O (Oh!)

Johnson, Ashley S. She's the Fairest Little Flower Dear Old Dixie Ever Grew (Knew)

Johnson, Billy The Moon Has His Eyes on You

Johnson, Bob Where There's Life, There's Bud

Johnson, Buddy Since I Fell for You

Johnson, "Buster" The Wang, Wang Blues

Johnson, Chic G'Bye Now; Oh Gee, Oh Gosh, Oh Golly I'm in Love

Johnson, Daniel The Carrier Dove

Johnson, Edward Jersey Bounce

Johnson, Enotris Long Tall Sally

Johnson, General Patches (I'm Depending on You); Want Ads

Johnson, George Stomp

Johnson, George W. I'll Be Good to You; When You and I Were Young, Maggie

Johnson, Herbert Face to Face

Johnson, Holly Two Tribes

Johnson, Howard E. Am I Wasting My Time on (over) You; At the Moving Picture Ball; Bring Back My Daddy to Me; (What'll We Do on a) Dew-Dew-Dewy Day; Feather Your Nest; Georgia; Gid-ap, Garibaldi; He May Be Old. But He's Got Young Ideas; I Don't Want To Get Well (I'm in Love with a Beautiful Nurse); I Know I Got More Than My Share; (I Scream, You Scream, We All Scream for) Ice Cream; I'd Like To See the Kaiser with a Lily in His Hand; Ireland Must Be Heaven, for My Mother Came from There; Just Like Washington Crossed the Delaware, General Pershing Will Cross the Rhine; M-O-T-H-E-R (A Word That Means the World to Me); Rockaway; Siam; Sweet Lady; There's a Broken Heart for Every Light on Broadway; What Do You Want To Make Those Eyes at Me For; When the Moon Comes over the Mountain; Where Do We Go from Here; You'd Never Know the Old Home Town of Mine

Johnson, J. C. Believe It Beloved; Dusky Stevedore; The Joint Is Jumpin'

Johnson, J. Rosamond Congo Love Song; Dry Bones; Lazy Moon; Lift Ev'ry Voice and Sing; The Maiden with the Dreamy Eyes; My Castle on the Nile; Oh, Didn't He Ramble; Old Flag Never Touched the Ground; Roll Them Cotton Bales; Under the Bamboo Tree

Johnson, James P. Charleston; Old-Fashioned Love; There's No Two Ways About Love

Johnson, James Weldon Dry Bones; Lift Ev'ry Voice and Sing; My Castle on the Nile; Old Flag Never Touched the Ground; Roll Them Cotton Bales

Johnson, Janice Booggie Oogie Oogie

Johnson, Jimmy P. If I Could Be with You One Hour To-night

Johnson, Laurie Lock Up Your Daughters

Johnson, Louis A. I'll Be Good to You; Stomp; Sweet Love

Johnson, Mrs. James G. Come, Oh, Come to Me

Johnson, Ronald Jay Rocky

Johnson, Val Stomp

Johnson, William Tuxedo Junction

Johnston, Archibald Baby Mine

Johnston, Arthur Between a Kiss and a Sigh; Black Moonlight; Cocktails for Two; The Day You Came Along; Down the Old Ox Road; I'm a Little Blackbird Looking for a Bluebird; I'm Sittin' High on a Hill Top; Just One More Chance; Learn To Croon; Mandy Make Up Your Mind; Marahuana; The Moon Got in My Eyes; Moon Song (That Wasn't Meant for Me); My Old Flame; One, Two, Button Your Shoe; Pennies from Heaven; So Do I; Song of the South; Thanks; Thanks a Million

Johnston, Bruce I Write the Songs

Johnston, Patricia I'll (I) Remember April

Johnston, Tom Long Train Runnin'

Johnstone, Davey I Guess That's Why They Call It the Blues

Johnstone, Gordon There Is No Death

Jolson, Al The Anniversary Song; Avalon; Back in Your Own Back Yard; Bagdad; California, Here I Come; Dirty Hands, Dirty Face; The Egg and I; Golden Gate; Harding, You're the Man for Us; I'll Say She Does; Keep Smiling at Trouble; Me and My Shadow; 'N Everything; Seventh Heaven; Sonny Boy; Stella; There's a Rainbow Round My Shoulder; Yoo-Hoo; You Ain't Heard Nothing Yet

Jones, Agnes Unchain My Heart

Jones, Alan Rankin Easy Street; Over You

Jones, Biff Suddenly There's a Valley

Jones, Booker T. Green Onions

Jones, Columbia Just Another Day in Paradise

Jones, David, *see* David Bowie

Jones, Earl C. Everybody Two-Step; The Harbor of Love; I Wonder Where My Lovin' Man Has Gone; On Mobile Bay; That Old Girl of Mine;

Jones, Evan The Pushbike Song

Jones, Graham When You and I Were Dancing

Jones, Howard Life in One Day; No One Is To Blame; Things Can Only Get Better

Jones, Idris The Pushbike Song

Jones, Isham If You Were Only Mine; I'll Never Have To Dream Again; I'll See You in My Dreams; Indiana Moon; It Had To Be You; Meet Me in Bubble Land; On the Alamo; The One I Love Belongs to Somebody Else; Spain; Swingin' Down the Lane; There Is No Greater Love; The Wooden Soldier and the China Doll; You're in the Army Now; You've Got Me Crying Again

Jones, J. S., Esq. A Yankee Ship and a Yankee Crew

Jones, Jimmy Handy Man

Jones, John Paul Whole Lotta Love

Jones, Joseph You Talk Too Much

Jones, Kenneth Only One You

Jones, Mai We'll Keep a Welcome

Jones, Marshall Fire; Love Rollercoaster

Jones, Michael I Want To Know What Love Is; Urgent; Waiting For a Girl Like You

Jones, Morgan Heart of a Teenage Girl; The Stranger

Jones, Ollie Send for Me; Step by Step

Jones, Paul Five-Four-Three-Two-One

Jones, Quincy Miss Celie's Blues (Sister); P.Y.T. (Pretty Young Thing); Yah Mo B There

Jones, Rickie Lee Chuck E's in Love

Jones, Sidney The Amorous Goldfish; Chin, Chin, China-man; Chon Kina; Six Little Wives

Jones, Stan Ghost Riders in the Sky, or, a Cowboy Legend; Wringle Wrangle

Jones, Tom The Honeymoon Is Over; Much More; My Cup Runneth Over; Never Say No; Soon It's Gonna Rain; Try To Remember

Jonson, Ben Drink to Me Only with Thine Eyes

Joplin, Scott Easy Winners; The Entertainer; Maple Leaf Rag

Jordan, Archie Drifter

Jordan, Cindy Jose Cuervo

Jordan, Jack Little Red Monkey

Jordan, Jim Schaefer Is the One Beer

Jordan, Joe Original Dixieland One-Step

Jordan, Julian The Song That Reached My Heart

Jordan, Leroy L. The Cisco Kid; Gypsy Man; Summer; Why Can't We Be Friends

Jordan, Louis Is You Is or Is You Ain't My Baby

Jordan, Robert English Country Gardens

Jordan, Roy I'm Gonna Move to (the) Outskirts of Town

Josephs, Wilfred The British Empire

Joshua, Lyn We'll Keep a Welcome

Jourdan, Michel Free Again

Joyner, Carole Young Love

Judge, Jack It's a Long (Long) Way to Tipperary

Judson, J. G. Won't You Be My Sweetheart

Julian, Don The Jerk

Julien, Michael Kiss Me, Honey Honey, Kiss Me

Jurgens, Dick Careless; Elmer's Tune

Jurmann, Walter All God's Chillun Got Rhythm; Cosi Cosa; San Francisco

Justis, William Raunchy

Justman, Seth Centerfold; Freeze-Frame

Kabalevsky, Dmitri Colas Breugnon

Kaempfert, Berthold Danke Schöen; Spanish Eyes; Strangers in the Night; Wooden Heart

Kahal, Irving By a Waterfall; I Can Dream, Can't I; I Left My Sugar Standing in the Rain (and She Melted Away); I'll Be Seeing You; It Was Only a Sun Shower; Let a Smile Be Your Umbrealla on a Rainy (Rainy) Day; (There Ought To Be a) Moonlight Saving Time; The Night Is Young and You're So Beautiful; Roam On (My) Little Gipsy Sweetheart; There's Something About a Rose (That Reminds Me of You); Three's a Crowd; Wedding Bells Are Breaking Up That Old Gang of Mine; When I Take My Sugar to Tea; You Brought a New Kind of Love to Me

Kahan, Stanley The Girl with the Golden Braids

Kahn, Art You Don't Like It—Not Much

Kahn, Donald A Beautiful Friendship; The G.I. Jive

Kahn, Grace LeBoy I Wish I Had a Girl

Kahn, Gus Ain't We Got Fun; All God's Chillun Got Rhythm; Around the Corner and Under the Tree; Beloved; Beside a Babbling Brook; Bimini Bay; But I Do—You Know I Do; Carioca; Carolina in the Morning; Charley, My Boy; Chloe; Coquette; Day Dreaming; Dream a Little Dream of Me; Flying Down to Rio; For My Sweetheart; Goofus; Guilty; Hangin' on the Garden Gate; Here We Are; Honolulu; The Hour of Parting; How Strange; I Never Knew (That Roses Grew); I Wish I Had a Girl; I Wonder Where My Baby Is Tonight; I'll Never Be the Same; I'll Say She Does; I'll See You in My Dreams; I'm Bringing a Red, Red, Rose; I'm Sittin' High On a Hill Top; I'm Through with Love; Isn't She the Sweetest Thing; It Had To Be You; It's Foolish But It's Fun; I've Had My Moments; Josephine; (Just a) Little Street Where Old Friends Meet; Liza (All the Clouds'll Roll Away); Love Me Forever; Love Me or Leave Me; Makin' Whoopee; Memories; Music Makes Me; My Baby Just Cares for Me; My Buddy; My Isle of Golden Dreams; My Sweetie's Turned Me Down; 'N Everything; No, No, Nora; Nobody's Sweetheart Now; On the Alamo; On the Good Ship Mary Ann; The One I Love Belongs to Somebody Else; One Night of Love; Orchids in the Moonlight; Persian Rug; Pretty Baby; Roses for Remembrance; Sailin' Away on the Henry Clay; Sailin' On; San Francisco; Sittin' in a Corner; Some Sunday Morning; Sometime; Spain; Swingin' Down the Lane; Thanks a Million; That Certain Party; Toot Toot Tootsie (Goo'Bye); Ukulele Lady; The Waltz You Saved for Me; When Lights Are Low; When My Ship Comes In; When You and I Were Seventeen; When You Come to the End of the Day; Where the Morning Glories Grow; Where the Shy Little Violets Grow; With All My Heart; Yes Sir, That's My Baby; You Ain't Heard Nothing Yet; You Stepped Out of a Dream; Your Eyes Have Told Me So; You've Got Everything

Kahn, Larry Ev'rywhere

Kahn, Murl Petticoats of Portugal

Kahn, Roger Wolfe Crazy Rhythm

Kaihau, Maewa Now Is the Hour

Kailimai, Henry On the Beach at Waikiki

Kaiser, Kurt Blest Be the Tie That Binds

Kalimar, Henry On the Shore at Lei Lei

Kalman, Emmerich Dear Eyes That Haunt Me; Hey Gypsy (Play Gypsy) (Komm Tzizany); Just a Voice To Call Me, Dear; Love Has Wings; Love's Own Sweet Song, or, Sari Waltz; My Faithful Stradivari; Play Gypsies—Dance Gypsies; Sigh by Night; Softly Thro' the Summer Night; Throw Me a Rose; We Two Shall Meet Again; You Are Mine Evermore

Kalmar, Bert All Alone Monday; All the Quakers Are Shoulder Shakers Down in Quaker Town; Dancing the Devil Away; The Egg and I; Ev'ryone Says "I Love You"; The Ghost of the Violin; Hello, Hawaii, How Are You; Hooray for Captain Spalding; I Gave You Up Just Before You Threw Me Down; I Love You So Much; I Wanna Be Loved by You; In the Land of Harmony; I've Been Floating Down the Old Green River; Keep On Doin' What You're Doin'; A Kiss To

Build a Dream On; Mandy 'n' Me; Moonlight on the Rhine; My Sunny Tennessee; Nevertheless (I'm in Love with You); Oh! What a Pal Was Mary; Over and Over Again; Puppchen; The Same Old Moon; She's Mine, All Mine; Since Maggie Dooley Learned the Hooley Hooley; So Long, Oo-Long, How Long You Gonna Be Gone?; Take Your Girlie to the Movies If You Can't Make Love at Home; Thinking of You; Three Little Words; Timbuctoo; Up in the Clouds; Watching the Clouds Roll By; Where Did You Get That Girl; Where Do They Go When They Row, Row, Row; Who's Sorry Now; You Said It

Kamen, Michael   Edge of Darkness

Kander, John   All That Jazz; Believe; Cabaret; City Lights; Class; The Grass Is Always Greener; The Happy Time; If You Could See Her; Life Is; The Life of the Party; Married; Maybe This Time; Meeskite; Mein Herr; Mister Cellophane; Money (Money); The Money Song; My Coloring Book; My Own Best Friend; Razzle Dazzle; The Top of the Hill; Two Ladies; Under the Roller Coaster; Wallflower; Why Can't I Speak; Willkommen

Kane, Kieran   Don't Worry 'Bout Me Baby

Kanner, Hal   I Guess I'll Get the Papers and Go Home

Kanski, Edward   My Grandma's Advice

Kanter, Hal   Move Over Darling

Kantner, Paul   Jane

Kaper, Bronislaw   All God's Chillun Got Rhythm; Cosi Cosa; Gloria, or, Theme from Butterfield 8; Hi Lili Hi Lo; Invitation; On Green Dolphin Street; San Francisco; Somebody Up There Likes Me; Take My Love

Kaplan, Bert   Horsey, Keep Your Tail Up

Kaplan, Saul   Rhythm Is Our Business

Karas, Anton   The Third Man Theme, or, The Harry Lime Theme

Karger, Fred   From Here to Eternity

Karges, Carlo   99 Luftballons

Karlin, Fred   Come Saturday Morning; For All We Know

Karlson, Keith   Everything's Al'Right

Karmen, Steve   When You Say Bud, You've Said It All

Karr, Harold   Mutual Admiration Society; A New-Fangled Tango

Kasha, Al   The Morning After, or, Song from *The Poseidon Adventure;*   We May Never Love Like This Again

Kassel, Art   Around the Corner and Under the Tree; Doodle Doo Doo; Sobbin' Blues

Katrivanov, D.   The Story of Tina

Katscher, Robert   Elizabeth; Oh Donna Clara; Tell Me I'm Forgiven; When Day Is Done

Kaufman, Al   Ask Anyone Who Knows; How Many Hearts Have You Broken

Kaufman, Paul   Poetry in Motion

Kavelin, Al   I Give You My Word

Kay, Julian   When the Circus Came to Town

Kaye, Buddy   "A"—You're Adorable; Boys Cry; Full Moon and Empty Arms; If You Catch a Little Cold; I'll Close My Eyes; Little Lulu; (It's Gonna Be) A Long, Long Winter;

Next Time; A Penny a Kiss, A Penny a Hug; Sweet William; This Is No Laughing Matter; Till the End of Time

Kaye, Max   Fanfare Boogie

Kaye, Sammy   Remember Pearl Harbor; Until Tomorrow

Keady, John Thomas   As the Backs Go Tearing By

Keagy, Kelly   Sister Christian

Kearney, Ramsey   Emotions

Kehner, Clarence Way   Bobby Sox (Socks) to Stockings

Keidel, Hal   Hi-Diddle-Diddle

Keiser, Bob (Robert A.), *see* **Robert King**

Keith, E. Austin   Sometime You'll Wish Me Back Again; When I'm Gone You'll Soon Forget

Keith, Larry   Blaze of Glory; This Time I'm in It for Love

Keith, Marilyn   Nice 'n' Easy; Yellow Bird

Keith, Vivian   Before the Next Teardrop Falls

Keithley, E. Clinton   Garland of Old Fashioned Roses

Kélar, Béla   Hungarian Dance No. 5

Kellem, Milton   Gonna Get Along Without Ya Now

Keller, Jack   Breaking in a Brand New Broken Heart; Easy Come, Easy Go; Everybody's Somebody's Fool; My Heart Has a Mind of Its Own; Run to Him

Keller, James   867-5309/Jenny

Keller, Jerry   Almost There; Here Comes Summer; A Man and a Woman; Turn Down Day

Kellette, John William   I'm Forever Blowing Bubbles

Kelley, C.   Two Silhouettes in the Moonlight

Kelly, Dan   Home on the Range, or, Oh, Give Me a Home Where the Buffalo Roam

Kelly, John T.   I Long To See the Girl I Left Behind

Kelly, John W.   Slide Kelly Slide; Throw Him Down McCloskey

Kelly, Keith   Tease Me

Kelly, Paul   Personally

Kelly, Tom   Like a Virgin

Kemp, Wayne   One Piece at a Time

Kenbrovin, Jean   I'm Forever Blowing Bubbles

Kendal, Alec   I'm Twenty-One Today; That's the Reason Noo I Wear a Kilt

Kendis, James   Come Out of the Kitchen, Mary Ann; Feather Your Nest; Gypsy Dream Rose; I Know What It Means To Be Lonesome; If I Had My Way; Nat'an, Nat'an, Nat'an, Tell Me for What Are You Waitin', Nat'an; Underneath the Russian Moon; When It's Night-Time in Italy, It's Wednesday over Here; Won't You Fondle Me

Kennedy, Hamilton   The Chestnut Tree; How Can You Buy Killarney; Ole Faithful; Tina

Kennedy, Harry   Cradle's Empty, Baby's Gone; A Flower from Mother's Grave; Molly and I and the Baby; Say "Au Revoir" But Not "Goodbye"

Kennedy, Jimmy   All Our Tomorrows; And Mimi; April in Portugal; At the Cafe Continental; Beside My Caravan; Bird on the Wing; Cafe in Vienna; The Chestnut Tree; The Cokey Cokey, or, The Hokey Cokey; The Coronation Waltz; Did

Your Mother Come from Ireland; The General's Fast Asleep; A Handsome Territorial; Harbor Lights; Home Town; An Hour Never Passes; Isle of Capri; Istanbul (Not Constantinople); Love Is Like a Violin; Misty Islands of the Highlands; My Prayer; My Song Goes Round the World; Never Goodbye; Oh Donna Clara; Oh Nicholas Don't Be So Ridiculous; Play to Me, Gypsy; Poor Little Angeline; Red Sails in the Sunset; Roll Along Covered Wagon; Serenade in the Night; South of the Border (Down Mexico Way); The Spice of Life; St. Mary's in the Twilight; Stay in My Arms, Cinderalla; The Sunset Trail; Sweet Heartaches; The Teddy Bear's Picnic; Ten Pretty Girls; There's a Boy Coming Home on Leave; There's No Other Love; Washing on the Siegfried Line; Why Did She Fall for the Leader of the Band

Kennedy, Michael   Heartbeat—It's a Loveboat

Kennedy, Tom   The Voice of R.K.O.

Kenner, Chris   I Like It Like That

Kennerley, Paul   Born To Run

Kennett, Karl   Just As the Sun Went Down; Just One Girl; Stay in Your Own Back Yard; Zizzy, Ze Zum, Zum

Kenney, Charles Lamb   The Vagabond

Kennick, T.   You Naughty, Naughty Men

Kenny, Charles   Cathedral in the Pines; Gone Fishin', Leanin' on the Ole Top Rail; Love Letters in the Sand; Make Believe Island; There's a Gold Mine in the Sky; While a Cigarette Was Burning

Kenny, Gerard   I Could Be So Good for You; I Made It Through the Rain

Kenny, Nick   Cathedral in the Pines; Gone Fishin'; Leanin' on the Old Top Rail; Love Letters in the Sand; Make Believe Island; My Cabin of Dreams; There's a Gold Mine in the Sky; While a Cigarette Was Burning

Kent, Arthur   Bring Me Sunshine; Don't Go to Strangers; Wonder When My Baby's Coming Home

Kent, Charlotte   Overnight

Kent, L.   Hold Tight—Hold Tight

Kent, Walter   Ah But It Happens; Gertie from Bizerte; I Never Mention Your Name (Oh No); I'll Be Home for Christmas; I'm Gonna Live Till I Die; (There'll Be Blue Birds over) The White Cliffs of Dover

Kenton, Stanley   And Her Tears Flowed Like Wine

Keppell, Lady Caroline   Robin Adair

Kerker, Gustave   Little Birdies Learning How To Fly; She Is the Belle of New York; Teach Me How To Kiss

Kern, Jerome   All in Fun; All the Things You Are; All Through the Day; And Russia Is Her Name; Babes in the Wood; Bill; Bojangles of Harlem; Can I Forget You; Can't Help Lovin' Dat Man; Can't Help Singing; Cleopatterer; Dancing Time; Day Dreaming; Dearly Beloved; Don't Ever Leave Me; D'Ya Love Me?; A Fine Romance; The Folks Who Live on the Hill; Go, Little Boat; Ha-Cha-Cha; Have a Heart; Here Am I; High, Wide, and Handsome; How'd You Like To Spoon With Me; I Dream Too Much; I Found You and You Found Me; I Watch the Love Parade; I Won't Dance; I'm Old-Fashioned; In Egern on the Tegern See; In Love in Vain; In Love with Love; In the Heart of the Dark; I've Told Every Little

Star; The Jockey on the Carousel; Just Let Me Look at You; Ka-Lu-A; Kiss a Four Leaf Clover; The Last Time I Saw Paris; Leave It to Jane; Left All Alone Again Blues; Long Ago and Far Away; Look For the Silver Lining; Lovely To Look At; Make Believe; More and More; Nestin' Time in Flatbush; The Night Was Made for Love; Nobody Else But Me; Nodding Roses; An Old-Fashioned Wife; Ol'Man River; On the Shore at Lei Lei; Once in a Blue Moon; One Moment Alone; One More Dance; Our Song; A Pal Like You; Pick Yourself Up; Poor Pierrot; Raggedy Ann; Rolled into One; Sally; Same Sort of Girl; Shadow of the Moon; She Didn't Say Yes (She Didn't Say No); Shufflin' Sam; The Siren's Song; Smoke Gets in Your Eyes; Some Sort of Somebody; The Song Is You; The Sun Shines Brighter; Sunny; Sure Thing; The Sweetest Sight That I Have Ever Seen; The Sweetest Thing in Life; They Didn't Believe Me; The Things I Want; Till ('Til) the Clouds Roll By; The Touch of Your Hand; Try To Forget; 'Twas Not So Long Ago; Two Hearts Are Better Than One; Two Little Bluebirds; Up with the Lark; Waltz in Swing Time; The Way You Look Tonight; What's Good About Good Night; When the Spring Is in the Air; Whip-Poor-Will; The Whistling Boy; Who; Whose Baby Are You; Why Do I Love You; Why Don't They Dance the Polka Anymore; Why Was I Born; Wild Rose; Will You Marry Me Tomorrow, Maria; A Year from Today; Yesterdays; You Are Love; You Couldn't Be Cuter; You Know and I Know (and We Both Understand); You Never Knew About Me; You Said Something; You Were Never Lovelier; You're Devastating; You're Here and I'm Here

Kern, Jim   Shut the Door (They're Comin' Through the Window)

Kernfeld, A.   The Pied Piper

Kerr, Harry D.   Do You Ever Think of Me; Neapolitan Nights; Song of the Islands

Kerr, Jim   Alive and Kicking

Kerr, Richard   I'll Never Love This Way Again; Looks Like We Made It; Mandy; No Night So Long

Kessel, Barney   Swedish Pastry

Kester, Max   Love Locked Out; Turn Erbert's Face to the Wall, Mother

Ketèlbey, Albert William (William Aston)   Bells Across the Meadow; In a Chinese Temple Garden; In a Monastery Garden; In a Persian Market

Key, Francis Scott   The Star Spangled Banner

Keyes, James   Sh-Boom

Keyser, Lillian   Jamaica Farewell

Khan, Chaka   Sweet Thing

Khent, Allyson R.   Sixteen Candles

Khoury, G.   Sea of Love

Kiallmark, George   Araby's Daughter; The Old Oaken Bucket

Kibbe, Guy   At the Codfish Ball

Kibble, Perry   Boogie Oogie Oogie

Kidd, Johnny   Shakin' All Over

Kihn, Greg   Jeopardy

Kilgore, Merle   Wolverton Mountain

Killen, Buddy Watchin' Girls Go By

Killion, Leo Hut Sut Song

Kilmer, Joyce Trees

Kim, Andy Rock Me Gently; Sugar Sugar

Kimball, Jennie Almost Over You

Kind, John A. Glover I Do Like To Be Beside the Seaside

King, Ben E. Stand by Me

King, C.M. Esq. A Yankee Ship and a Yankee Crew

King, Carole Go Away Little Girl; I Feel the Earth Move; It's Too Late; Jazz Man; The Loco-Motion; (You Make Me Feel Like) A Natural Woman; Nightingale; So Far Away; Sweet Seasons; Take Good Care of My Baby; Up on the Roof; Will You (Still) Love Me Tomorrow; You've Got a Friend

King, Charles E. The Hawaiian Wedding Song; Song of the Islands

King, Claude Wolverton Mountain

King, Denis Galloping Home

King, Irving, *see also* **Reginald Connelly** *and* **Jimmy Campbell** Chick Chick Chicken; The More We Are Together; Show Me the Way To Go Home

King, Jack Any Time's The Time To Fall in Love; How Am I To Know

King, Kenneth Everyone's Gone to the Moon; It's Good News Week

King, Mark Something About You

King, Pearl I Hear You Knocking

King, Pee Wee Bonaparte's Retreat; Slow Poke; Tennessee Waltz; You Belong to Me

King, Robert A. Beautiful Ohio; Dreamy Alabama; Fashionette; I Ain't Nobody's Darling; (I Scream, You Scream, We All Scream for) Ice Cream; Keep Your Skirts Down, Mary Ann; Lafayette—We Hear You Calling; Moonlight on the Colorado; While Strolling Through the Park One Day, or, The Fountain in the Park; Why Did I Kiss That Girl

King, Roy I'll Pray for You

King, Stoddard There's a Long, Long Trail

King, Wayne Beautiful Love; Goofus; Josephine; The Waltz You Saved for Me

King, William Atwell, Jr. Sweet Love

Kingsley, Charles Oh That We Two Were Maying

Kingsley, Gershon Popcorn

Kipling, Rudyard Danny Deever; Mother o' Mine; On the Road to Mandalay; Recessional

Kipner, Nat Too Much, Too Little, Too Late

Kipner, Stephen Hard Habit To Break; Heart Attack; Physical; Twist of Fate

Kipps, Charles, Jr. Walk Away from Love

Kirk, Reece Our Love Is on the Fault Line

Kirkman, Terry Cherish

Kisco, Charles It's a Lonesome Old Town (When You're Not Around)

Kittredge, Walter Tenting on the Old Camp Ground, or, Tenting Tonight

Klages, Raymond Climbing Up the Ladder of Love; Doin' the Raccoon; Hugs and Kisses; Just You, Just Me; Once in a Lifetime; Trail of Dreams; What Do I Care

Klauber, Marcy I Get the Blues When It Rains

Kleban, Edward And . . . ; At the Ballet; Dance: Ten, Looks: Three; Hello Twelve, Hello Thirteen, Hello Love; I Can Do That; I Hope I Get It; The Music and the Mirror; Nothing; One; Surprise, Surprise; Tits and Ass; What I Did for Love

Klein, Gary Bobby's Girl

Klein, Lou Daddy; A Gay Caballero; If I Had My Way; She Lived Next Door to a Firehouse

Klein, Manuel It's a Long Lane That Has No Turning

Kleinauf, Henry Johnson Rag

Kleinsinger, George Tubby the Tuba

Klenner, John Down the River of Golden Dreams; Heartaches; Just Friends; Smoke Dreams; Whisper That You Love Me

Klickmann, F. Henri Sweet Hawaiian Moonlight; Waters of Perkiomen

Klohr, John N. The Billboard (March)

Knapp, Mrs. Joseph F., *see* **Phoebe Palmet**

Knauff, George P. Wait for the Wagon

Kneass, Nelson Sweet Alice, or, Ben Bolt, or, Don't You Remember

Knight, Baker Never Be Anyone Else But You; The Wonder of You

Knight, Charles Here We Are, Here We Are, Here We Are Again

Knight, Holly Better Be Good to Me; Love Is a Battlefield; Love Touch (Theme from *Legal Eagles*); Never

Knight, Jerry Crush On You

Knight, Joseph Philip Rocked in the Cradle of the Deep

Knipe, Frederic Listen to the Radio

Knipper, Lev Meadowlands, or, Cavalry of the Steppes

Kniss, Richard L. Sunshine on My Shoulders

Knobloch, Fred Why Not Me

Knopfler, Mark Going Home; Money for Nothing; Private Investigations; Sultans of Swing; Walk of Life

Knox, Buddy Party Doll

Knox, Collie Night May Have Its Sadness

Kocher, Conrad For the Beauty of the Earth

Koda, Michael Smokin' in the Boys' Room

Koehler, Charles Leave Me with a Smile

Koehler, Ted Animal Crackers in My Soup; As Long as I Live; Between the Devil and the Deep Blue Sea; By the Shalimar; Don't Worry 'Bout Me; Dreamy Melody; Get Happy; Happy as the Day Is Long; Hitting the Bottle; I Gotta (I've Got a) Right To Sing the Blues; I Love a Parade; Ill Wind (You're Blowin' Me No Good); I'm Shooting High; I've Got My Fingers Crossed; I've Got the World on a String; Kickin' the Gong Around; Let's Fall in Love; Lovely Lady; The March of Time; Music Music Everywhere (But Not a Song in My Heart); Out in the Cold Again; Picture Me Without You; Some Sunday Morning; Stop! You're Breaking My Heart; Stormy Weather; There's No Two Ways About Love; Truckin'; What Are You Doing the Rest of Your Life; When Lights Are Low; When the Sun Comes Out; Wrap Your Troubles in Dreams (and Dream Your Troubles Away)

Koenig, Martha Careless Love

Koger, George Vieni, Vieni

Kohlman, Churchill Cry

Kolber, Larry I Love How You Love Me; Patches

Kome, Hal Real Goodness from Kentucky Fried Chicken

Koninsky, Sadie Eli Green's Cakewalk

Konto, Frank Ride Captain Ride

Konyn, Georges Pigalle; Two Loves Have I

Kooper, Al This Diamond Ring

Koplow, Don Howard Oh Happy Day

Korb, Nathan The Little Shoemaker

Kornfeld, Artie The Rain, the Park, and Other Things

Korr, M.L. Meadowlands, or, Cavalry of the Steppes

Kortchmar, Daniel Dirty Laundry; Somebody's Baby

Kortlander, Max Tell Me

Kosloff, Ira I Want You, I Need You, I Love You

Kosma, Joseph Autumn Leaves

Kossman, Moe The Swingin' Shepherd Blues

Kostelanetz, André Moon Love; On the Isle of May

Kötscher, Edmund Liechtensteiner Polka

Kountz, Richard The Sleigh

Kramer, Alex C. Candy; Comme Çi, Comme Ça; Far Away Places; High on a Windy Hill; It All Comes Back to Me Now; It's Love, Love, Love; Love Somebody; My Sister and I; No Other Arms, No Other Lips; That's the Beginning of the End; The Way That the Wind Blows

Krampf, Craig Oh Sherrie

Kreisler, Fritz Caprice Viennois; I'm in Love; Letter Song; Liebesfreud; Liebeslied; The Old Refrain; Schön Rosmarin; Stars in My Eyes; Tambourin Chinois; Who Can Tell

Kresa, Helmy That's My Desire

Kretzmer, Herbert Goodness Gracious Me; Yesterday When I Was Young

Krieger, Henry And I Am Telling You I'm Not Going; Cadillac Car; Dancing Is Everything; Dream Girls; Fabulous Feet; I Remember How It Was; Man in the Moon; One Night Only; When I First Saw You; William's Song

Krieger, Robert Hello, I Love You (Won't You Tell Me Your Name); Light My Fire

Kriegsman, James J. Joey

Kristofferson, Kris For the Good Times; Help Me Make It Through the Night; Loving Her Was Easier (Than Anything I'll Ever Do Again); Me and Bobby McGee

Krondes, Jimmy The End (of the Rainbow)

Krueger, Bennie Sunday

Kruger, Jerry I Heard You Cried Last Night

Kuhn, Lee All That Glitters Is Not Gold

Kuller, Sid The Tenement Symphony

Kummer, Clare Dearie

Kunneke, Edward Goodnight (I'm Only a Strolling Vagabond)

Kurtz, Manny In a Sentimental Mood; The Whole World Is Singing My Song

Kusik, Larry (Theme from) The Godfather (Waltz); Love Theme from *Romeo and Juliet*, or, A Time for Us; Speak Softly Love

Kyle, Frances When I Saw Sweet Nellie Home, or, I Was Seeing Nellie Home, or, Aunt Dinah's Quilting Party

La Bounty, Bill Hot Rod Hearts; This Night Won't Last Forever

Lacalle, Joseph M. Amapola, or, Pretty Little Poppy

Lacome, Paul Estudiantina

Lafarge, Guy La Seine

LaForge, Frank Little Star, or, Estrellita; Summer Dreams

Lago, Mario Aurora

Lai, Francis Albert Look Around (You'll Find Me There); (Theme from) Love Story, or, Where Do I Begin; A Man and a Woman

Laidlow, Betty St. Louis Woman

Laine, Cleo He Was Beautiful

Laine, Denny Mull of Kintyre

Laine, Frankie We'll Be Together Again

Laird-Clowes, Nicholas William Life in a Northern Town; Love Parade

Lake, Frank Bless 'Em All

Lake, Sol The Lonely Bull

LaKind, Bobby One By One

Lala You Give Good Love

Lamb, Arthur J. Any Old Port in a Storm; Asleep in the Deep; A Bird in a Gilded Cage; The (Little) Bird on Nellie's Hat; Jennie Lee; The Mansion of Aching Hearts; A Picnic for Two; When the Bell in the Lighthouse Rings Ding Dong; When the Birds in Georgia Sing of Tennessee; When the Mocking Birds Are Singing in the Wildwood; When You've Had a Little Love You Want a Little More; You Splash Me and I'll Splash You

Lamb (Spaulding), Henry The Volunteer Organist

Lamb, Joseph Sensation Rag

Lambert, Dennis Ain't No Woman Like the One I've Got; Country Boy You Got Your Feet in L.A.; Don't Pull Your Love; It Only Takes a Minute; Nightshift; We Built This City

"Lambrecht" Lonely Ballerina

Lamm, Robert William Does Anybody Really Know What Time It Is

Lampe, Carl G. Close to You

Lampe, J. Bodewalt Creole Belle; Mysterioso Pizzicato; A Vision of Salome

Lampert, Diane Break It to Me Gently

Land, Leon Lay Down Your Arms

Lane, Burton The Begat; Come Back to Me; Dancing on a Dime; Everything I Have Is Yours; Feudin' and Fightin'; (I Like New York in June) How About You; How Are Things in Glocca Morra; How Could You Believe Me When I Said I Love You When You Know I've Been a Liar All My Life; Hurry It's Lovely Up Here; I Hear Music; I Left My Hat in Haiti; If This Isn't Love; The Lady's in Love with You; Look to the Rainbow; Necessity; Oh, Me, Oh My, Oh You; Old Devil Moon; On a Clear Day You Can See Forever; Says My Heart; Stop! You're Breaking My Heart; Swing High, Swing Low; That Great Come and Get It Day; There's A Great Day Coming, Mañana; Tonight or Never; Too late Now; What Are You Doing the Rest of Your Life; What Did I Have That I Don't Have; When I'm Not Near the Girl I Love; When the Idle Poor Become the Idle Rich

Lane, Edward Bless You (for Being an Angel)

Lane, Grace Clinging Vine

Lane, Ken Everybody Loves Somebody

Lane, Ronnie Itchycoo Park

Laney, King Why Don't You Believe Me

Lang, John Broken Wings; Kyrie

Lang, Robert Do You Believe in Love

Langdon, Chris Rose, Rose I Love You

Langdon, Dory Pepe

Langdon, Gee A Letter to a Soldier

Lange, Arthur Sally, Irene and Mary; We're Going Over

Lange, Gustav Flower Song (Blumenlied)

Lange, Henry Hot Lips

Lange, Johnny Blue Shadows on the Trail; Clancy Lowered the Boom; I Lost My Sugar in Salt Lake City; Mule Train; Somebody Bigger Than You and I; Uncle Remus Said

Lange, Lee Cara Mia

Lange, Robert John "Mutt" Loverboy; When the Going Gets Tough, the Tough Get Going

Langford, Gordon March from "The Colour Suite"

Laparcerie, Miarka Love Is Like a Violin

LaPread, Ronald Sr. Sweet Love

Lara, Augustin Granada; You Belong to My Heart (Now and Forever), or, Solamente Una Vez

Lara, Maria Teresa Be Mine Tonight

Lardner, Ring June Moon

La Rocca, James D. At the Jazz Band Ball; Barnyard Blues; Bluin' the Blues; Clarinet Marmalade; Original Dixieland One-Step; Ostrich Walk

La Rosa, Julius Eh Cumpari

Larranaga, Robert A Scrumpdillyishus Day

Larson, Glen Big Man; Down by the Station

Larue, Jacques Cherry Pink and Apple Blossom White; Padre

La Russo, Andrea Dress You Up

Lashley, Lou S. Oh You Million Dollar Baby

Laska, Edward The Alcoholic Blues; How'd You Like To Spoon with Me

Lasley, David Blue Side; Jo Jo; Lead Me On

Lateiner, Joseph Mazel Tov

Latham, Dwight B. And the Great Big Saw Came Nearer

Latouche, John Ballad for Americans; Cabin in the Sky; Lazy Afternoon; Taking a Chance on Love

Lauder, Mike I Didn't Know I Loved You

Laudern, Harry The End of the Road; For the Noo, or, Something in the Bottle for the Morning; I Love a Lassie, or, Ma Scotch Bluebell; It's Nice To Get Up in the Morning; Roamin' in the Gloamin'; She Is Ma Daisy; Stop Yer Tickling, Jock!; That's the Reason Noo I Wear a Kilt; Tobermory; We Parted on the Shore; Wedding o' Sandy McNab; A Wee Deoch-an-Doris

Lauper, Cyndi She Bop; Time After Time

Laurie, Linda Leave Me Alone (Ruby Red Dress)

Lavere, Frank Have You Heard; Pretend

La Voie, Kent Me and You and a Dog Named Boo

Lawlor, Charles B. The Irish Jubilee; The Sidewalks of New York, or, East Side, West Side

Lawnhurst, Vee Accent on Youth

Lawrence, Alfred J. Come Along My Mandy; Kitty the Telephone Girl

Lawrence, Charles And Her Tears Flowed Like Wine

Lawrence, Jack All or Nothing At All; Beyond the Sea; Choo Choo Train; Concerto for Two; Delicado; Foolin' Myself; Hold My Hand; Huckleberry Duck; If I Didn't Care; In an Eighteenth Century Drawing Room; In the Moon Mist; Johnson Rag; Linda; Moonlight Masquerade; Play, Fiddle, Play; The Poor People of Paris; (By the) Sleepy Lagoon (Valse Serenade); Sunrise Serenade; Symphony; Tenderly; Vagabond Dreams; What Will I Tell My Heart; With the Wind and the Rain in Your Hair; Yes My Darling Daughter

Lawrence, Stephen You Take My Breath Away

Lawrence, Trevor I'm So Excited

Lawson, Herbert Happy Any Time

Lax, Roger Cuddle In; Hangin' Out the Window

Layton, J. Turner After You've Gone; The Bombo-Shay; Dear Old Southland; Sweet Emalina, My Gal; 'Way Down Yonder in New Orleans

Lazarus, Emma Give Me Your Tired, Your Poor

Lazarus, Frank Just Like That

Lea, James Coz I Love You; Merry Xmas Everybody

Leach, Jimmy The Little Boy That Santa Claus Forgot; Some Day Soon

Leader, Mickey Dance with a Dolly

Leander, Mike Early in the Morning; I Love You Love Me Love

Leavitt, Michael Bennett Little Footsteps

Leavitt, William My Baby's Comin' Home

Le Baron, William Deep in Your Eyes; I'm in Love; Letter Song; Little Girls, Good Bye; On Miami Shore, or, Golden Sands of Miami; Who Can Tell; You Are Free

Lebieg, Earl Sleep

Le Bon, Simon Charles   Hungry Like the Wolf; The Reflex; Union of the Snake; The Wild Boys

Lebowsky, Stan   The Wayward Wind

LeBoy, Grace   On the Good Ship Mary Ann

Le Brunn, George   If It Wasn't for the 'ouses in Between; It's a Great Big Shame; Liza Johnson; Oh Isn't It Singular

Le Clerq, Arthur   I Bought Myself a Bottle of Ink

Lecuona, Ernesto   African Lament (Lamento Africano); (You Are) Always in My Heart; Andalucia; At the Crossroads; The Breeze and I; Jungle Drums (Canto Karabali); Malagueña; Maria My Own; The Peacock; Say "Si Si"; Siboney; Two Hearts That Pass in the Night

Lecuona, Marguerita   Babalu; Taboo

Ledbetter, Huddie   Goodnight Irene

Ledru, Jack   Kiss and Run

Lee, Alfred   Champagne Charley Was His Name; The Daring Young Man (on the Flying Trapeze)

Lee, Bert   Ain't It Ni-Ice; And the Great Big Saw Came Nearer; Brahn Boots; Good Bye-ee; Hello, Hello, Who's Your Lady Friend; Hoch, Caroline; Josh-Ua; Knees Up Mother Brown; My Little Deitcher Girl; My Word You Do Look Queer; Olga Pulloffski; Paddy McGinty's Goat; Sing Brothers; Stop and Shop at the Co-Op Shop; With Her Head Tucked Underneath Her Arm

Lee, David   Goodness Gracious Me

Lee, Jim   Let's Dance

Lee, Larry   Fourteen Carat Mind; Jackie Blue

Lee, Leonard   Let the Good Times Roll

Lee, Lester   Blue Gardenia; Dreamer with a Penny; The Man from Laramie; Pennsylvania Polka; Sabre Dance

Lee, Martin   Angelo; Save Your Kisses for Me

Lee, Marvin   Livery Stable Blues

Lee, Nancy   The Stroll

Lee, Orrie   Waltzing Matilda

Lee, Peggy   He's a Tramp; I Don't Know Enough About You; It's a Good Day; Mañana (Is Soon Enough for Me)

Leeds, Milton   Misirlou; Perfidia; You, You, You Are the One

Leeson, Mike   For Your Eyes Only

Leeves, Reverend William   Auld Robin Gray, or, When the Sheep Are in the Fold

Leeway, Joe   Hold Me Now; King for a Day; Lay Your Hands on Me

Lefébure-Wély, Louis Alfred   The Monastery Bells

Leggett, Steve   Beer, Beer, Glorious Beer

Legrand, Michel   Brian's Song; Happy, or, Love Theme from *Lady Sings the Blues;* (If It Takes Forever) I Will Wait for You; Just a Piece of Sky; Pieces of Dreams; The Summer Knows, or, Theme from *Summer of '42;* Watch What Happens; What Are You Doing the Rest of Your Life; The Windmills of Your Mind, or, Theme from *The Thomas Crown Affair*

Lehak, Ned   You Forgot Your Gloves

Lehár, Franz   Girls, Girls, Girls; The Gold and Silver (Waltz); Gypsy Maiden; Love and Wine; Maxim's; Merry Widow Waltz, or, I Love You So; My Little Nest of Heavenly Blue, or, Frasquita Serenade (Blaues Himmelbett), or, Farewell My Love, Farewell; Pierette and Pierrot; Pretty Edelweiss; Say Not Love Is a Dream; Vilia; Waltz; The White Dove; Yours Is My Heart Alone

Lehman, Johnny   Night; Why Does It Get So Late So Early

Lehman, Kenny   Dance, Dance, Dance (Yowsah, Yowsah, Yowsah)

Lehmann, Liza   In a Persian Garden; There Are Fairies at the Bottom of Our Garden

Leiber, Jerry   Baby I Don't Care; Black Denim Trousers; Charlie Brown; Don't; Hound Dog; I Keep Forgettin' (Every Time You're Near); I Who Have Nothing; Is That All There Is; Jailhouse Rock; Kansas City; Love Potion Number Nine; On Broadway; Ruby Baby; Spanish Harlem; Stand by Me; There Goes My Baby; Yakety Yak

Leibert, Richard   Come Dance with Me

Leibling, Howard   California Nights

Leibowitz, Joseph   The Wedding Samba

Leidzen, Erik   Swedish Rhapsody

Leigh, Carolyn   Angelina; (To) Be a Performer; C'est la Vie; Dimples; Firefly; Give a Little Whistle; Here's to Us; Hey Look Me Over; How Little It Matters, How Little We Know; I Won't Grow Up; I'm Flying; I've Got Your Number; I've Gotta Crow; (On) The Other Side of the Tracks; Pass Me By; Poor Little Hollywood Star; Real Live Girl; Step to the Rear; Tender Shepherd; What Takes My Fancy; Witchcraft; You Bring Out the Lover in Me; Young At Heart

Leigh, Fred W.   The Army of Today's Alright; Captain Gingah; Don't Dilly Dally on the Way; The Galloping Major; Jolly Good Luck to the Girl Who Loves a Soldier; Little Bit off the Top; A Little of What You Fancy; Poor John; Put on Your Ta Ta Little Girlie; Waiting at the Church, or, My Wife Won't Let Me; Why Am I Always the Bridesmaid

Leigh, Mitch   Dulcinea; I'm Only Thinking of Him; The Impossible Dream, or, The Quest; Man of La Mancha; Sarava

Leigh, Richard   Don't It Make My Brown Eyes Blue

Leigh, Rowland   I Give My Heart; Just Once for All Time; Live, Laugh and Love; Oh Donna Clara; Tell Me I'm Forgiven

Leip, Hans   Lili (Lilli) Marlene

Leka, Paul   Na Na Hey Hey Kiss Him Goodbye

Leleiohaku   Hawaiian War Chant

Lemare, Jules   Sweet and Lovely

Lemon, Laura G.   My Ain Folk

Lemon, Mary Mark   Paddy

Lenghurst, Pearl   Be-Bop Baby

Lengsfelder, Hans   Perdido

Lennon, John   All My Loving; All You Need Is Love; And I Love Her; Baby You're a Rich Man; Beautiful Boy; Being for the Benefit of Mister Kite; Blackbird; Can't Buy Me Love; Come Together; A Day in the Life; Day Tripper; Dear Prudence; Do You Want To Know a Secret; Eight Days a Week; Eleanor Rigby; Fame; Fixing a Hole; The Fool on the Hill; Get Back; Getting Better; Girl; Give Peace a Chance; Good

Day Sunshine; Good Morning, Good Morning; Good Night; Got To Get You into My Life; A Hard Day's Night; Hello Goodbye; Hello Little Girl; Help!; Helter Skelter; Here, There and Everywhere; Hey Jude; I Am the Walrus; I Feel Fine; I Saw Her Standing There; I Should Have Known Better; I Want To Hold Your Hand; I Will; If I Fell; I'll Follow the Sun; I'll Keep You Satisfied; I'm a Loser; I'm Looking Through You; In My Life; It's Only Love; Julia; Lady Madonna; Let It Be; (With) A Little Help from My Friends; The Long and Winding Road; Love Me Do; Lovely Rita (Meter Maid); Lucy in the Sky with Diamonds; Magical Mystery Tour; Michelle; Nobody Told Me; Norwegian Wood; Nowhere Man; Ob-La-Di Ob-La-Da; Paperback Writer; Penny Lane; Please Please Me; P.S. I Love You; Revolution; Sergeant Pepper's Lonely Hearts Club Band; She Loves You; She Said She Said; She's a Woman; She's Leaving Home; (Just Like) Starting Over; Strawberry Fields Forever; Thank You Girl; Ticket To Ride; Watching the Wheels; We Can Work It Out; Whatever Gets You Thru the Night; When I'm Sixty-Four; Wild Honey Pie; Woman; A World Without Love; Yellow Submarine; Yesterday; Your Mother Should Know; You've Got To Hide Your Love Away

Lennon, Julian   Too Late for Goodbyes; Valotte

Lennox, Annie   Here Comes the Rain Again; Sweet Dreams (Are Made of This)

Lenoir, Jean   Speak to Me of Love

Lenox, Jean   I Don't Care

Leo, Frank   Watching the Trains Come In; Where Do Flies Go in the Winter Time

Leon, Harry   After Tonight We Say ''Goodbye''; Arm in Arm; A Bedtime Story; Broken Hearted Clown; Goodbye Hawaii; In a Golden Coach; Liszt, Chopin and Mendelssohn; The Little Drummer Boy; Love Me Forever; Me and the Old Folks at Home; Sally

Leonard, Anita   A Sunday Kind of Love

Leonard, Duke   Josephine Please No Lean on the Bell

Leonard, Eddie   Ida, Sweet as Apple Cider; Oh! Didn't It Rain; Roll Dem Roly Boly Eyes

Leonard, Mark   Missing You

Leonard, Michael   I'm All Smiles; Why Did I Choose You

Leonard, Patrick   Live To Tell

Leoncavallo, Ruggiero   La Mattinata ('Tis the Day); Vesti la Giubba

Leontovich, M.   Carol of the Bells

Leprevost, Gabriel   For All Eternity

Leray, Ken   Together We Are Beautiful

Lerios, Cory   Cool Love; Love Will Find a Way

Lerner, Alan Jay   (It's) Almost Like Being in Love; Ascot Gavotte; Camelot; Coco; Come Back to Me; Come to Me, Bend to Me; The Day Before Spring; Follow Me; Gabrielle; Get Me to the Church on Time; Gigi; God's Green World; Green-Up Time; The Heather on the Hill; Here I'll Stay; How Could You Believe Me When I Said I Love You When You Know I've Been a Liar All My Life; How To Handle a Woman; Hurry It's Lovely Up Here; A Hymn to Him; I Could Have Danced All Night; I Left My Hat in Haiti; I Love You This Morning; I Loved You Once in Silence; I Remember It Well;

I Still See Elisa; I Talk to the Trees; I Wonder What the King Is Doing Tonight; If Ever I Would Leave You; I'll Go Home with Bonnie Jean; I'm an Ordinary Man; I'm Glad I'm Not Young Anymore; I've Grown Accustomed to Her Face; Just You Wait; The Lusty Month of May; The Night They Invented Champagne; On a Clear Day You Can See Forever; On the Street Where You Live; (I Don't Understand) The Parisians; The Rain in Spain; Say a Prayer for Me Tonight; She Is Not Thinking of Me (Waltz at Maxim's); Show Me; The Simple Joys of Maidenhood; Thank Heaven for Little Girls; Then You May Take Me to the Fair; There But for You Go I; They Call the Wind Maria; Too Late Now; What Did I Have That I Don't Have; What Do (the) Simple Folk Do; Why Can't the English; With a Little Bit of Luck; Without You; Wouldn't It Be Lovely; You Did It; You Haven't Changed At All

Lerner, Sammy   Is It True What They Say About Dixie; A Little Co-operation from You; (I'm) Popeye the Sailor Man

Lerner, Sol   Gangway

Le Royal, A.   Good Luck, Good Health, God Bless You

LeRoyer, Pierre C.M.N.   (Theme from) Borsalino

Leslie, Edgar   All the Quakers Are Shoulder Shakers Down in Quaker Town; America I Love You; Among My Souvenirs; Blue (and Broken Hearted); By the River Sainte Marie; Come On, Papa; Crazy People; Dirty Hands, Dirty Face; For Me and My Gal; (He'd Have To Get Under,) Get Out and Get Under (To Fix Up His Automobile); Hello, Hawaii; How Are You; In a Little Gypsy Tea Room; In the Gold Fields of Nevada; It Looks Like Rain in Cherry Blossom Lane; Kansas City Kitty; A Little Bit Independent; Lovely; Me and Jane in a Plane; Mistakes; Moon Over Miami; The Moon Was Yellow; Moonlight on the Rhine; Oh! What a Pal Was Mary; Oh You Million Dollar Doll; On the Gin, Gin, Ginny Shore; On Treasure Island; (Home in) Pasadena; Robins and Roses; Rolling Stones—All Come Rolling Home Again; Romance; Rose of the Rio Grande; Sadie Salome, Go Home; Shepherd of the Hills; Since Maggie Dooley Learned the Hooley Hooley; Take Your Girlie to the Movies If You Can't Make Love at Home; When Alexander Takes His Ragtime Band to France; When You Played the Organ and I Sang ''The Rosary''

Leslie, Ernest   Rock Me to Sleep, Mother

Leslie, Henry   I'd Like To See the Kaiser with a Lily in His Hand

Leslie-Smith, Kenneth   One Love Forever

Lessing, Edith   Oh You Circus Day

Lester, Walter   Since I Don't Have You

Letters, William   Flanagan; Has Anybody Here Seen Kelly; Molly O'Morgan

Levant, Oscar   Blame It on My Youth; If You Want the Rainbow (You Must Have the Rain); Keep Sweeping the Cobwebs off the Moon; Lady Play Your Mandolin

Levay, Sylvester   Fly Robin Fly; Get Up and Boogie

Leveen, Raymond   Ti-Pi-Tin

Leven, Mel   My Quiet Village

Levenson, Robert   My Belgian Rose

Levey, Harold   Hurdy Gurdy Man; Lovely Lady

Levi, Maurice   Airy, Fairy Lillian

Levin, Ira   She Touched Me

Levine, Gerry   Evermore

Levine, Irwin   Candida; Knock Three Times; (Say Has Anybody Seen) My Sweet Gypsy Rose; This Diamond Ring; Tie a Yellow Ribbon Round the Ole Oak Tree

Levine, Joe   Yummy Yummy Yummy

Levinson, Jerry   Under a Blanket of Blue

Levinson, Lou   Here in My Heart

Levison, Jay   G'Bye Now

Levitin, Lee Oskar   The Cisco Kid; Gypsy Man; Summer; Why Can't We Be Friends

Levy, Eunice   Ko Ko Mo (I Love You So)

Levy, Marcy   Lay Down Sally

Levy, Morris   My Boy Lollipop

Levy, Sol P.   That Naughty Waltz

Lewie, Jona   Stop the Cavalry

Lewin, Lionel H.   Birds in the Night

Lewine, Richard   I Gotta Have You

Lewis, Al   All American Girl; As Long as You're Not in Love with Anyone Else; Why Don't You Fall in Love with Me; Blueberry Hill; The Breeze (That's Bringing My Honey Back to Me); The Finger of Suspicion Points at You; Gonna Get a Girl; Got the Bench, Got the Park, But I Haven't Got You; Invitation to a Broken Heart; Ninety-Nine Out of a Hundred (Want To Be Loved); No! No! A Thousand Times No!; (Potatoes Are Cheaper—Tomatoes Are Cheaper) Now's the Time To Fall in Love; On the Bumpy Road to Love; Rose O'Day; Tears on My Pillow; Way Back Home; When I'm the President (We Want Cantor); You Gotta Be a Football Hero (To Get Along with the Beautiful Girls)

Lewis, Bunny   Let's Talk About Love; No Greater Love; A Voice in the Wilderness

Lewis, Calvin H.   When a Man Loves a Woman

Lewis, David   Secret Lovers

Lewis, Edna   Judy's Turn To Cry; Lipstick on Your Collar

Lewis, Harold   This Little Piggie Went to Market

Lewis, Henry   The Bombo-Shay

Lewis, Huey   Heart of Rock and Roll; I Want a New Drug; If This Is It; The Power of Love; Stuck with You

Lewis, Ken   Tossing and Turning

Lewis, Matthew Gregory   On the Banks of Allan Water

Lewis, Meade   Honky Tonk Train Blues

Lewis, Morgan   A House with a Little Red Barn; How High the Moon; The Old Soft Shoe

Lewis, Richard A.   Get a Job

Lewis, Roger   Down by the Winegar Woiks; The Oceana Roll; One Dozen Roses

Lewis, Samuel M.   Absence Makes the Heart Grow Fonder (for Somebody Else); Arrah Go On, I'm Gonna Go Back to Oregon; At Last; Beautiful Lady in Blue; Cryin' for the Carolines; Daddy Long Legs; Dinah; Don't Cry, Frenchy, Don't Cry; Don't Wait 'Til the Night Before Christmas; Five Foot Two, Eyes of Blue (Has Anybody Seen My Girl?); For All We Know; Gloomy Sunday; Got Her off My Hands (But Can't Get Her off My Mind); Happy Go Lucky Lane; Have a Little Faith in Me; Hello, Central, Give Me No Man's Land; How Ya Gonna Keep 'Em Down on the Farm (After They've Seen Paree); How'd You Like To Be My Daddy; Huckleberry Finn; I Kiss Your Hand, Madame; I'd Love To Fall Asleep and Wake Up in My Mammy's Arms; If I knock the "L" out of Kelly; I'll Be Happy When the Preacher Makes You Mine; I'm All Bound 'Round with the Mason-Dixon Line; I'm Sitting on Top of the World (Just Rolling Along—Just Rolling Along); In a Little Spanish Town; In Shadowland; Just a Baby's Prayer at Twilight; Just Friends; Keep Sweeping the Cobwebs off the Moon; Laugh, Clown, Laugh; Love—What Are You Doing to My Heart; Meet Me at the Station, Dear; My Barney Lies Over the Ocean (Just the Way He Lied to Me); My Little Girl; My Mammy; My Mother's Rosary; Oh, How I Wish I Could Sleep Until My Daddy Comes Home; Old Pal Why Don't You Answer Me; Put Away a Little Ray of Golden Sunshine; Put Me To Sleep with an Old-Fashioned Melody; Revenge; Rock-a-Bye Your Baby with a Dixie Melody; Sam, You Made the Pants Too Long; (On the) Street of Dreams; That Mellow Melody; There's a Cradle in Caroline; There's a Little Lane Without a Turning on the Way to Home Sweet Home; This Time It's Love; Tuck Me to Sleep in My Old 'Tucky Home; Way Down in Iowa I'm Going To Hide Away; When You're a Long, Long Way from Home; Where Did Robinson Crusoe Go with Friday on Saturday Night?; Why Do They All Take the Night Boat to Albany; Why Don't You Answer Me; You're a Million Miles from Nowhere When You're One Little Mile from Home

Lewis, Stan   I'll Be Home

Lewis, Ted   When My Baby Smiles at Me

Lewis, Terry   Tender Love; What Have You Done for Me Lately

Lewis, Wayne   Secret Lovers

Leybourne, George   The Daring Young Man (on the Flying Trapeze)

Libbey, Dee   Mangos

Lieberman, John   Friendship Is for Keeps

Liebling, Howard   Sunshine, Lollipops and Rainbows

Lief, Max   She's Such a Comfort to Me

Lief, Nathaniel   She's Such a Comfort to Me

Lieurance, Thurlow   By the Waters of Minnetonka

Lightfoot, Gordon   For Lovin' Me; If You Could Read My Mind; Sundown; The Wreck of the Edmund Fitzgerald

Liliuokalani, Queen   Aloha Oe, or, Farewell to Thee

Lilley, Joseph J.   Jingle Jangle Jingle

Lillie, Muriel   Susannah's Squeaking Shoes

Lilly, R.P.   Plant a Watermelon on My Grave and Let the Juice Soak Through; That's Where My Money Goes

Limbo, Sonny   Just Another Day in Paradise; Key Largo

Lincke, Paul   Amina; (The) Glow Worm; Siamese Patrol; Spring, Beautiful Spring, or, Chimes of Spring

Lincoln, Harry J.   Midnight Fire-Alarm

Lind, Bob   Elusive Butterfly

Lind, Jon   Crazy for You

Lind, W. Murdock   Whistling Rufus

Linde, Dennis   Burning Love; Goodbye Marie

Lindeman, Edith   I Know; Little Things Mean a Lot

Lindsay, Jennie   Always Take Mother's Advice

Lindsay, John   Asia

Lindsey, Mort   Girl Talk

Lindsey, Ted   Too Many Lovers

Lindt, R.   Liechtensteiner Polka

Lindup, Dave   Itinerary of an Orchestra

Lindup, Mike   Something About You

Lingard, William Horace   Captain Jinks of the Horse Marines

Link, Harry   I'm Just Wild About Animal Crackers; I've Got a Feeling I'm Falling; The Kiss That You've Forgotten (Is the Kiss I Can't Forget); These Foolish Things (Remind Me of You); You're the One I Care For

Link, Peter   Why Can't I Touch You

Linley, George   Ever of Thee; Thou Art Gone from My Gaze; Well-a-Day

Linton, William B.   Easier Said Than Done

Linzer, Sandy   Dawn (Go Away); Fresh; Let's Hang On; A Lover's Concerto; Mornin' Beautiful; Native New Yorker; Workin' My Way Back to You

Lippman, Sidney   "A"—You're Adorable; Chickery Chick; It Couldn't Be True (Or Could It); Laroo Laroo Lilli Bolero; Little Lulu; My Sugar Is So Refined; Too Young; Who Do You Think You Are

Lipton, Dan   My Girl's a Yorkshire Girl; Oh Oh Antonio; Put Me Amongst the Girls; She's a Lassie from Lancashire

Lipton, Leonard   Puff the Magic Dragon

Lisbona, Edward B.   I Once Had a Heart, Margarita; It's My Mother's Birthday Today; The Shoemaker's Serenade; When the Guardsman Started Crooning on Parade

Liszt, Franz   Hungarian Rhapsody No. 2; Liebesträume

Little, George A.   Hawaiian Butterfly

Little, Jack   Hold Me; Jealous; (In) A Shanty in Old Shanty Town; Ting-a-Ling, or, The Waltz of the Bells; You're a Heavenly Thing

Littman, Julian   Strut

Lively, Bob   St. Louis Woman

Livgren, Kerry   Dust in the Wind

Livingston, Alan W.   I Taut I Taw a Puddy-Tat

Livingston, Fud   I'm Through with Love

Livingston, Jay   Almost in Your Arms; Another Time, Another Place; Bonanza; Bonne Nuit—Goodnight; Buttons and Bows; Copper Canyon; Dear Heart; Golden Earrings; Home Cooking; I'd Like To Baby You; In the Arms of Love; Love Song from *Houseboat*, or, Almost in Your Arms; Marshmallow Moon; Mr. Lucky; Misto Cristofo Columbo; Mona Lisa; My Beloved; Silver Bells; Streets of Laredo, or, The Cowboy's Lament; Tammy; To Each His Own; (Theme from) Vertigo; Whatever Will Be, Will Be, or, Que Sera, Sera

Livingston, Jerry   Baby Baby Baby; Ballad of Cat Ballou; Bibbidi-Bobbodi-Boo; Chi-Baba Chi-Baba (My Bambino Go to Sleep); Cinderella; Close to You; (When It's) Darkness on

the Delta; A Dream Is a Wish Your Heart Makes; Go, Go, Go, Go; Hanging Tree; Hawaiian Eye; I Like It—I Like It; I'm a Big Girl Now; It's the Talk of the Town; Just a Kid Named Joe; Lawman; Mairzy Doats; Moonrise on the Lowlands; The Navy Gets the Gravy and the Army Gets the Beans; (This Is) The Story of a Starry Night; The Twelfth of Never; A Very Merry Un-Birthday to You; Wait Until Dark; Wake the Town and Tell the People; Young Emotions

Livingston, Miss Hattie   The Young Folks At Home

Livraghi, R.   A Man Without Love

Llenas, Francois   A Day in the Life of a Fool

Llewellyn, Ray   Highway Patrol

Lloyd, Harry   I Just Fall in Love Again

Lloyd, Robert   Good Morning, Mister Zip-Zip-Zip

Lloyd, Rosie   B-I-Double L-Bill

Lockard, R.   Iowa Corn Song

Locke, Edward   Song of the Soul

Locke, Matthew   Believe Me If All Those Endearing Young Charms; My Lodging (It) Is on the Cold Ground

Lockhart, Eugene   The World Is Waiting for the Sunrise

Lockton, Edward   I'll Walk Beside You

Lockyer, Malcolm   Friends and Neighbours; Pathfinder's March

Loder, Edward James   The Brave Old Oak

Lodge, Henry   Temptation Rag

Loeb, John Jacob   Boo-Hoo; Get Out Those Old Records; Got the Jitters; Masquerade; Reflections in the Water; Sailboat in the Moonlight; Seems Like Old Times; Sweetie Pie

Loesser, Frank   Adelaide; Adelaide's Lament; Anywhere I Wander; Baby It's Cold Outside; (It's) Been a Long Day; Big "D"; Bloop Bleep; (See What) The Boys in the Back Room (Will Have); Brotherhood of Man; A Bushel and a Peck; Can't Get Out of This Mood; Dancing on a Dime; Dolores; Fugue for Tinhorns; Grand Old Ivy; Guys and Dolls; Happy To Keep His Dinner Warm; Heart and Soul; Hoop-Dee-Doo; How Sweet You Are; How To; I Believe in You; I Don't Want To Walk Without You, Baby; I Hear Music; I Said No; I Wish I (We) Didn't Have To Say Good Night; I Wish I Didn't Love You So; I Wish I Were Twins; If I Were a Bell; I'll Know; I'll Never Let a Day Pass By; I'm Hans Christian Andersen; In My Arms; Inchworm; I've Never Been in Love Before; Jingle Jangle Jingle; Joey, Joey, Joey; Just Another Polka; Kiss the Boys Goodbye; The Lady's in Love with You; Let's Get Lost; Love from a Heart of Gold; Luck Be a Lady; Make a Miracle; The Moon of Manakoora; The Most Happy Fella; "Murder" He Says; My Darling, My Darling; My Time of Day; No Two People; (Where Are You) Now That I Need You; The Oldest Established (Permanent Floating Crap Game in New York); (I'd Like To Get You) On a Slow Boat to China; Once in Love with Amy; Paris Original; Pernambuco; Praise the Lord and Pass the Ammunition; Rodger Young; Sand in My Shoes; Say It (Over and Over Again); Says My Heart; A Secretary Is Not a Toy; Sit Down, You're Rockin' the Boat; Small Fry; Somebody, Somewhere; Spring Will Be a Little Late This Year; Standing on the Corner; Strange Enchantment; Take Back Your Mink; Tallahassee; They're Either

Too Young or Too Old; Thumbelina; Two Sleepy People; The Ugly Duckling; We're the Couple in the Castle; What Do You Do in the Infantry?; Why Fight the (That) Feeling; A Woman in Love; Wonderful Copenhagen

Loewe, Frederick   (It's) Almost Like Being in Love; Ascot Gavotte; Camelot; Come to Me, Bend to Me; The Day Before Spring; Follow Me; Get Me to the Church on Time; Gigi; God's Green World; The Heather on the Hill; How To Handle a Woman; A Hymn to Him; I Could Have Danced All Night; I Love You This Morning; I Loved You Once in Silence; I Remember It Well; I Still See Elisa; I Talk to the Trees; I Wonder What the King Is Doing Tonight; If Ever I Would Leave You; I'll Go Home with Bonnie Jean; I'm an Ordinary Man; I'm Glad I'm Not Young Anymore; I've Grown Accustomed to Her Face; Just You Wait; The Lusty Month of May; The Night They Invented Champagne; On the Street Where You Live; (I Don't Understand) The Parisians; The Rain in Spain; Say a Prayer for Me Tonight; She Is Not Thinking of Me, (Waltz at Maxim's); Show Me; The Simple Joys of Maidenhood; Somehow; Thank Heaven for Little Girls; Then You May Take Me to the Fair; There But For You Go I; They Call the Wind Maria; What Do (the) Simple Folk Do; Why Can't the English; With a Little Bit of Luck; Without You; Wouldn't It Be Loverly; You Did It; You Haven't Changed At All

Lofthouse, Charlie (L. Charles)   Mama Don't Want No Peas an' Rice an' Cocoanut Oil

Logan, Frederick Knight   The Missouri Waltz; Pale Moon

Logan, Harold   I'm Gonna Get Married; Personality; Stagger Lee

Loggins, Dave   Morning Desire; Roll On Eighteen Wheeler

Loggins, Kenny   Danny's Song; Footloose; Heart To Heart; I'm Alright, or, (Theme from) Caddyshack; What a Fool Believes

Lohner, Fritz   Yours Is My Heart Alone

Löhr, Hermann   Little Grey Home in the West; Rose of My Heart; Where My Caravan Has Rested

Loman, Jules   Goodbye Sue

Lomas, Barbara   Express

Lomax, Alan   Tom Dooley, or, Tom Dula

Lomax, John   Goodnight Irene

Lombardo, Carmen   Boo-Hoo; Coquette; Get Out Those Old Records; Jungle Drums (Canto Karabali); Powder Your Face with Sunshine; Return to Me; Sailboat in the Moonlight; Seems Like Old Times; Snuggled on Your Shoulder, Cuddled in Your Arms; The Sweetest Music This Side of Heaven; Sweethearts on Parade

London, Mark   To Sir with Love

Long, Andy Iona   South Sea Island Magic

Long, Burt   Cindy Oh Cindy

Long, Jimmy   That Silver-Haired Daddy of Mine

Long, John P.   I Can't Do My Belly Bottom Button Up; Sing, Everybody Sing; What D'Yer Think of That

Longfellow, Henry Wadsworth   The Arrow and the Song; Excelsior; I Heard the Bells on Christmas Day; The Rainy Day; The Sea Hath Its Pearls; Stars of the Summer Night; The Village Blacksmith

Longstaffe, Ernest   When the Sergeant Major's on Parade

Lonsdale, T.S.   Tommy, Make Room for Your Uncle; Whoa, Emma

Lookofsky, Mike   Walk Away, Renee

Lopez, Gilbert   Happy, Happy Birthday, Baby

Lopez, Ray   Livery Stable Blues

Lopez, Vincent   Knock, Knock, Who's There

Lorber, Samuel   Where Were You When I Was Falling in Love

Lord, Jon   Smoke on the Water

Lordan, Jerry   Apache; Atlantis; Diamonds; A Girl Like You; I'm Just a Baby; I've Waited So Long; Scarlet O'Hara; Who Could Be Bluer; Wonderful Land

Lorenz, Gordon   There's No One Quite Like Grandma

Lorenzo, Ange   Sleepy Time Gal

Lorick, Robert   Dancing Is Everything; Fabulous Feet; I Remember How It Was; Man in the Moon; William's Song

Lorraine, William   December and May, or, Mollie Newell Don't Be Cruel; Salome

Lotz, Mark   Boomerang

Loucheim, Stuart F.   Mixed Emotions

Loudermilk, John D.   Abilene; Ebony Eyes; Indian Reservation; A Rose and a Baby Ruth; Sad Movies Make Me Cry; Waterloo

Loughnane, Lee   No Tell Lover

Louiguy, R.S., see Luis Guglielmi

Love, Mike   Do It Again; Getcha Back; Good Vibrations; Surfin' Safari

Loveday, Carroll   That's My Desire

Lovell, Herbie   Jamaica Farewell

Lovell, R.   Anchors Aweigh

Lover, Samuel   The Low-Backed Car; Widow Machree

Lovett, LeRoy   After the Lights Go Down Low

Lovett, Winfred   Kiss and Say Goodbye

Lowe, Bernie   Swingin' School; (Let Me Be Your) Teddy Bear; Teenage Prayer; Wild One

Lowe, Bert   I Love You (Sweetheart of All My Dreams)

Lowe, Chris   West End Girls

Lowe, Jim   Gambler's Guitar for Another Day

Lowell, Frances   Such a Li'l Fellow

Lowen, Eric   We Belong

Lown, Bert   Bye Bye Blues; You're the One I Care For

Lowry, F.   Whispering Bells

Lowry, Reverend Robert   All the Way My Saviour Leads Me; Hide Thou Me; I Need Thee Every Hour; Something for Jesus; We're Marching to Zion; Where Is My (Wander'ing) Boy Tonight

Luban, Francice   El Choclo

Lubin, Francia   A Gay Ranchero; Say "Si Si"

Lubin, Joe   Move Over Darling; The Shoemaker's Serenade; Till Stars Forget To Shine

Luboff, Norman   Yellow Bird

Lucas, Carrol   How Soon

Lucas, Clarence   The Perfect Song; The Song of Songs

Lucas, E.V.   When We've Wound Up the Watch on the Rhine

Lucas, Jimmy   I Love, I Love, I Love My Wife, But Oh You Kid

Lucas, Reggie Grant   Borderline; The Closer I Get to You; Never Knew Love Like This Before

Lucchesi, Roger   The Portuguese Washerwomen

Lucia, Peter Jr.   Crimson and Clover

Luders, Gustav   Heidelberg Stein Song; The Message of the Violet; My Gal Is a High Born Lady; The Tale of a Bumble Bee; The Tale of the Kangaroo; The Tale of the Seashell; The Tale of the Turtle Dove

Ludlow, Ben   Fifty Million Times a Day

Lukather, Steve   I Won't Hold You Back; Turn Your Love Around

Luke, Jemima   I Think When I Read That Sweet Story

Lully, Jean   Au Clair de la Lune

Lummis, Charles F.   The Star

Luna, Gabriel   Time Was, or, Dreaming

Lunceford, Jimmie   (If I Had) Rhythm in My Nursery Rhymes; Rhythm Is Our Business

Lunsford, Orville   All American Boy

Lunt, Stephen Broughton   She Bop

Lurie, Elliot   Brandy (You're a Fine Girl)

Lusini, Mauro   Son of a Travelin' Man

Lutcher, Nellie   He's a Real Gone Guy; Hurry On Down (to My House)

Luther, Frank   Barnacle Bill the Sailor

Luther, Martin   A Mighty Fortress Is Our God, or, Ein' Feste Berg

Lutz, Meyer W., *see* **Wilhelm Meyer-Lutz**

Lutz, Michael G.   Smokin' in the Boy's Room

Lyall, William   Magic

Lyle, Graham   Heart on My Sleeve; We Don't Need Another Hero; What's Love Got To Do with It; When I'm Dead and Gone

Lyle, Kenneth   The Army of Today's Alright; Here We Are, Here We Are, Here We Are Again; Jolly Good Luck to the Girl Who Loves a Soldier

Lyman, Abe   (What Can I Say, Dear) After I Say I'm Sorry; I Cried for You (Now It's Your Turn to Cry Over Me); Mandalay; Mary Lou; Tenderly

Lymon, Frank   Why Do Fools Fall in Love

Lyn, Merril   I Give You My Word

Lynd, Eve   Time Alone Will Tell

Lynn, Cheryl   Got To Be Real

Lynne, Jeff   Don't Bring Me Down; Shine a Little Love; Strange Magic; Sweet Talkin' Woman; Telephone Line; Xanadu

Lynton, Everett   I Never See Maggie Alone; Primrose Hill

Lyon, Del   The One Rose That's Left in My Heart

Lyte, Henry Francis   Abide with Me, or, Fast Falls the Eventide

Lyttelton, Humphrey   Bad Penny Blues

MacBoyle, Darl   "Forever" Is a Long, Long Time; To Have, To Hold, To Love

MacCarthy, Harry   The Bonnie Blue Flag

MacColl, Ewan   The First Time Ever I Saw Your Face

MacColl, Kirsty   They Don't Know

MacDermot, Galt   African Waltz; Aquarius; Be-In; Easy To Be Hard; Frank Mills; Good Morning Starshine; Hair; Let the Sunshine In; Manchester; Where Do I Go

MacDonald, Ballard   Beautiful Ohio; Bend Down, Sister; Bring Back Those Minstrel Days; Clap Hands, Here Comes Charley; Down in Bom-Bombay; Hot Heels; I Wish I Had My Old Girl Back Again; If I Should Plant a Tiny Seed of Love; (Back Home Again in) Indiana; It Takes a Little Rain with the Sunshine To Make the World Go Round; I've Got the Time—I've Got the Place, But It's Hard To Find the Girl; The Land of My Best Girl; The Little House upon the Hill; Nights of Gladness; On the Mississippi; Parade of the Wooden Soldiers; Piney Ridge; Play That Barbershop Chord (Mister Jefferson Lord); Rose of Washington Square; She Is the Sunshine of Virginia; Somebody Loves Me; There's a Girl in the Heart of Maryland (with a Heart That Belongs to Me); Three Wonderful Letters from Home; Tip-Top Tipperary Mary; The Trail of the Lonesome Pine; Wilson, That's All!

MacDonald, Ralph   Just the Two of Us

MacDonough, Glen   Absinthe Frappé; Al Fresco; Ask Her While the Band Is Playing; Bandana Land; I Can't Do the Sum; A Knot of Blue; Love Is Like a Cigarette; Rose of the World; Toyland

MacDowell, Edward   Thy Beaming Eyes; To a Water Lily; To a Wild Rose; Woodland Sketches

MacFadyen, Iaian A.   Scottish Soldier Green Hill

MacFarren, Mrs. Natalia   Lullaby; Songs My Mother Taught Me

MacGimsey, Robert   Shadrack (Meshack, Abednigo)

MacGregor, J. Chalmers   It Must Be Jelly, 'Cause Jam Don't Shake Like That

MacLean, Ross   Too Fat Polka

MacLellan, Gene   Put Your Hand in the Hand; Snowbird

MacMurrough, Dermot   Macushla

MacNeil, Michael   Alive and Kicking

MacPherson, Harry   Roll Along Prairie Moon

McBroom, Amanda   The Rose

McCarey, Leo   An Affair To Remember

McCarron, Charles   Blues My Naughty Sweetie Gives to Me; Down in Honky Tonky Town; Down Where the Swanee River Flows; Fido Is a Hot Dog Now; Oh! How She Could Yacki, Hacki, Wicki, Wacki, Woo; Poor Pauline

McCarthey, Peter Michael   Lily the Pink

McCarthy, Charles When Your Old Wedding Ring Was New

McCarthy, Daniel The Hat Me Father Wore

McCarthy, James Still I'm Sad

McCarthy, Joseph (In My Sweet Little) Alice Blue Gown; Beatrice Fairfax, Tell Me What To Do; Castle of Dreams; Following the Sun Around; I Found the End of the Rainbow; I Miss You Most of All; If We Can't Be the Same Old Sweethearts, We'll Just Be the Same Old Friends; If You're in Love You'll Waltz; I'm Always Chasing Rainbows; I'm in the Market for You; In All My Dreams I Dream of You; Ireland Must Be Heaven, for My Mother Came from There; Irene; The Kinkajou; My Baby's Arms; My Lovin' Honey Man; Norway; Oui, Oui Marie; Rambling Rose; The Ranger's Song; Rio Rita; Shave and a Haircut, Bay Rum; That's How I Need You; There's a Garden in Old Italy; There's a Little Spark of Love Still Burning; They Go Wild Simply Wild over Me; Underneath the Arches; What Do You Want To Make Those Eyes at Me For; When I Get You Alone Tonight; Why Try To Change Me Now; You Made Me Love You (I Didn't Want To Do It); You're Always in My Arms (But Only in My Dreams)

McCartney, Linda Another Day; Band on the Run; Helen Wheels; Jet; Let 'Em In; Listen To What the Man Said; Live and Let Die; My Love; Silly Love Songs; Uncle Albert/ Admiral Halsey

McCartney, Paul All My Loving; All You Need Is Love; And I Love Her; Another Day; Baby You're a Rich Man; Band on the Run; Being for the Benefit of Mister Kite; Blackbird; Can't Buy Me Love; Come Together; Coming Up— Live at Glasgow; A Day in the Life; Day Tripper; Dear Prudence; Do You Want To Know a Secret; Ebony and Ivory; Eight Days a Week; Eleanor Rigby; Fixing a Hole; The Fool on the Hill; Get Back; Getting Better; Girl; Give Peace a Chance; Good Day Sunshine; Good Morning, Good Morning; Good Night; Goodnight Tonight; Got To Get You into My Life; A Hard Day's Night; Helen Wheels; Hello Goodbye; Hello Little Girl; Help!; Helter Skelter; Here, There and Everywhere; Hey Jude; I Am the Walrus; I Feel Fine; I Saw Her Standing There; I Should Have Known Better; I Want To Hold Your Hand; I Will; If I Fell; I'll Follow the Sun; I'll Keep You Satisfied; I'm a Loser; I'm Looking Through You; In My Life; It's Only Love; Jet; Julia; Lady Madonna; Let 'Em In; Let It Be; Listen To What the Man Said; (With) A Little Help from My Friends; Live and Let Die; The Long and Winding Road; Love in the Open Air; Love Me Do; Lovely Rita (Meter Maid); Lucy in the Sky with Diamonds; Magical Mystery Tour; Maybe I'm Amazed; Michelle; Mull of Kintyre; My Love; No More Lonely Nights; Norwegian Wood; Nowhere Man; Ob-La-Di Ob-La-Da; Paperback Writer; Penny Lane; Please Please Me; P.S. I Love You; Revolution; Say Say Say; Sergeant Pepper's Lonely Hearts Club Band; She Loves You; She Said She Said; She's a Woman; She's Leaving Home; Silly Love Songs; Strawberry Fields Forever; Thank You Girl; Ticket To Ride; Uncle Albert/ Admiral Halsey; We All Stand Together; We Can Work It Out; When I'm Sixty-Four; Wild Honey Pie; A World Without Love; Yellow Submarine; Yesterday; Your Mother Should Know; You've Got To Hide Your Love Away

McClary, Thomas Sweet Love

McClintock, Harry Kirby Hallelujah, I'm a Bum

McCluskey, Andy If You Leave

McCormack, Keith Sugar Shack

McCormick, Charles Natural High

McCormick, Jonas 19

McCormick, Randy Real Love; Suspicions

McCosh, D.S. Hear Dem Bells

McCoy, Joe Why Don't You Do Right

McCoy, Rose Marie Don't Be Angry; I Beg of You; If I May

McCoy, Van Baby I'm Yours; The Hustle

McCray, Don Accidentally on Purpose

McCree, Junie Carrie, or, Carrie Marry Harry; Let's Go into a Picture Show; Nora Malone (Call Me by Phone); Put Your Arms Around Me Honey (Hold Me Tight); Take Me Up with You, Dearie

McCreery, John The American Star

McCulloch, James Hot Child in the City

McDaniel, Mel Goodbye Marie

McDaniels, Gene (That's the Time I) Feel Like Makin' Love

McDermott, Robert Transatlantic Lullaby

McDill, Bob Amanda; Falling Again; Good Ole Boys Like Me; It Must Be Love; Why Don't You Spend the Night

McDonald, Michael Heart to Heart; One by One; What a Fool Believes; Yah Mo B There; You Belong to Me

McDowell, Ronnie Watchin' Girls Go By

McEachern, Malcolm The Changing of the Guard

McFadden, Gene Ain't No Stoppin' Us Now

McFarland, J. Leslie Little Children; Stuck on You

McGavisk, James Gee, But It's Great To Meet a Friend from Your Old Home Town

McGear, M. Thank U Very Much

McGee, Parker American Music; I'd Really Love To See You Tonight; If You Ever Change Your Mind

McGhee, Thomas Abie My Boy; Chick Chick Chicken; I Want Some Money

McGill, Josephine Duna

McGlennon, Felix Actions Speak Louder Than Words; And Her Golden Hair Was Hanging Down Her Back; Comrades; Sons of the Sea

McGough, Roger Lily the Pink

McGowan, Richard J. Root, Hog, or Die

McGranahan, James Come, Oh, Come to Me; Sometime We'll Understand

McGrane, Paul Juke Box Saturday Night

McGrath, Terence Along Came Caroline

McGuffie, Bill Sweet September

McHugh, Jimmy As the Girls Go; The Bad Humor Man; Bandana Babies; Blue Again; Candlelight and Wine; Can't Get Out of This Mood; Cinderella Brown; Clear out of This World; Comin' In on a Wing and a Prayer; Cuban Love Song; Dig You Later (A Hubba-Hubba-Hubba); Diga Diga Do; Dinner at Eight; Doin' the New Low-Down; Don't Blame Me; Dream, Dream, Dream; Exactly Like You; Futuristic

Rhythm; Go Home and Tell Your Mother; Here Comes Heaven Again; Hey Young Fella Close Your Old Umbrella; (What Has Become of) Hinky Dinky Parlay Voo; Hooray for Love; How Blue the Night; I Can't Believe That You're in Love with Me; I Can't Give You Anything But Love; I Couldn't Sleep a Wink Last Night; I Don't Care Who Knows It; I Feel a Song Coming On; I Got Lucky in the Rain; I Hit a New High; I Wish I (We) Didn't Have To Say Good Night; I Won't Dance; I'm in the Mood for Love; I'm Shooting High; It's a Most Unusual Day; It's the Darndest Thing; I've Got My Fingers Crossed; Let's Get Lost; Lost in a Fog; Lovely Lady; Lovely To Look At; (This Is) A Lovely Way To Spend an Evening; "Murder" He Says; The Music Stopped; My Dream of the Big Parade; My Own; On the Sunny Side of the Street; Picture Me Without You; Say a Prayer for the Boys Over There; Say It (Over and Over Again); Singin' the Blues; South American Way; Thank You for a Lovely Evening; Too Young To Go Steady; When My Sugar Walks down the Street, All the Birdies Go Tweet-Tweet-Tweet; Where Are You; With All My Heart; You Say the Nicest Things, Baby; You're a Sweetheart; You're an Angel

McIntosh, Robbie   Pick Up the Pieces

McIntyre, Lani   The One Rose That's Left in My Heart

McIntyre, Mark   The Money Tree

McIntyre, Owen   Pick Up the Pieces

McIntyre, Roy   Jamaica Farewell

McKay, Albert   Best of My Love

McKee, Frank W.   Cecile Waltz

McKenna, William C.   Has Anybody Here Seen Kelly

McKinley, Ray   My Guy's Come Back

McKuen, Rod   Jean; Love's Been Good to Me; Seasons in the Sun; The World I Used To Know

McLaren, Ivor   Gentlemen, the King

McLean, Don   (Bye Bye) American Pie; Castles in the Air; Vincent

McLellan, C.M.S.   By the Saskatchewan; My Beautiful Lady, or, The Kiss Waltz

McLeod, Marilyn   Let the Heartaches Begin; Love Hangover; That Same Old Feeling

McManus, Patrick   American Made

McMichael, Ted   Hut Sut Song

McNally, Leonard   The Lass of Richmond Hill

McPhail, Lindsay   San

McPherson, James   Jane

McPherson, R.C.   All In Down and Out; Josephine, My Joe

McRae, Floyd F.   Sh-Boom

McRae, Teddy   Traffic Jam

McTell, Ralph   Streets of London

McVea, Jack   Open the Door, Richard

McVie, Christine   Don't Stop; Got a Hold on Me; Hold Me; Say You Love Me; Think About Me; You Make Lovin' Fun

Maalfrid, Lea   You Could Have Been with Me

Macaulay, Tony   Alibis; Build Me Up Buttercup; Don't Give

Up on Us; Gasoline Alley Bred; Home Lovin' Man; Last Night I Didn't Get To Sleep At All; Let the Heartaches Begin; Lights of Cincinnati; Love Grows; That Same Old Feeling; You Won't Find Another Fool Like Me

Macbeth, Allan   Forget-Me-Not

Mack, Andrew   Heart of My Heart (I Love You), or, The Story of the Rose; My Pearl's a Bowery Girl

Mack, Cecil   All In Down and Out; Charleston; Down Among the Sugar Cane; He's a Cousin of Mine; If He Comes In, I'm Going Out; Old-Fashioned Love; S-H-I-N-E; Teasing; That Minor Strain; That's Why They Call Me "Shine"; You're in the Right Church, But the Wrong Pew

Mack, Ronald   He's So Fine

Mackay, Charles   Baby Mine; Cheer, Boys, Cheer

Mackay, David   That's Livin' Alright

Mackeben, Theo   I Give My Heart

Mackechnie, A.L.   For All Eternity

MacKenzie, Len   (I'm) Chiquita Banana

Macklin, Cecil   Too Much Mustard (Très Moutarde)

Maclagan, T.   Captain Jinks of the Horse Marines

Macy, J.C.   Goodnight, Little Girl, Goodnight

Madara, John   One-Two-Three; You Don't Own Me

Madden, Edward   Blue Bell; By the Light of the Silvery Moon; The Chanticleer Rag; Consolation; Daddy's Little Girl; Down in Jungle Town; I'd Rather Be a Lobster Than a Wise Guy; I've Taken Quite a Fancy to You; (Look Out for) Jimmy Valentine; The Lanky Yankee Boys in Blue; The Leader of the German Band; A Little Boy Called "Taps"; (On) Moonlight Bay; My Cousin Caruso; Please Come and Play in My Yard; She Waits by the Deep Blue Sea; Silver Bell; Starlight; Two Blue Eyes; Two Little Baby Shoes; Way Down in My Heart, or, I've Got a Feeling for You; When You Wore a Pinafore; A Wise Old Owl

Madden, Frank   Maybe

Madison, Nat   My Cabin of Dreams

Madonna   Into the Groove; Live To Tell; Lucky Star

Madriguera, Enrico   Adios

Maeder, James Gaspard   You'll Meet Me, Won't You

Magenta, Guy   Once in Every Lifetime

Magidson, Herb   Conchita, Marquita, Lolita, Pepita, Rosita, Juanita Lopez; The Continental; Enjoy Yourself, It's Later Than You Think; Gone with the Wind; Good Night Angel; Here's to Romance; I'll Buy That Dream; I'll Dance at Your Wedding; I'm Stepping Out with a Memory Tonight; It's Time To Say Goodnight; Linger in My Arms a Little Longer Baby; (I'm Afraid) The Masquerade Is Over; Midnight in Paris; Music, Maestro, Please; A Needle in a Haystack; The Organ Grinder; Say a Prayer for the Boys Over There; Singin' in the Bathtub; Twinkle, Twinkle, Little Star; Violins from Nowhere

Magine, Frank   By the Shalimar; Dreamy Melody

Magness, Cliff   All I Need

Maguire, Sylvester   If I Had a Thousand Lives To Live

Mahoney, Jack   Bing! Bang! Bing 'Em on the Rhine; Every Day Will Be Sunday When the Town Goes Dry; A Ring on the Finger Is Worth Two on the Phone; When You Wore a Tulip and I Wore a Big Red Rose; While Others Are Building Castles in the Air (I'll Build a Cottage for Two)

Maiden, Tony Sweet Thing

Maker, Frederick Beneath the Cross of Jesus

Malcolm, Frederick Nice People (with Nice Habits); Oh Charley Take It Away

Malie, Tommie Jealous; Looking at the World Through Rose-Colored Glasses

Malkin, Norman Hay Mister Banjo

Mallet, David Rule, Britannia

Mallette, Wanda Just Another Woman in Love

Malloy, David Drivin' My Life Away; Gone Too Far; I Love a Rainy Night; Love Will Turn You Around; Real Love; Someone Could Lose a Heart Tonight; Step by Step; Suspicions

Malneck, Matt Eeny Meeny Miney Moe; Goody Goody; If You Were Mine; I'll Never Be the Same; I'm Through with Love; Pardon My Southern Accent; Stairway to the Stars (Park Avenue Fantasy)

Malotte, Albert Hay Ferdinand the Bull; The Lord's Prayer; Song of the Open Road

Malpadi, N. La Musica Prohibita

Maltby, Richard Jr. Baby Baby Baby; Capped Teeth and Caesar Salad; I Want It All; Lounging At the Waldorf; Romance; The Story Goes On; Unexpected Song

Malvin, Arthur Let Me Be Your Sugar Baby

Mamberg, Jerry I Love Rock 'n' Roll

Manchester, Melissa Midnight Blue; Whenever I Call You "Friend"

Mancini, Henry Baby Elephant Walk; Breakfast at Tiffany's; (Theme from) Charade; Days of Wine and Roses; Dear Heart; The Great Imposter; (Theme from) Hatari; In the Arms of Love; Life in a Looking Glass; Mr. Lucky; Moment to Moment; Moon River; (Theme from) Peter Gunn; (Theme from) The Pink Panther; The Sweetheart Tree; There's Enough To Go Around; (Theme from) Two for the Road; Wait Until Dark

Mandel, John Emily; (Song from) M*A*S*H; The Shadow of Your Smile

Mandel, Mel African Waltz

Mangione, Chuck Feels So Good; Give It All You Got

Manilow, Barry Copacabana (At the Copa); Could It Be Magic; Even Now; I Made It Through the Rain; It's a Miracle

Manker, Sidney Raunchy

Manlio, Tito Anema e Core (With All My Heart and Soul)

Mann, Barry Blame It on the Bossa Nova; Footsteps; Here You Come Again; I Love How You Love Me; Just Once; Kicks; Never Gonna Let You Go; On Broadway; Patches; Somewhere Out There; (You're My) Soul and Inspiration; Who Put the Bomp (in the Bomp Ba Bomp Ba Bomp); You've Lost That Lovin' Feelin'

Mann, Billy Shut the Door (They're Comin' Through the Window)

Mann, Dave Boutonniere; Dearie; Don't Go to Strangers;

Downhearted; No Moon At All; Somebody Bad Stole De Wedding Bell; There! I've Said It Again

Mann, Kal Bristol Stomp; The Cha Cha Cha; Let's Twist Again; Loddy Lo; South Street; Swingin' School; (Let Me Be Your) Teddy Bear; Twistin' U.S.A.; The Wah-Watusi; Wild One

Mann, Manfred Five-Four-Three-Two-One

Mann, Paul And So Do I; The Finger of Suspicion Points at You; Invitation to a Broken Heart; Put Your Dreams Away for Another Day; They Say

Mann, Rita Passing Strangers

Manne, Joe Meet Me in Bubble Land

Manners, Henry We Could Make Such Beautiful Music (Together)

Manners, Zeke Pennsylvania Polka

Manney, Charles F. O Cuba (Tu)

Manning, Dick Allegheny Moon; Don't Stay Away Too Long; Fascination; Gilly Gilly Ossenfeffer; The Hawaiian Wedding Song; Hot Diggity (Dog Ziggity Boom); Ivy Rose; Jilted; Mama Teach Me To Dance; The Morning Side of the Mountain; O Dio Mio; Papa Loves Mambo; La Plume de Ma Tante; Secretly; Takes Two To Tango; While the Angelus Was Ringing

Manning, Kathleen Lockhart In the Luxembourg Gardens

Manston, Frere Abergavenny

Manston, Irene Jezamine

Mantovani, A.P. Toyshop Ballet

Manus, Jack Midnight Masquerade

Manzanero, Canche A. It's Impossible

Manzarek, Raymond Hello, I Love You (Won't You Tell Me Your Name); Light My Fire

Marais, Josef A-Round the Corner (Beneath the Berry Tree); John Anderson, My Jo

Marascalco, John Good Golly Miss Molly

Marbet, Rolf Call Me Darling

Marble, E.S. Eileen Allanna

Marcello, Marco Marcelliano Angel's Serenade

Marchetti, F.D. Fascination, or, Valse Tzigane

Marcotte, Don I Think of You; I'm (Dreaming) Thinking Tonight of My Blue Eyes

Marcucci, Robert P. Why

Marcus, Sol Ask Anyone Who Knows; I Don't Want To Set the World on Fire; Till Then; When the Lights Go On Again (All Over the World)

Mares, Paul Farewell Blues; Make Love to Me; Milenberg Joys; Tin Roof Blues

Maresca, Ernie Runaround Sue; The Wanderer

Margetson, E.J. Tommy, Lad

Margis, Alfred Valse Bleue

Maria, Antonio A Day in the Life of a Fool

Marie, Gabriel La Cinquantaine

Marinos, Jimmy Talking in Your Sleep

Marion, Dave Her Eyes Don't Shine Like Diamonds; Only One Girl in the World for Me

Marion, George Jr. The Ladies Who Sing with the Band; My Future Just Passed; My Sweeter Than Sweet; Rastus on Parade; Sigh by Night; When the Nylons Bloom Again

Marion, Will Who Dat Say Chicken in Dis Crowd

Mark, Lowell Look Around (You'll Find Me There)

Markes, Lawrence W. I Tipped My Hat and Slowly Rode Away

Marks, Charley Where Do You Work-a John

Marks, Edward B. December and May, or, Mollie Newell Don't Be Cruel; His Last Thoughts Were of You; The Little Lost Child; Mother Was a Lady, or, If Jack Were Only Here; No One Ever Loved You More Than I

Marks, Gerald All of Me; Is It True What They Say About Dixie; That's What I Want for Christmas; You're the One (You Beautiful Son-of-a-Gun)

Marks, Godfrey Sailing (,Sailing) (over the Bounding Main)

Marks, Guy Loving You Has Made Me Bananas

Marks, John D. I Heard the Bells on Christmas Day; Rudolph the Red-Nosed Reindeer

Marks, Larry Along the Navajo Trail

Marks, Walter Bajour; How Could I Be So Wrong; I've Got To Be Me; Words, Words, Words

Markush, Fred Take Me in Your Arms

Markwell, Mark Secretly

Marley, Bob I Shot the Sheriff

Marlow, Ric A Taste of Honey

Marriott, Steve Itchycoo Park

Marsala, Joe And So To Sleep Again; Don't Cry, Joe; Little Sir Echo

Marsden, Gerrard Don't Let the Sun Catch You Crying; Ferry 'Cross the Mersey; I'm the One

Marsh, Roy K. I Never Knew I Could Love Anybody Like I'm Loving You

Marsh, Simeon Butler Jesus, Lover of My Soul

Marshall, Charles I Hear You Calling Me

Marshall, Ed Venus

Marshall, Henry I. Be My Little Baby Bumblebee; Malinda; Mary, You're a Little Bit Old-Fashioned; On the 5:15; You Can't Stop Me from Loving You

Marshall, Jim In America

Marshall, Sherman Then Came You

Martens, Frederick Herman Gesù Bambino; Júrame (Promise, Love); Grant Those Glances; O Cuba (Tu); Princesita

Martin, Bill Congratulations; Puppet on a String; Saturday Night; Till We Two Are One

Martin, Easthope Come to the Fair; Evensong

Martin, Freddy I Look at Heaven; Tonight We Love

Martin, Herbert I'm All Smiles; Why Did I Choose You

Martin, Hugh The Boy Next Door; Buckle Down, Winsocki; Connecticut; Ev'ry Time; Have Yourself a Merry Little Christmas; Home Sweet Heaven; Love; An Occasional Man; Pass That Peace Pipe; Shady Lady Bird; That's How I Love the Blues; The Trolley Song; Wish I May; You'd Better Love Me (While You May)

Martin, J.D. I Still Do

Martin, Larry Till We Two Are One

Martin, Lennie Since I Don't Have You

Martin, Nichola Now Those Days Are Gone

Martin, R. Once Upon a Wintertime

Martin, Sam You Call Everybody Darling

Martine, Layng Jr. Should I Do It

Martinoli, Carlos Love Me with All Your Heart

Martins, Rudy Ninety-Six Tears

Marvell, Holt These Foolish Things (Remind Me of You); The World Is Mine (Tonight)

Marvin, Hank B. Dancing Shoes; Foot Tapper; Gee Whiz, It's You; Genie with the Light Brown Lamp; Geronimo; I Could Easily Fall; On the Beach; Rise and Fall of Flingle Bunt; Sam; Shindig; Time Drags By

Marx, Richard Ask Any Mermaid; Crazy; What About Me

Marzials, Theophile Twickenham Ferry

Mascagni, Pietro Intermezzo

Mascheroni, Angelo For All Eternity

Maschwitz, Eric At the Balalaika; Climbing Up; Goodnight Vienna; He Wears a Pair of Silver Wings; Mademoiselle de Paris; A Nightingale Sang in Berkeley Square; Room Five Hundred and Four

Masefield, John Roadways

Mason, Barbara Yes, I'm Ready

Mason, Barry Delilah; Don't Turn Around; Here It Comes Again; The Last Waltz; Love Grows; Love Is All; A Man Without Love; Turn Around

Mason, Gerry I'll Think of You

Mason, James H. I Dig Rock and Roll Music

Mason, John Open the Door, Richard

Mason, Lowell From Greenland's Icy Mountains; Joy to the World, or, Antioch; My Faith Looks Up to Thee; Safely Through Another Week; Work For the Night Is Coming

Mason, Marilyn Love Takes Time

Mason, Mrs. Caroline A. Do They Miss Me at Home

Massenet, Jules Aragonaise; Élégie; Méditation

Masser, Michael Do You Know Where You're Going To, or, Theme from *Mahogany;* Greatest Love of All; If Ever You're in My Arms Again; It's My Turn; Saving All My Love for You; Tonight I Celebrate My Love; Touch Me in the Morning

Massey, Guy The Prisoner's Song

Massey, Louise My Adobe Hacienda

Masters, Frankie Scatterbrain

Matassa, C. Just a Dream

Mather, Robert Sexy Eyes

Mathieson, Gregg Heaven Knows; Telefone

Matkosky, Dennis Maniac

Matson, Vera Love Me Tender

Mattei, Titto 'Tis Not True

Matthews, Artie Weary Blues

Matthews, David We're Gonna Change the World

Matthews, J. Sherrie   Hey, Rube!

Matthews, Red-Chuck   White Silver Sands

Maurer, J. Ward   Get Wildroot Cream-Oil Charlie

Maurice, Peter   Silver Hair and Heart of Gold

Maxfield, Mike   The Cruel Sea

Maxwell, Robert   Ebb Tide; Shangri-La

May, Brian   Flash

May, Hans   Break of Day; Love Steals Your Heart; My Song Goes Round the World; Starlight Serenade; Throw Open Wide Your Window; The Windsor Waltz

May, Johnny   Now and Forever

May, Winifred   Jalousie (Jealousy)

Maybrick, Michael, *see* **Stephen Adams**

Mayer, Henry   My Melody of Love; Now

Mayerl, Billy   Autumn Crocus; Did Tosti Raise His Bowler Hat When He Said Goodbye; Hollyhock; Marigold

Mayfield Curtis   He Don't Love You Like I Love You; It's All Right; Let's Do It Again; Look into Your Heart; Sparkle; Um, Um, Um, Um, Um, Um

Mayfield, Percy   Hit the Road Jack

Mayhew, Billy   It's a Sin To Tell a Lie

Mayne, Martyn   I Remember the Cornfields

Mayo, Sam   I Know Where the Flies Go in the Wintertime

Mayo, Will H.   Where the Chicken Got the Axe

Mazzini, Pietro   For All Eternity; Se Saran Rose, or, Melba Waltz

Meacham, F.W.   American Patrol (We Must Be Vigilant)

Meade, Norman   One Way Love

Meadows, Fred   You Were Only Foolin'

Meadows, Jack   Big Head

Meara, D.O.   Buy a Broom, or, The Bavarian Girl's Song

Mears, John   I Found the End of the Rainbow

Medley, Philip   Twist and Shout

Medora, John   At the Hop

Meek, Joe   Don't You Think It's Time; Globetrotter; Ice Cream Man; Robot; Telstar

Meekaaeel, Muhammed   Ladies Night

Mehlinger, Artie   Hiawatha's Melody of Love

Meilhac, H.   Toreador Song

Meinken, Fred   The Wabash Blues

Meisner, Randy   Take It to the Limit

Melcher, Terry   Getcha Back; Move Over Darling

Mellencamp, John Cougar   Hurt So Good; Jack and Diane; R.O.C.K. in the USA (A Salute to 60's Rock); Small Town

Mellin, Robert   I'm Yours; My One and Only Love; Stranger on the Shore; You, You, You

Mellish, Colonel R.   Drink to Me Only with Thine Eyes

Mellor, Tom   Come Along My Mandy; I Wouldn't Leave My Little Wooden Hut for You; Kitty the Telephone Girl; When It's Apple Blossom Time in Normandy

Melody, Lord, *see* **Fitzroy Alexander**

Melrose, Walter   High Society (March); Make Love to Me; Tin Roof Blues

Melsner, Irving   Roses in the Rain

Melson, Joe   Blue Bayou; Cryin'; Only the Lonely (Know the Way I Feel); Running Scared

Melville, C.J. Whyte   Drink, Puppy, Drink

Mencher, Murray (Ted Murry)   Don't Break the Heart That Loves You; Flowers for Madame; Follow the Boys; An Old Water Mill; On the Bumpy Road to Love; Ro-Ro-Rollin' Along; Throw Another Log on the Fire; You Can't Pull the Wool over My Eyes

Mendelssohn, Felix   Hark the Herald Angels Sing; O Word of God Incarnate; On Wings of Song; Spring Song; Wedding March

Mendelssohn, Fred   Don't Be Angry

Mendez, Ricardo Lopez   Amor; Stars in Your Eyes

Mendonca, Newton   Desafinado (Slightly Out of Tune)

Mendoza y Cortéz, Quirino   Cielito Lindo (Ay, Ay, Ay, Ay)

Menendez, Nilo   Green Eyes

Menken, Alan   Little Shop of Horrors; Somewhere That's Green; Suddenly Seymour

Menten, Dale   A Scumpdillyishus Day

Mercer, Johnny   Ac-cent-tchu-ate the Positive; And So to Bed; And the Angels Sing; Any Place I Hang My Hat Is Home; Arthur Murray Taught Me Dancing in a Hurry; Aunt Jemima and Your Uncle Cream of Wheat; Autumn Leaves; Baby Doll; The Bad Humor Man; Barefoot in the Park; Bilbao Song; Blues in the Night; Bob White (Whatcha Gonna Swing Tonight); (Theme from) Charade; Come Rain or Come Shine; Cuckoo in the Clock; Day Dreaming; Day In—Day Out; Days of Wine and Roses; Dearly Beloved; Dream (When You're Feeling Blue); Early Autumn; Eeny Meeny Miney Mo; Emily; The Fleet's In; Fools Rush In; The G.I. Jive; Goody Goody; Have You Got Any Cares, Baby; Here Come the British (Bang! Bang!); Here Come the Waves; Hit the Road to Dreamland; Hooray for Hollywood; How Little We Know; I Remember You; I Wanna Be Around; I Wonder What Became of Me; If I Had My Druthers; If You Were Mine; I'm an Old Cowhand (from the Rio Grande); I'm Building Up to an Awful Let-Down; I'm Like a Fish Out of Water; I'm Old Fashioned; In the Cool, Cool, Cool of the Evening; Jeepers Creepers; Jubilation T. Cornpone; June Comes Around Every Year; Laura; Lazy Bones; Legalize My Name; Let's Take the Long Way Home; Lost; Love in a Home; Love Is Where You Find It; Love of My Life; Love with the Proper Stranger; Midnight Sun; Mister Meadowlark; Moment to Moment; Moon River; My Shining Hour; Namely You; Not Mine; On the Atchison, Topeka, and the Santa Fe; One for My Baby (and One More for the Road); Out of This World; Pardon My Southern Accent; P.S. I Love You; Ride, Tenderfoot, Ride; Ridin' on the Moon; Satin Doll; Skylark; Sobbin' Women; Something's Gotta Give; Spring, Spring, Spring; Sunday, Monday or Always; The Sweetheart Tree; Tangerine; That Old Black Magic; This Time the Dream's on Me; Too Marvelous for Words; (I Had Myself a) True Love; Wait and See; The Waiter and the Porter and the Upstairs Maid; What's Good for General Bullmoose; When a Woman Loves a Man; When the World Was Young (Ah, the Apple Tree); You Have Taken My Heart; You Must Have Been a Beautiful Baby; You Were Never Lovelier; You've Got Me Where You Want Me

Mercury, Freddie   Bohemian Rhapsody; Crazy Little Thing Called Love; Killer Queen

Merenstein, Charles   Handy Man

Merriam, Charles D.   Fly Like an Eagle

Merrick, Mahlon   To Look Sharp

Merrill, Alan   I Love Rock 'n' Roll

Merrill, Bob   (It Was) Always You; Belle, Belle, My Liberty Belle; Candy and Cake; Did You Close Your Eyes (When We Kissed); (How Much Is That) Doggie in the Window; Don't Rain on My Parade; Funny Girl; Honeycomb; If I Knew You Were Comin' I'd've Baked a Cake; I'm the Greatest Star; It's Good To Be Alive; Look At 'Er; Love Makes the World Go Round, or, Theme from *Carnival;* Make Yourself Comfortable; Mambo Italiano; Mira; My Truly, Truly Fair; People; Pittsburgh, Pennsylvania; Promise Me a Rose; Sparrow in the Tree Top; Staying Young; Sunshine Girl; A Sweet Old-Fashioned Girl; Take Me Along; Theme from *The Wonderful World of the Brothers Grimm;* Tina Marie; Walkin' to Missouri; You Are Woman (I Am Man)

Merrill, George   How Will I Know

Mersey, Robert D.   Jungle Boogie

Merson, Billy   The Photo of the Girl I Left Behind; The Spaniard That (Who) Blighted My Life

Mertz, Paul M.   I'm Glad There Is You

Meshel, Billy   (Theme from) The Godfather (Waltz)

Meskill, Jack   Au Revoir, Pleasant Dreams; (It Happened) On the Beach at Bali Bali; Rhythm of the Rain; Smile, Darn Ya, Smile; There's Danger in Your Eyes, Cherie; Wonderful You

Messager, André   Fortunio's Song (Fortunio); The Garden of Love; Long Ago in Alcala

Messenheimer, Sam   Singing a Vagabond Song

Metcalf, Gerald   Prisoner of Hope

Metcalf, John W.   Absent

Metcalf, Steven   Lean on Me

Methven, Florence   When You Look in the Heart of a Rose

Metz, Theodore M.   (There'll Be) A Hot Time in the Old Town (Tonight)

Meyer, Charles   Suddenly There's a Valley

Meyer, George W.   Bring Back My Daddy to Me; Bring Back My Golden Dreams; Brown Eyes—Why Are You Blue; Dear Old Rose; Everything Is Peaches Down in Georgia; For Me and My Gal; A Girlie Was Made To Love; Hiawatha's Melody of Love; Honey-Love; I'm a Little Blackbird Looking for a Bluebird; I'm Awfully Glad I Met You; In the Land of Beginning Again; Just Like Washington Crossed the Delaware, General Pershing Will Cross the Rhine; Mandy Make Up Your Mind; My Mother's Rosary; My Song of the Nile; A Ring on the Finger Is Worth Two on the Phone; Since Maggie Dooley Learned the Hooley Hooley; Sittin' in a Corner; Somebody Else, It's Always Somebody Else; The Mellow Melody; That Was Before I Met You; There Are Such Things; There'll Be a Hot Time for the Old Men When the Young Men Go to War; There's a Dixie Girl Who's Longing For a Yankee Doodle Boy; There's a Little Lane Without a Turning on the Way to Home Sweet Home; Tuck Me to Sleep in My Old 'Tucky Home; Way Down in Iowa I'm Going To Hide Away; When You're a Long, Long Way from Home; Where Did Robinson Crusoe Go with Friday on Saturday Night?; You Taught Me How To Love You, Now Teach Me To Forget; You're Dancing on My Heart

Meyer, Joseph   California, Here I Come; Clap Hands, Here Comes Charley; Crazy Rhythm; A Cup of Coffee, a Sandwich and You; Falling in Love with You; Golden Gate; Happy Go Lucky Lane; Headin' for Louisville; I Wish I Were Twins; If You Knew Susie, Like I Know Susie; It's Time To Say Goodnight; A Little More Love; My Honey's Lovin' Arms; Passe

Meyerbeer, Giacomo   Coronation March

Meyer-Lutz, Wilhelm   Skirt Dance (*as* Meyer W. Lutz)

Meyers, Billy   Bugle Call Rag; Nobody's Sweetheart Now

Meyers, Richard   Hold My Hand

Michael, George   Careless Whisper; Everything She Wants; I'm Your Man; Wake Me Up Before You Go-Go

Michaels, Sidney   Hic, Haec, Hoc

Michels, Walter   San

Mickens, Robert   Celebration

Middlebrooks, Ralph   Fire; Love Rollercoaster

Midnight, Charlie   Living in America

Migliacci, Francesco   Addio Addio, or, Goodbye; Son of a Travelin' Man; Volare, or, Nel Blu, Dipinto Di Blu

Miles, Alfred Hart   Anchors Aweigh

Miles, C. Austin   (He Walks with Me) In the Garden

Miles, Dick   The Coffee Song (They've Got an Awful Lot of Coffee in Brazil)

Miles, John   Music

Millan, Armando Oliveros   My Toreador

Millard, Harrison   Angel's Serenade; My Ideal; Viva l'America: Home of the Free; Waiting

Miller, Anne Stratton   Boats of Mine

Miller, Charles   The Cisco Kid; Gypsy Man; Summer; When Your Love Grows Cold; Why Can't We Be Friends; You Remind Me of the Girl That Used To Go to School with Me

Miller, Eddie   Release Me

Miller, Frank   Greenfields; If You're Irish Come into the Parlour; Marianne; Memories Are Made of This

Miller, Glenn   Moonlight Serenade

Miller, Helen   Follow the Gleam

Miller, Henry S.   The Cat Came Back

Miller, Herb   Night

Miller, Ned   Dark Moon; Sunday; Why Should I Cry Over You; You Don't Like It—Not Much

Miller, Robin   Choo-Choo Honeymoon; The Sailor of My Dreams

Miller, Roger   Dang Me; England Swings (Like a Pendulum Do); Hand for the Hog; How Blest We Are; King of the Road; Muddy Water

Miller, Ronald   For Once in My Life; Heaven Help Us All; I've Never Been to Me; A Place in the Sun; Robert and Elizabeth; Touch Me in the Morning; Yester-Me, Yester-You, Yesterday

Miller, Sonnie   Got a Date with an Angel

Miller, Sonny By Candlelight; Don't Ring-a Da Bell; Russian Rose; Seventeen Candles; Silver Wings in the Moonlight; Starlight Serenade; Till Stars Forget To Shine; Where the Waters Are Blue

Miller, Steve Abracadabra; The Joker; Rock'n Me

Miller, William Daddy's Home

Milligan, Spike The Snow Goose

Milliken, Richard Alfred The Groves of Blarney

Millöcker, Carl I Give My Heart

Mills, A.J. By the Side of the Zuyder Zee; Do You Remember the Last Waltz; Everybody's Crazy on the Foxtrot; Fall In and Follow Me; Just Like the Ivy; Ship Ahoy, or, All the Nice Girls Love a Sailor; Take Me Back to Dear Old Blighty; What Ho She Bumps; Why Did I Leave My Little Back Room

Mills, Annette The Badge from Your Coat; Boomps-a-Daisy; The Feather in Her Tyrolean Hat

Mills, Gordon I'll Never Get Over You; I'm the Lonely One; It's Not Unusual

Mills, Irving Blue Lou; Blues in My Heart; Boneyard Shuffle; Caravan; (What Has Become of) Hinky Dinky Parlay Voo; I Let a Song Go Out of My Heart; In a Sentimental Mood; It Don't Mean a Thing If It Ain't Got That Swing; Lovesick Blues; Minnie the Moocher, or, The Ho De Ho Song; Mood Indigo; Moonglow; Nobody Knows What a Red Head Mama Can Do; The Organ Grinder's Swing; Prelude to a Kiss; Ring Dem Bells; Riverboat Shuffle; Rockin' in Rhythm; Sidewalks of Cuba; Solitude; Sophisticated Lady; Straighten Up and Fly Right; There's No Two Ways About Love; When My Sugar Walks Down the Street, All the Birdies Go Tweet-Tweet-Tweet

Mills, Jay Ev'ry Day Away from You

Mills, Kerry Any Old Port in a Storm; At a Georgia Camp Meeting; Happy Days in Dixie; Let Bygones Be Bygones; The Longest Way 'Round Is the Sweetest Way Home; Meet Me in St. Louis, Louis; Rastus on Parade; Red Wing; Take Me Around Again; When the Bees Are in the Hive; Whistling Rufus

Mills, Nat Nice People (with Nice Habits)

Mills, Wilfred My Ain Folk

Milman, Henry Hart Ride On, Ride On

Milne, A.A. Christopher Robin at Buckingham Palace; Christopher Robin Is Saying His Prayers

Milton, Jay Travelin' Band

Mindel, David Richard (Our Love) Don't Throw It All Away

Miner, Raynard (Your Love Has Lifted Me) Higher and Higher

Minnigerode, Meade The Whiffenpoof Song

Minor, George Bringing in the Sheaves

Minucci, Ulpio Domani (Tomorrow)

Miron (Michrovsky), Issacher Tzena, Tzena, Tzena

Misraki, Paul I Love To Sing

Mitchell, Charles You Are My Sunshine

Mitchell, J.F. Never Take No for an Answer

Mitchell, James Jr. Float On

Mitchell, Joni Both Sides Now; Chelsea Morning; Michael from Mountains

Mitchell, Mel Petticoats of Portugal

Mitchell, Paul Tryin' To Love Two

Mitchell, Sidney D. All My Life; Bluin' the Blues; Laughing Irish Eyes; Mammy's Chocolate Soldier; A Melody from the Sky; Seventh Heaven; She Wouldn't Do What I Asked Her To; Sugar; Toy Trumpet; Twilight on the Trail; Would You Rather Be a Colonel with an Eagle on Your Shoulder, or a Private with a Chicken on Your Knee?; You Do the Darndest Things, Baby; You Turned the Tables on Me

Mitchell, Steve Jump (For My Love)

Mitchell, Willie Let's Stay Together

Mittenthal, Joseph What's the Use of Loving If You Can't Love All the Time

Mizell, Alphonso J. ABC; I Want You Back; Mama's Pearl

Mizzy, Vic The Jones Boy; My Dreams Are Getting Better All the Time; Take It Easy; Three Little Sisters; The (Whole) World Is Singing My Song

Mockridge, Cyril It's a Woman's World

Modugno, Domenico Addio, Addio, or, Goodbye; Ciao Ciao Bambina; Volare, or, Nel Blu, Dipinto Di Blu

Moeller, Tommy Concrete and Clay

Moffat, John Still Doin' Time

Mogol Al-Di-La; Help Yourself; I Who Have Nothing

Mogulesco, Sigmund Mazel Tov

Mohr, Halsey K. Liberty Bell—It's Time To Ring Again; Piney Ridge; They're Wearing 'Em Higher in Hawaii

Mohr, Joseph Silent Night, Holy Night

Moll, Billy Gid-ap, Garibaldi; (I Scream, You Scream, We All Scream for) Ice Cream; Moonlight on the Colorado; Ro-Ro-Rollin' Along; Wrap Your Troubles in Dreams (and Dream Your Troubles Away)

Möller, Friedrich The Happy Wanderer

Molloy, James Lyman The Kerry Dance; Love's Old Sweet Song; The Vagabond

Molneck, Matt Shangri-La

Moman, Chips (Hey Won't You Play) Another Somebody Done Somebody Wrong Song

Monaco, James V. An Apple for the Teacher; April Played the Fiddle; Beatrice Fairfax, Tell Me What To Do; Crazy People; Dirty Hands, Dirty Face; East Side of Heaven; Go Fly a Kite; Hang Your Heart on a Hickory Limb; I Can't Begin To Tell You; I Miss You Most of All; If We Can't Be the Same Old Sweethearts, We'll Just Be the Same Old Friends; I'm Making Believe; My Heart Is Taking Lessons; Oh You Circus Day; On the Sentimental Side; Only Forever; Pigeon Walk; (I've Got) A Pocketful of Dreams; Red Lips Kiss My Blues Away; Rhythm on the River; Row, Row, Row; Shave and a Haircut, Bay Rum; Six Lessons from Madame LaZonga; Sweet Potato Piper; That Sly Old Gentleman from Featherbed Lane; That's for Me; Through; Too Romantic; What Do You Want To Make Those Eyes At Me For; You Know You Belong to Somebody Else; You Made Me Love You (I Didn't Want To Do It); You're Gonna Lose Your Gal

Monckton, Lionel Arcady Is Ever Young; The Boy Guessed Right; Bring Me a Rose; Come to the Ball; The Girl with a Brogue; Little Miss Melody; Moonstruck; My Dear Little

Cingalee; The Pearl of Sweet Ceylon; The Pipes of Pan; The Pipes of Pan Are Calling; (Oh I Love) Society; The Soldiers in the Park; The Temple Bell; Tony from America; The Toy Monkey, or, I'm a Monkey on a Stick; Toy Town; Try Again Johnnie; Under the Deodar; When You Are in Love; Whisper to Me

Monk, Thelonious   Fifty-Second Street Theme

Monk, William Henry   Abide with Me, or, Fast Falls the Eventide

Monnot, Marguerite A.   Dis-Donc, Dis-Donc; If You Love Me (I Won't Care); Irma La Douce; Just Come Home; Milord; Our Language of Love; The Poor People of Paris

Monod, F.   La Seine

Monroe, Bill   Kentucky Waltz

Monroe, Vaughn   Racing with the Moon

Montgomery, Bob   Misty Blue

Montgomery, Garth   (I'm) Chiquita Banana

Montgomery, James   Angels from the Realms of Glory; Forever with the Lord

Montgomery, Marshall   Pal of My Cradle Days

Montgomery, Reggie   Gee, But I'd Like To Make You Happy; My Kid's a Crooner

Monti, Vittorio   Czardas

Montieth, A.   Whosoever Will May Come

Montrose, Percy   (Oh, My Darling) Clementine

Moody, Philip   Ça C'est Paris

Moody, Russell   Wear My Ring Around Your Neck

Moore, Charles   Call Round Any Old Time

Moore, Daniel   My Maria; Shambala

Moore, Dudley   Duddly Dell

Moore, Elizabeth Evelyn   Laroo Laroo Lilli Bolero

Moore, Fleecie   Caldonia (What Makes Your Big Head So Hard)

Moore, Hal   Patsy Ory Ory Aye (A-Workin' on the Railroad)

Moore, John Charles   Has Anybody Here Seen Kelly

Moore, Marvin   The Four Walls; The Green Door; I Dreamed

Moore, Phil   Blow Out the Candle; Shoo-Shoo Baby

Moore, Raymond   Sweet Marie; When Sweet Marie Was Sweet Sixteen

Moore, Robin   The Ballad of the Green Berets

Moore, Thomas   Araby's Daughter; Believe Me If All Those Endearing Young Charms; Canadian Boat Song; The Girl I Left Behind Me, or, Brighton Camp; The Harp That Once Thro' Tara's Halls; Let Erin Remember the Days of Old; Mary's Tears; The Minstrel Boy (to the War Has Gone); My Heart and Lute; Oft in the Stilly Night; Rich and Rare Were the Gems She Wore; There's Nothing True But Heaven; 'Tis the Last Rose of Summer

Moore, Warren   My Girl Has Gone; The Tracks of My Tears

Moorhouse, Alan   Boom Bang-A-Bang; The World Cup March

Mora, Helene   Kathleen

Moraine, Lyle L.   Christmas Island

Morakis, Takis   Boy on a Dolphin

Morales, Carlton   Valotte

Morales, Noro   Bim Bam Boom

Moran, Edward P.   The Morning After the Night Before; No Wedding Bells for Me; Put On Your Slippers and Fill Up Your Pipe

Morbelli, R.   Botch-A-Me

More, Julian   Dis-Donc, Dis-Donc; Irma La Douce; Our Language of Love

Morehead, Jim   Sentimental Me

Morelle, Ray   Bouquet (I Shall Always Think of You)

Moret, Neil   Cherry (as Charles N. Daniels); Chloe (as Charles N. Daniels); Hiawatha; Mickey; Moonlight and Roses (Bring Mem'ries of You) (as Charles N. Daniels); On Mobile Bay; Peggy; Persian Rug (as Charles N. Daniels); (I Got a Woman Crazy for Me) She's Funny That Way; Song of the Wanderer; You Tell Me Your Dream, or, I Had a Dream, Dear (as Charles N. Daniels)

Moretti, Raoul   Under a Roof in Paree

Morey, Larry   Ferdinand the Bull; Heigh-Ho; I'm Wishin'; One Song; Some Day My Prince Will Come; (Just) Whistle While You Work; With a Smile and a Song; The World Owes Me a Living

Morgan, Carey   The Argentines, the Portuguese and the Greeks; Blues My Naughty Sweetie Gives to Me; Bugle Call (Rag); My Greenwich Village Sue; My Own Iona; Sipping Cider Thru' (Through) a Straw

Morgan, Dennis   All Roads Lead to You; Crackers; Fooled by a Feeling; I Was Country When Country Wasn't Cool; I Wouldn't Have Missed It for the World; Kansas City Lights; Nobody; Wish You Were Here; Years

Morgan, Diana   Transatlantic Lullaby

Morgan, Freddy   Hey Mister Banjo

Morgan, George   Candy Kisses

Morgan, James   Don't Bite the Hand That's Feeding You

Morgan, Mary H.   Bless This House

Morgan, Mrs. John P.   Still as the Night

Morgan, Reginald   Count Your Blessings; Down Forget-Me-Not Lane

Morgan, Russ   Does Your Heart Beat for Me; So Tired; Somebody Else Is Taking My Place; You're Nobody 'Til Somebody Loves You

Morley, Thomas   Now Is the Month of Maying

Moroder, Giorgio   Call Me; Flashdance (What a Feeling); Heaven Knows; I Feel Love; Love To Love You Baby; On the Radio; Son of My Father; Take My Breath Away; The Wanderer

Morosco, Oliver   My Wonderful Dream Girl

Moross, Jerome   Lazy Afternoon

Morricone, Ennio   The Good, the Bad and the Ugly

Morris, Doug   Sweet Talkin' Guy

Morris, George Pope   My Mother's Bible; Open Thy Lattice Love; Woodman Spare That Tree

Morris, Harry B.   "Algy," the Piccadilly Johnny with the Little Glass Eye

Morris, Ken   Mister Moon You've Got a Million Sweethearts; Primrose Hill

Morris, Lee   Blue Velvet

Morris, Lily   Why Am I Always the Bridesmaid

Morris, Steveland   The Tears of a Clown

Morrison, Danny   Blaze of Glory

Morrison, Gerard   How Can You Buy Killarney

Morrison, J.   Hail Purdue

Morrison, James   Hello, I Love You (Won't You Tell Me Your Name); Light My Fire

Morrison, Van   Brown Eyed Girl; Domino; Gloria

Morrissey, Will   Covered Wagon Days (March); I'd Like To Be a Sister to a Brother Just Like You

Morrow, Geoff   Can't Smile Without You; In Thoughts of You

Morrow, Morton   One More Kiss; When the Poppies Bloom Again

Morse, Dolly, *see* **Theodora Morse**

Morse, Theodora (Dorothy Terris, Dolly Morse)   Siboney; Three O'Clock in the Morning; (My) Wonderful One

Morse, Theodore F. (D.A. Esrom)   Arrah Wanna; Blue Bell; Consolation; Daddy's Little Girl; Dear Old Girl; Down in Jungle Town; The Good Old U.S.A.; Hail, Hail, the Gang's All Here; Hurray for Baffin's Bay; I'd Rather Be a Lobster Than a Wise Guy; It's Great To Be a Soldier Man; I've Taken Quite a Fancy to You; Just a Little Rocking Chair and You; Keep a Little Cozy Corner in Your Heart for Me; Keep on the Sunny Side; The Lanky Yankee Boys in Blue; The Leader of the German Band; A Little Boy Called "Taps"; Longing For You; M-O-T-H-E-R (A Word That Means the World to Me); Nobody's Little Girl; One Called "Mother" and the Other "Home Sweet Home"; Please Come and Play in My Yard; She Waits by the Deep Blue Sea; She's the Fairest Little Flower Dear Old Dixie Ever Grew (Knew); Starlight; Two Blue Eyes; Two Little Baby Shoes; Two Little Boys; Way Down in My Heart, or, I've Got a Feeling for You; We'll Knock the Heligo—into Heligo—Out of Heligoland; When You Wore a Pinafore; Where the Southern Roses Grow; A Wise Old Owl; Won't You Be My Honey

Morse, Woolson   Ask the Man in the Moon; Love Will Find a Way; A Pretty Girl

Morton, Ferdinand Joseph "Jelly Roll"   Grandpa's Spells; Jelly Roll Blues; King Porter Stomp; Milenberg Joys; Wild Man Blues; Wolverine Blues

Morton, George   The Leader of the Pack

Morton, Hugh   Little Birdies Learning How To Fly; She Is the Belle of New York; Teach Me How To Kiss

Morton, Lionel   Juliet

Morton, Ray   A Cage in the Window

Moscheles, Ignaz   The Merry Swiss Boy

Mosley, Robert   Sha La La

Moss, Jon   Church of the Poison Mind; Do You Really Want To Hurt Me; It's a Miracle; Karma Chameleon; Miss Me Blind; Time (Clock of the Heart)

Moss, Katie   The Floral Dance

Moss, Neil   Holding Back the Years

Mösser, Peter   Morgen—One More Sunrise

Mossman, Ted   Full Moon and Empty Arms; Till the End of Time

Motzan, Otto   After the Dance; Bright Eyes; Mandy 'n' Me

Moy, Sylvia   I Was Made To Love Her; My Cherie Amor; Uptight (Everything's Alright)

Mozart, Wolfgang Amadeus   Away with Melancholy; (Theme from) Elvira Madigan; The Marriage of Figaro (Overture)

Mtume, James   The Closer I Get to You; Never Knew Love Like This Before

Mueller, Bill   That Daffydill Rag

Mueller, Frank   That Daffydill Rag

Mueller, Gus   The Wang, Wang Blues

Mueller, Mark   Nothin' At All

Muir, Lewis F.   Here Comes My Daddy Now—Oh Pop—Oh Pop—Oh Pop; Hitchy-Koo; Mammy Jinny's Jubilee; Play That Barbershop Chord (Mister Jefferson Lord); Ragtime Cowboy Joe; Waiting for the Robert E. Lee

Mullaly, W.S.   The Mottoes Framed Upon the Wall

Mullan, Richard   He; If I Lost You; I'll Find You; My September Love

Mullen, J.B.   Down on the Brandywine

Mullen, R.A.   Baby's Prayer

Mumy, Billy   Bless the Beasts and Children

Munro, Bill   When My Baby Smiles at Me

Munro, Ronnie   All Over Italy; Gertie the Girl with the Gong

Munson, Eddie   Ida, Sweet As Apple Cider

Murden, Orlando   For Once in My Life

Murdoch, Richard   Much Binding in the Marsh

Mure, Billy   Patsy Ory Ory Aye (A-Workin' on the Railroad)

Murphey, Michael   Carolina in the Pines; Disenchanted; Wildfire

Murphy, C.W.   Flanagan; Has Anybody Here Seen Kelly; Hold Your Hand Out Naughty Boy; I Live in Trafalgar Square; Let's All Go Down the Strand; Little Yellow Bird; My Girl's a Yorkshire Girl; Oh Oh Antonio; Put Me Amongst the Girls; She's a Lassie from Lancashire

Murphy, J.B.   Nicodemus Johnson

Murphy, Joseph   A Handful of Earth from (My Dear) Mother's Grave

Murphy, Owen   Señora

Murphy, Ralph   Half the Way; He Got You

Murphy, Stanley   Be My Little Baby Bumblebee; Malinda; Oh! How She Could Yacki, Hacki, Wicki, Wacki, Woo; On the 5:15; Put On Your Old Grey Bonnet; She Took Mother's Advice; They Always Pick On Me; What's the Good of Being Good—When No One's Good to Me

Murphy, Walter   A Fifth of Beethoven

Murrah, Roger   Southern Rains; We're in This Love Together

Murray, Alan   I'll Be Good Because of You; I'll Walk Beside You

Murray, Fred   Boiled Beef and Carrots; Ginger You're Barmy; I'm Henery the Eighth (I Am); Little Bit off the Top; Our Lodger's Such a Nice Young Man

Murray, Jack P.   Do the New York; Happy-Go-Lucky You and Broken-Hearted Me; Two Loves Have I

Murray, James Ramsey   Away in (a) the Manger, or, Luther's Cradle Hymn; Daisy Deane

Murray, Jean   Splish Splash

Murray, John P.   Flapperette; If I Love Again

Murray, Maurice   Crazy Heart

Murray, Mitch   The Ballad of Bonnie and Clyde; Billy Don't Be a Hero; How Do You Do It; I Like It; I'm Telling You Now; The Night Chicago Died

Murrells, Norman   The House of Bamboo

Murry, Ted, *see* **Murray Mencher**

Murtagh, Elaine   Dance On; In Summer

Murtagh, Valerie   Dance On; In Summer

Musarurgwa, August Machon   Skokiaan

Muse, Clarence   When It's Sleepy Time Down South

Musel, Bob   Band of Gold; The Homecoming Waltz

Musker, Frank   Every Woman in the World; Heaven on the Seventh Floor; Modern Girl

Mussorgsky, Modeste   A Night on Bald Mountain; Pictures at an Exhibition

Mustacchi, Joseph   Milord

Myddleton, W.H.   Down South

Myers, Dan (J. Richard Myers)   Dandy Jim of Caroline

Myers, David   Jack in the Box

Myers, Frank   You and I

Myers, Henry   In Chichicastenango

Myers, Michael   I'm in the Mood for Dancing

Myers, Randy James   Put a Little Love in Your Heart

Myers, Richard   Jericho; My Darling; Spread a Little Happiness

Myers, Sherman   Butterflies in the Rain; Just Humming Along; Moonlight on the Ganges; The Queen Was in the Parlour

Myers, Stanley   Cavatina; Children of Rome

Myrow, Josef   Autumn Nocturne; The Five O'Clock Whistle; Haunting Me; If I'm Lucky; On the Boardwalk in Atlantic City; Somewhere in the Night; Wilhelmina; You Do; You Make Me Feel So Young

Mysels, George   One Little Candle

Mysels, Maurice   I Want You, I Need You, I Love You

Mysels, Sammy   Red Silk Stockings and Green Perfume; The Singing Hills; We Three—My Echo, My Shadow and Me

Nägeli, Hans Georg   Blest Be the Tie That Binds; Dennis; Life Let Us Cherish, or, Snatch Fleeting Pleasures

Nakamura, Hachidai   Sukiyaki

Nance, Jack   It's Only Make Believe

Napier-Bell, Simon   You Don't Have To Say You Love Me

Napper, Pat   The Army Game

Napton, Johnny   My Devotion

Nascimbene, Mario   Song of the Barefoot Contessa

Naset, C.   Dreamy Melody

Nash, Johnny   Hold Me Tight; I Can See Clearly Now (the Rain Has Gone)

Nash, N. Richard   Sarava

Nash, Ogden   Speak Low

Nathan, Caspar   Meet Me in Bubble Land

Nathan, Charles   Say You're Mine Again

Navarro, Dan   We Belong

Nazelles, René   Under a Roof in Paree

Neale, Reverend John Mason   Come, Ye Faithful, Raise the Strain; Good King Wenceslas; Jerusalem the Golden

Neary, Brian   We Were Meant To Be Loved

Neat, John   She's a Lassie from Lancashire

Neely, Henry M.   Mem'ries, or, Golden Memory Days

Neiburg, Al J.   (When It's) Darkness on the Delta; I'm Confessin' That I Love You; It's a Hap-Hap-Happy Day; It's the Talk of the Town; Moonrise on the Lowlands; Under a Blanket of Blue

Neidlinger, William Harold   The Birthday of a King

Neil, Christopher   All I Need Is a Miracle

Neil, Fred   Everybody's Talkin', or, Theme from *Midnight Cowboy*

Nelson, Benjamin   There Goes My Baby

Nelson, Earl   Harlem Shuffle

Nelson, Edward G.   Auf Wiedersehn, My Dear; I Apologize; Josephine Please No Lean on the Bell; The Pal That I Loved Stole the Gal I Loved; Peggy O'Neil; Pretty Kitty Kelly; Ten Little Fingers and Ten Little Toes—Down in Tennessee; When Yankee Doodle Learns To Parlez Vous Francais

Nelson, Ox   I'm Looking for a Guy Who Plays Alto and Baritone and Doubles on a Clarinet and Wears a Size Thirty-Seven Suit

Nelson, Prince   I Feel for You; I Wanna Be Your Lover; Kiss; Let's Go Crazy; Manic Monday; Purple Rain; Raspberry Beret; Stand Back; When Doves Cry

Nelson, Sidney   Mary of Argyle; The Rose of Allandale

Nelson, Steve   A Bouquet of Roses; Frosty the Snow Man; Peter Cottontail

Nelson, Willie   Angel Flying Too Close to the Ground; A Good-Hearted Woman; On the Road Again

Nemo, Henry   Don't Take Your Love from Me; I Let a Song Go Out of My Heart

Nero, Paul   The Hot Canary

Nesbitt, Harry   Carolina; Georgia's Gotta Moon; Tears on My Pillow; Without That Certain Thing

Nesbitt, Max   Carolina; Georgia's Gotta Moon; Tears on My Pillow; Without That Certain Thing

Netson, James   The Greatest Mistake of My Life

Neubach, Ernst   My Song Goes Round the World

Neumann, Klaus Gunter   Wonderland by Night

Nevin, Ethelbert   Little Boy Blue; Mighty Lak' a Rose; Narcissus; Oh That We Two Were Maying; The Rosary

Nevins, Al   Twilight Time

Nevins, Morty   These Things I Offer You (for a Lifetime); Twilight Time

New, Derek   The Point of No Return

Newbury, M.   Funny, Familiar, Forgotten Feelings

Newcomb, Billy   The Big Sunflower

Newell, Norman   Adios, My Love, or, The Song of Athens; By the Fountains of Rome; Forget Domani; Jeannie; The Melba Waltz; More, or, Theme from *Mondo Cane;* My Thanks to You; Nice To Know You Care; Our Love Story; A Portrait of My Love; Say Wonderful Things; Song of Capri; That's How a Love Song Was Born; The White Rose of Athens

Newley, Anthony   The Candy Man; (Theme from) Goldfinger; Gonna Build a Mountain; The Good Old Bad Days; The Joker; Look at That Face; Nothing Can Stop Me Now!; Once in a Lifetime; The People Tree; Someone Nice Like You; What Kind of Fool Am I; Where Would You Be Without Me; Who Can I Turn To (When Nobody Needs Me); (On) A Wonderful Day Like Today

Newman, Alfred   Airport Love Theme; Anastasia; The Best of Everything; The Moon of Manakoora; (Theme from) Spellbound; Through a Long and Sleepless Night

Newman, Charles   Flowers for Madame; If You Were Only Mine; I'll Never Have To Dream Again; I'm a-Comin' a-Courtin' Corabelle; Pigalle; Six Lessons from Madame LaZonga; Sweethearts on Parade; Why Don't We Do This More Often; The Wooden Soldier and the China Doll; You Can't Pull the Woll over My Eyes; You've Got Me Crying Again

Newman, Greatrex   Spread a Little Happiness

Newman, Herb   The Wayward Wind

Newman, Joel   Kisses Sweeter Than Wine

Newman, John Henry   Lead, Kindly Light

Newman, Lionel   Again; I Met Her on Monday; Never

Newman, Randy   Mama Told Me Not To Come; Short People

Newton, Eddie   Casey Jones

Newton, Eileen   Somewhere a Voice Is Calling

Newton, John   Safely Through Another Week

Newton, Wood   Bobbie Sue

Nicholls, Billy   Without Your Love

Nicholls, Horatio   Adeline; Among My Souvenirs; Amy, Wonderful Amy; Back to Those Happy Days; The Badge from Your Coat; Bathing in the Sunshine; A Bedtime Story; Blue Eyes; Bouquet (I Shall Always Think of You); City of Laughter, City of Tears; Delilah; Delyse; Down Forget-Me-Not Lane; The Golden West; Gypsy Melody; Heart of a Rose; It Costs So Little; Janette; Just Like a Thief; Let's All Go to the Music Hall; Liszt, Chopin and Mendelssohn; Mistakes; My Inspiration Is You; Omaha; Persian Rosebud; Picador; Playthings; Riviera Rose; Romany Rose; Shanghai; Shepherd of the Hills; Sunny Havana; That Old Fashioned Mother of Mine; The Toy Drum Major; When the Guards Are on Parade; The Whispering Pines of Nevada

Nicholls, Roger   I Won't Last a Day Without You; Let Me Be the One; Rainy Days and Mondays

Nichols, Alberta   Harlem Moon; Padam, Padam; (It Will Have To Do) (Until) Till the Real Thing Comes Along

Nichols, Billy   Do It (Till You're Satisfied)

Nichols, Dan   You, You're the One

Nichols, George A.   I've Waited Honey, Waited Long for You

Nicholson, M.   Marie from Sunny Italy

Nicks, Stephanie   Rhiannon

Nicks, Stevie   Dreams; Gypsy; If Anyone Falls; Leather and Lace; Sara; Stand Back

Nicolai, Otto   The Merry Wives of Windsor (Overture)

Nielsen, Rick   I Want You To Want Me

Nightingale, Fred   Sugar and Spice

Nihi, Diane   Glory of Love (Theme from *The Karate Kid Part II*)

Nims, Walter   Precious and Few

Nitzsche, Jack   Up Where We Belong

Nix, Robert   Imaginary Lover; So into You

Noble, Harry   Hold Me, Thrill Me, Kiss Me

Noble, John Avery   Hawaiian War Chant; My Little Grass Shack in Kealakekua, Hawaii; A Song of Old Hawaii

Noble, Ray   Brighter Than the Sun; By the Fireside; Cherokee; Good Night, Sweetheart; I Found You; I Hadn't Anyone Till You; I'll Be Good Because of You; Love Is the Sweetest Thing; Love Locked Out; The Touch of Your Lips; The Very Thought of You

Noel, Art   If You Ever Go to Ireland; Nursie; What More Can I Say; You Don't Have To Tell Me, I Know

Nolan, Bob   Cool Water; Tumbling Tumbleweeds

Nolan, Kenny   I Like Dreamin'; Lady Marmalade; My Eyes Adored You

Nolan, Michael   Little Annie Roonie

Noll, Albert W.   Doan Ye Cry, Mah Honey

Norman, Jim Ed   Disenchanted

Norman, Leo   Fantasia on a Nursery Song

Norman, Monte   Dis-Donc, Dis-Donc; Irma La Douce; Our Language of Love

Norman, Morty   The James Bond Theme

Norman, Pierre   When I Take My Sugar to Tea; You Brought a New Kind of Love to Me

North, Alex   Unchained Melody

North, Bobby   Do I Worry

North, Michael   Lords of the Air

Norton, Carolina   Juanita

Norton, Daniel   Gee!

Norton, Frederick   Any Time Is Kissing Time; The Cobbler's Song; The Robbers' Chorus; The Robbers' March

Norton, George A.   The Memphis Blues; My Melancholy Baby; That's Gratitude

Norvas, Bill   Make Love to Me

Norwood, Dennise   The Garden of Eden

Norworth, Jack   Come Along My Mandy; Good Evening, Caroline; Honey Boy; Shine On Harvest Moon; Smarty; Take Me Out to the Ball Game

Novello, Ivor   And Her Mother Came Too; Fly Home, Little Heart; Fold Your Wings; Glamorous Night; I Can Give You the Starlight; Keep the Home Fires Burning (Till the Boys

Come Home); The Little Damozel; Love Is My Reason; Man of My Heart; Music in May (Careless Rapture); My Dearest Dear; My Life Belongs to You; Night May Have Its Sadness; Primrose; Rose of England; Shine Through My Dreams; Some Day My Heart Will Awake; Take Your Girl; The Violin Began To Play; Waking or Sleeping; Waltz of My Heart; We'll Gather Lilacs; When the Gypsy Played

Nugent, Maude   Sweet Rosie O'Grady

Nunez, Alcide   Livery Stable Blues

Nyro, Laura   And When I Die; Blowin' Away; I Never Meant To Hurt You; Save the Country; Stoned Soul Picnic; Stoney End; Sweet Blindness; Time and Love; Timer; Wedding Bell Blues

Oakeley, Frederick   Adeste Fideles, or, O Come All Ye Faithful

Oakey, Phil   Don't You Want Me

Oakland, Ben   The Champagne Waltz; Do the New York; If I Love Again; I'll Dance at Your Wedding; I'll Take Romance; Jave Jive; Sidewalks of Cuba; Twinkle, Twinkle, Little Star

Oakman, Peter   A Picture of You

Oates, John   I Can't Go for That (No Can Do); Maneater; Out of Touch; Possession Obsession; Sara Smile; She's Gone; You Make My Dreams

O'Brien, Billy   With My Shillelagh Under My Arm

O'Brien, Bob   A Zoot Suit

O'Brien, John   We'll Knock the Heligo—Into Heligo—Out of Heligoland

Ocean, Billy   Caribbean Queen; Loverboy; Suddenly; There'll Be Sad Songs (To Make You Cry); When the Going Gets Tough, the Tough Get Going

O'Connor, Caleb W.   Down the Field (March)

O'Connor, Desmond   How Lucky You Are; Let's Keep It That Way; Roll Me Over; Till All Our Dreams Come True; When You're in Love

O'Connor, Frederick   The Old House

O'Connor, Robert   Move In a Little Closer Baby

O'Connor, Shamus   MacNamara's Band

O'Day, Alan   Angie Baby

O'Dea, James   Hiawatha; Sammy

O'Dell, Kenny   Behind Closed Doors

Odette, Marcelene   Full Moon

O'Donnell, Charles   My Pony Boy

O'Dowd, George ("Boy George")   Church of the Poison Mind; Do You Really Want To Hurt Me; It's a Miracle; Karma Chameleon; Miss Me Blind; Time (Clock of the Heart)

Offenbach, Jacques   Apache Dance; Barcarolle; Can Can

O'Flynn, Charles   Jungle Drums (Canto Karabali); Roses Are Forget-Me-Nots; Smile, Darn Ya, Smile; Swingin' in a Hammock

Ogdon, Ina Duley   Brighten the Corner Where You Are

O'Hara, Fiske   Ireland Is Ireland to Me

O'Hara, Geoffrey   Give a Man a Horse He Can Ride; K-K-K-Katy; Leetle Bateese; There Is No Death; The Wreck of the "Julie Plante"

O'Hara, James   Grandpa (Tell Me 'Bout the Good Old Days); Older Women

O'Hara, Mark   Two Tribes

Ohman, Phil   Lost

O'Hogan, Betsy   Old Father Thames

O'Keefe, Donald   At the End of the Day

O'Keefe, Lester   There's No Other Love

O'Keefe, Walter   Little by Little

O'Kun, Lan   The Minute Waltz

Olcott, Chauncey   Isle o' Dreams; Mother Machree; My Wild Irish Rose; When Irish Eyes Are Smiling

Oldfield, Mike   19

Oldham, Andrew   As Tears Go By

Oldham, Richard   I Love the Name of Mary

Oldham, Spooner   Cry Like a Baby

Olias, Lotar   Blue Mirage; You, You, You

Oliphant, Thomas   Santa Lucia

Oliveira, Aloysio   Tico Tico

Oliveira, Louis   Dindi

Oliver, Henry Kemble   See, Gentle Patience Smiles on Pain

Oliver, Herbert   The Dancing Lesson; Down Vauxhall Way

Oliver, Joseph   Canal Street Blues; Chimes Blues; Snag It; Snake Rag; Sugar Foot Stomp, or, Dipper Mouth Blues; West End Blues

Oliver, Sy   Opus (Number) One; Yes Indeed

Oliver, Vic   Prelude to the Stars

Olivieri, Dino   I'll Be Yours (J'Attendrai)

Oliviero, N.   More, or, Theme from *Mondo Cane*

Olman, Abe   Down Among the Sheltering Palms; Oh Johnny, Oh Johnny, Oh!

Olsen, Ole   G'Bye Now; Oh Gee, Oh Gosh, Oh Golly I'm in Love; You're in the Army Now

Omartian, Michael S.   Get Used to It; She Works Hard for the Money

Onivas, D., *see* **Domenico Savino**

Ono, Yoko   Whatever Gets You Thru the Night

Onorati, Henry   The Little Drummer Boy

Openshaw, John   June Brought the Roses; Love Sends a Little Gift of Roses

Oppenheim, David   Child Love; Hold Me; When a Lady Meets a Gentleman Down South

Oppenheimer, George   I Feel a Song Coming On

Orange, Walter Lee   Nightshift; Sweet Love

Orbison, Roy   Blue Bayou; Cryin'; Oh Pretty Woman; Only the Lonely (Know the Way I Feel); Running Scared; That Lovin' You Feelin' Again

Ordway, John P.   Twinkling Stars Are Laughing Love

O'Reilly, P.J.   For You Alone

Orlob, Harold   Ask the Stars; How Can You Tell; I Was a

Very Good Baby; I Wonder Who's Kissing Her Now; I'll Remember You; Waiting

Orlowski, Anne   Rubber Ball

Ormont, David   The Hippopotamus Song, or, Mud, Glorious Mud

Ornadel, Cyril   If I Ruled the World; A Portrait of My Love

Ortolani, Riziero   Forget Domani; More, or, Theme from *Mondo Cane;* Seventh Dawn

Ory, Edward   Muskrat Ramble

Orzabal, Roland   Everybody Wants To Rule the World; Head Over Heels; Shout

Osborn, Arthur   The Cannon Song

Osborne, Gary Anthony   Little Jeannie; Part-Time Lover

Osborne, Jeffrey   On the Wings of Love

Osborne, Nat   As Long as the Shamrock Grows Green; Take Me Back to the Garden of Love

Osborne, Tony   The Secrets of the Seine; The Streets of Sorrento; Turkish Coffee; Windows of Paris

Osborne, Victor R.   Dance (Disco Heat)

Osborne, Will   Beside an Open Fireplace; Between Eighteenth and Nineteenth on Chestnut Street; Roses Are Forget-Me-Nots

Osser, Abe   The Miss America Pageant

Osser, Edna   I Dream of You; I'll Always Be with You

Osterman, Jack   Can't You Understand

O'Sullivan, Gilbert   Alone Again (Naturally); Claire; Get Down; Ooh Baby; Why Oh Why Oh Why?

O'Sullivan, Ray   No Matter How I Try; Nothing Rhymed

Otcasek, Richard   Drive; Shake It Up; Tonight She Comes; You Might Think

Oteo, Alfonso Esparza   Mi Viejo Amor

Otis, Clyde   The Boll Weevil Song; It's Just a Matter of Time; A Rockin' Good Way (To Mess Around and Fall in Love); The Stroll

Otis, Shuggie   Strawberry Letter #23

O'Toole, Mark   Two Tribes

Oungst, Webb M.   They Gotta Quit Kickin' My Dog (Dawg) Around, or, The Missouri Houn' Dawg Song

Overstreet, Paul   Same Ole Me

Overstreet, W. Benton   There'll Be Some Changes Made

Owen, Anita   Daisies Won't Tell; Sweet Bunch of Daisies

Owen, Fuzzy   Dear John Letter

Owen, Randy   Feels So Right; Mountain Music

Owens, Buck   Crying Time

Owens, Harry   Blue Shadows and White Gardenias; Cocoanut Grove; Dancing Under the Stars; Down Where the Trade Winds Blow; Linger Awhile; Sweet Leilani; To You Sweetheart, Aloha

Owens, Jack   Cynthia's in Love; Hi Neighbor; How Soon; Hut Sut Song

Owens, Kelly   I Beg of You

Owens, Robert Dale   'Tis Home Where'er the Heart Is

Owens, Tex   Cattle Call

Oxenford, Edward   Thy Sentinel Am I

Oxon, S.   Kafoozelum

Pace, D.   A Man Without Love

Pack, David   All I Need; Biggest Part of Me; How Much I Feel; You're the Only Woman

Paderewski, Ignace   Cracovienne Fantastique; Minuet in G

Padilla, José   My Spanish Rose; My Toreador; Paree!; Princesita; Valencia; Who'll Buy My Violets

Pafumy, J.   Rumba Rumba

Page, Clifford N.   Anchored

Page, James   Whole Lotta Love

Page, Martin   These Dreams; We Built This City

Page, Richard   Broken Wings; Kyrie

Paice, Ian   Smoke on the Water

Paich, David   Africa; Got To Be Real; Lady Love Me One More Time; Lowdown; Rosanna

Paine, Robert Thomas (Treat)   Adams and Liberty, or, The Boston Patriotic Song; The Green Mountain Farmer

Paisiello, Giovanni   Hope Told a Flattering Tale

Paiva, Jararaca   Mama Yo Quiero (I Want My Mama)

Paiva, Vincente   Mama Yo Quiero (I Want My Mama)

Paley, Herman   Sweet Little Buttercup; When It's Night Time Down in Burgundy; Won't You Fondle Me

Paley, Lou   Come to the Moon

Palitz, Morty   While We're Young

Palladino, Ralph   Do What You Do

Palmer, Bee   Please Don't Talk About Me When I'm Gone

Palmer, David   Nightingale

Palmer, Donald   Jazz Man

Palmer, Florrie   Morning Train (Nine to Five); When He Shines

Palmer, Horatio Richmond   Yield Not to Temptation

Palmer, Jack   Aunt Jemima (Silver Dollar); Everybody Loves My Baby, But My Baby Don't Love Nobody But Me; I Found a New Baby; Jumpin' Jive; Silver Dollar (Down and Out)

Palmer, John E.   (Casey Would Waltz with the Strawberry Blonde While) The Band Played On

Palmer, King   Eleventh Hour Melody

Palmer, Ray   My Faith Looks Up to Thee

Palmer, Robert   Addicted to Love

Palmer, Wally   Talking in Your Sleep

Palmet, Phoebe (Mrs. Joseph F. Knapp)   Open the Gates of the Temple

Palomero, M.E.   Princesita

Pankow, James C.   Just You 'n' Me (Babe); Old Days

Panzer, Marty   Even Now; It's a Miracle; Through the Years

Panzeri, M.   Ferryboat Serenade; For the First Time (Come Prima); A Man Without Love

Panzuti, V.   (I Don't Care) Only Love Me

Paoli, Gino   You're My World

Paramor, Norrie   The Frightened City; Let's Talk About Love; Lonely; Mañana Pasado Mañana; Once Upon a Dream; The Savage; A Voice in the Wilderness

Pardove, Joaquin   Negra Consentida (My Pet Brunette)

Paranteau, Zoel   Some Day I'll Find You

Parish, Mitchell   All My Love; Belle of the Ball; Blue Without You; A Blues Serenade; Ciao Ciao Bambina; Corrine Corrina; La Cucaracha; Deep Purple; Does Your Heart Beat for Me; Don't Be That Way; Dream, Dream, Dream; Emaline; Hands Across the Table; The Lamp Is Low; Let Me Love You Tonight; Lilacs in the Rain; Mademoiselle de Paris; Moonlight Serenade; One Morning in May; The Organ Grinder's Swing; Riverboat Shuffle; Ruby; A Sentimental Gentleman from Georgia; Serenata; Sidewalks of Cuba; Sleigh Ride; Sophisticated Lady; Sophisticated Swing; Stairway to the Stars (Park Avenue Fantasy); Star Dust; Stars Fell on Alabama; Sweet Lorraine; Take Me in Your Arms; Tzena, Tzena, Tzena; Volare, or, Nel Blu, Dipinto Di Blu

Parissi, Robert   Play That Funky Music

Park, Phil   Wish Me Luck As You Wave Me Goodbye

Parker, Brian   Concrete and Clay

Parker, Dorothy   How Am I To Know; I Wished on the Moon

Parker, Eula   The Village of Saint Bernadette

Parker, Henry   Jerusalem

Parker, John   Hard Habit To Break

Parker, Judy   December 1963 (Oh What a Night); Who Loves You

Parker, Ray, Jr.   Ghostbusters; I Still Can't Get Over Loving You; The Other Woman; A Woman Needs Love (Just Like You Do); You Can't Change That

Parker, Ross   Blue Ribbon Gal; Blue Skies Are Round the Corner; The Girl in the Alice Blue Gown; Hang on the Bell Nellie; I Shall Always Remember You Smiling; I Shall Be Waiting; I Won't Tell a Soul (That I Love You); I'll Make Up for Everything; Memories Live Longer Than Dreams; Monday, Tuesday, Wednesday; There'll Always Be an England; There's a Land of Begin Again; Your Heart and My Heart

Parker, Sol   This Love of Mine

Parks, C. Carson   Somethin' Stupid

Parks, Larry   Bread and Butter

Parks, Weldon   Dancing Machine

Parman, Cliff   Pretend

Parnell, Jack   The Kiss; The White Suit Samba

Parnes, Paul   Happiness Is

Parr, John   St. Elmo's Fire (Man in Motion)

Parr-Davies, Harry   Happy Ending; I Leave My Heart in an English Garden; In My Little Snapshot Album; It's in the Air; Mary Rose; My Paradise; Never Say Goodbye; Pedro the Fisherman; Sing As We Go; Smile When You Say ''Goodbye''; The Sweetest Song in the World; Where the Blue Begins; Wish Me Luck As You Wave Me Goodbye

Parris, Fredericke L.   Lost in the Fifties Tonight (In the Still of the Night)

Parsons, Alan   Don't Answer Me; Eye in the Sky; Games People Play; Prime Time; Time

Parsons, Bill   All American Boy

Parsons, Donovan   I Travel the Road; She's Such a Comfort to Me

Parsons, Geoffrey   Eternally, or, Terry's Theme; The Good Companions; If You Go (Away); If You Love Me (I Won't Care); The Little Shoemaker; Mama; Mandolin Serenade; Oh My Papa, or, O Mein Papa; La Seine; Smile; (Theme from) La Strada, or, Stars Shine in Your Eyes

Partichela, F.A.   Mexican Hat Dance

Parton, Des   Sad Sweet Dreamer

Parton, Dolly   Baby I'm Burning; Heartbreak Express; I Will Always Love You; 9 to 5; Two Doors Down

Partridge, Don   Rosie

Pascal, Milton   I Wanna Get Married

Pascoe, Richard W.   Little Town in the Ould County Down; That Tumble-Down Shack in Athlone

Pash, Warren   Private Eyes

Pasquale, Charles   Magic Is the Moonlight

Paterson, A.B. "Banjo"   Waltzing Matilda

Paterson, James   Come on Eileen

Patterson, Lover   There Goes My Baby

Patton, Robin   Hold Me

Paul, Alan   Love Must Be Free

Paul, Clarence   Fingertips (Part II); Until You Come Back to Me (That's What I'm Gonna Do)

Paul, Gene   Did Tosti Raise His Bowler Hat When He Said Goodbye

Paul, Mark   Softly, Softly

Paul, Olga   Meadowlands, or, Cavalry of the Steppes

Pauling, Lowman   Dedicated to the One I Love

Paull, E. T.   Ben Hur Chariot Race (March); Midnight Fire-Alarm

Paulton, Harry   At Midnight on My Pillow Lying; Dear Mother, in Dreams I See Her; Lullaby; A Soldier's Life; What the Dickie-Birds Say

Paxton, Tom   (The) Last Thing on My Mind

Payan, Jose   A Summer Evening in Santa Cruz

Payne, Jack   Blue Pacific Moonlight

Payne, John Howard   Home Sweet Home

Payne, Leon   I Love You Because

Payton, David   Magic

Peacock, Thomas Love   March of the Men of Harlech

Peacock, Trevor   Gossip Calypso; Mrs. Brown You've Got a Lovely Daughter; Mystery Girl; That's What Love Will Do

Pearl, Leslie   You Never Gave Up on Me

Pearson, Johnny   Sleepy Shores; Today I Met My Love

Pease, Harry   I Don't Want To Get Well (I'm in Love with a Beautiful Nurse); Josephine Please No Lean on the Bell; The Pal That I Loved Stole the Gal That I Loved; Peggy O'Neil; Pretty Kitty Kelly; Ten Little Fingers and Ten Little Toes—Down in Tennessee

Peck, Samuel Minturn   If You Love Me Darling, Tell Me with Your Eyes

Peek, Joseph   I Would Be True

Peel, Graham   In Summertime on Brendon

Pellesier, Victor   He Who His Country's Liv'ry Wears; When a Woman Hears the Sound of the Drum and Fife

Pelosi, Don   Angel of the Great White Way; Broken Hearted Clown; The Ferry Boat Inn; It Happened in Adano; The Little Drummer Boy; Little Old Mill; Love Me Forever; Nursie; Old Ship of Mine; The Stars Will Remember; When the Poppies Bloom Again; When You Lose the One You Love; You Don't Have To Tell Me, I Know

Penn, Arthur A.   Carissima; It's a Long Lane That Has No Turning; The Lamplit Hour; The Magic of Your Eyes; Smilin' Through; Sunrise and You

Penn, Dan   Cry Like a Baby

Penn, William   The Honeysuckle and the Bee

Penner, Joe   Doin' the Ducky Wuck

Pennington, James   Take Me Down

Penny, Lee   My Adobe Hacienda

Penridge, Stan   Beth

Penzabene, Rodger   I Wish It Would Rain

Pepper, Buddy   Pillow Talk; Vaya Con Dios

Pepper, Harry S.   Carry Me Back to Green Pastures; Don't Tell a Soul; Goodbye to All That; Please Don't Mention It; Rags, Bottles or Bones

Percy, Florence, *see* **Elizabeth Allen**

Peretti, Hugo   Can't Help Falling in Love (with You); The Lion Sleeps Tonight, or, Wimoweh

Perkins, Barney   Want Ads

Perkins, Carl Lee   Blue Suede Shoes

Perkins, Cy   They Gotta Quit Kickin' My Dog (Dawg) Around, or, The Missouri Houn' Dawg Song

Perkins, Frank   Emaline; A Sentimental Gentleman from Georgia; Stars Fell on Alabama

Perkins, Ray   Lady Luck Show

Perkins, William H.   At the End of a Beautiful Day

Perren, Frederick J.   ABC; Boogie Fever; Heaven Must Be Missing an Angel; Hot Line; I Want You Back; Makin' It; Mama's Pearl; Reunited

Perricone, Jack A.   Run Joey Run

Perronet, Edward   All Hail the Power of Jesus' Name

Perry, Barney   Walking in Rhythm

Perry, Greg S.   Want Ads

Perry, Jimmy   Who Do You Think You Are Kidding Mister Hitler

Perry, Stephen   Don't Stop Believin'; Foolish Heart; Oh Sherrie; Open Arms; Separate Ways; Who's Crying Now

Pestalozza, Alberto   Ciribiribin

Petch, Frank   The Crystal Gazer

Peterik, James M.   Burning Heart; Eye of the Tiger; Search Is Over; Vehicle

Peters, Ben   Before the Next Teardrop Falls; Burgers and Fries; Kiss an Angel Good Morning'

Peterson, Betty   My Happiness

Pether, Henry E.   Poor John; Waiting at the Church, or, My Wife Won't Let Me

Petkere, Bernice   Close Your Eyes; Lullaby of the Leaves

Petrie, Henry W.   As Deep as the Deep Blue Sea; Asleep in the Deep; Davy Jones' Locker; I Don't Want To Play in Your Yard; Where the Sunset Turns the Ocean's Blue to Gold; Where the Twilight Comes To Kiss the Rose Goodnight; You Can't Play in Our Yard Any More

Petrillo, Caesar   Jim

Pettis, Jack   Bugle Call Rag

Petty, Norman   Almost Paradise; Everyday; It's So Easy; Peggy Sue; That'll Be the Day; True Love Ways

Petty, Tom   Don't Do Me Like That; Stop Draggin' My Heart Around

Peyton, Dave   I Ain't Got Nobody

Pfaff, Warren   Pan Am Makes The Goin' Great

Pfrimmer, Donald   By Now; Drifter

Phelps, S.D.   Something for Jesus

Phile, Philip   Hail Columbia, or, New Federal Song; The President's March

Philipp, Adolph   Alma Where Do You Live

Philleo, Estelle   Out Where the West Begins

Phillips, A. Fred   Goodbye, Little Girl of My Dreams

Phillips, C.   Double Vision

Phillips, Charlie   Sugartime

Phillips, Donald   Melody from the Sea; The Old Pi-anna Rag

Phillips, Fred   Got Her off My Hands (But Can't Get Her off My Mind); Got the Bench, Got the Park, But I Haven't Got You; She Lived Next Door to a Firehouse

Phillips, Harry   Goodnight Children, Everywhere

Phillips, James John T.   The Little Shoemaker

Phillips, John   California Dreamin'; Creque Alley; Go Where You Wanna Go; Look Through My Window; Monday Monday; (Are You Going to) San Francisco (Be Sure to Wear Some Flowers in Your Hair); Twelve Thirty, or, Young Girls Are Coming to the Canyon

Phillips, Michele Gilliam   California Dreamin'; Creque Alley

Phillips, Mike   North to Alaska

Phillips, Montague F.   The Fishermen of England; Sing Joyous Bird

Phillips, Pam   Nobody Loves Me Like You Do

Phillips, Van   The Two of Us

Philp, James   The Jewel of Asia

Photoglou, James   We Were Meant To Be Loved

Piaf, Edith   If You Love Me (I Won't Care); Just Come Home; La Vie en Rose

Piantadosi, Al   Baby Shoes; The Curse of an Aching Heart; I Didn't Raise My Boy To Be a Soldier; If You had All the World and Its Gold; In All My Dreams I Dream of You; I've Lost All My Love for You; My Lovin' Honey Man; My Mariuccia Take a Steamboat; On the Shores of Italy; Pal of My Cradle Days; Send Me Away with a Smile; That's How I

Need You; What a Wonderful Mother You'd Be; When You Play in the Game of Love; When You're in Love with Someone Who Is Not in Love with You

Piccolo, Stephen Self Control

Pickett, Bobby Monster Mash

Pickett, Ken Grandad

Pickett, Phil It's a Miracle; Karma Chameleon; Move Away

Pickhall, Marjorie Duna

Picone, Vito Little Star

Pierce, Conrad Back on My Mind Again

Pierce, John Cool Love

Pierce, Marvin Fire; Love Rollercoaster

Pierce, Webb I Don't Care

Pierné, Gabriel March of the Tin Soldiers

Pierpoint, Folliott For the Beauty of the Earth

Pierpont, J.S. Jingle Bells, or, The One Horse Open Sleigh; Little White Cottage

Pike, Mashall S. Home Again; Little White Cottage

Pilcer, Harry The Gaby Glide

Pindar, Peter, *see* **John Wolcott**

Pinder, Mike Simple Game

Pinera, Carlos Ride Captain Ride

Pinkard, Maceo Congratulations; Gimme a Little Kiss, Will Ya, Huh?; Here Comes the Showboat; Jazz Baby's Ball; Mammy o' Mine; Sugar; Sweet Georgia Brown; Them There Eyes

Pinkard, Sandy Blessed Are the Believers; You're the Reason God Made Oklahoma

Pinsuti, Ciro Bedouin Love Song; The Sea Hath Its Pearls

Pippin, Steve This Time I'm in It for Love

Piron, Armand J. I Wish I Could Shimmy Like My Sister Kate

Pirroni, Marco Stand and Deliver

Piston, Walter The Incredible Flutist

Pitchford, Dean Almost Paradise; Don't Call It Love; Fame; Footloose; I Wanna Hear It from Your Lips; Let's Hear It for the Boy; You Should Hear How She Talks About You

Pitney, Gene He's a Rebel

Pitts, Tom I Never Knew I Could Love Anybody Like I'm Loving You

Pitts, William S. The Little Brown Church (in the Vale)

Pixley, Frank Heidelberg Stein Song; The Message of the Violet; The Tale of a Bumble Bee; The Tale of the Kangaroo; The Tale of the Seashell; The Tale of the Turtle Dove

Planché, James Robinson Love's Ritornella, or, Gentle Zitella; Rise, Gentle Moon

Planquette, Robert The Regiment of Sambre and Meuse

Plant, Robert Whole Lotta Love

Plante, Jacques Domino

Plater, Bobby Jersey Bounce

Plumb, Edward Love Is a Song That Never Ends

Pober, Leon (La La) Colette; Tiny Bubbles

Pockriss, Lee Calcutta; Catch a Falling Star; Itsy Bitsy Teenie Weenie Yellow Polkadot Bikini; Johnny Angel; My Heart Is an Open Book; Playground in My Mind; Sitting in the Back Seat; Starlight; Tracy; When Julie Comes Around

Poe, Coy The Object of My Affection; What's the Reason (I'm Not Pleasin' You)

Pointer, Anita I'm So Excited

Pointer, June I'm So Excited

Pointer, Ruth I'm So Excited

Pola, Eddie Caramba It's the Samba; The Girl with the Dreamy Eyes; I Didn't Slip, I Wasn't Pushed, I Fell; I Love the Way You Say "Goodnight"; I Said My Pajamas (and Put On My Prayers); I Was in the Mood; I'm Gonna Wash My Hands of You; The Longest Walk; Marching Along Together; Till the Lights of London Shine Again; The Wedding of Mister Mickey Mouse

Poldini, Eduard Poupée Valsante

Poll, Ruth Becase of Rain

Polla, W.C. Dancing Tambourine

Pollack, Benny Make Love to Me; Peckin'; Tin Roof Blues

Pollack, Jeanne La Pachanga

Pollack, Lew Angela Mia; Buddha; Charmaine; Cheatin' on Me; Diane; I'm Missin' Mammy's Kissin'—and I Know She's Missin' Mine; (Who's Wonderful, Who's Marvelous?) Miss Annabelle Lee; My Yiddishe Momme; Seventh Heaven; Sing, Baby, Sing; Toy Trumpet; Two Cigarettes in the Dark; You Do the Darndest Things, Baby

Pollavicini, V. You Don't Have To Say You Love Me

Pollock, Channing I Love Love; My Man

Pomeranz, David Tryin' To Get the Feelin' Again

Pomeroy, George S. The Whiffenpoof Song

Pomus, Jerome "Doc" Can't Get Used to Losing You; Little Sister; Save the Last Dance for Me; Surrender; Suspicion; Teenager in Love

Ponce, Manuel M. Little Star, or, Estrellita; Summer Dreams

Ponce, Phil Dancing Tambourine

Ponchielli, Amilcare Dance of the Hours

Poncia, Vini You Make Me Feel Like Dancing

Ponella, Frank The Old Grey Mare (She Ain't What She Used To Be)

Poniatowski, Prince Josef The Yeoman's Wedding Song

Pope, Pauline Racing with the Moon

Popp, Andre Love Is Blue; The Portuguese Washerwomen

Popplewell, Jack The First Lullaby; If I Should Fall in Love Again

Porcaro, Jeff Africa

Porcaro, Steve Human Nature

Poree, Anita Boogie Down; Keep on Truckin'

Portal, Otillio Sweet and Gentle

Porte, A. Nazareth

Portela, Raul Lisbon Antigua, or, In Old Lisbon

Porter, Cole Abracadabra; Ace in the Hole; After You (Who); Alladin; All of You; All Through the Night; Allez-Vous En; (I'm) Always True to You in My Fashion; Another Op'nin,

Another Show; Anything Goes; At Long Last Love; Be a Clown; Begin the Beguine; Blow, Gabriel, Blow; Brush Up Your Shakespeare; Bulldog! Bulldog! Bow, Wow, Wow; Ça, C'est L'Amour; Can-Can; C'est Magnifique; Close; Do I Love You; Don't Fence Me In; Don't Look At Me That Way; Down in the Depths on the Ninetieth Floor; Dream Dancing; Easy To Love; Ev'ry Time We Say Goodbye; Everything I Love; Experiment; Friendship; From Now On; From This Moment On; Get Out of Town; The Great Indoors; The Gypsy in Me; He's a Right Guy; Hey, Baby, Hey (I'm Nuts About You); How Could We Be Wrong; How's Your Romance; I Am in Love; I Am Loved; I Concentrate on You; I Get a Kick Out of You; I Happen To Like New York; I Hate Men; I Love Paris; I Love You; I Love You Samantha; I Want To Go Home; I'm a Gigolo; I'm in Love Again; In the Still of the Night; It All Belongs to You (The Laugh of the Town); It's All Right with Me; It's De-Lovely; I've a Shooting Box in Scotland; I've Got My Eyes on You; I've Got You on My Mind; I've Got You Under My Skin; Josephine; Just One of Those Things; Katie Went to Haiti; Ladies in Waiting; Let's Be Buddies; Let's Do It (Let's Fall in Love); Let's Misbehave; Little One; Love for Sale; Love of My Life; Mind If I Make Love to You; Miss Otis Regrets; Most Gentlemen Don't Like Love; My Heart Belongs to Daddy; Night and Day; Nobody's Chasing Me; Old-Fashioned Garden; Paree; Paris Loves Lovers; The Physician; A Picture of Me Without You; Rap Tap on Wood; Ridin' High; Rolling Home; Rosalie; Should I Tell You I Love You; Siberia; So in Love (Am I); So Near and Yet So Far; Stereophonic Sound; Swingin' the Jinx Away; Thank You So Much Mrs. Lowsborough—Goodbye; Tomorrow; Too Bad; Too Darn Hot; True Love; Two Little Babes in the Wood; Use Your Imagination; Well, Did You Evah; What Is This Thing Called Love; When I Was a Little Cuckoo; Where Have You Been; Who Wants To Be a Millionaire; Why Can't You Behave; Why Should I Care; Why Shouldn't I; Without Love; Wunderbar; You Can Do No Wrong; You Do Something to Me; You Don't Know Paree (Paris); You Irritate Me So; You'd Be So Nice To Come Home To; You're Just Too Too; You're Sensational; You're the Top; You've Got That Thing

Porter, David   Soul Man

Porter, Jake   Ko Ko Mo (I Love You So)

Poser, Freddie   Where Did My Snowman Go

Posford, George   At the Balalaika; Goodnight Vienna; The London I Love; Ordinary People; Room Five Hundred and Four; The World Is Mine (Tonight)

Post, Mike   Greatest American Hero (Believe It or Not)

Poterat, Louis   I'll Be Yours (J'Attendrai)

Potter, Brian   Ain't No Woman Like the One I've Got; Country Boy You Got Your Feet in L.A.; Don't Pull Your Love; It Only Takes a Minute

Pottier, Eugène   L'Internationale

Poulton, George R.   Aura Lee

Poulton, Harry   Darkest the Hour

Pounds, Mrs. Jessie Brown   Beautiful Isle of Somewhere

Powell, Felix   Pack Up Your Trouble in Your Old Kit Bag and Smile, Smile, Smile

Powell, Johnny   Will I What

Powell, Lester   You Are My First Love

Powell, Mel   My Guy's Come Back

Powell, Teddy   (Take Me Back to My) Boots and Saddle; Snake Charmer

Powell, W.C.   Sweet Violets

Powers, Chester, Jr.   (Let's) Get Together

Prado, Miguel   Time Was, or, Dreaming

Prado, Perez   Patricia

Praetorius, Michael   Lo, How a Rose E'er Blooming

Prager, Stephen   Fly Robin Fly; Get Up and Boogie

Pratt, Charles E.   Don't Go Out Tonight, Boy

Pratt, Michael   A Handful of Songs; The Little White Bull; Rock with the Cavemen; Water, Water

Prentice, Charles   Why Is the Bacon So Tough

Presley, Elvis   All Shook Up; Don't Be Cruel; Heartbreak Hotel; Love Me Tender

Presley, Reg   Little Girl

Preston, Billy   Nothing from Nothing; Outa-Space; Space Race; Will It Go Round in Circles; You Are So Beautiful

Preston, Leroy   My Baby Thinks He's a Train

Prestopino, Greg   Break My Stride

Prestwood, Hugh   The Sound of Goodbye

Prevert, Jacques   Autumn Leaves

Previn, Andre   Coco; Gabrielle; Like Young; (Theme from) Valley of the Dolls; You're Gonna Hear from Me

Previn, Dory   Come Saturday Morning; (Theme from) Valley of the Dolls; You're Gonna Hear from Me

Price, Alan   The House of the Rising Sun; The House That Jack Built; I'm Crying; Time and Tide (Theme from *Plague Dogs*)

Price, Chilton   Slow Poke; You Belong to Me

Price, George   Angel Child

Price, Lloyd   I'm Gonna Get Married; Personality; Stagger Lee

Price, Roma   That Lovin' You Feelin' Again

Priest, Stephen   Fox on the Run

Prift, Clarence   Lullaby in Rhythm

Prima, Louis   Sing, Sing, Sing, Sing; A Sunday Kind of Love

Primrose, Joe   St. James Infirmary

Prince, see Prince Nelson

Prince, Hugh   Beat Me, Daddy, Eight to the Bar; Boogie Woogie Bugle Boy; I Guess I'll Get the Papers and Go Home; Rum Boogie (Rhumboogie)

Pritchard, Henry   I Don't Want To Love You (Like I Do); Kentucky; Take Care (When You Say "Te Quiero")

Procter, Adelaide   The Lost Chord

Proffitt, Josephine   My Sugar Is So Refined

Prokofieff, Serge   Love of Three Oranges (March); Peter and the Wolf

Propheter, George   Wait Till the Tide Comes In

Prosen, Sidney   Till I Waltz Again with You

Provost, Heinz   Intermezzo (A Love Story) (Souvenir de Vienne)

Pryor, Arthur   Razzazza Mazzazza; The Whistler and His Dog

Puccini, Giacomo   Musetta's Waltz

Puccitta, Vincenzo   Strike the Cymbal

Puck, Harry   The Little House upon the Hill; Where Did You Get That Girl

Pugh, Phillip   Then Came You

Purcell, Edward C. (Edward Purcell Cockram)   Passing By

Purcell, Harold   The Moment I Saw You; Never Say Goodbye; Pedro the Fisherman; You Happen Once in a Lifetime

Purcell, Henry   Lilliburlero

Purdy, W.T.   On Wisconsin

Purvis, Katharine E.   When the Saints Go Marching In

Putman, Curly   The Green Green Grass of Home; My Elusive Dreams

Putman, James S.   I'll Be Ready When the Great Day Comes

Puzey, Robert   I'm In the Mood for Dancing

Quadling, Lew   Careless; Do You Care; Sam's Song

Queen, John   Just Because She Made Dem Goo-Goo Eyes

Quick, C.E.   Come Go with Me

Quillen, Charles W.   Back on My Mind Again; By Now; I Wouldn't Have Missed It for the World

Quilter, Roger   Now Sleeps the Crimson Petal

Quinn, Dan W.   The Same Sweet Girl Today

Quinn, Derek   Over You

Quittenton, Martin   Maggie May/Reason To Believe

Rabbitt, Eddie   B B B Burnin' Up with Love; Drivin' My Life Away; Gone Too Far; I Love a Rainy Night; Someone Could Lose a Heart Tonight; Step by Step; A World Without Love; Suspicions

Rabin, Trevor   Owner of a Lonely Heart

Rabinowitz, Harry   Love for Lydia

Race, Steve   Nicola; Ring Ding

Rachmaninoff, Sergei   Eighteenth Variation on a Theme by Paganini; Piano Concerto, No.2; Prelude in C# minor

Radclyffe-Hall, Marguerite   The Blind Ploughman

Radford, Dave   It's Tulip Time in Holland; Where the Black-Eyed Susans Grow

Rado, James   Aquarius; Be-In; Easy To Be Hard; Frank Mills; Good Morning Starshine; Hair; Let the Sunshine In; Manchester; Where Do I Go

Raff, Joachin   Cavatina

Rafferty, Gerry   Baker Street; Home and Dry; Stuck in the Middle (with You)

Raglan, Robert   Can This Be Love

Ragni, Gerome   Aquarius; Be-In; Easy To Be Hard; Frank Mills; Good Morning Starshine; Hair; Let the Sunshine In; Manchester; Where Do I Go

Ragovoy, Jerry   Time Is on My Side

Rainger, Ralph   Blue Hawaii; Easy Living; Faithful Forever; The Funny Old Hills; Here Lies Love; The Hills of Old Wyomin'; I Have Eyes (To See With); I Wish on the Moon; If I Should Lose You; (It's) June in January; Love in Bloom; Miss Brown to You; Moanin' Low; Please; Sweet Is the Word for You; Thanks for the Memory; With Every Breath I Take; You Started Something; You're a Sweet Little Headache

Rains, Chuck   Disenchanted; A Headache Tomorrow (Or a Heartache Tonight)

Rainsford, Lee   We're Through

Raksin, David   (Theme from) The Bad and the Beautiful; Laura; Theme from Ben Casey

Raleigh, Ben   Dungaree Doll; Laughing on the Outside (Crying on the Inside); She's a Fool; Tell Laura I Love Her; Wonderful Wonderful; You Walk By

Ralton, Harry   I Remember the Cornfields

Ram, Buck   For the First Time (Come Prima); The Great Pretender; I'll Be Home for Christmas; (You've Got) The Magic Touch; Only You (and You Alone); Twilight Time

Ramin, Sid   Music To Watch Girls By; The Patty Duke Theme (Cousins)

Ramirez, Roger "Ram"   Lover Man (Oh Where Can You Be)

Ramos, Silvano R.   El Rancho Grande

Ramsey, Harold   Her Name Is Mary

Rand, Ande   Only You (and You Alone)

Rand, Lionel   Let There Be Love

Randall, James Ryder   Maryland, My Maryland, or, Tannenbaum, O Tannenbaum!

Randall, Michael   All of My Life

Randazzo, Teddy   Goin' Out of My Head; Hurts So Bad; It's Gonna Take a Miracle

Randell, Denny   Let's Hang On; A Lover's Concerto; Native New Yorker; Swearin' to God; Workin' My Way Back to You

Randolph, Eugene   A Tear Fell

Randolph, Zilner Trenton   Ol' Man Mose

Rankin, Jeremiah Eames   God Be with You Till We Meet Again

Rans, Robert   Dance with Me; Material Girl

Ransom, R.L. Jr.   Dazz

Rapee, Erno   Angela Mia; Charmaine; Diane

Raposo, Joe   Sing (Sing a Song)

Rappolo, Leon   Farewell Blues; Milenberg Joys

Rasbach, Oscar   Trees

Rascel, Renato   Arrivederci Roma

Raskin, Gene   Those Were the Days

Raskin, Willie   Fifty Million Frenchmen Can't Be Wrong; I Found a Rose in the Devil's Garden; I'm Waiting for Ships That Never Come In; (When) They Cut Down the Old Pine Tree; Wedding Bells Are Breaking Up That Old Gang of Mine

Rath, Fred   Just a Girl That Men Forget

Rauch, Fred   Answer Me (My Love)

Ravasino, D.   Tell Me You're Mine

Ravel, Maurice   Bolero; Daphnis et Chloé; Pavanne for a Dead Infanta (Princess)

Raven, Carol   La Cumparsita; Look at Me; The Peacock

Ravenge, Lucia   Lonely Footsteps

Rawicz, Maryan   Spinning Wheel

Ray, Cyril   Gentlemen, the King

Ray, Edward   Hearts of Stone

Ray, Harry   Special Lady

Ray, Johnnie   The Little White Cloud That Cried

Ray, Lillian   The Sunshine of Your Smile

Ray, Maude Louise   My Task

Rayburn, Gene   Hop Scotch Polka

Raye, Don   Beat Me, Daddy, Eight to the Bar; Boogie Woogie Bugle Boy; Cow-Cow Boogie; Domino; He's My Guy; The House of Blue Lights; I'll (I) Remember April; Irresistible You; Lovely Lauana; Milkman Keep Those Bottles Quiet; Mister Five by Five; The Music Makers; (If I Had) Rhythm in My Nursery Rhymes; Rum Boogie (Rhumboogie); Scrub Me Mama with a Boogie Beat; Short, Fat and 4F; Star Eyes; They Were Doing the Mambo; This Is My Country; You Don't Know What Love Is

Raymonnd, Tony   Airy, Fairy Lillian

Raymonde, Ivor   I Only Want To Be with You; Stay Awhile

Raynor, Hal   Doin' the Ducky Wuck

Razaf, Andy   Ain't Misbehavin'; Blue Turning Grey Over You; Christopher Columbus; Dusky Stevedore; Honeysuckle Rose; In the Mood; It's Make Believe Ballroom Time; The Joint Is Jumpin'; Keepin' Out of Mischief Now; Memories of You; S'posin'; Stomping at the Savoy; That's What I Like About the South; Twelfth Street Rag; What Did I Do To Be So Black and Blue

Rea, Chris   Fool (If You Think It's Over)

Read, John   Granny's Old Arm-Chair; Whoa, Emma

Reader, Ralph   On (the) Crest of a Wave; Strollin'

Reardon, Jack   The Good Life; La Strada Del' Amore

Reaves, Erell   Fairy on the Clock; Lady of Spain

Reb, Johnny   Goober Peas

Rebennack, Malcolm   Right Place Wrong Time (as Dr. John)

Record, Eugene   Oh Girl

Redding, Edward C.   End of a Love Affair

Redding, Otis   (Sittin' on) The Dock of the Bay; Respect; Sweet Soul Music

Reddy, Helen   I Am Woman

Redi, P.G.   Non Dimenticar

Redington, Ginny   You, You're the One

Redman, Don   Cherry; How'm I Doin' (Hey Hey); I Gotcha

Redmond, John   Christmas in Killarney; Dream, Dream, Dream; The Gaucho Serenade; I Came, I Saw, I Congad; I Let a Song Go Out of My Heart

Redner, Lewis H.   O Little Town of Bethlehem

Reed, Bert   In the Quartermaster's Stores

Reed, David Jr.   All for (the) Love of You; Eli Green's Cakewalk; The Handicap March; Love Me and the World Is

Mine; Mister Johnson, Don't Get Gay; My Heart Has Learned To Love You, Now Do Not Say Goodbye

Reed, Les   Daughter of Darkness; Delilah; Don't Bring Me Your Heartaches; Here It Comes Again; It's Not Unusual; The Last Waltz; Leave a Little Love; Love Is All; Tell Me When; Turn Around

Reed, Nancy Binns   Oh Happy Day

Reeves, Billy   Shew (Shoo) Fly, Don't Bother Me

Reger, Max   Maria Wiegenlied

Reginald, Dwight K.   Snookeroo

Regney, Noel   Dominique

Reichardt, Alexander   Thou Art So Near and Yet So Far

Reichart, Heinz   My Little Nest of Heavenly Blue, or, Frasquita Serenade (Blaues Himmelbett), or, Farewell, My Love, Farewell

Reichner, Bix   Papa Loves Mambo; Stop Beating 'Round the Mulberry Bush; Teenage Prayer; You Better Go Now

Reid, Billy   Anything I Dream Is Possible; The Bridge of Sighs; Coming Home; The Gypsy; I Still Believe; I'll Close My Eyes; I'm Walking Behind You; It's a Pity To Say Goodnight; Reflections on the Water; Snowy White Snow and Jingle Bells; This Is My Mother's Day; A Tree in the Meadow

Reid, Clarence   Rockin' Chair

Reid, Donald   Green Years; Remember Pearl Harbor; Years Ago

Reid, Harold   Don't Wait On Me

Reid, Ivan   When I'm Gone I Won't Forget

Reid, Jerry   Guitar Man

Reid, Keith   A Whiter Shade of Pale

Reid, Michael   Inside; Stranger in My House

Reid, Terry   Friends

Reine, Johnny   Don't Ring-a Da Bell; Scottish Samba

Reine, Michael   Give Her My Love; The Homing Waltz; The Rose I Bring You; The Wedding of Lilli Marlene; The Windsor Waltz

Reinhard, Keith   You Deserve a Break Today; You, You're the One

Reinhardt, Heinrich   Day Dreams; Fountain Fay; Two Little Love Bees

Reisch, Walter   Tell Me Why You Smile Mona Lisa; Two Hearts in Three Quarter Time

Reisfeld, Bert   Call Me Darling; The Three Bells

Reisner, C. Francis   Goodbye Broadway, Hello France

Relf, Bob   Harlem Shuffle

Relfe, John   Mary's Dream, or, Sandy's Ghost

Rellegro, Don   The Green Cockatoo

Renard, Jean   Losing You

Renaud, Z.   Under Hawaiian Skies

Rene, Leon   I Lost My Sugar in Salt Lake City; Someone's Rocking My Dream Boat; When It's Sleepy Time Down South; When the Swallows Come Back to Capistrano

Rene, Malou   Tossin' and Turnin'

Rene, Otis   Someone's Rocking My Dream Boat; When It's Sleepy Time Down South

Renis, Tony   All of You

Resnick, Arthur   Good Lovin'; Under the Boardwalk; Yummy Yummy Yummy

Revaux, Jacques   My Way

Revel, Harry   Afraid To Dream; And So to Bed; A Boy and a Girl Were Dancing; By a Wishing Well; College Rhythm; Did You Ever See a Dream Walking; Doin' the Uptown Lowdown; Don't Let It Bother You; From the Top of Your Head to the Tip of Your Shoes; Goodnight My Love; Head Over Heels in Love; (Lookie, Lookie, Lookie,) Here Comes Cookie; I Feel Like a Feather in the Breeze; I Played Fiddle for the Czar; I'm Humming, I'm Whistling, I'm Singing; Love Thy Neighbor; The Loveliness of You; Many Moons Ago; May I; May I Have the Next Romance with You; Never in a Million Years; Paris in the Spring; She Reminds Me of You; A Star Fell Out of Heaven; Stay as Sweet as You Are; Sweet as a Song; Take a Number from One to Ten; There's a Lull in My Life; Underneath the Harlem Moon; Wake Up and Live; When I'm with You; With My Eyes Wide Open I'm Dreaming; Without a Word of Warning; You Can't Have Everything; You Gotta Eat Your Spinach, Baby; You Hit the Spot; You're My Past, Present and Future; You're Such a Comfort to Me

Revil, Rudi   The Little Shoemaker

Rew, Kimberley   Walking on Sunshine

Rexford, Eben E.   Only a Pansy Blossom; Silver Threads Among the Gold

Reynolds, Burt   I Don't Think I'm Ready for You

Reynolds, Dorothy   Free as Air; Salad Days

Reynolds, Ellis   I'm Confessin' That I Love You

Reynolds, Herbert   Auf Wiedersehn; Nodding Roses; On the Shore at Lei Lei; They Didn't Believe Me

Reynolds, Isaac G.   Won't You Be My Little Girl

Rhodes, Nick   Hungry Like the Wolf; A View to a Kill; The Wild Boys

Rhodes, Sandra   The Clown

Rhodes, Stan   A Sunday Kind of Love

Ricca, Louis   Dream, Dream, Dream; Goodbye Sue

Rice, Lieutenant Gitz   Dear Old Pal of Mine; Keep Your Head Down, "Fritzie Boy"

Rice, Max   Smile, Darn Ya, Smile

Rice, Seymoure   You Tell Me Your Dream, or, I Had a Dream, Dear

Rice, Thomas Dartmouth "Daddy"   (Jump) Jim Crow

Rice, Tim   All Time High; Don't Cry for Me, Argentina; Everything's Alright; I Don't Know How To Love Him; I Know Him So Well; Jesus Christ Superstar; One More Angel in Heaven

Rich, Charlie   Every Time You Touch Me (I Get High)

Rich, Fred   I'm Just Wild About Animal Crackers

Rich, Max   My Blue Bird Was Caught in the Rain; Wonderful You

Richard, Cliff   Bachelor Boy; Don't Talk to Him; On the Beach

Richard, Keith   Angie; As Tears Go By; Emotional Rescue; Get Off My Cloud; Honky Tonk Women; It's Only Rock 'n Roll (But I Like It); Nineteenth Nervous Breakdown; Paint It Black; (I Can't Get No) Satisfaction; Start Me Up

Richards, Deke   ABC; I Want You Back; Love Child; Mama's Pearl

Richards, Dick   Down on the Farm in Harvest Time

Richards, Henry Brinley   Warblings at Eve

Richards, Jack   He

Richards, Johnny   Young at Heart

Richardson, Arthur   Too Fat Polka

Richardson, Cindy   Almost Over You

Richardson, David   Wildflower

Richardson, J.P.   Chantilly Lace; Running Bear

Richie, Lionel Jr.   All Night Long (All Night); Endless Love; Hello; Just To Be Close to You; Miss Celie's Blues (Sister); Missing You; My Love; Oh No; Penny Lover; Running with the Night; Sail On; Say You, Say Me; Stuck On You; Sweet Love; Three Times a Lady; Truly; We Are the World; You Are

Richman, Daniel   Alone at a Table for Two

Richman, Harry   C'est Vous (It's You); (Who's Wonderful, Who's Marvelous?) Miss Annabelle Lee; (There Ought To Be a) Moonlight Saving Time; Muddy Water; Ro-Ro-Rollin' Along; (I Don't Believe It But) Say It Again; Singing a Vagabond Song; There's Danger in Your Eyes, Cherie; Walkin' My Baby Back Home

Richmond, Frank J.   Take Me Back to Your Heart Again

Richmond, Paul   Shining Star

Ricks, Lee   Cement Mixer (Put-ti Put-ti)

Ricotti, Frank   Music Machine

Riddle, Nelson   (Theme from) The Untouchables

Ridge, Antonia   The Happy Wanderer

Ridgeley, Andrew   Careless Whisper

Ridgewell, Charles   Billy Muggins; If Those Lips Could Only Speak; I'm Shy, Mary Ellen, I'm Shy

Riefoli, Raffaele   Self Control

Riesenfeld, Hugo   Westward Ho!—The Covered Wagon March

Riggs, T. Lawrason   I've a Shooting Box in Scotland

Rigual, Carlos   Love Me with All Your Heart

Rigual, Mario   Love Me with All Your Heart

Riley, E.   Iowa Corn Song

Riley, Melvin   Oh Sheila

Riley, Michael   The Music Goes 'Round and 'Round

Riley, Robert S.   Just Walking in the Rain

Rimbault, Edward F.   How Dry I Am

Rimsky-Korsakov, Nikolai   Capriccio Espagnol; Flight of the Bumble Bee; Scheherazade; Song of India

Rines, Joe   Use Ajax the Foaming Cleanser

Ringle, Dave   Funny Bunny Hug; Ragging the Scale; The Wabash Blues

Ringwald, Roy   I Hear Music

Rinker, Al   Ready, Willing, and Able

Rio, Chuck   Tequila

Rios, Carlos   Dancing on the Ceiling

Riperton, Minnie Lovin' You

Risbrook, Louis Express

Risbrook, William Express

Risco, Arthur Goodbye Sally

Ritenour, Lee Is It You

Ritter, Alf It Costs So Little

Rivers, Johnny Poor Side of Town

Roach, Joseph Maloy One Little Candle

Robbins, Ayn Gonna Fly Now, or, Theme from *Rocky*

Robbins, C.A. Washington and Lee Swing

Robbins, Everett 'Tain't Nobody's Business If I Do

Robbins, Kent I Don't Think She's in Love Anymore

Robbins, Marty Don't Worry; My Woman, My Woman, My Wife; El Paso; A White Sport Coat and a Pink Carnation

Robbins, Vic Goodbye Hawaii

Robé, Harold Dear Old Pal of Mine

Robeldo, Julian Three O'Clock in the Morning

Robert, Camille Madelon

Roberti, Roberto Aurora

Roberts, Allan Dreamer with a Penny; Either It's Love or It Isn't; Into Each Life Some Rain Must Fall; Johnny Doughboy Found a Rose in Ireland; Prove It by the Things You Do (It's Easy To Say); Put the Blame on Mame; Sabre Dance; That's Good Enough for Me; Tired; To Know You (Is To Love You); You Always Hurt the One You Love; You Can't See the Sun When You're Crying

Roberts, Austin I.O.U.

Roberts, Bruce The Lucky One; Main Event/the Fight; Making Love; No More Tears (Enough Is Enough); You Should Be Mine (The Woo Woo Song); You're the Only One

Roberts, C. Luckeyth Moonlight Cocktail; Rockaway

Roberts, Johnny My Boy Lollipop

Roberts, Lee G. Smiles

Roberts, Paddy Angel of the Great White Way; The Ballad of Bethnal Green; The Belle of Barking Creek; The Book; Evermore; The Good Companions; Got'n Idea; The Heart of a Man; Horsey, Horsey; In Love for the Very First Time; It's a Boy; Johnny Is the Boy for Me; Lay Down Your Arms; Meet Me on the Corner; Pickin' a Chicken; Softly, Softly; That Dear Old Gentleman; Three Brothers; You Are My First Love

Roberts, Paul There's a Star Spangled Banner Waving Somewhere

Roberts, Rhoda The Swingin' Shepherd Blues

Roberts, Richard You Are the Woman

Robertson, Brian A. Silent Running (On Dangerous Ground); Wired For Sound

Robertson, Dick Goodnight Wherever You Are; A Little on the Lonely Side; We Three—My Echo, My Shadow and Me

Robertson, Don The Happy Whistler; Humming Bird; Please Help Me I'm Falling; Ringo

Robertson, Jaime The Weight

Robey, Don Share Your Love with Me

Robin, Leo Beyond the Blue Horizon; Blue Hawaii; Bye Bye Baby; Diamonds Are a Girl's Best Friend; Did You Ever Ride on a Rainbow; Easy Living; Faithful Forever; For Every Man There's a Woman; The Funny Old Hills; A Gal in Calico; Give Me a Moment Please; Hallelujah!; Here Lies Love; The Hills of Old Wyomin'; Hooray for Love; I Can't Escape from You; I Have Eyes (To See With); If I Should Lose You; If I Were King; In Love in Vain; It Was Written in the Stars; Jericho; (It's) June in January; A Little Girl from Little Rock; Lost in Loveliness; Louise; Love in Bloom; Love Is Just Around the Corner; Miss Brown to You; Moonlight and Shadows; My Heart and I; My Ideal; No Love, No Nothing; Oh But I Do; (I'd Love To Spend) One Hour with You; One Love; Paree!; Please; Prisoner of Love; Rainy Night in Rio; Sweet Is the Word for You; Thanks for the Memory; This Is the Moment; Through a Thousand Dreams; True Blue Lou; Two Hearts Are Better Than One; Up with the Lark; We Will Always Be Sweethearts; What's Good About Goodbye; Whispers in the Dark; With Every Breath I Take; You Started Something; You're a Sweet Little Headache; Zing a Little Zong

Robin, Sid Flying Home; Undecided

Robinson, Avery Two Hearts in Three Quarter Time; Water Boy

Robinson, Earl Ballad for Americans; Black and White; The Hills of Old Wyomin', Hold Tight—Hold Tight; The House I Live In

Robinson, Eric Jay Dance (Disco Heat)

Robinson, Harry Hoots Mon

Robinson, J. Russell Aggravatin' Papa (Don't You Try To Two-Time Me); Half-Way to Heaven; Is I in Love? I Is; Margie; Mary Lou; Memories of France; Original Dixieland One-Step; (Lena from) Palesteena

Robinson, Jessie Mae I Went to Your Wedding; Keep It a Secret

Robinson, Lilla Cayley (The) Glow Worm

Robinson, Sharon New Attitude

Robinson, William "Smokey" Jr. Being with You; Cruisin'; Happy, or, Love Theme from *Lady Sings the Blues;* My Girl Has Gone; My Guy; The One Who Really Loves You; Shop Around; The Tears of a Clown; The Tracks of My Tears

Robison, Carson J. Barnacle Bill the Sailor; Carry Me Back to the Lone Prairie; The Runaway Train

Robison, Willard A Cottage for Sale; Head Low

Robyn, Alfred George My San Domingo Maid

Rocco, Tommy A Little Good News; Sounds Like Love

Rochinski, Stanley Powder Your Face with Sunshine

Rock, Joseph Since I Don't Have You

Rodde, Leroy W. Have You Heard

Rodde, Roy Why Don't You Believe Me

Roden, Robert F. Down by the Silvery Rio Grande; My Little Georgia Rose; There's a Dixie Girl Who's Longing For a Yankee Doodle Boy; Where the Twilight Comes To Kiss the Rose Goodnight

Rodgers, Jimmie It's Over; Mule Skinner Blues

Rodgers, Mary   The Boy from . . . ; Man to Man Talk; Very Soft Shoes

Rodgers, Nile   Dance, Dance, Dance (Yowsah, Yowsah, Yowsah); Good Times; Upside Down; We Are Family

Rodgers, Richard   All At Once; All At Once You Love Her; Any Old Place with You; Are You My Love; Babes in Arms; Bali Ha'i; Bewitched, Bothered and Bewildered; Bloody Mary; Blue Moon; The Blue Room; Bye and Bye; Can't You Do a Friend a Favor; Carousel Waltz; The Circus Is on Parade; Climb Ev'ry Mountain; A Cockeyed Optimist; Dancing on the Ceiling; Dites-moi Pourquoi; Do I Hear a Waltz; Do I Hear You Saying ''I Love You''; Do I Love You Because You're Beautiful; Do It the Hard Way; Do-Re-Mi; Don't Marry Me; Down by the River; Edelweiss; Ev'ry Sunday Afternoon; Ev'rybody's Got a Home But Me; Ev'rything I've Got (Belongs to You); Falling in Love with Love; A Fellow Needs a Girl; From Another World; The Gentleman Is a Dope; Getting To Know You; The Girl Friend; Give It Back to the Indians; Glad To Be Unhappy; Happy Christmas, Little Friend; Happy Talk; Have You Met Miss Jones; Hello Young Lovers; Here in My Heart; Honey Bun; How Can You Forget; How Was I To Know; A Hundred Million Miracles; I Cain't Say No; I Could Write a Book; I Didn't Know What Time It Was; I Enjoy Being a Girl; I Have Dreamed; I Haven't Got a Worry in the World; I Like To Recognize the Tune; I Married an Angel; I Want a Man; I Whistle a Happy Tune; I Wish I Were in Love Again; I'd Rather Be Right; If I Loved You; I'll Tell the Man in the Street; I'm Gonna Wash That Man Right Outa My Hair; I'm in Love with a Wonderful Guy; In My Own Little Corner; In Our Little Den of Iniquity; Isn't It Kinda Fun; Isn't It Romantic; It Might as Well Be Spring; It Never Entered My Mind; It's a Grand Night for Singing; It's Easy To Remember (and So Hard To Forget); It's Got To Be Love; I've Got Five Dollars; Johnny One Note; June Is Bustin' Out All Over; Kansas City; Keep It Gay; The Lady Is a Tramp; A Little Birdie Told Me So; Little Girl Blue; Loneliness of Evening; The Lonely Goatherd; Love Look Away; Love Never Went to College; A Lovely Night; Lover; Manhattan; Many a New Day; March of the (Royal) Siamese Children; Maria; Mimi; Moon of My Delight; The Most Beautiful Girl in the World; Mountain Greenery; My Favorite Things; My Funny Valentine; My Heart Stood Still; My Lucky Star; My Romance; No Other Love; No Strings; Nobody Told Me; Nobody's Heart (Belongs to Me); Oh What a Beautiful Mornin'; Oklahoma; On a Desert Island with Thee; On Your Toes; Out of My Dreams; Over and Over Again; People Will Say We're in Love; Poor Jud (Is Daid); Quiet Night; Sentimental Me; Shall We Dance; A Ship Without a Sail; Sing for Your Supper; Sixteen Going on Seventeen; Slaughter on Tenth Avenue (Ballet); So Far; So Long, Farewell; Soliloquy; Some Enchanted Evening; Something Wonderful Soon (Maybe Not Tomorrow); The Sound of Music; Spring Is Here; Strangers; Sunday; The Surrey with the Fringe on Top; Sweet Peter; The Sweetest Sounds; Take the Moment; The Tartar Song; Ten Cents a Dance; Ten Minutes Ago; That's for Me; There Is Nothin' Like a Dame; There's a Small Hotel; This Can't Be Love; This Nearly Was Mine; This Was a Real Nice Clambake; Thou Swell; To Keep My Love Alive; Too Good for the Average Man; A Tree in the Park; Wait Till You See Her; Way Out West; We Kiss in a Shadow; We're Gonna Be All Right; What's the Use of Wond'rin'; When I Marry Mister Snow; When the Children Are Asleep; Where or When; Where's That Rainbow; Why Can't I; Why Do I; Why Do You Suppose; With a Song in My Heart; You Are Beautiful; You Are Never Away; You Are Sixteen; You Are Too Beautiful; You Have Cast Your Shadow on the Sea; You Mustn't Kick It Around; You Took Advantage of Me; You'll Never Walk Alone; Younger Than Springtime; Yours Sincerely; You've Got To Be (Carefully) Taught; Zip

Rodin, Gil   Big Noise from Winnetka

Rodney, Don   The Four Winds and the Seven Seas

Rodney, Paul   Calvary

Rodor, Jean   Under the Bridges of Paris

Rodriguez, Augustin   Yours, or, Quiéreme Mucho

Rodriquez, G.H. Matos   La Cumparsita

Roe, Tommy   Dizzy; Sheila

Roemheld, Heinz   Ruby

Rogan, Jimmy   Stardust on the Moon; When a Gypsy Makes His Violin Cry

Rogan, K.C.   You'll Always Be My Lifetime Sweetheart

Rogers, Alexander   Bon Bon Buddy; I May Be Crazy, But I Ain't No Fool; Let It Alone; Nobody; Rockaway

Rogers, Dick   Between Eighteenth and Nineteenth on Chestnut Street; Harlem Nocturne; I Guess I'll Get the Papers and Go Home

Rogers, E.W.   Ask a Policeman; Call Round Any Old Time; Following in Father's Footsteps; My Friend the Major; When a Fellah Has Turned Sixteen

Rogers, Eric   Startime

Rogers, Gabby   Goodnight Children, Everywhere

Rogers, Howard E.   If He Can Fight Like He Can Love, Good Night Germany

Rogers, James H.   The Star

Rogers, Kay   A Hundred Pounds of Clay; Our Favourite Melodies

Rogers, Kenny   Crazy; Love Will Turn You Around; What About Me

Rogers, Randall Jay   Love's Found You and Me

Rogers, Robert Cameron   The Rosary

Rogers, Robert E.   My Girl Has Gone

Rogers, Smokey   Gone

Rohusuke, El   Sukiyaki

Roig, Gonzalo   Yours, or, Quiéreme Mucho

Rolfe, Sam   The Ballad of Paladin

Rollins, Don   The Race Is On

Rollins, Walter E.   Frosty the Snow Man; Peter Cottontail

Rolls, Jack   You Can't Do That 'Ere

Roma, Caro   Can't Yo' Heah Me Callin', Caroline; In the Garden of My Heart

Roma, Del   I Will Follow Him

Roman, Frank   Rambling Wreck from Georgia Tech

Roman, Vatro   Anna

Romberg, Sigmund Auf Wiedersehn; The Big Back Yard; Close as Pages in a Book; Dance, My Darlings; Deep in My Heart, Dear; The Desert Song; Drinking Song; Faithfully Yours; Fascination; Golden Days; It's a Wonderful World; Jump Jim Crow; Just We Two; The Little Church Around the Corner; Lost in Loveliness; Lover Come Back to Me; Marianne; Mother; Nina Rosa; One Alone; One Kiss; The Riff Song; The Road to Paradise; Romance; Serenade; Serenade of Love; Silver Moon; Softly, As in a Morning Sunrise; Song of Love; Stouthearted Men; Wanting You; When Hearts Are Young; When I Grow Too Old To Dream; When She Walks in the Room; Will You Remember (Sweetheart); Your Land and My Land

Rome, Harold J. Along with Me; Call Me Mister; Everybody Loves Somebody; Fanny; F.D.R. Jones; Little Surplus Me, or, Surplus Blues; Meadowlands, or, Cavalry of the Steppes; Military Life, or, The Jerk Song; Miss Marmelstein; The Money Song; (All of a Sudden) My Heart Sings; Once Knew a Fella; South America Take It Away; Wish You Were Here; Yuletide, Park Avenue

Romeo, Tony I Think I Love You

Romero, Ricardo Chiapanecas (While There's Music There's Romance)

Ronald, Landon Down in the Forest

Roncoroni, Joe My Love and Devotion

Ronell, Ann Linda; Who's Afraid of the Big Bad Wolf; Willow Weep for Me

Ronklyn, George My Mariuccia Take a Steamboat

Root, George Frederick The Battle Cry of Freedom; Free as a Bird; The Hazel Dell; Just Before the Battle, Mother; Rosalie the Prairie Flower (as Wurzel); There's Music in the Air; Tramp, Tramp, Tramp; The Vacant Chair, or, We Shall Meet But We Shall Miss Him

Roper, Irene Can This Be Love

Roper, Terence Can This Be Love

Roppolo, Leon Make Love to Me; Tin Roof Blues

Rosa, Malia Forever and Ever

Rosas, Juventino Over the Waves

Rose, Arthur Lambeth Walk

Rose, Billy Back in Your Own Back Yard; Barney Google; Cheerful Little Earful; Clap Hands, Here Comes Charley; Come On, Spark Plug!; A Cup of Coffee, a Sandwich and You; Does the Spearmint Lose Its Flavor on the Bedpost Overnight; Don't Bring Lulu; Fifty Million Frenchmen Can't Be Wrong; Follow the Swallow; Golden Gate; Got the Jitters; Great Day; Here Comes the Showboat; Hot Heels; The House Is Haunted; I Can't Get the One I Want (Those I Get I Don't Want); I Found a Million Dollar Baby in a Five and Ten Cent Store; I Got a "Code" in My "Dose"; I Wanna Be Loved; I Wonder Who's Dancing with You Tonight; I'd Rather Be Blue Over You (Than Happy with Somebody Else); If I Had a Girl Like You; If You Want the Rainbow (You Must Have the Rain); In the Middle of the Night; It Happened in Monterey; It's Only a Paper Moon; I've Got a Feeling I'm Falling; Me and My Shadow; More Than You Know; The Night Is Young and You're So Beautiful; Overnight; Poor Papa (He's Got Nuthin' At All); Suddenly; That Old Gang of Mine;

There's a Rainbow Round My Shoulder; Tonight You Belong to Me; Too Many Parties and Too Many Pals; Without a Song; Would You Like To Take a Walk; You Beautiful So and So; You Tell Her, I S-t-u-t-t-e-r; Yours for a Song; You've Gotta (Got To) See Mamma Ev'ry Night, Or You Can't See Mamma at All

Rose, David Dance of the Spanish Onion; Holiday for Strings; One Love; Our Waltz; (Theme from) Sea Hunt; Serenade to a Lemonade; The Stripper

Rose, Ed Baby Shoes; Buddha; He Walked Right In, Turned Around and Walked Right Out Again; Oh Johnny, Oh Johnny, Oh!; Take a Car; Take Me Around Again

Rose, Fred Be Honest with Me; Crazy Heart; 'Deed I Do; The End of the World; Honest and Truly; Jimtown Blues; Kaw-Liga; Tweedle-O-Twill; Under Hawaiian Skies

Rose, Vincent Avalon; Blueberry Hill; Linger Awhile; Love Tales; The Umbrella Man

Rosenberg, George M. (George Rosey) The Handicap March; The Honeymoon (March)

Rosenberg, Lee Too Much

Rosenfeld, Monroe H. And Her Golden Hair Was Hanging Down Her Back; B-I-Double L-Bill; Down at the Huskin' Bee; Down Where the Silv'ry Mohawk Flows; Gold Will Buy Most Anything But a True Girl's Heart; Johnny Get Your Gun; Just for the Sake of Our Daughter; Let Me Shake the Hand That Shook the Hand of Sullivan; She Was Happy Till She Met You; Take Back Your Gold; Those Wedding Bells Shall Not Ring Out; With All Her Faults I Love Her Still

Rosey, George, see **George M. Rosenberg**

Rosier, F.W. Crucifix

Rosner, George Nightingale

Rosoff, Charles Song of the Rose; When You and I Were Seventeen

Ross, Adrian Bohemia; Can It Be Love; Come to the Ball; Dollar Princesses; Fortunio's Song; Girls, Girls, Girls; The Golden Song; Goodnight (I'm Only a Strolling Vagabond); Gypsy Maiden; (Just) A Little Love, a Little Kiss; Little Miss Melody; Long Ago in Alcala; Love and Wine; Love, Here Is My Heart; Maxim's; Merry Widow Waltz, or, I Love You So; My Dear Little Cingalee; My Dream of Love; The Pearl of Sweet Ceylon; Six Little Wives; Try Again Johnnie; Under the Deodar; Vilia; A Waltz Dream; Whisper to Me

Ross, Alexander C. Tippecanoe and Tyler Too

Ross, Bernice White on White

Ross, Beverly Judy's Turn To Cry; Lollipop

Ross, Edward Jim

Ross, Jerry (You've Got To Have) Heart; Hernando's Hideaway; Hey There; I'll Never Be Jealous Again; I'm Not At All in Love; A Little Brains—A Little Talent; (When You're) Racing with the Clock; Rags to Riches; 7½ Cents; Shoeless Joe from Hannibal, Mo.; Steam Heat; Two Lost Souls; Whatever Lola Wants

Ross, Marshall Marching Strings

Ross, Marvin Webster Harden My Heart

Ross, Spencer Tzena, Tzena, Tzena

Rossetti, Christina A Birthday

Rossi, C.A.   The Good Companions

Rossi, Francis   What You're Proposing

Rossini, Gioacchino   The Barber of Seville (Overture); William Tell Overture

Rostill, John Henry   Genie with the Light Brown Lamp; I Could Easily Fall; Let Me Be There; Please Mister Please; Rise and Fall of Flingle Bunt; Time Drags By

Rota, Nino   (Theme from) The Godfather (Waltz); (Theme from) The Godfather (Part II); The Legend of the Glass Mountain; Love Theme from Romeo and Juliet, or, A Time for Us; Michael's Theme; Speak Softly Love; (Theme from) La Strada, or, Stars Shine in Your Eyes

Roth, David Lee   Jump

Roth, Murray   There's a Million Girlies Lonesome Tonight, and Still I'm All Alone

Rotha, M.   That's All I Want from You

Rothenberg, Walter   Now and Forever

Rothrock, Claire   Old Cape Cod

Rotter, Fritz   I Kiss Your Hand, Madame; Take Me in Your Arms; That's All I Want from You; When the White Lilacs Bloom Again

Roubanis, R.N.   Misirlou

Rourke, M.E.   A Lemon in the Garden of Love; Throw Me a Rose

Rousseau, Jean-Jacques   Rousseau's Dream

Rouzaud, René   The Poor People of Paris

Rowe, Josephine V.   Macushla

Rowe, Richard   Once Upon a Dream

Rowland, Edward   Hinky Dinky Parlay Voo, or, Mad'moiselle from Armentières

Rowland, Kevin   Come On Eileen

Rox, John   It's a Big, Wide, Wonderful World

Roy, Harry   Leicester Square Rag

Royal, Fred   Soft Winds

Royster, Joseph   If You Wanna Be Happy; Quarter to Three Waltz

Rozsa, Miklos   Lydia

Rubens, Paul   Bohemia; Can It Be Love; The Flying Dutchman; Here's to Love; I Love the Moon; Little Pink Petty from Peter; The Violin Song; Wonderful Eyes; Your King and Country Want You

Rubicam, Shannon   How Will I Know

Rubinstein, Anton   Melody in F

Rubinstein, Artur   Kamennoi Ostrow

Ruby, Harry   All Alone Monday; And He'd Say "Oo-La-La Wee-Wee"; Come On, Papa; Daddy Long Legs; Dancing the Devil Away; Do You Love Me; Ev'ryone Says "I Love You"; Give Me the Simple Life; Hooray for Captain Spalding; I Gave You Up Just Before You Threw Me Down; I Love You So Much; I Wanna Be Loved by You; Keep On Doin' What You're Doin'; A Kiss To Build a Dream On; Maybe It's Because; My Sunny Tennessee; Nevertheless (I'm in Love with You); Over and Over Again; Puppchen; The Same Old Moon; She's Mine, All Mine; So Long, Oo-Long, How Long You Gonna Be Gone?; Thinking of You; Three Little Words; Timbuctoo; Up in the Clouds; Watching the Clouds Roll By; What'll We Do on a Saturday Night When the Town Goes Dry; Where Do They Go When They Row, Row, Row; Who's Sorry Now

Ruby, Herman   (Does Your Mother Know You're Out) Cecilia; The Egg and I; I Can't Get the One I Want (Those I Get I Don't Want); I'll Always Be in Love with You; My Honey's Lovin' Arms; My Sunny Tennessee

Ruddy, Charles Louis   My Mother's Lullaby

Rudge, Myles   Hole in the Ground; Right Said Fred; A Windmill in Old Amsterdam

Rudolph, Richard   Lovin' You

Rugolo, Peter   (Theme from) Doctor Kildaire, or, Three Stars Will Shine Tonight

Ruick, Walter   Tampico

Ruiz, Gabriel   Amor; Cuanto Le Gusta; Stars in Your Eyes

Ruiz, Mariano   The Way of Love

Ruiz, Pablo   Sway

Rule, Bert L.   Have a Smile (for Everyone You Meet)

Rule, Herbert   Abie My Boy; I Want Some Money; Ours Is a Nice 'ouse Ours Is; Turned Up

Rule, James   All Over Nothing At All; Goodbye Sue

Rundgren, Todd   Hello It's Me; I Saw the Light; Love Is the Answer

Rushworth, Cedric   Down Sweetheart Avenue

Ruskin, Harry   I May Be Wrong, But I Think You're Wonderful

Russell, Ben   Katinka; Lonesome in the Moonlight; You Didn't Want Me When You Had Me

Russell, Bert   Hang On Sloopy; A Little Bit of Soap; One Way Love; Twist and Shout

Russell, Bob   At the Crossroads; Babalu; Ballerina; Brazil; Do Nothin' Till You Hear from Me; Don't Get Around Much Anymore; Full Moon; I Don't Know About You; Matinee; Would I Love You (Love You Love You)

Russell, Bobby   Better Homes and Gardens; He Ain't Heavy. . . . He's My Brother; Honey; Little Green Apples; The Night the Lights Went Out in Georgia

Russell, Graham   All Out of Love; Lost in Love; The One That You Love; Sweet Dreams

Russell, Harry   We Don't Want the Bacon, What We Want Is a Piece of the Rhine

Russell, Henry   The Brave Old Oak; Cheer, Boys, Cheer; A Life on the Ocean Wave; My Mother's Bible; The Old Arm Chair; Travelin' Band; Woodman Spare That Tree

Russell, James J.   Where the River Shannon Flows

Russell, Johnny   You'll Be Back Every Night in My Dreams

Russell, Kennedy   At Santa Barbara

Russell, Larry   Vaya Con Dios

Russell, Leon   Lady Blue; This Masquerade

Russell, Sidney Keith   B-I, Bi; Blue Gardenia; Frenesi; Maria Elena; Taboo; Time was, or, Dreaming; You Came a Long Way from St. Louis

Russo, Dan   Toot Toot Tootsie (Goo'Bye)

Rutherford, Mike   All I Need Is a Miracle; Invisible Touch; Silent Running (On Dangerous Ground); That's All

Rutherford, Robert   We've Got To Keep Up with the Joneses

Rutherford, Ruth   Love's Garden of Roses

Ruvin, Ralph   You're a Pink Toothbrush

Ryan, Ben   The Gang That Sang Heart of My Heart; Inka Dinka Doo; Love Tales; M-I-S-S-I-S-S-I-P-P-I; When Francis Dances with Me

Ryan, Desmond   Kattie (Katty) Avourneen

Ryan, Patti   Just Another Woman in Love

Ryan, Paul   I Will Drink the Wine

Ryerson, Frank   Blue Champagne

Ryskind, Morrie   Nobody Wants Me

Sablon, Jean   Passé

Sacco, Tony   The Breeze (That's Bringing My Honey Back to Me)

Sachs, Norman   African Waltz

Sade   Smooth Operator; The Sweetest Taboo

Sadler, Barry   The Ballad of the Green Berets

Safka, Melaine   Brand New Key; Lay Down (Candles in the Rain); Look What They've Done to My Song Ma

Safroni, Arnold   Imperial Echoes

Sager, Carole Bayer   A Groovy Kind of Love; Heartbreaker; Heartlight; I'd Rather Leave While I'm in Love; If You Remember Me; It's My Turn; Just for Tonight; Making Love; Midnight Blue; Nobody Does It Better; On My Own; On the Way to the Sky; That's What Friends Are For; Theme from *Ice Castles* (Through the Eyes of Love); They're Playing Our Song; Turn Around; When I Need You; You're the Only One

Saint-Saëns, Camille   Danse Macabre; My Heart at Thy Sweet Voice; The Swan

Sainte-Marie, Buffy   Until It's Time for You To Go; Up Where We Belong

Sallit, Norman   Here I Am (Just When I Thought I Was Over You)

Salmon, Arthur L.   Homing

Salter, William   Just the Two of Us

Salvador, Henri   Melodie d'Amour (Melody of Love)

Sam, Senora   I'll Be Good to You

Sammes, Mike   Out on the Edge of Beyond

Sampson, Edgar M.   Blue Lou; Don't Be That Way; Lullaby in Rhythm; Stomping at the Savoy

Sampson, Phil   I Loved 'Em Everyone

Samudio, Domingo   Wooly Bully

Samuel, Harold   Jogging Along the Highway

Samuels, Frank   Gypsy Dream Rose; Underneath the Russian Moon

Samuels, Walter G.   (Take Me Back to My) Boots and Saddle; True

Samwell, Ian   Fall in Love with You; Gee Whiz, It's You; High Class Baby; Never Mind; You Can Never Stop Me Loving You

Samwell-Smith, Paul   Still I'm Sad

Sananes, Charles   Till

Sanchez, Fernan   O Cuba (Tu)

Sanders, Alma M.   Little Town in the Ould County Down; That Tumble-Down Shack in Athlone

Sanders, George H.   Petite Tonkinoise

Sanders, Joe   Beloved

Sanders, Julio Cesar A.   Adios Muchachos

Sanders, Scott   Rolling Round the World

Sanders, Zell   Sally Go Round the Roses

Sanderson, James   Hail to the Chief

Sanderson, Wilfrid   The Company Sergeant Major; Friend o' Mine; Shipmates of Mine; Until

Sandler, Jacob   Eli Eli

Sandoval, Miguel   Eres Tu

Sandrich, Mark Jr.   Hic, Haec, Hoc

Sandwith, Mrs. M.T.E.   Clavelitos (Carnations)

Sanford, Chaz   Missing You; Talk To Me

Sanford, Dick   Red Silk Stockings and Green Perfume; The Singing Hills

Sanford, Ed   Smoke from a Distant Fire

Sanford, Harold   Mem'ries, or, Golden Memory Days

Sanford, James   Miss Lucy Neale

Sanicola, Henry   Mistletoe and Holly; This Love of Mine

Sankey, Ira David   Hiding in Thee; I Am Coming; The Ninety and Nine; Tell It Out Among the Nations (Heathen) That the Lord Is King; Tenderly Calling; Trusting Jesus, That Is All; When the Mists Have Rolled Away; Whosoever Will May Come

Sansone, Tony   Walk Away, Renee

Santley, Joseph H.   At the Moving Picture Ball; The Big Butter and Egg Man; Hawaiian Butterfly; Tamiami Trail; There's Yes, Yes, in Your Eyes

Santly, Henry W.   I'm Sitting Pretty in a Pretty Little City; You Said It

Santly, Lester   I'm Nobody's Baby

Santo, Johnny   Sleep Walk

Sapaugh, Thomas   Try a Little Kindness

Sargent, Epes   A Life on the Ocean Wave

Sarony, Leslie   Ain't It Grand To Be Bloomin' Well Dead; Coom Pretty One; The Dicky Bird Hop; Don't Do That to the Poor Puss Cat; The Flirtation Waltz; Forty-Seven Ginger Headed Sailors; I Lift Up My Finger and I Say Tweet Tweet; Jollity Farm; Mucking About the Garden (as Q. Cumber); Over the Garden Wall; Rhymes; Wheezy Anna; When a Soldier's on Parade; When the Guards Are on Parade

Saroyan, William   Come On-A-My House

Sarstedt, Peter   Where Do You Go to My Lovely

Satchell, Clarence   Fire; Love Rollercoaster

Saver, Robert   When It's Springtime in the Rockies

Saunders, Red   Hambone

Savino, Domenico (D. Onivas)   Indianola

Savitt, Jan   Now and Forever

Sawyer, Charles Carroll   Weeping, Sad, and Lonely, or, When This Cruel War Is Over

Sawyer, Jean   Painted Tainted Rose

Sawyer, Pamela Joan   Love Child; Love Hangover

Saxe, R.B.   A Rose in a Garden of Weeds

Saxon, David   There Must Be a Way

Sayer, Leo   Dreamin'; Living in a Fantasy; Long Tall Glasses (I Can Dance); You Make Me Feel Like Dancing

Sayers, Henry J.   Ta-Ra-Ra-Boom-Der-É (De-Ay)

Sayles, James M.   Star of the Evening

Sbarbaro, Anthony   At the Jazz Band Ball; Barnyard Blues; Bluin' the Blues; Clarinet Marmalade; Ostrich Walk

Scaggs, Boz   Breakdown Dead Ahead; Jo Jo; Look What You've Done to Me; Lowdown

Scales, Harvey   Disco Lady

Scanlan, William J.   Molly O!, or, Mavourneen; My Nellie's Blue Eyes; Peek-a-Boo; Remember Boy, You're Irish (Shane na Lown)

Scarborough, Skip   Love Ballad

Scarlett, Leroi   I Don't Want Another Sister

Schack, Marilyn   Java

Schaefer, Lloyd   Smoke Dreams

Schafer, Milton   She Touched Me

Schapiro, Herb   Dream Babies

Scharf, Stuart   (I'd Really) Like To Get To Know You

Scharf, Walter   Ben

Scharfenberger, Werner   Sailor (Your Home Is the Sea)

Scharwenka, Xavier   Polish Dance

Schertzinger, Victor   Arthur Murray Taught Me Dancing in a Hurry; Dream Lover; The Fleet's In; I Remember You; I'll Never Let a Day Pass By; Kiss the Boys Goodbye; Love Me Forever; Marcheta; (This Is) My Love Parade; My Wonderful Dream Girl; Not Mine; One Night of Love; Sand in My Shoes; Tangerine

Schiff, Steve   Don't You (Forget About Me)

Schifrin, Lalo   (Theme from) Mission: Impossible

Schless, Peter   On the Wings of Love

Schlitz, Don   The Gambler

Schmid, Johann C.   (Beautiful) Garden of Roses

Schmidt, Erwin R.   Carolina Sunshine; Drifting and Dreaming (Sweet Paradise)

Schmidt, Harvey   The Honeymoon Is Over; Much More; My Cup Runneth Over; Never Say No; Soon It's Gonna Rain; Try To Remember

Schmitz, Joseph   I Once Had a Heart, Margarita

Schnaars, James   Nothing Like Falling in Love

Schoch, Harriet   Ain't No Way To Treat a Lady

Schoebel, Elmer   Bugle Call Rag; Farewell Blues; Nobody's Sweetheart Now; Prince of Wails

Scholl, Jack   Isn't Love the Grandest Thing; My Little Buckaroo; An Old Water Mill; Throw Another Log on the Fire

Scholz, Tom   More Than a Feeling

Schonberger, John   Whispering

Schonberger, Malvin   Whispering

Schor, Neal   Don't Stop Believin'

Schraubstader, Carl   Last Night on the Back Porch—I Loved Her Best of All

Schroeder, Aaron   Because They're Young; A Big Hunk of Love; French Foreign Legion; Good Luck Charm; It's Now or Never; Mandolins in the Moonlight; Rubber Ball; Stuck on You; Time and the River

Schroeder, John   Don't Treat Me Like a Child; Little Miss Lonely; Walkin' Back to Happiness; You Don't Know

Schubert, Franz   Ave Maria; The Golden Song; Marche Militaire; Moment Musicale; Serenade

Schultze, Norbert   Lili (Lilli) Marlene

Schumann, Robert   The Happy Farmer; Träumerei; The Two Grenadiers

Schumann, Walter   (Theme from) Dragnet

Schuster, Ira   Did You Ever Get That Feeling in the Moonlight; Hold Me; Ten Little Fingers and Ten Little Toes— Down in Tennessee

Schuster, Joe   Dance of the Paper Dolls

Schütt, Edouard   À la Bien-Aimée, or, Papillons d' Amour

Schuyler, Thom   I Don't Know Where To Start; Love Will Turn You Around; Nothing Like Falling in Love

Schwabach, Kurt   Danke Schoen

Schwandt, Wilbur   Dream a Little Dream of Me

Schwartz, Arthur   After All, You're All I'm After; Alone Together; Alone Too Long; By Myself; Confession; Dancing in the Dark; A Gal in Calico; Goodbye to All That; Got a Bran' New Suit; Hammacher Schlemmer, I Love You; Haunted Heart; How Sweet You Are; I Guess I'll Have To Change My Plan; I Love Louisa; I See Your Face Before Me; If There Is Someone Lovelier Than You; I'll Buy You a Star; Look Who's Dancing; Louisiana Hayride; Love Is a Dancing Thing; Love Is the Reason; Lucky Seven; Make the Man Love Me; More Love Than Your Love; New Sun in the Sky; O Leo; Oh But I Do; Rainy Night in Rio; Seal It with a Kiss; She's Such a Comfort to Me; A Shine on Your Shoes; Something To Remember You By; That's Entertainment; Then I'll Be Tired of You; There's No Holding Me; They're Either Too Young or Too Old; This Is It; Through a Thousand Dreams; You and the Night and the Music; You Have Everything

Schwartz, Jean   Any Old Place I Can Hang My Hat Is Home Sweet Home to Me; Au Revoir, Pleasant Dreams; Back to the Carolina You Love; Bedelia; Chinatown, My Chinatown; Don't Put Me Off at Buffalo Any More; Goodbye Virginia; Hello, Central, Give Me No Man's Land; Hello, Hawaii, How Are You; I Love the Ladies; I'm All Bound 'Round with the Mason-Dixon Line; I'm Unlucky; Mister Dooley; My Guiding Star; My Irish Molly O; Rip Van Winkle Was a Lucky Man; Rock-a-Bye Your Baby with a Dixie Melody; Since Sister Nell Heard Paderewski Play; Sit Down, You're Rocking the Boat; Trust in Me; Why Do They All Take the Night Boat to Albany

Schwartz, Robert   Sweet Talkin' Guy

Schwartz, Stephen   All Good Gifts; Day by Day; Learn Your Lessons Well; Magic To Do; Spread a Little Sunshine

Schweers, John Arthur   Golden Tears

Scoggins, C.H.   Where the Silv'ry Colorado Wends Its Way

Scollard, Clinton   Sylvia

Scott, Andrew   Fox on the Run

Scott, Bennett   By the Side of the Zuyder Zee; Do You Remember the Last Waltz; Everybody's Crazy on the Foxtrot; Fall In and Follow Me; Ship Ahoy, or, All the Nice Girls Love a Sailor; Take Me Back to Dear Old Blighty

Scott, Bobby   He Ain't Heavy . . . He's My Brother; A Taste of Honey

Scott, Clement   Now Is the Hour; Oh Promise Me

Scott, Clifford   Honkey Tonk

Scott, Clive   Sky High

Scott, Cyril   Danse Nègre; Lotus Land

Scott, Emerson   Someone's Rocking My Dream Boat

Scott, Howard E.   The Cisco Kid; Gypsy Man; Summer; Why Can't We Be Friends

Scott, James   Brass in Pocket

Scott, John Prindle   Come, Ye Blessed; Ride On, Ride On

Scott, Johnnie   Maybe It's Because

Scott, Johnny   The Good Word (Theme from *Nationwide*)

Scott, Lady John (Alicia Ann Spottiswoode)   Annie Laurie

Scott, Marvin   Friends and Neighbours

Scott, Maurice   I've Got Rings on My Fingers, or, Mumbo Jumbo Jijjiboo J. O'Shea

Scott, Raymond   Huckleberry Duck; In an Eighteenth Century Drawing Room; Toy Trumpet; Twilight in Turkey (*as Harry Warnow*)

Scott, Richard   Why Lady Why

Scott, Ronnie   Abergavenny; It's a Heartache; Jezamine

Scott, Sir Walter   Ave Maria; Bonnie Dundee; Hail to the Chief

Scott, Tommy   Boys Cry

Scott, Winfield   Return to Sender; Tweedle Dee

Scotti, William   My Moonlight Madonna

Scotto, Vincent Baptiste   It's Delightful To Be Married; Petite Tonkinoise; Two Loves Have I; Under the Bridges of Paris; Vieni, Vieni

Scott-Wood, George   Shy Serenade

Seago, Eddie   Early in the Morning

Seals, Jimmy   Diamond Girl; Get Closer; I'll Play for You

Seals, Troy   I've Got a Rock 'n' Roll Heart; Red Neckin' Love Makin' Night; When We Make Love

Sears, Reverend Edmund Hamilton   It Came upon a Midnight Clear

Sebastian, John B.   Daydream; Did You Ever Have To Make Up Your Mind; Do You Believe in Magic; Summer in the City; Welcome Back

Sebastian, Mark   Summer in the City

Secunda, Sholom   Bei Mir Bist Du Schön (Means That You're Grand)

Sedaka, Neil   Bad Blood; Breaking Up Is Hard To Do; Calendar Girl; Frankie; The Immigrant; Laughter in the Rain; Little Devil; Lonely Night (Angel Face); Love in the Shadows; Love Will Keep Us Together; Should've Never Let You Go; Solitaire; That's When the Music Takes Me; Where the Boys Are; You Never Done It Like That

Seeger, Pete   Guantanamera; If I Had a Hammer; Turn! Turn! Turn!; Where Have All the Flowers Gone

Seger, Bob   We've Got Tonight

Seelen, Jerry   C'est Si Bon

Segal, Jack   Hard To Get; Scarlet Ribbons (for Her Hair); When Sonny Gets Blue

Seger, Bob   We've Got Tonight

Seiber, Matyas   By the Fountains of Rome

Seibert, T. Lawrence   Casey Jones

Seiler, Eddie   Ask Anyone Who Knows; I Don't Want To Set the World on Fire; Till Then; When the Lights Go On Again (All Over the World)

Seitz, Ernest   The World Is Waiting for the Sunrise

Selden, Albert   When I Fall in Love

Selden, Edgar   All That I Ask of You Is Love

Self, Ronnie   I'm Sorry

Sembello, Danny   Neutron Dance

Sembello, Michael   Maniac

Seneca, Joe   Break It to Me Gently

September, Anthony   Butterfly

Seraphine, Daniel   No Tell Lover

Seress, Rezso   Gloomy Sunday

Serota, Ronald   Three Times in Love

Serradell, Narciso   La Golondrina

Service, Paul   Disco Nights

Setser, Ed   I've Got a Rock 'n' Roll Heart

Settle, Mike   But You Know I Love You

Sexton, John   Auf Wiederseh'n Sweetheart; Why Worry

Seyler, Clifford   The Girl in the Crinoline Gown; I'm Tickled to Death I'm Single

Seymour, Rae H.   Summer Dreams

Seymour, Tot   Accent on Youth; Swingin' in a Hammock

Shackford, Charles   Let Bygones Be Bygones

Shaddick, Terry   Physical

Shafer, Bob   I Want You To Want Me To Want You

Shaftel, Arthur   Atlanta, Ga.; Just a Little Bit South of North Carolina; Love Is So Terrific

Shakespear, Nick   Will I What

Shakespeare, John Nichola   Little Bit o' Soul

Shakespeare, William   Bid Me Discourse; I Know a Bank Where the Wild Thyme Blows; Lo! Here the Gentle Lark; Sigh No More, Ladies

Shand, Terry   Dance with a Dolly; I Double Dare You; When the Circus Came to Town

Shank, Joe   Unsuspecting Heart

Shankar, Ravi   For All Mankind (Theme from *Gandhi*)

Shanklin, Wayne Big Hurt; Chanson d'Amour; Jezebel

Shannon, James Royce The Missouri Waltz; Too-ra-loo-ra-loo-ral, That's an Irish Lullaby

Shannon, Ronny Baby I Love You

Shaper, Hal Softly As I Leave You

Shaper, Harold There Goes My Lover

Shapiro, Dan I Wanna Get Married

Shapiro, Joe Round and Round

Shapiro, Ted If I Had You

Sharp, Martha Come Back When You Grow Up

Sharp, Todd Got a Hold on Me

Sharpe, Jack So Rare

Sharples, Winston It's a Hap-Hap-Happy Day

Sharron-Humak, Marti Jump (For My Love)

Shaver, Billy Joe (I'm Just an Old Chunk of Coal But) I'll Be a Diamond Someday

Shavers, Charles Undecided

Shaw, Artie Love of My Life; Traffic Jam

Shaw, David T. Columbia, the Gem of the Ocean, or, The Red, White and Blue

Shaw, Howard Stranger Than Fiction

Shaw, Knowles Bringing in the Sheaves

Shaw, Oliver Mary's Tears; There's Nothing True But Heaven

Shaw, Tommy Renegade

Shawn, Nelson Jim

Shay, Larry Everywhere You Go; Gee, But I'd Like To Make You Happy; Get Out and Get Under the Moon; A Sinner Kissed an Angel; When You're Smiling (the Whole World Smiles with You)

Shayne, Gloria Almost There; Goodbye Cruel World; The Men in My Little Girl's Life

Shea, John Cheer, Cheer for Old Notre Dame

Shea, Michael Cheer, Cheer for Old Notre Dame

Sheafe, M.W. Washington and Lee Swing

Shean, Al Mister Gallagher and Mister Shean

Shear, Jules All Through the Night

Shearing, George Lullaby of Birdland

Sheehy, Eleanor Beat Me, Daddy, Eight to the Bar

Sheeley, Sharon Dum Dum; Poor Little Fool

Shefter, Bert The Lamp Is Low

Sheldon, Ernie Baby the Rain Must Fall

Sheldon, Jon Limbo Rock

Shelley, Gladys How Did He Look

Sheppard, E.A. Any Old Iron

Sheppard, Jimmy Daddy's Home

Sheppard, Shep Honkey Tonk

Shepperd, Drey I Made It Through the Rain

Sheridan, Mark Who Were You with Last Night

Sheriden, Lee Angelo; Save Your Kisses for Me

Sherman, Al (What'll We Do on a) Dew-Dew-Dewy Day; Got the Bench, Got the Park, But I Haven't Got You; (Ho! Ho! Ha! Ha!) Me Too; Ninety-Nine Out of a Hundred (Want To Be Loved); No! No! A Thousand Times No!; (Potatoes Are Cheaper—Tomatoes Are Cheaper) Now's the Time To Fall in Love; (It Happened) On the Beach at Bali Bali; Save Your Sorrow for Tomorrow; When I'm the President (We Want Cantor); You Gotta Be a Football Hero (To Get Along with the Beautiful Girls)

Sherman, Alan Hello Mudduh, Hello Faddah

Sherman, Jimmy Lover Man (Oh Where Can You Be)

Sherman, Joe Graduation Day; Juke Box Baby; Ramblin' Rose

Sherman, Noel Graduation Day; Juke Box Baby; Morgen—One More Sunrise; Ramblin' Rose; Yesterday's Roses

Sherman, Richard M. Chim Chim Cher-ee; Chitty Chitty Bang Bang; Let's Get Together; A Spoonful of Sugar; Supercalifragilisticexpialidocious; You're Sixteen

Sherman, Robert B. Chim Chim Cher-ee; Chitty Chitty Bang Bang; Let's Get Together; A Spoonful of Sugar; Supercalifragilisticexpialidocious; You're Sixteen

Sherr, Jack Yours, or, Quiéreme Mucho

Sherrell, Doris Pony Ça C'est Paris

Sherrill, Billy Almost Persuaded; Every Time You Touch Me (I Get High); (If You Happen To See) The Most Beautiful Girl (in the World); My Elusive Dreams; Stand by Your Man; A Very Special Love Song

Sherrill, Billy Takin' It Easy

Sherrill, Mark Takin' It Easy

Sherrin, Ned Not So Much a Programme, More a Way of Life

Sherwin, Manning The Moment I Saw You; A Nightingale Sang in Berkeley Square; Who's Taking You Home Tonight; Wrap Yourself in Cotton Wool; You Happen Once in a Lifetime

Sherwin, William F. Fully Persuaded

Sherwood, Lew My Twilight Dream

Shield, William The Green Mountain Farmer

Shields, Larry At the Jazz Band Ball; Barnyard Blues; Bluin' the Blues; Clarinet Marmalade; Ostrich Walk

Shields, Ren Come Take a Trip in My Airship; Come to the Land of Bohemia; In the Good Old Summer Time; In the Merry Month of June; The Longest Way 'Round Is the Sweetest Way Home; Steamboat Bill; Up in a Balloon; Waltz Me Around Again Willie—'Round, 'Round, 'Round

Shilkret, Jack Make Believe

Shilkret, Nathaniel Down the River of Golden Dreams; Jeannine, I Dream of Lilac Time; (Look Down That) Lonesome Road

Shire, David Baby Baby Baby; I Want It All; It Goes Like It Goes; Night on Disco Mountain; Romance; The Story Goes On; Washington Square; With You I'm Born Again

Shirl, Jimmy Come to the Mardi Gras; I Believe; Made for Each Other; Meet Mister Callaghan; Sonata

Shisler, Charles Bring Me a Rose

Shorrock, Glenn Cool Change; Man on Your Mind

Shostakovich, Dmitri Age of Gold Ballet

Shull, Chester R. It's No Sin

Shuman, Alden   Seven Lonely Days

Shuman, Earl   Clinging Vine; Left Right Out of Your Heart; Seven Lonely Days

Shuman, Mort   Amsterdam; Can't Get Used To Losing You; Carousel; Desperate Ones; Here I Go Again; If We Only Have Love; Little Children; Little Sister; Madeleine; Marieke; Old Folks; Save the Last Dance for Me; Sons Of; Surrender; Suspicion; Teenager in Love; Timid Frieda

Sibelius, Jean   Finlandia; The Swan of Tuonela; Valse Triste

Sidney, George   Creole Belle

Sieczynski, Rudolf   Vienna Dreams; Wien, Du Stadt Meiner Träume

Siegel, Arthur   Love Is a Simple Thing; Monotonous

Siegel, Paul   Autumn Concerto

Sierra, G. Martinez   Ritual Fire Dance

Sievier, Bruce   Her Name Is Mary; Speak to Me of Love; You're Blasé

Sigidi   Take Your Time (Do It Right)

Sigler, Jack, Jr.   Love Can Make You Happy

Sigler, Maurice   Everything Stops for Tea; Everything's in Rhythm with My Heart; He's a Humdinger; I Saw Stars; I'm in a Dancing Mood; Jimmy Had a Nickel; Little Man, You've Had a Busy Day; My First Thrill; She Shall Have Music; Tell Me a Story; There Isn't Any Limit to My Love; This'll Make You Whistle

Sigman, Carl   Addio Addio, or, Goodbye; Answer Me (My Love); Arrivederci Roma; Ballerina; The Big Brass Band from Brazil; Careless Hands; Celery Stalks at Midnight; Civilization (Bongo Bongo Bongo); A Day in the Life of a Fool; The Day the Rains Came; Don't Ever Be Afraid To Go Home; Dream Along with Me (I'm on My Way to a Star); Ebb Tide; Eleventh Hour Melody; Enjoy Yourself, It's Later Than You Think; Funny Thing; Hop Scotch Polka; I Could Have Told You; It's All in the Game; Just Come Home; Little Rock Getaway; Losing You; (Theme from) Love Story, or, Where Do I Begin; A Marshmallow World; Matinee; Mountains Beyond the Moon; My Heart Cries for You; Passé; Pennsylvania 6-5000; There Is No Christmas Like a Home Christmas; Till; What Now My Love; You're My World

Signorelli, Frank   A Blues Serenade; I'll Never Be the Same; Stairway to the Stars (Park Avenue Fantasy)

Silbar, Jeff Alan   Where Were You When I Was Falling in Love

Silberman, L.   Abie My Boy; I Want Some Money; There You Are Then

Silesu, Lao   (Just) A Little Love, a Little Kiss; Love, Here Is My Heart

Silver, Abner   Angel Child; C'est Vous (It's You); Chasing Shadows; Farewell to Arms; Have You Forgotten So Soon; How Did He Look; I'm Goin' South; It Must Be Love; My Home Town Is a One Horse Town, But It's Big Enough for Me; My Love for You; No! No! A Thousand Times No!; (It Happened) On the Beach at Bali Bali; (I Don't Believe It But) Say It Again; Say It While Dancing; There Goes My Heart; With These Hands

Silver, Frank   Yes! We Have No Bananas

Silver, Maxwell   He Walked Right In, Turned Around and Walked Right Out Again

Silverman, Al   Tell Me That You Love Me Tonight

Silverman, Charles   Look Through Any Window

Silvers, Dolores Vicki   Learnin' the Blues

Silvers, Louis   April Showers; Weary River

Silvers, Phil   Nancy (with the Laughing Face)

Silvers, Sid   A Hundred Years from Now

Silverstein, Dave   Bend Down, Sister

Silverstein, Shel   A Boy Named Sue; The Unicorn

Silvestri, Alfred   Serenade, or, Rimpianto

Silvestre, Paul Armand   Berceuse

Simeone, Harry   The Little Drummer Boy

Simien, Sidney   My Toot Toot

Simmons, Charles   They Just Can't Stop It (The Games People Play)

Simmons, Pat   Black Water

Simms, Joseph   Ain't It a Shame

Simon, Carly   Anticipation; The Right Thing To Do; You're So Vain

Simon, Howard   As Long as I Live; Gonna Get a Girl

Simon, Joe   Get Down Get Down (Get On the Floor)

Simon, Moises   Marta, or, Rambling Rose of the Wildwood; The Peanut Vendor

Simon, Nat   And Mimi; Coax Me a Little Bit; The Gaucho Serenade; In My Little Red Book; Istanbul (Not Constantinople); The Mama Doll Song; No Can Do; The Old Lamp-Lighter; Poinciana; Sweet Heartaches

Simon, Norman J.   Look Around (You'll Find Me There)

Simon, Paul   The Boxer; Bridge Over Troubled Water; Fifty Ways To Leave Your Lover; The 59th Street Bridge Song, or, Feelin' Groovy; Gone At Last; Graceland; Homeward Bound; Kodachrome; Late In the Evening; Loves Me Like a Rock; Me an Julio Down by the Schoolyard; Mrs. Robinson; My Little Town; Red Rubber Ball; Scarborough Fair/Canticle, or, Parsley, Sage, Rosemary and Thyme; Slip Slidin' Away; The Sounds of Silence

Simons, Peter   United We Stand

Simons, Seymour   All of Me; Breezin' Along with the Breeze; Honey; Just Like a Gypsy

Simpkins, Lewis C.   Night Train

Simpson, Valerie   Ain't No Mountain High Enough; In Every Woman; Solid

Sinatra, Frank   I'm a Fool To Want You; Mistletoe and Holly; This Love of Mine

Sinclair, John L.   The Eyes of Texas (Are Upon You)

Sinding, Christian   Rustle of Spring

Sinfield, Pete   Have You Ever Been in Love; The Land of Make Believe

Singer, Artie   At the Hop

Singer, Bob   Unsuspecting Heart

Singer, Louis C.   One Meat Ball; Sleepy Serenade; Young and Warm and Wonderful

Singleton, Charles Don't Forbid Me; If I May; Spanish Eyes; Strangers in the Night

Siras, John Dance of the Paper Dolls; (In) A Shanty in Old Shanty Town

Sissle, Noble Bandana Days; I'm Just Wild About Harry; Love Will Find a Way; Shuffle Along; You Were Meant for Me

Skardina, Gary P. Jump (For My Love)

Skellern, Peter Our Jackie's Getting Married

Skelly, Alan Lily Dale

Skelly, Joseph P. A Boy's Best Friend Is His Mother; Strolling on the Brooklyn Bridge; Why Did They Dig Ma's Grave So Deep

Skidmore, Will E. It Takes a Long, Tall, Brown-Skin Gal

Skill, Mike Talking in Your Sleep

Skinner, Frank Head Low

Skinner, Terry Even the Nights Are Better; I Just Came Here To Dance; Touch Me When We're Dancing

Skleroy, Gloria I Just Fall in Love Again

Skylar, Sunny Amor; And So to Sleep Again; Atlanta, Ga.; Be Mine Tonight; Besame Mucho; Gotta Be This or That; Hair of Gold, Eyes of Blue; It Must Be Jelly, 'Cause Jam Don't Shake Like That; Just a Little Bit South of North Carolina; Love Is So Terrific; Love Me with All Your Heart; Too Many Times; Waitin' For the Train to Come In; You'll Always Be the One I Love; You're Breaking My Heart

Slack, Freddie The House of Blue Lights

Slade, Julian Free as Air; Salad Days

Slaney, Ivor Carlos' Theme; Georgian Rumba

Slate, Johnny Blaze of Glory

Slater, Jean You Can Never Stop Me Loving You

Slaughton, Reverend William Strike the Cymbal

Slay, Frank C., Jr. Buzz Buzz A-Diddle-It; Jump Over; Silhouettes

Sloan, P.F. The Eve of Destruction

Sloan, Reginald All Pals Together

Sloane, A. Baldwin Heaven Will Protect the Working Girl; Life Is Only What You Make It After All; When You Ain't Got No Money, Well, You Needn't Come 'Round

Small, Allan The Wedding Samba

Smalley, Victor H. The Lovin' Rag

Smalls, Charlie Believe in Yourself; Ease On down the Road; The Feeling We Once Had; He's the Wizard; Home; No Bad News

Smart, Henry Angels from the Realms of Glory

Smetana, Bedrich The Bartered Bride (Overture); Moldau

Smethurst, Allan Hev Yew Gotta Loight, Boy?

Smith, Arthur Beautiful Brown Eyes; Dueling Banjos

Smith, Beasley Beg Your Pardon; The Old Master Painter; That Lucky Old Sun

Smith, Billy Dawn Just Born To Be Your Baby; Step by Step

Smith, Carl (Your Love Has Lifted Me) Higher and Higher

Smith, Chris After All That I've Been to You; Ballin' the Jack; Beans Beans Beans; Come After Breakfast, Bring 'Long Your Lunch and Leave 'Fore Supper Time; Constantly; Down Among the Sugar Cane; Down in Honky Tonky Town; Fifteen Cents; He's a Cousin of Mine; If He Comes In, I'm Going Out; You're in the Right Church, But the Wrong Pew

Smith, Claydes Eugene Celebration; Cherish; Fresh; Joanna; Ladies Night; Misled

Smith, Colin Looking Around

Smith, Curt Head Over Heels

Smith, Dexter Ulysses Is His Name

Smith, E.S. Don't Let It Die

Smith, Edgar Heaven Will Protect the Working Girl; Kiss Me, Honey, Do; Life Is Only What You Make It After All; Ma Blushin' Rosie

Smith, Ethel Love Is Strange

Smith, George Totten Laughing Water

Smith, Harry B. Armorer's Song; Bright Eyes; Brown October Ale; Cupid and I; Dancing Fool; Day Dreams; Dear Eyes That Haunt Me; The Fortune Teller; Gypsy Love Song, or, Slumber On; I Wonder If You Still Care for Me; If Only You Were Mine; My Angeline; Play Gypsies—Dance Gypsies; Quiller Has the Brains; Romany Life; Same Sort of Girl; The Sheik of Araby; Star Light, Star Bright; Strollers We; There Once Was an Owl; To the Land of My Own (Small) Romance; Two Little Love Bees; We Two Shall Meet Again; When You're Wearing the Ball and Chain; Why Don't They Dance the Polka Anymore; A Woman Is Only a Woman, But a Good Cigar Is a Smoke; You Are Mine Evermore; You Belong to Me; You're Here and I'm Here; Yours Is My Heart Alone

Smith, Hubbard T. If You Love Me Darling, Tell Me with Your Eyes; Listen to My Tale of Woe

Smith, Hurricane Oh Babe, What Would You Say

Smith, J. Lester It Costs So Little

Smith, Jack Gimme a Little Kiss, Will Ya, Huh?

Smith, James Ain't Gonna Kiss You

Smith, Jerry Dean Truck Stop

Smith, John Stafford The Star Spangled Banner; To Anacreon in Heaven

Smith, Johnny I Can't Wait; Walk—Don't Run

Smith, Kenneth Leslie Always

Smith, Laura Little Sir Echo

Smith, Mike Bits and Pieces; Can't You See That She's Mine; Glad All Over

Smith, Pinetop Boogie Woogie

Smith, Richard B. The Breeze (That's Bringing My Honey Back to Me); When a Gypsy Makes His Violin Cry; Winter Wonderland

Smith, Robert Archibald Jessie, the Flow'r o' Dumblane

Smith, Robert B. The Angelus; Come Down Ma Evenin' Star; The Cricket on the Hearth; Day Dreams; Fountain Fay; I Might Be Your "Once-in-a-While"; Someone Like You; The Springtime of Life; Sweethearts; Two Little Love Bees; The Wooing of the Violin

Smith, Samuel Francis America (My Country 'Tis of Thee)

Smith, Victor With Your Love

Smith, Willie "The Lion"   Conversation on Park Avenue

Smotherman, Michael   Can You Fool (You Just Can't Forget Her); I'm Gonna Love You

Smyth, Carl   Our House

Snow, Mike   Rosetta

Snow, Phoebe   Poetry Man

Snow, Tom   Alibis; Don't Call It Love; He's So Shy; If Ever You're in My Arms Again; Let's Hear It for the Boy; Make a Move on Me; Somewhere Down the Road; You Should Hear How She Talks About You

Snyder, Eddie   The Girl with the Golden Braids; Love Theme from *Romeo and Juliet,* or, A Time for Us; Spanish Eyes; Strangers in the Night

Snyder, Ted   Beautiful Eyes; Dancing Fool; The Ghost of the Violin; How'd You Like To Be My Daddy; I Wonder If You Still Care for Me; In the Land of Harmony; It Must Be Love; Kiss Me, My Honey, Kiss Me; Meet Me at the Station, Dear; Moonlight on the Rhine; My Wife's Gone to the Country (Hurrah! Hurrah!); Next to Your Mother, Who Do You Love?; Oh, That Beautiful Rag; Roam On, (My) Little Gipsy Sweetheart; The Sheik of Araby; Take a Car; Take a Little Tip from Father; That Beautiful Rag; That Mysterious Rag; There's a Girl in This World for Every Boy and a Boy for Every Girl; Who's Sorry Now; You Beautiful So and So

Snyder, White   The Coal Black Rose

Soell, John B.   So Tired

Solieri, Joe   When Your Old Wedding Ring Was New

Solley, Pete   Talking in Your Sleep

Solman, Alfred   The (Little) Bird on Nellie's Hat; If I Had a Thousand Lives To Live; There's a Quaker Down in Quaker Town; When the Bell in the Lighthouse Rings Ding Dong; You Splash Me and I'll Splash You; You're More Than the World to Me

Solomon, Edward   All on Account of Liza

Soloviev-Sedoi, Vassili   Midnight in Moscow, or, Moscow Nights

Sommers, John Martin   Thank God I'm a Country Boy

Sondheim, Stephen   All I Need Is the Girl; America; Another Hundred People; Anyone Can Whistle; The Ballad of Sweeney Todd; Barcelonia; (Hats Off, Here They Come, Those) Beautiful Girls; Being Alive; The Boy from . . . . ; A Boy Like That; Broadway Baby; Children and Art; Chrysanthemum Tea; Comedy tonight; Company; Cool; Could I Leave You; Do I Hear a Waltz; Every Day a Little Death; Everybody Loves Louis; Everybody Ought To Have a Maid; Everybody Says Don't; Everything's Coming Up Roses; Finishing the Hat; Gee, Officer Krupke!; Getting Married Today; The Glamorous Life; God, That's Good; The God-Why-Don't-You-Love-Me Blues; Good Thing Going; I Feel Pretty; I Never Do Anything Twice; If Momma Was Married; I'm Still Here; Jet Song; Kiss Me; The Ladies Who Lunch; Let Me Entertain You; Liaisons; Little Lamb; A Little Priest; The Little Things You Do Together; Losing My Mind; Lovely; Maria; Merrily We Roll Along; The Miller's Son; Miracle Song; Mister Goldstone; Move On; Night Waltz; Not a Day Goes By; Not While I'm Around; Now; Old Friends; One Hand, One Heart; Please Hello; Pretty Lady; Pretty Women;

Putting It Together; Rose's Turn; Send in the Clowns; Side by Side by Side; Small World; Some People; Someone in a Tree; Something's Coming; Somewhere; Sorry—Grateful; Sunday; Take the Moment; Together Wherever We Go; To-night; Too Many Mornings; Waiting for the Girls Upstairs; We Do Not Belong Together; A Weekend in the Country; We're Gonna Be All Right; What Would We Do Without You; The Worst Pies in London; You Could Drive a Person Crazy; You Gotta Have a Gimmick; You Must Meet My Wife; You'll Never Get Away from Me

Sonin, Ray   Best of All; Gertie the Girl with the Gong; The Homecoming Waltz

Sosenko, Anna   Darling, Je Vous Aime Beaucoup; I'll Be Yours (J'Attendrai)

Sour, Robert   Body and Soul; I See a Million People; Walkin' by the River; We Could Make Such Beautiful Music (Together)

Sourire, Soeur   Dominique

Sousa, John Philip   The Belle of Pittsburgh (March); The Bride Elect; El Capitan (March); The Gladiator('s) March; Hands Across the Sea (March); High School Cadets; King Cotton March; The Liberty Bell; Manhattan Beach; Semper Fidelis; Stars and Stripes Forever; The Thunderer; Washington Post; What Was Your Name in the States?

South, Harry   The Sweeney

South, Joe   Down in the Boondocks; Games People Play; I Never Promised You a Rose Garden

Souther, John David   Best of My Love

Souvaine, Henry   Nobody Wants Me

Spaeth, Sigmund   Chansonette; Down South; My Little Nest of Heavenly Blue, or, Frasquita Serenade (Blaues Himmelbett), or, Farewell, My Love, Farewell; Serenade, or, Rimpianto

Spafford, H.C.   It Is Well with My Soul

Span, Norman ("King Radio")   Matilda

Sparks, Randy   Saturday Night; Today

Sparrow-Simpson, Reverend W.J.   The Crucifixion

Speaks, Oley   Morning; On the Road to Mandalay; Sylvia; When the Boys Come Home

Spear, Eric   Coronation Street; Meet Mister Callaghan

Spector, Lona   Sally Go Round the Roses

Spector, Phil   Be My Baby; Chapel of Love; Da Doo Ron Ron (When He Walked Me Home); Spanish Harlem; Then He Kissed Me; To Know Him Is To Love Him; You've Lost That Lovin' Feelin'

Speidel, Charles   Down by the Silvery Rio Grande

Spence, Lew   Nice 'n' Easy

Spencer, C. Mordaunt   The Rose of Tralee

Spencer, Frank   The Young Folks at Home

Spencer, Herbert   East of the Moon, West of the Stars; There's Egypt in Your Dreamy Eyes; Underneath the Stars

Spencer, Judy   Soft Summer Breeze

Spencer, Otis   Broadway Rose

Spencer, Richard   Color Him Father

Spencer, Robert   My Boy Lollipop

Spencer, Tim   Room Full (Roomful) of Roses

Spielman, Fred   It Only Hurts for a Little While; The Longest Walk; Paper Roses; The Shepherd Serenade

Spier, Larry   Memory Lane; Was It a Dream

Spikes, Benjamin   Some Day Sweetheart; Wolverine Blues

Spikes, John C.   Some Day Sweetheart; Wolverine Blues

Spilman, James E.   Flow Gently, Sweet Afton, or, Afton Water

Spina, Harold   Annie Doesn't Live Here Anymore; The Beat of My Heart; Haunted Ball Room; I Still Love To Kiss You Goodnight; It's Dark on Observatory Hill; It's So Nice To Have a Man Around the House; My Very Good Friend the Milkman; Would I Love You (Love You Love You)

Spinks, John   Your Love

Spiro, Harold   Nice One Cyril

Spoliansky, Mischa   The Canoe Song; Climbing Up; The Hour of Parting; The Melba Waltz; Song of Capri; Tell Me Tonight

Sporn, Murray   Java

Spotswood, W.   Hold Tight—Hold Tight

Spotti, Pino   I Want To Be Wanted

Spottiswoode, Alicia Ann, *see* **Lady John Scott**

Sprigato, Sylvester   It Isn't Fair

Springer, George E.   Lies

Springer, Philip   How Little It Matters, How Little We Know; Moonlight Gambler; Next Time; Sweet William; You Bring Out the Lover in Me

Springfield, Bobby   Some Memories Just Won't Quit

Springfield, Rick   Don't Talk to Strangers; Jessie's Girl; Love Somebody

Springfield, Tom   The Carnival Is Over; Georgy Girl; I'll Never Find Another You; Island of Dreams; Losing You; The Mogul Theme; Morning, Please Don't Come; Say I Won't Be There; A World of Our Own

Springsteen, Bruce   Blinded by the Light; Born in the U.S.A.; Dancing in the Dark; Glory Days; Hungry Heart; I'm on Fire; My Hometown

Squire, Chris   Owner of a Lonely Heart

Squire, W.H.   Lighterman Tom; Three for Jack; When You Come Home

St. Helier, Ivy   Coal Black Mammy

St. John, Dick   The Mountains High; Young and in Love

St. John, Ray   Smooth Operator

St. Lewis, Kenny   Boogie Fever; Heaven Must Be Missing an Angel; Hot Line

Stafford, Jim   Spiders and Snakes

Stahl, Felix   Many Times

Stainer, John   The Crucifixion

Stallman, Lou   It's Gonna Take a Miracle; Round and Round

Stamford, John J.   MacNamara's Band

Stammers, Frank   Ask the Stars; I'll Remember You

Stamper, Dave   Daddy Has a Sweetheart, and Mother Is Her Name; Garden of My Dreams; Lovely Lady; My Rambler Rose; 'Neath the South Sea Moon; Some Sweet Day; Sweet Sixteen; Throw Me a Kiss; Tulip Time

Standley, J.   It's in the Book

Stanford, Dok   Mistletoe and Holly

Stanford, Trevor   China Tea; Lucky Five; Passing Breeze; Roulette; Royal Event; Side Saddle; Snow Coach

Strange, Stanislaus   The Letter Song; My Hero; My Own United States; Sweet Thoughts of Home

Stanley, Eddie Y.   Botch-A-Me

Stanley, Edwin   That Naughty Waltz

Stanley, F.   Blue Bell Polka

Stanley, Ian   Everybody Wants To Rule the World; Shout

Stanley, Jack   You Better Keep Babying Baby (or Baby's Gonna Bye-Bye You)

Stanley, Ralph   Hi Tiddley Hi Ti Island; June Brought the Roses; Shufflin' Along

Stanley, Ray   Glendora

Stanley, Wynn   Sally, You Brought the Sunshine to Our Alley

Stanton, Albert   Abilene; The Lion Sleeps Tonight, or, Wimoweh

Stanton, Arnold   The Roving Kind

Stanton, Frank L.   Fat Li'l' Feller Wid His Mammy's Eyes; Just a-Wearyin' for You; Mighty Lak' a Rose; Morning

Stanton, Joan   Why

Stapp, Jack   Chattanoogie Shoe Shine Boy

Starr, Hattie   Little Alabama Coon

Starr, Ringo   Photograph

Stavely, Simon   Everything's Al'Right

Steals, Melvin   Could It Be I'm Falling In Love

Steals, Mervin   Could It Be I'm Falling in Love

Stebbins, George Coles   Saved by Grace; Saviour, Breathe an Evening Blessing; True-Hearted, Whole-Hearted, or, Peal Out the Watchword

Steel, M.   Along Came Caroline

Steele, Anne   See, Gentle Patience Smiles on Pain

Steele, C.T.   Happy Birds

Steele, Louis   Ivory Tower; Wanted

Steele, Porter   High Society (March)

Steele, Silas S.   Dandy Jim of Caroline; The Gum Tree Canoe (On Tom-Big-Bee River); The Rose of Alabama

Steele, Ted   Smoke Dreams

Steele, Tommy   A Handful of Songs; The Little White Bull; Rock with the Cavemen; Shiralee; Water, Water

Steels, Ted   How Can You Buy Killarney

Steffe, William   Battle Hymn of the Republic (Glory Hallelujah)

Stegall, Keith   Lonely Nights; Sexy Eyes; We're in This Love Together

Stegmeyer, Bill   A Symphony for Susan

Stein, Christopher   Heart of Glass; Rapture

Stein, Herman   I Gotcha

Stein, Jules   Sunday

Stein, William   Orange Colored Sky

Steinberg, Billy   Like a Virgin

Steinberg, Harry A.   Lovely Lady

Steinberg, Lewis   Green Onions

Steiner, Max   All This and Heaven Too; Allison's Theme from Parrish; As Long as I Live; Honey-Babe; It Can't Be Wrong; Lucy's Theme from Parrish; Sugarfoot; (Theme from) A Summer Place; Symphony Moderne; Tara's Theme

Steininger, Franz K.W.   Marching Along Together

Steinman, Jim   Making Love Out of Nothing At All; Read 'Em and Weep; Total Eclipse of the Heart

Stellman, Marcel   Johnny Is the Boy for Me; Maybe This Year

Stephens, Geoff   The Crying Game; Daddy Don't You Walk So Fast; Daughter of Darkness; Doctor's Orders; Knock, Knock, Who's There; Lights of Cincinnati; Like Sister and Brother; Tell Me When; There's a Kind of Hush; Winchester Cathedral; You Won't Find Another Fool Like Me

Stephens, Henry P.   All on Account of Liza

Stephens, Paul   Along Came Caroline

Stephens, Reed   There's a Kind of Hush

Stephens, Richard   Wheels

Stept, Sam H.   All My Life; Comes Love; Congratulations; Do Something; Don't Sit Under the Apple Tree (with Anyone Else But Me); I Came Here To Talk for Joe; I Fall in Love with You Every Day; I'll Always Be in Love with You; Laughing Irish Eyes; The Organ Grinder; Please Don't Talk About Me When I'm Gone; Sweet Heartache; That's My Weakness Now; This Is Worth Fighting For; When They Ask About You

Sterling, Andrew B.   Alexander (Don't You Love Your Baby No More); All Aboard for Blanket Bay; Close to My Heart; Do You Take This Woman for Your Lawful Wife?; Down Where the Cotton Blossoms Grow; Eyes of Blue, Eyes of Brown; Goodbye, Boys; Good-bye, Eliza Jane; Hannah, Won't You Open That Door?; I Wonder If She's Waiting; In the Evening by the Moonlight, Dear Louise; Just a Little Lovin'; Keep Your Skirts Down, Mary Ann; Last Night Was the End of the World; A Little Bunch of Shamrocks; Meet Me in St. Louis, Louis; My Old New Hampshire Home; On a Sunday Afternoon; On the Old Fall River Line; Rufus Rastus Johnson Brown (What You Goin' To Do When the Rent Comes 'Round); Strike Up the Band—Here Comes a Sailor; Take Me Back to New York Town; They're All Sweeties; Under the Anheuser Bush; Under the Yum Yum Tree; Wait 'Til the Sun Shines, Nellie; We're Going Over; When Kate and I Were Coming Thro' the Rye; When My Baby Smiles at Me; Where the Morning Glories Twine Around the Door; Where the Sweet Magnolias Grow; You'll Always Be the Same Sweet Girl

Stern, Henry R., *see* **S.R. Henry**

Stern, Jack   Rhythm of the Rain

Stern, Joseph W.   His Last Thoughts Were of You; The Little Lost Child; Mother Was a Lady, or, If Jack Were Only Here; No One Ever Loved You More Than I

Stern, Toni   Sweet Seasons

Stevens, Cat   Morning Has Broken; Peace Train; Wild World

Stevens, Even   B B B Burnin' Up with Love; Drivin' My Life Away; Gone Too Far; I Love a Rainy Night; Love Will Turn You Around; Someone Could Lose a Heart Tonight; Step by Step; Suspicions; When You're in Love with a Beautiful Woman; A World Without Love

Stevens, G.A.   On Mother Kelly's Doorstep

Stevens, George   I'm Shy, Mary Ellen, I'm Shy

Stevens, Leonard   I Faw Down an' Go Boom

Stevens, Mort   (Theme from) Hawaii Five-O

Stevens, Ray   Everything Is Beautiful; The Streak

Stevens, Richard John Samuel   Sigh No More, Ladies

Stevens, Shakin'   Oh Julie

Stevens, Steve   Eyes Without a Face

Stevenson, B.C.   Let Me Dream Again

Stevenson, Robert Louis   Boats of Mine

Stevenson, Sir John   Oft in the Stilly Night

Stevenson, William   Dancing in the Streets; Release Me

Stewart, Al   Come Closer to Me; I'll Never Love Again (La Borrachita); Song on the Radio; Time Passages

Stewart, Andy   Scottish Soldier Green Hill

Stewart, David   Here Comes the Rain Again; Sweet Dreams (Are Made of This)

Stewart, Dorothy   Now Is the Hour

Stewart, Eric   I'm Not in Love; The Things We Do for Love

Stewart, James E.   The Alabama Blossoms; Angel Gabriel; Good Sweet Ham; Jennie, the Flower of Kildare

Stewart, John C.   Daydream Believer

Stewart, Michael   The Colors of My Life; Come Follow the Band; Entire History of the World in Two Minutes and Thirty-Two Seconds; Hey There, Good Times; I Like Your Style

Stewart, Redd   Slow Poke; Tennessee Waltz; You Belong to Me

Stewart, Rod   Maggie May/ Reason To Believe; Tonight's the Night (It's Gonna Be Alright)

Stewart, Sam   Flat Foot Floogie (with the Floy Floy)

Stewart, Sandy   If Anyone Falls

Stewart, Sly   Everyday People; Family Affair; Hot Fun in the Summertime; Thank You Falettin Me Be Mice Elf Agin

Stewart, Steven   Smoke from a Distant Fire

Stieger, Jimmie   Looking At the World Through Rose-Colored Glasses

Stillman, Al   Bless 'Em All; The Breeze and I; Chances Are; Cockeyed Mayor of Kaunakakai; Enchanted Island; Happy Anniversary; (There's No Place Like) Home for the Holidays; I Believe; If Dreams Come True; In My Little Red Book; It's Not for Me To Say; Juke Box Saturday Night; Little Jack Frost Get Lost; Mama Yo Quiero (I Want My Mama); Moments To Remember; My Heart Reminds Me, or, And That Reminds Me; My One and Only Heart; No, Not Much; Now and Forever; Say "Si Si"; Song of the Blacksmith; The Way of Love; Who Needs You; You Alone, or, Solo Tu

Stills, Stephen   Southern Cross

Sting, *see* Gordon Sumner

Stinson, Donald Henry When the Wind Was Green

Stirling, Peter Lee Don't Turn Around; I Think of You

Stites, E.P. Trusting Jesus, That Is All

Stitzel, Mel Doodle Doo Doo; Make Love to Me; Tin Roof Blues

Stock, Larry Blueberry Hill; Did You Ever Get That Feeling in the Moonlight; The Morning Side of the Mountain; Tell Me a Story; The Umbrella Man; You Won't Be Satisfied (Until You Break My Heart); You're Nobody 'Til Somebody Loves You

Stoddard, George E. I Was a Very Good Baby; Waiting

Stoddard, Harry I Get the Blues When It Rains

Stodel, Jack Carolina

Stokes, Byron D. The Sweetheart of Sigma Chi

Stole, J.W. I Will Follow Him

Stoll, George Love on a Greyhound Bus

Stoller, Mike Baby I Don't Care; Black Denim Trousers; Charlie Brown; Don't; Hound Dog; I Keep Forgettin'; I Who Have Nothing; Is That All There Is; Jailhouse Rock; Kansas City; Love Potion Number Nine; On Broadway; Ruby Baby; Stand by Me; There Goes My Baby; Yakety Yak

Stoller, Rhet Match of the Day

Stoloff, Morris Song Without End

Stolz, Robert Don't Ask Me Why; It's Foolish But It's Fun; Tell Me Why You Smile Mona Lisa; Two Hearts in Three Quarter Time; The White Horse Inn; Your Eyes

Stone, Gregory Dark Eyes, or, Black Eyes; Let's Dance

Stone, Harry Chattanoogie Shoe Shine Boy

Stone, Helen Mexicali Rose

Stone, Jesse Idaho

Stone, John A. Sweet Betsy from Pike, or, Vilikens and His Dinah

Stone, Robert Gypsys, Tramps and Thieves

Stone, Russell We Do It

Stone, Samuel The Church's One Foundation

Stoner, Michael I Guess I'll Have To Dream the Rest; It's Make Believe Ballroom Time

Stookey, Paul I Dig Rock and Roll Music

Storball, Donald Cool Jerk

Storch, Eberhard Auf Wiederseh'n Sweetheart

Stordahl, Axel Day by Day; I Should Care

Stothart, Herbert April Blossoms; At the Balalaika; Cossack Love Song; or, Don't Forget Me; Cuban Love Song; The Donkey Serenade; How Strange; I Wanna Be Loved by You; The Rogue Song; Song of the Flame; The Song of the Shirt; When I'm Looking at You; Wildflower

Stott, H. Tweedle Dee—Tweedle Dum

Stott, Larry Chirpy Chirpy, Cheep Cheep

Stott, Walter Rotten Row

Stover, G.H. On the Beach at Waikiki

Strachey, Jack In a Party Mood; A Nightingale Sang in Berkeley Square; No Orchids for My Lady; These Foolish Things (Remind Me of You)

Straigis, Roy So Much in Love

Strange, William E. Limbo Rock

Stranks, Alan All; Break of Day; Love Steals Your Heart; No Orchids for My Lady

Straus, Oscar The Letter Song; Love's Roundelay; My Hero; Sweetest Maid of All; A Waltz Dream; We Will Always Be Sweethearts; While Hearts Are Singing

Strauss, Art Cinderella Sweetheart; Seventeen Candles

Strauss, Johann Artist's Life; The Blue Danube; Du und Du (You and You Waltz); Tales from (of) the Vienna Woods; A Thousand and One Nights; Vienna Life; Voices of Spring; Wine, Women and Song; With All My Heart

Strauss, Richard Also Sprach Zarathustra, or, Theme from *2001: A Space Odyssey;* Death and Transfiguration; Don Juan; Till Eulenspiegel; Waltzes

Stravinsky, Igor The Firebird Ballet Suite; Rites of Spring; Scenes de Ballet

Strayhorn, Billy Lush Life; Satin Doll; Take the "A" Train

Streisand, Barbra Evergreen, or, Love Theme from *A Star Is Born*

Strickland, Lily Ma Li'l Batteau; Mah Lindy Lou; My Lover Is a Fisherman

Stromberg, John Come Down My Evenin' Star; Kiss Me, Honey, Do; Ma Blushin' Rosie; My Best Girl's a New Yorker (Corker)

Strong, Barrett I Can't Get Next to You; I Heard It Through the Grapevine; I Wish It Would Rain; Just My Imagination (Running Away with Me); Papa Was a Rollin' Stone; Too Busy Thinking About My Baby; War

Strong, Mark The Ogo-Pogo

Strouse, Charles Applause; Born Too Late; Easy Street; Entire History of the World in Two Minutes and Thirty-Two Seconds; (It's) The Hard-Knock Life; Kids; Little Girls; (I've Got) A Lot of Livin' To Do; Maybe; N.Y.C.; Older and Wiser; Once Upon a Time; One Boy; Put On a Happy Face; Rosie; The Telephone Hour; Those Were the Days, or, Theme from *All in the Family;* Tomorrow; You've Got Possibilities

Strykert, Ron Down Under

Stuart, Allan La Rosita

Stuart, Jack So Tired

Stuart, Jamie Pick Up the Pieces

Stuart, Leslie I May Be Crazy; I Want To Be a Military Man; Lily of Laguna; Little Dolly Daydream; The Shade of the Palm; Soldiers of the Queen; Tell Me Pretty Maiden (Are There Any More at Home Like You) (*as* Thomas A. Barrett)

Stults, R.M. The Sweetest Story Ever Told, or, Tell Me That You Love Me

Sturdy, Leslie From the Time We Say Goodbye

Stutz, Carl Danger, Heartbreak Ahead; I Know; Little Things Mean a Lot

Styne, Jule All I Need Is the Girl; As Long as There's Music; Bells Are Ringing; Bye Bye Baby; Captain Hook's Waltz; Conchita, Marquita, Lolita, Pepita, Rosita, Juanita Lopez; Diamonds Are a Girl's Best Friend; Did You Ever Ride on a Rainbow; Don't Rain on My Parade; Ev'ry Street's a Boulevard in Old New York; Everything's Coming Up Roses; Fade Out—Fade In; Five Minutes More; Funny Girl; Hello, Hello There; Hold Me, Hold Me; How Do You Speak to an Angel; I Begged Her; I Don't Want To Walk Without You, Baby; I Fall In Love Too Easily; I Said No; I Still Get Jealous; If Momma Was Married; I'll Walk Alone; I'm Glad I Waited for You; I'm the Greatest Star; It's Been a Long, Long Time; It's Magic; It's the Same Old Dream; It's You or No One; (It Seems to Me) I've Heard That Song Before; Just in Time; Let It Snow, Let It Snow, Let It Snow; Let Me Entertain You; A Little Girl from Little Rock; Little Lamb; Long Before I Knew You; (It's Gonna Be) A Long, Long Winter; Make Someone Happy; Mister Goldstone; Never Never Land; Papa Won't You Dance with Me; The Party's Over; People; Put 'Em in a Box, Tie 'Em with a Ribbon (and Throw 'Em in the Deep Blue Sea); The River Song, or, Something's Always Happening on the River; Rose's Turn; Saturday Night Is the Loneliest Night of the Week; Say, Darling; Small World; Some People; Stay with the Happy People; There Goes That Song Again; The Things We Did Last Summer; Three Coins in the Fountain; Time After Time; Together Wherever We Go; When the One You Love (Simply Won't Love Back); You Are Woman (I Am Man); You Gotta Have a Gimmick; You'll Never Get Away from Me; You're My Girl; Zuyder Zee

Styne, Stanley   A Beautiful Friendship

Subano, Bruce   Bad Girls; Tell Me I'm Not Dreaming

Suessdorf, Karl   Moonlight in Vermont

Suesse, Dana   Ho Hum; Jazz Nocturne; My Silent Love; The Night Is Young and You're So Beautiful; Whistling in the Dark; You Oughta Be in Pictures; Yours for a Song

Sukman, Harry   Theme from *The Eleventh Hour*

Sullavan, Jeri   Rum and Coca-Cola

Sullivan, Alex   Kisses—The Sweetest Kisses of All

Sullivan, Arthur   Birds in the Night; Come, Ye Faithful, Raise the Strain; He Is an Englishman; I am the Captain of the Pinafore (What Never); I am the Monarch of the Sea; I'm Called Little Buttercup; Let Me Dream Again; The Long Day Closes; Looking Back; The Lost Chord; My Dearest Heart; Onward, Christian Soldiers; Tit-Willow; When I Was a Lad

Sullivan, Dan J.   You're as Welcome as the Flowers in May

Sullivan, Frank   Burning Heart; Eye of the Tiger; High on You; Search Is Over

Sullivan, Henry   I May Be Wrong, But I Think You're Wonderful; Mona Lisa; A Nice Cup of Tea

Sullivan, Joe   Little Rock Getaway

Sullivan, Joseph J.   Where Did You Get That Hat

Sullivan, Larry   Cinco Robles (Five Oaks)

Sullivan, Marion Dix   The Blue Juniata

Sullivan, Terry   One of the Ruins That Cromwell Knocked About a Bit; She Sells Sea-Shells (on the Seashore)

Summer, Donna   Bad Girls; Heaven Knows; I Feel Love; Love To Love You Baby; On the Radio; She Works Hard for the Money; The Wanderer

Summer, James S.   Twelfth Street Rag

Summerville, Slim   At the Codfish Ball

Sumner, Gordon "Sting"   Don't Stand So Close to Me; Every Breath You Take; Every Little Thing She Does Is Magic; Fortress Around Your Heart; If You Love Somebody Set Them Free; King of Pain; Money for Nothing; Wrapped Around Your Finger

Sunshine, Madeline   This Is Love

Sunshine, Marion   Mary, You're a Little Bit Old Fashioned; The Peanut Vendor

Surrey, Jean   Teen Angel

Surrey, Red   Teen Angel

Sussman, Bruce   Copacabana (At the Copa); I Made It Through the Rain

Sutherland, Gavin   Sailing

Sutton, Glen   Almost Persuaded

Sutton, Harry O.   I Don't Care

Svanoc, W.   Walk Right In

Swain, Charles   Old Friends and Old Times

Swan, Billy   I Can Help

Swan, Einar A.   Trail of Dreams; When Your Lover Has Gone

Swander, Don   Deep in the Heart of Texas

Swann, Donald   The Income Tax Collector

Swanstrom, Arthur M.   The Argentines, the Portuguese and the Greeks; Blues My Naughty Sweetie Gives to Me; Cross Your Fingers; My Greenwich Village Sue; Why (Is There a Rainbow in the Sky)

Sweeney, Chuck   Young Ideas

Sweet, Milo   Fight On

Swift, James Frederick   Sailing (Sailing) (Over the Bounding Main)

Swift, Kay   Can This Be Love; Can't We Be Friends; Fine and Dandy

Sylvester, Victor   The Golden Tango

Sylvia, Margo   Happy, Happy Birthday, Baby

Symes, Marty   By the River of (the) Roses; (When It's) Darkness on the Delta; How Many Hearts Have You Broken; I Have But One Heart; It's the Talk of the Town; There Is No Greater Love; Under a Blanket of Blue

Szinnyey, Stephen Ivor   When the Cherry Blossoms Fall

Tabet, Andre   Symphony

Tabrar, Joseph   Daddy Wouldn't Buy Me a Bow-Wow

Taccani, S. Paola   For the First Time (Come Prima)

Tagg, Eric   Is It You

Taggart, George   The Moth and the Flame

Taggart, Milton   When It's Springtime in the Rockies

Talbot, Howard   Arcady Is Ever Young; I Want To Marry a Man; The Pipes of Pan

Tallarico, Steve   Dream On

Talley, Lewis   Dear John Letter

Tannahill, Robert   Jessie, the Flow'r o' Dumblane

Tarney, Alan   Dreamin'; January, February; Little in Love;

Living in a Fantasy; We Don't Talk Anymore; Wired for Sound

Tarplin, Marvin   Cruisin; My Girl Has Gone; The Tracks of My Tears

Tate, Arthur F.   Somewhere a Voice Is Calling

Tate, James W.   A Bachelor Gay; Broken Doll; Ev'ry Little While; Give Me a Little Cosy Corner; I Was a Good Little Girl Till I Met You; If I Should Plant a Tiny Seed of Love; Paradise for Two; Somewhere in France with You

Tauber, Doris   Fooled; Them There Eyes

Tauber, Richard   My Heart and I; There Are Angels Outside Heaven

Taupin, Bernie   Bennie and the Jets; The Bitch Is Back; Crocodile Rock; Daniel; Don't Go Breaking My Heart; Don't Let the Sun Go Down on Me; Goodbye Yellow Brick Road; How You Gonna See Me Now; I Guess That's Why They Call It the Blues; Island Girl; Nikita; Philadelphia Freedom; Sad Songs (Say So Much); Snookeroo; Someone Saved My Life Tonight; Sorry Seems To Be the Hardest Word; Theme from a Non-Existent TV Series; These Dreams; We Built This City; Your Song

Taverner, Derek   Who Do You Think You Are Kidding Mister Hitler

Taylor, Andrew   Hungry Like the Wolf: The Reflex; Union of the Snake; A View to a Kill; The Wild Boys

Taylor, Bayard   Bedouin Love Song

Taylor, Charles   Cigarette

Taylor, Chip   Angel of the Morning; Wild Thing

Taylor, Earl   My Southern Rose

Taylor, Helen   Bless This House; Come to the Fair; I Love the Name of Mary; An Old Violin

Taylor, Herbert H.   In the Wildwood Where the Bluebells Grew

Taylor, Irving   Caramba It's the Samba; Everybody Loves Somebody; Knees Up Mother Brown; Kookie, Kookie, Lend Me Your Comb; Take It Easy; Three Little Sisters

Taylor, Jack   Band of Gold

Taylor, James   Celebration; Cherish; Don't Let Me Be Lonely Tonight; Fire and Rain; Fresh; Her Town Too; Joanna; Ladies Night; Misled; Only One; Shower the People

Taylor, James B.   Sparkling and Bright

Taylor, Jane   Twinkle, Twinkle, Little Star, or, Ah! Vous Diraije Maman, or, ABCDEFG, or, The Alphabet Song, or, Baa, Baa, Black Sheep, or, The Star

Taylor, John   Since I Don't Have You

Taylor, Leonard   There Goes My Lover

Taylor, Livingston   I Will Be in Love with You

Taylor, Michael C.   Rocky Mountain High; Sunshine on My Shoulders

Taylor, Nigel John   Hungry Like the Wolf; The Reflex; Union of the Snake; A View to a Kill; The Wild Boys

Taylor, R. Dean   Love Child

Taylor, Robert   Sha La La

Taylor, Roger Andrew   Hungry Like the Wolf; The Reflex; Union of the Snake; A View to a Kill; The Wild Boys

Taylor, Tell   Down by the Old Mill Stream; You're in the Army Now

Tchaikovsky, Peter   Chant sans Paroles; 1812 Overture; Marche Slav; None But the Lonely Heart; The Nutcracker Suite; Piano Concerto, No.1; Romeo and Juliet; Sleeping Beauty Waltz; Song Without Words; Waltz of the Flowers

Tchervanow, Ivor   The Sleigh

Teetor, Macy O.   Lost

Tempchin, Jack   One You Love; You Belong to the City

Temperton, Rodney   Baby, Come to Me; Boogie Nights; Give Me the Night; Miss Celie's Blues (Sister); Off the Wall; Rock With You; Sweet Freedom; Stomp; Thriller; Yah Mo B There

Temple, Edith   Count Your Blessings

Templeton, Alec   Bach Goes to Town

Tennant, Neil   West End Girls

Tennat, H.M.   My Time Is Your Time; When You and I Were Dancing

Tennille, Toni   Do That to Me One More Time; The Way I Want To Touch You

Tenny, Jack B.   Mexicali Rose

Tennyson, Alfred Lord   Come into the Garden, Maud; Now Sleeps the Crimson Petal; Sweet and Low

Tepper, Sid   Kewpie Doll; The Naughty Lady of Shady Lane; Red Roses for a Blue Lady; Travellin' Light

Terker, Arthur   (There's Something Nice About Everyone But) There's Everything Nice About You

Terriss, Dorothy, *see* **Theodora Morse**

Terry, Dewey Jr.   I'm Leaving It All Up to You; The Jolly Green Giant

Terry, Fred   Any Old Iron

Terry, George   Lay Down Sally

Terry, Robert Huntington   The Answer

Teschemacher, Edward   Because; Down Vauxhall Way; The Garden of Your Heart; I Know a Lovely Garden; I Wonder If Love Is a Dream; La Mattinata ('Tis the Day); O Flower Divine; Tommy, Lad; Until; Where My Caravan Has Rested

Testa, A.   I Want To Be Wanted

Thaler, Rudolf   Ciribiribin

Thayer, Pat   I Travel the Road

Thayer, William Armour   My Laddie

Theodorakis, Mikos   (Theme from) Zorba the Greek

Theoret, Sandy Mason   When I Dream

Thibaut, Giles   My Way

Thomas, Dennis Ronald   Celebration; Ladies Night

Thomas, Dick   I Lost the Best Pal That I Had; Sioux City Sue

Thomas, Edwin   A Warrior Bold

Thomas, Harry   Hold 'Em Joe

Thomas, Jimmie   Rockin' Robin

Thomas, John Rogers   Beautiful Isle of the Sea; The Belle of Mohawke Vale, or, Bonny (Bonnie) Eloise; The Cottage by the Sea; Croquet; Eileen Allanna; In Heavenly Love Abiding; Old Friends and Old Times; The Rose of Killarney; 'Tis But a Little Faded Flower; When the War Is Over, Mary

Thomas, Lester By the Sad Sea Waves

Thomas, Tim Why Can't We Live Together

Thomas, Wilfred Rose, Rose I Love You

Thomé, Francis Simple Aveu

Thompson, H.S. Annie Lisle; Cousin Jedediah; Lily Dale

Thompson, Harlan I Love You (Je t'Aime); Suppose I Had Never Met You

Thompson, Kay Love on a Greyhound Bus

Thompson, Richard Express

Thompson, Wayne The Letter

Thomson, James Give a Man a Horse He Can Ride; Rule, Britannia

Thorn, George Sweet and Gentle

Thornton, James The Bridge of Sighs; Don't Give Up the Old Love for the New; Going for a Pardon; The Irish Jubilee; My Sweetheart's the Man in the Moon; On the Benches in the Park; She May Have Seen Better Days; The Streets of Cairo; There's a Little Star Shining for You; When You Were Sweet Sixteen

Thorsen, Art It's in the Book

Throckmorton, James Fron I've Had a Lovely Time

Throckmorton, Sonny I Wish You Could Have Turned My Head

Tibbles, George Woody Woodpecker

Tierney, Harry (In My Sweet Little) Alice Blue Gown; Castle of Dreams; Following the Sun Around; I Found the End of the Rainbow; If You're in Love You'll Waltz; Irene; The Kinkajou; M-I-S-S-I-S-S-I-P-P-I; My Baby's Arms; The Ranger's Song; Rio Rita; You're Always in My Arms (But Only in My Dreams)

Tilley, Vesta Following in Father's Footsteps

Tillis, Mel Detroit City; Emotions; Ruby, Don't Take Your Love to Town

Tillman, Charles D. Life's Railway to Heaven; My Mother's Bible

Tillman, Floyd I Love You So Much It Hurts; Slippin' Around

Tilsley, Harry I Never See Maggie Alone

Timas, Ricky Cool It Now

Timberg, Sammy It's a Hap-Hap-Happy Day

Timm, Wladimir A. The Beer Barrel Polka

Timmons, Bobby Moanin'

Timothy, Al Kiss Me, Honey Honey, Kiss Me

Tinkaus, George J. Mammy's Little Kinky Headed Boy

Tinturin, Peter Foolin' Myself; What Will I Tell My Heart

Tiomkin, Dimitri Friendly Persuasion, or, Thee I Love; The Green Leaves of Summer; The Guns of Navarone; The High and the Mighty; (Theme from) High Noon (Do Not Forsake Me, Oh My Darling); Portrait of Jennie; (Theme from) Rawhide; Return to Paradise; Search for Paradise; Strange Are the Ways of Love; Strange Lady in Town; There's Never Been Anyone Else But You; The Unforgiven (The Need for Love); Wild Is the Wind

Titheradge, Dion And Her Mother Came Too

Tizol, Juan Caravan; Perdido

Tobani, Theodore Moses Hearts and Flowers

Tobias, Charles After My Laughter Came Tears; All Over the World; As Long as I Live; As the Years Go By; At Last; The Broken Record; Coax Me a Little Bit; Comes Love; (What'll We Do on a) Dew-Dew-Dewy Day; Don't Sit Under the Apple Tree (with Anyone Else But Me); Don't Sweetheart Me; Down Among the Sugar-Cane; Ev'ry Day Away from You; Faithfully Yours; Flowers for Madame; Get Out and Get Under the Moon; I Came Here To Talk for Joe; I Can Get It for You Wholesale; In the Valley of the Moon; Just Another Day Wasted Away; Love Ya; That Mama Doll Song; May I Sing to You; (Ho! Ho! Ha! Ha!) Me Too; Miss You; No Can Do; The Old Lamp-Lighter; An Old Water Mill; Rose O'Day; Somebody Loves You; Somewhere in Old Wyoming; That's Where I Came In; Those Lazy Hazy Crazy Days of Summer; Throw Another Log on the Fire; Time Waits for No One; Trade Winds; Two Tickets to Georgia; We Did It Before (and We Can Do It Again); When Your Hair Has Turned to Silver, I Will Love You Just the Same

Tobias, Fred Born Too Late; Good Timin'; One of Us Will Weep Tonight

Tobias, Harry At Your Command; If I Had My Life To Live Over; It's a Lonesome Old Town (When You're Not Around); Love Is All; Miss You; No Regrets; O-oo Ernest, Are You Earnest with Me?; Sail Along Silvery Moon; Sweet and Lovely

Tobias, Henry H. At Last; The Hippopotamus Song, or, Mud, Glorious Mud; Katinka; Miss You

Tolhurst, Kerryn Man on Your Mind

Tollerton, Nell Cruising Down the River

Tomer, William Gould God Be with You Till We Meet Again

Tomes, Jimmy Wheels

Tomlin, Pinky The Love Bug Will Bite You; Love Is All; The Object of My Affection; What's the Reason (I'm Not Pleasin' You)

Tomlinson, Ernest Dick's Maggot; Four Dances from Aladdin

Tomlinson, Ralph To Anacreon in Heaven

Toon, Earl Eugene Jr. Celebration; Ladies Night

Toplady, Augustus Montague Rock of Ages

Torch, Sidney Much Binding in the Marsh

Torme, Mel The Christmas Song, or, Merry Christmas to You, or, Chestnuts Roasting on an Open Fire; A Stranger in Town

Torok, Mitchell Mexican Joe

Torre, Janice Paper Roses

Toselli, Enrico Serenade; Serenade, or, Rimpianto

Tosti, Francesco Paolo Goodbye; My Ideal

Tourjee, Homer Won't You Be My Little Girl

Tours, Frank E. Mother o' Mine

Toussaint, Allen Holy Cow; I Like It Like That; Java; Mother-in-Law; Southern Nights

Touzet, Rene Let Me Love You Tonight; Made for Each Other

Towers, Leo After Tonight We Say "Goodbye"; Arm in Arm; A Bedtime Story; Goodbye Hawaii; Liszt, Chopin and Mendelssohn; Little Old Mill; Me and the Old Folks at Home;

Sally; Silver Wings in the Moonlight; The Stars Will Remember; When the Poppies Bloom Again

Towne, Billy   Never on Sunday

Townsend, Dave   Miss You Nights

Townsend, Ed   For Your Love; Let's Get It On

Townsend, John   Smoke from a Distant Fire

Townshend, Peter   Anyway, Anyhow, Anywhere; Let My Love Open the Door; My Generation; Pinball Wizard

Tozzi, Umberto   Gloria

Trace, Albert J.   You Call Everybody Darling

Trace, Ben L.   You Call Everybody Darling

Tracey, William   Bring Back My Daddy to Me; Funny Bunny Hug; Gee, But It's Great To Meet a Friend from Your Old Home Town; Give a Little Credit to Your Dad; In the Town Where I Was Born; Mammy o' Mine; Play That Barbershop Chord (Mister Jefferson Lord); Them There Eyes; There's a Million Girlies Lonesome Tonight, and Still I'm All Alone; You Better Keep Babying Baby (or Baby's Gonna Bye-Bye You)

Trader, Bill   (Now and Then) A Fool Such As I

Tranpani, Tulio   Cara Mia

Trask, W.S.   Say! Have You Taken Your Medicine Yet?

Travis, Merle   Sixteen Tons; Smoke! Smoke! Smoke! (That Cigarette)

Treadwell, George   There Goes My Baby

Tremayne, June   Don't Laugh at Me ('Cause I'm a Fool)

Trenet, Charles   Beyond the Sea; Boom; I Wish You Love; La Mer

Trent, Jackie   Color My World; Don't Sleep in the Subway; I Couldn't Live Without Your Love; Joanna; The Other Man's Grass (Is Always Greener); What Would I Be; Where Are You Now My Love

Trent, Jo'   I Just Roll Along Havin' My Ups and Downs; Muddy Water; My Kinda Love

Trevelyan, Arthur   Down in Poverty Row

Trevor, Huntley   Kitty the Telephone Girl; When It's Apple Blossom Time in Normandy

Trimachi, Bobbi   One Two Three Red Light

Trimachi, Sal   One Two Three Red Light

Tripp, Paul   Tubby the Tuba

Trivers, Barry   Do the New York; Two Loves Have I

Troubetzkay, Princess   My Laddie

Troup, Bob   Baby, Baby All the Time; (Get Your Kicks on) Route 66

Trout, Robert   Daddy

Troxel, Gary   Come Softly to Me

True, Christopher Mark   Why Have You Left the One You Left Me For?

True, Mark   Too Many Lovers

Tubbs, Pierre   Right Back Where We Started From

Tucci, Joseph William   Keep On Dancin'

Tucker, Henry   Star of the Evening; Sweet Genevieve; Weeping, Sad and Lonely, or, When This Cruel War Is Over

Tucker, Johnny   Dance of the Paper Dolls

Tucker, Michael   Fox on the Run

Tullar, Grant Colfax   Face to Face

Tunbridge, Joseph   Got a Date with an Angel; Hoch, Caroline; My Heart's To Let; Roll Away Clouds; Sing Brothers

Turk, Roy   After My Laughter Came Tears; Aggravatin' Papa (Don't You Try To Two-Time Me); Are You Lonesome Tonight; Contented; The Free and Easy Hour of Parting; Gimme a Little Kiss, Will Ya, Huh?; I Don't Know Why (I Just Do); I'll Follow You; I'll Get By (as Long as I Have You); I'm a Little Blackbird Looking for a Bluebird; I'm Gonna Charleston Back to Charleston; Just Another Day Wasted Away; Mandy Make Up Your Mind; Mean to Me; My Sweetie Went Away (She Didn't Say Where, When or Why); Oh! How I Laugh When I Think How I Cried About You; Walkin' My Baby Back Home; Where the Blue of the Night Meets the Gold of the Day; Why Dance; You Oughta See My Baby

Turnbow, Jay   Bread and Butter

Turner, John   Auf Wiederseh'n Sweetheart; Mama; Mandolin Serenade; Oh My Papa, or, O Mein Papa; Smile; (Theme from) La Strada, or, Stars Shine in Your Eyes

Turnier, Gary R.   Keep On Dancin'

Tuvin, Abe   A Gay Ranchero

Twemlow, Clifford   Convoy

Twiggs, Charles   Pop Goes the Weasel

"Twinkle"   Terry

Twitty, Conway   It's Only Make Believe

Twomey, Kathleen G.   Hey Jealous Lover; Johnny Doughboy Found a Rose in Ireland; Never Let Her Go; Serenade of the Bells; Wooden Heart

Tyler, Adele   Bobbie Sue

Tyler, Alvin O.   Java

Tyler, Daniel   Bobbie Sue

Tysh, Frederick   My Heart and I; Starlight Serenade; There Are Angels Outside Heaven

Tyson, Ian   Someday Soon

Udall, Lyn   Just As the Sun Went Down; Just One Girl; Stay in Your Own Back Yard; Zizzy, Ze Zum, Zum

Udell, Peter   First Thing Monday Mornin'; Hurting Each Other; I Got Love; Over the Hill; Save Your Heart for Me; Sealed with a Kiss; Why Am I Me

Uhr, Billy   Tears

Ulman, Abe   I'm Waiting for Ships That Never Come In

Ulmer, Georges   Pigalle

Ulvaeus, Bjorn   Dancing Queen; I Do, I Do, I Do, I Do, I Do; I Know Him So Well; SOS; When All Is Said and Done

Urbano, Al   Serenade of the Bells

Ure, Midge   Do They Know It's Christmas?; Vienna

Utrera, Adolfo   Green Eyes

Vacek, Karel   Beside My Caravan; Cafe in Vienna; Play to Me, Gypsy

Vale, Mike Crystal Blue Persuasion

Valens, Ritchie Donna

Valentine, Arthur A Bachelor Gay; Paradise for Two; Somewhere in France with You

Valentine, Gerald Oh Sheila

Vallance, Jim Heaven; Now and Forever (You and Me); Run to You; Summer of '69; What About Love

Vallee, Rudy Betty Co-Ed; Deep Night; Good Night, Sweetheart; I'm Just a Vagabond Lover; Oh Mama, or, The Butcher Boy; Vieni, Vieni

Vallins, John Too Much, Too Little, Too Late

Valverde, Estic Clavelitos (Carnations)

Valverde, Joaquin Clavelitos (Carnations)

Van, A. Double Vision

Van Alstyne, Egbert Back, Back, Back to Baltimore; Beautiful Love; Cneyenne; Drifting and Dreaming (Sweet Paradise); I'm Afraid To Come Home in the Dark; In the Shade of the Old Apple Tree; It Looks (to Me) Like a Big Night Tonight; Memories; Naughty Naughty Naughty; Navajo; Pretty Baby; Sailin' Away on the Henry Clay; San Antonio; That Old Girl of Mine; There Never Was a Girl Like You; What's the Matter with Father; When I Was Twenty-One and You Were Sweet Sixteen; Won't You Come Over to My House; Your Eyes Have Told Me So

Van Alystyne, Mrs. Alexander, *see* **Frances Jane Crosby**

Van Biene, August The Broken Melody

Van Boskerck, Francis Saltus Semper Paratus

Van Dam, Albert The Sentimental Touch

Van Halen, Alex Jump; Why Can't This Be Love

Van Halen, Edward Jump; Why Can't This Be Love

Van Heusen, Jimmy Ain't Got a Dime to My Name; All the Way; All This and Heaven Too; Apalachicola, Florida; Aren't You Glad You're You; As Long as I'm Dreaming; Blue Rain; The Boy's Night Out; But Beautiful; Call Me Irresponsible; Country Style; Darn That Dream; Deep in a Dream; (Just Say I'm a) Friend of Yours; Going My Way; Heaven Can Wait; Here's That Rainy Day; High Hopes; (And) His Rocking Horse Ran Away; If You Please; I'll Only Miss Her When I Think of Her; Imagination; The Impatient Years; It Could Happen to You; It's Always You; Life Is So Peculiar; Love and Marriage; Love Is the Darndest Thing; The Man with the Golden Arm; Moonlight Becomes You; My Heart Goes Crazy; My Heart Is a Hobo; My Kind of Town; Nancy (with the Laughing Face); Oh You Crazy Moon; Personality; Pocketful of Miracles; Polka Dots and Moonbeams; Put It There Pal; The Road to Morocco; The Second Time Around; Sleigh Ride in July; So Help Me; Suddenly It's Spring; Sunday, Monday or Always; Sunshine Cake; Swinging on a Star; (Love Is) The Tender Trap; Thoroughly Modern Millie; Wake Me When It's Over; Walking Happy; Where Love Has Gone; You Don't Have To Know the Language

Van Hoy, Rafe Baby I Lied; Can I See You Tonight; Sail Away; What's Forever For

Van Laar, Jan Sr. The Windmill's Turning

Van Leer, Thys Hocus Pocus

Van Loan, Paul Sally, Irene and Mary

Van Ness, Clarke Aunt Jemima (Silver Dollar); Silver Dollar (Down and Out)

Van Steeden, Peter Home

Van Warmer, Randy I Guess It Never Hurts To Hurt Sometimes; Just When I Needed You Most

Van Winkle, Joseph Mister Custer

Vancaire, Maurice The Song of Songs

Vance, Albert Disco Lady

Vance, Paul J. Calcutta; Catch a Falling Star; Itsy Bitsy Teenie Weenie Yellow Polkadot Bikini; Playground in My Mind; Run Joey Run; Starlight; Tracy; When Julie Comes Around

Vanda, Harry Love Is in the Air

Vandyke, Les Ain't That Funny; Applejack; As You Like It; Cupboard Love; Don't That Beat All; Don't You Know It; Forget Me Not; Get Lost; How About That; Poor Me; Someone Else's Baby; The Time Has Come; What Do You Want?; Who Am I

Vangelis (Theme from) Chariots of Fire

Vann, Teddy Loop de Loop

Vannelli, Gino Hurts To Be in Love; Living Inside Myself

Vannelli, Ross I Just Wanna Stop

Vantard, Henri Eugene Two Loves Have I

Varley, Bill Don't You Rock Me Daddy-O

Varna, H. Vieni, Vieni

Varnick, Ted In the Middle of an Island

Vassy, Kin Heed the Call

Vaughan, Frankie Don't Stop—Twist

Vaughan, Henry Calvary

Vaughn, Billy Trying

Vaughn, George Mule Skinner Blues

Vaughn, Jack Goodbye Jimmy Goodbye

Vaughn, Wayne Let's Groove

Vegas, Lolly Come and Get Your Love

Veitch, Trevor Gloria; Telefone

Vejvoda, Taromir The Beer Barrel Polka

Velazquez, Consuelo Besame Mucho

Velona, Tony Domani (Tomorrow); Lollipops and Roses; Music To Watch Girls By

Venis, Geoffrey Where Did My Snowman Go

Venosa, Arthur Little Star

Verde, Edoardo Ciao Ciao Bambina; Romantica

Verdi, Giuseppe Anvil Chorus

Verner, H. C. Won't You Be My Sweetheart

Vernor, F. Dudleigh The Sweetheart of Sigma Chi

Vernor, Max Where Was Moses When the Lights Went Out

Verscharen, Joseph Since I Don't Have You

Vicars, Harold The Song of Songs (as Moya)

Vienna, Franz I'm Gonna Wash My Hands of You; The Wedding of Mister Mickey Mouse

Vigil, Rafael Bad Boy

Villard (Gilles), Jean While the Angelus Was Ringing, or,

The Three Bells (Les Trois Cloches), or, The Jimmy Brown Song *(with different lyrics)*

Villipigue, Phil Lonely Street

Villoldo, A.G. El Choclo

Vimmerstedt, Sadie I Wanna Be Around

Vimont, F. Madrid

Vincent, Larry If I Had My Life To Live Over

Vincent, Nathaniel H. Give a Little Credit to Your Dad; I Know What It Means To Be Lonesome; Railroad Jim; La Veeda; (When It's Roundup Time in Texas) When the Bloom Is on the Sage

Vinton, Bobby Mister Lonely; My Melody of Love

Violinsky, Sol, *see* **Sol Ginsberg**

Vogel, Janet Since I Don't Have You

Vogler, Gerard Tell Me, Babbling Echo, or, The Request

Von Flotow, F. Ah! So Pure

von Suppé, Franz Light Cavalry (Overture); Poet and Peasant Overture

Von Tilzer, Albert The Alcoholic Blues; Au Revoir, But Not Good-Bye; Soldier Boy; Carrie, or, Carrie Marry Harry; Chili Bean (Eenie Meenie Minie Mo); Dapper Dan; Down Where the Swanee River Flows; "Forever" Is a Long, Long Time; Give Me the Moonlight, Give Me the Girl; Good Evening, Caroline; He's Our Al; Honey Boy; I May Be Gone for a Long, Long Time; I Used To Love You, But It's All Over Now; I'll Be with You in Apple Blossom Time; I'm the Lonesomest Gal in Town; It's the Irish in Your Eye, (It's the Irish in Your Smile); Kentucky Sue; Let's Go into a Picture Show; The Moon Has His Eyes on You; My Little Girl; Nora Malone (Call Me by Phone); Oh By Jingo, Oh By Gee, You're the Only Girl for Me; Oh! How She Could Yacki, Hacki, Wicki, Wacki, Woo; A Picnic for Two; Please Don't Take My Lovin' Man Away; Pucker Up Your Lips, Miss Lindy; Put On Your Slippers and Fill Up Your Pipe; Put Your Arms Around Me Honey (Hold Me Tight); Roll Along Prairie Moon; Smarty; Take Me Out to the Ball Game; Take Me Up with You, Dearie; Teasing; That's What the Daisy Said; Wait Till You Get Them Up in the Air, Boys; Waters of Venice, or, Floating Down the Sleepy Lagoon

Von Tilzer, Harry Alexander (Don't You Love Your Baby No More); All Aboard for Blanket Bay; All Alone; And the Green Grass Grew All Around; A Bird in a Gilded Cage; Close to My Heart; The Cubanola Glide; Do You Take This Woman for Your Lawful Wife?; Don't Take Me Home; Down on the Farm (They All Ask for You); Down Where the Cotton Blossoms Grow; Down Where the Wurzburger Flows; Goodbye, Boys; Good-bye, Eliza Jane; Hannah, Won't You Open That Door?; I Love, I Love, I Love My Wife, But Oh You Kid; I Want a Girl—Just Like the Girl That Married Dear Old Dad; I Wonder If She's Waiting; I'd Leave My Happy Home for You; In the Evening by the Moonlight, Dear Louise; In the Sweet Bye and Bye; Jennie Lee; Just a Little Lovin'; Last Night Was the End of the World; A Little Bunch of Shamrocks; The Mansion of Aching Hearts; My Old New Hampshire Home; On a Sunday Afternoon; On the Old Fall River Line; Pardon Me, My Dear Alphonse, After You, My Dear Gaston; Rufus Rastus Johnson Brown (What You Goin' To Do When the Rent Comes 'Round); The Scandal of Little Lizzie Ford; Take Me Back to New York Town; That Old Irish Mother of Mine; They Always Pick On Me; They're All Sweeties; Under the Anheuser Bush; Under the Yum Yum Tree; Wait 'Til the Sun Shines, Nellie; What's the Good of Being Good—When No One's Good to Me; When Kate and I Were Coming Thro' the Rye; When the Harvest Days Are Over, Jessie Dear; Where the Morning Glories Twine Around the Door; Where the Sweet Magnolias Grow; You'll Always Be the Same Sweet Girl

von Weber, Carl Maria Invitation to the Dance

Vosburgh, Dick Just Like That

Voss, Faye Sugar Shack

Voudouris, Roger Get Used to It

Voynow, Dick Riverboat Shuffle

Waaktaar, Pål Take On Me

Wachtel, Robert Her Town Too

Wade, Herman Avery I've Got a Pain in My Sawdust

Wade, Hugh Let It Be Soon; Time May Change

Wade, John Francis Adeste Fideles, or, O Come All Ye Faithful

Wade, Joseph Augustine Meet Me by Moonlight Alone

Waggner, George Mary Lou

Wagner, Dick How You Gonna See Me Now; Only Women Bleed; You and Me

Wagner, Josef Franz Under the Double Eagle (March)

Wagner, Richard Flying Dutchman (Overture); Pilgrim's Chorus; Wedding March

Wagner, Richard Allen Just As I Am

Waite, John Missing You

Waite, Ted I've Never Seen a Straight Banana

Waite, Wayne Brath There'll Be Sad Songs (To Make You Cry); When the Going Gets Tough, the Tough Get Going

Wakefield, Kathy One Hundred Ways

Wakley, Ronald Maybe This Year

Walbridge, A.D. Now I Lay Me Down To Sleep

Walden, Dana How 'Bout Us

Walden, Narada Michael Freeway of Love; How Will I Know; Who's Zoomin' Who

Waldteufel, Emile Estudiantina; The Skaters (Waltz)

Walker, Annie L. Work for the Night Is Coming

Walker, Barclay Good-Bye, Ma! Good-Bye, Pa! Good-Bye, Mule, or, Long Boy

Walker, Bee Hey Jealous Lover

Walker, Billy Joe B B B Burnin' Up with Love

Walker, Cindy Distant Dreams; I Don't Care; You Don't Know Me

Walker, Don Lost in Loveliness

Walker, George When It's All Goin' Out, and Nothin' Comin' In

Walker, James J. Will You Love Me in December As You Do in May

Walker, Jerry Jeff Mister Bo Jangles

Walker, Raymond Fido Is a Hot Dog Now; Funny Bunny Hug; Good Night, Nurse (Kiss Your Little Patient); Poor Pauline

Walker, Wayne P. Are You Sincere; Only the Heartaches

Walker, William Star in the East; Weeping Saviour

Wallace, Chester Moonlight on the Ganges

Wallace, J.L. Even the Nights Are Better; I Just Came Here To Dance; Touch Me When We're Dancing

Wallace, Oliver G. Der Fuehrer's Face; Hindustan; When I Saw an Elephant Fly

Wallace, Paul I Wish I Had My Old Girl Back Again

Wallace, Raymond Back Again to Happy-Go-Lucky Days; Ever So Goosey; Give Yourself a Pat on the Back; I'm Happy When I'm Hiking; Jolly Good Company; Old Father Thames; There's a Good Time Coming; When the Organ Played at Twilight (The Song That Reached My Heart); With My Shillelagh Under My Arm; You Can't Do That 'Ere

Wallace, Vincent Scenes That Are Brightest; Yes, Let Me Like a Soldier Fall

Wallace, William Ross The Sword of Bunker Hill

Wallace, William Vincent Sweet Spirit, Hear My Prayer

Waller, Jack Got a Date with an Angel; Hoch, Caroline; My Heart's To Let; Roll Away Clouds; Sing Brothers

Waller, Thomas "Fats" Ain't Misbehavin'; Blue Turning Grey over You; Honeysuckle Rose; I've Got a Feeling I'm Falling; The Joint Is Jumpin'; Keepin' Out of Mischief Now; The Ladies Who Sing with the Band; Lounging at the Waldorf; Squeeze Me; The Viper's Drag; What Did I Do To Be So Black and Blue; When the Nylons Bloom Again

Wallis, C. Jay All by Yourself in the Moonlight; Misery Farm

Walsh, Brock Automatic

Walsh, James Don't Have Any More, Mrs. Moore

Walter, Howard I Would Be True

Walter, Lee Special Lady

Ward, Carlos Express

Ward, Charles B. (Casey Would Waltz with the Strawberry Blonde While) The Band Played On; Only a Bowery Boy; Strike Up the Band—Here Comes a Sailor

Ward, Edward Always and Always; Lovely Lady

Ward, George Gee, But I'd Like To Make You Happy

Ward, Samuel Augustus America, the Beautiful

Ware, Dick Rock and Roll Waltz

Ware, L. Hold Tight—Hold Tight

Warfield, Charles Baby, Won't You Please Come Home

Waring, Anna In Heavenly Love Abiding

Waring, Fred I Hear Music

Waring, Tom So Beats My Heart for You; Way Back Home

Warman, Cy Sweet Marie

Warne, Peter Boom Bang-A-Bang

Warner, Frank Tom Dooley, or, Tom Dula

Warner, Henry Edward I've Got a Pain in My Sawdust

Warren, Diane Rhythm of the Night

Warren, Frank Indianola

Warren, Harry About a Quarter to Nine; Absence Makes the Heart Grow Fonder (for Somebody Else); An Affair To Remember; Am I in Love; At Last; Away Down South in Heaven; Baby Doll; Boulevard of Broken Dreams; By the River Sainte Marie; Chattanooga Choo Choo; Cheerful Little Earful; Chica Chica Boom Chic; Coffee in the Morning, Kisses at Night; Cryin' for the Carolines; Day Dreaming; Don't Give Up the Ship; Down Argentine Way; Fair and Warmer; Forty-Second Street; Gid-ap, Garibaldi; The Girl at the Ironing Board; The Girl Friend of the Whirling Dervish; Have a Little Faith in Me; Here We Are; Honolulu; I Found a Million Dollar Baby in a Five and Ten Cent Store; I Had the Craziest Dream; I Know Now; I Know Why; (Yi Yi Yi Yi) I Like You Very Much; I Love My Baby—My Baby Loves Me; I Only Have Eyes for You; I Wish I Knew; I'll Sing You a Thousand Love Songs; (You May Not Be an Angel But) I'll String Along with You; In Acapulco; It Happened in Sun Valley; I've Got a Gal in Kalamazoo; Jeepers Creepers; Keep Young and Beautiful; The Latin Quarter; The Little Things You Used To Do; Love Is Where You Find It; Lullaby of Broadway; Lulu's Back in Town; The More I See You; My Dream Is Yours; My Heart Tells Me; My One and Only Highland Fling; Nagasaki; No Love, No Nothing; Old Man Sunshine—Little Boy Bluebird; On the Atchison, Topeka, and the Santa Fe; Ooh That Kiss; (Home in) Pasadena; Pettin' in the Park; Remember Me; The Rose in Her Hair; Rose of the Rio Grande; The Rose Tattoo; September in the Rain; Serenade in Blue; Shadow Waltz; Shanghai Lil; She's a Latin from Manhattan; Shuffle Off to Buffalo; The Stanley Steamer; Summer Night; That's Amore; There Will Never Be Another You; This Heart of Mine; This Is Always; Three's a Crowd; Too Many Tears; The Torch Song; Wait and See; A Weekend in Havana; We're in the Money, or, The Gold Diggers' Song; Where Am I; Where Do You Work-a John; Where the Shy Little Violets Grow; With Plenty of Money and You; Wonder Bar; The Words Are in My Heart; Would You Like To Take a Walk; You Let Me Down; You Must Have Been a Beautiful Baby; You Wonderful You; You'll Never Know; Young and Healthy; You're Getting To Be a Habit with Me; You're My Everything; You've Got Me Where You Want Me; Zing a Little Zong

Warren, Mrs. Mercy The Liberty Song, or, Come, Join Hand in Hand, or, In Freedom We're Born

Warshauer, Frank It Isn't Fair

Washburn, Country Oh Monah; One Dozen Roses

Washburne, Henry S. The Grave of Bonaparte; The Vacant Chair, or, We Shall Meet But We Shall Miss Him

Washington, Carrol Mister Big Stuff

Washington, Ferdinand I'll Be Home

Washington, Leon Hambone

Washington, Ned Can't We Talk It Over; Cosi Cosa; Give a Little Whistle; Hi-Diddle-Dee-Dee (an Actor's Life for Me); The High and the Mighty; (Theme from) High Noon (Do Not Forsake Me, Oh My Darling); A Hundred Years from Today; I Don't Stand a Ghost of a Chance with You; I'm Getting Sentimental over You; I've Got No Strings; The Man from Laramie; My Foolish Heart; The Nearness of You; On Green Dolphin Street; (Theme from) Rawhide; Return to Paradise;

Search for Paradise; Singin' in the Bathtub; Smoke Rings; Song Without End; Stella by Starlight; Strange Are the Ways of Love; Strange Lady in Town; Sweet Heartache; Sweet Madness; The Unforgiven (The Need for Love); When I Saw an Elephant Fly; When You Wish upon a Star; Wild Is the Wind

Washington, Oscar   Night Train

Waterman, Pat   I Could Be So Good for You

Waters, Chris   Sexy Eyes

Waters, Roger   Another Brick in the Wall

Waters, Safford   The Belle of Avenoo A

Watkins, Morris W.   Roar, Lion, Roar

Watkins, Viola   Gee!

Watson, Deke   (I Love You) For Sentimental Reasons

Watson, John   Looking High, High, High

Watson, John G.   Goodnight to You All; Racing with the Moon

Watson, Michael   Anchored; Thy Sentinel Am I; Voices of the Woods, or, Welcome Sweet Springtime

Watson, Muriel   Goodnight to You All; Let's Keep It That Way; Sweetheart, We'll Never Grow Old

Watt, Tommy   Overdrive; Rock Bottom

Watters, Cyril   The Willow Waltz

Watts, Clem   If I Knew You Were Comin' I'd've Baked a Cake; You Call Everybody Darling

Watts, H. Grady   Blue Champagne

Watts, Isaac   At the Cross; Joy to the World, or, Antioch; O God, Our Help in Ages Past; We're Marching to Zion

Waxman, Franz   Mountains Beyond the Moon; (Theme from) Return to Peyton Place, or, The Wonderful Season of Love; Theme from Peyton Place

Wayburn, Ned   Come to the Moon; How Can You Tell

Wayne, Artie   Mahzel

Wayne, Bernie   Blue Velvet; Laughing on the Outside (Crying on the Inside); Vanessa; You Walk By

Wayne, Dottie   The Night Has a Thousand Eyes

Wayne, Jeff   War of the Worlds

Wayne, Jerry   I'll Be There

Wayne, Mabel   As Long as You're Not in Love with Anyone Else, Why Don't You Fall in Love with Me; Chiquita; Don't Wake Me Up, Let Me Dream; A Dreamer's Holiday; I Understand; In a Little Spanish Town; It Happened in Monterey; Little Man, You've Had a Busy Day; Ramona

Wayne, Sid   It's Impossible; Mangos; My Love for You; See You in September; Two Different Worlds

Weatherly, Frederick Edward   At Santa Barbara; Danny Boy; Friend o' Mine; The Holy City; Long Ago in Alcala; The Midshipmite; Mifanwy; Nancy Lee; Roses of Picardy; Three for Jack

Weatherly, Jim   (You're the) Best Thing That Ever Happened to Me; Midnight Train to Georgia; Neither One of Us (Wants To Be the First To Say Goodbye)

Weaver, Blue   Our Love (Don't Throw It All Away)

Weaver, Derek   Hold On to My Love

Webb, C.H.   Croquet

Webb, Chick   Stomping at the Savoy

Webb, George James   'Tis Dawn, the Lark Is Singing

Webb, Jim   All I Know; By the Time I Get to Phoenix; Didn't We; Galveston; Highwayman; It's a Sin When You Love Somebody; MacArthur Park; Up Up and Away, or, My Beautiful Balloon; Where's the Playground Susie; Wichita Lineman

Webb, Joy   It's an Open Secret

Webb, Roy   Roar, Lion, Roar

Webber, Andrew Lloyd   Capped Teeth and Caesar Salad; Don't Cry for Me, Argentina; Everything's Alright; Grizabella the Glamour Cat; I Don't Know How To Love Him; Jesus Christ Superstar; Memory; Mister Mistoffolees; One More Angel in Heaven; Unexpected Song

Webster, Joseph Philbrick   Lorena; Sweet By and By

Webster, Paul Francis   Airport Love Theme; Anastasia; April Love; Boy on a Dolphin; A Certain Smile; The Deadwood Stage; Doctor, Lawyer, Indian Chief; Friendly Persuasion, or, Thee I Love; Got the Jitters; The Green Leaves of Summer; The Guns of Navarone; Honey-Babe; How It Lies, How It Lies, How It Lies; I Got It Bad and That Ain't Good; I Speak to the Stars; I'll Remember Tonight; I'll Walk with God; Invitation; The Lamplighter's Serenade; Like Young; Love Is a Many-Splendored Thing; The Loveliest Night of the Year; Masquerade; Maverick; Memphis in June; My Moonlight Madonna; Padre; Rainbow on the River; (The Song of) Raintree County; Reflections in the Water; (Theme from) Return to Peyton Place, or, The Wonderful Season of Love; Secret Love; Seventh Dawn; The Shadow of Your Smile; Somewhere My Love, or, Lara's Theme; Sugarfoot; Tender Is the Night; Theme from Peyton Place; There's Never Been Anyone Else But You; The Twelfth of Never; Two Cigarettes in the Dark; A Very Precious Love; You Was

Webster, R.A.   Last Farewell

Webster, Reverend H.D.L.   Lorena

Webster, Warwick   Man in a Raincoat

Wechter, Cissy   Spanish Flea

Wechter, Julius   Spanish Flea; Up Cherry Street

Weeden, Howard   A Banjo Song

Weeks, Harold   Chong, He Come from Hong Kong; Hindustan

Weems, Ted   The Martins and the Coys; Oh Monah

Weersma, Melle   Penny Serenade

Weigall, Arthur   Susannah's Squeaking Shoes

Weil, Cynthia   All of You; Blame It on the Bossa Nova; Here You Come Again; He's So Shy; If Ever You're in My Arms Again; Just Once; Kicks; Never Gonna Let You Go; On Broadway; Running with the Night; Somewhere Down the Road; Somewhere Out There; (You're My) Soul and Inspiration; You've Lost That Lovin' Feelin'

Weill, Harry   Don't Leave Me, Dolly

Weill, Irving   (On the Shores of) Tripoli

Weill, Kurt   The Alabama Song, or, Moon of Alabama; All at Once; Bilbao Song; Cry, the Beloved Country; Get a Load of That; Green-Up Time; Here I'll Stay; It Never Was You;

Weinberg, Mortimer Where Do You Work-a John

Weinman, Bernard Too Much

Weinstein, Bobby Goin' Out of My Head; Hurts So Bad

Weinstein, Brian It's Gonna Take a Miracle

Weisberg, Dave Down by the Silvery Rio Grande

Weiser, Irving There I Go

Weisman, Ben Never Let Her Go; The Night Has a Thousand Eyes; Wooden Heart

Weiss, Donna Bette Davis Eyes

Weiss, George David Can Anyone Explain? (No! No! No!); Can't Help Falling in Love (with You); Cross Over the Bridge; A Girl! A Girl!, or, Zoom Ba Di Alli Nella; How Important Can It Be; I Don't See Me in Your Eyes Anymore; I Ran All the Way Home; I Want To Thank Your Folks; I'll Never Be Free; Jacques D'Iraq (Jock D'Rock); The Lion Sleeps Tonight, or, Wimoweh; Lullaby of Birdland; Mandolins in the Moonlight; Mister Wonderful; Oh What It Seemed To Be; Rumors Are Flying; Surrender; These Things I Offer You (for a Lifetime); Too Close for Comfort; What a Wonderful World; The Wheel of Fortune; Without You I'm Nothing

Weiss, Larry Bend Me, Shape Me; Rhinestone Cowboy

Weiss, Stephan And So Do I; Music Music Music; Put Your Dreams Away for Another Day; They Say; While You Danced, Danced, Danced

Weiss, Willoughby Hunter The Village Blacksmith

Weitz, Ted Goodness Knows How I Love You

Welch, Bruce Bachelor Boy; Dancing Shoes; Don't Talk to Him; Foot Tapper; Genie with the Light Brown Lamp; I Could Easily Fall; I Love You; On the Beach; Please Don't Tease; Please Mister Please; Rise and Fall of Flingle Bint; Shindig; Summer Holiday; Theme for Young Lovers; Time Drags By

Welch, Ed Shillingbury Tales; The Snow Goose

Welch, Robert L. Precious Love

Weldon, Frank Christmas in Killarney; Goodnight Wherever You Are; The Heart of a Fool; I Came, I Saw, I Congad; I Like Mountain Music; A Little on the Lonely Side

Weller, Fred Dizzy

Welles, Bob The Patty Duke Theme (Cousins)

Wells, Bryan A Place in the Sun; Yester-Me, Yester-You, Yesterday

Wells, Jack Joan of Arc, They Are Calling You

Wells, John Barnes Thumb Marks; Two Little Magpies

Wells, Robert The Christmas Song, or, Merry Christmas to You, or, Chestnuts Roasting on an Open Fire; From Here to Eternity; Mobile

Wendling, Pete All the Quakers Are Shoulder Shakers Down in Quaker Town; By the Sycamore Tree; Oh, How I Wish I Could Sleep Until My Daddy Comes Home; Oh! What a Pal Was Mary; Red Lips Kiss My Blues Away; Swingin' in a Hammock; Take Your Girlie to the Movies If You Can't Make Love at Home; There's Danger in Your Eyes, Cherie; (There's

Something Nice About Everyone But) There's Everything Nice About You; Wonderful You; Yaaka Hula Hickey Dula

Wenrich, Percy (On) Moonlight Bay; Put On Your Old Grey Bonnet; Rainbow; Sail Along Silvery Moon; She Took Mother's Advice; Silver Bell; Up in a Balloon; Way Out Yonder in the Golden West; When You Wore a Tulip and I Wore a Big Red Rose; Where Do We Go from Here

Wesley, Charles Hark the Herald Angels Sing; Jesus, Lover of My Soul

Wesley, Samuel The Church's One Foundation; In Heavenly Love Abiding

Weslyn, Louis Baby Rose; Send Me Away with a Smile

West, Arthur See, Saw, Margery Daw

West, Dottie I'd Like To Teach the World To Sing

West, Eugene Broadway Rose; You Know You Belong to Somebody Else

West, Keith Grocer Jack

West, Paul I'm on the Water Wagon Now

West-Oram, Jamie One Thing Leads to Another

Westendorf, Thomas P. Garfield Now Will Guide the Nation; I'll Take You Home Again Kathleen

Western, Johnny The Ballad of Paladin

Westlake, Clive Here I Go Again; I Close My Eyes and Count to Ten; Losing You

Weston, Harris Knees Up Mother Brown

Weston, Paul Autumn in Rome; Day by Day; The Gandy Dancers' Ball; I Should Care; Shrimp Boats

Weston, R.P. Ain't It Ni-Ice; And the Great Big Saw Came Nearer; Brahn Boots; Good Bye-ee; Hoch, Caroline; I'm Henery the Eighth (I Am); I've Got Rings on My Fingers, or, Mumbo Jumbo Jijjiboo J. O'Shea; My Word You Do Look Queer; Olga Pulloffski; Paddy McGinty's Goat; Sing Brothers; Sister Susie's Sewing Shirts for Soldiers; Stop and Shop at the Co-Op Shop; What a Mouth; When Father Papered the Parlour; With Her Head Tucked Underneath Her Arm

Weston, Willie Joan of Arc, They Are Calling You

Westover, Charles Runaway

Westphal, Frank C. Old Soldiers Never Die; When You Come to the End of the Day

Wetton, John Heart of the Moment

Wever, Ned Trust in Me

Wexler, Jerry (You Make Me Feel Like) A Natural Woman

Weydt, H.A. The Big Brown Bear

Wheeler, Billy Ed Coward of the County

Wheeler, Francis Dancing Fool; I Wonder If You Still Care for Me; It Was Only a Sun Shower; Let a Smile Be Your Umbrella on a Rainy (Rainy) Day; Roam On, (My) Little Gipsy Sweetheart; The Sheik of Araby; There's Something About a Rose (That Reminds Me of You)

Wheeley, Ken The Night the Floor Fell In

Whelan, James F. III Mad About You

Whipple, Sterling Prisoner of Hope

Whitcup, Leonard (Take Me Back to My) Boots and Saddle;

From the Vine Came the Grape (from the Grape Came the Wine); Snake Charmer; True

White, Alan   After the Lights Go Down Low

White, Barry   Can't Get Enough of Your Love Babe; I'm Gonna Love You Just a Little More Baby; Love's Theme; What Am I Gonna Do with You; You're the First, the Last, My Everything

White, Bert   Canadian Capers

White, Charles A.   Marguerite

White, Charles T.   Carry Me Back to Ole Virginny, or, De Floating Show; I'se Gwine Back to Dixie; Stop Dat Knocking at My Door

White, Cool (John Hodges)   Buffalo Gals (Won't You Come Out Tonight?), or, Lubly Fan

White, David   At the Hop; One-Two-Three; You Don't Own Me

White, Edward R.   The Crazy Otto Rag (Medley); Happiness Street (Corner Sunshine Square)

White, George   Cabin in the Cotton

White, Johnny   Ten Little Fingers and Ten Little Toes—Down in Tennessee

White, Joseph M.   Mammy's Little Kinky Headed Boy

White, Mark   Be Near Me

White, Maurice   Best of My Love; Let's Groove; Shining Star

White, P.   It's the Same Old Shillelagh

White, Peter   Time Passages

White, Tony Joe   Polk Salad Annie

White, Willie(y)   I'd Love To Be a Monkey in the Zoo; Oh! How I Laugh When I Think How I Cried About You

Whitehead, Joan   Ain't No Stoppin' Us Now

Whiteley, Ray   Back in the Saddle Again

Whiteman, Paul   (My) Wonderful One

Whitfield, Norman   Car Wash; I Can't Get Next to You; I Heard It Through the Grapevine; I Wanna Get Next to You; I Wish It Would Rain; Just My Imagination (Running Away with Me); Masterpiece; Papa Was a Rollin' Stone; Too Busy Thinking About My Baby; War

Whiting, George   Beautiful Eyes; Believe It Beloved; High upon a Hill Top; My Blue Heaven; My Wife's Gone to the Country (Hurrah! Hurrah!); West of the Great Divide

Whiting, Richard A.   Ain't We Got Fun; Beyond the Blue Horizon; Bimini Bay; Breezin' Along with the Breeze; Eadie Was a Lady; Give Me a Moment Please; Guilty; Have You Got Any Castles, Baby; Honey; Hooray for Hollywood; Horses; I Can't Escape from You; I Wonder Where My Lovin' Man Has Gone; I'm Like a Fish out of Water; It's Tulip Time in Holland; The Japanese Sandman; Louise; Mammy's (a) Little Coal Black Rose; Miss Brown to You; My Future Just Passed; My Ideal; My Sweeter Than Sweet; On the Good Ship Lollipop; (I'd Love To Spend) One Hour with You; Ride, Tenderfoot, Ride; (I Got a Woman Crazy for Me) She's Funny That Way; Sleepy Time Gal; Some Sunday Morning; Till We Meet Again; Too Marvelous for Words; True Blue Lou; Turn Out the Light; Ukulele Lady; When Did You Leave Heaven; When Shall We Meet Again; Where the Black-Eyed

Susans Grow; Where the Morning Glories Grow; You're an Old Smoothie

Whitlock, Tom   Take My Breath Away

Whitlock, William   Hop Scotch Polka; Take Your Time, Miss Lucy

Whitney, Howard   The Mosquito's Parade

Whitney, Joan   Candy; Comme Ci, Comme Ça; Far Away Places; High on a Windy Hill; It All Comes Back to Me Now; It's Love, Love, Love; Love Somebody; My Sister and I; No Other Arms, No Other Lips; So You're the One; That's the Beginning of the End; The Way That the Wind Blows

Whitsett, Carson   Why Not Me

Whitson, Beth Slater   Don't Wake Me Up, I'm Dreaming; Let Me Call You Sweetheart; Meet Me Tonight in Dreamland

Whittaker, Roger   Durham Town; Last Farewell; New World in the Morning; Why

Whymark, H.J.   Champagne Charley Was His Name

Whyte-Melville, G.T.   Goodbye

Whyton, Wally   Don't You Rock Me Daddy-O

Wickham, Vicki   You Don't Have To Say You Love Me

Wiener, Herb   It's My Party; Joey

Wiesenthal, T.V.   The Ingle Side

Wilbur, Richard   Glitter and Be Gay

Wilcox, Ella Wheeler   Laugh and the World Laughs with You

Wilde, Marty   Abergavenny; Bad Boy; Jezamine

Wildeblood, Peter   Meet the Family

Wilder, Alec   All the King's Horses; I'll Be Around; Is It Always Like This; It's So Peaceful in the Country; While We're Young

Wilder, Matthew   Break My Stride

Wilhousky, Peter J.   Carol of the Bells

Wilkin, John   G.T.O.

Wilkin, Marijohn   Waterloo

Wilkins, Ronnie   Son of a Preacher Man

Wilkinson, Dudley   Because of You

Willard, Mrs.   Rocked in the Cradle of the Deep

Willemetz, Albert   My Man; Valentine

Willet, Slim   Don't Let the Stars Get in Your Eyes

Williams, Alfred   Let Me Shake the Hand That Shook the Hand of Sullivan; The Monkey's Wedding

Williams, Arthur   Funny Thing; I Could Have Told You

Williams, Bernie   The Duke of Earl

Williams, Bert A.   Constantly; Let It Alone; Nobody; That's A Plenty; When It's All Goin' Out and Nothin' Comin' In

Williams, Charles   (Theme from) The Apartment; Devil's Gallop, or, Dick Barton Theme; The Dream of Olwen

Willams, Clarence   Baby, Won't You Please Come Home; Farewell to Storyville; Gulf Coast Blues; I Ain't Gonna Give Nobody None o' This Jelly Roll; Royal Garden Blues; Squeeze Me; Sugar Blues; Ugly Chile (You're Some Pretty Doll); West End Blues

Williams, Curley   Half As Much

Williams, Curtis Cherish; Earth Angel; Fresh; Joanna; Misled

Williams, Dave Whole Lot-ta Shakin' Goin' On

Williams, Edna I Don't Want Another Sister

Williams, Gene Wyoming Lullaby

Williams, George So Much in Love

Williams, Hank All My Rowdy Friends Have Settled Down; Cold Cold Heart; A Country Boy Can Survive; Dixie on My Mind; Hey Good Lookin'; Honky Tonkin'; I'm So Lonesome I Could Cry; Jambalaya (on the Bayou); Kaw-Liga; Lovesick Blues; Texas Women; There'll Be No Teardrops Tonight; Your Cheatin' Heart

Williams, Harry H. Back, Back, Back to Baltimore; Cheyenne; Don't Blame It All on Broadway; I'm Afraid To Come Home in the Dark; In the Shade of the Old Apple Tree; It Looks (to Me) Like a Big Night Tonight; It's a Long (Long) Way to Tipperary; Mickey; Naughty Naughty Naughty; Navajo; Oh You Cutie (You Ever Loving Child); Peggy; Rose Room; San Antonio; There Never Was a Girl Like You; What's the Matter with Father; When I Was Twenty-One and You Were Sweet Sixteen; Won't You Come Over to My House

Williams, Hugh, *see* **Will Grosz**

Williams, J.M. Corrine Corrina

Williams, James Fire; Love Rollercoaster

Williams, Jerry Givin' It Up for Your Love

Williams, Jimmy T. How Glad I Am

Williams, John Can You Read My Mind (Theme from *Superman*); (Theme from) Close Encounters of the Third Kind; (Theme from) The Empire Strikes Back; (Theme from) E.T. The Extra Terrestrial; (Theme from) Raiders of the Lost Ark; (Theme from) Star Wars

Williams, Lawrence Let Your Love Flow

Williams, M.B. My Mother's Bible

Williams, Mary Lou Camel Hop

Williams, Mason Classical Gas

Williams, Maurice Little Darlin'; Stay

Williams, Mentor Drift Away; When We Make Love

Williams, Milan Sweet Love

Williams, Paul Evergreen, or, Love Theme from *A Star Is Born;* I Won't Last a Day Without You; Rainy Days and Mondays; We've Only Just Begun; You and Me Against the World

Williams, Ralph G. Mister Big Stuff

Williams, Spencer Basin Street Blues; Careless Love; Dallas Blues; Everybody Loves My Baby, But My Baby Don't Love Nobody But Me; Farewell to Storyville; Georgia Grind; I Ain't Gonna Give Nobody None o' This Jelly Roll; I Ain't Got Nobody; I Found a New Baby; Royal Garden Blues; Shim-Me-Sha-Wabble; The Soft Shoe Shuffle; Tishomingo Blues; Twelfth Street Rag; When the Lights Are Low

Williams, Tex Smoke! Smoke! Smoke! (That Cigarette)

Williams, W.R. (Rossiter) I'd Love To Live in Loveland (with a Girl Like You)

Willis, Allee Blue Side; Lead Me On; Neutron Dance

Willis, Marvin Float On

Willis, Richard Storrs It Came upon a Midnight Clear; The Lone Fish (Meat) Ball

Willner, Dr. A.M. My Little Nest of Heavenly Blue, or Frasquita Serenade (Blaues Himmelbett), or, Farewell, My Love, Farewell; Pierette and Pierrot

Wills, Bob San Antonio Rose, or, Rose of San Antone

Wills, Johnnie Lee Rag Mop

Wills, William Gorman I'll Sing Thee Songs of Araby

Willson, Meredith Beautiful People of Denver; Chick-a-Pen; Dolce Far Niente; Gary, Indiana; Goodnight My Someone; I Ain't Down Yet; It's Beginning To Look (a Lot) Like Christmas; It's You; Keep-A-Hoppin'; Lida Rose; Marian the Librarian; May the Good Lord Bless and Keep You; My White Knight; Seventy-Six Trombones; Till There Was You; Trouble (in River City); You and I

Wilmot, Charles In the Twi-Twi-Twi-Light

Wilsh, Mike Juliet

Wilson, Al Down at the Old Swimming Hole; In the Little Red Schoolhouse

Wilson, Ann Dog and Butterfly; Magic Man; Never

Wilson, Anthony Brother Louie

Wilson, Brian Do It Again; Good Timin'; Good Vibrations; Help Me Rhonda; I Get Around; Sloop John B.; Surf City; Surfin' Safari

Wilson, Carl Good Timin'

Wilson, Ernest The Golden Tango

Wilson, Forrest Ko Ko Mo (I Love You So)

Wilson, Frank E. Boogie Down; Keep on Truckin'; Love Child; You've Made Me So Very Happy

Wilson, Irving M. Kid Days

Wilson, J.V. "Pinky" The Aggie War Hymn

Wilson, Jeffrey Let Me Love You Tonight; Still Right Here in My Heart

Wilson, Nancy Dog and Butterfly; Magic Man; Never

Wilson, Neil Cielito Lindo (Ay, Ay, Ay, Ay)

Wilson, Norro (If You Happen To See) The Most Beautiful Girl (in the World); Never Been So Loved in All My Life; Surround Me with Love; A Very Special Love Song

Wilson, Rob For All We Know

Wilson, Robert A Gordon for Me

Wilson, Ron Wipe Out

Wilson, Sandy I Could Be Happy with You; It's Never Too Late To Fall in Love; A Room in Bloomsbury; Sur la Plage; Won't You Charleston with Me

Wilson, Tony Emma; You Sexy Thing

Wilson, Wesley Gimme a Pigfoot (and a Bottle of Beer)

Wimperis, Arthur Arcady Is Ever Young; Bring Me a Rose; The Canoe Song; Gilbert the Filbert; The Girl with a Brogue; Here's to Love; If You Could Care for Me; I'll Make a Man of You; The Pipes of Pan; The Temple Bell; Tony from America

Windom, W.H. The Fatal Wedding

Wine, Toni Candida; A Groovy Kind of Love

Winegar, Frank When a Gypsy Makes His Violin Cry

Winfree, Dick   China Boy

Wingate, Philip   I Don't Want To Play in Your Yard; You Can't Play in Our Yard Any More

Winkler, Franz   Forever and Ever

Winkler, Gerhard   Answer Me (My Love)

Winnemore, A.F.   The Gum Tree Canoe (on Tom-Big-Bee River); Stop Dat Knocking at My Door

Winner, Joseph E.   Little Brown Jug (as R.A. Eastburn)

Winner, Septimus   Ellie Rhee, or, Carry Me Back to Tennessee; Listen to the Mocking Bird (as Alice Hawthorne); Oh Where, Oh Where, Has My Little Dog Gone, or, Der Deitcher's Dog; Ten Little Indians, or, Ten Little Injuns, or, Ten Little Niggers; What Is Home Without a Mother (as Alice Hawthorne); Whispering Hope

Winstone, Eric   Stage Coach

Winter, Edgar   Frankenstein

Winthrop, T.F.   Daisy Deane

Winwood, Steve   Higher Love; While You See a Chance

Wirges, William   (I'm) Chiquita Banana

Wirtz, Mark   Grocer Jack

Wisdom, Norman   Don't Laugh at Me ('Cause I'm a Fool)

Wise, Fred   "A"—You're Adorable; I Won't Cry Anymore; Little Lulu; Misirlou; Never Let Her Go; Nightingale; Wooden Heart; You, You, You Are the One

Wise, Jim   Choo-Choo Honeymoon; The Sailor of My Dreams

Wiseman, Scott   Have I Told You Lately That I Love You

Wisner, J.   Don't Throw Your Love Away

Withers, Bill   Ain't No Sunshine; Just the Two of Us; Lean on Me

Witmark, Frank M.   Zenda Waltzes

Witt, Max S.   The Moth and the Flame; My Little Georgia Rose

Wittstatt, Hans   Pepe

Wodehouse, P.G.   Bill; Cleopatterer; Ev'ry Little While; Go, Little Boat; Have a Heart; I Found You and You Found Me; Just a Voice To Call Me, Dear; Leave It to Jane; Ma Belle; March of the Musketeers; Nestin' Time in Flatbush; An Old-Fashioned Wife; A Pal Like You; Rolled into One; Shadow of the Moon; Shufflin' Sam; The Siren's Song; The Sun Shines Brighter; There's a Light in Your Eyes; There's Life in the Old Dog Yet; Throw Me a Rose; Till ('Til) the Clouds Roll By; A Year from Today; You Never Knew About Me; You Said Something

Wolcott, Charles   Sooner or Later (You're Gonna Be Comin' Around); Two Silhouettes; Without You

Wolcott, John (Peter Pindar)   Hope Told a Flattering Tale

Wolf, Don   Sleep Walk

Wolf, Ina   Sara; Who's Johnny ("Short Circuit" Theme)

Wolf, Jack   I'm a Fool To Want You

Wolf, Peter   Freeze-Frame; Sara; We Built This City

Wolf, Rennold   I Love Love; You Cannot Make Your Shimmy Shake on Tea

Wolfe, Jacques   De Glory Road; Shortnin' Bread

Wolfe, Steve   Beg, Steal or Borrow

Wolfert, David   Heartbreaker

Wolfson, Mack   The Crazy Otto Rag (Medley); Happiness Street (Corner Sunshine Square)

Woloshin, Sid   You Deserve a Break Today

Wonder, Stevie   Boogie On Reggae Woman; Go Home; Higher Ground; I Just Called To Say I Love You; I Was Made To Love Her; I Wish; Living for the City; Love Light in Flight; Master Blaster (Jammin'); My Cherie Amor; Part Time Lover; Superstition; Tell Me Something Good; That Girl; Uptight (Everything's Alright); You Are the Sunshine of My Life; You Haven't Done Nothing Yet

Wood, Arthur   Barwick Green (The Archers)

Wood, Bobby Ray   Half the Way; He Got You; Talkin' in Your Sleep

Wood, Clement   De Glory Road

Wood, Cyrus   The Lady in Ermine; Lovely Lady; When Hearts Are Young

Wood, Guy   French Foreign Legion; My One and Only Love; Till Then

Wood, Haydn   Bird of Love Divine; A Brown Bird Singing; It Is Only a Tiny Garden; Love's Garden of Roses; O Flower Divine; Roses of Picardy

Wood, J.T.   Wait Till the Clouds Roll By

Wood, Ken (Walter R. Moody)   The Happy Organ

Wood, Leo   Honest and Truly; Runnin' Wild; Somebody Stole My Gal

Wood, Roy   Blackberry Way; Fire Brigade

Woodard, Stgug   Let Me Love You Tonight

Woodbury, Isaac Baker   Be Kind to the Loved Ones at Home; The Rainy Day; Row Thy Boat Lightly; Stars of the Summer Night

Woode, Henri   Rosetta

Woodeforde-Finden, Amy   Kashmiri Love Song; Less Than the Dust; The Temple Bells; Till I Wake

Woodford, Terry   Angel in Your Arms

Woodley, Bruce   Red Rubber Ball

Woodman, H.F.   Row Thy Boat Lightly

Woodman, Jack   Got'n Idea; In Love for the Very First Time; Must Be Madison

Woodman, Raymond Huntington   A Birthday

Woods, Adam   One Thing Leads to Another

Woods, Guy   Shoofly Pie and Apple Pan Dowdy

Woods, Harry M.   Celebratin'; Dancing with My Shadow; Heigh-Ho Everybody, Heigh-Ho; I'll Never Say "Never Again" Again; I'm Goin' South; I'm Looking Over a Four Leaf Clover; Just an Echo in the Valley; Just Like a Butterfly (That's Caught in the Rain); Linger a Little Longer in the Twilight; A Little Kiss Each Morning, a Little Kiss Each Night; (Just a) Little Street Where Old Friends Meet; (Ho! Ho! Ha! Ha!) Me Too; My Hat's on the Side of My Head; The Old Kitchen Kettle; Over My Shoulder; Paddlin' Madelin' Home; Poor Papa (He's Got Nuthin' At All); River, Stay 'Way from My Door; Side by Side; So Many Memories; Try a Little Tenderness; We Just Couldn't Say Goodbye; (Ooh) What a Little Moonlight Can Do; When the Moon Comes over the Mountain; When the Red, Red Robin Comes Bob, Bob, Bobbin' Along

Woods, Orlando Express

Woods, Stuart Money Honey

Woodward, Matthew Pretty Edelweiss

Woodward, Rob Mouldy Old Dough

Woodworth, Samuel The Hunters of Kentucky; Love's Eyes; The Meeting of the Waters of Hudson and Erie; The Old Oaken Bucket

Wooley, Sheb The Purple People Eater

Woolfenden, Guy The Comedy of Errors

Woolfson, Eric Don't Answer Me; Eye in the Sky; Games People Play; Prime Time; Time

Woolley, Bruce Video Killed the Radio Star

Woolsey, Mary Hale When It's Springtime in the Rockies

Work, Henry Clay Father, Dear Father, Come Home with Me Now, or, Come Home, Father; Grafted into the Army; Grandfather's Clock; Kingdom Coming, or, The Year of Jubilo; Marching Through Georgia; Wake Nicodemus

Worsley, John Jack in the Box

Worth, Bobby Don't You Know; I Look at Heaven; Tonight We Love

Wotawa, E.J. Hail Purdue

Wreford, Reynall All

Wright, Adrian Don't You Want Me

Wright, Andrew When a Man Loves a Woman

Wright, Benjamin One Hundred Ways

Wright, Betty Where Is the Love

Wright, Dorothy Cinco Robles (Five Oaks)

Wright, Ellen Violets

Wright, Fred Howard (When It's Roundup Time in Texas) When the Bloom Is on the Sage

Wright, Gary Love Is Alive

Wright, Geoffrey Transatlantic Lullaby

Wright, Julian Ever So Goosey

Wright, Lawrence Are We Downhearted?—No!

Wright, Robert B. Always and Always; And This Is My Beloved; At the Balalaika; Baubles, Bangles and Beads; The Donkey Serenade; I'd Be Lost Without You; It's a Blue World; Jersey Bounce; Not Since Nineveh; Now; Strange Music; Stranger in Paradise; Sweet Danger

Wright, Stephen Jeopardy

Wrighton, W.T. Her Bright Smile Haunts Me Still

Wrubel, Allie As You Desire Me; Ev'rybody Has a Laughing Place; Fare Thee Well, Annabelle; Farewell to Arms; Flirtation Walk; Gone with the Wind; Good Night Angel; I Do Do Do Like You; I Met Her on Monday; I'll Buy That Dream; I'm a-Comin' a-Courtin' Corabelle; I'm Stepping Out with a Memory Tonight; The Lady from Twenty-Nine Palms; The Lady in Red; (I'm Afraid) The Masquerade Is Over; Mister (Mr.) and Mrs. Is the Name; Music, Maestro, Please; Why Does It Get So Late So Early; Why Don't We Do This More Often; Zip-A-Dee-Doo-Dah

Wulschner, Flora Forgotten

Wyche, Sid A Big Hunk of Love

Wyle, George Caramba It's the Samba; I Didn't Slip, I Wasn't Pushed, I Fell; I Love the Way You Say ''Goodnight''; I Said My Pajamas (and Put On My Prayers)

Wynette, Tammy Stand By Your Man

Yacich, Chris I Like Bananas Because They Have No Bones

Yakus, Milt Old Cape Cod

Yamin, Jamie Mary Ann

Yancy, Marvin This Will Be (an Everlasting Love)

Yarrow, Peter Day Is Done; Puff the Magic Dragon; Torn Between Two Lovers

Yellen, Jack Ain't She Sweet; Alabama Jubilee; All Aboard for Dixieland; Are You from Dixie, 'Cause I'm from Dixie Too; Are You Havin' Any Fun; Bagdad; A Bench in the Park; Cheatin' on Me; Crazy Words (Crazy Tune) (Vo-Do-De-O-Do); Forgive Me; Glad Rag Doll; Happy Days Are Here Again; Happy Feet; Happy in Love; Hard Hearted Hannah (the Vamp of Savannah); Hold My Hand; How's Every Little Thing in Dixie; I Forgive You; I Wonder What's Become of Sally; I'm the Last of the Red-Hot Mamas; I'm Waiting for Ships That Never Come In; It's Time To Say Goodnight; Louisville Lou, the Vampin' Lady; Lovin' Sam, the Sheik of Alabam'; Mama Goes Where Papa Goes; My Yiddishe Momme; She Don't Wanna; Sing, Baby, Sing; Song of the Dawn; Sweet and Hot; Who Cares; A Young Man's Fancy

Yeston, Maury The Germans at the Spa; My Husband Makes Movies; Nine; Only with You; Simple; Unusual Way

Yeudall, Robert Song of the Clyde

Yoell, Larry Please Believe Me

Yon, Pietro A. Gesù Bambino

Yorke, Peter Emergency Ward 10 Theme

Youmans, Vincent April Blossoms; Carioca; Drums in My Heart; Flying Down to Rio; Great Day; Hallelujah!; I Know That You Know; I Want To Be Happy; Keepin' Myself for You; Kinda Like You; More Than You Know; Music Makes Me; Oh Me! Oh My! Oh You!; Orchids in the Moonlight; Rise and Shine; So Do I; Sometimes I'm Happy; Tea for Two; Through the Years; Time on My Hands; Too Many Rings Around Rosie; Wildflower; Without a Song

Young, George Love Is in the Air

Young, Helen R. I Am Coming

Young, James Oliver 'Tain't What You Do (It's the Way That You Do It)

Young, Joe Absence Makes the Heart Grow Fonder (for Somebody Else); Along the Rocky Road to Dublin; Annie Doesn't Live Here Anymore; Arrah Go On, I'm Gonna Go Back to Oregon; Cryin' for the Carolines; Daddy Long Legs; Dinah; Don't Ask Me Why; Don't Blame It All on Broadway; Don't Cry, Frenchy, Don't Cry; Down in Dear Old New Orleans; Five Foot Two, Eyes of Blue (Has Anybody Seen My Girl?); Got Her off My Hands) But Can't Get Her off My Mind); Happy Go Lucky Lane; Have a Little Faith in Me; Hello, Central, Give Me No Man's Land; How Ya Gonna Keep 'Em Down on the Farm (After They've Seen Paree); How'd You Like To Be My Daddy; Huckleberry Finn; A

Hundred Years from Today; I Kiss Your Hand, Madame; I'd Love To Fall Asleep and Wake Up in My Mammy's Arms; If I Knock the "L" out of Kelly; I'll Be Happy When the Preacher Makes You Mine; I'm All Bound 'Round with the Mason-Dixon Line; I'm Gonna Sit Right Down and Write Myself a Letter; I'm Sitting on Top of the World (Just Rolling Along—Just Rolling Along); In a Little Spanish Town; In Shadowland; Just a Baby's Prayer at Twilight; Keep Sweeping the Cobwebs off the Moon; Laugh, Clown, Laugh; Life Is a Song, Let's Sing It Together; Lullaby of the Leaves; Meet Me at the Station, Dear; My Barney Lies over the Ocean (Just the Way He Lied to Me); My Mammy; Oh, How I Wish I Could Sleep Until My Daddy Comes Home; Old Pal Why Don't You Answer Me; Ooh That Kiss; Put Away a Little Ray of Golden Sunshine; Revenge; Rock-a-Bye Your Baby with a Dixie Melody; (In) A Shanty in Old Shanty Town; Sing an Old Fashioned Song (to a Young Sophisticated Lady); Snuggled on Your Shoulder, Cuddled in Your Arms; Take My Heart; There's a Cradle in Caroline; To a Sweet Pretty Thing; The Torch Song; Tuck Me To Sleep in My Old 'Tucky Home; Two Hearts in Three Quarter Time; Two Tickets to Georgia; Was That the Human Thing To Do; Way Down in Iowa I'm Going To Hide Away; Where the Angelus Is Ringing; When You're Away; Where Did Robinson Crusoe Go with Friday on Saturday Night?; Why Do They All Take the Night Boat to Albany; Why Don't You Answer Me; Yaaka Hula Hickey Dula; You Dropped Me Like a Red Hot Penny; You're a Heavenly Thing; You're a Million Miles from Nowhere When You're One Little Mile from Home; You're Gonna Lose Your Gal; You're My Everything

Young, John Jr.   Seventeen

Young, Kenny   Come Back and Shake Me; Under the Boardwalk

Young, Leon E.S.   Serenade

Young, Neil   Heart of Gold

Young Peter   I Give Thanks for You

Young, Rida Johnson   Ah! Sweet Mystery of Life; I'm Falling in Love with Someone; Italian Street Song; Jump Jim Crow; Mother; Mother Machree; My Dream Girl, I Loved You Long Ago; The Road to Paradise; Sometime; Tramp!

Tramp! Tramp! Along the Highway; When Love Is Young in Springtime; Will You Remember (Sweetheart)

Young, Russell   Crazy Love

Young, Stephen   Seven Bridges Road

Young, Victor   Around the World (in Eighty Days); Beautiful Love; Blue Star; The Call of the Far-Away Hills; Can't We Talk It Over; Can't You Understand; Golden Earrings; A Hundred Years from Today; I Don't Stand a Ghost of a Chance with You; Love Letters; My Foolish Heart; Sam, You Made the Pants Too Long; Stella By Starlight; (On the) Street of Dreams; Sweet Madness; Sweet Sue (Just You); When I Fall in Love

Yradier, Sebastian   Cielito Lindo (Ay, Ay, Ay, Ay); La Paloma (The Dove)

Yvain, Maurice   My Man; Throw Me a Kiss

Zacharias, Helmut   Tokyo Melody

Zager, Michael   Forgive Me Girl; I've Loved You for a Long Time

Zamecnik, J.S.   Neapolitan Nights

Zany, King   All She'd Say Was Umh Hum

Zaret, Hy   It All Comes Back to Me Now; My Sister and I; No Other Arms, No Other Lips; One Meat Ball; So You're the One; There I Go; Unchained Melody; Young and Warm and Wonderful

Zaritsky, Bernard   Little White Duck

Zawinul, Joe   Mercy Mercy Mercy

Zeller, Phil   On the South Side of Chicago

Ziegler, Richard A.   After the Lovin'

Zigman, Aaron   Crush on You

Zimmerman, Charles A.   Anchors Aweigh

Zimmerman, Leon   I'm Just a Vagabond Lover

Zoob, Dave   Sweet Lady

Zucca, Mlle. Mana   I Love Life; Nichavo!

Zwirn, Artie   Sorry (I Ran All the Way Home)

VIII

American and British Theatre, Film, Radio, and Television

"Screen play by Glotz, from a stage play by Motz, from a novel by Sock, from a story by Block, from a chapter by Rock, from a sentence by Stroke, from an idea by Croak, based on a Joe Miller joke."

Lyric by Sylvia Fine

This Part contains five divisions of American and British media: 1. Musical Theatre 2. Silent Films 3. Musical Films 4. Non-Musical Films (Dramatic Films with musical themes, title song or occasional song) 5. Radio and Television Shows and Programs

In each division, shows, films, radio program, and television program titles are listed alphabetically. In each entry, listed alphabetically, will be those song titles popular enough for inclusion in Part V. For further information about song popularity, refer to Authors' Notes at the front of this book. For more complete information about a particular song, refer to Part V; all song titles in this part are listed alphabetically in Part V.

In the case of musical theatre, the show title will be followed by the number of performances (when available) played by the original production on the New York Broadway stage, cited in parentheses. An asterisk in parentheses (*) signifies that the pro-

duction was still running during the first six months of 1987. For Off-Broadway productions that moved to the Broadway stage, the sum total of both runs will be indicated. For those shows which played in London only, or non-English speaking countries and London only, the number of performances played on the London stage will be cited in parentheses. In all instances the year of opening will be predominate over the London stage opening regardless of the production's origin. Non-musical plays with incidental music or one song are also included in this compilation. Unless indicated otherwise, this list will not include revival or substantially revised productions.

In the case of musical and non-musical films, the film title will be followed by the year of release in the United States, cited in parentheses. For films never released in the United States, the year of release in Great Britain will be used.

1. MUSICAL THEATRE

A total of 865 shows are represented in this division. For further information about this division, refer to notes at the beginning of this Part.

> Illic et cantant
> quidquid didicere theatris,
> et iactant facilis
> ad sua verba manus.

> They sing snatches of the songs learnt at the theatre, and accompany the words with ready gestures of the hand.
>
> Ovid Fasti 3,535

A to Z 1921 And Her Mother Came Too; Dapper Dan; Limehouse Blues

The Act (233) 1978 City Lights

Afgar (171) 1920 Dardanella; You'd Be Surprised

Africana (72) 1927 Here Comes the Showboat; I'm Comin' Virginia

After the Girl 1914 Wonderful Eyes

Ain't Misbehavin' (1,604) 1978 Ain't Misbehavin'; Black and Blue; Honeysuckle Rose; I Can't Give You Anything But Love; I'm Gonna Sit Right Down and Write Myself a Letter; It's a Sin To Tell a Lie; I've Got a Feeling I'm Falling; I've Got My Fingers Crossed; The Joint Is Jumpin'; Keepin' Out of Mischief Now; The Ladies Who Sing with the Band; Lounging at the Waldorf; Mean to Me; Squeeze Me; 'Tain't Nobody's Business If I Do; Two Sleepy People; The Viper's Drag; When the Nylons Bloom Again; You're Feet's Too Big

Airs and Graces (1917) Whisper to Me

All Aboard (108) 1913 Asia

All American (80) 1962 Once Upon a Time

All Clear 1937 Have You Met Miss Jones

All for Love (121) 1949 Dreamer With a Penny

All in Fun (3) 1940 It's a Big, Wide, Wonderful World

All the King's Horses (120) 1934 A Little White Gardenia

Allegro (315) 1947 A Fellow Needs a Girl; The Gentleman Is a Dope; So Far; You Are Never Away

Alma Where Do You Live (232) 1910 Alma Where Do You Live

Alone At Last (180) 1915 Pretty Edelweiss; Some Little Bug Is Going To Find You

Along Fifth Avenue (180) 1949 Maybe It's Because

Americana of 1926 (224) 1926 Nobody Wants Me; Sunny Disposish; That Lost Barbershop Chord

Americana of 1928 (12) 1928 My Kinda Love

Americana of 1932 (77) 1932 Brother, Can You Spare a Dime; Good Night Sweetheart

The Americans 1811 The Death of Nelson

America's Sweetheart (135) 1931 I've Got Five Dollars; I Want a Man

And On We Go 1936 The Night Is Young and You're So Beautiful

Andre Charlot's Revue of 1924 1924 Limehouse Blues; Night May Have Its Sadness; Parisian Pierrot; You Were Meant for Me

Andre Charlot's Revue of 1925 (138) 1925 A Cup of Coffee, a Sandwich and You; Poor Little Rich Girl; Susannah's Squeaking Shoes

Angel Face (57) 1919 I Might Be Your "Once-in-a-While"; Someone Like You

Angel in the Wings (308) 1947 The Big Brass Band from Brazil; Civilization

Animal Crackers (191) 1928 Hooray for Captain Spalding; Watching the Clouds Roll By

Annie (*) 1977 Easy Street; The Hard-Knock Life; Little Girls; Maybe; N.Y.C.; Tomorrow

Annie Get Your Gun (1,149) 1946 Anything You Can Do; Doin' What Comes Natur'lly; The Girl That I Marry; I Got Lost in His Arms; I Got the Sun in the Morning; I'm an Indian Too; My Defenses Are Down; There's No Business Like Show Business; They Say It's Wonderful; Who Do You Love, I Hope; You Can't Get a Man with a Gun

Anyone Can Whistle (9) 1964 Anyone Can Whistle; Everybody Says Don't; Miracle Song

Anything Goes (420) 1934 All Through the Night; Anything Goes; Blow Gabriel Blow; The Gypsy in Me; I Get a Kick out of You; You're the Top

Applause (900) 1970 based on the Bette Davis film *All About Eve,* and the original story by Mary Orr. Applause

Apple Blossoms (256) 1919 I'm in Love; Letter Song; Little Girls, Good Bye; Who Can Tell; You Are Free

The Arcadians (136) 1910 Arcady Is Ever Young; Bring Me a Rose; The Girl with a Brogue; The Pipes of Pan

Arms and the Girl (134) 1950 based on the Lawrence Langner and Armina Marshall play *The Pursuit of Happiness.* There Must Be Something Better Than Love

Around the World in Eighty Days (74) 1946 based on Jules Verne novel. Should I Tell You I Love You

Artists and Models, 1927 (151) 1927 Here Am I—Broken Hearted

As the Girls Go (420) 1948 As the Girls Go; I Got Lucky in the Rain; You Say the Nicest Things, Baby

As Thousands Cheer (400) 1933 Easter Parade; Happy Birthday to You; Heat Wave; How's Chances; Lonely Heart; Not for All the Rice In China

As You Were (143) 1920 If You Could Care for Me; Who Ate Napoleons with Josephine When Bonaparte Was Away

At Home Abroad (198) 1935 Got a Bran' New Suit; Love Is a Dancing Thing; O Leo

Babes in Arms (289) 1937 All At Once; Babes in Arms; I Wish I Were in Love Again; Johnny One Note; The Lady Is a Tramp; My Funny Valentine; Way Out West; Where or When; You Are My Lucky Star

Babes in Toyland (192) 1903 I Can't Do the Sum; The March of the Toys; Toyland

Babette (59) 1903 There Once Was an Owl

Baby (241) 1983 based on a story developed by Susan Yankowitz. Baby Baby Baby; I Want It All; Romance; The Story Goes On

Back Again 1918 A Good Man Is Hard To Find

Bajour (218) 1964 based on collected stories of Joseph Mitchell. Bajour; Words, Words, Words

Balalaika 1939 At the Balalaika

Ballroom (116) 1978 based on television program "Queen of the Stardust Ballroom." A Terrific Band and a Real Nice Crowd

The Band Wagon (260) 1931 Confession; Dancing in the Dark; I Love Louisa; New Sun in the Sky

Banjo Eyes (126) 1942 based on the John Cecil Holm and George Abbott play, *Three Men on a Horse.* We Did It Before (And We Can Do It Again); We're Having a Baby

Barefoot Boy with Cheek (108) 1947 based on novel by Max Shulman. Who Do You Think You Are

Barnum (854) 1980 The Colors of My Life; Come Follow the Band; I Like Your Style

Barry of Ballymore 1910 Mother Machree

Beatlemania (*) 1977 Roll Over Beethoven; I Want To Hold Your Hand; She Loves You; Help!; If I Fell; Can't Buy Me Love; Day Tripper; Yesterday; Eleanor Rigby; We Can Work It Out; Nowhere Man; A Day in the Life; Strawberry Fields Forever; Penny Lane; Magical Mystery Tour; Lucy in the Sky with Diamonds; Lady Madonna; The Fool on the Hill; Got To Get You into My Life; Michelle; Get Back; Come Together; With a Little Help from My Friends; All You Need Is Love; Revolution; Helter Skelter; Hey Jude; I Am the Walrus; The Long and Winding Road; Let It Be

The Beauty Shop (88) 1914 She Sells Sea-Shells (on the Seashore); When You're All Dressed Up and No Place to Go

The Beauty Spot 1917 M-I-S-S-I-S-S-I-P-P-I

The Believers (295) 1968 Where Do I Go from Here

The Belle of New York 1897 She Is the Belle of New York; Teach Me How To Kiss

Bells Are Ringing (924) 1956 Bells Are Ringing; Hello, Hello There; Just in Time; Long Before I Knew You; The Party's Over

Ben Franklin in Paris (215) 1964 Hic, Haec, Hoc

Best Foot Forward (326) 1941 Buckle Down Winsocki; Ev'ry Time; Shady Lady Bird; That's How I Love the Blues; wish I May (1963 revival)

The Best Little Whorehouse in Texas (1,584) 1978 A Lil' Ole Bitty Pissant Country Place

Betsy (39) 1926 Blue Skies

The Better 'Ole (353) 1918 What Do You Want To Make Those Eyes at Me For; When You Look in the Heart of a Rose

Betty (63) 1916 Can It Be Love (London production)

Between the Devil (93) 1937 By Myself; I See Your Face Before Me; You Have Everything

Big Boy (48) 1925 California, Here I Come; How I Love You; If You Knew Susie Like I Know Susie; It All Depends on You; Keep Smiling at Trouble

Big River (*) 1985 adapted from the novel *The Adventures of Huckleberry Finn* by Mark Twain. Hand for the Hog; How Blest We Are; Muddy Water

The Big Show (425) 1916 Poor Butterfly

Big Top 1941 Flamingo

Billion Dollar Baby (220) 1945 Bad Timing

The Billy Barnes Revue (199) 1959 Too Long at the Fair

Billy Rose's Aquacade 1939 Yours for a Song

Billy Rose's Crazy Quilt, *see* **Crazy Quilt**

The Bing Boys 1916 Another Little Drink Wouldn't Do Us Any Harm; If You Were the Only Girl in the World

The Bing Boys on Broadway 1918 First Love, Last Love, Best Love

The Bing Girls Are There 1917 Let the Great Big World Keep Turning

The Bird of Paradise 1915 On the Beach at Waikiki

Bitter Sweet (159) 1929 Dear Cafe; If Love Were All; I'll See You Again; Tokay; Zigeuner

The Black Crook (474) 1866 You Naughty, Naughty Men

Black Velvet 1938 Most Gentlemen Don't Like Love; My Heart Belongs to Daddy

Black Vanities 1940 Do I Love You; Let's Be Buddies

Blackbirds (of 1928) (518) 1928, 1932 Bandana Babies; Diga Diga Do; Doin' the New Low-Down; I Can't Give You Anything But Love

Blackbirds of 1930 (57) 1930 Memories of You

Blackbirds of 1933 (25) 1933 A Hundred Years from To-day

Blackbirds of 1934 (25) 1934 Rhapsody in Blue; St. James Infirmary

Blackbirds of 1936 1936 Aunt Jemima And Your Uncle Cream of Wheat

Bless the Bride 1947 I Was Never Kissed Before; Ma Belle Marguerita; This Is My Lovely Day

Bloomer Girl (654) 1944 Evelina; I Got a Song; Right As the Rain; T'morra, T'morra

Blossom Time (592) 1921 The Golden Song; Song of Love

The Blue Paradise (356) 1915 Auf Wiederseh'n

Bohemia 1896 Love Makes the World Go 'Round

The Bohemian Girl 1843 Then You'll Remember Me

Bolton's Revue 1948 No Orchids for My Lady

Bombo (219) 1921 April Showers; California, Here I Come; Dirty Hands, Dirty Face; I'm Goin' South; Toot Toot Tootsie; Who Cares

Bow Bells 1932 Mona Lisa; You're Blasé

The Boy 1917 Little Miss Melody

The Boy Friend (485) 1954 I Could Be Happy with You; It's Never Too Late To Fall in Love; A Room in Bloomsbury; Sur la Plage; Won't You Charleston with Me

The Boys from Syracuse (235) 1938 based on Shakespeare's *A Comedy of Errors*. Falling in Love with Love; Sing for Your Supper; This Can't Be Love; You Have Cast Your Shadow on the Sea

Bran Pie 1919 Chong, He Come from Hong Kong; Ja-Da

Bric-A-Brac 1915 Toy Town

Brigadoon (580) 1947 Almost Like Being in Love; Come to Me, Bend to Me; The Heather on the Hill; I'll Go Home with Bonnie Jean; There But For You Go I

The Brigand 1829 Love's Ritornella

Broadway Brevities of 1920 (105) 1920 The Moon Shines on the Moonshine

Brown of Harvard 1906 When Love Is Young in Springtime

Bubbling Brown Sugar 1976 God Bless the Child; Honeysuckle Rose; It Don't Mean a Thing If It Ain't Got That Swing; Love Will Find a Way; Sophisticated Lady; Stomping at the Savoy; Sweet Georgia Brown; Swing Low, Sweet Chariot; Take the "A" Train; There'll Be Some Changes Made

Bubbly 1917 Hawaiian Butterfly

Buddies (249) 1919 My Buddies

The Burgomaster (33) 1900 The Tale of the Kangaroo

Business As Usual 1914 When the Angelus Is Ringing; When We've Wound Up the Watch on the Rhine

Buzz Buzz 1918 K-K-K-Katy

By Jupiter (427) 1942 based on Julian F. Thompson play *The Warrior's Husband*. Ev'rything I've Got; Nobody's Heart; Wait Till You See Her

By the Beautiful Sea (270) 1954 Alone Too Long; More Love Than Your Love

Bye Bye Birdie (607) 1960 Kids; A Lot of Livin' To Do; Older and Wiser; One Boy; Put On a Happy Face; Rosie; The Telephone Hour

Cabaret (1,166) 1966 based on John Van Druten Play *I Am a Camera* and novel by Christopher Isherwood. Cabaret; If You Could See Her; Married; Meeskite; The Money Song; Willkommen

The Cabaret Girl 1921 Dancing Time; Ka-Lu-A

Cabin in the Sky (156) 1940 Cabin in the Sky; Taking a Chance on Love

La Cage aux Folles (*) 1983 based on the play of the same title by Jean Poiret. The Best of Times; I Am What I Am

Cairo 1921 The Chinaman's Song

Call Me Madam (644) 1950 The Best Thing for You; It's a Lovely Day Today; Marrying for Love; Something To Dance About; You're Just in Love

Call Me Mister (734) 1946 Along with Me; Call Me Mister; Hostess with the Mostes' on the Ball; Little Surplus Me; Military Life; South America, Take It Away; Yuletide, Park Avenue

Camelot (873) 1960 based on the T.H. White novel, *The Once and Future King*. Camelot; Follow Me; How To Handle a Woman; I Loved You Once in Silence; I Wonder What the King Is Doing Tonight; If Ever I Would Leave You; The Lusty Month of May; The Simple Joys of Maidenhood; Then You May Take Me to the Fair; What Do the Simple Folk Do

Can-Can (892) 1953 Allez-Vous En; Can-Can; C'est Magnifique; I Am in Love; I Love Paris; It's All Right with Me

Candide (73) 1956 based on satire by Voltaire. Glitter and Be Gay

Canterbury Tales (16) 1980 based on the translation of Geoffrey Chaucer by Nevill Coghill. I Have a Noble Cock

Carnival (719) 1961 based on film *Lili* and Paul Gallico's *The Seven Souls of Clement O'Reilly*. Always Always You; Love Makes the World Go Round; Mira

Carnival in Flanders (6) 1953 Here's That Rainy Day

Carousel (890) 1945 based on Ferenc Molnár play *Liliom*. The Carousel Waltz; If I Loved You; June Is Bustin' Out All Over; Soliloquy; This Was a Real Nice Clambake; What's the Use of Wond'rin'; When I Marry Mister Snow; When the Children Are Asleep; You'll Never Walk Alone

The Casino Girl (91) 1900 Sweet Annie Moore

The Cat and the Fiddle (395) 1931 Ha-Cha-Cha; I Watch the Love Parade; The Night Was Made for Love; One Moment Alone; Poor Pierrot; She Didn't Say Yes; Try To Forget

Cats (*) 1982 based on *Old Possum's Book of Practical Cats* by T.S. Eliot. Grizabella the Glamour Cat; Memory; Mister Mistoffolees

The Catch of the Season (104) 1905 Cigarette; Teasing

The Century Girl (200) 1916 You Belong to Me

Charlot Show of 1926 1926 A Cup of Coffee, A Sandwich and You

Chauve Souris (673) 1922 Parade of the Wooden Soldiers

Chauve Souris 1925 I Miss My Swiss, My Swiss Miss Misses Me; Oh, Katharina

Chee-Chee (31) 1928 based on Charles Petit novel *The Son of the Grand Eunuch*. Moon of My Delight; The Tartar Song

Cheep 1917 Where the Black-Eyed Susans Grow

The Cherry Girl 1903 Little Yellow Bird

Chicago (1947) 1975 All That Jazz; Class; Mister Cellophane; My Own Best Friend; Razzle Dazzle

Chin-Chin (295) 1914 Goodbye, Girls, I'm Through; It's a Long Way to Tipperary

A Chinese Honeymoon (376) 1902 Mister Dooley

The Chocolate Soldier (296) 1909 The Letter Song; My Hero

A Chorus Line (*) 1975 And . . . ; At the Ballet; Dance; Ten; Looks: Three; Hello Twelve, Hello Thirteen, Hello Love; I Can Do That; I Hope I Get It; The Music and the Mirror; Nothing; One; Tits and Ass; What I Did for Love

Chu Chin Chow (208) 1917 Any Time Is Kissing Time; The Cobbler's Song; The Robbers' Chorus; Robbers' March

The Cingalee (33) 1904 My Dear Little Cingalee; The Pearl of Sweet Ceylon

The Circus Princess (192) 1927 Dear Eyes That Haunt Me; We Two Shall Meet Again; You Are Mine Evermore

The Climax 1909 Song of the Soul

Clorindy, or, The Origin of the Cake Walk 1898 Who Dat Say Chicken in Dis Crowd

Clowns in Clover 1928 Forty-seven Ginger Headed Sailors

Cochrane's 1930 Revue 1930 With a Song in My Heart

Coco (332) 1969 Coco; Gabrielle

Company (690) 1970 Another Hundred People; Barcelona; Being Alive; Company; Getting Married Today; The Ladies Who Lunch; The Little Things You Do Together; Side by Side by Side; Sorry—Grateful; What Would We Do Without You; You Could Drive a Person Crazy

A Connecticut Yankee (418) 1927 based on novel by Mark Twain. Can't You Do a Friend a Favor (1943 production); My Heart Stood Still; On a Desert Island with Thee; Thou Swell; To Keep My Love Alive

Continental Varieties (77) 1934 Hands Across the Table

Conversation Piece (55) 1934 I'll Follow My Secret Heart; Regency Rakes

The Co-optimists 1925 Coal Black Mammy; The Girl in the Crinoline Gown; I Wonder Where My Baby Is Tonight; Remember; When the Sun Goes Down

Cordelia's Aspirations 1883 My Dad's Dinner Pail

Cotton Club Parade, 25th Edition 1934 As Long as I Live

Cotton Club Parade, 26th Edition 1935 Truckin'

Cotton Club Revue 1933 Stormy Weather

The Count of Luxembourg (120) Pierette and Pierrot; Say Not Love Is a Dream; Waltz

Countess Maritza (318) 1926 Hey Gypsy; Play Gypsies—Dance Gypsies

A Country Girl (112) 1902 Try Again Johnnie; Under the Deodar

A Country Sport 1893 Mamie, Come Kiss Your Honey

Courted into Court 1896 Mister Johnson, Turn Me Loose

The Cousin from Nowhere 1928 Goodnight

Crazy Quilt (67) 1931 I Found a Million Dollar Baby in a Five and Ten Cent Store; Would You Like To Take a Walk

Crazy with the Heat (99) 1941 With a Twist of the Wrist

Crest of the Wave 1938 Rose of England

Criss-Cross (206) 1926 Kiss a Four Leaf Clover

The Dairymaids (86) 1907 In the Twi-Twi-Twi-Light

Dames at Sea (575) 1968 Choo-Choo Honeymoon; The Sailor of My Dreams

Damn Yankees (1,019) 1955 based on Douglas Wallop novel *The Year the Yankees Lost the Pennant,* based on Goethe's Faust, ''which was the basis of Gounod's opera and Thomas Mann's novel and which, in turn, was based on Christopher Marlowe's *Dr. Faustus* which was also the inspiration of a Rembrandt etching and a cantata by Marius.'' Heart; A Little Brains—A Little Talent; Shoeless Joe from Hannibal, Mo.; Two Lost Souls; Whatever Lola Wants

Dancin' (*) 1978 Mr. Bojangles; Big Noise from Winnetka; Easy; Here You Come Again; Yankee Doodle Dandy; Stout Hearted Men; Under the Dougle Eagle; Dixie; When Johnny Comes Marching Home; Pack Up Your Troubles in Your Old Kit Bag; The Stars and Stripes Forever

Dancing Around (145) 1914 It's a Long Way to Tipperary

Dancing Mistress 1912 When You Are in Love

The Dancing Years 1939 I Can Give You the Starlight; My Dearest Dear; My Life Belongs to You; Primrose; Waltz of My Heart

The Day Before Spring (165) 1945 The Day Before Spring; God's Green World; I Love You This Morning; You Haven't Changed At All

A Day in Hollywood—a Night in the Ukraine (588) 1980 Just Like That

Dear Miss Phoebe 1950 I Leave My Heart in An English Garden

Dear World (132) 1969 based on Jean Giradoux play *The Madwoman of Chaillot.* And I Was Beautiful; Dear World; Each Tomorrow Morning; I Don't Want to Know; Kiss Her Now

Dearest Enemy (286) 1925 Bye and Bye; Here in My Arms; Sweet Peter

The Debutante (48) 1914 The Springtime of Life

The Defender (60) 1902 In the Good Old Summer Time

Demi-Tasse Revue 1918 How Can You Tell

The Desert Song (471) 1926 The Desert Song; One Alone; The Riff Song; Romance

Destry Rides Again (473) 1959 Once Knew a Fella

Dixie to Broadway (77) 1924 I'm a Little Blackbird Looking for a Bluebird; Mandy Make Up Your Mind

Do I Hear a Waltz? (220) 1965 based on Arthur Laurents play *The Time of the Cuckoo.* Do I Hear a Waltz; Take the Moment; We're Gonna Be All Right

Do Re Me (400) 1960 Make Someone Happy

Doing Our Bit (130) 1917 I'd Like To See the Kaiser with a Lily in His Hand

The Dollar Princess (228) 1909 Dollar Princesses; My Dream of Love

Dover Street to Dixie 1923 You've Gotta See Mamma Ev'ry Night or You Can't See Mamma at All

Drat! (1) 1972 Lean On Me

Drat! The Cat! (8) 1965 She Touched Me

The Dream Girl (117) 1924 My Dream Girl; I Loved You Long Ago

Dream Girls (1,521) 1982 based on the career of the sixties pop singing group *The Supremes*. And I Am Telling You I'm Not Going; Cadillac Car; Dream Girls; One Night Only; When I First Saw You

The DuBarry (87) 1932 I Give My Heart

Du Barry Was a Lady (408) 1939 Do I Love You; Friendship; Katie Went to Haiti; Well, Did You Evah

The Duchess of Dantzig (93) 1905 Wine of France

The Earl and the Girl (148) 1905 How'd You Like To Spoon With Me

Earl Carroll's Sketch Book of 1929 (400) 1929 You Beautiful So and So

Earl Carroll's Sketch Book of 1935 (207) 1935 At Last

Earl Carroll's Vanities of 1926 (Fifth Edition) (440) 1926 Climbing Up the Ladder of Love; Hugs and Kisses

Earl Carroll's Vanities of 1928 (Seventh Edition) (203) 1928 Once in a Lifetime (203) 1928 Once in a Lifetime

Earl Carroll's Vanities of 1930 (215) 1930 Good Night, Sweetheart; Hitting the Bottle; It's Great To Be In Love; The March of Time; Tonight or Never

Earl Carroll's Vanities of 1931 (278) 1931 Good Night, Sweetheart; It's Great To Be in Love; Tonight or Never

Earl Carroll's Vanities of 1932 (87) 1932 I'se Gotta Right To Sing the Blues; My Darling

Earl Carroll's Vanities of 1940 (25) 1940 Mama Yo Quiero

Early to Bed (382) 1943 The Ladies Who Sing with the Band; When the Nylons Bloom Again

East Is West 1919 Chinese Lullaby

East Wind (23) 1931 It's a Wonderful World

Eileen (64) 1917 Eileen; Thine Alone; When Shall I Again See Ireland

The Enchantress (72) 1911 To the Land of My Own Romance

Erminie 1886 At Midnight on My Pillow Lying; Darkest the Hour; Dear Mother, In Dreams I See Her; Lullaby; A Soldier's Life; What the Dickie-Birds Say

Eubie! (439) 1978 I'm Just Wild About Harry; Memories of You; Shuffle Along

Evergreen 1931 Dancing on the Ceiling

Everybody's Doing It 1911 Everybody's Doing It

Everybody's Welcome (139) 1931 based on Albert Hackett and Frances Goodrich play, *Up Pops the Devil*. As Time Goes By

Evita (1,568) 1979 Another Suitcase in Another Hall; Don't Cry for Me, Argentina

Face the Music (165) 1932 Let's Have Another Cup of Coffee; Manhattan Madness; On a Roof in Manhattan; Soft Lights and Sweet Music

Fade Out—Fade In (271) 1964 Fade Out—Fade In

Fanny (888) 1954 based on Marcel Pagnol trilogy. Fanny

Fantana (298) 1905 Tammany

The Fantasticks (*) 1960 loosely based on Edmond Rostand's *Les Romantiques*. Much More; Never Say No; Soon It's Gonna Rain; Try To Remember

Faust Up-to-Date 1890 Skirt Dance

Fiddler on the Roof (3242) 1964 based on stories of Shalom Aleichem. Anatevka; Do You Love Me; If I Were a Rich Man; Matchmaker, Matchmaker; Sabbath Prayer; Sunrise Sunset; To Life; Tradition

Fifty Miles from Boston (32) 1908 Harrigan; When We Are M-A-Double-R-I-E-D; You Do Something to Me

Fifty Million Frenchmen (254) 1929 Paree (What Did You Do to Me); You Do Something to Me; You Don't Know Paree (Paris); You've Got That Thing

Fine and Dandy (255) 1930 Can This Be Love; Fine and Dandy

Finian's Rainbow (723) 1947 The Begat; How Are Things in Glocca Morra; If This Isn't Love; Look to the Rainbow; Necessity; Old Devil Moon; That Great Come and Get It Day; When I'm Not Near the Girl I Love; When the Idle Poor Become the Idle Rich

Fiorello! (795) 1959 Home Again; I Love a Cop; Little Tin Box; Politics and Poker; Till Tomorrow; When Did I Fall in Love

The Firefly (120) 1912 Giannina Mia; Love Is Like a Firefly; Sympathy; When a Maid Comes Knocking at Your Heart

5064 Gerard 1914 He's a Rag Picker; Hors D'Oeuvres; I Want To Go Back to Michigan; Down on the Farm; Kitty the Telephone Girl; On the 5:15

The Five O'Clock Girl (280) 1927 Thinking of You; Up in the Clouds

The Fleet's Lit Up 1936 It's De-Lovely

Florodora (505) 1900 I Want To Be a Military Man; The Shade of the Palm; Tell Me Pretty Maiden

Flower Drum Song (600) 1958 based on C.Y. Lee novel. Don't Marry Me; A Hundred Million Miracles; I Enjoy Being a Girl; Love Look Away; Sunday; You Are Beautiful

Flying Colors (188) 1932 Alone Together; Louisiana Hayride; A Shine on Your Shoes

Flying Colours 1917 Arizona

Flying High (357) 1930 Thank Your Father

Follies (522) 1971 Beautiful Girls; Broadway Baby; Could I Leave You; The God-Why-Don't-You-Love-Me Blues; I'm Still Here; Losing My Mind; Too Many Mornings; Waiting for the Girls Upstairs

Follow Me (78) 1916 Oh Johnny, Oh Johnny, Oh!

Follow the Crowd 1915 The Girl on the Magazine Cover; I Love a Piano; Where Did Robinson Crusoe Go with Friday on Saturday Night

Follow The Girls (882) 1944 I Wanna Get Married

Follow Thru (403) 1929 Button Up Your Overcoat; Follow Thru; My Lucky Star; Then I'll Have Time for You; You Wouldn't Fool Me

Folly To Be Wise 1930 The King's Horses; Three Little Words

For the Love of Mike   1931   Got a Date with An Angel

The Fortune Teller   1898   The Fortune Teller; Gypsy Love Song; Romany Life

Forty-Five Minutes from Broadway   (90)   1906   Forty-Five Minutes from Broadway; Mary's a Grand Old Name; So Long Mary; Stand Up and Fight Like H---

Forty-Second Street   (*)   1980   based on the novel by Bradford Ropes and the MGM musical film. About a Quarter to Nine; Forty-Second Street; Lullaby of Broadway; Shadow Waltz; Shuffle Off to Buffalo; We're in the Money; Young and Healthy; You're Getting To Be a Habit with Me

Foxy Quiller   (50)   1900   Quiller Has the Brains

Frasquita   1923   My Little Nest of Heavenly Blue

The French Doll   (120)   1922   Do It Again

Friend and Foe   1881   Peek-a-Boo

Fritz Among the Gypsies   1882   Sweet Violets

Fun of the Fayre   1921   Ours Is a Nice 'Ouse, Ours Is; Whose Baby Are You

Funny Face   (244)   1927   The Babbitt and the Bromide; Funny Face; Let's Kiss and Make Up; My One and Only; 'S Wonderful

Funny Girl   (1,348)   1964   Don't Rain on My Parade; I'm the Greatest Star; People; You Are Woman

Funny Side Up   Comes Love; This Can't Be Love

A Funny Thing Happened on the Way to the Forum   (964)   1962   Comedy Tonight; Everybody Ought To Have a Maid; Lovely

Gang Way   1942   My Paradise

The Garrick Gaieties   (First Edition)   (174)   1925   Manhattan; Sentimental Me

The Garrick Gaieties   (Second Edition)   (43)   1926   Mountain Greenery

The Gate Revue   1939   Transatlantic Lullaby

Gay Divorce   (248)   1932   After You; How's Your Romance; I've Got You on My Mind; Night and Day

Gay Paree   (190)   1925   Collegiate; Oh! Boy, What a Girl

The Geisha   1896   The Amorous Goldfish; Chin, Chin, Chinaman; Chon Kina; The Jewel of Asia; The Toy Monkey

Gentlemen Prefer Blondes   (740)   1949 based on Anita Loos novel. Bye Bye Baby; Diamonds Are a Girl's Best Friend; A Little Girl from Little Rock

George M!   (435)   1968   Forty-Five Minutes from Broadway; Give My Regards to Broadway; Harrigan; Nellie Kelly, I Love You; Over There; So Long Mary; The Yankee Doodle Boy; You're a Grand Old Flag

George Washington, Jr.   (81)   1906   I Was Born in Virginia; If Washington Should Come to Life; You Can Have Broadway; You're a Grand Old Flag

George White's Music Hall Varieties   (72)   1932   Cabin in the Cotton; Let's Put Out the Lights and Go To Sleep

George White's Scandals of 1922   (88)   1922   I'll Build a Stairway to Paradise

George White's Scandals of 1924   (192)   1924   Somebody Loves Me

George White's Scandals of 1926   (424)   1926   The Birth of the Blues; Black Bottom; The Girl Is You and the Boy Is Me; Lucky Day

George White's Scandals of 1931   (Eleventh Edition)   (202)   1931   Life Is Just a Bowl of Cherries; My Song; That's Why Darkies Were Born; This Is the Missus; The Thrill Is Gone

George White's Scandals of 1939   (120)   1939   Are You Havin' Any Fun

Get a Load of This   1942   Wrap Yourself in Cotton Wool

The Girl Behind the Counter   (260)   1907   The Glow Worm; I Want To Marry a Man

The Girl Behind the Gun   (160)   1918   There's a Light in Your Eyes; There's Life in the Old Dog Yet

Girl Crazy   (272)   1930   Bidin' My Time; Boy! What Love Has Done to Me!; But Not for Me; Embraceable You; I Got Rhythm; Treat Me Rough

The Girl Friend   (409)   1926   The Blue Room; The Girl Friend; Mountain Greenery; Why Do I

The Girl from Utah   (120)   1914   Same Sort of Girl; They Didn't Believe Me; Why Don't They Dance the Polka Anymore

The Girl in Pink Tights   (115)   1954   Lost in Loveliness

The Girl of my Dreams   (40)   1911   Doctor Tinkle Tinker; Every Girl Loves Me But the Girl I Love

The Girls Against the Boys   (16)   1959   I Gotta Have You

Glamorous Night   1935   Fold Your Wings; Glamorous Night; Shine Through My Dreams; When the Gypsy Played

A Glance at New York   1848   The Folks Are All Waiting To See the Fast Steamer

The Glorious Days   1935   K-K-K-Katy; Lovely Lady; Swanee

The Glory of Columbia, Her Yeomanry   1803   He Who His Country's Liv'ry Wears; When a Woman Hears the Sound of the Drum and Fife

Godspell   (2,645, including OB run)   1971   based on Gospel According to St. Matthew. All Good Gifts; Day by Day; Learn Your Lessons Well

Going Greek   1937   A Little Co-operation from You

Going Up   (351)   1917   Going Up; If You Look in Her Eyes; The Tickle Toe

The Golden Apple   (173)   1954   Lazy Afternoon

Golden Rainbow   (385)   1968   based on Arnold Schulman play A Hole in the Head. How Could I Be Wrong; I've Got To Be Me

Good Boy   (253)   1928   I Wanna Be Loved by You

Good Morning, Dearie   (265)   1921   Ka-Lu-A; Look for the Silver Lining

The Good Mr. Best   1897   Mammy's Little Punkin Colored Coon

Good News   (551)   1927   The Best Things in Life Are Free; A Girl of the Pi Beta Phi; Good News; Lucky in Love; The Varsity Drag

Goodtime Charley   (104)   1975   Goodtime Charley

Grease   (3388)   1972   All Choked Up; Freddy My Love; Look at Me, I'm Sandra Dee

Great Day! (36) 1929 Great Day; More Than You Know; Without a Song

The Great Magoo (non-musical play) (11) 1932 It's Only a Paper Moon

Great Temptations (197) 1926 Valencia

The Great Waltz (298) 1934 With All My Heart

The Greenwich Village Follies, 1920 (192) 1920 I'll See You in C-U-B-A; When My Baby Smiles at Me

The Greenwich Village Follies, 1922 (216) 1922 Georgette; Sixty Seconds Every Minute, I Think of You

The Greenwich Village Follies, 1924 (127) 1924 I'm in Love Again

Guys and Dolls (1,200) 1950 based on Damon Runyon story *The Idyll of Miss Sarah Brown*. Adelaide's Lament; A Bushel and a Peck; Fugue For Tinhorns; Guys and Dolls; If I Were a Bell; I'll Know; I've Never Been in Love Before; Luck Be a Lady; My Time of Day; The Oldest Established; Sit Down, You're Rockin' the Boat; Take Back Your Mink

Gypsy (702) 1959 loosely based on memoirs of Gypsy Rose Lee. All I Need Is the Girl; Everything's Coming Up Roses; If Mama Was Married; Let Me Entertain You; Little Lamb; Mister Goldstone; Rose's Turn; Small World; Some People; Together Wherever We Go; You Gotta Have a Gimmick; You'll Never Get Away from Me

Gypsy Love (31) 1911 Gypsy Maiden; Love and Wine

H.M.S. Pinafore 1878 I Am the Captain of the Pinafore; I Am the Monarch of the Sea; I'm Called Little Buttercup

Hair (1,742, including OB run) 1968 Aquarius; Easy To Be Hard; Frank Mills; Good Morning Starshine; Hair; Let the Sunshine In; Manchester; Where Do I Go

Half a Sixpence (512) 1965 based on the H.G. Wells novel *Kipps*. Flash, Bang, Wallop; Half a Sixpence; If the Rain's Got To Fall

The Half Moon (48) 1920 Deep in Your Eyes

Hanky Panky (104) 1912 Oh You Circus Day

Happy Birthday (non-musical play) (564) 1946 I Haven't Got a Worry in the World

Happy Day 1916 Bohemia

Happy End 1929 Bilbao Song

Happy Hunting (412) 1956 Mutual Admiration Society; New Fangled Tango

The Happy Time (286) 1968 based on Samuel Taylor play and Robert L. Fontaine novel. The Happy Time; The Life of the Party

Harry Delmar's Revels (112) 1927 I Can't Give You Anything But Love (dropped)

Have a Heart (76) 1917 Have a Heart; You Said Something

Hazel Flagg (190) 1953 based on Ben Hecht film *Nothing Sacred*. Ev'ry Street's a Boulevard in Old New York; How Do You Speak to an Angel

Heads Up! (144) 1929 A Ship Without a Sail); Why Do You Suppose

The Heart of Paddy Whack 1914 A Little Bit of Heaven, Sure They Call It Ireland

Hello Daddy (198) 1928 Futuristic Rhythm

Hello, Dolly! (2,844) 1964 based on Thornton Wilder play *The Matchmaker*. Before the Parade Passes By; Dancing; Hello Dolly!; It Only Takes a Moment; It Takes a Woman; Put On Your Sunday Clothes; So Long Dearie

Hello, Yourself! (87) 1928 Jericho

Hellzapoppin' (1404) 1938 Boomps-a-Daisy

Her Soldier Boy (198) 1916 Mother; Pack Up Your Troubles in Your Old Kit Bag and Smile, Smile, Smile

Here and There 1917 For Me and My Gal

Here Goes the Bride (7) 1931 Hello, My Lover, Goodbye

Here's Howe (71) 1928 Crazy Rhythm

Hers To Hold 1943 Say a Prayer for the Boys Over There

Hi-De-Hi 1936 As Long As You're Not in Love with Anyone Else, Why Don't You Fall in Love with Me

Hi Diddle Diddle 1934 Miss Otis Regrets

Hide and Seek 1937 She's My Lovely

High Button Shoes (727) 1947 I Still Get Jealous; Papa Won't You Dance with Me; You're My Girl

High Jinks (213) 1913 All Aboard for Dixieland; The Bubble; Something Seems Tingle-Ingling

High Spirits (375) 1964 based on Noel Coward play *Blithe Spirit*. Home Sweet Heaven; You'd Better Love Me

High Time 1926 Mary Lou

Higher and Higher (108) Ev'ry Sunday Afternoon; From Another World; It Never Entered My Mind

Hip, Hip, Hooray (425) 1915 Ladder of Roses

His Honour the Mayor (104) 1906 Waltz Me Around Again Willie—'Round, 'Round, 'Round

Hit the Deck (352) 1927 based on Hubert Osborne play *Shore Leave*. Hallelujah!; Sometimes I'm Happy

Hitchy-Koo, 1917 (220) 1917 I May Be Gone for a Long, Long Time

Hitchy-Koo, 1918 (68) 1918 M-I-S-S-I-S-S-I-P-P-I

Hitchy-Koo, 1919 (56) 1919 Old-Fashioned Garden

Hodge Podge & Co. (73) 1899 A Picture No Artist Can Paint

Hold Everything! (413) 1928 Don't Hold Everything; To Know You Is To Love You; You're the Cream in My Coffee

Hold On to Your Hats (158) 1940 There's a Great Day Coming, Mañana

Hold Your Horses (88) 1933 If I Love Again

Home and Beauty 1937 A Nice Cup of Tea

Honeymoon Lane (364) 1926 The Little White House

The Honeymooners (72) 1907 If I'm Going To Die I'm Going To Have Some Fun; I'm a Popular Man

Hooray for What! (200) 1937 Down with Love; God's Country; Moanin' in the Mornin'; Napoleon's a Pastry

Hot Chocolates (219) 1929 Ain't Misbehavin'; What Did I Do To Be So Black and Blue

Houp-La 1916 Oh! How She Could Yacki, Hacki, Wicki, Wacki, Woo; Pretty Baby

House of Flowers (165) 1954 Can I Leave Off Wearin' My Shoes; House of Flowers; I Never Has Seen Snow; A Sleepin' Bee; Smellin' of Vanilla; Two Ladies in De Shade of De Banana Tree

How Now, Dow Jones (220) 1967 Step to the Rear

How To Succeed in Business Without Really Trying (1,095) 1961 based on Shepherd Mead novel. (It's) Been a Long Day; Brotherhood of Man; Grand Old Ivy; Happy To Keep His Dinner Warm; How To; I Believe in You; Love from a Heart of Gold; Paris Original; A Secretary Is Not a Toy

Hullo America 1917 Give Me the Moonlight, Give Me the Girl; Madelon

Hullo Ragtime 1911 Alexander's Ragtime Band; The Gaby Glide; Hitchy-Koo; Snooky Ookums; The Wedding Glide; You're My Baby

Hullo Tango 1913 Get Out and Get Under

I Can Get It for You Wholesale (300) 1962 based on Jerome Weidman novel. Miss Marmelstein

I Do! I Do! (560) 1966 based on Jan de Hartog play *The Fourposter*. The Honeymoon Is Over; My Cup Runneth Over

I Love My Wife (864) 1977 Hey There, Good Times

I Married an Angel (290) 1938 I Married an Angel; I'll Tell the Man in the Street; Spring Is Here

I'd Rather Be Right (290) 1937 Have You Met Miss Jones; I'd Rather Be Right

Illya Darling (320) 1967 based on film *Never on Sunday*. Never on Sunday

Inside U.S.A. (337) 1948 Haunted Heart

Irene (670) 1919 Alice Blue Gown; Castle of Dreams; Irene

Irma La Douce (527) 1960 Dis-Donc, Dis-Donc; Irma La Douce; Our Language of Love

The Isle o' Dreams (32) 1913 Isle o' Dreams; When Irish Eyes Are Smiling

It Happened in Nordland (154) 1904 Al Fresco; Bandana Land; A Knot of Blue

(It's a Bird, It's a Plane) It's Superman (129) 1966 based on comic strip "Superman." You've Got Possibilities

Jack O'Lantern (265) 1917 Come and Have a Swing with Me; Wait Till the Cows Come Home

Jacques Brel Is Alive and Well and Living in Paris (1,847) 1968 Amsterdam; Carousel; Desperate Ones; If We Only Have Love; Madeleine; Marieke; Old Folks; Sons of; Timid Frieda

Jamaica (558) 1957 Ain't It the Truth; Cocoanut Sweet; I Don't Think I'll End It All Today; Little Biscuit; Napoleon's a Pastry; Push Da Button; Savanna; Take It Slow, Joe; What Good Does It Do

Jerry's Girls (139) 1985 Before the Parade Passes By; The Best of Times; Bosom Buddies; Hello Dolly; I Don't Want To Know; If He Walked into My Life; It Only Takes a Moment; It Takes a Woman; Kiss Her Now; Mame; Milk and Honey; Movies Were Movies; Put On Your Sunday Clothes; So Long Dearie; Time Heals Everything; We Need a Little Christmas

Jesus Christ Superstar (711) 1971 Everything's Alright; I Don't Know How To Love Him; Jesus Christ Superstar

Jigsaw 1919 Swanee

Jill Darling 1934 I'm on a See-Saw

John Murray Anderson's Almanac (69) 1929 I May Be Wrong, But I Think You're Wonderful

John Murray Anderson's Almanac (227) 1953 Hold 'Em Joe

The Jolly Bachelors (84) 1910 Come Along My Mandy; Has Anybody Here Seen Kelly

Joseph and the Amazing Technicolor Dreamcoat (747) One More Angel in Heaven

Joy Bells 1918 Hindustan

Jubilee (169) 1935 Begin the Beguine; Just One of Those Things; A Picture of Me Without You; Shouldn't I

Jumbo (233) 1935 The Circus Is on Parade; Little Girl Blue; The Most Beautiful Girl in the World; My Romance; Over and Over Again

June Moon (273) 1929 based on Ring Lardner short story "Some Like 'Em Cold." June Moon

Katinka (220) 1915 Allah's Holiday; I Want To Marry a Male Quartet; Katinka; Rackety-Coo

Kean (92) 1961 based on Jean-Paul Sartre comedy and Alexandre Dumas play. Sweet Danger

Keep Off the Grass (44) 1940 Clear Out of This World

Kerry Gow 1883 A Handful of Earth from Mother's Grave

Kid Boots 1923 Alabamy Bound; Dinah; If You Knew Susie, Like I Know Susie; I'm Goin' South

Kiki 1921 Some Day I'll Find You

The King and I (1,246) 1951 based on Margaret Landon novel *Anna and the King of Siam*. Getting To Know You; Hello Young Lovers; I Have Dreamed; I Whistle a Happy Tune; March of the Siamese Children; Shall We Dance; Something Wonderful; We Kiss in a Shadow

King Dodo (64) 1902 The Tale of a Bumble Bee

King's Rhapsody 1949 Some Day My Heart Will Awake; Take Your Girl

Kismet (583) 1953 based on Edward Knoblock play. Not Since Nineveh; And This Is My Beloved; Baubles, Bangles and Beads; Stranger in Paradise

Kiss Me, Kate (1,077) 1948 based on Shakespeare's *The Taming of the Shrew*. Always True to You in My Fashion; Another Op'nin, Another Show; Brush Up Your Shakespeare; I Hate Men; So in Love; Too Darn Hot; Why Can't You Behave; Wunderbar

Knickerbocker Holiday (168) 1938 It Never Was You; September Song

Knights of Madness 1950 Your Heart and My Heart

La La Lucille (104) 1919 Nobody But You

Ladies First (164) 1918 Just Like a Gypsy

Lady Be Good (184) 1924 Fascinating Rhythm; The Half of It Dearie, Blues; The Man I Love (dropped); Oh, Lady Be Good; So Am I

The Lady in Ermine (232) 1922 The Lady in Ermine; When Hearts Are Young

Lady in the Dark (388) 1941 My Ship; Saga of Jenny; This Is New; Tschaikowsky

The Lady of the Slipper (232) 1912 Bagdad

Laffing Room Only (233) 1944 Feudin' and Fightin'

The Last of the Hogans 1891 Danny by My Side; Knights of the Mystic Star; Take a Day Off, Mary Ann

Latin Quarter 1950 C'est Si Bon; Clopin Clopant

The Laugh Parade (231) 1931 Ooh That Kiss; The Torch Song; You're My Everything

The Laughing Husband (48) 1914 You're Here and I'm Here

Leader of the Pack (120) 1985 Be My Baby; Chapel of Love; Da Doo Ron Ron; The Leader of the Pack

Leave It to Jane (167) 1917 Cleopatterer; Leave It to Jane; The Siren's Song; The Sun Shines Brighter

Leave It to Me (291) 1938 based on Samuel and Bella Spewack play *Clear All Wires*. From Now On; Get Out of Town; I Want To Go Home; Most Gentlemen Don't Like Love; My Heart Belongs to Daddy; Tomorrow

Lena Horne: The Lady and Her Music (333) 1981 As Long As I Live; Can't Help Lovin' Dat Man; From This Moment On; I Got a Name; I Want To Be Happy; If You Believe; I'm Glad There Is You; I'm Gonna Sit Right Down and Write Myself a Letter; Just One of Those Things; Push De Button; Stormy Weather; Watch What Happens; Where Or When

Lend an Ear (460) 1948 When Someone You Love Loves You; Who Hit Me

Let 'Em Eat Cake (90) 1933 Let 'Em Eat Cake; Mine

Let's Face It (547) 1941 based on Norma Mitchell and Russell Medcraft play *The Cradle Snatchers*. Ace in the Hole; Everything I Love; You Irritate Me So

Lew Leslie's International Revue (95) 1930 Cinderella Brown; Exactly Like You; On the Sunny Side of the Street

Lido Lady 1925 Here in My Arms; It All Depends on You

Life Begins at 8:40 (237) 1934 Fun To Be Fooled; Let's Take a Walk Around the Block; You're a Builder Upper

Lights Up 1940 Let the People Sing; You've Done Something to My Heart

Li'l Abner (693) 1956 based on comic strip characters created by Al Capp. If I Had My Druthers; Jubilation T. Cornpone; Love in a Home; Namely You; What's Good for General Bullmoose

Lilac Time, *see* **Blossom Time**

Linger Longer Letty (69) 1919 Oh By Jingo, Oh By Gee, You're the Only Girl for Me

Lisbon Story 1943 Never Say Goodbye; Pedro the Fisherman

Listen Lester (272) 1918 I Was a Very Good Baby; Waiting

The Little Dog Laughed 1939 Are You Havin' Any Fun; Franklin D. Roosevelt Jones; On the Outside Looking In; Run Rabbit Run

The Little Duchess (136) 1901 The Maiden with the Dreamy Eyes; Violets

Little Jessie James (453) 1923 I Love You; Suppose I Had Never Met You

Little Johnny Jones (52) 1904 Give My Regards to Broadway; Good-bye; Flo; Life's a Funny Proposition After All; The Yankee Doodle Boy

Little Mary Sunshine (1,143) 1959 Little Mary Sunshine

Little Me (257) 1962 based on Patrick Dennis novel. Be a Performer; Dimples; Here's to Us; I've Got Your Number; The Other Side of the Tracks; Poor Little Hollywood Star; Real Live Girl

The Little Millionaire (192) 1911 Barnum Had the Right Idea

Little Miss Bluebeard (175) 1923 I Won't Say I Will, But I Won't Say I Won't; Who'll Buy My Violets

Little Nellie Kelly 1922 Nellie Kelly, I Love You; You Remind Me of My Mother

A Little Night Music (601) 1973 based on Ingmar Bergman film *Smiles of a Summer Night*. Every Day a Little Death; The Glamorous Life; Liaisons; The Miller's Son; Night Waltz; Now; Send In the Clowns; A Weekend in the Country; You Must Meet My Wife

Little Shop of Horrors (*) 1983 based on the film by Roger Corman. Little Shop of Horrors; Somewhere That's Green; Suddenly Seymour

The Little Show (First Edition) (321) 1929 Can't We Be Friends; I Guess I'll Have To Change My Plan; Moanin' Low

Load of Coal 1929 Honeysuckle Rose

London Calling 1924 Parisian Pierrot

London Rhapsody 1937 Home Town

A Lonely Romeo (87) 1919 Any Old Place with You

Lost in the Stars (281) 1949 based on Alan Paton novel *Cry, the Beloved Country*. Cry, the Beloved Country; The Little Grey House; Lost in the Stars

Louisiana Purchase (444) 1940 Louisiana Purchase; Tomorrow Is a Lovely Day

Love Lies 1929 I Lift Up My Finger and I Say Tweet Tweet

Love Life (252) 1948 Green-Up Time; Here I'll Stay

Love Watches 1908 Good Night Dear

Lovely Lady (164) 1927 Lovely Lady

Love's Lottery (50) 1904 Sweet Thoughts of Home

Lucky (71) 1927 Dancing the Devil Away; The Same Old Moon

Lucky Girl (81) 1928 Crazy Rhythm

Mack and Mabel (66) 1974 Big Time; Time Heals Everything

The Mad Show (871) 1966 based on *Mad* Magazine. The Boy From. . .

Madame Sherry (231) 1910 The Birth of Passion; Every Little Movement

The Magic Melody (143) 1919 The Little Church Around the Corner

Maid in America (108) 1915 Floating down the Old Green River

The Maid of the Mountains (37) 1918 A Bachelor Gay; Love Will Find a Way; Paradise for Two

Make It Snappy (77) 1922 The Sheik of Araby

Malone's Night Off 1878 Such an Education Has My Mary Ann

Mame (1,508) 1966 based on Patrick Dennis novel *Auntie Mame* and Jerome Lawrence and Robert E. Lee play. Bosom Buddies; If He Walked into My Life; Mame; My Best Girl; Open a New Window; We Need a Little Christmas

Man of La Mancha (2,329, including OB run) 1965 based on the life and work of Miguel de Cervantes y Saavedra. Dulcinea; I'm Only Thinking of Him; The Impossible Dream; Man of La Mancha

The Man Who Owns Broadway (128) 1909 There's Something About a Uniform

Marinka (165) 1945 Sigh by Night

Maritza, *see* **Countess Maritza**

The Marriage Market (80) 1913 You're Here and I'm Here

Marrying Mary (43) 1906 He's a Cousin of Mine

Mary (219) 1920 The Love Nest; Mary

May Wine (213) 1935 based on Wallace Smith and Eric von Stroheim story. Dance, My Darlings

Mayfair and Montmartre 1921 Do It Again; Say It with Music

Maytime (492) 1917 Jump Jim Crow; The Road to Paradise; Will You Remember (Sweetheart)

The McSorleys 1882 I Never Drank Behind the Bar

Me and Bessie (453) 1975 After You've Gone; Gimme a Pigfoot; A Good Man is Hard To Find; A Hot Time in the Old Town; Nobody Knows You When You're Down and Out; 'Tain't Nobody's Business If I Do

Me and Juliet (358) 1953 Keep It Gay; No Other Love

Me and My Girl 1937 Lambeth Walk; Me and My Girl

The Me Nobody Knows (587, including OB run) 1970 Dream Babies

The Medal and the Maid (49) 1904 In Zanzibar; My Little Chimpanzee

Meet Mister Callaghan 1952 Meet Mister Callaghan

Meet The People (160) 1940 In Chichicastenango

Merrie England 1902 English Rose; Yeoman of England

Merrily We Roll Along (16) 1981 Good Thing Going; Merrily We Roll Along; Not a Day Goes By; Old Friends

The Merry Widow (416) 1907 Girls, Girls, Girls; Maxime's; Merry Widow Waltz; Vilia

Mexican Hayride (167) 1944 Abracadabra; I Love You

Michael Todd's Peep Show (278) 1950 Stay with the Happy People; Violins from Nowhere

The Midnight Rounders, 1921 (120) 1921 Ma! He's Making Eyes at Me; My Sunny Tennessee

The Midnight Sons (257) 1909 I've Got Rings on My Fingers **The Mikado** 1885 Tit-Willow

Milk and Honey (543) 1961 Chin Up, Ladies!; Mazel Tov; Milk and Honey; Shalom

Miss Calico 1926 I'm Comin' Virginia

Miss Dolly Dollars (56) 1905 A Woman Is Only a Woman, But a Good Cigar Is a Smoke

Miss Hook of Holland (119) 1907 The Flying Dutchman; Little Pink Petty from Peter

Miss Innocence (176) 1908 My Pony Boy; Shine On Harvest Moon

Miss Liberty (308) 1949 Give Me Your Tired, Your Poor; Homework; Just One Way To Say I Love You; Let's Take an Old-Fashioned Walk

Miss 1917 (48) 1917 Go, Little Boat

Miss Springtime (224) 1916 Throw Me a Rose

Mister Cinders 1929 Spread a Little Happiness

Mlle. Modiste (202) 1905 I Want What I Want When I Want It; Kiss Me Again; The Mascot of the Troop

The Most Happy Fella (676) 1956 based on Sidney Howard play *They Knew What They Wanted. Big ''D'';* Joey, Joey, Joey; The Most Happy Fella; Somebody, Somewhere; Standing on the Corner

Mother Goose (105) 1903 Always Leave Them Laughing When You Say Goodbye; Laughing Water

The Mousme 1911 The Temple Bell

Mr. Hamlet of Broadway (54) 1908 Beautiful Eyes

Mr. Manhattan 1913 When You're All Dressed Up and No Place To Go

Mr. Wonderful (383) 1956 Jacques D'Iraq; Mister Wonderful; Too Close for Comfort; Without You I'm Nothing

The Mulligan Guard 1873 The Mulligan Guard; Skidmore Fancy Ball

The Mulligan Guards' Nominee 1880 The Mulligan Braves; The Skidmore Masquerade

The Mulligan Guards' Picnic 1880 Locked Out After Nine

The Mulligan Guards' Surprise 1880 The Full Moon Union; Never Take the Horse Shoe from the Door

Murder at the Vanities (207) 1933 Sweet Madness

The Music Box Revue (313) 1921 Everybody Step; Say It with Music

The Music Box Revue of 1922 (273) 1922 Crinoline Days; Lady of the Evening

The Music Box Revue of 1923 1923 An Orange Grove in California; When You Walked Out Someone Else Walked Right In

The Music Box Revue of 1924 (184) 1924 All Alone; Unlucky in Love; What'll I Do

Music in the Air (342) 1932 In Egern on the Tegern See; I've Told Every Little Star; One More Dance; The Song Is You; When the Spring Is in the Air

The Music Man (1,375) 1957 Gary, Indiana; Goodnight My Someone; It's You; Lida Rose; Marian the Librarian; My White Knight; Seventy-Six Trombones; Till There Was You; Trouble

My Fair Lady (2,717) 1956 based on George Bernard Shaw play *Pygmalion.* Ascot Gavotte; Get Me to the Church on Time; A Hymn to Him; I Could Have Danced All Night; I'm an Ordinary Man; I've Grown Accustomed to Her Face; Just You Wait; On the Street Where You Live; The Rain in

Spain; Show Me; Why Can't the English; With a Little Bit of Luck; Without You; Wouldn't It Be Loverly; You Did It

My Maryland (312) 1927 based on Clyde Fitch play *Barbara Frietchie*. Mother; Silver Moon; Your Land and My Land

My One and Only 1983 Blah Blah Blah; How Long Has This Been Going On; I Can't Be Bothered Now; Kickin' the Clouds Away; My One and Only; Nice Work If You Can Get It; Soon; Strike Up the Band; 'S Wonderful

Nancy Brown (104) 1903 Navajo; Under the Bamboo Tree

Naughty Cinderella (121) 1925 Do I Love You

Naughty Marietta (136) 1910 Ah! Sweet Mystery of Life; I'm Falling in Love with Someone; Italian Street Song; Tramp! Tramp! Tramp! Along the Highway

New Faces of 1936 (193) 1936 You Better Go Now

New Faces of 1952 (365) 1952 I'm in Love with Miss Logan; Lizzie Borden; Love Is a Simple Thing; Monotonous

New Girl in Town (431) 1957 Based on Eugene O'Neill play *Anna Christie*. Did You Close Your Eyes; It's Good To Be Alive; Look at 'Er; Sunshine Girl

The New Moon (509) 1928 Lover Come Back to Me; One Kiss; Marianne; Softly, as in a Morning Sunrise; Stouthearted Men; Wanting You

The New Yorkers (168) 1930 The Great Indoors; I Happen To Like New York; Love for Sale; Where Have You Been

The New Ziegfeld Follies 1934 Wagon Wheels

Nice Going On 1932 You're an Old Smoothie

Nifties of 1923 (47) 1923 I Won't Say I Will, But I Won't Say I Won't

The Night Boat (148) 1920 Left All Alone Again Blues; My Spanish Rose; Whose Baby Are You

Nina Rosa (137) 1930 Nina Rosa; Serenade of Love

Nine (739) 1982 based on the film *8-1/2* by Federico Fellini. The Germans at the Spa; My Husband Makes Movies; Nine; Only with You; Simple; Unusual Way

Nine-Fifteen Revue (7) 1930 Get Happy

The 1940's Radio Hour (105) 1979 Ain't She Sweet; At Last; Blue Moon; Boogie Woogie Bugle Boy (From Company B); Chattanooga Choo Choo; Chiquita Banana; Have Yourself a Merry Little Christmas; I Got It Bad and That Ain't Good; I'll Be Seeing You; I'll Never Smile Again; Jingle Bells; Little Brown Jug; Rose of the Rio Grande; Strike Up the Band; That Old Black Magic

No, No, Nanette (321) 1925 based on Emil Nyitray and Frank Mandel play *My Lady Friends*. I Want To Be Happy; Tea for Two; Too Many Rings Around Rosie

No Strings (580) 1962 No Strings; Nobody Told Me; The Sweetest Sounds

Nobody Home (135) 1915 You Know and I Know

Nothing But Love (39) 1919 Ask the Stars; I'll Remember You

Nymph Errant 1933 Experiment; The Physician

The O'Brien Girl (164) 1921 Learn To Smile

Of Thee I Sing (441) 1931 Love Is Sweeping the Country; Of Thee I Sing; Who Cares; Wintergreen for President

Oh, Boy! (463) 1917 Nestin' Time in Flatbush; An Old-Fashioned Wife; A Pal Like You; Rolled into One; Till the Clouds Roll By; You Never Knew About Me

Oh Joy 1917 Till the Clouds Roll By

Oh, Kay! (256) 1926 Clap Yo' Hands; Dear Little Girl; Do Do Do; Fidgety Feet; Heaven on Earth; Maybe; Show Me the Town; Someone To Watch Over Me

Oh, Lady Lady (219) 1918 I Found You and You Found Me

Oh, Look! (68) 1918 I'm Always Chasing Rainbows

Oh, Please! (75) 1926 I Know That You Know

Okay For Sound 1936 The Fleet's in Port Again

Oklahoma! (2,248) 1943 based on Lynn Riggs play *Green Grow the Lilacs*. I Can't Say No; Kansas City; Many a New Day; Oh What a Beautiful Mornin'; Oklahoma; Out of My Dreams; People Will Say We're in Love; Poor Jud (Is Daid); The Surrey with the Fringe on Top

Old Chelsea 1943 Break of Day; My Heart and I; There Are Angels Outside Heaven

Old Lavender 1885 Poverty's Tears Ebb and Flow

Oliver! (774) 1963 based on Charles Dickens novel *Oliver Twist*. As Long as He Needs Me; Be Back Soon; Consider Yourself; Food Glorious Food; I'd Do Anything; Where Is Love; Who Will Buy; You've Got To Pick a Pocket or Two

Olivette 1881 The Torpedo and the Whale

On a Clear Day You Can See Forever (280) 1965 Come Back to Me; Hurry It's Lovely Up Here; On a Clear Day You Can See Forever; What Did I Have That I Don't Have

On the Town (197) 1944 Lucky To Be Me; New York, New York; Some Other Time; Ya Got Me

On the Twentieth Century (460) 1978 On the Twentieth Century

On with the Dance 1925 Poor Little Rich Girl

On with the Show 1926 I Can't Believe That You're in Love with Me

On with the Show 1933 Stormy Weather; When a Soldier's on Parade

On Your Toes (315) 1936 Glad To Be Unhappy; It's Got To Be Love; On Your Toes; Quiet Night; Slaughter on Tenth Avenue; There's a Small Hotel; Too Good for the Average Man

Once Upon a Mattress (460) 1959 based on the fairy tale of the Princess and the Pea. Man to Man Talk; Very Soft Shoes

One Dam Thing After Another Birth of the Blues; My Heart Stood Still

One Girl 1930 Time on My Hands

One Girl in a Million 1914 Moonlight on the Rhine

One Touch of Venus (567) 1943 Speak Low

The Only Girl (240) 1914 Tell It All Over Again; When You're Away; When You're Wearing the Ball and Chain

Orange Blossoms (95) 1922 A Kiss in the Dark

The Orchid (178) 1907 He Goes to Church on Sunday

Our Miss Gibbs (64) 1910 Moon Struck; Yip-I-Addy-I-Ay!

Out of This World (157) 1950 based on the Amphitryon legend. From This Moment On; I Am Loved; Nobody's Chasing Me; Use Your Imagination

Pacific Overtures (206) 1976 Chrysanthemum Tea; Please Hello; Pretty Lady; Someone in a Tree

Padlocks of 1927 (95) 1927 Hot Heels

Paint Your Wagon (289) 1951 I Still See Elisa; I Talk to the Trees; They Call the Wind Maria

The Pajama Game (1,063) 1954 based on Richard Bissell novel 7 1/2 *Cents.* Hernando's Hideaway; Hey There; I'll Never Be Jealous Again; I'm Not At All in Love; Racing with the Clock; 7 1/2 Cents; Steam Heat

Pal Joey (374) 1940 based on John O'Hara stories. Bewitched, Bothered and Bewildered; Do It the Hard Way; I Could Write a Book; In Our Little Den of Iniquity; You Mustn't Kick It Around; Zip

Panama Hattie (501) 1940 Let's Be Buddies

Pardon My English (46) 1933 Isn't It a Pity; Lorelei

Paris (195) 1928 Don't Look at Me That Way; Let's Do It; Let's Misbehave; Two Little Babes in the Wood

The Parisian Model (179) 1906 I Just Can't Make My Eyes Behave; It's Delightful To Be Married

Park Avenue (72) 1946 Goodbye to All That; There's No Holding Me

Passing Show of 1912 (136) 1912 The Wedding Glide

Passing Show of 1913 (116) 1913 Do You Take This Woman for Your Lawful Wife; You're Here and I'm Here

Passing Show of 1914 (133) 1914 Gilbert the Filbert; I'll Make a Man of You

Passing Show of 1915 (145) 1915 Ballin' the Jack

Passing Show of 1916 (140) 1916 Pretty Baby

Passing Show of 1917 (196) 1917 Good-bye, Broadway, Hello France

Passing Show of 1918 (124) 1918 I'm Forever Blowing Bubbles; Smiles

Passing Show of 1922 (85) 1922 Carolina in the Morning

Patrick's Day Parade 1874 Patrick's Day Parade

Peggy-Ann (333) 1926 Loosely based on Edgar Smith and A. Baldwin Sloane 1910 musical *Tillie's Nightmare.* A Little Birdie Told Me So; A Tree in the Park; Where's That Rainbow

Perchance To Dream 1945 Love Is My Reason; We'll Gather Lilacs

Peter Pan 1924 The Sweetest Things in Life

Peter Pan (152) 1954 based on Sir James M. Barrie play. Captain Hook's Waltz; I Won't Grow Up; I'm Flying; I've Gotta Crow; Never Never Land; Tender Shepherd; Wendy

Piccadilly Hayride 1947 The Coffee Song; Five Minutes More

Pickwick (56) 1965 based on the Dickens novel *Pickwick Papers.* If I Ruled the World

The Pink Lady (312) 1911 By the Saskatchewan; My Beautiful Lady

Pipe Dream (246) 1955 based on John Steinbeck novel *Sweet Thursday.* All At Once You Love Her; Ev'rybody's Got a Home But Me

Pippin (1,944) 1972 Magic To Do; Spread a Little Sunshine

Plain and Fancy (461) 1955 Young and Foolish

Please 1932 Louisiana Hayride

The Pleasure Seekers (72) 1913 Get Out and Get Under

Porgy and Bess (124) 1935 based on DuBose and Dorothy Heyward play *Porgy.* Bess, You Is My Woman Now; I Got Plenty O' Nuttin'; I Loves You Porgy; I'm on My Way; It Ain't Necessarily So; My Man's Gone Now; Oh, Bess, Oh Where's My Bess; Oh, I Can't Sit Down; Summertime; There's a Boat Dat's Leavin' Soon for New York; A Woman Is a Sometime Thing

Pot Luck 1920 Chili Bean

Present Arms (155) 1928 Do I Hear You Saying ''I Love You''; You Took Advantage of Me

The Prima Donna (72) 1908 If You Were I and I Were You

The Prince of Pilsen (143) 1903 Heidelberg Stein Song; The Message of the Violet; The Tale of the Seashell

The Prince of Tonight 1909 I Wonder Who's Kissing Her Now

Princess Nicotine 1894 Airy, Fairy Lillian

The Princess Pat (158) 1915 All for You; Love Is the Best of All; Neapolitan Love Song; Two Laughing Irish Eyes

Private Lives (non-musical play) (256) 1931 Some Day I'll Find You

Promises, Promises (1,281) 1968 based on Billy Wilder and I.A.L. Diamond screenplay *The Apartment.* A Fact Can Be a Beautiful Thing; I'll Never Fall in Love Again; Knowing When To Leave; Promises, Promises; Whoever You Are

The Provincetown Follies (63) 1935 Red Sails in the Sunset

The Punch Bowl 1923 It Ain't Gonna Rain No Mo'; What'll I Do

Purlie (688) 1970 Based on Ossie Davis play *Purlie Victorious.* I Got Love; First Thing Monday Mornin'

Push and Go 1915 By Heck; Chinatown, My Chinatown

The Quaker Girl (240) 1911 Come to the Ball; Tony from America

Queen High (378) 1926 Cross Your Heart; Gentlemen Prefer Blondes

The Ramblers (289) 1926 All Alone Monday

The Rebel Maid 1921 The Fishermen of England

Red, Hot and Blue! (183) 1936 Down in the Depths on the Ninetieth Floor; It's De-Lovely; Ridin' High

The Red Mill (274) 1906 Because You're You; Every Day Is Ladies' Day with Me; In Old New York; The Isle of Our Dreams; Moonbeams; When You're Pretty

The Red Widow (128) 1911 I Love Love

Redhead (452) 1959 Just for Once; Two Faces in the Dark

Reilly and the Four Hundred 1890 I've Come Here To Stay; Jolly Commodore; Maggie Murphy's Home; Taking In the Town

Revenge with Music (158) 1934 based on Pedro de Alarćon novel *The Three-Cornered Hat*. If There Is Someone Lovelier Than You; You and the Night and the Music

Rhapsody in Black (80) 1931 Harlem Moon; Till the Real Thing Comes Along

Right This Way (15) 1938 I Can Dream Can't I; I'll Be Seeing You

The Rink (204) 1984 Under the Roller Coaster; Wallflower

Rio Rita (494) 1927 Following the Sun Around; If You're in Love You'll Waltz; The Kinkajou; The Ranger's Song; Rio Rita

Rise and Shine, *see* **Take a Chance**

The Riviera Girl (78) 1917 Just a Voice To Call Me, Dear

The Roar of the Greasepaint—the Smell of the Crowd (232) 1965 The Joker; Look At That Face; Nothing Can Stop Me Now!; Where Would You Be Without Me; Who Can I Turn To; A Wonderful Day Like Today

Roberta (295) 1933 based on Alice Duer Miller novel *Gowns by Roberta*. Smoke Gets in Your Eyes; The Touch of Your Hand; Yesterdays; You're Devastating

Robin Hood 1890 Armorer's Song; Brown October Ale; Oh Promise Me

Robinson Crusoe Jr. (139) 1916 Where Did Robinson Crusoe Go with Friday on Saturday Night; Where the Black-Eyed Susans Grow; Yaaka Hula Hickey Dula

Roly-Boly Eyes (100) 1919 Ida, Sweet As Apple Cider

A Romance of Athlone 1899 My Wild Irish Rose

Rosalie (335) 1928 How Long Has This Been Going On

Rose Marie (557) 1924 The Door of My Dreams; Indian Love Call; Rose Marie; Totem Tom-Tom

The Rose of Algeria (40) 1909 Ask Her While the Band Is Playing; Love Is Like a Cigarette; Rose of the World

The Royal Vagabond (208) 1919 When the Cherry Blossoms Fall

Rufus LeMaire's Affairs (56) 1927 Bring Back Those Minstrel Days

A Runaway Girl 1898 The Boy Guessed Right; Society; The Soldiers in the Park

Runnin' Wild (213) 1923 Charleston; Old-Fashioned Love

Sadie Thompson (60) 1944 based on William Somerset Maugham short story "Miss Thompson" and the John Colton play, *Rain*. The Love I Long For

Sail Away (167) 1961 Sail Away; Why Do the Wrong People Travel

Sally (570) 1920 Look for the Silver Lining; Sally; Whippoor-will; Wild Rose

Sally in Our Alley (67) 1902 Sally in Our Alley; Under the Bamboo Tree

Salvation (239) 1969 Why Can't I Touch You

Samples 1916 Broken Doll

San Toy (65) 1900 Six Little Wives

Sarava (140) 1979 based on "Dona Flor and Her Two Husbands." Sarava

Sari (151) 1914 Love Has Wings; Love's Own Sweet Song; My Faithful Stradavari; Softly Thro' the Summer Night

Sauce Tartare 1949 La Seine

Say, Darling (332) 1958 based on Richard Bissell novel. Say, Darling; Something's Always Happening on the River

The Second Little Show (63) 1930 Lucky Seven; Sing Something Simple

See America First (15) 1916 I've Got a Shooting Box in Scotland

Serenade 1897 Cupid and I

Sergeant Brue (152) 1905 My Irish Molly-O

Set to Music (129) 1939 I Went to a Marvelous Party; Mad About the Boy; The Party's Over Now; The Stately Homes of England

Seven Lively Arts (183) 1944 Ev'ry Time We Say Goodbye; Scenes de Ballet; When I Was a Little Cuckoo

1776 (1,217) 1969 Momma Look Sharp

70, Girls, 70 (36) 1971 Believe

Shameen Dhu 1914 Too-ra-loo-ra-loo-ral, That's an Irish Lullaby

She Loves Me (301) 1963 based on Miklos Laslo play *Parfumerie* and the film *The Shop Around the Corner*. After All You're All I'm After; Dear Friend; She Loves Me; Will He Like Me

Shenandoah (1,050) 1975 Over the Hill; Why Am I Me

Shephard's Pie 1940 Who's Taking You Home Tonight

She's My Baby (71) 1928 How Was I To Know; My Lucky Star

Shoestring Revue (110) 1957 Entire History of the World in Two Minutes and Thirty-two Seconds

Show Boat (572) 1927 Based on Edna Ferber novel. Bill; Can't Help Lovin' Dat Man; Make Believe; Nobody Else But Me (1945 revival); Ol' Man River; Why Do I Love You; You Are Love

Show Girl (111) 1929 Liza

The Show Is On (237) 1936 By Strauss; I've Got Five Dollars; Little Old Lady; Now

Show of Shows 1929 Lady Luck Show; Singin' in the Bathtub

The Show of Wonders (209) 1916 Naughty, Naughty, Naughty

Shubert Gaities of 1919 (87) 1919 Jazz Baby's Ball

Shuffle Along of 1921 (504) 1921 Bandana Days; I'm Just Wild About Harry; Love Will Find a Way; Shuffle Along

Side by Side by Sondheim (390) 1977 Another Hundred People; Anyone Can Whistle; Barcelona; The Boy from. . . . ; Broadway Baby; Comedy Tonight; Company; Could I Leave You; Everybody Says Don't; Getting Married Today; I Never Do Anything Twice; If Momma Was Married; I'm Still Here; The Little Things You Do Together; Losing My Mind; Miracle Song; Pretty Lady; Send in the Clowns; Side by Side; We're Gonna Be All Right; You Could Drive a Person Crazy; You Gotta Have a Gimmick; You Must Meet My Wife

Sigh No More 1945 Matelot; Nina

Silk Stockings (477) 1955 based on film *Ninotchka*. All of You; Josephine; Paris Loves Lovers; Siberia; Stereophonic Sound; Too Bad; Without Love

The Silver Slipper (160) 1902 Tessie, You Are the Only, Only, Only

Simple Simon (135) 1930 Dancing on the Ceiling; Love Me or Leave Me; Ten Cents a Dance

Sinbad (164) 1918 Bagdad; Hello, Central, Give Me No Man's Land; How'd You Like To Be My Daddy; I'll Say She Does; My Mammy; Rock-A-Bye Your Baby with a Dixie Melody; Swanee

Sing for Your Supper (60) 1939 Ballad for Americans

Sing Out Sweet Land (102) 1945 Funny Bunny Hug

Sing Out the News (105) 1938 F.D.R. Jones

Singing Girl 1899 If Only You Were Mine

Singin' in the Rain (367) 1985 based on the MGM musical film. Blue Prelude; Fit As a Fiddle; I've Got a Feelin' You're Fooling; Love Is Where You Find It; Make 'Em Laugh; Singin' in the Rain; The Wedding of the Painted Doll; You Are My Lucky Star

Singin' the Blues (45) 1931 It's the Darndest Thing; Singin' the Blues

Sitting Pretty 1924 Shadow of the Moon; Shufflin' Sam; A Year from Today

The Skidmore Fancy Ball 1879 The Babies on Our Block; The Skidmore Fancy Ball

Skyscraper (248) 1965 based on Elmer Rice novel *Dream Girl*. I'll Only Miss Her When I Think of Her

Small Wonder (134) 1948 When I Fall in Love

Smiles (63) 1930 Time on My Hands; You're Driving Me Crazy

Snap 1922 Shufflin' Along

So Long Letty (96) 1916 So Long Letty

Some 1916 Ev'ry Little While

Some Colonel 1920 The Wooing of the Violin

Something for the Boys (422) 1943 He's a Right Guy

Sometime (283) 1918 Sometime

Song and Dance (474) 1985 Capped Teeth and Caesar Salad; Unexpected Song

Song of Norway (860) 1944 Now; Strange Music

Song of the Flame (219) 1925 Cossack Love Song; Song of the Flame

Sons O' Fun (742) 1941 Happy in Love

Sons O' Guns (295) 1929 Cross Your Fingers; Why (Is There a Rainbow in the Sky)

Sophisticated Ladies (767) 1981 Caravan; Don't Get Around Much Anymore; I Got It Bad and That Ain't Good; I Let a Song Go Out of My Heart; In a Sentimental Mood; It Don't Mean a Thing If It Ain't Got That Swing; Mood Indigo; Perdido; Rockin' in Rhythm; Satin Doll; Solitude; Sophisticated Ladies; Take the 'A' Train

The Sound of Music (1,443) 1959 loosely based on book by Maria Augusta Trapp, *The Trapp Family Singers*. Climb Ev'ry Mountain; Do Re Mi; Edelweiss; The Lonely Goatherd; Maria; My Favorite Things; Sixteen Going on Seventeen; So Long, Farewell; The Sound of Music; You Are Sixteen

South Pacific (1,925) 1949 based on James A. Michener novel *Tales of the South Pacific*. Bali Ha'i; Bloody Mary; A Cockeyed Optimist; Dites-moi Pourquoi; Happy Talk; Honey Bun; I'm Gonna Wash That Man Right Outa My Hair; I'm in Love with a Wonderful Guy; Some Enchanted Evening; There Is Nothin' Like a Dame; This Nearly Was Mine; Younger Than Springtime; You've Got To Be Taught

Spices of 1922 (73) 1922 'Way Down Yonder In New Orleans

Spread It Abroad 1935 These Foolish Things (Remind Me of You)

The Spring Chicken (66) 1906 A Lemon in the Garden of Love

Spring Is Here (104) 1929 Why Can't I; With a Song in My Heart; Yours Sincerely

The Spring Maid (192) 1910 Day Dreams; Fountain Fay; Two Little Love Bees

Squatter Sovereignty 1881 Paddy Duffy's Cart

St. Louis Woman (113) 1946 based on Arna Bontemps novel *God Sends Sunday*. Any Place I Hang My Hat Is Home; Come Rain or Come Shine; I Wonder What Became of Me (dropped); Legalize My Name; Ridin' on the Moon; True Love

Stags At Bay 1935 East of the Sun and West of the Moon

Stand Up and Sing 1931 There's Always Tomorrow

Star and Garter (609) 1942 The Girl on the Police Gazette

Stars in Your Eyes (127) 1939 This Is It

Stars on Ice (830) 1942 Juke Box Saturday Night

The Stepping Stones (241) 1923 In Love with Love; Once in a Blue Moon; Raggedy Ann

Stop Flirting I'll Build a Stairway to Paradise; Once in a Lifetime

Stop! Look! Listen! (105) 1915 The Girl on the Magazine Cover; I Love a Piano

Stop Press 1933 Easter Parade; How's Chances; You and the Night and the Music

Stop the World—I Want To Get Off (556) 1962 Gonna Build a Mountain; Someone Nice Like You; What Kind of Fool Am I

Streamline 1934 Other People's Babies

Street Scene (164) 1947 based on Elmer Rice play. Get a Load of That; Lonely House

The Streets of New York (84) 1963 Whoa, Emma

Streets of Paris (274) 1939 South American Way

Strike Me Pink (105) 1933 Let's Call It a Day; Strike Me Pink

Strike Up the Band (191) 1930 I've Got a Crush on You; The Man I Love; Soon; Strike Up the Band

The Strollers (70) 1901 Strollers We

A Stubborn Cinderella (88) 1909 When You First Kissed the Last Girl You Loved

The Student Prince (608) 1924 Deep in My Heart, Dear; Drinking Song; Golden Days; Just We Two; Serenade

The Student's Frolic 1884 The Vagabond

Sugar Babies (*) 1979 Cuban Love Song; Don't Blame Me; Exactly Like You; I Can't Give You Anything But Love; I Feel a Song Comin' On; I'm Shooting High; Let Me Be Your Sugar Baby; On the Sunny Side of the Street

Sunday in the Park with George (604) 1984 based on the life of the painter Georges Seurat. Children and Art; Everybody Loves Louis; Finishing the Hat; Move On; Putting It Together; Sunday; We Do Not Belong Together

Sunny (517) 1925 D'Ya Love Me; Paddlin' Madelin Home; Sunny; Two Little Bluebirds; Who

The Sunshine Girl (160) 1913 Here's to Love; You Can't Play Every Instrument in the Band

Sweeney Todd (557) 1979 The Ballad of Sweeney Todd; God, That's Good; Kiss Me; A Little Priest; Not While I'm Around; Pretty Women; The Worst Pies in London

Sweet Adeline (234) 1929 Don't Ever Leave Me; Here Am I; 'Twas Not So Long Ago; Why Was I Born

Sweet and Low (184) 1930 Cheerful Little Earful; Overnight; Would You Like To Take a Walk

Sweet Charity (608) 1966 based on Federico Fellini, Tullio Pinelli, Ennio Flaiano screenplay *Nights of Cabiria*. Baby Dream Your Dream; (Hey) Big Spender; Where Am I Going

Sweethearts (136) 1913 The Angelus; The Cricket on the Hearth; Sweethearts

Swingin' the Dream (13) 1939 based on Shakespeare play *A Midsummer Night's Dream*. Darn That Dream

Sybil (168) 1916 I Can Dance with Everyone But My Wife

Tails Up 1919 'N Everything

Take a Chance (243) 1932 Eadie Was a Lady; Rise and Shine; So Do I; Turn Out the Light; You're an Old Smoothie

Take Me Along (448) 1959 based on Eugene O'Neill play *Ah, Wilderness*. Promise Me a Rose; Staying Young; Take Me Along

The Talk of New York (157) 1907 I Want You; Under Any Old Flag At All; When a Fellow's on the Level with a Girl That's on the Square

Tangerine (337) 1921 Sweet Lady

The Tap Dance Kid (669) 1984 based on the novel *Nobody's Family Is Going To Change* by Louise Fitzhugh. Dancing Is Everything; Fabulous Feet; I Remember How It Was; Man in the Moon; William's Song

The Telephone Girl 1898 Little Birdies Learning How To Fly

Tell Her the Truth (11) 1932 based on James Montgomery play *Nothing But the Truth* and the Frederick Isham novel. Hoch, Caroline; Sing Brothers

Tell Me More (32) 1925 the original out-of-town title for

Tell Me More was *My Fair Lady*. Baby; Kickin' the Clouds Away; Tell Me More; Why Do I Love You

Tenderloin (216) 1960 based on Samuel Hopkins Adams novel. Artificial Flowers

That's a Pretty Thing 1934 La-Di-Da-Di-Da

That's the Ticket 1948 The Money Song

These Foolish Things 1938 Music, Maestro Please; Nice People; The Umbrella Man

They're Playing Our Song (1,082) 1979 Just for Tonight; They're Playing Our Song

The Third Little Show (136) 1931 Mad Dogs and Englishmen; When Yuba Plays the Rumba on His Tuba; You Forgot Your Gloves

This Is the Army (113) 1942 I Left My Heart at the Stage Door Canteen; I'm Getting Tired So I Can Sleep; My British Buddy; Oh, How I Hate To Get Up in the Morning; This Is the Army Mister Jones; With My Head in the Clouds

This Year of Grace (157) 1928 Dance Little Lady; A Room with a View; World Weary

This'll Make You Whistle 1936 I'm in a Dancing Mood; This'll Make You Whistle

The Three Musketeers (318) 1928 based on Alexandre Dumas novel. Ev'ry Little While; Ma Belle; March of the Musketeers

Three To Make Ready (327) 1946 The Old Soft Shoe

The Three Twins (288) 1908 Cuddle Up a Little Closer Lovely Mine; The Yama Yama Man

The Threepenny Opera (12) 1933 (95) 1954 Mack the Knife; Pirate Jenny

Three's a Crowd (272) 1930 All the King's Horses; Body and Soul; Something To Remember You By

Through the Years (20) 1932 based on Allan Langdon Martin and Jane Cowl play *Smilin' Through*. Drums in My Heart; Kinda Like You; Through the Years

Thumbs Up! (156) 1934 Autumn in New York; Zing Went the Strings of My Heart

Tillie's Nightmare (77) 1910 Heaven Will Protect the Working Girl; Life Is Only What You Make It After All

The Time, the Place and the Girl (32) 1907 Blow the Smoke Away

Tina 1915 The Violin Song

Tip-Toes (192) 1925 Looking for a Boy; Sweet and Low-Down; That Certain Feeling

Tonight at 8:30 (118) 1936 Has Anybody Seen Our Ship; Play Orchestra Play; You Were There

Tonight's the Night (108) 1914 They Didn't Believe Me

Too Many Girls (249) 1939 Give It Back to the Indians; I Didn't Know What Time It Was; I Like To Recognize the Tune; Love Never Went to College

Topsy and Eva (159) 1924 I Never Had a Mammy; Rememb'ring

Treasure Girl (68) 1928 Feeling I'm Falling; I've Got a Crush on You; K-ra-zy for You; Where's the Boy

A Tree Grows in Brooklyn (270) 1951 based on Betty Smith novel. I'll Buy You a Star; Look Who's Dancing; Love Is the Reason; Make the Man Love Me

A Trip to Chinatown 1892 After the Ball; The Bowery; Do, Do, My Huckleberry Do; Push Dem Clouds Away

Twirly-Whirly (244) 1902 Come Down Ma Evenin' Star

Two for the Show (124) 1940 A House with a Little Red Barn; How High the Moon

Two Little Girls in Blue 1921 Oh Me! Oh My! Oh You!

Two on the Aisle (279) 1951 Hold Me, Hold Me, Hold Me

Under the Counter (27) 1947 The Moment I Saw You

The Unsinkable Molly Brown (532) 1960 Beautiful People of Denver; Chick-a-Pen; Dolce Far Niente; I Ain't Down Yet; Keep-A-Hoppin'

Up and Doing 1938 Falling in Love with Love; Sing for Your Supper; This Can't Be Love

Up and Down Broadway (72) 1910 Chinatown, My Chinatown; Oh, That Beautiful Rag

Up in Central Park (504) 1945 The Big Back Yard; Close as Pages in a Book; When She Walks in the Room

U.S. 1918 Everything Is Peaches Down in Georgia

The Vagabond King (511) 1925 based on Justin Huntly McCarthy play *If I Were King*. Love Me Tonight; Only a Rose; Some Day; Song of the Vagabonds; Waltz Huguette

Vanderbilt Revue (13) 1930 Blue Again

The Velvet Lady (136) 1919 Spooky Ookum

Vera Violetta (112) 1911 The Gaby Glide

Veronique (81) 1905 The Garden of Love

Very Good Eddie (341) 1915 Babes in the Wood; Nodding Roses; On the Shore at Lei Lei; Some Sort of Somebody

Very Warm for May (59) 1939 All in Fun; All the Things You Are; In the Heart of the Dark

Virginia (60) 1937 Roll Away Clouds

Wake Up and Dream (136) 1929 I'm a Gigolo; Let's Do It; She's Such a Comfort to Me; What Is This Thing Called Love

Walk a Little Faster (119) 1932 April in Paris

Walking Happy (161) 1966 based on Harold Brighouse play *Hobson's Choice*. Walking Happy

A Waltz Dream (111) 1908 Love's Roundelay; Sweetest Maid of All; A Waltz Dream

Wang 1891 Ask the Man in the Moon; A Pretty Girl

Watch Your Step (175) 1914 Play a Simple Melody

Weekend (8) 1983 Cuddle In; Hangin' Out the Window

West Side Story (981) 1957 suggested by Shakespeare's *Romeo and Juliet*. America; A Boy Like That; Cool; Gee, Officer Krupke!; I Feel Pretty; Jet Song; Maria; One Hand, One Heart; Something's Coming; Somewhere; Tonight

What Makes Sammy Run? (540) 1964 based on Budd Schulberg novel. A Room Without Windows

What's in a Name (87) 1920 A Young Man's Fancy

When Johnny Comes Marching Home (71) 1909 My Own United States

When Sweet Sixteen (12) 1910 The Wild Rose

Where's Charley? (792) 1948 based on Brandon Thomas play *Charley's Aunt*. Make a Miracle; My Darling, My Darling; Once in Love with Amy; Pernambuco

The White Eagle (48) 1927 based on Edwin Milton Royle play *The Squaw Man*. Gather the Rose; Give Me One Hour; Regimental Song

White Horse Inn (223) 1936 Goodbye, Au Revoir, Auf Wiedersehn; The White Horse Inn; Your Eyes

Whoopee (379) 1928 based on the Owen Davis play *The Nervous Wreck*. I'm Bringing a Red, Red Rose; Love Me or Leave Me; Makin' Whoopee; My Blackbirds Are Bluebirds Now

The Wild Rose (61) 1926 I'm Unlucky; Look For the Silver Lining; We'll Have a Kingdom; Wild Rose

Wildcat (172) 1960 Angelina; Give a Little Whistle; Hey Look Me Over; What Takes My Fancy

The Wildflower 1923 April Blossoms; Bambalina; Wildflower

Will O' The Whispers 1927 The Man I Love; Miss Annabel Lee; My Blue Heaven; The Song Is Ended But the Melody Lingers On; When Day Is Done

Winged Victory (212) 1943 The Army Air Corps Song

Wish You Were Here (598) 1952 based on Arthur Kober play *Having a Wonderful Time*. Everybody Loves Somebody; Wish You Were Here

The Wiz (1,672) 1975 based on L. Frank Baum novel *The Wonderful Wizard of Oz*. Believe in Yourself; Ease On Down the Road; The Feeling We Once Had; He's the Wizard; Home; No Bad News

The Wizard of Oz (293) 1903 based on L. Frank Baum novel *The Wonderful Wizard of Oz*. Hurray for Baffin's Bay; Sammy

The Wizard of the Nile 1895 My Angeline; Star Light, Star Bright

Woman of the Year (770) 1981 based on the MGM film by Ring Lardner, Jr. The Grass Is Always Greener

The Wonder Bar (76) 1931 Elizabeth; Oh Donna Clara; Tell Me I'm Forgiven

Wonderful Town (559) 1953 based on Ruth McKenney stories and the Joseph Fields and Jerome Chodorov play *My Sister Eileen*. It's Love; Ohio; A Quiet Girl

Woodland (83) 1904 The Tale of the Turtle Dove

Words and Music 1935 Mad About the Boy; Mad Dogs and Englishmen

A Yankee at the Court of King Arthur, *see* **A Connecticut Yankee**

The Yankee Consul (115) 1904 Ain't It Funny What a Difference Just a Few Hours Make; My San Domingo Maid

The Yankee Girl (92) 1910 I've Got Rings on My Fingers

The Yankee Prince (28) 1908 Come On Down Town

The Yearling (3) 1965 based on Marjorie Kinnan Rawlings novel. I'm All Smiles; Why Did I Choose You

Yip! Yip! Yaphank (32) 1918 Mandy; Oh, How I Hate To Get Up in the Morning

Yokel Boy (208) 1939 The Beer Barrel Polka; Comes Love

You Never Know (78) 1938 based on Siegfried Geyer play *Candle Light*. At Long Last Love

You Said It (192) 1931 Sweet and Hot

Your Arms Too Short To Box with God (149) 1980 Come On Down

Your Own Thing (937) 1968 suggested by Shakespeare's *Twelfth Night*. Do Your Own Thing; When You're Young and in Love

You're a Good Man, Charlie Brown (1,597) 1967 based on Charles M. Schulz comic strip. You're a Good Man, Charlie Brown

You're in Love (167) 1917 You're in Love

Yours Is My Heart (36) 1946 Yours Is My Heart Alone

Ziegfeld Follies of 1908 (120) 1908 Shine On Harvest Moon

Ziegfeld Follies of 1909 (64) 1909 By the Light of the Silvery Moon

Ziegfeld Follies of 1911 (80) 1911 Be My Little Baby Bumblebee

Ziegfeld Follies of 1912 (88) 1912 Down in Dear Old New Orleans; Row, Row, Row

Ziegfeld Follies of 1913 (96) 1913 Isle d'Amour; A Little Love, A Little Kiss; Peg O'My Heart

Ziegfeld Follies of 1915 (104) 1915 Hello Frisco Hello

Ziegfeld Follies of 1916 (112) 1916 Oh! How She Could Yacki, Hacki, Wicki, Wacki, Woo

Ziegfeld Follies of 1919 (171) 1919 Mandy; My Baby's

Arms; A Pretty Girl Is Like a Melody; Sweet Sixteen; Tulip Time; Would You Rather Be a Colonel with an Eagle on Your Shoulder, or a Private with a Chicken on Your Knee?; You'd Be Surprised

Ziegfeld Follies of 1920 (123) 1920 All She'd Say Was Umh Hum; Hold Me; The Love Boat; Tell Me Little Gypsy

Ziegfeld Follies of 1921 (119) 1921 My Man; Second Hand Rose

Ziegfeld Follies of 1922 1922 Mister Gallagher and Mister Shean; My Rambler Rose; 'Neath the South Sea Moon; Some Sweet Day; Throw Me a Rose

Ziegfeld Follies of 1923 (333) 1923 Oh Gee, Oh Gosh, Oh Golly I'm in Love

Ziegfeld Follies of 1927 (167) 1927 Shaking the Blues Away

Ziegfeld Follies of 1931 (165) 1931 Do the New York; Half-Castle Woman; Shine On Harvest Moon

Ziegfeld Follies of 1934 (182) 1934 The House Is Haunted; The Last Round-Up; Suddenly; Wagon Wheels; What Is There To Say

Ziegfeld Follies of 1936–37 (112) 1936 I Can't Get Started; I Love the Likes of You; Words Without Music

Ziegfeld Follies of 1957 (123) 1957 Mangos

Ziegfeld Midnight Frolic, 1920 1920 Rose of Washington Square

Ziegfeld's American Revue of 1926 1926 Florida, the Moon and You

Zig-Zag 1917 Over There

Zorba (362) 1983 based on the novel by Nikos Kazantzakis. Life Is; The Top of the Hill; Why Can't I Speak

2. SILENT FILMS

''There never was a *silent* film. We'd finish a picture, show it in one of our projection rooms, and come out shattered. It would be awful. We'd have high hopes for the picture, work our heads off on it, and the result was always the same. Then we'd show it in a theatre, with a girl down in the pit pounding away at a piano, and there would be all the difference in the world. Without that music, there wouldn't have been a movie industry at all.''

Irving Thalberg

While most of the music used by the pianists and organists who accompanied silent movies was improvised, particularly from the classics, the following themes came to be associated with the films below, though there was no soundtrack as such. Non-specific silent standards including ''Mysterioso Pizzicato'' and ''Danse Macabre,'' too numerous to mention here, are listed alphabetically by title in Part V.

The Adventures of Pauline (serial) 1914 As Pearl White narrowly escaped her weekly encounters with death, pianists were playing ''Poor Pauline,'' a song by writer Charles McCarron and composer Raymond Walker, written for the occasion.

The Birth of a Nation 1915 Audiences swooned during the love scenes between Lillian Gish and Henry B. Walthall while hearing ''The Perfect Song,'' words by Clarence Lucas and music by James Carl Breil. Later, in 1928, ''Amos 'n' Andy'' chose for their opening radio theme this same melody.

The Covered Wagon 1923 Two songs are generally associated with this early western, "Covered Wagon Days," words and music by Will Morrissey and Joe Burrows and "Westward Ho!," words and music by R.A. Barnet and Hugo Rosenfeld.

Lilac Time 1928 Writer L. Wolfe Gilbert and composer Nathaniel Shilkret wrote especially for this film starring Colleen Moore, the song "Jeannine I Dream of Lilac Time."

Mickey 1918 For this film starring Mabel Normand, writers

Harry H. Williams and Neil Moret wrote, respectively, words and music to their title song of the same name.

Ramona 1927 This film adaptation of Helen Hunt Jackson's novel inspired writer L. Wolfe Gilbert and composer Mabel Wayne to write their title song. The film's star, Dolores Del Rio, promoted their song on a national personal appearance tour.

What Price Glory? 1926 Both words and music for "Charmaine" were written by Lew Pollack and Erno Rapee for this film, starring Victor McLaglen and Edmund Lowe.

3. MUSICAL FILMS

A total of 913 films are represented in this division. For further information about this division, refer to notes at the front of this Part.

Aaron Slick from Punkin Crick (1951) I'd Like To Baby You; Marshmallow Moon

After the Ball (1957) The Army of Today's Alright; Following in Father's Footsteps; Jolly Good Luck to the Girl Who Loves a Soldier

Alexander's Ragtime Band (1938) Alexander's Ragtime Band; All Alone; Blue Skies; Easter Parade; Everybody Step; Everybody's Doing It; Heat Wave; Lazy; Marie; Now It Can Be Told; Oh, How I Hate To Get Up in the Morning; A Pretty Girl Is Like a Melody; Remember; Say It with Music; That International Rag; When the Midnight Choo-Choo Leaves for Alabam'

Ali Baba Goes to Town (1937) Twilight in Turkey

Alice in Wonderland (1933) Alice in Wonderland

Alice in Wonderland (1951) Alice in Wonderland; I'm Late; A Very Merry UnBirthday to You

All the King's Horses (1935) A Little White Gardenia

Along Came Youth (1931) Any Time's the Time To Fall in Love; My Ideal

Along the Navajo Trail (1945) Along the Navajo Trail; Cool Water

Always a Bridesmaid (1943) Thanks for the Buggy Ride

Always in My Heart (1942) Always in My Heart

Always Leave Them Laughing (1949) By the Light of the Silvery Moon; Embraceable You

An American in Paris (1951) An American in Paris; By Strauss; Concerto in F; Embraceable You; I Got Rhythm; I'll Build a Stairway to Paradise; Liza; Nice Work If You Can Get It; Our Love Is Here To Stay; 'S Wonderful

Anchors Aweigh (1945) I Begged Her; I Fall in Love Too Easily; Jalousie; My Heart Sings

And the Angels Sing (1944) And the Angels Sing; His Rocking Horse Ran Away; It Could Happen to You

Andy Hardy Meets a Debutante (1940) Alone; I'm Nobody's Baby

Animal Crackers (1930) Collegiate; Hooray for Captain

Spalding; Some of These Days; Watching the Clouds Roll By

Annie Get Your Gun (1950) Anything You Can Do; Doin' What Comes Natur'lly; The Girl That I Marry; I Got Lost in His Arms; I Got the Sun in the Morning; I'm an Indian Too; My Defenses Are Down; There's No Business Like Show Business; They Say It's Wonderful; Who Do You Love, I Hope; You Can't Get a Man with a Gun

Anything Goes (1936) All Through the Night; Anything Goes; Blow Gabriel Blow; The Gypsy in Me; I Get a Kick Out of You; It's De-Lovely; My Heart and I; You're the Top

Anything Goes (1956) All Through the Night; Anything Goes; Blow Gabriel Blow; The Gypsy in Me; I Get a Kick Out of You; You're the Top

Apache Country (1952) Cold Cold Heart

Applause (1929) I've Got a Feeling I'm Falling; Yaaka Hula Hickey Dula

April in Paris (1953) April in Paris; I'm Gonna Ring the Bell Tonight; That's What Makes Paris Paree

April Love (1957) April Love

April Showers (1948) April Showers; Carolina in the Morning; It's Tulip Time in Holland

Around the World (1944) Candlelight and Wine

Artists and Models (1937) I Have Eyes; Stop! You're Breaking My Heart; Whispers in the Dark

At War with the Army (1950) The Navy Gets the Gravy and the Army Gets the Beans

Atlantic City (1944) On a Sunday Afternoon

Babes in Arms (1939) All At Once; Babes in Arms; God's Country; Good Morning; I Cried for You; I Wish I Were in Love Again; Ida, Sweet as Apple Cider; I'm Just Wild About Harry; Johnny One Note; The Lady Is a Tramp; My Funny Valentine; Way Out West; Where or When; You Are My Lucky Star

Babes in Toyland (1934) I Can't Do the Sum; The March of the Toys; Toyland; Who's Afraid of the Big Bad Wolf

Babes in Toyland (1961) The March of the Toys; Toyland

Babes on Broadway (1941) Franklin D. Roosevelt Jones; How About You; Mama Yo Quiero

Bachelor of Arts (1934) Easy Come, Easy Go

Balalaika (1939) At the Balalaika

Bambi (1942) Love Is a Song That Never Ends

The Band Wagon (1953) Dancing in the Dark; I Guess I'll Have to Change My Plan; I Love Louisa; Louisiana Hayride; New Sun in the Sky; A Shine on Your Shoes; That's Entertainment

The Barkleys of Broadway (1949) My One and Only Highland Fling; They Can't Take That Away from Me

Bathing Beauty (1944) Tico Tico

Beau James (1957) The Sidewalks of New York; Someone To Watch over Me; When We're Alone; Will You Love Me in December as You Do in May

Because You're Mine (1952) All the Things You Are; Because You're Mine; Granada; The Lord's Prayer; You Do Something to Me

Behind the Eight Ball (1942) Mister Five By Five

The Belle of New York (1952) Baby Doll

Belle of the Nineties (1934) My Old Flame

Belle of the Yukon (1944) Sleigh Ride in July

Belles on Their Toes (1952) Linger Awhile; Three O'Clock in the Morning; When You Wore a Tulip and I Wore a Big Red Rose; Whispering

Bells Are Ringing (1960) Bells Are Ringing; Hello, Hello There; Just in Time; Long Before I Knew You; The Party's Over

Bells of Capistrano (1927) America, the Beautiful; At Sundown; Don't Bite the Hand That's Feeding You; Forgive Me

The Benny Goodman Story (1956) And the Angels Sing; Avalon; Bugle Call Rag; China Boy; Goody Goody; I Got It Bad and That Ain't Good; If You Knew Susie Like I Know Susie; I'm Comin' Virginia; It's Been So Long; Jersey Bounce; Lullaby in Rhythm; Memories of You; Moonglow; On the Sunny Side of the Street; One O'Clock Jump; S-H-I-N-E; Sing, Sing, Sing, Sing; Stomping at the Savoy; Taking a Chance on Love; You Turned the Tables on Me

Best Foot Forward (1943) Buckle Down Winsocki; Ev'ry Time; Shady Lady Bird; That's How I Love the Blues; Wish I May

The Best Things in Life Are Free (1956) The Best Things in Life Are Free; The Birth of the Blues; Button Up Your Overcoat; Good News; Here Am I—Broken Hearted; If I Had a Talking Picture of You; I'm a Dreamer; It All Depends on You; Just a Memory; Just Imagine; Life Is Just a Bowl of Cherries; Lucky Day; My Sin; Sonny Boy; Sunny Side Up; The Thrill Is Gone; Together

Betty Co-Ed (1930) Betty Co-Ed

Betty Co-Ed (1946) Betty Co-Ed; Put the Blame on Mame

Big Boy (1930) Down South; The Handicap March

The Big Broadcast (1932) Crazy People; Here Lies Love; It Was So Beautiful; Kickin' the Gong Around; Please; Tiger Rag; Where the Blue of the Night Meets the Gold of the Day

The Big Broadcast of 1936 (1935) I Wished on the Moon; Miss Brown to You

The Big Broadcast of 1938 (1938) Thanks for the Memory

Big City Blues (1932) My Baby Just Cares for Me

The Big Pond (1930) You Brought a New Kind of Love to Me

The Big Sombrero (1949) My Adobe Hacienda

The Big Store (1940) The Tenement Symphony

Birth of the Blues (1941) The Birth of the Blues; By the Light of the Silvery Moon; Cuddle Up a Little Closer, Lovey Mine; The Memphis Blues; My Melancholy Baby; S-H-I-N-E; St. James Infirmary; St. Louis Blues; That's Why They Call Me ''Shine''; Tiger Rag; Wait 'Til the Sun Shines, Nellie; The Waiter and the Porter and the Upstairs Maid; Waiting at the Church

Bitter Sweet (1940) Dear Little Café; If Love Were All; I'll See You Again; Tokay; Zigeuner

Blonde Crazy (1931) When Your Lover Has Gone

Blondie of the Follies (1932) Three on a Match

Blue Hawaii (1961) Can't Help Falling in Love

Blue Skies (1929) I'll See You in C-U-B-A; You'd Be Surprised

Blue Skies (1946) All By Myself; Blue Skies; A Couple of Song and Dance Men; Everybody Step; Heat Wave; How Deep Is the Ocean; I'll See You in C-U-B-A; I've Got My Captain Working for Me Now; A Pretty Girl Is Like a Melody; Puttin' On the Ritz; Russian Lullaby; White Christmas; You Keep Coming Back Like a Song

The Blues Brothers I Love You Just the Way You Are; Minnie the Moocher; (Theme from) The Pink Panther; (Theme from) Rawhide

Blues in the Night (1941) Blues in the Night; This Time the Dream's on Me

Born to Dance (1936) Easy To Love; Hey, Babe, Hey!; I've Got You Under My Skin; Rap, Tap on Wood; Rolling Home; Swingin' the Jinx Away

Born To Sing (1942) Alone; Ballad for Americans; You Are My Lucky Star

Both Ends of the Candle April in Paris; Avalon; Bill; Body and Soul; Breezin' Along with the Breeze; Can't Help Lovin' Dat Man; Deep Night; Do Do Do; Don't Ever Leave Me; I Can't Give You Anything But Love; If You Were the Only Girl in the World; I'll Get By; I've Got a Crush on You; Just a Memory; The Love Nest; The Man I Love; More Than You Know; My Melancholy Baby; On the Sunny Side of the Street; The One I Love Belongs to Somebody Else; Someone To Watch Over Me; Something To Remember You By; Speak to Me of Love; Why Was I Born

The Boys from Syracuse (1940) Falling in Love with Love; Sing for Your Supper; This Can't Be Love; You Have Cast Your Shadow on the Sea

Brigadoon (1954) Almost Like Being in Love; Come to Me, Bend to Me; The Heather on the Hill; I'll Go Home with Bonnie Jean; There But For You Go I

Bright Lights (1931) Chinatown, My Chinatown

Broadway (1929) Dinah; I'm Just Wild About Harry

Broadway (1942) Alabamy Bound; The Darktown Strutters' Ball; I'm Just Wild About Harry; Some of These Days; Sweet Georgia Brown; Yes Sir, That's My Baby

Broadway Gondolier (1935) Lulu's Back in Town; The Rose in Her Hair

Broadway Melody (1929) Broadway Melody; Give My Regards to Broadway; The Wedding of the Painted Doll; You Were Meant for Me

Broadway Melody of 1936 (1935) Broadway Rhythm; Give My Regards to Broadway; I've Got a Feeling You're Fooling; You Are My Lucky Star

Broadway Melody of 1937 (1937) Yours and Mine

Broadway Melody of 1938 (1937) You Made Me Love You

Broadway Melody of 1940 (1940) Begin the Beguine; Give My Regards to Broadway; I Concentrate on You; I've Got My Eyes on You

Broadway Rhythm (1944) Amor; Irresistible You; Milkman Keep Those Bottles Quiet; Pretty Baby

Broadway Through a Keyhole (1933) Doin' the Uptown Lowdown; You're My Past, Present and Future

Broadway to Hollywood (1933) Come Down Ma Evenin' Star; Ma Blushin' Rosie

Buck Benny Rides Again (1940) Say It (Over and Over Again)

Buck Privates (1941) Boogie Woogie Bugle Boy; I'll Be with You in Apple Blossom Time

By the Beautiful Sea Alone Too Long

By the Light of the Silvery Moon (1953) Ain't We Got Fun; Be My Little Baby Bumblebee; By the Light of the Silvery Moon

Bye Bye Birdie (1963) Kids; A Lot of Livin' To Do; Older and Wiser; One Boy; Put On a Happy Face; Rosie; The Telephone Hour

Cabaret (1972) Cabaret; If You Could See Her; Married; Maybe This Time; Mein Herr; Money; Two Ladies; Willkommen

Cabin in the Sky (1943) Cabin in the Sky; Happiness Is a Thing Called Joe; S-H-I-N-E; Taking a Chance on Love

Cain and Mabel (1936) I'll Sing You a Thousand Love Songs

Calamity Jane (1953) The Deadwood Stage; Secret Love

Call Me Madam (1959) The Best Thing for You; Hostess with the Mostes' on the Ball; It's a Lovely Day Tomorrow; Marrying for Love; Something To Dance About; That International Rag; You're Just in Love

Call Me Mister (1951) Along with Me; Call Me Mister; Military Life; South America, Take It Away; Yuletide, Park Avenue

Call of the Canyon (1942) Boots and Saddle; The Call of the Canyon; Somebody Else Is Taking My Place

Camelot (1967) Camelot; Follow Me; How To Handle a Woman; I Loved You Once in Silence; I Wonder What the King Is Doing Tonight; If Ever I Would Leave You; The Lusty Month of May; The Simple Joys of Maidenhood; Then You May Take Me to the Fair; What Do the Simple Folk Do

The Camels Are Coming (1935) Who's Been Polishing the Sun

Can-Can (1960) Allez-vous En; C'est Magnifique; I Am in Love; I Love Paris; It's All Right with Me; Just One of Those Things; Let's Fall in Love; You Do Something to Me

Can't Help Singing (1944) Can't Help Singing; More and More

Captain January (1936) At the Codfish Ball

Carefree (1938) Change Partners; I Used To Be Color Blind; The Night Is Filled with Music

Careless Lady (1932) All of Me

Carolina Blues (1944) There Goes That Song Again

Carousel (1956) Carousel Waltz; If I Loved You; June Is Bustin' Out All Over; Soliloquy; This Was a Real Nice Clambake; What's the Use of Wond'rin'; When I Marry Mister Snow; When the Children Are Asleep; You'll Never Walk Alone

Casa Mañana (1951) Cielito Lindo; I Hear a Rhapsody

Casbah (1948) For Every Man There's a Woman; Hooray for Love; It Was Written in the Stars; What's Good About Goodbye

Casino de Paree (1935) About a Quarter to Nine; She's a Latin from Manhattan

The Cat and the Fiddle (1934) Ha-Cha-Cha; I Watch the Love Parade; The Night Was Made for Love; One Moment Alone; Poor Pierrot; She Didn't Say Yes; Try To Forget

Centennial Summer (1946) All Through the Day; In Love in Vain; Two Hearts Are Better Than One; Up with the Lark

The Champagne Waltz (1937) The Champagne Waltz

The Charm School I Feel Like a Feather in the Breeze; You Hit the Spot

Chasing Rainbows (1930) Happy Days Are Here Again

Check and Double Check (1930) Ring Dem Bells; Three Little Words

Children of Dreams (1931) If I Had a Girl Like You

Chip Off the Old Block (1944) My Song

The Chocolate Soldier (1941) The Letter Song; My Hero

Cinderella (1949) Bibbidi-Bobbodi-Boo; Cinderella; A Dream Is a Wish Your Heart Makes

Cinderella Jones (1946) When the One You Love Simply Won't Love Back

The Clock Strikes Eight (1935) In the Middle of a Kiss

Club Havana Besame Mucho; Tico Tico

Cockeyed Cavaliers (1934) Coquette

The Cockeyed World (1929) Hinky Dinky Parlay Voo; K-K-K-Katy; Over There; The Rose of No Man's Land; Semper Fidelis; You're the Cream in My Coffee

Cocoanut Grove (1938) Cocoanut Grove; Says My Heart; You Leave Me Breathless

College Coach (1933) Just One More Chance

College Humor (1933) Down the Old Ox Road; Learn To Croon

College Rhythm (1934) College Rhythm; Stay as Sweet as You Are; Take a Number from One to Ten

Collegiate (1936) I Feel Like a Feather in the Breeze; You Hit the Spot

Come Back to Me (1945) Here Comes Heaven Again

Come Out of the Pantry (1935) Everything Stops for Tea

Coney Island (1943) Put Your Arms Around Me Honey

A Connecticut Yankee (1931) Can't You Do a Friend a Favor; My Heart Stood Still; On a Desert Island with Thee; Thou Swell; To Keep My Love Alive

Copacabana (1947) Je Vous Aime; Tico Tico

Cover Girl (1944) Long Ago and Far Away; Sure Thing

Cow Town (1949) Powder Your Face with Sunshine

Cowboy Canteen (1944) Lazy River

Cowboy from Brooklyn (1938) Ride, Tenderfoot, Ride

Cowboy Serenade (1942) Cowboy Serenade

The Crooner (1932) Three's a Crowd

Cross My Heart (1946) Love Is the Darndest Thing

The Cuban Love Song (1931) Cuban Love Song

Cuban Pete (1946) The Breeze and I; Cuban Pete; El Cumbanchero

The Cuckoos (1930) All Alone Monday; Dancing the Devil Away; I Love You So Much

Curly Top (1935) Animal Crackers in My Soup

Daddy Long Legs (1955) Dream; Something's Gotta Give

Dames (1934) The Girl at the Ironing Board; I Only Have Eyes for You

Damn Yankees (1958) Heart; A Little Brains—A Little Talent; Shoeless Joe from Hannibal, Mo.; Two Lost Souls; Whatever Lola Wants

Damsel in Distress (1937) A Foggy Day; I Can't Be Bothered Now; Nice Work If You Can Get It; Things Are Looking Up

Dance Fools Dance (1931) The Free and Easy Hour of Parting; A Gay Caballero; Go Home and Tell Your Mother

The Dance of Life (1929) True Blue Lou

Dancing in the Dark (1950) Dancing in the Dark; I Love Louisa; New Sun in the Sky; Something to Remember You By

The Dancing Lady (1933) Everything I Have Is Yours

Dancing on a Dime (1940) Dancing on a Dime; I Hear Music

Dancing Pirate (1936) Are You My Love

Dancing Sweeties (1930) The Kiss Waltz

The Dancing Years (1939) I Can Give You the Starlight; My Dearest Dear; My Life Belongs to You; Primrose; Waltz of My Heart

A Date with Judy (1948) Cuanto Le Gusta; It's a Most Unusual Day

A Day at the Circus (1939) Lydia, the Tattooed Lady

A Day at the Races (1937) All God's Chillun Got Rhythm

Deep in My Heart (1954) Auf Wiederseh'n; Deep in My Heart, Dear; The Desert Song; Lover Come Back to Me; One Alone; One Kiss; Serenade; Softly, As in a Morning Sunrise; Stouthearted Men; When I Grow Too Old To Dream; Will You Remember (Sweetheart)

Delicious (1931) Blah, Blah, Blah; Delishious

Der Fuehrer's Face (1943) Der Fuehrer's Face

The Desert Song (1929) The Desert Song; The Riff Song; Romance

The Desert Song (1944) The Desert Song; One Alone; The Riff Song; Romance

The Desert Song (1952) The Desert Song; One Alone; The Riff Song; Romance

Diamond Horseshoe (1945) I Wish I Knew; In Acapulco; The More I See You

Dimples (1936) Picture Me Without You

Disc Jockey (1951) Oh Look At Me Now; The Ole Grey Goose; The Roving Kind

Dixie (1943) If You Please; Sunday, Monday or Always

Do You Love Me? (1946) Do You Love Me?

Doctor Dolittle (1967) Talk to the Animals

Doctor Rhythm (1938) My Heart Is Taking Lessons; On the Sentimental Side

Doll Face (1946) Dig You Later; Here Comes Heaven Again

The Dolly Sisters (1945) Arrah Go On; I'm Gonna Go Back to Oregon; Carolina in the Morning; The Darktown Strutters' Ball; Give Me the Moonlight, Give Me the Girl; I Can't Begin To Tell You; I'm Always Chasing Rainbows; Oh! Frenchy; On the Mississippi; Smiles

Don't Fence Me In (1945) Along the Navajo Trail; Don't Fence Me In; The Last Round-Up; My Little Buckaroo; Tumbling Tumbleweeds

Don't Knock the Rock (1957) Long Tall Sally

Double or Nothing (1937) The Moon Got in My Eyes

Down Argentine Way (1940) Down Argentine Way; Mama Yo Quiero; South American Way

Down Dakota Way (1949) Candy Kisses

Drum Crazy Cherokee; I Love My Baby; Indiana; Memories of You; Royal Garden Blues; Song of India; 'Way Down Yonder in New Orleans

Du Barry Was a Lady (1943) Do I Love You; Friendship; Katie Went to Haiti; Well, Did You Evah

Dumbo (1941) When I Saw an Elephant Fly

D'ye Ken John Peel (1932) Old Sam

The East Side of Heaven (1939) East Side of Heaven; Hang Your Heart on a Hickory Limb; That Sly Old Gentleman from Featherbed Lane

Easter Parade (1948) Better Luck Next Time; A Couple of Swells; Easter Parade; Everybody's Doing It; A Fella with an Umbrella; The Girl on the Magazine Cover; I Love a Piano; I Want To Go Back to Michigan—Down on the Farm; It Only Happens When I Dance with You; Shaking the Blues Away; Snooky Ookums; Steppin' Out with My Baby; When the Midnight Choo-Choo Leaves for Alabam'

Easy To Love (1953) Easy To Love

Easy To Wed (1946) Come Closer to Me

The Eddie Cantor Story (1954) Bye Bye Blackbird; How Ya Gonna Keep 'Em Down on the Farm; Ida, Sweet as Apple Cider; If You Knew Susie Like I Know Susie; Makin' Whoopee; Now's the Time To Fall In Love; Pretty Baby; Shine on

Harvest Moon; Yes Sir, That's My Baby; You Must Have Been a Beautiful Baby

Eddie Foy and the Seven Little Foys, *see* **The Seven Little Foys**

The Eddy Duchin Story (1956) Am I Blue; April Showers; The Blue Room; Body And Soul; Brazil; Exactly Like You; I'll Take Romance; It Must Be True; Just One of Those Things; Let's Fall in Love; The Man I Love; Margie; On the Sunny Side of the Street; S-H-I-N-E; Smiles; Star Dust; Three O'Clock in the Morning; Till We Meet Again; Time on My Hands; La Vie en Rose; What Is This Thing Called Love; Whispering; Will You Love Me in December As You Do in May; You're My Everything

Embarrassing Moments (1934) Brother, Can You Spare a Dime

The Emperor Waltz (1948) I Kiss Your Hand, Madame; The Whistler and His Dog

Ever Since Eve (1937) Shine On Harvest Moon

Evergreen (1935) Dancing on the Ceiling; Over My Shoulder

Every Night at Eight (1935) I Feel a Song Coming On; I'm in the Mood for Love

Everybody's Cheering Take Me Out to the Ball Game

Everything I Have Is Yours (1952) Everything I Have Is Yours

The Fabulous Dorseys (1947) At Sundown; Everybody's Doing It; Green Eyes; Marie; The Object of My Affection

Fancy Pants (1950) Home Cookin'

Fantasia (1940) Ave Maria; Dance of the Hours; A Night on Bald Mountain; The Nutcracker Suite; Rites of Spring; The Sorcerer's Apprentice; Waltz of the Flowers

Feather Your Nest (1937) Leaning on a Lamp Post

Ferdinand the Bull (1938) Ferdinand the Bull

Feudin', Fussin' and A-Fightin' (1948) Feudin' and Fightin'; Me and My Shadow; S'posin'

Fiddler on the Roof (1971) Anatevka; Do You Love Me; If I Were a Rich Man; Matchmaker, Matchmaker; Sabbath Prayer; Sunrise Sunset; To Life; Tradition

Fiesta (1947) La Golondrina

Fifty Million Frenchmen (1931) Paree (What Did You Do to Me); You Do Something to Me; You Don't Know Paree (Paris); You Remind Me of My Mother; You've Got That Thing

52nd Street (1937) I Still Love To Kiss You Goodnight

The Firefly (1937) The Donkey Serenade; Giannina Mia; Love Is Like a Firefly; Sympathy; When a Maid Comes Knocking at Your Heart

First a Girl (1936) Everything's in Rhythm with My Heart

First Love (1939) Amapola

The Five Pennies (1959) Billy Bailey Won't You Please Come Home; Indiana; The Music Goes 'Round and 'Round; Runnin' Wild

Flashdance (1983) (Theme from) Flashdance (What a Feeling); Maniac

The Fleet's In (1942) Arthur Murray Taught Me Dancing in a Hurry; The Fleet's In; I Remember You; Not Mine; Tangerine

Flirtation Walk (1934) Flirtation Walk; Mister and Mrs. Is the Name

Flower Drum Song (1962) Don't Marry Me; A Hundred Million Miracles; I Enjoy Being a Girl; Love Look Away; Sunday; You Are Beautiful

Flying Down to Rio (1933) Carioca; Flying Down to Rio; Music Makes Me; Orchids in the Moonlight

Folies Bergere (1935) I Don't Stand a Ghost of a Chance with You; Rhythm of the Rain

Follow the Band (1943) The Army Air Corps Song; He's My Guy; My Devotion

Follow the Boys (1944) Besame Mucho; Beyond the Blue Horizon; I Feel a Song Coming On; I'll Get By; I'll See You in My Dreams; I'll Walk Alone; Is You Is or Is You Ain't My Baby; Shoo-Shoo Baby; Some of These Days; Sweet Georgia Brown

Follow the Fleet (1936) Get Thee Behind Me Satan; I'm Putting All My Eggs in One Basket; Let Yourself Go; Let's Face the Music and Dance; We Saw the Sea

Follow Thru (1930) Button Up Your Overcoat

Footlight Parade (1933) By a Waterfall; Shanghai Lil

For Me and My Gal (1942) After You've Gone; Ballin the Jack; For Me and My Gal; How Ya Gonna Keep 'Em Down on the Farm; Oh You Beautiful Doll; Sailor's Hornpipe; When You Wore a Tulip and I Wore a Big Red Rose; Where Do We Go from Here

Forty-Second Street (1933) Forty-Second Street; Shuffle Off to Buffalo; Young and Healthy; You're Getting To Be a Habit with Me

Four Jills and a Jeep (1944) How Blue the Night

Freddie Steps Out (1946) Don't Blame Me

Free and Easy (1930) The Free and Easy Hour of Parting

Funny Face (1957) Clap Yo' Hands; Funny Face; How Long Has This Been Going On; Let's Kiss and Make Up; 'S Wonderful

Funny Girl (1968) Don't Rain on My Parade; Funny Girl; I'd Rather Be Blue over You; I'm the Greatest Star; My Man; People; You Are Woman

Funny Lady (1975) More Than You Know

A Funny Thing Happened on the Way to the Forum (1966) Comedy Tonight; Everybody Ought To Have a Maid; Lovely

G.I. Blues (1960) Blue Suede Shoes; Wooden Heart

The Galloping Major (1951) The Galloping Major

The Gang's All Here (1943) No Love, No Nothing

Gangway (1937) Gangway

Garden of the Moon (1938) The Girl Friend of the Whirling Dervish; Love Is Where You Find It; The Umbrella Man

The Gay City, *see* **Las Vegas Nights**

The Gay Divorcee (1934) The Continental; Don't Let It Bother You; A Needle in a Haystack; Night and Day

Gay Imposter (1938) Day Dreaming

Gay Purr-ee (1962) Little Drops of Rain

The Gay Ranchero (1948) A Gay Ranchero; Granada; You Belong to My Heart

Gentlemen Marry Brunettes (1955) Ain't Misbehavin'; Daddy; Have You Met Miss Jones; I Wanna Be Loved by You; I've Got Five Dollars; Miss Annabelle Lee; My Funny Valentine; You're Driving Me Crazy

Gentlemen Prefer Blondes (1953) Bye Bye Baby; Diamonds Are a Girl's Best Friend; A Little Girl from Little Rock

George White's Scandals (1934) Hold My Hand; Life Is Just a Bowl of Cherries; That's Why Darkies Were Born

George White's Scandals of 1935 (1935) It's Time To Say Goodnight

George White's Scandals of 1945 (1945) Life Is Just a Bowl of Cherries; Wishing (Will Make It So)

Get Hep to Love (1942) Siboney

Ghost Catchers (1944) These Foolish Things (Remind Me of You)

Gigi (1958) Gigi; I Remember It Well; I'm Glad I'm Not Young Anymore; The Night They Invented Champagne; The Parisians; Say a Prayer for Me Tonight; She Is Not Thinking of Me; Thank Heaven for Little Girls

Gilda (1946) Put the Blame on Mame

Girl Crazy (1932) Bidin' My Time; Boy! What Love Has Done to Me!; But Not for Me; Embraceable You; I Got Rhythm

Girl Crazy (1943) Bidin' My Time; Boy! What Love Has Done to Me!; But Not for Me; Embraceable You; Fascinating Rhythm; I Got Rhythm; Treat Me Rough

The Girl from Missouri (1934) A Hundred Years from Today; I've Had My Moments; Thank You for a Lovely Evening

Girl Rush (1955) A Occasional Man

Girls! Girls! Girls! (1962) Return to Sender

The Girls He Left Behind (1943) No Love, No Nothing

Girls' Town (1959) Lonely Boy

Give Me the Simple Life (1945) Give Me the Simple Life

Give Out, Sisters (1942) Pennsylvania Polka

Glad Rag Doll (1929) Glad Rag Doll

Glamorous Night (1935) Fold Your Wings; Glamorous Night; Shine Through My Dreams; When the Gypsy Played

The Glass Mountain (1950) The Legend of the Glass Mountain

The Glenn Miller Story (1954) American Patrol; At Last; Basin Street Blues; Bidin' My Time; Chattanooga Choo Choo; I Know Why; In the Mood; Moonlight Serenade; Pennsylvania 6-5000; A String of Pearls; Tuxedo Junction

Glorifying the American Girl (1930) At Sundown; Blue Skies; I'm Just a Vagabond Lover; Sam, the Old Accordion Man

Go Into Your Dance (1935) About a Quarter to Nine; The Little Things You Used To Do; She's a Latin from Manhattan

Godspell (1973) All Good Gifts; Day by Day; Learn Your Lessons Well

Going Hollywood (1933) Temptation; We'll Make Hay While the Sun Shines

Going My Way (1944) Going My Way; Swinging on a Star; Too-ra-loo-ra-loo-ral, That's an Irish Lullaby

Going Places (1938) Jeepers Creepers

Gold Diggers in Paris (1938) The Latin Quarter

Gold Diggers of Broadway (1929) Painting the Clouds with Sunshine; Tip Toe Through the Tulips

Gold Diggers of 1933 (1933) Pettin' in the Park; Shadow Waltz; We're in the Money

Gold Diggers of 1935 (1935) Lullaby of Broadway; The Words Are in My Heart

Gold Diggers of 1937 (1937) With Plenty of Money and You

The Golden Girl (1951) Never

The Goldwyn Follies (1938) I Love To Rhyme; I Was Doing All Right; Love Walked In; Our Love Is Here To Stay

Good News (1930) The Best Things in Life Are Free; Gee, But I'd Like To Make You Happy; A Girl of the Pi Beta Phi; The Varsity Drag

Good News (1947) The Best Things in Life Are Free; The French Lesson; Gee, But I'd Like To Make You Happy; A Girl of the Pi Beta Phi; Good News; Lucky in Love; The Varsity Drag

Goodnight Vienna (1932) Goodnight Vienna; Just Imagine; Pass That Peace Pipe

The Grasshopper and the Ants (1934) The World Owes Me a Living

Grease (1979) All Choked Up; Freddie My Love; Hopelessly Devoted to You; Look at Me, I'm Sandra Dee; You're the One That I Want

The Great American Broadcast (1941) Alabamy Bound; Give My Regards to Broadway

The Great Caruso (1951) The Loveliest Night of the Year

The Great Schnozzle Inka Dinka Doo

The Great Victor Herbert (1939) Absinthe Frappé; Ah! Sweet Mystery of Life; Al Fresco; All for You; I Might Be Your "Once in a While"; I'm Falling in Love with Someone; A Kiss in the Dark; Kiss Me Again; The March of the Toys; Neapolitan Love Song; Rose of the World; There Once Was an Owl; Thine Alone; To the Land of My Own Romance

The Great Waltz (1938) Du and Du; Tales from the Vienna Woods; Voices of Spring; With All My Heart

The Great Ziegfeld (1936) If You Knew Susie Like I Know Susie; It's Been So Long; My Man; A Pretty Girl Is Like a Melody; You (Gee, But You're Wonderful)

Gulliver's Travels (1940) Faithful Forever; It's a Hap-Hap-Happy Day

Guys and Dolls (1955) Adelaide; Adelaide's Lament; A Bushel and a Peck; Fugue For Tinhorns; Guys and Dolls; If I Were a Bell; I'll Know; I've Never Been in Love Before; Luck Be a Lady; My Time of Day; The Oldest Established; Sit Down, You're Rockin' the Boat; Take Back Your Mink; A Woman in Love

Gypsy (1962) All I Need Is the Girl; Everything's Coming Up Roses; If Momma Was Married; Let Me Entertain You; Little Lamb; Mister Goldstone; Rose's Turn; Small World; Some People; Together Wherever We Go; You Gotta Have a Gimmick; You'll Never Get Away from Me

Hair (1979) Aquarius; Black Boys, White Boys; Easy To Be Hard; Good Morning Starshine; Hair; Let the Sunshine In; Manchester; Where Do I Go

Hallelujah, I'm a Bum (1933) Hallelujah, I'm a Bum; You Are Too Beautiful

Hallelujah, I'm a Tramp, *see* **Hallelujah, I'm a Bum**

Hands Across the Border (1943) Cool Water

Hans Christian Andersen (1952) Anywhere I Wander; I'm Hans Christian Andersen; Inchworm; No Two People; Thumbelina; The Ugly Duckling; Wonderful Copenhagen

Happy Days (1930) La Golondrina

Happy-Go-Lucky (1943) Let's Get Lost; "Murder" He Says

A Hard Day's Night (1964) A Hard Day's Night

The Hard Way (1942) Am I Blue

The Harvey Girls (1946) On the Atchison, Topeka and the Santa Fe; Wait and See

Has Anybody Seen My Gal (1952) Five Foot Two, Eyes of Blue; Gimme a Little Kiss, Will Ya, Huh? It Ain't Gonna Rain No Mo'; Tiger Rag; When the Red, Red Robin Comes Bob, Bob, Bobbin' Along

Hats Off (1936) Twinkle, Twinkle, Little Star

Hawaii Calls (1938) Down Where the Trade Winds Blow

Head Over Heels (1936) Head Over Heels in Love; May I Have the Next Romance with You

Heads Up! (1930) A Ship Without a Sail

The Heart of a Man (1959) The Heart of a Man

Heart of the Rio Grande (1942) Cimarron; Deep in the Heart of Texas

The Heat's On (1943) The U.S. Field Artillery March

Hello, Dolly! (1970) Before the Parade Passes By; Hello, Dolly!; It Only Takes a Moment; It Takes a Woman; Put On Your Sunday Clothes; So Long Dearie

Hello Everybody (1933) Moon Song

Hello, Frisco, Hello (1943) Ragtime Cowboy Joe; You'll Never Know

Hellzapoppin' (1942) G'Bye Now

Help! (1965) Beethoven's Ninth Symphony; 1812 Overture; A Hard Day's Night; Help!; I Need You; Ticket To Ride; You're Gonna Lose That Girl; You've Got To Hide Your Love Away

Here Come the Waves (1944) Ac-cent-tchu-ate the Positive; Here Come the Waves; Let's Take the Long Way Home; That Old Black Magic

Here Comes Cookie (1935) Lazy Moon

Here Comes the Band (1935) Roll Along Prairie Moon

Here Comes the Groom (1951) Bonne Nuit—Goodnight; In the Cool, Cool, Cool of the Evening; Misto Cristofo Columbo

Here Is My Heart (1935) June in January; Love Is Just Around the Corner; With Every Breath I Take

Hey Boy! Hey Girl! (1947) Autumn Leaves; Fever; Lazy River

Hi, Buddy (1943) Take Me in Your Arms

Hi Gaucho (1936) Song of the Open Road

Hi, Good Lookin'! (1944) Aunt Hagar's Blues; Paper Doll

Hi Neighbor (1941) Deep in the Heart of Texas; Hi Neighbor

Hi' Ya Chum (1942) He's My Guy

High Society (1956) I Love You Samantha; Little One; Mind If I Make Love to You; True Love; Well, Did You Evah; Who Wants To Be a Millionaire; You're Sensational

High Society Blues (1930) I'm in the Market for You

High, Wide and Handsome (1937) Can I Forget You; The Folks Who Live on the Hill; High, Wide and Handsome; The Sweetest Sight That I Have Ever Seen; The Things I Want; Will You Marry Me Tomorrow, Maria

Higher and Higher (1944) Ev'ry Sunday Afternoon; From Another World; I Couldn't Sleep a Wink Last Night; It Never Entered My Mind; A Lovely Way To Spend an Evening; The Music Stopped

Hips Hips Hooray (1934) Keep On Doin' What You're Doin'

The Hit Parade (1937) Sweet Heartache; Was It Rain

Hit the Deck (1929) Hallelujah!; Keepin' Myself for You; More Than You Know; Sometimes I'm Happy

Hit the Deck (1955) Ciribiribin; Hallelujah!; I Know That You Know; Sometimes I'm Happy

Hitting a New High (1937) I Hit a New High

Hold That Ghost (1941) Aurora; Sleepy Serenade

Holiday in Havana (1949) I'll Take Romance; Made for Each Other

Holiday in Mexico (1946) I Think of You

Holiday Inn (1942) Abraham; Be Careful It's My Heart; Easter Parade; Happy Holiday; Let's Start the New Year Right; Plenty To Be Thankful For; White Christmas

Hollywood Canteen (1944) Don't Fence Me In; Tumbling Tumbleweeds; We're Having a Baby; What Are You Doing the Rest of Your Life

Hollywood Hotel (1938) Hooray for Hollywood; I'm Like a Fish out of Water

Hollywood Party (1934) I've Had My Moments

Hollywood Revue (of 1929) (1929) Prayer (*see* Blue Moon) Orange Blossom Time; Singin' in the Rain; While Strolling Through the Park One Day; You Were Meant for Me; Your Mother and Mine

Holy Terror (1931) For You; I'm a Dreamer

Honey (1930) Sing You Sinners

Honeychile (1950) Rag Mop

Honeymoon Lane (1931) The Little White House

Honeymoon Lodge (1943) As Long as You're Not in Love with Anyone Else, Why Don't You Fall in Love with Me;

Do I Worry; I Never Knew I Could Love Anybody Like I'm Loving You; I'm Through with Love

Honky Tonk (1929) I'm the Last of the Red-Hot Mamas

Honolulu (1939) Honolulu

Hooray for Love (1935) Hooray For Love; You're an Angel

Hoppity Goes to Town Be My Little Baby Bumblebee

Horse Feathers (1932) Ev'ryone Says "I Love You"

How To Succeed in Business Without Really Trying (1967) (It's) Been a Long Day; Brotherhood of Man; Grand Old Ivy; Happy To Keep His Dinner Warm; How To; I Believe in You; Love from a Heart of Gold; Paris Original; A Secretary Is Not a Toy

I Can't Give You Anything But Love, Baby (1940) I Can't Give You Anything But Love

I Could Go On Singing (1963) I Could Go On Singing

I Dood It (1943) Jericho; Star Eyes; Swinging the Jinx Away; Taking a Chance on Love

I Dream of Jeanie (1952) Come Where My Love Lies Dreaming; De Camptown Races; Jeanie with the Light Brown Hair; Lo! Here the Gentle Lark; My Old Kentucky Home; Oh! Susanna; Old Dog Tray; Old Folks at Home; On Wings of Song; Ring De Banjo

I Dream Too Much (1935) I Dream Too Much; The Jockey on the Carousel

I Married an Angel (1942) I Married an Angel; I'll Tell the Man in the Street; Spring Is Here

I See Ice (1938) In My Little Snapshot Album

I Surrender Dear (1948) I Surrender Dear

I Wonder Who's Kissing Her Now (1947) I Wonder Who's Kissing Her Now

Ice-Capades Revue (1942) The Army Air Corps Song; Song of the Islands; The U.S. Field Artillery March

Iceland (1942) There Will Never Be Another You

I'd Rather Be Rich (1964) Almost There

Idaho (1943) Idaho

If I Had My Way (1940) April Played the Fiddle; If I Had My Way

If I'm Lucky (1946) If I'm Lucky

If You Feel Like Singing Get Happy

I'll Be Your Sweetheart Daisy Bell; The Honeysuckle and the Bee; I'll Be Your Sweetheart

I'll Be Yours (1947) Granada

I'll Cry Tomorrow (1956) Happiness Is a Thing Called Joe; I'm Sitting on Top of the World; Sing You Sinners; When the Red, Red Robin Comes Bob, Bob, Bobbin' Along

I'll Get By (1950) I'll Get By; It's Been a Long, Long Time; I've Got the World on a String; MacNamara's Band; Once in a While; Taking a Chance on Love; There Will Never Be Another You; The Yankee Doodle Blues; You Make Me Feel So Young

I'll Remember April (1941) I'll Remember April

I'll See You in My Dreams (1951) Ain't We Got Fun; Carolina in the Morning; I Never Knew; I Wish I Had a Girl; I'll

See You in My Dreams; Love Me or Leave Me; Makin' Whoopee; Memories; My Buddy; No, No, Nora; Nobody's Sweetheart Now; The One I Love Belongs to Somebody Else; Pretty Baby; Swingin' Down the Lane; Toot Toot Tootsie; Ukulele Lady; Yes Sir, That's My Baby; Your Eyes Have Told Me So

I'll Take Romance (1937) I'll Take Romance

I'm Nobody's Sweetheart Now (1940) Nobody's Sweetheart Now

In Caliente (1935) The Lady in Red

In Old Sacramento (1946) I Can't Tell Why I Love You, But I Do; The Man That Broke the Bank at Monte Carlo; My Gal Is a High Born Lady; Speak to Me of Love; Strike Up the Band—Here Comes a Sailor

In Society (1945) Memory Lane; My Dreams Are Getting Better All the Time

In the Good Old Summertime (1949) I Don't Care; In the Good Old Summer Time; Meet Me Tonight in Dreamland; Play That Barbershop Chord; Put Your Arms Around Me Honey; Wait 'Til the Sun Shines, Nellie

Incendiary Blonde (1945) The Darktown Strutters' Ball; Ida, Sweet as Apple Cider; It Had To Be You; Oh By Jingo, Oh By Gee, You're the Only Girl for Me; Ragtime Cowboy Joe; Row, Row, Row; Sweet Genevieve; What Do You Want To Make Those Eyes at Me For

Innocents of Paris (1929) Louise; Valentine

Irene (1940) Alice Blue Gown; Castle of Dreams; Irene

Irma La Douce (1963) Dis-Donc, Dis-Donc; Irma La Douce; Our Language of Love

Is Everybody Happy (1929) Chinatown, My Chinatown; St. Louis Blues; Tiger Rag; 'Way Down Yonder in New Orleans

Is Everybody Happy (1943) Am I Blue; Cuddle Up a Little Closer, Lovey Mine; I'm Just Wild About Harry; On the Sunny Side of the Street; Pretty Baby

It Happened in Brooklyn (1947) It's the Same Old Dream; Time After Time

It Happened in Nordland (1904) Absinthe Frappé

It Happened in Sun Valley (1941) It Happened in Sun Valley

It Happened One Summer, *see* **State Fair**

It's a Date (1940) Hawaiian War Chant; Love Is All

It's A Great Life (1929) Let a Smile Be Your Umbrella on a Rainy Day; Pack Up Your Troubles in Your Old Kit Bag and Smile, Smile, Smile

It's Great To Be Young (1934) Rhythm Is Our Business

It's in the Air (1939) It's in the Air

It's Love Again (1936) It's Love Again

It's Magic (1948) It's Magic; It's You or No One; Put 'Em in a Box, Tie 'Em with a Ribbon and Throw 'Em in the Deep Blue Sea

Jack's the Boy (1932) The Flies Crawled Up the Window

Jailhouse Rock (1957) Baby I Don't Care; Jailhouse Rock

Jam Session (1944) Brazil; Cherokee; I Can't Give You Anything But Love; "Murder" He Says; St. Louis Blues

Jamboree (1957) Great Balls of Fire

Jazz Dance Ballin' the Jack; Royal Garden Blues

Jazz on a Summers Day Tea for Two

The Jazz Singer (1928) Blue Skies; Dirty Hands, Dirty Face; Kol Nidre; My Mammy; Toot Toot Tootsie

The Jazz Singer (1953) Lover

The Jazz Singer (1980) Hello Again

Jesus Christ Superstar (1973) Everything's Alright; I Don't Know How To Love Him; Jesus Christ Superstar

Jimmy and Sallie (1933) You're My Thrill

The Joe Louis Story (1942) I'll Be Around

Johnny Doughboy (1936) All My Life

Johnny Doughboy (1942) Johnny Doughboy Found a Rose in Ireland; All My Life

Jolson Sings Again (1949) After You've Gone; April Showers; Baby Face; Back in Your Own Backyard; California, Here I Come; Carolina in the Morning; Chinatown, My Chinatown; For Me and My Gal; Give My Regards to Broadway; I Only Have Eyes for You; I'm Just Wild About Harry; I'm Looking Over a Four Leaf Clover; Ma Blushin' Rosie; My Mammy; Pretty Baby; Rock-a-Bye Your Baby with a Dixie Melody; Sonny Boy; Swanee; Toot Toot Tootsie; You Made Me Love You

The Jolson Story (1946) About a Quarter to Nine; The Anniversary Song; April Showers; Avalon; Blue Bell; By the Light of the Silvery Moon; California, Here I Come; I Want a Girl—Just Like the Girl That Married Dear Old Dad; I'm Sitting on Top of the World; Is It True What They Say About Dixie; Let Me Sing and I'm Happy; Liza; Ma Blushin' Rosie; My Mammy; On the Banks of the Wabash Far Away; Rock-a-Bye Your Baby with a Dixie Melody; She's a Latin from Manhattan; The Spaniard That Blighted My Life; Swanee; There's a Rainbow Round My Shoulder; Toot Toot Tootsie; Waiting for the Robert E. Lee; When the Red, Red Robin Comes Bob, Bob, Bobbin' Along; When You Were Sweet Sixteen; You Made Me Love You

Joy of Living (1938) Just Let Me Look at You; What's Good About Good Night; You Couldn't Be Cuter

Juke Girl (1942) Someone's Rocking My Dream Boat

Jumbo (1964) The Circus Is on Parade; Little Girl Blue; The Most Beautiful Girl in the World; My Romance; Over and Over Again

Junior Prom (1946) My Heart Sings

Just for You (1952) Zing a Little Zong

Kansas City Kitty (1944) Kansas City Kitty; Tico Tico

Keep 'em Flying (1941) You Don't Know What Love Is

Keep Your Powder Dry I'll See You in My Dreams

Keep Your Seats Please (1937) When I'm Cleaning Windows

Kid Millions (1934) Mandy; When My Ship Comes In

The King and I (1956) Getting To Know You; Hello Young Lovers; I Have Dreamed; I Whistle a Happy Tune; March of the Siamese Children; Shall We Dance; Something Wonderful; We Kiss in a Shadow

King Creole (1959) Hard-Headed Woman

The King of Burlesque (1936) I'm Shooting High; I've Got My Fingers Crossed; Lovely Lady

King of Jazz (1930) A Bench in the Park; Happy Feet; It Happened in Monterey; Rhapsody in Blue; Song of the Dawn

King of the Cowboys (1943) A Gay Ranchero; I'm an Old Cowhand; The Red River Valley; Roll Along Prairie Moon; They Cut Down the Old Pine Tree

The King Steps Out (1936) Stars in My Eyes; Who Can Tell

King's Rhapsody (1956) Some Day My Heart Will Awake; Take Your Girl

Kismet (1955) And This Is My Beloved; Baubles, Bangles and Beads; Not Since Nineveh; Stranger in Paradise

Kiss Me, Kate (1953) Always True to You in My Fashion; Brush Up Your Shakespeare; From This Moment On; I Hate Men; So in Love; Too Darn Hot; Why Can't You Behave; Wunderbar

Kiss the Boys Goodbye (1941) I'll Never Let a Day Pass By; Kiss the Boys Goodbye; Sand in My Shoes

Kiss Them for Me (1959) Blue Moon; Don't Sit Under the Apple Tree; How About You; I've Got a Gal in Kalamazoo; Temptation; You Turned the Tables on Me

The Kissing Bandit (1948) Love Is Where You Find It

Knickerbocker Holiday (1944) It Never Was You; September Song; Zuyder Zee

Knock on Wood (1954) Knock on Wood

Ladies' Man (1947) Cocktails for Two; Holiday for Strings; Mama Yo Quiero

The Lady and the Tramp (1955) He's a Tramp

Lady Be Good (1941) Fascinating Rhythm; The Last Time I Saw Paris; Oh, Lady Be Good

Lady in the Dark (1944) Dream Lover; My Ship; Saga of Jenny; Suddenly It's Spring; This Is New; Tschaikowsky

Lady Sings the Blues (1972) All of Me; Don't Explain; Give Me a Pigfoot; God Bless the Child; Good Morning Heartache; Happy; I Cried for You; Lover Man; Mean to Me; My Man; Strange Fruit; 'Tain't Nobody's Business If I Do; Them There Eyes; You've Changed

Las Vegas Nights (1941) Dolores

Laughing Irish Eyes (1936) All My Life; Laughing Irish Eyes

Les Girls (1957) Ca, C'est L'Amour; Ladies in Waiting

Let's Dance (1950) Why Fight the Feeling

Let's Face It (1943) Ace in the Hole; Everything I Love; You Irritate Me So

Let's Fall in Love (1934) Let's Fall in Love

Life of the Party (1930) Somehow

Lights of Old Santa Fe (1954) Amor

Li'l Abner (1959) If I Had My Druthers; Jubilation T. Cornpone; Love in a Home; Namely You; What's Good for General Bullmoose

Lilacs in the Spring (1945) Lily of Laguna; We'll Gather Lilacs

Lili (1953) Hi Lili Hi Lo

Lillian Russell (1940)   The Band Played On

Lisbon Story (1944)   Never Say Goodbye; Pedro the Fisherman

Listen, Darling (1938)   On the Bumpy Road to Love; Zing Went the Strings of My Heart

A Little Bit of Heaven (1940)   A Little Bit of Heaven, Sure They Call It Ireland

Little Johnny Jones (1929)   Give My Regards to Broadway; Painting the Clouds with Sunshine; The Yankee Doodle Boy

Little Miss Broadway (1947)   That's Good Enough for Me

Little Nellie Kelly (1940)   It's a Great Day for the Irish; Singin' in the Rain

A Little Night Music (1979)   Every Day a Little Death; The Glamorous Life; Liaisons; Night Waltz; Now; Send in the Clowns; A Weekend in the Country; You Must Meet My Wife

Living It Up (1954)   Ev'ry Street's a Boulevard in Old New York

London Town, *see* **My Heart Goes Crazy**

Look For the Silver Lining (1949)   Just a Memory; A Kiss in the Dark; Look For the Silver Lining; Sunny; Time on My Hands; Whip-poor-will; Who; Wild Rose; The Yama Yama Man

Lord Byron of Broadway (1930)   Should I (Reveal); The Woman in the Shoe

Lost in the Stars (1974)   Cry the Beloved Country; The Little Grey House; Lost in the Stars

Louisiana Hayride (1944)   Put Your Arms Around Me Honey; Shortnin' Bread

Louisiana Purchase (1941)   Louisiana Purchase; Tomorrow Is a Lovely Day; You're Lonely and I'm Lonely

Love Happy (1949)   Gypsy Love Song; Willow Weep for Me

Love in Bloom (1935)   Here Comes Cookie

Love in the Rough (1930)   Go Home and Tell Your Mother

Love, Life and Laughter (1934)   Out in the Cold Cold Snow

Love Me or Leave Me (1955)   At Sundown; I'll Never Stop Loving You; It All Depends on You; Love Me or Leave Me; Mean to Me; Sam, the Old Accordion Man; Ten Cents a Dance; You Made Me Love You

Love Me Tonight (1932)   Isn't It Romantic; Love Me Tonight; Lover; Mimi

The Love Parade (1929)   Dream Lover; My Love Parade

Love Story (1944)   Cornish Rhapsody

Lovely To Look At (1952)   I Won't Dance; Lovely To Look At; Smoke Gets in Your Eyes; The Touch of Your Hand; Yesterdays; You're Devastating

Lover Come Back (1946)   Don't Tell Her; Just a Gigolo; Little White Lies; Sweet Jennie Lee; Where Is the Song of Songs for Me

Loving You (1957)   Teddy Bear

Lucky Boy (1929)   California, Here I Come; My Blackbirds Are Bluebirds Now; My Mother's Eyes

Lullaby of Broadway (1951)   I Love the Way You Say ''Goodnight''; Just One of Those Things; Lullaby of Broadway; Please Don't Talk About Me When I'm Gone; A Shanty in Old Shanty Town; Somebody Loves Me; You're Getting To Be a Habit with Me; Zing Went the Strings of My Heart

Make Believe Ballroom (1949)   I'm the Lonesomest Gal in Town

Make Mine Music (1946)   Make Mine Music; Two Silhouettes; Without You

Mame (1974)   Bosom Buddies; If He Walked into My Life; Mame; My Best Girl; Open a New Window; We Need a Little Christmas

Mammy (1930)   Let Me Sing and I'm Happy

Man About Town (1939)   Strange Enchantment

The Man from Music Mountain (1943)   I'm Thinking Tonight of My Blue Eyes

The Man from Oklahoma (1945)   I'm Beginning To See the Light

The Man from The Folies Bergere, *see* **Folies Bergere**

The Man I Love (1947)   Bill; Body and Soul; If I Could Be with You One Hour Tonight; Liza; The Man I Love; Why Was I Born

Man of La Mancha (1972)   Dulcinea; I'm Only Thinking of Him; The Impossible Dream; Man of La Mancha

Manhattan Angel (1949)   I'll Take Romance

Manhattan Parade (1932)   I Love a Parade

Manhattan Tower (1956)   Married I Can Always Get

Many Happy Returns (1934)   The Sweetest Music This Side of Heaven

Margie (1946)   Three O'Clock in the Morning

Marianne (1929)   Just You, Just Me

Mary Lou (1948)   Mary Lou

Mary Poppins (1964)   Chim Chim Cher-ee; A Spoonful of Sugar; Supercalifragilisticexpialidocious

Masquerade in Mexico (1945)   Adios, Mariquita Linda

Maytime (1937)   Jump Jim Crow; The Road to Paradise; Will You Remember (Sweetheart)

Me and Marlborough (1935)   All for a Shilling a Day; There's Something About a Soldier

Meet Danny Wilson (1952)   All of Me; A Good Man Is Hard to Find; How Deep Is the Ocean; I've Got a Crush on You; She's Funny That Way; That Old Black Magic; When You're Smiling; You're a Sweetheart

Meet Me in St. Louis (1944)   The Boy Next Door; Have Yourself a Merry Little Christmas; Look For the Silver Lining; Meet Me in St. Louis, Louis; Skip to My Lou; The Trolley Song; Under the Bamboo Tree

Meet Mister Callaghan (1953)   Meet Mr. Callaghan

Meet the People (1944)   I Like To Recognize the Tune

Melody For Two (1937)   September in the Rain

Melody Lane (1941)   Roll Dem Roly Boly Eyes; Song of the Islands

Melody Time (1948)   Blue Shadows on the Trail

The Merry Monihans (1944) I Hate To Lose You; I'm Always Chasing Rainbows; In My Merry Oldsmobile; Isle d' Amour; Rock-a-Bye Your Baby with a Dixie Melody; Rose Room; What Do You Want To Make Those Eyes at Me For; When You Wore a Tulip and I Wore a Big Red Rose

The Merry Widow (1934) Girls, Girls, Girls; Maxim's; The Merry Widow Waltz; Vilia

The Merry Widow (1952) Girls, Girls, Girls; Maxim's; The Merry Widow Waltz; Vilia

Mexicali Rose (1939) Mexicali Rose; El Rancho Grande; You're the Only Star in My Blue Heaven

Mexican Hayride (1948) Abracadabra; I Love You

Million Dollar Baby (1935) I Found a Million Dollar Baby in a Five and Ten Cent Store

Millions in the Air (1935) You Tell Her, I S-t-u-t-t-e-r

Mississippi (1935) Down by the River; It's Easy To Remember; Soon

Mr. Bug Goes to Town (1941) We're the Couple in the Castle

Mr. Dodd Takes the Air (1937) Am I In Love; Remember Me

Mr. Imperium (1951) You Belong to My Heart

Mr. Music (1950) Life Is So Peculiar

Monkey Business (1931) Ho Hum; When I Take My Sugar to Tea; You Brought a New Kind of Love to Me

Monte Carlo (1930) Beyond the Blue Horizon; Give Me a Moment Please

Moon over Las Vegas (1944) My Blue Heaven

Moon over Miami (1941) You Started Something

Moonlight and Cactus (1944) Down in the Valley; Home

Moonlight and Pretzels (1933) Ah, But Is It Love; Are You Making Any Money; Moonlight and Pretzels

Mother Wore Tights (1947) You Do

Moulin Rouge (1934) Boulevard of Broken Dreams; Coffee in the Morning, Kisses at Night

Murder at the Vanities (1934) Cocktails for Two; Marahuana

Music for Millions (1945) At Sundown

The Music Goes 'Round (1936) The Music Goes "Round and Round"

Music in My Heart (1940) It's a Blue World

Music in the Air (1935) I've Told Every Little Star; One More Dance; The Song Is You

The Music Man (1962) Gary, Indiana; Goodnight My Someone; It's You; Lida Rose; Marian the Librarian; My White Knight; Seventy-Six Trombones; Till There Was You; Trouble

My Blue Heaven (1950) My Blue Heaven

My Dream Is Yours (1949) Canadian Capers; I'll String Along with You; My Dream Is Yours; Someone Like You

My Fair Lady (1964) Ascot Gavotte; Get Me to the Church on Time; A Hymn to Him; I Could Have Danced All Night; I'm an Ordinary Man; I've Grown Accustomed to Her Face; Just You Wait; On the Street Where You Live; The Rain in Spain; Show Me; Why Can't the English; With a Little Bit of Luck; Without You; Wouldn't It Be Loverly; You Did It

My Gal Sal (1942) Come Tell Me What's Your Answer, Yes Or No; Mister Volunteer; My Gal Sal; On the Banks of the Wabash, Far Away

My Heart Goes Crazy (1946) My Heart Goes Crazy

My Man (1929) I'd Rather Be Blue over You; If You Want the Rainbow; My Man; Second Hand Rose

My Pal Trigger (1945) Harriet; Ole Faithful; El Rancho Grande

My Song Goes Round the World My Song Goes Round the World

My Wild Irish Rose (1947) Come Down Ma Evenin' Star; A Little Bit of Heaven, Sure They Call It Ireland; Mother Machree; My Nellie's Eyes; My Wild Irish Rose

Nancy Goes to Rio (1950) Embraceable You; Magic Is the Moonlight; Shine On Harvest Moon

Naughty Marietta (1935) Ah! Sweet Mystery of Life; I'm Falling in Love with Someone; Italian Street Song; Tramp! Tramp! Tramp! Along the Highway

The Naughty Nineties (1945) I'd Leave My Happy Home for You; Nora Malone; On a Sunday Afternoon

Neptune's Daughter (1949) Baby, It's Cold Outside

New Faces of 1937 (1937) Our Penthouse on Third Avenue; Peckin'

New Faces of 1954 (1954) C'est Si Bon; Monotonous

The New Moon (1930) Lover Come Back to Me; Marianne; One Kiss; Softly, As in a Morning Sunrise; Stouthearted Men; Wanting You

The New Moon (1940) Lover Come Back to Me; Marianne; One Kiss; Softly, As in a Morning Sunrise; Stouthearted Men; Wanting You

New Orleans (1947) Do You Know What It Means to Miss New Orleans

Night and Day (1946) Begin the Beguine; Easy To Love; I Get a Kick out of You; In the Still of the Night; I've Got You Under My Skin; Just One of Those Things; Let's Do It; Miss Otis Regrets; My Heart Belongs to Daddy; Night and Day; Old-Fashioned Garden; What Is This Thing Called Love; You Do Something to Me; You're the Top

A Night at the Opera (1935) Alone; Cosi Cosa

Nightclub Girl (1944) One O'Clock Jump; Peanut Song; Tiger Rag

A Night in Casablanca (1946) The Beer Barrel Polka; Moonlight Cocktail; Who's Sorry Now

The Night Is Young (1935) When I Grow Too Old To Dream

No Leave, No Love (1946) All the Time; Love on a Greyhound Bus

No, No, Nanette (1930) Dance of the Wooden Shoes

No, No, Nanette (1940) I Want To Be Happy; Tea for Two

Nothing But the Truth (1941) Do Something

Off the Beaten Track (1942) Mister Five By Five

Oh You Beautiful Doll (1949) Chicago; Come, Josephine, in My Flying Machine; I Want You To Want Me To Want

You; Ireland Must Be Heaven for My Mother Came from There; Oh You Beautiful Doll; Peg O' My Heart; There's a Broken Heart for Every Light on Broadway; When I Get You Alone Tonight

Oklahoma! (1955) I Cain't Say No; Kansas City; Many a New Day; Oh What a Beautiful Mornin'; Oklahoma; Out of My Dreams; People Will Say We're in Love; Poor Jud Is Daid; The Surrey with the Fringe on Top

The Old Homestead (1942) In the Town Where I Was Born

Oliver! (1968) As Long as He Needs Me; Be Back Soon; Consider Yourself; Food Glorious Food; I'd Do Anything; Where Is Love; Who Will Buy; You've Got To Pick a Pocket or Two

On a Clear Day You Can See Forever (1969) Come Back to Me; Hurry, It's Lovely Up Here; On a Clear Day You Can See Forever; What Did I Have That I Don't Have

On an Island with You (1948) The Wedding Samba

On Moonlight Bay (1951) Cuddle Up a Little Closer Lovey Mine; Every Little Movement; I'm Forever Blowing Bubbles; Moonlight Bay; Pack Up Your Troubles in Your Old Kit Bag and Smile, Smile, Smile; Tell Me; Till We Meet Again

On Stage Everybody (1945) Dance with a Dolly; Take Me in Your Arms

On the Avenue (1937) The Girl on the Police Gazette; I've Got My Love To Keep Me Warm; Slumming on Park Avenue; This Year's Kisses

On the Riviera (1951) Ballin' the Jack

On the Sunny Side of the Street (1951) Come Back to Sorrento; I Get a Kick Out of You; I Hadn't Anyone Till You; I May Be Wrong, But I Think You're Wonderful; I'm Gonna Live Till I Die; Let's Fall in Love; On the Sunny Side of the Street; Too Marvelous for Words

On the Town (1949) Lucky To Be Me; New York, New York; Some Other Time; Ya Got Me

On with the Show (1929) Am I Blue; Birmingham Bertha

On Your Toes (1939) Glad To Be Unhappy; It's Got To Be Love; On Your Toes; Quiet Night; Slaughter on Tenth Avenue; There's a Small Hotel; Too Good for the Average Man

One Hour with You (1932) One Hour with You; We Will Always Be Sweethearts

One Night of Love (1934) Ciribiribin; One Night of Love

One Sunday Afternoon (1948) Girls Were Made To Take Care of Boys; Mary, You're a Little Bit Old Fashioned; One Sunday Afternoon

Orchestra Wives (1942) American Patrol; At Last; Bugle Call Rag; I've Got a Gal in Kalamazoo; Serenade in Blue; Yours

Out of This World (1945) June Comes Around Every Year; Out of This World

Pagan Love Song (1950) Pagan Love Song

Paint Your Wagon (1969) I Still See Elisa; I Talk to the Trees; They Call the Wind Maria

Painting the Clouds with Sunshine (1951) The Birth of the Blues; Jalousie; Painting the Clouds with Sunshine; Tip

Toe Through the Tulips; Vienna Dreams; We're in the Money; With a Song in My Heart; You're My Everything

The Pajama Game (1957) Hernando's Hideaway; Hey There; I'll Never Be Jealous Again; I'm Not At All in Love; Racing with the Clock; 7 1/2 Cents; Steam Heat

Pal Joey (1957) Bewitched, Bothered and Bewildered; Do It the Hard Way; I Could Write a Book; I Didn't Know What Time It Was; In Our Little Den of Iniquity; The Lady Is a Tramp; My Funny Valentine; There's a Small Hotel; You Mustn't Kick It Around; Zip

Palm Springs (1936) The Hills of Old Wyomin'

Palmy Days (1931) Bend Down, Sister

Palooka, *see* **The Great Schnozzle**

Pan-Americana (1941) Babalu; Stars in Your Eyes

Panama Hattie (1942) Let's Be Buddies

Paramount on Parade (1930) Come Back to Sorrento; Sweeping the Clouds Away

Pardon My Sarong (1942) Do I Worry

Paris (1930) Among My Souvenirs

Paris Holiday (1958) April in Paris; The Last Time I Saw Paris

Paris Honeymoon (1938) The Funny Old Hills; I Ain't Got Nobody; I Have Eyes; You're a Sweet Little Headache

Paris in the Spring (1935) Paris in the Spring

Paris Love Song (1935) Paris in the Spring

Pennies from Heaven (1936) One, Two, Button Your Shoe; Pennies from Heaven; So Do I

People Are Funny (1946) Alouette; I'm in the Mood for Love

The Perils of Pauline (1947) I Wish I Didn't Love You So; Poor Pauline

Pete Kelly's Blue (1955) (What Can I Say, Dear) After I Say I'm Sorry; Bye, Bye, Blackbird; Hard Hearted Hannah; He Needs Me; I Never Knew; Pete Kelly's Blues; Somebody Loves Me; Sugar

Peter Pan (1953) The Second Star to the Right

Pigskin Parade (1936) You Do the Darndest Things, Baby

Pinocchio (1940) Give a Little Whistle; Hi-Diddle-Dee-Dee; I've Got No Strings; When You Wish upon a Star

The Pirate (1948) Be a Clown; Love of My Life; Nina; You Can Do No Wrong

Playboy of Paris (1930) My Ideal

Poor Little Rich Girl (1936) When I'm with You; You Gotta Eat Your Spinach, Baby

Porgy and Bess (1959) Bess, You Is My Woman Now; I Got Plenty o' Nuttin'; I Loves You Porgy; I'm on My Way; It Ain't Necessarily So; My Man's Gone Now; Oh Bess, Oh Where's My Bess; Oh, I Can't Sit Down; Summertime; There's a Boat Dat's Leavin' Soon for New York; A Woman Is a Sometime Thing

Presenting Lily Mars (1943) Broadway Rhythm

The Princess Comes Across (1936) Paris in the Spring

Priorities on Parade (1942) Conchita, Marquita, Lolita, Pepita, Rosita, Juanita Lopez

Private Buckaroo (1942) Don't Sit Under the Apple Tree; Three Little Sisters; You Made Me Love You

Public Nuisance No. 1 (1936) Me and My Dog

Purple Rain (1984) I Feel for You; Purple Rain

Puttin' On the Ritz (1930) Puttin' On the Ritz; Singing a Vagabond Song; There's Danger in Your Eyes, Cherie

Radio City Revels (1938) Good Night Angel

Rain or Shine (1930) Happy Days Are Here Again

Rainbow on the River (1936) Rainbow on the River

Rainbow Round My Shoulder (1952) Bye Bye Blackbird; She's Funny That Way; There's a Rainbow Round My Shoulder; 'Tis the Last Rose of Summer; Wrap Your Troubles in Dreams

The Rat Race (1960) At Sundown; Hot Lips; Lover; Out of Nowhere; The Wang-Wang Blues

Ready, Willing and Able (1937) Too Marvelous for Words

Rebecca of Sunnybrook Farm (1938) Toy Trumpet

Red, Hot and Blue! (1949) Down in the Depths on the Ninetieth Floor; It's De-Lovely; Now That I Need You; Ridin' High

Red-Headed Women (1932) Nobody's Sweetheart

Reveille with Beverly (1943) Big Noise from Winnetka; Cow-Cow Boogie; One O'Clock Jump; Take the "A" Train

Rhapsody in Blue (1945) An American in Paris; Bidin' My Time; Clap Yo' Hands; Concerto in F; Delishious; Do It Again; Embraceable You; Fascinating Rhythm; I Got Plenty o' Nuttin'; I Got Rhythm; I'll Build a Stairway to Paradise; It Ain't Necessarily So; Liza; Love Walked In; The Man I Love; Oh, Lady Be Good; Rhapsody in Blue; Somebody Loves Me; Someone To Watch Over Me; Summertime; Swanee; 'S Wonderful; The Yankee Doodle Blues

Rhythm Inn (1951) It's a Big, Wide, Wonderful World; With a Twist of the Wrist

Rhythm on the Range (1936) Empty Saddles; I Can't Escape from You; If You Can't Sing It You'll Have To Swing It; I'm an Old Cowhand; Mexicali Rose

Rhythm on the River (1940) Only Forever; Rhythm on the River; That's for Me

Rhythm Parade (1942) Sweet Sue; Wait 'Til the Sun Shines, Nellie

Rhythm Serenade I Love To Sing

Rich, Young and Pretty (1951) Dark Is the Night; There's Danger in Your Eyes, Cherie; We Never Talk Much; Wonder Why

Ride 'em Cowboy (1942) I'll Remember April

Ride, Tenderfoot Ride (1940) Eleven More Months and Ten More Days; Leanin' on the Ole Top Rail; Ride, Tenderfoot, Ride; The Woodpecker(s') Song

Riders of the Whistling Pines (1948) Hair of Gold, Eyes of Blue

Ridin' Down the Canyon (1942) In a Little Spanish Town; My Little Buckaroo

Riding High (1950) Sunshine Cake

Ridin' On a Rainbow (1941) Steamboat Bill

Rio Rita (1929) Following the Sun Around; If You're in Love, You'll Waltz; The Kinkajou; The Ranger's Song; Rio Rita; You're Always in My Arms

Rio Rita (1942) Following the Sun Around; If You're in Love You'll Waltz; The Kinkajou; The Ranger's Song; Rio Rita

The Road to Morocco (1942) Ain't Got a Dime to My Name; Moonlight Becomes You; The Road to Morocco

The Road to Rio (1947) Apalachicola, Florida; But Beautiful; You Don't Have To Know the Language

The Road to Singapore (1931) African Lament

The Road to Singapore (1940) Sweet Potato Piper; Too Romantic

The Road to Utopia (1945) Personality; Put It There, Pal

The Road to Zanzibar (1941) It's Always You

Roberta (1935) I Won't Dance; Lovely To Look At; Smoke Gets in Your Eyes; Yesterdays

Rock Around the Clock (1956) The Great Pretender; Only You; Rock Around the Clock

The Rogue Song (1930) The Rogue Song; The Song of the Shirt; When I'm Looking At You

Rolling in Money (1934) Coom Pretty One; The White Dove

Roman Scandals (1933) Keep Young and Beautiful

Romance and Rhythm (1938) Ride, Tenderfoot, Ride

Romance on the High Seas (1948) It's Magic; It's You or No One; Put 'Em in a Box, Tie 'Em with a Ribbon, and Throw 'Em in the Deep Blue Sea

Rosalie (1937) Close; In the Still of the Night; Rosalie; Show Me the Town; Why Should I Care

The Rose (1980) The Rose

Rose Marie (1936) Indian Love Call; Rose Marie; Some of These Days; Totem Tom-Tom

Rose Marie (1954) Indian Love Call; Rose Marie; Some of These Days; Totem Tom-Tom

Rose of the Rancho (1936) If I Should Lose You

Rose of Washington Square (1939) California, Here I Come; I'm Just Wild About Harry; I'm Sorry I Made You Cry; My Mammy; My Man; Pretty Baby; Rock-a-Bye Your Baby with a Dixie Melody; Rose of Washington Square; Toot Toot Tootsie

Royal Wedding (1951) How Could You Believe Me When I Said I Love You When You Know I've Been a Liar All My Life; I Left My Hat in Haiti; Too Late Now

Ruggles of Red Gap (1956) Did You Ever Ride on a Rainbow

Running Wild (1956) Runnin' Wild

Safety in Numbers (1930) My Future Just Passed

Sailors Three (1941) All Over the Place

Sally (1930) Look for the Silver Lining; Sally; Wild Rose

Sally in Our Alley (1931) Sally

Sally, Irene and Mary (1938) Sweet as a Song

Saludos Amigos (1942) Brazil; Tico Tico

San Antonio Rose (1941) Hi Neighbor; Hut Sut Song; San Antonio Rose

San Fernando Valley (1944) San Fernando Valley

Sanders of the River (1935) The Canoe Song

Satchmo the Great Indiana; Mack the Knife; What Did I Do To Be So Black and Blue

Saturday Night Fever (1977) A Fifth of Beethoven; How Deep Is Your Love; If I Can't Have You; Jive Talkin'; More Than a Woman; Night on Disco Mountain; Stayin' Alive; You Should Be Dancing

Say It with Music (1933) Love Is the Sweetest Thing

Say It with Songs (1929) Little Pal; Seventh Heaven

Second Chorus (1941) Love of My Life

Second Fiddle (1939) I Poured My Heart into a Song

Seven Brides for Seven Brothers (1954) Sobbin' Women; Spring, Spring, Spring

Seven Days Leave (1943) Can't Get Out of This Mood

The Seven Hills of Rome (1957) Arrivederci Roma; Jesabel; Memories Are Made of This; Temptation

The Seven Little Foys (1955) Chinatown, My Chinatown; Mary's a Grand Old Name; Row, Row, Row; The Yankee Doodle Boy

Shall We Dance (1937) Beginner's Luck; Let's Call the Whole Thing Off; Shall We Dance; Slap That Bass; They All Laughed; They Can't Take That Away from Me

She Done Him Wrong (1933) Easy Rider

She Loves Me Not (1934) After All, You're All I'm After; I'm Humming—I'm Whistling—I'm Singing; Love in Bloom

She Shall Have Music (1935) My First Thrill; She Shall Have Music; Why Did She Fall for the Leader of the Band

She's Working Her Way Through College (1952) As Time Goes By; With Plenty of Money and You

Shine On Harvest Moon (1944) Shine On Harvest Moon; Time Waits for No One; When It's Apple Blossom Time in Normandy

Shipmates Forever (1935) Don't Give Up the Ship

The Shocking Miss Pilgrim (1947) Aren't You Kind of Glad We Did; The Back Bay Polka; Changing My Tune; For You, For Me, For Evermore; One, Two, Three

Shoot the Works (1934) With My Eyes Wide Open I'm Dreaming

Show Boat (1929) Bill; Can't Help Lovin' Dat Man of Mine; Here Comes the Showboat; Lonesome Road; Ol' Man River

Show Boat (1936) Bill; Can't Help Lovin' Dat Man of Mine; Make Believe; Ol' Man River; You Are Love

Show Boat (1951) Bill; Can't Help Lovin' Dat Man of Mine; Make Believe; Nobody Else But Me; Ol' Man River; Why Do I Love You

Show Business (1944) Alabamy Bound; The Curse of an Aching Heart; Dinah; I Don't Want To Get Well; I Want a Girl—Just Like the Girl That Married Dear Old Dad; It Had To Be You; Makin' Whoopee; They're Wearing 'Em Higher in Hawaii

Show of Shows (1929) Lady Luck Show; Rock-a-Bye Your Baby with a Dixie Melody; Singin' in the Bathtub; You Were Meant for Me; Your Mother and Mine

Silk Stockings (1957) All of You; Josephine; Paris Loves Lovers; Siberia; Stereophonic Sound; Too Bad; Without Love

Silver Spurs (1945) Back in Your Own Back Yard; Tumbling Tumbleweeds; When It's Springtime in the Rockies

Since You Went Away (1937) The Dipsy Doodle; Together

Sincerely Yours (1955) Cornish Rhapsody; Embraceable You; The Man I Love; Swanee; Tea for Two

Sing a Jingle (1944) Beautiful Love; The Night We Called It a Day

Sing As We Go (1934) In My Little Bottom Drawer; Sing As We Go

Sing, Baby, Sing (1936) Sing, Baby, Sing; When Did You Leave Heaven; You Turned the Tables on Me

Sing Me a Love Song (1936) Summer Night; Your Eyes Have Told Me So

Sing You Sinners (1938) A Pocketful of Dreams; Small Fry

Sing Your Way Home (1945) I'll Buy That Dream

Singing Guns (1950) Mule Train

Singin' in the Corn (1946) Ma, He's Making Eyes At Me

Singin' in the Rain (1952) All I Do Is Dream of You; Fit as a Fiddle; Good Morning; I've Got a Feeling You're Fooling; Make 'Em Laugh; Should I (Reveal); Singin' in the Rain; The Wedding of the Painted Doll; Would You; You Are My Lucky Star

The Singing Fool (1928) I'm Sitting on Top of the World; It All Depends on You; Sonny Boy; There's a Rainbow Round My Shoulder

The Singing Hill (1941) Blueberry Hill; The Last Round-Up

The Singing Marine (1937) I Know Now

Singin' the Blues (1933) It's the Darndest Thing; Singin' the Blues; You Were Meant for Me

Sitting Pretty (1934) Did You Ever See a Dream Walking; Many Moons Ago; You're Such a Comfort to Me

Skirts Ahoy! (1952) Oh By Jingo, Oh By Gee, You're the Only Girl for Me

The Sky's the Limit (1943) My Shining Hour; One for My Baby and One More for the Road

Sleepy Lagoon (1943) Sleepy Lagoon

Sleepy Time Gal (1942) Sleepy Time Gal

Slightly French (1949) Let's Fall in Love

The Smiling Lieutenant (1931) While Hearts Are Singing

Smiling Through (1941) Through the Years

Snow White and the Seven Dwarfs (1937) Heigh-Ho; I'm Wishing; One Song; Some Day My Prince Will Come; Whistle While You Work; With a Smile and a Song

So Dear to My Heart (1948) Lavender's Blue

So Long Letty (1929) Am I Blue; Down Among the Sugar-Cane

So This Is College (1929) I Don't Want Your Kisses

Some Like It Hot (1959) By the Beautiful Sea; Down Among the Sheltering Palms; I Wanna Be Loved By You; I'm Through with Love; Runnin' Wild; Sweet Georgia Brown

Somebody Loves Me (1952) I Can't Tell Why I Love You, But I Do; I Cried for You; I'm Sorry I Made You Cry; Jealous; June Night; Rose Room; Smiles; Somebody Loves Me; The Wang-Wang Blues; 'Way Down Yonder in New Orleans

Something for the Boys (1944) He's a Right Guy; I Wish I Didn't Have To Say Good Night

Something To Shout About (1943) You'd Be So Nice To Come Home To

Son of a Paleface (1952) Am I in Love

A Song Is Born (1948) Heart and Soul

Song O' My Heart (1930) The Rose of Tralee

Song of Scheherazade (1947) Song of India

Song of Texas (1943) Mexicali Rose; Moonlight and Roses

Song of the Islands (1942) Blue Shadows and White Gardenias; Hawaiian War Chant; Song of the South

Song of the Sarong (1945) Lovely Luana

Song of the South (1946) Ev'rybody Has a Laughing Place; Sooner or Later; Uncle Remus Said; You'll Always Be the One I Love; Zip-A-Dee-Doo-Dah

Sons O' Guns (1936) Cross Your Fingers; Why (Is There a Rainbow in the Sky)

The Sound of Music (1965) Climb Ev'ry Mountain; Do Re Mi; Edelweiss; The Lonely Goatherd; Maria; My Favorite Things; Sixteen Going on Seventeen; So Long, Farewell; The Sound of Music; You Are Sixteen

South of Dixie (1944) Darkness on the Delta

South Pacific (1958) Bali Ha'i; Bloody Mary; A Cockeyed Optimist; Dites-moi Pourquoi; Happy Talk; Honey Bun; I'm Gonna Wash That Man Right Outa My Hair; I'm in Love with a Wonderful Guy; Some Enchanted Evening; There Is Nothin' Like a Dame; This Nearly Was Mine; Younger Than Springtime; You've Got To Be Taught

Sparkle (1976) Look In to Your Heart; Sparkle

Spring Is Here (1930) Cryin' for the Carolines; Have a Little Faith In Me; With a Song in My Heart

Spring Parade (1940) It's Foolish But It's Fun

Springtime in the Rockies (1942) Chattanooga Choo-Choo; I Had the Craziest Dream

St. Louis Blues (1958) Aunt Hagar's Blues; Beale Street Blues; Careless Love; The Memphis Blues; St. Louis Blues; Yellow Dog Blues

St. Louis Woman (1935) St. Louis Woman

Stand Up and Cheer (1934) Baby, Take a Bow; Stand Up and Cheer

A Star Is Born (1954) Black Bottom; I'll Get By; It's a New World; The Man That Got Away; The Peanut Vendor; Swanee; You Took Advantage of Me

A Star Is Born (1976) Evergreen

The Star Maker (1939) An Apple for the Teacher; Go Fly a Kite; Sunbonnet Sue

Star Spangled Rhythm (1942) Hit the Road to Dreamland; That Old Black Magic

Stardust on the Sage (1942) Good Night Sweetheart; Perfidia

Starlift (1951) I May Be Wrong, But I Think You're Wonderful; What Is This Thing Called Love; You Do Something to Me; You Oughta Be in Pictures; You're Gonna Lose Your Gal

Stars on Parade (1944) It's Love, Love, Love; When They Ask About You

Stars over Broadway (1935) Carry Me Back to the Lone Prairie; September in the Rain; Where Am I; You Let Me Down

State Fair (1945) Isn't It Kinda Fun; It Might as Well Be Spring; It's a Grand Night for Singing; That's for Me

State Fair (1962) Isn't It Kinda Fun; It Might as Well Be Spring; It's a Grand Night for Singing; That's for Me

Step Lively (1928) I'll Always Be in Love with You; My Inspiration Is You; There's a Cradle in Caroline

The Stooge (1952) I Feel a Song Coming On; I Feel Like a Feather in the Breeze; I'm Yours; Just One More Chance; Louise; Who's Your Little Who-Zis; With My Eyes Wide Open I'm Dreaming

Stork Club (1946) Doctor, Lawyer, Indian Chief

Stormy Weather (1943) Ain't Misbehavin'; Diga Diga Do; I Can't Give You Anything But Love; I Lost My Sugar in Salt Lake City; Stormy Weather; There's No Two Ways About Love

The Story of Vernon and Irene Castle (1939) By the Beautiful Sea; Chicago; Come Josephine in My Flying Machine; Cuddle Up a Little Closer, Lovey Mine; The Darktown Strutters' Ball; Hello, Hello, Who's Your Lady Friend; Oh You Beautiful Doll; Only When You're in My Arms; Too Much Mustard; Waiting for the Robert E. Lee; The Yama Yama Man

Stowaway (1936) Goodnight My Love; That's What I Want for Christmas

The Strawberry Blonde (1941) The Band Played On

Strictly Dynamite (1934) Oh Me, Oh My, Oh You

Strictly in the Groove (1942) Be Honest with Me; Elmer's Tune; Miss You; Somebody Else Is Taking My Place; You Are My Sunshine

Strike Me Pink (1936) Let's Call It a Day; Shake It Off; Strike Me Pink

Strike Up the Band (1940) I've Got a Crush on You; Our Love Affair; Soon; Strike Up the Band

The Strip (1951) Basin Street Blues; Don't Blame Me; A Kiss To Build a Dream On

The Student Prince (1927) Deep in My Heart, Dear; Drinking Song; Serenade

The Student Prince (1954) Deep in My Heart, Dear; Drinking Song; Golden Days; Serenade

Summer Holiday (1948) The Stanley Steamer

Summer Holiday (1962) Bachelor Boy; Foot Tapper; Next Time; Summer Holiday

Summer Stock (1950) Get Happy; You Wonderful You

Sun Valley Serenade (1941) At Last; Chattanooga Choo Choo; I Know Why; In the Mood; It Happened in Sun Valley

Sunbonnet Sue (1945) The Bowery; By the Light of the Silvery Moon; If I Had My Way; School Days; Sunbonnet Sue; While Strolling Through the Park One Day; Yip-I-Addy-I-Ay!

Sunny (1931) D'Ya Love Me; Sunny; Two Little Bluebirds; Who

Sunny (1941) D'Ya Love Me; Sunny; Who

The Sunny Side of the Street, *see* **On the Sunny Side of the Street**

Sunny Side Up (1929) If I Had a Talking Picture of You; I'm a Dreamer; Sunny Side Up; Turn On the Heat; You Find the Time, I'll Find the Place

Sunset in Wyoming (1941) Casey Jones

Susan Slept Here (1954) Hold My Hand

Swanee River (1940) Beautiful Dreamer; De Camptown Races; Jeanie With the Light Brown Hair; My Old Kentucky Home; Oh! Susanna; Old Black Joe; Ring De Banjo

Sweater Girl (1942) I Don't Want To Talk Without You; I Said No

Sweet Adeline (1935) Don't Ever Leave Me; Here Am I; 'Twas Not So Long Ago; Why Was I Born

Sweet and Low Down (1944) I'm Making Believe; I Found a New Baby

Sweet Charity (1969) Baby Dream Your Dream; (Hey) Big Spender; Where Am I Going

Sweet Music (1935) Fare Thee Well, Annabelle

Sweet Rosie O'Grady (1943) My Heart Tells Me

Sweethearts (1938) The Angelus; Sweethearts

Sweethearts On Parade (1930) Sweethearts on Parade; Yearning

Sweetie (1929) My Sweeter Than Sweet

Swing High (1930) It Must Be Love

Swing High, Swing Low (1937) Swing High, Swing Low

Swing in the Saddle (1931) Amor; By the River Saint Marie

The Swing Parade of 1946 1946 Caldonia; On the Sunny Side of the Street; Stormy Weather

Swing Time (1936) Bojangles of Harlem; A Fine Romance; Pick Yourself Up; Waltz in Swing Time; The Way You Look Tonight

Swingtime Johnny (1943) Boogie Woogie Bugle Boy; I May Be Wrong, But I Think You're Wonderful; When You and I Were Young, Maggie

Syncopation (1929) I'll Always Be in Love with You

Syncopation (1942) Do Something; You Made Me Love You

Take a Chance (1933) Eadie Was a Lady; It's Only a Paper Moon; Rise and Shine; Turn Out the Light

Take Me Back to Oklahoma (1940) You Are My Sunshine

Tars and Spars (1946) I'm Glad I Waited for You

Tea for Two (1950) Crazy Rhythm; Do Do Do; Here in My Arms; I Know That You Know; I Only Have Eyes for You; I Want to Be Happy; Oh Me! Oh My! Oh You!; Tea for Two

Tell Me Tonight (1933) Tell Me Tonight

Thank Your Lucky Stars (1943) How Sweet You Are; They're Either Too Young or Too Old

Thanks a Million (1935) I'm Sittin' High on a Hill Top; Thanks a Million

That Certain Age (1938) My Own

That Dangerous Age (1949) Song of Capri

That Girl from Paris (1937) Seal It with a Kiss

That Lady in Ermine (1948) This Is the Moment

That Midnight Kiss (1949) Down Among the Sheltering Palms; They Didn't Believe Me

That Night in Rio (1941) Chica Chica Boom Chic; I Like You Very Much

That Wonderful Urge (1949) It's Love, Love, Love

That's Right, You're Wrong (1939) Scatterbrain

That's the Spirit (1945) Baby, Won't You Please Come Home; How Come You Do Me Like You Do; Nola

There's No Business Like Show Business (1954) After You Get What You Want, You Don't Want It; Alexander's Ragtime Band; Heat Wave; A Man Chases a Girl; Play a Simple Melody; A Pretty Girl Is Like a Melody; Remember; There's No Business Like Show Business; When the Midnight Choo-Choo Leaves for Alabam'; You'd Be Surprised

Things Are Looking Up (1934) Things Are Looking Up

This Could Be the Night (1957) I Got It Bad and That Ain't Good; Taking a Chance on Love

This Is the Army (1943) God Bless America; I Left My Heart at the Stage Door Canteen; I'm Getting Tired So I Can Sleep; My British Buddy; Oh, How I Hate To Get Up in the Morning; This Is the Army Mister Jones

This Is the Life (1944) All or Nothing At All; With a Song in My Heart

This Time for Keeps (1947) Inka Dinka Doo

This Week of Grace (1933) Happy Ending; Mary Rose

This'll Make You Whistle (1939) I'm in a Dancing Mood; There Isn't Any Limit to My Love; This'll Make You Whistle

Thoroughly Modern Millie (1967) Thoroughly Modern Millie

Those Redheads from Seattle (1953) Baby Baby Baby

Thousands Cheer (1943) Daybreak; Heat Wave; Honeysuckle Rose; How's Chances

The Three Caballeros 1944 Baia; The Three Caballeros; You Belong to My Heart

Three Cheers for the Boys, *see* **Follow the Boys**

Three for the Show (1955) How Come You Do Me Like You Do; I've Got a Crush on You; Someone To Watch Over Me

Three Little Girls in Blue (1946) On the Boardwalk in Atlantic City; Somewhere in the Night; This Is Always; You Make Me Feel So Young

The Three Little Pigs (1933) Who's Afraid of the Big Bad Wolf

Three Little Words (1950) All Alone Monday; Horray For Captain Spalding; I Love You So Much; I Wanna Be Loved

By You; My Sunny Tennessee; Nevertheless; She's Mine, All Mine; So Long, Oo-Long; Thinking of You; Three Little Words; Where Did You Get That Girl; Who's Sorry Now

Thrill of a Romance (1945) I Should Care; Please Don't Say "No"

The Thrill of Brazil (1946) That's Good Enough for Me

Thumbs Up (1943) Zing Went the Strings of My Heart

Till the Clouds Roll By (1947) All the Things You Are; Can't Help Lovin' Dat Man; Cleopatterer; A Fine Romance; Go Little Boat; How'd You Like To Spoon with Me; I Won't Dance; Ka-Lu-A; The Last Time I Saw Paris; Leave It to Jane; Long Ago and Far Away; Look For the Silver Lining; Make Believe; Ol' Man River; One More Dance; Smoke Gets in Your Eyes; Sunny; They Didn't Believe Me; Till the Clouds Roll By; Who; Why Was I Born; Yesterdays

The Time, the Place and the Girl (1929) Doin' the Raccoon; If You Could Care for Me

The Time, The Place and The Girl (1946) Collegiate; Fashionette; A Gal in Calico; I Wonder Who's Kissing Her Now; Oh But I Do; Rainy Night in Rio; Through a Thousand Dreams

Tin Pan Alley (1940) Honeysuckle Rose; K-K-K-Katy; Moonlight Bay; Sheik of Araby

To Beat the Band (1935) Eeny Meeny Miney Mo; If You Were Mine

The Toast of New Orleans (1950) Be My Love

Together Again (1944) La Mer

The Tommy Steele Story (1957) A Handful of Songs

Too Many Girls (1940) Give It Back to the Indians; I Didn't Know What Time It Was; I Like To Recognize the Tune; Love Never Went to College

Too Much Harmony (1933) Black Moonlight; The Day You Came Along; Thanks

Top Hat (1935) Cheek to Cheek; Isn't This a Lovely Day; No Strings; The Piccolino; Top Hat, White Tie and Tails

Top of the Town (1937) Where Are You

Torch Song (1953) Blue Moon; Tenderly

Trail to San Antone (1943) By the River of Roses

Trocadero (1944) Shoo-Shoo Baby

Trouble in Store (1952) Don't Laugh At Me

True to the Army (1942) I Can't Give You Anything But Love

Tumbling Tumbleweeds (1935) Tumbling Tumbleweeds

Twenty Million Sweethearts (1934) Fair and Warmer; I'll String Along with You

Twilight on the Trail (1941) Cimarron; The Funny Old Hills

Two Blondes and a Redhead (1947) On the Sunny Side of the Street

Two for Tonight (1935) From the Top of Your Head to the Tip of Your Toes; Without a Word of Warning

Two Girls and a Sailor (1944) A-Tisket A-Tasket; Sweet and Lovely; Take It Easy

Two Latins from Manhattan (1941) Daddy

Two Tickets to Broadway (1951) There's No Tomorrow

Two Weeks with Love (1950) Aba Daba Honeymoon; By the Light of the Silvery Moon; My Hero; Row, Row, Row

Under the Clock (1948) If I Had You

The Unsinkable Molly Brown (1964) Beautiful People of Denver; Chick-a-Pen; Dolce Far Niente; I Ain't Down Yet; Keep-A-Hoppin'

Up in Central Park (1948) The Big Back Yard; Close as Pages in a Book; When She Walks in the Room

The Vagabond King (1930) If I Were King; Love Me Tonight; Only a Rose; Some Day; Song of the Vagabonds; Waltz Huguette

The Vagabond Lover (1929) Heigh-Ho Everybody, Heigh-Ho; If You Were the Only Girl in the World; I'm Just a Vagabond Lover; A Little Kiss Each Morning, a Little Kiss Each Night; Piccolo Pete

Variety Girl (1947) Tallahassee

Varsity Show (1937) Have You Got Any Castles, Baby

Vogues of 1938 (1937) That Old Feeling

Wabash Avenue (1950) Wilhelmina

Wagon Train (1940) Back in the Saddle Again

Waikiki Wedding (1937) Blue Hawaii; Sweet Is the Word for You; Sweet Leilani

Wait Till the Sun Shines Nellie (1952) Break the News to Mother; Goodbye Dolly Gray; It's a Long Way to Tipperary; Love's Old Sweet Song; On the Banks of the Wabash Far Away; Pack Up Your Trouble in Your Old Kit Bag and Smile Smile Smile; Wait 'Til the Sun Shines, Nellie

Wake Up and Dream (1934) What Is This Thing Called Love

Wake Up and Dream (1945) Give Me the Simple Life

Wake Up and Live (1937) Never in a Million Years; There's a Lull in My Life; Wake Up and Live

The Wall (1980) Another Brick in the Wall

Wedding Bells (1951) How Could You Believe Me When I Said I Love You When You Know I've Been a Liar All My Life; I Left My Hat in Haiti; Too Late Now

A Weekend in Havana (1941) A Weekend in Havana

Weekend Pass (1944) All Or Nothing At All

Welcome Stranger (1947) As Long as I'm Dreaming; Country Style; My Heart Is a Hobo

We're Going To Be Rich (1938) The Sweetest Song in the World

We're Not Dressing (1934) Goodnight My Love; Love Thy Neighbor; May I; She Reminds Me of You

West Side Story (1961) America; A Boy Like That; Cool; Gee, Officer Krupke!; I Feel Pretty; Jet Song; Maria; One Hand, One Heart; Something's Coming; Somewhere; Tonight

Wharf Angel (1934) Hello Frisco Hello; Oh You Beautiful Doll; Under the Yum Yum Tree; You Made Me Love You

What Lola Wants, *see* **Damn Yankees**

What's Buzzin' Cousin (1943) Short, Fat and 4F

What's Cookin'? (1942) Pack Up Your Trouble in Your Old Kit Bag and Smile, Smile, Smile

When Johnny Comes Marching Home (1942) This Is Worth Fighting For; When Johnny Comes Marching Home

When My Baby Smiles at Me (1948) When My Baby Smiles at Me

When the Boys Meet the Girls (1965) Bidin' My Time; Embraceable You; I Got Rhythm; Listen People

Where Do We Go from Here? (1945) All at Once

Where's Charley? (1952) Make a Miracle; My Darling, My Darling; Once in Love with Amy; Pernambuco

While I Live (1948) The Dream of Olwen

White Christmas (1954) Blue Skies; Count Your Blessings Instead of Sheep; Mandy; White Christmas

Whoopee (1930) Makin' Whoopee; My Baby Just Cares for Me

With a Song in My Heart (1952) Alabamy Bound; America, the Beautiful; Blue Moon; California, Here I Come; Chicago; Deep in the Heart of Texas; Dixie; Don't Sit Under the Apple Tree; Embraceable You; Get Happy; Give My Regards to Broadway; I'll Walk Alone; I'm Through with Love; Indiana; It's a Good Day; I've Got a Feeling You're Fooling; Stein Song; Tea for Two; That Old Feeling; They're Either Too Young or Too Old; With a Song in My Heart

The Wiz (1978) Believe in Yourself; Ease On Down the Road; The Feeling We Once Had; He's the Wizard; Home; No Bad News

The Wizard of Oz (1939) Ding Dong! The Witch Is Dead; If I Only Had a Brain; Over the Rainbow; We're Off To See the Wizard

Wonder Bar (1934) Wonder Bar

Words and Music (1948) Blue Moon; The Blue Room; I Wish I Were in Love Again; Johnny One Note; The Lady Is a Tramp; Lover; Mountain Greenery; On Your Toes; Slaughter on Tenth Avenue; There's a Small Hotel; This Can't Be Love; Thou Swell; Where or When; Where's That Rainbow; With a Song in My Heart

Xanadu (1980) Magic; Xanadu

Yankee Doodle Dandy (1942) Forty-Five Minutes from Broadway; Give My Regards to Broadway; Harrigan; I Was Born in Virginia; Mary's a Grand Old Name; Over There; So Long Mary; The Yankee Doodle Boy; You're a Grand Old Flag

Yellow Submarine (1968) All You Need Is Love; Eleanor Rigby; A Little Help from My Friends; Lucy in the Sky with Diamonds; Nowhere Man; Sergeant Pepper's Lonely Hearts Club Band; Yellow Submarine

Yentl (1985) Just a Piece of Sky

You Can't Have Everything (1937) Afraid To Dream; The Loveliness of You; You Can't Have Everything

You Were Meant for Me (1948) Ain't Misbehavin'; Ain't She Sweet; Crazy Rhythm; Good Night Sweetheart; If I Had You; I'll Get By; You Were Meant for Me

You Were Never Lovelier (1942) Dearly Beloved; I'm Old Fashioned; You Were Never Lovelier

You'll Find Out (1940) The Bad Humor Man

You'll Never Get Rich (1941) Dream Dancing; So Near and Yet So Far

Young at Heart (1954) Just One of Those Things; The Man I Love; Ready, Willing and Able; Someone To Watch Over Me; Young at Heart

Young Man of Music I May Be Wrong But I Think You're Wonderful; Too Marvelous for Words; The Very Thought of You; With a Song in My Heart

Young Man with a Horn (1950) The Very Thought of You; With a Song in My Heart

You're a Sweetheart (1937) You're a Sweetheart

You're My Everything (1949) Ain't She Sweet; California, Here I Come; Charleston; I Can't Begin To Tell You; I May Be Wrong, But I Think You're Wonderful; On the Good Ship Lollipop; Would You Like To Take a Walk; You're My Everything

Ziegfeld Follies (1946) The Babbitt and the Bromide; Limehouse Blues; Love; This Heart of Mine

Ziegfeld Girl (1941) I'm Always Chasing Rainbows; Minnie from Trinidad; Mister Gallagher and Mister Sheen; Whispering; You Stepped Out of a Dream

4. NON-MUSICAL FILMS

(Dramatic films with musical themes, title song, or occasional song) A total of 528 films are represented here. For further information about this section, refer to notes at the beginning of this Part.

Accent on Youth (1935) Accent on Youth

The Actress (1953) My Beautiful Lady

The Adventures of Sherlock Holmes (1939) I Do Like To Be Beside the Seaside

An Affair To Remember (1957) An Affair To Remember; There's a Gold Mine in the Sky

After Midnight (1950) Mona Lisa

Against All Odds (1984) (Theme from) Against All Odds (Take a Look at Me Now)

Airport (1970) Airport Love Theme

The Alamo (1960) The Green Leaves of Summer

Alfie (1966) Alfie

Alice Doesn't Live Here Anymore Daniel; I've Got a Crush on You; Where or When

Alice's Restaurant (1969) Alice's Restaurant

An Alligator Named Daisy (1955) In Love for the Very First Time

Aloha (1938) Aloha Oe

Amarcord (1972) Stormy Weather

American Gigolo (1980) Call Me

An American Tail (1986) Somewhere Out There

Anastasia (1956) Anastasia

Andy Hardy's Private Secretary (1941) I've Got My Eyes on You

Anna (1951) Anna; Non Dimenticar

Another Time, Another Place (1958) Another Time, Another Place

The Apartment (1959) (Theme from) The Apartment

Argentine Nights (1940) Rhumboogie

Around the World in Eighty Days (1958) Around the World (in Eighty Days)

Arthur (1981) Arthur's Theme (Best That You Can Do)

The Awakening (1928) Marie

Back To the Future (1985) The Power of Love

The Bad and the Beautiful (1953) (Theme from) The Bad and the Beautiful

Bad Lands of Dakota (1941) MacNamara's Band

Band of Thieves (1962) Lonely

The Barbarian (1933) Love Song of the Nile

Barbed Wire (1952) Ezekiel Saw De Wheel; Mexicali Rose

Barefoot in the Park (1967) Barefoot in the Park

Battle Cry (1954) Honey-Babe

Beat Girl (1960) Made You

The Beautiful Spy (1935) Olga Pulloffski

Because They're Young (1960) Because They're Young; Shazam

The Bells of St. Mary's (1946) Aren't You Glad You're You; The Bells of St. Mary's; In the Land of Beginning Again

Ben (1972) Ben

The Best of Everything (1959) The Best of Everything

The Best Years of Our Lives (1946) Among My Souvenirs; Lazy River

Between Two Women (1945) I'm in the Mood for Love

Beverly Hills Cop (1985) New Attitude

Big City (1948) Don't Blame Me

Blackboard Jungle (1955) Rock Around the Clock

The Blazing Sun (1950) Along the Navajo Trail

Blithe Spirit (1945) Waltz Theme

The Blue Angel (1930) Falling in Love Again

The Blue Angel (1959) Falling in Love Again

The Blue Veil (1951) I Couldn't Sleep a Wink Last Night; There'll Be Some Changes Made

Blues Brothers (1979) Rubber Biscuit

Bonnie and Clyde (1967) The Ballad of Bonnie and Clyde

Born Free (1966) Born Free

Born Yesterday (1951) I Can't Give You Anything But Love

Boys in the Band (1967) Anything Goes; The Look of Love

Boys' Night Out (1962) The Boys' Night Out

Brazil (1944) Brazil

Break the News (1941) It All Belongs to You

Breakfast at Tiffany's (1961) Breakfast at Tiffany's; Moon River

Brian's Song (1972) Brian's Song

The Bridge on the River Kwai (1957) Colonel Bogey March; The River Kwai March

Bright Eyes (1934) On the Good Ship Lollipop

Bright Eyes (1980) Bright Eyes

Bringing Up Baby (1938) I Can't Give You Anything But Love

Butch Cassidy and the Sundance Kid (1969) Raindrops Keep Fallin' on My Head

Butterfield 8 (1960) Gloria

The Caddy (1953) That's Amore

Caddyshack (1980) I'm Alright, or, (Theme from) Caddyshack

The Caine Mutiny (1954) I Can't Believe That You're in Love with Me

Calling Wild Bill Elliott (1942) Long Long Ago

Cameo Kirby (1930) Romance

Canyon Passage (1946) Ole Buttermilk Sky

Captain Carey, U.S.A. (1950) Mona Lisa

Car Wash (1977) Car Wash

Casablanca (1942) As Time Goes By

Casino Royale (1967) (Theme from) Casino Royale; The Look of Love

Catch Us If You Can (1965) Catch Us If You Can

Cavalcade (1933) Twentieth Century Blues

A Certain Smile (1958) A Certain Smile

The Champ (1979) If You Remember Me

Charade (1963) (Theme from) Charade

Chariots of Fire (1981) (Theme from) Chariots of Fire

Charlie Moon (1956) Out of Town

The Cherokee Strip (1940) My Little Buckaroo

Chitty Chitty Bang Bang (1968) Chitty Chitty Bang Bang

Christmas Holiday (1944) Always; Spring Will Be a Little Late This Year

Cinderella Swings It (1943) I Heard You Cried Last Night

Circus of Horrors (1960) Look for a Star

City Lights (1931) Who'll Buy My Violets

Clash By Night (1952) I Hear a Rhapsody

Clockwork Orange (1972) Singin' in the Rain

Close Encounters of the Third Kind (1977) (Theme from) Close Encounters of the Third Kind

College Scandal (1935) In the Middle of a Kiss

The Color of Money The Girl from Ipanema

The Color Purple (1985) Miss Celie's Blues (Sister)

Colorado (1940) De Camptown Races; Oh Susanna; Ring De Banjo

Colorado Sundown (1952) Down by the Riverside

Come to the Stable (1949) Through a Long and Sleepless Night

Confidential Agent (1945) Love Is the Sweetest Thing; Tip Toe Through the Tulips

Congress Dances (1931) Just Once for All Times; Live, Laugh and Love

Copper Canyon (1950) Copper Canyon

The Covered Wagon (1923) Covered Wagon Days; Westward Ho!—The Covered Wagon March

La Cucaracha (1934) La Cucaracha

The Dam Busters (1955) The Dam Busters

Dancin' Co-Ed (1939) Jungle Drums

Dangerous Moonlight (1941) Warsaw Concerto

Dark Passage (1947) How Little We Know

The Daughter of Rosie O'Grady (1950) The Daughter of Rosie O'Grady

Davy Crockett (1955) The Ballad of Davy Crockett

Days of Wine and Roses (1962) Days of Wine and Roses

Dead Reckoning (1947) Either It's Love or It Isn't

Dear Heart (1965) Dear Heart

Deliverance (1973) Dueling Banjos

Designing Woman (1957) There'll Be Some Changes Made

Desire (1936) Whispers in the Dark

Destry Rides Again (1939) The Boys in the Back Room; Once Knew a Fella

Diamonds Are Forever (1972) Diamonds Are Forever

Dinner at Eight (1933) Dinner at Eight; Don't Blame Me

Doctor No (1962) The James Bond Theme

La Dolce Vita (1959) Patricia

Don't Trust Your Husband (1948) Jealous

Down Mexico Way (1941) Maria Elena

Drag (1929) My Song of the Nile

Dreamland of Desire (1961) Adios, My Love, or, The Song of Athens

Dude Ranch (1931) Out of Nowhere

Dynamite (1929) How Am I To Know

Easy Living (1937) Easy Living

The Egg and I (1947) The Egg and I

Elvira Madigan (1967) (Theme from) Elvira Madigan

The Empire Strikes Back (1980) (Theme from) The Empire Strikes Back

Encore (1952) More Than You Know

Escape to Happiness (1939) Intermezzo

E.T. The Extra-Terrestrial (1982) (Theme from) E.T. The Extra-Terrestrial

Every Which Way But Loose (1979) Coca-Cola Cowboy; Every Which Way But Loose

Evil Under the Sun Anything Goes; It's D'Lovely; I've Got You Under My Skin; You Do Something to Me; You're the Top

Exodus (1960) (Theme from) Exodus

Expresso Bongo (1960) A Voice in the Wilderness

Faithful in My Fashion (1946) I Don't Know Why

Fame (1980) Fame

Fanny (1961) Fanny

Farewell Performance (1963) Ice Cream Man

Father Goose (1965) Pass Me By

The Feminine Touch (1941) Jealous

Ferry Across the Mersey (1965) Ferry 'Cross the Mersey

The Fighting Coast Guard (1951) Home on the Range; Semper Paratus

Fireworks (1953) Oh My Papa

Flame of the Barbary Coast (1945) Carrie; The Cubanola Glide

Flamingo Road (1949) If I Could Be with You One Hour Tonight

Follow the Boys (1962) Follow the Boys

Follow the Sun (1951) Love Is a Dancing Thing

Fools for Scandal (1938) How Can You Forget

Footloose (1984) Footloose

Forest Rangers (1942) Jingle Jangle Jingle

The French Lieutenant's Woman (1982) (Theme from) The French Lieutenant's Woman

Friendly Persuasion (1956) Friendly Persuasion

The Frightened City (1961) The Frightened City

From Hell to Heaven (1933) Please

From Here to Eternity (1953) From Here to Eternity

From Russia with Love (1963) From Russia with Love; The James Bond Theme

Fun at Saint Fanny's (1955) Anyone Can Be a Millionaire

Gaily Gaily (1970) There's Enough To Go Around

The Gay Desperado (1936) The World Is Mine (Tonight)

Georgy Girl (1966) Georgy Girl

Gandhi (1983) For All Mankind (Theme from *Gandhi*)

Ghostbusters (1984) Ghostbusters

The Girl from Jones Beach (1949) I Only Have Eyes for You

The Girl from Mexico (1939) Chiapanecas

Give My Regards to Broadway (1948) Give My Regards to Broadway; When Francis Dances with Me

Glory Alley (1952) St. Louis Blues

The Godfather (1972) (Theme from) The Godfather; Michael's Theme; Speak Softly Love

The Godfather, Part II (1974) (Theme from) The Godfather, Part II

Gold Mine in the Sky (1938) There's a Gold Mine in the Sky

Golden Earrings (1947) Golden Earrings

Goldfinger (1964) (Theme from) Goldfinger

Gone with the Wind (1939) Tara's Theme

The Good Companions (1957) The Good Companions

The Good, the Bad and the Ugly (1968) The Good, the Bad and the Ugly

The Graduate (1967) Mrs. Robinson; Scarborough Fair/ Canticle; The Sounds of Silence

The Great Imposter (1961) The Great Imposter

The Great John L. (1945) A Friend of Yours; When You Were Sweet Sixteen

The Great Race (1965) The Sweetheart Tree

Greatest American Hero (1981) (Theme from) Greatest American Hero (Believe It or Not)

Green Dolphin Street (1947) On Green Dolphin Street

The Guns of Navarone (1961) The Guns of Navarone

A Guy Named Joe (1944) I'll Get By

Halfway to Heaven (1929) Louise

Happy Anniversary (1959) Happy Anniversary

The Happy Ending (1970) What Are You Doing the Rest of Your Life

Hard To Get (1938) You Must Have Been a Beautiful Baby

Hatari (1962) Baby Elephant Walk; Hatari

Havana Rose (1951) Babalu

Have a Heart (1934) Lost in a Fog; Thank You for a Lovely Evening

Heart of the Rockies (1951) Wanderin'

Heaven Can Wait (1978) Ciribiribin; The Gladiator's Entry

Her Highness and the Bellboy (1945) Dream; Honey

Her Kind of Man (1946) Body and Soul; Something To Remember You By; Speak to Me of Love

Her Master's Voice (1936) With All My Heart

Here's to Romance (1935) Here's to Romance; Midnight in Paris

Hi Beautiful (1944) Don't Sweetheart Me; Singin' in the Rain

The High and the Mighty (1954) The High and the Mighty

High Noon (1952) (Theme from) High Noon

High Time (1960) The Second Time Around

Hired Wife (1940) Little Brown Jug

A Hole in the Head (1959) High Hopes

Home in Wyoming (1942) Tweedle-O-Twill

Houseboat (1958) Almost in Your Arms; Love Song from Houseboat

Hullabaloo (1940) Carry Me Back to Old Virginny; A Handful of Stars

The Hurricane (1937) The Moon of Manakoora

Hush Hush Sweet Charlotte (1965) Hush Hush Sweet Charlotte

I Cover the Waterfront (1933) I Cover the Waterfront

I Wake Up Screaming (1941) The Things I Love

I Was an American Spy (1951) Because of You

Ice Castles (1979) (Theme from) Ice Castles (Through the Eyes of Love)

Idiot's Delight (1938) How Strange

Idle on Parade (1959) I've Waited So Long

If I Were King (1938) If I Were King

I'll Be Seeing You (1944) I'll Be Seeing You

Illegal (1955) Can't We Talk It Over

In a Lonely Place (1950) I Hadn't Anyone Till You

Indian Territory (1950) Chattanoogie Shoe Shine Boy

Indiscreet (1931) Come to Me

Indiscretion of an American Wife (1954) Autumn in Rome

The Inn of the Sixth Happiness (1959) This Old Man

Intermezzo (1939) Intermezzo

Invitation (1952) Invitation

Istanbul (1957) When I Fall in Love

It's a Mad, Mad, Mad, Mad World (1963) It's a Mad, Mad, Mad, Mad World

It's a Pleasure (1945) Romance; Tico Tico

It's Great To Be Young (1952) Marching Strings; You Are My First Love

Ivy (1947) Ivy

Jack Ahoy (1935) My Hat's on the Side of My Head

Joan of the Ozarks (1942) The Wabash Blues

John and Julie (1955) John and Julie

Johnny Angel (1945) Memphis in June

The Joker Is Wild (1957) All the Way; Chicago

June Moon (1931) June Moon

Jungle Princess (1936) Moonlight and Shadows

Just for Fun (1963) The Night Has a Thousand Eyes

The Karate Kid Part II (1986) Glory of Love (Theme from *The Karate Kid Part II*)

Key Largo (1948) Moanin' Low

Kill That Story (1934) Two Cigarettes in the Dark

A King in New York (1957) Mandolin Serenade

King Solomon's Mines (1937) Climbing Up

Lady of the Pavements (1929) Where Is the Song of Songs for Me

Lady on a Train (1945) Gimme a Little Kiss, Will Ya, Huh?; Night and Day

The Las Vegas Story (1952) I Get Along Without You Very Well; My Resistance Is Low

The Last Musketeer (1952) Aura Lee; Down in the Valley

Laura (1944) Laura

Lawrence of Arabia (1962) (Theme from) Lawrence of Arabia

Leave It to Lester I'm Yours

Legal Eagles (1986) Love Touch (Theme from *Legal Eagles*)

The Lemon Drop Kid (1951) Silver Bells

Let's Get Married (1960) Do You Mind

Let's Make Music (1940) Big Noise from Winnetka

Lilac Time (1928) Jeannine, I Dream of Lilac Time

Limelight (1953) Eternally

Little Boy Lost (1953) Love Is Like a Violin

Live and Let Die (1973) Live and Let Die

Lizzie (1957) It's Not for Me To Say

Local Hero (1984) Going Home

Love Affair (1939) Wishing (Will Make It So)

Love, Honor and Behave (1938) Bei Mir Bist Du Schön

Love in the Afternoon (1957) Fascination

Love Is a Many-Splendored Thing (1955) Love Is a Many-Splendored Thing

Love Letters (1945) Love Letters

Love Me Forever (1935) On Wings of Song

Love Me Tender (1956) Love Me Tender

Love Story (1970) Where Do I Begin

Love with the Proper Stranger (1964) Love with the Proper Stranger

Lovers and Other Strangers (1970) For All We Know

Lydia (1941) Lydia

Ma He's Making Eyes at Me (1940) A Lemon in the Garden of Love; Me He's Making Eyes at Me

Macao (1952) One for My Baby and One More for the Road

The Magnificent Seven (1960) (Theme from) The Magnificent Seven

Mahogany (1976) Do You Know Where You're Going To

The Main Event (1979) Main Event/The Fight

Malaya (1950) Blue Moon; Temptation

A Man and a Woman (1966) A Man and a Woman

A Man Called Sullivan, *see* **The Great John L.**

A Man Could Get Killed (1966) Strangers in the Night

The Man from Laramie (1955) The Man from Laramie

The Man in the White Suit (1951) The White Suit Samba

The Man Who Knew Too Much (1956) Whatever Will Be, Will Be, or, Que Sera, Sera

The Man Who Shot Liberty Valance (1962) The Man Who Shot Liberty Valance

The Man with the Golden Arm (1955) The Man with the Golden Arm

Mannequin (1937) Always and Always

Margie (1940) Margie; (My) Wonderful One

Marjorie Morningstar (1958) A Very Precious Love

Marshmallow Moon (1951) My Beloved

M*A*S*H (1970) (Song from) M*A*S*H

The Mating Season (1951) When I Take My Sugar to Tea

Mickey (1918) Mickey

Midnight Cowboy (1969) Everybody's Talkin'; Midnight Cowboy

Midnight Express (1979) Chase

Mildred Pierce Oceana Roll

Mission to Moscow (1943) Mean to Me

Modern Times (1954) Smile

Mondo Cane (1963) More

Montana Moon (1930) The Moon Is Low

Montana Territory (1952) Down in the Valley

Moulin Rouge (1953) The Song from Moulin Rouge

Move Over Darling (1963) Move Over Darling

Mule Train (1950) Mule Train; The Old Chisholm Trail; Room Full of Roses

Murder on the Orient Express (1974) (Theme from) Murder on the Orient Express

My Foolish Heart (1949) My Foolish Heart

My Lucky Star (1938) By a Wishing Well

Nashville (1975) I'm Easy

Near the Rainbow's End (1930) Ro-Ro-Rollin' Along

Never a Dull Moment (1943) My Blue Heaven

Never on Sunday (1960) Never on Sunday

Never Say Goodbye (1946) Remember Me

A New Kind of Love (1963) (Theme from) A New Kind of Love

New Mexico (1951) Soldier, Soldier, Won't You Marry Me?

New York Town (1941) Love in Bloom; Yip-I-Addy-I-Ay!; You Oughta Be in Pictures

The Night Has a Thousand Eyes (1948) The Night Has a Thousand Eyes

Night Stage to Galveston (1952) The Eyes of Texas; The Yellow Rose of Texas

Night Without Stars (1951) If You Go

Nighttime in Nevada (1949) The Big Rock Candy Mountain

9 to 5 (1981) 9 to 5

No Trees in the Street (1958) Liza Johnson

Nob Hill (1945) I Don't Care Who Knows It

Norma Rae (1979) It Goes Like It Goes

North to Alaska (1960) North to Alaska

Now Voyager (1942) It Can't Be Wrong

The Odd Couple (1968) (Theme from) The Old Couple

An Officer and a Gentleman (1982) Up Where We Belong

Oklahoma Annie (1952) Have You Ever Been Lonely

The Old Barn Dance (1938) You're the Only Star in My Blue Heaven

Old Oklahoma Plains (1952) Look Down, Look Down That Lonesome Road; The Old Chisholm Trail

The Old West (1952) Somebody Bigger Than You and I

On the Beach (1959) On the Beach; Waltzing Matilda

On Wings of Song (1935) Love Me Forever

One Minute to Zero (1951) When I Fall in Love

One Touch of Venus (1948) Speak Low

Only Angels Have Wings Adios, Mariquita Linda; The Peanut Vendor

Only When I Laugh (1981) (You've Got To Have) Heart

Out of Africa (1986) (Theme from) Out of Africa

Overland Telegraph (1951) I'se Gwine Back to Dixie; Nelly Bly; Oh! Susanna

The Pagan (1929) Pagan Love Song

Paleface (1948) Buttons and Bows

Pandora and the Flying Dutchman (1952) How Am I To Know

Papa's Delicate Condition (1963) Call Me Irresponsible

Paper Moon (1973) It's Only a Paper Moon

The Parent Trap (1961) Let's Get Together

Parrish (1961) Allison's Theme; Lucy's Theme from Parrish

Pepe (1960) Pepe

Picnic (1956) Moonglow; (Theme from) Picnic

The Picture of Dorian Gray (1945) Little Yellow Bird

Pieces of Dreams (1970) Pieces of Dreams

Pillow Talk (1959) Pillow Talk

The Pink Panther (1964) (Theme from) The Pink Panther

Plague Dogs (1983) Time and Tide (Theme from *Plague Dogs*)

Play It Cool (1962) Once Upon a Dream

Pocketful of Miracles (1961) Pocketful of Miracles

Poseidon Adventure (1972) The Morning After

The Postman Always Rings Twice (1946) She's Funny That Way

The Prime of Miss Jean Brodie (1969) Jean

The Prize Fighter and the Lady (1933) You've Got Everything

Pursuit to Algiers Flow Gently, Sweet Afton; Loch Lomond

The Racket (1951) A Lovely Way To Spend an Evening

Rah-Rah-Daze (1930) So Beats My Heart for You

Raiders of the Lost Ark (1981) (Theme from) Raiders of the Lost Ark

The Rainmakers (1935) Isn't Love the Grandest Thing

Raintree County (1957) (The Song of) Raintree County

The Razor's Edge (1947) Mam'selle

Reaching for the Moon (1930) Reaching for the Moon

Reap the Wild Wind (1942) 'Tis But a Little Faded Flower

Return to Peyton Place (1958) (Theme from) Return to Peyton Place

Rhythmania (1931) Between the Devil and the Deep Blue Sea

Riders in the Sky (1949) Ghost Riders in the Sky

Rim of the Canyon (1949) You're the Only Star in My Blue Heaven

Ringside Maizie (1941) A Bird in a Gilded Cage

Road House (1949) Again; What a Little Moonlight Can Do

Roadie (1980) Drivin' My Life Away

Rockie IV (1986) Burning Heart

Rocky (1977) Gonna Fly Now

The Rodeo King and the Señorita (1951) Juanita; Strawberry Roan

Rolling Home to Texas (1941) Wabash Cannonball

Romance of the Rio Grande (1941) La Cucaracha

Romeo and Juliet (1969) Love Theme from Romeo and Juliet

Rose of the Rio Grande (1938) Song of the Rose

The Rose Tattoo (1955) The Rose Tattoo

Ruby Gentry (1953) Ruby

Saddle Pals (1941) Amapola

Sadie McKee (1934) All I Do Is Dream of You

San Antonio (1945) Some Sunday Morning

San Francisco (1936) San Francisco; Would You

The Sandpiper (1965) The Shadow of Your Smile

Santa Fe Trail (1940) Along the Santa Fe Trail

Saratoga Trunk (1944) As Long as I Live

Sea Wife (1957) I'll Find You

See Here, Private Hargrove (1944) In My Arms

Sentimental Journey (1945) Sentimental Journey

September Affair (1950) September Song

Serious Charge (1959) Living Doll

7 1/2% Solution (1977) I Never Do Anything Twice

Seventh Heaven (1937) Diane; Seventh Heaven

Shaft (1971) (Theme from) Shaft

Shane (1953) The Call of the Far-Away Hills

Shipyard Sally (1939) Wish Me Luck As You Wave Me Goodbye

Shiralee (1957) Shiralee

Shopworn Angel (1938) A Precious Little Thing Called Love

Sierra Sue (1941) Sierra Sue

The Singing Nun (1966) Dominique

Sink the Bismarck (1960) Sink the Bismarck

Sinner Take All (1937) I'd Be Lost Without You

Sioux City Sue (1946) Sioux City Sue; Some Day You'll Want Me To Want You; Yours

Six Lessons from Madame LaZonga (1941) Six Lessons from Madame LaZonga

Smart Girls Don't Talk (1948) The Stars Will Remember

Smilin' Through Smilin' Through

Somebody Up There Likes Me (1956) Somebody Up There Likes Me

Song of Love (1947) As the Years Go By

Song of Old Wyoming (1945) The Hills of Old Wyomin'

Song of Russia (1943) And Russia Is Her Name

Sooner or Later (1979) You Take My Breath Away

The Sophomore (1929) Little By Little

South Sea Sinner (1950) I'm the Lonesomest Gal in Town; It Had To Be You

Spellbound (1945) (Theme from) Spellbound

St. Elmo's Fire (1985) St. Elmo's Fire (Man in Motion); Love Theme from St. Elmo's Fire

Stand By Me (1986) Stand By Me

Star Wars (1977) (Theme from) Star Wars

The Sterile Cuckoo (1969) Come Saturday Morning

The Sting (1974) The Entertainer

The Story of G.I. Joe (1945) Linda

La Strada (1956) (Theme from) La Strada, or, Stars Shine in Your Eyes

Straight Is the Way (1933) A Hundred Years from Today

Strange Lady in Town (1955) Strange Lady in Town

Street Angel Angela Mia

Streets of Laredo (1949) Streets of Laredo

Strictly Dishonorable (1951) Everything I Have Is Yours

The Stripper (1963) The Stripper

The Subject Was Roses (1968) Albatross; Who Knows Where the Time Goes

Summer of '42 (1971) The Summer Knows

A Summer Place (1959) (Theme from) A Summer Place

The Sun Also Rises (1957) I Love You

Sunset Boulevard (1950) Charmaine

Sunshine Susie (1932) Today I Feel So Happy

Superman (1979) Can You Read My Mind

Suzy (1936) Did I Remember

Sweet Bird of Youth (1962) Ebb Tide

Sweetheart of Sigma Chi (1946) Five Minutes More; The Sweetheart of Sigma Chi

Sweetheart of the Fleet (1942) We Did It Before (and We Can Do It Again)

Tammy and the Bachelor (1957) Tammy

Tangier (1946) Polly Wolly Doodle; She'll Be Comin' Round the Mountain

Task Force (1949) If You Could Care for Me

Tender Is the Night (1961) Tender Is the Night

The Tender Trap (1955) The Tender Trap

Thank God It's Friday (1978) Last Dance

Thanks for the Memory (1938) Two Sleepy People

That Certain Feeling (1956) Hit the Road to Dreamland; That Certain Feeling

That's Life (1986) Life in a Looking Glass

That's My Boy (1951) Ballin' the Jack; I'm in the Mood for Love

Their Own Desire (1930) Blue Is the Night

The Third Man (1949) The Third Man Theme

Thirty Seconds Over Tokyo (1944) I Love You

This Could Be the Night (1957) Blue Moon; I'm Gonna Live Till I Die; I've Got You Under My Skin; Just You, Just Me; The Tender Trap

The Thomas Crown Affair (1968) The Windmills of Your Mind

Three Coins in the Fountain (1954) Three Coins in the Fountain

Three Daring Daughters (1948) The Dickey Bird Song

Three Flights Up The Kiss Waltz

Three Smart Girls Grow Up (1939) Because

Thunderdome (1985) We Don't Need Another Hero

Till the End of Time (1946) Till the End of Time

Times Square Lady (1935) The Object of My Affection

To Each His Own (1946) To Each His Own

To Have and Have Not (1945) Am I Blue; How Little We Know

To Sir with Love (1967) To Sir with Love

To the Victor (1948) La Vie en Rose

Tommy the Toreador (1959) The Little White Bull

Too Young To Know (1945) It's Only a Paper Moon

Top Gun (1986) Take My Breath Away

Top Man (1943) Wrap Your Troubles in Dreams

The Towering Inferno (1974) We May Never Love Like This Again

The Trail of the Lonesome Pine (1936) A Melody from the Sky; Twilight on the Trail

Trail Street (1947) You're Not the Only Pebble on the Beach

The Trespasser (1929) Love Your Magic Spell Is Everywhere

True Confession (1937) True Confession

True Grit (1969) True Grit

The Tulsa Kid (1940) Golden Slippers

Two for the Road (1967) (Theme from) Two for the Road

Two Guys from Milwaukee (1946) And Her Tears Flowed Like Wine

2001: A Space Odyssey (1968) Also Sprach Zarathustra

The Umbrellas of Cherbourg (1965) I Will Wait for You

Unchained (1955) Unchained Melody

Underwater (1955) Cherry Pink and Apple Blossom White

The Unfinished Dance (1947) Holiday for Strings

The Unforgiven (1960) The Unforgiven

Unholy Partners (1941) After You've Gone

The Uninvited (1944) Stella by Starlight

Untamed (1955) Chant of the Jungle

Urban Cowboy (1981) Could I Have This Dance

Utah Wagon Train (1951) Streets of Laredo

Valley of Fire (1951) On Top of Old Smokey

Valley of the Dolls (1968) (Theme from) Valley of the Dolls

Variety Time (1948) Babalu

Vertigo (1958) (Theme from) Vertigo

Viva Villa (1934) La Cucaracha

Voyage to the Bottom of the Sea (1961) Voyage to the Bottom of the Sea

Wait Until Dark (1968) Wait Until Dark

Walk on the Wild Side (1962) Walk on the Wild Side

Wallflower (1948) Ask Anyone Who Knows; I May Be Wrong But I Think You're Wonderful

The Way We Were (1973) The Way We Were

Weary River (1929) Weary River

West of Zanzibar (1954) West of Zanzibar

What a Whopper (1961) The Time Has Come

What Price Glory? (1926) Charmaine

What Price Glory? (1952) It's a Long Way to Tipperary; Oui, Oui, Marie; Pack Up Your Troubles in Your Old Kit Bag and Smile, Smile, Smile; Smiles

What's New Pussycat (1965) What's New Pussycat

When the Lights Go On Again (1942) When the Lights Go On Again

When You're in Love (1937) Minnie the Moocher; Our Song; The Whistling Boy

Where Love Has Gone (1964) Where Love Has Gone

Where The Boys Are (1960) Where the Boys Are

Whirlwind (1951) Tweedle-O-Twill

White Nights (1985) Say You, Say Me; Separate Lives (Love Theme from *White Nights*)

Who Done It (1942) He's My Guy; Mister Five by Five

The Wicked Lady (1946) Love Steals Your Heart

The Wild Blue Yonder (1951) The Thing

Willy Wonka (1972) The Candy Man

Winged Victory (1944) The Army Air Corps Song; The Whiffenpoof Song

Wives and Lovers (1963) (Theme from) Wives and Lovers

A Woman Commands (1932) Paradise

The Woman in Red (1984) I Just Called To Say I Love You

Wonderful Life (1964) On the Beach

The Wonderful World of the Brothers Grimm (1962) (Theme from) The Wonderful World of the Brothers Grimm

The World of Susie Wong (1961) How Can You Forget

Written on the Wind (1957) Temptation

Yanks (1980) (Theme from) Yanks

Yokel Boy (1942) Comes Love

You Light Up My Life (1977) You Light Up My Life

You Only Live Twice (1967) (Theme from) You Only Live Twice

Young Eagles (1930) Love, Here Is My Heart; Sunrise and You

The Young Ones (1961) The Savage

Youth on Parade (1943) (It Seems to Me) I've Heard That Song Before

Zorba the Greek (1964) (Theme from) Zorba the Greek

5. RADIO AND TELEVISION SHOWS AND PROGRAMS

A total of 73 radio and television programs are represented here. It is not the purpose of this list to indicate as many radio television themes as possible. Only those that have been commercially popular on their own standing are cited here. For further information about this section, refer to notes at the beginning of this Part.

> "That's what shepherds listened to in Arcadia
> Before somebody invented the radia."
>
> —*Ogden Nash*

Aladdin Aladdin

Alfred Hitchcock Presents Funeral March of a Marionette

All in the Family Those Were the Days

Amos'n' Andy The Perfect Song

Androcles and the Lion Strangers

Angie Different Worlds

Atlantic & Pacific Radio Hour Two Guitars

The Avengers The Avengers' Theme

Batman Batman Theme

BBC Radio News Imperial Echoes

Ben Casey Theme from Ben Casey

The Beverly Hillbillies Ballad of Jed Clampett

Bonanza Bonanza

Brideshead Revisited (Theme from) Brideshead Revisited

The British Empire (BBC) The British Empire

Cinderella Do I Love You Because You're Beautiful; In My Own Little Corner; Loneliness of Evening; A Lovely Night; No Other Love; Ten Minutes Ago

Come to Me Come to Me

Davy Crockett The Ballad of Davy Crockett

Doctor Finlay's Case-Book (BBC) March from "A Little Suite"

Doctor Kildaire (Theme from) Doctor Kildaire (Three Stars Will Shine Tonight)

Dragnet Dragnet

Dukes of Hazzard (Theme from) Dukes of Hazzard (Good Ol' Boys)

The Eleventh Hour Theme from The Eleventh Hour

Emergency Ward 10 (BBC) Emergency Ward 10 Theme

The F.B.I. The F.B.I.

Flame Trees of Thika (Theme from) Flame Trees of Thika

Fleischmann Hour My Time Is Your Time

Happy Days Happy Days

Have Gun, Will Travel The Ballad of Paladin

Hawaii Five-O (Theme from) Hawaii Five-O

I Love Lucy I Love Lucy

Jewel in the Crown (Theme from) Jewel in the Crown

Justice Hard To Get

The Late Show The Syncopated Clock

Looking Around (BBC) Looking Around

Love for Lydia (BBC) Love for Lydia

Maigret (BBC) The Maigret Theme

Makin' It Makin' It

The Man from U.N.C.L.E. (Theme from) The Man from U.N.C.L.E.

M*A*S*H (Song from) M*A*S*H

Maverick Maverick

Miami Vice (Theme from) Miami Vice

Million Dollar Movie Tara's Theme

Mission: Impossible (Theme from) Mission: Impossible

Mr. Lucky Mr. Lucky

M-Squad M-Squad

Nationwide (BBC) The Good Word

The Odd Couple (Theme from) The Odd Couple

Our Town Love and Marriage

Owen MD (BBC) Sleepy Shores

The Pallisers (BBC) The Pallisers

The Patty Duke Show The Patty Duke Theme (Cousins)

Peter Gunn (Theme from) Peter Gunn

The Philadelphia Story Tracy's Theme

Picture Parade (BBC) Picture Parade

Rawhide Rawhide

R.K.O. Radio Hour The Voice of R.K.O.

Rotten Row (BBC radio) Rotten Row

Sea Hunt (Theme from) Sea Hunt

Sesame Street Sing (Sing a Song)

77 Sunset Strip Kookie, Kookie, Lend Me Your Comb

Softly, Softly Softly, Softly Theme

Song for A Summer Night (Studio One) Song for a Summer Night

Steve Race (BBC) Dick's Maggot

The Strange World of Gurney Slade The Gurney Slade Theme

Stranger on the Shore (BBC) Stranger on the Shore

S.W.A.T. Theme from S.W.A.T.

Texaco Hour Near You

The Tonight Show Johnny's Theme

The Untouchables (Theme from) The Untouchables

Upstairs Downstairs (BBC) (Theme from) Upstairs Downstairs (The Edwardians)

Welcome Back Kotter Welcome Back

Wings Wings

Your Hit Parade Lucky Day; Happy Days Are Here Again

Z Cars (BBC) Z Cars Theme

IX

Thesaurus of Song Titles by Subject, Key Word, and Category

Very often there is a need by musical directors, arrangers, performers, and TV and radio programmers (when preparing theme programs or medleys for revue, nightclub, and cabaret acts as well as for large-scale productions in Vegas, concerts, and recordings) to have lists of selected songs relevant to a particular theme or idea.

A total of 2300 subject, key word, and category headings are listed alphabetically in this Part. All song titles are listed alphabetically under their respective headings. Unless indicated otherwise, generic headings will most often *not* be all-inclusive (e.g. Flower, *see* also Rose, Tulip, etc.). How-

ever, selected generic headings will be all-inclusive when the total number of songs entered is not unreasonable (e.g. Penny, *see* Money). Also, headings for countries or states will not include principal cities; thus "France" and "Paris" are listed separately and will not be cross-referenced.

It is not the purpose of these listings to indicate all songs relating to a particular subject, key word, or category. Only those songs selected for inclusion in Part V are entered here. For more complete information about a particular song, refer to Part V; all song titles here are listed alphabetically in Part V.

Abie   Abie My Boy

Abilene   Abilene

Abraham   Abraham; Abraham, Martin and John; Rock-a My Soul (in the Bosom of Abraham); We Are Coming, Father Abraham, 300,000 More

Absence   Absence Makes the Heart Grow Fonder; Absence Makes the Heart Grow Fonder (for Somebody Else); Absent

Acapulco   In Acapulco

Accent   Accent on Youth; Ac-cent-tchu-ate the Positive; Pardon My Southern Accent

Accident   Accidentally on Purpose

Accordion   Sam, the Old Accordion Man

Account   All on Account of Liza

Accustomed   I've Grown Accustomed to Her Face

Ace   Ace in the Hole

Ache, *see also* **Sick**   Blue Moon with Heartache; The Curse of an Aching Heart; Don't Bring Me Your Heartaches; Good Morning Heartache; Heartaches; Heartaches by the Number; I Know a Heartache When I See One; It's a Heartache; I've Got a Pain in My Sawdust; King of Pain; Let the Heartaches Begin; The Mansion of Aching Hearts; Only the Heartaches; See, Gentle Patience Smiles on Pain; Seven Year Ache; Sweet Heartache; Sweet Heartaches; You're a Sweet Little Headache

Across   Across the Alley from the Alamo; Across the Field; Bells Across the Meadow; Ferry 'Cross the Mersey; Hands Across the Sea; Hands Across the Table; Shenandoah, or, Across the Wide Missouri

Action   Actions Speak Louder Than Words; Solid Gold Easy Action

Actor   (To) Be a Performer; The Glamorous Life; Hi-Diddle-Dee Dee (An Actor's Life for Me)

Adair   My Sweet Adair; Robin Adair

Adam   Eve Cost Adam Just One Bone

Adano   It Happened in Adano

Add   Every Little Bit Added to What You've Got Makes Just a Little Bit More; I Can't Do the Sum

Address, *see* **Letter**

Adelaide   Adelaide; Adelaide's Lament

Adeline   Adeline; (You're the Flower of My Heart) Sweet Adeline

Admiral, *see* **Navy**

Admire   Mutual Admiration Society

Adore   "A"—You're Adorable; Love Forever I Adore You; My Eyes Adored You

Adventure   The Morning After, or, Song from the Poseidon Adventure

Advice   Always Take Mother's Advice; My Grandma's Advice; She Took Mother's Advice

Affair, *see also* **Court**   An Affair To Remember; End of a Love Affair; Family Affair; Odds and Ends (of a Beautiful Love Affair); Our Love Affair; 65 Love Affair; The Windmills of Your Mind, or, Theme from the Thomas Crown Affair

Affection   Just a Little Fond Affection; The Object of My Affection

Afraid   Afraid To Dream; Coward of the County; Don't Ever Be Afraid To Go Home; Fear Ye Not, O Israel; The Frightened City; I'm Afraid To Come Home in the Dark; Little Shop of Horrors; (I'm Afraid) The Masquerade Is Over; Mysterioso Pizzicato; Running Scared; Who's Afraid of the Big Bad Wolf

Africa   Africa; African Lament (Lamento Africano); African Sanctus; African Waltz; Congo Love Song; (Theme from) Out of Africa

Afternoon   Afternoon Delight; Afternoon of a Faun; Call Me Up Some Rainy Afternoon; Ev'ry Sunday Afternoon; Lazy Afternoon; On a Sunday Afternoon; One Sunday Afternoon

Again   Again; Alone Again (Naturally); And So To Sleep Again; (Every Time I Turn Around) Back in Love Again; Back in My Arms Again; Back in the Saddle Again; Back on My Mind Again; Blue Again; Calling to Her Boys Just Once Again; Do It Again; (Please) Do It Again; Do It Again; Falling Again; Fallin' in Love (Again); Falling in Love Again; The Fleet's in Port Again; Free Again; God Be with You Till We Meet Again; Happy Days Are Here Again; Hard Times Come Again No More; He Walked Right In, Turned Around and Walked Right Out Again; Hello Again; Here Comes Heaven Again; Here Comes the Rain Again; Here I Go Again; Here It Comes Again; Here We Are, Here We Are, Here We Are Again; Here You Come Again; Home Again; Home Again; Home Again Blues; I Just Fall in Love Again; I Wish I Had My Old Girl Back Again; I Wish I Were in Love Again; If Ever You're in My Arms Again; If I Love Again; If I Should Fall in Love Again; I'll Be with You When the Roses Bloom Again; I'll Never Be Jealous Again; I'll Never Fall in Love Again; I'll Never Have To Dream Again; I'll Never Love Again (La Borrachita); I'll Never Love This Way Again; I'll Never Say ''Never Again'' Again; I'll Never Smile Again; I'll See You Again; I'll Take You Home Again Kathleen; I'm in Love Again; I'm in Love Again; In the Land of Beginning Again; (Back Home Again in) Indiana; It's Love Again; It's Raining Again; Kiss Me Again, or, If I Were on the Stage; Left All Alone Again Blues; Let Me Dream Again; Let Us Be Sweethearts Over Again; Let's Do It Again; Let's Twist Again; Liberty Bell—It's Time To Ring Again; Loving Her Was Easier (Than Anything I'll Ever Do Again); Mary Dear, Some Day We Will Meet Again; Never Gonna Fall in Love Again; On the Road Again; Out in the Cold Again; Over and Over Again; Over and Over Again; Ready To Take a Chance Again; Rolling Stones—All Come Rolling Home Again; Say It (Over and Over Again); (I Don't Believe It But) Say It Again; Say You're Mine Again; Sometime You'll Wish Me Back Again; Take Me Around Again; Take Me Back to Your Heart Again; Tell It All Over Again; That Lovin' You Feelin' Again; There Goes That Song Again; There! I've Said It Again; There's a Land of Begin Again; Till I Waltz Again with You; Till the Lights of London Shine Again; Till We Meet Again; Try Again Johnnie; Tryin' To Get the Feelin' Again; Waltz Me Around Again Willie—'Round, 'Round, 'Round; We Did It Before (and We Can Do It Again);

We May Never Love Like This Again; We Two Shall Meet Again; We'll Be Together Again; We'll Meet Again; We'll Never Have To Say Goodbye Again; When Shall I Again See Ireland; When Shall We Meet Again; When the Lights Go On Again (All Over the World); When the Nylons Bloom Again; When The Poppies Bloom Again; When the Robins Nest Again; When the White Lilacs Bloom Again; When Will I See You Again; With You I'm Born Again; You Try Somebody Else, and I'll Try Somebody Else (We'll Be Back Together Again); You've Got Me Crying Again

Aggravate   Aggravatin' Papa (Don't You Try To Two-Time Me); You Irritate Me So

Ago, *see also* **Past**   All Those Years Ago; Dreams of Long Ago; Long Ago and Far Away; Long Ago in Alcala; Long Long Ago, or, The Long Ago; Long Time Ago, or, Shinbone Alley; My Dream Girl, I Loved You Long Ago; Ten Minutes Ago; 'Twas Not So Long Ago

Air   Air for the G String; The Air That I Breathe; Airy, Fairy Lillian; Castles in the Air; Folks That Put On Airs; Free as Air; In the Air Tonight; Introduction and Air to a Stained Glass Window; It's in the Air; The Lass with the Delicate Air, or, Young Molly Who Lives at the Foot of the Hill; Londonderry Air; Lords of the Air; Love in the Open Air; Love Is in the Air; On the Air; There's Music in the Air; Wait Till You Get Them Up in the Air, Boys; When the Spring Is in the Air; While Others Are Building Castles in the Air (I'll Build a Cottage for Two)

Air Force   The Army Air Corps Song, or, The U.S. Air Force Song; The Army, the Navy and the Air Force

Airplane, *see also* **Jet**   Airport Love Theme; Come, Josephine, in My Flying Machine; Come Take a Trip in My Airship; Going Up; The High and the Mighty; I'm an Airman; Leaving on a Jet Plane; Me and Jane in a Plane; Pan Am Makes the Goin' Great; Pilot Me; Take Me Up with You, Dearie; Trains and Boats and Planes; Wait Till You Get Them Up in the Air, Boys; Yellow Bird

Al   He's Our Al; In the Fall We'll All Go Voting for Al

Alabama   The Alabama Blossoms; Alabama Jubilee; The Alabama Song, or, Moon of Alabama; Alabamy Bound; Dreamy Alabama; Little Alabama Coon; Lovin' Sam, the Sheik of Alabam'; The Rose of Alabama; Stars Fell on Alabama; When the Midnight Choo-Choo Leaves for Alabam'

Aladdin, *see* **Magic**

Alamo   Across the Alley from the Alamo; On the Alamo

Alarm   Midnight Fire-Alarm

Alaska   North to Alaska

Albany   Why Do They All Take the Night Boat to Albany

Albatross   Albatross

Albert   The Lion and Albert; Uncle Albert/ Admiral Halsey

Album   In My Little Snapshot Album

Alcohol, *see also* **Wine**   The Alcoholic Blues; Another Little Drink Wouldn't Do Us Any Harm; Applejack; The Beer Barrel Polka; Beer, Beer, Glorious Beer; Blue Champagne; Brandy (You're a Fine Girl); Brown October Ale; Champagne Charley Was His Name; The Champagne Waltz; Cocktails for Two; Don't Have Any More, Mrs. Moore; Drinking Song;

(What Shall We Do with) The Drunken Sailor, or, Columbus, or, John Brown Had a Little Injun, or, Ten Little Indians; Every Day Will Be Sunday When the Town Goes Dry; For the Noo, or, Something in the Bottle for the Morning; Gimme a Pigfoot (and a Bottle of Beer); Have a Drink on Me; Heidelberg Stein Song; Here's to Us; Hitting the Bottle; How Dry I Am; I Never Drank Behind the Bar; I Will Drink the Wine; Ida, Sweet as Apple Cider; If You've Got the Time, We've Got the Beer; I'm on the Water Wagon Now; It's Always Fair Weather When Good Fellows Get Together, or, A Stein Song; Ka-Lu-A; Let's Have a Tiddley at the Milk Bar; Love Hangover; Lush Life; The Moon Shines on the Moonshine; Moonlight Cocktail; The Night They Invented Champagne; Pirate Song, or, Fifteen Men on a (the) Dead Man's Chest—Yo! Ho! Ho! and a Bottle of Rum; Rum Boogie (Rhumboogie); Rum and Coca-Cola; Schaefer Is the One Beer; Shave and a Haircut, Bay Rum; Sipping Cider Thru (Through) a Straw; (Maine) Stein Song; Tequila; There Is a Tavern in the Town; Under the Anheuser Bush; What'll We Do on a Saturday Night When the Town Goes Dry; When You Say Bud, You've Said It All; Where There's Life, There's Bud; Wonder Bar; You Cannot Make Your Shimmy Shake on Tea

Ale, *see* **Alcohol**

Alexander Alexander (Don't You Love Your Baby No More); Alexander's Ragtime Band; When Alexander Takes His Ragtime Band to France

Alfie Alfie

Ali Baba Ali Baba's Camel

Alice (In My Sweet Little) Alice Blue Gown; Alice in Wonderland; Alice, Where Art Thou; Alice's Restaurant; The Girl in the Alice Blue Gown; Sweet Alice, or, Ben Bolt, or, Don't You Remember

Allah, *see* **God**

Allan, *see* **Allen**

Allegheny Allegheny Moon

Allen Allan Water; Barbry (Barbara) Allen; On the Banks of Allan Water

Alley Across the Alley from the Alamo; Alley Cat; Creque Alley; Gasoline Alley Bred; Long Time Ago, or, Shinbone Alley; Sally in Our Alley; Sally, You Brought the Sunshine to Our Alley; The Sunshine of Paradise Alley

Alligator, *see* **Crocodile**

Allison Allison's Theme from Parrish

Alma Alma Where Do You Live

Alone, *see also* **Lone, Lonely, Lonesome** All Alone; All Alone; All Alone Monday; Alone; Alone Again (Naturally); Alone at a Table for Two; Alone Together; Alone Too Long; For You Alone; For You Alone; I Don't Like To Sleep Alone; I Never See Maggie Alone; I'll Walk Alone; Leave a Tender Moment Alone; Leave Me Alone (Ruby Red Dress); Left All Alone Again Blues; Let It Alone; Meet Me by Moonlight Alone; One Alone; One Moment Alone; Only You (and You Alone); Solitude; There's a Million Girlies Lonesome Tonight, and Still I'm All Alone; Thine Alone; Time Alone Will Tell; When I Get You Alone; Tonight; When We're

Alone, or, Penthouse Serenade; You Alone, or, Solo Tu; You'll Never Walk Alone; Yours Is My Heart Alone

Alphabet ABC; "A"—You're Adorable; The Alphabet Song; Take the "A" Train; Twinkle, Twinkle, Little Star, or, Ah! Vous Diraije Maman, or, ABCDEFG (The Alphabet Song)

Alphonse Pardon Me, My Dear Alphonse, After You, My Dear Gaston

Alsace Lorraine, My Beautiful Alsace Lorraine

Alto I'm Looking for a Guy Who Plays Alto and Baritone and Doubles on a Clarinet and Wears a Size Thirty-Seven Suit

Alvin Alvin's Harmonica

Always Always and Always; (You Are) Always in My Heart; Always in the Way; Always Leave Them Laughing When You Say Goodbye; Always Take Mother's Advice; (I'm) Always True to You in My Fashion; First, Last and Always; The Grass is Always Greener; I Shall Always Remember You Smiling; I Will Always Love You; If You Should Ever Need Me (You'll Always Find Me Here); I'll Always Be in Love with You; I'll always Be with You; I'm Always Chasing Rainbows; Is It Always Like This; It's Always Fair Weather When Good Fellows Get Together, or, A Stein Song; It's Always You; Married I Can Always Get; The Other Man's Grass (Is Always Greener); Our Country, May She Always Be Right; The River Song, or, Something's Always Happening on the River; Semper Fidelis; Semper Paratus; Somebody Else, It's Always Somebody Else; Sunday, Monday or Always; There'll Always Be an England; There's Always Something There To Remind Me; There's Always Tomorrow; They Always Pick On Me; This Is Always; We Will Always Be Sweethearts; Why Am I Always the Bridesmaid; You Always Hurt the One You Love; You'll Always Be My Lifetime Sweetheart; You'll Always Be the One I Love; You'll Always Be the Same Sweet Girl; You're Always in My Arms (But Only in My Dreams)

Amanda Amanda

Amaze Amazing Grace; Maybe I'm Amazed

America America (My Country 'Tis of Thee); America; America I Love You; America, the Beautiful; American Beauty Rose; An American Dream; An American in Paris; American Made; American Music; American Patrol (We Must Be Vigilant); (Bye Bye) American Pie; The American Star; Ballad for Americans; Born in the U.S.A.; God Bless America; God Bless the U.S.A.; The Good Old U.S.A.; (Theme from) Greatest American Hero (Believe It or Not); In America; Living in America; The Miss America Pageant; My Own United States; R.O.C.K. in the U.S.A.; See the U.S.A. in Your Chevrolet; South America Take It Away; South American Way; Surfin' U.S.A.; Tony from America; Twistin' U.S.A.; The U.S. Field Artillery March, or, the Caissons Go Rolling Along; Viva l'America; Home of the Free

Ammunition, *see* **Gun**

Amsterdam Amsterdam; A Windmill in Old Amsterdam

Amy Amy, Wonderful Amy; Once in Love with Amy

Anastasia Anastasia

Anchor, *see* **Boat**

Andalucia Andalucia

Angel And the Angels Sing; Angel Child; Angel Flying Too Close to the Ground; Angel Gabriel; Angel in Your Arms; Angel of the Great White Way; Angel of the Morning; Angela Mia; Angels from the Realms of Glory; Angels Meet Me at the Cross Roads; Angel's Serenade; Bless You (for Being an Angel); Earth Angel; Good Night Angel; Got a Date with an Angel; Hark the Herald Angels Sing; Heaven Must Be Missing an Angel; How Do You Speak to an Angel; I Married an Angel; (You May Not Be an Angel But) I'll String Along with You; Johnny Angel; Kiss an Angel Good Mornin'; Lonely Night (Angel Face); My Special Angel; One More Angel in Heaven; A Sinner Kissed an Angel; There Are Angels Outside Heaven; You're an Angel

Angelina Angelina; Angelina Baker; My Angeline; Poor Little Angeline

Angelo Angelo

Angie Angie; Angie Baby

Angry Don't Be Angry

Animal Animal Crackers in My Soup; Bless the Beasts and the Children; I'm Just Wild About Animal Crackers; Talk to the Animals

Ann Barbara Ann; Cape Ann; Come Out of the Kitchen, Mary Ann; Keep Your Skirts Down, Mary Ann; Mary Ann; On the Good Ship Mary Ann; Raggedy Ann; Such an Education, Has My Mary Ann, or, Sweet Mary Ann; Take a Day Off, Mary Ann

Anna Anna; Wheezy Anna

Annabelle Annabelle; Fare Thee Well, Annabelle; (Who's Wonderful, Who's Marvelous?) Miss Annabelle Lee

Annie Annie Doesn't Live Here Anymore; Annie Laurie; Annie Lisle; Annie's Song; Gentle Annie; I Must See Annie Tonight; Little Annie Roonie; Polk Salad Annie; Sweet Annie Moore; When the Corn Is Waving, Annie Dear

Anniversary, *see* **Marriage**

Answer The Answer; Answer Me (My Love); Come Tell Me What's Your Answer, Yes or No; Don't Answer Me; Love Is the Answer; Never Take No for an Answer; Old Pal Why Don't You Answer Me; One Less Bell To Answer; Question and Answer (Demande et Reponse); Why Don't You Answer Me

Anticipation Anticipation

Antonio Oh Oh Antonio

Anvil Anvil Chorus

Apache, *see* **Indian**

Apartment, *see* **House**

Apologize, *see* **Sorry**

Applause Applause; Baby, Take a Bow; Clap Hands, Here Comes Charley; Clap Yo' Hands; The Clapping Song, or, My Mother Told Me

Apple An Apple for the Teacher; Cherry Pink and Apple Blossom White; Don't Sit Under the Apple Tree (with Anyone Else But Me); Ida, Sweet as Apple Cider; I'll Be with You in Apple Blossom Time; In the Shade of the Old Apple Tree; Little Green Apples; One Bad Apple (Don't Spoil the Whole Bunch); Shoofly Pie and Apple Pan Dowdy; When

It's Apple Blossom Time in Normandy; When the World Was Young (Ah, the Apple Tree); Would God I Were a Tender Apple Blossom; You're De Apple of My Eye

Applejack, *see* **Alcohol**

April April Showers; April Fools; April in Paris; April in Portugal; April Love; April Played the Fiddle; April Showers; I'll (I) Remember April

Aquarius, *see* **Magic**

Araby Araby; Araby's Daughter; I'll Sing Thee Songs of Araby; (Theme from) Lawrence of Arabia; Arabian Dance; The Sheik of Araby

Arch Round the Marble Arch; Underneath the Arches

Archery, *see* **Arrow**

Argentina The Argentines, the Portuguese and the Greeks; Don't Cry for Me, Argentina; Down Argentine Way

Argyle Mary of Argyle

Arizona Arizona

Ark, *see* **Boat**

Arkansas The Arkansas Traveler

Armentières Hinky Dinky Parlay Voo, or, Mad'moiselle from Armentières

Armor Armorer's Song

Arms Almost in Your Arms; Angel in Your Arms; Arm in Arm; Babes in Arms; Back in My Arms Again; Come Home to My Arms; Farewell to Arms; Full Moon and Empty Arms; Granny's Old Arm-Chair; Here in My Arms; I Got Lost in His Arms; I'd Love To Fall Asleep and Wake Up in My Mammy's Arms; If Ever You're in My Arms Again; In My Arms; In the Arms of Love; Lay Down Your Arms; Let Me Linger Longer in Your Arms; Linger in My Arms a Little Longer Baby; Love Song from Houseboat, or, Almost in Your Arms; The Man with the Golden Arm; My Baby's Arms; My Honey's Lovin' Arms; No Other Arms, No Other Lips; The Old Arm Chair; Open Arms; Put Your Arms Around Me Honey (Hold Me Tight); Safe in the Arms of Jesus; Snuggled on Your Shoulder, Cuddled in Your Arms; Stay in My Arms, Cinderella; Take Me in Your Arms; Take Me in Your Arms (Rock Me a Little While); With Her Head Tucked Underneath Her Arm; With My Shillelagh Under My Arm; You're Always in My Arms (But Only in My Dreams)

Army, *see also* **Sergeant, Soldier,** etc. The Army Game; The Army of Today's Alright; The Army, the Navy, and the Air Force; Assembly; Captain Jinks of the Horse Marines; (Theme from) The French Lieutenant's Woman; The G.I. Jive; Grafted into the Army; He's 1-A in the Army (and A-1 in My Heart); The Marine's Hymn, or, From the Halls of Montezuma; The Navy Gets the Gravy and the Army Gets the Beans; The Regiment of Sambre and Meuse; Regimental Song; Reveille; Secret Army; Short, Fat, and 4F; 633 Squadron; Taps; Tatoo; There's a Boy Coming Home on Leave; This Is the Army Mister Jones; The U.S. Field Artillery March, or, The Caissons Go Rolling Along; What Do You Do in the Infantry?; You Don't Belong to the Regulars, You're Just a Volunteer; You're in the Army Now

Arrow The Arrow and the Song; Barwick Green (The Archers); Yeoman of England; The Yeoman's Wedding Song

Art Children and Art

Arthur Arthur Murray Taught Me Dancing in a Hurry; Arthur's Theme (Best That You Can Do)

Artificial Artificial Flowers

Artist Artist's Life; A Picture No Artist Can Paint

Ascot, *see* **Tie**

Ashamed I'm So Ashamed; Mamie (Don't You Feel Ashamie)

Asia Asia; The Jewel of Asia

Asleep, *see* **Sleep**

Assembly, *see* **Army, People**

Astrology, *see* **Magic**

Athens Adios My Love, or, The Song of Athens; The White Rose of Athens

Atlanta Atlanta, Ga.

Atlantic City On the Boardwalk in Atlantic City

Atlantis Atlantis

Aunt Aunt Hagar's Blues; Aunt Jemima (Silver Dollar); Aunt Jemima and Your Uncle Cream of Wheat; My Old Aunt Sally; (Go Tell Aunt Rhody) The Ole Grey Goose (Is Dead); La Plume de Ma Tante (The Pen of My Aunt); When I Saw Sweet Nellie Home, or I Was Seeing Nellie Home, or, Aunt Dinah's Quilting Party

Aura Lee Aura Lee

Aurora Aurora

Automobile, *see also* **Gasoline** Bus Stop; Cadillac Car; Car Wash; Chevy Van; Come On, Spark Plug!; Drive; Drivin' My Life Away; (He'd Have To Get Under,) Get Out and Get Under (To Fix Up His Automobile); G.T.O.; Hot Rod Heart; I'm Wild About Horns on Automobiles That Go "Ta-Ta-Ta-Ta"; In My Merry Oldsmobile; Keep On Truckin'; Love in an Automobile; Love On a Greyhound Bus; The Low-Backed Car; Omnibus; One Two Three Red Light; Overdrive; See the U.S.A. in Your Chevrolet; Sitting in the Back Seat; Take a Car; Texaco Star Theme (The Man Who Wears the Star); Traffic Jam; Truck Stop; Truckin'; You Could Drive a Person Crazy; You Drive Me Crazy; You're Driving Me Crazy (What Did I Do); Z Cars Theme

Autumn Autumn Concerto; Autumn Crocus; Autumn in New York; Autumn in Rome; Autumn Leaves; Autumn Nocturne; Autumn Serenade; Early Autumn

Avalon Avalon; Avalon Town

Avenger Batman Theme; The Avengers' Theme

Avenue The Belle of Avenoo A; Conversation on Park Avenue; Down Sweetheart Avenue; Electric Avenue; Our Penthouse on Third Avenue; Slaughter on Tenth Avenue; Slumming on Park Avenue; Stairway to the Stars (Park Avenue Fantasy); Yuletide, Park Avenue

Average Too Good for the Average Man

Awake, *see* **Wake**

Awful The Coffee Song (They've Got an Awful Lot of Coffee in Brazil); I'm Awfully Glad I Met You; I'm Building Up to an Awful Let-Down

Axe, *see* **Knife**

Babble Beside a Babbling Brook; Tell Me, Babbling Echo, or, The Request

Baby Alexander (Don't You Love Your Baby No More); Angie Baby; Babes in Arms; Babes in the Wood; The Babies on Our Block; Baby; Baby, Baby All the Time; Baby Baby Baby; Baby Baby Baby; Baby Blue Eyes; Baby Come Back; Baby, Come To Me; Baby Doll; Baby Don't Get Hooked on Me; Baby Dream Your Dream; Baby Elephant Walk; Baby Face; Baby I Don't Care; Baby I Lied; Baby I Love You; Baby I'm Yours; Baby It's Cold Outside; Baby Love; Baby Me; Baby I'm Burning; Baby Mine; Baby Rose; Baby Shoes; Baby, Take a Bow; Baby the Rain Must Fall; Baby We Can't Go Wrong; Baby, Won't You Please Come Home; Baby You're a Rich Man; Baby's Prayer; Bandana Babies; Bang Bang (My Baby Shot Me Down); Be-Bop Baby; Be My Baby; Be My Little Baby Bumblebee; Broadway Baby; Bye Bye Baby; Bye Bye Baby; Chi-Baba Chi-Baba (My Bambino Go to Sleep); Ciao Ciao Bambina; Cradle's Empty, Baby's Gone; Cry Like a Baby; Don't Worry 'Bout Me Baby; Dream Babies; Everybody Loves My Baby, But My Baby Don't Love Nobody But Me; Gesù Bambino; Happy, Happy Birthday, Baby; Have You Got Any Castles, Baby; Hello! Ma Baby; Hey, Babe, Hey (I'm Nuts About You); Hey Baby; High Class Baby; Honey-Babe; I Don't Want To Walk Without You, Baby; I Found a Million Dollar Baby in a Five and Ten Cent Store; I Found a New Baby; I Guess I'll Have to Telegraph My Baby; I Love My Baby—My Baby Loves Me; I Was a Very Good Baby; I Wonder Where My Baby Is Tonight; I'd Like To Baby You; I'm Gonna Love You Just a Little More Baby; I'm Just a Baby; I'm Nobody's Baby; Is You Is or Is You Ain't My Baby; It Ain't Me Babe; Jazz Baby's Ball; Juke Box Baby; Just a Baby's Prayer at Twilight; Just Born To Be Your Baby; Just You 'N' Me (Babe); Kentucky Babe; Let Me Be Your Sugar Baby; Love To Love You Baby; Ma Curly-Headed Babby; Molly and I and the Baby; Move In a Little Closer Baby; My Baby Just Cares for Me; My Baby Thinks He's a Train; My Baby's Arms; My Baby's Comin' Home; My Melancholy Baby; Oh Babe, What Would You Say; Oh Baby Mine (I Get So Lonely); Oh You Million Dollar Baby; One for My Baby (and One More for the Road); Ooh Baby; Other People's Babies; Pretty Baby; Rock-a-Bye (Hush-a-Bye) Baby; Rock-a-Bye Your Baby with a Dixie Melody; Rock Your Baby; A Rose and a Baby Ruth; Ruby Baby; Shoo-Shoo Baby; Since I Met You Baby; Sing, Baby, Sing; Sleep, Baby, Sleep, or, Irene's Lullaby; Somebody's Baby; Someone Else's Baby; Steppin' Out with My Baby; Take Good Care of My Baby; There Goes My Baby; Too Busy Thinking About My Baby; Two Little Babes in the Wood; Two Little Baby Shoes; Walkin' My Baby Back Home; We're Having a Baby; When My Baby Smiles at Me; Whose Baby Are You; Why Baby Why; Wonder When My Baby's Coming Home; Yes Sir, That's My Baby; You Better Keep Babying Baby (or Baby's Gonna Bye-Bye You); You Do the Darndest Things, Baby; You Gotta Eat Your Spinach, Baby; You Must Have Been a Beautiful Baby; You Oughta See My Baby; You're a Great Big Blue-Eyed Baby; You're My Baby

Bach, *see* **Music**

Bachelor Bachelor Boy; A Bachelor Gay

Back, *see also* **Return**   And Her Golden Hair Was Hanging Down Her Back; As the Backs Go Tearing By; The Big Back Yard; (See What) The Boys in the Back Room (Will Have); Getcha Back; Give Yourself a Pat on the Back; Go Way Bad and Sit Down; Holding Back the Years; I Won't Hold You Back; Last Night on the Back Porch—I Loved Her Best of All; Lookin' Out My Back Door; The Low-Backed Car; Sitting in the Back Seat; Stand Back; Stay in Your Own Back Yard; Step to the Rear; Texas in My Rear View Mirror; Why Did I Leave My Little Back Room; You'll Be Back Every Night in My Dreams

Bacon   We Don't Want the Bacon, What We Want Is a Piece of the Rhine; Why Is the Bacon So Tough

Bad, *see also* **Naughty**   (Theme from) The Bad and the Beautiful; Bad Bad Leroy Brown; Bad Blood; Bad Boy; Baby Boy; Bad Girls; The Bad Humor Man; Bad Moon Rising; Bad Penny Blues; Bad Time; Bad Timing; Big Bad John; The Good Old Bad Days; The Good, the Bad, and the Ugly; Hurts So Bad; I Got It Bad and That Ain't Good; No Bad News; One Bad Apple (Don't Spoil the Whole Bunch); Somebody Bad Stole De Wedding Bell; There's a Little Bit of Bad in Every Good Little Girl; Too Bad; Who's Afraid of the Big Bad Wolf; The Worst Pies in London; You're No Good

Badge   The Badge from Your Coat

Badinage   Badinage

Bag, *see also* **Baggage**   Pack Up Your Trouble in Your Old Kit Bag and Smile, Smile, Smile; Papa's Got a Brand New Bag

Bagdad   Bagdad; Bagdad; Bagdad

Baggage, *see also* **Bag**   Another Suitcase in Another Hall; In the Baggage Coach Ahead

Bagpipe   Irish Washerwoman, or, The Scotch Bagpipe Melody

Bake   Bake Dat Chicken Pie; If I Knew You Were Comin' I'd've Baked a Cake; This Was a Real Nice Clambake

Baker   Angelina Baker; Baker Street

Balalaika   At the Balalaika

Bald, *see* **Hair**

Bali Bali   (It Happened) On the Beach At Bali Bali

Ball, *see also* **Dance**   Great Balls of Fire; Hostess with the Mostes' on the Ball; The Lone Fish (Meat) Ball; One Meat Ball; Pinball Wizard; Red Rubber Ball; Take Me Out to the Ball Game; Wabash Cannonball; When You're Wearing the Ball and Chain

Ballerina   Ballerina; Lonely Ballerina; Dance Ballerina Dance

Ballet, *see* **Dance**

Balloon   Around the World (in Eighty Days); The Red Balloon; Up in a Balloon; Up Up and Away, or, My Beautiful Balloon

Baltimore   Back, Back, Back to Baltimore

Bamboo   The House of Bamboo; Smellin' of Vanilla (Bamboo Cage); Under the Bamboo Tree

Banana   The Banana Boat Song (Day-O); (I'm) Chiquita Banana; I Like Bananas Because They Have No Bones; I've Never Seen a Straight Banana; Lovin' You Has Made Me Bananas; Two Ladies in De Shade of De Banana Tree; Yes! We Have No Bananas

Band   Alexander's Ragtime Band; Ask Her While the Band Is Playing; At the Jazz Band Ball; Band of Gold; Band on the Run; (Casey Would Waltz with the Strawberry Blonde While) The Band Played On; The Big Brass Band from Brazil; Come Follow the Band; The Ladies Who Sing with the Band; The Leader of the German Band; MacNamara's Band; Rubberband Man; Sergeant Pepper's Lonely Hearts Club Band; Strike Up the Band; Strike Up the Band—Here Comes a Sailor; A Terrific Band and a Real Nice Crowd; Travelin' Band; When Alexander Takes His Ragtime Band to France; Why Did She Fall for the Leader of the Band; You Can't Play Every Instrument in the Band

Bandana   Bandana Babies; Bandana Days; Bandana Land

Bang   Bang Bang (My Baby Shot Me Down); Bing! Bang! Bing 'Em on the Rhine; Boom Bang-A-Bang; Flash, Bang, Wallop; Here Come the British (Bang! Bang!); Mister Kiss Kiss Bang Bang

Banjo   A Banjo Song; Banjo Song; Dueling Banjos; Hey Mister Banjo; Ring De Banjo

Bank, *see also* **Money, Shore**   I Know a Bank Where the Wild Thyme Blows; Loch Lomond, or, The Bonnie Bonnie Banks, or, Oh! Ye'll Take the High Road; The Man That (Who) Broke the Bank at Monte Carlo; On the Banks of Allan Water; On the Banks of the Old Raritan; On the Banks of the Wabash Far Away; Ye Banks and Braes o' Bonnie Doon

Banner, *see* **Flag**

Bar, *see* **Alcohol, Music**

Barbara   Barbara Ann; Barbry (Barbara) Allen

Barbecue   Struttin' With Some Barbecue

Barber   The Barber of Seville (Overture); The Five Cent Shave; Kookie, Kookie, Lend Me Your Comb; Lost Barber Shop Chord; Play That Barbershop Chord (Mister Jefferson Lord); Shave and a Haircut, Bay Rum; That Lost Barbershop Chord

Barcelona   Barcelona

Barefoot, *see* **Feet**

Baritone   I'm Looking for a Guy Who Plays Alto and Baritone and Doubles on a Clarinet and Wears a Size Thirty-Seven Suit

Bark, *see also* **Tree**   The Belle of Barking Creek

Barn   Barnyard Blues; A House with a Little Red Barn

Barnacle   Barnacle Bill the Sailor

Barney   Barney Google; My Barney Lies Over the Ocean (Just the Way He Lied to Me)

Barnum, *see* **Circus**

Barnyard, *see* **Barn**

Baron   Snoopy vs. The Red Baron

Barrel   The Battle of the Kegs; The Beer Barrel Polka

Barter   The Bartered Bride (Overture)

Basin Street   Basin Street Blues

Basket   I'm Putting All My Eggs in One Basket

Bass   The Big Bass Viol; Slap That Bass

Bat   Batman Theme

Bath   Bathing in the Sunshine; Singin' in the Bathtub

Battle   The Battle Cry of Freedom; Battle Hymn of the Republic; Battle of Britain; The Battle of New Orleans; The

Battle of the Kegs; Joshua Fit (Fought) de Battle of Jericho; Just Before the Battle, Mother; Love Is Like a Battlefield

Bavaria   Buy a Broom, or, The Bavarian Girl's Song

Bay   All Aboard for Blanket Bay; The Back Bay Polka; The Bay of Biscay O!; Bimini Bay; (Sittin' On) The Dock of the Bay; Galway Bay; Hurray for Baffin's Bay; (On) Moonlight Bay; On Mobile Bay; Sailing Down the Chesapeake Bay; Shave and a Haircut, Bay Rum

Bayou   Blue Bayou; Jambalaya (On the Bayou); Song of the Bayou

Beach, *see also* **Shore**   Love Letters in the Sand; Manhattan Beach; Miami Beach Rumba; Mister Sandman; On Miami Shore, or, Golden Sands of Miami; On the Beach; On the Beach; (It Happened) On the Beach At Bali Bali; On the Beach at Waikiki; Sand in My Shoes; Shifting, Whispering Sands; Till the Sands of the Desert Grow Cold; White Silver Sands; You're Not the Only Pebble on the Beach

Beads, *see* **Jewel**

Beam   Come, Oh Come with Me, the Moon Is Beaming; Moonbeams; Thy Beaming Eyes

Bean   Beans Beans Beans; Chili Bean (Eenie Meenie Minie Mo); Jumping Bean; The Navy Gets the Gravy and the Army Gets the Beans

Bear   The Big Brown Bear; For He's a Jolly Good Fellow, or, Malbrouk (Malbrough), or, We Won't Go Home Until Morning, or, The Bear Went over the Mountain; Grizzly Bear; The Preacher and the Bear; Running Bear; (Let Me Be Your) Teddy Bear; The Teddy Bear's Picnic

Beard, *see* **Hair**

Beast, *see* **Animal**

Beat   Beat It; Beat Me, Daddy, Eight to the Bar; The Beat of My Heart; Can't You Hear My Heart Beat; Does Your Heart Beat for Me; Don't That Beat All; Heartbeat—It's a Lovebeat; Scrub Me Mama With a Boogie Beat; So Beats My Heart for You; Stop Beating 'Round the Mulberry Bush; We Got the Beat

Beatrice   Beatrice Fairfax, Tell Me What to Do

Beautiful   America, the Beautiful; American Beauty Rose; And I Was Beautiful; At the End of a Beautiful Day; (Theme from) The Bad and the Beautiful; Beautiful Bird, Sing On; Beautiful Boy; Beautiful Brown Eyes; Beautiful Dreamer; Beautiful Eyes; A Beautiful Friendship; (Hats Off, Here They Come, Those) Beautiful Girls; Beautiful Isle of Somewhere; Beautiful Isle of the Sea; Beautiful Lady in Blue; Beautiful Love; A Beautiful Morning; Beautiful Ohio; Beautiful People of Denver; The Blue Danube (On the Beautiful Blue Danube); But Beautiful; By the Beautiful Sea; Do I Love You Because You're Beautiful; Everything Is Beautiful; A Fact Can Be a Beautiful Thing; For the Beauty of the Earth; (Beautiful) Garden of Roses; He Was Beautiful; I Don't Want To Get Well (I'm in Love with a Beautiful Nurse); If I Said You Had a Beautiful Body (Would You Hold It Against Me); Igy (What a Beautiful World); It Was So Beautiful (and You Were Mine); Keep Young and Beautiful; Lorraine, My Beautiful Alsace Lorraine; Mornin' Beautiful; The Most Beautiful Girl in the World; (If You Happen to See) The Most Beautiful Girl (in the World); My Beautiful Lady, or, The Kiss Waltz; My Beautiful Sarie Marais; The Night Is Young and You're So

Beautiful; Oh, That Beautiful Rag; Oh What a Beautiful Mornin'; Oh You Beautiful Doll; Odds and Ends (of a Beautiful Love Affair); Sleeping Beauty Waltz; Spring, Beautiful Spring, or, Chimes of Spring; That Beautiful Rag; Together We Are Beautiful; Too Beautiful To Last; Up Up and Away, or, My Beautiful Balloon; We Could Make Such Beautiful Music (Together); When You're in Love with a Beautiful Woman; You Are So Beautiful; You Are So Beautiful; You Are Too Beautiful; You Beautiful So and So; You Gotta Be a Football Hero (To Get Along with the Beautiful Girls); You Must Have Been a Beautiful Baby; You're the One (You Beautiful Son-of-a-Gun)

Bed, *see also* **Blanket**   And So to Bed; And So to Bed; Does the Spearmint Lose Its Flavor on the Bedpost Overnight; My Trundle Bed, or, Recollections of Childhood; Swingin' in a Hammock; That Sly Old Gentleman from Featherbed Lane; A Wet Sheet and a Flowing Sea

Bedelia   Bedelia

Bedouin   Bedouin Love Song

Bedtime, *see* **Sleep**

Bee, *see* **Bumblebee, Harvest, Sew**

Beef   Boiled Beef and Carrots

Beer, *see* **Alcohol**

Beethoven   Roll Over Beethoven

Before   Come After Breakfast, Bring 'Long Your Lunch and Leave 'Fore Supper Time; The Day Before Spring; Don't Wait 'Til the Night Before Christmas; I Gave You Up Just Before You Threw Me Down; I See Your Face Before Me; I Was Never Kissed Before; I'm Gonna Love That Guy (Like He's Never Been Loved Before); (It Seems to Me) I've Heard That Song Before; I've Never Been in Love Before; Just Before the Battle, Mother; Long Before I Knew You; The Morning After the Night Before; Never Knew Love Like This Before; That Was Before I Met You; To All the Girls I've Loved Before; Wake Me Up Before You Go-Go; We Did It Before (and We Can Do It Again)

Beg   Beg, Steal or Borrow; Beg Your Pardon; The Beggar's Opera; I Beg of You; I Begged Her

Begat, *see* **Birth**

Begin, *see also* **Birth, Start**   Begin the Beguine; I Can't Begin To Tell You; I'm Beginning To See the Light; In the Land of Beginning Again; It's Beginning To Look (a Lot) Like Christmas; Let the Heartaches Begin; (Theme from) Love Story, or, Where Do I Begin; Out Where the West Begins; Pick Yourself Up; Start Me Up; That's the Beginning of the End; There's a Land of Begin Again; The Violin Began To Play; We've Only Just Begun; Where the Blue Begins

Beginner   (I've Got) Beginner's Luck

Beguine, *see* **Dance**

Behave   I Just Can't Make My Eyes Behave; Why Can't You Behave

Behind   Behind Closed Doors; Get Thee Behind Me, Satan; The Girl I Left Behind Me, or, Brighton Camp; I Long To See the Girl I Left Behind; I Never Drank Behind the Bar; I'm Gonna Pin My Medal on the Girl I Left Behind; I'm Walking Behind You; The Photo of the Girl I Left Behind;

When De Moon Comes Up Behind the Hill; When I Leave the World Behind

Belgium   My Belgian Rose

Believe   Believe; Believe in Yourself; Believe It Beloved; Believe Me If All Those Endearing Young Charms; Blessed Are the Believers; Daydream Believer; Do You Believe in Love; Do You Believe in Magic; Don't Stop Believin'; (Theme from) Greatest American Hero (Believe It or Not); How Could You Believe Me When I Said I Love You When You Know I've Been a Liar All My Life; I Believe; I Believe in You; I Believe in You; I Believe There's Nothing Stronger Than Our Love; I Can't Believe That You're in Love with Me; I Still Believe; I'd Still Believe You True; I'm a Believer; I'm Making Believe; It's Make Believe Ballroom Time; It's Only Make Believe; The Land of Make Believe; Maggie May/ Reason To Believe; Make Believe; Make Believe; Make Believe Island; Please Believe Me; (I Don't Believe It But) Say It Again; They Didn't Believe Me; What a Fool Believes; Why Don't You Believe Me

Bell   Bell Bottom Trousers; Bells Across the Meadow; Bells Are Ringing; Blue Bell; The Blue Bell of Scotland; Blue Bell Polka; Carol of the Bells; Chimes Blues; Daisy Bell, or, A Bicycle Built for Two, or, Daisy, Daisy; Ding Dong! The Witch Is Dead; Don't Ring-a Da Bell; Hang on the Bell Nellie; Hear Dem Bells; I Heard the Bells on Christmas Day; I Love a Lassie, or, Ma Scotch Bluebell; If I Were a Bell; I'm a Ding Dong Daddy from Dumas; I'm Gonna Ring the Bell Tonight; In the Wildwood Where the Bluebells Grew; Jingle Bell Rock; Jingle Bells, or, The One Horse Open Sleigh; Jingle Jangle Jingle; Josephine Please No Lean on the Bell; Katy Bell; The Liberty Bell; Liberty Bell—It's Time To Ring Again; The Monastery Bells; Ding Dong Bell; No Wedding Bells for Me; Oh Peter Go Ring Dem Bells; One Less Bell To Answer; Ring-a-Ding Girl; Ring De Banjo; Ring Dem Bells; Ring Ding; Ring of Kerry; School Day (Ring! Ring! Goes the Bell); Serenade of the Bells; Silver Bells; Snowy White Snow and Jingle Bells; Somebody Bad Stole De Wedding Bell; Spring, Beautiful Spring, or, Chimes of Spring; The Temple Bell; The Temple Bells; Those Wedding Bells Shall Not Ring Out; Ting-a-Ling, or, The Waltz of the Bells; Wedding Bell Blues; Wedding Bells Are Breaking Up That Old Gang of Mine; Westminster Chimes; The Weymouth Chimes; When the Angelus Is Ringing; When the Bell In the Lighthouse Rings Ding Dong; While the Angelus Was Ringing, or, The Three Bells (Les Trois Cloches), or, The Jimmy Brown Song; Whispering Bells; Whittington Chimes

Belle   Belle, Belle, My Liberty Belle; The Belle of Avenoo A; The Belle of Barking Creek; The Belle of Mohawk Vale, or, Bonny Eloise; The Belle of Pittsburg; Belle of the Ball; Creole Belle; Lou(i)siana Belle; Ma Belle; Ma Belle Marguerita; She Is the Belle of New York

Belly   I Can't Do My Belly Bottom Button Up

Belong   I Belong to Glasgow; It All Belongs to You (The Laugh of the Town); Mister Volunteer, or, You Don't Belong to the Regulars, You're Just a Volunteer; My Heart Belongs to Daddy; My Heart Belongs to Me; My Life Belongs to You; Nobody's Heart (Belongs to Me); The One I Love Belongs to Somebody Else; She Belongs to Me; There's a Girl in the Heart of Maryland (with a Heart That Belongs to Me); To-

night You Belong to Me; Up Where We Belong; We Belong; We Do Not Belong Together; You Belong to Me; You Belong to Me; You Belong to Me; You Belong to My Heart (Now and Forever), or, Solamente Una Vez; You Belong to the City; You Know You Belong to Somebody Else

Beloved   And This Is My Beloved; Cry, the Beloved Country; My Beloved

Below, *see also* **Under**   Down Below

Ben   Ben; Ben Hur Chariot Race (March); Bennie and the Jets; Benny Heavens, Oh!; Sweet Alice, or, Ben Bolt, or, Don't You Remember

Bench   A Bench in the Park; Got the Bench, Got the Park, But I Haven't Got You; On the Benches in the Park; You're in the Right Church, But the Wrong Pew

Bend   Bend Down, Sister; Bend Me, Shape Me; By the Bend of the River; Come to Me, Bend to Me

Beneath, *see also* **Under**   Beneath the Cross of Jesus; 'Neath the South Sea Moon; Nothing New Beneath the Sun

Benefit   Being for the Benefit of Mister Kite

Beret, *see* **Hat**

Berkeley Square   A Nightingale Sang in Berkeley Square

Bertie   Burlington Bertie from Bow

Bess   Bess, You Is My Woman Now; Oh, Bess, Oh Where's My Bess

Best   Arthur's Theme (Best That You Can Do); The Best I Get Is Much Obliged to You; Best of All; The Best of Everything; Best of My Love; Best of My Love; The Best of Times; The Best of Times; The Best Thing for You; (You're the) Best Thing That Ever Happened to Me; Best Thing You've Ever Done; The Best Things in Life Are Free; A Boy's Best Friend Is His Mother; Diamonds Are a Girl's Best Friend; First Love, Last Love, Best Love; I Lost the Best Pal That I Had; The Land of My Best Girl; Last Night on the Back Porch—I Loved Her Best of All; Love Is the Best of All; My Best Girl; My Best Girl; My Best Girl's a New Yorker (Corker); My Own Best Friend; Pillsbury Says It Best; You're My Best Friend; You're the Best Break This Old Heart Ever Had

Bet *see* **Gambling**

Beth   Beth

Bethlehem   O Little Town of Bethlehem

Betsy   Sweet Betsy from Pike, or, Vilikens and His Dinah

Betty   Bette Davis Eyes; Betty Co-Ed

Bible   The Bible Tells Me So; My Mother's Bible; My Mother's Bible; (Theme from) Raiders of the Lost Ark

Bicycle   Daisy Bell, or, A Bicycle Built for Two, or, Daisy, Daisy; The Pushbike Song

Bide, *see* **Wait**

Big   And the Great Big Saw Came Nearer; The Big Back Yard; Big Bad John; The Big Bass Viol; The Big Brass Band from Brazil; The Big Brown Bear; The Big Butter and Egg Man; Big City; Big City Suite; Big "D"; Big Girls Don't Cry; Big Head; A Big Hunk of Love; Big Hurt; Big Mamou; Big Man; Big Noise from Winnetka; The Big Rock Candy Mountain; Big Shot; (Hey) Big Spender; The Big Sunflower; Big Time; The Biggest Aspidistra in the World; Biggest Part of Me;

Caldonia (What Makes Your Big Head So Hard); I'm a Big Girl Now; It Looks (to Me) Like a Big Night Tonight; It's a Big, Wide, Wonderful World; It's a Great Big Shame; Let the Great Big World Keep Turning; Mister Big Stuff; My Dream of the Big Parade; My Home Town Is a One Horse Town, But It's Big Enough for Me; El Rancho Grande; Somebody Bigger Than You and I; This Could Be the Start of Something Big; When Big Profundo Sang Low ''C''; When You Wore a Tulip and I Wore a Big Red Rose; Who's Afraid of the Big Bad Wolf; Your Feet's Too Big; You're a Great Big Blue Eyed Baby; You've Got Your Mother's Big Blue Eyes

Bikini Itsy Bitsy Teenie Weenie Yellow Polkadot Bikini

Bill Barnacle Bill the Sailor; B-I-Double L-Bill; Bill; Bill Bailey, Won't You Please Come Home; Billie Jean; Billy (for When I Walk); Billy; Billy Boy; Billy Don't Be a Hero; Billy Muggins; Brother Bill; Ode to Billy Joe; Rock-A-Billy; Steamboat Bill; Sweet William; Waltz Me Around Again Willie—'Round, 'Round, 'Round; Which Way You Goin' Billy; William Tell Overture; William's Song; Willie We Have Missed You

Bind Blest Be the Tie That Binds; Much Binding in the Marsh; My Mother Bids Me Bind My Hair

Bingo Balm of Gilead, or, Bingo

Bird, *see also* **Blackbird, Bluebird, Bob White, Canary, Cockatoo, Crow, Cuckoo, Dove, Eagle, Flamingo, Hummingbird, Lark, Magpie, Nest, Nightingale, Pigeon, Robin, Sparrow, Swallow, Thrush, Wing** Beautiful Bird, Sing On; Bird Dog; A Bird in a Gilded Cage; Bird of Love Divine; The (Little) Bird on Nellie's Hat; Bird on the Wing; Bird Songs at Eventide; Birds in the Night; The (Little) Bird on Nellie's Hat; A Brown Bird Singing; Chirpy Chirpy, Cheep Cheep; The Convict and the Bird; The Dickey Bird Song; The Dicky Bird Hop; Down in the Valley, or, Birmingham Jail, or, Bird in a Cage, or, Down on the Levee; Happy Birds; How I Love You (I'm Tellin' the Birds, I'm Tellin' the Bees); I Lift Up My Finger and I Say Tweet Tweet; Lady Bird; Let's All Sing Like the Birdies Sing; Listen to the Mocking Bird; A Little Bird Told Me; A Little Birdie Told Me So; Little Birdies Learning How To Fly; Little Yellow Bird; Lullaby of Birdland; Shady Lady Bird; She Was One of the Early Birds; Sing Joyous Bird; Sing Little Birdie; Snowbird; Thunderbirds Theme; Two Little Bluebirds; Warblings At Eve; What the Dickie-Birds Say; When My Sugar Walks Down the Street, All the Birdies Go Tweet-Tweet-Tweet; When the Birds Have Sung Themselves to Sleep; When the Birds in Georgia Sing of Tennessee; Whip-Poor-Will; (There'll Be Blue Birds Over) The White Cliffs of Dover; Yellow Bird

Birmingham Birmingham Bertha; Birmingham Rag; Down in the Valley, or, Birmingham Jail, or, Bird in a Cage, or, Down on the Levee

Birth *see also* **Baby, Begin** The Begat; The Birth of Passion; The Birth of the Blues; Born Free; Born in the U.S.A.; Born To Lose; Born To Run; Born Too Late; Born Yesterday; Evergreen, or, Love Theme from A Star Is Born; Friends and Lovers (Born To Each Other); I Was Born in Virginia, or, Ethel Levy's Virginia Song; In the Town Where I Was Born; Just Born To Be Your Baby; The Liberty Song, or, Come, Join Hand in Hand, or, In Freedom We're Born; My Gal Is

a High Born Lady; The Origin of Gunpowder, or, When Vulcan Forg'd the Bolts of Jove; That's How a Love Song Was Born; That's Why Darkies Were Born; The Town Where I Was Born; Why Was I Born; With You I'm Born Again

Birthday A Birthday; The Birthday of a King; Happy Birthday to You, or, Good Morning to All; Happy, Happy Birthday, Baby; It's My Mother's Birthday Today; A Very Merry Un-Birthday to You

Biscay The Bay of Biscay O!

Biscuit Little Biscuit

Bit And a Little Bit More; Bits and Pieces; Coax Me a Little Bit; Come a Little Bit Closer; Every Little Bit Added to What You've Got Makes Just a Little Bit More; I'm a Little Bit Fonder of You; Just a Little Bit South of North Carolina; A Little Bit Independent; A Little Bit Me, A Little Bit You; A Little Bit of Heaven, Sure They Call It Ireland; A Little Bit of Soap; Little Bit o' Soul; Little Bit off the Top; Mary, You're a Little Bit Old-Fashioned; One of the Ruins That Cromwell Knocked About a Bit; There's a Little Bit of Bad in Every Good Little Girl; With a Little Bit of Luck

Bitch The Bitch Is Back

Bite, *see* **Chew**

Black Black and Tan Fantasy; Black and White; Black and White Rag; Black Bottom; Black Denim Trousers; Black Is the Color of My True Love's Hair; Black Moonlight; Black Water; Blackberry Way; Coal Black Mammy; The Coal Black Rose; Dark Eyes, or, Black Eyes; Ebony and Ivory; Ebony Eyes; Long Cool Woman (in a Black Dress); Mammy's (a) Little Coal Black Rose; Baa, Baa, Black Sheep; Old Black Joe; Paint It Black; Sooty; That Old Black Magic; Two Lovely Black Eyes; A Walk in the Black Forest; What Did I Do To Be So Black and Blue; When the Black Sheep Returns to the Fold; Where the Black-Eyed Susans Grow

Blackbird Blackbird; Bye Bye Blackbird; If I Were a Blackbird; I'm a Little Blackbird Looking for a Bluebird; My Blackbirds Are Bluebirds Now

Blacksmith The Blacksmith Blues; Song of the Blacksmith; The Village Blacksmith

Blame Blame It on My Youth; Blame It on the Bossa Nova; Don't Blame It All on Broadway; Don't Blame Me; No One Is To Blame; Put the Blame on Mame; She Is More To Be Pitied Than Censured

Blanket All Aboard for Blanket Bay; Under a Blanket of Blue

Blaze Blaze Away (March); Blaze of Glory; Blaze of Glory

Bleed, *see* **Blood**

Bless, Blessing Bless 'Em All; Bless the Beasts and Children; Bless This House; Bless You (for Being an Angel); Blessed Are the Believers; Blest Be the Tie That Binds; Come, Ye Blessed; Count Your Blessings Instead of Sheep; God Bless America; God Bless Our Native Land; God Bless the Child; God Bless the USA; Good Luck, Good Health, God Bless You; Goodbye, Good Luck, God Bless You; Goodnight and God Bless You; How Blest We Are; May the Good Lord Bless and Keep You; Old Hundred(th) Doxology, or, Praise God, from Whom All Blessings Flow; Savior Breathe an Evening Blessing; We Gather Together (To Ask the Lord's Blessing), or, Prayer of Thanksgiving

Blind The Blind Ploughman; Blinded by the Light; I Used To Be Color Blind; Miss Me Blind; Sweet Blindness; Three Blind Mice

Block The Babies on Our Block; Let's Take a Walk Around the Block

Blockbuster Blockbuster

Blonde (Casey Would Waltz With the Strawberry Blonde While) The Band Played On; Gentlemen Prefer Blondes

Blood Bad Blood; Bloody Mary; Only Women Bleed; Scots Wha Hae Wi' Wallace Bled; Transfusion

Bloom Ain't It Grand To Be Bloomin' Well Dead; (When the) Bloom Is on the Rye, or, My Pretty Jane; I'll Be with You When the Roses Bloom Again; Lo, How a Rose E'er Blooming; Love in Bloom; A Room in Bloomsbury; (When It's Roundup Time in Texas) When the Bloom Is on the Sage; When the Nylons Bloom Again; When the Poppies Bloom Again; When the White Lilacs Bloom Again

Blossom The Alabama Blossoms; April Blossoms; A Blossom Fell; Cherry Pink and Apple Blossom White; Down Where the Cotton Blossoms Grow; I'll Be with You in Apple Blossom Time; It Looks Like Rain in Cherry Blossom Lane; Only a Pansy Blossom; Orange Blossom Time; When It's Apple Blossom Time in Normandy; When the Cherry Blossoms Fall; Would God I Were a Tender Apple Blossom

Blow Any Way the Wind Blows; Blow, Gabriel, Blow; Blow Out the Candle; Blow (Knock) the Man Down; Blow the Smoke Away; Blow Ye Winds, Heigh Ho; Blowin' Away; Blowin' in the Wind; Down Where the Trade Winds Blow; I Know a Bank Where the Wild Thyme Blows; Ill Wind (You're Blowin' Me No Good); I'm Forever Blowing Bubbles; The North Wind Doth Blow; The Way That the Wind Blows

Blue (In My Sweet Little) Alice Blue Gown; Am I Blue; As Deep as the Deep Blue Sea; Baby Blue Eyes: Beautiful Lady in Blue; Between the Devil and the Deep Blue Sea; Beyond the Blue Horizon; Blue (and Broken Hearted); Blue Again; The Blue Alsation Mountains; The Blue and the Gray, or, A Mother's Gift to Her Country; Blue Bayou; Blue Bell; The Blue Bell of Scotland; Blue Bell Polka; The Blue Bird of Happiness; Blue Champagne; The Blue Danube (On the Beautiful Blue Danube); Blue Eyes; Blue Gardenia; Blue Hawaii; Blue Is the Night; The Blue Juaniata; Blue Lou; Blue Mirage; Blue Monday; Blue Moon with Heartache; Blue on Blue; Blue Orchids; Blue Pacific Moonlight; Blue Prelude; Blue Rain; Blue Ribbon Gal; The Blue Room; Blue Shadows and White Gardenias; Blue Shadows on the Trail; Blue Side; Blue Skies; Blue Skies Are Round the Corner; Blue Star; Blue Suede Shoes; Blue Tango; Blue Turning Grey over You; Blue Velvet; Blue Without You; Blueberry Hill; Bluebird; The Bonnie Blue Flag; Brown Eyes—Why Are You Blue; Columbia, the Gem of the Ocean, or, The Red, White and Blue; Crystal Blue Persuasion; Don't It Make My Brown Eyes Blue; Dream (When You're Feeling Blue); Eyes of Blue, Eyes of Brown; Five Foot Two, Eyes of Blue (Has Anybody Seen My Girl?); Forever in Blue Jeans; From the Land of the Sky Blue Water; The Girl in the Alice Blue Gown; Hair of Gold, Eyes of Blue; Have You Ever Been Lonely (Have You Ever Been Blue); The House of Blue Lights; How Blue the Night; I Love a Lassie, or, Ma Scotch Bluebell; I'd Rather Be Blue over You (Than Happy with Somebody Else); I'm

(Dreaming) Thinking Tonight of My Blue Eyes; In the Blue of Evening; In the Wildwood Where the Bluebells Grew; It's a Blue World; Jackie Blue; Jimmy Crack Corn, or, The Blue Tail Fly; A Knot of Blue; Lady Blue; The Lanky Yankee Boys in Blue; Lavender's Blue (Diddle Diddle, or, Dilly Dilly); Little Boy Blue; Little Girl Blue; Love Is Blue; Midnight Blue; Mister Blue; Misty Blue; Mood Indigo; The Moon is Blue; Little Boy Blue; My Blue Heaven; My Little Nest of Heavenly Blue, or, Frasquita Serenade (Blaues Himmelbett), or, Farewell, My Love, Farewell; My Long-Tail Blue; My Nellie's Blue Eyes; Old Man Sunshine—Little Boy Bluebird; Once in a Blue Moon; Put 'Em in a Box, Tie 'Em with a Ribbon (and Throw 'Em in the Deep Blue Sea); Red Roses for a Blue Lady; Rhapsody in Blue; Roll On, Tulane, or, The Olive and Blue; Serenade in Blue; She Waits by the Deep Blue Sea; So Blue; Song Sung Blue; Three Shades of Blue; True Blue Lou; 'Twas off the Blue Canaries, or, My Last Cigar; Two Blue Eyes; Two Little Bluebirds; Two Little Girls in Blue; Under a Blanket of Blue; Valse Bleue; What Did I Do To Be So Black and Blue; When Sonny Gets Blue; When the Blue Sky Turns to Gold; Where the Blue Begins; Where the Blue of the Night Meets the Gold of the Day; Where the Sunset Turns the Ocean's Blue to Gold; Where the Waters Are Blue; (There'll Be Blue Birds over) The White Cliffs of Dover; Who Could Be Bluer; Whoever You Are, or, Sometimes Your Eyes Look Blue to Me; You're a Great Big Blue Eyed Baby; You're the Only Star in My Blue Heaven; You've Got Your Mother's Big Blue Eyes

Blueberry Blueberry Hill

Bluebird The Blue Bird of Happiness; Bluebird (Vola Colomba); Hello, Bluebird; I'm a Little Blackbird Looking for a Bluebird; My Blackbirds Are Bluebirds Now; My Blue Bird Was Caught in the Rain; Old Man Sunshine—Little Boy Bluebird; Two Little Bluebirds; (There'll Be Blue Birds over) The White Cliffs of Dover

Blush Ma Blushin' Rosie

Boardwalk On the Boardwalk in Atlantic City; Under the Boardwalk

Boat, *see also* **Row** Anchored; Anchored; Anchors Aweigh; The Banana Boat Song (Day-O); Boats of Mine; Canadian Boat Song; The Canoe Song; A Capital Ship; Cruising Down the River; De Boatman's Dance; Don't Give Up the Ship; The Ferry Boat Inn; Ferry 'Cross the Mersey; Ferryboat Serenade; The Fleet's In; The Fleet's in Port Again; The Folks Are All Waiting To See the Fast Steamer; Gangway; Go, Little Boat; The Gum Tree Canoe (on Tom-Big-Bee River); Has Anybody Seen Our Ship; Here Comes the Showboat; I Saw Three Ships Come Sailing; I'm Waiting for Ships That Never Come In; Jazzboat; Kon-Tiki; The Love Boat; Love Song from Houseboat, or, Almost in Your Arms; Michael (Row the Boat Ashore); The Morning After, or, Song from The Poseidon Adventure; I Saw Three Ships Come Sailing; My Mariuccia Take a Steamboat; My Ship; De Old Ark's a-Moverin'; Old Ship of Mine; (I'd Like To Get You) On a Slow Boat to China; On the Good Ship Lollipop; On the Good Ship Mary Ann; Paddlin' Madelin' Home; Red Sails in the Sunset; River Boat; Riverboat Shuffle; Rock the Boat; Row, Row, Row Your Boat (Round); Row Thy Boat Lightly; Sail Along Silvery Moon; Sail Away; Sail Away; Sail On; Sailboat in the Moonlight; Sailing; Sailing (,Sailing) (Over the Bounding Main); Sailing; Sailin' Away on the Henry Clay; Sailing Down the Chesapeake Bay; Sailin' On; Ship Ahoy, or, All the Nice Girls Love a Sailor; A Ship Without a Sail; Shipmates of Mine; Shrimp Boats; Sink the Bismarck; Sit Down, You're Rocking the Boat; Sit Down, You're Rockin' the Boat; Someone's Rocking My Dream Boat; Song of the Volga Boatman (Boatmen); SOS; The Stanley Steamer; Steamboat Bill; There's a Boat Dat's Leavin' Soon for New York; There's One Wide River To Cross, or, Noah's Ark; Tippecanoe and Tyler Too; Trains and Boats and Planes; Twickenham Ferry; Waiting for the Robert E. Lee; When My Dream Boat Comes Home; When My Ship Comes In; Why Do They All Take the Night Boat to Albany; The Wreck of the Edmund Fitzgerald; The Wreck of the ''Julie Plante''; The Wreck of (on) the Old (Southern) '97; A Yankee Ship and a Yankee Crew; Yellow Submarine

Bob   Bob White (Whatcha Gonna Swing Tonight); Bobbie Sue; Bobby Shafto; Bobby Sox (Socks) to Stockings; Bobby's Girl; Me and Bobby McGee; Robert and Elizabeth; Waiting for the Robert E. Lee; When the Red, Red Robin Comes Bob, Bob, Bobbin' Along

Body   Body and Soul; Comin' Thro' the Rye, or, If a Body Meet a Body; If I Said You Had a Beautiful Body (Would You Hold It Against Me); John Brown's Body; Shake Your Body (Down to the Ground)

Bohemia   Bohemia; Bohemian Rhapsody; Come to the Land of Bohemia

Boil   Boiled Beef and Carrots

Boll Weevil   The Boll Weevil Song

Bolt   The Origin of Gunpowder, or, When Vulcan Forg'd the Bolts of Jove; Sweet Alice, or, Ben Bolt, or, Don't You Remember

Bombay   Bombay Duckling (Kipling Theme); Down in Bom-Bombay

Bonanza   Bonanza

Bond, *see* **Money**

Bone   Boneyard Shuffle; Dry Bones; Eve Cost Adam Just One Bone; I Like Bananas Because They Have No Bones; Lazy Bones; Long Time Ago, or, Shinbone Alley; Rags; Bottles or Bones

Bongo   Civilization (Bongo Bongo Bongo)

Bonnet, *see* **Hat**

Bonnie   The Ballad of Bonnie and Clyde; The Belle of Mohawk Vale, or, Bonny Eloise; The Bonnie Blue Flag; Bonnie Doon; Bonnie Dundee; I'll Go Home with Bonnie Jean; Loch Lomond, or, The Bonnie Bonnie Banks, or O! Ye'll Take the High Road; My Bonnie Lies Over the Ocean, or, Bring Back My Bonnie to Me; Ye Banks and Braes O' Bonnie Doon

Boogie   Boogie Down; Boogie Fever; Boogie Nights; Boogie On Reggae Woman; Boogie Oogie Oogie; Boogie Woogie; Boogie Woogie Bugle Boy (from Company B); Bumble Boogie; Carle Boogie; Cow-Cow Boogie; Fanfare Boogie; Get Up and Boogie; I'm Your Boogie Man; Jungle Boogie; Rum Boogie; Scrub Me Mama with a Boogie Beat

Book   The Book; Close as Pages in a Book; I Could Write a Book; In My Little Red Book; In My Little Snapshot Album; It's in the Book; Marian the Librarian; My Coloring Book; My Heart Is an Open Book; Paperback Writer

Boom   Boom; Boom Bang-A-Bang; Clancy Lowered the Boom; I Faw Down an' Go Boom; Sh-Boom

Boomerang   Boomerang; My Boomerang Won't Come Back; Ricochet

Boondocks   Down in the Boondocks

Boot   (Take Me Back to My) Boots and Saddle; Brahn Boots; These Boots Are Made for Walking

Border   Borderline; South of the Border (Down Mexico Way)

Borrow   Beg, Steal or Borrow; Kookie, Kookie, Lend Me Your Comb

Bosom   Bosom Buddies; Rock-a My Soul (in the Bosom of Abraham); Tits and Ass

Boston   Adams and Liberty, or, The Boston Patriotic Song; Boston Come-All Ye

Bother   Bewitched, Bothered and Bewildered; Don't Let It Bother You; I Can't Be Bothered Now; Shew (Shoo) Fly, Don't Bother Me

Bottle, *see also* **Alcohol**   I Bought Myself a Bottle of Ink; Milkman Keep Those Bottles Quiet; Rags, Bottles or Bones; Time in a Bottle

Bottom   Bell Bottom Trousers; Black Bottom; I Can't Do My Belly Bottom Button Up; In My Little Bottom Drawer; Rock Bottom; There Are Fairies at the Bottom of Our Garden; Voyage to the Bottom of the Sea

Bough, *see* **Tree**

Boulevard   Boulevard of Broken Dreams; Ev'ry Street's a Boulevard in Old New York

Bounce   Jersey Bounce; On the Rebound

Bouquet   Bouquet (I Shall Always Think of You); Bouquet of Barbed Wire; A Bouquet of Roses

Boutonniere, *see* **Flower**

Bow   Baby, Take a Bow; Burlington Bertie from Bow; Buttons and Bows; The Heart Bow'd Down

Bowery   The Bowery; My Pearl's a Bowery Girl; Only a Bowery Boy

Bowl   A Bowl of Roses; Come, Landlord, Fill the Flowing Bowl; Life Is Just a Bowl of Cherries; (Poor) Tom Bowling, or, The Sailor's Epitaph

Box   I've a Shooting Box in Scotland; Jack in the Box; Jack in the Box Baby; Juke Box Baby; (In My) Little Tin Box; Put 'Em in a Box, Tie 'Em with a Ribbon (and Throw 'Em in the Deep Blue Sea)

Boy   Abie My Boy; Adios Muchachos; All American Boy; Au Revoir, But Not Goodbye, Soldier Boy; Bachelor Boy; Bad Boy; Bad Boy; Beautiful Boy; Billy Boy; Boogie Woogie Bugle Boy (from Company B); A Boy and a Girl Were Dancing; The Boy from . . . ; Boy from New York City; The Boy Guessed Right; A Boy Like That; A Boy Named Sue; The Boy Next Door; Boy on a Dolphin; Boy! What Love Has Done to Me; The Boys Are Coming Home Today; A Boy's Best Friend Is His Mother; Boys Cry; (See What) The Boys in the Back Room (Will Have); The Boys' Night Out; Boys of Summer; Calling to Her Boy Just Once Again; Can't You Take It Back and Change It For a Boy; Charley, My Boy;

Chattanoogie Shoe Shine Boy; Cheer, Boys, Cheer; China Boy; Country Boy You Got Your Feet in L.A.; Danny Boy; Dear Little Boy of Mine; Don't Go Out Tonight, Boy; A Dream of My Boyhood Days; The Drummer Boy of Shiloh; (Theme from) Dukes of Hazzard (Good Ol' Boys); Follow the Boys; The Girl Is You and the Boy Is Me; Girls Were Made To Take Care of Boys; Good Ole Boys Like Me; Goodbye, Boys; Good-Bye, Ma! Good-Bye, Pa! Good-Bye, Mule, or Long Boy; Hev Yew Gotta Loight, Boy?; Hold Your Hand Out Naughty Boy; Honey Boy; I Didn't Raise My Boy To Be a Soldier; I Was Looking for My Boy, She Said, or, Decoration Day; If a Girl Like You Loved a Boy Like Me; It's a Boy; Johnny Doughboy Found a Rose in Ireland; Johnny Is the Boy for Me; Keep the Home Fires Burning (Till the Boys Come Home); Keep Your Head Down, "Fritzie Boy"; Kiss the Boys Goodbye; The Lanky Yankee Boys in Blue; Lift Boy; Let's Hear It for the Boy; Little Boy Blue; A Little Boy Called "Taps"; The Little Boy That Santa Claus Forgot; The Little Drummer Boy; The Little Drummer Boy; Lonely Boy; Lonely Boy; Looking for a Boy; Loverboy; Mad About the Boy; Mammy's Little Kinky Headed Boy; Mary's Boy Child; The Merry Swiss Boy; (To the War Has Gone) The Minstrel Boy; Little Boy Blue; My Boy Lollipop; My Boyfriend's Back; My Laddie; My Pony Boy; Nature Boy; Oh! Boy, What a Girl; Oh Boys Carry Me 'Long; Oh Mamma, or, The Butcher Boy; Old Man Sunshine—Little Boy Bluebird; One Boy; Only a Bowery Boy; Remember Boy, You're Irish (Shane na Lown); Sailor Boys Have Talk to Me in English; Say a Prayer for the Boys Over There; Shoeshine Boy; Smokin' in the Boys' Room; Soldier Boy; Sonny Boy; Thank God I'm a Country Boy; There's a Boy Coming Home on Leave; There's a Dixie Girl Who's Longing for a Yankee Doodle Boy; There's a Girl in This World for Every Boy and a Boy for Every Girl; Tomboy; Tommy, Lad; Two Little Boys; Wait Till You Get Them Up in the Air, Boys; Water Boy; When I Was a Lad; When the Boys Come Home; Where Is My (Wand'ring) Boy Tonight; Where the Boys Are; Where's the Boy? Here's the Girl!; The Whistling Boy; The Wild Boys; (I Am) The Yankee Doodle Boy; You're Going Far Away, Lad, or, I'm Still Your Mother, Dear

Braids, *see* **Hair**

Brain, *see* **Think**

Brandywine Down on the Brandywine

Brass The Big Brass Band from Brazil; Brass in Pocket

Brave The Brave Old Oak; The Mulligan Braves

Brazil The Big Brass Band from Brazil; Brazil; The Coffee Song (They've Got an Awful Lot of Coffee in Brazil)

Bread Bread and Butter; Johnny Doughboy Found a Rose in Ireland; Mouldy Old Dough; Shortnin' Bread

Break, *see* **Broken**

Breakfast Breakfast at Tiffany's; Come After Breakfast, Bring 'Long Your Lunch and Leave 'Fore Supper Time

Breathe The Air That I Breathe; All Choked Up; Every Breath You Take; Saviour, Breathe an Evening Blessing; Take My Breath Away; Wheezy Anna; With Every Breath I Take; You Leave Me Breathless; You Take My Breath Away

Breeding Gasoline Alley Bred; Half-Breed; She Was Bred in Old Kentucky

Breeze, *see* **Wind**

Brian Brian's Song

Brick Another Brick in the Wall; Goodbye Yellow Brick Road

Bride, *see* **Marriage**

Bridge The Bridge of Sighs; Bridge over Troubled Water; Cross Over the Bridge; (Fifteen Miles (Years) on the) Erie Canal (Low Bridge!—Everybody Down); The 59th Street Bridge Song, or, Feelin' Groovy; Golden Gate; Knightsbridge March, or, In Town Tonight; London Bridge; The River Kwai March; Seven Bridges Road; Strolling on the Brooklyn Bridge; Under the Bridges of Paris

Brigade Fire Brigade

Bright Bright Eyes; Brighten the Corner Where You Are; Brighter Than the Sun; Her Bright Smile Haunts Me Still; In the Morning by the Bright Light; Scenes That Are Brightest; Sparkling and Bright; Star Light, Star Bright; The Sun Shines Brighter

Brighton The Girl I Left Behind Me, or, Brighton Camp

Bristol Bristol Stomp

Britain, Britannia, *see* **England**

Broadway, *see also* **Actor, Applause, Entertain** Angel of the Great White Way; Another Honky Tonk Night on Broadway; Another Op'nin', Another Show; Baby, Take a Bow; Broadway Baby; Broadway Melody; Broadway Rhythm; Broadway Rose; Carry Me Back to Ole Virginny, or, De Floating Show; Don't Blame It All on Broadway; Forty-Five Minutes from Broadway; Forty-Second Street; Give My Regards to Broadway; Good-Bye Broadway, Hello France; I Left My Heart at the Stage Door Canteen; Kiss Me Again, or, If I Were on the Stage; Lady Luck Show; Lullaby of Broadway; Matinee; (Don't Put Your Daughter on the Stage) Mrs. Worthington; On Broadway; There's a Broken Heart for Every Light on Broadway; There's No Business Like Show Business; You Can Have Broadway; You Don't Have To Be a Star (To Be in My Show)

Brogue, *see* **Talk**

Broken Blue (and Broken Hearted); Boulevard of Broken Dreams; Break It to Me Gently; Break It to Me Gently; Break My Stride; Break of Day; Break the News to Mother; Break Up To Make Up; Breakdance; Breakdown Dead Ahead; Breaking in a Brand New Broken Heart; Breaking Up Is Hard To Do; Broken Doll; Broken Hearted Clown; Broken-Hearted Melody; Broken Lady; The Broken Melody; The Broken Record; Broken Wings; Broken Wings; Danger, Heartbreak Ahead; Don't Break the Heart That Loves You; Don't Go Breaking My Heart; Happy-Go-Lucky You and Broken-Hearted Me; Hard Habit To Break; Heartbreak Hotel; Heartbreaker; Heartbreaker; Here Am I—Broken Hearted; How Can You Mend a Broken Heart; How Many Hearts Have You Broken; Invitation to a Broken Heart; (The Wreck of the) John B; The Man That (Who) Broke the Bank at Monte Carlo; The Merry-Go-Round Broke Down; Morning Has Broken; Nineteenth Nervous Breakdown; Only Love Can Break a Heart; Rambling Wreck from Georgia Tech; Stop! You're Breaking My Heart; That Tumble-Down Shack in Athlone; There's a Broken Heart for Every Light on Broadway; Wedding Bells Are Breaking Up That Old Gang of Mine; The Wheel of the Wagon Is Broken; Whose Little Heart Are You

Breaking Now; The Wreck of the Edmund Fitzgerald; The Wreck of the ''Julie Plante''; The Wreck of (on) the Old (Southern) '97; You Deserve a Break Today; You Won't Be Satisfied (Until You Break My Heart); You're Breaking My Heart; You're the Best Break This Old Heart Ever Had

Brook   Beside a Babbling Brook; Rebecca of Sunny-Brook Farm

Brooklyn   Strolling on the Brooklyn Bridge

Broom   Buy a Broom, or, The Bavarian Girl's Song; Chim Chim Cher-ee; Keep Sweeping the Cobwebs off the Moon; Love Is Sweeping the Country; Sweep; Sweeping the Clouds Away

Brother   Brother Bill; Brother, Can You Spare a Dime; Brother Louie; Brotherhood of Man; Emmet's Lullaby, or, Fritz, Our Cousin German, or, Brother's Lullaby; He Ain't Heavy . . . He's My Brother; I'd Like To Be a Sister to a Brother Just Like You; Like Sister and Brother; Sing Brothers; Theme from The Wonderful World of the Brothers Grimm; Three Brothers

Brown   Bad Bad Leroy Brown; Beautiful Brown Eyes; The Big Brown Bear; A Brown Bird Singing; Brown Eyed Girl; Brown Eyes—Why Are You Blue; Brown October Ale; Charlie Brown; Cinderella Brown; Don't It Make My Brown Eyes Blue; (What Shall We Do with) The Drunken Sailor, or, Columbus, or, John Brown Had a Little Injun, or, Ten Little Indians; Eyes of Blue, Eyes of Brown; Genie with the Light Brown Lamp; Golden Brown; The Hazel Dell; It Takes a Long, Tall, Brown-Skin Gal; Jeanie with the Light Brown Hair; John Brown's Body; Knees Up Mother Brown; The Little Brown Church (in the Vale); Little Brown Jug; Miss Brown to You; Mrs. Brown You've Got a Lovely Daughter; Nancy Brown; Rufus Rastus Johnson Brown (What You Goin' To Do When the Rent Comes 'Round); Sweet Georgia Brown; You're a Good Man, Charlie Brown

Brunette   Negra Consentida (My Pet Brunette)

Brush   Brush Up Your Shakespeare; You're a Pink Toothbrush

Bubble   The Bubble; I'm Forever Blowing Bubbles; Meet Me in Bubble Land; Tiny Bubbles

Buccaneer, *see* **Pirate**

Buckaroo, *see* **Cowboy**

Bucket   My Dad's Dinner Pail; The Old Oaken Bucket

Buckle   Buckle Down, Winsocki

Bud, *see also* **Alcohol**   Persian Rosebud; Rose in the Bud

Buddha, *see* **God**

Buddy, *See* **Friend**

Buffalo   Buffalo Gals (Won't You Come Out Tonight?), or, Lubly Fan; Don't Put Me Off at Buffalo Any More; Home on the Range, or, Oh, Give Me a Home Where the Buffalo Roam; Put Me Off at Buffalo; Shuffle Off to Buffalo

Bug   The Love Bug Will Bite You; Some Little Bug Is Going To Find You (Some Day); Thanks for the Buggy Ride

Bugle   Boogie Woogie Bugle Boy (from Company B); Bugle Call (Rag); Bugle Call Rag; Fugue for Tinhorns; I'm Wild About Horns on Automobiles That Go ''Ta-Ta-Ta-Ta''; Toy Trumpet; The Trumpeteer; When They Sound the Last All Clear

Build   Build Me Up Buttercup; Daisy Bell, or, A Bicycle Built for Two, or, Daisy, Daisy; Gonna Build a Mountain; The House That Jack Built; I'll Build a Stairway to Paradise; I'm Building Up to an Awful Let-Down; A Kiss To Build a Dream On; We Built This City; While Others Are Building Castles in the Air (I'll Build a Cottage for Two); You're a Builder Upper

Bull   Ferdinand the Bull; The Little White Bull; The Lonely Bull; My Toreador; Picador; Toreador Song; What's Good for General Bullmoose

Bulldog, *see* **Dog**

Bullet, *see* **Gun**

Bum, *see* **Hobo**

Bumblebee   Be My Little Baby Bumblebee; Bumble Boogie; The Flight of the Bumble Bee; The Honeysuckle and the Bee; How I Love You (I'm Tellin' the Birds, I'm Tellin' the Bees); A Sleepin' Bee; The Tale of a Bumble Bee; Two Little Love Bees; When the Bees Are in the Hive

Bump   On the Bumpy Road to Love; What Ho She Bumps

Bun   Hot Cross Buns

Bunch   Bunch of Roses; I've Got a Lovely Bunch of Cocoanuts; A Little Bunch of Shamrocks; One Bad Apple (Don't Spoil the Whole Bunch); Sweet Bunch of Daisies

Bunny, *see* **Rabbit**

Burger   Burgers and Fries

Burgundy   When It's Night Time Down in Burgundy

Burlington   Burlington Bertie from Bow

Burn, *see also* **Fire**   B B B Burnin' Up with Love; Baby I'm Burning; Burning Heart; Burning Love; There's a Little Spark of Love Still Burning; While a Cigarette Was Burning

Bury, *see* **Death**

Bus, *see also* **Automobile**   Bus Stop; Love on a Greyhound Bus

Bush   (Here We Go Round) The Mulberry Bush; Stop Beating 'Round the Mulberry Bush; Under the Anheuser Bush

Bushel   A Bushel and a Peck

Business   Rhythm Is Our Business; 'Tain't Nobody's Business If I Do; There's No Business Like Show Business

Bust   Busted; The Dam Busters (March); Ghostbusters; June Is Bustin' Out All Over

Busy   Little Man, You've Had a Busy Day; Too Busy Thinking About My Baby; Who Takes Care of the Caretaker's Daughter While the Caretaker's Busy Taking Care?

Butcher, *see* **Meat**

Butter   The Big Butter and Egg Man; Bread and Butter; Butterfingers; Gloria, or, Theme from Butterfield 8; I'm Called Little Buttercup; Ole Buttermilk Sky; Sweet Little Buttercup

Butterfly   Butterflies in the Rain; Butterly; Dog and Butterfly; Elusive Butterfly; Hawaiian Butterfly; I'd Be a Butterfly; Just Like a Butterfly (That's Caught in the Rain); The Moth and the Flame; Poor Butterfly

Button   Button Up Your Overcoat; Buttons and Bows; I Can't Do My Belly Bottom Button Up; One, Two, Button Your Shoe; Push De Button

Buy   Buy a Broom, or, The Bavarian Girl's Song; Can't Buy

Me Love; Daddy Wouldn't Buy Me a Bow-Wow; Gold Will Buy Most Anything But a True Girl's Heart; How Can You Buy Killarney; I Bought Myself a Bottle of Ink; I'll Buy That Dream; I'll Buy You a Star; Louisiana Purchase; Who Will Buy? Who'll Buy My Violets

Bygones, *see* **Past**

Cabaret At the Mississippi Cabaret; Cabaret

Cabin, *see* **House**

Cadet High School Cadets

Cafe Cafe in Vienna; Dear Little Café

Cage A Bird in a Gilded Cage; A Cage in the Window; Don't Go in the Lions' Cage Tonight; Down in the Valley, or, Birmingham Jail, or, Bird in a Cage, or, Down on the Levee

Cairo The Streets of Cairo

Cake Candy and Cake; Eli Green's Cakewalk; Golliwogg's Cake Walk; I Love To Dunk a Hunk of Sponge Cake; If I Knew You Were Comin' I'd've Baked a Cake; Let 'Em Eat Cake; Pillsbury Says It Best; Sunshine Cake; Take Me to the Midnight Cake Walk Ball

Calcutta Calcutta

Calendar Calendar Girl

Calico A Gal in Calico

California All the Gold in California; California Dreamin'; California Girls; California, Here I Come; California Nights; Hotel California; It Never Rains in Southern California; Twelve Thirty, or, Young Girls Are Coming to the Canyon

Call, *see also* **Telephone** Bugle Call (Rag); Bugle Call Rag; Call Me Darling; Call Me Irresponsible; Call Me Mister; The Call of the Canyon; The Call of the Far-Away Hills; Call Round Any Old Time; Calling All Workers (March); Calling to Her Boy Just Once Again; Can't Yo' Heah Me Callin', Caroline; Cattle Call; Crazy Little Thing Called Love; Creole Love Call; Don't Call It Love; First Call; Go Call the Doctor, or, Anti-Calomel; Happiness Is (Just) a Thing Called Joe; Heed the Call; I Guess That's Why They Call It the Blues; I Hear You Calling Me; I'll Come When You Call; I'm Called Little Buttercup; Indian Love Call; Joan of Arc, They Are Calling You; Just a Voice To Call Me, Dear; Lafayette—We Hear You Calling; Let Me Call You Sweetheart; Let's Call It a Day; Let's Call the Whole Thing Off; A Little Bit of Heaven, Sure They Call It Ireland; A Little Boy Called "Taps"; My Gal Sal, or, They Call Her Frivolous Sal; The Night We Called It a Day; One Called "Mother" and the Other "Home Sweet Home"; The Pipes of Pan Are Calling; A Precious Little Thing Called Love; Somewhere a Voice Is Calling; Tenderly Calling; That's Why They Call Me "Shine"; They Call the Wind Maria; What Is This Thing Called Love; When the Roll Is Called Up Yonder; Whenever I Call You "Friend"; You Call Everybody Darling; You Call It Madness (Ah, But I Call It Love)

Calvary Calvary

Camel Ali Baba's Camel; Camel Hop

Camelot Camelot

Camp At a Georgia Camp Meeting; De Camptown Races (Gwine To Run All Night); The Girl I Left Behind Me, or, Brighton Camp; Tenting on the Old Camp Ground, or, Tenting Tonight

Canada Canadian Boat Song; Canadian Capers; Canadian Sunset

Canal Canal Street Blues; (Fifteen Miles (Years) on the) Erie Canal (Low Bridge!—Everybody Down); The Meeting of the Waters of Hudson and Erie

Canary The Hot Canary; 'Twas Off the Blue Canaries, or, My Last Cigar

Candle Blow Out the Candle; Lay Down (Candles in the Rain); One Little Candle; Seventeen Candles; Sixteen Candles

Candlelight By Candlelight; Candlelight and Wine

Candy The Big Rock Candy Mountain; Candy; Candy and Cake; Candy Kisses; The Candy Man; Incense and Peppermints; Lollipop; Lollipops and Roses; Mammy's Chocolate Soldier; My Boy Lollipop; On the Good Ship Lollipop; The Peppermint Twist; A Rose and a Baby Ruth; Sunshine, Lollipops and Rainbows

Cane Down Among the Sugar Cane; Down Among the Sugar-Cane; (O) Hand Me Down My Walking Cane

Cannon, *see* **Gun**

Canoe, *see* **Boat**

Canteen I Left My Heart at the Stage Door Canteen

Canyon The Call of the Canyon; Copper Canyon; Twelve Thirty, or, Young Girls Are Coming to the Canyon

Cape Cape Ann; Cape Cod Girls; Old Cape Cod

Caper Canadian Capers

Capistrano When the Swallows Come Back to Capistrano

Capital A Capital Ship

Capri Isle of Capri; Song of Capri

Captain El Capitan (March); Captain Gingah; Captain Hook's Waltz; Captain Jinks of the Horse Marines; Captain Noah and His Floating Zoo; Hooray for Captain Spalding; I Am the Captain of the Pinafore (What Never); I've Got My Captain Working for Me Now; Ride Captain Ride; Wond'rous Love, or, Captain Kidd, or, Through All the World

Car, *see* **Automobile**

Caravan Beside My Caravan; Caravan; Caravans; I Pitch My Lonely Caravan at Night; Where My Caravan Has Rested

Careful Be Careful It's My Heart; You've Got To Be (Carefully) Taught

Careless Careless; Careless Hands; Careless (Kelly's) Love; Careless Love; Careless Whisper; Music in May (Careless Rapture)

Carlos, *see* **Charlie**

Carmen Carmen Etonense

Carnation Clavelitos (Carnations); A White Sport Coat and a Pink Carnation

Carnival, *see also* **Circus** The Carnival Is Over; Carnival of Venice; Love Makes the World Go Round, or, Theme from Carnival

Carolina Back to the Carolina You Love; Carolina; Carolina in the Morning; Carolina in the Pines; Carolina Moon; Carolina Sunshine; Cryin' for the Carolines; Dandy Jim of Caroline; An Evening in Caroline; Just a Little Bit South of North Carolina

Caroline Along Came Caroline; Can't Yo' Heah Me Callin', Caroline; Good Evening, Caroline; Hoch, Caroline; Sweet Caroline (Sweet Times Never Seemed So Good); There's a Cradle in Caroline

Carousel Carousel; Carousel Waltz; The Jockey on the Carousel; The Merry-Go-Round Broke Down

Carpenter, *see* **Wood**

Carrie Carrie, or, Carrie Marry Harry

Carrot Boiled Beef and Carrots

Cart Paddy Duffy's Cart

Casanova, *see* **Lover**

Casey (Casey Would Waltz with the Strawberry Blonde While) The Band Played On; Casey Jones

Casino, *see* **Gambling**

Cast, *see* **Throw**

Castle Castle of Dreams; Castles in the Air; Christopher Robin at Buckingham Palace; Have You Got Any Castles, Baby; Ivory Tower; My Castle on the Nile; Theme from Ice Castles (Through the Eyes of Love); We're the Couple in the Castle; When the Clock in the Tower Strikes Twelve; While Others Are Building Castles in the Air (I'll Build a Cottage for Two)

Cat, *see also* **Lion, Tiger** Alley Cat; Ballad of Cat Ballou; The Cat Came Back; Cat's in the Cradle; Don't Do That to the Poor Puss Cat; Grizabella the Glamour Cat; I Taut I Taw a Puddy-Tat; Kansas City Kitty; Kitten on the Keys; Matchstalk Men and Matchstalk Cats and Dogs; I Love Little Pussy; Stray Cat Strut; Three Little Kittens; (Theme from) The Pink Panther; The Waltzing Cat; What's New Pussycat

Catch Catch a Falling Star; Catch the Wind; Catch Us If You Can; Don't Let the Sun Catch You Crying; If You Catch a Little Cold; Isn't This a Lovely Day (To Be Caught in the Rain); My Blue Bird Was Caught in the Rain; Would You Catch a Falling Star

Cathedral, *see* **Church**

Cathy Cathy's Clown

Cattle Cattle Call

Cavalier The Spanish Cavalier

Cave Rock With the Cavemen

Cecile Cecile Waltz

Cecilia (Does Your Mother Know You're Out) Cecilia

Ceiling, *see* **Room**

Celebrate Celebratin'; Celebration; Tonight I Celebrate My Love

Celery Celery Stalks at Midnight

Cellophane Mister Cellophane

Cement Cement Mixer (Put-ti Put-ti)

Cent, *see* **Money**

Central, *see* **Telephone**

Century, *see* **Time**

Certain A Certain Smile; That Certain Feeling; That Certain Party; Without That Certain Thing

Ceylon The Pearl of Sweet Ceylon

Chain Chain Gang; Unchain My Heart; Unchained Melody; When You're Wearing the Ball and Chain

Chair Granny's Old Arm-Chair; (And) His Rocking Horse Ran Away; Just a Little Rocking Chair and You; The Old Arm Chair; (Ol') Rockin' Chair; Rockin' Chair; Sitting in the Back Seat; Take a Seat, Old Lady; The White House Chair; You're in the Right Church, But the Wrong Pew

Champagne, *see* **Alcohol**

Chance Chances Are; Give Peace a Chance; How's Chances; I Don't Stand a Ghost of a Chance with You; I Never Had a Chance; Just One More Chance; Ready To Take a Chance Again; Taking a Chance on Love; Treble Chance; While You See a Chance

Change Can't You Take It Back, and Change It for a Boy; Change Partners; Changes; Changing My Tune; The Changing of the Guard; Cool Change; I Guess I'll Have To Change My Plan; If You Ever Change Your Mind; Love Transformation; Shifting, Whispering Sands; There'll Be Some Changes Made; Time May Change; The Times They Are A-Changin'; We're Gonna Change the World; Why Try To Change Me Now; You Can't Change That; You Haven't Changed At All; You've Changed

Chant Chant of the Jungle; Hawaiian War Chant

Chapel, *see* **Church**

Charade (Theme from) Charade

Chariot Ben Hur Chariot Race (March); (Theme from) Chariots of Fire; Swing Low, Sweet Chariot

Charleston I'm Gonna Charleston Back to Charleston

Charlie Carlos' Theme; Champagne Charley Was His Name; Charley, My Boy; Charlie Brown; Charlie Is My Darlin'; Chuck E's in Love; Clap Hands, Here Comes Charley; Get Wildroot Cream-Oil Charlie; Goodtime Charley; Ma, Look At Charlie; Oh Charley Take It Away; You're a Good Man, Charlie Brown

Charlotte Hush Hush Sweet Charlotte

Charm Believe Me If All Those Endearing Young Charms; The Charming Young Widow I Met on the Train; Good Luck Charm; Snake Charmer

Chase Chasing Shadows; I'm Always Chasing Rainbows; A Man Chases a Girl; Nobody's Chasing Me

Cheap, *see* **Cost**

Cheat Cheatin' On Me; Who's Cheatin' Who; Your Cheatin' Heart

Cheek, *see* **Face**

Cheer Cheer, Boys, Cheer; Cheer, Cheer for Old Notre Dame; Cheerful Little Earful; Hooray for Captain Spalding; Stand Up and Cheer

Chelsea Chelsea Morning; Elsie from Chelsea

Cherie Cherie (Cherie, Je T'Aime); My Cherie Amor; There's Danger in Your Eyes, Cherie

Cherish Cherish; Cherish; Life Let Us Cherish, or, Snatch Fleeting Pleasures

Cherokee, *see* **Indian**

Cherry Cherry; Cherry; Cherry Pink and Apple Blossom White; Cherry Ripe; Down in the Old Cherry Orchard; I Gave My Love a Cherry, or, The Riddle Song; It Looks Like Rain

Chesapeake Sailing Down the Chesapeake Bay

in Cherry Blossom Lane; Life Is Just a Bowl of Cherries; Up Cherry Street; When the Cherry Blossoms Fall

Chesapeake Sailing Down the Chesapeake Bay

Chest Pirate Jenny, or, Fifteen Men on a (the) Dead Man's Chest—Yo! Ho! Ho! and a Bottle of Rum

Chester Chester (let Tyrants Shake Their Iron Rod)

Chestnut Between Eighteenth and Nineteenth on Chestnut Street; The Chestnut Tree; The Christmas Song, or, Merry Christmas to You, or, Chestnuts Roasting on an Open Fire

Chew Another One Bites the Dust; Chewing a Piece of Straw; Don't Bite the Hand That's Feeding You; The Love Bug Will Bite You

Cheyenne Cheyenne; Goodbye Ol' Paint, or, I Ride an Old Paint, or, I'm a-Leavin' Cheyenne

Chicago Chicago (That Toddlin' Town); The Night Chicago Died; On the South Side of Chicago

Chicken Bake Dat Chicken Pie; Chick; Chick-a-Pen; Chick Chick Chicken; The Chicken Reel; Chickery Chick; Hey Little Hen; Little Red Rooster; Pickin' a Chicken; Real Goodness from Kentucky Fried Chicken; Where the Chicken Got the Axe; Who Dat Say Chicken in Dis Crowd; Would You Rather Be a Colonel with an Eagle on Your Shoulder, or a Private with a Chicken on Your Knee?

Chief Doctor, Lawyer, Indian Chief; Hail to the Chief

Child Angel Child; Child Love; Don't Treat Me Like a Child; God Bless the Child; Hot Child in the City; The Little Lost Child; Love Child; Mary's Boy Child; My Trundle Bed, or, Recollections of Childhood; Oh You Cutie (You Ever Loving Child); Sometimes I Feel Like a Motherless Child; Ugly Chile (You're Some Pretty Doll); Wednesday's Child

Children All God's Chillun Got Rhythm; All God's Chillum Got Wings; Bless the Beasts and Children; Children and Art; Children of Rome; Goodnight Children, Everywhere; I Got (a Robe) Shoes, or, All God's Chillun Got Shoes; Little Children; March of the (Royal) Siamese Children; This Old Man, or, The Children's Marching Song (Nick, Nack, Paddy Whack); When the Children Are Asleep

Chili Chili Bean (Eenie Meenie Minie Mo)

Chime, *see* **Bell**

Chimpanzee, *see* **Monkey**

Chin Chin Up, Ladies!

China Chin, Chin, Chinaman; China Boy; China Tea; The Chinaman's Song; Chinatown; My Chinatown; Chinese Laundry Blues; Chinese Lullaby; Chon Kina; Chopsticks; In a Chinese Temple Garden; (Theme from) Murder on the Orient Express; Not for All the Rice in China; Chinese Dance; (I'd Like To Get You) On a Slow Boat to China; On a Street of Chinese Lanterns; We Three Kings of Orient (Are); The Wooden Soldier and the China Doll

Chipmunk The Chipmunk Song, or, Christmas Don't Be Late

Chocolate, *see* **Candy**

Choice Gentlemen Prefer Blondes; Janet's Choice; Why Did I Choose You

Choke, *see* **Breathe**

Chord, *see* **Music**

Chowder, *see* **Soup**

Christian Onward Christian Soldiers; Sister Christian

Christmas All I Want for Christmas (Is My Two Front Teeth); The Chipmunk Song, or, Christmas Don't Be Late; Christmas in Killarney; Christmas Island; Christmas Song, or, O Holy Night; The Christmas Song, or, Merry Christmas to You, or, Chestnuts Roasting on an Open Fire; Deck the Halls with Boughs of Holly; Do They Know It's Christmas; Does Santa Claus Sleep with His Whiskers; Don't Wait 'Til the Night Before Christmas; The First Nöel; God Rest You Merry Gentlemen; Good King Wenceslas; Happy Christmas, Little Friend; Happy Holiday; Hark the Herald Angels Sing; Have Yourself a Merry Little Christmas; Here Comes Santa Clause; Holly Holy; (There's No Place Like) Home for the Holidays; I Heard the Bells on Christmas Day; I Saw Mommy Kissing Santa Claus; I Saw Three Ships Come Sailing; I'll Be Home for Christmas; In Dulci Jubilo; It's Beginning To Look (a Lot) Like Christmas; Jingle Bell Rock; Jingle Bells, or, The One Horse Open Sleigh; The Little Boy That Santa Claus Forgot; Lonely Pup (in a Christmas Shop); Merry Xmas Everybody; Mistletoe and Holly; Rudolph the Red-Nosed Reindeer; Santa Claus Is Coming to Town; The Sleigh; Sleigh Ride; Sleigh Ride in July; Snowy White Snow and Jingle Bells; That's What I Want for Christmas; There Is No Christmas Like a Home Christmas; Twelve Days of Christmas; We Need a Little Christmas; White Christmas; Yuletide, Park Avenue

Christopher Christopher Columbus; Christopher Robin at Buckingham Palace; Christopher Robin Is Saying His Prayers; Misto Cristofo Columbus

Chrysanthemum Chrysanthemum Tea

Chuck, *see* **Charlie**

Chum, *see* **Friend**

Church, *see also* **Monastery, Prayer** At Trinity Church I Met My Doom; Cathedral in the Pines; Chapel of Love; Church of the Poison Mind; The Church's One Foundation; Crying in the Chapel; Get Me to the Church on Time; He Goes to Church on Sunday; I'll Be Happy When the Preacher Makes You Mine; In a Chinese Temple Garden; In the Chapel in the Moonlight; The Little Brown Church (in the Vale); The Little Church Around the Corner; A Little Priest; Open the Gates of the Temple; Papa Don't Preach; The Pope He Leads a Happy Life; The Preacher and the Bear; Son of a Preacher Man; The Temple Bell; The Temple Bells; Waiting at the Church, or, My Wife Won't Let Me; Walter, Walter (Lead Me to the Altar); Winchester Cathedral; You're in the Right Church, But the Wrong Pew

Cider, *see* **Alcohol**

Cigar, Cigarette, *see* **Smoke, Smoking**

Cincinnati Lights of Cincinnati

Cinderella Cinderella; Cinderella Brown; Cinderella Sweetheart; Stay in My Arms, Cinderella

Cindy Cindy; Cindy Oh Cindy

Circle The Circle Game; Will It Go Round in Circles

Circus, *see also* **Carnival** Barnum Had the Right Idea; Be a Clown; Broken Hearted Clown; Cathy's Clown; The Circus Is on Parade; The Clown; The Daring Young Man (on the Flying Trapeze); The Gladiator('s) March; The Gladiator's Entry; Laugh, Clown, Laugh; Oh You Circus Day; Send in the Clowns; The Tears of a Clown; When the Circus Came to Town

City   Big City; Big City Suite; City Lights; City of Laughter, City of Tears; City of New Orleans; Come On Down Town; Detroit City; Detroit Rock City; Doin' the Uptown Lowdown; Downtown; The Frightened City; The Holy City; I Lost My Sugar in Salt Lake City; I'm Sitting Pretty in a Pretty Little City; I'm the Urban Spaceman; In the Ghetto; Kansas City; Kansas City; Kansas City Kitty; Kansas City Lights; Living for the City; On the Boardwalk in Atlantic City; She Went to the City; Sioux City Sue; Summer in the City; Surf City; Trouble (in River City); We Built This City; You Belong to the City

Civilization   Civilization (Bongo Bongo Bongo)

Claire   Claire

Clam   This Was a Real Nice Clambake

Clancy   Clancy Lowered the Boom

Clap, *see* **Applause**

Clarinet   Clarinet Marmalade; I'm Looking for a Guy Who Plays Alto and Baritone and Doubles on a Clarinet and Wears a Size Thirty-Seven Suit

Clarksville   Last Train to Clarksville

Class, *see also* **School**   Class; High Class Baby

Clay   Concrete and Clay; A Hundred Pounds of Clay; Sailin' Away on the Henry Clay

Clean, *see* **Wash**

Clear   Clear Out of This World; I Can See Clearly Now (The Rain Has Gone); It Came Upon a Midnight Clear; On a Clear Day You Can See Forever; When the Mists Have Cleared Away; When They Sound the Last All Clear

Clementine   (Oh, My Darling) Clementine

Climb   Climb Ev'ry Mountain; Climbing Up; Climbing Up the Golden Stairs; Climbing Up the Ladder of Love; I'd Climb the Highest Mountain (If I Knew I'd Find You)

Cling, *see also* **Hold**   Clinging Vine; My Heart Still Clings to the Old First Love

Clock   Cuckoo in the Clock; England Swings (Like a Pendulum Do); Fairy on the Clock; Grandfather's Clock; (When You're) Racing with the Clock; (We're Gonna) Rock Around the Clock; The Syncopated Clock; Time (Clock of the Heart); When the Clock in the Tower Strikes Twelve

Close   (''near'') Angel Flying Too Close to the Ground; Close; Close as Pages in a Book; (Theme from) Close Encounters of the Third Kind; Close Enough to Perfect; Close to My Heart; Close to You; (They Long To Be) Close to You; The Closer I Get to You; Come a Little Bit Closer; Come Closer to Me; Cuddle Up a Little Closer, Lovey Mine; Don't Stand So Close to Me; Get Closer; Just To Be Close to You; Move in a Little Closer Baby

Close   (''shut'') Behind Closed Doors; Close Your Eyes; Did You Close Your Eyes (When We Kissed); Hey Young Fella Close Your Old Umbrella; I Close My Eyes and Count to Ten; I'll Close My Eyes; Just a Closer Walk with Thee; The Long Day Closes; Shut the Door (They're Comin' Through the Window); Too Close for Comfort

Clothes   Babooshka; Put On Your Sunday Clothes; There's Something About a Uniform; (Look for the) Union Label

Cloud   Get Off My Cloud; Kickin' the Clouds Away; The Little White Cloud That Cried; Liza (All the Clouds'll Roll Away); Painting the Clouds with Sunshine; Push Dem Clouds Away; Roll Away Clouds; Sweeping the Clouds Away; Till ('Til) the Clouds Roll By; Up in the Clouds; Wait Till the Clouds Roll By; Watching the Clouds Roll By; With My Head in the Clouds

Clover   Crimson and Clover; I'm Looking Over a Four Leaf Clover; Kiss a Four Leaf Clover; Maggie, the Cows Are in the Clover

Clown, *see* **Circus**

Club, *see* **People**

Clyde   The Ballad of Bonnie and Clyde; Song of the Clyde

Coach, *see also* **Train**   The Deadwood Stage; In a Golden Coach; Snow Coach; Stage Coach; The Surrey with the Fringe on Top; Thanks for the Buggy Ride

Coal   Coal Black Mammy; The Coal Black Rose; (I'm Just an Old Chunk of Coal But) I'll Be a Diamond Someday; Mammy's (a) Little Coal Black Rose

Coast   Gulf Coast Blues

Coat   The Badge from Your Coat; Button Up Your Overcoat; Man in a Raincoat; A White Sport Coat and a Pink Carnation

Coax   Coax Me a Little Bit

Cobbler, *see* **Shoes**

Coca-Cola   Coca-Cola Cowboy (Theme from Every Which Way But Loose); It's the Real Thing. Coke.; Rum and Coca-Cola; Things Go Better with Coke

Cockatoo   The Green Cockatoo

Cockeyed   Cockeyed Mayor of Kaunakakai; A Cockeyed Optimist

Cockle   Cockles and Mussels, Alive, Alive, O!, or, Sweet Molly Malone

Cocktail, *see* **Alcohol**

Cocoanut   Cocoanut Grove; Cocoanut Sweet; I've Got a Lovely Bunch of Cocoanuts; Mama Don't Want No Peas an' Rice an' Cocoanut Oil

Coffee   Coffee in the Morning, Kisses at Night; The Coffee Song (They've Got an Awful Lot of Coffee in Brazil); A Cup of Coffee, a Sandwich and You; I Love Coffee, I Love Tea; Java Jive; Let's Have Another Cup of Coffee; Turkish Coffee; You're the Cream in My Coffee

Coin, *see* **Money**

Cold, *see also* **Cool, Frost**   Baby, It's Cold Outside; Cold Cold Heart; I Got a ''Code'' in My Dose'' (Cold in My Nose); If You Catch a Little Cold; Little Jack Frost Get Lost; Massa's in De Cold (Cold) Ground; My Lodging It Is on the Cold Ground; Out in the Cold Again; Out in the Cold Cold Snow; Stone Cold Dead in the Market; Till the Sands of the Desert Grow Cold; When Your Love Grows Cold

Colette   (La La) Colette; Colette

Collar, *see* **Shirt**

College, *see* **School**

Colonel   Colonel Bogey (Bogie) March; The Colonel's Tune; Real Goodness from Kentucky Fried Chicken (re: Colonel Sanders); Would You Rather Be a Colonel with an Eagle on Your Shoulder, or a Private with a Chicken On Your Knee?

Colony   Old Colony Times

Color   Black Is the Color of My True Love's Hair; Color Him Father; Color My World; The Colors of My Life; Colours; I Used To Be Color Blind; Looking At the World Through Rose-Colored Glasses; Mammy's Little Pumpkin-Colored Coon(s); March from ''The Colour Suite''; My Coloring Book; Orange-Colored Sky

Colorado   Moonlight on the Colorado; Where the Silv'ry Colorado Wends Its Way

Columbia   Columbia, the Gem of the Ocean, or, The Red, White and Blue; Hail Columbia, or, New Federal Song

Columbus   Christopher Columbus; (What Shall We Do with) The Drunken Sailor, or, John Brown Had a Little Injun, or, Ten Little Indians, or, Columbus; Misto Cristofo Columbo

Comb, *see* **Hair**

Comedy   The Comedy of Errors; Comedy Tonight

Comfort   Consolation; Make Yourself Comfortable; She's Such a Comfort to Me; Too Close for Comfort; You're Such a Comfort to Me

Command   At Your Command; Simon Says

Commodore, *see* **Navy**

Companion, *see* **Friend**

Company   Boogie Woogie Bugle Boy (from Company B); Company; The Company Sergeant Major; Jolly Good Company

Comrade, *see* **Friend**

Concentrate, *see* **Think**

Concert   Concert in the Park

Concrete   Concrete and Clay

Confession   Confession; I'm Confessin' That I Love You; True Confession

Confidential   Confidentially

Congo, *see* **Africa**

Congratulations   Congratulations; Congratulations; Mazel Tov; Mazel Tov

Connecticut   Connecticut

Consider   Consider Yourself

Constant, *see* **Forever**

Constantinople   Constantinople; Istanbul (Not Constantinople)

Content, *see* **Satisfaction**

Contessa   Song of the Barefoot Contessa

Contraband   Ole Shady, or, The Song of the Contraband

Conversation, *see* **Talk**

Convict, *see* **Jail**

Cook   Home Cooking

Cookie   (Lookie, Lookie, Lookie) Here Comes Cookie; Little Biscuit

Cool   Cool; Cool Change; Cool It Now; Cool Jerk; Cool Love; Cool Night; Cool Water; I Was Country When Country Wasn't Cool; In the Cool, Cool, Cool of the Evening; Long Cool Woman (in a Black Dress)

Coon   All Coons Look Alike to Me; Coon! Coon! Coon!; Every Race Has a Flag But the Coon; Little Alabama Coon; Mammy's Little Pumpkin Colored Coon(s); Turkey in the Straw, or, Old Zip Coon; The Whistling Coon

Cooperation, *see also* **Help**   A Little Co-operation from You; Stop and Shop at the Co-Op Shop

Cop, *see* **Police**

Copacabana   Copacabana (At the Copa)

Copenhagen   Copenhagen; Wonderful Copenhagen

Copper   Copper Canyon

Coquette   Coquette

Corabelle   I'm a-Comin' a-Courtin' Corabelle

Corn   I Remember the Cornfields; Iowa Corn Song; Jimmy Crack Corn, or, The Blue Tail Fly; Way Down Yonder in the Cornfield; When the Corn is Waving, Annie Dear

Corner   A-Round the Corner (Beneath the Berry Tree); Around the Corner and Under the Tree; Blue Skies Are Round the Corner; Brighten the Corner Where You Are; Give Me a Little Cosy Corner; Happiness Street (Corner Sunshine Square); I Was Standing at the Corner of the Street; In a Cozy Corner; In My Own Little Corner; Keep a Little Cozy Corner in Your Heart for Me; The Little Church Around the Corner; Love is Just Around the Corner; Meet Me on the Corner; Meet Me on the Corner; Sittin' in a Corner; Standing on the Corner; The Three-Cornered Hat

Coronation   Coronation; Coronation March; Coronation Scot; Coronation Street; The Coronation Waltz

Cossack   Cossack Love Song, or, Don't Forget Me

Cost, *see also* **Money**   (How Much Is That) Doggie in the Window; Eve Cost Adam Just One Bone; It Costs So Little; (Potatoes Are Cheaper—Tomatoes Are Cheaper) Now's the Time To Fall in Love

Cottage, *see* **House**

Cotton   Cabin in the Cotton; Cotton Fields; Cotton Tail; Down Where the Cotton Blossoms Grow; King Cotton March; Peter Cottontail; Roll Out! Heave Dat Cotton; Roll Them Cotton Bales; Wrap Yourself in Cotton Wool

Count   Count Every Star; Count Me In; Count On Me Love; Count Your Blessings; Count Your Blessings Instead of Sheep; Don't Count the Rainy Days; I Close My Eyes and Count to Ten; Sound Off

Country   The Blue and the Gray, or, A Mother's Gift to Her Country; A Country Boy Can Survive; Country Boy You Got Your Feet in L.A.; Country Dance; Country Dance; Country Gardens; Country Matters; Country Road; Country Style; Cry, the Beloved Country; English Country Gardens; (This Is) God's Country; He Who His Country's Liv'ry Wears; I Was Country When Country Wasn't Cool; It's So Peaceful in the Country; A Lil' Ole Bitty Pissant Country Place; Love Is Sweeping the Country; My Wife's Gone to the Country (Hurrah! Hurrah!); Our Country, May She Always Be Right; Save the Country; Take Me Home Country Roads; Thank God I'm a Country Boy; This Is My Country; A Weekend in the Country; Your Dad Gave His Life for His Country; Your God Comes First, Your Country Next, Then Mother Dear; Your King and Country Want You

County   Coward of the County; Little Town in the Ould County Down; (The Song of) Raintree County

Couple, *see* **Two**

Court, see also **Affair** Frog Went a-Courtin', or, Frog He Would A-Wooing Go, or, Mister Frog Went a-Courtin'; Got a Date with an Angel; How'd You Like To Spoon with Me; Huggin' and Chalkin'; I'm a-Comin' a-Courtin' Corabelle; Last Date; Liaisons; My Last Date with You; Old Rosin the Beau; Pettin' in the Park; Too Young To Go Steady; The Wooing of the Violin; You Can't Get a Man with a Gun; You Should Be Mine (The Woo Woo Song)

Cousin Cousin Jedediah; Emmet's Lullaby, or, Fritz, Our Cousin German, or, Brother's Lullaby; He's a Cousin of Mine; My Cousin Caruso

Cover Covered Wagon Days (March); The Girl on the Magazine Cover; I Cover the Waterfront; Roll Along Covered Wagon; Westward Ho!—The Covered Wagon March

Cow Contented; (Whoopee Ti Yi Yo) Git Along Little Dog(g)ies; Holy Cow; I Could Go On Singing (Till the Cows Come Home); Maggie, the Cows Are in the Clover; Wait Till the Cows Come Home

Cowboy, see also **Boots, Horse, Saddle, West,** etc. Coca-Cola Cowboy (Theme from Every Which Way But Loose); Cowboy; Cowboy Serenade, or, My Last Cigarette; Everybody's Talkin', or, Theme from Midnight Cowboy; The Gaucho Serenade; A Gay Caballero; A Gay Ranchero; Ghost Riders in the Sky, or, A Cowboy Legend; I'm an Old Cowhand (from the Rio Grande); The Last Round-Up; Midnight Cowboy; My Little Buckaroo; Oh, Bury Me Not on the Lone Prairie, or, The Dying Cowboy; Ragtime Cowboy Joe; (Theme from) Rawhide; Rhinestone Cowboy; Streets of Laredo, or, The Cowboy's Lament; (When It's Roundup Time in Texas) When the Bloom Is on the Sage

Cozy Give Me a Little Cozy Corner; In a Cozy Corner; Keep a Little Cozy Corner in Your Heart for Me

Crack Jimmy Crack Corn, or, The Blue Tail Fly

Cracker Animal Crackers in My Soup; Crackers; I'm Just Wild About Animal Crackers

Cradle Away in (a) the Manger, or, Luther's Cradle Hymn; Cat's in the Cradle; Cradle's Empty, Baby's Gone; The Hand That Rocks the Cradle; Pal of My Cradle Days; Rocked in the Cradle of the Deep; There's a Cradle in Caroline

Crawl Did You Ever Think As the Hearse Rolls By, or, The Worms Crawl In, the Worms Crawl Out; The Flies Crawled up the Window

Crazy Crazy; Crazy Blues; Crazy for You; Crazy Heart; Crazy Little Thing Called Love; Crazy Love; The Crazy Otto Rag (Medley); Crazy People; Crazy Rhythm; Crazy Words (Crazy Tune) (Vo-Do-De-O-Do); Everybody's Crazy on the Foxtrot; Ginger You're Barmy; Hey, Habe, Hey (I'm Nuts About You); I Go Crazy; I Had the Craziest Dream; I May Be Crazy; I May Be Crazy, But I Ain't No Fool; K-ra-zy for You; Let's Go Crazy; Lovin' You Has Made Me Bananas; Maniac; Manic Monday; My Heart Goes Crazy; Oh Nicholas Don't Be So Ridiculous; Oh You Crazy Moon; (I Got a Woman Crazy for Me) She's Funny That Way; Silly Love Songs; Those Lazy Hazy Crazy Days of Summer; You Could Drive a Person Crazy; You Drive Me Crazy; You're Driving Me Crazy (What Did I Do)

Cream Aunt Jemima and Your Uncle Cream of Wheat; Cream of the Crop; Get Wildroot Cream-Oil Charlie; You're the Cream in My Coffee

Credit Give a Little Credit to Your Dad

Creek The Belle of Barking Creek

Creole Creole Belle; Creole Love Call; My Creole Sue

Crew, see **Boat**

Cricket The Cricket on the Hearth

Crimson, see **Red**

Crinoline Crinoline Days; The Girl in the Crinoline Gown

Crocodile Crocodile Rock; See You Later Alligator

Crocus Autumn Crocus

Croon Learn to Croon; My Kid's a Crooner; When the Guardsman Started Crooning on Parade

Crop, see **Harvest**

Croquet Croquet

Cross At the Cross; Beneath the Cross of Jesus; Cross Over the Bridge; Cross Your Fingers; Cross Your Heart; Dar's One More Ribber To Cross; I've Got My Fingers Crossed; Just Like Washington Crossed the Delaware, General Pershing Will Cross the Rhine; Hot Cross Buns; (Jesus Keep Me) Near the Cross; The Old Rugged Cross; One More River To Cross; Southern Cross; There's One Wide River To Cross, or, Noah's Ark

Cross Roads Angels Meet Me at the Cross Roads; At the Crossroads

Crow I've Gotta Crow; (Jump) Jim Crow

Crowd, see **People**

Crucifixion Crucifix; The Crucifixion; Were You There When They Crucified My Lord?

Cruel The Cruel Sea; December and May, or, Mollie Newell Don't Be Cruel; Don't Be Cruel; Goodbye Cruel World; Mean to Me; Weeping, Sad and Lonely, or, When This Cruel War Is Over

Cruise Cruisin'; Cruising down the River

Crusader Crusader's Hymn, or, Fairest Lord Jesus

Crush, see **Romance**

Cry After My Laughter Came Tears; And Her Tears Flowed Like Wine; As Tears Go By; The Battle Cry of Freedom; Before the Next Teardrop Falls; Big Girls Don't Cry; Boo-Hoo; Boys Cry; City of Laughter, City of Tears; Cry; Cry; Cry Like a Baby; Cry Me a River; The Cry of the Wild Goose; Cry, the Beloved Country; Cryin'; Cryin' for the Carolines; The Crying Game; Crying in the Chapel; Crying Time; (I'm) Dancing with Tears in My Eyes; Doan Ye Cry, Mah Honey; Don't Cry for Me, Argentina; Don't Cry, Frenchy, Don't Cry; Don't Cry Joe; Don't Let the Sun Catch You Crying; Golden Tears; I Ain't Gonna Grieve My Lord No More; I Cried for You (Now It's Your Turn To Cry over Me); I Heard You Cried Last Night; I Won't Cry Anymore; I'm Crying; I'm So Lonesome I Could Cry; I'm Sorry I Made You Cry; Judy's Turn To Cry; The Little White Cloud That Cried; Mary's Tears; My Heart Cried for You; Ninety-Six Tears; No More Tears (Enough Is Enough); O Dry Those Tears; Oh! How I Laugh When I Think How I Cried About You; Oh, Mary, Don't You Weep, Don't You Mourn; One of Us Will Weep Tonight; Play Me Hearts and Flowers (I Wanna Cry); Poverty's Tears Ebb and Flow; Prince of Wails; Read 'Em and Weep; Sad Movies Make Me Cry; Sad Songs (Say So

Much); Sobbin' Blues; Sobbin' Women; A Tear Fell; Tears; The Tears of a Clown; Tears on My Pillow; Tears on My Pillow; There'll Be No Teardrops Tonight; There'll Be Sad Songs (To Make You Cry); Too Many Tears; The Tracks of My Tears; Weeping, Sad and Lonely, or, When This Cruel War Is Over; Weeping Saviour; The Weeping Willer; When a Gypsy Makes His Violin Cry; When Doves Cry; While My Guitar Gently Weeps; Who's Crying Now; Why Should I Cry over You; Willow Weep for Me; You Can't See the Sun When You're Crying; You've Got Me Crying Again

Crystal Ballad of a Crystal Man; Crystal Blue Persuasion; The Crystal Gazer

Cuba Cuban Love Song; Cuban Overture; Cuban Pete; The Cubanola Glide; I'll See You in C-U-B-A; O Cuba (Tu)

Cuckoo Cuckoo in the Clock; When I Was a Little Cuckoo

Cuddle Cuddle In; Cuddle Up a Little Closer, Lovey Mine; Snuggled on Your Shoulder, Cuddled in Your Arms

Cup, see also **Butter (cup)** A Cup of Coffee, a Sandwich and You; Let's Have Another Cup of Coffee; My Cup Runneth Over; A Nice Cup of Tea; The World Cup March

Cupboard Cupboard Love

Cupid Cupid; Cupid and I

Curl, Curly, see **Hair**

Curse The Curse of an Aching Heart; The Curse of the Dreamer

Cut (When) They Cut Down the Old Pine Tree; Too Old To Cut the Mustard; You Can't Chop Your Poppa Up in Massachusetts

Cute Oh You Cutie (You Ever Loving Child); You Couldn't Be Cuter

Cymbal Strike the Cymbal

Cynthia Cynthia's in Love

Czar I Played Fiddle for the Czar

Dad, Daddy, see **Father**

Daffodil That Daffydill Rag

Dagger Dagger Dance

Daisy Boomps-a-Daisy; Daisies Won't Tell; Daisy Bell, or, A Bicycle Built for Two, or, Daisy, Daisy; Daisy Deane; Please Don't Eat the Daisies; She Is Ma Daisy; Sweet Bunch of Daisies; That's What the Daisy Said; Where the Lazy Daisies Grow

Dale Lily Dale

Dallas Dallas Blues

Dam The Dam Busters (March)

Dame There Is Nothin' Like a Dame

Dan Old Dan Tucker

Dance, see also **Ballerina** After the Ball; After the Dance; Arthur Murray Taught Me Dancing in a Hurry; At the Ballet; At the Codfish Ball; At the Devil's Ball; At the Hop; At the Jazz Band Ball; At the Moving Picture Ball; Ballin' the Jack; Begin the Beguine; Belle of the Ball; A Boy and a Girl Were Dancing; Breakdance; Camel Hop; Come Dance with Me; Come Dancing; Come to the Ball; Could I Have This Dance; Country Dance; A Couple of Song and Dance Men; Dagger

Dance; Dance (Disco Heat); Dance, Dance, Dance (Yowsah, Yowsah, Yowsah); Dance Hall Days; Dance Little Lady; Dance Me Loose; Dance, My Darlings; Dance of the Hours; Dance of the Paper Dolls; Dance of the Spanish Onion; Dance On; Dance: Ten; Looks: Three; Dance with a Dolly; Dance with Me; Dance with Me; Dance with Me Henry; Dance with Your Uncle Joseph; Dancing; Dancing Fool; Dancing Honeymoon; Dancing in the Dark; Dancing in the Dark; Dancing in the Streets; Dancing Is Everything; The Dancing Lesson; Dancing Machine; Dancing on a Dime; Dancing on the Ceiling; Dancing on the Ceiling; Dancing Queen; Dancing Shoes; Dancing Tambourine; Dancing the Devil Away; Dancing Time; Dancing Under the Stars; Dancing with My Shadow; (I'm) Dancing with Tears in My Eyes; Dancin' Your Memory Away; The Darktown Strutters' Ball; De Boatman's Dance; Devil's Gallop, or, Dick Barton Theme; The Dicky Bird Hop; Do You Want To Dance; The Doll Dance; Dream Dancing; Everybody Step; (Theme from) Flashdance (What a Feeling); The Floral Dance; Four Dances from Aladdin; The Gandy Dancers' Ball; The Grasshopper's Dance; Haunted Ball Room; I Can Dance with Everyone But My Wife; I Could Have Danced All Night; I Don't Wanna Dance; (When We Are Dancing) I Get Ideas; I Just Came Here To Dance; I Wonder Who's Dancing with You Tonight; I Won't Dance; I'll Dance at Your Wedding; I'm in a Dancing Mood; I'm in the Mood for Dancing; Invitation to the Dance; It Only Happens When I Dance with You; It's Make Believe Ballroom Time; Jazz Baby's Ball; Keep on Dancin'; The Kerry Dance; Last Dance; Let's Dance; Let's Dance; Let's Face the Music and Dance; Long Tall Glasses (I Can Dance); Look Who's Dancing; Love Is a Dancing Thing; Mama Teach Me To Dance; Mexican Hat Dance; Mick McGilligan's Ball; The Morris Dance; My Lady Loves To Dance; Neutron Dance; The Norwegian Dance; Dance of the Sugar-Plum Fairy; Arabian Dance; Chinese Dance; One More Dance; Papa Won't You Dance With Me; Phil the Fluter's Ball; Play Gypsies—Dance Gypsies; Polish Dance; Polovetsian Dances; Queen of the Hop; Ritual Fire Dance; Sabre Dance; The Safety Dance; Sailor's Hornpipe; Save the Last Dance for Me; Say It While Dancing; Scarf Dance; Scenes de Ballet; The Second Minuet; Shadow Dancing; Shall We Dance; Shall We Dance; Since Maggie Dooley Learned the Hooley Hooley; The Skidmore Fancy Ball; Skirt Dance; Slavonic Dances; Something To Dance About; Take Me to the Midnight Cake Walk Ball; Ten Cents a Dance; Touch Me When We're Dancing; Toyshop Ballet; When Frances Dances with Me; When You and I Were Dancing; While You Danced, Danced, Danced; Why Dance; Why Don't They Dance the Polka Anymore; Won't Somebody Dance with Me; You Make Me Feel Like Dancing; You Should Be Dancing; You're Dancing On My Heart

Dandy Dandy Jim of Caroline; Fine and Dandy

Danger Danger, Heartbreak Ahead; Silent Running (On Dangerous Ground); Sweet Danger; There's Danger in Your Eyes, Cherie; Without a Word of Warning

Daniel Daniel

Danny Danny Boy; Danny By My Side; Danny Deever; Danny's Song; Dapper Dan

Danube The Blue Danube (On the Beautiful Blue Danube); Waves of the Danube, or, Danube Waves

Dapper Dapper Dan

Dare The Daring Young Man (on the Flying Trapeze); I Double Dare You

Dark Dancing in the Dark; Dancing in the Dark; Dark Eyes, or, Black Eyes; Dark Is the Night; Dark Lady; Dark Moon; Darkest the Hour; (When It's) Darkness on the Delta; The Darktown Strutters' Ball; Daughter of Darkness; Edge of Darkness; Eyes That See in the Dark; I'm Afraid To Come Home in the Dark; In the Heart of the Dark; It's Dark on Observatory Hill; A Kiss in the Dark; On the Dark Side; That's Why Darkies Were Born; Two Cigarettes in the Dark; Two Faces in the Dark; Wait Until Dark; Whispers in the Dark; Whistling in the Dark

Dash The Dashing White Sergeant

Date, *see* **Court**

Daughter Araby's Daughter; Daughter of Darkness; The Daughter of Rosie O'Grady; Just for the Sake of Our Daughter; Lock Up Your Daughters; Mrs. Brown You've Got a Lovely Daughter; (Don Put Your Daughter on the Stage) Mrs. Worthington; She's the Daughter of Mother Machree; Who Takes Care of the Caretaker's Daughter While the Caretaker's Busy Taking Care?; Yes My Darling Daughter

Davenport Davenport Blues

David Ballad of Davy Crockett; Davy Jones' Locker; Little David, Play on Your Harp

Dawn, *see* **Morning**

Day, *see also* **Birthday** All Day and All of the Night; All for a Shilling a Day; All Through the Day; Another Day; Around the World (in Eighty Days); At the End of a Beautiful Day; At the End of the Day; Back Again to Happy-Go-Lucky Days; Back to Those Happy Days; Bandana Days; (It's) Been a Long Day; Break of Day; Bring Back Those Minstrel Days; Covered Wagon Days (March); Crinoline Days; Dance Hall Days; Dawn of a New Day; The Day After Tomorrow; The Day Before Spring; Day by Day; Day by Day; Day Dreaming; Day Dreaming; Day Dreams; Day In—Day Out; A Day in the Life; A Day in the Life of a Fool; Day Is Done; The Day the Rains Came; Day Tripper; The Day You Came Along; Daybreak; Daydream; Daydream Believer; Days of Wine and Roses; (What'll We Do on a Dew-Dew-Dewy Day; Don't Count the Rainy Days; A Dream of My Boyhood Days; Eight Days a Week; Eleven More Months and Ten More Days; Every Day a Little Death; Ev'ry Day Away from You; Every Day I Have the Blues; Every Day Is Ladies' Day with Me; Every Day Will Be Sunday When the Town Goes Dry; Everyday; Fifty Million Times a Day; A Foggy Day; Glory Days; Golden Days; Good Day Sunshine; The Good Old Bad Days; Graduation Day; Grandpa (Tell Me 'Bout the Good Old Days); Great Day; Happy as the Day Is Long; (Oh) Happy Day; Happy Days; Happy Days are Here Again; Happy Days in Dixie; A Hard Day's Night; Here's That Rainy Day; I Fall in Love with You Every Day; I Heard the Bells On Christmas Day; I Was Looking for My Boy, She Said, or, Decoration Day; I Won't Last a Day Without You; I'll Be Ready When the Great Day Comes; I'll Never Let a Day Pass By; Isn't This a Lovely Day (To Be Caught in the Rain); It's a Good Day; It's a Great Day for the Irish; It's a Hap-Hap-Happy Day; It's a Lovely Day Today; It's a Most Unusual Day; Just Another Day in Paradise; Just Another Day Wasted Away;

Kid Days; King for a Day; Let a Smile Be Your Umbrella on a Rainy (Rainy) Day; Let Erin Remember the Days of Old; Let's Call It a Day; Life in One Day; The Light of Other Days; Little Dolly Daydream; Little Man, You've Had a Busy Day; The Long Day Closes; Lucky Day; Make My Day; Many a New Day; Many Happy Returns of the Day; Mary, Dear, Some Day We Will Meet Again; Match of the Day; La Mattinata ('Tis the Day); Mem'ries, or, Golden Memory Days; Moving Day in Jungle Town; My Time of Day; Night and Day; The Night We Called It a Day; Not a Day Goes By; Now the Day Is Over; Now Those Days Are Gone; Oh Happy Day; Oh You Circus Day; Old Days; On a Clear Day You Can See Forever; One Fine Day, or, Un Bel Dí; Our Day Will Come; Pal of My Cradle Days; Patrick's Day Parade; A Perfect Day; Put Your Dreams Away for Another Day; The Rainy Day; Rainy Day Women #12 & 35; Rainy Days and Mondays; Rose O'Day; Salad Days; save It for a Rainy Day; School Day (Ring! Ring! Goes the Bell); School Days; A Scrumpdillyishus Day; Seven Lonely Days; She May Have Seen Better Days; Some Day; Some Day I'll Find You; Some Day I'll Find You; Some Day My Heart Will Awake; Some Day My Prince Will Come; Some Day Soon; Some Day Sweetheart; Some Day We'll Be Together; Some Day You'll Want Me To Want You; Some Days Are Diamonds (Some Days Are Stone); Some Little Bug Is Going To Find You (Some Day); Some of These Days; Some Sunny Day; Some Sweet Day; Someday Soon; Sunny Days; Take a Day Off, Mary Ann; That Great Come and Get It Day; That'll Be the Day; There's a Great Day Coming, Mañana; This Is My Lovely Day; This Is My Mother's Day; Those Lazy Hazy Crazy Days of Summer; Those Were the Days, or, Theme from All in the Family; Those Were the Days; Tomorrow Is a Lovely Day; Turn Down Day; Twelve Days of Christmas; Wasted Days, Wasted Nights; Well-a-Day; What a Diff'rence a Day Made (Makes); When Day Is Done; When the Harvest Days Are Over, Jessie Dear; When You Come to the End of the Day; Where Are the Friends of Other Days; Where the Blue of the Night Meets the Gold of the Day; While Strolling Through the Park One Day, or, The Fountain in the Park; (On) A Wonderful Day Like Today

Dean Nellie Dean

Death, *see also* **Bones** Ain't It Grand To Be Bloomin' Well Dead; Alknomook, or, The Death of the Cherokee Indian; And When I Die; At Trinity Church I Met My Doom; Breakdown Dead Ahead; The Deadwood Stage; Death and Transfiguration; The Death of Nelson; Did You Ever Think As the Hearse Rolls By, or, The Worms Crawl In the Worms Crawl Out; Ding Dong! The Witch Is Dead; Do It Or Die; Don't Let It Die; The Dying Poet; Every Day a Little Death; The Fatal Rose of Red; The Fatal Wedding; A Flower from Mother's Grave; Funeral March; Funeral March of a Marionette; Gloomy Sunday; The Grave of Bonaparte; A Handful of Earth from (My Dear) Mother's Grave; He's Dead But He Won't Lie Down; I'd Like To See the Kaiser with a Lily in His Hand; If I'm Going To Die I'm Going To Have Some Fun; I'm Gonna Live Till I Die; I'm Tickled to Death I'm Single; Live and Let Die; The Night Chicago Died; Oh, Bury Me Not on the Lone Prairie, or, The Dying Cowboy; Old Soldiers Never Die; (Go Tell Aunt Rhody) The Ole Grey Goose (Is Dead); Pavanne for a Dead Infanta (Princess); Pirate Song, or, Fifteen Men on a (the) Dead Man's Chest—Yo! Ho! Ho! and a Bottle of Rum; Plant a Watermelon on My Grave and Let the Juice Soak Through; Poor Jud (Is Daid); Root, Hog, or Die; Stone Cold Dead in the Market; There Is No Death; (Poor) Tom Bowling, or, The Sailor's Epitaph; When I Leave the World Behind; When I'm Dead and Gone; Why Did They Dig Ma's Grave So Deep; You Die If You Worry; (I'll Be Glad When You're Dead) You Rascal You

December   December and May, or, Mollie Newell Don't Be Cruel; December 1963 (Oh What a Night); Will You Love Me in December As You Do in May

Decorate   Deck the Halls with Boughs of Holly; I Was Looking for My Boy, She Said, or, Decoration Day; I'm Gonna Hire a Wino To Decorate Our Home; You Decorated My Life

Dedication, *see also* **Devotion**   Dedicated Follower of Fashion; Dedicated to the One I Love

Deep   As Deep as the Deep Blue Sea; Asleep in the Deep; Between the Devil and the Deep Blue Sea; Deep in a Dream; Deep in My Heart, Dear; Deep in the Heart of Texas; Deep in Your Eyes; Deep Night; Deep Purple; Deep River; Down in the Depths on the Ninetieth Floor; How Deep Is the Ocean; How Deep Is Your Love; Put 'Em in a Box, Tie 'Em with a Ribbon (and Throw 'Em in the Deep Blue Sea); Rocked in the Cradle of the Deep; She Waits by the Deep Blue Sea; Why Did They Dig Ma's Grave So Deep

Defense, *see* **Protect**

Delaware   Just Like Washington Crossed the Delaware, General Pershing Will Cross the Rhine

Delicate   The Lass with the Delicate Air, or, Young Molly Who Lives at the Foot of the Hill

Delicious, *see also* **Flavor**   Delishious; A Scrumpdillyishus Day

Delight   Afternoon Delight; It's Delightful To Be Married; Moon of My Delight

Delilah   Delilah; Delilah

Dell   Farmer in the Dell; The Hazel Dell

Delta   (When It's) Darkness on the Delta; Delta Dawn

Den   In Our Little Den of Iniquity

Denim, *see* **Dungaree**

Dennis   Dennis

Denver   Beautiful People of Denver

Depend   It All Depends on You; Patches (I'm Depending on You); You Can Depend on Me

Desert   Desert Moon; The Desert Song; On a Desert Island with Thee; Sahara; Till the Sands of the Desert Grow Cold

Desire   As You Desire Me; Desire; I Wanna Be Your Lover; Life's Desire; Morning Desire; That's My Desire

Desperate   Desperate Ones

Destruction   The Eve of Destruction

Detroit   Detroit City; Detroit Rock City

Devil   At the Devil's Ball; Between the Devil and the Deep Blue Sea; Dancing the Devil Away; Devil Woman; Devil's Gallop, or, Dick Barton Theme; Evil Hearted You; Get Thee Behind Me, Satan; He's a Devil in His Own Home Town; I Found a Rose in the Devil's Garden; Little Devil; Old Devil

Moon; Satan Takes a Holiday; Stand Up and Fight Like——; We'll Knock the Heligo—Into Heligo—Out of Heligoland; When You Come Back They'll Wonder Who the——You Are

Devotion, *see also* **Dedication**   Hopelessly Devoted to You; My Devotion; My Love and Devotion; My Love and Devotion

Dew   (What'll We Do on a) Dew-Dew-Dewy Day; The Foggy, Foggy Dew; Morning Dew

Diamond   Diamond Girl; Diamonds; Diamonds Are a Girl's Best Friend; Diamonds Are Forever; Fourteen Carat Mind; Her Eyes Don't Shine Like Diamonds; (I'm Just an Old Chunk of Coal But) I'll Be a Diamond Someday; Lucy in the Sky With Diamonds; Some Days Are Diamonds (Some Days Are Stone); This Diamond Ring

Diana   Diana

Diane   Diane; Jack and Diane

Dice, *see* **Gambling**

Die, *see* **Death**

Different   Ain't It Funny What a Difference Just a Few Hours Make; Different Worlds; Two Different Worlds; What a Diff'rence a Day Made (Makes)

Dig   Dig You Later (A Hubba-Hubba-Hubba); I Dig Rock and Roll Music; We're in the Money, or, The Gold Diggers' Song; Why Did They Dig Ma's Grave So Deep

Dilly   Don't Dilly Dally on the Way; Lavender's Blue (Diddle Diddle, or, Dilly Dilly)

Dime, *see* **Money**

Dimples   Dimples

Dinah   Dinah; I've Been Working on the Railroad, or, The Levee Song, or, Someone's in the Kitchen with Dinah; Sweet Betsy from Pike, or, Vilikens and His Dinah; When I Saw Sweet Nellie Home, or, I Was Seeing Nellie Home, or, Aunt Dinah's Quilting Party

Dinner, *see* **Supper**

Director   Our Director (March)

Dirty   Dirty Hands, Dirty Face; Dirty Laundry; Sooty

Distant, *see* **Far-Away**

Divine   Bird of Love Divine; O Flower Divine

Divorce   Dodging a Divorcee

Dixie   All Aboard for Dixieland; Are You from Dixie, 'Cause I'm from Dixie Too; (I Wish I Was in) Dixie, or, Dixie's Land; Dixie on My Mind; Happy Days in Dixie; Is It True What They Say About Dixie; I'se Gwine Back to Dixie; Original Dixieland One-Step; Rock-a-Bye Your Baby with a Dixie Melody; Seven or Eleven—My Dixie Pair o' Dice; She's the Fairest Little Flower Dear Old Dixie Ever Grew (Knew); There's a Dixie Girl Who's Longing For a Yankee Doodle Boy; When It's Night Time in Dixie Land

Dizzy   Dizzy; Dizzy Fingers; (Theme from) Vertigo

Dock   (Sittin' on) The Dock of the Bay

Doctor   (Theme from) Doctor Kildare, or, Three Stars Will Shine Tonight; Doctor, Lawyer, Indian Chief; Doctor Tinkle Tinker; Doctor Who Theme; Doctor's Orders; Go Call the Doctor, or, Anti-Calomel; The Physician; Theme from Ben Casey; Witch Doctor

Dodge   Dodging a Divorcee

Dog   Bird Dog; Bulldog! Bulldog! Bow, Wow, Wow; Daddy Wouldn't Buy Me a Bow-Wow; Dog and Butterfly; (How Much Is That) Doggie in the Window; Drink, Puppy, Drink; Fido Is a Hot Dog Now; (Whoopee Ti Yi Yo) Git Along Little Dog(g)ies; Hound Dog; Lonely Pup (in a Christmas Shop); Love on a Greyhound Bus; Mad Dogs and Englishmen; Matchstalk Men and Matchstalk Cats and Dogs; Me and My Dog; Me and You and a Dog Named Boo; Oh Where, Oh Where, Has My Little Dog Gone, or, Der Deitcher's Dog; Old Dog Tray; Puppy Love; Snoopy vs. The Red Baron; There's Life in the Old Dog Yet; They Gotta Quit Kickin' My Dog (Dawg) Around, or, The Missouri Houn' Dawg Song; Time and Tide (Theme from *Plague Dogs*); The Whistler and His Dog; Yellow Dog Blues

Doll, *see also* **(Teddy) Bear**   Baby Doll; Broken Doll; Dance of the Paper Dolls; Dance with a Dolly; The Doll Dance; Dungaree Doll; Glad Rag Doll; Guys and Dolls; Kewpie Doll; Living Doll; The Mama Doll Song; Oh You Beautiful Doll; Oh You Million Dollar Doll; Paper Doll; Party Doll; Poupée Valsante (Waltzing Doll); Rag Doll; Raggedy Ann; Satin Doll; Ugly Chile (You're Some Pretty Doll); (Theme from) Valley of the Dolls; The Wedding of the Painted Doll; The Wooden Soldier and the China Doll

Dollar, *see* **Money**

Dolly   Don't Leave Me, Dolly; Goodbye Dolly Gray; Hello Dolly; Little Dolly Daydream

Dolores   Dolores

Dolphin   Boy on a Dolphin; On Green Dolphin Street

Domino   Domino; Domino

Donegal   Back to Donegal; Dear Old Donegal

Donkey   The Donkey Serenade; Good-Bye, Ma! Good-Bye, Pa! Good-Bye, Mule, or, Long Boy; Little Donkey; The Little White Donkey; Mule Skinner Blues

Donna   Donna; Oh Donna Clara; Who's Holding Donna Now

Doodle   Monkey Doodle Dandy; Polly Wolly Doodle; There's a Dixie Girl Who's Longing For a Yankee Doodle Boy; When Yankee Doodle Learns To Parlez-Vous Francais; Yankee Doodle; The Yankee Doodle Blues; (I Am) The Yankee Doodle Boy

Doom, *see* **Death**

Door   Behind Closed Doors; The Boy Next Door; Door of My (Her) Dreams; The Green Door; Hannah, Won't You Open That Door?; I Left My Heart at the Stage Door Canteen; Knockin' on Heaven's Door; Let My Love Open the Door; Lookin' Out My Back Door; Never Take the Horse Shoe from the Door; On Mother Kelly's Doorstep; Open the Door, Richard; River, Stay 'Way from My Door; She Lived Next Door to a Firehouse; Shut the Door (They're Comin' Through the Window); Stop Dat Knocking at My Door; Two Doors Down; Where the Morning Glories Twine Around the Door

Dope, *see* **Stupid**

Double, *see* **Two**

Dough, *see* **Bread, Money**

Dove   The Carrier Dove; La Paloma (The Dove); The Tale of the Turtle Dove; When Doves Cry; The White Dove

Dover   (There'll Be Blue Birds over) The White Cliffs of Dover

Down   After the Lights Go Down Low; All In Down and Out; All My Rowdy Friends Have Settled Down; All the Quakers Are Shoulder Shakers Down in Quaker Town; And Her Golden Hair Was Hanging Down Her Back; Are We Downhearted?—No!; Away Down South in Heaven; Bang Bang (My Baby Shot Me Down); Bend Down, Sister; Blow (Knock) the Man Down; Boogie Down; Buckle Down, Winsocki; Come Down Ma Evenin' Star; Come On Down; Come on Down Town; Cruising Down the River; Doin' the New Low-Down; Doin' the Uptown Lowdown; Don't Bring Me Down; Don't Bring Me Down; Don't Go Down the Mine; Don't Let the Sun Go Down on Me; Down Among the Sheltering Palms; Down Among the Sugar Cane; Down Among the Sugar-Cane; Down Argentine Way; Down at the Huskin' Bee; Down at the Old Swimming Hole; Down Below; Down by the O-Hi-O; Down by the Old Mill Stream; Down by the River; Down by the Riverside, or, Ain't Gwine Study War No More; Down by the Silvery Rio Grande; Down by the Station; Down by the Winegar Woiks; Down Forget-Me-Not Lane; Down in Bom-Bombay; Down in Dear Old New Orleans; Down in Honkey Tonky Town; Down in Jungle Town; Down in Poverty Row; Down in the Boondocks; Down in the Depths on the Ninetieth Floor; Down in the Forest; Down in the Glen; Down in the Old Cherry Orchard; Down in the Valley, or, Birmingham Jail, or, Bird in a Cage, or, Down on the Levee; Down on the Brandywine; Down on the Farm (They All Ask for You); Down on the Farm in Harvest Time; Down South; Down Sweetheart Avenue; Down the Field (March); Down the Mall; Down the Old Ox Road; Down the River of Golden Dreams; Down the Winding Road of Dreams; Down Under; Down Vauxhall Way; Down Went McGinty; Down Where the Cotton Blossoms Grow; Down Where the Silv'ry Mohawk Flows; Down Where the Swanee River Flows; Down Where the Trade Winds Blow; Down Where the Wurzburger Flows; Down with Love; Down Yonder; Downhearted; Downhearted Blues; Downtown; Ease on Down the Road; (Fifteen Miles (Years) on the) Erie Canal (Low Bridge!—Everybody Down); Everything Is Peaches Down in Georgia; Flying Down to Rio; Get Down; Get Down Get Down (Get on the Floor); Get Down Tonight; (It's Hard To) Go Down Easy; Go Down, Moses; Go Way Back and Sit Down; (O) Hand Me Down My Walking Cane; The Heart Bow'd Down; He's Dead But He Won't Lie Down; How Ya Gonna Keep 'Em Down on the Farm (After They've Seen Paree); Hurry On Down (to My House); I Ain't Down Yet; I Faw Down an' Go Boom; I Gave You Up Just Before You Threw Me Down; I Just Roll Along Havin' My Ups and Downs; I Want To Go Back to Michigan—Down on the Farm; I'm Building Up to an Awful Let-Down; I'm Gonna Sit Right Down and Write Myself a Letter; I'm Tying the Leaves So They Won't Come Down; I've Been Floating Down the Old Green River; Just As the Sun Went Down; Just Try To Picture Me (Back (Down) Home in Tennessee); Keep Your Head Down, "Fritzie Boy"; Keep Your Skirts Down, Mary Ann; Lay Down (Candles in the Rain); Lay Down Sally; Lay Down Your Arms; Let's All Go Down the Strand; Little Town in the Ould County Down; (Look Down That) Lonesome Road; Look Down, Look Down That Lonesome Road; Lowdown; Me and Julio Down by the Schoolyard; Meet Me Jenny When the Sun Goes Down; The Merry-Go-Round Broke Down; My Defenses Are Down; My Sweetie Turned Me Down; Nineteenth Nervous Breakdown; Nobody Knows You When You're Down and Out; Now I Lay Me Down To Sleep; Oh, I Can't Sit Down; Old Folks At Home (Way Down Upon the Swanee River); Sailing down the Chesapeake Bay; Shake Your Body (Down to the Ground); Silver Dollars (Down and Out); Sit Down, You're Rocking the Boat; Sit Down You're Rocking the Boat; The Sky Fell Down; Somewhere Down the Road; South of the Border (Down Mexico Way); Sweet and Low-Down; Swingin' Down the Lane; Take Me Down; Ten Little Fingers and Ten Little Toes—Down in Tennessee; There's a Quaker Down in Quaker Town; (When) They Cut Down the Old Pine Tree; Throw Him Down McCloskey; Tie Me Kangaroo Down Sport; Turn Down Day; Two Doors Down; Upside Down; (Theme from) Upstairs Downstairs, or, The Edwardians; Waters of Venice, or, Floating Down the Sleepy Lagoon; Way Down in Iowa I'm Going To Hide Away; Way Down in My Heart, or, I've Got a Feeling for You; Way Down in Old Indiana; Way Down Yonder in New Orleans; Way Down Yonder in the Cornfield; When a Lady Meets a Gentleman Down South; When It's Night Time Down in Burgundy; When It's Sleepy Time Down South; When My Sugar Walks Down the Street, All the Birdies Go Tweet-Tweet-Tweet; When the Leaves Come Tumbling Down; When the Sun Goes Down; The World Turned Upside Down, or, Derry Down; You Can't Keep a Good Man Down; You Let Me Down

Dozen, *see* **Twelve**

Drag   Kind of a Drag; Stop Draggin' My Heart Around; Time Drags By; The Varsity Drag; The Viper's Drag

Dragon   Puff the Magic Dragon; St. (Saint) George and the Dragonet

Drawer   In My Little Bottom Drawer

Dream   Afraid To Dream; All I Do Is Dream of You; All I Have To Do Is Dream; An American Dream; Anything I Dream Is Possible; As Long as I'm Dreaming; Au Revoir, Pleasant Dreams; Baby Dream Your Dream; Beautiful Dreamer; Boulevard of Broken Dreams; Bring Back My Golden Dreams; California Dreamin', Castle of Dreams; Come Where My Love Lies Dreaming; The Curse of the Dreamer; Darn That Dream; Day Dreaming; Day Dreaming; Day Dreams; Daydream; Daydream Believer; Dear Mother, in Dreams I See Her; Deep in a Dream; Did You Ever See a Dream Walking; Distant Dreams; Don't Fall in Love with a Dreamer; Don't Wake Me Up, I'm Dreaming; Don't Wake Me Up, Let Me Dream; The Door of My (Her) Dreams; Down the River of Golden Dreams; Down the Winding Road of Dreams; Dream (When You're Feeling Blue); A Dream; Dream a Little Dream of Me; Dream Along with Me (I'm on My Way to a Star); Dream Babies; Dream Dancing; Dream, Dream, Dream; Dream, Dream, Dream; Dream Girls; A Dream Is a Wish Your Heart Makes; Dream Lover; Dream Lover; A Dream of My Boyhood Days; The Dream of Olwen; Dream On; Dreamer with a Penny; A Dreamer's Holiday; Dreamin'; Dreaming; Dreaming; The Dreaming; Dreams; Dreams of Long Ago; Dreamy Alabama; Dreamy Melody; Drifting and Dreaming (Sweet Paradise); Face to Face with the Girl of My Dreams; Garden of My Dreams; Girl of My Dreams; The Girl with the Dreamy Eyes; Goodbye, Little Girl of My Dreams; Gypsy Dream Rose; Hit the Road to Dreamland; I Can Dream About You; I Can Dream, Can't I; I Dream of You; I Dream Too Much; I Dreamed; I Dreamt I Dwelt in Marble Halls; I Guess I'll Have To Dream the Rest; I Had the Craziest Dream; I Have Dreamed; I Like Dreamin'; I Love You (Sweetheart of All My Dreams); I Wonder If Love Is a Dream; If Dreams Come True; If You Are But a Dream; I'll Buy That Dream; I'll Never Have To Dream Again; I'll See You in My Dreams; I'm a Dreamer (Aren't We All); I'm (Dreaming) Thinking Tonight of My Blue Eyes; The Impossible Dream, or, The Quest; In All My Dreams I Dream of You; Island of Dreams; Isle o' Dreams; The Isle of Our Dreams; It Was a Dream; It's the Same Old Dream; Jeanie with the Light Brown Hair; Jeannine, I Dream of Lilac Time; Just a Dream; A Kiss To Build a Dream On; The Land of Golden Dreams; Let Me Dream Again; Li'l Darlin' (Don't Dream of Anybody But Me); Little Dolly Daydream; Lover of My Dreams, or, Mirabelle Waltz; The Maiden with the Dreamy Eyes; Mary's Dream, or, Sandy's Ghost; Meet Me Tonight in Dreamland; Memories Live Longer Than Dreams; The Miner's Dream of Home; My Cabin of Dreams; My Dream Girl, I Loved You Long Ago; My Dream Is Yours; My Dream of Love; My Dream of the Big Parade; My Dreams Are Getting Better All the Time; My Elusive Dreams; My Isle of Golden Dreams; My Rosary of Dreams; My Twilight Dream; My Wonderful Dream Girl; Once Upon a Dream; Out of My Dreams; Pieces of Dreams; (I've Got) A Pocketful of Dreams; Put Your Dreams Away for Another Day; Roses Bring Dreams of You; Rousseau's Dream; Sad Sweet Dreamer; The Sailor of My Dreams; Sailor Who Are You Dreaming of Tonight; Say Not Love Is a Dream; Shine Through My Dreams; Silver Dream Machine; Smoke Dreams; Someone's Rocking My Dream Boat; (On the) Street of Dreams; Summer Dreams; Sweet Dreams; Sweet Dreams (Are Made of This); Tell Me I'm Not Dreaming; There's Egypt in Your Dreamy Eyes; These Dreams; This Time the Dream's on Me; Through a Thousand Dreams; Till All Our Dreams Come True; Time Was, or, Dreaming; Trail of Dreams; Vagabond Dreams; Vienna Dreams; A Waltz Dream; Was It a Dream; What's the Use of Dreaming; When I Dream; When I Dream in the Gloaming of You; When I Grow Too Old To Dream; When My Dream Boat Comes Home; With My Eyes Wide Open I'm Dreaming; Warp Your Troubles in Dreams (and Dream Your Troubles Away); You Are the Ideal of my Dreams; You Can't Stop Me from Dreaming; You Make My Dreams; You Stepped Out of a Dream; You Tell Me Your Dream, or, I Had a Dream, Dear; You'll Be Back Every Night in My Dreams; Your Wildest Dreams; You're Always in My Arms (But Only in My Dreams)

Dress, *see also* **Gown, Petticoat, Skirt**   Dress You Up; Leave Me Alone (Ruby Red Dress); Long Cool Woman (in a Black Dress); Paris Original; When You Wore a Pinafore; When You're All Dressed Up and No Place To Go

Drift   Drift Away; Drifter; Drifting and Dreaming (Sweet Paradise)

Drill   Drill Ye Tarriers Drill

Drink, *see also* **Alcohol**   Drink, Puppy, Drink; Drink to Me Only With Thine Eyes; I Think I'll Just Stay Here and Drink; Sipping Cider Thru' (Through) a Straw

Drive, *see* **Automobile**

Drop, *see also* **Cry, Rain**   The Moon Drops Low; You Dropped Me like a Red Hot Penny

Drum The Drummer Boy of Shiloh; Drums in My Heart; Jungle Drums (Canto Karabali); The Little Drummer Boy; The Little Drummer Boy; Totem Tom-Tom; The Toy Drum Major; When a Woman Hears the Sound of the Drum and Fife

Drunk, *see* **Alcohol**

Dry Dry Bones; Every Day Will Be Sunday When the Town Goes Dry; Hoem and Dry; How Dry I Am; O Dry Those Tears; What'll We Do on a Saturday Night When the Town Goes Dry; You Never Miss the Water Till the Well Runs Dry, or, Waste Not, Want Not

Dublin Along the Rocky Road to Dublin

Duck Bombay Duckling (Kipling Theme); Disco Duck (Part 1); Doin' the Ducky Wuck; Huckleberry Duck; Little White Duck; The Ugly Duckling

Duel, *see* **Fight**

Duke The Duke of Earl; (Theme from) Dukes of Hazzard (Good Ol' Boys); How Stands the Glass Around, or, Wolfe's Song, or, Why, Soldiers, Why, or, The Duke of Berwick's March

Dumas I'm a Ding Dong Daddy from Dumas

Dumb Dum Dum; Dummy Song, or, I'll Take the Legs from Off the Table

Dumpling, *see* **Potato**

Dungaree Black Denim Trousers; Dungaree Doll; Forever in Blue Jeans

Dunk I Love To Dunk a Hunk of Sponge Cake

Durham Durham Town

Dust Another One Bites the Dust; Dust in the Wind; I've Got a Pain in My Sawdust; Keep Sweeping the Cobwebs Off the Moon; Less Than the Dust; My Old Man's a Dustman; Star Dust; Stardust on the Moon

Dwarf, *see* **People**

Dwell I Dreamt I Dwelt in Marble Halls

Eadie Eadie Was a Lady

Eagle Fly Like an Eagle; Love Touch (Theme from *Legal Eagles*); Under the Double Eagle (March); Would You Rather Be a Colonel with an Eagle on Your Shoulder, or a Private with a Chicken on Your Knee?

Ear, *see* **Hear**

Earl The Duke of Earl

Early Early Autumn; Early in de Mornin'; Early in the Morning; She Was One of the Early Birds; Why Does It Get So Late So Early

Earring Golden Earrings

Earth Earth Angel; For the Beauty of the Earth; Give Me Love (Give Me Peace on Earth); A Handful of Earth from (My Dear) Mother's Grave; Heaven on Earth; I Feel the Earth Move

East East of the Moon, West of the Stars; East of the Sun and West of the Moon; East Side of Heaven; The Sidewalks of New York, or, East Side, West Side; Star in the East

Easter Easter Parade

Easy Ease On Down the Road; Easier Said Than Done; Easy; Easy Come, Easy Go; Easy Come, Easy Go; Easy Going Me; Easy Living; Easy Rider; Easy Street; Easy Street; Easy To Be Hard; Easy To Love; Easy To Love; The Free and Easy Hour of Parting; (It's Hard To) Go Down Easy; I Could Easily Fall; I Fall in Love Too Easily; I'm Easy; It's Easy To Remember (and So Hard To Forget); It's So Easy; Loving Her Was Easier (Than Anything I'll Ever Do Again); Make It Easy on Yourself; Mama Don't Allow No Easy Riders Here; Nice 'n' Easy; Prove It by the Things You Do (It's Easy To Say); Solid Gold Easy Action; Take It Easy; Take It Easy on Me; Takin' It Easy

Eat Don't Bite the Hand That's Feeding You; Hungry Heart; Hungry Like the Wolf; Let 'Em Eat Cake; Maneater; Peter Peter Pumpkin Eater; The Purple People Eater; You Gotta Eat Your Spinach, Baby

Ebb, *see* **Sea**

Ebenezer Wal, I Swan!, or, Ebenezer Frye, or, Giddiap Napoleon, It Looks Like Rain

Ebony, *see* **Black**

Echo The Echo Told Me a Lie; Imperial Echoes; Just an Echo in the Valley; Little Sir Echo; Swiss (Echo) Song; Tell Me, Babbling Echo, or, The Request; We Three—My Echo, My Shadow and Me

Ecstasy Ecstasy Tango

Eden, *see* **Garden**

Education, *see* **School**

Edward Just Like Eddie; The Wreck of the Edmund Fitzgerald

Eel, *see* **Fish**

Egg The Big Butter and Egg Man; The Egg and I; I'm Putting All My Eggs in One Basket; Humpty Dumpty

Egypt There's Egypt in Your Dreamy Eyes

Eight Beat Me, Daddy, Eight to the Bar; Dinner at Eight; Eight by Ten; Eight Days a Week; 867-5309/Jenny; I'm Henery the Eighth (I Am); Roll On Eighteen Wheeler

Eighteen Between Eighteenth and Nineteenth on Chestnut Street; 1812 Overture; Eighteenth Variation on a Theme by Paganini; In an Eighteenth Century Drawing Room

Eighty Around the World (in Eighty Days)

Eileen Come On Eileen; Eileen (Alanna Asthore); Eileen Alanna

Eleanor Eleanor Rigby

Elephant Baby Elephant Walk; Nellie the Elephant; When I Saw an Elephant Fly

Eleven Eleven More Months and Ten More Days; Eleventh Hour Melody; Seven or Eleven—My Dixie Pair o' Dice; Theme from The Eleventh Hour

Eli Eli Eli; Eli Green's Cakewalk; Eli's Comin'

Eliza, *see also* **Liza** Good-bye, Eliza Jane; I Still See Elisa

Elizabeth, *see also* **Liza** Elizabeth; Elizabethan Serenade; Robert and Elizabeth; The Scandal of Little Lizzie Ford

Ellen Ellen Bayne; I'm Shy, Mary Ellen, I'm Shy

Ellie Ellie Rhee, or, Carry Me Back to Tennessee

Elmer Elmer's Tune

Eloise   The Belle of Mohawk Vale, or, Bonny Eloise

Elsie   Elsie from Chelsea

Elusive, *see* **Hide**

Elvira   Elvira; (Theme from) Elvira Madigan

Emaline   Emaline; Sweet Emalina, My Gal

Emblem   National Emblem (March)

Embrace, *see* **Hold**

Emergency   Emergency Ward 10 Theme

Emigrant   The Lament of the Irish Emigrant

Emily   Emily; See Emily Play

Emma   Emma; Whoa, Emma

Emmet   Emmet's Lullaby, or, Fritz, Our Cousin German, or, Brother's Lullaby

Emotion   Emotion; Emotional Rescue; Emotions; Mixed Emotions; Young Emotions

Empire   The British Empire; (Theme from) The Empire Strikes Back

Empty   Cradle's Empty, Baby's Gone; Empty Saddles; Full Moon and Empty Arms; The Vacant Chair, or, We Shall Meet But We Shall Miss Him

Enchanted   Disenchanted; Enchanted Island; Some Enchanted Evening; Strange Enchantment

Encounter   (Theme from) Close Encounters of the Third Kind

End   At the End of a Beautiful Day; At the End of the Day; The End (of the Rainbow); End of a Love Affair; The End of the Road; The End of the World; Endless Love; Finishing the Hat; Happy Ending; I Don't Think I'll End It All Today; I Found the End of the Rainbow; Last Night Was the End of the World; The Little White House (at the End of Honeymoon Lane); Love Is a Song That Never Ends; My Unfinished Symphony; Never Ending Song of Love; Odds and Ends (of a Beautiful Love Affair); Round on the End and High in the Middle, O-hi-o; The Song Is Ended But the Melody Lingers On; Song Without End; Stoney End; Take It to the Limit; That Lovely Weekend; That's the Beginning of the End; There Isn't Any Limit to My Love; Till the End of Time; We're Through; West End Blues; West End Girls; When Day Is Done; When You Come to the End of the Day; Wipe Out

England   Battle of Britain; Britannia Rag; The British Empire; British Grenadiers; England Swings (Like a Pendulum Do); English County Gardens; English Rose; The Fishermen of England; He Is an Englishman; Here Come the British (Bang! Bang!); I Leave My Heart in an English Garden; Mad Dogs and Englishmen; My British Buddy; Rose of England; Rule, Britannia; The Stately Homes of England; There'll Always Be an England; Why Can't the English; Ye Parliament of England; Yeoman of England

Enjoy   Enjoy Yourself; Enjoy Yourself, It's Later Than You Think; I Enjoy Being a Girl

Enter   The Gladiator's Entry; It Never Entered My Mind

Entertain   The Entertainer; Let Me Entertain You; That's Entertainment

Erie   (Fifteen Miles (Years) on the) Erie Canal (Low Bridge!—Everybody Down); The E-RI-EE; The Meeting of the Waters of Hudson and Erie

Erin, *see* **Ireland**

Ermine, *see* **Mink**

Ernest   Ernie; O-oo Ernest, Are You Earnest with Me?

Error, *see* **Mistake**

Escape   Escape; I Can't Escape from You

Eskimo   Never Do a Tango with an Eskimo

Establish   The Oldest Established (Permanent Floating Crap Game in New York)

Eternally, *see* **Forever**

Eternity, *see* **Forever**

Ethel   I Was Born in Virginia, or, Ethel Levy's Virginia Song

Evangeline   Evangeline

Eve, *see also* **Evening**   Eve Cost Adam Just One Bone

Evelina   Evelina

Evening   Abide with Me, or, Fast Falls the Eventide; Bird Songs at Eventide; Come Down Ma Evenin' Star; The Eve of Destruction; An Evening in Caroline; Evensong; Good Evening, Caroline; I Hear a Thrush at Eve; I'll Miss You in the Evening; In the Blue of Evening; In the Cool, Cool, Cool of the Evening; In the Evening by the Moonlight; In the Evening by the Moonlight, Dear Louise; In the Twi-Twi-Twi-Light; In Twilight Town; Just a Baby's Prayer at Twilight; Lady of the Evening; Late in the Evening; Linger a Little Longer in the Twilight; Loneliness of Evening; (This Is) A Lovely Way To Spend an Evening; My Twilight Dream; Oh Star of Eve; Saviour, Breathe an Evening Blessing; Some Enchanted Evening; St. Mary's in the Twilight; Star of the Evening; A Summer Evening in Santa Cruz; Thank You for a Lovely Evening; Twilight in Turkey; Twilight on the Trail; Twilight Time; Tyrolese Evening Hymn; Warblings at Eve; When the Organ Played at Twilight (The Song That Reached My Heart); Where the Twilight Comes To Kiss the Rose Goodnight

Event   Main Event/ The Fight; Royal Event

Eventide, *see* **Evening**

Everything   The Best of Everything; Dancing Is Everything; Don't Hold Everything; Everything Happens to Me; Everything I Have Is Yours; Everything I Love; Everything Is Beautiful; Everything Is Peaches Down in Georgia; Ev'rything I've Got (Belongs to You); Everything She Wants; Everything Stops for Tea; Everything's Al'Right; Everything's Alright; Everything's Coming Up Roses; Everything's Gonna Be All Right; Everything's in Rhythm with My Heart; I Just Want To Be Your Everything; I'll Make Up for Everything; 'N Everything; There Goes My Everything; (There's Something Nice About Everyone But) There's Everything Nice About You; Time Heals Everything; Uptight (Everything's Alright); You Can't Have Everything; You Have Everything; You're My Everything; You're the First, the Last, My Everything; You've Got Everything

Everywhere   Ev'rywhere; Everywhere You Go; Goodnight Children, Everywhere; Love (Your Magic Spell Is Everywhere); Music Music Everywhere (But Not a Song in My Heart)

Evil   Evil Hearted You

Exactly   Exactly Like You

Excelsior   Excelsior; Excelsior

Exhibition   Pictures at an Exhibition

Experiment   Experiment; Experiments with Mice

Explain   Can Anyone Explain? (No! No! No!); Don't Explain

Eye, *see also* **Blind, Cockeyed, Glasses**   "Algy," the Picadilly Johnny with the Little Glass Eye; Baby Blue Eyes; Beautiful Brown Eyes; Beautiful Eyes; Bette Davis Eyes; Blue Eyes; Bright Eyes; Bright Eyes; Brown Eyed Girl; Brown Eyes—Why Are You Blue; Can I See You Tonight; Can't Take My Eyes Off You; Close Your Eyes; (I'm) Dancing with Tears in My Eyes; Dark Eyes, or, Black Eyes; Dear Eyes That Haunt Me; Deep in Your Eyes; Did You Close Your Eyes (When We Kissed); Don't Make My Brown Eyes Blue; Don't Let the Stars Get in Your Eyes; Double Vision; Drink to Me Only with Thine Eyes; Ebony Eyes; Eye in the Sky; Eye of the Tiger; Eyes of Blue, Eyes of Brown; Eyes of Darkness; The Eyes of Texas (Are Upon You); Eyes That See in the Dark; Eyes Without a Face; Fat Li'l' Feller Wid His Mammy's Eyes; Five Foot Two, Eyes of Blue (Has Anybody Seen My Girl?); For Your Eyes Only; The Girl with the Dreamy Eyes; Green Eyes; Hair of Gold, Eyes of Blue; Hawaiian Eye; Her Eyes Don't Shine Like Diamonds; I Close My Eyes and Count to Ten; I Couldn't Sleep a Wink Last Night; I Don't See Me in Your Eyes Anymore; I Have Eyes (To See With); I Just Can't Make My Eyes Behave; I Only Have Eyes for You; If You Look in Her Eyes; If You Love Me Darling, Tell Me with Your Eyes; I'll Close My Eyes; I'm (Dreaming) Thinking Tonight of My Blue Eyes; It's the Irish in Your Eye, (It's the Irish in Your Smile); I've Got My Eyes on You; Just Because She Made Dem Goo-Goo Eyes; Laughing Irish Eyes; Love Eyes; Love Has Eyes; Love's Eyes; Lyin' Eyes; Ma! He's Making Eyes at Me; The Magic of Your Eyes; The Maiden with the Dreamy Eyes; The Moon Got in My Eyes; The Moon Has His Eyes on You; My Eyes Adored You; My Mother's Eyes; My Nellie's Blue Eyes; The Night Has a Thousand Eyes; The Night Has a Thousand Eyes; Private Eyes; Roll Dem Roly Boly Eyes; Sad Eyes; Sexy Eyes; Show the White of Yo' Eye; Smoke Gets in Your Eyes; Spanish Eyes; Star Eyes; Stars in My Eyes; Stars in Your Eyes; (Theme from) La Strada, or, Stars Shine in Your Eyes; Them There Eyes; Theme from Ice Castles (Through the Eyes of Love); There's a Light in Your Eyes; There's Danger in Your Eyes, Cherie; There's Egypt in Your Dreamy Eyes; There's Yes, Yes, in Your Eyes; Thy Beaming Eyes; Two Blue Eyes; Two Laughing Irish Eyes; Two Lovely Black Eyes; A Vision of Salome; What Do You Want to Make Those Eyes at Me For; When Irish Eyes Are Smiling; Where the Black-Eyed Susans Grow; Where'd You Get Those Eyes; Whoever You Are, or, Sometimes Your Eyes Look Blue to Me; With My Eyes Wide Open I'm Dreaming; Wonderful Eyes; You Can't Pull the Wool over My Eyes; Your Eyes; Your Eyes Have Told Me So; You're a Great Big Blue Eyed Baby; You're De Apple of My Eye; You've Got Your Mother's Big Blue Eyes

Ezekiel   Ezekiel Saw De Wheel

Face   Baby Face; Cheek to Cheek; Dimples; Dirty Hands, Dirty Face; Eyes Without a Face; Face to Face; Face to Face; Face to Face with the Girl of My Dreams; The First Time Ever I Saw Your Face; Funny Face; I See Your Face Before Me; I've Grown Accustomed to Her Face; Let's Face the Music and Dance; Lonely Night (Angel Face); Look at That Face; Nancy (with the Laughing Face); Powder Your Face with Sunshine; Put On a Happy Face; Take That Look off Your Face; Turn 'Erbert's Face to the Wall, Mother; Two Faces in the Dark

Fact, *see* **Truth**

Fade   After the Roses Have Faded Away; Fade Out—Fade In; A Faded Summer Love; 'Tis But a Little Faded Flower

Fair   Come to the Fair; Crusader's Hymn, or, Fairest Lord Jesus; Fair and Warmer; Fair Harvard; It Isn't Fair; It's Always Fair Weather When Good Fellows Get Together, or, A Stein Song; Lord Thomas and Fair Elinore; My Truly, Truly Fair; Scarborough Fair/ Canticle, or, Parsley, Sage, Rosemary and Thyme; Schön Rosmarin (Fair Rosmarin); She's the Fairest Little Flower Dear Old Dixie Ever Grew (Knew); Strawberry Fair; Then You May Take Me to the Fair; (Have I Stayed) Too Long at the Fair

Fairy   Airy, Fairy Lillian; Fairy on the Clock; Nobody Loves a Fairy When She's Forty; Dance of the Sugar-Plum Fairy; Oh, the Fairies, Whoa, the Fairies; There Are Fairies at the Bottom of Our Garden

Faith   Adeste Fideles, or, O Come All Ye Faithful; Come, Ye Faithful, Raise the Strain; Faith; Faith of Our Fathers; Faithful Forever; Faithfully Yours; Have a Little Faith in Me; Keeping the Faith; My Faith Looks Up to Thee; My Faithful Stradivari; Ole Faithful; Semper Fidelis

Fall   Abide with Me, or, Fast Falls the Eventide; Any Time's the Time To Fall in Love; Baby the Rain Must Fall; Before the Next Teardrop Falls; A Blossom Fell; Can't Help Falling in Love (with You); Catch a Falling Star; Could It Be I'm Falling in Love; Don't Fall in Love with a Dreamer; Fall In and Follow Me; Fall in Love with You; Falling Again; Fallin' in Love (Again); Falling in Love Again; Falling in Love with Love; Falling in Love with You; Falling Leaves; Feeling I'm Falling; Fooled Around and Fell in Love; A Hard Rain's A-Gonna Fall; I Could Easily Fall; I Didn't Slip, I Wasn't Pushed, I Fell; I Fall in Love Too Easily; I Faw Down an' Go Boom; I Just Fall in Love Again; I'd Love To Fall Asleep and Wake Up in My Mammy's Arms; If Anyone Falls; If I Fell; If I Should Fall in Love Again; If the Rain's Got To Fall; I'll Never Fall in Love Again; I'm Falling in Love with Someone; In the Fall We'll All Go Voting for Al; Into Each Life Some Rain Must Fall; It's Never Too Late to Fall in Love; I've Got a Feeling I'm Falling; Let's Do It (Let's Fall in Love); Let's Fall in Love; Never Gonna Fall in Love Again; The Night the Floor Fell In; Nothing Like Falling in Love; (Potatoes Are Cheaper—Tomatoes Are Cheaper) Now's the Time To Fall in Love; On the Old Fall River Line; Please Help Me I'm Falling; Raindrops Keep Fallin' on My Head; Rise and Fall of Flingle Bunt; A Rockin' Good Way (To Mess Around and Fall in Love); Since I Fell for You; The Sky Fell Down; A Star Fell Out of Heaven; Stars Fell on Alabama; Taking Somebody with Me When I Fall; A Tear Fell; When Did I Fall in Love; When I Fall in Love; When I Fall in Love; When the Cherry Blossoms Fall; When the Leaves Come Tumbling Down; Where Were You When I Was Falling in Love; Why Did She Fall for the Leader of the

Band; Why Do Fools Fall in Love; Would You Catch a Falling Star; Yes, Let Me Like a Soldier Fall

Fame   Fame

Familiar   Funny, Familiar, Forgotten Feelings

Family, *see also* **Folks**   Family Affair; Horace and No Relations; Meet the Family; Those Were the Days, or, Theme from All in the Family; Two Tribes; We Are Family

Fan   Buffalo Gals (Won't You Come Out Tonight?), or, Lubly Fan

Fancy   Fancy; Fancy Free; I've Taken Quite a Fancy to You; A Little of What You Fancy; No Strings (I'm Fancy Free); The Skidmore Fancy Ball; What Takes My Fancy; A Young Man's Fancy

Fanfare   Fanfare Boogie

Fanny   Fanny

Fantasy   Black and Tan Fantasy; Living in a Fantasy; Stairway to the Stars (Park Avenue Fantasy)

Far-Away   The Call of the Far-Away Hills; Distant Dreams; Far Away Places; Far Off I Hear a Lover's Flute; Gone Too Far; Long Ago and Far Away; Number Something Far Away Lane; On the Banks of the Wabash Far Away; Smoke from a Distant Fire; So Far Away; So Near and Yet So Far; There Is a Green Hill Far Away; Thou Art So Near and Yet So Far; You're Going Far Away, Lad, or, I'm Still Your Mother, Dear

Farewell, *see* **Goodbye**

Farm   Down on the Farm (They All Ask for You); Down on the Farm in Harvest Time; Farmer in the Dell; The Green Mountain Farmer; The Happy Farmer; How Ya Gonna Keep 'Em Down on the Farm (After They've Seen Paree); I Want To Go Back to Michigan—Down on the Farm; Jollity Farm; Misery Farm; Old MacDonald Had a Farm; Rebecca of SunnyBrook Farm

Fascination   Fascinating Rhythm; Fascination, or, Valse Tzigane; Fascination; Fascination

Fashion   (I'm) Always True to You in My Fashion; Country Style; Dedicated Follower of Fashion; Fashionette; Garland of Old Fashioned Roses; I Like Your Style; I'm Old Fashioned; Let's Take an Old-Fashioned Walk; March of the Mods; Mary, You're a Little Bit Old Fashioned; Old-Fashioned Garden; Old-Fashioned Love; An Old-Fashioned Wife; Put Me To Sleep with an Old-Fashioned Melody; Sing an Old Fashioned Song (To a Young Sophisticated Lady); A Sweet Old Fashioned Girl; That Old Fashioned Mother of Mine

Fast, *see also* **Hurry**   Abide with Me, or, Fast Falls the Eventide; Daddy Don't You Walk So Fast; The Folks Are All Waiting To See the Steamer; The General's Fast Asleep; Tammany Quickstep

Fat   Fat Li'l' Feller Wid His Mammy's Eyes; Short, Fat and 4F; Sweet Little Buttercup; Too Fat Polka; Tubby the Tuba

Fatal, *see* **Death**

Fate   Cast Your Fate to the Wind; Twist of Fate

Father, *see also* **Grandfather**   Aggravatin' Papa (Don't You Try To Two-Time Me); Beat Me, Daddy, Eight to the Bar; Bring Back My Daddy to Me; Color Him Father; Come On, Papa; Daddy; Daddy; Daddy Don't You Walk So Fast; Daddy Has a Sweetheart, and Mother Is Her Name; Daddy Long

Legs; Daddy Wouldn't Buy Me a Bow-Wow; Daddy, You've Been a Mother to Me; Daddy's Home; Daddy's Little Girl; Daddy's Little Girl; Don't You Rock Me Daddy-O; Everybody Works But Father; Faith of Our Fathers; Father, Dear Father, Come Home with Me Now, or, Come Home, Father; Following in Father's Footsteps; Give a Little Credit to Your Dad; (Theme from) The Godfather (Waltz); (Theme from) The Godfather (Part II); Good-Bye, Ma! Good-Bye, Pa! Good-Bye, Mule, or, Long Boy; The Hat Me Father Wore; Hello Mudduh, Hello Faddah; Here Comes My Daddy Now—Oh Pop—Oh Pop—Oh Pop; How'd You Like To Be My Daddy; I Want a Girl—Just Like the Girl That Married Dear Old Dad; I'm a Ding Dong Daddy from Dumas; The Landing of the Pilgrims, or, the Pilgrim Fathers; Mama Goes Where Papa Goes; Mamma Loves Papa—Papa Loves Mamma; My Dad's Dinner Pail; My Heart Belongs to Daddy; Oh, How I Wish I Could Sleep Until My Daddy Comes Home; Oh My Papa, or, O Mein Papa; Old Father Thames; Padre; Papa Don't Preach; Papa Loves Mambo; Papa Was a Rollin' Stone; Papa Won't You Dance with Me; Papa's Got a Brand New Bag; Poor Papa (He's Got Nuthin' At All); Since Father Went To Work; Son of My Father; Take a Little Tip from Father; Thank Your Father; That Silver-Haired Daddy of Mine; Wait Until Your Daddy Comes Home; We Are Coming, Father Abraham, 300,000 More; What's the Matter with Father; When Father Papered the Parlour; You Can't Chop Your Poppa Up in Massachusetts; Your Dad Gave His Life for His Country

Fatima   Our Lady of Fatima

Faun   Afternoon of a Faun

Favor   Can't You Do a Friend a Favor

Favorite   My Favorite Things; Our Favorite Melodies

Fay   Fountain Fay

Fear, *see* **Afraid**

Feather   The Feather in Her Tyrolean Hat; Feather Your Nest; I Feel Like a Feather in the Breeze; That Sly Old Gentleman from Featherbed Lane

February   January, February

Federal   Hail Columbia, or, New Federal Song

Feed   Don't Bite the Hand That's Feeding You

Feel   Can't Fight This Feeling; Did You Ever Get That Feeling in the Moonlight; Dream (When You're Feeling Blue); Every Time I Feel the Spirit; (That's the Time I) Feel Like Makin' Love; Feeling I'm Falling; The Feeling We Once Had; Feelings; Feels So Good; Feels So Right; The 59th Street Bridge Song, or, Feelin' Groovy; (Theme from) Flashdance (What a Feeling); Fooled by a Feeling; Funny, Familiar, Forgotten Feelings; Hooked on a Feeling; How Much I Feel; I Feel a Song Coming On; I Feel Fine; I Feel for You; I Feel Like a Feather in the Breeze; I Feel Love; I Feel Pretty; I Feel the Earth Move; I Got You (I Feel Good); I Understand Just How You Feel; I've Got a Feeling I'm Falling; I've Got a Feeling You're Fooling; Mamie (Don't You Feel Ashamie); Moonlight Feels Right; More Than a Feeling; (You Make Me Feel Like) A Natural Woman; Only the Lonely (Know the Way I Feel); Sometimes I Feel Like a Motherless Child; That Certain Feeling; That Lovin' You Feelin' Again; That Old Feeling; That Same Old Feeling; Today I Feel So Happy; Tryin' To Get the Feelin' Again; Way Down in My

Heart, or, I've Got a Feeling for You; Why Fight the (That) Feeling; You Make Me Feel Brand New; You Make Me Feel Like Dancing; You Make Me Feel So Young; You've Lost That Lovin' Feelin'

Feet　Barefoot in the Park; Country Boy You Got Your Feet in L.A.; Fabulous Feet; Fidgety Feet; Flat Foot Floogie (with the Floy Floy); Following in Father's Footsteps; Foot Trapper; Footloose; Footsteps; Gimme a Pigfoot (and a Bottle of Beer); Happy Feet; Head Over Heels; Head Over Heels in Love; High Heel Sneakers; Hot Heels; The Lass with the Delicate Air, or, Young Molly Who Lives at the Foot of the Hill; Little Footsteps; Lonely Footsteps; On Your Toes; Song of the Barefoot Contessa; Steptoe and Son; Sugar Foot Stomp, or, Dipper Mouth Blues; Sugarfoot; Ten Little Fingers and Ten Little Toes—Down In Tennessee; (Everybody Ought To Know How To Do) The Tickle Toe; Tiger Feet; Tip Toe Through the Tulips (with Me); Tired of Toein' the Line; Your Feet's Too Big

Felix　Felix Kept On Walking

Fellow　Fat Li'l' Feller Wid His Mammy's Eyes; A Fella with an Umbrella; A Fellow Needs a Girl; For He's a Jolly Good Fellow, or, Malbrouk (Malbrough), or, We Won't Go Home Until Morning, or, The Bear Went over the Mountain; Hey Young Fella Close Your Old Umbrella; I'm Looking for a Nice Young Fellow Who Is Looking for a Nice Young Girl; It's Always Fair Weather When Good Fellows Get Together, or, A Stein Song; The Most Happy Fella; Once Knew a Fella; Such a Li'l Fellow; When a Fellah Has Turned Sixteen; When a Fellow's on the Level with a Girl That's on the Square

Fence, *see also* **Gate**　Don't Fence Me In; Leanin' on the Ole Top Rail

Ferdinand　Ferdinand the Bull

Ferry, *see* Boat

Festival　Beaulieu Festival Suite

Feud　Feudin' and Fightin'

Fever　Boogie Fever; Fever; Night Fever

Few　Ain't It Funny What a Difference Just a Few Hours Make; Precious and Few

Fiction, *see* **Story**

Fiddle, *see* **Violin**

Field　Across the Field; Cotton Fields; Down the Field (March); Greenfields; I Remember the Cornfields; In the Gold Fields of Nevada; Love Is Like a Battlefield; 'Mid the Green Fields of Virginia; The Pesky Sarpent, or, (On) Springfield Mountain; Strawberry Fields Forever; The U.S. Field Artillery March, or, The Caissons Go Rolling Along; Way Down Yonder in the Cornfield; We've a Million In the Field

Fife, *see* **Flute**

Fifteen　(Fifteen Miles (Years) on the) Erie Canal (Low Bridge!—Everybody Down); Fifteen Cents; Pirate Song, or, Fifteen Men On a (the) Dead Man's Chest—Yo! Ho! Ho! and a Bottle of Rum

Fifty　Fifty Million Frenchmen Can't Be Wrong; Fifty Million Times a Day; Fifty Ways to Leave Your Lover; Lost in the Fifties Tonight (In the Still of the Night); We've Been Chums for Fifty Years

Fifty-Nine　The 59th Street Bridge Song, or, Feelin' Groovy

Fifty-Two　Fifty-Second Street Theme

Fight　The Boxer; Can't Fight This Feeling; Dueling Banjos; The Duelists; Feudin' and Fightin'; Fight On; Glory of Love (Theme from *The Karate Kid Part II*); He Fought for a Cause He Thought Was Right; If He Can Fight Like He Can Love, Good Night Germany; Joshua Fit (Fought) de Battle of Jericho; Kung Fu Fighting; Main Event/The Fight; Stand Up and Fight Like H---; This Is Worth Fighting For; We Fight Tomorrow, Mother; Why Fight the (That) Feeling

Fill　Come, Landlord, Fill the Flowing Bowl; Let My Song Fill Your Heart; The Night Is Filled with Music; Put On Your Slippers and Fill Up Your Pipe

Find　A Good Man Is Hard To Find; I Found a Million Dollar Baby in a Five and Ten Cent Store; I Found a New Baby; I Found a Rose in the Devil's Garden; I Found the End of the Rainbow; I Found You; I Found You and You Found Me; I Found You in the Rain; I'd Climb the Highest Mountain (If I Knew I'd Find You); If You Should Ever Need Me (You'll Always Find Me Here); I'll Find You; I'll Never Find Another You; I've Got the Time—I've Got the Place, But It's Hard To Find the Girl; Johnny Doughboy Found a Rose in Ireland; Look Around (You'll Find Me There); Love Is Where You Find It; Love Is Where You Find It; Love's Found You and Me; Pathfinder's March; Some Day I'll Find You; Some Day I'll Find You; Some Little Bug Is Going To Find You (Some Day); You Find the Time, I'll Find the Place; You Won't Find Another Fool Like Me; You'll Never Find Another Love Like Mine

Fine　Fine and Dandy; A Fine Romance; He's So Fine; I Feel Fine; One Fine Day, or, Un Bel Dì

Finger, *see* **Hand**

Finland　Finlandia

Fire, *see also* **Burn**　(Theme from) Chariots of Fire; The Christmas Song, or, Merry Christmas to You, or, Chestnuts Roasting on an Open Fire; Fire; Fire and Rain; Fire Brigade; Fire in the Morning; The Firebird Ballet Suite; (Theme from) Flame Trees of Thika; Great Balls of Fire; I Don't Want To Set the World On Fire; I'm on Fire; I'm Playing with Fire; Keep the Home Fires Burning (Till the Boys Come Home); Kiss of Fire; Light My Fire; Love Theme from St. Elmo's Fire; The Man with the Ladder and the Hose; Midnight Fire-Alarm; The Moth and the Flame; My Old Flame; The Old Flame Flickers and I Wonder Why; Ritual Fire Dance; She Lived Next Door to a Firehouse; Sitting on a Fire Barred Gate; Smoke from a Distant Fire; Song of the Flame; St. Elmo's Fire (Man in Motion); Three on a Match; Throw Another Log on the Fire; Too Many Irons in the Fire; The Torch Song; Wildfire

Firefly　Firefly; Love Is Like a Firefly

Fireplace　Beside an Open Fireplace; The Cricket on the Hearth

Fireside　By the Fireside

First, *see* **One**

Fish, *see also* **Mermaid**　The Amorous Goldfish; At the Codfish Ball; Cape Cod Girls; The Eel; The Fishermen of England; Gone Fishin'; I'm Like a Fish Out of Water; The Lone Fish (Meat) Ball; Minnie the Mermaid, or, A Love Song in Fish Time; Pedro the Fisherman; Shrimp Boats; Three Little Fishes

Five Cinco Robles (Five Oaks); A Fifth of Beethoven; The Five Cent Shave; Five Foot Two, Eyes of Blue (Has Anybody Seen My Girl?); Five-Four-Three-Two-One; Five Hundred Miles, or, Railroader's Lament; Five Minutes More; The Five O'Clock Whistle; Forty-Five Minutes from Broadway; Four or Five Times; Hawaii Five-O; I Found a Million Dollar Baby in a Five and Ten Cent Store; In the Year 2525; I've Got Five Dollars; Lucky Five; Mister Five by Five; Morning Train (Nine To Five); 9 to 5; Room Five Hundred and Four; 65 Love Affair; Take Five

Fix Fixing a Hole; (He'd Have To Get Under,) Get Out and Get Under (To Fix Up His Automobile); How Can You Mend a Broken Heart

Flag And the Monkey Wrapped Its Tail Around the Flagpole; The Bonnie Blue Flag; Every Race Has a Flag But the Coon; Old Flag Never Touched the Ground; The Star Spangled Banner; Stars and Stripes Forever; There's a Star Spangled Banner Waving Somewhere; Under Any Old Flag At All

Flame, *see* **Fire**

Flamingo Flamingo; Pretty Flamingo

Flapper Flapperette

Flash Flash; Flash, Bang, Wallop; (Theme from) Flashdance (What a Feeling)

Flat Flat Foot Floogie (with the Floy Floy); McNally's Row of Flats

Flatbush Nestin' Time in Flatbush

Flatter Hope Told a Flattering Tale

Flavor, *see also* **Delicious** Does the Spearmint Lose Its Flavor on the Bedpost Overnight; A Taste of Honey; Under the Yum Yum Tree; Viceroy Gives You All the Taste All the Time; The Worst Pies in London; Yummy Yummy Yummy

Flea, *see* **Fly**

Fleet, *see also* **Boat** The Fleet's In; The Fleet's in Port Again

Fling My One and Only Highland Fling

Flirt Flirtation Walk; The Flirtation Waltz; Portrait of a Flirt

Flo Good-bye, Flo

Float Captain Noah and His Floating Zoo; Carry Me Back to Ole Virginny, or, De Floating Show; Float On; I've Been Floating Down the Old Green River; The Oldest Established (Permanent Floating Crap Game in New York); Waters of Venice, or, Floating Down the Sleepy Lagoon

Flood Captain Noah and His Floating Zoo

Floor Down in the Depths on the Ninetieth Floor; Get Down Get Down (Get on the Floor); Heaven on the Seventh Floor; The Night the Floor Fell In

Florida Apalachicola, Florida; Florida, the Moon and You

Flow And Her Tears Flowed Like Wine; Come, Landlord, Fill the Flowing Bowl; Down Where the Silv'ry Mohawk Flows; Down Where the Swanee River Flows; Down Where the Wurzburger Flows; Flow Gently, Sweet Afton, or, Afton Water; If the Waters Could Speak As They Flow; Let Your Love Flow; Old Hundred(th) Doxology, or, Praise God, From Whom All Blessings Flow; Poverty's Tears Ebb and Flow; A Wet Sheet and a Flowing Sea; Where the River Shannon Flows

Flower, *see also* **Aspidistra, Bloom, Blossom, Bluebell, Bouquet, Butter(cup), Carnation, Chrysanthemum, Crocus, Daffodil, Daisy, Forget-Me-Not, Gardenia, Lilac, Lily, Lotus, Magnolia, Marigold, Orchid, Pansy, Rose, Sunflower, Tulip, Violet, Wild(flower)** Artificial Flowers; Boutonniere; The Floral Dance; A Flower from Mother's Grave; Flower Song (Blumenlied); Flowers for Madame; Garland of Old Fashioned Roses; Hearts and Flowers; House of Flowers; Jennie, the Flower of Kildare; Jessie, the Flow'r o' Dumblane; Now Sleeps the Crimson Petal; Waltz of the Flowers; O Flower Divine; Play Me Hearts and Flowers (I Wanna Cry); Rosalie the Prairie Flower; (Are You Going to) San Francisco (Be Sure To Wear Some Flowers in Your Hair); She's the Fairest Little Flower Dear Old Dixie Ever Grew (Knew); (You're the Flower of My Heart) Sweet Adeline; The Sweetest Flower the Garden Grew; 'Tis But a Little Faded Flower; Wallflower; Waltz of the Flowers; Where Have All the Flowers Gone; You're as Welcome as the Flowers in May

Flute Far Off I Hear a Lover's Flute; The Incredible Flutist; Tom, Tom, the Piper's Son; Phil the Fluter's Ball; Piccolo Pete; The Pied Piper; The Pipes of Pan; The Pipes of Pan Are Calling; Sweet Potato Piper; When a Woman Hears the Sound of the Drum and Fife

Fly, *see also* **Firefly** Angel Flying Too Close to the Ground; Come, Josephine, in My Flying Machine; The Daring Young Man (on the Flying Trapeze); The Flies Crawled Up the Window; The Flight of the Bumble Bee; Fly Home, Little Heart; Fly Like an Eagle; Fly Me to the Moon, or, In Other Words; Fly Robin Fly; Flying Down to Rio; Flying Dutchman (Overture); The Flying Dutchman; Flying Home; Go Fly a Kite; Gonna Fly Now, or, Theme from Rocky; I Know Where the Flies Go in the Wintertime; I'm Flying; Jimmy Crack Corn, or, The Blue Tail Fly; Little Birdies Learning How To Fly; Love Light in Flight; Rumors Are Flying; Shew (Shoo) Fly, Don't Bother Me; Shoofly Pie and Apple Pan Dowdy; The Spanish Flea; Straighten Up and Fly Right; When I Saw an Elephant Fly; Where Do Flies Go in the Winter Time?

Fog, *see also* **Mist** A Foggy Day; The Foggy, Foggy Dew; Lost in a Fog; Those Lazy Hazy Crazy Days of Summer

Fold Auld Robin Gray, or, When the Sheep Are in the Fold; Centerfold; Fold Your Wings; When the Black Sheep Returns to the Fold

Folks, *see also* **Family, People** The Folks Are All Waiting To See the Fast Steamer; Folks That Put On Airs; The Folks Who Live on the Hill; I Want to Thank Your Folks; Me and the Old Folks at Home; My Ain Folk; Old Folks; Old Folks at Home (Way Down Upon the Swanee River); Some Folks; What Do (the) Simple Folk Do; The Young Folks at Home

Follow Come Follow the Band; Dedicated Follower of Fashion; Fall In and Follow Me; Follow Me; Follow the Boys; Follow the Gleam; Follow the Swallow; Follow Thru; Following in Father's Footsteps; Following the Sun Around; I Will Follow Him; I'll Follow My Secret Heart; I'll Follow the Sun; I'll Follow You

Fond Absence Makes the Heart Grow Fonder; Absence Makes the Heart Grow Fonder (for Somebody Else); I'm a Little Bit Fonder of You; Just a Little Fond Affection

Fondle, *see* **Hold**

Food　Food Glorious Food; Grocer Jack; Hors d'Oeuvres

Fool　April Fools; Can You Fool—(You Just Can't Forget Her); Dancing Fool; A Day in the Life of a Fool; Don't Laugh at Me ('Cause I'm a Fool); Everybody's Somebody's Fool; Fool (If You Think It's Over); Fool Number One; The Fool on the Hill; (Now and Then) A Fool Such As I; A Fool Was I; Fooled; Fooled Around and Fell in Love; Fooled by a Feeling; Foolin' Myself; Foolish Heart; Fools Rush In; Fun To Be Fooled; The Heart of a Fool; I May Be Crazy, But I Ain't No Fool; I'm a Fool To Care; I'm a Fool To Want You; It's Foolish But It's Fun; I've Got a Feeling You're Fooling; My Foolish Heart; Poor Little Fool; She's a Fool; These Foolish Things Remind Me of You; What a Fool Believes; What Kind of Fool; What Kind of Fool Am I; Who Do You Think You Are Kidding Mister Hitler; Why Do Fools Fall in Love; You Were Only Foolin'; You Won't Find Another Fool Like Me; You Wouldn't Fool Me, Would You; Young and Foolish

Foot, *see* **Feet**

Football　You Gotta Be a Football Hero (To Get Along with the Beautiful Girls)

Forbid　Don't Forbid Me; La Musica Prohibita (Forbidden Music); The Sweetest Taboo; Taboo

Foreign　French Foreign Legion

Forest, *see* **Tree, Wood**

Forever　Constantly; Diamonds Are Forever; Eternally, or, Terry's Theme; Faithful Forever; For All Eternity; Forever; Forever and Ever; Forever in Blue Jeans; "Forever" Is a Long, Long Time; Forever with the Lord; From Here to Eternity; (If It Takes Forever) I Will Wait for You; I'm Forever Blowing Bubbles; Love Forever I Adore You; Love Me Forever; Love Me Forever; Now and Forever; Now and Forever; Now and Forever (You and Me); On a Clear Day You Can See Forever; One Love Forever; Only Forever; Stars and Stripes Forever; Strawberry Fields Forever; This Night Won't Last Forever; This Will Be (An Everlasting Love); What's Forever For; You Are My First Love; You Belong to My Heart (Now and Forever), or, Solamente Una Vez

Forge　The Origin of Gunpowder, or, When Vulcan Forg'd the Bolts of Jove

Forget　Can I Forget You; Can You Fool—(You Just Can't Forget Her); Cossack Love Song, or, Don't Forget Me; Don't You (Forget About Me); Forget Domani; Forgotten; Funny, Familiar, Forgotten Feelings; Have You Forgotten So Soon; How Can You Forget; I Keep Forgettin' (Every Time You're Near); I'll Forget You; It's Easy To Remember (and So Hard To Forget); Just a Girl That Men Forget; The Kiss That You've Forgotten (Is the Kiss I Can't Forget); The Little Boy That Santa Claus Forgot; Non Dimenticar (Don't Forget; Till Stars Forget To Shine; To Be Forgotten; Try To Forget; Unforgettable; When I'm Gone I Won't Forget; When I'm Gone You'll Soon Forget; When You Know You're Not Forgotten; When You Know You're Not Forgotten by the Girl You Can't Forget; You Forgot Your Gloves; You Taught Me How To Love You, Now Teach Me To Forget

Forget-Me-Not　Down Forget-Me-Not Lane; Forget-Me-Not; Forget Me Not; Roses Are Forget-Me-Nots

Forgive　Forgive Me; Forgive Me Girl; Forgive My Heart; I

Forgive You; Mercy Mercy Mercy; Tell Me I'm Forgiven; The Unforgiven (The Need for Love)

Fortress　Fortress Around Your Heart; A Mighty Fortress Is Our God, or, Ein' Feste Burg

Fortune　The Fortune Teller; The Wheel of Fortune

Forty　Forty-Five Minutes from Broadway; Forty-Second Street; Forty-Seven Ginger Headed Sailors; Forty Years On; Nobody Loves a Fairy When She's Forty; The Summer Knows, or, Theme from Summer of '42

Foundation　The Church's One Foundation

Fountain　By the Fountains of Rome; Fountain Fay; Three Coins in the Fountain; While Strolling Through the Park One Day, or, The Fountain in the Park

Four　Five-Four-Three-Two-One; Four American Indian Songs; Four Dances from Aladdin; Four Indian Love Lyrics; Four or Five Times; The Four Walls; The Four Winds and the Seven Seas; Fourteen Carat Mind; I Want To Marry a Male Quartet; I'm Looking Over a Four Leaf Clover; Kiss a Four Leaf Clover; The Lobster Quadrille; Positively Fourth Street; Room Five Hundred and Four; When I'm Sixty-Four

Fox　Fox; Fox on the Run

Frame, *see* **Picture**

France　Don't Cry, Frenchy, Don't Cry; Fifty Million Frenchmen Can't Be Wrong; French Foreign Legion; The French Lesson; (Theme from) The French Lieutenant's Woman; Good-Bye Broadway, Hello France; I Like Your Old French Bonnet; La Marseillaise; Memories of France; Oh! Frenchy; Somewhere in France with You; Somewhere in France with You; When Alexander Takes His Ragtime Band to France; When Yankee Doodle Learns to Parlez Vous Francais; Wine of France

Frances　When Frances Dances with Me

Frank　Frank Mills; Frankenstein; Frankie; Frankie and Johnnie (Johnny) (Were Lovers); Franklin D. Roosevelt Jones

Fred　Freddy My Love; Right Said Fred

Free　The Best Things in Life Are Free; Born Free; Fancy Free; Free Again; The Free and Easy Hour of Parting; Free as Air; If You Love Somebody Set Them Free; I'll Never Be Free; Love Must Be Free; No Strings (I'm Fancy Free); People Got To Be Free; Set Me Free; Viva l'America—Home of the Free; You Are Free

Freedom　The Battle Cry of Freedom; Freedom Come, Freedom Go; The Liberty Song, or, Come, Join Hand in Hand, or, In Freedom We're Born; A Little Bit Independent; Philadelphia Freedom; Release Me; Sing a Song of Freedom; Spirit of Independence; Sweet Freedom

Friday　Where Did Robinson Crusoe Go with Friday on Saturday Night?

Frieda　Timid Frieda

Friend, *see also* **Neighbor, Partner**　All My Rowdy Friends Have Settled Down; All Pals Together; Be My Life's Companion; A Beautiful Friendship; Bon Bon Buddy; Bosom Buddies; A Boy's Best Friend Is His Mother; Budweiser's a Friend of Mine; Can't We Be Friends; Can't You Do a Friend a Favor; Comrades; Dear Friend; Dear Old Pal of Mine; Diamonds Are a Girl's Best Friend; Friend o' Mine; (Just Say

I'm a) Friend of Yours; Friendly Persuasion; Friends; Friends and Lovers (Born to Each Other); Friends and Neighbours; Friendship; Friendship Is for Keeps; The Gang That Sang Heart of My Heart; Gee, But It's Great To Meet a Friend from Your Old Home Town; Gee, But It's Great To Meet a Friend from Your Old Home Town; The Girl Friend; (She's) The Girl Friend of the Whirling Dervish; The Good Companions; Hail, Hail, the Gang's All Here; Happy Christmas, Little Friend; Hello, Hello, Who's Your Lady Friend; He's Me Pal; I Lost the Best Pal That I Had; If We Can't Be the Same Old Sweethearts, We'll Just Be the Same Old Friends; Just Friends; Let's Be Buddies; (With) A Little Help from My Friends; (Just a) Little Street Where Old Friends Meet; Mate O' Mine; My Boyfriend's Back; My British Buddy; My Buddies; My Buddy; My Friend the Major; My Friend the Sea; My Own Best Friend; My Very Good Friend the Milkman; Oh! What a Pal Was Mary; Old Friends; Old Friends and Old Times; Old Pal Why Don't You Answer Me; A Pal Like You; Pal of My Cradle Days; The Pal That I Loved Stole the Gal That I Loved; Playmates; Playmates; Power to All Our Friends; Put It There Pal; Shipmates of Mine; That's What Friends Are For; Too Many Parties and Too Many Pals; We've Been Chums for Fifty Years; What a Friend We Have in Jesus; Whenever I Call You ''Friend''; Where Are the Friends of Other Days; Why Can't We Be Friends; You're a Friend of Mine; You're My Best Friend; You've Got a Friend

Fringe   The Surrey with the Fringe on Top

Fritz   Emmet's Lullaby, or, Fritz, Our Cousin German, or, Brother's Lullaby

Frivolous   My Gal Sal, or, They Call Her Frivolous Sal

Frog   Frog Went a-Courtin', or, Frog He Would a-Wooing Go, or, Mister Frog Went a-Courtin'

Front   All I Want for Christmas (Is My Two Front Teeth)

Frost   Frosty the Snow Man; Little Jack Frost Get Lost

Fruit, *see also* **Apple, Peach,** etc.   Strange Fruit

Full   Full Moon; Full Moon and Empty Arms; The Full Moon Union; Fully Persuaded; Heart Full of Soul; Room Full (Roomful) of Roses

Fun   Ain't We Got Fun; All in Fun; Are You Havin' Any Fun; Fun To Be Fooled; Girls Just Want To Have Fun; Hot Fun in the Summertime; If I'm Going To Die I'm Going To Have Some Fun; Isn't It Kinda Fun; It's Foolish But It's Fun; You Make Lovin' Fun

Funeral, *see* **Death**

Funky   Funkytown; Play That Funky Music

Funny, *see also* **Comedy, Humor**   Ain't It Funny What a Difference Just a Few Hours Make; Ain't That Funny; Funny Bunny Hug; Funny Face; Funny, Familiar, Forgotten Feelings; Funny Girl; Funny How Love Can Be; The Funny Old Hills; Funny Thing; Funny Way of Laughing; Life's a Funny Proposition After All; My Funny Valentine; (I Got a Woman Crazy for Me) She's Funny That Way

Future   The Fortune Teller; The Future Mrs. 'Awkins; Futuristic Rhythm; My Future Just Passed; Whatever Will Be, Will Be, or, Que Sera, Sera; The Wheel of Fortune; When Will I Be Loved; When Will I See You Again; Where Am I Going; You're My Past, Present and Future

Gabriel   Angel Gabriel; Blow, Gabriel, Blow

Gabrielle   Gabrielle; The Gaby Glide

Gal   Blue Ribbon Gal; Buffalo Gals (Won't You Come Out Tonight?), or, Lubly Fan; For Me and My Gal; A Gal in Calico; I'm the Lonesomest Gal in Town; It Takes a Long, Tall, Brown-Skin Gal; I've Got a Gal in Kalamazoo; My Gal Is a High-Born Lady; My Gal Sal, or, They Call Her Frivolous Sal; The Pal That I Loved Stole the Gal That I Loved; Sleepy Time Gal; Somebody Stole My Gal; Sweet Emalina, My Gal; You're Gonna Lose Your Gal

Gallop, *see* **Dance, Horse**

Gambling   Ace in the Hole; (Theme from) Casino Royale; Domino; Domino; The Gambler; Gambler's Guitar; The Man That (Who) Broke the Bank at Monte Carlo; Moonlight Gambler; The Oldest Established (Permanent Floating Crap Game in New York); Politics and Poker; Roulette; Seven or Eleven—My Dixie Pair o' Dice; Solitaire; You Wanna Bet

Game   The Army Game; The Crying Game; Games People Play; Games People Play; (Theme from) Harry's Game; It's All in the Game; The Name Game; The Oldest Established (Permanent Floating Crap Game in New York); The Power Game; Simple Game; Take Me Out to the Ball Game; They Just Can't Stop It (The Games People Play); When You Play in the Game of Love

Gang   Chain Cang; The Gang That Sang Heart of My Heart; Hail, Hail, the Gang's All Here; The Leader of the Pack; That Old Gang of Mine; Wedding Bells Are Breaking Up That Old Gang of Mine

Ganges   Moonlight on the Ganges

Garden   Better Homes and Gardens; Come into the Garden, Maud; Country Gardens; English Country Gardens; A Garden in the Rain; The Garden of Eden; The Garden of Love; Garden of My Dreams; (Beautiful) Garden of Roses; The Garden of Your Heart; Hangin' On the Garden Gate; I Found a Rose in the Devil's Garden; I Know a Lovely Garden; I Leave My Heart in an English Garden; I Never Promised You a Rose Garden; In a Chinese Temple Garden; In a Monastery Garden; In a Persian Garden; In an Old Dutch Garden; (He Walks with Me) In the Garden; In the Garden of My Heart; In the Garden of Tomorrow; In the Luxembourg Gardens; It Is Only a Tiny Garden; A Lemon in the Garden of Love; Love's Garden of Roses; Mucking About the Garden; Old-Fashioned Garden; Over the Garden Wall; A Rose in a Garden of Weeds; Royal Garden Blues; The Sweetest Flower the Garden Grew; Take Me Back to the Garden of Love; Thank God for a Garden; There Are Fairies at the Bottom of Our Garden; There's a Garden in Old Italy; You Planted a Rose in the Garden of Love

Gardenia   Blue Gardenia; Blue Shadows and White Gardenias; A Little White Gardenia

Garland, *see* **Flower**

Gary   Gary, Indiana

Gasoline   Classical Gas; Gasoline Alley Bred

Gaston   Pardon Me, My Dear Alphonse, After You, My Dear Gaston

Gate, *see also* **Fence**   Golden Gate; Hangin' On the Garden

Gate; Open the Gates of the Temple; Sitting on a Fire Barred Gate

Gather   Gather the Rose; We Gather Together (To Ask the Lord's Blessing), or, Prayer of Thanksgiving; We'll Gather Lilacs

Gaucho, *see* **Cowboy**

Gay   A Bachelor Gay; A Gay Caballero; A Gay Ranchero; Glitter and Be Gay; Keep It Gay; Mister Johnson, Don't Get Gay

Gaze, *see* **Look**

Gazette, *see* **Magazine**

Gem, *see* **Jewel**

General   The General's Fast Asleep; Just Like Washington Crossed the Delaware, General Pershing Will Cross the Rhine; What's Good for General Bullmoose

Generation, *see* **People**

Genevieve   Sweet Genevieve

Genie, *see* **Magic**

Gentle, Gently   Break It to Me Gently; Break It to Me Gently; Dear Hearts and Gentle People; Flow Gently, Sweet Afton, or, Afton Water; Gentle Annie; Gentle on My Mind; Lo! Here the Gentle Lark; Love's Ritornella, or, Gentle Zitella; Rise, Gentle Moon; Rock Me Gently; See, Gentle Patience Smiles on Pain; Sweet and Gentle; While My Guitar Gently Weeps

Gentleman   The Gentleman Is a Dope; Gentlemen Prefer Blondes; Gentlemen, the King; God Rest You Merry Gentlemen; Most Gentlemen Don't Like Love; A Sentimental Gentleman from Georgia; That Dear Old Gentleman; That Shy Old Gentleman from Featherbed Lane; The Three Caballeros; When a Lady Meets a Gentleman Down South

George   Georgie Porgie; St. (Saint) George and the Dragonet

Georgette   Georgette; Georgy Girl

Georgia   At a Georgia Camp Meeting; Atlanta, Ga.; Everything Is Peaches Down in Georgia; Georgia; Georgia Grind; Georgia on My Mind; Georgian Rumba; Georgia's Gotta Moon; Marching Through Georgia; Midnight Train to Georgia; My Little Georgia Rose; The Night the Lights Went Out in Georgia; Rambling Wreck from Georgia Tech; A Sentimental Gentleman from Georgia; Sweet Georgia Brown; Trabling Back to Georgia; Two Tickets to Georgia; When the Birds in Georgia Sing of Tennessee

Germany   Emmet's Lullaby, or, Fritz, Our Cousin German, or, Brother's Lullaby; The Germans at the Spa; If He Can Fight Like He Can Love, Good Night Germany; Keep Your Head Down, ''Fritzie Boy''; The Leader of the German Band

Geronimo, *see* **Indian**

Gertie   Gertie from Bizerte; Gertie the Girl with the Gong

Ghetto, *see* **City**

Ghost   The Ghost of the Violin; Ghost Riders in the Sky, or, A Cowboy Legend; Ghostbusters; I Don't Stand a Ghost of a Chance with You; Mary's Dream, or, Sandy's Ghost; Spooky Ookum

Giant   The Jolly Green Giant

Gift   All Good Gifts; The Blue and the Gray, or, A Mother's Gift to Her Country; Love Sends a Little Gift of Roses

Gigi   Gigi

Gigolo   I'm a Gigolo; Just a Gigolo

Gilbert   Gilbert the Filbert

Ginger   Forty-Seven Ginger Headed Sailors; Ginger You're Barmy

Girl   All American Girl; All I Need Is the Girl; Any Little Girl, That's a Nice Little Girl, Is the Right Little Girl for Me; Are You There (with Another Girl); As the Girls Go; Bad Girls; (Hats Off, Here They Come, Those) Beautiful Girls; Big Girls Don't Cry; Bobby's Girl; A Boy and a Girl Were Dancing; Brandy (You're a Fine Girl); Brown Eyed Girl; Buy a Broom, or, The Bavarian Girl's Song; Calendar Girl; California Girls; Cape Cod Girls; Daddy's Little Girl; Daddy's Little Girl; Dear Little Girl; Dear Old Girl; Diamond Girl; Diamonds Are a Girl's Best Friend; Dream Girls; Every Girl Loves Me But the Girl I Love; Face to Face with the Girl of My Dreams; A Fellow Needs a Girl; Five Foot Two, Eyes of Blue (Has Anybody Seen My Girl?); Forgive Me Girl; Funny Girl; Georgy Girl; Gertie the Girl with the Gong; Girl; A Girl! A Girl!, or, Zoom Ba Di Alli Nella; The Girl at the Ironing Board; Girl Don't Come; The Girl Friend; The Girl Friend of the Whirling Dervish; The Girl from Ipanema; The Girl I Left Behind Me, or, Brighton Camp; The Girl I Loved in Sunny Tennessee; The Girl in the Alice Blue Gown; The Girl in the Crinoline Gown; The Girl Is Mine; The Girl Is You and the Boy Is Me; A Girl Like You; Girl of My Dreams; A Girl of the Pi Beta Phi; The Girl on the Magazine Cover; The Girl on the Police Gazette; Girl Talk; The Girl That I Marry; The Girl with a Brogue; The Girl with the Dreamy Eyes; The Girl with the Flaxen Hair; The Girl with the Golden Braids; A Girlie Was Made To Love; Girls, Girls, Girls; Girls Just Want To Have Fun; Girls Were Made To Take Care of Boys; Give Me the Moonlight, Give Me the Girl; Go Away Little Girl; Gold Will Buy Most Anything But a True Girl's Heart; Gonna Get a Girl; Goodbye, Girls, I'm Through; Goodbye, Little Girl, Goodbye; Goodbye, Little Girl of My Dreams; Goodnight, Little Girl, Goodnight; Heart of a Teenage Girl; Heaven Will Protect the Working Girl; Hello Little Girl; I Enjoy Being a Girl; I Long To See the Girl I Left Behind; I Want a Girl—Just Like the Girl That Married Dear Old Dad; I Was a Good Little Girl Till I Met You; I Wish I Had a Girl; I Wish I Had My Old Girl Back Again; I'd Love To Live in Loveland (with a Girl Like You); If a Girl Like You Loved a Boy Like Me; If I Had a Girl Like You; If You Were the Only Girl in the World; I'm a Big Girl Now; I'm Gonna Pin My Medal on the Girl I Left Behind; I'm Looking for a Nice Young Fellow Who Is Looking for a Nice Young Girl; Island Girl; I've Got the Time—I've Got the Place, But It's Hard To Find the Girl; Jessie's Girl; Jolly Good Luck to the Girl Who Loves a Soldier; Just a Girl That Men Forget; Just One Girl; Kitty the Telephone Girl; The Land of My Best Girl; Little Girl; Little Girl; Little Girl Blue; A Little Girl from Little Rock; Little Girls; Little Girls, Good Bye; A Man Chases a Girl; Material Girl; Me and My Girl; The Men in My Little Girl's Life; Modern Girl; The Most Beautiful Girl in the World; (If You Happen To See) The Most Beautiful Girl (in the World); Music To Watch Girls By; My Best

Girl; My Best Girl; My Best Girl's a New Yorker (Corker); My Dream Girl, I Loved You Long Ago; My Girl Has Gone; My Girl's a Yorkshire Girl; My Kind of Girl; My Little Deitcher Girl; My Little Girl; My Pearl's a Bowery Girl; My Wonderful Dream Girl; Mystery Girl; Nobody's Little Girl; Oh! Boy, What a Girl; Oh By Jingo, Oh By Gee, You're the Only Girl for Me; Oh Girl; Only One Girl in the World for Me; The Photo of the Girl I Left Behind; Poor Little Rich Girl; A Pretty Girl; A Pretty Girl Is Like a Melody; Put Me Amongst the Girls; Put On Your Ta Ta Little Girlie; A Quiet Girl; A Quiet Girl; Real Live Girl; Rich Girl; Ring-a-Ding Girl; Rose of Lucerne, or, The Swiss Toy Girl; Same Sort of Girl; The Same Sweet Girl Today; Ship Ahoy, or, All the Nice Girls Love a Sailor; Sunshine Girl; A Sweet Old-Fashioned Girl; Take Your Girl; Take Your Girlie to the Movies If You Can't Make Love at Home; Ten Pretty Girls; Thank Heaven for Little Girls; Thank You Girl; That Girl; That Old Girl of Mine; There Never Was a Girl Like You; There's a Dixie Girl Who's Longing For a Yankee Doodle Boy; There's a Girl in the Heart of Maryland (with a Heart That Belongs to Me); There's a Girl in This World for Every Boy and a Boy for Every Girl; There's a Little Bit of Bad in Every Good Little Girl; There's a Million Girlies Lonesome Tonight, and Still I'm All Alone; To All the Girls I've Loved Before; Twelve Thirty, or, Young Girls Are Coming to the Canyon; Two Little Girls in Blue; Uptown Girl; Use Ta Be My Girl; Waiting for a Girl Like You; Waiting For the Girls Upstairs; Watchin' Girls Go By; West End Girls; When a Fellow's on the Level with a Girl That's on the Square; When I'm Not Near the Girl I Love; When You First Kissed the Last Girl You Loved; When You Know You're Not Forgotten by the Girl You Can't Forget; Where Did You Get That Girl?; Where's the Boy? Here's the Girl!; (She's the Girlfriend of) The Whirling Dervish; Why Did I Kiss That Girl; Won't You Be My Little Girl; You Gotta Be a Football Hero (To Get Along with the Beautiful Girls); You Remind Me of the Girl That Used To Go to School with Me; You'll Always Be the Same Sweet Girl; Young Girl; You're My Girl

Glad Aren't You Glad You're You; Aren't You Kind of Glad We Did; Glad All Over; Glad Rag Doll; Glad To Be Unhappy; How Glad I Am; I'm Awfully Glad I Met You; I'm Glad I Waited for You; I'm Glad I'm Not Young Anymore; I'm Glad There Is You; Nights of Gladness; (I'll Be Glad When You're Dead) You Rascal You

Gladiator The Gladiator('s) March; The Gladiator's Entry

Glamorous The Glamorous Life; Glamorous Night; Grizabella the Glamour Cat

Glance, *see* **Look**

Glasgow Coming Up (Live at Glasgow); I Belong to Glasgow

Glass, *see also* **Crystal** ''Algy,'' the Piccadilly Johnny with the Little Glass Eye; Heart of Glass; How Stands the Glass Around, or, Wolfe's Song, or, Why, Soldiers, Why, or, The Duke of Berwick's March; Introduction and Air to a Stained Glass Window; The Legend of the Glass Mountain; Life In a Looking Glass

Glasses Judy in Disguise (with Glasses); Long Tall Glasses (I Can Dance); Looking At the World Through Rose Colored Glasses

Glen Down in the Glen

Glendora Glendora

Glide The Cubanola Glide; The Gaby Glide; The Wedding Glide

Glitter All That Glitters Is Not Gold; Glitter and Be Gay

Gloaming In the Gloaming; Roamin' in the Gloamin'; When I Dream in the Gloaming of You

Globe, *see* **World**

Glocca Morra How Are Things in Glocca Morra

Gloom Gloomy Sunday

Gloria Gloria; Gloria, or, Theme from Butterfield 8; Gloria

Glory Angels from the Realms of Glory; Beer, Beer, Glorious Beer; Blaze of Glory; Blaze of Glory; Food Glorious Food; Glory Days; The Glory of Love; Glory of Love (Theme from *The Karate Kid Part II*); De Glory Road; The Hippopotamus Song, or, Mud, Glorious Mud; The Land of Hope and Glory; O That Will Be Glory for Me, or, The Glory Song; Where the Morning Glories Grow; Where the Morning Glories Twine Around the Door

Glove, *see* **Hand**

Glow (The) Glow Worm; Moonglow

Goat The Lonely Goatherd; Paddy McGinty's Goat

God Allah's Holiday; Buddha; God Be with You Till We Meet Again; God Bless America; God Bless Our Native Land; God Bless the Child; God Bless the USA; God Only Knows; God Rest You Merry Gentlemen; God Save the King (Queen); God, That's Good; The God-Why-Don't-You-Love-Me Blues; (This Is) God's Country; God's Green World; Good Luck, Good Health, God Bless You; Good-bye, Good Luck, God Bless You; Goodnight and God Bless You; Holy! Holy! Lord God Almighty; I Got (a Robe) Shoes, or, All God's Chillun Got Shoes; I'll Walk with God; A Mighty Fortress Is Our God, or, Ein' Feste Burg; Nearer, My God, to Thee; O Dio Mio; O God, Our Help in Ages Past; O Word of God Incarnate; Old Hundred(th) Doxology, or, Praise God, from Whom All Blessings Flow; The Son of God Goes Forth to War; Swearin' to God; Thank God for a Garden; Thank God I'm a Country Boy; Vaya Con Dios; When Buddha Smiles; Would God I Were a Tender Apple Blossom; Your God Comes First, Your Country Next, Then Mother Dear; You're the Reason God Made Oklahoma

Godfather, *see* **Father**

Gold Age of Gold Ballet; All That Glitters Is Not Gold; All the Gold in California; And Her Golden Hair Was Hanging Down Her Back; Band of Gold; A Bird in a Gilded Cage; Bring Back My Golden Dreams; Climbing Up the Golden Stairs; Down the River of Golden Dreams; The Girl with the Golden Braids; The Gold and Silver (Waltz); Gold Will Buy Most Anything But a True Girl's Heart; Golden Brown; Golden Days; Golden Earrings; Golden Gate; (Oh Dem) Golden Slippers; The Golden Song; The Golden Tango; Golden Tears; De Golden Wedding; The Golden West; (Theme from) Goldfinger; Hair of Gold, Eyes of Blue; Heart of Gold; If You Had All the World and Its Gold; In a Golden Coach; In the Gold Fields of Nevada; Jerusalem the Golden; The Land of Golden Dreams; Love from a Heart of Gold; The Man with the Golden Arm; Mem'ries, or, Golden Memory Days; Mister Goldstone; My Isle of Golden Dreams; On Miami Shore, or, Golden Sands of Miami; Power of Gold; Put Away a Little Ray of Golden Sunshine; She Got the Goldmine I Got the Shaft; Silver Hair and Heart of Gold; Silver Threads Among the Gold; Sister Golden Hair; Solid Gold Easy Action; Take Back Your Gold; There's a Gold Mine in the Sky; Way Out Yonder in the Golden West; We're in the Money, or, The Gold Diggers' Song; When the Blue Sky Turns to Gold; Where the Blue of the Night Meets the Gold of the Day; Where the Sunset Turns the Ocean's Blue to Gold

Goldfish, *see* **Fish**

Gone, *see also* **Leave**   After the Love Has Gone; After You've Gone; Cradle's Empty, Baby's Gone; Everyone's Gone to the Moon; Gone; Gone At Last; Gone Fishin'; Gone with the Wind; He's a Real Gone Guy; I Can See Clearly Now (the Rain Has Gone); I May Be Gone for a Long, Long Time; I Wonder Where My Lovin' Man Has Gone; Love Is Here and Now You're Gone; (To the War Has Gone) The Minstrel Boy; My Girl Has Gone; My Man's Gone Now; My Wife's Gone to the Country (Hurrah! Hurrah!); Now Those Days Are Gone; Oh Where, Oh Where, Has My Little Dog Gone, or, Der Deitcher's Dog; Please Don't Talk About Me When I'm Gone; She's Gone; So Long, Oo-Long, How Long You Gonna Be Gone); Thou Art Gone from My Gaze; The Thrill Is Gone; When I'm Dead and Gone; When I'm Gone I Won't Forget; When Your Lover Has Gone; Where Have All the Flowers Gone; Where Love Has Gone

Gong   Gertie the Girl with the Gong; Kickin' the Gong Around

Good   All Good Gifts; Are the Good Times Really Over; Better Be Good to Me; (Theme from) Dukes of Hazzard (Good Ol' Boys); Feels So Good; For He's a Jolly Good Fellow, or, Malbrouk (Malbrough), or, We Won't Go Home Until Morning, or, The Bear Went over the Mountain; For the Good Times; God, That's Good; The Good Companions; Good Day Sunshine; Good Evening, Caroline; Good Golly Miss Molly; A Good Hearted Woman; Good King Wenceslas; The Good Life; Good Lovin'; Good Luck Charm; Good Luck, Good Health, God Bless You; A Good Man Is Hard To Find; Good Morning; Good Morning, Good Morning; Good Morning Heartache; Good Morning, Mister Zip-Zip-Zip; Good Morning Starshine; Good News; Good News; Good Night; Good Night Angel; Good Night Dear; Good Night Ladies, or, Merrily We Roll Along; Good Night, Nurse (Kiss Your Little Patient); Good Night, Sweetheart; The Good Old Bad Days; The Good Old U.S.A.; Good Ole Boys Like Me; Good Sweet Ham; The Good, the Bad and the Ugly; Good Thing Going; Good Times; Good Timin'; Good Timin'; Good Vibrations; The Good Word (Theme from Nationwide); Goodnight (I'm Only a Strolling Vagabond); Goodnight and God Bless You; Goodnight Children, Everywhere; Goodnight Irene; Goodnight, Little Girl, Goodnight; Goodnight My Love; Goodnight My Someone; Goodnight to You All; Goodnight Tonight; Goodnight Vienna; Goodnight Wherever You Are; Goodtime Charley; Goody Goody; Grandpa (Tell Me 'Bout the Good Old Days); Happy Birthday to You, or, Good Morning to All; Hey Good Lookin'; Hey There, Good Times; Hurt So Good; I Could Be So Good for You; I Got It Bad and That Ain't Good; I Got You (I Feel Good); I Love the Way You Say "Goodnight"; I Still Love To Kiss You Goodnight; I Was a Good Little Girl Till I Met You; I Was a Very Good Baby; I Wish I (We) Didn't Have To Say Good Night;

If He Can Fight Like He Can Love, Good Night Germany; I'll Be Good Because of You; I'll Be Good to You; Ill Wind (You're Blowin' Me No Good); In Good Old New York Town; In the Good Old Summer Time; It Was a Very Good Year; It's a Good Day; It's a Pity To Say Goodnight; It's Always Fair Weather When Good Fellows Get Together, or, A Stein Song; It's Good News Week; It's Good To Be Alive; It's Time To Say Goodnight; Jolly Good Company; Jolly Good Luck to the Girl Who Loves a Sailor; Kiss an Angel Good Mornin'; Let the Good Times Roll; A Little Good News; Love's Been Good to Me; May the Good Lord Bless and Keep You; My Old Kentucky Home (Good Night); My Very Good Friend the Milkman; Oh Lady Be Good; On the Good Ship Lollipop; On the Good Ship Mary Ann; A Rockin' Good Way (To Mess Around and Fall in Love); So Long (It's Been Good To Know Yuh); Sweet Caroline (Sweet Times Never Seemed So Good; Take Good Care of My Baby; Tell Me Something Good; That's Good Enough for Me; There's a Good Time Coming; There's a Little Bit of Bad in Every Good Little Girl; Too Good for the Average Man; What Good Does It Do; What's Good About Good Night; What's Good About Goodbye; What's Good for General Bullmoose; What's the Good of Being Good—When No One's Good to Me; Where the Twilight Comes To Kiss the Rose Goodnight; A Woman Is Only a Woman, But a Good Cigar Is a Smoke; You Can't Keep a Good Man Down; You Give Good Love; You're a Good Man, Charlie Brown; You're No Good

Goodbye   Addio Addio, or, Goodbye; Addio, Mia Bella Napoli; Adios; Adios, Mariquita Linda; Adios Muchachos; Adios My Love, or, The Song of Athens; After Tonight We Say "Goodbye"; Aloha Oe, or, Farewell to Thee; Always Leave Them Laughing When You Say Goodbye; (Bye Bye) American Pie; Arrivederci Roma; Au Revoir But Not Goodbye; Au Revoir, But Not Good-Bye, Soldier Boy; Au Revoir, Pleasant Dreams; Auf Wiedersehn; Auf Wiedersehn, My Dear; Auf Wiederseh'n Sweetheart; Bye Bye Baby; Bye Bye Baby; Bye Bye Blackbird; Bye Bye Blues; Bye Bye Love; Ciao Ciao Bambina; Did Tosti Raise His Bowler Hat When He Said Goodbye; Ev'ry Time We Say Goodbye; Fare Thee Well, Annabelle; The Farewell; Farewell Blues; Farewell to Arms; Farewell to Storyville; From the Time We Say Goodbye; Good Bye-ee; Goodbye; Goodbye; Goodbye, Au Revoir, Auf Wiedersehn; Goodbye, Boys; Good-Bye Broadway, Hello France; Goodbye Cruel World; Goodbye Dolly Gray; Goodbye, Eliza Jane; Good-bye, Flo; Goodbye, Girls, I'm Through; Good-bye, Good Luck, God Bless You; Goodbye Hawaii; Goodbye Jimmy Goodbye; Goodbye, Little Girl, Goodbye; Goodbye, Little Girl of My Dreams; Goodbye, Liza Jane; Good-Bye, Ma! Good-Bye, Pa! Good-Bye, Mule, or, Long Boy; Goodbye Marie; Goodbye, My Lady Love; Good-Bye, My Lover Good-Bye; G'Bye Now; Goodbye Ol' Paint, or, I Ride an Old Paint, or, I'm a-Leavin' Cheyenne; Goodbye, Rose; Goodbye Sally; Goodbye Stranger; Goodbye Sue; Goodbye to All That; Goodbye to All That; Goodbye Virginia; Goodbye Yellow Brick Road; Hello Goodbye; Hello, My Lover, Goodbye; In the Sweet Bye and Bye; I've Just Come Back To Say Goodbye; Jamaica Farewell; Kiss and Say Goodbye; Kiss the Boys Goodbye; Last Farewell; Little Girls, Good Bye; My Heart Has Learned To Love You, Now Do Not Say Goodbye; My Last Goodbye; My Little Nest of

Heavenly Blue, or, Frasquita Serenade (Blaues Himmelbett), or, Farewell, My Love, Farewell; Na Na Hey Hey Kiss Him Goodbye; Neither One of Us (Wants To Be the First To Say Goodbye); Never Can Say Goodbye; Never Goodbye; Never Say Goodbye; Say "Au Revoir" But Not "Goodbye"; Sayonara; Smile When You Say "Goodbye"; So Long, Farewell; So Long (It's Been Good To Know Yuh); So Long Letty; So Long Mary; So Long, Oo-Long, How Long You Gonna Be Gone?; The Sound of Goodbye; Thank You So Much Mrs. Lowsborough—Goodbye; Too Late for Goodbyes; Toot Toot Tootsie (Goo'Bye); We Just Couldn't Say Goodbye; We'll Never Have To Say Goodbye Again; What's Good About Goodbye; Wish Me Luck As You Wave Me Goodbye; You Better Keep Babying Baby (or Baby's Gonna Bye-Bye You)

Goodness   Goodness Gracio s Me; Goodness Knows How I Love You; Real Goodness from Kentucky Fried Chicken

Goodnight, *see* **Night**

Goofy   Goofus

Goose   The Cry of the Wild Goose; Ever So Goosey; Mother Goose's Melodies; (Go Tell Aunt Rhody) The Ole Grey Goose (Is Dead); The Snow Goose

Gordon   A Gordon for Me

Gospel   De Gospel Train

Gossip, *see* **Talk**

Gown, *see also* **Dress**   (In My Sweet Little) Alice Blue Gown; The Girl in the Alice Blue Gown; The Girl in the Crinoline Gown

Grace   Amazing Grace; Goodness Gracious Me; Graceland; Saved by Grace

Graduation, *see* **School**

Granada   Granada

Grand   Bei Mir Bist Du Schön (Means That You're Grand); Grand Old Ivy; Grande Valse Brilliante; I'm an Old Cowhand (from the Rio Grande); Isn't Love the Grandest Thing; It's a Grand Night for Singing; Mary's a Grand Old Name; El Rancho Grande; Rose of the Rio Grande

Grandfather   Grandad; Grandfather's Clock; Grandpa (Tell Me 'Bout the Good Old Days); Grandpa's Spells

Grandmother   Granny's Old Arm-Chair; My Grandma's Advice; There's No One Quite Like Grandma

Granite, *see* **Stone**

Grant   Mirami Asi, or, Grant Those Glances, or, Look At Me; President Grant's March

Grape   From the Vine Came the Grape (from the Grape Came the Wine); I Heard It Through the Grapevine

Grass   And the Grass Won't Pay No Mind; And the Green Grass Grew All Around; The Grass Is Always Greener; Grazin' in the Grass; The Green Green Grass of Home; My Little Grass Shack in Kealakekua, Hawaii; The Other Man's Grass (Is Always Greener)

Grasshopper   The Grasshopper's Dance

Grateful, *see* **Thank You**

Grave, *see* **Death**

Gravy   The Navy Gets the Gravy and the Army Gets the Beans

Gray   auld Robin Gray, or, When the Sheep Are in the Fold; The Blue and the Gray, or, A Mother's Gift to Her Country; Blue Turning Grey Over You; Darling Nelly Gray; Goodbye, Dolly Gray; Little Grey Home in the West; The Little Grey House; The Old Grey Mare (She Ain't What She Used To Be); (Go Tell Aunt Rhody) The Ole Grey Goose (Is Dead); Put On Your Old Grey Bonnet

Grease   Grease

Great   And the Great Big Saw Came Nearer; Angel of the Great White Way; Gee, But It's Great to Meet a Friend from Your Old Home Town; Great Balls of Fire; Great Day; the Great Imposter; The Great Indoors; The Great Pretender; (Theme from) Greatest American Hero (Believe It or Not); Greatest Love of All; The Greatest Mistake of My Life; I'll Be Ready When the Great Day Comes; I'm the Greatest Star; In the Great Somewhere; It's a Great Big Shame; It's a Great Day for the Irish; It's a Great Day for the Irish; It's Great To Be a Soldier Man; It's Great To Be in Love; Let the Great Big World Keep Turning; No Greater Love; Pan Am Makes the Goin' Great; That Great Come and Get It Day; There Is No Greater Love; there's a Great Day Coming, Mañana; West of the Great Divide; You're a Great Big Blue Eyed Baby

Greece   The Argentines, the Portuguese and the Greeks; (Theme from) Zorba the Greek

Green   And the Green Grass Grew All Around; As Long as the Shamrock Grows Green; The Ballad of Bethnal Green; The Ballad of the Green Berets; Berwick Green (The Archers); Carry Me Back to Green Pastures; Eli Green's Cakewalk; Evergreen, or, Love Theme from A Star Is Born; God's Green World; The Grass Is Always Greener; The Green Cockatoo; The Green Door; Green Eyes; the Green Green Grass of Home; Green Grow the Lilacs; The Green Leaves of Summer; The Green Mountain Farmer; Green Onions; Green-Up Time; Green Years; Greenfields; Greensleeves (Green Sleeves); If the Moon Turns Green; I've Been Floating Down the Old Green River; The Jolly Green Giant; Little Green Apples; 'Mid the Green Fields of Virginia; Mountain Greenery; On Green Dolphin Street; The Other Man's Grass (Is Always Greener); Polly Perkins of Paddington Green; Red Silk Stockings and Green Perfume; Scottish Soldier Green Hill; Somewhere That's Green; There Is a Green Hill Far Away; The Wearin' o' the Green; When the Wind Was Green; Wintergreen for President

Greenland   From Greenland's Icy Mountians

Greenwich Village   My Greenwich Village Sue

Grenadier   British Grenadiers; The Two Grenadiers

Greyhound, *see* **Dog**

Grieve, *see* **Cry**

Grind   The Organ Grinder; The Organ Grinder's Swing

Grocer   Grocer Jack

Groom, *see* **Marriage**

Groovy   The 59th Street Bridge Song, or, Feelin' Groovy; Groovin'; A Groovy Kind of Love; Let's Groove

Ground   Angel Flying Too Close to the Ground; Higher Ground; Hole in the Ground; Massa's in De Cold (Cold) Ground; My Lodging (It) Is on the Cold Ground; Old Flag Never Touched the Ground; Shake Your Body (Down to the

Ground); Silent Running (On Dangerous Ground); Tenting on the Old Camp Ground, or, Tenting Tonight

Grove, see **Tree**

Grow Absence Makes the Heart Grow Fonder; Absence Makes the Heart Grow Fonder (for Somebody Else); And the Green Grass Grew All Around; As Long as the Shamrock Grows Green; Come Back When You Grow Up; Down Where the Cotton Blossoms Grow; Everything's Coming Up Roses; Green Grow the Lilacs; I Never Knew (That Roses Grew); I Won't Grow Up; In the Wildwood Where the Bluebells Grew; I've Grown Accustomed to Her Face; Love Grows; She's the Fairest Little Flower Dear Old Dixie Ever Grew (Knew); The Sweetest Flower the Garden Grew; Sweetheart, We'll Never Grow Old; Till the Sands of the Desert Grow Cold; When I Grow Too Old To Dream; When Your Love Grows Cold; Where the Lazy Daisies Grow; Where the Morning Glories Grow; Where the Shy Little Violets Grow; Where the Southern Roses Grow; Where the Sweet Magnolias Grow

Guard The Changing of the Guard; The Mulligan Guard; The Skidmore Guard; Thy Sentinel Am I; When the Guards Are on Parade; When the Guardsman Started Crooning on Parade

Guess The Boy Guessed Right; I Guess I'll Get the Papers and Go Home; I Guess I'll Have To Change My Plan; I Guess I'll Have To Dream the Rest; I Guess I'll Have To Telegraph My Baby; I Guess It Never Hurts To Love Sometimes; I Guess That's Why They Call It the Blues

Guide Garfield Now Will Guide the Nation; My Guilding Star

Guilty Guilty; Guilty

Guitar, see also **Banjo, Mandolin** Gambler's Guitar; Guitar Man; My Heart and Lute; Two Guitars; Ukulele Lady; While My Guitar Gently Weeps

Gulf Gulf Coast Blues

Gum Does the Spearmint Lose Its Flavor on the Bedpost Overnight; Double Your Pleasure; The Gum Tree Canoe (on Tom-Big-Bee River)

Gun, see also **Bang, Shot** The Cannon Song; The Guns of Navarone; Johnny Get Your Gun; Momma Look Sharp; Old Sam (Pick Up Tha' Musket); The Origin of Gunpowder, or, When Vulcan Forg'd the Bolts of Jove; Peter Gunn; Pistol Packin' Mama; Praise the Lord and Pass the Ammunition; Rubber Bullets; The Torpedo and the Whale; The U.S. Field Artillery March, or, The Caissons Go Rolling Along; Wabash Cannonball; You Can't Get a Man with a Gun; You're the One (You Beautiful Son-of-a-Gun)

Guy, see also **Fellow** A Guy Is a Guy; Guys and Dolls; He's a Real Gone Guy; He's My Guy; I'd Rather Be a Lobster Than a Wise Guy; I'm Gonna Love That Guy (Like He's Never Been Loved Before); I'm in Love with a Wonderful Guy; I'm Looking For a Guy Who Plays Alto and Baritone and Doubles on Clarinet and Wears a Size Thirty-Seven Suit; My Guy; My Guy's Come Back; Some Guys Have All the Luck; Sweet Talkin' Guy; This Guy's in Love With You

Gypsy Gypsy; The Gypsy; Gypsy Dream Rose; The Gypsy in Me; Gypsy in My Soul; Gypsy Love Song, or, Slumber On; Gypsy Maiden; Gypsy Man; Gypsy Melody; Gypsys, Tramps and Thieves; He's a Gypsy from Poughkeepsie; Hey

Gypsy (Play Gypsy) (Komn Tzizany); In a Little Gypsy Tea Room; Just Like a Gypsy; (Say Has Anybody Seen) My Sweet Gypsy Rose; Play Gypsies—Dance Gypsies; Play to Me, Gypsy; Tell Me Little Gypsy; The Waltz of the Gypsies; The Water Gypsies; When a Gypsy Makes His Violin Cry; When the Gypsy Played

Habit Nice People (with Nice Habits); You're Getting To Be a Habit with Me

Hagar Aunt Hagar's Blues

Hail All Hail the Power of Jesus' Name; Hail Columbia, or, New Federal Song; Hail, Hail, the Gang's All Here; Hail Purdue; Hail to the Chief

Hair, see also **Barber, Blonde, Brunette, Redhead** And Her Golden Hair Was Hanging Down Her Back; Aqua Velva Man; Black Is the Color of My True Love's Hair; Does Santa Claus Sleep with His Whiskers; The Girl with the Flaxen Hair; The Girl with the Golden Braids; Hair; Hair of Gold, Eyes of Blue; I'm Gonna Wash That Man Right Outa My Hair; Jeanie with the Light Brown Hair; Kookie, Kookie, Lend Me Your Comb; Long-Haired Lover from Liverpool; Ma Curly-Headed Babby; Mammy's Little Kinky-Headed Boy; My Mother Bids Me Bind My Hair; A Night on Bald Mountain; The Rose in Her Hair; (Are You Going to) San Francisco (Be Sure To Wear Some Flowers in Your Hair); Scarlet Ribbons (for Her Hair); Shall I Have It Bobbed or Shingled; Silver Hair and Heart of Gold; Sister Golden Hair; That Silver-Haired Daddy of Mine; To Look Sharp; When Your Hair Has Turned to Silver, I Will Love You Just the Same; With the Wind and the Rain in Your Hair; Wooly Bully

Haircut, see **Barber**

Haiti I Left My Hat in Haiti; Katie Went to Haiti

Half Half a Sixpence; Half as Much; Half-Breed; Half-Caste Woman; The Half of It Dearie, Blues; Half the Way; Half-Way to Heaven; 7½ Cents

Hall Another Suitcase in Another Hall; Dance Hall Days; Deck the Halls with Boughs of Holly; The Harp That Once Thro' Tara's Halls; I Dreamt I Dwelt in Marble Halls; Let's All Go to the Music Hall; The Marine's Hymn, or, From the Halls

Hallelujah Hallelujah!; Hallelujah Chorus; Hallelujah, I'm a Bum

Ham Good Sweet Ham

Hammer If I Had a Hammer; Sledgehammer

Hammock, see **Bed, Swing**

Hand Careless Hands; Clap Hands, Here Comes Charley; Clap Yo' Hands; Cross Your Fingers; Dirty Hands, Dirty Face; Dizzy Fingers; Don't Bite the Hand That's Feeding You; The Finger of Suspicion Points at You; Fingertips (Part II); (Theme from) Goldfinger; Got Her off My Hands (But Can't Get Her off My Mind); Hand for the Hog; (O) Hand Me Down My Walking Cane; The Hand That Rocks the Cradle; A Handful of Earth from (My Dear) Mother's Grave; A Handful of Songs; Hands Across the Sea (March); Hands Across the Table; Handy Man; He's Got the Whole World in His Hand (Hands); Hold My Hand; Hold My Hand; Hold Your Hand Out Naughty Boy; I Kiss Your Hand; Madame; I Lift Up My Finger and I Say Tweet Tweet; I Want To Hold Your Hand; I'd Like To See the Kaiser with a Lily in His Hand; I'm an Old Cowhand (from the Rio Grande); I'm Gonna Wash My Hands of You; I've Got My Fingers Crossed; I've Got Rings on My Fingers, or, Mumbo Jumbo Jijjiboo J. O'Shea; Lay Your Hands on Me; Let Me Shake the Hand That Shook the Hand of Sullivan; The Liberty Song, or, Come, Join Hand in Hand, or, In Freedom We're Born; One Hand, One Heart; Put It There Pal; Put Your Hand in the Hand; Put Your Hands Together; A Ring on the Finger Is Worth Two on the Phone; Second Hand Rose; Slow Hand; Ten Little Fingers and Ten Little Toes—Down In Tennessee; Thumb Marks; Thumbelina; Time on My Hands; The Touch of Your Hand; Walk Hand in Hand; Wish Me Luck As You Wave Me Goodbye; With a Twist of the Wrist; With These Hands; Wrapped Around Your Finger; You Forgot Your Gloves; You Need Hands

Handicap   The Handicap March

Handle   How To Handle a Woman

Handsome   A Handsome Territorial; Hey Good Lookin'

Handy   Handy Man

Hang   And Her Golden Hair Was Hanging Down Her Back; Any Old Place I Can Hang My Hat Is Home Sweet Home to Me; Any Place I Hang My Hat Is Home; Hang On Sloopy; Hang On the Bell Nellie; Hang Your Heart on a Hickory Limb; Hangin' On the Garden Gate; Hangin' Out the Window; Hanging Tree; Let's Hang On; You Keep Me Hangin' On; You've Got Me Dangling on a String

Hangover, see Alcohol

Hanky Panky   Hanky Panky

Hannah   Hannah!; Hannah, Won't You Open That Door?; Hard Hearted Hannah (the Vamp of Savannah); Oh Miss Hannah

Happen   Ah But It Happens; (You're the) Best Thing That Ever Happened to Me; Don't Tell Her (What's Happened to Me); Everything Happens to Me; The Happening; I Happen To Like New York; It Could Happen to You; It Happened in Adano; It Happened in Monterey; It Happened in Sun Valley; It Only Happens When I Dance with You; (If You Happen To See) The Most Beautiful Girl (in the World); The River Song, or, Something's Always Happening on the River; Something Is Happening; Something's Always Happening on the River; Watch What Happens; You Happen Once in a Lifetime

Happiness   The Blue Bird of Happiness; Happiness; Happiness Is; Happiness Is (Just) a Thing Called Joe; Happiness Street (Corner Sunshine Square); Inn of the Sixth Happiness; My Happiness; Spread a Little Happiness; Walkin' Back to Happiness

Happy, see also Joy, Satisfied   Back to Those Happy Days; For He's a Jolly Good Fellow, or, Malbrouk (Malbrough), or, We Won't Go Home Until Morning, or, The Bear Went over the Mountain; Gee, But I'd Like To Make You Happy; Get Happy; Glad To Be Unhappy; Happy, or, Love Theme from Lady Sings the Blues; Happy Anniversary; Happy as the Day Is Long; Happy Birds; Happy Birthday to You, or, Good Morning to All; Happy Christmas, Little Friend; (Oh) Happy Day; Happy Days; Happy Days Are Here Again; Happy Days in Dixie; Happy Ending; The Happy Farmer; Happy Feet; Happy, Happy Birthday, Baby; Happy Holiday; Happy in Love; The Happy Organ; Happy Talk; The Happy Time; Happy To Keep His Dinner Warm; Happy Together; The

Happy Wanderer; The Happy Whistler; I Could Be Happy with You; I Want To Be Happy; I Whistle a Happy Tune; I'd Leave My Happy Home for You; I'd Rather Be Blue over You (Than Happy with Somebody Else); If You Wanna Be Happy; I'll Be Happy When the Preacher Makes You Mine; I'm Happy When I'm Hiking; It's a Hap-Hap-Happy Day; Jolly Commodore; Jolly Good Company; Jolly Good Luck to the Girl Who Loves a Soldier; The Jolly Green Giant; Let Me Sing and I'm Happy; Love Can Make You Happy; Many Happy Returns of the Day; The Most Happy Fella; The Jolly Miller; Oh Happy Day; The Pope He Leads a Happy Life; Put On a Happy Face; She Was Happy Till She Met You; Sometimes I'm Happy; Stay with the Happy People; (I Wanna Go Where You Go, Do What You Do) Then I'll Be Happy; Today I Feel So Happy; Walking Happy; You've Made Me So Very Happy

Happy-Go-Lucky   Back Again to Happy-Go-Lucky Days; Happy-Go-Lucky Lane; Happy-Go-Lucky Me; Happy-Go-Lucky You and Broken-Hearted Me

Harbor   Harbor Lights; The Harbor of Love; Remember Pearl Harbor

Hard   Breaking Up Is Hard To Do; Caldonia (What Makes Your Big Head So Hard); Do It the Hard Way; Easy To Be Hard; (It's Hard To) Go Down Easy; A Good Man Is Hard To Find; A Hard Day's Night; Hard Habit To Break; Hard-Headed Woman; Hard Hearted Hannah (the Vamp of Savannah); (It's) The Hard-Knock Life; A Hard Rain's A-Gonna Fall; Hard Times Come Again No More; Hard To Get; Hard To Say I'm Sorry; Harden My Heart; It's Easy To Remember (and So Hard To Forget); I've Got the Time—I've Got the Place, But It's Hard To Find the Girl; She Works Hard for the Money; Sorry Seems To Be the Hardest Word; When the Going Gets Tough the Tough Get Going

Hare, see Rabbit

Harem   In My Harem

Harlem   Bojangles of Harlem; Harlem Moon; Harlem Nocturne; Harlem Shuffle; Spanish Harlem; Underneath the Harlem Moon

Harm   Another Little Drink Wouldn't Do Us Any Harm; Not While I'm Around

Harmonica   Alvin's Harmonica

Harmony   In the Land of Harmony

Harp   The Harp That Once Thro' Tara's Halls; I Took My Harp to a Party; Little David, Play on Your Harp

Harriet   Harriet

Harry   Carrie, or, Carrie Marry Harry; Harry; (Theme from) Harry's Game; I'm Just Wild About Harry; The Third Man Theme, or, The Harry Lime Theme

Harvest   Cream of the Crop; Down at the Huskin' Bee; Down on the Farm in Harvest Time; Harvest of Love; Shine On Harvest Moon; When the Harvest Days Are Over, Jessie Dear

Hat   Any Old Place I Can Hang My Hat Is Home Sweet Home to Me; Any Place I Hang My Hat Is Home; The Ballad of the Green Berets; (Hats Off, Here They Come, Those) Beautiful Girls; The (Little) Bird on Nellie's Hat; Did Tosti Raise His Bowler Hat When He Said Goodbye; The Feather in Her Tyrolean Hat; Finishing the Hat; The Hat Me Father Wore;

Hats Off to Me; I Left My Hat in Haiti; I Like Your Old French Bonnet; I Tipped My Hat and Slowly Rode Away; (Theme from) Jewel in the Crown; Mexican Hat Dance; My Hat's on the Side of My Head; Put On Your Old Grey Bonnet; Raspberry Beret; She Wore a Yellow Ribbon, or, All Round My Hat (Round Her Neck) I (She) Wore a Yellow Ribbon; The Sun Has Got His Hat On; Sunbonnet Sue; The Three-Cornered Hat; The Toor-ie on His Bonnet; Top Hat, White Tie and Tails; Where Did You Get That Hat; The Windmills of Your Mind, or, Theme from The Thomas Crown Affair

Hate   I Hate Men; I Hate To Lose You; Oh, How I Hate To Get Up in the Morning

Haunt   Dear Eyes That Haunt Me; Haunted Ball Room; Haunted Heart; Haunting Me; Her Bright Smile Haunts Me Still; The House Is Haunted

Havana   Sunny Havana; A Weekend in Havana

Hawaii, *see also* **Nonsense** (e.g. **Yaaka Hula Hickey Dula**) Aloha Oe, or, Farewell to Thee; Blue Hawaii; Goodbye Hawaii; (Theme from) Hawaii Five-O; Hawaiian Butterfly; Hawaiian War Chant; The Hawaiian Wedding Song; Hello, Aloha! How Are You?; Hello, Hawaii, How Are You; Honolulu; My Little Grass Shack in Kealakekua, Hawaii; On the Beach at Waikiki; A Song of Old Hawaii; Sweet Hawaiian Moonlight; They're Wearing 'Em Higher in Hawaii; Under Hawaiian Skies

Hay   A Load of Hay; Louisiana Hayride; A Needle in a Haystack; We'll Make Hay While the Sun Shines

Haze, *see* **Fog**

Hazel, *see* **Brown**

Head   Caldonia (What Makes Your Big Head So Hard); Forty-Seven Ginger Headed Sailors; From the Top of Your Head to the Tip of Your Shoes; Goin' Out of My Head; Hard-Headed Woman; Head Low; Head Over Heels; Head over Heels in Love; A Headache Tomorrow (Or a Heartache Tonight); Headed for Heartache; Headin' for Louisville; I Wish You Could Have Turned My Head; Keep Your Head Down, "Fritzie Boy"; Ma Curly Headed Babby; Mammy's Little Kinky-Headed Boy; My Hat's on the Side of My Head; Nobody Knows What a Red Head Mama Can Do; Puddin' Head Jones; Put Your Head on My Shoulder; Raindrops Keep Fallin' on My Head; Sleepy Head; With Her Head Tucked Underneath Her Arm; With My Head in the Clouds; You Go to My Head; You're a Sweet Little Headache

Health, *see also* **Ache, Doctor, Hospital, Sick,** etc.   Good Luck, Good Health, God Bless You; I Don't Want To Get Well (I'm in Love with a Beautiful Nurse); Ill Wind (You're Blowin' Me No Good); Sexual Healing; Some Little Bug Is Going To Find You (Some Day); Time Heals Everything; Young and Healthy

Hear   Big Noise from Winnetka; Can't Yo' Heah Me Callin' Caroline; Can't You Hear My Heart Beat; Cheerful Little Earful; Couldn't Hear Nobody Pray; Do I Hear a Waltz; Do I Hear You Saying "I Love You"; Do Nothin' Till You Hear from Me; Far Off I Hear a Lover's Flute; Have You Heard; Hear Dem Bells; I Hear a Rhapsody; I Hear a Symphony; I Hear a Thrush at Eve; I Hear Music; I Hear Music; I Hear You Calling Me; I Hear You Knocking; I Heard It Through

the Grapevine; I Heard the Bells on Christmas Day; I Heard You Cried Last Night; I Wanna Hear It from Your Lips; (It Seems to Me) I've Heard That Song Before; Lafayette—We Hear You Calling; Let's Hear It for the Boy; Listen People; Listen to My Tale of Woe; Listen to the Mocking Bird; Listen to the Radio; Listen to What the Man Said; Since Sister Nell Heard Paderewski Play; The Sound of Goodbye; The Sound of Music; Sounds Like Love; Stereophonic Sound; Sweet Spirit, Hear My Prayer; The Sweetest Sounds; T.S.O.P. (The Sound of Philadelphia); When a Woman Hears the Sound of the Drum and Fife; When They Sound the Last All Clear; Wired for Sound; You Ain't Heard Nothing Yet; You Should Hear How She Talks About You; You're Gonna Hear from Me

Hearse, *see* **Death**

Heart, *see also* **Sweetheart**   Absence Makes the Heart Grow Fonder; Absence Makes the Heart Grow Fonder (for Somebody Else); (You Are) Always in My Heart; Anema e Core (With All My Heart and Soul); Anyone Who Had a Heart; Are We Downhearted?—No!; Be Careful It's My Heart; Be Still My Heart; The Beat of My Heart; Blue (and Broken Hearted); Blue Moon with Heartache; Blues in My Heart; Breaking in a Brand New Broken Heart; Broken Hearted Clown; Broken-Hearted Melody; Burning Heart; Can't You Hear My Heart Beat; Close to My Heart; Cold Cold Heart; Crazy Heart; Cross Your Heart; The Curse of an Aching Heart; Danger, Heartbreak Ahead; Dear Heart; Dear Hearts and Gentle People; Dearest, You're the Nearest to My Heart; Deep in My Heart, Dear; Deep in the Heart of Texas; Does Your Heart Beat for Me; Don't Break the Heart That Loves You; Don't Bring Me Your Heartaches; Downhearted; Downhearted Blues; A Dream Is a Wish Your Heart Makes; Drums in My Heart; Everything's in Rhythm with My Heart; Evil Hearted You; Fly Home, Little Heart; Foolish Heart; Forgive My Heart; Fortress Around Your Heart; The Gang That Sang Heart of My Heart; The Garden of Your Heart; Gold Will Buy Most Anything But a True Girl's Heart; A Good Hearted Woman; Good Morning Heartache; Hang Your Heart on a Hickory Limb; Happy-Go-Lucky You and Broken-Hearted Me; Hard Hearted Hannah (the Vamp of Savannah); Harden My Heart; Haunted Heart; Have a Heart; A Headache Tomorrow (Or a Heartache Tonight); Headed for Heartache; (You've Got To Have) Heart; Heart and Soul; Heart and Soul; Heart Attack; The Heart Bow'd Down; Heart Full of Soul; The Heart of a Fool; The Heart of a Man; Heart of a Rose; Heart of a Teenage Girl; Heart of Glass; Heart of Gold; Heart of Mine; Heart of My Heart (I Love You), or, The Story of the Rose; Heart of Oak; Heart of Rock and Roll; Heart of the Night; Heart of the Night; Heart of My Sleeve; Heart to Heart; Heartaches; Heartaches by the Number; Heartbeat—It's a Lovebeat; Heartbreak Express; Heartbreak Hotel; Heartbreaker; Heartbreaker; Heartlight; Hearts; Hearts and Flowers; Hearts of Stone; Here Am I—Broken Hearted; Here in My Heart; He's 1-A in the Army (and A-1 in My Heart); Hot Rod Heart; How Can You Mend a Broken Heart; How Many Hearts Have You Broken; Hungry Heart; I Give My Heart; I Have But One Heart; I Know a Heartache When I See One; I Leave My Heart in an English Garden; I Left My Heart at the Stage Door Canteen; I Left My Heart in San Francisco; I Let a Song Go Out of My Heart; I Once Had a Heart, Margarita; I Poured My Heart into a song; If I Give My Heart to You; I'll Follow My Secret Heart; In the Garden of My Heart; In the Heart of the Dark; Invitation to a Broken Heart; It's a Heartache; I've a Longing in My Heart for You, Louise; I've Got a Rock 'n' Roll Heart; Jealous Heart; Keep a Little Cozy Corner in Your Heart for Me; Left Right Out of Your Heart; Let My Song Fill Your Heart; Let the Heartaches Begin; Lonely Heart; Look into Your Heart; Love from a Heart of Gold; Love, Here Is My Heart; Love Me with All Your Heart; Love Steals Your Heart; Love—What Are You Doing to My Heart; Man of My Heart; The Mansion of Aching Hearts; Music Music Everywhere (But Not a Song in My Heart); My Dearest Heart; My Foolish Heart; My Heart and I; My Heart and I; My Heart at Thy Sweet Voice; My Heart Belongs to Daddy; My Heart Belongs to Me; My Heart Cries for You; My Heart Goes Crazy; My Heart Has a Mind of Its Own; My Heart Has Learned To Love You, Now Do Not Say Goodbye; My Heart Is a Hobo; My Heart Is an Open Book; My Heart Is Taking Lessons; My Heart Reminds Me, or, And That Reminds Me; (All of a Sudden) My Heart Sings; My Heart Still Clings to the Old First Love; My Heart Stood Still; My Heart Tells Me; My Heart's To Let; My One and Only Heart; Nobody's Heart (Belongs to Me); None But the Lonely Heart; One Hand, One Heart; The One Rose That's Left in My Heart; Only Love Can Break a Heart; Only the Heartaches; Open Up Your Heart (and Let the Sunshine In); Owner of a Lonely Heart; Peg o' My Heart; Play Me Hearts and Flowers (I Wanna Cry); Put a Little Love in Your Heart; Queen of Hearts; Rose of My Heart; Save Your Heart for Me; Says My Heart; Sergeant Pepper's Lonely Hearts Club Band; Silver Hair and Heart of Gold; So Beats My Heart for You; Some Day My Heart Will Awake; Someone Could Love a Heart Tonight; The Song from Moulin Rouge, or, Where Is Your Heart; The Song That Reached My Heart; Still Right Here in My Heart; Stop Draggin' My Heart Around; Stop! You're Breaking My Heart; Stouthearted Men; (You're the Flower of My Heart) Sweet Adeline; Sweet Heartache; Sweet Heartaches; Take Back the Heart You Gave; Take Me Back to Your Heart Again; Take My Heart; There Goes My Heart; There's a Broken Heart for Every Light on Broadway; There's a Girl in the Heart of Maryland (with a Heart That Belongs to Me); There's Where My Heart Is Tonight; This Heart of Mine; Time (Clock of the Heart); 'Tis Home Where'er the Heart Is; Total Eclipse of the Heart; True-Hearted, Whole-Hearted, or, Peal Out the Watchword; Two Hearts Are Better Than One; Two Hearts in Three Quarter Time; Two Hearts That Pass in the Night; Unchain My Heart; Unsuspecting Heart; Waltz of My Heart; Way Down in My Heart, or, I've Got a Feeling For You; What Will I Tell My Heart; When a Maid Comes Knocking at Your Heart; When Hearts Are Young; When the Organ Played at Twilight (The Song That Reached My Heart); When You Look in the Heart of a Rose; While Hearts Are Singing; Whose Little Heart Are You Breaking Now; With a Song in My Heart; With All My Heart; With All My Heart; Wooden Heart; The Words Are in My Heart; You Belong to My Heart (Now and Forever), or, Solamente Una Vez; You Have Taken My Heart; You Won't Be Satisfied (Until You Break My Heart); Young at Heart; Your Cheatin' Heart; Your Heart and My Heart; You're Breaking My Heart; You're Dancing on My Heart; You're the Best Break This Old Heart Ever Had; Yours Is My Heart Alone;

You've Done Something to My Heart; Zing Went the Strings of My Heart

Hearth, *see* **Fireplace**

Heat, *see* **Hot**

Heather   The Heather on the Hill

Heaven   All This and Heaven Too; All This and Heaven Too; Away Down South in Heaven; Bali Ha'i; East Side of Heaven; Half-Way to Heaven; Heaven; Heaven Can Wait; Heaven Help Us All; Heaven Knows; Heaven Must Be Missing an Angel; Heaven Must Have Sent You; Heaven On Earth; Heaven on the Seventh Floor; Heaven Will Protect the Working Girl; Hello, Central, Give Me Heaven; Here Comes Heaven Again; Home Sweet Heaven; I Look at Heaven; In Heavenly Love Abiding; Ireland Must Be Heaven, for My Mother Came from There; Knockin' on Heaven's Door; Life's Railway to Heaven; A Little Bit of Heaven, Sure They Call It Ireland; My Blue Heaven; My Little Nest of Heavenly Blue, or, Frasquita Serenade (Blaues Himmelbett), or, Farewell, My Love, Farewell; One More Angel in Heaven; Outside of Heaven; Pennies from Heaven; Seventh Heaven; Seventh Heaven; Shangri-La; Somebody Up There Likes Me; The Spacious Firmament on High; A Star Fell Out of Heaven; The Sweetest Music This Side of Heaven; Thank Heaven for Little Girls; There Are Angels Outside Heaven; There's Nothing True But Heaven; Timbuctoo; To Anacreon in Heaven; Too Much Heaven; When Did You Leave Heaven; You'll Never Get to Heaven; You're a Heavenly Thing; You're the Only Star in My Blue Heaven

Heavy   He Ain't Heavy—He's My Brother; The Weight

Heed   Heed the Call

Heel, *see* **Feet**

Heidelberg   Heidelberg Stein Song

Helen   Helen Wheels

Hell, *see* **Devil**

Hello   Good-Bye Broadway, Hello France; Hello; Hello Again; Hello, Aloha! How Are You?; Hello, Bluebird; Hello, Central, Give Me Heaven; Hello, Central, Give Me No Man's Land; Hello Dolly; Hello Frisco Hello; Hello Goodbye; Hello, Hawaii, How Are You; Hello, Hello There; Hello, Hello, Who's Your Lady Friend; Hello, I Love You (Won't You Tell Me Your Name); Hello It's Me; Hello Little Girl; Hello! Ma Baby; Hello Mudduh, Hello Faddah; Hello, My Lover, Goodbye; Hello Swanee, Hello; Hello Twelve, Hello Thirteen, Hello Love; Hello Young Lovers; Please Hello; Shalom; Ship Ahoy, or, All the Nice Girls Love a Sailor; To You Sweetheart, Aloha; Voices of the Woods, or, Welcome Sweet Springtime; Welcome Back; Welcome to My World; We'll Keep a Welcome; Willkommen; Yoo-Hoo; You're as Welcome as the Flowers in May

Help, *see also* **Cooperation**   Can't Help Falling in Love (with You); Can't Help Lovin' Dat Man; Can't Help Singing; Heaven Help Us All; Help!; Help Me Make It Through the Night; Help Me Rhonda; Help Yourself; I Can Help; I Can't Help It; I Can't Help Myself; (With) A Little Help from My Friends; O God, Our Help in Ages Past; Please Help Me I'm Falling; So Help Me; So Help Me; SOS

Hen, *see* **Chicken**

Henry Dance with Me Henry; I'm Henery the Eighth (I Am); John Henry; The John Henry Blues; Sailin' Away on the Henry Clay

Herald Hark the Herald Angels Sing

Herbert Turn 'Erbert's Face to the Wall, Mother

Hero Billy Don't Be a Hero; (Theme from) Greatest American Hero (Believe It or Not); My Hero; We Don't Need Another Hero; You Gotta Be a Football Hero (To Get Along with the Beautiful Girls)

Hiawatha, *see* **Indian**

Hide Elusive Butterfly; Hernando's Hideaway; Hide Thou Me; Hideaway; Hiding in Thee; My Elusive Dreams; Way Down In Iowa I'm Going To Hide Away; You Can't Pull the Wool over My Eyes; You've Got To Hide Your Love Away

High Ain't No Mountain High Enough; All Time High; Every Time You Touch Me (I Get High); The High and the Mighty; High Barbaree; High Class Baby; High Heel Sneakers; High Hopes; (Theme from) High Noon (Do Not Forsake Me, Oh, My Darling); High on a Windy Hill; High on You; High School Cadets; High Society (March); High upon a Hill Top; High, Wide and Handsome; (Your Love Has Lifted Me) Higher and Higher; Higher Ground; Higher Love; How High the Moon; I Hit a New High; I Lift Up My Finger and I Say Tweet Tweet; I'd Climb the Highest Mountain (If I Knew I'd Find You); I'm Shooting High; I'm Sittin' High on a Hill Top; Lift Boy; Lift Ev'ry Voice and Sing; Loch Lomond, or, The Bonnie Bonnie Banks, or, Oh! Ye'll Take the High Road; Looking High, High, High; The Mountains High; My Gal Is a High Born Lady; Natural High; Ridin' High; Rocky Mountain High; Roll Out! Heave Dat Cotton; Round on the End and High in the Middle, O-hi-o; Sky High; The Spacious Firmament on High; Swing High, Swing Low; Take Me High; They're Wearing 'Em Higher in Hawaii; The Tide Is High

Highlands Misty Islands of the Highlands; My One and Only Highland Fling

Highway, *see* **Road**

Hike, *see* **Walk**

Hill Blueberry Hill; The Call of the Far-Away Hills; The Folks Who Live on the Hill; The Fool on the Hill; The Funny Old Hills; The Heather on the Hill; High on a Windy Hill; High upon a Hill Top; The Hills of Home; The Hills of Old Wyomin'; I'm Sittin' High on a Hill Top; It's Dark on Observatory Hill; The Lass of Richmond Hill; The Lass with the Delicate Air, or, Young Molly Who Lives at the Foot of the Hill; The Little House upon the Hill; Mocking Bird Hill; Over the Hill; Primrose Hill; Scottish Soldier Green Hill; Shepherd of the Hills; The Singing Hills; The Sword of Bunker Hill; There Is a Green Hill Far Away; The Top of the Hill; When De Moon Comes Up Behind De Hill

Hindustan Hindustan

Hippopotamus The Hippopotamus Song, or, Mud, Glorious Mud

History Entire History of the World in Two Minutes and Thirty-Two Seconds

Hit Hit and Miss; Hit the Road Jack; Hit the Road to Dreamland; Hitting the Bottle; I Hit a New High; Pepsi-Cola Hits the Spot; Who Hit Me; You Hit the Spot

Hobo Gypsys, Tramps and Thieves; Hallelujah, I'm a Bum; He's a Rag Picker; He's a Tramp; The Lady Is a Tramp; My Heart Is a Hobo

Hog, *see* **Pig**

Hold, *see also* **Cling, Cuddle, Hug** Don't Hold Everything; Embraceable You; Got a Hold Me; Hold Back the Dawn; Hold 'Em Joe; Hold Me; Hold Me; Hold Me; Hold Me; Hold Me, Hold Me, Hold Me; Hold Me Now; Hold Me, Thrill Me, Kiss Me; Hold Me Tight; Hold My Hand; Hold My Hand; Hold On; Hold On to My Love; Hold Tight—Hold Tight; Hold Your Hand Out Naughty Boy; Holding Back the Years; I Don't Want To Put a Hold on You; I Want To Hold Your Hand; I Won't Hold You Back; If I Said You Had a Beautiful Body (Would You Hold It Against Me); Put Your Arms Around Me Honey (Hold Me Tight); Squeeze Me; There's No Holding Me; To Have, To Hold, To Love; Who's Holding Donna Now; Won't You Fondle Me

Hole Ace in the Hole; Down at the Old Swimming Hole; Fixing a Hole; Hole in the Ground

Holiday Allah's Holiday; A Dreamer's Holiday; Happy Holiday; Holiday for Strings; (There's No Place Like) Home for the Holidays; The Policeman's Holiday; Satan Takes a Holiday; Summer Holiday; Take a Day Off, Mary Ann

Holland, *see also* **Tulip, Windmill** Flying Dutchman (Overture); The Flying Dutchman; In an Old Dutch Garden; It's Tulip Time in Holland; Little Dutch Mill; My Old Dutch

Holly, *see* **Christmas**

Hollywood Hooray for Hollywood; Poor Little Hollywood Star

Holy Christmas Song, or, O Holy Night; Holly Holy; The Holy City; Holy Cow; Holy! Holy! Lord God Almighty; Silent Night, Holy Night

Home, *see also* **House** Any Old Place I Can Hang My Hat Is Home Sweet Home to Me; Any Place I Hang My Hat Is Home; Baby, Won't You Please Come Home; Be Kind to the Loved Ones at Home; Better Homes and Gardens; Bill Bailey, Won't You Please Come Home; The Boys Are Coming Home Today; Call Me (Come Back Home); Come Home Dewey, We Won't Do a Thing to You; Come Home to My Arms; Come, Landlord, Fill the Flowing Bowl; Coming Home; Da Doo Ron Ron (When He Walked Me Home); Daddy's Home; Do They Miss Me at Home; Don't Ever Be Afraid To Go Home; Don't Take Me Home; Everybody's Got a Home But Me; Father, Dear Father, Come Home with Me Now, or, Come Home, Father; Fly Home, Little Heart; Flying Home; For He's a Jolly Good Fellow, or, Malbrouk (Malbrough), or, We Won't Go Home Until Morning, or, The Bear Went over the Mountain; Galloping Home; Gee, But It's Great To Meet a Friend from Your Old Home Town; Go Home; Go Home and Tell Your Mother; Goin' Home; Going Home; The Green Green Grass of Home; He Brought Home Another; He's a Devil in His Own Home Town; The Hills of Home; The Hills of Old Wyomin'; Home; Home; Home Again; Home Again; Home Again Blues; Home and Dry; Home Cooking; (There's No Place Like) Home for the Holidays; Home Lovin' Man; Home on the Range, or, Oh, Give Me a Home Where the Buffalo Roam; Home Sweet Heaven; Home Sweet Home; Home Town; The Homecoming Waltz; Homesick; Homesick—That's All; Homeward Bound; Homework; Homing; The Homing Waltz; A House Is a Home;

A House Is Not a Home; I Could Go On Singing (Till the Cows Come Home); I Guess I'll Get the Papers and Go Home; I Ran All the Way Home; I Want To Go Home; I'd Leave My Happy Home for You; I'll Be Home; I'll Be Home for Christmas; I'll Go Home with Bonnie Jean; I'll Take You Home Again Kathleen; I'm Afraid To Come Home in the Dark; I'm Gonna Hire a Wino To Decorate Our Home; Indian Reservation; (Back Home Again in) Indiana; I've Got Sixpence (As I Go Rolling Home); Just Come Home; Just Try To Picture Me (Back Down) Home in Tennessee); Keep the Home Fires Burning (Till the Boys Come Home); Let's Take the Long Way Home; Little Grey Home in the West; The Longest Way 'Round Is the Sweetest Way Home; Love in a Home; Maggie Murphy's Home; The Miner's Dream of Home; My Baby's Comin' Home; My Home Town Is a One Horse Town, But It's Big Enough for Me; My Hometown; My Lodging (It) Is on the Cold Ground; My Old Kentucky Home (Good Night); My Old New Hampshire Home; Oh, How I Wish I Could Sleep Until My Daddy Comes Home; Oh! I Must Go Home Tonight; Old Folks at Home (Way Down Upon the Swanee River); One Called ''Mother'' and the Other ''Home Sweet Home''; Our Lodger's Such a Nice Young Man; Paddlin' Madelin' Home; Rolling Home; Rolling Stones—All Come Rolling Home Again; Rufus Rastus Johnson Brown (What You Goin' To Do When the Rent Comes 'Round); Sadie Salome, Go Home; Sailor (Your Home Is the Sea); She's Leaving Home; Show Me the Way To Go Home; Sorry (I Ran All the Way Home); The Stately Homes of England; Sweet Thoughts of Home; Take Me Home; Take Me Home; Take Me Home Country Roads; Take Your Girlie to the Movies If You Can't Make Love at Home; Tell Me Pretty Maiden (Are There Any More at Home Like You); The Tenement Symphony; There Is No Christmas Like a Home Christmas; There's a Boy Coming Home on Leave; There's a Little Lane Without a Turning on the Way to Home Sweet Home; Three Wonderful Letters from Home; 'Tis Home Where'er the Heart Is; Tuck Me to Sleep in My Old 'Tucky Home; Viva l' America: Home of the Free; Wait Till the Cows Come Home; Wait Until Your Daddy Comes Home; Walkin' My Baby Back Home; Way Back Home; We'll Have a Jubilee in My Old Kentucky Home; What Is Home Without a Mother; When I Saw Sweet Nellie Home, or, I Was Seeing Nellie Home, or, Aunt Dinah's Quilting Party; When Johnny Comes Marching Home; When My Dream Boat Comes Home; When the Boys Come Home; When You Come Home; When You're a Long, Long Way from Home; Who Takes Care of the Caretaker's Daughter While the Caretaker's Busy Taking Care?; Who's Taking You Home Tonight; Wonder When My Baby's Coming Home; Won't You Waltz ''Home Sweet Home'' with Me; You'd Be So Nice To Come Home To; You'd Never Know the Old Home Town of Mine; The Young Folks at Home; You're a Million Miles from Nowhere When You're One Little Mile from Home

Honest, see **Truth**

Honey, see **Sugar**

Honeymoon The Aba Daba Honeymoon; Choo-Choo Honeymoon; Dancing Honeymoon; Honeymoon; The Honeymoon (March); The Honeymoon Is Over; The Little White House (at the End of Honeymoon Lane); When the Honeymoon Was Over

Honeysuckle The Honeysuckle and the Bee; Honeysuckle Rose

Hong Kong Chong, He Come from Hong Kong; Hong Kong Blues

Honky Tonk Another Honky Tonk Night on Broadway; Down in Honky Tonky Town; Honkey Tonk; Honky Tonk Train Blues; Honky Tonk Women; Honky Tonkin'

Honolulu, see **Hawaii**

Hook Baby Don't Get Hooked on Me; Captain Hook's Waltz; Hooked on a Feeling; Hooked on Music

Hop, see also **Dance** Keep-A-Hoppin'

Hope, see **Wish**

Horizon, see **Sky**

Horn, see **Bugle**

Horse, see also **Saddle** All the King's Horses; Captain Jinks of the Horse Marines; Devil's Gallop, or, Dick Barton Theme; Galloping Home; The Galloping Major; Gid-ap, Garibaldi; Give a Man a Horse He Can Ride; Goodbye Ol' Paint, or, I Ride an Old Paint, or, I'm a-Leavin' Cheyenne; (And) His Rocking Horse Ran Away; The Horse; A Horse with No Name; Horses; Horsey, Horsey; Horsey, Keep Your Tail Up; Jingle Bells, or, The One Horse Open Sleigh; The Jockey on the Carousel; The King's Horses; Light Cavalry (Overture); Livery Stable Blues; Meadowlands, or, Cavalry of the Steppes; My Home Town Is a One Horse Town, But It's Big Enough for Me; My Pony Boy; Never Take the Horse Shoe from the Door; The Old Grey Mare (She Ain't What She Used To Be); Pony Time; Ride On, Ride On; Ride, Tenderfoot, Ride; Stop the Cavalry; The Unicorn; Wal, I Swan!, or, Ebenezer Frye, or, Giddiap Napoleon, It Looks Like Rain; The White Horse Inn; Wild Horses

Hose The Man with the Ladder and the Horse

Hospital, see also **Doctor, Medicine, etc.** Emergency Ward 10 Theme; Good Night, Nurse (Kiss Your Little Patient); I Don't Want To Get Well (I'm in Love with a Beautiful Nurse); (Song from) M*A*S*H; Nursie; St. James Infirmary

Hostess, see **Party**

Hot, see also **Fever, Warm** Dance (Disco Heat); The Heat Is On; Heat of the Moment; Heat Wave; (Love Is Like a) Heat Wave; The Hot Canary; Hot Child in the City; Hot Diggity (Dog Ziggity Boom); Hot Fun in the Summertime; Hot Heels; Hot Line; Hot Lips; Hot Love; Hot Rod Hearts; Hot Stuff; (There'll Be) A Hot Time in the Old Town (Tonight); I'm the Last of the Red-Hot Mamas; Hot Cross Buns; Pease Porridge Hot; Steam Heat; Sweet and Hot; There'll Be a Hot Time for the Old Men When the Young Men Go to War; Too Darn Hot; Too Hot; Turn On the Heat; You Dropped Me Like a Red Hot Penny

Hot Dog Fido Is a Hot Dog Now

Hotel The Ferry Boat Inn; Hotel California; Inn of the Sixth Happiness; There's a Small Hotel; The White Horse Inn

Hour, see **Time**

House, see also **Home, Porch** (Theme from) The Apartment; Bless This House; Cabin in the Cotton; Cabin in the Sky; Come On-A-My House; The Cottage by the Sea; A Cottage for Sale; The Cottage of My Mother; The House by the Side of the Road; The House I Live In; A House Is a Home; The House Is Haunted; A House Is Not a Home; The House of

Bamboo; The House of Blue Lights; House of Flowers; The House of the Rising Sun; The House That Jack Built; A House with a Little Red Barn; Hurry on Down (to My House); I Wouldn't Leave My Little Wooden Hut for You; If It Wasn't for the 'ouses in Between; In Our Little Den of Iniquity; In the House of Too Much Trouble; In the Little Red School-house; It's So Nice To Have a Man Around the House; Jailhouse Rock; Just a Cottage Small—by a Waterfall; Limehouse Blues; The Little Grey House; The Little House upon the Hill; The Little Old Log Cabin in the Lane; Little Old Sod Shanty; Little White Cottage; The Little White House (at the End of Honeymoon Lane); Lonely House; Love Song from Houseboat, or, Almost in Your Arms; The Mansion of Aching Hearts; McNally's Row of Flats; My Adobe Hacienda; My Cabin of Dreams; My Little Grass Shack in Kealakekua, Hawaii; The Old House; Our House; Our Penthouse on Third Avenue; Ours Is a Nice 'ouse Ours Is; (In) A Shanty in Old Shanty Town; She Lived Next Door to a Firehouse; Somebody's Coming to My House; Stranger in My House; Sugar Shack; That Tumble-Down Shack in Athlone; This Ole House; When the Bell in the Lighthouse Rings Ding Dong; When We're Alone, or, Penthouse Serenade; While Others Are Building Castles in the Air (I'll Build a Cottage for Two); The White House Chair; Within the Cellar's Depth I Sit; Won't You Come Over to My House

Houston Houston

Huckleberry Do, Do, My Huckleberry Do; Huckleberry Duck; Huckleberry Finn

Hudson The Meeting of the Waters of Hudson and Erie; The Voice of the Hudson

Hug Funny Bunny Hug; Huggin' and Chalkin'; Hugs and Kisses; A Penny a Kiss, A Penny a Hug

Humdinger He's a Humdinger

Humming I'm Humming, I'm Whistling, I'm Singing; Just Humming Along

Hummingbird Humming Bird

Humor The Bad Humor Man; Humoresque

Hundred Another Hundred People; Five Hundred Miles; A Hundred Million Miracles; A Hundred Pounds of Clay; A Hundred Years from Now; A Hundred Years from Today; Ninety-Nine Out of a Hundred (Want To Be Loved); Old Hundred(th) Doxology, or, Praise God, from Whom All Blessings Flow; One Hundred Ways; Room Five Hundred and Four; We Are Coming, Father Abraham, 300,000 More

Hungary Hungarian Dances; Hungarian Rhapsody No. 2

Hunk A Big Hunk of Love; I Love To Dunk a Hunk of Sponge Cake

Hunt Hunt Theme (Tantivy! Tantivy! Tantivy!), or, A-Hunting We Will Go; The Hunters of Kentucky; (Theme from) Sea Hunt

Hurry, see also **Fast** Arthur Murray Taught Me Dancing in a Hurry; Fools Rush In; Hurry It's Lovely Up Here; Hurry On Down (to My House); You Can't Hurry Love

Hurt Big Hurt; Do You Really Want To Hurt Me; Hurt; Hurt So Good; Hurting Each Other; Hurts So Bad; Hurts To Be in Love; I Guess It Never Hurts To Hurt Sometimes; I Love You So Much It Hurts; I Never Meant To Hurt You; It Only

Hurts for a Little While; Love Hurts; Mama, Look a Booboo; You Always Hurt the One You Love

Husband, see **Marriage**

Hush, see **Quiet**

Husk Down at the Huskin' Bee

Hut, see **House**

Ice From Greenland's Icy Mountains; Theme from Ice Castles (Through the Eyes of Love)

Ice Cream (I Scream, You Scream, We All Scream for) Ice Cream; Ice Cream Man

Ida Ida, Sweet As Apple Cider

Idaho Idaho

Idea, see also **Inspiration, Think,** etc. Got'n Idea; He May Be Old, But He's Got Young Ideas; (When We Are Dancing) I Get Ideas; Young Ideas

Ideal My Ideal; My Ideal; You Are the Ideal of My Dreams

Illinois In Dear Old Illinois

Imagination, see also **Believe, Fantasy, Pretend** Blue Mirage; Imaginary Lover; Imagination; I've Got To Use My Imagination; Just Imagine; Just My Imagination (Running Away with Me); S'posin'; Suppose I Had Never Met You; Use Your Imagination; Why Do You Suppose

Immigrant The Immigrant

Impatient The Impatient Years

Imperial Imperial Echoes

Important How Important Can It Be

Impossible Anything I Dream Is Possible; The Impossible Dream, or, The Quest; It's Impossible; (Theme from) Mission: Impossible; Possibly; You've Got Possibilities

Imposter, see **Pretend**

Incense, see **Perfume**

Inch Inchworm

Income, see **Money**

Incredible The Incredible Flutist

Independence, see **Freedom**

India Song of India

Indian Alknomook, or, The Death of the Cherokee Indian; Along the Navajo Trail; Apache; Apache Dance; The Belle of Mohawk Vale, or, Bonny Eloise; Cherokee; Doctor, Lawyer, Indian Chief; Down Where the Silv'ry Mohawk Flows; (What Shall We Do with) The Drunken Sailor, or, Columbus, or, John Brown Had a Little Injun, or, Ten Little Indians; Four American Indian Songs; Four Indian Love Lyrics; Geronimo; Give It Back to the Indians; Half-Breed; Hiawatha; Hiawatha's Melody of Love; I'm an Indian Too; Indian Love Call; Indian Reservation; Indian Summer; Keem-O-Sabe; Navajo; The Savage; Sioux City Sue; Ten Little Indians, or, Ten Little Injuns, or, Ten Little Niggers; Tobacco's But an Indian Weed; Totem Tom-Tom

Indiana Can't Get Indiana off My Mind; Gary, Indiana; (Back Home Again in) Indiana; Indiana Moon; Indianola; Way Down in Old Indiana

Indigo, see **Blue**

Indoors, *see* **Outside**

Inez   Mama Inez

Iniquity   In Our Little Den of Iniquity

Ink   I Bought Myself a Bottle of Ink

Inn, *see* **Hotel**

Inspiration, *see also* **Idea**   My Inspiration Is You; (You're My) Soul and Inspiration; You're the Inspiration

Introduction   Introduction and Air to a Stained Glass Window

Invent   The Night They Invented Champagne

Invitation   Invitation; Invitation to a Broken Heart; Invitation to the Dance

Iona   My Own Iona

Iowa   Iowa Corn Song; Way Down in Iowa I'm Going To Hide Away

Ipanema   The (Boy) Girl from Ipanema

Ireland   Come Back to Erin; Did Your Mother Come from Ireland; Galway Bay; If You Ever Go to Ireland; If You're Irish Come into the Parlour; Ireland Is Ireland to Me; Ireland Must Be Heaven, for My Mother Came from There; The Irish Jubilee; Irish Washerwoman, or, The Scotch Bagpipe Melody; It's a Great Day for the Irish; It's the Irish in Your Eye, (It's the Irish in Your Smile); It's the Same Old Shillelagh; Johnny Doughboy Found a Rose in Ireland; The Lament of the Irish Emigrant; Laughing Irish Eyes; Let Erin Remember the Days of Old; A Little Bit of Heaven, Sure They Call It Ireland; My Irish Molly O; My Wild Irish Rose; Remember Boy, You're Irish (Shane na Lown); That Old Irish Mother of Mine; Too-ra-loo-ra-loo-ral, That's an Irish Lullaby; Two Laughing Irish Eyes; When Irish Eyes Are Smiling; When Shall I Again See Ireland; With My Shillelagh Under My Arm

Irene   Goodnight Irene; Irene; Sally, Irene and Mary; Sleep, Baby, Sleep, or, Irene's Lullaby

Irma   Irma La Douce

Iron   Any Old Iron; Chester (Let Tyrants Shake Their Iron Rod); The Girl at the Ironing Board; Too Many Irons in the Fire

Irresistible   Irresistible You

Irresponsible   Call Me Irresponsible

Island   Christmas Island; Enchanted Island; Hi Tiddley Hi Ti Island; In the Middle of an Island; Island Girl; Island of Dreams; Islands in the Stream; Make Believe Island; Misty Islands of the Highlands; On a Desert Island with Thee; On Treasure Island; Rock Island Line; Song of the Islands; South Sea Island Magic; Thunder Island

Isle   Beautiful Isle of Somewhere; Beautiful Isle of the Sea; Isle d'Amour (Isle of Love); Isle of Capri; Isle o' Dreams; Isle of Innisfree; The Isle of Our Dreams; My Isle of Golden Dreams; On the Isle of May

Israel   Fear Ye Not, O Israel

Istanbul   Istanbul (Not Constantinople)

Italy   All Over Italy; Italian Street Song; Mambo Italiano; Marie from Sunny Italy; On the Shores of Italy; There's a Garden in Old Italy; When It's Night-Time in Italy, It's Wednesday over Here

Ivory   Ebony and Ivory; Ivory Tower

Ivy   Grand Old Ivy; Ivy Rose; Just Like the Ivy

Jack   Ballin' the Jack; Cu-Tu-Gu-Ru (Jack, Jack, Jack); Frère Jacques; Grocer Jack; Hit the Road Jack; The House That Jack Built; Jack and Diane; Jack in the Box; Jack in the Box; Jacques D'Iraq (Jock D'Rock); Little Jack Frost Get Lost; Jack and Jill; Jack Sprat; Little Jack Horner; Mother Was a Lady, or, If Jack Were Only Here; Three for Jack

Jackie   Jackie Blue; Our Jackie's Getting Married

Jail   Chain Gang; The Convict and the Bird; Down in the Valley, or, Birmingham Jail, or, Bird in a Cage, or, Down on the Levee; Folsom Prison (Blues); Jailhouse Rock; Prisoner of Hope; Prisoner of Love; The Prisoner's Song; When You're Wearing the Ball and Chain

Jam, *see also* **Jelly Roll**   C-Jam Blues; Clarinet Marmalade; It Must Be Jelly, 'Cause Jam Don't Shake Like That; Lady Marmalade; Master Blaster (Jammin'); Traffic Jam

Jamaica   Jamaica Farewell; Jamaican Rumba

James, *see* **Jim**

Jane   (When the) Bloom Is on the Rye, or, My Pretty Jane; Good-bye, Eliza Jane; Goodbye, Liza Jane; I'se Your Nigger If You Want Me, Liza Jane; Jane; Leave It to Jane; Li'l Liza Jane; Me and Jane in a Plane; My Sunshine Jane; Susan Jane

Janet   Janet; Janet's Choice; Janette

January   January, February; (It's) June in January

Japan   The Japanese Sandman; A Japanese Sunset

Jazz   All That Jazz; At the Jazz Band Ball; Jazz Baby's Ball; Jazz Man; Jazz Me Blues; Jazz Nocturne; Jazzboat

Jealous   All the World Will Be Jealous of Me; Hey Jealous Lover; I Still Get Jealous; I'll Never Be Jealous Again; Jalousie (Jealousy); Jealous; Jealous Heart

Jean   Billie Jean; I'll Go Home with Bonnie Jean; Jean; Jean; Jeanie with the Light Brown Hair; Jeannie; Jeannine, I Dream of Lilac Time

Jeans, *see* **Dungaree**

Jed   Ballad of Jed Clampett

Jelly, *see* **Jam**

Jelly Roll   I Ain't Gonna Give Nobody None o' This Jelly Roll; Jelly Roll Blues

Jemima   Aunt Jemima (Silver Dollar); Aunt Jemima and Your Uncle Cream of Wheat

Jennie   867-5309/Jenny; Jennie Lee; Jennie, the Flower of Kildare; Little Jeannie; Meet Me Jenny When the Sun Goes Down; Pirate Jenny; Portrait of Jennie; Saga of Jenny; Sweet Jennie Lee

Jericho   Jericho; Joshua Fit (Fought) de Battle of Jericho

Jerk   Cool Jerk; The Jerk; Military Life, or, The Jerk Song

Jersey   Jersey Bounce

Jerusalem   Jerusalem; Jerusalem; Jerusalem the Golden

Jessie   Jesse; Jessie, the Flow'r o' Dumblane; Jessie's Girl; When the Harvest Days Are Over, Jessie Dear

Jesus   All Hail the Power of Jesus' Name; Beneath the Cross of Jesus; Crusader's Hymn, or, Fairest Lord Jesus; Jesus Christ

Superstar; Jesus, Lover of My Soul; (Jesus Keep Me) Near the Cross; Safe in the Arms of Jesus; Something for Jesus; Steal Away to Jesus; Trusting Jesus, That Is All; What a Friend We Have in Jesus

Jet, *see also* **Airplane** Bennie and the Jets; Jet; Jet Song; Leaving on a Jet Plane

Jewel Baubles, Bangles and Beads; Columbia, the Gem of the Ocean, or, The Red, White and Blue; (Theme from) Jewel in the Crown; The Jewel of Asia; Rhinestone Cowboy; Rich and Rare Were the Gems She Wore

Jezamine Jezamine

Jezebel Jezebel

Jill Jack and Jill

Jilt Jilted

Jim Dandy Jim of Carolines; Dinner for One, Please James; Goodbye Jimmy Goodbye; The James Bond Theme; Jim; Jim Along, Josey; (Jump) Jim Crow; Jimmy Crack Corn, or, The Blue Tail Fly; Jimmy Had a Nickel; (Look Out for) Jimmy Valentine; Jimtown Blues; Lucky Jim; Railroad Jim; St. James Infirmary; They Were All Out of Step But Jim; While the Angelus Was Ringing, or, The Three Bells, or, The Jimmy Brown Song

Jinny Mammy Jinny's Jubilee

Jinx, *see* **Luck**

Jitters, *see* **Shake**

Jive The G.I. Jive; Java Jive; Jive Talkin'; Jumpin' Jive

Joan Joan of Arc, They Are Calling You

Joanna Joanna; Joanna

Job, *see* **Work**

Jockey, *see* **Horse**

Joe Don't Cry, Joe; Happiness Is (Just) a Thing Called Joe; Hold 'Em Joe; I Came Here To Talk for Joe; Joe Turner Blues; Just a Kid Named Joe; Mexican Joe; Ode to Billy Joe; Old Black Joe; Ragtime Cowboy Joe; Shoeless Joe from Hannibal, Mo.; Take It Slow, Joe

Joey Joey; Joey, Joey, Joey; Run Joey Run

Jog, *see* **Run**

John Abraham, Martin and John; "Algy," the Piccadilly Johnny with the Little Glass Eye; Big Bad John; Dear John Letter; (What Shall We Do with) The Drunken Sailor, or, Columbus, or, John Brown Had a Little Injun, or, Ten Little Indians; Frankie and Johnnie (Johnny) (Were Lovers); John and Julie; John Anderson, My Jo; (The Wreck of the) John B; John Brown's Body; John Henry; The John Henry Blues; (D'Ye Ken) John Peel; Johnny Angel; Johnny Doughboy Found a Rose in Ireland; Johnny Get Your Gun; Johnny Is My Darling; Johnny Is the Boy for Me; Johnny One Note; Johnny Remember Me; Johnny Schmoker; Johnny's Theme, or, Here's Johnny; Oh Johnny, Oh Johnny, Oh!; Poor John; Sloop John B.; When Johnny Comes Marching Home; Where Do You Work-a John; Who's Johnny ("Short Circuit" Theme)

Join The Liberty Song, or, Come, Join Hand in Hand, or, In Freedom We're Born

Joint The Joint Is Jumpin'

Joker The Joker; The Joker

Jolly, *see* **Happy**

Jones Casey Jones; Davy Jones' Locker; F.D.R. (Franklin D. Roosevelt) Jones; Have You Met Miss Jones; The Jones Boy; Me and Mrs. Jones; Puddin' Head Jones; This Is the Army Mister Jones; We've Got To Keep Up with the Joneses

Jordan Roll, Jordan, Roll

Joseph Dance with Your Uncle Joseph

Josephine Come, Josephine, in My Flying Machine; Josephine; Josephine; Josephine, My Jo; Josephine Please No Lean on the Bell; Who Ate Napoleons with Josephine When Bonaparte Was Away

Joshua Josh-Ua; Joshua Fit (Fought) de Battle of Jericho

Josita Josita

Journey, *see* **Travel**

Jove The Origin of Gunpowder, or, When Vulcan Forg'd the Bolts of Jove

Joy, *see also* **Ecstasy** Joy to the World, or, Antioch; Joy to the World; Milenberg Joys; The Simple Joys of Maidenhood; Sing Joyous Bird

Juanita Juanita

Jubilation, Jubilee Alabama Jubilee; The Irish Jubilee; Jubilation T. Cornpone; Kingdom Coming, or, The Year of Jubilo; Mammy Jinny's Jubilee; We'll Have a Jubilee in My Old Kentucky Home

Jud Poor Jud (Is Daid)

Judy Judy in Disguise (with Glasses); Judy's Turn To Cry

Jug Little Brown Jug

Juice Plant a Watermelon on My Grave and Let the Juice Soak Through

Juke Box, *see* **Record**

Julia Julia

Julie John and Julie; Oh Julie; When Julie Comes Around; The Wreck of the "Julie Plante"

Juliet Juliet; Juliet Bravo; Love Theme from Romeo and Juliet, or, A Time for Us; Romeo and Juliet

Julio Me and Julio Down by the Schoolyard

July Sleigh Ride in July

Jump (Jump) Jim Crow; The Joint Is Jumpin'; Jump; Jump (For My Love); Jump Over; Jumpin' at the Woodside; Jumping Bean; Jumpin' Jive; Keep-A-Hoppin'; One O'Clock Jump

June (I Like New York in June) How About You; In the Merry Month of June; June Brought the Roses; June Comes Around Every Year; (It's) June in January; June Is Bustin' Out All Over; June Moon; June Night (Just Give Me a June Night, the Moonlight and You); Memphis in June; (Give Me) A Night in June; One Night in June

Jungle Chant of the Jungle; Down in Jungle Town; Jungle Boogie; Jungle Drums (Canto Karabali); Moving Day in Jungle Town; Surfin' Safari

Kaiser I'd Like To See the Kaiser with a Lily in His Hand

Kalamazoo I've Got a Gal in Kalamazoo

Kangaroo The Tale of the Kangaroo; Tie Me Kangaroo Down Sport

Kansas Kansas City; Kansas City; Kansas City Kitty; Kansas City Lights

Kate I Wish I Could Shimmy Like My Sister Kate; Katie Went to Haiti; Katinka; Katinka; Kattie (Katty) Avourneen; Katy Bell; K-K-K-Katy; When Kate and I Were Coming Thro' the Rye

Katherine Oh, Katharina

Kathleen I'll Take You Home Again Kathleen; Kathleen; Kathleen Mavourneen

Keg, *see* **Barrel**

Kelly Careless (Kelly's) Love; Has Anybody Here Seen Kelly; If I Knock the ''L'' out of Kelly; Nellie Kelly, I Love You; On Mother Kelly's Doorstep; Pete Kelly's Blues; Pretty Kitty Kelly; Slide Kelly Slide

Kent Knocked 'Em in the Old Kent Road

Kentucky Clare De Kitchen, or, De Kentucky Screamer; The Hunters of Kentucky; Kentucky; Kentucky Babe; Kentucky Sue; Kentucky Waltz; My Old Kentucky Home (Good Night); Real Goodness from Kentucky Fried Chicken; She Was Bred in Old Kentucky; Sweet Kentucky Lady; Tuck Me To Sleep in My Old 'Tucky Home; We'll Have a Jubilee in My Old Kentucky Home

Kettle Be Like the Kettle and Sing; Polly Put the Kettle On; The Old Kitchen Kettle

Key, *see also* **Piano** Brand New Key; Key Largo

Khartoum Khartoum

Kick Alive and Kicking; I Get a Kick Out of You; Kickin' the Clouds Away; Kickin' the Gong Around; Kicks; (Get Your Kicks on) Route 66; They Gotta Quit Kickin' My Dog (Dawg) Around, or, The Missouri Houn' Dawg Song; You Mustn't Kick It Around

Kid The Cisco Kid; Glory of Love (Theme from *The Karate Kid Part II*); I Love, I Love, I Love My Wife, But Oh You Kid; I Love My Wife, But Oh You Kid; Just a Kid Named Joe; Kid Days; Kids; My Kid's a Crooner; Wond'rous Love, or, Captain Kidd, or, Through All the World

Kill, *see also* **Murder** Killer Queen; Killing Me Softly with His Song; Overkill; Video Killed the Radio Star; A View to a Kill

Killarney Christmas in Killarney; How Can You Buy Killarney; Killarney; The Rose of Killarney

King All the King's Horses; L'Arlèsienne (March of the Kings); The Birthday of a King; Come, Thou Almighty King; Gentlemen, the King; God Save the King (Queen); Good King Wenceslas; I Am the Monarch of the Sea; I Wonder What the King Is Doing Tonight; If I Ruled the World; If I Were King; King Cotton March; King for a Day; King of Pain; King of the Road; King Porter Stomp; The King's Horses; The King's Navee; Old King Cole; Tell It Out Among the Nations (Heathen) That the Lord Is King; Waltz Huguette, or, The Vagabond King Waltz; We Three Kings of Orient (Are); When You Are a King; Your King and Country Want You

Kingdom Kingdom Coming, or, The Year of Jubilo; We'll Have a Kingdom

Kiss Ain't Gonna Kiss You; Any Little Kiss; Any Time Is Kissing Time; Il Bacio, or, The Kiss Waltz; Besame Mucho (Kiss Me Much); Between a Kiss and a Sigh; Botch-A-Me; Candy Kisses; Coffee in the Morning, Kisses at Night; Did You Close Your Eyes (When We Kissed); Gimme a Little Kiss, Will Ya, Huh?; Good Night, Nurse (Kiss Your Little Patient); Hold Me, Thrill Me, Kiss Me; Hugs and Kisses; I Don't Want Your Kisses; I Kiss Your Hand, Madame; ('Til) I Kissed You; I Saw Mommy Kissing Santa Claus; I Still Love To Kiss You Goodnight; I Threw a Kiss in the Ocean; I Was Never Kissed Before; I Wonder Who's Kissing Her Now; I'm Missin' Mammy's Kissin'—And I Know She's Missin' Mine; In the Middle of a Kiss; Kiss; The Kiss; Kiss a Four Leaf Clover; Kiss an Angel Good Mornin'; Kiss and Let's Make Up; Kiss and Run; Kiss and Say Goodbye; Kiss Her Now; A Kiss in the Dark; Kiss Me; Kiss Me Again, or, If I Were on the Stage; Kiss Me, Honey, Do; Kiss Me, Honey Honey, Kiss Me; Kiss Me, My Honey, Kiss Me; Kiss Me Sweet; Kiss of Fire; Kiss on My List; The Kiss That You've Forgotten (Is the Kiss I Can't Forget); Kiss the Boys Goodbye; A Kiss To Build a Dream On; The Kiss Waltz; Kiss You All Over; Kisses Sweeter Than Wine; Kisses—The Sweetest Kisses of All; Last Kiss; Let's Kiss and Make Up; A Little Kiss Each Morning, a Little Kiss Each Night; (Just) A Little Love, a Little Kiss; Mama from the Train, or, A Kiss, A Kiss; Mamie, Come Kiss Your Honey; Mister Kiss Kiss Bang Bang; My Beautiful Lady, or, The Kiss Waltz; Na Na Hey Hey Kiss Him Goodbye; One Kiss; One More Kiss; Ooh That Kiss; Paper Kisses; Peckin'; A Penny a Kiss, A Penny a Hug; Prelude to a Kiss; Pucker Up Your Lips, Miss Lindy; Red Lips Kiss My Blues Away; Red Neckin' Love Makin' Night; Save Your Kisses for Me; Seal It with a Kiss; Sealed with a Kiss; A Sinner Kissed an Angel; Teach Me How To Kiss; Then He Kissed Me; They Kissed, I Saw Them Do It; This Year's Kisses; Throw Me a Kiss; We Kiss in a Shadow; When You First Kissed the Last Girl You Loved; Where the Twilight Comes To Kiss the Rose Goodnight; Why Did I Kiss That Girl

Kitchen Clare De Kitchen, or, De Kentucky Screamer; Come Out of the Kitchen, Mary Ann; I've Been Working on the Railroad, or, The Levee Song, or, Someone's in the Kitchen with Dinah; The Old Kitchen Kettle

Kite Being for the Benefit of Mister Kite; Go Fly a Kite

Kitten, *see* **Cat**

Kitty Kansas City Kitty; Kitty the Telephone Girl; Pretty Kitty Kelly

Knee Knees Up Mother Brown; Would You Rather Be a Colonel with an Eagle on Your Shoulder, or a Private with a Chicken on Your Knee?

Knife Dagger Dance; Mack the Knife, or, Theme from The Threepenny Opera, or, Morit'at; Sabre Dance; The Sword of Bunker Hill; The Valley of Swords; Where the Chicken Got the Axe

Knight Knights of the Mystic Star; Knightsbridge March, or, In Town Tonight; My White Knight

Knock Blow (Knock) the Man Down; (It's) The Hard-Knock Life; I Hear You Knocking; If I Knock the ''L'' out of Kelly; Knock, Knock, Who's There; Knock, Knock, Who's There; Knock on Wood; Knock on Wood; Knock Three Times; Knocked 'Em in the Old Kent Road; Knockin' on Heaven's Door; One of the Ruins That Cromwell Knocked About a Bit; Rap Tap on Wood; Stop Dat Knocking at My Door; We'll Knock the Heligo—Into Heligo—Out of Heligoland; Whar

Did You Cum From, or, Knock a Nigger Down; When a Maid Comes Knocking at Your Heart

Knot   A Knot of Blue

Kodachrome, *see* **Photograph**

Lace   Chantilly Lace; Leather and Lace

Lad, *see* **Boy**

Ladder   Climbing Up the Ladder of Love; Ladder of Roses; The Man with the Ladder and the Hose

Lady, *see also* **Woman**   Ain't No Way To Treat a Lady; Beautiful Lady in Blue; Broken Lady; Chin Up, Ladies!; Dark Lady; Disco Lady; Eadie Was a Lady; Every Day Is Ladies' Day with Me; Good Night Ladies, or, Merrily We Roll Along; Goodbye, My Lady Love; Happy, or, Love Theme from Lady Sings the Blues; Hello, Hello, Who's Your Lady Friend; I Love the Ladies; Ladies in Waiting; Ladies Night; The Ladies Who Lunch; The Ladies Who Sing with the Band; Lady; Lady Bird; Lady Blue; The Lady from Twenty-Nine Palms; The Lady in Ermine; The Lady in Red; The Lady Is a Tramp; Lady Love Me One More Time; Lady Luck Show; Lady Madonna; Lady Marmalade; Lady of Spain; Lady of the Evening; Lady Play Your Mandolin; Lady Willpower; The Lady's in Love with You; Lay, Lady, Lay; Little Old Lady; Louisville Lou, the Vampin' Lady; Lovely Lady; Lovely Lady; Lovely Lady Let the Roses See You Today; Luck Be a Lady; Lydia the Tattooed Lady; Mother Was a Lady, or, If Jack Were Only Here; My Beautiful Lady, or, The Kiss Waltz; My Gal Is a High-Born Lady; My Lady Lou; My Lady Loves To Dance; Mystery Lady; The Naughty Lady of Shady Lane; Nelly Was a Lady; No Orchids for My Lady; Oh, Lady Be Good; Our Lady of Fatima; Pretty Lady; Red Roses for a Blue Lady; Shady Lady Bird; She's a Lady; Sigh No More, Ladies; Sing an Old-Fashioned Song (to a Young Sophisticated Lady); Sophisticated Lady; Special Lady; Strange Lady in Town; Sweet Kentucky Lady; Sweet Lady; Take a Seat, Old Lady; That Lady; Three Times a Lady; Two Ladies; Two Ladies in De Shade of De Banana Tree; Ukulele Lady; When a Lady Meets a Gentleman Down South; Why Lady Why; You Are My Lady

Lagoon   (By the) Sleepy Lagoon (Valse Serenade); Waters of Venice, or, Floating Down the Sleepy Lagoon

Laguna   Lily of Laguna

Lake   I Lost My Sugar in Salt Lake City; There's a Lovely Lake in London

Lamb, *see* **Sheep**

Lament   Adelaide's Lament; Five Hundred Miles, or, Railroader's Lament; The Lament of the Irish Emigrant; Streets of Laredo, or, The Cowboy's Lament

Lamp   Genie with the Light Brown Lamp; The Lamp Is Low; The Lamplighter's Serenade; The Lamplit Hour; Leaning on a Lamp Post; The Old Lamp-Lighter

Lancashire   She's a Lassie from Lancashire

Land   Alice in Wonderland; Bandana Land; Come to the Land of Bohemia; Dear Old Southland; (I Wish I Was in) Dixie, or, Dixie's Land; From the Land of the Sky Blue Water; God Bless Our Native Land; Graceland; Hello, Central, Give Me No Man's Land; Hit the Road to Dreamland; I'd Love To Live in Loveland (with a Girl Like You); In Shadowland; In the Land of Beginning Again; In the Land of Harmony; In the Louisiana Lowlands; The Land of Golden Dreams; The Land of Hope and Glory; The Land of Make Believe; The Land of My Best Girl; The Landing of the Pilgrims, or, The Pilgrim Fathers; Lotus Land; Lullaby of Birdland; Meadowlands, or, Cavalry of the Steppes; Meet Me in Bubble Land; Meet Me Tonight in Dreamland; Moonrise on the Lowlands; Never Never Land; Original Dixieland One-Step; The Rose of No-Man's Land; Shadowland; There's a Land of Begin Again; To the Land of My Own (Small) Romance; Toyland; We'll Knock the Heligo—Into Heligo—Out of Heligoland; When It's Night Time in Dixie Land; Winter Wonderland; Wonderful Land; Wonderland by Night; Woodland Sketches; Your Land and My Land

Landlord, *see* **Home**

Lane   Down Forget-Me-Not Lane; Happy Go Lucky Lane; It Looks Like Rain in Cherry Blossom Lane; It's a Long Lane That Has No Turning; The Little Old Log Cabin in the Lane; The Little White House (at the End of Honeymoon Lane); Memory Lane; The Naughty Lady of Shady Lane; Number Something Far Away Lane; Penny Lane; Swingin' Down the Lane; That Sly Old Gentleman from Featherbed Lane; There's a Little Lane Without a Turning on the Way to Home Sweet Home

Language, *see* **Talk**

Lantern, *see* **Light**

Laramie   The Man from Laramie

Laredo   Streets of Laredo, or, The Cowboy's Lament

Lark   Lo! Here the Gentle Lark; Mister Meadowlark; Skylark; 'Tis Dawn, the Lark Is Singing; Up With the Lark

Lass   I Love a Lassie, or, Ma Scotch Bluebell; It Was a Lover and His Lass; The Lass of Richmond Hill; The Lass with the Delicate Air, or, Young Molly Who Lives at the Foot of the Hill; She's a Lassie from Lancashire

Last   At Last; At Last; At Long Last Love; Cowboy Serenade, or, My Last Cigarette; Do You Remember the Last Waltz; First, Last and Always; First Love, Last Love, Best Love; Gone At Last; His Last Thoughts Were of You; I Couldn't Sleep a Wink Last Night; I Heard You Cried Last Night; I Won't Last a Day Without You; I'm the Last of the Red-Hot Mamas; Last Dance; Last Date; Last Farewell; The Last Hope; Last Kiss; Last Night I Didn't Get To Sleep At All; Last Night on the Back Porch—I Loved Her Best of All; Last Night Was Made for Love; Last Night Was the End of the World; Last Night When We Were Young; The Last of the Hogans; The Last Round-Up; The Last Thing on My Mind; The Last Time I Saw Paris; Last Train to Clarksville; The Last Waltz; My Last Date with You; My Last Goodbye; Save the Last Dance for Me; The Things We Did Last Summer; This Night Won't Last Forever; 'Tis the Last Rose of Summer; Too Beautiful To Last; Took the Last Train; 'Twas off the Blue Canaries, or, My Last Cigar; When They Sound the Last All Clear; When You First Kissed the Last Girl You Loved; Who Were You with Last Night; You're the First, the Last, My Everything

Late   Born Too Late; The Christmas Song, or, Christmas Don't Be Late; Have I Told You Lately That I Love You; I'm Late; It's Never Too Late To Fall in Love; It's Too Late; Late in the Evening; The Pardon Came Too Late; Spring Will Be a Little Late This Year; Too Late Now; Too Late for Goodbyes; Too Much, Too Little, Too Late; What Have You Done For Me Lately; Why Does It Get So Late So Early

Later   Dig You Later (A Hubba-Hubba-Hubba); Enjoy Yourself, It's Later Than You Think; See You Later Alligator; Sooner or Later (You're Gonna Be Comin' Around)

Latin   The Latin Quarter; She's a Latin from Manhattan

Lattice   Open Thy Lattice Love

Laugh   After My Laughter Came Tears; Always Leave Them Laughing When You Say Goodbye; City of Laughter, City of Tears; Don't Laugh at Me (,'Cause I'm a Fool); Ev'rybody Has a Laughing Place; Funny Way of Laughing; It All Belongs to You (The Laugh of the Town); Laugh and the World Laughs with You; Laugh, Clown, Laugh; Laughing Irish Eyes; Laughing on the Outside (Crying on the Inside); The Laughing Policeman; Laughing Water; Laughter in the Rain; Life, Love and Laughter; Live, Laugh and Love; Make 'Em Laugh; (Ho! Ho! Ha! Ha!) Me Too; Nancy (With the Laughing Face); Oh! How I Laugh When I Think How I Cried About You; They All Laughed; This Is No Laughing Matter; Twinkling Stars Are Laughing Love; Two Laughing Irish Eyes

Laundry   Chinese Laundry Blues; Dirty Laundry

Laura   Laura; Tell Laura I Love Her; Think of Laura

Laurie   Annie Laurie

Lavender, *see* **Blue**

Law, *see also* **Lawyer**   Do You Take This Woman for Your Lawful Wife?; Lawman; Legalize My Name; Love Touch (Theme from *Legal Eagles*); Mother-in-Law

Lawrence   (Theme from) Lawrence of Arabia

Lawyer   Doctor, Lawyer, Indian Chief

Lay   Lay Down (Candles in the Rain); Lay Down Sally; Lay Down Your Arms; Lay, Lady, Lay; Lay Your Hands on Me; Now I Lay Me Down to Sleep; While She Lays

Layla   Layla

Lazy   Lazy; Lazy Afternoon; Lazy Bones; Lazy Lou'siana Moon; Lazy Moon; (Up a) Lazy River; Those Lazy Hazy Crazy Days of Summer; Where the Lazy Daisies Grow

Lead   All Roads Lead to You; All the Way My Saviour Leads Me; Lead, Kindly Light; Lead Me On; Misled; One Thing Leads to Another; The Path That Leads the Other Way; The Pope He Leads a Happy Life; Walter, Walter (Lead Me to the Altar)

Leader   The Leader of the German Band; The Leader of the Pack; Why Did She Fall for the Leader of the Band

Leaf, *see* **Tree**

Lean   Lean On Me; Lean On Me; Leaning on a Lamp Post; Leanin' on the Ole Top Rail

Learn   Learn To Croon; Learn To Smile; Learn Your Lessons Well; Learnin' the Blues; Little Birdies Learning How To Fly; My Heart Has Learned To Love You, Now Do Not Say Goodbye; Since Maggie Dooley Learned the Hooley Hooley; When Yankee Doodle Learns To Parlez Vous Francais

Leather   Leather and Lace

Leave, *see also* **Gone**   Always Leave Them Laughing When You Say Goodbye; Can I Leave Off Wearin' My Shoes; Come After Breakfast, Bring 'Long Your Lunch and Leave 'Fore Supper Time; Could I Leave You; Don't Ever Leave Me; Don't Leave Me, Dolly; Don't Leave Me This Way; Exodus; Fifty Ways To Leave Your Lover; The Free and Easy Hour of Parting; The Girl I Left Behind Me, or, Brighton Camp; Goodbye, Ol' Paint, or, I Ride an Old Paint, or, I'm a-Leavin' Cheyenne; The Hour of Parting; How Can I Leave Thee; I Leave My Heart in an English Garden; I Left My Hat in Haiti; I Left My Heart at the Stage Door Canteen; I Left My Heart in San Francisco; I Left My Sugar Standing in the Rain (and She Melted Away); I Long To See the Girl I Left Behind; I Wouldn't Leave My Little Wooden Hut for You; I'd Leave My Happy Home for You; I'd Rather Leave While I'm in Love; If Ever I Would Leave You; If You Leave; If You Leave Me Now; I'm Gonna Pin My Medal on the Girl I Left Behind; I'm Leaving It All Up to You; Knowing When To Leave; Leave a Little Love; Leave a Tender Moment Alone; Leave It to Jane; Leave Me Alone (Ruby Red Dress); Leave Me with a Smile; Leaving on a Jet Plane; Left All Alone Again Blues; Left Right Out of Your Heart; Love Me or Leave Me; The One Rose That's Left in My Heart; The Photo of the Girl I Left Behind; She Went to the City; She's Leaving Home; Should've Never Let You Go; Softly As I Leave You; There's a Boat Dat's Leavin' Soon for New York; There's a Boy Coming Home on Leave; Until It's Time for You To Go; When Did You Leave Heaven; When I Leave the World Behind; When the Midnight Choo-Choo Leaves for Alabam'; Why Did I Leave My Little Back Room; Why Have You Left the One You Left Me For?; (Oh Why, Oh Why Did I Ever Leave) Wyoming; You Leave Me Breathless

Lee   Jennie Lee; Mandy Lee; (Who's Wonderful, Who's Marvelous?) Miss Annabelle Lee; Nancy Lee; Stagger Lee; Sweet Jennie Lee; Waiting for the Robert E. Lee; Washington and Lee Swing

Left, *see* **Leave**

Leg   Daddy Long Legs; Dummy Song, or, I'll Take the Legs from off the Table; Legs; Shinbone Alley

Legal, *see* **Law**

Legend, *see* **Story**

Legion   French Foreign Legion

Lei Lei   On the Shore at Lei Lei

Leicester   Leicester Square Rag

Leilani   Sweet Leilani

Lemon   A Lemon in the Garden of Love; Lemon Tree; Limehouse Blues; Serenade to a Lemonade; The Third Man Theme, or, The Harry Lime Theme

Lena   (Lena From) Palesteena

Leo   O Leo

Leroy   Bad Bad Leroy Brown

Lesson   The Dancing Lesson; The French Lesson; Learn Your Lessons Well; My Heart Is Taking Lessons; Six Lessons from Madame La Zonga

Letter   Dear John Letter; I'm Gonna Sit Right Down and Write Myself a Letter; The Letter; The Letter Song; Letter Song;

The Letter That Never Came; A Letter to a Soldier; Love Letters; Love Letters in the Sand; Please Mister Postman; P.S. I Love You; P.S. I Love You; Return to Sender; Strawberry Letter #23; Take a Letter, Maria; Three Wonderful Letters from Home

Levee Down in the Valley, or, Birmingham Jail, or, Bird in a Cage, or, Down on the Levee

Liberty Adams and Liberty, or, The Boston Patriotic Song; Belle, Belle, My Liberty Belle; The Liberty Belle; Liberty Bell—It's Time To Ring Again; The Liberty Song, or, Come, Join Hand in Hand, or, In Freedom We're Born; The Man Who Shot Liberty Valance

Library, *see* **Book**

Lie Baby I Lied; The Echo Told Me a Lie; How Could You Believe Me When I Said I Love You When You Know I've Been a Liar All My Life; It's a Sin To Tell a Lie; Lies; Little White Lies; Lyin' Eyes

Liechtenstein Liechtensteiner Polka

Lift, *see* **High**

Light, *see also* **Moonlight** After the Lights Go Down Low; Blinded by the Light; By the Light of the Silvery Moon; City Lights; Every Night There's a Light; Genie with the Light Brown Lamp; Harbor Lights; Heartlight; Hev Yew Gotta Loight, Boy?; The House of Blue Lights; I Saw the Light; I'm Beginning To See the Light; I'm Gonna Get Lit Up (When the Lights Go On in London); In the Morning by the Bright Light; Jeanie with the Light Brown Hair; Kansas City Lights; The Keeper of the Eddystone Light, or, The Eddystone Light; The Lamplighter's Serenade; The Lamplit Hour; Lead, Kindly Light; Let's Put Out the Lights and Go to Sleep; Light Cavalry (Overture); Light My Fire; The Light of Other Days; Lighterman Tom; Lightnin' Strikes; The Lightning Tree; Lights of Cincinnati; Lights Out; The Lord Is My Light; Love Light in Flight; The Night the Lights Went Out in Georgia; The Old Lamp-Lighter; On a Street of Chinese Lanterns; One Two Three Red Light; Party Lights; Row Thy Boat Lightly; Soft Lights and Sweet Music; Star Light, Star Bright; Starlight; Starlight; Starlight Serenade; Stella By Starlight; There's a Broken Heart for Every Light on Broadway; There's a Light in Your Eyes; Till the Lights of London Shine Again; Travellin' Light; Turn Out the Light; When Lights Are Low; When the Bell in the Lighthouse Rings Ding Dong; When the Lights Are Low; When the Lights Go On Again (All Over the World); Where Was Moses When the Lights Went Out; You Light Up My Life

Lilac Green Grow the Lilacs; Jeannine, I Dream of Lilac Time; The Lilac Tree, or, Perspicacity; Lilacs in the Rain; We'll Gather Lilacs; When the White Lilacs Bloom Again

Lillian Airy, Fairy Lillian; Lili (Lilli) Marlene; Lily Dale; Lily of Laguna; Lily of the Valley; Lily the Pink; Shanghai Lil; The Wedding of Lilli Marlene

Lily I'd Like To See the Kaiser with a Lily in His Hand; To a Water Lily

Limb, *see* **Tree**

Limbo Limbo Rock

Lime, *see* **Lemon**

Limit, *see* **End**

Linda Adios, Mariquita Linda; Linda

Lindy By the Watermelon Vine, Lindy Lou; Mah Lindy Lou; Pucker Up Your Lips, Miss Lindy

Line Borderline; Hot Line; I'm All Bound 'Round with the Mason-Dixon Line; On the Old Fall River Line; Our Love Is on the Fault Line; Rock Island Line; Telephone Line; Tired of Toein' the Line; Washing on the Siegfried Line; Wichita Lineman

Linger, *see also* **Stay** Let Me Linger Longer in Your Arms; Linger a Little Longer in the Twilight; Linger Awhile; Linger in My Arms a Little Longer Baby; Lingering Lovers; The Song Is Ended But the Melody Lingers On

Lining Look for the Silver Lining

Lion Don't Go in the Lions' Cage Tonight; The Lion and Albert; The Lion Sleeps Tonight, or, Wimoweh; Roar, Lion, Roar; Wondering Where the Lions Are

Lips, *see also* **Kiss** Hot Lips; I Wanna Hear It from Your Lips; If Those Lips Could Only Speak; Lipstick on Your Collar; No Other Arms, No Other Lips; Pucker Up Your Lips, Miss Lindy; Red Lips Kiss My Blues Away; The Touch of Your Lips

Lisa I'm Not Lisa; Mona Lisa; Mona Lisa; Tell Me Why You Smile Mona Lisa

Lisbon, *see also* **Portugal** Lisbon Antigua, or, In Old Lisbon

Listen, *see* **Hear**

Little "Algy," the Piccadilly Johnny with the Little Glass Eye; (In My Sweet Little) Alice Blue Gown; Amapola, or, Pretty Little Poppy; And a Little Bit More; Another Little Drink Wouldn't Do Us Any Harm; Any Little Girl, That's a Nice Little Girl, Is the Right Little Girl for Me; Any Little Kiss; Be My Little Baby Bumblebee; The (Little) Bird on Nellie's Hat; Brylcreem, A Little Dab'll Do Ya; Cheerful Little Earful; Coax Me a Little Bit; Come a Little Bit Closer; Crazy Little Thing Called Love; Cuddle Up a Little Closer, Lovey Mine; Daddy's Little Girl; Daddy's Little Girl; Dance Little Lady; Dear Little Boy of Mine; Dear Little Café; Dear Little Girl; Dream a Little Dream of Me; (What Shall We Do with) The Drunken Sailor, or, Columbus, or, John Brown Had a Little Injun, or, Ten Little Indians; Every Day a Little Death; Every Little Bit Added to What You've Got Makes Just a Little Bit More; Every Little Movement (Has a Meaning All Its Own); Every Little Thing She Does Is Magic; Ev'ry Little While; Ev'ry Little While; Fat Li'l' Feller Wid His Mammy's Eyes; Fly Home, Little Heart; Gimme a Little Kiss, Will Ya, Huh?; (Whoopee Ti Yi Yo) Git Along Little Dog(g)ies; Give a Little Credit to Your Dad; Give a Little Whistle; Give a Little Whistle; Give Me a Little Cosy Corner; Go Away Little Girl; Go, Little Boat; Good Night, Nurse (Kiss Your Little Patient); Goodbye, Little Girl, Goodbye; Goodbye, Little Girl of My Dreams; Goodnight, Little Girl, Goodnight; Happy Christmas, Little Friend; Have a Little Faith in Me; Have Yourself a Merry Little Christmas; Hello Little Girl; Hey Little Hen; A House with a Little Red Barn; How Little It Matters, How Little We Know; How We Know; How's Every Little Thing in Dixie; I Love the Little Things; I Say a Little Prayer; I Was a Good Little Girl Till I

Met You; I Wouldn't Leave My Little Wooden Hut for You; If You Catch a Little Cold; I'm a Little Bit Fonder of You; I'm a Little Blackbird Looking for a Bluebird; I'm Called Little Buttercup; I'm Gonna Love You Just a Little More Baby; I'm Sitting Pretty in a Pretty Little City; In a Little Gypsy Tea Room; In a Little Spanish Town; In My Little Bottom Drawer; In My Little Red Book; In My Little Snapshot Album; In My Own Little Corner; In Our Little Den of Iniquity; In the Little Red Schoolhouse; In Zanzibar—My Little Chimpanzee; It Costs So Little; It Only Hurts for a Little While; It Takes a Little Rain with the Sunshine To Make the World Go Round; I've Told Every Little Star; Just a Little Bit South of North Carolina; Just a Little Fond Affection; Just a Little Lovin'; Just a Little Rocking Chair and You; Keep a Little Cozy Corner in Your Heart for Me; Leave a Little Love; Leetle Bateese; Li'l Darlin' (Don't Dream of Anybody But Me); Li'l Liza Jane; A Lil' Ole Bitty Pissant Country Place; Li'l Red Riding Hood; Linger a Little Longer in the Twilight; Linger in My Arms a Little Longer Baby; Little Alabama Coon; Little Annie Roonie; A Little Bird Told Me; A Little Birdie Told Me So; Little Birdies Learning How To Fly; Little Biscuit; A Little Bit Independent; A Little Bit Me, A Little Bit You; A Little Bit of Heaven, Sure They Call It Ireland; A Little Bit of Soap; Little Bit o' Soul; Little Bit off the Top; Little Boy Blue; A Little Boy Called "Taps"; The Little Boy That Santa Claus Forgot; A Little Brains—A Little Talent; The Little Brown Church (in the Vale); Little Brown Jug; A Little Bunch of Shamrocks; Little by Little; Little Children; The Little Church Around the Corner; A Little Co-operation from You; The Little Damozel; Little Darlin'; Little David, Play on Your Harp; Little Devil; Little Dolly Daydream; Little Donkey; Little Drops of Rain; The Little Drummer Boy; The Little Drummer Boy; Little Dutch Mill; Little Footsteps; Little Girl; Little Girl; Little Girl Blue; A Little Girl from Little Rock; Little Girls; Little Girls, Good Bye; A Little Good News; Little Green Apples; Little Grey Home in the West; The Little Grey House; (With) A Little Help from My Friends; The Little House upon the Hill; Little in Love; Little Jack Frost Get Lost; Little Jeannie; A Little Kiss Each Morning, A Little Kiss Each Night; Little Lamb; The Little Lost Child; (Just) A Little Love, a Little Kiss; A Little Lovin'; Little Lulu; Little Man, You've Had a Busy Day; Little Mary Sunshine; Little Miss Lonely; Little Miss Melody; A Little More Love; Little Mother of Mine; A Little of What You Fancy; Little Old Lady; The Little Old Log Cabin in the Lane; Little Old Mill; Little Old Sod Shanty; A Little on the Lonely Side; Little One; Little Pink Petty from Peter; A Little Priest; Little Red Monkey; Little Red Rooster; Little Rock Getaway; The Little Shoemaker; Little Shop of Horrors; Little Sir Echo; Little Sister; Little Star, or, Estrellita; Little Star; (Just a) Little Street Where Old Friends Meet; Little Surplus Me, or, Surplus Blues; Little Things Mean a Lot; The Little Things You Do Together; The Little Things You Used To Do; (In My) Little Tin Box; Little Town in the Ould County Down; The Little White Bull; The Little White Cloud That Cried; Little White Cottage; The Little White Donkey; Little White Duck; A Little White Gardenia; The Little White House (at the End of Honeymoon Lane); Little White Lies; Little Yellow Bird; Lonely Little Robin; Love Me Little, Love Me Long; Love Sends a Little Gift of Roses; Ma Li'l Batteau; Mammy's (a) Little Coal Black Rose;

Mammy's Little Kinky-Headed Boy; Mammy's Little Pumpkin-Colored Coon; March from "A Little Suite"; Mary Had a Little Lamb; Mary, You're a Little Bit Old-Fashioned; The Men in My Little Girl's Life; I Love Little Pussy; Little Bo-Peep; Little Boy Blue; Little Jack Horner; Little Miss Muffet; Little Tommy Tucker; Mary Had a Little Lamb; Three Little Kittens; Move In a Little Closer Baby; My Dear Little Cingalee; My Little Buckaroo; My Little Deitcher Girl; My Little Georgia Rose; My Little Girl; My Little Grass Shack in Kealakekua, Hawaii; My Little Nest of Heavenly Blue, or, Frasquita Serenade (Blaues Himmelbett), or, Farewell, My Love, Farewell; My Little Town; Nobody's Little Girl; O Little Town of Bethlehem; Oh Where, Oh Where, Has My Little Dog Gone, or, Der Deitcher's Dog; Old Man Sunshine—Little Boy Bluebird; On a Little Street in Singapore; One Little Candle; Petite Fleur; Petite Tonkinoise; The Petite Waltz; Poor Little Angeline; Poor Little Fool; Poor Little Hollywood Star; Poor Little Rich Girl; A Precious Little Thing Called Love; Put a Little Love in Your Heart; Put Away a Little Ray of Golden Sunshine; Put On Your Ta Ta Little Girlie; Roam On (My) Little Gipsy Sweetheart; The Scandal of Little Lizzie Ford; She's the Fairest Little Flower Dear Old Dixie Ever Grew (Knew); Shine a Little Love; Sing Little Birdie; Six Little Wives; Some Little Bug Is Going To Find You (Some Day); Spread a Little Happiness; Spread a Little Sunshine; Spring Will Be a Little Late This Year; Such a Li'l Fellow; Sweet Little Buttercup; Sweet Little Sixteen; Take a Little Tip from Father; Take Me in Your Arms (Rock Me a Little While); Tell Me Little Gypsy; Ten Little Fingers and Ten Little Toes—Down in Tennessee; Ten Little Indians, or, Ten Little Injuns, or, Ten Little Niggers; Thank Heaven for Little Girls; There's a Little Lane Without a Turning on the Way to Home Sweet Home; There's a Little Spark of Love Still Burning; There's a Little Star Shining for You; This Little Piggie Went to Market; Three Little Fishes; Three Little Sisters; Three Little Words; 'Tis But a Little Faded Flower; Too Much, Too Little, Too Late; Try a Little Kindness; Try a Little Tenderness; Twinkle, Twinkle, Little Star, or, Ah! Vous Diraije Maman, or, ABCDEFG (The Alphabet Song); Twinkle, Twinkle, Little Star; Two Little Babes in the Wood; Two Little Baby Shoes; Two Little Bluebirds; Two Little Boys; Two Little Girls in Blue; Two Little Love Bees; Two Little Magpies; Wake Up Little Susie; We Néed a Little Christmas; (Ooh) What a Little Moonlight Can Do; When I Was a Little Cuckoo; When You've Had a Little Love You Want a Little More; Where the Shy Little Violets Grow; Who's Your Little Who-Zis; Whose Little Heart Are You Breaking Now; Why Did I Leave My Little Back Room; With a Little Bit of Luck; Won't You Be My Little Girl; You're a Million Miles from Nowhere When You're One Little Mile from Home; You're a Sweet Little Headache; You're (You'se) Just a Little Nigger, Still You're Mine, All Mine; Zing a Little Zong

Liverpool Long-Haired Lover from Liverpool

Liza All on Account of Liza; Goodbye, Liza Jane; I'se Your Nigger If You Want Me, Liza Jane; Li'l Liza Jane; Liza (All the Clouds'll Roll Away); Liza Johnson; Lizzie Borden

Load Get a Load of That; A Load of Hay

Lobster I'd Rather Be a Lobster Than a Wise Guy; The Lobster Quadrille

Lock, *see also* **Key**　Lock Up Your Daughters; Locked Out After Nine; Love Locked Out

Locker　Davy Jones' Locker

Lodging, *see* **Home**

Log, *see* **Wood**

Logic, *see* **Think**

Lola　Whatever Lola Wants

Lollipop, *see* **Candy**

London　I'm Gonna Get Lit Up (When the Lights Go On in London); London Bridge; London by Night; The London I Love; London Pride; Londonderry Air; Maybe It's Because I'm a Londoner; Streets of London; There's a Lovely Lake in London; Till the Lights of London Shine Again; The Worst Pies in London

Lone, *see also* **Alone**　Carry Me Back to the Lone Prairie; The Lone Fish (Meat) Ball; Oh, Bury Me Not on the Lone Prairie, or, The Dying Cowboy

Lonely, *see also* **Alone**　Don't Let Me Be Lonely Tonight; Have You Ever Been Lonely (Have You Ever Been Blue); I Pitch My Lonely Caravan At Night; I'm the Lonely One; Little Miss Lonely; A Little on the Lonely Side; Loneliness of Evening; Lonely; Lonely Ballerina; (I'm Just a) Lonely Boy; Lonely Boy; The Lonely Bull; Lonely Footsteps; The Lonely Goatherd; Lonely Heart; Lonely House; Lonely Little Robin; Lonely Night (Angel Face); Lonely Nights; Lonely Pup (in a Christmas Shop); Lonely Street; Mister Lonely; No More Lonely Nights; None But the Lonely Heart; Oh Baby Mine (I Get So Lonely); Only the Lonely (Know the Way I Feel); Owner of a Lonely Heart; Saturday Night Is the Loneliest Night of the Week; Sergeant Pepper's Lonely Hearts Club Band; Seven Lonely Days; Weeping, Sad and Lonely, or, When This Cruel War Is Over; You're Lonely and I'm Lonely

Lonesome, *see also* **Alone**　Are You Lonesome Tonight; I Know What It Means To Be Lonesome; I'm So Lonesome I Could Cry; I'm the Lonesomest Gal in Town; It's a Lonesome Old Town (When You're Not Around); Lonesome and Sorry; Lonesome in the Moonlight; (Look Down That) Lonesome Road; Look Down, Look Down That Lonesome Road; Oh Lonesome Me; There's a Million Girlies Lonesome Tonight, and Still I'm All Alone; The Trail of the Lonesome Pine; What Are We Doing Lonesome

Long　All Night Long (All Night); All the Live-Long Day (and the Long, Long Night); Alone Too Long; As Long as He Needs Me; As Long as I Live; As Long as I Live; As Long as I'm Dreaming; As Long as the Shamrock Grows Green; As Long as the World Rolls On; As Long as There's Music; As Long as You're Not in Love with Anyone; At Long Last Love; (It's) Been a Long Day; (They Long To Be) Close to You; Daddy Long Legs; Don't Stay Away Too Long; Dreams of Long Ago; ''Forever'' Is a Long, Long Time; Good-Bye, Ma! Good-Bye, Pa! Good-Bye, Mule, or, Long Boy; Happy As the Day Is Long; How Long; How Long Has This Been Going On; How Long, How Long Blues; I Long To See the Girl I Left Behind; I May Be Gone for a Long, Long Time; I'll Get By (as Long as I Have You); It Takes a Long, Tall, Brown-Skin Gal; It's a Long Lane That Has No Turning; It's a Long (Long) Way to Tipperary; It's Been a Long, Long Time; It's Been So Long; I've a Longing in My Heart for You, Louise; I've Loved You for a Long Time; I've Waited

Honey, Waited Long for You; I've Waited So Long; Let Me Linger Longer in Your Arms; Let's Take the Long Way Home; Linger a Little Longer in the Twilight; Linger in My Arms a Little Longer Baby; Long Ago and Far Away; Long Ago in Alcala; The Long and Winding Road; Long Before I Knew You; Long Cool Woman (in a Black Dress); The Long Day Closes; Long-Haired Lover from Liverpool; Long Live Love; Long Long Ago, or, The Long Ago; (It's Gonna Be) A Long, Long Winter; Long Tall Glasses (I Can Dance); Long Tall Sally; Long Time Ago, or, Shinbone Alley; Long Train Runnin'; Longer; The Longest Time; The Longest Walk; The Longest Way 'Round Is the Sweetest Way Home; Longing for You; Longing for You; The Love I Long For; Love Me Little, Love Me Long; Memories Live Longer Than Dreams; My Dream Girl, I Loved You Long Ago; My Long-Tail Blue; No Night So Long; Sam, You Made the Pants Too Long; A Smile Will Go a Long, Long Way; So Long Dearie; So Long, Farewell; So Long (It's Been Good To Know Yuh); So Long Letty; So Long Mary; So Long, Oo-Long, How Long You Gonna Be Gone?; There's a Dixie Girl Who's Longing for a Yankee Doodle Boy; There's a Long, Long Trail; Through a Long and Sleepless Night; (Have I Stayed) Too Long at the Fair; 'Twas Not So Long Ago; When You're a Long, Long Way from Home; You Came a Long Way from St. Louis

Look, *see also* **Watch**　(Theme from) Against All Odds (Take a Look at Me Now); The Crystal Gazer; Don't Look at Me That Way; (Lookie, Lookie, Lookie) Here Comes Cookie; Hey Good Lookin'; Hey Look Me Over; How Did He Look; I Was Looking for My Boy, She Said, or, Decoration Day; If You Look in Her Eyes; I'm a Little Blackbird Looking for a Bluebird; I'm Looking for a Guy Who Plays Alto and Baritone and Doubles on a Clarient and Wears a Size Thirty-Seven Suit; I'm Looking for a Nice Young Fellow Who Is Looking for a Nice Young Girl; I'm Looking Over a Four Leaf Clover; I'm Looking Through You; It Looks (to Me) Like a Big Night Tonight; It's Beginning To Look (a Lot) Like Christmas; It's Dark on Observatory Hill; (Look Out for) Jimmy Valentine; Just Let Me Look At You; Life In a Looking Glass; Look At That Face; Look Down, Look Down That Lonesome Road; Look for a Star; Look for the Silver Lining; Look into Your Heart; The Look of Love; Look Through Any Window; Look Through My Window; Look to the Rainbow; Look What They've Done to My Song Ma; Look What You've Done to Me; Look Who's Dancing; Looking Around; Look At the World Through Rose-Colored Glasses; Looking Back; Looking for a Boy; Looking High, High, High; Lookin' Out My Back Door; Looks Like We Made It; Love Look Away; Lovely To Look At; Ma, Look At Charlie; Mama, Look a Booboo; Mirame Asi, or, Grant Those Glances, or, Look At Me; Momma Look Sharp; My Faith Looks Up to Thee; My Word You Do Look Queer; Oh Look At Me Now; On the Outside Looking In; Peek-a-Boo; Search for Paradise; Search Is Over; Take That Look off Your Face; Things Are Looking Up; Things Are Looking Up; Thou Art Gone from My Gaze; To Look Sharp; The Way You Look Tonight; When I'm Looking at You; When You Look in the Heart of a Rose; Whoever You Are, or, Sometimes Your Eyes Look Blue to Me

Loose　Dance Me Loose; Every Which Way But Loose; Footloose; Mister Johnson, Turn Me Loose

Lord   Crusader's Hymn, or, Fairest Lord Jesus; Forever with the Lord; Holy! Holy! Lord God Almighty; I Ain't Gonna Grieve My Lord No More; The Lord Is My Light; Lord Randall; Lord Thomas and Fair Elinore; Lords of the Air; The Lord's Prayer; May the Good Lord Bless and Keep You; Milord; My Sweet Lord; Play That Barbershop Chord (Mister Jefferson Lord); Praise the Lord and Pass the Ammunition; ('Tis Me, O Lord) Standin' in the Need of Pray'r; Tell It Out Among the Nations (Heathen) That the Lord Is King; We Gather Together (To Ask the Lord's Blessing), or, Prayer of Thanksgiving; Were You There When They Crucified My Lord?

Lorelei   Lorelei

Lorena   Lorena

Lorraine   Lorraine, My Beautiful Alsace Lorraine; Sweet Lorraine

Los Angeles   Country Boy You Got Your Feet in L.A.

Lose   Born To Lose; Can't Get Used to Losing You; Does the Spearmint Lose Its Flavor on the Bedpost Overnight; Get Lost; I Almost Lost My Mind; I Don't Want To Lose Your Love; I Got Lost in His Arms; I Lost My Sugar in Salt Lake City; I Lost the Best Pal That I Had; I'd Be Lost Without You; If I Lost You; If I Should Lose You; I'm a Loser; I've Lost All My Love for You; Let's Get Lost; Little Jack Frost Get Lost; The Little Lost Child; Losing My Mind; Losing You; Lost; Lost Barber Shop Chord; The Lost Chord; Lost in a Fog; Lost in Love; Lost in Loveliness; Lost in the Fifties Tonight (In the Still of the Night); Lost in the Stars; The Love I Lost (Part I); Perdido (Lost); (Theme from) Raiders of the Lost Ark; Someone Could Lose a Heart Tonight; That Lost Barbershop Chord; Two Lost Souls; Waterloo; What Did I Have That I Don't Have; When I Lost You; When You Lose the One You Love; Where Am I; Where Am I Going; You're Gonna Lose Your Gal; You've Lost That Lovin' Feelin'

Lost, *see* **Lose**

Lotus   Lotus Land

Lou   Blue Lou; Brother Louie; By the Watermelon Vine, Lindy Lou; Louie Louie; Louisville Lou, the Vampin' Lady; Mah Lindy Lou; Mary Lou; My Honey Lou; My Lady Lou; Skip to My Lou; True Blue Lou

Loud   Actions Speak Louder Than Words

Louis   Everybody Loves Louis

Louisa   I Love Louisa

Louise   In the Evening by the Moonlight, Dear Louise; I've a Longing in My Heart for You, Louise; Louise

Louisiana   In the Louisiana Lowlands; Lazy Lou'siana Moon; Lou(i)siana Belle; Louisiana Hayride; Louisiana Purchase

Louisville   Headin' for Louisville; Louisville Lou, the Vampin' Lady

Lounge, *see* **Rest**

Lovely   Hurry It's Lovely Up Here; I Know a Lovely Garden; If There Is Someone Lovelier Than You; Isn't This a Lovely Day (To Be Caught in the Rain); It's a Lovely Day Today; It's De-Lovely; I've Got a Lovely Bunch of Cocoanuts; I've Had a Lovely Time; Lost in Loveliness; The Loveliest Night of the Year; The Loveliness of You; Lovely; Lovely; Lovely Lady; Lovely Lady; Lovely Lady Let the Roses See You

Today; Lovely Luana; A Lovely Night; Lovely Rita (Meter Maid); Lovely To Look At; (This Is) A Lovely Way To Spend an Evening; Mrs. Brown You've Got a Lovely Daughter; She's My Lovely; Thank You for a Lovely Evening; That Lovely Weekend; There's a Lovely Lake in London; This Is My Lovely Day; Tomorrow Is a Lovely Day; Two Lovely Black Eyes; Where Do You Go to My Lovely; Wouldn't It Be Lovely; You Were Never Lovelier

Lover   Casanova; Don Juan; Dream Lover; Dream Lover; Easy Lover; Everybody Loves a Lover; Far Off I Hear a Lover's Flute; Fifty Ways To Leave Your Lover; Frankie and Johnnie (Johnny) (Were Lovers); Friends and Lovers (Born To Each Other); Good-Bye, My Lover, Good-Bye; Hello, My Lover, Goodbye; Hello Young Lovers; Hey Jealous Lover; I Wanna Be Your Lover; I'm Just a Vagabond Lover; Imaginary Lover; It Was a Lover and His Lass; Jesus, Lover of My Soul; Lingering Lovers; Long-Haired Lover from Liverpool; Lover; Lover Come Back to Me; Lover Man (Oh Where Can You Be); Lover of My Dreams, or, Mirabelle Waltz; Loverboy; A Lover's Concerto; My Lover Is a Fisherman; My Restless Lover; No Tell Lover; Part Time Lover; Part-Time Lover; Secret Lovers; Theme for Young Lovers; There Goes My Lover; Too Many Lovers; Torn Between Two Lovers; When Your Lover Has Gone; (Theme from) Wives and Lovers; You Bring Out the Lover in Me

Low   After the Lights Go Down Low; Clancy Lowered the Boom; Doin' the New Low-Down; Doin' the Uptown Lowdown; (Fifteen Miles (Years) on the) Erie Canal (Low Bridge!—Everybody Down); Head Low; In the Louisiana Lowlands; The Lamp Is Low; The Low-Backed Car; Lowdown; Moanin' Low; The Moon Drops Low; The Moon Is Low; Moonrise on the Lowlands; My Resistance Is Low; Speak Low; Sweet and Low; Sweet and Low-Down; Swing High, Swing Low; Swing Low, Sweet Chariot; When Big Profundo Sang Low ''C''; When Lights Are Low; When the Lights Are Low

Luana   Lovely Luana

Luck, *see also* **Chance, Happy-Go-Lucky**   (I've Got) Beginner's Luck; Better Luck Next Time; Good Luck Charm; Good Luck, Good Health, God Bless You; Good-bye, Good Luck, God Bless You; How Lucky You Are; I Got Lucky in the Rain; If I'm Lucky; I'm Unlucky; Jolly Good Luck to the Girl Who Loves a Soldier; Lady Luck Show; Luck Be a Lady; Lucky Day; Lucky Five; Lucky in Love; Lucky Jim; The Lucky One; Lucky Seven; Lucky Star; Lucky To Be Me; Mahzel; (Mister) Mr. Lucky; My Lucky Star; My Lucky Star; Never Take the Horse Shoe from the Door; Rip Van Winkle Was a Lucky Man; Some Guys Have All the Luck; Swingin' the Jinx Away; That Lucky Old Sun; Three on a Match; Unlucky in Love; Wish Me Luck As You Wave Me Goodbye; With a Little Bit of Luck; You Are My Lucky Star

Lucy   I Love Lucy; Lucille; Lucy in the Sky with Diamonds; Lucy's Theme from Parish; Miss Lucy Neale; Put Your Shoes On, Lucy; Santa Lucia; Take Your Time, Miss Lucy

Lulu   Don't Bring Lulu; Little Lulu; Lulu's Back in Town

Lunch   Come After Breakfast, Bring 'Long Your Lunch and Leave 'Fore Supper Time; The Ladies Who Lunch

Lush, *see also* **Alcohol**   Lush Life

Lust   The Lusty Month of May

Lute, *see* **Guitar**

Luther   Away in (a) the Manger, or, Luther's Cradle Hymn

Luxembourg   In the Luxembourg Gardens

Lydia   Love for Lydia; Lydia; Lydia the Tattooed Lady

Machine   Automatic; Come, Josephine, in My Flying Machine; Dancing Machine; Music Machine; Silver Dream Machine

Mack   Mack the Knife, or, Theme from the Threepenny Opera, or, Morit'at

Mad   It's a Mad, Mad, Mad, Mad World; Mad About the Boy; Mad About You; Mad Dogs and Englishmen; Manhattan Madness; Sweet Madness; You Call It Madness (Ah, But I Call It Love)

Madame   Flowers for Madame; I Kiss Your Hand, Madame; Six Lessons from Madame LaZonga

Madeleine   Madeleine; Paddlin' Madelin' Home

Madelon   Madelon

Mademoiselle   Hinky Dinky Parlay Voo, or, Mad'moiselle from Armentières; The Little Damozel; Mademoiselle de Paris; Mam'selle

Madness, *see* **Mad**

Madonna   Lady Madonna; My Moonlight Madonna

Madrid   Madrid

Maestro, *see* **Music**

Magazine   The Girl on the Magazine Cover; The Girl on the Police Gazette

Maggie   I Never See Maggie Alone; Maggie May; Maggie May/ Reason To Believe; Maggie Murphy's Home; Maggie, the Cows Are in the Clover; Since Maggie Dooley Learned the Hooley Hooley; When You and I Were Young, Maggie

Magic, *see also* **Ghost**   Abracadabra; Aladdin; Aquarius; Could It Be Magic; The Crystal Gazer; Danse Macabre; Ding Dong! The Witch Is Dead; Do You Believe in Magic; Every Little Thing She Does Is Magic; The Fortune Teller; Four Dances from Aladdin; Genie with the Light Brown Lamp; Grandpa's Spells; He's the Wizard; Hocus Pocus; It's Magic; Knight of the Mystic Star; Love (Your Magic Spell Is Everywhere); Magic; Magic; Magic Is the Moonlight; Magic Man; Magic Moments; The Magic of Your Eyes; Magic To Do; (You've Got) The Magic Touch; Magical Mystery Tour; Pinball Wizard; Puff the Magic Dragon; Shazam; The Sorcerer's Apprentice; South Sea Island Magic; (Theme from) Spellbound; Strange Magic; That Old Black Magic; We're Off To See the Wizard; The Wheel of Fortune; Witch Doctor; Witchcraft; You Can Do Magic

Magnificent   C'est Magnifique; (Theme from) The Magnificent Seven

Magnolia   Where the Sweet Magnolias Grow

Magpie   Two Little Magpies

Mahogany, *see* **Wood**

Maid   Everybody Ought To Have a Maid; Lovely Rita (Meter Maid); My San Domingo Maid; Sweetest Maid of All; The Waiter and the Porter and the Upstairs Maid; When a Maid Comes Knocking at Your Heart; Why Am I Always the Bridesmaid

Maiden   Gypsy Maiden; Like a Virgin; The Maiden with the Dreamy Eyes; A Maiden's Prayer; The Simple Joys of Maidenhood; Tell Me Pretty Maiden (Are There Any More at Home Like You)

Mail, *see* **Letter**

Maine   (Maine) Stein Song

Major   The Company Sergeant Major; The Galloping Major; My Friend the Major; The Toy Drum Major; When the Sergeant Major's on Parade

Male, *see* **Man**

Malinda   Malinda

Mall   Down the Mall; On the Mall

Malone   Cockles and Mussels, Alive, Alive, O!, or, Sweet Molly Malone; Nora Malone (Call Me by Phone)

Mame   Mame; Mamie (Don't You Feel Ashamie); Mamie, Come Kiss Your Honey; Put the Blame on Mame

Mammy   Coal Black Mammy; The Coal Black Rose; Fat Li'l' Feller Wid His Mammy's Eyes; I Never Had a Mammy; I'd Love To Fall Asleep and Wake Up in My Mammy's Arms; I'm Missin' Mammy's Kissin'—and I Know She's Missin' Mine; Mammy Jinny's Jubilee; Mammy o' Mine; Mammy's Chocolate Soldier; Mammy's (a) Little Coal Black Rose; Mammy's Little Kinky-Headed Boy; Mammy's Little Pumpkin-Colored Coon(s); My Mammy

Mamou   Big Mamou

Man, *see also* **Fellow, Gentleman, Guy**   Aqua Velva Man; Ask the Man in the Moon; Baby You're a Rich Man; The Bad Humor Man; Ballad of a Crystal Man; The Big Butter and Egg Man; Big Man; Blow (Knock) the Man Down; Brotherhood of Man; The Candy Man; Can't Help Lovin' Dat Man; The Chinaman's Song; A Couple of Song and Dance Men; The Daring Young Man (on the Flying Trapeze); De Boatman's Dance; For All Mankind (Theme from *Gandhi*); For Every Man There's a Woman; Frosty the Snow Man; Give a Man a Horse He Can Ride; A Good Man Is Hard To Find; Guitar Man; Gypsy Man; Handy Man; Harding, You're the Man for Us; The Heart of a Man; Hello, Central, Give Me No Man's Land; Home Lovin' Man; Hurdy Gurdy Man; I Hate Men; I Want a Man; I Want a Military Man; I Want To Marry a Male Quartet; I Want To Marry a Man; I Wonder Where My Lovin' Man Has Gone; Ice Cream Man; I'll Make a Man of You; I'll Tell the Man in the Street; I'm a Popular Man; I'm an Airman; I'm an Ordinary Man; I'm Gonna Wash That Man Right Outa My Hair; I'm the Urban Spaceman; I'm Your Boogie Man; I'm Your Man; An Innocent Man; It's Great To Be a Soldier Man; It's So Nice To Have a Man Around the House; The Japanese Sandman; Jazz Man; Just a Girl That Men Forget; Lawman; Lighterman Tom; Listen to What the Man Said; Little Man, You've Had a Busy Day; Lover Man (Oh Where Can You Be); Mad Dogs and Englishmen; Magic Man; Make the Man Love Me; A Man and a Woman; A Man Chases a Girl; The Man from Laramie; (Theme from) The Man from U.N.C.L.E.; The Man I Love; Man in a Raincoat; Man in the Moon; Man of La Mancha; Man of My Heart; Man of Mystery; Man on Your Mind; The Man That (Who) Broke the Bank at Monte Carlo; The Man

That Got Away; Man to Man Talk; The Man Who Shot Liberty Valance; The Man with the Golden Arm; The Man with the Ladder and the Hose; A Man Without Love; Maneater; March of the Men of Harlech; Matchstalk Men and Matchstalk Cats and Dogs; The Men in My Little Girl's Life; Milkman Keep Those Bottles Quiet; Mister Sandman; Mister Tambourine Man; My Lovin' Honey Man; My Man; My Man's Gone Now; My Old Man's a Dustman; My Sweetheart's the Man in the Moon; My Very Good Friend the Milkman; Nowhere Man; An Occasional Man; Ol' Man Mose; Ol' Man River; Old Man Sunshine—Little Boy Bluebird; The Other Man's Grass (Is Always Greener); Our Lodger's Such a Nice Young Man; Pedro the Fisherman; Piano Man; Pirate Song, or, Fifteen Men on a (the) Dead Man's Chest—Yo! Ho! Ho! and a Bottle of Rum; Please Don't Take My Lovin' Man Away; Please Mister Postman; Poetry Man; The Policeman's Holiday; (I'm) Popeye the Sailor Man; Ramblin' Man; Rip Van Winkle Was a Lucky Man; Rock with the Cavemen; The Rose of No Man's Land; Rubberband Man; Sam, the Old Accordion Man; Son of a Preacher Man; Son of a Travelin' Man; Song of the Volga Boatman (Boatmen); Soul Man; St. Elmo's Fire (Man in Motion); Stand By Your Man; Stouthearted Men; There'll Be a Hot Time for the Old Men When the Young Men Go to War; The Third Man Theme, or, The Harry Lime Theme; This Old Man, or, The Children's Marching Song (Nick, Nack, Paddy Whack); Too Good for the Average Man; Travelin' Man; The Umbrella Man; A Utah Man Am I; Walk Like a Man; When a Man Loves a Woman; When a Woman Loves a Man; Where Did My Snowman Go; Wichita Lineman; Wild Man Blues; Woodman Spare That Tree; Woodman, Woodman, Spare That Tree; The Yama Yama Man; Yesterday Man; You Are Woman (I Am Man); You Can't Get a Man with a Gun; You Can't Keep a Good Man Down; You Naughty, Naughty Men; A Young Man's Fancy; You're a Good Man, Charlie Brown

Manaña, *see* **Tomorrow**

Manchester   Manchester

Mandalay   Mandalay; On the Road to Mandalay

Mandolin   Lady Play Your Mandolin; Mandolin Serenade; Mandolins in the Moonlight

Mandy   Come Along My Mandy; Mandy; Mandy; Mandy 'n' Me; Mandy Lee; Mandy Make Up Your Mind

Manager   Away in (a) the Manager, or, Luther's Cradle Hymn

Mango   Mangos

Manhattan, *see* **New York**

Mansion, *see* **House**

Maple, *see* **Tree**

Marble   I Dreamt I Dwelt in Marble Halls; Round the Marble Arch

Mardi Gras   Come to the Mardi Gras

Mare, *see* **Horse**

Margarita   I Once Had a Heart, Margarita; Ma Belle Marguerita; Margaritaville; Marguerite

Margery   See, Saw, Margery Daw

Margie   Margie

Maria   Ave Maria; Ave Maria; Maria; Maria; Maria Elena; Maria My Own; Maria Wiegenlied; My Maria; My Mariuc-

cia Take a Steamboat; Take a Letter, Maria; They Call the Wind Maria; Will You Marry Me Tomorrow, Maria

Marian   Marian the Librarian

Marianne   Marianne; Marianne

Marie   Goodbye Marie; Marie; Marie from Sunny Italy; Oui, Oui, Marie; Rose Marie; Sweet Marie; Tina Marie; When Sweet Marie Was Sweet Sixteen

Marigold   Marigold

Marijuana   Marahuana; The Reefer Song

Marine, *see* **Army**

Marionette, *see* **Puppet**

Market, *see* **Store**

Marmalade, *see* **Jam**

Marriage, *see also* **Bachelor, Divorce, Honeymoon, Mrs., Widow**   The Anniversary Song; The Anniversary Waltz; Band of Gold; The Bartered Bride (Overture); Because I'm Married Now (I Would If I Could But I Can't); The Bride Elect; Carrie, or, Carrie Marry Harry; Do You Take This Woman for Your Lawful Wife?; Don't Marry Me; The Farmer in the Dell (The Bride Cuts the Cake); The Fatal Wedding; Get Me to the Church on Time; Getting Married Today; The Girl That I Marry; De Golden Wedding; Happy Anniversary; The Hawaiian Wedding Song; I Can Dance with Everyone But My Wife; I Love, I Love, I Love My Wife, But Oh You Kid; I Love My Wife, But Oh You Kid; I Married an Angel; I Wanna Get Married; I Want a Girl—Just Like the Girl That Married Dear Old Dad; I Want To Marry a Male Quartet; I Want To Marry a Man; I Went to Your Wedding; If Momma Was Married; I'll Be Happy When the Preacher Makes You Mine; I'll Dance at Your Wedding; I'm Gonna Get Married; It's Delightful To Be Married; Love and Marriage; The Marriage of Figaro (Overture); Married; Married I Can Always Get; Marry Me; Marrying for Love; Matchmaker, Matchmaker; The Merry Wives of Windsor (Overture); The Monkey's Wedding; My Husband Makes Movies; My Wife's Gone to the Country (Hurrah! Hurrah!); My Woman, My Woman, My Wife; No Wedding Bells for Me; O Soldier, Won't You Marry Me?; An Old-Fashioned Wife; Our Jackie's Getting Married; Six Little Wives; Soldier, Soldier, Won't You Marry Me?; Somebody Bad Stole De Wedding Bell; This Diamond Ring; Those Wedding Bells Shall Not Ring Out; Tony's Wife; Waiting at the Church, or, My Wife Won't Let Me; Walter, Walter, (Lead Me to the Altar); Wedding Bell Blues; Wedding Bells Are Breaking Up That Old Gang of Mine; The Wedding Glide; Wedding March; Wedding March (Bridal Chorus); The Wedding of Lilli Marlene; The Wedding of Mister Mickey Mouse; Wedding o' Sandy McNab; The Wedding of the Painted Doll; Wedding of the Rose; Wedding of the Winds; Wedding Ring; The Wedding Samba; When I Marry Mister Snow; When We Are M-a-double-r-i-e-d; When Your Old Wedding Ring Was New; When You're Wearing the Ball and Chain; Why Am I Always the Bridesmaid; Will You Marry Me Tomorrow, Maria; (Theme from) Wives and Lovers; The Yeoman's Wedding Song; You Must Meet My Wife

Marsh   Much Binding in the Marsh

Marshmallow   Marshmallow Moon; A Marshmallow World

Martha   Marta, or, Rambling Rose of the Wildwood

Martin Abraham, Martin and John; The Martins and the Coys

Marvelous I Went to a Marvelous Party; (Who's Wonderful, Who's Marvelous?) Miss Annabelle Lee; Too Marvelous for Words

Mary The Bells of St. Mary's; Bloody Mary; Come Out of the Kitchen, Mary Ann; Her Name Is Mary; I Love the Name of Mary; I'm Shy, Mary Ellen, I'm Shy; Keep Your Skirts Down, Mary Ann; Little Mary Sunshine; Mary; Mary Ann; Mary, Dear, Some Day We Will Meet Again; Mary Had a Little Lamb; Mary Lou; Mary of Argyle; Mary-Rose; Mary Rose; Mary, You're a Little Bit Old-Fashioned; Mary's a Grand Old Name; Mary's Boy Child; Mary's Dream, or, Sandy's Ghost; Mary's Tears; Mary Had a Little Lamb; Mistress Mary Quite Contrary; Oh, Mary, Don't You Weep, Don't You Mourn; Oh! What a Pal Was Mary; On the Good Ship Mary Ann; Proud Mary; Sally, Irene and Mary; So Long Mary; St. Mary's in the Twilight; Such an Education Has My Mary Ann, or, Sweet Mary Ann; Take a Day Off, Mary Ann; Tip-Top Tipperary Mary; When the War Is Over, Mary

Maryland Maryland, My Maryland, or, Tannenbaum, O Tannenbaum!; There's a Girl in the Heart of Maryland (with a Heart That Belongs to Me)

Mascot The Mascot of the Troop

Mash (Song from) M*A*S*H; Mashed Potato Time; Monster Mash

Mason-Dixon Line I'm All Bound 'Round with the Mason-Dixon Line

Masquerade Masquerade; (I'm Afraid) The Masquerade Is Over; Midnight Masquerade; Moonlight Masquerade; The Skidmore Masquerade; This Masquerade

Massachusetts Massachusetts; You Can't Chop Your Poppa Up in Massachusetts

Master Massa's in De Cold (Cold) Ground; Master Blaster (Jammin'); The Old Master Painter

Masterpiece Masterpiece

Match Match of the Day; Three on a Match

Matchmaker, *see* **Marriage**

Matelot Matelot

Matilda Matilda; Waltzing Matilda

Matter Country Matters; How Little It Matters, How Little We Know; It's Just a Matter of Time; No Matter How I Try; Oh! Dear, What Can the Matter Be; That's All That Matters; This Is No Laughing Matter; To Whom It Concerns; What Does It Matter; What's the Matter with Father

Maud Come into the Garden, Maud

Maverick Maverick

Maxim Maxim's Maxina; She Is Not Thinking of Me (Waltz at Maxim's)

May December and May, or, Mollie Newell Don't Be Cruel; The Lusty Month of May; Maggie May; Maggie May/Reason To Believe; Music in May (Careless Rapture); Now Is the Month of Maying; Oh That We Two Were Maying; On the Isle of May; One Morning in May; Will You Love Me in December As You Do in May; You're as Welcome as the Flowers in May

Maybellene Maybellene

Mayor Cockeyed Mayor of Kaunakakai

Meadow Bells Across the Meadow; Meadowlands, or, Cavalry of the Steppes; Mister Meadowlark; A Tree in the Meadow

Meat The Lone Fish (Meat) Ball; Oh Mama, or, The Butcher Boy; One Meat Ball

Medal I'm Gonna Pin My Medal on the Girl I Left Behind

Medicine I Want a New Drug; Love Potion Number Nine; Say! Have You Taken Your Medicine Yet?; A Spoonful of Sugar

Meet At a Georgia Camp Meeting; (Theme from) Close Encounters of the Third Kind; Comin' Thro' the Rye, or, If a Body Meet a Body; Gee, But It's Great To Meet a Friend from Your Old Home Town; God Be with You Till We Meet Again; Have a Smile (for Everyone You Meet); Have You Met Miss Jones; I Met Her on Monday; I Was a Good Little Girl Till I Met You; I'd Love To Meet That Old Sweetheart of Mine; I'm Awfully Glad I Met You; Liaisons; (Just a) Little Street Where Old Friends Meet; Mary Ann, Some Day We Will Meet Again; Meet Me at the Station, Dear; Meet Me by Moonlight Alone; Meet Me in Bubble Land; Meet Me in St. Louis, Louis; Meet Me Jenny When the Sun Goes Down; Meet Me on the Corner; Meet Me on the Corner; Meet Me Tonight in Dreamland; Meet Mister Callaghan; Meet the Family; The Meeting of the Waters of Hudson and Erie; She Was Happy Till She Met You; Since I Met You Baby; That Was Before I Met You; Till We Meet Again; Today I Met My Love; The Vacant Chair, or, We Shall Meet But We Shall Miss Him; We Two Shall Meet Again; When a Lady Meets a Gentleman Down South; When Shall We Meet Again; Where the Blue of the Night Meets the Gold of the Day; You Must Meet My Wife; You'll Meet Me, Won't You

Melancholy Away with Melancholy; My Melancholy Baby

Melba The Melba Waltz; Se Saran Rose, or, Melba Waltz

Melinda Me and My Melinda

Melisands Melisands in the Wood

Mellow Have You Never Been Mellow; Mellow Yellow; That Mellow Melody

Melody, *see also* **Tune** Broadway Melody; Broken-Hearted Melody; The Broken Melody; Dreamy Melody; Eleventh Hour Melody; Gypsy Melody; Hiawatha's Melody of Love; Just Like a Melody Out of the Sky; Little Miss Melody; Melodie d' Amour (Melody of Love); Melody; Melody from the Sea; A Melody from the Sky; Melody in F; Melody of Love; My Melody of Love; Our Favourite Melodies; Play a Simple Melody; A Pretty Girl Is Like a Melody; Put Me to Sleep with an Old-Fashioned Melody; Rock-a-Bye Your Baby with a Dixie Melody; The Song Is Ended But the Melody Lingers On; That Mellow Melody; Tokyo Melody; Unchained Melody

Melt I Left My Sugar Standing in the Rain (and She Melted Away); Melting Pot

Memory, *see also* **Forget, Remember** Dancin' Your Memory Away; I'm Stepping Out with a Memory Tonight; Just a Memory; Memories; Mem'ries, or, Golden Memory Days; Memories Are Made of This; Memories Live Longer Than Dreams; Memories of France; Memories of You; Memory; Memory Lane; Moonlight and Roses (Bring Me Mem'ries of

You); So Many Memories; Some Memories Just Won't Quit; Thanks for the Memory

Memphis   Going to Memphis; Memphis; The Memphis Blues; Memphis in June

Mend, *see* **Fix**

Mention   Oh No, We Never Mention Her; Please Don't Mention It

Mercy   Mercy Mercy Mercy

Mermaid   Ask Any Mermaid; Minnie the Mermaid, or, A Love Song in Fish Time

Merry   The Christmas Song, or, Merry Christmas to You, or, Chestnuts Roasting on an Open Fire; God Rest You Merry Gentlemen; Good Night Ladies, or, Merrily We Roll Along; Have Yourself a Merry Little Christmas; In My Merry Oldsmobile; In the Merry Month of June; Merrily We Roll Along; The Merry Swiss Boy; Merry Widow Waltz, or, I Love You So; The Merry Wives of Windsor (Overture); Merry Xmas Everybody; A Very Merry Un-Birthday to You

Merry-Go-Round, *see* **Carousel**

Mersey   Ferry 'Cross the Mersey

Mess   Messing About on the River; A Rockin' Good Way (To Mess Around and Fall in Love)

Message   The Message of the Violet; Message to Michael; Message Understood

Mexico   Mexicali Rose; Mexican Hat Dance; Mexican Joe; Mexico; South of the Border (Down Mexico Way)

Miami   Miami Beach Rumba; (Theme from) Miami Vice; Moon Over Miami; On Miami Shore, or, Golden Sands of Miami

Michael   Message to Michael; Michael (Row the Boat Ashore); Michael from Mountains; Michael's Theme; Mick McGilligan's Ball; Mickey; Mickey; The Wedding of Mister Mickey Mouse

Michelle   Michelle

Michigan   I Want To Go Back to Michigan—Down on the Farm

Middle   In the Middle of a Kiss; In the Middle of an Island; In the Middle of the Night; Round on the End and High in the Middle, O-hi-o; Stuck in the Middle (with You)

Midnight, *see also* **Twelve**   At Midnight on My Pillow Lying; Celery Stalks at Midnight; Everybody's Talkin', or, Theme from Midnight Cowboy; In the Midnight Hour; It Came upon a Midnight Clear; Midnight Blue; Midnight Cowboy; Midnight Fire-Alarm; Midnight in Moscow, or, Moscow Nights; Midnight in Paris; Midnight Masquerade; Midnight Sun; Midnight Train to Georgia; Take Me to the Midnight Cake Walk Ball; When the Midnight Choo-Choo Leaves for Alabam'

Mighty, *see* **Strong**

Mile   (Fifteen Miles (Years) on the) Erie Canal (Low Bridge!—Everybody Down); Five Hundred Miles, or, Railroader's Lament; Within a Mile of Edinburgh; You're a Million Miles from Nowhere When You're One Little Mile from Home

Milenberg   Milenberg Joys

Military   I Want a Military Man; Marche Militaire; Military Life, or, The Jerk Song; Polonaise Militaire

Milk   Let's Have a Tiddley at the Milk Bar; Milk and Honey; Milkman Keep Those Bottles Quiet; My Very Good Friend the Milkman; No Milk Today; Ole Buttermilk Sky

Mill, *see also* **Windmill**   Down by the Old Mill Stream; Little Old Mill; The Miller's Son; The Jolly Miller; Old Mill Wheel

Millie   Thoroughly Modern Millie

Million   Fifty Million Frenchmen Can't Be Wrong; Fifty Million Times a Day; A Hundred Million Miracles; I Found a Million Dollar Baby in a Five and Ten Cent Store; I See a Million People; Mister Moon, You've Got a Million Sweethearts; Never in a Million Years; Oh You Million Dollar Baby; Oh You Million Dollar Doll; One in a Million You; Thanks a Million; There's a Million Girlies Lonesome Tonight, and Still I'm All Alone; We've a Million in the Field; You're a Million Miles from Nowhere When You're One Little Mile from Home

Millionaire, *see* **Money**

Mimi   And Mimi; Mimi

Mind, *see also* **Think**   Always on My Mind; And the Grass Won't Pay No Mind; Back on My Mind Again; Can You Read My Mind; Can't Get Indiana off My Mind; Church of the Poison Mind; Did You Ever Have To Make Up Your Mind; Dixie on My Mind; Do You Mind; Fourteen Carat Mind; Gentle on My Mind; Georgia on My Mind; Got Her off My Hands (But Can't Get Her off My Mind); I Almost Lost My Mind; If You Could Read My Mind; If You Ever Change Your Mind; It Never Entered My Mind; I've Got You on My Mind; (The) Last Thing on My Mind; Losing My Mind; Mandy Make Up Your Mind; Man on Your Mind; Mind If I Make Love to You; My Heart Has a Mind of Its Own; Never Mind; Nineteenth Nervous Breakdown; Playground in My Mind; Suspicious Minds; The Windmills of Your Mind, or, Theme from The Thomas Crown Affair; You Were on My Mind

Mine   Don't Go Down the Mine; The Miner's Dream of Home; She Got the Goldmine I Got the Shaft; There's a Gold Mine in the Sky

Mink   The Lady in Ermine; Take Back Your Mink

Minnetonka   By the Waters of Minnetonka

Minnie   Minnie from Trinidad; Minnie the Mermaid, or, A Love Song in Fish Time; Minnie the Moocher, or, The Ho De Ho Song

Minor   That Minor Strain

Minstrel   Bring Back Those Minstrel Days; (To the War Has Gone) The Minstrel Boy; The Minstrel's Return from the War

Minute, *see* **Time**

Miracle   All I Need Is a Miracle; Gonna Take a Miracle; A Hundred Million Miracles; It's a Miracle; It's a Miracle; It's Gonna Take a Miracle; Make a Miracle; Miracle Song; Miracles; Miracles; Pocketful of Miracles

Mirage, *see* **Imagination**

Mirror   Life in a Looking Glass; The Music and the Mirror; Reflections; Reflections in the Water; Reflections on the Water; Texas in My Rear View Mirror

Misbehave   Ain't Misbehavin'; Let's Misbehave

Mischief Keepin' Out of Mischief Now

Misery Misery Farm

Miss Do They Miss Me at Home; Do You Know What It Means To Miss New Orleans; Good Golly Miss Molly; Have You Met Miss Jones; Heaven Must Be Missing an Angel; Hit and Miss; I Could Never Miss You (More Than I Do); I Miss My Swiss, My Swiss Miss Misses Me; I Miss You Most of All; I Wouldn't Have Missed It for the World; I'll Miss You in the Evening; I'll Only Miss Her When I Think of Her; I'm in Love with Miss Logan; I'm Missin' Mammy's Kissin'— and I Know She's Missin' Mine; Little Miss Lonely; Little Miss Melody; Little Miss Muffet; The Miss America Pageant; (Who's Wonderful, Who's Marvelous?) Miss Annabelle Lee; Miss Brown to You; Miss Celie's Blues (Sister); Miss Lucy Neale; Miss Marmelstein; Miss Me Blind; Miss Otis Regrets; Miss You; Miss You Nights; Missing You; Missing You; Little Miss Muffet; Oh! How I Miss You Tonight; Oh Miss Hannah; Pucker Up Your Lips Miss Lindy; Take Your Time, Miss Lucy; Willie We Have Missed You; You Never Miss the Water Till the Well Runs Dry, or, Waste Not, Want Not

Mission, *see* **Work**

Mississippi At the Mississippi Cabaret; M-I-S-S-I-S-S-I-P-P-I; Mississippi Mud; Mississippi Suite; Mister and Mississippi; On the Mississippi

Missouri The Missouri Waltz; Shenandoah, or, Across the Wide Missouri; Shoeless Joe from Hannibal, Mo.; They Gotta Quit Kickin' My Dog (Dawg) Around, or, The Missouri Houn' Dawg Song; Walkin' to Missouri

Mrs. Don't Have Any More, Mrs. Moore; The Future Mrs. 'Awkins; Me and Mrs. Jones; Mister and Mrs. Is the Name; Mrs. Brown You've Got a Lovely Daughter; Mrs. Robinson; Señora; Thank You So Much Mrs. Lowsborough—Goodbye; This Is the Missus; Who Threw the Overalls in Mrs. Murphy's Chowder

Mist In a Mist; In the Moon Mist; Misty; Misty Blue; Misty Islands of the Highlands; When the Mists Have Cleared Away; When the Mists Have Rolled Away

Mistake The Comedy of Errors; The Greatest Mistake of My Life; It's a Mistake; Mistakes

Mister Being for the Benefit of Mister Kite; Call Me Mister; Frog Went a-Courtin', or, Frog He Would a-Wooing Go, or, Mister Frog Went a-Courtin'; Good Morning, Mister Zip-Zip-Zip; Hey Mister Banjo; If You Can't Sing It You'll Have To Swing It (Mister Paganini); Meet Mister Callaghan; Mister and Mississippi; Mister (Mr.) and Mrs. Is the Name; Mister Big Stuff; Mister Blue; Mister Bo Jangles (Bojangles); Mister Cellophane; Mister Custer; Mister Dooley; Mister Dumpling; Mister Five by Five; Mister Gallagher and Mister Shean; Mister Goldstone; Mister Johnson, Don't Get Gay; Mister Johnson, Turn Me Loose; Mister Kiss Kiss Bang Bang; Mister Lonely; (Mister) Mr. Lucky; Mister Meadowlark; Mister Mistoffolees; Mister Moon You've Got a Million Sweethearts; Mister Sandman; Mister Tambourine Man; Mister Volunteer, or, You Don't Belong to the Regulars, You're Just a Volunteer; Mister Wonderful; Misto Cristofo Columbo; Monsieur Dupont; Play That Barbershop Chord (Mister Jefferson Lord); Please Mister Please; Please Mister Post-

man; Please Mister Sun; This Is the Army Mister Jones; The Wedding of Mister Mickey Mouse; When I Marry Mister Snow; Who Do You Think You Are Kidding Mister Hitler

Mistletoe, *see* **Christmas**

Mistress Mistress Mary Quite Contrary

Misty, *see* **Mist**

Mix Cement Mixer; Mixed Emotions

Moan Moanin'; Moanin' in the Mornin'; Moanin' Low

Mobile Mobile; On Mobile Bay

Mocking Bird Listen to the Mocking Bird; Mocking Bird; Mocking Bird Hill; When the Mocking Birds Are Singing in the Wildwood

Modern, *see* **New**

Mohawk, *see* **Indian**

Molly Cockles and Mussels, Alive, Alive, O!, or, Sweet Molly Malone; December and May, or, Mollie Newell Don't Be Cruel; Good Golly Miss Molly; The Lass with the Delicate Air, or, Young Molly Who Lives at the Foot of the Hill; Mollie Darling; Molly and I and the Baby; Molly O!, or, Mavourneen; Molly O'Morgan; Molly on the Shore; My Irish Molly O

Moment, *see* **Time**

Mona Mona Lisa; Mona Lisa; Oh Monah; Tell Me Why You Smile Mona Lisa

Monarch, *see* **King**

Monastery In a Monastery Garden; The Monastery Bells

Monday All Alone Monday; Blue Monday; First Thing Monday Mornin'; I Don't Like Mondays; I Met Her on Monday; Manic Monday; Monday Monday; Monday, Tuesday, Wednesday; Rainy Days and Mondays; Sunday, Monday or Always

Money, *see also* **Cost, Poor, Spend** Ain't Got a Dime to My Name; All for a Shilling a Day; Any Bonds Today?; Anyone Can Be a Millionaire; Are You Making Any Money; Aunt Jemima (Silver Dollar); Baby You're a Rich Man; Bad Penny Blues; Brother, Can You Spare a Dime; Dancing on a Dime; Dollar Princesses; Dreamer with a Penny; Fifteen Cents; The Five Cent Shave; Half a Sixpence; I Found a Million Dollar Baby in a Five and Ten Cent Store; I Want Some Money; If I Was a Millionaire; If I Were a Rich Man; If Money Talks, It Ain't on Speaking Terms with Me; The Income Tax Collector; I've Got Five Dollars; I've Got Sixpence (As I Go Rolling Home); Jimmy Had a Nickel; Love and a Dime; Mack the Knife, or, Theme from The Threepenny Opera, or, Morit'at; Minnie the Moocher, or, The Ho De Ho Song; Money (Money); Money for Nothing; Money Honey; The Money Song; The Money Tree; Sing a Song of Sixpence; Oh You Million Dollar Baby; Oh You Million Dollar Doll; Pennies from Heaven; A Penny a Kiss, A Penny a Hug; Penny Lane; Penny Lover; Penny Serenade; Poor Little Rich Girl; Rags to Riches; Rich and Rare Were the Gems She Wore; Rich Girl; 74 Cents; She Works Hard for the Money; Silver Dollar (Down and Out); Ten Cents a Dance; That's Where My Money Goes; This Is Worth Fighting For; Three Coins in the Fountain; We're in the Money, or, The Gold Diggers' Song; When the Idle Poor Become the Idle Rich; When the Values Go Up;

When You Ain't Got No Money, Well, You Needn't Come Around; Who Wants To Be a Millionaire; With Plenty of Money and You; The World Owes Me a Living; You Dropped Me Like a Red Hot Penny

Monkey   And the Monkey Wrapped Its Tail Around the Flagpole; I'd Love To Be a Monkey in the Zoo; In Zanzibar—My Little Chimpanzee; Little Red Monkey; Monkey Doodle Dandy; The Monkey's Wedding; The Toy Monkey, or, I'm a Monkey on a Stick

Monotonous   Monotonous

Monsieur, *see* **Mister**

Monster   Monster Mash

Monte Carlo   The Man That (Who) Broke the Bank at Monte Carlo

Monterey   It Happened in Monterey

Month   Eleven More Months and Ten More Days; In the Merry Month of June; The Lusty Month of May; Now Is the Month of Maying

Mood   Can't Get Out of This Mood; I Was in the Mood; I'm in a Dancing Mood; I'm in the Mood for Dancing; I'm in the Mood for Love; In a Party Mood; In a Sentimental Mood; In the Mood; Mood Indigo; Moody River; Moonlight Mood; Sunny Disposish

Moon   The Alabama Song, or, Moon of Alabama; Allegheny Moon; Ask the Man in the Moon; Bad Moon Rising; Blue Moon; Blue Moon with Heartache; By the Light of the Silvery Moon; Carolina Moon; Come, Oh Come with Me, the Moon Is Beaming; Come to the Moon; Dark Moon; Desert Moon; East of the Moon, West of the Stars; East of the Sun and West of the Moon; Everyone's Gone to the Moon; Florida, the Moon and You; Fly Me to the Moon, or, In Other Words; Full Moon; Full Moon and Empty Arms; The Full Moon Union; Georgia's Gotta Moon; Get Out and Get Under the Moon; Harlem Moon; How High the Moon; I Love the Moon; I Used To Sigh for the Silvery Moon; I Wished on the Moon; If the Moon Turns Green; In the Moon Mist; In the Valley of the Moon; Indiana Moon; It's Only a Paper Moon; June Moon; Keep Sweeping the Cobwebs off the Moon; Lazy Lou'siana Moon; Lazy Moon; Man in the Moon; Many Moons Ago; Marshmallow Moon; Me and the Moon; Mister Moon You've Got a Million Sweethearts; The Moon Drops Low; The Moon Got in My Eyes; The Moon Has His Eyes on You; The Moon Is Blue; The Moon Is Low; Moon Love; The Moon of Manakoora; Moon of My Delight; Moon over Miami; Moon River; The Moon Shines on the Moonshine; Moon Song (That Wasn't Meant for Me); The Moon Was Yellow; Moonbeams; Moonglow; Moonrise on the Lowlands; Moonstruck; Mountains Beyond the Moon; My Sweetheart's the Man in the Moon; 'Neath the South Sea Moon; No Moon At All; Oh You Crazy Moon; Old Devil Moon; Once in a Blue Moon; Pale Moon; Racing with the Moon; Reaching for the Moon; Reaching for the Moon; Ridin' on the Moon; Rise, Gentle Moon; Roll Along Prairie Moon; Roll On Silver Moon, or, The Silver Moon; Sail Along Silvery Moon; The Same Old Moon; Shadow of the Moon; Shame On the Moon; Shine On Harvest Moon; Shine On Victory Moon; Silver Moon; Stardust on the Moon; Swanee River Moon; Underneath the Harlem Moon; Underneath the Russian Moon; Wabash Moon;

When De Moon Comes Up Behind De Hill; When the Moon Comes over the Mountain

Moonlight   All by Yourself in the Moonlight; Au Clair de la Lune; Black Moonlight; Blue Pacific Moonlight; By the Light of the Silvery Moon; Clair de Lune; Did You Ever Get That Feeling in the Moonlight; Give Me the Moonlight, Give Me the Girl; In the Chapel in the Moonlight; In the Evening by the Moonlight; In the Evening by the Moonlight, Dear Louise; June Night (Just Give Me a June Night, the Moonlight and You); Lonesome in the Moonlight; Magic Is the Moonlight; Mandolins in the Moonlight; Meet Me by Moonlight Alone; Moonlight and Pretzels; Moonlight and Roses (Bring Me Mem'ries of You); Moonlight and Shadows; (On) Moonlight Bay; Moonlight Becomes You; Moonlight Cocktail; Moonlight Feels Right; Moonlight Gambler; Moonlight in Vermont; Moonlight Masquerade; Moonlight Mood; Moonlight on the Colorado; Moonlight on the Ganges; Moonlight on the Rhine; (There Ought To Be a) Moonlight Saving Time; Moonlight Serenade; Moonlight Sonata; My Moonlight Madonna; Orchids in the Moonlight; Polka Dots and Moonbeams; Sailboat in the Moonlight; Shadows in the Moonlight; Sweet Hawaiian Moonlight; Two Silhouettes in the Moonlight; (Ooh) What a Little Moonlight Can Do

Moose   What's Good for General Bullmoose

Mop   Rag Mop

Morgen   Morgen—One More Sunrise

Morning   Angel of the Morning; At Dawning; A Beautiful Morning; Beloved, It Is Morn; Carolina in the Morning; Chelsea Morning; Coffee in the Morning, Kisses at Night; Come Saturday Morning; Dawn (Go Away); Dawn of a New Day; Daybreak; Delta Dawn; Each Tomorrow Morning; Early in de Mornin'; Early in the Morning; Fire in the Morning; First Thing Monday Mornin'; For He's a Jolly Good Fellow, or, Malbrouk (Malbrough), or, We Won't Go Home Until Morning, or, The Bear Went over the Mountain; For the Noo, or, Something in the Bottle for the Morning; Good Morning; Good Morning, Good Morning; Good Morning Heartache; Good Morning, Mister Zip-Zip-Zip; Good Morning Starshine; Happy Birthday to You, or, Good Morning to All; Hold Back the Dawn; I Got the Sun in the Morning; I Love You This Morning; In the Morning by the Bright Light; It's Nice To Get Up in the Morning; Kiss an Angel Good Mornin'; Let It Rain! Let It Pour! (I'll Be in Virginia in the Morning); A Little Kiss Each Morning, a Little Kiss Each Night; Moanin' in the Mornin'; Morning; The Morning After, or, Song from The Poseidon Adventure; The Morning After the Night Before; Mornin' Beautiful; Morning Desire; Morning Dew; Morning Has Broken; Morning of My Life; Morning, Please Don't Come; The Morning Side of the Mountain; Morning Train (Nine to Five); New World in the Morning; Oh, How I Hate To Get Up in the Morning; Oh What a Beautiful Mornin'; One Morning in May; Seventh Dawn; Softly, As in a Morning Sunrise; Some Sunday Morning; Some Sunday Morning; Song of the Dawn; Three O'Clock in the Morning; 'Tis Dawn the Lark Is Singing; Too Many Mornings; Touch Me in the Morning; Where the Morning Glories Grow; Where the Morning Glories Twine Around the Door; The White Dawn Is Stealing

Morocco   The Road to Morocco

Morris   The Morris Dance

Moscow   Midnight in Moscow, or, Moscow Nights

Mose   Mysterious Mose; Ol' Man Mose

Moses   Go Down, Moses; Where Was Moses When the Lights Went Out

Mosquito   The Mosquito's Parade

Moth, *see* **Butterfly**   The Moth and the Flame

Mother, *see also* **Grandmother**   Always Take Mother's Advice; And Her Mother Came Too; The Blue and the Gray, or, A Mother's Gift to Her Country; A Boy's Best Friend Is His Mother; Break the News to Mother; (Does Your Mother Know You're Out) Cecilia; The Clapping Song, or, My Mother Told Me; The Cottage of My Mother; Daddy Has a Sweetheart, and Mother Is Her Name; Daddy You've Been a Mother to Me; Dear Mother, in Dreams I See Her; Did Your Mother Come from Ireland; A Flower from Mother's Grave; Go Home and Tell Your Mother; Good-Bye, Ma! Good-Bye, Pa! Good-Bye, Mule, or, Long Boy; A Handful of Earth from (My Dear) Mother's Grave; Hello Mudduh, Hello Faddah; I Saw Mommy Kissing Santa Claus; If Momma Was Married; I'm the Last of the Red-Hot Mamas; Ireland Must Be Heaven, for My Mother Came from There; It's My Mother's Birthday Today; Just Before the Battle, Mother; Knees Up Mother Brown; Little Mother of Mine; Look What They've Done to My Song Ma; Ma! He's Making Eyes at Me; Ma, Look At Charlie; Mama; The Mama Doll Song; Mama Don't Allow No Easy Riders Here; Mama Don't Want No Peas an' Rice an' Cocoanut Oil; Mama from the Train, or, A Kiss, A Kiss; Mama Goes Where Papa Goes; Mama Inez; Mama, Look a Booboo; Mama Teach Me To Dance; Mama Told Me Not To Come; Mama Yo Quiero (I Want My Mama); Mama's Pearl; Mamma Loves Papa—Papa Loves Mamma; Momma Look Sharp; Mother; Mother; M-O-T-H-E-R (A Word That Means the World to Me); Mother Goose's Melodies; Mother Machree; Mother o' Mine; Mother Was a Lady, or, If Jack Were Only Here; Mother-in-Law; Mother Bids Me Bind My Hair; My Mother's Bible; My Mother's Bible; My Mother's Eyes; My Mother's Lullaby; My Mother's Rosary; My Yiddishe Momme; Next to Your Mother, Who Do You Love?; Nobody Knows What a Red Head Mama Can Do; Oh Mama, or, The Butcher Boy; Oh Mamma Mia; On Mother Kelly's Doorstep; One Called "Mother" and the Other "Home Sweet Home"; Pistol Packin' Mama; Rock Me to Sleep, Mother; She Took Mother's Advice; She's the Daughter of Mother Machree; Sometimes I Feel Like a Motherless Child; Songs My Mother Taught Me; Tell Mother I'll Be There; That Old Fashioned Mother of Mine; That Old Irish Mother of Mine; That Wonderful Mother of Mine; This Is My Mother's Day; Turn 'Erbert's Face to the Wall, Mother; We Fight Tomorrow, Mother; What a Wonderful Mother You'd Be; What Is Home Without a Mother; Whisper Your Mother's Name; Why Did They Dig Ma's Grave So Deep; You Remind Me of My Mother; Your God Comes First, Your Country Next, Then Mother Dear; Your Mother and Mine; Your Mother Should Know; You're Going Far Away, Lad, or, I'm Still Your Mother, Dear; You've Got Your Mother's Big Blue Eyes; You've Gotta (Got To) See Mamma Ev'ry Night or You Can't See Mamma At All

Motion   Poetry in Motion; St. Elmo's Fire (Man in Motion)

Mottoe   The Mottoes Framed Upon the Wall

Mountain   Ain't No Mountain High Enough; Anyone Can Move a Mountain; The Big Rock Candy Mountain; The Blue Alsation Mountains; Climb Ev'ry Mountain; For He's a Jolly Good Fellow, or, Malbrook (Malbrough), or, We Won't Go Home Until Morning, or, The Bear Went over the Mountain; From Greenland's Icy Mountains; Go Tell It on the Mountain Gonna Build a Mountain; The Green Mountain Farmer; I Like Mountain Music; I'd Climb the Highest Mountain (If I Knew I'd Find You); The Legend of the Glass Mountain; Michael from Mountains; The Morning Side of the Mountain; Mountain Greenery; Mountain Music; Mountain of Love; Mountains Beyond the Moon; The Mountains High; Mountains of Mourne; A Night on Bald Mountain; Night on Disco Mountain; On Top of Old Smokey; The Pesky Sarpent, or, (On) Springfield Mountain; Rocky Mountain High; She'll Be Comin' Round the Mountain (When She Comes); Smoky Mountain Rain; These Are My Mountains; We All Went Up Up Up the Mountain; When It's Springtime in the Rockies; When the Moon Comes over the Mountain; (There'll Be Blue Birds over) The White Cliffs of Dover; Wolverton Mountain

Mouse   Thank You Falettin Me Be Mice Elf Agin; Three Blind Mice; The Wedding of Mister Mickey Mouse

Mouth, *see also* **Kiss, Lips, Teeth**   Sugar Foot Stomp, or, Dipper Mouth Blues; What a Mouth

Move   Anyone Can Move a Mountain; Every Little Movement (Has a Meaning All Its Own); I Feel the Earth Move; Make a Move on Me; Move Away; Move In a Little Closer Baby; Move On; Move Over Darling; Moving Day in Jungle Town; Movin' On; De Old Ark's a-Moverin'; Something (in the Way She Moves)

Movie, *see also* **Hollywood**   At the Moving Picture Ball; Freeze-Frame; If I Had a Talking Picture of You; Let's Go into a Picture Show; Matinee; My Husband Makes Movies; Sad Movies Make Me Cry; Take Your Girlie to the Movies If You Can't Make Love at Home; You Oughta Be in Pictures

Mud   The Hippopotamus Song, or, Mud, Glorious Mud; Mississippi Mud; Muddy Water; Muddy Water

Mulberry   (Here We Go Round) The Mulberry Bush; Stop Beating 'Round the Mulberry Bush

Mule, *see* **Donkey**

Mumble, *see* **Talk**

Murder, *see also* **Kill**   "Murder" He Says; (Theme from) Murder on the Orient Express; Outbreak of Murder; Slaughter on Tenth Avenue (Ballet); Strange Fruit; You Can't Chop Your Poppa Up in Massachusetts

Murphy   Maggie Murphy's Home; Oh Murphy; Who Threw the Overalls in Mrs. Murphy's Chowder

Music, *see also* **Beat, Harmony, Melody, Play, Swing, Tune,** etc.   American Music; As Long as There's Music; Bach Goes to Town; Beat Me, Daddy, Eight to the Bar; Chiapanecas (While There's Music There's Romance); Do-Re-Mi; Eighteenth Variation on a Theme by Paganini; Hooked On Music; I Dig Rock and Roll Music; I Hear Music; I Hear Music; I Like Mountain Music; I Love Music (Part 1); I Want To Marry a Male Quartet; Johnny One Note; Let the Music

Play; Let's All Go to the Music Hall; Let's Face the Music and Dance; Life Is Nothing Without Music; Lost Barber Shop Chord; The Lost Chord; Make Mine Music; Moment Musicale; Mountain Music; Music; The Music and the Mirror; The Music Goes 'Round and 'Round; Music in May (Careless Rapture); Music Machine; Music, Maestro, Please; The Music Makers; Music Makes Me; Music Music Everywhere (But Not a Song in My Heart); Music Music Music; The Music Stopped; Music To Watch Girls By; La Musica Prohibita (Forbidden Music); The Night Is Filled with Music; Pianissimo; Play That Barbershop Chord (Mister Jefferson Lord); Play That Funky Music; Rock and Roll Music; Say It with Music; She Shall Have Music; Soft Lights and Sweet Music; The Sound of Music; Sound Off; The Sound of Silence; Strange Music; Sweet Sixteen Bars; Sweet Soul Music; The Sweetest Music This Side of Heaven; Take Five; That Lost Barbershop Chord; That's When the Music Takes Me; There's Music in the Air; Classical Gas; Treble Chance; Tschaikowsky; Two Hearts in Three Quarter Time; We Could Make Such Beautiful Music (Together); When Big Profundo Sang Low ''C''; Words Without Music; You and the Night and the Music; You Can't Play Every Instrument in the Band

Musket, *see* **Gun**

Musketeer March of the Musketeers

Muskrat Muskrat Ramble

Mussel Cockles and Mussels, Alive, Alive, O!, or, Sweet Molly Malone

Mustard Too Much Mustard (Très Moutarde); Too Old To Cut the Mustard

Mutual Mutual Admiration Society

Mystery Ah! Sweet Mystery of Life; Mystery Lady; Magical Mystery Tour; Man of Mystery; Mysterioso Pizzicato; Mysterious Mose; Mystery Girl; That Mysterious Rag

Mystic, *see* **Magic**

Nadia Nadia's Theme, or, The Young and the Restless

Nagasaki Nagasaki

Nancy Nancy (with the Laughing Face); Nancy Brown; Nancy Lee; Nancy Till

Napoleon Bonaparte's Retreat; The Grave of Bonaparte; Napoleon's a Pastry; Wal, I Swan!, or, Ebenezer Frye, or, Giddiap Napoleon, It Looks Like Rain; Who Ate Napoleons with Josephine When Bonaparte Was Away

Narcissus Narcissus

Nathan Nat'an, Nat'an, Nat'an, Tell Me for What Are You Waitin', Nat'an

Nation Garfield Now Will Guide the Nation; The Good Word (Theme from Nationwide); National Emblem (March); Tell It Out Among the Nations (Heathen) That the Lord Is King

Native God Bless Our Native Land; Native New Yorker

Natural Alone Again (Naturally); Doin' What Comes Natur'lly; Natural High; (You Make Me Feel Like) A Natural Woman

Nature Human Nature; Nature Boy

Naughty Blues My Naughty Sweety Gives to Me; Hold Your Hand Out Naughty Boy; The Naughty Lady of Shady Lane; Naughty Naughty Naughty; That Naughty Waltz; You Naughty, Naughty Men

Navajo, *see* **Indian**

Navy, *see also* **Sailor,** etc. The Army, the Navy and the Air Force; Here Come the Waves; I Am the Captain of the Pinafore (What Never); I Am the Monarch of the Sea; Jolly Commodore; The Navy Gets the Gravy and the Army Gets the Beans; Uncle Albert/Admiral Halsey

Nazareth Nazareth

Neapolitan Neapolitan Love Song; Neapolitan Nights

Near And the Great Big Saw Came Nearer; Be Near Me; Dearest, You're the Nearest to My Heart; I Keep Forgettin' (Every Time You're Near); (Jesus Keep Me) Near the Cross; Near You; Nearer, My God, to Thee; The Nearness of You; So Near and Yet So Far; This Nearly Was Mine; Thou Art So Near and Yet So Far; When I'm Not Near the Girl I Love

Necessary It Ain't Necessarily So

Neck Red Neckin' Love Makin' Night; She Wore a Yellow Ribbon, or, All Round My Hat (Round Her Neck) I (She) Wore a Yellow Ribbon; Wear My Ring Around Your Neck

Ned (Old) Uncle Ned

Needle A Needle in a Haystack

Neighbor Friends and Neighbours; Hi Neighbor; Love Thy Neighbor

Nellie The (Little) Bird on Nellie's Hat; Darling Nelly Gray; Hang on the Bell Nellie; My Nellie's Blue Eyes; Nellie Dean; Nellie Kelly, I Love You; Nellie the Elephant; Nelly Bly; Nelly Was a Lady; Since Sister Nell Heard Paderewski Play; Wait 'Til the Sun Shines, Nellie; When I Saw Sweet Nellie Home, or, I Was Seeing Nellie Home, or, Aunt Dinah's Quilting Party

Nelson The Death of Nelson

Nervous Nineteenth Nervous Breakdown

Nest Feather Your Nest; The Love Nest; My Little Nest of Heavenly Blue, or, Frasquita Serenade (Blaues Himmelbett), or, Farewell, My Love, Farewell; Nestin' Time in Flatbush; When the Robins Nest Again

Nevada In the Gold Fields of Nevada; The Whispering Pines of Nevada

New Brand New Key; Breaking in a Brand New Broken Heart; Dawn of a New Day; Doin' the New Low-Down; Don't Give Up the Old Love for the New; From the New World Symphony; Got a Bran' New Suit; Hail Columbia, or, New Federal Song; I Found a New Baby; I Hit a New High; I Want a New Drug; It's a New World; Let's Start the New Year Right; Many a New Day; Method of Modern Love; Modern Girl; Modern Woman; New Attitude; A New-Fangled Tango; (Theme from) A New Kind of Love; New Sun in the Sky; New World in the Morning; Nothing New Beneath the Sun; Open a New Window; Original Dixieland One-Step; Papa's Got a Brand New Bag; Paris Original; Symphony Moderne; There's a New World; This Is New; Thoroughly Modern Millie; What's New; What's New Pussycat; When Your Old Wedding Ring Was New; You Brought a New Kind of Love to Me; You Make Me Feel Brand New

New Hampshire My Old New Hampshire Home

New Jersey Jersey Bounce

New Orleans The Battle of New Orleans; City of New Orleans; Do You Know What It Means to Miss New Orleans; Down in Dear Old New Orleans; 'Way Down Yonder in New Orleans

New York, *see also* **Brooklyn, Flatbush,** etc. Autumn in New York; Boy from New York City; Conversation on Park Avenue; Do the New York; Ev'ry Street's a Boulevard in Old New York; (I Like New York in June) How About You; I Happen To Like New York; In Good Old New York Town; In Old New York, or, The Streets of New York; Manhattan; Manhattan Beach; Manhattan Madness; Manhattan Serenade; My Best Girl's a New Yorker (Corker); Native New Yorker; New York, New York; New York City; The Oldest Established (Permanent Floating Crap Game in New York); On a Roof in Manhattan; She Is the Belle of New York; She's a Latin from Manhattan; The Sidewalks of New York, or, East Side, West Side; Slumming on Park Avenue; Stairway to the Stars (Park Avenue Fantasy); Take Me Back to New York Town; There's a Boat Dat's Leavin' Soon for New York; Yuletide, Park Avenue

News Break the News to Mother; Good News; I Guess I'll Get the Papers and Go Home; It's Good News Week; A Little Good News; No Bad News; Washington Post

Nicaragua Managua Nicaragua

Nicholas Oh Nicholas Don't Be So Ridiculous

Nicole Nicola

Nigger, *see also* **Coon** I'se Your Nigger If You Want Me, Liza Jane; Ten Little Indians, or, Ten Little Injuns, or, Ten Little Niggers; That's Why Darkies Were Born; Whar Did You Cum From, or, Knock a Nigger Down; You're (You'se) Just a Little Nigger, Still You're Mine, All Mine

Night, *see also* **Dark, Evening, Tonight** All Day and All of the Night; All Night Long (All Night); All the Live-Long Day (and the Long Long Night); All Through the Night; All Through the Night; All Through the Night; Another Honky Tonk Night on Broadway; Another Saturday Night; Birds in the Night; Blue Is the Night; Blues in the Night; Bonne Nuit—Goodnight; Boogie Nights; The Boys' Night Out; California Nights; Christmas Song, or, O Holy Night; Coffee in the Morning, Kisses at Night; Cool Night; Dark Is the Night; De Camptown Races (Gwine To Run All Night); December 1963 (Oh What a Night); Deep Night; Disco Nights; Does the Spearmint Lose Its Flavor on the Bedpost Overnight; Don't Wait 'Til the Night Before Christmas; Even the Nights Are Better; Every Night There's a Light; Give Me the Night; Glamorous Night; Good Night; Good Night Angel; Good Night Dear; Good Night Ladies, or, Merrily We Roll Along; Good Night, Nurse (Kiss Your Little Patient); Good Night, Sweetheart; Goodnight (I'm Only a Strolling Vagabond); Goodnight and God Bless You; Goodnight Children, Everywhere; Goodnight Irene; Goodnight, Little Girl, Goodnight; Goodnight My Love; Goodnight My Someone; Goodnight to You All; Goodnight Tonight; Goodnight Vienna; Goodnight Wherever You Are; A Hard Day's Night; Heart of the Night; Heart of the Night; Help Me Make It Through the Night; How Blue the Night; I Could Have Danced All Night; I Couldn't Sleep a Wink Last Night; I Heard You Cried Last Night; I Love a Rainy Night; I Love the Nightlife (Disco 'Round); I Love the Way You Say "Goodnight"; I Pitch My

Lonely Caravan at Night; I Still Love To Kiss You Goodnight; I Wish I (We) Didn't Have To Say Good Night; If He Can Fight Like He Can Love, Good Night Germany; In the Middle of the Night; In the Still of the Night; It Looks (to Me) Like a Big Night Tonight; It's a Grand Night for Singing; It's a Pity To Say Goodnight; It's Time To Say Goodnight; Jazz Nocturne; Juke Box Saturday Night; June Night (Just Give Me a June Night, the Moonlight and You); Ladies Night; Last Night I Didn't Get To Sleep At All; Last Night on the Back Porch—I Loved Her Best of All; Last Night Was Made for Love; Last Night Was the End of the World; Last Night When We Were Young; A Little Kiss Each Morning, a Little Kiss Each Night; London By Night; Lonely Night (Angel Face); Lonely Nights; Lost in the Fifties Tonight (In the Still of the Night); The Loveliest Night of the Year; A Lovely Night; The Market on Saturday Night; Midnight in Moscow, or, Moscow Nights; Miss You Nights; The Morning After the Night Before; My Old Kentucky Home (Good Night); Neapolitan Nights; Night; Night and Day; The Night Chicago Died; Night Fever; The Night Has a Thousand Eyes; The Night Has a Thousand Eyes; (Give Me) A Night in June; The Night Is Filled with Music; The Night Is Young and You're So Beautiful; Night May Have Its Sadness; A Night on Bald Mountain; Night on Disco Mountain; Night Owls; The Night the Floor Fell In; The Night the Lights Went Out in Georgia; The Night They Invented Champagne; Night Train; Night Waltz; The Night Was Made for Love; The Night We Called It a Day; Nights in White Satin; Nights of Gladness; Nightshift; No More Lonely Nights; No More Nights; No Night So Long; Nocturne; Oft in the Stilly Night; One Night in June; One Night of Love; One Night Only; One of These Nights; Overnight; Quiet Night; Rainy Night in Rio; Red Neckin' Love Makin' Night; Rhythm of the Night; Running with the Night; Saturday Night; Saturday Night; Saturday Night Is the Loneliest Night of the Week; Separate Lives (Love Theme from *White Nights*); Serenade in the Night; Shades of Night; Sharing the Night Together; Sigh By Night; Silent Night, Holy Night; Softly Thro' the Summer Night; Somewhere in the Night; Song for a Summer Night; Southern Nights; Stars of the Summer Night; Still As the Night; (This Is) The Story of a Starry Night; Strangers in the Night; Summer Night; Tender Is the Night; This Night Won't Last Forever; A Thousand and One Nights; Through a Long and Sleepless Night; Tonight's the Night (It's Gonna Be Alright); Twistin' the Night Away; Two Hearts That Pass in the Night; Wasted Days Wasted Nights; Whatever Gets You Thru the Night; What'll We Do On a Saturday Night When the Town Goes Dry; What's Good About Good Night; When It's Night Time Down in Burgundy; When It's Night Time in Dixie Land; When It's Night-Time In Italy, It's Wednesday Over Here; Where Did Robinson Crusoe Go with Friday on Saturday Night?; Where the Blue of the Night Meets the Gold of the Day; Where the Twilight Comes To Kiss the Rose Goodnight; Who Were You with Last Night; Why Do They All Take the Night Boat to Albany; Why Don't You Spend the Night; Wonderland by Night; Work for the Night Is Coming; You and the Night and the Music; You'll Be Back Every Night in My Dreams; You've Gotta (Got To) See Mamma Ev'ry Night, or You Can't See Mamma At All

Nightingale Nightingale; Nightingale; A Nightingale Sang in Berkeley Square

Nile   Love Songs of the Nile; My Castle on the Nile; My Song of the Nile

Nina   Nina; Nina Never Knew; Nina Rose

Nine   About a Quarter to Nine; The Lady from Twenty-Nine Palms; Locked Out After Nine; Love Potion Number Nine; Morning Train (Nine to Five); Nine; 9 To 5; The Ninety and Nine; 99 Luftballons; Ninety-Nine Out of a Hundred (Want To Be Loved); Summer of '69

Nineteen   Between Eighteenth and Nineteenth on Chestnut Street; 19; Nineteenth Nervous Breakdown

Ninety   Down in the Depths on the Ninetieth Floor; The Ninety and Nine; 99 Luftballons; Ninety-Nine Out of a Hundred (Want To Be Loved); Ninety-Six Tears; The Wreck of (on) the Old (Southern) '97

Nineveh   Not Since Nineveh

Noah   Captain Noah and His Floating Zoo; There's One Wide River To Cross, or, Noah's Ark

Nobody   Couldn't Hear Nobody Pray; Everybody Loves My Baby, But My Baby Don't Love Nobody But Me; I Ain't Gonna Give Nobody None o' This Jelly Roll; I Ain't Got Nobody; I Ain't Nobody's Darling; I'm Nobody's Baby; Nobody; Nobody; Nobody But You; Nobody Does It Better; Nobody Else But Me; Nobody Knows and Nobody Seems To Care; Nobody Knows De Trouble I've Seen; Nobody Knows, Nobody Cares; Nobody Knows What a Red Head Mama Can Do; Nobody Knows You When You're Down and Out; Nobody Loves Me Like You Do; Nobody Loves a Fairy When She's Forty; Nobody Loves Me Like You Do; Nobody Told Me; Nobody Told Me; Nobody Wants Me; Nobody's Chasing Me; Nobody's Heart (Belongs to Me); Nobody's Little Girl; Nobody's Sweetheart Now; 'Tain't Nobody's Business If I Do; Who Can I Turn To (When Nobody Needs Me); You're Nobody 'Til Somebody Loves You

Noël, *see* **Christmas**

Noise, *see* **Hear**

Nonsense   The Aba Daba Honeymoon; Alley-Oop; Be-Bop Baby; Beep Beep; Bibbidi-Bobbodi-Boo; Bim Bam Boom; Blah, Blah, Blah; Bloop Bleep; Boola Boola; Buzz Buzz A-Diddle-It; The Cha Cha Cha; Chi-Baba Chi-Baba (My Bambino Go to Sleep); Chica Chica Boom Chic; Chim Chim Cheree; Chitty Chitty Bang Bang; Crazy Words (Crazy Tune) (Vo-Do-De-O-Do); Da Doo Ron Ron (When He Walked Me Home); Dig You Later (A Hubba-Hubba-Hubba); Diga Diga Doo; The Dipsy Doodle; Dis-Donc, Dis-Donc; Do Wah Diddy Diddy; Doo Wacka Doo; Doodle Doo Doo; Eeny Meeny Miney Mo; Fiddle Faddle; A Girl! A Girl!, or, Zoom Ba Di Alli Nella; (Whoopee Ti Yi Yo) Git Along Little Dog(g)ies; Ha-Cha-Cha; Heebie Jeebies; Heigh-Ho; Helter Skelter; Hey-Ba-Ba-Re-Bop; Hi-Diddle-Dee-Dee (an Actor's Life for Me); Hi-Diddle-Diddle; Hi Lili Hi Lo; Hi Tiddley Hi Ti Island; Hic, Haec, Hoc; Hinky Dinky Parlay Voo, or, Mad' moiselle from Armentières; (What Has Become of) Hinky Dinky Parlay Voo; Hitchy-Koo; Ho Hum; Hocus Pocus; *see also* **Honky Tonk;** Hoop-Dee-Doo; Hot Diggity (Dog Ziggity Boom); Huckle-Buck; Hut Sut Song; Inka Dinka Doo; I've Got Rings on My Fingers, or, Mumbo Jumbo Jijjiboo J. O'Shea; Ja-Da; Jeepers Creepers; La-Di-Da-Di-La; Laroo Laroo Lilli Bolero; Loddy Lo; Lolly Too Dum; Loop de Loop; Mairzy Doats;

Na Na Hey Hey Kiss Him Goodbye; Oh! How She Could Yacki, Hacki, Wicki, Wacki, Woo; Ob-La-Di Ob-La-Da; The Ogo-Pogo; Patsy Ory Ory Aye (A-Workin' on the Railroad); Rackety-Coo!; Razzazza Mazzazza; Shadrack (Meshack, Abednigo); Shim-Me-Sha-Wabble; Shinaniki Da; Supercalifragilisticexpialidocious; Ta-Ra-Ra—Boom-Der-É (De-Ay); This Old Man, or, The Children's Marching Song (Nick, Nack, Paddy Whack); Tiggerty Boo; Ti-Pi-Tin; Tweedle-O-Twill; Wah Hoo; Who Put the Bomp (in the Bomp Ba Bomp Ba Bomp); Wig Wam Bam; Wringle Wrangle; Yaaka Hula Hickey Dula; Yakety Yak; The Yama Yama Man; Yip-I-Addy-I-Ay!; Zip-A-Dee-Doo-Dah; Zizzy, Ze Zum, Zum

Noon, *see also* **Twelve**   (Theme from) High Noon (Do Not Forsake Me, Oh My Darling)

Nora   No, No, Nora; Nora Malone (Call Me by Phone)

Normandy   When It's Apple Blossom Time in Normandy

North   Just a Little Bit South of North Carolina; Life in a Northern Town; The North Wind Doth Blow; North to Alaska; Northwest Passage; There's No North or South Today

Norway   Norway; The Norwegian Dance; Norwegian Wood

Nose   I Got a "Code" in my "Dose" (Cold in My Nose); Rudolph the Red-Nosed Reindeer

Note, *see* **Music**

Nothing   All or Nothing At All; All Over Nothing at All; Do Nothin' Till You Hear from Me; I Believe There's Nothing Stronger Than Our Love; I Can't Think Ob Nuthin' Else But You; I Got Plenty o' Nuttin'; I Who Have Nothing; I'll Stop At Nothing; Life Is Nothing Without Music; Money for Nothing; No Love, No Nothing; Nothing; Nothin' At All; Nothing Can Stop Me Now; Nothing from Nothing; Nothing Like Falling in Love; Nothing New Beneath the Sun; Nothing Rhymed; Poor Papa (He's Got Nuthin' At All); There Is Nothin' Like a Dame; There's Nothing True But Heaven; When It's All Goin' Out and Nothin' Comin' In; Without You I'm Nothing; You Ain't Heard Nothing Yet; You Ain't Seen Nothing Yet; You Haven't Done Nothing Yet

Notre Dame   Cheer, Cheer for Old Notre Dame

Now   (Theme from) Against All Odds (Take A Look At Me Now); Ain't No Stoppin' Us Now; Bess, You Is My Woman Now; Both Sides Now; By Now; Cool It Now; Even Now; Everybody's Doing It (Now); Father, Dear Father, Come Home with Me Now, or, Come Home, Father; Fido Is a Hot Dog Now; (Now and Then) A Fool Such As I; From Now On; Garfield Now Will Guide the Nation; Go Now; Gonna Fly Now, or, Theme from Rocky; G'Bye Now; Here Comes My Daddy Now—Oh Pop—Oh Pop; How You Gonna See Me Now; A Hundred Years from Now; I Can See Clearly Now (the Rain Has Gone); I Can't Be Bothered Now; I Know Now; I Need You Now; I Used To Love You, But It's All Over Now; I Wonder Who's Kissing Her Now; If You Leave Me Now; I'm a Big Girl Now; I'm on the Water Wagon Now; I'm Telling You Now; It All Comes Back to Me Now; It's Now or Never; I've Got My Captain Working for Me Now; Keepin' Out of Mischief Now; Kiss Her Now; Love Is Here and Now You're Gone; My Blackbirds Are Bluebirds Now; My Heart Has Learned To Love You, Now Do Not Say Goodbye; My Man's Gone Now; Nobody's Sweetheart Now; Nothing Can Stop Me Now; Now; Now;

Now; Now; Now and Forever; Now and Forever; Now and Forever (You and Me); Now I Lay Me Down To Sleep; Now Is the Hour; Now Is the Month of Maying; Now It Can Be Told; Now Sleeps the Crimson Petal; (Where Are You) Now That I Need You; Now the Day Is Over; Now Those Days Are Gone; (Potatoes Are Cheaper—Tomatoes Are Cheaper) Now's the Time To Fall in Love; Oh Look At Me Now; The Party's Over Now; Ten Thousand Years from Now; That's My Weakness Now; The Time Has Come; Too Late Now; What Now My Love; What the World Needs Now Is Love; Where Are You Now My Love; Who Can It Be Now?; Who's Crying Now; Who's Holding Donna Now; Who's Sorry Now; Whose Little Heart Are You Breaking Now; Why Try To Change Me Now; You Belong to My Heart (Now and Forever), or, Solamente Una Vez; You Better Go Now, You're in the Army Now; You're My Past, Present and Future

Nurse, *see* **Hospital**

Nursery Fantasia on a Nursery Song; (If I Had) Rhythm in My Nursery Rhymes

Nutcracker The Nutcracker Suite

Nuts, *see* **Crazy**

Oak, *see* **Tree**

Object, *see* **Thing**

Observe, *see* **Look**

Occasional An Occasional Man

Ocean, *see* **Sea**

October Brown October Ale

Odd (Theme from) Against All Odds (Take a Look At Me Now); (Theme from) The Odd Couple; Odds and Ends (of a Beautiful Love Affair); Space Oddity

Ode, *see* **Story**

Off Can I Leave Off Wearin' My Shoes; Can't Get Indiana off My Mind; Can't Take My Eyes Off You; Don't Put Me Off at Buffalo Any More; Dummy Song, or, I'll Take the Legs from off the Table; Far Off I Hear a Lover's Flute; Get Off My Cloud; Got Her off My Hands (But Can't Get Her off My Mind); Hats Off to Me; Keep Sweeping the Cobwebs off the Moon; Let's Call the Whole Thing Off; Little Bit off the Top; Off the Wall; Put Me Off at Buffalo; Shake It Off; Shuffle Off to Buffalo; Sound Off; Take a Day Off, Mary Ann; Take That Look off Your Face; 'Twas off the Blue Canaries, or, My Last Cigar; We're Off To See the Wizard

Officer, *see* **General, Police, Sergeant,** etc.

Ohio Beautiful Ohio; Down by the O-Hi-O; Ohio; Round on the End and High in the Middle, O-hi-o

Oil Mama Don't Want No Peas an' Rice an' Cocoanut Oil

Oklahoma Oklahoma; You're the Reason God Made Oklahoma

Old Any Old Iron; Any Old Place I Can Hang My Hat Is Home Sweet Home to Me; Any Old Place with You; Any Old Port in a Storm; The Brave Old Oak; Call Round Any Old Time; Carry Me Back to Old Virginny; Carry Me Back to Ole Virginny, or, De Floating Show; Cheer, Cheer for Old Notre Dame; Dear Old Donegal; Dear Old Girl; Dear Old Pal of Mine; Dear Old Rose; Dear Old Southland; Don't Give

Up the Old Love for the New; Down at the Old Swimming Hole; Down by the Old Mill Stream; Down in Dear Old New Orleans; Down in the Old Cherry Orchard; Down the Old Ox Road; (Theme from) Dukes of Hazzard (Good Ol' Boys); Ev'ry Street's a Boulevard in Old New York; For Old Time's Sake; The Funny Old Hills; Garland of Old Fashioned Roses; Gee, But It's Great To Meet a Friend from Your Old Home Town; Get Out Those Old Records; The Good Old Bad Days; The Good Old U.S.A.; Good Ole Boys Like Me; Goodbye Ol' Paint, or, I Ride an Old Paint, or, I'm a-Leavin' Cheyenne; Grand Old Ivy; Grandpa (Tell Me 'Bout the Good Old Days); Granny's Old Arm-Chair; He May Be Old, But He's Got Young Ideas; Hey Young Fella Close Your Old Umbrella; The Hills of Old Wyomin'; (There'll Be) A Hot Time in the Old Town (Tonight); I Like Your Old French Bonnet; I Love You in the Same Old Way—Darling Sue; I Want a Girl—Just Like the Girl That Married Dear Old Dad; I Wish I Had My Old Girl Back Again; I'd Love To Meet That Old Sweetheart of Mine; If We Can't Be the Same Old Sweethearts, We'll Just Be the Same Old Friends; I'm an Old Cowhand (from the Rio Grande); I'm Old-Fashioned; In an Old Dutch Garden; In Dear Old Illinois; In Good Old New York Town; In Old New York, or, The Streets of New York; In the Good Old Summer Time; In the Shade of the Old Apple Tree; It Seems Like Old Times; It's a Lonesome Old Town (When You're Not Around); It's the Same Old Dream; It's the Same Old Shillelagh; I've Been Floating Down the Old Green River; Knocked 'Em in the Old Kent Road; Leanin' on the Ole Top Rail; Let Erin Remember the Days of Old; Let's Take an Old-Fashioned Walk; A Lil' Ole Bitty Pissant Country Place; Lisbon Antigua, or, In Old Lisbon; Little Old Lady; The Little Old Log Cabin in the Lane; Little Old Mill; Little Old Sod Shanty; (Just a) Little Street Where Old Friends Meet; Little Town in the Ould County Down; Love's Old Sweet Song; Mary, You're a Little Bit Old Fashioned; Mary's a Grand Old Name; Me and the Old Folks at Home; Mi Viejo Amor (An Old Love); Old King Cole; There Was an Old Woman Who Lived in a Shoe; Mouldy Old Dough; My Heart Still Clings to the Old First Love; My Old Aunt Sally; My Old Dutch; My Old Flame; My Old Kentucky Home (Good Night); My Old Man's a Dustman; My Old New Hampshire Home; De Old Ark's a-Moverin'; The Old Arm Chair; Old Black Joe; Old Cape Cod; The Old Chisholm Trail; Old Colony Times; Old Dan Tucker; Old Days; Old Devil Moon; Old Dog Tray; Old-Fashioned Garden; Old-Fashioned Love; An Old-Fashioned Wife; Old Father Thames; Old Flag Never Touched the Ground; The Old Flame Flickers and I Wonder Why; Old Folks; Old Folks at Home (Way Down upon the Swanee River); Old Friends; Old Friends and Old Times; The Old Granite State; The Old Grey Mare (She Ain't What She Used To Be); Old Grimes; The Old House; Old Hundred(th) Doxology, or, Praise God, from Whom All Blessings Flow; The Old Kitchen Kettle; The Old Lamp-Lighter; Old MacDonald Had a Farm; Ol' Man Mose; Ol' Man River; Old Man Sunshine, Little Boy Bluebird; The Old Master Painter; Old Mill Wheel; The Old Oaken Bucket; Old Pal Why Don't You Answer Me; The Old Pi-anna Rag; The Old Piano Roll Blues; The Old Refrain; Old Rosin the Beau; The Old Rugged Cross; Old Sam (Pick Up Tha' Musket); Old Ship of Mine; The Old Soft Shoe; Old Soldiers Never Die; The "Ol" Song; The Old Spinning Wheel; (Gimme Dat) Old Time Religion; Old Timer; An Old Violin; An Old Water Mill; Older and Wiser; Older Women; The Oldest Established (Permanent Floating Crap Game in New York); Ole Buttermilk Sky; Ole Faithful; (Go Tell Aunt Rhody) The Ole Grey Goose (Is Dead); Ole Shady, or, The Song of the Contraband; On the Banks of the Old Raritan; On the Old Fall River Line; On Top of Old Smokey; Pack Up Your Trouble in Your Old Kit Bag and Smile, Smile, Smile; Poor Old Slave; Put Me to Sleep with an Old-Fashioned Melody; Put On Your Old Grey Bonnet; (Ol') Rockin' Chair; Sam, the Old Accordion Man; The Same Old Auld Lang Syne; The Same Old Moon; Same Ole Me; Seems Like Old Times; (In) A Shanty in Old Shanty Town; She Was Bred in Old Kentucky; She's the Fairest Little Flower Dear Old Dixie Ever Grew (Knew); Sing an Old Fashioned Song (to a Young Sophisticated Lady); Somewhere in Old Wyoming; A Song of Old Hawaii; A Sweet Old Fashioned Girl; Sweetheart, We'll Never Grow Old; Take a Seat, Old Lady; Take Me Back to Dear Old Blighty; Tell Me the Old, Old Story; Tenting on the Old Camp Ground, or, Tenting Tonight; That Dear Old Gentleman; That Lucky Old Sun; That Old Black Magic; That Old Fashioned Mother of Mine; That Old Feeling; That Old Gang of Mine; That Old Girl of Mine; That Old Irish Mother of Mine; That Same Old Feeling; That Sly Old Gentleman from Featherbed Lane; There'll Be a Hot Time for the Old Men When the Young Men Go to War; There's a Garden in Old Italy; There's Life in the Old Dog Yet; (When) They Cut Down the Old Pine Tree; They're Either Too Young or Too Old; This Old Man, or, The Children's Marching Song (Nick, Nack, Paddy Whack); This Ole House; Tie a Yellow Ribbon Round the Ole Oak Tree; Too Old To Cut the Mustard; Tuck Me to Sleep in My Old 'Tucky Home; Turkey in the Straw, or, Old Zip Coon; (Old) Uncle Ned; Under Any Old Flag at All; Way Down in Old Indiana; We Came from the Same Old State; Wedding Bells Are Breaking Up That Old Gang of Mine; We'll Have a Jubilee in My Old Kentucky Home; When I Grow Too Old To Dream; When Your Old Wedding Ring Was New; A Windmill in Old Amsterdam; A Wise Old Owl; The Wreck of (on) the Old (Southern) '97; You'd Never Know the Old Home Town of Mine; You're an Old Smoothie; You're the Best Break This Old Heart Ever Had

Olga   Olga Pulloffski

Olive   Roll On, Tulane, or, The Olive and Blue

Omaha   Omaha

Once, *see* **One**

One   Ain't No Woman Like the One I've Got; Another One Bites the Dust; Be Kind to the Loved Ones at Home; Calling to Her Boy Just Once Again; The Church's One Foundation; Coom Pretty One; Dar's One More Ribber To Cross; Dedicated to the One I Love; Desperate Ones; Dinner for One, Please James; Do That to Me One More Time; Eve Cost Adam Just One Bone; The Feeling We Once Had; First Call; First, Last and Always; First Love, Last Love, Best Love; The First Lullaby; The First Noël; First Thing Monday Mornin'; First Time; The First Time Ever I Saw Your Face; Five-Four-Three-Two-One; Fool Number One; For Once in My Life; For the First Time (Come Prima); Give Me One Hour; The Harp That Once Thro' Tara's Halls; He's 1-A in the Army (and A-1 in My Heart); I Can't Get the One I Want (Those I Get I Don't Want); I Have But One Heart; I Know

a Heartache When I See One; (Just One Way To Say) I Love You; I Loved You Once in Silence; I Might Be Your "Once-in-a-While"; I Once Had a Heart, Margarita; If I Could Be with You One Hour Tonight; I'm Putting All My Eggs in One Basket; I'm the Lonely One; I'm the One; I'm Tickled to Death I'm Single; I'm Twenty-One Today; In Love for the Very First Time; Jingle Bells, or, The One Horse Open Sleigh; Johnny One Note; Just Once; Just One Girl; Just One More Chance; Just One of Those Things; Just One Way To Say I Love You; Lady Love Me One More Time; Let Me Be the One; Life in One Day; Little One; Love in the First Degree; Love Plus One; The Lucky One; Morgen—One More Sunrise; My First Thrill; My Heart Still Clings to the Old First Love; My Home Town Is a One Horse Town, But It's Big Enough for Me; My One and Only; My One and Only Heart; My One and Only Highland Fling; My One and Only Love; Neither One of Us (Wants To Be the First To Say Goodbye); Nice One Girl; Oh Isn't It Singular; Once Ev'ry Year; Once in a Blue Moon; Once in a Lifetime; Once in a Lifetime; Once in a While; Once in Every Lifetime; Once in Love with Amy; Once Knew a Fella; Once upon a Dream; Once upon a Time; Once upon a Wintertime; One; One Alone; One Bad Apple (Don't Spoil the Whole Bunch); One Boy; One by One; One Called "Mother" and the Other "Home Sweet Home"; One Dozen Roses; One Fine Day, or, Un Bel Di; One for My Baby (and One More for the Road); One Hand, One Heart; (I'd Love To Spend) One Hour with You; One Hundred Ways; The One I Love Belongs to Somebody Else; One in a Million You; One Kiss; One Less Bell To Answer; One Little Candle; One Love; One Love Forever; One Meat Ball; One Moment Alone; One More Angel in Heaven; One More Dance; One More Kiss; One More River To Cross; One More Time; One Morning in May; One Night in June; One Night of Love; One Night Only; One O'Clock Jump; One of the Ruins That Cromwell Knocked About a Bit; One of Those Nights; One of Us Will Weep Tonight; One Piece at a Time; The One Rose That's Left in My Heart; One Song; One Sunday Afternoon; The One That You Love; One Thing Leads to Another; One, Two, Button Your Shoe; One, Two, Three; One—Two—Three; One Two Three Red Light; One Way Love; The One Who Really Loves You; One You Love; Only One Girl in the World for Me; Only One; Only One You; Opus (Number) One; Original Dixieland One-Step; Rolled Into One; Schaefer Is the One Beer; She Was One of the Early Birds; So You're the One; Soliloquy; Soliloquy; Solitaire; Still the One; Take a Number From One to Ten; There Once Was an Owl; (There's Something Nice About Everyone But) There's Everything Nice About You; There's One Wide River To Cross, or, Noah's Ark; A Thousand and One Nights; Till We Two Are One; Time Waits for No One; Two Hearts Are Better Than One; The Unicorn; When I First Saw You; When I Was Twenty-One and You Were Sweet Sixteen; When the One You Love (Simply Won't Love Back); When You First Kissed the Last Girl You Loved; When You Lose the One You Love; While Strolling Through the Park One Day, or, The Fountain in the Park; Why Have You Left the One You Left Me For?; Wild One; (My) Wonderful One; Yesterday Once More; You Always Hurt the One You Love; You Are My First Love; You Happen Once in a Lifetime; You, You, You Are the One; You, You're the One; You'll Always Be the One I Love; Your God Comes First, Your

Country Next, Then Mother Dear; You're a Million Miles from Nowhere When You're One Little Mile From Home; You're the First, the Last, My Everything; You're the One (You Beautiful Son-of-a-Gun); You're the One I Care For; You're the One That I Want; You're the Only One

Onion Dance of the Spanish Onion; Glass Onion; Green Onions

Onward Onward, Christian Soldiers

Open Beside an Open Fireplace; The Christmas Song, or, Merry Christmas to You, or, Chestnuts Roasting on an Open Fire; Hannah, Won't You Open That Door?; It's an Open Secret; Jingle Bells, or, The One Horse Open Sleigh; Let My Love Open the Door; Love in the Open Air; My Heart Is an Open Book; Open a New Window; Open Arms; Open the Door, Richard; Open the Gates of the Temple; Open Thy Lattice Love; Open Up Your Heart (and Let the Sunshine In); Song of the Open Road; Throw Open Wide Your Window; With My Eyes Wide Open I'm Dreaming

Optimist A Cockeyed Optimist

Orange Love of Three Oranges (March); Orange Blossom Time; Orange Colored Sky; An Orange Grove in California; Tangerine

Orchard, see **Tree**

Orchestra Itinerary of an Orchestra; Play Orchestra Play; Suite No. 1 for Small Orchestra

Orchid The Biggest Aspidistra in the World; Blue Orchids; No Orchids for My Lady; Orchids in the Moonlight

Order Doctor's Orders

Ordinary I'm an Ordinary Man; Ordinary People

Organ The Happy Organ; The Organ Grinder; The Organ Grinder's Swing; The Volunteer Organist; When the Organ Played at Twilight (The Song That Reached My Heart); When You Played the Organ and I Sang ''The Rosary''

Orient, see **China**

Origin, see **Birth**

Original see **New**

Ostrich Ostrich Walk

Otis Miss Otis Regrets

Otto The Crazy Otto Rag (Medley)

Out All In Down and Out; All Out of Love; Blow Out the Candle; The Boys' Night Out; Can't Get Out of This Mood; (Does Your Mother Know You're Out) Cecilia; Clear Out of This World; Come Out of the Kitchen, Mary Ann; Day In—Day Out; Desafinado (Slightly Out of Tune); Did You Ever Think As the Hearse Rolls By, or, The Worms Crawl In, the Worms Crawl Out; Don't Go Out Tonight, Boy; Fade Out—Fade In; (He'd Have To Get Under,) Get Out and Get Under (To Fix Up His Automobile); Get Out and Get Under the Moon; Get Out of Town; Get Out Those Old Records; Goin' Out of My Head; Hangin' Out the Window; He Walked Right In, Turned Around and Walked Right Out Again; I Get a Kick Out of You; I Let a Song Go Out of My Heart; I Went Out of My Way; If He Comes In, I'm Going Out; If I Knock the ''L'' out of Kelly; I'm Gonna Wash That Man Right Outa My Hair; I'm Like a Fish Out of Water; I'm Stepping Out with a Memory Tonight; (Look Out for) Jimmy Valentine; Just Like a Melody Out of the Sky; Keepin' Out of Mischief

Now; Left Right Out of Your Heart; Let's Put Out the Lights and Go to Sleep; Lights Out; Locked Out After Nine; Lookin' Out My Back Door; Love Locked Out; Love Will Find Out the Way; Love You Inside and Out; Making Love Out of Nothing At All; The Night the Lights Went Out in Georgia; Nobody Knows You When You're Down and Out; Out in the Cold Again; Out in the Cold Cold Snow; (Theme from) Out of Africa; Out of My Dreams; (You Came Along From) Out of Nowhere; Out of This World; Out of Touch; Out of Town; Out on the Edge of Beyond; Out There in the Sunshine With You; Out Where the West Begins; Outa-Space; Reach Out and Touch; Reach Out for Me; Reach Out I'll Be There; Roll Out! Heave Dat Cotton; She's Out of My Life; Silver Dollar (Down and Out); Somewhere Out There; A Star Fell Out of Heaven; Steppin' Out; Steppin' Out with My Baby; Take Me Out to the Ball Game; Tell It Out Among the Nations (Heathen) That the Lord Is King; They Were All Out of Step But Jim; Those Wedding Bells Shall Not Ring Out; Time Don't Run Out on Me; Turn Out the Light; Way Out West; We Can Work It Out; We'll Knock the Heligo—Into Heligo—Out of Heligoland; When It's All Goin' Out and Nothin' Comin' In; When the Sun Comes Out; When You Walked Out Someone Else Walked Right In; Where Was Moses When the Lights Went Out; Wipe Out; You Bring Out the Lover in Me

Outbreak Outbreak of Murder

Outcast The Outcast Unknown

Outside Baby, It's Cold Outside; Come Outside; The Great Indoors; I'm Gonna Move to (the) Outskirts of Town; Laughing on the Outside (Crying on the Inside); On the Outside Looking In; Outside of Heaven; There Are Angels Outside Heaven

Over Almost Over You; Am I Wasting My Time on (over) You; Are the Good Times Really Over; Blue Turning Grey over You; Bridge over Troubled Water; Can't We Talk It Over; The Carnival Is Over; Come On Over; Cross Over the Bridge; Does the Spearmint Lose Its Flavor on the Bedpost Overnight; Fool (If You Think It's Over); For He's a Jolly Good Fellow, or, Malbrouk (Malbrough), or, We Won't Go Home Until Morning, or, The Bear Went over the Mountain; (There's No) Gettin' Over Me; Glad All Over; Head Over Heels; Head over Heels in Love; Here I Am (Just When I Thought I Was Over You); Hey Look Me Over; The Honeymoon Is Over; I Cried for You (Now It's Your Turn To Cry over Me); I Just Want To Go Back and Start the Whole Thing Over; I Still Can't Get Over Loving You; I Used To Love You, But It's All Over Now; I'd Rather Be Blue over You (Than Happy with Somebody Else); If I Had My Life To Live Over; I'll Never Get Over You; I'm Getting Sentimental over You; I'm Looking Over a Four Leaf Clover; It's Over; Jump Over; June Is Bustin' Out All Over; Kiss You All Over; Let Us Be Sweethearts Over Again; (I'm Afraid) The Masquerade Is Over; Moon Over Miami; Move Over Darling; My Barney Lies Over the Ocean (Just the Way He Lied to Me); My Bonnie Lies Over the Ocean, or, Bring Back My Bonnie to Me; My Cup Runneth Over; Now the Day Is Over; Over and Over; Over and Over Again; Over and Over Again; Over My Shoulder; Over the Garden Wall; Over the Hill; Over the Rainbow; Over the Waves; Over There; Over You; Over You; Overdrive; Overkill; Overnight; The Party's Over; The Party's Over Now; Roll Me Over; Roll

Over Beethoven; Sailing (, Sailing) (Over the Bounding Main); Say a Prayer for the Boys Over There; Say It (Over and Over Again); Shakin' All Over; Someone To Watch Over Me; (Just Like) Starting Over; Stop and Think It Over; Tell It All Over Again; They Go Wild Simply Wild Over Me; Wake Me When It's Over; We Shall Overcome; Weeping, Sad and Lonely, or, When This Cruel War Is Over; We're Going Over; When It's Night-Time in Italy, It's Wednesday over Here; When the Harvest Days Are Over, Jessie Dear; When the Honeymoon Was Over; When the Lights Go On Again (All Over the World); When the Moon Comes over the Mountain; When the War Is Over; Mary; (There'll Be Blue Birds over) The White Cliffs of Dover; Why Should I Cry over You; Won't You Come Over to My House; You Can't Pull the Wool over My Eyes

Overalls, *see* **Pants**

Overcoat, *see* **Coat**

Owl, *see* **Wise**

Ox   Down the Old Ox Road; Hadyn's Ox Minuet

Pacific   Blue Pacific Moonlight

Pack, *see also* **Gang**   Pack Up Your Trouble in Your Old Kit Bag and Smile, Smile, Smile; Pistol Packin' Mama

Paddle, *see* **Boat**

Paddy   Paddy Duffy's Cart; Paddy McGinty's Goat

Pagan   Pagan Love Song

Paganini, *see* **Music**

Page, *see* **Book**

Pail, *see* **Bucket**

Pain, *see* **Ache**

Paint   Goodbye Ol' Paint, or, I Ride an Old Paint, or, I'm a-Leavin' Cheyenne; Masterpiece; The Old Master Painter; Paint It Black; Painted Tainted Rose; Painting the Clouds with Sunshine; A Picture No Artist Can Paint; The Wedding of the Painted Doll

Pair, *see* **Two**

Pajamas, *see* **Sleep**

Pal, *see* **Friend**

Palace, *see* **Castle**

Pale   Pale Moon; A Whiter Shade of Pale

Palm, *see* **Tree**

Pan   The Pipes of Pan; The Pipes of Pan Are Calling; Shoofly Pie and Apple Pan Dowdy

Pansy   Only a Pansy Blossom

Panther, *see* **Cat**

Pants, *see also* **Dungaree, Suit**   Bell Bottom Trousers; Black Denim Trousers; Brass in Pocket; I've Got a Pocketful of Dreams; Pocketful of Miracles; Sam, You Made the Pants Too Long; Short Shorts; Who Threw the Overalls in Mrs. Murphy's Chowder; You've Got To Pick a Pocket or Two

Papa, *see* **Father**

Paper   Dance of the Paper Dolls; I Guess I'll Get the Papers and Go Home; It's Only a Paper Moon; Paper Doll; Paper Kisses; Paper Mache; Paper Roses; Paperback Writer; When Father Papered the Parlour

Parade   Before the Parade Passes By; The Circus Is on Parade; Don't Rain on My Parade; Easter Parade; I Love a Parade; I Watch the Love Parade; Love Parade; The Mosquito's Parade; My Dream of the Big Parade; (This Is) My Love Parade; Parade of the Wooden Soldiers; Patrick's Day Parade; Picture Parade; The Pullman Porter's on Parade; Rastus On Parade; South Rampart Street Parade; Sweethearts On Parade; When a Soldier's on Parade; When the Guards Are on Parade; When the Guardsman Started Crooning on Parade; When the Sergeant Major's on Parade

Paradise   Almost Paradise; Almost Paradise; Drifting and Dreaming (Sweet Paradise); I'll Build a Stairway to Paradise; Just Another Day in Paradise; My Paradise; Paradise (Waltz); Paradise for Two; Return to Paradise; The Road to Paradise; Search for Paradise; Stranger in Paradise; The Sunshine of Paradise Alley

Pardon, *see* **Sorry**

Paris   An American in Paris; April in Paris; Ca C'est Paris; How Ya Gonna Keep 'Em Down on the Farm (After They've Seen Paree); I Love Paris; The Last Time I Saw Paris; Mademoiselle de Paris; Midnight in Paris; Paree!; Paris in the Spring; Paris Loves Lovers; Paris Original; Parisian Pierrot; (I Don't Understand) The Parisians; The Poor People of Paris; That's What Makes Paris Paree; Under a Roof in Paree; Under Paris Skies; Under the Bridges of Paris; Windows of Paris; You Don't Know Paree (Paris)

Park   Barefoot in the Park; A Bench in the Park; Concert in the Park; Conversation on Park Avenue; Got the Bench, Got the Park, But I Haven't Got You; Itchycoo Park; MacArthur Park; On the Benches in the Park; Pettin' in the Park; The Rain, the Park and Other Things; Slumming on Park Avenue; The Soldiers in the Park; Stairway to the Stars (Park Avenue Fantasy); A Tree in the Park; While Strolling Through the Park One Day, or, The Fountain in the Park; Yuletide, Park Avenue

Parliament   Ye Parliament of England

Parlour   If You're Irish, Come into the Parlour; The Queen Was in the Parlour; When Father Papered the Parlour

Parsley, *see* **Seasonings**

Parting, *see* **Leave**

Partner   Change Partners; Changing Partners

Party   Hostess with the Mostes' on the Ball; I Took My Harp to a Party; I Went to a Marvelous Party; In a Party Mood; It's My Party; The Life of the Party; Party All the Time; Party Doll; Party Lights; Party Time; The Party's Over; The Party's Over Now; Shindig; That Certain Party; Too Many Parties and Too Many Pals; When I Saw Sweet Nellie Home, or, I Was Seeing Nellie Home, or, Aunt Dinah's Quilting Party

Pasadena   (Home in) Pasadena

El Paso   El Paso

Pass   Before the Parade Passes By; An Hour Never Passes; I Passed By Your Window; I'll Never Let a Day Pass By; My Future Just Passed; Pass Me By; Pass That Peace Pipe; Passe; Passing Breeze; Passing By; Passing Strangers; Praise the

Lord and Pass the Ammunition; Two Hearts That Pass in the Night

Passage   Northwest Passage; Time Passages

Passion   The Birth of Passion

Past, *see also* **Ago**   O God, Our Help in Ages Past; Let Bygones Be Bygones; Let Bygones Be Bygones; You're My Past, Present and Future

Pastry   Napoleon's a Pastry; Swedish Pastry; Who Ate Napoleons with Josephine When Bonaparte Was Away

Pasture   Carry Me Back to Green Pastures

Pat   Give Yourself a Pat on the Back

Patch   Patches; Patches (I'm Depending on You)

Path   The Path That Leads the Other Way; Pathfinder's March

Patience   See, Gentle Patience Smiles on Pain

Patient, *see* **Hospital**

Patricia   Patricia

Patrick   Patrick's Day Parade

Patrol, *see also* **Police**   American Patrol (We Must Be Vigilant); Highway Patrol; Siamese Patrol

Paul   Paul Temple Theme

Paula   Hey Paula

Pauline   Poor Pauline

Pay   And the Grass Won't Pay No Mind

Pea   Goober Peas; Mama Don't Want No Peas an' Rice an' Cocoanut Oil

Peace   Give Me Love (Give Me Peace on Earth); Give Peace a Chance; It's So Peaceful in the Country; Pass That Peace Pipe; Peace Train; Shalom

Peach   Everything Is Peaches Down in Georgia; If You Don't Want My Peaches, You'd Better Stop Shaking My Tree

Peacock   The Peacock; The White Peacock

Peanut   The Peanut Vendor

Pearl   Mama's Pearl; My Pearl's a Bowery Girl; The Pearl of Sweet Ceylon; Remember Pearl Harbor; The Sea Hath Its Pearls; A String of Pearls

Peasant, *see* **Poor**

Pebble, *see* **Rock**

Peck   A Bushel and a Peck; Peckin'

Peculiar, *see* **Strange**

Pedro, *see* **Peter**

Peek, *see* **Watch**

Peg   Peg o' My Heart; Peggy; Peggy O'Neil; Peggy Sue

Pen   La Plume de Ma Tante (The Pen of My Aunt)

Pence, *see* **Money**

Pennsylvania   Pennsylvania Polka; Pennsylvania 6-5000; Pittsburgh, Pennsylvania

Penny, *see* **Money**

Penthouse, *see* **House**

People *see also* **Company, Gang**   Another Hundred People; Assembly; Beautiful People of Denver; Crazy People; Dear Hearts and Gentle People; Everyday People; For All Mankind (Theme from *Gandhi*); Games People Play; Games Peo-

ple Play; Human Nature; I See a Million People; Let the People Sing; Listen People; March of the Dwarfs; My Generation; Nice People (with Nice Habits); No Two People; Ordinary People; Other People's Babies; People; People Got To Be Free; The People Tree; People Will Say We're in Love; Personally; The Poor People of Paris; The Purple People Eater; Sergeant Pepper's Lonely Hearts Club Band; Short People; Smiley's People; Some People; Stay with the Happy People; A Terrific Band and a Real Nice Crowd; They Just Can't Stop It (The Games People Play); Three's a Crowd; Two Sleepy People; Wake the Town and Tell the People; Was That the Human Thing To Do; What Do (the) Simple Folk Do; Who Dat Say Chicken in Dis Crowd; Why Do the Wrong People Travel; You Could Drive a Person Crazy; You're Only Human (Second Wind)

Pepper   Sergeant Pepper's Lonely Hearts Club Band

Peppermint, *see* **Candy**

Perfect   Close Enough to Perfect; A Perfect Day; The Perfect Song; Practice Makes Perfect

Performer, *see* **Actor**

Perfume   Incense and Perfume; Red Silk Stockings and Green Perfume; Shave and a Haircut, Bay Rum

Perhaps   Perhaps, Perhaps, Perhaps

Permanent   The Oldest Established (Permanent Floating Crap Game in New York)

Persia   In a Persian Garden; In a Persian Market; Persian Rosebud; Persian Rug

Person, *see* **People**

Personality   Personality; Personality; Sunny Disposish; With All Her Faults I Love Her Still

Persuasion   Almost Persuaded; Coax Me a Little Bit; Crystal Blue Persuasion; Friendly Persuasion, or, Thee I Love; Fully Persuaded; (Theme from) The Persuaders

Petal, *see* **Flower**

Peter   Cuban Peter; Little Pink Petty from Peter; Peter Peter Pumpkin Eater; Oh Peter Go Ring Dem Bells; Pedro the Fisherman; Pete Kelly's Blues; Peter and the Wolf; Peter Cottontail; (Theme from) Peter Gunn; Piccolo Pete; Sweet Peter

Petersbourgh   Petersbourgh Sleighride

Petite, *see* **Little, Small**

Petticoat   Petticoats of Portugal

Petting, *see* **Court**

Petty   Little Pink Petty from Peter

Phil   Phil the Fluter's Ball

Philadelphia   Philadelphia Freedom; T.S.O.P. (The Sound of Philadelphia)

Phoenix   By the Time I Get to Phoenix

Photograph   Freeze-Frame; In My Little Snapshot Album; Kodachrome; The Photo of the Girl I Left Behind; Photograph

Physician, *see* **Doctor**

Pianissimo, *see* **Music, Quiet**

Piano   I Love a Piano; Kitten on the Keys; The Old Pi-anna

Rag; The Old Piano Roll Blues; Piano Man; The Singing Piano

Picardy   Roses of Picardy

Piccolo, *see* **Flute**

Pick   He's a Rag Picker; Old Sam (Pick Up Tha' Musket); Pick Up the Pieces; Pick Yourself Up; Pickin' a Chicken; They Always Pick on Me; You've Got To Pick a Pocket or Two

Picnic   (Theme from) Picnic; A Picnic for Two; Stoned Soul Picnic; The Teddy Bear's Picnic

Picture, *see also* **Photograph**   At the Moving Picture Ball; Freeze-Frame; If I Had a Talking Picture of You; Just Try To Picture Me (Back (Down) Home in Tennessee); Let's Go into a Picture Show; Masterpiece; The Mottoes Framed Upon the Wall; Picture Me Without You; A Picture No Artist Can Paint; A Picture of Me Without You; A Picture of You; Picture Parade; The Picture That's Turned to (Toward) the Wall; Pictures at an Exhibition; Pictures in the Sky; Portrait of a Flirt; Portrait of Jennie; A Portrait of My Love; You Oughta Be in Pictures

Pie   (Bye Bye) American Pie; Bake Dat Chicken Pie; The Pied Piper; Shoofly Pie and Apple Pan Dowdy; Sweetie Pie; Wild Honey Pie; The Worst Pies in London

Piece   Bits and Pieces; Chewing a Piece of Straw; Just a Piece of Sky; One Piece at a Time; Pick Up the Pieces; Pieces of Dreams; We Don't Want the Bacon, What We Want Is a Piece of the Rhine

Pig   Gimme a Pigfoot (and a Bottle of Beer); Hand for the Hog; Root, Hog, or Die; This Little Piggie Went to Market

Pigeon   Pigeon Walk

Pilgrim   The Landing of the Pilgrims, or, the Pilgrim Fathers; Pilgrims' Chorus

Pillow   At Midnight on My Pillow Lying; Pillow Talk; Tears on My Pillow; Tears On My Pillow

Pilot, *see* **Airplane**

Pin   I'm Gonna Pin My Medal on the Girl I Left Behind

Pinball   Pinball Wizard

Pine, *see* **Tree**

Pink   Cherry Pink and Apple Blossom White; Lily the Pink; Little Pink Petty from Peter; (Theme from) The Pink Panther; Pink Shoelaces; Strike Me Pink; A White Sport Coat and a Pink Carnation; You're a Pink Toothbrush

Pipe, *see* **Flute, Smoke**

Piper, *see* **Flute**

Pirate   Pirate Jenny; Pirate Song, or, Fifteen Men on a (the) Dead Man's Chest—Yo! Ho! Ho! and a Bottle of Rum; The Scarlet Buccaneer

Pistol, *see* **Gun**

Pitch   I Pitch My Lonely Caravan at Night

Pittsburgh   The Belle of Pittsburgh (March); Pittsburgh, Pennsylvania

Pity   Isn't It a Pity; It's a Pity To Say Goodnight; She Is More To Be Pitied Than Censured; Sympathy; Tusk

Place   All Over the Place; Another Time, Another Place; Any Old Place I Can Hang My Hat Is Home Sweet Home to Me; Any Place I Hang My Hat Is Home; Any Old Place with You; Ev'rybody Has a Laughing Place; Far Away Places; (There's No Place Like) Home for the Holidays; I Know a Place; I've Got the Time—I've Got the Place, But It's Hard To Find the Girl; A Lil' Ole Bitty Pissant Country Place; A Place in the Sun; (Theme from) Return to Peyton Place, or, The Wonderful Season of Love; Right Place Wrong Time; Somebody Else Is Taking My Place; (Theme from) A Summer Place; Theme from Peyton Place; When You're All Dressed Up and No Place To Go; You Find the Time, I'll Find the Place

Plan   I Guess I'll Have To Change My Plan

Plant   If I Should Plant a Tiny Seed of Love; Plant a Watermelon on My Grave and Let the Juice Soak Through; You Planted a Rose in the Garden of Love

Play   (Hey Won't You Play) Another Somebody Done Somebody Wrong Song; April Played the Fiddle; Ask Her While the Band Is Playing; (Casey Would Waltz with the Strawberry Blonde While) The Band Played On; Games People Play; Games People Play; Hey Gypsy (Play Gypsy); I Don't Want To Play in Your Yard; I Played Fiddle for the Czar; I'll Play for You; I'm Looking For a Guy Who Plays Alto and Baritone and Doubles on a Clarinet and Wears a Size Thirty-Seven Suit; I'm Playing with Fire; Lady Play Your Mandolin; Let the Music Play; Little David, Play on Your Harp; Play a Simple Melody; Play, Fiddle, Play; Play Gypsies—Dance Gypsies; Play Me Hearts and Flowers (I Wanna Cry); Play Orchestra Play; Play That Barbershop Chord (Mister Jefferson Lord); Play That Funky Music; Play to Me, Gypsy; Playthings; Please Come and Play in My Yard; See Emily Play; Since Sister Nell Heard Paderewski Play; They Just Can't Stop It (The Games People Play); They're Playing Our Song; The Violin Began To Play; When the Gypsy Played; When the Organ Played at Twilight (The Song That Reached My Heart); When You Play in the Game of Love; When You Played the Organ and I Sang "The Rosary"; When Yuba Plays the Rumba on His Tuba; Yiddle on Your Fiddle, or, Play Some Ragtime; You Can't Play Every Instrument in the Band; You Can't Play in Our Yard Any More

Playground   I'm on a See-Saw; Playground in My Mind; Where's the Playground Susie

Playmate, *see* **Friend**

Plea   Just As I Am Without One Plea

Pleasant   Au Revoir, Pleasant Dreams

Please   Baby, Won't You Please Come Home; Bill Bailey, Won't You Please Come Home; Dinner for One, Please James; (Please) Do It Again; Give Me a Moment Please; If You Please; Josephine Please No Lean on the Bell; May I; May I Have the Next Romance with You; May I Sing to You; Morning, Please Don't Come; Music, Maestro, Please; Please; Please Be Kind; Please Believe Me; Please Come and Play in My Yard; Please Don't Go; Please Don't Mention It; Please Don't Say "No"; Please Don't Take My Lovin' Man Away; Please Don't Talk About Me When I'm Gone; Please Don't Tease; Please Go 'Way and Let Me Sleep; Please Hello; Please Help Me I'm Falling; Please Mister Please; Please Mister Postman; Please Mister Sun; Please Please Me; What's the Reason (I'm Not Pleasin' You)

Pleasure   Double Your Pleasure; Life Let Us Cherish, or, Snatch Fleeting Pleasures

Plenty   I Got Plenty o' Nuttin'; Plenty To Be Thankful For; That's A Plenty; With Plenty of Money and You

Plough, *see* **Work**

Plum   Dance of the Sugar-Plum Fairy; Plum Pudding

Pocket, *see* **Pants**

Poet   The Dying Poet; Poet and Peasant Overture

Poetry, *see also* **Rhyme**   Poetry in Motion; Poetry Man

Point   The Finger of Suspicion Points at You; The Point of No Return

Poison   Church of the Poison Mind

Poker, *see* **Gambling**

Poland   Polish Dance

Police, *see also* **Patrol**   Ask a Policeman; Gee, Officer Krupke!; The Girl on the Police Gazette; I Love a Cop; I Shot the Sheriff; The Laughing Policeman; Lawman; M-Squad; The Policeman's Holiday

Polish, *see* **Shine**

Politics   Politics and Poker

Polkadot   Itsy Bitsy Teenie Weenie Yellow Polkadot Bikini; Polka Dots and Moonbeams

Polly   Polly Put the Kettle On; Polly Perkins of Paddington Green; Polly Wolly Doodle

Pomp   Pomp and Circumstance

Pony, *see* **Horse**

Poor   Don't Do That to the Poor Puss Cat; Down in Poverty Row; Give Me Your Tired, Your Poor; Poet and Peasant Overture; Poor Butterfly; Poor John; Poor Jud (Is Daid); Poor Little Angeline; Poor Little Fool; Poor Little Hollywood Star; Poor Little Rich Girl; Poor Me; Poor Old Slave; Poor Papa (He's Got Nuthin' at All); Poor Pauline; The Poor People of Paris; Poor Pierrot; Poor Side of Town; Poverty's Tears Ebb and Flow; Salad Days; Slumming on Park Avenue; (Poor) Tom Bowling, or, The Sailor's Epitaph; When the Idle Poor Become the Idle Rich

Pop, *see also* **Father**   Pop Goes the Weasel

Popcorn   Popcorn

Pope, *see* **Church**

Popeye   (I'm) Popeye the Sailor Man

Poppy   Amapola, or, Pretty Little Poppy; When the Poppies Bloom Again

Popular   I'm a Popular Man

Porch   Last Night on the Back Porch—I Loved Her Best of All

Porridge   Pease Porridge Hot

Port   Any Old Port in a Storm; The Fleet's in Port Again

Porter, *see* **Train**

Portrait, *see* **Picture**

Portugal   April in Portugal; The Argentines, the Portuguese and the Greeks; Petticoats of Portugal; The Portuguese Washerwoman

Positive   Ac-cent-tchu-ate the Positive; Positively Fourth Street

Possible, *see* **Impossible**

Postman, *see* **Letter**

Pot   Melting Pot

Potato   Burgers and Fries; Mashed Potato Time; Mister Dumpling; (Potatoes Are Cheaper—Tomatoes Are Cheaper) Now's the Time To Fall in Love; Sweet Potato Piper

Potion, *see* **Medicine**

Potomac   All Quiet Along the Potomac Tonight

Poughkeepsie   He's a Gypsy from Poughkeepsie

Pound   A Hundred Pounds of Clay

Pour, *see also* **Rain**   I Poured My Heart into a Song

Poverty, *see* **Poor**

Powder   Powder Your Face with Sunshine

Power   All Hail the Power of Jesus' Name; The Power Game; Power of Gold; The Power of Love; Power to All Our Friends

Practice   Practice Makes Perfect

Prairie   Carry Me Back to the Lone Prairie; Oh, Bury Me Not on the Lone Prairie, or, The Dying Cowboy; Roll Along Prairie Moon; Rosalie the Prairie Flower

Praise   Old Hundred(th) Doxology, or, Praise God, from Whom All Blessings Flow; Praise the Lord and Pass the Ammunition

Prayer   Baby's Prayer; Christopher Robin Is Saying His Prayers; Comin' In on a Wing and a Prayer; Couldn't Hear Nobody Pray; I Said My Pajamas (and Put On My Prayers); I Say a Little Prayer; I'll Pray for You; Just a Baby's Prayer at Twilight; The Lord's Prayer; A Maiden's Prayer; My Prayer; Sabbath Prayer; Say a Prayer for Me Tonight; Say a Prayer for the Boys Over There; ('Tis Me, O Lord) Standin' in the Need of Pray'r; Sweet Spirit, Hear My Prayer; Teenage Prayer; We Gather Together (To Ask the Lord's Blessing), or, Prayer of Thanksgiving

Preacher, *see* **Church**

Precious   Precious and Few; A Precious Little Thing Called Love; Precious Love; A Very Precious Love

Prefer, *see* **Choice**

Prelude   Blue Prelude; Prelude to a Kiss; Prelude to the Stars

Present, *see* **Now**

President   President Grant's March; The President's March; When I'm the President (We Want Cantor); The White House Chair; Wintergreen For President

Pretend, *see also* **(Make) Believe, Fantasy, Imagination**   The Great Imposter; The Great Pretender; It's Make Believe Ballroom Time; It's Only Make Believe; Pretend

Pretty   Amapola, or, Pretty Little Poppy; (When the) Bloom Is on the Rye, or, My Pretty Jane; Coom Pretty One; I Feel Pretty; I'm Sitting Pretty in a Pretty Little City; Oh Pretty Woman; P.Y.T. (Pretty Young Thing); Pretty Baby; Pretty Edelweiss; Pretty Flamingo; A Pretty Girl; A Pretty Girl Is Like a Melody; Pretty Kitty Kelly; Pretty Lady; Pretty Women; Tell Me Pretty Maiden (Are There Any More at Home Like You); Ten Pretty Girls; To a Sweet Pretty Thing; Ugly Chile (You're Some Pretty Doll); When You're Pretty

Pretzel   Moonlight and Pretzels

Pride   London Pride

Priest, *see* **Church**

Primrose, *see* **Rose**

Prince   Prince of Wails; Some Day My Prince Will Come

Princess   Dollar Princesses; Pavanne for a Dead Infanta (Princess); Princesita

Prison, Prisoner, *see* **Jail**

Private   Private Eyes; Private Investigations; Would You Rather Be a Colonel with an Eagle on Your Shoulder, or a Private with a Chicken on Your Knee?

Program   Not So Much a Programme, More a Way of Life

Prohibition, *see* **Alcohol**

Promise   I Never Promised You a Rose Garden; Júrame (Promise, Love); Oh Promise Me; Promise Her Anything But Give Her Love; Promise Me a Rose; Promises Promises

Proper   Love with the Proper Stranger

Proposition   Life's a Funny Proposition After All; What You're Proposing

Protect   Heaven Will Protect the Working Girl; My Defenses Are Down; Not While I'm Around; Safe in the Arms of Jesus; Safely Through Another Week; The Safety Dance

Proud   Proud Mary

Prove, *see* **Truth**

Prudence   Dear Prudence

Pucker, *see* **Kiss**

Pudding   Plum Pudding; Puddin' Head; Puddin' Head Jones

Puff, *see* **Smoke**

Pull   Don't Pull Your Love; You Can't Pull the Wool over My Eyes

Pumpkin   Mammy's Little Pumpkin Colored Coon(s); Peter Peter Pumpkin Eater

Puppet   Funeral March of a Marionette; I've Got No Strings; Puppchen; Puppet on a String

Puppy, *see* **Dog**

Purchase, *see* **Buy**

Pure   Ah! So Pure

Purple   Deep Purple; The Purple People Eater; Purple Rain

Purpose   Accidentally On Purpose

Push   I Didn't Slip, I Wasn't Pushed, I Fell; Push De Button; Push Dem Clouds Away; The Pushbike Song

Quaker   All the Quakers Are Shoulder Shakers Down in Quaker Town; There's a Quaker Down in Quaker Town

Quarter, *see also* **Money**   About a Quarter to Nine; In the Quatermaster's Stores; The Latin Quarter; Quarter to Three Waltz; Two Hearts in Three Quarter Time

Quartette, *see* **Four**

Queen   Caribbean Queen (No More Love on the Run); Dancing Queen; God Save the King (Queen); Killer Queen; Queen of Hearts; Queen of the Hop; The Queen Was in the Parlour; Soldiers of the Queen

Queer   My Word You Do Look Queer

Question   Question and Answer (Démande et Réponse)

Quick, *see* **Fast**

Quiet, *see also* **Soft**   All Quiet Along the Potomac Tonight; Careless Whisper; Hush Hush Sweet Charlotte; I Loved You Once in Silence; Milkman Keep Those Bottles Quiet; Rock-a-Bye (Hush-a-Bye) Baby; My Quiet Village; My Silent Love; Pianissimo; A Quiet Girl; A Quiet Girl; Quiet Night; Shifting, Whispering Sands; Silent Night, Holy Night; Silent Running (On Dangerous Ground); The Sounds of Silence; There's a Kind of Hush; When Stars Are in the Quiet Skies; Whisper That You Love Me; Whisper to Me; Whisper Your Mother's Name; Whispering; Whispering Bells; Whispering Hope; The Whispering Pines of Nevada; Whispers in the Dark

Quit, *see* **Stop**

Rabbit   Bunny Hop; Cotton Tail; Funny Bunny Hug; The March Hare; Peter Cottontail; Run Rabbit Run

Raccoon   Doin' the Raccoon

Race   Ben Hur Chariot Race (March); De Camptown Races (Gwine To Run All Night); Every Race Has a Flag But the Coon; The Race Is On; (When You're) Racing with the Clock; Racing with the Moon; Space Race

Rachel   Reuben and Rachel, or, Reuben, Reuben, I've Been Thinking

Radio   Listen to the Radio; On the Air; On the Radio; Sleepin' with the Radio On; Song on the Radio; Turn Your Radio On; Video Killed the Radio Star; The Voice of R.K.O.; The WRNS March

Rag   He's a Rag Picker; Rag Doll; Rag Mop; Raggedy Ann; Ragging the Scale; Rags, Bottles or Bones; Rags to Riches

Rail, *see* **Fence, Train**

Railroad, *see* **Train**

Rain, *see also* **Storm**   April Showers; Baby the Rain Must Fall; Because of Rain; Blue Rain; Butterflies in the Rain; Call Me Up Some Rainy Afternoon; Come Rain or Come Shine; The Day the Rains Came; Don't Count the Rainy Days; Don't Rain on My Parade; Fire and Rain; A Garden in the Rain; A Hard Rain's A-Gonna Fall; Here Comes the Rain Again; Here's That Rainy Day; I Can See Clearly Now (The Rain Has Gone); I Found You in the Rain; I Get the Blues When It Rains; I Got Lucky in the Rain; I Left My Sugar Standing in the Rain (and She Melted Away); I Love a Rainy Night; I Made It Through the Rain; I Wish It Would Rain; If the Rain's Got To Fall; If You Want the Rainbow (You Must Have the Rain); Into Each Life Some Rain Must Fall; Isn't This a Lovely Day (To Be Caught in the Rain); It Ain't Gonna Rain No Mo'; It Looks Like Rain in Cherry Blossom Lane; It Never Rains in Southern California; It Takes a Little Rain with the Sunshine To Make the World Go Round; It Was Only a Sun Shower; It's Raining Again; Just Like a Butterfly (That's Caught in the Rain); Just Walking in the Rain; Laughter in the Rain; Lay Down (Candles in the Rain); Let a Smile Be Your Umbrella on a Rainy (Rainy) Day; Let It Rain! Let It Pour! (I'll Be in Virginia in the Morning); Lilacs in the Rain; Little Drops of Rain; Man in a Raincoat; My Blue Bird Was Caught in the Rain; Oh! Didn't It Rain; Purple Rain; Rain; Rain; Rain Forest; The Rain in Spain; The Rain, the Park and Other Things; Raindrops; Raindrops Keep Fallin' on My Head; (The Song of) Raintree County; The Rainy Day; Rainy Day Women #12 & 35; Rainy Days and Mondays; Rainy Night in Rio; Rhythm of the Rain; Rhythm of the Rain; Right As the Rain; Roses in the Rain; Running Between the Raindrops; Save It for a Rainy Day; September in the Rain; Shower the People; Singing' in the Rain; Smoky Mountain Rain; Soon It's Gonna Rain; Southern Rains; Wal, I Swan!, or, Ebenezer Frye, or, Giddiap Napoleon, It Looks Like Rain; Was It Rain; Who'll Stop the Rain; With the Wind and the Rain in Your Hair

Rainbow   Did You Ever Ride on a Rainbow; The End (of the Rainbow); I Found the End of the Rainbow; If You Want the Rainbow (You Must Have the Rain); I'm Always Chasing Rainbows; I've Got the World on a String; Look to the Rainbow; Over the Rainbow; Rainbow; Rainbow; Rainbow on the River; De Rainbow Road; Rainbow Stew; Sing a Rainbow; Sunshine, Lollipops and Rainbows; There's a Rainbow Round My Shoulder; Where's That Rainbow; Why (Is There a Rainbow in the Sky)

Raise   Come, Ye Faithful, Raise the Strain; Did Tosti Raise His Bowler Hat When He Said Goodbye; I Didn't Raise My Boy To Be a Soldier

Ramble   Marta, or, Rambling Rose of the Wildwood; Muskrat Ramble; My Rambler Rose; Oh, Didn't He Ramble; Ramblin' Man; Ramblin' Rose; Ramblin' Rose; Rambling Wreck from Georgia Tech

Ramona   Ramona

Ranch   El Rancho Grande

Range   Home on the Range, or, Oh, Give Me a Home Where the Buffalo Roam

Ranger   The Ranger's Song; The Yellow Rose of Texas, or, Song of the Texas Rangers

Rapture   Music in May (Careless Rapture); Rapture

Rare   Rich and Rare Were the Gems She Wore; So Rare

Rascal   (I'll Be Glad When You're Dead) You Rascal You

Raspberry   Raspberry Beret

Rastus   Rastus On Parade; Rufus Rastus Johnson Brown (What You Goin' To Do When the Rent Comes 'Round)

Rattle   Shake, Rattle and Roll

Raunchy   Raunchy

Ray, *see* **Sunshine**

Reach   Reach Out and Touch; Reach Out for Me; Reach Out I'll Be There; Reaching for the Moon; Reaching for the Moon; The Song That Reached My Heart; When the Organ Played at Twilight (The Song That Reached My Heart)

Read   Can You Read My Mind; I Think When I Read That Sweet Story; If You Could Read My Mind; Read 'Em and Weep; The Wind Cannot Read

Rear, *see* **Back**

Reason, *see also* **Think**   (I Love You) For Sentimental Reasons; Love Is My Reason; Love Is the Reason; That's the Reason Noo I Wear a Kilt; What's the Reason (I'm Not Pleasin' You); You're the Reason God Made Oklahoma; You're the Reason I'm Living

Rebecca   Rebecca of Sunny-Brook Farm

Rebel   He's a Rebel

Rebound, *see* **Bounce**

Recognize   I Like To Recognize the Tune; You'd Never Know the Old Home Town of Mine

Recollection, *see* **Remember**

Record   (Hey Won't You Play) Another Somebody Done Somebody Wrong Song; The Broken Record; Get Out Those Old Records; Juke Box Baby; Juke Box Saturday Night; Stereophonic Sound

Red, *see also* **Rose**   Columbia, the Gem of the Ocean, or, The Red, White, and Blue; Crimson and Clover; The Fatal Rose of Red; A House with a Little Red Barn; I'm Bringing a Red, Red Rose; I'm the Last of the Red-Hot Mamas; In My Little Red Book; In the Little Red Schoolhouse; The Lady in Red; Leave Me Alone (Ruby Red Dress); Li'l Red Riding Hood; Little Red Monkey; Little Red Rooster; My Love Is Like a Red, Red Rose; Nobody Knows What a Red Head Mama Can Do; Now Sleeps the Crimson Petal; One Two Three Red Light; Raspberry Beret; The Red Balloon; Red Lips Kiss My Blues Away; Red Neckin' Love Makin' Night; The Red River Valley; Red Roses for a Blue Lady; Red Rubber Ball; Red Sails in the Sunset; Red Silk Stockings and Green Perfume; Red Wing; Roses Are Red, My Love; Rudolph the Red-Nosed Reindeer; Scarlet O'Hara; Scarlet Ribbons (for Her Hair); The Scarlet Buccaneer; Sink Red Sun; Snoopy vs. The Red Baron; The Song from Moulin Rouge, or, Where Is Your Heart; Though Your Sins Be as Scarlet; When the Red, Red Robin Comes Bob, Bob, Bobbin' Along; When You Wore a Tulip and I Wore a Big Red Rose; You Dropped Me Like a Red Hot Penny

Redhead   Nobody Knows What a Red Head Mama Can Do

Refine   My Sugar Is So Refined

Reflection, *see* **Mirror**

Refrain   The Old Refrain

Regards   Give My Regards to Broadway

Regency   Regency Rakes

Regiment, *see* **Army**

Regret   Miss Otis Regrets; No Regrets

Regular   Mister Volunteer, or, You Don't Belong to the Regulars, You're Just a Volunteer

Reindeer, *see* **Christmas**

Relations, *see* **Family**

Release, *see* **Freedom**

Religion   (Gimme Dat) Old Time Religion

Remember, *see also* **Forget, Memory**   An Affair To Remember; Deja Vu; Did I Remember; Do You Remember the Last Waltz; I Remember How It Was; I Remember It Well; I Remember the Cornfields; I Remember You; I Shall Always Remember You Smiling; If You Remember Me; I'll (I) Remember April; I'll Remember Tonight; I'll Remember You; I'm Stepping Out with a Memory Tonight; It's Easy To Remember (and So Hard To Forget); Johnny Remember Me; Let Erin Remember the Days of Old; Moments To Remember; My Heart Reminds Me, or, And That Reminds Me; My Trundle Bed, or, Recollections of Childhood; Remember Boy, You're Irish (Shane Na Lown); Remember Me; Remember Pearl Harbor; Rememb'ring; Reminiscing; Roses for Remembrance; She Reminds Me of You; Something To Remember You By; The Stars Will Remember; Sweet Alice, or, Ben Bolt, or, Don't You Remember; Then You'll Remember Me; There's Always Something There To Remind Me; There's Something About a Rose (That Reminds Me of You); These Foolish Things Remind Me of You; Try To Remember; Will You Remember (Sweetheart); You Remind Me of My Mother; You Remind Me of the Girl That Used To Go to School with Me

Renee   Walk Away, Renee

Renegade   Renegade

Rent, *see* **Home**

Republic   Battle Hymn of the Republic

Rescue, *see* **Save**

Reservation   Indian Reservation

Resistance   My Resistance Is Low

Respect   Respect

Rest   God Rest You Merry Gentlemen; I Guess I'll Have To Dream the Rest; Let the Rest of the World Go By; Lounging at the Waldorf; What Are You Doing the Rest of Your Life; What Are You Doing the Rest of Your Life; Where My Caravan Has Rested

Restaurant   Alice's Restaurant; I Left My Heart at the Stage Door Canteen; Real Goodness from Kentucky Fried Chicken; The Waiter and the Porter and the Upstairs Maid; You Deserve a Break Today; You, You're the One

Restless   My Restless Lover; Nadia's Theme, or, The Young and the Restless

Retreat   Bonaparte's Retreat; Retreat

Return   Arrah Go On, I'm Gonna Go Back to Oregon; Baby Come Back; Baby, Won't You Please Come Home; Back Again to Happy-Go-Lucky Days; Back, Back, Back to Baltimore; (Every Time I Turn Around) Back in Love Again; Back in My Arms Again; Back in the Saddle Again; Back in Your Own Back Yard; Back on My Mind Again; Back to Donegal; Back to the Carolina You Love; Back to Those Happy Days; Be Back Soon; Bill Bailey, Won't You Please Come Home; The Bitch Is Back; (Take Me Back to My) Boots and Saddle; The Boys Are Coming Home Today; The Breeze (That's Bringing My Honey Back to Me); Bring Back My Daddy to Me; Bring Back My Golden Dreams; Bring Back Those Minstrel Days; Can't You Take It Back and Change It for a Boy; Carry Me Back to Green Pastures; Carry Me Back to Old Virginny; Carry Me Back to Ole Virginny, or, De Floating Show; Carry Me Back to the Lone Prairie; The Cat Came Back; Come Back and Shake Me; Come Back to Erin; Come Back to Me; Come Back to Sorrento; Come Back When You Grow Up; Come Home, Dewey, We Won't Do a Thing to You; Come Home to My Arms; Don't Take Me Home; Ellie Rhee, or, Carry Me Back to Tennessee; (Theme from) The Empire Strikes Back; Father, Dear Father, Come Home with Me Now, or, Come Home, Father; Get Back; Give It Back to the Indians; Hard Times Come Again No More; Here Comes Heaven Again; I Just Want To Go Back and Start the Whole Thing Over; I Want To Go Back to Michigan—Down on the Farm; I Want To Go Home; I Want You Back; I Wonder If She'll Ever Come Back to Me; I'm Going Back to Himazas; (Back Home Again in) Indiana; I'se Gwine Back to Dixie; It All Comes Back to Me Now; I've Just Come Back To Say Goodbye; Just Come Home; Keep the Home Fires Burning (Till the Boys Come Home); Looking Back; Lover Come Back to Me; Lulu's Back in Town; Many Happy Returns of the Day; The Minstrel's Return from the War; My Baby's Comin' Home; My Bonnie Lies Over

the Ocean, or, Bring Back My Bonnie to Me; My Boomerang Won't Come Back; My Guy's Come Back; Oh, How I Wish I Could Sleep Until My Daddy Comes Home; Oh! I Must Go Home Tonight; The Point of No Return; Return To Me; (Theme from) Return to Peyton Place, or, The Wonderful Season of Love; Return to Sender; Right Back Where We Started From; Rolling Stones—All Come Rolling Home Again; Show Me the Way To Go Home; Sometime You'll Wish Me Back Again; Take Back the Heart You Gave; Take Back Your Gold; Take Back Your Mink; Take Me Back to the Garden of Love; Take Me Back to Your Heart Again; There's a Boy Coming Home on Leave; Trabling Back to Georgia; Turn Back the Universe and Give Me Yesterday; Until You Come Back to Me (That's What I'm Gonna Do); Wait Till the Cows Come Home; Wait Until Your Daddy Comes Home; Walkin' Back to Happiness; Walkin' My Baby Back Home; Way Back Home; Welcome Back; When Johnny Comes Marching Home; When My Dream Boat Comes Home; When the Black Sheep Returns to the Fold; When the Boys Come Home; When the One You Love (Simply Won't Love Back); When the Swallows Come Back to Capistrano; When You Come Back; When You Come Back They'll Wonder Who the——You Are; When You Come Home; Wonder When My Baby's Coming Home; Workin' My Way Back to You; You Keep Coming Back Like a Song; You Try Somebody Else, and I'll Try Somebody Else (We'll Be Back Together Again); You'd Be So Nice To Come Home To

Reuben   Reuben and Rachel, or, Reuben, Reuben, I've Been Thinking

Revenge   Revenge

Reverie   My Reverie; Reverie

Revival   Revival

Revolution, *see* **War**

Rhine   Bing! Bang! Bing 'Em on the Rhine; Just Like Washington Crossed the Delaware, General Pershing Will Cross the Rhine; Moonlight on the Rhine; We Don't Want the Bacon, What We Want Is a Piece of the Rhine; When We've Wound Up the Watch on the Rhine

Rhinestone, *see* **Jewel**

Rhody   (Go Tell Aunt Rhody) The Ole Grey Goose (Is Dead)

Rhonda   Help Me Rhonda

Rhyme   I Love To Rhyme; Nothing Rhymed; Rhymes; (If I Had) Rhythm In My Nursery Rhymes

Rhythm   All God's Chillun Got Rhythm; Broadway Rhythm; College Rhythm; Crazy Rhythm; Everything's in Rhythm with My Heart; Fascinating Rhythm; Futuristic Rhythm; I Got Rhythm; Lullaby in Rhythm; (If I Had) Rhythm in My Nursery Rhymes; Rhythm Is Our Business; Rhythm of the Night; Rhythm of the Rain; Rhythm of the Rain; Rhythm on the River; Rockin' in Rhythm; The Syncopated Clock; Walking in Rhythm

Ribbon   Blue Ribbon Gal; Put 'Em in a Box, Tie 'Em with a Ribbon (and Throw 'Em in the Deep Blue Sea); Scarlet Ribbons (for Her Hair); She Wore a Yellow Ribbon, or, All Round My Hat (Round Her Neck) I (She) Wore a Yellow Ribbon; Tie a Yellow Ribbon Round the Ole Oak Tree

Rice   Mama Don't Want No Peas an' Rice an' Cocoanut Oil; Not for All the Rice in China

Rich, *see* **Money**

Richard Devil's Gallop, or, Dick Barton Theme; Dick's Maggot; Open the Door, Richard

Richmond The Lass of Richond Hill

Ricochet, *see* **Boomerang**

Riddle I Gave My Love a Cherry, or, The Riddle Song

Ride Did You Ever Ride on a Rainbow; Easy Rider; Ghost Riders in the Sky, or, A Cowboy Legend; Give a Man a Horse He Can Ride; Goodbye Ol' Paint, or, I Ride an Old Paint, or, I'm a-Leavin' Cheyenne; I Tipped My Hat and Slowly Rode Away; Li'l Red Riding Hood; Louisiana Hayride; Mama Don't Allow No Easy Riders Here; Petersbourgh Sleighride; Ride Captain Ride; Ride Like the Wind; Ride On, Ride On; Ride, Tenderfoot, Ride; Ridin' High; Ridin' on the Moon; Sleigh Ride; Sleigh Ride in July; Thanks for the Buggy Ride

Ridiculous, *see* **Crazy**

Right All Right; The Boy Guessed Right; Feels So Right; Have I the Right; He Fought for a Cause He Thought Was Right; He Walked Right In, Turned Around and Walked Right Out Again; He's a Right Guy; (If Loving You Is Wrong) I Don't Want To Be Right; I Gotta (I've Got a) Right To Sing the Blues; I'd Rather Be Right; I'm Gonna Sit Right Down and Write Myself a Letter; I'm Gonna Wash That Man Right Outa My Hair; Left Right Out of Your Heart; Let's Start the New Year Right; Love So Right; Moonlight Feels Right; Our Country, May She Always Be Right; Right as the Rain; Right Back Where We Started From; Right Place Wrong Time; Right Said Fred; The Right Thing To Do; The Second Star to the Right; Still Right Here in My Heart; Straighten Up and Fly Right; Treat Her Right; Walk Right In; When You Walked Out Someone Else Walked Right In; Why Don't You Do Right; You're in the Right Church, But the Wrong Pew

Ring, *see also* **Bell** If the Phone Doesn't Ring, It's Me; I've Got Rings on My Fingers, or, Mumbo Jumbo Jijjiboo J. O'Shea; A Ring on the Finger Is Worth Two on the Phone; Ringo; Smoke Rings; This Diamond Ring; Too Many Rings Around Rosie; Wear My Ring Around Your Neck; Wedding Ring; When Your Old Wedding Ring Was New

Rio de Janeiro Flying Down to Rio; Rainy Night in Rio

Rio Grande Rose of the Rio Grande

Ripe Cherry Ripe

Rise Bad Moon Rising; The House of the Rising Sun; Moonrise on the Lowlands; Morgen—One More Sunrise; Rise and Fall of Flingle Bunt; Rise; Rise and Shine; Rise, Gentle Moon; Softly, As in a Morning Sunrise; Sunrise and You; Sunrise Serenade; Sunrise Sunset; When De Moon Comes Up Behind De Hill; When the Moon Comes over the Mountain; The World Is Waiting for the Sunrise

Rita Lovely Rita (Meter Maid); Rio Rita

Rite Rites of Spring; Ritual Fire Dance

Ritz Puttin' On the Ritz

River, *see* **Colorado,** etc. By the Bend of the River; By the River of (the) Roses; By the River Sainte Marie; Cruising Down the River; Cry Me a River; Dar's One More Ribber To Cross; Deep River; Down by the River; Down by the Riverside, or, Ain't Gwine Study War No More; Down by the Silvery Rio Grande; Down the River of Golden Dreams; Down Where the Swanee River Flows; The Gum Tree Canoe (on Grande); I've Been Floating Down the Old Green River; (Up a) Lazy River; Messing About on the River; Moody River; Moon River; Old Folks at Home (Way Down Upon the Swanee River); Ol' Man River; On the Old Fall River Line; One More River To Cross; Rainbow on the River; The Red River Valley; Rhythm on the River; Rio Rita; River Boat; The River Kwai March; The River Song, or, Something's Always Happening on the River; River, Stay 'Way from My Door; Riverboat Shuffle; Riviera Rose; Shenandoah, or, Across the Wide Missouri; Something's Always Happening on the River; Swanee River Moon; There's One Wide River To Cross, or, Noah's Ark; Time and the River; Trouble (in River City); Walkin' by the River; We Parted by the River; Weary River; Where the River Shannon Flows; Yellow River

Road All Roads Lead to You; Along the Rocky Road to Dublin; Caminito; Country Road; Down the Old Ox Road; Down the Winding Road of Dreams; Ease On Down the Road; The End of the Road; Freeway of Love; De Glory Road; Goodbye Yellow Brick Road; Highway Patrol; Highwayman; Hit the Road Jack; Hit the Road to Dreamland; The House by the Side of the Road; I Travel the Road; Jogging Along the Highway; King of the Road; Knocked 'Em in the Old Kent Road; Loch Lomond, or, The Bonnie Bonnie Banks, or, Oh! Ye'll Take the High Road; (Look Down That) Lonesome Road; The Long and Winding Road; Look Down, Look Down That Lonesome Road; On the Bumpy Road to Love; On the Road Again; On the Road to Mandalay; One for My Baby (and One More for the Road); De Rainbow Road; The Road to Morocco; The Road to Paradise; Roadways; (Get Your Kicks on) Route 66; Seven Bridges Road; Somewhere Down the Road; Song of the Open Road; Take Me Home Country Roads; Tramp! Tramp! Tramp! Along the Highway; (Theme from) Two for the Road

Roam, *see* **Wander**

Roar Roar, Lion, Roar

Roast, *see also* **Cook** The Christmas Song, or, Merry Christmas to You, or, Chestnuts Roasting on an Open Fire

Robber Gypsys, Tramps and Thieves; Just Like a Thief; The Robbers' Chorus; The Robbers' March; The Rogue Song; You've Got to Pick a Pocket or Two

Robe I Got (a Robe) Shoes, or, All God's Chillun Got Shoes

Robert, *see* **Bob**

Robin Auld Robin Gray, or, When the Sheep Are in the Fold; Christopher Robin at Buckingham Palace; Christopher Robin Is Saying His Prayers; Fly Robin Fly; Lonely Little Robin; Robin Adair; Robins and Roses; Rockin' Robin; When the Red, Red Robin Comes Bob, Bob, Bobbin' Along; When the Robins Nest Again; Where Did Robinson Crusoe Go with Friday on Saturday Night; Won't You Tell Me Why, Robin

Robot Mr. Roboto; Robot

Rock, *see also* **Stone** Along the Rocky Road to Dublin; The Big Rock Candy Mountain; Crocodile Rock; Detroit Rock City; Don't You Rock Me Daddy-O; Gonna Fly Now, or, Theme from Rocky; The Hand That Rocks the Cradle; Heart of Rock and Roll; (And) His Rocking Horse Ran Away; I Dig Rock and Roll Music; I Love Rock 'n' Roll; It's Only

Rock 'n Roll (But I Like It); It's Still Rock and Roll to Me; I've Got a Rock 'n' Roll Heart; Jailhouse Rock; Just a Little Rocking Chair and You; Limbo Rock; A Little Girl from Little Rock; Little Rock Getaway; Love on the Rocks; Loves Me Like a Rock; Rock-a-Bye (Hush-a-Bye) Baby; Rock-A-Billy; Rock-a-Bye (Hush-a-Bye) Baby; Rock-a-Bye Your Baby with a Dixie Melody; Rock-a My Soul (in the Bosom of Abraham); Rock 'n Me; Rock and Roll Music; Rock and Roll Waltz; (We're Gonna) Rock Around the Clock; The Rock Beside the Sea; Rock Bottom; R.O.C.K. in the U.S.A. (A Salute to 60's Rock); Rock Island Line; Rock Love; Rock Me Amadeus; Rock Me Gently; Rock Me to Sleep, Mother; Rock of Ages; Rock On; Rock the Boat; Rock with Me; Rock with the Cavemen; Rock Your Baby; Rockaway; Rocked in the Cradle of the Deep; (Ol') Rockin' Chair; Rockin' Chair; A Rockin' Good Way (To Mess Around and Fall in Love); Rockin' In Rhythm; Rockin' Robin; Rocky; Rocky Mountain High; Sit Down, You're Rocking the Boat; Sit Down, You're Rockin' the Boat; Someone's Rocking My Dream Boat; Take Me in Your Arms (Rock Me a Little While); That's Rock 'N' Roll; When It's Springtime in the Rockies; You're Not the Only Pebble on the Beach

Rod Chester (Let Tyrants Shake Their Iron Rod); Hot Rod Hearts

Rodger Rodger Young

Rogue, *see* **Robber**

Roll As Long as the World Rolls On; Cimarron (Roll On); Did You Ever Think As the Hearse Rolls By, or, The Worms Crawl In, the Worms Crawl Out; Good Night Ladies, or, Merrily We Roll Along; Heart of Rock and Roll; I Dig Rock and Roll Music; I Just Roll Along Havin' My Ups and Downs; I Love Rock 'n' Roll; I'm Sitting on Top of the World (Just Rolling Along—Just Rolling Along); It's Only Rock 'n Roll (But I Like It); It's Still Rock and Roll to Me; I've Got a Rock 'n' Roll Heart; I've Got Sixpence (As I Go Rolling Home); Let the Good Times Roll; Like a Rolling Stone; Liza (All the Clouds'll Roll Away); Merrily We Roll Along; The Oceana Roll; The Old Piano Roll Blues; Papa Was a Rollin' Stone; Rock and Roll Music; Rock and Roll Waltz; Roll Along Covered Wagon; Roll Along Prairie Moon; Roll Away Clouds; Roll Dem Roly Boly Eyes; Roll, Jordan, Roll; Roll Me Over; Roll on Eighteen Wheeler; Roll On Silver Moon, or, The Silver Moon; Roll On, Tulane, or, The Olive and Blue; Roll Out! Heave Dat Cotton; Roll Over Beethoven; Roll Them Cotton Bales; Rolled into One; Rolling Home; Rolling Round the World; Rolling Stones—All Come Rolling Home Again; Ro-Ro-Rollin' Along; Shake, Rattle and Roll; That's Rock 'N' Roll; Till the Clouds Roll By; The U.S. Field Artillery March, or, The Caissons Go Rolling Along; Wait Till the Clouds Roll By; Watching the Clouds Roll By; When the Mists Have Rolled Away; When the Roll Is Called Up Yonder

Rollercoaster Love Rollercoaster; Under the Roller Coaster

Romance Chiapanecas (While There's Music There's Romance); Crush on You; A Fine Romance; Here's to Romance; How's Your Romance; I'll Take Romance; Isn't It Romantic; I've Got a Crush on You; Liaisons; May I Have the Next Romance with You; My Romance; Romance; Romance; Romance; Romantica; Teenage Crush; This Is Romance; To the Land of My Own (Small) Romance; Too Romantic

Rome Arrivederci Roma; Autumn in Rome; By the Fountains of Rome; Children of Rome

Roof Dancing on the Ceiling; On a Roof in Manhattan; Tin Roof Blues; Under a Roof in Paree; Up on the Roof

Room Another Brick in the Wall; The Blue Room; (See What) The Boys in the Back Room (Will Have); Dancing on the Ceiling; Dancing on the Ceiling; The Four Walls; Haunted Ball Room; In a Little Gypsy Tea Room; In an Eighteenth Century Drawing Room; In Our Little Den of Iniquity; It's Make Believe Ballroom Time; The Mottoes Framed upon the Wall; Off the Wall; Over the Garden Wall; The Picture That's Turned to (Toward) the Wall; Room Five Hundred and Four; Room Full (Roomful) of Roses; A Room in Bloomsbury; A Room with a View; A Room Without Windows; Rose Room; Smokin' in the Boys' Room; Tommy, Make Room for Your Uncle; Turn 'Erbert's Face to the Wall, Mother; Wallflower; When Father Papered the Parlour; When She Walks in the Room; Why Did I Leave My Little Back Room

Rooster, *see* **Chicken**

Rosalie Rosalie; Rosalie the Prairie Flower

Rosary My Mother's Rosary; My Rosary of Dreams; The Rosary; When You Played the Organ and I Sang "The Rosary"

Rose After the Roses Have Faded Away; American Beauty Rose; Baby Rose; A Bouquet of Roses; A Bowl of Roses; Bring Me a Rose; Bring Me a Rose; Broadway Rose; Bunch of Roses; By the River of (the) Roses; The Coal Black Rose; Cracklin' Rosie; The Daughter of Rosie O'Grady; Days of Wine and Roses; Dear Old Rose; English Rose; Everything's Coming Up Roses; The Fatal Rose of Red; (Beautiful) Garden of Roses; Garland of Old Fashioned Roses; Gather the Rose; Goodbye, Rose; Gypsy Dream Rose; Heart of a Rose; Heart of My Heart (I Love You), or, The Story of the Rose; Honeysuckle Rose; I Found a Rose in the Devil's Garden; I Never Knew (That Roses Grew); I Never Promised You a Rose Garden; I'll Be with You When the Roses Bloom Again; I'm Bringing a Red, Red Rose; Ivy Rose; Johnny Doughboy Found a Rose in Ireland; June Brought the Roses; Ladder of Roses; Lida Rose; Lo, How a Rose E'er Blooming; Lollipops and Roses; Looking at the World Through Rose-Colored Glasses; Love Sends a Little Gift of Roses; Lovely Lady Let the Roses See You Today; Love's Garden of Roses; Ma Blushin' Rosie; Mammy's(a) Little Coal Black Rose; Marta, or, Rambling Rose of the Wildwood; Mary Rose; Mary Rose; Mexicali Rose; Mighty Lak' a Rose; Moonlight and Roses (Bring Me Mem'ries of You); My Belgian Rose; My Little Georgia Rose; My Love Is Like a Red, Red Rose; My Rambler Rose; My Southern Rose; My Spanish Rose; (Say Has Anybody Seen) My Sweet Gypsy Rose; My Wild Irish Rose; Nina Rosa; Nodding Roses; One Dozen Roses; The One Rose That's Left in My Heart; Only a Rose; Painted Tainted Rose; Paper Roses; Persian Rosebud; Primrose; Primrose Hill; Promise Me a Rose; Rambling Rose; Ramblin' Rose; Red Roses for a Blue Lady; Riviera Rose; Robins and Roses; Romany Rose; Room Full (Roomful) of Roses; Rosanna; The Rose; A Rose and a Baby Ruth; The Rose I Bring You; A Rose in a Garden of Weeds; The Rose in Her Hair; Rose in the Bud; Rose Marie; Rose O'Day; The Rose of Alabama; The Rose of Allandale; Rose of England; The Rose of Killarney; Rose of Lucerne, or, The Swiss Toy Girl; Rose of My Heart; The Rose of No Man's Land; Rose of the Rio Grande; Rose of the World; The Rose of Tralee; Rose of Washington Square; Rose Room; Rose, Rose I Love You; The Rose Tattoo; Roses Are Forget-Me-Nots; Roses Are Red, My Love; Roses Bring Dreams of You; Roses for Remembrance; Roses in the Rain; Roses of Picardy; Rose's Turn; Rosetta; Rosetta; Rosie; Rosie; La Rosita; Russian Rose; Sally Go Round the Roses; San Antonio Rose, or, Rose of San Antone; Schön Rosmarin (Fair Rosmarin); Se Saran Rose, or, Melba Waltz; Second Hand Rose; Song of the Rose; Sweet Rosie O'Grady; There's Something About a Rose (That Reminds Me of You); Throw Me a Rose; Tiger Rose; 'Tis the Last Rose of Summer; To a Wild Rose; Too Many Rings Around Rosie; La Vie en Rose; Wedding of the Rose; When You Look in the Heart of a Rose; When You Wore a Tulip and I Wore a Big Red Rose; Where the Southern Roses Grow; Where the Twilight Comes To Kiss the Rose Goodnight; The White Rose of Athens; The Wild Rose; Wild Rose; Yankee Rose; The Yellow Rose of Texas, or, Song of the Texas Rangers; Yesterday's Roses; You Planted a Rose in the Garden of Love

Rosemary, *see* **Seasonings**

Rotten   Rotten Row

Roulette, *see* **Gambling**

Roundelay   Love's Roundelay

Round-Up, *see* **Cowboy**

Route, *see* **Road**

Row   Down in Poverty Row; McNally's Row of Flats; Michael (Row the Boat Ashore); Rotten Row; Row, Row, Row; Row, Row, Row Your Boat (Round); Row Thy Boat Lightly; Where Do They Go When They Row, Row, Row

Royal   I Have a Noble Cock; March of the (Royal) Siamese Children; Royal Event; Royal Garden Blues

Rubber   Red Rubber Ball; Rubber Ball; Rubber Bullets; Rubberband Man

Ruby   Ruby; Ruby Baby; Ruby, Don't Take Your Love to Town

Rudolph   Rudolph the Red-Nosed Reindeer

Rug   Persian Rug

Rugged   The Old Rugged Cross

Ruin   One of the Ruins That Cromwell Knocked About a Bit

Rule   Everybody Wants To Rule the World; If I Ruled the World; Rule, Britannia

Rum, *see* **Alcohol**

Rumania   Rumanian Rhapsody

Rumor   Rumors Are Flying

Run   Band on the Run; Born To Run; De Camptown Races (Gwine To Run All Night); Caribbean Queen (No More Love on the Run); Fox on the Run; (And) His Rocking Horse Ran Away; I Ran All the Way Home; Jogging Along the Highway; Just My Imagination (Running Away with Me); Kiss and Run; Long Train Runnin'; My Cup Runneth Over; Run Joey Run; Run Rabbit Run; Run to Him; Run to You; Run-

around Sue; Runaway; The Runaway Train; Running Bear; Running Between the Raindrops; Running Scared; Runnin' Wild; Running with the Night; Silent Running (On Dangerous Ground); Sorry (I Ran All the Way Home); Time Don't Run Out on Me; Walk—Don't Run; You Never Miss the Water Till the Well Runs Dry, or, Waste Not, Want Not

Rush, *see* **Hurry**

Russia   And Russia Is Her Name; From Russia with Love; Russian Lullaby; Russian Rag; Russian Rose; Underneath the Russian Moon

Ruth   A Rose and a Baby Ruth

Rye   (When the) Bloom Is on the Rye, or, My Pretty Jane; Comin' Thro' the Rye, or, If a Body Meet a Body; When Kate and I Were Coming Thro' the Rye

Sabbath   Sabbath Prayer

Sabre, *see* **Knife**

Sad   By the Sad Sea Waves; By the Sad Sea Waves; Night May Have Its Sadness; Sad Eyes; Sad Movies Make Me Cry; Sad Songs (Say So Much); Sad Sweet Dreamer; Save Your Sorrow for Tomorrow; Still I'm Sad; There'll Be Sad Songs (To Make You Cry); Valse Triste; Weeping, Sad and Lonely, or, When This Cruel War Is Over

Saddle   Back in the Saddle Again; (Take Me Back to My) Boots and Saddle; Empty Saddles; Side Saddle

Sadie   Sadie Salome, Go Home

Safari, *see* **Jungle**

Safe, Safety, *see* **Protect**

Saga, *see* **Story**

Sage, *see* **Seasonings**

Sahara, *see* **Desert**

Sail, *see* **Boat**

Sailor   Barnacle Bill the Sailor; (What Shall We Do with) The Drunken Sailor, or, Columbus, or, John Brown Had a Little Injun, or, Ten Little Indians; Forty-Seven Ginger-Headed Sailors; The Midshipmite; (I'm) Popeye the Sailor Man; Sailor (Your Home Is the Sea); Sailor Boys Have Talk to Me in English; The Sailor of My Dreams; Sailor Who Are You Dreaming of Tonight; Sailor's Hornpipe; Ship Ahoy, or, All the Nice Girls Love a Sailor; Strike Up the Band—Here Comes a Sailor; (Poor) Tom Bowling, or, The Sailor's Epitaph

Saint   The Bells of St. Mary's; By the River Sainte Marie; Come, Ye Saints; St. Elmo's Fire (Man in Motion); St. (Saint) George and the Dragonet; St. James Infirmary; St. Mary's in the Twilight; The Village of Saint Bernadette; When the Saints Go Marching In

St. Louis   Meet Me in St. Louis, Louis; St. Louis Blues; St. Louis Woman; You Came a Long Way from St. Louis

Sake   For Old Times' Sake; Just for the Sake of Our Daughter

Salad   Capped Teeth and Caesar Salad; Polk Salad Annie; Salad Days

Sale   A Cottage for Sale; I Can Get It for You Wholesale; Love for Sale

Sally   Goodbye Sally; I Wonder What's Become of Sally; Lay Down Sally; Long Tall Sally; My Gal Sal, or, They Call Her

Frivolous Sal; My Old Aunt Sally; Sally; Sally; Sally Go Round the Roses; Sally in Our Alley; Sally, Irene and Mary; Sally, You Brought the Sunshine to Our Alley

Salome Sadie Salome, Go Home; Salome; A Vision of Salome

Salt Lake City I Lost My Sugar in Salt Lake City

Sam Lovin' Sam, the Sheik of Alabam'; Oh Sam; Old Sam (Pick Up Tha' Musket); Sam; Sam, the Old Accordion Man; Sam, You Made the Pants Too Long; Sammy; Sam's Song; Shufflin' Sam

Samantha I Love You Samantha

Sambo Ching A Ring Chaw, or, Sambo's Address to His Bred'ren

San Antonio San Antonio; San Antonio Rose, or, Rose of San Antone

San Domingo My San Domingo Maid

San Fernando San Fernando Valley

San Francisco Hello Frisco Hello; I Left My Heart in San Francisco; San Francisco; (Are You Going to) San Francisco (Be Sure To Wear Some Flowers in Your Hair)

San Jose Do You Know the Way to San Jose

Sand, *see* **Beach**

Sandra Look At Me, I'm Sandra Dee

Sandwich A Cup of Coffee, a Sandwich and You

Sandy Mary's Dream, or, Sandy's Ghost; Wedding o' Sandy McNab

Santa Barbara At Santa Barbara

Santa Claus Does Santa Claus Sleep with His Whiskers; Here Comes Santa Claus; I Saw Mommy Kissing Santa Claus; The Little Boy That Santa Claus Forgot; Santa Claus Is Coming to Town

Santa Cruz A Summer Evening in Santa Cruz

Santa Fe Along the Santa Fe Trail; On the Atchison, Topeka, and the Santa Fe

Sara Sara

Sari Love's Own Sweet Song, or, Sari Waltz

Saskatchewan By the Saskatchewan

Satan, *see* **Devil**

Satin Nights in White Satin; Satin Doll

Satisfaction Contended; Do It (Till You're Satisfied); I'll Keep You Satisfied; Just To Satisfy You; (I Can't Get No) Satisfaction; Satisfied; You Won't Be Satisfied (Until You Break My Heart)

Saturday Another Saturday Night; Come Saturday Morning; Juke Box Saturday Night; The Market on Saturday Night; Saturday Night; Saturday Night; Saturday Night Is the Loneliest Night of the Week; What'll We Do on a Saturday Night When the Town Goes Dry; Where Did Robinson Crusoe Go with Friday on Saturday Night?

Savannah Hard Hearted Hannah (the Vamp of Savannah); Savanna; Sweet Savannah

Save Brother, Can You Spare a Dime; Emotional Rescue; God Save the King (Queen); (There Ought To Be a) Moonlight Saving Time; Rescue the Perishing; Save It for a Rainy Day; Save the Country; Save the Last Dance for Me; Save Your

Heart for Me; Save Your Kisses for Me; Save Your Sorrow for Tomorrow; Saved by Grace; Saving All My Love for You; Someone Saved My Life Tonight; The Waltz You Saved for Me; Woodman Spare That Tree; Woodman, Woodman, Spare That Tree

Saviour All the Way My Saviour Leads Me; Saviour, Breathe an Evening Blessing; Weeping Saviour

Savoy Stomping at the Savoy

Saw And the Great Big Saw Came Nearer; I've Got a Pain in My Sawdust

Scale Ragging the Scale

Scandal The Scandal of Little Lizzie Ford

Scared, *see* **Afraid**

Scarf Scarf Dance

Scarlet, *see* **Red**

School, *see also* **Lesson, Teach** An Apple for the Teacher; Betty Co-Ed; Brush Up Your Shakespeare; College Life; College Rhythm; Collegiate; Estudiantina; Freshie; Gaudeamus Igitur; A Girl of the Pi Beta Phi; Graduation Day; Harper Valley P.T.A.; High School Cadets; The Homecoming Waltz; Homework; In the Little Red Schoolhouse; Love Never Went to College; Me and Julio Down by the Schoolyard; School Day (Ring! Ring! Goes the Bell); School Days; Smokin' in the Boys' Room; Such an Education, Has My Mary Ann, or, Sweet Mary Ann; The Sweetheart of Sigma Chi; Swingin' School; To Sir with Love; The Varsity Drag; The Whiffenpoof Song; You Remind Me of the Girl That Used To Go to School with Me

Scot Coronation Scot

Scotland The Blue Bell of Scotland; Hop Scotch Polka; I Love a Lassie, or, Ma Scotch Bluebell; Irish Washerwoman, or, The Scotch Bagpipe Melody; I've a Shooting Box in Scotland; Scots Wha Hae Wi' Wallace Bled; Scottish Samba; Scottish Soldier Green Hill; That's the Reason Noo I Wear a Kilt

Scream Clare De Kitchen, or, De Kentucky Screamer; (I Scream, You Scream, We All Scream for) Ice Cream

Scrub, *see* **Wash**

Sea As Deep as the Deep Blue Sea; Beautiful Isle of the Sea; Between the Devil and the Deep Blue Sea; Beyond the Sea; By the Beautiful Sea; By the Sad Sea Waves; By the Sad Sea Waves; Columbia, the Gem of the Ocean, or, The Red, White, and Blue; The Cottage by the Sea; The Crest of a Wave; The Cruel Sea; Ebb Tide; The Four Winds and the Seven Seas; Hands Across the Sea (March); Heat Wave; (Love Is Like a) Heat Wave; Here Come the Waves; How Deep Is the Ocean; I Am the Monarch of the Sea; I Do Like To Be Beside the Seaside; I Threw a Kiss in the Ocean; A Life on the Ocean Wave; Melody from the Sea; La Mer (the Sea); My Barney Lies Over the Ocean (Just the Way He Lied to Me); My Bonnie Lies Over the Ocean, or, Bring Back My Bonnie to Me; My Friend the Sea; 'Neath the South Sea Moon; The Oceana Roll; On the Crest of a Wave; Over the Waves; Poverty's Tears Ebb and Flow; Put 'Em in a Box, Tie 'Em with a Ribbon (and Throw 'Em in the Deep Blue Sea); The Rock Beside the Sea; Sailor (Your Home Is the Sea); The Sea Hath Its Pearls; (Theme from) Sea Hunt; Sea of Love; Seashore; She Sells Sea-Shells (on the Seashore); She Waits by the

Deep Blue Sea; Sons of the Sea; South Sea Island Magic; Surf City; Surfin' Safari; Surfin' U.S.A.; Sussex by the Sea; The Tale of the Seashell; The Tide Is High; Time and Tide (Theme from *Plague Dogs*); Transatlantic Lullaby; Voyage to the Bottom of the Sea; Wait Till the Tide Comes In; Waves of the Danube, or, Danube Waves; We Saw the Sea; A Wet Sheet and a Flowing Sea; What Are the Wild Waves Saying; When the Sunset Turns the Ocean's Blue to Gold; You Have Cast Your Shadow on the Sea

Seal   Seal It with a Kiss; Sealed with a Kiss

Search, *see* **Look**

Season   (Theme from) Return to Peyton Place, or, The Wonderful Season of Love; Seasons in the Sun; Sweet Seasons

Seasonings, *see also* **Pepper, Salt, Sugar**   I Know a Bank Where the Wild Thyme Blows; I Lost My Sugar in Salt Lake City; Scarborough Fair/Canticle, or, Parsley, Sage, Rosemary and Thyme; Smellin' of Vanilla (Bamboo Cage); The Spice of Life; Sugar and Spice; (When It's Roundup Time in Texas) When the Bloom Is on the Sage

Seat, *see* **Chair**

Second, *see* **Time, Two**

Secret   Do You Want To Know a Secret; I'll Follow My Secret Heart; It Is No Secret; It's an Open Secret; Keep It a Secret; Secret Army; Secret Love; Secret Lovers; Secretly; The Secrets of the Seine; Your Secret's Safe with Me

Secretary   A Secretary Is Not a Toy

See-Saw   I'm on a See-Saw; See, Saw, Margery Daw; See Saw Majory Daw

Seed   If I Should Plant a Tiny Seed of Love

Seine   The Secrets of the Seine; La Seine

Send   Heaven Must Have Sent You; Love Sends a Little Gift of Roses; Return to Sender; Send for Me; Send in the Clowns; Send Me Away with a Smile; You Send Me

Sensational   Sensation Rag; You're Sensational

Sentimental   (I Love You) For Sentimental Reasons; I'm Getting Sentimental over You; In a Sentimental Mood; On the Sentimental Side; A Sentimental Gentleman from Georgia; Sentimental Journey; Sentimental Me; Sentimental Me; The Sentimental Touch

September   My September Love; See You in September; September in the Rain; September Song; Sweet September; Valse Septembre

Serenade   Angel's Serenade; Autumn Serenade; A Blues Serenade; Cowboy Serenade, or, My Last Cigarette; The Donkey Serenade; Elizabethan Serenade; Ferryboat Serenade; The Gaucho Serenade; The Lamplighter's Serenade; Mandolin Serenade; Manhattan Serenade; Moonlight Serenade; My Little Nest of Heavenly Blue, or, Frasquita Serenade (Blaues Himmelbett), or, Farewell, My Love, Farewell; Penny Serenade; Serenade; Serenade; Serenade; Serenade, or, Rimpianto; Serenade; Serenade for Strings (Suite); Serenade in Blue; Serenade in the Night; Serenade of Love; Serenade of the Bells; Serenade to a Lemonade; Serenata; The Shepherd Serenade; The Shoemaker's Serenade; Shy Serenade; (By the) Sleepy Lagoon (Valse Serenade); Sleepy Serenade; Starlight Serenade; Sunrise Serenade; When We're Alone, or, Penthouse Serenade

Sergeant   The Company Sergeant Major; The Dashing White Sergeant; Sergeant Pepper's Lonely Hearts Club Band; When the Sergeant Major's on Parade

Seven   Forty-Seven Ginger Headed Sailors; The Four Winds and the Seven Seas; Heaven on the Seventh Floor; Lucky Seven; (Theme from) The Magnificent Seven; Seven Bridges Road; 7½ Cents; Seven Lonely Days; Seven or Eleven—My Dixie Pair o' Dice; Seven Year Ache; Seventh Dawn; Seventh Heaven; Seventh Heaven; The Wreck of (on) the Old (Southern) '97

Seventeen   At Seventeen; Seventeen; Seventeen Candles; Sixteen Going On Seventeen; When You and I Were Seventeen

Seventy   Seventy-Six Trombones

Seville   The Barber of Seville (Overture)

Sew   Look for the Silver Lining; A Needle in a Haystack; Silver Threads Among the Gold; Sister Susie's Sewing Shirts for Soldiers; When I Saw Sweet Nellie Home, or, I Was Seeing Nellie Home, or, Aunt Dinah's Quilting Party

Seymour   Suddenly Seymour

Shack, *see* **House**

Shade, Shadow   Blue Shadows and White Gardenias; Blue Shadows on the Trail; Chasing Shadows; Dancing with My Shadow; In Shadowland; In the Shade of the Old Apple Tree; In the Shadows; Love in the Shadows; Me and My Shadow; Moonlight and Shadows; The Naughty Lady of Shady Lane; Ole Shady, or, The Song of the Contraband; The Shade of the Palm; Shades of Night; Shadow Dancing; Shadow of the Moon; The Shadow of Your Smile; Shadow Waltz; Shadowland; Shadows in the Moonlight; Shady Lady Bird; Silhouette; Three Shades of Blue; Two Ladies In De Shade of De Banana Tree; Two Silhouettes; Two Silhouettes in the Moonlight; We Kiss in a Shadow; We Three—My Echo, My Shadow, and Me; A Whiter Shade of Pale; You Have Cast Your Shadow on the Sea

Shaft   (Theme from) Shaft; She Got the Goldmine I Got the Shaft

Shake   All Shook Up; All the Quakers Are Shoulder Shakers Down in Quaker Town; Chester (Let Tyrants Shake Their Iron Rod); Come Back and Shake Me; Got the Jitters; If You Don't Want My Peaches, You'd Better Stop Shaking My Tree; It Must Be Jelly, 'Cause Jam Don't Shake Like That; Let Me Shake the Hand That Shook the Hand of Sullivan; Put It There Pal; Shake It; Shake It Off; Shake It Up; Shake, Rattle and Roll; Shake Your Body (Down to the Ground); (Shake Shake Shake) Shake Your Booty; Shakin' All Over; Shaking the Blues Away; Whole Lot-ta Shakin' Goin' On; You Cannot Make Your Shimmy Shake on Tea

Shakespeare   Brush Up Your Shakespeare

Shalimar   By the Shalimar

Shame   Ain't It a Shame; Ain't That a Shame; It's a Great Big Shame; Shame; Shame On the Moon

Shamrock   As Long as the Shamrock Grows Green; A Little Bunch of Shamrocks

Shanghai   Shanghai; Shanghai; Shanghai Lil

Shangri-La   Shangri-La

Shanty, *see* **House**

Shape   Bend Me, Shape Me

Share   I Know I Got More Than My Share; Share Your Love with Me; Sharing the Night Together

Sharon   My Sharona

Sharp   Momma Look Sharp; to Look Sharp

Shave, *see* **Barber**

Shawl   My Shawl

Sheep   Auld Robin Gray, or, When the Sheep Are in the Fold; Little Lamb; Baa, Baa, Black Sheep; Little Bo-Peep; Mary Had a Little Lamb; Shepherd of the Hills; The Shepherd Serenade; The Swingin' Shepherd Blues; Tender Shepherd; When the Black Sheep Returns to the Fold; Wrap Yourself in Cotton Wool; You Can't Pull the Wool over My Eyes

Sheik   Lovin Sam, the Sheik of Alabam'; The Sheik of Araby

Sheila   Oh Sheila; Sheila

Shell, *see* **Sea**

Shelter   Down Among the Sheltering Palms

Shepherd, *see* **Sheep**

Sheriff, *see* **Police**

Sherry   Oh Sherrie; Sherry

Shilling, *see* **Money**

Shiloh   The Drummer Boy of Shiloh

Shimmy   I Wish I Could Shimmy Like My Sister Kate; You Cannot Make Your Shimmy Shake on Tea

Shin   Long Time Ago, or, Shinbone Alley

Shine, *see also* **Glitter**   Chattanoogie Shoe Shine Boy; Come Rain or Come Shine; (Theme from) Doctor Kildare, or, Three Stars Will Shine Tonight; Her Eyes Don't Shine Like Diamonds; I Don't Care If the Sun Don't Shine; The Moon Shines on the Moonshine; My Shining Hour; Rise and Shine; S-H-I-N-E; Shine; Shine a Little Love; Shine On Victory Moon; A Shine on Your Shoes; Shine Through My Dreams; Shining Star; Shining Star; Sparkle; Sparkling and Bright; (Theme from) La Strada, or, Stars Shine in Your Eyes; The Sun Shines Brighter; That's Why They Call Me "Shine"; There's a Little Star Shining for You; Till Stars Forget To Shine; Till the Lights of London Shine Again; Twinkle, Twinkle, Little Star, or, Ah! Vous Diraije Maman, or, ABCDEFG (The Alphabet Song); Twinkle, Twinkle, Little Star; Twinkling Stars Are Laughing Love; Wait 'Til the Sun Shines, Nellie; We'll Make Hay While the Sun Shines; When He Shines; Who's Been Polishing the Sun

Ship, *see* **Boat**

Shirt   Lipstick on Your Collar; Sister Susie's Sewing Shirts for Soldiers; The Song of the Shirt; The Song of the Shirt

Shoe, *see also* **Boot**   Baby Shoes; Blue Suede Shoes; Can I Leave Off Wearin' My Shoes; Chattanoogie Shoe Shine Boy; The Cobbler's Song; Dancing Shoes; From the Top of Your Head to the Tip of Your Shoes; (Oh Dem) Golden Slippers; High Heel Sneakers; I Got (a Robe) Shoes, or, All God's Chillun Got Shoes; The Little Shoemaker; There Was an Old Woman Who Lived in a Shoe; Never Take the Horse Shoe from the Door; The Old Soft Shoe; One, Two, Button Your Shoe; Pink Shoelaces; Put On Your Slippers and Fill Up Your Pipe; Put Your Shoes On, Lucy; Sand in My Shoes; A Shine on Your Shoes; Shoe Shine Boy; Shoeless Joe from Hannibal, Mo.; The Shoemaker's Serenade; Shoestring; The Soft Shoe Shuffle; Susannah's Squeaking Shoes; Two Little Baby Shoes; Very Soft Shoes; The Woman in the Shoe

Shop, *see* **Store**

Shore, *see also* **Bank**   Bam, Bam, Bamy Shore; Gulf Coast Blues; Michael (Row the Boat Ashore); Molly on the Shore; On Miami Shore, or, Golden Sands of Miami; On the Gin, Gin, Ginny Shore; On the Shore at Lei Lei; On the Shores of Italy; Seashore; She Sells Sea-Shells (on the Seashore); Sleepy Shores; Stranger on the Shore; (On the Shores of) Tripoli; We Parted on the Shore

Short   Short, Fat and 4F; Short People; Short Shorts; Shortnin' Bread; Who's Johnny ("Short Circuit" Theme)

Shot   Bang Bang (My Baby Shot Me Down); Big Shot; I Shot the Sheriff; I'm Shooting High; In My Little Snapshot Album; I've a Shooting Box in Scotland; The Man Who Shot Liberty Valance

Shoulder   All the Quakers Are Shoulder Shakers Down in Quaker Town; Over My Shoulder; Put Your Head on My Shoulder; Snuggled on Your Shoulder, Cuddled in Your Arms; Sunshine on My Shoulders; There's a Rainbow Round My Shoulder; Would You Rather Be a Colonel with an Eagle on Your Shoulder, or a Private with a Chicken on Your Knee?

Shout, *see* **Talk**

Show, *see* **Broadway**

Showboat, *see* **Boat**

Shower, *see* **Rain**

Shrimp, *see* **Fish**

Shuffle   Boneyard Shuffle; Harlem Shuffle; Riverboat Shuffle; Shuffle Along; Shuffle Off to Buffalo; Shufflin' Along; Shufflin' Sam; The Soft Shoe Shuffle

Shut, *see* **Close**

Shy   He's So Shy; I'm Shy, Mary Ellen, I'm Shy; Shy Serenade; Timid Frieda; Where the Shy Little Violets Grow

Siam   March of the (Royal) Siamese Children; Siam; Siamese Patrol

Siberia   Siberia

Sicily   Sicilian Hymn (O Sanctissima)

Sick, *see also* **Ache, Fever**   Homesick; Homesick—That's All; Lovesick Blues; Lovesick Blues; Mama, Look a Booboo; My Resistance Is Low

Side   Blue Side; By The Side of the Zuyder Zee; Danny by My Side; Down by the Riverside, or, Ain't Gwine Study War No More; East Side of Heaven; The House by the Side of the Road; I Do Like To Be Beside the Seaside; The Ingle Side; Keep on the Sunny Side; A Little on the Lonely Side; The Morning Side of the Mountain; My Hat's on the Side of My Head; On the Dark Side; On the Sentimental Side; On the South Side of Chicago; On the Sunny Side of the Street; (On) The Other Side of the Tracks; Poor Side of Town; Side by Side; Side by Side; Side Saddle; The Sidewalks of New York, or, East Side, West Side; (Keep Your) Sunny Side Up; The Sweetest Music This Side of Heaven; Time Is on My Side; Walk on the Wild Side; The World Turned Upside Down, or, Derry Down

Sidewalk, *see* **Street**

Sierra   Sierra Sue

Sigh Between a Kiss and a Sigh; The Bridge of Sighs; The Bridge of Sighs; I Used To Sigh for the Silvery Moon; Sigh by Night; Sigh No More, Ladies

Silence, *see* **Quiet**

Silhouette, *see* **Shade, Shadow**

Silk Red Silk Stockings and Green Perfume

Silly, *see* **Crazy**

Silver Aunt Jemina (Silver Dollar); By the Light of the Silvery Moon; Down by the Silvery Rio Grande; Down Where the Silv'ry Mohawk Flows; The Gold and Silver (Waltz); He Wears a Pair of Silver Wings; I Used To Sigh for the Silvery Moon; Look for the Silver Lining; Roll On, Silver Moon, or, The Silver Moon; Sail Along Silvery Moon; Silver Bell; Silver Bells; Silver Dollar (Down and Out); Silver Dream Machine; Silver Hair and Heart of Gold; Silver Moon; Silver Threads Among the Gold; Silver Wings in the Moonlight; That Silver-Haired Daddy of Mine; When Your Hair Has Turned to Silver, I Will Love You Just the Same; Where the Silv'ry Colorado Wends Its Way; White Silver Sands

Simon Simple Simon; Simon Says; Simon the Cellarer; Simonetta

Simple, Simply Give Me the Simple Life; Love Is a Simple Thing; Simple; Simple Simon; Play a Simple Melody; Simple Aveu; Simple Game; The Simple Joys of Maidenhood; Sing Something Simple; They Go Wild Simply Wild over Me; What Do (the) Simple Folk Do; When the One You Love (Simply Won't Love Back)

Sin It's a Sin To Tell a Lie; It's a Sin When You Love Somebody; It's No Sin; My Sin; Sing You Sinners; A Sinner Kissed an Angel; Though Your Sins Be As Scarlet

Sincerely Are You Sincere; Sincerely; Yours Sincerely

Singapore On a Little Street in Singapore

Single, *see* **One**

Sink Sink Red Sun; Sink the Bismarck

Sioux City Sioux City Sue

Sir Little Sir Echo; To Sir with Love

Sister Bend Down, Sister; I Don't Want Another Sister; I Wish I Could Shimmy Like My Sister Kate; I'd Like To Be a Sister to a Brother Just Like You; Like Sister and Brother; Little Sister; Miss Celie's Blues (Sister); My Sister and I; Since Sister Nell Heard Paderewski Play; Sister Christian; Sister Golden Hair; Sister Susie's Sewing Shirts for Soldiers; Three Little Sisters

Sit, *see also* **Chair** (Sittin' on) The Dock of the Bay; Don't Sit Under the Apple Tree (with Anyone Else But Me); Go Way Back and Sit Down; I'm Gonna Sit Right Down and Write Myself a Letter; I'm Sittin' High on a Hill Top; I'm Sitting on Top of the World (Just Rolling Along—Just Rolling Along); I'm Sitting Pretty Little City; Oh, I Can't Sit Down; Sit Down, You're Rocking the Boat; Sit Down, You're Rocking the Boat; Sitting by the Window; Sittin' in a Corner; Sitting in the Back Seat; Sitting on a Fire Barred Gate; Within the Cellar's Depth I Sit

Six Half a Sixpence; Inn of the Sixth Happiness; I've Got Sixpence (As I Go Rolling Home); Sing a Song of Sixpence; Ninety-Six Tears; Seventy-Six Trombones; 633 Squadron; Six Lessons From Madame LaZonga; Six Little Wives

Sixteen Only Sixteen; Only Sixteen; Sixteen Candles; Sixteen Going On Seventeen; Sixteen Tons; Sweet Little Sixteen; Sweet Sixteen; Sweet Sixteen Bars; When a Fellah Has Turned Sixteen; When I Was Twenty-One and You Were Sweet Sixteen; When Sweet Marie Was Sweet Sixteen; When You Were Sweet Sixteen; You Are Sixteen; You're Sixteen

Sixty R.O.C.K. in the U.S.A. (A Salute to 60's Rock); 65 Love Affair; Sixty Seconds Every Minute, I Think of You; Summer of '69; When I'm Sixty-Four

Size I'm Looking For a Guy Who Plays Alto and Baritone and Doubles on a Clarinet and Wears a Size Thirty-Seven Suit

Skate The Skaters (Waltz)

Skin It Takes a Long, Tall, Brown-Skin Gal; I've Got You Under My Skin; Mule Skinner Blues

Skip Skip to My Lou

Skirt Keep Your Skirts Down, Mary Ann; Skirt Dance; They're Wearing 'Em Higher In Hawaii

Sky Beyond the Blue Horizon; Blue Skies; Blue Skies Are Round the Corner; Cabin in the Sky; Eye in the Sky; From the Land of the Sky Blue Water; Ghost Riders in the Sky, or, A Cowboy Legend; Just a Piece of Sky; Just Like a Melody Out of the Sky; Lucy in the Sky with Diamonds; A Melody from the Sky; New Sun in the Sky; Ole Buttermilk Sky; On the Way to the Sky; Pictures in the Sky; The Sky Fell Down; Sky High; Skylark; Skyliner; There's a Gold Mine in the Sky; Under Hawaiian Skies; Under Paris Skies; When Stars Are in the Quiet Skies; When the Blue Sky Turns to Gold; Why (Is There a Rainbow in the Sky)

Slap Slap That Bass

Slaughter, *see* **Murder**

Slave Poor Old Slave

Sleep, *see also* **Bed, Dream, Goodnight** And So to Sleep Again; Asleep in the Deep; At Midnight on My Pillow Lying; A Bedtime Story; Brahms' Lullaby; Chi-Baba Chi-Baba (My Bambino Go to Sleep); Does Santa Claus Sleep with His Whiskers; Don't Sleep in the Subway; The General's Fast Asleep; Give Me Your Tired, Your Poor; Gypsy Love Song, or, Slumber On; Ho Hum; I Couldn't Sleep a Wink Last Night; I Don't Like To Sleep Alone; I Said My Pajamas (and Put On My Prayers); I'd Love To Fall Asleep and Wake Up in My Mammy's Arms; If You Talk in Your Sleep, Don't Mention My Name; I'm Getting Tired So I Can Sleep; The Japanese Sandman; Last Night I Didn't Get to Sleep At All; Let's Put Out the Lights and Go to Sleep; The Lion Sleeps Tonight, or, Wimoweh; Lullaby of Broadway; Mister Sandman; Now I Lay Me Down to Sleep; Now Sleeps the Crimson Petal; Oh, How I Wish I Could Sleep Until My Daddy Comes Home; Please Go 'Way and Let Me Sleep; Put Me to Sleep with an Old-Fashioned Melody; Rock-a-Bye (Hush-a-Bye) Baby; Rock Me to Sleep, Mother; Russian Lullaby; Sleep; Sleep, Baby, Sleep, or, Irene's Lullaby; Sleep Walk; Sleeping Beauty Waltz; A Sleepin' Bee; Sleepin' with the Radio On; Sleepy Head; (By the) Sleepy Lagoon (Valse Serenade); Sleepy Serenade; Sleepy Shores; Sleepy Time Gal; So Tired; So Tired; Talkin' in Your Sleep; Talking in Your Sleep; Then I'll Be Tired of You; Through a Long and Sleepless Night; Tired; Too-ra-loo-ra-loo-ral, That's an Irish Lullaby; Tired of Toein' the Line; Tossin' and Turnin'; Tossing and Turning; Tuck Me to Sleep in My Old 'Tucky Home; Two Sleepy People; Waking or Sleeping; Waters of Venice, or, Floating Down the Sleepy Lagoon; Weary River; When It's Sleepy Time Down South; When the Birds Have Sung Themselves to Sleep; When the Children Are Asleep; World Weary; Wyoming Lullaby

Sleeve Heart on My Sleeve

Sleigh Jingle Bells, or, The One Horse Open Sleigh; Petersbourgh Sleighride; The Sleigh; Sleigh Ride; Sleigh Ride in July

Slide Slide Kelly Slide; Slip Slidin' Away

Slip I Didn't Slip, I Wasn't Pushed, I Fell; Slip Slidin' Away; Slippin' Around

Slipper, *see* **Shoe**

Slow I Tipped My Hat and Slowly Rode Away; (I'd Like To Get You) On a Slow Boat to China; Slow Hand; Slow Poke; Take It Slow, Joe; Time Drags By

Slumber, *see* **Sleep**

Sly That Sly Old Gentleman from Featherbed Lane

Small If I Should Plant a Tiny Seed of Love; It Is Only a Tiny Garden; Itsy Bitsy Teenie Weenie Yellow Polkadot Bikini; Just a Cottage Small—By a Waterfall; A Lil' Ole Bitty Pissant Country Place; Small Fry; Small Town; Small World; Suite No. 1 for Small Orchestra; There's a Small Hotel; Thumbelina; Tiny Bubbles; To the Land of My Own (Small) Romance

Smart, *see* **Think**

Smell Smellin' of Vanilla (Bamboo Cage)

Smile Can't Smile Without You; A Certain Smile; Have a Smile (for Everyone You Meet); Her Bright Smile Haunts Me Still; I Shall Always Remember You Smiling; I'll Never Smile Again; I'm All Smiles; It's the Irish in Your Eyes, (It's the Irish in Your Smile); Keep Smiling at Trouble; Learn To Smile; Leave Me with a Smile; Let a Smile Be Your Umbrella on a Rainy (Rainy) Day; Pack Up Your Trouble in Your Old Kit Bag and Smile, Smile, Smile; Sara Smile; See, Gentle Patience Smiles on Pain; Send Me Away with a Smile; The Shadow of Your Smile; Smile; Smile, Darn Ya, Smile; Smile When You Say "Goodbye"; A Smile Will Go a Long, Long Way; Smiles; Smiley's People; Smilin' Through; The Sunshine of Your Smile; Teeth 'n' Smiles; Tell Me Why You Smile Mona Lisa; When Buddha Smiles; When Irish Eyes Are Smiling; When My Baby Smiles at Me; When You're Smiling (The Whole World Smiles with You); With a Smile and a Song

Smoke, Smoking Blow the Smoke Away; Cigarette; Cowboy Serenade, or, My Last Cigarette; Lost Like a Cigarette; On Top of Old Smokey; Pass That Peace Pipe; Puff the Magic Dragon; Put On Your Slippers and Fill Up Your Pipe; Smoke Dreams; Smoke from a Distant Fire; Smoke Gets in Your Eyes; Smoke on the Water; Smoke Rings; Smoke! Smoke! Smoke! (That Cigarette); Smokin' in the Boys' Room; Smoky Mokes; Smoky Mountain Rain; Sound Off for Chesterfield; Three on a Match; Tobacco's But an Indian Weed; 'Twas off the Blue Canaries, or, My Last Cigar; Two Cigarettes in the Dark; Viceroy Gives You All the Taste All the Time; While

a Cigarette Was Burning; A Woman Is Only a Woman, But a Good Cigar Is a Smoke

Snake The Pesky Sarpent, or, (On) Springfield Mountain; Snake Charmer; Snake Rag; Spiders and Snakes; Union of the Snake; The Viper's Drag

Snapshot, *see* **Photograph**

Snatch, *see* **Take**

Sneaker, *see* **Shoe**

Snow Frosty the Snow Man; I Never Has Seen Snow; Let It Snow, Let It Snow, Let It Snow; Out in the Cold Cold Snow; Snow Coach; The Snow Goose; Snowbird; Snowy White Snow and Jingle Bells; When I Marry Mister Snow; Where Did My Snowman Go

Soak Plant a Watermelon on My Grave and Let the Juice Soak Through

Soap A Little Bit of Soap

Sob, *see* **Cry**

Society Folks That Put on Airs; High Society (March); Mutual Admiration Society; (Oh I Love) Society; Well, Did You Evah; We've Got To Keep Up with the Joneses

Socks Bobby Sox (Socks) to Stockings

Sod Little Old Sod Shanty

Soft Come Softly to Me; Killing Me Softly with His Song; The Old Soft Shoe; Soft Lights and Sweet Music; The Soft Shoe Shuffle; Soft Winds; Softly As I Leave You; Softly, As in a Morning Sunrise; Softly, Softly; Softly, Softly Theme; Softly Thro' the Summer Night; Speak Softly; Speak Softly Love; Very Soft Shoes

Soldier Au Revoir, But Not Good-Bye, Soldier Boy; How Stands the Glass Around, or, Wolfe's Song, or, Why, Soldiers, Why, or, The Duke of Berwick's March; I Didn't Raise My Boy To Be a Soldier; It's Great To Be a Soldier Man; Jolly Good Luck to the Girl Who Loves a Soldier; A Letter to a Soldier; Mammy's Chocolate Soldier; March of the Tin Soldiers; O Soldier, Won't You Marry Me?; Old Soldiers Never Die; Onward, Christian Soldiers; Parade of the Wooden Soldiers; Scottish Soldier Green Hill; Sister Susie's Sewing Shirts for Soldiers; Soldier Boy; Soldier, Soldier, Won't You Marry Me?; Soldiers' Chorus; The Soldiers in the Park; A Soldier's Life; Soldiers of the Queen; There's Something About a Soldier; There's Something About a Uniform; The Warrior; A Warrior Bold; When a Soldier's on Parade; The Wooden Soldier and the China Doll; Yes, Let Me Like a Soldier Fall

Solid Solid; Solid Gold Easy Action

Soliloquy, *see* **One**

Somebody Everybody Loves Somebody; Everybody Loves Somebody; Everybody's Somebody's Fool; I'd Rather Be Blue over You (Than Happy with Somebody Else); If You Love Somebody Set Them Free; It's a Sin When You Love Somebody; Love Somebody; Love Somebody; The One I Love Belongs to Somebody Else; Some Sort of Somebody; Somebody; Somebody Bad Stole De Wedding Bell; Somebody Bigger Than You and I; Somebody Else Is Taking My Place; Somebody Else, It's Always Somebody Else; Somebody Love Me; Somebody Loves You; Somebody Somewhere; Somebody Stole My Gal; Somebody Up There Likes Me; Somebody's Baby; Somebody's Coming to My House; Somebody's Watching Me; Taking Somebody with Me When I Fall; Won't Somebody Dance with Me; You Know You Belong to Somebody Else; You Try Somebody Else, and I'll Try Somebody Else (We'll Be Back Together Again); You're Nobody 'Til Somebody Loves You

Someone   Goodnight My Someone; If There Is Someone Lovelier Than You; I'm Falling in Love with Someone; I've Been Working on the Railroad, or, The Levee Song, or, Someone's in the Kitchen with Dinah; Make Someone Happy; Someone Could Lose a Heart Tonight; Someone Else's Baby; Someone in a Tree; Someone Like You; Someone Nice Like You; Someone Saved My Life Tonight; Someone To Watch Over Me; Someone's Rocking My Dream Boat; When Someone You Love Loves You; When You Walked Out Someone Else Walked Right In; When You're in Love With Someone Who Is Not in Love With You

Something   Do Something; For the Noo, or, Something in the Bottle for the Morning; Number Something Far Away Lane; The River Song, or, Something's Always Happening on the River; Sing Something Simple; Something (in the Way She Moves); Something About You; Something Better to Do; Something for Jesus; Something Is Happening; Something Seems Tingle-Ingling; Somethin' Stupid; Something To Dance About; Something To Remember You By; Something Wonderful; Something's Always Happening on the River; Something's Coming; Something's Gotta Give; Tell Me Something Good; There Must Be Something Better Than Love; There's Always Something There To Remind Me; (There's Something Nice About Everyone But) There's Everything Nice About You; There's Something About a Rose (That Reminds Me of You); There's Something About a Soldier; There's Something About a Uniform; This Could Be the Start of Something (Big); Wanna Be Startin' Somethin'; You Do Something to Me; You Said Something; You Started Something; You've Done Something to My Heart

Sometime, *see* **Time**

Somewhere   Beautiful Isle of Somewhere; In the Great Somewhere; Somebody, Somewhere; Somewhere; Somewhere a Voice Is Calling; Somewhere Along the Way; Somewhere Down the Road; Somewhere in France with You; Somewhere in Old Wyoming; Somewhere in the Night; Somewhere My Love, or, Lara's Theme; Somewhere Out There; Somewhere That's Green; There's a Star Spangled Banner Waving Somewhere

Son   The Miller's Son; Tom, Tom, the Piper's Son; My Son, My Son; Son of a Preacher Man; Son of a Travelin' Man; The Son of God Goes Forth to War; Son of My Father; Son, This Is She; Sonny Boy; Sons Of; Sons of the Sea; Steptoe and Son; When Sonny Gets Blue; You're the One (You Beautiful Son-of-a-Gun)

Soon   Be Back Soon; Have You Forgotten So Soon; How Soon; It's Too Soon To Know; Let It Be Soon; Mañana (Is Soon Enough for Me); Some Day Soon; Someday Soon; Soon; Soon (Maybe Not Tomorrow); Soon It Will Be Sunday; Soon It's Gonna Rain; Sooner or Later (You're Gonna Be Comin' Around); There's a Boat Dat's Leavin' Soon for New York

Sophisticated   Sing an Old Fashioned Song (to a Young Sophisticated Lady); Sophisticated Lady; Sophisticated Swing

Sorcerer, *see* **Magic**

Sorrento   Come Back to Sorrento; The Streets of Sorrento

Sorry   (What Can I Say, Dear) After I Say I'm Sorry; Are You Sorry; Beg Your Pardon; Going for a Pardon; Hard To Say I'm Sorry; I Apologize; I'm Sorry; I'm Sorry; I'm Sorry I Made You Cry; Lonesome and Sorry; The Pardon Came Too Late; Pardon Me, My Dear Alphonse, After You, My Dear Gaston; Pardon My Southern Accent; Sorry (I Ran All the Way Home); Sorry—Grateful; Sorry Seems To Be the Hardest Word; Who's Sorry Now

Soul   Anema e Core (With All My Heart and Soul); Body and Soul; Don't Tell a Soul; Gypsy in My Soul; Heart and Soul; Heart and Soul; Heart Full of Soul; I Won't Tell a Soul (That I Love You); It Is Well with My Soul; Jesus, Lover of My Soul; Little Bit o' Soul; Rock-a My Soul (in the Bosom of Abraham); Song of the Soul; (You're My) Soul and Inspiration; Soul Man; Stoned Soul Picnic; Sweet Soul Music; Two Lost Souls

Sound, *see* **Hear**

Soup   Animal Crackers in My Soup; Pease Porridge Hot; Who Threw the Overalls in Mrs. Murphy's Chowder

South   Away Down South in Heaven; Dear Old Southland; Down South; I'm Goin' South; It Never Rains in Southern California; Just a Little Bit South of North Carolina; My Southern Rose; 'Neath the South Sea Moon; On the South Side of Chicago; Pardon My Southern Accent; Song of the South; South America Take It Away; South American Way; South of the Border (Down Mexico Way); South Rampart Street Parade; South Sea Island Magic; South Street; Southern Cross; Southern Nights; Southern Rains; That's What I Like About the South; There's No North or South Today; When a Lady Meets a Gentleman Down South; When It's Sleepy Time Down South; Where the Southern Roses Grow; The Wreck of (on) the Old (Southern) '97

Souvenir   Among My Souvenirs; Souvenir

Space   I'm the Urban Spaceman; Outa-Space; Space Oddity; Space Race; The Spacious Firmament on High

Spain   Dance of the Spanish Onion; España (Rhapsody); España (Tango); In a Little Spanish Town; Lady of Spain; My Spanish Rose; The Rain in Spain; The Spaniard That (Who) Blighted My Life; The Spanish Cavalier; Spanish Eyes; Spanish Flea; Spanish Harlem

Spare, *see* **Save**

Spark   Come On, Spark Plug!; There's a Little Spark of Love Still Burning

Sparkle, *see* **Shine**

Sparrow   Sparrow in the Tree Top

Speak, *see also* **Talk**   Actions Speak Louder Than Words; How Do You Speak to an Angel; I Speak to the Stars; If Money Talks, It Ain't on Speaking Terms with Me; If the Waters Could Speak As They Flow; If Those Lips Could Only Speak; Speak Low; Speak Softly; Speak Softly Love; Speak to Me of Love; When Yankee Doodle Learns To Parlez Vous Francais; Why Can't I Speak

Spearmint, *see* **Gum**

Special   My Special Angel; Special Lady; A Very Special Love; A Very Special Love Song

Spell, *see* **Magic**

Spend   (Hey) Big Spender; (This Is) A Lovely Way To Spend an Evening; (I'd Love To Spend) One Hour with You; Why Don't You Spend the Night

Spice, *see* **Seasonings**

Spider   Spiders and Snakes

Spin   The Old Spinning Wheel; Spinning Wheel; Spinning Wheel

Spinach   You Gotta Eat Your Spinach, Baby

Spirit   Every Time I Feel the Spirit; Spirit of Independence; Sweet Spirit, Hear My Prayer

Splash, *see* **Water**

Splendor   Love Is a Many-Splendored Thing

Spoil   One Bad Apple (Don't Spoil the Whole Bunch)

Sponge   I Love To Dunk a Hunk of Sponge Cake

Spoon, *see also* **Court**   A Spoonful of Sugar

Sport   Tie Me Kangaroo Down Sport; A White Sport Coat and a Pink Carnation

Spot   Pepsi-Cola Hits the Spot; You Hit the Spot

Spread   Spread a Little Happiness; Spread a Little Sunshine

Spring   Another Spring; The Day Before Spring; It Might as Well Be Spring; Paris in the Spring; The Pesky Sarpent, or, (On) Springfield Mountain; Rites of Spring; Rustle of Spring; Spring, Beautiful Spring, or, Chimes of Spring; Spring Is Here; Spring Song; Spring, Spring, Spring; Spring Will Be a Little Late This Year; The Springtime of Life; Suddenly It's Spring; Voices of Spring; Voices of the Woods, or, Welcome Sweet Springtime; When It's Springtime in the Rockies; When Love Is Young in Springtime; When the Spring Is in the Air; The Year's at the Spring; Younger Than Springtime

Spy   The James Bond Theme; (Theme from) The Pink Panther

Squad, *see* **Police**

Square   Happiness Street (Corner Sunshine Square); I Live in Trafalgar Square; Leicester Square Rag; A Nightingale Sang in Berkeley Square; Rose of Washington Square; When a Fellow's on the Level with a Girl That's on the Square

Squeak   Susannah's Squeaking Shoes

Squeeze, *see* **Hold**

Stable, *see* **Horse**

Stage *see also* **Broadway, Coach**   The Deadwood Stage; Stage Coach

Stain   Introduction and Air to a Stained Glass Window

Stair   Climbing Up the Golden Stairs; I'll Build a Stairway to Paradise; Upstairs Downstairs; Stairway to the Stars (Park Avenue Fantasy); (Theme from) Upstairs Downstairs, or, The Edwardians; The Waiter and the Porter and the Upstairs Maid; Waiting for the Girls Upstairs

Stand   Don't Stand So Close to Me; How Stands the Glass Around, or, Wolfe's Song, or, Why, Soldiers, Why, or, The Duke of Berwick's March; I Can't Stand It; I Don't Stand a Ghost of a Chance With You; I Left My Sugar Standing in the Rain (and She Melted Away); I Saw Her Standing There; I Was Standing at the Corner of the Street; My Heart Stood Still; Stand and Deliver; Stand Back; Stand by Me; Stand by Your Man; Stand Up and Fight Like H——; ('Tis Me, O Lord) Standin' in the Need of Pray'r; Standing on the Corner; United We Stand; We All Stand Together

Stanley   The Stanley Steamer

Star   The American Star; Ask the Stars; Blue Star; Catch a Falling Star; Come Down Ma Evenin' Star; Count Every Star; Dancing Under the Stars; (Theme from) Doctor Kildare, or, Three Stars Will Shine Tonight; Don't Let the Stars Get in Your Eyes; Dream Along with Me (I'm on My Way to a Star); East of the Moon, West of the Stars; Evergreen, or, Love Theme from A Star Is Born; Good Morning Starshine; I Can Give You the Starlight; I Saw Stars; I Speak to the Stars; I'll Buy You a Star; I'm the Greatest Star; It Was Written in the Stars; I've Told Every Little Star; Jesus Christ Superstar; Knights of the Mystic Star; Little Star, or, Estrellita; Little Star; Look for a Star; Lost in the Stars; Lucky Star; My Guiding Star; My Lucky Star; My Lucky Star; Oh Star of Eve; Poor Little Hollywood Star; Prelude to the Stars; The Second Star to the Right; Shining Star; Shining Star; Stairway to the Stars (Park Avenue Fantasy); The Star; Star Dust; Star Eyes; A Star Fell Out of Heaven; Star in the East; Star Light, Star Bright; Star of the Evening; The Star Spangled Banner; (Theme from) Star Wars; Stardust on the Moon; Starlight; Starlight; Starlight Serenade; Stars and Stripes Forever; Stars Fell on Alabama; Stars in My Eyes; Stars in Your Eyes; Stars of the Summer Night; The Stars Will Remember; Startime; Stella By Starlight; (This Is) The Story of a Starry Night; (Theme from) La Strada, or, Stars Shine in Your Eyes; Swinging on a Star; Texaco Star Theme (The Man Who Wears the Star); There's a Little Star Shining for You; There's a Star Spangled Banner Waving Somewhere; Till Stars Forget to Shine; Twinkle, Twinkle, Little Star, or, Ah! Vous Diraije Maman, or, ABCDEFG (The Alphabet Song); Twinkle, Twinkle, Little Star; Twinkling Stars Are Laughing Love; Underneath the Stars; Video Killed the Radio Star; (Theme from) The Way to the Stars; When Stars Are in the Quiet Skies; When You Wish upon a Star; Would You Catch a Falling Star; You Are My Lucky Star; You Don't Have To Be a Star (To Be in My Show); You're the Only Star in My Blue Heaven

Start, *see also* **Begin**   I Can't Get Started (with You); I Don't Know Where To Start; I Just Want To Go Back and Start the Whole Thing Over; Let's Start the New Year Right; Right Back Where We Started From; Start Me Up; (Just Like) Starting Over; This Could Be the Start of Something (Big); Wanna Be Startin' Somethin'; When the Guardsman Started Crooning on Parade; You Started Something

State   The Old Granite State; State of Shock; The Stately Homes of England; We Came from the Same Old State; What Was Your Name in the States?

Station, *see* **Train**

Stay, *see also* **Linger**   Come Sta'; Don't Stay Away Too Long; Here I'll Stay; I Think I'll Just Stay Here and Drink; I've Come Here To Stay; Let's Stay Together; Make Love Stay; Our Love Is Here To Stay; River, Stay 'Way from My Door; Stay; Stay as Sweet as You Are; Stay Awhile; Stay in My Arms, Cinderella; Stay in Your Own Back Yard; Stay with the Happy People; Stayin' Alive; Staying Young; (Have I Stayed) Too Long at the Fair

Steady, *see* **Court**

Steal   Beg, Steal or Borrow; Love Steals Your Heart; The Pal That I Loved Stole the Gal That I Loved; Somebody Bad

Stole De Wedding Bell; Somebody Stole My Gal; Steal Away; Steal Away to Jesus; The White Dawn Is Stealing

Steam　My Mariuccia Take a Steamboat; The Stanley Steamer; Steam Heat; Steamboat Bill

Stein, *see* **Alcohol**

Stella　Stella; Stella By Starlight

Step　Everybody Step; Everybody Two-Step; Following in Father's Footsteps; Footsteps; I'm Stepping Out with a Memory Tonight; Little Footsteps; On Mother Kelly's Doorstep; Original Dixieland One-Step; Step by Step; Step by Step; Step to the Rear; Steppin' Out; Steppin' Out with My Baby; Steptoe and Son; Tammany Quickstep; They Were All Out of Step But Jim; You Stepped Out of a Dream

Stephanie　Stephanie—Gavotte

Stevedore　Dusky Stevedore

Stick　The Toy Monkey, or, I'm a Monkey on a Stick

Still　Be Still My Heart; Her Bright Smile Haunts Me Still; I Still Believe; I Still Can't Get Over Loving You; I Still Do; I Still Get a Thrill (Thinking of You); I Still Get Jealous; I Still Love To Kiss You Goodnight; I Still See Elisa; I Wonder If You Still Care for Me; I'd Still Believe You True; I'm Still Here; In the Still of the Night; It's Still Rock and Roll to Me; Lost in the Fifties Tonight (In the Still of the Night); My Heart Still Clings to the Old First Love; My Heart Stood Still; Oft in the Stilly Night; Still as the Night; Still Doin' Time; Still I'm Sad; Still Right Here in My Heart; Still the One; There's a Little Spark of Love Still Burning; There's a Million Girlies Lonesome Tonight, and Still I'm All Alone; Will You (Still) Love Me Tomorrow; With All Her Faults I Love Her Still; You're Going Far Away, Lad, or, I'm Still Your Mother, Dear; You're (You'se) Just a Little Nigger, Still You're Mine, All Mine

Stockholm　Stockholm

Stockings　Bobby Sox (Socks) to Stockings; Red Silk Stockings and Green Perfume; When the Nylons Bloom Again

Stomp　Bristol Stomp; King Porter Stomp; Stomp; Stomping at the Savoy; Sugar Foot Stomp, or, Dipper Mouth Blues

Stone, *see also* **Rock**　Hearts of Stone; Like a Rolling Stone; Mister Goldstone; The Old Granite State; Papa Was a Rollin' Stone; Rolling Stones—All Come Rolling Home Again; Some Days Are Diamonds (Some Days Are Stone); Stone Cold Dead in the Market; Stoned Soul Picnic; Stoney End

Stop　Ain't No Stoppin' Us Now; Bus Stop; Don't Stop; Don't Stop Believin'; Don't Stop 'Til You Get Enough; Don't Stop—Twist; Everything Stops for Tea; I Can't Stop Loving You; I Just Wanna Stop; If You Don't Want My Peaches, You'd Better Stop Shaking My Tree; I'll Never Stop Loving You; I'll Stop at Nothing; The Music Stopped; Nothing Can Stop Me Now; Some Memories Just Won't Quit; Stop and Shop at the Co-Op Shop; Stop and Think It Over; Stop Beating 'Round the Mulberry Bush; Stop Dat Knocking at My Door; Stop Draggin' My Heart Around; Stop! In the name of Love; Stop the Cavalry; Stop Your Tickling, Jock!; Stop! You're Breaking My Heart; They Gotta Quit Kickin' My Dog (Dawg) Around, or, The Missouri Houn' Dawg Song; They Just Can't Stop It (The Games People Play); Truck Stop; Whoa, Emma; Who'll Stop the Rain; You Can Never Stop Me Loving You;

You Can't Stop Me from Dreaming; You Can't Stop Me from Loving You

Store　I Found a Million Dollar Baby in a Five and Ten Cent Store; I'm in the Market for You; In a Persian Market; In the Quartermaster's Stores; Little Shop of Horrors; Lonely Pup (in a Christmas Shop); Lost Barber Shop Chord; The Market on Saturday Night; The Peanut Vendor; Play That Barbershop Chord (Mister Jefferson Lord); She Sells Sea-Shells (on the Seashore); Shop Around; Stone Cold Dead in the Market; Stop and Shop at the Co-Op Shop; That Lost Barbershop Chord; This Little Piggie Went to Market; Toyshop Ballet

Storm, *see also* **Rain**　Any Old Port in a Storm; Lightnin' Strikes; The Lightning Tree; Stormy Weather; Thunder Island; Thunderbirds Theme; The Thunderer

Story　A Bedtime Story; Ghost Riders in the Sky, or, A Cowboy Legend; Heart of My Heart (I Love You), or, The Story of the Rose; Hope Told a Flattering Tale; I Love To Tell the Story; I Think When I Read That Sweet Story; Intermezzo (A Love Story) (Souvenir de Vienne); The Legend of the Glass Mountain; Listen to My Tale of Woe; (Theme from) Love Story, or, Where Do I Begin; Love Tales; Ode to Billy Joe; Our Love Story; Saga of Jenny; Shillingbury Tales; The Story Goes On; (This Is) The Story of a Starry Night; Story of My Life; The Story of Tina; Stranger Than Fiction; The Sweetest Story Ever Told, or, Tell Me That You Love Me; The Tale of a Bumble Bee; The Tale of the Kangaroo; The Tale of the Seashell; The Tale of the Turtle Dove; Tales from (of) the Vienna Woods; Tell Me a Story Tell Me the Old, Old Story

Storyville　Farewell to Storyville

Straight　I've Never Seen a Straight Banana; Straighten Up and Fly Right

Strain　Come, Ye Faithful, Raise the Strain; That Minor Strain

Strand　Let's All Go Down the Strand

Strange, Stranger　Don't Go to Strangers; Don't Talk to Strangers; Goodbye Stranger; How Strange; Life Is So Peculiar; Love Is Strange; Love with the Proper Stranger; Passing Strangers; Strange Are the Ways of Love; Strange Enchantment; Strange Fruit; Strange Interlude; Strange Lady in Town; Strange Magic; Strange Music; The Stranger; Stranger in My House; Stranger in Paradise; A Stranger in Town; Stranger on the Shore; Stranger Than Fiction; Strangers; Strangers in the Night; Wayfarin' Stranger

Straw　Chewing a Piece of Straw; Sipping Cider Thru' (Through) a Straw; Turkey in the Straw, or, Old Zip Coon

Strawberry　(Casey Would Waltz with the Strawberry Blonde While) The Band Played On; Strawberry Fair; Strawberry Fields Forever; Strawberry Letter #23; Strawberry Roan

Stream　Down by the Old Mill Stream; Islands in the Stream

Street　Baker Street; Basin Street Blues; Beale Street Blues; Between Eighteenth and Nineteenth on Chestnut Street; Canal Street Blues; Coronation Street; Dancing in the Streets; Easy Street; Easy Street; Ev'ry Street's a Boulevard in Old New York; The 59th Street Bridge Song, or, Feelin' Groovy; Fifty-Second Street Theme; Forty-Second Street; Happiness Street (Corner Sunshine Square); I Was Standing at the Corner of the Street; I'll Tell the Man in the Street; In Old New York, or, The Streets of New York; Italian Street Song; Kookie,

Kookie, Lend Me Your Comb (77 Sunset Strip); (Just a) Little Street Where Old Friends Meet; Lonely Street; On a Little Street in Singapore; On a Street of Chinese Lanterns; On Green Dolphin Street; On the Street Where You Live; On the Sunny Side of the Street; Positively Fourth Street; Sidewalks of Cuba; The Sidewalks of New York, or, East Side, West Side; South Rampart Street Parade; South Street; (On the) Street of Dreams; La Strada Del' Amore (The Street of Love); The Streets of Cairo; Streets of Laredo, or, The Cowboy's Lament; Streets of London; The Streets of Sorrento; Twelfth Street Rag; Up Cherry Street; When My Sugar Walks Down the Street, All the Birdies Go Tweet-Tweet-Tweet

Strike (Theme from) The Empire Strikes Back; Lightnin' Strikes; Moonstruck; Strike Me Pink; Strike the Cymbal; Strike Up the Band; Strike Up the Band—Here Comes a Sailor; When the Clock in the Tower Strikes Twelve

String, *see also* **Violin** Air for the G String; Holiday for Strings; (You May Not Be an Angel But) I'll String Along with You; I've Got No Strings; I've Got the World on a String; Marching Strings; No Strings (I'm Fancy Free); No Strings; Puppet on a String; Serenade for Strings (Suite); Shoestring; Skiffling Strings; A String of Pearls; You've Got Me Dangling on a String; Zing Went the Strings of My Heart

Strip Kookie, Kookie, Lend Me Your Comb (77 Sunset Strip); The Streak; The Stripper; You Gotta Have a Gimmick

Stripe Stars and Stripes Forever

Stroll, *see* **Walk**

Strong The High and the Mighty; I Believe There's Nothing Stronger Than Our Love; A Mighty Fortress Is Our God, or, Ein' Feste Burg; Only the Strong Survive; Treat Her Rough

Strut, *see* **Walk**

Stuck Stuck in the Middle (with You); Stuck On You; Stuck on You; Stuck with You; You'll Never Get Away from Me

Study Down by the Riverside, or, Ain't Gwine Study War No More

Stuff Hot Stuff; Mister Big Stuff

Stupid The Gentleman Is a Dope; Somethin' Stupid

Stutter, *see* **Talk**

Style, *see* **Fashion**

Submarine, *see* **Boat**

Subway, *see* **Train**

Sudden (All of a Sudden) My Heart Sings; Suddenly; Suddenly; Suddenly It's Spring; Suddenly Seymour; Suddenly There's a Valley

Suede Blue Suede Shoes

Sugar Down Among the Sugar Cane; Down Among the Sugar-Cane; I Left My Sugar Standing in the Rain (and She Melted Away); I Lost My Sugar in Salt Lake City; Let Me Be Your Sugar Baby; Milk and Honey; My Sugar Is So Refined; Dance of the Sugar-Plum Fairy; A Spoonful of Sugar; Sugar; Sugar and Spice; Sugar Blues; Sugar Foot Stomp, or, Dipper Mouth Blues; Sugar Shack; Sugar Sugar; Sugar Town; Sugarfoot; Sugartime; A Taste of Honey; When I Take My Sugar to Tea; When My Sugar Walks Down the Street, All the Birdies Go Tweet-Tweet-Tweet; Wild Honey Pie

Suit, *see also* **Coat, Pants** Got a Bran' New Suit; I'm Looking for a Guy Who Plays Alto and Baritone and Doubles on

a Clarinet and Wears a Size Thirty-Seven Suit; Tuxedo Junction; The White Suit Samba; A Zoot Suit

Suitcase, *see* **Baggage**

Sullivan Let Me Shake the Hand That Shook the Hand of Sullivan

Sultan Sultans of Swing

Sum, *see* **Add**

Summer Boys of Summer; A Faded Summer Love; The Green Leaves of Summer; Here Comes Summer; Hot Fun in the Summertime; In Summer; In Summertime on Brendon; In the Good Old Summer Time; In the Summertime; Indian Summer; My Summer Love; Soft Summer Breeze; Softly Thro' the Summer Night; Song for a Summer Night; Stars of the Summer Night; Sumer Is Icumen In; Summer; Summer Dreams; A Summer Evening in Santa Cruz; Summer Holiday; Summer in the City; Summer Is A-Comin' In; The Summer Knows, or, Theme from Summer of '42; Summer Night; Summer of '69; (Theme from) A Summer Place; Summer Set; Summertime; Summertime Summertime; The Things We Did Last Summer; Those Lazy Hazy Crazy Days of Summer; 'Tis the Last Rose of Summer

Sun Arise, O Sun; Brighter Than the Sun; Don't Let the Sun Catch You Crying; Don't Let the Sun Go Down on Me; East of the Sun and West of the Moon; Following the Sun Around; The Girl I Loved in Sunny Tennessee; The House of the Rising Sun; I Don't Care If the Sun Don't Shine; I Got the Sun in the Morning; I'll Follow the Sun; It Was Only a Sun Shower; Just As the Sun Went Down; Keep on the Sunny Side; Marie from Sunny Italy; Meet My Jenny When the Sun Goes Down; Midnight Sun; Morgen—One More Sunrise; My Sunny Tennessee; New Sun in the Sky; Nothing New Beneath the Sun; On the Sunny Side of the Street; A Place in the Sun; Please Mister Sun; Rebecca of Sunny-Brook Farm; Seasons in the Sun; Sink Red Sun; Softly, As in a Morning Sunrise; Some Sunny Day; The Sun Has Got His Hat On; The Sun Shines Brighter; Sunbonnet Sue; Sunny; Sunny; Sunny Days; Sunny Disposish; Sunny Havana; (Keep Your) Sunny Side Up; Sunrise and You; Sunrise Serenade; Sunrise Sunset; That Lucky Old Sun; Wait 'Till the Sun Shines, Nellie; We'll Make Hay While the Sun Shines; When the Sun Comes Out; When the Sun Goes Down; Who's Been Polishing the Sun; The World Is Waiting for the Sunrise; You Can't See the Sun When You're Crying

Sun Valley It Happened in Sun Valley

Sunday Every Day Will Be Sunday When the Town Goes Dry; Ev'ry Sunday Afternoon; Gloomy Sunday; He Goes to Church on Sunday; Never on Sunday; On a Sunday Afternoon; One Sunday Afternoon; Put On Your Sunday Clothes; Some Sunday Morning; Some Sunday Morning; Soon It Will Be Sunday; Sunday; Sunday; A Sunday Kind of Love; Sunday, Monday, or Always

Sundown, *see* **Sunset**

Sunflower The Big Sunflower; Sunflower

Sunset At Sundown; Canadian Sunset; A Japanese Sunset; Red Sails in the Sunset; Sundown; Sunrise Sunset; The Sunset Trail; When the Sun Goes Down; Where the Sunset Turns the Ocean's Blue to Gold

Sunshine Ain't No Sunshine; Bathing in the Sunshine; Bring

Me Sunshine; Carolina Sunshine; Good Day Sunshine; Happiness Street (Corner Sunshine Square); It Takes a Little Rain with the Sunshine To Make the World Go Round; Let the Sunshine In; Little Mary Sunshine; My Sunshine Jane; Old Man Sunshine—Little Boy Bluebird; Open Up Your Heart (and Let the Sunshine In); Out There in the Sunshine with You; Painting the Clouds with Sunshine; Powder Your Face with Sunshine; Put Away a Little Ray of Golden Sunshine; Sally, You Brought the Sunshine to Our Alley; She Is the Sunshine of Virginia; Spread a Little Sunshine; Sunshine Cake; Sunshine Girl; Sunshine, Lollipops and Rainbows; The Sunshine of Paradise Alley; The Sunshine of Your Smile; Sunshine on My Shoulders; Walking on Sunshine; We'll Sing in the Sunshine; You Are My Sunshine; You Are the Sunshine of My Life

Super Jesus Christ Superstar

Superstition Superstition

Supper Come After Breakfast, Bring 'Long Your Lunch and Leave 'Fore Supper Time; Dinner at Eight; Dinner for One, Please James; Happy To Keep His Dinner Warm; My Dad's Dinner Pail; Sing for Your Supper

Suppose, *see* **Imagination**

Sure Are You Sure; How Can I Be Sure; (Are You Going to) San Francisco (Be Sure To Wear Some Flowers in Your Hair); Sure Thing

Surf, *see* **Sea**

Surplus Little Surplus Me, or, Surplus Blues

Surprise Surprise, Surprise; You'd Be Surprised

Surrender I Surrender Dear; Never Surrender; Surrender; Surrender

Surrey, *see* **Coach**

Survive A Country Boy Can Survive; Help Me Make It Through the Night; I Will Survive; Only the Strong Survive

Susan Bobbie Sue; A Boy Named Sue; Goodbye Sue; I Love You in the Same Old Way—Darling Sue; If You Knew Susie, Like I Know Susie; Kentucky Sue; My Creole Sue; My Greenwich Village Sue; Oh! Susanna; Peggy Sue; Runaround Sue; Sierra Sue; Sioux City Sue; Sister Susie's Sewing Shirts for Soldiers; Sunbonnet Sue; Susan Jane; Susannah's Squeaking Shoes; Suzanne; Sweet Sue (Just You); A Symphony for Susan; Wake Up Little Susie; Where's the Playground Susie

Suspicion The Finger of Suspicion Points at You; Suspicion; Suspicious; Suspicious Minds

Sussex Sussex by the Sea

Swallow Follow the Swallow; When the Swallows Come Back to Capistrano

Swan The Swan; The Swan of Tuonela; Wal, I Swan!, or, Ebenezer Frye, or, Giddiap Napoleon, It Looks Like Rain

Swanee Down Where the Swanee River Flows; Hello Swanee, Hello; Old Folks at Home (Way Down Upon the Swanee River); Swanee; Swanee River Moon

Swear Swearin' to God

Sweden Swedish Pastry; Swedish Rhapsody

Sweep, *see* **Broom**

Sweet Ah! Sweet Mystery of Life; Ain't She Sweet; (In My

Sweet Little) Alice Blue Gown; Any Old Place I Can Hang My Hat Is Home Sweet Home to Me; Cockles and Mussels, Alive, Alive, O!, or, Sweet Molly Malone; Cocoanut Sweet; Dolce Far Niente; Drifting and Dreaming (Sweet Paradise); Flow Gently, Sweet Afton, or, Afton Water; Good Sweet Ham; Home Sweet Heaven; Home Sweet Home; How Sweet It Is (To Be Loved by You); How Sweet You Are; Hush Hush Sweet Charlotte; I Think When I Read That Sweet Story; Ida, Sweet as Apple Cider; In the Sweet Bye and Bye; Isn't She the Sweetest Thing; Kiss Me Sweet; Kisses Sweeter Than Wine; Kisses—The Sweetest Kisses of All; The Longest Way 'Round Is the Sweetest Way Home; Love Is the Sweetest Thing; Love's Old Sweet Song; Love's Own Sweet Song, or, Sari Waltz; My Heart at Thy Sweet Voice; My Sweet Adair, (Say Has Anybody Seen) My Sweet Gypsy Rose; My Sweet Lord; My Sweeter Than Sweet; One Called ''Mother'' and the Other ''Home Sweet Home''; The Pearl of Sweet Ceylon; Sad Sweet Dreamer; The Same Sweet Girl Today; Soft Lights and Sweet Music; Some Sweet Day; Stay as Sweet as You Are; Such an Education Has My Mary Ann, or, Sweet Mary Ann; (You're the Flower of My Heart) Sweet Adeline; Sweet Alice, or, Ben Bolt, or, Don't You Remember; Sweet and Gentle; Sweet and Hot; Sweet and Lovely; Sweet and Low; Sweet and Low-Down; Sweet Annie Moore; Sweet as a Song; Sweet Betsy from Pike, or, Vilikens and His Dinah; Sweet Blindness; Sweet Bunch of Daisies; Sweet By and By; Sweet Caroline (Sweet Times Never Seemed So Good); Sweet Danger; Sweet Dreams; Sweet Dreams (Are Made of This); Sweet Emalina, My Gal; Sweet Freedom; Sweet Genevieve; Sweet Georgia Brown; Sweet Hawaiian Moonlight; Sweet Heartache; Sweet Heartaches; Sweet Is the Word for You; Sweet Jennie Lee; Sweet Kentucky Lady; Sweet Lady; Sweet Leilani; Sweet Life; Sweet Little Buttercup; Sweet Little Sixteen; Sweet Lorraine; Sweet Love; Sweet Love; Sweet Madness; Sweet Marie; A Sweet Old-Fashioned Girl; Sweet Peter; Sweet Potato Piper; Sweet Rosie O'Grady; Sweet Savannah; Sweet Seasons; Sweet September; Sweet Sixteen; Sweet Sixteen Bars; Sweet Soul Music; Sweet Spirit, Hear My Prayer; Sweet Sue (Just You); Sweet Talkin' Guy; Sweet Talkin' Woman; Sweet Thing; Sweet Thoughts of Home; Sweet Violets; Sweet Violets; Sweet William; The Sweetest Flower the Garden Grew; Sweetest Maid of All; The Sweetest Music This Side of Heaven; The Sweetest Sight That I Have Ever Seen; The Sweetest Song in the World; The Sweetest Sounds; The Sweetest Story Ever Told, or, Tell Me That You Love Me; The Sweetest Taboo; The Sweetest Thing in Life; Sweetie Pie; There's a Little Lane Without a Turning on the Way to Home Sweet Home; They're All Sweeties; To a Sweet Pretty Thing; Voices of the Woods, or, Welcome Sweet Springtime; When I Saw Sweet Nellie Home, or, I Was Seeing Nellie Home, or, Aunt Dinah's Quilting Party; When I Was Twenty-One and You Were Sweet Sixteen; When Sweet Marie Was Sweet Sixteen; When You Were Sweet Sixteen; Where the Sweet Magnolias Grow; Won't You Waltz ''Home Sweet Home'' with Me; You'll Always Be the Same Sweet Girl; You're a Sweet Little Headache

Sweetheart Auf Wiederseh'n Sweetheart; Blues My Naughty Sweetie Gives to Me; Cinderella Sweetheart; Daddy Has a Sweetheart, and Mother Is Her Name; Don't Sweetheart Me; Down Sweetheart Avenue; For My Sweetheart; Good Night,

Sweetheart; I Love You (Sweetheart of All My Dreams); I'd Love To Meet That Old Sweetheart of Mine; If We Can't Be the Same Old Sweethearts, We'll Just Be the Same Old Friends; If You See My Sweetheart; I'll Be Your Sweetheart; I'm in Love with Two Sweethearts; Let Me Call You Sweetheart; Let Us Be Sweethearts Over Again; Mister Moon You've Got a Million Sweethearts; My Sweetheart's the Man in the Moon; My Sweetie Turned Me Down; My Sweetie Went Away (She Didn't Say Where, When Or Why); Nobody's Sweetheart Now; Some Day Sweetheart; The Sweetheart of Sigma Chi; The Sweetheart Tree; Sweetheart, We'll Never Grow Old; Sweethearts; Sweethearts on Parade; To You Sweetheart, Aloha; We Were Sweethearts for Many Years; We Will Always Be Sweethearts; Will You Remember (Sweetheart); Won't You Be My Sweetheart; You'll Always Be My Lifetime Sweetheart; You're a Sweetheart

Swell A Couple of Swells; Thou Swell

Swim Down at the Old Swimming Hole

Swing Bob White (Whatcha Gonna Swing Tonight); Come and Have a Swing with Me); England Swings (Like a Pendulum Do); If You Can't Sing It You'll Have To Swing It (Mister Paganini); It Don't Mean a Thing If It Ain't Got That Swing; The Organ Grinder's Swing; Sophisticated Swing; Sultans of Swing; Sway; Swing High, Swing Low; Swing Low, Sweet Chariot; Swingin' Down the Lane; Swingin' in a Hammock; Swinging on a Star; Swingin' School; The Swingin' Shepherd Blues; Swingin' the Jinx Away; Waltz in Swing Time; Washington and Lee Swing

Switzerland I Miss My Swiss, My Swiss Miss Misses Me; The Merry Swiss Boy; Rose of Lucerne, or, The Swiss Toy Girl; Swiss (Echo) Song

Sword, *see* **Knife**

Sylvia Sylvia

Sympathy, *see* **Pity**

Syncopation, *see* **Rhythm**

Table Alone at a Table for Two; Dummy Song, or, I'll Take the Legs from off the Table; Hands Across the Table; You Turned the Tables on Me

Taboo, *see* **Forbid**

Tail And the Monkey Wrapped Its Tail Around the Flagpole; Cotton Tail; Horsey, Keep Your Tail Up; Jimmy Crack Corn, or, The Blue Tail Fly; My Long-Tail Blue; Peter Cottontail; Top Hat, White Tie and Tails

Take (Theme from) Against All Odds (Take a Look At Me Now); Always Take Mother's Advice; Can't You Take It Back and Change It for a Boy; Come Take a Trip in My Airship; Do You Take This Woman for Your Lawful Wife?; Don't Take Me Home; Don't Take Your Love from Me; Dummy Song, or, I'll Take the Legs from off the Table; Every Breath You Take; Girls Were Made To Take Care of Boys; I Took My Harp to a Party; I'll Take Romance; I'll Take You Home Again Kathleen; I'll Take You There; It Only Takes a Minute; It Only Takes a Moment; It Takes a Little Rain With the Sunshine To Make the World Go Round; It Takes a Long, Tall, Brown-Skin Gal; It Takes a Woman; It's Gonna Take a Miracle; Let's Take a Walk Around the

Block; Let's Take an Old-Fashioned Walk; Let's Take the Long Way Home; Life Let Us Cherish, or, Snatch Fleeting Pleasures; Loch Lomond, or, the Bonnie Bonnie Banks, or, Oh! Ye'll Take the High Road; My Heart Is Taking Lessons; My Mariuccia Take a Steamboat; Never Take No for an Answer; Never Take the Horse Shoe From the Door; Oh Charley Take It Away; Please Don't Take My Lovin' Man Away; Ready To Take a Chance Again; Ruby, Don't Take Your Love to Town; Satan Takes a Holiday; Say! Have You Taken Your Medicine Yet?; She Took Mother's Advice; Snag It; Somebody Else Is Taking My Place; South America Take It Away; Take a Car; Take a Day Off, Mary Ann; Take a Letter, Maria; Take a Little Tip from Father; Take a Number from One to Ten; Take a Seat, Old Lady; Take Back the Heart You Gave; Take Back Your Gold; Take Back Your Mink; Take Care (When You Say "Te Quiero"); Take Five; Take Good Care of My Baby; Take It Easy; Take It Easy on Me; Take It Slow, Joe; Take It to the Limit; Take Me Along; Take Me Around Again; Take Me Back to Dear Old Blighty; Take Me Back to New York Town; Take Me Back to the Garden of Love; Take Me Back to Your Heart Again; Take Me Down; Take Me High; Take Me High; Take Me Home Country Roads; Take Me in Your Arms; Take Me in Your Arms (Rock Me a Little While); Take Me Out to the Ball Game; Take Me to the Midnight Cake Walk Ball; Take Me Up with You, Dearie; Take My Breath Away; Take My Heart; Take My Love; Take On Me; Take That Look off Your Face; Take the "A" Train; Take the Moment; Take Your Girl; Take Your Girlie to the Movies If You Can't Make Love at Home; Take Your Time, Miss Lucy; Takes Two To Tango; Taking a Chance on Love; Taking in the Town; Takin' It Easy; That's When the Music Takes Me; Then You May Take Me to the Fair; They Can't Take That Away From Me; Took the Last Train; What Takes My Fancy; When Alexander Takes His Ragtime Band to France; When I Take My Sugar to Tea; Who Takes Care of the Caretaker's Daughter While the Caretaker's Busy Taking Care?; Who's Taking You Home Tonight; Why Do They All Take the Night Boat to Albany; With Every Breath I Take; Would You Like To Take a Walk; You Have Taken My Heart; You Take My Breath Away; You Took Advantage of Me

Tale, *see* **Story**

Talent A Little Brains—A Little Talent

Talk, *see also* **Babble, Scream, Speak** Can't We Talk It Over; Conversation on Park Avenue; Don't Talk to Him; Don't Talk to Strangers; Everybody's Talkin', or, Theme from Midnight Cowboy; Girl Talk; The Girl with a Brogue; Gossip Calypso; Grandpa (Tell Me 'Bout the Good Old Days); Happy Talk; I Came Here To Talk for Joe; I Heard It Through the Grapevine; I Just Called To Say I Love You; I Never Mention Your Name (Oh No); I Talk to the Trees; If I Had a Talking Picture of You; If You Talk in Your Sleep, Don't Mention My Name; It's the Talk of the Town; Jive Talkin'; The Language of Love; Let's Talk About Love; Live To Tell; Man to Man Talk; More Than I Can Say; Never Said a Mumblin' Word; Nobody Told Me; Our Language of Love; Pardon My Southern Accent; Pillow Talk; Please Don't Talk About Me When I'm Gone; Sad Songs (Say So Much); Sailor Boys Have Talk to Me in English; Say It Isn't So; Say Say Say; Say You, Say Me; Shout; Sweet Talkin' Guy; Sweet Talkin' Woman; Talk to Me; Talk to the Animals; Talkin' in Your Sleep; Talking in Your Sleep; Tell Her About It; Tell Me I'm Not Dreaming; Twist and Shout; We Don't Talk Anymore; We Never Talk Much; Yakety Yak; You Don't Have To Know the Language; You Should Hear How She Talks About You; You Talk Too Much; You Tell Her, I S-t-u-t-t-e-r

Tall   It Takes a Long, Tall, Brown-Skin Gal; The Jolly Green Giant; Long Tall Glasses (I Can Dance); Long Tall Sally

Tallahassee   Tallahassee

Tambourine   Dancing Tambourine; Mister Tambourine Man

Tammany   Tammany; Tammany Quickstep

Tammy   Tammy

Tan   Black and Tan Fantasy

Tangerine, see **Orange**

Tap   Foot Trapper; A Little Boy Called ''Taps''; Taps

Tara   The Harp That Once Thro' Tara's Halls; Tara's Theme

Task   My Task

Taste, see **Flavor**

Tattoo   Lydia the Tattooed Lady; The Rose Tattoo; Tattoo

Tavern, see **Alcohol**

Tax, see **Money**

Tea   China Tea; Chrysanthemum Tea; Everything Stops for Tea; I Love Coffee, I Love Tea; In a Little Gypsy Tea Room; A Nice Cup of Tea; Tea for Two; When I Take My Sugar to Tea; You Cannot Make Your Shimmy Shake on Tea

Teach, see also **School**   Arthur Murray Taught Me Dancing in a Hurry; I'd Like To Teach the World To Sing; Mama Teach Me To Dance; Songs My Mother Taught Me; Teach Me How To Kiss; Teach Me Tonight; You Taught Me How To Love You, Now Teach Me To Forget; You've Got To Be (Carefully) Taught

Teacher, see **School**

Tear, see also **Cry**   As the Backs Go Tearing By; Torn Between Two Lovers

Tease   Please Don't Tease; Tease Me; Teasing; Temptation; Temptation Rag

Teenager   Heart of a Teenage Girl; Teen Angel; Teenage Crush; Teenage Prayer; Teenager in Love

Teeth   All I Want for Christmas (Is My Two Front Teeth); Capped Teeth and Caesar Salad; Teeth 'n' Smiles; You're a Pink Toothbrush

Telegraph   I Guess I'll Have To Telegraph My Baby

Telephone   Call Me; Call Me (Come Back Home); Call Me Up Some Rainy Afternoon; Hello, Central, Give Me Heaven; Hello, Central, Give Me No Man's Land; Hello Frisco Hello; Hello, Hawaii, How Are You; Hot Line; If the Phone Doesn't Ring, It's Me; I've Got Your Number; Kitty the Telephone Girl; Nora Malone (Call Me by Phone); A Ring on the Finger Is Worth Two on the Phone; Something Seems Tingle-Ingling; Telefone; The Telephone Hour; Telephone Line; Telstar

Television   Theme from a Non-Existent TV Series; Video Killed the Radio Star

Temple, see **Church**

Ten   Dance: Ten; Looks: Three; (What Shall We Do with) The Drunken Sailor, or, Columbus, or, John Brown Had a

Little Injun, or, Ten Little Indians; Eight By Ten; Eleven More Months and Ten More Days; Emergency Ward 10 Theme; I Close My Eyes and Count to Ten; I Found a Million Dollar Baby in a Five and Ten Cent Store; Slaughter on Tenth Avenue; Take a Number from One to Ten; Ten Cents a Dance; Ten Little Fingers and Ten Little Toes—Down in Tennessee; Ten Little Indians, or, Ten Little Injuns, or, Ten Little Niggers; Ten Minutes Ago; Ten Pretty Girls; Ten Thousand Years from Now

Tender   Leave a Tender Moment Alone; Love Me Tender; Tender Is the Night; Tender Love; Tender Shepherd; (Love Is) The Tender Trap; Tenderly; Tenderly; Tenderly Calling; Try a Little Tenderness; Would God I Were a Tender Apple Blossom

Tenement, see **Home**

Tennessee   Ellie Rhee, or, Carry Me Back to Tennessee; The Girl I Loved in Sunny Tennessee; Just Try To Picture Me (Back (Down) Home in Tennessee); My Sunny Tennessee; Ten Little Fingers and Ten Little Toes—Down in Tennessee; Tennessee Waltz; When the Birds in Georgia Sing of Tennessee

Tent, see **Camp**

Terrific   Love Is So Terrific; A Terrific Band and a Real Nice Crowd

Territory   A Handsome Territorial

Terry   Eternally, or, Terry's Theme; Terry

Tessie   Tessie, You Are the Only, Only, Only

Texas   Deep in the Heart of Texas; The Eyes of Texas (Are upon You); Texas in My Rear View Mirror; Texas Women; (When It's Roundup Time in Texas) When the Bloom Is on the Sage; The Yellow Rose of Texas, or, Song of the Texas Rangers

Thames   Old Father Thames

Thank You   Danke Schöen; I Give Thanks for You; I Want To Thank Your Folks; My Thanks to You; Plenty To Be Thankful For; Sorry—Grateful; Thank God for a Garden; Thank God I'm a Country Boy; Thank Heaven for Little Girls; Thank U Very Much; Thank You Falettin Me Be Mice Elf Agin; Thank You for a Lovely Evening; Thank You Girl; Thank You So Much Mrs. Lowsborough—Goodbye; Thank You Very Much; Thank Your Father; Thanks; Thanks a Million; Thanks for the Buggy Ride; Thanks for the Memory; That's Gratitude

Thanksgiving   We Gather Together (To Ask the Lord's Blessing), or, Prayer of Thanksgiving

Thick   (Love Is) Thicker Than Water

Thief, see **Robber**

Thing, see also **Everything, Something,** etc.   All the Things You Are; All Things Love Thee, So Do I; The Best Thing for You; (You're the) Best Thing That Ever Happened to Me; Best Thing You've Ever Done; The Best Things in Life Are Free; Come Home, Dewey, We Won't Do a Thing to You; Crazy Little Thing Called Love; Do Your Own Thing; Every Little Thing She Does Is Magic; A Fact Can Be a Beautiful Thing; First Thing Monday Mornin'; Funny Thing; Happiness Is (Just) a Thing Called Joe; How Are Things in Glocca Morra; How's Every Little Thing in Dixie; I Just Want To

Go Back and Start the Whole Thing Over; I Love the Little Things; Isn't Love the Grandest Thing; Isn't She the Sweetest Thing; It Don't Mean a Thing If It Ain't Got That Swing; It's the Darndest Thing; It's the Real Thing. Coke.; It's Your Thing; Just One of Those Things; (The) Last Thing on My Mind; Let's Call the Whole Thing Off; Little Things Mean a Lot; The Little Things You Do Together; The Little Things You Used To Do; Love Is a Dancing Thing; Love Is a Many-Splendored Thing; Love Is a Simple Thing; Love Is the Darndest Thing; Love Is the Sweetest Thing; My Favorite Things; The Object of My Affection; One Thing Leads to Another; P.Y.T. (Pretty Young Thing); Playthings; A Precious Little Thing Called Love; Prove It by the Things You Do; The Rain, the Park and Other Things; The Right Thing To Do; Say Wonderful Things; Sure Thing; Sweet Thing; The Sweetest Thing in Life; There Are Such Things; These Foolish Things Remind Me of You; These Things I Offer You (for a Lifetime); The Thing; Things Are Looking Up; Things Are Looking Up; Things Can Only Get Better; Things Go Better with Coke; The Things I Love; The Things I Want; The Things We Did Last Summer; The Things We Do for Love; Till the Real Thing Comes Along; To a Sweet Pretty Thing; (It Will Have To Do) Until the Real Thing Comes Along; Was That the Human Thing To Do; What Is This Thing Called Love; Wild Thing; Without That Certain Thing; A Woman Is a Sometime Thing; You Do the Darndest Things, Baby; You Say the Nicest Things, Baby; You Sexy Thing; You're a Heavenly Thing; You've Got That Thing

Think, *see also* **Mind, Reason, Understand, Wise** Bouquet (I Shall Always Think of You); Did You Ever Think As the Hearse Rolls By, or, The Worms Crawl In, the Worms Crawl Out; Do You Ever Think of Me; Don't Think Twice, It's All Right; Don't You Think It's True; Enjoy Yourself, It's Later Than You Think; Fool (If You Think It's Over); Here I Am (Just When I Thought I Was Over You); I Can't Think Ob Nuttin' Else But You; I Concentrate on You; I Don't Think I'll End It All Today; I Don't Think I'm Ready for You; I Don't Think She's in Love Anymore; I May Be Wrong, But I Think You're Wonderful; I Still Get a Thrill (Thinking of You); I Think I Love You; I Think I'll Just Stay Here and Drink; I Think of You; I Think of You; I Think When I Read That Sweet Story; If I Only Had a Brain; I'll Only Miss Her When I Think of Her; I'll Think of You; I'm Only Thinking of Him; I'm (Dreaming) Thinking Tonight of My Blue Eyes; A Little Brains—A Little Talent; Logical Song; The Logical Song; Losing My Mind; Méditation; My Baby Thinks He's A Train; Oh! How I Laugh When I Think How I Cried About You; Quiller Has the Brains; Reuben and Rachel, or, Reuben, Reuben, I've Been Thinking; Scatterbrain; She Is Not Thinking of Me (Waltz at Maxim's); Sixty Seconds Every Minute, I Think of You; Smarty; Stop and Think It Over; Sweet Thoughts of Home; Think About Me; Think of Laura; Thinking of You; Too Busy Thinking About My Baby; The Very Thought of You; What D'Yer Think of That; Who Do You Think You Are; Who Do You Think You Are Kidding Mister Hitler; You Might Think

Thirteen Hello Twelve, Hello Thirteen, Hello Love

Thirty Twelve Thirty, or, Young Girls Are Coming to the Canyon

Thousand If I Had a Thousand Lives to Live; I'll Sing You a Thousand Love Songs; The Night Has a Thousand Eyes; The Night Has a Thousand Eyes; No! No! A Thousand Times No!; Ten Thousand Years From Now; A Thousand and One Nights; Through a Thousand Dreams; We Are Coming, Father Abraham, 300,000 More

Thread, *see* **Sew**

Three (Theme from) Close Encounters of the Third Kind; Dance: Ten; Looks: Three; (Theme from) Doctor Kildaire, or, Three Stars Will Shine Tonight; Five-Four-Three-Two-One; I Saw Three Ships Come Sailing; Knock Three Times; Love of Three Oranges (March); Mack the Knife, or, Theme from The Threepenny Opera, or, Morit'at; Three Little Kittens; One, Two, Three; One-Two-Three; One Two Three Red Light; Our Penthouse on Third Avenue; Quarter to Three Waltz; 633 Squadron; Strawberry Letter #23; The Third Man Theme, or, The Harry Lime Theme; Three Blind Mice; Three Brothers; The Three Caballeros; Three Coins in the Fountain; The Three-Cornered Hat; Three for Jack; Three Little Fishes; Three Little Sisters; Three Little Words; Three O'Clock in the Morning; Three on a Match; Three Shades of Blue; Three Times a Lady; Three Times in Love; Three Wonderful Letters from Home; Three's a Crowd; Treble Chance; Two Hearts in Three Quarter Time; We Are Coming, Father Abraham, 300,000 More; We Three Kings of Orient (Are); We Three— My Echo, My Shadow, and Me; While the Angelus Was Ringing, or, The Three Bells (Les Trois Cloches), or, The Jimmy Brown Song

Thrill Hold Me, Thrill Me, Kiss Me; Thriller; I Still Get a Thrill (Thinking of You); My First Thrill; The Thrill Is Gone; You're My Thrill

Throw Cast Your Fate to the Wind; (Our Love) Don't Throw It All Away; Don't Throw Your Love Away; I Gave You Up Just Before You Threw Me Down; I Threw a Kiss in the Ocean; Our Love (Don't Throw It All Away); Put 'Em in a Box, Tie 'Em with a Ribbon (and Throw 'Em in the Deep Blue Sea); Throw Another Log on the Fire; Throw Him Down McCloskey; Throw Me a Kiss; Throw Me a Rose; Throw Open Wide Your Window; Who Threw the Overalls in Mrs. Murphy's Chowder; You Have Cast Your Shadow on the Sea

Thrush I Hear a Thrush at Eve

Thumb, *see* **Hand**

Thunder, *see* **Storm**

Thyme, *see* **Seasonings**

Ticket, *see* **Broadway, Travel**

Tickle I'm Tickled to Death I'm Single; Stop Yer Tickling, Jock!; (Everybody Ought To Know How To Do) The Tickle Toe

Tide, *see* **Sea**

Tie Ascot Gavotte; Blest Be the Tie That Binds; I'm Tying the Leaves So They Won't Come Down; Put 'Em in a Box, Tie 'Em with a Ribbon (and Throw 'Em in the Deep Blue Sea); Tie a Yellow Ribbon Round the Ole Oak Tree; Tie Me Kangaroo Down Sport; Top Hat, White Tie and Tails

Tiffany's Breakfast at Tiffany's

Tiger Eye of the Tiger; Tiger Feet; Tiger Rag; Tiger Rose

Tight Hold Me Tight; Hold Tight—Hold Tight; Put Your Arms Around Me Honey (Hold Me Tight); Tighten Up; Uptight (Everything's Alright)

Time, *see also* **Clock, Midnight, Month, Noon, Year,** etc. About a Quarter to Nine; Ain't It Funny What a Difference Just a Few Hours Make; All the Time; All Time High; Am I Wasting My Time on (over) You; Another Time, Another Place; Any Time; Any Time is Kissing Time; Any Time's the Time To Fall in Love; Are the Good Times Really Over; As Time Goes By; Baby, Baby All the Time; (Every Time I Turn Around) Back in Love Again; Bad Time; Bad Timing; The Best of Times; Better Luck Next Time; Bidin' My Time; Big Time; By the Time I Get to Phoenix; Call Round Any Old Time; Come After Breakfast, Bring 'Long Your Lunch and Leave 'Fore Supper Time; Crying Time; Dance of the Hours; Dancing Time; Darkest the Hour; Did It in a Minute; Do That to Me One More Time; Does Anybody Really Know What Time It Is; Don't You Think It's Time; Down on the Farm in Harvest Time; Entire History of the World in Two Minutes and Thirty-Two Seconds; Ev'ry Time; Every Time I Feel the Spirit; Ev'ry Time We Say Goodbye; Every Time You Touch Me (I Get High); Everytime You Go Away; (That's the Time I) Feel Like Makin' Love; Fifty Million Times a Day; First Time; The First Time Ever I Saw Your Face; Five Minutes More; The Five O'Clock Whistle; For Old Times' Sake; For the First Time (Come Prima); For the Good Times; ''Forever'' Is a Long, Long Time; Forty-Five Minutes from Broadway; Four or Five Times; The Free and Easy Hour of Parting; From the Time We Say Goodbye; From This Moment On; Get Me to The Church on Time; Give Me a Moment Please; Give Me One Hour; Good Times; Good Timin'; Good Timin'; Goodtime Charley; Green-Up Time; The Happy Time; Hard Times Come Again No More; Heat of the Moment; Here's to the Next Time; Hey There, Good Times; Hot Fun in the Summertime; (There'll Be) A Hot Time in the Old Town (Tonight); An Hour Never Passes; The Hour of Parting; I Didn't Know What Time It Was; I Guess It Never Hurts To Hurt Sometimes; I Keep Forgettin' (Every Time You're Near); I Know Where the Flies Go in the Wintertime; I May Be Gone for a Long, Long Time; I Need Thee Every Hour; If I Could Be with You One Hour Tonight; If You've Got the Time, We've Got the Beer; I'll Be with You in Apple Blossom Time; In an Eighteenth Century Drawing Room; In Love for the Very First Time; In the Good Old Summer Time; In the Midnight Hour; In the Summertime; It Only Hurts for a Little While; It Only Takes a Moment; It Only Takes a Minute; It Seems Like Old Times; It's Been a Long, Long Time; It's Just a Matter of Time; It's Make Believe Ballroom Time; Its Time to Say Goodnight; It's Tulip Time in Holland; I've Got the Time—I've Got the Place, But It's Hard To Find the Girl; I've Had a Lovely Time; I've Had My Moments; I've Loved You for a Long Time; Jeannine, I Dream of Lilac Time; Just in Time; Just Once for All Time; Knock Three Times; Lady Love Me One More Time; The Lamplit Hour; The Last Time I Saw Paris; Leave a Tender Moment Alone; Let the Good Times Roll; Liberty Bell—It's Time To Ring Again; Long Time Ago, or, Shinbone Alley; The Longest Time; Love Takes Time; Love Theme from Romeo and Juliet, or, A Time for Us; Magic Moments; Many Times; The

March of Time; Mashed Potato Time; Maybe This Time; Minnie the Mermaid, or, A Love Song in Fish Time; Minute by Minute; Ten Minute Waltz; The Moment I Saw You; Moment Musicale; Moment to Moment; Moments to Remember; (There Ought To Be a) Moonlight Saving Time; Hickory, Dickory, Dock; My Dreams Are Getting Better All the Time; My Shining Hour; My Time Is Your Time; My Time of Day; Nestin' Time in Flatbush; Next Time; No! No! A Thousand Times No!; Now Is the Hour; (Potatoes Are Cheaper—Tomatoes Are Cheaper) Now's the Time To Fall in Love; Old Colony Times; Old Friends and Old Times; (Gimme Dat) Old Time Religion; Old Times; On the Twentieth Century; Once in a Lifetime; Once in a Lifetime; Once in a While; Once in Every Lifetime; Once upon a Time; Once upon a Wintertime; (I'd Love To Spend) One Hour with You; One Moment Alone; One More Time; One O'Clock Jump; One Piece at a Time; Orange Blossom Time; Part-Time Lover; Part Time Lover; Party All the Time; Party Time; Pony Time; Prime Time; Quarter to Three Waltz; Right Place Wrong Time; Rock of Ages; The Second Time Around; Seems Like Old Times; Sixty Seconds Every Minute, I Think of You; Sleepy Time Gal; Some Other Time; Sometime; Sometime; Sometime We'll Understand; Sometime You'll Wish Me Back Again; Sometimes I Feel Like a Motherless Child; Sometimes I'm Happy; The Springtime of Life; Startime; Stay Awhile; Still Doin' Time; Sugartime; Summertime; Summertime Summertime; Sweet Caroline (Sweet Times Never Seemed So Good); Take Me in Your Arms (Rock Me a Little While); Take the Moment; Take Your Time (Do It Right); Take Your Time, Miss Lucy; The Telephone Hour; Ten Minutes Ago; Theme from The Eleventh Hour; Then I'll Have Time for You; There'll Be a Hot Time for the Old Men When the Young Men Go to War; There'll Come a Time; There'll Come a Time; There's a Good Time Coming; These Things I Offer You (for a Lifetime); This Is the Moment; This Time I'm in It for Love; This Is Love; This Time the Dream's on Me; Three O'Clock in the Morning; Three Times a Lady; Till the End of Time; Time; Time (Clock of the Heart); Time After Time; Time After Time; Time Alone Will Tell; Time and Love; Time and the River; Time and Tide (Theme from *Plague Dogs*); Time Don't Run Out on Me; Time Drags By; The Time Has Come; Time Heals Everything; Time in a Bottle; Time Is on My Side; Time Marches On; Time May Change; Time on My Hands; Time Passages; Time Waits for No One; Time Was, or, Dreaming; Time Will Reveal; Timer; The Times of Your Life; The Times They Are a-Changin'; Too Many Times; Tulip Time; Tulsa Time; Twelve Thirty, or, Young Girls Are Coming to the Canyon; Twentieth Century Blues; Twilight Time; Two Hearts in Three Quarter Time; Until It's Time for You To Go; Viceroy Gives You All the Taste All the Time; Voices of the Woods, or, Welcome Sweet Springtime; Waltz in Swing Time; When Alexander Takes His Ragtime Band to France; When It's Apple Blossom Time in Normandy; When It's Night Time Down in Burgundy; When It's Night Time in Dixie Land; When It's Night-Time in Italy, It's Wednesday over Here; When It's Sleepy Time Down South; When It's Springtime in the Rockies; When Love Is Young in Springtime; (When It's Roundup Time in Texas) When the Bloom Is on the Sage; Where Do Flies Go in the Winter Time?; Who Knows Where the Time Goes; Whoever

You Are, or, Sometimes Your Eyes Look Blue to Me; A Woman Is a Sometime Thing; A Wonderful Time Up There; You Didn't Have To Tell Me—I Knew It All the Time; You Find the Time, I'll Find the Place; You Happen Once in a Lifetime; You'll Always Be My Lifetime Sweetheart; Younger Than Springtime; You're Only Human (Second Wind)

Timid, *see* **Shy**

Tin (In My) Little Tin Box; March of the Tin Soldiers; Tin Roof Blues

Tina The Story of Tina; Tina; Tina Marie

Tinhorn, *see* **Bugle**

Tiny, *see* **Small**

Tip From the Top of Your Head to the Tip of Your Shoes; I Tipped My Hat and Slowly Rode Away; Take a Little Tip from Father; Tip Toe Through the Tulips (with Me); Tip-Top Tipperary Mary; Tippecanoe and Tyler Too

Tipperary It's a Long (Long) Way to Tipperary; Tip-Top Tipperary Mary

Tired, *see* **Sleep**

Tobacco, *see* **Smoke, Smoking**

Today Any Bonds Today?; The Army of Today's Alright; The Boys Are Coming Home Today; Getting Married Today; A Hundred Years from Today; I Don't Think I'll End It All Today; I'm Going To See You Today; I'm Twenty-One To-day; It's a Lovely Day Today; It's My Mother's Birthday Today; Lovely Lady Let the Roses See You Today; No Milk Today; The Same Sweet Girl Today; There's No North or South Today; Today; Today I Feel So Happy; Today I Met My Love; (On) A Wonderful Day Like Today; A Year from Today; You Deserve a Break Today

Toe, *see* **Feet**

Together Alone Together; Come Together; (Let's) Get Together; Happy Together; It's Always Fair Weather When Good Fellows Get Together, or, A Stein Song; Let's Get Together; Let's Stay Together; Let's Work Together; Life Is a Song, Let's Sing It Together; The Little Things You Do Together; Love Will Keep Us Together; Marching Along Together; The More We Are Together; Put Your Hands Together; Putting It Together; Sharing the Night Together; Some Day We'll Be Together; Together; Together We Are Beautiful; Together Wherever We Go; Togetherness; We Could Make Such Beautiful Music (Together); We Do Not Belong Together; We Gather Together (To Ask the Lord's Blessing), or, Prayer of Thanksgiving; We'll Be Together Again; We're in This Love Together; Why Can't We Live Together; You Try Somebody Else, and I'll Try Somebody Else (We'll Be Back Together Again)

Tokyo Tokyo Melody

Tom Lighterman Tom; Lord Thomas and Fair Elinore; Little Tommy Tucker; Tom, Tom, the Piper's Son; (Poor) Tom Bowling, or, The Sailor's Epitaph; Tom Dooley, or, Tom Dula; Tomboy; Tommy, Lad; Tommy, Make Room for Your Uncle; The Windmills of Your Mind, or, Theme from The Thomas Crown Affair

Tomato (Potatoes Are Cheaper—Tomatoes Are Cheaper) Now's the Time To Fall in Love

Tomorrow All Our Tomorrows; The Day After Tomorrow; Domani; Each Tomorrow Morning; A Headache Tomorrow (Or a Heartache Tonight); In the Garden of Tomorrow; It's Almost Tomorrow; Love Me Tomorrow; Mañana (Is Soon Enough for Me); Mañana Pasado Mañana; Save Your Sorrow for Tomorrow; Soon (Maybe Not Tomorrow); There's a Great Day Coming, Mañana; There's Always Tomorrow; There's No Tomorrow; Till Tomorrow; T'morra, T'morra; Tomor-row; Tomorrow; Tomorrow Is a Lovely Day; Until Tomor-row; We Fight Tomorrow, Mother; Will You (Still) Love Me Tomorrow; Will You Marry Me Tomorrow, Maria

Ton Sixteen Tons

Tonight, *see also* **Evening, Night** After Tonight We Say ''Goodbye''; All Quiet Along the Potomac Tonight; Anyone Who Isn't Me Tonight; Are You Lonesome Tonight; Be Mine Tonight; Bob White (Whatcha Gonna Swing Tonight); Buf-falo Gals (Won't You Come Out Tonight), or, Lubly Fan; Comedy Tonight; (Theme from) Doctor Kildare, or, Three Stars Will Shine Tonight; Don't Go in the Lions' Cage To-night; Don't Go Out Tonight, Boy; Don't Let Me Be Lonely Tonight; Get Down Tonight; Goodnight Tonight; A Head-ache Tomorrow (Or a Heartache Tonight); Hoo-oo Ain't You Coming Out Tonight; I Must See Annie Tonight; I Wish That You Were Here Tonight; I Wonder What the King Is Doing Tonight; I Wonder Where My Baby Is Tonight; I Wonder Where She Is Tonight; I Wonder Who's Dancing with You Tonight; I'd Really Love To See You Tonight; If I Could Be with You One Hour Tonight; I'll Remember Tonight; I'm Gonna Ring the Bell Tonight; I'm Stepping Out with a Mem-ory Tonight; I'm (Dreaming) Thinking Tonight of My Blue Eyes; In the Air Tonight; It Looks (to Me) Like a Big Night Tonight; Just for Tonight; Knightsbridge March, or, In Town Tonight; Let Me Love You Tonight; Let Me Love You To-night; The Lion Sleeps Tonight, or, Wimoweh; Lost in the Fifties Tonight (In the Still of the Night); Love Me Tonight; Meet Me Tonight in Dreamland; Oh! How I Miss You To-night; Oh! I Must Go Home Tonight; One of Us Will Weep Tonight; Sailor Who Are You Dreaming of Tonight; Say a Prayer for Me Tonight; Someone Could Lose a Heart To-night; Someone Saved My Life Tonight; Teach Me Tonight; Tenting on the Old Camp Ground, or, Tenting Tonight; There'll Be No Teardrops Tonight; There's a Million Girlies Lonesome Tonight, and Still I'm All Alone; There's Where My Heart Is Tonight; Tonight; Tonight I Celebrate My Love; Tonight or Never; Tonight She Comes; Tonight We Love; Tonight You Belong to Me; Tonight's the Night (It's Gonna Be Alright); The Way You Look Tonight; We've Got To-night; We've Got Tonight; When I Get You Alone Tonight; Where Is My (Wand'ring) Boy Tonight; Who's Taking You Home Tonight; The World Is Mine (Tonight)

Tony Tony From America; Tony's Wife

Top From the Top of Your Head to the Tip of Your Shoes; High upon a Hill Top; I'm Sittin' High on a Hill Top; I'm Sitting on Top of the World (Just Rolling Along—Just Roll-ing Along); Leanin' on the Ole Top Rail; Little Bit off the Top; On Top of Old Smokey; Sparrow in the Tree Top; The Surrey with the Fringe on Top; Tip-Top Tipperary Mary; Top Hat, White Tie and Tails; The Top of the Hill; Top of the World; Top of the World; Topsy; You're the Top

Torch, *see* **Fire**

Toreador, *see* **Bull**

Torpedo, *see* **Gun**

Touch Every Time You Touch Me (I Get High); Invisible Touch; Love Touch (Theme from *Legal Eagles*); (You've Got) The Magic Touch; Old Flag Never Touched the Ground; Out of Touch; Reach Out and Touch; The Sentimental Touch; She Touched Me; Touch Me in the Morning; Touch Me When We're Dancing; The Touch of Your Hand; The Touch of Your Lips; (Theme from) The Untouchables; The Way I Want To Touch You; We All Stand Together; Why Can't I Touch You; Won't You Fondle Me

Tour, *see* **Travel**

Tower, *see* **Castle**

Town All the Quakers Are Shoulder Shakers Down in Quaker Town; Avalon Town; Bach Goes to Town; Chicago (That Toddlin' Town); Chinatown, My Chinatown; Come On Down Town; The Darktown Strutters' Ball; De Camptown Races (Gwine To Run All Night); Doin' the Uptown Lowdown; Down in Honky Tonky Town; Down in Jungle Town; Downtown; Durham Town; Every Day Will Be Sunday When the Town Goes Dry; Funkytown; Gee, But It's Great To Meet a Friend from Your Old Home Town; Get Out of Town; Her Town Too; He's a Devil in His Own Home Town; Home Town; (There'll Be) A Hot Time in the Old Town (Tonight); I'm Gonna Move to (the) Outskirts of Town; I'm the Lonesomest Gal in Town; In a Little Spanish Town; In Good Old New York Town; In the Town Where I Was Born; In Twilight Town; It All Belongs to You (The Laugh of the Town); It's a Lonesome Old Town (When You're Not Around); It's the Talk of the Town; Jimtown Blues; Knightsbridge March, or, In Town Tonight; Life in a Northern Town; Little Town in the Ould County Down; Lulu's Back in Town; Moving Day in Jungle Town; My Hometown; My Home Town Is a One Horse Town, But It's Big Enough for Me; My Kind of Town; My Little Town; O Little Town of Bethlehem; Out of Town; Poor Side of Town; Ruby, Don't Take Your Love to Town; Santa Claus Is Coming to Town; (In) A Shanty in Old Shanty Town; Show Me the Town; Small Town; Strange Lady in Town; A Stranger in Town; Sugar Town; Take Me Back to New York Town; Taking in the Town; There Is a Tavern in the Town; There's a Quaker Down in Quaker Town; The Town Where I Was Born; Toy Town; Uptown Girl; Wake the Town and Tell the People; What'll We Do on a Saturday Night When the Town Goes Dry; When the Circus Came to Town; You'd Never Know the Old Home Town of Mine

Toy, *see also* **Doll,** etc. March of the Tin Soldiers; The March of the Toys; Rose of Lucerne, or, The Swiss Toy Girl; A Secretary Is Not a Toy; The Toy Drum Major; The Toy Monkey, or, I'm a Monkey on a Stick; Toy Town; Toy Trumpet; Toyland; Toyshop Ballet

Trace Traces

Track, *see* **Train**

Tracy Tracy; Tracy's Theme

Trade Down Where the Trade Winds Blow

Tradition Tradition

Traffic, *see* **Automobile, Travel**

Tragedy Tragedy

Trail Along the Navajo Trail; Along the Sante Fe Trail; Blue Shadows on the Trail; The Old Chisholm Trail; On the Trail; The Sunset Trail; Tamiami Trail; There's a Long, Long Trail; Trail of Dreams; The Trail of the Lonesome Pine; Twilight on the Trail

Train The Charming Young Widow I Met on the Train; Chattanooga Choo-Choo; Choo-Choo Honeymoon; Choo-Choo Train; De Gospel Train; Don't Sleep in the Subway; Down by the Station; Express; Five Hundred Miles, or, Railroader's Lament; Heartbreak Express; Honky Tonk Train Blues; I've Been Working on the Railroad, or, The Levee Song, or, Someone's in the Kitchen with Dinah; King Porter Stomp; Last Train to Clarksville; Life's Railway to Heaven; Long Train Runnin'; Mama from the Train, or, A Kiss, A Kiss; Meet Me at the Station, Dear; Midnight Train to Georgia; Morning Train (Nine to Five); Mule Train; (Theme from) Murder on the Orient Express; My Baby Thinks He's a Train; Night Train; On the Atchison, Topeka, and the Sante Fe; On the 5:15; (On) The Other Side of the Tracks; Patsy Ory Ory Aye (A-Workin' on the Railroad); Peace Train; The Pullman Porter's on Parade; Railroad Jim; The Runaway Train; Take a Car; Take the "A" Train; Took the Last Train; The Tracks of My Tears; Trains and Boats and Planes; The Trolley Song; Tuxedo Junction; The Waiter and the Porter and the Upstairs Maid; Waitin' for the Train To Come In; Watching the Trains Come In; When the Midnight Choo-Choo Leaves for Alabam'

Tralee The Rose of Tralee

Tramp, *see* **Hobo**

Transformation, *see* **Change**

Trap (Love Is) The Tender Trap

Trapeze, *see* **Circus**

Travel, *see also* **Wander** All Aboard for Blanket Bay; All Aboard for Dixieland; The Arkansas Traveler; Around the World (in Eighty Days); Come Take a Trip in My Airship; Day Tripper; Don't Put Me Off at Buffalo Any More; Homeward Bound; I Travel the Road; Magical Mystery Tour; Pan Am Makes the Goin' Great; Sentimental Journey; Son of a Travelin' Man; Ticket to Ride; Trabling Back to Georgia; Traffic Jam; Travelin' Band; Travelin' Man; Travelin' Light; Two Tickets to Georgia; Voyage to the Bottom of the Sea; Wayfarin' Stranger; The Wayworn Traveller; Why Do the Wrong People Travel

Tray Old Dog Tray

Treasure On Treasure Island

Treat Don't Treat Me Like a Child; Treat Her Right; Treat Me Rough; Why Do You Treat Me Like You Do

Tree, *see also* **Wood** Around the Corner and Under the Tree; Autumn Leaves; The Brave Old Oak; By the Sycamore Tree; Carolina in the Pines; Cathedral in the Pines; The Chestnut Tree; Cinco Robles (Five Oaks); Cocoanut Grove; Deck the Halls with Boughs of Holly; Don't Sit Under the Apple Tree (with Anyone Else But Me); Down Among the Sheltering Palms; Down in the Forest; Down in the Old Cherry Orchard; Falling Leaves; (Theme from) Flame Trees of Thika; The Green Leaves of Summer; The Gum Tree Canoe (on Tom-

Big-Bee River); Hang Your Heart on a Hickory Limb; Hanging Tree; Heart of Oak; I Talk to the Trees; If You Don't Want My Peaches, You'd Better Stop Shaking My Tree; I'm Looking Over a Four Leaf Clover; I'm Tying the Leaves So They Won't Come Down; In the Shade of the Old Apple Tree; Kiss a Four Leaf Clover; The Lady from Twenty-Nine Palms; Lemon Tree; The Lightning Tree; The Lilac Tree, or, Perspicacity; The Little Old Log Cabin in the Lane; Lullaby of the Leaves; Maple Leaf Rag; Mountain Greenery; The Old Oaken Bucket; An Orange Grove in California; The Palm Trees, or, The Palms; The People Tree; Piney Ridge; Rain Forest; (The Song of) Raintree County; The Shade of the Palm; Someone in a Tree; The Song of the Trees; Sparrow in the Tree Top; The Sweetheart Tree; (When) They Cut Down the Old Pine Tree; Tie a Yellow Ribbon Round the Ole Oak Tree; The Trail of the Lonesome Pine; A Tree in the Meadow; A Tree in the Park; Trees; Two Ladies in De Shade of De Banana Tree; Under the Bamboo Tree; Under the Yum Yum Tree; A Voice in the Wilderness; A Walk in the Black Forest; The Weeping Willer; When the Leaves Come Tumbling Down; When the World Was Young (Ah, the Apple Tree); The Whispering Pines of Nevada; The Willow Waltz; Willow Weep for Me; Woodman Spare That Tree; Woodman, Woodman, Spare That Tree

Trinidad   Minnie from Trinidad

Trinity   At Trinity Church I Met My Doom

Trip, *see* **Travel**

Trolley, *see* **Train**

Trombone   Seventy-Six Trombones

Troop   The Mascot of the Troop

Trouble   Bridge Over Troubled Water; In the House of Too Much Trouble; Keep Smiling at Trouble; Nobody Knows De Trouble I've Seen; Pack Up Your Trouble in Your Old Kit Bag and Smile, Smile, Smile; Trouble; Trouble (in River City); Wrap Your Troubles in Dreams (and Dream Your Troubles Away); You've Got Your Troubles

Trousers, *see* **Pants**

Truck, *see* **Automobile**

Trucking, *see* **Walk**

Trudie   Trudie

True, *see* **Truth**

Trumpet, *see* **Bugle**

Trust   Trust In Me; Trusting Jesus, That Is All

Truth, *see also* **Sincerely**   Ain't It the Truth; (I'm) Always True to You in My Fashion; Be Honest with Me; Black Is the Color of My True Love's Hair; A Fact Can Be a Beautiful Thing; Gold Will Buy Most Anything But a True Girl's Heart; Honest and Truly; Honesty; Hurrah! for Hayes and Honest Ways; I Honestly Love You; I Love You Truly; I Would Be True; I'd Still Believe You True; If Dreams Come True; Is It True What They Say About Dixie; It Couldn't Be True (or Could It); It Must Be True (You Are Mine, All Mine); My Truly, Truly Fair; No Honestly!; Prove It by the Things You Do (It's Easy to Say); Say It Isn't So; There's Nothing True But Heaven; Till All Our Dreams Come True; 'Tis Not True; True Blue Lou; True Confession; True Grit; True-Hearted, Whole-Hearted, or, Peal Out the Watchword; (I Had Myself

a) True Love; True Love; True Love Ways; Truly; When a Fellow's on the Level with a Girl That's on the Square; You Can't Be True, Dear

Tuba   Tubby the Tuba; When Yuba Plays the Rumba on His Tuba

Tuesday   Monday, Tuesday, Wednesday

Tulip   It's Tulip Time in Holland; Tip Toe Through the Tulips (with Me); Tulip Time; When You Wore a Tulip and I Wore a Big Red Rose

Tulsa   Tulsa Time

Tune, *see also* **Melody**   Changing My Tune; The Colonel's Tune; Crazy Words (Crazy Tune) (Vo-Do-De-O-Do); Desafinado (Slightly Out of Tune); Elmer's Tune; I Like To Recognize the Tune; I Whistle a Happy Tune; That Mesmerizing Mendelssohn Tune

Turkey   Turkey in the Straw, or, Old Zip Coon; Turkish Coffee; Twilight In Turkey

Turn   (Every Time I Turn Around) Back in Love Again; Blue Turning Grey over You; Don't Turn Around; He Walked Right In, Turned Around and Walked Right Out Again; I Cried for You (Now It's Your Turn To Cry over Me); I Wish You Could Have Turned My Head; If the Moon Turns Green; It's a Long Lane That Has No Turning; It's My Turn; Judy's Turn To Cry; Let the Great Big World Keep Turning; Love Will Turn You Around; My Sweetie Turned Me Down; The Picture That's Turned to (Toward) the Wall; Rose's Turn; There's a Little Lane Without a Turning on the Way to Home Sweet Home; Tossin' and Turnin'; Tossing and Turning; Turn Around; Turn Around; Turn Back the Universe and Give Me Yesterday; Turn Down Day; Turn 'Erbert's Face to the Wall, Mother; Turn Your Love Around; Turn Your Radio On; Turned Up; When a Fellah Has Turned Sixteen; When the Blue Sky Turns to Gold; When Your Hair Has Turned to Silver, I Will Love You Just the Same; Where the Sunset Turns the Ocean's Blue to Gold; Who Can I Turn To (When Nobody Needs Me); The Windmill's Turning; The World Turned Upside Down, or, Derry Down; You Turned the Tables on Me

Turtle   The Tale of the Turtle Dove

Tuxedo, *see* **Suit**

Twelve   Hello Twelve, Hello Thirteen, Hello Love; One Dozen Roses; The Twelfth of Never; Twelfth Street Rag; Twelve Days of Christmas; Twelve Thirty, or, Young Girls Are Coming to the Canyon; When the Clock in the Tower Strikes Twelve

Twenty   I'm Twenty-One Today; In the Year 2525; The Lady from Twenty-Nine Palms; On the Twentieth Century; Strawberry Letter #23; Twentieth Century Blues; When I Was Twenty-One and You Were Sweet Sixteen

Twice, *see* **Two**

Twilight, *see* **Evening**

Twinkle, *see* **Shine**

Twins, *see* **Two**

Two   Aggravatin' Papa (Don't You Try To Two-Time Me); All I Want for Christmas (Is My Two Front Teeth); Alone at a Table for Two; B-I-Double L-Bill; Cocktails for Two; Concerto for Two; A Couple of Song and Dance Men; A Couple of Swells; Daisy Bell, or, A Bicycle Built for Two, or, Daisy,

Daisy; Don't Think Twice, It's All Right; Double Vision; Double Your Pleasure; Entire History of the World in Two Minutes and Thirty-Two Seconds; Everybody Two-Step; Five Foot Two, Eyes of Blue (Has Anybody Seen My Girl?); Five-Four-Three-Two-One; Forty-Second Street; I Double Dare You; I Never Do Anything Twice; I Wish I Were Twins; I'm in Love with Two Sweethearts; I'm Looking for a Guy Who Plays Alto and Baritone and Doubles on a Clarinet and Wears a Size Thirty-Seven Suit; Just the Two of Us; Just We Two; No Two People; Oh That We Two Were Maying; (Theme from) The Odd Couple; One, Two, Button Your Shoe; One, Two, Three; One-Two-Three; One Two Three Red Light; Paradise for Two; A Picnic for Two; A Ring on the Finger Is Worth Two on the Phone; Second Hand Rose; The Second Minuet; The Second Rhapsody; The Second Star to the Right; The Second Time Around; Seven or Eleven—My Dixie Pair o' Dice; The Summer Knows, or, Theme from Summer of '42; Takes Two To Tango; Tea for Two; There's No Two Ways About Love; Till We Two Are One; Torn Between Two Lovers; Tryin' To Love Two; Two Blue Eyes; Two Cigarettes in the Dark; Two Different Worlds; Two Doors Down; Two Faces in the Dark; (Theme from) Two for the Road; The Two Grenadiers; The Two Guitars; Two Hearts Are Better Than One; Two Hearts in Three Quarter Time; Two Hearts That Pass in the Night; Two Ladies; Two Ladies in De Shade of De Banana Tree; Two Laughing Irish Eyes; Two Little Babes in the Wood; Two Little Baby Shoes; Two Little Bluebirds; Two Little Boys; Two Little Girls in Blue; Two Little Love Bees; Two Little Magpies; Two Lost Souls; Two Lovely Black Eyes; Two Loves Have I; The Two of Us; Two Silhouettes; Two Silhouettes in the Moonlight; Two Sleepy People; Two Tickets to Georgia; Two Tribes; Under the Double Eagle (March); We Two Shall Meet Again; We're the Couple in the Castle; While Others Are Building Castles in the Air (I'll Build a Cottage for Two); (Theme from) You Only Live Twice; You're Only Human (Second Wind); You've Got To Pick a Pocket or Two

Typewriter, *see* **Write**

Tyrant   Chester (Let Tyrants Shake Their Iron Rod)

Ugly   The Good, the Bad and the Ugly; Ugly Chile (You're Some Pretty Doll); The Ugly Duckling

Ukulele, *see* **Guitar**

Umbrella   A Fella with an Umbrella; Hey Young Fella Close Your Old Umbrella; Let a Smile Be Your Umbrella on a Rainy (Rainy) Day; The Umbrella Man

Uncle   Aunt Jemima and Your Uncle Cream of Wheat; Dance with Your Uncle Joseph; (Theme from) The Man from U.N.C.L.E.; Tommy, Make Room for Your Uncle; Uncle Albert/ Admiral Halsey; (Old) Uncle Ned; Uncle Remus Said

Under, *see also* **Beneath**   Around the Corner and Under the Tree; Dancing Under the Stars; Don't Sit Under the Apple Tree (with Anyone Else But Me); Down Under; (He'd Have To Get Under,) Get Out and Get Under (To Fix Up His Automobile); Get Out and Get Under the Moon; I've Got You Under My Skin; Under a Blanket of Blue; Under a Roof in Paree; Under Any Old Flag At All; Under Hawaiian Skies; Under Paris Skies; Under the Anheuser Bush; Under the

Bamboo Tree; Under the Boardwalk; Under the Bridges of Paris; Under the Deodar; Under the Double Eagle (March); Under the Roller Coaster; Under the Yum Yum Tree; Underneath the Arches; Underneath the Harlem Moon; Underneath the Russian Moon; Underneath the Stars; With Her Head Tucked Underneath Her Arm; With My Shillelagh Under My Arm

Understand, *see also* **Explain**   Can't You Understand; I Understand; I Understand Just How You Feel; Message Understood; (I Don't Understand) The Parisians; Sometime We'll Understand; Why Don't They Understand; You Know and I Know (and We Both Understand)

Unfinished, *see* **End**

Unhappy, *see* **Happy**

Uniform, *see* **Clothes**

Union   The Full Moon Union; Part of the Union; (Look For the) Union Label; Union of the Snake

United   Reunited; United We Stand

Universe, *see* **World**

Unusual   It's a Most Unusual Day; It's Not Unusual; Unusual Way

Up   All Shook Up; B B B Burnin' Up with Love; Break Up To Make Up; Breaking Up Is Hard To Do; Build Me Up Buttercup; Call Me Up Some Rainy Afternoon; Chin Up, Ladies!; Climbing Up; Come Back When You Grow Up; Coming Up (Live at Glasgow); Did You Ever Have To Make Up Your Mind; Doin' the Uptown Lowdown; Don't Give Up on Us; Don't Give Up the Old Love for the New; Don't Give Up the Ship; Don't Wake Me Up, I'm Dreaming; Don't Wake Me Up, Let Me Dream; Dress You Up; The Flies Crawled Up the Window; (He'd Have To Get Under,) Get Out and Get Under (To Fix Up His Automobile); Get Up and Boogie; Going Up; Green-Up Time; Hurry It's Lovely Up Here; I Can't Do My Belly Bottom Button Up; I Gave You Up Just Before You Threw Me Down; I Just Roll Along Havin' My Ups and Downs; I Won't Grow Up; I'd Love To Fall Asleep and Wake Up in My Mammy's Arms; I'll Make Up for Everything; I'm Building Up to an Awful Let-Down; I'm Leaving It All Up to You; It's Nice To Get Up in the Morning; Lock Up Your Daughters; Mandy Make Up Your Mind; Upstairs Downstairs; My Faith Looks Up to Thee; Oh, How I Hate To Get Up in the Morning; Open Up Your Heart (and Let the Sunshine In); Pick Up the Pieces; Pick Yourself Up; Put On Your Slippers and Fill Up Your Pipe; Shake It Up; Somebody Up There Likes Me; Stand Up and Cheer; Stand Up and Fight Like H——; Start Me Up; Straighten Up and Fly Right; Strike Up the Band; Strike Up the Band—Here Comes a Sailor; (Keep Your) Sunny Side Up; Take Me Up with You, Dearie; Things Are Looking Up; Things Are Looking Up; Tighten Up; Turned Up; Up Cherry Street; Up in a Balloon; Up in the Clouds; Up on the Roof; Up Up and Away, or, My Beautiful Balloon; Up Where We Belong; Up with the Lark; Upside Down; (Theme from) Upstairs Downstairs, or, The Edwardians; Uptight (Everything's Alright); Uptown Girl; Wait Till You Get Them Up in the Air, Boys; The Waiter and the Porter and the Upstairs Maid; Waiting for the Girls Upstairs; Wake Me Up Before You Go-Go; Wake Up and Live; Wake Up Little Susie; We All Went Up Up Up the Mountain; Wedding Bells Are Breaking Up That Old Gang of Mine; When De Moon Comes Up Behind De Hill; When the Roll Is Called Up Yonder; When the Values Go Up; When You're All Dressed Up and No Place to Go; A Wonderful Time Up There; The World Turned Upside Down, or, Derry Down; You Can't Chop Your Poppa Up in Massachusetts; You're a Builder Upper

Upon   The Eyes of Texas (Are Upon You); High Upon a Hill Top; It Came Upon a Midnight Clear; The Little House Upon the Hill; The Mottoes Framed Upon the Wall; Old Folks at Home (Way Down Upon the Swanee River); Once Upon a Dream; Once Upon a Time; Once Upon a Wintertime; When You Wish Upon a Star

Urban, *see* **City**

Utah   A Utah Man Am I

Vacant, *see* **Empty**

Vagabond, *see also* **Wander**   Goodnight (I'm Only a Strolling Vagabond); I'm Just a Vagabond Lover; Song of the Vagabonds; The Vagabond; Vagabond Dreams; Waltz Huguette, or, The Vagabond King Waltz

Vain   In Love in Vain; You're So Vain

Valencia   Valencia

Valentine   (Look Out For) Jimmy Valentine; My Funny Valentine; Valentine

Valleri   Valleri

Valley   Down in the Valley, or, Birmingham Jail, or, Bird in a Cage, or, Down on the Levee; Harper Valley P.T.A.; In the Valley of the Moon; It Happened in Sun Valley; Just an Echo in the Valley; Lily of the Valley; The Little Brown Church (in the Vale); The Red River Valley; San Fernando Valley; Suddenly There's a Valley; The Valley of Swords; (Theme from) Valley of the Dolls; Valley Valparaiso

Vamp   Hard Hearted Hannah (The Vamp of Savannah); Louisville Lou, the Vampin' Lady; The Vamp

Vanessa   Vanessa

Vanilla, *see* **Seasonings**

Variation   Eighteenth Variation on a Theme by Paganini

Velvet   Blue Velvet

Vendor, *see* **Store**

Venice   Carnival of Venice; Waters of Venice, or, Floating Down the Sleepy Lagoon

Venus   Venus

Vermont   Moonlight in Vermont

Vibration   Good Vibrations

Victory   Easy Winners; Shine On Victory Moon; The Victors; What Does It Take (To Win Your Love); The World Cup March

Vienna   Cafe in Vienna; Goodnight Vienna; Intermezzo (A Love Story) (Souvenir de Vienne); Tales from (of) the Vienna Woods; Vienna; Vienna Dreams; Vienna Life

View   A Room with a View; Texas in My Rear View Mirror; A View to a Kill

Village   My Greenwich Village Sue; My Quiet Village; The Village Blacksmith; The Village of Saint Bernadette

Vine   By the Watersmelon Vine, Lindy Lou; Clinging Vine; From the Vine Came the Grape (from the Grape Came the Vine); I Heard It Through the Grapevine

Vinegar   Down by the Winegar Woiks

Violet   The Message of the Violet; Sweet Violets; Sweet Violets; Violets; Where the Shy Little Violets Grow; Who'll Buy My Violets

Violin, *see also* **String**   April Played the Fiddle; The Big Bass Viol; Fit as a Fiddle (and Ready for Love); The Ghost of the Violin; I Played Fiddle for the Czar; Love Is Like a Violin; My Faithful Stradivari; Pizzicati; Play, Fiddle, Play; Ragtime Violin; The Violin Began To Play; The Violin Song; Violins From Nowhere; When a Gypsy Makes His Violin Cry; The Wooing of the Violin; Yiddle on Your Fiddle, or, Play Some Ragtime

Virginia   Carry Me Back to Old Virginny; Carry Me Back to Ole Virginny, or, De Floating Show; Goodbye Virginia; I Was Born in Virginia, or, Ethel Levy's Virginia Song; I'm Comin' Virginia; Let It Rain! Let It Pour! (I'll Be in Virginia in the Morning); 'Mid the Green Fields of Virginia; She Is the Sunshine of Virginia

Vision, *see* **Eye**

Voice   Just a Voice To Call Me, Dear; Lift Ev'ry Voice and Sing; My Heart at Thy Sweet Voice; Somewhere a Voice Is Calling; A Voice in the Wilderness; The Voice of R.K.O.; The Voice of the Hudson; Voices of Spring; Voices of the Woods, or, Welcome Sweet Springtime

Volunteer   Mister Volunteer, or, You Don't Belong to the Regulars, You're Just a Volunteer; The Volunteer Organist

Vote   In the Fall We'll All Go Voting for Al

Vulcan   The Origin of Gunpowder, or, When Vulcan Forg'd the Bolts of Jove

Wabash   On the Banks of the Wabash Far Away; The Wabash Blues; Wabash Cannonball; Wabash Moon

Wagon   Covered Wagon Days (March); I'm on the Water Wagon Now; Roll Along Covered Wagon; Wagon Wheels; Wait for the Wagon; Westward Ho!—The Covered Wagon March; The Wheel of the Wagon Is Broken

Waikiki, *see* **Hawaii**

Wail, *see* **Cry**

Wait   Anticipation; Bidin' My Time; Don't Wait On Me; Don't Wait 'Til the Night Before Christmas; The Folks Are All Waiting To See the Fast Steamer; Heaven Can Wait; I Can't Wait; I Shall Be Waiting; (If It Takes Forever) I Will Wait for You; I Wonder If She's Waiting; I'm Glad I Waited for You; I'm Waiting for Ships That Never Come In; I've Waited Honey, Waited Long for You; I've Waited So Long; Just You Wait; Ladies in Waiting; Love Won't Let Me Wait; Nat'an, Nat'an, Tell Me for What Are You Waitin', Nat'an; She Waits by the Deep Blue Sea; Time Waits for No One; Wait; Wait and See; Wait for Me; Wait for the Wagon; Wait 'Til the Sun Shines, Nellie; Wait Till the Clouds Roll By; Wait Till the Cows Come Home; Wait Till the Tide Comes In; Wait Till You Get Them Up in the Air, Boys; Wait Till You See Her; Wait Until Dark; Wait Until Your Daddy Comes

Home; Waiting; Waiting; Waiting at the Church, or, My Wife Won't Let Me; Waiting for a Girl Like You; Waiting for the Girls Upstairs; Waiting for the Robert E. Lee; Waitin' for the Train To Come In; The World Is Waiting for the Sunrise

Waiter, *see* **Restaurant**

Wake Arise, O Sun; Don't Wake Me Up, I'm Dreaming; Don't Wake Me Up, Let Me Dream; I'd Love To Fall Asleep and Wake Up in My Mammy's Arms; Reveille; Rise and Shine; Some Day My Heart Will Awake; Till I Wake; Wake Me Up Before You Go-Go; Wake Me When It's Over; Wake Nicodemus; Wake the Town and Tell the People; Wake Up and Live; Wake Up Little Susie; Waking Or Sleeping

Waldorf Lounging at the Waldorf

Walk Baby Elephant Walk; Billy (For When I Walk); Da Doo Ron Ron (When He Walked Me Home); Daddy Don't You Walk So Fast; Did You Ever See a Dream Walking; Eli Green's Cakewalk; Felix Kept On Walking; Flirtation Walk; Golliwogg's Cake Walk; Goodnight (I'm Only a Strolling Vagabond); (O) Hand Me Down My Walking Cane; He Walked Right In, Turned Around and Walked Right Out Again; I Don't Want To Walk Without You, Baby; If He Walked into My Life; I'll Walk Alone; I'll Walk Beside You; I'll Walk with God; I'm Happy When I'm Hiking; I'm Walkin'; I'm Walking Behind You; (He Walks with Me) In the Garden; Just a Closer Walk with Thee; Just Walking in the Rain; Keep On Truckin'; Lambeth Walk; Let's Take a Walk Around the Block; Let's Take an Old-Fashioned Walk; The Longest Walk; Love Walked In; On the Boardwalk in Atlantic City; Ostrich Walk; Pigeon Walk; Sleep Walk; Sleep Walk; Stray Cat Strut; The Stroll; Strollers We; Strollin'; Strolling on the Brooklyn Bridge; Strut; Struttin' with Some Barbecue; Take Me to the Midnight Cake Walk Ball; These Boots Are Made for Walking; Tramp, Tramp, Tramp; Tramp! Tramp! Tramp! Along the Highway; Truckin'; Walk Away from Love; Walk Away, Renee; Walk—Don't Run; Walk Hand in Hand; A Walk in the Black Forest; Walk Like a Man; Walk of Life; Walk On By; Walk on the Wild Side; Walk Right In; Walkin' Back to Happiness; Walkin' by the River; Walking Happy; Walking In Rhythm; Walkin' My Baby Back Home; Walking On Sunshine; Walkin' to Missouri; When My Sugar Walks Down the Street, All the Birdies Go Tweet-Tweet-Tweet; When She Walks in the Room; When You Walked Out Someone Else Walked Right In; While Strolling Through the Park One Day, or, The Fountain in the Park; Would You Like To Take a Walk; You Walk By; You'll Never Walk Alone

Wall, *see* **Room**

Walrus I Am the Walrus

Walter Walter, Walter (Lead Me to the Altar)

Wander, *see also* **Vagabond** Anywhere I Wander; The Happy Wanderer; Home on the Range, or, Oh, Give Me a Home Where the Buffalo Roam; Roam On, (My) Little Gipsy Sweetheart; Roamin' in the Gloamin'; The Roving Kind; Song of the Wanderer; The Wanderer; The Wanderer; Wanderin'; Where Is My (Wand'ring) Boy Tonight

War, *see also* **Battle** Down by the Riverside, or, Ain't Gwine Study War No More; Hawaiian War Chant; (To the War Has Gone) The Minstrel Boy; The Minstrel's Return from the War; Revolution; The Son of God Goes Forth to War; (Theme from) Star Wars; There'll Be a Hot Time for the Old Men When the Young Men Go to War; War; War of the Worlds; Waterloo; Weeping, Sad and Lonely, or, When This Cruel War Is Over; When the War Is Over, Mary

Ward, *see* **Hospital**

Warm Fair and Warmer; Happy To Keep His Dinner Warm; I've Got My Love To Keep Me Warm; Young and Warm and Wonderful

Warn, *see* **Danger**

Warrior, *see* **Soldier**

Warsaw (Theme from the) Warsaw Concerto

Wash, *see also* **Laundry** Car Wash; I'm Gonna Wash My Hands of You; I'm Gonna Wash That Man Right Outa My Hair; Irish Washerwoman, or, The Scotch Bagpipe Melody; The Portuguese Washerwomen; Scrub Me Mama with a Boogie Beat; Use Ajax the Foaming Cleanser; Washboard Blues; Washing on the Siegfried Line; When I'm Cleaning Windows

Washington If Washington Should Come to Life; Just Like Washington Crossed the Delaware, General Pershing Will Cross the Rhine; Rose of Washington Square; Washington and Lee Swing; Washington Post; Washington Square

Waste Am I Wasting My Time on (over) You; Just Another Day Wasted Away; Wasted Days Wasted Nights; You Never Miss the Water Till the Well Runs Dry, or, Waste Not, Want Not

Watch Somebody's Watching Me; Someone To Watch Over Me; True-Hearted, Whole-Hearted, or, Peal Out the Watchword; Watch What Happens; Watchin' Girls Go By; Watching the Clouds Roll By; Watching the Trains Come In; Watching the Wheels; When We've Wound Up the Watch on the Rhine

Water, *see also* **Float, Flood, Flow,** etc. Allan Water; Black Water; Bridge Over Troubled Water; By the Waters of Minnetonka; Cool Water; Flow Gently, Sweet Afton, or, Afton Water; From the Land of the Sky Blue Water; If the Waters Could Speak As They Flow; I'm Like a Fish Out of Water; I'm on the Water Wagon Now; Laughing Water; The Meeting of the Waters of Hudson and Erie; Muddy Water; Muddy Water; On the Banks of Allan Water; Reflections in the Water; Reflections on the Water; Smoke on the Water; Splish Splash; (Love Is) Thicker Than Water; To a Water Lily; Water Boy; The Water Gypsies; Water, Water; Waterloo; Waters of Perkiomen; Waters of Venice, or, Floating Down the Sleepy Lagoon; Where the Waters Are Blue; You Never Miss the Water Till the Well Runs Dry, or, Waste Not, Want Not; You Splash Me and I'll Splash You

Waterfall By a Waterfall; Just a Cottage Small—By a Waterfall

Waterfront I Cover the Waterfront

Watermelon By the Watermelon Vine, Lindy Lou; Plant a Watermelon on My Grave and Let the Juice Soak Through

Wave, *see* **Hand, Sea**

Weak That's My Weakness Now

Wear Can I Leave Off Wearin' My Shoes; The Hat Me Father Wore; He Wears a Pair of Silver Wings; He Who His Country's Liv'ry Wears; I'm Looking for a guy Who Plays Alto and Baritone and Doubles on a Clarinet and Wears a

Size Thirty-Seven Suit; Rich and Rare Were the Gems She Wore; (Are You Going to) San Francisco (Be Sure To Wear Some Flowers in Your Hair); She Wore a Yellow Ribbon, or, All Round My Hat (Round Her Neck) I (She) Wore a Yellow Ribbon; Texaco Star Theme (The Man Who Wears the Star); That's the Reason Noo I Wear a Kilt; They're Wearing 'Em Higher in Hawaii; Wear My Ring Around Your Neck; The Wearin' o' the Green; When You Wore a Pinafore; When You Wore a Tulip and I Wore a Big Red Rose; When You're Wearing the Ball and Chain

Weary, *see* **Sleep**

Weasel   Pop Goes the Weasel

Weather   It's Always Fair Weather When Good Fellows Get Together, or, A Stein Song; Stormy Weather

Wedding, *see* **Marriage**

Wednesday   Monday, Tuesday, Wednesday; Wednesday's Child; When It's Night-Time in Italy, It's Wednesday Over Here

Weed   A Rose in a Garden of Weeds; Tobacco's But an Indian Weed; Tumbling Tumbleweeds

Week   Eight Days a Week; It's Good News Week; Safely Through Another Week; Saturday Night Is the Loneliest Night of the Week; That Lovely Weekend; A Weekend in Havana; A Weekend in the Country

Weep, *see* **Cry**

Weight, *see* **Heavy**

Welcome, *see* **Hello**

Well, *see* **Healthy, Wishing Well**

Wendy   Wendy

West   East of the Moon, West of the Stars; East of the Sun and West of the Moon; The Golden West; Little Grey Home in the West; Northwest Passage; Out Where the West Begins; The Sidewalks of New York, or, East Side, West Side; Way Out West; Way Out Yonder in the Golden West; West End Blues; West End Girls; West of the Great Divide; West of Zanzibar (Jambo); Westminster Chimes; Westminster Waltz; Westward Ho!—The Covered Wagon March

Wet   A Wet Sheet and a Flowing Sea

Whale   The Torpedo and the Whale

Wheat   Aunt Jemima and Your Uncle Cream of Wheat

Wheel   Ezekiel Saw De Wheel; Helen Wheels; Old Mill Wheel; The Old Spinning Wheel; Roll on Eighteen Wheeler; Spinning Wheel; Spinning Wheel; Wagon Wheels; Watching the Wheels; The Wheel of Fortune; The Wheel of the Wagon Is Broken; Wheels

Whiskers, *see* **Beard**

Whisper, *see* **Quiet**

Whistle   Anyone Can Whistle; The Five O'Clock Whistle; Give a Little Whistle; Give a Little Whistle; The Happy Whistler; I Whistle a Happy Tune; I'm Humming, I'm Whistling, I'm Singing; This'll Make You Whistle; (Just) Whistle While You Work; The Whistler and His Dog; The Whistling Boy; The Whistling Coon; Whistling in the Dark; Whistling Rufus

White   Angel of the Great White Way; Black and White; Black and White Rag; Blue Shadows and White Gardenias; Bob

White (Whatcha Gonna Swing Tonight); Cherry Pink and Apple Blossom White; Columbia, the Gem of the Ocean, or, The Red, White and Blue; The Dashing White Sergent; The Little White Bull; The Little White Cloud That Cried; Little White Cottage; The Little White Donkey; Little White Duck; A Little White Gardenia; The Little White House (at the End of Honeymoon Lane); Little White Lies; My White Knight; Nights in White Satin; Separate Lives (Love Theme from *White Nights*); Show the White of Yo' Eye; Snowy White Snow and Jingle Bells; Top Hat, White Tie and Tails; When the White Lilacs Bloom Again; White Christmas; (There'll Be Blue Birds over) The White Cliffs of Dover; The White Dawn Is Stealing; The White Dove; The White Horse Inn; The White House Chair; White On White; The White Peacock; The White Rose of Athens; White Silver Sands; A White Sport Coat and a Pink Carnation; The White Suit Samba; White Wings; A Whiter Shade of Pale

Whoopee   Makin' Whoopee

Wide   High, Wide and Handsome; It's a Big, Wide, Wonderful World; Shenandoah, or, Across the Wide Missouri; There's One Wide River To Cross, or, Noah's Ark; Throw Open Wide Your Window; With My Eyes Wide Open I'm Dreaming

Widow   The Charming Young Widow I Met on the Train; The Merry Widow Waltz, or, I Love You So; Widow Machree

Wife, *see* **Marriage**

Wild   The Cry of the Wild Goose; I Know a Bank Where the Wild Thyme Blows; I'm Just Wild About Animal Crackers; I'm Just Wild About Harry; I'm Wild About Horns on Automobiles That Go "Ta-Ta-Ta-Ta"; In the Wildwood Where the Bluebells Grew; Marta, or, Rambling Rose of the Wildwood; My Wild Irish Rose; Runnin' Wild; They Go Simply Wild Over Me; To a Wild Rose; Walk on the Wild Side; What Are the Wild Waves Saying; When the Mocking Birds Are Singing in the Wildwood; The Wild Boys; Wild Honey Pie; Wild Horses; Wild Is the Wind; Wild Man Blues; Wild One; The Wild Rose; Wild Rose; Wild Thing; Wild Wind; Wild World; Wildfire; Wildflower; Wildflower; Your Wildest Dreams

William, *see* **Bill**

Willow, *see* **Tree**

Willpower   Lady Willpower; Ready, Willing and Able

Win, *see* **Victory**

Wind   Any Way the Wind Blows; Blow Ye Winds, Heigh Ho; Blowin' in the Wind; The Breeze (That's Bringing My Honey Back to Me); The Breeze and I; Breezin' Along with the Breeze; Cast Your Fate to the Wind; Catch the Wind; Down Where the Trade Winds Blow; Dust in the Wind; The Four Winds and the Seven Seas; Gone With the Wind; High on a Windy Hill; I Feel Like a Feather in the Breeze; Ill Wind (You're Blowin' Me No Good); The North Wind Doth Blow; Passing Breeze; Ride Like the Wind; Soft Summer Breeze; Soft Winds; They Call the Wind Maria; Trade Winds; The Way That the Wind Blows; The Wayward Wind; Wedding of the Winds; When the Wind Was Green; Wild Is the Wind; Wild Wind; The Wind Cannot Read; Windy; With the Wind and the Rain in Your Hair; Written on the Wind; You're Only Human (Second Wind)

Winding Down the Winding Road of Dreams; The Long and Winding Road; Where the Morning Glories Twine Around the Door; Where the Silv'ry Colorado Wends Its Way

Windmill A Windmill in Old Amsterdam; The Windmills of Your Mind, or, Theme from the Thomas Crown Affair; The Windmill's Turningt

Window A Cage in the Window; (How Much Is That) Doggie in The Window; The Flies Crawled Up the Window; Hangin' Out the Window; I Passed by Your Window; Introduction and Air to a Stained Glass Window; Look Through Any Window; Look Through My Window; Open a New Window; A Room Without windows; Shut the Door (They're Comin' Through the Window); Sitting by the Window; Throw Open Wide Your Window; When I'm Cleaning Windows; Windows of Paris; Windows of the World

Windsor The Merry Wives of Windsor (Overture); The Windsor Waltz

Wine And Her Tears Flowed Like Wine; Candlelight and Wine; Days of Wine and Roses; Down on the Brandywine; From the Vine Came the Grape (from the Grape Came the Wine); I Will Drink the Wine; I'm Gonna Hire a Wino To Decorate Our Home; Kisses Sweeter Than Wine; Love and Wine; Wine of France; Wine, Women, and Song

Wing All God's Chillun Got Wings; Bird on the Wing; Broken Wings; Broken Wings; Comin' In on a Wing and a Prayer; Fold Your Wings; He Wears a Pair of Silver Wings; If I Only Had Wings; Love Has Wings; On the Wings of Love; On Wings of Song; Red Wing; Silver Wings in the Moonlight; White Wings; Wings

Winner, *see* **Victory**

Winnetka Big Noise from Winnetka

Winter, *see also* **Cold, Snow,** etc. I Know Where the Flies Go in the Wintertime; If Winter Comes; (It's Gonna Be) A Long, Long Winter; Once upon a Wintertime; Where Do Flies Go in the Winter Time?; Winter; Winter Wonderland; Wintergreen for President

Wire Bouquet of Barbed Wire; Wired For Sound

Wisconsin On Wisconsin

Wise, *see also* **Think** I'd Rather Be a Lobster Than a Wise Guy; Nightowls; Older and Wiser; There Once Was an Owl; A Wise Old Owl

Wish, *see also* **Desire** (I Wish I Was in) Dixie, or, Dixie's Land; A Dream Is a Wish Your Heart Makes; High Hopes; Hope Told a Flattering Tale; I Hope I Get It; I Wish; I Wish I Could Shimmy Like My Sister Kate; I Wish I (We) Didn't Have To Say Good Night; I Wish I Didn't Love You So; I Wish I Had a Girl; I Wish I Had My Old Girl Back Again; I Wish I Knew; I Wish I Were in Love Again; I Wish I Were Twins; I Wish It Would Rain; I Wish That You Were Here Tonight; I Wish You Could Have Turned My Head; I Wish You Love; I Wished on the Moon; I'm Wishing; The Land of Hope and Glory; The Last Hope; Oh, How I Wish I Could Sleep Until My Daddy Comes Home; Prisoner of Hope; Sometime You'll Wish Me Back Again; When You Wish upon a Star; Whispering Hope; Who Do You Love, I Hope; Wish I May; Wish Me Luck As You Wave Me Goodbye; Wish You Were Here; Wish You Were Here; Wishing (Will Make It So); Wishin' and Hopin'; Yearning (Just for You)

Wishing Well By a Wishing Well; You Never Miss the Water Till the Well Runs Dry, or, Waste Not, Want Not

Witch, *see* **Magic**

Wizard, *see* **Magic**

Woe Listen to My Tale of Woe

Wolf Hungry Like the Wolf; Peter and the Wolf; Who's Afraid of the Big Bad Wolf; Wolverine Blues

Woman, *see also* **Belle, Dame, Doll, Gal, Lady, Lass, Madame, Mademoiselle, Maid, Maiden** Ain't No Woman Like the One I've Got; Along Comes a Woman; Bess, You Is My Woman Now; Boogie on Reggae Woman; Cherchez la Femme; Devil Woman; Do You Take This Woman for Your Lawful Wife?; Every Woman in the World; For Every Man There's a Woman; (Theme from) The French Lieutenant's Woman; A Good-Hearted Woman; Half-Caste Woman; Hard-Headed Woman; Honky Tonk Women; How To Handle a Woman; I Am Woman; In Every Woman; Irish Washerwoman, or, The Scotch Bagpipe Melody; It Takes a Woman; It's a Woman's World; Just Another Woman in Love; Just Like a Woman; Long Cool Woman (in a Black Dress); A Man and a Woman; Modern Woman; More Than a Woman; Older Women; The Other Woman; Texas Women; There Was an Old Woman Who Lived in a Shoe; My Woman, My Woman, My Wife; (You Make Me Feel Like) A Natural Woman; Oh Pretty Woman; Only Women Bleed; The Portuguese Washerwomen; Pretty Women; Rainy Day Women #12 & 35; She's a Woman; (I Got a Woman Crazy for Me) She's Funny That Way; The Siren's Song; Sobbin' Women; St. Louis Woman; Sweet Talkin' Woman; This Woman; When a Man Loves a Woman; When a Woman Hears the Sound of the Drum and Fife; When a Woman Loves a Man; When You're in Love With a Beautiful Woman; Wine, Women and Song; Woman; Woman in Love; A Woman in Love; The Woman in the Shoe; A Woman Is a Sometime Thing; A Woman Is Only a Woman, But a Good Cigar Is a Smoke; A Woman Needs Love (Just Like You Do); Women Do Know How To Carry On; You Are the Woman; You Are Woman (I Am Man); You're the Only Woman

Wonder I Wonder, I Wonder, I Wonder; I Wonder If Love Is a Dream; I Wonder If She'll Ever Come Back to Me; I Wonder If She's Waiting; I Wonder If You Still Care for Me; I Wonder What Became of Me; I Wonder What the King Is Doing Tonight; I Wonder What's Become of Sally; I Wonder Where My Baby Is Tonight; I Wonder Where My Lovin' Man Has Gone; I Wonder Where She Is Tonight; I Wonder Who's Dancing with You Tonight; I Wonder Who's Kissing Her Now; The Old Flame Flickers and I Wonder Why; What's the Use of Wond'rin'; When You Come Back They'll Wonder Who the——You Are; Winter Wonderland; Wonder Bar; The Wonder of You; Wonder When My Baby's Coming Home; Wonder Why; Wondering Where the Lions Are; Wond'rous Love, or, Captain Kidd, or, Through All the World

Wonderful Amy, Wonderful Amy; I May Be Wrong, But I Think You're Wonderful; I'm in Love with a Wonderful Guy; It's a Big, Wide, Wonderful World; It's a Wonderful World; (Who's Wonderful, Who's Marvelous?) Miss 'Annabelle Lee; Mister Wonderful; My Wonderful Dream Girl; (Theme from) Return to Peyton Place, or, The Wonderful Season of Love; Say Wonderful Things; Something Wonderful; 'S Wonderful; That Wonderful Mother of Mine; Theme from The Wonderful World of The Brothers Grimm; They Say It's Wonderful; Three Wonderful Letters from Home; What a Wonderful Mother You'd Be; What a Wonderful World; Wonderful Copenhagen; (On) A Wonderful Day Like Today; Wonderful Eyes; Wonderful Land; (My) Wonderful One; A Wonderful Time up There; Wonderful Wonderful; Wonderful You; You (Gee But You're Wonderful); You Wonderful You; Young and Warm and Wonderful

Wonderland Alice in Wonderland; Wonderland By Night

Woo, *see* **Court**

Wood, *see also* **Tree** Babes in the Wood; The Deadwood Stage; Do You Know Where You're Going To, or, Theme from Mahogany; I Wouldn't Leave My Little Wooden Hut for You; If I Were a Carpenter; In the Wild Wood Where the Bluebells Grew; Jumpin' at the Woodside; Knock On Wood; Knock On Wood; Marta, or, Rambling Rose of the Wildwood; Melisands in the Wood; Norwegian Wood; Parade of the Wooden Soldiers; Rap Tap on Wood; Tales from (of) the Vienna Woods; Throw Another Log on the Fire; Two Little Babes in the Wood; Voices of the Woods, or, Welcome Sweet Springtime; When the Mocking Birds Are Singing in the Wildwood; Wooden Heart; The Wooden Soldier and the China Doll; Woodland Sketches; Woodman Spare That Tree; Woodman, Woodman, Spare That Tree

Woodpecker The Woodpecker(s') Song; Woody Woodpecker

Wool, *see* **Sheep**

Word, *see also* **Write** Actions Speak Louder Than Words; Crazy Words (Crazy Tune) (Vo-Do-De-O-Do); Fly Me to the Moon, or, In Other Words; The Good Word (Theme from Nationwide); I Give You My Word; M-O-T-H-E-R (A Word That Means the World to Me); My Word You Do Look Queer; Never Said a Mumblin' Word; O Word of God Incarnate; Song Without Words; Sorry Seems To Be the Hardest Word; Sweet Is the Word for You; Three Little Words; Too Marvelous for Words; True-Hearted, Whole-Hearted, or, Peal Out the Watchword; Without a Word of Warning; Words; The Words Are in My Heart; Words Without Music; Words, Words, Words

Work The Blind Ploughman; Calling All Workers (March); Everybody Works But Father; Get a Job; Heaven Will Protect the Working Girl; Heigh-Ho; I've Been Working on the Railroad, or, The Levee Song, or, Someone's in the Kitchen With Dinah; I've Got My Captain Working for Me Now; Let's Work Together; (Theme from) Mission: Impossible; My Task; Nice Work If You Can Get It; Patsy Ory Ory Aye (A-Workin' On the Railroad); A Secretary Is Not a Toy; She Works Hard for the Money; Since Father Went to Work; Want Ads; We Can Work It Out; Where Do You Work-a John; (Just) Whistle While You Work; Work for the Night is Coming; Workin' My Way Back to You

World Across the Universe; All Over the World; All the World Will Be Jealous of Me; Around the World (in Eighty Days); As Long As the World Rolls On; The Biggest Aspidistra in the World; Clear Out of This World; Color My World; Dear World; Different Worlds; The End of the World; Entire History of the World in Two Minutes and Thirty-Two Seconds; Every Woman in the World; Everybody Wants To Rule the

World; From Another World; From the New World Symphony; Globetrotter; God's Green World; Goodbye Cruel World; He's Got the Whole World in His Hand (Hands); I Don't Want To Set the World on Fire; I Haven't Got a Worry in the World; I Wouldn't Have Missed It for the World; I'd Like To Teach the World To Sing; If I Ruled the World; If You Had All the World and Its Gold; If You Were the Only Girl in the World; Igy (What a Beautiful World); I'm Sitting on Top of the World (Just Rolling Along—Just Rolling Along); It Takes a Little Rain with the Sunshine To Make the World Go Round; It's a Big, Wide, Wonderful World; It's a Blue World; It's a Mad, Mad, Mad, Mad World; It's a New World; It's a Woman's World; It's a Wonderful World; I've Got the World on a String; Joy to the World, or, Antioch; Joy to the World; Last Night Was the End of the World; Laugh and the World Laughs with You; Let the Great Big World Keep Turning; Let the Rest of the World Go By; Looking at the World Through Rose Colored Glasses; Love Makes the World Go 'Round; Love Makes the World Go Round, or, Theme from Carnival; Love Me and the World Is Mine; Make the World Go Away; A Marsh-mallow World; The Most Beautiful Girl in the World; (If You Happen To See) The Most Beautiful Girl (in the World); M-O-T-H-E-R (A Word That Means the World to Me); My Song Goes Round the World; New World in the Morning; Only One Girl in the World for Me; Out of This World; Rolling Round the World; Rose of the World; Small World; The Sweetest Song in the World; Tell All the World; That International Rag; Theme from The Wonderful World of the Brothers Grimm; There's a Girl in This World For Every Boy and a Boy For Every Girl; There's a New World; Top of the World; Transatlantic Lullaby; Two Different Worlds; War of the Worlds; We Are the World; Welcome to My World; We're Gonna Change the World; What a Wonderful World; What the World Needs Now Is Love; When I Leave the World Behind; When the Lights Go On Again (All Over the World); When the World Was Young (Ah, the Apple Tree); When You're Smiling (The Whole World Smiles with You); The Whole World Is Singing My Song; Wild World; Windows of the World; Wond'rous Love, or, Captain Kidd, or, Through All the World; The World Cup March; World Gets in the Way; The World I Used To Know; The World Is Mine (Tonight); The World Is Singing My Song; The World Is Waiting for the Sunrise; A World of Our Own; The World Owes Me a Living; The World Turned Upside Down, or, Derry Down; World Weary; A World Without Love; A World Without Love; You and Me Against the World; You're More Than the World to Me; You're My World

Worm Did You Ever Think As the Hearse Rolls By, or, The Worms Crawl In, the Worms Crawl Out; (The) Glow Worm; Inchworm

Worry Do I Worry; Don't Worry; Don't Worry; Don't Worry 'Bout Me; Don't Worry 'Bout Me Baby; I Haven't Got a Worry in the World; Why Worry; You Die If You Worry

Wrap And the Monkey Wrapped Its Tail Around the Flagpole; Wrap Your Troubles in Dreams (and Dream Your Troubles Away); Wrap Yourself in Cotton Wool; Wrapped Around Your Finger

Wreck, *see* **Broken**

Write, *see also* **Book, Letter,** etc.   I Bought Myself a Bottle of Ink; I Could Write a Book; I Write the Songs; I'm Gonna Sit Right Down and Write Myself a Letter; It Was Written in the Stars; Paperback Writer; La Plume de Ma Tante (The Pen of My Aunt); The Typewriter; Written on the Wind

Wrong   (Hey Won't You Play) Another somebody Done Somebody Wrong Song; Baby We Can't Go Wrong; Fifty Million Frenchmen Can't Be Wrong; How Could I Be So Wrong; How Could We Be Wrong; (If Loving You Is Wrong) I Don't Want To Be Right; I May Be Wrong, But I Think You're Wonderful; It Can't Be Wrong; Right Place Wrong Time; Why Do the Wrong People Travel; You Can Do No Wrong; You're in the Right Church, But the Wrong Pew

Wurzburger   Down Where the Wurzburger Flows

Wyoming   The Hills of Old Wyomin'; Somewhere in Old Wyoming; (Oh Why, Oh Why Did I Ever Leave) Wyoming; Wyoming Lullaby

Yankee   The Lanky Yankee Boys in Blue; There's a Dixie Girl Who's Longing For a Yankee Doodle Boy; When Yankee Doodle Learns to Parlez-Vouz Francais; Yankee Doodle; The Yankee Doodle Blues; (I Am) The Yankee Doodle Boy; Yankee Rose; A Yankee Ship and a Yankee Crew; (Theme from) Yanks

Yard, *see also* **Fence, Gate**   Back in Your Own Back Yard; The Big Back Yard; Boneyard Shuffle; I Don't Want To Play in Your Yard; Me and Julio Down by the Schoolyard; Please Come and Play in My Yard; Stay in Your Own Back Yard; You Can't Play in Our Yard Any More

Year   All Those Years Ago; As the Years Go By; (Fifteen Miles (Years) on the) Erie Canal (Low Bridge!—Everybody Down); Forty Years On; Green Years; Holding Back the Years; A Hundred Years from Now; A Hundred Years from Today; The Impatient Years; In the Year 2525; It Was a Very Good Year; June Comes Around Every Year; Kingdom Coming, or, The Year of Jubilo; Let's Start the New Year Right; The Loveliest Night of the Year; Maybe This Year; Never in a Million Years; Once Ev'ry Year; Seven Year Ache; Spring Will Be a Little Late This Year; Ten Thousand Years from Now; This Year's Kisses; Through the Years; Through the Years; We Were Sweethearts for Many Years; We've Been Chums for Fifty Years; A Year from Today; Years; Years Ago; The Year's at the Spring

Yearn, *see* **Wish**

Yellow   Goodbye Yellow Brick Road; Itsy Bitsy Teenie Weenie Yellow Polkadot Bikini; Little Yellow Bird; Mellow Yellow; The Moon Was Yellow; She Wore a Yellow Ribbon, or, All Round My Hat (Round Her Neck) I (She) Wore a Yellow Ribbon; Tie a Yellow Ribbon Round the Ole Oak Tree; Yellow Bird; Yellow Dog Blues; Yellow River; The Yellow Rose of Texas, or, Song of the Texas Rangers; Yellow Submarine

Yes   Come Tell Me What's Your Answer, Yes or No; Oui, Marie; Say ''Si Si''; She Didn't Say Yes (She Didn't Say No); There's Yes, Yes, in Your Eyes; Yeah Yeah; Yes, I'm Ready; Yes Indeed; Yes, Let Me Like a Soldier Fall; Yes My Darling Daughter; Yes Sir, That's My Baby; Yes! We Have No Bananas

Yesterday, *see also* **Last (Night)**   Born Yesterday; Only Yesterday; Turn Back the Universe and Give Me Yesterday; Yesterday; Yesterday Man; Yesterday Once More; Yesterday When I Was Young; Yesterdays; Yesterday's Roses; Yester-Me, Yester-You, Yesterday

Yiddish   My Yiddishe Momme; That's Yiddishe Love

Yonder   Down Yonder; 'Way Down Yonder in New Orleans; Way Down Yonder in the Cornfield; Way Out Yonder in the Golden West; When the Roll Is Called Up Yonder

Yorkshire   My Girl's a Yorkshire Girl

Young   Accent on Youth; Arcady Is Ever Young; Because They're Young; Believe Me If All Those Endearing Young Charms; Blame It on My Youth; The Charming Young Widow I Met on the Train; The Daring Young Man (on the Flying Trapeze); He May Be Old, But He's Got Young Ideas; Hello Young Lovers; Hey Young Fella Close Your Old Umbrella; I'm Glad I'm Not Young Anymore; I'm Looking for a Nice Young Fellow Who Is Looking for a Nice Young Girl; Keep Young and Beautiful; The Lass with the Delicate Air, or, Young Molly Who Lives at the Foot of the Hill; Last Night When We Were Young; Like Young; Nadia's Theme, or, The Young and the Restless; The Night Is Young and You're So Beautiful; Our Lodger's Such a Nice Young Man; P.Y.T. (Pretty Young Thing); Rodger Young; Sing an Old-Fashioned Song (to a Young Sophisticated Lady); Staying Young; Theme for Young Lovers; There'll Be a Hot Time for the Old Men When the Young Men Go to War; They're Either Too Young or Too Old; Too Young; Too Young To Go Steady; Twelve Thirty, or, Young Girls Are Coming to the Canyon; When Hearts Are Young; When Love Is Young in Springtime; When the World Was Young (Ah, the Apple Tree); When You and I Were Young, Maggie; When You're Young and in Love; While We're Young; Yesterday When I Was Young; You Make Me Feel So Young; Young and Foolish; Young and Healthy; Young and in Love; Young and Warm and Wonderful; Young At Heart; Young Emotions; The Young Folks at Home; Young Girl; Young Ideas; Young Love; A Young Man's Fancy; Younger Than Springtime

Youth, *see* **Young**

Yummy, *see* **Flavor**

Zanzibar   In Zanzibar—My Little Chimpanzee; West of Zanzibar

Zion   We're Marching to Zion

Zoo   Captain Noah and His Floating Zoo; I'd Love To Be a Monkey in the Zoo

Zuyder Zee   By the Side of the Zuyder Zee; Zuyder Zee

X

Lyric Key Lines

This Part contains a total of 3,025 lyric key lines listed alphabetically, and their song titles. Included for reference are a combination of lyric first lines from either the chorus, refrain and/or verse (when they are not the title of the song), first and second lines (when the first line is or includes the title of the song, but for one of several reasons indicated below, the second line is of relevant value and therefore cited), and key lines (when neither the title nor first lyric line). It is not the purpose of this list to include all first, second, or key lines associated with any given song, as that list is endless. Only those that in the authors' judgment are commonly referred to are entered here. In some cases, both a first, and second or key line may be used when considered appropriate.

Typically, a lyric first line is sufficient to identify a song (e.g. ''City sidewalks, busy sidewalks dressed in holiday style'' . . . ''Silver Bells'').

Very often a title may also be the first lyric line but only one word or so vague in meaning that an extended first line is necessary for positive identification (e.g. ''Once upon a time a girl with moonlight in her eyes'' . . . ''Once Upon a Time''). Most commonly, however, is the instance where the title is the first line, but the second line of lyric is generally forgotten or misquoted (e.g. ''Beautiful Dreamer, wake unto me, Starlight and dew-drops are waiting for thee'' . . . ''Beautiful Dreamer''). Lastly, a key line, when not the title or first line, is the one most remembered and necessary to reference the title of the song (e.g. ''And we are his sisters and his cousins and aunts'' . . . ''I Am the Monarch of the Sea'').

For more complete information about a particular song, refer to Part V; all song titles in this Part may be found in Part V.

A beautiful lady in blue, We met just like two shadows do **Beautiful Lady in Blue**

A bell rings high in the steeple, tho' there's no steeple in view **Ah But It Happens**

A boy and a girl were dancing The same as we're dancing tonight **A Boy and a Girl Were Dancing**

A boy found a dream upon a distant shore **Amapola**, or, **Pretty Little Poppy**

A boy is born in hard time Mississippi **Living for the City**

A bully ship and a bully crew, Doo-da, doo-da! **De Camptown Races (Gwine To Run All Night)**, or, **Sacramento**

A camp meeting took place, by the colored race **At a Georgia Camp Meeting**

A capital ship for an ocean trip Was the ''Walloping Window-Blind'' **A Capital Ship**

A captain bold from Halifax, who dwelt in country quarters **The Hunters of Kentucky**

A chair is still a chair even when there's no one sitting there **A House is Not a Home**

A cigarette that bears a lipstick's traces **These Foolish Things (Remind Me of You)**

A country dance was being held in a garden **Polka Dots and Moonbeams**

A fair-haired boy in a foreign land At sunrise was to die **The Pardon Came Too Late**

A fellow needs a girl to sit by his side at the end of a weary day **A Fellow Needs a Girl**

A fine romance! With no kisses! A fine romance, my friend, this is! **A Fine Romance**

A foggy day in London town Had me low and had me down **A Foggy Day**

A fool there was and he made his pray'r **From Now On**

A gal is a thing that a man's gotta have, That we can well believe **Bless 'Em All**

A Gay Ranchero, a caballero can always find someone to pet **A Gay Ranchero**

A good man is hard to find, You always get the other kind **A Good Man Is Hard To Find**

A heart that longs for you, Two arms that will be true **These Things I Offer You (For a Lifetime)**

A heart that's true, there are such things; A dream for two **There Are Such Things**

A house ain't a home 'til you bake in the oven **Pillsbury Says It Best**

A hubba, hubba, hubba, hello Jack **Dig You Later (A Hubba-Hubba-Hubba)**

A hundred and one pounds of fun **Honey Bun**

A kiss on the hand may be quite continental **Diamonds Are a Girl's Best Friend**

A law made a distant moon ago here **Camelot**

A lady known as Paris, Romantic and charming, Has left her old companions and faded from view **The Last Time I Saw Paris**

A life on the ocean wave! A home on the rolling deep! **A Life on the Ocean Wave**

A little bird told me that you love me and I believe that you do **A Little Bird Told Me**

A little maiden climbed on an old man's knee **After the Ball**

A long, long time ago on graduation day **Roses Are Red, My Love**

A lovely night, a lovely night, A finer night you know you'll never see **A Lovely Night**

A man wants to smell like a man **Aqua Velva Man**

A man was walking up and down, To find a place where he could dine in town **One Meat (Fish) Ball**

A moment after dark around the park **The Lamplighter's Serenade**

A passing policeman found a little child **The Little Lost Child**

A penny for a spool of thread, A penny for a needle **Pop Goes the Weasel**

A portrait of Jennie more precious to me **Portrait of Jennie**

A redder berry on the thorn, A deeper yellow on the corn **Beloved, It is Morn**

A rose must remain with the sun and the rain or its lovely promise won't come true **To Each His Own**

A sailboat in the moonlight, and wouldn't that be heaven **Sailboat in the Moonlight**

A sexton stood one Sabbath eve within a belfry grand **Those Wedding Bells Shall Not Ring Out**

A slave to my bride of the jungle **African Lament (Lamento Africano)**

A song of love is a sad song, Hi Lili Hi Lili Hi Lo **Hi Lili Hi Lo**

A Spanish cavalier stood in his retreat, And on his guitar play'd a tune, dear **The Spanish Cavalier**

A sweet Tuxedo girl you see, Queen of swell society **Ta-Ra-Ra-Boom-Der-É (De-Ay)**

A tear fell when I saw you in the arms of someone new **A Tear Fell**

A time for us someday there'll be when chains are torn by courage born **Love Theme from *Romeo and Juliet*, or, A Time for Us**

A time to be reapin' A time to be sowin' **The Green Leaves of Summer**

A very precious love, is what you are to me, A stairway to the star **A Very Precious Love**

A winning way, a pleasant smile **Little Annie Roonie**

A year from today when I come back to you The sun will be shining the sky will be blue **A Year From Today**

A-gwine down to New Orleans I got up on de landin' **My Old Aunt Sally**

A-well-a, bless my soul, What's wrong with me? I'm itching like a man on fuzzy tree **All Shook Up**

"Aba, daba, daba, daba, daba, daba, dab," Said the Chimpie to the Monk **The Aba Daba Honeymoon**

Ach du lieber Augustin, Augustin, Augustin **O (Ach) Du Lieber Augustin**

Across the morning sky All the birds are leaving **Who Knows Where the Time Goes**

Adeste, fideles, laeti, triumphantes **Adeste Fideles, or, O Come All Ye Faithful**

Adios, Mariquita Linda I'll remember you standing here **Adios, Mariquita Linda**

Afraid to dream, Afraid that you may not be there **Afraid To Dream**

After long enough of being alone, ev'ryone must face their share of loneliness **Only Yesterday**

After the ball is over, after the break of morn **After the Ball**

After the dance the chimes ring out ding dong **After the Dance**

Again, This couldn't happen again **Again**

Ah look at all the lonely people! **Eleanor Rigby**

Ah my heart is thine This is the time to come and take it **My Heart at Thy Sweet Voice**

Ain't no sunshine when she's gone. It's not warm when she's away **Ain't No Sunshine**

Al-Di-La means you are far above me, Very far **Al-Di-La**

Alas, my love, you do me wrong To cast me off discourteously **Greensleeves (Green Sleeves)**

All alone Monday Singing the blues, All alone Tuesday reading the News **All Alone Monday**

All alone, all at sea! Why does nobody care for me **A Ship Without a Sail**

All at once my lucky star was glowing **All At Once**

All by myself alone at home a-feeling blue **I Wonder, I Wonder, I Wonder**

All day I've faced a barren waste without the taste of water **Cool Water**

All day, all night, Marianne, Down by the seaside siftin' sand **Marianne**

All hail, to dear old Texas A and M Rally around Maroon and White **The Aggie War Hymn**

All I know is I wanna sigh, when you're standing near I get a Humpty Dumpty feelin' **Am I in Love**

All I want is a party doll, To come along with me, when I'm feelin' wild **Party Doll**

All I want is a room in Bloomsbury, Just a room that will do For you and me **A Room in Bloomsbury**

All I want is a room somewhere, Far away from the cold night air **Wouldn't It Be Loverly**

All in vain I've been dreaming of a love that's beaming **Marta, or, Rambling Rose of the Wildwood**

All my future plans, Dear, will suit your plans   **The Blue Room**

All of a sudden my heart sings When I remember little things   **(All of a Sudden) My Heart Sings**

All of me why not take all of me, Can't you see I'm no good without you   **All of Me**

All our friends keep knocking at the door   **I Don't Want To Walk Without You, Baby**

''All quiet along the Potomac,'' They say, Except now and then a stray picket is shot   **All Quiet Along the Potomac Tonight**

All that I ask is love All that I want is you   **All That I Ask of You Is Love**

All the chapel bells were ringing in the little valley town   **While the Angelus Was Ringing,** or, **The Three Bells (Les Trois Cloches), or The Jimmy Brown Song**

All the cowhands wanna marry Harriet, Harriet's handy with a lariat   **Harriet**

All the darkies will be there, Don't forget to curl your hair   **De Golden Wedding**

All the girls are crazy 'bout a certain little lad   **Oh Johnny, Oh Johnny, Oh!**

All the little flowers nod their pretty heads   **She Is the Sunshine of Virginia**

All things come home at eventide, Like birds that weary of their roaming   **Homing**

All through the day I dream about the night, I dream about the night, Here with you   **All Through the Day**

All through the night there's a little brown bird singing   **A Brown Bird Singing**

All we do is go out walking when the sun shines bright and gay   **(What'll We Do on a) Dew-Dew-Dewy Day**

All you do is push de button up de elevator   **Push De Button**

All you Preachers Who delight in panning the dancing teachers   **I'll Build a Stairway to Paradise**

Allegheny moon, I need your light To help me find romance tonight   **Allegheny Moon**

Alone Alone with a sky of romance above   **Alone**

Alone at a table for two Alone in our old rendezvous   **Alone at a Table for Two**

Alone in my quiet village I pray you will be returning some day to me   **My Quiet Village**

Alone together, Beyond the crowd, Above the world We're not too proud   **Alone Together**

Alouette, gentille Alouette, Alouette, je te plumerai   **Alouette**

Always and always I'll go on adoring the glory and wonder of you   **Always and Always**

Always get that mood indigo, Since my baby said goodbye   **Mood Indigo**

Am I blue? Am I blue? Ain't these tears in these eyes tellin' you?   **Am I Blue**

Am I fool number one, or am I fool number two   **Fool Number One**

Am I in love can it be so   **Who Can Tell**

America, I love you, You're like a sweetheart of mine   **America I Love You**

An old cowpoke went riding out one dark and windy day   **Ghost Riders in the Sky,** or, **A Cowboy Legend**

An old man gazed on a photograph in the locket he's worn for years   **Two Little Girls in Blue**

Anastasia, tell me who you are, Are you someone from another star?   **Anastasia**

Anatevka, Anatevka, Underfed, overworked Anatevka   **Anatevka**

And here's to you, Mrs. Robinson, Jesus loves you more than you will know   **Mrs. Robinson**

And I feel just as happy as a big sunflow'r   **The Big Sunflower**

And I wake up in the morning with my hair down in my eyes and she says, ''Hi''   **Little Green Apples**

And now we are aged and gray, Maggie, And the trials of Life nearly done   **When You and I Were Young, Maggie**

And the song they sang was Hiawatha's melody Just a golden memory   **Hiawatha's Melody of Love**

And then he holds my hand, (Mm) And then I understand (Mm)   **Paradise (Waltz)**

And then she said, ''Just because you've become a young man now''   **Shop Around**

And they called it puppy love, Oh, I guess they'll never know   **Puppy Love**

And this law, I will maintain, Until my dying day, Sir   **Country Gardens,** or, **Vicar of Bray**

And we are his sisters and his cousins and his aunts   **I Am the Monarch of the Sea**

And when I told them How beautiful you are   **They Didn't Believe Me**

Angela mia You are my angel dear, The Heavens sent you down to me from up above   **Angela Mia**

Angels from the realms of glory, Wing your flight o'er all the earth   **Angels from the Realms of Glory**

Angie, Angie, when will those clouds all disappear?   **Angie**

Another bride another June Another sunny honeymoon   **Makin' Whoopee**

Another hundred people just got off of the train   **Another Hundred People**

Anyone can whistle, that's what they say, easy   **Anyone Can Whistle**

April in Paris, chestnuts in blossom, holiday tables under the trees   **April in Paris**

April love is for the very young, Ev'ry star's a wishing star that shines for you   **April Love**

Are the stars out tonight? I don't know if it's cloudy or bright   **I Only Have Eyes for You**

Are we really happy here with this lonely game we play   **This Masquerade**

Are you going to Scarborough Fair? Parsley, sage, rosemary and thyme   **Scarborough Fair/Canticle,** or, **Parsley, Sage, Rosemary and Thyme**

Are you lonesome tonight Do you miss me tonight Are you sorry we drifted apart   **Are You Lonesome Tonight**

Are you sleeping, are you sleeping, Brother John, brother John **Frère Jacques**

Are you sorry? Really sorry? Do you think of me now and then? **Are You Sorry**

Around the world I've searched for you, I traveled on when hope was gone to keep our rendezvous **Around the World (in Eighty Days)**

As beats the ocean surf upon the sand **So Beats My Heart for You**

As I approach the prime of my life **This Is All I Ask**

As I cruised out one evening upon a night's career **The Roving Kind**

As I look at you a thought goes through my mind **You Oughta Be in Pictures**

As I love thee, so you love me At ev'ning morning, caring **Ich Liebe Dich (I Love Thee)**

As I stroll along I hear melodies **Music Music Everywhere (But Not a Song in My Heart)**

As I walk along the Bois Boolong With an independent air **The Man That (Who) Broke the Bank at Monte Carlo**

As I walked out in the streets of Laredo, As I walked down in Laredo one day **Streets of Laredo, or, The Cowboy's Lament**

As I was a-gwine down the road, Tired team and a heavy load **Turkey in the Straw, or, Old Zip Coon**

As I was lumb'ring down de street **Buffalo Gals (Won't You Come Out Tonight?), or, Lubly Fan**

As I was motivatin' over the hill, I saw Maybelline in a Coupe de Ville **Maybelline**

As I was walking down the street one day, A man came up to me, and asked me what the time was that was on my watch **Does Anybody Really Know What Time It Is**

As I was walking down the street **Buffalo Gals (Won't You Come Out Tonight?), or, Lubly Fan**

As I was walking one morning for pleasure **(Whoopee Ti Yi Yo) Git Along Little Dog(g)ies**

As I went out one morning to take the pleasant air **Lolly Too Dum**

As I went out walking, upon a fine day, I got awful lonesome, as the day passed away **On Top of Old Smokey, or, Little Mohee**

As I write this letter, send my love to you **P.S. I Love You**

As long as there's music and words of romance, The spell of a theme starts you to dream **As Long As There's Music**

As the backs go tearing by On the way to do or die **As the Backs Go Tearing By**

As the blackbird in the spring, 'Neath the willow tree **Aura Lee**

As the girls go So goes all creation **As the Girls Go**

As time goes on I realize just what you mean to me **Color My World**

Ask any mermaid you happen to see, What's the best tuna? Chicken of the Sea **Ask Any Mermaid**

At eighty-eight, he seemed the fatherly kind **Dimples**

At the Balalaika Where there is magic in the sparkling wine **At the Balalaika**

At the old concert hall on the Bow'ry, 'Round a table were seated one night **She Is More To Be Pitied Than Censured**

At the opera I like to be with Freddie **Rolled into One**

At the villa of the Baron De Signac **Liaisons**

Attend the tale of Sweeney Todd. His skin was pale and his eye was odd **The Ballad of Sweeney Todd**

Au clair de la lune, mon ami Pierrot **Au Clair de la Lune**

Aunt Jemima pancakes without her syrup, is like a ship without a sail **Aunt Jemima (Silver Dollar)**

Autumn in New York why does it seem so inviting? **Autumn in New York**

Autumn in Rome, my heart remembers fountains where children played **Autumn in Rome**

Avast! belay! hurray for Baffin's Bay! **Hurray for Baffin's Bay**

Away from Mississippi's vale, Wid my ole had dar for a sail **The Rose of Alabama**

Away in a manger, no crib for His bed, The little Lord Jesus laid down his sweet head **Away in (a) Manger, or, Luther's Cradle Hymn**

Away out here they got a name for rain, and wind, and fire **They Call the Wind Maria**

Away with the music of Broadway! Be off with your Irving Berlin! **By Strauss**

Ay, ay, ay, ay! Sing, sorrow never! **Cielito Lindo (Ay, Ay, Ay, Ay)**

Ay Marieke Marieke I loved you so much **Marieke**

Babe, we are well met, As in a spell met, I lift my helmet, Sandy **Thou Swell**

Baby's good to me you know, She's happy as can be, You know, She said so **I Feel Fine**

Baby, Here's a five and dime, Baby, Now's about the time **A String of Pearls**

Baby, let me be your lovin' teddy bear. Put a chain around my neck and lead me anywhere **(Let Me Be Your) Teddy Bear**

Baby, won't you please come home 'Cause your mamma's all alone **Baby, Won't You Please Come Home**

Back home in Tennessee Just try to picture me Right on my mother's knee **Just Try To Picture Me (Back [Down] Home in Tennessee)**

Backward, turn backward, oh Time in your flight! **Rock Me to Sleep, Mother**

Bad news, Go 'way! Call 'round some day **I Can't Be Bothered Now**

Bang! went the bridge lamp, down went the table **(And) His Rocking Horse Ran Away**

Basin Street is the street where the elite, always meet **Basin Street Blues**

Be like I, Hold your head up high **The Blue Bird of Happiness**

Be my love, for no one else can end this yearning **Be My Love**

Be sure it's true, when you say, "I love you"   **It's a Sin To Tell a Lie**

Be wise, be smart, behave my heart, don't upset your cart when she's close   **Too Close for Comfort**

Beautiful changes in diff'rent keys Beautiful changes and harmonies   **Changes**

Beautiful Dreamer, wake unto me, Starlight and dew-drops are waiting for thee   **Beautiful Dreamer**

Beautiful love, you're all a mystery! Beautiful love, what have you done to me?   **Beautiful Love**

Because of you, the skies are blue, Beloved   **Beloved**

Because they're all sweeties sweet, sweet sweeties I can't keep away from the girls   **They're All Sweeties**

Because they've told me I can't behold ye till weddin' music starts playin'   **Come to Me, Bend to Me**

Because you come to me with naught save love   **Because**

Bedelia, I want to steal ya, Bedelia, I love you so   **Bedelia**

Bee-dle-dee dee dee dee, Two ladies   **Two Ladies**

Before the parade passes by, I'm gonna go and taste Saturday's high life   **Before the Parade Passes By**

Before you half remember what her smile was like   **Kiss Her Now**

Behind a grammer school-house In a double tenement   **Maggie Murphy's Home**

Believe you must believe. When days are dark and dim you must believe   **Believe**

Bells ring, birds sing Sun is shining No more pining   **Bye Bye Blues**

Beneath the cross of Jesus I fain would take my stand   **Beneath the Cross of Jesus**

Besame Besame mucho; Each time I cling to your kiss I hear music divine   **Besame Mucho (Kiss Me Much)**

Beside a shady nook, A moment's bliss we took   **It Must Be True (You Are Mine, All Mine)**

Better coffee a millionaire's money can't buy   **Chock Full O' Nuts Is That Heavenly Coffee**

Beyond the blue horizon, Waits a beautiful day   **Beyond the Blue Horizon**

Beyond the busy highway, Beyond the city strife   **Feudin' and Fightin'**

Big wheel keep on turnin', Proud Mary keep on burnin'   **Proud Mary**

Bill, I love you so. I always will   **Wedding Bell Blues**

Black, black, black is the color of my true love's hair; Her lips are wondrous rosy fair   **Black Is the Color of My True Love's Hair**

Blackbird singing in the dead of night   **Blackbird**

Blah, blah, blah, blah moon, Blah, blah, blah above   **Blah, Blah, Blah**

Bless 'em all, Bless 'em all, The long and the short and the tall   **Bless 'Em All**

Bless the beasts and the children, for in this world they have no voice   **Bless the Beasts and Children**

Blest be the tie that binds My collar to my shirt. I'm wasting

no dollars In buying new collars To hide that ring of dirt   **Blest Be the Tie That Binds**

Blow me a kiss from across the room, Say I look nice when I'm not   **Little Things Mean a Lot**

Blow, tropic wind, Sing a song thru the tree   **Poinciana**

Blue because we're parted, Blue and broken hearted   **Blue (and Broken Hearted)**

Blue Monday how I hate Blue Monday, Have to work like a slave all day   **Blue Monday**

Blue moon you saw me standing alone Without a dream in my heart   **Blue Moon**

Blue rain Falling down on my window pane   **Blue Rain**

Blue Spanish eyes Teardrops are falling from your Spanish eyes   **Spanish Eyes**

Blues, Twentieth Century Blues are getting me down   **Twentieth Century Blues**

Bongo, bongo, bongo, I don't want to leave the Congo, Oh, no, no, no, no, no!   **Civilization (Bongo Bongo Bongo)**

Boo-hoo, you've got me crying for you   **Boo-Hoo**

Born free, as free as the wind blows, as free as the grass grows   **Born Free**

Born from a world of tyrants, beneath the western sky   **British Grenadiers,** or, **Free America**

Born on a mountain top in Tennessee   **Ballad of Davy Crockett**

Born to lose, I've lived my life in vain; Ev'ry dream has only brought me pain   **Born To Lose**

Bought a ticket the other night, The Union Station was lit up bright   **Love on a Greyhound Bus**

Bows and flows of angel hair, and ice cream castles in the air   **Both Sides Now**

Boy, boy, crazy boy, Get cool, boy   **Cool**

Brand new state! Brand new state, gonna treat you great!   **Oklahoma**

Bright was the day, bells ringing gay   **I Love You in the Same Old Way—Darling Sue**

Bring a drink of water, Leroy   **Going to Memphis**

Bring the good old bugle, boys, we'll sing another song   **Marching Through Georgia**

Broadway Rose, there's a tear in your eye   **Broadway Rose**

Broadway's turning into Coney, Champagne Charlie's drinking gin   **Give It Back to the Indians**

Broder let us leabe, Buera lan for Hettee   **Ching A Ring Chaw,** or, **Sambo's Address to His Bred'ren**

Broken-hearted melody, Once you were our song of love   **Broken-Hearted Melody**

Brylcreem makes men's hair look neat   **Brylcreem, A Little Dab'll Do Ya**

Buddha, does he really love me, Buddha, is he thinking of me   **Buddha**

Build your dreams to the stars above but when you need someone true to love   **Don't Go to Strangers**

But along came Bill, Who's not the type at all. You'd meet him on the street and never notice him   **Bill**

But it stopped short never to go again, When the old man died **Grandfather's Clock**

But, oh, Jane! doesn't look the same, When she left the village she was shy **And Her Golden Hair Was Hanging Down Her Back**

By a wishing well, I was standing there And I wished I could find someone who would care **By a Wishing Well**

Bye, bye, baby Time to hit the road to dreamland **Hit the Road to Dreamland**

Bye bye mein lieber Herr, Farewell mein lieber Herr **Mein Herr**

Call Roto-Rooter, that's the name, and away go troubles down the drain **Roto-Rooter**

Can I forget you? Or will my heart remind me that once we walked in a moonlit dream? **Can I Forget You**

Can it be the trees that fill the breeze with rare and magic perfume? **Love in Bloom**

Can our love be passé when you seem kind of lost without me **Passé**

"Candy," I call my sugar "Candy" Because I'm sweet on "Candy" **Candy**

Candy kisses wrapped in paper mean more to you than any of mine **Candy Kisses**

Can't figure out why I ever wanted to roam **Just a Little Bit South of North Carolina**

Can't help singing of a promise that April is bringing **Can't Help Singing**

Can't we simply pass the time of day? **My Heart Goes Crazy**

Can't we two go walkin' together out beyond the valley of trees? **The Heather on the Hill**

Can't you see I love you? Please don't break my heart in two **Wooden Heart**

Can't you see the rain and hail am fastly falling, Alexander? **Alexander (Don't You Love Your Baby No More)**

Carefully dressed, carefully coached, Diamond braceleted, emerald broached **Poor Little Hollywood Star**

Careless Now that you've got me loving you **Careless**

Castles were crumbling And daydreams were tumbling, December was battling with June **Changing My Tune**

Catch a falling star and put it in your pocket, Never let it fade away **Catch a Falling Star**

Catch me the smile you smile and I'll make this big world my tiny island **Cocoanut Sweet**

'Cause honest and truly, I'm in love with you **Honest and Truly**

'Cause I don't care, I don't mind Anywhere that she goes you'll find **(Ho! Ho! Ha! Ha!) Me Too**

Chances are 'cause I wear a silly grin, The moment you come into view **Chances Are**

Charming, romantic, the perfect cafe **Dear Friend**

Chatter me, With your flattery. You know the reason why I'm teasy **Coax Me a Little Bit**

Cherry, Cherry, ain't it a shame, That you can't be sweet as your name **Cherry**

Chestnuts roasting on an open fire, Jack Frost nipping at your

nose **The Christmas Song**, or, **Merry Christmas to You,** or, **Chestnuts Roasting on an Open Fire**

Chicago, Chicago that toddlin' town Chicago, Chicago I'll show you around **Chicago (That Toddlin' Town)**

Chick-a-pen goan' to have to whop you right on top-a your head **Chick-a-Pen**

Chickery chick cha-la cha-la, check-a la romey in a bananika **Chickery Chick**

Chicks and ducks and geese better scurry **The Surrey with the Fringe on Top**

Chin up, ladies! Look around the horizon **Chin Up, Ladies!**

China boy go sleep, Close your eyes, don't peep **China Boy**

Chinatown, my Chinatown, Where the lights are low, Hearts that know no other land **Chinatown, My Chinatown**

Chong, he come from Hong Kong where Chineeman play all-ee day on a drum **Chong, He Come from Hong Kong**

Christmas, Christmas time is near, Time for toys and time for cheer **The Chipmunk Song**, or, **Christmas Don't Be Late**

Cigarette holder which wigs me over her shoulder, she digs me **Satin Doll**

Cimarron, roll on, To my lonely song, Carry me away, From the skies of gray **Cimarron (Roll On)**

Cinco robles, cinco cerros, my sweetheart Five oaks and five hills away **Cinco Robles (Five Oaks)**

Cinderella, Cinderella, All I hear is Cinderella from the moment that I get up **Cinderella**

Cindy, oh, Cindy, Cindy, don't let me down, Write me a letter soon **Cindy Oh Cindy**

Ciribiribin He waits for her each night beneath her balcony **Ciribiribin**

City sidewalks, busy sidewalks dressed in holiday style **Silver Bells**

Clap-a yo' hand! Slap-a yo' thigh! Hallelujah **Clap Yo' Hands**

Climb ev'ry mountain, search high and low, Follow ev'ry byway, ev'ry path you know **Climb Ev'ry Mountain**

Climbing up the ladder of love to find a heart that's meant for me **Climbing Up the Ladder of Love**

Close your eyes and I'll kiss you, tomorrow I'll miss you **All My Loving**

Close your eyes and kiss a four leaf clover, whisper tenderly **Kiss a Four Leaf Clover**

Close your eyes, Lena, my darling, While I sing your lullaby **Emmet's Lullaby**, or, **Fritz, Our Cousin German,** or, **Brother's Lullaby**

Close your eyes rest your head on my shoulder and sleep **Close Your Eyes**

Clothes must play a part To light on eye, to win a heart **Lovely To Look At**

Cold, empty bed, Springs hard as lead, Pains in my head **What Did I Do To Be So Black and Blue**

Colored folks work on de Mississippi, Colored folks work while de white folks play **Ol' Man River**

Come all ye young sailor men, listen to me **Boston Come-All Ye**

Come along, get you ready, wear your bran', bran' new

gown   **(There'll Be) A Hot Time in the Old Town (To-night)**

Come along with me down to the old swimming hole   **Down at the Old Swimming Hole**

Come away with me Lucille In my merry Oldsmobile   **In My Merry Oldsmobile**

Come back to the shores of Honolulu, I'm so lonely here without you   **Under Hawaiian Skies**

Come closer to me, so I can see heaven in your eyes   **Come Closer to Me**

Come come come into my arms. Let me know the wonder of all of you   **Could It Be Magic**

Come down, come down from your ivory tower   **Ivory Tower**

Come fill my cup, come fill up my can   **Bonnie Dundee**

Come into the garden, Maud, For the black bat, Night is flown   **Come into the Garden, Maud**

Come on and dance, I feel so happy, Come on and dance, We'll make it snappy!   **Dancing Fool**

Come on and—Ease on down—Ease on down the Road!   **Ease on Down the Road**

Come on, people! Come on, children! Come on down to the glory river   **Save the Country**

Come on, you children, gather around   **Clap Yo' Hands**

Come Saturday morning I'm going away with my friend   **Come Saturday Morning**

Come sit thee near; Place thyself upon my knee   **On a Desert Island with Thee**

Come softly, darling. Come softly, darling   **Come Softly to Me**

Come they told me pa-rum pum pum pum A new born King to see   **The Little Drummer Boy**

Come to me, bend to me kiss me good day! Darlin', my darlin', 'tis all I can say   **Come to Me, Bend to Me**

Come to me, my sweet princess, to my heart I would thee press   **In a Persian market**

Come to us, we've waited so long for you   **The Siren's Song**

Come with me, my love, to the sea, the sea of love   **Sea of Love**

Come, cheer up, my lads, 'tis to glory we steer   **Heart of Oak**

Come, come, ye Saints, no toil nor labor fear   **Come, Ye Saints**

Come, join hand in hand, brave Americans all   **The Liberty Song, or, Come, Join Hand in Hand, or, In Freedom We're Born**

Come, listen, all you gals and boys, I'm just from Tuckyhoe   **(Jump) Jim Crow**

Consider yourself at home, consider yourself one of the family   **Consider Yourself**

Contented! with you with me I'm contented   **Contented**

Could be Who knows There's something due any day   **Something's Coming**

Could he say "I love you?" No, the best he could do Was to whistle it   **The Whistling Boy**

Cracklin' Rosie, get on board, we're gonna ride till there ain't no more to go   **Cracklin' Rosie**

Cradle me where southern skies can watch me with a million eyes   **Lullaby of the Leaves**

Creole babies walk along with rhythm in their thighs   **Underneath the Harlem Moon**

Crump don't 'low no easy riders here   **The Memphis Blues**

Cynthia as flighty as a summer breeze her smile is sunlight thru the trees   **Cynthia's in Love**

Daddy always thought that he married beneath him   **At the Ballet**

Daddy, dear old daddy, You've been more than a daddy to me   **Daddy, You've Been a Mother to Me**

Daddy wore a happy smile, When his bride came down the aisle   **Cathedral in the Pines**

Daisy, Daisy, give me your answer true   **Daisy Bell, or, A Bicycle Built for Two, or, Daisy, Daisy**

Daisy is darling, Iris is sweet, Lily is lovely, Blossom's a treat   **American Beauty Rose**

Dance ballerina dance And do your pirouette in rhythm with your aching heart   **Ballerina**

Dance, dance, dance, little lady! Youth is fleeting to the rhythm beating In your mind   **Dance Little Lady**

Dance: Ten; Looks: Three, And I'm still on unemployment   **Dance: Ten; Looks: Three**

Dancing in the dark Till the tune ends   **Dancing in the Dark**

Daniel is trav'ling tonight on a 'plane   **Daniel**

Dans les jardins d'mon père, les lauriers sont fleurìs   **Auprès de Ma Blonde**

Dark is the night, sad is my heart, Blue is the moon, it's over!   **Dark Is the Night (C'est Fini)**

Dark moon, Away up high in the sky, Oh tell me why   **Dark Moon**

Dark on observatory hill. And I'd like to recite you a poem that I wrote   **It's Dark on Observatory Hill**

Darling, I am growing old, Silver threads among the gold   **Silver Threads Among the Gold**

Darling, Je vous aime beaucoup, Je ne sais pas What to do   **Darling, Je Vous Aime Beaucoup**

Darling Sue, dear, How I miss your laughing   **I Love You in the Same Old Way—Darling Sue**

Darling you and I know the reason why a summer sky is blue   **You and I**

Darn that dream I dream each night, you say you love me and you hold me tight   **Darn That Dream**

Dashing thro' the snow, In a one-horse open sleigh   **Jingle Bells, or, The One Horse Open Sleigh**

Dat you, Sambo? yes I cum, Don't you hear de Banjo—tum, tum, tum   **The Coal Black Rose**

Day after day, alone on a hill, The man with the foolish grin is keeping perfectly still   **The Fool on the Hill**

Day after day I must face a world of strangers where I don't belong, I'm not that strong   **I Won't Last a Day Without You**

Day after day, we will always be sweethearts, The same as the day we began   **We Will Always Be Sweethearts**

Day by day, Day by day, Oh, dear Lord, three things I pray   **Day by Day**

Day by day I'm falling more in love with you   **Day by Day**

Day is ending, Birds are wending Back to the shelter of   **My Blue Heaven**

Day-o, Day-o, Day delight and I wanna go home   **The Banana Boat Song (Day-O)**

Days can be sunny, With never a sigh   **I Got Rhythm**

De Camptown ladies sing dis song, doo-dah, doo-dah!   **De Camptown Races (Gwine To Run All Night)**

De floating scow ob ole Virginia Dat I worked from day to day   **Carry Me Back to Old Virginny**

De massa run, ha! ha! De darky stay, ho! ho!   **Kingdom Coming, or, The Year of Jubilo**

Dear little girl, I love you, Dear little girl   **Sally**

Dear little rose, with your heart of gold   **When You Look in the Heart of a Rose**

Dear old Southland I hear you calling me. And I long how I long to roam back to my old Kentucky home   **Dear Old Southland**

Dear one the world is waiting for the sunrise   **The World Is Waiting for the Sunrise**

Dear Sir or Madam will you read my book? It took me years to write, will you take a look?   **Paperback Writer**

Dearest I love you always think of you First thing each morning and last thing at night.   **Dearest, You're the Nearest to My Heart**

Dearest love, do you remember, When we last did meet   **Weeping, Sad and Lonely, or, When This Cruel War Is Over**

Dearest one: I write what I'm afraid to speak   **Yours Sincerely**

Dearie, my Dearie Nothing's worth while, but dreams of you   **Dearie**

Dearly beloved, how clearly I see, Somewhere in Heaven you were fashioned for me   **Dearly Beloved**

Deep in my heart, dear, I have a dream of you Fashioned of starlight   **Deep in My Heart, Dear**

Deep music fills the night deep in the heart of Harlem   **Harlem Nocturne**

Deep river, my home is over Jordan   **Deep River**

Deep within my heart lies a melody, A song of old San Antone   **San Antonio Rose, or, Rose of San Antone**

Desmond has a barrow in the market place   **Ob-La-De Ob-La-Da**

Deux par deux, Deux par deux, Voilà le vrai bonheur   **I Watch the Love Parade**

Did I remember to tell you I adore you, And I am living for you alone?   **Did I Remember**

Did you ever think as the hearse rolls by, that sooner or later you're going to die   **Did You Ever Think as the Hearse Rolls By, or, The Worms Crawl In, the Worms Crawl Out**

Did you say, "I've got a lot to learn?"   **Teach Me Tonight**

Dinah is there anyone finer in the state of Carolina   **Dinah**

Dinner for one, please James, Madam will not be dining, Yes, you may bring the wine in   **Dinner for One, Please James**

Dis ole hammer killed John Henry, Made music sweet and it did amuse   **The John Henry Blues**

Dites-moi Pourquoi La vie est belle   **Dites-Moi Pourquoi**

Dizzy, I'm so dizzy, my head is spinnin' like a whirlpool   **Dizzy**

Do I love you because you're beautiful? Or are you beautiful because I love you?   **Do I Love You Because You're Beautiful**

Do I love you, do I? Doesn't one and one make two?   **Do I Love You**

Do it the hard way, And it's easy sailing   **Do It the Hard Way**

Do me wrong, do me right. Tell me lies but hold me tight   **Don't Let Me Be Lonely Tonight**

Do not fear my little darling, And I will take you right home   **The Little Lost Child**

Do not wait until some deed of greatness you may do   **Brighten the Corner Where You Are**

Do nothin' till you hear from me. Pay no attention to what's said   **Do Nothin' Till You Hear from Me**

Do you believe in mermaids, a lot of people do   **Ask Any Mermaid**

Do you care? Is there a change for me?   **Do You Care**

Do you love me? Do I what? Do you love me? Do I love you?   **Do You Love Me**

Do you recall a year ago tonight?   **Blueberry Hill**

Do you remember sweet Betsy from Pike? 'Crossed the big mountains with her lover Ike   **Sweet Betsy from Pike, or, Vilikens and His Dinah**

Do you want to dance and hold my hand; Tell me you're my lover man   **Do You Want To Dance**

Do yuh hear that whistle down the line? I figure that it's engine number forty nine   **On the Atchison, Topeka and the Santa Fe**

Doe a deer, a female deer, Ray a drop of golden sun   **Do-Re-Mi**

Does he love me? It's too soon to know   **It's Too Soon to Know**

Dogs got to bark, a mule's got to bray   **Never Say No**

Don't blame me for falling in love with you   **Don't Blame Me**

Don't Don't that's what you say Each time that I hold you this way   **Don't**

Don't even go to a movie show if you are not at my side   **Keepin' Out of Mischief Now**

Don't ever leave me, now that you're here! Here is where you belong   **Don't Ever Leave Me**

Don't know why there's no sun up in the sky, stormy weather   **Stormy Weather**

Don't let it bother you when things go wrong If you're glum just hum   **Don't Let It Bother You**

Don't let the sun go down on me although I search myself it's always someone else I see   **Don't Let the Sun Go Down on Me**

Don't save your kisses, just pass them around   **A Hundred Years from Today**

Don't settle for some of the taste, some of the time **Viceroy Gives You All the Taste All the Time**

Don't talk of stars burning above. If you're in love, show me! **Show Me**

Don't throw bouquets at me, Don't please my folks too much **People Will Say We're in Love**

Don't whisper things to me you don't mean **The Night Has a Thousand Eyes**

Don't worry 'bout me It's all over now. Tho I may be blue I'll manage somehow **Don't Worry**

Don't worry 'bout me, I'll get along. Forget about me be happy, my love **Don't Worry 'Bout Me**

Don't you hear my heart whisper thru your window **Emaline**

Don't you know I have fallen in love with you **Don't You Know**

Don't you know I love you so I won't be happy until you're mine **Make Love to Me**

Double your pleasure, Double your fun, with double good, double good, Doublemint Gum **Double Your Pleasure**

Down Among the Sheltering Palms, Oh honey, wait for me Oh honey, wait for me **Down Among the Sheltering Palms**

Down at the races keeping cases, we don't care a rap **The Handicap March**

Down beside the Dardanella Bay, Where oriental breezes play **Dardanella**

Down in the jungles lived a maid, Of royal blood though dusky shade **Under the Bamboo Tree**

Down in the valley, the valley so low, Hang your head over, hear the wind blow **Down in the Valley,** or, **Birmingham Jail,** or, **Bird in a Cage,** or, **Down on the Levee**

Down on the Mississippi floating, Long time I trabbel o'er the way **Nelly Was a Lady**

Down the Rock Island Line it is a mighty good road **Rock Island Line**

Down the trail of dreams, I'm with you once again **Trail of Dreams**

Down to the depths, up to the heights, giddy with joy, crazy with fear **(Theme from) Vertigo**

Down where the trade winds play; Down where you lose a day **Trade Winds**

Dozens of girls would storm up, I had to lock my door **Embraceable You**

Dream along with me. I'm on my way to a star, Come along **Dream Along with Me**

Dream of me while the moon softly beams **Au Revoir, Pleasant Dreams**

Dream when you're feeling blue, Dream that's the thing to do **Dream (When You're Feeling Blue)**

Dreary days are over. Life's a fourleaf clover **Long Ago and Far Away**

Drifting and dreaming, While shadows fall. Softly at the twilight **Drifting and Dreaming (Sweet Paradise)**

Drink a bit, laugh a bit, love a bit more, I can supply your need **Half-Caste Woman**

Drinkin' rum and Coca-Cola, Go down "Point Koomahnah" **Rum and Coca-Cola**

Du bist mein kleines Puppchen, My pretty little Puppchen **Puppchen**

Du, du liegst mir im Herzen, du, du liegst mir im Sinn **Du, Du, Liegst Mir im Herzen**

Dusk, and the shadows falling O'er land and sea **Somewhere a Voice Is Calling**

D'ya love me? (Um-hu!) D'ya mean it? (Um-hu!) **D'Ya Love Me?**

D'ye ken John Peel with his coat so gay **(D'Ye Ken) John Peel**

Each time I see a crowd of people **Maybe You'll Be There**

Each time we have a quarrel it almost breaks my heart **Teen-ager in Love**

East is east and west is west and the wrong one I have chose **Buttons and Bows**

East Side, West Side, All around the town **The Sidewalks of New York,** or, **East Side, West Side**

Edelweiss, Edelweiss, Ev'ry morning you greet me **Edelweiss**

E'er since Miss Susan Johnson lost her jockey, Lee **Yellow Dog Blues**

Eighteen hundred and ninety-one, that's the year that I begun **Patsy Ory Ory Aye (A-Workin' on the Railroad)**

Ein' feste Burg ist unser Gott, Ein' gute Wehr und Waffen **A Mighty Fortress Is Our God,** or, **Ein' Feste Burg**

Eleanor Rigby, picks up the rice in the church where a wedding has been **Eleanor Rigby**

Embrace me, My sweet embraceable you **Embraceable You**

Emotions, what are you doin' Oh, don't you know You'll be my ruin **Emotions**

Empty saddles in the old corral, Where do ya ride tonight? **Empty Saddles**

Ev'ry day a little death In the parlor, in the bed, In the curtains in the silver **Every Day a Little Death**

Ev'ry day for a week we would try to feel the motion, feel the motion down the hill **Nothing**

Ev'ry honey bee fills with jealousy when they see you out with me **Honeysuckle Rose**

Ev'ry little breeze is sighing of love undying at sundown **At Sundown**

Ev'ry little breeze seems to whisper "Louise" **Louise**

Ev'ry little while I find I'm missing you, Wonder if you miss me too **Ev'ry Little While**

Ev'ry morning Ev'ry evening Ain't we got fun **Ain't We Got Fun**

Ev'ry mornin' find me moanin' Cause of all the trouble I see **Moanin'**

Ev'ry star up in the sky, Seems to wink as we go by Mary Ann **Mary Ann**

Ev'ry Sunday afternoon and Thursday night We'll be free as birds in flight **Ev'ry Sunday Afternoon**

Ev'ry time it rains, it rains pennies from heaven **Pennies from Heaven**

Ev'ry time you're near a rose Aren't you glad you've got a nose **Aren't You Glad You're You**

Ev'rybody doesn't like something, but nobody doesn't like Sara Lee **Nobody Doesn't Like Sara Lee**

Ev'rybody hand in hand, Swingin' down the lane **Swingin' Down the Lane**

Ev'rybody has a sweetheart underneath the rose **My Sweetheart's the Man in the Moon**

Ev'rybody's gonna have religion in glory? **A Wonderful Time Up There**

Ev'rybody's lookin' for the big Bajour! **Bajour**

Ev'rybody's talking about Bagism, Shagism, Dragism, Madism, Ragism, Tagism **Give Peace a Chance**

Ev'ryone knows She's a rambling rose She's a beauty growing wild **Rambling Rose**

Ev'rything is peaches down in Georgia, What a peach of a clime, For a peach of a time **Everything Is Peaches Down in Georgia**

Ev'rything is rosy, When I'm with my Rosie **Rosie**

Ev'rythin's up to date in Kansas City, They've gone about as fur as they c'n go! **Kansas City**

Ev'rytime I look at you I don't understand **Jesus Christ Superstar**

Evening shadows make me blue When each weary day is through **My Happiness**

Ever since I first met you, I've been in love with love **In Love with Love**

Every morning at seven o'clock There were twenty terriers a-working on the rock **Drill Ye Terriers Drill**

Every morning at the mine you could see him arrive **Big Bad John**

Everybody's going out and having fun **Oh Lonesome Me**

Everything is beautiful in its own way, Like a starry summer night **Everything Is Beautiful**

Eyes of fire and dew, Eyes of darkest hue **Dark Eyes**, or, **Black Eyes**

Ezekiel saw de wheel, 'way up in de middle ob de air **Ezekiel Saw De Wheel**

Fair Harvard! thy sons to thy jubilee throng, And with blessings surrender thee o'er **Fair Harvard**

Faith of our fathers, living still In spite of dungeon, fire and sword **Faith of Our Fathers**

Faithful, remember that whatever I do **Faithful Forever**

Falling in love again, Never wanted to; What am I to do? Can't help it! **Falling in Love Again**

Falling in love with love is falling for make believe **Falling in Love with Love**

Falling leaf, and fading tree, Lines of white on a sullen sea **Goodbye**

Far above Cayuga's Waters, With its waves of blue **Far Above Cayuga's Waters**, or, **Annie Lisle**

Fare thee well I know you're leaving **He Don't Love You Like I Love You**

Farewell, Mother, you may never Press me to your heart again **Just Before the Battle, Mother**

Fascinating rhythm You've got me on the go! Fascinating rhythm I'm all a quiver **Fascinating Rhythm**

Fascination captured my heart When you smiled at me and I first felt the thrill **Fascination**

Father and I went down to camp, Along with Captain Gooding **Yankee Doodle**

Father, dear father, come home with me now! The clock in the steeple strikes one **Father, Dear Father, Come Home With Me Now**, or, **Come Home, Father**

Fee fee fi fi fo fo fum I smell the smoke in the auditorium **Charlie Brown**

Ferdinand, Ferdinand, the Bull with the delicate "ego" **Ferdinand the Bull**

Feudin' and fussin' and a-fightin' Sometimes it gets to be excitin' **Feudin' and Fightin'**

Fight that team across the field, Show them Ohio's here **Across the Field**

Fill the steins to dear old Maine, Shout till the rafters ring! **(Maine) Stein Song**

Find a wheel and it goes 'round 'round 'round as it skims along with a happy sound **Round and Round**

Finer things are for the finer folk, Thus society began **Too Good for the Average Man**

Firm, united let us be, Ral'ying round our liberty **Hail Columbia**, or, **New Federal Song**

First the tide rushes in **Ebb Tide**

First time that I saw you, girl I knew that I just had to make you mine **Dizzy**

First you get some gravel. Pour it in the vout **Cement Mixer (Put-ti Put-ti)**

First you put your two knees close up tight **Ballin' the Jack**

First you say you do and then you don't **Undecided**

Fish got to swim and birds got to fly, I got to love one man till I die **Can't Help Lovin' Dat Man**

Five foot two, eyes of blue, But oh! what those five foot could do **Five Foot Two, Eyes of Blue (Has Anybody Seen My Girl?)**

Flies in the buttermilk, two by two **Skip to My Lou**

Flow river, flow Down to the sea **By the Saskatchewan**

Fly away, fly away Kentucky Babe, fly away to rest **Kentucky Babe**

"Fly away!" Said my carefree heart, "To the place where my daydreams start **Malagueña**

Fly me to the moon, and let me play among the stars **Fly Me to the Moon**, or, **In Other Words**

Flying home to a place that's always sunny **Flying Home**

Food, glorious food! Hot sausage and mustard! **Food Glorious Food**

Fools rush in, so here I am Very glad to be unhappy **Glad To Be Unhappy**

For all we know we may never meet again, Before you go Make this moment sweet again **For All We Know**

For ev'ry man there's a woman, For ev'ry life there's a plan **For Every Man There's a Woman**

For I bring a little white gardenia As refreshing as a day in May   **A Little White Gardenia**

For it is Mary, Mary, plain as any name can be   **Mary's a Grand Old Name**

For I've got beginner's luck. The first time that I'm in love, I'm in love with you   **(I've Got) Beginner's Luck**

For once in my life I have someone who needs me, someone I've needed so long   **For Once in My Life**

For some girls are quickly forgotten, And gone with the dawn of the day   **I'm Just a Vagabond Lover**

For the benefit of Mr. Kite there will be a show tonight on trampoline   **Being for the Benefit of Mister Kite**

For there's a change in the weather There's a change in the sea   **There'll Be Some Changes Made**

For those who fancy coloring books and lots of people do   **My Coloring Book**

For we need a little Christmas, Right this very minute   **We Need a Little Christmas**

For when I walk I always walk with Billy 'Cause Billy knows just where to walk   **Billy (For When I Walk)**

For when my baby smiles at me my heart goes roaming to paradise   **When My Baby Smiles at Me**

Frankie and Johnnie were lovers, oh, Lordie how they could love!   **Frankie and Johnnie (Johnny) (Were Lovers)**

Freddy my love, I miss you more than words can say   **Freddy, My Love**

Free an' easy that's my style Howdy do me watch me smile   **Any Place I Hang My Hat Is Home**

Frère Jacques, frère Jacques, Dormez-vous, dormez-vous   **Frère Jacques**

From Greenland's icy mountains, From India's coral strand   **From Greenland's Icy Mountains**

From la Sierra Morena, Cielito Lindo, From high descending   **Cielito Lindo (Ay, Ay, Ay, Ay)**

From now on, no more philand'ring, No more hot spots, no scatterbrain   **From Now On**

From the calm Pacific waters, To the rough Atlantic shore   **Wabash Cannonball**

From the halls of Montezuma, to the shores of Tripoli   **The Marine's Hymn**, or, **From the Halls of Montezuma to the Shores of Tripoli**

From the Island of Manhattan to the Coast of Gold   **Of Thee I Sing**

From this valley they say they are going   **The Red River Valley**

Full moon and empty arms. The moon is there for us to share but where are you?   **Full Moon and Empty Arms**

Funniest pair of eyes I've ever seen   **What Do You Want To Make Those Eyes at Me For**

Funny, Did ya hear that? Funny! Yes, the guy said   **Funny Girl**

Funny, you're a stranger who's come here, Come from another town   **Small World**

Gaze on those glist'ning lights below and above   **Paris Loves Lovers**

Gee but I'd give the world to see that old gang of mine   **That Old Gang of Mine**

Gee, it's all fine and dandy, Sugar Candy, when I've got you   **Fine and Dandy**

Gee! It's great, after bein' out late   **Walkin' My Baby Back Home**

Gentleman Jack's a ladies man, He can make love like no one can   **Cu-Tu-Gu-Ru (Jack, Jack, Jack)**

Georgia, Georgia, the whole day through, just an old sweet song keeps Georgia on my mind   **Georgia on My Mind**

Get out from that kitchen and rattle those pots and pans   **Shake, Rattle and Roll**

Get out of town Before it's too late, my love   **Get Out of Town**

Get Wildroot Cream Oil, Charlie, It Keeps your hair in trim   **Get Wildroot Cream-Oil Charlie**

Getting to know you, getting to know all about you   **Getting To Know You**

Gigi, Am I a fool without a mind or have I merely been too blind to realize?   **Gigi**

Gimme a little kiss will ya huh? What are ya gonna miss will ya huh?   **Gimme a Little Kiss, Will Ya, Huh?**

Gimme dat ol' time religion, gimme dat ol' time religion   **(Gimme Dat) Old Time Religion**

Gin a body meet a body, Comin' thro' the rye   **Comin' Thro' the Rye**, or, **If a Body Meet a Body**

Git along little taxi you can keep the change   **Way Out West**

Give a little whistle, Ring a little bell   **Give a Little Whistle**

Give a rouse, then, in the Maytime, For a life that knows no fear!   **It's Always Fair Weather When Good Fellows Get Together**, or, **A Stein Song**

Give me a kiss to build a dream on and my imagination will thrive upon that kiss   **A Kiss To Build a Dream On**

Give me five minutes more, Only five minutes more   **Five Minutes More**

Give me my ranch and my cattle, Far from the great city's rattle   **El Rancho Grande**

Give me somebody to dance for. Give me somebody to show   **The Music and the Mirror**

Give my regards to Broadway, Remember me to Herald Square   **Give My Regards to Broadway**

Give up the fond embrace, Pass up that pretty face   **The Back Bay Polka**

Gloria is but a kiss in the night, one brief caress   **Gloria**, or, **Theme from** *Butterfield 8*

Gloria, it's not Marie it's Gloria. It's not Cherie, it's Gloria   **Gloria**

Go fly a kite and tie your troubles to the tail   **Go Fly a Kite**

Go tell Aunt Rhody That the old grey goose in dead   **(Go Tell Aunt Rhody) The Ole Grey Goose (Is Dead)**

Go tell it on the mountain, over the hills and everywhere   **Go Tell It on the Mountain**

Go to sleep, go to sleep, my baby, my baby, my baby   **Emmet's Lullaby**, or, **Fritz, Our Cousin German**, or, **Brother's Lullaby**

Go while the going is good, Knowing when to leave may be the smartest thing that anyone can learn. Go **Knowing When To Leave**

God bless you, you make me feel brand new, for God blessed me with you **You Make Me Feel Brand New**

God didn't make little green apples and it don't rain in Indianapolis in the summertime **Little Green Apples**

God, I hope I get it, I hope I get it **I Hope I Get It**

Going barefoot in the park where it says, "Keep off the grass" **Barefoot in the Park**

Going down the Stoney End, I never wanted to go down the Stoney End **Stoney End**

Goin' steady, goin' steady, goin' steady, steady for good **The Telephone Hour**

Goin' steady, you know it, man, Goin' steady, it's crazy, man! **The Telephone Hour**

Golden Gate, I'm comin' to ya, Golden Gate, sing hallelujah **Golden Gate**

Gone are the days when I'd answer the bell **When the Nylons Bloom Again**

Gone are the days when my heart was young and gay **Old Black Joe**

Gone with the wind, Just like a leaf that has blown away **Gone with the Wind**

Gonna get a girl because I ought to have a girl **Gonna Get a Girl**

Gonna take a sentimental journey, Gonna set my heart at ease **Sentimental Journey**

Gonna tell Aunt Mary 'bout Uncle John **Long Tall Sally**

Good King Wenceslas looked out, On the feast of Stephen **Good King Wenceslas**

Good morning, heartache, you old gloomy sight **Good Morning Heartache**

Good morning, Mister Zip-Zip-Zip, With your hair cut just as short as mine **Good Morning, Mister Zip-Zip-Zip**

"Good morrow, good morrow, good morrow," said she **The Nightingale**

Good news! You're bound to do me good, Come right here to me **Good News**

Good night angel Thanks for another evening in heaven! **Good Night Angel**

Good times and bum times, I've seen 'em all and, my dear, I'm still here **I'm Still Here**

Goodbye means our affair is ended **Once in a While**

Goodbye my Blue Bell, Farewell to you **Blue Bell**

Goodbye New York town, goodbye Miss Liberty **Good-Bye Broadway, Hello France**

Goodbye, Rose, the Autumn leaves are falling **Goodbye, Rose**

Got a date with an angel, Got to meet her at seven **Got a Date with an Angel**

Got a good reason for taking the easy way out **Day Tripper**

Got a little rhythm, A rhythm, a rhythm That pit-a-pats through my brain **Fascinating Rhythm**

Got a new dance and it goes like this **The Peppermint Twist**

Got along without ya before I met ya **Gonna Get Along Without Ya Now**

Got de St. Louis Blues jes as blue as ah can be **St. Louis Blues**

Got on board a westbound seven forty seven **It Never Rains in Southern California**

Grab and cab and go down To where the band is playing **Sweet and Low-Down**

Granada tierra ensangrentada en tardes de toros **Granada**

Gray skies are gonna clear up, Put on a happy face **Put On a Happy Face**

Guten Abend, gut' nacht! Mit Rosen bedacht **Lullaby**, or, **Wiegenlied**, or, **Schlummerlied**

Gwine to lay down my sword and shield, down by the riverside **Down by the Riverside**, or, **Ain't Gwine Study War No More**

Gwineter th'ow the dice away Li'l Liza Jane **Li'l Liza Jane**

Hail, Columbia, happy land, Hail, ye heroes, heav'n born band **Hail Columbia**, or, **New Federal Song**

Hail! Hail to old Purdue! All hail to our Old Gold and Black! **Hail Purdue**

Hail to the victors valiant. Hail to the conq'ring Heroes **The Victors**

Haircut, simply terrible, Necktie, the worst! **You've Got Possibilities**

Half a pound of tupenny rice, Half a pound of treacle **Pop Goes the Weasel**

Half of what I say is meaningless **Julia**

Hands across the table, while the lights are low, Tho' you hush your lips **Hands Across the Table**

Hang down your head, Tom Dooley, Hang down your head and cry **Tom Dooley**, or, **Tom Dula**

Happy, happy birthday, baby, Although you're with somebody new **Happy, Happy Birthday, Baby**

Happy talk, keep talkin' happy talk **Happy Talk**

Has anybody seen Colette? Where did she go? **(La La) Colette**

Has anybody seen our ship The H.M.S. "Peculiar" **Has Anybody Seen Our Ship**

Has she got naughty eyes? Yes, she has got naughty eyes **That Certain Party**

Haul out the holly, Put up the tree before my spirit falls again **We Need a Little Christmas**

Have no use for other sweets of any kind, since the day you came around **Honeysuckle Rose**

Have you discovered in your attic you're dramatic, acrobatic, operatic? **(To) Be a Performer**

Have you forgotten so soon, That lovely night in June, our graduation dance **Have You Forgotten So Soon**

Have you heard I married an angel, I'm sure that the change'll be awf'lly good for me **I Married an Angel**

Have you heard? The coast of Maine just got hit by a hurricane **Well, Did You Evah**

Have you heard? Who's kissing him now Do you think he's blue **Have You Heard**

Have you met Miss Jones? "Someone said as we shook hands **Have You Met Miss Jones**

Have you met my good friend Charley? Well you've heard of him no doubt **Clap Hands, Here Comes Charley**

Hawaii isles of beauty Where skies are blue and love is true **Song of the Islands**

He always sings raggy music to the cattle, As he swings back and forward in the saddle **Ragtime Cowboy Joe**

He came from somewhere back in her long ago **What a Fool Believes**

He clasped his hands, then raised his eyes, And prayed before he died **The Drummer Boy of Shiloh**

He dances overhead on the ceiling, near my bed **Dancing on the Ceiling**

He doesn't act as tho' he cares **As Long as He Needs Me**

He gave her kisses and promised the moon **Sunshine Girl**

He goes on the prowl each night Like an alley cat **Alley Cat**

He got O-no sideboard He one spinal cracker He bag production He got walrus gumboot **Come Together**

He is an Englishman! For he himself has said it, And it's greatly to his credit, That he is an Englishman! **He Is an Englishman**

He just plays chords, that make you feel grand **Sam, the Old Accordion Man**

He made the night a little brighter Wherever he would go **The Old Lamp-Lighter**

He makes his own dreams, His own paradise **The Man with the Golden Arm**

He may be a great big Gen'ral, May be a Sergeant Major **There's Something About a Soldier**

He means to marry me Monday, What shall I do? I'd rather die **Kiss Me**

He said he had to work, so I went to the show alone **Sad Movies Make Me Cry**

He says "murder," he says Ev'ry time we kiss, He says, "murder" **"Murder" He Says**

He stood and looked at me And I was beautiful **And I Was Beautiful**

He took a hundred pounds of clay and then He said, "Hey! Listen, I'm gonna fix this world today **A Hundred Pounds of Clay**

He was a jerk before he got into the service **Military Life, or, The Jerk Song**

Hear Aunt Hagar's children harmonizing, Hear that sweet melody **Aunt Hagar's Blues**

Hear my lullaby in rhythm, Dream your dreams and wander with 'em **Lullaby in Rhythm**

Here my voice where you are! Take a train; Steal a car **Come Back to Me**

Hear the sweet voice of the child, Which the night-winds repeat as they roam! **Father, Dear Father, Come Home with Me Now, or, Come Home, Father**

Hearken, hearken, music sounds afar **Funiculi—Funicula**

Heart and soul, I fell in love with you. Heart and soul, the way a fool would do **Heart and Soul**

Heart of my heart I love that melody **The Gang That Sang Heart of My Heart**

Heart of oak are our ships, heart of oak are our men **Heart of Oak**

Hearts made of stone will never break, For the love you have for them, they just won't take **Hearts of Stone**

Heavenly shades of night are falling, it's twilight time **Twilight Time**

Heigh! Nelly, Ho! Nelly, listen, lub, to me **Nelly Bly**

Heigh-Ho, Heigh-Ho, To make your troubles go, Just keep on singing all day long **Heigh-Ho**

Hello darkness, my old friend, I've come to talk with you again **The Sounds of Silence**

Hello! How are you? Howza folks? What's new? **The Babbitt and the Bromide**

Hello, young lovers, Whoever you are, I hope your troubles are few **Hello Young Lovers**

Help! I need somebody. Help! Not just anybody **Help!**

Hep Hep There goes the Johnson Rag Hoy Hoy There goes the latest shag Ho Ho **Johnson Rag**

Here, a sheer hulk, lies poor Tom Bowling, The Darling of our crew **(Poor) Tom Bowling, or, The Sailor's Epitaph**

Here am I just a slave to love Waiting for your caress **What Do I Care**

Here and there and ev'rywhere **A Girl of the Pi Beta Phi**

Here comes heaven again Get that angel face **Here Comes Heaven Again**

Here I am lonely tired and lonely crying for home in vain **Just Like a Butterfly (That's Caught in the Rain)**

Here I go again, Again I've got that yen, and I'm all in a tizzy **Here I Go Again**

Here I go again I hear those trumpets blow again **Taking a Chance on Love**

Here I stand with head in hand, Turn my face to the wall **You've Got to Hide Your Love Away**

Here in this enchanted place; Here, enclosed in your embrace **Here**

Here is the Drag, See how it goes. Down on the heels, up on the toes **The Varsity Drag**

Here, making each day of the year changing my life with a wave of her hand **Here, There and Everywhere**

Here we are, just you and I, Two hearts filled with one sensation **Here's to Romance**

Here we are, out of cigarettes, Holding hands and yawning **Two Sleepy People**

Here we are you and I Let the world hurry by **Here We Are**

Here's success to Port, Drink it down, drink it down **Drink It Down, Drink It Down**

Here's to good old Yale, drink it down, drink it down **Balm of Gilead, or, Bingo**

Here's to the ladies who lunch, Ev'rybody laugh **The Ladies Who Lunch**

Here's to us, my darling, my dear **Here's to Us**

Heroes are threading Through meadowlands so widely spreading **Meadowlands, or, Cavalry of the Steppes**

He's a real Nowhere Man, Sitting in his Nowhere Land, Making all his nowhere plans for nobody **Nowhere Man**

He's a tramp, but they love him; Breaks a new heart ev'ry day **He's a Tramp**

He's just a sentimental gentleman from Georgia, Georgia, Gentle to the ladies all the time **A Sentimental Gentleman from Georgia**

He's stone cold dead in the market, I kill nobody but my husband **Stone Cold Dead in the Market**

He's such a good egg He's a regular guy **The Egg and I**

Hey there! Georgy girl, Swinging down the street so fancy free **Georgy Girl**

Hey! listen to my story 'bout a gal named Daisy Mae **Daddy**

Hey, Babe, hey, Babe, How you doin' today, Babe? **Hey, Babe, Hey (I'm Nuts About You)**

Hey, baby! I ain't askin' much of you **A Big Hunk of Love**

Hey, buds below, up is where to grow, Up with which below can't compare with **Hurry It's Lovely Up Here**

Hey, did you happen to see the most beautiful girl in the world? And if you did was she crying, crying? **(If You Happen To See) The Most Beautiful Girl (in the World)**

Hey, diddle, diddle, the cat and the fiddle, the cow jumped over the moon **Hey, Diddle, Diddle**

Hey, don't worry, I've been lied to **Minute by Minute**

Hey, good lookin', Say, what's cookin'? Do you feel like bookin' Some fun tonight? **Hey, Good Lookin'**

Hey Jude don't make it bad, take a sad song and make it better **Hey Jude**

Hey, little girl, comb your hair, fix your makeup, soon he will open the door **(Theme from) Wives and Lovers**

Hey, look me over, lend me an ear, Fresh out of clover, mortgaged up to here **Hey Look Me Over**

Hey, Mister Tambourine Man, play a song for me **Mister Tambourine Man**

Hey now, ev'rybody in the union hall **Pony Time**

Hi there, neighbor Goin' my way **(This Is) God's Country**

Hi-Diddle-Diddle, And the cat and the fiddle, And the cow jumped over the moon **Hi-Diddle-Diddle**

Hic, haec, hoc, In vino veritas **Hic, Haec, Hoc**

Hide your heart from sight, Lock your dreams at night **It Could Happen to You**

Hig row, de boatmen row, floatin' down de river de Ohio **De Boatmen's Dance**

High on a hill was a lonely goatherd, lay-ee-odl, lay-ee-odl, lay-ee-oo **The Lonely Goatherd**

Hold it, flash, bang, wallop, what a picture **Flash, Bang, Wallop**

Hold me in your arms, dear, dream with me **Melodie d'Amour (Melody of Love)**

Hold me, hold me, never let me go until you've told me **Hold Me, Thrill Me, Kiss Me**

Hold my hand! No matter what the weather **Hold My Hand**

Hold that Tiger, Hold that tiger **Tiger Rag**

Hold tight hold tight hold tight Foo-ra-de-ack-a-sa-ki Want some seafood Mama **Hold Tight—Hold Tight**

Hold your hoss, here they come, Rat-tat-tat goes the drum **The Circus Is on Parade**

Holding hands at midnight 'Neath a starry sky **Nice Work If You Can Get It**

Hon, don't you hear that trombone moan? Just listen to that saxophone **Royal Garden Blues**

Honestly, I thought you wouldn't; Naturally, you thought you couldn't **Aren't You Kind of Glad We Did**

Honey I love you too much. Need your lovin' too much **Too Much**

Honey, mascara your eyebrow and come with me **Sophisticated Swing**

Honeycomb wontcha be my baby? Honeycomb be my own **Honeycomb**

Hop-a-long, Sal, where you goin'? You look mighty fine- **Keep-A-Hoppin'**

Hot diggity dog ziggity boom! What you do to me! It's so new to me **Hot Diggity (Dog Ziggity Boom)**

How are things in Glocca Morra? Is that little brook still leaping there? **How Are Things in Glocca Morra**

How can you forget when you lie awake and dream at night? **How Can You Forget?**

How cold, the wind that whispers you are gone **(Theme from) The Godfather (Part II)**

How dear to my heart are the scenes of my childhood **The Old Oaken Bucket**

How do you solve a problem like Maria? **Maria**

How does it feel to be one of the beautiful people **Baby You're a Rich man**

How far away are you? How many lonely sighs, dear? **No Other Love**

How I love the kisses of Dolores Ay, ay, ay Dolores **Dolores**

How I miss that sweet lady with her old country touch **Mama from the Train, or, A Kiss, A Kiss**

How little I knew until very lately **Without Love**

How little we know how much to discover what chemical forces flow **How Little It Matters, How Little We Know**

How lovely to sit here in the shade With none of the woes of man and maid **I'm Glad I'm Not Young Anymore**

How much is that doggie in the window? The one with the waggely tail **(How Much Is That) Doggie in the Window**

How stands the glass around? For shame, ye take no care, my boys **How Stands the Glass Around, or, Wolfe's Song, or, Why, Soldiers, Why, or, The Duke of Berwick's March**

How the world can change, it can change like that **Married**

How to apply for a job, How to advance from the mail room **How To**

How to handle a woman, There's a way, said a wise old man **How To Handle a Woman**

How'd you like to take a trip and be carefree **A Dreamer's Holiday**

Huckleberry Finn, If I were Huckleberry Finn, I'd do the things he did **Huckleberry Finn**

Hugs and kisses, from someone like you I'll say this is, like dreams coming true **Hugs and Kisses**

Humming bird, mockingbird, listen to me **Can't Help Singing**

Hurrah! Hurrah! for Southern Rights, Hurrah! **The Bonnie Blue Flag**

Hurrah! Hurrah! We bring the jubilee! **Marching Through Georgia**

Hurray for the flag of the free **Stars and Stripes Forever**

Hush now, don't explain! Just say you'll remain **Don't Explain**

I am a lineman for the county, And I drive the main road **Wichita Lineman**

I am a Utah man, sir, and I live across the green **A Utah Man Am I**

I am dejected, I am depressed, Yet resurrected and sailing the crest **I Am in Love**

I am he as you are he as you are me and we are all together **I Am the Walrus**

I am just a little girl who's looking for a little boy **Looking for a Boy**

I am not such a clever one About the latest fads **I'm Old Fashioned**

I am the Captain of the Pinafore! And a right good captain too! **I Am the Captain of the Pinafore (What Never)**

I am the monarch of the sea, The ruler of the Queen's Navee **I Am the Monarch of the Sea**

I am twice as happy as a millionaire **Please Go 'Way and Let Me Sleep**

I am weak but Thou art strong, Jesus, keep me from all wrong **Just a Closer Walk with Thee**

I begged her, I pleaded, I told her, "Baby come out of your shell" **I Begged Her**

I believe for ev'ry drop of rain that falls a flower grows **I Believe**

I came from ole Virginny, from the county Acomac **Maple Leaf Rag**

I came from the town of Mira beyond the bridges of Saint Claire **Mira**

I came to town de udder night, I hear de noise, den saw de fight **Old Dan Tucker**

I can be happy, I can be sad, I can be good or I can be bad **It All Depends on You**

I can only give you love that lasts forever **That's All**

I can see a swath of sinners settin' yonder **Learn Your Lessons Well**

I can see He's happier without me **He's a Right Guy**

I can see, no matter how near you'll be, You'll never belong to me **I Can Dream, Can't I**

I can't light no more of your darkness **Don't Let the Sun Go Down on Me**

I can't show my face, Can't go anyplace **It's the Talk of the Town**

I can't sleep I can't eat get a pail and soak my feet **I Got a "Code" in My "Dose" (Cold in My Nose)**

I can't wait until next Sunday morning **I'll Be Happy When the Preacher Makes You Mine**

I come from Alabama with my banjo on my knee **Oh! Susanna**

I come to the garden alone, while the dew is still on the roses **(He Walks with Me) In the Garden**

I could cry salty tears; Where have I been all these years? **How Long Has This Been Going On?**

I could learn my ABC's Bring home A's instead of D's **(If I Had) Rhythm in My Nursery Rhymes**

I could show the world how to smile, I could be glad all of the while **If I Had You**

I couldn't sleep a wink last night because we had that silly fight **I Couldn't Sleep a Wink Last Night**

I couldn't sleep a wink last night just a-thinking of you **Tossin' and Turnin'**

I cried for you, Now it's your turn to cry over me **I Cried for You (Now It's Your Turn To Cry over Me)**

I didn't know what time it was, Then I met you **I Didn't Know What Time It Was**

I didn't raise my boy to be a soldier, I brought him up to be my pride and joy **I Didn't Raise My Boy To Be a Soldier**

I dig rock 'n' roll music and I love to get the chance to play and sing it **I Dig Rock and Roll Music**

I dim all the lights and I sink in my chair **Deep in a Dream**

I don't believe in frettin' and grievin' **Give Me the Simple Life**

I don't care if the sun don't shine, I get my lovin' in the evenin' time **I Don't Care If the Sun Don't Shine**

I don't have plans and schemes and I don't have hopes and dreams **Since I Don't Have You**

I don't know how to love him, what to do how to move him **I Don't Know How To Love Him**

I don't know what day it is, Or if it's dark or fair **A Ship Without a Sail**

I don't know why, but I'm feeling so sad **Lover Man (Oh Where Can You Be)**

I don't know why I am so very shy, I always was demure- **How'd You Like To Spoon with Me?**

I don't know why I love you like I do **I Don't Know Why (I Just Do)**

I don't know why I should cry over you, sigh over you **Why Should I Cry Over You**

I don't know why they redesigned me **What Did I Have That I Don't Have**

I don't like men, Women I don't like too **I Do Do Do Like You**

I don't like your peaches, they are full of stones **I Like Bananas Because They Have No Bones**

I don't want a genius for a husband Or a man who's big financially **That's Good Enough for Me**

I don't want my arms around you, no, not much! **No, Not Much**

I don't want my heart to be broken 'cause it's the only one I've got **I Beg of You**

I don't want to love you Please don't let me care **I Don't Want To Love You (Like I Do)**

I don't want to set the world on fire I just want to start a flame in your heart **I Don't Want To Set the World on Fire**

I don't want you to feel when you go out for a meal **I've Got My Eyes on You**

I don't want you, but I'd hate to lose you **Between the Devil and the Deep Blue Sea**

I dreaded ev'ry morning, Until without a warning, You arrived bringing heaven to my door **What a Diff'rence a Day Made (Makes)**

I dream of Jeanie with the light-brown hair, Borne like a vapour on the summer air **Jeanie with the Light Brown Hair**

I dream too much, but if I dream too much I only dream to touch your heart again **I Dream Too Much**

I dreamed about a reefer five feet long, a might immense, but not too strong **The Viper's Drag**

I dreamed that I was Queen of France, and at a royal palace dance **I Dreamed**

I dreamt I dwelt in marble halls, With vassals and serfs at my side **I Dreamt I Dwelt in Marble Halls**

I drove a herd of cattle down From old Nebraska way **Sioux City Sue**

I fall in love with you ev'ry day. The thrill is always new ev'ry day **I Fall in Love with You Every Day**

I feel, I feel, I feel, I feel like a morning star **Shew (Shoo) Fly, Don't Bother Me**

I feel pretty, oh, so pretty I feel pretty and witty and bright! **I Feel Pretty**

I fell in love last night At a moonlight masquerade **Moonlight Masquerade**

I fell in love with you first time I looked into them there eyes **Them There Eyes**

I fetch his slippers, Fill up the pipe he smokes **Boy! What Love Has Done to Me!**

I forgive you all you've done to hurt me tho you did desert me **I Forgive You**

I found my thrill on Blueberry Hill, On Blueberry Hill when I found you **Blueberry Hill**

I gave my heart to you in old Lisbon that night **Lisbon Antigua**, or, **In Old Lisbon**

I gave my love a cherry that has no stone, I gave my love a chicken that has no bone **I Gave My Love a Cherry**, or, **The Riddle Song**

I get high when I see you go by, my oh my **It's Only Love**

I get too hungry For dinner at eight **The Lady Is a Tramp**

I give her all my love, That's all I do **And I Love Her**

I give in to you! Why do I? I'm as easy as pie **Why Do I**

I give to you and you give to me True love, true love **True Love**

I give you my word I'll never love again, I give you my word this is my first and last romance **I Give You My Word**

I got a shoe, you got a shoe, All God's chillun got shoes **I Got (a Robe) Shoes**, or, **All God's Chillun Got Shoes**

I got rhythm, I got music, I got my man Who could ask for anything more? **I Got Rhythm**

I got spurs that jingle jangle jingle, As I go ridin' merrily along **Jingle Jangle Jingle**

I got to Kansas City on a Frid'y **Kansas City**

I grieve my Lord From day to day I left de straight And narrow way **I Ain't Gonna Grieve My Lord No More**

I guess I'll get the papers and go home. Like I've been doing ever since we've been apart **I Guess I'll Get the Papers and Go Home**

I had a girl, Donna was her name **Donna**

I had the craziest dream last night, yes I did; I never dreamt it could be **I Had the Craziest Dream**

I have a true confession to make to you alone **True Confession**

I have been a rover, I have walked alone **Love's Been Good to Me**

I have been just like a weary river that keeps winding endlessly **Weary River**

I have dreamed thee too long, Never seen thee or touched thee **Dulcinea**

I have eyes for you to give you dirty looks **Ev'rything I've Got (Belongs to You)**

I have mixed emotions when it comes to loving you **Mixed Emotions**

I have often walked down this street before **On the Street Where You Live**

I hear a bird, Londonderry bird **How Are Things in Glocca Morra**

I hear a voice, It's Angelina. I see a face, It's Angelina **Angelina**

I hear most when I look at you, A beautiful theme of ev'ry dream I ever knew **The Song Is You**

I hear music, I hear melodies, Sparkling song of love tingle from your touch **I Hear Music**

I hear music Mighty fine music, The murmur of a morning breeze up there **I Hear Music**

I hear the cottonwoods whisp'rin' above **Tammy**

I hear the sound of music, Your fav'rite kind of music **My Heart Reminds Me**, or, **And That Reminds Me**

I heard the bells on Christmas Day Their old familiar carols play **I Heard the Bells on Christmas Day**

I just came from Mexico, Where they all drink Texico **There's a Great Day Coming, Mañana**

I just want the right to love you all of my life **All Of My Life**

I knew a man Bojangles and he danced for you, in worn out shoes **Mister Bo Jangles (Bojangles)**

I knew it from the start Love would play a part **That Certain Feeling**

I know a certain feller by the name of Andy Gooch **Shut the Door (They're Comin' Through the Window)**

I know a little bit about a lot of things **I Don't Know Enough About You**

I know a merry place Far from intrusion. It's just the very place For your seclusion **Here in My Arms**

I know a place where dreams are born, and time is never planned **Never Never Land**

I know an angel on the East side of heaven Who lives in a third story room   **East Side of Heaven**

I know an island, my dear, An island to where lovers steer   **Isle d'Amour (Isle of Love)**

I know I'm only dreaming, Blow the smoke away   **Blow the Smoke Away**

I know what it means to be lost in the dark   **I Know**

I know you don't know what I'm going through   **Hurts So Bad**

I laughed at sweethearts I met at school   **My Heart Stood Still**

I laughed the day I saw you leave   **(What Can I Say, Dear) After I Say I'm Sorry**

I left her by the river Sainte Marie We pledged our love until eternity   **By the River Sainte Marie**

I left my heart in San Francisco. High on a hill, it calls to me   **I Left My Heart in San Francisco**

I like music old or new   **Music Makes Me**

I likes to do what takes my fancy   **What Takes My Fancy**

I live for the good of my nation, and my sons are all growing low   **Old Rosin the Beau**

I look to you all See the love there that's sleeping   **While My Guitar Gently Weeps**

I look at you and suddenly, something in your eyes I see   **Old Devil Moon**

I love Bosco, it's rich and choc'laty   **I Love Bosco**

I love her in the morning And I love her at night   **Last Night on the Back Porch—I Loved Her Best of All**

I love I love I love my calendar girl Yeah sweet calendar girl   **Calendar Girl**

I love my baby, My baby loves me Don't know nobody As happy as we   **I Love My Baby—My Baby Loves Me**

I love Paris in the springtime, I love Paris in the fall   **I Love Paris**

I love the looks of you, the lure of you   **All of You**

I love the mornin' glories growin' and the breezes softly blowin'   **Atlanta, Ga.**

I love those dear hearts and gentle people Who live in my home town   **Dear Hearts and Gentle People**

I love to do my work, Never complain   **Ev'ry Sunday Afternoon**

I love to go a-wandering, Along the mountain track   **The Happy Wanderer**

I love to rhyme, Mountaineers love to climb   **I Love To Rhyme**

I love to tell the story Of unseen things above   **I Love to Tell the Story**

I love you as I never lov'd before   **When You Were Sweet Sixteen**

"I love you" Hums the April breeze "I love you" echo the hills   **I Love You**

I love you, I love you, is all that I can say   **I Love You (Je t'aime)**

I love you so much it hurts me, Darlin' that's why I'm so blue   **I Love You So Much It Hurts**

I love you that's what my heart is saying   **Cuban Love Song**

I love you, there's nothing to hide It's better than burning inside   **There! I've Said It Again**

I love you this morning, My heart sings, What a day!   **I Love You This Morning**

I love you, Samantha, and my love will never die   **I Love You Samantha**

I love your funny face, Your sunny, funny face   **Funny Face**

I love your lovin' arms, They hold a world of charms   **My Honey's Lovin' Arms**

I loved you once in silence And mis'ry was all I knew   **I Loved You Once in Silence**

I made up things to say on my way to you   **I've Told Every Little Star**

I make up things to say on my way to you   **I've Told Ev'ry Little Star**

I married many men, a ton of them, because I was untrue to none of them   **To Keep My Love Alive**

I met you in a garden in an old Kentucky town   **When You Wore a Tulip and I Wore a Big Red Rose**

I miss the thrill of grammar school romances   **Homesick— That's All**

I miss you since you went away, dear   **Miss You**

I need someone to love me Need somebody to carry me home to San Francisco   **Hong Kong Blues**

I need to laugh and when the sun is out I've got something I can blab about   **Good Day Sunshine**

I need your love so badly, I love you, oh, so madly   **I Don't Stand a Ghost of a Chance with You**

I never cared much for moonlit skies, I never wink back at fireflies   **I'm Beginning To See the Light**

I never had a mammy a mammy to rock me to sleep   **I Never Had a Mammy**

I never has seen snow, all the same I know, snow ain't so beautiful   **I Never Has Seen Snow**

I never knew I could love anybody, Honey, like I'm loving you; I couldn't realize what a pair of eyes And a baby smile could do   **I Never Knew I Could Love Anybody Like I'm Loving You**

I never knew that roses grew, Of if skies were blue or gray   **I Never Knew (That Roses Grew)**

I never meant to hurt you, I'm not that way at all   **I Never Meant To Hurt You**

I offer you congratulations I really mean it from my heart   **Congratulations**

I often wonder why you came to me, Brought such a flame to me then let it die   **If I Love Again**

I once had a girl, or should I say she once had me   **Norwegian Wood**

I peeked in to say goodnight And then I heard my child in pray'r   **Scarlet Ribbons (For Her Hair)**

I ran all the way home Just to say I'm sorry   **Sorry (I Ran All the Way Home)**

I ran around with my own little crowd   **I Didn't Know About You**

I read the news today oh boy about a lucky man who made the grade   **A Day in the Life**

I realize the way your eyes deceived me   **Paper Roses**

I really need this job. Please, God, I need this job   **I Hope I Get It**

I really want to see you, really want to be with you   **My Sweet Lord**

I remember all my life raining down as cold as ice   **Mandy**

I remember the bliss Of that wonderful kiss   **Do Do Do**

I remember you, You're the one who made my dreams come true   **I Remember You**

I ride an old Paint, I lead an old Dan, I'm goin' to Montan' for to throw the hoolihan   **Goodbye Ol' Paint,** or, **I Ride an Old Paint,** or, **I'm a-Leavin' Cheyenne**

I rode by a house with the windows lighted up Lookin' bright than a Christmas tree   **Ev'rybody's Got a Home But Me**

I said "No" He said "Please" I said "No" He said "Please"   **I Said No**

I saw a man with his head bowed low His heart had no place to go   **There But For You Go I**

I saw a youth and maiden on a lonely city street   **Take Back Your Gold**

I saw buddies true, marching two by two   **My Dream of the Big Parade**

I saw stars I heard a birdie sing so sweet, so sweet   **I Saw Stars**

I saw the harbor lights They only told me we were parting   **Harbor Lights**

I saw the old homestead and faces I love   **The Miner's Dream of Home**

I saw you last night and got that old feeling   **That Old Feelin**

I saw you standing in the sun and you were something to see   **That's for Me**

I see a bad moon rising; I see trouble on the way   **Bad Moon Rising**

I see stars in your eyes When my lips beg your lips to surrender   **Stars in Your Eyes**

I shall marry the miller's son, Pin my hat on a nice piece of property   **The Miller's Son**

I should care, I should go around weeping   **I Should Care**

I shouldn't mind if you find someone new But I do   **But I Do—You Know I Do**

I sit alone in the golden daylight, But all I see is a silver sky   **All Through the Day**

I stand at your gate and the song that I sing is of moonlight   **Moonlight Serenade**

I started out to go to Cuba, Soon I was at Miami Beach   **Miami Beach Rumba**

I still get jealous when they look at you. I may not show it, but I do   **I Still Get Jealous**

I tell you ev'ry street's a boulevard in old New York   **Ev'ry Street's a Boulevard in Old New York**

I think I'm gonna be sad, I think it's today, Yeh!   **Ticket To Ride**

I think of you with ev'ry breath I take and ev'ry breath becomes a sigh   **With Every Breath I Take**

I thought I'd found the man of my dreams   **Can't We Be Friends**

I thought love's game was over lady luck had gone away   **Taking a Chance on Love**

I told the witch doctor I was in love with you   **Witch Doctor**

I told this heart of mine Our love could never be   **My Heart Has a Mind of Its Own**

I took each word he said as gospel truth, The way a silly little child would   **Can't We Be Friends**

I took my harp to a party But nobody asked me to play   **I Took My Harp to a Party**

I took one look at you, That's all I meant to do   **My Heart Stood Still**

I touch your hand And my arms grow strong   **Younger Than Springtime**

I used to be the apple of your eye   **You Turned the Tables on Me**

I used to play around with hearts that hastened at my call   **Poor Little Fool**

I used to visit all the very gay places   **Lush Life**

I used to walk with you along the avenue   **Somewhere Along the Way**

I walk under ladders, Number thirteen doesn't scare me   **Ridin' on the Moon**

I walked along the streets of Hong King town, up and down   **Love Is a Many-Splendored Thing**

I walked away and said "goodbye", I was hasty, wasn't I?   **I'll Never Say "Never Again" Again**

I wandered today to the hill, Maggie   **When You and I Were Young, Maggie**

I wanna be around, to pick up the pieces, when somebody breaks your heart   **I Wanna Be Around**

I wanna get married, I wanna get spliced I long to be knotted   **I Wanna Get Married**

I want to be a good little wife in the good old fashioned way   **An Old-Fashioned Wife**

I want to be happy, but I won't be happy till I make you happy, too   **I Want To Be Happy**

I want to be like that gal on the river Who sang her songs to the ships passing by   **Lorelei**

I want to be no one but me   **Nobody Else But Me**

I want to go home to old Topeka and cry "Eureka, I'm here to stay!"   **I Want To Go Home**

I want to tell you all a story 'bout a Harper Valley widowed wife   **Harper Valley P.T.A.**

I was a stranger in the city, Out of town where the people I knew   **A Foggy Day**

I was all right for awhile, I could smile for awhile   **Cryin'**

I was alone, I took a ride, I didn't know what I would find there   **Got To Get You into My Life**

I was born to love, and my poor mother worked the mines   **Stoney End**

I was born in Alabama, My master's name was Meal **Miss Lucy Neale**

I was born on a farm out in I-o-way **Goofus**

I was created for one man alone; It wasn't easy to find **Don't Ever Leave Me**

I was doing all right Nothing but rainbows in my sky **I Was Doing All Right**

I was justified when I was five raisin' cane I spit in your eye **The Bitch is Back**

I was layin' 'round town, just spendin' my time **Strawberry Roan**

I was never able to recite a fable That would make the party bright **You Were Never Lovelier**

I was standing on the corner when I heard my bulldog bark **Stagger Lee**

I was up with the lark this morning, I love the dawn of the day **Up with the Lark**

I watch the love parade, gaily going by **I Watch the Love Parade**

I went down to the St. James Infirmary; To see my baby there **St. James Infirmary**

I went out of my way to get into a lot of trouble **I Went Out of My Way**

I went strolling down by the river, feeling very sad inside **The Little White Cloud That Cried**

I went to de creek I couldn't git across **Clare De Kitchen,** or, **De Kentucky Screamer**

I will gather stars out of the blue for you, for you **For You**

I will shout, And I'll dance, And I'll wake up early in de morn **Angel Gabriel**

I will sing you a song, And it won't be very long **The Streets of Cairo**

I wish I knew someone like you could love me **I Wish I Knew**

I wish I was in de land ob cotton, Old times dar am not forgotten **(I Wish I Was in) Dixie,** or, **Dixie's Land**

I wished on the moon for something I never knew **I Wished on the Moon**

I woke up singing this morning got out of the right side of bed **It's a Most Unusual Day**

I won't dance! Don't ask me **I Won't Dance**

I won't grow up. I don't want to go to school **I Won't Grow Up**

I won't kiss your hand, Madam, Crazy for you though I am **My Romance**

I wonder what he'll think of me! I guess he'll call me ''The old man!'' **Soliloquy**

I wonder what the King is doing tonight? What merriment is the King pursuing tonight? **I Wonder What the King Is Doing Tonight**

I wonder who's kissing her now, Wonder who's teaching her how **I Wonder Who's Kissing Her Now**

I work at the Palace Ballroom, But, gee, that palace is cheap **Ten Cents a Dance**

I would be true, for there are those who trust me **I Would Be True**

I would fall in love with the proper stranger If I heard the bells and the banjos ring **Love with the Proper Stranger**

I'd do anything for you, dear, anything **I'd Do Anything**

I'd kiss you if I dared, I want to but I'm scared **Alone Too Long**

I'd like to swim in a clear blue stream Where the water is icy cold **Much More**

I'd rather be a sparrow than a snail. Yes I would. If I could, I surely would **El Condor Pasa (If I Could)**

I'd rather be right than influential, I'd rather be right than wealthy and wise **I'd Rather Be Right**

I'd work for you, I'd slave for you, I'd be a beggar or a knave for you **(It Will Have To Do) Until the Real Thing Comes Along**

I'll be down to get you in a taxi, Honey **The Darktown Strutters' Ball**

I'll be so happy to keep his dinner warm while he goes onward **Happy To Keep His Dinner Warm**

I'll be yours, My world may be lonely but, I'll await your return **I'll Be Yours (J'Attendrai)**

I'll build a stairway to Paradise With a new step ev'ry day **I'll Build a Stairway to Paradise**

I'll buy you a diamond ring my friend if it makes you feel alright **Can't Buy Me Love**

I'll close my eyes to ev'ryone else if you'll open your heart to me **I'll Close My Eyes**

I'll go my way by myself This is the end of romance **By Myself**

I'll know when my love comes along; I'll know then and there **I'll Know**

I'll never forget the moment we kissed the night or the hayride **Magic Moments**

I'll never love again if you forget me My heart won't let me love some one new **I'll Never Love Again (La Borrachita)**

I'll never smile again Until I smile at you **I'll Never Smile Again**

I'll pretend I'm free from sorrow **There'll Be No Teardrops Tonight**

I'll sing thee songs of Araby, And tales of fair Cashmere **I'll Sing Thee Songs of Araby**

I'll sing you a song, a good song of the sea To me way, ay, blow the man down **Blow (Knock) the Man Down**

I'll spend my days chasing after sunshine **Following the Sun Around**

I'll take romance, While my heart is young and eager to fly **I'll Take Romance**

I'll take you home again, Kathleen, Across the ocean wild and wide **I'll Take You Home Again Kathleen**

I'll try to explain to friends dear, The Reason we two are apart **What Will I Tell My Heart**

I'll walk alone because, to tell you the truth, I'll be lonely **I'll Walk Alone**

I'm a bitch I'm a bitch oh the bitch is back Stone cold sober as a matter of fact **The Bitch Is Back**

I'm a Ding Dong Daddy from Dumas, You ought to see me do my stuff **I'm a Ding Dong Daddy from Dumas**

I'm a rovin' cowboy, far away from home **Carry Me Back to the Lone Prairie**

I'm a sentimental sap, that's all **You Took Advantage of Me**

I'm a travelin' man And I've made a lot of stops All over the world **Travelin' Man**

I'm a Yankee Doodle Dandy, A Yankee Doodle, do or die **(I Am) The Yankee Doodle Boy**

I'm always chasing rainbows, Watching clouds drifting by **I'm Always Chasing Rainbows**

I'm an old cowhand from the Rio Grande But my legs ain't bowed and my cheeks ain't tanned **I'm an Old Cowhand (from the Rio Grande)**

I'm as corny as Kansas in August, I'm as normal as blueberry pie **I'm in Love with a Wonderful Guy**

I'm as restless as a willow in a windstorm **It Might As Well Be Spring**

I'm bidin' my time; 'Cause that's the kinda guy I'm **Bidin' My Time**

I'm blue ev'ry Monday, Thinking over Sunday **Sunday**

I'm bringing you kisses from over the sea **Hello, Aloha! How Are You?**

I'm called little Buttercup, Dear little Buttercup, Though I could never tell why **I'm Called Little Buttercup**

I'm Chiquita Banana and I've come to say, I come from little island down equator way **(I'm) Chiquita Banana**

I'm coming back to you, my Hula Lou, Beside the sea at Waikiki **Yaaka Hula Hickey Dula**

I'm comin' home, I've done my time **Tie a Yellow Ribbon Round the Old Oak Tree**

I'm coming, I'm coming, for my heart is bending low **Old Black Joe**

I'm coming Virginia I'm coming to stay Don't hold it agin' me for runnin' away **I'm Comin' Virginia**

I'm dancing with my honey, My honey's close to me **I Haven't Got a Worry in the World**

I'm dreaming now of Hallie, Sweet Hallie, sweet Hallie **Listen to the Mocking Bird**

I'm dreaming of a white Christmas, Just like the ones I used to know **White Christmas**

I'm fixing a hole where the rain gets in and stops my mind from wandering **Fixing a Hole**

I'm flying high, but I've got a feeling I'm falling, falling for nobody else but you **I've Got a Feeling I'm Falling**

I'm flying. Look at me way up high, suddenly here am I, I'm flying **I'm Flying**

I'm getting married in the morning Ding! dong! the bells are gonna chime **Get Me to the Church on Time**

I'm glad I waited for you But then what else could I do? **I'm Glad I Waited for You**

I'm goin' to buy a paper doll that I can call my own **Paper Doll**

I'm goin' to Tishomingo, because I'm sad today, I wish to linger, way down old Dixie way **Tishomingo Blues**

I'm gonna be a shady lady bird I've got an awful lot to learn **Shady Lady Bird**

I'm gonna catch the midnight train 'Cause all my sins are taken away **(O) Hand Me Down My Walking Cane**

I'm gonna love you Like nobody's loved you, Come rain or come shine **Come Rain or Come Shine**

I'm gonna wait till the midnight hour, That's when my love comes tumbling down **In the Midnight Hour**

I'm gwine away by the light of the moon, Want all the children for to follow me **In the Morning by the Bright Light**

I'm happy on the prairie all the day singing lay-lee-o-lay **The Funny Old Hills**

I'm in love with a dolly named Glendora **Glendora**

I'm in love with a sweet little girlie, only one **Just One Girl**

I'm in love with you Honey, Say you love me too **Honey**

I'm in the seventh heaven! It's easy to guess My baby said "Yes!" **Seventh Heaven**

I'm jist a girl who cain't say no, I'm in a turrible fix **I Cain't Say No**

I'm just a Broadway Baby, walking off my tired feet **Broadway Baby**

I'm just a poor, wayfaring stranger trav'ling through this world of woe **Wayfarin' Stranger**

I'm just a wild rose, Not a prim and mild rose **Wild Rose**

I'm just a woman, a lonely woman waitin' on the weary shore **Am I Blue**

I'm just breezin' along with the breeze Trailin' the rails roamin' the seas **Breezin' Along with the Breeze**

I'm just like left over "K" rations Excess war commodity **Little Surplus Me,** or, **Surplus Blues**

I'm leavin' it all up to you, You decide what you're gonna do **I'm Leaving It All Up to You**

I'm looking for that lost barber shop chord—Where can it be? **That Lost Barbershop Chord**

I'm looking rather seedy now while holding down my claim **Little Old Sod Shanty**

I'm looking through you, where did you go? I thought I knew you, what did I know? **I'm Looking Through You**

I'm making up for all the years that I waited, I'm compensated at last **Soon**

I'm Mister Blue, when you say you love me, Then prove it by goin' out on the sly **Mister Blue**

I'm nobody's baby I wonder why, Each night and day I pray the Lord up above **I'm Nobody's Baby**

I'm not much to look at, nothin' to see **(I Got a Woman Crazy for Me) She's Funny That Way**

I'm not scared of dyin', and I don't really care **And When I Die**

I'm old fashioned, I love the moonlight, I love the old fashioned things **I'm Old Fashioned**

I'm older and wiser, I've grown up today **Older and Wiser**

I'm on a see-saw. You throw me up and you throw me down **I'm on a See-Saw**

I'm on the outside lookin' in, And I wanna be, and I wanna be back on the inside with you   **On the Outside Looking In**

I'm on the road to anywhere Let me travel on!   **Song of the Open Road**

I'm reaching for the moon Just reaching for the moon   **Reaching for the Moon**

I'm saving my money to buy you a rainbow   **Rainbow**

I'm sentimental, so I walk in the rain   **Why Try to Change Me Now**

I'm so afraid of night, 'cause I'm too romantic   **Too Romantic**

I'm so lonely and blue, when I'm without you   **Without You**

I'm so young and you're so old. This my darling I've been told   **Diana**

I'm sorry dear so sorry, dear, I'm sorry I made you cry   **I'm Sorry I Made You Cry**

I'm sorry, so sorry That I was such a fool   **I'm Sorry**

I'm the greatest star. I am by far, But no one knows it   **I'm the Greatest Star**

I'm the most happy fella In the whole Napa Valley   **The Most Happy Fella**

I'm the Sheik of Araby, Your love belongs to me   **The Sheik of Araby**

I'm through with moanin' in the mornin', moonin' in the evenin'   **Moanin' in the Mornin'**

I'm thru with love, I'll never fall again, Said "Adieu" to love   **I'm Through with Love**

I'm walking on the air, dear, For life is fair, dear, to lovers   **Why Do I Love You**

I'm walkin', yes indeed, and I'm talkin' 'bout you and me   **I'm Walkin'**

I'm watchin' Sis go pit-a-pat   **I Can Do That**

I'm wild again, Beguiled again, A simpering, whimpering child again   **Bewitched, Bothered and Bewildered**

I'm wishing for the one I love to find me today   **I'm Wishing**

I'm world weary, world weary, Living in a great big town   **World Weary**

I'm wrackin' my brain to think of a name to give to this tune so Frankie can croon   **Opus (Number) One**

I'm yours, heart and soul I am yours Can't you see it in my eyes   **I'm Yours**

I'se got a gal an' you got none, Li'l Liza Jane   **Li'l Liza Jane**

I've an awf'lly funny feelin' that this thought that's been a-stealin'   **You've Changed**

I've been away from you a long time I never thought I'd miss you so   **Swanee**

I've been blue all day My man's gone away   **Gulf Coast Blues**

I've been married and married, and often I've sighed   **To Keep My Love Alive**

I've come again to see you, I'll sing another song   **Take Your Time, Miss Lucy**

I've flown around the world in a plane; I've settled revolutions in Spain   **I Can't Get Started (with You)**

I've found a new baby, I've found a new girl   **I Found a New Baby**

I've got a crush on you, Sweetie Pie. All the day and nighttime hear me sigh   **I've Got a Crush on You**

I've got a dog, and I've got a cat   **Gee, But I'd Like to Make You Happy**

I've got a mule, her name is Sal, Fifteen miles on the Erie Canal   **(Fifteen Miles [Years] on the) Erie Canal (Low Bridge! Everybody Down)**

I've got five dollars; I'm in good condition; And I've got ambition   **I've Got Five Dollars**

I've got me ten fine toes to wiggle in the sand   **Pass Me By**

I've got my eyes on you, So best beware where you roam   **I've Got My Eyes on You**

I've got ten little fingers, and ten little toes, Down in Tennessee, Waiting there for me   **Ten Little Fingers and Ten Little Toes—Down In Tennessee**

I've got the Dallas Blues and the Main Street heart disease   **Dallas Blues**

I've got the world on a string, sittin' on a rainbow, Got the string around my finger   **I've Got the World on a String**

I've got the You-don't-know-the-half-of-it-dearie blues!   **The Half of It, Dearie, Blues**

I've got those "God, Why don't you love me, oh you do I'll see you later" blues   **The God-Why-Don't-You-Love-Me Blues**

I've got to stand tall You know a man can't crawl   **Cathy's Clown**

I've got you under my skin, I've got you deep in the heart of me   **I've Got You Under My Skin**

I've got you, you've got me, Who cares how rough the road may be   **On the Bumpy Road to Love**

I've got your number, I know you inside out   **I've Got Your Number**

I've gotta crow! I'm just the cleverest fellow 'twas ever my fortune to know   **I've Gotta Crow**

I've grown accustomed to her face, She almost makes the day begin   **I've Grown Accustomed to Her Face**

I've had a million dreams that never came true   **You Stepped Out of a Dream**

I've interviewed Pablo Picasso And a countess named de Frasso   **Zip**

I've just got here, thro' Paris, from the sunny southern shore   **The Man That (Who) Broke the Bank at Monte Carlo**

I've lost all my love for you The one bit of joy I knew   **I've Lost All My Love for You**

I've never wanted wealth untold; my life has one design   **Band of Gold**

I've no proof when people say you're more or less aloof   **You're Sensational**

I've often heard my daddy speak of Ireland's lakes and dells   **Ireland Must Be Heaven, for My Mother Came from There**

I've seen the lights of gay Broadway, Old Market Street down by the Frisco Bay   **Beale Street Blues**

I've thrown away my toys, even my drum and trains   **On the Good Ship Lollipop**

I've told ev'ry little star, Just how sweet I think you are, why haven't I told you? **I've Told Every Little Star**

I've written you a song, A beautiful routine (I hope you like it) **Blah, Blah, Blah**

Ice cream, cold cream, benzine, gasoline **Who Threw the Overalls in Mrs. Murphy's Chowder**

If a picture paints a thousand words, then why can't I paint you? **If**

If buttercups buzz'd after the bee, if boats were on land, churches on sea **The World Turned Upside Down, or, Derry Down**

If ever I would leave you It wouldn't be in summer **If Ever I Would Leave You**

If ever the devil was born without a pair of horns it was you **Jezebel**

If her eyes are blue as skies, That's Peggy O'Neil **Peggy O'Neil**

If I am fancy free, And love to wander **Gypsy in My Soul**

If I could make a wish I think I'd pass **The Air That I Breathe**

If I could stick my pen in my heart, I would spill it all over the stage **It's Only Rock 'n' Roll (But I Like It)**

If I expected love when first we kissed **Blame It on My Youth**

If I fell in love with you would you promise to be true **If I Fell**

If I had a girl like you, I wouldn't care if the whole world knew **If I Had a Girl Like You**

If I had a nickel, I know what I would do **That's How Much I Love You**

If I had a talking picture of you-oo, I would run it ev'ry time I felt blue-oo **If I Had a Talking Picture of You**

If I had it, you could have it, but honey, I ain't got it **Silver Dollar (Down and Out)**

If I lose my head beg your pardon For things that I've said **Beg Your Pardon**

If I love again, I'll find other charms; But I'll make believe, You are in my arms **If I Love Again**

If I loved you, time and again I would try to say All I'd want you to know **If I Loved You**

If I ruled the world ev'ry day would be the first day of spring **If I Ruled the World**

If I should lose you the stars would fall from the sky **If I Should Lose You**

If I should suddenly start to sing Or stand on my head or anything **Things Are Looking Up**

If I should take a notion to jump into the ocean **'Tain't Nobody's Business If I Do**

If I told a lie, If I made you cry **I Apologize**

If I were a little bird, I'd fly from tree to tree **Careless Love**

If I were hang'd on the highest hill **Mother o' Mine**

If I'm lucky you will tell me that you care that we'll never be apart **If I'm Lucky**

If it's true that love affairs are all arranged in Heaven **Looking for a Boy**

If little, little David hadn't grabbed that stone A-lyin' there on the ground **Good Timin'**

If music is no longer lovely, If laughter is no longer lilting **I Don't Want to Know**

If my friends should ask for me, Here at home is where I'll be **Breaking in a Brand New Broken Heart**

If the nightingales could sing like you They'd sing much sweeter than they do **You Brought a New Kind of Love to Me**

If there is a Cinderella, looking for a steady fella **A Blues Serenade**

If there's a gleam in her eye each time she straightens your tie **The Lady's in Love with You**

If there's something to be done and it's got you on the run **Let Your Fingers Do the Walking**

If they asked me I could write a book **I Could Write a Book**

If, Yankees, you would have a song, a deuced nation fine one **Yankee Doodle**

If you ain't wrong you're right If you ain't dark it's light **Gotta Be This or That**

If you believe, within your heart you'll know **Believe in Yourself**

If you can hear me calling, dear, Come to me **Come to Me**

If you could see her thru my eyes, You wouldn't wonder at all **If You Could See Her**

If you ever go to Trinidad, They make you feel so very glad **Rum and Coca-Cola**

If you ever plan to motor west Travel my way, take the highway that's the best **(Get Your Kicks on) Route 66**

If you hear a song in blue like a flower crying for the dew **Prelude to a Kiss**

If you lak-a-me, lak I lak-a-you, And we lak-a both the same **Under the Bamboo Tree**

If you like-a Ukulele Lady, Ukulele Lady like-a you **Ukulele Lady**

If you look in the heart in the heart of a fool, You will see bitter tears bitter tears **The Heart of a Fool**

If you miss the train I'm on, you will know that I am gone **Five Hundred Miles, or, Railroader's Lament**

If you promise me a rose, I go out and buy a pot **Promise Me a Rose**

If you search for love that's true, then you must find La Strada del Amore **La Strade Del' Amore (The Street of Love)**

If you see me walkin' down the street and I start to cry each time we meet **Walk On By**

If you want a suit that's nifty don't pay twenty-seven fifty **I Can Get It for You Wholesale**

If you want to go down to Mexico, Go, my child **God's Green World**

If you want toys like other little boys In your neighborhood **Don't Wait 'Til the Night Before Christmas**

If you were mine I could be a ruler of kings **If You Were Mine**

If you were only mine I know the sun would shine for me **If You Were Only Mine**

If your world falls flat on its face today **Each Tomorrow Morning**

If you're ever in a jam, Here I am **Friendship**

If you're fond of sand dunes and salty air **Old Cape Cod**

If you're gonna give me good kisses like that   **A Rockin' Good Way (To Mess Around and Fall in Love)**

If you're in love you'll waltz, To waltz is but a dream For there's a simple charm   **If You're in Love You'll Waltz**

If you're romantic, chum Pack up your duds and come to Acapulco   **In Acapulco**

If you're smart do something foolish just for once!   **Just for Once**

If you've been in Havana You have heard a dreamy tune   **Siboney**

If you've found another guy who satisfies you more than I do   **Run to Him**

If you've got it, You don't need it   **The Money Song**

Imagination is funny, it makes a cloudy day sunny   **Imagination**

Imagine me with my head on your shoulder   **I'll Buy That Dream**

In a cavern, in a canyon, excavating for a mine   **(Oh, My Darling) Clementine**

In a dinky honky tonky village in Texas   **Beat Me, Daddy, Eight to the Bar**

In a little Spanish town, 'Twas on a night like this, Stars were peek-a-booing down   **In a Little Spanish Town**

In a mountain greenery, Where God paints the scenery   **Mountain Greenery**

In a perfect world, I would wave my hand, and ev'ry one would understand   **Billy**

In a sentimental mood I can see the stars come thru my room   **In a Sentimental Mood**

In Alabam' at the Muscles Shoals Dam, I saw the great John Henry   **The John Henry Blues**

In Cuba, each merry maid wakes up with this serenade   **The Peanut Vendor**

In dulci jubilo Now sing with hearts aglow!   **In Dulci Jubilo**

In Egern on the Tegern See where we have our home, We watch the sunset fade away   **In Egern on the Tegern See**

In eighteen and fourteen we took a little trip   **The Battle of New Orleans**

In every job that must be done There is an element of fun   **A Spoonful of Sugar**

In good King Charles's golden days   **Country Gardens, or, Vicar of Bray**

In good old Colony times When we were under the king   **Old Colony Times**

In heavenly love abiding, No change my heart shall fear   **In Heavenly Love Abiding**

In Lim'rick city he was brought up, And Dublin was his station   **Barbry (Barbara) Allen**

In May of Nineteen Forty-one, the war had just begun   **Sink the Bismarck**

In my little red book, I see somehow all the girls that I knew   **In My Little Red Book**

In my solitude you haunt me With reveries of days gone by   **Solitude**

In my sweet little Alice Blue Gown, When I first wandered down in to town   **(In My Sweet Little) Alice Blue Gown**

In our schooldays, merry schooldays, We were happy girls and boys   **It's Delightful To Be Married**

In Penny Lane there is a barber showing photographs   **Penny Lane**

In Scarlet town where I was born, there was a fair maid dwellin'   **Barbry (Barbara) Allen**

In Sloppy Joe's, in Havana I lingered quenching my thirst   **Mama Inez**

In some Cuban town you stop watching an old maker of shawls   **My Shawl**

In some secluded rendezvous, That overlooks the Avenue   **Cocktails for Two**

In Spain they say "Si, Si"; In France you'll hear "Wee, Wee"   **Say "Si Si"**

In sunny Roseland, where summer breezes are playing   **Rose Room**

In that dear little town in the ould County Down, It will linger way down in my heart   **Little Town in the Ould County Down**

In the evening by the moonlight, you can hear those darkies singing   **In the Evening by the Moonlight**

In the evening when I sit alone a-dreaming   **(You're the Flower of My Heart) Sweet Adeline**

In the garden of tomorrow, Will the roses be more fair?   **In the Garden of Tomorrow**

In the gloaming, O my darling! When the lights are dim and low   **In the Gloaming**

In the movie plays of now-a-days, a romance always must begin in June   **A Cup of Coffee, a Sandwich and You**

In the prison cell I sit, Thinking, mother dear, of you   **Tramp, Tramp, Tramp**

In the region where the roses always bloom   **Ida, Sweet as Apple Cider**

In the shadows, let me come and sing to you   **Shadow Waltz**

In the sky the bright stars glittered, on the bank the pale moon shone   **When I Saw Sweet Nellie Home, or, I Was Seeing Nellie Home, or, Aunt Dinah's Quilting Party**

In the spring a young man's fancy lightly turns to love   **A Young Man's Fancy**

In the spring when the feeling was chronic And my caution was leaving you flat   **You Took Advantage of Me**

In the still of the night, As I gaze from my window   **In the Still of the Night**

In the town where I was born lived a man who sailed to sea   **Yellow Submarine**

In Shadowland I feel your welcome hand In dreamy shadowland You're by my side   **In Shadowland**

In the Valley Valparaiso looking at the lonely sunset   **Valley Valparaiso**

In this world of ordinary people   **I'm Glad There Is You**

In your heart, my sweet white dove, Let me build my only throne   **The White Dove**

Inchworm, inchworm, measuring the marigolds   **Inchworm**

Indiana moon, I miss you Indiana moon I'm blue **Indiana Moon**

Into each life some rain must fall, But too much is fallin' in mine **Into Each Life Some Rain Must Fall**

Irene, a little bit of salt and sweetness, Irene, a dainty slip of rare completeness **Irene**

Is it a sin, Is it a crime Loving you, dear, Like I do? **Guilty**

Is it an earthquake or simply a shock? Is it the good turtle soup or merely the mock? **At Long Last Love**

Is it worth waiting for? If we live 'til eighty-four **Food Glorious Food**

Is that all there is? Is that all there is? If that's all there is my friends then let's keep dancing **Is That All There Is?**

Is there anybody going to listen to my story **Girl**

Is this the little girl I carried? Is this the little boy at play? **Sunrise Sunset**

Isn't it romantic? Music in the night, A dream that can be heard **Isn't It Romantic**

Isn't it rich? Are we a pair? Me here at last on the ground, you in mid-air **Send in the Clowns**

Isn't it warm, isn't it rosy, side by side by side **Side By Side By Side**

Isn't she cute! Isn't she sweet! She's gentle and mentally nearly complete **The Girl Friend**

Iss ve not der Supermen? Aryan pure Supermen? **Der Fuehrer's Face**

Is das nicht ein Schnitzelbank? Ja, das ist ein Schnitzelbank **Schnitzelbank**

It ain't necessarily so, De t'ings dat yo' li'ble To read in de Bible **It Ain't Necessarily So**

It ain't so much a question of not knowing whut to do **I Cain't Say No**

It came from nowhere the night that we met **Moon Song (That Wasn't Meant for Me)**

It came upon the midnight clear, That glorious song of old **It Came upon a Midnight Clear**

It is ten weary years since I left England's shore **The Miner's Dream of Home**

It isn't fair for you to taunt me, How can you make me care this way **It Isn't Fair**

It may be for years, and it may be forever **Kathleen Mavourneen**

It must have been moonglow, Way up in the blue **Moonglow**

It only takes a moment, For your eyes to meet and then **It Only Takes a Moment**

It seems we stood and talked like this before **Where or When**

It takes a woman, all powdered and pink, To joyously clean out the drain in the sink **It Takes a Woman**

It was a lucky April shower, It was the most convenient door **I Found a Million Dollar Baby (in a Five and Ten Cent Store)**

It was just a neighborhood dance **Oh What It Seemed To Be**

It was just another very uneventful ordinary morning, in old New York **Suddenly**

It was so beautiful, so wonderful, So gorgeous, so divine **It Was So Beautiful (and You Were Mine)**

It was twenty years ago today, that Sgt. Pepper taught the band to play **Sergeant Pepper's Lonely Hearts Club Band**

It wasn't love, but c'est la vie but that is life **C'est la Vie**

It's a beautiful day, ain't it? So exciting and gay, ain't it? **Call Me Mister**

It's a big holiday ev'rywhere, for the Jones family **F.D.R. Jones**

It's a funny thing, I look at you I get a thrill I never knew **Isn't It a Pity**

It's a grand night for singing! The moon is flying high **It's a Grand Night for Singing**

It's a lesson too late for the learning, made of sand **The Last Thing on My Mind**

It's a most unusual day Feel like throwing my worries away **It's a Most Unusual Day**

It's a new world I see A new world for me! **It's a New World**

It's a time for joy, a time for tears, a time we'll treasure thru the years **Graduation Day**

It's a very ancient saying, But a true and honest thought **Getting to Know You**

It's an old, old, old variation On the very oldest of themes **Words without Music**

It's been a hard day's night, And I've been working like a dog **A Hard Day's Night**

It's cherry pink and apple blossom white, When your true lover comes your way **Cherry Pink and Apple Blossom White**

It's Chesterfield you ought to buy, we kid you not, they satisfy **Sound Off**

It's cost me a lot, but there's one thing that I've got It's my man **My Man**

It's easy to say you love me, Easy to say you're true **Prove It by the Things You Do (It's Easy To Say)**

It's getting better all the time I used to get mad at my school **Getting Better**

It's got to be love, It couldn't be tonsillitis **It's Got To Be Love**

It's June in January because I'm in love **(It's) June in January**

It's knowing that your door is always open and your path is free to walk **Gentle on My Mind**

It's love at last but I can see this love cannot belong to me **Bad Timing**

It's nine o'clock on a Saturday, The regular crowd shuffles in **Piano Man**

It's not the pale moon that excites me, that thrills and delights me **The Nearness of You**

It's only human for anyone to want to be in love **In Love in Vain**

It's only love and that is all, why should I feel the way I do? **It's Only Love**

It's only me from over the sea, said Barnacle Bill, the Sailor **Barnacle Bill the Sailor**

It's a priest. Have a little priest. Is it really good? Sir, it's too good, At least   **A Little Priest**

It's quarter to three, There's no one in the place except you and me   **One for My Baby (and One More for the Road)**

It's somebody else's moon above, not mine   **Not Mine**

It's the big back yard of the city It's a great cool lawn with a tree   **The Big Back Yard**

It's the real thing, in the back of your mind   **It's the Real Thing. Coke**

It's the story of a very unfortunate Memphis man   **Hong Kong Blues**

It's the wrong time, and the wrong place   **It's All Right with Me**

It's three o'clock in the morning, We've danced the whole night thru   **Three O'Clock in the Morning**

It's very clear Our love is here to stay   **Our Love Is Here To Stay**

It's you in the sunrise. It's you in my cup   **It's You**

Ivy Rose Ivy Rose, I'm in love with you Cling to me like a vine   **Ivy Rose**

Ja, das ist die Liechtensteiner Polka mein Schatz!   **Liechtensteiner Polka**

Ja-Da, Ja-Da, Ja-Da, Ja-Da, Jing, Jing, Jing   **Ja-Da**

Jean, Jean, roses are red, All the leaves have gone green   **Jean**

Jenny made her mind up when she was three   **Saga of Jenny**

Jeremiah was a bullfrog, Was a good friend of mine   **Joy to the World**

Jerusalem the golden, With milk and honey blest!   **Jerusalem the Golden**

Jesus Christ, Jesus Christ, who are you? What have you sacrificed?   **Jesus Christ Superstar**

Jesus, Lover of my soul, Let me to Thy bosom fly   **Jesus, Lover of My Soul**

Jesus loves the little children, All the little children of the world   **Everything is Beautiful**

Jilted, I've been jilted, You found a new love   **Jilted**

Jim O'Shea was cast away Upon an Indian isle   **I've Got Rings on My Fingers,** or, **Mumbo Jumbo Jijjiboo J. O'Shea**

Jimmie crack corn and I don't care   **Jimmy Crack Corn,** or, **The Blue Tail Fly**

Jimmy kissed me in the springtime, Tommy kissed me in the fall   **Joey**

Joan of Arc, Joan of Arc, Do your eyes, from the skies, see the foe?   **Joan of Arc, They Are Calling You**

John Brown's body lies a mould'ring in the grave   **John Brown's Body**

Johnnie get your gun, get your gun, get your gun   **Over There**

Johnny Angel How I love him, He's got something that I can't resist   **Johnny Angel**

Johnny is a joker (He's a bird.) A very funny joker   **Bird Song**

(Johnny, you're too young) But I'm gonna get married (You're so smart) My name she'll carry   **I'm Gonna Get Married**

Johnson Flood Mississippi Mud Black Bottom I got 'em   **Johnson Rag**

Jojo was a man who thought he was a loner But he knew it couldn't last   **Get Back**

Jolly boating weather, And a hay-harvest breeze   **Carmen Etonense,** or, **Eton Boating Song**

Josephine please no lean on the bell, When you moosh please no poosh on the bell   **Josephine Please No Lean on the Bell**

Joshua fit de battle ob Jericho   **Joshua Fit (Fought) de Battle of Jericho**

Juba dis an' Juba dat Juba killed a yellow cat   **Juba Dance**

June is bustin' out all over! All over the meadow and the hill!   **June Is Bustin' Out All Over**

Jungle Drums, Through the black of night, Send your message to me   **Jungle Drums**

Just a gigolo, Ev'rywhere I go, People know the part I'm playing   **Just a Gigolo**

Just a kid named Joe What his second name is I don't know   **Just a Kid Named Joe**

Just a song at twilight, when the lights are low   **Love's Old Sweet Song**

Just a-wearyin' for you, All the time a-feelin' blue   **Just A-Wearyin' for You**

Just another day, guess I'll go my weary way   **I Guess I'll Get the Papers and Go Home**

Just arrived on the seventeen, Tho't I'd see the old gang again   **A Stranger in Town**

Just as I am, without one plea, But that Thy blood was shed for me   **Just As I Am Without One Plea**

Just before the battle, Mother, I am thinking most of you   **Just Before the Battle, Mother**

Just break the news to Mother; She knows how dear I love her   **Break the News to Mother**

Just close your eyes, forget your sighs a little while   **Dream, Dream, Dream**

Just imagine that he loves me dearly   **Just Imagine**

Just in time I found you just in time Before you came, my time was running low   **Just in Time**

Just kiss me once, then kiss me twice, Then kiss me once again   **It's Been a Long, Long Time**

Just let me hear some of that rock and roll music, Any old way you choose it   **Rock and Roll Music**

Just let me sing my song, My song divine   **Song of the Soul**

Just like a Gipsy I've wander'd my whole life thru   **Just Like a Gypsy**

Just once in a lifetime A man knows a moment One wonderful moment   **Once in a Lifetime**

Just one more chance, To prove it's you alone I care for   **Just One More Chance**

Just picture a penthouse 'way up in the sky, With hinges on chimneys for stars to go by   **When We're Alone,** or, **Penthouse Serenade**

Just say that I'm a friend of yours And maybe they won't get wise   **(Just Say I'm a) Friend of Yours**

Just two little love birds all alone   **In Our Little Den of In-iquity**

Just walking in the rain Getting soaking wet, Torturing my heart   **Just Walking in the Rain**

Just we two, if they knew how in the waltz we woo   **Just We Two**

Just what makes that little ol' ant think he'll move that rubber tree plant   **High Hopes**

Just yesterday morning they let me know you were gone   **Fire and Rain**

K-K-K-Katy, beautiful Katy, You're the only g-g-g-girl that I adore   **K-K-K-Katy**

Kathleen Mavourneen! The grey dawn is breaking   **Kathleen Mavourneen**

Katie went to Haiti, Stopped off for a rest. Katie met a natie   **Katie Went to Haiti**

Keep it gay, keep it light, keep it fresh, keep it fair   **Keep It Gay**

Keep your sunny side up, up! Hide the side that gets blue   **(Keep Your) Sunny Side Up**

Kids! I don't know what's wrong with these kids today!   **Kids**

Kind friends, your pity pray bestow On one who stands before you, And listen to my tale of woe   **Constantinople**

Kiss today goodbye, The sweetness and the sorrow   **What I Did for Love**

L'aventure c'est pour les loups   **(Theme from) Borsalino**

L.A.'s fine, the sun shines most the time and the feelin' is lay back   **I Am, I Said**

La plume de ma tante Est sur le bureau de mon oncle   **La Plume de Ma Tante (The Pen of My Aunt)**

La Veeda, Life of Spain, Eyes that shine Like stars in the sky   **La Veeda**

Ladies and gentlemen, When my heart is sick   **Tomorrow**

Lady madonna chidren at your feet wonder how you manage to make ends meet   **Lady Madonna**

Lady Willpower, it's now or never. Give your love to me and I'll shower your heart   **Lady Willpower**

Landlord, fill the flowing bowl, until it doth run over   **Come, Landlord, Fill the Flowing Bowl**

Languid and plaintive, Hear the chant of the jungle   **Chant of the Jungle**

Last night as I got home about a half past ten   **Take a Letter, Maria**

Last night I said these words to my girl   **Please Please Me**

Last night we met and I dream of you yet   **With the Wind and the Rain in Your Hair**

Last night when we were young, Love was a star, a song unsung   **Last Night When We Were Young**

Laura and Tommy were lovers, He wanted to give her ev'rything   **Tell Laura I Love Her**

Laura is the face in the misty night Footsteps that you hear down the hall   **Laura**

Lavender blue, dilly, dilly, lavender green. If I were king, dilly, dilly, I'd need a queen   **Lavender's Blue (Diddle, Diddle, or, Dilly, Dilly)**

Lay, lady, lay, lay across my big brass bed   **Lay, Lady, Lay**

Lazy moon! come out soon! Make my poor heart beat warmer   **Lazy Moon**

Lead, kindly Light, amid th' encircling gloom, Lead Thou me on   **Lead, Kindly Light**

Learn to croon If you want to win your heart's desire   **Learn To Croon**

Leave you? Leave you? How could I leave you? How could I go it alone?   **Could I Leave You?**

Leaves come tumb'ling down, Round my head   **A Faded Summer Love**

Left a good job in the city, Workin' for the man ev'ry night and day   **Proud Mary**

Les we go to de golden wedding, All de darkies will be there   **De Golden Wedding**

Let every good fellow now fill up his glass, Vive la compagnie   **Vive La Compagnie, or, Vive L'Amour**

Let every good fellow now join in a song, Vive la compagnie!   **Vive La Compagnie, or, Vive L'Amour**

Let it rain and thunder! Let a million firms go under!   **Who Cares**

Let martial note In triumph float   **Stars and Stripes Forever**

Let me ride on a trail In the hills of old Wyomin'   **The Hills of Old Wyomin'**

Let me sing you a song of a gargle, A lotion to me very dear   **Beer, Beer, Glorious Beer**

Let me take you down, 'cos I'm going to Strawberry Fields   **Strawberry Fields Forever**

Let me whisper "Dolce Far Niente" My darling   **Dolce Far Niente**

Let someone start believing in you Let him hold out his hand   **Watch What Happens**

Let the drums roll out! Let the trumpet call! While the people shout! Strike up the band   **Strike Up the Band**

Let tyrants shake their iron rod, And Slav'ry clank her galling chains   **Chester (Let Tyrants Shake Their Iron Rod)**

Let's all get up and dance to a song that was a hit before your Mother was born   **Your Mother Should Know**

Let's be quiet as a mouse and build a lovely little house for Wendy   **Wendy**

Let's face the music, our love is over   **Addio Addio, or, Goodbye**

Let's get lost, lost in each others arms   **Let's Get Lost**

Let's go down by the grapevine, Drink my Daddy's wine, Get happy   **Sweet Blindness**

Let's meet on the road to Morocco Instead of the tunnel of love   **The Road to Morocco**

Let's take a boat to Bermuda Let's take a plane to Saint Paul   **Let's Get Away from It All**

Let's twist again like we did last summer   **Let's Twist Again**

Lies that made me happy, Lies that made me blue   **Lies**

Life can't go on without that certain thing   **Without That Certain Thing**

Life has just begun. Jack has found his Jill   **'S Wonderful**

Life is just a bowl of cherries, Don't make it serious, Life's too mysterious **Life Is Just a Bowl of Cherries**

Life's great, life's grand, Future all planned **Ridin' High**

Lights are bright, Pianos making music all the night **I Wonder What Became of Me**

Like a ghost sent to plague you, I'll be there **I'll Be There**

Like a port in a storm, Like a breeze when you're warm **You're Such a Comfort to Me**

Like a ship at sea, I'm just lost in a fog **Lost in a Fog**

Like all fools, I believed what I wanted to believe **You Are Too Beautiful**

Like the roses need their fragrance **That's How I Need You**

Lindy, Lindy, Sweet as the sugar cane **By the Watermelon Vine, Lindy Lou**

Listen people to what I say, I say ev'rybody's got to have their day **Listen People**

Listen to my tale of woe, It's terribly sad, but true **Oh, Lady Be Good**

Listen to the rhythm of the falling rain, telling me just what a fool I've been **Rhythm of the Rain**

Listen to yo' daddy warn you, 'Fore you start a travelin' **A Woman Is a Sometime Thing**

Listen while I get you told Stop messin' round, sweet jelly roll **Aggravatin' Papa (Don't You Try To Two-Time Me)**

Little biscuit I'm your oven. Little apple I'm your tree **Little Biscuit**

Little darling, It's been a long, cold, lonely winter **Here Comes the Sun**

Little drops of rain, Little grains of sand, Make the mighty ocean And the pleasant land **Little Drops of Rain**

Little man you're crying, I know why you're blue **Little Man, You've Had a Busy Day**

Little old Lady, passing by, Catching ev'ry one's eye **Little Old Lady**

Little one, I was so gloomy, Felt that life sure would undo me **Little One**

Little sister, don't you kiss me once or twice then say it's very nice **Little Sister**

Living for you is easy living, It's easy to live, when you're in love **Easy Living**

Liza, Liza, skies are gray **Liza (All the Clouds'll Roll Away)**

Lollipop, lollipop, Oh, lolli, lolli, lolli **Lollipop**

Long ago and far away, I dreamed a dream one day And now that dream is here beside me **Long Ago and Far Away**

Long before I knew you Long before I met you I was sure I'd find you someday, somehow **Long Before I Knew You**

Long distance, information, Give me Memphis, Tennessee **Memphis**

Look ahead, look astern, look a-weather and a-lee **High Barbaree**

Look at me again, dear; Let's hold hands and then, dear **Sentimental Me**

Look at me I'm as helpless as a kitten up a tree **Misty**

Look at me, I'm Sandra Dee, Lousy with virginity **Look at Me, I'm Sandra Dee**

Look at that face just look at it, Look at that fabulous face of yours **Look at That Face**

Look at them shufflin', a shufflin' down **Muskrat Ramble**

Look at this, this is cookin', it's a meal **Real Goodness from Kentucky Fried Chicken**

Look for the silver lining whene'er a cloud appears in the blue **Look for the Silver Lining**

Look for the union label, when you are buying a coat, dress, or blouse **(Look For the) Union Label**

Look here, Alexander, I was only fooling **Alexander (Don't You Love Your Baby No More)**

Look, look, look to the rainbow, Follow it over the hill and stream **Look to the Rainbow**

Look! Look! My heart is an open book. I love nobody but you **My Heart Is an Open Book**

Look, Ma'am, an invitation. Look, Ma'am, delivered by hand **A Weekend in the Country**

Look out of the window, please, ay, ay, ay **Ay, Ay, Ay**

Lord Thomas rose early one morning in May and dress'd himself in blue **Lord Thomas and Fair Elinore**

Lost a heart as good as new Lost the moment I met you **Lost**

Love is a dancing thing, Gay as a Mayday, I'm in the heyday of it **Love Is a Dancing Thing**

Love is a many splendored thing, It's the April rose that only grows in the early Spring **Love Is a Many-Splendored Thing**

Love is ev'rywhere Its music fills the air **A Melody from the Sky**

Love is funny, or it's sad, or it's quiet, or it's mad **But Beautiful**

Love is just game that two are playing **You Are Free**

Love is like a never ending melody **Desafinado (Slightly Out of Tune)**

Love is lovelier the second time around, Just as wonderful with both feet on the ground **The Second Time Around**

Love is so terrific, such a funny feeling, Makes you wanna cuddle and cling **Love Is So Terrific**

Love is sweeping the country, Waves are hugging the shore **Love Is Sweeping the Country**

Love laughs at a king, kings don't mean a thing **(On the) Street of Dreams**

Love letters straight from your heart Keep us so near while apart **Love Letters**

Love me, love me, say you do. Let me fly away with you **Wild Is the Wind**

Love me tender, love me sweet; Never let me go **Love Me Tender**

Love walked right in and drove the shadows away **Love Walked In**

Love! love! Hooray for love! Who is ever too blasé for love? **Hooray for Love**

Love, here is my heart, One rose for your hair **Love, Here Is My Heart**

Love, look at the two of us, Strangers in many ways **For All We Know**

Love, love me, darlin', Come and go with me   **Come Go with Me**

Love, love me do, you know I love you   **Love Me Do**

Love, oh love, oh careless love!   **Careless Love**

Lovely lady, when you fall in love Fall in love with me   **Lovely Lady**

Lovely Rita meter maid. Nothing can come between us   **Lovely Rita (Meter Maid)**

Lovely to look at, Delightful to know and heaven to kiss   **Lovely To Look At**

Lover, one lovely day, Love came, planning to stay   **On Green Dolphin Street**

Lover, when I'm near you And I hear you speak my name   **Lover**

Lullaby of Birdland that's what I always hear when you sigh   **Lullaby of Birdland**

''M'' is for the million things she gave me   **M-O-T-H-E-R (A Word That Means the World to Me)**

Ma, he's making eyes at me! Ma, he's awful nice to me!   **Ma! He's Making Eyes at Me**

Mad about the boy, I know it's stupid to be mad about the boy   **Mad About the Boy**

Madrid, Madrid, Madrid, Pedazo de la España en que nací   **Madrid**

Mairzy doats and dozy doats and liddle lamzy divey   **Mairzy Doats**

Make of our hands One hand   **One Hand, One Heart**

Malbrouck has gone to battle, Mironton, mironton, mirontaine   **For He's a Jolly Good Fellow**, or, **Malbrouk (Malbrough)**, or, **We Won't Go Home Until Morning**, or, **The Bear Went Over the Mountain**

Mama don't want no peas, no beans, no cocoanut oil, Just a bottle of brandy handy all the while   **Mama Don't Want No Peas an' Rice an' Cocoanut Oil**

Mama take this bade off of me; I can't use it anymore   **Knockin' on Heaven's Door**

Mama, I want to tell you that I'll always love you   **Mama**

Mamma love Papa, Papa love Mamma, Ev'rything's dandy, sweet as can be   **Mamma Loves Papa—Papa Loves Mamma**

Mammy Mammy The sun shines East, the sun shines West   **My Mammy**

Mammy's little baby loves short'nin', short'nin',   **Shortnin' Bread**

Man that I love he has left me in this town   **Gulf Coast Blues**

Mangos, papaya, chestnuts from the fire   **Mangos**

Manischewitz is the wine for you, Manischewitz lets the flavor through   **Man Oh Manischewitz**

Many a new face will please my eye, Many a new love will find me   **Many a New Day**

Many a tear has to fall, but it's all in the game   **It's All in the Game**

Many are the hearts that a weary tonight   **Tenting on the Old Camp Ground**, or, **Tenting Tonight**

Many moons ago, It was on a night like this When we sealed our love with one sweet kiss   **Many Moons Ago**

Many queens I have seen On the stage and the screen Who, would never do   **Nobody But You**

Many years ago in old Sorrento A certain ditty was quite the thing   **Chi-Baba Chi-Baba (My Bambino Go to Sleep)**

March went out like a lion, A whippin' up the water in the bay   **June Is Bustin' Out All Over**

Maria. I've just met a girl named Maria   **Maria**

Matchmaker, Matchmaker, make me a match, Find me a find, catch me a catch   **Matchmaker, Matchmaker**

Matinee, seats for two, I was there, where were you?   **Matinee**

Matt Casey formed a social club that beat the town for style   **(Casey Would Waltz with the Strawberry Blonde While) The Band Played On**

Maxwellton's braes are bonnie, where early fa's the dew   **Annie Laurie**

May I be the only one to say I Really fell in love the day I First set eyes on you   **May I**

May the Lord protect and defend you   **Sabbath Prayer**

Maybe I hang around here a little more than I should   **I Honestly Love You**

Maybe I should have saved those leftover dreams   **Here's That Rainy Day**

Maybe I'm right, and maybe I'm wrong, And maybe I'm weak, and maybe I'm strong   **Nevertheless**

Maybe this time I'll be lucky. Maybe this time he'll stay   **Maybe This Time**

Maybe you'll think of me, When you are all alone   **Maybe**

Me and Missus Jones, we've got a thing going on   **Me and Mrs. Jones**

Me and my shadow strolling down the avenue   **Me and My Shadow**

Me donkey want water, Hold 'em Joe; Spring 'round the corner, Hold 'em Joe   **Hold 'Em Joe**

Meet me unerneath our little tree in the park!   **A Tree in the Park**

Mem'ries I recall of all your pretty little love tales   **Love Tales**

Mem'ries light the corners of my mind   **The Way We Were**

Mem'ry takes me back away To an early childhood day-   **Whip-Poor-Will**

Memphis in June, A shady veranda Under a Sunday blue sky   **Memphis in June**

Men of Harlech! In the Hollow, Do ye hear like rushing billow   **March of the Men of Harlech**

Met a gal in calico Down in Santa Fe   **A Gal in Calico**

Met the girl I love in a town 'way down in Dixie 'Neath the stars above   **Bonaparte's Retreat**

Michael wakes you up with sweets, He takes you up streets and the rain comes down   **Michael from Mountains**

Michelle ma belle. These are words that go together well, my Michelle   **Michelle**

Mickey, pretty Mickey, With your hair of raven hue   **Mickey**

'Mid pleasures and Palaces though we may roam **Home Sweet Home**

Midnight One more night without sleepin' **The Green Door**

Mimi, You funny little good for nothing Mimi, Am I the guy? **Mimi**

Mine eyes have seen the glory of the coming of the Lord **Battle Hymn of the Republic**

Mine, love is mine, Whether it rain or storm or shine **Mine**

Minnesota, hats off to thee **The Rouser**

Miss Otis regrets she's unable to lunch today, Madame **Miss Otis Regrets**

Missed the Saturday dance, Heard they crowded the floor **Don't Get Around Much Anymore**

Mister Paganini Please play my rhapsody **If You Can't Sing It You'll Have To Swing It (Mister Paganini)**

Mister Shylock was stingy; I was miserly, too **I've Got Five Dollars**

Mister "X" may we ask you a question? **(In My) Little Tin Box**

Mistress Murphy gave a party just about a week ago **Who Threw the Overalls in Mrs. Murphy's Chowder**

Mm-Mm-Mm Would you like to take a walk? **Would You Like To Take a Walk**

Mm-Mm-Mm-Mm-Mm I'm hummin' Cause my daily work is thru **I'm Humming, I'm Whistling, I'm Singing**

Mona Lisa, Mona Lisa men have named you **Mona Lisa**

Monday was my wedding day, Tuesday I was married **(Go Tell Aunt Rhody) The Ole Grey Goose (Is Dead)**

Money grows on trees, the desert starts to freeze **The Moon Is Blue**

Money makes the world go around, the world go around **Money (Money)**

Moody river, More deadly Than the vainest knife **Moody River**

Moon over Miami, Shine on my love and me **Moon Over Miami**

Moon shinin' on the river Come along, my Liza **Liza (All the Clouds'll Roll Away)**

Morning has broken like the first morning, Blackbird has spoken like the first bird **Morning Has Broken**

Most people live on a lonely island Lost in the middle of a foggy sea **Bali Ha'i**

Mother, may I go out dancing? **Yes My Darling Daughter**

Mrs. Lovett's meat pies, Savory and sweet pies **God, That's Good**

Music soothes the savage That's a well-known phrase **Sweet Potato Piper**

Musical guys have crowned it king. Up to their eyes they're drowned in Swing time, swing time **Waltz in Swing Time**

My baby's arms, Hold all my charms, My baby's eyes of blue **My Baby's Arms**

My Bonnie lies over the ocean, my Bonnie lies over the sea **My Bonnie Lies Over the Ocean,** or, **Bring Back My Bonnie to Me**

My boy, Bill! (I will see that he's named after me, I will!) **Soliloquy**

My Boy Lollipop, You made my heart go giddyup **My Boy Lollipop**

My Cherie Amor, lovely as a summer day **My Cherie Amor**

My country, 'tis of thee, Sweet land of liberty, Of thee I sing **America (My Country 'Tis of Thee)**

My evening star I wonder who you are **Come Down Ma Evenin' Star**

My faith looks up to Thee, Thou Lamb of Calvary **My Faith Looks Up to Thee**

My father sent me to old Rutgers And resov'd that I should be a man **On the Banks of the Old Raritan**

My friends all know it, how I adore him **Teenage Prayer**

My funny Valentine, Sweet comic Valentine, You make me smile with my heart **My Funny Valentine**

My gal and I, we had a fight And I'm all by myself **Runnin' Wild**

My girl said goodbye, My, oh my, My girl didn't cry **Big Girls Don't Cry**

My girl's the kind of girl for steady company **The Girl Friend**

My grandfather's clock was too large for the shelf, So it stood ninety years on the floor **Grandfather's Clock**

My heart is sad and lonely, For you I sigh, for you, dear, only **Body and Soul**

My Heart is young in April It's filled with love and laughter **Autumn Concerto**

My heart went leaping the day you came along **The Day You Came Along**

My house is made of flowers, the warm winds carpet the floor **House of Flowers**

My life began when Happy smiled, Sweet like candy to a child **Happy,** or, **Love Theme from** *Lady Sings the Blues*

My little Margie, I'm always thinking of you **Margie**

My love don't give me presents. I know that she's no peasant **She's a Woman**

My love I'll never find the words, my love **You Make Me Feel Brand New**

My love lives for your love, for your smile, for your sigh, my beloved **My Beloved**

My loving you meant only heartaches **Heartaches**

My lucky moon above was shinin', knock on wood **Knock On Wood**

My man's gone now, ain't no use a-listenin' For his tired footsteps climbing up de stairs **My Man's Gone Now**

My mother's name was Mary, she was so good and true **Mary's a Grand Old Name**

My old flame, I can't even think of his name **My Old Flame**

My ol' gran'ma she once told me, Don't believe all you hear or see **All That Glitters Is Not Gold**

My one and only, What am I gonna do if you turn me down **My One and Only**

My prayer is to linger with you At the end of the day **My Prayer**

My pretty Jane! my pretty Jane! Ah! never never look so shy **(When the) Bloom Is on the Rye,** or, **My Pretty Jane**

My Rio, Rio by the sea-o **Flying Down to Rio**

My romance doesn't have to have a moon in the sky **My Romance**

My ship has sails that are made of silk, The decks are trimmed with gold **My Ship**

My sin was loving you Not wisely but too well **My Sin**

My song won't appeal to a lover of art **My Song**

My sweet Katinka, Oh where can she be? **Katinka**

My sweetheart, You're gorgeous, you're gorgeous, you're gorgeous **The Broken Record**

My sweetheart's the man in the moon, I'm going to marry him soon **My Sweetheart's the Man in the Moon**

My wife and I live all alone, In a little brown hut, we call our own **Little Brown Jug**

My wonderful one, Whenever I'm dreaming, Love's lovelight a-gleaming, I see **(My) Wonderful One**

My Yiddishe Momme, I need her more than ever now **My Yiddishe Momme**

Name your heart's desire, Presto! It's done! **There's No Holding Me**

Napoleon's a pastry. Bismark is a herring. Alexander's a creme de cocoa mixed with rum **Napoleon's a Pastry**

'Neath the same old moon That shines above **The Same Old Moon**

Nelly was a lady, last night she died; toll de bell for Lubly Nell, my dark Virginia bride **Nelly Was a Lady**

N-E-S-T-L-É-S, Nestlés makes the very best choc'late **Nestlés**

Never comb your hair Sunny! Leave the breezes there Sunny! **Sunny**

Never felt like this until I kissed you **('Til) I Kissed You**

Never thought I'd fall, But now I hear love call **I'm Getting Sentimental over You**

Never treats me sweet and gentle the way he should **I Got It Bad and That Ain't Good**

Never try to bind me, Never hope to know **Waltz Huguette,** or, **The Vagabond King Waltz**

New York, New York, a helluva town, The Bronx is up but the Battery's down **New York, New York**

Nicodemus, the slave, was of African birth, And was bought for a bagful of gold **Wake Nicodemus**

Night and day you are the one Only you beneath the moon and under the sun **Night and Day**

Night and stars above that shine so bright **Caravan**

Night and you, and blue Hawaii, the night is heavenly and you are heaven to me **Blue Hawaii**

Night, Here comes the night, Another night to dream about you **Night**

Night in Madrid, blue and tender; Spanish moon makes silver splendor **Lady of Spain**

No doubt you've seen the maiden with the dimple in her chin **The Maiden with the Dreamy Eyes**

No love, no nothin', Until my baby comes homes **No Love, No Nothing**

No moon at all What a night, Even lightnin' bugs have dimmed their light **No Moon at All**

No one can buy tomorrow, No one can sell their sorrow **(Theme from) The Godfather (Waltz)**

No one to talk with, all by myself **Ain't Misbehavin'**

No other love have I, Only my love for you, Only the dream we knew, No other love **No Other Love**

No strings, no strings except our own devotion **No Strings**

No tears no fears Remember there's always tomorrow **We'll Be Together Again**

No use talkin', no use of talkin' You'll start in dog-walkin' no matter where **Royal Garden Blues**

Nobody but you, Nobody will do **Nobody But You**

Nobody feels any pain Tonight as I stand inside the rain **Just Like a Woman**

Nobody knows the trouble I've seen, nobody knows but Jesus **Nobody Knows De Trouble I've Seen**

Nobody told me Love was made of lightning **Nobody Told Me**

Nobody's heart belongs to me, Heigh-ho! Who cares? **Nobody's Heart (Belongs to Me)**

Nola is like a dream come true, She's sweet and unaffected **Nola**

Non dimenticar means don't forget you are my darling **Non Dimenticar (Don't Forget)**

North of Labrador we'll see the sun divide the midnight with the moon **Regimental Song**

Not a soul down on the corner, That's a pretty certain sign **Wedding Bells Are Breaking Up That Old Gang of Mine**

Not to worry, Not to worry, I may not be smart, but I ain't dumb **Not While I'm Around**

Nothin' says lovin' like somethin' from the oven **Pillsbury Says It Best**

Nothing to do to save his life call his wife in **Good Morning, Good Morning**

Nothing's gonna harm you, Not while I'm around **Not While I'm Around**

Nothing's impossible I have found, for when my chin is on the ground **Pick Yourself Up**

Now, as the sweet imbecilities Tumble so lavishly Onto her lap **Now**

Now at last the door of my dreams Is swinging wide **The Door of My (Her) Dreams**

Now Clancy was a peaceful man if you know what I mean **Clancy Lowered the Boom**

Now ev'rybody's happy, And ev'ryone's gay, cause ev'ry little mammy and pappy is swingin' the Jinx away **Swingin' the Jinx Away**

Now here's a story 'bout Minnie, the Moocher **Minnie the Moocher,** or, **The Ho De Ho Song**

Now how I came to get this hat 'tis very strange and funny **Where Did You Get That Hat**

Now I'm a feller with a heart of gold, And the ways of a gentleman **Smoke! Smoke! Smoke! (That Cigarette)**

Now in the summer of life sweetheart **Will You Love Me in December As You Do in May**

Now it's time to say good night Good night Sleep tight **Good Night**

Now I've got a guy and his name is Dooley **Pink Shoelaces**

Now, I've been happy lately, Thinkin' about the good things to come **Peace Train**

Now, Not someday but now Let's taste ev'ry bit of bliss **Now**

Now, now, soldier, won't you marry me? For O the fife and drum **Soldier, Soldier, Won't You Marry Me?**

Now of late, the daily papers say the government's cash is low **Why Should I Care**

Now old Adam was the first in history **Waterloo**

Now poets may sing of the dear Fatherland **Down Where the Wurzburger Flows**

Now since my baby left me I've found a new place to dwell **Heartbreak Hotel**

Now that I've lost ev'rything to you you say you wanna start something new **Wild World**

Now that I've met you, Love, can you see I'm just a slave and a dreamer, schemer **Beautiful Love**

Now the day is over, Night is drawing nigh **Now the Day Is Over**

Now the first is number one Oh! the army's lots of fun **Roll Me Over**

Now the Gypsy band, Rest their caravan, Where a hill conceals the sun **Play, Fiddle, Play**

Now the sunshine lingers there And the roses bloom as fair **My Old New Hampshire Home**

Now when I wake up In the afternoon **No Bad News**

Now you got to have friends. You know the feelin's, oh so strong **Friends**

Now you say you're lonely, You cry the long night thru **Cry Me a River**

O beautiful for spacious skies, For amber waves of grain **America, the Beautiful**

O dry those tears, And calm those fears, Life is not made for sorrow **O Dry Those Tears**

O Evergreen, O Evergreen! How faithful are your branches! **Maryland, My Maryland, or, Tannenbaum, O Tannenbaum!**

O Genevieve, I'd give the world To live again the lovely past! **Sweet Genevieve**

O Genevieve, sweet Genevieve, The days may come, the days may go **Sweet Genevieve**

O I was born down ole Varginee Long time ago **Long Time Ago, or, Shinbone Alley**

O Leo, O Lai-ee! I'm yodelling away **O Leo**

O little town of Bethlehem, How still we see thee lie! **O Little Town of Bethlehem**

O-hoi ye-ho, Ho-ye-ho, Who's for the ferry? **Twickenham Ferry**

Of all the girls that are so smart, There's none like pretty Sally **Sally in Our Alley**

Of all the love I have won or have lost there is one love I should never have crossed **I'm a Loser**

Of all the wives as e'er you know, Yeo ho! lads! ho! Yeo ho! Yeo ho! **Nancy Lee**

Of thee I sing, baby, Summer, Autumn, Winter, Spring, baby **Of Thee I Sing**

"Oh, bury me not on the lone prairie! These words came low and mournfully **Oh, Bury Me Not on the Lone Prairie, or, The Dying Cowboy**

Oh come back my darling Chiquita, The chapel on the hill, covered with dew **Chiquita**

Oh for a year on a desert island with thee, Out in the sheer middle of the sea **On a Desert Island with Thee**

Oh go 'way man, I can hypnotize this nation **Maple Leaf Rag**

Oh God, our help in ages past, Our hope for years to come **O God, Our Help in Ages Past**

Oh he don't know what it's all about **Cockeyed Mayor of Kaunakakai**

Oh I got plenty o' nuttin', an' nuttin's plenty fo' me **I Got Plenty o' Nuttin'**

Oh I was born in Mobile town, a-workin' on the levee **I've Been Working on the Railroad, or, The Levee Song, or, Someone's in the Kitchen with Dinah**

Oh life is so peculiar. You get so wet in the rain **Life Is So Peculiar**

Oh Lord why did you send the darkness to me? **Willow Weep for Me**

Oh my heart is beating wildly And it's all because you're here **When I'm Not Near the Girl I Love**

Oh my wonderful one, how I adore you thru the day and the night **Tell Me You're Mine**

Oh the buzzin' of the bees in the cigarette trees **The Big Rock Candy Mountain**

Oh the E-ri-ee was a-rising, And the gin was getting low **The E-ri-ee**

Oh the golden sands of old Miami shore **On Miami Shore, or, Golden Sands of Miami**

Oh the Martins and the Coys, They were reckless mountain boys **The Martins and the Coys**

Oh the night that I struck New York, I went out for a quiet walk **The Bowery**

Oh the world owes me a living. Deedle, diedle, doedle, diedle dum **The World Owes Me a Living**

Oh tico tico tick! Oh tico tico tock! This tico tico he's the cuckoo in my clock **Tico Tico**

Oh white folk jis as sure as fate, Dat Carolina is de nullify state **Dandy Jim of Caroline**

Oh woman oh woman don't treat me so mean **Hit the Road Jack**

Oh yeh, I'll tell you something, I think you'll understand **I Want To Hold Your Hand**

Oh yes, I'm the great pretender, Pretendin' I'm doin' well **The Great Pretender**

Oh! daddy, squeeze me and squeeze me again **Squeeze Me**

Oh! don't you remember Sweet Alice, Ben Bolt—Sweet Alice with hair so brown? **Sweet Alice,** or, **Ben Bolt,** or, **Don't You Remember**

Oh! gimme a horse a great big horse, and gimme a buckaroo and let me Wah Hoo **Wah Hoo**

Oh! how we danced on the night we were wed **The Anniversary Song**

Oh! I want to go back to that tumble down shack Where the wild roses bloom 'round the door **That Tumble-Down Shack in Athlone**

Oh! in Dixie's land I'll take my stand, And lib and die in Dixie **(I Wish I Was in) Dixie,** or, **Dixie's Land**

Oh! I'se from Lucianna as you all know **Jim Along, Josey**

Oh! me, Oh! my, Oh! you! I don't know what to do **Does the Spearmint Lose It's Flavor on the Bedpost Overnight**

Oh! Mister Gallagher Hello what's on your mind this morning **Mister Gallagher and Mister Shean**

Oh! My name was Robert Kidd, as I sailed, as I sailed **Won-d'rous Love,** or, **Captain Kidd,** or, **Through All the World**

Oh! my poor Nelly Gray, they have taken you away **Darling Nelly Gray**

Oh! my soul, my soul am agwine for to rest **Angel Gabriel**

Oh! Oh! That funny bunny hug (It's the latest, it's the greatest and the up-to-datest) **Funny Bunny Hug**

Oh! the weather outside is frightful But the fire is so delightful **Let It Snow, Let It Snow, Let It Snow**

Oh, by gosh, by golly, It's time for mistletoe and holly **Mistletoe and Holly**

Oh, come to the church in the wildwood, Oh, come to the church in the dale **The Little Brown Church (in the Vale)**

Oh, de ol' ark's a-moverin', a-moverin', a-moverin' **De Old Ark's a-Moverin'**

Oh, dem golden slippers! Oh, dem golden slippers! Golden slippers I'se gwine to wear **(Oh Dem) Golden Slippers**

Oh, do it again, I may say, "No, no, no, no, no," But do it again **(Please) Do It Again**

Oh, do, do, do what you've done, done, done before, baby **Do Do Do**

Oh, Dunderbeck, oh, Dunderbeck, how could be so mean **Rambling Wreck from Georgia Tech,** or, **Dunderbeck**

Oh, give me a home where the buffalo roam **Home on the Range,** or, **Oh, Give Me a Home Where the Buffalo Roam**

Oh, give me something to remember you by, When you are far away from me, dear **Something To Remember You By**

Oh, he floats through the air with the greatest of ease **The Daring Young Man (on the Flying Trapeze)**

Oh, I went down South for to see my Sal **Polly Wolly Doodle**

Oh, I will take you back, Kathleen, To where your heart will feel no pain **I'll Take You Home Again Kathleen**

Oh, I'd love to be an Oscar Mayer Wiener, That is what I'd truly like to be **The Wiener Song (I Wish I Were an Oscar Mayer Wiener)**

Oh, it's a long, long while from May to December **September Song**

Oh, it's a very merry confectionery, scrumpdillyishus day **A Scrumpdillyishus Day**

Oh, it's beer, beer, beer, That makes you feel so queer **In the Quartermaster's Stores**

Oh, Jimmy, farewell! Your brothers fell Way down in Alabarmy **Grafted into the Army**

Oh, let me go, let me go, let me go, lover **Let Me Go Lover**

Oh, let me live on Broadway, where the lights are all aglow **There's a Broken Heart for Every Light on Broadway**

Oh, Man up in the Moon, Won't you be ready soon? **Shadow of the Moon**

Oh, my father was the keeper of the Eddystone Light, He slept with a mermaid one fine night **The Keeper of the Eddystone Light,** or, **The Eddystone Light**

Oh, my golden slippers am laid away, Kase I don't 'spect to wear 'em till my wedding day **(Oh Dem) Golden Slippers**

Oh, my man I love him so, he'll never know **My Man**

Oh, oh, oh, oh, gee, Man, oh, oh, gee **Gee!**

Oh, oh, what good does it do a guy to know that June is in the sky? **What Good Does It Do**

Oh, Paddy, dear, and did ye hear the news that's goin' round? **The Wearin' o' the Green**

Oh, promise me that some day you and I will take our love together to some sky **Oh Promise Me**

Oh, Rat-a-tat-a-tat-a-tu **Little Star**

Oh, Rose Marie, I love you! I'm always dreaming of you **Rose Marie**

Oh, say can you see, by the dawn's early light **The Star Spangled Banner**

Oh, sentimental me and poor romantic you **Sentimental Me**

Oh, Shenandoah, I long to hear you Away, you rolling river **Shenandoah,** or, **Across the Wide Missouri**

Oh, sweet and lovely lady, be good! Oh lady, be good to me! **Oh, Lady Be Good**

Oh, the fact'ries may be rearing With a boom-a-lack-a, zoom-a-lack-a whee! **Everything Stops for Tea**

Oh, the games people play now, ev'ry night and ev'ry day, now **Games People Play**

Oh, the moonlight's fair tonight along the Wabash **On the Banks of the Wabash Far Away**

Oh, the old church bells are ringing, and the mocking birds are singing **Where the Sunset Turns the Ocean's Blue to Gold**

Oh, the old gray mare, she ain't what she used to be **The Old Grey Mare**

Oh, the rain comes a pitter, patter, And I'd like to be safe in bed **Till ('Til) the Clouds Roll By**

Oh, the shark has pretty teeth, dear And he shows them pearly white **Mack the Knife,** or, **Theme from** *The Threepenny Opera,* or, **Morit'at**

Oh, the wayward wind is a restless wind **The Wayward Wind**

Oh, those Wabash Blues, I know I got my dues **The Wabash Blues**

Oh, we'll rally 'round the flag, boys, we'll rally once again **The Battle Cry of Freedom**

Oh, what a time I had with Minnie the Mermaid **Minnie the Mermaid, or, A Love Song in Fish Time**

Oh, what was your name in the States? Was it Thompson or Johnson or Bates? **What Was Your Name in the States?**

Oh, where have you been, Billy Boy, Billy Boy? **Billy Boy**

Oh, why don't you work like other men do? **Hallelujah, I'm a Bum**

Oh, woe is me. What goes with me? **Home Cooking**

Oh, you can kiss me on a Monday, a Monday, a Monday is very, very good **Never on Sunday**

Oh, you land and leany Chili Beanie eenie minnie mo **Chili Bean (Eenie Meenie Minie Mo)**

Oklahoma, where the wind comes sweepin' down the plain **Oklahoma**

Old Abe Lincoln keeps kicking up a fuss **Root, Hog, or Die**

Old Deacon Splivins, his flock was givin' The way of livin' right **Aunt Hagar's Blues**

Old Grimes is dead, that good old man, We ne'er shall see him more **Old Grimes**

Old King Cole was a merry old soul, And a merry old soul was he **Old King Cole (Mother Goose's Melodies)**

Old MacDonald had a farm, E-I-E-I-O **Old MacDonald Had a Farm**

Ol' man river, dat ol' man river, He must know sumpin, but don't say nothin' **Ol' Man River**

Old Man Sunshine listen, you! Never tell me, "Dreams come true!" **But Not for Me**

Old Noah, he built himself an ark **One More River To Cross**

Old Noah, he did build an ark **There's One Wide River to Cross, or, Noah's Ark**

Old Peter Minuit had nothing to lose, When he bought the Isle of Manhattan **Give It Back to the Indians**

Ole buttermilk sky, I'm keeping my eye peeled on you **Ole Buttermilk Sky**

Ole Faithful, we rode the range together **Ole Faithful**

On a clear day Rise and look around you And you'll see who you are **On a Clear Day You Can See Forever**

On a day like today We passed the time away **Love Letters in the Sand**

On a hill far away stood an old rugged cross **The Old Rugged Cross**

On a lone barren isle where the wild roaring billow **The Grave of Bonaparte**

On a picnic morning Without a warning I looked at you and somehow I knew **(Theme from) Picnic**

On a Sunday morn, sat a maid forlorn **Wait 'Til the Sun Shines, Nellie**

On a tree by a river a little tom-tit Sang "Willow, tit-willow, tit-willow **Tit-Willow**

On a weekend pass I wouldn't have had time To get home and marry that baby of mine **Ebony Eyes**

On a wonderful day like today I defy any cloud to appear in the sky **(On) A Wonderful Day Like Today**

On one summer's day Sun was shining fine **Bill Bailey, Won't You Please Come Home**

On Shiloh's dark and bloody ground, The dead and wounded lay **The Drummer Boy of Shiloh**

On Springfield Mountain there did dwell A Loveli youth; I knowed him well **The Pesky Sarpent, or, (On) Springfield Mountain**

On Sunday night, 'tis my delight And pleasure don't you see **Maggie Murphy's Home**

On that great Come-And-Get-It day, Won't it be fun when worry is done and money is hay **That Great Come and Get It Day**

On the boardwalk in Atlantic City, We will walk in a dream **On the Boardwalk in Atlantic City**

On the first day of Christmas My true love sent to me, A partridge in a pear tree **The Twelve Days of Christmas**

On the first day of May It is moving day **Mountain Greenery**

On the Good Ship Lollipop It's a sweet trip to a candy shop **On the Good Ship Lillipop**

On the other side of the tracks, That is where I'm goin' to be **(On) The Other Side of the Tracks**

On, Wisconsin, On, Wisconsin. Plunge right thru that line **On Wisconsin**

Once a jolly swagman camped by a billabong **Waltzing Matilda**

Once a wand'ring ne'er-do-well, Just a vagrant roving fellow, I went my way **You Are Love**

Once his hopes were high as the sky, Once a dream was easy to buy **Midnight Cowboy**

Once I had a man as sweet as he could be **Baby, Baby All the Time**

Once I had a secret love That lived within the heart of me **Secret Love**

Once I heard a father ask his soldier son, "Why can't you advance like the other boys have done?" **Would You Rather Be a Colonel with an Eagle on Your Shoulder, or a Private with a Chicken on Your Knee?**

Once I laughed when I heard you saying That I'd be playing solitaire **It Never Entered My Mind**

Once I strayed 'Neath the window of a lovely, lovely lady **Penny Serenade**

Once I was a lady's maid way down in Drury Lane **Bell Bottom Trousers**

Once in a lifetime, someone comes along Bringing happiness for two **Once in a Lifetime**

Once in a while will you try to give one little thought to me **Once in a While**

Once in the dear dead days beyond recall **Love's Old Sweet Song**

Once there lived side by side, two little maids **I Don't Want To Play in Your Yard**

Once there was a thing called spring, when the world was writing verses like yours and mine **Spring Is Here**

Once there were green fields, kissed by the sun **Greenfields**

Once upon a time a girl with moonlight in her eyes **Once Upon a Time**

Once upon a time, before I took up smiling, I hated the moonlight! **Blue Moon**

Once upon a time there was a tavern, Where we used to raise a glass or two **Those Were the Days**

Once we walked alone Down by the river All the world our own **Down by the River**

Once, yes, once for a lark. Twice, though, loses the spark **I Never Do Anything Twice**

One boy, one special boy, One boy to go with, to talk with and walk with **One Boy**

One bright and guiding light that taught me wrong from right **My Mother's Eyes**

One day I met a Jane all the way from Spain lovely land of joy **My Spanish Rose**

One day, little girl, the sadness will leave your face **True Grit**

One day when I had nothing to do for an hour **I Got Lucky in the Rain**

One day you'll look to see I've gone **I'll Follow the Sun**

One dream in my heart, One love to be living for **This Nearly Was Mine**

One hot day in the old Fall River Mister Andrew Borden died **Lizzie Borden**

One love will never die as long as I live **One Love**

One moment alone That's all we have known, And yet it seemed paradise **One Moment Alone**

One more time Just one more time Let me do the thing that I used to do **One More Time**

One night I was late Came home from a date **Rock and Roll Waltz**

One night of love, When two hearts are one, A night to have and hold **One Night of Love**

One night the moon was so mellow Rosita met young Manuelo **Ti-Pi-Tin**

One singular sensation ev'ry little step she takes **One**

One song, I have but one song, One song, only for you **One Song**

Only you can make this world seem right **Only You (and You Alone)**

Onward, Christian soldiers, Marching as to war With the cross of Jesus Going on before **Onward, Christian Soldiers**

Ooh I need your love babe, guess you know it's true **Eight Days a Week**

Ooh, you came out of a dream, Peaches and Cream, Lips like strawberry wine **You're Sixteen**

Ooover and a over I tried to prove my love for you **Personality**

Ordinary mothers lead ordinary lives **The Glamorous Life**

Oriental moonbeams thru a willow tree, Sprinkle light in Silv'ry rays **China Boy**

Oui Oui Marie, will you do this for me **Oui, Oui, Marie**

Our father who art in heaven, Hallowed be Thy name **The Lord's Prayer**

Our hour and I'll be meeting you **My Last Date with You**

Our Jimmy has gone for to live in a tent **Grafted into the Army**

Our little dream castle with ev'ry dream gone **A Cottage for Sale**

Our love affair is a wondrous thing, That we'll rejoice in remembering **An Affair To Remember**

Our romance won't end on a sorrowful note, Though by tomorrow you're gone **They Can't Take That Away from Me**

Our waltz is music fashioned in Heaven, Angels composed it for us to dance to **Our Waltz**

Out in God's green world you'll find All the joy your heart has designed **God's Green World**

Out of my dreams and into your arms I long to fly **Out of My Dreams**

Out of the darkness you suddenly appeared **The Moon Got in My Eyes**

Out on ol' Smoky, ol' Smoky so low **On Top of Old Smokey**

Out on the plains Down near Santa Fe, I met a cowboy **Cow-Cow Boogie**

Out where the bright lights are glowing You're drawn like a moth to a flame **The Four Walls**

Over hill, over dale, as we hit the dusty trail **The U.S. Field Artillery March, or, The Caissons Go Rolling Along**

Over the quiet hills Slowly the shadows fall **Bird Songs at Eventide**

Overnight, I found you and overnight, I lost you **Overnight**

Pack up all my care and woe Here I go singing low **Bye Bye Blackbird**

Paddy Mack drove a hack Up and down Broadway **Where Do We Go from Here**

Paint your initials on my jeans, So ev'ryone in town will know we go aroun' together **Dungaree Doll**

Pal of my cradle days, I've needed you always, Since I was a baby upon your knee **Pal of My Cradle Days**

Pale moon shining on the fields below **When It's Sleepy Time Down South**

Pardon me, boy, is that the Chattanooga Choo-choo, Track twenty-nine, Boy, you can gimme a shine **Chattanooga Choo Choo**

Pardon me, miss, but I've never done this with a real live girl **Real Live Girl**

Paree, I still adore you, Paree, I'm longing for you **Paree!**

Paris loves lovers, For lovers it's heaven above **Paris Loves Lovers**

(Parlez-Moi d'Amour) Speak to me of love and say what I'm longing to hear **Speak to Me of Love**

Peas! Peas! Peas! Peas! Eating goober peas! **Goober Peas**

Peg O' My Heart, I love you, Don't let us part, I love you **Peg o' My Heart**

Peggy O'Neil is a girl who could steal Any heart, Anywhere, anytime **Peggy O'Neil**

Pennies in a stream, falling leaves, a sycamore **Moonlight in Vermont**

People keep on learnin' Soldiers keep on warrin' **Higher Ground**

People, people who need people Are the luckiest people in the world **People**

People try to put us down (Talkin' 'bout my generation) **My Generation**

Pepsi-Cola hits the spot, Twelve full ounces, that's a lot **Pepsi-Cola Hits the Spot**

Per fa' l'amore ce voglio' le figliole **A Girl! A Girl!**, or, **Zoom Ba Di Alli Nella**

Perfect song of loving hearts united **The Perfect Song**

Pernambuco, unbelievable town Where the crops go to seed and the bank Is in need **Pernambuco**

Phone rings, door chimes, in comes Company! **Company**

Picture a happy home when supper time is near **The Sweetest Thing in Life**

Picture yourself in a boat on a river with tangerine trees and marmalade skies **Lucy in the Sky with Diamonds**

Play to me beneath the summer moon **Zigeuner**

Please don't be offended if I preach to you a while **Look for the Silver Lining**

Please don't say ''No'' say ''Maybe'' Or say ''Come back in the Spring'' **Please Don't Say No**

Please forgive this platitude, But I like your attitude **Fine and Dandy**

Please lend your little ear to my pleas **Please**

Please lock me away, and don't allow the day here inside **A World Without Love**

Please, Mister Postman look and see is there a letter in your bag for me? **Please Mister Postman**

Please play for me That sweet melody Called Doodle Doo Doo **Doodle Doo Doo**

Please take your medicine, Dear World **Dear World**

Poetry in motion, Walkin' by my side; Her lovely locomotion keeps my eyes open wide **Poetry in Motion**

Poinciana, your branches speak to me of love **Poinciana**

Poor Johnny One Note Sang out with gusto And just overloaded the place **Johnny One Note**

Pore Jud is daid, Pore Jud Fry is daid! **Poor Jud (Is Daid)**

Pretend you're happy when you're blue. It isn't very hard to do **Pretend**

Pretty lady in the pretty garden, can't-cher stay? **Pretty Lady**

Pretty women fascinating sipping coffee, dancing **Pretty Women**

Proudly swept the raincloud by the cliff **Aloha Oe**, or, **Farewell to Thee**

Pull up an easy chair and sit yourself down **The Money Tree**

Put on your Sunday clothes when you feel down and out **Put On Your Sunday Clothes**

Put your arms around me child, Like when you bumped your shin **The Feeling We Once Had**

Put your head on my shoulder, Hold me in your arms, baby **Put Your Head on My Shoulder**

Quiet night, and all around the calm and balmy weather **Quiet Night**

Racing with the moon high up in the midnight blue **Racing with the Moon**

Rain Let us cuddle while the Rain pitter patters **Rain**

Raindrops keep fallin' on my head, and just like the guy whose feet are too big for his bed **Raindrops Keep Fallin' on My Head**

Raindrops on roses and whiskers on kittens **My Favorite Things**

Ramona, I hear the mission bells above **Ramona**

Remember the Christmas morning long ago **The Happy Time**

Remember the times we've had, dear, Remember our vows so true **Rememb'ring**

Return to me, Oh, my dear, I'm so lonely; Hurry back, hurry back **Return to Me**

Riding one morning, my fare I'd just paid **Elsie from Chelsea**

Rio Rita, Life is sweeter, Rita, When you are near **Rio Rita**

Roar, lion roar and wake the echoes of the Hudson Valley! **Roar, Lion, Roar**

Robins and roses and maybe a tree, A few morning glories, A cottage two stories high **Robins and Roses**

Rock of ages, cleft for me! Let me hide myself in Thee **Rock of Ages**

Rock'd in the cradle of the deep, I lay me down in peace to sleep **Rocked in the Cradle of the Deep**

Roll Green Wave, roll them down the field! **Roll On, Tulane**, or, **The Olive and Blue**

Roll, Jordan, roll, I want to go to Heav'n when I die, To hear Jordan roll **Roll, Jordan, Roll**

Roll up—Roll up for the Mystery Tour **Magical Mystery Tour**

Romance didn't thrill you, Wasn't it a shame? **I Heard You Cried Last Night**

Roses are shining in Picardy in the hush of the silver dew **Roses of Picardy**

'Round de meadows am a-ringing, de darkies' mournful song Massa's in De Cold (Cold) Ground Down in de cornfield, hear dat mournful sound **Massa's in De Cold (Cold) Ground**

Round her neck she wore a yellow ribbon **She Wore a Yellow Ribbon**, or, **All Round My Hat (Round Her Neck) I (She) Wore a Yellow Ribbon**

Round my Indiana homestead wave the cornfields **On the Banks of the Wabash Far Away**

Rumors are flying that you've got me sighing, That I'm in a crazy kind of a daze **Rumors Are Flying**

'S wonderful! 'S marvelous! You should care for me! **'S Wonderful**

Sad times May follow your tracks, Bad times May bar you from Saks **Ace in the Hole**

Sadness just makes me sigh, I've come to say goodbye **Farewell Blues**

Sail! home as straight as an arrow, My yacht shoots along on the crest of the sea **White Wings**

Sailing, sailing, over the bounding main, For many a stormy wind shall blow ere Jack comes home again **Sailing**, or, **Sailing, Sailing, over the Bounding Main**

Salagadoola Menchicka boola Bibbidi-bobbodi-boo **Bibbidi-Bobbodi-Boo**

Samantha, you're all I'll ever adore   **I Love You Samantha**

Sand in my shoes, Sand from Heaven, Calling me to that ever so heavenly shore   **Sand in My Shoes**

Saviour, breathe an evening blessing Ere repose our spirits seal   **Saviour, Breathe an Evening Blessing**

Savoy, the home of sweet romance   **Stomping at the Savoy**

Saw a gal with golden hair dancin' as I played   **The Girl with the Golden Braids**

Say "au revoir" but not "goodbye," For parting brings a bitter sigh   **Say "Au Revoir" But Not "Goodbye"**

Say "au revoir" but not "goodbye," Tho' we must part, love cannot die   **Say "Au Revoir" But Not "Goodbye"**

Say, darkies, hab you seen de massa, Wid de muffstash on his face   **Kingdom Coming, or, The Year of Jubilo**

Say, darling, May I offer you an invitation   **Say, Darling**

Say! have you seen the carioca? It's not a foxtrot or a polka   **Carioca**

Say, it's only a paper moon, Sailing over a cardboard sea   **It's Only a Paper Moon**

Say not love is a dream! Say not that hope is vain   **Say Not Love Is a Dream**

Schaefer is the one beer to have, when you're having more than one   **Schaefer Is the One Beer**

Screen celebs and stage satellites, Social debs and High hatellites   **Doin' the Uptown Lowdown**

Seated one day at the organ, I was weary and ill at ease   **The Lost Chord**

See the pretty apple top of the tree!   **On Your Toes**

See the setting sun, the evening's just begun and love is in the air   **Be Mine Tonight**

See the tree, how big it's grown, but friend, it hasn't been too long, it wasn't big   **Honey**

See the U.S.A. in your Chevrolet, American is asking you to call   **See the U.S.A. in Your Chevrolet**

Serenade in the night 'neath a fair lady's window   **Serenade in the Night**

Set my hands upon the plough, My feet upon the sod   **The Blind Ploughman**

Seven lonely days make one lonely week   **Seven Lonely Days**

Seven or eleven means ev'rything to me Means I'm gonna see my Mammy   **Seven or Eleven—My Dixie Pair o' Dice**

Shades of night are falling and I'm lonely   **Me and My Shadow**

Shades of night are falling, Hear the lovebirds calling from the trees above   **Shades of Night**

Shadows fall on the prairie. Day is done and the sun is slowly fading out of sight   **The Call of the Far-Away Hills**

Shake it off with rhythm, Don't let trouble ride you   **Shake It Off**

Shall we dance? On a bright cloud of music shall we fly?   **Shall We Dance**

Shall we dance, or keep on moping? Shall we dance, and walk on air?   **Shall We Dance**

Shall we never more behold thee; Never hear thy winning voice again   **Gentle Annie**

Shalom, The nicest greeting I know; Shalom, Means twice as much as hello   **Shalom**

She didn't say "Yes," She didn't say "No," She didn't say "Stay," She didn't say "Go,"   **She Didn't Say Yes**

She is more to be pitied than censured, She is more to be helped than despised   **She Is More To Be Pitied Than Censured**

She lightens my sadness, she livens my days, She bursts with a kind of madness my well-ordered ways   **You Must Meet My Wife**

She never saw the streets of Cairo, On the Midway she had never strayed   **The Streets of Cairo**

She said I know what it's like to be dead   **She Said She Said**

She shall have music wherever she goes, With plenty of rhythm to tickle her toes   **She Shall Have Music**

She takes just like a woman, yes, she does. She makes love just like a woman   **Just Like a Woman**

She touched me, she put her hand near mine and then she touched me   **She Touched Me**

She walks like you. She talks like you   **She Reminds Me of You**

She was a child of the valley, An innocent maiden was she   **No! No! A Thousand Times No!**

She was afraid to come out of the locker, She was as nervous as she could be   **Itsy Bitsy Teenie Weenie Yellow Polka-dot Bikini**

She was bred in old Kentucky, Where the meadow grass is blue   **She Was Bred in Old Kentucky**

Sherry baby, Sherry baby, Sherry can you come out tonight   **Sherry**

She's got a halfback at Pennsylvania, She's got a quarterback at Yale   **All American Girl**

She's got eyes of blue I never cared for eyes of blue   **That's My Weakness Now**

She's got that, she's got this Can she hug, can she kiss?   **Oh! Boy, What a Girl**

She's my sweetheart! I'm her beau! She's my Annie! I'm her Joe!   **Little Annie Roonie**

She's so gay tonight She's like spring tonight She's a rollicking, frolicking thing tonight   **She Is Not Thinking of Me (Waltz at Maxim's)**

She's the sweetest rose of color This darkey ever knew   **The Yellow Rose of Texas, or, Song of the Texas Rangers**

She's the yellow Rose of Texas I'm longing for to see   **The Yellow Rose of Texas, or, Song of the Texas Rangers**

Shine, little glow-worm, glimmer   **The Glow Worm**

Shipmates, stand together, Don't give up the ship   **Don't Give Up the Ship**

Shoe shine boy, you work hard all day, shoe shine boy, got no time to play   **Shoe Shine Boy**

Shoofly pie and apply pan dowdy makes your eyes light up, your tummy say "howday"   **Shoofly Pie and Apple Pan Dowdy**

Should I reveal exactly how I feel Should I confess I love you   **Should I (Reveal)**

Should your career need a springboard, Here is the best in the land **The Ladies Who Sing with the Band**

Shout to Jehovah, all the earth; Serve ye Jehovah with gladness **Old Hundred(th) Doxology,** or, **Praise God, from Whom All Blessings Flow**

Show me now how two hearts know when they are meant to be as one **Almost Paradise**

Show me the way to go home, I'm tired and I wanna go to bed **Show Me the Way To Go Home**

Shufflin' Sam says "Hurry, honey, git yer shoes!" **Shufflin' Sam**

Siam, I'm so lonesome where I am If you love your Omar Khayam **Siam**

Sierra Sue, I'm sad and lonely The rocks and hills are lonely, too **Sierra Sue**

Since you're gone the stars, the moon, the sun in the sky **Gone**

Sing for your supper and you'll get breakfast, Songbirds always eat **Sing for Your Supper**

Sing, sing a song of mazel tov, keep mazel at your side **Mazel Tov**

Sing! Sing a song. Sing out loud, sing out strong **Sing (Sing a Song)**

Singing, "Bell-bottomed trousers, coats of navy blue" **Bell Bottom Trousers**

Sinner hear what I'm sayin' Sinner you been swingin' not prayin' **Walk on the Wild Side**

Sit there and count your fingers, what can you do? **Little Girl Blue**

Sitting by the roadside on a summer's day **Goober Peas**

Sittin' in the morning sun, I'll be sittin' when the evenin' come **Sittin' on the Dock of the Bay**

Sixteen candles make a lovely sight But not as bright as your eyes tonight **Sixteen Candles**

Skeeters am a hummin' on de honeysuckle vine **Kentucky Babe**

Sky so vast is the sky with far away clouds just wandering by **Dindi**

Slap that bass, slap it till it's dizzy **Slap That Bass**

Sleep, my child, and peace will attend thee, all through the night **All Through the Night**

Sleep, Sleep, Sleep. How we love to sleep **Sleep**

Sleepy time gal, You're turning night into day **Sleepy Time Gal**

Slumber on, my little gypsy sweetheart; Dream of the field and the grove **Gypsy Love Song,** or, **Slumber On**

Small fry, Struttin' by the pool room; Small fry, Should be in the schoolroom **Small Fry**

Smellin' of vanilla, smellin' of rose, decked 'n' dolled in our finest clothes **Smellin' of Vanilla (Bamboo Cage)**

Smile, darn ya, smile, You know this old world is a great world after all **Smile, Darn Ya, Smile**

Smile the while you kiss me sad adieu **Till We Meet Again**

Smile tho your heart is aching, Smile even tho it's breaking **Smile**

Snap your fingers, walk aroun' a bit **College Rhythm**

So far away! Doesn't anybody stay in one place anymore? **So Far Away**

So goodbye yellow brick road Where the dogs of society howl **Goodbye Yellow Brick Road**

So here am I watchin' and waitin' for my bluebird **My Blue Bird Was Caught in the Rain**

So I just roll along Havin' my ups, Havin' my downs **I Just Roll Along Havin' My Ups and Downs**

So I went bowling, over the rolling, over the rolling sea **Three for Jack**

So love thy neighbor, Walk up and say "How be ya!" **Love Thy Neighbor**

So many sweet songs still to be sung **I Don't Think I'll End It All Today**

So much life to be lived, So much to be tried **You Deserve a Break Today**

So rare, You're like the fragrance of blossoms fair **So Rare**

So, take a letter, Maria, Address it to my wife **Take a Letter, Maria**

So Winter froze the river, and winter birds don't sing **Time and Love**

So you met someone who set you back on your heels **Goody Goody**

Soft o'er the fountain, ling'ring falls the southern moon **Juanita**

Soft summer breeze, lazy old stream, cotton clouds up high **Soft Summer Breeze**

Soft winds whisper sweet words to my love **Soft Winds**

Some day my prince will come, Some day I'll find my love **Some Day My Prince Will Come**

Some day sweetheart, you may be sorry for what you've done to my poor heart **Some Day Sweetheart**

Some day when I'm awf'ly low, When the world is cold **The Way You Look Tonight**

Some enchanted evening, You may see a stranger **Some Enchanted Evening**

Some folks like to get away Take a holiday from the neighborhood **New York State of Mind**

Some folks say dat a nigger won't steal! But I cotch one in my cornfield **Whar Did You Cum From,** or, **Knock a Nigger Down**

Some men plough the open plain, Some men sail the brine **My Truly, Truly Fair**

Some Niggers they have but one coat, But you see I've got two **My Long-Tail Blue**

Some people are born to be doctors, Some are born to be lumberjacks **Just Born To Be Your Baby**

Some people think it came from Tennessee **Rock-A-Billy**

Some think the world is made for fun and frolic **Funiculì—Funiculà**

Somebody hold me too close, Somebody hurt me too deep **Being Alive**

Somebody loves me I wonder who, I wonder who she can be **Somebody Loves Me**

Somebody, somewhere wants me and needs me That's very wonderful to know **Somebody, Somewhere**

Someday he'll come along, The man I love; And he'll be big and strong, The man I love **The Man I Love**

Someday, I don't know how, She'll bring her love to me **Dream Lover**

Someday I'll find you, Moonlight behind you **Some Day I'll Find You**

Someday, some way, you'll realize that you've been blind **It's Just a Matter of Time**

Someday we'll build a home on a hilltop high, You and I **The Folks Who Live on the Hill**

Someone had to pick the cotton, Someone had to plant the corn **That's Why Darkies Were Born**

Somethin's cookin' that rates an ovation **My Guy's Come Back**

Something familiar, something peculiar, Something for ev-'ryone, a comedy tonight! **Comedy Tonight**

Something in the way she moves Attracts me like no other lover **Something (In the Way She Moves)**

Sometimes, clearly, I see two faces in the dark **Two Faces in the Dark**

Sometimes I wonder why I spend the lonely night Dreaming of a song? **Star Dust**

Sometimes I'm happy, Sometimes I'm blue, My disposition depends on you **Sometimes I'm Happy**

Sometimes in the morning when shadows are deep **My Cup Runneth Over**

Sometimes you win, sometimes you lose, and sometimes the blues get a hold of you **Sweet Seasons**

Sometimes your eyes look blue to me, Although I know they're really green **Whoever You Are,** or, **Sometimes Your Eyes Look Blue to Me**

Somewhere beyond the sea Somewhere waiting for me **Beyond the Sea**

Somewhere over the rainbow way up high **Over the Rainbow**

Somewhere the sun is shining, Somewhere the songbirds dwell **Beautiful Isle of Somewhere**

Somewhere there's music, How faint the tune! **How High the Moon**

Sonata, my Sonata, I hear your haunting theme and I begin to dream **Sonata**

Song of songs, song of memory, And broken melody of love and life **The Song of Songs**

Song of the South, your music weaves a magic spell **Song of the South**

Song of toil and danger, Will you serve a stranger And bow down to Burgundy? **Song of the Vagabonds**

Song sung blue, ev'rybody knows one **Song Sung Blue**

Songs were made to sing while we're young, Ev'ry day is spring **While We're Young**

Sons of the thief, sons of the saint **Sons Of**

Soon or late, maybe, If you wait, maybe **Maybe**

Soon the lonely nights will be ended **Soon**

Soon you leave me, This night is flying **Can I Forget You**

Southern trees bear a strange fruit, blood on the leaves and blood at the root **Strange Fruit**

Sowing in the morning, Sowing seeds of kindness **Bringing in the Sheaves**

Speak low when you speak love our summer days wither away too soon **Speak Low**

Speak softly love and hold me warm against your heart **Speak Softly Love**

Spending these lonesome evenings With nothing to do but live in dreams that I make up, All by myself **Why Was I Born?**

Spirit move me Ev'rytime I'm near you **Could It Be Magic**

Splish splash, I was takin' a bath 'Long about a Saturday night **Splish Splash**

Spring is here! Why doesn't my heart go dancing? **Spring Is Here**

Spring was never waiting for us, girl, it ran one step ahead as we followed in the dance **MacArthur Park**

Stand Navy out to sea, Fight our battle cry **Anchors Aweigh**

Stand Old Ivy! Stand firm and strong **Grand Old Ivy**

Stand well back, I'm coming through nothing can stop me now **Nothing Can Stop Me Now!**

Stardust on the moon, What night for love, With such ecstasy above **Stardust on the Moon**

Stars fade out of the skies Just to rest in her eyes **I Dream Too Much**

Stars hung suspended above a floating yellow moon **Wonderland by Night**

Stars in my eyes tell how I feel, For this tender passion is real **Stars in My Eyes**

Start spreadin' the news, I'm leaving today **Theme from New York, New York**

Still as the night, Deep as the sea, Should be your love for me **Still as the Night**

Still half a sixpence Is better than half a penny **Half a Sixpence**

Stop oh yes, wait a minute Mister Postman **Please Mister Postman**

Strange enchantment fills the moonrise, There's a breeze like sandalwood and wine **Strange Enchantment**

Strange music in my ears, only now as you spoke did it start **Strange Music**

Stumbling all around, Stumbling all around, Stumbling all around so funny **Stumbling**

Such a feelin's comin' over me, there is wonder in most ev-'rything I see **Top of the World**

Suddenly it happened to me, Suddenly the thrill went through me **Suddenly**

Sugar in the mornin', sugar in the evenin', Sugar at supper time **Sugartime**

Sugar, ah, honey, honey, You are my candy girl And you've got me wanting you **Sugar Sugar**

Summer dreams, where do they go when winter comes? **Summer Dreams**

Summertime an' the livin' is easy **Summertime**

Sunday, sweet Sunday, with nothing to do, Lazy and lovely, my one day with you **Sunday**

Sunrise, Sunset, Sunrise, Sunset, Swiftly flow the days **Sunrise Sunset**

Sure, I've got rings on my fingers, Bells on my toes **I've Got Rings on My Fingers**, or, **Mumbo Jumbo Jijjiboo J. O'Shea**

Surry down to a stoned soul picnic. There'll be lots of time and wine **Stoned Soul Picnic**

Suzanne takes you down to her place near the river **Suzanne**

Swanee, How I love you, How I love you, my dear old Swanee **Swanee**

Sweet and low, sweet and low, wind of the western sea **Sweet and Low**

Sweet Hawaiian moonlight fair Guard my dear one sleeping there **Sweet Hawaiian Moonlight**

Sweet Indian maiden, Since first I met you, I can't forget you **Cherokee**

Sweet lady, Make believe I've won your hand **Sweet Lady**

Sweet Leilani Heavenly Flower, Nature fashioned roses kissed with dew **Sweet Leilani**

Sweet Peter, sweet Peter Had a wife and couldn't cheat her **Sweet Peter**

Sweet Rosie O'Grady, my dear little Rose **Sweet Rosie O'Grady**

Sweet thing, let me tell you 'bout The world and the way things are **He's the Wizard**

Sweet violets, Sweeter than all the roses **Sweet Violets**

Sweetest li'l feller, Ev'rybody knows **Mighty Lak' a Rose**

Sweethearts make love in the park, They hide away in the dark **If I Had a Girl Like You**

Sweetie pie, Little bit sugar, little bit honey **Sweetie Pie**

Swift, swift as a shot Bold, bold as the wind **Canadian Sunset**

Swing high, swing low upon the trapeze **Over and Over Again**

Swing low, sweet chariot, Comin' for to carry me home! **Swing Low, Sweet Chariot**

Symphony, symphony of love Music from above, How does it start? **Symphony**

'Tain't my brother, nor my sister, but it's me, oh Lord **('Tis Me, O Lord) Standin' in the Need of Pray'r**

'Tention folks, speak of jokes, This is one on me **Stumbling**

'Tho we gotta say goodbye for the summer, Darling I'll promise you this **Sealed with a Kiss**

'Tis advertised in Boston, New York and Buffalo **Blow Ye Winds, Heigh Ho**

'Tis the last rose of summer Left blooming alone All her lovely companions are faded and gone! **'Tis the Last Rose of Summer**

T'was a sunny day in June, And the birds were all in tune **Dear Old Girl**

'Twas in Trafalgar's bay We saw the Frenchmen lay **The Death of Nelson**

'Twas just a garden in the rain, Close to a little leafy lane **A Garden in the Rain**

'Twas not so long ago that Pa was Mother's beau **'Twas Not So Long Ago**

'Twas on a sunny morning, The brightest of the year **Johnny Is My Darling**

'Twas on the good ship Cuspidor we sailed through Baffin's Bay **Hurray for Baffin's Bay**

'Twas on the Isle of Capri that I found her **Isle of Capri**

Taboo, taboo, Remember she isn't for you **Taboo**

Take a number from one to ten Double it and add a million **Take a Number from One to Ten**

Take away the breath of flowers, It would surely be a sin **It's No Sin**

Take back the heart that thou gavest, What is my anguish to thee? **Take Back the Heart You Gave**

Take back your gold, for gold can never buy me; Take back your bribe, and promise you'll be true **Take Back Your Gold**

Take back your samba Ay! your rhumba Ay! your conga Ay, yay, yay! **South America Take It Away**

Take good care of my baby Please don't ever make her blue **Take Good Care of My Baby**

Take me along, if you luv-a-me **Take Me Along**

Take me down, down, down where the Wurzburger flows, flows, flows **Down Where the Wurzburger Flows**

Take my heart, it's your forever, Tell me yours is mine alone **Take My Heart**

Take one fresh and tender kiss. Add one stolen night of bliss **Memories Are Made of This**

Take out the papers and the trash, or you don't get no spending cash **Yakety Yak**

Take to the highway won't you lend me your name **Country Road**

Take your share of trouble Face it and don't complain **If You Want the Rainbow (You Must Have the Rain)**

Takin' the shade out of the sun Whatever made me think that I was number one? **Easy Come, Easy Go**

Talk to him, please, Mister Sun, Speak to him, Mister Rainbow **Please Mister Sun**

Talk to me baby whisper in my ear **Ko Ko Mo (I Love You So)**

Talkin' to myself and feelin' old, sometime I'd like to quit **Rainy Days and Mondays**

Tall and tan and young and lovely **The Girl from Ipanema**

Tangerine She is all they claim With her eyes of night and lips as bright as flame **Tangerine**

Tell me, tell me, tell me, Oh, who wrote the Book of Love? **Book of Love**

Tell me the tales that to me were so dear **Long Long Ago**, or, **The Long Ago**

Tell me what's good about goodnight? Find me the fun in being lonely **What's Good About Good Night**

Tell me where she is Tell me where she goes **Don't Tell Her (What's Happened to Me)**

Tell me why you keep fooling, little coquette? **Coquette**

Tell ya what I'm thinkin', honestly and true **Why Am I Me**

Ten cents a dance; That's what they pay me **Ten Cents a Dance**

Ten million soldiers to war have gone, Who may never return again **I Didn't Raise My Boy To Be a Soldier**

Ten minutes ago, I saw you, I looked up when you came thru the door **Ten Minutes Ago**

Tender shepherd, tender shepherd, watches over all his sheep **Tender Shepherd**

Tenderly hold me, kiss and enfold me **Tenderly**

Thank heaven for little girls! For little girls get bigger ev'ry day **Thank Heaven for Little Girls**

Thanks for all the lovely delight I found in your embrace **Thanks**

Thanks for the memory of candlelight and wine, Castles on the Rhine **Thanks for the Memory**

That certain feeling, The first time I met you **That Certain Feeling**

That old Bilbao moon, I won't forget it soon **Bilbao Song**

That old black magic has me in its spell **That Old Black Magic**

That's life, That's what people say, You're ridin' high in April, Shot down in May **That's Life**

That's what you get for lovin' me **For Lovin' Me**

That's where my money goes, to buy me baby clothes **That's Where My Money Goes**

That's why you can trust your car, to the man who wears the star **Texaco Star Theme (The Man Who Wears the Star)**

The ''Good Time Coming'' is almost here! It was long, long, long on the way! **Wake Nicodemus**

The air seems fresh, the lights grow bright, The walls are charged with dynamite **When She Walks in the Room**

The ballroom was filled with fashion's throng **A Bird in a Gilded Cage**

The beam in your eyes the smile of your face **The Loveliness of You**

The bird with feathers of blue, Is waiting for you **Back in Your Own Back Yard**

The birds are humming 'go feather your nest **Feather Your Nest**

The birds of the forest are calling for thee **Gypsy Love Song,** or, **Slumber On**

The boat rides we would take, The moonlight on the lake **The Things We Did Last Summer**

The Bow'ry, the Bow'ry, They say such things, and they do strange things **The Bowery**

The breeze and I are saying with a sigh that you no longer care **The Breeze and I**

The breeze is chasing the zephyr, the moon is chasing the sea **Nobody's Chasing Me**

The breeze kissed your hair Knowing you were fair **One Moment Alone**

The briar's in bud, the sun going down **Twickenham Ferry**

The brightest paper valentine has nothin' on this heart of mine **It's Good To Be Alive**

The cherry on the top of the sundae **Big Time**

The Church's one foundation Is Jesus Christ her Lord **The Church's One Foundation**

The clown with his pants falling down **That's Entertainment**

The crowd sees me out dancing, carefree and romancing **Laughing on the Outside (Crying on the Inside)**

The days of wine and roses Laugh and run away Like a child at play **Days of Wine and Roses**

The Dipsy Doodle's a thing to beware. The Dipsy Doodle will get in your hair **The Dipsy Doodle**

The evening breeze caressed the trees tenderly **Tenderly**

The falling leaves drift by the window **Autumn Leaves**

The favorite doesn't always win, No matter what the odds **Sure Thing**

The first Noël, the angels did say, Was to certain poor shepherds in fields as they lay **The First Noël**

The frog he would a-wooing go, M-m, m-m . . . Whether his mother would let him or no, M-m, m-m **Frog Went a-Courtin',** or, **Frog He Would a-Wooing Go,** or, **Mister Frog Went a-Courtin'**

The hills are alive with the sound of music, With songs they have sung for a thousand years **The Sound of Music**

The hour was sad I left the maid, A ling'ring farewell taking **The Girl I Left Behind Me,** or, **Brighton Camp**

The hours I spent with thee, dear heart, Are as a string of pearls to me **The Rosary**

The house I live in, A plot of earth, a street, The grocer and the butcher **The House I Live In**

The it's time for parting, and my tears are starting **Leave Me with a Smile**

The lady comes to the gate, Dressed in lavender and leather **Albatross**

The last time I saw Paris Her heart was warm and gay, I heard the laughter of her heart in ev'ry street cafe **The Last Time I Saw Paris**

The leaves of brown came tumbling down, remember? **September in the Rain**

The leopard's pappy got the gout from eatin' too much speckled trout **Uncle Remus Said**

The look of love is in your eyes, a look your smile can't disguise **The Look of Love**

The Lord above gave man an arm of iron **With a Little Bit of Luck**

The Lord made Adam, the Lord made Eve, He made 'em both a little bit naive **The Begat**

The loveliness of Paris Seems somehow sadly gay **I Left My Heart in San Francisco**

The many happy evenings I spent, when but a lad **Paddy Duffy's Cart**

The miller's big dog lay on the barn-floor, And Bingo was his name **Balm of Gilead,** or, **Bingo**

The mist of May is in the gloamin', and all the clouds are holdin' still **The Heather on the Hill**

The moon belongs to ev'ryone **The Best Things in Life Are Free**

The moon descends and so to bed. The music ends and so to bed　**And So to Bed**

The more I read the papers The less I comprehend　**Our Love Is Here To Stay**

The more I'm with you, the more I can see My love is yours alone　**Everything I Have Is Yours**

The most beautiful girl in the world Picks my ties out, eats my candy, Drinks my brandy　**The Most Beautiful Girl in the World**

The mountain's high and the valley's so deep, Can't get across to the other side　**The Mountain's High**

The music's sweet, the lights are low, Playin' a song on the radio　**Dum Dum**

The New Year's Eve we did the town, the day we tore the goalpost down　**Moments to Remember**

The night in Manhattan was the start of it　**Manhattan Serenade**

The night is bitter, The stars have lost their glitter　**The Man That Got Away**

The night is like a lovely tune　**My Foolish Heart**

The night is young, the skies are clear And if you want to go walking, dear　**It's De-Lovely**

The night they invented champagne, It's plain as it can be They thought of you and me!　**The Night They Invented Champagne**

The object of my affection can change my complexion　**The Object of My Affection**

The odds were a hundred to one against me　**They All Laughed**

The old home town looks the same as I step down from the train　**The Green Green Grass of Home**

The other night, dear, as I lay sleeping　**You Are My Sunshine**

The pale moon was rising above the green mountain　**The Rose of Tralee**

The pen of my aunt is on the bureau of my uncle　**La Plume de Ma Tante (The Pen of My Aunt)**

The people in the ballroom were stuffy and arty　**The Waiter and the Porter and the Upstairs Maid**

The Pope he leads a jolly life, jolly, life, He's free from every day care and strife, care and strife　**The Pope He Leads a Happy Life**

The prettiest gal that ever I saw Was sucking cider through a straw　**Sipping Cider Thru' (Through) a Straw**

The rain in Spain stays mainly in the plain　**The Rain in Spain**

The rolling tide that brings you to me　**Adios My Love,** or, **The Song of Athens**

The sentimental touch can fill a heart with such sweet madness　**The Sentimental Touch**

The shades of night were falling fast, As thro' an Alpine village pass'd　**Excelsior**

The ship goes sailing down the bay, good-bye, my lover, good-bye　**Good-Bye, My Lover, Good-Bye**

The sky's full of rain, clouds are all black and you're on a train without any track　**When the One You Love (Simply Won't Love Back)**

The sleepless nights, The daily fights, The quick toboggan when you reach the heights　**I Wish I Were in Love Again**

The son of God goes forth to war, A kingly crown to gain　**The Son of God Goes Forth to War**

The song of a robin sings Through years of endless springs　**Stella by Starlight**

The song for a summer night is a song your heart sings when you're in love　**Song for a Summer Night**

The sons of the Prophet are hardy and bold And quite unaccustomed to fear　**Abdulla Bulbul Ameer**

The spacious firmament on high, With all the blue ethereal sky　**The Spacious Firmament on High**

The stars shine above you, Yet linger awhile　**Linger Awhile**

The summer days are ending in the valley　**The White Rose of Athens**

The summer smiles, the summer knows, And unashamed, she sheds her clothes　**The Summer Knows,** or, **Theme from** *Summer of '42*

The sun comes up, I think about you. The coffee cup, I think about you　**Losing My Mind**

The sun shines bright in my old Kentucky home　**My Old Kentucky Home (Good Night)**

The sweetest sounds I'll ever hear Are still inside my head　**The Sweetest Sounds**

The tears I cried for you could fill an acean　**Everybody's Somebody's Fool**

The things I get are what I never seem to want　**The Things I Want**

The things we planned, Goodbye to all that. We built on sand　**Goodbye to All That**

The tide will turn, life is a dream come true　**When Someone You Love Loves You**

The touch of your lips upon my brow; Your lips that are cool and sweet　**The Touch of Your Lips**

The Union forever, Hurrah, boys, hurrah!　**The Battle Cry of Freedom**

The very thought of you And I forget to do The little ordinary things　**The Very Thought of You**

The very thought of you makes my heart sing　**My One and Only Love**

The volley was fired at sunrise, Just after break of day　**The Pardon Came Too Late**

The warden threw a party in the county jail　**Jailhouse Rock**

The way you wear your hat, The way you sip your tea　**They Can't Take That Away from Me**

The wheel of fortune goes spinning around; will the arrow point my way　**The Wheel of Fortune**

The world is lyrical, Because a miracle Has brought my lover to me!　**Dancing on the Ceiling**

The worst person I know, Mother-in-Law, Mother-in-Law　**Mother-in-Law**

The years creep slowly by, Lorena　**Lorena**

Thee I love, More than the meadows so green and still　**Friendly Persuasion,** or, **Thee I Love**

Them that's got shall get, Them that's not shall lose **God Bless the Child**

Then cherish her with care, And smooth her silv'ry hair **A Boy's Best Friend Is His Mother**

Then you may take me to the fair if you do all the things you promise **Then You May Take Me to the Fair**

There ain't nothin' I can do, nor nothin' I can say **'Tain't Nobody's Business If I Do**

There are blues that you get from worry There are blues that you get from pain **Blues My Naughty Sweetie Give to Me**

There are eyes of blue, There are brown eyes too **The Maiden with the Dreamy Eyes**

There are girls just ripe for some kissin' And I mean to kiss me a few! **(I've Got) A Lot of Livin' To Do**

There are places I'll remember all my life, though some have changed **In My Life**

There are smiles that make us happy **Smiles**

There are times ev'ry day, as you work or you play, when a pause would be welcome to you **Fifty Million Times a Day**

There goes my baby with someone new **Bye Bye Love**

There goes the girl I dreamed all thru school about **My Future Just Passed**

There is a brotherhood of man, A benevolent brotherhood of man **Brotherhood of Man**

There is a charm I can't explain, About a girl I've seen **The Big Sunflower**

There is a flower within my heart, Daisy, Daisy! **Daisy Bell, or, A Bicycle Built for Two, or, Daisy, Daisy**

There is a green hill far away, Without a city wall **There Is a Green Hill Far Away**

There is a house in New Orleans, They call the Rising Sun **The House of the Rising Sun**

There is a lady sweet and kind, Was never face so pleas'd my mind **Passing By**

There is a melody Forever haunting me **A Song of Old Hawaii**

There is a railroad around lover's lane And the conductor is you **Any Old Place with You**

There is a tavern in the town, in the town, And there my true love sits him down, sits him down **There Is a Tavern in the Town**

There is a danger in my loving you, Danger in your letting me **Sweet Danger**

There is no trick to a Can-Can, it is so simple to do **Can-Can**

There must be a place, a place where love has gone **Where Love Has Gone**

There must be a way To help me forget that we're through **There Must Be a Way**

There never was a gal I could love Like I love my Josephine **Josephine**

There ought to be a moonlight saving time So I could love that girl of mine **(There Ought To Be a) Moonlight Saving Time**

There she is My old gal there he is my old pal **Here Am I— Broken Hearted**

There was a boy, a very strange, enchanted boy **Nature Boy**

There was a frog lived in a pool, sing song Kitty, won't you Ki me oh **Kemo-Kimo**

There was a little Dutchman, his name was Johnny Vorbeck **Rambling Wreck from Georgia Tech, or, Johnny Vorbeck**

There was a man like you and me, as simple as a man could ever be **The Syncopated Clock**

There was a man, walked through the town To see what he could find around **The Lone Fish (Meat) Ball**

There was once a simple maiden came to New York on a trip **And Her Golden Hair Was Hanging Down Her Back**

There were bells on the hill, but I never heard them ringing **Till There Was You**

There were ninety and nine that safely lay In the shelter of the field **The Ninety and Nine**

There will be many other nights like this **There Will Never Be Another You**

There'll be life, there'll be love, there'll be laughter **Life, Love and Laughter**

There's a bright golden haze on the meadow **Oh What a Beautiful Mornin'**

There's a broken heart for ev'ry light on Broadway, A million tears for every gleam, they say **There's a Broken Heart for Every Light on Broadway**

There's a charming Irish lady with a roguish winning way **Bedelia**

There's a cheerful little earful Gosh I miss it something fearful **Cheerful Little Earful**

There's a church in the valley by the wildwood **The Little Brown Church (in the Vale)**

There's a cocoanut grove where life is entrancing **Cocoanut Grove**

There's a day we feel gay If the weather's fine **On a Sunday Afternoon**

There's a doctor livin' in your town, There's a lawyer and an Indian too **Doctor, Lawyer, Indian Chief**

There's a far land, I'm told, Where I'll find a field of gold **Here I'll Stay**

There's a garden, what a garden, Only happy faces bloom there **The Beer Barrel Polka**

There's a guy named Jack from a country called Iraq **Jacques D'Iraq (Jock D'Rock)**

There's a land of beginning again, Where skies are always blue **In the Land of Beginning Again**

There's a land that is fairer than day, And by faith we can see it afar **In the Sweet Bye and Bye**

There's a long, long trail a-winding In to the land of my dreams **There's a Long, Long Trail**

There's a low green valley on the old Kentucky shore **Darling Nelly Gray**

There's a man in the funny papers we all know, Alley Oop Oop Oop Oop Oop **Alley-Oop**

There's a place for us. Somewhere a place for us **Somewhere**

There's a place that I know where the sweet tulips grow **Tulip Time**

There's a rainbow 'round my shoulder, And a sky of blue above **There's a Rainbow Round My Shoulder**

There's a rainbow on the river The skies are clearing **Rainbow on the River**

There's a rose that grows on "No Man's Land" And it's wonderful to see **The Rose of No Man's Land**

There's a saying old Says that love is blind **Someone To Watch Over Me**

There's a small hotel With a wishing well: I wish that we were there together **There's a Small Hotel**

There's a somebody I'm longing to see. I hope that he turns out to be **Someone To Watch Over Me**

There's a story the gypsy knows is true **Golden Earrings**

There's a time in each year that we always hold dear **In the Good Old Summer Time**

There's a whole new way of livin', Pepsi helps supply the drive **Pepsi's Got a Lot To Give, You've Got a Lot To Live**

There's a yellow rose in Texas That I am going to see **The Yellow Rose of Texas, or, Song of the Texas Rangers**

There's a young man that I know, His age is twenty-one **Someday Soon**

There's always a Joker in the pack, There's always a lonely clown **The Joker**

There's an inn in Indiana with a very goodly clientele **The Ladies Who Sing with the Band**

There's an old spinning wheel in the parlor Spinning dreams of the long, long ago **The Old Spinning Wheel**

There's an old-time melody, I heard long ago **My Mother's Rosary**

There's been a change in me! I have a lovely disposition, That's very strange in me **I Married an Angel**

There's dew upon the ground, and not a soul in sight **Walkin' by the River**

There's fryers and broilers and Detroit barbecue ribs **The House of Blue Lights**

There's got to be a morning after if we can hold on through the night **The Morning After, or, Song from *The Poseidon Adventure***

There's just one place for me, near you **Near You**

There's Malichevsky, Rubenstein, Arensky and Tschaikowsky **Tschaikowsky**

There's music in the air When the infant morn is nigh; And faint its blush is seen **There's Music in the Air**

There's no land so grand as my land **The Yankee Doodle Blues**

There's no place in the world for the angry young man, with his working class ties and his radical plans **Angry Young Man**

There's nothing left for me, Of days that used to be **Among My Souvenirs**

There's nothing you can do that can't be done **All You Need Is Love**

There's nothin' you can do to turn me away, Nothin' anyone can say **The Right Thing To Do**

There's romance in the air, They're such a loving pair **The Wooden Soldier and the China Doll**

There's something about an Aqua Velva Man **Aqua Velva Man**

There's a kiss that you get from Baby, There's the kiss that you get from Dad **Kisses—The Sweetest Kisses of All**

There's the perfume of a million flowers **A Song of Old Hawaii**

These are the eyes that watched him as he walked away **My Coloring Book**

These days ev'ry fellow has a sweetheart **I Wish I Had a Girl**

They all laughed at Christopher Columbus When he said the world was round **They All Laughed**

They asked me how I knew My true love was true **Smoke Gets in Your Eyes**

They call her hard hearted Hannah, the vamp of Savannah, the meanest gal in town **Hard Hearted Hannah (The Vamp of Savannah)**

They call it a teenage crush, They don't know how I feel **Teenage Crush**

They call me the moonlight gambler. I've gambled for love and lost **Moonlight Gambler**

They call us Babes in arms, But we are Babes in armour **Babes in Arms**

They have a new expression along old Harlem way **The Joint Is Jumpin'**

They say into your early life romance came **Sophisticated Lady**

They say, Rube you're like a dream, not always what you seem **Ruby**

They say that the seasons are four **(Theme from) Return to Peyton Place, or, The Wonderful Season of Love**

They say we're young and we don't know, We won't find out till we grow **I Got You Babe**

They try to tell us we're too young **Too Young**

They're really rockin' in Boston, In Pittsburgh, P.A. **Sweet Little Sixteen**

They're writing songs of love, But not for me **But Not for Me**

They've got an awful lot of coffee in Brazil **The Coffee Song (They've Got an Awful Lot of Coffee in Brazil)**

Things are looking up! I've been looking the landscape over **Things Are Looking Up**

Things go better with Coca-Cola, Things go better with Coke **Things Go Better with Coke**

Things look swell, Things look great, Gonna have the whole world on a plate **Everything's Coming Up Roses**

Think of what you're losing By constantly refusing to dance with me **I Won't Dance**

Think of an evening in June, Under a crystal like moon **Avalon Town**

This can't be love because I feel so well **This Can't Be Love**

This is a man who thinks with his heart, His heart is not always wise **Something Wonderful**

This is for the people who never rode the train **Down by the Station**

This is it, my great romance, I want to hang on to this one big chance **This Is It**

This is my first affair, so, please be kind **Please Be Kind**

This is new—I was merely existing. This is new And I'm living at last **This Is New**

This is not a sad song, a sad song, to sing when you're alone **Song Sung Blue**

This is romance There's a sky to invite us, And a moon to excite us **This Is Romance**

This is the end of a beautiful friendship it ended a moment ago **A Beautiful Friendship**

This is the land of milk and honey This is the land of sun and song **Milk and Honey**

This is the moment, This is the time, Why don't we take it and make it sublime? **This Is the Moment**

This is the waltz from Africa, A swingin' version of a dance **African Waltz**

This isn't sometimes, this is always. This isn't maybe, this is always **This Is Always**

This land is mine, God gave this land to me **(Theme from) Exodus**

This love of mine Goes on and on, Tho' life is empty Since you have gone **This Love of Mine**

This lovely day will lengthen into ev'nin **I'll (I) Remember April**

This night has music the sweetest music, It echoes something within my heart **Yours, or, Quiéreme Mucho**

This ole house once knew my children; this ole house once knew my wife **This Ole House**

This old man, he play'd one, He play'd nick-nack on my drum **This Old Man, or, The Children's Marching Song (Nick, Nack, Paddy Whack)**

This time we almost made the pieces fit, didn't we, girl? **Didn't We**

This was a real nice clambake, We're mighty glad we came **This Was a Real Nice Clambake**

This will be my shining hour, Calm and happy and bright **My Shining Hour**

This word so sweet that I repeat Means I adore you **Amor**

Tho' it's a fickle age, With flirting all the rage **Ain't Misbehavin'**

Tho my eyes may wander to and fro or yonder **(It Was) Always Always You**

Tho we said "goodbye," when the moon is high **Does Your Heart Beat for Me**

Tho you belong to somebody else **Tonight You Belong to Me**

Those fingers in my hair That sly, come hither stare **Witchcraft**

Thou swell! Thou witty! Thou sweet! Thou grand! **Thou Swell**

Thou wilt come no more, gentle Annie, Like a flow'r thy spirit did depart **Gentle Annie**

Though April showers may come your way **April Showers**

Though I know that we meet ev'ry night **With a Song in My Heart**

Though new young blossoms are born each May **'Twas Not So Long Ago**

Though you say we're through, I'll always love you **You Can Depend on Me**

Three brothers down in Rio had a noisy fam'ly trio **The Big Brass Band from Brazil**

Three little chillun lyin' in bed; Two wuz sick and de other 'most dead! **Shortnin' Bread**

Three little words, Oh, what I'd give for that wonderful phrase **Three Little Words**

Three on a match is sure unlucky for me Our affair has been a riddle since we're three **Three on a Match**

Through the clouds, gray with years, Over hills, wet with tears **Follow Me**

Thru the trees comes autumn with her serenade **Autumn Serenade**

Thy beaming eyes Are Paradise To Me, my love, to me **Thy Beaming Eyes**

Till black is white, Till day is night, Till moon stops shining And wrong is right **Till Then**

Till the end of time, Long as stars are in the blue **Till the End of Time**

Till then my darling please wait for me, Till then no matter when it will be **Till Then**

Time after time I tell myself that I'm So lucky to be loving you **Time After Time**

Time heals ev'rything, Tuesday, Thursday, Time heals ev'rything, April, August **Time Heals Everything**

Time was, when we had fun on the schoolyard swings **Time Was, or, Dreaming**

Tits and ass. Bought myself a fancy pair **Dance: Ten; Looks: Three**

To dream the impossible dream, to fight the unbeatable foe **The Impossible Dream or, The Quest**

To ev'rything (turn, turn, turn) There is a season (turn, turn, turn) **Turn! Turn! Turn!**

To keep my love, you must be leaner **Oh, Katharina**

To know, know, know you is to love, love, love you **To Know You Is To Love You**

To lead a better life I need my love to be here **Here, There and Everywhere**

To Life, To Life, L'chaim! L'chaim, L'chaim, To Life! **To Life, or, L'Chaim**

To look sharp, ev'ry time you shave, to feel sharp, And be on the ball **To Look Sharp**

To show affection In your direction You know I'm fit and able **My One and Only**

To spend one night with you in our old rendezvous **That's My Desire**

To the knights in the days of old **Follow the Gleam**

To the Lairds of Convention 'twas Claver'se who spoke **Bonnie Dundee**

To you, beautiful lady, I raise my eyes **My Beautiful Lady,** or, **The Kiss Waltz**

Tobacco's but an Indian weed, grows green at morn, cut down at eve **Tobacco's But an Indian Weed**

Tommy Mottola Lives on the road; He lost his lady Two months ago **Cherchez la Femme**

Tonight I heard the wild goose cry Winging North in the lonely sky **The Cry of the Wild Goose**

Tonight I mustn't think of her **Music, Maestro, Please**

Tonight Just let me look at you, Don't talk, don't break the spell **Just Let Me Look at You**

Tonight, while all the world is still Here I stand **Serenata**

Tony's wife, the boys in Havana love Tony's wife **Tony's Wife**

Too late now to forget your smile; The way we cling when we've danced awhile **Too Late Now**

Too many mornings, waking and pretending I reach for you **Too Many Mornings**

Took a walk and passed your house late last night **Silhouettes**

Toolin' down the Highway doin' seventy nine! **Transfusion**

Toot, Toot, Tootsie, Goodbye! Toot, Toot, Tootsie, don't cry **Toot Toot Tootsie (Goo'Bye)**

Toyland! Toyland! Little girl and boy land **Toyland**

Tra la! It's May! The lusty month of May! **The Lusty Month of May**

Tramp, tramp, tramp! the boys are marching, Cheer up, comrades, they will come **Tramp, Tramp, Tramp**

Tramping feet with traffic meet, and fill the street with booming and zooming **The Beat of My Heart**

Troubles really are bubbles, they say, And I'm bubbling over today! **Where's That Rainbow**

Trust in me all you do; Have the faith I have in you **Trust in Me**

Try not to get worried, try not to turn on to problems that upset you **Everything's Alright**

Try to remember the kind of September when life was slow and oh, so mellow **Try To Remember**

Try to see it my way, Do I have to keep on talking till I can't go on? **We Can Work It Out**

Tuck me to sleep in my old 'Tucky home Cover me with Dixie skies and leave me there alone **Tuck Me To Sleep in My Old 'Tucky Home**

Turn on the heat. Start in to strut. Wiggle and wobble and warm up the hut **Turn On the Heat**

Twas a calm, still night, And the moon's pale light **Lily Dale**

Tweedlee, Tweedlee, Tweedlee Dee, I'm as happy as can be **Tweedle Dee**

Twenty-one great tobaccos, make twenty wonderful smokes **Chesterfield, Twenty-one Great Tobaccos**

Twilight descends ev'rything ends til tomorrow tomorrow **Till Tomorrow**

Twilight soon will fade, I'll meet you at the masquerade **Masquerade**

Two cigarettes in the dark He strikes a match 'til the spark clearly thrilled me **Two Cigarettes in the Dark**

Two drummers sat at dinner, in a grand hotel one day **Mother Was a Lady,** or, **If Jack Were Only Here**

Two German officers crossed the Rhine, Parlay Voo **Hinky Dinky Parlay Voo**

Two hearts beat with a joi complete **Two Hearts in Three Quarter Time**

Two hearts that pass in the night, in the magical light of the moon **Two Hearts That Pass in the Night**

Two silhouettes together in the afterglow **Two Silhouettes**

Underneath the Russian moon, Stars shining bright We'd meet each night **Underneath the Russian Moon**

Unforgettable, That's what you are, Unforgettable tho near or far **Unforgettable**

Up a lazy river by the old mill run **(Up a) Lazy River**

Up in Harlem at a table for two, Well, there were the four of us baby, me, your big feet and you **Your Feet's Too Big**

Up in Harlem ev'ry Saturday night **Gimme a Pigfoot (and a Bottle of Beer)**

Up in the mornin' and out to school, The teacher is teachin' the Golden Rule **School Day (Ring! Ring! Goes the Bell)**

Up to de washin' soap, Down to de watah once mo' **Washboard Blues**

Up where the smoke is all billered and curled **Chim Chim Cher-ee**

Use Ajax the foaming cleanser, Floats the dirt right down the drain! **Use Ajax the Foaming Cleanser**

Vamp and swing along, keep a-doing it **The Vamp**

Venus, if you will, Please send a little girl for me to thrill **Venus**

Vilia, Oh, Vilia, enchanting the night, Fashioned of stardust **Vilia**

Violets, who'll buy my violets? Take these Cupid eyes of blue **Who'll Buy My Violets**

Volare, Oh, oh, Cantare, oh, oh, oh, oh! **Volare,** or, **Nel Blu, Dipinto Di Blu**

Wabash moon keep shining On the one who waits for me **Wabash Moon**

Wait till you see her, see how she looks, Wait till you hear her laugh **Wait Till You See Her**

Waiting around for the girls upstairs, after the curtain came down **Waiting for the Girls Upstairs**

Wake up and live Don't mind the rainy patter **Wake Up and Live**

Waking skies At sunrise Ev'ry sunset too **Memories Of You**

Walk hand in hand with me thru' all eternity Have faith, believe in me **Walk Hand in Hand**

Walk right in, set right down, Daddy let your mind roll on **Walk Right In**

Walkin' with mah baby, she's got great big feet **Caldonia (What Makes Your Big Head So Hard)**

765

Wang, wang blues, She's gone and left me with the wang, wang blues **The Wang, Wang Blues**

Wave your little hand and whisper, "So long, dearie" **So Long Dearie**

Way back in my childhood I heard a story so true **Cotton Tail**

Way down among Brazilians coffee beans grow by the billions **The Coffee Song (They've Got an Awful Lot of Coffee in Brazil)**

Way down upon the Swanee River, Far, far away **Old Folks At Home**

We are a band of brothers, and native to the soil **The Bonnie Blue Flag**

We are the men of Texaco, We wear the Texaco Star **Texaco Star Theme (The Man Who Wears the Star)**

We can never know about the days to come **Anticipation**

We come from ev'ry quarter, From North, South, East and West **Good Morning, Mister Zip-Zip-Zip**

We come on the sloop, "John B," My grandfather and me **(The Wreck of the) John B**

We could hear the darkies singing as she said farewell to me **The Girl I Love in Sunny Tennessee**

We could make believe I love you, Only make believe that you love me **Make Believe**

We don't have to march with the infantry, Ride with the cavalry, shoot with the artillery **The King's Navee**

We from childhood played together **Comrades**

We gather together to ask the Lord's blessing, He chastens and hastens His will to make known **We Gather Together (To Ask the Lord's Blessing)**, or, **Prayer of Thanksgiving**

We got sunlight on the sand, We got moonlight on the sea **There Is Nothin' Like a Dame**

We had a quarrel, a teenage quarrel **A Rose and a Baby Ruth**

We had to have something new, a dance to do up here in Harlem **Truckin'**

We have nothing to remember so far so far **So Far**

We have one hour, my love, for at midnight we must part **Eleventh Hour Melody**

We hunted and we halloed, And the first thing that we found **Cape Ann**

We kiss in a shadow, We hide from the moon **We Kiss in a Shadow**

We met at nine. We met at eight. I was on time. No, you were late **I Remember It Well**

We plow the fields and scatter the good seed on the land **All Good Gifts**

We shall meet, but we shall miss him, There will be one vacant chair **The Vacant Chair**, or, **We Shall Meet, But We Shall Miss Him**

We skipped the light fandango, Turned cartwheels 'cross the floor **A Whiter Shade of Pale**

We strolled the lane, together; Laughed at the rain, together **Together**

We sure like girls, all kinds of girls, From Annie to Veronica **Alvin's Harmonica**

We thought that love was over, that we were really through **We Just Couldn't Say Goodbye**

We three kings of Orient are; Bearing gifts we traverse afar **We Three Kings of Orient (Are)**

We two were sweethearts But we said goodbye **Just Friends**

We used to spend the spring together before we learned to walk **The Most Beautiful Girl in the World**

We were comrades, comrades, ever since we were boys **Comrades**

We were forty miles from Albany, Forget it I never shall **The E-ri-ee**

We were waltzing together, to a dream melody **Changing Partners**

We'd like to know A little bit about you For our files **Mrs. Robinson**

We'll always be bosom buddies, friends, sisters and pals **Bosom Buddies**

We'll gather lilacs in the spring again, And walk together down a shady lane **We'll Gather Lilacs**

We'll have a blue room, A new room, For two room **The Blue Room**

We'll have Manhattan The Bronx and Staten Island too **Manhattan**

We'll melt in Syria, freeze in Siberia, Negligee in Timbuktu **Any Old Place with You**

We'll ride in a great big balloon, And airships that fly to the moon **Meet Me in St. Louis, Louis**

We're all pals together, Comrades, Birds of a feather **The Ranger's Song**

We're at nineteen Moonbeam Terrace, overlooking Starlight Square **We're the Couple in the Castle**

We're Regency Rakes, and each of us takes A personal pride In the thickness of his hide **Regency Rakes**

We're so proud, here we are at the Waldorf where folks sit around all day **Lounging at the Waldorf**

We're tenting tonight on the old camp ground, Give us a song to cheer **Tenting on the Old Camp Ground**, or, **Tenting Tonight**

We've just been introduced, I do not know you well **Shall We Dance**

We've played the game of stay away But it costs more than I can pay **I Surrender Dear**

Wear my ring around your neck, To tell the world you're mine by heck **Wear My Ring Around Your Neck**

Weary, my heart was weary, Alone and dreary, The day before Spring **The Day Before Spring**

Weddin' bells are dandy, Mandy make up your mind **Mandy Make Up Your Mind**

Wednesday morning at five o'clock as the day begins **She's Leaving Home**

Weep no more, my lady, Oh! weep no more today! **My Old Kentucky Home (Good Night)**

Weeping, sad and lonely, Hopes and fears how vain! **Weeping, Sad and Lonely**, or, **When This Cruel War Is Over**

Well, a hard headed woman, a soft hearted man Been the cause of trouble ever since the world began **Hard-Headed Woman**

Well, come along boys, and listen to my tale **The Old Chisholm Trail**

Well, good mornin', Captain **Mule Skinner Blues**

Well I feel so stange, well, up on my word **All Choked Up**

Well I never felt more like singing the blues 'cause I never thought that I'd ever lose your love **Singin' the Blues**

Well, I saw my baby walking, With another man today **See You Later Alligator**

Well, I saw the thing a-comin' out of the sky **The Purple People Eater**

Well I think I'm going out of my head Yes I think I'm going out of my head over you **Goin' Out of My Head**

Well I'm a-write a little letter, gonna mail it to my local D.J. **Roll Over Beethoven**

Well, it's one for the money, two for the show, three to get ready, now go, cat, go! **Blue Suede Shoes**

Well, let's take it from the top and grab some wheels **Kookie, Kookie, Lend Me Your Comb**

Well, my daddy left home when I was three **A Boy Named Sue**

Well, she was just seventeen, You know what I mean **I Saw Her Standing There**

Well, What are we gonna tell your mama? **Wake Up Little Susie**

Well, what do you know! She smiled at me in my dreams last night **My Dreams Are Getting Better All the Time**

Well, you give me all your lovin' and your turtledovin' **That'll Be the Day**

Well, you see how we communicate with words! words! words! **Words, Words, Words**

Were his days a little dull? Were his nights a little wild? **If He Walked into My Life**

Were not the sinful Mary's tears An off'ring worthy Heav'n **Mary's Tears**

What a day this has been! What a rare mood I'm in! **(It's) Almost Like Being in Love**

What a diff'rence a day made, Twenty four little hours **What a Diff'rence a Day Made (Makes)**

What a friend we have in Jesus, All our sins and griefs to bear! **What a Friend We Have in Jesus**

What a lovely day What a lovely day For a dip in the sea **Sur La Plage**

What a wonderful feelin' More than I can explain **Down Among the Sugar-Cane**

What are the joys of white men here What are his pleasures say? **Bonja Song**

What did I have that I don't have? What did he like that I lost track of? **What Did I Have That I Don't Have**

What do the simple folk do to help them escape when they're blue? **What Do (the) Simple Folk Do**

What do they do on a rainy night in Rio? What do they do when there is no starry sky? **Rainy Night in Rio**

What do you get when you fall in love **I'll Never Fall in Love Again**

What goes up must come down, Spinning wheel got to go 'round **Spinning Wheel**

What good is sitting alone in your room? Come hear the music play **Cabaret**

What is it that we're living for? Applause, Applause **Applause**

What is so rare as a day in June? **So Rare**

What makes the robin sing? My love, My love **My Love, My Love**

What now my love Now that you left me How can I live thru another day **What Now My Love**

What say, let's be buddies, What say, let's be pals **Let's Be Buddies**

What shall we do with the drunken sailor **(What Shall We Do with) The Drunken Sailor, or, Columbus, or, John Brown Had a Little Injun, or, Ten Little Indians**

What the world needs now is love, sweet love. It's the only thing that there's just too little of **What the World Needs Now Is Love**

What would you do if I sang out of tune **(With) A Little Help from My Friends**

What's good about goodbye? What's fair about farewell? **What's Good About Goodbye**

What's it all about, Alfie? Is it just for the moment we live? **Alfie**

What's that light that is beckoning? **Song of the Flame**

What's the use of wond'rin' if he's good or if he's bad **What's the Use of Wond'rin'**

What's this dull town to me? Robin's not near **Robin Adair**

Wheel about, an' turn about, An' do jis so **(Jump) Jim Crow**

When a bee lies sleepin' in the palm o' your hand **A Sleepin' Bee**

When a fellow loves a maiden And that maiden doesn't love him **La Cucaracha**

When a lad, I stood one day by a cottage far away **She Was Bred in Old Kentucky**

When a man begins to angle and a heart he tries to entangle **D'Ya Love Me?**

When a zither starts to play, you'll remember yesterday **The Third Man Theme, or, The Harry Lime Theme**

When April blossoms bloom, they'll bloom for me **April Blossoms**

When are you gonna come down When are you going to land **Goodbye Yellow Brick Road**

When breezes blow petticoats of Portugal, There's quite a show **Petticoats of Portugal**

When day is done and shadows fall, I dream of you **When Day Is Done**

When day is gone And night comes on, Until the dawn what do I do? **Dream Dancing**

When first I saw the lovelight in your eye **When You Were Sweet Sixteen**

When Francis dances with me, Hully Gee, I'm as gay as can be **When Francis Dances with Me**

When from out the shades of night **Come Down Ma Evenin' Star**

When he don't sweet talk anymore **That's the Beginning of the End**

When he'd say play something hot-sky I would play a hot Ka-sot-sky **I Played Fiddle for the Czar**

When hearts are young, When love's a star, a song unsung **When Hearts Are Young**

When I come home at half past three, My wife don't want no part of me **Oh Murphy**

When I find myself in times of trouble Mother Mary comes to Me **Let It Be**

When I get older losing my hair, many years from now **When I'm Sixty-Four**

When I get to the bottom I go back to the top of the slide **Helter Skelter**

When I go to sleep I never count sheep **Linda**

When I have a brand new hairdo With my eyelashes all in curl **I Enjoy Being a Girl**

When I hear a song I close my eyes and I belong to Simonetta **Simonetta**

When I hear that serenade in blue, I'm somewhere in another world alone with you **Serenade in Blue**

When I hug you and when I squeeze you **You Don't Like It—Not Much**

When I marry Mister Snow. The flowers'll be buzzin' with the hum of bees **When I Marry Mister Snow**

When I see you ev'ry day, I say mm-mm **Hello Little Girl**

When I take you out, tonight, with me **The Surrey with the Fringe on Top**

When I think of home, I think of a place where there's Love overflowing **Home**

When I think of Tom, I think about a night When the earth smelled of summer **Hello Young Lovers**

When I want a melody lilting through the house **By Strauss**

When I want you in my arms, when I want you and all your charms **All I Have To Do Is Dream**

When I was a bachelor, I lived all alone, I worked at the weaver's trade **The Foggy, Foggy Dew**

When I was a kid about half past three **'Tain't What You Do (It's the Way That You Do It)**

When I was a lad I served a term As office boy to an attorney's firm **When I Was a Lad**

When I was a little bitty baby my mama would rock me in the cradle **Cotton Fields**

When I was a young man and never been kissed **Kisses Sweeter Than Wine**

When I was just a little girl I asked my mother, "What will I be?" **Whatever Will Be, Will Be**, or, **Que Sera, Sera**

When I was seven years of age I used to go to school **M-I-S-S-I-S-S-I-P-P-I**

When I was young and simple (I don't recall the date) **I Never Do Anything Twice**

When I was young, I used to wait on master and give him his plate **Jimmy Crack Corn**, or, **The Blue Tail Fly**

When I was young I'd listen to the radio waitin' for my fav'rite songs **Yesterday Once More**

When I was younger, so much younger than today **Help!**

When I went romancin' I gied no thought to any weddin' ring **My One and Only Highland Fling**

When I woke up this mornin' you were on my mind And you were on my mind **You Were on My Mind**

When I worked in the mill, Wearin' at the loom, I'd gaze absent-minded at the roof **If I Loved You**

When I'm blue lonesome too What am I gonna do **Follow the Swallow**

When Irish eyes are smiling, sure it's like a morn in Spring **When Irish Eyes Are Smiling**

When Israel was in Egypt's land, Let my people go! **Go Down, Moses**

When it's fish day in Germany you can't get shaved in Massachusetts **When It's Night-Time in Italy, It's Wednesday Over Here**

When it's moonlight in Ka-lu-a, Night like this is divine **Ka-Lu-A**

When it's twilight on the trail And I jog along The world is like a dream **Twilight on the Trail**

When I've suffered intensely and enjoyed it immensely **Then I'll Have Time for You**

When John Henry was about three days old **John Henry**

When Liberty Valance rode to town the women folk would hide **The Man Who Shot Liberty Valance**

When the lights are low, you steal into my heart And linger like a melody **When Lights Are Low**

When love comes in and takes you for a spin, oo la la-la **C'est Magnifique**

When Madame Pompadour was on a ballroom floor **Personality**

When Missus O'Leary's cow kicked the lantern **Put the Blame on Mame**

When my juke-box baby takes the floor 'round the old juke-box in the candy store **Juke Box Baby**

When orchids bloom in the moonlight and lovers vow to be true **Orchids in the Moonlight**

When other lips and other hearts their tales of love shall tell **Then You'll Remember Me**

When Roto-Rooter comes, That's when your troubles go **Roto-Rooter**

When skies were dark came Noah's Ark, Amen **Great Day**

When somebody loves you, it's no good unless he loves you all the way **All the Way**

When song birds are singing Here's all they keep singing **Heigh-Ho Everybody, Heigh-Ho**

When suddenly you sight someone for whom you yearn **Ça, C'est L'Amour**

When Sunny gets blue her eyes get gray and cloudy **When Sunny Gets Blue**

When the angelus is ringing in the belfry on the hill **When the Angelus Is Ringing**

When the big brass band began to play Pretty music so gay, hats were then thrown away **At a Georgia Camp Meeting**

When the children are asleep, we'll sit and dream The things that ev'ry other dad and mother dream **When the Children Are Asleep**

When the circus came to town All the clowns were tumbling down **When the Circus Came to Town**

When the corn is waving, Annie dear, O meet me by the stile **When the Corn Is Waving, Annie Dear**

When the day is hotly quiet And the breeze seems not to blow **Shifting, Whispering Sands**

When the deep purple falls over sleepy garden walls **Deep Purple**

When the golden sun sinks in the hills **Little Grey Home in the West**

When the idle poor become the idle rich, You'll never know just who is who, or who is which **When the Idle Poor Become the Idle Rich**

When the moon comes over the mountain Ev'ry beam, brings a dream dear of you **When the Moon Comes Over the Mountain**

When the moon hits your eye like a big pizza pie, that's amore **That's Amore (That's Love)**

When the night falls silently, the night falls silently on forests dreaming **The Glow Worm**

When the noisy town Lets its window down Lets its windows down **A Tree in the Park**

When the scented night of summer covers Field and city with her veil of blue **(Just) A Little Love, a Little Kiss**

When the sky is a bright canary yellow **A Cockeyed Optimist**

When the sun comes out and that rain stops beatin' on my window pane **When the Sun Comes Out**

When the sun goes down, the tide goes out **Mississippi Mud**

When the sun in the mornin' peeps over the hill **Mocking Bird Hill**

When the sun in the sky Bids the daytime goodbye **My Cabin of Dreams**

When the values go up, up up! And the prices go down, down, down! **When the Values Go Up**

When the world's in a minor key And life is a trifle blah **Dancing**

When there's a sun above I always find Romantic thoughts of love never entered my mind **Hey, Good Lookin'**

When they begin the Beguine it brings back the sound of music so tender **Begin the Beguine**

When they go Parlay Voo and Parlay Vee Zis for you and Zat for me **Fifty Million Frenchmen Can't Be Wrong**

When this old world starts getting me down **Up on the Roof**

When this world began It was heaven's plan **Somebody Loves Me**

When trouble troubles you, sing, baby sing! **Sing, Baby, Sing**

When Washington and Lee's men fall in line **Washington and Lee Swing**

When we fought the Yankees and annihilation was near **Jubilation T. Cornpone**

When we go waltzing, One, two, three **One, Two, Three**

When we have out victory, And we've added to our history **When the Lights Go On Again (All Over the World)**

When we kiss my heart's on fire, Burning with a strange desire **Surrender**

When we're sent to dear Siberia, To Siber-i-eer-i-a **Siberia**

When Whippoorwills call and ev'ning is nigh I hurry to my blue heaven **My Blue Heaven**

When will I see you again? When will we share precious moments? **When Will I See You Again**

When you are down with the blues, It means that devil got into your shoes **Dancing the Devil Away**

When you do the Kinkajou, You dance before you think you do **The Kinkajou**

When you flyin' too high, like birds sweepin' de sky **Two Ladies in De Shade of De Banana Tree**

When you hear dem-a bells go ding, ling, ling **(There'll Be) A Hot Time in the Old Town (Tonight)**

When you held your hand to my heart **Lover**

When you just give love and never get love You'd better let love depart **Since I Fell for You**

When you shall see flowers that lie on the plan **The Touch of Your Hand**

When you sit down one day, look over yourself and say, "You're very good" **Rap Tap on Wood**

When you walk through a storm, hold your head up high And don't be afraid of the dark **You'll Never Walk Alone**

When you want a true lover send for me, send for me **Send for Me**

When your money's gone, friends have turned you down **Dallas Blues**

When you're a Jet you're a Jet all the way **Jet Song**

When you're all alone Any old night And you're feeling out of tune **Get Out and Get Under the Moon**

When you're alone Who cares for starlit skies **When Your Lover Has Gone**

When you're down and out Lift up your head and shout **Great Day**

When you're down and troubled and you need some love and care **You've Got a Friend**

When you're weary, feelin' small, When tears are in your eyes, I'll dry them all **Bridge over Troubled Water**

When you've grown up my dear And are as old as I **Toyland**

Whenever I feel afraid I hold my head erect **I Whistle a Happy Tune**

Whenever it's early twilight I watch till a star breaks through **It's Always You**

Whenever skies look grey to me And trouble begins to brew **I Concentrate on You**

Whenever we kiss I worry and wonder **The Song from Moulin Rouge,** or, **Where Is Your Heart**

Where are the simple joys of maidenhood? **The Simple Joys of Maidenhood**

Where do all the flies go in the winter time? Early in November, up the walls they climb **Where Do Flies Go in the Winter Time?**

Where do I begin to tell the story of how great a love can be **(Theme from) Love Story,** or, **Where Do I Begin**

Where do they go The smoke rings I blow each night **Smoke Rings**

Where do you go in your dreams, can you fly **Dream Babies**

Where has the time all gone to Haven't done half the things we want to **Some Other Time**

Where have you been all the day, Randall, my son? **Lord Randall**

Where is love? Does it fall from skies above? **Where Is Love?**

Where shall I go, when I go where I go **Song of the Wanderer**

Where the deep blue pearly waters wash upon white silver sands **White Silver Sands**

Where there's life there's Bud, In a penthouse or a bungalow, where the bright sun shines or candles glow **Where There's Life, There's Bud**

Where they do not care for money And though you may think it funny **In Chichicastenango**

Where will I find a treasure, like the love from a heart of gold? **Love from a Heart of Gold**

Where'd you get those eyes? Where'd you get those lips? Where'd you get those dimples, honey? **Where'd You Get Those Eyes**

Where's that guy with the bugle **If He Walked into My Life**

Where's that rainbow you hear about? Where's that lining they cheer about? **Where's That Rainbow**

Where's that Tiger! Where's that Tiger! **Tiger Rag**

Wherever we go, Whatever we do, We're gonna go through it together **Together Wherever We Go**

Wherever we go, wherever you may wonder in your life **Let Me Be There**

Whether you are here or yonder, whether you are false or true **More Than You Know**

While plodding on our way, the toilsome road of life **A Boy's Best Friend Is His Mother**

While riding in my Cadillac What, to my surprise **Beep Beep**

While strolling down the street one eve upon more pleasure bent **Just Tell Them That You Saw Me**

While tearing off A game of golf I may make a play for the caddy **My Heart Belongs to Daddy**

While the shot and shell were screaming upon the battlefield **Break the News to Mother**

While the train rolled onward a husband sat in tears **In the Baggage Coach Ahead**

Whip-poor-will, I used to love to hear you call to me **Whip-Poor-Will**

Whispering while you cuddle near me, Whispering so no one can hear me **Whispering**

''White Wings'', they never grow weary, they carry me cheerily over the sea **White Wings**

Who cares If the sky cares to fall in the sea? **Who Cares**

Who day and night must scramble for a living **Tradition**

Who d'ya think is coming to town You'll never guess who **Miss Brown to You**

Who has an itch to be filthy rich? **Who Wants To Be a Millionaire**

Who hit me? Where am I and what happened? **Who Hit Me?**

Who knows how long I've loved you **I Will**

Who needs you, to drive me out of my mind? **Who Needs You**

Who put the bomp in the bomp ba bomp ba bomp, Who put the ram in the ramalama ding-dong **Who Put the Bomp (in the Bomp Ba Bomp Ba Bomp)**

Who stole my heart away? Who makes me dream all day? **Who**

Who threw the overalls in Mistress Murphy's chowder? Nobody spoke so he shouted all the louder **Who Threw the Overalls in Mrs. Murphy's Chowder**

Who will buy this wonderful morning? Such a sky you never did see **Who Will Buy?**

Who's sorry now? Who's sorry now? Whose heart is aching for breaking each vow? **Who's Sorry Now**

Who's that coming down the street? **The Organ Grinder's Swing**

Who's that knocking at my door? **Barnacle Bill the Sailor**

Who's the most important man this country ever knew **Barney Google**

Who's the swiniest swine in the world? **Captain Hook's Waltz**

Why am I happy? Why am I gay? Me and my baby just moved out today **Happiness Street (Corner Sunshine Square)**

Why are people gay All the night and day **Love Is Sweeping the Country**

Why are the stars always winkin' and blinkin' above? **Elmer's Tune**

Why, baby, why don't you treat me like you used to do? **Why Baby Why**

Why dance? Let us stroll through the garden where no one is near **Why Dance**

Why did someone nice like you Have to love someone like me? **Someone Nice Like You**

Why did ya' say goodbye to me **Footsteps**

Why do birds sing so gay And lovers await the break of day? **Why Do Fools Fall in Love**

Why do I cry darling thrill me **You Bring Out the Lover in Me**

Why do I love you? Why do you love me? Why should there be two happy as we? **Why Do I Love You**

Why do you suppose that robins have red breasts And cats meow? **Why Do You Suppose**

Why don't we get along ev'rything I do is wrong **What's the Reason (I'm Not Pleasin' You)**

Why must I meet you in a secret rendezvous? **Secretly**

Why should I care when my sweetheart is there? **Why Should I Care**

Why this feeling? Why this glow? Why the thrill when you say "Hello!" **Mister Wonderful**

Why was I born? Why am I living? What do I get? What am I giving? **Why Was I Born?**

Why'd you tell me this While you look for my reaction **You Belong to Me**

Will I ever find the girl in my mind The one who is my ideal **My Ideal**

Will I? Won't I? Do I? Don't I? **Legalize My Name**

Will there be rain will there be storm **The Way That the Wind Blows**

Will you come with me, my Phillis dear, To yon blue mountain free? **Wait for the Wagon**

Willie Fitzgibbons who used to sell ribbons And stood up all day on his feet **Waltz Me Around Again Willie—'Round, 'Round, 'Round**

Willowy ladies, Billowy gowns, Avenues, buildings and parks **Beautiful People of Denver**

Winds may blow o'er the icy sea, I'll take with me the warmth of thee **A Taste of Honey**

Wise men say only fools rush in **Can't Help Falling in Love (with You)**

Wish I could lose those weary blues My tired heart can't love no more **Weary Blues**

Wish we didn't have to meet secretly, Wish we didn't have to kiss secretly **Secretly**

With a million neon rainbows burning below me **Down in the Depths on the Ninetieth Floor**

With a smile and a song, Life is just a bright sunny day **With a Smile and a Song**

With a song in my heart I behold your adorable face **With a Song in My Heart**

With a twist of the wrist with your lips that insist, With that come hither look in your eye **With a Twist of the Wrist**

With her red silk stockings and her green perfume She blew into the man's town **Red Silk Stockings and Green Perfume**

With my eyes wide open I'm dreaming, Can it be true I'm holding you Close to my heart? **With My Eyes Wide Open I'm Dreaming**

With someone like you, A pal good and true **Let the Rest of the World Go By**

With these hands I will cling to you, I'm yours forever and a day **With These Hands**

Without a song the day would never end; Without a song the road would never bend **Without a Song**

Without love, what is a woman? A pleasure unemployed **Without Love**

Woke up, it was a Chelsea morning, and the first thing that I heard **Chelsea Morning**

Woman, I can remember a woman **Daughter of Darkness**

Won't you stop and take a little time out with me **Take Five**

Won't you tell me when we will meet again **Sunday, Monday, or Always**

Won'tcha come along with me, To the Mississippi? **Basin Street Blues**

Woodman, spare that tree! Touch not a single bough **Woodman Spare That Tree**

Would you like to be the love of my life for always, And always watch over me? **Love of My Life**

Would you like to ride in my beautiful balloon? **Up, Up and Away,** or, **My Beautiful Balloon**

Wouldn't anybody care to meet a sweet old fashioned girl? **A Sweet Old Fashioned Girl**

Y'heave ho! My lads, the wind blows free **Sailing,** or, **Sailing, Sailing over the Bounding Main**

Yankee Rose so true, How we all love you **Yankee Rose**

Ye banks and braes o' bonnie Doon, How can ye bloom sae fresh and fair? **Ye Banks and Braes O' Bonnie Doon**

Ye gentlemen and ladies fair, who grace this famous city **The Hunters of Kentucky**

Yellow bird, up high in banana tree **Yellow Bird**

Yes, C.C. Rider, Girl, see what you have done, yes, yes, yes **C.C. Rider**

Yes it means I'm in love again. Had no lovin' since you know when **I'm in Love Again**

Yes, it's a good day for singin' a song **It's a Good Day**

Yes! let me like a Soldier fall, Upon some open plain **Yes, Let Me Like a Soldier Fall**

Yes, they'll all come to meet me, arms reaching smiling sweetly **The Green Green Grass of Home**

Yesterday, all my troubles seemed so far away **Yesterday**

Yesterday morning I did see blossoms on the apple tree **Green-Up Time**

Yesterdays, Yesterdays, Days I knew as happy sweet sequester'd days **Yesterdays**

Yield not to temptation, For yielding is sin **Yield Not to Temptation**

You ain't nothin' but a Hound Dog, cryin' all the time **Hound Dog**

You always hurt the one you love, The one you shouldn't hurt at all **You Always Hurt the One You Love**

You and I should never try to argue it never gets us anyplace **You Do the Darndest Things, Baby**

You and the night and the music fill me with flaming desire **You and the Night and the Music**

You and your smile had a strange invitation **Invitation**

You are beautiful, small and shy. You are the girl whose eyes met mine **You Are Beautiful**

You are from another world, oh, so strangely sweet **From Another World**

You are love, here in my arms where you belong **You Are Love**

You are my love and my life, You are my inspiration **Just You 'N' Me (Babe)**

You are my lucky star I saw you from afar **You Are My Lucky Star**

You are my song of love, melody immortal **Song of Love**

You are my special angel Sent up from above **My Special Angel**

You are never away from your home in my heart; There is never a day when you don't play a part **You Are Never Away**

You are sixteen, going on seventeen, Baby, it's time to think! **Sixteen Going on Seventeen**

You are the promised kiss of springtime That makes the lonely winter seem long **All the Things You Are**

You are there, exciting and fair, While I'm so dull tonight **Just Let Me Look at You**

You are too beautiful, my dear, to be true, And I am a fool for beauty **You Are Too Beautiful**

You are woman, I am man. You are smaller So I can be taller than **You Are Woman (I Am Man)**

You ask where I live, here's the address I give **The Four Winds and the Seven Seas**

You better watch out, you better not cry **Santa Claus Is Coming to Town**

You came along from out of nowhere. You took my heart and found it free **(You Came Along from) Out of Nowhere**

You came, I was alone, I should have known you were temptation **Temptation**

You can bring Pearl she's a darn nice girl but don't bring Lulu **Don't Bring Lulu**

You can dance ev'ry dance with the guy who gave you the eye **Save the Last Dance for Me**

You can shake an apple off an apple tree **Stuck on You**

You can take a silver dollar and drop it on the ground **Silver Dollar (Down and Out)**

You can take the moon, Gather up the stars and the robins that sing merrily **Put 'Em in a Box, Tie 'Em with a Ribbon (And Throw 'Em in the Deep Blue Sea)**

You can tell me when you open the door You can tell if there's love in a home **Love in a Home**

You can't do a thing but put the bite on my toes **Little Jack Frost Get Lost**

You can't have everything, Be satisfied with the little you may get **You Can't Have Everything**

You coax the blues right out of the horn, Mame **Mame**

You couldn't be cuter Plus you couldn't be smarter **You Couldn't Be Cuter**

You deserve a gal who's willin' Namely me **Namely You**

You do something to me. Something that simply mystifies me **You Do Something to Me**

You don't have to prove to me You're beautiful to strangers **You Belong to Me**

You don't need anybody to hold you **I'll Keep You Satisfied**

You go to my head and you linger like a haunting refrain **You Go to My Head**

You gotta bend down, sister, Bend down sister; If you want to keep thin **Bend Down, Sister**

You had plenty money nineteen twen'y two **Why Don't You Do Right**

You have cast your shadow on the sea, On both the sea and me **You Have Cast Your Shadow on the Sea**

You have loved lots of girls in the sweet long ago **I Wonder Who's Kissing Her Now**

You have the cool clear eyes of a seeker of wisdom and truth **I Believe in You**

You have to understand the way I am, Mein Herr **Mein Herr**

You hit the spot like a balmy breeze on a night in May **You Hit the Spot**

You keep goin' your way, I'll keep goin' my way **River, Stay 'Way from My Door**

You keep sayin' you got somethin' for me **These Boots Are Made for Walking**

You know I can be found sitting home all alone **Don't Be Cruel**

You know that it would be untrue; You know that I would be a liar **Light My Fire**

You know the feeling of something half remembered **Laura**

You leave me breathless, you heavenly thing. You look so wonderful You're like a breath of spring **You Leave Me Breathless**

You let me think that I'm your one big love **Kiss and Run**

You made me cry when you said goodbye Ain't that a shame! **Ain't That a Shame**

You made me what I am today, I hope you're satisfied **The Curse of an Aching Heart**

You make me feel so young, You make me feel so spring has sprung **You Make Me Feel So Young**

You may think, Looking at the four of us **Regency Rakes**

You might wake up some mornin', to the sound of something moving past your window in the wind **Elusive Butterfly**

You must remember this, a kiss is still a kiss, A sigh is just a sigh **As Time Goes By**

You must take the "A" train To go to Sugar Hill way up in Harlem **Take the "A" Train**

You ole fire I'm mad with desire, You're my favorite one **Blowin' Away**

You ought to see my Cindy She lives away down South **Cindy**

You oughta be in pictures, You're wonderful to see **You Oughta Be in Pictures**

You say eether and I say eyether **Let's Call the Whole Thing Off**

You say the nicest things, baby Who could help but fall in love with you **You Say the Nicest Things, Baby**

You say yes, I say no, You say stop, I say go, go, go, **Hello Goodbye**

You say you want a revolution Well you know **Revolution**

You see this guy, this guy's in love with you **This Guy's in Love with You**

You seek bluebirds Don't take blackbirds **Follow Thru**

You shake my nerves and you rattle my brain Too much love drives a man insane **Great Balls of Fire**

You sinners drop ev'rything, Let dat harmony ring **Sing You Sinners**

You start to light her cigarette And all at once you love her **All at Once You Love Her**

You stepped out of a dream, You are too wonderful to be what you seem! **You Stepped Out of a Dream**

You talk too much, you worry me to death, You talk too much, you even worry, my pet **You Talk Too Much**

You tell me you love me, you say you'll be true **Butterfly**

You think I don't love you, Oh, but I do! **Oh But I Do**

You think you've lost your love, Well I saw her yesterday-yi-yay **She Loves You**

You thrill me you chill me with shivers of joy **Charley, My Boy**

You took my kisses and you took my love, you taught me how to care **All of Me**

You walk by, enchanting as a dream **You Walk By**

You walked in to the party like you were walking onto a yacht **You're So Vain**

You went away and left me long time ago **I Hear You Knocking**

You were never lovelier, You were never so fair **You Were Never Lovelier**

You will shout when it hits you, Yes indeed **Yes Indeed**

You wouldn't believe where I been; the cities and towns I been in **It's a Miracle**

You you you, I'm in love with you you you, I could be so true true true **You, You, You**

You'd be so easy to love, So easy to idolize **Easy To Love**

You'll always be the one I love, Ev'ry hour, ev'ry day, ev'ry year **You'll Always Be the One I Love**

You'll never get away from me, You can climb the highest tree, I'll be there somehow **You'll Never Get Away from Me**

You'll never know how much I really love you **Do You Want To Know a Secret**

You'll never miss the water till your well runs dry **Joe Turner Blues**

You'll wonder where the yellow went, when you brush your teeth with Pepsodent! **You'll Wonder Where the Yellow Went**

You're a grand old flag, You're a high flying flag **You're a Grand Old Flag**

You're a sweet little headache But you are lots of fun, I've a good mind to spank you, Then thank you for all you've done **You're a Sweet Little Headache**

You're always sorry, you're always grateful, You're always wond'ring what might have been **Sorry—Grateful**

You're as cute as you can be, Baby! **Baby**

You're as pleasant as the morning and refreshing as the rain **Scatterbrain**

You're bound to fall For the bugle call, You're gonna brag 'Bout that bugle call rag **Bugle Call Rag**

You're clear out of this world. When I'm looking at you I hear out of this world **Out of This World**

You're deep, just like a chasm. You've no enthusiasm **You're Blasé**

You're from Big D I can guess by the way you drawl and the way you dress **Big "D"**

You're just too charming! You're just too great! **You're Just Too Too**

You're mean to me. Why must you be mean to me? **Mean to Me**

You're more than life to me More than eternity **More**

You're my best girl and nothing you do is wrong **My Best Girl**

You're near, that moment's here, I'm almost in your arms! **Almost in Your Arms**

You're nobody's sweetheart now, They don't baby you somehow **Nobody's Sweetheart Now**

You're not a dream, you're not an angel, you're a man **Until It's Time for You To Go**

You're sixteen, you're beautiful, and you're mine **You're Sixteen**

You're so delishious And so caprishious **Delishious**

You're so ugly, oh, so ugly You're some ugly chile **Ugly Chile (You're Some Pretty Chile)**

You're the cream in my coffee You're the salt in my stew **You're the Cream in My Coffee**

You're the kind of a girl that men forget, Just a toy to enjoy for awhile **Just a Girl That Men Forget**

You're the one I care for, You're the one and therefore I hope you care for me **You're the One I Care For**

You're walking along the street, or you're at a party **This Could Be the Start of Something (Big)**

You've always been with me Though we were far apart **Along with Me**

You've been good to me, you made me glad when I was blue **Thank You Girl**

You've changed, that sparkle in your eye is gone **You've Changed**

You've got the magic touch, it makes me glow so much **(You've Got) The Magic Touch**

You've got to accenttchuate the positive, Eliminate the negative **Ac-cent-tchu-ate the Positive**

You've got to hate and fear **You've Got To Be (Carefully) Taught**

You've got to hand it to Little Mary Sunshine, Little Mary is the sunshine of the sun **Little Mary Sunshine**

You've got to see Mama ev'ry night, or you can't see Mamma at all, You've got to kiss Mamma, treat her right, or she won't be home when you call **You've Gotta (Got to) See Mamma Ev'ry Night, Or You Can't See Mamma At All**

You've gotta hold me, hold me, hold me, hold me, baby **Hold Me, Hold Me, Hold Me**

You've heard all about your raggy melody **Ja-Da**

You, you, you are my true love **You, You, You Are the One**

You, you're the one, you are the only reason **You, You're the One**

Young girl, get out of my mind, my love for you is way out of line **Young Girl**

Younger than springtime are you, Softer than starlight are you **Younger Than Springtime**

Your eyes don't shine like they used to shine **(I'm Afraid) The Masquerade Is Over**

Your heart's lost it's quiver, Your life's a bore **Abracadabra**

Your poise! Your pose! That cute fantastic nose! **You Couldn't Be Cuter**

Your sweet expression, The smile you gave me, The way you looked when we met **It's Easy To Remember (and So Hard To Forget)**

Yours sincerely The one who loves you dearly **Yours Sincerely**

Yours till the stars lose their glory! **Yours,** or, **Quiéreme Mucho**

Zing, zing, zing a little zong with me, I know we're not beside the Zuider Zee **Zing a Little Zong**

Zip! Walter Lippman wasn't brilliant today **Zip**